LAW&RIGHTS

Summaries of UK Legislation 2016-17

Volume 1

LAW&RIGHTS

Summaries of UK Legislation 2016-17

Volume 1

Compiled from authoritative sources
Edited by Public Services Publishing Ltd
PO Box 68848, London SE26 9BX

www.lawandrights.co.uk
www.publicservicespublishing.co.uk

 **Public Services Publishing**

Published by Public Services Publishing Ltd

Copyright © Public Services Publishing Ltd 2016

ISBN for this volume 978-0-9955104-0-1

ISBN for the set 978-0-9955104-2-5

Printed by Charlesworth Press, Wakefield

Contents
Volume 1

Environmental Law

National Security

Nationality and Immigration

Taxation

The Justice System

See Volume 2 for–

Cars and Driving

Consumer Rights

Family Law

Health and Welfare

Housing

Individual Rights

Planning Law

Social Security

ANIMALS

ANIMALS

CONTROL OF DOGS: ENGLAND AND WALES

1 Introduction

This Note brings together various enactments relating to the control of dogs. In particular, the provisions relating to the control of stray and dangerous dogs, dogs who kill, injure, or worry livestock, and the control and destruction of dogs bred for fighting are described below.

S.37 of the Local Government Act 1988 enables the Secretary of State to provide by regulations for the establishment and administration of a dog registration scheme by local authorities, or such other organisations as he may, after consulting with them, designate.

As to Public Open Space Protection Orders (which have replaced Dog Control Orders) in England and Wales, see the Note on **Anti-Social Behaviour in England and Wales.**

2 Control of stray dogs

Under the Control of Dogs Order 1992, dogs (other than packs of hounds or dogs being used for sporting purposes, for destroying vermin, or as sheepdogs) must, while on a highway or place of public resort, wear a collar bearing the name and address of the owner.

3 Seizure and delivery of stray dogs

Ss.149 to 151 of the Environmental Protection Act 1990 deal with the control of stray dogs *inter alia* by their seizure and delivery to a local authority officer.

S.149(1) provides for every local authority to appoint an officer for the purpose of discharging the functions imposed or conferred on it by s.149 for dealing with stray dogs found in its area.

"Local authority" for these purposes means, in relation to England, a district council, London borough council, the Common Council of the City of London, or the Council of the Isles of Scilly; or in Wales, a county or county borough council.

Among the functions imposed or conferred by s.149 are the following. Where the officer has reason to believe that any dog found in a public place or on any other land or premises is a stray dog, he must (if practicable) seize the dog and detain it but, where he finds it on land or other premises which is not a public place, only with the consent of the owner or occupier of the land or premises (s.149(3)). Where any dog so seized wears a collar bearing the address of any person, or the owner of the dog is known, the officer must serve on the person whose address is on the collar, or on the owner, a notice in writing stating that the dog has been seized and where it is being kept and stating that the dog will be disposed of if it is not claimed within seven clear days after the service of the notice and the amounts for which he would be liable under s.149(5) (s.149(4)). The amounts for which a person claiming to be the owner of the seized dog is liable (and which he must pay in order to have the dog returned to him) are the amount of the expenses incurred by reason of the dog's detention and such further sum as is for the time being prescribed. The sum of £25 has been prescribed for this purpose by the Environmental Protection (Stray Dogs) Regulations 1992 (the 1992 Regulations).

4 Disposal of stray dogs

Where any dog seized under s.149 of the 1990 Act has been detained for seven clear days after the seizure, or where a notice has been served under s.149(4), seven clear days have elapsed since the service of the notice, and the owner has not claimed the dog and paid the amounts due under s.149(5), the officer may dispose of the dog—

(a) by selling it or giving it to a person who will, in his opinion, care properly for the dog;

(b) by selling it or giving it to an establishment for the reception of stray dogs; or

(c) by destroying it in a manner to cause it as little pain as possible.

No dog seized under s.149 must be sold or given for the purposes of vivisection (s.149(6)).

Where a dog is disposed of under (a) or (b) above to a person acting in good faith, the ownership of the dog will be vested in the recipient (s.149(7)).

5 Register of stray dogs

S.149(8) of the 1990 Act provides that the officer must keep a register of the dogs seized under s.149. The register must contain prescribed particulars which are set out in the 1992 Regulations. The register must be available at all reasonable times for inspection by the public, free of charge. Notwithstanding the foregoing, the officer may cause a dog detained under s.149 to be destroyed before the expiration of the seven-day period mentioned above where he is of the opinion that this should be done to avoid suffering.

6 Duty of person who finds a stray dog

Under s.150 of the 1990 Act, the finder of a stray dog who takes possession of it must forthwith either return the dog to its owner or take it to the officer of the local authority for the area in which it was found and must inform the officer of the local authority where the dog was found.

Where a dog has been taken under s.150 to an officer of a local authority, the dog may be dealt with in either of the following ways.

(1) If the finder wants to keep the dog, he must inform the officer of the fact and must furnish his name and address, and the officer, having complied with the prescribed procedure, must allow the finder to remove the dog. The 1992 Regulations prescribe the procedure for this purpose; *inter alia* the officer must keep a record containing a brief description of the dog (including any distinctive physical characteristics or markings, tattoos, or scars); the information recorded on a tag or collar worn by or, which is otherwise carried by, the dog; the name and address of the finder. The 1992 Regulations also require the officer where the owner of the dog can be identified and readily contacted, to make reasonable attempts to contact him and afford him a reasonable opportunity to collect the dog. Also, the officer must make all such enquiries as he considers appropriate in the circumstances of the case to ascertain that the finder is a fit and proper person to keep the dog, and that he is able to feed and care for it. The officer must also inform the finder orally and in writing that he is obliged to keep the dog (if unclaimed by the owner) for not less than one month. Failure to comply with that obligation is an offence. In Scotland, a person who keeps a dog by virtue of this provision for a period of two months without its being claimed by the person who has right to it will at the end of that period become the owner of the dog (s.150(4)).

(2) If the finder does not want to keep the dog, the officer must, unless he has reason to believe that the dog is not a stray, treat it as if it had been seized by him under s.149 (see **4 Disposal of stray dogs**, above).

7 Prohibition on dogs bred for fighting

S.1 of the Dangerous Dogs Act 1991 makes provision relating to the control and destruction of dogs bred for fighting, namely the pit bull terrier, the Japanese Tosa, and any dog of the type designated by the Secretary of State, being of a type appearing to him to be bred for fighting or to have the characteristics of dogs bred for that purpose. The Dogo Argentino and the Fila Braziliero have been so designated.

S.1(2) of the Act forbids any person to–
(a) breed or breed from such a dog;
(b) sell or exchange such a dog or offer, advertise, or expose, such a dog for sale or exchange;
(c) make or offer to make a gift of such a dog or advertise or expose such a dog as a gift;
(d) allow such a dog of which he is the owner, or of which he is for the time being in charge, to be in a public place without being muzzled and kept on a lead; or
(e) abandon such a dog of which he is the owner or, for the time being in charge of such a dog, allow it to stray.

For the purpose of the 1991 Act, where a dog is owned by a person who is under 16, any reference to its owner includes a reference to the head of the household, if any, of which that person is a member (or, in Scotland, to the person who has his actual care and control).

Contravention of any of the above-mentioned prohibitions is an offence, except that, where paragraphs (b) and (c) above are concerned, no person will be guilty of an offence for publishing an advertisement to the order of another which he did not himself devise, nor will he be convicted if he can also show that he did not know and had no reasonable cause to suspect that the advertisement related to a dog to which the prohibitions apply.

S.2 of the 1991 Act empowers the Secretary of State where it appears to him that dogs of any type to which s.1 above does not apply present a serious danger to the public, by order, to impose in relation to dogs of that type restrictions corresponding, with such modifications, if any, as he thinks appropriate, to all or any of those mentioned in paragraphs (d) and (e) above. He is also empowered to create offences in relation to such dogs.

No-one is allowed to have possession or custody of any dog to which s.1 applies, except in pursuance of the power of seizure conferred by the provisions of the 1991 Act or in accordance with an order for its destruction made under those provisions (s.1(3)).

8 Exemption schemes

The Dangerous Dogs Act 1991 provides that the Secretary of State may provide that the prohibition on possession or custody of a dog bred for fighting is not to apply in such cases and subject to compliance with such conditions as are specified in an exemption scheme (s.1(5)).

The Dangerous Dogs Exemption Schemes (England and Wales) Order 2015 sets out the exemption scheme for these purposes. In order to be exempted, the dog must–
(a) be neutered;
(b) be permanently identifiable (i.e., microchipped);
(c) have third party insurance which insures against the death of, or bodily injury caused to any person by the dog (other than a member of the policyholder's family who resides permanently with him or certain employees);
(d) have a certificate of exemption from the Agency (i.e., Heybrush Enterprises Ltd.) all the conditions of which are complied with.

The fee for the certificate of exemption referred to in (d) above is currently £77 plus VAT (Dangerous Dogs

Exemption Schemes (England and Wales) Order 2015). The conditions to be complied with are that the owner must–

- notify the Agency of any change of address of the dog for 30 days or more, and of its death or export;
- produce the certificates of exemption and insurance when required;
- keep the dog in sufficiently secure conditions to prevent its escape;
- keep the dog muzzled and on a lead when in a public place; and
- provide access to the dog for the purpose of reading a microchip.

The Dangerous Dogs (Amendment) Act 1997, s.4 extends the application of the 1991 Order so that the requirements of the exemption scheme in paragraphs (a) to (d) above now also apply to dogs in respect of which an order has been made under either s.4A(1) or s.4B(3) of the 1991 Act (see **12 Destruction of dangerous dogs**, below).

9 Control of dangerous dogs

A magistrates' court in England or Wales has power to order that a dog which appears to it to be dangerous and not kept under proper control, be kept under proper control or be destroyed (Dogs Act 1871, s.2).

Where a dog is found to have injured cattle or poultry or chased sheep, it may be dealt with as a dangerous dog under s.2 of the 1871 Act (Dogs Act 1906, s.1(4)).

Where a court makes an order under s.2 of the 1871 Act directing a dog to be destroyed it may (in Scotland, must) also appoint a person to undertake the dog's destruction and require any person having custody of the dog to deliver it up for that purpose. The court may also, if it thinks fit, make an order disqualifying the owner from having custody of a dog for a specified period (see **14 Disqualification from keeping a dog**, below).

Under s.3(1) of the 1991 Act it is an offence to permit a dog, of any breed, to be dangerously out of control in any place whether or not a public place. A dog is to be regarded as dangerously out of control on any occasion on which there are grounds for reasonable apprehension that it will injure any person or assistance dog, whether or not it actually does so, but references to a dog causing injury or there being grounds for reasonable apprehension that it will do so, do not include references to any case in which the dog is being used for a lawful purpose by a constable or a person in the service of the Crown. The owner of the dog or anyone else who had charge of the dog at the relevant time is made guilty of the offence, and the Act makes it an aggravated offence if whilst out of control, the dog causes injury to any person or assistance dog. It is a defence for the owner of the dog if he was not at the material time in charge of it, to prove that the dog was, at the material time, in the charge of a person whom he reasonably believed to be a fit and proper person to be in charge of it.

S.3(5) of the 1991 Act declares for the avoidance of doubt that an order under s.2 of the 1871 Act may (a) be made whether or not the dog is shown to have injured any person; and (b) specify the measures to be taken for keeping the dog under proper control, whether by muzzling, keeping on a lead, excluding it from specified places or otherwise. If it appears to a court on a complaint under s.2 of the 1871 Act that the dog to which the complaint relates is a male and would be less dangerous if neutered, the court may under s.2 make an order requiring it to be neutered.

A person guilty of an offence of allowing a dog to be dangerously out of control is liable on summary conviction to imprisonment for a term not exceeding six months or an unlimited fine or both. A person guilty of an aggravated offence is liable–

(a) on summary conviction, to imprisonment for a term not exceeding six months or an unlimited fine or both;

(b) on conviction on indictment to imprisonment for a term of up to 14 years if a person dies as a result of being injured; 5 years in any other case where a person is injured; or 3 years in any case where an assistance dog is injured (whether or not it dies), or a fine or both.

10 Destruction of dangerous dogs

Where a person is convicted of an offence under s.1 of the 1991 Act or an offence under an order made under s.2 of the 1991 Act (see **9 Prohibition on dogs bred for fighting**, above), or under s.3 of the 1991 Act, the court (Dangerous Dogs Act 1991, s.4(1))–

(1) may (and, subject to s.4(1A) below, must, in the case of an offence under s.1 or an aggravated offence under s.3) order the destruction of any dog in respect of which the offence was committed; and

(2) may order the offender to be disqualified, for such a period as the court thinks fit, from having custody of a dog.

However, nothing in s.4(1) requires the court to order a dog's destruction if the court is satisfied that (a) it is not a danger to public safety, and (b) in the case of a dog born before 30th November 1991, there is a good reason why it has not been exempted under the Dangerous Dogs Compensation and Exemption Schemes order 1991 (see **10 Exemption schemes**, above) (s.4(1A)). In deciding whether a dog would constitute a danger to public safety, the court must consider (i) the temperament of the dog and its past behaviour, and (ii) whether the owner of the dog, or the person for the time being in charge of it, is a fit and proper person to be in charge of the dog, and may consider any other relevant circumstances (s.4(1B)).

Where a court makes an order for the destruction of a dog owned by a person other than the offender, the owner may appeal to the Crown Court against the order (s.4(2)). A dog must not be destroyed until the end of the period for giving notice of appeal against the conviction or against the order; and if notice of appeal is given within that period, until the appeal is determined or withdrawn and unless the offender, and if different, the owner of the dog gives notice to the court that made the order that there is to be no appeal (s.4(3)). Where a court makes an order for the destruction of a dog, it may appoint a person to undertake the destruction of the dog and require any person having custody of it to deliver it up for that purpose and order the offender to pay such sum as the court may determine to be the reasonable expenses of destroying the dog and of keeping it pending its destruction (s.4(4)).

Any person who is disqualified may, at any time after the end of the period of one year beginning with the date of the order, apply to the court that made it (or a magistrates' court acting for the same petty sessions area as that court) for a direction terminating the disqualification (s.4(6)). The court may having regard to the applicant's character, his conduct since the disqualification was imposed and any other circumstances of the case, grant or refuse the application; and order the applicant to pay all or any part of the costs of the application. Where an application is refused no further application can be made before the end of the period of one year beginning with the date of the refusal (s.4(7)).

Where a person is convicted of an offence under s.1 or an aggravated offence under s.3 above, but the court does not order the dog's destruction, the court must order that, unless the dog is exempted under the Dangerous Dogs Compensation and Exemption Scheme Order 1991 (see **10 Exemption schemes**, above) from the prohibition contained in s.1(3) within a two month period (which the court may extend) it must be destroyed (s.4A(1) to (3)).

Where a person is convicted under s.3 of the offence of permitting a dog to be dangerously out of control (see above), the court may order that, unless the dog's owner keeps it under proper control, it will be destroyed. The court may specify measures that should be taken to control the dog (e.g., muzzling) and, if the dog is male, may require it to be neutered (s.4A(4) and (5)).

Where a dog is seized under s.5 (see below), and it appears to a justice of the peace that no one is to be prosecuted (whether because the owner cannot be found or any other reason), or that the dog cannot be released into the owner's custody without the owner contravening s.1(3) of the Act (see **9 Prohibition on dogs bred for fighting**, above), he may still order the destruction of the dog and, subject to s.4B(2), must do so if the dog is of a fighting breed described in s.1 (s.4B(1)). However, the justice need not order the dog's destruction if he is satisfied (a) that the dog is not a danger to the public, or (b) that, in the case of a dog born before 30th November 1991, there is a good reason why the dog has not been exempted under the above Compensation and Exemption Schemes Order (s.4B(2)). In the case of a dog to which (b) applies, the justice must order that, unless the dog obtains exemption under the Order (see **10 Exemption schemes**, above) within a two month period, it will be destroyed (s.4B(3)).

11 Other enforcement provisions

A constable or local authority officer (e.g., a dog warden or nominated person) is empowered to seize (Dangerous Dogs Act 1991, s.5)–

   (a) any dog which appears to him to be a dog to which s.1 of the 1991 Act applies and which is in a public place;
   (b) any dog in a public place which appears to him to be a dog to which an order under s.2 of the 1991 Act applies and in respect of which an offence against the order has been or is being committed;
   (c) any dog in any public place (whether or not a dog to which s.2 of the 1991 Act or such an order applies) which appears to him to be dangerously out of control; and
   (d) any dog not in a public place (whether or not a dog to which s.2 of the 1991 Act or such an order applies) which appears to him to be dangerously out of control.

If a justice of the peace is satisfied by information on oath that there are reasonable grounds for believing that an offence under the 1991 Act is being or has been committed or that evidence of the commission of such an offence is to be found, on any premises he may issue a search warrant authorising a constable to enter those premises and seize any dog or any other thing found there which is evidence of the commission of such an offence (s.5(2)).

The Secretary of State has the power under s.7 of the 1991 Act to make an order prescribing the kind of muzzle or lead to be used for the purposes of complying, in the case of a dog of any type, with ss.1 or 2 of the 1991 Act. References to a dog being muzzled are references to its being securely fitted with a muzzle sufficient to prevent it biting any person, and references to its being kept on a lead are references to its being securely held on a lead by a person who is not less than 16 years old.

12 Disqualification from keeping a dog

Where a court makes an order under s.2 of the 1871 Act directing a dog to be destroyed (see **11 Control of dangerous dogs**, above) it may also, if it thinks fit, make an order disqualifying the owner from having custody of a dog for a specified period.

Any person who fails to comply with an order under s.2 of the 1871 Act to keep a dog under proper control or fails to comply with an order to deliver a dog up for destruction commits an offence and a court may disqualify him from having custody of a dog for a specified period (Dangerous Dogs Act 1989, s.1(1), (3), and (7)).

There is a right of appeal to the Crown Court against any order made under s.2 of the 1871 Act or under s.1(1) of the 1989 Act (1989 Act, s.1(2) and (7)).

A person who is disqualified from having custody of a dog by virtue of an order made under s.1(1) or (3) may, at any time after the end of the period of one year beginning with the date of the order, apply for a direction terminating the disqualification. The court may, having regard to the applicant's character, his conduct since the disqualification was imposed, and any other circumstances of the case, grant or refuse such an application. Where such an application is refused, no further application will be entertained for one year from the date of the refusal (1989 Act, s.1(4) and (5)).

13 Injury done by dogs to livestock

Where a dog kills or injures livestock, any keeper of it is liable for the damage unless the livestock is killed or injured on land on which it has strayed by a dog either belonging to the occupier or present on the land with the authority of the occupier (Animals Act 1971 (the 1971 Act), ss.3 and 5(4)). For the purposes of the 1971 Act, livestock means cattle, horses, asses, mules, hinnies, sheep, pigs, goats, and deer not in the wild state, and poultry. Poultry means the domestic varieties of fowls, turkeys, geese, ducks, guinea-fowls, pigeons, peacocks, and quails (1971 Act, s.11).

Under the Dogs (Protection of Livestock) Act 1953, the owner or person in charge of a dog that worries livestock (as defined) on agricultural land is liable to prosecution, but the owner will not be convicted if he proves that the dog was in the charge of some other person, whom he reasonably believed to be a fit and proper person to be in charge of the dog. No offence under the Act is committed if the livestock is trespassing on the land concerned and the dog is owned by, or in the charge of, the occupier or a person authorised by him, provided that the person concerned does not cause the dog to attack the livestock (s.1). A dog found on agricultural land worrying livestock may be seized by a police officer (s.2). For the purposes of this Act, livestock means cattle (i.e., bulls, cows, oxen, heifers, or calves), sheep, goats, swine, horses, asses, mules, or poultry (i.e., domestic fowls, turkeys, geese, or ducks) (s.3(1)).

The Secretary of State also has power, under s.13 of the Animal Health Act 1981, to make orders *inter alia* for the muzzling and keeping of dogs under control and for the seizure and detention of dogs with a view to the prevention of the worrying of animals. The Control of Dogs Order 1992 (made under s.13) provides for the wearing by dogs of collars while in a highway or in a place of public resort, and for exemptions from this requirement.

14 Killing of or injury to dogs worrying livestock

In any civil proceedings against a person for killing or causing injury to a dog, it will be a defence to prove that the defendant was acting for the protection of livestock (as defined by s.11 of the 1971 Act–see **13 Injury done by dogs to livestock**, above) which he was entitled to protect and that notice of the killing or injury was given to the police within 48 hours.

A person is entitled to protect livestock if–

(i) it, or the land on which it is, belongs to him or to a person under whose authority he is acting, and the circumstances are not such that liability for killing or injuring straying livestock would be excluded by s.5(4) of the 1971 Act (see **13 Injury done by dogs to livestock**, above), and

(ii) the dog is worrying or about to worry the livestock and there are no other means of stopping it, or the dog has been worrying livestock, has not left the vicinity and is not under control, and there are no means of ascertaining to whom it belongs.

For the purpose of condition (i), land belongs to a person if he is the occupier (1971 Act, s.9).

15 Fouling

The Dogs (Fouling of Land) Act 1996 was repealed by s.65 of the Clean Neighbourhoods and Environment Act 2005 and replaced by Dog Control Orders under s.55 of the 2005 Act, which provision has now also been repealed and replaced by Public Open Spaces Protection Orders, for which see the Note on **Anti-Social Behaviour in England and Wales**.

16 Microchipping

From April 2016, all keepers of dogs in England and Wales must have their dog microchipped with their and their dog's details recorded on a reunification database (Microchipping of Dogs (England) Regulations 2015, Microchipping of Dogs (Wales) Regulations 2015). For further details see the Note on **Pets: Ownership, Health and Welfare**.

17 Authorities

Statutes–

Animals Act 1971

Animal Health Act 1981

Clean Neighbourhoods and Environment Act 2005

ANIMALS

Dangerous Dogs Acts 1989 and 1991, and Amendment Act 1997

Dogs Act 1871 and 1906 to 1928

Dogs (Protection of Livestock) Act 1953

Environmental Protection Act 1990

Local Government Act 1988

Statutory Instruments–

Control of Dogs Order 1992 (S.I. 1992 No. 901)

Controls on Dogs (Non-application to Designated Land) (Wales) Order 2007 (S.I. 2007 No 701)

Controls on Dogs (Non-application to Designated Land) Order 2009 (S.I. 2009 No 2829)

Dangerous Dogs (Designated Types) Order 1991 (S.I. 1991 No. 1743)

Dangerous Dogs Exemption Schemes (England and Wales) Order 2015 (S.I. 2015 No. 138)

Environmental Protection (Stray Dogs) Regulations 1992 (S.I. 1992 No. 288)

Microchipping of Dogs (England) Regulations 2015 (S.I. 2015 No. 108)

Microchipping of Dogs (Wales) Regulations 2015 (S.I. 2015 No. 1990)

CONTROL OF DOGS: SCOTLAND

1 Introduction

This Note brings together various enactments relating to the control of dogs. In particular, the provisions relating to the control of stray and dangerous dogs, dogs who kill, injure, or worry livestock, and the control and destruction of dogs bred for fighting are described below.

S.37 of the Local Government Act 1988 enables the Secretary of State to provide by regulations for the establishment and administration of a dog registration scheme by local authorities, or such other organisations as he may, after consulting with them, designate.

2 Dog control notices

Each local authority must appoint at least one authorised officer for the purposes of the Control of Dogs (Scotland) Act 2010. If it comes to the attention of such an officer that a dog has, on at least one occasion been out of control (whoever is in charge of the dog at the time), he may serve on the proper person a written "dog control notice" requiring them to bring and keep the dog under control (s.1). The "proper person" is the owner (or if under 16, the person with parental responsibility for the owner), or if the owner is not apparent after reasonable enquiry or it would not be reasonable to serve a notice on them, any person aged at least 16 who appears to have day-to-day charge of the dog.

A dog is "out of control" if (s.1(3))–
   (a))it is not being kept under control effectively and consistently (by whatever means) by the proper person,
   (b) its behaviour gives rise to alarm, or apprehensiveness on the part of any individual for his or some other person's safety, or the safety of an animal other than the dog in question, and
   (c) the individual's alarm or apprehensiveness is, in all the circumstances, reasonable.

A dog control notice may only apply to one dog (s.1(8)).

A notice must require the owner to–
   (d) keep the dog under control;
   (e) keep the authority notified of any change of name or address;
   (f) ensure an electronic transponder is implanted in the dog within 14 days (or satisfy the authority that the dog already has such a device);
   (g) be present and in charge of the dog whenever it is in a public place (or have an entrusted person present and in charge); and
   (h) take such other steps as may be specified by the officer which in his opinion are steps which must be taken if the dog is to be brought and kept under control or would be conducive to so doing.

The form of control notice is prescribed by the Control of Dogs (Scotland) Act 2010 (Prescribed Form of Notice) Order 2011.

An appeal against a notice (or a term of a notice) may be made to the sheriff (s.3). Local authorities are to monitor the effectiveness of such notices and enforce their terms (s.4). Failure to comply with a notice is an offence which may lead to a fine, a disqualification order barring a person from owning or keeping a dog, and the dog's destruction (s.5).

A local authority may discharge a notice of its own accord, or on application by the person subject to it. If it decides not to discharge it, an appeal may be made to the sheriff (s.7).

3 The Scottish dog control database

The Scottish Ministers, after consultation with local authorities and with such other persons as they think appropriate, may by order provide for the establishment, maintenance, operation, management and control of a national database of dog control notices, and for the appointment of a database operator (Control of Dogs (Scotland) Act 2010, s.8).

4 Control of stray dogs

Under the Control of Dogs Order 1992, dogs (other than packs of hounds or dogs being used for sporting purposes, for destroying vermin, or as sheepdogs) must, while on a highway or place of public resort, wear a collar bearing the name and address of the owner.

5 Seizure and delivery of stray dogs

Ss.149 to 151 of the Environmental Protection Act 1990 deal with the control of stray dogs *inter alia* by their seizure and delivery to a local authority officer.

S.149(1) provides for every local authority to appoint an officer for the purpose of discharging the functions imposed or conferred on it by s.149 for dealing with stray dogs found in its area.

"Local authority" for these purposes means the council for a local government area.

Among the functions imposed or conferred by s.149 are the following. Where the officer has reason to believe that any dog found in a public place or on any other land or premises is a stray dog, he must (if practicable) seize the dog and detain it but, where he finds it on land or other premises which is not a public place, only with the consent of the owner or occupier of the land or premises (s.149(3)). Where any dog so seized wears a collar bearing the address of any person, or the owner of the dog is known, the officer must serve on the person whose address is on the collar, or on the owner, a notice in writing stating that the dog has been seized and where it is being kept and stating that the dog will be disposed of if it is not claimed within seven clear days after the service of the notice and the amounts for which he would be liable under s.149(5) (s.149(4)). The amounts for which a person claiming to be the owner of the seized dog is liable (and which he must pay in order to have the dog returned to him) are the amount of the expenses incurred by reason of the dog's detention and such further sum as is for the time being prescribed. The sum of £25 has been prescribed for this purpose by the Environmental Protection (Stray Dogs) Regulations 1992 (the 1992 Regulations).

6 Disposal of stray dogs

Where any dog seized under s.149 of the 1990 Act has been detained for seven clear days after the seizure, or where a notice has been served under s.149(4), seven clear days have elapsed since the service of the notice, and the owner has not claimed the dog and paid the amounts due under s.149(5), the officer may dispose of the dog–
  (a) by selling it or giving it to a person who will, in his opinion, care properly for the dog;
  (b) by selling it or giving it to an establishment for the reception of stray dogs; or
  (c) by destroying it in a manner to cause it as little pain as possible.
No dog seized under s.149 must be sold or given for the purposes of vivisection (s.149(6)).
Where a dog is disposed of under (a) or (b) above to a person acting in good faith, the ownership of the dog will be vested in the recipient (s.149(7)).

7 Register of stray dogs

S.149(8) of the 1990 Act provides that the officer must keep a register of the dogs seized under s.149. The register must contain prescribed particulars which are set out in the 1992 Regulations. The register must be available at all reasonable times for inspection by the public, free of charge. Notwithstanding the foregoing, the officer may cause a dog detained under s.149 to be destroyed before the expiration of the seven-day period mentioned above where he is of the opinion that this should be done to avoid suffering.

8 Duty of person who finds a stray dog

Under s.150 of the 1990 Act, the finder of a stray dog who takes possession of it must forthwith either return the dog to its owner or take it to the officer of the local authority for the area (see **5 Seizure and delivery of stray dogs**, above) in which it was found and must inform the officer of the local authority where the dog was. A dog may also be taken to the police station which is nearest to the place in which it was found.

Where a dog has been taken under s.150 to an officer of a local authority, the dog may be dealt with in either of the following ways.
  (1) If the finder wants to keep the dog, he must inform the officer of the fact and must furnish his name and address, and the officer, having complied with the prescribed procedure, must allow the finder to remove the dog. The 1992 Regulations prescribe the procedure for this purpose; *inter alia* the officer must keep a record containing a brief description of the dog (including any distinctive physical characteristics or markings, tattoos, or scars); the information recorded on a tag or collar worn by or, which is otherwise carried by, the dog; the name and address of the finder. The 1992 Regulations also require the officer where the owner of the dog can be identified and readily contacted, to make reasonable attempts to contact him and afford him a reasonable opportunity to collect the dog. Also, the officer must make all such enquiries as he considers appropriate in the circumstances of the case to ascertain that the finder is a fit and proper person to keep the dog, and that he is able to feed and care for it. The officer must also inform the finder orally and in writing that he is obliged to keep the dog (if unclaimed by the owner) for not less than one month. Failure to comply with that obligation is an offence. A person who keeps a dog by virtue of this provision for a period of two months without its being claimed by the person who has right to it will at the end of that period become the owner of the dog (s.150(4)).
  (2) If the finder does not want to keep the dog, the officer must, unless he has reason to believe that the dog is not a stray, treat it as if it had been seized by him under s.149 (see **5 Seizure and delivery of stray dogs**, above).

9 Prohibition on dogs bred for fighting

S.1 of the Dangerous Dogs Act 1991 makes provision relating to the control and destruction of dogs bred for fighting, namely the pit bull terrier, the Japanese Tosa, and any dog of the type designated by the Secretary of State, being of a type appearing to him to be bred for fighting or to have the characteristics of dogs bred for that purpose. The Dogo Argentino and the Fila Braziliero have been so designated.

S.1(2) of the Act forbids any person to–

(a) breed or breed from such a dog;

(b) sell or exchange such a dog or offer, advertise, or expose, such a dog for sale or exchange;

(c) make or offer to make a gift of such a dog or advertise or expose such a dog as a gift;

(d) allow such a dog of which he is the owner, or of which he is for the time being in charge, to be in a public place without being muzzled and kept on a lead; or

(e) abandon such a dog of which he is the owner or, for the time being in charge of such a dog, allow it to stray.

For the purpose of the 1991 Act, where a dog is owned by a person who is under 16, any reference to its owner includes a reference to the head of the household, if any, of which that person is a member (or, in Scotland, to the person who has his actual care and control).

Contravention of any of the above-mentioned prohibitions is an offence, except that, where paragraphs (b) and (c) above are concerned, no person will be guilty of an offence for publishing an advertisement to the order of another which he did not himself devise, nor will he be convicted if he can also show that he did not know and had no reasonable cause to suspect that the advertisement related to a dog to which the prohibitions apply.

S.2 of the 1991 Act empowers the Secretary of State where it appears to him that dogs of any type to which s.1 above does not apply present a serious danger to the public, by order, to impose in relation to dogs of that type restrictions corresponding, with such modifications, if any, as he thinks appropriate, to all or any of those mentioned in paragraphs (d) and (e) above. He is also empowered to create offences in relation to such dogs.

No-one is allowed to have possession or custody of any dog to which s.1 applies, except in pursuance of the power of seizure conferred by the provisions of the 1991 Act or in accordance with an order for its destruction made under those provisions (s.1(3)).

10 Exemption schemes

The Dangerous Dogs Act 1991 provides that the Secretary of State may provide that the prohibition on possession or custody of a dog bred for fighting is not to apply in such cases and subject to compliance with such conditions as are specified in an exemption scheme (s.1(5)).

Part III of the Dangerous Dogs Compensation and Exemption Schemes Order 1991, sets out the exemption scheme for these purposes. In order to be exempted, the dog must–

(a) be neutered;

(b) be permanently identifiable;

(c) have third party insurance which insures against the death of, or bodily injury caused to any person by the dog (other than a member of the policyholder's family who resides permanently with him or certain employees);

(d) have a certificate of exemption from the Agency (i.e., Heybrush Enterprises Ltd.) all the conditions of which are complied with.

The fee for the certificate of exemption referred to in (d) above is currently £77 plus VAT (Dangerous Dogs (Fees) (Scotland) Order 2013). The conditions to be complied with are that the owner must–

– notify the Agency of any change of address of the dog for 30 days or more, and of its death or export;

– produce the certificates of exemption and insurance when required;

– keep the dog in sufficiently secure conditions to prevent its escape;

– keep the dog muzzled and on a lead when in a public place; and

– provide the Agency with evidence that the dog has been tattooed in the prescribed manner; and, on request to display the dog's tattoo.

The Dangerous Dogs (Amendment) Act 1997, s.4 extends the application of the 1991 Order so that the requirements of the exemption scheme in paragraphs (a) to (d) above now also apply to dogs in respect of which an order has been made under either s.4A(1) or s.4B(3) of the 1991 Act (see **12 Destruction of dangerous dogs**, below).

11 Control of dangerous dogs

Where a dog is out of control and dangerous and serving a dog control notice (see **2 Dog control notices**, above) would be inappropriate, a local authority may apply to a sheriff for the dog's destruction (Control of Dogs (Scotland) Act 2010, s.9).

Where a dog is found to have injured cattle or poultry or chased sheep, it may be dealt with as a dangerous dog under s.9 of the 2010 Act).

Where a court makes an order under s.9 of the 2010 Act directing a dog to be destroyed it must also appoint a person to undertake the dog's destruction and require any person having custody of the dog to deliver it up for that purpose. The court may also, if it thinks fit, make an order disqualifying the owner from having custody of a dog for a specified period (see **14 Disqualification from keeping a dog**, below).

Under s.3(1) of the 1991 Act it is an offence to permit a dog, of any breed, to be dangerously out of control in any place whether or not a public place. A dog is to be regarded as dangerously out of control on any occasion on which there are grounds for reasonable apprehension that it will injure any person or assistance dog, whether or not it actually does so, but references to a dog causing injury or there being grounds for reasonable apprehension that it will do so, do not include references to any case in which the dog is being used for a lawful purpose by a constable or a person in the service of the Crown. The owner of the dog or anyone else who had charge of the dog at the relevant time is made guilty of the offence, and the Act makes it an aggravated offence if whilst out of control, the dog causes injury to any person or assistance dog. It is a defence for the owner of the dog if he was not at the material time in charge of it, to prove that the dog was, at the material time, in the charge of a person whom he reasonably believed to be a fit and proper person to be in charge of it.

A person guilty of an offence of allowing a dog to be dangerously out of control is liable on summary conviction to imprisonment for a term not exceeding six months or a fine not exceeding level 5 on the standard scale or both. A person guilty of an aggravated offence is liable–

(a) on summary conviction, to imprisonment for a term not exceeding six months or a fine not exceeding the statutory maximum or both;

(b) on conviction on indictment, to imprisonment for a term not exceeding two years or a fine or both.

12 Destruction of dangerous dogs

Where a person is convicted of an offence under s.1 of the 1991 Act or an offence under an order made under s.2 of the 1991 Act (see **9 Prohibition on dogs bred for fighting**, above), or under s.3 of the 1991 Act, the court (Dangerous Dogs Act 1991, s.4(1))–

(1) may (and, subject to s.4(1A) below, must, in the case of an offence under s.1 or an aggravated offence under s.3) order the destruction of any dog in respect of which the offence was committed; and

(2) may order the offender to be disqualified, for such a period as the court thinks fit, from having custody of a dog.

However, nothing in s.4(1) requires the court to order a dog's destruction if the court is satisfied that (a) it is not a danger to public safety, and (b) in the case of a dog born before 30th November 1991, there is a good reason why it has not been exempted under the Dangerous Dogs Compensation and Exemption Schemes order 1991 (see **10 Exemption schemes**, above) (s.4(1A)). In deciding whether a dog would constitute a danger to public safety, the court must consider (i) the temperament of the dog and its past behaviour, and (ii) whether the owner of the dog, or the person for the time being in charge of it, is a fit and proper person to be in charge of the dog, and may consider any other relevant circumstances (s.4(1B)).

Where a court makes an order for the destruction of a dog owned by a person other than the offender, the owner may appeal to the Crown Court against the order (in Scotland, appeal must be made within the period of seven days beginning with the date of the order either to the High Court of Justiciary (following a conviction on indictment), or to the Sheriff Appeal Court, (following a summary conviction)) (s.4(2), (9)). A dog must not be destroyed until the end of the period for giving notice of appeal against the conviction or against the order (in Scotland, until the end of the period of seven days beginning with the date of the order); and if notice of appeal is given within that period, until the appeal is determined or withdrawn and unless the offender, and if different, the owner of the dog gives notice to the court that made the order that there is to be no appeal (s.4(3), (9)). Where a court makes an order for the destruction of a dog, it may appoint a person to undertake the destruction of the dog and require any person having custody of it to deliver it up for that purpose and order the offender to pay such sum as the court may determine to be the reasonable expenses of destroying the dog and of keeping it pending its destruction (s.4(4)).

Any person who is disqualified may, at any time after the end of the period of one year beginning with the date of the order, apply to the court that made it (or a magistrates' court acting for the same petty sessions area as that court) for a direction terminating the disqualification (s.4(6)). The court may having regard to the applicant's character, his conduct since the disqualification was imposed and any other circumstances of the case, grant or refuse the application; and order the applicant to pay all or any part of the costs of the application. Where an application is refused no further application can be made before the end of the period of one year beginning with the date of the refusal (s.4(7)).

Where a person is convicted of an offence under s.1 or an aggravated offence under s.3 above, but the court does not order the dog's destruction, the court must order that, unless the dog is exempted under the Dangerous Dogs Compensation and Exemption Scheme Order 1991 (see **10 Exemption schemes**, above) from the prohibition contained in s.1(3) within a two month period (which the court may extend) it must be destroyed (s.4A(1) to (3)).

Where a person is convicted under s.3 of the offence of permitting a dog to be dangerously out of control (see above), the court may order that, unless the dog's owner keeps it under proper control, it will be destroyed. The court may specify measures that should be taken to control the dog (e.g., muzzling) and, if the dog is male, may require it to be neutered (s.4A(4) and (5)).

Where a dog is seized under s.5 (see below), and it appears to a sheriff that no one is to be prosecuted (whether because the owner cannot be found or any other reason), or that the dog cannot be released into the owner's custody without the owner contravening s.1(3) of the Act (see **9 Prohibition on dogs bred for fighting**, above), he may still order the destruction of the dog and, subject to s.4B(2), must do so if the dog is of a fighting breed described in s.1 (s.4B(1)). However, the sheriff need not order the dog's destruction if he is satisfied (a) that the dog is not a danger to the public, or (b) that, in the case of a dog born before 30th November 1991, there is a good reason why the dog has not been exempted under the above Compensation and Exemption

Schemes Order (s.4B(2)). In the case of a dog to which (b) applies, the sheriff must order that, unless the dog obtains exemption under the Order (see **10 Exemption schemes**, above) within a two month period, it will be destroyed (s.4B(3)).

13 Other enforcement provisions

A constable or local authority officer (e.g., a dog warden or nominated person) is empowered to seize (Dangerous Dogs Act 1991, s.5)–

(a) any dog which appears to him to be a dog to which s.1 of the 1991 Act applies and which is in a public place;

(b) any dog in a public place which appears to him to be a dog to which an order under s.2 of the 1991 Act applies and in respect of which an offence against the order has been or is being committed;

(c) any dog in any public place (whether or not a dog to which s.2 of the 1991 Act or such an order applies) which appears to him to be dangerously out of control;

(d) any dog not in a public place (whether or not a dog to which s.2 of the 1991 Act or such an order applies) which appears to him to be dangerously out of control.

If a justice of the peace or sheriff is satisfied by evidence on oath, that there are reasonable grounds for believing that an offence under the 1991 Act is being or has been committed or that evidence of the commission of such an offence is to be found, on any premises he may issue a search warrant authorising a constable to enter those premises and seize any dog or any other thing found there which is evidence of the commission of such an offence (s.5(2)).

The Secretary of State has the power under s.7 of the 1991 Act to make an order prescribing the kind of muzzle or lead to be used for the purposes of complying, in the case of a dog of any type, with ss.1 or 2 of the 1991 Act. References to a dog being muzzled are references to its being securely fitted with a muzzle sufficient to prevent it biting any person, and references to its being kept on a lead are references to its being securely held on a lead by a person who is not less than 16 years old.

14 Disqualification from keeping a dog

Under the Control of Dogs (Scotland) Act 2010, a court may disqualify a person from owning or keeping a dog where they fail to comply with a dog control notice (s.5(2)(a)) or when a dog which they have owned or kept is ordered to be destroyed (s.9(5)). Application for a disqualification to be discharged may be made to the court which made the order, and if refused an appeal may be made to the Sheriff Appeal Court or sheriff principal, as appropriate (s.11).

15 Injury done by dogs to livestock

Under the Dogs Acts 1906 the owners of a dog will be liable for injury done to any cattle or poultry by that dog. The person seeking damages will not be required to show a previous mischievous propensity in the dog, or to show negligence on the part of the owner. The occupier of any premises where the dog was kept or permitted to live or remain at the time the injury was suffered will be presumed to be the owner of the dog, unless he proves he was not the owner of the dog at that time (s.1). The expression "cattle" includes horses, mules, asses, sheep, goats, and swine; and "poultry" includes domestic fowls, turkeys, geese, ducks, guinea-fowls, pigeons, pheasants, and partridges (s.7).

The Secretary of State also has power, under s.13 of the Animal Health Act 1981, to make orders *inter alia* for the muzzling and keeping of dogs under control and for the seizure and detention of dogs with a view to the prevention of the worrying of animals. The Control of Dogs Order 1992 (made under s.13) provides for the wearing by dogs of collars while in a highway or in a place of public resort, and for exemptions from this requirement.

16 Killing of or injury to dogs worrying livestock

In any civil proceedings against a person for killing or causing injury to a dog, it will be a defence to prove that the defendant was acting for the protection of livestock which he was entitled to protect and that notice of the killing or injury was given to the police within 48 hours (Civic Government (Scotland) Act 1982, s.129).

A person is entitled to protect livestock if–

(i) it, or the land on which it is, belongs to him or to a person under whose authority he is acting, and the circumstances are not such that the livestock was killed or injured on land on to which it had strayed and either the dog belonged to the occupier or its presence on the land was authorised by the occupier; and

a person killing or causing injury to a dog will be deemed to act for the protection of any livestock if–

(ii) the dog is worrying or about to worry the livestock and there are no other means of stopping it, or the dog has been worrying livestock, has not left the vicinity and is not under control, and there are no means of ascertaining to whom it belongs.

17 Fouling–Scotland

In Scotland provision as to dog fouling is made by the Dog Fouling (Scotland) Act 2003. If a dog defecates on any land as defined under s.2, it will be an offence for the person in charge of the dog at the time to fail to remove the faeces from the land unless (i) he has a reasonable excuse for failing to do so, or (ii) the owner, occupier or other person controlling the land has consented (generally or specifically) to his failing to do so (s.1).

The Act applies to any public open place, other than agricultural land (s.2). This includes any covered place open to the air on at least one side.

No offence is committed by (s.3)–

(a) a blind person in charge of a dog being used for that person's guidance;

(b) a person in charge of a working dog being used for the driving or tending of sheep or cattle;

(c) a person in charge of any dog being used on official duties by a member of the armed forces, HM Revenue and Customs, or the police;

(d) a person in charge of a dog being used in emergency rescue work; or

(e) a disabled person with a physical impairment which affects their mobility, manual dexterity, physical co-ordination or ability to lift, carry or otherwise move everyday objects, who is in charge of a dog trained to assist the person with any such impairment.

Enforcement is by means of fixed penalty notices issued by the local authority or the police. Every local authority must appoint at least one person to issue such notices in their area (ss.4 and 5). The amount of the fixed penalty is 20% of Level 1 on the standard scale or such other amount as the Scottish Ministers may prescribe. 20% of Level 1 is currently £40. The penalty is payable to the local authority. A penalty which remains unpaid 28 days after the penalty notice was issued, is increased by a further 10% of Level 1 (i.e., by £20). A person served with a penalty notice may request a hearing from the local authority (s.8) and a penalty will not be increased whilst a hearing is pending. If the authority (or police) determine that the offence to which the notice relates was not committed, or that the notice should not have been issued to the person named in it, then it may be withdrawn and any fixed penalty which has been paid must be repaid (s.13).

18 Authorities

Statutes–

Animal Health Act 1981

Civic Government (Scotland) Act 1982

Control of Dogs (Scotland) Act 2010

Dangerous Dogs Acts 1989 and 1991, and Amendment Act 1997

Dog Fouling (Scotland) Act 2003

Dogs Act 1871 and 1906 to 1928

Environmental Protection Act 1990

Local Government Act 1988

Statutory Instruments–

Control of Dogs Order 1992 (S.I. 1992 No. 901)

Control of Dogs (Scotland) Act 2010 (Prescribed Form of Notice) Order 2011 (S.S.I. 2011 No. 39)

Dangerous Dogs Compensation and Exemption Schemes Order 1991, as amended (S.I. 1991 Nos. 1744, 2297, and 2636)

Dangerous Dogs (Designated Types) Order 1991 (S.I. 1991 No. 1743)

Dangerous Dogs (Fees) (Scotland) Order 2013 (S.S.I. 2013 No. 178)

Environmental Protection (Stray Dogs) Regulations 1992 (S.I. 1992 No. 288)

PETS: OWNERSHIP, HEALTH AND WELFARE

1 Contents

This Note deals with a number of matters concerning the ownership of pets, including—
  A: Pets shops and the sale and keeping of pets
  B: Dangerous pets
  C: Animal boarding and breeding establishments
  D: Rabies and quarantine
  E: Pets—entering the UK from abroad
For provisions concerning the control of dogs and the keeping of certain breeds of dangerous dogs, see the Note on **Control of Dogs**.

A: PET SHOPS AND THE SALE AND KEEPING OF PETS

2 Regulation of pet shops

The Pet Animals Act 1951 regulates the sale of pets in pet shops and elsewhere.

S.1 of the Act provides that no person may keep a pet shop (whether on commercial premises or in a private house) without a licence granted by the local authority. In deciding whether to grant a licence, the authority must have regard to the need to ensure that—
  (a) animals will be kept in suitable accommodation;
  (b) they will be adequately supplied with food and drink;
  (c) mammals will not be sold too young;
  (d) all reasonable precautions will be taken to prevent the spread of disease; and
  (e) steps will be taken to guard against fire or other emergencies.

Licences may be granted subject to conditions and an appeal lies to a magistrates' court against the refusal of a licence or against any condition contained in it.

The prohibition in s.1 does not apply to the keeping or selling of pedigree animal bred by the person himself, or the sale of the offspring of a pet animal (s.7).

A local authority may authorise any of its officers or any vet to inspect licensed pet shops in its area (s.4).

Where a person is convicted of an offence under the Act or certain other legislation relating to the keeping of animals the court may disqualify them, for such period as it thinks fit, from holding a pet shop licence (s.5).

S.2 of the Pet Animals Act 1951 makes it an offence to sell animals as pets in a street or public place or from a market stall.

The Breeding and Sale of Dogs (Welfare) Act 1999 provides that the keeper of a licensed pet shop is guilty of an offence if he removes a dog's collar with its identity tag or badge (see **13 Offences**, below) before sale (s.8(3)).

3 Sale of puppies and kittens—Scotland

In Scotland, people who sell young cats or dogs under 84 days of age must obtain a licence from a local authority. Pet dealers who do not live in Scotland can obtain a licence from the City of Edinburgh Council. A licence lasts for a maximum of three years. A licence is not required (Licensing of Animal Dealers (Young Cats and Young Dogs) (Scotland) Regulations 2009, Reg. 3)—
  (i) by a person who holds a breeding licence granted under the Breeding of Dogs Act 1973;
  (ii) by a person who holds a pet shop licence granted under the Pet Animals Act 1951;
  (iii) in relation to the sale of a young cat or dog kept at an animal sanctuary, animal rehabilitation centre or an animal re-homing centre;
  (iv) in relation to the sale by a person of the offspring of a cat or dog kept by that person as a pet; or
  (v) by a person who sells no more than two young cats or two young dogs (or one of each) in any 12 month period.
A licence will include the following mandatory conditions, namely that the licence holder (Reg. 8)—
  (a) must not, without reasonable excuse, keep a cat or dog which is less than eight weeks of age at any time unless it is accompanied by its mother;
  (b) must not keep more than the maximum permitted number of animals;
  (c) must ensure that all young cats and dogs acquired by him (i) receive a physical examination by a vet within 24 hours of his acquiring them; (ii) have a unique number assigned to them to allow them to be individually identified; and (iii) are accompanied by a written record containing specified information;
  (d) must ensure that any disease or parasitic infection of a young cat or dog is treated within 24 hours of identification, whether after the physical examination by a vet or otherwise;
  (e) must retain for no less than three years from the date of sale of a young cat or dog a copy of the written record referred to in (c)(iii) above;
  (f) must ensure that the licensing authority is permitted to inspect at any reasonable time any place or equipment used in, or in connection with, the acquisition, sale, transport or keeping of animals to which

the licence relates and any documents held by or on behalf of the licence holder relating to such animals;

(g) must accede to any reasonable request for information from the licensing authority relating to the undertaking by the licence holder of any activities referred to in (c) above;

(h) must provide the number of the animal dealing licence which he holds and the name and telephone number of the licensing authority in any advertisement or information issued by or on his behalf; and

(i) must, prior to delivery of a young cat or dog to a purchaser, exhibit the animal dealing licence (or a copy) to the purchaser.

A licence holder who acquires a young cat or dog which is to be sold must keep the animal separately from any other animal kept by him for not less than 10 days from the date of acquisition (Reg. 15). The animal must be examined by a vet during the first 24 hours of this period.

A licence holder must transport a young cat or dog directly from the premises specified in the animal dealing licence to its purchaser in Scotland (Reg. 16).

These provisions are enforced by the local authority.

4 Offering animals as prizes

In Scotland, it is an offence to offer or give an animal as a prize (except where offered or given in a family context) (Animal Health and Welfare (Scotland) Act 2006, s.31).

In England and Wales it is, subject to limited exceptions, an offence to enter into an arrangement with a person reasonably believed to be under 16, who is not accompanied by an adult, whereby an animal is to be won as a prize (Animal Welfare Act 2006, s.11).

5 Pets not to be sold to children

In England and Wales, it is an offence to sell an animal as a pet to anyone whom the seller has reasonable cause to believe is under the age of 16 (Animal Welfare Act 2006, s.11).

In Scotland, it is an offence to sell an animal to anyone under the age of 16 (Animal Health and Welfare (Scotland) Act 2006, s.30).

6 Electronic collars–Wales

In Wales, it is an offence to attach an electronic collar (i.e., one designed to administer an electric shock) to a dog or cat, or to cause such a collar to be used or be responsible for a dog or cat wearing such a collar (Animal Welfare (Electronic Collars) (Wales) Regulations 2010).

7 Codes of practice

A number of codes of practice have been made under the Animal Welfare Act 2006. A person's failure to comply with a provision of a code of practice does not of itself render him liable to proceedings of any kind, however in any proceedings against a person for an offence under the 2006 Act or regulations made under it–

(a) failure to comply with a relevant provision of a code of practice may be relied upon as tending to establish liability; and

(b) compliance with a relevant provision of such a code of practice may be relied upon as tending to negative liability.

For England, codes of practice have been issued in respect of the–

 − Welfare of Privately Kept Non-Human Primates;
 − Welfare of Cats;
 − Welfare of Dogs; and
 − Welfare of Horses, Ponies, Donkeys and their Hybrids.

B: DANGEROUS PETS

8 Dangerous wild animals as pets

The Dangerous Wild Animals Act 1976 prohibits the keeping of dangerous wild animals, except under the authority of a licence granted by a local authority. Exceptions apply in the case of licensed zoos, licensed pet shops (see 2 **Regulation of pet shops**, above), circuses and certain scientific premises (ss.1 and 5). The Schedule to the 1976 Act lists the wild animals that are classified as "dangerous" for the purposes of the Act. The list includes dangerous snakes and spiders; crocodiles and alligators; badgers; non-domesticated cattle; sheep and goats; and monkeys and apes.

An application for a licence for keeping dangerous wild animals must specify the species of animal and the number of each species that the applicant wishes to keep and the premises where they will be kept. No-one under 18 may apply for a licence.

A licence will not be granted unless an authority is satisfied that–

(a) the applicant is a suitable person to hold such a licence;

(b) any animal will be kept in secure and suitable accommodation and will be supplied with adequate food, drink and bedding;

(c) the animal will be able to exercise (where appropriate);

(d) proper steps will be taken to protect the animal in case of fire or other emergency; and

(e) all reasonable precautions will be taken to prevent and control the spread of infectious disease.

A licence will come into force immediately upon being granted and will remain in force for two years (s.2 as amended by the Legislative Reform (Dangerous Wild Animals) (Licensing) Order 2010).

9 Microchipping—England and Wales

From April 2016, all keepers of dogs in England and Wales must have their dog microchipped with their and their dog's details recorded on a reunification database (Microchipping of Dogs (England) Regulations 2015, Microchipping of Dogs (Wales) Regulations 2015).

The duty is imposed on every "keeper" of a dog. A dog breeder is considered the first keeper of a puppy if the breeder owns the bitch that gave birth to the puppy. Accordingly the breeder is under a duty to have such a puppy microchipped. In relation to an assistance dog, until the dog stops working as an assistance dog, the body responsible for its training and allocation is the keeper; after the dog has stopped working as an assistance dog, the person with whom it normally resides will be the keeper.

Where a dog is transferred to a new keeper, the new keeper must, unless the previous keeper has already done so, record their full name, address and contact telephone number (if any) and any change in the dog's name with the database on which the dog's details are recorded. From 6th April 2016 no keeper may transfer a dog to a new keeper until it has been microchipped unless they have a certificate from a vet stating that the dog should not be microchipped for reasons of the animal's health (Reg. 8(2)).

An authorised person may (Reg. 12)—

(a) serve on the keeper of a dog which is not microchipped a notice requiring him to have the dog microchipped within 21 days;

(b) where the keeper of a dog has failed to comply with such a notice, without the consent of the keeper—
   (i) arrange for the dog to be microchipped; and
   (ii) recover the cost of doing so from him;

(c) take possession of a dog without the consent of the keeper for the purpose of checking whether it is microchipped or for the purpose of microchipping it.

An authorised person for these purposes is a police or community support officer, or any person authorised by the Secretary of State, Welsh Ministers or a local authority (Reg. 11).

Offences are generally punishable with a fine not exceeding Level 2 on the standard scale (as to the standard scale, see the Notes on **Treatment of Offenders**).

10 Dangerous dogs

Provisions relating to the Dangerous Dogs Acts will be found in the Notes on **Control of Dogs**.

C: ANIMAL BOARDING AND BREEDING ESTABLISHMENTS

11 Boarding establishments

The Animal Boarding Establishments Act 1963 regulates the keeping of boarding establishments for looking after other people's cats and dogs.

Under s.1 of the Act, no person may keep a boarding establishment for animals without a licence issued by the appropriate local authority. Anyone disqualified from keeping such an establishment, from keeping a pet shop (see **2 Regulation of pet shops**, above), or from having custody of animals (i.e., because they have been convicted of cruelty to an animal) will not be granted a licence. If a person already holds a licence, they may lose it if they are convicted of an offence under certain legislation relating to animals, and may be disqualified from holding a licence for such time as the court thinks fit.

In deciding whether to grant a licence, an authority must have regard in particular to the need to ensure that the animals will be suitable accommodated, fed, exercised and protected from disease and fire and that a proper register of animals with arrival and departure dates is kept.

It is an offence to keep a boarding establishment without a licence or to fail to comply with licence conditions.

A local authority may authorise any of its officers or any vet to inspect licensed boarding establishments and any such person has powers of entry and inspection at reasonable times (s.2).

12 Breeding of dogs

The Breeding of Dogs Act 1973, as amended by the Breeding and Sale of Dogs (Welfare) Act 1999 (which does not apply in Wales, see below), provides that it is an offence to keep a breeding establishment for dogs (i.e., any premises, including a private house, where the business of breeding dogs for sale is carried on) without a licence granted by the local authority. People who are disqualified from keeping such an establishment or are disqualified from keeping a pet shop or boarding establishment (see **2 Regulation of pet shops**, and **11 Boarding establishments**, above) or from having custody of an animal will not be granted licences (s.1).

In deciding whether to grant a licence, an authority must have regard to the need to secure that (s.1(4))–

(a) the dog will be suitably accommodated, fed, attended to, exercised, and visited;

(b) the dog will be protected from disease and fire;

(c) appropriate steps will be taken to ensure that dogs will be properly looked after when being taken to and from the establishment;

(d) bitches do not give birth to more than six litters each and do not give birth more than once a year.

Accurate records must be kept (s.1(4)(h)) and the Breeding of Dogs (Licensing Records) Regulations 1999 and the corresponding Scottish Regulations prescribe the form that such records must take. Any licence granted must contain conditions that will ensure that these objectives are attained.

On an application for a new licence, the authority must arrange for the premises to be inspected both by a vet and by an officer of the authority. In any other case, they must arrange for one or other of the two to inspect the premises (s.1(2A)). Following such an inspection, the authority must arrange for a report to be made about the premises, the applicant, and any other relevant matter and must consider that report before deciding whether to grant a licence (s.1(2B)).

In Wales the requirements concerning the licensing of persons involved in the breeding of dogs are contained in the Animal Welfare (Breeding of Dogs) (Wales) Regulations 2014 which replace the requirements contained in the Breeding of Dogs Act 1973. Subject to qualifying criteria (i.e. if a person is disqualified from keeping a boarding establishment), any person wishing to breed dogs in Wales must obtain a licence from their local authority under the Regulations. A person who breeds dogs without a licence commits an offence under s.13(6) of the Animal Welfare Act 2006 and is liable to imprisonment for a term of up to six months, a fine or both (Reg. 22). The Regulations are enforced by the local authority (Reg. 27). Any person who is aggrieved by the refusal to grant or renew, or the decision to revoke, a licence may appeal to a magistrates' court within 28 days beginning with the day following the date on which the decision is notified (Reg. 19). Subject to certain exclusions concerning, for example, scientific procedures a person carries on the activity of dog breeding for these purposes if that person keeps on premises three or more breeding bitches and (Reg. 5)–

(i) breeds on those premises three or more litters of puppies in any twelve month period;

(ii) advertises for sale from those premises a puppy or puppies born from three or more litters of puppies for sale in any twelve month period;

(iii) supplies from those premises a puppy or puppies born from three or more litters of puppies in any twelve month period; or

(iv) advertises a business of breeding or selling puppies from those premises.

To apply for a licence an applicant must submit (Reg. 7)–

(v) an application in a form and manner approved by the local authority;

(vi) a draft enhancement and enrichment programme;

(vii) a draft socialisation programme;

(viii) details of the anticipated number of adult dogs and puppies to be present on the premises at any one time; and

(ix) such supporting documentation as the authority reasonably requires.

The applicant must also pay any appropriate fee (Reg. 12).

13 Offences

It is an offence to keep a boarding establishment without a licence or to fail to comply with any licence conditions. A local authority may authorise any of its officers or a vet to inspect licensed premises (s.2). The Breeding of Dogs Act 1991 authorises justices of the peace to issue warrants authorising the search of premises by officers of the local authority or by a vet if there are reasonable grounds for suspecting that an unlicensed breeding establishment for dogs is being carried on (s.1).

The keeper of a licensed dog breeding establishment is guilty of an offence if he (s.8(1))–

(a) sells a dog other than at a licensed breeding establishment, licensed pet shop, or a Scottish rearing establishment;

(b) sells a dog otherwise than to the keeper of a licensed pet shop or Scottish rearing establishment knowing or believing that the animal will be resold;

(c) sells a dog less than eight weeks old otherwise than to a licensed pet shop or Scottish rearing establishment;

(d) sells to the keeper of a licensed pet shop or Scottish rearing establishment a dog not born at a licensed breeding establishment; or

(e) sells to the keeper of a licensed pet shop or Scottish rearing establishment a dog which, when delivered, is not wearing a collar with an identity tag or badge indicating the breeding establishment at which it was born and other prescribed information (see below).

Similar duties are placed on the keepers of Scottish rearing establishments (s.8(2)).

The keeper of a licensed pet shop is guilty of an offence if he removes a dog's collar with its identity tag or badge before sale (s.8(3)).

For the purposes of s.8, the Sale of Dogs (Identification Tag) Regulations and the corresponding Scottish

ANIMALS

Regulations prescribe additional information that must be displayed on an identity tag or badge. This additional information consists of the dog's date of birth and the identifying number, if any, allocated by the breeding establishment at which it was born.

D: RABIES AND QUARANTINE

14 Quarantine for imported animals

Under the Animal Health Act 1981 Orders may be made for the purpose of preventing the introduction of rabies into Great Britain. An Order may require animals capable of carrying rabies to be quarantined.

The Rabies (Importation of Dogs, Cats and Other Mammals) Order 1974, treated as made under the 1981 Act, controls the landing from abroad of dogs, cats and certain other mammals.

Note.–Pet animals are not subject to the requirements of the Rabies Order if they meet the requirements of EU Regulation No 576/2013 and the Non-Commercial Movement of Pet Animals Order 2011: see E: PETS–ENTERING THE UK FROM ABROAD, below.

The Rabies Order provides that a licence must be obtained before an animal may be landed in Great Britain (Art. 4). Only specified ports and airports may be used (including the Channel Tunnel), although in exceptional circumstances or in an emergency other ports and airports may be used.

Immediately on landing, the animal must be handed over to an authorised carrying agent and quarantined for four months at its owner's expense at such premises and subject to such conditions as may be specified in the licence (Art. 5). The above does not apply to certain animals where a licence has been granted for them to be used in scientific research or for them to be brought into a zoo. The Secretary of State (or Scottish or Welsh Ministers) may authorise the release of an animal from quarantine, or waive its period of quarantine, if satisfied that such a release will present negligible risk of the introduction of rabies into or spread of rabies within Great Britain. Only authorised premises may be used for quarantine and during the quarantine period a dog or cat must be vaccinated against rabies at its owner's expense unless it has already been vaccinated and blood tested in connection with the pet travel scheme (Art. 6). Whilst in quarantine, an animal may not normally be moved from the authorised premises except to similar premises (Art. 7).

If an animal is not detained and quarantined as required, or there is reason to believe that an animal has been landed in Great Britain in contravention of the Order, an inspector may require the animal to be quarantined immediately. An inspector may also seize and destroy any animal landed in contravention of the Order (Art. 13).

It is an offence to land or attempt to land in Great Britain an animal the landing of which is prohibited, or to fail to comply with the provisions of the Order or of any licence (Art. 16).

A constable may arrest without a warrant a person whom he reasonably suspects to be committing or to have committed an offence in breach of an Order. Constables also have power to enter, by force if necessary, any boat, aircraft or vehicle to search for animals (Animal Health Act 1981, s.62).

E: PETS–ENTERING THE UK FROM ABROAD

15 The Pet Travel Scheme: introduction

The Non-Commercial Movement of Pet Animals Order 2011, made under EC Regulation No. 998/2003 (itself now repealed and replaced by EU Regulation No. 576/2013), creates certain exemptions from the requirements for pets to be quarantined under the Rabies (Importation of Dogs, Cats and Other Mammals) Order 1974 (see **14 Quarantine for imported animals**, above). Wild animals cannot be moved under these provisions. The animals covered by these provisions are defined in EU Regulation No. 576/2013 as (Annex 1)–

(i) domestic dogs and domestic cats (Part A of Annex 1);
(ii) ferrets (Part A of Annex 1); and
(iii) invertebrates (except bees, bumble bees, molluscs and crustaceans), ornamental aquatic animals, amphibia, reptiles, birds (except poultry covered by other EU legislation), rodents, and rabbits (other than those intended for food production) [set out in Part B of Annex 1 but not covered by the following paragraphs].

The rules (the Pet Travel Scheme), as described in the following paragraphs, are complicated but in essence for a dog, cat or ferret (a pet animal of a species listed in Part A of Annex 1) to be admitted to Great Britain from an approved country (see **18 Approved countries**, below) without quarantine it must–

(a) be microchipped (or identified by a tattoo which was applied on or before 3rd July 2011) and vaccinated against rabies;
(b) the vaccination must have been *after* the pet was microchipped and administered as per the vaccine manufacturer's data sheet;
  Note.–for any documents issued after the 29th December 2014 the animal must be at least 12 weeks old before the completion of the initial vaccination course.
(c) the pet must have an EU Pet Passport or Official Veterinary Health Certificate from a vet certifying the microchip and vaccination;
(d) at least 21 days must have passed since the vaccination (the day of vaccination counts as day 0 not day 1);
(e) entry to Great Britain must be by an approved route and with an approved transport company;

17

(f) a dog must have been treated for the *Echinococcus multilocularis* (EM) tapeworm between 1 and 5 days before its arrival and the treatment must have been recorded in its passport or Official Health Certificate.

For travel from any other country (an unlisted country), the requirements are—

(g) as (a) to (c) above;

(h) a blood sample for a blood test must have been taken at least 30 days after vaccination and the pet must have passed the blood test;

(i) the EU Pet Passport or Official Veterinary Health Certificate must certify the microchip, vaccination and blood test result;

(j) a waiting period of three months must have passed since the date the blood sample was taken; and

(k) as (e) and (f) above

Note.—If a pet was successfully blood tested and issued with an EU pet passport before it left Great Britain or other EU country to go to an unlisted country, the three-month waiting period before re-entering Great Britain will not apply (but all other rules still apply, including the requirement for the blood sample to be taken at least 30 days after vaccination).

The number of pets that can be moved between EU Member States – including into and out of Great Britain – under EU Regulation No. 576/2013 is limited to five per person, unless they are taking part in a competition, show or sporting event (see below). If a person has more than five pets there are additional rules, these include: travelling from a registered premises; using an authorised transporter; and registering the movement on the TRACES system. If a person is travelling with pets (aged over six months) and has written evidence that they are registered to attend a show, competition or sporting event, or training for such an event, they can continue to travel under the Pet Travel Scheme.

The Scheme applies to all dogs, cats and ferrets travelling with their owners. If a person brings a dog, cat or ferret into Great Britain in order to sell it or pass it to a new owner, it cannot travel under the Scheme. If the journey began outside the EU that person must sign a declaration confirming that they do not intend to sell or transfer ownership of the pet. The format of the declaration is contained in Annex IV to Implementing EU Regulation No. 577/2013 on the model identification documents for the non-commercial movement of dogs, cats and ferrets, the establishment of lists of territories and third countries and the format, layout and language requirements of the declarations attesting compliance with certain conditions provided for in EU Regulation No. 576/2013.

If a person is not able to accompany their pet then they (or a person they have authorised in writing) must travel within five days of the pet's movement. This rule applies both to travel within the EU and for movements from outside the EU.

Note.—The commercial movements of pets and the health status of pets being transported for commerce or trade is covered under the Balai Directive 92/65.

16 When quarantine is not required

Under the Non-Commercial Movement of Pet Animals Order 2011 as read with EU Regulation No. 576/2013, domestic dogs, domestic cats and ferrets may be brought into Great Britain from an EU Member State or a permitted country (see **18 Approved countries**, below) without being quarantined if the animal—

(a) is identified (see **19 Identification of animals**, below);

(b) has been vaccinated against rabies;

(c) in the case of dogs and cats from Malaysia, has been microchipped and has a health certificate in respect of Nipah disease;

(d) in the case of cats from Australia, has been microchipped and has a health certificate in respect of Hendra disease; and

(e) in the case of a dog, complies with specified requirements as to *Echinococcus multilocularis* (tapeworm).

17 Means of transport and approved routes

Dogs, cats and ferrets brought into Great Britain must be brought in using an approved carrier (Non-Commercial Movement of Pet Animals Order 2011, Art. 11). Carriers must be approved by the Animal and Plant Health Agency and must comply with strict requirements.

Only certain (approved) routes can be used to bring pet dogs, cats and ferrets into Great Britain under the Pet Travel Scheme. The routes are approved by the Animal and Plant Health Agency.

18 Approved countries

The approved countries from which dogs, cats and ferrets will not be quarantined, provided they have been microchipped and vaccinated against rabies, are contained in Implementing EU Regulation No. 577/2013 on the model identification documents for the non-commercial movement of dogs, cats and ferrets, the establishment of lists of territories and third countries and the format, layout and language requirements of the declarations attesting compliance with certain conditions provided for in EU Regulation No. 576/2013 as follows (Annex II)—

(a) EU Member States;

(b) Andorra, Faroes Islands, Greenland, Iceland, Liechtenstein, Monaco, Norway, San Marino, Switzerland or the Vatican; and

(c) Antigua and Barbuda, Argentina, Aruba, Ascension, Australia, Azores, Bahrain, Barbados, Belarus, Bermuda, Bonaire, St Eustatius and Saba (the BES Islands), Bosnia and Herzegovina, British Virgin Islands, Canada, Cayman Islands, Chile, Curaçao, Falkland Islands, Fiji, French Polynesia, Guam, Hawaii, Hong Kong, Jamaica, Japan, Malaysia, Macedonia, Mauritius, Mayotte, Mexico, Montserrat, New Caledonia, New Zealand, Russian Federation, St Helena, St Kitts and Nevis, St Lucia, St Maarten, St Pierre et Miquelon, St Vincent and the Grenadines, Singapore, Taiwan, Trinidad and Tobago, United Arab Emirates, the USA, Vanuatu, and Wallis and Fortuna.

19 Identification of animals

All dogs, cats and ferrets must have a microchip implanted in their bodies and the carrier must have adequate facilities for checking pets.

The minimum qualifications for microchipping of dogs, cats and ferrets for the purposes of pet travel between Member States and third countries are set out in the Non-Commercial Movement of Pet Animals Order 2011. *Inter alia*, the requirements are that the person be a veterinary surgeon or a veterinary nurse acting under the direction of a veterinary surgeon, or a student of veterinary surgery or a student veterinary nurse and in either case are acting under the direction of a veterinary surgeon. Adequate training and assessment concerning implantation is also required (Art. 10A).

20 Health of animals

After being microchipped, the animal must have been vaccinated against rabies. Vaccination must take place after the age of three months and any necessary booster injection must also have been given. Following vaccination, and at least six months before it is brought into Great Britain, the animal's blood must be tested for rabies antibodies. The Minister (or the Scottish or Welsh Ministers) will publish a list of recognised laboratories to carry out such tests.

In addition to the above requirements, dogs must also be treated by a vet for tapeworm between 48 and 24 hours prior to embarkation for Great Britain (unless coming from Finland, Ireland, Malta or Norway).

21 Documentation

A dog, cat or ferret entering Great Britain from another EU Member State must be accompanied by a pet passport issued by an authorised vet or third country certificate issued by an official vet. A new style passport was introduced in December 2014, however, existing passports still remain valid for the lifetime of the pet. Therefore, if a person already has a passport for their pet they do not need to get a new one.

The passport must be stamped and signed by a vet to show that the animal has been vaccinated against rabies and is free of ticks (see **20 Health of animals**, above). A dog, cat or ferret entering Great Britain from a permitted country outside the EU (i.e., one of the countries listed in (b) and (c) of **18 Approved countries**, above) must be accompanied by a Third Country Health Certificate giving this information.

The Animal and Plant Health Agency approves carriers who may bring animals into Great Britain and agrees with them a "Required Method of Operation". Under this, the carrier, after carrying out the necessary checks, must give the person in charge of the animal a certificate stating that the animal complies with the provisions of the Non-Commercial Movement of Pet Animals Order 2011 and EU Regulation No. 576/2013. *Guidance for Authorised Pet Carriers and Checkers from 29th December 2014* has been produced and is available at <www.gov.uk/government/uploads/system/uploads/attachment_data/file/382820/pets-checks-pt44.pdf>.

22 Duties at port of arrival

Anyone importing a dog, cat or ferret must produce, on demand, all required health certificates (see **21 Documentation**, above). An authorised officer may carry out any necessary checks and searches to ensure compliance with these provisions.

23 Enforcement

Local authorities are responsible for enforcing the Non-Commercial Movement of Pet Animals Order 2011 (Art. 13). Note that the Common Council of the City of London is the enforcement authority for all London boroughs (Art. 3).

24 Guidance

Guidance on the Pet Travel Scheme has been produced (4th August 2014) by the Department for Environment, Food & Rural Affairs and the Animal & Plant Health Agency. A helpline is in operation and may be contacted on tel. 0370 241 1710 or e-mail: pettravel@ahvla.gsi.gov.uk.

25 Authorities

Statutes–

Animal Boarding Establishments Act 1963

Animal Health Act 1981

Animal Health and Welfare (Scotland) Act 2006

Animal Welfare Act 2006

Breeding and Sale of Dogs (Welfare) Act 1999

Breeding of Dogs Acts 1973 and 1991

Dangerous Wild Animals Act 1976

Pet Animals Act 1951

EU Legislation–

Regulation (EU) No. 576/2013 on the non-commercial movement of pet animals

Regulation (EU) No. 577/2013 on the model identification documents for the non-commercial movement of dogs, cats and ferrets, the establishment of lists of territories and third countries and the format, layout and language requirements of the declarations attesting compliance with certain conditions provided for in EU Regulation No. 576/2013

Statutory Instruments–

Animal Welfare (Breeding of Dogs) (Wales) Regulations 2014 (S.I. 2014 No. 3266)

Animal Welfare (Electronic Collars) (Wales) Regulations 2010 (S.I. 2010 No. 943)

Breeding of Dogs (Licensing Records) Regulations (S.I. 1999 No. 3192)

Breeding of Dogs (Licensing Records) (Scotland) Regulations (S.S.I. 1999 No. 176)

Legislative Reform (Dangerous Wild Animals) (Licensing) Order 2010 (S.I. 2010 No. 839)

Licensing of Animal Dealers (Young Cats and Young Dogs) (Scotland) Regulations 2009 (S.S.I. 2009 No. 141)

Microchipping of Dogs (England) Regulations 2015 (S.I. 2015 No. 108)

Microchipping of Dogs (Wales) Regulations 2015 (S.I. 2015 No. 1990)

Non-Commercial Movement of Pet Animals Order 2011, as amended (S.I. 2011 No. 2883, 2012 No. 2897 and 2014 No. 3158)

Rabies (Importation of Dogs, Cats an Other Mammals) Order 1974, as amended (S.I. 1974 No. 2211, 1977 No. 361, 1984 No. 1182, 1986 No. 2062, 1990 No. 2371, 1999 No. 3443, 2000 No. 1298, 2001 No. 6, 2003 No. 229, 2011 No. 2883 and 2014 No. 3158)

Sale of Dogs (Identification Tags) Regulations 1999 (S.I. 1999 No. 3191)

Sale of Dogs (Identification Tags) (Scotland) Regulations 1999 (S.S.I. 1999 No. 177)

ANIMALS

PROTECTION OF WILDLIFE: ENGLAND AND WALES

A: INTRODUCTION

1 Scope of the Note

This Note is concerned with Part I of the Wildlife and Countryside Act 1981, as amended by the Countryside and Rights of Way Act 2000.

B: PROTECTION OF BIRDS

2 Protection of wild birds, their nests, and eggs

Subject to a number of exceptions, s.1(1) of the Wildlife and Countryside Act 1981 provides that a person is guilty of an offence if he intentionally–

  (a) kills, injures, or takes any wild bird;

  (b) takes, damages, or destroys the nest of any wild bird while that nest is in use or is being built;

  (c) takes, damages or destroys the nest of a wild bird included in Sch. ZA1: birds which re-use their nest (the Schedule includes the Golden Eagle, White-tailed Eagle and Osprey); or

  (d) takes or destroys any egg of any wild bird.

S.1(2) makes it an offence for any person to have in his possession or control–

  (e) any live or dead wild bird or any part of, or anything derived from, such a bird; or

  (f) any egg of a wild bird or any part of such an egg;

unless he can show (s.1(3)) that the bird or egg has not been killed, taken, or sold, or had been lawfully killed or taken; or (s.1(3ZA) that the egg was in the possession or control of any person, before 28th September 1982. "Wild bird" means any bird of a kind which is ordinarily resident in or is a visitor to the European territory of any EU Member State in a wild state but does not include poultry or, except in ss.5 and 16, any game bird (s.27), and, for the purposes of s.1 only, does not include any bird which is shown to have been bred in captivity (s.1(6)). A bird is not to be treated as so bred unless its parents were lawfully in captivity when the egg was laid (s.27).

It is an offence, under s.1(5), if any person intentionally or recklessly (a) disturbs any such wild bird while it is building a nest or is in, on, or near a nest containing eggs or young, or (b) disturbs dependent young of such a bird. See also, **15 Civil sanctions**, below.

For the purposes of ss.1 and 2, "close season" is defined by s.2(4) and its length depends upon the species involved. The Secretary of State is given power, by order, to vary the close season for any wild bird and to specify any period not exceeding 14 days as a period of special protection for any wild birds included in Part II of Schedule I or Part I of Schedule 2 (s.2(5) and (6)).

3 Areas of special control

Under s.3, of the Wildlife and Countryside Act 1981 the Secretary of State may by order take measures to protect wild birds, their nests, and eggs in any area specified in the order either at all times or during specified periods. The killing or taking of birds within Part II of Schedule 2 and certain acts of authorised persons are excepted from such control, and the making of any such order will not affect the exercise of the rights of any person in respect of any land in an area so specified as owner, lessee, occupier, or licensee.

4 Exceptions

Exceptions to s.1 of the Wildlife and Countryside Act 1981 are contained in ss.2 and 4. The killing or taking of a bird listed in Part I of Schedule 2, or the injuring of such a bird in an attempt to kill it, outside the close season for that bird (except, in England and Wales, on Sundays in any area prescribed for this purpose by order of the Secretary of State) is not an offence (s.2(1) and 3)).

A bird listed in Part II of Schedule 2, including the nest or egg of such a bird, may be destroyed or taken by an authorised person at any time (s.2(2)). An "authorised person" means the owner or occupier, of the land on which the action authorised is taken; or any person authorised in writing by the local authority for the area, or by one of certain specified bodies (s.27).

By virtue of s.4, nothing in s.1 or in any order made under s.3 makes unlawful–

  (a) anything done in pursuance of a requirement by the Minister of Agriculture or the Secretary of State for Wales under s.98 of the Agriculture Act 1947 or under or in pursuance of an order made under ss.21 or 22 of the Animal Health Act 1981, or, except in relation to a wild bird included in Schedule 1 or the nest or egg of such a bird, anything done under, or in pursuance of an order made under any other provision of the Act;

  (b) the taking of a disabled bird to tend and release it or the killing of a seriously disabled bird if there is no reasonable chance of its recovery;

  (c) any act made unlawful by s.1 or an order under s.3 which is the incidental result of a lawful operation and could not reasonably have been avoided.

A person may not rely on a defence provided for in paragraph (b) above where the disability was caused by his own unlawful act (s.4(2)(a) and (b)).

Notwithstanding the provisions of s.1, or of an order made under s.3, an authorised person is not guilty of an offence by reason of the killing or injuring of any wild bird, other than a bird included in Schedule 1, if he shows that his action was necessary for the purpose of (a) preserving public health or air safety, (b) preventing the spread of disease, or (c) preventing serious damage to livestock, foodstuffs for livestock, crops, vegetables, fruit, growing timber, fisheries, or inland waters (s.4(3)).

An authorised person will not be regarded as showing that any action of his was necessary for a purpose mentioned in s.4(3)(c) (see (c) above) unless he shows that there was no other satisfactory solution (s.4(4)).

Further, an authorised person will not be entitled to rely on the defence provided by s.4(3)(c) as respects any action taken at any time for any purpose mentioned in paragraph (c) above, if it had become apparent, before that time, that the action would prove necessary for that purpose and either (i) a licence under s.16 (see E: MISCELLANEOUS, below) authorising that action had not been applied for by him as soon as reasonably practicable after that fact had become apparent or (ii) an application by him for such a licence had been determined, and (b) unless he notified the agriculture Minister as soon as reasonably practicable after that time that he had taken the action (s.4(4) to (6)).

5 Other offences

S.5, of the Wildlife and Countryside Act 1981 as amended, prohibits the use of certain methods of killing or taking wild birds or knowingly causing or permitting such methods to be employed.

Part 1 of Schedule 3 contains a list of birds which may not be sold alive or shown in competition unless the bird has been bred in captivity and ringed or marked in accordance with the Wildlife and Countryside (Ringing of Certain Birds) Regulations 1982; this list includes most of the smaller birds including finches and linnets; *inter alia* the sale or possession for sale or showing of any live wild bird not in this list is an offence (s.6(1) and (3)). S.6(2) covers the sale of dead wild birds.

S.7 provides for the registration and ringing or marking of the birds listed in Schedule 4, if kept in captivity, in accordance with the Wildlife and Countryside (Registration and Ringing of Certain Captive Birds) (England) Regulations 2015, or (Wales) Regulations 2003. To keep or possess such a bird otherwise than in accordance with these provisions is an offence.

S.8 provides that, subject to certain exceptions, any person who keeps or confines any bird, other than poultry, in a cage or other receptacle which is not sufficient in height, length, or breadth to permit the bird to stretch its wings freely commits an offence.

See also, **12 Civil sanctions**, below.

6 Restriction on the use of lead shot

The Environmental Protection (Restriction on the Use of Lead Shot) (England) Regulations 1999 and (Wales) Regulations 2002 make it an offence to use lead shot for the purposes of shooting with a shot gun (Reg. 3)—

(a) on or over any area below the high-water mark of ordinary spring tides;

(b) on or over any specified site of special scientific interest; or

(c) any specified wild bird.

Schedule 1 to the Regulations specifies the areas to which the prohibition in (b) applies. The birds to which the prohibition in (c) applies are Coot, Ducks, Geese, and Moorhen; and in England only, Swans and Common Lapwing (Sch. 2). Lead shot is defined as shot made either of lead or of any alloy or compound comprised of more than 1% lead (Reg. 2).

C: PROTECTION OF OTHER ANIMALS

7 Wild animals

S.9 of the Wildlife and Countryside Act 1981 contains provisions for the protection of the wild animals listed in Schedule 5 to that Act. Subject only to the exceptions mentioned in that section or in s.10, it is an offence for any person (a) intentionally to kill, injure, or take any such animal or (b) to have in his possession or control any such animal whether alive or dead, or any part of, or anything derived from, such an animal unless he can show that the animal has not been killed, taken, or sold in contravention of the law (s.9(1), (2), and (3)). It is also an offence for any person to intentionally or recklessly damage or destroy a shelter used by a wild animal included in Schedule 5, to disturb any such animal while using such a shelter (s.9(4)), or to sell or to have in his possession for the purpose of sale any live or dead wild animal included in Schedule 5, or any part of, or anything derived from, such an animal (s.9(5)(a)). Wild animal means any animal (other than a bird) which is or (before it was killed or taken) was living wild (s.27).

By virtue of s.10(1) to (3), nothing in s.9 makes unlawful—

(a) anything done in pursuance of a statutory requirement;

(b) anything done within a dwelling house;

(c) the taking of a disabled animal to tend and release it, or the killing of a seriously disabled animal if there is no reasonable chance of its recovery;

(d) any act made unlawful by s.9 which was the incidental result of a lawful operation and could not reasonably have been avoided.

A person may not rely on a defence provided for in paragraph (b) or (d) above as respects anything done in relation to a bat otherwise than in the living area of a dwelling house unless he had notified the Nature Conservancy Council of the proposed action or operation and allowed them a reasonable time to advise him as to whether it should be carried out and, if so, the method to be used (s.10(5)). A person may not rely on a defence provided for in paragraph (c) above where the disability was caused by his own unlawful act (s.10(3)(a) and (b)).

Notwithstanding anything in s.9, an authorised person is not guilty of an offence by reason of the killing or injuring of a wild animal included in Schedule 5 if he shows that his action was necessary for the purpose of preventing serious damage to livestock, foodstuffs for livestock, crops, vegetables, fruit, growing timber or any other form of property or to fisheries, unless it had become apparent, before that time, that the action would prove necessary and a licence under s.16, authorising that action, had not been applied for as soon as reasonably practicable after that fact had become apparent or an application for such a licence had been determined (s.10(4) and (6)).

S.11, as amended, prohibits the use of certain methods of killing or taking wild animals or knowingly causing or permitting such methods to be employed.

See also, **15 Civil sanctions**, below.

8 Cruelty to wild animals

The Wild Mammals (Protection) Act 1996 makes it an offence for any person to mutilate, kick, beat, nail or otherwise impale, stab, burn, crush, drown, drag or asphyxiate any wild animal with intent to inflict unnecessary suffering (s.1). There are exceptions for mercy killings; the reasonably swift and humane killing of animals injured or taken in the course of lawful shooting, hunting, coursing or pest control activity; and the lawful use of traps, snares, or poisonous substances, etc.

Animals which are not living in a wild state, or are under the control of man whether on a permanent or temporary basis, or are of a kind commonly domesticated in the UK, are protected from harm by the Animal Welfare Act 2006. See also **11 Circus animals**, below.

9 Badgers

The Protection of Badgers Act 1992 makes special provision for badgers by introducing five specific offences, namely–

(a) wilfully killing, taking or injuring a badger (or attempting to do so) (s.1);

(b) cruelty to badgers (including the use of badger tongs), and digging for badgers (except as permitted by the Act) (s.2);

(c) intentionally or recklessly interfering with badger setts by damaging or destroying them obstructing an entrance, causing a dog to enter a sett, or disturbing a badger occupying a sett (s.3);

(d) selling, possessing or offering for sale live badgers, except in accordance with the Act (s.4);

(e) marking or ringing a badger, unless licensed to do so (s.5).

There are general exceptions, including mercy killings and authorised scientific research; and specific exceptions, including an exception from (a) and (c) above for the prevention of serious damage to land, crops, poultry or any other forms of property (ss.6 to 8). Licences may be granted allowing, in specified circumstances, acts which would otherwise be offences under the Act, e.g., for the purpose of preventing the spread of disease (s.10).

An act which would be an offence under s.3, or which would breach a licence condition under s.10, may in England be dealt with by way of civil sanction (Environmental Civil Sanctions (England) Order 2010). The civil sanctions which are available are fixed and variable monetary penalties, compliance, restoration and stop notices (see **15 Civil sanctions**, below), and enforcement undertakings.

10 Hunting with dogs

From 18th February 2005, the Hunting Act 2004 makes it an offence to hunt a wild mammal with a dog (s.1). The following categories of hunting are exempt from this ban (Sch. 1)–

(a) Stalking a wild mammal or flushing it out from cover for the purpose of–

    (i) protecting livestock, game birds, wild birds, food for livestock, crops, growing timber, fisheries, other property or the biological diversity of an area;

    (ii) obtaining meat to be used for human or animal consumption; or

    (iii) participation in a field trial (other than a hare coursing event).

The stalking or flushing out must not involve the use of more than two dogs, must not involve the use of a dog below ground unless the conditions of Sch. 1 para. 2 (see (b) below) are met, and reasonable steps must be taken for the wild mammal to be shot dead as soon as it is found or flushed out (para. 1).

(b) The use of dogs below ground for the purpose of protecting game birds or wild birds being preserved for shooting. The stalking or flushing out must not involve the use of more than one dog below ground, and reasonable steps must be taken for the wild mammal to be flushed out from below ground as soon as possible and be shot dead as quickly as possible thereafter. Also the dog must be protected from injury and be treated in accordance with any code of conduct issued or approved by the Secretary of State (para. 2).

(c) The hunting of rats or rabbits (paras.3 and 4).

(d) The retrieval of hares which have been shot (para. 5).

(e) Falconry, i.e. flushing a wild mammal from cover if undertaken to enable a bird of prey to hunt that wild mammal (para. 6).

(f) The recapture of a wild mammal if it has escaped or been released from captivity. The wild mammal must be recaptured or shot dead as soon as possible, the dogs must be controlled so as not to prevent or obstruct this, and the animal should not have been released for the purpose of being hunted (para. 7).

(g) The rescue of a wild mammal if the hunter reasonably believes it is injured as long as no more than two dogs are used, dogs are not used below ground, and action is taken as soon as possible to relieve the animal's suffering (para. 8).

(h) Hunting for research and observation purposes as long as no more than two dogs are used, the hunting must take place above ground, and the dogs are controlled to ensure that they do not injure the animal (para. 9).

In each of the above exemptions, the hunting must take place on land which belongs to the hunter or which he has been given permission to use by the owner or occupier. All dogs used in the course of exempted hunting must be kept under close control. It is an offence for a person knowingly to permit their land to be used for the commission of an offence under s.1; similarly it is an offence for a person to allow their dog to be used in the commission of such an offence (s.3). It is a defence to a charge under s.1 that the person accused reasonably believed the hunting was exempt (s.4).

S.5 of the Hunting Act 2004 creates a number of offences in relation to hare coursing including participating in, attending, or knowingly facilitating a hare coursing event, or allowing land to be used for such an event (s.5(1)). S.5(2) provides that it is an offence for a person to be responsible for a dog which participates in such an event.

An offence (whether in relation to hunting or hare coursing) is punishable on summary conviction by an unlimited fine.

11 Circus animals

The operation of a travelling circus is an activity which may not be carried on in England except under the authority of a licence issued by the Secretary of State under the Animal Welfare Act 2006 (Welfare of Wild Animals in Travelling Circuses (England) Regulations 2012, Reg. 3). The fee for the issue of a licence is £389.36, plus an inspection fee of £72.53 per hour, plus any actual travel, accommodation and other reasonable expenses of an inspector (Reg. 8).

Before a licence can be granted, the Secretary of State must be satisfied that certain conditions are or will be met, and will continue to be met. These conditions require an operator to–

(a) give the Secretary of State written notice before acquiring a new wild animal for use in the travelling circus;

(b) notify the Secretary of State of tour itineraries;

(c) provide the Secretary of State with a stock list, and individual animal records;

(d) make group and individual care plans for all wild animals in the travelling circus;

(e) require access to wild animals to be restricted to competent persons and the presence at all times of sufficient staff to ensure animal and public safety and a competent person in overall charge of the animals;

(f) require the appointment of a lead veterinary adviser and quarterly visits by a suitable veterinary surgeon; and

(g) require the operator to take all reasonable steps to meet the needs of wild animals in the travelling circus, with specific requirements for the display, training, performance, environment and transportation of wild animals in the circus.

D: PROTECTION OF PLANTS

12 Wild plants

S.13(1) of the Wildlife and Countryside Act 1981 provides that a person is guilty of an offence if he (a) intentionally picks, uproots, or destroys any wild plant included in Schedule 8 or (b) not being an authorised person (see above), intentionally uproots any wild plant not included in that Schedule. "Wild plant" means any plant which is or (before it was picked, uprooted, or destroyed) was growing wild and is of a kind which ordinarily grows in Great Britain in a wild state (s.27). A person will not be guilty of this offence if he shows that his action, although made unlawful by s.13(1), was an incidental result of a lawful operation and could not reasonably have been avoided. S.13(2)(a) makes it an offence for any person to sell or have in his possession for sale any live or dead wild plant included in Schedule 8, or any part of, or anything derived from, such a plant.

See also, **15 Civil sanctions**, below.

E: MISCELLANEOUS

13 General provisions

S.14 of the Wildlife and Countryside Act 1981 prohibits the introduction of new species of animals or plants.

It is an offence for a person—

(a) to release or allow to escape into the wild any animal which is of a kind which is not ordinarily resident in, and is not a regular visitor to, Great Britain in a wild state, or which is included in Part I of Schedule 9; or

(b) to plant or otherwise cause to grow in the wild any plant which is included in Part II of Schedule 9.

Further, it is an offence to sell any such an animal or plant (or anything from which such an animal or plant can be reproduced or propagated) if it has been prescribed by the Secretary of State (s.14ZA). The Wildlife and Countryside Act 1981 (Prohibition on Sale etc. of Invasive Non-native Plants) (England) Order 2014 prescribes five aquatic plants which may not be sold in England. These are: floating water primrose; floating pennywort; parrot's feather; Australian swamp stone-crop; and water fern.

Under s.16, licences giving exemption, for specified purposes, from certain specified restrictions imposed by Part I of the 1981 Act may be granted by the Secretary of State, each of the Nature Conservancy Councils, or the Minister for Agriculture, Fisheries and Food.

S.18 makes it an offence for any person to attempt to commit an offence under Part I or to have in his possession for the purposes of committing such an offence anything capable of being used for the commission of the offence.

S.22 empowers the Secretary of State by order to vary Schedules 1 to 6, 8 and 9. A number of Orders have been made under this provision.

S.23 deals with advisory bodies and their functions, and s.24 gives to the Nature Conservancy Councils acting jointly certain advisory functions.

S.25 requires every local authority to bring to the attention of the public, and of schoolchildren in particular, the effect of the provisions of Part I, as well as any Order made under Part I which affects the whole or any part of that area. Part I extends to the Isles of Scilly as if the Isles were a county and the Council of the Isles were a county council (s.27(4)).

See also, **14 Civil sanctions**, below.

14 Civil sanctions

Many of the criminal offences in the Wildlife and Countryside Act 1981 mentioned in this Note may, in England, be dealt with by way of civil sanction instead. The main civil sanctions which are available are variable monetary penalty, compliance notice, restoration notice, and stop notice (Environmental Civil Sanctions (England) Order 2010).

A variable monetary penalty may be imposed, or a compliance or restoration notice served, by Natural England where it is satisfied beyond reasonable doubt that an offence under the 1981 Act has been committed.

A variable monetary penalty cannot exceed the maximum amount of any fine which could be imposed if criminal proceedings were brought. Natural England must first serve a notice of intent to impose the penalty and the recipient of the notice has 28 days to make representations and objections. The recipient may also offer a third party undertaking to benefit any third party affected by the offence (Natural England may accept or reject such an undertaking). After 28 days, Natural England must, taking into account any third party undertaking, decide whether to issue the variable monetary penalty. It may not issue a penalty where it is satisfied that, by reason of any defence, the recipient would not be convicted of the offence to which the notice relates.

A compliance or restoration notice will require the recipient to either take specified steps within a specified time frame to ensure that the offence does not continue or recur (a compliance notice) or that the position is restored so far as is possible to what it would have been had the offence not been committed (a restoration notice)

A stop notice may be served where a person is carrying on an activity (or is likely to do so) which Natural England reasonable believes is causing, or will cause, or presents a significant risk of causing serious harm to human health or the environment (including the heath of animals and plants) and involves or is likely to involve the commission of an offence under the 1981 Act. The notice will prohibit the person from carrying on the activity until specified steps have been taken to remove or reduce the harm or risk of harm.

An appeal against a penalty or a compliance, restoration or stop notice may be made to the First-tier Tribunal *inter alia* on the grounds of error of fact or law, or unreasonableness of the amount of the penalty.

Note.–A compliance notice is not an available remedy in the case of an offence under s.5 (see **5 Other offences**, above), or s.11(1) (see **7 Wild animals**, above).

15 Control of horses–Wales

A local authority in Wales has power to seize, impound and dispose of horses which are in public places (such as on the public highway) without lawful authority, or are on other land without the consent of the occupier of the land. In the case of private land, the local authority must be satisfied that the horse is there without the consent of the occupier of the land and that the occupier consents to the local authority seizing and impounding it (Control of Horses (Wales) Act 2014, ss.1 and 2). For these purposes "horse" includes a pony, donkey, mule or any other equine animal (s.9).

Within 24 hours of a seizure the local authority must post a written notice at or near the place where the horse was seized stating the date and time it was seized and detailing how contact may be made with the local authority. It must also, within 24 hours of seizure, inform the local police of its actions and give notice to anyone who appears to be the owner or a person acting on behalf of the owner of the horse (s.3). Reasonable steps must be taken to establish the identity of the owner of the horse as soon as reasonably practicable following its seizure and if, within 7 days of seizing a horse the local authority ascertains that a person who has not already been given written notice, is the owner of the horse, he must also be given a written notice within 24 hours. The requirements for notices are set out in s.3 and must set out the local authority's powers to dispose of impounded horses.

The owner of the horse is liable to pay the local authority any costs reasonably incurred in its seizure and impounding and in feeding and maintaining it whilst impounded. The local authority is not required to return a horse until such costs are paid (s.4).

A local authority's power to sell or otherwise dispose (including by arranging for its destruction) of a horse arise if neither the owner of the horse nor a person acting on his behalf contacts them within 7 days of the notice being given to a person or posted under s.3, or if the owner does not pay the costs of seizure under s.4 within 7 days of being required to do so.

The local authority may also recover any costs it incurs in relation to any arrangements for the disposal or destruction of the horse. Where there are no proceeds, the local authority may seek to obtain its costs of disposal from the owner. Where there are proceeds, but the costs exceed the amount of the proceeds, the owner is liable to pay the local authority the amount of that excess (s.5).

The local authority must keep a register, open to public inspection, of all horses seized under these provisions (s.6).

Where the owner of a horse disputes the amount the local authority claims in relation to the costs of seizure or disposal, he may, within 7 days of receiving notice of those costs, refer the dispute to the Welsh Ministers for resolution (s.7).

16 Authorities

Statutes–

Animal Welfare Act 2006

Control of Horses (Wales) Act 2014

Countryside and Rights of Way Act 2000

Hunting Act 2004

Protection of Badgers Act 1992

Wildlife and Countryside Act 1981

Wildlife and Countryside (Amendment) Act 1991

Wild Mammals (Protection) Act 1996

Statutory Instruments–

Environmental Civil Sanctions (England) Order 2010, as amended (S.I. 2010 No. 1157 and 2015 No. 664)

Environmental Protection (Restriction on Use of Lead Shot) (England) Regulations 1999, as amended (S.I. 1999 No. 2170, 2002 No. 2102, and 2003 No. 2512)

Environmental Protection (Restriction on Use of Lead Shot) (Wales) Regulations 2002 (S.I. 2002 No. 1730)

Welfare of Wild Animals in Travelling Circuses (England) Regulations 2012 (S.I. 2012 No. 2932)

Wildlife and Countryside Act 1981 (Amendment) Regulations 1995 and 2004 (S.I. 1995 No. 2825 and 2004 No. 1487)

Wildlife and Countryside Act 1981 (Amendment) (Wales) Regulations 2004 (S.I. 2004 No. 1733)

Wildlife and Countryside Act 1981 (Prohibition on Sale etc. of Invasive Non-native Plants) (England) Order 2014 (S.I. 2014 No. 538)

Wildlife and Countryside (Registration and Ringing of Certain Captive Birds) (England) Regulations 2015 (S.I. 2015 No. 618)

Wildlife and Countryside (Registration and Ringing of Certain Captive Birds) (Wales) Regulations 2003, as amended (S.I. 2003 No. 3235 and 2009 No. 1733)

Wildlife and Countryside (Ringing of Certain Birds) Regulations 1982 (S.I. 1982 No. 1220)

PROTECTION OF WILDLIFE: SCOTLAND

A: INTRODUCTION

1 Scope of the Note

This Note is concerned with Part I of the Wildlife and Countryside Act 1981, as amended by the Nature Conservation (Scotland) Act 2004.

B: PROTECTION OF BIRDS

2 Protection of wild birds, their nests, and eggs

In Scotland, subject to a number of exceptions, s.1(1) of the Wildlife and Countryside Act 1981, as amended provides that a person is guilty of an offence if he intentionally or recklessly–

(a) kills, injures, or takes any wild bird;

(b) takes, damages, destroys or otherwise interferes with the nest of any wild bird while that nest is in use or is being built;

(c) damages, destroys or otherwise interferes with any nest habitually used by any wild bird included in Sch. A1 to the Act;

(d) obstructs or prevents any wild bird from using its nest; or

(e) takes or destroys any egg of any wild bird.

Sch. A1 to the Act currently includes the White-tailed Eagle and Golden Eagle (s.1(1)(ba) and the Wildlife and Countryside Act 1981 (Variation of Schedules A1 and 1A) (Scotland) Order 2013).

S.1(2) makes it an offence for any person to have in his possession or control–

(f) any live or dead wild bird or any part of, or anything derived from, such a bird; or

(g) any egg of a wild bird or any part of such an egg;

unless he can show (s.1(3))–

(h) the bird or egg had not been killed or taken, or had lawfully been killed or taken at or from a place in Scotland;

(i) the bird, egg or other thing had lawfully been sold at a place in Scotland; or

(j) the bird, egg or other thing had been killed at, taken from or sold outside Scotland and that act would not have been unlawful in Scotland or at the place at which the act took place.

It is an offence, under s.1(5), if any person intentionally or recklessly (a) disturbs any such wild bird while it is building a nest or is in, on, or near a nest containing eggs or young, or (b) disturbs dependent young of such a bird.

It is also an offence, under s.1(5A), (5B) if any person intentionally or recklessly disturbs any wild bird included in Sch. 1 or intentionally or recklessly harasses any wild bird included in Sch. 1A. Sch. 1A currently includes the White-tailed Eagle, Golden Eagle, Hen Harrier and Red Kite (s.1(5B) and the Wildlife and Countryside Act 1981 (Variation of Schedules A1 and 1A) (Scotland) Order 2013).

"Wild bird" means any bird of a kind which is ordinarily resident in or is a visitor to the European territory of any EU Member State in a wild state but does not include poultry or, except in ss.5 and 16, any game bird (s.27), and, for the purposes of s.1 only, does not include any bird which is shown to have been bred in captivity unless it has been released for conservation purposes, or is a partridge, pheasant, mallard or red grouse born in captivity and fully released for any purpose (s.1(6), as amended by the Wildlife and Natural Environment (Scotland) Act 2011). A bird is not to be treated as so bred unless its parents were lawfully in captivity when the egg was laid (s.27).

3 Exceptions

Exceptions to s.1 of the Wildlife and Countryside Act 1981 are contained in ss.2 and 4, as amended. The killing or taking of a bird listed in Part I of Sch. 2, or the injuring of such a bird in an attempt to kill it, outside the close season for that bird is not an offence where the person who kills or takes the bird has either a legal right to do so or permission from a person with such a right (s.2(1) and (3)). The exception does not apply to the killing or taking of certain specified birds on a Sunday or on Christmas Day.

It is also not an offence for person with a legal right or permission to do so to take for the purposes of breeding grey or red-legged partridge or common pheasant, or the egg of such a bird, during a period of 28 days after the start of the close season for those birds (a process sometimes referred to as "catching up")(s.2(3B)), or to take a red grouse for the purpose of preventing the spread of disease where it is intended to release the bird after no more than 12 hours (s.2(3C)).

By virtue of s.4, nothing in s.1 makes unlawful–

(a) anything done in pursuance of a requirement by the Scottish Ministers, under s.39 of the Agriculture (Scotland) Act 1948 (pest control) or under or in pursuance of an order made under ss.21 or 22 of the Animal Health Act 1981, or, except in relation to a wild bird included in Sch. 1 or the nest or egg of such a bird, anything done under, or in pursuance of an order made under any other provision of the Act;

(b) the taking of a disabled bird to tend and release it or the killing of a seriously disabled bird if there is no reasonable chance of its recovery;

(c) any act made unlawful by s.1 ("an unlawful act") if he shows that each of the conditions specified in s.4(2A) was satisfied in relation to the carrying out of the unlawful act.

A person may not rely on a defence provided for in paragraph (b) above where the disability was caused by his own unlawful act (s.4(2)(a) and (b)).

The conditions in s.2(2A) are—

(a) the unlawful act was the incidental result of a lawful operation or other activity;

(b) the person who carried it out took reasonable precautions to avoid an unlawful act or did not foresee (and could not have reasonably foreseen) the incidental performance of an unlawful act; and

(c) the person performing the unlawful act took reasonable steps to minimise the damage or disturbance to the wild bird, nest or egg.

Notwithstanding the provisions of s.1, an authorised person is not guilty of an offence by reason of the killing or injuring of any wild bird, other than a bird included in Sch. 1, if he shows that his action was necessary for the purpose of (a) preserving public health or air safety, (b) preventing the spread of disease, or (c) preventing serious damage to livestock, foodstuffs for livestock, crops, vegetables, fruit, growing timber, fisheries, or inland waters (s.4(3)). An authorised person will not be regarded as showing that any action of his was necessary for a purpose mentioned in s.4(3) unless he shows that there was no other satisfactory solution (s.4(4)).

Further, an authorised person will not be entitled to rely on the defence provided by s.4(3) as respects any action taken at any time for any purpose mentioned in that subsection, if it had become apparent, before that time, that the action would prove necessary for that purpose and either (i) a licence under s.16 (see E: MISCELLANEOUS, below) authorising that action had not been applied for by him as soon as reasonably practicable after that fact had become apparent or (ii) an application by him for such a licence had been determined, and (b) unless he notified the agriculture Minister as soon as reasonably practicable after that time that he had taken the action (s.4(4) to (6)).

4 Other offences

S.5, of the Wildlife and Countryside Act 1981 as amended, prohibits the use of certain methods of killing or taking wild birds or knowingly causing or permitting such methods to be employed.

Part 1 of Schedule 3 contains a list of birds which may not be sold alive or shown in competition unless the bird has been bred in captivity and ringed or marked in accordance with the Wildlife and Countryside (Ringing of Certain Birds) Regulations 1982; this list includes most of the smaller birds including finches and linnets; *inter alia* the sale or possession for sale or showing of any live wild bird not in this list is an offence (s.6(1) and (3)). S.6(2) covers the sale of dead wild birds.

S.7 provides for the registration and ringing or marking of the birds listed in Schedule 4, if kept in captivity, in accordance with the Wildlife and Countryside (Registration and Ringing of Certain Captive Birds) (Scotland) Regulations 2009. To keep or possess such a bird otherwise than in accordance with these provisions is an offence.

S.8 provides that, subject to certain exceptions, any person who keeps or confines any bird, other than poultry, in a cage or other receptacle which is not sufficient in height, length, or breadth to permit the bird to stretch its wings freely commits an offence.

5 Restriction on the use of lead shot

The Environmental Protection (Restriction on Use of Lead Shot) (Scotland) (No. 2) Regulations 2004 prohibit the use of lead shot for the purpose of shooting with a shot gun on or over wetlands. Wetland are defined as any area of marsh, fen, peatland or water, whether natural or artificial, permanent or temporary, with water that is static or flowing, fresh, brackish or salt, including areas of marine water the depth of which at low tide does not exceed six metres.

C: PROTECTION OF OTHER ANIMALS

6 Wild animals

Subject only to the exceptions mentioned in ss.9 or 10 of the Wildlife and Countryside Act 1981 (as amended by the Nature Conservation (Scotland) Act 2004), it is an offence for any person (a) intentionally or recklessly to kill, injure, or take any such animal or (b) to have in his possession or control any such animal whether alive or dead, or any part of, or anything derived from, such an animal unless he can show that (s.9(1), (2), and (3))—

(a) the animal has not been unlawfully killed or taken at or from a place in Scotland;

(b) the animal or other thing had not been unlawfully sold at a place in Scotland; or

(c) the animal or other thing had been killed at, taken from or sold at a place outside Scotland and the act of killing, taking or sale would not have been unlawful in Scotland if it had been committed there or the animal or other thing had been lawfully brought from the place where it was killed, taken or sold.

It is an offence for any person intentionally or recklessly to damage or destroy a shelter used by a wild animal included in Schedule 5, to disturb any such animal while using such a shelter (s.9(4)), or intentionally or recklessly disturbs or harasses any wild animal included in Sch. 5 as a dolphin, whale, porpoise or basking shark

ANIMALS

(s.9(5A)). It is also an offence to sell or to have in his possession for the purpose of sale any live or dead wild animal included in Schedule 5, or any part of, or anything derived from, such an animal (s.9(5)(a)). Anyone who knowingly causes or permits an unlawful act under s.9 is also guilty of an offence (s.9(5A)). Wild animal means any animal (other than a bird) which is or (before it was killed or taken) was living wild (s.27).

By virtue of s.10(1) to (3), nothing in s.9 makes unlawful–

(a) anything done in pursuance of a requirement by the Minister of Agriculture, Fisheries and Food, the Secretary of State for Wales, or the Scottish Ministers, under s.97 of the Agriculture Act 1947 or s.39 of the Agriculture (Scotland) Act 1948 (see above), or under, or in pursuance of, an order made under the Animal Health Act 1981;

(b) anything done within a dwelling house;

(c) the taking of a disabled animal to tend and release it, or the killing of a seriously disabled animal if there is no reasonable chance of its recovery;

(d) any act made unlawful by s.9 if he shows that certain conditions were met or the unlawful act was carried out in relation to an animal bred and lawfully held in captivity.

A person may not rely on a defence provided for in paragraph (b) or (d) above as respects anything done in relation to a bat otherwise than in the living area of a dwelling house unless he had notified the Nature Conservancy Council of the proposed action or operation and allowed them a reasonable time to advise him as to whether it should be carried out and, if so, the method to be used (s.10(5)). A person may not rely on a defence provided for in paragraph (c) above where the disability was caused by his own unlawful act (s.10(3)(a) and (b)).

Notwithstanding anything in s.9, an authorised person is not guilty of an offence by reason of the killing or injuring of a wild animal included in Schedule 5 if he shows that his action was necessary for the purpose of preventing serious damage to livestock, foodstuffs for livestock, crops, vegetables, fruit, growing timber or any other form of property or to fisheries, unless it had become apparent, before that time, that the action would prove necessary and a licence under s.16, authorising that action, had not been applied for as soon as reasonably practicable after that fact had become apparent or an application for such a licence had been determined (s.10(4) and (6)). An authorised person cannot rely on the defence under s.10(4) unless he notified the Scottish Ministers as soon as reasonably practicable after taking the action (s.10(4A)).

Ss.11 to 11F prohibit the use of certain methods of killing or taking wild animals or knowingly causing or permitting such methods to be employed.

A person using a snare must have an identification number, be trained in the setting and use of snares, and attach identification tags to snares (s.11A). A person who sets a snare must ensure that it is inspected at least every 24 hours to see whether there is an animal caught in the snare, and whether the snare is free. If an animal is found to be caught then it must be released or removed. If the snare is found not to be free-running then it must be removed or mended to make it free-running (s.11B). A person with an identification number must keep a record of their snaring activities and produce it to a constable if asked (s.11E). A person who without reasonable excuse while on any land has in his possession a snare or sets a snare on that land without the authorisation of the owner or occupier of the land is guilty of an offence (s.11C).

The Snares (Training) (Scotland) Order 2015 makes provision as to the bodies which have been approved to issue training certificates. The Snares (Identification Numbers and Tags) (Scotland) Order 2012 provides that application for an identification number must be made in person at a police station and that there is a fee of £20, and provides that the tag to be attached to a snare must identify whether it is intended for brown hares, rabbits or foxes.

7 Hares and rabbits

It is an offence for any person intentionally or recklessly to kill, injure or take any wild animal included in the Wildlife and Countryside Act 1981 Schedule 5A in the close season, or (without a legal right, or permission from a person who has such a right) any wild animal in Schedule 6A at any time. Schedule 5A relates to mountain and brown hares and Schedule 6A to those hares and rabbits (ss.10A, 11G). It is a defence if the accused can show that the animal in question was too seriously disabled to recover, and that the disability to the animal was not caused by his unlawful act (ss.10B, 11H).

It is an offence to possess, control, sell or offer to sell, possess or transport for the purpose of selling any wild animal or part of a wild animal which has been killed or taken in contravention of sections 10A or 11G (s.11I)

Basically, the phrase "without a legal right, or permission from a person who has such a right", means poaching.

8 Cruelty to wild animals

The Wild Mammals (Protection) Act 1996 makes it an offence for any person to mutilate, kick, beat, nail or otherwise impale, stab, burn, crush, drown, drag or asphyxiate any wild animal with intent to inflict unnecessary suffering (s.1). There are exceptions for mercy killings; the reasonably swift and humane killing of animals injured or taken in the course of lawful shooting, hunting, coursing or pest control activity; and the lawful use of traps, snares, or poisonous substances, etc.

Animals which are not living in a wild state, or are under the control of man whether on a permanent or temporary basis, or are of a kind commonly domesticated in the UK, are protected from harm by the Animal Health and Welfare (Scotland) Act 2006.

ANIMALS

9 Badgers

The Protection of Badgers Act 1992 makes special provision for badgers by introducing five specific offences, namely–
- (a) wilfully killing, taking or injuring a badger (or attempting to do so) (s.1);
- (b) cruelty to badgers (including the use of badger tongs), and digging for badgers (except as permitted by the Act) (s.2);
- (c) intentionally or recklessly interfering with badger setts by damaging or destroying them obstructing an entrance, causing a dog to enter a sett, or disturbing a badger occupying a sett (s.3);
- (d) selling, possessing or offering for sale live badgers, except in accordance with the Act (s.4);
- (e) marking or ringing a badger, unless licensed to do so (s.5);
- (f) knowingly causing or permitting any of the above offences.

There are general exceptions, including mercy killings and authorised scientific research; and specific exceptions, including an exception from (a) and (c) above for the prevention of serious damage to land, crops, poultry or any other forms of property (ss.6 to 8). Licences may be granted allowing, in specified circumstances, acts which would otherwise be offences under the Act, e.g., for the purpose of preventing the spread of disease (s.10).

10 Hunting with dogs

From 1st August 2002, the Protection of Wild Mammals (Scotland) Act 2002 makes it an offence for a person to deliberately hunt a wild mammal with a dog. It is also an offence for an owner of a dog to allow someone else to hunt with it, and for an owner or occupier of land to knowingly permit someone to hunt on that land (s.1).

A "wild mammal" does not include a rabbit or a rodent (s.10(1)). To "hunt" includes to search for or course. There are exceptions which allow–
- (a) stalking, searching and flushing from cover for the purpose of (s.2)–
    - (i) protecting livestock, ground-nesting birds, timber, fowl, game birds or crops from attack by wild mammals;
    - (ii) providing food for consumption;
    - (iii) protecting human health;
    - (iv) preventing the spread of disease;
    - (v) controlling the number of a pest species (i.e., fox, hare, mink, stoat, and weasel); or
    - (vi) controlling the number of a particular species in order to safeguard its welfare;

    but only if the target wild mammal is shot or killed by a bird of prey once it is safe to do so.

    A dog under control may be used to flush out a fox or mink for the above purposes provided, the fox or mink is shot as soon as reasonably possible after being flushed. An offence is not committed if a dog kills a pest species whilst flushing it.
- (b) use of a dog under control to stalk or flush out a wild mammal to provide quarry for sport involving the use of a bird of prey, firearm or shotgun (i.e., falconry and shooting) (s.3).
- (c) use of a dog by an authorised person to search for or catch a wild mammal where there is no intention of harming that wild mammal (s.4).
- (d) use of a dog under control to (s.5)–
    - (i) retrieve a hare which has been shot;
    - (ii) locate a wild mammal which has escaped or been released from captivity (but only if the mammal is captured or shot once located); or
    - (iii) retrieve or locate a wild mammal which is reasonably believed to be seriously injured or orphaned.

    Paragraph (ii) does not apply to a fox or hare. It also does not apply to a deer, boar or mink unless it has escaped from a farm or zoo. It does not apply to any mammal deliberately released for the purpose of being hunted.

    An orphaned fox must be killed by a single dog, or otherwise killed as humanely as possible.
- (e) any other "excepted activity" designated by the Scottish Ministers (s.6).

An offence is punishable on summary conviction by six months imprisonment, a fine not exceeding level 5 on the standard scale, or both (s.8). As to the standard scale, see the Note on **Treatment of Offenders**.

11 Marine Wildlife Watching Code

Scottish Natural Heritage must prepare and issue a Scottish Marine Wildlife Watching Code, setting out recommendations, advice and information relating to commercial and leisure activities involving the watching of marine wildlife (Nature Conservation (Scotland) Act 2004, s.51).

D: PROTECTION OF PLANTS

12 Wild plants

S.13(1) of the Wildlife and Countryside Act 1981 has been amended by Sch. 6 to the Nature Conservation (Scotland) Act 2004 so that a person is guilty of an offence if he (a) intentionally or recklessly picks, uproots, or destroys any wild plant included in Schedule 8 or any seed or spore attached to any such wild plant, or (b) not being an authorised person (see above), intentionally or recklessly uproots any wild plant not included in that Schedule. "Wild plant" means any plant (including fungi) which is or (before it was picked, uprooted, or destroyed) was growing wild and is of a kind which ordinarily grows in Great Britain in a wild state (s.27).

S.13(2)(a) makes it an offence for any person to sell or have in his possession for sale any live or dead wild plant included in Schedule 8, or any part of, or anything derived from, such a plant.

A person is not be guilty of this offence if he shows that (s.13(3))–

(a) the unlawful act was the incidental result of a lawful operation or other activity;

(b) the person who carried out the lawful operation or other activity took reasonable precautions to avoid carrying out the unlawful act or did not foresee and could not have reasonably foreseen that the unlawful act would be an incidental result of carrying out the lawful operation or other activity; and

(c) the person who carried out the unlawful act took reasonably practical steps to minimise the damage to the wild plant.

Anyone who knowingly causes or permits to be done an act which is unlawful under s.13 is guilty of an offence (s.13(3A)).

E: MISCELLANEOUS

13 General provisions

S.14 of the Wildlife and Countryside Act 1981 (as amended by the Nature Conservation (Scotland) Act 2004, Sch. 6) prohibits the introduction of new species of animals or plants. It is an offence for a person to–

(a) release or allow to escape into the wild (i) any animal of a type specified by the Scottish Ministers, or (ii) any animal to a place outside its native range, or (iii) otherwise causes any animal to be out of the control of any person at a place out side its native range (s.14(1)).

(b) plant or causes to grow in the wild any wild plant which is included in Part 2 of Sch. 9 or a hybrid of any plant included in that Part (s.14(2)).

(c) keep, possess, or have under their control any specified type of invasive animal(s.14ZC)

Exceptions to the prohibitions in s.14(1) and (2) are contained in the Wildlife and Countryside Act 1981 (Exceptions to section 14) (Scotland) Order 2012; the animals which are specified for the purposes of (a) and (c) are listed in the Wildlife and Countryside Act 1981 (Keeping and Release and Notification Requirements) (Scotland) Order 2012.

There is also a prohibition on the sale of invasive animals or plants (s.14A)).

The Scottish Ministers may require certain people to notify them of the presence of an invasive animal or invasive plant at a place outwith the native range of that plant or animal. Notification can only be required where the Scottish Ministers consider that the person or type of person to be subject to the requirement has, or should have, knowledge of, or is likely to encounter, the specified invasive animal or plant (s.14B).

The Scottish Ministers may issue codes of practice for the purpose of providing practical guidance in respect of the release, keeping, sale and notification offences in the 1981 Act, and in respect of species control agreements and species control orders (and related offences), and related matters (s.14C). Guidance in such a code of practice is not binding but it can be taken into account in determining any question in any proceedings, and in a criminal prosecution for a relevant offence the court may have regard to compliance with the code when deciding whether or not the accused is liable for the offence.

The Scottish Ministers, Scottish Natural Heritage, the Scottish Environment Protection Agency or the Forestry Commissioners may, after giving any owner or occupier it has identified at least 42 days in which to enter into a voluntary agreement, make a species control order for any premises where they are satisfied of the presence on the premises of an invasive animal or plant at a place outwith its natural range (s.14D). An emergency species control order may be made without agreement or notice where the making of the order is urgently necessary. An emergency order will expire 49 days after it is made, to allow sufficient time for the making of a non-emergency order if appropriate (s.14E). A control order will specify what must be done by whom and by when in order to control or eradicate an invasive species, may specify preventative measures and may provide for who is to pay for control and eradication measures, which may include the owner or occupier of the premises subject to the order (s.14F). An appeal against an order may be made to the sheriff within 28 days (s.14H).

Possession of any pesticide containing a prescribed active ingredient is an offence under s.15A(1) of the Wildlife and Countryside Act 1981 Act. A person guilty of an offence under s.15A(1) is liable on summary conviction to imprisonment for a term not exceeding six months or to a fine not exceeding level 5 on the standard scale (currently £5,000), or to both.

The Possession of Pesticides (Scotland) Order 2005 prescribes types of ingredients of pesticides for the purposes of s.15A as: Aldicarb, Alphachloralose, Aluminium phosphide, Bendiocarb, Carbofuran, Mevinphos, Sodium cyanide and Strychnine.

Under s.16, licences giving exemption, for specified purposes, from certain specified restrictions imposed by Part 1 of the 1981 Act may be granted by the Scottish Ministers (who may delegate their power to Scottish Natural Heritage or a local authority).

S.18 makes it an offence for any person to attempt to commit an offence under Part 1 or to have in his possession for the purposes of committing such an offence anything capable of being used for the commission of the offence. Ss.18A and 18B make employers and owners vicariously responsible for employees, managers etc., subject to a defence of due diligence.

S.22 empowers the Scottish Ministers by order to vary Schedules A1 to 6, 8 and 9. A number of Orders have been made under this provision.

S.23 deals with advisory bodies and their functions, and s.24 gives to the Nature Conservancy Councils acting jointly certain advisory functions.

S.25 requires every local authority to bring to the attention of the public, and of schoolchildren in particular, the effect of the provisions of Part I, as well as any Order made under Part I which affects the whole or any part of that area.

14 Scottish Fossil Code

Scottish Natural Heritage must prepare and issue the Scottish Fossil Code, setting out recommendations, advice and information relating to fossils (Nature Conservation (Scotland) Act 2004, s.52).

15 Authorities

Statutes–

Animal Health and Welfare (Scotland) Act 2006

Nature Conservation (Scotland) Act 2004

Protection of Badgers Act 1992

Protection of Wild Mammals (Scotland) Act 2002

Wildlife and Countryside Act 1981

Wildlife and Countryside (Amendment) Act 1991

Wildlife and Natural Environment (Scotland) Act 2011

Wild Mammals (Protection) Act 1996

Statutory Instruments–

Environmental Protection (Restriction on Use of Lead Shot) (Scotland) (No. 2) Regulations 2004, as amended (S.S.I. 2004 No. 358 and 2013 No. 349)

Possession of Pesticides (Scotland) Order 2005 (S.S.I. 2005 No. 66)

Snares (Identification Numbers and Tags) (Scotland) Order 2012 (S.S.I. 2012 No, 282)

Snares (Training) (Scotland) Order 2015 (S.S.I. 2015 No. 377)

Wildlife and Countryside Act 1981 (Amendment) Regulations 1995 (S.I. 1995 No. 2825)

Wildlife and Countryside Act 1981 (Exceptions to section 14) (Scotland) Order 2012, as amended (S.S.I. 2012 Nos. 173 and 205)

Wildlife and Countryside Act 1981 (Keeping and Release and Notification Requirements) (Scotland) Order 2012, as amended (S.S.I. 2012 Nos. 174 and 226

Wildlife and Countryside Act 1981 (Variation of Schedules A1 and 1A) (Scotland) Order 2013 (S.S.I. 2013 No. 31)

Wildlife and Countryside (Registration and Ringing of Certain Captive Birds) (Scotland) Regulations 2009 (S.S.I. 2009 No. 419)

Wildlife and Countryside (Ringing of Certain Birds) Regulations 1982 (S.I. 1982 No. 1220)

EDUCATION

EDUCATION

ENGLAND AND WALES

INTRODUCTION TO THE EDUCATION SECTION

1 Introduction

This Note gives a brief overview of the responsibility at local and national level for education matters.

2 Principal addresses

The following are the principal addresses–

Department for Children, Schools and Families
Sanctuary Buildings,
Great Smith Street,
London SW1P 3BT   (Tel: 0870 000 2288)

Department for Innovation, Universities and Skills
Sanctuary Buildings,
Great Smith Street,
London SW1P 3BT   (Tel: 01928 794666)

Teachers' Pensions
Capita Hartshead
Mowden Hall
Darlington
DL3 9EE   (Tel: 01325 745000)

Qualifications and Curriculum Authority
83 Piccadilly
London
W1J 8QA   (Tel: 020 7509 5555)

Office for Standards in Education, Children's Services and Skills
Royal Exchange Buildings
St Ann's Square
Manchester
M2 7LA   (Tel: 08456 404045 or 08456 404040)

Welsh Executive
Crown Building,
Cathays Park,
Cardiff CF10 3NQ   (Tel: 0122 282 5111)

3 The legislation

The "Education Acts" are the Education Act 1996 (the principal Act); the Education Act 1973 and 1980; the Education (Fees and Awards) Act 1983; the Further Education Act 1985 (except ss.4 and 5); the Education Act 1986; the Education (No. 2) Act 1986; the Education Reform Act 1988; the Further and Higher Education Act 1992; the Education Act 1994; the Education Act 1997; the Education (Schools) Act 1997; the Teaching and Higher Education Act 1998; the School Standards and Framework Act 1998, the Education Act 2002, the Higher Education Act 2004, the Education Act 2005, the Learner Travel (Wales) Measure 2008, the Education and Skills Act 2008, the Apprenticeship, Skills, Children and Learning Act 2009, the Healthy Eating in Schools (Wales) Measure 2009, the Children, Schools and Families Act 2010, the Academies Act 2010, the Education (Wales) Measure 2011, the Education Act 2011, the Education (Wales) Act 2014, Part 3 and s.100 of the Children and Families Act 2014, and the Education (Wales) Act 2014.

4 Central administration

Under s.10 of the Education Act 1996, the Secretary of State is responsible for promoting the education of the people of England and Wales.

The Secretary of State is required to exercise his powers in respect of those bodies in receipt of public funds which (a) carry responsibility for securing that the required provision for primary, secondary, or further education is made in schools, or institutions within the further education sector in, or in any area of England and Wales, or (b) which conduct such schools or institutions in England and Wales, for the purpose of promoting primary, secondary, and further education. Among other things, he must do so with a view to improving standards, encouraging diversity, and increasing opportunities for choice (s.11).

5 Devolution–Wales

The Government of Wales Act 2006 provides for legislative competence to be devolved to the Welsh Assembly in certain fields, one of which–Field 5–is education and training. This covers–
  (a) the categories of school that may be maintained by local authorities;
  (b) the establishment and discontinuance of schools maintained by local authorities, their change from one category to another and their alteration in other respects;
 (ba) conduct and governance of schools maintained by local authorities, including the allocation of functions, property, rights and liabilities relating to such schools;
 (bb) securing collaboration between persons or bodies with functions relating to schools maintained by local authorities;
 (bc) the establishment of, and involvement with, bodies to carry out activities relating to education or training or exercise education functions on behalf of local authorities;
  (c) the admission of pupils to schools maintained by local authorities;
  (d) the regulation of schools that are not maintained by local authorities and of relevant independent educational institutions;
  (e) school attendance, the behaviour of pupils at school, school discipline and the exclusion of pupils from school (including the duties of parents in connection with those matters);
  (f) the making of arrangements for the provision of education for persons of compulsory school age who have been excluded from schools or who for any other reason would not otherwise receive suitable education;
  (g) entitlement to primary, secondary and further education and to training;
  (h) the provision of services that are intended to encourage, enable or assist people to participate effectively in education or training, to take advantage of opportunities for employment, or to participate effectively in the life of their communities;
  (i) food and drink provided on school premises or provided for children at a place where they receive education or childcare;
  (j) Arrangements for persons to travel to and from the places where they receive nursery, primary, secondary or further education or training, and in the case of people within (q) below, higher education;
  (k) securing the provision of facilities for post-16 education or training;
  (l) the establishment and dissolution of further education institutions and bodies that conduct such institutions; and their conduct and functions, property, rights and liabilities, property held by any person for the purposes of such an institution; and the governance and staff of such institutions;
 (m) securing collaboration between bodies that conduct institutions concerned with the provision of further education, or between one or more such bodies and other persons or bodies that have functions relating to education or training in Wales;
  (n) provision of financial resources for and in connection with education or training provided by further education institutions; post-16 education or training provided otherwise than by such institutions; and the carrying out of research relating to such education or training;
  (o) the inspection of–
      (i) schools;
      (ii) relevant independent educational institutions;
      (iii) education or training provided by institutions concerned with the provision of further education;
      (iv) pre-16 education or training, or post-16 education or training, provided otherwise than by any of the above institutions;
      (v) the training of teachers and specialist teaching assistants for schools;
      (vi) services of the kinds mentioned (h) above;
  (p) provision of advice and information in connection with, and the carrying out of studies in relation to pre- or post-16 education or training, the training of teachers and specialist teaching assistants for schools, and services of the kinds mentioned in (h) above;
  (q) education and training for–
      (i) those who have a greater difficulty in learning than the majority of people of their age;
      (ii) those who have, or have had a physical or mental impairment, or a progressive health condition (such as cancer, multiple sclerosis or HIV infection) where it is at a stage involving no physical or mental impairment;
  (r) provision for children or young people of facilities for social or physical training, or educational activities.
  In relation to any of the above matters, the Welsh Assembly now has the power to make an Assembly Measure, instead of the matter being legislated for by Act of Parliament.

6 Local authorities

The local authorities with responsibility for education are (Education Act 1996, s.579)–
  (a) the county council for a county in England having a county council;
  (b) the district council for a district in England which is not in a county having a county council;
  (c) London borough councils;

(d) the Common Council of the City of London (in its capacity as a local authority);

(e) the county council for a county in Wales;

(f) the county borough council for a county borough in Wales.

The term "local education authority" is no longer used.

In England, local authorities are responsible for further education as well as schools (s.13). A local authority has a specific statutory duty to promote high standards and fulfilment of learning potential for those under the age of 20 (and, in England, those aged 20 but under 25 and for whom an EHC plan is maintained) (s.13A). In England there is also a duty to ensure fair access to opportunity for education and training.

A local authority must also secure that (Education Act 1996, s.18A, not yet in force in Wales)–

(a) enough suitable education is provided to meet the reasonable needs of children subject to youth detention in their area;

(b) enough suitable education and training is provided to meet the reasonable needs of persons who are over compulsory school age but under 19 and subject to youth detention in their area.

This local authority duty does not apply to young people in Young Offender Institutions whose education is the responsibility of, in England, the Secretary of State (under s.86), and in Wales of the Welsh Ministers (under the Learning and Skills Act 2000, s.32).

7 Support services: provision by local authorities

In addition to their responsibilities in respect of schools, local authorities in England have a duty to make available to young people (i.e., aged 13 to 19) and relevant young adults for whom they are responsible such services as they consider appropriate to encourage, enable or assist them to engage and remain in education or training. A relevant young adult is a person aged 20 to 24 years who has a learning difficulty (Education and Skills Act 2008, s.68). This is done through the service known as the Connexions services. A local authority can fulfil the duty to make services available either by providing them itself or by making arrangements with others, which could include other local authorities. The Secretary of State has the power to give directions about certain matters (specified in s.68) to a local authority relating to the exercise of its duty to make support services available (2008 Act, s.69). The Connexions service provider may enter into, as part of the Connexions service, a learning and support agreement with a young person aged 13 to 19 (2008 Act, s.71). This includes a young person who is not participating, or at risk of not participating, in education or training as required by s.2 of the 2008 Act (duty to participate in education or training). A learning and support agreement comprises agreement by a young person to comply with certain requirements, and agreement by the Connexions service provider to provide specified support (which may include financial support or an incentive payment) on condition that the young person complies with those requirements. It does not amount to a legally binding contract and the young person must be involved in negotiating the agreement. A local authority is required to ensure that Connexions support has been offered to a young person to whom the duty to participate in education or training applies, before taking enforcement action for failure to comply with the duty imposed by s.2.

8 Inspection of education establishments

The Education Act 2005, s.2 provides that Her Majesty's Chief Inspector of Schools in England has a duty to keep the Secretary of State informed about, *inter alia*, the quality of education provided in schools. Similar provisions apply to Wales (s.20). The Act provides for the regular inspection of schools by inspection teams led by registered inspectors (see the Note on **Education: Standards and Inspection: England and Wales**).

9 Organisation of the system

The statutory system of public education is organised in three progressive stages known as primary, secondary, and further education, and it is the duty of local authorities to contribute to the spiritual, moral, mental, and physical development of the community by securing that efficient education throughout those stages is available to meet the needs of the population of their areas (Education Act 1996, ss.1 and 13).

10 Unreasonable exercise of functions

The Secretary of State has a general power to prevent, by giving such directions as appear to him to be expedient, the unreasonable exercise of functions by any local authority, or by the governors of any community, foundation or voluntary school or community or foundation special school, or a maintained nursery school (Education Act 1996, s.496). The Secretary of State may also make an order declaring an authority or governors, as the case may be, in default if he is satisfied, on complaint by any person, that they have failed to discharge a duty imposed on them, and may give directions, enforceable by a mandatory order, to secure its execution (s.497).

If a local authority is failing in any respect to perform its function to an adequate standard (or at all), the Secretary of State may give it directions as to the performance of its functions, or direct that a function be exercised by him or a person nominated by him and that the authority comply with any instructions of his or of his nominee in relation to the exercise of that function. Again, these directions are enforceable by a mandatory order (s.497A).

11 Research

Under s.526 of the Education Act 1996, local authorities may make provision for conducting or assisting the conduct of research for the purpose of improving the educational facilities provided for their areas.

12 Welfare of children and consultation with pupils

The Education Act 2002, s.175, provides that a local authority must make arrangements for ensuring that their education functions are exercised with a view to safeguarding and promoting the welfare of children. A local authority, in considering what arrangements are required to be made by them concerning welfare, must have regard to any guidance issued by the Secretary of State or the National Assembly for Wales. It is also the duty of a local authority, in the exercise of any of their schools functions, to have regard to any guidance from the Secretary of State, or the National Assembly for Wales, about consultation with pupils in connection with the taking of decisions affecting them. Such guidance must provide for a pupil's views to be considered in the light of his age and understanding (Education Act 2002, s.176 amended by the Education and Inspections Act 2006, Sch. 18 Pt 6).

13 Looked after children

The governing body of a maintained school in England and Wales (i.e., a community or foundation school; voluntary school, including both voluntary aided and voluntary controlled; community or foundation special school; and maintained nursery school) must designate a member of staff as having responsibility for promoting the educational achievement of looked after children who are registered pupils at the school.

The responsibilities of the designated person include both pupils who are looked after by a local authority and those who are "relevant children" or "former relevant children" (i.e., children who are no longer looked after but have been at some point since the age of 16). The designated person is also responsible for promoting the educational achievement of children and young persons at the school who have equivalent legal status under the laws of Scotland or Northern Ireland (Children and Young Persons Act 2008, s.20).

The Designated Teacher (Looked After Pupils etc) (England) Regulations 2009 provide that a designated teacher for these purposes must be a qualified teacher.

14 Financial assistance for education and childcare

The former wide variety of powers for making financial assistance available for purposes connected with education are, in many cases, repealed by the Education Act 2002 (see especially s.18 in this regard) and replaced by a single broad power. Thus, by s.14, the Secretary of State or Welsh Assembly may give, or make arrangements for the giving of, financial assistance to any person for–

(a) the provision or proposed provision of education, educational services, childcare, or services related to child care;

(b) enabling any person to undertake a course of education or higher education within the further education sector and providing for his maintenance while he undertakes such a course;

(c) the promotion of: learning or research, the use of educational buildings or facilities for purposes other than education;

(d) the provision of training for teachers or non-teaching staff;

(e) promoting the recruitment or retention of teachers or non-teaching staff;

(f) remuneration of teachers or non-teaching staff.

Such financial assistance may be given on such terms as the Secretary of State or Welsh Assembly considers appropriate (s.16) and arrangements may be made for such financial assistance to be provided other than by the Secretary of State or Welsh Assembly (s.17). It should be noted that assistance extends beyond the UK (s.14(2), (3)). Financial assistance may be given in any form (s.15).

Authorities

Children and Young Persons Act 2008

Education Acts 1962 to 2009

Government of Wales Act 2006

Designated Teacher (Looked After Pupils etc) (England) Regulations 2009 (S.I. 2009 No. 1538)

Education (Pupil Referral Units) (Application of Enactments) Regulations 1994, as amended (S.I. 1994 No. 2103 and 1996 No. 2087)

SCHOOLS: ADMISSION AND ATTENDANCE
ENGLAND AND WALES

1 Introduction

This Note sets out the ways in which schools can set admission policies, including the rules as to parental preference. It also covers school attendance and the measures which can be taken to improve attendance rates, such as school attendance orders, education supervision orders, and penalty notices.

A: GENERAL PROVISIONS

2 Parent's duty and compulsory school age

It is the duty of the parent of every child of compulsory school age to cause him to receive, either by regular attendance at school or otherwise, efficient full-time education suitable to his age, ability, and aptitude, and to any special educational needs he may have (Education Act 1996, s.7). "Compulsory school age" means (s.8) any age between 5 and 16 years, subject to the appropriate school-leaving date.

A pupil ceases to be of compulsory school age on the school leaving date for any calendar year–
   (a) if he reaches the age of 16 after that date but before the beginning of the school year next following;
   (b) if he is 16 on that date; or
   (c) (unless (a) applies) if that date is the school leaving date next following his sixteenth birthday.

Under the Education (School Leaving Date) Order 1997, the school leaving date for 1998 and subsequent years is the last Friday in June.

As a general rule, pupils will be admitted to school only at the beginning of a term, but a child unable to enter a school at the beginning of the term owing to illness or other circumstances beyond the parent's control, or because his parents were then resident at a place from which a school was not reasonably accessible, may enter during the currency of a term (s.433).

3 Children to be educated in accordance with parents' wishes

In carrying out their functions under the Education Acts, the Secretary of State and local authorities must have regard to the general principle that, so far as is compatible with the provision of efficient instruction and training and the avoidance of unreasonable public expenditure, pupils are to be educated in accordance with the wishes of their parents (Education Act 1996, s.9).

B: SCHOOL ADMISSIONS

4 Selection of pupils

Ss.99 to 103 of the School Standards and Framework Act 1998 and s.39 of the Education and Inspections Act 2006 contain provisions relating to the selection of pupils.

S.39 of the 2006 Act provides that no admission arrangements for a maintained school may make provision for selection by ability (meaning general ability in any particular subject or subjects) unless–
   (a) they make provision for a permitted form of such selection (see below); or
   (b) the school is a grammar school.

S.99(2) of the 1998 Act permits the following forms of selection by ability: pre-existing arrangements authorised by s.100 (see below); selection authorised by s.101 (see below); and selection of pupils over school age.

No admission arrangements for a maintained school may make provision for selection on aptitude for a particular subject (e.g., art), unless they provide for a permitted form of such selection and, under s.99(4), the only forms of selection by aptitude permitted are those authorised by either s.100 (pre-existing arrangements–see below), or s.102 (aptitude for particular subject–see below).

Where a school's admission arrangements for the 1997-98 school year made provision for some pupils to be admitted by ability or by aptitude (and have at all times since then continued to do so) the school admission arrangements may continue to make such provision so long as the proportion of selective admissions in any relevant age group does not exceed the "permitted proportion" and there is no significant change in the basis of selection (s.100, amended by the Education and Inspections Act 2006, s.53). The "permitted proportion", in relation to any relevant age group, means the lowest proportion of selective admissions provided for by the school's admission arrangements at any time since the beginning of the 1997-1998 school year (s.100(1A), inserted by the Education and Inspections Act 2006, s.53(3)). The Education (Proportion of Selective Admissions) Regulations 1998 specify that, when making this calculation, the total number of pupils admitted in an age group will be taken to be equal to the number of pupils in that age group which it is or was intended to admit to the school.

Schools may make arrangements to secure that in any year the pupils admitted in any relevant age group to a maintained school in England and Wales represent all levels of ability among applicants in that age group with no level of ability being substantially over-represented or under-represented (pupil banding). Once a pupil has been allocated to a particular ability band, no further selection process can be carried out for the purpose of deciding whether he should be admitted to the school (s.101, amended by the 2006 Act, s.54). In Wales, the introduction of banding arrangements under s.101 (as amended by the Education Act 2002, Sch. 21, para. 109) is not permitted unless proposals for a school to have such arrangements have been published, and fallen to be implemented, under any enactment.

In England, admission authorities of maintained schools may introduce three additional forms of banding: the first across the full ability range of children applying to any of two or more schools in a local authority area; the second across the full ability range of the relevant age group within the local authority area; and the third across the full ability range of the relevant age group within England. Where, in England, the admission authority is the local authority, it must secure the consent of the governing body before introducing such arrangements (s.100(1A), inserted by the School Standards and Inspections Act 2006).

S.102(1) permits maintained schools to select pupils for admission to the school by reference to their aptitude for one or more prescribed subjects where (a) the school's admission authority are satisfied that the school has a specialism in the subjects concerned; and (b) the proportion of selective admission in any relevant age group does not exceed 10%. The School Admissions (Admission Arrangements and Co-ordination of Admission Arrangements) (England) Regulations 2012 prescribe the following subjects for the purposes of s.102: modern foreign languages; the performing and visual arts; physical education or sport; and (but only if the school made provision for selection by aptitude in relation to them in 2007-08 and each subsequent year) design and technology, and information technology.

S.102(1) does not in itself permit pupils to be tested on their general ability, or on their aptitude outside the subject in question, but a school's admission arrangements may provide both for selection on aptitude under s.102 and on ability under s.101 (see above), in which case pupils may be tested on their general ability.

Where schools do select up to 10% of their intake by reference to their aptitude in a prescribed subject, they are able to admit up to 10% by aptitude irrespective of any banding arrangements adopted (s.101(5), as amended by the 2006 Act, s.54(1)).

Where a selective school is a grammar school, ss.105 to 109 (see **5 Grammar schools**, below) prescribe the procedure for altering its admission arrangements so that it no longer has selective arrangements and its admission arrangements may not be altered except in accordance with those sections. The Education (Substituted Grammar Schools) Regulations 1999 provide for cases where a maintained school has been established in substitution for one or more former grammar schools. The Secretary of State may designate such a school as a grammar school.

5 Grammar schools

Where a maintained school is a grammar school, ss.105 to 109 of the School Standards and Framework Act 1998 prescribe the procedures for altering the school's admission arrangements so that it is no longer a selective school (s.104).

Where the Secretary of State was satisfied that a maintained school had selective admission arrangements at the beginning of the 1997-98 school year, he could by order designate the school as a grammar school. A school had selective admission arrangements for these purposes if its admission arrangements made provision for all (or substantially all) of its pupils to be selected by reference to general ability, with a view to admitting pupils of only high ability (s.104).

S.105 allows the Secretary of State to make regulations for ballots of parents to be held, at their request, for determining whether grammar schools should retain selective admission arrangements. The Education (Grammar School Ballots) Regulations 1998 make provision for the holding of such ballots. A ballot may relate to all grammar schools within a relevant local authority area (an "area ballot") or to a group of schools, or to a single "stand alone" grammar school (and a ballot relating to a group of schools or to a single school is referred to as a "feeder school ballot" (Reg. 11). Schedule 1 to the Regulations lists the local authorities where area ballots may take place, while Schedules 2 and 3 list, respectively, the groups of schools and stand alone schools that may be the subject of a feeder school ballot.

No ballot may be held unless a request for a ballot is made by means of a petition sent to Electoral Reform (Ballot Services) Ltd (ERBS), whose address is Independence House, 33 Clarendon Street, London N8 0NW (Tel. 020 8365 8909). In the case of an area ballot, a petition must be signed by at least 20% of eligible parents. A parent will be an eligible parent for these purposes if (a) he is registered as a parent of a child of compulsory school age who is a pupil at a school maintained by the local authority for the area in question; (b) he is resident in the area in question and is a registered parent of a child of compulsory school age attending an independent school or alternative provision Academy in that area; or (c) he is a parent resident in the area whose child is below compulsory school age, or is below the age of 16 and is being educated at home; or is of compulsory school age and is attending a school (whether a state school, an independent school, or an alternative provision Academy) which is outside the local authority's area (Reg. 4). Parents who come within category (c) must register with the ERBS and provide evidence of eligibility before they may sign a petition.

In the case of feeder school ballots, a petition must also be signed by at least 20% of eligible parents. A parent is eligible for these purposes if he is a parent of a child who is a pupil at a school which is a feeder school for the stand alone grammar school or for the group of schools in respect of which the petition is being held. A parent whose child is older than the normal age for transfer to the grammar school or schools concerned is not eligible. A "feeder school" is defined as a school from which at least five pupils have transferred to the grammar school or schools concerned during the school year in question and the preceding two years. Pupils who are over the normal transfer age when they transfer are disregarded for these purposes (Reg. 6).

Petitions are only valid for the school year in which they are held. ERBS will determine whether a petition is valid and will then notify all relevant bodies, including the local authority for the area, the governing body for each grammar school affected, and the governing bodies of all other relevant schools in the area (including feeder schools where the petition relates to a feeder school ballot) (Reg. 10).

All parents who were eligible to sign the petition for a ballot will also be eligible to vote in the ballot, together, in the case of an area ballot, with parents within category (c) above who have registered with ERBS within four weeks of notification being given that a ballot will take place (Reg. 12).

Ballot papers will ask parents if they are in favour of the school or schools listed on the ballot paper introducing new admission arrangements which will admit children of all abilities (Reg. 13).

Each ballot will be a secret postal ballot and each parent will have one vote, irrespective of the number of children he has and the number of different schools those children attend. ERBS must ensure that ballot papers are returned no later than ten weeks from the date on which notice has been given by that body that a ballot will be held and at least five weeks from the date on which papers are sent to parents (Reg. 14).

Where the result of a ballot is that a school or schools should retain selective admission arrangements, no further ballot may be held relating to that same area, group of schools, or school, as the case may be, for the next five years (Reg. 16). Where the result of a ballot is that a school or schools should end selective admissions, that change must be introduced in either the second or third school year after the result is announced (depending on whether the result is announced before or after 31st December in any school year) (Reg. 17).

Regulations 18 and 20 prescribe that certain information must be given to parents who are considering whether to ask for a ballot. If ten or more parents notify ERBS that they are planning to raise a petition, ERBS will *inter alia* provide them with a list of feeder schools and calculate the number of parents who would need to sign a petition. Governing bodies are also required to provide relevant information to ERBS (Reg. 19). Schools must also provide parents organising petitions or disseminating information prior to a ballot with lists of the names and addresses of parents who would be eligible to vote in a ballot, but a parent may request that his name and address should be omitted from such a list (Reg. 20).

S.107 prohibits expenditure from being incurred by a local authority or a school maintained by an authority for the purpose of seeking to influence (whether by written material or otherwise) requests for ballots or the outcome of a ballot. S.107 does not, however, prohibit expenditure on publishing or otherwise providing (a) fairly presented factual material; or (b) fair and reasonable assessments of the likely consequences of a ballot being in favour of a school or schools ceasing to be selective; or (c) an accurate statement of an authority or school's intentions or proposals in the event of such a result.

Where the result of a ballot shows a simple majority of votes cast in favour of the school or schools concerned ceasing to be selective, the admission authority must revise their admission arrangements so that they cease to be selective and, once this has been done, the Secretary of State must revoke the order made under s.104 above which designates the school or schools concerned as grammar schools (s.108).

S.109 allows governing bodies of grammar schools to themselves end selective admission arrangements, even where a ballot has not been held. Governing bodies may end selection by ability altogether, or may make provision for selection under ss.101 or 102 to reflect all ability levels or aptitude for a particular subject (see **4 Selection of pupils** above). Any such revision of admission arrangements will be one of the alterations to a maintained school which is prescribed for the purposes of s.18 of the 2006 Act (see the Note on **Schools: Provision and Governance** at para **9 Alteration of schools: England**).

In the case of grammar schools which are community schools, proposals to end selective admission arrangements are to be published by the governing body rather than by the local authority. The Education (Proposals for Grammar Schools to Cease to have Selective Admission Arrangements) Regulations 1999 make provision where proposals are published by the governing body. In particular, such proposals will have no effect if a valid petition requesting a ballot to decide whether the school should retain selective admission arrangements is received after the proposals are published by a governing body but before they are decided, or a valid petition has already been received when the proposals are published but the ballot result date has not yet occurred (Reg. 4).

6 Parental preference

Every local authority must make arrangements for enabling parents to express a preference as to the school their child is to attend, or preferences for more than one school (which may be outside the local authority area in which he lives) and to give their reasons for that preference or preferences (School Standards and Framework Act 1998, s.86 (as amended by the Education Act 2002, Sch. 4 and the Education and Inspections Act 2006, s.42)). In England, local authorities must provide advice and assistance to parents of children living in their area to help them in the formulation of their preference on a school for their child (s.86(1A)). Advice and assistance includes providing parents with good, easy to understand information and advice about the schools in their area, and neighbouring areas where applicable, in a form that fits the needs of the parent. This might include how the admission arrangements work and the level of priority their child will have for a place, whether their child will be entitled to school transport and how that will work if the child does not live within walking distance of the school, and whether the school has any special features that may of interest to the parent (Explanatory Notes to Education and Inspections Act 2006, s.42).

The authority and the governing body of a maintained school must comply with any such preference unless (1998 Act, s.86)–

EDUCATION

(a) compliance would prejudice the provision of efficient education or the efficient use of resources (including the duty placed on local authorities and governing bodies to limit infant class sizes–see H: CLASS SIZES, below);

(b) the child has been permanently excluded from two or more schools, the latest exclusion being within the last two years (see **7 Children permanently excluded from two or more schools**, below);

(c) the arrangements for admission to the preferred school are based wholly on selection by reference to ability or aptitude and are so based with a view to admitting only pupils with high ability or aptitude, and compliance would be incompatible with selection under those arrangements; or

(d) where a parent has expressed more than one preference, the child is offered admission to one of the preferred schools. In such a case, any other preferred school is not obliged to offer admission to that child.

Local authorities must also make arrangements to enable a young person to apply for a place at a school, independently of his or her parents, either to study in the sixth form or, if they are above compulsory school age, to study at any level of education (for example to re-sit their GCSEs). Parents also have the right to apply to schools on behalf of their children (s.86A). The duty to comply with the preference is subject to the same exceptions as set out in (a) to (d) above (s.86B).

Note.–The parent's right of choice does not apply in relation to nursery schools; to children who will not have attained the age of five at the time of their proposed admission to school; to special schools; or to children with special educational needs (1998 Act, s.98).

The authority must make arrangements enabling a parent (parent or child in relation to a sixth form) to appeal against any decision of the authority as to the school his child is to attend or against any refusal by the governing body of a community or voluntary controlled school to admit the child to such a school. The governors of a foundation or voluntary aided school have a similar duty to arrange for appeals against their refusal of admission of a child to their school. Joint arrangements for this purpose may be made by the governors of two or more foundation or voluntary aided schools maintained by the same authority (s.94 of the 1998 Act, amended by he Education and Inspections Act 2006, s.51(1)). Any refusal to transfer a pupil already admitted to a secondary school to that school's sixth form also carries a right of appeal (s.94(1A)).

The constitution of the appeal panel for an appeal pursuant to any arrangements made under s. 94 is provided for by regulations. Under the School Admissions (Appeals Arrangements) (England) Regulations 2012 (and the equivalent 2005 Welsh Regulations), an appeal under s.94 will be to an appeal panel, consisting of a minimum of three (and in Wales not more than five) members appointed by the authority or governing body from (a) persons eligible to be lay members; and (b) persons who have experience in education, are acquainted with educational conditions in the area of the authority or are parents of registered pupils at a school. At least one member of the panel must be a lay member and at least one must be a person falling within (b). A person is eligible to be a lay member if he has no personal experience in the management of any school or the provision of education in any school (disregarding any such experience as a governor or in a voluntary capacity).

See also **13 Admissions codes of practice**, below.

7 Children permanently excluded from two or more schools

The duty imposed under ss.86 and 86B of the School Standards and Framework Act 1998 (see **6 Parental preference**, above) does not apply in the case of a pupil who has been permanently excluded from two or more schools, the latest such exclusion having taken place within the preceding two years (s.87). However, a child is not to be regarded as having been so excluded if (1998 Act s.87(4), as amended by Education Act 2002, Sch 4)–

(a) he was reinstated as a pupil at the school following a direction given in accordance with s. 52 of the Education Act 2002;

(b) on a review of his exclusion it was decided that it would not be practical to reinstate him but that it would otherwise have been appropriate so to do;

(c) he was below school age at the time of his exclusion.

In a case where s.87 applies to a child, there is no right for the child's parent to appeal against a school's refusal to admit him and, in addition, the governing body of a community or voluntary controlled school may appeal against any decision of the local authority that a child to whom s.87 applies should be admitted to that school (1998 Act, s.95). This does not apply in relation to a decision by or on behalf of a local authority in England to admit to a school a child who is looked after by a local authority in England (s.95(2A), inserted by the Education and Inspections Act 2006, s.48(2)). There is provision for references in such cases to be made to an adjudicator (s.95A, as so inserted). Local authorities must notify the governing body of a community or voluntary controlled school that a decision has been made to admit a looked after child who has been permanently excluded from two or more schools. On receipt of the notification, the governing body has seven days to refer the matter to the adjudicator. Such a reference can only be made where the admission of the child would cause serious prejudice to the provision of efficient education or the efficient use of resources. If the adjudicator agrees that serious prejudice would be caused, the decision to admit the child to the school ceases to have effect but the adjudicator may, with the agreement of the local authority that looks after the child, determine that another school should admit the child. The adjudicator cannot name another school if the child has been permanently excluded from the school or if the admission of the child to the school would cause serious prejudice. There is a power under s.95A to make regulations as to the consultation which must be carried out by the adjudicator and the information which must be provided by the admission authority.

The procedure to be followed on an appeal by a governing body against the admission of a child to whom s.87 applies is set out in the School Admission Appeals Code (see further **6 Parental preference**, above).

8 School admission arrangements–introduction

The admission authority for a school year will, before the beginning of each school year, determine the admission arrangements which are to apply for that year (School Standards and Framework Act 1998, s.89). In the case of a community or voluntary controlled schools the admission authority is the local authority (although some such schools may be given delegated power to determine their own admission arrangements) and in the case of foundation or voluntary aided schools it is the governing body (s.88).

No admission arrangements for a maintained school may require or authorise any interview with an applicant for admission to the school, or his parents, where the interview is to be taken into account (to any extent) in determining whether the applicant is to be admitted to the school (ss.88A and 88R). However, interviews are allowed which are intended to assess suitability for a boarding place at a school with boarding accommodation, and schools with permissible selective admission arrangements may conduct assessments to ascertain an applicant's aptitude (ss.88A(2), (3), 88R(2), (3)).

Community and voluntary controlled schools in England must comply with any decision to admit a child made by their local authority (if it is the school's admission authority) (School Standards and Framework Act 1998, s.88(1A) inserted by the Education and Inspections Act 2006, s.43(1)).

The duty to comply with a local authority's decision to admit does not affect the governing body's right to appeal to an independent appeal panel against the admission of any child who has been twice permanently excluded, nor the requirement for the local authority to seek governing body consent to the introduction of pupil banding to the school's admission arrangements (s.88(1B) as so inserted).

9 Determining admission arrangements–Wales

Before determining the admission arrangements that are to apply for a particular school year, an admission authority in Wales must consult (School Standards and Framework Act 1998, s.89(2))–
(a) whichever of the governing body and the local authority are not the admission authority;
(b) the admission authorities for all other maintained schools in the relevant area (see definition below) or other schools that may be prescribed;
(c) the governing bodies for all community and voluntary controlled schools in the relevant area;
(d) the admission authorities for maintained schools of any prescribed description.
(e) in the case of a foundation or voluntary school which has a religious character, such body or person representing the religion or religious denomination in question as may be prescribed.

Once such consultations have been carried out, the admission authority must determine their proposed arrangements. Admission authorities may be required to publish their reasons for making a determination in certain circumstances (1998 Act, s.89(4)(fa)).

A determination under s.89 by the admission authority must include a determination of the number of pupils in each relevant age group that it is intended to admit to the school in that year and, in the case of a school at which boarding accommodation is provided, a determination of the number of pupils in each relevant age group that it is intended to admit as boarders, or otherwise than as boarders (s.89A, added by the Education Act 2002, s.47).

The governing body of any maintained school must comply with a determination by the local authority that a child should be admitted in accordance with the application of the area's co-ordinated admissions scheme (s.89C(3A), inserted by the Education and Inspections Act 2006, s.43(3)).

The Education (Determination of Admission Arrangements) (Wales) Regulations 2006 set out the procedure admission authorities should follow when determining their admission arrangements. All Welsh admission authorities must complete the consultation required by s.89 before 1 March in the determination year in the same way as in England. There is also a duty in Wales to have regard to the indicated admission number for each relevant age group when determining the number of pupils to be admitted in any school year in any relevant age group. The indicated admission number is the number calculated in accordance with the capacity assessment method set out in the guidance document "Measuring the capacity of schools in Wales". This guidance is available on the Welsh Assembly's website at <www.learning.gov.uk> (Reg. 4).

Where the admission arrangements in Wales are for a primary school, the duty to consult other admission authorities in the relevant area only applies to the authorities for other primary schools (Reg. 5). An admission authority which is a local authority must consult every neighbouring local authority. An admission authority which is the governing body for a school must consult any other local authority whose area falls within or adjoins the relevant area for consultation (Reg. 6). A governing body which is an admission authority has the power to suspend consultation requirements in certain circumstances (Reg. 7). The consultation must relate to all of the proposed admission arrangements, except any arrangements which cannot be introduced or altered except by means of statutory proposals (Reg. 8). A written copy of the proposed admission arrangements must be sent to each admission authority that must be consulted and asked for comments (Reg. 9). There are also requirements for notifying other admission authorities about the final admission arrangements (Reg. 10).

In Wales, details about admission arrangements which provide for selection of pupils by ability must be published in a local newspaper; so must the situation where the admission authority has determined an admission number for a relevant age group which is lower than the current indicated admission number (Reg. 11). An admission authority must also publish additional information under Reg. 11 to provide, on request, further details relating to its admission arrangements and to the parents' right of objection (Reg. 12).

The Education (Variation of Admission Arrangements) (Wales) Regulations 2013 prescribe that an admission authority may vary the admission arrangements they have set out for a particular school year in order to give effect to the School Admissions Code; to implement proposals approved by the Welsh Ministers, or to correct any omission or misprint in the admission arrangements.

10 Determining admission arrangements–England

Rather than statutory annual consultations as to admission arrangements (as is the case in Wales), in England the Secretary of State has a power to prescribe the consultation process by regulations which may set out who must be consulted, how often consultation must take place and the circumstances in which no, or partial, consultation is required (School Standards and Framework Act 1998, ss.88B to 88G). The School Admissions (Admission Arrangements and Co-ordination of Admission Arrangements) (England) Regulations 2012 have been made for this purpose and apply from the academic year 2013-2014 (see below).

There is power to restrict the alteration of admission arrangements following the establishment or expansion of a school (s.88G).

The 2012 Regulations make provision for admission arrangements for school years 2013-2014 onwards. The Regulations require all admission authorities to ensure that they complete the consultation required for each school year before 1st March in the "determination year" (defined as the school year beginning two years prior to the school year which the arrangements will be for). In addition, every such authority must take all steps necessary to ensure that they will have determined these admission arrangements before 15th April in that determination year (Reg. 17). Schools which are their own admission authority do not have to consult on a proposal to increase or to keep the same admission number, but if the admission authority is the local authority, the governing body of the school must be consulted (Reg. 14). No consultation is needed if there has been no change to admission arrangements in the previous seven years (Reg. 15).

Those who must be consulted are (Reg. 12)–
(a) whichever of the governing body and the local authority are not the admission authority;
(b) the admission authorities for all other schools in the relevant area (for primary schools, only other primary schools);
(c) where the admission authority for the school is the local authority, any neighbouring local authority;
(d) parents of children aged 2-18 resident in the relevant area;
(e) such other persons in the relevant area who appear to the admission authority to have an interest in the proposed admission arrangements; and
(f) in the case of a foundation or voluntary school which is designated as having a religious character, the body or person representing the religion or religious denomination in question.

A local authority must publish, on their website and in a newspaper circulating in its locality, information relating to the admission arrangements for maintained schools in their area. The prescribed information includes the fact that certain parents may object to the adjudicator on the ground that a school's admission arrangements do not comply with the School Admissions Code or Part 3 of the School Standards and Framework Act 1998 (see **15 Alteration and variation of, and objections to admissions in England,** below) (Reg. 18).

11 Co-ordination of admission arrangements

Ss.89B and 89C of the 1998 Act (added by the Education Act 2002) concern the co-ordination of admission arrangements to maintained schools. They provide that regulations may be made requiring LEAs to co-ordinate the admission arrangements for school in their areas and also requiring consultations to be undertaken with a view to securing compatibility of admission arrangements between different LEAs where reasonably practicable. The School Admissions (Admission Arrangements and Co-ordination of Admission Arrangements) (England) Regulations 2012 Regs. 26 to 32 and the School Admissions (Common Offer Date) (Wales) Regulations 2013 make provision in this regard.

12 Objection to admissions

Where admission arrangements have been determined by an admissions authority, parents may object to those arrangements (School Standards and Framework Act 1998, s.90 as amended by the Education and Inspections Act 2006, s.41(8)). Any such objection will, in England, be referred to an adjudicator (appointed by the Secretary of State under s.25 of the Act) and, in Wales, will be referred directly to the Welsh Ministers. The decision of the adjudicator or the ministers on the objection will be binding on the admission authority and on all the persons entitled to object and, where necessary an admission authority must revise their admission arrangements in such a way as to give effect to the objection.

An adjudicator must provide, on request by the Secretary of State, advice on such matters relating to the admission of pupils to relevant schools as may be specified by the Secretary of State. The adjudicator may request information from the admission authorities of community, foundation or voluntary schools and the proprietors of other relevant schools so as to enable him to comply with the request. Those from whom the adjudicator requests information must provide that information (s.25(3A)-(3D), inserted by the Education and Inspections Act 2006, s.163).

On a referral of an objection to a school's admission arrangements the adjudicator can consider whether it would be appropriate for changes to be made to any aspect of the admission arrangements, whether or not he would be required to do so for the purpose of determining the objection (s.90(5A), amended by the Education and Inspections Act 2006, s.47(2)).

The adjudicator (in relation to England) or the Welsh Assembly (in relation to Wales) must publish a report in relation to any decision on referred admission arrangements. The report must include the decision on the objection, any decision on whether any changes should be made to the admission arrangements and the reason(s) for the decisions. The report may specify the modifications to be made to the admission arrangements (s.90(5B) and (5C), as so inserted).

Decisions of the adjudicator (in relation to England) or the Welsh Assembly (in relation to Wales) are binding on the admission authority and on people by whom an objection may be made. Any changes required by the adjudicator or Secretary of State (in relation to England) or the Welsh Assembly (in relation to Wales) must be implemented by the admission authority (s.90(8), inserted by the Education and Inspections Act 2006, s.47(4)).

There is also a restriction on the alteration of admission arrangements following the adjudicator's decision (s.90A, inserted by the Education and Inspections Act 2006, s.46(3)). Determinations by the adjudicator will generally remain effective for a prescribed number of school years or lesser period as determined by the adjudicator.

The School Admissions (Admission Arrangements and Co-ordination of Admission Arrangements) (England) Regulations 2012 and the Education (Objections to Admission Arrangements) (Wales) Regulations 2006 set out the criteria under which objections to admissions may be made (see 15 **Alteration and variation of, and objections to admissions in England,** below).

13 Admissions codes of practice

The Secretary of State and Welsh Ministers may issue and from time to time revise codes for school admissions and school admissions appeals containing such provision as they think appropriate for admission authorities in the exercise of their functions. The codes may impose requirements and may include guidelines setting out aims, objectives and other matters in relation to the discharge of their functions by local authorities and governing bodies. Any such code must be published (School Standards and Framework Act 1998, s.84 amended by the Education and Inspections Act 2006, s.40).

The current Codes were published in December 2014 (England) (Appeals Code in February 2012) and July 2013 (Wales) (Appeals Code in January 2014). In particular, the Codes specify that in drawing up admission arrangements, admission authorities must ensure that they—

(a) are clear in the sense of being free from doubt and easily understood;

(b) are objective and based on known facts;

(c) are procedurally fair and are also equitable for all groups of children (including those with special educational needs, disabilities, those in public care, or who may be a young carer);

(d) provide parents or carers with easy access to helpful admissions information;

(e) comply with all relevant legislation, including on infant class sizes and on equal opportunities.

Matters of procedure of appeal panels and decision making in appeals are provided for in the Codes. *Inter alia,* admission authorities must allow appellants at least ten school days from the date of notification that their application was unsuccessful, to prepare and submit their written appeal to the admission authority. In circumstances where a young person has a right of appeal (i.e., in respect of admission to a school sixth-form or admission to a school other than the school sixth-form by a young person who is above compulsory school age) that right is in addition to the parent's right of appeal. Appeal panels must make every effort to allow appellants the opportunity to appear in person, make oral representations and clarify or supplement their written appeal. Appellants may be accompanied or represented by a friend, adviser, interpreter or signer who may speak on their behalf at the hearing.

In reaching a decision, the appeal panel must consider whether the relevant oversubscription criteria for the school and coordinated admission arrangements were correctly and impartially applied to the child concerned and whether or not there would be prejudice caused by the additional admission of the child. The panel must also consider whether the appellant's grounds for the child to be admitted outweigh any prejudice to the school. The panel must take into account the appellant's reasons for expressing a preference for the particular school (e.g. why they want that school in particular and what it can offer the child that others cannot).

The School Admissions Code for England is available at <https://www.gov.uk/government/publications/school-admissions-code--2> and the Appeals Code at <https://www.gov.uk/government/publications/school-admissions-appeals-code>. The corresponding Welsh Codes covering admissions and appeals are available at <http://wales.gov.uk/topics/educationandskills/schoolshome/admissions-and-appeals-code>.

14 Admissions and the local authority

A local authority in Wales must, in accordance with regulations, establish for its area an admission forum to advise, *inter alia*, admission authorities for maintained schools in the area on matters connected with the determination of admission arrangements and other matters connected with the admission of pupils. Admission forums have the power to prepare and publish reports on matters connected with admissions to maintained schools in their area. It also enables them to request from the local authority, neighbouring authorities, and governing bodies, any information they require to fulfil this function and there is a duty on those bodies to comply with such a request. (School Standards and Framework Act 1998, s.85A added by the Education Act 2002, s. 46, and amended by the Education and Inspections Act 2006, s.41).

The Education (Admission Forums) (Wales) Regulations 2003 contain provisions for the establishment of admission forums.

Admission forums must be notified by admission authorities of their admission arrangements following determination; be notified by an admission authority of any referral it has made to the adjudicator for a variation of its admission arrangements; and be notified by the relevant admission authority of the effect of any adjudicator's determination following such a referral (the School Standards and Framework Act 1998, s.89(10) amended by the Education and Inspections Act 2006, s.41(7)).

Regulations may require the publication by a LEA, governing body of a foundation or voluntary aided school of such information relating to admissions as may be prescribed, and may make provision as to the time by and manner in which the information is to be published (s.92 of the 1998 Act as substituted by the 2002 Act, Sch 4).

The School Information (England) Regulations 2008 set out in detail the information local authorities (and school governors where appropriate) are required to publish concerning their policy and arrangements for primary and secondary education, and the time and manner of publication. Corresponding provision is made for Wales by the School Information (Wales) Regulations 2011.

15 Alteration and variation of, and objections to admissions

The School Admissions (Admission Arrangements and Co-ordination of Admission Arrangements) (England) Regulations 2012 prescribe the circumstances in which an admission authority may vary the admission arrangements they have determined for a particular academic year. An admission authority may vary the admission arrangements under which pupils are to be admitted to school to the extent that such variation is necessary to give effect to any of the following (Reg. 19)–

(a) the School Admissions Code;

(b) mandatory requirements of Part 3 of School Standards and Framework Act 1998;

(c) a determination of the adjudicator regarding admission arrangements; or

(d) a correction to any misprint in the admission arrangements.

Objections to determined admission arrangements may be referred to the Adjudicator. The 2012 Regulations prescribe the types of objections that may not be referred (Reg. 21), the time limits within which objections must be made (Reg. 23), that an objection may not raise the same or substantially the same issue in relation to admission arrangements which has been the subject of an adjudicator decision within the previous two years (Reg. 22), and that objections cannot be anonymous (Reg. 24). An admission authority must provide any of the information set out in Sch. 1, if requested to do so by the adjudicator (Reg. 25).

In Wales, the Education (Objections to Admission Arrangements) (Wales) Regulations 2006 apply. Here, the right of governing bodies to object to admission arrangements is limited so that they cannot object to the arrangements for any other community or voluntary controlled school in the relevant area, nor can they object to admission arrangements for their own school unless the objection relates to the determination of the admission number for the school (Reg. 4). Any objection must be received within six weeks after the notification that the arrangements have been determined or, where the objection is by a parent, six weeks following the publication of relevant details in a local newspaper, unless it was not reasonably practicable for it to have been received earlier (Reg. 5). The parents who are eligible to make an objection are defined in Reg. 6. Guidance is available on the Welsh Assembly's website at <www.learning.wales.gov.uk>. The types of objections a parent may make are set out in Reg. 7. A parental objection may only be determined by the Welsh Assembly if five or more parents make the same or substantially the same objection to the same admission arrangements (Reg. 8). The way in which Welsh Assembly decisions on objections are to be published is dealt with by Reg. 9. When an objection to a school's admission arrangements has been decided, no further objection to the school's arrangements for that school year or the following year may be made on the same issue (Reg. 10). Where an objection has been upheld against the admission arrangements of an admission authority, another relevant admission authority may revise its admission arrangements to achieve consistency with the decision upholding the objection (Reg. 11).

16 Admission of looked after children

The School Admissions (Admission Arrangements and Co-ordination of Admission Arrangements) (England) Regulations 2012 prescribe the actions to be taken and the circumstances in which an admission authority for a maintained school must give priority to a "relevant looked after child" (a child who is looked after by a local authority within the meaning of s.22 of the Children Act 1989).

Admission authorities must give priority in their oversubscription criteria to relevant looked after children, subject to certain exceptions (Reg. 7). Grammar schools which select pupils on the basis of highest ranked results need not give priority to relevant looked after children (Reg. 8). The Regulations also deal with the admission of looked after children at schools designated as having a religious character (Reg. 9), at schools which have made provision in their admission arrangements for selection by ability or aptitude since the beginning of the 1997-1998 school year (Reg. 10) and at schools which make provision for selection by banding (Reg. 11).

Similar provision is made for Wales by the Education (Admission of Looked After Children) (Wales) Regulations 2009.

17 Education otherwise than at school

Under s.19 of the Education Act 1996, a local authority has a duty to make arrangements for the provision of suitable full-time or part-time education otherwise than at school for children of compulsory school age (and may make such arrangements for young persons over that age but under 18) who by reason of illness, exclusion from school or otherwise may not, for any period, receive suitable education unless such arrangements are made.

18 Power to direct admission of child to a school

A local authority may give directions to the governing body of a school for which they are not the admission authority specifying a school to which a child should be admitted, provided that school is a reasonable distance from the child's home and the child has not been permanently excluded from it (School Standards and Framework Act 1998, s.96 as amended by the Education Act 2000, Sch. 4 and the Education and Inspections Act 2006, s.51(2)). This power arises where a child has either been refused admission to each school within a reasonable distance of his home and/or has been permanently excluded from a school. A direction under s.96 may not specify a school where the child's admission would prejudice efficient education or the efficient use of resources, as a consequence of the duty to limit infant class sizes (see the Note on **Schools: Provision and Governance**). Once a direction has been issued under s.96, a governing body must comply with it, but may still exclude a child on disciplinary grounds once he has become a pupil.

Before giving a direction under s.96, the local authority must consult the child's parents and the governing body of the school they propose to specify in the direction. The governing body may, within 15 days of receiving notice that a direction to admit is to be made, refer the matter to adjudicator in England or the Assembly in Wales (s.97, amended by the Education and Inspections Act 2006, s.49).

A local authority in England can, in relation to a child looked after by them, direct an admission authority (after first consulting it) to admit the child to a school, unless it is one from which the child has been permanently excluded (s.97A, inserted by the Education and Inspections Act 2006, s.50(1)). The procedure for giving direction under s.97A is set out in s.97B. Regulations may be made in England to requiring the adjudicator to undertake consultation or an admission authority to provide information (s.97C, inserted by the 2006 Act, s.51(3)). The Welsh Assembly has the power to make regulations about admission of looked after children under s.97D (inserted by the 2006 Act, s.52).

C: SCHOOL ATTENDANCE

19 School sessions in the year

The Education (School Day and School Year) (England) Regulations 1999 provide that, in each school year (as defined), a school must meet for not less than 380 sessions (i.e., half days), reduced to 378 in 2010-11 and 2011-12. This requirement does not however apply to a nursery class. A school year means the period beginning with the first school term to begin after July and ending with the beginning of the first such term to begin after the following July. The Education (School Day and School Year) (Wales) Regulations 2003 make similar provision for Wales.

In England, the governing body, in the case of all maintained schools, must determine the times of the school sessions and regulations may make provision as to the procedure to be followed where the governing body proposes to change any of those times (2002 Act, s.32(1)(b), (2)(b), (3)(a)). In the case of a foundation, voluntary aided or foundation special school the governing body will also determine the dates and times when the school terms and holidays are to begin and end (s.32(2)(a)); in the case of a community, voluntary controlled or community special school or maintained nursery school, the dates when the school terms and holidays are to begin and end will be determined by the local authority (s.32(1)(a)).

In Wales, the local authority must determine the term dates for each community, voluntary controlled or community special school or maintained nursery school in its area; and the governing body of a foundation or voluntary aided school must determine the term dates for its school (s.32A). In doing so, local authorities and governing bodies must co-operate and co-ordinate with each other to ensure that the dates set are the same (or as close as possible to being the same) for every maintained school in Wales. Section 32A(5) provides that local authorities must notify the Welsh Ministers of the school term dates determined. The Education

(Notification of School Term Dates) (Wales) Regulations 2014 provide that the notice must be sent at least two school years in advance. Therefore, the first term dates which local authorities have determined and which must be notified to the Welsh Ministers are for the school year 2016/2017. The Regulations also make provision in relation to the form and content of the notifications, the period in which notification must be given and the procedure for notification. The Welsh Ministers have the power to direct a local authority or governing body to set different school term dates (s.32B). They may do this where, for example, a special event is taking place which means that it might be desirable for a *particular* school or set of schools to be on holiday at a different time; or where an area has different term dates to the rest of Wales. The times of school sessions in Wales are generally determined by the governing body although a local authority can alter school session times where it is satisfied that to do so would promote sustainable modes of travel or improve the efficiency and effectiveness of travel arrangements (s.32C).

The Education (School Sessions and Charges and Remissions Policies) (Information) (England) Regulations 1999 *inter alia* require head teachers of all maintained schools in England to make available to parents of their pupils and other persons information about the times at which each school session begins and ends on a school day. The information must be available for inspection at the school at all reasonable times on a school day and for distribution without charge to parents on request.

The Education (School Curriculum and Related Information) Regulations 1989, as amended require the governing bodies of maintained schools to publish with their annual report (as to which see the Note on **Schools: Provision and Governance** at para **38 Governors' reports**) information about the dates of the school terms and half-term holidays for the next school year.

20 Registration of pupils

The proprietor of every school, i.e., the persons responsible for the management of the school (in the case of a community, foundation or voluntary school or community or foundation special school, the governing body), must cause a register of all pupils at the school to be kept in accordance with regulations (Education Act 1996, s.434).

The Education (Pupil Registration) (England) Regulations 2006 and (Wales) Regulations 2010 provide for the registration of pupils at all schools in England and Wales, including independent schools, and apply to all pupils in any school, including those not of compulsory school age.

An admission register and, except in respect of boarders at an independent school, an attendance register must be kept at every school, including a pupil referral unit (see above). The admission register must contain the names of all pupils in the school with particulars as to sex; the name and address of every person known to the proprietor of the school to be a parent of the pupil, and particulars of any parent with whom the pupil normally resides (this fact must be recorded against the name of the parent); a note of at least one telephone number at which the parent can be contacted in an emergency; and the pupil's date of birth, date of admission or re-admission, and previous school. At a school which includes boarders, the register must show whether each pupil of compulsory school age is a boarder or not.

The name of a pupil must be included in the register from the beginning of the first day on which the school has agreed, or has been notified, that the pupil will attend the school (Reg. 5(3)).

Names are to be deleted from the admission register only on certain prescribed grounds. *Inter alia,* where a pupil has been continuously absent for a period of four weeks, his name may be deleted but only after both the school and the local authority have failed, after reasonable enquiry, to locate the pupil. The attendance register must be marked at the beginning of each morning session and once during the afternoon session to show the names of those present, absent or attending an approved educational activity, and, in the case of an absence, whether that absence is authorised or unauthorised, as the case may be.

Where a pupil is registered at more than one school his name may only be deleted from the admission register of a school which he has ceased to attend where the proprietor of any or every other school at which the pupil is registered gives his consent (except where the pupil has died, been permanently excluded or is of no fixed abode) (Reg. 8(1)(c)). Before deleting a pupil's name from the admission register on the ground that they have not returned from a leave of absence, both the proprietor and the local authority must have failed, after reasonable enquiry, to ascertain where the pupil is (Reg. 8(1)(f)). A pupil's name may be deleted from the admission register on the ground that he has been continuously absent without authorisation for 20 school days provided the proprietor does not have reasonable grounds to believe that the pupil is unable to attend the school by reason of sickness or unavoidable cause (Reg. 8(1)(h)). The name of a pupil who is detained in pursuance of a final court order or order of recall may only be deleted from the register where that order is for a period of not less than four months and where the proprietor does not have reasonable grounds to believe that the pupil will return to school at the end of that period (Reg. 8(1)(i)). Where a pupil is a boarder at a maintained school or an Academy in England, the pupil's name must be deleted from the admission register where payment of the boarding charges by their parents remains outstanding at the end of the term to which those charges relate (Reg. 8(1)(o)).

An "approved educational activity" is one which takes place outside school premises and which is (a) approved by a person authorised by the school's proprietor and supervised by an authorised person and (b) of an educational nature (including work experience permitted under s.560 during the last year of compulsory schooling (see the Note on **Schools: Admission and Attendance**) and a sporting activity). Where a pupil is attending such an activity, the nature of the activity must also be noted in the register.

Regular returns must be made to the local authority showing the name and address of every registered day pupil of compulsory school age who fails to attend school regularly or is absent for a continuous period of more than ten school days, except where such absence is due to illness covered by a medical certificate.

The requirement to make a return to the local authority also applies where a pupil's name is deleted under certain provisions of Reg. 8(1) and applies as soon as the grounds for deletion are met and in any event before the pupil's name is deleted (Reg. 12(3)).

Entries in the registers must be made in ink and corrections must not obliterate the original entry. Registers must be preserved for a period of at least three years. Where a register is kept by means of a computer that register must be backed-up in the form of an electronic, micro-fiche or printed copy not less than once a month (Reg. 15(2)).

21 Leave of absence

Under the Education (Pupil Registration) (England) Regulations 2006 and (Wales) Regulations 2010, leave of absence must not be granted to enable a pupil to undertake employment, whether paid or unpaid, during school hours except employment in entertainment or abroad under a licence granted under ss.25 or 37 of the Children and Young Persons Act 1963 (see the Note on **Employment of Children**) (Reg. 7).

A pupil may be marked in the attendance register as unable to attend due to exceptional circumstances where the school site, or part of it, is closed, or where transport normally provided for that pupil by the school or the local authority is unavailable (Reg. 6(1)). Where a pupil is attending another school at which he is a registered pupil he must be marked in the attendance register as attending an approved educational activity (Reg. 6(4)).

In England, leave of absence (e.g., for a holiday during term time) may not be given to a pupil except where an application has been made by the parent in advance and the proprietor of the school considers that there are exceptional circumstances relating to the application (Reg. 7).

22 School attendance targets

S.63 of the School Standards and Framework Act 1998 enables regulations to be made requiring governing bodies of schools to secure that annual targets are set for reducing the level of absences on the part of pupils. Provision made by regulations under this section may relate to absences authorised under s.434 of the Education Act 1996, or to absences which are not so authorised, or to both (s.63(3A) of the 1998 Act).

Under the Education (School Attendance Targets) (England) Regulations 2007 the Secretary of State may require the governing body of a maintained school to set absence targets to reduce levels of absence for pupils in a particular group, levels of absence for a particular reason or levels of persistent absence. Each particular level must be higher that the national average and it must be an appropriate target to set.

The School Performance and Absence Targets (Wales) Regulations 2011 require the governing body of every maintained school providing secondary education to set final, reviewed and provisional targets in respect of pupils' unauthorised absence from school for one and two years ahead respectively. Information concerning these targets and the actual unauthorised absence rate must be published every year with the annual report.

23 School attendance orders and education supervision orders

A local authority must make arrangements to enable it to establish (so far as is possible) the identities of children in their area who are of compulsory school age but are not registered pupils at a school, and are not receiving suitable education otherwise than at a school. In doing so a local authority must have regard to any guidance given from time to time by the Secretary of State. A "suitable education", in relation to a child, means efficient full-time education suitable to his age, ability and aptitude and to any special educational needs he may have (Education Act 1996, s.436A, amended by the Education and Inspections Act 2006, s.4).

If it appears to the local authority that a child of compulsory school age in their area is not receiving suitable education, either by regular attendance at school or otherwise, they must serve a notice in writing on the parent requiring him to satisfy them, within a specified period of not less than 15 days, that the child is receiving such education. If he fails to do so and in their opinion it is expedient that the child should attend school they must, in the form prescribed by the Education (School Attendance Order) Regulations 1995 (S.I. No. 2090, as amended by 2010/1142), serve on the parent a school attendance order requiring him to have the child registered at a school named in the order (s.437). The authority must, before serving the order, inform the parent of their intention to do so and specify the school they propose to name or one or more suitable alternative schools. If the parent selects one of the specified schools within the prescribed period that school must be named in the order. If, within the period, the parent applies for the child to be admitted to a school maintained by an authority other than the one mentioned in the notice and he notifies the authority that served the notice of his application, the school of the parent's choice will be named in the order provided that the child has been offered a place at that school. Where a maintained school is named in an order, the authority must inform the governing body and the head teacher, (and in the case of a maintained school, the local authority), who must admit the child to the school (s.438).

The above requirements are subject to certain reservations (s.439), namely, an authority may not name in a school attendance order–

(i) a school at which the admission of a child under the order would result in the number in the child's age group determined in accordance with s.89 of the 1998 Act being exceeded (see **8 School admission**

EDUCATION

arrangements–introduction, above), being exceeded, unless the authority is responsible for determining the admission arrangements for that school;

(ii) a school from which the child concerned is permanently excluded;

(iii) a school other than the school or schools determined in accordance with a direction by the Secretary of State under s.439(8).

In the case of a child for whom they maintain an EHC plan or a statement of special educational needs, the authority must specify in the attendance order the school named in that plan or SEN statement (s.441).

If at any time while an order is in force the parent applies for the child to be admitted to a maintained school other than that named in the order, and the child is offered a place there, the authority must amend the order by substituting that school for the one previously named. If a school is applied for which is not a maintained school, the authority must comply with the parent's request to amend the order provided that the child is either (i) offered a place at the school and the authority are required to pay the fees by virtue of regulations made under s.18(3) or (ii) is offered a place as a result of the application and the school is suitable to his age, ability, and aptitude and to any special educational needs he may have (s.440). The authority must also comply with a parent's request to revoke a school attendance order if they are satisfied that the child is receiving suitable education otherwise than at school, unless the name of a school or other institution is specified in an EHC plan or special educational needs statement for the child (s.442).

Where an authority decide to specify a particular maintained school in a school attendance order, they must, before serving the notice, give notice in writing of their decision to the governing body and head teacher of the school and if another authority are responsible for determining the admission arrangements for the school, to that authority. A governing body or authority receiving such notice may, within 15 days of receiving it, apply to the Secretary of State for a direction (s.439(6) and (7)).

It is an offence for a parent to fail to comply with a school attendance order unless he can prove that the child is receiving suitable education otherwise than at school (s.443). The parent is also guilty of an offence if either (s 444, as amended)–

(a) a child of compulsory school age who is a registered pupil at a school fails to attend regularly; or

(b) knowing that such a child is failing to attend school regularly, he fails to cause him to do so.

The offence in (a) is punishable with a fine not exceeding level 3 on the standard scale, and the offence in (b) with a fine not exceeding level 4. As to the standard scale, see the Note on **Treatment of Offenders**, para **68 Maximum fines**. A penalty notice can be issued in respect of (a), (see **24 Penalty notices**, below).

Before instituting proceedings for an offence under ss.443 or 444, a local authority must consider whether it would be appropriate (instead of or as well as instituting the proceedings) to apply for an education supervision order (see below) with respect to the child. The court before which a person is either convicted of an offence under s.443 or charged with an offence under s.444 may direct the local authority instituting the proceedings to apply for an education supervision order unless, having consulted the local authority, they decide that the child's welfare would be adequately safeguarded without the making of an education supervision order. Where the local authority apply for an education supervision order with respect to a child who is the subject of a school attendance order, and the court decides that s.36(3) of the Children Act 1989 (see below) prevents it from making the order, the court may direct that the school attendance order shall cease to be in force (s.447).

Under s.36 of the Children Act 1989 a local authority may, in certain circumstances, after consulting the social services committee of the appropriate local authority, apply to the court for an education supervision order placing a child under the supervision of a designated local authority. A court may only make an education supervision order if it is satisfied that the child concerned is of compulsory school age and is not being properly educated (s.36(3)). For this purpose a child is being properly educated only if he is receiving efficient full-time education suitable to his age, ability, and aptitude and any special educational needs he may have. Where he is the subject of a school attendance order in force under s.437 of the 1996 Act which has not been complied with, or is a registered pupil at a school which he is not attending regularly, unless it is proved that he is being properly educated it will be assumed that he is not, and the local authority must, before instituting proceedings, consider whether it would be appropriate to apply for an education supervision order. Such an order cannot be made with respect to a child who is in the care of a local authority. Where a school attendance order was in force immediately before the making of the education supervision order, the former will cease to have effect.

24 Penalty notices

Where an "authorised officer" has reason to believe that a person has committed an offence under s.444(1) of the Education Act 1996 by failing to secure the regular attendance at school of a registered pupil (see **23 School attendance orders and education supervision orders**, above sub-paragraph (a)), he may issue that person with a penalty notice (s.444A).

A penalty notice may also be issued in England in respect of the presence of an excluded pupil in a public place under the Education and Inspections Act 2006, ss.103 and 105.

An "authorised officer" for these purposes is (s.105)–

(a) a policeman;

(b) an officer of the local authority in England authorised by the local authority to give penalty notices; or

(c) a head teacher of a relevant school in England or a member of staff of a relevant school who is authorised by the head teacher to give penalty notices.

The provision relates to maintained schools, pupil referral units, Academies, city technology colleges, and city colleges for the technology of the arts.

It is also an offence for a parent to fail to secure regular attendance of a child at "alternative educational provision" e.g., where a child has been excluded and provision has been arranged away from the school (Education Act 1996, s.444ZA inserted by Education Act 2005, s.116). Where it is considered that a person has committed this offence, a penalty notice may be issued under s.444A of the 1996 Act). "Alternative educational provision" means–

(a) education provided by a local authority for a child otherwise than at a school or at his home; and
(b) education at a place outside the premises of the school at which the child is a registered pupil and which the child is required to attend for the purpose of instruction or training (Reg. 3).

The penalty notice will offer the person to whom it is given the opportunity of discharging any liability to conviction for the offence by paying a penalty within a prescribed period. The penalty is payable to the local authority who must use the proceeds to meet the costs of issuing such notices, enforcing notices and prosecuting those who do not pay (s.444A(5) and Reg. 21).

The Education (Penalty Notices) (England) Regulations 2007 and (Wales) Regulations 2013 prescribe the necessary details for the operation of the penalty notice scheme under s.444A of the Education Act 1996 and (England only) s.105 of the Education and Inspections Act 2006. The amount of penalty is £60, where the amount is paid within 21 days of receipt of the notices and £120 where the amount is paid after 21 days but within 28 days of receipt of the notice (Reg. 4). If the notice is unpaid or paid in part at the end of the 28-day period, the local authority must decide whether to prosecute for the original offence or withdraw the notice. The local authority must draw up and consult on a code of conduct for the issuing of penalty notices (Regs. 14-17).

Codes of conduct under the now revoked Education (Penalty Notices) (England) Regulations 2004 continue in force for penalty notices issued under s.444A of the 1996 Act, but they are not automatically extended to penalty notices issued under s.105 of the 2006 Act.

25 Authorities

Statutes–

Education Acts 1962 to 2008

Education and Inspections Act 2006

School Standards and Framework Act 1998

Statutory Instruments for England and Wales–

Education (Aptitude for Particular Subjects) Regulations 1999, as amended (S.I. 1999 No. 258 and 2006 No. 3408)

Education (Grammar School Ballots) Regulations 1998, as amended (S.I. 1998 No. 2876 and 2012 No. 979)

Education (Proportion of Selective Admissions) Regulations 1998 (S.I. 1998 No. 2229)

Education (Proposals for Grammar Schools to Cease to have Selective Admission Arrangements) Regulations 1999 (S.I. 1999 No 2103)

Education Relevant Areas for Consultation on Admission Arrangements) Regulations 1999, as amended (S.I. 1999 No. 124, and 2010 No. 1172)

Education (School Attendance Order) Regulations 1995, as amended (S.I. 1995 No. 2090 and 2010 Nos. 1142 and 1172)

Education (School Leaving Date) Order 1997 (S.I. 1997 No. 1970)

Education (Substituted Grammar Schools) Regulations 1999 (S.I. 1999 No. 2102)

Statutory Instruments applying only to England–

Education Act 1996 (Amendment of Section 19) (England) Regulations 2007 (S.I. 2007 No. 1507)

Education (Penalty Notices) (England) Regulations 2007, as amended (S.I. 2007 No. 1867, 2012 No. 1046, and 2013 No. 757)

Education (Pupil Registration) (England) Regulations 2006, as amended (S.I. 2006 No. 1751, 2007 No 603, 2010 No. 1725, 2011 No. 1625, 2012 No. 1033, and 2013 No. 756)

Education (School Attendance Targets) (England) Regulations 2007, as amended (S.I. 2007 No. 2261 and 2010 No. 2838)

Education (School Day and School Year) (England) Regulations 1999, as amended (S.I. 1999 No. 3181, 2010 No. 604, and 2011 No. 154)

Education (School Sessions and Charges and Permissions Policies) (Information) (England) Regulations 1999 (S.I. 1999 No. 2255)

School Admissions (Admission Arrangements and Co-ordination of Admission Arrangements) (England) Regulations 2012, as amended (S.I. 2012 No. 8 and 2014 No. 2886)

School Admissions (Appeals Arrangements) (England) Regulations 2012 (S.I. 2012 No. 9)

School Information (England) Regulations 2008, as amended (S.I. 2008 No. 3093 2010 Nos. 1172 and 1874, 2012 Nos. 979 and 1124, 2013 Nos. 758 and 2912, 2014 No. 2103, and 2015 No. 902)

Statutory Instruments applying only to Wales–

Education (Admission Appeals Arrangements) (Wales) Regulations 2005, as amended (S.I. 2005 No. 1398, 2009 Nos. 823 and 1500, and 2013 No. 2535)

Education (Admission Forums) (Wales) Regulations 2003 (S.I. 2003 No. 2962)

Education (Admission of Looked After Children) (Wales) Regulations 2009 (S.I. 2009 No. 821)

Education (Determination of Admission Arrangements) (Wales) Regulations 2006 (S.I. 2006 No. 174)

Education (Notification of School Term Dates) (Wales) Regulations 2014 (S.I. 2014 No. 1249)

Education (Objections to Admission Arrangements) (Wales) Regulations 2006 (S.I. 2006 No 176)

Education (Penalty Notices) (Wales) Regulations 2013 (S.I. 2013 No. 1983)

Education (Pupil Registration) (Wales) Regulations 2010 (S.I. 2010 No. 1954)

Education (School Day and School Year) (Wales) Regulations 2003, as amended (S.I. 2003 No. 3231, 2006 No. 1262, 2008 No. 1739, 2011 No. 149, and 2012 No. 248)

Education (Variation of Admission Arrangements) (Wales) Regulations 2013 (S.I. 2013 No. 1140)

School Admissions (Common Offer Date) (Wales) Regulations 2013 (S.I. 2013 No. 1144)

School Information (Wales) Regulations 2011 (S.I. 2011 No. 1944)

School Performance and Absence Targets (Wales) Regulations 2011 (S.I. 2011 No. 1945)

SCHOOLS: CURRICULUM AND EXAMS
ENGLAND AND WALES

1 Contents

This Note deals principally with the National Curriculum and the exceptions to it. The Note also covers provision of religious education and more general provisions such as those relating to political indoctrination, sex education, charging policies in the State sector, and external examinations.

This Note has been structured as follows–
A: The School Curriculum
B: Religious Worship and Education
C: General Provisions relating to Education at Schools (discipline, political indoctrination, sex education, charging etc.)
D: External examinations

A: THE SCHOOL CURRICULUM

2 Introduction

The Secretary of State (as respects all maintained schools, as defined–see the Note on **Schools: Provision and Governance: England and Wales** at para 17 **Categories of schools**), every local authority (as respects every school maintained by them), and every governing body or head teacher of a maintained school (as respects that school) must exercise their functions (including, in particular, those conferred on them by Part V of the 1996 Act with respect to religious education and religious worship (not applicable in the case of maintained nursery schools), and the National Curriculum) with a view to securing that the curriculum for the school is a balanced and broadly based curriculum which (Education Act 2002, ss.78 and 79 for England; ss.99 and 100 for Wales)–
(a) promotes the spiritual, moral, cultural, mental, and physical development of pupils at the school and of society; and
(b) prepares such pupils for the opportunities, responsibilities, and experiences of later life.

In relation to Wales, most of the functions of the Secretary of State have been transferred to the Welsh Ministers and references to the Secretary of State should be construed as references to the Welsh Ministers (Government of Wales Act 1998, s.43; and the National Assembly for Wales (Transfer of Functions) Order 1999 (S.I. No. 672)).

3 Innovative projects

The Education Act 2002 contains powers to facilitate "innovative projects" by qualifying bodies. For these purposes "qualifying bodies" are–
(a) a local authority;
(b) an education action forum;
(c) the governing body of a qualifying school (i.e., community, foundation or voluntary school or special school; maintained nursery school; city technical college; city college for the technology of the arts; or Academy); and
(d) the proprietor of an approved special school.

Such projects must, in the opinion of the Secretary of State or the Welsh Ministers, contribute to the raising of educational standards achieved by children (s.1). On the application of a qualifying body, the Secretary of State or Welsh Ministers may, for a limited period, suspend, relax, or modify educational requirements imposed by legislation, or confer new powers on the qualifying body. The Secretary of State or Welsh Ministers must refuse such an application if it is likely to have a detrimental effect on the education of children with special educational needs (s.2). These powers have now expired in relation to England but apply for Wales until February 2019.

4 The National Curriculum

S.80 of the Education Act 2002 provides that the curriculum for every maintained school in England must comprise a basic curriculum which includes (2002 Act, s.80)–
(a) provision for religious education for all registered pupils at the school (but this does not apply to pupils who are under compulsory school age or to pupils at a maintained special school); and
(b) a curriculum for all registered pupils at the school who have ceased to be young children for the purposes of the Childcare Act 2006 (see the Note on **Child Minding and Day Care for Young Children**) but are not over compulsory school age (to be known as the National Curriculum for England);
(c) in the case of a secondary school, provision for sex education for all registered pupils at the school; and
(d) in the case of a special school, provision for sex education for all registered pupils at the school who are provided with secondary education.

For Wales the basic curriculum is the same as for England, with the addition of (s.101, as amended by the Basic Curriculum for Wales (Amendment) Orders (S.I. 2003 No. 932 and 2008 No. 1899))–

(e) provision for personal and social education for all registered pupils at the school who are of compulsory school age; and

(f) provision for work-related education for all registered pupils at the school during the third and fourth key stages.

In relation to any maintained school and any school year, the local authority and the governing body must exercise their functions with a view to securing, and the head teacher must secure, that the National Curriculum for England (or Wales) as subsisting at the beginning of that year is implemented (ss.88 and 109).

In relation to implementation of the assessment arrangements for the National Curriculum, schools and local authorities are required to implement these as they exist at a given point in time (rather than as they are at the start of a school year) (s.88(1A)).

The governing body of a qualifying school, which is a maintained school (i.e., a community, foundation, or voluntary school; or community or foundation special school) of a prescribed description satisfying prescribed criteria, may apply to the Secretary of State or Welsh Ministers for exemption from, or modification of, a national curriculum provision (ss.6 and 7). An application must be in a specified form, contain certain information and can only be made by the governing body after consultation with the LEA, parents and other appropriate persons (s.8). If the school ceases to be a qualifying school, the Secretary of State or Welsh Ministers may, without a further application, revoke any exemption order or restrict any conferred exemption (s.9).

5 The early years foundation stage and foundation phase

England

In England, the Early Years Foundation Stage has replaced the Foundation Stage for young children who are receiving early years provision. Early years provision means the provision of childcare for a young child (a young child being a child aged from birth up to the 1st September following his fifth birthday). For detail as to the Early Years Foundation Stage, see the Note on **Child Minding and Day Care for Young Child**.

Wales

In Wales, the foundation stage has been renamed the foundation phase (see definition below). For the foundation phase the National Curriculum must comprise areas of learning (as to which see below) and may specify in relation to them (Education Act 2002, s.104)–

(a) the knowledge, skills and understanding which pupils of different abilities and maturities are expected to have by the end of the foundation phase ("the early learning goals");

(b) the matters, skills and processes which are required to be taught to pupils of different abilities and maturities during the foundation phase (the "educational programmes"); and

(c) assessment arrangements.

The foundation phase is the period beginning with the "relevant time" and ending at the same time as the school year in which the age of seven is attained. The "relevant time" in the case of a child who is provided with funded nursery education before the age of three is the third birthday; in the case of a child provided with funded nursery education after he has attained three years of age, the time when he is first provided with such education; and in the case of a child who is not provided with any funded nursery education, when he first receives primary education other than nursery education (2002 Act, s.102).

The Welsh Ministers must establish a complete National Curriculum for the foundation phase as soon as is reasonably practicable and revise it when they consider it necessary or expedient to do so (s.108). "Areas of learning" may be specified and the Education (National Curriculum) (Foundation Phase) (Wales) Order 2014 and National Curriculum (Educational Programmes for the Foundation Phase and Programmes of Study for the Second and Third Key Stages) (Wales) Order 2013 do so. The assessment arrangements that must be carried out by in relation to each pupil in the foundation phase are set out in the National Curriculum (Desirable Outcomes, Educational Programmes and Baseline and End of Phase Assessment Arrangements for the Foundation Phase) (Wales) Order 2015 (S.I. No. 1596).

In relation to any maintained nursery school and any school year, the local authority and the governing body must exercise their functions with a view to securing and the head teacher must secure, that the National Curriculum as subsisting at the beginning of that year, so far as it relates to the foundation phase, is implemented (s.110).

6 The key stages

The first key stage (in England) begins at the same time as the school year in which the pupil attains the age of six, and ends at the same time as the school year in which the majority of pupils in his class (i.e. the teaching group in which he is regularly taught in that subject or a group designated by the head teacher where there are two or more such groups) attain the age of seven. In Wales it has been replaced by the Foundation Phase (see **5 The early years foundation stage and foundation phase,** above). The second key stage begins at the same time as the school year in which the majority attain the age of eight and ends at the same time as the school year when the majority attain the age of eleven. The third key stage begins at the same time as the school year in which the majority attain the age of twelve and ends at the same time as the school year in which the majority attain the age of fourteen. The fourth key stage starts at the same time as the school year in which the majority attain the age of fifteen and ends at the same time as the school year in which the majority cease to be of compulsory school age (Education Act 2002, England, s.82; Wales, s.103).

7 Curriculum requirements for the second and third key stages

For the second, and third key stages the National Curriculum comprises the core and other foundation subjects. The core subjects for these three key stages are: mathematics, English, science and, for Welsh-speaking schools, Welsh. The foundation subjects for these three key stages are: design and technology, computing, physical education, history, geography, art and design, and music. In addition, for the second key stage in England, a modern foreign language is a foundation subject; and for the third key stage in England and Wales, citizenship and a modern foreign language are foundation subjects (2002 Act, England, s.84; Wales, s.105). The Secretary of State and Welsh Ministers can revise this curriculum whenever they consider it necessary or expedient to do so, and can specify in relation to each of the foundation subjects such attainment targets, programmes of study and assessment arrangements as they considers appropriate (Education Act 2002, England, s.87; Wales, s.108).

The National Curriculum for the first key stage is disapplied where the Foundation Stage (England) or the Foundation Phase (Wales) applies instead.

8 Curriculum requirements for the fourth key stage

Ss.85 and 85A of the Education Act 2002 (substituted by the Education and Inspections Act 2006, s.74) of the Education Act 2002 defines the curriculum for the fourth key stage for England. The National Curriculum for England comprises–
  (a) the core and other foundation subjects;
  (b) work-related learning; and
  (c) in relation to any pupil, such other courses of study as are necessary to satisfy the entitlements conferred on him by s.85(5) and s.85A (see below).

The National Curriculum for England specifies programmes of study in relation to each of the core and other foundation subjects for the fourth key stage (s.85(2)). The core subjects for the fourth key stage in England are mathematics, English and science (s.85(3)).

The other foundation subjects for the fourth key stage are computing, physical education and citizenship (s.85(4)).

A pupil in the fourth key stage is entitled, if he so elects, to follow a course of study in science which leads to such qualification or set of qualifications as the governing body may choose from among those (s.85(5))–
  (a) approved under s.98 of the Learning and Skills Act 2000 for the purposes of s.96 of that Act; and
  (b) specified by the Secretary of State by order for the purposes of this subsection.

The Education (National Curriculum) (Science at Key Stage 4) (England) Order 2007 specifies two sets of qualifications for those purposes. The first entitles a pupil to take a course of study which leads to a combined Science GSCE. The second set of qualifications is three separate GCSE qualifications in the sciences of Physics, Chemistry and Biology.

"Work-related learning" means planned activity designed to use the context of work to develop knowledge, skills and understanding useful in work, including learning through the experience of work, learning about work and working practices and learning the skills for work (s.85(7)).

A pupil in the fourth key stage is also entitled to follow a course of study in a subject within each of the four entitlement areas or follow a course of study within an entitlement area specified by the Secretary of State (s.85A(1)). The entitlement areas are (s.85A(2))–
  (a) arts, comprising: art and design, music, dance, drama, and media arts;
  (b) design and technology;
  (c) humanities, comprising: geography and history; and
  (d) modern foreign languages, comprising any modern foreign language specified in an order made by the Secretary of State or, if the order so specifies, any modern foreign language (The Education (National Curriculum) (Languages) (England) Order 2013 No. 2230 and (Wales) Order 2008 No. 1408 do specify "any modern foreign language").

A "course of study" means (s.85A(6))–
  (a) in relation to a subject within an entitlement area, a course of education or training which leads to such qualification as the governing body may choose from among those approved;
  (b) in relation to an entitlement area, a course of education or training which leads to such qualification as the governing body may choose from among those specified by the Secretary of State by order.

In relation to courses of study within the specified entitlement areas, the governing body of a maintained school must consider whether it would be appropriate to make any collaboration arrangements (s.85A(4)). "Collaboration arrangements" means (s.85A(5)) –
  (a) arrangements made with the governing body of one or more other maintained schools; and
  (b) arrangements made, with one or more further education bodies.

The core subjects in Wales are mathematics, English, science and, in Welsh-speaking schools, Welsh. The foundation subjects are physical education and, in non-Welsh-speaking schools, Welsh (2002 Act, s.106). Any provision of s.106 can be amended by order by the Welsh Ministers (s.107). The Learning and Skills (Wales) Measure 2009 inserts provisions in the 2002 Act concerning the curriculum in maintained schools in Wales by expanding it to include the local curriculum entitlements of pupils in key stage 4. The Education (Local Curriculum for Pupils in Key Stage 4) (Wales) Regulations 2009 make provision as to the formation of the local curriculum (including the minimum number of course of study at NQF level 2), the elections a pupil may make, the head teacher's decision as to entitlement, and the head teacher's decision to remove an entitlement.

9 Exceptions

To enable development work or experiments to be carried out, the Secretary of State or Welsh Ministers may direct, in respect of a particular maintained school, that the National Curriculum is not to apply or is to apply with specified modifications. In certain cases the agreement of the governing body and the local authority, is required before such a direction can be given (Education Act 2002, England, s.90; Wales, s.111).

Regulations may also provide that specified provisions of the National Curriculum are not to apply or are to apply with modifications (England, s.91; Wales, s.112).

The special educational provision for any pupil specified in a statement under s.324 of the Education Act 1996 (see the Note on **Special Educational Provision and Special Schools: England and Wales**, at para **19 Statement of child's special educational needs**) of his special education needs may exclude the application of the National Curriculum or apply it with modifications (England, s.92; Wales, s.113).

Regulations may enable a head teacher of a maintained school to make temporary exceptions to the application of the National Curriculum to individual pupils. The Secretary of State (or Welsh Ministers) must consult any persons with whom consultation appears to him to be desirable before making any regulations under this section (England, s.93; Wales, s.114). Where a head teacher gives or varies a direction under such regulations, he must supply certain specified information concerning that direction to the governing body, the local authority by which the school is maintained and the pupil's parent (England, s.94; Wales, s.115). The parent of the pupil concerned may appeal to the governing body against such a direction (England, s.95; Wales, s.116).

10 Key stage exceptions

In England, the National Curriculum (Exceptions for First, Second, Third and Fourth Key Stages) (England) Regulations 2013 provide for the current programmes of study, attainment targets and assessment arrangements for all national curriculum subjects (except for English, mathematics and science for pupils in years 1, 2, 5 and 6) to cease to apply at all four key stages in maintained schools for the 2013/14 school year, and also for the 2014/15 and 2015/16 school years in relation to key stage 4 English, mathematics and science, and in relation to the programme of study for science for year 11 pupils for the school year 2016/17. During this period schools will continue to be required to teach all subjects of the national curriculum, but teachers will have the freedom to teach a programme of study of their choice, as part of a broad and balanced curriculum. By the time a disapplication for a particular subject expires, a new curriculum for that subject will be in place which schools will be required to teach.

The Education (National Curriculum) (Exceptions) Wales Regulations 1991 provide an exception to the provisions of the National Curriculum relating to Welsh which applies in respect of pupils admitted to a school in the final year of the third key stage or in any year of the fourth key stage, other than those who have studied Welsh for at least 38 weeks during the period of three years immediately preceding their admission to the school.

The Education (National Curriculum for Wales) Disapplication of Science at Key Stage 4) Regulations 2006 disapply the requirement in the National Curriculum for Wales for pupils to study science if the head teacher of the school is satisfied that the pupil is pursuing a course leading to an approved external qualification from the National Qualifications Framework at entry level, level 1 or level 2.

11 Procedure for making regulations and orders

Where the Secretary of State proposes to make orders under the 2002 Act ss.82, 83, 84, or 87, or regulations under s.91, he must give notice of the proposal to specified bodies and persons, giving them a reasonable opportunity to submit evidence and make representations about the issues arising. The Secretary of State must publish, in such manner as in his opinion is likely to bring them to the notice of persons having a special interest in education, a draft of the proposed order or regulations and a summary of the views expressed during the consultation. He must allow not less than one month for the submission of evidence and representations on the issues arising, after the expiry of which period he can make the order or regulations with or without modifications (s.96).

12 Establishment of National Curriculum

The Secretary of State and Welsh Ministers must each set (i) such attainment targets, (ii) such programmes of study, and (iii) such assessment arrangements as they consider appropriate for each subject (2002 Act, ss.87 and 108). Such an order may not require (ss.87(4) and 108(4))–

(a) that any particular period or periods of time should be allocated during any key stage to the teaching of any programme of study or any matter, skill, or process forming part of it; or

(b) that provision of any particular kind should be made in school timetables for the periods to be allocated to such teaching during any such stage.

In England, from 1st September 2014 (1st September 2015 for English and mathematics) the Education (National Curriculum) (Attainment Targets and Programmes of Study) (England) Order 2013/2232, as amended by 2014/1941, 2014/3285 and 2015/900, gives effect to the Framework Document, which contains new programmes of study and attainment targets for core and other foundation subjects at all four key stages (except that there are no attainment targets at key stage 4). The Framework Document is available at <www.gov.uk/government/ collections/national-curriculum>. S.I. 2014/3285 which amends the 2013 Order gives effect to a revised Framework Document from 2016, with a new key stage 4 programme of study for science that will apply to year 10 pupils in 2016/17 and to all pupils in key stage 4 from 2017 onwards. It also provides that those Orders which contain the current key stage 4 programmes of study for science will continue to apply to all pupils in key stage 4 up to 2016, and to year 11 pupils only in 2016/17. The revised Framework Document can be found at <https://www.gov.uk/government/publications/national-curriculum-in-england-framework-for-key-stages-1-to-4>.

For Wales, the attainment targets are set out in a number of documents published by the Welsh Ministers, as listed in the Education (National Curriculum) (Attainment Targets and Programmes of Study) (Wales) Order 2008, as amended (S.I. 2008/1409, 2008/1787, and 2015/1601) and the National Curriculum (Educational Programmes for the Foundation Phase and Programmes of Study for the Second and Third Key Stages) (Wales) Order 2013/434.

In England, assessment arrangements are specified by the Secretary of State by order under s.87(3)(c). The Education (National Curriculum) (Key Stage 1 Assessment Arrangements) (England) Order 2004/2783, as amended by 2010/677, 2010/1172, 2011/2392, 2011/3057, 2012/765, 2013/1513, 2014/2103 and 2015/900) specifies the assessment arrangements for the core subjects in the final year of the first key stage, as they apply to maintained schools in England. The Education (National Curriculum) (Specified Purpose) (England) Order 2015/901 specifies an additional purpose for which assessment arrangements may be made: determining the suitability of test materials for use in National Curriculum tests at key stages 1 and 2. The Education (National Curriculum) (Key Stage 2 Assessment Arrangements) (England) Order 2003 (S.I. No. 1038, as amended by S.I. 2009/1585, 2010/290, 2010/677, 2011/2392, 2012/765, 2012/838, 2013/1513, 2014/2103 and 2015/900) specifies in relation to maintained schools the assessment arrangements for the core subjects in the final year of the second key stage. The Education (National Curriculum) (Key Stage 3 Assessment Arrangements) (England) Order 2003 (S.I. 2003/1039 as amended by 2008/3081, 2009/1585, 2010/677, 2011/2392, 2012/765, 2014/2103 and 2015/900) provides for teacher assessment of pupils in maintained schools in England in the final year of the third key stage in the above-mentioned subjects. There is no longer any provision for pupil tests at key stage 3; attainment is judged purely on the basis of assessment.

In Wales, the first key stage has been removed from the National Curriculum as it is now covered by the Foundation Phase. Assessment arrangements may be specified by the Welsh Ministers. Corresponding provision in Wales is made for key stage 2 by the National Curriculum (Key Stage 2 Assessment Arrangements) (Wales) Order 2004/2915, as amended by 2011/1937. It provides for pupils to be assessed by a teacher and not by tests. Similarly, the National Curriculum (Key Stage 3 Assessment Arrangements) (Wales) Order 2005, as amended (S.I. 2005/1394, 2008/1899, and 2011/1937) applies for Welsh schools in relation to key stage 3. The Education (National Curriculum) (Assessment Arrangements for Reading and Numeracy) (Wales) Order 2013 provides for assessment arrangements for reading and numeracy for pupils who attend schools maintained by a local authority (other than any established in a hospital) in Wales. The National Curriculum (Assessment Arrangements for the Foundation Phase and the Second and Third Key Stages) (Wales) Order 2014 (S.I. 2014/1999) places a statutory duty on schools to assess throughout the year the overall standards in literacy and numeracy of pupils undertaking the Foundation phase and second and third key stages. The National Curriculum (Moderation of Assessment Arrangements for the Second and Third Key Stages) (Wales) Order 2015/1309 provides for moderation provisions which apply in relation to all statutory teacher assessments of pupils in maintained schools other than special schools maintained by local authorities in the final year of the second and third key stages. *Inter alia*, the Order places a duty on a head teacher of a maintained school to make arrangements to ensure that their school joins a school moderation cluster group and that the group meets at least once every school year in the spring or summer school terms. The Order also sets out the purpose of a school moderation cluster group which may contain schools from more than one local authority area.

13 Education and training to satisfy entitlements

Young people who are over compulsory school age, but have not yet had their 19th birthday have an extra core entitlement to a course of study in each of maths, English, and computing (Education Act 1996, ss.17A, 17C).

14 School performance targets

The Secretary of State may make regulations which require the governing body of a maintained school to secure that annual targets are set in respect of the performance of pupils in public examinations, National Curriculum assessments, and the attainment of external qualifications. The Regulations may require such targets and the past performance of pupils in the particular examinations, assessments, or in connection with the attainment of the particular qualifications to which such targets relate, to be published (Education Act 1997, s.19).

In England, the regulations which made provision in this respect were revoked with effect from 1st September 2011.

The School Performance and Absence Targets (Wales) Regulations 2011 provide for performance targets to be set by all maintained schools in Wales where education is provided for pupils in the second, third and fourth key stages. Provisional, reviewed and final targets for the current, next and next but one years must be set in respect of *inter alia* the core subjects and must be published in the school's annual report.

15 The Office of Qualifications and Examinations Regulation

S.127 of the Apprenticeship, Skills, Children and Learning Act 2009 provides for the establishment of a Non-Ministerial Department in England known as the Office of Qualifications and Examinations Regulation (Ofqual). In discharging its functions, Ofqual has five objectives. These are (s.128)–

(1) the qualifications standards objective. Ofqual must secure that regulated qualifications (a) give a reliable indication of knowledge, skills and understanding; and (b) indicate a consistent level of attainment (including over time) between comparable regulated qualifications and a consistent level of attainment (but not over time) between regulated qualifications and comparable unregulated qualifications (including those awarded outside the UK).

(2) the assessment standards objective. Ofqual must promote the development and implementation of regulated assessment arrangements which (a) give a reliable indication of achievement, and (b) indicate a consistent level of attainment (including over time) between comparable assessments.

(3) the public confidence objective. Ofqual must promote public confidence in regulated qualifications and assessment arrangements.

(4) the awareness objective. Ofqual must promote awareness and understanding of the range of regulated qualifications available, the benefits of regulated qualifications to learners, employers and institutions within the higher education sector, and the benefits of recognition to bodies awarding or authenticating qualifications.

(5) the efficiency objective. Ofqual must ensure that regulated qualifications are provided efficiently and that any relevant sums payable for the award or authentication of a regulated qualification represent value for money.

For a qualification to be a "regulated qualification", it must (s.130)–

(a) not be a foundation, first or higher degree;

(b) be awarded or authenticated in England;

(c) be awarded or authenticated by a body which is recognised by Ofqual.

Ofqual must recognise an awarding body in respect of the award or authentication of a specified qualification, or description of qualification, if the awarding body has applied for recognition in the respect in question, and it meets the applicable criteria for recognition (s.132). The criteria may include fee-capping criteria (i.e., limiting the amount a recognised body may charge for the award or authentication of a qualification in respect of which the body is recognised, or for a service provided in connection with such a qualification) (s.135). However, Ofqual may impose a fee capping condition only if satisfied that the limit is necessary in order to secure value for money (s.136).

Ofqual may decide that a certain qualification, or qualifications falling within a certain description, is or are subject to the accreditation requirement. The effect of this is that a recognised body cannot award or authenticate any form of such a qualification unless the particular form is individually accredited (s.138).

The Secretary of State may make an order specifying the minimum requirements in respect of knowledge, skills or understanding that someone must be able to demonstrate to gain a particular qualification or a qualification of a particular description (s.141). He may only specify minimum requirements in relation to qualifications which are, or are likely to be, approved for public funding for people under 19 and may make an order only if satisfied that it is necessary to do so in order to ensure that the curriculum is appropriate for the ages of the people likely to be studying for the qualification.

Ofqual may impose a monetary penalty on an awarding body (up to a maximum of 10% of the body's turnover) or withdraw recognition in respect of some or all of the qualifications in respect of which a body is recognised, if the body has breached a condition of recognition (ss.151A to 152). A body may appeal to the First-tier Tribunal against a decision to impose a penalty or as to the amount of the penalty.

Similar functions in relation to schools in Wales are now carried out be the Welsh Ministers.

16 Qualifications Wales

Qualifications Wales has two principal aims (Qualifications Wales Act 2015, s.3)–

(1) ensuring that qualifications, and the Welsh qualification system, are effective for meeting the reasonable needs of learners in Wales; and

(2) promoting public confidence in qualifications and in the Welsh qualification system.

In considering what is appropriate for the purpose of achieving its principal aims, Qualifications Wales must have regard to–

(a) the desirability of promoting sustainable growth in the Welsh economy;

(b) the desirability of promoting and facilitating the use of the Welsh language;

(c) the range and nature of qualifications available, and of their assessment arrangements;

(d) the reasonable requirements of employers, higher education institutions and the professions regarding education and training (including as to required standards of practical competence);

(e) whether the knowledge, skills and understanding required to be demonstrated for the purpose of determining whether a person is to be awarded a qualification reflect current knowledge and best practice;

(f) whether qualifications indicate a consistent level of attainment with that indicated by whatever Qualifications Wales considers to be comparable qualifications, whether awarded in Europe or elsewhere;

(g) whether qualifications are provided efficiently and so as to secure value for money;

(h) the respective roles played by, and responsibilities of, awarding bodies, learning providers, Qualifications Wales and the Welsh Ministers; and any other persons exercising functions that Qualifications Wales considers relevant for the purpose of the Welsh qualification system.

Qualifications Wales must recognise an awarding body in respect of the award of a specified qualification, or description of qualification, if the awarding body has applied for recognition and meets the applicable criteria for recognition which Qualifications Wales has set (s.8).

B: RELIGIOUS WORSHIP AND EDUCATION

17 Duty to provide religious education

Local authorities, governing bodies and head teachers must ensure that religious education is given in accordance with the provision for such education included in the school's basic curriculum by virtue of s.80 of the Education Act 2002 (1998 Act, s.69).

18 Community, foundation and voluntary schools without a religious character

In the case of community, foundation and voluntary schools without a religious character, all schools in those categories must follow the agreed syllabus, adopted by the local authority under the 1996 Act. This syllabus must be drawn up by a local authority in consultation with a conference of representatives of religious bodies and teachers' associations in the area. It is the authority's duty to convene conferences from time to time to reconsider any agreed syllabus and a conference must be convened no later than five years from the date on which any agreed syllabus was adopted (s.375 and Sch. 31 to the Act). Former grant-maintained schools which, prior to September 1999, were following the agreed syllabus of a different local authority may continue to follow their current syllabus which must be non-denominational) until a date specified by the Secretary of State or until the governing body so determine, if earlier. A general duty is imposed on local authorities to provide facilities for a child at a secondary school to receive at the school (but at no cost to the school or to the authority) religious education in accordance with the tenets of a particular religious denomination where arrangements cannot conveniently be made for the child to be withdrawn from the school to receive religious education elsewhere (Sch. 31, para. 2) (see also **22 Exceptions and special arrangements**, below).

19 Foundation and controlled schools with a religious character

In the case of foundation and controlled schools which have a religious character, the governors must provide up to two sessions a week of religious education under arrangements requested by the parents or, subject to such arrangements, in accordance with an agreed syllabus adopted by the school. Former grant-maintained schools may continue to follow their existing syllabus until a date specified by the Secretary of State or, if earlier, until a date agreed by the governing body (Sch. 31, para. 3).

For these purposes, a foundation or voluntary school has a religious character if it has been designated as having such a character by order of the Secretary of State. The Religious Character of Schools (Designation Procedure) Regulations 1998 set out the procedure to be followed by the Secretary of State in making an order designating a school as having a religious character.

20 Voluntary aided schools with a religious character

Religious education at a voluntary aided school with a religious character must be in accordance with either (i) the school's trust deed; or (ii) the tenets of the religion or denomination on which the school's religious character is based; or (iii) the wishes of parents as regards the pupils concerned following any agreed syllabus adopted by the local authority. The religious education given to pupils at such schools is under the general control of the governing body (Sch. 31, para 4).

21 Collective worship

Under s.398 of the 1996 Act, attendance or non-attendance at any place of religious worship must not be made a condition of a pupil attending a maintained school.

Subject to s.71 of the 1998 Act (see **23 Exceptions and special arrangements**, below), each pupil attending a community, foundation or voluntary school must, on each school day, take part in an act of collective worship (s.70). It is the duty of the local authority, governing body and head teacher to ensure that s.70 is complied with.

22 Nature of collective worship

Schedule 20 to the 1998 Act prescribes the arrangements for, and the contents of, collective worship. In the case of community, foundation and voluntary schools, there may be a single act of worship or separate acts for pupils of different ages or in different groups or classes. Where a school does not have a religious character (see **19 Foundation and controlled schools with a religious character**, above) arrangements for collective worship are to be made by the head teacher in consultation with the governors. If the school is a foundation school with a religious character or a voluntary school, arrangements are made by the governors after consultation with the head teacher. Collective worship must normally take place on school premises but may take place elsewhere on special occasions (para. 2).

In the case of community schools and foundation schools without a religious character, collective worship should be wholly or mainly of a broadly Christian character, which means that it must reflect the broad traditions of Christian belief but not be distinctive of any particular denomination. Not every act of worship need comply with this provision, provided that, during any school term, most acts do so comply. In deciding whether non-Christian worship should take place, or the extent to which worship should comply with Christian beliefs and traditions, regard may be had to the family backgrounds of pupils and to their ages and aptitudes (para. 3).

The requirement that collective worship should be wholly or mainly Christian does not apply where a standing advisory council on religious education has decided under s.394 of the 1996 Act that it is not appropriate for this requirement to apply in the case of a particular school or in the case of any class or description of pupils at any school. In such a case, the collective worship must not be distinctive of any Christian or other religious denomination, but may be distinctive of a particular faith (para. 4).

In the case of a foundation school with a religious character, and all voluntary schools, the required collective worship should be in accordance with the school's trust deed or (if the trust deed does not cover this subject) worship should be in accordance with the religion or denomination specified in relation to that school by the Secretary of State in the order designating the school as one having a religious character (see **19 Foundation and controlled schools with a religious character**, above) (para. 5).

23 Exceptions and special arrangements

If the parent of a pupil at a community, foundation or voluntary school requests that he be wholly or partly excused from receiving religious education at the school and/or attending collective worship there, the pupil must be excused until this request is withdrawn. In the case of a non sixth form pupil, a parent may request that the pupil be excused. A sixth-form pupil attending a maintained school may withdraw himself from religious worship. A governing body of a maintained school is required to make arrangements for giving sixth form pupils who are boarders, if they so request, a reasonable opportunity to attend religious education in accordance with the tenets of a particular religion.

If a parent of a child so excused wants him to receive alternative religious education (of a kind not provided at the school) during the times when he is so excused and he cannot with reasonable convenience be sent to another community, foundation or voluntary school where he would receive this education, he may be withdrawn from school for such periods of time as are reasonably necessary to enable him to receive such education elsewhere. The local authority must first be satisfied that this will only interfere with the pupil's attendance at his school at the beginning or end of a school session. If the school is a boarding school, the governors must arrange for the pupil to receive alternative religious education outside school hours and to attend alternative worship on Sundays or other days observed by his religion. Any expenditure incurred by the governors must not be met by them or by the local authority (School Standards and Framework Act 1998, s.71, amended by the Education and Inspections Act 2006, s.55).

C: GENERAL PROVISIONS RELATING TO EDUCATION AT SCHOOLS

24 Political indoctrination

The local authority (if appropriate), governing body, and head teacher of any maintained school or community or foundation special school must forbid (a) the pursuit of partisan political activities by junior pupils (i.e., pupils under the age of 12); and (b) the promotion of partisan political views in the teaching of any subject in the school (Education Act 1996, s.406). They must also secure, as far as reasonably practicable, that, where political issues are brought to the attention of pupils while they are at school or taking part in extra-curricular activities provided or organised for them by or on behalf of the school, they are offered a balanced presentation of opposing views (s.407).

25 Sex education

The local authority (if appropriate), governing body, and head teacher of any maintained school or community or foundation special school, must take such steps as are reasonably practicable to secure that where sex education is given to any registered pupils it is given in such a manner as to encourage those pupils to have due regard to moral considerations and the value of family life (Education Act 1996, s.403).

The Secretary of State must issue guidance designed to secure that when sex education is given to pupils at maintained schools (s.403(1A), added by the Learning and Skills Act 2000, s.148)–

(a) they learn about the nature of marriage and its importance for family life and the bringing up of children; and

(b) they are protected from teaching and materials which are inappropriate having regard to their age and religious and cultural background.

26 Charges in maintained schools

Part VI Chapter III (ss.449 to 462) of the Education Act 1996 makes provision for the charges that are prohibited and those that are permitted in maintained schools. For this purpose, a maintained school is any school maintained by a local authority (s.449).

Prohibited charges–No charge is to be made in respect of admission to any school (s.450), nor for education provided for registered pupils during school hours (s.451, as amended by the Education and Inspections Act 2006, s.56). Regulations may be made to prescribe the circumstances under which charges can be made for singing and musical instrument tuition (s.451(3), as substituted by the Education and Inspections Act 2006, s.56). The Charges for Music Tuition (England) Regulations 2007 prescribe the circumstances in which a charge may be made for tuition in singing or in playing a musical instrument given during school hours. Regulations may also be made to prescribe the circumstances under which charges can be made for early years provision (s.451(2A), added by the Childcare Act 2006, s.17: see the Note on **Child Minding and Day Care for Young Children** at para **28 Charges**).

No charge is to be made in respect of the entry of a registered pupil at any maintained school for any prescribed public examination in any syllabus for that examination for which the pupil has been prepared at the school (s.453) although wasted fees may be recovered from a pupil's parent where the pupil fails without good reason to meet any examination requirement of the syllabus (s.453(2)). The Education (Prescribed Public Examinations) (England) Regulations 2010 (for Wales, the Education (Prescribed Public Examinations) Regulations 1989) specify the public examinations which are prescribed for this purpose.

Neither the parent nor the pupil at any such school will be required to pay for or supply any materials, books, instruments, or other equipment (not including clothing (s.462(1)) required in connection with the education provided for the pupil at the school, or in connection with any syllabus for a prescribed public examination for which the pupil has been prepared at the school, unless the parent has indicated that he wishes the article to be owned by him or the pupil (s.454(1) and (2)).

No charge is to be made in respect of transport provided for a pupil at a maintained school where the transport is either incidental to education provided for the pupil at the school or is provided to enable him to meet any examination requirement for any syllabus for which he has been prepared at the school (s.454(3)).

Transport is incidental to education provided for pupils at the school if it is provided for the purpose of carrying those pupils to or from any part of the school premises in which education is provided for them, from or to any other part of those premises, or to or from any place outside the school premises in which education is provided for those pupils under arrangements made by or on behalf of the governing body or the local authority, from or to the school premises or any other such place (s.454(4)).

Permitted charges.–Under s.455, a charge, referred to as a regulated charge, may be made for a registered pupil at a maintained school in respect of certain optional extras, namely–

(a) education or transport other than education or transport in respect of which no charge may be made by virtue of ss.451 or 454 (see above) or s.509 (transport to enable pupils to attend school–see the Note on **Health and Welfare in Schools**);

(b) entry for a public examination in any syllabus for that examination otherwise than in circumstances in which by virtue of s.453(1) (see above) no charge may be made;

(c) board and lodging provided for any such pupil on a residential trip.

No charge may be made in respect of (a) or (b) unless the education or transport is provided, or the pupil is entered for the examination in that syllabus, by agreement with his parent; and a regulated charge must not exceed the cost of the provision of the optional extra (excluding any costs attributable to the provision of teaching staff) or the board and lodging in question (ss.455 and 456). However–

(a) where the optional extra consists of tuition in playing a musical instrument, the costs of its provision will include costs, or an appropriate proportion of the costs, attributable to the provision of teaching staff employed to provide the tuition; and

(b) in Wales, where transport is provided under the Learner Travel (Wales) Measure 2008, s.6 (see the Note on **Financial and Other Assistance to Pupils** at para **11 Travel to school in Wales**), the charge may exceed the cost of provision.

Charging policy.–Every local authority and every governing body must determine and keep under review a charging policy and, if they make a charge, a remissions policy in respect of optional extras and board and lodging charges in respect of residential trips. The remissions policy must provide for complete remission of any charges otherwise payable in respect of board and lodging provided for a pupil on a residential trip if the education provided on the trip is education in respect of which, by virtue of s.451 (see above), no charge is to be made and his parent is in receipt of–

(a) income support; or

(b) an income-based jobseeker's allowance; or

(c) any other benefit or allowance, or entitled to any tax credit under the Tax Credits Act 2002 or element of such a tax credit as may be prescribed for this purpose in such circumstances as may be so prescribed,

in respect of any period wholly or partly comprised in the time spent on the trip (s.457 as amended by the Education Act 2002, s.200).

For these purposes, the Education (Residential Trips) (Prescribed Tax Credits) (England) Regulations 2003 and the Education (Remission of Charges Relating to Residential Trips) (Wales) Regulations 2003 extend this remission of charges to parents who are–

(d) in receipt of support under Part VI of the Immigration and Asylum Act 1999;

(e) receiving child tax credit but not working tax credit and have an income of not more than £16,190;

(f) state pension credit so long as the claimant is receiving the guarantee credit; or

(g) in Wales, in receipt of universal credit.

Board and lodging charges–The general rule is that, where any registered pupil at a maintained school is provided at the school with board and lodging at the expense of a local authority, charges will be payable in respect of the board and lodging by the parent of the pupil concerned to that authority.

Exceptions to the general rule are where board and lodging are provided for the pupil at a school maintained by a local authority, and under arrangements made by that authority, on the ground that, in the opinion of the authority, education suitable to the pupil's age, ability, and aptitude and to any special educational needs he may have cannot otherwise be provided by the authority for him. In these circumstances, the whole of the charges payable will be remitted by the local authority.

Where the local authority are satisfied that payment of the full charges payable would involve financial hardship to the parent of the pupil concerned, they will remit or pay so much of the charges as they consider necessary to avoid hardship to the parent (s.458).

27 Information about charging and remission policies

The Education (School Sessions and Charges and Remissions Policies) (Information) (England) Regulations 1999 *inter alia* require the head teacher of every maintained school, and the relevant local authority in England, to make available information about the charging and remissions policies determined by the governing body and the authority respectively. The information must be available for distribution without charge to parents of pupils at the school on request, and for reference by parents and others at the school, at the authority's office, and in public libraries in the area of the authority.

28 Careers education guidance

Part VII of the Education Act 1997 places a duty on local authority maintained schools and special schools to provide a programme of impartial careers guidance for pupils in England aged between 13 and 18 (s.42A and the Careers Guidance in Schools Regulations 2013, S.I. No. 709) and in Wales aged between 14 and 19 (s.43 and the Education (Extension of Careers Education) (Wales) Regulations 2001, S.I. No. 1987).

In England, the guidance must be given by someone other than a teacher or other person employed at the school and must include information on all 16 to 18 education or training options, including apprenticeships.

Schools and institutions in Wales and further education institutions in England must also provide pupils with access to guidance materials relating to careers education and to career opportunities (s.45).

29 Work experience

S.560, as amended by s.112 of the School Standards and Framework Act 1998, enables local authorities in England and Wales to arrange for children under school-leaving age to have work experience, as part of their education, during the last year of compulsory schooling. It provides that enactments prohibiting or regulating the employment of children shall not apply to the employment of a child in his last two years of compulsory schooling if the employment is in pursuance of arrangements made by a local authority or by a school's governing body.

30 Health and welfare of school pupils

For the provisions concerning health and general welfare of school pupils, see the Note on **Health and Welfare in Schools**.

31 Local authority duties in respect of recreation

S.507A of the Education Act 1996 (inserted by s.6 of the Education and Inspections Act 2006) imposes a duty on LEAs in respect of providing recreational and training facilities for children under 13 in England. S.507B (inserted by s.6 of the Education and Inspections Act 2006) imposes similar obligations in England to promote the well-being of persons aged 13-19 (and of persons aged up to 25 with learning difficulties) by securing access for them to sufficient educational and recreational leisure-time activities and facilities, so far as is reasonably practicable. In performing its duty under s.507B, the authority is required to ascertain from young people in the authority's area their views on existing provision and the need for any additional provision, and to take those views into account. Before taking any action the authority is also required to take steps to assess whether it is beneficial for other agencies and individuals to provide services in its place and, where appropriate, to secure that those services are provided by such agencies or individuals. S.507B also includes the power to levy charges and places a requirement on authorities to have regard to any guidance given by the Secretary of State when exercising its functions under the section.

Similar duties in respect of Wales are applied by s.508 (amended by s.6 of and Sch.1 to the Education and Inspections Act 2006).

D: EXTERNAL EXAMINATIONS

32 Introduction

S.402 of the 1996 Act imposes on the governing body of every maintained school a duty to secure that each registered pupil is entered at the appropriate time for each prescribed public examination for which he is being prepared at the school at the time in question, in each syllabus for which he is being so prepared, unless they or the parent requests that they should not. The Education (Prescribed Public Examinations) (England) Regulations 2010 (for Wales, the Education (Prescribed Public Examinations) Regulations 1989) specify the public examinations prescribed for this purpose.

In England and Wales, the main external examinations for pupils in secondary schools are those for the General Certificate of Secondary Education, and those for the Advanced and Advanced Supplementary level examinations.

The Learning and Skills Act 2000 s.96 provides that no course of study leading to a qualification authenticated by an outside person is to be—

(a) provided by a maintained school; or

(b) funded by a local authority or by the Learning and Skills Council for England or the National Assembly for Wales;

for pupils of compulsory school age (or above that age but under 19) unless the qualification is for the time being approved by the Secretary of State or Welsh Ministers or by a body designated by them.

S.127 of the Apprenticeship, Skills, Children and Learning Act 2009 provides for the establishment of a Non-Ministerial Department in England known as the Office of Qualifications and Examinations Regulation (Ofqual). See **15 The Office of Qualifications and Examinations Regulation,** above. In Wales, Qualifications Wales exercises regulatory functions in relation to qualifications awarded in Wales (Qualifications Wales Act 2015, s.3) (see **16 Qualifications Wales,** above).

33 General Certificate of Secondary Education

The General Certificate of Secondary Education (G.C.S.E.) is a single system of examinations mainly intended for pupils aged 16 years, with a single scale of grades from A down to G. Grades A, B, and C have standards at least as high as the former General Certificate of Education Ordinary level grades A, B, and C or the former Certificate of Education Grade 1. Grades D, E, F, and G are at least as high as the former Certificate of Secondary Education Grades 2 to 5. Candidates who do not reach Grade G in a subject will be ungraded and that subject will not be recorded on the Certificate.

The examinations are designed, principally, for pupils in the last year of statutory secondary education but are also available to candidates for further education and to private candidates. There is no minimum or maximum age of entry.

34 General Certificate of Education (G.C.E.) Advanced Levels

The General Certificate of Education Advanced level ("A Level") and Advanced Supplementary level ("AS level") examinations are designed mainly for pupils who have spent two years in the sixth form. There are five pass grades (A to E). The AS level examinations, for which a new two-year course was introduced in September 1987, are intended to broaden the studies of A level students by allowing them to study more subjects after the age of 16. A course of study for AS level requires about half the work of an A level course but at the same standard, and two AS level passes are roughly equivalent to one A level pass at a comparable grade.

35 Examining boards

There are three unitary examining boards who each offer A Level, GCSE, and GNVQ qualifications. The three are—

AQA (the Assessment and Qualifications Alliance);

The Edexcel Foundation; and

OCR (Oxford, Cambridge and RSA Examination.

36 Authorities

Statutes—

Apprenticeship, Skills, Children and Learning Act 2009

EDUCATION

Education Acts 1962 to 2009

Education and Inspections Act 2006

Learning and Skills Act 2000

Learning and Skills (Wales) Measure 2009

Qualifications Wales Act 2015

School Standards and Framework Act 1998

Statutory Instruments–

Charges for Music Tuition (England) Regulations 2007 (S.I. 2007 No. 2239)

Education (Amendment of the Curriculum Requirements for Fourth Key Stage) (England) Order 2003 (S.I. 2003 No, 2946)

Education (Local Curriculum for Pupils in Key Stage 4) (Wales) Regulations 2009, as amended (S.I. 2009, No. 3256 and 2014 No. 42)

Education (National Curriculum) (Assessment Arrangements for Reading and Numeracy) (Wales) Order 2013 (S.I. 2013 No. 433)

Education (National Curriculum) (Exceptions) (Wales) Regulations 1991 (S.I. 1991 No. 1657)

Education (National Curriculum for Wales) Disapplication of Science at Key Stage 4) Regulations 2006 (S.I. 2006 No. 1335)

Education (National Curriculum) (Foundation Phase) (Wales) Order 2014, as amended (S.I. 2014 No. 1996 and 2015 No. 1596)

Education (National Curriculum) (Science at Key Stage 4) (England) Order 2007, as amended (S.I. 2007 No. 2241 and 2016 No. 432)

Education (Prescribed Public Examinations (England) Regulations 2010 (S.I. 2010 No. 2327)

Education (Prescribed Public Examinations Regulations 1989 (S.I. 1989 No. 377)

Education (Remission of Charges Relating to Residential Trips) (Wales) Regulations 2003, as amended (S.I. 2003 No. 860, 2011 No. 706, and 2013 No. 2731)

Education (Residential Trips) (Prescribed Tax Credits) (England) Regulations 2003, as amended (S.I. 2003 No. 381, 2005 No. 1014, and 2011 No. 730)

Education (School Sessions and Charges and Remissions Policies) (Information) (England) Regulations 1999 (S.I. 1999 No. 2255)

National Curriculum (Exceptions for First, Second, Third and Fourth Key Stages) (England) Regulations 2013, as amended (S.I. 2013 No. 1487 and 2014 Nos. 1866 and 3286)

School Performance and Absence Targets (Wales) Regulations 2011 (S.I. 2011 No. 1945)

SCHOOLS: DISCIPLINE AND EXCLUSION
ENGLAND AND WALES

1 Introduction

The Note is concerned with the responsibility for discipline and behaviour policy in schools, when children may be excluded, and the consequences of exclusion, including parenting contracts and parenting orders and pupil referral units.

2 Responsibility for discipline

S.88 of the Education and Inspections Act 2006 requires the governing body of a maintained school to ensure that policies designed to promote good behaviour and discipline on the part of pupils are pursued at the school. In particular, the governing body must make and keep under review a written statement of general principles to which the head teacher is to have regard. Where the governing body wants the behaviour policy to include particular measures or address particular issues, they must notify the head teacher. The governing body may give the head teacher further guidance. Before making or revising the statement of principles, the governing body must consult the head teacher; parents of pupils registered at the school; registered pupils; and any people who work at the school who it is considered appropriate to consult. The governing body must have regard to national guidance when carrying out its functions, as provided by the Secretary of State. and Welsh Assembly. These provisions apply to all maintained schools (community; foundation; voluntary; community special; foundation special; maintained nursery), pupil referral units and non-maintained special schools.

3 Determination by head teacher of behaviour policy

The head teacher must determine measures that promote self-discipline and a proper regard for authority, encourage good behaviour and respect for others, prevent bullying, secure that tasks are completed, and generally secure an acceptable standard of behaviour by pupils. These measures constitute the school's behaviour policy (Education and Inspections Act 2006, s.89(1)).

The head teacher must follow the governing body's statement of principles and have regard to any notification or guidance given by it (s.89(2)).

The head teacher must determine what standard of behaviour should be regarded as acceptable in so far as it is not determined by the governing body (s.88(3)).

The measures determined by the head teacher must include the making of rules and provision for disciplinary penalties (s.89(4)).

The head teacher may determine measures to regulate the behaviour of pupils when they are not on school premises or under the control or charge of a member of the school staff (s.89(5)).

The head teacher must set out the behaviour policy in a written document and publicise it by making it generally known to staff, pupils and parents, in particular, by bringing it to their attention at least once a year (s.89(6)).

A "disciplinary penalty" is a penalty imposed on a pupil by any school at which education is provided for him, where his conduct falls below the standard which could reasonably be expected of him because (for example) he fails to follow a school rule or an instruction given by a member of staff (s.90).

The enforcement of disciplinary penalties is dealt with by s.90. This section does not legitimise corporal punishment (s.91(10)).

The conditions that make the detention of a pupil outside school sessions lawful are set out in s.92. In the case of a detention during a break between school sessions on the same day (for example, a detention at lunchtime), the head teacher must have made the school's policy on detention outside of school sessions known within school and to parents. In other cases, for example evening or weekend detention, three further conditions apply in addition to this, namely that the pupil is below the age of 18, that the detention is on a "permitted day of detention" and that [in Wales only] the pupil's parent has been given at least 24 hours' notice. In considering whether the imposition of a detention is reasonable regard must be had to whether suitable travelling arrangements can reasonably be made by the pupil's parent. A "permitted day of detention" is a school day (other than one on which the school has given the pupil leave of absence); a Saturday or Sunday during the school term (other than weekends preceding or following half-term breaks); and a non-teaching work day that may fall in or out of the school term.

The Education (Excluded Days of Detention) (England) Regulations 2007 specify what days may not be permitted days of detention for the purposes of s.92 in relation to England.

4 Power of members of staff to use force

A member of staff may use reasonable force to prevent a pupil from committing an offence, causing personal injury, damaging property or doing something that prejudices discipline at the school (Education and Inspections Act 2006, s.93). The power to use force extends to members of staff at any school at which the pupil is receiving education (s.92(2)). The use of this power is restricted to when both the member of staff and the pupil are on school premises or in other situations where the member of staff has lawful control or charge of the pupil involved (s.92(3)). This section does not legitimise corporal punishment. (s.92(4)).

5 Defence where confiscation lawful

Staff are protected against civil or criminal liability where a lawfully confiscated item is retained or disposed of (Education and Inspections Act 2006, s.94).

As to searches for weapons under the Education Act 1996, s.550AA, see the Note on **Offensive Weapons and Firearms**. In England, the power of search is wider and includes other items such as controlled drugs, alcohol, stolen property, any article which a member of staff reasonably suspects has been, or is likely to be, used to commit an offence or to cause personal injury to, or damage to the property of, any person, including the pupil being searched, and any other item which the school rules identify as one for which a search can be undertaken. There is also a power to make regulations to add to the list of prohibited items for which a search may be made (Education Act 1996, ss.550ZA to 550ZD).

6 Abolition of corporal punishment

S.548 of the Education Act 1996 (substituted by the School Standards and Framework Act 1998, s.131) makes provision as to corporal punishment of pupils in England and Wales. Where in any proceedings it is shown that corporal punishment has been given to a pupil under 18 (including a child at a nursery school) by, or on the authority of, a member of staff at any school (including an independent school—see the Note on **Independent Schools**), giving the punishment cannot be justified on the ground that it was done in pursuance of a right exercisable by the member of staff by virtue of his position as such. In this context, giving corporal punishment means doing anything for the purposes of punishing the pupil concerned (whether or not there are also other reasons) which apart from any justification would constitute battery. It is irrelevant whether the punishment takes place at the school or at another place where education is being provided or elsewhere. Action to avert immediate danger of personal injury to, or immediate danger to the property of, any person (including the pupil concerned) is not to be taken as giving corporal punishment.

7 Exclusion from school

Ss.51A and 52 of the Education Act 2002 deals with the power to exclude pupils at a maintained school, pupil referral unit or Academy on disciplinary grounds.

The head teacher of a maintained school, teacher in charge of a pupil referral unit, or principal in charge of an Academy may exclude a pupil from the establishment for a fixed period or permanently.

The School Discipline (Pupil Exclusions and Reviews) (England) Regulations 2012, the Education (Pupil Exclusions and Appeals) (Maintained Schools) (Wales) Regulations 2003, and the Education (Pupil Exclusions and Appeals) (Pupil Referral Units) (Wales) Regulations 2003 all make similar provision with regard to exclusions. The references below are to the School Discipline (Pupil Exclusions and Reviews) (England) Regulations 2012 which require that—

(a) where a head teacher/teacher in charge/principal (the "head teacher") excludes a pupil, he must without delay take reasonable steps to inform the pupil's parent, or the pupil himself if he is 18 or over, of the period of the exclusion, the reasons for it, and the means by which representations about the exclusion may be made (Regs. 5, 14, 23);

(b) if the exclusion –
    (i) is permanent;
    (ii) will result in the pupil missing a public examination or a National Curriculum test, or
    (iii) takes the total exclusions for that pupil to more than 5 school days in any term,
then the head teacher must also inform the responsible body (i.e., for a maintained school, the governing body; for a pupil referral unit, the management committee; and for an Academy, the proprietor) and the local authority.

Those bodies must also be informed about any other exclusions, and the reasons for them, once a term. The Secretary of State may request such information from the local authority (Reg. 11);

(c) where a responsible body are informed of an exclusion—
    (i) within (b)(i), (ii) above; or
    (ii) which would take the total exclusions for that pupil to more than 15 school days in any term or 5 days and the parent (or pupil over 18) wishes to make representations,
they are under a duty to consider the circumstances of that exclusion and any representations made to them by the pupil's parent, the pupil himself if he is 18 or over, or the local authority (except that an Academy may restrict a local authority to observer status) (Regs. 6, 15, 24). The responsible body must consider whether or not the pupil should be reinstated and where they consider that the pupil should be reinstated, they must in addition consider whether he should be reinstated immediately, or reinstated by a particular date (and, in Wales, whether it is practical for a head teacher to comply with a direction requiring reinstatement).

(d) The responsible body must act within—
    (i) 15 school days in the case of a permanent exclusion; an exclusion for a fixed period which would

cause the pupil's total number of days of exclusion to exceed 15 school days in any term; or an exclusion where the pupil would, as a result of the exclusion, lose an opportunity to take a public examination or a National Curriculum test; or

(ii) 50 school days in the case of an exclusion for a fixed period where the pupil would, as a result of the exclusion, be excluded for a total of more than 5school days but not more than 15 school days in any term; and the pupil's parent (or the pupil himself if he is 18 or over) has made representations under regulation.

(iii) where a pupil has been excluded in circumstances in which they would, as a result of the exclusion, lose an opportunity to take a public examination or a National Curriculum test, the governing body must (so far as it is reasonably practicable) act before the date of that examination or test.

If the responsible body decides not to reinstate a pupil who has been permanently excluded and the parent (or pupil himself if he is 18 or over) applies for a review, the local authority (in relation to a maintained school or a pupil referral unit), or the proprietor (in relation to an Academy), must make arrangements for a review of that decision by a review panel (Regs. 7, 16, 25). When applying for a review, the parent or pupil may request the local authority (or proprietor) to appoint a special educational needs expert to advise the review panel. A panel may uphold the decision not to reinstate the pupil, recommend that that decision is reconsidered, or if it considers that the decision of the responsible body was flawed when considered in the light of the principles applicable on an application for judicial review, quash the decision and direct the responsible body to reconsider the matter (s.51A(4)).

In England, if, following a decision by the panel to quash the governing body's original decision, the governing body—

(1) reconsider the exclusion and decide not to reinstate the pupil; or

(2) fail to reconsider the exclusion within 10 days,

the review panel may order that the local authority are to make an adjustment to the school's budget share for the funding period during which the exclusion occurs in the sum of £4,000 (or in the case of an Academy, order the proprietor to make a payment to the local authority in the sum of £4,000). Such a decision is binding.

In the exercise of any of these functions, regard must be had to any guidance given from time to time by the Secretary of State; and, in establishing any fact this must be done on the balance of probabilities.

In England, the head teacher of a school must inform the local authority in whose area a permanently excluded pupil resides, if it is different form the school's local authority, that the pupil has been permanently excluded.

As to parenting contracts and parenting orders in case of exclusion from school, see 10 **Parenting contracts**, and see 11 **Parenting orders**, below.

8 Duty of governing body or proprietor where pupil excluded for fixed period

There is a duty for schools to provide suitable full-time education to temporarily excluded pupils. They are expected to send work home for the pupil to complete. The Secretary of State may prescribe exceptions to this duty (Education and Inspections Act 2006, s.100).

The Education (Provision of Full-Time Education for Excluded Pupils) (England) Regulations 2007 provide—

(a) that the duty of school governing bodies and local authorities to provide suitable full-time education for excluded pupils is to apply from the sixth school day of exclusion (Regs. 3 and 4);

(b) exceptions to that duty for pupils in Year 11 who have no further examinations to take, and for pupils with a statement of special educational needs specifying fewer hours' education than the number of hours provided for pupils in full-time education (Reg. 5).

Note.—Consecutive periods of exclusion must be treated as one period for the purpose of providing suitable alternative education, such education must therefore be provided no later than the sixth school day of the exclusion, regardless of whether the pupil was excluded for one period of six days or more or two or more consecutive fixed periods of less than six days (Regs. 3(3) and 4(3)).

9 Duty of parent in relation to excluded pupil

Where a pupil has been excluded from a relevant school in England, his head teacher must give the pupil's parent a notice containing prescribed information including the day on which full-time education will be provided to the excluded pupil. It must set out the days on which the parent is subject to the duty to ensure that the pupil is not in a public place during school hours (see below). That responsibility will not exceed five days. The notice can be served by any effective method (Education and Inspections Act 2006, s.104).

Where a pupil has been excluded, either for a fixed period or permanently, and notice has been given to a parent of the pupil, there is a duty on the parent to ensure that the excluded pupil is not present in a public place during normal school hours on a day which is one of the first five school days to which the exclusion relates and is specified in the notice (or, in the case of an exclusion for a fixed period of five days or less, on any of the days to which the exclusion relates which is specified in the notice). The parent commits an offence if he fails in this duty, but has a defence if he shows that he had a reasonable justification for the failure. The sanction faced by a parent, if found guilty, is a fine not exceeding level 3 on the standard scale. Only a local authority can institute proceedings against the parent (s.103).

The Education (Provision of Full-Time Education for Excluded Pupils) (England) Regulations 2007 provide in relation to the notice to be given to parents under s.104 of the 2006 Act (about the full-time education to be provided following the exclusion, and the days on which the parent is required by s.103 of the 2006 Act to ensure that the pupil is not in a public place during school hours without reasonable justification) for the time by which the notice must be given (Reg. 6), and for the information it must contain (Reg. 7).

A penalty notice may be given to a parent in respect of the presence of an excluded pupil in public place (s.105). The Secretary of State may make regulations about the administration of penalty notices (s.106) (see the Note on **Schools: Admission and Attendance: England and Wales**).

10 Parenting contracts

Where a pupil has (Anti-social Behaviour Act 2003, s.19)–
(a) been excluded from school on disciplinary grounds for a fixed period or permanently (see **7 Exclusion from school**, above); or
(b) failed to attend regularly at a school where he is a registered pupil,
the local authority or governing body may enter into a parenting contract with a parent of the pupil. This is a document which contains a statement by the parent agreeing to comply with requirements specified in the document, and a statement by the local authority or governing body agreeing to support the parent for the purpose of complying with those requirements. The requirements may include a requirement to attend a counselling or guidance programme. The purpose of the contract is to improve the behaviour of the pupil (where he has been excluded) and ensure regular attendance (where this has not been the case).

This provision applies to community, foundation and voluntary schools, community or foundation special schools, maintained nursery school, pupil referral units, Academies, city technology colleges, and city colleges for the technology of the arts.

An alternative trigger to enable schools and local authorities to enter, in certain circumstances, into parenting contracts with parents where the pupil has not been excluded is provided by s.19(1A) (inserted by the Education and Inspections Act 2006, s.97(2)). These circumstances are where the school or local authority have reason to believe that a pupil has engaged in behaviour which–
(a) has caused or is likely to cause significant disruption to the education of other pupils or significant detriment to the welfare of that pupil or other pupils or to the health or safety of any staff; or
(b) forms part of a pattern of behaviour which (if continued) could lead to the pupil being excluded.
Such behaviour can take place at school, or elsewhere if reasonable for the school to regulate it (s.19(1B), as so inserted).

Further provision as to parenting contracts is made by the Education (Parenting Contracts and Parenting Orders) (England) Regulations 2007 (see **11 Parenting orders**, below).

11 Parenting orders

Where a pupil has (Anti-social Behaviour Act 2003, s.20)–
(a) been excluded from school on disciplinary grounds for a fixed period or permanently (see **7 Exclusion from school**, above); and
(b) in the case of a fixed period exclusion it is the second such exclusion in a 12 month period; and
(c) application is made within the relevant period,
then a "relevant body" can apply to a magistrates' court for a parenting order to be made in respect of a parent of the pupil. A "relevant body" means a local authority and the governing body of any relevant school in England at which the pupil to whom the application relates is a pupil, or from which he has been excluded (Anti-social Behaviour Act 2003, s.20(2), amended by the Education and Inspections Act 2006 s.98(3) and (6)).

There is a further ground on which an application for a parenting order can be made where the pupil has behaved in such a way that he could have been excluded permanently or for a fixed period and any other conditions specified in regulations are met. Any policy that the school might have to restrict exclusions or to restrict exclusions in certain circumstances is not relevant in this context; the relevant factor is the seriousness of the misbehaviour (2003 Act, s.20(2A) and (2B), inserted by the 2006 Act, s.98(4)).

The court can make a parenting order under s.20 if it is satisfied that the type of behaviour described in s.20(2A) has occurred and that making the order would be desirable in the interests of improving the pupil's behaviour (s.20(3), substituted by the 2006 Act, s.98(5)).

The "relevant period" is–
(d) in the case of a pupil excluded for a fixed period, the later of (i) 40 days from when the exclusion was considered by the governing body (or if it was not considered, from the day the exclusion began) or (ii) six months after a parenting contract began;
(e) in the case of a permanent exclusion, the later of (i) 40 days from when an appeal panel upheld the exclusion (or if there was no appeal, from the last day on which an appeal could have been made) or (ii) six months after a parenting contract began.
A parenting order requires the parent to comply, for a period not exceeding 12 months, with specified requirements and requires attendance on a counselling or guidance programme for up to three months. If a parenting order has been made previously, attendance on the programme may, but need not, be required. If the

court is satisfied that a residential programme is likely to be more effective than a non-residential one in improving the behaviour of the pupil and that any consequent interference in family life is proportionate in all the circumstances, then it may require the parent to attend a residential programme.

In deciding whether to make a parenting order, the court will take into account any refusal by the parent to enter into a parenting contract and any failure to comply with any contract which has been entered into (s.21). Where the pupil is under 16, the court must also consider information about family circumstances and the likely effect of an order on those circumstances. The court will also take into account any failure by the parent, without reasonable excuse, to attend a reintegration interview under s.102 of the Education and Inspections Act 2006 when requested to do so (Anti-social Behaviour Act 2003, s.21(1A), as inserted by the Education and Inspections Act 2006, s.99).

A parent can appeal against the making of a parenting order to the Crown Court (s.22).

The Secretary of State may be regulations make provision for which local authority should have the power to enter into a parenting contract or apply for an order when the child lives in one authority but attends school in another; which school should have the power to apply for an order where the pupil has been permanently excluded; requirements to consult and share information; and how the costs associated with a parenting order should be met (Anti-social Behaviour Act 2003, s.22A, inserted by the Education and Inspections Act 2006, s.99(3)).

The Education (Parenting Contracts and Parenting Orders) (England) Regulations 2007 make provision in relation to parenting orders and parenting contracts. They prescribe conditions to be fulfilled before an application can be made for a parenting order (Reg. 3). They also prescribe the condition in respect of both permanent and fixed term exclusions (namely that the application must be made within the relevant period) (Reg. 4), and the condition where it appears that the pupil has engaged in behaviour warranting exclusion (again the application must also be made within the relevant period) (Reg. 5). A local authority is restricted from entering into a parenting contract or applying for a parenting order under certain circumstances (Reg. 7) and there is a limit on the power of a governing body of a relevant school to apply for a parenting order (Reg. 8). Relevant bodies who may enter into parenting contracts or apply for parenting orders must consult one another before doing so (Reg. 9). They must also seek from one another information which they reasonably consider may be relevant to enable them to decide whether or not to enter into a parenting contract or apply for a parenting order, to avoid multiple contracts and orders in relation to the same child, and to determine the content of a contract or order (Reg. 10).

Similar provision is made for Wales by the Education (Parenting Orders) (Wales) Regulations 2006.

12 Reintegration interviews

The Secretary of State and the Welsh Assembly may make regulations specifying (Education and Inspections Act 2006, s.102(1))–

(a) the circumstances in which maintained schools, academies, city technology colleges and city colleges for the technology of the arts must arrange reintegration interviews with the parents of temporarily excluded pupils; and

(b) the procedures and time limits connected with such an interview.

These interviews are aimed at engaging with the parent to assist with the reintegration of a pupil excluded for a fixed period and to promote an improvement in his behaviour.

The Education (Reintegration Interview) (Wales) Regulations 2010 prescribe the circumstances in which a head teacher must request the parents of an excluded pupil of compulsory school age to attend such a reintegration interview, and the procedure by which the interview must be arranged. A head teacher must request an interview with a parent of a pupil of compulsory school age who has been excluded from a primary school for any fixed period, or from a secondary school for a fixed period of six or more school days. The parent must be an individual who resides with the child. The head teacher need not make such a request if the exclusion starts within 10 days of the end of the summer term or the pupil is expected to leave the school for a reason other than his behaviour (Reg. 3).

The request must be made by a notice in writing and must contain specific information (Reg. 4). A notice from a head teacher under these Regulations may be combined with a notice informing the parent of the exclusion (under regulations made under the Education Act 2002, s.52(3)(a)) (Reg. 5).

The notice may be delivered to the parent, left at his usual or last known address, or sent in a prepaid properly addressed letter. It may be sent by e-mail if the parent has agreed to use e-mail to receive notices (Education Act 1996, s.572).

The equivalent regulations for England have been revoked.

13 Pupil referral units

Each local authority is required to make arrangements for the provision of suitable full-time or part-time education at school or otherwise than at school for those children of compulsory school age who by reason of illness, exclusion from school (see **7 Exclusion from school**, above), or otherwise, may not for any period receive suitable education unless such arrangements are made for them. A school established and maintained by a local authority which is specially organised to provide education for such children and which is not a county or special school is known as a pupil referral unit. A local authority has a discretion to secure the provision of boarding

EDUCATION

accommodation at any pupil referral unit (Education Act 1996, s.19).

In England, local authorities must provide permanently excluded pupils from relevant schools with suitable full-time education. A relevant school is a maintained school, an academy, a city technology college or a city college for the technology of the arts (Education Act 1996, s.19(3A), inserted by the Education and Inspections Act 2006, s.101).

The Secretary of State may make regulations requiring local authorities to establish management committees for their pupil referral units (Education Act 1997, s.48). The Education (Pupil Referral Units) (Management Committees etc.) (England) Regulations 2007 (S.I. No. 2978 as amended by 2009 No. 1924 and 2012 Nos. 1825, 2404 and 3158) have been made and provide for such committees to have parent, staff, authority appointed, community and sponsor members, and that the number of community members must out number all the other members. A community member is a person who lives or works in the community served by the unit or who, in the opinion of the committee, is committed to the good government and success of the unit. The 2007 Regulations also set out the matters which a local authority can and cannot delegate to a management committee.

14 Children with behavioural difficulties

S.527A of the Education Act 1996 (inserted by the Education Act 1997, s.9) requires local authorities to prepare, and from time to time review, a statement setting out the arrangements made or proposed to be made by the authority in connection with the education of children with behavioural difficulties. In particular, the statement must include details of (a) the arrangements made by the authority for the provision of advice and resources to schools maintained by the authority or special schools in the authority's area, and (b) the arrangements made by the authority to meet requests from such schools for support and assistance in connection with the promotion of good behaviour and discipline on the part of pupils; and (c) any other arrangements made by the authority to assist children with behavioural difficulties to find places at suitable schools. The statement must also deal with the interaction between the arrangements made by the authority under s.527A and those made by them for pupils with behavioural difficulties who also have special educational needs. In England, a statement made by an authority under s.527A must (unless the authority has been excepted) be published and must be revised at prescribed intervals (see the Local Authority (Behaviour Support Plans) Regulations 1998, as amended (S.I. 1998 No. 644, 2001 Nos. 606, 828, and 3710, 2003 No. 3082, and 2005 No. 617)).

15 Off-site provision to improve behaviour

The governing body of a maintained school in England (other than a nursery school) may require a pupil to attend at any place outside the school premises for the purpose of receiving educational provision which is intended to improve the behaviour of the pupil (Education Act 2002, s.29A). A governing body imposing a requirement that a pupil attend off-site provision must give written notice of the requirement to the relevant person (i.e., the pupil's parent (where the pupil is under 18) or the pupil), and, where the pupil has a statement of special educational needs, to the local authority maintaining the statement. They must keep the off-site provision requirement under review by holding review meetings, at such intervals as they consider appropriate having regard to the needs of the pupil, for as long as the requirement remains in effect. Parents, pupils (aged over 18) and local authorities (for pupils with a statement of special educational needs) can request a review meeting and the governing body must then hold such a meeting if one has not been held in the previous 10 weeks. Following each review meeting, the governing body must decide whether they should continue to require the pupil to attend off-site provision and, if so, for how long (Education (Educational Provision for Improving Behaviour) Regulations 2010).

16 Authorities

Statutes–
Anti-social Behaviour Act 2003

Education Acts 1962 to 2006

Education and Inspections Act 2006

School Standards and Framework Act 1998

Statutory Instruments applying only to England–
Education (Educational Provision for Improving Behaviour) Regulations 2010, as amended (S.I. 2010 No. 1156, 2012 No. 2532, and 2014 No. 2301)

Education (Excluded Days of Detention) (England) Regulations 2007 (S.I. 2007 No. 1304)

Education (Parenting Contracts and Parenting Orders) (England) Regulations 2007, as amended (S.I. 2007 No. 1869, 2010 No. 1172, and 2012 No. 1033)

Education (Provision of Full-Time Education for Excluded Pupils) (England) Regulations 2007, as amended (S.I. 2007 No. 1870, 2012 No. 1033, and 2014 Nos. 2103 and 3216)

School Discipline (Pupil Exclusions and Reviews) (England) Regulations 2012 (S.I. 2012 No. 1033)

Statutory Instruments applying only to Wales–

Education (Parenting Orders) (Wales) Regulations 2006, as amended (S.I. 2006 No. 1277 and 2010 No. 1142)

Education (Pupil Exclusions and Appeals) (Maintained Schools) (Wales) Regulations 2003, as amended (S.I. 2003 No. 3227 and 2004 No. 1805)

Education (Pupil Exclusions and Appeals) (Pupil Referral Units) (Wales) Regulations 2003, as amended (S.I. 2003 No. 3246 and 2004 No. 1805)

Education (Pupil Referral Units) (Appeals Against Permanent Exclusion) (Wales) Regulations 2003 (S.I. 2003 No. 287)

Education (Reintegration Interview) (Wales) Regulations 2010 (S.I. 2010 No. 2953)

Education (School Performance and Unauthorised Absence Targets) (Wales) Regulations 1999 (S.I. 1999 No. 1811)

Education (Variation of Admission Arrangements) (Wales) Regulations 2006 (S.I. 2006 No. 177)

HEALTH AND WELFARE IN SCHOOLS
ENGLAND AND WALES

Contents

This Note has been arranged as follows–
   A: School medical and dental examinations and treatment
   B: Child guidance service
   C: Cleanliness
   D: Health of teachers
   E: School meals and milk
   F: School premises
   G: Diseases

A: SCHOOL MEDICAL AND DENTAL EXAMINATIONS AND TREATMENT

I Overview

The National Health Service Act 2006 contains provision for the medical and dental inspection and treatment of pupils. Local authorities must make accommodation available for such inspection and treatment (2006 Act, Sch. 1, para. 5, and the School Premises (England) Regulations 2012, Reg. 5; Education (School Premises) Regulations 1999, Reg. 5 (for Wales).

Local authorities have a duty to make arrangements for encouraging and assisting pupils to take advantage of the provision for such inspection and treatment made for them, unless the parent of any pupil objects in writing, in which case the pupil must not be encouraged or assisted to do so (Education Act 1996, s.520).

S.80 of the 2006 Act makes provision for the Secretary of State to make available to local authorities health facilities and the services of persons providing health services so far as is reasonably necessary and practicable to enable them to discharge their functions. S.82 requires health and local authorities to co-operate in exercising their respective functions and, by s.254 of the 1996 Act, a local social services authority may permit the use of its premises, furniture, and equipment by a local authority.

Similar provision for Wales is contained in the National Health Service (Wales) Act 2006.

In addition, in all non-maintained special schools, by virtue of the Education (Non-Maintained Special Schools) (England) Regulations 1999, Sch, para 9, provision must be made for–
   (a) the care and supervision of the health of the pupils by appropriately qualified persons (where a school provides for pupils with a particular type of disability, those persons must have experience relevant to that disability);
   (b) the maintenance of medical and dental records;
   (c) the medical and dental inspection at appropriate intervals of the pupils, and their medical and dental treatment.

Medical examinations may be required in order to assess whether a child has special educational needs (see the Note on **Special Educational Provision and Special Schools: England and Wales**).

B: CHILD GUIDANCE SERVICE

2 General

Local authorities, as part of their general responsibilities for the education of pupils and of their duties to ascertain which children have special educational needs, may provide a child guidance service to give help and advice about behavioural, emotional, and learning difficulties in children. Educational psychologists, psychiatrists, and social workers may be employed in this service.

3 Counselling services–Wales

Every local authority must make reasonable provision for an independent counselling service in respect of the health, emotional and social needs of secondary school pupils in its area; other persons belonging to the authority's area who have attained the age of 11 but not the age of 19; pupils in their final year at primary school; and such other primary school pupils as the Welsh Ministers may specify (School Standards and Organisation (Wales) Act 2013, s.92).

C: CLEANLINESS

4 Statutory provisions

S.521 of the Education Act 1996 provides that a local authority may, by directions in writing applying either to all schools they maintain or to schools named in the directions, authorise a medical officer to cause examinations of the persons and clothing of pupils to be made whenever he thinks such examinations are necessary in the interests of cleanliness. If the person or clothing of any pupil is found on examination to be infested with vermin or in a foul condition, the parent may be required to see that proper cleansing is effected. If the parent fails to do this, a medical officer may order the cleansing to be carried out under arrangements made by the local authority. If examination or cleansing cannot be done immediately, a medical officer may direct that the pupil be suspended from school. If, after cleansing, the pupil again becomes verminous, the parent may be fined. No girl may be examined or cleansed except by a duly qualified medical practitioner or by a woman authorised by a local authority (ss.522 to 524).

In other educational establishments (as defined in s.135) under the management of education authorities; however, it is the education authority (not a medical officer) which will direct that a pupil or young person be excluded, and in the case of a young person, it is he (not his parent) who will be required to effect the cleansing and who may be fined.

D: HEALTH OF TEACHERS

5 Fitness for employment

By virtue of the Education (Health Standards) (England) Regulations 2003 (and (Wales) Regulations 2004), a teacher may not be appointed nor continue in employment unless the employing authority is satisfied as to his health and physical capacity (Regs 6 and 7).

E: SCHOOL MEALS AND MILK

6 Introduction

S.512 of the Education Act 1996 (as substituted by the Education Act 2002, s.201) empowers a local authority to provide registered pupils at any school maintained by the authority, other persons who receive education at such a school, and children who receive relevant funded nursery education, with milk, meals and other refreshments. Such provision is to be made either on the school premises or at any other place where education is being provided. A local authority must exercise this power for any person if—

(a) prescribed requirements are met;
(b) a request for the provision of school lunches for that person has been made; and
(c) either that person is eligible for free school lunches (see **7 Free lunch and milk**, below) or, in the case of a registered pupil at a maintained school, it would not be unreasonable for the authority to provide the lunches.

In England, the only prescribed requirement for the purpose of (a) above is that, in the case of children who have not attained compulsory school age but receive nursery education, they must be receiving it either full-time or for a period which spans the lunch break (Education (School Lunches) (Prescribed Requirements) (England) Order 2003). In Wales, the requirement is that the child must be present for two full sessions in the day (School Lunches (Prescribed Requirement) (Wales) Order 2005).

A local authority may charge for milk, meals, etc. In England, if they do charge they must charge every person the same price for the same quantity of the same item (1996 Act, s.512ZA inserted by the 2002 Act, s.201 and amended by the Education and Inspections Act 2006, s.87), except where a person is eligible for free milk or lunches for specified reasons (1996 Act, s.512ZB, as so inserted). In Wales, local authorities and governing bodies have the option to charge different pupils different prices for the same quantity of the same item. Such "flexible charging" is intended to enable local authorities and governing bodies to charge less for school meals provided to children of families on low incomes but not eligible for free school meals in order to encourage them to take school meals (1996 Act, s.512ZA, as amended). In both England and Wales, the price charged for an item must not exceed the cost of providing that item.

S.512(5) provide that a local authority must provide such facilities as they consider appropriate for pupils to consume food and drink they have brought to school.

The Secretary of State may transfer from a local authority to a governing body the responsibility to provide school lunches and, to certain pupils, free lunches and milk (1996 Act, s.512A, added by the 1998 Act, s.116). The Education (Transfer of Functions Concerning School Lunches etc) (England) (No. 2) Order 1999 imposes on governing bodies of maintained schools in England whose budget share includes an amount for meals and other refreshment the duty to provide school lunches (including free lunches for those who qualify for them). The Order also requires the governing bodies of former grant-maintained and grant-maintained special schools in England to provide free school milk.

A local authority may make arrangements with the proprietors of a school not maintained by the authority for milk, meals, and other refreshment to be provided for pupils attending the school (s.513).

In a non-maintained special school, the governing body has duties similar to those imposed by s.512 of the 1996 Act with regard to providing facilities for the consumption of food and drink which pupils bring to school, the remitting of charges, and the provision of milk, meals, and other refreshment free of charge in the middle of the day to pupils whose parents are receiving the relevant benefit (Education (Non-Maintained Special Schools) (England) Regulations 1999 (S.I. No. 2257), Sch, para 12).

In Wales, a local authority must ensure that a supply of drinking water is available, free of charge, on the premises of any maintained school (Healthy Eating in Schools (Wales) Measure 2009, s.5).

In Wales, a local authority or governing body of a maintained school which provides school meals or milk under s.512 must encourage the take-up of school meals and milk, and take reasonable steps to ensure that every pupil who is entitled to receive school lunches and milk free of charge under section 512ZB (see **7 Free lunch and milk**, below) does receive them (2009 Measure, s.6).

7 Free lunch and milk

All government-funded schools (i.e., maintained schools, academies, free schools and pupil referral units) must offer free school meals to every infant pupil i.e., those in reception, year 1 or year 2 (Education Act 1996, ss.512ZB(4A), 512B).

A child will be entitled to a free school lunch (and free milk where milk is provided) if they meet other prescribed requirements or if their parent is in receipt of (s.512ZB(4))–

- (a) universal credit
- (b) income support;
- (c) income-based jobseeker's allowance;
- (d) income-related employment and support allowance;
- (e) support provided under the Immigration and Asylum Act 1999 Part 6; or
- (f) any other prescribed benefit, allowance or tax credit.

A person will also be entitled to a free school lunch if they themselves are in receipt of (a), (b), (c) or (f) above.

For the purposes of (f), a person in receipt of child tax credit based on annual income not exceeding £16,105 and who does not receive working tax credit will be entitled to free school meals (Education (Free School Lunches) (Prescribed Tax Credits) (England) Order 2003 and (Wales) Order 2003. So too will a child of a parent who is in receipt of the guarantee credit part of the state pension credit (Education (Free School Lunches) (State Pension Credit) Order 2005 and (Wales) Order 2005). A child of a parent entitled to working tax credit during the four week period immediately after their employment ceases, or after they start to work for less than 16 hours per week, is also entitled to free school lunches (Education (Free School Lunches) (Working Tax Credit) (England) Order 2009 and (Wales) Order 2009).

In Wales, a local education authority or governing body must take reasonable steps to ensure that a pupil cannot be identified as a pupil who receives a school lunch or milk free of charge by any person other than an authorised person (s.512ZC of the 1996 Act, added by the Healthy Eating in Schools (Wales) Measure 2009).

In Wales, a local authority also has a duty to provide breakfasts free of charge on each school day for pupils at maintained primary schools if the governing body of the school has made a written request to them for breakfasts to be provided and 90 days have passed since the authority received the request (School Standards and Organisation (Wales) Act 2013, s.88).

8 Nutritional standards

Under s.114A of the School Standards and Framework Act 1998 (inserted by the Education Act 2006), regulations may prescribe nutritional standards or requirements to be complied with in the provision of school lunches for pupils at maintained schools in England (whether the lunches are provided on or off school premises and whether they are provided in pursuance of any statutory requirement or otherwise).

In England, the Requirements for School Food Regulations 2014 set nutritional standards for school lunches in maintained schools. Food is divided into five groups, namely–

- – fruit and vegetables;
- – meat, fish, eggs, beans and other non dairy sources of protein;
- – starchy foods;
- – milk and dairy foods; and
- – drinks.

School lunches must include (or not include) these foods at a frequency as specified in the Regulations. For example, meat products may not be provided more than once a week in primary schools and twice a week in secondary schools; no more than two portions of food that has been deep-fried, batter-coated or breadcrumb-coated may be provided each week; no more than two portions of food which includes pastry may be provided each week; confectionery must not be provided, and salt must not be available to add to food after the cooking process is complete. Other food provided on school premises before 6pm on a school day must also comply with the Regulations, but confectionary, snacks, cakes or biscuits provided by a boarding school as part of an evening meal need not comply. The Regulations also do not apply to food provided–

- (a) at parties or celebrations to mark religious or cultural occasions;
- (b) at fund-raising events;
- (c) as rewards for achievement, good behaviour or effort;
- (d) for use in teaching food preparation and cookery skills, including where the food prepared is served to pupils as part of a school lunch; or
- (e) on an occasional basis by parents or pupils.

In Wales the Healthy Eating in Schools (Wales) Measure 2009, s.4 makes similar provision. The Healthy Eating in Schools (Nutritional Standards and Requirements) (Wales) Regulations 2013 (which apply to local authorities and governing bodies of maintained schools in Wales) set out the types of food and drink that can, and cannot, be provided during the school day and define the nutrient content of school lunches.

In Wales, both local authorities and governing bodies of maintained schools must take action to promote healthy eating and drinking by registered pupils (Healthy Eating in Schools (Wales) Measure 2009, s.1).

F: SCHOOL PREMISES

9 Standard of premises

The School Premises (England) Regulations 2012 and (for Wales) the Education (School Premises) Regulations 1999 contain provisions concerning accommodation of schools in England and Wales maintained by local authorities. The Regulations cover *inter alia* the numbers of washrooms that must be provided for both pupils and staff, and provisions relating to lighting, acoustics, water supplies, staff accommodation, and medical accommodation. The regulations also specify the sleeping, eating and living accommodation that must be provided for boarding school pupils.

G: DISEASES

10 Infections, contaminations and notifiable diseases

The Health Protection (Notification) Regulations 2010 (and the equivalent Regulations in respect of Wales) enables a local authority to require that a child is kept away from school where a local authority is satisfied that (Reg. 2)–
    (a) the child is or may be contaminated;
    (b) the infection or contamination is one which presents or could present significant harm to human health;
    (c) there is a risk that the child might infect or contaminate others;
    (d) it is necessary to keep the child away from school in order to remove or reduce that risk;
    (e) keeping the child away from school is a proportionate response to the risk to others presented by the child.
The local authority must serve a notice on the child's parent giving prescribed information requiring the parent to keep the child away from school. It must also, as soon as reasonably practicable after serving the notice, inform the headteacher of the child's school that it has served such a notice in relation to the child. The duration of the requirement to keep the child away from school can last up to a maximum of 28 days and the parent may request that the local authority review the notice at any time before the requirement lapses. It is an offence for a parent to fail without reasonable excuse to comply with such a notice.

A local authority may by serving notice on a headteacher of a school require the headteacher to provide it with a list of the names, addresses and contact telephone numbers for all the pupils of the school in cases where it is satisfied that a person who is or has recently been on the school's premises is or may be infected or contaminated. The requirements that need to be satisfied before a notice is served are in similar terms to those set out in (b)–(d) above (Reg. 3).

11 Authorities

Statutes–
Education Act 1996

Health Services Act 1980

Healthy Eating in Schools (Wales) Measure 2009

National Health Service Act 2006

National Health Service (Wales) Act 2006

School Standards and Framework Act 1998

School Standards and Organisation (Wales) Act 2013

Statutory Instruments–
Education (Free School Lunches) (Prescribed Tax Credits) (England) Order 2003, as amended (S.I. 2003 No. 383 and 2011 No. 728)

Education (Free School Lunches) (Prescribed Tax Credits) (Wales) Order 2003, as amended (S.I. 2003 No. 879 and 2011 No. 710)

Education (Free School Lunches) (State Pensions Credit) Order 2005 (S.I. 2005 No. 885)

Education (Free School Lunches) (State Pension Credit) (Wales) Order 2005 (S.I. 2005 No. 3110)

Education (Free School Lunches) (Working Tax Credit) (England) Order 2009 (S.I. 2009 No. 830)

Education (Free School Lunches) (Working Tax Credit) (Wales) Order 2009 (S.I. 2009 No. 1673)

EDUCATION

Education (Health Standards) (England) Regulations 2003 (S.I. 2003 No. 3139)

Education (Health Standards) (Wales) Regulations 2004 (S.I. 2004 No. 2733)

Education (Non-Maintained Special Schools) (England) Regulations 1999 (S.I. 1999 No. 2257)

Education (School Lunches) (Prescribed Requirements) (England) Order 2003 (S.I. 2003 No. 382)

Education (School Premises) Regulations 1999 (S.I. 1999 No. 2)

Education (Transfer of Functions Concerning School Lunches etc) (England) (No. 2) Order 1999 (S.I. 1999 No. 2164)

Health Protection (Local Authority Powers) Regulations 2010 (S.I. 2010 No. 657)

Healthy Eating in Schools (Nutritional Standards and Requirements) (Wales) Regulations 2013, as amended (S.I. 2013 Nos. 1984 and 2750)

Requirements for School Food Regulations 2014, as amended (S.I. 2014 Nos. 1603 and 3001)

School Lunches (Prescribed Requirement) (Wales) Order 2005 (S.I. 2005 No. 1208)

School Premises (England) Regulations 2012 (S.I. 2012 No. 1943)

INDEPENDENT SCHOOLS IN ENGLAND AND WALES

1 Preliminary

This Note deals with the registration and inspection of independent schools, with the establishment of Academies, and the abolition of corporal punishment in independent schools.

This Note is structured as follows–

A: Registration
B: Inspection
C: Academies
D: Corporal punishment
E: Provision of information
F: Staff at schools with a religious character.

Note.–The provisions of the Education Act 2002 and the Education and Skills Act 2008 described in this Note have been extended so as to apply also to alternative provision Academies that are not independent schools (Education Act 2002, s.156AA; Education and Skills Act 2008, s.93A).

2 Introduction

An "independent school" means any school at which–

(a) full-time education is provided for five or more pupils of compulsory school age; or
(b) at least one pupil of that age for whom an EHC plan or a statement of special educational needs is maintained, or who is looked after by a local authority,

and which is not a school maintained by a local authority or a non-maintained special school (Education Act 1996 s.463, as substituted by Education Act 2002, s.172). In effect, all former direct grant schools in England and Wales which have not become maintained schools are included in the definition of independent schools.

In England, the registration and inspection provisions apply to "independent educational institutions", which includes independent schools as defined above, with provision to extend them in the future to independent educational institutions that provide part-time education–

(a) for at least 12.5 hours a week, for at least 28 weeks, during an academic year at the end of which the person is under the age of 12; or
(b) for at least 15 hours a week, for at least 28 weeks, during an academic year at the end of which the person is aged 12 or over,

and which does not amount to full-time education.

In Wales, the functions of the Secretary of State are carried out by the National Assembly, and references below to the Secretary of State should be read accordingly.

A: REGISTRATION

3 General

Part 4 of the Education and Skills Act 2008 and Part 10 of the Education Act, provide for the registration of independent schools in England and Wales respectively.

An independent school must be registered in the register of independent schools, which is open to public inspection. Separate registers are kept for England and Wales. Breach of this provision is an offence punishable on summary conviction by imprisonment for up to 51 weeks (England) or 6 months (Wales) or a fine (unlimited), or both (Education and Skills Act 2008, s.96; Education Act 2002, s.159).

4 The procedure for applying for registration in England

Where an application for registration is made in England, the Chief Inspector of Schools will inspect the school and make a report to the Secretary of State on the extent to which the independent school standards are, and are likely to continue to be, met in relation to the school (Education and Skills Act 2008, s.99). This report will be taken into account in determining the application for registration. As to the standards, see **6 Standards and enforcement,** below. A fee, based on the number of pupils, is payable in respect of an inspection: see the Education (Independent Educational Provision in England) (Inspection Fees) Regulations 2009.

The Secretary of State may make regulations prescribing the particulars to be furnished to him by proprietors of such schools on application for registration and subsequently (ss.98 and 123). The Secretary of State may order the name of any school to be deleted from the register where information requested is not supplied. The regulations may, in particular, require the proprietor of a school to provide such information as is required by the local authority for the purpose of determining whether the school is a children's home within the meaning of the Care Standards Act 2000.

The Education (Independent Educational Provision in England) (Provision of Information) Regulations 2010 have made for the above-mentioned purposes and make provision for annual returns (see **8 Particulars to be furnished,** below).

5 Material changes—England

The proprietor of a registered independent educational institution must seek prior approval from the Secretary of State for any change which is defined as a "material" change (Education and Skills Act 2008, s.102). for a special institutions (i.e., those specially organised to make provision for students with special educational needs) a material change which requires prior approval is a change of proprietor, a change of address or any change in the institution's registered details. For any other institution, a material change is a change which results in either the introduction of boarding provision or the institution becoming a special institution (s.101).

6 Standards and enforcement

Regulations may be made prescribing standards for independent schools as to (Education and Skills Act 2008, s.94 (England); Education Act 2002, 157 (Wales))–

(a) the quality of education provided;
(b) the spiritual, moral, social and cultural development of pupils;
(c) the welfare, health and safety of pupils;
(d) the suitability of proprietors and staff;
(e) premises and accommodation;
(f) the provision of information;
(g) complaints procedures; and
(h) (England only) the quality of the leadership and management.

The Education (Independent School Standards) (England) Regulations 2014 and (Wales) 2003 have been made under this power. The Secretary of State (or Welsh Assembly) can at any time require the Chief Inspector of Schools to inspect an independent school (2008 Act, s.109; 2002 Act, s.163).

Wales

If the Welsh Assembly is satisfied at any time that a registered independent school is not meeting any one or more of the independent school standards, then (2002 Act, s.165)–

(i) if there is a risk of serious harm to the welfare of pupils, the authority may, after the expiry of an appeal period, remove the school from the register;
(ii) if (i) does not apply, a notice may be served identifying the standards which are not being met and requiring the proprietor to submit an action plan specifying the steps that will be taken to ensure compliance together with a timetable for taking those steps.

An action plan may be rejected or approved. If it is rejected (or if no plan is submitted at all), then the school may be removed from the register or an order may be made requiring the proprietor to–

(iii) stop using any part of the school premises for all, or any specified purposes;
(iv) close any part of the school's operations; or
(v) stop the admission of any new pupils, or pupils of a specified description.

Failure to comply with an order may result in the school being removed from the register and is also an offence punishable on summary conviction by imprisonment for up to six months or an unlimited fine, or both.

Appeals in relation to registration may be made to the First-tier Tribunal (2002 Act, s.166).

England

Where the Secretary of State considers that an independent educational institution is not meeting one or more of the required standards, he may serve a notice on the proprietor requiring him to provide an action plan (2008 Act, s.114). The purpose of the action plan is to address the failure to meet the required standards. On receipt of a plan, the Secretary of State may approve it, with or without modifications or reject it, in which case he can request a further action plan. The Secretary of State may take enforcement action against an institution. where the proprietor has either (s.115)–

(a) been required to provide an action plan within the last three years but has failed to provide one or failed to comply with a plan that has been approved; or
(b) where the Secretary of State is satisfied in the light of at least one inspection report that the institution has failed to meet the required standards for a continuous period of at least two years despite an action plan having been provided by the proprietor.

If the Secretary of State decides to take enforcement action he must inform the proprietor, who has a right of appeal. The forms of enforcement action available to the Secretary of State are–

(c) removing the institution from the register (s.116); or
(d) imposing a restriction short of de-registration, namely (s.117)–
    (i) requiring the cessation of the use of part of the premises for all or for specified purposes;
    (ii) closing part of the institution's operation; and/or
    (iii) stopping the admission of new students or new students of a specified description.

Failing to comply with a restriction is an offence (s.118).

Where a student at an institution is suffering, or is at risk of suffering, significant harm, the Secretary of State may apply to a justice of the peace for an emergency order imposing an immediate restriction on, or deregistering, an independent educational institution,. An order may be made without notice to the proprietor with a copy of it being served on him as soon as reasonably practicable after the order is made, together with a copy of any written statement provided in support of the application and a notice explaining the right of appeal (ss.120, 122). Where the institution concerned has students with special educational needs, the Secretary of State must inform all relevant local education authorities of the order (so that they may take any action they deem necessary) (s.122).

There are rights of appeal against deregistration and other measures to the First-tier Tribunal.

7 Suitability of proprietors and staff—England and Wales

The Secretary of State may deregister an independent educational institution if it allows a person who is subject to a barring or disqualifying order to carry out certain activities in relation to the institution. The activities include acting as a proprietor, acting on a body of persons named as proprietor or carrying out specified work (Education and Skills Act 2008, s.119).

In Wales, the Welsh Ministers may remove a school from the register where they are satisfied that any person who, in relation to the school, carries out work of a prescribed kind is subject to a direction, order or decision made under any prescribed enactment having effect in any part of the UK (Education Act 2002, s.169).

The Education (Independent Educational Provision in England) (Unsuitable Persons) Regulations 2009 and the Education (Independent Schools) (Unsuitable Persons) (Wales) Regulations 2009, provide that an independent school can be removed from the register if the Secretary of State or Welsh Ministers are satisfied that a person who is subject to a direction, order or decision prescribed by those Regulations has been carrying out any work (in Wales "regular" work i.e., for more than 2 days in any 30 day period) which gives that person the opportunity, in consequence of anything that person is permitted or required to do in connection with the work, to have contact with a student at the institution or a child or vulnerable adult within the meaning of the Safeguarding Vulnerable Groups Act 2006 (Reg.2). An institution may also be removed from the register if its proprietors are subject to such a prescribed direction, order or decision.

Under the Education and Skills Act 2008, s.128 (in Wales, the Education Act 2002, ss.167A-167D) the Secretary of State (or Welsh Ministers) can prohibit unsuitable people from participating in the management of independent schools. In England, the grounds for such a prohibition are set out in the Independent Educational Provision in England (Prohibition on Participation in Management) Regulations 2014 which provide that a person can be prohibited if—

(a) they have been convicted of, or given a caution for, an offence which is relevant to their suitability to take part in the management of an independent school; or

(b) they have engaged in conduct which—

    – is aimed at undermining the fundamental British values of democracy, the rule of law, individual liberty, and mutual respect and tolerance of those with different faiths and beliefs;

    – has been found to be in breach of professional standards by a professional body; or

    – is so inappropriate that, in the opinion of the Secretary of State, it makes a person unsuitable to take part in the management of an independent school; and

(c) because of that conviction, caution or conduct, the Secretary of State considers that they are unsuitable to take part in the management of an independent school.

See further the Notes on **Teachers' Qualifications and Employment** and **Protection of Children and Young Persons.** at B: EMPLOYMENT TO WORK WITH CHILDREN.

8 Particulars to be furnished

The Education (Independent Educational Provision in England) (Provision of Information) Regulations 2010, and the Independent Schools (Provision of Information) (Wales) Regulations 2003 (the English, and Welsh Regulations respectively) prescribe the particulars to be furnished to the Secretary of State or appropriate Registrar of Independent Schools, both when applying for registration and subsequent to registration.

The Regulations prescribe the information to be contained in an application for registration (e.g., details of the proprietor, age range and sex of the pupils, layout of the premises, religious ethos of the school, employee details, etc), in an initial return (if one is requested by the Secretary of State), and in an annual return. In England, Academies do not need to make initial or annual returns and need to provide less information in an application.

In Wales, where the proprietor of an independent school ceases to use a person's services on the grounds of that person's unsuitability to work with children, or their health where it raises an issue concerning the safety and welfare of children, then that fact must be reported to the Independent Barring Board within one month (Welsh Regulations, Reg. 6). [As to the power to bar persons from being teachers or persons in relevant work in schools, the Note on **Teachers' Qualifications and Employment**].

Provision is made for a school to be deleted from the register for failing to provide the prescribed particulars (English Regulations, Reg. 6; Welsh Regulations, Reg. 7).

9 Independent schools with a religious character

The Religious Character of Schools (Designation Procedure) (Independent Schools) (England) Regulations 2003 set out the procedure to be followed by the Secretary of State in making an order designating an independent school as having a religious character under the School Standards and Framework Act 1998 s.69. The proprietor of an independent school may apply to the Secretary of State for him to make such an order (Reg. 4). If a school's proprietor applies for an order designating an independent school as having a religious character after it has admitted its first pupils, the Secretary of State may make an order if (a) below applies and at least one of (b) to (d) applies. He may designate the school if he is not satisfied that any of (b) to (d) apply but, having regard to any representations made by a religious body on behalf of the school, he is satisfied that (a) applies (Reg. 5)–

(a) he is satisfied that the school is conducted, or education is provided, in accordance with the tenets of one or more religious denomination; and

(b) some or all of the premises occupied by the school were provided on trust in connection with the provision of education or the conduct of an educational institution in accordance with the tenets of one or more religious denomination; or

(c) at least one member of the governing body is appointed to represent the interests of one or more religious denomination; or

(d) the school's governing instrument provides for it to be conducted, that education be provided, in accordance with the tenets of one or more religious denomination.

If a school's proprietor applies for an order before the admission of its first pupils, the Secretary of State must designate the school as a school which has a religious character (so as to allow the recruitment of appropriate staff) if (Reg. 5(2A))–

(e) he has been given the name and address of the school;

(f) he is satisfied that the conduct or education at the school will be in accordance with the tenets of one or more religious denomination; and

(g) at least one of conditions (b) to (d) above are met.

If at least one of the conditions (b) to (d) are not met but the Secretary of State has been given the name and address of the school and is satisfied that the conduct or education at the school will be in accordance with the tenets of one or more religious denomination, he may, having regard to any representations made by any religious body on behalf of the school, designate the school as having a religious character.

The Secretary of State may revoke the designation of any school where he considers it appropriate to do so (Reg. 6).

Note.–Reference to education being provided in accordance with the tenets of one or more religious denomination does not require that all education be provided in accordance with those tenets (Reg. 5(3)).

Similar provisions apply in Wales under the Independent Schools (Religious Character of Schools) (Designation Procedure) (Wales) Regulations 2003, with application being made to the Welsh Assembly.

B: INSPECTION

10 Inspection of independent schools

Independent schools are liable to inspection by the Chief Inspectors of Education for England and Wales respectively (Education and Skills Act 2008, s.108 (England); Education Act 2002, ss.163, 164 (Wales)).

The Secretary of State or Welsh registration authority may, at any time, require the Chief Inspector for England or Wales to inspect any registered independent school or arrange for the inspection of such a school by a body approved by the registration authority for these purposes (2008 Act, s.109; 2002 Act, s.163).

When conducting an inspection the Chief Inspector must make a report on the extent to which the school meets the standard or standards to which the inspection relates.

The person conducting the inspection in England or Wales has (2008 Act, s.110; 2002 Act, s.164)–

(a) a right of entry to the premises of the school; and

(b) a right to inspect and take copies of any records kept by the school and any other documents containing information relating to the school which are required for the purposes of the inspection.

It is an offence intentionally to obstruct a person in the exercise of his functions in relation to the inspection. A person guilty of this offence is liable on summary conviction to a fine not exceeding level 4 on the standard scale.

In Wales, the Independent Schools (Publication of Inspection Reports) (Wales) Regulations 2003 set out the manner in which a report of an inspection of an independent school by the Chief Inspector or one or more registered inspectors is to be published when publication is required by the registration authority.

Provision for the inspection of independent schools is also made under the Children Act 1989. S.87 of that Act requires the proprietor or other person responsible for conducting an independent school to safeguard and promote the welfare of any child for whom it provides accommodation. The National Care Standards Commission (in England) and Welsh Assembly must ensure that this is done, and must report any failure to do so. For this purpose, the authority may, under the National Care Standards Commission (Inspection of Schools and Colleges) Regulations 2002 (for England) or the Inspection of Boarding Schools and Colleges (Powers and Fees) (Wales) Regulations 2002, authorise a person to inspect the premises, the children themselves, or the relevant records which are required to be kept.

Note.–In England the Secretary of State can approve inspectorates (in addition to Ofsted) to undertake inspections of independent educational institutions (but not Academies, city technology colleges, or city colleges for the technology of the arts) (Education and Skills Act 2008, s.106). The Independent Inspectorates (Education and Boarding Accommodation) Regulations 2014 (S.I. No. 2158) specify the matters which the Secretary of State must take into account in deciding whether or not to approve such a body.

C: ACADEMIES

11 General

Under s.1 of the Academies Act 2010 (which replaces similar provisions in s.482 of the Education Act 1996), the Secretary of State may enter into "Academy arrangements" with any person that take the form of an Academy agreement or arrangements for Academy financial assistance given by the Secretary of State through grant funding under s.14 of the Education Act 2002. An Academy may be either an Academy school, a 16-19 Academy or an alternative provision Academy. Academies have largely replaced city technology colleges and city colleges for the technology of the arts set up by the Education Reform Act 1988.

Academy arrangements are those under which the person undertakes to establish, maintain, and carry on or provide for the carrying on of, an independent educational institution in England with a balanced and broadly based curriculum (see the Note on **Schools: Curriculum and Exams** at para **4 The National Curriculum**). There is no longer a requirement to have an emphasis on a particular subject area or areas. The institution must provide education for pupils of different abilities who are wholly or mainly drawn from the area in which it is situated. No charge may be made for admission to, attendance at, or (unless specifically specified in the terms of the Academy arrangements) education provided at an Academy.

In respect of an Academy agreement the Secretary of State agrees to make payments to the other party in consideration of the undertakings outlined above. The funding agreement for an Academy so far as relating to current expenditure must provide for payments by the Secretary of State to the Academy for at least seven years, or indefinitely but terminable on seven years' written notice. The funding agreement may make provision for the repayment of capital grants to the Secretary of State in the event of the termination of the funding agreement, although this is not obligatory (s.2).

In deciding whether to enter into Academy arrangements in relation to an additional school, the Secretary of State must take into account what the impact of establishing the additional school would be likely to be on maintained schools, Academies and institutions within the further education sector in the area in which the additional school is (or is proposed to be) situated (s.9).

For each academic year the Secretary of State must publish a report containing information on Academy arrangements entered into and the performance of Academies during that year (s.11).

12 Conversion of schools into Academies

The governing body of a maintained school may apply for an Academy order to be made in respect of the school, or the Secretary of State may make an Academy order if the school is eligible for intervention under the Education and Inspections Act 2006 (see the Note on **Education: Standards and Inspection**). An Academy order is an order for the purpose of enabling the school to be converted in to an Academy. In the case of a foundation or voluntary school that has a foundation, the governing body must consult the foundation before making an application and may make such an application only with the consent of the trustees of the school and the person(s) by whom the foundation governors are appointed. Before a maintained school is converted into an Academy, the school's governing body must consult such persons as they think appropriate. The consultation may take place before or after an Academy order, or an application for an Academy order, has been made in respect of the school but must take place before the Academy arrangements are entered into. The Secretary of State must also consult before making an Academy order. A maintained school is "converted into" an Academy if Academy arrangements (see **13 General**, above) are entered into in relation to the school or a school that replaces it (Academies Act 2010, ss.3–5).

13 Effect of an Academy order

The local authority must cease to maintain the school on the conversion date on which the school, or a school that replaces it, opens as an Academy (Academies Act 2010, s.6(1)) and the relevant independent school standards (as defined in s.157(2) of the Education Act 2002 (see **6 Standards in independent schools**, above)) that are applicable to the Academy are to be treated as met in relation to the Academy on the conversion date (s.6(2)).

Objection to admission arrangements at an Academy may be referred to an adjudicator in the same way as for maintained schools: see the Note on **Schools: Admission and Attendance** at para **12 Alteration and variation of, and objections to admissions**.

D: CORPORAL PUNISHMENT

14 Abolition of corporal punishment

S.548 of the Education Act 1996 (as substituted by s.131 of the School Standards and Framework Act 1998) abolished corporal punishment in all schools in England and Wales, including independent schools. It is no longer lawful for any teacher or staff member to administer corporal punishment to a child under 18, whether on or off school premises. "Corporal punishment" is defined as any punishment which would, apart from any justification, constitute battery. However, corporal punishment will not be treated as being given to a child if it is done to avert an immediate danger of personal injury to any person (including the child himself) or immediate danger to the property of any person (including the child).

E: PROVISION OF INFORMATION

15 Requirement to provide information

Under s.537 of the 1996 Act, the proprietor of any independent school or alternative provision Academy may be required by the Secretary of State by regulations to provide such information about the school as may be prescribed.

Under s.537A, regulations may require the proprietor of any independent school to provide such individual pupil information as may be prescribed.

The Secretary of State may also require the proprietor of any city technology college or city college for the technology of the arts to provide prescribed persons with prescribed categories of information published under s.537(7) of the 1996 Act. (See also the Note on **Schools: Provision and Governance** at para **47 Other information about schools**.)

F: STAFF AT SCHOOLS WITH A RELIGIOUS CHARACTER

16 Employment of teachers

In the case of an independent school with a religious character, preference may be given, in connection with the appointment, pay or promotion of all teachers (not simply religious education teachers) to those whose religious opinion accord with the school's religion or denomination or to those who attend religious worship in accordance with those tenets or who are willing to teach religious education in accordance with them. In addition, regard may be had in connection with the termination of employment or engagement of any teacher at the school to conduct which is incompatible with the school's religion or denomination (School Standards and Framework Act 1998, s.124A).

A voluntary controlled or foundation schools with a religious character which has converted into an Academy must have one-fifth of its total number of teachers including the principal as "reserved" teachers i.e., selected for their fitness and competence to give religious education in accordance with the tenets of the religion or religious denomination of the school, and who are appointed on such grounds (s.124AA).

A school has a religious character if it has been designated by the Secretary of State as having such a character (ss.69 and 124B).

17 Authorities

Statutes–
Academies Act 2010

Children Act 1989

Education Acts 1962 to 2008

School Standards and Framework Act 1998

Statutory Instruments–
Education (Independent Educational Provision in England) (Inspection Fees) Regulations 2009, as amended (S.I. 2009 No. 1607 and 2010 1002)

Education (Independent Educational Provision in England) (Provision of Information) Regulations 2010, as amended (S.I. 2010 No 2919, 2012 No. 939, and 2014 No. 2103)

Education (Independent Educational Provision in England) (Unsuitable Persons) Regulations 2009, as amended (S.I. 2009 No. 1633 and 2010 No. 2920)

Education (Independent School Standards) (England) Regulations 2014 (S.I. 2014 No. 3283)

Education (Independent Schools) (Unsuitable Persons) (Wales) Regulations 2009 (S.I. 2009, No. 2558)

Independent Educational Provision in England (Prohibition on Participation in Management) Regulations 2014 (S.I. 2014 No. 1977)

Independent School Standards (Wales) Regulations 2003, as amended (S.I. 2003 No. 3234, 2005 No. 2929, 2007 No. 947, and 2009 No. 2544)

Independent Schools (Provision of Information) (Wales) Regulations 2003, as amended (S.I. 2003 No. 3230, 2007 No. 947, and 2009 No. 2544)

Independent Schools (Religious Character of Schools) (Designation Procedure) (Wales) Regulations 2003 (S.I. 2003 No. 3233)

Independent Schools (Publication of Inspection Reports) (Wales) Regulations 2003 (S.I. 2003 No. 3232)

Inspection of Boarding Schools and Colleges (Powers and Fees) (Wales) Regulations 2002 (S.I. 2002 No. 3161)

National Care Standards Commission (Inspection of Schools and Colleges) Regulations 2002 (S.I. 2002 No. 552)

Religious Character of Schools (Designation Procedure) (Independent Schools) (England) Regulations 2003, as amended (S.I. 2003 No. 2314 and 2004 No. 2262)

SCHOOLS: PROVISION AND GOVERNANCE
ENGLAND AND WALES

1 Introduction

The Note is structured as follows–

A: Provision of schools

B: Establishment, alteration and closure of schools

C: Status and government of schools

D: Constitution of governing bodies in England

E: Constitution of governing bodies in Wales

F: Reports and parents' meetings

G: Class sizes

H: School and pupil records and information

In relation to Wales, most of the functions of the Secretary of State have been transferred to the Welsh Ministers and references to the Secretary of State should be construed as references to the Ministers (Government of Wales Act 1998, s.43; and the National Assembly for Wales (Transfer of Functions) Order 1999 (S.I. No. 672)).

A: PROVISION OF SCHOOLS

2 Duty of local authority

It is the duty of every local authority to secure that there are available in their area sufficient schools to provide primary education for all pupils of the appropriate ages and to provide secondary education for all pupils of the appropriate ages (Education Act 1996, s.14). The dividing line between primary and secondary education is not a fixed age, but lies at such point between 10½ and 12 years as may be suitable to the pupil's requirements. This allows the transfer to be made at the beginning of a school year (s.2).

In carrying out the duty imposed by s.14, the local authority are required to have regard, in particular, to the following points–

(a) The need for securing that (except in the case of special schools) primary and secondary education are provided in separate schools.

(b) The need to secure that special educational provision is made for pupils having special educational needs (see the Note on **Special Educational Provision and Special Schools: England and Wales**).

(c) The expediency of securing the provision of boarding accommodation, either in boarding schools or otherwise, for pupils for whom education as boarders is considered by their parents and by the authority to be desirable (s.14(6)).

A local authority have no duty to provide education for children under the age of five (s.14(4)). Where they do provide such education, it is normally provided in a nursery school or in a nursery class in a primary school. S.17 empowers local authorities to establish and maintain any such school or class.

When exercising their functions as to the provision of schools in their area, local authorities in England must do so with a view to securing diversity in the provision of schools and increasing opportunities for parental choice (s.14(3A), inserted by the Education and Inspections Act 2006, s.2).

3 Early years provision

English local authorities must ensure that free early years provision is made available by providers who are under a duty to provide the Early Years Foundation Stage (see the Note on **Schools: Curriculum and Exams: England and Wales** at para **The early years foundation stage and foundation phase**). This covers children who at the start of term are–

(a) aged three; or

(b) aged two if–

– the child's parent is entitled to working tax credit because their annual income does not exceed £16,190;

– the child has a statement of educational needs made under the Education Act 1996, s.324 or has had an education, health and care plan made for him under the Children and Families Act 2014, s.37;

– the child is entitled to disability living allowance;

– the child has previously been looked after by the local authority and is no longer looked after because an adoption order; a special guardianship order; or a child arrangement order has been made.

The provision must be available for each child for a period of 570 hours per year and during no fewer than 38 weeks in the year (Local Authority (Duty to Secure Early Years Provision Free of Charge) Regulations 2013).

4 Duty to consider parental representations

Local authorities in England must respond to parental representations in relation to the exercise of their functions as to the provision of schools (under the Education Act 1996, s.14). They must consider what action to take in response to such representations and provide a statement to the parent setting out any action which they propose to take in response or, where relevant, their reasons for taking no action, in each case having regard to guidance from the Secretary of State. The guidance to authorities will set out how local authorities might reasonably respond to parental representations on the opportunities for choice and the diversity of schools in their area.

5 Rationalisation of school places

The Secretary of State and Welsh Ministers have the power to direct local authorities to make proposals to "rationalise" school places (School Standards and Framework Act 1998, s.34, and Sch. 7; School Standards and Organisation (Wales) Act 2013, s.57). This power may be exercised either where the provision of primary. or secondary education in an area is excessive or where there are or will be insufficient places in an area. They may then direct an authority to make proposals to establish, alter or discontinue schools or to direct the governing body of any foundation or voluntary school to make proposals to alter the school.

6 School premises

The School Premises (England) Regulations 2012 and (for Wales) the Education (School Premises) Regulations 1999 prescribe standards to which the premises of schools maintained by a local authority must conform, and specify requirements *inter alia* as to the land for buildings, recreation areas, and playing fields, and as to the teaching accommodation, washrooms, medical accommodation, study areas, and staff accommodation, and, in the case of schools with boarders, sleeping and living accommodation.

The disposal, and change of use, of land by maintained schools is also covered by the School Standards and Framework Act 1998 (s.77 and of Sch. 22, Part A1, as amended or inserted by the Education and Inspections Act 2006, s.36, Sch. 4). The modifications relate to foundation, voluntary and foundation special schools, and separate the procedures in England for the disposal of playing field land and non-playing field land.

7 Primary and secondary education

In general, education is provided in primary schools for children aged between 5 and 11 and in secondary schools for children aged between 11 and 16.

"Primary education" means (Education Act 1996, s.2(1), as amended by the 2002 Act, s.156)–
   (a) full or part-time education provided to children between the age of two and compulsory school;
   (b) full-time education suitable for the requirements of children over compulsory school age but under 10½; and
   (c) full-time education suitable for the requirements of children between 10½ and 12 whom it is expedient to educate together with children under that age.
"Secondary education" means (1996 Act, s.2 as amended by the 2002 Act, s.177)–
   (d) full-time education suitable for the requirements of children over the age of 12;
   (e) full-time education suitable for the requirements of children between 10½ and 12 whom it is expedient to educate together with children over that age;
   (f) full-time education suitable for the requirements of pupils over compulsory school age, but under the age of 19 which is provided at a school at which education within (d) or (e) is also provided, or at an institution maintained by an LEA, or which is an Academy;
   (g) full-time education which is provided partly at a school and partly at any other kind of establishment or institution.
"Secondary education" includes vocational, social, physical and recreational training (s.177(3) of the 2002 Act).

B: ESTABLISHMENT, ALTERATION AND CLOSURE OF SCHOOLS

8 Procedure for establishing a new school: England

The Education and Inspections Act 2006 deals with the establishment of new schools in England. A local authority which is of the view that there is a need for a new school in their area must seek proposals for the establishment of an Academy (s.6A). The local authority must specify a date by which proposals must be submitted and after that date must notify the Secretary of State of the steps taken to satisfy this duty and the proposals that have been submitted (or that there have been no proposals). The notification to the Secretary of State must identify a site for the school and any other matters prescribed by regulations.

A local authority may, if the Secretary of State consents, publish a notice inviting proposals (other than from local authorities) for the establishment of a new foundation, voluntary, or foundation special school, or Academy. This applies to secondary schools, primary schools and special schools (s.7). Sch.2 has effect in relation to the consideration, approval, and implementation of proposals. It provides for the proposals to be decided by the local authority or adjudicator, in place of the school organisation committee and adjudicator.

Before publishing a notice under s.7, local authorities must consult such people as they consider appropriate, and in discharging this duty they must have regard to any guidance given by the Secretary of State (s.9).

Local authorities may–

(a) with the consent of the Secretary of State, publish proposals (otherwise than under s.7) for a new community, foundation, or community or foundation special school which is not to be one providing education suitable only to the requirements of persons above compulsory school age nor a replacement for an infant or junior school (s.10);

(b) without any need for consent publish proposals for (s.11)–

(i) a new community or foundation primary school to replace a maintained infant and a maintained junior school;

(ii) the establishment of a new voluntary aided school;

(iii) a new foundation or voluntary controlled school resulting from an existing religious school changing or losing its religious designation;

(iv) a new foundation or voluntary controlled school with a religious character replacing an existing religious school, resulting from the reorganisation of faith schools in an area; and

(v) for a new community or foundation school where following publication of a s.7 notice no proposals are approved by the local authority, no Academy arrangements are entered into, or no proposals are received.

A new maintained school may be a member of a federation from the outset (s.12).

Regulations may modify ss.7 to 12 and Sch.2 where a school is proposed to be situated in an area different from that of the local authority who published the notice under s.7, or, if the proposals are published outside a competition (that is, under ss.10 or 11), different from that of the local authority who it is proposed should maintain the school (s.13).

The power of a local authority to establish and maintain a school within the area of another local authority does not apply if the other local authority is situated in Wales (s.14).

9 Alteration of schools: England

Where a local authority or the governing body of a maintained school proposes to make certain alterations to the school, and the proposals are ones that those bodies may make, they must publish statutory proposals to do so (Education and Inspections Act 2006, s.19).

The alterations that may be proposed by a local authority are (s.19(2))–

(a) in the case of community schools, community special schools or maintained nursery schools, those that are prescribed in regulations;

(b) in the case of foundation schools or voluntary schools, an enlargement of the premises, an increase in the number of pupils in any relevant age group, the establishment or discontinuance of special educational needs provision, or the establishment of provision suitable for pupils over compulsory school age; and

(c) in the case of foundation special schools, an enlargement of the premises, an increase in the number of pupils for whom the school is organised to make provision, or a change in the type of special educational needs for which the school is organised to make provision.

Regulations may prescribe the alterations to maintained schools that require the publication of statutory proposals (s.18(1)). Alterations which include a change in the category of the school; the acquisition by a foundation or foundation special school of a foundation; and any change in a school's instrument of government which results in the majority of governors being foundation governors must be published(s.18(2)).

Note.–A maintained school may not change, acquire or lose a religious character; change category to a community or community special school; change category from a mainstream school to a special school or from a special school to a mainstream school; or change category from a maintained nursery school to any other kind of school or from any other kind of school to a maintained nursery school (s.18(4)).

There are certain restrictions on the powers of governing bodies to publish foundation proposals except with the consent of the school's existing trustees, and of anyone by whom the foundation governors are appointed (s.20).

Regulations may make provision about the publication and determination of proposals under s.19 (s.21). Such regulations must provide for the proposals to be determined by the governing body, and not be referred to the adjudicator. This applies only if the proposals do not involve the acquisition of a foundation or a change to the instrument of government which results in the majority of governors being foundation governors. Similar provision is made in respect of proposals for a change of category from community special school to foundation special school (s.22). Regulations made under s.21 must make provision in connection with the referral of certain proposals to the adjudicator (s.23).

Regulations may also make provision in connection with the implementation of approved proposals for the alteration of schools (including arrangements under which the duty to implement the proposals may be removed, or the proposals modified) (s.24). Regulations may in particular make provision corresponding to the provisions of Schedule 2 governing the implementation of proposals for the establishment or discontinuance of schools (s.24(7)). A school's change of category is not to be taken as authorising any change in the religious character of the school (s.24(8)).

10 Establishment and alteration of schools: Wales

No new foundation school or foundation special school may be established in Wales (School Standards and Organisation (Wales) Act 2013, s.40).

Where a local authority in Wales proposes to (ss.41-42, 44)–

(a) establish a new or community or community special school;

(b) make any regulated alteration (see below) to a community school or maintained nursery school;

(c) open or close the sixth form of a voluntary or foundation school; or

(d) increase or reduce the capacity of a voluntary or foundation school without a religious character,

they must publish their proposals.

Similarly, a governing body planning to make a regulated alteration to a foundation or voluntary school, or any person seeking to establish a new voluntary school, must publish their proposals (ss.41-42)

For these purposes a "regulated alteration" is (s.40 and Sch. 2)–

– in relation to a maintained school, any alteration in the site of the school, or a change from same-sex to mixed sex (or vice versa), or (except in relation to maintained nursery schools) a change in the age range of the school, sixth form provision, or, the language medium;

– for community, foundation and voluntary schools, an alteration which would enlarge the school numbers by 25% or 200 pupils, or alter boarding provision, pupil banding, or provision of special educational needs or the type of such provision;

– for special schools, an alteration to boarding provision, the type of special education for which provision is made, or an increase of 10% in pupil numbers; and

– for maintained nursery schools, a change to special educational provision or the type of such provision, a change of language medium, or an increase in teaching space of 50% or more.

Before publishing any proposals the relevant body or promoters must consult on its proposals in accordance with the School Organisation Code. The Code can be accessed from the Welsh Government's website at <www.wales.gov.uk>. Any person can object in writing to proposals within 28 days of the publication date (s.49).

Where proposals relate to sixth form education or the relevant local authority has objected to them, the proposals require approval by the Welsh Ministers. Where there have been objections to proposals (made by a person other than the local authority), but they do not require the approval of the Welsh Ministers, they will require approval by the relevant local authority. Provided they do not require the Welsh Ministers' approval, a local authority will determine its own proposals (ss.50-53).

No alteration may be made to a maintained school that changes the religious character of the school or causes a school to acquire or lose a religious character (s.40(5)).

11 Closure of schools in England

The Education and Inspections Act 2006 provides for the publication of statutory proposals where a local authority or school governing body wish to close a maintained school in England, including maintained mainstream schools, special schools and nursery schools (s.15(1)). A governing body of a voluntary, foundation or foundation special school may publish proposals for the closure of their school (s.15(2)). Regulations will prescribe the information to be contained within the proposals and the publication arrangements (s.15(3)). The body formulating proposals to close a rural primary school must have regard to: the impact on the community of the closure, the availability and cost (to the local authority) of transport for pupils to other schools; any increase in the use of motor vehicles; and the likely effect of such an increase, and any alternatives to school closure. The body must also have regard to guidance issued by the Secretary of State (s.15(4)). Governing bodies must submit their published proposals to local authorities in accordance with regulations (s.15(5)). Sch.2 has effect in relation to the consideration, approval and implementation of school closure proposals.

The 2006 Act provides for consultation where the local authority or the governing body propose to close a rural primary school or special school. The body proposing to close the school must consult the following before publishing the proposals (s.16)–

(a) registered parents of registered pupils at the school;

(b) in the case of a rural primary school, the local authority and the district council or parish council for the area;

(c) in the case of a community or foundation special school, any local authority that maintains and EHC plan or a statement of special educational needs for any registered pupil at the school; and

(d) any other persons the body deem appropriate.

The Secretary of State, if he considers it expedient to do so in the interests of the health, safety or welfare of pupils at a school, may direct a local authority to discontinue a community or foundation special school on a date specified in the direction (s.17).

12 Regulations pertaining to school organisation in England

In England, the School Organisation (Establishment and Discontinuance of Schools) (England) Regulations 2013 prescribe various matters relating to proposals for the establishment and discontinuance of schools pursuant to the provisions contained in Part 2 (ss.7-17) of the Education and Inspections Act 2006.

The School Organisation (Prescribed Alterations to Maintained Schools) (England) Regulations 2013 prescribe various matters relating to prescribed alterations to maintained schools in England pursuant to Part 2 (ss.7-17) of the Education and Inspections Act 2006.

13 Closure of schools in Wales

A local authority may make proposals to discontinue a community, community special, foundation or voluntary school, or a maintained nursery school; and the governing body of a foundation or voluntary school may make proposals to discontinue that school (School Standards and Organisation (Wales) Act 2013, ss.43, 44).

The procedure for publication and consultation on proposals to discontinue a school are the same as for proposals establishing or altering a school (see **10 Establishment and alteration of schools: Wales**, above).

The governing body of a foundation or voluntary school must give at least two years notice to the Welsh Ministers and the local authority of any proposals to discontinue a school. If expenditure (other than on repairs) has been incurred on the school premises by the Welsh Ministers or the local authority, the Welsh Ministers consent to the notice must first be obtained. If a governing body, having given two years notice to discontinue, is unable or unwilling to operate the school for the full two year period, the local authority may take over the running as a community school for the remainder of the period (s.80).

The Welsh Ministers may direct a local authority to discontinue (without the need for proposals under s.44) a community special school if they consider it expedient to do so in the interests of health, safety or welfare of pupils. Before doing so the Welsh Ministers are required to consult specified persons and give notice to the governing body and head teacher (s.81).

14 Removal of foundations in England

Governing bodies of certain schools with foundations may publish proposals to remove the foundation or to reduce the proportion of governors appointed by the foundation (Education and Inspections Act 2006, s.25). This may apply to foundation and foundation special schools where the school was established pursuant to proposals implemented under the Education and Inspections Act 2006 or the school acquired its foundation pursuant to proposals implemented under the 2006 Act.

Regulations may make provision about the publication and determination of proposals under s.25 (s.26) and about the implementation of proposals published under s.25 (s.27). The School Organisation (Removal of Foundation, Reduction in Number of Foundation Governors and Ability of Foundation to Pay Debts) (England) Regulations 2007 have been made for this purpose.

15 Restriction on establishment, alteration or discontinuance of schools in England

The opening or closure of maintained schools, or the making of prescribed alterations to them, is prohibited in England without the publication and determination of statutory proposals (Education and Inspections Act 2006, s.28).

The prohibition does not apply where the Secretary of State has issued a direction to the local authority to close a community or foundation special school, or to close a school in special measures, or where the governing body of a foundation or voluntary school give notice that they intend to close the school (s.28(3)).

It is prohibited to make, without the publication and determination of statutory proposals, an alteration which involves the removal of a foundation or the reduction in the proportion of governors appointed by the foundation so that they no longer constitute a majority (s.28(4)).

16 School forums and funding

S.47A of the School Standards and Framework Act 1998 Act (as inserted by the 2005 Act) imposes an obligation on local authorities to establish schools forums and provides for the constitution and function of schools forums to be set out in regulations. The Schools Forums (England) Regulations 2012 provide for the constitution of a schools forum in every local authority in England, including the election of schools members, the election or selection of Academies members, the appointment of non-schools members, their meetings and proceedings (Regs. 3–8). A local authority is required to consult their schools forum before entering into certain contracts for supplies or services and also annually in respect of specified financial issues relating to the schools budget including, *inter alia*, arrangements for the education of pupils with special educational needs. The schools forum must inform the governing bodies of schools maintained by the local authority of any consultation carried under these provisions (Regs. 9–11). A local authority is required to pay the expenses of their schools forum out of the schools budget and the reasonable expenses of its members (Regs. 12, 13).

S.57 of, and Sch. 5 to, the Education and Inspections Act 2006 contain provisions relating to the duties and powers of local authorities in relation to the financing of maintained schools and the role of schools forums.

S.48 of, and Sch.14 to, the 1998 Act place a duty on a local authority to establish a scheme which deals with matters connected to the financing of maintained schools. All local authorities have existing schemes. Sch.5 to the 2006 Act amends the duty to establish to one that requires a local authority to maintain such a scheme and enables regulations to be made governing the approval of revisions to such schemes.

S.49 of the 1998 Act places a duty on local authorities to provide the schools they maintain with a delegated budget share. This is amended by Sch.5 to the 2006 Act to enable regulations to be made that require local authorities to give all new schools budget shares from a date determined in accordance with regulations by the schools forum or the Secretary of State or Assembly.

Sch.15 to the 1998 Act makes provision for the circumstances under which a local authority may withdraw delegated budget responsibility from a maintained school and the process it must follow in doing so. There is no appeal to the Secretary of State or Assembly against the withdrawal of their right to a delegated budget.

C: STATUS AND GOVERNMENT OF SCHOOLS

17 Categories of schools

Part II of the School Standards and Framework Act 1998 set out a new framework for maintained primary, secondary and special schools. As from 1st September 1999 (the date fixed by the School Standards and Framework (Appointed Day) Order 1998), schools maintained by local authorities have been divided into the following categories–
   (a) community schools;
   (b) foundation schools;
   (c) voluntary schools, comprising voluntary aided schools and voluntary controlled schools;
   (d) community special schools; and
   (e) foundation special schools.
The Education Act 2002 has added (see s.39(1))–
   (f) maintained nursery schools.
In addition to the above, there are also independent schools (see the Note on **Independent Schools**). If a maintained school converts to become an Academy under the Academies Act 2010, the local authority must cease to maintain it and it will be treated as an independent school.

18 Changing the category of a school

Schools may change from one category to another (School Standards and Framework Act 1998, s.35, and Sch. 8). The Education (Change of Category of Maintained Schools) (England) Regulations 2000 make provision for community, voluntary controlled, voluntary aided and foundation schools in England to become another type of school within those categories, and for a community special school to become a foundation special school and vice versa. Similar provisions apply in Wales (except that schools cannot become foundation schools and a foundation or voluntary school which has a religious character cannot become a community school) under the School Standards and Organisation (Wales) Act 2013, s. 45; and the Government of Maintained Schools (Change of Category) (Wales) Regulations 2015.

19 Kinds of foundation and voluntary school

S.21 of the School Standards and Framework Act 1998 defines the different kinds of foundation and voluntary schools and the types of foundation.
There may be three kinds of foundation school–
   (i) those having a foundation otherwise than under the 1998 Act;
   (ii) those belonging to a group of schools for which a foundation body acts under s.21; and
   (iii) those not falling within (i) or (ii).
There may also be three kinds of voluntary controlled or voluntary aided schools–
   (1) those having a foundation otherwise than under the 1998 Act;
   (2) those belonging to a group of schools for which a foundation body acts under s.21; and
   (3) those not falling within (1) or (2) but which were previously voluntary schools or grant-maintained schools which were voluntary schools before becoming grant-maintained.
For these purposes, the term "foundation" in relation to a foundation or voluntary school means any body of persons (whether incorporated or not, but excluding the school's governing body) which holds land on trust for the purposes of the school, or a foundation body. A "foundation body" is a corporate body, established under s.21, which holds the property of at least three foundation or voluntary schools for the purposes of the schools and appoints foundation governors for those schools.

20 Foundation bodies

The Foundation Body Regulations 1999 make provision for the establishment, membership and functions of foundation bodies and the steps to be taken in connection with schools joining a foundation body. The governing bodies of the three or more schools wishing to set up a foundation body for those schools must apply to the Secretary of State for his consent to the establishment of the body. An instrument of government must then be adopted for the body and the governors of each school in the group must appoint a member of their governing body to be a governor member of the foundation body. The governors of each school must also nominate persons to be community members of the body. Community members must be persons with interests in the business or local community, or both, but must have no connection with any of the schools in the group (whether as parents, staff or otherwise), nor be an elected member of or employed by the local authority. Any land held by the schools in the group must be transferred to the foundation body, which must hold land and other property for those schools and must appoint foundation governors to every school in the group.

A school may only join an established foundation body with the agreement of the governors of all the existing schools in the group and with the consent of the Secretary of State.

21 Requirements as to foundations

Foundations of foundation and foundation special schools *not* established under the 1998 Act, and the charity trustees of those foundations, must have specified characteristics (School Standards and Framework Act 1998, s.23A, inserted by Education and Inspections Act 2006, s.33). The Secretary of State has power, in certain circumstances, to remove and appoint charity trustees (School Standards and Framework Act 1998, s.23B, inserted by the Education and Inspections Act 2006, s.33).

The School Organisation (Requirements as to Foundations) (England) Regulations 2007 (S.I. No. 1287) provide that such a foundation must be either a company limited by guarantee or by shares registered under the Companies Act 1985 or a body incorporated by Royal Charter. The Regulations also set out who may not be a trustee, and the power of the Secretary of State to remove any trustee.

22 Parent councils

The governing body of a foundation school in England with a foundation which appoints the majority of governors to the school's governing body must establish a parent council (Education Act 2002, s.23A, inserted by the Education and Inspections Act 2006, s.34). The majority of members of the Council must be parents of registered pupils at the school (parent members). People other than parent members may only be members of a parent council where the parent members consent to them being members and appoint them as such in accordance with the regulations. The purpose of the parent council is to advise the governing body on matters relating to the conduct of the school, and the governing body's exercise of their powers to provide community facilities, etc (under the Education Act 2002, s.27).

The School Governance (Parent Council) (England) Regulations 2007 set out the people that the parent members must include. There is discretion on the governing body as to the manner in which people are appointed or elected to the parent council and the term for which they should serve as members (Reg. 3(3)). People other than parents of registered pupils may be members of the parent council provided the majority of members are parents (Reg. 3(4) and (5)).

D: CONSTITUTION OF GOVERNING BODIES IN ENGLAND

23 Governance in England

Each maintained school has a governing body which must be a body corporate constituted in accordance with regulations (Education Act 2002, s.19, Schedule 1).

Arrangements for the temporary government of new schools, i.e., until such time as the governing body is constituted for the school under an instrument of government, must be made by the local authority (s.34 and the School Governance (New Schools) (England) Regulations 2007). All governing bodies of new schools must be constituted in accordance with the School Governance (Constitution) (England) Regulations 2012 ("the Constitution Regulations"). The instrument of government of a school must specify the size of the membership of the governing body (Reg. 28) which must have at least 7 governors including the head teacher, two parent governors, one staff and one local authority governor (Reg. 13). The procedure for making and varying an instrument of government, and the contents of such instruments, are dealt with in s.20 of the Education Act 2002 and in Part 5 of the Constitution Regulations.

The School Governance (Roles, Procedures and Allowances) (England) Regulations 2013 deal with the procedures to be adopted by governing bodies in all maintained schools (including maintained nursery schools) in England.

24 Types of governor

The categories of governor, namely–
- –parent governor,
- –local authority governor,
- –staff governor,
- –foundation governor,
- –partnership governors; and
- –community governor,

are defined in Part 2 of the Constitution Regulations.

A *parent governor* is normally a person elected to the governing body by parents of pupils registered at the school and who is himself a parent when elected.

A *local authority governor* is one nominated by the local authority; and appointed as a governor by the governing body having, in the opinion of the governing body, met any eligibility criteria that they have set.

A *staff governor* is elected by those paid to work at the school and must himself be so working when elected.

Upon ceasing to work at the school a staff governor will be disqualified from continuing to hold office. There must be at least one staff governor (in addition to the head teacher).

Foundation governors are persons, appointed to the governing body otherwise than by a local authority who, in the case of schools with a particular religious character, are appointed for the purpose of ensuring that that character is preserved and developed; or who, where a school has a trust deed, are appointed to ensure that the school is conducted in accordance with that deed, or who would, in the opinion of the person entitled to appoint them, be capable of achieving the purposes for which they are appointed as a foundation governor.

Partnership governors are, for schools having a religious character, governors nominated by the appropriate diocesan authority of the Church of England or Roman Catholic Church or other appropriate religious body; and for non-religious schools are nominated by parents of registered pupils at the school or by such other persons in the community served by the school as the governing body consider appropriate.

Community governors are those appointed by the governing body as people who live and work in the community served by the school or who are, in the opinion of the governing body, committed to the good government and success of the school.

25 Number of governors and requirements for holding office, etc

Part 3 of the Constitution Regulations specifies the composition of governing bodies for various types of schools. The circumstances in which a person is qualified for or disqualified from holding or continuing in office as a governor are set out in Part 4 of, and Schedule 4 to, the Constitution Regulations. Amongst other specified matters, a governor must be aged 18 or over, and must not be a bankrupt or a disqualified company director or be convicted of certain criminal offences. Where a governor was elected or appointed before 1st April 2016 and does not hold an enhanced criminal record certificate, the governing body must apply for one by 1st September 2016. Where a governor is elected or appointed on or after 1st April 2016 and does not hold an enhanced criminal record certificate, the governing body must apply for one within 21 days after the appointment or election (Reg. 16A). Resignation and removal procedures are also specified in Part 4. With certain exceptions, a governor is to hold office for four years from the date of election or appointment (Reg. 18). The local authority must make sure that every governor is provided, free of charge, with appropriate information to discharge his functions as a governor, and must also ensure that free training is made available to each governor for the effective discharge of those functions (Education Act 2002, s.22).

In prescribed cases, the governing bodies of two or more maintained schools; or of an existing federation and of one or more maintained schools; or of two or more existing federations; may provide for their respective schools to be federated. Such federated schools are to have one single instrument of government (s.24 and see **30 Collaboration between schools**, below). Certain statutory provisions may be amended by regulations in their application to federated schools (s.25).

The School Governance (Federations) (England) Regulations 2012 set out the circumstances in which a federation can be established or in which a school can join an existing federation. At least two schools can federate in accordance with s.24 of the Education Act 2002. The procedure for federation are set out in Regs.6-13 and, under Reg.13, on the day the schools federate, their governing bodies are dissolved, the governing body of the federation is incorporated and all assets and liabilities are transferred to the governing body of the federation.

26 Qualifications and disqualifications for governors

Local authority, foundation, parent and partnership governors are only eligible to be appointed where they have the skills required to contribute to the effective governance and success of the school (School Governance (Constitution) (England) Regulations 2012, Regs 6, 8, 9, Sch. 1).

Provision as to qualifications for and disqualifications from the office of school governor, for the resignation and removal of governors and for their term of office is made by Schedule 4 which provides, *inter alia*, that–

(a) no person may be a governor if he is a pupil at the school or unless he is aged 18 or over at the date of his election;

(b) no person may hold more than one governorship at the same school, but the fact that a person is qualified to be elected or appointed as a governor of a particular category does not disqualify him from election or appointment in any other category;

(c) a person cannot be a parent governor if they are an elected member of a local authority or paid to work at the school for more than 500 hours in any 12 months;

(d) a person cannot be a local authority governor if they are eligible to be a staff governor;

(e) a person cannot be a partnership governor if they are a parent of a pupil, elected local authority member, employed by the local authority in education functions or eligible to be a staff governor;

(f) a governor (other than a governor who is such by virtue of his office), who without the consent of the governing body fails to attend meetings for a continuous period of six months will be disqualified;

(g) a person will be disqualified from being a governor if they–

(i) have had their estate sequestrated and the sequestration has not been discharged, annulled or reduced, or if they have been made the subject of a bankruptcy or debt relief restrictions order or an interim order;

(ii) are subject to a disqualification under the Company Directors Disqualification Act 1986 or to an order under the Insolvency Act 1986 s.429(2)(b);

(iii) have been removed from office as a charity trustee on the grounds of misconduct or mismanagement;

(iv) are included in the list of teachers and workers with children whose employment is prohibited or restricted;

(f) a person will be disqualified from being a governor if they have been convicted of an offence and sentenced to–

(i) not less than three months' imprisonment (whether or not suspended) without the option of a fine, within the last five years;

(ii) not less than two and a half years' imprisonment within the last 20 years;

(iii) not less than five years' imprisonment at any time;

(iv) a fine following conviction for nuisance or disturbance, on local authority or grant-maintained school premises, under the Education Act 1996 s.547 or the Further and Higher Education Act 1992 s.85A within the last five years.

A person will also be disqualified from being a governor if they refuse a request by the clerk to the governing body to make an application for a criminal records certificate.

27 Additional requirements for foundation and voluntary schools

The governing body of a foundation school or a foundation special school which, in either case, does not have a foundation, must include at least two (but no more than one quarter of the total) partnership governors.

The governing body of a foundation school or a foundation special school which, in either case, has a foundation but which is not a qualifying foundation school, must include at least two (but no more than 45 per cent of the total) foundation governors.

The governing body of a qualifying foundation school must include such number of foundation governors as to outnumber all the other governors by up to two. A "qualifying" foundation school is one that acquired its status under s.23A of the School Standards and Framework Act 1998.

The governing body of a voluntary aided school must include such number of foundation governors as to outnumber all the other governors by two.

The governing body of a voluntary controlled school must include at least two (but no more than one quarter of the total) foundation governors.

In calculating the number of governors required in order to comply with these requirements, the number is to be rounded up or down to the nearest whole number.

28 Responsibility for conduct of schools

The conduct of a maintained school is to be under the direction of the school's governing body which is to conduct the school with a view to promoting high standards of educational achievement there (Education Act 2002, s.21(1), (2)). The governing body of a maintained school must also make arrangements for ensuring that its functions relating to the conduct of the school are exercised with a view to safeguarding and promoting the welfare of children who are pupils at the school (s.175(2)). Such a governing body, in the exercise of any function relating to the conduct of the school, must have regard to any guidance given by the Secretary of State (or the Welsh Assembly) about consultation with pupils in connection with the taking of decisions affecting them. Any such guidance must provide for a pupil's views to be considered in the light of his age and understanding (s.176, amended by the Education and Inspections Act 2006, s.167).

In discharging its functions, the governing body must comply with the instrument of government (see **23 Governance in England**, above) and, subject to any other statutory provision, with any relevant trust deed (s.21(4)).

29 Duties of governing bodies

The governing body of a maintained school in England and Wales must promote the well-being of pupils at the school when discharging its functions relating to the conduct of the school (s.21(5)(a), inserted by the Education and Inspections Act 2006, s.38(1)). Well-being is defined in relation to pupils at a school in England, as relating to the matters mentioned in s.10(2) of the Children Act 2004 (s.21(8)(a), as so inserted). For pupils at a schools in Wales, well-being is defined as relating to the matters mentioned in s.25(2) of the Children Act 2004 (s.21(8)(b), as so inserted). In both ss.10(2) and 25(2) of the Children Act 2004 the matters are–

(a) physical and mental health and emotional well-being;

(b) protection from harm and neglect;

(c) education, training and recreation;

(d) the contribution made by them to society; and

(e) social and economic well-being

The governing body of a maintained school in England must promote community cohesion when discharging its functions relating to the conduct of the school (s.21(5)(b), inserted by the Education and Inspections Act 2006, s.38(1)). The governing body of a maintained school in England and Wales must have regard to any relevant Children and Young People's Plan (CYPP) in exercising its functions in relation to the conduct of the school (s.21(6), as so inserted). A relevant CYPP is defined (in s.21(9)(a), as so inserted) in relation to a school in England, as a plan published by the local authority under s.17 of the Children Act 2004 or, in relation to a local authority that is exempt from the requirements in that section, a similar plan setting out the authority's strategic plan for their delivery of children's services. The Children and Young People's Plan (England) Regulations 2005 (S.I. No. 2149) exempt local authorities that are classified as "excellent" under Comprehensive Performance Assessment from the requirement to produce a statutory plan. A relevant CYPP is defined (in s.21(9)(b), as so inserted) in relation to a school in Wales, as a plan published by the local authority under s.26 of the Children Act 2004 or, in relation to a local authority that is exempt from the requirements in that section, a similar plan setting out the authority's strategic plan for their delivery of children's services. Under the Children and Young People's Plan (Wales) Regulations 2007 (S.I. No. 2316) there are no exemptions from the requirement to publish a plan.

Governing bodies of maintained schools in England must, in the discharge of their functions, have regard to any views expressed by parents of registered pupils. It will be for individual schools to determine how and when to seek the views of parents. This does not apply to governing bodies of maintained schools in Wales (s.21(7), as so inserted).

With regard to the limit on the power to provide community facilities (Education Act 2002, s.28), governing bodies must take into account the CYPP and the views of parents, in each case in providing extended services for the wider community (s.28(4A)-(4C), inserted by the Education and Inspections Act 2002, s.38(2)).

The governing body of a school must establish, and publicise, procedures for dealing with all complaints relating to the school other than complaints falling to be dealt with by procedures established by virtue of other statutory provisions (s.29(1)).

The School Governance (Roles, Procedures and Allowances) (England) Regulations 2013 provide that the functions of the governing body include the following core functions–

(a) ensuring that the vision, ethos and strategic direction of the school are clearly defined;
(b) ensuring that the head teacher performs his or her responsibilities for the educational performance of the school; and
(c) ensuring the sound, proper and effective use of the school's financial resources.

The 2013 Regulations also provide that in exercising their functions the governing body must act with integrity, objectivity and honesty and in the best interests of the school; and be open about the decisions they make and the actions they take and in particular be prepared to explain their decisions and actions to interested parties. The governing body must appoint a clerk with a view to ensuring their efficient functioning and must have regard to advice from the clerk as to the nature of their functions. The head teacher's responsibilities include the internal organisation, management and control of the school; and the educational performance of the school, and they are accountable to the governing body for the performance of all their responsibilities and must comply with any reasonable direction of the governing body.

The Education (School Government) (Terms of Reference) (Wales) Regulations 2000 lay down a number of principles which are to serve as terms of reference for governing bodies, and also set out the respective roles and responsibilities of governing bodies and head teachers in similar terms to the 2013 Regulations. In Wales, the governing body and the head have an express duty to exercise their respective functions to promote equal opportunities and good relations between people of different racial groups and different genders, and the head teacher must also formulate a policy for the secular curriculum of the school, for adoption by the governing body.

30 Collaboration between schools

In England, regulations may enable the governing bodies of two or more maintained schools to arrange for any of their functions to be discharged jointly or by a joint committee of theirs (Education Act 2002, s.26). The School Governance (Collaboration) (England) Regulations 2003 have been made under this provision and deal with the establishment, membership and proceedings of such joint committees.

In Wales, the Education (Wales) Measure 2011 gives education bodies (for pupils under the age of 19) collaboration powers and imposes a duty on such bodies to consider from time to time whether the exercise of its powers of collaboration would further the "collaboration objective" i.e., the effective and efficient use of public resources by the body in respect of the provision of education and training suitable to the requirements of persons who have not attained the age of 19 (ss.1-9).

31 Provision of community facilities by governing body

The governing body of a maintained school has power to provide any facilities or services whose provision furthers any charitable purpose for the benefit of pupils at the school or their families, or people working or living in the school's locality (Education Act 2002, s.27(1)). A governing body may incur expenditure for this purpose and may also charge for any services or facilities provided (s.27(2), (3)). Schedule 3 introduces a new s.51A into the 1998 Act; both Schedule 3 and s.51A make provision for expenditure incurred by a governing body under s.27 of the 2002 Act. However, there are limitations on this power. Thus a governing body cannot, under s.27, do anything which it is unable to do by virtue of a prohibition or restriction on its powers contained in the school's instrument of government, and it must be satisfied that the exercise of powers under s.27 will not, to a significant extent, interfere with any performance of certain statutory duties (s.28(1), (3)). Before exercising any powers under s.27 a governing body in Wales (but not England) must consult, amongst others, the LEA, the staff of the school, and the parents of registered pupils of the school (s.28(4)). A governing body must establish, and publicise, procedures for dealing with all complaints relating to the provision of facilities or services under s.27(1) (s.29(1)).

32 Power to form companies

The governing body of a maintained school may form, or take part in forming, companies to: provide services or facilities for any schools; make, or facilitate the making of, arrangements for such provision by other persons; exercise relevant local authority functions, or enter into an agreement to establish an Academy. The governing body may, for specified purposes, invest in such companies, and may form, or take part in forming, companies to purchase services for that school and other participating schools. It may also become a member of such a company and provide staff to any such company (Education Act 2002, s.11). The School Companies Regulations 2002 govern the operation of such companies, called "school companies", and deal *inter alia* with who may be admitted to membership of school companies, remuneration of directors of such companies and the supervising authority for a school company.

A governing body can only exercise any of these powers with the consent of the local authority and if it has a delegated budget within the meaning of the Schools Standards and Framework Act 1998 (s.12). Where he considers it expedient to do so for purposes connected to any function of his relating to education, the Secretary of State may form, or take part in forming, or invest in, companies to carry on activities to secure those purposes or facilitate their achievement (s.13).

33 Parent governor representatives on education committees

Regulations may be made requiring local authority education committees to include representatives of parent governors at maintained schools (Education Act 1996, s.499). The Parent Governor Representatives (England) Regulations 2001 and the corresponding Welsh Regulations require local authorities to appoint between two and five parent governor representatives to each committee which carries out any functions conferred on the authority in its capacity as a local authority. Local authorities are responsible for making arrangements for the election of representatives. Elections must be by secret ballot, with all parent governors at schools maintained by the relevant authority being eligible to stand for election and to vote.

Parent governor representatives will be entitled to vote on matters relating to schools maintained by the authority and on matters relating to pupils at such schools.

34 Instruments of government

Every maintained school is required to have an "instrument of government" setting out the constitution of the governing body and other matters relating to the school (Education Act 2002, s.20). The School Governance (Constitution) (England) Regulations 2003 set out the matters that must be contained in the instrument of government. These include (Reg. 29)–
   (a) the name of the school and the category of school to which it belongs;
   (b) the name of the governing body of the school and the manner in which the governing body is to be constituted, including the make-up of the governors (see above) their numbers, and where the term of office is to be less than 4 years, the length of that term;
   (c) where the school has foundation governors (see **24 Types of governor**, above), the name of any body or person entitled to appoint/remove such governors;
   (d) where the school has sponsor governors, the name of any sponsor entitled to nominate governors;
   (e) where the school is a maintained special school, the name of any body entitled to nominate a community governor; and
   (f) where the school is a foundation or voluntary school with a religious character, a description of the school's ethos.
The instrument of government must comply with any trust deed relating to the school (Reg. 29(3)).

The governing body must prepare a draft of the instrument of government and submit it to the local authority for their approval. In the case of a school with foundation governors, the foundation governors, any trustees of the school, and (in the case of a church school) the appropriate diocesan authority must approve the draft first (Reg. 30).

The governing body or a local authority may review the instrument of government at any time (Reg. 31).

E: CONSTITUTION OF GOVERNING BODIES IN WALES

35 Government of maintained schools in Wales

The Government of Maintained Schools (Wales) Regulations 2005 set out the arrangements for the constitution of governing bodies of maintained schools, including maintained nursery schools, in Wales. All governing bodies of schools in Wales must be constituted in accordance with these Regulations.

Part 2 describes the various categories of governor. These are broadly the same as in England (see **24 Types of governor**, above) but in Wales there are also the categories of teacher governors and representative governors in community special schools.

Part 3 of the Welsh Regulations sets out the general principles by which the size and composition of school governing bodies are to be determined, and Part 4 deals with qualifications and term of office.

The remainder of the Regulations deal with the procedure for making, reviewing and varying instruments of government and the content of instruments (Part 5); enabling governors appointed or elected to office on or before 31st October 2005 to continue in office when an instrument of government made in accordance with the Regulations comes into effect (Part 6); the appointment and removal of officers of the governing body, and their functions, (Part 7); meetings and proceedings of the governing body (Part 8); the circumstances in which a governor may be suspended from meetings for up to six months (Reg. 49); delegation of governing body functions (Regs 50 to 52); the establishment and proceedings of committees of governing bodies, including clerking arrangements, convening meetings, quorum, voting, and publication of minutes (Part 9); and conflicts of interest (Part 10).

A local authority must enter into a partnership agreement with the governing body of a school it maintains, setting out how the authority and governors are to discharge their respective functions (Maintained Schools (Partnership Agreements) (Wales) Regulations 2007).

Provision for federation of maintained schools in Wales is contained in the Education (Wales) Measure 2011 and the Federation of Maintained Schools (Wales) Regulations 2014 which provides both for governing bodies to decide that two or more schools federate (s.10), and for local authorities to propose federations of schools (s.11). In addition, the Welsh Ministers may direct the federation of schools causing concern (s.16). Schools which are federated will have a single governing body (s.13). Governing bodies of federated schools must be constituted in accordance with the 2014 Regulations.

The Parent Governor Representatives and Church Representatives (Wales) Regulations 2001 make provision for representatives of parent governors at maintained schools to be included in education overview and scrutiny committees of local authorities in Wales.

36 Information and training for governors

Local authorities have a duty to provide such information to governors of maintained schools in Wales as is needed to enable them to carry out their functions, and must ensure that there is made available to every governor, free of charge, such training as it considers necessary for the effective discharge of their functions (Education (Wales) Measure 2011, s.22).

A local authority must also inform the body which appoints the clerk to a governing body that it may ask the local authority to provide a person to act as the clerk (s.23). The appointing body must ensure that anyone appointed as clerk has completed prescribed training to a prescribed standard (s.24). Local authorities have a duty to secure the training they see as necessary for clerks to governing bodies (s.25).

The training requirements for governors and clerks at maintained schools in Wales are set out in the Government of Maintained Schools (Training Requirements for Governors) (Wales) Regulations 2013 (S.I. 2013 No. 2124 as amended by 2014 No. 2225), and the Government of Maintained Schools (Clerk to a Governing Body) (Wales) Regulations 2013 (S.I. No. 2127). The required content of the training is set out in documents published by the Welsh Ministers.

37 School Councils

In Wales, under the School Councils (Wales) Regulations 2005, maintained schools must set up school councils which provide pupils with the opportunity to discuss and make representations on matters relating to the school.

F: REPORTS AND PARENTS' MEETINGS

38 Governors' reports

Once in every school year the governing body of a maintained school must prepare a report, a "governors' report", dealing with matters to be specified in regulations. Regulations may also specify to whom copies of such a report are to be made available and in what language or languages, and in what form, they are to be produced (Education Act 2002, s.30). The Education (Governors' Annual Reports) (England) Regulations 1999 set out the information to be contained in such reports in relation to maintained schools in England.

Inter alia, a report must contain–
   (a) the names of the existing governors and the category of governor to which each belongs;
   (b) a financial statement indicating the sum made available to the governors and how, in general terms, such sum was spent (including details of any travelling and subsistence allowances paid to the governors in that year);
   (c) in the case of a school with pupils aged 15 or over, information about pupils leaving the school, or employment or training taken up by school leavers;
   (d) a general description of arrangements made for the security of pupils and staff at the school;

(e) the number of pupils of compulsory school age registered at the school;

(f) a statement on the school's whole staff development policy

(g) a summary of the policy on pupils with special educational needs and of changes to the policy during the year, and a statement on the success of the governing body in implementing that policy;

(h) specified details as to pupils in the final year of the first, second and third key stages; and

(i) details of GCE "A" and "AS" examinations taken by pupils aged 16, 17, or 18.

It is for the governors to decide the language or languages in which the report is to be produced and the form it will take, but they must comply with any direction given in the regulations.

S.317(6) of the 1996 Act (added by the Special Educational Needs and Disability Act 2001, s.14(2)) specifies that information about disabled pupils, e.g., concerning access and steps taken to prevent less favourable treatment, must be included in the annual report. The governors' report may be combined with any other document whose preparation by the governing body is required by or under any enactment.

The governors must take such steps as are reasonably practicable to secure that all parents and employees at the school receive (free of charge) a copy of the report. Copies must also be available for inspection at the school and, where there is a parents' meeting (see **39 Annual parents' meetings (England)**, below), copies must be given to parents at least two weeks before the meeting (Reg. 5).

The School Governors' Annual Reports (Wales) Regulations 2011 contain similar provisions. Here, reports must also describe the steps taken by governors to develop or strengthen the school's links with the community (including the police), give details of absences, the school's performance in literacy and numeracy tests, a summary of the school development plan, and list the school's sporting aims and achievements, but need not include details about school security. In place of (f) and (g) above, a Welsh report must include information about any reviews of policies or strategies adopted by the governing body. Also, in Wales parents need not be provided with a copy of the full report if they have been provided with a summary report and informed that they can request a copy of the full report if they wish.

39 Annual parents' meetings (England)

Once in every school year the governing body of a school in England must hold an annual parents' meeting which is open to all parents of registered pupils at the school, the head teacher and other persons who may be invited by the governing body (Education Act 2002, s.33(1)). The purpose of the meeting is to provide an opportunity for discussion of the manner in which the school has been, and is to be, conducted, and of any other matters relating to the school raised by parents of registered pupils (s.33(2)). Regulations may make provision as to circumstances in which a governing body are to be exempt from the obligation to hold such an annual meeting (s.33(3)).

The Education (Annual Parents' Meetings) (Exemptions) (England) Regulations 2003 exempt community special and foundation special schools from the requirement to hold an annual parents' meeting if the school is established in a hospital or is a boarding school and the governors consider that it would be impractical to hold such a meeting (Reg. 4). Where a school has had an Ofsted inspection and has held a parents' meeting to discuss the Ofsted report prior to the governing body drawing up an action plan, no annual parents' meeting need be held in the 12 months following that parent's meeting (Reg. 5).

If a school holds a meeting (or series of meetings) to which all parents are invited where they have the opportunity to discuss the manner in which the school has been and is to be conducted, and the school's performance, and where at least two governors (including one non-staff governor) attend, then no annual parent's meeting need be held in the school year in which that meeting (or series of meetings) is held (Reg. 6).

A school will also be exempt from the requirement to hold an annual parent's meeting in any year in which it gives parents, with their copy of the governor's report, a notice asking whether they require an annual parent's meeting to be held and the parents of fewer than 15 registered pupils respond (Reg. 7).

40 Parents' meetings (Wales)

In Wales, a governing body must hold a parents' meeting if the following four conditions are met (School Standards and Organisation (Wales) Act 2013, s.94)–

(a) it receives a petition requesting a meeting from whichever is the lower of: the parents of 10% of registered pupils, or the parents of 30 registered pupils;

(b) the meeting is for the purpose of discussing a matter relating to the school;

(c) that there will be no more than three such meetings in a school year; and

(d) that there are enough school days left in the school year in which to hold the meeting.

Upon receipt of a request the governing body must inform parents of registered pupils at the school of the date and purpose of the meeting and must hold it within 25 days.

G: CLASS SIZES

41 Limits on infant class sizes

Part I (ss.1, 2 and 4) of the 1998 Act gives the Secretary of State power to impose limits on class sizes for infant classes (i.e., classes where the majority of the pupils attain the ages of five, six or seven during the school year).

S.1 of the 1998 Act gives the Secretary of State power to impose a limit on class size and to specify the school years in relation to which any such limit is to have effect. Any limit imposed under s.1 will specify the maximum number of pupils that a class may contain while an ordinary teaching session (i.e., not a school assembly or other activity usually conducted with a large group of pupils) is conducted by a single school teacher. Once a limit has been imposed, it is the duty of authorities and governing bodies of schools affected to secure that the limit is complied with. The School Admissions (Infant Class Sizes) (England) Regulations 2012 and the School Admissions (Infant Class Sizes) (Wales) Regulations 2013 both impose a limit of 30 pupils in an infant class while an ordinary teaching session is conducted by a single school teacher (or, where there is more than one school teacher, a maximum of 30 pupils for each teacher).

42 Excepted children

Where certain types of children (known as "excepted children") cannot be educated in another infant class without prejudicing efficient education or the efficient use of resources, those children are not to be counted for the purposes of determining whether the limit of 30 is exceeded. Excepted children are—

(a) children whose statement of special educational needs specifies that they be educated at a particular school and who are admitted to that school outside a normal admission round;

(b) children who are looked after by a local authority and who are admitted to that school outside a normal admission round, and children who have ceased to be looked after ("previously looked after children") as a result of being adopted or being placed with a family or given a special guardian;

(c) children initially refused admission to a school, who are subsequently offered a place outside a normal admission round by a direction of an admission appeal panel;

(d) children who the local authority have confirmed cannot gain a place at any other suitable school within a reasonable distance of their home because they moved into the area outside a normal admission round;

(e) children who are registered pupils at special schools but who receive some tuition at a mainstream school;

(f) children with special educational needs who are normally educated in a special unit in a mainstream school but who receive some tuition in a non-special class;

(g) children of armed forces personnel who are admitted outside the normal admission round (in Wales, from the 2014/15 school year only);

(h) children whose twin or other siblings from a multiple birth are admitted as non-excepted pupils (in Wales, from the 2014/15 school year only).

(i) in Wales, pupils admitted outside a normal admission round for whom education at a school of a particular religious character is desired;

(j) in Wales, pupils admitted after the first day of the school year where the school has not yet reached its admission number but has organised classes so that the admission of the child would mean the school having to take relevant measures; and

(k) in Wales, children for whom education at a Welsh speaking school is desired, where the school concerned is the only one within a reasonable distance of the child's home;

43 Use of school premises

The articles of government of every county and maintained special school must provide for the use of school premises outside the time of school sessions to be under the control of the governing body. Control must be exercised subject to any direction of the local authority and having regard to the desirability of school premises being made available, when not in use by the school, for use by members of the local community (Education Act 1996, s.149).

H: SCHOOL AND PUPIL RECORDS AND INFORMATION

44 School records

Under the Education (Pupil Information) (England) Regulations 2005, it is the duty of the governing body of every school to keep a curricular record in respect of every registered pupil, and to update it at least once a year (Reg. 4). This is a formal record of a pupil's academic achievements, his other skills and abilities and his progress in school. It does not include the pupil's personal education plan or EHC plan which are instead included in a pupil's educational record.

Copies of a pupil's curricular record must be provided to another school which is considering admitting the pupil, but copies of National Curriculum assessments or a pupil's educational record may only be provided once a pupil has transferred to the new school (Regs. 5 and 9).

The right of a pupil to gain access to his record is governed by the Data Protection Act 1998 (see the Note on **The Data Protection Act 1998**). The disclosure of information contained in educational records which could not be disclosed to the pupil under the 1998 Act is prohibited (Reg. 5).

Similar provisions apply in Wales by virtue of the Pupil Information (Wales) Regulations 2011.

45 Individual pupils' achievements

The Education (Pupil Information) (England) Regulations 2005 and the Head Teacher's Report to Parents and Adult Pupils (Wales) Regulations 2011, require head teachers of schools to provide information about individual pupils' achievements.

Head teachers are required to provide reports each school year on their pupils' progress and achievements, free of charge to the parent of each pupil; and where the pupil is aged over 18, to the pupil and if there are special circumstances to the parent of such a pupil. In the case of a pupil who is over compulsory school age and who is proposing to leave the school, or has already left it, a report need not be provided for his parents (although the pupil himself will receive a school leaver's report–see below). The information so provided must include details of the National Curriculum levels of attainment and public examination results (Reg. 6).

The head teacher must provide a school leaver with a school leaver's report being a record of his qualifications and other school achievements (Reg. 8).

A pupil's educational record must be made available free of charge to a parent on request, and a copy supplied on payment of a fee (not exceeding the cost of supply) (Education (Pupil Information) (England) Regulations 2005, Reg. 5; Education (Pupil Information) (Wales) Regulations 2011, Reg. 5).

46 Information on National Curriculum assessments and school examination results

The Education (School Performance Information) (England) Regulations 2007 contain detailed provisions relating to the provision of information to the Secretary of State by schools maintained by local authorities and Academies. Such information relates to the various key stage assessments.

Proprietors of city technology colleges, non-maintained special schools and independent schools must also provide specified information to the Secretary of State if so requested.

Similar provision about the provision of information to the Welsh Ministers is made in relation to schools in Wales by the School Performance Information (Wales) Regulations 2011.

47 Other information about schools

The Secretary of State has the power to make regulations requiring the proprietor of every independent (see the Note on **Independent Schools**) and the governing body of every school which is (a) maintained by a local authority, or (b) a special school not maintained by a local authority, to provide prescribed information with a view to (Education Act 1996, s.537)–
  (a) assisting parents in choosing schools for their children;
  (b) increasing public awareness of the quality of education provided and the educational standards achieved in schools; and
  (c) assisting in assessing the efficiency with which the schools' financial resources are managed.

Such information must not name any pupil to which it relates. The Secretary of State may publish, or arrange to have published, such information as is provided, or require local authorities to publish prescribed categories of such information. He may also require the governing bodies of maintained schools, or local authorities, or the proprietor of any city technology college or city college for the technology of the arts, to provide prescribed persons with prescribed categories of information so published.

The School Information (England) Regulations 2008 *inter alia* require local authorities to publish for each school year a composite prospectus of admission information for schools in their area maintained by them (not including special schools), Academy schools, and city colleges for the technology of the arts. An authority may publish a single composite prospectus covering all their schools, or they may produce separate prospectuses, each covering part of the total area. Separate prospectuses may be produced for primary and secondary schools. The School Information (Wales) Regulations 2011 make similar provision for all maintained schools in Wales and provide for a composite prospectus for each area or separate prospectuses for primary, middle and secondary schools.

The Regulations also prescribe the information which individual schools must include on their website, such as a Special Educational Needs information report, charging and remissions policy, behaviour policy, and the school's most recent key stages 2 and 4 results.

48 Individual pupil information

S.537A (added by the Education Act 1997, s.20 and substituted by the School Standards and Framework Act 1998) gives the Secretary of State power to make regulations requiring the proprietor of every independent school or alternative provision Academy, and the governing body of every maintained or non-maintained special school, to provide such "individual pupil information" relating to past or present pupils as may be prescribed. The Education (Information About Individual Pupils) (England) Regulations 2013 (and the corresponding (Wales) Regulations 2007), which have been made under s.537A, dictate that information on the educational achievements of pupils is to be provided.

Information provided under s.537A may be passed on by the Secretary of State to prescribed bodies or persons, but no information received under s.537A may be published in any form which includes the name of any pupil to which it relates. The Education (Individual Pupil Information) (Prescribed Persons) (England)

Regulations 2009 (and the corresponding (Wales) Regulations 2004) prescribe the bodies and persons who may be provided with "individual pupil information". These include local authorities, the Joint Council for Qualifications and OFSTED.

The Education (Information About Individual Pupils) (England) Regulations 2013 further provide that the governing bodies of maintained schools, non-maintained special schools, and city technology colleges and academies must supply personal information about pupils, on matters as diverse as their ethnicity, whether pupils have special educational needs and if so what type, whether a pupil has been awarded a bursary, and whether a school has received top-up funding in respect of a pupil. Details are also required as to the pupil's learning aims, which are courses of study leading to a qualification awarded or authenticated by a body recognised by the Office of Qualifications and Examinations Regulation. Personal details as to excluded pupils must also be provided, as well as the exclusion start date, the type of exclusion, the reason for exclusion and the number of sessions to which the exclusion applies. Maintained schools must provide the information to their local authority; other schools must provide it directly to the Secretary of State.

The Secretary of State may collect individual information about children receiving education funded by the local authority otherwise than at a school (which includes children in hospital and those taught by voluntary providers) (Education Act 1996, s.537B, inserted by the Education and Inspections Act 2006, s.164).

In Wales, The Education (Information About Individual Pupils) (Wales) Regulations 2007 require the governing body of a maintained school to provide individual pupil information in machine readable format about pupils, including sixth formers, including ethnicity, fluency in Welsh, excluded pupils, special educational needs, and (for sixth formers) details as to the courses they are studying and screening for basic skills.

In terms of early years provision in England, the Childcare (Provision of Information About Young Children) (England) Regulations 2009 prescribe the individual child information that early years providers (including early years childminder agencies and childminders registered with them) can be required to supply to the Secretary of State and their local authority.

49 Information about children receiving funded education outside school

Regulations may make provision requiring a person who provides funded education to give to the relevant person such individual child information as may be prescribed (Education Act 1996, s.537B, inserted by the Education and Inspections Act 2006, s.164). The "relevant person" means the Secretary of State and other prescribed persons.

The Education (Information About Children in Alternative Provision) (England) Regulations 2007 prescribe the supply of individual data items about children receiving education which is funded by the local authority outside mainstream schools. The providers of such education must supply such information to either the Secretary of State or the local authority which is funding such education, when required to do so. Similar provision is made by the Education (Information About Children in Alternative Provision) (Wales) Regulations 2009.

50 Biometric information

Automated fingerprint, iris, face and palm vein recognition systems are used in schools for a variety of purposes including controlling access to school buildings, monitoring attendance, recording the borrowing of library books and cashless catering. The processing of such biometric information is subject to the provisions of the Data Protection Act 1998 (see the Note on **The Data Protection Act 1998**), but whilst that Act requires the data subject (i.e., the child) to be notified about the processing of his or her personal data, and in most cases to consent to it, there is no requirement, in the case of a person aged under 18, for consent also to be obtained from their parents.

The Protection of Freedoms Act 2012 provides that schools, 16-19 Academies, and further education institutions must notify the parents of a child that they intend to process the child's biometric information and that the parents may object, in writing, to that processing. The information may only be processed if no parent objects to it and the written consent of one parent is obtained. Consent under this provision is only required if the information is to be used for the purposes of an automated biometric recognition system, such as a fingerprint recognition system (s.26). The biometric data must not be processed if the child objects to its processing, irrespective of the child's age, maturity or ability to understand. This is the case even if consent has been given by a parent to the information being processed (s.26(5)). If there is an objection to the processing of biometric data, the school must ensure that reasonable alternative means are available by which the child may do, or be subject to, anything which the child would have been able to do, or be subject to, had their biometric information been processed (s.26(7)).

The school is not required to notify a parent, or obtain their consent if they are satisfied that (s.27)–
   (a) the parent cannot be found;
   (b) the parent lacks capacity to object or (as the case may be) consent to the processing of the child's biometric information;
   (c) the welfare of the child requires that the parent is not contacted; or
   (d) it is otherwise not reasonably practicable to notify the parent or (as the case may be) obtain their consent.

51 Authorities

Statutes–

Apprenticeship, Skills, Children and Learning Act 2009,

Education Acts 1962 to 2006

Education and Inspections Act 2006

Education (Wales) Measure 2011

Protection of Freedoms Act 2012

School Standards and Framework Act 1998

School Standards and Organisation (Wales) Act 2013

Statutory Instruments for England and Wales–
Foundation Body Regulations 1999 (S.I. 1999 No. 1502)

Statutory Instruments applying only to England–
Annual Parents' Meetings (Exemptions) (England) Regulations 2003 (S.I. 2003 No. 1921)

Childcare (Provision of Information About Young Children) (England) Regulations 2009, as amended (S.I. 2009 No. 1554, 2010 No. 677, 2012 No. 765, 2014 Nos. 2103 and 3197, and 2015 No. 1696)

Education (Change of Category of Maintained Schools) (England) Regulations 2000, as amended (S.I. 2000 No. 2195, 2003 No. 2136, 2005 No. 1731, and 2006 Nos. 1164 and 1507)

Education (Governors' Annual Reports) (England) Regulations 1999, as amended (S.I. 1999 No. 2157, 2002 Nos. 1171 and 2214, and 2005 No. 845)

Education (Individual Pupil Information) (Prescribed Persons) (England) Regulations 2009, as amended (S.I. 2009 No. 1563 2010 Nos. 677, 1940, and 1941, 2012 Nos. 765, 956 and 979, 2013 Nos. 235 and 1193, and 2014 No. 2103)

Education (Information About Children in Alternative Provision) (England) Regulations 2007, as amended (S.I. 2007 Nos. 1065 and 3224, 2010 Nos. 677, 1939 and 1941, 2012 Nos. 756, 765 and 979, and 2014 No. 2103)

Education (Information About Individual Pupils) (England) Regulations 2013, as amended (S.I. 2013 No. 2904, 2014 Nos. 852 and 2103, and 2015 No. 971)

Education (Pupil Information) (England) Regulations 2005, as amended (S.I. 2005 No. 1437, 2007 No. 3224, 2008 No. 1747, 2010 Nos. 677 and 1941, 2012 Nos. 765 and 979, 2013 No. 3212, 2014 No. 2103, and 2015 Nos. 902 and 971)

Education (School Performance Information) (England) Regulations 2007, as amended (S.I. 2007 No. 2324, 2008 Nos. 364 and 1727, 2010 No. 677, 2012 Nos. 765 and 1274, 2013 Nos. 1759 and 3212, 2014 No. 2103, and 2015 Nos. 902 and 1566)

Local Authority (Duty to Secure Early Years Provision Free of Charge) Regulations 2013, as amended (S.I. 2013 No. 3193 and 2014 No. 1705)

Maintained Schools (Partnership Agreements) (Wales) Regulations 2007 (S.I. 2007 No. 3066)

Parent Governor Representatives (England) Regulations 2001, as amended (S.I. 2001 No. 478, 2003 No. 2045, and 2010 No. 1172)

School Companies Regulations 2002, as amended (S.I. 2002 No.2978, 2003 No. 2049, 2004 No. 3264, 2006 No. 2198, 2009 No. 1924, 2010 Nos. 1172 and 1939, 2012 Nos. 979 and 2404, and 2014 No. 2923)

School Admissions (Infant Class Sizes) (England) Regulations 2012, as amended (S.I. 2012 No. 10 and 2014 Nos. 852 and 2103)

School Governance (Collaboration) (England) Regulations 2003, as amended (S.I. 2003 No. 1962, 2013 No. 1624, and 2015 No. 883)

School Governance (Constitution) (England) Regulations 2012, as amended (S.I. 2012 No. 1034, 2014 Nos. 1257 and 1959, 2015 No. 883, and 2016 No. 204)

School Governance (Federations) (England) Regulations 2012, as amended (S.I. 2012 No. 1035, 2013 No. 1624, 2014 Nos. 1257 and 1959, 2015 No. 1554, and 2016 No. 204)

School Governance (New Schools) (England) Regulations 2007, as amended (S.I. 2007 No. 958, 2010 No. 1172, 2012 Nos. 1033 and 2404, 2013 No. 235, and 2015 No. 883)

School Governance (Parent Council) (England) Regulations 2007 (S.I. 2007 No. 1330)

School Governance (Roles, Procedures and Allowances) (England) Regulations 2013, as amended (S.I. 2013 Nos. 1624 and 2688 and 2014 No. 1257)

School Information (England) Regulations 2008, as amended (S.I. 2008 No. 3093 2010 Nos. 1172 and 1874, 2012 Nos. 979 and 1124, 2013 Nos. 758 and 2912, 2014 No. 2103, and 2015 No. 902)

School Organisation (Establishment and Discontinuance of Schools) (England) Regulations 2013, as amended (S.I. 2013 No. 3109 and 2014 No. 2103)

School Organisation (Prescribed Alterations to Maintained Schools) (England) Regulations 2013, as amended (S.I. 2013 No. 3110 and 2014 No. 2103)

School Organisation (Removal of Foundation, Reduction in Number of Foundation Governors and Ability of Foundation to Pay Debts) (England) Regulations 2007, as amended (S.I. 2007 No. 3475 and 2012 No. 956)

School Premises (England) Regulations 2012 (S.I. 2012 No. 1943)

Schools Forums (England) Regulations 2012, as amended (S.I. 2012 Nos. 2261 and 2991, 2013 No. 3104 and 2014 No. 3352)

Statutory Instruments applying only to Wales–

Education (Individual Pupil Information) (Prescribed Persons) (Wales) Regulations 2004, as amended (S.I. 2004 No. 549 and 2005 No. 3239)

Education (Information About Children in Alternative Provision) (Wales) Regulations 2009, as amended (S.I. 2009 No. 3355 and 2010 No. 2431)

Education (Information About Individual Pupils) (Wales) Regulations 2007, as amended (S.I. 2007 No. 3562, 2011 No. 2325, and 2013 No. 3137)

Education (Parent Governor Representatives) (Wales) Regulations 1999 (S.I. 1999 No. 1900)

Education (School Premises) Regulations 1999, as amended (S.I. 1999 No. 2 and 2012 No. 1943)

Federation of Maintained Schools (Wales) Regulations 2014, as amended (S.I. 2014 Nos. 1132 and 1609)

Government of Maintained Schools (Change of Category) (Wales) Regulations 2015 (S.I. 2015 No. 1521)

Government of Maintained Schools (Wales) Regulations 2005, as amended (S.I. 2005 Nos. 2914 and 3200, 2006 No. 873, 2007 No. 944, 2009 No. 2544, 2010 Nos. 638 and 1142, 2013 No. 2124, and 2014 No. 1609)

Head Teacher's Report to Parents and Adult Pupils (Wales) Regulations 2011, as amended (S.I. 2011 No. 1943, 2013 No. 437, and 2014 No. 1998)

Parent Governor Representatives and Church Representatives (Wales) Regulations 2001, as amended (S.I. 2001 No. 3711, 2005 No. 2913, 2010 No. 1142, and 2013 No. 3005)

Pupil Information (Wales) Regulations 2011 (S.I. 2011 No. 1942)

School Admissions (Infant Class Sizes) (Wales) Regulations 2013, as amended (S.I. 2013 No. 1141 and 2014no. 852)

School Councils (Wales) Regulations 2005 (S.I. 2005 No. 3200)

School Government (Terms of Reference) (Wales) Regulations 2000, as amended (S.I. 2000 No. 3027, and 2005 No. 2913)

School Governors' Annual Reports (Wales) Regulations 2011, as amended (S.I. 2011 No. 1939, 2013 Nos. 437 and 1561, and 2014 No. 2677)

School Information (Wales) Regulations 2011, as amended (S.I. 2011 No. 1944 and 2013 No. 437)

School Performance Information (Wales) Regulations 2011 (S.I. 2011 No. 1963)

SPECIAL EDUCATIONAL PROVISION AND SPECIAL SCHOOLS
ENGLAND AND WALES

1 Contents

This Note covers the provisions for the education of children and young persons up to the age of 25 with special educational needs (special educational provision) in Wales (Part A) and England (Part B). Part C deals with Special schools and their staff and the Disabled Persons (Services, Consultation and Representation) Act 1986 which apply to both England and Wales.

2 Discrimination legislation

Part 6 (ss.85 to 99) of the Equality Act 2010 contains provisions dealing with discrimination, harassment and victimisation in respect of the admission and treatment of school pupils and further and higher education students. The provisions apply to the responsible body (i.e. local authority, governing body, education authority, proprietor or manager) of such an establishment. Schools and further and higher education institutions for these purposes are (ss.85, 91)–

(a) schools in England and Wales, i.e., schools maintained by a local authority, independent educational institutions (other than special schools) and special schools (not maintained by a local authority);

(b) schools in Scotland, i.e., schools managed by an education authority, independent schools, and schools in respect of which the managers are for the time being receiving grants under s.73(c) or (d) of the Education (Scotland) Act 1980;

(c) universities, any other institution within the higher education sector and institutions within the further education sector in England and Wales;

(d) universities, designated institutions and colleges of further education in Scotland.

For more information on these provisions and discrimination in schools and further and higher education institutions generally, see the Note on **Discrimination and Equality Law.**

A: WALES

3 The legislation

This Part of this Note is arranged as follows–

1: Special educational provision
2: Special educational needs
3: Further and higher education
4: Approval of independent schools

The principal provisions governing the provision of education for children and young persons with special educational needs in Wales are to be found in the Education Act 1996, Part IV (ss.312 to 349), as amended by the School Standards and Framework Act 1998 and as supplemented and amended by the Special Educational Needs and Disability Act 2001. Unless otherwise indicated, the provisions referred to below are the provisions of Part IV of the 1996 Act.

The Learning and Skills Act 2000 governs the provision of education for persons with learning difficulties who are over compulsory school age but under the age of 25 (see 3: FURTHER AND HIGHER EDUCATION, below).

4 Duty of parents to secure the education of their children

It is the duty of the parent of every child of compulsory school age to cause him to receive efficient full-time education suitable to his age, ability, and aptitude, and to any special educational needs he may have, either by regular attendance at school or otherwise (s.7).

1: SPECIAL EDUCATIONAL PROVISION

5 Meaning of special educational provision

Special educational provision means, in the case of a child aged two years or over, educational provision which is additional to, or otherwise different from, that made generally for children of his age in schools maintained by the local authority (other than special schools–see below) in their area; and, in the case of a child under two years of age, educational provision of any kind (s.312(4)).

The term child includes any person under 19 years of age who is registered as a pupil at a school (s.312(5)).

6 Duty of local authorities and other bodies to secure special educational provision

The 1996 Act provides that it is the duty of every local authority to secure that there is available for their area sufficient schools for providing primary and secondary education and, in fulfilling that duty a local authority must, in particular, have regard to the need for securing that special educational provision is made for pupils who have special educational needs (see below) (s.14(6)(b)).

A local authority must arrange for the parent of any child in their area with special educational needs to be provided with advice and information about matters relating to those needs (s.332AA(1)) (these are usually known as parent partnership services). The authority must take appropriate steps for making the services provided under s.332AA(1) known to parents of children in their area, head teachers and proprietors of schools in their area and any other relevant people (s.332AA(4)).

S.316 (as substituted by the 2001 Act, s.1) applies to a child with special educational needs who should be educated in a school (s.316(1)). If no statement is maintained under s.324 (see **19 Statement of child's special educational needs**, below) for that child, he must be educated in a mainstream school (s.316(2)). If a statement is maintained under s.324 the child must still be educated in a mainstream school unless that is incompatible with the wishes of his parent or the provision of efficient education for other children (s.316(3)). Where a local authority name a maintained school in a statement, the governing body cannot rely on the exception concerning the provision of efficient education for other children to refuse admission to the statemented child (s.316A(7)).

"Mainstream" school means any school other than: a special school; or an independent school which is not a city technology college, a city college for the technology of the arts or an Academy (see the Note on **Special Educational Provision and Special Schools: England and Wales**) (s.316(4)).

S.316 allows a child to be educated in an independent school which is not a mainstream school or in a non-maintained special school (see **42 Special schools: Introduction**, below) if the cost is met otherwise than by the local authority (s.316A(1) added by the 2001 Act, s.1). A child is not required by s.316(2) to be educated in a mainstream school during any period when he is admitted to a special school for an assessment of his educational needs under s.323 or following a change in his circumstances (see **43 Maintained special schools**, below), nor when he remains admitted to a special school in prescribed circumstances following an assessment there; nor when he is admitted to a community or foundation special school established in a hospital (s.316A(2)).

It is specifically provided by s.316A(3) that s.316 does not affect the operation of either s.348 which is concerned with the provision of special education at non-maintained schools, or paragraph 3 of Schedule 27 which is concerned with a parent's right to express a preference for a maintained school.

If a local authority decide to make a statement for a child under s.324 (see **19 Statement of child's special educational needs**, below) but do not name the parent's preferred school in that statement, the authority must comply with s.316(3) (see above) and can only rely on the exception in s.316(3)(b) (provision of efficient education for other children), in relation to their mainstream schools as a whole, if they can show that there are no reasonable steps which they could take to prevent such an incompatibility (s.316A(4), (5)). In relation to a particular mainstream school, a local authority can only rely on the exception in s.316(3)(b) if they can show that there are no reasonable steps which they or another authority can take in relation to the school to prevent the incompatibility (s.316A(6)).

To the extent that it appears necessary or desirable for the purpose of co-ordinating provision for children with special educational needs, the governing bodies of community, foundation and voluntary schools and maintained nursery schools must, in exercising functions relating to the provision for such children, consult the local authority and the governing bodies of other such schools (s.317(3)). They must designate a member of the staff at the school (to be known as the "special educational needs co-ordinator" or "SENCO") as having responsibility for co-ordinating the provision for pupils with special educational needs (s.317(3A), inserted by the Education and Inspections Act 2006, s.173). Regulations may require the governing bodies to ensure that special educational needs co-ordinators have prescribed qualifications or prescribed experience (or both), and confer on the governing bodies of those schools other functions relating to special educational needs co-ordinators (s.317(3B), as so inserted).

The Welsh Ministers may direct local authorities to consider making regional provision for children with special educational needs, or direct local authorities and governing bodies to make arrangements or proposals for regional provision. Regional provision may involve the provision of education at a school maintained by one local authority for children from other authorities, or the provision of goods and services by one local authority to other authorities or schools (School Standards and Organisation (Wales) Act 2013, ss.64-70).

Where a child who has special educational needs (see **13 Meaning of special educational needs**, below) is being educated in a community, foundation or voluntary school, or a maintained nursery school, those concerned with the making of special educational provision for the child must secure that the child engages in the activities of the school together with children who do not have special educational needs, so far as is reasonably practicable and compatible with (a) the child receiving the special educational provision which his learning difficulty calls for, (b) the provision of efficient education for the children with whom he will be educated, and (c) the efficient use of resources (s.317(4)).

7 Review of arrangements for special educational provision

A local authority must keep under review the arrangements made by them for special educational provision and, in doing so, must, to the extent that it appears necessary or desirable for the purpose of co-ordinating provision for children with special educational needs, consult the governing bodies of community, foundation and voluntary schools, community and foundation special schools, and maintained nursery schools in their area (s.315).

8 Special educational provision otherwise than in schools

Where a local authority are satisfied that it would be inappropriate for the special educational provision (or any part of the special educational provision) which a learning difficulty of a child in their area calls for, to be made in a school, they may arrange for the provision (or, as the case may be, for that part of it) to be made otherwise than in a school. Before making any such arrangement as described above, a local authority must consult the child's parent (s.319).

9 Provision of education at non-maintained schools

Where special education provision in respect of a child with special educational needs is made at a school which is not a maintained school and either the name of the school is specified in a statement in respect of the child under s. 324 (see **19 Statement of child's special educational needs**, below) or the local authority are satisfied that his interests require the necessary special educational provision to be made for him at a school which is not a maintained school and that it is appropriate for the child to be provided with education at the particular school, the authority must pay the whole of the fees payable in respect of the education provided for him at the school. If board and lodging are provided for the child at the school and the authority are satisfied that the necessary special educational provision cannot be provided for the child unless board and lodging are also provided, they must also pay the whole of the fees payable in respect of the board and lodging.

Maintained school for the above purpose means a school maintained by a local authority, a grant-maintained school, and a grant-maintained special school (s.348).

10 Provision outside England and Wales for certain children

A local authority may make such arrangements as they think fit for enabling a child for whom they maintain a statement under s.324 (see **19 Statement of child's special educational needs**, below) to attend an institution outside England and Wales which specialises in providing for children with special needs. For this purpose, the term children with special needs means children who have particular needs which would be special educational needs if those children were in England and Wales.

The arrangements which a local authority may make in this connection include contributing to or paying (a) fees charged by the institution, (b) expenses reasonably incurred in maintaining a child whilst it is at the institution or travelling to or from it, (c) his travelling expenses, and (d) expenses reasonably incurred by any person accompanying a child while he is travelling or staying at the institution.

The powers given to a local authority by the above-mentioned provisions are without prejudice to any other powers of a local authority to give financial assistance (s.320).

11 Information as to schools and admission arrangements

The governors of each school maintained by a local authority must publish such information as respects the school as may be required by regulations made by the Secretary of State (School Standards and Framework Act 1998, s.92). S.317(5) of the 1996 Act makes similar provision with respect to the annual report of the governing body of a community, foundation or voluntary school as to the information it should contain about the implementation of the governing body's policy for pupils with special educational needs.

The Education (Special Educational Needs) (Information) (Wales) Regulations 1999, made *inter alia* for the above-mentioned purposes, provide that the governing body of each community, foundation or voluntary school and the governing body of every community or foundation special school other than a special school established in a hospital must publish information on the matters specified in Schedule 1 and Schedule 2, respectively, to the Regulations. Included in the information to be published under those Schedules is (a) basic information about the school's special educational provision; (b) information about the school's policies for the identification, assessment, and provision for all pupils with special educational needs, and (c) information about the school's staffing policies and partnerships with bodies beyond the school.

The Regulations further provide that the governing body of each community or foundation special school which is established in a hospital must publish information about the matters specified in Schedule 3 to the Regulations. Included in the information which must be provided by such schools is (a) information as to how children with special educational needs are identified and their needs determined, (b) how the progress of such children is monitored, and (c) arrangements for providing access by such pupils to a balanced and broadly based curriculum.

The information referred to above must be published in a single document (a) for distribution (free of charge) *inter alia* to parents of pupils or prospective pupils and (b) for reference at the school.

Local authorities are also under a duty to publish information about special educational provision especially regarding its financing and the authority's broad aims concerning such educational provision (see the Special Educational Needs (Provision of Information by Local Authorities) (Wales) Regulations 2002).

12 School attendance orders

S.437 makes provision for the serving of school attendance orders on the parents of a child of compulsory school age if it appears to the local authority that the child is not receiving suitable education (see the Note on **Schools: Provision and Governance: England and Wales**).

2: SPECIAL EDUCATIONAL NEEDS

13 Meaning of special educational needs

Under s.312(1), a child has special educational needs if he has a learning difficulty which calls for special educational provision to be made for him.

S.312(2) provides that a child has a learning difficulty if—
(a) he has a significantly greater difficulty in learning than the majority of children of his age; or
(b) he has a disability which either prevents or hinders him from making use of educational facilities of a kind generally provided in schools, within the area of the local authority concerned; or
(c) he is under the age of five years and is, or would be if special educational provision were not made for him, likely to fall within paragraph (a) or (b) when over that age.

A child is not to be taken as having a learning difficulty solely because the language (or form of language) in which he is, or will be, taught is different from a language (or form of language) which has at any time been spoken in his home (s.312(3)).

14 Code of Practice

S.313 enables the Welsh Ministers to issue and, from time to time revise, a code of practice giving practical guidance in respect of the discharge by maintained schools and maintained nursery schools of their functions regarding children with special educational needs. When exercising those functions, the above-mentioned authorities and bodies must have regard to the provisions of the Code. On any appeal, the Special Educational Needs Tribunal for Wales will have regard to any provision of the Code which appears to it to be relevant to any question arising on appeal.

The Code of Practice for Wales is available at <http://learning.wales.gov.uk/resources>.

15 Duties of governing bodies, etc., in relation to pupils with special educational needs

The governing body of a community, foundation or voluntary school or a maintained nursery school must—
(a) in exercising their functions in relation to the school, use their best endeavours to secure that, if any registered pupil has special educational needs, the special educational provision which his learning difficulty calls for is made;
(b) where the head teacher or the chairman of the governing body (or the governor designated for the purposes of s.317) has been informed by the local authority that a registered pupil has special educational needs, secure that those needs are made known to all who are likely to teach him;
(c) secure that the teachers in the school are aware of the importance of identifying, and providing for, those registered pupils who have special educational needs (s.317(1) and (2)).

If a child for whom no statement is maintained (see **19 Statement of child's special educational needs**, below) is a registered pupil at a community, foundation or voluntary school, or a maintained nursery school, or a pupil referral unit, and special educational provision is made for him of which his parent has not previously been informed then, in the case of a pupil referral unit, the local education must ensure that the head teacher informs the parent of the special educational provision, and in any other case the parent must be so informed by the governing body (s.317A). A similar provision applies to special educational provision made during the course of nursery education (School Standards and Framework Act 1998, s.123(3A) and (3B)).

16 Identification and assessment of children with special educational needs

By virtue of s.321, a local authority must exercise their powers with a view to securing that of the children for whom they are responsible, they identify those among them who have special educational needs and for whom it is necessary for the authority to determine the special educational provision which any learning difficulty they may have calls for.

A local authority are responsible for a child if he is in their area and—
(a) he is a registered pupil at a maintained school or a maintained nursery school; or
(b) education is provided for him at a school which is not a maintained school but is so provided at the expense of the authority; or
(c) he does not come within (a) or (b) above but is a registered pupil at a school and has been brought to the authority's attention as having (or probably having) special educational needs; or
(d) he is not a registered pupil at a school, is not under the age of two or over compulsory school age and has been brought to their attention as having (or probably having) special educational needs.

(Any reference in this Note, therefore, to a child for whom an authority is responsible for the above purposes excludes a child under the age of two.)

S.322 provides that where it appears to a local authority that any Health Authority or a local authority could, by taking any specified action, help in the exercise of any of their functions under Part IV, they may request that help, specifying the action in question. Any authority who is so requested must comply with the request unless they consider that the help requested is not necessary for the purpose of the exercise by the local authority of those functions or, in the case of a Health Authority, if that authority consider it is not reasonable for them to comply with the request, having regard to the resources available to them for the purpose of the exercise of their functions.

17 Assessments of special educational needs

Ss.323, 329, 329A and Schedule 26 together with the Education (Special Educational Needs) (Wales) Regulations 2002 deal with the making of an assessment of the educational needs of a child. An assessment may be made–
  (a) on the initiative of the local authority (s.323);
  (b) at the request of the child's parent (s.329); or
  (c) at the request of a responsible body (s.329A).

Where the authority are of the opinion that a child for whom they are responsible has, or probably has, special educational needs which call for them to determine the special educational provision that should be made for him, they are under a duty to make an assessment of those needs (s.323(3)).

The procedure is for the authority (i) to decide whether to make an assessment, (ii) if they so decide, to make an assessment, and (iii) in appropriate cases, to make a statement. At each stage, certain consultation procedures must be followed.

Before making the assessment, however, they must serve notice on the child's parent informing him that they are considering whether to do so, of the procedure to be followed in making it, of the name of the officer from whom further information may be obtained, and of the parent's right to make representations, and submit written evidence, to the authority within a specified period of not less than 29 days beginning with the date on which the notice is served (s.323(1)). When the period specified has expired, the authority must decide whether or not to make an assessment, taking into account any representations made or evidence submitted to them (s.323(3)). If the authority decide to make an assessment, they must then inform the child's parent in writing of their decision and of their reasons for making it (s.323(4)). If the local authority decide not to assess the educational needs of the child concerned, they must notify his parent in writing of their decision (s.323(6)).

The Education (Special Educational Needs) (Wales) Regulations 2002 provide that, where the authority notify a parent of their decision to make an assessment, they must send copies of the notification to the health authority, if the child is registered at a school, the head teacher of that school, and if the child receives education from an early education provider, to the head of special educational needs at that provider (Reg. 6).

For the purpose of making an assessment, the authority must seek (Regs. 7 to 10)–
  (a) advice from the child's parents;
  (b) educational advice (usually obtained from the child's head teacher);
  (c) medical advice from a doctor designated or nominated by the health authority;
  (d) psychological advice from an educational psychologist; and
  (e) any other advice which they consider desirable in the case in question,
and consider the advice so obtained.

In addition to this advice, they must take into consideration representations made, or evidence submitted by, the child's parent (Reg. 11).

The authority may require the child's attendance at an examination. They must give notice to the parent of the purpose, time, and place of the examination and inform him of his right to be present at the examination (1996 Act, Sch. 26, para. 4). If a parent fails to bring the child for examination, then (unless the child is over compulsory school age at the appropriate time), the parent is guilty of an offence (Sch. 26, para. 5).

Under s.329, if the parent of a child for whom a local authority are responsible but for whom no statement (see below) is maintained by the authority asks the authority to arrange for an assessment to be made of the child's educational needs, and such an assessment has not been made within six months of the request, the authority must comply with the request if it is necessary for them to make such an assessment (s.329(1)). The procedure that will be followed in making such an assessment is the same as for the making of an assessment initiated by the local authority.

Responsible bodies, i.e., maintained schools, maintained nursery schools, pupil referral units, independent schools and non-maintained special schools, also have the right to ask the local authority to carry out an assessment or reassessment of a registered pupil to determine whether the child needs a statement of special educational needs, where no assessment or reassessment has taken place within the previous six months. The local authority must inform a parent of such a request and of the parent's rights before they decide whether or not they will comply with the request. The local authority must also inform a parent and the school of their decision concerning the request within six weeks of receiving the request and if they decide not to assess the child's educational needs, the authority must give the parent and the school the reason for the decision. The parent may appeal to the Special Educational Needs Tribunal for Wales against the decision not to assess the child's needs (s.329A and the Education (Special Educational Needs) (Wales) Regulations 2002, Reg. 12).

18 Assessment of educational needs of children under two years of age

In the case of a child under the age of two years, the authority may make an assessment with the parent's consent and must do so at the parent's request. The assessment may be made in such manner as the authority consider appropriate (s.331).

EDUCATION

19 Statement of child's special educational needs

Ss.324, 326, Schedule 27, and the Education (Special Educational Needs) (Wales) Regulations 2002 deal with the making of a statement of the special educational needs of a child where the authority are of the opinion that they ought to determine the special education provision that should be made for him, and with appeals against statements.

S.324(1) provides that, if, in the light of an assessment under s.323 of any child's educational needs and of any representations made by the child's parent in pursuance of Schedule 27, it is necessary for the local authority to determine the special educational provision which any learning difficulty he may have calls for, the authority will make and maintain a statement of his special educational needs.

The special educational provision specified in a statement under s.324 may include such information as may be prescribed. The statement must *inter alia* give details of the authority's assessment of the special educational needs of the child, and specify the special educational provision to be made for the purpose of meeting those needs. *Inter alia* the Education (Special Educational Needs) (Wales) Regulations 2002 provide that the statement must specify the special educational provision in terms of facilities and equipment, staffing arrangements, curriculum, or otherwise which the authority consider appropriate to meet those needs, and in particular, the type of school and name of a particular school which the authority consider would be appropriate for the child or whether the child should be provided with education otherwise than at school, and any additional non-educational provision to be made available (Reg. 16 and Schedule 2 to the Regulations). If however the child's parent has made suitable arrangements for the special educational provision to be made for the child (e.g., by paying for a place at an independent school), then the name of a school or institution does not have to be specified in the statement by the local authority (s.324(2) to (4A)).

Before making a statement, the authority must serve on the parent a notice accompanying a copy of the proposed statement and a written explanation of the effect of paragraph 4 of Schedule 27. Broadly, paragraph 4 of Schedule 27 makes provision for the procedure that will be followed if a parent on whom a copy of a proposed statement has been served under s.324 (see above) disagrees with any part of the proposed statement. Within 15 days of receiving a copy of the proposed statement, the parent may make representations to the authority and/or require the authority to arrange a meeting (or meetings) with an officer of the authority to discuss the statement. If, after such a meeting, the parent disagrees with any part of the assessment, he may within 15 days after any such meeting (or the last of such meetings) require the authority to arrange one or more further meetings with the person who gave the advice in connection with the assessment which is relevant to the subject of the disagreement.

The authority may, after considering the representations made to them, make the statement in the form originally proposed or make it in a modified form (Sch. 27, para. 5(2)). The parent must be informed of their decision and, if it was that a statement should be made, be served with a copy of the statement. The parent must be told of his right of appeal against the special educational provision specified in the statement and of the name of the person to whom he may apply for information and advice about the child's special educational needs (Sch. 27, para. 6).

20 Resolution of disputes and appeals

A local authority must make arrangements to avoid or resolve disagreements between authorities (on the one hand) and parents of children (on the other) about the exercise by authorities of special educational needs functions (s.332BA(1)). They must also make arrangements to avoid or resolve, in each relevant school, disagreements between parent and proprietor about the special educational needs provision made for a relevant child (s.332BA(2)). Such arrangements must be made known to parents of children in the local authority's area and to head teachers and proprietors of schools and other appropriate persons in that area, and must provide for the appointment of independent persons to facilitate the avoidance or resolution of disagreements (s.332BA(6), (3)).

These arrangements cannot affect a parent's entitlement to appeal to the Special Educational Needs Tribunal for Wales ("the Tribunal") (s.332BA(7)).

A tribunal known as the Special Educational Needs Tribunal was established under the 1996 Act. It is empowered to exercise the jurisdiction conferred on it by Part III of the 1996 Act (s.333(1)).

If the Tribunal makes an order, the local authority concerned must comply with the order within a prescribed period beginning on the date when the order was made (s.336A(1)).

An appeal can be made by a child as well as by the child's parents, on the same or different grounds (s.332ZA). The Welsh Ministers may by regulations provide for a child to have a person (known as a "case friend") to make representations on his behalf to avoid or resolve disputes with the local education authority, or to exercise a right of appeal on behalf of the child (s.332ZC). A local education authority must arrange for an independent advocacy service to be available in their area, and for a child or a case friend for a child to be referred to the service should they request it. For these purposes, "independent advocacy services" are services intended to provide advice and assistance to a child who is considering whether to appeal to the Tribunal, who has made or intends to make an appeal, or who is taking part in or intending to take part in dispute resolution arrangements (s.332BB).

21 Appeals against contents of statements

Under s.326, every local authority must make arrangements for enabling the parent of a child for whom they maintain a statement under s.324 (see above) to appeal, following the first or any subsequent assessment of the child's educational needs under s.323 (see **17 Assessment of special educational needs**, above), against the special educational provision specified in the statement. Such an appeal lies to the Tribunal (see above) (s.326(1)). S.326(1) and (1A) (inserted by the Special Educational Needs and Disability Act 2001, s.10 and Schedule 1, para 19) make it clear that there is a right to appeal to the Tribunal against a decision to name a particular school.

The Tribunal can either dismiss the appeal, order the authority to amend the statement, or order the authority to cease to maintain the statement (s.326(3)).

An appeal can be made by a child as well as by the child's parents, on the same or different grounds (s.332ZA).

22 Appeal against decision not to make a statement

If after making an assessment under s.323 (see **17 Assessment of special educational needs**, above) of the educational needs of any child for whom no statement is maintained under s.324 (see **19 Statement of child's special educational needs**, above), the local authority do not propose to make such a statement, they must give notice in writing to the child's parent of their decision. In such a case, the child's parent may appeal to the Tribunal against the decision. On such an appeal, the Tribunal may dismiss the appeal, or order the local authority to make and maintain such a statement, or remit the case to the authority for them to reconsider whether, having regard to any observations made by the Tribunal, it is necessary for the authority to determine the special educational provision which any learning difficulty the child may have calls for (s.325).

An appeal can be made by a child as well as by the child's parents, on the same or different grounds (s.332ZA).

23 Unopposed appeals

If a parent or a child has appealed to the Tribunal under s.325 (decision not to make a statement), ss.328, (reviews of educational needs), ss.329, 329A (assessment of needs), or paragraph 8(3) of Schedule 27 (substitution of named school for school named by parent) against the decision of a local authority and the authority notify the Tribunal that they will not oppose the appeal, then the appeal is treated as having been determined in favour of the parent and the Tribunal does not have to make an order (s.326A(1) to (3)). Before the end of a prescribed period the local authority must comply with the parent's wishes (s.326A(4)).

24 Mandatory review of statements

S. 328(1) provides that regulations may prescribe the frequency with which assessments under s.323 are to be repeated in respect of children for whom statements are maintained under s.324.

Also, where the parent of a child for whom a statement is maintained under s.324 (see **19 Statement of child's special educational needs**, above) asks the local authority arrange for an assessment to be made in respect of a child under s.323 (see **17 Assessment of special educational needs**, above) then, if such an assessment has not been made within the period of six months ending with the date of the request and it is necessary for the authority to make a further assessment under that section, the authority must comply with the request. If the authority determine not to comply with the request, they must give notice to that effect to the parent and the parent may appeal to the Tribunal against the determination. On such an appeal, the Tribunal may dismiss the appeal or order the authority to arrange for an assessment to be made in respect of the child under s.323 (s.328(2) to (4)).

An appeal can be made by a child as well as by the child's parents, on the same or different grounds (s.332ZA).

A statement under s.324 must be reviewed by the local authority (a) on the making of an assessment in respect of the child concerned under s.323 and (b) in any event, within the period of 12 months beginning with the making of the statement or, as the case may be, with the previous review (s.328(5)).

The Education (Special Educational Needs) (Wales) Regulations 2002 provide that where an authority carry out an annual review of a statement under s.328 (other than when the child is in his 10th year of compulsory education–see below), the authority must require the head teacher of the child's school to submit a report to them (Reg. 20). The head teacher, when preparing the report, must seek advice from the child's parent and any other person he considers appropriate and from any person the authority consider appropriate on a number of specified matters, including–

    (a) the child's progress towards meeting the objectives and targets specified in the statement;
    (b) the application of the provisions of the National Curriculum to the child;
    (c) progress made since the last statement as to the child's behaviour and attitude to learning;
    (d) whether the statement continues to be appropriate and whether any amendments should be made to it; and
    (e) whether the authority should cease to maintain the statement.

A meeting must be held by the head teacher, to which the above-mentioned persons must be invited together with a representative of the authority and a staff member who teaches the child if appropriate, at which the matters mentioned above will be discussed. The report will be completed after that meeting. When the head teacher submits his report, he must at the same time send copies to the child's parent, the persons from whom he sought advice, and other persons whom he or the authority think appropriate. The authority will review the statement in the light of the report and make recommendations as to the steps which ought to be taken, including whether the authority should amend or cease to maintain the statement (Reg. 20). Amendments made to the 1996 Act by the Special Needs and Disability Act 2001, s.10 and Schedule 1, Part 1, give a parent the right to a meeting with the local authority to discuss any proposed change to the statement following a review, and local authorities must make arrangements for a parent to express a preference for a maintained school when a change to the school referred to in a statement is proposed following a review.

Regulation 21 provides for the procedure where the review is the first review commenced where the child is in his 10th year of compulsory schooling. The authority are required to prepare a report. The procedure is similar to that provided by Regulation 20. A representative of the Careers Service will attend the meeting. The report will be completed after the meeting is held and the head teacher must send copies to the parents and other persons as he or the authority think appropriate. The authority will review the statement in the light of the report and any other information or advice they consider relevant and will make written recommendations and prepare a transition plan. Copies of the recommendations and the transition plan will be sent to the head teacher and persons mentioned above. A "transition plan" is a document which sets out the appropriate arrangements for a young person during the period beginning with the commencement of his tenth year of compulsory education and ending when aged 19, including arrangements for special educational provision and for any other necessary provision, for suitable employment and accommodation for leisure activities, and which will facilitate a satisfactory transition from childhood to adulthood.

Similar provision is made for the review of a statement of a child who does not attend a school (Reg.22).

25 Access of local authority to certain schools

Where a local authority maintain a statement for a child under s.324 (see **19 Statement of a child's special educational needs**, above) and, in pursuance of that statement, education is provided for the child at a school maintained by another local authority or at an independent school or alternative provision Academy, any person authorised by the first local authority is entitled to have access at any reasonable time to the premises of any such school to monitor the special educational provision made in pursuance of that statement for the child at the school (s.327).

26 Children under five years of age who may have special educational needs

S.332 provides that it is the duty of a Health Authority or a National Health Service trust who, in the course of exercising any of their functions in relation to a child under the age of five years, of whom they form the opinion that he has (or probably has) special educational needs to inform the child's parent of their opinion. After giving the parent an opportunity to discuss that opinion with an officer of the Health Authority or the trust, the Authority or trust must bring the matter to the attention of the appropriate local authority.

If the Health Authority or the trust are of the opinion that a particular voluntary organisation is likely to be able to give the parent advice or assistance with any special educational needs that the child may have, they must inform the parent accordingly (s.332(2)).

3: FURTHER AND HIGHER EDUCATION

27 Post-16 learning

The assessment of special educational needs under s.324 of the 1996 Act only applies to a child at school (i.e., up to the age of 16). However, the Learning and Skills Act 2000 ss.139A and 140 provide that, where a statement of special educational needs has been maintained under s.324, and the Welsh Ministers believe that the person concerned will leave school at the end of his last year of compulsory schooling to receive post-16 education or training or higher education, then an assessment must be conducted during the last year of compulsory schooling. The assessment will set out the person's needs and the provision required to meet them (s.140(4)).

Where a person is receiving, or is likely to receive, post-16 education or training, but does not have an existing statement of special educational needs (e.g., because learning difficulties have developed shortly before or after leaving school), the Welsh ministers have the power to conduct an assessment on anyone up to the age of 25 (s.140(3)).

4: APPROVAL OF INDEPENDENT SCHOOLS

28 Requirements for approval

The Education (Special Educational Needs) (Approval of Independent Schools) Regulations 1994 prescribe the requirements to be complied with by an independent school in Wales as a condition of its approval as a school suitable for the admission of children for whom statements of special educational needs are maintained under s.324, and while such an approval is in force. Included in the requirements for Wales are—

(a) a requirement that the proprietor of the school be a fit and proper person so to act;

(b) the teaching staff must be suitable and sufficient in number for the purposes of securing the provision of education appropriate to the ages, abilities, aptitudes, and special educational needs of the children at the school; and in this connection such teaching staff must include a head teacher;

(c) in the case of an independent school which is also a boarding school, there must be employed staff suitable and sufficient in number for the purposes of securing the proper care and supervision of the boarders, and of attending to their welfare and, for this purpose, a head of care must be appointed (the head of care must be a separate appointment from that of head teacher); and

(d) the premises of the school must, as a rule, conform to the standards prescribed by regulations from time to time in force under s.542 of the 1996 Act and applicable in the case of a school maintained by a local authority.

These requirements do not apply to independent schools which are Academies, city technology colleges or city colleges for the technology of the arts (Reg. 2A).

B: ENGLAND

29 Introduction

In England, statements of special educational needs for children (made under the Education Act 1996, s.324) and learning difficulty assessments for young people (made under the Learning and Skills Act 2000, s.139A) have been replaced by 0-25 Education, Health and Care plans (EHC plans) for both children and young people (made under the Children and Families Act 2014, Part 3).

30 When a child or young person has special educational needs

A child or young person has special educational needs if they have a learning difficulty or disability which calls for special educational provision to be made for them (Children and Families Act 2014, s.19).

A child of compulsory school age or a young person has a learning difficulty or disability if they have–

(a) a significantly greater difficulty in learning than the majority of others of the same age, or

(b) a disability which prevents or hinders them from making use of facilities of a kind generally provided for others of the same age in mainstream schools or mainstream post-16 institutions.

A child under compulsory school age has a learning difficulty or disability if they are likely to be within (a) or (b) above when of compulsory school age (or would be likely, if no special educational provision were made).

Note.–A child or young person does not have a learning difficulty or disability solely because the language in which they are or will be taught is different from the language they speak at home.

31 Identifying those with special educational needs

Local authorities have a duty to identify all those children and young people in their area who have or may have special educational needs or disabilities (Children and Families Act 2014, s.21).

In practise, children and young people can be brought to the attention of the local authority by their parents, their school or college, or by a social worker, doctor, health visitor, teacher, early years professional or a further education tutor.

Where a clinical commissioning group, NHS Trust or NHS Foundation Trust, in carrying out their functions in relation to a child under compulsory school age, are of the opinion that the child has or probably has special educational needs or a disability they must tell the child's parents and give them the chance to discuss this with an officer of the group or trust. They must then tell the appropriate local authority. They must also tell the parent if they think a particular voluntary organisation is likely to be able to give them advice or assistance in respect of their child's special educational needs or disability (s.22).

Once a child or young person has been identified by the authority, or brought to its attention by any person, as someone who has or may have special educational needs, then the local authority is responsible for that child or young person (s.24).

32 Assessment of needs

A child's parent, a young person or a person acting on behalf of a school or post-16 institution may request a local authority to undertake an EHC needs assessment i.e., an assessment of the educational, health care and social care needs of the child or young person (Children and Families Act 2014, s.36).

When a request is made, or a local authority otherwise becomes responsible for a child or young person, the authority must determine (in consultation with the child's parent, a young person) whether it may be necessary for special educational provision to be made for the child or young person in accordance with an EHC plan.

If it decides that it is not necessary for special educational provision to be made for the child or young person in accordance with an EHC plan it must notify the child's parent or the young person of the decision and of the reasons for making it.

If, having received and considered a request for an assessment, a local authority decides not to carry one out, the child's parents or the young person may appeal against that decision to the First-tier Tribunal (s.51). See **41**

Appeals and mediation, below.

Generally, decisions as to whether or not it is not necessary for special educational provision to be made for a child or young person in accordance with an EHC plan, or whether or not to conduct an EHC needs assessment, must be made by a local authority within 6 weeks (Special Educational Needs and Disability Regulations 2014, Regs. 4 and 5).

Detailed provision as to the people to be consulted, and matters to be taken into account, when undertaking EHC needs assessments are contained in the Special Educational Needs and Disability Regulations 2014, Part 2.

33 Preparation of education, health and care plan

If an assessment indicates that a child or young person requires an EHC plan for their special educational provision then the local authority is under a duty to make sure that an EHC plan is prepared and then implemented (Children and Families Act 2014, s.37). The EHC plan should specify the short and long term outcomes that it is designed to help the child or young person to achieve and the special educational, health and social care provision that will be made to support them (e.g., access to specialist teaching, speech and language therapy provision, and short breaks).

The child's parent or the young person must be consulted about the content of the plan during its preparation and may make representations about its content and request the authority to secure that a particular school or other institution is named in the plan (s.38). The school or institution must be–
- (a) a maintained school;
- (b) a maintained nursery school;
- (c) an Academy;
- (d) an institution within the further education sector in England;
- (e) a non-maintained special school; or
- (f) an institution approved by the Secretary of State (under s.41) being an independent special school or a special post-16 institutions.

The local authority must secure that the EHC plan names the school or other institution requested unless (s.39)–
- (g) it is unsuitable for the age, ability, aptitude or special educational needs of the child or young person concerned; or
- (h) the attendance of the child or young person at the requested school or other institution would be incompatible with either the provision of efficient education for others, or the efficient use of resources.

If either (g) or (h) applies, the authority must name a school or other institution which it thinks would be appropriate for the child or young person, or specify the type of school or other institution which it thinks would be appropriate for the child or young person.

If the child's parent or the young person have not specified a particular school or institution, the EHC plan must name the specific institution or type of institution that the local authority considers appropriate (s.40).

The detailed contents of EHC Plans are prescribed by the Special Educational Needs and Disability Regulations 2014.

34 Children and young people in detention

Where a child or young person under 19 is detained in a young offender institution, secure training centre or secure children's home, similar provisions for the assessment of needs and making of EHC plans are contained in the Children and Families Act 2014, Part 3 (ss.70-75).

The Special Educational Needs and Disability (Detained Persons) Regulations 2015 require local authorities to work together with other bodies to assess the education, health and care needs of children and young people with special educational needs, whether they are in or have been released from custody and to develop EHC plans where necessary, specifically relating to post-detention needs and provision.

35 Duty to implement EHC plan

Where an EHC plan is maintained for a child or young person, the local authority must make sure that the special educational provision set out in it is made, and the responsible commissioning body must arrange any specified health care provision, but they need not make that provision themselves if the child's parent or the young person makes alternative, suitable arrangements (Children and Families Act 2014, s.42).

Where a school or institution is named in an EHC plan, it must admit the child or young person (s.43).

Although the duty in relation to EHC plans only extends until a young person reaches the age of 25, a local authority has the power to maintain an EHC plan for a young person until the end of the academic year in which they become 25 (s.46).

36 Reviewing and re-assessing and ceasing to maintain EHC plans

A local authority must to review a child or young person's EHC plan at least every 12 months (Children and Families Act 2014, s.44). It must also reassess a plan if requested to do so by the child's parent or the young person, or by the governing body, proprietor or principal of the school, post-16 institution or other institution which the child or young person attends. It may also make a re-assessment of needs at any other time if it thinks it necessary.

A review will consider whether the provision in the EHC plan is meeting the child or young person's assessed needs and whether they are making progress towards the outcomes identified. A re-assessment means undertaking the assessment process again, e.g., when a child or young person's needs have changed significantly.

A local authority may only stop maintaining an EHC plan if they are no longer responsible for that child or young person, for example if the child or young person has moved to another area, or they consider that it is no longer necessary for the EHC plan to be maintained (s.45). When deciding whether a young person aged over 18 no longer requires the special educational provision specified in their EHC plan, a local authority must have regard to whether the educational or training outcomes specified in the plan have been achieved.

The detailed procedure for the review of EHC Plans is set out in the Special Educational Needs and Disability Regulations 2014.

37 Mainstream education

A local authority must secure that and EHC plan provides for a child or young person to be educated in a maintained nursery school, mainstream school or mainstream post-16 institution, unless that is incompatible with either the wishes of the child's parent or the young person, or the provision of efficient education for others and there are no reasonable steps that could be taken to overcome this (Children and Families Act 2014, s.33).

If the incompatibility cannot be overcome, the EHC plan can provide for the child or young person to be educated in a special school or a special post-16 institution such as an independent specialist provider. The Secretary of State may approve independent schools that are specially organised to make special educational provision for children with special educational needs, and special post-16 institutions (s.41 and the Special Educational Needs and Disability Regulations 2014, Part 5). Independent schools which have such approval may then be specified in an EHC plan.

Where a child or young person has special educational needs but does not have an EHC plan they must be educated in a maintained nursery school, mainstream school or mainstream college except where (s.34)–

(a) it is agreed that they are admitted to a special school or special post-16 institution to be assessed for an EHC plan;
(b) it is agreed that they are admitted to a special school or special post-16 institution following a change in their circumstances;
(c) they are admitted to a special school which is established in a hospital; or
(d) where they are admitted to a Special Academy whose Academy arrangements allow it to admit children or young people with special educational needs who do not have an EHC plan.

A child or young person (with or without an EHC plan) may be educated in an independent school, a non-maintained special school or a special post-16 institution, if the cost is not to be met by a local authority or the Secretary of State (ss.33(6), 34(3)).

Where a child with special educational needs is being educated in a maintained nursery school or a mainstream school, the school must enable the child to take part in the activities of the school with other children as far as is reasonably practicable and so long as this ensures the child gets the special educational provision they need, does not damage the education of the other children and does not mean an inefficient use of resources (s.35).

A local authority may arrange for special educational provision to be made for a child or young person otherwise than in a school, college or provider of relevant early years education, but only if it is satisfied that it would be inappropriate for provision to be made in one of those settings and they have consulted the child's parent or the young person (s.61).

A local authority may also arrange special education provision for a child or young person with an EHC plan outside England and Wales in an institution that specialises in providing for special educational needs (s.62).

38 Duties of schools, etc

The governing body of a school (or proprietor of an Academy or management committee of a pupil referral unit) must use their best endeavours to secure that the special educational provision that is called for by a pupil or student's special educational needs is made (Children and Families Act 2014, s.66).

Mainstream schools, (including Academy and nursery schools) must also ensure that they have a member of staff designated as Special Educational Needs (SEN) co-ordinator with responsibility for co-ordinating special educational provision for children and young people with special educational needs in their school (s.67). The co-ordinator must be a qualified teacher working at the school (or the head or acting head) and must hold a postgraduate qualification in special educational needs co-ordination known as "The National Award for Special Educational Needs Co-ordination" (Special Educational Needs and Disability Regulations 2014, Reg. 49).

Where a child or young person does not have an EHC plan, the governing bodies of maintained schools (or proprietor of an Academy or management committee of a pupil referral unit) must tell a child's parent, or the young person, when special educational provision is being made for the child or young person (s.68). (This does not need to happen if the child or young person has an EHC plan since parents of children with EHC plans and young people who have EHC plans will already be aware that special educational provision is being made.)

Governing bodies of maintained schools (and proprietors of Academies) must prepare a report containing "special educational needs information" i.e., information about the implementation of the governing body's or proprietor's policy for pupils at the school with special educational needs, and information as to the arrangements for the admission of disabled pupils to the school; the steps taken to prevent less favourable treatment of disabled pupils; the facilities provided to assist access to the school by disabled pupils; and the accessibility plan which schools must publish under the Equality Act 2010 (s.69 and the Special Educational Needs and Disability Regulations 2014, Sch. 1). The report must be published on the school's website (Reg. 52).

The Secretary of State must issue a Code of Practice giving guidance to local authorities, the governing bodies, proprietors, management committees, and other bodies on the exercise of their functions under the Children and Families Act 2014. These bodies must have regard to the Code when carrying out those functions, as must those who help them carry out those functions. The First-tier Tribunal must also have regard to any provision in the Code that it considers to be relevant to any question arising out of a special educational needs appeal with which it is dealing (s.77). The current code is the "Special Educational Needs and Disability Code of Practice: 0 to 25 years" which came into force on the 1st April 2015 and is available at–
<www.gov.uk/government/publications/send-code-of-practice-0-to-25>.

39 Advice and information

A local authority must publish information about the services they expect to be available for children and young people with special educational needs and disabilities. This is called the "local offer" and the authority must keep it under review and revise as necessary. The local offer must include information about the provision the local authority expects to be available both inside and outside its own area for children and young people with special educational needs and disabilities, whether or not they have EHC plans (Children and Families Act 2014, s.30).

The local offer must include–
(a) special educational, health care and social care provision;
(b) other educational provision;
(c) training provision;
(d) provision to assist in preparing children and young people for adulthood and independent living (such as finding employment or obtaining accommodation);
(e) arrangements for children and young people to travel to schools or post-16 education (including further education colleges, sixth form colleges, independent specialist providers and training providers); and
(f) providers of relevant early years education.

A local authority must also make arrangements for providing advice and information about special educational needs and disabilities to children, young people and the parents of children in its area with those needs, and to make the providers of the advice known to those people, schools, colleges and others they consider appropriate (s.32).

40 Fees, personal budgets and direct payments

Where a local authority is responsible for a child or young person with special educational needs, and special educational provision is made for him or her at a school, post-16 institution or provider of relevant early years education, the local authority must pay the fees for the education and training received where the institution is named in the EHC plan. This also applies if there is no EHC plan and the local authority is satisfied the child or young person requires special educational provision and that it is appropriate for them to receive it at the institution in question. Where board and lodging are provided for the child or young person at such a school or college or place where relevant early years education is provided, the local authority must pay those fees if it is satisfied that special educational provision cannot be made there unless board and lodging are provided (Children and Families Act 2014, s.63).

Where a local authority maintains an EHC plan, or has decided to make an EHC plan, for a child or young person it must, if asked to do so by the child's parent or the young person, prepare a personal budget for that child or young person (s.49). A personal budget is an amount available to secure particular provision set out in the EHC plan. It can take the form of direct payments which families can spend themselves, or notional budgets which they can devise with the local authority and which the local authority can spend on their behalf at their direction by arranging the provision in the EHC plan, or a combination of both. Detailed provision as to personal budgets and direct payments is contained in the Special Educational Needs (Personal Budgets) Regulations 2014.

41 Appeals and mediation

A child's parent or a young person have a right of appeal to the First-tier Tribunal in relation to the following matters (Children and Families Act 2014, s.51)–
(a) a decision of a local authority not to secure an EHC needs assessment for the child or young person;
(b) a decision of a local authority, following an EHC needs assessment, that it is not necessary for special educational provision to be made for the child or young person in accordance with an EHC plan;
(c) where an EHC plan is maintained for the child or young person–
    (i) the child's or young person's special educational needs as specified in the plan;
    (ii) the special educational provision specified in the plan;

(iii) the school or other institution named in the plan, or the type of school or other institution specified in the plan;

(iv) if no school or other institution is named in the plan, that fact;

(d) a decision of a local authority not to secure a re-assessment of the needs of the child or young person following a request to do so;

(e) a decision of a local authority not to secure the amendment or replacement of an EHC plan it maintains for the child or young person following a review or re-assessment;

(f) a decision of a local authority to cease to maintain an EHC plan for the child or young person.

After making a decision in relation to an assessment or a plan or after the plan is made, amended or replaced a local authority must inform parents and young people, of their right to mediation about educational, health and social care issues (s.52). Mediation is different to an appeal, in that it seeks to resolve matters through agreement between parents/young people and local authorities rather than through a judicial decision. The mediator must be independent, i.e., they cannot be an employee of a local authority.

When a parent or young person wishes to bring an appeal about a decision of a local authority, or the content of an EHC plan (but not an appeal only about the school or other institution named in an EHC plan or the type of school or other institution specified in an EHC plan, or the fact that an EHC plan does not name a school or other institution), they may do so *only* if an independent mediation adviser has provided them with information about mediation and how it might help and given them a certificate to the effect that (s.55)–

(a) they have decided not to pursue mediation;

(b) they have pursued and completed mediation and still wish to pursue an appeal.

Where a mediation certificate is required, the parent or young person must contact the mediation adviser within two months of receiving the written notice of the local authority's decision, and inform the him that they wish to appeal and whether or not they wish to pursue mediation (Special Educational Needs and Disability Regulations 2014, Reg. 33). Where they do want to go to mediation, this must generally be arranged within 30 days (Regs. 35 and 36).

C: PROVISIONS APPLICABLE TO ENGLAND AND WALES

42 Special schools: introduction

Special schools are schools which are specially organised to make special educational provision for pupils with special educational needs. Special schools are either maintained by local authorities, in which case they will be either community special schools or foundation special schools, an Academy, or will be non-maintained but approved by the Secretary of State under s.342.

The Secretary of State or Welsh Ministers may, under s.342, approve any school specially organised to make special educational provision for pupils with special educational needs, not being a community or foundation school, and may give their approval before or after the school is established. Regulations may make provision as to the requirements which are to be complied with as a condition of approval for such a school (see below). Regulations will also make provision for the requirements to be complied with by such a school while it is approved by virtue of the above-mentioned provisions and for the withdrawal of such a school, at the request of the proprietor or on the grounds that there has been a failure to comply with any prescribed requirement (s.342(4)).

In cases of urgency e.g., where it appears that a pupil at the school in question is suffering or is likely to suffer significant harm, the Secretary of State or Welsh Ministers may apply to a justice of the peace for an order for the withdrawal of approval of a non-maintained special school (s.342A) and the Non-Maintained Special Schools (England) Regulations 2015 make such provision (Reg. 5). This would have the practical effect of closing the school immediately. The justice of the peace may only make an order if it appears to him that a pupil at the school is suffering or likely to suffer significant harm.

The Education (Grant) Regulations 1990 allow the Secretary of State to make grants to persons other than local authorities to set up and maintain special schools (Reg. 6).

43 Maintained special schools

The School Organisation (Establishment and Discontinuance of Schools) (England) Regulations 2007 make provision in relation to the establishment, alteration and discontinuance of maintained special schools.

A local authority may publish proposals for the establishment of a community special school without the consent of the Secretary of State, if on the day when the competition notice is published, the authority have a current performance rating of 4 (Reg. 9). If the performance rating is 3 or 2, consent is needed. The matters to which the Secretary of State will have regard in determining whether to give consent include the extent of diversity among local schools, and–

(a) the range of curricular specialisms;

(b) the range of extended services;

(c) general standards of attainment;

(d) the range of special educational needs specialisms; and

(e) the availability of boarding or respite provision, within local schools. The manner in which proposals for the establishment, alteration or discontinuance of a maintained special school must be publicised, and the consultation requirements, are set out in the Regulations in detail.

The Education (Maintained Special Schools) (Wales) Regulations 1999 make provision in relation to the establishment, alteration and discontinuance of maintained special schools in Wales.

No child may be admitted to a maintained special school unless (a) a statement of special educational needs is maintained for him (see **19 Statement of child's special educational needs**, above); or (b) he is admitted for the purpose of assessing his needs and his admission has been agreed by the local authority, the school's head teacher, his parent, and every other person whose advice must be sought under the Education (Special Educational Needs) Regulations 2001 (see **17 Assessments of special educational needs**, above); or (c) he is admitted following a change in his circumstances with the agreement of the local authority, head teacher and parent (and his admission under this criterion must be reviewed at the end of the term). A child requiring hospital treatment may be admitted to a special school established in a hospital.

44 Standards in non-maintained special schools

The Schedule to the Non-Maintained Special Schools (England) Regulations 2015 provides for conditions of approval and continuing requirements for non-maintained special schools. These include approval by the Secretary of State of the number and categories of children provided for in the school and the special educational provision. No non-maintained special school may be conducted for profit. Provision must be made for the care and supervision of the health of the pupils (see the Note on **Health and Welfare in Schools**) and for every pupil attending the school to attend religious worship and receive religious education, or to be withdrawn from such worship or from receiving such education, in accordance with the wishes of their parents. Sixth form students may withdraw from collective worship. Arrangements must be in place to actively promote the fundamental British values of democracy, the rule of law, individual liberty, and mutual respect and tolerance of those with different faiths and beliefs. Pupils of secondary school age must also receive sex education, or be excused from such education at the request of their parents. In non-maintained schools, facilities must be provided for consumption of milk, meals, and refreshment; maintained special schools are subject to the provisions concerning school meals and milk set out in the Note on **Health and Welfare in Schools**. In addition, the governing body, in the case of a non-maintained school, must make such arrangements for safeguarding and promoting the welfare of the pupils at the school as will have been approved by the Secretary of State. All special schools maintained by local authorities must conform to the standards for school premises set out in the School Premises (England) Regulations 2012 and (for Wales) the Education (School Premises) Regulations 1999. These regulations relate to facilities, lighting and acoustics, playing space, etc.

45 Qualifications of teachers

The Education (School Teachers' Qualifications) (England) Regulations 2003 set out the qualifications required of teachers of the blind, or deaf, or blind and deaf in special schools.

46 Inspection of special schools

Special schools fall within the categories of schools for which the Chief Inspectors of England and Wales respectively are required to secure that regular inspections are made. For details of the requirements see the Note on **Education: Standards and Inspection: England and Wales**.

47 Information about special schools

The School Information (England) Regulations 2008 and the corresponding Welsh Regulations of 2011 set out for maintained special schools the information about schools and admission procedures required to be published under s.414 of the Education Act 1996. The Education (Non-Maintained Special Schools) (England) Regulations 2011 require the governing body of a non-maintained special school to publish a prospectus containing information about the school (Sch., Pt. 2, para 33).

48 The Disabled Persons (Services, Consultation and Representation) Act 1986

A local authority are required to seek the opinion of the appropriate officer as to whether a child is or is not a disabled person where they (Disabled Persons (Services, Consultation and Representation) Act 1986, s.5)–
  (a) have made a statement under s.7 of the 1981 Act, s.168 of the 1993 Act or s.324 of the 1996 Act, or have maintained an EHC plan under s.37 of the Children and Families Act 2014 in respect of a child at the time when it is due to be reviewed (or, if it is has been reviewed, when they institute a re-assessment of it); or
  (b) make a statement or EHC plan in respect of a child over 14 years of age; or
  (c) maintain a statement or EHC plan in respect of a child whom the appropriate officer has considered not to be a disabled person pursuant to (a) above but they have reason to believe the child's mental or physical condition has since significantly changed.
The appropriate officer means the officer appointed for the purposes of the section by the local authority for

the area in which the child is ordinarily resident.

Where the opinion has been given that the child is a disabled person (in which case he is then called a "disabled student") and it appears that he will cease to receive full-time education either in school or in a further education establishment on a particular date, and will be under the age of 19 years and 8 months before that date, the local authority responsible for the school which the child is about to leave, or which he attended immediately before he ceased to receive full-time education at school, must notify the appropriate officer in writing not more than 12 months nor less than 8 months before that date. The appropriate officer must then arrange for the social services authority to assess the needs of the disabled person in accordance with the welfare enactments.

S.6 of the 1986 Act requires local authorities, for the purpose of performing their duties under s.5, to keep under review the dates when children opined to be disabled are expected to cease to receive full-time education at school or, as the case may be, at a further education establishment.

49 Authorities

Statutes–

Disabled Persons (Services, Consultation and Representation) Act 1986

Education Act 1996

Education and Inspections Act 2006

Equality Act 2010

Learning and Skills Act 2000

School Standards and Framework Act 1998

School Standards and Organisation (Wales) Act 2013

Special Educational Needs and Disability Act 2001

Statutory Instruments–

Education (Grant) Regulations 1990, as amended (S.I. 1990 No. 1989, 1991 No. 1975, 1994 No. 2102, 1997 Nos. 678 and 2961, and 1998 No. 86)

Education (Maintained Special Schools) (Wales) Regulations 1999, as amended (S.I. 1999 No. 1780, 2009 No. 48, and 2011 No. 190)

Education (School Premises) Regulations 1999 (S.I. 1999 No. 2)

Education (Special Educational Needs) (Approval of Independent Schools) Regulations 1994, as amended (S.I. 1994 No. 651, 1998 No. 417, 2001 No. 783, 2002 No. 2072, 2005 No. 2929, 2008 No. 1701, and 2010 Nos. 1142 and 2431) (applies only to Wales)

Education (Special Educational Needs) (Information) (Wales) Regulations 1999 (S.I. 1999 No. 1442)

Education (Special Educational Needs) (Wales) Regulations 2002, as amended (S.I. 2002 No. 152, 2003 No. 1717, and 2010 No. 1142)

Education (School Teachers' Qualifications) (England) Regulations 2003, as amended (S.I. 2003 No. 1662, 2007 No. 2782, 2009 No. 3156, and 2012 Nos. 431 and 1736)

Non-Maintained Special Schools (England) Regulations 2015 (S.I. 2015 No. 728)

School Information (England) Regulations 2008, as amended (S.I. 2008 No. 3093 2010 Nos. 1172 and 1874, 2012 Nos. 979 and 1124, 2013 Nos. 758 and 2912, 2014 No. 2103, and 2015 No. 902)

School Information (Wales) Regulations 2011 (S.I. 2011 No. 1944)

School Organisation (Establishment and Discontinuance of Schools) (England) Regulations 2007, as amended (S.I. 2007 Nos. 1288, 3224 and 3464, 2009 Nos. 1556 and 2984, 2010 Nos. 1172 and 1941, 2012 No. 956, and 2013 No. 235)

School Premises (England) Regulations 2012 (S.I. 2012 No. 1943)

Special Educational Needs and Disability (Detained Persons) Regulations 2015 (S.I. 2015 No. 62)

Special Educational Needs and Disability Regulations 2014, as amended (S.I. 2014 Nos. 1530 and 2096, and 2015 Nos. 359 and. 971)

Special Educational Needs (Personal Budgets) Regulations 2014, as amended (S.I. 2014 Nos. 1652 and 2096)

Special Educational Needs (Provision of Information by Local Authorities) (Wales) Regulations 2002, as amended (S.I. 2002 No. 157, 2005 No. 2913, and 2010 No. 1142)

EDUCATION: STANDARDS AND INSPECTION
ENGLAND AND WALES

1 Introduction

This Note covers the provisions as to the standards of performance expected of schools and those as to intervention in, and special measures for, schools which are underperforming. The inspection regime for schools, local authorities and other educational bodies are also covered.

A: SCHOOL STANDARDS

2 Duties in relation to high standards

Local authorities have a specific duty to promote high standards. They must exercise their functions with a view to promoting the fulfilment by every child of his educational potential and, in the case of local authorities in England, with a view to ensuring fair access to educational opportunity, as well as with a view to promoting high standards (Education Act 1996 Act, s.13A, as substituted by the Education and Inspections Act 2006 s.1). This section applies to—

(a) children of compulsory school age (whether at school or otherwise); and

(b) children under or over that age who are registered as pupils at schools maintained by the authority.

3 Provisions with respect to England

School performance targets are set by the governing bodies of every maintained school which provides education for Key Stage 2 pupils, Key Stage 4 pupils, or pupils with special educational needs (Education (School Performance Targets) (England) Regulations 2004 (as amended)) (see the Note on **Schools: Curriculum and Exams: England and Wales** at para 14 **School performance targets**). The local authority must send a list of the targets for each school in their area to the Secretary of State by the 31st January in each school year.

4 Provisions with respect to Wales

A local authority in Wales must, every three years, prepare and publish a plan setting out the authority's strategy for discharging its functions in relation to children and relevant young persons (Children Act 2004 s.26, and the Children and Young People's Plan (Wales) Regulations 2007). The content of a plan is not prescribed but will be determined by each authority having regard to guidance issued by the Welsh Ministers.

The Welsh Ministers have a power to issue guidance to school authorities setting out how they are to improve the standards of education in schools (School Standards and Organisation (Wales) Act 2013, s.33). School authorities have a duty to comply with any such guidance (s.34).

Part 4 (ss. 84 to 87) of the 2013 Act establishes a statutory requirement for local authorities to have Welsh in education strategic plans in place. A Welsh in education strategic plan is a plan which contains (s.84)—

(a) a local authority's proposals on how it will carry out its education functions to improve the planning of the provision of education through the medium of Welsh in its area and improve the standards of Welsh medium education and of the teaching of Welsh;

(b) the local authority's targets for improving the planning of the provision of Welsh medium education in its area and for improving the standards of that education and of the teaching of Welsh;

(c) a report on the progress made to meet the targets contained in the previous plan or previous revised plan.

Each local authority will be required to submit its Welsh in education strategic plan to Welsh Ministers for approval (s.85). S.86 further provides that the Welsh Ministers may require a local authority to carry out an assessment of the demand among parents in its area for Welsh medium education for their children. The Welsh in Education Strategic Plans and Assessing Demand for Welsh Medium Education (Wales) Regulations 2013 provide for the circumstances in which a local authority will be required to carry out a Welsh medium education assessment and the questions and information to be included in such an assessment. Welsh Ministers have the power to make regulations which will make further provisions on matters such as the form and content of a Welsh in education strategic plan, its timing and duration, keeping the plan under review, consultation and submission of the plan for approval to the Welsh Ministers and its publication. Regulations may also make provision enabling a joint plan by two or more local authorities (s.87). The Welsh in Education Strategic Plans and Assessing Demand for Welsh Medium Education (Wales) Regulations 2013 provide, *inter alia*, for the duration of the plan; the form and content of the plan; the date for submission of the plan to the Welsh Ministers for approval; and, the date on which the plan must be published.

The governing body of a maintained school must draw up a school development plan in order to assist it to exercise its responsibility for conducting the school with a view to promoting high standards of educational achievement (Education (School Development Plans) (Wales) Regulations 2014, Reg. 3). The matters which must be covered by a plan are set out in the Schedule to the Regulations. The governing body must monitor and review the progress made by the school during each school year against the school's development plan and must revise the plan at least annually and in any event no later than the date on which it was last prepared or revised; and also following an inspection by Her Majesty's Inspectorate for Education and Training Wales (Reg. 6).

5 School improvement partners

A local authority in England must appoint, in relation to each of their maintained schools, an accredited person (to be known as a "school improvement partner") to provide advice to the governing body and head teacher of the school with a view to improving standards at the school (Education and Inspections Act 2006, s.5).

6 Special measures

The School Inspections Act 1996 (the Inspections Act) (as amended by the Education Act 2002, Sch 21) provides for the special measures that may be taken in relation to certain schools which are failing to give an acceptable standard of education. Broadly, if a report either after a s.10 inspection of a school (see the Note on **Schools: Curriculum and Exams: England and Wales**) or on an inspection of a school by a member of the inspectorate under s.14 of the Inspections Act is sent to the appropriate authority stating that the inspector or, as the case may be, the member of the inspectorate is of the opinion that special measures are required to be taken in relation to a school (i.e., a community, foundation or voluntary school or community or foundation special school, or maintained nursery school), the appropriate authority (as defined) must prepare a written statement of the action they propose to take in the light of the report and the period in which they propose to take it (s.17). Regulations (under s.19) may make provision for monitoring the measures taken by the school for improving the standard of education at the school in question. Under such regulations, the Secretary of State may also require the Chief Inspector to conduct further inspections. If a school, as a result of any such further inspection, is found to require special measures and the grounds are substantially different from the earlier inspection, the regulations may make provision corresponding to any of the provisions made by Chapter II of Part I of the Inspections Act.

7 Intervention in schools by local authorities in England

In England, a maintained school becomes eligible for intervention if the governing body has received a formal performance standards and safety warning notice and has failed satisfactorily to comply with the notice within "the compliance period" (Education and Inspections Act 2006, s.60). The compliance period is defined as beginning on the day on which the warning notice is given (or, where the governing body make representations in writing to the Chief Inspector against the warning notice, from the date the warning notice is confirmed by him) and ending 15 working days from that date (s.60(10)). The local authority must have provided reasonable notice to the governing body that it proposed to exercise its powers of intervention. The school is not eligible for intervention if the governing body of the school has made a representation to the Chief Inspector and the warning notice has not been confirmed by him under.

The circumstances in which a local authority may give a warning notice to a maintained school are set out in s.60(2). A local authority may issue a warning when standards of pupil performance are unacceptably low; or when there is a serious breakdown in management or governance so as to impair standards; or when safety of pupils or staff is threatened. Clarification of the standards of pupil performance is set out in s.60(3). A warning notice may also be issued where an order about teachers' pay and conditions has not been complied with (s.60A).

A warning notice must set out the reasons for the warning, the action to be taken by the governing body, the compliance period and the action that the local authority plans to take should the governing body fail to take the necessary action set out in the warning notice (s.60(4)).

There is a duty on local authorities to inform the governing body of the school that they are able to make representations to the Chief Inspector within the compliance period against the issuing of the warning notice (s.60(5)).

The local authority must give copies of the formal warning notice, at the same time as issuing it to the governing body of the school, to the Chief Inspector, the head teacher, in the case of a Church of England school or a Roman Catholic Church school, the appropriate diocesan authority and, in the case of a foundation or voluntary school, the person who appoints the foundation governors (s.60(6)).

The governing body of a school that has received a warning notice from the local authority must submit a written representation to the Chief Inspector within the compliance period. This written representation should also be copied to the local authority (s.60(7)).

The Chief Inspector must consider any representations made by a governing body regarding the issuing of a warning notice (s.60(8)). The Chief Inspector must give written notice to the governing body of his decision whether or not the warning notice is justified. This notice should also be copied to the local authority and other individuals specified by the Secretary of State in guidance (s.60(9)).

In England, a maintained school is a community, foundation or voluntary school; a community or foundation special school; or a maintained nursery school (Education and Inspections Act 2006, s.59).

8 School requiring significant improvement in England

A maintained school in England is eligible for intervention if, following an inspection, the Chief Inspector has given a notice under s.13(3)(a) of the Education Act 2005 that the school requires significant improvement, as defined by s.44 of that Act (Education and Inspections Act 2006, s.61).

Where there is a further inspection, a school is only eligible for intervention under s.61 if, following the inspection, the notice to the Secretary of State has not been superseded by either a report that the school no longer requires significant improvement or an additional notice to the Secretary of State that the school requires special measures (s.61(b)).

9 School requiring special measures in England

A maintained school in England is eligible for intervention if, following an inspection, the Chief Inspector has given a notice under s.13(3)(a) of the Education Act 2005 that the school requires special measures, as defined by s.44 of the 2005 Act (see 6: SCHOOLS CAUSING CONCERN, below) (Education and Inspections Act 2006, s.62).

Where there is a further inspection, a school is only eligible for intervention under s.62 if, following the inspection, the notice to the Secretary of State has not been superseded by a report stating that the school no longer requires special measures (s.62(b)).

10 Powers available to a local authority on intervention in England

Local authorities in England may direct the governing body of a maintained school to take certain steps if the school is eligible for intervention, including requiring the governing body to contract with another party for the provision of advisory services to the governing body; collaborate with the governing body of another school; collaborate with a further education college; or create or join a federation. This power does not apply if the school has not complied with a formal warning issued by the local authority under s.60A (Education and Inspections Act 2006, s.63(1)).

Before using their powers, the local authority must consult the governing body of the school; in the case of a church school, foundation or voluntary, the appropriate diocesan authority and in the case of other foundation or voluntary schools, the body that appoints the foundation governors (s.63(2)).

If a school has not complied with a warning notice issued by the local authority and therefore becomes eligible for intervention, s.63(3) provides that the power of the local authority to require a governing body to enter into arrangements can only be exercised within two months of the end of the compliance period.

Local authorities in England have the power to appoint additional governors at a maintained school which is subject to special measures, in need of significant improvement or at which the governing body have not complied with a formal warning, provided the Secretary of State has not already appointed additional governors under s.67 (see 11 Powers of the Secretary of State to intervene in schools in England, below) (s.64).

Local authorities have the power to appoint a specially constituted governing body in place of the existing governors at a school that is eligible for intervention. The specially constituted governing body is known as an "Interim Executive Board"; and the power may only be exercised with the consent of the Secretary of State and the governing body must be given written notice of the exercise of the power. Before using the power the local authority must consult the governing body of the school; in the case of a church school, foundation or voluntary, the appropriate diocesan authority and in the case of other foundation or voluntary schools, the body that appoints the foundation governors (s.65).

Local authorities may suspend a school's right to a delegated budget if the school is eligible for intervention under the 2006 Act (s.66).

11 Powers of the Secretary of State to intervene in schools in England

In England, the Secretary of State may appoint additional governors to the governing body of a school that is eligible for intervention (Education and Inspections Act 2006, s.67(1)).

Before using this power, the Secretary of State must consult the local authority; the governing body of the school; in the case of a foundation or voluntary school which is a Church of England or Roman Catholic school, the appropriate diocesan authority; and in the case of other foundation or voluntary schools, the person or persons who appoint the foundation governors (s.67(2)).

The Secretary of State has the power to direct the closure of a school if that school requires special measures (under s.62); has failed to comply with a performance standards or safety warning notice (issued under s.60), or has been identified as requiring significant improvement by the Chief Inspector and has been issued with a notice to improve (s.68).

The Secretary of State may appoint a governing body to consist of interim executive members called an "Interim Executive Board" to conduct a school that is eligible for intervention in place of the normal governing body.

The Secretary of State may direct a local authority to consider giving a warning notice to a governing body if he thinks that there are reasonable grounds for it to do so. The Secretary of State's direction must be in writing and the authority must give a written response, copied to Her Majesty's Chief Inspector of Schools within 10 working days. If the authority agree to issue a warning notice they must do so – copied to the Secretary of State – within five working days of their response to the Secretary of State and withdraw any previous warning notice given to the governing body under s.60. If the authority decides not to issue a warning notice they must set out the reasons for the decision in their response to the Secretary of State and he may then direct them to give the warning notice (s.69A). There is a similar power for the Secretary of State to direct a local authority to consider giving a teachers' pay and conditions warning notice to a governing body (s.69B).

12 Duty of local authority to have regard to guidance in England

Local authorities must have regard to guidance issued by the Secretary of State when exercising any of their functions as to intervention in schools (Education and Inspections Act 2006, s.72).

13 Intervention in schools in Wales

The School Standards and Organisation (Wales) Act 2013 sets out the following grounds for intervention in the conduct of a maintained school (s.2)–

1 The standards of performance of pupils at the school are unacceptably low. For this purpose, the standards of performance of pupils are low if they are low by reference to any one or more of the following–
   (a) the standards that the pupils might in all the circumstances reasonably be expected to attain;
   (b) where relevant, the standards previously attained by them;
   (c) the standards attained by pupils at comparable schools.
2 There has been a breakdown in the way the school is managed or governed.
3 The behaviour of pupils at the school or any action taken by those pupils or their parents is severely prejudicing, or is likely to severely prejudice, the education of any pupils at the school.
4 The safety of pupils or staff of the school is threatened (whether by a breakdown of discipline or otherwise).
5 The governing body or head teacher has failed, or is likely to fail, to comply with a duty under the Education Acts.
6 The governing body or head teacher has acted, or is proposing to act, unreasonably in the exercise of any of its or his or her functions under the Education Acts.
7 Her Majesty's Chief Inspector of Education and Training in Wales has given a notice under the Education Act 2005, s.37(2) that the school requires significant improvement and that notice has not been superseded by–
   (a) his giving notice that special measures are required to be taken in relation to the school, or
   (b) a subsequent inspection report stating that the school no longer requires significant improvement.
8 Her Majesty's Chief Inspector of Education and Training in Wales has given a notice under the Education Act 2005, s.37(2) that special measures are required to be taken in relation to the school, and that notice has not been superseded by a subsequent inspection report stating that the school no longer requires special measures.

If one or more of grounds 1 to 6 exist, the local authority may give a warning notice to the governing body of the school specifying (s.3)–
   (a) the grounds for intervention;
   (b) the reasons why the authority is satisfied that the grounds exist;
   (c) the action the authority requires the governing body to take in order to deal with the grounds for intervention;
   (d) the period within which the action is to be taken by the governing body ("the compliance period");
   (e) the action the authority is minded to take if the governing body fails to take the required action.

If after having been given a warning notice the governing body of the school has failed to comply, or secure compliance, with the notice to the authority's satisfaction within the compliance period, then the local authority may intervene in the school.

Note.– If a local authority–
   (a) if it is satisfied that grounds 7 or 8 exist and not less than 10 days have elapsed since the giving of the notice referred to in those grounds; or
   (b) one or more of grounds 1 to 6 exist and that there is a related risk to health and safety of any person that calls for urgent action,
then it does not have to comply with the warning notice procedure before exercising its powers of intervention.

The Welsh Ministers also have power to intervene if the local authority fails to act (s.11).

14 Powers available on intervention in Wales

Where a power of intervention applies (see **13 Intervention in schools in Wales**, above), an authority may exercise the following powers contained in the School Standards and Organisation (Wales) Act 2013. They may–
   (a) direct the governing body of a school to make arrangements or enter into a contract for the provision of advisory services or to collaborate in accordance with the Education (Wales) Measure 2011, s.5(2), so as to improve the school's performance (s.5);
   (b) appoint additional governors to the governing body of a maintained school (s.6);
   (c) appoint a specially constituted governing body (known as an "interim executive board") in place of the existing governors to take over the running of the school (s.7);
   (d) suspend a school's right to a delegated budget (s.8); or

(e) issue such directions to the governing body or head teacher of a school it maintains as it thinks appropriate, and take any other steps (s.9).

If the Welsh Ministers intervene, they have similar powers to (a), (b), (c) and (e) above (ss.12-14, 17), and may also–

(e) direct that schools be federated (s.15); or

(f) direct closure of a school (s.16).

15 Powers of the Welsh Ministers to intervene in local authorities

The School Standards and Organisation (Wales) Act 2013 sets out the following grounds for intervention by the Welsh Ministers in the conduct by a local authority of its education functions. That the local authority (s.21)–

(1) has failed, or is likely to fail, to comply with a duty that is an education function;

(2) has acted, or is proposing to act, unreasonably in the exercise of an education function; or

(3) is failing, or is likely to fail, to perform an education function to an adequate standard.

If one or more of the grounds exists the Welsh Ministers must follow a similar warning notice procedure as for intervention in schools. If action is still needed following a warning notice the Welsh Ministers may–

(a) direct the local authority to obtain advisory services from a third party (s.24);

(b) direct a local authority to use the services of a third party to carry out its functions (s.25);

(c) direct that a local authority's functions are carried out by the Welsh Ministers or by a person nominated by them (s.26);

(d) issue such directions to the local authority as it thinks appropriate, and take any other steps (s.28).

Directions under (b) or (c) may relate to any of the local authority's education functions, not just those to which the power to intervene relates (s.27).

16 Powers of the Secretary of State to intervene in local authorities

S.497A of the Education Act 1996 (inserted by the School Standards and Framework Act 1998, s.8 and widened in scope by the Education Act 2002, s.60) gives the Secretary of State additional powers to secure the proper performance of a local authority's education functions. If they are satisfied (either on a complaint by an interested person or otherwise) that an authority is failing in any respect to perform any educational functions to an adequate standard, or at all, they may direct the authority or an officer of the authority to secure that that function is performed in such a way as to achieve the objectives specified in the direction. They may also give the authority or an officer such directions as they think expedient and such directions may require that any contract or other arrangements made by the authority with that person contains such terms and conditions as may be specified.

Where the Secretary of State is contemplating giving directions to a local authority, the authority must give them and any person authorised by them for the purpose all such assistance as they are reasonably able to give (1998 Act s.497AA, inserted by the 2002 Act, s.61).

17 Education action zones and education action forums

S.10 of the 1998 Act (as amended by the Education Act 2002, s.187 and Sch 15) permits the Secretary of State to establish education action zones, which are local clusters of schools working together to improve standards. An education action zone will initially be set up for three years, but may be extended for a further two years by order of the Secretary of State. A school may not be included in an action zone without the consent of the governing body.

An order establishing an action zone must also provide for the establishment of an Education Action Forum for the zone. This is to be a corporate body, and its members must include one person appointed by the governing body of each of the participating schools (unless a governing body chooses not to make such an appointment), and one or two persons appointed by the Secretary of State (unless he chooses not to appoint) (1998 Act s.11A, inserted by 2002 Act, s.187 and Sch 15). An Education Action Forum may add to the zone any eligible school (i.e., a maintained school, a nursery school, a pupil referral unit, or an independent school (1998 Act s.10(1A), as so inserted) or any new school which has a temporary governing body. A school may only be added in accordance with procedural requirements specified in Regulations and with the consent of the governing body of the School and the Secretary of State (s.11B, as so inserted). A participating school may be removed from the Education Action Zone in accordance with specified procedures and with the consent of the Secretary of State (s.11C, as so inserted). Any changes must be notified to the Secretary of State (s.11D, as so inserted). Schedule 1 to the 1998 Act, together with the Education Action Forum (Proceedings) Regulations 1998 set out the manner in which a Forum must conduct its affairs. The main object of a Forum is the improvement of educational standards at each school participating in the zone concerned. In particular, a Forum may discharge on behalf of a school's governing body specific functions relating to the conduct of that school. A Forum may also, with the consent of the Secretary of State, carry on any other activities which it considers will promote the provision of, or access to, education whether in a participating school or otherwise (s.12(1A), as so inserted).

18 Home-School agreements

Ss.110 and 111 of the School Standards and Framework Act 1998 make provision for home-school arrangements, which are defined as agreements specifying–

    (a) the school's aims and values;

    (b) the school's responsibilities with regard to the education of its pupils;

    (c) the responsibilities which the parents of pupils are expected to discharge; and

    (d) the school's expectations as regards the conduct of its pupils.

Every school is required to adopt a home-school agreement for the school, together with a "parental declaration", which is a document to be used by parents to record that they take note of the school's aims, values and responsibilities and that they acknowledge and accept the parental responsibilities and the school's expectations of its pupils. A school's governing body must take reasonable steps to secure that the parental declaration is signed by every registered parent of a pupil at the school who is or qualifying school age. However, a governing body is not required to seek a parent's signature if, having regard to any special circumstances relating to the parent or pupil in question, they consider that it would be inappropriate to do so.

Where a governing body consider that a pupil has sufficient understanding of the home-school agreement as it relates to him, they may invite him to sign the parental declaration instead of his parent.

Before adopting a home-school agreement or parental declaration, the governing body must consult parents of registered pupils together with such other persons a may be prescribed.

S.111 requires a school's governing body to have regard to any guidance given from time to time by the Secretary of State. Neither a governing body nor a local authority may ask a parent to sign a parental declaration before their child is admitted to a school, or make signing of a declaration a condition of a child's admission to a school. Similarly, a child may not be excluded from a school because of a parent's failure to sign a declaration.

A breach of a home-school agreement does not give rise to any legal liability.

B: SCHOOL INSPECTORS AND INSPECTIONS

I: INTRODUCTION

19 Introduction

The Education Act 2005 and the Education and Inspections Act 2006 make provision for the inspection of schools. The Learning and Skills Act 2000 extended inspection to the further education sector.

Under s.I of the Act, Her Majesty may by Order in Council appoint a person to be Her Majesty's Chief Inspector of Schools (the Chief Inspector) in England and others to serve as HM Inspectors (HMI) on his staff. Under s.52 of the 2000 Act, the Secretary of State may appoint a Chief Inspector of Adult Learning.

For inspection of independent schools, see the Note on **Independent Schools** and for inspection of schools in Scotland, see the Note on **Schools: Scotland**.

2: SCHOOL INSPECTORS AND SCHOOL INSPECTIONS: ENGLAND

20 The Office for Standards in Education, Children's Services and Skills

The Office for Standards in Education, Children's Services and Skills, is established by s.112 of the Education and Inspections Act 2006. Schedule 11 sets out in detail how the Office will be constituted: that it will comprise a chairman and between five and 10 members (all to be appointed by the Secretary of State) and the Chief Inspector. The Schedule contains further detail about the terms of appointment of the chairman and members other than the Chief Inspector, including provision for their remuneration and the payment of pensions, allowances and gratuities

The Office has the function of determining the strategic priorities, objectives and targets for the Chief Inspector in connection with the performance of his functions, and to secure that the Chief Inspectors functions are performed efficiently and effectively.

21 Her Majesty's Chief Inspector of Education, Children's Services and Skills

The office of Her Majesty's Chief Inspector of Education, Children's Services and Skills (the Chief Inspector) is established by s.113 of the Education and Inspections Act 2006 which also abolished the office of Her Majesty's Chief Inspector of Schools in England. The Chief Inspector's terms of appointment are determined by the Secretary of State. A term of office may be no more than five years, though a previous post-holder is not barred from re-appointment. Further provisions about the Chief Inspector and other inspectors are set out in s.115 and Sch.12.

The Office for Standards in Education, Children's Services and Skills and Her Majesty's Chief Inspector of Education, Children's Services and Skills (Allocation of Rights and Liabilities) Order 2007 makes provision for the allocation of rights and liabilities as between the Office and the Chief Inspector.

The Chief Inspector has a general duty to keep the Secretary of State informed about the quality and standards, improvement, user-focus and efficiency and effectiveness of the activities within his remit. He must provide information or advice on matters relating to those activities at the Secretary of State's request and may give advice to the Secretary of State of his own volition. Further functions may be assigned him by the Secretary of State (Education and Inspections Act 2006, s.118).

The Chief Inspector must perform his functions in such a way as to encourage improvement in the performance of the activities within his remit. The Chief Inspector must discharge his functions efficiently and effectively and with regard to the needs of users of services within his remit (s.119).

Any of the functions of the Chief Inspector may be fulfilled by: any Her Majesty's Inspector (HMI); any other member of the staff of the Office for Standards in Education, Children's Services and Skills; or any additional inspector (Education and Inspections Act 2006, Sch. 12, paras. 9, 11 and 12). The exceptions to this are that a report concluding that special measures are required must be personally authorised by the Chief Inspector or an HMI specifically authorised to do so and that an additional inspector cannot conduct an inspection unsupervised by an HMI unless he has previously conducted such an inspection to the satisfaction of an HMI.

22 Reports made by the Chief Inspector

For the purposes of the law of defamation, a report made by Her Majesty's Chief Inspector of Education, Children's Services and Skills (the Chief Inspector) is privileged unless shown to have been made with malice. A report may be published solely by electronic means (Education and Inspections Act 2006, s.151).

The Chief Inspector may (to the extent he considers it appropriate) combine the reports of inspections carried out under two or more of his inspection functions, and to produce them as a combined report. He can also make a combined report which includes a report made by another person (s.152).

23 Matters to be covered in a report

Under s.5 of the Education Act 2005 (duty to inspect certain schools in England at particular intervals), a report by Her Majesty's Chief Inspector of Education, Children's Services and Skills (the Chief Inspector) must cover (Education Act 2005, s.5 as amended)–
  (a) the quality of the education provided in the school;
  (b) how far the education provided in the school meets the needs of the range of pupils, including in particular the needs of those with a disability and those with special educational needs;
  (c) the educational standards achieved in the school;
  (d) the quality of the leadership in and management of the school, including whether the financial resources made available to the school are managed effectively;
  (e) the spiritual, moral, social and cultural development of the pupils at the school;
  (f) the contribution made by the school to the well-being of those pupils; and
  (g) the contribution made by the school to community cohesion.

24 Use of information by the Chief Inspector

The information obtained in connection with one of Her Majesty's Chief Inspector of Education, Children's Services and Skills' functions may be used in connection with any other of his functions (Education and Inspections Act 2006, s.153).

25 Annual reports to the Secretary of State

The Chief Inspector must make an annual report to the Secretary of State, who in turn must lay this report before Parliament. The Chief Inspector has the power to make such other reports as he considers appropriate. He may publish any report he makes in whatever manner he considers appropriate (Education and Inspections Act 2006, s.121).

26 Inspections

The Chief Inspector has a duty to inspect every school in England mentioned below and, having performed the inspection, to make a written report of the inspection (Education Act 2005, s.5)–
  (a) community, foundation and voluntary schools (see the Note on **Schools: Provision and Governance: England and Wales**);
  (b) community and foundation special schools (see the Note on **Special Educational Provision and Special Schools: England and Wales**);
  (c) maintained nursery schools;
  (d) academies, city technology colleges and city colleges for the technology of the arts (see the Note on **Independent Schools**); and
  (e) special schools which are not community or foundation special schools but are approved by the Secretary of State under s.342 of the Education Act 1996 (see the Note on **Special Educational Provision and Special Schools: England and Wales**).

Schools that are in the process of closing need not be inspected if the Chief Inspector decides that no useful purpose would be served by such an inspection.

Schools may be exempted from inspection or subject only to a "short" inspection: see **27 Exemption and short inspections**, below.

A registered inspector conducting an inspection must report on the matters set out in s.5: see **23 Matters to be covered in a report**, paras (a)-(g), above.

An inspection under s.5 must not extend to denominational education or the content of collective worship (which is inspected under s.48—see **43 Inspection of religious education**, below).

The Education (School Inspection) (England) Regulations 2005 requires the Chief Inspector to inspect each school to which s.5 applies every five years (Reg. 3).

The appropriate authority responsible for the school must take reasonably practical steps to notify parents and any other prescribed people of the time an inspection by the Chief Inspector is to take place (s.6). For these purposes, the 2005 Regulations prescribe that the following people must be notified (Reg. 4)—

(a) in the case of a school maintained by a local authority and which has a delegated budget, whoever appears to be an appropriate officer of the local authority;

(b) in the case of a school maintained by a local authority and which does not have a delegated budget, the chairman of the governing body;

(c) in the case of a voluntary school, the person who appoints the school's foundation governors and, in the case of a voluntary aided school, the appropriate diocesan authority (if different);

(d) in the case of a special school which is not maintained by a local authority, any local authority which is paying fees in respect of the education of anyone at that school;

(e) in the case of any school at which a registered pupil is a child who is looked after by the local authority, a person appearing to them to be an appropriate officer of that local authority; and

(f) in the case of a secondary school, the Secretary of State.

During an inspection, the Chief Inspector must have regard to the views of (s.7)—

(g) the head teacher;

(h) the governing body of a maintained school;

(i) the proprietor of the school if there is one;

(j) any person prescribed for the purposes of s.6 (see (a) to (f) above);

(k) the school's staff; and

(l) the school's pupils and their parents.

The Chief Inspector may inspect any school in England, even when he is not required to do so under the Act (s.8). Where the Chief Inspector chooses to inspect a school under s.8, that inspection may be treated as an inspection under s.5 (s.9).

The Chief Inspector may publish an interim statement (known as a "health check") where the he considers that a school's performance is such that it is appropriate to defer a routine inspection of the school for at least a year. The statement must set out the Chief Inspector's opinion that inspection can be deferred and the reasons for that opinion. It is made on the basis of information available at the time and does not prevent the Chief Inspector from inspecting the school at any time if this is deemed necessary in light of changed circumstances. An interim statement cannot be used to defer an inspection beyond the end of the maximum period allowed between scheduled inspections (s.10A).

When inspecting a school under ss.5 or 8, the Chief Inspector has at all reasonable times a right of entry to the school premises and certain associated premises as well as a right to inspect, and take copies of, any records kept by the school.

It is an offence intentionally to obstruct the Chief Inspector in relation to the inspection of a school. A person guilty of this offence is liable on summary conviction to a fine not exceeding level 4 on the standard scale. As to the standard scale, see the Note on **Treatment of Offenders** at para **68 Maximum fines: the "standard scale"**.

27 Exemption and short inspections

Where a school receives the highest grading ("outstanding") in an inspection by the Chief Inspector under s.5 of the 2005 Act (see **26 Inspections**, above), then it will be exempted from further routine inspection (Education (Exemption from School Inspection) (England) Regulations 2012). The exemption does not apply to maintained nursery schools, special schools and pupil referral units and is subject to the school maintaining its high standards. The Chief Inspector will regularly risk assess all exempt schools – if performance deteriorates significantly or if parents lose confidence or register specific concerns, he will be able to re-inspect the school (under s.8) and may choose to treat that inspection as an inspection under s.5.

If a school is rated "good" at its last s.5 inspection, then instead of its next full s.5 inspection it will have a "short" s.8 inspection to determine whether it needs a full inspection (the same applies to a school which is a successor to a predecessor school which was rated "good" or better at its last s.5 inspection). If there is significant concern that the school may no longer be "good", the short inspection may recommend that a full inspection takes place. Equally, if there is strong evidence to indicate that a school is likely to be "outstanding", a full inspection may also be recommended, following which the school may then become exempt (Education (School Inspection) (England) Regulations 2005, Reg. 3). Schools which are "outstanding" but in a category which cannot be exempt (see above) will also receive a short inspection rather than a full one.

28 Publication of inspection reports

The Chief Inspector may arrange for any report of an inspection carried out by him under the Education Act

2005 to be published in the manner he considers appropriate, including by electronic means. A report published by the Chief Inspector is privileged, with regard to the law of defamation, unless the publication is shown to have been made with malice (s.11).

29 Where a school causes or has caused concern

If, on completion of an inspection under the Education Act 2005, s.5, the Chief Inspector thinks special measures are required in relation to a school or that a school requires significant improvement (see 6: SCHOOLS CAUSING CONCERN, below), he must do the following (s.13)–

- (a) send a draft of the report of the inspection to the governing body in the case of a maintained school, and in the case of any other school, to the proprietor of the school; and
- (b) consider any comments on the draft that are made by the governing body or proprietor (the Education (School Inspection) (England) Regulations 2005 provide that the governing body or proprietor have five working days to comment on the draft report (Reg. 5)).

If special measures or a significant improvement are required, he must–

- (a) give a notice in writing to that effect to the Secretary of State, the local authority in the case of a maintained school, and in the case of any other school, to the proprietor of the school; and
- (b) state his opinion in the report of the inspection.

30 Reports and measures: maintained schools

The Chief Inspector must ensure that a copy of the report of any inspection of a maintained school under the Education Act 2005, s.5 is sent to the appropriate authority for the school (i.e., the governing body of a maintained school or, if it does not have a delegated budget, the local authority). Copies of the report must also be sent to (s.14)–

- (a) the head teacher of the school;
- (b) whichever of the local authority and the governing body are not the appropriate authority;
- (c) in the case of a school having foundation governors, the person who appoints them and (if different) the appropriate appointing authority (i.e., the diocesan authority for a church school or the person who appoints foundation governors for a non-church school); and
- (d) anyone else that may be prescribed.

Similar provisions apply to copies of interim statements deferring a routine inspection (s.14A).

The appropriate authority must make a copy of the report available for inspection by members of the public, provide a copy of the report to anyone who asks for one, and take reasonable steps to ensure that every registered parent of a registered pupil at the school receives a copy within five working days from the time the report was received (s.14, and the Education (School Inspection) (England) Regulations 2005, Reg. 6). A fee may be charged for a second copy or where a copy of the report is provided to a non-parent (Reg. 8).

When a school requires special measures or significant improvement (see 6: SCHOOLS CAUSING CONCERN, below), the local authority has a duty on to prepare a written statement of the action it proposes to take, and the timetable for this action. Where the local authority proposes to take no action in response to the inspection report, its statement must set out its reasons for not doing so. The local authority must send its statement to the Secretary of State, the Chief Inspector and, in the case of a voluntary-aided school, the person who appoints foundation governors and, if different, the diocesan authority (s.15). The Education (School Inspection) (England) Regulations 2005 provide that the local authority must prepare the statement of action referred to above within 10 working days (Reg. 7).

31 Reports and measures: non-maintained schools

The Chief Inspector must ensure that a copy of the report of any inspection of a non-maintained school under the Education Act 2005, s.5 is sent to the proprietor of the school. In the case of a special school which is not a community or foundation special school the proprietor must send a copy of any report sent to him to any local authority that is paying fees in respect of the attendance of a registered pupil at the school (s.16). Similar provisions apply to copies of interim statements deferring a routine inspection (s.16A).

The proprietor must make this report available for inspection by members of the public, provide a copy of the report to anyone who asks for one and take reasonable steps to ensure that every registered parent of a registered pupil at the school receives a copy within five working days from the time the report was received (s.16, and the Education (School Inspection) (England) Regulations 2005, Reg. 6).

A fee may be charged (not exceeding the cost of supply) where a copy of the report is provided to anyone who asks for one (Reg. 8).

When a school requires special measures or significant improvement (see 6: SCHOOLS CAUSING CONCERN, below), the proprietor of the school has a duty on to prepare a written statement of the action he proposes to take, and the timetable for this action. The Education (School Inspection) (England) Regulations 2005 provide this statement of action must be prepared within 10 working days (Reg. 7). Copies of this statement must be sent to the Chief Inspector, any other prescribed persons and, in the case of a special school which is not a community or foundation special school, any local authority which is paying for a pupil to be at the school (s.17).

32 Her Majesty's Inspectorate of Education and Training in Wales

The Education Act 2005 makes provision for the appointment of Her Majesty's Chief Inspector for Education and Training in Wales (the Chief Inspector) and HMI in Wales (s.19 and Sch.2).

The appointment (and removal from office on grounds of incapacity or misconduct) is made by Her Majesty (in practice on a recommendation by the Welsh First Minister). It is for the Chief Inspector to determine the terms and conditions of appointment of HMI, subject to the approval of the Assembly.

The Chief Inspector in Wales has the general duty of keeping the Assembly informed about (s.20)–
  (a) the quality of the education provided by schools in Wales;
  (b) how far that education meets the needs of the range of pupils at those schools;
  (c) the educational standards achieved;
  (d) the quality of the leadership and management of schools, including whether the financial resources made available are managed efficiently;
  (e) the spiritual, moral, social and cultural development of the pupils; and
  (f) the contribution made by schools to the well-being of the pupils.

33 Reports to the Assembly

The Chief Inspector must make an annual report to the Welsh Assembly which must publish it. The Chief Inspector may also make and publish other reports as he considers appropriate (Education Act 2005, s.21).

34 The power to establish an advisory panel

The Welsh Assembly has the power to establish a panel to advise it on any matter relating to the Chief Inspector's functions. The power includes the appointment of members, remuneration and allowances, the preparation of reports and a requirement for the Chief Inspector for Wales and the panel to co-operate with each other (Education Act 2005, s.22).

35 Power of entry and inspection

The Chief Inspector's rights of entry to schools and rights to inspect documents for the purposes of inspection are set out in the Education Act 2005, s.23. These rights extend to other premises where pupils aged 15 or over (but who are still of compulsory school age) receive part of their education. It is an offence intentionally to obstruct the Chief Inspector when carrying out his duties. A person guilty of this offence is liable on summary conviction to a fine not exceeding level 4 on the standard scale. As to the standard scale, see the Note on **Treatment of Offenders** at para **68 Maximum fines: the "standard scale"**.

The Chief Inspector can arrange for any school to be inspected by HMI, and for an inspection to be monitored (see **37 Duty to arrange regular inspections**, below) (s.24).

36 Registered inspectors

Any person inspecting a school in Wales (see **37 Duty to arrange regular inspections**, below) must be a member of HMI or a registered inspector. When deciding on an application for registration the Chief Inspector must have regard to the extent to which he intends to use HMI or registered inspectors to carry out inspections and the extent to which there is a need for registered inspectors in any region of Wales (Education Act 2005, s.25). Under the Education (School Inspection) (Wales) Regulations 2006, there is a prescribed fee of £150 which must accompany an application for registration (Reg. 5).

The conditions to be satisfied before the Chief Inspector can remove the name of an inspector from the register, and before he can impose or vary conditions to which the registration of an inspector is subject, are set out in s.26.

There is a right of appeal to a tribunal constituted under s.27 in relation to a registration decision taken by the Chief Inspector. The tribunal must confirm a decision to refuse to renew a person's registration made on the ground of a reduced need or no need for registered inspectors in Wales if the tribunal is satisfied that the refusal was in fact on that ground.

The requirements for the constitution of tribunals, their procedure and staffing are set out in Sch.3.

37 Duty to arrange regular inspections

The schools that must be inspected are (Education Act 2005, s.28)–
  (a) community, foundation and voluntary schools (see the Note on **Schools: Provision and Governance: England and Wales**);

(b) community and foundation special schools (see the Note on **Special Educational Provision and Special Schools: England and Wales**);

(c) maintained nursery schools; and

(d) special schools which are not community or foundation special schools but are approved by the Secretary of State under s.342 of the Education Act 1996 (see the Note on **Special Educational Provision and Special Schools: England and Wales**).

The Education (School Inspection) (Wales) Regulations 2006 prescribe that inspections must be carried out in respect of every school at least once within a seven year period beginning on 1 September 2016 and ending on 31 August 2023 and at least once within every subsequent six year period beginning on the expiry of the previous period, or in the case of a school which has not previously been inspected, within six years of the date on which pupils were first admitted to the school (Reg. 6).

Where an inspection is arranged, the appropriate authority (that is the governing body of a maintained school or a local authority if the school does not have a delegated budget – Reg. 4) must take reasonably practicable steps to notify (Reg. 7)–

(a) in the case of a maintained school which has a delegated budget, a person appearing to them to be an appropriate officer of the local authority;

(b) in the case of a maintained school which does not have a delegated budget, the chairman of the governing body;

(c) in the case of a school which has foundation governors, the person who appoints those governors and, in the case of a voluntary aided school which is a Church in Wales school, a Church of England school or a Roman Catholic school, the appropriate diocesan authority (if different);

(d) in the case of a non-maintained special school, the Welsh Assembly or any local authority if the Assembly or authority are paying fees in respect of the provision of education to any person at the school;

(e) in the case of any school at which a registered pupil is a child who is looked after by the local authority, a person appearing to them to be an appropriate officer of that local authority; and

(f) in the case of a secondary school, such members of the local business community as the appropriate authority think fit, having regard, in particular, to the desirability of notifying members who employ, or have recently employed, former pupils of the school, of the time when the inspection is to take place.

Schools that are in the process of closing need not be inspected if the Chief Inspector decides that no useful purpose would be served by such an inspection.

A registered inspector conducting an inspection in Wales must report on the same areas as an inspector in England (see **26 Inspections**, above).

Inspections may be carried out by HMI or a registered inspector; the choice is at the Chief Inspector's discretion. Further details on the following are provided by Sch.4–

(a) selection of inspectors;

(b) the composition of inspection teams;

(c) enrolment of people who may act as inspection team members;

(d) training for inspections;

(e) meetings with parents of schools being inspected (the arrangements to be made by the appropriate authority for a meeting with parents prior to an inspection are set out in Reg. 8 of the 2006 Welsh Regulations);

(f) rights of entry for the purposes of inspection;

(g) the offence of obstructing an inspector or an inspection team; and

(h) replacement of an inspector during the course of an inspection.

38 Publication of inspection reports

Any report of an inspection (see **36 Duty to arrange regular inspections**, above) made by a registered inspector may be published in the manner that the Chief Inspector considers appropriate, including by electronic means.

39 Inspections and reports: all schools

A registered inspector or a member of the Inspectorate must write a written report and summary report following completion of a school inspection under s.28 (Education Act 2005, s.33). The required procedure in relation to the report of an inspection carried out by a registered inspector or an HMI who is of the view that a school requires significant improvement or special measures (see 6: SCHOOLS CAUSING CONCERN, below) is set out in ss.34-35.

A school inspection by a registered inspector must be carried out within a time specified in regulations made by the Assembly; the period allowed for the making of an inspection report must be specified in regulations too. The Chief Inspector may extend those times but notice of any extension must be given.

Under the Education (School Inspection) (Wales) Regulations 2006, an inspection must be completed within two weeks and a report of the inspection must be completed within 35 working days of the date on which the inspection was completed. The appropriate authority (that is the governing body of a maintained school or a local authority if the school does not have a delegated budget – Reg. 4) or proprietor must take reasonably practicable steps to ensure that a summary of the report is received by parents within 10 working days from the receipt of it by them (this does not apply to independent schools which are subject to regulation under the Education Act 2002) (Reg. 9).

40 Reports and measures: maintained schools

Where an inspection of a maintained school identifies that the school requires significant improvement or special measures (see 6: SCHOOLS CAUSING CONCERN, below), the Chief Inspector is required to inform the Assembly and the local authority of this in writing without delay (Education Act 2005, s.37).

In the case of maintained schools, school inspection reports and summaries must be made available to the appropriate authority for the school (i.e., the governing body, or if the school does not have a delegated budget, the local authority). Copies of the report and summary must be sent by the person who made the report to (s.38)–

(a) the Chief Inspector;

(b) the head teacher;

(c) whichever of the local authority and the governing body are not the appropriate authority;

(d) in the case of a school having foundation governors, to the person who appoints them and the appropriate appointing authority; and

(e) any other person that may be prescribed.

The appropriate authority must–

(f) make a copy of any report and summary sent to the authority available for inspection by members of the public at reasonable times and places;

(g) provide a copy of the report and summary, free of charge or in prescribed cases on payment of such fee as they think fit, to any person who asks for one; and

(h) take such steps as are reasonably practicable to make sure that every registered parent of a registered pupil at the school receives a copy of the summary within the prescribed period following receipt of the report by the authority.

If the inspection is a s.28 inspection or is carried out by a member of the Inspectorate, and the school provides full-time education suitable for pupils over compulsory school age, the person making the report must send a copy (together with a copy of the summary, if there is one) to the National Council for Education and Training for Wales (s.38).

The cases in which fees may be charged for inspection reports, summaries and action plans are set out in the Education (School Inspection) (Wales) Regulations 2006 (Reg. 12).

Where a report of an inspection states that special measures are required or that the school requires significant improvement (see 6: SCHOOLS CAUSING CONCERN, below), the school's governing body or, where the school does not have a delegated budget, the local authority, must prepare a written statement of action setting out the steps it proposes to take in the light of the report. Regulations made by the Assembly will set out the periods for preparing a written statement and the periods for sending them to specified persons, including the Assembly (s.39).

Under the Education (School Inspection) (Wales) Regulations 2006, the appropriate body (that is the governing body of a maintained school or a local authority if the school does not have a delegated budget – Reg. 4) or proprietor must prepare an action plan within 20 working days from the date on which they receive the report and send copies to those people and bodies entitled to receive them within the period specified (this varies according to whether or not the school has been identified as a school causing concern (this does not apply to independent schools which are subject to regulation under the Education Act 2002) (Reg. 10).

Where a local authority receives a copy of a report from a governing body under s.39, it too must prepare (within either 10 or 12 days: see Reg. 11) a written statement of the action it intends to take. (s.40).

41 Reports and measures: non-maintained schools

In the case of a report of a s.28 inspection of a school other than a maintained school, the person making the report must send a copy of the report, together with the summary of it, to the proprietor of the school and (unless the person making it is a member of the Inspectorate) to the Chief Inspector (Education Act 2005, s.41). If the report states that the person making it is of the opinion that special measures are required to be taken in relation to the school or that the school requires significant improvement (see 6: SCHOOLS CAUSING CONCERN, below) and either that person is a member of the Inspectorate or the report states that the Chief Inspector agrees with his opinion, a copy of the report and summary must be sent to the Assembly. Where a member of the Inspectorate makes the report, he must send a copy of the report, together with the summary of it, to the proprietor of the school and to the Assembly.

In the case of a special school which is not a community or foundation special school, the proprietor of the school must send a copy of any report and summary sent to him to any local authority that is paying fees in respect of the attendance of a registered pupil at the school.

The proprietor of the school must also–

(a) make any report and summary sent to him available for inspection by members of the public at reasonable times and places;

(b) provide a copy of the report and summary, free of charge or in prescribed cases on payment of such fee as he thinks fit, to any person who asks for one; and

(c) take such steps as are reasonably practicable to make sure that every registered parent of a registered pupil at the school receives a copy of the summary within a prescribed period following receipt of the report by the authority.

The cases in which fees may be charged for inspection reports, summaries and action plans are set out in the Education (School Inspection) (Wales) Regulations 2006 (Reg. 12).

Where a report of any inspection states that a school requires special measures or requires significant improvement (see 6: SCHOOLS CAUSING CONCERN, below, the proprietor must prepare a written statement of action setting out the steps he proposes to take in the light of the report. Regulations made by the Assembly will set out the periods for preparing these written statements and the periods for sending them to specified persons, including the Assembly (s.42). The Education (School Inspection) (Wales) Regulations 2006 have been made for this purpose, in particular Reg. 10 (see **40 Reports and measures: maintained schools,** above).

6: SCHOOLS CAUSING CONCERN

42 Categories of schools causing concern

Special measures are required to be taken in relation to a school if (Education Act 2005, s.44)–

(a) the school is failing to give its pupils an acceptable standard of education; and

(b) the people responsible for leading, managing or governing the school are not demonstrating the capacity to secure the necessary improvement in the school.

A school requires significant improvement if, although not defined by the above, it is performing significantly less well than it might in all the circumstances reasonably be expected to perform.

Where sixth forms require significant improvement, similar inspection and reporting measures apply (Learning and Skills Act 2000, s.113 and Sch.7, as amended by the Education Act 2005, s.46 and Sch.5) (see 10: INSPECTION OF FURTHER EDUCATION, below).

7: OTHER INSPECTIONS: ENGLAND AND WALES

43 Inspection of religious education

It is the duty of the governing body of any voluntary or foundation school in England which has been designated (under the School Standards and Framework Act 1998, s.69(3)) by the Secretary of State as having a religious character to make sure that any denominational education given to pupils and the content of the school's collective worship are inspected (Education Act 2005, s.48).

The Education (School Inspection) (England) Regulations 2005 prescribe that when choosing a person to carry out an inspection under s.48 the foundation governors or the governing body must consult with (Reg. 9)–

(a) in the case of a school designated as Church of England or Roman Catholic, the appropriate diocesan authority;

(b) in the case of a school designated as Jewish, the Jewish Studies Education Inspection Service;

(c) in the case of a school designated as Methodist, the Education Secretary to the Methodist Church;

(d) in the case of a school designated as Muslim, the Association of Muslim Schools;

(e) in the case of a school designated as Sikh, the Network of Sikh Organisations; and

(f) in the case of a school designated as Seventh Day Adventist, the Education Department of the British Union Conference of the Seventh Day Adventist.

An inspection under s.48 must be carried out by 1 August 2009 and every five years thereafter (Reg. 10). Inspections are to be carried out within a time-span of 10 working days, and when the inspection has been completed, the person conducting it must prepare a written report. The report must be prepared within 15 working days of the completion of the inspection (Reg. 11).

The report must be sent to the governing body of the school concerned. The governing body must (s.49)–

(a) make any such report available for inspection by members of the public, at reasonable times and places;

(b) take reasonably practicable steps to secure that every parent of a registered pupil at the school for whom the school provides denominational education or who takes part in acts of collective worship (the content of which falls to be inspected under s.48) receives a copy of the report as soon as is reasonably practicable; and

(c) provide a copy of the report to anyone else who asks for one (the governing body may charge a fee for providing a copy of the report to such a person (Reg. 12)).

In England, "Denominational education", in relation to a school, means religious education which is required by s.80(1)(a) or 101(1)(a) of the Education Act 2002 to be included in the school's basic curriculum, but is not required by any Act to be given in accordance with an agreed syllabus (s.47).

Inspection of religious education in Wales is provided for in a similar way under s.50 and Sch.6.

The Education (School Inspection) (Wales) Regulations 2006 provide for such inspections to take place at least once within a seven year period beginning on 1 September 2016 and ending on 31 August 2023 and at least once within every subsequent six year period beginning on the expiry of the previous period, or, where there has been no previous inspection, within six years from when the school first admitted pupils (Reg. 14). There is provision for consultation with the appropriate diocesan authority in the choice of inspector (Reg. 15). The 2006 Regulations prescribe the periods within which such inspections are to be carried out, and inspection report and action plans are to be prepared, and an action plan is to be sent to those entitled to receive a copy of it (Reg. 16). A fee (not exceeding the cost of supply) may be charged for a copy of an inspection report, summary or action plan (Reg. 17).

In Wales "denominational education", in relation to a school, means religious education which is required by 101(1)(a) of the Education Act 2002 to be included in the school's basic curriculum, but is not required by any Act, to be given in accordance with an agreed syllabus (2006 Regulations, Reg. 13).

44 Local authority inspections

Where a local authority requires information about any matter in connection with a school which it maintains, and it is not reasonably practicable for it to obtain the information in any other way, it may inspect the school for the purpose of obtaining the information and has a right of entry to do this (Education Act 2005, s.51).

In Wales, any local authority may provide a school inspection service for schools within its area. Such a service – providing for the inspection of schools under ss.28 or 50 by officers of the authority – may, in addition to providing for the inspection of schools which are maintained by it, provide for the inspection of other schools. The full cost of providing the service must be recovered by way of charges made by the authority to those using the service (s.52).

The Education (School Inspection) (Wales) Regulations 2006, make provision in relation to local authority school inspection services and require an authority to keep accounts in respect of such a service (Reg. 18).

45 Inspection of child minding, day care and nursery education

The inspection of child minding, day care and nursery education is dealt with by Part 10A of the Children Act 1989. As to child minding and day care, see the Note on **Child Minding and Day Care for Young Children**.

The Education (Inspection of Nursery Education) (Wales) Regulations 2015 provide that funded nursery education must be inspected by a registered nursery education inspector at intervals of six years. The Children's Centres (Inspections) Regulations 2010 provide that inspections in England be carried out every five years.

46 Inspection of independent schools

The inspection of independent schools is covered by the Education Act 2002. See the Note on **Independent Schools**.

47 Inspection of careers services in Wales

The Chief Inspector for Education and Training in Wales has a general duty to keep the Welsh Assembly informed about the quality of "relevant services" provided in Wales in pursuance of arrangements made or directions given by the Assembly under s.10 of the Employment and Training Act 1973, i.e., careers services (s.55).

Inspections must be carried out at least once within a seven year period beginning on 1 September 2016 and ending on 31 August 2023 and at least once within every subsequent six year period beginning on the expiry of the previous period. If there has been no previous inspection, the first inspection must be within six years from when the careers provision was first made (Inspection of Careers and Related Services (Wales) Regulations 2006, Reg. 4). The Chief Inspector may, and when asked to do so by the Assembly, must–

(a) give advice to the Assembly on matters relating to the provision of careers services in Wales; and

(b) inspect any provider of careers services.

An inspection of any provider of careers services comprises a review of the way in which he is discharging his responsibilities, having regard to any guidance given by the Assembly with respect to the provision of careers services.

Where a "relevant provider" who provides a careers service to which s.55 applies also provides in Wales education, training or an advisory service in pursuance of arrangements made by the Assembly under s.2 of the Employment and Training Act 1973 or with the assistance of a grant or loan made under s.12(1) of the Industrial Development Act 1982, the Chief Inspector has the general duty of keeping the Assembly informed about the quality of those education, training or advisory services. The Chief Inspector must inspect any relevant provider under this section at six yearly intervals (s.56, and the Inspection of Careers and Related Services (Wales) Regulations 2006, Reg. 4)).

In conducting an inspection, the inspector or inspectors must act in accordance with any instructions or guidelines from the Welsh Assembly.

Provision is made for rights of entry for inspectors, including rights to inspect records and documents and to take copies as required for the purposes of an inspection. It is an offence to obstruct an inspector or a person

assisting him. When the inspection has been completed, the Chief Inspector must–
- (c) prepare a written report on the inspection within a prescribed period;
- (d) send a copy of the report to the person inspected, the Assembly, any prescribed person and any other person whom he considers appropriate; and
- (e) publish the report in the prescribed manner or, if none is prescribed, in such manner as the Chief Inspector considers appropriate.

The Assembly may make regulations which require a person inspected under ss.55 or 56 to prepare a written statement in response to an inspection report (and to set out matters to be covered in the statement), set out the timescale for its preparation and describe its publication arrangements (s.57).

48 Inspection of schools providing accommodation

Provision for the inspection of schools and colleges providing accommodation is made by the Children Act 1989 which requires the "relevant person" to safeguard and promote the welfare of any child for whom the school provides accommodation (whether on its own premises or elsewhere) (s.87). The relevant person is–
- (a) the proprietor of an independent school or alternative provision Academy and any other person responsible for conducting such a school or Academy;
- (b) the governing body of any other school or institution; or
- (c) in the case of an institution conducted by a further education corporation, that corporation.

Her Majesty's Chief Inspector (in England) must ensure that this is done, and must report any failure to do so to–
- (a) the Secretary of State (in the case of an independent school or alternative provision Academy);
- (b) the local authority (in the case of a special school maintained by that authority);
- (c) the local authority (in the case of a school not within (a) or (b)) in whose area the school is situated.

In Wales, the Welsh Assembly must ensure compliance and report any failure to–
- (d) the local authority which maintains the school (in the case of a special school) or in whose area the school is situated (other non-independent schools).

For this purpose, the Secretary of State (or Assembly) may, under the National Care Standards Commission (Inspection of Schools and Colleges) Regulations 2002 (for England) or the Inspection of Boarding Schools and Colleges (Powers and Fees) (Wales) Regulations 2002, authorise a person to inspect the premises, the children themselves or the relevant records required to be kept. The Secretary of State can prescribe national minimum standards for safeguarding and promoting the welfare of children accommodated in boarding schools (s.87C).

49 Other inspections in England

The Secretary of State and Her Majesty's Chief Inspector of Education, Children's Services and Skills (the Chief Inspector) may make arrangements for the inspection of secure training centres. Under s.146 of the Education and Inspections Act 2006, the functions of inspecting secure training centres will become exercisable solely by the Chief Inspector.

The Secretary of State may make regulations requiring the Chief Inspector to inspect "relevant functions" of a local authority on such occasions or at such intervals as the regulations specify. "Relevant functions" are defined by Part 3 of the Care Standards Act 2000, as adoption and fostering functions (Education and Inspections Act 2006, s.147).

The Secretary of State may make regulations requiring a local authority in England to pay a fee to the Office for Standards in Education, Children's Services and Skills in respect of its "relevant functions". The Chief Inspector may make a scheme setting the fee level for periods when no regulations made by the Secretary of State are in force. "Relevant functions" are defined in Part 3 of the Care Standards Act 2000 as adoption and fostering functions (Education and Inspections Act 2006, s.155).

Her Majesty's Chief Inspector of Education, Children's Services and Skills (Fees and Frequency of Inspections) (Children's Homes etc.) Regulations 2015 apply to England only and prescribe fees that are to be paid to the Chief Inspector and the frequency of inspections of certain establishments and agencies. Part 2 of the Regulations prescribe the registration fees which are payable in respect of voluntary adoption agencies, adoption support agencies, children's homes, residential family centres, fostering agencies, holiday schemes for disabled children and providers of social work services. Part 3 prescribes the variation fees which are payable in respect of all these establishments and agencies with the exception of holiday schemes for disabled children. Part 4 prescribes the annual fees which are payable by all the above establishments and agencies (including holiday schemes for disabled children) but with the exception of providers of social work services. That Part also prescribes the annual fees which are payable by boarding schools, residential colleges, residential special schools and in respect of local authority adoption and fostering functions. Part 5 of the Regulations prescribes the frequency of inspection in relation to children's homes, residential family centres, voluntary adoption agencies, adoption support agencies, fostering agencies and holiday schemes for disabled children.

Certain functions of the Commission for Social Care Inspection are also transferred to the Chief Inspector under s.148 of the Education and Inspections Act 2006). This section relates to the registration of children's homes, residential family centres, fostering agencies, voluntary adoption agencies and adoption support agencies.

Finally, Sch.13 to the Education and Inspections Act 2006 is brought into effect by s.149. The Schedule defines the interaction between the Chief Inspector and the existing inspection authorities.

50 Power to investigate complaints by parents about schools in England

Her Majesty's Chief Inspector of Education, Children's Services and Skills (the Chief Inspector) may investigate complaints by parents about schools in England (Education Act 2005, ss.11A-11C inserted by the Education and Inspections Act 2006, s.160).

The Chief Inspector may investigate certain written complaints about matters of a prescribed description relating to schools, for the purpose of deciding whether to take further action, and in particular whether to use his existing inspection functions. The schools which are covered are: community, foundation and voluntary schools; community and foundation special schools; maintained nursery schools; Academies; city technology colleges; city colleges for the technology of the arts; and special schools which are not community or foundation special schools but are for the time being approved by the Secretary of State (s.11A).

The Education (Investigation of Parents' Complaints) (England) Regulations 2007 prescribe various matters in relation to the handling by Ofsted of parents' complaints. In particular, they set out the areas of complaint which are qualifying complaints, consistent with Ofsted's functions, and provide that a complaint cannot be considered if there is an alternative statutory route other than the school's complaints procedure. These Regulations also set out the general rule that a complaint cannot be considered unless the school's complaints procedure has first been exhausted, subject to the Chief Inspector's discretion to waive this requirement.

The governing body of a school (which, for a non-maintained school, is for these purposes the proprietor of the school) and/or local authority, in the case of a maintained school, must make specified information and other information relevant to the investigation of complaints available to the Chief Inspector on request (s.11B).

The preparation and distribution of any report made by the Chief Inspector as a result of an investigation of a qualifying complaint under s.11B may make a report (s.11C).

8: INSPECTION OF LOCAL AUTHORITY EDUCATION FUNCTIONS IN ENGLAND

51 Inspection and review of functions

Chapter 4 of Part 8 of the Education and Inspections Act 2006 makes provision for the Her Majesty's Chief Inspector of Education, Children's Services and Skills (the Chief Inspector) to undertake inspections and annual reviews of the performance of local authorities' functions, and sets out which of those functions are within the Chief Inspector's remit for these purposes. The Chief Inspector's powers of inspection and review include powers in relation to the exercise by local authorities of their general powers to promote the economic and social well-being of their areas under the Local Government Act 2000 (Education and Inspections Act 2006, s.135).

52 Inspection of local authorities in England

Her Majesty's Chief Inspector of Education, Children's Services and Skills (the Chief Inspector) has a number of general inspection duties in respect of the performance of local authorities' functions. The Chief Inspector may carry out an inspection of the performance of the functions, including anything done in pursuance of those functions under arrangements made by the local authority. In carrying out his inspection the Chief Inspector must also inspect any related activities. The Chief Inspector must also carry out an inspection of a specified local authority where the Secretary of State requests him to do so (Education and Inspections Act 2006, s.136).

53 Reports of inspections

Her Majesty's Chief Inspector of Education, Children's Services and Skills (the Chief Inspector) must make a written report of any inspection of a local authority conducted under s.136 of the Education and Inspections Act 2006 (see 52 Inspection of local authorities in England, above). The Chief Inspector must send a copy of the report to the local authority and the Secretary of State. The local authority must prepare a written statement setting out the action it proposes to take in the light of the report and the timetable for doing so. The authority must publish the report, and action plan, in accordance with regulations to be made by the Secretary of State. The Chief Inspector may publish the report in such manner as he considers appropriate (Education and Inspections Act 2006, s.137).

The Education and Inspections Act 2006 (Inspection of Local Authorities) Regulations 2007 prescribe the manner and period within which a local authority in England must publish an inspection report and a written statement of proposed action following an inspection by the Chief Inspector.

54 Annual reviews of local authorities in England

Her Majesty's Chief Inspector of Education, Children's Services and Skills (the Chief Inspector) must undertake an annual review of local authorities' performance of functions and of related activities (see 51 Inspection and review of functions, above). Having carried out such a review, the Chief Inspector must award a performance rating for each authority (Education and Inspections Act 2006, s.138).

55 Power of entry to inspect local authorities

Her Majesty's Chief Inspector of Education, Children's Services and Skills (the Chief Inspector) has a power of entry for the purpose of carrying out inspections of local authorities under s.136 of the Education and Inspections Act 2006 (see **52 Inspection of local authorities in England**, above) or annual reviews of local authorities under s.138 (see **54 Annual reviews of local authorities in England**, above). The inspector may at any reasonable time enter any premises for the purposes of the inspection or review, though his power does not extend to domestic premises (see s.159) unless those premises are a school (s.139).

Any person who is authorised to exercise a power of entry or inspection on behalf of the Chief Inspector must, if required to do so, produce evidence of his authority to exercise the power (s.150).

56 Power to inspect documents

Where Her Majesty's Chief Inspector of Education, Children's Services and Skills (the Chief Inspector) exercises his power of entry for the purpose of carrying out inspections of local authorities, he may require the production of documents, including computer records; inspect, take copies or remove them from the premises; inspect computers; and inspect the state and management of the premises (s.140 of the Education and Inspections Act 2006).

A person who, without reasonable excuse, obstructs the exercise of these powers or fails to comply with a requirement under s.140, is guilty of an offence and liable on summary conviction to a fine not exceeding level 4 on the standard scale (s.140(9)). As to the standard scale, see the Note on **Treatment of Offenders** at para **68 Maximum fines: the "standard scale"**.

57 Power to require information

Her Majesty's Chief Inspector of Education, Children's Services and Skills (the Chief Inspector) may at any time ask for information relating to the functions he inspects or related activities, from a local authority in England, or anyone delivering those functions under arrangements made by the local authority (Education and Inspections Act 2006, s.141).

A person who, without reasonable excuse, fails to comply with requirements of s.141 is guilty of an offence and is liable, on summary conviction, to a fine not exceeding level 4 on the standard scale (s141(4)). As to the standard scale, see the Note on **Treatment of Offenders** at para **68 Maximum fines: the "standard scale"**.

58 Inspection of CAFCASS functions

Her Majesty's Chief Inspector of Education, Children's Services and Skills (the Chief Inspector) must inspect the performance of the Children and Family Court Advisory and Support Service (CAFCASS). The Chief Inspector is required to produce a written report of any inspection and send copies to the Secretary of State and CAFCASS. The Chief Inspector must publish the report in such a manner as he considers appropriate (Education and Inspections Act 2006, s.143).

59 Power of entry to inspect CAFCASS

Her Majesty's Chief Inspector of Education, Children's Services and Skills (the Chief Inspector) has the power to enter any premises occupied by Children and Family Court Advisory and Support Service (CAFCASS) and any organisations or individuals contracted to carry out functions on behalf of CAFCASS. The Chief Inspector does not have the right to enter private dwellings. The power of entry may be exercised at reasonable times only (Education and Inspections Act 2006, s.144).

Any person who is authorised to exercise a power of entry or inspection on behalf of the Chief Inspector must, if required to do so, produce evidence of his authority to exercise the power (s.150).

60 Power to inspect documents at CAFCASS

Her Majesty's Chief Inspector of Education, Children's Services and Skills (the Chief Inspector) has the power to inspect, take copies of or take away documents held by the Children and Family Court Advisory and Support Service (CAFCASS) or documents relating to the performance of CAFCASS functions which he considers relevant for the purposes of the inspection. The powers may be exercised at reasonable times only (Education and Inspections Act 2006, s.145).

9: INSPECTION OF LOCAL AUTHORITY EDUCATION FUNCTIONS IN WALES

61 Inspection of local authorities

S.38 of the Education Act 1997 gives power to the Chief Inspector of Schools in England and the Chief Inspector of Education and Training in Wales to inspect local authorities. Each Chief Inspector is also under a duty to inspect an authority when requested to do so by the Secretary of State or Welsh Assembly (as the case may be).

An inspection of an authority in England under s.38 will consist of a review of the way in which the authority is performing any of its local authority functions.

An inspection in Wales consists of a review of the way in which the authority is performing any of its local authority functions and also of the functions conferred on the authority relating to education, training or youth support services.

The inspection will be conducted by one of HMI or by an additional inspector authorised under the Education Act 2005 but he may be assisted by such other persons as the Chief Inspector thinks fit.

On completion of an inspection under s.38, the inspector must make a written report and send copies to the authority in question and to the Secretary of State. On receipt of the report, the authority concerned must prepare a written statement of the action it proposes to take in the light of the report and the period within which it proposes to take it. The Education (Publication of Local Authority Inspection Reports) Regulations 1998 prescribe the manner in which reports and local authority statements are to be published. *Inter alia*, copies of both must be sent to local newspapers and to public libraries and copies must also be made available to members of the public on demand at a charge not exceeding the cost of supply.

S.40 (as substituted by the Education Act 2002, s.180) makes provision about the rights of entry of inspectors carrying out inspections of local authorities under s.38 of the 1997 Act and their right to inspect documents. As well as premises of the local authority and schools maintained by it, rights of entry extend to other premises (but not to private houses) on which education is being provided under arrangements made by the authority. The right of entry is accompanied by rights to inspect and copy records and documents including computer records. It is an offence wilfully to obstruct an inspector who is seeking to exercise any of the rights under s.40.

10: INSPECTION OF FURTHER EDUCATION IN ENGLAND

62 Education and training in England

Her Majesty's Chief Inspector of Education, Children's Services and Skills (the Chief Inspector) may inspect both further education and work-based training as well as such other education or training as may be prescribed by regulations made by the Secretary of State (Education and Inspections Act 2006, s.123(1)). The training which may be inspected can include the training of teachers and trainers (s.123(2)).

The Education and Inspections Act 2006 (Prescribed Education and Training etc) Regulations 2007 make provision for the inspection of education and training by the Chief Inspector. Certain education is prescribed for the purposes of s.123, thereby bringing it within the remit of the Chief Inspector, including education or training in dance or drama. Action plans must be published following an inspection and report by the Chief Inspector. Where the Chief Inspector carries out an area inspection under s.128 (see **66 Area inspections**, below), he may direct the Council or a local authority to prepare an action plan.

63 Inspection of education and training

Her Majesty's Chief Inspector of Education, Children's Services and Skills (the Chief Inspector) must inspect the education and training that is within his remit and is specified by the Secretary of State. When he has completed an inspection, he has a duty to make a written report on it, stating whether the education and training inspected is of a quality adequate to meet the reasonable needs of those receiving it. The Chief Inspector must arrange for the report to be published, and send copies to specified recipients and to anyone else he considers appropriate (Education and Inspections Act 2006, s.124).

64 Inspection of further education institutions

Her Majesty's Chief Inspector of Education, Children's Services and Skills (the Chief Inspector) must inspect all further education institutions. When the Chief Inspector has completed the inspection, he has a duty to report on it (Education and Inspections Act 2006, s.125). S.125(1A), as inserted by the Education Act 2011 s.42, provides that the duty to inspect may not apply to prescribed categories of institution in prescribed circumstances. The Further Education Institutions (Exemption from Inspection) (England) Regulations 2012 provide that an institution within the further education sector and a 16 to 19 Academy will be exempt from routine inspection where the institution's overall effectiveness has been awarded the highest grade in its most recent inspection under s.125 (Regs. 3, 4).

The Chief Inspector may inspect any education or training (s.126(1)); this applies even if he is not required to do so under the 2006 Act (s.126(2)).

65 Action plans

The action to be taken after all inspections (other than inspections commissioned under s.126(2) of the Education and Inspections Act 2006) is set out in s. 127 of the 2006 Act. The provider of the education and training inspected must provide a written action plan together with a timetable setting out when the action will be taken. The person must publish the plan within a period prescribed by regulations made by the Secretary of State and send copies to those people listed. Her Majesty's Chief Inspector of Education, Children's Services and Skills may waive the requirement for an action plan.

66 Area inspections

Her Majesty's Chief Inspector of Education, Children's Services and Skills (the Chief Inspector) must, if requested by the Secretary of State to do so, carry out an inspection covering the whole of a specified area. He will be under a duty to inspect the quality and availability of provision in that area for people aged 15 or over but under 19 as well as the standards they achieve. Included in the scope of the inspections are those who will reach the age of 15 in the current school year. The Chief Inspector may carry out such inspections without being requested to do so (Education and Inspections Act 2006, s.128).

67 Reports of area inspections

Her Majesty's Chief Inspector of Education, Children's Services and Skills (the Chief Inspector) must make a written report on completing an area inspection. He must also make arrangements for the report to be published and sent to the Secretary of State and each local authority whose area is wholly or partly within the area subject to the inspection. Copies may be sent to anyone else the Chief Inspector considers appropriate (Education and Inspections Act 2006, s.129).

68 Action plans following area inspections

The Secretary of State may require a local authority to prepare a written action plan, together with a timetable setting out when the action will be taken by them. They must publish the plan within a specified period and send copies to a list of people to be prescribed by regulations (Education and Inspections Act 2006, s.130).

69 Power of entry

Her Majesty's Chief Inspector of Education, Children's Services and Skills has (the Chief Inspector) the power of entry when conducting of further education and training, except those commissioned by providers. Any right to access an employer's premises can only be exercised if reasonable notice has been given in writing (Education and Inspections Act 2006, s.131).

Any person who is authorised to exercise a power of entry or inspection on behalf of the Chief Inspector must, if required to do so, produce evidence of his authority to exercise the power (s.150).

70 Power to inspect documents

Where Her Majesty's Chief Inspector of Education, Children's Services and Skills (the Chief Inspector) exercises his power of entry for the purpose of carrying out an inspection (see **69 Power of entry**, above), he may require the production of documents, including computer records, and inspect and take copies of documents and remove them from the premises under inspection. He may also inspect computers and may require assistance from someone operating a computer. Obstruction of this power, or that under s.131, without reasonable excuse is an offence for which a person is liable on summary conviction to a fine not exceeding level 4 on the standard scale (Education and Inspections Act 2006, s.132). The penalty also applies if someone fails to comply with any requirement under s.132. As to the standard scale, see the Note on **Treatment of Offenders** at para **68 Maximum fines: the "standard scale"**.

71 Framework for inspections

A framework or frameworks which lay out a common set or sets of principles which cover all inspections conducted under Chapter 3 of Part 8 of the Education and Inspections Act 2006 (inspection of further education and training) must be established by Her Majesty's Chief Inspector of Education, Children's Services and Skills. He may revise the framework but he must publish any revised framework (Education and Inspections Act 2006, s.133).

11: INSPECTION OF FURTHER EDUCATION IN WALES

72 The conduct of inspections in Wales

In Wales, responsibility for the inspection of further education and training rests solely with the Chief Inspector of Education and Training in Wales (Learning and Skills Act 2000, s.75).

The conduct of inspections in Wales is set out in s.77. Inspections in Wales must be carried out every six years (Inspection of Education and Training (Wales) Regulations 2001, Reg.2). The Chief Inspector of Education and Training in Wales has power over area inspections on Wales (s.83).

73 Additional provisions relating to Wales

The Chief Inspector for Wales may (and the Welsh Assembly may direct him to) carry out a survey across the whole of Wales or a specified part of it on matters concerned with post-16 education or training policy. He may also carry out a comparative study of the provision made outside Wales in respect of specified matters relating to such education or training (Learning and Skills Act 2000, s.85).

The Secretary of State or Her Majesty's Chief Inspector of Education, Children's Services and Skills may also request the Chief Inspector for Wales to inspect any education or training provided in Wales under the Employment and Training Act 1973, s.2 (responsibility for making arrangements for education or training to help those without work find employment has not been devolved to the Welsh Assembly) (2000 Act, s.82, amended by Education and Inspections Act 2006, Sch. 14).

74 Authorities

Statutes–

Children Act 1989

Education Acts 1997, 2002 and 2005

Education and Inspections Act 2006

Learning and Skills Act 2000

School Standards and Framework Act 1998

School Standards and Organisation (Wales) Act 2013

Statutory Instruments–

Children and Young People's Plan (Wales) Regulations 2007, as amended (S.I. 2007 No. 2316 and 2010 No. 1142)

Children's Centres (Inspections) Regulations 2010 (S.I. 2010 No. 1173)

Education and Inspections Act 2006 (Inspection of Local Authorities) Regulations 2007(S.I. 2007 No. 462)

Education and Inspections Act 2006 (Prescribed Education and Training etc) Regulations 2007 (S.I 2007 No. 464)

Education (Exemption from School Inspection) (England) Regulations 2012 (S.I. 2012 No. 1293)

Education (Inspection of Nursery Education) (Wales) Regulations 2015, as amended (S.I. 2015 No. 1599 and 2016 No. 135)

Education (Investigation of Parents' Complaints) (England) Regulations 2007, as amended (S.I. 2007 No. 1089 and 2008 No. 1723)

Education (Publication of Local Authority Inspection Reports) Regulations 1998, as amended (S.I. 1998 No. 880, 2001 No. 3710, 2005 No. 761, and 2013 No. 235)

Education (School Development Plans) (Wales) Regulations 2014 (S.I. 2014 No. 2677)

Education (School Inspection) (England) Regulations 2005, as amended (S.I. 2005 No. 2038, 2008 No. 1723, 2009 No. 1564, 2010 No. 1941, and 2012 No. 756, and 2015 Nos. 170 and 1639)

Education (School Inspection) (Wales) Regulations 2006, as amended (S.I. 2006 No. 1714, 2010 No. 1436, 2014 No. 1212, and 2016 No. 135)

Further Education Institutions (Exemption from Inspection) (England) Regulations 2012 (S.I. 2012 No. 2576)

Her Majesty's Chief Inspector of Education, Children's Services and Skills (Fees and Frequency of Inspections) (Children's Homes etc.) Regulations 2015 (S.I. 2015 Nos. 551 and 971, and 2016 No. 322)

Inspection of Boarding Schools and Colleges (Powers and Fees) (Wales) Regulations 2002 (S.I. 2002 No. 3161)

Inspection of Careers and Related Services (Wales) Regulations 2006, as amended (S.I. 2006 No. 3103, 2010 No. 1436, 2014 No. 1212, and 2016 No. 135)

Inspection of Education and Training (Wales) Regulations 2001, as amended (S.I. 2001 No. 2501, 2004 No. 783, 2010 No. 1436, and 2014 No. 1212)

National Care Standards Commission (Inspection of Schools and Colleges) Regulations 2002 (S.I. 2002 No. 552)

Office for Standards in Education, Children's Services and Skills and Her Majesty's Chief Inspector of Education, Children's Services and Skills (Allocation of Rights and Liabilities) Order 2007 (S.I. 2007 No. 600)

ADDITIONAL SUPPORT FOR LEARNING AND SPECIAL SCHOOLS: SCOTLAND

1 Introduction

In Scotland, provision is made for children and young people with additional support needs by the Education (Additional Support for Learning) (Scotland) Act 2004. References to young people are to those aged 16 or 17, still receiving school education (s.29(2)).

In addition, the Standards in Scotland's Schools etc Act 2000 imposes a specific duty on education authorities to provide places in mainstream schools for children with special educational needs unless there are exceptional circumstances (see **16 Placing requests**, below).

2 Additional support needs

A child or young person has additional support needs where, ordinarily, he is unlikely to benefit from school education without additional support (Education (Additional Support for Learning) (Scotland) Act 2004, s.1).

A child or young person is deemed to have additional support needs if they are looked after by a local authority (within the meaning of the Children (Scotland) Act 1995, s.17(6)) unless an education authority form the view that the child or young person is, or is likely to be, able without the provision of additional support to benefit from school education provided to or to be provided for them (s.1(1A), (1B)).

"Additional support" means–
- (a) in relation to a pre-school child, a child of school age or a young person, provision (whether or not educational provision) which is additional to, or otherwise different from, the education provided generally; and
- (b) in relation to a child under school age other than a pre-school child, such provision (whether or not educational provision) as is appropriate in the circumstances.

3 Co-ordinated support plans

A child or young person requires a co-ordinated support plan if (Education (Additional Support for Learning) (Scotland) Act 2004, s.2)–
- (a) the education authority is responsible for that person's education;
- (b) their needs arise from complex or multiple factors;
- (c) they have enduring additional support needs; and
- (d) those needs require significant additional support to be provided.

4 Children and young people who lack capacity

Children and young people have the same rights as parents unless they lack capacity when their parents will act on their behalf.

For the purposes of the Education (Additional Support for Learning) (Scotland) Act 2004, a child or young person lacks capacity to do something if he is incapable of doing it as a result of mental illness, developmental disorders or learning disabilities, or an inability to communicate because of a physical disability. If a communication deficiency can be improved by some form of assistance, that child or young person does not lack capacity (s.3).

5 Duties and powers of education authorities

Every education authority must–
- (a) make adequate and efficient provision for each child and young person having additional support needs for whom it is responsible; and
- (b) keep under consideration those additional support needs and the adequacy of those arrangements.

The duty in (a) above does not require the education authority to do anything which it does not otherwise have the power to do, or would result in unreasonable expenditure being incurred (Education (Additional Support for Learning) (Scotland) Act 2004, s.4).

In exercising any of their functions in connection with the provision of school education, every education authority must take into account the additional support needs of children and young people and must provide such additional support as is appropriate for each child.

In addition, where a child is brought to their attention education authorities have a duty (unless the child's parent does not consent) to–
- (a) establish whether a child has additional support needs, and
- (b) provide such additional support as is appropriate for the child,

if that child–
- (c) is under school age (unless the child is a prescribed pre-school child),
- (d) belongs to the authority's area, and
- (e) appears to have additional support needs arising from a disability (defined by s.6 of the Equality Act 2010

as arising from physical or mental impairment which has a substantial and long-term adverse effect on his ability to carry our normal day-to-day activities),

An education authority has a discretionary power to provide additional support for children and young people other those to whom the education authority has a duty (s.5).

6 Establishment of additional support needs

Every education authority must make appropriate arrangements for identifying from among the children and young people for whose school education it is responsible those who have additional support needs, and those having additional support needs who require a co-ordinated support plan. The education authority must also make appropriate arrangements for identifying which particular additional support needs the children and young people have.

The people eligible to make a reasonable request to the education authority to establish whether any child or young person has additional support needs or requires a co-ordinated support plan are–
(a) in the case of a child, the child's parent; and
(b) in the case of a young person, the young person or the young person's parent.

Where a child or young person for whose school education an education authority is responsible comes to the attention of the authority as having, or appearing to have, additional support needs, or having such needs and requiring, or appearing to require, a co-ordinated support plan, the education authority must establish whether the child or young person does have additional support needs or requires a co-ordinated support plan, unless the authority considers it unreasonable to do so (Education (Additional Support for Learning) (Scotland) Act 2004, s.6). Every education authority must in particular consider whether each child or young person looked after by a local authority for whose school education they are responsible requires a co-ordinated support plan (s.6(1A)).

A similar request may be made in relation to children and young people for whose school education an education authority is not responsible (s.7).

7 Assessments and examinations

Where an education authority is establishing whether a child or young person has additional support needs or requires a co-ordinated support plan, or proposes to review any such plan, and the appropriate person requests that the education authority arranges for the child or young person to undergo an assessment or examination, the education authority must comply with the assessment request unless the request is unreasonable. An assessment or examination includes educational, psychological or medical assessment or examination.

The appropriate person means the person making the request, the child's parent, the young person or the young person's parent. The assessment or examination must be carried out by whoever the education authority considers appropriate (Education (Additional Support for Learning) (Scotland) Act 2004, s.8).

A request may also be made at any time for a process of educational, psychological or medical assessment or examination for the purpose of considering the additional support needs of a child or young person (s.8A).

8 Contents of co-ordinated support plans

Where an education authority establishes that a child or young person for whose school education it is responsible requires a co-ordinated support plan, it must prepare such a plan which must contain (Education (Additional Support for Learning) (Scotland) Act 2004, s.9)–
(a) a statement of the education authority's conclusions as to the factors from which the additional support needs arise, the educational objectives sought, the additional support required by the child or young person to achieve those objectives, and who should provide the support;
(b) a nomination of a school to be attended by the child or young person;
(c) the name and other appropriate contact details of the officer of the authority responsible for the discharge of the authority's duty or, if that duty is to be discharged by another person, the identity of that other person; and
(d) the name and other appropriate contact details of an officer of the authority from whom the child's parent, the young person or the young person's parent can obtain advice and further information.

Every education authority must keep under consideration the adequacy of any co-ordinated support plans for any children or young people for whose school education they are responsible. Reviews must be carried out every 12 months. A review may be carried out sooner if the child's parent, young person or young person's parent so requests, or if the authority considers it necessary or expedient to do so because of a significant change in the child's or young person's circumstances.

In reviewing any co-ordinated support plan the education authority must establish whether the child or young person for whom the plan was prepared still requires such a plan and either continue it with any appropriate changes or discontinue it (s.10).

Where an education authority proposes to establish whether any child or young person requires a co-ordinated support plan or to review any such plan, the education authority must inform the child's parents, young person, young person's parents or any independent or grant-maintained school involved of–
(a) their proposal;
(b) the outcome; and

(c) the rights they have to refer the outcome to a tribunal (see **14 Reference to a tribunal**, below).

The education authority must distribute the plan or amended plan to the appropriate person, ensure that additional support is provided by them for the child or young person in accordance with the plan or amended plan, seek to ensure that additional support is provided for the child or young person in accordance with the plan or amended plan by any person identified in the plan, co-ordinate the provision of additional support for the child or young person and inform everyone who will be involved in the provision of additional support for the child or young person of the matters contained in the plan or amended plan.

The Scottish Ministers may by regulations make further provision as to co-ordinated support plans (s.11). The Additional Support for Learning (Co-ordinated Support Plan) (Scotland) Amendment Regulations 2005 prescribe the form and content of a co-ordinated support plan for a child or young person with additional support needs. The regulations also prescribe time limits and exceptions to such limits for responding to requests to establish whether a plan is required, for the preparation and review of a plan, and for responding to requests for an early review of a plan (Regs 4 to 7), arrangements for keeping the plan (Reg. 8), arrangements for the transfer of a plan to another education authority (Reg. 9), arrangements for the disclosure without explicit consent of the plan to specified people or in specified circumstances (Reg. 10) and arrangements for the discontinuance, retention and destruction of a plan (Reg. 11).

9 The exchange of information

When establishing whether any child or young person has additional support needs and requires a co-ordinated support plan, preparing such a plan or determining what provision to make for additional support, the education authority has a duty to consider (Education (Additional Support for Learning) (Scotland) Act 2004, s.12)–

(a) relevant advice and information from appropriate agencies;

(b) the views of the child, the child's parent, the young person or the young person's parent;

(c) any relevant advice or information provided to the authority by or on behalf of the child or young person; and

(d) any other relevant advice and information in the authority's possession or control.

No later than 12 months before the child or young person ceases school education or as soon as reasonably practicable after the education authority becomes aware that the child will cease school education it must–

(a) request from such appropriate agency or agencies as the authority think fit (if any) such information as the authority considers appropriate concerning any provision likely to be made for the child or young person on ceasing to receive school education and take account of it; and

(b) seek the views of the child, the child's parent or the young person or the young person's parent and take account of them.

No later than six months before the date on which any child or young person to whom the Act relates is expected to cease receiving school education or as soon as reasonably practicable after the education authority is aware that the child or young person is leaving school, the education authority must exchange information with other appropriate agencies (s.13). In doing so, an authority has a duty to seek and take account of the child's views in relation to any information to be provided (unless the authority are satisfied that the child lacks capacity to express a view).

10 Action on a change in school education

The Scottish Ministers may issue regulations for the taking of specified action in connection with changes in a child's or young person's school education (Education (Additional Support for Learning) (Scotland) Act 2004, s.13).

The Additional Support for Learning (Changes in School Education) (Scotland) Regulations 2005 provide that the following changes in the school education of children and young people are specified changes for the purposes of the Act–

(a) where a child under school age starts school;

(b) where a child begins primary education;

(c) where a child begins secondary education;

(d) where a child changes school other than under (a)-(c) above; and

(e) where an education authority ceases to be responsible for the school education of a child or young person (Reg. 2).

Education authorities must seek advice and information from appropriate agencies to assist them in establishing the additional support needs of children and young people, determining what provision to make for additional support or considering the adequacy of such support (Reg. 3). Education authorities must also consider which agencies might require information in order to make arrangements for additional support for the child or young person and provide them with this information (Reg. 4).

11 Supporters and advocacy

A young person or a child's parents may be accompanied by another person at any meetings they may have with an education authority, including meetings at school. This other person may act as a supporter or may speak or make representations on behalf of the young person or child's parents. There is no requirement for education authorities to provide or pay for any supporters or advocacy services (Education (Additional Support for Learning) (Scotland) Act 2004, s.14).

The Scottish Ministers must secure the provision of an advocacy service to be available on request and free of charge to support parents and young people in Tribunal proceedings. "Advocacy services" are services whereby another person conducts discussions with or makes representations to the Tribunal or any other person involved in the proceedings on behalf of parent or young person (s.14A).

12 Mediation and dispute resolution

There is a duty on education authorities to arrange for independent mediation services to be provided, free of charge, to parents of children or young people. Mediation services will seek to avoid or resolve disagreements between the authority and parents or young people (Education (Additional Support for Learning) (Scotland) Act 2004, s.15).

The Scottish Ministers may, by regulations, require education authorities to put in place free arrangements to resolve disputes between the authority and any parents or young people (s.16). The Additional Support for Learning Dispute Resolution (Scotland) Regulations 2005 have been made under this provision and provide for an application for referral to be made to the Scottish Ministers.

Parents or young people are not compelled to refer disagreements to a mediation service and their entitlement to make a reference to a tribunal is not affected by their use of mediation or their pursuance of dispute resolution under any regulations made.

13 Appeals

Additional Support Needs Tribunals for Scotland are established under the Education (Additional Support for Learning) (Scotland) Act 2004 (s.17). Schedule 1 makes provision for–
   (a) the appointment of the president and panels;
   (b) the constitution of tribunals;
   (c) the terms of office and the removal from office;
   (d) allowances for tribunal members;
   (e) the administration of tribunal functions;
   (f) staff, property and services;
   (g) finance arrangements;
   (h) rules of procedure, practice directions and evidence;
   (i) tribunal decisions;
   (j) the annual report and the disclosure of information; and
   (k) allowances for attendance at hearings.
The Scottish Ministers are responsible for appointing a president to head up the tribunals and may, by regulations, make further provision in connection with the tribunals and the president (s.17).

Any person who has made a reference to a tribunal, may appeal the decision of the tribunal to the Court of Session on a point of law (s.21).

14 Reference to a tribunal

If an education authority is responsible for providing school education for the child or young person, then the child's parent, the young person or the young person's parent may make a reference to a tribunal in relation to an education authority's–
   (a) decision on whether or not a co-ordinated support plan is required or continues to be required;
   (b) failure to prepare a co-ordinated support plan in the required time;
   (c) decision about information contained in a co-ordinated support plan;
   (d) decision to refuse a placing request to a specified school, in particular circumstances; and
   (e) failure to comply with its duties in terms of post-school transitions.
Where information in the co-ordinated support plan is referred to a tribunal there cannot be a further reference on the same information until an updated plan is issued following its next review.

References relating to a refusal of a placing request can be made to a tribunal if a co-ordinated support plan has been prepared for the child or young person concerned, or a plan is about to be prepared or if a reference has been made to the tribunal over the decision that a plan is not required (Education (Additional Support for Learning) (Scotland) Act 2004, s.18).

15 Powers of a tribunal

The tribunal may either confirm the education authority's decision that a co-ordinated support plan is needed, or not needed, or overturn the decision and direct the authority to take specific action within a specified time. This also applies where the education authority has decided not to comply with a request to review a co-ordinated support plan earlier than the required 12-month period.

Where a reference relates to the education authority's failure to prepare a plan or its failure to conduct or complete a review of the plan within the time required, the tribunal can require the authority to rectify this.

Where a reference relates to an education authority's refusal of a placing request, then the tribunal must consider the statutory grounds of refusal and the appropriateness of the refusal for the individual child or young person.

Tribunals must take account of the code of practice published by the Scottish Ministers under s.27 (Education (Additional Support for Learning) (Scotland) Act 2004, s.19).

The Scottish Ministers may extend that which can be referred to a tribunal under s.18(1) and extend the tribunals' powers as well as enable the president of the tribunals to reject certain references without a hearing (s.20).

16 Placing requests

Making placing requests and appealing decisions relating to placements for children and young people with additional support needs is dealt with by the Education (Additional Support for Learning) (Scotland) Act 2004, s.22 and Sch.2).

There is a duty on the education authority to comply with a parent's (or young person's) request to place the child or young person with additional support needs in a specified school. The request can be for a special school (public or independent) or a mainstream school. If the specified school is an independent special school, in Scotland or elsewhere in the UK, the education authority must pay for it (para.2 of Sch.2).

In certain circumstances the duty to comply with a parent's or young person's request does not apply. There is an assumption that the education will be provided in a mainstream school unless certain circumstances exist (Sch. 2, para 3).

S.15 of the 2000 Act places a duty on education authorities to provide education for all children in mainstream schools unless education in a mainstream school–
   (a) would not be suited to the child's ability or aptitude;
   (b) would be incompatible with the provision of efficient education for the children with whom the child would be educated; or
   (c) would result in unreasonable public expenditure being incurred which would not ordinarily be incurred.

S.15 also provides that it is to be presumed that those circumstances arise only exceptionally. However, where such circumstances do arise, an authority may not provide education for the child in a mainstream school without taking account of the views of the child and the child's parents.

Under the Education (School and Placing Information) (Scotland) Regulations 2012, education authorities are required to advertise and make available *inter alia* certain information about schools, including special schools, to enable parents to make placing requests for their children.

Parents or a young person may appeal a placing decision to the education authority's appeal committee and then to the sheriff (Sch.2, paras 5 to 7). Where an authority (or appeal committee) fail to make a decision on a placing request within strict time limits (see the Additional Support for Learning (Placing Requests and Deemed Decisions) (Scotland) Regulations 2005), then they will be deemed to have refused the request, so allowing the next step in the appeal process to be taken.

17 Teachers in special schools

The Requirements for Teachers (Scotland) Regulations 2005 prescribe that teachers employed to teach pupils who are hearing or visually impaired or both must possess an appropriate qualification (Regs 5, 6 and 7). There is an exception where the teacher is in the process of obtaining the appropriate qualification but that person must not teach without it for more than five years (Reg. 8).

18 Other agencies

Where an appropriate agency (that is another local authority, a health board or someone specified in an Order issued by the Scottish Ministers) could help the education authority to perform its functions under the Education (Additional Support for Learning) (Scotland) Act 2004, the education authority may specify what help it needs and ask the agency for help. The agency cannot decline help unless the request is incompatible with that agency's own duties or the performance of the request would prejudice the discharge of its functions (Education (s.23).

The Additional Support for Learning (Appropriate Agencies) (Scotland) Order 2005 specifies further appropriate agencies that an education authority may ask for help. These are–
   (a) the colleges of further education and higher education institutions set out in Sch.2 to the Further and Higher Education (Scotland) Act 2005;
   (b) the Scottish Agricultural College; and
   (c) the Skills Development Scotland Co. Ltd.

The Additional Support for Learning (Appropriate Agency Request Period and Exceptions) (Scotland) Regulations 2005 specify 10 weeks within which a request for help must be met, although there are specified exceptions to this time limit. The request can only be made in relation to the exercise of the education authority's functions under the Act.

19 Standards in special schools

The Scottish Ministers may make regulations which set standards and make requirements of special schools (Education (Additional Support for Learning) (Scotland) Act 2004, s.24).

The School Premises (General Requirements and Standards) (Scotland) Regulations 1967 prescribe *inter alia* the standards for educational accommodation, playing space, etc., in special schools (excluding child guidance clinics). However buildings and sites may be approved notwithstanding that they do not meet these standards, where it is impracticable or unreasonable for them to meet them.

20 Attendance outside the United Kingdom

An education authority may make arrangements for a child or young person with additional support needs to attend a school or other appropriate establishment outside the UK (Education (Additional Support for Learning) (Scotland) Act 2004, s.25).

21 Publication of information

There is a duty on education authorities to publish, keep under review and potentially revise certain information listed in the Education (Additional Support for Learning) (Scotland) Act 2004. The Scottish Ministers can, by regulations, add to the list of information to be published (s.26).

The Additional Support for Learning (Publication of Information) (Scotland) Regulations 2005 adds to the list of information to be published (Reg. 2). The information may be published in electronic and printed form as well as any other format, such as video or audio, reasonably required without fee (Reg. 4).

The Scottish Ministers must, each year, collect from each education authority information on (s.27A)–

(a) the number of children and young persons for whose school education the authority are responsible having additional support needs;

(b) the principal factors giving rise to the additional support needs of those children and young persons;

(c) the types of support provided to those children and young persons; and

(d) the cost of providing that support.

The Scottish Ministers must publish the information collected each year.

The Scottish Ministers may, by Order, specify certain persons from whom parents and young people can obtain further advice, information and support in relation to the provision for additional support needs, including support and advocacy services (s.26(2)(i)). The Additional Support for Learning (Sources of Information) (Scotland) Order 2010 specifies Children in Scotland: Working for Children and Their Families (trading as Enquire-the Scottish national advice service for additional support for learning), the Scottish Independent Advocacy Alliance, and the Govan Law Centre Trust.

22 Closure of special schools

The provisions of s.22A and the Education (Publication and Consultation Etc.) (Scotland) Regulations 1981 apply to the closure, alteration, etc., of special schools (see the Note on **Schools: Scotland**).

23 Authorities

Statutes–

Education (Additional Support for Learning) (Scotland) Acts 2004 and 2009

Standards in Scotland's Schools etc. Act 2000

Statutory Instruments–

Additional Support for Learning (Appropriate Agencies) (Scotland) Order 2005, as amended (S.S.I. 2005 No. 325, 2010 Nos. 143 and 276, and 2015 No. 153)

Additional Support for Learning (Appropriate Agency Request Period and Exceptions) (Scotland) Regulations 2005 (S.S.I. 2005 No. 264)

Additional Support for Learning (Changes in School Education) (Scotland) Regulations 2005 (S.S.I. 2005 No. 265)

Additional Support for Learning (Co-ordinated Support Plan) (Scotland) Amendment Regulations 2005, as amended (S.S.I. 2005 No. 518, 2010 Nos. 149 and 275, and 2013 No. 147)

Additional Support for Learning Dispute Resolution (Scotland) Regulations 2005, as amended (S.S.I. 2005 No. 501, and 2010 Nos. 144 and 275)

Additional Support for Learning (Placing Requests and Deemed Decisions) (Scotland) Regulations 2005 (S.S.I. 2005 No. 515)

Additional Support for Learning (Publication of Information) (Scotland) Regulations 2005 (S.S.I. 2005 No. 267)

Additional Support for Learning (Sources of Information) (Scotland) Order 2010, as amended (S.S.I. 2010 Nos. 145 and 276, 2011 No. 102, and 2014 No. 103)

Education (Publication and Consultation Etc.) (Scotland) Regulations 1981, as amended (S.I. 1981 No. 1558, 1987 No. 2076, 1988 No. 107, and 1989 No. 1739)

Education (School and Placing Information) (Scotland) Regulations 2012 (S.S.I. 2012 No. 130)

Requirements for Teachers (Scotland) Regulations 2005 (S.S.I. 2005 No. 355)

School Premises (General Requirements and Standards) (Scotland) Regulations 1967, as amended (S.I. 1967 No. 1199, 1973 No. 522, 1976 No. 475, 1979 No. 1186, 1980 No. 100, 1982 No. 965, and S.S.I. 2005 No. 517)

INDEPENDENT SCHOOLS IN SCOTLAND

1 Preliminary

This Note deals with the registration and inspection of independent schools, with the establishment of Academies, and the abolition of corporal punishment in independent schools.

2 Introduction

An "independent school" means any school at which full-time education is provided for pupils of compulsory school age and which is not a public school, a grant-aided school, or a self-governing school (Education (Scotland) Act 1980, s.135(1), as amended by the Self-Governing Schools etc. (Scotland) Act 1989, Sch. 10 and the School Education (Ministerial Powers and Independent Schools) (Scotland) Act 2004).

3 General

Part V of the Education (Scotland) Act 1980 provides for the registration of independent schools in Scotland.

An independent school must be registered in the register of independent schools, which is open to public inspection. Breach of this provision is an offence punishable on summary conviction by imprisonment for up to 6 months or a fine not exceeding level 4 on the standard scale, or both (Education (Scotland) Act 1980, s.101). As to the standard scale, see the Note on **Treatment of Offenders** at para 35 **Maximum fines and the "standard scale"**).

4 The procedure for applying for registration in Scotland

The procedure for application for registration as an independent school in Scotland is set out in s.98A of the Education (Scotland) Act 1980 (inserted by the School Education (Ministerial Powers and Independent Schools) (Scotland) Act 2004, s.4).

Any person intending to open and run an independent school must apply to the Scottish Ministers for registration. The Scottish Ministers may define by regulations the form an application for registration is to take, and the information which it is to include. The Registration of Independent Schools (Scotland) Regulations 2006 have been made for this purpose.

The Scottish Ministers must be satisfied when considering an application for registration that (s.98A(3))–
   (a) efficient and suitable instruction will be provided at the school, having regard to the ages and sex of the pupils who shall be attending the school;
   (b) the welfare of such pupils will be adequately safeguarded and promoted;
   (c) the proprietor of the school is a proper person to be the proprietor of an independent school and every proposed teacher in the school is a proper person to be a teacher in any school;
   (d) the proposed school premises are suitable for use as a school; and
   (e) the accommodation to be provided at the school premises is adequate and suitable taking account of the number, sex and ages of the pupils.

When determining whether a person is a proper person to be a proprietor or teacher consideration must be had to whether that person is disqualified from being such a proprietor or teacher.

If the Scottish Ministers are satisfied as to these matters they may then grant an application for registration. They may also register an independent school subject to conditions.

If they decide to refuse an application to register an independent school because they are not satisfied as to (c), (d) or (e) above, the Scottish Ministers may make a disqualification order (s.98B, as inserted).

Should the Scottish Ministers make a disqualification order they are required to notify the proprietor, the Registrar and any other person or body they think fit (s.98C). Where the Scottish Ministers make an order disqualifying a proposed teacher from being a teacher at any school (under s.98B(5)), they are also required to notify the proposed teacher, the Registrar, and any other person or body they think fit. There is a right of appeal to the sheriff principal by a proprietor against a decision made by the Scottish Ministers to refuse an application, to set conditions on registration, or to make a disqualification order. There is also a right of appeal by a proposed teacher against a disqualification order relating to that teacher.

The Registrar must record in the register–
   (a) in relation to every application for registration of an independent school, such information as the Scottish Ministers may direct;
   (b) in relation to any conditions on the carrying on of a registered school, such information (including information relating to any variation and revocation of such conditions) as the Scottish Ministers may direct;
   (c) every order of an Independent Schools Tribunal or the Scottish Ministers imposing any disqualification; and
   (d) in relation to every registered school, such information which is to be furnished to the Registrar as the Scottish Ministers may direct.

Where an order removing any disqualification is made by the Scottish Ministers or the sheriff principal, the Registrar must remove the order imposing that disqualification from the register (s.98(2), as substituted by the 2004 Act, s.3).

5 Standards in independent schools–Scotland

If the Scottish Ministers are satisfied at any time that a registered independent school or provisionally registered school is objectionable on the grounds of (Education (Scotland) Act 1980, s.99(1) and (1A), inserted by the School Education (Ministerial Powers and Independent Schools) (Scotland) Act 2004, s.5(2))–

(a) failure to provide efficient and suitable instruction;

(b) unsuitability of the school premises;

(c) the inadequacy or unsuitability of the accommodation;

(d) a condition imposed by the Scottish Act on the carrying on of the school not being or has not been complied with;

(e) any part of the school premises disqualified from being used as a school;

(f) any accommodation provided at the school premises disqualified from being used as such;

(g) the proprietor of the school is disqualified from being the proprietor of an independent school, disqualified from working with children, a person prescribed by the Scottish Ministers in regulations or otherwise not a proper person to be the proprietor of an independent school;

(h) a teacher in the school is disqualified from being a teacher in any school, disqualified from working with children, a person prescribed by the Scottish Ministers in regulations or otherwise not a proper person to be a teacher in any school; or

(j) the proprietor of the school has not furnished information required, or notified a change in such particulars to the Registrar,

the Scottish Ministers must serve on the proprietor of the school a notice of complaint (s.99). The Scottish Ministers need not do this where they are satisfied that they need to make an order under s.100(2) of the Scottish Act urgently referring the complaint to an Independent Schools Tribunal (s.99(1B), inserted by the 2004 Act, s.5(2)).

A notice of complaint must (s.99(1C), inserted by the 2004 Act, s.5(2))–

(a) state the ground of the complaint together with the full particulars of the matter complained of; and

(b) specify the measures which in the opinion of the Scottish Ministers are necessary to remedy the matter and the period within which those measures must be taken.

The proprietor of a registered school may appeal to the sheriff principal against a notice of complaint (s.99(3)).

The Scottish Ministers can make an order directing the Registrar to remove the school from the register as the result of a notice of complaint in three circumstances (s.100, as amended by the 2004 Act, s.5(3))–

(a) after a notice of complaint has been served on the proprietor and no appeal has been made, or alternatively where an appeal has been made but refused, and the period in the notice has expired and the Scottish Ministers are not satisfied that the proprietor has taken satisfactory action to remedy the matter;

(b) where a notice of complaint has been served, an appeal has been lodged but no decision has yet been made and where, pending that decision, the Scottish Ministers are satisfied that there is a serious risk of harm to any pupil attending the school; or

(c) Scottish Ministers are satisfied that urgent action is required.

In addition to the power to remove a school from the register, the Scottish Ministers may make disqualification orders with regard to school premises or accommodation, school proprietors and teachers. Orders can also be made imposing or varying conditions on the number, age or sex of pupils.

When the Scottish Ministers make an order they are required to notify the proprietor, the Registrar and any other person or body they think fit. Where the order is one to disqualify a teacher, the Scottish Ministers must also notify that teacher. There is a right of appeal against disqualification orders.

Any proprietor disqualified from being a proprietor, or any teacher disqualified from being a teacher, will unless specifically stated otherwise, be disqualified from being both a proprietor of an independent school and a teacher at any school.

The enforcement of orders is dealt with by s.101 (as amended by the 2004 Act, s.5(4)) which provides for the following offences–

(a) running an independent school that is not registered;

(b) using school premises, any part of such premises, or accommodation subject to a disqualification order;

(c) acting as the proprietor of an independent school when disqualified from doing so by an order; and

(d) endeavouring to get a position as a teacher, accept such a position, or teach in any school, whilst being disqualified from being a teacher (s.101(3A) of the Scottish Act, inserted by s.5(4)(b) of the 2004 Act).

Application may be made to the Scottish Ministers for the removal of a disqualification order (s.102). The Scottish Ministers must inform the person, the Registrar and any other person or body they think fit of any decision they reach on an application to remove a disqualification. There is an appeal to the sheriff principal within 28 days of the applicant being notified of the decision by the Scottish Ministers to refuse to remove a disqualification (s.102(1A), inserted by the 2004 Act, s.6). The appeals procedure is set out in s.103 (substituted by the 2004 Act, s.6).

The whole registration, complaints and enforcement procedure under the Scottish Act also extends to proprietors which are bodies corporate as well as individuals (s.103A, inserted by s the 2004 Act, s.7).

6 Suitability of proprietors and staff–Scotland

Two of the grounds upon which the Scottish Ministers may find that a registered independent school is objectionable are that (Education (Scotland) Act 1980, s.99(1) and (1A), inserted by the School Education (Ministerial Powers and Independent Schools) (Scotland) Act 2004, s.5(2))–

    (a) the proprietor of the school is disqualified from being the proprietor of an independent school, disqualified from working with children, disqualified by regulations, or otherwise not a proper person to be the proprietor of an independent school; or

    (b) that a teacher is in a similar position.

    Where a Scottish independent school is found to be objectionable the Scottish Ministers must serve on the proprietor of the school a notice of complaint and the measures necessary to remedy these matters (s.99 of the Education (Scotland) Act 1980).

    Disqualification orders can also be made with regard to proprietors or teachers against which there is a right of appeal. Any proprietor disqualified from being a proprietor, or any teacher disqualified from being a teacher, will, unless specifically stated otherwise, be disqualified from being both a proprietor of an independent school and a teacher at any school (s.100(2)(e) and s.101 of the Scottish Act, amended by s.5(3) and (4) of the 2004 Act) (see **5 Standards in independent schools–Scotland**, above).

    Independent schools in Scotland are required to submit an annual return to the registrar. One of the matters which it must contain is a statement that criminal record certificates have been obtained, and are in accordance with the school's child protection policy and procedure, in respect of any teachers and others in child care positions employed for the first time in, or re-employed by or in the school, within the previous 12 months (Registration of Independent Schools (Scotland) Regulations 2005, Sch. 2).

7 Particulars to be furnished

    The Registration of Independent Schools (Scotland) Regulations 2005 prescribe the particulars to be furnished to the Registrar of Independent Schools, both when applying for registration and subsequent to registration.

    The Regulations prescribe the information to be contained in an application for registration (e.g., details of the proprietor, age range and sex of the pupils, layout of the premises, religious ethos of the school, employee details, etc), in an initial return (if one is requested by the Secretary of State), and in an annual return.

8 Abolition of corporal punishment

    The Standards in Scotland's Schools etc. Act 2000, s.16 abolished corporal punishment in all schools in Scotland. It is no longer lawful for any teacher or staff member to administer corporal punishment to a child under 18, whether on or off school premises. "Corporal punishment" is defined as any punishment which would, apart from any justification, constitute physical assault. However, corporal punishment will not be treated as being given to a child if it is done to avert an immediate danger of personal injury to any person (including the child himself) or immediate danger to the property of any person (including the child).

9 Authorities

Statutes–

Education (Scotland) Acts 1980 and 1981

School Education (Ministerial Powers and Independent Schools) (Scotland) Act 2004

Self-Governing Schools etc. (Scotland) Act 1989

Standards in Scotland's Schools etc Act 2000

Statutory Instruments–

Registration of Independent Schools (Scotland) Regulations 2006 (S.S.I. 2006 No. 324)

SCHOOLS IN SCOTLAND

1 Introduction

The main Act governing school education in Scotland is the Education (Scotland) Act 1980, together with the other Acts listed in the **Authorities**, below. References in this Note are to sections of, or Schedules to, the 1980 Act unless otherwise stated.

This Note has been structured as follows–

A: Provision of schools
B: Government of public schools
C: Standards in schools
D: Inspection of schools
E: Inspection of education authorities
F: School attendance
G: Information about schools
H: General provisions
 (religious instruction, corporal punishment,
 pupil records, etc.)
I: School premises
J: Teachers' qualification and employment
K: Nursery education

A: PROVISION OF SCHOOLS

2 Education authorities

The education authorities in Scotland are the councils for the local government areas (Education (Scotland) Act 1980, s.135). They are required under s.1 to secure the provision of adequate and efficient school education (other than schooling in nursery schools and classes, which they are empowered to provide) and further education for their area. They are also empowered, and, in the case of pupils at school, required, to secure the provision of adequate facilities for social, cultural, and recreational activities, and for physical education and training. The standards and general requirements to which education authorities are to conform in discharging their functions under s.1 may be prescribed by regulations (s.2).

3 Duties of education authorities

It is the right of every child of school age to be provided with school education by, or by virtue of arrangements made by, an education authority (Standards in Scotland's Schools etc Act 2000, s.1); and it is the duty of every education authority to secure for their area adequate and efficient provision of school education and further education (Education (Scotland) Act 1980, s.1).

For children under school age, the duty to provide school education only applies to the extent required by the Children and Young People (Scotland) Act 2014 (1980 Act, s.1(1A)) (see **50 Provision of school education for children under school age**, below).

In fulfilling their duty to secure adequate and efficient school education, education authorities must determine how much public school accommodation is required, taking account of all the schools suitable and available for the purpose.

An education authority must maintain and keep efficient every public school and other education establishment under their management, and from time to time must provide such additional accommodation as may be necessary for the above purpose (1980 Act, s.17) (see further I: SCHOOL PREMISES, below).

Education authorities must also secure for pupils in attendance at schools in their areas the provision of adequate facilities for social, cultural, and recreative activities, and for physical education and training.

Where school education is provided to a child or young person by, or under arrangements made by, an education authority, the authority must secure that the education is directed to the development of the personality, talents and physical and mental ability of the child or young person to their fullest potential. In doing so an authority must have due regard, so far as is reasonably practicable, to any views of the child or young person in decisions significantly affecting them, taking account of their age and maturity (Standards in Scotland's Schools etc Act 2000, s.2).

4 Duty in relation to promotion of health

The Scottish Ministers must endeavour to ensure that schools managed by education authorities, grant-aided schools and hostels provided and maintained by education authorities for pupils, are health-promoting. Further, education authorities must endeavour to ensure that schools managed by them and hostels provided and maintained by them for pupils, are health-promoting. The managers of a grant-aided school must also endeavour to ensure that the school is health-promoting. In carrying out its duty, an education authority or, as the case may be, the managers of a grant-aided school, must have regard to any guidance issued by the Scottish Ministers. A school or hostel is "health-promoting" if it provides (whether on its own or in conjunction with Health Boards, parents or any other person) activities and an environment and facilities which promote the physical, social, mental and emotional health and well-being of pupils in attendance at the school or residing in the hostel (Standards in Scotland's Schools etc Act 2000, s.2A inserted by the Schools (Health Promotions and Nutrition) (Scotland) Act 2007, s.1).

Under s.5 of the 2000 Act (inserted by the 2007 Act, s.2), an annual statement of health promotion must be made by the education authority.

5 Food and drink: nutritional requirements

Education authorities and managers of grant aided schools have a duty to ensure that food or drink provided for pupils must comply with nutritional requirements specified by the Scottish Ministers (Education (Scotland) Act 1980, ss.56A-56D inserted by the Schools (Health Promotion and Nutrition) (Scotland) Act 2007, s.3).

Education authorities must also consider the nutritional requirements in situations where they enter into an arrangement with regard to a pupil's education in an independent school (ss.49(2ZA), 50(1ZA) and 50A of the 1980 Act, amended or inserted by the 2007 Act, s.5).

Specific duties are placed on education authorities to require the promotion of school lunches and to require the protection of the identity of those receiving free school lunches (1980 Act, ss.53A and 53B inserted by the 2007 Act, ss.7 and 8).

Education authorities also have a duty to take into consideration any sustainable development guidance issued by Scottish Ministers when providing food and drinks (or related services) in schools (1980 Act, s.56E inserted by the 2007 Act, s.9).

6 Charging of fees

Under s.3, an education authority may not, with limited exceptions, charge fees for school education in schools under their management. S.11 of the 1989 Act prohibits charging fees in respect of school education provided at self-governing schools.

School education means progressive education appropriate to the requirements of pupils in attendance at schools, regard being had to the age, ability, and aptitude of such pupils, and includes—
  (a) activities in nursery schools and nursery classes of a kind suitable for pupils who are under school age;
  (b) provision for special education needs (see the Note on **Additional Support for Learning and Special Schools: Scotland**);
  (c) the teaching of Gaelic in Gaelic-speaking areas.

S.3 does not apply to the provision of school education for children under school age (s.3(7)), however fees may still not be charged if the education authority have a duty to provide such education (see **27 School age**, below).

7 Types of schools

There are five main types of school in Scotland (s.135, as amended by 1989 Act, Sch. 10)—
  (1) *Public schools*, i.e., schools under the management of an education authority.
  (2) *Grant-aided schools*, i.e., schools other than public schools, self-governing schools, or technology academies, in respect of which grants are made by the Scottish Ministers to the managers of the school other than grants in aid of the employers' superannuation contribution.
  (3) *Self-governing schools*, i.e., schools maintained by the Scottish Ministers under s.1 of the 1989 Act, for which an application for self-governing status has been approved by them pursuant to s.16 of that Act and which have a board of management incorporated under s.19(2) (see **13 Self-governing status**, below).
  (4) *Technology academies*, i.e., independent schools providing secondary education and having a broad curriculum with an emphasis on science and technology, established and carried on by a person in consideration of a payment by the Scottish Ministers by an agreement under s.68 of the 1989 Act (see the Note on **Independent Schools**).
  (5) *Other independent schools*, i.e., schools at which full-time education is provided for pupils of school age, not being public schools, grant-aided schools, or self-governing schools.

8 Changes in educational provision

The Schools (Consultation) (Scotland) Act 2010 contains provisions which set out a consultation procedure in respect of proposed school closures and certain other proposals affecting schools. The Act also makes specific provision for closure proposals for rural schools and establishes a system of Ministerial call-in, in relation to school closure decisions.

Sections 1 to 11 of the Act concern the process whereby local authorities consult on proposals for closures or other changes to schools that require consultation. When a local authority has formulated a "relevant proposal", it must comply with the consultation process set out in the Act. A "relevant proposal" is defined as a proposal to (Sch. 1)–

(a) permanently discontinue a school or discontinue all the nursery classes in a school or a stage of education in a school (apart from a nursery class);

(b) permanently discontinue the provision of Gaelic medium education in all the nursery classes in a school that also provides a nursery class through English medium education or in a stage of education (apart from a nursery class) in a school that also provides the stage of education through English medium education;

(c) permanently discontinue the provision of English medium education in all the nursery classes in a school that also provides a nursery class through Gaelic medium education or in a stage of education (apart from a nursery class) in a school that also provides the stage of education through Gaelic medium education;

(d) establish a new school or a new stage of education in a school;

(e) relocate (in whole or in part) a school or nursery class;

(f) vary any admission arrangements for a school;

(g) change the school commencement date of a primary school;

(h) vary the arrangements for the transfer of pupils from a primary school to a secondary school;

(i) vary arrangements for the constitution of a special class in a school other than a special school;

(j) discontinue arrangements for the provision of transport by the education authority for pupils attending a denominational school;

(k) change a denominational school into a non-denominational school;

(l) discontinue a further education centre which is managed by the education authority.

A "stage of education" is defined as a yearly stage of a primary or secondary education, a nursery class in a school or a special class in a school which is not itself a special school.

The initial requirements as to consultation are to (s.1)–

(i) prepare an educational benefits statement;

(ii) prepare and publish a proposal paper;

(iii) give notice of the proposal to the relevant consultees (see below) and invite representations;

(iv) hold, and give notice of, a public meeting;

(v) involve Her Majesty's Inspectors (HMIE).

The consultees include the parents of the pupils at any affected school; the pupils of the school in so far as the local authority considers them to be of a suitable age and understanding; the Parent Council of the school; the staff and any trade union representative of them; and, any other users of the school the local authority considers relevant. Parents of any children expected to attend any affected school within 2 years of the date of publication of the proposal paper will also be consultees (Sch. 2). The consultation period is a period of at least 6 weeks that starts on the day (or last day) on which the notice required is given, that runs continuously, and includes at least 30 school days of any affected school (s.6). Following compliance with the initial requirements in (i) to (v) above, the local authority must then review the proposal and prepare and publish a consultation report (ss.9, 10). A local authority may proceed with a relevant proposal only after the expiry of 3 weeks starting with the day on which the consultation report is published (s.11). In exercising its functions, a local authority must have regard to any guidance issued by the Scottish Ministers (s.19) and the Scottish Ministers may by regulations make such provision as they consider necessary or expedient for the purposes of, or in connection with, the Act (s.20).

Where a decision is made not to implement a closure proposal in relation to a school, no further closure proposal can be made in respect of that school for a further five years unless there is a significant change in the school's circumstances (s.2A).

Additional requirements apply when authorities are considering a closure proposal concerning a rural school. The local authority must have special regard to the following factors (i) the likely effect on the community if the closure proposal is implemented, and (ii) the likely effect caused by any different travelling arrangements that may be required in consequence of the proposal (s.12). Where an education authority is formulating a closure proposal as respects a rural school it must (s.12A)–

(a) identify its reasons for formulating the proposal;

(b) consider whether there are any reasonable alternatives to the proposal as a response to those reasons; and

(c) assess, for the proposal and each of the identified alternatives (i) the likely educational benefits of the implementation of the proposal, or as the case may be, alternative; (ii) the likely effect of each on the local community; and (iii) the likely effects of any different travelling arrangements that may be required.

Additional consultation requirements also apply to proposals for the closure of a rural school (s.13). In the Act, a "rural school" is a school which is designated as such by its inclusion in the list of rural schools maintained by the Scottish Ministers (s.14).

The Scottish Ministers may "call-in" a decision taken by an authority after the consultation procedures set out in the Act have been completed. Where a local authority have decided to implement a closure proposal it must notify the Scottish Ministers of that decision within 6 working days starting on and including the day on which the decision was made and supply the Scottish Ministers with a copy of the proposal paper and of the consultation report. The Scottish Ministers then have eight weeks in which to issue a call-in notice to the education authority (s.15). The Scottish Ministers may issue a call-in notice where it appears to them that the local authority may have failed (i) in a significant regard to comply with the requirements imposed on it by or under the Act so far as they are relevant in

EDUCATION

relation to the closure proposal, or (ii) to take proper account of a material consideration relevant to its decision to implement the proposal (s.17). Where the Scottish Ministers issue a call-in notice as respects a closure proposal they must refer the proposal to the Convener of the School Closure Review Panels who will constitute a Panel to consider the closure proposal (s.17A).

Following a review of a closure proposal the School Closure Review Panel may (s.17C)–
(a) refuse to consent to the proposal;
(b) refuse to consent to the proposal and remit it to the education authority for a fresh decision as to implementation; or
(c) grant consent to the proposal, either subject to conditions or unconditionally.

An appeal may be made to the sheriff against a decision of a School Closure Review Panel by the education authority or a relevant consultee in relation to the closure proposal, but only on a point of law (s.17D).

An education authority must also obtain the consent of the Scottish Ministers before implementing any proposal relating to a denominational school transferred to it under s.16(1) of the 1980 Act or provided by the authority under s.17(2) of that Act which (a) would if implemented have the effect that all or some of the pupils attending the school would no longer be able to receive denominational education of the kind provided in it (1980 Act, s.22C), or (b) is a proposal to discontinue or amalgamate the school or part of it, to change the site or the arrangements for admission, or to disapply the arrangements for admission, or to disapply the arrangements for its management as a denominational school (1980 Act, s.22D).

B: GOVERNMENT OF PUBLIC SCHOOLS

9 Parental involvement

Under the Scottish Schools (Parental Involvement) Act 2006 it is the duty of Scottish Ministers and education authorities to promote the involvement of parents of pupils in attendance at public schools in the education provided to those pupils by the schools (s.1).

Each education authority must prepare a document called "strategy for parental involvement" containing their general policies for implementing their parental involvement duties, having regard to how that strategy will promote equal opportunities (s.2).

Note.–The School Boards (Scotland) Act 1988 has been repealed by the Scottish Schools (Parental Involvement) Act 2006 and school boards have been replaced by parent councils and combined parent councils. See **10 Parent forums and parent councils**, below.

10 Parent forums and parent councils

The parents of the pupils at a public school constitute the "parent forum" of the school which may be represented by a body known as a "parent council" (Scottish Schools (Parental Involvement) Act 2006, s.5).

The education authority must notify the parent forum in writing of its intention to prepare a scheme for the establishment of a parent council for the school, inviting them to indicate, within a reasonable period, a preference as to how the council should be constituted (s.6). The notification must include an invitation to indicate that there should be no such scheme or that such a scheme should be prepared by a body other than the education authority.

The members of the parent council must be members of the school's parent forum or people who are co-opted to the council by the members (s.7).

The functions of a parent council are to support those managing the school in their endeavours to raise the standards and quality of education in the school and to develop the pupils to their fullest potential. The parent council may make representations to the head teacher and education authority about the arrangements in the school to support parents in getting involved in their own child's education, and that of all the pupils at the schools generally. It may also make representations to the education authority about the arrangements in the authority's area to support parents in getting involved in their child's education and in the education provided to all pupils attending public schools in the authority's area. The parent council's other functions are to promote contact between the school, the parent forum, pupils and others; to report at least annually to the parent forum on its activities; to seek, collate and report the views of the parent forum on specified matters; and, to review its constitution and amend it as necessary, seeking the agreement of the forum members (s.8(1)).

In addition, a parent council established for a primary school is to promote contact between the parent forum of the school and such providers of nursery education to prospective pupils of the school as the parent council considers appropriate (s.8(2)).

The parent council may make representations to the head teacher, education authority or others as appropriate (s.8(4)). Representations made by a parent council to Her Majesty's Inspectorate of Education are covered by s.8(5) and (6).

Parent councils must have regard to any guidance issued to them by the education authority (s.8(13)).

A head teacher has both the duty and the right either to attend or, if he so elects, to be represented at any meeting of that council. Parent council meetings are to be open to the public except where matters are being discussed on a confidential basis (s.9).

A parent council may raise funds by any means (other than by borrowing) and may receive gifts, and may expend any sums so received at its discretion. It must, however, keep proper accounts. Where a parent council ceases to exist, any property belonging to it passes to the education who must use it for the benefit of the school (s.10).

11 Duties, reports, appointments and complaints

The education authority for a school's area has a duty to give advice and information on any matter to a parent council when the council reasonably requests it (s.11(1)). An education authority must also take appropriate steps to ensure that the head teacher and staff of each school in their area are available to give advice and information to a parent council on what is being done by those managing the school to promote parental involvement in education there, and in giving such advice and information in a manner consistent with the authority's duties under the Scottish Schools (Parental Involvement) Act 2006 (s.11(2)).

The head teacher of a school must also, if requested to do so by a parent council, give advice to the council on any matter falling within his area of responsibility (s.11(3)).

An education authority must, in respect of each financial year, determine an allocation of a reasonable sum of money within the authority's budget that is reasonably required by the council for meeting its administrative, training and other expenses (s.11(4)).

An education authority may provide a parent council with services or accommodation (s.11(5)). It must also inform a parent council about the school's arrangements for consultation between parents and teachers and the council may make representations concerning those arrangements to the authority or to the head teacher (s.11(6)).

An education authority must give advice and information to any parent of a pupil in attendance at a public school in their area when that parent reasonably requests it from them on any matter relating to the education provided to that pupil (s.12).

The head teacher of a public school must, at least once a year, report to any parent council or combined parent council or, if no such council has been established, to the parent forum, evaluating the performance of the school and stating what his objectives and ambitions are for the school (s.13).

An education authority must inform the Scottish Ministers and the parent council about the authority's procedures for filling any post, other than on an acting basis, of head teacher or deputy head teacher of a school and also about any change they make to their appointment process (s.14).

The Parental Involvement in Headteacher and Deputy Headteacher Appointments (Scotland) Regulations 2007 provide for parental involvement in the process relating to the appointment of headteachers and deputy headteachers. The Regulations require an education authority to involve the parent council, as the representative body within each school of parents of pupils at that school, in specified stages of the appointment process.

An education authority must establish a complaints procedure in relation to the exercise by the authority of, or failure by them to exercise, any of their functions under the Scottish Schools (Parental Involvement) Act 2006 (s.15).

12 Combined parent councils

Where a majority in each of the parent forums of two or more schools decide that they wish to have a combined council to cover the interests of the schools involved, s.16(1) and (2) set out how a combined council may be set up. The members of the parent forum at each school must be told in writing of the proposal and given a specific but reasonable timeframe in which to give their response to the proposal. The decision is to be based on the response of the majority of parent members of each of the forums responding within that period. Arrangements to establish a combined council can be made at any time, including where a parent council has already been set up (s.16(3)). However, an existing parent council ceases to exist when a combined council is established (Scottish Schools (Parental Involvement) Act 2006, s.16(4)).

A school can withdraw from a combined parent council by giving notice of the proposed decision to withdraw to each member of the parent forum. The decision is to be made on the basis of the views of the majority of members responding within the relevant notice period (s.17).

13 Self-governing status

Under Part 1 of the Self-Governing Schools etc (Scotland) Act 1989 responsibility for the management of a state-funded school could be transferred from the education authority to a board of management where proposals to that effect were supported by the parents of children attending the school and approved by the Secretary of State (now the Scottish Ministers). The Standards in Scotland's Schools etc Act 2000 repealed Part 1 of the 1989 Act and s.17 of the 2000 Act further provides that the Scottish Ministers may by order provide that any school that has become self-governing will revert to education authority control.

C: STANDARDS IN SCHOOLS

14 Raising standards

Ss.3 to 7 of the Standards in Scotland's Schools etc Act 2000 contain an "improvement framework" for Scottish schools.

Under s.3, the Scottish Ministers must endeavour to secure improvements in the quality of the school education which is provided for Scotland, and must exercise their powers in relation to such provision with a view to raising educational standards. A similar duty is placed on educational authorities.

From time to time the Scottish Ministers, after consulting the education authorities and other persons having an interest in the matter, are required to define, by order, priorities in educational objectives for school education in Scotland and to define and publish measures of performance in respect of those priorities (s.4). The Education (National Priorities) (Scotland) Order 2000 defines priorities in education for the purposes of s.4 as follows–

(a) to raise standards of educational attainment for all in schools, especially in the core skills of literacy and numeracy, and to achieve better levels in national measures of achievement including examination results;

(b) to support and develop the skills of teachers, the self-discipline of pupils and to enhance school environments so that they are conducive to teaching and learning;

(c) to promote equality and help every pupil benefit from education, with particular regard paid to pupils with disabilities and special educational needs, and to Gaelic and other lesser used languages;

(d) to work with parents to teach pupils respect for self and one another and their interdependence with other members of their neighbourhood and society and to teach them the duties and responsibilities of citizenship in a democratic society; and

(e) to equip pupils with the foundation skills, attitudes and expectations necessary to prosper in a changing society and to encourage creativity and ambition.

15 Annual statement of improvement objectives

An education authority must publish an "annual statement of education improvement objectives", after consulting parents, teachers, other school employees, and after giving children and young people an opportunity to express their views (2000 Act, s.5). Each annual statement must include an account of the ways in which or the circumstances in which–

(a) the authority will seek to involve parents in promoting their children's education;

(b) they will, in providing school education, encourage equal opportunities; and

(c) they will provide "Gaelic medium education" (i.e., teaching in Gaelic) and (where this is provided) of the ways in which they will seek to develop the provision of such education.

Education authorities are also required to publish an annual report as to their success in meeting the objectives as set out in their annual statement.

16 School development plans

Each education authority must ensure that there is prepared for each school an annual development plan which takes account of the objectives and strategy for parental involvement in the authority's annual statement of education improvement objectives and sets objectives for the school (including objectives as to the involvement of a pupil's parents in the education provided to the pupil and to the school's pupils generally) and which contains a statement of the education authority's ambitions for the school (Standards in Scotland's Schools, etc Act 2000, s.6, amended by the Scottish Schools (Parental Involvement) Act 2006, s.3). Such plans must be prepared after consultation with teachers, other school employees, parents and any parent council or combined parent council established for the school. In particular, the plan must include an account of the ways in which, and extent to which, the head teacher will consult the school's pupils and seek to involve them when decisions need to be made about the everyday running of the school. After 12 months, a report on the implementation of the plan must also be prepared.

Parents of school pupils must have access to the development plan and report, upon request and without cost, and are entitled to receive summary copies of both of them.

17 Review of school performance

S.7 of the 2000 Act requires an education authority to define and publish measures and standards of performance for schools managed by them, and to monitor the quality of education provided by reference to these measures and standards. If an education authority concludes that a school is not performing satisfactorily, it must take such steps as appear to it to be requisite to remedy the matter.

The quality of education includes the extent to which a pupil's parents are involved in the education provided to the pupil (s.7, amended by the Scottish Schools (Parental Involvement) Act 2006, s.4).

18 Delegation schemes

S.8 of the 2000 Act places on a statutory footing the system known as "devolved school management". Education authorities are required to have a scheme for delegating to head teachers the preparation of the school's development plan and such other functions as the authority think fit.

D: INSPECTION OF SCHOOLS

19 School inspections

The Scottish Ministers may require an inspection of any educational establishment at such intervals as they think appropriate. They may also require a special inspection of any school whenever they consider such an inspection to be desirable. In addition, they may, from time to time, require an inspection of any other educational establishment. Inspections are made by Her Majesty's Inspectors or any person appointed by the Scottish Ministers for these purposes (or both) (Education (Scotland) Act 1980, s.66(1)).

If requested to do so by the Scottish Ministers, Her Majesty's Inspectors or any person appointed by the Scottish Ministers shall give advice to the Scottish Ministers on specific matters. Also, the Inspectors may, at the Scottish Ministers' request, inspect and report on a school or class of schools in relation to a specific matter (s.66(1AA) of the 1980 Act, inserted by the Standards in Scotland's Schools etc. Act 2000, s.11).

20 Codes of practice in relation to school inspections

The Scottish Ministers may, from time to time, prepare, approve and issue codes of practice for the purposes of giving practical guidance on matters relating to inspections under s.66 of the Education (Scotland) Act 1980 (see **19 School inspections**, above) and promoting what appears to them to be desirable practices.

These codes of practice do not apply to the inspection of further education establishments (s.66A of the 1980 Act, inserted by the Standards in Scotland's Schools etc. Act 2000, s.12).

21 Scottish Ministers' power to make schools act

If, after an inspection of a public school or a grant-aided school under s.66(1) or s.66(1AA) of the 1980 Act, Her Majesty's Inspectors find that, having been given sufficient opportunity to improve in relation to a matter identified under s.66(1), the "relevant person" is failing or has failed to take satisfactory action to do so; and, having regard to the seriousness of that failure, an enforcement direction is justified, they must make a reference to the Scottish Ministers.

"Relevant person" means the education authority in relation to a public school and the managers of the school in relation to a grant-aided school.

A reference to the Scottish Ministers must be in writing, specify the failure and include recommendations as to the action which, in the opinion of the Inspector, the relevant person should take to remedy or prevent the recurrence of that failure. The Inspector must inform the relevant person of the making of that reference (s.66B of the 1980 Act, inserted by the School Education (Ministerial Powers and Independent Schools) (Scotland) Act 2004, s.1).

Where, on a reference under s.66B, it appears to the Scottish Ministers that the relevant person is failing or has failed to take satisfactory action to improve in relation to the matter mentioned in s.66B; and an enforcement direction is justified, they may serve a preliminary notice on the relevant person.

A preliminary notice is a notice which—
(a) informs the relevant person of the apparent failure; and
(b) requires the relevant person to submit to the Scottish Ministers, within a specified timeframe, a written response which states that the person has not so failed and gives reasons supporting that statement, or states that the person has so failed but gives reasons why an enforcement direction should not be given (s.66C of the 1980 Act, inserted by the School Education (Ministerial Powers and Independent Schools) (Scotland) Act 2004, s.1).

Where a preliminary notice is served under s.66C and the time specified in it has expired but it still appears to the Scottish Ministers that the relevant person is failing or has failed to take satisfactory action to improve and, having regard to the seriousness of that failure, action is justified, they may give the relevant person an enforcement direction.

An enforcement direction is a direction in writing by the Scottish Ministers requiring the relevant person to take action calculated to remedy or prevent the recurrence of the failure within a specified timeframe (s.66D of the 1980 Act, inserted by the School Education (Ministerial Powers and Independent Schools) (Scotland) Act 2004, s.1).

E: INSPECTION OF EDUCATION AUTHORITIES

22 Inspection of education authority

Her Majesty's Inspectors, or any person appointed by the Scottish Ministers for inspection purposes must inspect an education authority when asked to do so by the Scottish Ministers to review the way in which the authority is exercising its functions in relation to the provision of school education.

The education authority must assist whoever is carrying out the inspection (Standards in Scotland's Schools etc. Act 2000, s.9).

23 Codes of practice in relation to inspection of education authority

The Scottish Ministers may, for the purposes of giving practical guidance in relation to inspections of education authorities (see **21 Inspection of education authority**, above) and promoting what appear to them to be desirable practices, prepare, approve and issue codes of practice (Standards in Scotland's Schools etc. Act 2000, s.10).

24 Scottish Ministers' power to make education authorities act

Where an education authority has failed to improve, an Inspector may refer it to the Scottish Ministers. The Scottish Ministers may in turn issue a preliminary notice to the authority, which may be followed by enforcement directions. The process is identical in relation to education authorities as for schools (see **21 Scottish Ministers' power to make schools act**, above) (Standards in Scotland's Schools etc. Act 2000, ss.10A-10C inserted by the School Education (Ministerial Powers and Independent Schools) (Scotland) Act 2004, s.2).

F: SCHOOL ATTENDANCE

25 Pupils to be educated in accordance with the wishes of their parents

In the exercise and performance of their powers and duties under the principal Act, the Scottish Ministers, education authorities, and boards of management of self-governing schools must have regard to the general principle that, so far as is compatible with the provision of suitable instruction and training and the avoidance of unreasonable public expenditure, pupils are to be educated in accordance with their parent's wishes (s.28 and the 1989 Act, s.10 and Sch. 2).

26 Placing in schools

Ss.28A to 28H, as inserted by s.1 of the 1981 Act and as amended by the 1996 Act, deal with the placing of children in schools.

S.28A(1) imposes a duty on an education authority to comply with a written request (a placing request) by a parent of a qualifying child to place his child in a school (not including a nursery school or a nursery class in a school) specified in the request (the specified school), if it is under their management, unless one of the specified grounds for refusal is shown to apply. A child will generally be a "qualifying child" for these purposes if he is of school age or his fifth birthday falls before the March following the start of the school year (see s.28A(6)). In carrying out their duty, the authority must have regard to any guidance given by the Scottish Ministers. The duty does not apply (s.28A(3))–

(a) if placing the child in the specified school would–
 (i) make it necessary to employ an additional teacher or give rise to significant expenditure on extending or otherwise altering the school's accommodation or facilities or be seriously detrimental to the continuity of the child's education; or
 (ii) be likely to be seriously detrimental to order and discipline in the school, or to the educational well-being of pupils; or
 (iii) assuming that pupil numbers remain constant, make it necessary, at the beginning of a future stage of the child's primary education, for the authority to create an additional class, or additional composite class, in the school or to employ an additional teacher at that school;
 (iv) otherwise have the consequence that the capacity of the school would be exceeded in terms of pupil numbers.
(b) if the education normally provided at the school is not suited to the child's age, ability, or aptitude;
(c) if the authority have already required the child to discontinue his attendance at the school;
(d) if, where the school is a special school, the child does not have special educational needs requiring the education or special facilities normally provided there; or
(e) if, where the school is single-sex, the child is not of the sex provided for.

Also, the duty does not apply where the acceptance of the placing request in respect of a child from outside of the school's catchment area would prevent the education authority from retaining reserved places at the school (s.28(3A), as inserted by the 1996 Act, s.33).

The authority must inform the parent in writing of their decision, and, if the request is refused, must also give him written reasons for their decision and inform him of his right to refer their decision to an appeal committee set up in accordance with s.28D and Schedule A1 (see below) (s.28A(4)).

S.28B requires an authority to publish, or otherwise make available, information as to their placing arrangements, such other matters as are prescribed by the Education (School and Placing Information) (Scotland) Regulations 2012, and such other matters as the authority consider necessary or expedient for the purposes of their functions under the principal Act. *Inter alia* they must (i) inform the parent of the general effect of s.28A(1) and (2) (see above), of the school in which the child is proposed to be placed under their placing arrangements, and of the parent's right to make a placing request; (ii) formulate guidelines to be followed by them as respects placing in schools generally or, if they think it necessary, in any particular school in the event of there being more placing requests in respect of certain schools (or that particular school) than there are places available; and (iii) supply on request by a parent any information about any school under their management which has been prescribed by or determined in accordance with the Education (School and Placing Information) (Scotland) Regulations 2012.

S.28C provides for an appeal against a refusal of a placing request to be referred to an appeal committee set up under s.28D. A reference must be lodged with the appeal committee within 28 days of the receipt by the parent of the education authority's decision (on good cause being shown, this time limit may be ignored by the committee).

A parent who has made a reference under s.28C may appeal to the sheriff having jurisdiction where the specified school is situated against the decision of an appeal committee on that reference in accordance with the provisions of s.28F.

By virtue of s.28G, a school pupil who is over the school age (see below) and under the age of 18 (referred to in the Act as a young person) may himself exercise the right to make a placing request under the foregoing provisions, with the same right of appeal.

27 School age

Under the principal Act, it is the duty of the parent of every child of school age to provide efficient education for him suitable to his age, ability, and aptitude, either by causing him to attend a public school regularly or by other means (s.30). A person is of school age if he has attained the age of five but not the age of 16, subject to provisions as to the appropriate school commencement date and summer or winter leaving date (s.31). For the purposes of s.31, a child who does not attain the age of five on a school commencement date will be deemed not to have attained that age until the school commencement date next following the fifth anniversary of his birth, but an education authority must, in respect of each school commencement date fixed by them, also fix the "appropriate latest date", i.e., the latest following date (which must not be more than six months and seven days) on or before which a child must attain the age of five in order to come within the category of children whom the authority consider of sufficient age to commence attendance at a public primary school at that school commencement date.

S.32 provides that an education authority must fix a school commencement date (which may be different for different schools) for the commencement of attendance at primary schools in their area; any such date may be either a calendar date of fixed by reference to the occurrence of a particular annual event.

The summer leaving date is 31st May and the winter leaving date is the first day of the Christmas holiday period for a pupil attending a school and 21st December for any other person. Pupils reaching the age of 16 years on or after 1st March and before 1st October in any year may leave at the summer leaving date; those reaching 16 on or after 1st October and before 1st March may leave at the winter leaving date (s.33).

28 Exemptions from attendance

An education authority have discretion to exempt a pupil over 14 years of age from school attendance (on such conditions as to further attendance up to the appropriate leaving date as they think fit) if they are satisfied that attendance would cause exceptional hardship by reason of his home circumstances (s.34).

29 Exclusion of pupils

The Schools General (Scotland) Regulations 1975 (the 1975 Regulations) provide that an education authority or the board of management of a self-governing school (see 13 **Self-governing status**, above) may not exclude a pupil from a school to which he has been admitted except where (Reg. 4)–
  (a) they are of the opinion that the parent of the pupil refuses or fails to comply, or to allow the pupil to comply, with the rules, regulations, or disciplinary requirements of the school; or
  (b) they consider that in all the circumstances to allow the pupil to continue his attendance at the school would be likely to be seriously detrimental to order and discipline in the school or the educational well-being of the pupils there.

Where a decision has been taken under Regulation 4 to exclude a pupil from school, notice of the decision and the date (which must be within seven days after the date of the decision) and time when, and the place where, the head teacher, other teacher of the school, or an officer of the education authority or a member of the board of management of a self-governing school will be available to discuss the decision must be given to the parent of the pupil (or, if the pupil is a young person, be given to the pupil himself for the purpose of discussion with him).

Within eight days of the date of the decision, the education authority *inter alia* must, unless the pupil has been re-admitted to school or the parent or pupil, as the case may be, has already indicated that he does not wish to take the matter to appeal, inform the parent or the pupil, as the case may be, of the reasons for the decision to exclude, the conditions with which the pupil and his parent (or either of them) are required to comply as conditions precedent to the re-admission of the pupil, and the right to refer the decision to an appeal committee set up and maintained under s.28D in accordance with the provisions of s.28H. Further appeal may be made to the sheriff in accordance with the provisions of s.28F (see 26 **Placing in schools**, above).

A pupil aged between 16 and 18 can appeal in his own right against his exclusion from school and, under s.41

of the 2000 Act, this right is extended to all pupils with "legal capacity" under s.2 of the Age of Legal Capacity (Scotland) Act 1991 (and there is a presumption that a child aged 12 or over will be sufficiently mature to have legal capacity).

30 Admission of children under school age to primary school

Under s.38 of the 2000 Act, a parent of a child below school age may request an education authority to admit that child to a primary school class and the authority must comply with this request if the education provided in such a class is suited to the child's ability and aptitude. There is no duty on an authority, however, to place such a child in any particular school.

31 Number of school days

The 1975 Regulations provide that every school under the management of an education authority must open for at least 190 days (excluding Saturdays and Sundays) in the school year, unless this is prevented by circumstances outside the authority's control (Reg. 5).

32 Registration of pupils

The 1975 Regulations provide that registers must be kept at every school of admissions and withdrawals in respect of each school year and of daily attendance (or of periods of residence, in the case of pupils residing at a boarding school) (Reg. 9 and Sch. 1).

33 Failure to secure attendance

It is an offence for a parent of a child of school age to fail, without reasonable excuse, to secure his child's regular attendance at the school which the child has been attending unless the authority have consented to the child's withdrawal. Such consent must not be unreasonably withheld (s.35). If the authority consider that such an offence has been committed, they must serve a notice on the parent requiring him to appear before them and explain the reason for the child's absence from school. If he fails to satisfy them that he had a reasonable excuse (see below), they may either prosecute him or warn him and defer for not more than six weeks their decision whether to prosecute. In the latter event, they may, if the child is still of school age, make a school attendance order (see below) requiring his attendance at the school he was attending, or, if he has changed residence, at a school attended by children in his neighbourhood (s.36).

Where a child of school age has not attended a public school in the area in which he is residing, or has been withdrawn from such a school with the authority's consent, or has been excluded by them from such a school, then, if the authority are not satisfied that the parent is providing efficient and suitable education for the child, they must serve a notice on the parent requiring him to provide (orally or in writing) such information as they may require regarding the means, if any, he has adopted for providing education. If the parent fails to satisfy the authority that he is providing suitable and efficient education for the child or that there is reasonable excuse for his failure to do so, they must make an attendance order (s.37).

An attendance order is an order in writing requiring the parent of the child to cause the child to attend a school named in the order, being either a public school or any other school the managers of which are willing to receive the child. In an attendance order, a school at which the parent will be required to pay fees may not be named unless at the request of the parent, nor may a special school be named unless the child is a recorded child (see the Note on **Additional Support for Learning and Special Schools: Scotland**). Before making an attendance order, the authority must take into account any views expressed by the parent as to which school he desires his child to attend. If aggrieved by the order, the parent may within 14 days appeal to the sheriff, whose decision will be final (s.38). An order remains in force (subject to any amendment or variation of it), unless revoked by the authority or annulled by the sheriff, so long as the child is of school age (s.40). Failure to comply with an order without reasonable excuse constitutes an offence (s.41).

34 Reasonable excuses

For the purposes of ss.35 to 37 and 41, the following are deemed to be reasonable excuses (s.42(1), as amended by the 1981 Act, s.2).

   (a) There is not within walking distance (i.e., two miles for a child under eight years of age, and three miles for others) a public or other school whose managers are willing to receive the child and provide him with free education, and either–
      (i) no arrangements have been made by the education authority under ss.50 or 51 for transport, boarding accommodation, or other special facilities (see the Note on **Health and Welfare in Schools**), or
      (ii) any arrangements so made are such as to involve walking more than the said walking distance.
   (b) Sickness.
   (c) Other circumstances accepted by the authority or the court as affording a reasonable excuse.

Only paragraphs (b) and (c) above will apply where the authority, having proposed to place a child in a school which is not within walking distance but for which an offer of suitable arrangements of the kind referred to in ss.50 and 51 (see the Note on **Health and Welfare in Schools**) has been made, have, nevertheless, in consequence of a placing request, placed the child in another school [which may be a school which is not within walking distance].

35 Education otherwise than at school

If an education authority are satisfied that by reason of prolonged ill-health or any extraordinary circumstances a pupil is unable to attend a suitable school, or it would be unreasonable to expect him to attend school, they may make special arrangements for him to be educated elsewhere (s.14, as substituted by the 2000 Act, s.40).

An education authority must also make alternative arrangements for a child who has been permitted to stay away from school in order to give assistance at home because a family member is ill or infirm. Alternative arrangements (whether within or outside a school) must also be made "without undue delay" for pupils who have been excluded from a public school in the authority's area.

S.14 also allows the Scottish Ministers to issue guidance as to the circumstances in which parents may choose to educate their children at home.

G: INFORMATION ABOUT SCHOOLS

36 Provision of information

S.28I of the principal Act (as inserted by s.17 of the Education (Schools) Act 1992), empowers the Scottish Ministers to make regulations requiring, in respect of every school for the management of which an education authority is responsible, the education authority, and in respect of any other school the board of management (if there is one) or the managers, to provide them and other prescribed persons with such information about the school as may be prescribed (including information about the continuing education of pupils leaving the school, or the employment or training taken up by such pupils on leaving). In exercising this power they must do so with a view to making available information which is likely to–

(a) assist parents in choosing schools for their children;

(b) increase public awareness of the quality of education provided and the educational standards achieved in schools; and

(c) assist in assessing the degree of efficiency with which the financial resources of the school are managed.

Such information must not name any pupil to whom it relates.

The Scottish Ministers may publish, or arrange to have published, information provided in accordance with such regulations, or require an education authority to publish such information at such times and in such form as they may specify. The Scottish Ministers may also make regulations requiring education authorities to provide to prescribed persons such information or categories of information as may be prescribed (s.28J).

The Education (School and Placing Information) (Scotland) Regulations 2012, as amended, provide for the publication of basic, school, and supplementary information, provisions as to placing requests, and the form in which such information is to be made available.

The Scottish Ministers may also make regulations requiring that prescribed information and reports about pupils attending any school (other than a grant-aided school, an independent school, or a nursery school) must be supplied to the parents of such pupils at prescribed times and in a prescribed form and manner (s.28K of the principal Act, as inserted by the Education (Schools) Act 1992).

H: GENERAL PROVISIONS

37 Limit on class sizes

The Education (Lower Primary Class Sizes) (Scotland) Regulations 1999 impose a limit on class sizes for primary 1, 2 and 3 classes at schools managed by local education authorities. The limit is set at a maximum of 30 pupils in a class at any time while an ordinary teaching session is conducted by a single qualified teacher (or, where there is more than one teacher, a maximum of 30 pupils per teacher). However, where certain types of children ("excepted pupils") cannot be educated at the school in another class without prejudicing efficient education or the efficient use of resources, they will not be counted for the purpose of ascertaining whether the limit is exceeded. Excepted pupils include certain children with additional support needs; children initially refused a place at a school but subsequently offered a place outside a normal placing round; and children who have moved into the area outside a normal placing round and who cannot gain a place at any other suitable school within a reasonable distance of their home.

In respect of the school year beginning in 2011, the limit for primary 1 classes is reduced from 30 to 25.

38 Sex education

Under s.56 of the 2000 Act, the Scottish Ministers may issue guidance to education authorities about the manner in which education about sexual matters is to be conducted. Authorities must have regard to such guidance.

39 Medical examinations

An education authority may require the parents of a pupil attending a school managed by them to submit that pupil for a medical or dental inspection. Where the pupil is aged between 16 and 18, the authority may require the pupil himself to submit to an examination (s.57 of the 1980 Act). It is an offence for a parent to refuse to submit his child for an examination (although it is not an offence for a pupil aged between 16 and 18 to refuse to undergo an examination). Under s.131A (added by s.57 of the 2000 Act), an examination, inspection or treatment may only be carried out on a child who has "legal capacity" (i.e., a child who is considered to have sufficient understanding–normally a child of 12 or over) if the child himself consents.

40 Religious observances and religious instruction

S.8 sanctions the continuation of the custom in public schools in Scotland for religious observance to be practised and religious instruction to be given to pupils whose parents do not object. This custom may not be discontinued by an education authority unless and until a resolution to do so, passed by the authority, has been approved by a majority of local government electors in the area, voting by ballot at a poll taken for the purpose. Every public school and grant-aided school must be open to pupils of all denominations, and pupils withdrawn by their parents from religious observance or instruction in the school must not be placed at any disadvantage as regards their secular instruction (s.9). A pupil who is a boarder at a public school or other education establishment managed by an education authority must, at the request of the pupil's parent, be permitted to attend religious worship in accordance with the tenets of his parent's denomination on Sundays or other days exclusively set apart for religious observance, or to receive religious instruction in such tenets outside the working hours of the school (s.10).

41 Corporal punishment

S.16 of the 2000 Act makes provision for the abolition of corporal punishment of all school pupils in Scotland (including pupils attending independent schools, other than nursery schools) by providing that where in any proceedings it is shown that corporal punishment has been given to a pupil by, or on the authority of, a member of the staff, giving the punishment cannot be justified on the ground that it was done in pursuance of a right exercisable by the member of staff by virtue of his position as such. Giving corporal punishment means doing anything for the purposes of punishing the pupil concerned (whether or not there are also other reasons for doing it) which apart from any justification would constitute physical assault upon the person. Action to avert immediate danger of personal injury to, or immediate danger to the property of, any person (including the pupil concerned) is not to be taken as giving corporal punishment.

The effect of s.16 is that, while independent schools may no longer administer corporal punishment, private nursery schools may continue to do so, subject to the common law.

42 Pupil records

The Pupils' Educational Records (Scotland) Regulations 2003 require an education authority and the board of management of a self-governing school to give parental access to educational records held by them relating to the education of school pupils (including former pupils) which originated from or were supplied by a teacher or other employee or the child concerned or a parent (Reg. 3(1)).

The requirement does not apply to information–
   (i) contained in a copy of a reference given to a person requesting it in connection with a pupil's application for employment, education, or training;
   (ii) contained in a record of needs under s.60 of the principal Act (as to which see (see the Note on **Additional Support for Learning and Special Schools: Scotland**) or a co-ordinated support plan (under the Education (Additional Support for Learning) (Scotland) Act 2004;
   (iii) which is data to which the Data Protection Act 1984 applies;
   (iv) to the extent that disclosure would be likely in the authority's opinion to cause significant distress or harm to the pupil or any other person (Regs 3 and 6).

Where a parent has been given access to information he may request the authority to correct or erase information which he can show to be inaccurate (Reg. 10).

Records must be made available for inspection free of charge within 15 school days. A fee (not exceeding the cost of supply and subject to the maximum chargeable under the Date Protection Act 1998) may be charged if a copy is requested. A second identical or similar request by a parent need not be complied with unless there has been a change of circumstances or a reasonable interval has elapsed since the first request (Reg. 5). Where a pupil changes schools, his new school may request, free of charge, a copy of his educational records.

43 Safety of pupils

The Schools (Safety and Supervision of Pupils) (Scotland) Regulations 1990 require every education authority and the board of management of a self-governing school to take reasonable care for the safety of pupils when under their charge and, specifically, to secure that, in any primary school attended by 50 or more pupils, or any special school, pupils are supervised by at least one adult when in a playground during any break time.

The Grants for Improvement of School Security (Scotland) Regulations 1997 enable the Scottish Ministers to pay grants to local authorities in respect of expenditure incurred by them in improving school security and protecting pupils, staff and other persons in schools against violence. Grants may also be paid for training persons in connection with that purpose. Before a grant may be paid, the Scottish Ministers must be satisfied that the education authority have prepared a safety strategy for their schools and have an action plan to implement that strategy.

44 School education in social work establishments

S.14A, as inserted by s.12 of the 1981 Act, empowers an education authority to provide for their area school education in any social work establishment provided by a local authority under s.59 of the Social Work (Scotland) Act 1968 wholly or mainly for children under school age, by making available the services of a teacher employed by the education authority and by providing *inter alia* appropriate equipment.

45 Work experience

Ss.123 and 125 empower an education authority to arrange for children under school leaving age to have work experience, as part of their education, during the last year of compulsory schooling. The provisions are similar to those of the Education Act 1996 s.560 for England and Wales (see the Note on **Employment of Children**).

I: SCHOOL PREMISES

46 Standards for educational premises

It is the duty of an education authority to secure that the premises and equipment of any educational establishment under their management conform to the standards and requirements applicable to that establishment and, in particular, that the premises and equipment of all educational establishments under their management are maintained in such a condition as to conduce to the good health and safety of all persons occupying or frequenting the premises or using the equipment (s.19).

J: TEACHERS' QUALIFICATION AND EMPLOYMENT

47 Introduction

Employment as a teacher in schools is normally restricted to teachers registered or conditionally registered by the General Teaching Council for Scotland and holding a qualification appropriate to the post (see **48 General Teaching Council for Scotland**, below).

48 General Teaching Council for Scotland

The Council is constituted under the Public Services Reform (General Teaching Council for Scotland) Order 2011. It comprises 19 elected representatives of the teachers, 11 members nominated by local authorities, Universities Scotland, the further education sector, parent councils, and by the Churches, and 7 members appointed by the Council itself.

The main functions of the Council are to (Art.4)–
(a) keep the register of teachers;
(b) establish (and review and change as necessary) the standards of education and training appropriate to school teachers; and the standards of conduct and professional competence expected of a registered teacher;
(c) investigate the fitness to teach of individuals who are, or who are seeking to be, registered;
(d) keep itself informed of the education and training of individuals undertaking courses for the education and training of teachers;
(e) consider, and to make recommendations to the Scottish Ministers about, matters relating to teachers' education, training, career development and fitness to teach; and the supply of teachers (except matters of remuneration or conditions of service); and
(f) keep such other registers of other individuals working in educational settings as it thinks fit.

The principal aims of the Council are to (Art.5)–
(g) contribute to improving the quality of teaching and learning; and
(h) maintain and improve teachers' professional standards.

49 Registration

The General Teaching Council for Scotland must make and publish rules governing the operation of the register, in particular in relation to the procedure for inclusion in the register and setting out registration

EDUCATION

criteria (Public Services Reform (General Teaching Council for Scotland) Order 2011, Art. 15).

The Council must include an individual in the register if it is satisfied that the registration criteria are met, that the individual is not unfit to teach and that the Council's rules, or the provision on barred individuals, do not otherwise prevent the individual from being registered (Art. 16).

Registration is dependent on an individual either obtaining a recognised teaching qualification (as determined by the Council), or satisfying the Council that they have the education, training or experience to warrant registration (Art. 17).

The Council must investigate a person's fitness to teach in specified circumstances, and has a discretion to investigate in other cases (Art. 18). Where an individual is considered unfit to teach, their registration must either be refused, or they must be removed from the register.

An individual may not be registered if they are barred from regulated work with children. If a registered individual becomes barred from such work they must be removed from the register (Art. 19).

For special additional qualifications for teachers in further education, see the Note on **Further and Higher Education**.

The Requirements for Teachers (Scotland) Regulations 2005 require education authorities to employ an adequate number of registered teachers with appropriate skills and knowledge (Regs. 3 and 4). Teachers employed to teach pupils who are hearing or visually impaired or both must possess an appropriate qualification (Regs. 5, 6 and 7). There is an exception where the teacher is in the process of obtaining the appropriate qualification but that person must not teach without it for more than five years (Reg. 8).

K: NURSERY EDUCATION

50 Provision of early learning and childcare for children under school age

Under s.1 of the Education (Scotland) Act 1980 (see **3 Duties of education authorities**, above), an education authority has a duty to secure school education for children under school age to the extent required by the Children and Young People (Scotland) Act 2014.

The 2014 Act provides that an education authority must secure that the mandatory amount (see below) of early learning and childcare is made available for each eligible pre-school child belonging to its area (s.47). An "eligible pre-school child" is one who–

(a) is under school age,
(b) has not started at a primary school (other than at a nursery class in such a school), and
(c) either (i) is aged 2 or over and is or has been at any time since their second birthday looked after by a local authority, or the subject of a kinship care order, or had a parent appointed guardian; or (ii) is within such age range, or is of such other description, as the Scottish Ministers may by order specify (see below).

If a child qualifies *only* by reason of being looked after by a local authority, that authority may, after assessing the child's needs, make alternative arrangements in relation to the child's education and care where that would better safeguard or promote the child's wellbeing (s.49).

The Provision of Early Learning and Childcare (Specified Children) (Scotland) Order 2014 prescribes children as being eligible to receive the mandatory amount of early learning and childcare from the start of the term following their third birthday until, generally, they are first eligible to attend primary school (when the general duty to provide school education applies). In addition, 2 year olds with a parent in receipt of one or more qualifying benefits (income support, income-based jobseeker's allowance, income-related employment and support allowance, incapacity benefit, severe disablement allowance, State pension credit, universal credit, child tax credit payable in certain circumstances, and support provided under Part VI of the Immigration and Asylum Act 1999) are eligible from the first term after their second birthday; or, the first term after their parent starts receiving out of work benefits. Once a 2 year old child has started early learning and childcare, they will remain an eligible pre-school child even if their parent subsequently ceases to be in receipt of a qualifying benefit.

The "mandatory amount" of early learning and childcare for these purposes is 600 hours per year (s.48) which must be provided for at least 38 weeks of every calendar year in sessions of between 2.5 hours and 8 hours in duration (s.51). An education authority must have regard to the desirability of ensuring that the method by which it makes early learning and childcare available is flexible enough to allow parents an appropriate degree of choice when deciding how to access the service (s.52).

Such school education must be provided without payment of fees (Standards in Scotland's Schools etc Act 2000, s.33), however where an education authority provides school education in addition to that which is prescribed (e.g., for younger children) they may charge a fee.

School education for children under school age may be provided in a nursery school, in a nursery class in a school, or at some other establishment with which the education authority have made arrangements for the purpose of fulfilling their duty to provide such education (2000 Act, s.33(3)).

An education authority may make such arrangements as it thinks fit for (2000 Act, s.37)–

(a) conveying children, without charge between their homes and the school or establishment they are attending;
(b) making bicycles or other suitable forms of transport available to parents for the purpose of conveying children between their homes and the school or establishment they are attending, or paying money allowances instead; or

156

(c) paying, in whole or in part, the reasonable travelling expenses of children.

Where a parent of a child under school age requests that their child be admitted to a class (other than a nursery class) in a primary school, the authority must, if the school education normally provided in the class is suited to the ability and aptitude of the child, admit the child to such a class (2000 Act, s.38) (see **30 Admission of children under school age to primary school**, above).

51 Authorities

Statutes–

Children and Young People (Scotland) Act 2014

Education Act 1996

Education (Amendment) (Scotland) Act 1984

Education (No. 2) Act 1986

Education (Schools) Act 1992

Education (Scotland) Acts 1980, 1981 and 1996

Local Government (Scotland) Act 1994

School Education (Ministerial Powers and Independent Schools) (Scotland) Act 2004

Schools (Consultation) (Scotland) Act 2010

Schools (Health Promotions and Nutrition) (Scotland) Act 2007

Scottish Schools (Parental Involvement) Act 2006

Standards in Scotland's Schools etc Act 2000

Statutory Instruments–

Education (Lower Primary Class Sizes) (Scotland) Regulations 1999, as amended (S.I. 1999 No. 1080, 2005 No. 517, and 2010 No. 326)

Education (National Priorities) (Scotland) Order 2000 (S.I. 2000 No. 443)

Education (School and Placing Information) (Scotland) Regulations 2012 (S.S.I. 2012 No. 130)

Grants for Improvement in School Education (Scotland) Regulations 1998 (S.I. 1998 No. 3051)

Grants for Improvement of School Security (Scotland) Regulations 1997 (S.I. 1997 No. 965)

Parental Involvement in Headteacher and Deputy Headteacher Appointments (Scotland) Regulations 2007 (S.I. 2007 No. 132)

Provision of Early Learning and Childcare (Specified Children) (Scotland) Order 2014, as amended (S.S.I. 2014 No. 196 and 2015 No. 268)

Public Services Reform (General Teaching Council for Scotland) Order 2011 (S.S.I. 2011 No. 215)

Pupils' Educational Records (Scotland) Regulations 2003, as amended (S.S.I. 2003 No. 581, and 2005 No. 517)

Raising of the School Leaving Age (Scotland) Regulations 1972 (S.I. 1972 No. 59)

Requirements for Teachers (Scotland) Regulations 2005, as amended (S.S.I. 2005 No. 355 and 2011 No. 215)

Schools General (Scotland) Regulations 1975, as amended (S.I. 1975, No. 1135, 1982 Nos. 56 and 1735, 1987 No. 290, 1993 No. 1604, 1994 No. 351, and S.S.I. 2003 No. 581)

Schools (Safety and Supervision of Pupils) (Scotland) Regulations 1990, as amended (S.I. 1990 No. 295 and 1994 No. 351)

EDUCATION

EMPLOYMENT

EMPLOYMENT

EMPLOYMENT PROTECTION: INTRODUCTION

1 The legislation

The Employment Rights Act 1996 is a consolidating enactment which repealed most of the then existing employment legislation.

The Employment Tribunals Act 1996 consolidated provisions relating to employment tribunals and the Employment Appeal Tribunal. This Act was originally named the Industrial Tribunals Act 1996 but s.1 of the Employment Rights (Dispute Resolution) Act 1998 re-named industrial tribunals as employment tribunals and the name of the 1996 Act was consequently changed.

The law relating to employment protection is dealt with in separate Notes, each of which covers one Part of the Act and related legislation. The Notes cover the following topics–

> Terms of Employment;
> Rights Arising in the Course of Employment;
> Maternity Rights;
> Part-time, Fixed-term and Agency Workers;
> Termination of Employment;
> Unfair Dismissal;
> Redundancy;
> Insolvency of Employers;
> Public Interest Disclosure;
> Employment Tribunals, ACAS, and the Employment Appeal Tribunal.

2 Application of the Employment Rights Act 1996

Most of the provisions of the Employment Rights Act 1996 apply all employees. Much of the Act also applies, with modifications, to members of the armed forces (including the provisions as to unfair dismissal–see the Note on **Unfair Dismissal** (s.192)).

Certain categories of employees are excluded from some of the provisions of the Act (ss. 198 to 200). These excluded categories and the categories excluded by virtue of other provisions of the Act or other enactments are dealt with in more detail in the relevant Notes.

The Act extends to the whole of Great Britain.

3 Restrictions on contracting out

The general rule is that provision in any agreement which purports to exclude or limit the operation of any provision of the Employment Rights Act 1996 or precludes any person from complaining to, or bringing proceedings under the Act before, an employment tribunal is void. This rule does not apply to (Employment Rights Act 1996, s.203, as amended by s.9 of the Employment Rights (Dispute Resolution) Act 1998)–

(a) any provision in a collective agreement excluding rights to guarantee payments under s.28 if an order under s.35 is currently in force in respect of that provision (see the Note on **Rights Arising in the Course of Employment**);

(b) any provision in a dismissal procedures agreement excluding rights under s.94 if that provision is not to have effect unless an order under s.110 is for the time being in force in respect of it (see the Note on **Unfair Dismissal**);

(c) any agreement to refrain from instituting or continuing any proceedings before an employment tribunal where a conciliation officer has taken action in accordance with s.18(2) and (3) of the Employment Tribunals Act (see the Note on **Employment Tribunals, ACAS, and the Employment Appeal Tribunal**);

(d) any agreement to refrain from proceeding, presenting, or continuing any proceedings specified in s.18 of the above Act (except in relation to proceedings by virtue of an order under s.3–see the Note on **Employment Tribunals, ACAS, and the Employment Appeal Tribunal**) if the conditions regulating settlement agreements under that Act are satisfied in relation to the agreement (*inter alia* the agreement must be in writing and relate to the particular proceedings, the employee must have received advice from a relevant independent adviser identified in the agreement, and there must be in force at the time an insurance policy covering the risk of a claim by the employee in respect of loss arising in consequence of the advice); or

(e) any provision in an agreement if an order under s.157 (order of exemption from redundancy provisions of Part XI of the Act–see the Note on **Redundancy**) is for the time being in force in respect of it.

Any attempt to exclude or limit the operation of any provision in Part 1 of Pensions Act 2008 (automatic enrolment of employees in a pension scheme: see the Note on **Occupational Pension Schemes: General Provisions**) or to preclude a person from bringing proceedings under s.55 of that Act (i.e., enforcement of the right not to suffer detriment in relation to automatic enrolment) before an employment tribunal will also be void (2008 Act, s.58).

4 General interpretation

In the Employment Rights Act 1996, except so far as the context otherwise requires, the following terms have the meanings given below.

Contract of Employment means a contract of service or apprenticeship, whether express or implied and (if it is express) whether oral or in writing.

Effective Date of Termination (of a contract of employment) has the meaning given by s.97, as to which see the Note on **Unfair Dismissal**.

Employee means an individual who has entered into or works under (or, where the employment has ceased, worked under) a contract of employment.

Employer, in relation to an employee, means the person by whom the employee is (or, in the case where the employment has ceased, was) employed.

Employment means, except for the purpose of s.171 (redundancy payments for certain public servants), employment under a contract of employment.

Job, in relation to an employee, means the nature of the work which he is employed to do in accordance with his contract and the capacity and place in which he is so employed.

Week means, in relation to an employee whose remuneration is calculated weekly by a week ending with a day other than Saturday, a week ending with that other day, and, in relation to any other employee, a week ending with Saturday (s.235).

5 "Continuous employment"

In order to qualify for certain rights under the Employment Rights Act 1996, an employee must have been employed for a minimum period of "continuous employment" ascertained in accordance with the rules set out in ss.210 to 219. The principal rules are summarised below.

Except so far as otherwise provided by ss.215 to 217, a week which does not count under the provisions of s.212 breaks the continuity of a period of employment; and a person's employment during any period will, unless the contrary is shown, be presumed to have been continuous (s.210).

Any week during the whole or part of which the employee's relations with the employer are governed by a contract of employment counts in computing a period of employment (s.212(1)).

S.212(3) applies to periods in which there is no contract of employment. If in any week the employee is, for the whole or part of the week–

(a) incapable of work in consequence of sickness or injury, or

(b) absent from work on account of a temporary cessation of work, or

(c) absent from work in circumstances such that, by arrangement or custom, he is regarded as continuing in the employment of his employer for all or any purposes,

that week will, notwithstanding that it does not fall under s.212(1), count as a period of employment (s.212(3)). But not more than 26 weeks will count under (a) or (subject to s.212(2)–see below) (d) above between any periods which fall under s.212(1) (s.212(4)).

Where in a week or any part of a week an employee takes part in a strike, that week does not count in computing a period of employment but the continuity of the period of employment is not broken (s.216(1)).

A change of employer does not break the continuity of a period of employment where (a) there has been a transfer of a trade, business, or undertaking; (b) an Act of Parliament has modified the contract of employment and some other corporate body is substituted as the employer; (c) the employer dies, and the employee is taken into the employment of the personal representatives or trustees of the deceased; (d) there is a change in the partners, personal representatives, or trustees who constitute the employer; (e) the new employer is at the time of the change an associated employer of the original employer; (f) the employee in a school maintained by a local authority moves to another school maintained by the same authority or a maintained school where the governors of that school and not the local authority are the teacher's employers; or (g) the employee is undergoing professional training which involves being employed successively by a number of different health service employers, and he moves from one such employer to another (s.218).

The Employment Protection (Continuity of Employment) Regulations 1996 provide for the preservation of the continuity of a dismissed employee's period of employment where he is reinstated or re-engaged as a result of–

(a) the presentation of a complaint to an employment tribunal under s.111 of the Act;

(b) the making of a claim in accordance with a dismissal procedures agreement designated by an order under s.110 of the Act;

(c) any action taken by a conciliation officer under the Employment Tribunals Act 1996, ss.18A-18C;

(d) the making of a relevant settlement agreement (i.e., an agreement authorised under s.203 of the Act settling a complaint arising out of dismissal; or an agreement to refrain from instituting or continuing any proceedings before an employment tribunal for which that tribunal has jurisdiction); or

(e) the making of an agreement to submit a dispute to arbitration in accordance with a scheme under the Trade Union and Labour Relations (Consolidation) Act 1992 s.212A (see the Note on **Employment Tribunals, ACAS, and the Employment Appeal Tribunal**, at para 21 **ACAS arbitration scheme**) (arbitration in unfair dismissal cases).

The Regulations also provide that an employee's continuity of employment will not be broken where a dismissed employee is reinstated or re-engaged on condition that he repays any redundancy payment or equivalent payment already paid to him in respect of his dismissal, provided that the reinstatement or re-engagement is a consequence of one of the above-mentioned courses of action.

6 Normal working hours and a week's pay

Calculating the extent of an employee's right to certain payments under the Act involves the calculation of his normal working hours and of the amount of his week's pay. For the purpose of calculating the amount payable to an employee for certain purposes, the amount of a week's pay may not exceed £479 (which sum may be varied by order) (Employment Rights Act 1996, s.227).

Where an employee is entitled to overtime pay when employed for more than a fixed number of hours in a week or other period, the fixed number of hours are his normal working hours. However, in such a case, if the contract of employment fixes the number, or the minimum number, of hours to be worked in that period, and that number or minimum number of hours exceeds the number of hours without overtime, that number or minimum number of hours are the normal working hours and not the number of hours without overtime (s.234).

Where an employee's remuneration does not vary according to the amount of work done, the amount of his week's pay is the amount payable by the employer under the contract of employment in force on the calculation date (as defined) for a full week's work (s.221(2)).

Where the employee's remuneration does vary according to work done, the amount of his week's pay is the amount of remuneration for the number of normal working hours in a week calculated at the average hourly rate of remuneration payable by the employer in respect of the period of 12 weeks (a) ending on the calculation date, where this is the last day of the week, or (b) in any other case, ending with the last complete week before the calculation date (s.221(3)).

Where there are normal working hours for an employee, but the contract of employment in force on the calculation date provides that the employee must work during those hours on days of the week or at times of the day which differ from week to week or over a longer period so that the remuneration payable for, or apportionable to, any week varies, then the amount of his week's pay is the amount of remuneration for the average weekly number of normal working hours at the average hourly rate of remuneration (s.222).

Where there are no normal working hours for an employee, the amount of his week's pay is the amount of his average weekly remuneration in the period of 12 weeks (a) ending on the calculation date, where this is the last day of the week, or (b) in any other case, ending with the last complete week before the calculation date. In calculating the average weekly remuneration, no account is to be taken of a week in which no remuneration was payable, and remuneration in earlier weeks must be brought in so as to bring the number of weeks of which account is taken up to 12 (s.224).

7 Recoupment of social security benefit

S.16 of the Employment Tribunals Act 1996 establishes machinery whereby the Secretary of State may make regulations for the recoupment from an employer of sums paid by way of jobseeker's allowance, income-related employment and support allowance or income support paid to an employee out of a prescribed part of an amount awarded by an employment tribunal in certain proceedings brought by an employee against an employer. S.16 applies to payments which are the subject of proceedings before employment tribunals and which are—

(a) payments of wages or compensation for loss of wages,
(b) payments under certain sections of the Trade Union and Labour Relations (Consolidation) Act 1992,
(c) payments by employers to employees under specified sections or parts of the Employment Rights Act 1996, or
(d) payments of similar nature to those mentioned in paragraph (b) or (c),

and to payments in pursuance of a protective award under s.189 of the 1992 Act (see the Note on **Unfair Dismissal**).

The Employment Protection (Recoupment of Benefits) Regulations 1996 have effect under s.16 of the Employment Tribunals Act 1996. The awards affected are those made because of unfair dismissal, failure to make guarantee payments, failure to pay remuneration for periods when the employee is suspended on medical grounds, and protective awards in respect of redundancies. The Regulations set out the procedure for the determination of the amount of benefit which is recoverable and for the review of that determination by the relevant statutory authority. The employer must pay the prescribed amounts to the Department for Work and Pensions and pay the balance of the award to the employee.

Note. –Employers do not have to repay any benefit where a settlement is reached without a tribunal hearing, either with or without the help of a conciliation officer of the Advisory, Conciliation and Arbitration Service.

8 Death of employee or employer

Ss.206 and 207 of the Employment Rights Act 1996 make detailed provision for the purpose of supplementing and modifying the Act's provisions as respects the death of an employee or employer. In general, the institution or continuance of tribunal proceedings in respect of the rights of employees (and matters connected therewith) under the Act is not affected by the death of the employer or the employee. Such proceedings are taken over by the personal representatives of the deceased employee or employer, as the case may be.

9 Employee shareholders

The "employee shareholder" is a new employment status introduced on 1st September 2013 (Employment Rights Act 1996, s.205A, added by the Growth and Infrastructure Act 2013, s.31). Employee shareholders have reduced employment rights compared to other employees, but in return receive shares in their employer company which are treated favourably for tax.

An individual is an "employee shareholder" if (s.205A(1))–

(1) the company and the individual agree that the individual is to be an employee shareholder;

(2) in consideration of that agreement, the company issues or allots to the individual fully paid up shares in the company or in its parent undertaking, which have a value, on the day of issue or allotment, of no less than £2,000;

(3) the company gives the individual a written statement of the particulars of the status of employee shareholder and of the rights which attach to the shares; and

(4) the individual gives no consideration other than by entering into the agreement.

The statement referred to in (3) above must–

(a) state that, as an employee shareholder, the individual will not have certain specified employment rights (see below);

(b) set out the different notice periods that would apply to the individual in relation to maternity, paternity, adoption and parental leave;

(c) state whether any voting rights attach to the employee shares;

(d) state whether the employee shares carry any rights to dividends;

(e) state whether the employee shares would, if the company were wound up, confer any rights to participate in the distribution of any surplus assets;

(f) if the company has more than one class of shares and any of the rights referred to in (c) to (e) above attach to the employee shares, explain how those rights differ from the equivalent rights that attach to the shares in the largest class (or next largest class if the class which includes the employee shares is the largest);

(g) state whether the employee shares are redeemable and, if they are, at whose option;

(h) state whether there are any restrictions on the transferability of the employee shares and, if there are, what those restrictions are;

(i) state whether any of the requirements of ss.561 and 562 of the Companies Act 2006 are excluded in the case of the employee shares (existing shareholders' right of pre-emption); and

(j) state whether the employee shares are subject to drag-along rights or tag-along rights and, if they are, explain the effect of the shares being so subject.

An agreement between a company and an individual that the individual is to become an employee shareholder will be of no effect unless, before it is made, the individual, having been given the above statement, receives advice from a relevant independent adviser as to the terms and effect of the proposed agreement, and a seven day cooling off period has passed since the day on which the individual received the advice. Any reasonable costs incurred by the individual in obtaining the advice (whether or not the individual becomes an employee shareholder) must be met by the company.

The main employment rights forfeited by an employee shareholder are the right–

(a) to make a request to undertake study or training (see the Note on **Rights Arising in the Course of Employment**);

(b) to make a request for flexible working (see the Note on **Rights Arising in the Course of Employment**);

(c) not to be unfairly dismissed (see the Note on **Unfair Dismissal**); and

(d) to a redundancy payment (see the Note on **Redundancy**).

These are dealt with in each individual Note.

10 Authorities

Statutes–

Employment Relations Act 1999

Employment Rights Act 1996

Employment Rights (Dispute Resolution) Act 1998

Employment Tribunals Act 1996

Statutory Instruments–

Employment Protection (Continuity of Employment) Regulations 1996, as amended (S.I. 1996 No. 3147, 2001 No. 1188, 2013 No. 1956, and 2014 No. 386)

Employment Protection (Recoupment of Benefits) Regulations, as amended 1996 (S.I. 1996 No. 2349, 2008 No. 2683, 2010 No. 2429, and 2013 No. 630)

CONDUCT OF EMPLOYMENT AGENCIES, EMPLOYMENT BUSINESSES AND GANGMASTERS

A: EMPLOYMENT AGENCIES AND BUSINESSES

1 The legislation

The Employment Agencies Act 1973 made provision for regulating the conduct of private employment agencies and employment businesses by means of a system of licensing. This system of licensing was repealed by the Deregulation and Contracting Out Act 1994 (the 1994 Act). In its place the Secretary of State has been given power to issue prohibition orders prohibiting a person from carrying on an employment agency in specified circumstances (see **3 Prohibition orders**, below); this provision and its related provisions (i.e., ss.3A, 3B, 3C, and 3D), being inserted in the 1973 Act by the 1994 Act. The provisions of the 1973 Act, as amended by the above-mentioned Acts are described below.

The Care Standards Act 2000 makes special provision for the regulation of agencies in England and Wales which supply registered nurses, midwives or health visitors (see **8 Nurses agencies**, below).

2 Definitions

S.13(1) to (3) of the Act contains *inter alia* the following definitions.

"Employment Agency" is defined to mean the business (whether or not carried on with a view to profit and whether or not carried on in conjunction with any other business) of providing services (whether by the provision of information or otherwise) for the purpose of finding persons employment with employers or of supplying employers with persons for employment by them.

The reference to providing services does not include–
  (i) publishing a newspaper or other publication unless it is published wholly or mainly for the said purpose;
  (ii) the display by any person of advertisements on any premises occupied by him otherwise than for the said purpose; or
  (iii) providing a programme service within the meaning of the Broadcasting Act 1990.

"Employment Business" is defined to mean the business (whether or not carried on with a view to profit and whether or not carried on in conjunction with any other business) of supplying persons in the employment of the person carrying on the business, to act for, and under the control of, other persons in any capacity.

"Employment" includes (a) employment by way of a professional engagement or otherwise under a contract for services; and (b) the reception in a private household of a person under an arrangement whereby that person is to assist in the domestic work of the household in consideration of receiving hospitality and pocket money or hospitality only.

3 Prohibition orders

On application by the Secretary of State, an employment tribunal may by order prohibit a person from carrying on, or being concerned with the carrying on of (a) any employment agency or employment business; or (b) any specified description of employment agency or employment business (s.3A(1)). Such an order is referred to as a prohibition order and may either prohibit a person from engaging in an activity altogether or prohibit him from doing so otherwise than in accordance with specified conditions. A prohibition order will be made for a period beginning with the date of the order and ending (a) on a specified date, or (b) on the happening of a specified event but, in either case, not more than ten years later (s.3A(3)). Subject to s.3A(5) and (6) (see below), an employment tribunal will not make a prohibition order in relation to any person unless it is satisfied that he is, on account of his misconduct or for any other sufficient reason, unsuitable to do what the order prohibits (s.3A(4)).

An employment tribunal may make a prohibition order in relation to a body corporate if it is satisfied that (a) any director, secretary, manager, or similar officer of the body corporate, (b) any person who performs on behalf of the body corporate any of the functions mentioned in (a), or (c) any person in accordance with whose directions or instructions the directors of the body corporate are accustomed to act, is unsuitable, on account of his misconduct or for any other sufficient reason, to do what the order prohibits (s.3A(5)).

An employment tribunal may make a prohibition order in relation to a partnership if it is satisfied that any member of the partnership, or any manager employed by the partnership, is unsuitable, on account of his misconduct or any other sufficient reason, to do what the order prohibits (s.3A(6)).

For the purposes of s.3A(4) (see above), where an employment agency or employment business has been improperly conducted, each person who was carrying on, or concerned with the carrying on of, the agency or business at the time, will be deemed to have been responsible for what happened unless he can show that it happened without his connivance or consent and was not attributable to any neglect on his part (s.3A(7)).

Any person who, without reasonable excuse, fails to comply with a prohibition order will be guilty of an offence (s.3B).

S.3C provides that, on application by the person to whom a prohibition order applies, an employment tribunal may vary or revoke the order if the tribunal is satisfied that there has been a material change of circumstances since the order was last considered. The tribunal may not, on an application under s.3C, so vary a prohibition order as to make it more restrictive.

The Secretary of State will be a party to any proceedings before an employment tribunal with respect to an application under s.3C, and will be entitled to appear and be heard.

When making a prohibition order or disposing of an application under s.3C, an employment tribunal may, with a view to preventing the making of vexatious or frivolous applications, by order prohibit the making of an application, or a further application, in relation to the prohibition order before such date as the tribunal may specify.

S.3D provides for the making of an appeal against a prohibition order. An appeal will lie to the Employment Appeal Tribunal on a question of law arising from any decision of, or arising in proceedings before, an employment tribunal under ss.3A or 3C (see above). No other appeal will lie from a decision of an employment tribunal under ss.3A or 3C, and s.11 of the Tribunals and Inquiries Act 1991 (appeals from certain tribunals to the High Court or Court of Session) will not apply to proceedings before an employment tribunal under ss.3A or 3C (see above).

4 Regulations for the conduct of agencies

S.5 of the Act empowers the Secretary of State to make regulations to secure the proper conduct of employment agencies and businesses and to protect the interests of persons availing themselves of their services. No regulations are to be made by the Secretary of State without prior consultation with such bodies as appear to him to be representative of the interests concerned (s.12(2)).

The Conduct of Employment Agencies and Employment Businesses Regulations 2003 impose duties on persons who carry on employment agencies and businesses.

Inter alia, the Regulations prohibit–

(a) any requirement for work-seekers to use additional services of an agency or business or connected undertaking for which the Act does not prohibit the charging of fees or the hiring or purchasing of goods; and where a worker does take up any such additional services he must be able to give notice to cancel or withdraw from those services without incurring any detriment or penalty (Reg. 5);

(b) subjecting or threatening to subject a work-seeker to any detriment on the ground that they have terminated or given notice to terminate any contract between them and the agency or business, or in the case of a business have taken up or propose to take up employment with someone else (Reg. 6);

(c) the introduction or supply of a work-seeker to a hirer to perform duties normally performed by a striking worker, or duties normally performed by any other worker who the hirer has assigned to perform the duties of a striking worker (the prohibition does not apply in the case of unofficial strikes or other unofficial industrial action) (Reg. 7);

(d) the agency from paying, making arrangements for payment, or introduce the hirer to someone connected with the agency who will pay, the work-seeker his remuneration arising from employment with the hirer (Reg. 8);

(e) any term which prevents, unless a "transfer fee" is paid, a temporary worker taking up a permanent job with the hirer or a company to which the hirer has introduced them, or being supplied by a different employment business (Reg. 10);

(f) withhold or threaten to withhold any payment from a work-seeker in respect of work done on grounds of non-receipt of payment from the hirer, failure of the work-seeker to provide authenticated time sheets, the work-seeker not having worked during a period other than that to which the payment relates, or any matter within the control of the employment business (Reg. 12).

The Regulations also make provision as to notification to work-seekers of any charges which may arise, the right of work-seekers to cancel or withdraw from additional services provided by the Agency, and for the agreement of the work-seeker as to the terms on which work will be obtained for him (Regs 13 to 16).

The agency or business must obtain sufficient information from the hirer to enable them to select a suitable work-seeker for the position (Reg. 18). They must also obtain confirmation of the identity of the work-seeker, and that he has the experience, training and qualifications, and any authorisation which the hirer considers are necessary, or which are required by law or by any professional body, to work in the position which the hirer seeks to fill (Reg. 19).

The agency or business must take all reasonably practicable steps to ensure that the work-seeker and hirer are aware of any requirements laid down by law or by any professional body which must be satisfied in relation to the position, and must make all reasonably practicable enquiries to ensure that it would not be detrimental to the interests of either the work-seeker or the hirer for the work-seeker to work in the position sought to be filled (Reg. 20(1)). Where a business receives information which gives it reasonable grounds to believe that a work-seeker is unsuitable for the position filled, it must inform the hirer and end the supply of the work-seeker to the hirer. Where such information indicates that a work-seeker *may* be unsuitable but does not give gives it reasonable grounds to believe that a work-seeker *is* unsuitable, it must without delay inform the hirer of the information and commence such further enquiries as are reasonably practicable. If the further enquiries confirm that the work-seeker is unsuitable the hirer must be informed and the supply of the work-seeker ended (Reg. 20(2)-(4)). Where an agency supplies a work-seeker to a hirer, it must inform the hirer of any information it receives or obtains within three months from the date of the introduction which indicates that the work-seeker is or may be unsuitable for the position (Reg. 20(5)-(6)).

Where professional qualifications are required for the position, or a work-seeker will be working with vulnerable persons, the agency or business must obtain copies of the relevant qualifications or authorisations, obtain two references from non-relatives of the work-seeker, and take all other reasonably practicable steps to confirm that the work-seeker is suitable for the position concerned. Where all reasonably practicable steps have been taken to comply with these requirements but the agency or business have been unable to do so fully, they must comply with the requirements to the extent they are able to do so, inform the hirer that they have been unable to fully comply, and give details of the steps taken (Reg. 22). There are special provisions relating to an au pair (Reg. 24).

Every advertisement issued or caused to be issued by an agency or employment business must mention in relation to each position it advertises whether it is for temporary or permanent work (Reg. 27(1)). Neither an agency or employment business may issue or cause to be issued an advertisement about positions which hirers seek to fill unless the agency or employment business has information about specific positions of all types to which the advertisement relates and, in relation to each such position, has the authority to find work-seekers for that position or issue the advertisement concerned (Reg. 27(2)). Every advertisement issued in which rates of pay are given must state the nature of the work, the location at which the work-seeker would be required to work, and the minimum experience, training or qualifications required in order to receive those rates of pay (Reg. 27(3)). An agency or employment business must not advertise a GB vacancy (i.e. either for a specific position, or for a generic position the duties of which are ordinarily to be performed in Great Britain) in an EEA State other than the UK unless it (Reg. 27A)–

(i) advertises the vacancy in English in Great Britain at the same time as it advertises the vacancy in the other EEA State; or

(ii) has advertised the vacancy in English in Great Britain in the period of 28 days ending with the day on which it advertises the vacancy in the other EEA State.

The above requirement does not apply if the GB vacancy is for a worker to act solely for, and under the control of, the agency or employment business itself. Breach of the requirement constitutes a criminal offence under s.5 of the Employment Agencies Act 1973 and may also give rise to an action in damages. It is a defence in any proceedings that the agency or employment business believed, on reasonable grounds, that advertising the GB vacancy in English in Great Britain would be disproportionate having regard to the likelihood that such advertising would result in an application from a person with the skills required to fill the vacancy. In respect of a contravention, the Secretary of State also has the power to invoke s.3A of the Employment Agencies Act 1973 which provides for the employment tribunal, on application by the Secretary of State, to make an order prohibiting an individual or individuals from running or being involved in the running of an employment agency or employment business for up to 10 years.

5 Refusal of agency services: trade unions

The Employment Relations Act 1999 (Blacklist) Regulations 2010 prohibit the compilation, use, sale or supply of blacklists ("prohibited lists") containing details of trade union members and activists whose purpose is to discriminate against workers on grounds of trade union membership or trade union activities. A person has a right of complaint to an employment tribunal against an employment agency if that agency refuses any of its services for a reason which relates to a prohibited list and either (Reg. 6(1))–

(a) the employment agency contravenes the prohibition contained in the Regulations in relation to that list; or

(b) the employment agency relies on information supplied by a person who contravenes the prohibition contained in the Regulations in relation to that list and knows or ought reasonably to know that information relied on is supplied in contravention of that prohibition.

An employment agency will be taken to refuse a person a service if that person makes use of the service and the agency (Reg. 6(2))–

(c) refuses or deliberately omits to make the service available to that person;

(d) causes that person not to make use of the service or to cease to make use of it; or

(e) does not provide that person the same service, on the same terms, as it provides to others.

Generally, an employment tribunal cannot consider a complaint unless it is presented within three months beginning with the date of the conduct to which the complaint relates, however, it may consider a complaint out of time if it considers that it is just and equitable to do so (Reg. 7(1), (2)). The date of the conduct to which a claim relates will be taken to be, in the case of an actual refusal, the date of the refusal, or in the case of conduct causing a person not to make use of a service or to cease to make use of it, the date of that conduct. In the case of a deliberate omission to make a service available, the date will be the end of the period within which it was reasonable to expect the person to act. In the case of failure to provide the same service on the same terms as is provided to others, the date will be the last date on which the service was in fact provided (Reg. 7(4)).

An employment tribunal, on finding a complaint is well-founded, must make a declaration to that effect and may make an order requiring the respondent to pay compensation or make a recommendation that the respondent take action to obviate or reduce the adverse effect on the complainant of any conduct to which the complaint relates (Reg. 8). An award of compensation will not be less than £5,000. However, an award can be increased if the respondent fails without reasonable justification to comply with a recommendation or reduced where the tribunal considers that the conduct of the complainant was such that it would be just and equitable to reduce the award. The amount of compensation will also be reduced or further reduced by the amount of any compensation awarded under s.140 of the 1992 Act in respect of the same refusal. The total amount of compensation cannot exceed £65,300. Where a person is pursuing a complaint before the employment tribunal, that person is permitted to apply to the Court for orders restraining or preventing the compilation, use, sale or supply of the blacklist in question (Reg. 13(4)).

6 Restriction on the charging of fees to persons seeking employment

S.6 of the Act provides that, except in such cases or classes of case as the Secretary of State may prescribe, no person carrying on an employment agency or business may request or directly or indirectly receive—
- (a) from any person any fee for providing services (whether by provision of information or otherwise) for finding or seeking to find him employment;
- (b) from any employee any fee for providing services (whether by provision of information or otherwise) for finding or seeking to find another person with a view to the employee acting for and under the control of that other person; or
- (c) from a second person for providing services (whether by provision of information or otherwise) for finding or seeking to find a third person with a view to the second person becoming employed by the first person and acting for and under the control of the third person.

The Conduct of Employment Agencies and Employment Businesses Regulations 2003 prescribe those occupations in the entertainment and fashion and sports industries in respect of which the workers may be charged fees, except where a fee is charged to the employer or where the employer and agent are connected with each other. Any fee charged by the agency must consist only of a charge or commission payable out of the work-seekers employment (up front fees are prohibited).

Where a fee is charged by an Agency for inclusion of information about the work-seeker in a publication, there is a 7-day cooling off period (30 days for performers within the entertainment industry) (Reg. 26).

7 Inspection of premises

An officer duly authorised by the Secretary of State may—
- (a) enter and inspect any relevant business premises (i.e., (i) premises used or to be used for or in connection with the carrying on of an employment agency or employment business, (ii) any other premises which the officer has reasonable cause to believe are or have been used for or in connection with an employment agency or business, and (iii) any other premises used for carrying on any business by a person who also carries on or has carried on an employment agency or business if the officer has reasonable cause to believe that records or other documents relating to the employment agency or business are kept there);
- (b) inspect any records or other documents kept in pursuance of the Act or regulations made thereunder; and
- (c) obtain from any person on the premises information for the purposes of ascertaining whether the provisions of the Act or regulations are being complied with.

If a record or other document or information is not kept at the premises being inspected, the officer may require any person on the premises to inform where and by whom it is kept and to make arrangements, if it is reasonably practicable to do so, for it to be inspected by or furnished to the officer at the premises at a time specified by the officer.

No information so obtained must, however, be disclosed without the consent of the person by whom it was provided except to the Secretary of State for the purpose of the exercise of his functions under the Act, or for the institution of criminal proceedings pursuant to or arising out of the Act or for the purposes of any hearing under the Act (s.9).

8 Exceptions

S.13(7) of the Act sets out those agencies and business services which are expressly excluded from the scope of the Act, as follows—
- (a) duly certified businesses carried on exclusively to obtain employment for (i) former members of the armed forces or (ii) persons released from a prison, detention centre, or young offender's institution;
- (b) services ancillary to the letting for hire of any aircraft, vessel, vehicle, plant or equipment;
- (c) the exercise of any of their functions by a local authority, a police and crime commissioner, a chief constable, the London Fire and Emergency Planning Authority, or the Broads Authority or a National Park Authority;
- (d) services provided by any organisation of employers or organisation of workers for its members, or provided in pursuance of arrangements made or a direction given under s.10 of the Employment and Training Act 1973;
- (e) services provided by an appointments board or service controlled by one or more universities;
- (f) any prescribed business or service, or prescribed class of business or service, or service carried on or provided by prescribed persons or classes of persons.

  The Employment Agencies Act 1973 (Exemptions) Regulations 1976 prescribe the persons or classes of persons whose businesses or services are exempted from the provisions of the Act. These include—

(i) charities;

(ii) certain colleges of education and other institutions of further education in England and Wales;

(iii) specified professional organisations;

(iv) bodies comprising representatives of industrial training boards and representatives of employers' organisations, workers' organisations, or any joint body comprising such organisations;

(v) the British Council; and

(vi) the Crown Agents for Overseas Governments and Administrations.

9 Nurses agencies

Employment agencies in England and Wales which supply, or provide services for the purpose of supplying, registered nurses, midwives or health visitors may be regulated by the Health and Social Care Act 2008 in England or the Care Standards Act 2000 in Wales (see the Notes on **Regulation of Health and Social Care**). The main difference between England and Wales is that in Wales employment agencies which supply nurses *must* be registered, whilst in England only an agency that actually provides a regulated activity (such as nursing care) needs to be registered. Consequently, an employment agency in England that supplies nurses to another organisation which provides the regulated activity does not need to be registered. This also means that, in England, agencies which supply nurses to work for people in their own homes usually do not need to be registered with the Care Quality Commission.

Any person who carries on such an agency which does need to be registered must do so with either the Care Quality Commission (in England) or the Welsh Assembly. The Health and Social Care Act 2008 (Regulated Activities) Regulations 2010 (for England) and the Nurses Agencies (Wales) Regulations 2003 make detailed provision as to the regulation of such agencies including requirements as to the fitness of people to carry on or manage an agency, the conduct of agencies, and the fitness of nurses supplied by an agency. In particular, no nurse must be supplied by the agency unless (2010 Regulations, Reg. 21)–

(a) she is of integrity and good character;

(b) she has the qualifications, skills and experience which are necessary for the work which she is to perform;

(c) she is physically and mentally fit for that work; and

(d) full and satisfactory information is available in relation to her in respect of specified matters (see below).

The specified matters referred to above are (Sch. 3)–

1. proof of identity including a recent photograph;

2. a criminal record certificate or enhanced criminal record certificate, as appropriate (see the Note on **Criminal Record Checks**) together with, where applicable, suitability information relating to children or vulnerable adults;

3. satisfactory evidence of conduct in previous employment concerned with the provision of services relating to (a) health or social care; or (b) children or vulnerable adults;

4. where a person has been previously employed in a position whose duties involved work with children or vulnerable adults, satisfactory verification, so far as reasonably practicable, of the reason why their employment in that position ended;

5. satisfactory documentary evidence of any relevant qualification;

6. a full employment history, together with a satisfactory written explanation of any gaps in employment;

7. satisfactory information about any physical or mental health conditions which are relevant to the person's ability to carry on, manage or work for the purposes of, the regulated activity.

Additionally in Wales, the selection of a nurse for supply must be made by or under the supervision of a nurse. Every nurse supplied by the agency acting as an employment business must be instructed that when working for a service user she must at all times wear identification showing her name, the name of the agency and a recent photograph.

B: GANGMASTERS

10 The licensing of gangmasters

In order to protect gang-service workers, the Gangmasters (Licensing) Act 2004 provides for the licensing of activities involving the supply or use of workers in connection with (s.3)–

(a) agricultural work;

(b) gathering shellfish; and

(c) processing and packaging agricultural products, shellfish and fish.

It is an offence to act as a gangmaster without being licensed (ss.6 and 12). However, the Secretary of State may specify circumstances in which a licence is not required (s.6(2)) and the Gangmasters Licensing (Exclusions) Regulations 2013 have been made for this purpose. They exclude, *inter alia*, the supply of workers to process or pack produce if the workers are supplied to catering establishments, shops, wholesale markets and distribution warehouses. Specific exclusions also apply to certain supplies of agricultural workers, shellfish gatherers and bodies corporate.

The 2004 Act applies to work where a person acts as a gangmaster (whether they are in the UK or elsewhere) in relation to work that takes place in the UK or coastal waters (s.5). The Act applies to England

and Wales, Scotland and Northern Ireland (s.30).

11 The procedure for licensing gangmasters

The procedure for licensing gangmasters is set out in the Gangmasters (Licensing Conditions) Rules 2009.

The rules specify the information to be provided by an applicant (r.3), and the licence conditions that apply to all licence holders (r.4 and the Schedule).

One of the requirements for obtaining or keeping a licence is that the licence holder and anyone specified in the licence must be "fit and proper". An applicant is fit and proper if he complies with the obligations contained in Reg.8(2) of the Gangmasters (Licensing Authority) Regulations 2015 which include the avoidance of exploitation of workers as respects their recruitment, use or supply; and compliance with any obligations imposed by or under any enactment in so far as they relate to, or affect the conduct of, the licence holder.

A specified licence fee, which varies with the turnover of the business, is payable as is a charge for any inspection of the business which may be required as part of the application process (r.6).

12 When a person "acts as a gangmaster"

A person "acts as a gangmaster", and therefore needs to be licensed, where he ("A") provides a worker to do work for another person ("B"). It is irrelevant whether–
(a) the worker works under a contract with A or is supplied to him by another person. It does not matter whether A supervises the work or not;
(b) the worker is supplied directly under arrangements between A and B, or indirectly under arrangements involving one or more intermediaries, i.e., the supply of labour by sub-contract gangmasters falls within the 2004 Act and so requires a licence;
(c) A supplies the worker himself or procures that the worker is supplied by a secondary labour-provider;
(d) the work is done under the control of A, B or an intermediary, i.e., it does not matter who is controlling the work performed by the worker; or
(e) the work done for B is for the purposes of a business carried on by him or in connection with services provided by him to another person, i.e., arrangements such as a subcontractor supplying workers to a main gangmaster who is engaged by a third-party client fall within the terms of the 2004 Act.

A person also acts as a gangmaster if he uses workers to do work to which the Act applies in connection with services provided by him to another person (i.e., he supplies a service to B e.g., clearing a field of peas, rather than supplying the workers to B to do the job). There are other provisions designed to close potential loopholes whereby arrangements could otherwise be structured so as to avoid the provisions of the Act (see s.4).

An unlicensed gangmaster will still commit an offence under the 2004 Act even though the worker he uses has no right to be, or to work, in the United Kingdom (s.26(2)).

A person who is supplied workers by an unlicensed gangmaster also commits an offence unless he can prove that he took all reasonable steps to satisfy himself that the gangmaster was acting under the authority of a valid licence and he did not know and had no reasonable grounds for suspecting that the gangmaster did not have a valid licence (s.13, not in force in relation to gathering shellfish).

13 The Gangmasters Licensing Authority

The Gangmasters (Licensing) Act 2004 establishes the Gangmasters Licensing Authority (the Authority) (s.1), whose main functions are to–
(a) undertake the licensing process;
(b) inspect licensees and review their activities;
(c) act as an information source to specified persons; and
(d) keep under review the operation of the 2004 Act and perform any other functions prescribed by the Secretary of State.

It is for the Secretary of State to direct the Authority (s.2) and to determine other matters. To this end, the Gangmasters (Licensing Authority) Regulations 2015 make provision for the constitution, structure and other matters relating to the operation of the Gangmasters Licensing Authority.

The Authority must establish and maintain a register of licensed gangmasters, which must be available for public inspection (s.11).

14 Appeals

An appeals procedure against any decision of the Gangmasters Licensing Authority (see **13 Gangmasters Licensing Authority**, above) is provided for by the Gangmasters (Licensing) Act 2004, s.10.

The Gangmasters (Appeals) Regulations 2006 make provision for the procedure for appealing against a decision to refuse to grant a licence, to impose conditions to which a licence is subject, to modify or revoke a licence, or to refuse to transfer a licence.

15 Authorities

Statutes–

Care Standards Act 2000

Deregulation and Contracting Out Act 1994

Employment Agencies Act 1973

Employment Protection Act 1975

Employment Relations Act 1999

Gangmasters (Licensing) Act 2004

Statutory Instruments–

Conduct of Employment Agencies and Employment Businesses Regulations 2003, as amended (S.I. 2003 No. 3319, 2005 No. 2114, 2006 No. 3221, 2007 No. 3575, 2010 No. 1782, 2014 No. 3351, and 2016 No. 510)

Employment Agencies Act 1973 (Exemption) Regulations 1976 and (Exemption) (No. 2) Regulations 1979 and 1984 (S.I. 1976 No. 710, 1979 No. 1741, and 1984 No. 978)

Employment Relations Act 1999 (Blacklists) Regulations 2010, as amended (S.I. 2010 No. 493 and 2014 No. 386)

Gangmasters (Appeals) Regulations 2006 (S.I. 2006 No. 662)

Gangmasters (Licensing Authority) Regulations 2015 (S.I. 2015 No. 805)

Gangmasters (Licensing Conditions) Rules 2009 (S.I. 2009 No. 307)

Gangmasters Licensing (Exclusions) Regulations 2013, as amended (S.I. 2013 No. 2216 and 2014 No. 2124)

Health and Social Care Act 2008 (Regulated Activities) Regulations 2010 (S.I. 2010 No. 781)

Nurses Agencies (Wales) Regulations 2003, as amended (S.I. 2003 No. 2527, 2006 No. 3251, 2009 Nos. 1824 and 2541, and 2012 No. 2404)

DISCRIMINATION AT WORK AND EQUALITY OF TERMS

1 Introduction

The Equality Act 2010, which applies to England and Wales and Scotland, harmonised discrimination legislation concerning sex, race and disability including in relation to employment and work.

The 2010 Act provides protection from discrimination in respect of what are defined as "protected characteristics", namely (s.4)–

(a) age;

(b) disability;

(c) gender reassignment;

(d) marriage and civil partnership;

(e) pregnancy and maternity;

(f) race;

(g) religion or belief;

(h) sex; and

(i) sexual orientation.

The conduct that is prohibited by the Act in respect of the protected characteristics, and the discrimination and equality provisions concerning areas such as services and public functions, premises and education, are more fully described in the Note on **Discrimination and Equality Law**.

Schedule 9 to the 2010 Act contains exceptions to certain provisions of the Act dealing with work. These relate, *inter alia*, to occupational requirements, religious requirements, and the armed forces. There are also certain exceptions contained in that Schedule relating to age contravention, for example, in relation to payment of the minimum wage: see **14 Exceptions**, below.

A: WORK

2 Employment: discrimination and victimisation

The Equality Act 2010 prohibits an employer (A) from discriminating or victimising against a person (B) (s.39(1), (3))–

(a) in the arrangements A makes for deciding to whom to offer employment;

(b) as to the terms on which A offers B employment;

(c) by not offering B employment.

The above provisions deal with applicants for employment. In respect of employees, A must not discriminate or victimise against an employee of his (B) (s.39(2), (4))–

(d) as to B's terms of employment;

(e) in the way A affords B access, or by not affording B access, to opportunities for promotion, transfer or training or for receiving any other benefit, facility or service;

(f) by dismissing B;

(g) by subjecting B to any other detriment.

The reference to dismissing B includes a reference to the termination of B's employment (s.39(7))–

(i) by the expiry of a period (including a period expiring by reference to an event or circumstances);

(ii) by an act of B's (including giving notice) in circumstances such that B is entitled, because of A's conduct, to terminate the employment without notice.

Paragraph (i) above does not apply if, immediately after the termination, the employment is renewed on the same terms (s.39(8)).

"Employment" means employment under a contract of employment, a contract of apprenticeship or a contract personally to do work. It also includes Crown employment, and employment as a relevant member of the House of Commons or House of Lords staff (s.83(2)).

3 Pregnancy and maternity discrimination

In respect of pregnancy and maternity discrimination and work cases, a person discriminates against a woman if, in the protected period (see below) in relation to a pregnancy of hers, the person treats her unfavourably because of the pregnancy or because of an illness suffered by her as a result of it (s.18(2)). For the purposes of s.18(2), if the treatment of a woman is in implementation of a decision taken in the protected period, the treatment is to be regarded as occurring in that period, even if the implementation is not until after the end of that period (s.18(4)). A person also discriminates against a woman if they treat her unfavourably because she is on compulsory maternity leave or because of the exercise or intended exercise of the right to ordinary or additional maternity leave (s.18(3), (4)). The protected period, in relation to a woman's pregnancy, begins when the pregnancy begins, and ends (s.18(6))–

(a) if she has the right to ordinary and additional maternity leave, at the end of the additional maternity leave period or (if earlier) when she returns to work after the pregnancy;

(b) if she does not have that right, at the end of the period of 2 weeks beginning with the end of the pregnancy.

4 Gender reassignment discrimination

In relation to gender reassignment discrimination and cases of absence from work, a person (A) discriminates against a transsexual person (B) if, in relation to an absence of B's that is because of gender reassignment, A treats B less favourably than A would treat B if (Equality Act 2010, s.16(2))–
  (i) B's absence was because of sickness or injury; or
  (ii) B's absence was for some other reason and it is not reasonable for B to be treated less favourably.
A person's absence is because of gender reassignment if it is because the person is proposing to undergo, is undergoing or has undergone a process (or part of a process) for the purpose of reassigning the person's sex by changing physiological or other attributes of sex (s.16(3)).

5 Employment: harassment

An employer is prohibited under the Equality Act 2010 from harassing a person who is an employee of theirs or a person who has applied to them for employment (s.40(1)).
The provisions which made an employer liable for the harassment of his employees by a third party (such as a customer) have been repealed.

6 Adjustments for disabled persons

A duty to make reasonable adjustments in respect of "interested" disabled persons (i.e., employees and applicants for employment) applies to an employer (Equality Act 2010, s.39(5), Sch. 8). The descriptions of disabled persons for the purposes of the provisions of the Act concerning work (including occupational pension schemes) are contained in Part 2 of Schedule 8 to the Act. The duty comprises three separate requirements.

First Requirement
Where a provision, criterion or practice of a person puts a disabled person at a substantial disadvantage in relation to a relevant matter in comparison with persons who are not disabled, there is a requirement to take such steps as it is reasonable to have to take to avoid the disadvantage.

Second Requirement
Where a physical feature puts a disabled person at a substantial disadvantage in relation to a relevant matter in comparison with persons who are not disabled, there is a requirement to take such steps as it is reasonable to have to take to avoid the disadvantage.

Third Requirement
Where a disabled person would, but for the provision of an auxiliary aid, be put at a substantial disadvantage in relation to a relevant matter in comparison with persons who are not disabled, there is a requirement to take such steps as it is reasonable to have to take to provide the auxiliary aid.

Regulations may, *inter alia*, prescribe matters to be taken into account in deciding whether it is reasonable for a person to take a step for the purposes of these provisions or persons to whom the requirements will not apply (s.22).
A failure to comply with any of the requirements amounts to a failure to comply with a duty to make reasonable adjustments and a person discriminates against a disabled person if he fails to comply with that duty in relation to that disabled person. A failure to comply with this duty is not actionable by virtue of another provision of the Act: the person discriminated against will be the claimant as the duty applies in respect of that person only and another body cannot legally challenge the failure (s.21).
A person is not subject to a duty to make reasonable adjustments if that person does not know and could not reasonably be expected to know (Sch. 8, Pt. 3))–
  (a) in the case of an applicant or potential applicant, that an interested disabled person is or may be an applicant for the work in question;
  (b) in any other case referred to in Part 3 of Schedule 8 (i.e. an applicant for membership of a trade organisation or for the conferment of a relevant qualification), that an interested disabled person has a disability and is likely to be placed at the disadvantage referred to in the first, second or third requirements.
A person has a disability if (s.6(1))–
  (c) they have a physical or mental impairment; and
  (d) the impairment has a substantial and long-term effect on their ability to carry out normal day-to-day activities.
A reference to a disabled person includes a person who has had a disability (s.6(2)).
S.6 is supplemented by Schedule 1 to the Act which deals with determination of disability and gives guidance. The effect of an impairment is deemed to be a long-term effect if it has lasted for at least 12 months or is likely to last at least 12 months or for the rest of the life of the affected person (i.e., where the affected person is suffering from a terminal illness and unlikely to live 12 months, they are still protected by the Act). Any impairment that is likely to recur is treated as having a long-term effect (Sch. 1, para. 2). Regulations may make provision for a condition of a prescribed description to be, or not to be, an impairment or for an effect of a prescribed description on the ability of a person to carry out normal day-to-day activities to be treated as being, or as not being, a substantial adverse effect (Sch. 1, paras 1, 4). Regulations may also provide for persons of

prescribed descriptions to be treated as having disabilities (Sch. 1, para. 7). By virtue of the Equality Act 2010 (Disability) Regulations 2010 the following are to be treated as not amounting to an impairment (Regs. 3, 4)–

    (i) addictions to alcohol, nicotine or any other substance (other than those medically caused);

    (ii) other specified conditions namely a tendency to start fires; a tendency to steal; a tendency to physical or sexual abuse of other persons; exhibitionism; and voyeurism.

In addition, the condition known as seasonal allergic rhinitis (hayfever) will not in itself be treated as an impairment (although it may be taken into account where it aggravates the effect of another condition). The Regulations also exclude tattoos and a piercing of the body for decorative or other non-medical purposes from the definition of severe disfigurement (Reg. 5). Where a child under six years of age has an impairment which does not have a substantial and long-term adverse effect on the ability of that child to carry out normal day-to-day activities, that impairment is to be taken as having a substantial and long-term adverse effect on the ability of that child to carry out normal day-to-day activities where it would normally have such an effect on the ability of a person aged six or over to carry out such activities (Reg. 6). A person is deemed to have a disability where that person is certified by a consultant ophthalmologist as blind, severely sight impaired or partially sighted (Reg. 7).

Severe disfigurement is to be treated as having a substantial adverse affect on a person's ability to carry out normal day-to-day activities. However, regulations may provide that in prescribed circumstances a severe disfigurement is not to be treated as having that effect, in particular in relation to deliberately acquired disfigurement (see above) (Sch. 1, para. 3).

An impairment is to be treated as having a substantial adverse affect on a person's ability to carry out normal day-to-day activities if measures (i.e. medical treatment) are being taken to treat or correct it and, but for those measures, it would be likely to have that effect (Sch. 1, para. 5).

Cancer, HIV infection and multiple sclerosis are each a disability (Sch. 1, para. 6).

Certain progressive serious illnesses (such as cancer, multiple sclerosis, muscular dystrophy or HIV infection) will be taken to be an impairment which has a substantial adverse effect if a person with the condition has an impairment which is not having a substantial adverse effect but is likely to result in the person having an impairment with such an effect (Sch. 1, para. 8).

A question as to whether a person had a disability at the relevant time is to be determined as if the provisions of, or made under, the 2010 Act were in force when the act complained of was done and had been in force at the relevant time (Sch. 1, para. 9).

The appropriate Minister may issue guidance giving examples of effects which it would, or would not, be reasonable, in relation to particular activities, to regard as substantial adverse effects; or substantial adverse effects which it would, or would not, be reasonable to regard as long-term (Sch. 1, Pt. 2).

7 Contract workers

The Equality Act 2010 prohibits a principal from discriminating against or victimising a contract worker (s.41(1), (3))–

    (a) as to the terms on which the principal allows the worker to do the work;

    (b) by not allowing the worker to do, or to continue to do, the work;

    (c) in the way the principal affords the worker access, or by not affording the worker access, to opportunities for receiving a benefit, facility or service; or

    (d) by subjecting the worker to any other detriment.

A principal must not, in relation to contract work, harass a contact worker (s.41(2)). A "principal" is defined as a person who makes work available for an individual who is employed by another person and supplied by that other person in furtherance of a contract to which the principal is a party (whether or not that other person is a party to it) (s.41(5)). The definition can therefore include an employment agency. A "contract worker" is an individual supplied to a principal in furtherance of such a contract mentioned above (s.41(6)).

A duty to make reasonable adjustments in respect of disabled persons applies to a principal as well as to the employer of a contract worker (s.41(4)). As to the duty to make reasonable adjustments see **6 Adjustments for disabled persons**, above.

8 Specific areas of employment

The following provisions apply to specific occupations or professions insofar as they deal with discrimination, victimisation and harassment under the Equality Act 2010.

Police

For the purposes of the provisions of the Equality Act 2010 concerning employment, holding the office of constable or an appointment as a police cadet will be treated as employment (s.42)–

    (a) by the chief officer, in respect of any act done by the chief officer in relation to a constable, appointment to the office of constable, or in relation to a police cadet or appointment as one;

    (b) by the responsible authority, in respect of any act done by the authority in relation to a constable, appointment to the office of constable, or in relation to a police cadet or appointment as one.

Partnerships and limited liability partnerships

A firm (in respect of the position of partner) or a limited liability partnership (in respect of the position of member), including a proposed firm or limited liability partnership, must not discriminate against or victimise a person (ss.44(1), (5), 45(1), (5))–

    (a) in the arrangements it makes for deciding to whom to offer a position as a partner or member;

    (b) as to the terms on which it offers the person a position as a partner or a member;

    (c) by not offering the person a position as a partner or a member.

A firm or limited liability partnership must not discriminate against or victimise a partner or a member (ss.44(2), (6), 45(2), (6))–

    (d) as to the terms on which a person is a partner or a member;

    (e) in the way it affords a partner or a member access, or by not affording them access, to opportunities for promotion, transfer or training or for receiving any other benefit, facility or service;

    (f) by expelling a partner or a member;

    (g) by subjecting a partner or a member to any other detriment.

A firm or limited liability partnership must not harass a partner or member or a person who has applied for such a position (ss.44(3), 45(3)).

A duty to make reasonable adjustments in respect of disabled persons applies to a firm or limited liability partnership, including any such proposed firm or partnership (ss.44(7), 45(7)). As to the duty to make reasonable adjustments see **6 Adjustments for disabled persons**, above.

Barristers and advocates

A barrister must not discriminate against or victimise a person (s.47(1), (4))–

    (a) in the arrangements they make for deciding to whom to offer a pupillage or tenancy;

    (b) as to the terms on which they offer a person a pupillage or tenancy;

    (c) by not offering a person a pupillage or tenancy.

A barrister must not discriminate against or victimise a person who is a pupil or tenant (s.47(2), (5))–

    (d) as to the terms on which a person is a pupil or tenant;

    (e) in the way they afford a pupil or tenant access, or by not affording access, to opportunities for promotion, transfer or training or for receiving any other benefit, facility or service;

    (f) by terminating the pupillage;

    (g) by subjecting a person to pressure to leave chambers;

    (h) by subjecting a person to any other detriment.

A barrister is also prohibited, in relation to a pupillage or tenancy, from harassing the pupil or tenant or a person who has applied for a pupillage or tenancy (s.47(3)). The above provisions also apply to a barrister's clerk or a person who carries out the functions of a barrister's clerk (s.47(8)).

A person who has instructed a barrister must not, in relation to that instruction, discriminate against the barrister by subjecting them to a detriment; harass the barrister; or, victimise the barrister (s.47(6)).

A duty to make reasonable adjustments in respect of disabled persons applies to a barrister (s.47(7)).

Similar provisions concerning discrimination, victimisation and harassment apply in respect of an advocate and a person who is a devil or a member of a stable (s.48).

Office holders

A person who has the power to make an appointment to a personal office must not discriminate against or victimise a person (s.49(3), (5))–

    (a) in the arrangements they make for deciding to whom to offer the appointment;

    (b) as to the terms on which they offer the person the appointment;

    (c) by not offering the person the appointment.

A "personal office" is an office or post to which a person is appointed to discharge a function personally under the direction of another person and in respect of which the appointed person is entitled to remuneration (s.49(2)). For these purposes a person is not to be taken to be entitled to remuneration merely because the person is entitled to payments in respect of expenses incurred or by way of compensation for loss of income or benefits (s.49(11)). A person is to be regarded as discharging functions personally under the direction of another person if that other person is entitled to direct the person as to when and where to discharge the functions (s.49(10)).

A person who has the power to make an appointment to a personal office must not, in relation to the office, harass a person seeking, or being considered for, the appointment (s.49(4)).

A person who is a "relevant person" (see below) in relation to a personal office must not discriminate against or victimise a person appointed to the office (s.49(6), (8))–

    (d) as to the terms of the person's appointment;

    (e) in the way the relevant person affords the appointed person access, or by not affording them access, to opportunities for promotion, transfer or training or for receiving any other benefit, facility or service;

    (f) by terminating the person's appointment;

    (g) by subjecting the person to any other detriment.

The "relevant person" will, *inter alia*, be the person who has the power in relation to the matter to which the conduct in question relates (s.52).

A relevant person is also prohibited, in relation to a personal office, from harassing a person appointed to it (s.49(7)).

A duty to make reasonable adjustments in respect of disabled persons applies to a person who has the power to make an appointment to a personal office and a relevant person in relation to that office (s.49(9)).

EMPLOYMENT

Certain offices, including political offices, are deemed to be excluded offices for the purposes of the above provisions. Work to which other provisions of the 2010 Act apply are also excluded. Those provisions are s.39 (employment (see **2 Employment: discrimination and victimisation,** above)), s.41 (contract work (see **8 Contract workers,** above)), s.44 (partnerships), s.45 (limited liability partnerships), s.47 (barristers), s.48 (advocates) and s.55 (employment services (see **9 Employment service-providers,** below)) (Sch. 6).

Similar provisions to those dealing with appointments to personal offices also apply to appointments to public offices (s.50). A public office is defined as an–
- (i) office or post, appointment to which is made by a member of the executive;
- (ii) office or post, appointment to which is made on the recommendation of, or subject to the approval of, a member of the executive;
- (iii) office or post, appointment to which is made on the recommendation of, or subject to the approval of the, House of Commons, House of Lords, National Assembly for Wales or Scottish Parliament.

The same exclusions set out in Schedule 6 to the Act apply (see above).

9 Employment service-providers

The Equality Act 2010 prohibits a person concerned with the provision of an employment service (an "employment service-provider") from discriminating against or victimising a person (s.55(1), (4))–
- (a) in the arrangements the service-provider makes for selecting persons to whom to provide, or to whom to offer to provide, the service;
- (b) as to the terms on which the service-provider offers to provide the service to the person;
- (c) by not offering to provide the service to the person.

The provision of an employment service includes, *inter alia*, the provision of a service for finding employment for people or for supplying employers with people to do work. It also includes the provision of vocational training and vocational guidance or making arrangements for the provision of such training or guidance (s.56(2)).

An employment service-provider is also prohibited, in relation to the provision of an employment service, from discriminating against or victimising a person (s.55(2), (5))–
- (d) as to the terms on which the service-provider provides the service to the person;
- (e) by not providing the service to the person;
- (f) by terminating the provision of the service;
- (g) by subjecting the person to any other detriment.

An employment service-provider must not, in relation to the provision of an employment service, harass a person who asks the service-provider to provide the service or a person for whom the service-provider provides the service (s.55(3)).

A duty to make reasonable adjustments in respect of disabled persons applies to an employment service-provider except in relation to the provision of a vocational service (s.56(6)). "Vocational training" means training for employment or work experience (s.56(6)). As to the duty to make reasonable adjustments see **6 Adjustments for disabled persons,** above.

10 Trade organisations

The Equality Act 2010 prohibits a trade organisation from discriminating against or victimising a person (s.57(1), (4))–
- (a) in the arrangements it makes for deciding to whom to offer membership of the organisation;
- (b) as to the terms on it is prepared to admit the person as a member;
- (c) by not accepting the person's application for membership.

A trade organisation must not discriminate against or victimise a person (s.57(2), (5))–
- (d) in the way it affords a person access, or by not affording a person access, to opportunities for receiving a benefit, facility or service;
- (e) by depriving a person of membership;
- (f) by varying the terms on which a person is a member;
- (g) by subjecting a person to any other detriment.

A trade organisation must not, in relation to membership of it, harass a member or an applicant for membership (s.57(3)).

A duty to make reasonable adjustments in respect of disabled persons applies to a trade organisation (s.57(6)). As to the duty to make reasonable adjustments see **6 Adjustments for disabled persons,** above.

A trade organisation is defined as an organisation of workers, an organisation of employers, or any other organisation whose members carry on a particular trade or profession for the purposes of which the organisation exists (s.57(7)).

11 Local authority members

In respect of the carrying out of local authority official business, the authority concerned must not discriminate against or victimise a member of the authority (Equality Act 2010, s.58(1), (3))–
- (a) in the way the authority affords the member access, or by not affording the member access, to

opportunities for training or for receiving any other facility;

(b) by subjecting the member to any other detriment.

A member is not subjected to a detriment for the purposes of these provisions only because the member is (s.58(4))–

(c) not appointed or elected to an office of the authority;

(d) not appointed or elected to, or to an office of, a committee or sub-committee of the authority;

(e) not appointed or nominated in exercise of an appointment power of the authority.

A local authority must not, in relation to a member's carrying out of official business, harass the member (s.58(2)).

A duty to make reasonable adjustments in respect of disabled persons applies to a local authority (s.59(6)). As to the duty to make reasonable adjustments see **6 Adjustments for disabled persons**, above.

For the purposes of s.58 a "local authority" means (s.59(2))–

(i) a county council in England;

(ii) a district council in England;

(iii) the Greater London Authority;

(iv) a London borough council;

(v) the Common Council of the City of London;

(vi) the Council of the Isles of Scilly;

(vii) a parish council in England;

(viii) a county council in Wales;

(ix) a community council in Wales;

(x) a county borough council in Wales;

(xi) a council constituted under s.2 of the Local Government etc. (Scotland) Act 1994;

(xii) a community council in Scotland.

12 Enquiries about disability and health

S.60 of the Equality Act 2010 deals with health enquiries by a person during a process of recruitment. A person to whom an application for work is made must not ask about the health of the applicant (s.60(1))–

(a) before offering work to the applicant;

(b) where a person is not in a position to offer work to the applicant, before including the applicant in a pool of applicants from whom the person intends (when in a position to do so) to select a person to whom to offer work.

A contravention of the above provisions is enforceable by the Commission for Equality and Human Rights under the Equality Act 2006 (as to which see the Note on **Discrimination and Equality Law**) (s.60(2)). A person does not contravene a disability provision merely by asking about an applicant's health, but that person's reliance on information given in response may be a contravention of such a provision and the applicant may have a claim for disability discrimination in an employment tribunal (s.60(3)–(5)).

Health questions are permitted in limited circumstances. A question is permitted in so far as asking the question is necessary for the purpose of (s.60(6))–

(i) establishing whether an applicant will be able to comply with a requirement to undergo an assessment or establishing whether a duty to make reasonable adjustments is or will be imposed on a person in relation to an applicant in connection with a requirement to undergo an assessment;

(ii) establishing whether the an applicant will be able to carry out a function that is intrinsic to the work concerned;

(iii) monitoring diversity in the range of persons applying to a person for work;

(iv) taking action to which s.158 of the Act (the concept of positive action) would apply if references in that section to persons who share (or do not share) a protected characteristic were references to disabled persons (or persons who are not disabled) and the reference to the characteristic were a reference to a disability;

(v) if a person applies in relation to the work a requirement to have a particular disability, establishing whether the applicant has that disability.

Paragraph (v) above applies only if a person shows that, having regard to the nature or context of the work, the requirement is an occupational requirement and the application of the requirement is a proportionate means of achieving a legitimate aim (s.60(8)).

13 Working beyond retirement

The right of employees to request to work beyond retirement age has been removed due to the phasing out of the default retirement age from April 2011 (see the Employment Equality (Repeal of Retirement Age Provisions) Regulations 2011).

14 Exceptions

S.83, Sch. 9 to the Equality Act 2010 contains exceptions to the work provisions contained in Part 5 of the Act. These include the following:

Occupational requirements

A person does not contravene certain provisions of the Act by applying in relation to work a requirement to have a particular protected characteristic if he can show that, having regard to the nature or context of the work (Sch. 9, para. 1)–

(a) it is an occupational requirement;

(b) the application of the requirement is a proportionate means of achieving a legitimate aim;

(c) the person to whom he applies the requirement does not meet it, or he has reasonable grounds for not being satisfied that the person meets it.

Religious requirements relating to sex, marriage etc.

A person does not contravene certain provisions of the Act by applying in relation to employment a particular requirement including a requirement to be of a particular sex; not to be married or a civil partner; not to be married to a person of the same sex; not to be a transsexual person; or a requirement relating to sexual orientation if he can show that (Sch. 9, para. 2)–

(a) the employment is for the purposes of an organised religion;

(b) the application of the requirement engages the compliance or non-conflict principle (see below);

(c) the person to whom he applies the requirement does not meet it, or he has reasonable grounds for not being satisfied that the person meets it.

The application of a requirement engages the compliance principle if it is applied so as to comply with the doctrines of the religion and a requirement engages the non-conflict principle if, because of the nature or context of the employment, the requirement is applied so as to avoid conflicting with the strongly held religious convictions of a significant number of the religion's followers.

Armed forces

The armed forces are exempt from certain provisions of the Act in respect of the arrangements it makes for deciding to whom to offer employment (or by not offering employment) and in respect of the way it affords access to opportunities for promotion, transfer or training or for receiving any other benefit, facility or service. A person does not contravene these provisions by applying in relation to service in the armed forces a relevant requirement if he shows that the application is a proportionate means of ensuring the combat effectiveness of the armed forces. A relevant requirement is a requirement to be a man or a requirement not to be at transsexual person (Sch. 9, para. 4).

Employment services

An employment service-provider does not contravene provisions concerning the arrangements made for selecting persons, or on the terms a service is provided under s.55(1) or (2) (see **9 Employment service-providers**, above) if he can show that he acted in reliance on a statement made to him by a person with the power to offer the work in question to the effect that his action would be lawful and it was reasonable for him to rely on that statement (Sch. 9, para. 5).

The National Minimum Wage

It is not an age contravention for a person to pay a young worker at a lower rate than that at which the person pays an older worker if the hourly rate for the national minimum wage for a person of the young worker's age is lower than that for a person of the older worker's age, and the rate at which the young worker is paid is below the single hourly rate (Sch. 9, para. 11). It is not an age contravention for a person to pay an apprentice who does not qualify for the national minimum wage at a lower rate than the person pays an apprentice who does (Sch. 9, para. 12).

Redundancy and benefits based on length of service

It is not an age contravention for a person to give a qualifying employee an enhanced redundancy payment of an amount less than that of an enhanced redundancy payment which the person gives to another qualifying employee, if each amount is calculated on the same basis (Sch. 9, para. 13). It is not an age contravention for a person to be put at a disadvantage when compared with another person in relation to the provision of a benefit, facility or service in so far as the disadvantage is because he has a shorter period of service than the other person. However, if his period of service exceeds 5 years, a person may rely on these provisions only if he reasonably believes that doing so fulfils a business need (Sch. 9, para. 10).

Insurance etc.

It is not an age contravention for an employer to make arrangements for, or afford access to, the provision of insurance or a related financial service to an employee for a period which ends when the employee attains whichever is the greater of 65 years of age and the state pension age (Sch. 9, para. 14). It is not a contravention of Part 5 of the Act, so far as relating to relevant discrimination, to do anything in relation to an annuity, life insurance policy, accident insurance policy or similar matter involving the assessment of risk if that thing is done by reference to actuarial or other data from a source on which it is reasonable to rely, and it is reasonable to do it (Sch. 9, para. 20).

Maternity leave benefits

A person will not contravene certain provisions of the Act so far as relating to pregnancy and maternity by depriving a woman who is on maternity leave of any benefit from the terms of her employment relating to pay (non-contractual payments) (Sch. 9, para. 17).

Benefits depending on marital status

A person does not contravene Part 5 of the Act, so far as relating to sexual orientation, by doing anything which prevents or restricts a person who is not married from having access to a benefit, facility or service the right to which accrued before 5th December 2005 (the day on which s.1 of the Civil Partnership Act 2004 came into force), or which is payable in respect of periods of service before that date. Further, a person will not contravene Part 5, so far as relating to sexual orientation, by providing married persons and civil partners (to the exclusion of all other persons) with access to a benefit, facility or service (Sch. 9, para. 18).

Provision of services to the public

Certain provisions of the Act will not be contravened in relation to the provision of a benefit, facility or service to a person where the provider is concerned with the provision (for payment or not) of a benefit, facility or service of the same description to the public (Sch. 9, para. 19).

Contributions to personal pension schemes

A Minister of the Crown may by order provide that it is not an age contravention for an employer to maintain or use, with respect to contributions to personal pension schemes, practices, actions or decisions relating to age which are of a specified description (Sch. 9, para. 16).

B: EQUALITY OF TERMS

I: SEX EQUALITY

15 Sex equality: relevant types of work

Ss.64–71 of the Equality Act 2010 contain provisions dealing with sex equality and work. The provisions apply where (s.64(1))–
  (a) a person (A) is employed on work that is equal to the work that a comparator of the opposite sex (B) does; or
  (b) a person (A) holding a personal or public office does work that is equal to the work that a comparator of the opposite sex (B) does.
The references to the work that B does are not restricted to work done contemporaneously with the work done by A (s.64(2)). If A is employed, B is a comparator if (s.79(3))–
  (i) B is employed by A's employer or by an associate of A's employer; and
  (ii) A and B work at the same establishment.
B will also be a comparator if (s.79(4))–
  (iii) B is employed by A's employer or by an associate of A's employer;
  (iv) B works at an establishment other than the one at which A works; and
  (v) common terms apply at the establishments (either generally or as between A and B).
If A holds a personal or public office, B is a comparator if (s.79(5))–
  (vi) B holds a personal or public office; and
  (vii) the person responsible for paying A is also responsible for paying B.

16 The meaning of "equal work"

For the purposes of the provisions concerning sex equality and work contained in the Equality Act 2010, the work of a person (A) is like that of another person (B) if it is (s.65(1))–
  (a) like B's work;
  (b) rated as equivalent to B's work;
  (c) of equal value to B's work.
A's work is like B's work if (s.65(2))–
  (d) A's work and B's work are the same or broadly similar;
  (e) such differences as there are between their work are not of practical importance in relation to the terms of their work;
On a comparison of one person's work with another's for the purposes of (d) and (e) above, it is necessary to have regard to the frequency with which differences between their work occur in practice and the nature and extent of the differences (s.65(3)). A's work will be rated as equivalent to B's if a job evaluation study (s.65(4))–
  (f) gives an equal value to A's job and B's job in terms of the demands made on a worker;
  (g) would give an equal value to A's job and B's job in those terms were the evaluation not made on a sex-specific system.
A system is sex-specific if, for the purposes of one or more of the demands made on a worker, it sets values for men different from those it sets for women (s.65(5)).
A's work is of equal value to B's if it is neither like B's work nor rated as equivalent to B's work but nevertheless equal to B's work in terms of the demands made on A by reference to factors such as effort, skill and decision-making (s.65(6)).

17 Sex equality clause

If the terms of a person's work do not, by whatever means, include a sex equality clause they are to be treated as including one (Equality Act 2010, s.66(1)). A sex equality clause is a provision that has the following effect (s.66(2))–
- (a) if a term of work of a person (A) is less favourable to them than a corresponding term of another person (B) is to B, A's term is modified so as not to be less favourable;
- (b) if A does not have a term which corresponds to a term of B's that benefits B, A's terms are modified so as to include such a term.

Paragraph (a) above applies to a term of A's relating to membership of or under an occupational pension scheme only in so far as a sex equality rule (see **18 Sex equality rule-pensions**, below) would have effect in relation to the term (s.66(3)).

In the case of work which has been rated as equivalent to B's work (see **16 The meaning of "equal work"**, above), a reference in paragraph (b) above to a term includes a reference to such terms (if any) as have not been determined by the rating of the work (as well as those that have) (s.66(4)).

A sex equality clause does not have effect in relation to terms of work affected by compliance with laws regulating the employment of women or the appointment of women to personal or public offices, neither does such a clause have effect in relation to terms of work affording special treatment to women in connection with pregnancy or childbirth (Sch. 7, paras. (1), (2)).

The 2010 Act contains the defence of material factor, in that the sex equality clause in A's terms will have no effect in relation to a difference between A's terms and B's terms if the responsible person shows that the difference is because of a material factor reliance on which (s.69(1))–
- (c) does not involve treating A less favourably because of A's sex than the responsible person treats B; and
- (d) if the factor is within the provision described below, is a proportionate means of achieving a legitimate aim.

A factor falls within these provisions if A shows that, as a result of the factor, A and persons of the same sex doing work equal to A's are put at a particular disadvantage when compared with persons of the opposite sex doing work equal to A's (s.69(2)). The long-term objective of reducing inequality between men's and women's terms of work is always to be regarded as a legitimate aim (s.69(3)).

18 Sex equality rule–pensions

The Equality Act 2010 provides that if an occupational pension scheme does not include a sex equality rule it is to be treated as including one (s.67(1)). A sex equality rule is a provision that has the following effect (s.67(2))–
- (a) if a relevant term of work of a person (A) is less favourable to them than it is to another person (B), the term is modified so as not to be less favourable;
- (b) if a term confers a relevant discretion capable of being exercised in a way that would be less favourable to A than to B, the term is modified so as to prevent the exercise of the discretion in that way.

A term is relevant if it is (s.67(3), (5))–
- (c) a term on which persons become members of the scheme; or
- (d) a term on which members of the scheme are treated (including a reference to the term as it has effect for the benefit of dependants of members).

A discretion is relevant if its exercise in relation to the scheme is capable of affecting (s.67(4), (6))–
- (e) the way in which persons become members of the scheme; or
- (f) the way in which members of the scheme are treated (including a reference to the way they are treated as the scheme has effect for the benefit of dependants of members).

If the effect of a relevant matter on persons of the same sex differs according to their family, marital or civil partnership status, a comparison for the purposes of these provisions of the effect of that matter on persons of the opposite sex must be with persons who have the same status (s.67(7)). A relevant matter is a relevant term, a term conferring a relevant discretion, or the exercise of a relevant discretion in relation to an occupational pension scheme (s.67(8)).

A sex equality rule will have no effect in relation to a difference between A and B in the effect of a relevant matter if the trustees or managers of the scheme in question show that the difference is because of a material factor which is not the difference of sex (s.69(4)). As to the defence of material factor see **17 Sex equality clause**, above.

The trustees or managers of an occupational pension scheme may by resolution make consequential sex equality alterations to the scheme (s.68).

There are certain exceptions in relation to the application of the sex equality rule. For example, in respect of state retirement pensions where a man and a woman are eligible, in prescribed circumstances, to receive different amounts by way of pension (Sch. 7, Pt. 2). Permitted exceptions to the sex equality rule are contained in the Equality Act (Age Exceptions for Pension Schemes) Order 2010. These concern bridging pensions which are paid to men before they reach state pension age; indexation paid with a member's pension equivalent to the payments to which a person of the opposite sex would be entitled as part of the State additional pension; and, the use of actuarial factors which differ for men and women in relation to the calculation of employer's contributions in certain circumstances and the provision of certain benefits.

2: PREGNANCY AND MATERNITY EQUALITY

19 Maternity equality clause

Where a woman is employed or holds a personal or public office, if the terms of the woman's work do not, by whatever means, include a maternity equality clause, they are to be treated as including one (Equality Act 2010, ss. 72, 73(1)). The effect of such a clause will be to modify a term of the woman's work that provides for maternity-related pay to be calculated by reference to her pay at a particular time, where each of the following three conditions are satisfied (s.74(1)–(4))–

    (a) after the time referred to above, but before the end of the protected period (see below) (i) her pay increases, or (ii) it would have increased had she not been on maternity leave;

    (b) the maternity-related pay is not (i) what her pay would have been had she not been on maternity leave, or (ii) the difference between the amount of statutory maternity pay to which she is entitled and what her pay would have been had she not been on maternity leave;

    (c) the terms of her work do not provide for the maternity-related pay to be subject to (i) an increase as is mentioned in paragraph (a)(i) above, or (ii) an increase that would have occurred as mentioned in paragraph (a)(ii) above.

The modification referred to above is a modification to provide for the maternity-related pay to be subject to any increase as mentioned in paragraph (a)(i) above, or any increase that would have occurred as mentioned in paragraph (a)(ii) above (s.74(5)). Maternity-related pay is pay (other than statutory maternity pay) to which a woman is entitled as a result of being pregnant or in respect of times when she is on maternity leave (s.74(9)).

The protected period, in relation to a woman's pregnancy, begins when the pregnancy begins, and ends (s.18(6))–

    (d) if she has the right to ordinary and additional maternity leave, at the end of the additional maternity leave period or (if earlier) when she returns to work after the pregnancy;

    (e) if she does not have that right, at the end of the period of 2 weeks beginning with the end of the pregnancy.

In relation to pay, a term of a woman's work that provides for pay within paragraphs (f) to (h) below but does not provide for her to be given the pay in circumstances in which she would have been given it had she not been on maternity leave, is also modified so as to provide for her to be given it in circumstances in which it would normally be given (s.74(6)). Pay is within these provisions if it is (s.74(7))–

    (f) pay (including pay by way of bonus) in respect of times before the woman is on compulsory maternity leave;

    (g) pay by way of bonus in respect of times when she is on compulsory maternity leave;

    (h) pay by way of bonus in respect of times after the end of the protected period.

A term of a woman's work that provides for pay after the end of the protected period but does not provide for it to be subject to an increase to which it would have been subject had she not been on maternity leave is modified so as to provide for it to be subject to the increase (s.74(8)).

In the case of a term relating to membership of or rights under an occupational pension scheme, a maternity equality clause has only such effect as a maternity equality rule would have (s.73). As to the maternity equality rule see **20 Maternity equality rule-pensions**, below.

As to maternity rights generally see the Note on **Maternity Rights**.

20 Maternity equality rule-pensions

If an occupational pension scheme does not include a maternity equality rule it is to be treated as including one (Equality Act 2010, s.75(1)). If a relevant term does not treat time when the woman is on maternity leave as it treats time when she is not, the term is modified so that it does so (s.75(3)). If a term confers a relevant discretion capable of being exercised so that time when she is on maternity leave is treated differently from time when she is not, the term is modified so as not to allow the discretion to be exercised in that way (s.75(4)). A term is relevant if it is (s.75(5))–

    (a) a term relating to membership of the scheme;

    (b) a term relating to the accrual of rights under the scheme;

    (c) a term providing for the determination of the amount of a benefit payable under the scheme.

A discretion is relevant if its exercise is capable of affecting (s.75(6))–

    (d) membership of the scheme;

    (e) the accrual of rights under the scheme;

    (f) the determination of the amount of a benefit payable under the scheme.

The above provisions do not require the woman's contributions to the scheme in respect of time when she is on maternity leave to be determined otherwise than by reference to the amount she is paid in respect of that time (s.75(7)). Therefore, contributions will be related to actual pay.

3: DISCLOSURE OF INFORMATION

21 Discussions about pay

The Equality Act 2010 contains provisions designed to protect people who discuss their pay with colleagues with a view to finding out if differences exist that are related to a protected characteristic (as to which see 1

Introduction, above). A term of a person's work that purports to prevent or restrict the person from disclosing or seeking to disclose information about the terms of that person's work is unenforceable against them in so far as the person makes or seeks to make a relevant pay disclosure (s.77(1)). A term of a person's work that purports to prevent or restrict the person from seeking disclosure of information from a colleague about the terms of the colleague's work is unenforceable against the person in so far as they seek a relevant pay disclosure from the colleague (or former colleague) (s.77(2)). A disclosure is a relevant pay disclosure if made for the purpose of enabling the person who makes it, or the person to whom it is made, to find out whether or to what extent there is, in relation to the work in question, a connection between pay and having, or not having, a particular protected characteristic (s.77(3)). The following are to be treated as protected acts for the purposes of the relevant victimisation provision (s.77(4))–

(a) seeking a disclosure that would be a relevant pay disclosure;
(b) making or seeking to make a relevant pay disclosure;
(c) receiving information disclosed in a relevant pay disclosure.

The relevant victimisation provision is s.27 of the 2010 Act in relation to employment or appointment to a personal or public office (s.77(5)). As to victimisation generally see the Note on **Discrimination and Equality Law**.

S.78 (not yet in force) provides that regulations may require employers to publish information relating to the pay of employees for the purpose of showing whether, by reference to factors of such description as is prescribed, there are differences in the pay of male and female employees.

C: OCCUPATIONAL PENSION SCHEMES

22 The non-discrimination rule

A non-discrimination rule is implied into all occupational pension schemes by the Equality Act 2010 s.61. A non-discrimination rule is a provision by virtue of which a responsible person must not discriminate against another person in carrying out any of their functions in relation to the occupational pension scheme and must not harass or victimise another person in relation to the scheme (s.61(2)). The following are responsible persons (s.61(4))–

(a) the trustees or managers of the scheme;
(b) an employer whose employees are, or may be, members of the scheme;
(c) a person exercising an appointing function in relation to an office the holder of which is, or may be, a member of the scheme.

A non-discrimination rule will not have effect in relation to an occupational pension scheme in so far as an equality rule has effect in relation to it (s.61(10)). As to the equality rules see **18 Sex equality rule-pensions** and see **20 Maternity equality rule-pensions**, above. A non-discrimination rule does not apply in relation to a person who is a pension credit member of a scheme (i.e. as a result of a court order) (s.61(5)). It is not a breach of a non-discrimination rule for the employer, trustees or managers of a scheme to maintain or use in relation to the scheme rules, practices, actions or decisions relating to age which are of a description specified by Ministerial order (s.61(8)). The Equality Act (Age Exceptions for Pension Schemes) Order 2010 contains permitted exceptions for occupational pension schemes to the non-discrimination rule which relate, *inter alia*, to employer contributions to personal pension schemes and rules, practices, actions and decisions relating to differences in the amount of age related benefit under occupational pension schemes.

A duty to make reasonable adjustments in respect of disabled persons applies to a responsible person (s.61(11)). As to the duty to make reasonable adjustments see **6 Adjustments for disabled persons**, above.

The trustees or managers may by resolution make non-discrimination alterations to a scheme (s.62). Such a resolution may be made where other rules prevent the non-discrimination rule taking effect.

D: ENFORCEMENT

I: EMPLOYMENT TRIBUNALS

23 Jurisdiction

An employment tribunal has jurisdiction to determine (Equality Act 2010, s.120(1)–(4))–

(a) a complaint relating to a contravention of Part 5 (work) of the Equality Act 2010;
(b) a complaint relating to a contravention of s.108 (relationships that have ended), s.111 (instructing, causing or inducing contraventions), or s.112 (aiding contraventions) of the Act that relates to Part 5;
(c) an application by a responsible person (see **22 The non-discrimination rule**, above) for a declaration as to the rights of that person and a worker in relation to a dispute about the effect of a non-discrimination rule;
(d) an application by the trustees or managers of an occupational pension scheme for a declaration as to their rights and those of a member in relation to the effect of a non-discrimination rule.

If it appears to a court in which proceedings are pending that a claim or counter-claim relating to a non-discrimination rule could be more conveniently determined by an employment tribunal, the court may strike out the claim or counter-claim (s.122(1)). If in proceedings before a court a question arises about a non-discrimination rule, the court may, whether or not on an application by a party to the proceedings, (s.122(2))–

(i) refer the question, or direct that it be referred by a party to the proceedings, to an employment tribunal for determination, and

(ii) stay or sist the proceedings in the meantime.

An employment tribunal will have jurisdiction to determine a question that is referred to it by virtue of s.122 (s.120(4)).

In proceedings before an employment tribunal on a complaint relating to a breach of a non-discrimination rule, the employer is to be treated as a party and is accordingly entitled to appear and be heard (s.120(5)). Nothing in s.120 affects such jurisdiction as the High Court, the county court, the Court of Session or the sheriff has in relation to a non-discrimination rule (s.120(6)).

Paragraphs (a) and (b) above do not apply to a complaint relating to an act done when the complainant was serving as a member of the armed forces unless the complainant has made a service complaint about the matter and the complaint has not been withdrawn (s.121(1)).

24 Time limits

Proceedings on a complaint within s.120 (see **23 Jurisdiction**, above) may not be brought after the end of the period of three months starting with the date of the act to which the complaint relates or such other period as the employment tribunal thinks just and equitable (Equality Act 2010, s.123(1)). The period is extended to six months in respect of certain armed forces cases falling within s.121(1) (s.123(2)). For these purposes, conduct extending over a period is to be treated as done at the end of the period and failure to do something is to be treated as occurring when the person in question decided on it (s.123(3)). In the absence of evidence to the contrary, a person is to be taken to decide on failure to do something when the person does an act inconsistent with doing it or if the person does no inconsistent act, on the expiry of the period in which the person might reasonably have been expected to do it (s.123(4)).

25 Remedies

If an employment tribunal finds that there has been a contravention of a provision referred to in the Equality Act 2010 s.120(1) (see **23 Jurisdiction**, above) the tribunal may (s.124(2))–

(a) make a declaration as to the rights of the complainant and the respondent in relation to the matters to which the proceedings relate;

(b) order the respondent to pay compensation to the complainant;

(c) make an appropriate recommendation.

An "appropriate recommendation" is a recommendation that within a specified period the respondent takes specified steps for the purposes of obviating or reducing the adverse effect on the complainant of any matter to which the proceedings relate (s.124(3)).

If the tribunal finds that a contravention is established by virtue of s.19 of the Act (indirect discrimination (see the Note on **Discrimination and Equality Law**)) but is satisfied that the provision, criterion or practice was not applied with the intention of discriminating against the complainant it must not make an order under paragraph (b) above unless it first considers whether to act under paragraphs (a) or (c) above (s.124(4), (5)).

If a respondent fails, without reasonable excuse, to comply with an appropriate recommendation the tribunal may, if an order was made under paragraph (b) above, increase the amount of compensation paid or, if no such order was made, make one (s.124(7)).

Additional remedies are available to a tribunal in respect of contraventions referred to in s.120(1) relating to the terms on which persons become members of an occupational pension scheme or the terms on which members of an occupational pension scheme are treated. In addition to which anything may be done by a tribunal under s.124, a tribunal may also by order declare (s.126(2))–

(d) if the complaint relates to the terms on which persons become members of a scheme, that the complainant has a right to be admitted to the scheme;

(e) if the complaint relates to the terms on which members of the scheme are treated, that the complainant has a right to membership of the scheme without discrimination.

An order made under paragraphs (d) or (e) above may make provision as to the terms on which or the capacity in which the claimant is to enjoy the admission or membership and may have effect in relation to a period before the order is made (s.126(4)).

2: EQUALITY OF TERMS

26 Jurisdiction and references to tribunal

An employment tribunal has jurisdiction to determine a complaint relating to a breach of an equality clause or rule (Equality Act 2010, s.127(1)). The jurisdiction conferred includes jurisdiction to determine a complaint arising out of a breach of an equality clause or rule (s.127(2)). An employment tribunal also has jurisdiction to determine (s.127(3)–(5))–

(a) an application by a responsible person for a declaration as to the rights of that person and a worker in relation to a dispute about the effect of an equality clause or rule;

(b) an application by the trustees or managers of an occupational pension scheme for a declaration as to their rights and those of a member in relation to a dispute about the effect of an equality rule;

(c) a question that relates to an equality clause or rule and is referred to the tribunal by virtue of s.128(2) (see below).

In proceedings before an employment tribunal on a complaint relating to a breach of an equality rule, the employer is to be treated as a party and is accordingly entitled to appear and be heard (s.127(8)). Nothing in the above provisions affects such jurisdiction as the High Court, the county court, the Court of Session or the sheriff has in relation to an equality clause or rule (s.127(9)). The provisions do not apply to a complaint relating to an act done when the complainant was serving as a member of the armed forces unless the complainant has made a service complaint about the matter and the complaint has not been withdrawn (s.127(6)).

If in proceedings before a court a question arises about an equality clause or rule, the court may (whether or not on an application by a party to the proceedings) refer the question, or direct that it be referred by a party to the proceedings, to an employment tribunal for determination and stay or sist the proceedings in the meantime (s.128(2)).

27 Time limits

Proceedings on a complaint or application may be brought to an employment tribunal after the end of the qualifying period. In standard cases, the qualifying period will be the period of six months beginning with the last day of employment. In concealment cases, the period will be six months beginning with the day on which the worker discovered (or could with reasonable diligence have discovered) the qualifying fact (i.e. a fact relevant to the complaint without knowledge of which the person concerned could not reasonably have been expected to bring the proceedings). In incapacity cases, the period will be six months beginning with the day on which the worker ceased to have the incapacity. If a complaint or application relates to terms of service in the armed forces, the qualifying period is extended to nine months (Equality Act 2010, ss. 129, 130).

28 Remedies

In proceedings before a court or employment tribunal on a complaint relating to a breach of an equality clause, other than a breach with respect to membership of, or rights under, an occupational pension scheme, the court or tribunal may if it finds that there has been such a breach (Equality Act 2010, s.132(1), (2))–

(a) make a declaration as to the rights of the parties in relation to the matters to which the proceedings relate;

(b) order an award by way of arrears of pay or damages in relation to the complainant.

In proceedings relating to a breach of an equality rule or a breach of an equality clause with respect to membership of, or rights under, an occupational pension scheme if the court or tribunal finds that there has been such a breach (s.133(1), (2))–

(c) it may make a declaration as to the rights of the parties in relation to the matters to which the proceedings relate;

(d) it must not order arrears of benefits or damages or any other amount to be paid to the complainant.

If a breach relates to a term on which persons become members of a scheme, the court or tribunal may declare that the complainant is entitled to be admitted to the scheme with effect from a specified date. A court or tribunal may also declare, if a breach relates to a term on which members of the scheme are treated, that the complainant is, in respect of a specified period, entitled to secure the rights that would have accrued if the breach had not occurred (s.133(4), (6)).

Similar provisions to those contained in s.132 above apply on a complaint by a pensioner member of a scheme relating to a breach of an equality clause or rule with respect to a term on which the member is treated (s.134).

29 Equal pay audits

Where an employer is found by an employment tribunal to have committed an equal pay breach the tribunal must (unless an exception applies–see below) require the employer to undertake an equal pay audit i.e., a systematic evaluation of their pay and reward systems to ensure that further breaches do not occur or that existing breaches do not continue. The audit will need to identify any differences in pay (including non-contractual pay) between men and women doing equal work in the same employment, provide reasons for any differences, and set out an action plan for eliminating those differences, where they cannot be explained or justified otherwise than by reference to gender (Equality Act 2010, s.139A, added by the Enterprise and Regulatory Reform Act 2013, s.98).

A tribunal must not order an audit to be carried out if (Equality Act 2010 (Equal Pay Audits) Regulations 2014, Regs. 3 and 4)–

(a) the information which would be required to be included in an audit is already available from an audit which has been completed by the respondent in the previous three years;

(b) it is clear without an audit whether any action is required to avoid equal pay breaches occurring or continuing;

(c) the breach gives no reason to think that there may be other breaches;

(d) the disadvantages of an audit outweigh the benefits;

(e) (until 1st October 2024) the respondent is a micro-business (i.e., has fewer than 10 employees), or a new business (i.e., established in the 12 months prior to the claim).

3: THE COMMISSION FOR EQUALITY AND HUMAN RIGHTS

30 General

The Commission for Equality and Human Rights (CEHR) is established by s.1 of the Equality Act 2006 and its constitution is set out in s.2 and Sch.1, see further the Note on **Discrimination and Equality Law** at para **31 The Commission for Equality and Human Rights**, *et seq.*

The CEHR may issue a Code of Practice containing practical guidance with a view to ensuring or facilitating compliance with the law (i.e. the Equality Act 2010), and promoting equality of opportunity for disabled people and people who have had a disability, (Equality Act 2006, s.14 as amended by the Equality Act 2010). If a provision of a code of practice appears to a court, tribunal or other body hearing any proceedings to be relevant, it must take that provision into account, but a failure on a person's part to observe any provision of a Code does not in itself make a person liable to any proceedings (s.15(4)). The existing Code issued by the Commission for Equality and Human Rights under s.14 before its amendment (Disability Discrimination Act 1995 Code of Practice for Trade Organisations, Qualifications Bodies and General Qualifications Bodies) will remain in place for those bodies. The Equality Act 2010 Codes of Practice (Services, Public Functions and Associations, Employment, and Equal Pay) Order 2011 brings into force the Equality Act 2010 Code of Practice on Employment and the Equality Act 2010 Code of Practice on Equal Pay. The Employment Code covers provisions in the 2010 Act which make it unlawful to discriminate against, harass or victimise a person at work or in employment services, and restrict the circumstances in which potential employees can be asked questions about health and disability. The Code also covers provisions in the Act relating to unenforceable terms in contracts. The Equal Pay Code covers provisions in the Act relating to equal pay between men and women; pregnancy and maternity pay; and provisions making it unlawful for an employment contract to prevent an employee disclosing his or her pay.

Codes are available from the Commission's website at <www.equalityhumanrights.com>.

31 Enforcement powers of the CEHR

The CEHR has the power to conduct investigations. Such investigations may be into (Equality Act 2006, s.20)–

(a) the commission of an unlawful act under the Equality Act 2010;

(b) compliance with a requirement of an unlawful act notice issued under s.21; or

(c) compliance with the terms of an agreement entered into under s.23.

Investigations may only be carried out if the CEHR suspects that the person concerned may have committed an unlawful act. The provisions relating to the terms of reference, representations, evidence, reports and recommendations and effects of recommendations in respect of CEHR inquiries, investigation and assessments are set out in Sch.2 to the Act. As to the issue of unlawful act notices and the additional enforcement powers of the CEHR see the Note on **Discrimination and Equality Law** at para **34 Enforcement powers of the Commission for Equality and Human Rights**, *et seq.*

The Commission has power to assist an individual who is or may become party to legal proceedings if those proceedings relate or may relate (wholly or partly) to a provision of the equality enactments (which includes the Equality Act 2010), and the individual alleges that he has been the victim of behaviour contrary to a provision of those equality enactments (s.28). When a person who has been assisted by the Commission becomes entitled to have his costs/expenses repaid to him by another party, the Commission may recover its expenses out of the costs awarded or paid by agreement (2006 Act, s.29).

Nothing in the Equality Act 2006 affects the right of a person to bring proceedings under the Equality Act 2010 in respect of a contravention of that Act where they have entitlement to do so (2006 Act, s.24A(4)).

E: SUPPLEMENTAL

32 Ships, hovercraft and offshore work

Part 5 (work) of the Equality Act 2010 as summarised in this Note applies in relation to work on ships and hovercraft, and seafarers, only in such circumstances as are prescribed (Equality Act 2010, s.81). The Equality Act 2010 (Work on Ships and Hovercraft) Regulations 2011 prescribe the circumstances in which Part 5 of the Act applies to seafarers working on UK ships and hovercraft or on ships and hovercraft from other EEA States. The Regulations provide that it is not unlawful to differentiate in relation to pay where a person applied for work, or was recruited, as a seafarer outside Great Britain and is not a British Citizen or a national of another EEA State or designated state (Reg. 5).

Her Majesty may by Order in Council provide that in the case of persons in offshore work specified provisions of Part 5 apply (with or without modification) (s.82). The Equality Act 2010 (Offshore Work) Order 2010 provides that Part 5 applies to offshore work as if the work were taking place in Great Britain unless it –

(a) takes place in the Northern Irish Area as defined by the Civil Jurisdiction (Offshore Activities) Order 1987; or

(b) is in connection with a ship which is in the course of navigation or a ship which is engaged in dredging or fishing.

33 Authorities

Statutes–

Equality Act 2006

Equality Act 2010

Statutory Instruments–

Employment Equality (Repeal of Retirement Age Provisions) Regulations 2011 (S.I. 2011 No. 1069)

Equality Act (Age Exceptions for Pension Schemes) Order 2010 as amended (S.I. 2010 Nos. 2133, and 2285, and 2015 No. 1985)

Equality Act 2010 (Disability) Regulations 2010 (S.I. 2010 No. 2128)

Equality Act 2010 (Equal Pay Audits) Regulations 2014 (S.I. 2014 No. 2559)

Equality Act 2010 (Offshore Work) Order 2010 (S.I. 2010 No. 1835)

Equality Act 2010 (Sex Equality Rule) (Exceptions) Regulations 2010, as amended (S.I. 2010 No. 2132, 2014 No. 1711, and 2015 No. 1985)

Equality Act 2010 (Work on Ships and Hovercraft) Regulations 2011 (S.I. 2011 No. 1771)

Equality Act 2010 Codes of Practice (Services, Public Functions and Associations, Employment, and Equal Pay) Order 2011 (S.I. 2011 No. 857)

EMPLOYMENT TRIBUNALS, ACAS, AND THE EMPLOYMENT APPEAL TRIBUNAL

1 The legislation

This Note is concerned with the institutions established by statute for the resolution of disputes relating to employment. The relevant law is contained in–
- (a) the Employment Tribunals Act 1996, which is concerned with employment tribunals, the role of conciliation officers, and the Employment Appeal Tribunal; and
- (b) ss.191 to 214 and 247 to 253 of the Trade Union and Labour Relations (Consolidation) Act 1992, which is concerned with the Advisory, Conciliation, and Arbitration Service (ACAS).

A: EMPLOYMENT TRIBUNALS

2 Introduction

Employment tribunals are now established under s.1 of the Employment Tribunals Act 1996. Their jurisdiction extends to references, complaints, applications, and appeals under *inter alia* the Employment Act 1980, the Trade Union and Labour Relations (Consolidation) Act 1992, the Employment Rights Act 1996, the National Minimum Wage Act 1998, the Employment Relations Act 1999, the Transfer of Undertakings Regulations 2006, and the Pensions Act 2008.

3 Procedural rules

S.7 of the Employment Tribunals Act 1996 makes provision *inter alia* for the making of regulations governing the procedure before employment tribunals and with respect to the composition of such tribunals. The Employment Tribunals (Constitution and Rules of Procedure) Regulations 2013 (which apply throughout England, Scotland, and Wales) lay down the composition of, and the rules of procedure before tribunals.

The above Regulations set out in Schedules the rules which apply to proceedings before them, as follows–
- (a) Schedule 1 sets out the procedure before employment tribunals which applies in all cases other than those covered by Schedules 2 or 3;
- (b) Schedule 2 sets out the modifications which apply in cases involving national security;
- (c) Schedule 3 sets out the rules of procedure which apply to equal value claims.

The overriding objective of the rules is to enable tribunals to deal with cases justly (rule 2).

4 Pre-hearing reviews

S.9 of the Employment Tribunals Act 1996 and Rules of Procedure, rule 53 authorise a preliminary consideration of proceedings (a pre-hearing review) before an employment tribunal. If, upon review, the tribunal concludes that that any party has no reasonable prospect of success, it may require that party to pay a deposit of an amount not exceeding £1,000 if they wish to continue to participate in the proceedings (rule 39). A claim may be struck out if (rule 37)–
- (a) it is scandalous, vexatious, or has no reasonable prospect of success;
- (b) it has been conducted in a scandalous, unreasonable or vexatious manner;
- (c) there has been non-compliance with a tribunal order or practice direction.
- (d) it has not been actively pursued; or
- (e) it is no longer possible to have a fair hearing.

A deposit not exceeding £1,000 may also be required if a party wishes to pursue a specific allegation or argument within proceedings.

Where an award of costs is subsequently made against a party who has paid a deposit, the deposit will be used in full or part settlement of the award (rule 39).

5 Restricted reporting

A tribunal may at any stage of the proceedings, on its own initiative or on application, make an order with a view to preventing or restricting the public disclosure of any aspect of those proceedings so far as it considers necessary in the interests of justice, or in order to protect the human rights of any person. A private hearing may also be ordered to protect confidential information i.e., where evidence is likely to consist of information which could not be disclosed without contravening a statutory prohibition, or which has been obtained in confidence, or which could cause substantial injury to an undertaking (rule 50 and Employment Tribunals Act 1996 s.10A).

In particular, restricted reporting orders may be made–
- (a) in cases involving allegations of sexual misconduct, to prevent those making or affected by allegations of sexual misconduct from being identified (s.11);

(b) in cases under the Disability Discrimination Act 1995 where evidence of a personal nature is likely to be heard by the tribunal (s.12).

This means that if any identifying matter is published in a newspaper or periodical or included in a television or radio programme, in contravention of a restricted reporting order, the proprietor, publisher or editor will be guilty of an offence.

6 National security cases

S.10 of the Employment Tribunals Act 1996 and Rules of Procedure, rule 94 provide that, in cases which concern matters of national security, a tribunal may sit in private, exclude the applicant or his representative from all or any part of the proceedings, conceal the identity of witnesses, or keep secret the reasons for its decision. Modified rules of procedure in such cases are set out in the Employment Tribunals (Constitution and Rules of Procedure) Regulations 2013 Sch. 2.

Where an applicant's representative is excluded, the Attorney General (in Scotland, the Advocate General) may appoint a special advocate to represent the applicant's interests (Sch. 2 rule 8).

S.10B additionally provides that, where a case concerns national security, it is an offence to publish anything which would identify any witness whose identity has been concealed, or to reveal the reasons behind a tribunal's decision which has been kept secret under s.10.

7 Composition of tribunals

There is a President of the Employment Tribunals (England and Wales) and a President of the Employment Tribunals (Scotland) who determine the number of tribunals to be set up in their respective jurisdictions (rules 5 and 7).

Each tribunal consists of an Employment Judge, who must be legally qualified (i.e., he must be a person who satisfies the judicial-appointment eligibility condition within the meaning of the Tribunals, Courts and Enforcement Act 2007, s.50 on a five year basis, or be a Scottish Advocate or solicitor or Northern Irish barrister or solicitor, also of five years standing), and two other members, one selected from a panel of persons appointed by the Secretary of State after consulting any organisation or association of organisations representing employers and the other from a panel appointed by the Secretary of State after consultation with any organisation or association of organisations representing employees (rule 9).

The composition of a panel is modified in cases involving national security (see rule 10).

8 Single member tribunals

Certain proceedings may be heard by an Employment Judge acting alone. These include proceedings (Employment Tribunals Act 1996, s.4(3) as amended)–
   (a) on a complaint under ss.68A, 87 or 192 (unauthorised deduction of trade union subscriptions or trade union political fund contributions), or an application under ss.161, 165 or 166 of the 1992 Act (interim relief, variation of an Order etc.,);
   (b) on a complaint under the Pension Schemes Act 1993, s.126;
   (c) on an application under ss.11, 163 or 170 of the 1996 Act (right to receive statement of employment particulars, or a statement of changes to those particulars, and right to an itemised pay statement);
   (d) on a complaint under ss.23, 34, 111 or 188 of the 1996 Act (deductions from wages, guarantee payments, unfair dismissal, insolvency payment, etc.,) (or under s.70(1) relating to s.64 (suspension on medical grounds)) or on an application under ss.128, 131 or 132 of that Act (interim relief for unfair dismissal);
   (e) under the Transfer of Undertakings (Protection of Employment) Regulations 2006, Reg. 15(10) (failure to pay compensation–see the Note on **Transfer of Undertakings**);
   (f) proceedings on a complaint under the National Minimum Wage Act 1998, ss.11 or 19C;
   (g) proceedings on a complaint under the Working Time Regulations 1998, Reg. 30 relating to an amount due under ibid Regs. 14(2) or 16(1);
   (h) proceedings on a complaint under the Merchant Shipping (Working Time: Inland Waterways) Regulations 2003, Reg. 18 relating to an amount due under ibid Reg.11;
   (i) proceedings on a complaint under the Civil Aviation (Working Time) Regulations 2004, Reg. 18 relating to an amount due under ibid Reg. 4;
   (j) proceedings on a complaint under the Fishing Vessels (Working Time: Sea-fishermen) Regulations 2004, Reg. 19 relating to an amount due under ibid Reg. 11;
   (k) in respect of which a tribunal has jurisdiction by virtue of an order under s.3 of the Act (order conferring jurisdiction on tribunal in respect of damages for breach of contract–see below);
   (l) in which the parties have given their written consent to the proceedings being heard by an Employment Judge acting alone (whether or not they have subsequently withdrawn it);
   (m) in which the person (or, where more than one, each of the persons) against whom the proceedings are brought does not, or has ceased to, contest the case;

Regulations made under s.7 may provide that any act which is required or authorised by regulations to be done by a tribunal and is of a description specified by the regulations may be done by the Employment Judge acting alone (s.4(6) as amended by the 1998 Act).

9 Determination without a hearing

S.7(3A) and (3AA) of the Employment Tribunals Act 1996 empowers the Secretary of State to make employment procedure regulations authorising the determination of tribunal proceedings without any hearing in prescribed circumstances. The effect of this provision is that cases may be determined on the basis of written evidence alone, where both parties consent to this, or where the person against proceedings are brought presents no response to the proceedings or does not contest the case. Once consent has been given, it cannot subsequently be withdrawn. Regulations may also authorise the determination of proceedings without hearing anyone other than the persons by whom the proceedings are brought (or their representatives) where (a) the party against whom the proceedings are brought has done nothing to contest the case, or (b) the applicant is not seeking any relief which a tribunal has a power to give, or is not entitled to such relief (s.7(3B) as so inserted). Finally, regulations may authorise the determination of proceedings without hearing anyone other than the parties concerned where the tribunal is, on undisputed facts, bound to dismiss the case because of the decision of a superior court, or where the proceedings relate only to a preliminary issue (s.7(3C) as so inserted).

10 Jurisdiction of employment tribunals

S.3 of the Employment Tribunals Act 1996 gives the appropriate Minister power, by order, to provide that proceedings in respect of any claim to which the section applies or any such claim of a description specified in the order (other than for damages or for a sum due in respect of personal injuries) may be brought before an employment tribunal.

S.3 applies to any of the following claims–

(a) a claim for damages for breach of a contract of employment or other contract connected with employment;

(b) a claim for a sum due under such a contract;

(c) a claim for the recovery of a sum in pursuance of any enactment relating to the terms or performance of such a contract;

being, in each case, a claim such that a court in England and Wales or Scotland, as the case may be, would under the law for the time being in force have jurisdiction to hear and determine an action in respect of the claim.

An order under s.3 may provide that a tribunal must not order the payment of an amount exceeding such sum as may be specified in the order as to the maximum sum which a tribunal may order to be paid. An order under s.3 may include provisions as to the manner and time in which proceedings are to be brought under that section, and may make different provision in respect of different types of claims (s.8).

The Employment Tribunals Extension of Jurisdiction (England and Wales) Order 1994 and the corresponding Order for Scotland enables an employee to bring a claim for damages for breach of his contract of employment, or for a sum due under that contract, before an employment tribunal if the claim arises or is outstanding on the termination of his employment. The Order also enables an employer to make such a claim against an employee where the employee has claimed against him under the Order. Articles 3 and 4 of the Order exclude from the above provisions the categories of claim specified in Article 5, namely, claims relating to living accommodation, intellectual property (which includes copyright, rights in performances, moral rights, design right, registered designs, patents, and trade marks), obligations of confidence, and a term which is a covenant in restraint of trade.

An employee's complaint about a contractual claim must normally be presented within a period of three months beginning with the effective date of termination (as defined in s.97(1) of the 1996 Act) (see the Note on **Unfair Dismissal**). An employer's complaint about a contractual claim must be presented within six weeks of receiving a copy of an originating application relating to the employee's complaint. Where the tribunal is satisfied that it was not reasonably practicable for the complaint to be presented within the above period, the complaint may be presented within such further period as the tribunal considers reasonable (Arts 7 and 8).

An employment tribunal must not in any proceedings in respect of a contract claim, or in respect of a number of contract claims relating to the same contract, order the payment of an amount exceeding £25,000 (Art. 10).

11 Compulsory conciliation

Generally, a prospective claimant must submit the details of their claim to ACAS before they can lodge the claim at an employment tribunal (Employment Tribunals Act 1996, s.18A). This applies to all "relevant proceedings" i.e., those (s.18)–

(a) arising out of a contravention or alleged contravention of any of the following provisions of the 1992 Act, namely, ss.66, 68A, 70C, 87, 137, 138, 145A, 145B, 146, 168, 168A, 169, 170, 174, 189, 192 or Sch A1 para 156 (rights in relation to trade union membership);

(b) arising out of a contravention or alleged contravention of any of the following provisions of the 1996 Act, namely, ss.11, 23, 34, 63I, 70, 70A, 80(1), 80H, 93, 111, 163 or 177 or Parts V, or VI (see the Notes on **Rights Arising in the Course of Employment** and **Unfair Dismissal**);

(c) arising out of a contravention or alleged contravention of ss.11, 19D(1)(a) or 24 of the National Minimum Wage Act 1998 (see the Note on **Wages**);

(d) under the Pensions Act 2008, s.56;

(e) under ss.120 or 127 of the Equality Act 2010;

(f) under the Safety Representatives and Safety Committees Regulations 1977, Reg. 11;

(g) under the Employment Tribunals Extension of Jurisdiction (England and Wales) Order 1994, Art. 6;

(h) under the Employment Tribunals Extension of Jurisdiction (Scotland) Order 1994, Art. 6;

(i) under the Health and Safety (Consultation with Employees) Regulations 1996, Sch. 2 para 2;

(j) arising under the Working Time Regulations 1998, Reg. 30;

(k) arising under the Transnational Information and Consultation of Employees Regulations 1999 (S.I. No. 3323), Regs. 27 or 32;

(l) arising out of a contravention or alleged contravention of the Part-time Workers (Prevention of Less Favourable Treatment) Regulations 2000;

(m) arising out of a contravention or alleged contravention of the Fixed-term Employees (Prevention of Less Favourable Treatment) Regulations 2002 (see Note [8] 4A);

(n) under the Merchant Shipping (Hours of Work) Regulations 2002, Reg. 22;

(o) under the Flexible Working (Procedural Requirements) Regulations 2002, Reg. 15;

(p) under the Merchant Shipping (Working Time: Inland Waterways) Regulations 2003, Reg. 18;

(q) under the Civil Aviation (Working Time) Regulations 2004, Reg. 18;

(r) under the Fishing Vessels (Working Time: Sea-fishermen) Regulations 2004, Reg. 19;

(s) arising under the Information and Consultation of Employees Regulations 2004, Regs 29 or 33 (right of employee information and consultation representatives to time off and not to suffer detriment);

(t) under the Occupational and Personal Pension Schemes (Consultation by Employers and Miscellaneous Amendment) Regulations 2006, Sch, paras 4 or 8;

(u) under the European Cooperative Society (Involvement of Employees) Regulations 2006, Regs 30 or 34;

(v) under the Companies (Cross-Border Mergers) Regulations 2007, Regs 45 or 51;

(w) under the Cross-border Railway Services (Working Time) Regulations 2008, Reg. 17;

(x) under the Ecclesiastical Offices (Terms of Service) Regulations 2009, Reg. 9;

(y) under the European Public Limited-Liability Company (Employee Involvement) (Great Britain) Regulations 2009, Regs 28 or 32;

(z) arising out of a contravention, or alleged contravention of the Agency Workers Regulations 2010, Reg 18;

(z1) under the Employee Study and Training (Procedural Requirements) Regulations 2010, Reg. 17;

(z2) under the Employment Relations Act 1999 (Blacklists) Regulations 2010, Regs 5, 6 or 9;

(z3) under the Exclusivity Terms in Zero Hours Contracts (Redress) Regulations 2015, Reg. 3.

A person may be exempted from the need to inform ACAS before starting tribunal proceedings in prescribed cases, including where (s.18A(7) and the Employment Tribunals (Early Conciliation: Exemptions and Rules of Procedure) Regulations 2014)–

(i) the requirement is complied with by another person instituting relevant proceedings relating to the same matter;

(ii) proceedings that are not "relevant proceedings" are instituted by means of the same form as proceedings that are;

(iii) s.18B applies (see below) because ACAS has been contacted by a person against whom relevant proceedings are being instituted;

(iv) a claim for unfair dismissal is accompanied by a claim for interim relief; or

(v) the claim is against the Security Service, the Secret Intelligence Service or GCHQ.

To satisfy the requirement for early conciliation, a prospective claimant must either send a completed early conciliation form (see 12 **Procedure**, below) to ACAS (by post or email), or telephone ACAS, in each case giving the name and address of themselves and of the prospective respondent (Reg. 5, Sch. 1).

Where s.18A applies, an ACAS conciliation officer is required to try and achieve a settlement to the dispute, within a prescribed period, so that employment tribunal proceedings can be avoided (s.18A(3)). If during that time the conciliation officer concludes that a settlement is not possible, or the period expires with no settlement having been reached, the officer must issue a certificate to the prospective claimant. A claimant cannot to lodge a claim with a tribunal without such a certificate (s.18A(8)). The conciliation officer can, however, continue to try and achieve a settlement to the dispute after the prescribed period has expired (s.18A(5)).

Where a prospective claimant is no longer employed by the employer, the conciliation officer may attempt to promote either their reinstatement or re-engagement or, if the individual does not want that, or it is not practicable, attempt to achieve an agreement between the parties on the level of compensation to be paid by the employer (s.18A(9)).

ACAS must also promote settlement in certain cases where s.18A does not apply e.g.,–

(a) where a person contacts ACAS requesting the services of a conciliation officer in a matter that might otherwise result in employment tribunal proceedings against them even though the prospective claimant has not contacted ACAS (s.18B(1)); or

(b) where the prospective claimant contacts ACAS, even though they are exempted under s.18A(7) (see above) from the requirement to provide information to ACAS (s.18B(2)).

Where an application instituting relevant proceedings has been presented to an employment tribunal, and a copy of it has been sent to a conciliation officer, the conciliation officer must still endeavour to promote a settlement if requested to do so by both the person by whom and the person against whom the proceedings are brought, or if, in the absence of any such request, he considers that he could act with a reasonable prospect of success (s.18C).

In all cases, the conciliation officer must have regard to the desirability of encouraging the use of any other procedures available for the settlement of grievances (s.18(6)).

Matters communicated to a conciliation officer in performing his functions under ss.18A to 18C are not admissible in evidence before a tribunal except with the consent of the person who communicated them (s.18(7)).

12 Procedure

For proceedings in England and Wales, all applications must be made on the prescribed form. An interactive version of the form, which may be completed online, can be found at—
<https://www.employmenttribunals.service.gov.uk/employment-tribunals>

Alternatively, completed forms may be posted to Employment Tribunal Central Office (England and Wales), PO Box 10218, Leicester LE1 8EG. All other case related correspondence should be sent to the office that has been allocated the claim For a full list of regional offices, see—
<www.justice.gov.uk/tribunals/employment/venues>

Tribunal procedure enquiries may be answered on a public enquiry line (tel: 0300 123 1024).

For proceedings in Scotland, applications by post should be sent to the Employment Tribunals Central Office Scotland, PO Box 27105, Glasgow G2 9JR (tel: 0141 354 8574). Claim forms can also be sent online (see above).

In most cases, following the making of an application, the Secretary will send a copy of the application to the respondent, who has 21 days in which to enter an appearance if he wishes to take part in the proceedings.

There is power for a tribunal to hold a pre-hearing assessment (see **4 Pre-hearing reviews**, above).

Where an application proceeds to a hearing, the hearing is normally held in public and is to be conducted in such manner as the tribunal considers most suitable to the clarification of the issues before it and generally to the just handling of the proceedings, but, so far as appears appropriate, the tribunal must seek to avoid formality. A party may appear before the tribunal in person or be represented by any person he desires to represent him.

13 Fees

An application will be rejected if not accompanied either by the required fee, or by an application for remission of the fee (Employment Tribunals (Constitution and Rules of Procedure) Regulations 2013, Rule 11). If a remission application is refused in part or in full, the Tribunal will send the claimant a notice specifying a date for payment of the Tribunal fee and the claim will be rejected if the fee is not paid by the date specified.

There are two fee scales, one for individuals presenting their claim to the Tribunal alone, and one for two or more individuals presenting their claims together as a "fee group". Each scale is then broken down into two fee levels (defined in the Fees Order as Types A and B). Type A comprises the simpler types of tribunal case (as set out in Schedule 2 to the Order) such as unpaid wages, redundancy pay, holiday pay and notice pay. Type B claims are the more complex cases, such as unfair dismissal, discrimination, equal pay and whistleblowing, which therefore attract a higher fee (Employment Tribunals and the Employment Appeal Tribunal Fees Order 2013).

One fee is payable when the claim is presented, and one in advance of hearing (Sch.2, Table 3).

Individuals	Type A Case	Type B Case
Issue fee	£160	£250
Hearing fee	£230	£950

For claimants presenting their claims together as part of a fee group, the level of fee varies with the size of the group (Sch. 2, Table 4)—

Type A Case Fee groups	2-10 claimants	11-200 claimants	Over 200 claimants
Issue fee	£320	£640	£960
Hearing fee	£460	£920	£1,380

Type B Case Fee groups	2-10 claimants	11-200 claimants	Over 200 claimants
Issue fee	£500	£1,000	£1,500
Hearing fee	£1,900	£3,800	£5,700

The following additional fees may also be payable (Sch.1 and Reg. 4)—
   – Reconsideration of a default judgment: £100 (Type A or B);
   – Reconsideration of a judgment following a final hearing: £100 (Type A); £350 (Type B);
   – Dismissal following withdrawal: £60 (Type A or B);
   – An employer's contract claim made by way of application as part of the response to the employee's contract claim: £160 (Type A only);
   – A fee of £600 is payable by the respondent when a case is listed for judicial mediation.

On appeal to the Employment Appeal Tribunal, the fee structure is simpler. There is no distinction between Type A and Type B cases, nor between individuals and groups. The fees are (Regs. 13, 14)—
   (a) £400 payable on the making of the appeal;

(b) £1,200 payable by an appellant before the hearing to determine the appeal

Fees may be remitted (i.e., waived), on application by the applicant to the Tribunal (Reg. 17 and Sch. 3). Remission is on the same basis as for county court fees: see the Note on **The County Court**, at para **21 Fee remissions and reductions.**

14 Costs

Where, in the opinion of the tribunal (rule 76)–

(i) a party (or their representative) has acted vexatiously, abusively, disruptively or otherwise unreasonably in either the bringing of the proceedings (or part) or the way that the proceedings (or part) have been conducted; or

(ii) any claim or response had no reasonable prospect of success,

the tribunal may make an award of costs against that party in respect of the costs incurred by the other party. Such a costs order may order the payment of–

(a) the other party's costs, not exceeding £20,000;

(b) the whole or a specified part of the other party's costs, as assessed by the Tribunal (or by a court);

(c) a specified amount as reimbursement of all or part of a Tribunal fee paid by the receiving party;

(d) a specified amount in respect of necessary and reasonably incurred expenses of the other party or of a witness; or

(e) an amount agreed between the parties.

*Note.–*The amount paid under (b) to (e) may exceed the £20,000 specified in (a).

An award may also be made in respect of costs incurred as a result of a party requesting a postponement or the adjournment of a hearing.

15 Enforcement of judgments

S.7(1) of the Employment Tribunals Act 1996 and the Employment Tribunals (Enforcement of Orders under the Civil Jurisdiction and Judgments Act 1982) (Scotland) Regulations 1995 provide for the issue of copies of, and certificates in connection with, orders for the payment of a sum of money (money orders) issued by Scottish employment tribunals, in order to enable an interested party to secure the recognition or enforcement of that order in another state which is a contracting state under the 1968 and 1988 Conventions on Jurisdiction and Enforcement of Judgments in Civil and Commercial Matters. The Regulations also prescribe the manner of application for, and form of, a certificate in respect of money orders issued by Scottish employment tribunals, in order to enable an interested party to secure enforcement of that order in another part of the UK under Schedule 6 to the Civil Jurisdiction and Judgments Act 1982.

16 Financial penalties on employers–aggravating behaviour

Where there has been a breach of a worker's employment rights and the tribunal considers that, in the circumstances, the employer's behaviour in committing the breach had one or more aggravating features. the tribunal has a discretion to impose a financial penalty on the employer (Employment Tribunals Act 1996 s.12A, added by the Enterprise and Regulatory Reform Act 2013, s.16).

The features which tribunals should take into consideration when determining whether a breach had aggravating features are not prescribed: it is for the tribunal to decide, taking into account any factors which it considers relevant, including the circumstances of the case and the employer's particular circumstances. The tribunal should only take into account information of which it has become aware during its consideration of the claim. A non-exhaustive list of factors which an employment tribunal may consider in deciding whether to impose a financial penalty could include the size of the employer; the duration of the breach of the employment right; or the behaviour of the employer and of the employee. A tribunal may be more likely to find that the employer's behaviour in breaching the law had aggravating features where the action was deliberate or committed with malice, the employer was an organisation with a dedicated human resources team, or where the employer had repeatedly breached the employment right concerned. The tribunal may be less likely to find that the breach had aggravating features where an employer has been in operation for only a short period of time, is a micro business, has only a limited human resources function, or the breach was a genuine mistake.

If the tribunal has made a non-financial award to the claimant (e.g.' an order for reinstatement) then any financial penalty imposed under s.12A must be at least £100 and cannot exceed £5,000 (s.12A(3)). If the remedy awarded by the tribunal to the claimant is a financial award (e.g., compensation) then any financial penalty imposed must be set at 50% of the amount of the claimant's financial award subject to a minimum of £100 and a maximum of £5,000 (s.12A(4), (5)).

In deciding whether to order an employer to pay a penalty, and how much the penalty should be, the tribunal must have regard to the employer's ability to pay (s.12A(2)).

17 Financial penalties on employers–non-payment of an award

A financial penalty may be imposed on an employer who fails to pay (Employment Tribunals Act 1996, ss.37A to 37D)—

    (a) an award made by an Employment Tribunal (including as to costs and sums to cover preparation);

    (b) costs (in Scotland, expenses) awarded against them to cover a worker's Employment Tribunal fee;

    (c) sums due under an ACAS conciliated settlement.

The procedure for imposing a penalty can start as soon as the time for appealing the Employment Tribunal decision has expired without an appeal being made (s.37B). The employer will be given a warning notice of the intention is to impose a financial penalty on them (s.37E). They will then have 28 days either to pay the whole unpaid amount of the award or settlement sum or to set out their case as to why no financial penalty should be imposed.

The amount of the penalty is based on the total amount that remains unpaid to the worker, including interest on the award payable on the last date for responding to the warning notice, as well as any amount the employer has been told to pay by way of employment tribunal fees. The penalty will be 50% of the sum owed with a minimum of £100 and a maximum of £5,000 (s.37F). Where an employer has defaulted on an agreement to pay by instalments, the penalty will be based on the whole amount still unpaid (s.37D).

Where a penalty notice has been issued the amount of the penalty can be reduced by 50% if both the penalty and the whole unpaid amount are paid within 14 days of the penalty notice (s.37F).

An employer may appeal a notice, or the amount of the penalty, to an Employment Tribunal within 28 days beginning with the day the penalty notice was served (s.37G).

B: ACAS

18 Introduction

The Advisory, Conciliation, and Arbitration Service (ACAS) is charged with the general duty of promoting the improvement of industrial relations (Trade Union and Labour Relations (Consolidation) Act 1992, s.209, as amended by the Employment Relations Act 1999, s.26).

ACAS operates under the direction of its council which consists of a full-time chairman and a minimum of nine other members. All are appointed by the Secretary of State, three of them after consultation with appropriate employers' organisations and a further three after consultation with appropriate organisations representing workers (1992 Act, s.248).

ACAS may, in any case in which it thinks it appropriate to do so, but subject to directions by the Secretary of State, charge a fee for exercising a function in relation to any person. No liability to pay a fee will arise on the part of any person, unless ACAS has notified that person that a fee may or will be charged. Where a function is exercised in relation to two or more persons the fee chargeable will be apportioned among them as ACAS thinks appropriate (1992 Act, s.251(A), as inserted by the 1993 Act, s.44).

19 Conciliation in trade disputes

S.210 of the Trade Union and Labour Relations (Consolidation) Act 1992 defines the role of ACAS in conciliation. Where a trade dispute exists or is apprehended, ACAS may, at the request of one or more parties to the dispute or otherwise, offer its assistance with a view to bringing about a settlement. Such assistance may be by way of conciliation or other means and may include the appointment of an outsider to offer similar assistance. In exercising such functions, ACAS must have regard to the desirability of encouraging the parties to a dispute to use any appropriate agreed procedures for negotiation or the settlement of disputes.

ACAS is required to appoint officers to act as conciliation officers under any enactment in respect of matters which are or could be the subject of proceedings before an employment tribunal (1992 Act, s.211).

20 Arbitration

Where a trade dispute exists or is apprehended, ACAS may, at the request of one or more parties to the dispute and with the consent of all of them, refer all or any of the matters to which the dispute relates for settlement to an arbitrator (in Scotland, an arbiter) or to the Central Arbitration Committee. ACAS must not refer a dispute for arbitration unless conciliation and any other agreed procedures for settlement have failed or there is a special reason which justifies arbitration as an alternative to those procedures (Trade Union and Labour Relations (Consolidation) Act 1992, s.212).

21 ACAS arbitration scheme

S.212A of the Trade Union and Labour Relations (Consolidation) Act 1992 (inserted by s.7 of the 1998 Act) empowers ACAS to prepare an arbitration scheme for the settlement of disputes under Part X of the Employment Rights Act 1996 (i.e., unfair dismissal cases—see the Note on **Unfair Dismissal**). Any such scheme must be approved by the Secretary of State. The ACAS Arbitration Scheme (Great Britain) Order 2004 has been made under this provision. Where the parties to any unfair dismissal dispute voluntarily agree in writing to submit the dispute to arbitration in accordance with the ACAS scheme, the dispute will be referred to the arbitration of a person appointed by ACAS (not being an ACAS officer or employee). Arbitration conducted in accordance with the ACAS scheme is not subject to the Arbitration Act 1996, but some of the provisions of the scheme are based on modifications of that Act.

Where an arbitrator orders that an employee should be re-instated, or otherwise re-employed, provision is made for such an order to be enforced by an employment tribunal.

An agreement to submit a dispute to arbitration in accordance with the ACAS scheme removes the dispute from the jurisdiction of employment tribunals (although an agreement to submit a dispute to arbitration otherwise than in accordance with the ACAS scheme will not remove the jurisdiction of the tribunals (1998 Act, s.8).

22 Advice and inquiry

ACAS may, on request or otherwise, advise employers, employers' associations, workers, and trade unions on matters concerned with or affecting or likely to affect industrial relations and may publish general advice thereon (1992 Act, s.213, as substituted by the Trade Union Reform and Employment Rights Act 1993, s.43).

23 Financial penalties on employers

As to financial penalties on employers who fail to pay sums due under an ACAS conciliated settlement, see **17 Financial penalties on employers–non-payment of an award**, above.

24 Codes of Practice

ACAS may issue Codes of Practice containing such practical guidance as it thinks fit for the purpose of promoting the improvement of industrial relations (Trade Union and Labour Relations (Consolidation) Act 1992, s.199(1)), and is required to publish Codes on the disclosure of information by employers (under ss.181 and 182 of the 1992 Act) to trade unions for the purpose of collective bargaining and on the time off to be granted to trade union officials and trade union members (under ss.168 and 170 of the 1992 Act). The procedure to be followed in issuing such a Code is laid down in s.200 of the 1992 Act; *inter alia* a Code of Practice may not be issued unless it is approved by the Secretary of State and Parliament. ACAS may from time to time revise any Code of Practice it has issued (1992 Act, s.201).

In addition to Codes of Practice issued by ACAS under s.199(1), s.203 of the 1992 Act empowers the Secretary of State, after consultation with ACAS, to issue such Codes of Practice containing practical guidance as he thinks fit for the purpose of promoting the improvement of industrial relations or of promoting what appears to him to be desirable practices in relation to the conduct by trade unions of ballots and elections. A Code of Practice issued by the Secretary of State also requires the approval of Parliament.

Failure on a person's part to observe any provision of a Code does not render him liable to any proceedings but the Code is admissible in evidence and any relevant provision may be taken into account in determining the question at issue (1992 Act, s.207).

In consequence of the above-mentioned provisions, a number of Codes of Practice have been issued and reference is made to them in the relevant Notes in the Employment Section. Codes of Practice issued under these provisions are available at <http://www.acas.org.uk>.

C: EMPLOYMENT APPEAL TRIBUNAL

25 General

S.87 of the Employment Protection Act 1975 established the Employment Appeal Tribunal, which is continued in existence under s.20 of the Act. The Appeal Tribunal consists of judges of the High Court and Court of Appeal, at least one judge of the Court of Session, and other members appointed for their special knowledge or experience of industrial relations, as representatives of either employers or workers (s.22).

Ss.21 to 37 of the Act make provision for the membership, sittings, proceedings, and powers of the Tribunal. Subject to certain exceptions, proceedings before the Tribunal must be heard by a judge and either two or four appointed members, so that in either case there is an equal number of persons whose knowledge or experience of industrial relations is as representatives of employers or workers. However with the consent of the parties proceedings before the Tribunal may be heard by a judge and one appointed member or by a judge and three appointed members. Proceedings on an appeal from an employment tribunal consisting of an Employment Judge acting alone must be heard by a judge alone unless a judge directs that the proceedings be heard otherwise (s.28).

26 Rules of procedure

The Lord Chancellor, after consultation with the Lord President of the Court of Session, is empowered to make rules with respect to the proceedings before the Appeal Tribunal (s.30). The procedure for the institution, hearing, and disposal of cases before the Tribunal is prescribed by the Employment Appeal Tribunal Rules 1993. As with employment tribunals, the Rules include provision for the use of the Tribunal's discretionary powers to prevent those making or affected by allegations of sexual misconduct from being identified and to make a restricted reporting order having effect (if not revoked earlier) until promulgation of their decision (s.31). The Rules also include provision to restrict publicity in disability cases in which evidence of a personal nature is likely to be heard (s.32).

Under s.21, appeals lie to the Tribunal on questions of law arising in proceedings before, or from any decision of an employment tribunal under, or by virtue of, the Acts and Regulations mentioned above (see **2 Introduction**).

The Employment Appeal tribunal also has jurisdiction to hear appeals from decisions of the Central Arbitration Committee under the Transnational Information and Consultation of Employees Regulations 1999 (S.I. No. 3323) and to hear first instance complaints under those Regulations (which relate to European Works Councils: see the Note on **Rights Arising in the Course of Employment**).

An appeal on a question of law lies (with the consent of the Tribunal or the Court concerned) from the Tribunal to the Court of Appeal or the Court of Session, as appropriate (s.37).

27 Restriction of proceedings orders

Under s.33, the Tribunal may, if on an application by the Attorney General or the Lord Advocate, it is satisfied that any person has habitually and persistently and without any reasonable ground instituted vexatious proceedings, or made vexatious applications, before the Certification Officer, in an employment tribunal or the Tribunal itself, make a "restriction of proceedings order". Such an order prohibits that person from instituting or continuing proceedings without the leave of the Tribunal.

28 Authorities

Statutes–

Civil Jurisdiction and Judgments Act 1982

Employment Relations Act 1999

Employment Rights (Dispute Resolution) Act 1998

Employment Tribunals Act 1996

Trade Union and Labour Relations (Consolidation) Act 1992

Statutory Instruments–

ACAS Arbitration Scheme (Great Britain) Order 2004, as amended (S.I. 2004 No. 753, 2006 No. 2405, 2013 No. 1956, and 2014 No. 386)

Employment Appeal Tribunal Rules 1993, as amended (S.I. 1993 No. 2854, 1996 No. 3216, 2001 Nos. 1128 and 1476, 2004 No. 2526, 2005 No. 1871, and 2013 No. 1693)

Employment Tribunals and the Employment Appeal Tribunal Fees Order 2013, as amended (S.I. 2013 Nos. 1893 and 2302, 2014 Nos. 468, 513 and 590, and 2015 No. 414)

Employment Tribunals (Constitution and Rules of Procedure) Regulations 2013, as amended (S.I. 2013 No. 1237, 2014 Nos. 271, 468, 611, and 787, and 2016 No. 271)

Employment Tribunals (Early Conciliation: Exemptions and Rules of Procedure) Regulations 2014, as amended (S.I. 2014 Nos.254 and 847)

Employment Tribunals (Enforcement of Orders under the Civil Jurisdiction and Judgments Act 1982) (Scotland) Regulations 1995 (S.I. 1995 No. 1717)

Employment Tribunals Extension of Jurisdiction (England and Wales) Order 1994 (S.I. 1994 No. 1623)

Employment Tribunals Extension of Jurisdiction (Scotland) Order 1994 (S.I. 1994 No. 1624)

EMPLOYERS LIABILITY: COMPULSORY INSURANCE

1 Employers liable to compulsory insurance

The Employers' Liability (Compulsory Insurance) Act 1969 and the Regulations made thereunder provide for the compulsory insurance of employees by employers as follows. Every employer, (except certain "public" employers such as local authorities (other than parish or community councils), the police, NHS bodies, and nationalised undertakings), carrying on any business in Great Britain must insure against liability for bodily injury or disease sustained by his employees and arising out of and in the course of their employment in Great Britain in that business, but not including injury or disease suffered or contracted outside Great Britain (ss.1 and 3). "Employee" means an individual who works under a contract of service or apprenticeship, but the Act does not require the employer to insure employees who are close relatives (as defined) (s.2).

The Employers' Liability (Compulsory Insurance) Regulations 1998 specify additional employers who are exempted from the requirements of the Act. They include–

(a) any employer holding a certificate issued by a government department stating that claims established against that employer in respect of any liability to such employees as are mentioned in s.1 (see above) will be met, to the extent to which the employer cannot satisfy them, out of money provided by Parliament;

(b) any foreign or Commonwealth government;

(c) any inter-governmental organisation having by virtue of any statute or Order in Council the legal capacities of a body corporate;

(d) any subsidiary of a nationalised industry;

(e) a number of other specified statutory bodies including managing committees of approved probation homes or hostels, and probation committees;

(f) licensees within the meaning of the Nuclear Installations Act 1965 in respect of liability to pay compensation for any breach of duty to prevent injury arising from nuclear matter;

(g) any employer to the extent he is required to insure against liability for bodily injury sustained by his employee who is carried in or upon a vehicle or who is entering or getting on to, or alighting from, a vehicle, and where that bodily injury is caused by, or arises out of, the use by the employer of a vehicle on the road; and

(h) a limited company run by its owner who is the sole employee of the company.

2 Prohibited conditions

The Employers' Liability (Compulsory Insurance) Regulations 1998 prohibit for the purposes of the Act certain conditions in policies of insurance which would entitle insurers to deny liability under the policy, and provide that the amount for which an employer is required to insure is £5m. in respect of claims relating to any one or more of his employees arising out of any one occurrence (but, in the case of a company with subsidiaries, this requirement will be satisfied if the company maintains insurance for itself and its subsidiaries for £5m. in respect of claims relating to any one or more of its own employees and to any one or more of its subsidiaries' employees arising out of any one occurrence). They also require insurers entering into contracts of insurance with employers for the purposes of the Act to issue certificates of insurance in a prescribed form and require employers to permit inspectors authorised by the Secretary of State to inspect the policy of insurance (or a copy). Employers must display copies of the certificates at each of their premises for the information of their employees and must produce or send the certificates (or copies) to an officer of the Health and Safety Executive, if so required. From 1st October 2008, the requirement to "display" the certificate will be satisfied if it is made available in electronic form and each employee to whom it relates has access to it in that form. The Regulations apply the statutory requirements to employees not ordinarily resident in Great Britain but who are present in Great Britain in the course of employment there for a continuous period of at least 14 days. The requirement for certificates of insurance to be retained for at least 40 years is repealed with effect from 1st October 2008.

3 Offences

It is an offence for an employer not to be insured in accordance with the Act on any day, and where the offence is committed by a corporation with the consent or connivance of, or facilitated by the neglect of, any officer of the corporation, such an officer will be liable as well as the corporation (Employers' Liability (Compulsory Insurance) Act 1969, s.5).

4 Authorities

Employers' Liability (Compulsory Insurance) Act 1969

Employers' Liability (Compulsory Insurance) Regulations 1998, as amended (S.I. 1998 No. 2573, 1999 No. 1820, 2000 No. 253, 2003 No. 1615, 2004 No. 2882, 2008 No. 1765, 2009 No. 801, 2010 No. 677, 2011 No. 686, 2012 No. 765, and 2013 No. 1466)

EMPLOYMENT OF CHILDREN

1 Introduction

The main provisions as to employment of children are contained in Part II of the Children and Young Persons Act 1933, Part III of the Children and Young Persons (Scotland) Act 1937 (the 1937 Act), and Part II of the Children and Young Persons Act 1963, as amended by the Regulations listed in **10 Authorities**, below.

A child means a person who is not over compulsory school age (as to which (for England and Wales), see the Note on **Schools: Admission and Attendance: England and Wales** at para **2 Parent's duty and compulsory school age**; and (for Scotland), see the Note on **Schools: Scotland** at para **27 School age**).

2 General provisions

Under s.18 of the Children and Young Persons Act 1933, as amended by the Children (Protection at Work) Regulations 1998, no child may be employed–
  (a) so long as he is under the age of 14;
  (b) before the end of school hours or for more than two hours on any day he is required to be at school;
  (c) before 7 am or after 7 pm on any day;
  (d) for more than two hours on a Sunday;
  (e) to do any work other than "light work" (see below);
  (f) for more than eight hours (or five hours in the case of a child under 15) on any day on which he is not required to attend school and which is not a Sunday;
  (g) for more than 12 hours in any week in which he is required to attend school;
  (h) for more than 35 hours (25 hours in the case of a child under 15) in any week in which he is not required to attend school;
  (i) for more than four hours in any day without a rest break of one hour; or
  (j) at any time in a year unless at that time he has had, or could still have, at least two weeks during a school holiday without employment.

For the purposes of (e) above, "light work" means work which, on account of the inherent nature of the tasks which it involves and the particular conditions under which they are performed, is not harmful to a child's safety, health or development, and is not harmful to their school attendance or participation in work experience under s.560 of the Education Act 1996 (see **5 Work experience**, below) or to their capacity to benefit from the instruction received or the experience gained.

Similar provision is made for Scotland by s.28 of the 1937 Act.

3 Local variations

A local authority may make byelaws which modify the above provisions and authorise–
  (1) the employment, on an occasional basis, of children aged 13 by their parents or guardians in light agricultural or horticultural work;
  (2) the employment of children for not more than one hour before the beginning of school hours on any day on which they are required to attend school;
  (3) the employment of children aged 13 in categories of light work (see **2 General provisions**, above) specified in the bylaws.

A local authority may also make byelaws imposing additional restrictions to those set out in (a) to (i) above. Such byelaws may–
  (a) prohibit absolutely the employment of children in any specified occupation;
  (b) prescribe the age below which children are not to be employed;
  (c) prescribe the number of hours each day or week, and the times of day, for which children may be employed;
  (d) prescribe meal and rest intervals, holidays and half-holidays, and any other conditions to be observed in relation to the employment of children.

Byelaws made under s.18 may apply generally to an authority's area, or may distinguish between children of different ages, between boys and girls, and between different localities, trades, occupations, and circumstances.

The above provisions, and any byelaws made under them, do not affect children who do anything under the provisions of the 1933 and 1963 Acts (see **7 Employment in entertainment, sport or modelling**, below).

4 Education and employment

If it appears to a local authority (in Scotland, an education authority) that any child who is a registered pupil at a county, voluntary, or special school is being employed in such a manner as to affect his health or education, the authority may serve written notice on the employer prohibiting him from employing the child or imposing such restrictions on his employment of the child as appear to them expedient in the interests of the child (Education Act 1996, s.559; Education (Scotland) Act 1962, s.137).

5 Work experience

S.560 of the Education Act 1996 provides that, subject to certain exceptions, the enactments prohibiting or regulating the employment of children in England and Wales do not apply to the employment of a child in his two last years of compulsory schooling where the employment is arranged or approved by the local authority, or the governing body of a school on behalf of such an authority, with a view to providing the child with work experience as a part of his education. For these purposes a child is taken to be in his last two years of compulsory schooling from the beginning of the last two years at his school during the whole or part of which he is of compulsory school age (see 1 **Introduction**, above). Similar provision is made for Scotland by ss.123 and 125 of the Education (Scotland) Act 1980 in relation to a child in his last year of compulsory schooling.

6 Street trading

The expression street trading includes hawking newspapers, matches, flowers, and other articles, playing, singing, or performing for profit, shoe blackening, and other similar occupations carried on in streets or public places (Children and Young Persons Act 1933, s.30).

No child may engage or be employed in street trading, except where a local authority has made byelaws authorising children of 14 years of age or over to be employed by their parents in street trading (s.20(1)). The byelaws must contain provisions determining the days and hours during which and the places at which they may be so employed (s.20(3)).

A local authority may make byelaws regulating or prohibiting street trading by persons under the age of 18. Such byelaws may *inter alia* provide for licences, and determine the hours and days during which, and the places at which, such persons may engage in street trading but may not authorise a child to engage, or be employed, on a Sunday (s.29(2) and (3)).

Identical provision is made for Scotland in ss.30 and 37 of the Children and Young Persons (Scotland) Act 1937.

7 Employment in entertainment, sport or modelling

The following provisions apply to England, Wales, and Scotland.

Under s.37 of the Children and Young Persons Act 1963 (as amended), a child may not, except under a licence granted by the local authority in whose area he resides or, if he does not reside in Great Britain, by the local authority in whose area the applicant for the licence resides or has his place of business, take part in–

(1) any performance in connection with which a charge is made (whether for admission or otherwise);
(2) any performance in licensed premises within the meaning of the Licensing Act 2003 or the Licensing (Scotland) Act 2005, or in premises in respect of which a club is registered under either of those Acts;
(3) any broadcast performance or any performance included in a cable programme service;
(4) any performance recorded (by whatever means) with a view to its use in a broadcast or such a service, or in a film intended for public exhibition.

A child is treated as taking part in a performance if he takes the place of a performer in any rehearsal or in any preparation for the recording of the performance (s.37(1) and (2)).

A licence is also required for a child to take part in a sport, or work as a model, where payment in respect of his doing so, other than for defraying expenses, is made to him or to another person.

A licence is not required for any child to take part in a performance if no payment in respect of his taking part in the performance, other than defraying expenses, is made to him or to another person, and–

(a) in the six months preceding the performance he has not taken part in other such performances on more than three days; or
(b) the performance is given under arrangements made by a school, or by a body of persons approved by the Secretary of State or the local authority in whose area the performance takes place (s.37(3)).

The power of a local authority to grant a licence is subject to such restrictions and conditions as the Secretary of State may by regulations prescribe (see below). A licence may not be granted unless the local authority is satisfied that the child is fit, that proper provision has been made to secure his health and kind treatment, and that his education will not suffer (s.37(4)). A licence must specify the times, if any, during which the child may be absent from school for the purposes authorised by the licence (s.37(7)).

Note.–The restrictions on the circumstances in which a local authority could issue a performance licence to a child under the age of 14 have been removed.

The Children (Performances and Activities) (England) Regulations 2014, (Scotland) Regulations 2014, and (Wales) Regulations 2015 make provision for the obtaining of a licence for a child to do anything to which s.37 applies. Where the child is to take part in a performance, the licence must be obtained by the person responsible for the production of the performance. Where the child is taking part in a sporting event, or is modelling, the organiser of the event, or, as the case may be, the person engaging the child as a model, must obtain the licence. The licence must be applied for at least 21 days before the event in question. The licensing authority may make such enquiries as they consider necessary and may in particular require a report from the child's head teacher or require the child to have a medical examination. A licence will not be granted unless the authority is satisfied that the child's education will not suffer and that suitable arrangements have been made for the child's education during the currency of the licence.

The Regulations cover applications for licences; restrictions on the grant of licences; restrictions and conditions applying to all licences and concerning *inter alia* education, earnings, chaperones, accommodation, travel arrangements, and breaks in performances; restrictions on *inter alia* the maximum number and length of performances and rehearsals daily, and the earliest and latest hour that a child can be present at the place of performance or rehearsal.

In Wales, a licence must not be granted for a child who attends school unless a letter has been obtained from the head teacher (or it is not practicable to do so) (Reg. 14).

8 Dangerous performances

No person under the age of 16 and no child aged 16 may take part in any performance for which a licence is required in which his life or limbs are endangered. It is an offence to cause or procure, or as a parent allow, such a performance (Children and Young Persons Act 1933, s.23 and Children and Young Persons (Scotland) Act 1937, s.33).

No child under 12 years of age may be trained to take part in performances of a dangerous nature, and no child who has attained that age may be trained to take part in such performances except under the terms of a licence granted by the local authority for that purpose (Children and Young Persons Act 1933, s.24, Children and Young Persons (Scotland) Act 1937, s.34, and Children and Young Persons Act 1963, s.41).

9 Employment in entertainments abroad

It is an offence for a person having the custody, charge, or care of any child to allow him, or for any person to cause or procure any child, to go abroad–
  (a) for the purpose of singing, playing, performing, being exhibited, or taking part in any broadcast or recorded performance for profit, or
  (b) for the purpose of taking part in a sport, or working as a model, where payment in respect of his doing so, other than for expenses, is made to him or another person,

unless a licence has been granted in respect of him by a justice of the peace. A licence may be granted to any child who is 14 years or over, subject to such restrictions and conditions as the justice thinks fit, only if the justice is satisfied that the application for the licence is made by or with the consent of the applicant's parent or guardian; that he is going abroad to fulfil a particular engagement; that he is fit for the purpose and proper provision has been made for securing his health, kind treatment, and adequate supervision while abroad; and that he has been given a copy of his contract of employment or similar document drawn up in a language understood by him (Children and Young Persons Act 1933, ss.25 and 26, and Children and Young Persons Act 1963, s.42(1)).

A licence may be granted under s.25 to a child under the age of 14 provided (Children and Young Persons Act 1963, s.42(2))–
  (c) the engagement which he is to fulfil is for acting and the application for the licence is accompanied by a declaration that the part he is to act cannot be taken except by a person of about his age; or
  (d) the engagement is for dancing in a ballet which does not form part of an entertainment of which anything other than ballet or opera also forms part and the application for the licence is accompanied by a declaration that the part he is to dance cannot be taken except by a child of about his age; or
  (e) the engagement is for taking part in a performance the nature of which is wholly or mainly musical or which consists only of opera and ballet and the nature of his part in the performance is wholly or mainly musical.

10 Authorities

Statutes–

Children and Young Persons Acts 1933 to 1963

Children and Young Persons (Scotland) Acts 1937 to 1963

Education Act 1996

Education (Scotland) Acts 1962 and 1980

Statutory Instruments–

Children (Performances and Activities) (England) Regulations 2014 (S.I. 2014 No. 3309)

Children (Performances and Activities) (Scotland) Regulations 2014 (S.S.I. 2014 No. 372)

Children (Performances and Activities) (Wales) Regulations 2015 (S.I. 2015 No. 1757)

Children (Protection at Work) Regulations 1998 (S.I. 1998 No. 276)

Children (Protection at Work) Regulations 2000 (S.I. 2000 Nos. 1333 and 2548)

Children (Protection at Work) (Scotland) Regulations 2000 (S.S.I. 2000 No. 149)

EMPLOYMENT OF PERSONS FROM ABROAD

1 Introduction

This Note deals with the illegal employment in the United Kingdom of persons from abroad. For guidance as to when persons from abroad may legally work in the United Kingdom, see the Immigration Section, and in particular see the Note on **The Immigration Rules**.

2 EU Member States

Generally, nationals of EU Member States have free movement throughout the EU and can seek employment in any Member State. However, the Accession Treaties for new Member States may provide for existing Member States to derogate from this position so as to regulate access to their labour markets for a limited period: see **3 New EU Member State–2013**, below.

Note.–the derogation period for Bulgaria and Romania ended on 31st December 2013.

3 New EU Member State–2013

Croatia joined the EU on 1st July 2013. Unless excepted, a national of Croatia who, until the end of the "accession period" (i.e., 30th June 2018), wishes to work in the UK requires a worker authorisation document (Accession of Croatia (Immigration and Worker Authorisation) Regulations 2013, Regs.2 and 8).

Authorisation to work in the UK is not required by a national of Croatia who (Reg. 2)–

   (a) has leave to enter or remain in the UK under the Immigration Act 1971 where that leave is not subject to any condition restricting employment;

   (b) was legally working in the UK on 30th June 2013 and had been legally working in the UK without interruption throughout the period of 12 months ending on that date (and a such a person who legally works in the UK without interruption for a period of 12 months falling partly or wholly after 30th June 2013 ceases to be an accession State national subject to worker authorisation at the end of that period of 12 months);

   (c) is also a national of the UK or any other EEA State other than Croatia;

  (ca) is the spouse, civil partner, or child under the age of 18 of a person who has leave to enter or remain in the UK that allows that person to work in the UK;

   (d) is the spouse or civil partner of a UK national or of a person settled in the UK;

   (e) has a permanent right of residence under the Immigration (European Economic Area) Regulations 2006;

   (f) is a family member of an EEA national who has a right to reside in the UK under the 2006 EEA Regulations, unless that EEA national is subject to worker authorisation or is a student or former student within (h) below;

  (fa) is the spouse, civil partner, or descendant of an accession state national subject to worker authorisation who has a right to reside in the UK (provided in the case of a descendant that he is under 21 or dependent on the national subject to authorisation);

   (g) is a highly skilled person and hold a registration certificate that includes a statement that they have unconditional access to the UK labour market;

   (h) is in the UK as a student, does not work for more than 20 hours a week (unless the work is part of a course of vocational training or during the student's vacation) and holds a registration certificate that includes a statement that they are a student who has access to the UK labour market within these limits;

   (i) are a posted worker; or

   (j) is a member of a diplomatic mission, family member of such a person, or a person otherwise entitled to diplomatic immunity.

An employer who employs an accession State national subject to worker authorisation during the accession period will be guilty of an offence if the employee does not hold an accession worker authorisation document or that document is subject to conditions that preclude him from taking up the employment (Reg. 11). It be a defence to prove that before the employment began there was produced to the employer a document that appeared to him to be an accession worker authorisation document that authorised the worker to take up the employment or a document that appeared to him to be a registration certificate issued to the worker and the registration certificate contained a statement that the worker had unconditional access to the UK labour market.

These defences are not available if the employer did not check and take a copy of the document, or knew that employment of the worker would constitute an offence.

4 Restriction on employment of persons from abroad

S.15 of the Immigration, Asylum and Nationality Act 2006 provides for the payment of a penalty by anyone who employs a person who is subject to immigration control if–

   (a) that person has not been granted leave to enter or remain in the UK; or

(b) that person's leave is not valid, has ceased to have effect, or is subject to a condition precluding him from taking up employment.

The maximum penalty is £20,000–see below (Immigration (Employment of Adults Subject to Immigration Control) (Maximum Penalty) Order 2008, art. 2).

An employer is however excused from paying a penalty if he shows that he has complied with any prescribed requirements in relation to the employment. The Immigration (Restrictions on Employment) Order 2007 specifies these requirements.

The Home Office *Code of Practice on Preventing Illegal Working: Civil Penalty Scheme for Employers* provides for two levels of penalty. Level I (where the employer has not been found to be employing illegal workers within the previous three years) has a starting point for the calculation of the civil penalty of £15,000 before reductions are applied. Level 2 (for second or subsequent breaches within three years) has a starting point of £20,000. For both Levels, if there is evidence that the employer reported suspected illegal workers the penalty will be reduced by £5,000; and if there is evidence that the employer actively co-operated with the authorities there will be also be a reduction of £5,000. There is a minimum penalty of £5,000 (Level I) or £10,000 (Level 2) however if it is a first breach (i.e., Level I) and there is evidence of effective document checking practices as well as mitigation for reporting and co-operation, an employer will be given a warning notice rather than a penalty.

There is a fast payment option for a Level I penalty which reduces the amount of the civil penalty by 30% if payment is received in full within 21 days of the penalty being imposed. This is not available for Level 2 penalties (second or subsequent breaches within three years).

5 Excusal from penalty

An employer is excused from paying a penalty under the Immigration, Asylum and Nationality Act 2006, s.15 if he can show that, before the employment began (Immigration (Restrictions on Employment) Order 2007, Art. 6(1))–

(a) the prospective employee provided to him certain documents;
(b) the employer took all reasonable steps to check the validity of the documents and retained a record of the date on which any check was made;
(c) the employer took copies of the documents (which must be kept for two years after the end of the employment);
(d) the employer is satisfied that any photograph on a document is that of the employee;
(e) all reasonable steps are taken to check that the prospective employee is the rightful owner of the document.

A further requirement, if the employee or prospective employee is a student who has permission to work for a limited number of hours per week during term time whilst studying in the UK, is that the employer must obtain and retain details of the term and vacation dates of the course that the employee or prospective employee is undertaking (Reg. 6(2)).

The Immigration (Restrictions on Employment) Order 2007 specifies the documents which an employer may accept for the purpose of providing him with an excusal from the penalty under s.15.

List A contains the range of documents which may be accepted for checking purposes for a person who has a *permanent* right to work in the UK. These documents provide the employer with an excusal for the duration of the employment. List B contains the range of documents which may be accepted for checking purposes for a person who has a *temporary* right to work in the UK. These documents provide an excusal only for a limited period. List A includes–

(1) a UK passport describing the holder, or a person named in the passport as a child of the holder, as a British citizen, or a citizen of the United Kingdom and Colonies having the right of abode in the UK;
(2) a passport or national identity card showing that the holder, or a person named in the passport as the child of the holder, is a national of an EEA country or Switzerland;
(3) a registration certificate or document certifying permanent residence issued by the Home Office to a national of the EEA or Switzerland;
(4) a permanent residence card issued by the Home Office to the family member of a national of a EEA country or Switzerland;
(5) a current biometric immigration document issued by the Home Office to the holder which indicates that the person named in it is allowed to stay indefinitely in the UK, or has no time limit on their stay in the UK;
(6) a current passport endorsed to show that the holder is exempt from immigration control, is allowed to stay indefinitely in the UK, has the right of abode in the UK, or has no time limit on their stay in the UK;
(7) a current Immigration Status Document issued by the Home Office to the holder with an endorsement indicating that the person named in it is allowed to stay indefinitely in the UK or has no time limit on their stay in the UK, when produced in combination with an official document giving the person's permanent National Insurance Number and their name issued by a Government agency or a previous employer;
(8) a full birth (or adoption) certificate issued in the UK which includes the name(s) of at least one of the holder's (adoptive) parents, when produced in combination with an official document giving the person's permanent National Insurance Number and their name issued by a Government agency or a previous employer;

(9) a birth or adoption certificate issued in the Channel Islands, the Isle of Man or Ireland, when produced in combination with an official document giving the person's permanent National Insurance Number and their name issued by a Government agency or a previous employer;

(10) certificate of registration or naturalisation as a British citizen, when produced in combination with an official document giving the person's permanent National Insurance Number and their name issued by a Government agency or a previous employer.

In the case of a passport, the employer must also copy (in a format which cannot be subsequently altered) any pages containing personal details (including nationality), a photograph or signature of the holder, and date of expiry, and the details and endorsements described above. All other documents must be photocopied or scanned in their entirety (Art. 6).

List B is for employees with a temporary right to work in the UK and provide excusal only for a limited period. Employers must conduct follow-up checks as specified by the Order. Generally, these will be required when the employee's permission to be in the UK and to do the work in question expires, as evidenced by the document or combination of documents produced for the right to work check. In respect of documents issued by the Home Office which do not give an expiry date (work-permitted Application Registration Cards and Certificates of Application–List B Part 2) the duration of the statutory excuse will be six months from the date of verification by the Home Office Employer Checking Service.

List B includes–

Part 1

(1) a current passport endorsed to show that the holder is allowed to stay in the UK and is allowed to do the type of work in question.

(2) a current biometric immigration document issued by the Home Office to the holder which indicates that the person named in it is allowed to stay in the UK and is allowed to do the work in question.

(3) a current residence card (including an accession residence card or a derivative residence card) issued by the Home Office to a non-European Economic Area national who is a family member of a national of a European Economic Area country or Switzerland or who has a derivative right of residence.

(4) a current immigration status document containing a photograph issued by the Home Office to the holder with an endorsement indicating that the person named in it is allowed to stay in the UK and is allowed to do the work in question, when produced in combination with an official document giving the person's permanent National Insurance Number and their name issued by a Government agency or previous employer.

Part 2

(1) a certificate of application issued by the Home Office under the Immigration (European Economic Area) Regulations 2006, Reg. 17(3) or 18A(2), to a family member of a national of a European Economic Area country or Switzerland stating that the holder is permitted to take employment which is less than 6 months old, together with a Positive Verification Notice from the Home Office Employer Checking Service;

(2) an application registration card issued by the Home Office stating that the holder is permitted to take the employment in question, together with a Positive Verification Notice from the Home Office Employer Checking Service;

(3) a Positive Verification Notice issued by the Home Office Employer Checking Service to the employer or prospective employer which indicates that the named person may stay in the UK and is permitted to do the work in question.

If an employer has any concerns about the validity of a document presented to them they can contact the Sponsorship, Employer and Education Helpline on 0300 123 4699.

Enquiry forms for the Home Office Employer Checking Service can be downloaded from <www. gov.uk/government/publications/employer-checking-service-form-check-employees-right-to-work>.

6 Employment of skilled non-EEA migrants

Employers can only recruit skilled non-EEA migrants from abroad if they have completed a resident labour market test and can show that no suitably qualified settled worker can fill the job. The requirement therefore applies to the majority of skilled jobs (i.e., those which are filled under Tier 2 of the Points Based System (see the Note on **The Immigration Rules**)) and an employer will not be able to sponsor a skilled non-EEA migrant until the test has been completed. The requirement is subject to certain exemptions (see below).

The resident labour market test

In order to complete a resident labour market test for a job vacancy specific advertising requirements must be satisfied. The advertisement must include–

(a) the job title;

(b) the main duties and responsibilities of the job (job description);

(c) the location of the job;

(d) an indication of the salary package or salary range or terms on offer;

(e) the skills, qualifications and experience needed; and

(f) the closing date for applications (unless the job is part of the organisation's rolling recruitment programme in which case the advertisement must state the period of such programme).

All vacancies must be advertised to settled workers for 28 calendar days. This requirement can be fulfilled by either—

(g) advertising the vacancy for a single continuous period, with a minimum closing date of 28 calendar days from the date the advertisement first appeared; or

(h) advertising the vacancy in two stages, where each stage lasts no less than 7 calendar days and both stages added together total a minimum of 28 calendar days.

All jobs must be advertised at the appropriate rate of pay for that job in the UK to ensure there has been a genuine attempt to fill the vacancy with a resident worker. In circumstances where a migrant worker is hired, he must be paid at or above the rate advertised.

If a settled worker applies for the job but does not have the necessary qualifications, experience or skills, the employer cannot refuse to employ them unless he specifically requested those qualifications, experience or skills in the job advertisement.

Exemptions

An employer will not have to complete a resident labour market test if the job is on the shortage occupation list. If an occupation is on that list it means that there are not enough resident workers to fill the available jobs in that particular occupation. The shortage occupation list is updated regularly: see <www.gov.uk/government/uploads/system/uploads/attachment_data/file/308513/shortageoccupationlistapril14.pdf>. Additionally, an employer does not have to complete a resident labour market test if the job is an intra-company transfer. Other exemptions apply including—

(a) a migrant who is already employed by the employer and has permission to stay in the UK under, *inter alia*, the International Graduates Scheme or other similar schemes or has permission to stay under the post-study worker category of Tier 1 (see the Note on **The Immigration Rules**);

(b) a migrant who has current leave to be in the UK as a post-graduate doctor or dentist and is undertaking further training;

(c) intra-company transfers; and

(d) jobs here the salary will be £153,500 or more.

Certain jobs in the creative sector do not have to be advertised in Jobcentre Plus, but the other resident labour market test requirements must still be met. The exemption from advertising in Jobcentre Plus also applies in other limited circumstances including certain PhD level jobs, pupillage positions for trainee barristers, "milkround" graduate recruitment exercises, and jobs where the salary package is at least £71,600 or where there will be stock exchange disclosure requirements.

Tier 2 and 5 of the points-based system – policy guidance for sponsors gives detailed guidance on the above requirements and is available at <www.gov.uk/government/publications/sponsor-a-tier-2-or-5-worker-guidance-for-employers>.

7 Codes of Practice

In addition to the Home Office *Code of Practice on Preventing Illegal Working: Civil Penalty Scheme for Employers* (see **4 Restriction on employment of persons from abroad**, above), the Home Office have produced a *Code of Practice for Employers: Avoiding Unlawful Discrimination while Preventing Illegal Working* (May 2014). It aims to provide employers with guidance on avoiding a penalty under s.15 whilst at the same time avoiding unlawful race discrimination.

8 Criminal employment offences

It is a criminal offence to employ a person knowing that they are an adult subject to immigration control who has not been granted leave to enter or remain (unless granted permission to work by the Secretary of State), or whose leave to remain is invalid, has ceased to have effect (whether by reason of curtailment, revocation, cancellation, passage of time or otherwise) or is subject to a condition preventing him from accepting the employment (Immigration, Asylum and Nationality Act 2006, s.21).

9 Provision of information by HM Revenue and Customs

Under the Nationality, Immigration and Asylum Act 2002, s.130, HM Revenue and Customs can supply information to the Secretary of State (i.e., the Home Office) where it reasonably suspects that—

(a) a person does not have leave to enter or remain in the UK; or

(b) a person does not have permission to work in the UK.

HM Revenue and Customs can also supply information to the Secretary of State for the purpose of establishing where that person is if the Secretary of State reasonably suspects that that person has undertaken work in the UK in breach of—

(c) a condition attached to his leave to enter the UK;

(d) a restriction imposed on entry to the UK; or

(e) a restriction imposed in a deportation order.

HM Revenue and Customs can supply information to the Secretary of State for the purpose of—

(f) determining whether an applicant for naturalisation is of good character;

(g) applying the rules as to maintenance and accommodation in the case of an applicant for entry clearance.

10 Authorities

Statutes–

Asylum and Immigration Act 1996

Immigration, Asylum and Nationality Act 2006

Nationality, Immigration and Asylum Act 2002

Statutory Instruments–

Accession of Croatia (Immigration and Worker Authorisation) Regulations 2013 (S.I. 2013 No. 1460)

Immigration (Employment of Adults Subject to Immigration Control) (Maximum Penalty) Order 2008, as amended (S.I. 2008 No. 132 and 2014 No. 1262)

Immigration (Restrictions on Employment) Order 2007, as amended (S.I. 2007 No. 3290, 2009 No. 2908, 2012 No. 1547, and 2014 No. 1183)

Home Office Code of Practice on Preventing Illegal Working: Civil Penalty Scheme for Employers (May 2014)

Home Office Code of Practice for Employers: Avoiding Unlawful Discrimination while Preventing Illegal Working (May 2014)

EMPLOYMENT MEDICAL ADVISORY SERVICE

1 Purposes of the Service

S.55 of the Health and Safety at Work etc. Act 1974 continues the Employment Medical Advisory Service, which is maintained for the following purposes–

(a) securing that the Secretary of State, the Health and Safety Executive, (in Scotland, Scottish Enterprise and Highlands and Islands Enterprise), and others concerned with the health of persons employed, or seeking or training for employment, can be kept informed of, and adequately advised on, matters of which they ought respectively to take cognizance concerning the safeguarding and improvement of the health of those persons;

(b) giving information and advice on health to such persons; and

(c) acting for other purposes in connection with the Secretary of State's functions relative to employment.

The Health and Safety Executive is responsible for maintaining the service and may, for the above-mentioned purposes and for assisting employment medical advisers in the performance of their functions, investigate related problems or arrange or make payments for such investigations and for this purpose provide and maintain laboratories and other services. The Executive must appoint employment medical advisers who must be fully registered medical practitioners (s.56).

2 Availability of school medical records

It is the duty of the Secretary of State to ensure that each Health Authority makes available to an employment medical adviser on request such particulars of the school medical record of a person under 18 years of age as he may reasonably need for the efficient performance of his functions. The disclosure of information so obtained, except for the performance of those functions, is not permitted without that person's consent (Health and Safety at Work etc. Act 1974 s.60).

3 Fees

S.57 of the Health and Safety at Work etc. Act 1974 empowers the Secretary of State, after consultation with the maintaining authority, to make regulations fixing the fees payable to the Health and Safety Executive for medical examinations and surveillance carried out by employment medical advisers which are required under certain regulations relating to lead and asbestos in the workplace, ionising radiation, substances hazardous to health and work in compressed air.

4 Authorities

Health and Safety at Work etc. Act 1974

Employment Medical Advisory Services (Factories Act Orders etc. Amendment) Order 1973, as amended (S.I. 1973 No. 36, 1980 No. 1248, and 1985 No. 1333)

Health and Safety (Miscellaneous Fees) Regulations 1997 (S.I. 1997 No. 2505)

HEALTH AND SAFETYAT WORK: GENERAL

A: INTRODUCTION

Contents

This Note deals with the health, safety, and welfare of persons at work. In particular, it covers general duties and details certain health and safety regulations.

This Note is arranged as follows–

A: Introduction
B: General duties
C: Health and safety regulations
D: Health and Safety Executive
E: Enforcement
F: Environment and Safety Information Act 1988
G: Employers' Liability (Defective Equipment) Act 1969

1 Health and Safety at Work etc. Act 1974

The Health and Safety at Work etc. Act 1974 introduced a comprehensive and integrated system of law dealing with the health, safety, and welfare of persons at work. Duties are placed on all persons connected with health and safety at work, whether as employers, employees, or self-employed, or as manufacturers and suppliers of plant and materials, and protection is given to members of the public affected by the activities of persons at work.

The Act and the regulations made under it provide for the progressive repeal of existing statutory provisions relating to health and safety at work and for their replacement by a new system of regulations and approved codes of practice operating in combination with the other provisions of Part 1 of the Act and designed to maintain or improve the standards of health, safety, and welfare established by or under such legislation.

In consequence, and in accordance with European Community (EC) Directives, regulations have been made which provide for a comprehensive scheme of health and safety requirements relevant to workplaces. They also make provision for the progressive repeal of many of the provisions of the above-mentioned Acts and for their replacement. The regulations include the–

- Health and Safety (Display Screen Equipment) Regulations 1992;
- Management of Health and Safety at Work Regulations 1999;
- Manual Handling Operations Regulations 1992;
- Personal Protective Equipment at Work Regulations 1992;
- Workplace (Health, Safety and Welfare) Regulations 1992;
- Health and Safety (Safety Signs and Signals) Regulations 1996; and the
- Provision and Use of Work Equipment Regulations 1998.

These Regulations are dealt with below together with other health and safety Regulations e.g., the Control of Noise at Work Regulations 2005 and the Work at Height Regulations 2005 which are also of general application. The Health and Safety Executive, established by the Act, is responsible for the enforcement of the relevant statutory provisions (i.e., Part 1 of the Act, any regulations made under Part 1, and the existing statutory provisions set out in Schedule 1 to the Act) except where responsibility for enforcement has been given to local authorities or to the Secretary of State (see E: ENFORCEMENT, below).

This Note deals with those aspects of the Act and the regulations made thereunder which are of general application to workplaces. Part II of the Act, which is concerned with the Employment Medical Advisory Service, is dealt with in the Note on **Employment Medical Advisory Service**. Protection for "whistleblowers" who draw attention to breaches of health and safety legislation in the workplace is dealt with in the Note on **Public Interest Disclosure**.

2 Application of the Act

The relevant provisions of the Health and Safety at Work etc. Act 1974 extend to the whole of Great Britain. The provisions of Parts I, II, and IV (i.e., ss. 1 to 59 and 80 to 82) are also applied (by the Health and Safety at Work etc. Act 1974 (Application outside Great Britain) Order 2013), with certain exceptions, to wells, offshore installations and pipelines, and pipelines within territorial waters and areas designated under the Continental Shelf Act 1964 and to certain work connected with those installations and pipelines, as well as to construction works, diving operations, works connected with the production of energy from water or wind, coal gasification and certain other activities within territorial waters, and to mines within territorial waters or extending beyond them.

Nothing in Part 1 of the Act applies in relation to a person by reason only that he employs another, or is himself employed, as a domestic servant in a private household (s.51).

3 Application to the Crown

The Crown is bound by Part 1 of the Health and Safety at Work etc. Act 1974, except ss.21 to 25 (which concern certain powers of inspectors to issue notices and deal with imminent danger (see E: ENFORCEMENT, below)) and ss.33 to 42 (which deal with offences under the Act). Ss.33 to 42 do, however, apply to persons in public service of the Crown (s.48). By virtue of s.2 of the National Health Service (Amendment) Act 1986, a health authority is not regarded as the servant or agent of the Crown, or as enjoying any status, immunity, or privilege of the Crown, and premises used by a health authority will not be regarded as property of or property held on behalf of the Crown.

4 Definitions

Ss.52 and 53 of the Health and Safety at Work etc. Act 1974 contain the definitions for the purposes of Part I. In particular (i) "work" means work as an employee or as a self-employed person; (ii) an employee is at work throughout the time when he is in the course of his employment but not otherwise; (iii) a self-employed person is at work throughout such time as he devotes to work as a self-employed person; (iv) an "employee" means an individual who works under a contract of employment (and related expressions are to be construed accordingly); (v) a "self-employed person" means an individual who works for gain or reward otherwise than under a contract of employment; and (vi) a reference to personal injury includes any disease and any impairment of a person's physical or mental condition.

The Health and Safety (Training for Employment) Regulations 1990 extend the meaning of "work" for the purposes of Part I of the Act to include relevant training (i.e., work experience provided pursuant to a training course or programme, or training for employment, or both, except if (a) the immediate provider of the relevant training is an educational establishment (namely, a university, college, school, or similar educational or technical institute) and it is provided on a course run by the establishment; or (b) received under a contract of employment. The meaning of "work" is also extended so as to provide that a person provided with relevant training is at work throughout the time when he would be in the course of his employment if he were in such training under a contract of employment, but not otherwise. A person provided with relevant training is treated as an employee of the person whose undertaking (whether carried on by him for profit or not) is for the time being the immediate provider to that person of the training.

5 Power to repeal certain health and safety provisions

Under s.37 of the Deregulation and Contracting Out Act 1994, the Secretary of State has power to make regulations which repeal, or as the case may be, revoke any existing statutory provision for the purposes of Part I of the Act, or any provision of regulations made under s.15 of the Act (see below), which has effect in place of a statutory provision under Part I. Before making any such regulations, the Secretary of State must consult the Health and Safety Executive and such other persons as he considers appropriate.

6 General principles of Part I

S.1 of the Health and Safety at Work etc. Act 1974 sets out the general principles underlying the provisions of Part I, which are aimed at–
  (a) securing the health, safety, and welfare of persons at work;
  (b) protecting persons other than persons at work against risks to health and safety arising out of, or in connection with, the activities of persons at work, including risks attributable to the manner of conducting an undertaking, the plant or substances used, and the condition of the premises; and
  (c) controlling the keeping and use of dangerous substances and preventing their unlawful acquisition, possession, and use.

B: GENERAL DUTIES

7 Duties of employers to their employees

S.2 of the Health and Safety at Work etc. Act 1974 requires employers to ensure, so far as is reasonably practicable, the health, safety, and welfare of their employees at work.

The matters to which this duty extends include–
  (a) the provision and maintenance of plant and systems of work that are, so far as is reasonably practicable, safe and without risks to health;
  (b) arrangements for ensuring, so far as is reasonably practicable, safety and absence of risk to health in connection with the use, handling, storage, and transport of articles and substances;
  (c) the provision of such information, instruction, training, and supervision as is necessary to ensure, so far as is reasonably practicable, the health and safety at work of employees;
  (d) so far as is reasonably practicable, as regards any place of work under the employer's control, the maintenance of means of access to and egress from it that are safe and without such risks; and
  (e) the provision and maintenance of a working environment for employees that is so far as is reasonably practicable, safe, without risks to health, and adequate as regards facilities and arrangements for their welfare at work.

Under s.2(3), employers are required to prepare, revise when necessary, and bring to the attention of their employees a written statement of their policy in these matters and the organisation and arrangements for carrying it out. The Employers' Health and Safety Policy Statements (Exception) Regulations 1975 except from the requirements of s.2(3) an employer with less than five employees.

The Safety Representatives and Safety Committees Regulations 1977 (the 1977 Regulations) provide for recognised trade unions to appoint safety representatives to represent employees in consultations with employers on health and safety matters. A person so appointed must, so far as is reasonably practicable, either have been employed by his employer throughout the preceding two years or have had at least two years' experience in similar employment (Reg. 3). Every employer must consult any such representatives with a view to the making and maintenance of arrangements which will enable him and his employees to co-operate effectively in promoting and developing measures to ensure the health and safety at work of the employers, and checking the effectiveness of such measures (s.2(6)).

The functions of safety representatives under the 1977 Regulations include: investigating potential hazards and dangerous occurrences at workplaces and complaints by an employee relating to his health, safety or welfare at work; and representing employees at consultations at the workplace with health and safety inspectors (Reg. 4). Safety representatives are also given powers under the Regulations which entitle them to carry out inspections (Reg. 5).

An employer must permit safety representatives to take time off with pay during working hours to carry out their functions and to receive the necessary training (Reg. 4(2)). Regulation 11 provides that industrial tribunals have jurisdiction to hear complaints by safety representatives relating to time off with pay.

An employer must, if requested in writing to do so by any two safety representatives, establish a safety committee within three months of the request being made and in accordance with the provisions of s.2(7) of the Act and Regulation 9. Such safety committees have the function of keeping under review the measures taken to protect the health and safety of employees.

The Health and Safety (Consultation with Employees) Regulations 1996, which apply where there are employees not represented by safety representatives appointed by trade unions under the 1977 Regulations, contain similar provisions to those in the 1977 Regulations, requiring employers in such situations to consult either employees directly or representatives elected by them.

S.9 of the Act forbids employers to charge employees for anything required by the Act to be done for their health and safety.

8 Duties of employers and the self-employed to persons other than employees

Under s.3(1) of the Health and Safety at Work etc. Act 1974, employers are required to ensure, so far as is reasonably practicable, that the conduct of their undertakings will not expose persons not in their employment to risks to their health and safety; under s.3(2) self-employed people who conduct undertakings of a prescribed description (see below) are similarly required to ensure that they do not endanger themselves or such other persons; and, under s.3(3) employers and self-employed persons may, in prescribed circumstances, be required to provide information to the public as to possible dangers.

A self-employed person's undertaking will be of a "prescribed description" for these purposes if it involves the carrying out of any activity which is listed in the Schedule to the Health and Safety at Work etc. Act 1974 (General Duties of Self-Employed Persons) (Prescribed Undertakings) Regulations 2015; or although not listed in the Schedule may pose a risk to the health and safety of another person (other than the self-employed person carrying it out or their employees). The listed activities are those which carry a high risk, namely those concerned with: agriculture (including forestry), asbestos, construction, gas, genetically modified organisms, and railways.

9 Duties of persons concerned with premises to persons other than their employees

S.4 of the Health and Safety at Work etc. Act 1974 imposes a duty on persons who have, to any extent in connection with the carrying on by them of a trade, business, or other undertaking, control of non-domestic premises made available to others who are not their employees for use as a place of work or a place where they may use plant or substances provided for their use there. It is the duty of any such person to take such measures as it is reasonable for a person in his position to take to ensure, so far as is reasonably practicable, that the premises, all means of access thereto and egress therefrom available for use by persons using the premises, and any plant or substances in the premises of, as the case may be, provided for use there, is or are safe and without risks to health. Where a person has, by virtue of any contract or tenancy, an obligation of any extent in relation to (i) the maintenance or repair of any such premises or any means of access thereto or egress therefrom, or (ii) the safety or absence or risks to health arising from plant or substances in any such premises, that person is to be treated as being a person who has control of the matters to which his obligation extends. The duty applies in relation to those premises and other non-domestic premises used in connection with them and is also imposed on persons who have control of the means of access to or egress from such premises or control of any plant or substance in such premises.

10 Duty in relation to harmful emissions into the atmosphere

The Control of Asbestos in the Air Regulations 1990, made under s.1(1)(b) of the Act (see **6 General principles**

of Part I, above, at (b)) impose a limit value (*viz*, an amount not exceeding 0.1 milligram of asbestos per cubic metre of air) for the discharge from certain defined premises of asbestos in to the air during the use of asbestos.

For other legislation concerning atmospheric pollution, see the Note on **Air Pollution**.

11 Duties of manufacturers, designers, importers, or suppliers

S.6 of the Health and Safety at Work etc. Act 1974 (as amended by the Consumer Protection Act 1987, Sch. 3) imposes a duty on designers, manufacturers, importers, or suppliers of any article of fairground equipment to ensure that it is safe and without risks to health when set, used, cleaned, or maintained (or, in the case of substances used, handled, processed, stored, or transported); to this end, they must carry out any necessary testing, inspection, and research and provide the necessary information and instruction. Persons who install or erect plant are under a duty to ensure, so far as is reasonably practicable, that it is not installed or erected so as to make it unsafe when properly used.

In the case of suppliers under leases, hire-purchase, or conditional sale or credit sale agreements, the "effective supplier" (i.e., dealer) and not the "ostensible supplier" (i.e., financing institution) is responsible for carrying out these requirements (s.6(9) and the Health and Safety (Leasing Arrangements) Regulations 1992).

12 Duties of employees

S. 7 of the Health and Safety at Work etc. Act 1974 requires an employee to take reasonable care at work for the health and safety of himself and others who may be affected by his acts and omissions at work and to co-operate with employers in meeting statutory requirements.

13 Duty not to interfere

S.8 of the Health and Safety at Work etc. Act 1974 provides that no person must intentionally or recklessly interfere with or misuse anything provided under the relevant statutory provisions for health, safety, or welfare at work.

C: HEALTH AND SAFETY REGULATIONS

14 Introduction

Under s.15 of the Health and Safety at Work etc. Act 1974 (as substituted by the Employment Protection Act 1975, Sch. 15) *inter alia* the following health and safety regulations have been made.

Note.–Breach of a duty imposed by a statutory instrument containing health and safety regulations is not actionable except to the extent that regulations under the Health and Safety at Work etc. Act 1974, s.47 so provide (s.47, as amended by the Enterprise and Regulatory Reform Act 2013, s.69).

15 Confined spaces

The Confined Spaces Regulations 1997 impose requirements and prohibitions with respect of the health and safety of persons carrying out work in confined spaces (as defined in Regulation 2(1)) where there is a risk of a serious injury (including loss of consciousness) arising from a fire or explosion; drowning, or asphyxiation.

Inter alia, the Regulations prohibit the entry into a confined space for the purpose of carrying out work where it is reasonably practicable to carry out the work by other means; require work in a confined space to be carried out only in accordance with a safe system of work; and impose requirements regarding the preparation and implementation of adequate arrangements for the emergency rescue of any person working in a confined space. The Regulations do not apply to activities on-board a ship, in an underground mine, or a diving operation.

16 Construction work: health, safety and welfare

The Construction (Design and Management) Regulations 2015 impose requirements with respect to the health, safety and welfare of persons carrying out construction work (including any building, civil engineering or engineering construction work, but not including any mining works). It is the duty of every dutyholder (which includes clients, designers and contractors), to comply with the provisions of the Regulations insofar as they affect him or any person at work under his control, or relate to matters which are within his control. Every person at work is under a duty to co-operate with any person on whom any duty or requirement is imposed by the Regulations and, when working under another person's control, to report to that person any defect which he believes may endanger the health or safety of himself or another person (Reg. 8).

The specific health and safety requirements imposed on construction work by the Regulations are as follows.

Safe places of work–There must, so far as is reasonably practicable, be suitable and sufficient safe access to, and egress from, every workplace and to any other place provided for the use of persons at work. Every workplace must, so far as is practicable, be made and kept safe and steps must be taken to ensure that no person gains access to any place that is unsafe. So far as is practicable, and having regard to the work carried on, every workplace must have sufficient working space and be so arranged that it is suitable for any person working there (Reg. 17).

Stability of structures –All practical steps must be taken where necessary to prevent danger to any person, to ensure that any new or existing structure does not collapse if, due to the carrying out of construction work, it may become unstable; or is in a temporary state of weakness or instability. Any buttress, temporary support or other structure must be of such design and so installed and maintained as to withstand any foreseeable loads which may be imposed on it, and must only be used for the purposes for which it is so designed, installed and maintained (Reg. 19).

Demolition or dismantling –Steps must be taken to ensure that the demolition or dismantling of any structure is planned and carried out in such a manner as to prevent danger or, where it is not practicable to prevent it, to reduce danger to as low a level as is reasonably practicable. Such demolition or dismantling must be planned and recorded in writing before the demolition or dismantling work begins (Reg. 20).

Explosives –So far as is reasonably practicable, explosives must be stored, transported and used safely and securely. An explosive charge may only be used or fired if suitable and sufficient steps have been taken to ensure that no-one is exposed to risk of injury from the explosion or from projected or flying material caused by the explosion (Reg. 21).

Excavations –All practical steps must be taken to prevent danger arising from excavations including, where necessary, the provision of supports or battering. Suitable and sufficient steps must be taken to prevent any person, work equipment, or any accumulation of material from falling into any excavation and, where necessary, to prevent any part of an excavation or ground adjacent to it from being overloaded by work equipment or material. Construction work must not be carried out in an excavation where any supports or battering have been provided unless specified steps are taken (Reg. 22).

Cofferdams and caissons –Every cofferdam or caisson must be of suitable design and construction; appropriately equipped so that workers can gain shelter or escape if water or materials enter it; and properly maintained. They must not be used unless specified steps are taken (Reg. 23).

Energy distribution installations. –Where necessary to prevent danger, energy distribution installations must be suitably located, checked and clearly indicated (Reg. 25)

Prevention of drowning – Where, in the course of construction work, a person is at risk of falling into water or other liquid with a risk of drowning, suitable and sufficient steps must be taken to prevent, so far as is reasonably practicable, the person falling; minimise the risk of drowning in the event of a fall; and ensure that suitable rescue equipment is provided, maintained and, when necessary, used so that a person may be promptly rescued in the event of a fall. Suitable and sufficient steps must be taken to ensure the safe transport of any person conveyed by water to or from a place of work. Any vessel used to convey any person by water to or from a place of work must not be overcrowded or overloaded. (Reg. 26).

Traffic routes – A construction site must be organised in such a way that, so far as is reasonably practicable, pedestrians and vehicles can move without risks to health or safety. Traffic routes must be suitable for the persons or vehicles using them, sufficient in number, in suitable positions and of sufficient size. Each traffic route must be indicated by suitable signs where necessary for reasons of health or safety; regularly checked; and properly maintained. No vehicle is to be driven on a traffic route unless, so far as is reasonably practicable, that traffic route is free from obstruction and permits sufficient clearance. (Reg. 27).

Vehicles –Steps must be taken to prevent or control the unintended movement of any vehicle and to ensure that the person driving, operating or directing the vehicle warns persons who are at risk from it. Vehicles used for construction work must be driven, operated, towed and loaded in a safe manner and no person may remain in a vehicle during the loading or unloading of loose material unless a safe place is provided for him (Reg. 28).

Fire risk, etc –Steps must be taken to prevent the risk of injury to any person arising from fire or explosion, flooding, or any substance liable to cause asphyxiation (Reg. 29).

Emergency routes and exits –Where necessary, a sufficient number of emergency routes and exits must be provided leading to a place of safety. Any such route and exit must be kept free from obstruction and, where necessary, provided with emergency lighting. All routes and exits must be indicated by suitable signs (Reg. 31).

Emergency procedures – Where necessary in the interests of the health or safety of a person on a construction site, suitable and sufficient arrangements for dealing with any foreseeable emergency must be made and, where necessary, implemented, and those arrangements must include procedures for any necessary evacuation of the site or any part of it. Steps must be taken to ensure that persons are familiar with these arrangements and that those arrangements are tested at suitable intervals (Reg. 30).

Fire detection and fire-fighting –Suitable and sufficient fire-fighting equipment, fire detectors and alarm systems must be provided on sites and must be tested at regular intervals. Every person working on a site must, so far as practicable, be instructed in the use of fire-fighting equipment and where a work activity may give rise to a particular risk of fire, a person must not carry out work unless suitably instructed. Fire-fighting equipment which is not designed to come into use automatically must be easily accessible. Fire-fighting equipment must be indicated by suitable signs. (Reg. 32).

Welfare facilities –Various welfare facilities must be provided on sites, including sanitary conveniences, washing and rest facilities, drinking water and cloakroom facilities. Changing facilities must also be provided for persons who have to wear special clothing at work (Sch. 2).

Fresh air –Steps must be taken to ensure that, so far as is practicable, every workplace or approach thereto has sufficient fresh or purified air and any machinery used for this purpose must be capable of giving visible or audible warning of any machine failure (Reg. 33).

Temperature and weather protection –Steps must be taken to ensure that, so far as practicable, the temperature of any indoor workplace is reasonable having regard to the purpose for which that place is used. Outdoor workplaces must be arranged so as to give as much protection as possible from adverse weather having regard to the purpose for which the site is used; and any protective clothing or work equipment provided for the use of any person at work there (Reg. 34).

Lighting –There must be suitable and sufficient lighting in every workplace and approach thereto which must be, so far as is reasonably practicable, by natural light. The colour of artificial lighting provided must not adversely affect or change the perception of health and safety signs or signals. Secondary lighting must be provided in places where the failure of the primary artificial lighting would lead to health or safety risks (Reg. 35).

Good order and security–Every part of a site must, so far as practicable, be kept in good order and in a reasonable state of cleanliness. No timber or other material with projecting nails may be used in any work where the nails may cause danger. Where necessary in the interests of health and safety, a construction site shall, so far as is reasonably practicable and in accordance with the level of risk posed, either have its perimeter identified by suitable signs and be so arranged that its extent is readily identifiable or be fenced off or both (Reg. 18).

Training –Every contractor must provide every worker carrying out construction work under his control with any information and training which he needs for the particular work to be carried out safely and without risk to health. A contractor must not employ or appoint a person to work on a construction site unless that person has, or is in the process of obtaining, the necessary skills, knowledge, training and experience to carry out the tasks allocated to them in a manner that secures the health and safety of any person working on the construction site (Reg. 15).

Additional duties apply where the work involves particular risks (Sch. 3).

17 Construction work: design and management

The Construction (Design and Management) Regulations 2015 impose requirements on a client (i.e., a person who seeks or accepts the services of another which may be used in the carrying out of a project for him or carries out a project himself) to take reasonable steps to ensure that the arrangements made for managing a project (including the allocation of sufficient time and other resources) by persons with a duty under the Regulations (including the client himself) are suitable to ensure that (Reg. 4)–

    (a) the construction work can be carried out so far as is reasonably practicable without risk to the health and safety of any person; and

    (b) the necessary welfare facilities (see **16 Construction work: health, safety and welfare**, above) are provided.

No designer may start work in relation to a project unless any client for the project is aware of his duties under these Regulations (Reg. 9). Every designer must, in preparing or modifying a design which may be used in construction work avoid foreseeable risks to the health and safety of any person–

    (c) carrying out or liable to be affected by construction work;

    (d) maintaining or cleaning a structure;

    (e) using a structure designed as a workplace.

In discharging this duty, the designer must eliminate hazards which may give rise to risks, or if that is not possible must, so far as is reasonably practicable–

    (f) take steps to reduce or, if that is not possible, control the risks through the subsequent design process;

    (g) provide information about those risks to the principal designer; and

    (h) ensure appropriate information is included in the health and safety file.

18 Display screen equipment

The Health and Safety (Display Screen Equipment) Regulations 1992, implement EC Directive No. 90/270/EEC, and lay down the minimum requirements for work with display screen equipment. The Regulations do not apply to or in relation to drivers' cabs or control cabs for vehicles or machinery; display screen equipment on board a means of transport or mainly intended for public operation; portable systems not in prolonged use; calculators, cash registers or any equipment having a small data or measurement display required for direct use of the equipment; or window typewriters.

Under the Regulations every employer is required to perform a suitable and sufficient analysis of those workstations used by users (or provided for by him for use by operators) in order to assess risks, and to review assessments when necessary. An employer must reduce risks identified by assessments to the lowest extent reasonably practicable (Reg. 2). Regulation 1 defines workstation to mean an assembly comprising–

    (a) display screen equipment i.e., any alphanumeric or graphic display screen, regardless of the display process involved (whether provided with software determining the interface between the equipment and its operator or user, a keyboard or any other input device);

(b) any optional accessories to the display screen equipment;

(c) any disk drive, telephone, modem, printer, document holder, work chair, work desk, work surface or other item peripheral to the display screen equipment; and

(d) the immediate work environment around the display screen equipment.

For these purposes, a user is an employee who habitually uses display screen equipment as a significant part of his normal work (whether at his own employer's workstation; a workstation at home; or at another employer's workstation); and an operator is a self-employed person (i.e., a self-employed agency "temp") who habitually uses display screen equipment as a significant part of his normal work.

In addition, an employer must ensure that any workstation meets the requirements laid down in the Schedule to the Regulations (Reg. 3). *Inter alia* the Schedule provides that the image on the screen be stable, with no flickering or other forms of instability, the screen must swivel and tilt easily and freely; the keyboard be tiltable and separate from the screen so as to allow the operator or user to find a comfortable working position avoiding fatigue in the arms or hands; the work desk or work surface has a sufficiently large, low-reflectance surface and allow a flexible arrangement of the screen, keyboard, documents and related equipment; the work chair be stable, adjustable in height, and a footrest be made available to any operator or user who wishes one; there are satisfactory lighting conditions; and the employer take into account certain principles when selecting software.

Further, Regulation 4 imposes a duty on every employer to plan the activities of users at work in his undertaking so that their daily work on the screen is periodically interrupted by such breaks or changes of activity as reduce their workload at that equipment.

Every employer is required to ensure that users are provided with an appropriate eye and eyesight test on request; further tests at regular intervals, unless the user declines; additional tests on request for users who experience visual difficulties; and special corrective appliances where the test shows these are needed and normal ones cannot be used (Reg. 5). An employer must provide health and safety training for users of workstations. He must also provide operators and users with information on all aspects of health and safety relating to their workstations, and on the measures taken to comply with the Regulations (Regs. 6 and 7).

The Health and Safety Executive may, by a certificate in writing, exempt the home forces or the visiting forces from any of the requirements imposed by the Regulations in the interests of national security (Reg. 8).

19 Artificial light at work

The Control of Artificial Optical Radiation at Work Regulations 2010 impose a duty on employers to carry out a specific form of risk assessment where work is carried out which could expose employees to levels of artificial optical radiation (i.e., artificial light) that could create a reasonably foreseeable risk of adverse health effects to the eyes or skin and where those risks have not already been eliminated or controlled (Reg. 3). Where a risk assessment is necessary the Regulations also impose duties to–

(a) eliminate, or where this is not reasonably practicable, to reduce to as low a level as is reasonably practicable the risk of adverse health effects to the eyes or skin of the employee as a result of exposure to artificial optical radiation where this risk has been identified in the risk assessment (Reg. 4(1));

(b) devise an action plan comprising technical and organisational measures to prevent exposure to artificial optical radiation exceeding the exposure limit values where the risk assessment indicates that employees are exposed to levels of artificial optical radiation that exceed the exposure limit values (Reg. 4(3));

(c) take action in the event that the exposure limit values are exceeded despite the implementation of the action plan and measures to eliminate or reduce so far as is reasonably practicable the risk of exposure (Reg. 4(5));

(d) demarcate, limit access to, and provide for appropriate signs in those areas where levels of artificial optical radiation are indicated in the risk assessment as exceeding the exposure limit values (Reg. 4 (6) and (7);

(e) provide information and training if the risk assessment indicates that employees could be exposed to artificial optical radiation which could cause adverse health effects to the eyes or skin of the employee (Reg. 5); and

(f) provide health surveillance and medical examinations in certain cases (Reg. 6).

20 Electricity at work

The Electricity at Work Regulations 1989 impose (in Part II) general health and safety requirements with respect to electricity at work upon employers, self-employed persons, and employees. Part III of the Regulations imposes specific requirements upon the managers of mines and quarries which are not covered here.

Broadly speaking, the Regulations impose a duty upon every employer and self-employed person to comply with the provisions of the Regulations in so far as they relate to matters which are within his control; and impose upon every employee the duty to co-operate with his employer so far as is necessary to enable any duty placed on that employer by the provisions of the Regulations to be complied with, and to comply with the provisions of the Regulations in so far as they relate to matters which are within his control.

In particular, Part II provides *inter alia* that all systems must at all times be of such construction and be maintained as to prevent, so far as practicable, danger; no electrical equipment be put into use where its strength and capability may be exceeded in such a way as may give rise to danger; electrical equipment which may reasonably foreseeably be exposed to mechanical damage, the effects of the weather, natural hazards, temperature or pressure, or wet, dirty, dusty or corrosive conditions, or any flammable or explosive substance, including dusts, vapours, or gases, be of such construction or as necessary protected as to prevent, so far as is reasonably practicable, danger arising from such exposure; precautions be taken either by earthing or by suitable means, to prevent danger arising when any conductor (other than a circuit conductor) which may reasonably foreseeably become charged as a result of either the use of a system, or fault in a system, becomes so charged; adequate precautions be taken to prevent electrical equipment, which has been made dead in order to prevent danger while work is carried out on or near that equipment, from becoming electrically charged during that work if danger may thereby arise; no person be engaged in any work activity on or so near any live conductor (other than one suitably covered with insulating material so as to prevent danger) that danger may arise unless it is unreasonable in all the circumstances for it to be dead, and it is reasonable in all the circumstances for him to be at work on or near it while it is live, and suitable precautions (including where necessary the provision of suitable protective equipment) are taken to prevent injury; for the purposes of enabling injury to be prevented, adequate working space, means of access, and lighting be provided at all electrical equipment in which or near which work is being done in circumstances which may give rise to danger; and any person engaged in any work activity where technical knowledge or experience is necessary to prevent danger, be competent to prevent such danger.

The Health and Safety Executive may, by a certificate in writing, exempt *inter alia* any person, system, or process, or class of persons, systems, or processes from the requirements imposed by the Regulations provided that they are satisfied that no person's health, safety, and welfare will thereby be prejudiced (Reg. 30).

21 Fire precautions

Every employer must ensure that he complies with the requirements as to fire safety contained in the Regulatory Reform (Fire Safety) Order 2005 (for England and Wales) and the Fire (Scotland) Act 2005.

22 First-aid

Under the Health and Safety (First-Aid) Regulations 1981, an employer must provide, or ensure that there are provided, adequate and appropriate equipment and facilities and an adequate and appropriate number of suitable persons for rendering first-aid to his employees if they are injured or become ill at work. A person will not be suitable for this purpose unless he has undergone such training and has such qualifications as may be appropriate in the circumstances of that case. In the case of the absence of such a person, in temporary and exceptional circumstances, or where, having regard to the nature and location of the undertaking and the number of its employees, it is adequate and appropriate so to do, the employer must appoint a person to take charge of the first-aid equipment and facilities and of any situation relating to an injured or ill employee who will need help from a doctor or nurse (Reg. 3).

An employer must inform his employees of the first-aid arrangements he has made (Reg. 4).

23 Hazardous substances

The Control of Substances Hazardous to Health Regulations 2002 (generally known as the COSHH Regulations) impose duties on employers to protect their employees, and any other persons who may be affected, from exposure to substances hazardous to health. Employees are also under a duty to protect themselves from such exposure. The Regulations also apply to a self-employed person as if he were both an employer and an employee. The substances covered by the Regulations are listed in Schedules to them, together with prohibitions on the use of prescribed substances in particular processes, monitoring, fumigation and surveillance requirements.

24 Safety helmets: exemption for Sikhs

Turban-wearing Sikhs are exempt from legal requirements to wear a safety helmet in all workplaces, either as workers or visitors, subject to certain exclusions (see below) (Employment Act 1989 s.11, as amended by the Deregulation Act s.6). This does not remove the requirement for an employer to assess the risk to his employees, nor to make available any protective equipment, including head protection, considered to be necessary following the risk assessment. The decision not to wear appropriate head protection in accordance with the exemption is to be made by the turban-wearing Sikh individual. The liability of persons in respect of a Sikh who chooses to benefit from the exemption is limited to the extent that the injury, loss or damage would have been sustained by the Sikh even if he had been wearing a safety helmet in compliance with the requirement (s.11(4)). These provisions exclude turban-wearing Sikhs from relying upon the exemption in circumstances where the Sikh individual is providing, or is training to provide, an urgent response to hazardous occupational situations, such as fire or riots, where the wearing of a safety helmet is considered necessary to protect the Sikh from a risk of injury or the Sikh is a member of, or a person providing support to, Her Majesty's Forces and is taking part in, or is training in how to take part in, a military operation where the wearing of a safety helmet is necessary to protect the Sikh from a risk of injury (s.11(5)).

25 Work at height

The Work at Height Regulations 2005 implement EC Directive Council Directive 89/655/EEC concerning the minimum safety and health requirements for the use of work equipment by workers at work. They—
   (a) impose duties relating to the organising and planning of work at height (Reg. 4);
   (b) require that persons at work be competent, or supervised by competent persons (Reg. 5);
   (c) prescribe steps to be taken to avoid risk from work at height (Reg. 6 and Sch. 1);
   (d) impose duties relating to the selection of work equipment (Reg. 7);
   (e) impose duties in relation to particular work equipment (Reg. 8 and Schs 2 to 6);
   (f) impose special provision for people working at height while engaged in dock operations (Reg. 8A);
   (g) impose duties for the avoidance of risks from fragile surfaces, falling objects and danger areas (Reg. 9 to 11);
   (h) require the inspection of certain work equipment and of places of work at height (Reg. 12 and 13 and Sch 7); and
   (i) impose duties on persons at work (Reg. 14).

26 Information

The Health and Safety Information for Employees Regulations 1989 impose a duty on an employer to furnish his employees with information relating to health, safety, and welfare by means of posters or leaflets approved by the Health and Safety Executive. The employer must, in relation to each of his employees (a) ensure that the approved poster is kept displayed in a readable condition at a place which is reasonably accessible to the employee while he is at work, and in such a position in that place as to be easily seen and read by that employee; (b) give to the employee an approved leaflet, or (c) give to the employee information as to how the information referred to in (a) or (b) may be obtained (Reg. 4). The poster or, where a leaflet or information is provided a written notice accompanying that leaflet or information, must specify the name and address of the enforcing authority (see E: ENFORCEMENT, below) for the premises and the address of the employment medical advisory service for the area in which the premises are situated (Reg. 5).

The Health and Safety Executive may grant exemption certificates to certain persons if *inter alia* having regard to the circumstances of the case it is satisfied that the health, safety, and welfare of the persons who are likely to be affected by the exemption will not be prejudiced in consequence of it (Reg. 6).

The Health and Safety Executive may, by a certificate in writing, exempt the home forces or the visiting forces from any of the requirements imposed by the Regulations in the interests of national security (Reg. 14).

27 Lifts

The Lifts Regulations 1997 implement EC Directive 95/16/EC and apply to lifts which permanently serve buildings or constructions, and to specified safety components for use in such lifts. The Regulations do not, *inter alia*, apply to lifts or components placed on the market and put into service before 1st July 1997. Persons who install lifts or who manufacture or import safety components (the "responsible persons" (as defined)) must comply with certain requirements designed to ensure that all lifts comply with relevant safety standards. In addition, the appropriate conformity assessment procedure must be carried out; a declaration of conformity drawn up; and a CE marking affixed to the product. A lift installer must take steps to ensure the proper operation and safe use of the lift.

28 Lifting equipment

The Lifting Operations and Lifting Equipment Regulations 1998 implement parts of EC Directive 89/655 and apply to equipment for lifting and lowering loads and to any operation concerned with the lifting and lowering of loads. *Inter alia*, employers must ensure that equipment is of adequate strength and stability for each load (Reg. 4); that equipment for lifting persons is such as to prevent a person being crushed, trapped, struck or falling from it (Reg. 5); that equipment is positioned or installed so as to reduce the risk of a person being struck by the equipment or its load (Reg. 6); that machinery is marked to indicate its safe working load (Reg. 7); that lifting operations are properly planned by a competent person and are appropriately supervised (Reg. 8); that equipment is examined after installing, or after assembly on a new site; and that equipment subject to deterioration is thoroughly examined at prescribed intervals (every six months in the case of equipment for lifting persons) and reports made of the examination (Regs. 9 and 10).

29 Management of health and safety

The Management of Health and Safety at Work Regulations 1999 implement EC Directive No. 89/391/EEC, and make additional provision with respect to the health and safety of persons at work generally. The Regulations do not apply to—
   (a) the normal ship-board activities (i.e., the construction, reconstruction or conversion of a ship outside, but not inside, Great Britain; and the repair of a ship except when in dry dock) of a ship's crew; and
   (b) Regulations 3(4), (5), 10(2) and 19 do not apply to occasional or short-term work involving work regarded as not being harmful, damaging or dangerous to young people in a family undertaking.

The Regulations *inter alia* impose the following obligations on employers (and self-employed persons who fall within s.3(2) of the 1974 Act: see **8 Duties of employers and the self-employed to persons other than employees**, above).

Risk assessment.–Every employer and relevant self-employed person is required to make an assessment of the health and safety risks to which his undertaking gives rise, for the purpose of identifying the measures he needs to take to comply with his obligations under the health and safety legislation (Reg. 3(1) and (2)).

An employer who employs, or is to employ, a young person must take particular account of certain specified matters when making or reviewing a risk assessment, namely (Reg. 3(5))–

(i) the inexperience, lack of awareness of risks and immaturity of young persons;
(ii) the fitting-out and layout of the workplace and the workstation;
(iii) the nature, degree and duration of exposure to physical, biological and chemical agents;
(iv) the form, range and use of work equipment and the way in which it is handled;
(v) the organisation of processes and activities;
(vi) the extent of the health and safety training provided or to be provided to young persons;
(vii) the risks from certain specified agents, processes and work (listed in the Annex to Council Directive 94/33/EC on the protection of young people at work, as amended by Directive 2014/27/EU).

Where the employer employs five or more employees, he must record the significant findings of the assessment and any group of his employees identified by it as being especially at risk (Reg. 3(6)).

Health and safety arrangements.–Every employer is also required to give effect to such arrangements as are appropriate (having regard to the nature of his activities and the size of his undertaking) for the effective planning, organisation control, monitoring, and review of the preventive and protective measures. Where the employer has five or more employees he must also record the above-mentioned arrangements (Reg. 5).

Co-operation and co-ordination.–Two or more employers who share a workplace or an employer who shares a workplace with a self-employed person or persons are required to co-operate with those other persons so far as is necessary to enable them to comply with their statutory health and safety obligations and to co-ordinate the measures he takes to comply with his statutory health and safety obligations with those of the other employers and/or self-employed persons concerned. (Reg. 11)

Persons working in host employers' or self-employed persons' undertakings.–Every employer and every self-employed person must ensure that the employer of any employees from an outside undertaking, and any self-employed persons working in their respective undertakings, and any employee from an outside undertaking is provided with specified health and safety instructions and information (Reg. 12).

Temporary workers.–Every employer and every self-employed person must provide temporary workers in his undertaking with health and safety information before they commence their duties (Reg. 15).

Risk assessments for new or expectant mothers.–Regulation 16 provides that, where the persons working in an undertaking include women of child bearing age, a risk assessment by an employer under Regulation 3(1) (see above) must include an assessment of the risk to the health and safety of a new or expectant mother from any processes or working conditions, or physical, biological or chemical agents while at work.

If an individual employee is at risk an employer must, if it is reasonable to do so and is the only way to avoid such risk, alter her working conditions or hours of work, or where this is not reasonable or would not avoid the risk, he must, subject to s.67 of the Employment Rights Act 1996 (see the Note on **Maternity Rights** at para **14 Right to offer alternative work**), suspend her as long as it is necessary to avoid the risk. However the employer need not take any action until the expectant mother or new mother (as the case may be) has informed him in writing that she is pregnant, has given birth within the previous six months, or is breastfeeding (Regs. 16 and 18). In relation to an agency worker, if it is not reasonable to alter the working conditions or hours of work, or if that would not avoid the risk, the hirer must without delay inform the temporary work agency, who must then end the supply of that agency worker to the hirer (Reg. 16A).

Similar provision as to suspension is made by Regulation 17 with respect to a new or expectant mother who works at night, provided that she produces a medical certificate stating that it is necessary for her health or safety that she should not work at night. Where an agency worker produces such a certificate, the hirer must without delay inform the temporary work agency, who must then end the supply of that agency worker to the hirer (Reg. 17A).

Breach of a duty imposed by regulations 16, 16A, 17 or 17A is, so far as it causes damage, actionable by the new or expectant mother (Reg. 22).

Protection of young persons.–Regulation 19 provides that every employer must ensure that young persons (defined by Reg. 2(2) as those under 18) employed by him are protected from any risks to their health or safety which are a consequence of their lack of experience, immaturity or lack of awareness. In particular, a young person must not be employed to do work–

(a) beyond their physical or psychological capacity;
(b) involving harmful exposure to agents which are toxic, carcinogenic, cause heritable genetic damage or harm to the unborn child or which in any other way chronically affect human health;
(c) involving harmful exposure to radiation;

(d) involving the risk of accidents which it can reasonably be assumed cannot be avoided by young persons owing to their insufficient attention to safety or lack of experience or training;

(e) in which there is a risk to health from extreme temperatures, noise or vibration.

This does not prevent the employment of a young person who is over the school leaving age in work which is necessary for his training, is supervised by a competent person, and where any risk is reduced to the lowest level reasonably practicable.

Further requirements.–Every employer is also required to–

(a) ensure that employees are provided with health surveillance appropriate to the risks identified by the risk assessment (Reg. 6);

(b) appoint an adequate number of competent persons (as defined) to assist him to comply with his obligations under the health and safety legislation (Reg. 7);

(c) establish and give effect to procedures to be followed in the event of serious and imminent danger to persons at work in his undertaking and to provide his employees with specified heath and safety information (Regs. 8 and 10);

(d) arrange any necessary contacts with external services as regards first aid, emergency medical care and rescue work (Reg. 9); and

(e) consider his employees' capabilities as regards health and safety when entrusting tasks to them and to ensure that, in specified circumstances, his employees are provided with adequate health and safety training (Reg. 13).

The Regulations also impose two requirements upon employees, namely, to use machinery, equipment, dangerous substances, transport equipment, means of production and safety devices in accordance with any relevant training and instructions, and to inform their employers or any specified fellow employees of dangerous work situations and shortcomings in those employers' health and safety arrangements (Reg. 14).

30 Manual handling

The Manual Handling Operations Regulations 1992 implement EC Directive No. 90/269/EEC, and impose from 1st January 1993, health and safety requirements for the manual handling of loads where there is a risk particularly of back injury to workers. For these purposes manual handling operations means any transporting or supporting of a load (including the lifting, putting down, pushing, pulling, carrying or moving thereof) by hand or by bodily force. Injury does not include injury caused by any toxic or corrosive which (a) has leaked or spilled from a load; (b) is present on the surface of a load but has not leaked or spilled from it; or (c) is a constituent part of a load; and load includes any person and any animal.

The Regulations require every employer and self-employed person–

(a) so far as reasonably practicable, to avoid the need to undertake any manual handling operations at work which involve a risk of injury; or

(b) where it is not reasonably practicable to avoid the need to undertake such operations at work:

    (i) to make a suitable and sufficient assessment of all such manual handling operations to be undertaken, having regard to (a) the tasks (e.g., whether they involve excessive movement of loads or unsatisfactory bodily movement or posture); (b) the loads (e.g., whether they are heavy or bulky or unwieldy); (c) the working environment (e.g., whether there are space constraints preventing good posture or conditions causing ventilation problems or gusts of wind); (d) the individual capability (e.g., whether the job requires unusual strength, height, or requires special information or training for its safe performance); (e) and other factors (whether movement or posture is hindered by personal protective equipment or by clothing),

    (ii) to take appropriate steps to reduce the risk of injury arising out of undertaking any manual handling operations to the lowest level reasonably practicable, and

    (iii) to take appropriate steps to provide any of those who are undertaking any such manual handling operations with general indications and, where it is reasonably practicable to do so, precise information on the weight of each load, and the heaviest side of any load whose centre of gravity is not positioned centrally.

In determining whether there is a risk of injury and the steps to be taken to reduce that risk, regard must be had to the physical suitability of the employee to carry out the operations; his clothing, footwear and other personal effects; his knowledge and training; the results of any health surveillance and of any relevant risk assessment (under the Management of Health and Safety at Work Regulations 1999, see **29 Management of health and safety**, above); and whether the employee is within a group of employees identified by such an assessment as being especially at risk. In addition, the Regulations require every employee to make full and proper use of any system of work provided for his use by his employer in compliance with paragraph (b)(ii) above.

The Health and Safety Executive may, by a certificate in writing, exempt the home forces or the visiting forces from any of the requirements imposed by the Regulations in the interests of national security (Reg. 6).

31 Noise

Under the Control of Noise at Work Regulations 2005 (which implement EC Directive 2003/10), every employer must eliminate at source, or if that is not possible, reduce the risk of damage to the hearing of his employees from exposure to noise to the lowest level reasonably practicable (Reg. 6). The Regulations set out lower and upper "exposure action values" and "exposure limit values" for an employee's daily or weekly personal noise exposure and for peak sound pressure (Reg. 4). If the lower exposure action value is reached, the employer must take specified action to reduce the risk caused by the exposure. If the upper value is reached, further specified action must be taken to reduce the risk. When any of his employees is likely to be exposed to noise at or above the lower exposure action value, an employer is required to ensure that a risk assessment is carried out so as to identify the measures which need to be taken to comply with the duties under the Regulations; risk assessments must be reviewed when there is reason to suspect that the assessment is no longer valid or there has been a significant change in the work to which the assessment relates (Reg. 5).

An employer is required to provide suitable and efficient personal hearing protectors to employees likely to be exposed to certain levels of noise; to ensure that hearing protection zones (as defined) are demarcated and identified and no employee of his enters any such zone without personal hearing protectors (Reg. 7). Employees at risk must be placed under suitable health surveillance (including hearing tests) and if hearing damage occurs, consideration must be given to assigning the employee to other work where there is no noise exposure risk (Reg. 9). An employer must also provide each of his employees who is likely to be exposed to levels of noise above the lower exposure action value with information, instruction, and training on *inter alia* the risk of damage to his hearing and the steps he can take to minimise the risk (Reg. 10). The Regulations (except Reg. 9) also apply to certain self-employed persons (i.e., those who fall within the Health and Safety at Work Act 1974 s.3(2) – see **8 Duties of employers and the self-employed to persons other than employees**, above (Reg. 3(3)).

32 Vibration

Under the Control of Vibration at Work Regulations 2005 (which implement EC Directive 2002/44), every employer must protect employees who may be exposed to risk from vibration at work. The Regulations apply to both hand-arm and whole body vibration. An employer must eliminate at source, or if that is not possible, reduce the risk to his employees from exposure to vibration to the lowest level reasonably practicable (Reg. 6).

The Regulations set out daily "exposure limit values" and "exposure action values" (Reg. 4). Where the "action value" is reached, specified action must be taken to reduce the risk. The "limit value" is the level of daily exposure which must not be exceeded except in specified circumstances.

Where there is a likelihood that employees will be exposed to risk from vibration, an employer must carry out a suitable and sufficient risk assessment (Reg. 5). The assessment must be reviewed when there is reason to suspect that it is no longer valid or there has been a significant change in the work to which it relates. Employees at risk must be placed under suitable health surveillance and if an identifiable disease or adverse health effect due to exposure to vibration occurs, consideration must be given to assigning the employee to other work where there is no exposure risk (Reg. 7). An employer must also provide each of his employees who is likely to be exposed to vibration at or above the exposure action value with information, instruction, and training on *inter alia* safe working practices to minimise exposure to vibration (Reg. 8). The Regulations (except Reg. 7) also apply to certain self-employed persons (i.e., those who fall within the Health and Safety at Work Act 1974 s.3(2) – see **8 Duties of employers and the self-employed to persons other than employees**, above (Reg. 3(5)).

33 Personal protective equipment

The Personal Protective Equipment at Work Regulations 1992 implement EC Directive No. 89/656/EEC, and impose health and safety requirements with respect to the provision for, and use by, persons at work of personal protective equipment. These Regulations apply to all personal protective equipment to which the Regulations apply from 1st January 1993. Personal protective equipment means all equipment which is intended to be worn or held by a person at work and which protects him against one or more risks to his health or safety, and any addition or accessory designed to meet that objective. These Regulations do not apply in relation to personal protective equipment which is ordinary working clothes which do not specifically protect the health and safety of the wearer, an offensive weapon within the meaning of the Prevention of Crime Act 1953 used for self-defence; portable devices for detecting and signalling risks and nuisances; personal protective equipment used for protection while travelling on a road within the meaning of the Road Traffic Act 1988 and the Roads (Scotland) Act 1984; and equipment used during the playing of competitive sports. Nor do these Regulations apply where any of the following Regulations apply and in respect of any risk to a person's health or safety for which any of them require the provision or use of personal protective equipment, namely, the Noise at Work Regulations 1989, the Construction (Head Protection) Regulations 1989 (see above), the Control of Lead Work Regulations 2002, the Ionising Radiations Regulations 1999, the Control of Asbestos at Work Regulations 2002, and the Control of Substances Hazardous to Health Regulations 2002.

The Regulations require employers to ensure suitable personal protective equipment is provided for their employees and also require self-employed persons to ensure suitable personal protective equipment is provided for themselves. Personal protective equipment is suitable if–

(a) it is appropriate for the risks involved, the conditions at the place where exposure to the risk may occur, and the period for which it is worn;

(b) it takes account of ergonomic requirements and the state of health of the person or persons who may wear it and of the characteristics of their workstations;

215

(c) it is capable of fitting the wearer correctly, if necessary, after adjustments within the range for which it is designed;

(d) so far as is practicable, it is effective to prevent or adequately control the risk or risks involved without increasing overall risk;

(e) it complies with any enactment which implements in Great Britain any provision on design or manufacture with respect to health or safety in any relevant Community Directive listed in Schedule 1 to the Regulations which is applicable to that item of personal protective equipment (Reg. 4).

Where necessary to ensure that equipment is hygienic and otherwise free of risk to health, personal protective equipment must be provided for the sole use of the person using it.

The Regulations also require every employer and self-employed person—

(a) to ensure that where the presence of more than one risk to health or safety makes it necessary for his employee to wear or use simultaneously more than one item of personal protective equipment, such equipment is compatible and continues to be effective against the risk or risks in question;

(b) to assess any such personal protective equipment as mentioned above, so as to determine whether the equipment intended to be provided will be suitable and compatible with other equipment which may need to be worn simultaneously;

(c) to maintain (including replace or clean as appropriate) any personal protective equipment provided in an efficient state, in efficient working order, and in good repair; and

(d) to ensure that appropriate accommodation is provided for personal protective equipment when it is not being used (Regs. 5 to 8).

Regulation 9 requires the employer to ensure that an employee is provided with such information, instruction and training as is adequate and appropriate to enable him to know the risks which the equipment will avoid or limit, the purpose for which and the manner in which the equipment is to be used, and any action to be taken to ensure that the equipment remains in an efficient state, and must ensure that such information is kept available to employees. Where appropriate, and at suitable intervals, demonstrations in the wearing of personal protective equipment must be organised. Regulation 10(1) requires every employer to take all reasonable steps to ensure that any equipment provided to his employees is properly used.

Regulation 10(2) to (4) also requires every employee and self-employed person to make full and proper use of any personal protective equipment provided and to take all reasonable steps to ensure that it is returned to the accommodation provided for it after use.

Every employee who has been provided with personal protective equipment is placed under a duty to report any loss of or obvious defect in that equipment (Reg. 11).

The Health and Safety Executive may, by a certificate in writing, exempt the home forces or the visiting forces from any of the requirements imposed by the Regulations in the interests of national security (Reg. 12).

34 Reporting of injuries, diseases and dangerous occurrences

The Reporting of Injuries, Diseases and Dangerous Occurrences Regulations 2013 impose duties on those responsible for the activities of persons at work, including self-employed persons, to notify the enforcing authority under the Health and Safety at Work Act 1974 immediately when the following events arising out of or in connection with work occur i.e., where—

(a) there is an accident (including an act of violence against a person) involving workers which gives rise to certain specified injuries (Reg. 4);

(b) there is an accident after which non-workers are taken to a hospital (Reg. 5);

(c) there is an accident resulting in a fatality (Reg. 6);

(d) there is a dangerous occurrence (see below);

(e) a person who undertakes a specific kind of work, contracts a specified disease (Regs. 8-10)

The specified injuries for the purposes of (a) above include—

− fractures, other than to fingers, thumbs or toes;

− amputations;

− partial or total loss of sight;

− crush injuries to the head or torso causing damage to the brain or internal organs in the chest or abdomen;

− burns (including scalding) which cover more than 10% of the body's total surface area or which cause significant damage to the eyes, respiratory system or other vital organs;

− any degree of scalping requiring hospital treatment;

− loss of consciousness caused by head injury or asphyxia; or

− any other injury arising from working in an enclosed space which leads to hypothermia or heat-induced illness or which requires resuscitation or admittance to hospital for more than 24 hours.

The occupational diseases which must be reported are (Reg. 8) −

− Carpal Tunnel Syndrome, where the person's work involves regular use of percussive or vibrating tools;

− cramp in the hand or forearm, where the person's work involves prolonged periods of repetitive movement of the fingers, hand or arm;

− occupational dermatitis, where the person's work involves significant or regular exposure to a known skin sensitizer or irritant;

− Hand Arm Vibration Syndrome, where the person's work involves regular use of percussive or vibrating tools, or the holding of materials which are subject to percussive processes, or processes causing vibration;

- occupational asthma, where the person's work involves significant or regular exposure to a known respiratory sensitizer; and
- tendonitis or tenosynovitis in the hand or forearm, where the person's work is physically demanding and involves frequent, repetitive movements.

Dangerous occurrences (specified in Schedule 2) include structural collapses, fires and explosions, release of flammable liquids and gases, escapes of hazardous substances, and other specific occurrences in relations to mines, quarries and transport systems.

Notification of an injury, fatality or dangerous occurrence must be by the quickest practicable means, and must be followed by a report on an approved form within ten days (Sch. 1).

Where a person at work is incapacitated for routine work for more than seven consecutive days (excluding the day of the accident), the responsible person must as soon as practicable and, in any event, within 15 days of the accident send a report to the relevant enforcing authority (Reg. 4(2)).

Where an employee who suffered a reportable injury at work subsequently dies within one year of the date of the accident, the employer must inform the enforcing authority of the death without delay, whether or not the accident was reported under Regulation 4 (Reg. 6).

The above reporting requirements do not, however, apply to the reporting of events covered by certain other legislation, e.g., the Nuclear Installations Act 1965 or the Ionising Radiations Regulations 1999 (Reg. 14).

Reports can be made online at:
<www.hse.gov.uk/riddor/report.htm>.

35 Safety signs, warning signs and signals

The Health and Safety (Safety Signs and Signals) Regulations 1996 implement EC Directive No. 92/58/EEC and impose requirements in relation to the provision of safety signs and signals. The Directive has been updated by Directive 2014/27/EU in order to align it to Regulation (EC) No 1272/2008 on the classification, labelling and packaging of substances and mixtures.

Safety signs must be provided where the risk assessment made under Regulation 3 of the Management of Health and Safety at Work Regulations 1999 (see **29 Management of health and safety**, above) indicates that the risks cannot be avoided in other ways. Fire safety signs must also be provided where they are required to comply with the provision of any enactment (Reg. 4). The signs to be used are set out in Schedule 1 to the Regulations.

In certain circumstances, hand signals must be used to guide persons carrying out manoeuvres which create a risk to the health or safety of persons at work. Schedule 1 specifies the signals to be used.

Areas, rooms or enclosures used for the storage of significant quantities of hazardous substances or mixtures must be indicated by a suitable warning sign taken from Schedule 1 to the Regulations, or marked as provided in that Schedule, unless the labelling of individual packages or containers is adequate for this purpose. If there is no equivalent warning sign to warn about hazardous chemical substances or mixtures, the relevant hazard pictogram, as laid down in Annex V to Regulation (EC) No. 1272/2008 on the classification, labelling and packaging of substances and mixtures, must be used (Sch. 1, Pt. 1 para. 12). Containers used at work for chemical substances or mixtures classified as hazardous according to the criteria for any physical or health hazard class in accordance with Regulation (EC) 1272/2008, and containers used for storage of such hazardous substances or mixtures, together with the visible pipes containing or transporting such hazardous substances or mixtures, must be labelled with the relevant hazard pictograms in accordance with that Regulation (Sch. 1, Pt. 3, para. 1). This does not apply to containers used at work for brief periods nor to containers whose contents change frequently, provided that alternative adequate measures are taken, in particular for information and/or training which guarantee the same level of protection.

Employers are required to ensure that employees receive suitable and sufficient instruction and training in the meaning of safety signs and the measures to be taken in connection with such signs (Reg. 5).

36 Work equipment

The Provision and Use of Work Equipment Regulations 1998 implement EC Directive 89/655/EEC, and impose requirements upon employers in respect of work equipment provided for or used by their employees at work, upon self-employed persons, persons having control of equipment or of persons using equipment, and persons who have control of the way in which work equipment is used. "Work equipment" means any machinery, appliance, apparatus, tool, or installation for use at work (whether exclusively or not). "Use" in relation to work equipment means any activity involving work equipment and includes starting, stopping, programming, setting, transporting, repairing, modifying, maintaining, servicing and cleaning.

The Regulations impose requirements in respect of the following matters.

(1) *General Duties (Regs. 4 to 10)* Regulations 4 to 10 require every employer to ensure that: work equipment is so constructed or adapted as to be suitable for the purpose for which it is used or provided; in selecting work equipment, regard be had to the working conditions and to the risks to the health and safety of persons which exist on the premises or undertaking in which that work equipment is to be used and any risk posed by the use of that work equipment, and work equipment is used only for operations for which, and under conditions for which, it is

suitable (Reg. 4); work equipment is maintained in an efficient state, in efficient working order and in good repair, and where any machinery has a maintenance log, the log is kept up to date (Reg. 5); work equipment is inspected after installation and before use, or after assembly at a new site, and equipment exposed to conditions causing deterioration is inspected at suitable intervals and each time that exceptional circumstances occur which may jeopardise the equipment's safety (Reg. 6); where the use of work equipment is likely to involve a specific risk to health or safety, the use of that work equipment is restricted to those persons given the task of using it, and repairs, modifications, maintenance or servicing of that equipment is restricted to those persons who have been specifically designated to perform operations of that description for which they would have received adequate training (Reg. 7); all persons who use work equipment have available to them adequate health and safety information and where appropriate, written instructions pertaining to the use of the work equipment (which may include the conditions in which and the methods by which the equipment may be used, foreseeable abnormal situations and the action to be taken if such a situation were to occur, and any conclusions to be drawn from experience in using the equipment), and all such information be readily comprehensible to those concerned (Reg. 8); all persons who use work equipment or who supervise or manage the use of work equipment have received adequate training for purposes of health and safety, including training in the methods which may be adopted when using the equipment, any risks which such use may entail and precautions to be taken (Reg. 9); and any item of work equipment provided for use in the premises or undertaking of the employer complies with the essential requirements of any enactment which implements in Great Britain any of the relevant Community Directives listed in Schedule 1 to the Regulations which is applicable to that item of work equipment (Reg. 10).

(2) *Specific Duties (Regs. 11 to 24)* Regulations 11 to 24 require every employer to ensure that: measures are taken which are effective to prevent access to any dangerous part of machinery or to any rotating stock-bar, or to stop the movement of any dangerous part of machinery or rotating stock-bar before any part of a person enters a danger zone. These measures include the provision of such information, instruction, training and supervision as is necessary and (a) the provision of fixed guards enclosing every dangerous part or rotating stock-bar where and to the extent that it is practicable to do so, but where or to the extent that it is not, then (b) the provision of other guards or protection devices where and to the extent that it is practicable to do so, but where or to the extent that it is not, then (c) the provision of jigs, holders, push-sticks or similar protection appliances used in conjunction with the machinery where and to the extent that it is practicable to do so (Reg. 11); measures are taken to ensure that the exposure of a person using work equipment to any risk to his health from any specified hazard (i.e., any article or substance falling or being ejected from work equipment, rupture or disintegration of parts of work equipment, work equipment catching fire or overheating, and an unintended or premature discharge of any article or of any gas, dust, liquid, vapour or other substance, or an unintended explosion) is either prevented or, where that is not reasonably practicable, adequately controlled. The measures to be taken include providing measures to minimise the effects of the hazard as well as to reduce the likelihood of the hazard occurring. Personal protective equipment may be appropriate where a risk remains that cannot otherwise be eliminated. This provision does not apply where any of the following Regulations require measures to be taken to prevent or control such a risk, namely, the Noise at Work Regulations 1989, the Construction (Head Protection) Regulations 1989 (see above), and the Control of Lead at Work Regulations 2002, the Ionising Radiations Regulations 1999, the Control of Asbestos at Work Regulations 2002, and the Control of Substances Hazardous to Health Regulations 2002 (Reg. 12); work equipment, parts of work equipment and any article or substance produced, stored or used in work equipment which, in each case is at a high or very low temperature has protection where appropriate so as to prevent injury to any person by burn, scald, or sear (Reg. 13); where appropriate, there are controls for starting or making a significant change in operating conditions, the equipment is provided with one or more accessible controls, and the equipment is provided with one or more accessible emergency stop controls, unless it is not necessary by reason of the nature of the hazards and the time taken to come to a complete stop (Regs. 14 to 16); the controls be clearly visible and identifiable, including by appropriate marking where necessary; except where necessary, controls must not be placed where any person using them might be exposed to risk; that where appropriate, so far as reasonably practicable, the operator of the equipment is able to see from the control position that no-one is at risk from the result of the operation of that control; systems of work are effective to ensure that, when equipment is about to start, no person is in a place where he would be exposed to risk as a result of the equipment starting, but where neither of these is practicable, that an audible, visible or other suitable warnings is given whenever the equipment is about to start (Reg. 17(1) to (3)); a person exposed to risk has sufficient time and suitable means to avoid that risk (Reg. 17(4)); so far as reasonably practicable, all control systems of work equipment are safe (i.e., their operation does not create any increased risk to health or safety, they ensure, so far as reasonably practicable, that any fault in or damage to any part of the system or the loss of supply of any source of energy used by the equipment cannot result in additional or increased risk to health or safety, and they do not impede the operation of any stop or emergency stop control) and are chosen making due allowance for the failures, faults and constraints to be expected in the planned circumstances of use (Reg. 18); where appropriate work equipment is provided with suitable means to isolate it from all its sources of energy (Reg. 19); work equipment is stabilised by clamping or otherwise where necessary for purposes of health and safety (Reg. 20); suitable and sufficient lighting, which takes account of the operations to be carried out, is provided at any place where a person uses work equipment (Reg. 21); appropriate measures are taken to ensure that work equipment is so constructed or adapted that, so far as is reasonably practicable, maintenance operations which involve a risk to health or safety can be carried out while the equipment is shut down and, in other cases, that maintenance operations can be carried out without exposing the person carrying them out to a risk to his health, or safety or that appropriate measures can be taken for the protection of any person carrying out maintenance operations which involve a risk to his health or safety (Reg. 22); work equipment is marked in a clearly visible manner with any marking appropriate for reasons of health and safety (Reg. 23); and work equipment incorporates any warnings or warning devices which are appropriate for reasons of health and safety (i.e., they must be unambiguous, easily perceived and easily understood) (Reg. 24).

(3) *Mobile Equipment (Regs. 25 to 30)* Regulations 25 to 30 make provision in relation to mobile work equipment. *Inter alia*, employers must ensure that no employee is carried by mobile equipment unless it is suitable for carrying people and incorporates safety features (Reg. 25); that equipment that might roll over is stabilised and that there is a restraining system to prevent persons from being crushed (Reg. 26); that fork lift trucks are adapted or equipped so as to reduce the risk of overturning (Reg. 27); that self-propelled equipment may not be started by unauthorised persons, have devices for braking and stopping, and have features to prevent a collision with other such equipment (Reg. 28); that remote-controlled self-propelled equipment stops automatically once it leaves its control range (Reg. 29); and that drive shafts are safe (Reg. 30).

37 Workplace

The Workplace (Health, Safety and Welfare) Regulations 1992 implement EC Directive No. 89/654/EEC, and impose requirements with respect to health, safety, and welfare of persons in a workplace upon every employer, any person who has to any extent control of a workplace, and any person who is deemed to be the occupier of a factory for the purposes of s.175(5) of the Factories Act 1961. For these purposes a workplace means any premises or part of premises which are not domestic premises and are made available to any person as a place of work, and includes any place within the premises to which such person has access while at work and any room, lobby, corridor, staircase, road, or other place used as a means of access to or egress from that place of work other than a public road. The requirements cover many aspects of health, safety, and welfare in the workplace and will apply to all places of work except those places of work which relate to means of transport, are construction sites, sites where extraction of mineral resources or exploration for them is carried out, temporary work sites, and workplaces in agricultural or forestry land away from main buildings. As respects the latter two cases the requirements relating to sanitary conveniences, washing facilities, and drinking water (Regs. 20 to 22–see *Facilities* below) will apply but only so far as it is reasonably practicable.

The Regulations impose requirements in respect of the following matters.

(1) *Working Environment (Regs. 5 to 11)* Regulations 5 to 11 require that–
  (a) effective and suitable provision be made to ensure that every enclosed workplace is ventilated by a sufficient quantity of fresh or purified air;
  (b) the temperature in all workplaces inside buildings be reasonable and that a sufficient number of thermometers be provided (see further below);
  (c) every workplace have suitable and sufficient lighting and which must, as far as is reasonably practicable, be by natural light;
  (d) all furniture, furnishings, fittings, surfaces of floors, and walls and ceilings of all workplaces be kept sufficiently clean;
  (e) every room where persons work have sufficient floor area, height, and unoccupied space for purposes of health, safety, and welfare (and no room must be so overcrowded as to cause risk to the health or safety of persons at work in it, and the number of persons employed at any one time must not be such that the amount of cubic space allowed for each is less than 11 cubic metres); and
  (f) every workstation be so arranged that it is suitable both for any person at work in the workplace who is likely to work at that workstation and for any work of the undertaking which is likely to be done there (in the case of outdoor workstations, protection must be provided from adverse weather).

The Workplace (Health, Safety and Welfare) Regulations 1992 Approved Code of Practice suggests a minimum temperature in workrooms of at least 16°C – or 13°C if much of the work indoors involves severe physical effort. These temperatures are not however legal requirements; the employer's essential duty is to determine what reasonable comfort will be in the particular circumstances.

(2) *Safety (Regs. 12 to 19)* Regulations 12 to 19 require that every floor and the surface of every traffic route be of a construction such that the floor or surface is suitable for the purpose for which it is used i.e., the floor or surface must have no hole or slope, or be uneven or slippery so as to expose any person to a risk to his health or safety and every floor must have an effective means of drainage where necessary; so far as reasonably practicable, measures be taken to ensure that persons are protected from falling objects and from falling from a height or into a dangerous substance (any area where there is any such risk must be clearly indicated); every window or other transparent or translucent surface be of safety material and be appropriately marked; no window, skylight, or ventilator which is capable of being opened be likely to be opened, closed, or adjusted in a manner which exposes any person performing such operation to a risk to his health or safety; all windows and skylights in a workplace be of a design or be so constructed that they may be cleaned safely; every workplace must be organised in such a way that pedestrians and vehicles can circulate in a safe manner; doors and gates be

suitably constructed i.e., sliding doors must have a device to prevent them coming off their tracks during use, powered doors must have features to prevent them causing injury by trapping any person, and any doors which are capable of opening by being pushed from either side, be of such a construction as to provide when closed a clear view of the space close to both sides; escalators and moving walkways to function safely, be equipped with any necessary safety devices, and be fitted with one or more emergency stop controls which are easily identifiable and readily accessible.

(3) *Facilities (Regs. 20 to 25A)* Regulations 20 to 25A require that: suitable and sanitary conveniences be provided at readily accessible places i.e., the rooms containing them must be adequately ventilated and lit, kept in a clean and orderly condition, and separate rooms containing conveniences be provided for men and women except where and so far as each convenience is in a separate room the door of which is capable of being secured from inside (in the case of workplaces which are not new workplaces, and to which the Factories Act 1961 applied before these Regulations came into force, there must be at least one suitable water closet for use per every 25 females, and one per every 25 males); suitable and sufficient washing facilities, including showers if required by the nature of the work or for health reasons, be provided at readily accessible places, including a supply of hot and cold, or warm water (running so far as practicable), soap, and towels; an adequate supply of wholesome drinking water be provided for all persons at work in the workplace; suitable and sufficient accommodation be provided for the clothing of any person at work which is not worn during working hours, and for special clothing which is worn by any person at work but which is not taken home. Suitable and sufficient rest facilities must be provided at readily accessible places, with arrangements to protect non-smokers from discomfort caused by tobacco smoke. There must be facilities for pregnant or nursing mothers to rest, and facilities for persons at work to eat meals. Rest rooms and areas must be equipped with adequate numbers of tables and seating with backs for the number of persons likely to use them at any one time. They must also have adequate and suitable seating for the number of disabled persons at work.

Where necessary, those parts of the workplace used or occupied directly by disabled persons must be organised to take account of them (including in particular doors, passageways, stairs, showers, washbasins, toilets and workstation).

The Health and Safety Executive may, by a certificate in writing, exempt the home forces or the visiting forces from any of the requirements imposed by the Regulations in the interests of national security (Reg. 26).

D: THE HEALTH AND SAFETY EXECUTIVE

38 Duties and powers

S.10 of the Health and Safety at Work etc. Act 1974 establishes the Health and Safety Executive, which is responsible to the Secretary of State for administering Part 1 of the Act. The duties of the Executive include duties to undertake research, provide information and advice relating to health and safety matters, develop policies relating to such matters, and submit proposals for new regulations to, and carry out the directions of, the Secretary of State. The Executive is responsible *inter alia* for the enforcement of the statutory requirements (s.18). The Health and Safety Executive may investigate and make a special report on any accident or other occurrence or situation it considers necessary or expedient to investigate for any of the general purposes of Part 1, or may direct others to carry out such an investigation and report. With the consent of the Secretary of State, the Executive may order an inquiry into such matters (s.14).

39 Codes of practice

The Executive may, with the consent of the Secretary of State and after consulting such government departments or other bodies as are appropriate, approve and issue codes of practice containing guidance of safety matters (s.16). S.17 defines the status of such codes in legal proceedings; they do not constitute statutory requirements, but failure to observe the provisions of a code may be used as evidence of a breach of the statutory requirements to which the code is relevant. Codes of Practice have been issued on *inter alia* the Health and Safety (First-Aid) Regulations 1981, the Management of Health and Safety at Work Regulations 1999, Provision and Use of Work Equipment Regulations 1998, and the Workplace (Health, Safety and Welfare) Regulations 1992.

40 Guidance booklets

A number of Guidance Booklets have been prepared by the Health and Safety Executive. Each Booklet is intended to give a general framework. They are not to be regarded as an authoritative interpretation of the law. They can be bought as hard copies, or downloaded for free. A full list can be found at–
<www.hse.gov.uk/pubns/books/index-hsg-ref.htm>.

41 Addresses

The Health and Safety Executive has its head office at Redgrave Court, Merton Road, Bootle, Merseyside, L20

7HS and there are area offices throughout Great Britain. See <www.hse.gov.uk/contact/maps/>.

E: ENFORCEMENT

42 Responsible authorities

It is the duty of the Health and Safety Executive to make adequate arrangements for the enforcement of the relevant statutory provisions except to the extent that some other authority or class of authorities is made so responsible by such provisions or by regulations (Health and Safety at Work etc. Act 1974, s.18). The relevant statutory provisions means Part I of the 1974 Act, any regulations made under Part I, and existing statutory provisions set out in Schedule 1; these include the Mines and Quarries Acts 1954 to 1971 (with limited exceptions), the Agriculture (Safety, Health and Welfare Provisions) Act 1956, the Factories Act 1961 (with one exception not relevant to this Note), and the Offices, Shops and Railway Premises Act 1963.

The Health and Safety (Enforcing Authority) Regulations 1998 provide that where the main activity carried on in non-domestic premises is specified in Schedule 1 to the Regulations, the local authority for the area in which those premises are situated will be the enforcing authority for them (Reg. 3). The activities specified in Schedule 1 are the sale or storage of goods for retail or wholesale distribution (subject to certain exceptions); the display or demonstration of goods for the purposes of offer or advertisement for sale; office activities; catering services; provision of residential accommodation; consumer services provided in shop premises except dry cleaning or radio, television, or motor repairs; cleaning in coin operated units in launderettes and similar premises; certain cosmetic or therapeutic treatments; subject to exceptions, sports, cultural, or recreational activities; the hiring out of pleasure craft for use on inland waters; the care, treatment, accommodation, or exhibition of animals (but not horse breeding or horse training at a stable or an agricultural activity or veterinary surgery); the activities of an undertaker (except where the main activity is embalming or the making of coffins); church worship or religious meetings; car parking facilities at an airport; and the provision of childcare or playgroup or nursery facilities.

The local authorities concerned are, in England, the councils of districts, unitary authorities and London boroughs, the Common Council of the City of London, the Sub-Treasurer of the Inner Temple, the Under-Treasurer of the Middle Temple, and the Council of the Isles of Scilly; in Wales, the councils of a county or county borough; and, in Scotland, the council for each local government area.

The Regulations provide exceptions where the Executive is the enforcing authority for premises occupied by certain specified bodies (Reg. 4) and also provide for arrangements enabling responsibility for enforcement of the statutory provisions described above to be transferred, in particular cases, from a local authority to the Executive or from the Executive to a local authority, and for the assignment of responsibility in cases of uncertainty (Regs. 5 and 6).

43 Inspectors

Every enforcing authority is empowered to appoint inspectors to carry into effect the relevant statutory provisions. S.20 of the Health and Safety at Work etc. Act 1974 sets out the powers of an inspector. *Inter alia* an inspector may at any reasonable time (or, in a situation which is or may be dangerous at any time) enter premises which he has reason to believe it is necessary for him to enter, may examine and investigate, and direct that premises be left undisturbed for so long as is reasonably necessary for the purpose of examination and investigation, may take samples of substances found in any premises he has power to enter, and may require the production of, inspect, and take copies of documents in specified cases.

44 Improvement and prohibition notices

If an inspector considers that a person is contravening one or more of the relevant statutory provisions or has contravened one or more of those provisions in circumstances that make it likely that the contravention will continue or be repeated, he may, under s.21 of the Health and Safety at Work etc. Act 1974, serve on that person an improvement notice requiring him to remedy the contravention or the matters occasioning it within a specified period.

Under s.22, if an inspector considers that activities to or in relation to which any relevant statutory provisions apply which are being carried on or are likely to be carried on, involve, or will involve, a risk of serious personal injury, he may issue a prohibition notice requiring that the action in question must not be carried on unless the matter specified in the notice and any associated contraventions of specified provisions have been remedied. The notice takes effect at the end of the period specified in it or, if the notice so declares, immediately.

S.23 contains provisions supplementary to those of ss.21 and 22. S.24 provides for appeals against improvement or prohibition notices; such an appeal is to be made to an industrial tribunal (see the Note on **Employment Tribunals, ACAS, and the Employment Appeal Tribunal**).

45 Sources of imminent danger

S.25 of the Health and Safety at Work etc. Act 1974 empowers an inspector to render harmless, by destruction or otherwise, an article or substance found by him in any premises which he has power to enter if he believes that it is a source of imminent danger of serious personal injury. Before any article that forms part of a batch of similar articles or any substance is rendered harmless by the inspector, he must, if it is practicable for him to do so, take a sample thereof and give to a responsible person at the premises at which it was found a portion of that sample. He must thereafter give to such a responsible person and to the owner of the article or substance a written report relating to his actions.

In order to facilitate the exercise of the powers or duties of an enforcing authority or inspector, an HM Revenue and Customs officer may seize and detain any imported article or substance for up to two working days (s.25A, as inserted by the Consumer Protection Act 1987, Sch. 3).

46 Obtaining and disclosure of information

The Executive may, with the consent of the Secretary of State, obtain from any person any information needed by the Executive or enforcing authorities in order to carry out their functions (Health and Safety at Work etc. Act 1974, s.27). In order to facilitate the exercise of the powers or duties of an enforcing authority or inspector, the Commissioners of Revenue and Customs may disclose any relevant information to them (s.27A, as inserted by the Consumer Protection Act 1987, Sch. 3). S.28 prohibits the disclosure of such information without the consent of the person furnishing it, except in specified circumstances (e.g., disclosure to Government departments, enforcing authorities, water authorities, and the police).

47 Offences under the Act: criminal proceedings

S.33 and Sch. 3A of the Health and Safety at Work etc. Act 1974 lists offences created under the Act (which include failure to discharge duties under ss.2 to 7, contravention of ss.8 or 9 or of health and safety regulations, and obstruction of inspectors) and the penalties which may be imposed. In most cases, the maximum penalty on summary conviction is an unlimited fine or imprisonment for up to six months. For more serious cases, which are tried on indictment, the maximum punishment is generally imprisonment for up to two years or an unlimited fine, or both.

Provision is made *inter alia* in relation to offences which are due to the fault of a person other than the person primarily liable (s.36) and the circumstances in which directors or other officers of a company or other body may be personally liable (s.37). In any proceedings under the Act, or under the regulations made under it, the onus is on the accused to prove that it was not practicable or reasonably practicable to do more than was in fact done or that there was no better practicable means than the one used to satisfy the statutory requirements (s.40). Under s.42, the court may, in addition to or instead of imposing a penalty, require the convicted person to remedy the cause of the offence.

F: THE ENVIRONMENT AND SAFETY INFORMATION ACT 1988

48 Provisions of the Act

The Environment and Safety Information Act 1988 provides for the keeping of public registers of certain statutory notices concerning health, safety, and environmental protection. It applies *inter alia* to notices under ss.21 and 22 (see **44 Improvement and prohibition notices**, above).

S.1 of the Act requires that the register be adequately indexed so as to enable entries relating to any particular premises (or, where the notice does not relate to any particular premises, to any particular person) to be located; that the register and the index be made available for inspection by the public free of charge at all reasonable hours; and that on request, and upon payment of a reasonable fee, copies of the entries on the register be supplied to any person inspecting it. Each entry in the register must state sufficient particulars to convey the substance of the notice to which it relates.

Entries must be made by the authority concerned on the register within 14 days of service of the notice (where there is a right of appeal against the notice, 14 days from the expiry of the period allowed for appeal or the disposal of the appeal, as the case may be) and must be kept on the register for a period of not less than three years from the date of the service of the notice (s.3).

S.4 makes provision for the protection of trade secrets which would otherwise be liable to be disclosed by such a register.

G: EMPLOYERS' LIABILITY (DEFECTIVE EQUIPMENT) ACT 1969

49 Provisions of the Act

Where an employee suffers personal injury in the course of his employment in consequence of a defect in equipment provided by his employer for the purpose of the employer's business and the defect is attributable wholly or partly to the fault of a third party, the injury is deemed under the Employers' Liability (Defective Equipment) Act 1969 to be attributable to negligence on the part of the employer. Any contracting-out of this provision is prohibited. The Act binds the Crown and applies throughout Great Britain.

50 Authorities

Statutes–

Deregulation and Contracting Out Act 1994

Employer's Liability (Defective Equipment) Act 1969

Environment and Safety Information Act 1988

Health and Safety at Work etc. Act 1974

Health and Safety (Offences) Act 2008

National Health Service (Amendment) Act 1986

Statutory Instruments–

Confined Spaces Regulations 1997, as amended (S.I. 1997 No. 1713 and 1997 No. 2776)

Construction (Design and Management) Regulations 2015 (S.I. 2015 No. 51)

Control of Artificial Optical Radiation at Work Regulations 2010, as amended (S.I. 2010 No. 1140, and 2014 No. 469)

Control of Asbestos in the Air Regulations 1990 (S.I. 1990 No. 556)

Control of Noise at Work Regulations 2005, as amended (S.I. 2005 No. 1643, 2009 No. 693, 2014 No. 469, and 2015 No. 1637)

Control of Substances Hazardous to Health Regulations 2002, as amended (S.I. 2002 No. 2677, 2003 No. 978, 2004 No. 3386, 2006 No. 2739, 2008 No. 960, 2014 No. 469, and 2015 Nos. 21 and 1637)

Control of Vibration at Work Regulations 2005, as amended (S.I. 2005 No. 1093, 2014 No. 469, and 2015 No. 1637)

Electricity at Work Regulations 1989, as amended (S.I. 1989 No. 635, 1996 No. 192, and 1997 No. 1993)

Employers Health and Safety Policy Statement (Exception) Regulations 1975 (S.I. 1975 No. 1584)

Health and Safety at Work etc. Act 1974 (Application outside Great Britain) Order 2013 (S.I. 2013 No. 240)

Health and Safety at Work etc. Act 1974 (General Duties of Self-Employed Persons) (Prescribed Undertakings) Regulations 2015 (S.I. 2015 No. 1583)

Health and Safety (Consultation with Employees) Regulations 1996, as amended (S.I. 1996 No. 1513, 1997 No. 1840, 1999 No. 3242, 2005 No. 1541, S.S.I. 2006 No. 457, S.I. 2013 No. 1471, and 2014 No. 431)

Health and Safety (Display Screen Equipment) Regulations 1992, as amended (S.I. 1992 No. 2792 and 2002 No. 2174)

Health and Safety (Enforcing Authority) Regulations 1998, as amended (S.I. 1998 No. 494, 2005 Nos. 1541 and 2929, S.S.I. 2006 Nos. 457 and 2739, S.I. 2007 No. 320, 2008 No. 960, 2009 No. 693, 2011 No. 3058, 2013 No. 602, 2014 Nos. 469 and 1638, and 2015 No. 21)

Health and Safety (First-Aid) Regulations 1981, as amended (S.I. 1981 No. 917, 1989 No. 1671, 1997 No. 2776, 1999 No. 3242, 2002 No. 2174, 2013 No. 1512, and 2015 No. 1637)

Health and Safety Information for Employees Regulations 1989, as amended (S.I. 1989 No. 682, 1995 No. 2923, and 2009 No. 606)

Health and Safety (Leasing Arrangements) Regulations 1992 (S.I. 1992 No. 1524)

Health and Safety (Safety Signs and Signals) Regulations 1996, as amended (S.I. 1996 Nos. 341 and 2092, 1999 No. 3242, 2005 No. 1643, S.S.I. 2006 No. 457, S.I. 2014 No. 469, and 2015 No. 21)

Health and Safety (Training for Employment) Regulations 1990 (S.I. 1990 No. 1380)

Lifting Operations and Lifting Equipment Regulations 1998, as amended (S.I. 1998 No. 2307, 2002 No. 2174, 2013 No. 448, 2015 No. 1637)

Lifts Regulations 1997, as amended (S.I. 1997 No. 831, 2014 No. 469, and 2015 No. 1630)

Management of Health and Safety at Work Regulations 1999, as amended (S.I. 1999 No. 3242, 2003 No. 2457, 2005 No. 1541, S.S.I. 2006 No. 457, S.I. 2013 No. 1667, and 2015 Nos. 21 and 1637)

Manual Handling Operations Regulations 1992, as amended (S.I. 1992 No. 2793, 2002 No. 2174, and 2015 No. 1637)

Personal Protective Equipment at Work Regulations 1992, as amended (S.I. 1992 No. 2966, 1994 Nos. 3017, and 3246, 1999 No. 860, 2002 No. 2174, 2005 No. 1643, 2006 No. 2739, 2013 No. 448, and 2015 Nos. 1630 and 1637)

Provision and Use of Work Equipment Regulations 1998, as amended (S.I. 1998 No. 2306, 2002 No. 2174, 2005 Nos. 735 and 1093, 2006 No. 2739, 2007 No. 320, 2013 No. 448, 2015 No. 1637)

Reporting of Injuries, Diseases and Dangerous Occurrences Regulations 2013, a amended (S.I. 2013 No. 1471, 2014 No. 1638, and 2015 No. 1637)

Safety Representatives and Safety Committees Regulations 1977, as amended (S.I. 1977 No. 500, 1992 No. 2051, 1996 No. 1513, 1997 No. 1840, 1999 Nos. 860 and 3242, 2006 No. 594, and S.S.I. 2006 No. 457, S.I. 2008

No. 960, 2012 No. 199, 2013 No. 1471, and 2014 Nos. 431 and 469)

Work at Height Regulations 2005, as amended (S.I. 2005 No. 735, 2007 Nos. 114, 320, 2013 No. 1512, and 2015 No. 1637)

Workplace (Health, Safety and Welfare) Regulations 1992, as amended (S.I. 1992 No. 3004, 1995 No. 2036, 1996 No. 1592, 2002 No. 2174, 2005 No. 735, 2007 No. 320, and 2013 No. 448)

HOLIDAYS

1 General

The Working Time Regulations 1998 for the first time provided employees with a statutory right to paid annual leave (Reg. 13) by implementing in the UK the provisions of EC Directive 2003/88. The amount of paid leave is four weeks in each leave year (see the Note on **Working Time Restrictions** at para 13 **Annual leave**). The Work and Families Act 2006 gives the Secretary of State a power to confer on workers a prescribed amount of annual leave which is more generous than that provided for by the Directive (s.13).

In general, there is no statutory requirement that an employee should be entitled to take a day off work on days designated as bank holidays or on days recognised as customary public holidays.

Entitlement to holidays and holiday pay in addition to that provided for by the Working Time Regulations or under the 2006 Act is dependent upon—

(a) the terms of employment agreed by the employer and employee including any implied term based on previous practice in that establishment or on the custom in that particular trade or industry;

(b) the terms of any voluntary agreement between the employers' association and the trade union for the trade or industry in question;

(c) any minimum holidays fixed by the Agricultural Wages Board for Scotland (see the Note on **Wages**);

S.1 of the Employment Rights Act 1996 includes a requirement that any terms and conditions relating to holidays (including public holidays) and holiday pay should be included in the written statement which the employer must give to the employee not later than two months after he begins work (see the Note on **Terms of Employment**).

2 Common law and bank holidays

In England and Wales, Christmas Day and Good Friday are common law holidays.

The Banking and Financial Dealings Act 1971 fixes the days which are to be bank holidays in the United Kingdom and provides that, by Royal Proclamation, other days in the special circumstances of any year and additional special days may be appointed as bank holidays. Days regularly fixed as bank holidays by Royal Proclamation are marked * below.

3 England and Wales

* New Year's Day (if this is a Sunday, a substitute day will be announced by the Government, after consultation with interested organisations)
Easter Monday
* The first Monday in May (Early May Bank Holiday)
The last Monday in May (Spring Bank Holiday)
The last Monday in August (Summer Bank Holiday)
26th December, if it is not a Sunday
27th December in a year in which 25th or 26th December is a Sunday

4 Scotland

New Year's Day, (or the 3rd January if the 1st is a Sunday)
2nd January (or the 3rd January if the 2nd is a Sunday)
Good Friday
The first Monday in May (Early May Bank Holiday)
* The last Monday in May (Spring Bank Holiday)
The first Monday in August (Summer Bank Holiday)
St Andrew's Day (30th November), or, if it falls on a weekend, the following Monday
Christmas Day, if it is not a Sunday, or, if it is a Sunday, 26th December
* 26th December, (if this is a Sunday, or if Christmas Day falls on a Sunday, a substitute day will be announced by the Government)

5 Authorities

Banking and Financial Dealings Act 1971

Employment Rights Act 1996

St Andrew's Day Bank Holiday (Scotland) Act 2007

Work and Families Act 2006

Working Time Regulations 1998, as amended (S.I. 1998 No. 1833, 1999 Nos. 3242 and 3372, and 2001 No. 3256)

INSOLVENCY OF EMPLOYERS

1 The legislation

Part XII of the Employment Rights Act 1996 contains provisions relating to the protection of employees in relation to certain payments due to them from their employers or payable by the employers for their benefit. The Insolvency Act 1986 and the Bankruptcy (Scotland) Act 1985 establish the priority of certain debts for repayment on insolvency; these debts include certain payments due to employees.

Unless otherwise stated, references to sections in this Note are to sections of the Act.

A: EMPLOYEES' RIGHTS ON INSOLVENCY OF EMPLOYER

2 Interpretation

For the purposes of Part XII of the Employment Rights Act 1996, in England and Wales, an employer is taken to be insolvent if, but only if–

(a) he has been adjudged bankrupt or has made a composition or arrangement with his creditors;

(b) he has died and his estate falls to be administered in accordance with an order under s.421 of the Insolvency Act 1986;

(c) where the employer is a company, a winding up or administration order is made, a resolution for voluntary winding up is passed with respect to it, a receiver or manager of its undertaking is duly appointed, possession is taken (by or on behalf of the holders of any debentures secured by a floating charge) of any property of the company subject to that charge, or any voluntary arrangement proposed for the purposes of Part I of the 1986 Act is approved under that Part (s.183).

In Scotland, an employer is taken to be insolvent if, but only if–

(1) an award of sequestration is made on his estate or he executes a trust deed for his creditors or enters into a composition contract;

(2) he has died and a judicial factor appointed under s.11A of the Judicial Factors (Scotland) Act 1889 is required to divide his insolvent estate among his creditors; or

(3) where the employer is a company, a winding up order or an administration order is made, a resolution for voluntary winding up is passed with respect to it, a receiver of its undertaking is duly appointed, or a voluntary arrangement proposed for the purposes of Part I of the 1986 Act is approved under that Part (s.183).

There are certain definitions (e.g., of employee and employer) which apply to Part XII and generally throughout the Act. These provisions are dealt with in the Note on **Employment Protection: Introduction**.

3 Exceptions

The provisions of Part XII of the Employment Rights Act 1996 do not apply to share fishermen or merchant seamen (s.199(2) and (4)) or to employment where under his contract of employment the employee ordinarily works outside the territory of the member States of the European Communities and of Iceland and Norway (s.196(7)).

4 Employee's application to Secretary of State

S.182(1) of the Employment Rights Act 1996 provides that where an employer has become insolvent, the employment of the employee has been terminated and, on the appropriate date (see below), the employer owed to his employee any part of a debt to which the section applies, the employee may apply in writing to the Secretary of State for settlement of what is owing to him out of the National Insurance Fund.

S.182 applies to the following–

(a) any arrears of pay in respect of one or more (but not more than eight) weeks (including a guarantee payment, remuneration on suspension on medical grounds or on maternity grounds, any payment for time off under Part VI of the Act (see the Note on **Rights Arising in the Course of Employment**) or s.169 of the Trade Union and Labour Relations (Consolidation) Act 1992 (the 1992 Act) (payment for time off to carry out trade union duties), or remuneration under a protective award under s.189 of the 1992 Act (see the Note on **Redundancy**);

(b) any amount which the employer is liable to pay the employee for the minimum period of notice required under s.86 of the Act (see the Note on **Terms of Employment**), or for failure to give such notice;

(c) any holiday pay–

(i) in respect of a period or periods of holiday not exceeding six weeks in all, and

(ii) to which the employee became entitled during the 12 months ending with the relevant date;

(d) any basic award of compensation for unfair dismissal within the meaning of s.118 (see the Note on **Unfair Dismissal**);

(e) any reasonable sum by way of reimbursement of any fee or premium paid by an apprentice or articled clerk.

The appropriate date for these purposes means–

(1) in relation to arrears of pay and to holiday pay, the date on which the employer became insolvent;

(2) in relation to a protective award under s.189 of the Trade Union and Labour Relations (Consolidation) Act 1992 and a basic award of compensation for unfair dismissal, whichever is the latest of (i) the date on which the employer became insolvent, (ii) the date of termination of employment, and (iii) the date on which the award was made;

(3) in relation to any other debt, whichever is the later of the date on which the employer became insolvent and the date of termination of employment (s.185).

The amount which may be paid by the Secretary of State is limited, where the amount of that debt is referable to a period of time, to a sum calculated at a maximum rate of £479 a week (s.186).

Where a relevant officer (e.g., a trustee in bankruptcy or a receiver) has been appointed in connection with the employer's insolvency, the Secretary of State must not make any payment until he has received a statement from the relevant officer of the amount of the debt owed, unless he is satisfied that he does not need a statement in order to determine the amount owed to the employee (s.187).

A person who has applied for a payment under s.182 may, within three months of the date on which the Secretary of State's decision was communicated to him (or, if that is not reasonably practicable, within such further period as is reasonable), present a complaint to an employment tribunal that the Secretary of State has failed to make a payment or has paid less than should have been paid. The tribunal may then decide the amount of any payment which it finds the Secretary of State ought to make (s.188).

5 Unpaid contributions to occupational pension schemes

If, on an application made to him in writing by the persons competent to act in respect of an occupational pension scheme, the Secretary of State is satisfied that an employer has become insolvent and when he did so there remained unpaid relevant contributions (see below) falling to be paid by him to the scheme, then, subject to certain conditions, the Secretary of State will pay into the fund the sum which, in his opinion, is payable (Pension Schemes Act 1993 (the 1993 Act) s.124(1)). The Secretary of State, before making such a payment, must have received a statement from the relevant officer (e.g., a trustee in bankruptcy, a liquidator or a receiver) of the amount remaining unpaid (1993 Act s.125(2) and (3)), although the Secretary of State may dispense with this requirement if he is satisfied that no such statement is necessary (1993 Act, s.125(5)).

Relevant contributions are those contributions which an employer is to pay to an occupational pension scheme either on his own account or on behalf of an employee and a contribution is not to be treated as falling to be paid on behalf of an employee unless an equal sum has been deducted from the employee's pay by way of a contribution (1993 Act, s.124(2)). The sum payable in respect of an employer's unpaid contributions on his own account is the least of—

(a) the balance of contributions remaining unpaid on insolvency in respect of the 12 months immediately preceding that date;

(b) the amount certified by an actuary to be necessary to meet the scheme's liability to the employees on dissolution;

(c) an amount equal to 10% of the total amount of remuneration paid or payable to the employees for the 12 months immediately preceding the insolvency (remuneration includes holiday pay, statutory sick pay, statutory maternity pay, and guarantee payments) (1993 Act s.124(3) and (4)).

Where the scheme in question is a money purchase scheme, the sum payable in respect of the employer's unpaid contributions is the lesser of the amounts mentioned in (a) and (c) above (1993 Act s.124(3A) as inserted by the Pensions Act 1995, s.90).

Any sum payable under the 1993 Act s.124 in respect of unpaid contributions on behalf of an employee must not exceed amounts deducted from his pay in respect of his contributions to the scheme during the 12 months immediately preceding the employer's insolvency (1993 Act s.124(5)).

Persons who are competent to act in respect of an occupational pension scheme and who have applied under s.124 to the Secretary of State for a payment, may complain to an employment tribunal that he has not made such a payment or that any payment made is less than the required amount. Such a complaint must be made within three months of the Secretary of State's decision, or within a further reasonable period. If the tribunal finds that the Secretary of State should have made a payment it must declare both that fact and the amount which it finds should be paid (1993 Act s.126).

6 Transfer to Secretary of State of rights and remedies

Where the Secretary of State makes any payment to an employee in pursuance of s.182 of the Employment Rights Act 1996, the employee's rights and remedies in respect thereof are transferred to the Secretary of State (including any right to be paid in priority to other creditors of the employer) together with an entitlement to be paid in priority to any other unsatisfied claim of the employee and the benefit of any decision of an employment tribunal requiring an employer to pay that debt to the employee (s.189).

7 Power of the Secretary of State to obtain information

The Secretary of State may, by written notice require an employer to provide information and require any person having custody or control of relevant records to produce them for the purpose of determining whether an application under s.182 is well-founded (Employment Rights Act 1996, s.190).

B: PREFERENTIAL DEBTS ON INSOLVENCY

8 Priority of certain debts due to employee

S.386 of, and Schedule 6 to, the Insolvency Act 1986 and s.51 of, and Schedule 3 to, the Insolvency Act 1985 specify the categories of debts which have preference in the distribution of the estate of an individual who is insolvent or on the winding up of a company. The last category so specified (category 5) is "Remuneration of employees" and debts within this category have preference over the debts of ordinary creditors. A summary of the provisions of the 1985 and 1986 Acts is contained in the Note on **Bankruptcy**.

The following *inter alia* qualify as preferred debts within category 5–
   (1) so much of any amount which is owed by the debtor to a person who is or has been an employee of the debtor and is payable by way of remuneration in respect of the whole or any part of the period of four months next before the relevant date (as defined by s.387 of the 1986 Act and para. 7 of Sch. 3 to the 1985 Act) as does not exceed the sum of £800;
   (2) any amount owed by way of accrued holiday remuneration, in respect of any period of employment before the relevant date, to any person whose employment by the debtor has been terminated whether before, on, or after that date; and
   (3) so much of any amount ordered (whether before or after the relevant date) to be paid by the debtor under the Reserve Forces (Safeguard of Employment Act) 1985 in respect of the debtor's default (before the relevant date) in the discharging of his duty under that Act as does not exceed the sum of £800.

The figures in paragraphs (1) and (3) are prescribed by the Insolvency Proceedings (Monetary Limits) Order 1986 and the Bankruptcy (Scotland) Regulations 2008, Reg. 10.

9 Interpretation

A sum is payable by a debtor by way of remuneration in respect of a period if–
   (a) it is paid by way of wages or salary in respect of services rendered to the debtor in that period;
   (b) it is paid by way of wages or salary in respect of holiday or of absence from work through sickness or other good cause in that period;
   (c) it is a guarantee payment under s.28 of the Act (employee without work to do–see the Note on **Rights Arising in the Course of Employment**);
   (d) it is remuneration on suspension on medical grounds under s.64 of the Act (see the Note on **Rights Arising in the Course of Employment**);
   (e) it is any payment for time off under s.53 or s.56 (see the Note on **Rights Arising in the Course of Employment: Time Off**) or s.169 of the 1992 Act;
   (f) it is remuneration under a protective award made by an employment tribunal under s.189 of the 1992 Act (redundancy dismissal with compensation–see the Note on **Redundancy**).

Where a person's employment is terminated by or in consequence of his employer's liquidation or bankruptcy or by or in consequence of a specified event (e.g., the appointment of a receiver), the employee is entitled to the holiday pay which has accrued in respect of the period of his employment even if he has not completed the period of employment which would qualify him to take a holiday under his contract of employment.

10 Authorities

Statutes–

Bankruptcy (Scotland) Act 1985

Employment Rights Act 1996

Insolvency Acts 1985 and 1986

Pensions Act 1995

Pension Schemes Act 1993

Trade Union and Labour Relations (Consolidation) Act 1992

Statutory Instruments–

Bankruptcy (Scotland) Regulations 2008, as amended (S.S.I. 2008 Nos. 82 and 334 and 2010 No. 367)

Insolvency Proceedings (Monetary Limits) Order 1986, as amended (S.I. 1986 No. 1996, 2004 No. 547, 2009 No. 465 and 2015 No. 26)

MATERNITY RIGHTS

A: PRELIMINARY

1 Introduction

Part VIII of the Employment Rights Act 1996, as substituted by Schedule 4 to the Employment Relations Act 1999, provides for a general right of maternity leave for an employee who is pregnant or has given birth to a child, irrespective of the length of time she has been employed by her employer. The provisions implement requirements of the Pregnant Workers' Directive (Council Directive 92/85/EEC). Part VIII has been supplemented by Part II of the Maternity and Parental Leave etc. Regulations 1999.

The basic provisions are that—
(a) an employee is entitled to 26 weeks "ordinary" maternity leave;
(b) in addition, those employees who have been continuously employed by their employer for at least 26 weeks are entitled to "additional" maternity leave following on from their ordinary leave giving them a total leave period of 52 weeks;
(c) the Act and Regulations protect employees who are dismissed or subjected to detriment because they are pregnant, have given birth, or have taken advantage of their right to take maternity leave;
(d) Part VII of the Act confers on employees who have been suspended from work on maternity grounds the right to be offered any alternative available work and the right to be paid during a period of suspension.

These provisions are dealt with in detail in the following paragraphs.

Certain definitions and provisions (e.g., the method of calculating a period of continuous employment) which apply to Part VIII and throughout the Act are to be found in the Note on **Employment Protection Introduction**. In addition, the term "childbirth", when used in Part VIII, means the birth of a living child or a stillbirth occurring after 24 weeks of pregnancy. The "expected week of childbirth" means the week, beginning with midnight between Saturday and Sunday, in which it is expected that childbirth will occur (s.235).

The Equality Act 2010 brings in to force provisions dealing with pregnancy and maternity equality, whereby, *inter alia*, if the terms of a woman's work do not include a maternity equality clause, they are to be treated as including one (s.73). In particular, the maternity equality clause provisions contained in the 2010 Act deal with the calculation of maternity-related pay: see the Note on **Discrimination at Work and Equality of Terms**.

B: THE RIGHT TO MATERNITY LEAVE

2 Ordinary maternity leave

The general rule is that all pregnant employees, regardless of their length of service with their employer, are entitled to ordinary maternity leave of 26 weeks (Employment Rights Act 1996, s.71 and the Maternity and Parental Leave etc. Regulations 1999, Reg. 7).

To exercise her entitlement to ordinary maternity leave, an employee must, not later than the 15th week before her expected week of childbirth, give notice to her employer of the expected week of childbirth and the date on which she intends to start her leave (Reg. 4). Notice of this last date must be given in writing, if her employer so requests. This date may be changed, provided she notifies the employer at least 28 days before the date varied, or 28 days before the new date, whichever is the earlier, or if that is not reasonably practicable, as soon as is reasonably practicable. An employer may ask for a certificate from a doctor or midwife giving the expected week of birth.

An employee may choose when she wishes to start her maternity leave, but she may not begin it earlier than the beginning of the 11th week before the start of the expected week of birth (Reg. 4(2)(b)).

Maternity leave will, however, start automatically if the woman is absent from work with a pregnancy-related illness at any time in the 4 weeks prior to the expected week of birth or if she actually gives birth before her leave is due to begin (Reg. 6).

S.71 does not confer any right on an employee to be paid during her maternity leave. However, an employee may be entitled to receive statutory maternity pay during her ordinary maternity leave (see the Note on **Statutory Maternity, Paternity, Adoption and Parental Pay, and Maternity Allowance**) and may also be entitled under her contract of employment to receive all or part of her normal pay during her absence.

3 Compulsory maternity leave

An employer must not allow certain employees to work during a "compulsory maternity leave period" (Employment Rights Act 1996, s.72). Regulation 8 of the Maternity and Parental Leave etc. Regulations 1999 provides that, for the purposes of s.72, the compulsory leave period which applies to employees entitled to ordinary maternity leave is a two week period following the date of birth.

It is an offence for an employer to contravene s.72. So far as it causes damage, an employee can also bring a civil claim for any breach (Health and Safety at Work etc. Act 1974 (Civil Liability) (Exceptions) Regulations 2013, Reg. 2).

4 Additional maternity leave

S.73 of the Employment Rights Act 1996 provides that an employee who satisfies prescribed conditions may also take "additional" maternity leave following on immediately after the end of her ordinary maternity leave (Maternity and Parental Leave etc. Regulations 1999, Reg. 6(3)). The additional leave period lasts for a further 26 weeks from the end of the ordinary maternity leave (Reg. 7).

5 Right to return to work, etc

An employee who exercises her right to take either ordinary or additional maternity leave is entitled to the benefit of the terms and conditions of employment (other than those regarding pay) which would have applied to her if she had not been absent. She is also bound by any obligations arising under those terms and conditions (Maternity and Parental Leave etc. Regulations 1999, Reg. 9).

An employee taking ordinary or additional maternity leave is entitled to return from leave to the same job in which she was employed before her absence, or, if it is not reasonably practicable for her employer to permit her to return to that job, to another job which is both suitable and appropriate for her to do in the circumstances. However, this right does not apply if the employee is made redundant during her maternity leave (see **7 Redundancy during maternity**, below). An employee's right to return to her own job, or to another suitable job, is a right to return on terms and conditions as to remuneration no less favourable than would have been applicable to her had she not been absent, and with her seniority, pension rights and similar rights as they would have been had she not been absent, and otherwise on terms and conditions no less favourable than those which would have been applicable to her had she not been absent from work (Regs 18 and 18A).

6 Curtailment of maternity leave

A woman entitled to ordinary or additional maternity leave ("statutory maternity leave") may curtail that leave in order to enable them or their spouse, civil partner or partner to take shared parental leave (as to which, see the Note on **Statutory Maternity, Paternity, Adoption and Parental Pay, and Maternity Allowance**). Similar provisions apply to allow curtailment of statutory adoption leave.

The Maternity and Adoption Leave (Curtailment of Statutory Rights to Leave) Regulations 2014 lay down the procedure which a mother/adopter must follow in order to curtail their statutory leave. This involves a mother/adopter giving her employer notice to end her maternity/adoption leave on a specified date (at least 8 weeks in the future), together with a notice of entitlement to shared parental leave (or a declaration that her partner has given their employer notice of their entitlement to shared parental leave and the mother consents to the leave her partner intends to take).

If the curtailment notice is given before the baby is born, it may be revoked in the six weeks following the birth. Otherwise, a notice can only be revoked if the mother's/adopter's partner dies, or of it is discovered in the 8 weeks following the notice that neither the mother/adopter nor their partner has any entitlement to shared parental leave.

The Curtailment Regulations are modified for an employee who is a parental order parent so as to recognise that the leave relates to the birth of a child born with the help of a surrogate (Paternity, Adoption and Shared Parental Leave (Parental Order Cases) Regulations 2014, S.I. No. 3096).

7 Redundancy during maternity

Regulation 10 of the Maternity and Parental Leave etc. Regulations 1999 applies where, during an employee's ordinary or additional maternity leave, it is not practicable, because of redundancy, for her employer to continue to employ her under her existing employment contract. If there is a suitable available vacancy, the employee is entitled to be offered (before the end of her existing contract) alternative employment with her employer or his successor, or with an associated employer, under a new contract of employment which begins immediately after the end of her old contract. The new employment offered must be both suitable and appropriate for the employee, and its provisions as to the capacity and place in which she is to be employed and as to the other terms and conditions of her employment must not be substantially less favourable to her than if she had continued to be employed under the previous contract. For provisions relating to redundancy generally, see the Note on **Redundancy**.

8 Return to work

An employer who is notified under Regulation 4 (see **2 Ordinary maternity leave**, above) of the start date of an employee's ordinary maternity leave period must, within 28 days, notify her of the date her additional maternity leave period will end (the additional leave follows on from the ordinary leave) (Maternity and Parental Leave etc. Regulations 1999, Reg. 7(6) and (7)).

An employee who intends to return to work early (i.e., before her additional maternity leave is over) must give her employer at least eight weeks' notice of the date on which she intends to return (16 weeks notice in the case of an employee shareholder (as to whom see the Note on **Employment Protection Introduction**, at para **9**

Employee shareholders)). If she attempts to return to work early without giving this notice, her employer is entitled to postpone her return to a date which will mean that he does have eight weeks' notice (but an employer may not postpone an employee's return to a date after the end of her relevant maternity leave period) (Reg. 11). An employee whose return to work has been postponed in this way has no right to be paid until the date to which her return has been postponed.

Note.–If an employer fails to give an employee notice of the date her maternity leave period ends (see Reg. 7(6), above), then Regulation 11 does not apply and he cannot prevent her from returning to work early (Reg. 11(5)).

Note.– An employee may carry out up to 10 days' work for her employer during her statutory maternity leave period (but not during the first two weeks after the birth) without bringing her maternity leave to an end (Reg. 12A).

9 Contractual right to maternity leave

An employee's contract of employment may give her a contractual right to take maternity leave. In a case where an employee has rights under the Act and the Regulations (statutory rights) as well as rights under her contract (contractual rights), she may not exercise both sets of rights separately, but may, in taking leave, take advantage of whichever rights are, in any particular respect, the more favourable. The provisions of the Act and of the Regulations will apply, subject to any necessary modifications, to the exercise of the composite right (i.e., the most favourable rights from the statutory and contractual rights) as they apply to the exercise of the statutory right (Maternity and Parental Leave etc. Regulations 1999, Reg. 21).

10 Protection from detriment

Under s.47C of the Employment Rights Act 1996 (added by the 1999 Act, Schedule 4 Part III) and Regulation 19 of the Maternity and Parental Leave etc. Regulations 1999, an employee has the right not to be subjected to any detriment by any act, or deliberate failure to act, by her employer done because she is pregnant; has given birth; has taken or sought to take either ordinary, compulsory or additional maternity leave; or has availed herself of the benefits of any of the terms and conditions of her employment preserved by s.71 and Regulation 9 (see **2 Ordinary maternity leave**, above) during her maternity leave period. The term "detriment" does not include dismissal (but see **11 Unfair dismissal**, below).

An employee is also protected from being subjected to detriment if she–

(a) fails to return to work after a period of ordinary or additional maternity leave where her employer has failed to notify her of the date her maternity leave period ends (i.e., under Reg. 7, see **8 Return to work,** above) and she reasonably believes that it has not ended, or her employer gives her less than 28 days' notice of the date her maternity leave period ends and it is not reasonably practicable for her to return on that date (Reg. 19(2)(ee)); or

(b) undertook, considered undertaking, or refused to undertake work in accordance with Reg. 12A (see **8 Return to work,** above).

11 Unfair dismissal

An employee who is dismissed is entitled to be regarded for the purposes of Part X of the Act (unfair dismissal–see the Note on **Unfair Dismissal**) as unfairly dismissed if the reason or principal reason for the dismissal is *inter alia* that she (Employment Rights Act 1996, s.99 (as substituted by the 1999 Act, Schedule 4 Part III) and the Maternity and Parental Leave etc. Regulations 1999, Reg. 20)–

(a) is pregnant, or has given birth, or has taken or sought to take, or has availed herself of the benefits of ordinary or additional maternity leave; or

(b) is redundant and Regulation 10 (see **7 Redundancy during maternity**, above) has not been complied with; or

(c) failed to return to work after a period of ordinary or additional maternity leave where her employer had failed to notify her of the date her maternity leave period was to end (i.e., under Reg. 7, see **8 Return to work**, above) and she reasonably believed that it had not ended, or her employer gave her less than 28 days' notice of the date her maternity leave period was to end and it was not reasonably practicable for her to return on that date; or

(d) undertook, considered undertaking, or refused to undertake work in accordance with Reg. 12A (see **8 Return to work**, above).

An employee will also be regarded as unfairly dismissed if the reason for the dismissal is redundancy and the circumstances of the redundancy applied equally to one or more other employees in the undertaking who held positions similar to that held by the employee who have not been dismissed, and it is shown that the reason for selecting the employee was one of the reasons specified in (a) above (Reg. 20(2)).

An employee will not be regarded as unfairly dismissed if it is not reasonably practicable for a reason other than redundancy for the employer to permit her to return to a suitable and appropriate job and she either accepts or unreasonably refuses an offer of such a job from an associated employer (Reg. 20(6) and (7)). The specific small employer exemption has been repealed.

C: RIGHTS ON SUSPENSION FROM WORK ON MATERNITY GROUNDS

12 Introduction

Part VII of the Employment Rights Act 1996 confers two rights on employees who are suspended on maternity grounds. The term "maternity grounds" is to be construed in accordance with s.66 (see **13 Suspension from work on maternity grounds**, below).

13 Suspension from work on maternity grounds

For the purposes of the Employment Rights Act 1996 Part VII, s.66 provides that an employee is suspended on maternity grounds where, in consequence of—

    (a) any requirement imposed by or under any relevant provision of any enactment or of any instrument made under any enactment, or

    (b) any recommendation in any relevant provision of a code of practice issued or approved under s.16 of the Health and Safety at Work etc. Act 1974,

she is suspended from work by her employer on the ground that she is pregnant, has recently given birth or is breastfeeding a child (s.66(1)). The relevant provisions for the respective purposes of (a) and (b) above are Regulations 16(3) and 17 of the Management of Health and Safety at Work Regulations 1999, as amended (see the Note on **Health and Safety at Work General**) (the Suspension from Work (on Maternity Grounds) Order 1994).

For the purposes of Part VII, an employee will be regarded as suspended from work only if, and so long as, she continues to be employed by her employer, but is not provided with work or (disregarding alternative work for the purposes of s.67 (see below)) does not perform the work she normally performed before the suspension (s.66(3)).

14 Right to offer alternative work

Where an employer has available suitable alternative work for an employee, the employee has a right to be offered to be provided with it before being suspended on maternity grounds (Employment Rights Act 1996, s.67(1)).

For such work to be suitable for an employee for the purposes of s.67, (a) the work must be of a kind which is both suitable in relation to her and appropriate for her to do in the circumstances; and (b) the terms and conditions applicable to her for performing the work, if they differ from the corresponding terms and conditions applicable to her for performing the work she normally performs under her contract of employment, must not be substantially less favourable to her than those corresponding terms and conditions (s.67(2)).

An employee may present a complaint to an employment tribunal, within three months beginning with the first day of suspension (or such further period as the tribunal considers reasonable in a case where it is satisfied that it was not reasonably practicable for the complaint to be presented within the three-month period), that her employer has failed to offer to provide her with alternative work in contravention of s.67(1) (see above) (s.70(1) and (2)). Where the tribunal finds the complaint well-founded it may make an award of compensation to be paid by the employer to the employee. The amount of the compensation will be such as the tribunal considers just and equitable in all the circumstances having regard to the infringement of the complainant's right under s.67(1) by the employer's failure complained of and to any loss sustained by the complainant which is attributable to that failure (s.70(6) and (7)).

Where the supply of an agency worker to a hirer is ended on maternity grounds and the temporary work agency has available suitable alternative work, the agency worker has a right to be offered to be proposed for such alternative work (subject to completion of a qualifying period (see the Note on **Part-time, Fixed-term, and Agency Workers**) (s.68B(1), (2)). These provisions will not apply—

    (a) where the agency worker has confirmed in writing that she no longer requires the work-finding services of the temporary work agency, or

    (b) beyond the original intended duration, or likely duration, whichever is the longer, of the assignment which ended when the supply of the agency worker to the hirer was ended on maternity grounds (s.68B(3)).

For the right to present a complaint to an employment tribunal in these circumstances see **15 Right to remuneration**, and **17 Right to remuneration: agency workers**, below.

15 Right to remuneration

For the period of any suspension under s.66, an employee is entitled to be paid remuneration by her employer while she is so suspended. An employee is not entitled to remuneration if her employer offered to provide her with suitable alternative work for the purpose of s.67 (see above) and she unreasonably refused to perform that work (Employment Rights Act 1996, s.68(2)). The amount of remuneration payable will be a week's pay in respect of each week of the period of suspension; and if in any week remuneration is payable in respect of part only of that week, the amount of the week's pay will be reduced proportionately (s.69(1)). Any remuneration payable under s.68(1) (i.e., the statutory remuneration), will not affect any right of an employee in relation to remuneration under her contract of employment (her contractual remuneration) but any contractual remuneration paid by an employer to an employee in respect of any period will go towards discharging the employer's liability under s.68 in respect of that period; and, conversely, any payment of statutory remuneration in discharge of an employer's liability under s.68 in respect of any period will go towards discharging any obligation of the employer to pay contractual remuneration in respect of that period (s.69(2) and (3)). An employee may present a complaint to an employment tribunal that her employer has failed to pay the whole or any part of remuneration to which she is entitled under s.68, in respect of any day, before the end of three months beginning with that day, or within such further period as the tribunal considers reasonable in a case where it is satisfied that it was not reasonably practicable for the complaint to be presented with that period (s.70(1) and (2)). Where a tribunal finds a complaint under s.70 well-founded the tribunal will order the employer to pay the complainant the amount of remuneration which it finds is due to her (s.70(3)).

16 Right to remuneration: agency workers

Where the supply of an agency worker to a hirer is ended on maternity grounds, that agency worker is entitled, subject to completion of a qualifying period (see the Note on **Part-time, Fixed-term, and Agency Workers**), to be paid remuneration by the temporary work agency. However, this entitlement will not arise if–
  (a) the temporary work agency has offered to propose the agency worker to a hirer that has alternative work available which is suitable alternative work, or proposed the agency worker to a hirer that has suitable alternative work available, and that hirer has agreed to the supply of that agency worker, and
  (b) the agency worker has unreasonably refused the offer or to perform that work (s.68C).
The amount of remuneration payable will be a week's pay in respect of each week for which remuneration is payable in accordance with s.68C; and if in any week remuneration is payable in respect of part only of that week, the amount of the week's pay will be reduced proportionally (s.69A(1)). A right to remuneration payable under s.68C (i.e., the statutory remuneration), will not affect any right of the agency worker in relation to remuneration under the contract with the temporary work agency (her contractual remuneration) but any contractual remuneration paid by the temporary work agency to an agency worker in respect of any period will go towards discharging the agency's liability under s.68C in respect of that period; and, conversely, any payment of statutory remuneration in discharge of a temporary work agency's liability under s.68C in respect of any period will go towards discharging any obligation of the agency to pay contractual remuneration in respect of that period (s.69A(2), (3)).

An agency worker may present a complaint to an employment tribunal that the temporary work agency has failed to pay the whole or any part of remuneration to which she is entitled under s.68C, in respect of any day, before the end of three months beginning with the day on which the supply of the agency worker to the hirer was ended on maternity grounds, or within such further period as the tribunal considers reasonable in a case where it is satisfied that it was not reasonably practicable for the complaint to be presented within that period (s.70A(1) and (2)). Where a tribunal finds a complaint under s.70A well-founded the tribunal will order the temporary work agency to pay the complainant the amount of remuneration which it finds is due to her (s.70A(3)).

17 Authorities

Employment Relations Act 1999

Employment Rights Act 1996

Equality Act 2010

Health and Safety at Work etc. Act 1974 (Civil Liability) (Exceptions) Regulations 2013 (S.I. 2013 No. 1667)

Maternity and Adoption Leave (Curtailment of Statutory Rights to Leave) Regulations 2014, as amended (S.I. 2014 Nos. 3052 and 3096, and 2015 No. 552)

Maternity and Parental Leave etc. Regulations 1999, as amended (S.I. 1999 No. 3312, 2001 No. 4010, 2002 No. 2789, 2006 No. 2014, 2008 No. 1966, 2013 Nos. 283, 388, and 591, and 2014 No. 3221)

Suspension from Work (on Maternity Grounds) Order 1994, as amended (S.I. 1994 No. 2930 and 1999 No. 3242)

PART-TIME, FIXED-TERM AND AGENCY WORKERS

A: PART-TIME WORKERS

1 Introduction

The Part-time Workers (Prevention of Less Favourable Treatment) Regulations 2000 are made under s.19 of the Employment Relations Act 1999 and implement Council Directive 97/81/EC (the Part Time Work Directive), as extended by Directive 98/23/EC.

The Regulations are concerned with less favourable treatment of part-time workers in contract terms and conditions. Part-time workers are given the right not to be treated less favourably than full-time workers of the same employer who work under the same type of contract. In addition, workers who change from full-time to part-time work with the same employer are to be treated no less favourably than they were before they became part-time.

2 The basic rights

As a result of the Part-time Workers (Prevention of Less Favourable Treatment) Regulations 2000–

   (a) part-timers must not receive a lower basic rate of pay than comparable full-time workers employed by the same employer;

   (b) part-timers should also receive the same hourly rate of overtime pay as comparable full-timers, once they have worked more than normal full-time hours;

   (c) part-timers must not be treated less favourably than full-timers when it comes to qualifying for sick pay or maternity pay or being allowed access to an occupational pension scheme or training and promotion;

   (d) in the case of contractual entitlement to holidays, maternity and paternity leave, and careers breaks, part-timers should have the same contractual rights, on a pro rata basis, as comparable full -timers;

   (e) when selecting candidates for redundancy, part-timers should not be treated less favourably than full-timers.

In all the above cases, less favourable treatment of part-timers will be allowed if an employer can justify the treatment on objective grounds (e.g., to achieve a business objective).

To claim under the Regulations, part-timers must be able to identify a comparable full-time worker who is receiving more favourable treatment (see **4 Comparable full-time workers**, below).

3 Application of the Regulations

The Part-time Workers (Prevention of Less Favourable Treatment) Regulations 2000 apply to all "workers". This includes not only those who work under a contract of employment, but also individuals who have entered into any other contract, whether oral or written, whereby they undertake to perform personally work or other services for another party to the contract whose status is not that of a client or customer of any profession or business undertaking carried on by the individual (Reg. 1). The Regulations apply to all employers: there is no exemption for small employers.

A part-time worker is defined as a worker who is paid by reference to the time he works and who, having regard to the custom and practice of the employer's workplace, is not identifiable as a full-time worker (Reg. 2).

4 Comparable full-time workers

A "comparable full-time worker" is defined (Part-time Workers (Prevention of Less Favourable Treatment) Regulations 2000, Reg. 2) as a full-time worker employed by the same employer under the same type of contract, who is engaged in the same or broadly similar work having regard, where relevant, to whether they have a similar level of qualifications, skills and experience and who works, or is based, at the same workplace as the part-time worker. Where there is no comparable full-time worker at the same workplace, comparison may be made with workers employed by the same employer at other workplaces, provided that they satisfy the other requirements.

5 Less favourable treatment of part-time workers

A part-time worker has the right not to be treated by his employer less favourably than the employer treats a comparable full-time worker (Part-time Workers (Prevention of Less Favourable Treatment) Regulations 2000, Reg. 5)–

   (a) as regards the terms of his contract; or

   (b) by being subjected to any other detriment by any act, or deliberate failure to act, of his employer.

The right conferred by Regulation 5 only applies if the less favourable treatment is on the ground that the worker is part-time and cannot be justified on objective grounds.

In determining whether a part-time worker has been treated less favourably than a comparable full-time worker, the pro-rata principle should be applied unless it is inappropriate–this being defined (Reg. 1) to mean that where a comparable full-time worker receives pay or any other benefit, a part-time worker should receive or be entitled to receive not less than the proportion of that pay or other benefit that the number of his weekly hours bears to the number of weekly hours of the comparable full-time worker (e.g., if a part-time worker works two days a week and a full-time worker works five days a week, the part-timer should receive two fifths of the full-timers' rate of pay).

A part-time worker paid at a lower rate for overtime worked by him in a period than a full-time worker is or would be paid for overtime in the same period is not, for that reason, to be regarded as treated less favourably than the comparable full-time worker where the total number of hours worked by the part-timer in the period, including the overtime, does not exceed the number of hours the full-timer is required to work in that period, disregarding absences from work and overtime (Reg. 5(4)).

6 Workers becoming part-time

The Part-time Workers (Prevention of Less Favourable Treatment) Regulations 2000 apply to a full-time worker who becomes a part-timer, and to a full-time worker who returns to work part-time (whether to the same job or to a job at the same level) after an absence of less than 12 months (e.g., maternity leave), whether it is a different contract or a varied contract and regardless of whether it is the same type of contract. In these cases, the worker becoming part-time or returning to work part-time after an absence does not have to find a comparable full-time worker but may instead compare their treatment as a part-time worker with the treatment they received under their previous full-time contract (Regs. 3 and 4).

7 Right to receive written statement of reasons for less favourable treatment

If a part-time worker believes that his employer may have treated him less favourably than a comparable full-time worker, he may ask his employer for a written statement, giving reasons for the treatment in question. That statement must be provided by the employer within 21 days of the worker's request and is admissible in evidence at an employment tribunal during any proceedings under the Regulations (Part-time Workers (Prevention of Less Favourable Treatment) Regulations 2000, Reg. 6).

8 Unfair dismissal

An employee who is dismissed will be regarded as unfairly dismissed (see the Note on **Unfair Dismissal**) if the reason, or principal reason, for dismissal is that the employee has, amongst other things (Part-time Workers (Prevention of Less Favourable Treatment) Regulations 2000, Reg. 7)–
  (a) brought tribunal proceedings under the Regulations;
  (b) alleged that the employer has infringed the Regulations;
  (c) requested from his employer a written statement of reasons; or
  (d) refused to forego his rights under the Regulations.
A worker also has the right not to be subjected to any detriment by any act, or deliberate failure to act, on the part of his employer done on one of the above grounds.

9 Complaint to an employment tribunal

A worker may present a complaint to a tribunal that his employer has infringed a right conferred on him by the Part-time Workers (Prevention of Less Favourable Treatment) Regulations 2000, Regulation 5 (see **5 Less favourable treatment of part-time workers**, above) or has subjected him to any detriment under Regulation 7 (see **8 Unfair dismissal**, above). Any such complaint will not normally be considered unless it is presented within three months of the date of the treatment or detriment complained of. In the case of a less favourable contract term, the treatment will be regarded as taking place throughout the period during which the contract term applies.

Where a tribunal decides that a complaint is well-founded, it may–
  (a) make a declaration as to the complainant's rights;
  (b) order the employer to pay compensation; and/or
  (c) recommend that the employer take action to avoid the adverse effect on the complainant of any matter to which the complaint relates.
Any compensation awarded by a tribunal must take into account any loss suffered by the worker, including expenses reasonably incurred by him and the loss of any benefit which he might reasonably be expected to have had but for the infringement. However, compensation awarded for less favourable treatment under Regulation 5 will not include compensation for injury to the worker's feelings.

Failure on the part of the employer to comply with any recommendation made by a tribunal may lead to the tribunal increasing the amount of compensation paid to the worker.

10 Restrictions on contracting out

Regulation 9 of the Part-time Workers (Prevention of Less Favourable Treatment) Regulations 2000 provides that s.203 of the Employment Rights Act 1996 (see the Note on **Employment Protection: Introduction**) applies to the Regulations. The effect of this is that any agreement between an employer and worker that the

Regulations will not apply, or will apply in a modified form, is void and will not therefore prevent a worker from taking action under the Regulations.

B: FIXED-TERM WORKERS

11 Introduction

The Fixed-term Employees (Prevention of Less Favourable Treatment) Regulations 2002 are made under ss.45 and 51 of the Employment Act 2002 and implement Council Directive 99/70/EC (the Fixed-term Work Directive).

The Regulations are concerned with less favourable treatment of fixed-term employees in contract terms and conditions. Fixed-term employees are given the right not to be treated less favourably than permanent employees of the same employer doing similar work. In addition, the regulations also provide that when a fixed-term employee who has been continuously employed on fixed-term contracts for four years or more is re-engaged on a fixed-term contract without his continuity being broken, the new contract will in certain circumstances have effect as a permanent contract.

12 The right not to be treated less favourably

A fixed-term employee has the right not to be treated by his employer less favourably than a comparable permanent employee (Fixed-term Employees (Prevention of Less Favourable Treatment) Regulations 2002, Reg. 3)–
    (a) with regard to the terms of his employment contract, including in particular, terms as to–
        (i) any period of service qualification relating to any particular condition of service;
        (ii) the opportunity to receive training; and
        (iii) the opportunity to secure a permanent position;
   or
    (b) by being subjected to any other detriment by an act, or deliberate failure to act, of his employer.

The right in (a) only applies if the less favourable treatment is on the ground that the employee is a fixed-term employee and the treatment is not justified on objective grounds. A term will be regarded as justified on objective grounds if the terms of the fixed-term employee's contract of employment, taken as a whole, are at least as favourable as the terms of a comparable permanent employee's contract (Reg. 4).

13 The "pro rata principle"

In deciding whether a fixed-term employee has been treated less favourably than a permanent employee, the "pro rata principle" will be applied unless it is inappropriate to do so (Fixed-term Employees (Prevention of Less Favourable Treatment) Regulations 2002, Reg.3(5)). This means that where a comparable permanent employee receives, or is entitled to, pay or any other benefit, a fixed-term employee is entitled to receive, or be entitled to, such proportion of that pay or other benefit as is reasonable in the circumstances, having regard to the length of his contract of employment and to the terms on which the pay or other benefit is offered (Reg. 1(2)).

14 Comparable employees

An employee is a comparable permanent employee in relation to a fixed-term employee if, at the time of the treatment alleged to be less favourable to the fixed-term employee (Fixed-term Employees (Prevention of Less Favourable Treatment) Regulations 2002, Reg. 2)–
    (a) both employees work for the same employer, in the same or broadly similar work, having regard where relevant to whether they have a similar level of qualification and skills; and
    (b) they both work at the same establishment (or where there is no comparable permanent employee at the same establishment as the fixed-term employee, at different establishments, but where (a) is still satisfied).

An employee cannot be a comparable employee if his employment has ceased (Reg.2(2)).

15 Written statement of reasons for less favourable treatment

A fixed-term employee who considers that he has been treated less favourably than a permanent employee can ask his employer for a written statement giving particulars of the reasons for the treatment. Such a statement must be produced within 21 days and is admissible as evidence in tribunal proceedings. If no statement is provided, or the statement is evasive or equivocal, the tribunal may draw any inference which it considers to be just and reasonable (Fixed-term Employees (Prevention of Less Favourable Treatment) Regulations 2002, Reg. 5).

Note.–Reg. 5 does not apply where a fixed-term employee has been dismissed and is entitled to a written statement of reasons for his dismissal under s.92 of the 1996 Act (see the Note on **Termination of Employment** at para **4 Written statement of reasons for dismissal**).

16 Unfair dismissal and the right not to be subjected to detriment

An employee has the right not to be subjected to any detriment by any act, or deliberate failure to act, of his employer on specified grounds. An employee who is dismissed will be regarded as unfairly dismissed if the reason, or principal reason, for the dismissal is a specified reason. The specified reasons and grounds are that the employee (Fixed-term Employees (Prevention of Less Favourable Treatment) Regulations 2002, Reg. 6)–

(a) brought proceedings against the employee under the Fixed-term Employees (Prevention of Less Favourable Treatment) Regulations 2002;

(b) requested a written statement of reasons under the Regulations;

(c) gave evidence or information in connection with proceedings brought by any employee under the Regulations;

(d) did anything under the regulations in relation to the employer or anyone else;

(e) alleged that the employer had infringed the Regulations;

(f) refused, or proposed to refuse, to forgo a right given to him by the Regulations;

(g) declined to serve a workforce agreement for the purpose of the Regulations;

(h) performed functions or activities as a representative (or candidate) of the workforce in relation to a workforce agreement.

It is also a specified ground or reason that the employer believes or suspects that the employee has done or intends to do any of the things listed above.

17 Complaint to an employment tribunal

Where an employee has a right under the Regulations, he may bring a complaint to an employment tribunal that it has been infringed (Fixed-term Employees (Prevention of Less Favourable Treatment) Regulations 2002, Reg. 7). A complaint must generally be brought within three months of the alleged infringement, although a tribunal may consider an out of time complaint if it considers that it would be just and equitable to do so.

Where it finds a complaint well founded, a tribunal may–

(a) make a declaration as to the rights of the employee and the employer in relation to the subject matter of the complaint;

(b) order the employer to pay compensation to the employee; and/or

(c) recommend that the employer take such steps as the tribunal considers reasonable for the purpose of obviating or reducing the adverse effect on the employee of the matter to which the complaint relates.

In calculating any compensation the tribunal must have regard both to the infringement and to any loss attributable to it, but must take account of the duty of the employee to mitigate his loss. Loss will include any expenses reasonably incurred in consequence of the infringement and loss of any benefit which the employee might reasonably have expected to have had but for the infringement. Compensation must not include any amount in respect of injury to feelings. Where the employee is himself partly responsible for the infringement, the compensation may be reduced accordingly.

Where an employer fails to comply with a recommendation of the tribunal under (c) above, the tribunal may order him to pay compensation or increase the amount of compensation already awarded.

18 Successive fixed-term contracts

When a fixed-term employee has been continuously employed on fixed-term contracts for four years or without his continuity being broken, his contract will have effect as a permanent contract unless renewal on a fixed-term basis can be objectively justified. Periods of continuous employment before 10th July 2002 are disregarded for these purposes (Fixed-term Employees (Prevention of Less Favourable Treatment) Regulations 2002, Reg. 8).

A workplace agreement (as to which see Schedule 1 to the Regulations) may modify this provision by providing–

(a) the maximum total periods for which employees may be continuously employed on fixed-term contracts or successive fixed-term contracts;

(b) the maximum number of successive fixed-term contracts and renewals under which employees may be employed; and

(c) the objective grounds which will justify the renewal of a fixed-term contract or the engagement of employees under successive fixed-term contracts.

If an employee considers that he is, by virtue of these provisions, a permanent employee, he can request a written statement from his employer to confirm the position. The employer must, within 21 days, provide such a statement or a statement as to why his contract remains fixed-term (Reg. 9). An employee may make a complaint to an industrial tribunal if no statement is provided or if the employer contends that the contract is still fixed-term.

19 Restrictions on contracting out

Regulation 10 of the Fixed-term Employees (Prevention of Less Favourable Treatment) Regulations 2002 provides that s.203 of the 1996 Act (see the Note on **Employment Protection: Introduction**) applies to the

Regulations. The effect of this is that any agreement between an employer and employee that the Regulations will not apply, or will apply in a modified form, is void and will not therefore prevent an employee from taking action under the Regulations.

20 Exclusions

The Fixed-term Employees (Prevention of Less Favourable Treatment) Regulations 2002 do not apply to service in the armed forces (other than associations formed under the Reserve Forces Act 1996) (Reg. 14).

The Regulations do not have effect in relation to fixed-term employees undergoing a period of work experience not exceeding one year as part of a higher education course (Reg. 18).

The Regulations do not have effect in relation to employment under a fixed-term contract where the employee is an agency worker, except in relation to entitlement to statutory sick pay (Reg. 19).

The Regulations do not have effect in relation to employment where the employee is an apprentice (Reg. 20).

C: AGENCY WORKERS

21 Introduction

The Agency Workers Regulations 2010 implement Council Directive 2008/104/EC on temporary agency work. The Directive establishes a general framework for protection of temporary agency workers. The Regulations provide certain rights for temporary agency workers including in relation to basic working and employment conditions.

22 Definitions

An "agency worker" means an individual who (Agency Workers Regulations 2010, Reg. 3(1))–
  (a) is supplied by a temporary work agency to work temporarily for and under the supervision and direction of a hirer; and
  (b) has a contract with the agency which is a contract of employment, or any other contract with the agency to perform work and services personally.

An individual will be treated as having been supplied by a temporary work agency to work temporarily for and under the supervision of the hirer if (Reg. 3(3))–
  (a) the agency initiates or is involved as an intermediary in the making of the arrangements that lead to the individual being supplied to work temporarily for and under the supervision of the hirer; and
  (b) the individual is supplied by an intermediary, or one of a number of intermediaries, to work temporarily for and under the supervision of the hirer.

An individual will not be regarded as an agency worker if (Reg. 3(2))–
  (a) the contract the individual has with the agency has the effect that the status of the agency is that of a client or customer of a profession or business undertaking carried on by the individual; or
  (b) there is a contract, by virtue of which the individual is available to work for the hirer, having the effect that the status of the hirer is that of a client or customer of a profession or business undertaking carried on by the individual.

An individual is not prevented from being an agency worker because the temporary work agency supplies the individual through one or more intermediaries or because the individual is employed by, or otherwise has a contract with one, or more intermediaries (Reg. 3(5)).

A "temporary work agency" means a person engaged in the economic activity, public or private, whether or not operating for profit, and whether or not carrying on such activity in conjunction with others of (Reg. 4(1))–
  (a) supplying individuals to work temporarily for and under the supervision and direction of hirers; or
  (b) paying for, or receiving or forwarding payment for, the services of individuals who are supplied to work temporarily for and under the supervision and direction of hirers.

A person is not a temporary work agency if they are engaged in the economic activity of paying for, or receiving or forwarding payments for, the services of individuals regardless of whether the individuals are supplied to work for hirers (Reg. 4(2)).

23 Rights of agency workers

Subject to completion of a qualifying period (see **24 Qualifying period**, below), an agency worker is entitled to the same basic working and employment conditions at the time such qualifying period commenced as the worker would be entitled to for doing the same job had they been recruited by the hirer other than by using the services of a temporary work agency (Agency Workers Regulations 2010, Reg. 5(1)). The basic working and employment conditions are (Reg. 5(2))–
  (a) where the agency worker would have been recruited as an employee, the relevant terms and conditions that are ordinarily included in the contracts of employees of the hirer;
  (b) where the agency worker would have been recruited as a worker, the relevant terms and conditions that

are ordinarily included in the contracts of workers of the hirer.

The provisions concerning entitlement are deemed to have been complied with where (Reg. 5(3))–

(c) an agency worker is working under the same relevant terms and conditions as an employee who is a comparable employee; and

(d) the relevant terms and conditions of that comparable employee are terms and conditions ordinarily included in the contracts of employees, who are comparable employees of the hirer.

An employee is a comparable employee in relation to an agency worker if at the time when a breach of the agency worker's rights is alleged to take place (Reg. 5(4))–

(i) both that employee and the agency worker are working for and under the supervision and direction of the hirer and engaged in the same or broadly similar work having regard, where relevant, to whether they have a similar level of qualification and skills; and

(ii) the employee works or is based at the same establishment as the agency worker, or, where there is no comparable employee working or based at that establishment who satisfies the requirements of (i) above, works or is based at a different establishment and satisfies those requirements.

"Relevant terms and conditions" are terms and conditions relating to (Reg. 6(1))–

(a) pay;

(b) the duration of working time;

(c) night work;

(d) rest periods;

(e) rest breaks; and

(f) annual leave.

"Pay" means any sums payable to a worker of the hirer in connection with the worker's employment, including any fee, bonus, commission, holiday pay or other emolument referable to the employment. However, pay does not include certain payments or rewards including (Reg. 6(3))–

(a) any payment by way of occupational sick pay;

(b) any payment by way of a pension, allowance or gratuity in connection with the worker's retirement or as compensation for loss of office;

(c) any payment in respect of maternity, paternity or adoption leave;

(d) any payment referable to the worker's redundancy;

(e) any payment or reward made pursuant to a financial participation scheme (such as a distribution of shares or options);

(f) any bonus, incentive payment or reward which is not directly attributable to the amount or quality of work done by a worker, and which is given to a worker for a reason other than the amount or quality of work done such as to encourage the worker's loyalty or to reward the worker's long-term service;

(g) any payment for time off for carrying out trade union duties;

(h) any payment by way of an advance under an agreement for a loan or by way of an advance of pay;

(i) any payment in respect of expenses incurred by the worker in carrying out the employment;

(j) any payment to the worker otherwise than in that person's capacity as a worker.

Any monetary value attaching to any payment or benefit in kind furnished to a worker will not be treated as pay except any voucher or stamp of fixed value expressed in monetary terms and capable of being exchanged for money, goods or services (Reg. 6(4)).

To the extent it relates to pay, Regulation 5 is disapplied in relation to an agency worker who has a permanent contract of employment with a temporary work agency provided a number of conditions are fulfilled. The conditions relate to the form and terms of the permanent contract and for a minimum amount of pay to be paid to the agency worker between assignments (Regs. 10, 11).

24 The qualifying period

The right of an agency worker in relation to the basic working and employment conditions (see **23 Rights of agency workers**, above) do not apply unless the worker has completed a qualifying period. To complete such period the agency worker must work in the same role with the same hirer for 12 continuous calendar weeks, during one or more assignments (Agency Workers Regulations 2010, Reg, 7(2)). The agency worker works in the same role unless (Reg. 7(3))–

(a) he has started a new role with the same hirer, whether supplied by the same or by a different temporary work agency;

(b) the work or duties that make up the whole or the main part of that new role are substantively different from the work or duties that made up the whole or the main part of the previous role; and

(c) the temporary work agency has informed the agency worker in writing of the type of work he will be required to do in the new role.

Any week during the whole or part of which an agency worker works during an assignment is counted as a calendar week (Reg. 7(4)). There are specific rules for calculating whether any weeks completed with a particular hirer are continuous. Where the worker has certain specified breaks, either between assignments or during an assignment where the worker is not working, but returns to work in the same role with the same hirer, any continuous weeks during which the worker worked for that hirer before the break will be carried forward and treated as continuous with any weeks during which the worker works for the hirer after the break.

This will apply where, *inter alia*, the break is (Reg. 7(5) to (12))–

    (i) for any reason and the break is not more than six calendar weeks;

    (ii) wholly due to the fact that the worker is incapable of working in consequence of sickness or injury (such sickness or injury must be 28 calendar weeks or less, not due to pregnancy, childbirth, or maternity and subject to medical evidence being provided if required);

    (iii) related to pregnancy, childbirth or maternity and is at a time in a protected period (see the Note on **Maternity Rights**);

    (iv) wholly for the purpose of taking time off for leave, whether statutory or contractual, to which the worker is entitled (i.e., adoption, paternity and ordinary, compulsory or additional maternity leave);

    (v) wholly due to the fact the worker is required to attend as a juror and the break is 28 calendar weeks or less;

    (vi) wholly due to a temporary cessation in the hirer's requirement for any worker to be present at the establishment and work in a particular role, for a pre-determined period of time according to the established custom and practices of the hirer;

    (vii) wholly due to a strike, lock out or other industrial action at the hirer's establishment.

Where an agency worker has completed the qualifying period with a particular hirer, the rights conferred by the Regulations apply and continue to apply to that worker in relation to that hirer unless the worker is no longer working in the same role (see (a) to (c), above) with the hirer or there is a break between assignments, or during an assignment, when the agency worker is not working (i.e., a break to which paragraphs (i) to (vii), above do not apply) (Reg. 8).

In certain circumstances an agency worker will be treated as having completed the qualifying period from the time at which he would have completed that period but for the structure of the assignment or assignments mentioned in (a) to (c), below. This provision applies when an agency worker has (Reg. 9(3))–

    (a) completed two or more assignments;

    (b) completed at least one assignment with the hirer and one or more earlier assignments with hirers connected to that hirer;

    (c) worked in more than two roles during an assignment with the hirer, and on at least two occasions has worked in a role that was not the "same role" as the previous role within the meaning of Reg. 7(3).

The following must also apply for the worker to be treated as having completed the qualifying period (Reg. 9(4))–

    (i) the most likely explanation for the structure of the assignment, or assignments, is that the hirer or the temporary work agency supplying the worker to the hirer (or one or more hirers connected to that hirer if applicable), intended to prevent the worker from being entitled to, or from continuing to be entitled to, the rights conferred in respect of the basic working and employment conditions;

    (ii) the worker would be entitled to, or would continue to be entitled to, the rights mentioned in (i) above in relation to the hirer, but for that structure.

25 Access to collective facilities, amenities and access to employment

During an assignment (see **24 The qualifying period**, above) an agency worker has the right to be treated no less favourably than a comparable worker in relation to the collective facilities and amenities provided by the hirer. This includes, in particular, (Agency Workers Regulations 2010, Reg. 12(1), (2))–

    (a) canteen or other similar facilities;

    (b) child care facilities; and

    (c) transport services.

For these purposes an individual is a comparable worker to an agency worker if at the time when a breach of this right is alleged to take place (Reg. 12(4))–

    (a) both that individual and the agency worker are working for and under supervision and direction of the hirer and engaged in the same or broadly similar work having regard, where relevant, to whether they have a similar level of qualification and skills;

    (b) that individual works or is based at the same establishment as the agency worker, or, where there is no comparable worker working or based at that establishment who satisfies the requirements of (a) above, works or is based at a different establishment and satisfies those requirements; and

    (c) that individual is an employee of the hirer or, where there is no employee satisfying the requirements of (a) and (b) above, is as worker of the hirer and satisfies those requirements.

An agency worker has, during an assignment, the right to be informed by the hirer of any relevant vacant posts with the hirer, in order to give that agency worker the same opportunity as a comparable worker to find permanent employment with the hirer. The hirer may inform the agency worker of such posts by a general announcement in a suitable place in the hirer's establishment (Reg. 13).

26 Liability of temporary work agency and hirer

Both a temporary work agency and a hirer can be found liable for a breach of an agency worker's rights in relation to basic working and employment conditions (see **23 Rights of agency workers**, above) (Agency Workers Regulations 2010, Reg. 14(1), (2)). A temporary work agency will not be liable for such a breach where it is established that the agency (Reg. 14(3))–

(a) obtained, or had taken reasonable steps to obtain, relevant information from the hirer (i) about the basic working and employment conditions in force at the hirer, (ii) if needed to assess compliance with Reg. 5 about the relevant terms and conditions under which an employee of the hirer is working where that employee is considered to be a comparable employee to the agency worker and those terms and conditions are ordinarily included in such a comparable employee's contract, and (iii) which explains why the employee is considered a comparable employee;

(b) where it has received such information, has acted reasonably in determining what the agency worker's basic working and employment conditions should be at the end of the qualifying period and during the period after that, until the agency worker ceases to be entitled to the rights conferred by the Regulations; and

(c) ensured that where it has responsibility for applying those basic working and employment conditions to the agency worker, that worker has been treated in accordance with the determination described in (b), above,

and to the extent that the temporary work agency is not liable under these provisions, the hirer will be liable.

27 Restrictions on contracting out

Regulation 15 of the Agency Workers Regulations 2010 provides that s.203 of the 1996 Act (see the Note on **Employment Protection: Introduction**) applies to the Regulations. The effect of this is that any agreement between an employer and employee that the Regulations will not apply, or will apply in a modified form, is void and will not therefore prevent an employee from taking action under the Regulations.

28 Right to receive information

An agency worker who considers that the hirer or a temporary work agency may have treated him in a manner which infringes a right in relation to basic working and employment conditions (see **23 Rights of agency workers**, above) may make a written request to the temporary work agency for a written statement containing information relating to the treatment in question (Agency Workers Regulations 2010, Reg. 16(1)). The agency must, within 28 days of receiving such a request, provide the worker with a written statement setting out (Reg. 16(2))–

(a) relevant information relating to the basic working and employment conditions of workers of the hirer;

(b) the factors the temporary work agency considered when determining the basic working and employment conditions which applied to the agency worker at the time when the breach of the right is alleged to have taken place, and

(c) where the temporary work agency seeks to rely on compliance with the relevant part of the Regulations by reason of the fact that the worker is working under the same relevant terms and conditions as an employee who is a comparable employee, information which explains the basis on which it is considered that an individual is a comparable employee and which describes the terms and conditions which apply to that employee.

Where a worker has not been provided with such a statement within 30 days of making the request, he may make a written request to the hirer for a written statement containing information relevant to the basic working and employment conditions of workers of the hirer (Reg. 16(3)).

An agency worker who considers that the hirer may have treated him in a manner infringing rights concerning access to facilities, amenities and employment (see **25 Access to collective facilities, amenities and access to employment**, above) may make a written request to the hirer for a written statement containing information relating to the treatment in question (Reg. 16(5)). The hirer must provide the worker with such a statement within 28 days setting out (Reg. 16(6))–

(a) all relevant information relating to the rights of a comparable worker in respect of the rights concerning collective access to facilities and amenities or employment as the case may be; and

(b) particulars of the reasons for the treatment of the agency worker in respect of the rights conferred.

Where it appears to a tribunal that a temporary work agency or hirer deliberately or without reasonable excuse failed to provide information, or that a statement provide is evasive or equivocal, it may draw an inference which it considers just and equitable to draw, including an inference that the right in question has been infringed (Reg. 16(8)).

29 Unfair dismissal and the right not to be subjected to detriment

An agency worker who is an employee and is dismissed will be regarded as unfairly dismissed if the reasons, or grounds for, dismissal are (Agency Workers Regulations 2010, Reg. 17)–

(a) that the agency worker brought proceedings under the 2010 Regulations; gave evidence or information in connection with such proceedings brought by an agency worker; made a request for a written statement; otherwise did anything under the Regulations in relation to a temporary work agency, hirer, or any other person; alleged that a temporary work agency or hirer had breached the Regulations; or refused (or proposed to refuse) to forgo a right conferred by the Regulations; or

(b) that the hirer or a temporary work agency believed or suspected that the agency worker has done or intended to do any of the things mentioned in (a) above.

An agency worker has the right not to be subjected to any detriment by, or as a result of, any act, or any deliberate failure to act, of a temporary work agency or the hirer, done on a ground specified in (a) or (b) above.

30 Complaints to employment tribunals

An agency worker may present a complaint to an employment tribunal that a temporary work agency or the hirer has infringed a right conferred on that worker in respect of basic working and employment conditions, access to facilities, amenities or employment, or the right not to be subjected to detriment. An agency worker may also present a complaint that a temporary work agency has breached a term of the contract of employment or breached a duty under the Regulations in respect of permanent contracts which provide for pay between assignments (Agency Workers Regulations 2010, Reg. 18(2), (3)).

An employment tribunal will not consider a complaint unless it is presented before the end of the period of three months beginning with the date of the alleged infringement, detriment or breach to which it relates (or if a series of acts or failures, the last such act or failure). In the case of an alleged infringement of the right concerning access to employment, the time limit is calculated from the date the person or persons (whether or not employed by the hirer) were informed of the vacancy (Reg. 18(4)). A tribunal has discretion to consider a complaint out of time if it considers that it is just and equitable to do so (Reg. 18(5)).

Where an employment tribunal finds that a complaint is well-founded it will take such of the following steps as it considers just and equitable–

(a) make a declaration as to the rights of the complainant in relation to the matters to which the complaint arises;

(b) order the respondent to pay compensation to the complainant;

(c) recommend that the respondent take, within a specified period, action appearing to the tribunal to be reasonable, in all the circumstances of the case, for the purpose of obviating or reducing the adverse effect on the complainant of any matter to which the complaint arises (Reg. 18(8)).

The amount of compensation awarded will be such as the tribunal considers just and equitable in all the circumstances having regard to the infringement or breach to which the complaint relates and any loss which is attributable to the infringement. The loss will be taken to include any expenses reasonably incurred by the complainant in consequence of the infringement or breach, and loss of any benefit which the complainant might reasonably be expected to have had but for the infringement or breach (Reg. 18(10), (11)). In respect of infringement of rights relating to the basic working and employment conditions or permanent contracts providing for pay between assignments, the amount of compensation will be not less than two weeks' pay unless the tribunal consider it just and equitable to reduce that amount (Reg. 18(12), (13)). An additional award of up to £5,000 may be awarded where it orders the respondent to pay compensation and where the tribunal finds that Reg. 9(4) applies (structure of assignments, see **24 The qualifying period**, above) (Reg. 18(14)).

31 Special classes of person

The Agency Workers Regulations 2010 have effect in relation to (Reg. 21)–

(a) Crown employment;

(b) service as a member of the armed forces of the Crown;

(c) persons in Crown employment;

(d) persons in service as a member of the armed forces of the Crown,

as they have effect in relation to other employment and other employees.

The Regulations also have effect in relation to employment as a relevant member of staff of the House of Lords or House of Commons as they have effect in relation to other employment (Regs. 22, 23).

For the purposes of the Regulations, the holding, otherwise than under a contract of employment, of the office of constable or an appointment as a police cadet will be treated as employment, under a contract of employment, by the relevant officer (Reg. 24).

32 Authorities

Employment Act 2002

Employment Relations Act 1999

Agency Workers Regulations 2010, as amended (S.I. 2010 No. 93, 2011 No. 1941, 2012 No. 2397, and 2014 No. 386)

Fixed-term Employees (Prevention of Less Favourable Treatment) Regulations 2002, as amended (S.I. 2002 No. 2034, 2006 No. 594, 2008 No. 2776, 2012 No. 3112, 2014 No. 386, and 2015 No. 971)

Part-time Workers (Prevention of Less Favourable Treatment) Regulations 2000, as amended (S.I. 2000 No. 1551, 2001 No. 1107, 2002 No. 2035, 2005 No. 2240, 2006 No. 594, and 2014 No. 386)

PUBLIC INTEREST DISCLOSURE

1 Introduction

The Public Interest Disclosure Act 1998 protects individual workers who make certain disclosures of information in the public interest and allows such individuals (popularly referred to as "whistleblowers") to bring proceedings in employment tribunals against their employers in the event of dismissal or other actions taken against them by their employers. S.1 of the Act inserts a new Part IVA (ss.43A to 43L) into the Employment Rights Act 1996. Part IVA is entitled "Protected Disclosures" and defines the categories of disclosure that qualify for protection under the Act.

2 Disclosures qualifying for protection

For the purposes of Part IVA of the Employment Rights Act 1996, a disclosure made by a worker will only be protected if it falls into one of the categories of "protected disclosure" i.e., it is a disclosure made by a "worker" (see **3 Meaning of "worker"**, below) which, in the reasonable belief of the worker is made in the public interest and, tends to show one or more of the following (s.43B(1))–
  (a) that a criminal offence either has been committed, is being committed, or is likely to be committed;
  (b) that a person has failed, is failing, or is likely to fail to comply with any legal obligation to which he is subject;
  (c) that a miscarriage of justice has occurred, is occurring, or is likely to occur;
  (d) that the health or safety of any individual has been, is being, or is likely to be endangered;
  (e) that the environment has been, is being, or is likely to be damaged; or
  (f) that information tending to show any matter falling within (a) to (e) above has been, is being, or is likely to be deliberately concealed.

For these purposes, it is immaterial whether the matters disclosed occurred, are occurring, or are likely to occur in the UK or elsewhere (s.43B(2)). It is also immaterial that the person receiving the information is already aware of it (s.43L(3)).

A disclosure is not protected if a criminal offence is committed by the person in making it (e.g., if the disclosure would breach the Official Secrets Act) (s.43B(3)).

A disclosure of information in respect of which a claim of legal professional privilege could be made in legal proceedings is not protected if made by a legal advisor to whom information has been disclosed in the course of giving legal advice (s.43B(4)).

3 Meaning of "worker"

The protection applies only to disclosures made by "workers". The Employment Rights Act 1996 extends this term to cover not only employees and independent contractors providing services other than in a professional- or business-client relationship, but also agency workers, homeworkers, NHS doctors, dentists and other staff, student nurses and midwives, and trainees on work experience or similar schemes. In the case of an agency worker, the "employer" for these purposes will be the person who substantially determines the terms on which he is employed (s.43K, as amended by the Protected Disclosures (Extension of Meaning of Worker) Order 2015/491).

4 Disclosure to employer or other responsible person

A worker will be protected if he makes his disclosure either to his employer or, where the worker reasonably believes that the matter relates solely to the conduct of someone other than the employer or is a matter for which someone other than his employer is legally responsible, to that other person. A worker who, in accordance with a procedure authorised by his employer, makes a qualifying disclosure to another person (e.g., a health and safety representative or a union official) will be treated for the purposes of the Act as if he had made the disclosure to his employer (Employment Rights Act 1996, s.43C).

5 Disclosure to others

A worker is protected if he makes a disclosure in the course of obtaining legal advice or, in the case of workers employed by government appointed bodies, if he makes a disclosure to the sponsoring government department (Employment Rights Act 1996, ss.43D and 43E).

A worker will also be protected if the disclosure is made to a person or body prescribed by an order made by the Secretary of State and the worker reasonably believes that the information disclosed, together with any allegations contained in it, are substantially true (s.43F). The Public Interest Disclosure (Prescribed Persons) Order 2014 prescribes, in relation to specified matters, a number of persons and bodies for these purposes, including–
  – a member of the House of Commons, the Lord Advocate, Scotland, and the Welsh Ministers;
  – auditors appointed to audit the accounts of bodies under the Local Audit and Accountability Act 2014; the Accounts Commission for Scotland (and auditors appointed by them to audit the accounts of local government, and health service bodies, local policing bodies, chief constables and the Metropolitan

Police), Audit Scotland, the Auditor Generals for Wales and Scotland, the Comptroller and Auditor General, and the Standards Commission for Scotland and the Chief Investigating Officer;
- the Certification Officer;
- the Charity Commission for England and Wales, and Office of the Scottish Charity Regulator;
- the Chief Executives of the Criminal Cases Review and Scottish Criminal Cases Review Commissions;
- the Children's Commissioner, Children's Commissioner for Wales, the Commissioner for Children and Young People in Scotland, and Her Majesty's Chief Inspector of Education, Children's Services and Skills;
- the Civil Aviation Authority;
- the Care Inspectorate, Care Quality Commission, Care Council for Wales, Monitor, the National Health Service Trust Development Authority, and Healthcare Improvement Scotland;
- the Commissioners of Revenue and Customs, Revenue Scotland (for devolved taxes), and the Keeper of the Registers of Scotland (for the Scottish land and buildings transaction tax);
- the Water Services Regulation Authority and Water Industry Commission for Scotland;
- the Environment Agency and SEPA;
- the Financial Conduct Authority, Prudential Regulation Authority, Financial Reporting Council Limited and its conduct committee, the Payment Systems Regulator, and the Bank of England;
- the Competition and Markets Authority, Gas and Electricity Markets Authority, and Director of the Serious Fraud Office;
- the Food Standards Agency;
- the General Chiropractic Council, General Dental Council, General Medical Council, General Optical Council, General Osteopathic Council, General Pharmaceutical Council, Health and Care Professions Council, and the Nursing and Midwifery Council;
- the Health and Safety Executive;
- the Homes and Communities Agency and Scottish Housing Regulator;
- elected local policing bodies, Police and Crime Panels, the Independent Police Complaints Commission, and the National Crime Agency;
- the Information Commissioner and Scottish Information Commissioner;
- local authorities responsible for health and safety and consumer protection legislation;
- the NSPCC and any of its officers;
- the Office of Communications;
- the Office for Nuclear Regulation;
- the Office of Qualifications and Examinations Regulation;
- the Pensions Regulator;
  the Office of Rail Regulation;
  the Scottish Social Services Council; and
- the Secretaries of State for Business, Innovation and Skills; Education; and Transport.

In all cases, disclosure to these bodies may only be made in respect of matters which are the statutory responsibility of the individual or body concerned. MPs are prescribed persons in relation to all matters.

The cases in which a worker will be protected if he makes a wider disclosure (e.g., to the media) are set out in s.43G. A worker will only be protected under this section in the following circumstances–

(i) he reasonably believes that the information disclosed and the allegations made are substantially true;
(ii) the disclosure is not made for personal gain;
(iii) the worker has previously disclosed the same information to his employer or to one of the individuals or bodies prescribed for the purposes of s.43F (see above) or has not done this because he reasonably believed that (a) any such disclosure would lead to action being taken against him by his employer or, (in a case where there is no prescribed statutory individual or body to whom disclosure could have been made), (b) disclosure to his employer would lead to the concealment or destruction of evidence; and
(iv) it is reasonable in all the circumstances for disclosure to be made, taking into account the identity of the person to whom disclosure is made; the seriousness of the matter disclosed; any duty of confidentiality owed by the worker; any action already taken by the employer or statutory body or individual to whom disclosure ahs already been made; and the extent to which the worker, in making any prior disclosure to his employer, complied with any procedures laid down by the employer.

6 Disclosure of exceptionally serious failure

In respect of exceptionally serious matters, a worker may still be protected even if he makes a disclosure which is not protected under any of the provisions outlined in previous paragraphs. The worker must reasonably believe the matters disclosed to be true; the disclosure must not be made for personal gain; and, in all the circumstances, it must be reasonable for the disclosure to be made (Employment Rights Act 1996, s.43H).

7 Contractual duties of confidentiality

Any provision in an agreement between a worker and an employer, including an agreement not to bring proceedings under the Employment Rights Act 1996 or for breach of contract, is void insofar as it purports to prevent a worker from making protected disclosure (s.43J).

8 Rights of workers

Ss.2 to 9 of the Public Interest Disclosure Act 1998 amend the Employment Rights Act 1996 so as to set out the rights of workers who have made protected disclosures.

S.2 inserts a new s.47B into Part V of the 1996 Act (see the Note on **Rights Arising in the Course of Employment: Detriment**). Under s.47B, a worker has the right not to be subjected to any detriment by any act, or deliberate failure to act, by the employer, done on the ground that the worker has made a protected disclosure. S.47B therefore protects employed workers from actions short of dismissal and protects other workers (who are not technically employees) from any action taken by the employer (e.g., termination of their contracts).

S.48 of the 1996 Act allows a worker to present a complaint to an employment tribunal if he has been subjected to a detriment in contravention of s.47B. A tribunal may make an award of compensation although, in the case of a worker who is not an employee and whose contract has been terminated, compensation must not exceed that which would have been payable under the 1996 Act if the worker had been an employee who had been unfairly dismissed (see the Note on **Unfair Dismissal**) (s.49, as amended by s.4 of the 1998 Act). If it appears to the tribunal that the protected disclosure was not made in good faith, the tribunal may, if it considers it just and equitable in all the circumstances to do so, reduce any award it makes to the worker by no more than 25% (s.49(6A)).

S.103A of the 1996 Act, as inserted by s.5 of the 1998 Act, provides that an employee who is dismissed will automatically be regarded for the purposes of the 1996 Act as being unfairly dismissed if the reason for his dismissal was that he had made a protected disclosure. Similarly, s.6 inserts a new s.105(6A) into the 1996 Act which confers on employees the right not to be selected for redundancy for making a protected disclosure (the effect being that a person who is selected for redundancy for this reason will be regarded as unfairly dismissed: see the Note on **Unfair Dismissal** at para 15 **Dismissal on ground of redundancy**).

An employee who has been unfairly dismissed or unfairly selected for redundancy for making a protected disclosure may bring a claim to an employment tribunal even though he has not been employed for the normal minimum qualifying period of one year or is above the normal age limit for bringing a claim (ss.108(ff) and 109(ff) of the 1996 Act, each as inserted by s.7 of the 1998 Act).

Where the reason (or principal reason) for the dismissal is that the complainant made a protected disclosure, and it appears to the tribunal that the disclosure was not made in good faith, the tribunal may, if it considers it just and equitable in all the circumstances to do so, reduce any award it makes to the complainant by no more than 25% (s.123(6A)).

S.127B, as inserted by s.8 of the 1998 Act, allows regulations to be made determining the compensation that may be awarded when an employee is unfairly dismissed or unfairly selected for redundancy in breach of the Act. The Public Interest Disclosure (Compensation) Regulations 1999 remove the normal monetary limits on compensation that may be awarded under the 1996 Act.

9 Exceptions

Although the Public Interest Disclosure Act 1998 applies to civil servants, it does not apply to members of the armed forces or to those involved in national security (ss.191 and 193 of the Employment Rights Act 1996, as amended by s.10 of the 1998 Act and Sch. 8 of the Employment Relations Act 1999). S.200 of the 1996 Act (as amended by s.13 of the 1998 Act) also specifically excludes police officers from the scope of the Public Interest Disclosure Act 1998. The Act does not apply to people who normally work outside Great Britain (s.196 of the 1996 Act as amended by s.12 of the 1998 Act).

10 Protection for applicants for employment in the health service

The Employment Rights 1996 s.49B, as inserted by s.149 of the Small Business, Enterprise and Employment Act 2015, gives the Secretary of State the power to make regulations prohibiting defined NHS employers from discriminating against job applicants because it appears to the NHS employer that the applicant has made a protected disclosure (within the meaning given by s.43A of the Employment Rights Act 1996). For these purposes, an NHS employer discriminates against an applicant if the employer refuses the applicant's application or in some other way treats the applicant less favourably than it treats or would treat other applicants in relation to the same contract, office or post. An applicant means an individual who applies to the NHS employer for a contract of employment, a contract to do work personally, or appointment to an office or post.

11 Authorities

Statutes–
Employment Relations Act 1999

Employment Rights Act 1996

Public Interest Disclosure Act 1998

Statutory Instruments–
Public Interest Disclosure (Compensation) Regulations 1999 (S.I. 1999 No. 1548)

Public Interest Disclosure (Prescribed Persons) Order 2014, as amended (S.I. 2014 Nos. 2418 and 3294, and 2015 Nos. 1407 and 1981)

REDUNDANCY

A: INTRODUCTION

1 The legislation

This Note is concerned with the law relating to redundancy. The relevant law is contained in–

(a) Part XI of the Employment Rights Act 1996, which requires employers to make lump sum compensation payments, termed redundancy payments, to employees dismissed because of redundancy and, in certain circumstances, to employees who have been laid off or kept on short-time for a substantial period; and

(b) ss.188-198 of the Trade Union and Labour Relations (Consolidation) Act 1992, which are concerned with redundancy handling procedures.

The redundancy provisions extend throughout Great Britain. Certain definitions and provisions (e.g., the method of calculating a period of continuous employment), which apply to this Part and throughout the whole Act are to be found in the Note on **Employment Protection: Introduction**.

Unless otherwise stated, any references to sections are references to sections of the Act.

B: ENTITLEMENT TO REDUNDANCY PAYMENT

2 Entitled employees

Subject to the exceptions below, where an employee has been continuously employed by his employer for at least two years and is dismissed by that employer by reason of redundancy or is laid off or kept on short time the employee may be entitled to a redundancy payment (Employment Rights Act 1996, ss.135 and 155).

The Redundancy Payments Office Holders Regulations 1965, and the corresponding Scottish Regulations of 1966, apply the 1996 Act, with the necessary modifications, to certain office holders, including (in England and Wales) justices' clerks, registrars of births and deaths, and rent officers, and (in Scotland) chief constables. The Redundancy Payments Termination of Employment Regulations 1965 apply the Act to a chief constable or a chief or assistant chief officer of a fire brigade who becomes redundant as a result of an amalgamation of police forces or combination of fire brigades.

3 Excluded employees

Certain categories of employees are not entitled to redundancy payments under the Employment Rights Act 1996, including the following–

(a) employees who benefit under alternative schemes which are the subject of exemption orders made by the Secretary of State under s.157;

(b) Crown servants (s.159);

(c) a domestic servant in a private household where the employer is a close relative of the employee (s.161);

(d) dock workers to whom s.5 of the Dock Work Act 1989 and the Dock Work (Compensation Payment Scheme) Regulations 1989 (S.I. No. 1111) apply);

(e) share fishermen (s.199(2)); and

(f) employee shareholders (as to whom see Note the Note on **Employment Protection: Introduction** at para **9 Employee shareholders**)) (s.205A(2)(d)).

4 Dismissal by reason of redundancy

Where an employee who has been continuously employed for two years or more is dismissed by his employer by reason of redundancy, he will normally be entitled to a redundancy payment (Employment Rights Act 1996, s.155). The meaning of dismissal for these purposes is similar to its meaning for the purposes of the unfair dismissal provisions of Part X (see the Note on **Unfair Dismissal**, at para **4 Meaning of dismissal**) (s.136(1)).

The dismissal of an employee is to be taken as being a dismissal by reason of redundancy if it is attributable wholly or mainly to (s.139(1))–

(a) the fact that the employer has ceased (whether permanently or temporarily and for whatever cause), or intends to cease, to carry on the business for the purposes of which the employee was employed by him, or has ceased, or intends to cease, to carry on that business in the place where the employee was so employed, or

(b) the fact that the requirements of that business for employees to carry out work of a particular kind, or for employees to carry out work of a particular kind in the place where the employee was so employed, have ceased or diminished or are expected to cease or diminish.

For these purposes the business of the employer together with the business or businesses of his associated employers are to be treated as one unless either condition (a) or (b) above would be satisfied without so treating them (s.139(2)). The activities carried on by a local authority in relation to schools maintained by it and the activities carried on by the governors of those schools will in like manner normally be treated as one business (s.139(3)).

In certain circumstances (e.g., on the death of an employer or on the employer's bankruptcy), there will be an implied or constructive dismissal. In these circumstances, the employee will be treated as being dismissed by reason of redundancy if his contract is not renewed or if he is not re-engaged (e.g., by his employer's personal representatives) and the circumstances in which his contract is not renewed or he is not re-engaged are wholly or mainly attributable to one or other of the facts specified in paragraphs (a) and (b) above (s.139(4)).

Except as provided by s.140 (see **7 The notice period**, below), an employee will not be entitled to a redundancy payment by reason of dismissal where his conduct was such as to entitle the employer to dismiss him without notice. Where the employer does give the notice required by the employee's contract, he must include a statement to the effect that the employee's conduct was such as to justify dismissal without notice (s.140(1)).

5 Lay-off and short-time

An employee may be entitled to a redundancy payment if he is laid off or kept on short-time. For the purposes of Part XI, an employee is laid off during any week in which he is employed under a contract on such terms and conditions that his remuneration depends on his being provided with work by his employer and, in that week, he is not provided with any such work and is therefore not entitled to any remuneration. An employee is treated as being kept on short-time for any week if, by reason of a diminution in the work provided by his employer, his remuneration for that week is less than half a week's pay (Employment Rights Act 1996, s.147). The amount of a week's pay is calculated in accordance with the provisions of ss.221 to 229 (see the Note on **Employment Protection: Introduction**).

An employee will be entitled to a redundancy payment by reason of being laid off or kept on short-time only if he gives written notice to his employer of his intention to claim such a payment and, before service of that notice—

(a) he has been laid off or kept on short-time for four or more consecutive weeks and the last such week ended on the date of service of the notice or ended not more than four weeks before that date, or

(b) he has been laid off or kept on short-time for a series of six or more weeks (of which not more than three were consecutive) within a 13-week period, where the last week of the series ended on the date of the service of the notice, or within the preceding four-week period (s.148).

The employee must, in addition to serving a notice of intention to claim a redundancy payment, terminate his contract of employment by giving one week's notice (or the minimum notice required under his contract, if greater) within a specified period (s.150). An employee will still not be entitled to a payment in pursuance of his notice of intention to claim if (i) on the date of service of the notice of termination it was reasonably to be expected that within the succeeding four weeks he would enter upon a period of at least 13 weeks during which he would not be laid off or kept on short-time for any week and (ii) the employer, within seven days of service of the notice of intention to claim gives written notice to the employee that he contests his claim. If, however, the expectation mentioned at (i) is not fulfilled, the employee does not lose his entitlement (s.152).

An employee is not entitled to a redundancy payment by reason of being laid off or kept on short-time if he is dismissed by his employer, although he may still be entitled to a redundancy payment in respect of the dismissal itself (s.151).

6 Renewal of contract or re-engagement

An employee will not be entitled to a redundancy payment if he unreasonably refuses an offer, made by his employer or an associated employer before the termination of his contract, to renew his contract or to re-engage him under a new contract, such renewal or re-engagement to take effect within four weeks of the termination of his previous contract. The terms and conditions of the new or renewed contract (including the capacity and place in which the employee will work) must either correspond with their counterparts in the previous contract or if they do differ (wholly or in part), the offer must constitute an offer of suitable employment in relation to that employee (Employment Rights Act 1996, s.141(1) and (3)). However, in the latter circumstances, the employee is entitled to a trial period of four weeks under the new contract. If, during this period, the employee, for whatever reason, terminates the contract or if the employer, for a reason connected with or arising out of the change of employment, dismisses the employee, he will be treated as though he had been dismissed by reason of redundancy on the date on which his previous contract ended (s.138(1) to (4)). However, where it is the employee who has terminated the new contract, he will not be entitled to a redundancy payment unless his decision to do so was a reasonable one (s.141(4)). The trial period may be for a longer period by written agreement between the employee and employer for any necessary retraining of the former under the new contract (s.138(6)).

As to the situation where a change occurs in the ownership of a business, see the Note on **Transfer of Undertakings** and the Transfer of Undertakings (Protection of Employment) Regulations 1981 (as amended).

The Redundancy Payments (Continuity of Employment in Local Government, etc.) (Modification) Order 1999 enables the re-engagement of a person currently in a relevant government service in another such service to be treated as continuous service for the purposes of the redundancy provisions. The Redundancy Payments (National Health Service) (Modification) Order 1993 makes similar provision in relation to persons employed in relevant health services.

7 The notice period

An employee who leaves his job voluntarily after notice of redundancy has been served but before his period of notice is due to expire does not lose his right to a redundancy payment, provided that he gives his employer notice in writing and his employer does not object. There is a right of appeal to an employment tribunal if the employer's consent is thought to have been unreasonably withheld (Employment Rights Act 1996, s.142).

Where an employee is dismissed during such a notice period for reasons of misconduct which justify dismissal without notice (other than taking part in a strike), he may apply to an employment tribunal, which may, if it considers that it is just and equitable to do so in all the circumstances, determine that he should be paid the whole or part of the redundancy payment to which he would otherwise have been entitled (s.140(1) and (3)).

An employee who takes part in a strike during the notice period and is dismissed for doing so is still entitled to any redundancy payment which would have been due to him on the expiry of his notice (s.140(2)).

The employer may, however, serve a notice on the employee requesting him to return to work after the strike and to remain at work beyond the date when his notice would have expired for as many days as were lost by the strike. If the employee does not attend for work on each of the required number of extra days, the employer will be entitled to contest any liability to pay him a redundancy payment in respect of the dismissal. In these circumstances, the employee may apply to a tribunal, which will consider whether he had reasonable grounds for failing to comply with the request and, if it finds this to be the case, may order full or part payment to be made by the employer (s.143).

C: PROCEDURE FOR HANDLING REDUNDANCIES

8 Introduction

Ss.188 to 198 of the Trade Union and Labour Relations (Consolidation) Act 1992 deal with the procedure for handling redundancies. Certain of these provisions are described below.

For the purposes of ss.188 to 198, references to dismissal as redundant are references to dismissal for a reason not related to the individual concerned or for a number of reasons all of which are not so related; and for the purposes of any proceedings, where any employee is or is proposed to be dismissed it must be presumed, unless the contrary is proved, that he is or is proposed to be dismissed as redundant (s.195, as substituted by the 1993 Act, s.34).

9 Duty to consult representatives

Where an employer is proposing to dismiss as redundant 20 or more employees at one establishment within a period of 90 days or less, the employer must consult about the dismissals all the persons who are appropriate representatives (see below) of any of the employees who may be affected by the proposed dismissals or by measures taken in connection with those dismissals. The consultation must begin in good time and in any event—
- (1) where the employer is proposing to dismiss 100 or more employees at one establishment within a period of 90 days or less, at least 45 days, and
- (2) otherwise, at least 30 days,

before the first of the dismissals takes effect.

In determining how many employees an employer is proposing to make redundant, no account must be taken of employees in respect of whose proposed dismissals consultation has already begun.

The appropriate representatives of any employees are—
- (a) where there is an independent trade union recognised by the employer, representatives of that union, or
- (b) in any other case, whichever of the following employee representatives the employer chooses—
    - (i) those appointed or elected by affected employees (other than for the purposes of being consulted about redundancies) who, having regard to the purposes for and method by which they were appointed or elected, have authority from those employees to receive information and to be consulted about proposals on their behalf;
    - (ii) employee representatives elected by affected employees for the purpose of being consulted about redundancies in an election satisfying s.188A(1) (see 11 **Election of representatives**, below).

The employer must allow the appropriate representatives access to the employees affected and must afford to those representatives such accommodation and other facilities as may be appropriate.

Where there has been a delay on the part of the employees affected to elect representatives, the employer will be treated as complying with the above requirements if he complies with them as soon as is reasonably practicable after the election of those representatives, provided that the employer had invited the employees who may be affected to elect such employee representatives long enough before the time when the consultation is required under the above provisions.

10 The consultation requirements

As part of the consultation, the employer must make written disclosure—
- (i) in a document delivered or sent by post to the appropriate representatives or, if the employer has invited

affected employees to elect representatives and they have failed to do so within a reasonable time, to each affected employee; or

(ii) in the case of representatives from a trade union, in a document sent by post to the union at its head or main office.

The disclosure must give—

(a) the reasons for his proposals;

(b) the number and descriptions of employees whom it is proposed to dismiss as redundant;

(c) the total number of employees of any such description employed at the establishment in question;

(d) the proposed method of selecting the employees who may be dismissed;

(e) the proposed method of carrying out the dismissals, with due regard to any agreed procedure, including the period over which the dismissals are to take effect; and

(f) the proposed method of calculating the amount of any redundancy payments to be made (otherwise than in compliance with an obligation imposed by virtue of any enactment) to employees who may be dismissed.

The consultation required must also include consultation about ways of—

(i) avoiding dismissals,

(ii) reducing the numbers of employees to be dismissed, and

(iii) mitigating the consequences of the dismissals,

and must be undertaken by the employer with a view to reaching agreement with the appropriate representatives.

If it is not reasonably practicable, due to special circumstances, for the employer to comply with the above requirements (other than the mode of conveying written disclosure), he must take such steps towards compliance as are practicable in those circumstances. Where the decision leading to the proposed dismissals is that of a person controlling the employer (directly or indirectly), a failure on the part of that person to provide information to the employer must constitute special circumstances rendering it not reasonably practicable for the employer to comply with such a requirement (Trade Union and Labour Relations (Consolidation) Act 1992, s.188, as amended by the 1993 Act, s.34 and the (Protection of Employment) Regulations).

11 Election of representatives

The requirements of the Trade Union and Labour Relations (Consolidation) Act 1992 s.188A(1), which need to be satisfied with regard to the election of employee representatives under s.188(1B) (see **9 Duty to consult representatives**, above), are that—

(a) the employer must make such arrangements as are reasonably practicable to ensure that the election is fair;

(b) the employer must determine the number of representatives to be elected, having regard to the interests of all affected employees and the number and classes of those employees;

(c) the employer must determine whether the affected employees should be represented either by representatives of all of those employees or of particular classes of affected employees;

(d) the term of office of the representatives must be sufficient as to enable information to be given and consultations to be completed;

(e) candidates for election must be affected employees at the date of the election;

(f) no affected employee must be unreasonable excluded from standing for election;

(g) all affected employees on the date of the election must be entitled to vote, and may vote for as many candidates as there are representatives to be elected;

(h) the election must be conducted so that so far as reasonably practicable voting is secret, and the votes must be counted accurately.

For the purposes of s.188, persons are employee representatives if they have been elected by employees for the specific purpose of being consulted about proposed dismissals, or, having been elected or appointed by employees (whether before or after the dismissals have been proposed) for some other purpose, it is appropriate for the employer to consult them. In either case, the representatives must be employed by the employer at the time when they are elected or appointed (s.196, as amended by the (Protection of Employment) Regulations).

12 Complaint by representatives and protective award

Where an employer has failed to comply with any requirement of the Trade Union and Labour Relations (Consolidation) Act 1992 ss.188 or 188A, a complaint may be presented to an employment tribunal on that ground—

(a) in the case of a failure relating to the election of employee representatives, by any of the affected employees or by any of the employees who have been dismissed as redundant;

(b) in the case of any other failure relating to employee representatives, by any of the representatives to whom the failure related;

(c) in the case of a failure relating to trade union representatives, by the trade union concerned; and

(d) in any other case, by any of the employees who have been or may be dismissed as redundant.

If the employer relies on special circumstances to justify non-compliance, he must show that such circumstances existed and that he did, in fact, take such steps to comply as were reasonably practicable in those circumstances. If the tribunal finds the complaint well-founded, it will so declare and may also make a protective award, i.e., an award that the employer pay remuneration for the protected period (see below) to such descriptions of employees as may be specified. The protective award is designed to ensure that remuneration is paid from the date of the award or of the first of the dismissals, whichever is earlier, for a period (the protected period) considered just and equitable, but not for more than 90 days or 30 days, whichever is the appropriate period under s.188. The complaint must be lodged before the date on which the last of the dismissals to which the complaint relates becomes effective, or during the period of three months beginning with that date, or within such further period as the tribunal considers reasonable where it is satisfied that it was not reasonably practicable for the complaint to be presented during that time (1992 Act, s.189, as amended by the (Protection of Employment) Regulations).

Remuneration during the protected period is at the employee's weekly rate of pay (or *pro rata*) as assessed under ss.190 and 191 of the 1992 Act. To be eligible under the award, an employee must have been entitled to be paid under his contract of employment or by right of a period of notice; and he will have no entitlement if he is employed during the protected period and is either fairly dismissed (other than for redundancy) or unreasonably terminates his employment and, but for that, would still have been employed. Where the employer offers (whether before or after the previous employment ends) to renew the employee's contract, or to re-engage him under a new contract, in either case taking effect before or during the protected period–

(1) the renewed provisions, or those of the renewed contract, as to capacity and place of employment and other terms and conditions, would not differ from those of the previous contract; or

(2) the said provisions would differ from those of the previous contract, but the employment offered is suitable for the employee;

then unreasonable refusal of the offer by the employee will disentitle him to any remuneration under a protective award for the period involved. If, however, the employee's contract is renewed, or he is re-engaged under paragraph (2), there must be provision for a trial period (whether or not there has been a previous trial period) of the new arrangements lasting 4 weeks from the end of the previous employment or such longer period as may be agreed for the purpose of retraining.

If, during the trial period, either the employee acting reasonably for whatever cause, or the employer, in connection with the changed circumstances, terminates the contract of employment, then the employee remains entitled under the award (1992 Act, s.190, as amended by the 1993 Act; and s.191).

An employee may complain to an employment tribunal of non-payment of remuneration by his employer under a protective award. The complaint must be lodged within three months from the date of failure to pay, or within such further period as the tribunal considers reasonable where it is satisfied that it was not reasonably practicable for the complaint to be presented within that time. If the complaint is upheld, the employer will be ordered to remunerate the complainant as the tribunal directs (1992 Act, s.192).

13 Duty to notify Secretary of State

When proposing to make 20 or more employees redundant (under s.188 of the Trade Union and Labour Relations (Consolidation) Act 1992 (see above)), an employer must give written notice of the fact to the Secretary of State *before* giving notice to terminate an employee's contract of employment. Where there are between 20 and 99 proposed redundancies, the notice must be given at least 30 days before the first of those dismissals takes effect; where there are 100 or more proposed redundancies the notice period is increased to 45 days. The notice *inter alia* must, where appropriate under s.188, identify the representatives to be consulted and state when consultations with them began, and must be in such form and contain such other particulars as may be directed. Where there are representatives to be consulted under s.188, the employer must give to each of them a copy of the above notice. After its receipt, the employer may be required to provide further information (1992 Act, s.193, as amended). Failure to give notice under s.193 is an offence (1992 Act, s.194).

14 Collective agreements

Where a collective agreement is in force providing for alternative employment for employees to whom the agreement relates if they are dismissed as redundant by an employer to whom it relates, or for the handling of redundancies, the Secretary of State may, on the application of all the parties and if satisfied that the arrangements under the agreement are generally at least as favourable as those outlined above, by order adapt, modify, or exclude any of the latter provisions both in their application to all or any of those employees and in their application to any other employees of such an employer (Trade Union and Labour Relations (Consolidation) Act 1992, s.198).

15 Excluded employees

By virtue of ss.282 to 284 of the Trade Union and Labour Relations (Consolidation) Act 1992 (as, amended by the 1993 Act), ss.188 to 198 of that Act (see above) do not apply to–

(a) the expiry of a fixed term contract of three months or less (unless the employee is being dismissed by reason of redundancy before the point at which it was agreed in the contract that it would expire); or

(b) employment as a share fisherman.

Where under his contract of employment an employee works, or in the case of a prospective employee would ordinarily work, outside Great Britain, ss.193 and 194 (duty to notify Secretary of State of redundancies— see paragraph 11, above) do not apply (s.285, as amended by the 1999 Act).

16 Employees being transferred from one employer to another

Where there is likely to be a transfer under the Transfer of Undertakings (Protection of Employment) Regulations 2006 (see the Note on **Transfer of Undertakings**) and—

(a) the transferee is proposing to dismiss as redundant 20 or more employees at one establishment within a period of 90 days or less; and

(b) the individuals who work for the transferor and who are to be (or are likely to be) transferred to the transferee's employment under the transfer include one or more individuals who may be affected by the proposed dismissals, or by measures taken in connection with the proposed dismissals,

then the transferee (i.e., the new employer) may elect to consult, or to start to consult, representatives of affected transferring individuals about the proposed dismissals before the transfer takes place, provided that the transferor (i.e., the old employer) agrees (Trade Union and Labour Relations (Consolidation) Act 1992, s.198A). The provisions of ss.188-198 described in the previous paragraphs will then apply as if the transferring individuals were already employees of the new employer.

D: REDUNDNACY PAYMENTS

17 Calculation of payments

The amount of a redundancy payment is calculated by starting at the end of the period of continuous service and reckoning backwards the number of years falling within that period, as follows (Employment Rights Act 1996, s.162)—

For each year of service while aged less than 22 years	half a week's pay
For each year of service while aged at least 22 years but less than 41 years	one week's pay
For each year of service while aged at least 41 years	one and a half week's pay

The amount of a week's pay is calculated in accordance with the provisions of ss.220 to 226 (see the Note on **Employment Protection: Introduction**), and is subject to a limit of £479. Reckonable service is limited to the last 20 years before redundancy (s.162(3)).

For both men and women, the amount payable is reduced by one-twelfth for every complete month by which their age exceeds 64 (s.162(4) and (5)).

On the making of any redundancy payment (otherwise than in pursuance of a tribunal decision specifying the amount of payment to be made), an employer must provide the employee with a written statement indicating how the amount of the payment has been calculated (s.165(1)).

The Redundancy Payments Pensions Regulations 1965 prescribe the conditions under which employers of certain employees who are entitled to a pension or similar allowance on or soon after the termination of their employment by reason of redundancy may exclude or reduce their liability to make redundancy payments.

The Redundancy Payments Statutory Compensation Regulations 1965 provide that a redundancy payment due to an employee shall be set off against compensation due to him under certain statutory provisions in force immediately before 6th December 1965 (e.g., those affecting employees of nationalised industries and local authorities).

Note.–The Income and Corporation Taxes Act 1988 (s.579) provides that any redundancy payment under the Act, or the corresponding amount of any other employer's payment made to an employee under an approved scheme, is normally exempt from income tax; and the employer's redundancy payment is allowable for tax purposes as a business expense.

18 Resolution of disputes

Any question as to the right of an employee to a redundancy payment or as to the amount of such payment may be determined by an employment tribunal (see the Note on **Employment Tribunals, ACAS, and the Employment Appeal Tribunal**) and, for the purposes of such a reference, an employee will be presumed to have been dismissed by reason of redundancy unless the contrary is proved (Employment Rights Act 1996, s.163(1) and (2)).

Except where a written claim for payment has been submitted to the employer, or a reference has been made to a tribunal concerning entitlement to or the amount of, a payment, or a complaint about his dismissal has been made by the employee under s.111 of the Act (see the Note on **Unfair Dismissal**), an application to a tribunal should be made within six months of the date of termination of employment. But the right to a redundancy payment will not be lost if such a claim, reference, complaint, or application is submitted within the following six-month period and it appears to the tribunal to be just and equitable for the employee to receive such a payment, having regard to the reason for his failure to take any such step within the initial six-month period (s.164).

Where a tribunal determines that an employee has a right to a redundancy payment it may also order the employer to pay him such amount as it considers appropriate in all the circumstances to compensate him for any financial loss sustained by him which is attributable to the non-payment of the redundancy payment (s.163(5)).

19 National Insurance Fund

The National Insurance Fund has been established *inter alia* for the purpose of making payments to certain employees.

An employee may apply to the Secretary of State for payment out of the fund after he has taken all reasonable steps (other than legal proceedings) to recover any payment which he claims the employer is liable to pay to him under a redundancy agreement, if the employer either refuses or fails to pay the whole or part of the payment, or is insolvent and the whole or part remains unpaid (Employment Rights Act 1996, s.166). As to the law relating to the rights of an employee on the insolvency of his employer: see the Note on **Insolvency of Employers**.

20 Authorities

Statutes–

Employment Relations Act 1999

Employment Rights Act 1996

Trade Union and Labour Relations (Consolidation) Act 1992

Trade Union Reform and Employment Rights Act 1993

Statutory Instruments–

Redundancy Payments (Continuity of Employment in Local Government, etc.) (Modification) Order 1999, as amended (S.I. 1999 No. 2277, 2000 No. 1042, 2001 No. 866, 2002 Nos. 532, and 1397, 2004 Nos. 664, 1682 and 3168, 2005 Nos. 772, 2929 and 3226, 2007 No. 3224, 2008 Nos. 2250 and 2831, 2009 Nos. 462 and 801, 2010 Nos. 903 and 1172, 2012 Nos. 666 and 2733, 2013 Nos. 1465 and 1784, and 2015 No. 916)

Redundancy Payments (National Health Service) (Modification) Order 1993, as amended (S.I. 1993 No. 3167 and 2000 No. 694, 2002 No. 2469, 2004 No. 696, and 2005 Nos. 445, 1622 and 2078)

Redundancy Payments Office Holders Regulations 1965 (S.I. 1965 No. 2007)

Redundancy Payments Office Holders (Scotland) Regulations 1966 (S.I. 1966 No. 1436)

Redundancy Payments Pensions Regulations 1965 (S.I. 1965 No. 1932)

Redundancy Payments Statutory Compensation Regulations 1965 (S.I. 1965 No. 1988)

Redundancy Payments Termination of Employment Regulations 1965 (S.I. 1965 No. 2022)

RIGHTS ARISING IN THE COURSE OF EMPLOYMENT

Contents

This and other Notes in the Employment Section cover the law relating to—
A: Guarantee payments
B: Suspension from work on medical grounds
C: The right of employees not to suffer detriment
D: Time off work
E: Leave for domestic and family reasons
F: European works councils
G: Paternity and adoption leave
H: Information and Consultation

I The legislation

Parts III, V, VI, VII, VIII and 8A of the Employment Rights Act 1996, as amended, deal with the law relating to the following rights of employees—
(a) the right to guarantee payments (Part III);
(b) the right to remuneration on suspension on medical grounds (Part VII);
(c) the right not to suffer detriment (Part V);
(d) the right to time off for other specified purposes (Part VI);
(e) the right to leave for family and domestic reasons (Part VIII); and
(f) the right to paternity and adoption leave (Part VIII); and
(g) the right to request flexible working (Part 8A).

Share fishermen; and members of the police service are generally excluded from all the rights provided for under the above Parts (ss.199(2), and 200).

The rights of employees to be informed and consulted about certain matters are contained in the Employment Relations Act 2004.

Certain definitions (e.g., normal working hours) and provisions (e.g., the method of calculating a period of continuous employment and a week's pay) which apply to employment law generally are set out in the Note on **Employment Protection: Introduction**.

Unless otherwise stated, any references to sections are references to sections of the Act.

Note.–The law relating to the rights of an employee in connection with trade union membership and activities has been consolidated in the Trade Union and Labour Relations (Consolidation) Act.

A: GUARANTEE PAYMENTS

2 Right to guarantee payment

An employee who has been continuously employed for not less than one month is thereafter entitled to a guarantee payment for a workless day if that is a day during any part of which he would normally be required to work but throughout that day he is not provided by his employer with work for which he is employed by reason of a diminution in the requirements of the employer's business for work of the kind the employee is employed to do or any other occurrence affecting the normal working of the employer's business in relation to such work. "Day" means the period of 24 hours from midnight to midnight, but where a period of employment begun on one day extends or normally extends over midnight into the following day, that period will be treated as falling wholly on the day during which the greater part of the period of employment falls (ss.28 and 29(1)).

However an employee is not entitled to a guarantee payment if—
(a) the failure to provide him with work occurs in consequence of a strike, lockout, or other industrial action involving any employee of his employer or of an associated employer;
(b) he unreasonably refuses an offer of suitable alternative work (whether or not he is contracted to perform that work);
(c) he does not comply with reasonable requirements imposed by his employer with a view to ensuring that his services are available (ss.29(2) and (3));
(d) they are covered by an exemption order: see **5 Exemption orders**, below.

3 Calculation of guarantee payment

The guarantee payment payable to an employee for any working day is calculated by multiplying the actual number of his normal working hours on that day by the guaranteed hourly rate.

Generally, the guaranteed hourly rate is calculated by dividing the employee's weekly pay by the number of working hours in a normal week's employment; the average for the last 12 weeks is taken if the normal hours vary from week to week. Where his employment has been for a period of less than 12 weeks, the number of hours must be assessed by taking account either (a) of the average number of normal working hours in a week which the employee could expect under his contract, or (b) of the average number of such hours worked by fellow employees engaged in comparable employment by the same employer, whichever of these is the more appropriate factor to be considered in the circumstances (s.30).

The amount of a guarantee payment for any day must not exceed £26.00. A guarantee payment is payable only in respect of a specified number of days in any three-month period; usually the number of days (up to a maximum of five) normally worked in a week under the employee's contract at the relevant time. If the employee's contract has been varied, or replaced by a new contract, in connection with a period of short-time working, the guarantee payment is calculated by reference to the last day on which the original contract was in force (s.31).

Remuneration paid by an employer to an employee under a contractual obligation in respect of a workless day goes towards discharging any liability of the employer to pay a guarantee payment in respect of that day, and the converse applies (s.32).

4 Complaint to employment tribunal

An employee may complain to an employment tribunal within the period of three months (which may be extended by the tribunal) after his employer fails to pay the whole or any part of a guarantee payment to which the employee is entitled. If the tribunal finds the complaint well-founded, it will order the employer to the pay the employee the amount due (s.34).

5 Exemption orders

Where employees are covered by a collective agreement or an agricultural wages order (see the Note on **Wages**) which entitles them to guaranteed remuneration, the appropriate Minister may, on the application of all the parties to the agreement or, as the case may be, of the body which made the wages order, make an order excluding those employees from entitlement to a guarantee payment under s.28 (s.35). A number of exemption orders have been made in this connection, the latest being the Guarantee Payments (Exemption) (No. 30) Order 1996 (S.I. No. 2132).

B: SUSPENSION FROM WORK ON MEDICAL GROUNDS

6 Rights to remuneration

An employee who is suspended from work on medical grounds because of any requirement imposed by or under a provision of an enactment or regulations made under an enactment or any recommendation made under a code of practice under the Health and Safety at Work etc. Act 1974 (see the Note on **Health and Safety at Work**) specified in s.64(2) of the Act, is entitled to be remunerated by his employer for a maximum period of 26 weeks (s.64).

However an employee is not entitled to remuneration under s.64–

(a) unless he has been continuously employed for a period of not less than one month, ending with the day before that on which the suspension begins; or

(b) in respect of any period during which he is incapable of work by reason of disease, or bodily or mental disablement; or

(c) in respect of any period during which he was offered by his employer suitable alternative work (whether or not he is contracted to perform that work), and he has unreasonably refused to perform that work; or

(d) in respect of any period during which he does not comply with reasonable requirements imposed by his employer with a view to ensuring that his services are available (s.65).

Any contractual remuneration paid by an employer to an employee in respect of any period will go towards his liability under s.64 and the converse applies (s.69).

7 Complaint to employment tribunal

An employee may present a complaint to an employment tribunal within the period of three months (which may be extended by the tribunal) after his employer has failed to pay the whole or any part of remuneration which is due to him under s.64. If the tribunal finds the complaint to be well-founded, it will order the employer to pay the amount due (s.70).

C: THE RIGHT OF EMPLOYEES NOT TO SUFFER DETRIMENT

8 Right not to suffer detriment

An employee has the right not to be subjected to any detriment by any act, or any deliberate failure to act, by his employer in various specified situations where the employee is seeking to utilise an employment right. These cases are–

in health ad safety cases

in working time cases under the Working Time Regulations 1998

when making a public interest disclosure

for taking leave for family or domestic reasons, or taking paternity or adoption leave

by bringing proceedings or exercising their rights under the Part-time Workers (Prevention of Less Favourable Treatment) Regulations 2000 or the Fixed-term Employees (Prevention of Less Favourable Treatment) Regulations 2002

by reason of making an application, exercising rights, or bringing proceedings under the provisions relating to flexible working

by reason of making an application, exercising rights, or bringing proceedings under the provisions relating to study or training

by refusing to accept an offer from the employer for them to become an employee shareholder

in connection with the taking of shared parental leave;

by reason of his being an employee representative

by reason of his being a European Works Council member

by reason of his activities in relation to trade union recognition

by reason of his being a trustee of an occupational pension scheme

by reason of his being an information and consultation representative

This right is covered fully in the separate note on the right of employees not to suffer detriment.

D: TIME OFF WORK

9 Introduction

Ss.50 to 63K provide that an employer must allow an employee time off work for any of the following purposes, namely—

(a) to carry out certain public duties;

(b) where the employee has been given notice of dismissal by reason of redundancy, to look for new employment or make arrangements for training for new employment;

(c) in the case of a pregnant employee, to receive ante-natal care and, in the case of an employee who has a qualifying relationship with a pregnant woman, to accompany her to ante-natal appointments;

(d) in the case of an employee who is a representative for the purposes of Part IV of the Trade Union and Labour Relations (Consolidation) Act 1992 (redundancies) (see the Note on **Redundancy**) or Regulations 9, 13 and 15 of the Transfer of Undertakings (Protection of Employment) Regulations 2006) (see the Note on **Transfer of Undertakings**), or a candidate in an election for such representatives, to perform his functions as such a representative or candidate;

(e) a Works Council member;

(f) in the case of an employee who is a trustee of an occupational pension scheme, to perform his duties as a trustee and to undergo relevant training;

(g) in the case of certain employees aged 16 or 17, to undertake study or training; and

(h) an information and consultation representative.

These provisions are covered fully in the separate note on the right to time off work

E: LEAVE FOR FAMILY AND DOMESTIC REASONS

10 Introduction

The Employment Relations Act 1999 gives employees new rights to take unpaid "parental" leave to care for a child for whom they are responsible or to deal with an unexpected family emergency.

Part 8A of the Employment Rights Act 1996 (inserted by the Employment Act 2002, s.47) gives an employee the right to ask for a contractual variation of the terms and conditions of their employment in order to request flexible working.

These rights are covered fully in the separate Note on **Rights Arising in the Course of Employment: Leave for Domestic and Family Reasons, and Flexible Working**.

F: EUROPEAN WORKS COUNCILS

11 Background

The European Works Council Directive 1994/45/EC provides for the establishment in "Community-scale undertakings" or "Community-scale groups of undertakings" of European Works Councils or procedures for the purpose of informing and consulting employees on certain matters. This Directive was extended to cover the UK by Directive 97/74/EC and has been implemented by the Transnational Information and Consultation of Employees Regulations 1999 which apply to the whole of the UK, including Northern Ireland (Reg. 1).

A "Community-scale undertaking" is an undertaking with at least 1,000 employees within the Member States and at least 150 employees in each of at least two Member States. A "Community-scale group of undertakings" is a group with at least 1,000 employees within the Member States and at least two group undertakings in different Member States each with at least 150 employees.

The Regulations apply to undertakings where–
(a) the central management is situated in the UK;
(b) the central management is not situated in any Member State but its representative agent is situated in the UK; or
(c) neither the central management nor the representative agent is situated in a Member State but the undertaking has more employees at an establishment in the UK than in any other Member State.

Where (b) or (c) applies, only certain of the provisions of the Regulations will apply to the undertaking (see Reg. 4).

Note.–An "undertaking" need not necessarily be a company. It could, for example, be a partnership.

12 Formation of a European Works Council agreement

The Regulations provide for a European Works Council agreement to result from negotiations between the central management of the business concerned and employee representatives (Reg. 9). The process may be initiated by the central management or at the written request of at least 100 employees (or representatives of at least 100 employees) in at least two Member States.

Negotiations on behalf of employees are to be carried out by a "special negotiating body" consisting of–
(i) at least one member from each Member State in which the undertaking has an establishment;
(ii) one additional member from a Member State in which the undertaking employs at least 25, but not more than 50 per cent of its employees;
(iii) two additional members from a Member State in which the undertaking employs at least 50, but not more than 75 per cent of its employees;
(iv) three additional members from a Member State in which the undertaking employs at least 75 per cent of its employees.

The UK members of a special negotiating body are to be elected by a ballot conducted in accordance with the Regulations (Regs. 13 and 14) unless a "consultative committee" exists, in which case that committee will nominate members to the special negotiating body. A "consultative committee" is a committee which represents all the undertaking's UK employees; whose normal functions include or comprise the carrying out of an information and consultation function; which is able to carry out that function without interference from the UK management (or central management, if different); and whose members were all elected by ballot (Reg. 15).

The central management and the special negotiating body are under a duty to negotiate in a spirit of co-operation with a view to reaching a written agreement on the detailed arrangements for the information and consultation of employees (Reg. 17). They may decide to establish an "information and consultation procedure" instead of a European Works Council (Reg. 17(3)).

13 Contents of a European Works Council agreement

Where it is decided to establish a European Works Council, the agreement establishing it must set out–
(a) the undertakings covered by the agreement;
(b) the composition of the council, terms of office, etc;
(c) the functions of the council and the procedure for information and consultation with it;
(d) the venue, frequency and duration of its meetings;
(e) its financial and material resources; and
(f) the duration of the agreement and procedure for its re-negotiation.

If it is decided to establish an information and consultation procedure instead of a Works Council, the agreement establishing it must specify the method by which representatives are to enjoy the right to meet to discuss the information conveyed to them. That information must relate in particular to transnational questions which significantly affect the interests of employees (Reg. 17).

14 Default provisions

The Transnational Information and Consultation of Employees Regulations 1999 contain default provisions which will apply if (Reg. 18)–
(a) the central management and special negotiating body agree that they should; or
(b) the central management refuses to commence negotiations within six months of receiving a request (see **12 Formation of a European Works Council agreement**, above); or
(c) the parties have failed to reach an agreement within three years of the request for negotiations being made.

These default provisions are contained in the Schedule to the Regulations and provide that the Council will have, *inter alia*, a right to be informed and consulted about–
(i) the structure, economic and financial situation of the business;
(ii) the probable development of the business and of production and sales;
(iii) the situation and probable trend of employment and investments; and
(iv) substantial changes concerning organisation, new working methods or production procedures, transfers of production, mergers, cutbacks or closures, and collective redundancies.

15 Enforcement provisions

If an agreement is reached between the central management and the special negotiating body as to the establishment of a European Works Council (or information and consultation procedure), but because of a failure of the central management it is not established (or not fully established), a complaint may be brought before the Central Arbitration Committee (CAC) who may make an order specifying the steps to be taken by the central management and imposing a penalty (Reg. 20).

Similarly, where a European Works Council (or information and consultation procedure) is established, but the terms of its operation are not complied with, a complaint may be brought before the CAC who may make an order specifying the steps which the party in default is required to take and the period for compliance. If the defaulter is the central management, the applicant may, within three months beginning with the date on which the decision is made, apply to the Employment Appeal Tribunal for a penalty notice to be issued (Reg. 21).

The maximum penalty under Regulations 20 and 21 is £75,000 (Reg. 22).

16 Consequential employment rights

An employee who is–
  (i) a member of a special negotiating body;
  (ii) a member of a European Works Council;
  (iii) an information and consultation representative; or
  (iv) a candidate in an election for someone who will become (i), (ii) or (iii),
has consequential employment rights arising from his position in relation to (Regs 25 to 32)–
  (a) time off work to perform his duties;
  (b) not being subjected to detriment because of his position; and
  (c) not being unfairly dismissed.

G: PATERNITY AND ADOPTION LEAVE

17 Introduction

Part VIII of the Employment Rights Act 1996, as amended by the Employment Act 2002, makes provision for paternity leave (ss.80A to 80E). The Act is supplemented by the Paternity and Adoption Leave Regulations 2002.

Part VIII of the Employment Rights Act 1996, as amended by the Employment Act 2002, makes provision for adoption leave (ss.75A to 75D). The Act is supplemented by the Paternity and Adoption Leave Regulations 2002.

The Shared Parental Leave Regulations 2014 introduce an entitlement for employees who are mothers, fathers, adopters, or prospective adopters, or the partners of mothers or adopters, or prospective adopters, to take shared parental leave in the first year of their child's life or in the first year after the child's placement for adoption.

These provisions are covered fully in the separate note on Paternity and Adoption Leave, and Shared Parental Leave.

H: INFORMATION AND CONSULTATION

18 The right of employees to be informed and consulted

EC Directive 2002/14 on the Information and Consultation of Employees establishes a general framework setting out minimum requirements for the information to be given to, and consultation to be undertaken with, employees throughout the European Union. This Directive is implemented in the UK by the Employment Relations Act 2004 (s.42) and the Information and Consultation of Employees Regulations 2004.

The provisions on information and consultation apply to undertakings with at least 50 employees (Reg. 3 and Sch. 1).

Where 10% of its employees so request (subject to a minimum of 15 and a maximum of 2,500 employees), an employer must enter into negotiations as to the information and consultation procedures to be adopted. A request must be in writing and sent to the Central Arbitration Committee (Reg. 7). In the absence of a negotiated agreement between employer and employees, standard information and consultation provisions apply.

19 The standard provisions

Under the standard provisions the employer must arrange for the holding of a ballot of its employees to elect information and consultation representatives (Reg. 19). There must be one representative for every 50 employees, with a minimum of 2 and a maximum of 25 representatives.

The employer must provide the representatives with information on (Reg. 20)–
  (a) recent and probable development of the undertaking's activities and economic situation;
  (b) the situation, structure, and probable development of employment within the undertaking and any anticipatory measures envisaged, particularly where there is a threat to employment;

257

(c) decisions likely to lead to substantial changes in work organisation or in contractual relations (although this duty ceases once an employer is under a duty to consult employee representatives under the provisions dealing with redundancy (see the Note on **Redundancy**) or transfer of undertakings (see the Note on **Transfer of Undertakings**).

In the case of (b) and (c), the representatives must be consulted as well as informed. Such consultation must be conducted in such a way as to ensure that the timing, method and content of the consultation are appropriate and so that representatives can meet the employer at the relevant level of management and obtain a reasoned response to any opinion they express. In the case of (c), consultation must be with a view to reaching agreement on decisions within the scope of the employer's powers.

The regulations specifically provide that the parties must work in a spirit of co-operation and with due regard for their reciprocal rights and obligations, taking into account the interests of both the undertaking and the employees (Reg. 21).

The employer is not required to disclose information or documents which, judged objectively, would seriously harm the functioning of, or would be prejudicial to, the undertaking (Reg. 26).

20 Disputes and penalties

Complaints about the operation of the consultation and information provisions by an employer may be made to the Central Arbitration Committee by an information and consultation representative (or if they have not been appointed yet, by an employee or employee's representative) (Reg. 22). The Committee has the power to order the employer to take steps to comply with the provisions. Penalty notices (to a maximum of £75,000) may also be issued.

The Committee can also make a declaration as to whether an employer is correct is not disclosing material under Regulation 26 (see **19 The standard provisions**, above) and order such disclosure (Reg. 26(3)).

21 Authorities

Statutes–
Employment Relations Act 1999

Employment Rights Act 1996

Statutory Instruments–
Information and Consultation of Employees Regulations 2004, as amended (S.I. 2004 No. 3426, 2006 Nos. 514 and 2405, 2009 No. 3348, 2010 No. 93, 2013 No. 1956, and 2014 No. 386)

Paternity and Adoption Leave Regulations 2002, as amended (S.I. 2002 No. 2788, 2003 No. 921, 2004 No. 923, 2005 No. 2114, 2006 No. 2014, 2007 No. 2014, 2008 No. 1966, 2011 No. 1740 and 2014 Nos. 2112, 3096, and 3206)

Shared Parental Leave Regulations 2014, as amended (S.I. 2014 No. 3050, and 2015 No. 552)

Transnational Information and Consultation of Employees Regulations 1999, as amended (S.I. 1999 No. 3323, 2004 Nos. 1079 and 2518, 2006 No. 2059, 2009 Nos. 2401 and 3348, 2010 No. 1088, 2013 No. 1956, and 2014 No. 386)

RIGHTS ARISING IN THE COURSE OF EMPLOYMENT: DETRIMENT

1 Right not to suffer detriment in health and safety cases

An employee has the right not to be subjected to any detriment by any act, or any deliberate failure to act, by his employer done on the ground that—

(a) having been designated by the employer to carry out activities in connection with preventing or reducing risks to health and safety at work, he carried out, or proposed to carry out, any such activities;

(b) being a representative of workers on matters of health and safety at work, or a member of a safety committee, (i) in accordance with established statutory arrangements or (ii) by reason of being acknowledged as such by the employer, he performed, or proposed to perform, any functions as such a representative or a member of such a committee;

(c) being an employee at a place where—
   (i) there was no such representative or safety committee, or
   (ii) there was such a representative or committee but it was not reasonably practicable for the employee to raise the matter by those means,
he brought to his employer's attention, by reasonable means, circumstances connected with his work which he reasonably believed were harmful or potentially harmful to his health and safety;

(d) in circumstances of danger which he reasonably believed to be serious and imminent and which he could not reasonably have been expected to avert, he left, or proposed to leave, or (while the danger persisted) refused to return to, his place of work or any dangerous part of his place of work; or

(e) in circumstances of serious and imminent danger, he took, or proposed to take, appropriate steps to protect himself or other persons from the danger. However, an employee will not be regarded as having been subjected to any detriment in these circumstances where the employer shows that it was, or would have been, so negligent for the employee to take the steps which he took, or proposed to take, that a reasonable employer might have treated him as the employer did (s.44).

S.44 does not apply where the detriment in question amounts to dismissal (s.44(4)).

2 Right not to suffer detriment in working time cases

An employee has the right not to be subjected to any detriment by any act, or deliberate failure to act, by his employer done on the ground that the worker—

(a) refused to comply with a requirement which the employer imposed in contravention of the Working Time Regulations 1998;

(b) refused to forgo a right conferred on him by those Regulations;

(c) failed to sign a workforce agreement for the purposes of those Regulations, or to enter into, or agree to vary or extend, any other agreement with his employer which is provided for in those Regulations;

(d) being a representative of members of the workforce for the purposes of Schedule 1 to those Regulations, or a candidate in an election in which any person elected will, on being elected, be such a representative, performed any functions or activities as such a representative or candidate;

(e) brought proceedings against the employer to enforce a right conferred on him by those Regulations; or

(f) alleged that the employer had infringed such a right (s.45A).

S.45A does not apply where a worker is an employee and the detriment in question amounts to dismissal (s.45A(4)).

As to the Working Time Regulations, see the Note on **Working Time Restrictions**.

3 Right not to suffer detriment for making a protected disclosure

An employee has the right not to be subjected to any detriment by any act, or deliberate failure to act, done by an employer on the ground that the employee concerned has made a protected disclosure under the Public Interest Disclosure Act 1998 (s.47B, added by the 1998 Act, s.2). As to protected public interest disclosures, see the Note on **Public Interest Disclosure**.

4 Right not to suffer detriment for taking leave for family or domestic reasons, or taking paternity or adoption leave

An employee has the right not to be subjected to any detriment by any act, or deliberate failure to act, by an employer done on the ground that they (s.47C, as added by the 1999 Act, Schedule 4; and the Paternity and Adoption Leave Regulations 2002, Reg. 28)—

(a) are pregnant;

(b) have given birth;

(c) have taken maternity leave;

(d) have taken parental leave or time off to deal with a family emergency (i.e., under s.57A: see the Note on

Rights Arising in the Course of Employment: Leave for Domestic and Family Reasons, and Flexible Working);

   (e) have taken paternity or ordinary or additional adoption leave, or their employer believes that they are likely to take ordinary or additional adoption leave;

   (f) have taken time off to accompany to an ante-natal appointment: (i.e., under s.57ZE: see the Note on **Rights Arising in the Course of Employment: Time Off**), or their employer believes that they are likely to take such time off; or

   (g) have taken time off to attend an adoption appointment (i.e., under ss.57ZJ or 57ZL), or their employer believes that they are likely to take such time off.

S.47C does not apply where the detriment amounts to dismissal (Reg. 28(2)).

An employee also has the right not to be subjected to any detriment for considering, undertaking, or not undertaking, any work for the employer whilst on adoption leave (Reg. 28(1)(bb)).

An agency worker has a right not to be subjected to a detriment by the temporary work agency or hirer on the ground that they took or sought to take time off for an ante-natal appointment, or to accompany to such an appointment under ss.57ZA or 57ZG (s.47C, as amended by the Children and Families Act 2014, s.129(1): see the Note on **Rights Arising in the Course of Employment: Time Off**).

5 Part-time and fixed-term employees

Part-time and fixed-term employees have a right not to be subjected to any detriment by any act, or deliberate failure to act, by an employer by reason of their bringing proceedings or exercising their rights under the Part-time Workers (Prevention of Less Favourable Treatment) Regulations 2000 or the Fixed-term Employees (Prevention of Less Favourable Treatment) Regulations 2002 (see the Note on **Part-time, Fixed-term, and Agency Workers**).

6 Right not to suffer detriment–flexible working

An employee has the right not to be subjected to any detriment by any act, or deliberate failure to act, by an employer by reason of their making an application, exercising their rights, or bringing proceedings under the provisions relating to flexible working (see the Note on **Rights Arising in the Course of Employment: Leave for Domestic and Family Reasons, and Flexible Working**) (s.47D).

7 Right not to suffer detriment–study or training

An employee has the right not to be subjected to any detriment by any act, or any deliberate failure to act, by an employer by reason of their making an application, exercising their rights, or bringing proceedings under the provisions relating to study or training (see the Note on **Rights Arising in the Course of Employment: Time Off**) (ss.47A, 47F).

There is a similar right where the employee is seeking to participate in education or training under the Education and Skills Act 2008, ss.27-28 (duty of under-18s to participate in education or training) (s.47AA).

8 Right not to suffer detriment–employee shareholders

An employee has the right not to be subjected to a detriment by any act, or any deliberate failure to act, by their employer done on the ground that the employee refused to accept an offer by the employer for them to become an employee shareholder (s.47G, as added by the Growth and Infrastructure Act 2013, s.31). As to employee shareholders, see the Note on **Employment Protection: Introduction** at para **9 Employee shareholders**).

9 Right not to suffer detriment–shared parental leave

An employee is entitled not to be subjected to any detriment by any act, or any deliberate failure to act, by an employer because the employee took, sought to take, or made use of the benefits of, shared parental leave; the employer believed that the employee was likely to take shared parental leave; or, the employee undertook, considered undertaking, or refused to undertake work during shared parental leave (Shared Parental Leave Regulations 2014, Reg. 42).

10 Right of employee representatives not to suffer detriment

An employee has the right not to be subjected to any detriment by any act, or any deliberate failure to act, by his employer done on the ground that, being–

   (a) an employee representative for the purposes of Part IV of the Trade Union and Labour Relations (Consolidation) Act 1992 (redundancies) (see the Note on **Redundancy**) or Regulations 9, 13 and 15 of the Transfer of Undertakings (Protection of Employment) Regulations 2006 (see the Note on **Transfer of Undertakings**); or

   (b) a candidate in an election for such representatives,

he performed, or proposed to perform, any functions or activities as such a representative or candidate (s.47(1)). This section does not apply where the detriment in question amounts to a dismissal (s.47(2)).

An employee who participates in an election for the representatives mentioned in (a) above has a similar right not to be subjected to detriment (s.47(1A), as inserted by the Collective Redundancies and Transfer of Undertakings (Protection of Employment) (Amendment) Regulations 1999 (S.I. No. 1925).

11 European Works Council members, etc

An employee who is—
(i) a member of a special negotiating body;
(ii) a member of a European Works Council;
(iii) an information and consultation representative; or
(iv) a candidate in an election for someone who will become (i), (ii) or (iii),
has the right not to be subjected to any detriment by any act, or deliberate failure to act, by his employer on one of a number of specified grounds relating to the performance of the functions or activities of his position (Transnational Information and Consultation of Employees Regulations 1999, Reg. 31).

The provisions do not apply where the detriment in question amounts to a dismissal (Reg. 32(3)).

As to European Works Councils generally, see the Note on **Rights Arising in the Course of Employment.**

12 Right of workers not to suffer detriment—union recognition

A worker has a right not to be subjected to any detriment by his employer as a result of his (Sch. A1, para 156)—
(a) acting with a view to obtaining or preventing recognition of a union by his employer;
(b) acting with a view to obtaining or preventing the ending of bargaining arrangements;
(c) indicating his support for or opposition to such recognition or the ending of such bargaining arrangements;
(d) influencing or seeking to influence other workers to vote, abstain, or vote in a particular way in a ballot under Schedule A1 on one of the above matters, or himself voting in such a ballot.

13 Right not to suffer detriment—pensions

An employee has the right not to be subjected to any detriment by any act, or any deliberate failure to act, by his employer done on the ground that, being a trustee of a relevant occupational pension scheme which relates to his employment, the employee performed (or proposed to perform) any functions as such a trustee (Employment Rights Act 1996, s.46(1)). This section does not apply where the detriment in question amounts to a dismissal (s.46(2)).

A worker has the right not to be subjected to any detriment by an act done on specified grounds in relation to enrolment in a pension scheme under the Pensions Act 2008, Part 1 (see the Note on **Occupational Pension Schemes: General Provisions**). For example, this right would protect a worker who might have been denied promotion or training opportunities because of their decision not to opt out of pension scheme membership (Pensions Act 2008, s.55).

14 Right of information and consultation representatives not to suffer detriment

An employee who is an information and consultation representative under the provisions relating to information and consultation of employees has the right not to be subjected to any detriment by any act, or any deliberate failure to act, by his employer done on the ground that he performed (or proposed to perform) any functions as such a representative (Information and Consultation of Employees Regulations 2004, Reg. 32). The right extends to employees who are negotiating representatives (i.e., employees elected or appointed to negotiate information and consultation procedures with an employer), employees' representatives, and candidates to be a representative.

All employees, whether or not they are representatives, have a right not to suffer detriment by reason of their taking part in information and consultation procedures (e.g., by voting in an election for a representative).

15 Complaint to employment tribunal

An employee may complain to an employment tribunal that he has been subjected to a detriment in contravention of ss.44, 45A, 46, 47, 47B, 47C, 47D or of Regulation 31 of the Transnational Information and Consultation of Employees Regulations 1999. The complaint must be made within three months beginning with the date of the act or failure to act to which the complaint relates or, where that act or failure is part of a series of similar acts or failures, the last of them, or within such further period as the tribunal considers reasonable. For these purposes, the date of the act means the last day of that period, and a deliberate failure to act is to be treated as done when it was decided on, and, in the absence of evidence establishing the contrary, an employer will be taken to decide on a failure to act when he does an act inconsistent with doing the failed act or, if he has done no such inconsistent act, when the period expires within which he might reasonably have been expected to do the failed act if it was to be done (s.48, and the Transnational Information and Consultation of Employees Regulations 1999, Reg. 32). Where the tribunal finds that a complaint is well-founded, it will make a declaration to that effect and may make an award of compensation to be paid to the complainant in respect of the act or failure to act complained of. The amount of the compensation awarded will be such as the tribunal considers just and equitable in all the circumstances having regard to the infringement complained of and to any loss which is attributable to the act or failure which infringed his right. The loss may include any expenses reasonably incurred by the complainant in consequence of the act or failure complained of, and loss of any benefit which he might reasonably be expected to have had but for that act or failure. An employee is under a duty to mitigate his loss, and the tribunal must reduce the amount of the compensation by such proportion as it considers just and equitable, where it finds that the act or failure complained of was to any extent caused or contributed to by action of the complainant (s.49, and the Transnational Information and Consultation of Employees Regulations 1999, Reg. 32).

16 Zero hours contracts

A person working on a zero hours contract has the right not to be unfairly dismissed or subjected to a detriment because they have breached a provision of a the contract which prohibits them from doing work under another contract or arrangement (Exclusivity Terms in Zero Hours Contracts (Redress) Regulations 2015).

The right not to suffer any detriment in these circumstances is subject to "early conciliation" meaning that a prospective claimant wishing to take a case to an employment tribunal must first contact the Advisory, Conciliation and Arbitration Service ("Acas") about their dispute and consider conciliation before presenting a claim to a tribunal (Employment Tribunals Act 1996, s.18(1)(z3)).

As to zero hours contracts, see the Note on **Terms of Employment** at para 12 **Exclusivity in zero hours contracts**.

17 Authorities

Statutes–

Children and Families Act 2014

Employment Relations Act 1999

Employment Rights Act 1996

Pensions Act 2008

Statutory Instruments–

Exclusivity Terms in Zero Hours Contracts (Redress) Regulations 2015, as amended (S.I. 2015 Nos. 2021 and 2054)

Information and Consultation of Employees Regulations 2004, as amended (S.I. 2004 No. 3426, 2006 Nos. 514 and 2405, 2009 No. 3348, 2010 No. 93, 2013 No. 1956, and 2014 No. 386)

Paternity and Adoption Leave Regulations 2002, as amended (S.I. 2002 No. 2788, 2003 No. 921, 2004 No. 923, 2005 No. 2114, 2006 No. 2014, 2007 No. 2014, 2008 No. 1966, 2011 No. 1740 and 2014 Nos. 2112, 3096, and 3206)

Shared Parental Leave Regulations 2014, as amended (S.I. 2014 No. 3050, and 2015 No. 552)

Transnational Information and Consultation of Employees Regulations 1999, as amended (S.I. 1999 No. 3323, 2004 Nos. 1079 and 2518, 2006 No. 2059, 2009 Nos. 2401 and 3348, 2010 No. 1088, 2013 No. 1956, and 2014 No. 386)

RIGHTS ARISING IN THE COURSE OF EMPLOYMENT: LEAVE FOR DOMESTIC AND FAMILY REASONS, AND FLEXIBLE WORKING

1 Introduction

The Employment Relations Act 1999 gives employees new rights to take unpaid leave to care for a child for whom they are responsible or to deal with an unexpected family emergency. These rights are described in detail in this Note.

2 Parental leave

Part VIII of the 1996 Act (ss.71 to 80E) gives the Secretary of State the power to make regulations giving employees the right to take unpaid "parental leave" to care for children. Part III of the Maternity and Parental Leave etc. Regulations 1999 (the Regulations) has been made under this power.

3 Entitlement to leave

Regulation 13 provides that an employee who has been continuously employed by his employer for at least one year and who has, or who expects to have, responsibility for a child is entitled to take parental leave to care for that child. The right to take parental leave applies to anyone who has parental responsibility for a child within the meaning of the Children Act 1989 or the Children (Scotland) Act 1995, and to anyone registered as the child's father under the Births and Deaths Registration Act 1953 or the Registration of Births, Deaths and Marriages (Scotland) Act 1965.

4 Extent of entitlement

An employee is entitled to take 18 weeks' leave for each child. Where the number of hours worked each week varies, or where an employee works some weeks but not others, a week's leave is calculated by dividing the total of the periods for which he is normally required to work in a year by 52 (Reg. 14).

An employee must take his full entitlement to parental leave before the child's 18th birthday (Reg. 15).

5 Procedures for taking leave

Employers and employees may agree their own procedures for taking parental leave through individual, workforce or collective agreements. Where a workforce or collective agreement forms part of an employee's contract, the provisions of that agreement will apply. Where there is no applicable workforce or collective agreement, the Regulations contain (in Schedule 2) certain default provisions which will apply instead. These are as follows–

(i) an employee must, if required by his employer, provide evidence of his entitlement to leave (e.g., evidence of a child's date of birth, or evidence of parentage (and of previous employment where Reg. 13(1A) applies));

(ii) an employee must give his employer at least 21 days' notice of his intention to take leave and give beginning and end dates. If the employee is an expectant father wishing to take leave when his child is born, he must specify the expected week of the birth and the duration of the leave he intends to take;

(iii) where the employee gives notice of his intention to take leave, the employer may, within seven days, give notice in turn postponing that leave for up to six months (but not beyond the child's 18th birthday) on the ground that the employer's business would be unduly disrupted by the employee taking leave during that period. However, an employer may not postpone an employee's leave where the employee is a father wishing to take leave after the birth of his child, or where the employee is adopting a child and wishes to take leave immediately after the child is placed with him;

(iv) leave must be taken in multiples of one week, except where the child in question is entitled to a disability allowance, in which case leave may be taken in multiples of one day;

(v) an employee must not take more than four weeks leave for any one child in any one year (a year being a 12 month period beginning on the date on which the employee first became entitled to take parental leave for that child, with each successive twelve month period beginning on the anniversary of that date).

6 Terms and conditions of employment during periods of leave

Regulation 17 provides that an employee who takes parental leave is entitled, during leave periods, to the benefit of his employer's implied obligations to him of trust and confidence, and any terms of employment relating to (i) notice of termination of the contract; (ii) compensation for redundancy; and (iii) disciplinary or grievance procedures. Equally, the employee is bound, during that period, by his implied obligation to his employer of good faith, and any terms and conditions of employment relating to (i) notice of termination of his contract by him; (ii) disclosure of confidential information; (iii) the acceptance of gifts or other benefits; and (iv) the employee's participation in any other business (Reg. 17).

7 Right to return to work after parental leave

An employee who takes parental leave is entitled to return to the same job that he had before his absence if the period of leave was four weeks or less, which was—

(a) an isolated period of leave, or
(b) the last of two or more consecutive periods of statutory leave which did not include—

    (i) any period of parental leave of more than four weeks; or
    (ii) any period of statutory leave which when added to any other period of statutory leave (excluding parental leave) taken in relation to the same child means that the total amount of statutory leave taken in relation to that child totals more than 26 weeks.

An employee who takes more than four weeks leave is entitled to return either to the same job, or if it is not reasonably practicable for the employer to permit him to return to the same job, to another job which is both suitable and appropriate for him.

Where parental leave of up to four weeks follows on immediately after a period of additional maternity leave (lasting up to 52 weeks from the date of the birth—see the Note on **Statutory Maternity, Paternity, Adoption and Parental Pay, and Maternity Allowance**) a woman is entitled to return to the same job, unless it is not reasonably practicable for her to do so. In these circumstances, she is entitled to return to another job which is both suitable and appropriate for her (Reg. 18).

The right to return is a right to return with seniority, pension rights and similar rights as they would have been if the employee had not been absent (Reg. 18A).

An employee has the right not to be subjected to detriment or to be dismissed for exercising his right to parental leave (Regs 19 and 20) (see the Notes on **Rights Arising in the Course of Employment: Detriment**, and **Unfair Dismissal**).

8 Contractual right to parental leave

Where an employee's contract of employment already gives a right to parental leave, the employee may not exercise the right under the Regulations and the contractual right separately, but may take advantage of whichever right is, in any particular respect, the more favourable (Reg. 21).

9 Complaint to a tribunal

An employee may present a complaint to an industrial tribunal that his employer has unreasonably postponed a period of parental leave requested by him or has prevented the employee from taking such leave. Any such complaint must be made within three months of the date (or the last date) of the matters complained of or within such further period as the tribunal considers reasonable. Where a tribunal finds a complaint to be well-founded, it must make a declaration to that effect, and make an award of compensation of an amount that it considers just and equitable, having regard to the employer's behaviour and any loss sustained by the employee (s.80).

10 Time off for dependants

S.57A of the Act (inserted by s.8 of, and Schedule 4 Part II to, the 1999 Act) provides that an employee is entitled to be permitted by his employer to take a reasonable amount of time off during working hours in order to take necessary action (s.57A(1))—

(a) to assist when a dependant falls ill, gives birth or is injured or assaulted;
(b) to make arrangements for the provision of care for a dependant who is ill or injured;
(c) in consequence of a dependant's death;
(d) because of the unexpected disruption or termination of arrangements for the care of a dependant (e.g. where a child minder fails to turn up); and
(e) to deal with an unexpected incident involving a child of the employee occurring while the child is at school or college.

For all the above purposes, a "dependant" is an employee's spouse, child or parent, or any person living in the employee's household (other than an employee, tenant or lodger) (s.57A(3)). For the purposes of (a) and (b) above, the term "dependant" also includes any other person who reasonably relies on the employee for help if they fall ill or are injured or assaulted, and for the purposes of (a), (b), and (d) above, any person who reasonably relies on the employee to make care arrangements for them.

An employee will not be entitled to time off unless he (i) tells his employer of the reason for his absence as soon as reasonably practicable and, (ii) except where (i) cannot be complied with until the employee returns to work, tells his employer how long he expects to be absent.

There is no prescribed limit to the amount of time off that may be taken under s.57A, except that it must be a "reasonable" period. *Time off for Dependants–A short guide for employers and employees*, formerly produced by the Department for Business, Enterprise and Regulatory Reform (2007) but now no longer available stated, in Section 5, that "for most cases, one or two days should be sufficient to deal with the problem". For example, if a child falls ill "the leave should be enough to help the employee cope with the immediate crisis", e.g., taking the child to see a doctor and arranging long term care, but "the employee is not entitled to take two weeks' leave to look after a sick child".

There is no right under s.57A to be paid during a period of absence and any entitlement to pay will depend on the terms of an employee's contract.

S.57B allows an employee to present a complaint to an employment tribunal that his employer has unreasonably refused to permit him to take time off as required by s.57A. Any such complaint must be presented within three months of the date of the refusal, or within such further period as the tribunal considers reasonable. Where a tribunal finds a complaint to be well-founded, it must make a declaration to that effect and may make an award of compensation of such amount as it considers just, having regard to the employer's default and any loss suffered by the employee.

11 Right to request flexible working: introduction

Part 8A of the Employment Rights Act 1996 (inserted by the Employment Act 2002, s.47) gives an employee the right to ask for a contractual variation of the terms and conditions of their employment in order to request flexible working. Prior to the coming into force of provisions of the Children and Families Act 2014, the right had applied to parents and carers only. This restriction has been removed by the 2014 Act.

The employee must be a "qualifying employee" which means that the employee must (s.80F(8))–
  (a) satisfy such conditions as to duration of employment as the Secretary of State may specify by regulations (see 13 **Conditions to be satisfied**, below); and
  (b) not be an agency worker.

An employee shareholder (see the Note on **Employment Protection: Introduction**, at para **9 Employee shareholders**) does not have the right to make an application to request flexible working although they still have a limited right to make an application within 14 days beginning with the day on which the employee shareholder concerned returns to work from a period of parental leave (1996 Act, s.205A(8)).

12 Variations which may be requested

A variation may be requested if it relates to (Employment Rights Act 1996, s.80F(1)(a))–
  (a) the hours a person is required to work;
  (b) the time a person is required to work;
  (c) where, as between home and an employer's premises, a person is required to work; or
  (d) such other aspects of the terms and conditions of a person's employment as the Secretary of State may specify by regulations.

13 Conditions to be satisfied

An application must (Employment Rights Act 1996, s.80F(2))–
  (a) state that it is an application to request flexible working;
  (b) specify the change applied for and the date it is proposed the change should become effective;
  (c) explain what effect the employee thinks the change will have on the employer and how, in their opinion, such an effect might be dealt with.

The Flexible Working Regulations 2014 requires an employee to have 26 weeks of continuous employment in order to make a flexible working application (Reg. 3). An application must be in writing, must be dated and must state if any previous flexible working applications have been made and, if so, when (Reg. 4).

Only one application can be made in any 12 month period (s.80F(4)).

14 Procedure following an application

A flexible working application is taken as made on the day it is received. Any such application is received, unless the contrary is proved (Flexible Working Regulations 2014, Reg. 5)–
  (a) where the application is sent by electronic transmission (and the employer has agreed that an application can be sent by such means, has specified an electronic address and form to be used), on the day of transmission;
  (b) if sent by post, on the day on which it would have been delivered in the ordinary course of post; and
  (c) if it is delivered personally, on the day of delivery.

The employer is under a duty to deal with the application in a reasonable manner and to notify the employee of the decision on the application within the decision period (see below) (Employment Rights Act 1996, s.80G(1)(a), (aa)). A Code of Practice on handling in a reasonable manner requests to work flexibly has been issued by ACAS under s.199 of the Trade Union and Labour Relations (Consolidation) Act 1992.

There is a requirement on the employer to notify the employee of its decision within three months beginning on the date that the application is made. This period can be extended by agreement between the employer and employee (s.80G(1B), (1C)).

There are circumstances in which the employer can treat a flexible working request as withdrawn. They are where an employee fails to attend two consecutive meetings to discuss the request or an appeal with their employer without good reason (s.80G(1D)). The employer must notify the employee that the employer has decided to treat that conduct of the employee as a withdrawal of the application.

15 Grounds for refusal

An application may be refused on the following grounds (Employment Rights Act 1996, s.80G(1)(b))–
(i) the burden of additional costs;
(ii) detrimental effect on the ability to meet customer demand;
(iii) inability to re-organise work among existing staff;
(iv) inability to recruit additional staff;
(v) detrimental impact on quality;
(vi) detrimental impact on performance;
(vii) insufficiency of work during the periods the employee proposes to work;
(viii) planned structural changes; and
(ix) such other grounds as the Secretary of State may specify.

16 Appeals

Where an employer allows an employee to appeal a decision to reject an application, the reference to the decision on the application (see **14 Procedure following an application**, above) is a reference to the decision on the appeal, or if more than one appeal is allowed, the decision on the final appeal (Employment Rights Act 1996, s.80G(1A)).

17 Complaints to an employment tribunal

An employee who has made an application may present a complaint to an employment tribunal that (Employment Rights Act 1996, s.80H(1))–
(a) an employer has failed to deal with the application in a reasonable manner, or failed to notify the employee of the decision on the application within the decision period, or failed to refuse the application on one of the applicable grounds;
(b) a decision by the employer to reject the application was based on incorrect facts; or
(c) the employer's notification under s.80G(1D) (application treated as having been withdrawn) was given in circumstances that did not satisfy one of the requirements in that section (i.e. the employer sought to treat the employee's flexible working request as withdrawn without having grounds to do so).
No complaint may be made in respect of an application which has been disposed of by agreement or withdrawn (s.80H(2)). An employee may make a complaint under paragraph (c) above as soon as the employer has informed the employee that it is treating the request as withdrawn. In the case of an application which has not been disposed of by agreement or withdrawn, no complaint under paragraphs (a) or (b) above may be made until (s.80H(3))–
(d) the employer notifies the employee of the employer's decision on the application, or
(e) if the decision period applicable to the application comes to an end without the employer notifying the employee of the employer's decision on the application, the end of the decision period (as to which see **14 Procedure following an application**, above).
The maximum amount of compensation that may be awarded where a complaint is well founded is 8 weeks' pay (Flexible Working Regulations 2014, Reg. 6). The maximum amount of a weeks' pay that may be taken into account is £479. The tribunal may also make an order that the employer reconsider the application (Employment Rights Act 1996, s.80I).
As an alternative to tribunal proceedings, ACAS operates an arbitration scheme to help resolve flexible working time disputes. The scheme is voluntary and so can only be used where both parties agree. Details are contained in the ACAS (Flexible Working) Arbitration Scheme (Great Britain) Order 2004.

18 Authorities

Statutes–
Children and Families Act 2014
Employment Relations Act 1999
Employment Rights Act 1996

Statutory Instruments–
ACAS (Flexible Working) Arbitration Scheme (Great Britain) Order 2004, as amended (S.I. 2004 No. 2333, 2011 No. 1043, 2013 No. 1956, and 2014 No. 386)
Flexible Working Regulations 2014 (S.I. 2014 No. 1398)
Maternity and Parental Leave etc. Regulations 1999, as amended (S.I. 1999 No. 3312, 2001 No. 4010, 2002 No. 2789, 2006 No. 2014, 2008 No. 1966, 2013 Nos. 283, 388, and 591, and 2014 No. 3221)

RIGHTS ARISING IN THE COURSE OF EMPLOYMENT: PATERNITY AND ADOPTION LEAVE AND SHARED PARENTAL LEAVE

A: PATERNITY LEAVE

1 Introduction

Part VIII of the Employment Rights Act 1996, as amended by the Employment Act 2002, makes provision for paternity leave (ss.80A to 80E). The Act is supplemented by the Paternity and Adoption Leave Regulations 2002.

Paternity leave is absence from work for the purpose of caring for a child or supporting the child's mother or adopter (Regs. 4(1) and 8(1)). An employee is not entitled to be absent from work in respect of paternity leave in relation to a child under these provisions if the employee has taken any shared parental leave in respect of that child (Reg. 4(1A)). As to shared parental leave see **17 The shared parental leave regulations**, below.

2 Entitlement to paternity leave: birth

To be eligible for paternity leave, a person must (s.80A and Reg. 4)–
(a) be either–
    (i) the father of the child and have or expect to have responsibility for the child's upbringing; or
    (ii) married to, the civil partner or the partner of the child's mother, but not the child's father, and have or expect to have the main responsibility (apart from that of the mother) for the child's upbringing; and
(b) have been continuously employed for a period of at least 26 weeks ending with the week preceding the 14th week before the expected week of the child's birth;

Where a child is born before the 14th week before the expected week of birth, condition (b) above is modified accordingly (Reg. 4(3)).

An employee is not entitled to paternity leave however if they have taken any shared parental leave in respect of the child (Reg. 4(1A)).

"Partner" means a person, whether or not of the same sex, who lives with the child's mother and the child in an enduring family relationship but who is not a close relative of the mother (Reg. 2).

3 Entitlement to paternity leave: adoption

To be eligible for paternity leave on adopting a child, a person must (s.80B and Reg. 8)–
(a) be either married to, the civil partner or the partner of a child's adopter and have, or expect to have, the main responsibility (apart from that of the adopter) for the upbringing of the child; and
(b) have been in employment continuously for a period of at least 26 weeks ending with the week in which the adopter is notified of being matched with the child for the purposes of adoption.

An employee is not entitled to be absent from work in respect of paternity leave in relation to a child under these provisions if the employee has taken any shared parental leave in respect of that child (Reg. 8(1A)). As to shared parental leave see **17 The shared parental leave regulations**, below.

"Partner" means a person, whether or not of the same sex, who lives with the adopter and the child in an enduring family relationship but who is not a close relative of the adopter (Reg. 2).

The provisions as to paternity leave are modified slightly when a child is adopted from overseas. Such children are not "placed" for adoption and so the references in the legislation to the date of placement are replaced by references to the date of the child's entry into Great Britain, and references to the person with whom a child is placed are replaced by references to the child's adopter. In such cases, the following paragraphs should be read with those modifications.

The Paternity and Adoption Leave Regulations 2002 are modified so as to provide different triggers and qualification points where the employee is a parental order parent so as to recognise that the leave relates to the birth of a child born with the help of a surrogate and not an adoption (Paternity, Adoption and Shared Parental Leave (Parental Order Cases) Regulations 2014, S.I. No. 3096).

4 Notice and evidential requirements

An employee must give his employer notice of his intention to take leave, specifying (Regs 6 and 10)–
(a) the expected week of the child's birth, or the date on which the adopter was notified of having been matched with the child and the expected date of the placement;
(b) the length of the period of leave the employee has chosen to take (see **5 Period of leave**, below); and
(c) the date on which the employee has chosen to begin his leave.

The notice should be given to the employer in or before the 15th week before the expected week of the child's birth, or no more than 7 days after the date on which the adopter is notified of having been matched with the child. In either case, where this is not reasonably practicable, notice must be given as soon as it is reasonably practicable.

An employer may also request a declaration from the employee that his absence will be for the purpose specified in Regulation 4(1) or 8(1) (see 1 **Introduction**, above) and that the employee satisfies the conditions for entitlement.

5 Period of leave

An employee may take either one or two (consecutive) weeks' leave (Regs 5 and 9).

Leave may generally only be taken in the 56 days following a child's birth or placement with the adopter. Where the child is born early, the leave must be taken before the end of 56 days from the first day of the expected week of its birth.

An employee may choose to begin the leave on–
  (a) the date on which the child is born or placed with the adopter;
  (b) a date a specified number of days after the date in (a); or
  (c) a predetermined date which is not later than the first day of the expected week of birth or the date on which the child is expected to be placed with the adopter.

An employee may vary the date chosen as the date on which paternity leave is to begin provided he gives his employer notice. Generally, this means 28 days notice before the day the leave is to begin, or if that is not reasonably practicable, as soon as is reasonably practicable.

Where an employee has chosen to start his leave on a particular predetermined date and the child is not born or placed for adoption on or before that date, he must vary his choice of date to a later date or choose option (a) or (b).

If option (a) has been chosen and the employee is at work on that day, his paternity leave will begin on the next day.

6 Terms and conditions of employment

An employee who takes paternity leave is entitled during the leave period to the benefit of the terms and conditions of his employment (other than those regarding pay) which would have applied if he had not been absent. He is also bound by any obligations arising under those terms and conditions (Reg. 12). At the end of his leave, he is generally entitled to return to the job in which he was employed before his absence, with seniority, pension rights and similar rights as they would have been if he had not been absent, and on terms and conditions no less favourable than those which would have applied if he had not been absent (Regs 13 and 14). An employee who returns to work after a period of paternity leave which was (Reg. 13)–
  (a) an isolated period of leave; or
  (b) the last of two or more consecutive periods of statutory leave which did not include any–
    (i) period of parental leave of more than four weeks; or
    (ii) period of statutory leave which when added to any other periods of statutory leave (excluding parental leave) taken in relation to the same child means that the total amount of statutory leave taken in relation to that child totals more than 26 weeks,
is entitled to return from leave to the job in which he was employed before his absence. An employee who returns to work after a period of paternity leave not falling within the description in paragraph (a) or (b) above is entitled to return from leave to the job in which he was employed before his absence, or, if it is not reasonably practicable for the employer to permit him to return to that job, to another job which is both suitable for him and appropriate for him to do in the circumstances.

B: ADOPTION LEAVE

7 Introduction

Part VIII of the Employment Rights Act 1996, as amended by the Employment Act 2002, makes provision for adoption leave (ss.75A to 75D). The Act is supplemented by the Paternity and Adoption Leave Regulations 2002.

8 Entitlement to adoption leave

To be eligible for adoption leave in respect of a child a person must (s.75A and Reg. 15)–
  (a) be the child's adopter;
  (b) have notified the adoption agency that he agrees that the child should be placed with him and on the date of the placement.

Adoption leave is also available where a child is placed with prospective adopters under the Children Act 1989, s.22C (i.e., with local authority foster parents who are prospective adopters).

9 Notice and evidential requirements

An employee must give his employer notice of his intention to take adoption leave, specifying (Reg. 17)–

(a) the date on which the child is expected to be placed with him for adoption; and

(b) the date on which he has chosen his adoption leave to begin (see **10 Period of leave**, below).

The notice should be given to the employer no more than seven days after the date on which the adopter is notified of having been matched with the child or where this is not reasonably practicable, soon as it is reasonably practicable.

Where the employer requests it, the employee must also provide one or more documents from the adoption agency giving details of–

(i) the name and address of the adoption agency;

(ii) the date on which the employee was notified that he had been matched with the child; and

(iii) the date on which the agency expects to place the child with him.

An employer, when notified of the start date of an employee's ordinary adoption leave period must, within 28 days, notify him of the date that his additional adoption leave period will end (Reg. 17(7)).

10 Period of leave

An employee's ordinary adoption leave period is 26 weeks (Reg. 18). An employee with whom a child is placed for adoption, who takes ordinary adoption leave, and whose leave does not terminate early (see below) will be entitled to additional adoption leave of a further 26 weeks (Reg. 20).

An employee may choose to begin the leave on (Reg. 16)–

(a) the date on which the child is placed with him for adoption; or

(b) a predetermined date which is no more than 14 days before the date on which the child is expected to be placed with him for adoption and no later than that date.

An employee may vary the date chosen as the date on which adoption leave is to begin provided he gives his employer notice. Generally, this means 28 days notice before the day the leave is to begin, or if that is not reasonably practicable, as soon as is reasonably practicable (Reg. 17(4)).

If option (a) has been chosen and the employee is at work on that day, his adoption leave will begin on the next day (Reg. 18(3)).

An employee may carry out up to 10 days' work for his employer during the statutory adoption leave period without bringing his adoption leave to an end (Reg. 21A).

An adoption leave period will terminate early if the placement does not take place, the child dies, or the child is returned to the adoption agency. Generally, the leave period will end eight weeks after the happening of the terminating event (Reg. 22).

Where an employee is dismissed during a period of ordinary or additional leave, the leave period ends at the date of the dismissal (Reg. 24).

11 Terms and conditions of employment

An employee who takes adoption leave is entitled during the leave period to the benefit of the terms and conditions of his employment (other than those regarding pay) which would have applied if he had not been absent. He is also bound by any obligations arising under those terms and conditions (Reg. 19). At the end of his leave, he is generally entitled to return to the job in which he was employed before his absence, with seniority, pension rights and similar rights as they would have been if he had not been absent, and on terms and conditions no less favourable than those which would have applied if he had not been absent (Regs 26 and 27). The provisions contained in Regs 26 and 27 are on similar terms to those for paternity leave (Regs 13 and 14): see **6 Terms and conditions of employment**, above.

12 Redundancy during adoption leave

Regulation 23 applies where, during an employee's ordinary or additional adoption leave, it is not practicable, because of redundancy, for a person's employer to continue to employ them under their existing employment contract. If there is a suitable available vacancy, the employee is entitled to be offered (before the end of their existing contract) alternative employment with the employer or his successor, or with an associated employer, under a new contract of employment which begins immediately after the end of the old contract. The new employment offered must be both suitable and appropriate for the employee, and its provisions as to the capacity and place in which he is to be employed and as to the other terms and conditions of his employment must not be substantially less favourable to him than if he had continued to be employed under the previous contract. For provisions relating to redundancy generally, see the Note on **Redundancy**.

13 Return to work

An employee who intends to return to work early (i.e., before his additional adoption leave is over) must give his employer at least eight weeks' notice of the date on which he intends to return (16 weeks in the case of an employee shareholder (as to whom see the Note on **Employment Protection: Introduction**, at para **9 Employee shareholders**)). If he attempts to return to work early without giving this notice, his employer is entitled to postpone his return to a date which will mean that he does have eight weeks' notice (but an employer may not postpone an employee's return to a date after the end of the additional adoption leave period) (Reg. 25). An employee whose return to work has been postponed in this way has no right to be paid until the date to which his return has been postponed.

Note.–If an employer fails to give an employee notice of the date his additional adoption leave period ends (see **9 Notice and evidential requirements**, above, Reg. 17(7)), then Regulation 25 does not apply and the employer cannot prevent him from returning to work early (Reg. 25(5)).

C: PROVISIONS COMMON TO PATERNITY AND ADOPTION LEAVE

14 Protection from detriment

Under s.47C (added by the 1999 Act, Schedule 4 Part III) and Regulation 28, an employee has the right not to be subjected to any detriment by any act, or deliberate failure to act, by his employer done because he has taken or sought to take paternity or adoption leave. The term "detriment" does not include dismissal (but see **15 Unfair dismissal**, below). As to detriment, see the Note on **Rights Arising in the Course of Employment: Detriment.**

An employee is also protected from being subjected to detriment if he–
- (a) fails to return to work after a period of additional adoption leave where his employer has failed to notify him of the date the leave period ends and he reasonably believes that it has not ended, or his employer gives him less than 28 days' notice of the date his additional adoption leave period ends and it is not reasonably practicable for him to return on that date (Reg. 28(1)(c)); or
- (b) undertook, considered undertaking, or refused to undertake work in accordance with Reg. 21A (see **10 Period of leave**, above).

15 Unfair dismissal

Under s.99 (as substituted by the 1999 Act, Schedule 4 Part III) and Regulation 29, an employee who is dismissed is entitled to be regarded for the purposes of Part X of the Act (unfair dismissal–see the Note on **Unfair Dismissal**) as unfairly dismissed if the reason or principal reason for the dismissal is *inter alia* that–
- (a) the employee took or sought to take paternity or adoption leave;
- (b) the employer believed that the employee was likely to take ordinary or additional adoption leave;
- (c) the employee failed to return to work after a period of additional adoption leave where his employer had failed to notify him of the date his additional adoption leave period was to end (i.e., under Reg. 17, see **9 Notice and evidential requirements**, above) and he reasonably believed that it had not ended, or his employer gave him less than 28 days' notice of the date his additional adoption leave period was to end and it was not reasonably practicable for him to return on that date;
- (d) the employee undertook, considered undertaking, or refused to undertake work in accordance with Reg. 21A (see **10 Period of leave**, above); or
- (e) the employee took or sought to take time off under s.57ZE (see the Note on **Rights Arising in the Course of Employment: Time Off**, at para 5 **Time off to accompany to ante-natal appointment**) or the employer believed that he was likely to take such time off.

An employee will also be regarded as unfairly dismissed if the reason for the dismissal is redundancy and the circumstances of the redundancy applied equally to one or more other employees in the undertaking who held positions similar to that held by the employee who have not been dismissed, and it is shown that the reason for selecting the employee was one of the reasons specified above (Reg. 29(2)).

An employee will not be regarded as unfairly dismissed if it is not reasonably practicable for a reason other than redundancy for the employer to permit him to return to a suitable and appropriate job and he either accepts or unreasonably refuses an offer of such a job from an associated employer (Reg. 29(4) and (5)). The specific small employer exemption has been repealed.

16 Contractual rights to paternity or adoption leave

Where a person is entitled to a statutory right to paternity or adoption leave and also has a contractual right to such leave, he cannot exercise both rights but can choose to exercise whichever is the most favourable to him (Reg. 30).

D: SHARED PARENTAL LEAVE

17 The Shared Parental Leave Regulations

The Shared Parental Leave Regulations 2014 introduce an entitlement for employees who are mothers, fathers, adopters, or prospective adopters, or the partners of mothers or adopters, or prospective adopters, to take shared parental leave in the first year of their child's life or in the first year after the child's placement for adoption. The right to shared parental leave is a statutory right for employees with a partner who is working or has recently been working (whether employed or self-employed). The Regulations are made in exercise of powers inserted into the Employment Rights Act 1996 (ss.75E to 75K) by the Children and Families Act 2014, s.117(1). Part 2 of the

Regulations confer the right to take shared parental leave (birth) where a mother who is entitled to statutory maternity leave, statutory maternity pay, or maternity allowance, curtails that leave, pay or allowance period. The balance of the leave, pay, or allowance period can be taken as shared parental leave if the other conditions for entitlement are satisfied. For adoptions, Part 3 of the Regulations confers the right to take shared parental leave (adoption) where an adopter who is entitled to statutory adoption leave or statutory adoption pay curtails that leave or pay period. The balance of the leave or pay period can be taken as shared parental leave if the other conditions for entitlement are satisfied. The right to take shared parental leave (birth) and the right to take shared parental leave (adoption) have effect in relation to children whose expected week of birth begins on or after 5th April 2015 or in relation to children placed for adoption on or after 5th April 2015.

18 Entitlement to shared parental leave: birth

S.75E of the Employment Rights Act 1996 and Part 2 of the Shared Parental Leave Regulations 2014 deal with entitlement to shared parental leave in relation to birth. In the paragraphs below, "P" means the father of the child, or the person who at the date of the child's birth is married to, or the civil partner or the partner of, the mother. Note that, for these purposes, a "partner" can be a person (whether of a different sex or the same sex) who lives with the mother and the child in an enduring family relationship but is not the mother's child, parent, grandchild, grandparent, sibling, aunt, uncle, niece or nephew (Reg. 3(1)).

Mother's entitlement

A mother ("M") is entitled to be absent from work to take shared parental leave to care for her child if she satisfies the conditions specified below and P satisfies the further conditions specified below (Reg. 4). M must–
   (a) satisfy the continuity of employment test (see **23 Continuity of employment test**, below);
   (b) have, at the date of the child's birth, the main responsibility for the care of the child (apart from the responsibility of P);
   (c) be entitled to statutory maternity leave in respect of the child;
   (d) have ended any entitlement to statutory maternity leave by curtailing that leave (and that leave remains curtailed) or, where M has not curtailed that leave, has returned to work before the end of her statutory maternity leave;
   (e) have complied with the notice requirements concerning entitlement to shared parental leave (see **21 Notice of entitlement to shared parental leave**, below);
   (f) have complied with the requirements of evidence for the employer; and
   (g) have given a period of leave notice (see **22 Entitlement to particular periods of leave**, below).
P must–
   (h) satisfy the employment and earnings test; and
   (i) have, at the date of the child's birth, the main responsibility for the care of the child (apart from the responsibility of M).
Note that entitlement is not affected by the number of children born or expected as a result of the same pregnancy.

P's entitlement

For P to be entitled to be absent from work to take shared parental leave he must satisfy the conditions below and M must satisfy the further conditions below (Reg. 5). P must–
   (a) satisfy the continuity of employment test;
   (b) have, at the date of the child's birth, the main responsibility for the care of the child (apart from the responsibility of M);
   (c) have complied with requirement as to notice to employer of entitlement to shared parental leave;
   (d) have complied with the requirements of evidence for the employer; and
   (e) have given a period of leave notice.
M must–
   (f) have, at the date of the child's birth, the main responsibility for the care of the child (apart from the responsibility of P);
   (g) be entitled to statutory maternity leave, statutory maternity pay, or maternity allowance in respect of the child; and
   (h) where–
         (i) she is entitled to statutory maternity leave, have ended any entitlement to statutory maternity leave by curtailing that leave (and that leave remains curtailed) or, where she has not curtailed that leave, has returned to work before the end of her statutory maternity leave;
         (ii) she is not entitled to statutory maternity leave but is entitled to statutory maternity pay, she has curtailed the maternity pay period (and that period remains curtailed); or
         (iii) she is not entitled to statutory maternity leave but is entitled to maternity allowance, she has curtailed the maternity allowance period (and that period remains curtailed).

19 Entitlement to shared parental leave: adoption

S.75G of the Employment Rights Act 1996 and Part 3 of the Shared Parental Leave Regulations 2014 deal with entitlement to shared parental leave in relation to adoption. In the paragraphs below "A" means the person with whom the child is, or is expected to be, placed for adoption, or, in a case where two people have been matched jointly, whichever of them has elected to be the child's adopter for the purposes of the Paternity and Adoption Leave Regulations 2002. "AP" means the person who at the date that the child is placed for adoption is married to, or the civil partner or the partner of, A. For the definition of "partner" see **18 Entitlement to shared parental leave: birth**, above.

A's entitlement

A is entitled to be absent from work to take shared parental leave to care for her child if she satisfies the conditions specified below and AP satisfies the further conditions specified below (Reg. 20). A must–

(a) satisfy the continuity of employment test (see **23 Continuity of employment test**, below);

(b) have, at the date of the child's placement for adoption, the main responsibility for the care of the child (apart from the responsibility of AP);

(c) be entitled to statutory adoption leave in respect of the child;

(d) have ended any entitlement to statutory adoption leave by curtailing that leave (and that leave remains curtailed) or, where A has not curtailed that leave, has returned to work before the end of her statutory adoption leave;

(e) have complied with the notice requirements concerning entitlement to shared parental leave (see **21 Notice of entitlement to shared parental leave**, below);

(f) have complied with the requirements of evidence for the employer; and

(g) have given a period of leave notice (see **22 Entitlement to particular periods of leave**, below).

AP must–

(h) satisfy the employment and earnings test; and

(i) have, at the date of the child's placement for adoption, the main responsibility for the care of the child (apart from the responsibility of AP).

Note that entitlement is not affected by the number of children placed for adoption through a single placement.

AP's entitlement

For AP to be entitled to be absent from work to take shared parental leave he must satisfy the conditions below and A must satisfy the further conditions below (Reg. 21). AP must–

(a) satisfy the continuity of employment test;

(b) have, at the date of the child's placement for adoption, the main responsibility for the care of the child (apart from the responsibility of A),

(c) have complied with requirement as to notice to employer of entitlement to shared parental leave;

(d) have complied with the requirements of evidence for the employer; and

(e) have given a period of leave notice.

A must–

(f) have, at the date of the child's placement for adoption, the main responsibility for the care of the child (apart from the responsibility of AP);

(g) be entitled to entitled to statutory adoption leave or statutory adoption pay in respect of the child; and

(h) where–

(i) A is entitled to statutory adoption leave, A has ended any entitlement to statutory adoption leave by curtailing that leave (and that leave remains curtailed) or, where A has not curtailed in that way, A has returned to work before the end of the statutory adoption leave, or

(ii) where A is not entitled to statutory adoption leave but is entitled to statutory adoption pay, A has curtailed the adoption pay period (and that period remains curtailed).

The Employment Rights Act 1996 ss.75G and 75H and the Shared Parental Leave Regulations 2014 are modified so as to apply to adoptions from overseas (by the Employment Rights Act 1996 (Application of Sections 75G and 75H to Adoptions from Overseas) Regulations 2014, S.I. No. 3091, and the Shared Parental Leave and Paternity and Adoption Leave (Adoptions from Overseas) Regulations 2014, S.I. No. 3092); and to parental order parents i.e., parents whose child is born with the help of a surrogate (Employment Rights Act 1996 (Application of Sections 75A, 75B, 75G, 75H, 80A and 80B to Parental Order Cases) Regulations 2014, S.I. No 3095, and the Paternity, Adoption and Shared Parental Leave (Parental Order Cases) Regulations 2014, S.I. No. 3096).

20 Amount and periods of shared parental leave

Eligible employees will be able to share up to 50 weeks of shared parental leave which can be taken at any time between the birth (or placement for adoption) of a child and the child's first birthday. The leave can be taken discontinuously in minimum periods of one week and must be taken in complete weeks, with the employee returning to work between periods of leave (Shared Parental Leave Regulations 2014, Regs. 6, 7 (birth); 22, 23 (adoption)). See **22 Entitlement to particular periods of leave**, below.

21 Notice of entitlement to shared parental leave

Both M and P must, not less than eight weeks before the start date of the first period of shared parental leave to be taken, give their employer a written notice of entitlement and intention to take shared parental leave which contains specified information and is accompanied by specified declarations set out in Regulations 8 and 9 of the Shared Parental Leave Regulations 2014. The specified information must include, *inter alia*, the total amount of shared parental leave available, the child's expected week of birth and the child's date of birth (see below), and how much shared parental leave M and P each intend to take. Where a notice is given before the child is born, M and P must give the child's date of birth to the employer as soon as reasonably practicable after the birth of the child and, in any event, before the first period of shared parental leave to be taken. Where M or P gives such a notice their employer may request within 14 days beginning with the date on which that notice was given a copy of the child's birth certificate and the name and address of either M or P's employer, whichever is applicable (Reg. 10). Both M and P may give their employer a written notice to vary a notice given under the above provisions in order to vary how much shared parental leave M and P each intend to take (Reg. 11). There is no limit on the number of notices to vary that may be given.

Regulations 24 and 25 contain similar provisions in the case of adoption. The notice of entitlement and intention to take shared parental leave must, *inter alia*, contain the date that A was notified of having been matched for adoption with the child, the date that the child is expected to be placed for adoption with A and the date of the placement. The employer may request evidence, in the form of one or more documents issued by the adoption agency that matched A with the child of, *inter alia*, the name and address of the adoption agency, the date that A was notified of having been matched for adoption with the child and the date on which the adoption agency expects to place the child with A (Reg. 26). Similar provisions as to variation of notices are contained in Reg. 27.

Where a notice is to be given under these Regulations it may be given by electronic communication, where the person who is to receive the notice has agreed that the notice may be given in this way, or by post or by personal delivery (Reg. 46).

22 Entitlement to particular periods of leave

M or P may only be absent from work to take a period of shared parental leave if she or he gives the employer a written notice which sets out the start and end dates of each period of shared parental leave requested in that notice (Shared Parental Leave Regulations 2014, Reg. 12). Such a notice must be given not less than eight weeks before the start date of the first period of shared parental leave requested. A notice may be given at the same time as a notice of entitlement and intention to take shared parental leave is given to the employer, but not before, and may provide notice of more than one period of leave. If the notice is given before the child is born it must contain a start date for the leave which is the day on which the child is born or which is expressed as a number of days following the date of the child's birth and contain an end date expressed as a number of days following the date of the child's birth. Where an employee gives a notice under Regulation 12 which requests one continuous period of shared parental leave, the employee is entitled to take that period of leave (Reg. 13). In respect of a notice which requests discontinuous periods of shared parental leave, in the two weeks beginning with the date the notice was given the employer who received the notice may (i) consent to the periods of leave requested; (ii) propose alternative dates for the periods of leave; or (iii) refuse the periods of leave requested without proposing alternative dates. Where in the two weeks beginning with the date the notice was given the employer (iv) agrees to the periods of leave requested in that notice; or (v) agrees with the employee alternative dates for the periods of leave, the employee is entitled to take the leave on the dates agreed. Where no agreement has been reached, the employee is entitled to take the total amount of leave requested in the notice as a continuous period of leave (Reg. 14). There are provisions dealing with variations of period of leave (Reg. 15) and modification of the eight week requirement for notices where a child is born early (Reg. 17). Entitlement to shared parental leave in the event of the death of the mother, father, partner or the child are contained in Reg. 19 of, and Sch. 2 to, the Regulations.

A cap on the number of notices to book shared parental leave means that an employee may take no more than three periods of leave, unless an employer agrees to allow more periods of leave or to accept more than three notices to book leave (Reg. 16).

Similar provisions concerning adoption are contained in Regulations 28 to 33. Entitlement to shared parental leave in the event of a disrupted placement or the death of adopter, adopter's partner or child are contained in Reg. 34 of, and Sch. 2 to, the Regulations.

23 Continuity of employment test

For the purposes of entitlement to shared parental leave, an employee satisfies the continuity of employment test if the employee (Shared Parental Leave Regulations 2014, Reg. 35)–
   (a) has been continuously employed with an employer for a period of not less than 26 weeks ending with the relevant week (see below); and
   (b) remains in continuous employment with that employer until the week before any period of shared parental leave taken by the employee.

For shared parental leave (birth) the "relevant week" means the week immediately preceding the 14th week before the expected week of birth and for shared parental leave (adoption) the week in which the person with whom the child is, or is expected to be, placed for adoption was notified of having been matched for adoption with the child.

24 Employment and earnings test

An individual satisfies the employment and earnings test if that individual (Shared Parental Leave Regulations 2014, Reg. 36(1))–

(a) has been engaged in employment as an employed or self-employed earner for any part of the week in the case of at least 26 of the 66 weeks immediately preceding the calculation week (see below); and

(b) has average weekly earnings of not less than the amount set out in s.35(6A) of the Social Security Contributions and Benefits Act 1992 (i.e., the maternity allowance threshold: for the current amount see the Note on **Statutory Maternity, Paternity, Adoption and Parental Pay, and Maternity Allowance**, at para **7 Qualifications for maternity allowance**) in relation to the tax year preceding the tax year containing the calculation week.

For shared parental leave (birth) the "calculation week" means the expected week of birth and for shared parental leave (adoption) the week in which the person with whom the child is, or is expected to be, placed for adoption was notified of having been matched for adoption with the child. An individual's average weekly earnings are determined by dividing by 13 the specified payments made, or treated as being made, to or for the benefit of that individual, in the 13 weeks (whether or not consecutive) in the period of 66 weeks immediately preceding the calculation week in which the payments are greatest (Reg. 36(2)). Where an individual receives any pay after the end of that period in respect of any week falling within that period, the average weekly amount is to be determined as if such sum had been paid in that period (Reg. 36(3)).

25 Work during shared parental leave

An employee may carry out work for the employer during a period of shared parental leave without bringing the period of leave to an end, however, such work must not be more than 20 days (known as "touch-in" days) for each employer during the period in which shared parental leave may be taken. For these purposes, any work carried out on any day constitutes a day's work. "Work" means any work done under the contract of employment and includes training or any activity undertaken for the purposes of keeping in touch with the workplace. Contact to discuss an employee's return to work or any other reasonable contact from time to time between an employer and an employee does not constitute work for these purposes (Shared Parental Leave Regulations 2014, Reg. 37).

26 Right to return to work

Where an employee returns to work after a period of shared parental leave which, when added to any other period of relevant statutory leave taken by the employee in relation to the child, means that the total amount of statutory leave taken by the employee in relation to the child is 26 weeks or less, the employee is entitled to return from leave to the job in which the employee was employed before the absence, except where para. (b) below applies. Where an employee returns to work after a period of shared parental leave which (Shared Parental Leave Regulations 2014, Reg. 40)–

(a) when added to any other period of relevant statutory leave taken by the employee in relation to the child, means that the total amount of relevant statutory leave taken by the employee in relation to the child is more than 26 weeks; or

(b) was the last of two or more consecutive periods of relevant statutory leave which included a period of parental leave of more than four weeks, a period of additional maternity leave, or a period of additional adoption leave,

the employee is entitled to return from leave to the job in which the employee was employed before the absence, or, if it is not reasonably practicable for the employer to permit the employee to return to that job, to another job which is both suitable for the employee and appropriate for the employee to do in the circumstances.

27 Terms and conditions during leave

An employee who takes shared parental leave is, during any period of leave, entitled to the benefit of all of the terms and conditions of employment which would have applied if the employee had not been absent, and bound by any obligations arising under those terms and conditions (Shared Parental Leave Regulations 2014, Reg. 38).

28 Authorities

Statutes–
Children and Families Act 2014

Employment Relations Act 1999

Employment Rights Act 1996

Statutory Instruments–
Paternity and Adoption Leave Regulations 2002, as amended (S.I. 2002 No. 2788, 2003 No. 921, 2004 No. 923, 2005 No. 2114, 2006 No. 2014, 2007 No. 2014, 2008 No. 1966, 2011 No. 1740 and 2014 Nos. 2112, 3096, and 3206)

Shared Parental Leave Regulations 2014, as amended (S.I. 2014 No. 3050, and 2015 No. 552)

RIGHTS ARISING IN THE COURSE OF EMPLOYMENT: TIME OFF

1 Introduction

Ss.50 to 63K of the Employment Rights Act 1996 provide that an employer must allow an employee time off work for any of the following purposes, namely–
   (a) to carry out certain public duties;
   (b) where the employee has been given notice of dismissal by reason of redundancy, to look for new employment or make arrangements for training for new employment;
   (c) in the case of a pregnant employee, to receive ante-natal care and, in the case of an employee who has a qualifying relationship with a pregnant woman, to accompany her to ante-natal appointments;
   (d) in the case of an employee who is a representative for the purposes of Part IV of the Trade Union and Labour Relations (Consolidation) Act 1992 (redundancies) (see the Note on **Redundancy**) or Regulations 9, 13 and 15 of the Transfer of Undertakings (Protection of Employment) Regulations 2006 (see the Note on **Transfer of Undertakings**), or a candidate in an election for such representatives, to perform his functions as such a representative or candidate;
   (e) a Works Council member;
   (f) in the case of an employee who is a trustee of an occupational pension scheme, to perform his duties as a trustee and to undergo relevant training;
   (g) in the case of certain employees aged 16 or 17, to undertake study or training; and
   (h) an information and consultation representative.
These provisions are described below.
An employer must also allow an employee time off work to carry out trade union duties and to take part in trade union activities.

2 Time off for public duties

An employee must be given time off during working hours for his duties as a justice of the peace; or as a member of a local authority (including a National Parks Authority or the Broads Authority); a statutory tribunal; an NHS trust or health authority (in Scotland, a health board); boards of visitors for prisons (in Scotland, visiting committees for prisons), remand centres, and young offender institutions; the managing or governing bodies of certain educational establishments; the Environment Agency or Scottish Environment Protection Agency or Scottish Water; sewerage authorities and Water Industry Consultative Committees; and the Education Workforce Council. The duties of such a member are defined as attendance at meetings of the body or its committees or sub-committees or doing anything generally approved by the body for the purpose of the discharge of its functions or those of its committees or sub-committees. The extent to which such time off is permitted for any of these purposes is that which is reasonable in all the circumstances, taking account of how much time off is necessary to perform the duties generally and also for the particular duty, how much time off had already been granted to the employee for trade union duties and activities and the circumstances of the employer's business and the effect of the employee's absence on the running of that business (s.50). S.50 does not apply to merchant seamen (s.199).

3 Time off to look for work

An employee under notice of dismissal for redundancy (see the Note on **Redundancy** at para **4 Dismissal by reason of redundancy**) is entitled before the notice expires to reasonable time off with pay during working hours to seek employment or to arrange for training for future employment. To qualify for this, the employee must have been continuously employed for at least two years by the date when the notice expires (or the end of his minimum period of notice (see the Note on **Termination of Employment**), if that would be later). The maximum amount payable is two-fifths of a week's pay (ss.52 and 53). Any right of an employee to remuneration under his contract is not affected by these provisions and any contractual remuneration paid to an employee in respect of a period of time off under s.52 goes towards discharging any liability to pay remuneration under that section. Conversely, any payment under s.52 goes towards any contractual liability to pay remuneration (s.53(7)). S.52 does not apply to merchant seamen (s.199).

4 Time off for ante-natal care

A pregnant employee has the right not to be unreasonably refused time off work to keep an appointment at any place for the purpose of receiving ante-natal care. The appointment must have been made on the advice of a registered medical practitioner, midwife, or health visitor, and she must produce, if so requested by her employer, a certificate from one of them stating that she is pregnant and an appointment card (but neither a certificate nor an appointment card need be produced in respect of her first appointment) (s.55). She is entitled to be paid remuneration at the appropriate hourly rate for the period of her absence (s.56). A right to any amount under s.55 does not affect an employee's right to remuneration under her contract of employment. Any contractual remuneration paid to an employee in respect of a period of time off goes towards discharging any liability under s.55 and, conversely, any payment under s.55 goes towards discharging any contractual liability to pay remuneration (s.56(5) and (6)).

An agency worker is entitled to be permitted by their temporary work agency and hirer, subject to the completion of a qualifying period (see the Note on **Part-time, Fixed-term, and Agency Workers**), to take time off during their working hours in order to enable her to keep such an appointment (s.57ZA). An agency worker who is permitted to take time off is entitled to be paid remuneration by the temporary work agency for the period of absence at the appropriate hourly rate (s.57ZB). An agency worker may present a complaint to an employment tribunal that the temporary work agency has unreasonably refused to permit her to take time off as required by these provisions or has failed to pay the whole or part of any amount to which she is entitled (s.57ZC).

5 Time off to accompany to ante-natal appointment

An employee who has a qualifying relationship (see below) with a pregnant woman or her expected child is entitled to be permitted by their employer to take time off during the employee's working hours in order that they may accompany the woman when she attends an ante-natal care appointment (Employment Rights Act 1996 s.57ZE, as inserted by the Children and Families Act 2014 s.127(1)). Time off may not be taken on more than two occasions and, on each of those occasions, the maximum time off during working hours to which the employee is entitled is six and a half hours. The appointment must have been made on the advice of a registered medical practitioner, registered midwife or registered nurse. The employer can request the employee to give the employer a declaration signed by the employee concerning the ante-natal appointment in question. A person has a qualifying relationship with a pregnant woman or her expected child if they–

(a) are the husband or civil partner of the pregnant woman;

(b) being of a different sex or the same sex, live with the woman in an enduring family relationship but are not a relative of the woman;

(c) are the father of the expected child;

(d) are a parent of the expected child by virtue of s.42 or s.43 of the Human Fertilisation and Embryology Act 2008; or

(e) are a potential applicant for a parental order under s.54 of the Human Fertilisation and Embryology Act 2008 in respect of the expected child.

The entitlement therefore applies to intended parents in a surrogacy arrangement if they meet the required criteria. The above provisions also apply to agency workers, and references to the employer are to be read as the temporary work agency and the hirer (s.57ZG).

An employee or agency worker (see above) may present a complaint to an employment tribunal that their employer has unreasonably refused to let them take time off as required by s.57ZE. A complaint must be presented before the end of the period of three months beginning with the day of the appointment in question, or within such further period as the tribunal considers reasonable in a case where it is satisfied that it was not reasonably practicable for the complaint to be presented before the end of that period. If the complaint is substantiated, the tribunal must make an order to this effect and must award compensation of twice the hourly salary of the employee or agency worker for the period of absence, the calculation day being the day of the appointment (ss.57ZF, 57ZH).

6 Time off for employee representatives

An employee who is an employee representative for the purposes of Part IV of the Trade Union and Labour Relations (Consolidation) Act 1992 (redundancies) (see the Note on **Redundancy**) or Regulations 9, 13 and 15 of the Transfer of Undertakings (Protection of Employment) Regulations 2006 (see the Note on **Transfer of Undertakings**), or who is a candidate in an election for such representatives, will be entitled to be allowed reasonable time off with pay during working hours in order to perform his functions as a representative or candidate (s.61).

7 Time off for European Works Council members, etc

An employee who is–

(i) a member of a special negotiating body;

(ii) a member of a European Works Council;

(iii) an information and consultation representative; or

(iv) a candidate in an election for someone who will become (i), (ii) or (iii),

is entitled to be permitted by his employer to take reasonable paid time off during working hours in order to perform his functions (Transnational Information and Consultation of Employees Regulations 1999, Regs. 25 and 26).

As to European Works Councils generally, see the Note on **Rights Arising in the Course of Employment**.

8 Time-off for occupational pension scheme trustees

The employer in relation to an occupational pension scheme must permit an employee of his who is a trustee of the scheme to take time off during the employee's working hours for the purpose of performing any of his duties as such a trustee, or undergoing training relevant to the performance of those duties. The amount of time off which an employee is permitted to take must be such as is reasonable in all the circumstances, having regard, in particular, to both the time required for the performance of the duties of a trustee and the undergoing of relevant training and the circumstances of the employer's business and the effect of the employee's absence on the running of the business (s.58). An employer who permits an employee to take time off under s.58 must pay him for the time taken off pursuant to the permission (s.59). A right to be paid under s.59 does not affect any right of an employee in relation to remuneration under his contract of employment. Any contractual remuneration paid to an employee in respect of time off under s.58 goes towards discharging the employer's liability and, conversely, any payment under s.59 goes towards discharging any liability of the employer to pay contractual remuneration.

9 Time off for study or training

Note.–These provisions apply only in Wales and Scotland. In England they have been replaced by a duty on young people to undertake education or training if they have not achieved a set level of qualification.

Wales and Scotland

S.63A of the Act (inserted by s.32 of the Teaching and Higher Education Act 1998) provides that employees aged 16 or 17, who are not in full-time secondary or further education and who have not attained a standard of achievement prescribed by regulations (see below) are entitled to be permitted by their employer to take time off during working hours to undertake study or training (whether on or off the employer's premises) leading to a relevant qualification. For these purposes, a "relevant qualification" means an external academic or vocational qualification awarded or authenticated by a prescribed body, which would be likely to enhance the employee's employment prospects (whether with his employer or otherwise). The right granted under s.63A also applies to an employee aged 18 who began studying or training for a relevant qualification while he was aged 16 or 17.

The amount of time off which an employee is to be permitted to take under s.63A, and the occasions on which, and any conditions subject to which, time off may be so taken, are those that are reasonable in all the circumstances having regard, in particular, to the requirements of the employee's study or training and the circumstances of the employer's business, including the effect on the business of the employee's time off.

Under s.63B (inserted by the 1998 Act, s.33) an employee entitled to time off under s.63A is also entitled to be paid the appropriate hourly rate for that time. Any contractual pay paid to an employee for a period of time off under s.63A goes towards discharging the employer's liability to pay contractual pay for that period.

The Right to Time Off for Study or Training Regulations 2001 and the equivalent Scottish Regulations set out the standard of achievement which is prescribed for the purposes of s.63A (i.e., an employee who has not achieved this standard is entitled to time off for study or training). *Inter alia*, an employee who has not previously achieved grades A* to C in five GCSE examinations (or the Scottish Qualifications Authority Standard Grades at grades 1 to 3 in five subjects), or who has not obtained certain vocational qualifications, will be entitled to time off.

S.63D (inserted by the Apprenticeship, Skills, Children and Learning Act 2009) provides a right for qualifying employees to request their employer to allow them to undertake study or training. A qualifying employee is an employee who has been continuously employed for a period of not less than 26 weeks (Employee Study and Training (Qualifying Period of Employment) Regulations 2010, Reg. 2) and who is not an employee shareholder (see the Note on **Employment Protection: Introduction**, at para **9 Employee shareholders**). The request, which must be in writing (Employee Study and Training (Eligibility, Complaints and Remedies) Regulations 2010, Reg. 4), has to be considered by the employer and accepted unless one of the specified reasons for refusal applies. The request must be for study or training that is intended to improve an employee's effectiveness at work and the performance of the employer's business (s.63D(4)). The request may be for training of any sort, including study or training that is undertaken outside the place of work with an external training provider, or in-house training provided by the employer, and it is not essential that the training lead to the award of a qualification of any sort. Employees whose learning needs are already catered for in other ways (e.g., under s.63A, see above), cannot make an application under s.63D. Agency workers are also excluded. An employee's application must give the following details of the proposed study or training–

    (i) its subject matter;
    (ii) where and when it would take place;
    (iii) who would provide or supervise it;
    (iv) what qualification (if any) it would lead to,

and explain how the employee thinks the proposed study or training would improve their effectiveness in the employer's business, and the performance of the employer's business (s.63E(4)). The procedure to be followed by an employer in dealing with an application is set out in the Employee Study and Training (Procedural Requirements) Regulations 2010.

An employer may refuse a request only where certain permissible business reasons apply (s.63F). These permissible grounds for refusal are–

    (a) that the proposed study or training would not improve the employee's effectiveness in the employer's business, or the performance of the employer's business;
    (b) the burden of additional costs;

(c) detrimental effect on ability to meet customer demand;

(d) inability to re-organise work among existing staff;

(e) inability to recruit additional staff;

(f) detrimental impact on quality;

(g) detrimental impact on performance;

(h) insufficiency of work during the periods the employee proposes to work;

(i) planned structural changes;

(j) any other grounds specified by the Secretary of State in regulations.

An employee may complain to an employment tribunal where the employer has failed to comply with the duties concerning the consideration of a request (including procedural requirements) and where the employer's decision to refuse a request, or part of it, is based on incorrect facts (s.63I).

10 Time off for information and consultation representatives

An employee who is an information and consultation representative under the provisions relating to information and consultation of employees is entitled to paid time off work during working hours to perform his functions (Information and Consultation of Employees Regulations 2004, Reg. 27). The right extends to employees who are negotiating representatives, i.e., employees elected or appointed to negotiate information and consultation procedures with an employer.

11 Complaint to employment tribunal

An employee may complain to an employment tribunal that his employer has failed to grant him time off as prescribed by ss.50, 52, 55, 58, 59, 61 or 63A, or has failed to pay him or her the whole of any amount of any sum required to be paid under ss.53, 56, 59, 62, and 63B.

The complaint must be made within three months (or such longer period as the tribunal may allow) of the failure. The complainant, if successful, may be awarded compensation for any loss, and, where appropriate, the tribunal will order the payment by the employer of any pay found to be due to the employee (ss.51, 54, 57, 60, 61, and 63C).

Similarly, in relation to European Works Councils, an employee may make a complaint that his employer has failed to grant him time off or has failed to pay him as required by Regulations 25 and 26 of the Transnational Information and Consultation of Employees Regulations 1999: Reg. 27.

12 Authorities

Statutes–

Children and Families Act 2014

Employment Relations Act 1999

Employment Rights Act 1996

Statutory Instruments–

Employee Study and Training (Eligibility, Complaints and Remedies) Regulations 2010 (S.I. 2010 No. 156)

Employee Study and Training (Procedural Requirements) Regulations 2010, as amended (S.I. 2010 No. 155 and 2014 No. 431)

Employee Study and Training (Qualifying Period of Employment) Regulations 2010 (S.I. 2010 No. 800)

Information and Consultation of Employees Regulations 2004, as amended (S.I. 2004 No. 3426, 2006 Nos. 514 and 2405, 2009 No. 3348, 2010 No. 93, 2013 No. 1956, and 2014 No. 386)

Right to Time Off for Study and Training Regulations 2001, as amended (S.I. 2001 No. 2801 and 2010 No. 1172)

Right to Time Off for Study and Training (Scotland) Regulations 1999, as amended (S.I. 1999 No. 1058, S.S.I. 2001 Nos. 211 and 298 and S.I. 2010 No. 1172)

Transnational Information and Consultation of Employees Regulations 1999, as amended (S.I. 1999 No. 3323, 2004 Nos. 1079 and 2518, 2006 No. 2059, 2009 Nos. 2401 and 3348, 2010 No. 1088, 2013 No. 1956, and 2014 No. 386)

SUNDAY WORKING:
RIGHTS OF SHOP AND LICENSED BETTING OFFICE WORKERS

A: PRELIMINARY

1 Introduction

The Sunday employment of shop workers is regulated by the Employment Rights Act 1996 Part IV, which also regulates the employment of betting office workers on Sundays. The Act has been amended by the Employment Relations Act 1999.

As originally enacted, Part IV of the 1996 Act applied only to England and Wales. However, the Sunday Working (Scotland) Act 2003 extends many of the provisions to Scotland.

B: SHOP WORKERS

2 Definitions

For the purposes of the Employment Rights Act 1996, a shop includes any premises where any retail trade or business is carried on. Retail trade includes the business of a barber or hairdresser, that of hiring goods other than for use in the course of a trade or business, and retail sales by auction (Employment Rights Act 1996, s.232).

3 Commencement date

For the purposes of Part IV of the Employment Rights Act 1996, so far as it relates to shop workers, the commencement date means 26th August 1994 in England and Wales, and 6th April 2004 in Scotland.

These dates are important for many of the provisions of Part IV, for example, it is important for the purpose of establishing which shop workers are protected shop workers (see **5 Meaning of protected shop worker**, below) and, in particular, for determining the effect of certain contracts of employment of shop workers (see **15 Effect of rights on contract of employment**, below).

4 Workers to whom Part IV applies

Part IV of the Employment Rights Act 1996 applies to a "protected shop worker" and an "opted-out shop worker", and, in certain circumstances to a shop worker who is proposing to become an opted-out shop worker.

5 Meaning of protected shop worker

A shop worker in England and Wales (but not Scotland) is to be regarded as a protected shop worker if, and only if, the following provisions apply to him, namely–
- (a) on the day before the commencement date (see **3 Commencement date**, above), he was employed as a shop worker to work only on Sunday,
- (b) he has been continuously employed during the period beginning with that day and ending with the appropriate date (see below), and
- (c) throughout that period, or throughout every part of it during which his relations with his employer were governed by a contract of employment, he was a shop worker (Employment Rights Act 1996, s.36(1) and (2)).

In addition, a shop worker in England, Wales or Scotland will be a protected shop worker if, under his contract of employment, he is not, and may not be, required to work on any Sunday and would not be so required even if the provisions of Part IV were disregarded (s.36(3)).

For the purposes of (b) above, the appropriate date means–
- (1) where the employee is dismissed or made redundant for refusing Sunday work (see **10 Right not to be dismissed for refusing Sunday work**, below), the effective date of termination (s.101(4)) (see below);
- (2) where the employee suffers a detriment for refusing Sunday work (see **10 Right not to be dismissed for refusing Sunday work**, below), the date of the act or failure to act (s.45(9))(see below);
- (3) where the employee's contract is unenforceable to the extent that it requires him to do shop work on a Sunday or requires the employer to provide him with shop work on a Sunday or where the employee ceases to be a protected worker because he has given an opting-in notice and expressly agrees as mentioned in s.36(5) (see **6 Opting-in notice**, below), the day on which the agreement is entered into (s.37(5));
- (4) in relation to a shop worker to whom s.38 (see below) applies, any time in relation to which the contract is to be enforced (s.38(3)); and
- (5) in relation to a shop worker to whom s.39 (see below) applies, the end of the period in respect of which the remuneration is paid or the benefit accrues (s.39(5)).

In relation to appropriate date (1) above, the effective date of termination, in any case falling within s.96(1) (see below), means the day with effect from which the employee is treated by s.91 as being dismissed. Where, under s.96(1), a woman is not permitted to return to work after childbirth and is employed as a shop worker under her contract of employment on the last day of her maternity leave period, she is to be treated for the purposes of the Act as if she had been employed as a shop worker on the day with effect from which she is treated as dismissed (s.96(6)).

In relation to appropriate date (2) above, the date of the act means, where the act extends over a period, the first day of the period, and a deliberate failure to act will be treated as done when it was decided on (s.45(10)).

Where on the day before the commencement date (see above) an employee's relations with his employer have ceased to be governed by a contract of employment, he will be regarded as satisfying condition (a) (conditions for shop worker to be regarded as a protected shop worker) above, if—

  (a) that day falls in a week which counts as a period of employment with the employer under s.212(2) or (3) (absence from work because of sickness, pregnancy, etc.) or under regulations made under s.219 (reinstatement or re-engagement of dismissed employee), and
  (b) on the last day before the commencement date on which his relations with his employer were governed by a contract of employment, the employee was a shop worker and was not employed to work only on Sunday (s.36(4)).

Note.—A protected shop worker has the right to refuse to work on a Sunday, without the need to serve a notice of objection to Sunday working (see below), unless he has served an opting-in notice on his employer and complied with the statutory requirements relating to opting-in notices, as to which, see below. Any other shop worker, not employed to work on a Sunday only, has the right to refuse to work on a Sunday provided that he serves on his employer a notice of objection to Sunday working (see below) and fulfils the statutory requirements relating to the giving of such a notice.

6 Opting-in notice

A shop worker will not be protected if (Employment Rights Act 1996, s.36(5))—

  (a) on or after the commencement date (see **3 Commencement date**, above), he has given his employer an opting-in notice; and
  (b) after giving that notice, he has expressly agreed with the employer to do shop work on Sunday or on a particular Sunday.

The opting-in notice must be in writing, signed, and dated by the shop worker, and in it, he must expressly state that he wishes to work on Sunday or that he does not object to Sunday working (s.36(6)).

7 Notice of objection to Sunday working

A shop worker who, under his contract of employment—

  (a) is or may be required to work on Sunday (whether or not as a result of previously giving an opting-in notice); but
  (b) is not employed to work only on Sunday,

may at any time give his employer written notice (an "opting-out" notice), signed and dated by him, to the effect that he objects to Sunday working (Employment Rights Act 1996, s.40).

[The notice takes effect three months after it has been served. This period is termed the notice period (see below). During the notice period, the employee must continue working under his contract as originally agreed, thus, he must work on a Sunday if required to do so by his employer.]

8 Opted-out shop worker

A shop worker is to be regarded as opted-out if, and only if (Employment Rights Act 1996, s.41(1))—

  (a) he has given his employer an opting-out notice (see above),
  (b) he has been continuously employed during the period beginning with the day on which the notice was given and ending with the appropriate date (see below), and
  (c) throughout that period, or throughout every part of it during which his relations with his employer were governed by a contract of employment, he was a shop worker.

For the purposes of (b) above, the "appropriate date" is normally the date on which the shop worker expressly agrees with his employers to do shop work on Sunday or on a particular Sunday (s.43(5)).

A shop worker is not an opted-out shop worker if, after giving the opting-out notice concerned, he has given his employer an opting-in notice, and after giving that opting-in notice, he has expressly agreed with his employer to do shop work on Sunday or on a particular Sunday (s.41(2)).

9 Meaning of notice period

In relation to an opted-out shop worker, notice period means the period of three months beginning with the day on which the opting-out notice concerned was given (see **7 Notice of objection to Sunday working**, above) (Employment Rights Act 1996, s.41(3)).

10 Right not to be dismissed for refusing Sunday work

The dismissal of a protected or opted-out shop worker by his employer will be regarded for the purposes of Part X of the Employment Rights Act 1996 (see the Note on **Unfair Dismissal**) as unfair if the reason for it (or the principal reason) was that the shop worker refused, or proposed to refuse, to do shop work on Sunday or on a particular Sunday (Employment Rights Act 1996, s.101(1)). This provision will not apply in relation to an opted-out shop worker where the reason (or principal reason) for the dismissal was that he refused, or proposed to refuse, to do shop work on any Sunday or Sundays falling before the end of the notice period (see above) (s.101(2)).

The dismissal of a shop worker by his employer will also be regarded for the purposes of Part X of the Act (see above) as unfair if the reason for it (or the principal reason) was that the shop worker gave, or proposed to give, an opting-out notice to the employer (s.101(3)).

Where the reason or principal reason for the dismissal of a protected or opted-out shop worker was that he was redundant, but it is shown (a) that the circumstances constituting the redundancy applied equally to one or more other employees in the same undertaking who held positions similar to that held by him and who have not been dismissed by the employer, and (b) that the reason (or the principal reason) for which he was selected for dismissal was that specified in s.101(1) (see above), then, for the purposes of Part X of the Act, the dismissal will be regarded as unfair (s.105(4)). Similarly, the dismissal of a shop worker will be unfair if the reason (or principal reason) is that specified in s.101(3) (see above) (s.105(4)).

11 Exclusion of ss.108 and 109

S.94 of the Employment Rights Act 1996 (see the Note on **Unfair Dismissal**) will apply to a dismissal regarded as unfair by virtue of s.101 (see above) regardless of the period for which the employee has been employed and of his age; accordingly ss.108 and 109 (which provide a qualifying period and an upper age limit) will not apply to such a dismissal (Employment Rights Act 1996, ss.108(3) and 109(2)).

12 Right not to suffer detriment for refusing Sunday work

A protected or opted-out shop worker has the right not to be subjected to any detriment by any act, or any deliberate failure to act, by his employer done on the ground that the shop worker refused, or proposed to refuse, to do shop work on Sunday or on a particular Sunday (Employment Rights Act 1996, s.45(1)). A shop worker who has given, or proposes to give, his employer an opting-out notice has a similar right (s.45(3)). However, s.45(1) will not apply to anything done in relation to an opted-out shop worker on the ground that he refused, or proposed to refuse, to do shop work on any Sunday or Sundays falling before the end of the notice period (see **9 Meaning of notice period**, above) (s.45(2)). S.45(1) and (3) do not apply where the detriment amounts to dismissal (s.45(4)).

A shop worker who does not work on Sunday or on a particular Sunday is not to be regarded as having been subject to any detriment by–
(a) any failure to pay remuneration in respect of shop work on a Sunday which he has not done,
(b) any failure to provide him with any other benefit, where that failure results from the application, in relation to a Sunday on which the employee has not done shop work, of a contractual term under which the extent of that benefit varies according to the number of hours worked by the employee or the remuneration of the employee, or
(c) any failure to provide him with any work, remuneration, or other benefit which by virtue of s.38 or 39 (see below) the employer is not obliged to provide (s.45(5)).

Where an employer offers to pay a specified sum to any one or more employees who are protected or opted-out shop workers or who, under their contracts of employment, are not obliged to do shop work on Sunday, if they agree to do shop work on Sunday or on a particular Sunday–
(a) an employee to whom the offer is not made is not to be regarded for the purposes of s.45(1) as having been subjected to any detriment by any failure to make the offer to him or to pay him that sum, and
(b) an employee who does not accept the offer is not to be regarded for those purposes as having been subjected to any detriment by any failure to pay him that sum (s.45(6) to (8)).

13 Proceedings for contravention of s.45

An employee may present a complaint to an employment tribunal (see the Note on **Rights Arising in the Course of Employment: Detriment**) that he has been subjected to a detriment in contravention of s.45 (s.48(1)).

14 Employer's duty to give explanatory statement

Where a person becomes a shop worker to whom s.40 applies (see **7 Notice of objection to Sunday working**, above), his employer is under a duty, before the end of the period of two months beginning with the day on which that person becomes such a shop worker, to give him a written statement in the prescribed form (see below) (Employment Rights Act 1996, s.42(1)).

If an employer fails to comply with the above requirement, and the shop worker, on giving the employer an opting-out notice, becomes an opted-out shop worker, the notice period under s.41(3) (see **9 Meaning of notice period**, above) will be one month (instead of three months) (s.42(2)).

An employer will not be regarded as failing to comply with his duty under s.42(1) (see above), in any case where, before the end of the two-month period referred to in that paragraph, the shop worker has given him an opting-out notice (s.42(3)).

The prescribed form, which may be amended by order, is as follows (s.42(4))–

"STATUTORY RIGHTS IN RELATION TO SUNDAY SHOP WORK

You have become employed as a shop worker and are or can be required under your contract of employment to do the Sunday work your contract provides for.

However, if you wish, you can give a notice, as described in the next paragraph, to your employer and you will then have the right not to work in or about a shop on any Sunday on which the shop is open once three months have passed from the date on which you gave the notice.

Your notice must–

    be in writing;

    be signed and dated by you;

    say that you object to Sunday working.

For three months after you give the notice, your employer can still require you to do all the Sunday work your contract provides for. After the three month period has ended, you have the right to complain to an employment tribunal if, because of your refusal to work on Sundays on which the shop is open, your employer–

    dismisses you,

    or does something else detrimental to you, for example, failing to promote you.

Once you have the rights described, you can surrender them only by giving your employer a further notice, signed and dated by you, saying that you wish to work on Sunday or that you do not object to Sunday working and then agreeing with your employer to work on Sundays or on a particular Sunday."

15 Effect of rights on contract of employment

Any contract of employment under which a shop worker in England and Wales who satisfies condition (a) for being regarded as a protected worker (see **5 Meaning of protected shop worker**, above) was employed on 25th August 1996 is unenforceable to the extent that it requires him to do shop work on Sunday on or after the commencement date, or requires the employer to provide the shop worker with shop work on Sunday on or after that date (Employment Rights Act 1996, s.37(1)).

Any agreement entered into after the commencement date (see **3 Commencement date**, above) between a protected shop worker (in England, Wales or Scotland: see **5 Meaning of protected shop worker**, above) and his employer is unenforceable to the extent that it requires the shop worker to do work on Sunday or requires the employer to provide the shop worker with shop work on Sunday (s.37(2)), except where, after giving an opting-in notice, a protected shop worker expressly agrees with his employer to do shop work on Sunday or on a particular Sunday (see s.36(5) under **6 Opting-in notice**, above), and so ceases to be protected. In such a case, his contract will be taken to be varied to the extent necessary to give effect to the terms of the agreement (s.37(3)).

Where a shop worker in England, Wales or Scotland gives his employer an opting-out notice, the contract of employment under which he was employed immediately before he gave that notice becomes unenforceable to the extent that it requires the shop worker to do shop work on Sunday after the end of the notice period (see **9 Meaning of notice period**, above), or requires the employer to provide the shop worker with shop work on Sunday after the end of that period (s.43(1)).

Any agreement entered into between an opted-out shop worker and his employer will be unenforceable to the extent that it requires the shop worker to do shop work on Sunday after the end of the notice period (see above) or requires the employer to provide him with shop work on Sunday after that period (s.43(2)), except that where, after giving an opting-in notice, the [previously opted-out] shop worker expressly agrees with his employer to do shop work on Sunday or on a particular Sunday (in accordance with s.41(2)), and so ceases to be opted out. In such a case, his contract will be taken to be varied to the extent necessary to give effect to the terms of the agreement (s.43(3)).

S.38, which does not apply in Scotland, makes provision for the effect of the contract of a shop worker in the following circumstances–

  (a) under his contract of employment he satisfies the following condition for being regarded as a protected worker, namely, (a) of s.36(1) (see **5 Meaning of protected shop worker**, above) and was employed on 25th August 1994, and the employer is, or may be, required to provide him with shop work for a specified number of hours each week, and

  (b) under that contract, the shop worker was or might have been required to work on Sunday before the commencement date, and

  (c) the shop worker has done shop work on Sunday in that employment (whether or not before the commencement date), but has, on or after the commencement date, ceased to do so.

In the above circumstances, so long as the shop worker remains a protected shop worker, that contract will not be regarded as requiring the employer to provide him with shop work on weekdays in excess of the hours normally worked by the shop worker on weekdays before he ceased to do shop work on Sunday.

S.39, which does not apply in Scotland, provides for the effect of a shop worker's contract in the following circumstances–

(a) on 25th August 1994, the shop worker was employed under a contract of employment under which he satisfies condition (a) of s.36(1) (see **5 Meaning of protected shop worker**, above) and was or might have been required to work on Sunday before that date, and

(b) the shop worker has done shop work on Sunday in that employment (whether or not before the commencement date) but has, on or after the commencement date, ceased to do so, and

(c) it is not apparent from the contract what part of the remuneration payable, or of any other benefit accruing, to the shop worker was intended to be attributable to shop work on Sunday.

In the above-mentioned circumstances, so long as the shop worker remains a protected shop worker, that contract will be regarded as enabling the employer to reduce the amount of remuneration paid, or the extent of the other benefit provided, to the shop worker, in respect of any period, by the proportion which the hours of shop work which (apart from Part IV), the shop worker could have been required to do on Sunday in the period (the contracted Sunday hours) bears to the aggregate of those hours and the hours of work actually done by the shop worker in this period (s.39(2) and (3)).

Where, under the contract of employment, the hours of work actually done on weekdays in any period would be taken into account in determining the contractual Sunday hours, they will be taken into account in determining the contractual Sunday hours for the purpose of the above-mentioned provision (s.39(4)).

16 Restrictions on contracting out of the provisions covering employment of shop workers on Sunday

S.203(1) of the Employment Rights Act 1996 provides that any provision in any agreement (whether a contract of employment or not) will be void in so far as it purports (a) to exclude or limit the operation of any provision of Part IV, or (b) to preclude any person from presenting a complaint to an employment tribunal by virtue of any provision of this Part.

However, the above provision does not apply to an agreement to refrain from presenting or continuing with a complaint where (a) a conciliation officer has taken action under s.18 of the Employment Tribunals Act 1996, or the conditions regulating settlement agreements under that Act are satisfied in relation to the agreement (for a description of these provisions, see the Note on **Employment Tribunals, ACAS, and the Employment Appeal Tribunal** at para **11 Compulsory Conciliation**).

C: BETTING WORKERS

17 Application to betting office workers

The provisions of Part IV of the Employment Rights Act 1996 apply equally to betting workers in England, Wales and Scotland, with appropriate modifications.

For the purposes of Part IV, betting work means (a) work at a track for a bookmaker on a day on which the bookmaker acts as such at the track, being work which consists of or includes dealing with betting transactions, and (b) work in a licensed betting office in England or Wales on a day on which the office is open for use for the effecting of betting transactions (s.233(2)).

Betting worker means an employee who, under his contract of employment, is required to do betting work or may be required to do such work (s.232(1)).

For the purposes of Part IV, so far as it relates to betting workers, commencement date for workers in England and Wales means 3rd January 1995, and for workers in Scotland, means 6th April 2004.

Part IV provides for two types of betting worker, the protected betting worker, and the opted-out betting worker, in the same terms as it provides for a protected shop worker and an opted-out shop worker (see **5 Meaning of protected shop worker**, and see **8 Opted-out shop worker**, above).

The reader is therefore asked when referring to betting workers, to substitute protected betting worker or opted-out betting worker in the provisions described above for shop workers.

18 Authorities

Employment Relations Act 1999

Employment Rights Act 1996

Sunday Working (Scotland) Act 2003

TERMINATION OF EMPLOYMENT

1 Introduction

Part IX of the Employment Rights Act 1996 (the Act), as amended by the Employment Relations Act 1999, governs the manner of termination of contracts of employment.

Certain definitions and provisions (e.g., the method of calculating a period of continuous employment, normal working hours, and a week's pay) which apply to this Part and throughout the Act are to be found in the Note on **Employment Protection: Introduction**. For the purpose of Part IX, and in particular s.92 below, the meaning of the effective date of termination in relation to a contract of employment is given in the Note on **Unfair Dismissal** at para **5 Effective date of termination**.

Certain mariners and seamen, are not entitled to the benefit of the rights under ss.86 to 91 below; and share fishermen, and members of the police service are not entitled to written statements of reasons for dismissal under s.92 below (ss.199 and 200).

Unless otherwise stated, any references to sections are reference to sections of the Act.

2 Minimum period of notice

The period of notice required to be given by an *employer* to terminate the contract of employment of a person who has been continuously employed for one month or more is not less than–

(a) one week, if the employee has been continuously employed for less than two years,

(b) one week for each year of continuous employment, if he has been continuously employed for two years or more but less than 12 years, and

(c) 12 weeks, if he has been continuously employed for 12 years or more (s.86(1)).

The period of notice required to be given by an *employee* who has been continuously employed for one month or more is not less than one week (s.86(2)).

The above requirements supersede any provision for shorter notice contained in any contract of employment with a person who has been continuously employed for one month or more, but either party may waive his right to notice on any occasion, or may accept payment in lieu of notice (s.86(3)).

If a person's contract of employment is for a term certain of one month or less, but he has been continuously employed for three months or more, the contract has effect as if it were for an indefinite period and the minimum period of notice required from employer and employee is as stated above (s.86(4)).

The Act expressly preserves the right of either party to a contract of employment to terminate the contract without notice by reason of such conduct of the other party as would have enabled him to do so before the passing of the Act (s.86(6)).

If an employer fails to give the notice required by s.86, the rights conferred by s.87 (see below) will be taken into account in assessing his liability for breach of the contract (s.91(5)).

3 Employee's rights during period of notice

During a period of notice (whether given by employer or employee) to terminate the employment of a person who has been employed for one month or more, the employer must pay the employee in accordance with the provisions of ss.88 to 91. The provisions of ss.88 to 91 will not apply however, if the contract of employment requires the employer to give a notice which is at least one week longer than is required by the Act (s.87).

Ss.88 to 91 protect an employee against loss of pay during the period of notice in respect of sickness, injury, pregnancy, childbirth, absence on adoption, parental or paternity leave, failure by his employer to provide him with work, or absence on holiday authorised by the terms of his employment, but not if he takes part in a strike after having given notice and before the contract ends. Nor is he entitled to pay in respect of leave granted at his own request. Directions are also given for dealing with the contingency where the employer, or the employee, breaks the contract before the expiration of the period of notice (s.91).

4 Written statement of reason for dismissal

An employee whose contract of employment–

(a) is terminated by his employer, with or without notice; or

(b) if for a limited term, terminates by virtue of a limiting event without being renewed under the same contract;

may require his employer to provide a written statement of particulars of the reasons for his dismissal within 14 days of receiving the request for it (s.92(1) and (2)). To qualify, the employee must have completed one year of continuous employment ending with the effective date of termination (s.92(3) as amended by the Unfair Dismissal and Statement of Reasons for Dismissal (Variation of Qualifying Period) Order 1999). Employment is for a "limited term" if it is not intended to be permanent and the contract provides for it to terminate by virtue of a "limiting event", such as the expiry of a term, the performance of a specific task, or the occurrence of a specific event (s.235).

However, an employee is entitled to a written statement without having to request it irrespective of whether she has been employed for any period, if she is dismissed—

(c) at any time while she is pregnant;

(d) after childbirth; or

(e) while on adoption leave,

in circumstances in which her ordinary or additional maternity or adoption leave period ends by reason of the dismissal (s.92(4) and (4A)). A written statement so provided is admissible in evidence in any proceedings (s.92(5)). Unreasonable refusal to provide one, or the provision of one containing inadequate or untrue particulars of reasons, may form the subject of a complaint by the employee to an employment tribunal. Such a complaint must be presented within the time limits for presentation of a complaint of unfair dismissal under s.111 of the Act (see the Note on **Unfair Dismissal** at para **27 Complaint to employment tribunal**). If the tribunal upholds the complaint, it may declare what it considers were the employer's reasons for the dismissal and will award the employee a sum equal to two weeks' pay to be paid by the employer (s.93).

Authorities

Employment Relations Act 1999

Employment Rights Act 1996

Unfair Dismissal and Statement of Reasons for Dismissal (Variation of Qualifying Period) Order 1999 (S.I. 1999 No. 1436)

TERMS OF EMPLOYMENT

1 Introduction

This Note deals with–
  (a) the provisions of Part 1 of the Employment Rights Act 1996 which oblige employers to provide their employees with written particulars of employment (ss.1 to 4) as well as itemised pay statements (s.8), but subject to exceptions in both cases, and prescribe the manner in which these duties are to be enforced;
  (b) the provisions of the Social Security Contributions and Benefits Act 1992 which provides for the effect of statutory maternity, paternity and adoption pay on contractual remuneration (see Part C, below);
  (c) the provisions of the Employment Act 2008 (failure to comply with a code of practice); and
  (d) zero hours workers.
  Certain definitions and provisions (e.g., the method of calculating a period of continuous employment) which apply to this Part and throughout the Employment Rights Act 1996 are to be found in the Note on **Employment Protection: Introduction**.

A: EMPLOYMENT PARTICULARS

2 Excluded employees

The following categories of employees are not entitled to written statements under the Employment Rights Act 1996, ss.1 to 4–
  (a) employees whose employment continues for less than one month (s.198);
  (b) certain mariners (s.199(1)).
  Ss.1 to 4, however, will apply to an employee who at any time comes or ceases to come within one of the excluded categories mentioned above, as if his employment with his employer terminated or began at that time. In such a case, the obligation to specify the date on which his employment actually began under s.1(3) (see below) is not affected (s.5).

3 Written particulars of employment

Not later than two months after an employee begins work, the employer must supply him with a written statement which (subject to certain conditions) may be given in instalments before the end of the two-month period (Employment Rights Act 1996, s.1(1) and (2)), identifying the names of the employer and the employee, specifying the date when the employment began, and specifying the date on which the employee's period of continuous employment began (taking into account any employment with a previous employer which counts towards that period) (s.1(3)). The statement must also give the following particulars of the terms of employment as at a specified date not more than one week before the statement is given (s.1(4))–
  (a) the scale or rate of remuneration, or the method of calculating remuneration;
  (b) the intervals at which remuneration is paid (that is, whether weekly or monthly or with reference to some other period);
  (c) any terms and conditions relating to hours of work (including any relating to normal working hours);
  (d) any terms and conditions relating to–
      (i) entitlement to holidays (including public holidays) and holiday pay (the particulars given being sufficient to enable the employee's entitlement, including entitlement to accrued holiday pay on termination of employment, to be precisely calculated);
      (ii) incapacity for work due to sickness or injury, including any provisions for sick pay;
      (iii) pensions and pension schemes;
  (e) the length of notice which the employee is obliged to give and entitled to receive to terminate his contract of employment;
  (f) the title of the job which the employee is employed to do or a brief description of the work;
  (g) where the employment is not intended to be permanent, the period for which it is expected to continue or, if it is for a fixed term, the date when it is to end;
  (h) either the place of work or, where the employee is required or permitted to work at various places, an indication of that and of the address of the employer;
  (j) any collective agreements which directly affect the terms and conditions of the employment including, where the employer is not a party, the persons by whom they were made, and
  (k) where the employee is required to work outside the UK for a period of more than one month–
      (i) the period for which he is to so work,
      (ii) the currency in which he will be paid,
      (iii) any additional remuneration payable, and any benefits provided, by reason of his being required to work outside the UK, and
      (iv) any terms and conditions relating to his return to the UK.

Paragraph (d)(iii) above does not apply where there is a pension scheme established under an Act of Parliament, the provisions of which require information to be given to new employees of their rights under the scheme (s.1(5)).

If there are no particulars to be entered under any of the heads of paragraph (d) or (k) above, or under any of the other paragraphs of s.1(3) or s.1(4) above, that fact must be stated (s.2(1)). The particulars required by s.1(3) above, together with the matters specified by paragraphs (a) to (c), head (i) of paragraph (d) and paragraphs (f) and (h) must all be included in a single document (s.2(4)). Where, within two months of the commencement of his employment, an employee is to begin work outside the UK for a period of more than one month, the statement under s.1 must be given to him before he leaves the UK (s.2(5)). However, details of pensions and sickness entitlement may be given by reference to any other reasonably accessible document, and details of notice entitlement by reference to the provisions of the law or to those of any reasonably accessible collective agreement which governs this matter (s.2(2) and (3)).

A statement must be given under s.1 notwithstanding that a person's employment ends before the period within which the statement is required to be given (s.2(6)).

The statement must also (s.3(1) and s.3(5))–

(1) specify any disciplinary rules applicable, or refer to a reasonably accessible document which does so;

(1A) specify any procedure applicable to the taking of disciplinary decisions relating to the employee, or to a decision to dismiss the employee, or refer to a reasonably accessible document which does so;

(2) specify (i) a person to whom the employee can apply if dissatisfied with any disciplinary decision relating to him, or any decision to dismiss him, and (ii) a person to whom he can apply to seek redress of a grievance arising from his employment, and, in each case, the mode of application;

(3) explain (or refer to a document easily available to the employee which explains) any further steps consequent upon such application; and

(4) state whether a contracting-out certificate is in force in respect of the employment stating that the employment is contracted-out for the purposes of Part III of the Pension Schemes Act 1993.

Paragraphs (1) to (3) do not apply to any rules, disciplinary decisions, decisions to dismiss, grievances, or procedures relating to health and safety at work (s.3(2)).

Where an employer issues an employee with a document, such as a contract of employment or letter of engagement, which contains the particulars required in a written statement under s.1, there is no need for the employer to issue a separate written statement under that section (s.7A).

The exemption from some of these provisions which previously applied to small employers no longer applies.

4 Changes in terms of employment

If any change is made in any of the matters particulars of which are required to be included in a statement, the employer must notify the employee of the nature of the change, within one month, by further written statement; if the change results from the employee being required to work outside the United Kingdom for more than one month, the further written statement must be given before the employee leaves, if this is earlier (Employment Rights Act 1996, s.4(1) and (3)).

A statement under s.4(1) may refer the employee to some other reasonably accessible document for a change in any of the matters specified in paragraph (d)(ii) and (iii) above, or specified in (1) and (3) above. A statement may also refer the employee to the law or to the provisions of any accessible collective agreement for a change in paragraph (e) above (s.4(4) and (5)).

No statement need be given under s.1 where there has been (a) a change in the employer's name but not his identity, or (b) a change in the employer's identity in such circumstances that the continuity of the employee's period of employment is not broken, and (in either case) the change does not involve any change in the terms (other than the names of the parties) included in the original statement; but a statement of the change must be given under s.4(1) (s.4(6)). A written statement of the change of an employer's identity must specify the date on which the employee's period of continuous employment began (s.4(8)).

5 Enforcement of rights under ss.1 to 4

Where an employee has not received a written statement within the prescribed period or is dissatisfied as to the sufficiency or accuracy of the particulars included, he may require the matter to be referred to an employment tribunal.

The tribunal has power to determine what particulars the written statement should have included to satisfy the Act's requirements and, where the employer has issued a statement, may confirm or amend the particulars or substitute others. The complaint must be made within three months beginning with the date on which the employment ceased or within such further period as the tribunal considers reasonable in cases where it is satisfied that it was not reasonably practicable for the application to be made within the three month period (Employment Rights Act 1996, ss.11 and 12).

Where there are tribunal proceedings in relation to another employment matter (see below), and the employer is found to be in breach of either s.1 or s.4, the tribunal must, unless it would be unjust or inequitable–

(a) if it finds in favour of the employee, but makes no award in relation to the employee's claim, make an award of two weeks' pay, or if it considers it just and equitable, four weeks' pay in relation to the breach of s.1 or s.4;

(b) if it finds in favour of the employee, and makes an award in relation to the employee's claim, also make an additional award of two weeks' pay, or if it considers it just and equitable, four weeks' pay in relation to the breach of s.1 or s.4.

This provision for additional compensation applies where the tribunal proceedings relate to any of the matters specified in the Employment Act 2002, Schedule 5. This covers most tribunal proceedings such as unfair dismissal, redundancy, equal pay, discrimination, working time, etc.

B: ITEMISED PAY STATEMENTS

6 Right to itemised pay statement

Subject to certain exceptions (as noted above), every employee is entitled to be provided by his employer with a written itemised pay statement when, or before, any payment of wages or salary is made to him. The statement must show the gross amount of any wages or salary, the amounts of any variable deductions and (unless they are dealt with as indicated in s.9–see below) the amount of any fixed deductions, the net amount of wages or salary payable, and, where different parts of the net amount are paid differently, the amount and method of each part-payment (Employment Rights Act 1996, s.8).

Separate particulars of a fixed deduction need not be included, provided that the amount of the deduction is included in the total of such deductions which is given and that the employee has, before or with the pay statement, been supplied with a written standing statement of fixed deductions detailing the amount of each deduction, the intervals at which it is to be made, and its purpose. An employer may amend the standing statement by written notice to the employee, but any such amendment must be incorporated in the consolidated statement which the employer must re-issue every 12 months (s.9).

7 Excluded employees

Share fishermen, certain merchant seamen, and members of the police service are not entitled to itemised pay statements under s.8 (Employment Rights Act 1996, ss.199(2) and 200(1)).

8 Enforcement of rights under s.8

If an employer does not provide the necessary pay statement or does not provide one which satisfies the requirements of s.8 (see above), the employee may require reference to be made to an employment tribunal of any question (excluding questions relating only to accuracy of an amount in a statement of pay or fixed deductions) as to what particulars should have been in such a statement. When a statement has been given and there is a query as to its particulars, either party may require such a reference. Where the employment has ceased, the application requiring a reference must be made within three months of the date on which it ended or, within such further period as the tribunal considers reasonable in cases where it is satisfied that it was not reasonably practicable for the application to be made within the three-month period. If, on a reference, the tribunal finds that the employer has not provided any of the above statements as required, or that a statement does not contain the specified particulars relating to a deduction, it will so declare and, if it also finds that unnotified deductions (i.e., deductions for which no statements have been provided, whether or not such deductions were in breach of the contract of employment) have been made during the 13 weeks preceding the application, it may order the employer to pay the employee a sum not exceeding the total amount of those unnotified deductions (Employment Rights Act 1996, ss.11 and 12).

The amount so paid is limited by s.26 of the Act, which provides that the aggregate of such a sum and the amount ordered to be paid under s.24 of the Act (see the Note on **Wages**) by an employment tribunal in respect of a particular deduction must not exceed the amount of that deduction.

Note.–Part II of the Act includes provisions governing the maximum amount of the deductions which may be made from wages by employers, and the right of access to employment tribunals over claims relating to such deductions (see **Wages**).

C: EFFECT OF STATOTORY MATERNITY, PATERNITY AND ADOPTION PAY

9 Effect of statutory maternity pay on contractual remuneration

Paragraph 3 of Schedule 13 to the Social Security Contributions and Benefits Act 1992 and the Statutory Maternity Pay (General) Regulations 1986 (see the Note on **Statutory Maternity, Paternity, Adoption and Parental Pay, and Maternity Allowance**) provide that any entitlement to statutory maternity pay will not affect any right of a woman in relation to "contract remuneration", which means any sums payable under a contract of service by way of remuneration, for incapacity for work due to sickness or injury; and by reason of pregnancy or confinement. However–

(a) any contractual remuneration paid to a woman by an employer in respect of a week in the maternity pay period (see the Note on **Statutory Maternity, Paternity, Adoption and Parental Pay, and Maternity Allowance**) will go towards discharging any liability of his to her in respect of that week; and

(b) any statutory maternity pay paid to a woman who is an employee of his in respect of a week in the maternity pay period will go towards discharging any liability of that employer to pay contractual remuneration to her in respect of that week.

10 Effect of statutory paternity and adoption pay on contractual remuneration

The effect of statutory paternity and adoption pay on contractual remuneration is similar to that described above for statutory maternity pay. S.171ZG of the Social Security Contributions and Benefits Act 1992 and the Statutory Paternity and Statutory Adoption Pay (General) Regulations 2002 (S.I. No. 2822) (see the Note on **Statutory Maternity, Paternity, Adoption and Parental Pay, and Maternity Allowance**) provide that any entitlement to statutory paternity pay will not affect any right of a person in relation to "contract remuneration", which means any sums payable under the contract of service by way of remuneration, for incapacity for work due to sickness or injury, or by reason of the birth or adoption of a child. However—

(a) any contractual remuneration paid to a person by an employer in respect of a week in the paternity pay period (see the Note on **Statutory Maternity, Paternity, Adoption and Parental Pay, and Maternity Allowance**) will go towards discharging any liability of his to him in respect of that week; and

(b) any statutory paternity pay paid to a person who is an employee of his in respect of a week in the paternity pay period will go towards discharging any liability of that employer to pay contractual remuneration to him in respect of that week.

S.171ZP and the 2002 Regulations make similar provision in respect of statutory adoption pay.

D: NON-COMPLIANCE WITH A STATUTORY CODE OF PRACTICE

11 Effect of non-compliance

Where in proceedings before an employment tribunal it appears to the tribunal that (Trade Union and Labour Relations Act 1992, s.207A)—

(a) the claim concerns a matter to which a relevant Code of Practice applies;

(b) either the employer or employee has failed to comply with that Code in relation to that matter; and

(c) that failure was unreasonable,

then the tribunal may, if it considers it just and equitable in all the circumstances to do so, increase or decrease (depending on whether it is the employer or employee at fault) any award it makes to the employee by no more than 25%.

A "relevant" Code of practice for these purposes is one issued under the enactments listed in Schedule A2 to the Act. This covers all the main tribunal jurisdictions including—

- equal pay equality clauses;
- sex, race, religious, disability, and age discrimination;
- trade union membership and activities;
- unauthorised deductions and payments;
- detriment;
- unfair dismissal;
- redundancy payments; and
- working time.

E: ZERO HOURS WORKERS

12 Exclusivity in zero hours contracts

The Employment Rights Act 1996 s.27A(3), as inserted by the Small Business, Enterprise and Employment Act 2015 s.153, renders unenforceable a provision in a zero hours contract which prohibits a worker from working for another employer. A "zero hours contract" means a contract of employment or other worker's contract under which (i) the undertaking to do or perform work or services is an undertaking to do so conditionally on the employer making work or services available to the worker, and (ii) there is no certainty that any such work or services will be made available to the worker (s.27A(1)). When an employment tribunal considers mutuality of obligation in terms of determining the employment status of an individual working under a zero hours contract, the employment tribunal can ignore the prohibition on exclusivity terms in s.27A(3) (s.27A(4)). This avoids any risk that by prohibiting exclusivity terms in zero hour contracts, individuals who might have been held to be "employees" by virtue of such exclusivity clauses, could lose that status and their eligibility to certain rights. Exclusivity terms are rendered void and unenforceable against workers for other purposes. S.27B(1) gives the Secretary of State power to make regulations to further ensure that zero hours workers are not restricted from working for another employer.

13 Authorities

Employment Act 2008

Employment Relations Act 1999

Employment Rights Act 1996

Social Security Contributions and Benefits Act 1992

Employment Act 2002 (Dispute Resolution) Regulations 2004 (S.I. 2004 No. 752)

TRANSFER OF UNDERTAKINGS

1 Introduction

This Note deals with the provisions of the Transfer of Undertakings (Protection of Employment) Regulations 2006 which implement Council Directive 2001/23/EC on the approximation of the law of Member States relating to the safeguarding of employee's rights in the event of transfers or mergers of undertakings, businesses, or parts of businesses. It also deals with the effect on pensions of such a transfer.

Where an undertaking is transferred many aspects of the law relating to employment may be relevant, for example, the law relating to termination of employment, or unfair dismissal: these aspects of the law are dealt with in other Notes in the Employment Section. In particular, the provisions of the Employment Rights Act 1996 (the 1996 Act) relating to continuity of employment are dealt with in the Note on **Employment Protection: Introduction**.

2 Scope of the regulations

The Transfer of Undertakings (Protection of Employment) Regulations 2006 apply to a relevant transfer, i.e., (Reg. 3)–
  (a) the transfer of an undertaking or business (or part of an undertaking or business) situated immediately before the transfer in the UK, to another person where there is a transfer of an economic entity which retains its identity; or
  (b) a service provision change i.e., a situation in which–
      (i) activities cease to be carried on by a person ("the client") on his own behalf and are instead carried on for him by a contractor;
      (ii) activities cease to be carried on by a contractor and are instead carried on by another contractor; or
      (iii) activities cease to be carried on by a contractor and are instead carried on by the client himself.

The transfer (a) may be effected by a series of two or more transactions; and (b) may take place whether or not any property is transferred to the transferee by the transferor. References in (b) to activities being carried out instead by another person (including the client) are to activities which are fundamentally the same as the activities carried out by the person who has ceased to carry them out.

In the case of a service provision change, the provisions only apply if there is an organised group of employees in Great Britain whose principal purpose is to carry out the activities concerned on behalf of the client; the client intends that, following the service provision change, the activities will be carried on by the transferee (other than in connection with a single specific event or task of short-term duration); and the activities concerned do not consist wholly or mainly of the supply of goods for the client's use.

The Regulations apply to any employee (i.e., any individual who works for another person, whether under a contract of service or apprenticeship or otherwise, but not including anyone who provides services under a contract for services).

Any provision of any agreement (whether a contract of employment or not) is void in so far as it purports to exclude or limit the operation of the Regulations (except in so far as the Regulations themselves provide that such an agreement may be made) or to preclude any person from presenting a complaint to an employment tribunal (Reg. 18).

3 Effect of a relevant transfer

A relevant transfer does not operate so as to terminate the contract of employment of any person employed by the transferor in the undertaking or part transferred. Instead, the contract takes effect after the transfer as if made with the new employer and all related rights and liabilities (but not is so far as they relate to occupational pension schemes) are also transferred (Transfer of Undertakings (Protection of Employment) Regulations 2006, Regs. 4 and 10).

However, where the employee informs the transferor or the transferee that he objects to becoming employed by the transferee, the transfer will operate so as to terminate his contract of employment with the transferor but he will not be treated, for any purpose, as having been dismissed by the transferor (Reg. 4(8)).

The above provisions are without prejudice to any right of an employee (apart from the Regulations) to terminate his contract of employment without notice if a substantial change is made in his working conditions to his detriment and in such a case the employee will be treated as dismissed by the employer(Reg. 4(9)).

Any collective agreement made by the transferor with a trade union recognised by him in respect of any employee whose contract is preserved by Regulation 4 is deemed, except in so far as it relates to occupational pension schemes, to have been made with the transferee. For these purposes, any provisions of an occupational pension scheme which do not relate to benefits for old age, invalidity, or survivors will be treated as not being part of the occupational pension scheme (Regs. 5 and 10).

Regulation 6 makes provision for the situation where, after a relevant transfer, the undertaking or part of the undertaking transferred maintains an identity distinct from the remainder of the transferee's undertaking.

Where, before such a transfer, an independent trade union is recognised by the transferor in respect of employees of any description who are transferred, then, after the transfer, the union is deemed to have been recognised by the transferee to the same extent in respect of those employees (and any such agreement may be varied or rescinded accordingly).

Note.–Where the transferor is subject to insolvency proceedings at the time of the transfer, the Regulations do not operate to transfer to the new employer liability for any sums payable to employees by the Secretary of State under statutory schemes.

4 Dismissal of employee because of relevant transfer

Where, either before or after a relevant transfer, any employee of the transferor or transferee is dismissed, that employee is treated for the purposes of Part X of the 1996 Act (see the Note on **Unfair Dismissal**) as unfairly dismissed if the sole or principal reason for the dismissal is the transfer (Transfer of Undertakings (Protection of Employment) Regulations 2006, Reg. 7(1)).

Where the sole or principal reason for a dismissal is an economic, technical or organisational reason entailing changes in the workforce of either the transferor or the transferee before or after a relevant transfer, then Reg. 7(1) does not apply and the dismissal will either be regarded as having been for redundancy or else for a substantial reason of a kind such as to justify the dismissal of an employee holding the position the employee held (Reg. 7(2) and (3)).

Regulation 7(1) does not apply (Reg. (7(5) and (6))–
  (i) to any dismissal which is required by reason of the application of s.5 of the Aliens Restriction (Amendment) Act 1919) (Reg. 8(5)); or
  (ii) to the dismissal of an employee if the application of the unfair dismissal provisions of the Employment Rights Act 1996 (i.e., s.94) to the dismissal of the employee are excluded by or under any provision of that Act, the Employment Tribunals Act 1996, or the Trade Union and Labour Relations (Consolidation) Act 1992 (see the Note on **Unfair Dismissal**).

5 Duty to inform and consult representatives

Where a relevant transfer is to take place, an employer must inform the appropriate representatives of any affected employees (see below) long enough beforehand to enable consultations to take place between him and those representatives (Transfer of Undertakings (Protection of Employment) Regulations 2006, Reg. 13). He must inform them of–
  (a) the date or proposed date of the transfer and the reasons for it;
  (b) the legal, economic, and social implications of the transfer for the affected employees; and
  (c) what measures, if any, he envisages will be taken, in connection with the transfer, in relation to the affected employees.

Where information is to be supplied by an employer this must include suitable information relating to the use of agency workers (if any) by that employer (Reg. 13(2A)).

An affected employee is an employee of the transferor or transferee who may be affected by the transfer or by connected measures (Reg. 13(1)). The appropriate representatives of any employees are (Reg. 13(3))–
  (d) where there is an independent trade union recognised by the employer, representatives of that union, or
  (e) in any other case, whichever of the following employee representatives the employer chooses–
      (i) those appointed or elected by affected employees (other than for the purposes of being informed and consulted about a transfer) who, having regard to the purposes for and method by which they were appointed or elected, have authority from those employees to receive information and to be consulted about proposals on their behalf;
      (ii) employee representatives elected by affected employees for the purpose of being consulted about the transfer in an election satisfying the requirements of Regulation 14(1) (these requirements are identical to those which apply in relation to the election of representatives in connection with collective redundancies–see the Note on **Redundancy**, at para 11 **Election of representatives**).

Where an employer envisages that he will, in connection with the transfer, be taking measures in relation to any such employees, he must consult all the persons who are appropriate representatives of any of the affected employees with a view to seeking their agreement to measures to be taken, and must consider any reply to their representations, and, if he rejects any of them, he must state his reasons (Reg. 13(6) and (7)). The employer must allow the appropriate representatives access to the affected employees and must afford them such accommodation and other facilities as may be appropriate (Reg. 13(8)).

If there are special circumstances rendering it not reasonably practicable for an employer to perform one of these duties, he must take all steps toward performing that duty as are reasonably practicable in the circumstances (Reg. 13(9)), but on complaint to an employment tribunal that he has failed to fulfil his duty to inform or consult, it is for the employer to show that there were such special circumstances and he took such steps (Reg. 15(2)).

Note.–Where there are no existing appropriate representatives and the employer has not invited any of the affected employees to elect employee representatives, an employer with fewer than 10 employees (i.e., a micro-business) can inform and consult directly with all the affected employees (Reg. 13A).

6 Complaint to a tribunal

A complaint as to an employer's failure to comply with the Transfer of Undertakings (Protection of Employment) Regulations 2006 as to information for and consultation with employee representatives may be made to an employment tribunal as follows–
(i) in the case of a failure relating to the election of employee representatives, by any employees who are affected employees;
(ii) in the case of any other failure relating to employee representatives, by the employee representatives concerned;
(iii) in the case of a failure relating to trade union representatives, by the trade union concerned, or,
(iv) in any other case, by any employees who are affected employees.

A complaint must be made within three months of the transfer or, if that is not reasonably practicable, within such longer period as the tribunal considers reasonable (Reg. 15(12)). If the tribunal finds the complaint to be well-founded, it may order the employer to pay compensation to specified classes of affected employees or, if the transferor proves that he was unable to perform his duty because the transferee had failed to give him the information necessary to enable him to do so, it may order the transferee to pay compensation to those employees of the transferor affected. The compensation payable must not exceed thirteen week's pay for each affected employee (Regs. 15(7), (8), 16(3)).

7 Pensions

An employee who becomes the employee of a new employer by virtue of a transfer to which the Transfer of Undertakings (Protection of Employment) Regulations 1981 apply, and who had actual or contingent rights in relation to an occupational pension scheme immediately before the transfer, has certain rights in relation to the new employer (Pensions Act 2004, ss.257, 258).

The new employer is required to secure that the employee is, or is eligible to become, an active member of the new employer's occupational pension scheme and, if it is a money purchase scheme, to make "relevant contributions" to it. Alternatively, the new employer must make such contributions to a stakeholder pension scheme of which the employee is a member (or offer to contribute to a stakeholder scheme of which he is eligible to be a member).

The Transfer of Employment (Pension Protection) Regulations 2005 prescribe requirements for a non money purchase (Defined Benefit) occupational pension arrangement. They also provide the level and detail of relevant contributions to be made to a money purchase (Defined Contribution) occupational or stakeholder pension arrangement which the new employer may offer.

8 Authorities

Pensions Act 2004

Transfer of Employment (Pension Protection) Regulations 2005 (S.I. 2005 No. 649)

Transfer of Undertakings (Protection of Employment) Regulations 2006, as amended (S.I. 2006 No. 246, 2009 No. 592, 2010 No. 93, and 2014 Nos. 16, 386 and 853)

UNFAIR DISMISSAL

A: UNFAIR DISMISSALS

1 The legislation

This Note deals with the right not to be unfairly dismissed. Part X of the Employment Rights Act 1996 gives employees (subject to certain exceptions listed below) the general right not to be unfairly dismissed and makes provision for the remedies available to an employee who is unfairly dismissed.

Part X does not apply to share fishermen and members of the police force (ss.199 and 200).

2 Right not to be unfairly dismissed

Subject to exceptions employees have the right not to be unfairly dismissed by their employers (Employment Rights Act 1996, s.94).

In addition to the employees in those employments which are entirely excluded from the provisions of Part X, s.94 does not apply to the dismissal of an employee if—

(a) he has not been continuously employed for at least two years (s.108(1)) (unless the dismissal is automatically unfair: see **3 Automatically unfair dismissals**, below); or

(b) he was dismissed by reason of any such requirement as is referred to in s.64(2) (see the Note on **Rights Arising in the Course of Employment**) and was not continuously employed for a period of not less than one month ending with the effective date of termination (s.108(2)); or

(c) he is an employee shareholder (as to whom see the Note on **Employment Protection: Introduction**), unless the dismissal—

    (i) is regarded as automatically unfair;

    (ii) amounts to a contravention of the Equality Act 2010; or

    (ii) is one to which para (b) above applies.

Note.—The two year period referred to in (a) above is reduced to one year if the employment began before 6th April 2012.

There is no qualifying time period for bringing a claim if the reason for the dismissal is, or relates to, the employee's political opinions or affiliation (s.108(4)). However such a dismissal is not automatically unfair.

3 Automatically unfair dismissals

Even though paragraph (a) or (c) above applies to a person, they will still be unfairly dismissed if it is shown that the reason or principal reason for the dismissal or, in a redundancy case, for selecting the employee for dismissal, was an inadmissible reason i.e., was for a reason specified in—

(a) s.98B (dismissal because of jury service, unless the employee's absence was likely to cause substantial injury to the employer's undertaking and the employee unreasonably refused or failed to apply for excusal from or a deferral of the obligation to attend in pursuance of being so summoned);

(b) s.99 (dismissal on ground of pregnancy, or on ground of taking maternity leave or leave for family or domestic reasons);

(c) s.100 (dismissal in health and safety cases, below);

(d) s.101 (dismissal of shop workers or betting workers who refuse Sunday work);

(e) s.101A (dismissal in working time cases, below);

(ea) s.101B (dismissal in connection with study or training, below);

(f) s.102 (dismissal of trustees of occupational pension schemes);

(g) s.103 (dismissal of employee representatives);

(h) s.103A (dismissal of employees making protected disclosures);

(i) s.104 (dismissal on ground of assertion of statutory right);

(j) s.104A (dismissal in connection with the National Minimum Wage);

(k) s.104B (dismissal in connection with tax credits);

(l) s.104C (dismissal in connection with flexible working);

(la) s.104D (dismissal in connection with pension scheme membership);

(lb) s.104E (dismissal in connection with study or training);

(lc) s.104F (dismissal in connection with trade union blacklists);

(ld) s.104G (dismissal in connection with employee shareholder status);

(m) s.105 (dismissal on ground of redundancy);

(n) s.238A of the Trade Union and Labour Relations (Consolidation) Act 1992 (dismissal in connection with industrial action);

(o) s.152(1) of the 1992 Act (dismissal relating to trade union membership);

(p) paragraphs 161 or 162 of Schedule A1 to the 1992 Act (dismissals relating to union recognition);

(q) the Part-time Workers (Prevention of Less Favourable Treatment) Regulations 2000, Reg. 7; or the Fixed-term Employees (Prevention of Less Favourable Treatment) Regulations 2002, Reg 6(1));

(r) s.12 of the Employment Relations Act 1999 (dismissal of a worker for exercising his right to be accompanied to a disciplinary or grievance hearing, or his right to accompany another worker to such a hearing;

(s) the Employment Equality (Age) Regulations 2006 Sch. 6 para 13 (dismissal of a worker for exercising his right to be accompanied to a meeting or an appeal about his working beyond retirement age, or accompanying a person to such a meeting or appeal);

(t) Regulation 30 of the Information and Consultation of Employees Regulations 2004 (dismissal of an employee for a reason connected with the rights granted by those Regulations);

(u) Regulation 17 of the Agency Workers Regulations 2010 (dismissal of agency worker for a reason connected with the rights granted by those Regulations); or

(v) Regulation 29 paras (1)(a) or (b) of the European Public Limited-Liability Company (Employee Involvement) (Great Britain) Regulations 2009 (S.I. No. 2009/2401) (dismissal for exercising rights under the 2009 Regulations).

For these purposes a redundancy case is a case where the reason or principal reason for the dismissal was that the employee was redundant but the equal application of the circumstances to non-dismissed employees required by s.153 (see **15 Dismissal on ground of redundancy**, below) is also shown (1992 Act, s.154, as amended by the 1993 Act, Sch. 7 and the Employment Rights Act 1996, Sch. 1).

Where a dismissal procedures agreement is designated by an order of the Secretary of State, the provisions of that agreement relating to dismissal will have effect in substitution for any rights under s.94. However, a dismissal procedures agreement may include a provision that it will not apply to dismissals of particular descriptions (e.g., dismissal in connection with pregnancy) (s.110, as amended by s.12 of the 1998 Act). The Advisory, Conciliation and Arbitration Service (ACAS) may, in accordance with any dismissal procedures agreement, refer any matter to the arbitration of a person appointed by ACAS for the purpose (s.212B of the 1992 Act, inserted by Sch. 1 to the 1998 Act).

4 Meaning of dismissal

An employee is treated as dismissed, for the purposes of the Employment Rights Act 1996 Part X, if, but only if (s.95(1))–

(1) his employer terminates his contract of employment, with or without notice; or

(2) he is employed under a limited term contract which terminates by virtue of a limiting event without being renewed under the same contract (see below); or

(3) the employee terminates the contract, with or without notice, in circumstances such that he is entitled so to do without notice by reason of the employer's conduct.

Where an employer gives notice of termination to an employee and, within that period of notice, the employee gives notice to the employer to terminate the contract of employment on a date earlier than the date on which the employer's notice is due to expire, the employee is deemed to have been dismissed by his employer, and the reasons for the dismissal will be taken to be the reasons given by the employer (s.95(2)).

Employment is for a "limited term" if it is not intended to be permanent and the contract provides for it to terminate by virtue of a "limiting event", such as the expiry of a term, the performance of a specific task, or the occurrence of a specific event (s.235).

5 Effective date of termination

The general rule is that the effective date of termination of a contract of employment means (Employment Rights Act 1996, s.97(1))–

(a) in relation to an employee whose contract is terminated by notice (whether given by the employer or by the employee), the date on which that notice expires;

(b) in relation to an employee whose contract is terminated without notice, the date on which the termination takes effect; and

(c) in relation to an employee who is employed under a limited term contract which terminates by virtue of a limiting event without being renewed under the same contract, the date on which that term expires.

Where the contract is terminated by the employer and the notice required to be given by him under s.86 (see the Note on **Termination of Employment**) would if duly given on the material date, expire on a date later than the effective date of termination (applying the general rule) then, for the purposes of s.92 (see the Note on **Termination of Employment**), s.108(1) (see **2 Right not to be unfairly dismissed**, above), and s.119(1) (see below), the later date will be treated as the effective date of termination in relation to the dismissal. For this purpose, the material date is the date when notice of termination was given or (where no notice was given) the date when the contract was terminated (s.97(2) and (3)).

Where the contract is terminated by the employee and (i) the material date does not fall during a period of notice of termination given by the employer, and (ii) had the contract been terminated not by the employee but by notice given on the material date by the employer, that notice would have been required (by s.86) to expire on a date later than the effective date of termination (applying the general rule) then, for the purposes of ss.108(1) and 119(1), the later date will be treated as the effective date of termination in relation to the dismissal. For this purpose, the material date means the date when notice of termination was given by the employee or (where no notice was given) the date when the contract was terminated by the employee (s.97(4) and (5)).

6 Fairness of dismissal

In determining whether a dismissal was fair or unfair, it is for the employer to show (a) what was the reason (or, if there was more than one, the principal reason) for the dismissal, and (b) that it was a reason falling within s.98(2) (see below) or some other substantial reason of a kind such as to justify the dismissal of an employee holding the position which that employee held (Employment Rights Act 1996, s.98(1)). S.98(2) lists the following reasons–

(1) a reason related to the capability (assessed by reference to skill, aptitude, health, or any other physical or mental quality) or qualifications of the employee for performing work of the kind which he was employed by the employer to do;

(2) a reason related to the conduct of the employee;

(3) that the employee was redundant; or

(4) that the employee could not continue to work in the position which he held without contravention (either on his part or on that of his employer) of a duty or restriction imposed by or under an enactment.

Where the employer has fulfilled the requirements of s.98(1) then, subject to ss.152, 153 and 238 of the 1992 Act (see below), the determination of the question whether the dismissal was fair or unfair, having regard to the reason shown by the employer, will depend on whether in the circumstances (including the size and administrative resources of the employer's undertaking) the employer acted reasonably or unreasonably in treating it as a sufficient reason for dismissing the employee; and that question will be determined in accordance with equity and the substantial merits of the case (s.98(4) and (6)).

For the law relating to dismissal of an employee on the transfer of an undertaking, see the Note on **Transfer of Undertakings**.

7 Dismissal in health and safety cases

S.100 provides that the dismissal of an employee by his employer will be regarded as having been unfair if the reason for it (or, if more than one, the principal reason) was one of the reasons specified in s.100(1)(a) to (e), which are similar to those described in s.44(1)(a) to (e) (see the Note on **Rights Arising in the Course of Employment: Detriment**).

8 Dismissal in working time cases

S.101A provides that the dismissal of an employee is to be regarded as unfair if the reason for it (or, if more than one, the principal reason) is that the employee–

(a) refused to comply with a requirement of the employer which contravened the Working Time Regulations 1998 (see the Note on **Working Time Restrictions**);

(b) refused to forgo a right conferred on him by those Regulations;

(c) failed to sign a workforce agreement for the purposes of the Regulations, or to enter into, or agree to vary or extend, any other agreement with his employer which is provided for in those Regulations; or

(d) being a representative of the workforce for the purposes of the Regulations, or a candidate in an election of representatives, performed any function or activities as a representative or candidate.

9 Dismissal of trustees of occupational pension schemes

A dismissal will be regarded as unfair where the reason for it (or, if more than one, the principal reason) was that the employee, being a trustee of an occupational pension scheme relevant to his employment, performed or proposed to perform any functions as such a trustee (s.102).

10 Dismissal of employee representatives

A dismissal will be regarded as unfair where the reason for it (or, if more than one, the principal reason) was that the employee, being an employee representative for the purposes of Part IV of the 1992 Act or Regulations 9, 13 and 15 of the Transfer of Undertakings (Protection of Employment) Regulations 2006 (see the Note on **Transfer of Undertakings**), or a candidate in elections for such representatives, performed, or proposed to perform, any functions as an employee representative or candidate (s.103(1)).

A dismissal will also be unfair if the reason (or principal reason) for it is that the employee took part in an election of employee representatives for the purposes of Part IV of the 1992 Act or Regulations 9, 13 and 15 of the 2006 Regulations (s.103(2)).

11 Dismissal of European Works Council members, etc

A person who is dismissed and who is–

(i) a member of a special negotiating body;

(ii) a member of a European Works Council;

(iii) an information and consultation representative; or

(iv) a candidate in an election for someone who will become (i), (ii) or (iii), will generally be regarded as unfairly dismissed if the reason, or principal reason, for the dismissal is that he performed any functions or activities as such a member, representative or candidate or he (or a person acting on his behalf) made a request for paid time-off work to carry out his functions, or proposed to do so (Transnational Information and Consultation of Employees Regulations 1999, Reg. 28).

As to European Works Councils generally, see the Note on **Rights Arising in the Course of Employment.**

12 Dismissal relating to trade union membership

By virtue of s.152 of the 1992 Act, the dismissal of an employee by his employer will be regarded as having been unfair if the reason for it (or, if more than one, the principal reason) was that the employee (s.152(1))–
- (a) was, or proposed to become, a member of an independent trade union;
- (b) had taken part, or proposed to take part, in the activities of such a union at an appropriate time (as defined by s.152(2)), which is in the same terms as s.146 of the 1992 Act;
- (ba) had made use, or proposed to make use, of trade union services at an appropriate time;
- (bb) had failed to accept an offer made in contravention of ss.145A or 145B (inducements relating to union membership or activities); or
- (c) was not a member of any trade union, or of a particular trade union, or of one of a number of particular trade unions, or had refused or proposed to refuse to become or remain a member.

A refusal, or proposed refusal, on the part of the employee to comply with a requirement that, in the event of his failure to become or ceasing to remain a member of a trade union, he must make one or more payments, or his objection, or proposed objection, to a provision under which a sum or sums would in the event be deducted from his pay, will be treated as a reason falling within (c) above (1992 Act, s.152(3)).

Note.–the qualifying period and upper age limit for unfair dismissal protection (see **2 Right not to be unfairly dismissed**, above) do not apply to dismissals regarded as unfair under s.152 (s.154).

13 Dismissals relating to union recognition

A dismissal will be unfair if the reason (or a main reason) for it is that the employee (Sch. A1, para 161)–
- (a) acted with a view to obtaining or preventing the recognition of a union, or securing or preventing the ending of bargaining arrangements; or
- (b) voted, or sought to influence the votes of other employees, in a ballot as to union recognition or bargaining arrangements; or
- (c) indicated his support or opposition to such recognition or arrangements.

As to the application of this provision to workers at sea, see the Employment Relations (Offshore Employment) Order 2000 (S.I. No. 1828).

14 Dismissal of employees making protected disclosures

A dismissal will be regarded as unfair if the reason for it (or, if more than one, the principal reason) is that the employee made a protected disclosure (see the Note on **Public Interest Disclosure**) (s.103A).

15 Dismissal on ground of redundancy

A dismissal will be regarded as unfair where the reason for dismissal was redundancy and it is shown that the reason applied equally to other employees holding similar positions who were not dismissed and the reason for selection of that employee for dismissal was one of those specified in s.152(1) (see above) (1992 Act, s.153).

A dismissal will also be regarded as unfair where the reason for dismissal was redundancy and it is shown that the reason applied equally to other employees holding similar positions who were not dismissed and the reason for selection of that employee for dismissal was an inadmissible reason (s.105). For the inadmissible reasons, see **3 Automatically unfair dismissals**, above.

Note.–the qualifying period and upper age limit for unfair dismissal protection (see **2 Right not to be unfairly dismissed**, above) do not apply to dismissals regarded as unfair under s.153 (s.154).

16 Dismissal on ground of pregnancy, or on ground of taking maternity leave or leave for family or domestic reasons

S.99 (as substituted by the 1999 Act) and Regulation 20 of the Maternity and Parental Leave etc. Regulations 1999, provide that an employee will be treated as unfairly dismissed if the reason (or, if there is more than one, the principal reason) for her dismissal is–
- (a) that she is pregnant;
- (b) that she has given birth to a child and her maternity leave period is ended by that dismissal;
- (c) in consequence of any statutory requirement or any recommendation in any relevant code of practice, as defined in s.66 (suspension on the ground that she is pregnant, has recently given birth, or is breastfeeding a child – see the Note on **Maternity Rights**);
- (d) where her contract of employment was terminated after the end of the maternity leave period, she took, or

availed herself of the benefits of, ordinary or additional maternity leave;

(e) that she took or sought to take parental leave or other time off for domestic reasons under s.57A of the Act (see the Note on **Rights Arising in the Course of Employment: Time-Off**);

(ee) that she failed to return after a period of ordinary or additional maternity leave where her employer did not notify of the date on which that period would end and she reasonably believed that it had not ended, or her employer gave her less than 28 days' notice of the day the period would end and it was not reasonably practicable for her to return on that date (see the Note on **Maternity Rights**);

(eee) the fact that she undertook, considered undertaking or refused to undertake work for her employer during her statutory maternity leave period;

(f) she declined to sign a workforce agreement for the purposes of the Maternity and Parental Leave etc. Regulations 1999, or acted as a representative of the workforce for the purposes of negotiating a workforce agreement under the Regulations;

(g) that her maternity leave period is ended by the dismissal and the reason (or, if there is more than one, the principal reason for her dismissal) is that she is redundant and Regulation 10 (right to be offered suitable alternative employment where redundancy is during maternity leave period – see the Note on **Maternity Rights**) has not been complied with.

An employee will not be regarded as unfairly dismissed if, for a reason other than redundancy, it is not reasonably practicable for her employer to permit her to return to a job which is both suitable and appropriate for her and she then accepts, or unreasonably refuses, a suitable and appropriate job offered by an associated employer (Maternity and Parental Leave etc. Regulations 1999, Reg. 20(7)).

The Shared Parental Leave Regulations 2014, Reg. 43 provides protection for an employee (both the mother and the partner) from unfair dismissal in connection with entitlement to shared parental leave for reasons connected with any of the following facts: (i) the employee took, sought to take, or made use of the benefits of, shared parental leave; (ii) the employer believed that the employee was likely to take shared parental leave; or (iii) the employee undertook, considered undertaking, or refused to undertake work during shared parental leave. As to shared parental leave, see the Note on **Rights Arising in the Course of Employment: Leave for Domestic and Family Reasons, and Flexible Working**.

17 Dismissal in connection with tax credits

The dismissal of an employee will be regarded as unfair if the reason for it was that the employee (s.104B)–

(a) was, or might be, entitled to a working tax credit;

(b) had taken or was proposing to take, action to enforce or otherwise secure a right conferred by tax credit regulations; or

(c) had taken action which resulted in a penalty being imposed on or proceedings being brought against the employer in connection with tax credits.

18 Dismissal in connection with flexible working

The dismissal of an employee will be regarded as unfair if the reason for it was that the employee made or proposed to make an application for flexible working; exercised or proposed to exercise a right in connection with flexible working; or brought, or alleged circumstances which would constitute grounds for bringing, proceedings against the employer in connection with flexible working (s.104C). As to flexible working, see the Note on **Rights Arising in the Course of Employment: Leave for Domestic and Family Reasons, and Flexible Working**.

19 Dismissal in connection with pension scheme membership

The dismissal of an employee will be regarded as unfair if the reason for it was that (s.104D)–

(a) any action was taken, or was proposed to be taken, with a view to enforcing in favour of the employee a requirement imposed by the Pensions Act 2008 Part 1 (automatic enrolment);

(b) the employer was prosecuted for an offence under the Pensions Act 2008, s.45 as a result of action taken for the purpose of enforcing such a requirement in favour of the employee; or

(c) any provision of the Pensions Act 2008 Part 1 Chapter 1 applies to the employee, or will or might apply.

20 Dismissal in connection with study or training

The dismissal of an employee will be regarded as unfair if the reason for it was that the employee made or proposed to make an application for time-off for study or training; exercised or proposed to exercise a right in connection with time-off for study or training; or brought, or alleged circumstances which would constitute grounds for bringing, proceedings against the employer in connection with time-off for study or training (s.104E). As to time-off for study or training, see the Note on **Rights Arising in the Course of Employment: Time-Off** at para **9 Time off for study or training**.

Dismissal will also be regarded as unfair if the reason for it is that, being a person entitled to be permitted to participate in education or training under the Education and Skills Act 2008, ss.27-28 (duty of under-18s to participate in education or training) the employee exercised, or proposed to exercise, that right (s.101B).

21 Dismissal in connection with trade union blacklists

The dismissal of an employee will be regarded as unfair if the reason for it was that the employer contravened the Employment Relations Act 1999 (Blacklists) Regulations 2010 prohibiting the compilation, use, sale or supply of blacklists containing details of trade union members and activists, or the employer (i) relies on information supplied by a person who contravenes the Regulations in relation to that list and (ii) knows or ought reasonably to know that the information relied on is supplied in contravention of the Regulations.

22 Dismissal in connection with employee shareholder status

The dismissal of an employee will be regarded as unfair if the reason for it was that the employee refused to accept an offer by the employer for him to become an employee shareholder (see the Note on **Employment Protection: Introduction** at para **9 Employee shareholders**) (s.104G).

23 Dismissal on ground of assertion of statutory right

The dismissal of an employee will be regarded as unfair if the reason for it was that the employee (a) brought proceedings against the employer to enforce a right of his which is a relevant statutory right; or (b) alleged that the employer had infringed such a right. A relevant statutory right is any right conferred by the Act, for which the remedy for its infringement is by way of a complaint or reference to an employment tribunal; the right conferred by s.86 of the Act (minimum period of notice (see the Note on **Termination of Employment**)) ;the rights conferred by the following provisions of the 1992 Act, namely, ss.68, 86, 146, 168, 169, and 170 (deductions from pay, union activities, and time off); and the rights conferred by the Working Time Regulations 1998 (see the Note on **Working Time Restrictions**). It is immaterial whether the employee has the right or not and whether it has been infringed or not, provided that he acted in good faith in seeking to assert it. Moreover, it will be unnecessary for the employee to specify the right that he sought to assert, provided it was made reasonably clear to the employer what the right claimed to have been infringed was (s.104).

24 Dismissal of replacement

Where an employee has been informed in writing by his employer that he is being engaged to replace another employee who is temporarily absent because of pregnancy, childbirth, or adoption leave he will not be regarded as unfairly dismissed if the reason for his dismissal was to give work to the first-mentioned employee. Similarly, if an employee is engaged to replace another employee who has been suspended from work on medical grounds or maternity grounds (within the meaning of Part VII) (suspension from work on maternity ground – see the Note on **Maternity Rights**), he will not be regarded as unfairly dismissed if he is dismissed in order to allow resumption of work by the other employee (s.106).

25 Dismissal in connection with industrial action

In a case where an employee complains of unfair dismissal by his employer because of (a) a lock-out by his employer, or (b) his involvement in an official strike or other industrial action, a tribunal has no power to decide whether his dismissal was fair or unfair unless other employees similarly involved in the lock-out or other industrial action at the time of the dismissal in the same establishment have not been dismissed, or, if dismissed, have been offered re-engagement within three months of their dismissal, and the complainant has not been re-engaged.

S.237 of the 1992 Act provides that an employee has no right to complain of unfair dismissal if at the time of the dismissal he was taking part in an unofficial strike or other unofficial industrial action unless it is shown that the reason or principal reason for dismissal or selection for dismissal was one of those specified in ss.99, 100, 103, or 103A of the Act (i.e., dismissal in maternity, health and safety, employee representative or protected disclosure cases–see **2 Right not to be unfairly dismissed**, above). A strike or other industrial action is unofficial in relation to an employee unless (a) he is a member of a trade union and the action is authorised or endorsed by that union (as determined by the provisions of s.20(2) of the 1992 Act); or (b) he is not a member of a trade union but there are among those taking part in the industrial action members of a trade union by which the action has been authorised or endorsed. Provided that, a strike or other industrial action will not be regarded as unofficial if none of those taking part in it is a member of a trade union.

S.238A (added by the Employment Relations Act 1999 and amended by the Employment Act 2004) allows employees to taking part in official industrial action to complain of unfair dismissal in certain additional cases. Employees taking part in official industrial action (described in s.238A as "protected industrial action") will be regarded as unfairly dismissed if the reason for the dismissal was the fact that they were taking part in the industrial action and one of the following circumstances applies–

  (a) the dismissal took place within twelve weeks of the day on which the employee began to take industrial action, not counting days when the employee was locked out (whether or not he was still taking this action when he was dismissed);

  (b) the dismissal took place after the end of the above twelve-week period, but the employee had stopped taking action before the end of that period;

  (c) the dismissal took place after the end of the twelve-week period and the employee was still taking action when dismissed but the employer had not taken reasonable steps to resolve the dispute.

In deciding whether the employer had taken reasonable steps to resolve the dispute, regard must be had to whether the employer or union had–

(i) complied with agreed procedures to resolve the dispute;

(ii) offered or agreed to begin or re-open negotiations after action had begun;

(iii) unreasonably refused a request to use conciliation or mediation services; and

(iv) where it had been agreed to use conciliation or mediation services, been committed to the process.

In assessing whether an employer has taken the above steps, the tribunal must not judge the merits of the dispute.

Note.–For these purposes, where dismissal is by notice, a dismissal takes place on the date notice of the dismissal is given, not the date the notice takes effect (s.238A(9)).

When bringing a complaint under s.238A, an employee will not be required to have been employed for a minimum of one year or to be under retirement age (see **2 Right not to be unfairly dismissed**, above).

26 Disciplinary procedures

S.10 of the 1999 Act gives workers (including agency workers and home workers) who have been required or invited to attend a disciplinary or grievance hearing (see below) a statutory right to be accompanied by a single companion, chosen by the worker, in any case where a worker makes a reasonable request to be accompanied. The companion must be either a trade union official (but not necessarily from the same union as the one recognised by the employer) or another of the employer's workers. The companion has the right to address the hearing in order to put the worker's case, sum up the case, and respond on the worker's behalf to any view expressed at the hearing, and to confer with the worker during the hearing. The employer does not have to permit the companion to answer questions on behalf of the worker. If a chosen companion is not available at the time proposed for the hearing, the employer must postpone the hearing to an alternative time chosen by the worker within the next five working days. An employer must allow a worker who has been chosen as another worker's companion paid time off to accompany that worker.

For the purposes of s.10, a "disciplinary hearing" is one which could result in–

(a) the administration of a formal warning to a worker by his employer;

(b) the taking of some other action by the employer; or

(c) the confirmation of a warning issued or of some other action taken.

A "grievance hearing" is a hearing which concerns the performance of a duty by an employer in relation to a worker (s.13(4) and (5)).

A worker may present a complaint to an employment tribunal if his employer fails to allow him to take a companion to a disciplinary or grievance hearing. Any such complaint must be presented within three months of the date of the failure, or within such further period as the tribunal considers reasonable in a case where it is satisfied that it was not reasonably practicable for the complaint to be presented during the three month period. Where the tribunal finds a complaint well founded, it must order the employer to pay compensation to the worker of an amount not exceeding two weeks' pay (as to the maximum amount allowed for a week's pay, see the Note on **Employment Protection: Introduction** at para **6 Normal working hours and a week's pay**) (s.11).

A worker has the right not to be subjected to any detriment by any act, or deliberate failure to act, by his employer done on the ground that he exercised his right under s.10 or accompanied or sought to accompany another worker (whether of the same employer or not) pursuant to a request under s.10. In addition, a worker who is dismissed will be regarded for the purposes of Part X as unfairly dismissed if the reason for the dismissal is that he exercised his right under s.10 or accompanied or sought to accompany another worker (s.12).

Any provision in an agreement (whether a contract of employment or another agreement) is void insofar as it purports to exclude or limit the rights granted by s.10 (s.14).

The Code of Practice (Disciplinary and Grievance Procedures) Order 2015 brought into effect the *ACAS Code of Practice on Disciplinary and Grievance Procedures* issued under s.199 of the Trade Union and Labour Relations (Consolidation) Act 1992. The Code recommends *inter alia* that employees should be told in writing of complaints against them and given the opportunity to state their case, and should have the right to be accompanied by a trade union representative or a fellow employee of their choice; that disciplinary action should not be taken until the case has been fully investigated; that, except for gross misconduct, no employee should be dismissed for a first breach of discipline; and that employees should have a right of appeal (normally to a manager not previously involved) against any penalty imposed. Legal action cannot be taken against an employer solely because he has not complied with one of the Code's provisions. However, employment tribunals may take into account, in determining whether an employee has been unfairly dismissed, whether the employer has complied with the provisions of the Code.

B: REMEDIES FOR UNFAIR DISMISSAL

27 Complaint to employment tribunal

Employment tribunals have jurisdiction to hear and determine complaints by persons who have been unfairly dismissed under the Act (s.111(1)). A complaint must generally be presented within three months of the effective date of termination although the tribunal may extend this period if it is satisfied that it was not reasonably practicable for the complaint to be presented within the specified time (s.111(2)).

Where a complainant was taking part in a strike and other employees also taking part in the strike have been offered re-engagement but the complainant has not, the period within which the complaint must be presented is six months (1992 Act, ss.238 and 239). The tribunal will also consider a complaint presented during a period of notice but before the effective date of termination (s.111(3)). The tribunal may consider a complaint in relation to prohibition on the keeping of trade union blacklists that is otherwise out of time if it considers it just and equitable to do so (s.111(5)).

A prospective claimant must submit the details of their claim to ACAS before they can lodge the claim at an employment tribunal (see the Note on **Employment Tribunals, ACAS, and the Employment Appeal Tribunal** at para 11 **Compulsory conciliation**).

28 Settlement agreements

Where an employer and employee discuss ending the employment relationship under a settlement agreement, an offer to terminate the employment relationship on agreed terms is not admissible as evidence in any subsequent unfair dismissal case. This applies to offers made by either the employer or employee, to the offer itself and also to the content of any negotiations about the offer, but does not apply where the employee claims to have been dismissed for an automatically unfair reason (s.111A).

Where either party has behaved improperly in making or negotiating the offer the tribunal may consider this as evidence in an unfair dismissal claim (s.111A(4)).

A settlement offer is admissible as evidence before a tribunal when determining costs or expenses in an unfair dismissal claim provided that the party which made the offer expressly reserved the right to refer to it in such a situation (s.111A(5)).

A *Code of Practice on Settlement Agreements* has been issued by the Advisory, Conciliation and Arbitration Service (Employment Code of Practice (Settlement Agreements) Order 2013, S.I. No. 1665) and is available at <http://www.acas.org.uk/settlementagreements>.

29 Remedies for unfair dismissal–introduction

Where an employment tribunal finds that a complaint of unfair dismissal under s.111 is well-founded, it must explain to the complainant what orders for reinstatement or re-engagement can be made, and ascertain whether he seeks such an order. If he does, the tribunal may make the order it considers appropriate. If an order for reinstatement or re-engagement is not granted, the tribunal must make a basic, compensatory, and, in certain circumstances, a special award of compensation (s.112).

30 Order for reinstatement

An order for reinstatement requires the employer to treat the employee as though he had not been dismissed and, on making such an order, the tribunal must specify (1) the amount payable by the employer for any benefit lost by the complainant as a result of the dismissal, including arrears of pay from cessation of employment to reinstatement, (2) any rights and privileges, including seniority and pension rights, which must be restored, and (3) the date by which the order must be complied with (s.114(1) and (2)). In particular, if the complainant, but for his dismissal, would have benefited from improved terms and conditions, the order will require him to be treated as if he had so benefited from the date on which he would have done so if not dismissed (s.114(3)).

31 Order for re-engagement

An order for re-engagement requires the employer (or his successor or an associated employer) to employ the complainant in employment which is comparable to his pre-dismissal employment or is otherwise suitable (s.115(1)). The tribunal must specify the terms of re-engagement, which are similar to those listed above for reinstatement, and also the employer's name, and the nature of, and remuneration for, the employment (s.115(2)).

32 Procedure of the tribunal

In deciding which of the two types of order to make, the tribunal must first consider reinstatement and take into account (i) whether the complainant wishes it, (ii) whether it is practicable (and the engagement of a permanent replacement of the dismissed employee is to be taken into account for this purpose only if the employer shows (a) that it was not practicable to carry on without such replacement or (b) that the replacement was engaged after the lapse of a reasonable period, without having heard from the dismissed employee that he wished to be reinstated or re-engaged and at the time when the employer engaged the replacement it was no longer reasonable for him to arrange for the dismissed employee's work to be done except by a permanent replacement), and (iii) where the complainant caused or contributed to his dismissal, whether it would be just to order reinstatement (s.116(1)). If the tribunal decides against reinstatement, it must consider re-engagement, taking into account similar considerations to those set out above for reinstatement, and, if it decides to make such an order, it must endeavour to ensure (except where there has been contributory fault by the complainant) that the terms are, as nearly as is reasonably practicable, not less favourable to the complainant than under reinstatement (s.116(2) to (4)). The Employment Protection (Continuity of Employment) Regulations 1997 provide for the preservation of continuity of employment where a dismissed employee is reinstated or re-engaged (see the Note on **Employment Protection: Introduction**).

33 Compensation for failure to comply with order

Where the employer has reinstated or re-engaged the complainant following an order by the tribunal, but has not fully complied with the terms of the order, the tribunal must make an award of compensation to the complainant against the employer for the loss involved (s.117(1)), subject to a limit of the lower of £78,962 or 52 x 1 week's pay (ss.123 and 124). If the employer does not reinstate or re-engage the complainant in accordance with an order, the complainant will be given a basic and a compensatory award. Further, unless the employer satisfies the tribunal that it was not practicable to comply with the order because it was not practicable for him to arrange for the dismissed employee's work to be done without engaging a permanent replacement, the tribunal must make an award of additional compensation of an amount equal to not less than 26 nor more than 52 weeks' pay (s.117(3), as amended by the 1999 Act, s.33).

Where the tribunal finds that a complainant has unreasonably prevented an order for reinstatement or re-engagement from being complied with, it will take that conduct into account as a failure on the part of the complainant to mitigate his loss (s.117(8)). The amount of an employee's week's pay is calculated in accordance with the provisions of ss.220 to 227 (see the Note on **Employment Protection: Introduction**), but for this purpose is subject to a limit of £479 (s.227).

Note.—Any adjustment of an award under s.123 is made after any increase in the award under s.31 (non-completion of statutory dismissal procedures) or s.38 (failure to give a written statement of particulars or of a change in particulars— see the Note on **Terms of Employment** at para 5 **Enforcement of rights under ss.1 to 4**) (s.124A).

34 Amount of compensation–introduction

Where an award of compensation is made because no order for reinstatement or re-engagement has been made, or where such an order has been made but the employer has not reinstated or re-engaged the employee in accordance with it, the award of compensation is to consist of a basic award calculated in accordance with ss.119 to 122, and a compensatory award calculated in accordance with ss.123 to 126 (s.118(1)).

The tribunal, in considering whether it would be just and equitable to reduce, or further reduce, any part of an award of compensation for a dismissal which is to be regarded as unfair by virtue of ss.152 or 153, must disregard any conduct or action of the complainant in so far as it constitutes–

(a) a breach, or proposed breach, of any requirement in a contract or other agreement that the complainant (i) must be or become a member of a particular union or of one of a number of such unions; (ii) must cease to be, or refrain from becoming, such a member; or (iii) must not take part in the activities of any trade union, or of a particular trade union, or of one of a number of such unions; or

(b) a refusal, or proposed refusal, to comply with a requirement that on failing to become or ceasing to remain a member of a trade union, he must make one or more payments, or an objection, or proposed objection, to a provision under which a sum or sums would in that event, be deducted from his pay (1992 Act, s.155).

Note.—Where in proceedings before an employment tribunal it appears to the tribunal that (Trade Union and Labour Relations Act 1992, s.207A)–

(a) the claim concerns a matter to which a relevant Code of Practice applies;

(b) either the employer or employee has failed to comply with that Code in relation to that matter; and

(c) that failure was unreasonable,

then the tribunal may, if it considers it just and equitable in all the circumstances to do so, increase or decrease (depending on whether it is the employer or employee at fault) any award it makes to the employee by no more than 25%. The *ACAS Code of Practice on Disciplinary and Grievance Procedures* (see **26 Disciplinary procedures**, above) is a relevant Code for these purposes.

35 The basic award

The basic award is calculated (in accordance with s.119) by ascertaining the total number of years for which the complainant has been continuously employed up to the effective date of termination and, reckoning backwards from that date, allowing (subject to a maximum of 20 years) one and a half weeks' pay for each of those years in which the complainant was aged up to 64 but not under 41, one week's pay for years when he was under 41 but not under 22, and half a week's pay for years when he was under 22 (s.119(1) to (3)).

Where the dismissal is to be regarded as unfair by virtue of ss.152 or 153 of the 1992 Act, the amount of the basic award (before any reduction under the provisions described below) must not be less than £5,853 (1992 Act, s.156(1); s.120). Similarly, where the dismissal is unfair by virtue of s.100(1)(a) or (b) (health and safety cases); s.101A(d) (working time cases); s.102(1) (occupational pension scheme trustee cases); or s.103 (employee representative cases), the minimum basic award is also £5,853 (s.120).

Where the tribunal finds that the main reason for the dismissal was redundancy and that, under s.141 of the Act, the claimant is not, or if he were otherwise entitled would not be, entitled to a redundancy payment, or that, under s.138, he is not treated as dismissed for the purposes of Part X of the Act, the amount of the basic award will be two weeks' pay (s.121). The amount of an employee's week's pay is calculated in accordance with the provisions of ss.220 to 227 (see the Note on **Terms of Employment**), but for this purpose is subject to a limit of £479 (s.227).

Where a dismissal is regarded as unfair by virtue of s.104F (keeping of prohibited trade union blacklists), whether or not the dismissal is unfair or regarded as unfair for any other reason, the amount of the basic award (before any reduction is made under s.122) will not be less than £5,000 (s.120(1C)). The award will be reduced or further reduced by the amount of any basic award in respect of the same dismissal under s.156 of the 1992 Act (minimum basic award in case of dismissal on grounds related to trade union membership or activities) (s.122(5)).

Where the tribunal considers that any conduct of the complainant before the dismissal (or, where the dismissal was with notice, before the notice was given) was such that it would be just and equitable to reduce or further reduce the amount of the basic award to any extent, the tribunal must reduce or further reduce that amount accordingly, but this provision does not apply where the reason or principal reason for the dismissal was that the employee was redundant unless the dismissal is to be regarded as unfair by virtue of s.153 of the 1992 Act or s.100(1) of the Act; in that event, it will apply only to so much of the basic award as is payable because of s.156(1) of the 1992 Act or because of s.120 of the Act (1992 Act, s.156(2), s.122(2) and (3)). Where the complainant has been awarded any amount in respect of the dismissal under a designated dismissal procedures agreement (see **3 Automatically unfair dismissals**, above), the tribunal must reduce (or further reduce) the amount of the basic award to such extent as it considers just and equitable (s.122(3A), inserted by the Employment Rights (Dispute Resolution) Act 1998, Sch.1).

Where the tribunal finds that the complainant has unreasonably refused an offer by the employer which if accepted would have had the effect of reinstating him in his employment in all respects as if he had not been dismissed, the tribunal must reduce or further reduce the amount of the basic award to such extent as it considers just and equitable having regard to that finding (s.122(1)).

36 The compensatory award

Subject to s.124, the general rule is that a compensatory award is such amount as the tribunal considers just and equitable in all the circumstances to compensate the complainant for the loss attributable to the employer's action in dismissing him (s.123(1)). This loss will include any expenses reasonably incurred by the complainant in consequence of the dismissal, and loss of any benefit which he might reasonably be expected to have had but for dismissal, but limited, in the case of a redundancy payment (whether made under the Act or otherwise), to the excess of such payment over the amount of the basic award (disregarding any reduction in the award under s.122). The complainant must, however, mitigate his loss as he would be required to do at common law. In determining how far the loss is attributable to the employer's action leading to dismissal, any pressure on him through industrial action must be ignored, and the question is to be determined as if no such pressure was exercised.

If the dismissal is found to have been caused or contributed to by any action of the complainant, he will suffer a reduction in his compensatory award, which will also be reduced by the excess of any redundancy payment received from the employer over the basic award (s.123(3) to (7)). S.124 imposes a limit of the lower of £78,962 or 52 x 1 week's pay on the amount of the award, which applies to the net amount of compensation after taking into account any payment made by the employer to the complainant or any reduction required by any enactment; save where the exception in s.124(4) applies. S.124(4) provides that, in the case of an award of compensation under s.117(3) (see **33 Compensation for failure to comply with order**, above) where an additional award falls to be made, the limits imposed by s.124 may be exceeded to the extent necessary to enable the award fully to reflect the amount specified as payable under s.114(2) or s.115(2) (see **30 Order for reinstatement**, and see **31 Order for re-engagement**, above), if that limit would otherwise reduce the amount of the compensatory award when added to the additional award. In addition, the limit does not apply if the reason for dismissing the employee, or selecting him for redundancy, was one of the reasons specified in s.100 or s.103A (i.e., dismissal in health and safety cases or dismissal for making a protected disclosure—see **7 Dismissal in health and safety cases**, and see **14 Dismissal of employees making protected disclosures**, above) (s.124(1A), added by the 1999 Act, s.37).

37 Prevention of dual compensation

Where compensation falls to be awarded in respect of any act under the Act relating to unfair dismissal and the Equality Act 2010 an employment tribunal must not award compensation under either of those Acts in respect of any loss or other matter which is or has been taken into account under the other by the tribunal (or another employment tribunal) in awarding compensation on the same or another complaint in respect of that act (s.126).

38 Awards against third parties

If, in proceedings before an employment tribunal the employer or the complainant claims that the employer was induced to dismiss the complainant by pressure which a trade union or other person exercised on him by calling, organising, procuring, or financing a strike or other industrial action, or by threatening to do so, and that the pressure was exercised because the complainant was not a member of any union, or of a particular trade union or of one of a number of particular trade unions, the employer or complainant may require the person who he claims exercised the pressure to be joined (in Scotland, sisted) as a party to the proceedings. Where any such person has been so joined and the tribunal makes an award of compensation, but finds the claim to be well-founded, it may make the award against that person instead of against the employer, or partly against that person and partly against the employer, as it considers just and equitable in the circumstances (1992 Act, s.160).

39 Interim relief

Under s.161 of the 1992 Act, an employee who complains to an employment tribunal that his dismissal is to be regarded as unfair by virtue of s.152 of the 1992 Act (see **12 Dismissal relating to trade union membership,** above) is entitled to apply to the tribunal for interim relief in the form of an order which, if granted, will enable him to be reinstated in his job or re-engaged by his former employer in another job pending the disposal of his complaint of unfair dismissal. If on the hearing of an application for interim relief the employer fails to attend before the tribunal, or states that he is unwilling either to reinstate the employee or re-engage him, the tribunal will make an order for the continuation of the employee's contract of employment.

An application under s.161 will not be entertained unless–

(a) it is presented to the tribunal before the end of the period of seven days immediately following the effective date of termination (whether before, on, or after that date); and

(b) in a case in which the employee relies on s.152(1)(a) or (b), before the end of that period the employee presents to the tribunal a certificate signed by an authorised official of the union concerned stating that on the date of the dismissal the employee was or had proposed to become a member of the union and that there appear to be reasonable grounds for supposing that the reason for his dismissal (or, if more than one, the principal reason) was one alleged in the complaint (1992 Act, ss.161 and 162).

Similarly, s.128 gives an employee the right to apply for interim relief, pending a determination of a complaint of unfair dismissal brought on the grounds specified in ss.100, 102, 103, 103A, or Schedule A1, paragraph 161, or the opening words of s.104F(1) (providing the conditions in (a) and (b) of that subsection have been met) (see **2 Right not to be unfairly dismissed,** above). An application for interim relief under s.128 will not be entertained unless it is presented to the tribunal before the end of the period of seven days immediately following the effective date of termination (whether before, on, or after that date). If granted, it will enable the employee to be reinstated in his job or re-engaged by his former employer in another job pending the disposal of his complaint of unfair dismissal. If on the hearing of an application for interim relief the employer fails to attend before the tribunal, or states that he is unwilling either to reinstate the employee or re-engage him, the tribunal will make an order for the continuation of the employee's contract of employment (s.129). An order under s.129 is an order that the contract of employment continue in force (a) for the purposes of pay or other benefit derived from the employment, seniority, pension rights and other similar matters and (b) for the purpose of determining for any purpose the period for which the employee has been continuously employed from the date of the termination until the determination or settlement of the complaint (s.130).

40 Authorities

Statutes–

Employment Act 2002

Employment Relations Acts 1999 and 2004

Employment Rights Act 1996

Employment Rights (Dispute Resolution) Act 1998

Trade Union and Labour Relations (Consolidation) Act 1992

Trade Union Reform and Employment Rights Act 1993

Statutory Instruments–

Code of Practice (Disciplinary and Grievance Procedures) Order 2015 (S.I. 2015 No. 649)

Employment Protection (Continuity of Employment) Regulations 1996, as amended (S.I. 1996 No. 3147, 2001 No. 1188, 2013 No. 1956, and 2014 No. 386)

Employment Protection (Employment in Aided Schools) Order 1981 (S.I. 1981 No. 847)

Employment Relations Act 1999 (Blacklists) Regulations 2010, as amended (S.I. 2010 No. 493 and 2014 No. 386)

Maternity and Parental Leave etc. Regulations 1999, as amended (S.I. 1999 No. 3312, 2001 No. 4010, 2002 No. 2789, 2006 No. 2014, 2008 No. 1966, and 2013 Nos. 283, 388, and 591)

Transnational Information and Consultation of Employees Regulations 1999, as amended (S.I. 1999 No. 3323, 2004 Nos. 1079 and 2518, 2006 No. 2059, 2009 Nos. 2401 and 3348, 2010 No. 1088, 2013 No. 1956, and 2014 No. 386)

Unfair Dismissal and Statement of Reasons for Dismissal (Variation of Qualifying Period) Order 2012 (S.I. 2012 No. 989)

WAGES

A: PROTECTION OF WORKERS IN RELATION TO THE PAYMENT OF WAGES

1 The legislation

The Employment Rights Act 1996 contains in Part II provisions for the protection of workers in relation to the payment of wages. The Act repealed *inter alia* the previous legislation in this field, contained in Part I of the Wages Act 1986. The Act has been amended by the Employment Rights (Dispute Resolution) Act 1998 and the Employment Relations Act 1999.

Part II imposes general restrictions on the deductions which may be made from wages and on the payments which an employer may receive from his workers as well as particular restrictions on such deductions and payments in retail employment. Part II extends to Crown employment, excluding service in the armed services of the Crown.

2 Definitions

For the purposes of the Employment Rights Act 1996 Part II, a worker is an individual who currently works (or formerly worked) under (s.230(2) and (3))–
(a) a contract of service or apprenticeship; or
(b) any other contract (whether express or implied and whether oral or in writing) whereby he undertakes to do or perform personally any work or services for another party to the contract whose status is not by virtue of the contract that of a client or customer of any profession or business undertaking carried on by the individual.

S.27 defines wages to mean any sum payable to a worker by his employer in connection with his employment including (s.27(1) and (2))–
(1) any fee, bonus, commission, holiday pay, or other emolument referable to his employment, whether payable under his contract or otherwise;
(2) statutory sick, maternity, paternity or adoption pay;
(3) any guarantee payment under s.28 of the Act (see the Note on **Rights Arising in the Course of Employment**);
(4) any payment for time off under Part VI of the Act (see the Note on **Rights Arising in the Course of Employment**) or under s.169 of the Trade Union and Labour Relations (Consolidation) Act 1992;
(5) remuneration on suspension on medical grounds or on maternity grounds under s.64 or 68 of the Act (see the Notes on **Rights Arising in the Course of Employment** and **Maternity Rights**);
(6) any sum payable in pursuance of an order for reinstatement or re-engagement under s.113 of the Act (see the Note on **Unfair Dismissal**);
(7) any sum payable under s.130 of the Act or s.164 of the 1992 Act (see the Note on **Unfair Dismissal**);
(8) remuneration under a protective award under s.189 of the 1992 Act (see the Note on **Redundancy**);
but excluding any of the following–
(a) any payment by way of an advance under an agreement for a loan or by way of an advance of wages (but the fact that such an advance is not treated as part of a worker's wages does not mean that a deduction from the worker's wages on account of the advance is exempted from the general restriction imposed by s.13(1) (see below));
(b) any payment in respect of expenses incurred by the worker in carrying out his employment;
(c) any payment by way of a pension, allowance, or gratuity in connection with the worker's retirement or as compensation for loss of office;
(d) any payment referable to the worker's redundancy;
(e) any payment to the worker otherwise than in his capacity as a worker.

Any payment by an employer to a worker by way of a non-contractual bonus is treated as wages of the worker payable to him on the day of payment of the bonus (s.27(3)).

Any payment in non-monetary form and benefits in kind received by a worker from his employer will be treated as wages only if they are in the form of vouchers, stamps, or similar documents which have a fixed value in monetary terms and are exchangeable for money, goods, or services (s.27(5)).

3 General restrictions

An employer must not make any deduction from the wages of any worker employed by him unless–
(a) it is required or authorised to be made by virtue of any statutory provision or any relevant provision of the worker's contract; or
(b) the worker has previously signified in writing his agreement or consent to the making of it (Employment Rights Act 1996, s.13(1)).

An employer must not receive any payment from any worker employed by him unless the payment satisfies one of the conditions set out in paragraphs (1) and (2) above (s.15(1)).

A provision of a worker's contract with his employer will qualify as a relevant provision for the purposes of s.13 and s.15 if either (s.13(2))–

(a) the provision is comprised in one or more written terms of the contract, and a copy of the contract was given to the worker by his employer at any time before the deduction in question was made by the employer (or, as the case may be, before the employer received the payment in question from the worker); or

(b) the provision is comprised in one or more terms of the contract (whether express or implied and whether oral or in writing) and both the existence and effect of the term or terms of the contract in relation to the worker were notified to him in writing by the employer prior to the making of the deduction or payment.

Certain deductions and payments are not subject to the above restrictions, including the following (ss.14 and 16)–

(1) a deduction or payment in reimbursement of an overpayment of wages or expenses by the employer;

(2) a deduction or payment made in consequence of any disciplinary proceedings which were held by virtue of any statutory provision;

(3) a deduction made in pursuance of a requirement imposed on the employer by a statutory provision to deduct and pay over to a public authority any amount due from a worker (e.g., in respect of income tax), provided that the amount of the deduction has been determined by the authority;

(4) any deduction made in pursuance of arrangements established by the worker's contract or with his prior agreement in writing, where the employer pays such a deduction over to a third party who notifies the employer of amounts due to them from the worker (e.g., trade union subscriptions);

(5) a deduction or payment made in any case where the worker has taken part in a strike or other industrial action and the deduction is made, or the payment has been required, by the employer on account of that fact;

(6) a deduction made (with the worker's prior agreement or consent signified in writing), or payment received by the employer, for the purpose of satisfying an order of a court or tribunal requiring the payment of any amount by the worker to the employer.

S.13 is without prejudice to any other statutory provision by virtue of which any sum payable to a worker by his employer but not falling within the definition of wages in s.27 (see above) is not to be subject to any deduction at the instance of the employer (s.13(7)). Where a certificate has been given by a worker to his employer for the purposes of s.86 of the Trade Union and Labour Relations (Consolidation) Act 1992 (the political fund), nothing in the worker's contract, or in any agreement or consent signified by the worker, is to be taken for these purposes as authorising the making of deductions in contravention of any obligation imposed on the employer in consequence of the giving of that certificate (Trade Union and Labour Relations (Consolidation) Act 1992, s.88(1) and (2), as amended by the Act, Sch. 1, para 56(5)).

4 Workers in retail employment

In addition to complying with the general restrictions set out in ss.13(1) and 15(1) of the Employment Rights Act 1996, an employer must comply with the further conditions set out in s.18 (in the case of a deduction) or s.20 (in the case of a payment) where the deduction or payment concerns a worker engaged in retail employment and is on account of a cash shortage or a stock deficiency. A deduction or payment made otherwise than in accordance with these additional conditions cannot be treated as having been lawfully made under s.13.

For the purpose of Part II, retail employment, in relation to a worker, means employment involving (whether on a regular basis or not) (i) the carrying out by the worker of retail transactions (defined as the sale, or supply of goods, or the supply of services, including financial services) directly with members of the public or with fellow workers or other individuals in their personal capacities, or (ii) the collection by the worker of amounts payable in connection with such retail transactions carried out by other persons (s.17(2)).

References in Part II to deductions or payments on account of cash shortages or stock deficiencies include references to a deduction or payment made or received on account of–

(a) any dishonesty or other conduct on the part of the worker which resulted in any such shortage or deficiency, or

(b) any other event in respect of which he (whether together with any other workers or not) has any contractual liability and which so resulted,

whether the amount of the deduction or payment is designed to reflect the exact amount of the shortage or deficiency or not (s.17(4)).

The conditions imposed by s.18 are that–

(1) the amount or aggregate amount of any deduction or deductions which may lawfully be made on account of cash shortages or stock deficiencies from the wages payable to a worker on any pay day must not exceed one-tenth of the gross amount of those wages (s.18(1)); and

(2) a deduction on account of a cash shortage or stock deficiency must not be made later than the end of the period of 12 months beginning with the date when the employer established the existence of the shortage or deficiency or (if earlier) the date when he ought reasonably to have done so; if the deduction is one of a series of deductions relating to the same shortage or deficiency, the first deduction in the series must have been made not later than the end of that period (s.18(2)).

S.19 takes account of the situation which may arise when a worker and his employer have agreed that the amount of his wages or any part of them is or may be determined by reference to the incidence of cash shortages or stock deficiencies. If, on any pay day, the gross amount of the worker's wages is in such a case less than it would have been had there been no such shortages or deficiencies, the following provisions apply–

(a) the amount of the difference in the worker's gross wages is treated as a deduction from that pay day's wages made on account of the cash shortages or stock deficiencies in question; and

(b) the normal amount of his gross wages is treated for the purposes of Part II as the gross amount of his wages on that pay day; and

(c) both the general restriction in s.13(1) and (if that restriction and s.18(2) are satisfied) the upper limit on the amount of any deduction imposed by s.18(1) (see above) will have effect in relation to the amount described in (a) above.

Under s.20, an employer will not be treated as having received a payment from a worker on account of a cash shortage or stock deficiency in accordance with s.15(1) unless he has before receiving the payment (s.20(1) and (2))–

(1) notified the worker in writing of the worker's total liability to him in respect of that shortage or deficiency; and

(2) required the worker to make the payment by means of a demand for payment which is in writing and is made on one of the worker's pay days.

Demand for payment in respect of a particular shortage or, in the case of a series of such demands, the first such demand, must not be made (s.20(3))–

(a) earlier than the first pay day of the worker following the date when he is notified of his total liability in accordance with paragraph (1) above or, where he is so notified on a pay day, earlier than that day, or

(b) later than the end of a period of 12 months beginning with the date when the employer established the existence of the shortage or deficiency or (if earlier) the date when he ought reasonably to have done so.

The maximum amount of the payment or payments which may be demanded of a worker on any one pay day in accordance with s.20 is one-tenth of the worker's gross wages payable on that day; and that maximum must be reduced by the amount of any deduction or deductions which are made from those wages in accordance with s.18(1) (s.21(1)). Once a lawful demand for payment has been made under s.20 on any pay day, it is not to be taken into account for the purpose of establishing the limit applicable under s.21(1) on any subsequent pay day, even though further requests for payment have to be made (s.21(2)).

In relation to a retail worker's final instalment of wages (i.e., either wages paid in respect of the last of a worker's periods of employment under his contract of employment, or an amount paid in lieu of notice, whichever is paid the later), s.18(1) does not operate to restrict the amount of any deduction which may be made from that final instalment, provided that it is made in accordance with s.13(1). Nothing in s.20 applies to any payment made on or after the date on which any such worker's final instalment of wages is paid, but s.15(1) must be observed and a payment will not be treated as having been received in accordance with s.15(1) if demand for it was not first made within the period of 12 months prescribed by s.20(3) (s.22).

In the case of a demand for payment in respect of a cash shortage or stock deficiency, no legal proceedings can be instituted by an employer to recover an amount after the end of the 12 months' period prescribed by s.20(3) unless he has within that period made a demand for payment which meets the conditions of s.20 (s.20(5)).

5 Complaints by workers to employment tribunals

Under s.23 of the Employment Rights Act 1996, a worker may complain to an employment tribunal–

(a) that a deduction from his wages has been made by his employer in contravention of the general restriction imposed by s.13(1) or outside the time limit of 12 months imposed by s.18(2), or

(b) that a payment has been received from him by his employer in contravention of s.15(1), or

(c) that, by means of one or more deductions from his wages on account of a cash shortage or stock deficiency, the employer has recovered from him an amount or an aggregate amount which exceeds the limit imposed by s.18(1), or

(d) that, in pursuance of one or more demands made (in accordance with s.20) on a particular day, he has made to his employer a payment or payments exceeding (or exceeding in aggregate) the limit imposed by s.21(1).

A complaint must normally be presented to the tribunal within the period of three months beginning with the date of the payment of wages from which the deduction was made, or with the date when the payment was received; but this period may be extended by the tribunal (s.23(2) and (4)). If a complaint relates to a series of deductions of payments, or is brought under (d) above and the payments there mentioned were made on different dates, the time limit runs from the date of the last in the series or the last of the payments so mentioned (s.23(3)). There is a limitation on how far back in time an employment tribunal is able to consider when determining whether a worker has suffered unauthorised deductions from their wages. The employment tribunal can only consider deductions from wages where the wages from which the deduction was made were paid within the previous two years before the worker brought their complaint in the tribunal (s.23(4A)). The limitation applies to complaints in relation to deductions from those wages that fall under s.27(1)(a) (see **2 Definitions**, above (para (1)), except for those wages specified in s.27(1)(b) to (j) (see **2 Definitions**, above (paras (2) to (8)) (s.23(4B)).

No complaint may be presented under s.23 in respect of any deduction made in contravention of s.86 of the Trade Union and Labour Relations (Consolidation) Act 1992 (deduction of political fund contribution where certificate of exemption or objection has been given) (s.23(5) as inserted by the 1998 Act).

Where a tribunal finds a complaint under s.23 well-founded, it may order the employer to pay to the worker the amount of any deduction made or payment received, in contravention of the above provisions (s.24(1)).

Where a tribunal makes such an order it may also order the employer to pay to the worker, in addition, such amount as it considers appropriate in all the circumstances to compensate the worker for any financial loss sustained by him which is attributable to the matter complained of (s.24(2)).

Where a deduction has been made in contravention of s.86 of the Trade Union and Labour Relations (Consolidation) Act 1992 (Rules as to political fund), no complaint may be brought under s.23 unless a declaration has been made (under s.87(2) of the 1992 Act) by a court, either before or after the date of payment of the wages from which the deduction was made, that the employer has failed to comply with the requirement under s.86. In such a case a complaint must be presented to the tribunal within the period of three months beginning with the date of the deduction or the declaration whichever is the later (1992 Act s.88, as amended by the Act, Sch. 1, para 56(5)).

Any provision in an agreement will be void in so far as it purports to exclude or limit the operation of any provision of Part II, except that a worker may agree to refrain from presenting or continuing with a complaint (a) where a conciliation officer has taken action in accordance with s.18 of the Employment Tribunals Act 1996 (see the Note on **Employment Tribunals, ACAS, and the Employment Appeal Tribunal**), or (b) if the conditions regulating settlement agreements are satisfied in relation to the agreement (*inter alia*, such an agreement must be in writing and relate to the particular complaint; the worker must have received independent legal advice; and there must be in force, a policy of insurance covering the risk of a claim by the worker in respect of loss arising in consequence of the advice) (s.203).

B: NATIONAL MINIMUM WAGE

6 Introduction

The National Minimum Wage Act 1998 provides for the payment of a national minimum wage, payable to most workers who work, or normally work, in the United Kingdom, regardless of the type of work they do. The Act, which applies to the whole of the United Kingdom, came into effect on 1st April 1999. As from this date workers covered by the Act have the right to be paid the minimum wage and may take action to enforce this right (see **15 Enforcement,** below).

The National Minimum Wage (Offshore Employment) Order 1999 provides that the Act applies to those who work, or ordinarily work, in the territorial waters or continental shelf sector of the United Kingdom whether or not they are British subjects, and to bodies corporate whether or not they are incorporated under UK law.

The provisions of the Act have been supplemented by the National Minimum Wage Regulations 2015, as amended, details of which are set out in the following paragraphs.

Figures given in this section are those effective from **1st April 2016**.

7 Application of the Act

The National Minimum Wage Act 1998 applies to all "workers". S.54 defines this term as an individual who has entered into, or works under (or, where the employment has ceased, worked under) a contract of employment or any other contract (whether express or implied and, if express, whether oral or written) whereby the individual undertakes to do or perform personally any work or services for another party to the contract whose status is not by virtue of the contract that of a client or customer of any profession or business undertaking carried on by the individual. A "contract of employment" means a contract of service or apprenticeship, whether express or implied and (if express) whether oral or in writing. Agency workers and home workers are also covered by the Act (see **18 Special classes of worker,** below).

8 Entitlement to and amount of the national minimum wage

S.1 of the National Minimum Wage Act 1998 provides that a person who qualifies for the national minimum wage must be paid by his employer in respect of his work in any "pay reference period" (see below) at a rate which is not less than the national minimum wage. The minimum wage is such hourly rate as the Secretary of State may from time to time prescribe (see below). The "pay reference period" is one month or, in the case of workers paid more frequently (e.g., weekly) that shorter period (National Minimum Wage Regulations 2015, Reg. 6).

Ss. 2 and 3 (as amended) allow the Secretary of State to make detailed regulations for determining–
  (a) the hourly rate at which a person is to be regarded as paid by his employer;
  (b) the extent to which young persons under 26 are to be covered by the Act; and
  (c) the extent to which the Act is to apply to persons over 26 who have recently started work for a new employer or who are undertaking certain schemes or further or higher education which requires attendance for a period of work experience.

Regulation 4 sets the hourly rate of the minimum wage for a worker aged 25 or above as being the National Living Wage of £7.20. Different rates apply to those under the age of 25 and certain other categories of workers (see **9 Workers who qualify at a different rate,** below). The following workers do not qualify for the minimum wage–
  (a) a person who is participating in a scheme designed to provide training, work experience or temporary

work, or to assist in the seeking or obtaining of work and which is, in whole or in part, made or funded by (Reg. 51)–
- the Secretary of State under the Employment and Training Act 1973, s.2; or the Jobseekers Act 1995, s.17B;
- the Scottish or Welsh Ministers under the Employment and Training Act 1973, s.2;
- the Chief Executive of Skills Funding;
- Scottish Enterprise or Highlands and Islands Enterprise under the Enterprise and New Towns (Scotland) Act 1990, s.2;
- the European Social Fund.

(b) a person who is participating in a trial period of work with an employer for a period of six weeks or less, as part of a scheme designed to provide training, work experience or temporary work, or to assist in the seeking or obtaining of work and funded as in (a) above (Reg. 52);

(c) a person who undertakes a higher or further education course, and before the course ends is required to attend a period of work experience not exceeding one year (Reg. 53);

(d) a worker participating in a traineeship in England which consists of a skills programme which includes a work experience placement and work preparation training, lasts no more than six months, is government funded, and is open to persons who on the first day of the traineeship have attained the age of 16 but not 25 years old (Reg. 54);

(e) a worker who is provided with accommodation and other benefits (which may include money) under certain not-for-profit schemes where before entry into the scheme the worker was homeless or residing in a hostel for homeless persons and (Reg. 55)–
   (i) was in receipt of, or entitled to universal credit, income, income-based jobseeker's allowance, income-related employment and support allowance; or
   (ii) was not entitled to receive any of those benefits only because he was not habitually resident in the UK.

(f) workers participating in various European programmes, such as Leonardo da Vinci, Youth in Action and Erasmus+ (Reg. 56).

(g) workers (e.g., au pairs) who live free of charge in their employer's family home; are treated as a member of that family; and who perform tasks which, if undertaken by a family member, would be considered domestic tasks (Reg. 57); and

(h) a worker who is a member of his employer's family; lives in the employer's family home; and shares in the tasks and activities of the family or participates in the running of the family business (Reg. 58).

9 Workers who qualify at a different rate

Different rates of national minimum wage apply to those under the age of 25 and certain other categories of workers. The hourly rate of the national minimum wage is (National Minimum Wage Regulations 2015, Reg. 4A)–
(a) £6.70 for a worker who is aged 21 years or over (but is not yet aged 25 years);
(b) £5.30 for a worker who is aged 18 years or over (but is not yet aged 21 years);
(c) £3.87 for a worker who is aged under 18 years;
(d) £3.30 for a worker to whom the apprenticeship rate applies (i.e. for those undertaking certain Government apprenticeship schemes if they are in the first 12 months of the scheme or are aged under 19).

Where the rate which is payable to a worker changes during a pay reference period (e.g., because a worker turns 22), the hourly rate payable to him for that period is that in force on the first day of the period (Reg. 4B).

10 Calculation of the hourly rate

The hourly rate paid to a worker in a pay reference period is determined by dividing the total remuneration paid in that pay reference period (after specified reductions have been made) by the number of hours worked (National Minimum Wage Regulations 2015, Reg. 7).

Part 5 of the Regulations sets out detailed rules for calculating the number of hours worked for the purposes of the Act and, for these purposes, hours worked are categorised as either "time work", "salaried hours work", "output work", or "unmeasured work".

"Salaried hours work" is work performed under a contract which entitles the worker to be paid for an ascertainable basic number of hours worked in a year, for which he is paid an annual salary in weekly or monthly instalments regardless of the number of hours actually worked in any particular week or month but is not paid in respect of those basic hours any additional amount (other than a performance payment), although he may be entitled to overtime pay if he works more than his basic hours (Reg. 21).

"Time work" is defined as work (not being salaried hours work) that is paid for under a worker's contract by reference to the hours spent working or by reference to output over a specified time period, or work that would be paid by reference to output but for the fact that the worker is paid by reference to the length of the period of time alone when his output is below a particular level (Reg.30).

"Output work" is work that does not come into the category of time work and which, but for the effect of the minimum wage legislation, would be paid for wholly by reference to the number of pieces produced by the worker or by reference to some other measure of output (e.g., sales figures) (Reg. 36).

"Unmeasured work" is any other work that is not time work, salaried hours work or output work (Reg. 44).

In addition to time spent actually working, time when a worker is required to be available for work at or near a workplace (but not at his home) is treated as either time work or salaried hours work, as the case may be, except that where a worker is permitted to sleep during these periods and is provided with suitable sleeping arrangements he will only be treated as working if he is awake for the purpose of working. Similarly, time spent travelling for work purposes is to be treated as either time work or salaried hours work, as the case may be, except where—

(a) the travelling is incidental to the work, to the extent that the travelling time is time when the worker would not otherwise be working and the work is not assignment work (i.e., work carried out at different places not belonging to the worker's employer); or

(b) the travelling is between the worker's home and his workplace or place where an assignment is carried out.

For the purposes of (a), travelling is deemed to be incidental to a worker's duties unless those duties necessarily involve travelling (e.g., a bus driver). Where a worker's hours vary, making it uncertain whether time spent travelling would otherwise be spent working, that time is to be treated for the purposes of (a) above as time when he would otherwise be working.

Time work does not include time when a worker is absent from work, unless it is for the purpose of travelling for work purposes (see above) or for receiving training approved by his employer (see below). A worker taking industrial action will be regarded as absent from work. Rest breaks taken by time workers are treated as absences from work, unless the breaks are taken during time which would otherwise be treated as working time (e.g., breaks taken while the worker is travelling in the course of his duties).

Time when a time worker or salaried hours worker is receiving approved training or is travelling between his workplace and a place where he receives such training is regarded as time spent working.

In the case of output work and unmeasured work, time spent travelling for work purposes is treated as working time, except where the travelling is between home and work.

The Regulations set out detailed rules for calculating the total number of hours worked in any pay reference period. In the case of time work, the total numbers of hours worked in a pay reference period is the total number of hours of time work done by a worker during that period (Reg. 31). In the case of salaried hours work, the numbers of hours worked in a pay reference period will normally be the basic number of hours in a year required under the worker's contract, divided by 52 or 12, according to whether the worker is paid weekly or monthly (Reg. 22). Where a worker has worked overtime, Regulation 26 specifies the hours to be taken into account. Regulations 36 to 43 contain rules for determining hours of output work, and Regulations 44 to 50 rules for unmeasured work. Generally, the number of hours worked for output work is calculated by reference to the "average hourly output rate" of workers employed by the employer to do that work. For unmeasured work, the number of hours worked will be the number of hours spent by the worker during the pay reference period doing that work.

11 Payments counting or not counting towards the minimum wage

For the purpose of the National Minimum Wage, the following payments made by an employer to a worker are not counted as remuneration (National Minimum Wage Regulations 2015, Reg. 10)—

(a) any payments by way of an advance under a loan agreement or by way of an advance of wages;

(b) any pension, allowance or gratuity in connection with the worker's retirement or loss of employment;

(c) any payment of an award made by a court or tribunal or to settle proceedings which might have been brought, except the payment of an amount due under the worker's contract;

(d) any redundancy payment;

(e) any payment by way of an award under a suggestion scheme;

(f) benefits in kind, other than living accommodation, even if a monetary value is attached to the benefit;

(g) vouchers, stamps, or similar documents provided by the employer, which are exchangeable for money, goods, or services;

(h) payments of expenses incurred by a worker in the course of his work; payments of allowances which are not attributable to a worker's performance; and payments of sums representing tips, service charges, gratuities or cover charges paid by customers.

Where living accommodation is provided for a worker, it is taken into account at a fixed daily rate of £5.35 (Regs 14-16).

12 The Low Pay Commission

Before making any regulations under ss.1 to 3 above, the Secretary of State must ask the body known as the Low Pay Commission for its views and the Commission must then make a report to the Prime Minister and the Secretary of State containing its recommendations. Further references to the Commission on any matters relating to the Act may be made at any time (National Minimum Wage Act 1998, ss.5 and 6).

Before making any recommendation, the Commission must, *inter alia*, consult organisations of employers' representatives and organisations of workers' representatives. The Commission must also, when considering what recommendations to make, have regard to the effect of the Act on the economy of the UK as a whole and on competitiveness (s.7).

13 Records

The Secretary of State may make regulations requiring employers to keep records for the purposes of the Act (National Minimum Wage Act 1998, s.9). Employers must keep records in a form which enables the information kept about a worker to be produced in a single document (National Minimum Wage Regulations 2015, Reg. 59). Records may be kept on computer and must be retained for at least three years. S.10 allows workers to inspect and copy these records. If an employer fails to comply with a worker's request under s.10, the worker can bring a complaint to an employment tribunal (s.11).

Regulations may confer on workers the right to be given by employers a national minimum wage statement, to enable them to determine whether they are receiving the minimum wage (this statement may be included in an itemised pay statement) (s.12).

14 Officers

The Secretary of State may (a) appoint enforcement officers to act for the purposes of the Act and/or (b) arrange for existing bodies to act for these purposes (National Minimum Wage Act 1998, s.13). S.14 grants enforcement officers wide powers to examine records held by employers; ask for explanations and records; and question employers.

Information obtained by an officer may, by or with the authority of the Secretary of State, be supplied to the HM Revenue and Customs (Finance Act 2000, s.148).

15 Enforcement

Ss.17 to 22 deal with enforcement of the National Minimum Wage Act 1998. If a worker who qualifies for the minimum wage is paid less than that wage during any pay reference period (see **8 Entitlement to and amount of the national minimum wage**, above), he will be entitled under his contract to be paid the difference between the pay he has actually received and the pay he would have received if he had been paid at a rate equal to the minimum wage (s.17). Where arrears have been outstanding over a period of time, the formula used to calculate them is adjusted to take account of the length of time that arrears have been owing. The effect of s.17 is that a worker who has not been paid the minimum wage may bring a civil claim for breach of contract as well as a complaint to an employment tribunal under Part II of the Employment Rights Act 1996 (unlawful deductions from wages–see **5 Complaints by workers to employment tribunals**, above).

S.18 deals with special classes of workers, such as home workers, agency workers and others who would not normally be regarded as having an employment contract. For the purposes of s.17, it will be assumed that there is or, as the case may be, was such a contract (s.18).

In addition to individual enforcement, an enforcement officer appointed under s.13 (see **14 Officers**, above) may serve a notice of underpayment requiring the employer to pay arrears to the worker or workers named in the notice. The notice may require employers to pay arrears relating to periods up to six years before the date of service of the notice (s.19, as substituted by the Employment Act 2008).

The notice of underpayment must require the employer to pay a financial penalty to the Secretary of State within 28 days of service of the notice (s.19A, as added by the 2008 Act) unless the Secretary of State has, by directions, specified circumstances in which a penalty is not to be imposed. The penalty is set at 200% of the total underpayment of the national minimum wage. The minimum penalty is £100 and the maximum penalty is £20,000 and, if the amount as calculated for any worker would be more than £20,000, the amount for the worker taken into account in calculating the financial penalty is to be £20,000. If the employer complies with the notice within 14 days of its service, the financial penalty is reduced by 50%. The notice of underpayment must contain a provision suspending the requirement to pay a penalty where proceedings have been instituted, or may be instituted against an employer in respect of a criminal offence (i.e., under s.31: see **17 Offences**, below) (s.19B, as so added).

An employer may appeal to an employment tribunal against a notice of underpayment on one or more of three main grounds, namely (s.19C, as so added)–

(a) at the date set out in the notice, no arrears were owing to any worker(s) named in the notice i.e., that the employer was compliant with the Act;

(b) any requirement in the notice to pay a sum to a worker was incorrect; either because no sum was due to that particular worker or that the sum specified in the notice was incorrect;

(c) either a notice included a penalty in circumstances that have been specified in directions under s.19A or that the amount of the penalty specified is incorrect.

If the employment tribunal allows an appeal under ground (a) it must rescind the notice. If it allows an appeal under either ground (b) or (c) it must rectify the notice.

Officers also have power to take civil action to recover arrears on behalf of a worker or workers (s.19D, as so added). Financial penalties are recoverable in the county court (or sheriff court in Scotland) (s.19E, as so added).

An officer may withdraw a notice of underpayment by serving notice of withdrawal on the employer where it appears to him that the notice wrongly includes or omits any requirement or is incorrect in any particular. Where a notice is withdrawn and no replacement notice is issued, any penalty which the employer has already paid in accordance with the withdrawn notice must be repaid with interest (s.19F, as so added). A replacement notice may be issued at the same time that a notice is withdrawn. It cannot include workers who were not contained in the withdrawn notice. Contravention of this requirement is a ground for appeal by an employer against the notice. The replacement notice may include arrears incurred after service of the withdrawn notice but before service of the replacement notice and must set out the material differences from the withdrawn notice. When a replacement notice is issued, the six years limitation period for including arrears is calculated from the date of service of the first notice rather than the date of service of the replacement notice. An officer may only issue one replacement notice (s.19G, as so added).

16 Right not to suffer unfair dismissal or other detriment

A workers has the right not to be subjected to any detriment (i.e., less favourable treatment) by any act, or deliberate failure to act, by an employer done on the ground that any action was taken, or proposed to be taken, by or on behalf of a worker with a view to enforcing his right to be paid the national minimum wage (National Minimum Wage Act 1998, s.23). Similarly, a worker must not be subjected to any detriment by his employer done on the ground that the employer has been prosecuted for an offence under the Act (see **17 Offences**, below) or on the ground that a worker qualifies, or might qualify, for the national minimum wage. For the purposes of s.23, it is immaterial whether or not a worker actually has any right under the Act, or whether or not that right has been infringed, as long as any claim made by the worker has been made in good faith.

S.23 does not apply where the detriment in question amounts to dismissal (but see s.25, below).

A worker may present a complaint to an employment tribunal under s.48 of the Employment Rights Act 1996 that he has been subjected to a detriment in contravention of s.23, above. Where a complaint is found to be well-founded, the tribunal may make an award of compensation under s.49 of the 1996 Act (see the Note on **Rights Arising in the Course of Employment** at para **7 Complaint to employment tribunal**). In the case of a worker who is not an employee, but whose contract has been terminated, specified compensation limits apply.

S.25 inserts a new section (s.104A) into the 1996 Act giving employees who are dismissed for any of the reasons specified in s.23, above, the right to bring a claim for unfair dismissal under Part X of the 1996 Act on the ground that they have been dismissed for asserting their statutory rights–see the Note on **Unfair Dismissal** at para **23 Dismissal on ground of assertion of statutory right**. Where any of the circumstances specified in s.23 applies, the dismissal will be regarded as automatically unfair and it will not be necessary for the employee to show that he has been employed for the normal qualifying period for unfair dismissals of two years.

17 Offences

In addition to enforcement through a notice of underpayment, an employer who refuses or wilfully neglects to pay the national minimum wage is guilty of an offence. An employer who fails to keep proper records, or who keeps false records, will also commit an offence (National Minimum Wage Act 1998, s.31).

18 Special classes of workers

Ss.34 and 35 of the National Minimum Wage Act 1998 deal with agency workers and home workers. Where an individual ("agency worker") is supplied by an agent to do work for another (the "principal") but is not, as respects that work, a worker because of the absence of a worker's contract between the individual and the agent or principal, and is also not a party to a contract under which he undertakes to perform work for a customer or client of a profession or business the individual carries on, the Act still applies to that individual as if there were a worker's contract between the individual and the person responsible for paying him (whether this is the agent or the principal) (s.34). Similarly, home workers (i.e., individuals who contract to perform work away from an employee's premises, whether or not that work is actually performed at home) are covered by the Act, even though they may in practice delegate their work to others (s.35).

S.41 gives the Secretary of State additional powers to deem individuals to be workers for the purposes of the Act.

Voluntary workers for charities, voluntary bodies, and associated fund-raising or statutory bodies, who receive expenses or certain benefits are not covered by the Act. Voluntary workers who receive some payment solely for the purpose of providing them with some means of subsistence (not including accommodation) are similarly not covered by the Act if they are placed by charities to work for other charities, voluntary organisations or associated bodies (s.44). Residential members of charitable religious communities are not covered unless the community is an independent school, an alternative provision Academy, or a college of further or higher education (s.44A, as added by the Employment Relations Act 1999, s.22).

Work undertaken by persons detained in prisons and removal centres or discharging fines is also excluded from the Act, even if those concerned receive some pay (ss.45, 45A, 45B).

19 Agricultural workers

Agricultural workers are within the scope of the National Minimum Wage Act 1998, but for additional provision for Scotland and Wales, see C: AGRICULTURAL WAGES, below.

20 Restrictions on contracting out

Any provision in any agreement (whether a worker's contract or not) is void in so far as it purports to exclude or limit the operation of the National Minimum Wage Act 1998 or to preclude a person from bringing proceedings under the Act before an employment tribunal (s.49).

C: AGRICULTURAL WAGES

21 Introduction

The wages of agricultural workers in Scotland and Wales, besides being affected by the provisions of Part II of the National Minimum Wage Act 1998, summarised above, are also subject to regulation under the Agricultural Wages (Scotland) Act 1949 and the Agricultural Sector (Wales) Act 2014. These Acts establish the Scottish Agricultural Wages Board and the Agricultural Advisory Panel for Wales to exercise powers to set minimum rates of wages, holidays, and other matters concerning employment in agriculture.

In both Acts, "agriculture" includes dairy-farming, the production of any consumable produce which is grown for sale or for consumption or other use for the purposes of a trade or business or of any other undertaking (whether carried on for profit or not), and the use of land as grazing, meadow, or pasture land or orchard or osier land, or for market gardens or nursery grounds.

Unless continued by Order of the Welsh Ministers, the Welsh Act will expire on 30th July 2018.

22 Rates of wages, and holidays

The Scottish Board are given power (Agricultural Wages (Scotland) Act 1949, s.3)–
(a) to fix minimum rates of wages for agricultural workers; and
(b) to direct that any such workers are to be entitled to be allowed by their employers holidays of such duration as may be specified in the direction.

The Scottish Board are bound to exercise their power under (a), and must do so by fixing, by order–
(1) minimum rates of wages for time workers and piece workers, respectively;
(2) separate minimum rates of time work which are intended to apply to piece workers with the object of securing for them a minimum rate of remuneration on a time work basis; and
(3) separate minimum rates of pay in respect of holidays.

The Welsh Panel have the function of preparing draft agricultural wages orders, consulting on such orders and submitting them to the Welsh Ministers for approval (Agricultural Sector (Wales) Act 2014, s.3).

In both Scotland and Wales, no minimum rate may be fixed lower than the national minimum wage (see B: NATIONAL MINIMUM WAGE, above) (1949 Act s.3(2B); 2014 Act s.3(5)). If the national minimum wage at any time becomes higher than the rate set under s.3, then the Scottish Board is to be taken as having made an order fixing the minimum rate at a rate equal to the national minimum wage (s.3(9)). There is no equivalent provision in Wales.

For the purposes of any minimum rate of wages, the Scottish Board and Welsh Panel are empowered to define the benefits or advantages (such as board and lodging or the occupation of a dwelling) which may be reckoned as payment of wages in lieu of payment in cash, and to determine the value at which those benefits and advantages are to be reckoned (1949 Act, s.7; 2014 Act, s.3(2)).

Information as to the current orders of the Scottish Board may be obtained from the Scottish Agricultural Wages Board, Pentland House, 47 Robbs Loan, Edinburgh EH14 1TY (tel: 0131 556 8400). Current rates for Wales are contained in the Agricultural Wages (Wales) Order 2016 (S.I. No. 107).

23 Enforcement of agricultural wages order

For the purposes of enforcing an agricultural wages order made under the 1949 or 2014 Acts, the enforcement provisions of the National Minimum Wage Act 1998 have effect (Agricultural Wages (Scotland) Act 1949, s.3A; Agricultural Sector (Wales) Act 2014, s.5) (see 15 Enforcement, above).

24 Enforcement of holiday orders

An employer must be prosecuted before a court of summary jurisdiction if he fails to allow holidays to an employee in accordance with an agricultural wages order (Agricultural Wages (Scotland) Act 1949, s.4; Agricultural Sector (Wales) Act 2014, s.6).

25 Learners and apprentices

Employers may not receive premiums in respect of learners except under an agreement approved by the Scottish Ministers (Agricultural Wages (Scotland) Act 1949, s.6).

26 Authorities

Statutes–

Agriculture (Miscellaneous Provisions) Act 1972

Agricultural Sector (Wales) Act 2014

Agricultural Wages (Scotland) Act 1949

Employment Relations Act 1999

Employment Rights Act 1996

Employment Rights (Dispute Resolution) Act 1998

National Minimum Wage Act 1998

Trade Union and Labour Relations (Consolidation) Act 1992

Statutory Instruments–

National Minimum Wage Act 1998 (Amendment) Regulations 1999 (S.I. 1999 No. 583)

National Minimum Wage (Offshore Employment) Order 1999 (S.I. 1999 No. 1128)

National Minimum Wage Regulations 2015, as amended (S.I. 2015 Nos. 621, 971, and 1724, and 2016 No. 68)

WORKING TIME RESTRICTIONS

1 Introduction

The Working Time Regulations 1998 implement Council Directives 93/104/EC and 94/33/EC on the organisation of working time and the protection of young people at work. *Inter alia*, the Regulations provide–

(a) the right for workers to receive four weeks' annual paid leave ;

(b) a limit of 48 hours in a week in which a worker can be required to work; and

(c) entitlement to weekly and daily rest periods and to a rest break during the working day.

The Regulations apply to most workers over school leaving age who are employed under a contract of employment, together with certain other workers who work under a contract whereby they undertake to personally perform any work or other services for another party to the contract, whose status is not by virtue of the contract that of client or customer of any profession or business undertaking carried on by the worker (e.g., agency workers). The Regulations do not cover the self-employed, or workers engaged in certain particular types of work (see **18 Excluded workers**, below). For the purposes of the Regulations, a "young worker" is a worker who is over compulsory school age, but under 18 (Reg. 2).

The Department for Business, Innovation and Skills have published guidance explaining the Regulations and advising employers on how to comply with them. This is only available online: see the links at <www.bis.gov.uk> in the Policies Section under Working Time. References in the following paragraphs to "BIS guidance" are to this online guidance.

2 Maximum weekly working time

Unless the employer has first obtained the worker's written agreement, a worker's working time, including overtime, in any applicable reference period (see below) must not exceed an average of 48 hours in each seven day period. For these purposes, "working time" is defined as any period when a worker is working at his employer's disposal and carrying out his activity or other duties, together with periods during which a worker is receiving relevant training and any other periods treated as working time under a workforce agreement or collective agreement. The BIS guidance advises that when a worker is permitted to be away from the workplace when "on-call" and accordingly free to pursue leisure activities, then on-call time is not "working time". In addition, lunch breaks spent at leisure are not working time and work done at home only counts if the work is being performed on a basis previously agreed with the employer. An employer must take all reasonable steps, in keeping with the need to protect the health and safety of workers, to ensure that this limit is complied with in the case of each worker to whom the provision applies and must keep up-to-date records of all workers who carry out work to which the limit does not apply because the worker has agreed that it should not (see above) (Reg. 4).

In calculating a worker's average working time, the normal averaging period (known as the "applicable reference period") is 17 weeks, although this is extended to 26 weeks in the case of certain workers to whom Regulation 21 applies (see below) and 52 weeks in the case of workers employed in offshore work (Reg. 25B). Workers and employers may also agree under a workforce or collective agreement (see **23 Collective and workforce agreements**, below) to extend the reference period to up to 52 weeks (Reg. 23). Where a worker has been employed for less than 17 weeks, the applicable reference period is the period of his employment. The formula for calculating average working hours takes account of periods of annual leave, sick leave and maternity, paternity, adoption, and parental leave, extra time being added to total hours worked to compensate for the worker's absence.

An agreement that the limit in Regulation 4 should not apply to a particular employee may either relate to a specific period or apply indefinitely and (subject to any provision in the agreement for a different notice period) will be terminable by the worker by giving at least seven days' notice in writing to his employer. Where an agreement provides for termination after a period of notice, that notice period must not exceed three months (Reg. 5).

3 Maximum weekly working time–young workers

A young worker's working time must not exceed eight hours in a day or 40 hours in a week (Reg. 5A). If, during any day or week, a young worker is employed by more than one employer, the number of hours he works for each employer must be aggregated to ensure that the limits are not exceeded. An employer must take all reasonable steps, in keeping with the need to protect the health and safety of workers, to ensure that these limits are not exceeded.

Regulation 5A does not apply to a young worker where (Reg.27A(1))–

(a) he is required to undertake work which is necessary either to maintain continuity of service or production or to respond to a surge in demand for a service or product; and

(b) no adult worker is available to perform the work; and

(c) performing the work will not adversely affect the young worker's education or training.

Regulation 5A does not apply to members of the armed forces (Reg. 25).

4 Maximum weekly working time–doctors in training

From 1st August 2004 a maximum weekly working time of 58 hours for doctors in training was introduced. This was subsequently reduced to 56 hours and from 1st August/1st November 2009 (depending on the NHS trust involved) until 31st July 2011 it is 52 hours (Reg. 25A).

The reference period for a doctor in training is also modified from that given in Regulation 4.

5 Night work

Regulation 6 provides that a night worker's normal hours of work in any applicable reference period must not exceed an average of 8 hours a night in any 24 hour period. For these purposes, "night time" in relation to a worker means a period of at least seven hours, including the period between midnight and 5 a.m. and a "night worker" is one who, as a normal course (i.e., on the majority of days), works at least three hours of his daily working time during night time, or who is likely, during night time, to work at least such proportion of his annual working time as may be specified for the purposes of the Regulations in a collective or workforce agreement. As with day workers (see above), the normal averaging period is 17 weeks. In addition, night workers whose work involves special hazards or heavy physical or mental strain are subject to an eight hour limit in each 24 hour period. The work of a night worker is to be regarded as involving special hazards, or heavy physical or mental strain, if it is identified as such in a collective or workforce agreement, or is recognised as such in a risk assessment made by the employer under Regulation 3 of the Management of Health and Safety at Work Regulations 1999 (see the Note on **Health and Safety at Work: General** at para **29 Management of health and safety**). A collective or workforce agreement (see below) may modify or exclude the application of Regulation 6 (Reg. 23).

6 Night work–young workers

An employer must ensure that no young worker works during a restricted period (Reg. 6A). A "restricted period" is the period between the hours of 10pm and 6am or, where the worker's contract provides for him to work after 10pm, the period between 11pm and 7am (Reg. 2).

Where a young worker is–

(a) required to undertake work which is necessary either to maintain continuity of service or production or to respond to a surge in demand for a service or product; and

(b) no adult worker is available to perform the work; and

(c) performing the work will not adversely affect the young worker's education or training,

then Regulation 6A does not apply if they are employed (Reg. 27A(2))–

(d) in a hospital or similar establishment; or

(e) in connection with cultural, artistic, sporting or advertising activities,

In addition, where (a) to (c) apply Regulation 6A does not apply, except in so far as it prohibits work between the hours of midnight and 4 a.m., in relation to a young worker employed in (Reg. 27A(3))–

(f) agriculture;

(g) retail trading;

(h) postal or newspaper deliveries;

(i) a catering business;

(j) a hotel, public house, restaurant, bar or similar establishment; or

(k) a bakery.

Where Regulation 6A does not apply and a young worker is accordingly required to work, he must be supervised by an adult worker where such supervision is necessary for the young worker's protection, and he must be allowed a compensatory rest period (Reg. 27A(4)).

Regulation 6A does not apply to members of the armed forces, who must also be allowed an appropriate period of compensatory rest (Reg. 25).

7 Health assessment and transfer of night workers to day work

An employer must not assign an adult worker to night work unless–

(a) the employer has ensured that the worker is given the opportunity of a free health assessment; or

(b) the worker had an assessment before being assigned to night work on an earlier occasion and the employer has no reason to believe that that assessment is no longer valid.

In the case of a worker who is over compulsory school age, but under 18, the free assessment must also include an assessment of the worker's capacities. For all workers, the opportunity of a free assessment must be made available at regular intervals. A night worker is entitled to be transferred, wherever possible, to non-night work where a registered medical practitioner has advised the employer that the worker is suffering from health problems connected with his night work (Reg. 7).

There is no prescribed procedure for conducting a health assessment, but the BIS guidance suggests that employers should construct a health questionnaire for workers to complete before beginning night work. This should be compiled with guidance from a qualified health care professional familiar with the nature of the employer's business and the effects of night working. Where answers to the questionnaire raise any doubts about an individual's fitness to work at night, the individual should be referred to a health care professional for further assessment. The guidance also suggests that questionnaires be completed on a regular basis.

8 Pattern of work

Where the pattern according to which an employer organises work is such as to put the health and safety of a worker employed by him at risk, in particular because the work is monotonous or the work-rate is pre-determined, the employer must ensure that the worker is given adequate rest breaks (Reg. 8).

9 Records

An employer must keep records to show that the limits specified in Regulations 4, 5A, 6, 6A and 7 are being complied with in the case of each worker employed by him. These records must be kept for two years (Reg. 9). Employers may be able to use existing records maintained for other purposes, such as pay, or they may need to make new arrangements, as appropriate.

Regulation 9 does not apply to members of the armed forces (Reg. 25).

10 Daily rest

An adult worker is entitled to a rest period of at least eleven consecutive hours in each 24 hour period of employment. In the case of a young worker, the minimum rest period is 12 hours in any 24 hour period, although this may be interrupted in the case of activities involving periods of work that are split up over the day or are of short duration (Reg. 10). A collective or workforce agreement (see **23 Collective and workforce agreements**, below) may modify or exclude the application of Regulation 10 (Reg. 23). Regulation 10 does not apply to young workers serving in the armed forces who, if required to work, must be allowed an appropriate period of compensatory rest (Reg. 25(2) and (3)).

11 Weekly rest

A worker is also entitled to an uninterrupted weekly rest period of at least 24 hours in each seven day period. However, an employer may replace this entitlement with two rest periods of at least 24 hours in each 14 day period, or one rest period of at least 48 hours in each such period. A young worker (see above) is entitled to a rest period of at least 48 hours in every seven days, although this may be interrupted in the case of activities involving periods of work that are split up over the day or are of short duration, and may be reduced where this is justified by technical or organisational reasons (but not to less than 36 hours). The minimum rest period to which a worker is entitled does not include any part of the daily rest period to which he is entitled under Regulation 10 (see **10 Daily rest**, above), except where this is justified by objective or technical reasons or reasons concerning the organisation of work.

For the above purposes, a seven or 14 day period is to be taken to begin at such times and on such days as may be provided for in an agreement or, where there is no relevant agreement, at the start of each week (i.e., midnight between Sunday and Monday) (Reg. 11).

Regulation 11 does not apply to young workers serving in the armed forces who, if required to work, must be allowed an appropriate period of compensatory rest (Reg. 25(2) and (3)).

A collective or workforce agreement (see **23 Collective and workforce agreements**, below) may modify or exclude the application of Regulation 11 (Reg. 23).

12 Rest breaks

Where a worker's daily working time is more than six hours, he is entitled to a rest break and the duration and terms on which a break is granted shall be in accordance with any provisions which are contained in a collective agreement or workforce agreement. Subject to the provisions of any such agreement, a rest break should be an uninterrupted period of at least 20 minutes and the worker is entitled to spend this period away from his workstation, if he has one.

Where a young worker's (see above) daily working time is more than four and a half hours, he is entitled to a rest break of at least 30 minutes, which should be consecutive if possible, and he is entitled to spend this away from his workstation if he has one (Reg. 12).

A collective or workforce agreement (see **23 Collective and workforce agreements**, below) may modify or exclude the application of Regulation 12 (Reg. 23).

13 Annual leave

For any leave year beginning on or after 1st April 2009, a worker is entitled to 5.6 weeks annual leave (i.e., 5 weeks and 3 days). From April 2009 therefore, the maximum entitlement is 28 days. The annual leave entitlement is reduced proportionately where a worker's employment begins after the start of the leave year (for leave during the first year of employment, also see **15 Dates on which leave is taken**, below) (Regs. 13 and 13A).

A worker's leave year, for the purposes of Regulation 13, begins on such date during the calendar year as may be provided for in a relevant agreement or, where there is no such agreement, the leave year will start–

  (a) on 1st October, if the worker started work with his employer on or before 1st October 1998 (and each subsequent leave year will start on the anniversary of that date); or
  (b) on the date the worker started employment, if the worker started work with his employer after 1st October 1998 (and each subsequent leave year will start on the anniversary of the date on which he started work).

Leave to which a worker is entitled under Regulation 13 may be taken in instalments, but it may only be taken in the leave year in respect of which it is due, and it may not be replaced by a payment in lieu, except where the worker's employment is terminated (see **14 Compensation relating to leave entitlement**, below).

There is no statutory entitlement to time off on public holidays but, where a contract entitles a worker to time off on such days, this can be used to discharge an employer's responsibility for providing leave under the Regulations.

14 Compensation relating to leave entitlement

Regulation 14 provides that, where a worker's employment is terminated during the course of a leave year and, as a result, he loses part of his entitlement to annual leave, he has a right to receive a payment in lieu of leave. The sum due may be decided by a workforce or collective agreement or, in the absence of such an agreement, the sum will be calculated in accordance with a formula set out in Regulation 14.

Regulation 14 also provides for an employer to be compensated where the proportion of leave taken by the worker exceeds the proportion of the leave year which has expired. Compensation may take the form of a payment, additional work, or some other form.

15 Dates on which leave is taken

A worker may take leave to which he is entitled (under Regs 13 and 13A) on such days as he may elect, by giving notice to his employer. The notice period should be at least twice the length of the period of leave to be taken. However, an employer may give notice to the worker requiring him to take all or part of his leave on specified days. The notice given by the employer should be at least twice the period of the leave to be taken. An employer may also refuse a worker permission to take leave requested, by giving notice to the worker within a period equivalent to the period of the leave requested (Reg. 15).

Any right or obligation under Regulation 15 may be varied or excluded by a workforce or collective agreement (see **23 Collective and workforce agreements**, below).

During the first year of employment only "accrued" leave may be taken (Reg. 15A). A worker's leave accrues at the rate of one twelfth of his entitlement (see **13 Annual leave**, above) on the first day of each month of that year (with fractions rounded up to the nearest half day).

16 Payment in respect of leave

Under Regulation 16, a worker is entitled to be paid for any period of annual leave to which he is entitled under Regulation 13 at the rate of a week's pay for each week of leave (Reg. 16(1)). A right to payment under Reg. 16(1) does not affect any right of a worker to remuneration under his contract ("contractual remuneration"), but Reg. 16(1) does not confer a right under that contract. This means that the right to payment in respect of annual leave provided for by the Working Time Regulations is not intended to operate in such a way so as to provide that right under a worker's contract. It is a separate statutory right. Any contractual remuneration paid under a contract in relation to a period of leave goes towards discharging an employer's liability under Regulation 16. Ss.221 to 224 of the Employment Rights Act 1996 (see the Note on **Employment Protection: Introduction** at para **6 Normal working hours and a week's pay**) apply for the purpose of determining the amount of a week's pay for the purpose of Regulation 16.

17 Entitlement under other provisions

Regulation 17 provides that where during any period a worker is entitled to a daily or weekly rest period, a rest break or annual leave both under a provision of the Regulations and under a separate provision (including a contractual provision), he may not exercise the two rights separately, but may take advantage of whichever right is the more favourable to him.

18 Excluded workers

The provisions on maximum weekly working time, night-working, daily and weekly rest periods, rest breaks and entitlement to paid annual leave do not apply to the following sectors of activity (Reg. 18)–

  (i) air, road, sea, inland waterway and lake transport;
  (ii) sea fishing; and
  (iii) the activities of certain services (e.g., police or armed forces) where the characteristics of the service inevitably conflict with the provisions of the Regulations.

As to workers in air transport, see **19 Civil aviation**, below; in road transport, see **20 Road transport**, below; and on fishing vessels, see **21 Fishing vessels**, below.

In addition, the Regulations do not apply to domestic servants in private households (Reg. 19) or to workers whose working time is not measured or pre-determined, or can be determined by the worker himself, e.g., managing executives and other persons with autonomous decision-making powers, family workers or workers officiating at religious services or in religious communities (Reg. 20).

Special provision is also made for the following workers (Reg. 21)—

(a) workers whose home and workplace are distant from one another (including cases where the worker is employed in offshore work), or who have different places of work distant from one another;

(b) workers engaged in security and surveillance activities, where a permanent presence is required to protect property or persons (e.g., security guards and caretakers);

(c) workers whose activities involve the need for continuity of service or production, as may be the case in relation to—

    (i) services provided by hospitals (including the activities of doctors in training), residential institutions, and prisons;

    (ii) work at docks and airports;

    (iii) press, radio, television, cinematographic production, postal and telecommunications services and civil protection services;

    (iv) gas, water and electricity production, transmission and distribution, household refuse collection and incineration;

    (v) industries in which work cannot be interrupted on technical grounds;

    (vi) research and development activities;

    (vii) agriculture;

    (viii) the carriage of passengers on regular urban transport services.

(d) workers in industries such as agriculture, tourism and postal services, where there are foreseeable surges of activity;

(e) workers whose activities are affected by unusual and unforseeable circumstances, exceptional events, or an accident or the imminent risk of one;

(f) workers in rail transport—

    (i) whose activities are intermittent;

    (ii) who spends his working time on board trains; or

    (iii) whose activities are linked to timetables to ensure continuity and regularity of traffic.

However, in all the above cases, a worker who is required to work during a rest period or rest break is entitled, wherever possible, to an equivalent period of compensatory rest or, in exceptional cases, where it is not possible for objective reasons to grant such rest, to such protection as may be appropriate to safeguard the worker's health and safety (Reg. 24).

A mobile worker (i.e., someone employed as travelling or flying personnel in road or air passenger transport services) is also excluded (if they are not already excluded by Reg. 18) from the provisions as to night-time work, daily and weekly rest, and rest periods (Reg. 24A). However such a worker is entitled to adequate rest, except where his activities are affected by the matters set out in Reg. 21 (see above). "Adequate rest" for this purpose means regular rest breaks sufficient to ensure that, as a result of fatigue or irregular working patterns, he does not cause injury to himself, fellow workers or others, and does not damage his health.

19 Civil aviation

Working time restrictions for those employed as members of cabin or flight crew on a civil aircraft by an undertaking established in the UK are governed by the Civil Aviation (Working Time) Regulations 2004.

These regulations provide, amongst other things, for four weeks annual leave, not less than seven days per month and 96 days per year as rest days (free from all employment duties including acting as a standby), and that no one should work as a crew member in any month if in the 12 month period expiring at the end of the previous month their aggregate block *flying* time exceeded 900 hours. There is a limit of 2,000 hours annual *working* time for crew members ("crew members" includes both cabin and flight crew). In limited circumstances, when calculating annual working time standby time is counted as half the time actually spent on standby (see Reg. 9A).

20 Road transport

Working time restrictions for mobile road transport workers and self-employed drivers are governed by the Road Transport (Working Time) Regulations 2005.

A "mobile worker" for these purposes is someone who is in the service of an undertaking which operates transport services for passengers or goods by road, for hire or reward or on his own account.

A "self-employed driver" for these purposes is someone whose main occupation is to transport passengers or goods by road for hire or reward under a Community licence or any other professional authorisation to carry out such transport, who is entitled to work for himself and who is not tied to an employer by an employment contract or by any other type of working hierarchical relationship, who is free to organise the relevant working activities, whose income depends directly on the profits made and who has the freedom, individually or through a co-operation between self-employed drivers, to have commercial relations with several customers.

The regulations provide, amongst other things, for a maximum working week of 60 hours (including overtime), subject to an average working week of 48 hours (measured over a 17 week period). No mobile worker must work for more than six hours without a break. Where working time is between six and nine hours, there must be a 30 minute break at some time during that period, and where working time exceeds nine hours there must be a 45 minute break. Breaks may be made up of separate periods of not less than 15 minutes.

21 Fishing vessels

Working time restrictions for workers on sea-going fishing vessels are governed by the Fishing Vessels Working Time) Regulations 2004.

The regulations provide, amongst other things, for a maximum working time (including overtime) of an average of 48 hours for each seven day period. A worker is entitled to "adequate" rest, defined as regular rest periods the duration of which are sufficiently long and continuous to ensure that, as a result of fatigue or other irregular working patterns, he does not cause injury to himself, to fellow workers, or to others, and that he does not damage his health. A worker's minimum rest periods must be 10 hours (divided into not more than two periods not more than 14 hours apart, one of which is at least six hours long) in any 24 hour period, and 77 hours in any seven day period.

Workers to whom the regulations apply are entitled to at least four weeks' paid annual leave.

22 Shift workers

Regulation 10(1) (daily rest period) does not apply to workers changing shift who cannot take a daily rest period between shifts. Regulation 11 (weekly rest periods) does not apply to shift workers changing shifts who cannot take a weekly rest period between the end of one shift and the start of the next one. Neither Regulations 10 or 11 apply to workers engaged in activities involving work split up over the day (e.g., cleaning staff) (Reg. 22).

23 Collective and workforce agreements

Many of the requirements of the Regulations may be modified or excluded by a collective or workforce agreement. A collective agreement is one made between an employer and an independent trade union, whereas a workforce agreement is an agreement between an employer and his workers (or their representatives) which satisfies the conditions set out in Schedule 1 to the Regulations. Schedule 1 provides that a workforce agreement may apply to the whole workforce, or to a group of workers within the workforce. Where the agreement applies to a group, that group must share a workplace, function or unit within the business. To be valid, a workforce agreement must–
  (i) be in writing;
 (ii) have been circulated in advance to the workers to whom it applies;
(iii) be signed by the elected representatives of the workforce or group in question; and
(iv) have effect for no more than five years.

Schedule 1 to the Regulations also sets out the requirements for the election of workforce representatives. The number of such representatives is to be determined by the employer; the candidates must be members of the workforce or group in question; and all members of that workforce or group must be eligible to vote. So far as is reasonably practicable, voting must take place in secret.

24 Young workers

Regulation 27 provides that the rules on daily rest periods and rest breaks do not apply in relation to a young worker where his employer requires him to undertake unforeseen work which is of a temporary nature; must be performed immediately; and which no adult worker is available to perform. The young worker must be allowed to take an equivalent period of compensatory rest within the following three weeks.

25 Enforcement

It is the duty of the Health and Safety Executive to make adequate arrangements for the enforcement of the above requirements except that (Reg. 28)–
  (a) the local authority is responsible for enforcement where workers are employed in premises for which a local authority is responsible, under the Health and Safety (Enforcing Authority) Regulations 1998 (see the Note on **Health and Safety at Work: General** at para **42 Responsible authorities**), for enforcing any of the relevant statutory provisions;
  (b) the civil aviation authority is responsible for enforcement where workers are civil aviation workers; and
  (c) the Driver and Vehicle Standards Agency (DVSA) is responsible for enforcement in relation to relevant road transport workers (i.e., mobile workers (see **18 Excluded workers**, above) to whom the domestic

driver's hours code, EC Regulation 3820/85, or the AETR Rules apply, as to all of which see the Note on **Drivers' Hours**).

An employer who fails to comply with any of the relevant requirements is guilty of an offence and liable on conviction to a fine (Reg. 29). Where an offence is due to the act or default of someone other than the person committing it, proceedings may be taken against that other person (Reg. 29A). Where an offence is committed by a company and is proved to have been committed with the consent of connivance of, or to have been attributable to any neglect on the part of, any director, manager, secretary or similar officer or someone purporting to act in such a capacity, proceedings may be taken against that person (Reg. 29B).

Proceedings in England and Wales can only be begun by an inspector, or by or with the consent of the Director of Public Prosecutions (Reg. 29C).

In addition to, or instead of imposing any punishment, a court may order a convicted person to take specified steps to remedy any matter which it appears to the court to be in his power to remedy (Reg. 29E).

26 Inspections

Each enforcement authority (i.e., the Health and Safety Executive, a local authority, the CAA or DVSA–see **25 Enforcement**, above) may appoint inspectors to enforce the provisions of the Regulations on their behalf (Sch. 3).

Inspectors have a power of entry into premises (and may take the police with them if they reasonably apprehend any serious obstruction). They may require the production of, and inspect and take copies of, any necessary records (except those protected by legal privilege).

An inspector may serve an improvement notices if he is of the opinion that a person is contravening the Regulations, or has contravened them in the past and is likely to do so again. If an inspector finds an activity which involves, or will involve a risk of serious personal injury, he may serve a prohibition notice prohibiting it. Appeals may be made against such notices to an employment tribunal.

27 Remedies

A worker may present a complaint to an employment tribunal that his employer has (Reg. 30)–
(a) refused to permit him to exercise any right he has under–
    (i) Regulations 10, 11, 12 or 13 (daily and weekly rest periods; rest breaks; and annual leave entitlement);
    (ii) Regulation 24 (compensatory rest periods); or
    (iii) Regulations 25, 27 and 27A (compensatory rest periods for young people); or
(b) failed to pay him the whole or part of any amount due to him under Regulations 14 or 16 (compensation related to entitlement to leave and payment in respect of periods of leave).

28 Restrictions on contracting -out

Any provision in an agreement (whether a contract of employment or not) is void insofar as it purports to exclude or limit the operation of any provision of the Working Time Regulations, save insofar as the Regulations provide for an agreement to have that effect, or to preclude a person from bringing proceedings under the Regulations before an employment tribunal (Reg. 35). Regulation 35 does not apply to any agreement to refrain from instituting or continuing proceedings where a conciliation officer has taken action under s.18 of the Employment Tribunals Act 1996 (conciliation–see the Note on **Employment Tribunals, ACAS, and the Employment Appeal Tribunal**), if certain conditions are satisfied in relation to the agreement.

29 Special classes of persons

Regulations 36 to 43 make special provision for specific types of workers, including members of the police and armed services, non-employed trainees, and agricultural workers.

30 Authorities

Civil Aviation (Working Time) Regulations 2004, as amended (S.I. 2004 No. 756, 2008 No. 960, and 2010 No. 1226)

Fishing Vessels Working Time) Regulations 2004, as amended (S.I. 2004 No. 1713 and 2013 No. 1956)

Road Transport (Working Time) Regulations 2005, as amended (S.I. 2005 No. 639, 2007 No. 853, and 2012 No. 991)

Working Time Regulations 1998, as amended (S.I. 1998 No. 1833, 1999 Nos. 3242 and 3372, 2001 No. 3256, 2002 No. 3128, 2003 No. 1684, 2004 No. 2516, 2005 No. 2241, 2006 Nos. 99, 594 and 2389, 2007 No. 2079, 2008 No. 960, 2009 Nos. 1567, 2766 and 3348, 2013 Nos. 1956 and 2228, and 2014 Nos. 107, 386, 431, 469, 480, 3229 and 3322)

ENVIRONMENTAL LAW

ENVIRONMENTAL LAW

AIR POLLUTION: ENGLAND AND WALES

I The legislation

The law relating to air pollution is contained, principally, in the Clean Air Act 1993, which is largely concerned with smoke control, and Part IV of the Environment Act 1995, which is concerned with air quality.

As to the climate change levy, see the Note on **Climate Change**.

2 Dark smoke

The occupier of a building commits an offence if dark smoke is emitted from a chimney of the building except where the emission lasts for not longer than the period and in the circumstances permitted by regulations. Certain defences are specified (Clean Air Act 1993, s.1). In addition, if dark smoke is emitted from any industrial or trade premises, the occupier and any person who causes or permits the emission commit an offence; it is a defence to prove that the contravention complained of was inadvertent and that all practicable steps had been taken to prevent or minimise the emission (s.2).

3 Smoke control areas

Under the Clean Air Act 1993 s.18, a local authority may by order (a smoke control order) declare the whole or part of the district of the authority to be a smoke control area. A smoke control order may–
  (i) make different provision for different parts of the smoke control area;
  (ii) limit the operation of s.20 (see below) to specified classes of buildings in the area; and
  (ii) may exempt specified buildings or classes of buildings or specified fireplaces or classes of fireplace in the area (see **6 Exempted fireplaces,** below) from the operation of s.20 upon such conditions as may be specified in the order.

In smoke control areas, subject to exemptions and limitations, the emission of smoke from chimneys is an offence. It is, however, a defence to prove that the emission of smoke was not caused by the use of any fuel other than a fuel declared by the Secretary of State to be an authorised fuel (see **5 Authorised fuels,** below) (s.20).

4 Grants for necessary adaptations

Provision is made, by the Clean Air Act 1993 s.25, for the payment of grants by local authorities towards the cost of any necessary adaptation, alteration, conversion, or replacement of appliances (including the provision of electrical or gas ignition for open fireplaces) in private dwellings (other than dwellings the erection or conversion of which began after 16th August 1964) after a smoke control area is declared. No grant is payable on the installation of a heating appliance which has been designated as unsuitable by a local authority or by the Secretary of State.

Local authorities may also make grants, at their discretion, towards the cost of such necessary works in churches, chapels, church and chapel halls, and any premises occupied for the purposes of a non-profit-making organisation whose main objects are charitable or are otherwise concerned with the advancement of religion, education, or social welfare (s.26).

5 Authorised fuels

For the purposes of the Clean Air Act 1993 certain fuels are "authorised fuels". Fuels are authorised if they are declared to be such by the Secretary of State (for England) or by the Smoke Control Areas (Authorised Fuels) (Wales) Regulations 2015. S.23 prohibits–
  (i) the acquisition of solid fuel, other than an authorised fuel, for use in a building or in a boiler or industrial plant in a smoke control area, unless it is to be used in an exempted building, fireplace, or boiler, or in exempted plant; and
  (ii) the retail sale of solid fuel, other than authorised fuel, for delivery to premises in a smoke control area; retail sale over the counter or to a customer who collects his own fuel is not prohibited.
The Secretary of State must publish lists of authorised fuels, and revised copies of the lists as soon as is reasonably practicable after any change is made to it (s.20(5B), (5ZB)).

6 Exempted fireplaces

The Secretary of State (for England) may exempt any class or description of fireplace from the provisions of s.20 (prohibition of smoke emissions in smoke control areas) if they are satisfied that such fireplaces can be used for burning fuel other than authorised fuels without producing any smoke or a substantial quantity of smoke. They must publish a list of those classes or descriptions of fireplace that are exempt (s.21).

For Wales, a series of Smoke Control Areas (Exempted Fireplaces) Orders, having effect under s.21, exempt certain fireplaces, subject to conditions, from the provisions of s.20. Further exemption Orders set out the exact classes of fireplaces which are exempted provided that they are installed, maintained, and operated so as to minimise the emission of smoke.

7 Smoke as a statutory nuisance

Under the Environmental Protection Act 1990, *inter alia* the following matters constitute statutory nuisances for the purposes of Part III of that Act–
  (a) smoke emitted from premises so as to be prejudicial to health or a nuisance;
  (b) fumes or gases emitted from premises so as to be prejudicial to health or a nuisance;
  (c) any dust, steam, smell, or other effluvia arising on industrial, trade, or business premises and being prejudicial to health or a nuisance.

As to the powers of local authorities and the courts to deal with statutory nuisances, see the Note on **Public Health: Nuisance, Diseases, etc**

8 Prevention of atmospheric pollution

Ss.30 to 32 of the Clean Air Act 1993 empower the Secretary of State to make regulations controlling the composition of any fuel used in motor vehicles, and imposing limits on the sulphur content of oil fuel used in furnaces or engines. The Motor Fuel (Composition and Content) Regulations 1999 have been made under these sections and implement European Council Directives 93/12/EEC and 98/70/EC (and updated by Commission Directive 2011/63/EU so as to reference the latest version of the industry fuel standards). The general distribution and sale of leaded petrol is prohibited, but suppliers and distributors may obtain "leaded petrol permits" from the Secretary of State authorising the distribution of leaded petrol to, and the sale of leaded petrol from, nominated filling stations. Such permits limit the amount of leaded petrol that a permit holder may distribute and sell during any calendar year.

S.33 makes it an offence to burn insulation from a cable to recover metal from it, unless the burning is part of a process subject to regulations under the Pollution Prevention and Control Act 1999, s.2.

9 Straw and stubble burning

S.152 of the Environmental Protection Act 1990 provides that the appropriate Minister may by regulations prohibit or restrict the burning of crop residues on agricultural land by persons engaged in agriculture. He may also provide exemptions from any prohibition or restriction so imposed. Crop residues means straw or stubble or any other crop residues.

The Crop Residues (Burning) Regulations 1993 have been made under s.152 and prohibit the burning of specified crop residues except for specified purposes. *Inter alia*, cereal straw and stubble and oil-seed rape residue may not be burnt except for the purpose of education or research, disease control or, in certain circumstances, the elimination of plant pests, or for the disposal of straw stacks or broken bales. Where one of these exceptions applies, the burning must comply with specified requirements including not being carried out on a Saturday, Sunday or Bank Holiday, or between the hours from one hour before sunset until sunrise.

The Heather and Grass etc. Burning (England) Regulations 2007 and (Wales) Regulations 2008 (made under the Hill Farming Act 1946) prohibit the burning of rough grass, heather, bracken, gorse and vaccinium without a licence outside the "burning season" (i.e., 1st October to 15th April (31st March in Wales) for upland areas, 1st November to 31st March (15th March in Wales) otherwise). The regulations also place restrictions on burning in the burning season, but do not apply to private or allotment gardens.

10 Asbestos in the air

The Control of Asbestos in the Air Regulations 1990 (made under the European Communities Act 1972 s.2(2)) makes provision for controlling environmental pollution by asbestos resulting from the working of products containing asbestos (Reg. 4). Any person undertaking–
  (a) activities involving the working of products containing asbestos must ensure that those activities do not cause significant environmental pollution by asbestos fibres or dust emitted into the air, or
  (b) the demolition of buildings, structures, and installations containing asbestos and the removal from them of asbestos or materials containing asbestos involving the release of asbestos fibres or dust into the air must ensure that significant environmental pollution is not caused thereby.

11 National air quality strategy

Part IV of the Environment Act 1995 requires the Secretary of State to prepare and publish a statement (referred to as "the strategy") containing policies with respect to the assessment or management of the quality of air.

The strategy may contain policies relating to the quality of air for implementing obligations of the UK under the Community Treaties or international agreements to which the UK is for the time being a party. The strategy must contain either a statement relating to the whole of Great Britain or one or two statements which between them relate to the whole of Great Britain and must be kept under review and may be modified from time to

time. In particular, the strategy must include–
   (a) statements with respect to air quality standards;
   (b) objectives for restricting the levels of substances present in the air; and
   (c) the measures local authorities and others must take for achieving those objectives.
   When preparing the strategy, the Secretary of State must consult the Environment Agency), such representatives of local government as he may consider appropriate, and such other bodies or persons he may consider appropriate (s.80). In discharging its pollution control functions, the Agency must have regard to the strategy (s.81).
   Schedule 11 provides supplementary provision in relation to air quality.
   In fulfilment of the requirement in Part IV, the Government has adopted the United Kingdom National Air Quality Strategy (Cm 3587). The Strategy sets out air quality standards, commitments to achieve air quality objectives throughout the United Kingdom, and the process by which those objectives will be achieved. The Air Quality Strategy aims to protect both health and the environment.

12 London air quality strategy

   The London Mayor must prepare and publish a London air quality strategy (Greater London Authority Act 1999, s.362) containing his proposals and policies for–
   (a) the implementation in Greater London of the national air quality strategy (see **12 National air quality strategy**, above);
   (b) the achievement in Greater London of prescribed air quality objectives; and
   (c) such other proposals and policies as he considers appropriate.
   The strategy must contain information about–
   (i) the air quality and likely future air quality in Greater London;
   (ii) measures to be taken by the Authority and Transport for London for the purpose of implementing the strategy; and
   (iii) measures which other bodies or persons are to be encouraged to take for the purpose of implementing the strategy.
   In preparing his strategy, the Mayor must have regard to action already taken by a local authority under the Environment Act 1995 ss.82 to 84 (see **13 Local authority reviews and designation of air quality management areas**, below), and must consult the Environment Agency and any local authority whose boundary adjoins Greater London.
   The Secretary of State may give the Mayor a direction as to the content of the strategy if he considers that it is likely to be detrimental to any area outside Greater London or because a direction is needed in order to implement the national air quality strategy.

13 Local authority reviews and designation of air quality management areas

   Each local authority must from time to time cause a review to be conducted of the quality for the time being, and the likely future quality, within the "relevant period", of air within the authority's area. The Air Quality (England) Regulations 2000 and the equivalent (Wales) Regulations 2000 each prescribe the relevant periods for different substances for these purposes. Where such a review is conducted, the local authority must also cause an assessment to be made as to whether the air quality standards and objectives are being achieved or are likely to be achieved within the relevant period in their area and must identify any parts of their area where those standards are not likely to be achieved (Environment Act 1995, s.82).
   If it appears that air quality standards or objectives are not being (or are not likely to be) achieved within the authority's area, they must by order designate as an air quality management area any part of their area in which it appears that those standards or objectives are not being (or are not likely to be) achieved within the relevant period (s.83). An action plan must then be prepared setting out how the authority intends to exercise its powers in relation to the designated area so as to achieve the prescribed air quality standards and objectives (s.84).
   The Local Authorities' Plans and Strategies (Disapplication) (England) Order 2005 disapplies for English local authorities which are rated as 4 stars or "excellent" the duty under s.84(2) of the Environment Act 1995 to prepare action plans in relation to air quality (Art. 8).

14 Reserve powers of the Secretary of State and the London Mayor

   The Secretary of State (in relation to England and Wales outside Greater London), the London Mayor (for Greater London) may conduct, or cause to be conducted or made within the area of a local authority, a review of the air quality within the relevant period, or an assessment of whether air quality standards or objectives are being achieved, or an identification of any parts of a local authority area in which it appears that those standards or objectives are not likely to be achieved within the relevant period, or an assessment of the respects in which it appears that air quality standards or objectives are not being achieved. After a review they may issue (in certain circumstances) directions to the local authority requiring them to take such steps as may be specified in the directions.
   The Secretary of State and London Mayor may also give directions to local authorities requiring them to take specified steps for the implementation of United Kingdom obligations under the Community Treaties or any international agreement to which the United Kingdom is for the time being a party (Environment Act 1995, s.85).

15 Authorities

Statutes–

Clean Air Act 1993

Environment Act 1995

Environmental Protection Act 1990

Statutory Instruments–

Air Quality (England) Regulations 2000, as amended (S.I. 2000 No. 928 and 2002 No. 3043)

Air Quality (Wales) Regulations 2000, as amended (S.I. 2000 No. 1940 and 2002 No. 3182)

Control of Asbestos in the Air Regulations 1990 (S.I. 1990 No. 556)

Crop Residues (Burning) Regulations 1993 (S.I. 1993 No. 1366)

Heather and Grass etc. Burning (England) Regulations 2007 (S.I. 2007 No. 2003)

Heather and Grass etc. Burning (Wales) Regulations 2008 (S.I. 2008 No. 1081)

Local Authorities' Plans and Strategies (Disapplication) (England) Order 2005, as amended (S.I. 2005 No. 157 and 2009 No. 714)

Motor Fuel (Composition and Content) Regulations 1999, as amended (S.I. 1999 No. 3107 2001 No. 3896, 2003 No. 3078. 2007 No. 1608, 2010 No. 3035, 2012 No. 2567, 2013 No. 2897, and 2015 Nos. 1630 and 1796)

Smoke Control Areas (Authorised Fuels) (Wales) Regulations 2015 (S.I. 2015 No. 1517)

AIR POLLUTION: SCOTLAND

1 The legislation

The law relating to air pollution is contained, principally, in the Clean Air Act 1993, which is largely concerned with smoke control, and Part IV of the Environment Act 1995, which is concerned with air quality.

As to the climate change levy, see the Note on **Climate Change**.

2 Dark smoke

The occupier of a building commits an offence if dark smoke is emitted from a chimney of the building except where the emission lasts for not longer than the period and in the circumstances permitted by regulations. Certain defences are specified (Clean Air Act 1993, s.1). In addition, if dark smoke is emitted from any industrial or trade premises, the occupier and any person who causes or permits the emission commit an offence; it is a defence to prove that the contravention complained of was inadvertent and that all practicable steps had been taken to prevent or minimise the emission (s.2).

3 Smoke control areas

Under the Clean Air Act 1993 s.18, a local authority may by order (a smoke control order) declare the whole or part of the district of the authority to be a smoke control area. A smoke control order may–
  (i) make different provision for different parts of the smoke control area;
  (ii) limit the operation of s.20 (see below) to specified classes of buildings in the area; and
  (ii) may exempt specified buildings or classes of buildings or specified fireplaces or classes of fireplace in the area (see **6 Exempted fireplaces**, below) from the operation of s.20 upon such conditions as may be specified in the order.

S.19 gives the Scottish Environment Protection Agency (SEPA) power, after consultation with a local authority, to direct the authority to submit proposals for bringing into operation one or more smoke control orders, within a prescribed period (being not less than six months). If no proposals are submitted or, if those submitted are unacceptable, SEPA may declare the authority in default and direct them to carry out proposals which the Agency has devised.

In smoke control areas, subject to exemptions and limitations, the emission of smoke from chimneys is an offence. It is, however, a defence to prove that the emission of smoke was not caused by the use of any fuel other than a fuel declared by the Scottish Ministers to be an authorised fuel (see **5 Authorised fuels**, below) (s.20).

4 Grants for necessary adaptations

Provision is made, by the Clean Air Act 1993 s.25, for the payment of grants by local authorities towards the cost of any necessary adaptation, alteration, conversion, or replacement of appliances (including the provision of electrical or gas ignition for open fireplaces) in private dwellings (other than dwellings the erection or conversion of which began after 16th August 1964) after a smoke control area is declared. No grant is payable on the installation of a heating appliance which has been designated as unsuitable by a local authority or by the Secretary of State.

Local authorities may also make grants, at their discretion, towards the cost of such necessary works in churches, chapels, church and chapel halls, and any premises occupied for the purposes of a non-profit-making organisation whose main objects are charitable or are otherwise concerned with the advancement of religion, education, or social welfare (s.26).

5 Authorised fuels

For the purposes of the Clean Air Act 1993 certain fuels are "authorised fuels". Fuels are authorised if they are declared to be such by the Scottish Ministers. S.23 prohibits–
  (i) the acquisition of solid fuel, other than an authorised fuel, for use in a building or in a boiler or industrial plant in a smoke control area, unless it is to be used in an exempted building, fireplace, or boiler, or in exempted plant; and
  (ii) the retail sale of solid fuel, other than authorised fuel, for delivery to premises in a smoke control area; retail sale over the counter or to a customer who collects his own fuel is not prohibited.

The Scottish Ministers must publish their lists of authorised fuels, and revised copies of the lists as soon as is reasonably practicable after any change is made to it (s.20(5B), (5ZB)).

6 Exempted fireplaces

The Scottish Ministers may exempt any class or description of fireplace from the provisions of s.20 (prohibition of smoke emissions in smoke control areas) if they are satisfied that such fireplaces can be used for burning fuel other than authorised fuels without producing any smoke or a substantial quantity of smoke. They must publish a list of those classes or descriptions of fireplace that are exempt (s.21).

7 Smoke as a statutory nuisance

Under the Environmental Protection Act 1990, *inter alia* the following matters constitute statutory nuisances for the purposes of Part III of that Act (which extends to Scotland, by virtue of the repeal of s.83 of that Act by the Environment Act 1995)–
(a) smoke emitted from premises so as to be prejudicial to health or a nuisance;
(b) fumes or gases emitted from premises so as to be prejudicial to health or a nuisance;
(c) any dust, steam, smell, or other effluvia arising on industrial, trade, or business premises and being prejudicial to health or a nuisance.

As to the powers of local authorities and the courts to deal with statutory nuisances, see the Note on **Public Health: Nuisance, Diseases, etc.**

8 Prevention of atmospheric pollution

Ss.30 to 32 of the Clean Air Act 1993 empower the Secretary of State to make regulations controlling the composition of any fuel used in motor vehicles, and imposing limits on the sulphur content of oil fuel used in furnaces or engines. The Motor Fuel (Composition and Content) Regulations 1999 have been made under these sections and implement European Council Directives 93/12/EEC and 98/70/EC (and updated by Commission Directive 2011/63/EU so as to reference the latest version of the industry fuel standards). The general distribution and sale of leaded petrol is prohibited, but suppliers and distributors may obtain "leaded petrol permits" from the Secretary of State authorising the distribution of leaded petrol to, and the sale of leaded petrol from, nominated filling stations. Such permits limit the amount of leaded petrol that a permit holder may distribute and sell during any calendar year.

S.33 makes it an offence to burn insulation from a cable to recover metal from it, unless the burning is part of a process subject to regulations under the Pollution Prevention and Control Act 1999, s.2.

10 Straw and stubble burning

S.152 of the Environmental Protection Act 1990 provides that the appropriate Minister may by regulations prohibit or restrict the burning of crop residues on agricultural land by persons engaged in agriculture. He may also provide exemptions from any prohibition or restriction so imposed. Crop residues means straw or stubble or any other crop residues.

11 Asbestos in the air

The Control of Asbestos in the Air Regulations 1990 (made under the European Communities Act 1972 s.2(2)) makes provision for controlling environmental pollution by asbestos resulting from the working of products containing asbestos (Reg. 4). Any person undertaking–
(a) activities involving the working of products containing asbestos must ensure that those activities do not cause significant environmental pollution by asbestos fibres or dust emitted into the air, or
(b) the demolition of buildings, structures, and installations containing asbestos and the removal from them of asbestos or materials containing asbestos involving the release of asbestos fibres or dust into the air must ensure that significant environmental pollution is not caused thereby.

12 National air quality strategy

Part IV of the Environment Act 1995 requires the Secretary of State to prepare and publish a statement (referred to as "the strategy") containing policies with respect to the assessment or management of the quality of air.

The strategy may contain policies relating to the quality of air for implementing obligations of the United Kingdom under the Community Treaties or international agreements to which the United Kingdom is for the time being a party. The strategy must contain either a statement relating to the whole of Great Britain or one or two statements which between them relate to the whole of Great Britain and must be kept under review and may be modified from time to time. In particular, the strategy must include–
(a) statements with respect to air quality standards;
(b) objectives for restricting the levels of substances present in the air; and
(c) the measures local authorities and others must take for achieving those objectives.

When preparing the strategy, the Secretary of State must consult the Scottish Environment Protection Agency, such representatives of local government as he may consider appropriate, and such other bodies or persons he may consider appropriate (s.80). In discharging its pollution control functions, each Agency must have regard to the strategy (s.81).

Schedule 11 provides supplementary provision in relation to air quality.

In fulfilment of the requirement in Part IV, the Government has adopted the United Kingdom National Air

Quality Strategy (Cm 3587). The Strategy sets out air quality standards, commitments to achieve air quality objectives throughout the United Kingdom, and the process by which those objectives will be achieved. The Air Quality Strategy aims to protect both health and the environment.

13 Local authority reviews and designation of air quality management areas

Each local authority must from time to time cause a review to be conducted of the quality for the time being, and the likely future quality, within the "relevant period", of air within the authority's area. The Air Quality (Scotland) Regulations 2000 prescribe the relevant periods for different substances for these purposes. Where such a review is conducted, the local authority must also cause an assessment to be made as to whether the air quality standards and objectives are being achieved or are likely to be achieved within the relevant period in their area and must identify any parts of their area where those standards are not likely to be achieved (Environment Act 1995, s.82).

If it appears that air quality standards or objectives are not being (or are not likely to be) achieved within the authority's area, they must by order designate as an air quality management area any part of their area in which it appears that those standards or objectives are not being (or are not likely to be) achieved within the relevant period (s.83). An action plan must then be prepared setting out how the authority intends to exercise its powers in relation to the designated area so as to achieve the prescribed air quality standards and objectives (s.84).

14 Reserve powers of SEPA

SEPA may conduct, or cause to be conducted or made within the area of a local authority, a review of the air quality within the relevant period, or an assessment of whether air quality standards or objectives are being achieved, or an identification of any parts of a local authority area in which it appears that those standards or objectives are not likely to be achieved within the relevant period, or an assessment of the respects in which it appears that air quality standards or objectives are not being achieved. After a review they may issue (in certain circumstances) directions to the local authority requiring them to take such steps as may be specified in the directions.

Authorities

Statutes–

Clean Air Act 1993

Environment Act 1995

Environmental Protection Act 1990

Statutory Instruments–

Air Quality (Scotland) Regulations 2000, as amended (S.S.I. 2000 No. 97, 2002 No. 297, and 2016 No. 162)

Control of Asbestos in the Air Regulations 1990 (S.I. 1990 No. 556)

Motor Fuel (Composition and Content) Regulations 1999, as amended (S.I. 1999 No. 3107 2001 No. 3896, 2003 No. 3078. 2007 No. 1608, 2010 No. 3035, 2012 No. 2567, 2013 No. 2897, and 2015 No. 1796)

ENVIRONMENTAL LAW

CLIMATE CHANGE

1 The 2050 target and carbon budgets

The Government has a duty to ensure that the UK carbon account for 2050 is at least 80% lower than the "1990 baseline" (Climate Change Act 2008, s.1). The baseline actually varies according to the greenhouse gas concerned. The targeted greenhouse gases, and their base years, are as follows–

- carbon dioxide (1990);
- methane (1990);
- nitrous oxide (1990);
- hydrofluorocarbons (1995);
- perfluorocarbons (1995); and
- sulphur hexafluoride (1995).

The Government must also set "carbon budgets" representing UK emissions for five year periods beginning with the period 2008-2012 (s.4), taking account of any "carbon units" which are credited or debited to the net UK carbon account under a system of "carbon accounting". The Act makes provision as to how to calculate whether the target for 2050 has been met and how carbon budgets are to be set. It requires that the carbon budget for 2018-2022 is set in a way that is consistent with an interim target to reduce emissions of greenhouse gases by at least 34% by 2020, against 1990 levels (s.5, as amended by the Climate Change Act 2008 (2020 Target, Credit Limit and Definitions) Order 2009). Before setting a carbon budget, the Government must to take into account advice from the Committee on Climate Change and any views of the devolved administrations (s.9). The following matters must be taken into account (s.10)–

- (a) scientific knowledge about climate change;
- (b) technology relevant to climate change;
- (c) economic circumstances, and in particular the likely impact of the decision on the economy and the competitiveness of particular sectors of the economy;
- (d) fiscal circumstances, and in particular the likely impact of the decision on taxation, public spending and public borrowing;
- (e) social circumstances, and in particular the likely impact of the decision on fuel poverty;
- (f) energy policy, and in particular the likely impact of the decision on energy supplies and the carbon and energy intensity of the economy;
- (g) differences in circumstances between England, Wales, Scotland and Northern Ireland;
- (h) European and international circumstances;
- (i) the estimated amount of reportable emissions from international aviation and international shipping for the budgetary period or periods in question.

The carbon budgets for the periods to 2018-2022 are set out in the Carbon Budgets Order 2009 and the provisions as to carbon accounting are contained in the Carbon Accounting Regulations 2009.

In Scotland, the Climate Change (Scotland) Act 2009 sets a target interim reduction for greenhouse gas emissions of 42% by 2020 (rather than the 34% target for the UK set out above) (s.2). Annual targets for the years 2023-2027 are set out in the Climate Change (Annual Targets) (Scotland) Order 2011 (S.S.I. No. 353) and as to carbon accounting in the Carbon Accounting Scheme (Scotland) Regulations 2010.

2 The Committee on Climate Change

The Committee on Climate Change is an independent, non-departmental public body. It has a duty to advise the Government on (Climate Change Act 2008, s.33)–

- (a) whether the 80% target for 2050 should be amended; and
- (b) if so, what the amended percentage should be.

It also has a duty to advise the Government, in relation to each budgetary period, on (ss.34 and 35)–

- (a) the level of the carbon budget for the period;
- (b) the extent to which the carbon budget for the period should be met by (i) reducing the amount of net UK emissions of targeted greenhouse gases, or (ii) the use of carbon units that may be credited to the net UK carbon account for the period;
- (c) the respective contributions towards meeting the carbon budget for the period that should be made by (i) the sectors of the economy covered by trading schemes (taken as a whole), and (ii) the sectors of the economy not so covered (taken as a whole);
- (d) the sectors of the economy in which there are particular opportunities for contributions to be made towards meeting the carbon budget for the period through reductions in emissions of targeted greenhouse gases; and
- (e) the consequences of treating emissions from international aviation and international shipping as UK emissions for the purposes of the targets and budgets in the Act.

The Committee must report to Parliament and the devolved legislatures each year on progress towards meeting the carbon budgets and targets (s.36).

The Scottish Ministers have the power to set up a Scottish Committee on Climate Change (Climate Change (Scotland) Act 2009, s.25, not yet in force).

3 Trading schemes

Trading schemes may be established to (Climate Change Act 2008, s.44)–
- (a) limit or encourage the limitation of activities that consist of the emission of greenhouse gas or that cause or contribute, directly or indirectly, to such emissions; or
- (b) encourage activities that consist of, or that cause or contribute, directly or indirectly, to reductions in greenhouse gas emissions or the removal of greenhouse gas from the atmosphere.

Activities are regarded as indirectly causing or contributing to greenhouse gas emissions if they involve, in particular (s.45)–
- (a) the consumption of energy;
- (b) the use of materials in whose production energy was consumed;
- (c) the disposal otherwise than for recycling of materials in whose production energy was consumed; or
- (d) the production or supply of anything whose subsequent use directly causes or contributes to greenhouse gas emissions.

Correspondingly, activities are regarded as indirectly causing or contributing to the reduction of greenhouse gas emissions if they involve a reduction under any of those heads.

4 Adaptation to climate change

The Climate Change Act 2008 recognises that in addition to taking measures designed to reduce climate change, adaptation to future climate change was also necessary. Accordingly the Government must lay reports before Parliament containing an assessment of the risks for the UK of the current and predicted impact of climate change (s.56). The Committee on Climate Change must advise on the preparation of each such report (s.57).

The Government also has a duty to lay programmes before Parliament addressing the risks identified in the most recent report and setting out (s.58)–
- (a) its objectives in relation to adaptation to climate change;
- (b) its proposals and policies for meeting those objectives; and
- (c) the time-scales for introducing those proposals and policies.

Where a report is laid under s.56 of the 2008 Act, the Scottish Ministers must lay a programme before the Scottish Parliament setting out *inter alia* their objectives in relation to adaptation to climate change and their proposals and policies for meeting those objectives, including timescales (Climate Change (Scotland) Act 2009, s.53).

5 The climate change levy

Schedule 6 to the Finance Act 2000 provides for a tax to be known as the climate change levy. The tax was introduced on 1st April 2001 and is charged on industrial and commercial use of energy (i.e., lighting, heating and power for appliances) subject to specified exceptions and reliefs as described in this Note.

6 Taxable supplies

The levy is charged on "taxable supplies", which are defined as the supply of a taxable commodity (Sch. 6, para 2). Taxable commodities are (Sch. 6, para 3)–
- (a) electricity;
- (b) any gas in a gaseous state that is of a kind supplied by a gas utility;
- (c) petroleum gas or other gaseous hydrocarbons in a liquid state;
- (d) coal and lignite;
- (e) coke and semi-coke of coal and lignite; and
- (f) petroleum coke.

The rate of levy varies according to the type of taxable commodity supplied (see **10 Registration and rate of levy**, below).

7 Exempted supplies–domestic and charity use

A supply is excluded from the levy if it is (Sch. 6, para 8)–
- (a) for domestic use; or
- (b) for charity use otherwise than in the course or furtherance of a business.

Where a supply is partly for domestic or charity use and partly not, if at least 60% of the supply is for domestic or charity use then the whole supply is treated as if it is for such a use. In any other case, the supply must be apportioned to determine the extent to which the supply is for domestic or charity use.

The following supplies are always for domestic use (Sch. 6 para 9)–
- (i) a supply of not more than one tonne of coal or coke held out for sale as a domestic fuel;
- (ii) a supply of gas or petroleum gas through pipes at a rate not exceeding 4397 kilowatt hours per month;
- (iii) a supply of liquid petroleum gas (LPG) in cylinders with a net weight less than 50kg where either fewer than 20 cylinders are supplied, or the LPG is not intended for re-sale by the recipient;

(iv) a supply of LPG not in cylinders to a person at premises where no more than two tonnes of such LPG may be stored;

(v) a supply of electricity not exceeding 1000 kilowatt hours per month.

If a supply does not come within (i) to (v) above, it will only be a supply for domestic use if it is for use in–

(vi) a building, or part of a building, consisting of a dwelling or a number of dwellings;

(vii) a building, or part of a building, used for "relevant residential purposes" (i.e., children's homes, old people's homes, rehabilitation centres, hospices, residential school accommodation, army barracks etc, monasteries, nunneries and similar establishments, and institutions which are the sole or main residence of at least 90% of their residents);

(viii) self-catering holiday accommodation; and

(ix) a caravan or houseboat.

Hospitals, prisons and hotels are specifically excluded from (vii) above.

8 Exempted supplies–transport

A supply of a taxable commodity is exempt from the levy if it is to be burned or consumed (Sch. 6, para 12)–

(a) to propel a train;

(b) to propel a non-railway vehicle (see below) while it is being used for, or for purposes connected with, transporting passengers;

(c) in a railway or non-railway vehicle while it is being used for, or for purposes connected with, transporting passengers;

(d) in a railway vehicle while it is being used for, or for purposes connected with, transporting goods;

(e) in a ship on a journey any part of which is outside territorial waters.

A "non-railway vehicle" is a ship, or any vehicle (other than a railway vehicle), designed or adapted to carry not less than 12 passengers.

Paragraphs (a) to (c) above do not apply to the transporting of passengers to, from or within a place of entertainment, recreation or amusement or a place of cultural, scientific, historical or similar interest.

9 Exempted supplies–miscellaneous exemptions

A supply of a taxable commodity will be exempt if–

(a) it is used to produce another energy product;

(b) the person to whom the supply is made has notified the supplier that he intends to export the commodity;

(c) the person to whom the supply is made has notified the supplier that he intends to use the commodity to supply another person (this exception does not apply to electricity or gas in a gaseous state);

(d) the person to whom the supply is made intends to use the commodity other than as a fuel (the Climate Change Levy (Fuel Use and Recycling Processes) Regulations 2005 prescribe the uses which are, and are not, to be taken as uses of a commodity as fuel);

(e) *(repealed from a date to be appointed)* it is made by a "fully exempt combined heat and power station" i.e., a power station certified by the Secretary of State as satisfying prescribed conditions as to performance levels. Similar provisions apply to "partially exempt" power stations, and also to certain other combined heat and power stations which have made a "CHP declaration";

(f) it is, subject to prescribed conditions, electricity made from certain renewable resources (e.g., wind and solar power);

(g) it is a supply for fuel use in a prescribed recycling process (the Climate Change Levy (Fuel Use and Recycling Processes) Regulations 2005 prescribe the relevant recycling processes); or

(h) it is a supply to be used in a mineralogical or metallurgical process (as defined).

10 Registration and rate of levy

The person liable to account for the levy is the person making the supply (Sch. 6, para 40). Such a person must register with the Commissioners of Revenue and Customs in accordance with the provisions of the Climate Change Levy (Registration and Miscellaneous Provisions) Regulations 2001.

The rate of levy varies according to the type of taxable commodity supplied. Rates applicable from 1st April 2014 (1st April 2015 in brackets) are as follows (Sch. 6, para 42)–

Taxable commodity	*Rate of levy (£)*
Electricity	0.00541per kwh (0.00554)
Gas supplied by a gas utility or in a gaseous state	0.00188per kwh (0.00193)
LPG or other liquid gaseous hydrocarbons	0.01210per kg (0.01240)
Any other taxable commodity (e.g., coal)	0.01476per kg (0.01512)

11 Reduced-rate supplies

Certain supplies may qualify as "reduced-rate" supplies. This reduced rate is available to energy intensive sites which negotiate a "climate change agreement" with the Secretary of State setting out energy efficiency targets to be attained by the sites. The reduced rate will be 20% of the full rate. The industries which qualify as energy intensive for these purposes, and which may therefore enter into climate change agreements, are set out in Schedule 6, para 51, as extended by the Climate Change Agreements (Energy-intensive Installations) Regulations 2006 (S.I. No. 59).

12 Authorities

Statutes–

Climate Change Act 2008

Climate Change (Scotland) Act 2009

Finance Act 2000

Statutory Instruments–

Carbon Accounting Regulations 2009 (S.I. 2009 No. 1257)

Carbon Accounting Scheme (Scotland) Regulations 2010, as amended (S.S.I. 2010 No. 216, S.I. 2011 No. 1043, S.S.I. 2015 No. 189, and 2016 No. 46)

Carbon Budgets Order 2009 (S.I. 2009 No. 1259)

Climate Change Act 2008 (2020 Target, Credit Limit and Definitions) Order 2009 (S.I. 2009 No. 1258)

Climate Change Levy (Registration and Miscellaneous Provisions) Regulations 2001, as amended (S.I. 2001 No. 7, 2005 No. 1716, and 2009 No. 1890)

Climate Change Levy (Fuel Use and Recycling Processes) Regulations 2005, as amended (S.I. 2005 No. 1715, 2011 No. 1715, and 2014 No. 844)

CONTROL OF NOISE

Contents

This Note deals with the laws which provide for the control of noise, or for the making of grants towards insulating buildings and dwellings from noise. The Note is organised as follows–

A: Statutory nuisances
B: Audible intruder alarms
C: Noise at night
D: Control of noise from work on construction sites
E: Noise in streets
F: Traffic noise
G: Noise from railways
H: European Noise Requirements

See also the Notes on **Anti-Social Behaviour**.

A: STATUTORY NUISANCES

1 Environmental Protection Act 1990 s.79

In England and Wales, and Scotland, under s.79 of the Environmental Protection Act 1990 (the 1990 Act), as amended by the Noise and Statutory Nuisance Act 1993 (the 1993 Act) s.2, and the Environment Act 1995 (the 1995 Act) ss.107 and 120, Schedules 17 and 24, there are two statutory nuisances specifically relating to noise, namely–

(a) noise emitted from premises so as to be prejudicial to health or a nuisance (s.79(1)(g)); and
(b) noise emitted from or caused by a vehicle, machinery, or equipment (which term includes a musical instrument) in a street, which is prejudicial to health or a nuisance (s.79(1)(ga)).

These statutory nuisances can be dealt with by both the local authority and a magistrates' court or, in Scotland, the sheriff, in accordance with ss.80 to 82 of the 1990 Act. The general provisions relating to the service of abatement notices and the bringing of summary proceedings by persons aggrieved by statutory nuisances are dealt with in the Note on **Public Health: Nuisances, Diseases, etc** and are not repeated here. However, provisions relating specifically to noise are dealt with in the following paragraphs.

2 Special provisions relating to s.79(1)(g)

Whether or not a local authority decide to take proceedings under s.80(4), they may abate the nuisance and do whatever may be necessary in execution of the abatement notice (s.81(3)). By virtue of the Noise Act 1996 s.10(7), where the statutory nuisance falls within s.70(1)(g) (noise emitted from premises) the powers of a local authority in England and Wales under s.81(3) specifically include the power to seize and remove any equipment which it appears is or has been used in the emission of the noise. Seized equipment may be retained for 28 days or until any proceedings are concluded. Where a person is convicted of a "noise offence" – which includes an offence under s.80(4) in relation to a statutory nuisance under s.79(1)(g) – the court may make a forfeiture order in respect of the equipment. Where a local authority do not bring proceedings, they may return the equipment to anyone who–

(a) appears to be the owner; and
(b) makes a claim for the return within six months of the expiry of 28 days from the date of seizure; and
(c) who pays such reasonable charge for the seizure, removal and retention as the authority may demand.

If no claim is made within the time period, the local authority may dispose of the equipment.

3 Special provisions relating to s.79(1)(ga)

In the case of a statutory nuisance within s.79(1)(ga), that (i) has not yet occurred, or (ii) arises from noise emitted from or caused by an unattended vehicle or unattended machinery or equipment, ss.80 and 80A of the 1990 Act (as inserted by the 1993 Act, s.3) provides that where a local authority is satisfied that noise amounting to a nuisance (including noise emitted from or caused by a vehicle, machinery, or equipment in a road), exists, or is likely to occur or recur, in the area of the local authority, the local authority shall serve a notice (a) requiring the abatement of the nuisance or prohibiting or restricting its occurrence or recurrence; and/or (b) requiring the execution of specified works and the taking of other steps necessary for the purpose of the notice or as may be specified in the notice. The notice must also specify the time or times within which the requirements of the notice are to be complied with (s.80(1)). However, s.80(1) does not apply to noise emitted from or caused by a vehicle, machinery or equipment in a street made by traffic (but see **17 Insulation of buildings**, below), by any naval, military, or air force of the Crown or by a visiting force (as defined), or by a political demonstration or a demonstration supporting or opposing a cause or campaign (s.79(6A) as inserted by the 1993 Act, s.2).

The notice is to be served on the person responsible for the nuisance or, if that person cannot be found or the nuisance has not yet occurred (and the noise in question is not road noise), on the owner or occupier of the premises from which the noise is emitted or would be emitted (s.80(2)). The person served with the notice may appeal against the notice to a magistrates' court (or a sheriff's court) within 21 days from service of the notice (s.80(3)). In the case of noise in a street (or, in Scotland, in a road) which has not yet occurred or is emitted from or caused by an unattended vehicle or unattended machinery or equipment, the notice must be served (a) where the person responsible for the vehicle, machinery, or equipment can be found, on that person; (b) where (i) that person cannot be found or (ii) the local authority determines that s.80A(2)(b) [i.e., this sub-paragraph] shall apply, by fixing the notice to the vehicle, machinery, or equipment (s.80A, as inserted by the 1993 Act, s.3).

Where a notice under s.80 in respect of road noise has not been complied with, the local authority may abate, the nuisance and do whatever may be necessary in execution of the notice (s.81(3)). The local authority may recover any expenses reasonably incurred in this connection from any person on whom the notice under s.80 was duly served or by whose act or default the nuisance was caused; and the court or the sheriff may apportion those expenses between such persons in such manner as it considers fair and reasonable (s.81(4)).

Where a nuisance which exists or has occurred within the area of a local authority, or which has affected any part of that area, appears to be wholly or partly caused by some act or default committed or taking place outside the area, the local authority for the affected area may act under s.80 as if the act or default were wholly within that area, except that any appeal must be heard by a magistrates' court or, in Scotland, the sheriff, having jurisdiction where the act or default is alleged to have taken place (s.81(2)).

4 Summary proceedings by persons aggrieved

By virtue of s.82 (as amended by the 1993 and 1995 Acts), a magistrates' court or a sheriff may act on a complaint (or a summary application) made by the occupier of any premises on the ground that in his capacity as occupier of the premises he is aggrieved by noise amounting to a nuisance. If the court is satisfied that the alleged nuisance exists, or that although abated, it is likely to recur on the same premises (or where the noise in question is in a street (or, in Scotland, a road) in the same street (or road)), it must make an order–

(a) requiring the person against whom the proceedings are taken to abate the nuisance, within a specified time and to execute any works necessary for that purpose; and/or

(b) prohibiting a recurrence of the nuisance, and requiring the defendant, within a specified time, to execute any works necessary to prevent the recurrence.

Proceedings under s.82 may be brought (a) against the person responsible for the nuisance or, if that person cannot be found, against the owner or occupier of the premises from which the noise is emitted, or would be emitted or (b) in the case of noise in a street (or, in Scotland, a road) emitted from or caused by an unattended vehicle or unattended machinery or equipment, against the person responsible for the vehicle, machinery, or equipment (s.82(4), as amended by the 1993 and 1995 Acts).

The Statutory Nuisance (Appeals) Regulations 1995 and the equivalent 1996 Scottish regulations make provision with respect to appeals to magistrates' courts or, in Scotland, to the sheriff, against abatement notices, and the suspension of such notices, served under ss.80 and 80A.

The above provisions do not apply to (a) noises made by aircraft (but see 27 **Insulation against airport noise and vibration**, below) or (b) noises made by traffic (but see 17 **Insulation of buildings**, below), by any naval, military, or air force of the Crown, or by visiting forces (as defined) or by a political demonstration supporting or opposing a cause or campaign (s.80(6A), as inserted by the 1993 Act, s.2).

B: AUDIBLE INTRUDER ALARMS

5 Alarm notification areas

The Clean Neighbourhoods and Environment Act 2005 gives powers to local authorities to deal with the annoyance caused by audible intruder alarms in their areas (ss.69 to 81). The regime enables a local authority to designate its area (or part of it) as an alarm notification area (s.69) and also to withdraw a designation made under s.69 (s.79).

6 Designation as an alarm notification area

The effect of a designation is that the occupier or owner of any premises (residential or non-residential) in the area must notify the local authority of the details of a key-holder for the premises (Clean Neighbourhoods and Environment Act 2005, s.71). The authority can then turn to that key-holder for assistance in silencing an alarm. It is an offence to fail to nominate or notify the local authority of the details of a key-holder. To be eligible to be a key-holder for residential premises a person must have a key for the premises where the alarm is situated, normally reside in the vicinity of the premises, have sufficient information to be able to silence the alarm (i.e., pass codes), agree to be a key-holder, and not be an occupier of the premises or a key-holding company (s.72). For business premises, the key-holder can be a key-holding company or the owner or occupier of the building.

If a person becomes aware that their nominated key-holder no longer satisfies the conditions to be eligible as a key-holder, they have 28 days in which to nominate another key-holder.

7 Offences under s.71: fixed penalty notices

An authorised officer of a local authority may issue a fixed penalty notice where it appears to him that an offence of failing to nominate or notify details of a key-holder has been committed, offering the offender an opportunity to discharge, by payment of a fixed penalty within 14 days, any liability to conviction for the offence (Clean Neighbourhoods and Environment Act 2005, s.73).

Local authorities may fix the amount of a fixed penalty for offences committed in their area at between £50 and £80 (in Wales, £75 and £150). Where they do not set an amount, a default penalty of £75 applies. In either case, a local authority may treat a penalty as having been paid if a lesser amount (but not less than £50) is paid before the end of such (shorter) period as it may specify (s.74).

An authorised officer of a local authority has the power to require the name and address of a person if he proposes to give him a fixed penalty notice. It is an offence for a person either to fail to give that information or to give false or inaccurate information (s.76).

8 Powers in relation to alarms

An authorised officer of a local authority has a power to enter premises (but not by force) in order to silence an intruder alarm in or on the premises where he is satisfied that–
(a) it has been sounding continuously for 20 minutes or intermittently for an hour;
(b) it is likely to give people living or working in the vicinity reasonable cause for annoyance; and
(c) if the premises are in an alarm notification area, reasonable steps have been taken to get the nominated key-holder to silence the alarm.

It should be noted that the use of this power is not limited to premises in an area which has been designated as an alarm notification area (Clean Neighbourhoods and Environment Act 2005, s.77).

An authorised officer may enter premises using reasonable force if necessary to silence an alarm following the issue of a warrant by a justice of the peace. Before issuing a warrant, the justice of the peace must be satisfied that conditions (a) to (c) are met and that entry to the premises cannot be gained without the use of force (s.78).

C: NOISE AT NIGHT

9 Noise Act 1996: introduction

The Noise Act 1996, which applies to England and Wales only, contains provisions enabling local authorities to take action to deal with noise emitted from residential buildings at night (i.e., the period between 11pm and 7am). In particular, the Act contains a new night noise offence (s.1).

The Noise Act is extended to licensed premises in by ss.84, 85 and Sch.1 of the Clean Neighbourhoods and Environment Act 2005.

10 Night-time noise

Under Noise Act 1996, s.2 (amended by s.84 and Sch.1 to the Clean Neighbourhoods and Environment Act 2005), an officer of a local authority may take reasonable steps to investigate a complaint made by an individual present in a dwelling at night that excessive noise is coming from another dwelling (the "offending dwelling") or any premises in respect of which a premises licence or a temporary event notice has effect (the "offending premises"). This is a discretionary power rather than a duty. For these purposes, references to noise coming from a dwelling includes noise coming from a garden, yard, or outhouse. A complaint under s.2 may be made by any means (e.g., by telephone). If, having investigated the complaint, the officer is satisfied that noise is coming from the offending dwelling or premises at night and that the noise, if measured inside the complainant's dwelling would exceed permitted levels he may serve a warning notice on the person who appears to be responsible for the noise (s.2(4)).

It is for the officer investigating the complaint to decide whether any noise, if it were measured from inside the complainant's dwelling, would or might exceed the permitted level and to decide whether to use a device to measure the noise (s.2(5)). S.5 empowers the Secretary of State (or Welsh Assembly) to give directions determining the maximum level of noise which may be emitted during night hours from any dwelling or other premises and different permitted levels may be determined for different circumstances and the level may be determined partly by reference to other levels of noise. The Secretary of State (or Welsh Assembly) may also approve devices used for the measurement of noise and, in any proceedings under the Act, a measurement of noise made by a device is not admissible as evidence of the noise level unless it is an approved device (s.6).

Where an offending dwelling or premises is within the area of another local authority area, the authority receiving a complaint may still investigate it (s.2(7)).

A warning notice must state that noise exceeding the permitted level is being emitted from the offending dwelling and that any person responsible for the noise may be guilty of an offence. The specified period must begin not earlier than ten minutes after the time of service of the notice and end with the following 7 a.m. (s.3(1) and (2)).

Where a complaint is in respect of a dwelling, the notice must be served on any person present at or near the offending dwelling who appears to be responsible for the noise, or if it is not reasonably practicable to identify a responsible person, the notice may be left at the dwelling (s.3(3)).

Where a complaint is in respect of other premises, a warning notice must be served by delivering it to the person who appears to the officer of the authority to be the responsible person in relation to the offending premises at the time the notice is delivered i.e., the licensee, designated premises supervisor or other person in charge (s.3(3A), inserted by s.84 and Sch.1 to the Clean Neighbourhoods and Environment Act 2005).

Once a warning notice has been served, any person responsible for excessive noise coming from the offending premises during the period specified in the notice is guilty of an offence, although it is a defence in the case of a dwelling to show that there is a reasonable excuse for the excessive noise (ss.4 and 4A). The offence is a summary one, punishable by a fine not exceeding in level 3 (dwellings) or level 5 (other premises) on the standard scale. As an alternative to prosecution, the officer of the authority may issue a fixed penalty notice to the person he believes has committed the offence. That person then has 14 days to pay the fixed penalty see below) before criminal proceedings can be begun (s.8, amended by s.82 of the Clean Neighbourhoods and Environment Act 2005).

As to the standard scale, see the Notes on **Treatment of Offenders**.

11 Amount of fixed penalty

A local authority may set the level of the fixed penalty (in lieu of liability to conviction for an offence) in its area at between £75 and £110 (in Wales, £100 and £150). A lesser amount (but not less than £60) can be accepted as full payment if payment is made early. Where no amount is specified by a local authority, the fixed penalty is set at £100.

Where the alleged offence relates to licensed premises, the amount of the fixed penalty is fixed at £500 (with no power for a local authority to set an alternative).

An authorised officer of a local authority has the power to require the name and address of a person if he proposes to give him a fixed penalty notice, and makes it an offence for that person either to fail to give that information or to give false or inaccurate information (s.8B, as so inserted).

12 Seizure of equipment

Once an offence has been committed under s.4 or s.4A, an officer of the local authority may enter the dwelling or other premises from which the noise is being emitted and may seize and remove any equipment which it appears to him is being or has been used in the emission of the noise (s.10, amended by (amended by the Clean Neighbourhoods and Environment Act 2005, s.84 and Sch.1). The Schedule to the Act gives authorities power to retain seized equipment for 21 days or until any criminal proceedings are finished. This power of retention does not, however, apply if a fixed penalty has been paid. In the event of a successful prosecution, a court may order the forfeiture of any related equipment. Before making such an order, the court must consider the value of the equipment and the likely financial and other effects on the offender of making the order. If no order for forfeiture is made, the court may direct the return, retention or disposal of the equipment, as it sees fit. If entry to a dwelling or other premises is refused, the local authority may obtain a warrant from a justice of the peace authorising an officer to enter the premises by force (s.10(4)).

D: CONTROL OF NOISE FROM CONSTRUCTION SITES

13 Control of Pollution Act 1974: construction sites

Ss.60 and 61 of the 1974 Act (which extend throughout Great Britain) give local authorities powers to specify requirements concerning noise before work starts on a construction site. In particular, they may specify the plant or machinery which is or is not to be used, the hours during which works may be carried out, and the permitted level of noise.

Various British Standards Institution Codes of Practice for noise control on construction and open sites have been approved as codes of practice *inter alia* for the carrying out of works which are subject to control under s.60 of the Act. Approval has been given by–
   – The Control of Noise (Code of Practice for Construction and Open Sites) (England) Order 2015 (S.I. No. 227);
   – The Control of Noise (Codes of Practice for Construction and Open Sites) (Wales) Order 2002 (S.I. No. 1795); and
   – The Control of Noise (Codes of Practice for Construction and Open Sites) (Scotland) Order 2002 (S.S.I. No. 104).

E: NOISE IN STREETS

14 Control of Pollution Act 1974: street noise

S.62 of the 1974 Act (as amended by the 1993 Act, s.7), which applies throughout Great Britain, prohibits the use of loudspeakers in a street between (a) 9 p.m. and 8 a.m. for any purpose; and (b) at any other time for the purpose of advertising an entertainment, trade, or business (s.62(1)), with the exception of loudspeakers fixed to a vehicle conveying a perishable commodity for human consumption (e.g., ice cream), which may be operated between noon and 7 p.m. if they operate otherwise than by means of words (e.g., by using a chime) and give no reasonable cause for annoyance. There are also exceptions for the use of loudspeakers at any time in case of emergency, or by the police or fire brigade, or in certain other specified circumstances (s.62(2) and (3)). The Secretary of State may by order amend the times specified in (a) above but those times may not be amended so as to permit the operation of a loudspeaker in a street at any time between the hours of nine in the evening and eight in the following morning (s.61(1A) and (1B), as inserted by the 1993 Act, s.7). Further, s.62(1) will not apply to the operation of a loudspeaker in accordance with a consent granted by a local authority under Schedule 2 to the 1993 Act (see below) (1974 Act, s.62(3A), as inserted by the 1993 Act, s.7).

15 Consent of local authorities to the operation of loudspeakers in streets or roads

Under s.8 of the 1993 Act, a local authority (see below) may resolve that Schedule 2 to the 1993 Act is to apply to its area. Under Schedule 2, on an application (in the form provided by the Schedule) made by any person, the local authority may consent to the operation in its area of a loudspeaker in contravention of s.62(1) of the 1974 Act. But such a consent will not be given to the operation of a loudspeaker in connection with any election or for the purposes of advertising any entertainment, trade, or business. A consent may be granted subject to such conditions as the local authority considers appropriate.

Local authority, for the above purpose, means in relation to England and Wales, a district or London borough council, the Common Council of the City of London, the Sub-Treasurer of the Inner Temple, or the Under Treasurer of the Middle Temple and, in relation to Scotland, a district or islands council.

16 Codes of practice for minimising noise

Codes of Practice, giving guidance on appropriate methods of minimising noise from ice-cream vans, burglar alarms, and model were respectively brought into force on 1st February 1982 by statutory instruments S.I. 1981 Nos. 1828, 1829, and 1830. In England, the Code of Practice on methods of minimising noise from ice-cream vans has been replaced by S.I. 2013 No. 2036; and that for burglar alarms has been repealed by S.I. 2014 No. 2123.

F: TRAFFIC NOISE

17 Insulation of buildings

The Noise Insulation Regulations 1975 and the corresponding Scottish Regulations of 1975 (made under s.20 and s.18 respectively of the Land Compensation Act 1973) and Land Compensation (Scotland) Act 1973 provide for the insulation of dwellings and other residential buildings against noise caused, or expected to be caused, by the use of new highways, existing highways to which carriageways are added, and certain other highways which have been altered as regards their location, width, or level.

18 Buildings to which the Regulations apply

The Regulations apply, subject to certain exceptions, to any dwelling or building used for residential purposes which will be not more than 300 metres from the nearest point on the carriageway of the highway, or additional carriageway thereof, or alteration thereof, as the case may be, if, on the basis of estimates made by the authority in accordance with the Regulations, it is found that the noise expected to be occasioned by the future use of the highway will, in the immediate vicinity of the most exposed window of the building, be at a level not less than that specified by the Regulations and will exceed, to the specified extent, the noise level prevailing before the work of construction or alteration was begun. The exceptions include any building first occupied after the date on which a highway of additional carriageway was first open to public traffic or, in the case of an altered highway, the date on which it was first open to public traffic after completion of the alterations.

19 Duties and powers of highway authorities

A highway authority are required to carry out, or (at the option of the building occupier) to make a grant in respect of the cost of carrying out, insulation work to prescribed standards in or to an eligible building only in the case of a new highway or additional carriageway first opened to public use after 16th October 1972. A highway authority have power to carry out such work or pay grant in respect of a highway which has been altered (otherwise than by resurfacing) in respect of its location, width, or level after 16th October 1969.

These powers may be used in order to mitigate noise caused by works of construction or alteration which are seriously affecting, or likely to affect for a substantial period, the enjoyment of any eligible building, even though the building would not qualify under the long-term provisions of the Regulations.

20 Grants

The amount of a grant will be equal to the actual cost incurred by the person to whom it is made in carrying out the work for which the highway authority accept responsibility under the Regulations or the reasonable cost which would have been incurred by the authority in so doing, whichever is the less. The person receiving the grant must complete the relevant work within 12 months from the date of accepting the offer of a grant. Where a building in respect of which an offer has been made is let, the insulation work may be carried out by the landlord or tenant even if the consent of the other party to the tenancy is required and is withheld.

21 Delegation to local authorities

Highway authorities may delegate to local authorities certain of their responsibilities under the Regulations, including those concerning the receipt of claims for grants from private owners and occupiers of buildings.

22 Movable homes

S.20A of the Land Compensation Act 1973 (added by the Planning and Compensation Act 1991) enables regulations to be made providing for payments to be made to persons living in caravans and houseboats which are or are likely to be affected by noise from the construction or use of a new or altered highway. The Highways Noise Payments and Movable Homes (England) Regulations 2000 provide for noise payments not exceeding £1,650 to be made to occupiers of caravans lawfully stationed on a protected site and to the occupiers of lawfully moored houseboats. To qualify for a payment, the caravan or houseboat must be within 300 metres of the highway in question. A payment will only be made if noise exceeds a prescribed level. Similar provisions apply in Wales (see the Highways Noise Payments (Movable Homes) (Wales) Regulations 2001). In England, the authority responsible for the highway works may prepare a map or list identifying the caravans and houseboats which may qualify. Any such list or map must be available for public inspection.

Claims must be made within six years of the end of the "qualifying period" as follows–

(a) In England, if the highway was constructed or altered so as to give rise to increased noise levels after 25th September 1990 but before 22nd November 1997, the qualifying period is the period of three years ending on 23rd November 2000 (so a claim must be made by 22nd November 2006). If the highway was built or altered after 22nd November 1997, the qualifying period is three years from the date it was first opened for traffic after construction or alteration (so a claim must be made within six years of that date). For claims for payments arising out of construction works, the qualifying period ends on the date when the enjoyment of the movable home has been seriously affected by noise caused by the works for six months (so a claim must be made within six years of that date) (Regs 2 and 8).

(b) In Wales, if the highway was constructed or altered so as to give rise to increased noise levels before 1st April 2001, the qualifying period is three years ending on that date (so a claim must be made by 31st March 2007). Where the construction or alteration is after 1st April 2001, the qualifying period ends two years after the road is first opened for traffic after construction or alteration (so a claim must be made within six years of that opening date). For claims for payments arising out of construction works, the qualifying period ends on the date when the enjoyment of the movable home has been seriously affected by noise caused by the works for six months (so a claim must be made within six years of that date) (Regs 3 and 8).

G: NOISE FROM RAILWAYS AND AIRPORTS

23 Noise insulation

The Noise Insulation (Railways and Other Guided Transport Systems) Regulations 1996 (made under s.20 of the Land Compensation Act 1973) provide for the insulation of dwellings and other residential buildings against noise caused, or expected by to caused by new works, additional works or altered works forming part of a railway or tramway system, or other system using a mode of guided transport. The Regulations do not apply to noise coming from ground-borne vibration.

24 Duty and power to carry out works

Where new works are constructed, or an existing system is added to, the authority responsible for the works must provide eligible buildings with insulation, or pay a grant for insulation works to be carried out when or after the relevant date (i.e., the date on which the works were first used after their completion) the movement of vehicles using, or expecting to use, the initial or additional works, causes or is expected to cause the noise level to increase to a prescribed level (Reg. 4). A discretionary power to provide such insulation or to pay a grant is given to the responsible authority where an existing system is altered or where any construction when or after the relevant date (see above) the movement of vehicles using, or expecting to use, the altered works, causes or is expected to cause the noise level to increase to a prescribed level (Reg. 5). The procedures to be used for ascertaining noise levels are described in a technical memorandum entitled *Calculation of Railway Noise 1995*, published by the Stationery Office and calculations will be based on the traffic flows expected under normal operating conditions within a period of 15 years from the date on which the works are first used (Reg. 9).

25 Buildings to which Regulations apply

To be eligible for insulation or grant, a building must be a dwelling or other building used for residential purposes which must be located within 300 metres of the relevant works. The following are *inter alia* not eligible buildings namely, any building subject to a compulsory purchase order or demolition order; a building that was first occupied as a dwelling or for residential purposes after the relevant date (see above); or any part of a building in respect of which a grant has been paid or is payable in respect of carrying out insulation work under any enactment other than the Land Compensation Act 1973 or any statutory instrument made under any such enactment or under the Noise Insulation Regulations 1975 (see F: NOISE FROM HIGHWAYS, above).

26 Grants

The amount of grant will be equal to the actual cost incurred by the claimant in carrying out the work, or the reasonable cost of carrying out the work, whichever is the less. The person receiving the grant must complete the work within 24 months of the date of accepting the offer of a grant (Regs 13 and 15). Where a building is let, the insulation work may be carried out by the landlord or tenant even if the consent of the other party to the tenancy is required and withheld (Reg. 11).

27 Insulation against airport noise and vibration

Under s.79 of the Civil Aviation Act 1982, the Secretary of State may, if it appears to him that buildings near a designated aerodrome require protection from noise and vibration attributable to the use of the aerodrome, make a scheme in relation to such buildings or classes of such buildings as he thinks fit, requiring the person for the time being managing the aerodrome to make grants towards the cost of insulating such buildings or parts of such buildings against noise.

Heathrow and Gatwick Airport were both designated for these purposes but the time limits for applications for grants have now passed.

H: EUROPEAN NOISE REQUIREMENTS

28 Lawnmowers and other outdoor equipment

The Noise Emission in the Environment by Equipment for use Outdoors Regulations 2001 provide for the permissible sound power level requirements of certain lawnmowers and lawn trimmers (as defined). Lawnmowers, for the purpose of the Regulations, are defined to mean any motorised equipment appropriate for the upkeep by cutting, by whatever method, of areas of grass used for recreational, decorative, or similar purposes, but excluding agricultural and forestry equipment. In particular, the Regulations prohibit, on or after 3rd July 2001, the placing on the market of any such lawnmower unless it conforms to the noise emission requirements set out in the Regulations.

The Regulations also apply to other machinery used outside (such as chainsaws) but do not apply to vehicles primarily used for carrying people.

29 Household appliances

The Household Appliances (Noise Emission) Regulations 1990, as amended (S.I. 1990 No. 161 and 1994 No. 1386) make provision regarding the information about noise emissions that must be contained in labels accompanying household appliances. Household appliances are defined in Regulation 2 and include any such appliance consisting of any machine, part of a machine, or installation manufactured principally for use in dwellings and, in particular, household appliances for upkeep, cleaning purposes, preparation and storage of foodstuffs, production and distribution of heat and cold and air conditioning.

No manufacturer or importer must market (i.e., supply by way of sale, lease, hire, or hire-purchase whether as principal or agent for another) any such appliance manufactured or imported by him in respect of which the requirements of Regulation 4 or of the EC Directive 86/594/EEC as implemented in the law of a member State other than the United Kingdom are not satisfied.

Regulation 4(1) provides that where a manufacturer or an importer of a household appliance, manufactured or imported by him on or after 28th February 1990, takes any steps to inform any person to whom the appliance is to be, or may be, marketed of the level of airborne noise emitted by the appliance, the level must be determined in accordance with Article 6(1) of the above-mentioned Directive which is set out in the Schedule to the Regulations.

The principal requirement of Article 6(1) is that the general test method used to determine the airborne noise emitted by household appliances must be accurate enough for the measurement uncertainties to produce standard deviations not exceeding 2 dB in the case of A-weighted sound power levels.

Regulation 4(1) is taken to have been satisfied if measurements for determining the level of airborne noise have been carried out in accordance with the relevant national standard.

Regulation 4(2) and (3) requires that the level of airborne noise emission be stated in a manner which is readily understandable by any person to whom it is to be, or may be, marketed and that where a label containing technical information other than in respect of the level of airborne noise emitted by the appliance is attached to the appliance, the level of airborne noise must be stated on that label.

It is a duty of weights and measures authorities to enforce the above Regulations (Reg. 6).

30 Noise mapping

Directive 2002/49/EC aims to define a common Europe-wide approach intended to avoid, prevent or reduce on a prioritised basis the harmful effects, including annoyance, due to exposure to environmental noise.

The Directive provides for data about environmental noise levels to be collected and to that end provides for "strategic noise mapping" in order to capture data on noise levels. Once data has been collected, action plans should address priorities in those areas most in need with a view to preventing and reducing environmental noise where necessary and particularly where exposure levels can induce harmful effects on human health and to preserve environmental noise quality where it is good.

The Directive applies to environmental noise to which humans are exposed in particular in built-up areas, in public parks or other quiet areas, in quiet areas in open country, near schools, hospitals and other noise-sensitive buildings and areas. It does not apply to noise that is caused by the exposed person himself, noise from domestic activities, noise created by neighbours, noise at work places or noise inside means of transport or due to military activities in military areas. "Environmental noise" means unwanted or harmful outdoor sound created by human activities, including noise emitted by means of transport, road traffic, rail traffic, air traffic, and from sites of industrial activity.

The "mapping" was undertaken during 2007 and noise action plans designed to manage noise issues and effects, including noise reduction in those areas have subsequently been prepared and adopted. Plans of noise sources have been prepared with such plans also aiming to protect quiet areas against an increase in noise. These areas must be identified in published form, kept under review, and revised if necessary.

The Directive is implemented in the UK by the Environmental Noise (England) Regulations 2006 (S.I. No. 2238 as amended by S.I. 2008 No. 375 and 2009 No. 1610); (Wales) (S.I. 2006 No. 2629 as amended by S.I. 2009 No. 47); and Scotland (S.S.I. 2006 No. 465).

31 Authorities

Statutes–
Civil Aviation Act 1982

Clean Neighbourhoods and Environment Act 2005

Control of Pollution Act 1974

Environment Act 1995

Environmental Protection Act 1990

European Communities Act 1972

Land Compensation Act 1973

Land Compensation (Scotland) Act 1973

Local Government, Planning and Land Act 1980

Noise Act 1996

Noise and Statutory Nuisance Act 1993

Statutory Instruments–
Highways Noise Payments and Movable Homes (England) Regulations 2000, as amended (S.I. 2000 Nos. 2887 and 3086, and 2001 No. 1803)

Highways Noise Payments (Movable Homes) (Wales) Regulations 2001 (S.I. 2001 No. 604)

Noise Emission in the Environment by Equipment for use Outdoors Regulations 2001, as amended (S.I. 2001 Nos. 1701 and 3958, 2005 No. 3525, 2007 No. 3224, 2009 No. 2748, and 2015 No. 98)

Noise Insulation (Railways and Other Guided Transport Systems) Regulations 1996 (S.I. 1996 No. 428)

Noise Insulation Regulations 1975, as amended (S.I. 1975 No. 1763 and 1988 No. 2000)

Noise Insulation (Scotland) Regulations 1975 (S.I. 1975 No. 460)

Statutory Nuisance (Appeals) Regulations 1995, as amended (S.I. 1995 No. 2644 and 2006 No. 771)

Statutory Nuisance (Appeals) (Scotland) Regulations 1996 (S.I. 1996 No. 1076)

FLOOD RISK MANAGEMENT: ENGLAND AND WALES

1 Introduction

The Flood Risk Regulations 2009 transpose Directive 2007/60/EC of the European Parliament and of the Council on the assessment and management of flood risks for England and Wales. The purpose of the Directive is to establish a framework for the assessment and management of flood risks, aiming at the reduction of adverse consequences for human health, the environment, cultural heritage and economic activity associated with floods in the community.

For the purposes of the Regulations it does not matter whether a flood has been caused by heavy rainfall, a river overflowing or its banks being breached, a dam overflowing or being breached, tidal waters or any other event (or combination of events). However, a flood does not include (Reg. 2)–

(a) a flood from a sewerage system unless wholly or partly caused by an increase in the volume of rainwater (including snow or other precipitation) entering or otherwise affecting the system; or

(b) a flood caused by a burst water main.

The Flood and Water Management Act 2010 defines a flood in similar terms (s.1).

2 Preliminary flood risk assessments

The Environment Agency is under a duty to prepare in relation to each river basin district a preliminary assessment map and report in relation to flooding from the sea, main rivers, and reservoirs (Flood Risk Regulations 2009, Reg. 9). Lead local flood authorities (i.e. the unitary authority for the area or the county council if there is no unitary authority) are also under a duty to prepare a preliminary assessment report in relation to flooding (Reg. 10) i.e., a report about past floods and the possible harmful consequences of future floods (Reg. 12(1)), and a preliminary assessment map i.e., a map showing the borders of river basins and sub-basins, any areas of coastline, topography, and the purposes for which the land in the area is used (Reg. 11(1)). Following these assessments, both the Environment Agency and lead local flood authorities are under a duty to identify areas at significant risk of flooding ("flood risk areas") (Regs 13, 14). The Environment Agency must publish such maps and reports prepared by the Agency and the lead local flood authorities for each river basin district (Reg. 15). The assessments and decisions concerning flood risk areas must be reviewed at least every six years (Regs 16, 17).

3 Flood hazard maps and flood risk maps

Part 3 of the Flood Risk Regulations 2009 imposes a duty on the Environment Agency and lead local flood authorities to prepare flood risk maps and flood hazard maps in relation to flood risk areas (as to which see **2 Preliminary flood risk assessments**, above). A flood hazard map is one which shows the likely extent of possible floods, the likely direction and speed of flow of such a flood, and whether the probability of a flood occurring is low, medium or high (Reg. 20). A flood risk map is one which shows, *inter alia*, the number of people living in the area who are likely to be affected in the event of flooding and the likely effect on human health, economic activity and the environment (including cultural heritage) (Reg. 21). The Agency must publish such maps (Reg. 22) and it and the lead local flood authorities must review them at least every six years (Regs 23, 24).

4 Flood risk management plans

The Environment Agency and lead local flood authorities are under a duty to prepare flood risk management plans in relation to each identified flood risk area (as to which see **2 Preliminary flood risk assessments**, above) (Regs 25, 26). A flood risk management plan must include details of (Reg. 27(2))–

(a) objectives for the purpose of managing the flood risk; and

(b) the proposed measures for achieving those objectives.

In setting objectives the plan must have regard to reducing the adverse consequences of flooding for human health, economic activity or the environment (including cultural heritage) (Reg. 27(3)). The measures must, in particular, include measures relating to (Reg. 27(4))–

(a) the prevention of flooding;

(b) the protection of individuals, communities and the environment against the consequences of flooding; and

(c) arrangements for forecasting and warning.

The Agency must publish the flood risk management plans prepared by it and lead local flood authorities (Reg. 28) and both the Agency and those authorities must review such plans at least every six years (Regs 29, 30).

The Flood and Water Management Act 2010 provides for the Environment Agency (for England) and the Welsh Ministers to develop a national flood and coastal erosion risk management strategy which must include an assessment of flood and coastal erosion risk (s.7). Local authorities must develop, maintain (which includes updating and reviewing), apply, and monitor the application of, a strategy for local flood risk in their area (ss.9 and 10).

5 Designation of features

The Environment Agency, local authorities and internal drainage boards may by notice to the owner designate "features" which affect flood or coastal erosion risk but which are not maintained or operated by them (Flood and Water Management Act 2010, s.30). A "feature" is defined as a structure, or a natural or man-made feature of the environment which could e.g., include walls, channels, culverts, sluices, raised ground and embankments (Sch. 1, para 4). Once designated by them, the body which carried out the designation becomes the "responsible authority" for that feature.

The responsible authority must monitor and enforce the designation and must consent to any alteration, removal or replacement of a feature. Consequently, a person should not alter, remove, or replace a designated structure or feature without the permission of the responsible authority. It is not an offence to carry out work without consent, but it is an offence not to comply with a subsequent enforcement notice (Sch. 1, paras 5, 6). If a person carries out works to alter, remove or replace a designated feature without obtaining consent, and the responsible authority considers that this increases an immediate and serious flood or coastal erosion risk that warrants emergency action, it may take such remedial action without the need to first serve an enforcement notice (para 12).

An authority has a power of entry onto land in order to (para 13)–
(a) establish whether a person has altered, removed or replaced a designated feature without consent;
(b) determine whether a person has complied with an enforcement notice;
(c) take the steps set out in an enforcement notice if the person on which it was served has not taken them; or
(d) to act in an emergency.

The authority must give at least 7 days notice to the occupier of the land and state the reason for entry, unless an emergency necessitates earlier intervention. An authority must pay compensation to a person in respect of damage to their land resulting from the exercise of the powers of entry, however no compensation is payable to a person who has altered, removed or replaced the feature without consent, or who has failed to comply with an enforcement notice, unless the authority has exercised its powers unreasonably in which case compensation will be paid in respect of any damage suffered as a result of the unreasonable use of powers irrespective of whether a notice has been contravened. This is in addition to any civil remedies that are available to someone who has suffered damage (para 14).

An owner of a designated feature may appeal against a designation notice; a decision in connection with a consent to alter, remove or replace a designated feature, refusal to cancel a designation; or receipt of an enforcement notice (para 15). The Designation of Features (Appeals) (England) Regulations 2012, and (Wales) Regulations 2012, confer jurisdiction on the First-tier Tribunal to consider such appeals and make provision for procedure and the powers of the First-tier Tribunal in determining appeals.

6 Deliberate flooding, etc

The Environment Agency and local authorities may carry out works that will or may cause flooding, coastal erosion, or an increase in water below ground if (Flood and Water Management Act 2010, ss.38, 39)–
(a) the work is in the interests of nature conservation, preservation of cultural heritage, or people's enjoyment of the environment or cultural heritage;
(b) consultation on the proposed works has been undertaken; and
(c) the benefits of the work will outweigh the harmful consequences.

The Incidental Flooding and Coastal Erosion (England) Order 2011 and (Wales) Order 2011 give the Environment Agency and local authorities powers of entry and compulsory purchase for these purposes and makes provision for payment of compensation.

7 Authorities

Statutes–
Flood and Water Management Act 2010

Statutory Instruments–
Designation of Features (Appeals) (England) Regulations 2012 (S.I. 2012 No. 1945)

Designation of Features (Appeals) (Wales) Regulations 2012 (S.I. 2012 No. 1819)

Flood Risk Regulations 2009, as amended (S.I. 2009, No. 3042, 2010 No. 1102, and 2011 No. 2880)

Incidental Flooding and Coastal Erosion (England) Order 2011 (S.I. 2011 No. 2855)

Incidental Flooding and Coastal Erosion (Wales) Order 2011 (S.I. 2011 No. 2829)

EC Legislation–
Flood Risk Directive, EC Council Directive 2007/60/EC

FLOOD RISK MANAGEMENT: SCOTLAND

1 Introduction

The Flood Risk Management (Scotland) Act 2009, makes provision concerning the assessment and management of flood risks, including provision for implementing European Parliament and Council Directive 2007/60/EC. The Scottish Ministers, the Scottish Environment Protection Agency (SEPA) and responsible authorities must exercise their flood risk related functions with a view to reducing overall flood risk and, in particular, to secure compliance with the Directive. "Responsible authorities" are local authorities, Scottish Water, the Forestry Commissioners, and the Cairngorms and Loch Lomond and The Trossachs National Park Authorities (s.5 and the Flood Risk Management (Designated Responsible Authorities) (Scotland) Order 2013).

The definition of "flood" specifically excludes a flood solely from a sewerage system but otherwise means the temporary covering by water from any source of land not normally covered by water. "Flood risk" means the combination of the probability of a flood and of the potential adverse consequences associated with a flood for human health, the environment, cultural heritage and economic activity (s.3).

2 Flood risk assessments

SEPA is under a duty to prepare a flood risk assessment for each flood risk management district providing an assessment of any flood risk for that district (Flood Risk Management (Scotland) Act 2009, s.9). A flood risk management district means (s.8)–

 (a) an area designated as a river basin district; or
 (b) such other area as the Scottish Ministers may designate by order, being such area as they consider appropriate and to which they assign one or more coastal areas or river basins.

An assessment must include, *inter alia*, an assessment of the potential adverse consequences of any future flood for human health, the environment, cultural heritage and economic activity in that district. It must also include maps of the flood risk management district and descriptions of previous flooding which has had significant adverse consequences or where such consequences may be envisaged (s.9). Every assessment must be reviewed at intervals of not less than six years (s.10). SEPA must make copies of the assessment available for public inspection (s.12).

SEPA is under a duty to identify potentially vulnerable areas for each flood risk management district for which it considers that significant flood risk exists or is likely to occur. It must prepare and submit to the Scottish Ministers a document identifying such risks (s.13). SEPA must also make available warnings where it considers that a flood is occurring, or is likely to occur in the near future (s.74).

Scottish Water is under a duty to assess flood risk for each potentially vulnerable area from sewerage systems. An assessment must identify where in the area it considers that a flood is likely to originate from a sewerage system and estimate the volume of sewerage which is likely to be released in the event of such a flood (s.16).

Local authorities must prepare a maps or maps which shows bodies of water and sustainable urban drainage systems in its area. Such map or maps must be made available for public inspection. Every local authority must assess these bodies of water to ascertain whether the condition of such bodies gives rise to a risk of flooding. A schedule of clearance and repair works must be prepared if an authority considers that those works would substantially reduce that risk. The schedule must be made available for public inspection (ss.17, 18).

SEPA must also assess whether alteration, enhancement or restoration of the natural features and characteristics of any river basin or coastal area in a flood risk management district could contribute to the management of flood risk for the district (s.20).

3 Flood hazard maps and flood risk maps

SEPA is under as duty to prepare flood hazard maps and flood risk maps for potentially vulnerable areas in each flood risk management district (as to which see **2 Flood risk assessments**, above). Flood hazard maps must show areas which could be flooded. The types of flood shown will have either a low, medium or high probability. Other information included will be the flood extent and water depths or water level (Flood Risk Management (Scotland) Act 2009, s.22). Flood risk maps must show the potential adverse consequences associated with each type of flood for which any information is shown in a flood hazard map. Such consequences include the number of inhabitants potentially affected, the type of economic activity which could be flooded and the protected areas or bodies of water potentially affected (s.23). Both flood hazard and flood risk maps must be reviewed at least every six years and copies of such maps must be made available for public inspection (ss.24, 25).

4 Flood risk management plans

A flood risk management plan must be prepared and submitted to the Scottish Ministers by SEPA for the potentially vulnerable areas in each flood management district (as to which see **2 Flood risk assessments**, above). A flood risk management plan must (Flood Risk Management (Scotland) Act 2009, s.27)–

 (a) set objectives for the management of flood risks for the potentially vulnerable areas; and

(b) identify measures to achieve those objectives in a way which it considers sustainable.

In setting objectives and identifying measures account must be taken of such matters as the impact of climate change on the occurrence of floods, flood risk assessments that have been prepared, and the benefits (including environmental, social and economic benefits) that are likely to be derived from implementing proposed measures (s.28).

The lead local authority for each local plan district must prepare a local flood risk management plan to supplement the relevant flood risk management plan. The local plan will consist of a supplementary and an implementation part. The supplementary part will include a summary of the objectives and measures contained in the relevant flood risk management plan. A draft of the supplementary part must be published and made available for public inspection. Any representations made must be taken into account before the plan is finalised. Once finalised, the local flood risk management plan must be published and copies of it made available for public inspection (ss.34 to 36). An interim report on the plan must be made between two and three years after it is finalised and a final report between five and six years afterwards. Such reports must contain an assessment of the progress made towards implementing the measures and copies of the reports must be made available for public inspection (ss.37, 38).

5 Local authority powers

Subject only to any express statutory prohibition, a local authority may do anything which it considers will contribute to the implementation of current measures described in any local flood risk management plan. It may also do anything it considers necessary to reduce an imminent risk of flooding which would be likely to have serious adverse consequences, or which it considers will otherwise manage flood risk in its area without affecting the implementation of the area's local flood risk management plan (Flood Risk Management (Scotland) Act 2009, s.56).

A local authority may make a flood protection scheme for the management of flood risk within its area (s.60). In making such a scheme, an authority must consider whether it is likely to have a significant effect on the environment and prepare an environmental statement where necessary (Flood Risk Management (Flood Protection Schemes, Vulnerable Areas and Local Plan Districts) (Scotland) Regulations 2010). An authority must keep a register of flood protection schemes (s.62). Once a flood protection scheme is confirmed, the Scottish Ministers must direct that any planning permission necessary for the scheme is deemed to be granted, subject to any planning conditions which they may specify.

6 Authorities

Statutes–
Flood Risk Management (Scotland) Act 2009

Statutory Instruments–
Flood Risk Management (Designated Responsible Authorities) (Scotland) Order 2013 (S.S.I. 2013 No. 314)

Flood Risk Management (Flood Protection Schemes, Vulnerable Areas and Local Plan Districts) (Scotland) Regulations 2010 (S.S.I. 2010 No. 426)

EC Legislation–
Flood Risk Directive, EC Council Directive 2007/60/EC

LITTER AND WASTE: ENGLAND AND WALES

1 Contents
This Note covers the main pieces of legislation relating to litter and waste on land

Reference should also be made to the Note on **Anti-Social Behaviour in England and Wales** which deals with nuisances which negatively affect a community's quality of life, such as litter, noise and graffiti.

2 Offences of leaving litter
It is an offence for a person to throw down, drop or otherwise deposit any litter and leaves it in any place which is open to the air and to which the public have access. It is immaterial whether the litter is left on land or in water. No offence is committed where the depositing of the litter is either authorised by law or done by or with the consent of the owner, occupier or other person having control of the place the litter is left. Only the owner, occupier or other person having control of the land can give consent. A person who is guilty of this offence is liable on summary conviction to a fine not exceeding level 4 on the standard scale (Environmental Protection Act 1990, s.87, amended by the Clean Neighbourhoods and Environment Act 2005, s.1.

In general, relevant land is land under the control of an authority or body mentioned above which is open to the air and is land to which the public are entitled or permitted to have access with or without payment (s.86).

3 Fixed penalty notices for litter
A fixed penalty notice may be given by an authorised officer of a litter authority to a person who he has reason to believe has committed an offence under s.87 (Environmental Protection Act 1990, s.88, amended). For this purpose, a litter authority is–
- (a) any principal litter authority, other than a county council, a regional council, or a joint board;
- (b) any county council, regional council or joint board designated by order by the Secretary of State in relation to such an area as is specified in the order (not being an area in a National Park);
- (c) any National Park Committee;
- (d) any Park board for any area in a National Park; and
- (e) the Broads Authority.

Where a person is given a notice under s.88 in respect of an offence, no proceedings will be begun before the end of 14 days following the date of the notice and a person will not be convicted of an offence if he pays the fixed penalty before the end of that period. The fixed penalty is payable to the litter authority whose officer gave the notice.

If an authorised officer of a litter authority plans to give a person a notice he may require the person to give him his name and address. A person commits an offence if he fails to do so or gives a false or inaccurate name or address. A person guilty of this offence is liable on summary conviction to a fine not exceeding level 3 on the standard scale.

4 Amount of fixed penalty for litter
The amount of a fixed penalty for litter that can be specified by a local authority must be between £50 and £80 (in Wales, between £75 and £150). If the litter authority has not specified an amount, the fixed penalty is £75 (Environmental Offences (Fixed Penalties) (Miscellaneous Provisions) Regulations 2007, (Wales) Regulations 2008, and the Environmental Protection Act 1990, s.88(6A)(b)).

The local authority may also specify that a lower amount will be accepted as full payment if it is paid within less than 14 days. The lower amount cannot be less than £50.

5 Duty to keep land and highways clear of litter
S.89(1) of the Environmental Protection Act 1990 places a duty on various bodies to ensure that "relevant" land in their area is kept, so far as practicable, clear of litter and refuse. The Secretary of State has issued a code of practice under s.89(7) which gives guidance as to the bodies responsible and the land which is "relevant" to each of them, as follows–

Principal litter authorities.–land, other than highway land, which is open to the air on at least one side, is under the direct control of the authority, and to which the public are entitled to have access;

Crown authorities.–their land which is open to the air and to which the public have access;

Designated statutory undertakers.–land under their direct control to which the public are permitted or are entitled to have access. The Litter (Statutory Undertakers) (Designation and Relevant Land) Order 1991 and Railways Act 1993 (Consequential Modifications) Order 1999 (S.I. No. 1443) designate certain transport related undertakings for this purpose, including those authorised to operate railways, and passenger transport executives. In relation to railways, "relevant" land includes land to which the public have no right of access (e.g., the track side);

Educational institutions.–land in the open air which is under the direct control of a body designated by the Litter (Designated Educational Institutions) Order 1991, including universities, publicly funded colleges of further and higher education, and maintained schools;

Highways.–London Borough and English District Councils, and Welsh county and county borough councils, have responsibility for highways maintainable at the public expense (other than a trunk road which is a special road). The Secretary of State has responsibility for trunk roads which are special roads and for certain other highways where the duty has been transferred to him from the local authority.

The Code of Practice also gives practical guidance as to the generally acceptable standards of cleanliness and target response times for dealing with litter.

6 Summary proceedings by persons aggrieved by litter

Any member of the public aggrieved by a breach of the duty imposed by s.89 (duty to keep land and highways clear of litter) may complain to a magistrates' court (Environmental Protection Act 1990, s.91). The court may, if the complaint is justified, make a *litter abatement order* requiring the defendant to clear the litter away or as the case may be clear the highway, within a time specified in the order. A code of practice under s.89(7) or a direction under s.89(6A) (see **5 Duty to keep land and highways clear of litter**, above), is admissible in evidence in any proceedings under s.91 (s.91(11)).

7 Community protection notices

Community protection notice are intended to deal with unreasonable, ongoing problems or nuisances which negatively affect a community's quality of life, such as litter, noise or graffiti. For these provisions, see the Note on **Anti-Social Behaviour in England and Wales** from para 19 **Community protection notices–introduction**.

8 Free distribution of printed matter

A person commits an offence if he distributes any free printed matter on "designated land" without the consent of a principal litter authority if he knows that the land has been so designated. Land may only be designated if the authority is satisfied that it is being defaced by the discarding of free printed matter which has been distributed there.

Fixed penalty notices may be issued in relation to this offence (Environmental Protection Act 1990, s.94B, Sch. 3A, inserted by the Clean Neighbourhoods and Environment Act 2005, s.23). The Secretary of State and Welsh Assembly may make regulations setting a maximum or minimum range within which the fixed penalty amount can be set (Sch. 3A, para 7). The range for England is £50 to £80, and for Wales £75 to £150. If the litter authority has not specified an amount, the fixed penalty is £75. The local authority may also specify that a lower amount will be accepted as full payment if it is paid within less than 14 days. The lower amount cannot be less than £50 (Environmental Offences (Fixed Penalties) (Miscellaneous Provisions) Regulations 2007, Reg. 2; (Wales) Regulations 2008, Reg. 3).

9 Abandoned shopping and luggage trolleys

A local authority may by resolution, apply to their area the scheme relating to abandoned shopping and luggage trolleys set out in Sch.4 to the 1990 Act (amended for England and Wales by the Clean Neighbourhoods and Environment Act 2005, ss.99 and 100) (Environmental Protection Act 1990, s.99). *Inter alia* the scheme gives an authority in England and Wales power to seize such trolleys and charge anyone believed to be their owner for removal, storage and disposal, whether or not they come forward to claim their return.

10 Application of Part IV to any description of animal droppings

The Secretary of State may, by order, apply the provisions of Part IV which apply to refuse to any description of animal droppings in all or in any prescribed circumstances subject to such modifications as appear to him to be necessary (Environmental Protection Act 1990, s.86(14)). By virtue of this provision the Litter (Animal Droppings) Order 1991 applies Part IV to dog faeces on the following descriptions of land which is not heath or woodland or used for the grazing of animals–

(a) any public walk or pleasure ground;

(b) any land, whether enclosed or not, on which there are no buildings or of which no more than 1/20th part is covered with buildings, and the whole or the remainder of which is laid out as a garden or is used for the purpose of recreation;

(c) any part of the seashore which is frequently used by large numbers of people and managed by the person having direct control of it as a tourist resort;

(d) any esplanade or promenade which is above the place to which the tide flows at mean high water springs;

(e) any land not forming part of the highway which is open to the air, which the public are permitted to use on foot only, and which provides access to retail premises;

(f) a trunk road picnic area;

(g) a picnic site; and

(h) land (whether above or below ground and whether or not consisting of or including buildings) forming or used in connection with off-street parking places.

11 Provision and maintenance of litter bins

The Litter Act 1983 gives local authorities in Great Britain power to provide and maintain receptacles for refuse or litter and imposes a duty on them to empty and clean bins so provided. (ss.5 and 7).

12 Interference with refuse tips and dustbins

It is an offence under s.60(1) of the Environmental Protection Act 1990 to sort over or disturb anything deposited at a place for the disposal of waste, or in a receptacle for waste, provided by a waste disposal contractor under arrangements made with a waste disposal authority.

13 Civic amenity sites

Under the Refuse Disposal (Amenity) Act 1978, unauthorised dumping is an offence (s.2). The 1978 Act also provides for the removal and disposal of abandoned vehicles.

The duty to provide civic amenity sites lies with waste disposal authorities (Environmental Protection Act 1990, s.51(1)(b)). Local authorities can require proof of residence, and charge or turn away those who cannot do so to prevent their sites being used by non-residents.

Note.–A "best value" local authority has the power to charge a person for providing a service to him if the authority is authorised, but not required, to provide that service and the person has agreed to its being provided (Local Government Act 2003, s.93); and the Localism Act 2011, s.1 gives a local authority a general power to act, which could also be used to charge for discretionary services. However, a charge may not be made to residents in England to visit a household waste recycling centre or to deposit household waste or recycling at such a centre, unless a charge was being made before 6th April 2015 (and such charges must be removed by 1st April 2020) (Local Government (Prohibition of Charges at Household Waste Recycling Centres) (England) Order 2015; Local Authorities (Prohibition of Charging Residents to Deposit Household Waste) Order 2015).

14 Accumulations of rubbish

Under s.34 of the Public Health Act 1961, as amended by s.26 of the Civic Amenities Act 1967, authorities are given power to remove accumulations of rubbish on any land in the open air in their area.

15 Waste electrical and electronic equipment

Special provisions apply to waste electrical and electronic equipment (WEEE). These provisions, contained in the Waste Electrical and Electronic Equipment Regulations 2013, aim to reduce waste from electrical and electronic equipment (EEE) encourage the separate collection of WEEE and its treatment, reuse, recovery, recycling and sound environmental disposal; make producers of EEE responsible for the environmental impact of their products; and improve the environmental performance of all those involved during the lifecycle of EEE.

The types of EEE covered by the Regulations until 31st December 2018 are (Schs 1 and 2)–

1. Large household appliances (e.g., fridges, freezers, cookers, microwave ovens, dishwashers, radiators, fans, etc);
2. Small household appliances (e.g., vacuum cleaners, toasters, clocks, irons, etc);
3. IT and telecommunications equipment (e.g., computers, printers, laptops, calculators, telephones, etc);
4. Consumer equipment (e.g., radios, televisions, hi-fis, video-cameras, etc);
5. Lighting equipment (e.g., sodium or fluorescent lamps, etc);
6. Electrical and electronic tools (with the exception of large-scale stationary industrial tools) (e.g., drills, saws, sewing machines, lawnmowers, etc);
7. Toys, leisure and sports equipment (e.g., electric trains, video games and consoles, etc);
8. Medical devices (with the exception of all implanted and infected products);
9. Monitoring and control instruments (e.g., smoke detectors, heating regulators, etc); and
10. Automatic dispensers (e.g., for hot drinks, money, etc).

From 1st January 2019 the categories change and will be (Schs 3 and 4)–

1. Temperature exchange equipment;
2. Screens, monitors and equipment containing screens having a surface area greater than 100cm^2.
3. Lamps;
4. Large equipment (any external dimension greater than 50cm) including but not limited to household appliances; IT and telecommunication equipment; consumer equipment; luminaires; equipment

reproducing sound or images, musical equipment; electrical and electronic tools; toys, leisure and sports equipment; medical devices; monitoring and control instruments; automatic dispensers equipment for generation of electric currents, but excluding any equipment included in categories 1 to 3;

5. Small equipment (no external dimension greater than 50cm) including but not limited to the items listed under 4. above excluding IT and telecommunication equipment; and

6. Small IT and telecommunication equipment (no external dimension greater than 50cm).

All goods covered by the Regulations must be marked with a crossed out wheeled bin symbol (Reg. 22) and a date mark (Reg. 23). A producer must also provide information on reuse and environmentally sound treatment for each new type of EEE that they put on the market (Reg. 24).

Producers of EEE are responsible for collecting, treating, recovering and disposing of an amount of WEEE equivalent to the amount of EEE that they produce. Such producers must join a producer compliance scheme who will arrange for the collection, treatment and recycling of WEEE. Responsibility for "historic" EEE (i.e., which was put on the market before 13th August 2005) is divided between current producers according to their market share.

Retailers who sell EEE to the public must ensure that their customers can return their WEEE free of charge. This will be on a one-for-one basis, as long as the new equipment is of similar type and has the same function as the old equipment (Reg. 42). Retailers can set up alternative collection systems as long as they are still convenient for customers. Retailers in turn return the WEEE, free of charge, to the producer compliance scheme.

A producer or distributor must not show a purchaser at the time of sale of new EEE the costs of financing the collection, treatment and environmentally sound disposal of WEEE from private households (Reg. 51).

16 Carrier bags

Regulations may be made requiring sellers of goods to charge for single-use carrier bags (whether plastic or paper) (Climate Change Act 2008, s.77, Sch. 6). The charge may be required both for bags supplied at the place where goods are sold, or for the purpose of delivering goods.

The regulations will define the meaning of "single use carrier bag" and may also set a minimum charge.

In Wales, the Single Use Carrier Bags Charge (Wales) Regulations 2010 provide that a charge of 5p must be made from 1st October 2011 for every single use carrier bag supplied new–

(a) at the place in Wales where the goods are sold, for the purpose of enabling the goods to be taken away;

(b) for the purpose of enabling the goods to be delivered to persons in Wales.

There are a number of exceptions to the charge, including bags used solely to contain unpackaged food, goods contaminated by soil, or packaged but uncooked fish, meat or poultry (or a combination of those items) in small bags; bags used to contain purchases made on board ships, trains, aircraft, coaches or buses; mail order dispatch or courier bags; paper bags of specified dimensions provided they do not have handles; and bags containing items supplied on a medical prescription.

In England, the Single Use Carrier Bags Charges (England) Order 2015 provides that from 5th October 2015 large shops ("sellers") must make a minimum charge of 5p (including any VAT) for each single use carrier bag supplied at the place in England where the goods are sold for the purpose of enabling the goods to be taken away *or* for the purpose of enabling the goods to be delivered to persons in England (Art. 3). A "seller" means a person who sells goods and employs 250 or more employees. For these purposes, the number of employees of a person is taken to be the number of that person's full-time equivalent employees (2015 Order, Sch. 1). A single use carrier bag means an unused bag made of lightweight plastic material with handles, other than an excluded bag. The following are excluded bags (Sch. 2)–

(a) unwrapped food bags;

(b) unwrapped loose seeds bags;

(c) unwrapped blades bags;

(d) prescription-only medicine bags;

(e) uncooked meat food bags;

(f) live aquatic creatures bags;

(g) returnable multiple reuse bags;

(h) woven plastic bags;

(i) transit goods bags.

Sellers are required to keep records and supply copies to the Secretary of State and to members of the public who ask for them (Sch. 3). Local authorities in England are responsible for enforcing the Order (Art. 5).

Note.–a bag does not need to be made of plastic in order to come within the definition of a "single use" carrier bag and so attract a charge.

17 Batteries

From 1st February 2010, a distributor of portable batteries (e.g., a retailer) must, at any place it supplies such batteries to end-users (Waste Batteries and Accumulators Regulations 2009, Reg. 31)–

(a) take back waste batteries at no charge; and

(b) inform end-users about the possibility of such take back at their sales points.

A producer of batteries must be a member of a "battery compliance scheme" i.e., a scheme which finances the collection, treatment and recycling of batteries. Such schemes will collect waste batteries from the distributors for appropriate disposal. No charge may be made for collection of waste batteries.

There are similar provisions, from May 2009, for no-charge take back of waste industrial batteries and car batteries. In the case of car batteries, the producer must collect waste batteries free of charge and within a reasonable time from the "final holder", that is the business, scrap metal dealer etc who has removed the battery from the car. Since January 2010, it has been illegal to dispose of waste industrial or car batteries in a landfill or by incineration.

18 Authorities

Statutes–

Civic Amenities Act 1967

Clean Neighbourhoods and Environment Act 2005

Climate Change Act 2008

Environment Act 1995

Environmental Protection Act 1990

Litter Act 1983

Pollution Prevention and Control Act 1999

Public Health Act 1961

Refuse Disposal (Amenity) Act 1978

Statutory Instruments–

Environmental Offences (Fixed Penalties) (Miscellaneous Provisions) Regulations 2007, as amended (S.I. 2007 No. 175 and 2012 No. 1151)

Environmental Offences (Fixed Penalties) (Miscellaneous Provisions) (Wales) Regulations 2008 (S.I. 2008 No. 663)

Litter (Animal Droppings) Order 1991 (S.I. 1991 No. 961)

Litter (Designated Educational Institutions) Order 1991 (S.I. 1991 No. 561)

Litter (Statutory Undertakers) (Designation and Relevant Land) Order 1991, as amended (S.I. 1991 No. 1043 and 1992 No. 406)

Local Authorities (Prohibition of Charging Residents to Deposit Household Waste) Order 2015 (S.I. 2015 No. 973)

Local Government (Prohibition of Charges at Household Waste Recycling Centres) (England) Order 2015 (S.I. 2015 No. 619)

Single Use Carrier Bags Charge (Wales) Regulations 2010, as amended (S.I. 2010 No. 2880, 2011 No. 2184, 2012 No. 1916, and 2013 No. 898)

Single Use Carrier Bags Charges (England) Order 2015 (S.I. 2015 No. 776)

Street Litter Control Notices Order 1991, as amended (S.I. 1991 No. 1324, and 1997 No. 632)

Waste Batteries and Accumulators Regulations 2009, as amended (S.I. 2009 No. 890, 2011 No. 988, S.S.I. 2011 No. 226, S.I. 2013 No. 3134, and 2015 Nos. 1360 and 1935)

Waste Electrical and Electronic Equipment Regulations 2013, as amended (S.I. 2013 No. 3113 and S.I. 2014 No. 1771)

LITTER AND WASTE: SCOTLAND

1 Contents

This Note covers the main pieces of legislation relating to litter and waste on
Reference should also be made to the Note on **Anti-Social Behaviour in Scotland** which deals with nuisances which negatively affect a community's quality of life, such as fly tipping and graffiti.

2 Offences of leaving litter

It is an offence for a person to throw down, drop or otherwise deposit in, into, or from any public open place (including buildings with at least one open side), or leave, anything which causes, or contributes to, or tends to lead to the defacement by litter of any public open place. There is an exception if the depositing and leaving of the litter was authorised by law or done with the consent of the owner, occupier, or other person or authority having control of the place in or into which that thing was deposited (Environmental Protection Act 1990, s.87).

S.87 also applies to certain specified places in so far as they are not public open places, namely—
  (i) any relevant road (see below), and any trunk road which is a special road;
  (ii) any place on relevant Crown land;
  (iii) any place on relevant land (see below)—
      (a) of a principal litter authority;
      (b) of any designated statutory undertaker;
      (c) of any designated educational institution; and
      (d) within a litter control area of a local authority.

Every public road other than a trunk road which is a special road, is a relevant road (s.86(9), (10)).

In general, relevant land is land under the control of an authority or body mentioned above which is open to the air and is land to which the public are entitled or permitted to have access with or without payment (s.86).

3 Fixed penalty notices for litter

A fixed penalty notice may be given by an authorised officer of a litter authority or a policeman to a person who he has reason to believe has committed an offence under s.87 (Environmental Protection Act 1990, s.88, amended). For this purpose, a litter authority is—
  (a) any principal litter authority, other than a county council, a regional council, or a joint board;
  (b) any county council, regional council or joint board designated by order by the Secretary of State in relation to such an area as is specified in the order (not being an area in a National Park);
  (c) any National Park Committee;
  (d) any Park board for any area in a National Park; and
  (e) the Broads Authority.

Where a person is given a notice under s.88 in respect of an offence, no proceedings will be begun before the end of 14 days following the date of the notice and a person will not be convicted of an offence if he pays the fixed penalty before the end of that period. The fixed penalty is payable to the litter authority whose officer gave the notice.

4 Amount of fixed penalty for litter

The amount of a fixed penalty for litter is £80 (see the Litter (Fixed Penalty) (Scotland) Order 2013), or such other amount as may be substituted by order.

5 Duty to keep land and highways clear of litter

S.89(1) of the Environmental Protection Act 1990 places a duty on various bodies to ensure that "relevant" land in their area is kept, so far as practicable, clear of litter and refuse. The Secretary of State has issued a code of practice under s.89(7) which gives guidance as to the bodies responsible and the land which is "relevant" to each of them, as follows—

Principal litter authorities.—land, other than highway land, which is open to the air on at least one side, is under the direct control of the authority, and to which the public are entitled to have access.
Crown authorities.—their land which is open to the air and to which the public have access;

Designated statutory undertakers.—land under their direct control to which the public are permitted or are entitled to have access. The Litter (Statutory Undertakers) (Designation and Relevant Land) Order 1991 and Railways Act 1993 (Consequential Modifications) Order 1999 (S.I. No. 1443) designate certain transport related undertakings for this purpose, including those authorised to operate railways, and passenger transport executives. In relation to railways, "relevant" land includes land to which the public have no right of access (e.g., the track side);

Educational institutions.–land in the open air which is under the direct control of a body designated by the Litter (Designated Educational Institutions) Order 1991, including universities, publicly funded colleges of further and higher education, and maintained schools;

Roads.–Councils and joint boards in whose area the relevant road is situated. The Secretary of State has responsibility for trunk roads which are special roads and for certain other highways where the duty has been transferred to him from the local authority.

The Code of Practice also gives practical guidance as to the generally acceptable standards of cleanliness and target response times for dealing with litter.

The Scottish Ministers may give such directions as they consider expedient for securing compliance by a person with their duty under s.89 (s.89(6A)). A person who receives such a direction must comply with it. Directions may be given generally or to specific people.

6 Litter control areas

The Scottish Ministers may, by order, prescribe descriptions of land which may be designated by a principal litter authority (other than a regional authority or joint board) as, or as part of, a litter control area (Environmental Protection Act 1990, s.90(1)).

The Litter Control Areas Order 1991 prescribes *inter alia* the following descriptions of land–

(a) car parks to which the public are entitled or permitted to have access;

(b) land forming a retail shopping development, other than the land which is retail floor space or ancillary space used directly within that retail floor space;

(c) land to which the public are entitled or permitted to have access, which is open to the air, and which forms part of a business or office park or an industrial or trading estate;

(d) land used as *inter alia* a cinema, concert hall, theatre, bingo hall, swimming bath, or gymnasium, or as an amusement arcade or centre;

(e) any part of an inland beach or the seashore which is frequently used by large numbers of people, and managed by the person having direct control of it as a tourist resort;

(f) land to which the public are entitled or permitted to have access, which is open to the air, and which is under the direct control of various specified statutory and non-statutory authorities;

(g) land forming, or forming part of, a camping or caravan site (including a mobile home site) which is used for more than 28 days in one year.

7 Summary proceedings by persons aggrieved by litter

Any member of the public aggrieved by a breach of the duty imposed by s.89 (duty to keep land and highways clear of litter) may complain to a sheriff (Environmental Protection Act 1990, s.91). The sheriff may, if the complaint is justified, make a *litter abatement order* requiring the defendant to clear the litter away or as the case may be clear the highway, within a time specified in the order. A code of practice under s.89(7) or a direction under s.89(6A) (see **5 Duty to keep land and highways clear of litter**, above), is admissible in evidence in any proceedings under s.91 (s.91(11)).

8 Summary proceedings by litter authorities

Where a principal litter authority are satisfied that, any relevant Crown land, any relevant land of a designated statutory undertaker or of an educational institution, or any such land within a litter control area of a local authority, is defaced by litter or refuse, or such defacement is likely to recur, they must serve a *litter abatement notice* imposing either a requirement that the litter be cleared within a time specified in the notice and/or a prohibition on permitting the land to become defaced by litter or refuse (Environmental Protection Act 1990, s.92). A code of practice under s.89(7) or a direction under s.89(6A) (see **5 Duty to keep land and highways clear of litter**, above), is admissible in evidence in any proceedings under s.92 (s.92(8)).

9 Street litter control notices

A principal litter authority may, with a view to the prevention of accumulations of litter or refuse in and around any street or open land adjacent to any street, issue street litter control notices imposing such reasonable requirements as the authority consider appropriate in the circumstances on the occupiers of commercial and retail premises which front onto a street. The Street Litter Control Notices Order 1991 prescribes the descriptions of commercial or retail premises in respect of which a street litter control notice may be issued and descriptions of land which may be included in an area of open land

10 Public registers

The principal litter authorities must maintain a register of designated litter control areas made under s.90 (see above) and of street litter control orders made under s.93 (see above) (Environmental Protection Act 1990, s.95(1)).

11 Abandoned shopping and luggage trolleys

A local authority may by resolution, apply to their area the scheme relating to abandoned shopping and luggage trolleys set out in Sch.4 to the 1990 Act (Environmental Protection Act 1990, s.99). *Inter alia* the scheme gives an authority power to seize such trolleys and charge their owners for their return.

12 Application of Part IV to any description of animal droppings

The Secretary of State may, by order, apply the provisions of Part IV which apply to refuse to any description of animal droppings in all or in any prescribed circumstances subject to such modifications as appear to him to be necessary (Environmental Protection Act 1990, s.86(14)). By virtue of this provision the Litter (Animal Droppings) Order 1991 applies Part IV to dog faeces on the following descriptions of land which is not heath or woodland or used for the grazing of animals–

(a) any public walk or pleasure ground;

(b) any land, whether enclosed or not, on which there are no buildings or of which no more than 1/20th part is covered with buildings, and the whole or the remainder of which is laid out as a garden or is used for the purpose of recreation;

(c) any part of the seashore which is frequently used by large numbers of people and managed by the person having direct control of it as a tourist resort;

(d) any esplanade or promenade which is above the place to which the tide flows at mean high water springs;

(e) any land not forming part of a public road which is open to the air, which the public are permitted to use on foot only, and which provides access to retail premises;

(f) a trunk road picnic area;

(g) a picnic site; and

(h) land (whether above or below ground and whether or not consisting of or including buildings) forming or used in connection with off-street parking places.

13 Provision and maintenance of litter bins

The Litter Act 1983 gives local authorities in Great Britain power to provide and maintain receptacles for refuse or litter and imposes a duty on them to empty and clean bins so provided. (ss.5 and 7).

14 Interference with refuse tips and dustbins

It is an offence under s.60(1) of the Environmental Protection Act 1990 to sort over or disturb anything deposited at a place for the disposal of waste, or in a receptacle for waste, provided by a waste disposal contractor under arrangements made with a waste disposal authority.

15 Civic amenity sites

Under the Refuse Disposal (Amenity) Act 1978, unauthorised dumping is an offence (s.2). The 1978 Act also provides for the removal and disposal of abandoned vehicles.

Local authorities are under a duty to provide places where household refuse may be deposited at all reasonable times free of charge by persons resident in their area and, on payment of such charges (if any) as the authority think fit, by other persons and, to dispose of refuse so deposited (Refuse Disposal (Amenity) Act 1978, s.1(1)). The local authority may determine what kinds of refuse may be deposited at any particular place and fix terms on which business refuse may be deposited; may provide plant and apparatus for the treatment and disposal of any such rubbish; and may sell or otherwise dispose of any such refuse (s.1(3)). A local authority may enter into an agreement with any other person for the provision by him of these facilities at any place under his control (s.1(4)).

16 Waste electrical and electronic equipment

Special provisions apply to waste electrical and electronic equipment (WEEE). These provisions, contained in the Waste Electrical and Electronic Equipment Regulations 2013, aim to reduce waste from electrical and electronic equipment (EEE) encourage the separate collection of WEEE and its treatment, reuse, recovery, recycling and sound environmental disposal; make producers of EEE responsible for the environmental impact of their products; and improve the environmental performance of all those involved during the lifecycle of EEE.

The types of EEE covered by the Regulations until 31st December 2018 are (Schs 1 and 2)–

1. Large household appliances (e.g., fridges, freezers, cookers, microwave ovens, dishwashers, radiators, fans, etc);

2. Small household appliances (e.g., vacuum cleaners, toasters, clocks, irons, etc);

3. IT and telecommunications equipment (e.g., computers, printers, laptops, calculators, telephones, etc);

4. Consumer equipment (e.g., radios, televisions, hi-fis, video-cameras, etc);

5. Lighting equipment (e.g., sodium or fluorescent lamps, etc);

6. Electrical and electronic tools (with the exception of large-scale stationary industrial tools) (e.g., drills,

saws, sewing machines, lawnmowers, etc);
7. Toys, leisure and sports equipment (e.g., electric trains, video games and consoles, etc);
8. Medical devices (with the exception of all implanted and infected products);
9. Monitoring and control instruments (e.g., smoke detectors, heating regulators, etc); and
10. Automatic dispensers (e.g., for hot drinks, money, etc).
From 1st January 2019 the categories change and will be (Schs 3 and 4)–
1. Temperature exchange equipment;
2. Screens, monitors and equipment containing screens having a surface area greater than 100cm^2.
3. Lamps;
4. Large equipment (any external dimension greater than 50cm) including but not limited to household appliances; IT and telecommunication equipment; consumer equipment; luminaires; equipment reproducing sound or images, musical equipment; electrical and electronic tools; toys, leisure and sports equipment; medical devices; monitoring and control instruments; automatic dispensers equipment for generation of electric currents, but excluding any equipment included in categories 1 to 3;
5. Small equipment (no external dimension greater than 50cm) including but not limited to the items listed under 4. above excluding IT and telecommunication equipment; and
6. Small IT and telecommunication equipment (no external dimension greater than 50cm).

All goods covered by the Regulations must be marked with a crossed out wheeled bin symbol (Reg. 22) and a date mark (Reg. 23). A producer must also provide information on reuse and environmentally sound treatment for each new type of EEE that they put on the market (Reg. 24).

Producers of EEE are responsible for collecting, treating, recovering and disposing of an amount of WEEE equivalent to the amount of EEE that they produce. Such producers must join a producer compliance scheme who will arrange for the collection, treatment and recycling of WEEE. Responsibility for "historic" EEE (i.e., which was put on the market before 13th August 2005) is divided between current producers according to their market share.

Retailers who sell EEE to the public must ensure that their customers can return their WEEE free of charge. This will be on a one-for-one basis, as long as the new equipment is of similar type and has the same function as the old equipment (Reg. 42). Retailers can set up alternative collection systems as long as they are still convenient for customers. Retailers in turn return the WEEE, free of charge, to the producer compliance scheme.

A producer or distributor must not show a purchaser at the time of sale of new EEE the costs of financing the collection, treatment and environmentally sound disposal of WEEE from private households (Reg. 51).

17 Carrier bags

There is a power to make regulations requiring suppliers of goods to charge for carrier bags (Climate Change (Scotland) Act 2009, s.88). S.88A, as inserted by the Regulatory (Reform) Scotland Act 2014 s.43 (offences relating to the supply of carrier bags), provides that a person authorised for the purpose by an enforcement authority may give a person a fixed penalty notice if the person so authorised has reason to believe that the person to whom the notice is given has committed a relevant offence (i.e., breached regulations made under s.88). Sch. 1A to the 2009 Act gives further details about the contents of penalty notices. *Inter alia*, such a notice must contain information concerning the amount of the fixed penalty, the payment deadline, the discounted amount and the discounted payment deadline. The maximum amount of the fixed penalty that may be prescribed is an amount equal to level 2 on the standard scale (as to the standard scale, see the Note on **Treatment of Offenders**). The payment deadline is the first working day occurring at least 28 days after the day on which the notice is given and the discounted payment deadline at least 14 days after the day on which notice is given. The Single Use Carrier Bags Charge (Fixed Penalty Notices and Amendment) (Scotland) Regulations 2015 set the level of the fixed penalty at £200, discounted to £100 if paid within 14 days.

The charge for a single use carrier bag is 5p. The Single Use Carrier Bags Charge (Scotland) Regulations 2014 contain a number of exceptions to the charge, including bags used solely to contain unpackaged food, goods contaminated by soil, or packaged but uncooked fish, meat or poultry (or a combination of those items) in small bags; bags used to contain purchases made on board ships, trains, aircraft, coaches or buses; mail order dispatch or courier bags; bags containing items supplied on a medical prescription; and bags for purchases made in prisons and other secure accommodation if the bag is necessary for reasons of security, good order, discipline or safety.

Note.–a bag does not need to be made of plastic in order to come within the definition of a "single use" carrier bag and so attract a charge.

18 Batteries

From 1st February 2010, a distributor of portable batteries (e.g., a retailer) must, at any place it supplies such batteries to end-users (Waste Batteries and Accumulators Regulations 2009, Reg. 31)–
(a) take back waste batteries at no charge; and
(b) inform end-users about the possibility of such take back at their sales points.

A producer of batteries must be a member of a "battery compliance scheme" i.e., a scheme which finances the collection, treatment and recycling of batteries. Such schemes will collect waste batteries from the distributors for appropriate disposal. No charge may be made for collection of waste batteries.

There are similar provisions, from May 2009, for no-charge take back of waste industrial batteries and car batteries. In the case of car batteries, the producer must collect waste batteries free of charge and within a reasonable time from the "final holder", that is the business, scrap metal dealer etc who has removed the battery from the car. Since January 2010, it has been illegal to dispose of waste industrial or car batteries in a landfill or by incineration.

19 Authorities

Statutes–

Environmental Protection Act 1990

Litter Act 1983

Refuse Disposal (Amenity) Act 1978

Statutory Instruments–

Litter (Animal Droppings) Order 1991 (S.I. 1991 No. 961)

Litter Control Areas Order 1991, as amended (S.I. 1991 No. 1325 and 1997 No. 633)

Litter (Designated Educational Institutions) Order 1991 (S.I. 1991 No. 561)

Litter (Fixed Penalty) (Scotland) Order 2013 (S.S.I. 2013 No. 315)

Litter (Statutory Undertakers) (Designation and Relevant Land) Order 1991, as amended (S.I. 1991 No. 1043 and 1992 No. 406)

Single Use Carrier Bags Charge (Fixed Penalty Notices and Amendment) (Scotland) Regulations 2015 (S.S.I. 2015 No. 159)

Single Use Carrier Bags Charge (Scotland) Regulations 2014, as amended (S.S.I. 2014 No. 161 and 2015 No. 159)

Street Litter Control Notices Order 1991, as amended (S.I. 1991 No. 1324, and 1997 No. 632)

Waste Batteries and Accumulators Regulations 2009, as amended (S.I. 2009 No. 890, 2011 No. 988, S.S.I. 2011 No. 226, S.I. 2013 No. 3134, and 2015 Nos. 1360, and 1935)

Waste Electrical and Electronic Equipment Regulations 2013, as amended (S.I. 2013 No. 3113 and S.I. 2014 No. 1771, and 2015 No. 1968)

NATIONAL SECURITY

NATIONAL SECURITY

COVERT SURVEILLANCE, SEARCHES, AND TELEPHONE TAPPING

Contents

This Note is organised into the following Parts–
- A: Covert Search and Surveillance of Property (under the Police Act 1997)
- B: Covert Surveillance of People (under the Regulation of Investigatory Powers Act 2000 Part II, and (Scotland) Act 2000)
- C: Interception of Communications (under the Regulation of Investigatory Powers Act 2000 Part I, and (Scotland) Act 2000)
- D: Acquisition and Disclosure of Communications Data (under the Regulation of Investigatory Powers Act 2000 Part I, and (Scotland) Act 2000)
- E: Disclosure of Encrypted Electronic Information (under the Regulation of Investigatory Powers Act 2000 Part III, and (Scotland) Act 2000)
- F: The Tribunal
- G: CCTV

1 Codes of Practice

There are a number of Codes of Practice governing the operation of the Regulation of Investigatory Powers Act 2000. These include–
- (a) Code of practice on the interception of communications;
- (b) Code of practice on the acquisition and disclosure of communications data;
- (c) Code of practice on the retention of communications data;
- (d) Code of practice on covert surveillance and property interference;
- (e) Code of practice on the use of covert human intelligence sources;
- (f) Code of practice for the investigation of protected electronic information; and
- (g) The Equipment Interference Code of Practice.

These Codes can be found online at either–
<https://www.gov.uk/government/collections/ripa-codes> or
 <https://www.gov.uk/government/publications/code-of-practice-for-covert-surveillance-and-property-interference>
and are also available from The Stationery Office.

Scottish codes in relation to (c) and (d) can be found at–
<www.gov.scot/Topics/archive/law-order/Police/policepowers/17206/7789>

A: COVERT SEARCH AND SURVEILLANCE OF PROPERTY

2 Introduction

The Police Act 1997 Part III (ss.91 to 108, and Sch. 7) puts covert entry upon and interference with property by the police, National Crime Agency, and HM Revenue and Customs upon a statutory footing for the first time. Previously, these matters were dealt with by Home Office Circular which gave guidance as to when such methods could be used and what authorisations were needed, but gave the police no protection against any criminal or civil liability they may incur in using them (e.g., for criminal damage for a forced covert entry, or for trespass). The circular will continue to apply in those instances where no criminal offence or civil wrong is involved, e.g., where covert surveillance is in a public place.

Covert surveillance of people under the Regulation of Investigatory Powers Act 2000 Part II is dealt with in Part B, below.

Telephone tapping and the interception of faxes and e-mails in the course of transmission over a telecommunications system are dealt with separately by Part I of the 2000 Act–see Part C, below.

References in Part A to sections are to sections of the 1997 Act, as amended by the Regulation of Investigatory Powers Act 2000.

3 Authorisations to interfere with property or wireless telegraphy

No entry or interference with property or with wireless telegraphy is unlawful if it is authorised by an authorisation having effect under Part III of the Police Act 1997 (s.92). The Act does not elaborate on what will be an interference with property or with wireless telegraphy, but it is envisaged that it will include the placing of listening devices on private property (i.e., bugging); of tracking devices on vehicles; and the jamming of private communications systems.

Where an authorising officer (see **4 Authorising officers**, below) believes that it is necessary for specified action to be taken for the purpose of preventing or detecting serious crime and that the taking of action is proportionate to what the action seeks to achieve, he may authorise such action to be taken in relation to specified property or in respect of wireless telegraphy. In considering an authorisation, he must take account of whether what the action seeks to achieve could be achieved by other means (s.93).

4 Authorising officers

Application for an authorisation must be made to an authorising officer. Authorising officers are the (Police Act 1997, s.93(5))–

  (a) chief constables in England, Scotland and Wales;
  (b) Chief or Deputy Chief Constable of the Police Service of Northern Ireland;
  (c) Commissioner or Assistant Commissioner of the Metropolitan Police;
  (d) Commissioner of Police for the City of London;
  (e) Chief Constable (or equivalent) of the ministry of defence police and the various armed forces police services;
  (f) Chief Constable of the British Transport Police;
  (g) Director General of the National Crime Agency, or any member of the staff of that Agency who is designated for the purposes by the Director General;
  (h) any officer designated by the Commissioners of Revenue and Customs;
  (ha) any senior immigration officer designated by the Secretary of State; and
  (i) the chair of the Competition and Markets Authority.

Where it is not reasonably practicable for an authorising officer to consider an application, provision is made for authorisation to be given by other specified officers (s.94).

5 Authorisations requiring approval

In certain circumstances, an authorisation needs the approval of a Commissioner (see **7 The Commissioners**, below) before it will have effect (Police Act 1997, s.97), although approval need not be sought where the authorised officer believes the case is one of urgency. Authorisations which need such approval include–

  (a) those relating to property wholly or mainly used as a dwelling, or a hotel bedroom, or which is an office; and
  (b) those which are likely to result in any person acquiring knowledge of–
         (i) matters subject to legal professional privilege;
         (ii) confidential personal information; or
         (iii) confidential journalistic material.

Matters subject to legal privilege include communications between a professional legal adviser and a client (or person representing the client) in connection with the giving of legal advice or in contemplation or for the purposes of legal proceedings. Legal privilege also includes communications between a professional legal adviser, his client (or representative) and any other person in connection with, contemplation of, or for the purposes of legal proceedings (s.98).

"Confidential personal information" includes information acquired or created in the course of a trade, business or profession and which is held in confidence. "Personal information" means information concerning an individual, whether living or dead, who can be identified from it and which relates to physical or mental health or spiritual counselling or assistance given or received, Information is held in confidence if it is held subject to an express or implied undertaking to hold it in confidence or to a restriction on disclosure or obligation of secrecy contained in any enactment (s.99).

"Confidential journalistic material" includes material acquired or created for the purposes of journalism which is held by the person who acquired or created it for those purposes, is held in confidence, and has been so held since it was first acquired or created for the purposes of journalism (s.100).

6 Form and duration of an authorisation

In general, an authorisation must be in writing and will last for three months. In cases of urgency, an authorisation may be given orally, but in such a case it will last only for 72 hours. Authorisations given in the absence of an authorising officer (see **4 Authorising officers**, above) will also only last for 72 hours. Authorisations may be renewed for a further period of three months (Police Act 1997, s.95(1) to (3)).

An authorisation must be cancelled by an authorising officer if he is satisfied that it is no longer necessary or proportionate (s.95(4) and (5)).

7 The Commissioners

Commissioners and a Chief Commissioner are appointed by the Prime Minister. They must a have judicial background and are appointed for a (renewable) term of three years (Police Act 1997, s.91). The commissioners' functions are–

  (a) to consider authorisations in sensitive cases (s.97, see **5 Authorisations requiring approval**, above);
  (b) to deal with complaints relating to interference with property where an authorisation has been granted (s.102);

(c) to quash authorisations where satisfied that, at the time an authorisation was given, there were no reasonable grounds for it to have been given (s.103);

(d) to cancel an authorisation where the reasonable grounds for its issue cease to apply (s.103(4));

(e) to order the destruction of records relating to information obtained by virtue of a quashed or cancelled authorisation, except as required for pending proceedings (s.103(3) and (5)).

Appeal against a commissioner's decision is to the Chief Commissioner (ss.104 and 106). Other than these appeal provisions, the decisions of the Chief Commissioner and the other Commissioners are not subject to appeal and may not be questioned in any court (s.91(10)).

B: COVERT SURVEILLANCE OF PEOPLE

8 Introduction

The Regulation of Investigatory Powers Act 2000 Part II (ss.26 to 48) (in Scotland, the Regulation of Investigatory Powers (Scotland) Act 2000) creates a system of authorisations regulating the use of surveillance and "covert human intelligence sources" (e.g., undercover operations) in relation to people. If an authorisation is obtained, the action will be lawful (s.27; Scottish Act, s.5). If no authorisation is obtained, then the action may breach Article 8 of the European Convention on Human Rights (the right to respect for private and family life) and so be unlawful by virtue of the Human Rights Act 1998, s.6 (action by a public authority incompatible with a Convention right). As to Article 8 and the Human Rights Act 1998, see the Note on **The Human Rights Act 1998**.

Note.– In matters concerning national security and the interests of the economic well-being of the UK authorisations are granted under the Regulation of Investigatory Powers Act 2000 for the whole of the UK, even if the conduct takes place in Scotland (s.46).

9 Types of surveillance

Surveillance may be either "directed" or "intrusive" (Regulation of Investigatory Powers Act 2000, s.26; Scottish Act, s.1).

"Directed" surveillance is pre-planned covert surveillance for the purpose of a specific operation or investigation which is not intrusive, but which is undertaken in such a manner as is likely to result in the obtaining of private information about a person (whether or not that person is specifically identified at the outset) (s.26(2); Scottish Act, s.1(2)).

Surveillance is "covert" if it is carried out in a manner calculated to ensure that the person(s) subject to the surveillance is unaware that it is or may be taking place (s.26(9); Scottish Act, s.1(8)).

"Intrusive" surveillance is covert surveillance carried out in relation to anything taking place on residential premises or in a private vehicle and which involves either a person or a device being inside the premises or vehicle or a device placed outside which consistently provides information of the same quality and detail as might be expected from a device inside the premises or vehicle (s.26(3) and (5); Scottish Act s.1(3) and (5)). The Regulation of Investigatory Powers (Extension of Authorisation Provisions: Legal Consultations) Order 2010 extends the definition of intrusive surveillance to include directed surveillance which takes place at certain types of specified premises used for legal consultations, such as police stations, solicitors' offices, courts and detention centres; and the Regulation of Investigatory Powers (Modification of Authorisation Provisions: Legal Consultations) (Scotland) Order 2015 provides that directed surveillance in relation to matters subject to legal privilege is also to be treated as if it were intrusive surveillance. The effect of this is that such surveillance becomes subject to the higher level of authorisation required for intrusive surveillance (see **15 Additional provisions relating to intrusive surveillance**, below).

A tracking device attached to a vehicle is specifically excluded from the definition of intrusive surveillance (s.26(4); Scottish Act, s.1(4)). Television detector apparatus is also specifically excluded (s.26(6); no Scottish equivalent).

Surveillance under Part II of the Act is subject to the provisions of the Covert Surveillance and Property Interference Code of Practice (see **1 Codes of Practice**, above). There is a separate Code for Scotland (available from The Stationery Office).

10 Covert human intelligence sources

A covert human intelligence source is a person who establishes or maintains a personal or other relationship with someone for the covert purpose of (Regulation of Investigatory Powers Act 2000, s.26(8); Scottish Act s.1(7))–

(a) using the relationship to obtain information, or provide access to it for someone else; or

(b) disclosing information obtained by the use of the relationship, or as a consequence of its existence.

A purpose is covert if the relationship is conducted in a manner that is calculated to ensure that one of the parties is unaware of that purpose (s.26(9); Scottish Act s.1(8)).

The conduct and use of such sources is subject to the provisions of the Covert Human Intelligence Sources Code of Practice (see **1 Codes of Practice**, above). There is a separate Code for Scotland (available from The Stationery Office).

11 Lawful conduct

Conduct will be lawful if it is authorised under Part II of the Regulation of Investigatory Powers Act 2000 or, in Scotland, under the Scottish Act (s.27; Scottish Act, s.5). In addition, no civil liability will arise in connection with any conduct which is incidental to any authorised conduct. Conduct may be authorised without any territorial restrictions.

Any authorisation by a local authority in England and Wales is subject to judicial approval. This approval requirement means that the grant or renewal of an authorisations or notice, can only come into effect if approved by a magistrates' court (s.32A). Before giving approval, the court must be satisfied that–

(a) there were reasonable grounds for the local authority to believe that covert surveillance or the use of a covert human intelligence source was necessary and proportionate;

(b) there remain reasonable grounds for so believing; and

(c) the "relevant conditions" which relate to the authorisation or notice are met i.e., the person making the authorisation was of the correct office, rank or position, and the authorisation or notice was not in breach of any restrictions imposed by the Secretary of State and satisfied any other conditions set out in any order made by him.

12 Authorisation

Grounds and manner of authorisation

Directed surveillance may be authorised if (Regulation of Investigatory Powers Act 2000, s.28; Scottish Act, s.6)–

(a) it is necessary on specified grounds; and

(b) it is proportionate to what is sought to be achieved.

In England and Wales, the specified grounds are–

(i) in the interests of national security;

(ii) for the purpose of preventing or detecting crime, or preventing disorder;

(iii) in the interests of the economic well-being of the United Kingdom;

(iv) in the interests of public safety;

(v) for the purpose of protecting public health;

(vi) for the purpose of assessing or collecting any tax, duty, levy, etc. payable to a government department; or

(vii) any other purpose specified by the Secretary of State by Order.

Under the Scottish Act, the specified grounds are (ii), (iv) and (v), above. Note that even though the conduct may take place in Scotland, an authorisation will be granted under the Regulation of Investigatory Powers Act 2000, not the Scottish Act, where the ground for the surveillance is (i), or (iii) (2000 Act, s.46).

The use of covert human intelligence sources may be authorised (s.29; Scottish Act, s.7) if, in addition to (a) and (b) above, there are specific arrangements in place regarding the use of the "source", covering such things as managing and supervising the source, keeping records of his use, and protecting his identity (see the Regulation of Investigatory Powers (Source Records) Regulations 2000 and the equivalent Scottish 2002 Regulations). The Secretary of State and Scottish Ministers have the power to impose additional requirements before an authorisation is granted or renewed under these provisions.

In England and Wales, any authorisation by a local authority under s.28 or s.29 is subject to judicial approval: see **11 Lawful conduct**, above.

Legal professional privilege

The Regulation of Investigatory Powers (Covert Human Intelligence Sources: Matters Subject to Legal Privilege) Order 2010 creates an enhanced regime of prior approval for activities involving conduct of a source, or the use of a source, to obtain, provide access to or disclose matters subject to legal privilege. In these circumstances an authorisation cannot be granted or renewed until approved either by the Secretary of State or by an ordinary Surveillance Commissioner. Approval may only be given if there are reasonable grounds for believing that the authorisation is necessary–

(i) in the interests of national security;

(ii) for the purpose of preventing or detecting serious crime; or

(iii) in the interests of the economic well-being of the UK.

The conduct must also be proportionate to what is sought to be achieved and certain arrangements must exist in relation to the, source, such as a person having day-to-day responsibility for dealing with the source and another person having general oversight of the use made of the source.

In Scotland, where a source may obtain, provide access to, or disclose communications subject to legal privilege, the approval of an ordinary Surveillance Commissioner must be obtained before the authorisation of the conduct or use of a source (Regulation of Investigatory Powers (Authorisation of Covert Human Intelligence Sources) (Scotland) Order 2014). The granting of such authorisations is limited to cases involving the prevention and detection of serious crime.

Undercover police officers

In Scotland, where the source is an undercover police officer, the authorising officer must be an Assistant Chief Constable or above, the Surveillance Commissioner must be notified that an authorisation is being made, and the prior approval of a surveillance commissioner is required if the authorisation is to extend beyond a period of 12 months.

Sources aged under 18

Special provisions apply to the use of sources aged under 18 (see the Regulation of Investigatory Powers (Juveniles) Order 2000 and the equivalent Scottish 2002 Regulations). An assessment of the nature and magnitude of any risk of physical injury or psychological distress to a juvenile source must be carried out before their use is authorised.

Intrusive surveillance

Intrusive surveillance may be authorised (s.32) if (a) and (b) above are satisfied. In this case the specified grounds are limited to those set out in (i) to (iii) above.

Length of authorisation

Authorisation for the use of a covert human intelligence source will generally last for 12 months (s.43). Where an authorisation is to be renewed beyond 12 months (3 months where the (Legal Privilege) Order 2010 applies), it becomes a "long term authorisation" and prior approval must be sought from a Surveillance Commissioner. In any other case, although prior approval is not needed, notice must be given (although not necessarily in advance) to a Surveillance Commissioner of the grant of an authorisation for the use of a relevant source (Regulation of Investigatory Powers (Covert Human Intelligence Sources: Relevant Sources) Order 2013, Regs. 4 and 5).

13 Authorities who may carry out surveillance, etc

Authorisations may be granted by officers of "relevant public authorities" (Regulation of Investigatory Powers Act 2000, s.30; Scottish Act, ss.6 and 7). Those public authorities which are relevant for these purposes are listed in s.46 and Schedule 1 to the Act (as extended by the Regulation of Investigatory Powers (Directed Surveillance and Covert Human Intelligence Sources) Orders 2003 to 2010); the Scottish Act, s.8; and the Regulation of Investigatory Powers (Authorisations Extending to Scotland) Order 2007.

Relevant authorities for the purposes of directed surveillance and covert human intelligence sources for the whole of the UK in matters relating to national security or the economic well-being of the UK are–

(a) the armed forces;

(b) the intelligence services;

(c) the revenue departments i.e., HM Revenue and Customs;

(d) the MoD Police;

(e) British Transport Police and the Civil Nuclear Constabulary;

(f) the National Crime Agency and Serious Fraud Office;

(g) various other government departments, including the departments of the Environment, Food and Rural Affairs (Defra Investigation Services only), Trade and Industry, and the Home Office (UK Border Agency only);

(h) The Charities Commission, Environment Agency, Financial Conduct Authority, Prudential Regulation Authority, Gambling Commission, Competition and Markets Authority, Police Ombudsman for Northern Ireland, the Health and Safety Executive, Care Quality Commission, Office of Communications, and the Gangmasters Licensing Authority.

Relevant authorities for the purposes of directed surveillance and covert human intelligence sources for England and Wales only are–

(i) police forces in England and Wales, the National Crime Agency, and the Serious Fraud Office;

(j) various other government departments, including the Home Office and the Ministry of Agriculture;

(k) the National Assembly for Wales;

(l) local authorities and fire authorities;

(m) the Food Standards Agency (not Northern Ireland).

Note that there is a restriction on individuals holding a prescribed office, rank or position (see **14 Authorising officers**, below) in any county council in England, a London borough council, the Common Council of the City of London in its capacity as a local authority, the Council of the Isles of Scilly, or any county council or county borough council in Wales. Such an individual may not grant an authorisation for the carrying out of directed surveillance unless it is for the purpose of preventing or detecting a criminal offence. The criminal offence which is sought to be prevented or detected must be one which is punishable, whether on summary conviction or on indictment, by a maximum term of at least six months of imprisonment, or would constitute an offence under ss.146, 147 or 147A of the Licensing Act 2003 (sale of alcohol to children); or s.7 of the Children and Young Persons Act 1933 or ss.91-92 of the Children and Families Act 2014 (sale of tobacco to, or purchase on behalf of, children) (Regulation of Investigatory Powers (Directed Surveillance and Covert Human Intelligence Sources) Order 2010, Reg. 7A).

In Scotland, relevant public authorities for the purposes of directed surveillance and covert human intelligence sources are (Scottish Act, s.8)–

(n) the Scottish Administration;

(o) the Police Service of Scotland;

(p) the Scottish Environment Protection Agency;

(q) the Police Investigations and Review Commissioner;

(r) certain NHS bodies in Scotland.

Certain other bodies are relevant authorities only for the purpose of directed surveillance. These include–

(s) a universal service provider (e.g., the Post Office);

(t) the Royal Pharmaceutical Society of Great Britain;

(u) (England and Wales only) certain NHS bodies;

(v) Her Majesty's Chief Inspector of Education, Children's Services and Skills in England;

(w) the Information Commissioner;

(x) the Department of Work and Pensions.

Intrusive surveillance will generally only be carried out by the police, armed forces, HM Revenue and Customs, or the intelligence services, although there is provision for the Secretary of State to grant an authorisation on behalf of a "designated" public authority (s.41). The Regulation of Investigatory Powers (Intrusive Surveillance) Order 2003 (S.I. No. 3174) designates the Northern Ireland Office for this purpose.

14 Authorising officers

Authorisations for directed surveillance or covert human intelligence sources are granted by persons prescribed by Order (Regulation of Investigatory Powers Act 2000, s.30). The Regulation of Investigatory Powers (Prescription of Offices, Ranks and Positions) Order 2000 (and the equivalent 2010 Scottish Order) prescribes, by reference to office, rank or position, those persons who may grant authorisations. For the police, authorisations must generally be made by officers of the rank of superintendent or above, although in urgent cases an inspector may grant an authorisation. Authorisation for the long term use of a covert human intelligence source (i.e., beyond 12 months) must be from a chief constable.

Authorisation for intrusive surveillance may only be granted by the Secretary of State (e.g., for applications from the intelligence services or others) or a senior authorising officer, i.e., a chief constable (or armed forces equivalent), the Director General of the National Crime Agency and any member of his staff designated by him, or a designated HM Revenue and Customs officer (s.32).

In Scotland, an authorisation for intrusive surveillance may only be granted by a chief constable, or by the Police Investigations and Review Commissioner (s.10(1)).

The procedures for the grant of authorisations (e.g., in the absence of the senior authorising officer) are similar to those under the Police Act 1997, Part III (see A: COVERT SEARCH AND SURVEILLANCE OF PROPERTY, above).

15 Additional provisions relating to intrusive surveillance

An authorisation for intrusive surveillance made by the police, National Crime Agency, Police Investigations and Review Commissioner, Competition and Markets Authority or HM Revenue and Customs must be notified to a surveillance commissioner (see 6 The Commissioners, above) (Regulation of Investigatory Powers Act 2000, s.35; Scottish Act, s.13. *Note* that in Scotland, Scottish surveillance commissioners are appointed for the purposes of the Scottish Act by s.2). The notice must state either that the approval of a commissioner is required before the grant of the authorisation will take effect, or that the case is one of urgency, together with the grounds for that belief. The Regulation of Investigatory Powers (Notification of Authorisations etc.) Order 2000 (and the equivalent Scottish Order) provide that the notice must also state–

(a) the grounds for belief that authorisation is necessary and the surveillance proportionate;

(b) the nature of the authorised conduct including the residential premises or private vehicle in relation to which the conduct is authorised and the identity, where known, of persons to be subject to the authorised conduct; and

(c) whether the conduct authorised is likely to lead to intrusion on the privacy of persons other than any person the subject of that conduct.

The commissioner must scrutinise the notice as soon as possible and decide whether or not to approve it.

A commissioner also has the power to quash or cancel an authorisation that has been granted and to order the destruction of records in connection with such a quashed or cancelled authorisation (s.37; Scottish Act, s.15).

There is a procedure for appealing against decisions of a surveillance commissioner to the Chief Surveillance Commissioner (ss.38 and 39; Scottish Act, ss.16 and 17).

C: INTERCEPTION OF COMMUNICATIONS

16 Introduction

The Regulation of Investigatory Powers Act 2000 makes provision for and in connection with the interception of communications sent by post or by means of telecommunication systems and amends s.45 of the Telecommunications Act 1984 (offences relating to interception and disclosure of messages by persons engaged in the running of a telecommunications system. Amongst other things, the Act–

– contains the offence of intentionally intercepting a communication in the course of its transmission by post or by means of a public (and, unless excluded, a private) telecommunication system;

– empowers the Secretary of State to authorise by warrant the interception of a communication so transmitted and specifies the circumstances in which such a warrant may be issued;

    — establishes a Tribunal to receive applications from persons who believe that communications sent to or by them have been intercepted and to investigate whether or not there has been a contravention of the Act; and

    — appoints a Commissioner to keep under review the carrying out by the Secretary of State of his functions under the Act.

A Code of Practice on "Interception of Communications" has been issued (see **I Codes of Practice**, above).

17 Prohibition on interception

S.1(1) of the Regulation of Investigatory Powers Act 2000 provides that a person who intentionally and without lawful authority intercepts a communication in the course of its transmission by post or by means of a "public" telecommunication system commits an offence. S.1(2) provides a similar offence in relation to a "private" telecommunication system (e.g., a hotel or office network) but provides additional exclusions from liability.

No proceedings in respect of an offence under s.1 may be instituted in England and Wales, except by or with the consent of the Director of Public Prosecutions (s.1(8)).

If the Communications Commissioner considers that a person has without lawful authority intercepted a communication in the course of its transmission by means of a public telecommunication system, but has not committed an offence under s.1(1) (i.e., it was not intentional) he may serve a monetary penalty notice. The maximum penalty is £50,000. An appeal against a notice may be made to the First-tier Tribunal (Regulation of Investigatory Powers (Monetary Penalty Notices and Consents for Interceptions) Regulations 2011).

18 Lawful authority for interception

Interception is not criminal if it is carried out with lawful authority. This is defined (Regulation of Investigatory Powers Act 2000, s.1(5)) as conduct authorised–

    (a) under ss.3 or 4 (see **19 Lawful interception without a warrant**, below);

    (b) by a warrant issued under s.5 (see **20 Warrants for interception**, below); or

    (c) by any other statutory power and relates to stored information (e.g., on a pager).

In addition, interception of a private telecommunications system does not give rise to criminal liability if it is carried out by a person with a right to control the operation or use of the system, or who has the express or implied consent of such a person to make the interception (s.1(6)).

19 Lawful interception without a warrant

Interception without a warrant is lawful if (Regulation of Investigatory Powers Act 2000, s.3)–

    (a) the parties to the communication have consented to its interception;

    (b) one of the parties to the communication has consented to the interception and surveillance under Part II of the Act (see B: COVERT SURVEILLANCE OF PEOPLE, above) has been authorised;

    (c) it is by or on behalf of a person who provides a postal or telecommunications service and it is connected with the provision or operation of that service (e.g. where the post office needs to open a letter to find a return address) or with the enforcement of any enactment relating to the use of that service; or

    (d) it is authorised by a designated person for certain purposes under the Wireless Telegraphy Act 2006.

S.4 lists further circumstances when interception without a warrant is authorised, including–

    (e) where the United Kingdom is required to give information under the Convention on Mutual Assistance in Criminal Matters between the Member States of the European Union;

    (f) where regulations so permit, for legitimate business purposes. The Telecommunications (Lawful Business Practice) (Interception of Communications) Regulations 2000 provide that interception is authorised for monitoring and recording communications for the purpose of establishing the existence of facts or compliance with regulatory practices or procedures, in the interests of national security, for preventing or detecting crime, detecting the unauthorised use of a telecommunications system, in order to secure or as an inherent part of, the effective operation of a system, and for monitoring, but not recording, free helplines providing counselling and support services anonymously; and

    (g) certain interceptions in prisons and high security psychiatric hospitals (in Scotland, state hospitals).

20 Warrants for interception

The Secretary of State may issue a warrant authorising or requiring the person to whom it is addressed to intercept, in the course of their transmission by post or by means of a telecommunication system, such communications as are described in the warrant. The warrant may also require the person to whom it is addressed to disclose the intercepted material in such manner as is described in the warrant (Regulation of Investigatory Powers Act 2000, s.5(1)). A warrant may also provide for the making of a request for assistance, or for the provision of assistance, under a mutual assistance agreement with another country.

However, a warrant must not be issued unless the Secretary of State considers that the conduct it authorises is proportionate to what is sought to be achieved, and it is necessary (s.5(2) and (3))–

    (a) in the interests of national security; or

(b) for the purpose of preventing or detecting serious crime;

(c) for the purpose, in circumstances appearing to the Secretary of State to be relevant to the interests of national security, of safeguarding the economic well-being of the United Kingdom, provided the information sought relates to the acts or intentions of persons outside the British Islands; or

(d) to give effect to the provisions of any international mutual assistance agreement relating to the prevention or detection of serious crime.

In considering whether a warrant is necessary, the Secretary of State must take into account whether the information which it is considered necessary to acquire could reasonably be acquired by other means (s.5(4)).

In Scotland, the power to issue a warrant where (b) or (d) applies rests with the Scottish Ministers (Scotland Act (Transfer of Functions to the Scottish Ministers etc.) Order 2007 (S.I. No. 2915, as amended)).

21 Application for a warrant

Application for a warrant may only be made by or on behalf of (Regulation of Investigatory Powers Act 2000, s.6)–

(a) The Director-General of the Security Service, the Chief of the Secret Intelligence Service, or the Director of GCHQ;

(b) The Director General of the National Crime Agency;

(c) chief constables in Scotland, the Chief Constable of the PSNI, and the Commissioner of Police for the Metropolis (but not chief constables in England and Wales, who make application through the National Crime Agency);

(d) the Commissioners of Revenue and Customs;

(e) the Chief of Defence Intelligence; and

(f) the competent authority requesting assistance under an international mutual assistance agreement.

22 Scope of warrants

A warrant must either (Regulation of Investigatory Powers Act 2000, s.8)–

(a) name or describe either one person as the interception subject or a single set of premises in relation to which the interception is to take place; or

(b) if it relates to specified material (as opposed to communications relating to a particular person or premises) sent or received outside the United Kingdom by a telecommunications system, be accompanied by a certificate from the Secretary of State as to the material the examination of which he considers necessary.

23 Issue and duration of warrants

Except in urgent cases, a warrant may be issued only under the hand of the Secretary of State (Regulation of Investigatory Powers Act 2000, s.7(1)). A warrant is normally valid for three months, but may be renewed by the Secretary of State   warrant issued in an emergency is valid for five working days (s.9(1) and (6)).

The Secretary of State must cancel a warrant at any time before its expiry, if he considers it to be no longer necessary (s.9(4)).

A copy of an interception warrant may be served on a person outside the UK, and may relate to conduct outside the UK (s.11(2A)).

24 Modification of warrants and certificates

A warrant may be modified by the Secretary of State (see **22 Scope of warrants**, above), and must be modified by him if at any time he considers that it includes factors which no longer need to be included (Regulation of Investigatory Powers Act 2000, s.10(1) and (2)).

A certificate may be modified to include in the certified material additional material where the Secretary of State considers the examination of such material to be necessary and must be modified to exclude material which he considers it is no longer necessary to examine (s.10(1) and (3)).

25 Safeguards

Where the Secretary of State issues a warrant, he has a duty to make such arrangements as he considers necessary for securing that–

(a) the extent to which any intercepted material is disclosed, the number of persons to whom any of the material is disclosed, the extent to which the material is copied, and the number of copies made of any of the material is limited to the minimum that is necessary and each copy made of any of that material is destroyed as soon as its retention is no longer necessary (Regulation of Investigatory Powers Act 2000, s.15(2) and (3));

(b) where a certificate is issued in relation to a warrant (see **22 Scope of warrants**, above), so much of the intercepted material as is not certified by the certificate is not read, looked at, or listened to by any person. In addition, material intercepted under a warrant should only be examined if it does not have as its purpose the identification of material contained in communications sent by, or intended for, an individual who is known to be in the British Islands and has not been selected by reference to such a person unless the Secretary of State certifies that it is necessary (s.16).

26 Complaints

S.65 of and Schedule 3 to the Regulation of Investigatory Powers Act 2000 establish the Tribunal which will investigate complaints under the Act.

Any person who believes that communications sent to him or by him have been intercepted in the course of transmission by post, or by a public telecommunication system, may apply to the Tribunal for an investigation. Also see **42 The Tribunal**, below.

27 The Interception of Communications Commissioner

The Prime Minister must appoint as Commissioner a person who holds or who has held high judicial office to carry out the following functions, namely (Regulation of Investigatory Powers Act 2000, s.57)–

(a) to keep under review the carrying out by the Secretary of State of the functions conferred on him by ss.1 to 11 of the Act, and the adequacy of any of the safeguards provided by s.15;

(b) to give to the Tribunal all such assistance as they may require to enable them to carry out their functions under the Act.

It is the duty of every person holding office under the Crown, and of every person employed by the police or the Post Office or in the running of a public telecommunication system to disclose or give to the Commissioner such documents or information as he may require to enable him to carry out his functions (s.58).

The Commissioner must make a report to the Prime Minister if it appears to him (i) that there has been a contravention of the provisions of the Act which has not been the subject of a report made to the Prime Minister by the Tribunal, or (ii) that any of the safeguards provided by the Act have proved inadequate. The Commissioner is also required to make annual and half-yearly reports to the Prime Minister who must lay before each House of Parliament a copy of such report, together with a statement as to whether any matter has been excluded from the copy. The Prime Minister, after consultation with the Commissioner, may exclude from the copy of a report any matter the publication of which it appears to him would be prejudicial to national security, to the prevention or detection of serious crime, the economic well-being of the United Kingdom, or the continued discharge of functions by a public authority (s.58).

28 Exclusion of evidence

The Regulation of Investigatory Powers Act 2000 prohibits the adducing of evidence or cross-examination of a witness in any court or tribunal which tends to suggest that an offence under s.1 of the Act has been or is to be committed by, or a warrant has been or is to be issued to, any of the following (s.17)–

(a) any person to whom a warrant is addressed;

(b) a person holding office under the Crown;

(c) any person employed by the police;

(d) any person providing or employed in providing a postal service; and

(e) any person providing a public telecommunications service or employed in providing such a service.

There are exceptions to the prohibition, in particular it does not apply (i) in relation to proceedings for a relevant offence, as defined in s.18(12), (ii) where the evidence is adduced or the question is asked for the purpose of establishing the fairness or unfairness of a dismissal on grounds of an offence under various provisions of the Act, or of conduct from which such an offence might be inferred, (iii) in relation to a suggestion that an offence under s.1 has been committed, where a person has been convicted of such an offence; or (iv) limited disclosures to prosecutors (to enable them to secure the fairness of the prosecution) or to judges alone (s.18).

29 Interference with electronic devices: prisons

The Prisons (Interference with Wireless Telegraphy) Act 2012 provides for the authorisation of interference with "wireless telegraphy" for the purpose of preventing, detecting or investigating the use of electronic communications devices (including mobile phones and other devices which are capable of accessing the internet or are otherwise capable of sending or receiving data) within prisons, young offender institutions and secure training centres. Authorisation is given by the Secretary of State or Scottish Ministers. The interference that may be carried out is for the collection of traffic data in relation to an electronic communication, which includes data comprised in, attached to or logically associated with an electronic communication and which identifies the person, apparatus or location to or from which the communication is transmitted; identifies apparatus through which the communication is transmitted; or identifies the time at which an event relating to the communication occurs. It does not include the content of the communication.

D: ACQUISITION AND DISCLOSURE OF COMMUNICATIONS DATA

30 Introduction

Ss. 21 to 25 of the Regulation of Investigatory Powers Act 2000 relate to the circumstances in which public authorities (such as the police) can require "communications data" to be provided to them. It relates to the *acquisition* of data as opposed to the *interception* of data (as to which see C: INTERCEPTION OF COMMUNICATIONS, above).

The definition of "communications data" expressly excludes the contents of a communication. It relates solely to information relating to the use of a communications system whether attached to a particular communication or existing independently. It includes, for example, any data which identifies any person, apparatus or location to or from which the communication is or may be transmitted. This could include data held by a telephone company on the numbers rung from a particular telephone, or data held by an internet service provider as to e-mails sent or received by a customer (but not their content) (s.21).

31 Authorisation for acquisition of data

An authorisation for the acquisition of data may be given only where it is *necessary* to obtain the data on one of the following grounds (Regulation of Investigatory Powers Act 2000, s.22(2))–
   (a) in the interests of national security;
   (b) for the purpose of preventing or detecting crime, or preventing disorder;
   (c) in the interests of the economic well-being of the UK so far as those interests are also relevant to the interests of national security;
   (d) in the interests of public safety;
   (e) for the purpose of protecting public health;
   (f) for the purpose of assessing or collecting any tax, duty, levy, etc payable to a government department;
   (g) for the purpose, in an emergency, of preventing death or injury or any damage to a person's physical or mental health, or of mitigating any such damage; or
   (h) any other purpose specified by the Secretary of State by Order. The Regulation of Investigatory Powers (Communications Data) Order 2010 specifies: assisting investigations into alleged miscarriages of justice, and assisting in identifying any person who has died otherwise than as a result of crime or who is unable to identify himself because of a physical or mental condition, other than one resulting from crime, or obtaining information about the next of kin or other connected persons of such a person or about the reason for his death or condition.

An authorisation may require a person to disclose data held by them and, if they are not already in possession of it, may require them to obtain the data (s.22(4)), but not to do anything which it is not reasonably practicable for them to do (s.22(7)). An authorisation may relate to conduct outside the UK (and may be given to a person outside the UK) (s.22(5A)). If an operator fails to provide the requested information, the Secretary of State may take court proceedings to obtain an order to force them to do so (e.g., an order for specific performance) (s.22(8)).

32 Grant of authorisations

The public authorities who may grant authorisations are (Regulation of Investigatory Powers Act 2000, s.25(1) and the Regulation of Investigatory Powers (Communications Data) Order 2010)–
   (a) a police force;
   (b) the National Crime Agency;
   (c) the Commissioners for Revenue and Customs;
   (d) any of the intelligence services;
   (e) any other public authority specified by the Secretary of State. The 2010 Order specifies the Financial Conduct Authority, Prudential Regulation Authority, Serious Fraud Office, Police Ombudsman for Northern Ireland, Independent Police Complaints Commission, Police Investigations and Review Commissioner, Ofcom, Gangmasters Licensing Authority, Immigration Service, Air, Marine and Rail Accident Investigation Branches, Gambling Commission, Information Commissioner, Criminal Cases Review Commission (and Scottish equivalent), and various emergency services e.g., coastguards, ambulance service, fire and rescue authorities, and NHS trusts. Other bodies (listed in the Order) can acquire data on a limited basis.

An authorisation lasts for one month, but may be renewed at any time before it expires (s.23(4) and (5)).

An authorisation must be cancelled as soon as it becomes no longer "necessary" or when the conduct required by the authorisation is no longer proportionate to what is sought to be achieved by obtaining the data (s.23(8)).

Local authority authorisations or notices to obtain communications data are subject to two restrictions under provisions in the Protection of Freedoms Act 2012. First, the use of directed surveillance powers by local authorities is subject to a "seriousness threshold". Second, the acquisition and disclosure of communications data, directed surveillance and use of covert human intelligence sources by local authorities is subject to a judicial approval mechanism.

The seriousness threshold (which will be prescribed by Order) will restrict local authority use of directed surveillance to the investigation of offences which attract a maximum custodial sentence of six months or more or which involve underage sales of alcohol and tobacco.

The approval requirement means that the grant or renewal of an authorisations or notice, can only come into effect if approved by a magistrates' court (in Scotland, a sheriff) (s.23A). Before giving approval, the court or sheriff must be satisfied that—

(a) there were reasonable grounds for the local authority to believe that obtaining communications data was necessary and proportionate;

(b) there remain reasonable grounds for so believing; and

(c) the "relevant conditions" which relate to the authorisation or notice are met i.e., the person making the authorisation was of the correct office, rank or position, and the authorisation or notice was not in breach of any restrictions imposed by the Secretary of State and satisfied any other conditions set out in any order made by him.

33 Reimbursement of costs

The Secretary of State has a duty to ensure that there are arrangements for "appropriate contributions" to be made towards the costs incurred by postal and telecommunications operators in complying with requests for data (Regulation of Investigatory Powers Act 2000, s.24).

E: DISCLOSURE OF ENCRYPTED ELECTRONIC INFORMATION

34 Introduction

Electronic data may be encrypted or password protected so that it can only be read by someone with a key to the encryption. Part III of the Regulation of Investigatory Powers Act 2000 sets out the circumstances in which a person may be required to disclose such a key.

35 Notices requiring disclosure of a key

The power to require disclosure of a key may only be used once the encrypted information has been, or when it is likely to be, obtained by the public authority requiring disclosure, and only where it has been obtained (Regulation of Investigatory Powers Act 2000, s.49)—

(a) by the exercise of a statutory power to seize, detain, inspect, search or otherwise to interfere with documents or property (e.g., under Part III of the Police Act 1997, see A: COVERT SEARCH AND SURVEILLANCE OF PROPERTY, above);

(b) by means of the exercise of a statutory power to intercept communications (see Part C, above);

(c) as a result of the acquisition and disclosure of communications data provisions (see Part D, above) or the surveillance provisions (see Part B, above) of the Regulation of Investigatory Powers Act 2000;

(d) as a result of any person providing or disclosing it under a statutory duty; or

(e) by any other lawful means (e.g., where it is handed over voluntarily).

If it is believed on reasonable grounds that any person is in possession of the key to the encrypted information and that—

(i) the imposition of a disclosure requirement is necessary and proportionate—

(1) for the purpose of securing the effective exercise or proper performance of a statutory power or duty;

(2) in the interests of national security;

(3) for the purpose of preventing or detecting crime; or

(4) in the interests of the economic well-being of the United Kingdom; and

(ii) that it is not reasonably practicable to obtain possession of the encrypted information in any other way;

then a person with "appropriate permission" may serve a notice imposing a disclosure requirement.

36 Appropriate permission to require disclosure

The authority required to impose a disclosure requirement varies according to the manner in which the encrypted information was (or is likely to be) obtained. The various levels of authority are given in Schedule 2 to the Regulation of Investigatory Powers Act 2000.

(a) If a judge gives permission for a disclosure requirement to be imposed, no further authority is needed. For these purposes "judge" means a circuit judge (in England and Wales), a sheriff (in Scotland), or a county court judge (in Northern Ireland).

(b) If the data has been obtained under a warrant (e.g., under Part I of the 2000 Act (see Part C, above) or under the Drug trafficking Act 1994) or under Part III of the Police Act 1997 (see Part A, above), then the authority for a disclosure requirement may be included in the original warrant or be given in writing subsequently. Authorisations may only be given by the police, HM Revenue and Customs, and persons holding office under the Crown.

(c) If the data has been lawfully obtained by the intelligence services without a warrant (e.g., under a directed surveillance authorisation, see Part B, above), the Secretary of State may give authorisation for a disclosure requirement.

(d) If the data has been lawfully obtained by other persons without a warrant (e.g., by the police under the Police and Criminal Evidence Act 1984), the police, HM Revenue and Customs and armed forces may give authorisation for a disclosure requirement. Where the encrypted data is obtained by someone other than those three, authority must be given by a judge.

(e) If the data has been obtained by the police, HM Revenue and Customs or the intelligence services without the exercise of statutory powers (e.g., where it has been voluntarily handed over) then the Secretary of State may give authorisation for a disclosure requirement in the case of the intelligence services, otherwise authority must be given by a judge.

37 Effect of a disclosure requirement

Where a notice imposing a disclosure requirement is served on someone who has both possession of the encrypted material and a means of accessing it and disclosing it in an intelligible form, then that person must use either provide the material in an intelligible form or, alternatively, make a disclosure of the key.

Where the notice is served on someone who is not in possession of the information, they must disclose the key, if that is in their possession. Where that person is no longer in possession of the key, they must provide any information which would facilitate the obtaining or discovery of the key or the putting of the encrypted data into an intelligible form (Regulation of Investigatory Powers Act 2000, s.50).

There are additional requirements where the key rather than an intelligible version of the information is sought (s.51). Such a direction made by the police, HM Revenue and Customs, or armed forces must be made by a senior officer (i.e. chief officer of police, or equivalent). A notice requiring a key may only be issued if there are special circumstances making it necessary (i.e., that the disclosure requirement would be defeated in whole or in part if the requirement to disclose a key were not included) and the direction is proportionate to what is sought to be achieved. In considering proportionality, regard must be had to what other information is also protected by the key in question and of any potential adverse effect on a business.

Where the police, HM Revenue and Customs, or armed forces serve a notice requiring disclosure of a key, they must also inform the Chief Surveillance Commissioner (or Intelligence Services Commissioner, as appropriate).

38 Reimbursement of costs

The Secretary of State has a duty to ensure that there are arrangements for "appropriate contributions" to be made towards the costs incurred by persons in complying with disclosure notices (Regulation of Investigatory Powers Act 2000, s.52).

39 Secrecy

A disclosure notice may contain a secrecy requirement requiring the person to whom it is given and any other person who becomes aware of it to keep secret the giving of the notice, its contents, and things done in pursuance of it (Regulation of Investigatory Powers Act 2000, s.54).

40 Non-compliance with a notice

Failure to comply with a disclosure notice is an offence. If it is shown that a person was in possession of a key before a notice was served, then he will be taken to be in possession of the key at all subsequent times unless he shows that he was not in possession of it by the time he was required to disclose it (Regulation of Investigatory Powers Act 2000, s.53).

Failure to comply with the secrecy requirements (tipping off) is also an offence (s.54(4)).

On summary conviction a person is liable to imprisonment for up to six months (two years on indictment, five years for tipping off) and/or a fine (unlimited in England and Wales, not exceeding the statutory maximum in Scotland) (unlimited on indictment). As to the statutory maximum, see the Note on **Treatment of Offenders** at para 35 **Maximum fines: the "standard scale"**.

41 Protection for keys disclosed to authorities

The authorities to whom a key is handed over are under a duty to ensure that (Regulation of Investigatory Powers Act 2000, s.55)—

(a) a key handed over pursuant to a notice is used only for obtaining access to, or putting into intelligible form, the encrypted information in relation to which the notice was issued;

(b) the uses to which a disclosed key is put are reasonable;

(c) the use and any retention of the key is proportionate to what is sought to be achieved;

(d) the number of persons to whom the key is disclosed or made available, and the number of copies made, is limited to the minimum necessary for the purpose of enabling the encrypted information to be put into an intelligible form;

(e) disclosed keys are stored in a secure manner;

(f) all records of a disclosed key are destroyed as soon as it is no longer needed for the purpose of enabling information to be put into an intelligible form.

Failure to comply with these requirements may lead to civil liability for any loss or damage which results (s.55(4)).

F: THE TRIBUNAL

42 The Tribunal

S.65 and Schedule 3 to the Regulation of Investigatory Powers Act 2000 establish the Tribunal whose members are appointed for a term of five years. Each member must satisfy the judicial-appointment eligibility condition on a 7-year basis.

The Tribunal has jurisdiction to hear complaints and other proceedings relating to matters arising under the Regulation of Investigatory Powers Act 2000 and the Regulation of Investigatory Powers (Scotland) Act 2000.

In relation to interception of communications under Part I of the Act, the Tribunal will investigate the conduct complained of and the authority for it, applying the principles that a court would apply on an application for judicial review (i.e., the procedure by which the High Court exercises its supervisory jurisdiction over the proceedings and decisions of inferior courts and other bodies and persons who carry out quasi-judicial functions) (s.67(3)).

On determining a complaint, the Tribunal will inform the complainant of their decision but this will be confined to a statement that they have or have not made a determination in his favour (s.68(4)). The Tribunal may (s.67(7))–

(a) make an award of compensation;
(b) if they think fit, make an order doing one or more of the following–
  (i) quashing or cancelling the relevant warrant or authorisation;
  (ii) directing the destruction of any records of information obtained in exercise of any power conferred by a warrant or authorisation, or held by any public authority in relation to any person.

The Tribunal must also make a report to the Prime Minister if the determination relates to a warrant or authorisation given or granted by the Secretary of State (s.68(5)).

The Tribunal also has jurisdiction in relation to complaints against the security and intelligence services.

The Tribunal is also the only appropriate tribunal for complaints under s.7 of the Human Rights Act 1998 (action by a public authority which is incompatible with right under the European Convention on Human Rights (see the Note on **The Human Rights Act 1998**).

The contact details for the Tribunal are–
The Investigatory Powers Tribunal
PO Box 33220
London SW1H 9ZQ
Tel: 0207 035 3711
More information about the Tribunal is available on its website at <www.ipt-uk.com>.

G: CCTV

43 Regulation of CCTV

The Secretary of State must prepare a code of practice containing guidance about surveillance camera systems i.e., closed circuit television, automatic number plate recognition systems, and any other systems for recording or viewing visual images for surveillance purposes (Protection of Freedoms Act 2012, s.29). The Protection of Freedoms Act 2012 (Code of Practice for Surveillance Camera Systems and Specification of Relevant Authorities) Order 2013 brings into force a code of practice for surveillance camera systems, which sets out guidance about the use of surveillance camera systems, and the use of images or information obtained by virtue of such systems. The Home Office code of practice is available at <www.gov.uk/government/publications/circular-0112013>. Local authorities and the police must have regard to the surveillance camera code when exercising any of their functions to which the code relates. A failure on the part of any person to act in accordance with any provision of the code does not of itself make that person liable to criminal or civil proceedings, but the code is admissible in evidence in any such proceedings and a court or tribunal may, in particular, take into account a failure by a relevant authority to have regard to the surveillance camera code in determining a question in any such proceedings (s.33).

The Secretary of State must appoint a person as the Surveillance Camera Commissioner who will have the functions of (s.34)–

(a) encouraging compliance with the surveillance camera code;
(b) reviewing the operation of the code, and
(c) providing advice about the code (including changes to it or breaches of it).

44 Authorities

Statutes–

Anti-terrorism, Crime and Security Act 2001

Police Act 1997

Prisons (Interference with Wireless Telegraphy) Act 2012

Regulation of Investigatory Powers Act 2000

Regulation of Investigatory Powers (Scotland) Act 2000

Statutory Instruments–

Protection of Freedoms Act 2012 (Code of Practice for Surveillance Camera Systems and Specification of Relevant Authorities) Order 2013, as amended (S.I. 2013 Nos. 1961 and 2318)

Regulation of Investigatory Powers (Authorisation of Covert Human Intelligence Sources) (Scotland) Order 2014 (S.S.I. 2014 No. 339)

Regulation of Investigatory Powers (Authorisations Extending to Scotland) Order 2007, as amended (S.I. 2007 Nos. 934 and 3224, 2009 Nos. 2748 and 3403, and 2014 No. 467)

Regulation of Investigatory Powers (Communications Data) Order 2010, as amended (S.I. 2010 No. 480, 2011 No. 2085, 2013 Nos. 472 and 602, 2014 No. 549, and 2015 No. 228)

Regulation of Investigatory Powers (Covert Human Intelligence Sources: Matters Subject to Legal Privilege) Order 2010 (S.I. 2010 No. 123)

Regulation of Investigatory Powers (Covert Human Intelligence Sources: Relevant Sources) Order 2013 (S.I. 2013 No. 2788)

Regulation of Investigatory Powers (Directed Surveillance and Covert Human Intelligence Sources) Orders 2003 to 2010, as amended (S.I. 2003 No. 3171, 2005 No. 1084, 2006 Nos. 594 and 1874, 2007 No. 1098, 2009 No. 462, 2010 No. 521, 2011 No. 2085, 2012 No. 1500, 2013 Nos. 472 and 2788, 2014 Nos. 467 and 549, and 2015 No. 937)

Regulation of Investigatory Powers (Extension of Authorisation Provisions: Legal Consultations) Order 2010 (S.I. 2010 No. 461)

Regulation of Investigatory Powers (Juveniles) Order 2000 (S.I. 2000 No. 2793)

Regulation of Investigatory Powers (Juveniles) (Scotland) Order 2002 (S.S.I. 2002 No. 206)

Regulation of Investigatory Powers (Modification of Authorisation Provisions: Legal Consultations) (Scotland) Order 2015 (S.S.I. 2015 No. 32)

Regulation of Investigatory Powers (Monetary Penalty Notices and Consents for Interceptions) Regulations 2011 (S.I. 2011 No. 1340)

Regulation of Investigatory Powers (Notification of Authorisations etc.) Order 2000 (S.I. 2000 No. 2563)

Regulation of Investigatory Powers (Notification of Authorisations etc.) (Scotland) Order 2000 (S.S.I. 2000 No. 340)

Regulation of Investigatory Powers (Prescription of Offices, Ranks and Positions) Order 2000, as amended (S.I. 2000 No. 2417, 2002 No. 1555)

Regulation of Investigatory Powers (Prescription of Offices, Ranks and Positions) (Scotland) Order 2010 (S.S.I. 2010 No. 350)

Regulation of Investigatory Powers (Source Records) Regulations 2000 (S.I. 2000 No. 2725)

Regulation of Investigatory Powers (Source Records) (Scotland) Regulations 2002 (S.S.I. 2002 No. 205)

Telecommunications (Lawful Business Practice) (Interception of Communications) Regulations 2000, as amended (S.I. 2000 No. 2699 and 2011 No. 1208)

PREVENTION OF TERRORISM

A: INTRODUCTION

1 The legislation

The Terrorism Act 2000 repeals and replaces much of the law relating to terrorism. In general, the Act applies to the whole of the UK. Additional provision is contained in the Terrorism Act 2006 and the Terrorism Prevention and Investigation Measures Act 2011.

2 Definition of "terrorism"

"Terrorism" is defined by the Act to mean (Terrorism Act 2000, s.1)–
- (a) the use or threat of action which–
    - (i) involves serious violence against a person;
    - (ii) involves serious damage to property;
    - (iii) endangers a person's life (other than the person committing the action);
    - (iv) creates a serious risk to the health or safety of the public or a section of the public; or
    - (v) is designed seriously to interfere with or disrupt an electronic system;
- (b) where the use or threat is designed to influence the government or an international governmental organisation or to intimidate the public or a section of the public; and
- (c) the use or threat is made for the purposes of advancing a political, religious, racial, or ideological cause.

The use or threat of action within (a) above which involves the use of firearms or explosives is terrorism whether or not it comes within (b) above (it would therefore cover the assassination of a key individual).

The definition expressly covers action taken outside the United Kingdom (s.1(4)(a)).

B: MEMBERSHIP AND FUNDING, ETC

3 Proscribed organisations

S.3 of the Terrorism Act 2000 provides for the proscription of organisations which the Secretary of State believes are concerned in terrorism. Proscribed organisations are listed in Schedule 2 to the Act. The Secretary of State may, by order, add or remove organisations form the list (s.3(3)). The list originally contained 14 organisations connected with terrorism in Northern Ireland but has been extended by the Terrorism Act 2000 (Proscribed Organisations) (Amendment) Orders 2001 to 2015 and the Proscribed Organisations (Name Changes) Orders 2010 to 2014 to include a further 64 organisations mainly connected with terrorism in the Middle East, but also including ETA and the Tamil Tigers.

There is an appeals procedure where deproscription is refused (see ss.5 to 10 and the Proscribed Organisations (Applications for Deproscription) Regulations 2006).

A group may be considered to promote or encourage terrorism (and so be liable to proscription) if its activities include the unlawful glorification of terrorism, or its activities are carried out in a manner that ensures that it is associated with statements containing unlawful glorification of terrorism (s.3(5A)).

4 Offences as to membership and support

A person is guilty of an offence if he–
- (a) belongs or professes to belong to a proscribed organisation (Terrorism Act 2000, s.11);
- (b) solicits or invites support for a proscribed organisation other than support with money or other property (see **8 Offences as to terrorist property**, below) (s.12(1));
- (c) arranges or assists in the arrangement or management of, or addresses, any meeting of three or more persons knowing that the meeting is to support a proscribed organisation, to further the activities of such an organisation, or to be addressed by a person belonging or professing to belong to such an organisation (s.12(2) and (3)); or
- (d) wears in a public place (as defined) any item of clothing, or wears, carries, or displays any article, in such a way as to arouse reasonable apprehension that he is a member or supporter of a proscribed organisation (s.13).

A person belonging to a proscribed organisation is not guilty of an offence if he shows that he became a member of it when it was not a proscribed organisation and that he has not since he became a member taken part in any of its activities at any time while it was a proscribed organisation (s.11(2)).

5 Offences as to encouragement of terrorism

It is an offence to encourage terrorism by publishing a statement which is a direct or indirect encouragement to commit, prepare or instigate acts of terrorism with the intention to encourage terrorism, or reckless as to whether it will do so (Terrorism Act 2006, s.1).

A statement which "glorifies" the commission or preparation of acts of terrorism (whether in the past, the future or generally) and from which members of the public could reasonably infer that such conduct should be emulated in existing circumstances, is specifically stated to be an indirect encouragement to terrorism and so an offence (s.1(3)). Glorification includes praise or celebration (s.20).

It is also an offence, with the intention to encourage terrorism, or reckless as to whether it will do so, to give, sell, lend or otherwise disseminate books and other publications, including material on the internet, that encourage people to engage in terrorism, or provide information that could be useful to terrorists (s.2).

Where a statement or publication contrary to ss.1 or 2 appears on the internet, a notice will be given to the publisher (i.e., the webmaster) giving them two working days to remove it, failing which they will be taken to have endorsed it (s.3).

6 Offences as to preparation for terrorist acts

It is an offence to prepare to commit or assist others to commit one or more acts of terrorism with the intent of committing or assisting others to commit such acts (Terrorism Act 2006, s.5).

It is an offence to direct, at any level, the activities of an organisation which is concerned in the commission of acts of terrorism (Terrorism Act 2000, s.56). It is also an offence to possess an article in circumstances which give rise to a reasonable suspicion that his possession is for a purpose connected with the commission, preparation or instigation of an act of terrorism (2000 Act, s.57).

It is an offence to collect or makes a record of information of a kind likely to be useful to a person committing or preparing an act of terrorism, or to possess a document or record containing information of that kind (s.58).

It is an offence to elicit or attempt to elicit information about an individual who is or has been a member of Her Majesty's forces, a member of any of the intelligence services, or a constable, which is of a kind likely to be useful to a person committing or preparing an act of terrorism, or to publish or communicates any such information (s.58A).

7 Training for terrorism

It is an offence to provide or receive instruction or training in the making or use of firearms, explosives, or other weapons (Terrorism Act 2000, s.54). There is a defence for a person to show that their action or involvement was wholly for a purpose other than assisting, preparing for or participating in terrorism.

It is an offence to provide instruction or training in specified skills knowing that a person receiving it intends to use those skills for or in connection with the commission or preparation of acts of terrorism or offences under the Council of Europe Convention on the Prevention of Terrorism or for assisting the commission or preparation by others of such acts or offences (Terrorism Act 2006, s.6).

The specified skills include the making, handling or use of a noxious substance; the use of any method or technique for doing anything else that is capable of being done for the purposes of terrorism; and the design or adaptation for the purposes of terrorism of any method or technique for doing anything.

Attendance at a place used for terrorist instruction or training (whether in the UK or elsewhere) whilst such instruction or training is being provided is also an offence if the person attending knows, believes, or could not reasonably have failed to understand that the instruction or training was for those purposes (s.8).

Note.–The Council of Europe Convention covers certain specified UK offences in relation to explosives, biological and chemical weapons, hostage-taking, hijacking/skyjacking, terrorist funds and similar offences and equivalent offences overseas.

8 Offences as to terrorist property

Part III of the Terrorism Act 2000 is concerned with terrorist property (and is not limited solely to money). terrorist property is defined as money or other property which is likely to be used for the purposes of terrorism, the proceeds of the commission of acts of terrorism and the proceeds of acts carried out for the purposes of terrorism (s.14).

The Act sets out a number of offences as follows–

(a) fundraising for the purposes of terrorism, which includes inviting the provision of, receiving, and providing money or property for those purposes (s.15);

(b) using money or property for the purposes of terrorism, which includes possessing money or property intending that it be used or reasonably suspecting that it may be used for such purposes (s.16);

(c) making money or property available to another (i.e., funding) knowing, or reasonably suspecting, that it will be used for the purposes of terrorism (s.17);

(ca) for an insurer under an insurance contract to make a payment to an insured party where the insurer knows, or has reasonable cause to suspect, that the payment is made in respect of money or property that has been, or is to be, handed over in response to a demand made wholly or partly for the purposes of terrorism (s.17A);

(d) being involved in an arrangement whereby terrorist property is retained or controlled by or on behalf of another person (e.g., money laundering) by concealment, removal from the UK, transfer to nominees, or in any other way (s.18);

(e) failing to disclose a belief or suspicion that another person has committed any of the above offences where that belief or suspicion arises from information which has come to a person's attention in the course of a trade, profession, or business or in the course of his employment (with an exception for legal privilege) (s.19); and

(f) tipping off a suspect or a third party that information about money laundering or terrorist financing has been disclosed to the authorities or that an investigation is being or may be carried out (s.21D).

9 Forfeiture

If a person is convicted of an offence under ss.15 to 18 of the Terrorism Act 2000 (see **8 Offences as to terrorist property**, above), the court may make a forfeiture order in respect of any money or other property which (s.23)–

(a) was in his possession or control at the time of the offence (or in the case of an offence under s.18, which related to the arrangement in question), and

(b) which had been used for the purposes of terrorism, or which he intended to use, or knew or had reasonable cause to suspect might be used, for the purposes of terrorism.

Where a person is convicted of an offence under s.17A the court may order the forfeiture of the amount paid under, or purportedly under, the insurance contract (s.23(5A)).

Where a criminal investigation has begun the High Court (in Scotland, the Court of Session) may make a restraint order prohibiting a person from dealing with property in respect of which a forfeiture order could later be made. A restraint order may be made once investigations have been begun, even though criminal proceedings have not yet been started.

Similar forfeiture provisions also apply where a person is convicted of (s.23A)–

(a) an offence under the Terrorism Act 2000, s.54 (weapons training), ss.57 to 58A (possessing things/collecting information for terrorist purposes), ss.59 to 61 (inciting terrorism abroad);

(b) an offence under the Terrorism Act 2006, ss.2,. 5, and 6 (dissemination of terrorist publications, preparation of terrorist acts, terrorism training);

(c) ancillary offences (aiding, abetting, counselling or procuring); and

(d) non-terrorist offences committed with a terrorist connection.

The proceeds of forfeiture may be used to compensate the victims of terrorism where the inadequacy of the offender's means preclude him from paying compensation under other powers.

10 Seizure of terrorist cash

Police, HM Revenue and Customs and immigration officers have the power in certain circumstances to seize and detain cash if they have reasonable grounds for suspecting that it is terrorist cash (Anti-terrorism, Crime and Security Act 2001, s.1 and Sch. 1). "Cash" includes currency, postal orders, cheques of any kind including travellers' cheques, bankers' drafts, bearer bonds and bearer shares, and other form of monetary instrument as the Secretary of State may specify by Order (Sch. 1, para. 1). "Terrorist cash" for these purposes is cash which is (s.1(1), Sch. 1 para. 1)–

(a) intended to be used for the purposes of terrorism;

(b) consists of the resources of an organisation which is proscribed; or

(c) is property earmarked as terrorist property (i.e., which has been obtained through terrorism).

Cash may be seized whether or not any proceedings have been brought for an offence in connection with it (s.1(2)).

Cash may be seized initially for a period of 48 hours (Sch. 1 para. 3). Within that time, application must be made to a magistrates' court for its continued detention or forfeiture. In Scotland, application is made to the sheriff. The court may order detention of the cash for up to three months and orders may be renewed up to a maximum of two years. The cash must be detained in an interest bearing account. Provision is made for the release of cash where the court is not satisfied that there are grounds for its continued detention.

Application may be made for the cash to be forfeited. The magistrates (or sheriff) may only grant an application if satisfied that the cash is terrorist cash. An appeal against forfeiture must be made within 30 days to the Crown Court (in Scotland, the sheriff principal) (Sch. 1 para. 7).

Where cash has been detained, a victim of terrorism to whom the cash belonged may apply to the court (or sheriff) for it to be returned to him (Sch. 1 para. 9).

Earmarked property (see above) may be traced even though it passes into the hands of other people and/or is converted into different property. It only ceases to be earmarked when it is acquired by someone in good faith, for value, and without notice that it was earmarked (Sch. 1 paras 11 to 16).

11 Freezing orders

The government (through the Treasury) may freeze the assets of overseas persons by "designating" them under the Terrorist Asset-Freezing etc Act 2010. Before making an order, the Treasury must–

(a) reasonably believe that the person is or has been involved in terrorist activity (or is owned or controlled directly or indirectly by, or is acting on behalf or at the direction of, such a person); and

(b) consider that it is necessary for the purpose of protecting members of the public from terrorism that financial restrictions should be applied in relation to the person.

A designation expires one year after being made unless renewed. An interim designation, which last up to 30 days, may be made based on "reasonable suspicion" rather than "reasonable belief"

The effect of designation is that it is an offence for a person to—

(c) deal with funds or economic resources owned, held or controlled by a designated person if the person who is dealing knows, or has reasonable cause to suspect, that they are owned, held or controlled by a designated person (s.11).

(d) make funds, financial services, or economic resources available (directly or indirectly) to, or for the benefit of, a designated person if the person making them available knows, or has reasonable cause to suspect, that they are being made available (directly or indirectly) to a designated person (ss.12 to 15).

There are limited exceptions, e.g., to allow frozen accounts to be credited with interest or other earnings due, or payments to be made which are due under contracts, agreements or obligations that were concluded or arose before the account became frozen (s.16). The Treasury may also grant a licence to allow a person to do an act which would otherwise be prohibited (s.17). It should be noted that an offence may be committed by a UK national or UK incorporated body even where the conduct in question (which may include acts or omissions) is wholly or partly outside the UK (s.33).

In order to monitor compliance, and detect evasion, the Treasury has the power to request information from a designated person (and others) as to (i) funds and economic resources owned, held or controlled by or on behalf of that person, (ii) any disposal of such funds or economic resources, and (iii) (so far as they may reasonably require) about expenditure by or on behalf of the designated person and for such person's benefit (s.20).

A designated person may appeal to the High Court or the Court of Session against a Treasury decision to make or vary, or not to vary or revoke, an interim or final designation, or a Treasury decision to renew a final designation (s.26).

C: INVESTIGATION OF TERRORISM

12 Cordons

Where it is considered expedient for the purposes of a terrorist investigation, the police have the power to cordon off an area (Terrorism Act 2000, s.33) for an initial period of up to 14 days, which may be extended to 28 days (s.35).

The effects of cordoning off an area are that the police may (s.36)—

(a) order a person to leave the area immediately;

(b) order a person to leave premises in or adjacent to the cordoned off area immediately;

(c) order a driver or person in charge of a vehicle in the area to move it from the area immediately;

(d) arrange for the removal of a vehicle from the area or its movement within the area;

(e) prohibit or restrict access to the area by people or vehicles.

13 Powers of search and seizure

For the purposes of a terrorist investigation, the police may apply for a warrant to enter specified premises (or all premises occupied or controlled by a specified person), to search them and any person found there, and to seize and retain any relevant material found during such a search (Terrorism Act 2000, s.37, and Sch. 5 para. 1). In Scotland, application is made by the procurator fiscal (under Sch. 5, para. 28).

Material is "relevant" for these purposes if it is likely to be of significant value to a terrorist investigation and must be seized in order to prevent it from being concealed, lost, damaged, altered, or destroyed.

Application for a warrant must be made to a justice of the peace (in Scotland, to a sheriff) who may grant it if satisfied that it is sought for the purposes of a terrorist investigation, that there are reasonable grounds for believing that there is material (other than excepted material) on the premises which is likely to be of substantial value to the investigation, and (where the application relates to residential premises) that a warrant is likely to be necessary in the circumstances of the case. In urgent cases, a warrant may be authorised by a police superintendent (Sch. 5, paras 15 and 31) but in this case, particulars must be notified to the Secretary of State as soon as is reasonably practicable.

Excepted material is material defined as "excluded" or "special procedure" material under the Police and Criminal Evidence Act 1984 and special procedures apply to applications for its production or access to it or for search warrants in respect of it (Sch. 5, paras 4 to 12).

Premises may also be searched for terrorist publications, which can be seized and forfeited (Terrorism Act 2006, s.28).

14 Power to require financial information

For the purposes of a terrorist investigation the police (in Scotland, the procurator fiscal) may apply to a circuit judge (in Scotland, a sheriff; in Northern Ireland, a county court judge) for an order requiring a financial institution to provide customer information (Terrorism Act 2000, s.38 and Sch. 6).

"Customer information" includes information as to whether a business relationship exists between the institution and a particular person and the dates when it began or ended, a customer's account number, full name, address or former address, date of birth, the identity of any person sharing an account with the customer, and any evidence as to identity obtained by the institution for the purposes of money laundering legislation (Sch. 6, para. 7).

S.38A and Schedule 6A (both added by the Anti-terrorism, Crime and Security Act 2001 s.3, Sch. 2) require a financial institution to provide details of the contents of an account under an "account monitoring order". Such an order may require details not obtainable under the Schedule 6 provisions and can last for up to 90 days.

15 Disclosure of information

The Anti-terrorism, Crime and Security Act 2001 permits the disclosure to the security services of information by a number of specified public authorities for the purposes of (s.17 and Sch. 4)–
  (a) any criminal investigation which is being carried out, whether in the UK or elsewhere;
  (b) any criminal proceedings which have or may be initiated, whether in the UK or elsewhere;
  (c) the initiation or ending of such an investigation or proceedings, or to aid a decision as to whether they should be initiated or ended.
Any disclosure must be proportionate to what is sought to be achieved by it (s.17(5)).

A separate provision provides that no obligation of secrecy prevents the disclosure by HM Revenue and Customs of information for any of the above purposes or (s.19)–
  (d) to help any of the intelligence services carry out their functions;
although a disclosure prohibited by the Data Protection Act 1998 remains prohibited (s.19(7)). Again, any disclosure must be proportionate to what is sought to be achieved by it. The requirement of proportionality is necessary as disclosure may affect a person's rights under the European Convention on Human Rights Articles 6 and 8.

16 Information about terrorism

It is an offence for a person not to disclose, as soon as reasonably practicable, any information which he knows or believes might be of material assistance in (Terrorism Act 2000 s.38B, added by the Anti-terrorism, Crime and Security Act 2001 s.117)–
  (a) preventing the commission of a terrorist act; or
  (b) securing the apprehension, prosecution or conviction of someone in the United Kingdom for an offence involving the commission, preparation or instigation of an act of terrorism.

17 Tipping off

Where a person knows, or has reasonable cause to suspect, that the police are conducting, or propose to conduct, a terrorist investigation, he will commit an offence if he discloses anything which is likely to prejudice the investigation or interferes with material which is likely to be relevant to it (s.39). There is an exception for disclosures made by professional legal advisers provided they are not made with a view to furthering a criminal purpose.

D: COUNTER-TERRORIST POWERS

18 Terrorism Prevention and Investigation Measures

The Secretary of State may issue a Terrorism Prevention and Investigation Measures notice (a "TPIM notice") imposing specified measures on a person if the following conditions are met (Terrorism Prevention and Investigation Measures Act 2011, s.3)–
  (a) the Secretary of State is satisfied, on the balance of probabilities, that the individual is, or has been, involved in terrorism-related activity ("relevant activity");
  (b) some or all of the relevant activity is new terrorism-related activity;
  (c) the Secretary of State reasonably considers that it is necessary, for purposes connected with protecting members of the public from a risk of terrorism, for TPIM to be imposed on the individual;
  (d) the Secretary of State reasonably considers that it is necessary, for purposes connected with preventing or restricting the individual's involvement in terrorism-related activity, for the specified TPIM to be imposed on the individual;
  (e) a court gives the Secretary of State permission, or the Secretary of State reasonably considers that the urgency of the case requires TPIM to be imposed without obtaining such permission.
The types of measures which may be imposed on an individual relate to (Sch. 1)–

Overnight residence
Requiring the individual to reside at or within a specified residence – either their own or a residence considered to be appropriate by the Secretary of State – and to remain there for a specified period or periods overnight.

Travel
Restrictions on an individual leaving the UK, or any area within the UK that is their place of residence. The

restrictions imposed may include a requirement not to leave the specified area without receiving permission from, or giving notice to, the Secretary of State, and a prohibition on possessing passports or international travel tickets without permission.

Exclusion
Restrictions on an individual entering specified areas or places (e.g., particular streets, localities or towns where it is believed their extremist contacts live or associate), or types of areas or places (e.g., internet cafés or airports).

Movement directions
Requiring the individual to comply with directions in relation to their movements given by a constable. The direction must be given either for the purpose of securing compliance with other specified measures or where the individual is being escorted by a constable as part of a condition imposed under the Act. Directions given under a movement directions measure may last for as long as the constable considers necessary up to a maximum of 24 hours.

Financial services
Restrictions on the individual's access to financial services, including having no more than one nominated financial account without permission, and not having more than a specified amount of cash.

Property
Restrictions on an individual's ability to transfer money or other property outside the UK without permission or, without giving notice. Conditions may also be imposed in relation to the transfer of property to or by the individual and requiring disclosure of details of any property of a specific description in which they have an interest or over which they may exercise any right.

Weapons and explosives
Prohibiting the making of an application for a firearm certificate or shot gun certificate, or the possession of an imitation firearm, offensive weapons or explosives.

Electronic communication device
Prohibiting the possession or use of electronic communications devices without permission, and impose conditions on such possession or use. Requirements may also be imposed on the individual in relation to other persons' possession or use of devices within the individual's residence.

Association
Restrictions on the individual's association or communication with other persons, in particular, a requirement not to associate or communicate with specified persons or persons of specified descriptions (e.g., persons living outside the UK) without permission, or not to associate with a list of named individuals (without permission), and that if they wish to associate with others, they must first give notice to the Secretary of State. Permission to associate or communicate with a specified person may be subject to conditions e.g., that they are escorted by a constable or someone else. This measure relates to association or communication by any means and whether directly or indirectly.

Work or studies
Restrictions on the individual's work or studies, in particular an individual could be prohibited from undertaking certain specified types of work or studies without permission.

Reporting
Require an individual to report to a particular police station at a time and in a manner notified to him or her in writing, and to comply with directions given by a constable in relation to that reporting.

Appointments
Require an individual to attend meetings with such persons as the Secretary of State may specify, at such locations and at such times as the Secretary of State (or specified person) may by notice require.

Photography
Require an individual to have their photograph taken.

Monitoring
Require an individual to cooperate with specified arrangements for enabling their movements, communications and other activities to be monitored. This may include a requirement to wear, use or maintain an electronic tag and associated apparatus, to comply with associated directions and to grant access to the residence for these purposes.

A TPIM notice will last for 12 months and may be renewed only once (s.5).

The power to issue a TPIM notice will expire after five years (i.e., on the 14th December 2016) unless renewed for a further five year period (s.21).

19 Arrest without warrant

The police may arrest without a warrant a person reasonably suspected of being a terrorist (s.41). A terrorist is defined as someone who has committed one of a number of specified terrorist offences, or who is or has been concerned in the commission, preparation or instigation of acts of terrorism (s.40(1)). Provisions relating to the treatment of detained persons are contained in Schedule 8 to the Act.

20 Notification requirements

A person over the age of 16 convicted of a terrorism offence (or an offence with a terrorism connection) and sentenced to 12 months or more imprisonment will be subject to a notification requirement upon their release (Counter-Terrorism Act 2008, Part 4). The offences in respect of which a notification requirement will be imposed include all the main terrorism offences under the Terrorism Acts 2000 and 2006 and the Anti-terrorism, Crime and Security Act 2001.

The notification requirement requires a person to notify the police of their name and any other names they use, date of birth, national insurance number, home address, other addresses where they regularly reside or stay, and any other information that may be prescribed. Changes of name or address and temporary addresses must also be notified. All information must be re-notified every 12 months. Notification must be made orally by attendance at a police station and fingerprints and/or photographs may be taken.

The period for which a person will be subject to a notification requirement varies, according to their age and the severity of the sentence they received, from 10 to 30 years.

Under the Counter-Terrorism Act 2008 (Foreign Travel Notification Requirements) Regulations 2009, a person to whom the notification requirements in Part 4 of the 2008 Act apply who intends to leave the UK for a period of three or more days is required to notify the police of their departure before they leave and of their return if they subsequently return to the UK. The notification of departure must usually be given seven days before the date of intended departure (Reg. 4) and the notification of return within the period of three days beginning with the day on which the person returns (Reg. 5). Notification is made by the person attending at their local police station and making an oral notification (Reg. 6).

Foreign travel restriction orders may also be imposed, prohibiting a person from visiting specified countries, or only allowing travel to specified countries, or banning foreign travel altogether. Such restriction orders are made by a magistrates' court (in Scotland a sheriff court) on application by the police.

21 Post-charge questioning

Ss.22 and 23 of the Counter-Terrorism Act 2008 allows a judge of the Crown Court in England and Wales to authorise questioning of a person about an offence for which they have been charged or after they have been officially informed that they may be prosecuted, or after the person has been sent for trial for the offence, where the offence is a terrorism offence (as defined in s.27) or where the judge considers the offence to have a terrorist connection (as defined in s.93). In Scotland, a sheriff may authorise questioning of a person about such an offence, for which they have been charged or when they have appeared on petition in respect of the offence. An authorisation must specify the period during which questioning is authorised and may impose such conditions as appear to be necessary in the interests of justice, which may include conditions as to the place where the questioning is to be carried out. A judge (or sheriff) can authorise post-charge questioning only if satisfied that further questioning of the person is necessary in the interests of justice, that the police investigation related to the suspect is being conducted diligently and expeditiously, and that it would not interfere unduly with the preparation of the person's defence to the charge in question or any other criminal charge. An authorisation begins when questioning pursuant to the authorisation begins and runs continuously from that time and is limited to a maximum of 48 hours before further authorisation must be sought. Codes of practice under s.66 of the Police and Criminal Evidence Act 1984 must make provision about post-charge questioning. Post-charge questioning is required to be video-recorded with sound (s.25) and must be conducted in accordance with the *Code of Practice for the Video Recording with Sound of Interviews of Persons Detained under Section 41 of, or Schedule 7 to, the Terrorism Act 2000 and Post Charge Questioning of Persons Authorised under Sections 22 or 23 of the Counter-Terrorism Act 2008* which is available from the Home Office.

22 Search of premises, persons and vehicles

The police may apply for a warrant to search specified premises for the purpose of making an arrest if they reasonably suspect that a person who is or has been concerned in the commission, preparation or instigation of acts of terrorism may be found there (s.42).

Ss.43 and 43A of the Terrorism Act 2000 permit a constable to stop and search a person whom he reasonably suspects to be a terrorist to discover whether he has in his possession anything which may constitute evidence that he is a terrorist; a vehicle carrying the person, or which the constable reasonably suspects of being used for the purposes of terrorism may also be stopped and searched.

S.47A of the Terrorism Act 2000 provides additional powers of stop and search of pedestrians and vehicles in a specified area which apply only where an officer of or above the rank of assistant chief constable (or equivalent rank in the metropolitan police area or the City of London) authorises their use on the ground that he reasonably suspects that an act of terrorism will take place and reasonably considers that the authorisation of is necessary to prevent such an act and that the area or place specified in the authorisation is no greater than is necessary and the duration of the authorisation is no longer than is necessary.

Any exercise of these stop and search powers must be conducted in accordance with the *Code of Practice (England, Wales and Scotland) for the Exercise of Stop and Search Powers under Sections 43 and 43A of the*

Terrorism Act 2000, and the Authorisation and Exercise of Stop and Search Powers Relating to Section 47A of, and Schedule 6B to, the Terrorism Act 2000 which is available from the Home Office.

23 Parking restrictions

The police may apply for an authorisation allowing them to prohibit or restrict parking in specified roads (s.48). Authorisation is given by a senior police officer (i.e., of the rank of assistant chief constable or above) and will only be granted where it is expedient for the prevention of acts of terrorism. An authorisation may last for up to 28 days and may be extended (s.50).

24 Port and border controls

The Terrorism Act 2000 s.53 and Schedule 7 contain provisions as to the port and border controls which may be exercised by police, immigration and HM Revenue and Customs officers.

There is a power to stop, question and detain people at a port or in a border area if it is believed that the person's presence in the area is connected with his–

(a) entering or leaving Great Britain or Northern Ireland;

(b) travelling by air within Great Britain or within Northern Ireland; or

(c) arrival by ship or plane at any place in Great Britain or Northern Ireland (whether the journey was from within or outside Great Britain and Northern Ireland).

Officers may require proof of identity and the production of certain documents and have the power to detain people for up to six hours (Sch. 7, paras 1 to 6, as amended by the 2001 Act). There are various provisions as to the searches of ships, aircraft and vehicles which may be made (see paras 7 to 10) and the property that may be detained (see para. 11).

Certain ports are "designated ports" for the purposes of the Act. Ships or aircraft which carry passengers for reward must use a designated port or seek approval in advance for the use of a different port. Carriers of passengers other than for reward may use non-designated ports provided they give at least 12 hours notice to the police in the area where the port is situated (para. 12).

The owners or agents of a ship or aircraft must also, on request, provide specified details about passengers, crew, goods and vehicles being carried (para. 17). The information which can be requested is specified in Schedule 7 to the Terrorism Act 2000 (Information) Order 2002 (S.I. No. 1945).

25 Retention of travel documents

Where the police have reasonable grounds to suspect that a person at a port, airport or international railway station in Great Britain intends to leave the country to become involved in terrorism-related activity outside the UK they may (Counter-Terrorism and Security Act 2015, Sch. 1 para 2(5))–

(a) require that person to hand over all travel documents in their possession;

(b) search for travel documents relating to that person and to take possession of any that are found;

(c) inspect any travel document relating to that person;

(d) retain any travel document relating to that person that is lawfully in police possession.

A "travel document" for these purposes is a passport or a ticket for travel to a place outside the UK.

Where a travel document relating to the person is in the possession of an immigration officer or customs official, the police may direct that officer or official to pass the document to them as soon as practicable, and in the meantime to retain it. An immigration officer or customs official who lawfully comes into possession of a travel document can also ask the police whether they want to give them a direction to pass the document on to them and can retain that document in the meantime (Sch. 1 paras 2(9), (3)).

When the police do retain a travel document, they must seek authorisation from a senior police officer for its continued retention, or else return it (Sch. 1, para 4).

The officer or official retaining a document must inform the person to whom it relates that they are suspected of intending to leave the country for the purpose of involvement in terrorism-related activity outside the UK, and that the police are therefore entitled to retain the document while the matter is considered by a senior police officer. If the authorisation is refused, the travel document must be returned to the person as soon as possible; if it is granted it may be retained for up to 14 days while (Sch. 1, para 5)–

(a) the Secretary of State considers whether to cancel the person's passport;

(b) consideration is given to charging the person with an offence;

(c) consideration is given to making the person subject to any order or measure to be made or imposed by a court, or by the Secretary of State, for purposes connected with protecting members of the public from a risk of terrorism; or

(d) steps are taken to carry out any of the actions mentioned in (a) to (c) above.

The 14 day period may be extended for up to a further 30 days on application to a district judge (in Scotland, a sheriff) (Sch.1, para 8) but the person to whom the document relates must be able to make representations and be represented at the hearing. However they or their representative may be excluded on specified grounds (such as national security or the hindrance of investigations).

If a travel document is still being retained by the police 72 hours after an authorisation has been given for its retention, a senior police officer must carry out a review of whether the decision to give authorisation was flawed (Sch. 1, para 6).

Where a power to retain a document is exercised against a person and such a power has already been exercised in relation to the same person on two or more occasions in the preceding six months, then the travel documents may be retained only for a period of 5 days (rather than 14). An extension up to a maximum of 30 days may be applied for, but will only be granted if the district judge/sheriff thinks that there are exceptional circumstances which justify the further use of these powers in relation to the same person (Sch. 1, para 13).

The Secretary of State may designate qualified immigration officers or customs officials as being "accredited", a status which gives them the same powers as the police to search for and seize travel documents (Sch. 1, para 17).

The Counter-Terrorism and Security Act 2015 (Code of Practice for Officers exercising functions under Schedule 1) Regulations 2015 (S.I. No. 217) makes further provision as to the exercise of these powers.

Note.-These power are also exercisable where a person travels within the UK from Great Britain to Northern Ireland for the purpose of involvement in terrorism outside the UK, but not where the person is travelling from Northern Ireland to Great Britain.

26 Temporary exclusion orders

A "temporary exclusion order" (TEO) requires the individual on whom it is imposed not to return to the UK unless their return is in accordance with a permit to return issued by the Secretary of State before the individual began the return, or the return is the result of the individual's deportation to the UK (Counter-Terrorism and Security Act 2015, s.2).

A TEO may only be imposed where the Secretary of State reasonably–
   (a) suspects that the individual is, or has been, involved in terrorism-related activity outside the UK;
   (b) considers that it is necessary, for purposes connected with protecting members of the public in the UK from a risk of terrorism, for a temporary exclusion order to be imposed on the individual;
   (c) considers that the individual is outside the UK;
and
   (d) the individual has the right of abode in the UK; and
   (e) a court has given the Secretary of State permission to make the order, or the Secretary of State reasonably considers that the urgency of the case requires a TEO to be imposed without obtaining such permission.

For these purposes, involvement in "terrorism-related activity" is any one or more of the following (s.14(4))–
   (f) the commission, preparation or instigation of acts of terrorism;
   (g) conduct that facilitates the commission, preparation or instigation of such acts, or is intended to do so;
   (h) conduct that gives encouragement to the commission, preparation or instigation of such acts, or is intended to do so;
   (i) conduct that gives support or assistance to individuals who are known or believed by the individual concerned to be involved in conduct falling within (f) above.

It is immaterial whether the acts of terrorism in question are specific acts of terrorism or acts of terrorism in general.

A court can consider an application for a TEO without the person concerned having knowledge of it. Where the court determines that any of the decisions of the Secretary of State that conditions (a) to (e) above are met is obviously flawed, then it must not give permission for the TEO, but otherwise it must give permission. Only the Secretary of State (not the person being made subject to the TEO) can appeal (s.3).

Notice of the imposition of a TEO must be given to the individual on whom it is imposed (the "excluded individual"), together with an explanation of the procedure for making an application for a permit to return. An order comes into force when notice of its imposition is given and remains in force for two years (unless revoked or otherwise brought to an end earlier) (s.4). Where a person's whereabouts are not known, and no address is available for correspondence with them or their representative, the notice will be deemed to have been given when the Secretary of State enters a record of the above circumstances and places the signed notice on the relevant file (Temporary Exclusion Orders (Notices) Regulations 2015, Reg. 3).

Where a TEO is made in a case of urgency, the Secretary of State must, immediately after giving notice of the imposition of the order, refer it to the court for it to consider whether or not her decisions as to (a) to (e) above being met were obviously flawed (Sch. 2). If any of the decisions is flawed, the TEO must be quashed, otherwise it must be confirmed.

An individual subject to a TEO may apply for a "permit to return" to the UK which, if granted, may be made subject to conditions and must state (s.5)–
   (a) the time at which, or period of time during which, they are permitted to arrive on return to the UK (e.g., on a specific flight);
   (b) the manner in which they are permitted to return to the UK; and
   (c) the place where they are permitted to arrive on return to the UK.

If an individual applies for a permit to return, the Secretary of State must issue one within a reasonable period, but may refuse the application if the individual is required to attend an interview with a police or immigration officer at a specified time and a place and fails to do so (s.6). A permit to return must be issued if the Secretary of State considers that the individual is to be deported to the UK (s.7).

Where an individual subject to a TEO returns to the UK, the Secretary of State may impose any or all of the following obligations upon them (s.9)–
- – to report to a police station;
- – to attend at appointments (which may for example include de-radicalisation programmes);
- – to notify the police of their place of residence and any change of address.

Once an individual subject to a TEO is back in the UK, he may apply to the court for a statutory review of the decision to impose the TEO, and any associated in-country measures (s.11).

27 The Authority to Carry Scheme

Carriers will not always be aware of a terrorism-related exclusion or deportation order or travel ban and so are not always in a position to deny boarding to a person subject to such an order. Under the Counter-Terrorism and Security Act 2015 (Authority to Carry Scheme) Regulations 2015 (made under the Counter-Terrorism and Security Act 2015, s.22) the Home Secretary has introduced an "Authority to Carry Scheme", which allows her to refuse a carrier authority to bring certain passengers to, or take them from, the UK, in accordance with the terms of the Scheme. The Scheme applies to all passenger air, ship and train carriers operating into and out of the UK that have been given written notice requiring submission of passenger data to e-Borders. Under the scheme carriers are required to seek authority to carry all passengers who fall within the scope of the scheme (see below). If the carrier does not seek such authority, or if the carrier brings to or takes from the UK a passenger in respect of whom authority has been denied, the carrier will be liable to a financial penalty (set out in the Authority to Carry Scheme (Civil Penalties) Regulations 2015) of up to £50,000.

A carrier to whom the Scheme applies is required to provide passenger data to e-Borders before departure. The submission of this information constitutes a request by the carrier for authority to carry all the passengers who come within the scope of the Scheme. The carrier will be notified by the Home Office via telephone of the details of any individual whom they do not have authority to carry to/from the UK. If no notification is received by a set time, carriers will automatically have authority to carry all the passengers. If, due to technical failure, the carrier is unable to send the data required it must decide if it wishes to carry passengers who have not been subject to pre-departure checks. The Home Office will liaise with the carrier to discuss appropriate next steps should the carrier have boarded an individual whom they would have been denied authority to carry. The carrier will however be liable to the financial penalty if it does not seek authority to carry in accordance with this Scheme, unless it can establish that it has a reasonable excuse for avoiding liability.

The scheme applies to all passengers and crew travelling, or expected to travel, to or from the UK on a carrier to which the scheme applies (but where a carrier provides information voluntarily, it only applies to passengers and crew in respect of whom information is provided).

Authority to carry *to the UK* may be refused in respect of–
- (a) individuals who are assessed by the Secretary of State to pose a direct threat to the security of an aircraft, ship or train or persons or property on board;
- (b) individuals who are the subject of a Temporary Exclusion Order;
- (c) individuals listed by the UN or EU as being subject to travel restrictions (to the extent the individual is seeking to travel in breach of those restrictions);
- (d) EEA nationals or accompanying/joining third country national family members of EEA nationals who are, or in relation to whom the Secretary of State is in the process of making, the subject of an exclusion or deportation order under the Immigration (European Economic Area) Regulations 2006;
- (e) third country nationals who have been excluded from the UK by the Secretary of State, or in relation to whom the Secretary of State is in the process of making an exclusion decision, under the immigration rules, rule 320(6);
- (f) third country nationals who are the subject of a deportation order or whom the Secretary of State is in the process of making the subject of a deportation order;
- (g) third country nationals who have been or would be refused a visa because of national security, and;
- (h) individuals who are using an invalid travel document that is, or appears to be, a passport or other document which has been lost, stolen or cancelled, has expired, was not issued by the government or authority by which it purports to have been issued or has undergone an unauthorised alteration.

Authority to carry *from the UK* may be refused in respect of the following persons–
- (a) individuals who pose a direct threat to the security of any aircraft, ship or train or persons or property on board;
- (b) individuals listed by the UN or EU as being subject to travel restrictions (to the extent the individual is seeking to travel in breach of those restrictions);
- (c) children (i.e., under the age of 18) whom the Secretary of State has reasonable grounds to believe are intending to leave the UK for the purposes of involvement in terrorism-related activity;
- (d) individuals whose travel documents are being retained under the Counter-Terrorism and Security Act 2015;
- (e) individuals who are the subject of post-custodial licence conditions preventing travel from the UK following a conviction for a terrorism-related offence;
- (f) individuals who are the subject of a travel measure preventing their travel outside the UK under the Terrorism Prevention and Investigation Measures Act 2011; and

(g) individuals in respect of whom the Secretary of State has cancelled a passport, or has not issued a passport to, on the basis that they have or may have been, or will or may become, involved in activities so undesirable that it is contrary to the public interest for the person to have access to passport facilities.

28 Dangerous pathogens and toxins

An occupier of premises has a duty to notify the Secretary of State before keeping or using any dangerous substance there (Anti-terrorism, Crime and Security Act 2001, s.59). A "dangerous substance" for these purposes is one listed in Schedule 5 to the Act (which lists various viruses, rickettsiae, bacteria and toxins and has been modified by SI 2007/926 and SI 2012/1466) or anything infected with or otherwise carrying such a substance (s.58). However, a substance will not be a dangerous substance if it satisfies prescribed conditions or is kept or used in prescribed circumstances. The Security of Pathogens and Toxins (Exceptions to Dangerous Substances) Regulations 2002 prescribe exceptions for pathogens kept and used for certain medical purposes and for toxins in limited circumstances.

The police can require an occupier of premises to provide details of the–
(a) security measures in place with relation to a dangerous substance (s.60);
(b) persons with access to a dangerous substance (s.61).

Directions may be given by the police requiring specified security measures to be taken (s.62); and by the Secretary of State requiring a substance to be disposed of where he has grounds for believing that security measures are not adequate (s.63), or requiring the occupier to deny specified people access to the substance (s.64). Where a person is denied access, they may appeal to the Pathogens Access Appeal Commission (and then, on a point of law, to the Court of Appeal or Court of Session) (s.70).

Under the Terrorism Act 2006, making or having possession of a radioactive device or material with the intention of using it in the course of or in connection with the commission or preparation of an act of terrorism or for the purposes of terrorism, or of making it available to be so used, or actually using it, is an offence (ss.9 and 10). Trespass on a nuclear site is also an offence (Serious Organised Crime and Police Act 2005, ss.128 and 129).

29 Duties of local authorities and others

In the exercise of their functions (other than any judicial functions), the following authorities and bodies must have due regard to the need to prevent people from being drawn into terrorism (Counter-Terrorism and Security Act 2015, s.26)–
(a) local authorities;
(b) governors of prisons and young offender institutions, providers of probation services, etc;
(c) educational bodies such as schools and universities, and child care agencies, but where they have a duty to do so proprietors or governing bodies of further and higher education institutions must have particular regard to the duty to ensure freedom of speech, and the importance of academic freedom;
(d) NHS bodies; and
(e) the police.

Guidance for authorities and bodies in relation to the exercise of this duty has been issued by the Secretary of State (Counter-Terrorism and Security Act 2015 (Risk of Being Drawn into Terrorism) (Guidance) Regulations 2015/1697) and is available at–
<www.gov.uk/government/publications/prevent-duty-guidance>.

Where the Secretary of State is satisfied that an authority has failed to discharge its duty under s.26, he may give it directions for the purpose of enforcing the performance of that duty and any such direction may be enforced by a mandatory order (s.30).

Higher and further education bodies have a duty to provide information to a monitoring authority to allow that authority to assess their compliance with the Prevent duty (s.32).

Every local authority must have a panel in place for its area for the purposes of assessing the extent to which individuals referred to it by the police are vulnerable to being drawn into terrorism (s.36).

The panel must prepare a support plan in respect of any identified individual whom the panel considers should be offered support and if that individual (or, if under 18, their parent or guardian) consents, the panel must make arrangements for support to be provided in accordance with the plan.

E: OFFENCES OVERSEAS

30 Conspiracy to commit offences abroad

A conspiracy is an agreement with any other person or persons to pursue a course of conduct which will necessarily amount to or involve the commission of an offence if carried out in accordance with the agreement (Criminal Law Act 1977, s.1(1)).

It is an offence to conspire in England and Wales to commit an act abroad which would be unlawful both under the law of England and Wales if carried out here, and under the law of the country where it is intended that the act be committed (1977 Act s.1A, as inserted by the Criminal Justice (Terrorism and Conspiracy) Act 1998, s.5).

The offence will have been committed if any party to the agreement (or their agent) does anything in relation to it in England and Wales before the formation of the agreement; or if someone becomes a party to the agreement in England and Wales; or if any party (or their agent) does, or omits to do, anything in England and Wales in pursuance of the agreement.

Similar provisions apply in Scotland by virtue of the Criminal Procedure (Scotland) Act 1995 s.11A, and in Northern Ireland under the Criminal Attempts and Conspiracy (Northern Ireland) Order 1983 Art. 9A (as inserted respectively by the Criminal Justice (Terrorism and Conspiracy) Act 1998, ss.7 and 6).

31 Inciting terrorism overseas

A person will commit an offence if they incite another person to commit an act of terrorism wholly or partly outside the UK and that act would, if committed in the UK, constitute a relevant offence. In England, Wales and Northern Ireland, the offences which are relevant are murder, certain offences against the person (wounding with intent, poisoning and causing explosions) and endangering life by damaging property. In Scotland, the relevant offences are murder, assault to severe injury and reckless conduct which causes actual injury (Terrorism Act 2000, ss.59 to 61).

32 Terrorist bombing overseas

A person may be convicted in the UK for carrying out an act of terrorism overseas if his action would have constituted one of a number of specified offences if carried out in the UK (Terrorism Act 2000, s.62). The specified offences relate to biological and chemical weapons, and causing explosions.

33 Fund-raising and money laundering overseas

A person may be convicted in the United Kingdom for any act which would be an offence under ss.15 to 18 (see **8 Offences as to terrorist property**, above) if carried out in the United Kingdom (Terrorism Act 2000, s.63).

34 Other terrorist offences committed overseas

A UK national or resident will commit an offence which can be prosecuted in the UK if, whilst abroad, he commits one of the offences specified in the Terrorism Act 2000, ss.63A and 63B, namely–

  (a) *deleted*;
  (b) directing a terrorist organisation;
  (c) possession of an article for terrorist purposes;
  (d) collection of information for terrorist purposes;
  (e) inciting terrorism overseas; or
  (f) an act of terrorism, or for the purposes of terrorism, which if committed in the UK would constitute a specified offence (i.e., murder, manslaughter, culpable homicide, rape, assault, kidnapping, abduction, false imprisonment, various offences against the person, criminal damage, various forgery and counterfeiting offences, malicious mischief, wilful fire-raising).

If *any* person (whether or not a UK national or resident)–

  (g) does anything outside the UK as an act of terrorism or for the purposes of terrorism;
  (h) that action is done to, or in relation to, a UK national, resident or protected person (e.g., diplomatic and consular staff); and
  (i) that act, if committed in the UK, would have constituted a specified act (i.e., murder, manslaughter, culpable homicide, rape, assault, kidnapping, abduction, false imprisonment, various offences against the person, various forgery and counterfeiting offences),

then he can be prosecuted for that offence in the UK (s.63C).

Similar jurisdiction for overseas offences also applies to terrorist attacks, or threats, against the residential or working premises, or vehicles, of protected persons (see above) when a protected person is in, or likely to be in, them (s.63D). The relevant offences in this case are criminal damage, malicious mischief, wilful fire-raising and (in Scotland) breach of the peace.

The Terrorism Act 2006 further provides that if *any* person (whether or not a UK national or resident) does anything outside the UK which if done in the UK would have been one of certain specified offences then they will be guilty of that offence in the UK. These specified offences are–

  (j) an offence under ss.1 to 6 of the 2006 Act so far as it relates to a Convention offence (encouragement of terrorism, dissemination of terrorist publications, preparation of terrorist acts, and training for terrorism);
  (k) an offence under ss.8 to 11 of the 2006 Act (attendance at a terrorist training camp, offences in relation to radioactive devices and materials, etc);
  (l) an offence under s.11(1) of the 2000 Act (membership of a prescribed organisation);
  (m) an offence under s.54 of the 2000 Act (weapons training);
  (n) conspiracy, incitement, or attempting to commit any of these offences, or aiding, abetting, counselling or procuring the commission of such an offence.

An offence under the Anti-terrorism, Crime and Security Act 2001 s.113 committed abroad can also be prosecuted in the UK if it is conducted (s.113A)–

(i) for the purpose of advancing a political, religious, racial, or ideological cause, and

(ii) by a UK national or resident, or

(iii) by any person in relation to a UK national resident or protected person.

S.113 relates to use of noxious substances or things to cause harm and intimidate which is designed to influence the government or an international governmental organisation or to intimidate the public or a section of the public and which has or is likely to have the effect of causing (a) serious violence against a person anywhere in the world; (b) serious damage to real or personal property anywhere in the world; (c) endangering human life or creating a serious risk to the health or safety of the public or a section of the public; or (d) inducing in members of the public the fear that the action is likely to endanger their lives or create a serious risk to their health or safety.

35 Authorities

Statutes–

Anti-terrorism, Crime and Security Act 2001

Counter-Terrorism Act 2008

Counter-Terrorism and Security Act 2015

Criminal Justice (Terrorism and Conspiracy) Act 1998

Criminal Law Act 1977

Serious Organised Crime and Police Act 2005

Terrorism Acts 2000 and 2006

Terrorism (Northern Ireland) Act 2006

Terrorism Prevention and Investigation Measures Act 2011

Terrorist Asset-Freezing etc Act 2010

Statutory Instruments–

Authority to Carry Scheme (Civil Penalties) Regulations 2015 (S.I. 2015 No. 957)

Counter-Terrorism Act 2008 (Foreign Travel Notification Requirements) Regulations 2009 (S.I. 2009 No. 2493)

Counter-Terrorism and Security Act 2015 (Authority to Carry Scheme) Regulations 2015 (S.I. 2015 No. 997)

Criminal Attempts and Conspiracy (Northern Ireland) Order 1983 (S.I. 1983 No. 1120)

Proscribed Organisations (Applications for Deproscription) Regulations 2006 (S.I. 2006 No. 2299)

Proscribed Organisations (Name Changes) Orders 2010 to 2013 (S.I. 2010 No. 34, 2011 No. 2688, 2013 Nos. 1795 and 2742, and 2014 Nos. 1612 and 2210)

Security of Pathogens and Toxins (Exceptions to Dangerous Substances) Regulations 2002 (S.I. 2002 No. 1281)

Temporary Exclusion Orders (Notices) Regulations 2015 (S.I. 2015 No. 438)

Terrorism Act 2000 (Proscribed Organisations) (Amendment) Orders 2001 to 2013 (S.I. 2001 No. 1261, 2002 No. 2724, 2005 No. 2892, 2006 No. 2016, 2008 Nos. 1645 and 1931, 2010 No. 611, 2011 No. 108, 2012 Nos. 1771 and 2937, 2013 Nos. 1746 and 3172, 2014 Nos. 927, 1624, and 3189, 2015 Nos. 55 and 959, and 2016 No. 391)

NATIONALITY AND IMMIGRATION

NATIONALITY AND IMMIGRATION

BRITISH NATIONALITY

Contents

This Note has been structured as follows–

A: INTRODUCTION

1 The legislation

The British Nationality Act 1981 introduced entirely new provisions in respect of citizenship and nationality to replace the system embodied in the British Nationality Act 1948 and later Nationality Acts. As a consequence of the fundamental change substantial amendments have been made to those provisions of the Immigration Act 1971 which concern the right of abode in the UK (see the Note on **Control of Immigration**). There are five kinds of citizenship or status under the 1981 Act, as amended, namely–

(a) British citizenship;
(b) British Overseas Territories citizenship (formerly British Dependent Territories citizenship)
(c) British Overseas citizenship;
(d) British subject, and
(e) Commonwealth citizen.

The British Nationality (Falkland Islands) Act 1983 provided for the acquisition of British citizenship by all those having a connection with the Falkland Islands on 1st January 1983.

The British Overseas Territories Act 2002 provides for the acquisition of British Citizenship by all those who were British Overseas Territories citizens on 21st May 2002 (except those who were British Overseas Territories citizens solely by reason of a connection with the Sovereign Bases in Cyprus). *Note.*–Except in C: BRITISH OVERSEAS TERRITORIES CITIZENSHIP, below, references in this Note to British Overseas Territories and citizens does *not* include reference to the Sovereign Bases in Cyprus and citizenship derived from them.

As to registration as British citizens of citizens of the former colony of Hong Kong, see **21 Registration as a British Citizen under the British Nationality (Hong Kong) Act 1990**, *et seq*, below.

Biometric information may be required when a person applies to become a British citizen either by registration or naturalisation.

References in this Note to sections or schedules are to the British Nationality Act 1981, unless otherwise stated.

2 Delegation of functions

Under s.43, as amended by the 1986 Order, the Secretary of State may delegate the exercise of any of his functions under the 1981 Act with respect to specified matters in cases concerning British citizens or British citizenship. The specified matters are registration and naturalisation, renunciation, resumption and deprivation of British citizenship, or British Overseas Territories citizenship, and renunciation and deprivation of the status of a British National (Overseas).

3 Extent

The 1981 Act extends to Northern Ireland (s.53(4)), and all its provisions, other than provisions relating to the amendment or repeal of certain of the provisions of the 1971 Act, extend to the Channel Islands, and the Isle of Man (which are together referred to in the 1981 Act as "the Islands"), and to the overseas territories (see below) (s.53(5)). The 1983 Act also extends to Northern Ireland, the Channel Islands, and the overseas territories (s.5(4) and (5)). In both Acts, except where the context otherwise requires, the term "the UK" means Great Britain, Northern Ireland, the Channel Islands, and the Isle of Man, taken together (s.50(1) of the 1981 Act and s.4(2) of the 1983 Act).

4 Children

For the purposes of the 1981 Act, the following general rules of interpretation apply, except where the context requires otherwise. These rules also apply for the purposes of the 1983 and 2002 Acts.

A person born outside the UK or an overseas territory aboard a ship or aircraft is deemed to have been born in the UK or that territory if at the time of his birth his father or mother was a British citizen (or British Overseas territories citizen) or if he would, but for this provision, have been born stateless, and if (in either case) at the time of the birth the ship or aircraft was registered in the UK or that territory or was an unregistered ship or aircraft of the government of the UK or that territory (s.50(7), (7A), (7B)). In any other case, a person born aboard a ship or aircraft will be regarded as born outside the UK and overseas territories.

S.50(9) provides that for the purposes of the Act a child's mother is the woman who gives birth to the child. The father of a child will be (a) the husband, at the time of the child's birth, of the woman who gives birth to the child; or (b) a person treated as the father of the child under the Human Fertilisation and Embryology Act 1990, s.28; or (c) where neither (a) nor (b) applies, any person who satisfies prescribed requirements as to proof of paternity (s.50(9A)). The prescribed requirements are set out in the British Nationality (Proof of Paternity) Regulations 2006 (S.I. 2006 No. 1496 and 2015 No. 1615) and are that the Secretary of State is satisfied that he is the natural father having regard to evidence such as birth certificates, DNA test reports and court orders. The expressions "parent" and "child", and "descended" are to be construed accordingly (s.50(9C)).

S.47 provides that a person born out of wedlock and legitimated by the subsequent marriage of his parents (i.e., if by the law of the place in which his father was domiciled at the time of the marriage, the marriage operated immediately or subsequently to legitimate him) will, as from the date of the marriage, be treated as if he had been born legitimate.

Provision is made, by s.48, for the citizenship of a child born after the death of his father or mother to be determined by the status of the parent in question at the time of that parent's death.

S.50(11) provides that a person is of full age if he has attained the age of 18, and of full capacity if he is not of unsound mind.

The Secretary of State is under a duty to make arrangements for ensuring that certain immigration and customs functions are discharged having regard to the need to safeguard and promote the welfare of children who are in the UK. The duty extends to any services provided by another person pursuant to arrangements made by the Secretary of State and which relate to the discharge of such functions, The functions are any—

    (a) function of the Secretary of State in relation to immigration, asylum or nationality;

    (b) function conferred by or by virtue of the Immigration Acts on an immigration officer;

    (c) general customs function of the Secretary of State;

    (d) customs function conferred on a designated customs official.

The Director of Border Revenue must also make arrangements for ensuring that his functions are discharged having regard to the need to safeguard and promote the welfare of children who are in the UK. The duty extends to any services provided by another person pursuant to arrangements made by the Director in the discharge of such a function (Borders, Citizenship and Immigration Act 2009, s.55).

5 "British subject" and "alien"

Following the passing of the 1981 Act, the term "British subject" means a person having the status of British subject under that Act, and the term "alien" means a person who is neither a Commonwealth citizen (as defined in s.37) nor a British protected person nor a citizen of the Republic of Ireland. The interpretation of these terms when they are used in legislation passed before or after the 1981 Act depends, in part, on whether the particular legislation is to be interpreted in relation to a time which fell before 1st January 1983 or in relation to a time which falls or fell after 31st December 1982; this aspect of the matter is dealt with by detailed rules set out in s.51.

B: BRITISH CITIZENSHIP

(1): ACQUISITION AFTER COMMENCEMENT

6 Good character

An application for registration of an adult or young person as a citizen of any description, or as a British subject under the following provisions, will not be granted unless the Secretary of State is satisfied that the adult

or young person is of good character (British Nationality Act 1981, s.41A). The provisions are–
- (a) ss.1(3), (3A) and (4), 3(1), (2) and (5), 4(2) and (5), 4A, 4C, 4D, 4G, 4H, 4I, 5, 10(1) and (2), 13(1) and (3) of the British Nationality Act 1981 (registration as British citizen);
- (b) ss.15(3) and (4), 17(1) and (5), 22(1) and (2), and 24 of that Act (registration as British overseas territories citizen, etc.);
- (c) s.27(1) of that Act (registration as British overseas citizen);
- (d) s.32 of that Act (registration as British subject);
- (e) s.1 of the Hong Kong (War Wives and Widows) Act 1996 (registration as British citizen); and
- (f) s.1 of the British Nationality (Hong Kong) Act 1997 (registration as British citizen).

An "adult or young person" means a person who has attained the age of 10 years at the time when the application was made.

For the purpose of assessing good character, section 4 of the Rehabilitation of Offenders Act 1974, which provides that a rehabilitated person in respect of a spent conviction is to be treated as if they had not committed or been charged with, prosecuted for or convicted of, or sentenced for the offence or offences which were the subject of the conviction, does not apply (UK Borders Act 2007, s.56A).

7 Acquisition by birth or adoption (s.1)

A person will be a British citizen if–
- (a) he was born in the UK on or after 1st January 1983;
- (b) he was born in the Falkland Islands on or after 1st January 1983; or
- (c) he was born in an overseas territory on or after 21st May 2002; and

at the time of the birth, his father or mother was a British citizen, or settled in the UK or that territory (s.1(1)). People who were citizens of those countries and territories on those dates, became British citizens on those dates.

In addition, a person born between 26th April 1969 and 1st January 1983, whose mother was a United Kingdom and Colonies citizen by virtue of having been born in the British Indian Ocean Territory, and who on 21st May 2002 was neither a British citizen nor a British Overseas Territories citizen became a British citizen on that date.

A person born in the UK or a qualifying territory on or after 13th January 2010 will be a British citizen if at the time of the birth his father or mother is a member of the armed forces (s.1(1A)). Where that is not the case when the child is born but a parent subsequently becomes a member of the armed forces while the child is still a minor, the child is entitled to be registered as a British citizen at that time. A "member of the armed forces" means a member of the regular forces within the meaning of the Armed Forces Act 2006 and a member of the reserve forces subject to service law by virtue of that Act. British overseas territory forces and British Commonwealth visiting forces are excluded from this definition (s.50(1A), (1B)).

"Settled" is, by virtue of s.1(8) of the 1981 Act, to be construed, unless the context otherwise requires, in accordance with the rules contained in s.50(2) to (4); it means, subject to exceptions for certain special cases, being ordinarily resident in the UK or, as the case may be, an overseas territory without being subject under the immigration laws to any restriction on the period for which the resident may remain. The exceptions are people who, while not being British citizens, are exempted from the restrictions on entry to the UK (or overseas territory, where appropriate) under specified provisions of s.8 of the 1971 Act (or the corresponding immigration laws of the relevant overseas territory) (s.50(2) and (3)).

A person to whom a child is born in the UK after commencement is regarded for the purposes of s.1(1) as being settled in the UK at the time of the birth if–
- (a) he would fail to be so regarded but for his being at that time entitled to an exemption under s.8(3) of the 1971 Act (which applies to people such as members of missions within the meaning of the Diplomatic Privileges Act 1964 and members of their families and households);
- (b) immediately before he became entitled to the exemption he was settled in the UK; and
- (c) he was ordinarily resident in the UK from the time when he became entitled to that exemption to the time of the birth (s.50(4)).

S.50(4) will not apply if at the time of the birth the child's father or mother is a person on whom any immunity from jurisdiction is conferred by or under the 1964 Act.

A new-born infant found abandoned in the UK or an overseas territory at any time after commencement will, unless the contrary is shown, be deemed to have been born in the UK or that territory after commencement to a parent who at the time of the birth was a British citizen or was settled in the UK or that territory (s.1(2)).

The following people born in the UK after commencement who are not British citizens by virtue of s.1(1), (1A) or (2) of the 1981 Act are entitled to be registered as British citizens–
- (a) a person whose father or mother, during his minority, becomes a British citizen or becomes settled in the UK (in this case, an application for registration must be made during the child's minority) (s.1(3));
- (b) a person whose father or mother, during his minority, becomes a member of the armed forces (again, an application for registration must be made during the child's minority);
- (c) a person who, as regards each of the first ten years of his life, was not absent from the UK for more than 90 days in any of those years (in this case, the application for registration may be made at any time after the person attains the age of ten years, and the Secretary of State has discretion to allow the registration even though the 90-day limit has been exceeded in any one or all of those years) (s.1(4) and (7)).

Where after commencement an order authorising the adoption of a minor who is not a British citizen is made by any court in the UK or an overseas territory, the minor will become a British citizen as from the date of the order if the adopter or, in the case of a joint adoption, one of the adopters is a British citizen on that date (s.1(5)). Where an adoption order to which s.1(5) applies is subsequently annulled, or otherwise ceases to have effect, the status of the adopted person as a British citizen is not affected (s.1(6)).

See also **6 Good character**, above.

8 Acquisition by descent (s.2)

A person born outside the UK and overseas territories after commencement will be a British citizen if at the time of the birth his father or mother–

(a) is a British citizen otherwise than by descent (s.2(1)(a));

(b) is a British citizen and is serving outside the UK and overseas territories (s.2(1)(b)) in (i) Crown service under the government of the UK or an overseas territory (s.2(2)(a)) or (ii) service of any description for the time being designated under s.2(3) for the purpose by the Secretary of State (s.2(2)(b)), and his or her recruitment for that service took place in the UK or overseas territory; or

(c) is a British citizen and is serving outside the UK and overseas territories in service under a Community institution, his or her recruitment for that service having taken place in a country which was a Community country at the time (s.2(1)(c)).

Crown service means the service of the Crown, whether within Her Majesty's dominions or elsewhere, and Crown service under the government of the UK means Crown service under Her Majesty's government in the UK, or under Her Majesty's government in Northern Ireland, the Scottish Administration or the Welsh Assembly Government (s.50).

The British Citizenship (Designated Service) Order 2006, as amended, has been made for the purposes of s.2(2)(b).

9 Meaning of British citizen "by descent" (s.14)

For the purposes of the 1981 Act, a British citizen is a British citizen "by descent" if and only if–

(a) he is a person born outside the UK after commencement who is a British citizen by virtue of s.2(1)(a) only (i.e., because his father or mother was a British citizen otherwise than by descent), or by virtue of registration under s.3(2) (acquisition of British citizenship by minors in certain cases–see below), or by virtue of registration under s.9 (Right to registration by virtue of father's citizenship, etc., now repealed); or

(b) subject to the exception described in s.14(2) (see below), he is a person born outside the UK before commencement who became a British citizen at commencement (see B: BRITISH CITIZENSHIP, 3: ACQUISITION AT COMMENCEMENT, below) and immediately before commencement–

　(i) was a citizen of the United Kingdom and Colonies by virtue of s.5 of the British Nationality Act 1948 (this section of the 1948 Act conferred citizenship of the United Kingdom and Colonies on a person who was born elsewhere than in the United Kingdom and Colonies on or after 1st January 1949 if his father was such a citizen at the time of the birth, provided that (s.5(1)), if the father was himself such a citizen by descent only, his citizenship was not passed on to his child unless (1) the child or his father was born in a protectorate, protected state, mandated territory, or trust territory, or in any place where the sovereign exercised jurisdiction over British subjects, or (2) the child was born in a place in a foreign country other than a place mentioned in (1) and the birth was registered at a UK consulate within one year of its occurrence, or later, with the Secretary of State's permission (the Secretary of State having had the power to dispense with the grant of his permission where a later registration was made without it), or (3) the child's father was, at the time of the birth, in Crown service under Her Majesty's Government in the UK, as defined in s.32 of the 1948 Act, or (4) the child was born in what was at the time of his birth a self-governing Commonwealth country to which a citizenship law had taken effect, and did not become a citizen of that county at birth); or

　(ii) was a person who, under any provision of the British Nationality Acts 1948 to 1965, was deemed for the purposes of the proviso to s.5(1) of the 1948 Act (see the four cases (1) to (4) described in para. (i) above) to be a citizen of the United Kingdom and Colonies by descent only, or would have been so deemed if male; or

　(iii) had the right of abode in the UK by virtue only of s.2(1)(b) of the 1971 Act as then in force (connection with UK through parent or grandparent), or had that right by virtue only of the said s.2(1)(b) and of s.2(1)(c) of the 1971 Act (citizens of the United Kingdom and Colonies settled and ordinarily resident for five years in the UK), or had that right by virtue only of being or having been the wife of a person who immediately before commencement had that right by virtue only of the said s.2(1)(b) or the said s.2(1)(b) and (c); or

　(iv) being a woman, was a citizen of the United Kingdom and Colonies as a result of her registration as such a citizen under s.6(2) of the 1948 Act by virtue of having been married to a man who at commencement became a British citizen by descent or would have done so but for his having died or ceased to be a citizen of the United Kingdom and Colonies as a result of a declaration of renunciation; or

(c) he is a British citizen by virtue of registration under s.3(1) (registration of minors at discretion of the Secretary of State–see **10 Acquisition by registration: minors,** below) and either–
  (i) his father or mother was a British citizen at the time of the birth; or
  (ii) his father or mother was a citizen of the United Kingdom and Colonies at that time and became a British citizen at commencement or would have done so but for his or her death; or
(d) he is a British citizen by virtue of registration under s.4B (see **12 Acquisition by registration–certain persons who have no other citizenship (s.4B)**, below); s.4C **(see 13 Acquisition by registration–certain persons born before 1983 (s.4C)**, below); s.5 (see **16 Acquisition by registration: nationals for the purposes of the Community Treaties,** below); or
(da) he is a British citizen by descent by virtue of ss.4F(3), 4G(2), 4H(2) or 4I(4) (see **15 Acquisition by children of unmarried parents,** below)
(e) subject to the exception described in s.14(2) (see below), being a woman born outside the UK before commencement, she is a British citizen as a result of her registration under s.8 (Registration by virtue of marriage, now repealed) by virtue of being or having been married to a man who at commencement became a British citizen by descent or would have done so but for his having died or ceased to be a citizen of the United Kingdom and Colonies as a result of a declaration of renunciation; or
(f) he is a British citizen by virtue of registration under s.10 (see **18 Registration following renunciation of citizenship of United Kingdom and Colonies,** below) who, having before commencement ceased to be a citizen of the United Kingdom and Colonies as a result of a declaration of renunciation, would, if he had not so ceased, have at commencement become a British citizen by descent by virtue of paragraph (b) above; or
(g) he is a British citizen by virtue of registration under s.13 (see **25 Resumption,** below), immediately before he ceased to be a British citizen as a result of a declaration of renunciation, was such a citizen by descent; or
(h) he is a person born in a British overseas territory after commencement who is a British citizen by virtue of paragraph 2 of Schedule 2 (see G: MISCELLANEOUS, 1: STATELESS PERSONS, below); or
(i) he is a person who is a British citizen by virtue of the application to him of any provision of the 1983 Act but not otherwise, who became a British citizen at commencement and who would not be a British citizen but for s.1(b)(ii) or (iii) of the 1983 Act (see B: BRITISH CITIZENSHIP, 3: ACQUISITION AT COMMENCEMENT, below); or
(j) he is a person who is a British citizen by virtue of the application to him of any provision of the 1983 Act, who became a British citizen at commencement, and who–
  (i) would have been a British citizen by descent if the 1983 Act had not been passed, and
  (ii) would not be a British citizen by virtue of the 1983 Act but for s.1(1)(b)(ii) or (iii) of the 1983 Act.

S.14(2) excepts certain people from the categories of British citizens by descent who would otherwise so qualify. A person born outside the UK before commencement is not a British citizen by descent under paragraph (b) or (c) above if his father was at the time of his birth serving outside the UK in either (i) Crown service under the government of the UK or service of any description at any time designated for the purpose by the Secretary of State, his recruitment for that service having taken place in the UK, or (ii) service under a Community institution, his recruitment to that service having taken place in a country which was then a member of the Communities.

Note.–A person who is a British citizen by virtue of being a British Overseas Territories citizen will be a British citizen by descent if, and only if, he was a British Overseas Territories citizen by descent before 21st May 2002 and, if he was also a British citizen at that date, he was a British citizen by descent.

10 Acquisition by registration–minors (s.3)

If while a person is a minor, an application is made for his registration as a British citizen, the Secretary of State may, if he thinks fit, cause him to be so registered (s.3(1)).

Under s.3(2), a person born outside the UK and overseas territories is entitled to be registered as a British citizen if an application for registration is made while he is a minor and if all the following requirements are fulfilled by either of the child's parents (s.3(3))–
(a) the parent in question was a British citizen by descent at the time of the birth; and
(b) the father or mother of the parent in question (i) was a British citizen otherwise than by descent at that time of the birth of the parent in question or (ii) became a British citizen otherwise than by descent at commencement, or would have become such a citizen otherwise than by descent at commencement but for his or her death; and
(c) as regards any period of three years ending with a date not later than the date of the birth (i) the parent in question was in the UK or an overseas territory at the beginning of that period and (ii) the number of days on which the parent in question was absent from the UK and the overseas territory in that period did not exceed 270.

In the case of a person born stateless, requirement (c) above need not be fulfilled (s.3(2)).

For all the purposes of the 1981 Act, only days for the whole of which a person was absent from the UK are to be taken into account (s.50(10)).

Under s.3(5) and (6), a person born outside the UK and overseas territories is entitled to be registered as a British citizen if an application for such registration is made while he is a minor, and if all the following requirements are satisfied, namely–

(a) that at the time of the minor's birth his father or mother was a British citizen by descent; and

(b) that the minor and his father and mother were in the UK or an overseas territory at the beginning of the period of three years ending with the date of the application and that, in the case of each of them, the number of days on which the person in question was absent from the UK and the overseas territories in that period does not exceed 270; and

(c) that the consent of the minor's father and mother to the registration has been signified in the prescribed manner.

In the following circumstances, the above rules are modified in the manner indicated.

(1) If the minor's father or mother died, or their marriage or civil partnership was terminated, on or before the date of the application for registration, or his father or mother were legally separated on that date, the references to his father and mother in requirement (b) above are to be read as references to his father or mother.

(2) If the minor's father or mother died on or before the date of the application, the reference to his father or mother in requirement (c) above is to be read as a reference to either of them.

(3) If the minor was born illegitimate, all the references in requirements (b) and (c) above are to be read as references to his mother.

See also **6 Good character**, above.

11 Acquisition by registration–British Overseas Territories citizens, etc. (ss.4 and 4A)

If an application is made to register as a British citizen a person who is a British Overseas Territories citizen (other than a person who is such a citizen by reason only of a connection with the Sovereign Bases in Cyprus, or who has previously renounced British citizenship), the Secretary of State may, if he thinks fit, cause that person to be so registered (s.4A, added by the British Overseas Territories Act 2002).

Otherwise, s.4, as amended by the 1986 Order, applies to any person who is of a British Overseas Territories citizen, a British National (Overseas), a British Overseas citizen, a British subject under the Act, or a British protected person. Such a person is entitled to be registered as a British citizen if all the following requirements are satisfied in his case (s.4(2)), namely–

(a) that he was in the UK at the beginning of the period of five years ending with the date of his application for registration (this requirement does not apply to an applicant who was, immediately before commencement, settled in the UK and that the number of days on which he was absent from the UK in that period does not exceed 450 (s.4(3))); and

(b) that the number of days on which he was absent from the UK in the last 12 months of that five-year period does not exceed 90; and

(c) that he was not at any time in that period of 12 months subject under the immigration laws to any restriction on the period for which he might remain in the UK; and

(d) that he was not at any time in that period of five years in the UK in breach of the immigration laws.

The Secretary of State may, for the purposes of s.4(2), if in the special circumstances of any particular case he thinks fit to do so, waive requirements (a) to (d) above, but not requirement (c) if the applicant was subject to a restriction of the kind therein mentioned on the date of the application (s.4(4)).

Under s.4(5), the Secretary of State, if satisfied that an applicant to whom s.4 applies has at any time served in service relevant for this purpose, may, if he thinks fit in the special circumstances of the case, cause him to be registered as a British citizen. Relevant service for this purpose means (i) Crown service under the government of an overseas territory or (ii) paid or unpaid service (not falling within (i)) as a member of any body established by law in an overseas territory members of which are appointed by or on behalf of the Crown.

For the purposes of (d) above, a person will be "in breach of immigration rules" if he is in the UK (British Nationality Act 1981, s.50A)–

(1) without the right of abode, or leave to enter or remain;

(2) does not have qualifying common travel area entitlement (citizen of the Republic of Ireland who arrived in the UK on a local journey);

(3) is not entitled to enter and remain as a member of the crew of a ship or aircraft;

(4) is not entitled to reside by virtue of any provision made under s.2(2) of the European Communities Act 1972; or

(5) does not have exemption (e.g., for diplomats).

S.2 of the 1983 Act, as amended by the 1986 Order, empowers the Secretary of State, at his discretion, to register a British Overseas Territories citizen, or a British National (Overseas), as a British citizen in either of the following cases.

(a) The person is a British Overseas Territories citizen by virtue of s.23 of the 1981 Act (see C: BRITISH OVERSEAS TERRITORIES CITIZENSHIP, 3: ACQUISITION AT COMMENCEMENT, below) or, having become such a citizen by virtue of that section, is a British National (Overseas), and the person or one of his parents was settled in the Falkland Islands either immediately before commencement or, in the case of a parent who died before commencement, was settled in the Falkland Islands immediately before his or her death.

(b) The person is a British Overseas Territories citizen by virtue of registration or naturalisation under the 1981 Act or, having become such a citizen by virtue of such registration or naturalisation, is a British National (Overseas), and either (i) that registration or naturalisation was effected in the Falkland Islands under the provisions of s.43 of the 1981 Act or (ii) the Secretary of State is satisfied that the registration or naturalisation was effected wholly or partly by reason of a connection which the person or some other person has with the Falkland Islands.

The procedure for registration under this provision is laid down in the British Nationality (General) Regulations 2003.

See also **6 Good character**, above.

12 Acquisition by registration—certain persons who have no other citizenship (s.4B)

If a person has the status of–
(a) British Overseas citizen;
(b) British subject (under the Nationality, Immigration and Asylum Act 2002);
(c) British protected person; or
(d) British National (Overseas),

then, if the Secretary of State is satisfied that they have no other citizenship or nationality and have not after the relevant date (4th July 2002 in the case of (a) to (c) above or 19th March 2009 in the case of (d) above) renounced, voluntarily relinquished, or lost through action or inaction, any citizenship or nationality, they are entitled to be registered as British citizens.

The procedure for registration under this provision is laid down in the British Nationality (General) Regulations 2003.

13 Acquisition by registration—certain persons born before 1983 (s.4C)

A person born before 1st January 1983 who would have become a British citizen by descent through his mother before 1st January 1983 had the rules for mothers been the same as for fathers, and who would have had a right of abode in the UK immediately before that date had he become a citizen, may apply for registration.

The procedure for registration under this provision is laid down in the British Nationality (General) Regulations 2003.

See also **6 Good character**, above.

14 Acquisition by registration—children born to members of the armed forces (s.4D)

A person born outside the UK and the qualifying territories on or after 13th January 2010 is entitled to be registered as a British citizen if an application for registration is made and the following conditions are satisfied–
(a) at the time of the person's birth, his father or mother was a member of the armed forces and serving outside the UK and the qualifying territories;
(b) if the person is a minor on the date of the application, the consent of his father and mother to his registration as a British citizen has been signified in the prescribed manner.

If the person's father or mother has died on or before the date of the application, the reference in (b) above is to be read as a reference to either of them. The Secretary of State may, in the special circumstances of the case, waive the need for the second condition to be satisfied.

See also **6 Good character**, above.

15 Acquisition by children of unmarried parents

A person born after 1st July 2006 is entitled to be registered as a British citizen if at the time of his birth his natural father was not marred to his mother, no one is treated as his father under the Human Fertilisation and Embryology Act 1990, and he has never been a British citizen, if–
(a) their had mother been married to their natural father at the time of their birth they would have been entitled to be registered as a British citizen under ss.1(3), 3(2) or (5) or Sch.2 paras 4 or 5 (s.4F);
(b) at any time after commencement of the 1981 Act, the person would automatically have become a British citizen at birth under that Act or the British Nationality (Falkland Islands) Act 1983, had their mother been married to their natural father at the time of the birth (s.4G);
(c) they were a citizen of the United Kingdom and Colonies immediately before commencement of the 1981 Act and would automatically have become a British citizen under the 1981 Act had their mother been married to their natural father at the time of the birth (s.4H);
(d) they are an eligible former British national or non-British national (as defined) and would have automatically become a British citizen under the 1981 Act had their mother been married to their natural father at the time of their birth (s.4I).

16 Acquisition by registration—nationals for the purposes of the Community Treaties (s.5)

A British Overseas Territories citizen who fails to be treated as a national of the UK for the purposes of the Community Treaties (e.g., a Gibraltarian) is entitled to be registered as a British citizen on making an application for registration.

See also **6 Good character**, above.

17 Acquisition by naturalisation (s.6)

British citizenship by naturalisation may be granted to a person who is of full age and capacity who fulfils specified requirements. Different requirements apply in the case of a person married to or the civil partner of a British citizen on the date of the application for naturalisation (s.6 and Sch.1).

The requirements are as follows. Every applicant must (Sch. 1, paras 1, 3(e))–

(a) be of good character;

(b) have a sufficient knowledge of the English, Welsh, or Scottish Gaelic language;

(c) have sufficient knowledge about life in the UK.

A person not married to or the civil partner of a British Citizen must also–

(d) in the event of being granted a certificate of naturalisation, either intend that his home (or his principal home) will be in the UK or intend to enter into, or continue in, Crown service under the government of the UK, or service under an international organisation of which the UK or Her Majesty's Government is a member, or service in the employment of a company or association established in the UK.

There are also residence requirements as follows. A person not married to or the civil partner of a British Citizen must either–

(e) have been in the UK at the beginning of the period of five years ending with the date of the application, and not have been absent from the UK in that period for more than 450 days; and

(f) not have been absent from the UK in the last 12 months for more than 90 days; and

(g) not at any time in the last 12 months have been subject under the immigration laws to any restriction on the period for which he might remain in the UK; and

(h) not have been in breach of UK immigration laws at any time in the last five years; or

(i) on the date of the application be serving outside the UK in Crown service under the government of the UK.

For a person married to or the civil partner of a British citizen on the date of the application the residence requirements are–

(j) that they were in the UK at the beginning of the period of three years ending with the date of the application, and have not been absent from the UK in that period for more than 270 days; and

(k) have not been absent from the UK in the last 12 months for more than 90 days; and

(l) have not at any time in the last 12 months been subject under the immigration laws to any restriction on the period for which they might remain in the UK; and

(m) have not been in breach of UK immigration laws at any time in the last three years.

The Secretary of State may, if in the special circumstances of any particular case he thinks fit, exercise a power to vary or waive the above requirements. In particular he may–

– waive the language and/or knowledge requirements if he considers that because of an applicant's age or physical or mental condition it would be unreasonable to expect them to fulfil them;

– where the applicant is or has been a member of the armed forces, treat him as fulfilling the requirement specified in (e) above even though he was not in the UK at the beginning of the five year period;

– treat an applicant as fulfilling the residence requirements despite being absent from the UK for more than the specified number of days; and

– treat requirement (h) as being fulfilled despite a breach of the immigration laws.

A person will (subject to the Secretary of State's power of waiver) be treated as having been absent from the UK during certain specified periods. These include (Sch. 1, para 9)–

(a) any period when he was in the UK and either was entitled to an exemption under s.8(3) or (4) of the 1971 Act (exemption for diplomatic agents and others– see the Note on **Control of Immigration** at para **2 Leave to enter or remain in the UK**) or was a member of the family and formed part of the household of such a person;

(b) any period when he was serving a sentence passed on him by a court in the UK or elsewhere, or detained in a hospital in the UK under a hospital order made in connection with his conviction of an offence, or detained under any power of detention conferred by the immigration laws of the UK.

The procedure for registration under these provisions is laid down in the British Nationality (General) Regulations 2003 which, for example, specify when a person will be deemed to have a sufficient knowledge of language and life in the UK. *Inter alia*, Reg. 5A provides that a person who has previously been accepted as having sufficient knowledge of the English language for the purposes of a grant of indefinite leave to remain by the Secretary of State will have such knowledge for the purposes of an application for naturalisation as a British citizen under s.6 of the 1981 Act. A person has sufficient knowledge about life in the UK if they have passed the "Life in the UK Test" or, if they are ordinarily resident outside the UK, a person designated by the Secretary of State has certified that they have sufficient knowledge about life in the UK for the purpose of an application for naturalisation.

18 Registration following renunciation of citizenship of United Kingdom and Colonies (s.10)

S.10(1) preserves for an indefinite period the effect of the law contained in the British Nationality Act 1964 relating to the resumption of citizenship of the United Kingdom and Colonies by people having an appropriate connection with the UK. That Act dealt with the case in which a person on becoming a citizen of a Commonwealth country was required by the laws of that country to renounce his citizenship of the United

Kingdom and Colonies. Such a person was given by the 1964 Act the right at a later date to re-acquire citizenship of the United Kingdom and Colonies by registration if he had a qualifying connection with the UK, e.g., if he, his father, or his father's father was born, or registered or naturalised as a citizen, in the UK. S.10 provides that any person is entitled to be registered as a British citizen if, immediately before commencement, he would (if he had applied for it) have been entitled, under s.1(1) of the 1964 Act, to be registered as a citizen of the United Kingdom and Colonies by virtue of having an appropriate qualifying connection with the UK (see below), or by virtue of having been married before commencement to a person who has, or would if living have, such a connection. A person can be registered only once under s.10 (s.10(3)). Any other person who ceased to be a citizen of the United Kingdom and Colonies before commencement as a result of renunciation may, if the Secretary of State thinks fit, be registered on application as a British citizen if the person has an appropriate qualifying connection with the UK, or has been married to or the civil partner of a person who has, or would if living have, such a connection (s.10(2)).

For the purposes of s.10, a person will be taken to have an appropriate qualifying connection with the UK if he, his father, or his father's father—

(a) was born in the UK; or

(b) is or was a person naturalised in the UK; or

(c) was registered as a citizen of the United Kingdom and Colonies in the UK or in a country which was a Commonwealth country at the time of registration (s.10(4)).

The procedure for registration under this provision is laid down in the British Nationality (General) Regulations 2003.

See also **6 Good character**, above.

(2): ACQUISITION AT COMMENCEMENT

19 The 1981 Act

S.11 contains the rules for determining which citizens of the United Kingdom and Colonies became British citizens at commencement. The general rule is that, with one exception, every person who immediately before commencement (a) was a citizen of the United Kingdom and Colonies, and (b) had the right of abode in the UK under the 1971 Act as then in force, became a British citizen at commencement (s.11(1)). The exception is a person who, as a stateless person from birth, was registered as a citizen of the United Kingdom and Colonies under s.1 of the British Nationality (No. 2) Act 1964 on the ground mentioned in s.1(a) of that Act (namely, that his mother was a citizen of the United Kingdom and Colonies at the time of his birth); but, under s.11(2), such a person did become a British citizen at commencement under s.11(1) or would have done so but for her death, or immediately before commencement he had the right of abode in the UK by virtue of s.2(1)(c) of the 1971 Act as then in force (i.e., by virtue of settlement in the UK, combined with at least five years' ordinary residence there as a citizen of the United Kingdom and Colonies).

Under s.11(3), a person who immediately before commencement was a citizen of the United Kingdom and Colonies by virtue of having been registered under s.12(6) of the 1948 Act under arrangements made by virtue of s.12(7) (registration as citizens of the United Kingdom and Colonies by UK High Commissioner in an independent Commonwealth country of certain people who, before 1st January 1949, were British subjects) became a British citizen at commencement if he was so registered on the basis of his descent in the male line from a person who was both possessed of one of the qualifications specified in s.12(1)(a) and (b) of the 1948 Act (birth or naturalisation in the United Kingdom and Colonies) and born or naturalised in the UK (s.11(3)). The joint effect of these two conditions is to exclude from the ambit of s.11(3) any person granted citizenship under the 1948 Act who relied on an ancestor possessing only the qualification specified in s.12(1)(c) of the 1948 Act (ancestor becoming British subject by reason of annexation of territory which was included in the United Kingdom and Colonies at commencement of the 1948 Act) or who relied on an ancestor who was born outside the UK or who was naturalised elsewhere than in the UK.

20 The 1983 Act

S.1 of the 1983 Act provides that a person became a British citizen at commencement if—

(a) he became a British Overseas Territories citizen at commencement under s.23 of the 1981 Act (see C: BRITISH OVERSEAS TERRITORIES CITIZENSHIP, 3: ACQUISITION AT COMMENCEMENT, below); and

(b) immediately before commencement either—

(i) he was a citizen of the United Kingdom and Colonies and he had that citizenship by virtue of his birth, naturalisation, or registration in the Falkland Islands; or

(ii) one of his parents, or a parent of one of his parents, was, or but for his death would have been, a citizen of the United Kingdom and Colonies, who so had that citizenship (s.1(b)(ii) of the 1983 Act); or

(iii) where the person is woman, she was, or had at any time been, the wife of a man who by virtue of (i) or (ii) above, became a British citizen at commencement or would have done so but for his death (s.1(b)(iii) of the 1983 Act).

21 Registration as a British Citizen under the British Nationality (Hong Kong) Act 1990

The British Nationality (Hong Kong) Act 1990 (the 1990 Act) provided for the acquisition of British citizenship by selected Hong Kong residents, their spouses, and minor children.

Under s.1(1), the Secretary of State set up a scheme to register as British citizens up to 50,000 people recommended to him by the Governor of Hong Kong under a scheme or schemes made and approved in accordance with Schedule 1 to the 1990 Act. The Scheme is not considered in detail as the time limit for registration ended on 30th June 1997 (s.1(2)).

A person registered under s.1 is treated for the purposes of the 1981 Act as a British citizen otherwise than by descent. The spouses and minor children of a person who is registered as a British citizen are treated for the purposes of the 1981 Act as British citizens by descent (see above). A British Overseas Territories citizen will cease to be such if he becomes a British citizen by virtue of the 1990 Act (s.2).

22 Registration as a British citizen under the Hong Kong (War Wives and Widows) Act 1996

The Hong Kong (War Wives and Widows) Act 1996 provides for the acquisition of British citizenship by certain women who are Hong Kong residents. Under the Act, the Secretary of State may, on an application made for the purpose, register as a British citizen any woman who, before the passing of the Act, was the recipient or intended recipient of a UK settlement letter if–
  (a) she has her residence, or principal residence, in Hong Kong;
  (b) where she is no longer married to the man in recognition of whose service the assurance was given, she has not remarried (s.1(1)).
A "UK settlement letter" means a letter written by the Secretary of State which–
  (a) confirmed the assurance given to the intended recipient that, in recognition of her husband's service, or her late or former husband's service, in defence of Hong Kong during the Second World War, she could come to the UK for settlement at any time; and
  (b) was sent by the Secretary of State to the Hong Kong Immigration Department for onward transmission to the intended recipient (whether or not she in fact received it) (s.1(2)).
A woman who is registered as a British citizen by virtue of this Act is treated for the purposes of the British Nationality Act 1981 as a British citizen otherwise than by descent (s.2(1)); and the following provisions of that Act will apply: s.37 (Commonwealth citizenship); s.41 (regulations); s.42 (registration and naturalisation: citizenship ceremony, oath and pledge); s.42B (registration and naturalisation: timing); s.44(1) and (2) (decisions involving exercise of discretion); s.45 (evidence); s.50 (interpretation); and s.51(3) (meaning of "citizen of the UK and Colonies" in other Acts and instruments) (s.2(3)).

See also **6 Good character**, above.

23 Registration as a British citizen under the Hong Kong Act 1997

S.1 of the 1997 Act provides for the registration as a British citizen of any person who is ordinarily resident in Hong Kong at the time of application and who was also ordinarily resident there immediately before 4th February 1997 and who either–
  (a) is a British Overseas Territories citizen only by virtue of a connection with Hong Kong and who would be stateless if he were not either a British Overseas Territories citizen or a British Overseas Territories citizen and a British National (Overseas); or
  (b) was on 4th February 1997 a British Overseas citizen, a British subject or a British protected person and who would otherwise have been stateless.
A person qualifying for citizenship by satisfying (b) above is treated as a British citizen by descent. A person qualifying for citizenship by satisfying (a) above is either a British citizen by descent or otherwise than by descent depending upon whether they were a British Overseas Territories citizen by descent or otherwise (s.2).

See also **6 Good character**, above.

(4): RENUNCIATION AND RESUMPTION

24 Renunciation (s.12)

Any British citizen of full age and capacity (for this purpose, any person who has married or formed a civil partnership is deemed to be of full age) may renounce his citizenship by making a declaration in the prescribed manner and, except in any of the circumstances mentioned below, the Secretary of State must register the declaration (s.12(1)), whereupon the person will cease to be a British citizen (s.12(2)). In time of war, however, the Secretary of State may withhold registration (s.12(4)).

A declaration under s.12 must not be registered unless the Secretary of State is satisfied that the person who made it will after the registration have or acquire some citizenship or nationality other than British citizenship. If the declaration is registered and in fact the person does not have any such citizenship or nationality on the date of registration and does not acquire some such citizenship or nationality within six months of that date, he will be, and be deemed to have remained, a British citizen notwithstanding the registration (s.12(3)).

Note.–There is nothing in UK law to prevent a person having another citizenship in addition to British citizenship.

25 Resumption (s.13)

A person who has ceased to be a British citizen as a result of a declaration of renunciation is entitled, if he wishes to resume that citizenship and makes the necessary application, to be registered as such a citizen, provided that (a) he is of full capacity, and (b) his renunciation of British citizenship was necessary to enable him to retain or acquire some other citizenship or nationality (s.13(1)). A person can exercise this right only once (s.13(2)). The Secretary of State is empowered (s.13(3)), if he thinks fit, to register as a British citizen a person who has ceased to be a British citizen as a result of a declaration of renunciation (for whatever reason made) and who applies for resumption of that citizenship.

See also **6 Good character**, above.

26 Regulations (s.41)

The British Nationality (General) Regulations 2003 contain general provisions for carrying into effect the purposes of the 1981 Act in respect of British citizenship, among other matters. Under s.41 (as applied by s.4(2) of the 1983 Act), the British Nationality (Falkland Islands) Regulations 1983 make provision for carrying into effect the purposes of the 1983 Act.

C: BRITISH OVERSEAS TERRITORIES CITIZENSHIP

27 Definition

Part II of the 1981 Act creates the form of citizenship known as British Overseas Territories citizenship. The overseas territories, listed in Schedule 6, as amended, are: Anguilla; Bermuda; British Antarctic Territory; British Indian Ocean Territory; British Virgin Islands; Cayman Islands; Falkland Islands; Gibraltar; Montserrat; Pitcairn, Henderson, Ducie and Oeno Islands; St Helena, Ascension and Tristan da Cunha; South Georgia and South Shetland Islands; the Sovereign Base Areas of Akrotiri and Dkehelia; and the Turks and Caicos Islands.

Note.–British Overseas Territories citizens–with the exception of those whose citizenship is solely by virtue of a connection with the Sovereign Bases in Cyprus–are also full British citizens: see B: BRITISH CITIZENSHIP, above.

The provisions of Part II follow very closely those in Part I relating to British citizenship; the principal differences mainly involve the substitution for references to the UK of references to an overseas territory, but there are some material variations in the details of the rules in certain areas, and attention to these is drawn below.

Note.–Under s.43, the Secretary of State may delegate to the Governor of any overseas territory the exercise of any of his functions under the 1981 Act with respect to specified matters in cases concerning British Overseas Territories citizens or British Overseas Territories citizenship. The specified matters are registration and naturalisation, and renunciation, resumption, and deprivation of British citizenship or British Overseas Territories citizenship. The exercise of any power under the 1981 Act to make rules or regulations cannot be delegated.

28 Hong Kong

The Hong Kong Act 1985 and the Hong Kong (British Nationality) Order 1986 *inter alia* provide that British Overseas Territories citizenship cannot be retained or acquired on or after 1st July 1997 by virtue of a connection with Hong Kong; and that people who were such citizens by virtue of any such connection could, before that date (or before the end of 1997 if born in that year), acquire a new form of British nationality the holders of which are known as British Nationals (Overseas) (see D: BRITISH NATIONALS (OVERSEAS), below).

As to the limited right to acquire full British citizenship, see B: BRITISH CITIZENSHIP, 4: HONG KONG, above.

(1): ACQUISITION AFTER COMMENCEMENT

29 Acquisition by birth or adoption (s.15)

Subject to the necessary modification, the provisions of s.15 are identical to those of s.1 (see **7 Acquisition by birth or adoption**, above). The definition of "settled" in s.50 applies for the purposes of s.15.

See also **6 Good character**, above.

30 Acquisition by descent (s.16)

S.16(1) confers British Overseas Territories citizenship on people born outside the overseas territories in circumstances similar to those which apply for the purposes of s.2(1), with the omission of the reference to service under a Community institution in s.2(1)(c) (see **8 Acquisition by descent**, above). Relevant service for the purpose of s.16 are (a) Crown Service under the government of an overseas territory, and (b) any description of service, designated by the Secretary of State, which he considers to be closely associated with the activities outside the overseas territories of the government of any overseas territory (s.16(2) and (3)). The British Overseas Territories Citizenship (Designated Service) Order 1982 designates certain kinds of service for this purpose.

31 Meaning of British Overseas Territories citizen "by descent" (s.25)

For the purposes of the 1981 Act, a British Overseas Territories citizen is such a citizen "by descent" if and only if he falls into one of the categories described in s.25, as follows–

(a) a person born outside the overseas territories after commencement who is a British Overseas Territories citizen by virtue of s.16(1) only (i.e., a person one of whose parents is such a citizen otherwise than by descent) or by virtue of registration under s.17(2) (provision corresponding exactly with s.3(2)) or s.21 (provision corresponding to s.9);

(b) subject to the exception described in s.25(2) (see below), a person born outside the overseas territories who became a British Overseas Territories citizen after commencement and who immediately before commencement was a citizen of the United Kingdom and Colonies, deemed to be such a citizen, in the circumstances described in paragraph (b)(i) and (ii) in the above summary of s.14;

(c) a British Overseas Territories citizen by virtue of registration under s.17(1) (registration of minor at the discretion of the Secretary of State–see below) in whose case provisions apply which correspond to those described in paragraph (c)(i) and (ii) in the above summary of s.14;

(d) subject to the exception described in s.25(2), a person born outside the overseas territories before commencement who became a British Overseas Territories citizen at commencement under s.23(1)(b) only (see below);

(e) subject to the exception described in s.25(2), a woman who became a British Overseas Territories citizen at commencement under s.23(1)(c) only (see below), and did so by virtue only of having been, immediately before commencement or earlier, the wife of a man who immediately after commencement was, or would but for his death have been, a British Overseas Territories citizen by descent by virtue of paragraph (b) or (d) above;

(f) subject to the exception described in s.25(2), a woman born outside the overseas territories before commencement who is a British Overseas Territories citizen as a result of registration under s.20 (Registration by virtue of marriage, now repealed) by virtue of being or having been married to a man who at commencement became such a citizen by descent or would have done so but for his having died or ceased to be a citizen of the United Kingdom and Colonies as a result of a declaration of renunciation;

(g) a British Overseas Territories citizen by virtue of registration under s.22 (see below) who, having before commencement ceased to be a citizen of the United Kingdom and Colonies as a result of a declaration of renunciation, would, if he had not so ceased, have at commencement become a British Overseas Territories citizen by descent by virtue of paragraph (b), (d), or (e) above;

(h) a British Overseas Territories citizen by virtue of registration under s.24 (see below) who, immediately before he ceased to be such a citizen as a result of a declaration of renunciation, was such a citizen by descent;

(i) a person born in the UK after commencement who is a British Overseas Territories citizen by virtue of paragraph 1 of Schedule 2 (see G: MISCELLANEOUS, 1: STATELESS PERSONS, below).

32 Acquisition by registration: minors (s.17)

The provisions of s.17 follow exactly those of s.3 (see **10 Acquisition by registration–minors (s.3)**, above), with only the necessary modifications.

See also **6 Good character**, above.

33 Acquisition by naturalisation (s.18)

The rules governing naturalisation as a British Overseas Territories citizen, set out in s.18(1) and (2) and paragraphs 5 to 8 and 9 of Schedule 1, are the same in all essential respects as those relating to naturalisation as a British citizen–see the summary of s.6(1) and (2) in **17 Acquisition by naturalisation (s.6)**, above). The language requirement is a sufficient knowledge of the English language or any other language recognised for official purposes in the relevant territory; and s.18(3) requires the applicant for naturalisation to specify in his application the overseas territory which is to be treated as the relevant territory for the purposes of his application.

(2): ACQUISITION AFTER COMMENCEMENT–SPECIAL CASES

34 Right to registration replacing right to resume citizenship of United Kingdom and Colonies (s.22)

S.22 makes provision corresponding to that of s.10 (see **18 Registration following renunciation of citizenship of United Kingdom and Colonies**, above), with modification. For the purposes of s.22, a person is taken to have an appropriate qualifying connection with an overseas territory if he, his father, or his father's father–

(a) was born in that territory; or

(b) is or was a person naturalised in that territory; or

(c) was registered as a citizen of the United Kingdom and Colonies in that territory; or

(d) became a British subject by reason of the annexation of any territory included in that territory.

See also **6 Good character**, above.

(3): ACQUISITION AT COMMENCEMENT

35 Categories of British Overseas Territories citizens at commencement

Under s.23, the following people became British Overseas Territories citizens at commencement–

(a) any person who was immediately before commencement a citizen of the United Kingdom and Colonies and who had that citizenship by his birth, naturalisation, or registration in an overseas territory (s.23(1)(a));

(b) any person who was immediately before commencement a citizen of the United Kingdom and Colonies, and was born to a parent (i) who at the time of the birth (the material time) was a citizen of the United Kingdom and Colonies, and (ii) who either had that citizenship at the material time by his birth, naturalisation, or registration in an overseas territory or was himself born to a parent who at the time of that birth so had that citizenship (s.23(1)(b) (in relation to any time before 1949, the above references to citizenship of the United Kingdom and Colonies should be read as if they were references to British nationality (s.23(6));

(c) any person who, being a woman, was immediately before commencement a citizen of the United Kingdom and Colonies and either was then, or had any time been, the wife of a man who under the provisions described in paragraph (a) or (b) above became a British Overseas Territories citizen at commencement or would have done so but for his death (s.23(1)(c));

(d) any person who was immediately before commencement a citizen of the United Kingdom and Colonies by virtue of registration under s.7 of the British Nationality Act 1948 (registration of minors at the Secretary of State's discretion) or s.1 of the British Nationality (No. 2) Act 1964 (person, stateless from birth, registered by virtue of his mother's citizenship of the United Kingdom and Colonies) if–

    (i) he was so registered otherwise than in an overseas territory; and

    (ii) his father or mother (in the case of a person registered under s.7) or his mother (in the case of a person registered under s.1 of the 1964 Act) was a citizen of the United Kingdom and Colonies at the time of the registration or would have been such a citizen but for his or her death, and became a British Overseas Territories citizen at commencement or would have done so but for his or her death (s.23(2));

(e) any person who immediately before commencement was a citizen of the United Kingdom and Colonies by virtue of having been registered under s.12(6) of the 1948 Act (see 17 The 1981 Act, above, at the second para. of the summary of s.11(3)) otherwise than in an overseas territory and was so registered on an application under s.12(6) of the 1948 Act based on his descent in the male line from a person who possessed one of the qualifications specified in s.12(1)(a), (b), or (c) of that Act (see the summary of s.11(3) above), if the person's ancestor–

    (i) was born or naturalised in an overseas territory; or

    (ii) became a British subject by reason of the annexation of any territory included in an overseas territory (s.23(3));

(f) any person who was immediately before commencement a citizen of the United Kingdom and Colonies by virtue of registration, otherwise than in an overseas territory, under s.1 of the British Nationality Act 1964 (resumption of citizenship), was so registered by virtue of having an appropriate qualifying connection with an overseas territory or, being a woman, by virtue of having been married to a person who at the time of the registration had or would, if then living, have had such a connection (s.23(4)). For these purposes, a person is taken to have such a connection if he, his father, or his father's father–

    (i) was born in an overseas territory; or

    (ii) is or was a person naturalised in an overseas territory; or

    (iii) was registered as a citizen of the United Kingdom and Colonies in an overseas territory; or

    (iv) became a British subject by reason of the annexation of any territory included in an overseas territory (s.23(5)).

(4): RENUNCIATION AND REDEMPTION

36 Application of ss.12 and 13

The provisions of ss.12 and 13 apply in relation to British Overseas Territories citizens and British Overseas Territories citizenship as they apply to British citizens and British citizenship (s.24).

See also **6 Good character**, above.

(5): REGULATIONS

37 Regulations

The British Nationality (British Overseas Territories) Regulations 2007 (S.I. No. 3139) contain general provisions for carrying into effect the purposes of the Act in respect of British Overseas Territories citizenship.

D: BRITISH NATIONALS (OVERSEAS)

38 Hong Kong

The Hong Kong Act 1985 provided that, as from 1st July 1997, the Crown would no longer have sovereignty or jurisdiction over any part of Hong Kong. The Schedule to the Act provided that provision could be made by order whereby British Overseas Territories citizenship could not be retained or acquired on or after 1st July 1997 by virtue of a connection with Hong Kong; and that people who were such citizens by virtue of any such connection could before that date (or before the end of 1997 if born in that year before 1st July 1997) acquire a new form of British nationality the holders of which are known as British Nationals (Overseas). The Hong Kong (British Nationality) Order 1986 has been made under this provision, and extends to Northern Ireland, the Channel Islands, the Isle of Man, and to all other overseas territories.

39 Acquisition of status

Article 4(1) of the 1986 Order created a new form of British nationality the holders of which are known as British Nationals (Overseas). Any person who was a British Overseas Territories citizen by virtue (wholly or partly) of having a connection (as defined below) with Hong Kong, who would not be such a citizen but for that connection, and who applied on or before the relevant date (see below) was entitled before 1st July 1997 (or before the end of 1997 if born in that year before that date) to be registered as a British National (Overseas) and to hold or be included in a passport appropriate to that status (Art. 4(2)). Such a person has the status of a Commonwealth citizen (see below) (1981 Act, s.37, as amended by Art. 7(3) of the 1986 Order). The relevant date for each applicant depended on the year of his birth, the last relevant date being 30th September 1997 (for those born in 1997 before the handover on 1st July). An application for registration made after the relevant date may be accepted if the applicant shows that there are special circumstances which justify his being so registered.

Whether a person had a "connection" with Hong Kong was determined in accordance with Article 2 of the 1986 Order, but is not covered in detail here as the last date for applications has now passed (see above).

40 Provisions for reducing statelessness

Article 6 of the 1986 Order contains provisions whereby certain people who might otherwise be rendered stateless by virtue of the 1986 Order may become British Overseas citizens. However, also see **23 Registration as British Citizen under the Hong Kong Act 1997**, above.

41 Renunciation

By Article 7(10) of the 1986 Order, the provisions of s.12 of the 1981 Act are applied in relation to British Nationals (Overseas) or the status of British Nationals (Overseas) as they apply to British citizens or the British citizenship.

42 Regulations

The British Nationality (Hong Kong) Regulations 1986 contain provisions concerning certain procedural and administrative matters for carrying into effect the provisions of the 1986 Order.

43 Deprivation

By Article 7(11) of the 1986 Order, the provisions of s.40 of the 1981 Act (deprivation of citizenship) are applied in relation to people registered as British Nationals (Overseas) and to the status of British Nationals (Overseas) as they apply in relation to British citizens and British citizenship (see below).

E: BRITISH OVERSEAS CITIZENSHIP

44 Introduction

Part III of the 1981 Act created the form of citizenship known as British Overseas citizenship. Any person who was a citizen of the United Kingdom and Colonies immediately before commencement and who did not at that date become either a British citizen or a British Overseas Territories citizen became a British Overseas citizen (s.26).

45 Renunciation (s.29)

The provisions of s.12 apply in relation to British Overseas citizens and British Overseas citizenship as they apply in relation to British citizens and British citizenship.

46 Regulations (s.41)

The British Nationality (General) Regulations 2003 contain provisions concerning procedural and administrative matters for carrying into effect the provisions of the 1981 Act concerning, among other matters, British Overseas citizenship.

F: BRITISH SUBJECTS

47 Continuance as British subjects of certain British subjects (s.30)

The following people became British subjects at commencement by virtue of s.30–

(a) any person who immediately before commencement was a British subject without citizenship by virtue of s.13 of the British Nationality Act 1948 (which provided that a person who was a British subject on 31st December 1948 and was, on that date, potentially a citizen of a Commonwealth country but was not at that date a citizen of the United Kingdom and Colonies or of a Commonwealth country, or of Eire, should remain a British subject at the commencement of the 1948 Act until he became a citizen of the United Kingdom and Colonies or of a Commonwealth country, or of Eire, or an alien);

(b) any person who immediately before commencement was a British subject by virtue of s.16 of the 1948 Act (which enabled certain people who had lost their status as British subjects before 1st January 1949 by reason of their parents' loss of British nationality to obtain the status of British subject under the 1948 Act);

(c) any person who immediately before commencement was a British subject by virtue of s.1 of the British Nationality Act 1965 (which entitled alien women who had been married to British subjects of certain descriptions, including British subjects without citizenship by virtue of s.13 or s.16 of the 1948 Act and certain citizens of Eire, to be registered as British subjects).

48 Continuance as British subjects of certain former citizens of Eire (s.31)

A woman who immediately before commencement was the wife of a British subject was entitled, on making application to be registered as a British subject if certain conditions were fulfilled. These provisions are not dealt with in detail as the time limit for the making of applications under them has expired.

49 Renunciation (s.34)

The provisions of s.12 apply in relation to British subjects and the status of a British subject as they apply to British citizens and British citizenship.

50 Loss of status as British subject (s.35)

A person who is a British subject otherwise than by virtue of s.31 (see **48 Continuance as British subjects of certain former citizens of Eire**, above) will cease to be such a subject if, in whatever circumstances and whether under the 1981 Act or otherwise, he acquires any other citizenship or nationality whatever.

51 Regulations (s.41)

The British Nationality (General) Regulations 2003 contain provisions concerning procedural and administrative matters for carrying into effect the provisions of the 1981 Act relating to *inter alia* the status of British subjects under the Act.

G: MISCELLANEOUS

(1): STATELESS PERSONS

52 Introduction

S.36 and Schedule 2 contain provisions for reducing statelessness, the principal beneficiaries of which are people who would otherwise have remained, or been born, stateless after commencement by reason of the 1981 Act's other provisions.

Provisions for reducing statelessness in the case of British Overseas Territories citizens who enjoy that status by virtue of a connection with Hong Kong and who might otherwise be rendered stateless on 1st July 1997 are contained in the 1986 Order (see D: BRITISH NATIONALS (OVERSEAS), above).

53 People born in the UK after commencement

A person born in the UK after commencement who would otherwise be born stateless will, if at the time of his birth his father or mother is a British Overseas Territories citizen, a British Overseas citizen, or a British subject, be a citizen or subject of that description. If the person is born legitimate and at the time of the birth each of his parents is a citizen or subject of a description mentioned above but not of the same description, he will be a citizen or subject of the same description so mentioned as each of them is respectively at that time; but he will not become a British subject under this provision if by virtue of the provision he becomes a citizen of one of those two descriptions (Sch. 2, para. 1).

54 People born in an overseas territory after commencement

Paragraph 2 of Schedule 2 provides for people born in an overseas territory after commencement who would otherwise be born stateless in exactly the same terms as paragraph 1 (see **53 People born in the UK after commencement,** above), subject only to the substitution of the term British citizen for British Overseas Territories citizen wherever the latter occurs in that paragraph.

55 People born in the UK or an overseas territory after commencement

A person born in the UK or an overseas territory after commencement is entitled, on making an application, to be registered as a British citizen or a British Overseas Territories citizen, according to the circumstances of the case, if all the following requirements are satisfied in his case, namely—
- (a) that he is and always has been stateless; and
- (b) that on the date of his application he was under the age of 22; and
- (c) that he was in the UK or an overseas territory (no matter which) at the beginning of the period of five years ending with that date and that the number of days on which he was absent both from the UK and the overseas territories in that period does not exceed 450 (or such larger number as the Secretary of State in the special circumstances of the case allows under para. 6).

An applicant satisfying all the above requirements will be registered as a British citizen in if the above-mentioned period of five years the number of days wholly or partly spent by him in the UK exceeds the number of days wholly or partly spent by him in the overseas territories; otherwise, he will be registered as a British Overseas Territories citizen (Sch. 2, para. 3).

56 People born outside the UK and the overseas territories after commencement

A person born outside the UK and the overseas territories after commencement is entitled, on making an application, to be registered as a British citizen, a British Overseas Territories citizen, a British Overseas citizen, or a British subject, according to the circumstances of the case, if all the following requirements are satisfied in his case, namely—
- (a) that the applicant is and always has been stateless, and
- (b) that at the time of the applicant's birth his father or mother was a citizen or subject of a description mentioned above, and
- (c) that the applicant was in the UK or an overseas territory (no matter which) at the beginning of the period of three years ending with the date of his application and that the number of days on which he was absent from both the UK and the overseas territories in that period does not exceed 270 (this number may be increased under para. 6).

A successful applicant will be registered as a British citizen, a British Overseas Territories citizen, or a British Overseas citizen, assuming that one of these citizenships has been relied on for the purposes of paragraph (b) above, and the choice in each case will depend on which of the three was so relied on; if the father or mother between them held more than one of those descriptions of citizenship, the applicant is entitled to nominate one of those so held in his application. In all other cases, the successful applicant will be registered as a British subject (Sch. 2, para. 4).

57 People born stateless before commencement

A person born stateless before commencement is entitled, on making an application for registration under paragraph 5, to be so registered if the circumstances are such that, if—
- (a) the 1981 Act had not been passed, and the enactments repealed or amended by the Act had continued in force accordingly, and
- (b) an application for the registration of the applicant under s.1 of the British Nationality (No. 2) Act 1964 (which provided for the acquisition of citizenship of the United Kingdom and Colonies by certain classes of people who would otherwise have been stateless) as a citizen of the United Kingdom and Colonies had been made on the date of his application,

the applicant would have been entitled under that section to be registered as such a citizen (Sch. 2, para. 5). An applicant so entitled will be registered as such a citizen as he would have become at commencement if, immediately before commencement, he had been registered as such a citizen on whichever of the three grounds mentioned in s.1 of the 1964 Act he would have been entitled to be so registered on in the circumstances described in paragraphs (a) and (b) above.

(2): COMMONWEALTH CITIZENSHIP

58 People who are Commonwealth citizens

S.37 provides that every person who—
- (a) under the British Nationality Acts 1981 and 1983 and the British Overseas Territories Act 2002 is a British citizen, a British Overseas Territories citizen, a British National (Overseas), a British Overseas

citizen, or a British subject; or

(b) under any enactment for the time being in force in any country mentioned in Schedule 3 is a citizen of that country;

has the status of a "Commonwealth citizen".

Schedule 3 may be amended, by Order in Council, by the addition or removal of any entry, or by the insertion of any additional entry. The last countries to be added to Schedule 3 were Cameroon and Mozambique (S.I. 1998/3161) and Rwanda (S.I. 2010/246). References in the 1981 Act to any country mentioned in Schedule 3 include references to the dependencies of that country (s.50(12)).

After commencement, no person is to have the status of a Commonwealth citizen or the status of a British subject otherwise than under the 1981 Act (s.37(4)).

(3): BRITISH PROTECTED PERSONS

59 People who are British protected persons

British protected persons are those who are declared by Order in Council to be so by virtue of their connection with a protectorate, or a protected state, or a former protectorate or trust territory. The British Protectorates, Protected States and Protected Persons Order 1982 defines who are to be protected persons for the purposes of the Act, and also provides for the registration as British protected persons of certain classes of stateless persons.

British protected persons are not Commonwealth citizens or British subjects under the 1981 Act, but they are not aliens.

(4): DEPRIVATION OF CITIZENSHIP

60 Grounds for deprivation

Under s.40, the Secretary of State may, provided that he is satisfied that it is conducive to the public good, by order deprive a citizen in one of the categories described below, of his citizenship status. The categories are (s.40(2))–

(a) a British citizen

(b) a British overseas territories citizen;

(c) a British Overseas citizen;

(d) a British National (Overseas);

(e) a British protected person; or

(f) a British subject.

No order may be made if it would make someone stateless (s.40(4)).

Where a person's citizenship status derives from his registration or naturalisation, the Secretary of State may deprive him of it if he is satisfied that it was obtained by means of fraud, false representation or concealment of a material fact (s.40(3)).

Before an order is made under s.40, the Secretary of State must give to the person concerned notice in writing specifying that he has decided to make an order, the reasons for the order, and that there is a right of appeal (s.40(5)). An appeal will be to an adjudicator under the Nationality, Immigration and Asylum Act 2002, s.81 (see the Note on **Control of Immigration** at B: IMMIGRATION APPEALS), unless the Secretary of State certifies that his decision was taken wholly or partly on grounds of national security or the interests of the relationship between the UK and another country, in which case the appeal will be to the Special Immigration Appeals Commission (see the Note on **Control of Immigration** at para **27 Special Immigration Appeals Commission**) (s.40A).

The above provisions apply in relation to British Nationals (Overseas) and the status of British Nationals (Overseas) (with the substitution of a reference to s.18 of the 1981 Act for s.6 of that Act in paragraph (a) above) and, in relation to British Overseas Territories citizens and British Overseas Territories citizenship, as they apply in relation to British citizens and British citizenship.

(5): GENERAL

61 Registration and naturalisation: general provisions (ss.42 to 42B)

A person will not be–

(a) registered as a British citizen, British overseas territories citizen, British Overseas citizen or British subject under any provision of the 1981 Act; or

(b) granted a certificate of naturalisation as a British citizen or British overseas territories citizen under any such provision of the 1981 Act,

unless–

(c) any requisite fee (see below) has been paid; and

(d) the person concerned has made the relevant citizenship oath and pledge specified in Schedule 5.

The Secretary of State may, if he thinks it appropriate, disapply these requirements in special circumstances (s.42(6)).

The Citizenship Oath and Pledge (Welsh Language) Order 2007 specifies the form of words in Welsh which may be used when making the citizenship oath (or affirmation) and pledge in Wales for the purpose of registration or naturalisation in accordance with these provisions.

62 Decisions involving exercise of discretion (s.44)

Any discretion vested by or under the 1981 Act or the 1983 Act in the Secretary of State, a Governor of a colony, or a Lieutenant Governor of one of the Islands must be exercised without regard to race, colour, or religion of any person who may be affected by its exercise. Nothing in s.44 affects the jurisdiction of any court to entertain proceedings of any description concerning the rights of any person under any provision of the 1981 Act.

(6): FEES

63 British Nationality Fees

The Immigration and Nationality (Fees) Regulations 2016 specify the fees payable in Great Britain and Northern Ireland in connection with applications made, *inter alia*, under the 1981 Act, as follows—

1	For registration as a British citizen where the applicant is aged 18 or over at the time the application is made	£1,041
2	For registration as a British overseas territories citizen, a British overseas citizen, a British subject or as a British protected person where the applicant is aged 18 or over at the time the application is made	£833
3	For registration as a British citizen where the person in respect of whom the application is made is a child at the time the application is made	£936
4	For registration as a British overseas territories citizen, a British overseas citizen, a British subject or as a British protected person where the person in respect of whom the application is made is a child at the time the application is made	£749
5	Application for naturalisation as a British citizen	£1,156
6	Application for naturalisation as a British overseas territories citizen	£925
7	Registration of a declaration of renunciation of British citizenship, of British overseas territories citizenship, of British overseas citizenship, of British National (Overseas) status, of the status of British subject or of the status of British protected person (where a person makes more than one declaration at the same time only one fee is payable)	£272
8	Supplying a certified copy of a notice, certificate, order, declaration, or entry, given, granted or made under the 1981 Act or any of the former nationality Acts or the British Nationality (Hong Kong) Act 1997	£272
9	Arrangement of a citizenship ceremony (including administration of a citizenship oath and pledge at the ceremony)	£80
10	Administration of a citizenship oath or oath and pledge, where not administered at a citizenship ceremony (except where the oath is administered by a justice of the peace, when it is free)	£5
11	Application for the review of an application for a certificate of registration or naturalisation, or for a certificate of entitlement, which has been refused by the Secretary of State	£272
12	Application for the amendment of a certificate of registration or naturalisation other than where the amendment is required to rectify an error made by the Secretary of State	£198
13	Application for a letter or other document confirming a person's nationality status or that a person is not a British citizen	£198
14	Application for a certificate of entitlement where the application is made in respect of a person who is in the UK at the time that the application is made	£272
15	Application for a certificate of entitlement where the application is made in respect of a person who is outside the UK at the time that the application is made	£472
16	Taking a record of a person's biometric information for the purposes of an application for registration or naturalisation	£19.20

(7): FORMS

64 Applications for British citizenship

The following forms of application for British citizenship have been issued by the Home Office, together with a full guide to the completion of the form in each case—

Form B: Application by a British Overseas Territories citizen, a British Overseas citizen, a British subject under the 1981 Act, or a British protected person

Form AN: Application for naturalisation

Form MN1: Application for registration of a child under 18

Enquiries should be addressed to the Home Office, Nationality Directorate, 3rd Floor, India Buildings, Water Street, Liverpool L2 0QN (tel: 0151 236 4723).

65 Authorities

Statutes–

Borders, Citizenship and Immigration Act 2009

British Nationality Act 1981

British Nationality (Falkland Islands) Act 1983

British Nationality (Hong Kong) Acts 1990 and 1997

British Overseas Territories Act 2002

Hong Kong Act 1985

Hong Kong (War Wives and Widows) Act 1996

Nationality, Immigration and Asylum Act 2002

Statutory Instruments–

British Citizenship (Deprivation) Rules 1982 (S.I. 1982 No. 988)

British Citizenship (Designated Service) Order 2006, as amended (S.I. 2006 No. 1390, and 2007 No. 744)

British Nationality (Falkland Islands) Regulations 1983 (S.I. 1983 No. 479)

British Nationality (General) Regulations 2003, as amended (S.I. 2003 Nos. 548 and 3158, 2004 No. 1726, 2005 Nos. 2114 and 2785, 2007 No. 3137, 2009 No. 3363, 2010 Nos. 677 and 785, 2012 No. 1588, 2013 No. 2541, 2014 No. 1465, and 2015 Nos. 681 and 1806)

British Nationality (Hong Kong) (Registration of Citizens) Regulations 1990 (S.I. 1990 No. 2211)

British Nationality (Hong Kong) Regulations 1986, as amended (S.I. 1986 No. 2175, 2003 No. 540, and 2007 No. 3137)

British Overseas Territories Citizenship (Designated Service) Order 1982, as amended (S.I. 1982 No. 1710 and 2008 No. 1240)

British Protectorates, Protected States and Protected Persons Order 1982, as amended (S.I. 1982 No. 1070 and 1983 No. 1699)

Citizenship Oath and Pledge (Welsh Language) Order 2007 (S.I. 2007 No. 1484)

Hong Kong (British Nationality) Order 1986, as amended (S.I. 1986 No. 948 and 1993 No. 1795)

Immigration and Nationality (Fees) Regulations 2016 (S.I. 2016 No. 226)

CONTROL OF IMMIGRATION

1 Introduction

The Immigration Act 1971, as amended, is the principal Act governing the control of immigration into, and the stay in the UK of persons who require leave to enter or remain here. Statutory instruments (see **55 Authorities**, below) which are made under the Act, make more detailed provision for the same purposes.

The Home Secretary is the Secretary of State generally responsible for the control of immigration. The Home Office includes an Immigration and Nationality Directorate, at Lunar House, Wellesley Road, Croydon, Surrey CR9 2BY which handles most questions in this field on the Home Secretary's behalf.

S.4 of, and Schedule 2 to, the Act confer on immigration officers (aided by medical inspectors) power to give or refuse leave to enter, and various ancillary powers for the enforcement of control at points of entry. S.4 also empowers the Secretary of State to give leave to remain in the UK and to vary the terms on which limited leave to enter has been granted.

This Note is arranged in Parts as follows:

PART I: STATUTORY PROVISIONS
A: Statutory provisions regulating a person's leave to enter and remain in the United Kingdom
B: Immigration Appeals
C: Removal of Persons from the United Kingdom
D: Criminal Proceedings and Other Sanctions
E: Supplementary
F: Asylum-seekers and Human Rights claims
G: Liability of carriers

PART II: FEES AND FORMS
H: Fees
I: Immigration forms

A: STATUTORY PROVISIONS REGULATING A PERSON'S LEAVE TO ENTER AND REMAIN IN THE UNITED KINGDOM

2 Right of abode in the United Kingdom

All persons who have the right of abode in the UK under the Act are free to live in, and to come and go into and from, the UK without let or hindrance. Those not having that right may live, work, and settle in the UK by permission and subject to such regulation of their entry, stay, and departure as is imposed by the Act. However, those settled in the UK on 1st January 1973, when the Act came fully into force, are treated as having indefinite leave to remain (Immigration Act 1971, s.1), unless they fall into a category of persons exempted from the Act's provisions relating to leave to enter or remain under any of the Act's provisions (e.g., s.8 – see **7 Exceptions from the requirement for leave**, below).

The following persons have the right of abode–
(a) a British citizen (see the Note on **British Nationality**); and
(b) a Commonwealth citizen (see the Note on **British Nationality**) who immediately before 1st January 1983 was a Commonwealth citizen having the right of abode by virtue of s.2(1)(d) or s.2(2) of the Act as then in force and has not ceased to be a Commonwealth citizen in the meanwhile.

S.2(1)(d) of the Act, as previously in force, provided that a Commonwealth citizen should have the right of abode if he was born to, or legally adopted by, a parent who at the time of the birth or adoption had citizenship of the UK and Colonies by his birth in the UK, the Channel Islands, or the Isle of Man (the Islands). S.2(2), as previously in force, provided for a woman to have the right of abode if she was a Commonwealth citizen and was then the wife of a citizen of the UK and Colonies or of a Commonwealth citizen entitled to the right of abode under any provision of s.2(1) as then in force or had at any time been married either to such a citizen or to a British subject who but for his death would on the date of commencement of the British Nationality Act 1948 (1st January 1949) have been such a citizen by virtue of s.2(1)(a) or (b), as then in force (but not by virtue of marriage to a British subject who was such a citizen and had the right of abode by virtue of settlement in the UK and ordinary residence there for five years by virtue of s.2(1)(c) of the 1971 Act or by virtue of marriage to a Commonwealth citizen having the right of abode by virtue of s.2(1)(d)).

3 Leave to enter or remain in the United Kingdom

S.3 of the Immigration Act 1971 provides *inter alia* that, except as otherwise provided by or under the Act, a person who is not a British citizen must not enter the UK unless given leave to do so. Leave may be given for a limited or for an indefinite period. Leave to remain in the UK may be given to a person already present there. Limited leave to enter or remain in the UK may be given, subject to conditions restricting the immigrant's employment or occupation in the UK, or requiring him to–

(i) maintain and accommodate himself and any dependants of his without recourse to public funds;

(ii) register with the police;

(iii) report to an immigration officer or the Secretary of State;

(iv) comply with conditions as to residence,

or a combination of these requirements.

S.3(3) provides for the variation of the conditions attached to a person's limited leave to enter or remain in the UK and further provides that, where the limit on the duration of a person's leave is removed, any condition attached to the leave will cease to apply. Once a person leaves the Common Travel Area (i.e., the UK, Republic of Ireland, Channel Islands and the Isle of Man), any leave that may have been granted will lapse and fresh leave to enter will need to be obtained if that person wishes to return (s.3(4)).

The power to give or refuse leave to enter the UK under the Act is exercised by immigration officers, and the power to give leave to remain in the UK or to vary any leave under s.3(3) (see above) is exercised by the Secretary of State (s.4).

4 Obtaining leave to enter or remain in advance

S.3A of the Immigration Act 1971 (inserted by the Immigration and Asylum Act 1999, s.1) allows the Secretary of State to make an order allowing arrangements to be made for individuals to be granted or refused leave to enter before their arrival in the UK. A person with advance leave (granted by a British Embassy or Commission overseas) will therefore be able to enter the country without further detailed examination by immigration officers. S.3A also provides that an order may be made allowing the issue of a visa (or other form of entry clearance) to have effect as leave to enter the UK (i.e., without the need for further examination by an immigration officer) and for leave not to lapse if a person leaves the Common Travel Area. It should be noted however that 1971 Act has been amended by the Asylum and Immigration (Treatment of Claimants, etc.) Act 2004 so that where a person's leave to enter derives from an entry clearance granted under s.3A, he may still be examined by an immigration officer for the purpose of establishing whether the leave should be cancelled on the grounds that the person's purpose in arriving in the UK is different from the purpose specified in the entry clearance (1971 Act, Sch. 2, para 2A(2A).

S.3B (inserted by s.2 of the 1999 Act) allows the Secretary of State to make further provision concerning the giving, refusing, or varying of leave to remain in the UK. In particular, an order may allow an individual leave to enter the UK and then re-enter without his leave to remain lapsing.

The Immigration (Leave to Enter or Remain) Order 2000 is made under these provisions and provides that an entry clearance will have effect as a leave to enter if it is endorsed with the conditions to which it is subject or with a statement that it is to have effect as indefinite leave to enter the UK. However, an entry clearance will not have effect as a leave to enter if it is endorsed on a convention travel document (i.e., a travel document for a refugee issued other than by the UK government) issued after 26th February 2004. The extent of the leave varies according to the type of entry clearance, as follows–

(a) a visit visa has effect, during its period of validity, as a leave to enter on an unlimited number of occasions for six months (or until the end of the visa's validity, if less);

(b) any other entry clearance has effect as a leave to enter on one occasion during its period of validity.

The Order also provides that leave to enter or remain in the UK which is conferred by means of an entry clearance (other than a visit visa) or which is given for a period exceeding six months will not lapse if the person goes to a country outside the common travel area. Leave will lapse however if a person stays outside the UK for a continuous period of two years (except that any period spent by a partner or child accompanying a member of HM Forces overseas will not count towards the calculation of the two year period (so that if the posting lasts more than two years and the partner or child do not return to the UK during that time, their leave will not lapse)).

Where a person has made a successful application for a biometric immigration document from overseas (see **6 Biometric registration,** below) and travels to the UK on a short term entry clearance vignette in order to collect their biometric immigration document in the UK, that vignette has effect as leave to enter for the period for which it has been endorsed.

5 Fingerprints and other physical data

The Nationality, Immigration and Asylum Act 2002 provides the power to fingerprint and gather physical data from people who make an immigration application (i.e., an application for entry clearance, a transit visa, leave to enter or remain in the UK, or variation of such leave) (s.126, as amended by the Immigration Act 2014). Biometric information can also be required from certain non-EEA family members of EEA nationals, and other non-EEA nationals who are able to enter or remain in the UK under an enforceable EU right. Regulations may require such an application to be accompanied by information about the applicant's external physical characteristics, including features of the iris and any other part of the eye. The "authorised persons", who can collect such data are the same as those set out in s.141(5) of the Immigration and Asylum Act 1999 and include police constables, immigration officers and prison officers.

The regulations may specify the form in which physical data should be provided, and the way in which it should be provided, and may deal with the effect of failure to cooperate with the provision of data by a person making an immigration application. They may also define further the role of the authorised person and deal with the retention and destruction of data.

The Immigration (Provision of Physical Data) Regulations 2006 are made under s.126 of the 2002 Act and make provision for a record of fingerprints and a face photograph to accompany an application either for entry clearance or for leave to enter the UK as a refugee. (Regs 2 and 3). If the application for entry clearance is not accompanied by a record of the applicant's fingerprints the application for entry clearance may be treated as invalid (Reg. 7). Where an applicant is under 16 a record of fingerprints may only be provided in the presence of a person aged 18 or over who is the applicant's parent or guardian or a person who takes responsibility for the applicant (Reg. 4(1)).

The Regulations also provide that biometric information may be retained only if the Secretary of State thinks that it is necessary to do so for use in connection with the exercise of a function under the Immigration Acts or in relation to nationality (Reg. 8) and he must take all reasonable steps to ensure that it is destroyed when he no longer thinks that it is necessary to retain it (Reg. 9). Biometric information which relates to a British or Commonwealth citizen who has a right of abode in the UK must be destroyed except that a photograph of a person who is registered or naturalised as a British citizen may be retained until they are issued with a UK passport describing them as a British citizen. Except in limited circumstances, any record of a person's fingerprints must be destroyed at the end of the period of ten years beginning with the date on which the fingerprints were provided (Reg. 10),

Under s.127 of the 2002 Act the Secretary of State may operate a scheme under which an individual may supply, or submit to the obtaining of, data (under a similar but voluntary scheme to that envisaged in s.126) about their external physical characteristics. Such voluntary provision of data may assist and accelerate that person's entry into the UK. There are safeguards regarding the use and retention of such data (s.127(2)).

S.141 of the Immigration and Asylum Act 1999 also provides a power to fingerprint certain people, in particular those who have had a negative immigration decision made against them, and asylum applicants. Those subject to fingerprinting under the 1999 Act are not also subject to the provisions of the 2002 Act.

For the circumstances when a person subject to immigration control must apply for the issue of a biometric immigration document see **6 Biometric registration**, below.

6 Biometric registration

A biometric immigration document is a record of fingerprints and a facial image, together with personal details of the holder and details of their leave to remain in the UK.

A person subject to immigration control must apply for the issue of a biometric immigration document where that person whilst in the UK makes an application for one of the following (Immigration (Biometric Registration) Regulations 2008, as amended)—

(a) for limited leave to remain for a period which, together with any preceding period of leave to enter or remain, exceeds a cumulative total of 6 months leave in the UK;

(b) for indefinite leave to remain;

(c) to replace a stamp, sticker or other attachment in a passport or other document which indicated that the applicant had been granted limited or indefinite leave to enter or remain in the UK;

(d) to replace a letter which indicated that the applicant had been granted limited or indefinite leave to enter or remain in the UK;

(e) to be recognised as a refugee or a person in need of humanitarian protection;

(f) to be recognised as a stateless person in accordance with Article 1 of the Stateless Convention;

(g) for a Convention Travel Document, Stateless Person's Travel Document or a Certificate of Travel and the applicant does not already hold a valid biometric immigration document; or

(h) as the dependant of a person who is making an application in accordance with (a), (b), (e) or (f), above.

Additionally, a person who has been notified on or after 1st December 2012 that the Secretary of State has decided to grant him leave to remain and was not required to apply for a biometric immigration document in respect of that leave will be required to apply for biometric immigration document.

A foreign national from a country listed in the Schedule to the Regulations, who is subject to immigration control, and who is applying for entry clearance which will have effect as leave to enter the UK for more than 6 months must apply for a biometric immigration document whilst overseas, and then collect it from a specified location within a prescribed time following their arrival in the UK. Successful applicants will be provided with a short term entry clearance vignette for use to travel to the UK to collect their biometric immigration document together with a. written decision informing them which Post Office branch to collect their biometric immigration document from, as well as how to arrange a different collection point.

If a person fails to comply with a requirement of the 2008 Regulations e.g., because they fail to notify the Secretary of State that the document has been lost or stolen, they may be issued with a penalty notice. The Immigration (Biometric Registration) (Objection to Civil Penalty) Order 2008 (S.I. 2008/2830, as amended by S.I. 2015/564) sets out the procedure for objecting to a civil penalty, and the Immigration (Biometric Registration) (Civil Penalty Code of Practice) Order 2015 (S.I. 2015/565) sets out the matters which the Secretary of State must consider when determining whether to issue a civil penalty notice.

7 Health charges

All non-EEA nationals applying for entry clearance or leave to remain in the UK for a limited period must generally pay an immigration health charge. The charge must be paid as part of the application process and a separate charge is payable in respect of each application made, including in respect of dependants (Immigration (Health Charge) Order 2015).

Health charge payers will be able to access the NHS in the same way as a permanent resident i.e., they will receive NHS care generally free of charge (but may be charged for services a permanent resident would also pay for, such as dental treatment).

For the amount of the health charge see **51 Fees–health charges**, below. The Secretary of State has a discretion to reduce, waive or refund the health charge.

No charge is payable by an applicant (Sch.2)–

(a) for entry clearance where if granted it would have effect on arrival in the UK as leave to enter for 6 months or less, or where the leave to enter which may be granted pursuant to that entry clearance would be for 6 months or less;

(b) for entry clearance under Appendix V to the immigration rules (i.e., visitors);

(c) for entry clearance or leave to remain as Tier 2 Intra-company Transfer Migrants;

(d) for leave to remain of any kind made by a child under the age of 18 years where the child is being looked after by a local authority;

(e) for leave to remain which relates to a claim for asylum or humanitarian protection;

(f) for leave to remain which relates to a claim that the person's removal from the UK would be contrary to the UK's obligations under article 3 of the Convention for the Protection of Human Rights and Fundamental Freedoms;

(g) for leave to remain which relates to the person's identification as a victim of human trafficking in accordance with the UK's obligations under the Council of Europe Convention on Action against Trafficking in Human Beings;

(h) for leave to remain outside the immigration rules with access to public funds under the Home Office policy known as the "Destitution Domestic Violence Concession" published on 2nd December 2013;

(i) for entry clearance or leave to remain as the dependant of a person who makes an application of a type mentioned in paras (c), (e), (f), (g) or (h);

(j) for entry clearance or leave to remain as the dependant of a member of Her Majesty's forces;

(k) for entry clearance or leave to remain as the dependant of a member of a force who is exempt from immigration control under s.8(4)(b) or (c) of the Immigration Act 1971;

(l) for entry clearance or leave to remain where provision for such entry clearance or leave has been made pursuant to an EU obligation; or

(m) who is a British Overseas Territory citizen resident in the Falkland Islands.

8 Exceptions from the requirement for leave

S.8 of the Immigration Act 1971 provides for the entry of members of the crew of a ship or aircraft for limited periods, without leave, and for the exemption from immigration control of diplomats and their families and of members of the home forces, Commonwealth forces, or visiting forces.

Under s.8(2), the Secretary of State may by order exempt from any provision of the 1981 Act relating to persons who are not British citizens such persons or classes of persons as may be specified in the order, either unconditionally or subject to such conditions as may be imposed under the order. S.8(5A) (inserted by the 1981 Act, s.39(4)), provides that an order made under s.8(2) may, as regards any person or class of persons to whom it applies, provide for that person or class to be, in specified circumstances, regarded (notwithstanding the order) as settled in the UK for the purposes of s.1(1) of the 1981 Act (acquisition of British citizenship by birth in the UK on or after 1st January 1983).

The Immigration (Exemption from Control) Order 1972 has been made under s.8(2). *Inter alia* consular officials and representatives of governments are exempted by the Order.

If a person ceases to be exempt, he is to be treated as if he had been given leave to remain in the UK for 90 days beginning with the day on which he ceased to be exempt. However, the period of deemed leave does not supersede any leave granted prior to the period of exemption if that leave still has more than 90 days to run upon cessation of the exemption (s.8A, inserted by the Immigration and Asylum Act 1999, s.7).

9 Exclusion from the United Kingdom

Under s.8B of the Immigration Act 1971 (inserted by the Immigration and Asylum Act 1999, s.8), certain persons may be excluded from the UK as a result of the UK's international obligations under United Nations Security Council resolutions and European Union Council resolutions. An excluded person must be refused leave to enter or remain in the UK.

Under the Immigration (Designation of Travel Bans) Order 2000, no exclusion may be made in a particular case which would be contrary to the UK's obligations under the European Convention on Human Rights or the 1951 Refugee Convention.

10 Nationals of the European Economic Area

S.7(1) of the 1988 Act provides that a person does not require leave under the Act to remain in the UK where he is entitled to do so by virtue of an enforceable European Community right, or any provision made under s.2(2) of the European Communities Act 1972. The Immigration (European Economic Area) Regulations 2006 (the EEA Regulations) have been made under s.2(2) of the 1972 Act and provide that a European Economic Area (EEA) national must be admitted to the UK if he produces, on arrival, a valid national identity card or passport issued by another EEA state (Reg. 11). The EEA States comprise all the States that are members of the European Community plus Norway, Iceland and Liechtenstein, and for the purposes of these Regulations only, Switzerland. There is a derogation from this provision in that nationals of newly joined Member States do not have a right to reside in the UK to look for work unless they are self-sufficient (for further details see the Note on **Employment of Persons From Abroad**).

A family member of an EEA national (being a spouse or civil partner, a direct descendant who is a child under 21 or a dependant, an older dependent direct relative, or certain extended family members treated as family members for the purposes of the Regulations) will also be admitted to the UK if he can produce such a valid national identity card or passport and, if required, proof of family membership. A family member of a national returning to the UK after a period of residence in an EEA state may also be admitted to the UK under the regulations if the UK national was employed or self-employed in the EEA state; the marriage/civil partnership (in the case of a spouse/civil partner) took place and the parties lived together in an EEA state; and the UK national, on his return to the UK, would, if he were an EEA national, be classed as a qualified person (see **11 EEA nationals–right of residence**, below) (Reg. 9). A family member who is not an EEA national must hold, if he is a visa national (i.e., a national or citizen of a country specified in the Appendix to the Rules) or a person seeking to install himself with an EEA national, an EEA family permit (a form of entry clearance) or residence document. An entry clearance officer must issue an EEA family permit, free of charge, to a person who is a family member of a qualified person (Reg. 12). A person will not be entitled to be admitted to the UK under Article 3 if his exclusion is justified on the grounds of public policy, public security, or public health (Reg. 21). Such a person may be excluded from entry or deported.

A person who is not entitled to reside in the UK as a result of any other provision of the EEA Regulations is nevertheless entitled to a derivative right to reside in the UK for as long as they are (Regs. 11, 15A)–

(a) the primary carer of an EEA national, who is both under the age of 18 and residing in the UK as a self sufficient person, where the denial of such a right would prevent the EEA national child from exercising his or her own right of residence;

(b) the child of an EEA national where they are in education in the UK and had entered the UK and begun to reside there at a time when their EEA national parent was residing as a worker;

(c) the primary carer of the child of an EEA national where requiring them to leave the UK would prevent the child from continuing to be educated in the UK.

Dependants of a primary carer within (a) or (c) also have rights of entry and residence where a refusal to confer such a right would prevent the primary carer from exercising his or her right of residence.

11 EEA nationals–right of residence

The 2006 Regulations give an initial 3 month right of residence, provided that the EEA national or family member does not become an unreasonable burden on the social assistance system (Reg. 13). "Qualified" persons (see below) and their family members have an extended right of residence for so long as they remain qualified (Reg. 14). A person who has resided in the UK under the Regulations for 5 years acquires a permanent right of residence (Reg. 15).

There is a derogation from this provision in that people from recently joined Member States do not have a right to reside in the UK to look for work unless they are self-sufficient (for further details see the Note on **Employment of Persons From Abroad**).

A qualified person for these purposes is an EEA national who is in the UK as (Reg. 6)–

(a) a worker;

(b) a self-employed person;

(c) a jobseeker;

(d) a self-sufficient person; or

(e) a student.

These terms are defined more closely in Regulation 4. A self-sufficient person or a student must have sufficient resources to avoid becoming a burden on the UK's social security system and must also be covered by sickness insurance in respect of all risks in the UK. A jobseeker (or worker who has become involuntarily unemployed) has aright to reside for up to 6 months in total, but once the 6 months is reached they cannot become "qualified" again until 12 months have elapsed, unless they are able to provide compelling evidence of a genuine prospect of engagement (or, in the case of a former worker, compelling evidence that they are seeking work and have a genuine chance of being engaged).

On production of a valid identity card or passport issued by an EEA state and proof that he is a qualified person, the Secretary of State will issue a registration certificate to a qualified person who applies for such a certificate. An EEA family permit, will be issued to a family member on proof that the person is a family member of an EEA national residing in the UK in accordance with the Regulations (Reg. 12). A registration certificate (or residence card if they are not an EEA national) will be issued to a family member of a qualified person on production of a valid identity card or passport where the EEA national has a permanent right of residence (Regs. 16 and 17). A person with a right of residence under Reg. 15A may apply to the Secretary of State for a derivative residence card (which may take the form of a stamp in the applicant's passport) (Reg. 18A). The Secretary of State may refuse to grant a registration certificate/residence card on grounds of public policy, public security, or public health (Reg. 20).

An EEA national or his family member has a right of appeal against a refusal to grant or withdrawal of a registration certificate/residence card (see B: IMMIGRATION APPEALS, below).

The Secretary of State may withdraw or refuse to renew residence documentation granted to an EEA national or a family member of such a person if revocation is justified on the grounds of public policy, public security, or public health, or if the person concerned has ceased to be a qualified person or the family member of a qualified person, as the case may be (Reg. 20). Any such decision must be based exclusively on the personal conduct of the individual concerned. A person's previous criminal convictions do not in themselves justify a decision on the ground of public policy or public security. A decision to refuse admission to the UK, or to refuse residence documentation, to a person on the grounds of public health may be justified only if a disease has epidemic potential or is one to which the Public Health (Control of Disease) Act 1984, s.38 applies (i.e., notifiable diseases: cholera, plague, relapsing fever, smallpox, and typhus). A disease contracted after a person has been in the UK for 3 months does not justify a decision to refuse to renew the permit or document or a decision to remove a person (Reg. 21).

For the provisions relating to the removal of an EEA national or his family member from the UK and for his right of appeal against such a removal, see C: REMOVAL OF PERSONS FROM THE UNITED KINGDOM, below, and see B: IMMIGRATION APPEALS, below.

Although Switzerland is not an EEA state, the provisions outlined in this paragraph also broadly apply to Swiss nationals (see the Immigration (Swiss Free Movement of Persons) (No. 3) Regulations 2002).

12 Certificate of entitlement to right of abode

A person seeking to enter the UK and claiming to have the right of abode must prove that he has that right by producing either–
    (a) a UK passport describing him as a British citizen or as a citizen of the UK and Colonies having the right of abode; or
    (b) a certificate of entitlement issued by or on behalf of the UK government certifying that he has such a right of abode (s.3(9), as substituted by the 1988 Act).

The procedure for applying for a certificate of entitlement to right of abode is laid down in the Immigration (Certificate of Entitlement to Right of Abode in the United Kingdom) Regulations 2006. A certificate ceases to have effect on the expiry of the passport or travel document to which it is affixed.

S.2 of the 1988 Act provides that any woman–
    (a) who has the right of abode under s.2(1)(b) of the Act as, or as having been, the wife of a man to whom she is or was polygamously married and who is or was such a citizen of the UK and Colonies, Commonwealth citizen, or British subject as is mentioned in s.2(2)(a) or (b) of the Act as previously in force; and
    (b) who has not before 1st August 1988 and since her marriage to the husband been in the UK,
will not be entitled to enter the UK in the exercise of the right of abode or to be granted a certificate of entitlement in respect of that right if there is another woman living (whether or not one to whom this provision applies) who is the wife or widow of the husband, and who is, or at any time since her marriage to the husband has been, in the UK, or has been granted a certificate of entitlement in respect of that right of abode or an entry clearance to enter the UK as the wife of the husband. A woman is not precluded by this provision from re-entering the UK if since her marriage she has at any time been in the UK and there was at that time no such other woman living as is described therein. Presence in the UK as a visitor or illegal immigrant is disregarded for this purpose.

13 Variation of leave

S.3C of the Immigration Act 1971 (inserted by the Immigration and Asylum Act 1999, s3) provides that, where a person who has been granted leave to enter or remain in the UK for a limited period applies in writing, before that period ends, to the Secretary of State for an extension of that leave, the leave will, where no decision has been taken on the application, be automatically extended to the point at which the appropriate period for appealing a refusal expires. This prevents a person from becoming an "overstayer" where they have made a valid application to remain. An application for variation of a person's leave to enter or remain in the UK may not be made while that leave is treated as continuing under s.3C (so successive applications for leave to remain may not be made).

Where a person's leave to enter or remain in the UK is varied so that he has no leave to enter or remain in the UK, or such leave is revoked, that person's leave is extended during any period when an appeal against the variation or revocation could be brought or such an appeal is pending. However, such extended leave will lapse if the person leaves the UK (s.3D, inserted by the Immigration, Asylum and Nationality Act 2006, s.11).

14 Registration with the police

The Immigration (Registration with Police) Regulations 1972 prescribe the procedure to be followed by an alien (see the Note on **British Nationality**) who has a limited leave to enter or remain in the UK, which is subject to a condition requiring him to register with the police, and prescribe the fee payable for the issue of a registration certificate. The Immigration Rules paras 325, 326 and Schedule 2 provide further details as to who is required to register.

15 Hotel registers

The Immigration (Hotel Records) Order 1972 provides that any person of 16 years or over who stays at any hotel or (subject to exemption for certain premises certified by the police for this purpose) any other premises, whether furnished or unfurnished, where lodging or sleeping accommodation is provided for reward must, on arrival, inform the person in charge of the premises of his name and nationality. If he is an alien, he must also state—

(a) on arrival, the number and place of issue of his passport, certificate of registration, or other document establishing his identity and nationality; and

(b) on or before departure, his next destination and, if it is known to him, his full address there.

The person in charge of such premises must require all persons aged 16 or over who stay at his premises to comply with the above obligations, and must keep for at least 12 months a record in writing of the date of arrival of such persons and of the particulars furnished by them. This record must at all times be open for inspection by any constable or by any other person authorised by the Secretary of State.

16 Common travel area

The UK, the Channel Islands, the Isle of Man, and the Republic of Ireland are collectively referred to in the Act as the common travel area. Arrival in and departure from the UK on a local journey from or to any of the Islands or the Republic of Ireland are not subject to control under the Act except in so far as any one of the Islands or the Republic of Ireland is excluded for specific purposes from the common travel area by order of the Secretary of State (s.1(3)).

S.9 of, and Schedule 4 to, the Act make special provision as to the operation of immigration control in relation to persons entering the UK from places within the common travel area and as to the effect in the UK of action taken under the laws of the Islands. In particular, s.9(4) provides that a person who is not a British citizen may not enter the UK without leave on a local journey from a place in the common travel area if either the Secretary of State so directs on the ground that his exclusion is conducive to the public good as being in the interests of national security or he has at any time been refused leave to enter and has not since then been given leave to enter or remain in the UK.

The Immigration (Control of Entry through the Republic of Ireland) Order 1972 imposes conditions and restrictions on specified persons who enter the Republic of Ireland from outside the common travel area and then enter the UK.

Certain visa nationals who a valid Republic of Ireland visa, and subsequent endorsement conferring permission to land in the Republic, may travel on to the UK and remain in the UK for the same duration as the Irish permission to land without the need to obtain a UK visa. This applies currently to visitors from India and the People's Republic of China (Immigration (Control of Entry through the Republic of Ireland) Order 1972, Art. 3A, Schedule).

17 Claimant's credibility–asylum and human rights claims

Where a person makes an asylum or human rights claim then, in deciding whether to believe a statement made by or on behalf of that person, the deciding authority will take account, as damaging the claimant's credibility, of any behaviour of a specified nature (Asylum and Immigration (Treatment of Claimants, etc.) Act 2004, s.8).

The behaviour which is specified for these purposes is any behaviour by the claimant which the deciding authority thinks is designed or likely to—

(a) conceal information;

(b) mislead;

(c) obstruct or delay the handling or resolution of the claim, or the taking of a decision in relation to the claimant.

The types of behaviour which are treated as coming within (a) and (b) above are: failing without reasonable explanation to produce a passport on request; producing a document which is not a valid passport as if it were; the destruction, alteration or disposal of a passport, ticket or other travel document without reasonable explanation; and a failure without reasonable explanation to answer a question asked by the deciding authority.

Other behaviour which will also be taken to have an adverse affect on a person's credibility includes—

(d) the failure by a claimant to take advantage of a reasonable opportunity to make an asylum or human rights claim whilst in a safe country;

(e) the failure by a claimant to make an asylum or human rights claim before being notified of an immigration decision, unless the claim relies wholly on matters arising after the notification;

(f) the failure by a claimant to make an asylum or human rights claim before being arrested under an immigration provision, unless there was no reasonable opportunity to do so or the claim relies wholly on matters arising after the arrest.

B: IMMIGRATION AND ASYLUM APPEALS

18 Introduction

Part 5 of the Nationality, Immigration and Asylum Act 2002 (ss.81 to 117, as amended by the Immigration Act 2014) sets out a new appeals procedure in connection with refusals of protection or human rights claims, or revocation of previously granted protection status. Appeals are dealt with by the First-tier tribunal. See **28 Appeal procedures**, below.

EEA nationals have rights of appeal under the Immigration (European Economic Area) Regulations 2006.

S.104 sets out when an appeal is pending and when it ends: an appeal ceases to be pending when it is finally determined, withdrawn, lapses, or is abandoned. An appeal is treated as abandoned if the appellant has left the UK, or has been granted leave to enter or remain in the UK; an appeal is treated as finally determined if a deportation order has been made. An appeal will be treated as pending if a further appeal may be made and until such further appeal is finally determined.

The Immigration (Notices) Regulations 2003 oblige the Secretary of State, immigration officers and entry clearance officers to provide a written notice of any decision which is appealable. A notice may be given either to the person concerned or to his representative. Any notice must contain a statement of the reasons for the decision in question and, if it relates to the giving of directions for a person to be removed from the UK, a statement of the country to which he will be removed. The notice must also contain full details of how to appeal.

19 Right of appeal

A right of appeal to the Tribunal only arises where the Secretary of State has decided to (Nationality, Immigration and Asylum Act 2002, s.82(1), as substituted by the Immigration Act 2014)—
(a) refuse a protection claim;
(b) refuse a human rights claim; or
(c) revoke a person's protection status.

A protection claim is defined as a claim that removal of the person from the UK would breach the UK's obligations under the Convention relating to the Status of Refugees done at Geneva on 28 July 1951 ("the Refugee Convention") or in relation to those who are eligible for a grant of humanitarian protection. Protection status is defined as the grant of leave to an individual as a refugee or a person eligible for humanitarian protection. This right of appeal is subject to the exceptions and limitations, such as to the place from which an appeal must be brought: see **23 Limitations on appeals from within the UK**, below.

20 Grounds of appeal

An appeal against an immigration decision can only be brought on one of the following grounds (Nationality, Immigration and Asylum Act 2002, s.84, as substituted by the Immigration Act 2014).

An appeal under s.82(1)(a) (refusal of protection claim, see **19 Right of appeal**, above) can only be brought on one or more of the following grounds—
(a) that removal of the appellant from the UK would breach the UK's obligations under the Refugee Convention;
(b) that removal of the appellant from the UK would breach the UK's obligations in relation to persons eligible for a grant of humanitarian protection;
(c) that removal of the appellant from the UK would be unlawful under s.6 of the Human Rights Act 1998 (public authority not to act contrary to Human Rights Convention).

An appeal under s.82(1)(b) (refusal of human rights claim) can only be brought on the ground that the decision is unlawful under s.6 of the Human Rights Act 1998.

An appeal under s.82(1)(c) (revocation of protection status) can only be brought on one or more of the following grounds—
(a) that the decision to revoke the appellant's protection status breaches the UK's obligations under the Refugee Convention;
(b) that the decision to revoke the appellant's protection status breaches the UK's obligations in relation to persons eligible for a grant of humanitarian protection.

21 One-stop procedure

The First-tier Tribunal must consider not only the decision being appealed against, but also any other decision in respect of which the appellant has a right of appeal, but must not consider a "new" matter (i.e., one not previously considered by the Secretary of State) unless the Secretary of State has given the Tribunal consent to do so (s.85). Where an immigration officer has required a statement from the person (under s.120) as to his reasons for wanting to enter or remain in the UK, any grounds on which he should be permitted to enter or remain, and any grounds on which he should not be removed or required to leave, the First-tier Tribunal must also consider any matter in the statement which could give rise to a right of appeal.

22 Decision of the First-tier Tribunal

The First-tier Tribunal must allow an appeal if it decides—

(a) that the decision appealed against was not made in accordance with the law (which includes the immigration rules); or

(b) that a discretion should have been exercised differently.

If neither of these paragraphs applies, it must dismiss the appeal (Nationality, Immigration and Asylum Act 2002, s.86).

23 Limitations on appeals from within the UK

An appeal under s.82(1)(a) (protection claim appeal, see **19 Right of appeal**, above), must be brought from outside the UK if (Nationality, Immigration and Asylum Act 2002, s.92, as amended by the Immigration Act 2014)—

(a) the claim to which it relates has been certified under s.94(1) or (7) (claim clearly unfounded or removal to safe third country, see below); or

(b) para 5(3)(a), 10(3), 15(3) or 19(b) of Schedule 3 to the Asylum and Immigration (Treatment of Claimants, etc) Act 2004 (removal of asylum seeker to safe third country) applies.

Otherwise, the appeal must be brought from within the UK.

An appeal under s.82(1)(b) (human rights claim appeal) where the claim to which the appeal relates was made while the appellant was in the UK, must be brought from outside the UK if—

(a) the claim to which the appeal relates has been certified under s.94(1) or (7) (claim clearly unfounded or removal to safe third country) or section 94B (certification of human rights claims made by persons liable to deportation), or

(b) para 5(3)(b) or (4), 10(4), 15(4) or 19(c) of Schedule 3 to the Asylum and Immigration (Treatment of Claimants, etc) Act 2004 (removal of asylum seeker to safe third country) applies.

Otherwise, the appeal must be brought from within the UK.

An appeal under s.82(1)(b) (human rights claim appeal) where the claim to which the appeal relates was made while the appellant was outside the UK, the appeal must be brought from outside the UK.

An appeal under s.82(1)(c) (revocation of protection status)—

(a) must be brought from within the UK if the decision to which the appeal relates was made while the appellant was in the UK;

(b) must be brought from outside the UK if the decision to which the appeal relates was made while the appellant was outside the UK.

If, after an appeal under s.82(1)(a) or (b) has been brought from within the UK, the Secretary of State certifies the claim to which it relates under s.94(1) or (7) or s.94B, the appeal must be continued from outside the UK.

Where a person has made a protection or human rights claim (or both) he can be barred from bringing an appeal if the Secretary of State certifies that the claim is clearly unfounded. This will be the case, unless the Secretary of State is satisfied that the claim is not clearly unfounded, if the applicant is entitled to reside in Albania, Bolivia, Bosnia-Herzegovina, Brazil, Ecuador, Gambia (in respect of men), Ghana (in respect of men), India, Jamaica, Kosovo, Liberia (in respect of men). Macedonia, Malawi (in respect of men), Mali (in respect of men), Mauritius, Moldova, Mongolia, Nigeria (in respect of men), Peru, Serbia and Montenegro, Sierra Leone (in respect of men), South Africa, South Korea, and Ukraine (s.94, and the Asylum (Designated States) Orders 2003 to 2010). The Secretary of State can add to or remove countries from this list either for all persons, or for certain descriptions of person (who can be defined by, for example, gender, language, race, religion, social or other group, or political opinion). The Secretary of State must also prescribe a European Common List of Safe Countries of Origin and a claim form a person from a country on that list will also be certified as clearly unfounded, unless the Secretary of State is satisfied otherwise (s.94A).

Where a human rights claim has been made by a person who is liable to deportation under—

(a) the Immigration Act 1971, s.3(5)(a) (Secretary of State deeming deportation conducive to public good); or

(b) the Immigration Act 1971, s.3(6) (court recommending deportation following conviction) (see **29 Administrative removal and deportation**, below),

the Secretary of State may certify the claim if he considers that, despite the appeals process not having been begun or not having been exhausted, removal of the person to the country or territory to which it is proposed they be removed, pending the outcome of an appeal in relation to their claim, would not be unlawful under s.6 of the Human Rights Act 1998 (public authority not to act contrary to Human Rights Convention). The grounds upon which the Secretary of State may certify a claim include (in particular) that the person to be deported would not, before the appeals process is exhausted, face a real risk of serious irreversible harm if removed to the country or territory to which it is proposed they be removed (s.94B).

24 Removal of right of appeal by certificate

Where a certificate is issued in any of the cases described below, then the right of appeal is effectively removed (Nationality, Immigration and Asylum Act 2002, ss.96 to 98). Where an appeal is already in progress when the certificate is issued, the appeal will lapse (s.99).

Earlier right of appeal

An appeal may not be brought, or continued, if the Secretary of State or an immigration officer certifies that (s.96)—

(a) the person was notified of their right to appeal against an earlier immigration decision (whether or not an appeal was brought or has been determined);

(b) the new appeal relates to a matter which could have been raised in an appeal against the earlier decision; and

(c) there is no satisfactory reason, in the opinion of the Secretary of State or an immigration officer, for that matter not being raised in an appeal against the earlier decision.

Also, an appeal cannot be made if the Secretary of State or an immigration officer certifies that—

(d) the person has previously been required to give details (under s.120) of all grounds of appeal under a one-stop notice (see **20 One-stop procedure**, above), the new appeal relates to a matter which should have been raised then, and there is no satisfactory reason why it was not.

National security

An appeal may not be brought, or continued, if the Secretary of State certifies that the immigration decision was taken by him or at his direction, wholly or partly on the ground that the person's removal is in the interests of (s.97)—

(a) national security; or

(b) the relationship between the UK and another state.

In addition an appeal may not be brought, or continued, if the Secretary of State certifies that the decision was taken wholly or partly in reliance on information which, in his opinion, should not be made public in the interests of national security, the relationship between the UK and another country, or otherwise in the public interest.

Note.—An application for judicial review may be made to the Special Immigration Appeals Commission in cases where there in no right of appeal because of a certificate issued under s.97 (Special Immigration Appeals Commission Act 1997, s.2E).

Public good

A certificate may remove a person's in country right of appeal against a decision of the Secretary of State to cancel their leave to enter or remain in the UK on the grounds that their presence in the UK would not be conducive to the public good (s.97B).

An appeal against a refusal of leave to enter the UK or a refusal of entry clearance cannot be made if the Secretary of State certifies that the decision was taken by him or at his direction, wholly or partly on the ground that exclusion or removal of the person from the UK is conducive to the public good (s.98). This provision does not prevent an appeal being brought under paras (b) or (c) of **20 Grounds of appeal**, above.

25 Human rights claims

Where a court or tribunal has to decide whether a decision made under the Immigration Acts—

(a) breaches a person's right to respect for private and family life under Article 8; and

(b) as a result would be unlawful under s.6 of the Human Rights Act 1998 (see the Note on **The Human Rights Act 1998**),

it must, in considering the public interest question (i.e., whether an interference with a person's right to respect for private and family life is justified) have regard (in particular) (Nationality, Immigration and Asylum Act 2002, s.117A, added by the Immigration Act 2014, s.19)—

(c) in all cases, to the considerations listed in s.117B, and

(d) in cases concerning the deportation of foreign criminals, to the considerations listed in s.117C.

Public interest considerations applicable in all cases (s.117B)

(1) The maintenance of effective immigration controls is in the public interest.

It is in the public interest, and in particular in the interests of the economic well-being of the UK, that persons who seek to enter or remain in the UK are—

(2) able to speak English;

(3) financially independent,

because such persons are not a burden on taxpayers, and are better able to integrate into society.

(4) Little weight should be given to a private life, or a relationship formed with a qualifying partner (i.e., a British citizen or someone settled in the UK), that is established by a person at a time when the person is in the UK unlawfully.

(5) Little weight should be given to a private life established by a person at a time when their immigration status is precarious.

(6) In the case of a person who is not liable to deportation, the public interest does not require their person's removal where they have a genuine and subsisting parental relationship with a qualifying child (i.e., under 18 and a British citizen or who has lived in the UK for 7 years), and it would not be reasonable to expect the child to leave the UK.

A "foreign criminal" is someone (s.117D(2))—

(a) who is not a British citizen,

(b) who has been convicted in the UK of an offence, and

(c) who—

(i) has been sentenced to a period of imprisonment of at least 12 months;

(ii) has been convicted of an offence that has caused serious harm; or

(iii) is a persistent offender.

Additional considerations in cases involving foreign criminals (s.117C)

(1) The deportation of foreign criminals is in the public interest.

(2) The more serious the offence committed by a foreign criminal, the greater is the public interest in deportation of the criminal.

(3) In the case of a foreign criminal who has not been sentenced to a period of imprisonment of four years or more, the public interest requires their deportation unless Exception 1 or Exception 2 applies.

(4) Exception 1 applies where–

(a) the criminal has been lawfully resident in the UK for most of his life,

(b) he is socially and culturally integrated in the UK, and

(c) there would be very significant obstacles to his integration into the country to which it is proposed he be deported.

(5) Exception 2 applies where the criminal has a genuine and subsisting relationship with a qualifying partner, or a genuine and subsisting parental relationship with a qualifying child, and the effect of his deportation on the partner or child would be unduly harsh.

(6) In the case of a foreign criminal who has been sentenced to a period of imprisonment of at least four years, the public interest requires deportation unless there are very compelling circumstances, over and above those described in Exceptions 1 and 2.

(7) paras (10 to (6) are to be taken into account only to the extent that the reason for the decision to deport was the offence or offences for which the criminal has been convicted.

26 EEA nationals

S.109 of the Nationality, Immigration and Asylum Act 2002 allows the Secretary of State to make regulations for appeals against any immigration decision made in respect of EEA nationals and their families. Such regulations will, in some cases, also cover non-EEA family members of UK nationals if the UK national is returning to the UK after a period of employment in an EEA state. The Immigration (European Economic Area) Regulations 2006 have been made under s.109 and provide for appeals on the ground that a the decision breaches the appellant's rights under the EU Treaties in respect of entry to or residence in the UK (Sch. 1, para 1).

An appeal under the regulations lies to the First-tier Tribunal, except that an appeal will lie to the Special Immigration Appeal Commission (see **27 Special Immigration Appeals Commission**, below) against a decision to remove a person from the UK on the ground that his removal is conducive to the public good as being in the interest of national security or of the relations between the UK and any other country. An appeal will also lie to the Commission if the Secretary of State certifies that the decision was taken wholly or partly in reliance on information which, in his opinion, should not be made public in the interests of national security, the relationship between the UK and another country, or otherwise in the public interest (Reg. 28).

A person claiming to be an EEA national may not appeal under the Regulations unless he produces a valid national identity card or valid passport issued by another EEA State.

An appeal under the 2006 Regulations will not prevent the Secretary of State from giving, or executing removal directions, but where a person is removed from the UK before their appeal is heard or finally determined they may apply for permission to be temporarily admitted to the UK in order to present their case in person (Reg. 29AA).

27 Special Immigration Appeals Commission

The Special Immigration Appeals Commission, is a body established under the Special Immigration Appeals Commission Act 1997 to hear appeals against decisions taken on the grounds of national security and/or for the public good. Prior to that Act, there was no right of appeal against decisions made on those grounds. The Commission must allow an appeal if it considers that the decision or action against which the appeal is brought was not in accordance with the law or with immigration rules, or, where the decision or action involved the exercise of a discretion by the Secretary of State, that the discretion should have been exercised differently. A further appeal on a question of law may be made to the appropriate appeal court.

28 Appeal procedures

The Tribunal Procedure (First-tier Tribunal) (Immigration and Asylum Chamber) Rules 2014 prescribe the procedure to be followed for appeals made under Part 5 of the 2002 Act.

Where an appellant makes an appeal within the UK, notice of appeal must be given not later than 14 days after the notice of the decision being appealed was sent to them. Where the appeal is made outside the UK, notice of appeal must be given within 28 days (Reg. 19). The First-tier Tribunal may extend these time limits in special cases (Regs. 4 and 20). The notice of appeal must set out the grounds for the appeal and contain specified particulars, such as whether the appellant will attend or be represented at any hearing, or needs an interpreter (Reg. 19). In most cases, an appeal hearing will take place (Reg. 25).

An appeal, only on a point of law, from a First-tier Tribunal decision may be made to the Upper Tribunal (Tribunals, Courts and Enforcement Act 2007, s.11).

Modified "fast track" rules apply where the appellant is in detention at specified detention centres: see the Fast Track Rules in the Schedule to the above 2014 Rules. In particular, the time limit for making appeals against decisions, and applications, in such cases is reduced to two days (Schedule, para 5).

C: REMOVAL OF PERSONS FROM
THE UNITED KINGDOM

29 Administrative removal and deportation

Those who have failed to observe conditions attached to their leave to enter or remain in the UK, overstayers, and those who have obtained leave by deception are subject to administrative removal procedures rather than to deportation. Deportation action will however continue to apply to cases where the Secretary of State considers a person's removal to be conducive to the public good (Immigration Act 1971, s.3(5)). In addition, a person who is not a British citizen will also be liable to be deported from the UK if, after he has attained the age of 17, he is convicted of an offence which is punishable with imprisonment and on his conviction he is recommended for deportation by a court empowered by the Act to do so (s.3(6)). Deportation action will also apply to the family members of those subject to deportation under s.3(5) or (6).

Where a claimant has an outstanding immigration appeal under s.82 of the 2002 Act (see **18 Right of appeal**, above), they cannot be removed or required to leave (2002 Act, s.78). However, any preparatory or interim action may be taken, including the giving of a direction for the claimant's removal and the making of a deportation order (although such an order cannot be made before the time for making an appeal against the immigration decision has expired: s.79).

The Secretary of State can require a person to take specified action where that action will or may enable a travel document to be obtained by or for that person and possession of such a document will facilitate their deportation or removal from the UK (Asylum and Immigration (Treatment of Claimants, etc.) Act 2004, s.35). The action that can be required is not specified, but include, for example, obtaining or providing documents or fingerprints, or attending at an Embassy or High Commission. Non-compliance will be an offence punishable with a fine or imprisonment.

30 Provisions relating to deportation

A decision to deport will first be notified to the potential deportee against which there may be a limited or full right of appeal. If the appeal is not made, or fails, the Secretary of State may, subject to what follows, make a deportation order against him (i.e., an order requiring him to leave and prohibiting him from entering the UK). Such an order will invalidate any leave to enter or remain in the UK given the deportee before the order is made or while it is in force (Immigration Act 1971, s.5(1)).

A deportation order made against a person may be revoked at any time by a further order of the Secretary of State, and will cease to have effect if the deportee becomes a British citizen (s.5(2)).

A deportation order will not be made against a person as belonging to the family of another person if more than eight weeks have elapsed since the person left the UK after the making of the deportation order against him; and a deportation order made on that ground will cease to have effect if the person ceases to belong to the family of the other person, or if the deportation order made against the other person ceases to have effect (s.5(3)).

For the purposes of deportation, the following persons are to be regarded as belonging to another person's family: in the case of a man, his wife, and his or her children under the age of 18 years; in the case of a woman, her husband and her or his children under the age of 18 years. (An adopted child, whether legally adopted or not, may be treated as the child of the adopter, and if legally adopted, will be regarded as the child only of the adopter; an illegitimate child (subject to the foregoing rule as to adoptions) will be regarded as the child of the mother; and "wife" includes each of two or more wives.) (s.5(4) as amended by the 1996 Act, Sch. 2).

Where a person is liable to deportation but, without a deportation order leaves the UK to live permanently abroad, the Secretary of State may make payments of such amounts as he may determine to meet that person's expenses in so leaving the UK, including travelling expenses for members of his family or household (s.5(6)).

S.7 provides that a Commonwealth citizen or a citizen of the Republic of Ireland who was such a citizen on 1st January 1973 and who was then ordinarily resident in the UK–

(a) will not be liable to deportation on the grounds either that his deportation is conducive to the public good or because another member of his family has been ordered to be deported if at the time of the Secretary of State's decision he had been ordinarily resident in the UK for the last five years; and

(b) cannot on conviction of an offence be recommended for deportation if at the time of the conviction he had for the last five years been ordinarily resident in the UK.

Commonwealth citizens and citizens of the Republic of Ireland who entered the UK on or after 1st January 1973 do not have this exemption from deportation.

Supplementary provisions as to the procedure to be followed in connection with deportation are contained in Schedule 3 to the Act.

Note.–An appeal against a decision to make a deportation order which has been certified as having been made on national security grounds should normally only be able to be brought from outside the UK. Where the appellant makes a human rights claim, it may be brought in country unless the Secretary of State certifies that removal would not breach the UK's obligations under the European Convention on Human Rights. An in-country appeal against that certificate may be made to the Special Immigration Appeals Commission, as may an application for judicial review of a decision which has been certified under s.97A (2002 Act, s.97A; Special Immigration Appeals Commission Act 1997, s.2E).

As to removal of asylum seekers, see **41 Protection of claimants from deportation**, below.

31 Automatic deportation

The Secretary of State must make a deportation order in respect of a "foreign criminal" unless certain exceptions apply (UK Borders Act 2007, s.32). A "foreign criminal" for these purposes means–

(a) a non-British Citizen who has been convicted in the UK of an offence; and

(b) who is sentenced to a period of imprisonment of at least 12 months or is sentenced to a period of imprisonment for a specified offence.

Deportation of a foreign criminal is conducive to the public good for the purposes of s.3(5)(a) of the 1971 Act. The exceptions where automatic deportation will not apply include where (s.33)–

(c) removal would breach a person's rights under the European Convention on Human Rights or the UK's obligations under the Refugee Convention;

(d) the Secretary of State thinks that the foreign criminal was under the age of 18 on the date of conviction;

(e) removal would breach the foreign criminal's rights under the Community treaties;

(f) the Secretary of State has received a valid extradition request in respect of the foreign criminal; and

(g) the foreign criminal is a "mentally disordered offender".

32 Administrative removal from the United Kingdom

A person may be removed from the UK under the authority of the Secretary of State or an immigration officer if they require leave to enter or remain in the UK but do not have it (Immigration and Asylum Act 1999, 10(1), as substituted by the Immigration Act 2014, s.1).

A family member of a person liable to be removed may also be removed if they are given written notice of the intention to remove them and (s.10(2))–

(a) the family member is a partner, adult dependent relative; child (or a child living in the same household as the person to be removed in circumstances where they have care of the child); or, where the person to be removed is a child, their parent; and

(b) where the family member has leave to enter or remain in the UK, that leave was granted on the basis of their family life with the person to be removed; or, where the family member does not have leave to enter or remain in the UK, in the opinion of the Secretary of State or immigration officer the family member would not, on making an application for such leave, be granted leave in his or her own right, but would be granted leave on the basis of his or her family life with the person to be removed if that person had leave to enter or remain; and

(c) the family member is neither a British citizen, nor entitled to enter or remain in the UK by virtue of an enforceable EU right or of any provision made under s.2(2) of the European Communities Act 1972.

A notice given to a family member under these provisions invalidates any leave to enter or remain in the UK previously given to them. A notice given to a family member may be given at any time prior to the removal of the person liable to removal, or during the eight weeks beginning with the date on which that person is removed (Immigration (Removal of Family Members) Regulations 2014, Reg. 3). Where a person's whereabouts are not known, and no address is available for correspondence with either them or their representative, the notice will be deemed to have been given when the Secretary of State or immigration officer enters a record of the above circumstances and places the signed notice on the relevant file. Where notice is deemed to have been so given and then the person is located, they must be given a copy of the notice and details of when and how it was deemed to be served as soon as is practicable (Reg. 4).

For the purposes of removing a person from the UK under these provisions, the Secretary of State or an immigration officer may give any such direction for the removal of the person as may be given under the Immigration Act 1971, Sch. 2 paras 8-10.

The Immigration (Removal Directions) Regulations 2000 allow directions to be given to owners, agents and captains of ships and aircraft and to Channel Tunnel operators requiring them to remove a named individual to his own country or to a country to which there is reason to believe he will be admitted.

33 Restriction on removal of children

Where a child is to be removed from or required to leave the UK, and a parent or carer of the child who is living in a household in the UK with them is also to be removed then, during the 28 days beginning with the day on which their appeal rights are exhausted (Nationality, Immigration and Asylum Act 2002, s.78A, added by the Immigration Act 2014, s.2)–

(a) the child may not be removed from or required to leave the UK; and

(b) the parent or carer may not be removed from or required to leave the UK if, as a result, no other parent or carer would remain in the UK

In such cases, the Secretary of State must consult the Independent Family Returns Panel on how best to safeguard and promote the welfare of the children of the family and, where it is proposed to detain a family in pre-departure accommodation, on the suitability of so doing, having particular regard to the need to safeguard and promote the welfare of the children of the family (Borders, Citizenship and Immigration Act 2009, s.54A, added by the Immigration Act 2014, s.3).

34 Removal of refugees

Where a person has been recognised as a refugee under the Geneva Convention on Refugees, that Convention prohibits their being returned to the border of a country where their life or freedom is at risk for a Convention reason. There is an exception for refugees regarded as a danger to the security of the host country or a danger to the community of that country having being convicted of a particularly dangerous crime. S.72 of the Nationality, Immigration and Asylum Act 2002 provides that for these purposes a particularly dangerous crime is one for which a person has been–

(a) convicted in the UK and sentenced to a minimum of two years' imprisonment;

(b) convicted outside the UK and sentenced to at least two years' imprisonment and if he had been convicted in the UK he could have been sentenced to at least two years; or

(c) convicted, within or outside the UK, of an offence specified by the Secretary of State by Order (Schedules 1-6 of the Nationality, Immigration and Asylum Act 2002 (Specification of Particularly Serious Crimes) Order 2004 list the offences that constitute serious crimes for these purposes).

The presumption that a person constitutes a danger to the community is rebuttable by that person (s.72(6)) but the gravity of their fear or the threat of persecution to them is irrelevant when considering whether or not they have rebutted the presumption (s.76(8)).

D: CRIMINAL PROCEEDINGS AND OTHER SANCTIONS

35 Offences

Ss.24 to 28 of the Immigration Act 1971 are concerned with criminal offences in connection with illegal entry, knowingly overstaying limited leave, harbouring of illegal entrants, and matters otherwise relating to the administration of the Act.

An illegal entrant is defined as a person who either unlawfully enters or seeks to enter in breach of a deportation order or of the immigration laws; or enters or seeks to enter by means which include deception by another person (s.33(1) as amended by the Asylum and Immigration Act 1996, Sch. 2).

It is an offence, *inter alia*, to–

(a) knowingly enter the UK in breach of a deportation order, or without leave;

(b) knowingly to remain beyond the time limited by leave or to fail to observe a condition of leave, such as reporting to an immigration officer when on temporary admission (s.24(1) of the Act);

(c) knowingly be concerned in or make arrangements for securing or facilitating the entry into the UK of an illegal entrant or asylum claimant (s.25, as amended by the 1996 Act);

(d) (for a non-British citizen) to use deception to obtain, or seek to obtain, leave to enter or remain in the UK, or to secure or seek to secure, the avoidance, postponement or revocation of enforcement action against him (including deportation) (s.24A, added by the Immigration and Asylum Act 1999, s.28); or

(e) to make a return, statement or representation which the entrant knows to be false or does not believe to be true, or to use false documents (s.26).

There is a defence to (c) above on the grounds that the person concerned has already reached the UK, or that the act was done be a person otherwise than for gain, or in the course of his employment by a bone fide organisation whose purpose it is to assist refugees (s.25(1A) to (1C)).

It is a defence for a refugee charged with an offence under (d) (s.24A, deception) or (e) (s.26, falsification of documents) above, to show that, having come to the UK directly from a country where his life or freedom was threatened (within the meaning of the Refugee Convention) he presented himself to the UK authorities without delay, showed good cause for his illegal entry or presence, and claimed asylum as soon as reasonably practicable after his arrival. If the refugee arrived in the UK via another country, he must also show that he could not reasonably have expected to be given protection there (1999 Act, s.31). A person cannot rely on this defence if his claim for asylum has been refused unless he can still show that he is a genuine refugee.

It is also an offence to employ a person knowing that they are an adult subject to immigration control who has not been granted leave to enter or remain (unless granted permission to), or whose leave to remain is invalid, has ceased to have effect or is subject to a condition preventing him from accepting the employment (Immigration, Asylum and Nationality Act 2006, s.21). See further the Note on **Employment of Persons From Abroad**.

36 Entering the UK without a passport

In certain circumstances, it is an offence to enter the UK without a valid passport. The Asylum and Immigration (Treatment of Claimants, etc.) Act 2004 provides that if a person attending an interview at which he is—

(1) seeking leave to enter or remain in the UK; or

(2) claiming asylum;

does not have with him (or produces within three days) a valid immigration document which satisfactorily establishes his identity and nationality or citizenship (i.e., a passport), then he will commit an offence (s.2). It will be a defence for a person to—

(a) prove that he is an EEA national (or family member);

(b) prove that they have a reasonable excuse for not having such a document;

(c) produce a false immigration document and prove that they used it for all purposes in connection with their journey to the UK; or

(d) prove that they travelled to the UK without at any stage in the journey having a valid immigration document.

The deliberate destruction or disposal of a document is not a reasonable excuse for not having it, unless the destruction or disposal was for a reasonable cause or beyond the control of the person charged with the offence.

37 Bank accounts

A bank or building society must not open a current account for a person who is in the UK, and requires leave to enter or remain in the UK but does not have it unless (Immigration Act 2014, s.40)—

(a) it has carried out an immigration "status check" in respect of the applicant, which has indicated that the person is not a "disqualified person" for whom an account should not be opened; or

(b) the bank or building society has been unable to carry out a status check because of circumstances that cannot reasonably be regarded as within its control.

"Opening an account" includes adding a person to an existing account, as well as opening an account in their name or in joint names, or for which they are identified as a signatory or beneficiary.

A "status check" means a check with a specified anti-fraud organisation or a specified data-matching authority (i.e., CIFAS). The Secretary of State has discretion as to who should be barred from opening current accounts as there will be some individuals who face legitimate barriers which prevent them from leaving the UK, even though they do not have leave to enter or remain here. Accordingly, the prohibition does not apply in the case of an account to be operated (or an account that is operated) by or for a person or body of a description specified in an order made by the Treasury. The Immigration Act 2014 (Bank Accounts) (Prohibition on Opening Current Accounts for Disqualified Persons) Order 2014 (S.I. No. 3086) provides that the prohibition does not apply in the case of an account to be operated (or an account that is operated) by or for a person or body who is not a charity, a consumer or a micro-enterprise (i.e., it only applies to "retail" banking).

38 Residential tenancies

As to the ban on a person occupying privately rented property as their only or main home if they are a "disqualified person" i.e., have entered the UK unlawfully, or have overstayed their leave to enter or remain, or who had a limited right to enter or remain in the UK which has expired, see the Notes on **Landlord and Tenant: Miscellaneous Provisions**.

E: SUPPLEMENTARY

39 Voluntary Leavers Scheme

S.58 of the Nationality, Immigration and Asylum Act 2002 enables the Secretary of State assist voluntary leavers and to assist individuals to decide whether to become voluntary leavers.

A "voluntary leaver" is someone who—

(a) is not a British citizen or EEA national;

(b) leaves the UK for a place where he hopes to take up permanent residence; and

(c) wishes to leave the UK and who the Secretary of State thinks it is in their interest to leave.

Payments may be made towards travelling and other expenses, expenses incurred on or shortly after arrival in the new place of residence, services designed to assist the voluntary leaver to settle in the new place of residence, and expenses in connection with a journey to prepare for, or to assess the possibility of becoming, a voluntary leaver.

40 Extension of Act

S.36 of the Immigration Act 1971 enables it to be extended by Order in Council to any of the Islands and such Orders have been made accordingly in respect of the Islands. S.37 extends the Act to Northern Ireland.

F: ASYLUM-SEEKERS AND HUMAN RIGHTS CLAIMS

41 Protection of claimants from deportation

The Secretary of State must prescribe a European Common List of Safe Countries of Origin (Nationality, Immigration and Asylum Act 2002, s.94A). A human rights or asylum claim from a person from a country on the list will automatically be considered as unfounded unless there are serious grounds for considering that the country in question is not safe in the particular circumstances of the applicant.

A person cannot be removed from or be required to leave the UK whilst they have an asylum claim pending (s.77). However, any preparatory or interim action may be taken, including the giving of a direction for the claimant's removal and the making of a deportation order, provided they are not implemented until the claim is finally decided. In addition, s.77 does not prevent claimants being removed to "safe countries", as described below.

First List of Safe Countries

S.77 does not prevent a person who has made a claim for asylum being removed from the UK to another EU Member State (or Norway, Iceland or Switzerland) if the Secretary of State certifies that in his opinion the claimant is not a national or citizen of the State to which he is being sent (Asylum and Immigration (Treatment of Claimants, etc.) Act 2004, Sch. 3, Part 2, as amended by the Asylum (First List of Safe Countries) (Amendment) Orders 2006/3393 and 2010/2802).

Sch. 3 also provides that, in deciding whether a person who has made an asylum or human rights claim may be removed from the UK, EU Member States, Norway, Iceland and Switzerland are to be regarded as places–

  (a) where a person's life and liberty is not threatened by reason of his race, religion, nationality, membership of a particular social group, or political opinion;
  (b) from which he will not be sent to another country in contravention of his rights under the European Convention on Human Rights; and
  (c) from which he will not be sent to another country otherwise than in accordance with the Refugee Convention.

Where it is proposed to remove a person from the UK under these provisions, no appeal can be brought under the Nationality, Immigration and Asylum Act 2002, s.92 (see **23 Limitations on appeals from within the UK**, above). In Human Rights Convention claims (s.92(4)(a)), the Secretary of State will certify that a claim is unfounded unless satisfied that the claim is not clearly unfounded.

Where a person is outside the UK, no appeal against an immigration decision can be made if it would be inconsistent with treating an EU Member State (or Norway, Iceland or Switzerland) as being a place where (a) to (c) above apply.

Second List of Safe Countries

S.77 does not prevent a person who has made a claim for asylum being removed from the UK to another State if the Secretary of State has specified that State and certifies that in his opinion the claimant is not a national or citizen of the State to which he is being sent (Asylum and Immigration (Treatment of Claimants, etc.) Act 2004, Sch. 3, Part 3).

Schedule 3 also provides that, in deciding whether a person who has made an asylum claim may be removed from the UK, such specified States are to be regarded as places–

  (a) where a person's life and liberty is not threatened by reason of his race, religion, nationality, membership of a particular social group, or political opinion; and
  (b) from which he will not be sent to another country otherwise than in accordance with the Refugee Convention.

The limitations on the right of appeal against such a decision are as outlined above.

Third List of Safe Countries

S.77 does not prevent a person who has made a claim for asylum being removed from the UK to another State if the Secretary of State has specified that State as safe for the purposes of the Refugee Convention and certifies that in his opinion the claimant is not a national or citizen of the State to which he is being sent (Asylum and Immigration (Treatment of Claimants, etc.) Act 2004, Sch. 3, Part 4).

Schedule 3 also provides that, in deciding whether a person who has made an asylum claim may be removed from the UK, such specified States are to be regarded as places–

  (a) where a person's life and liberty is not threatened by reason of his race, religion, nationality, membership of a particular social group, or political opinion; and
  (b) from which he will not be sent to another country otherwise than in accordance with the Refugee Convention.

The limitations on the right of appeal against such a decision are as outlined above, except that in Human Rights Convention claims (under s.92(4)(a)), no appeal may be made if the Secretary of State certifies that a claim is clearly unfounded.

Countries Safe for Individuals

S.77 does not prevent a person who has made a claim for asylum being removed from the UK to another State if the Secretary of State has specified that State in relation to that individual and certifies that in his opinion the claimant is not a national or citizen of the State to which he is being sent (Asylum and Immigration

(Treatment of Claimants, etc.) Act 2004, Sch. 3, Part 5).

The limitations on the right of appeal against such a decision are as outlined above.

The Immigration (Leave to Enter) Order 2001 provides that the Secretary of Sate may give or refuse leave to enter to asylum seekers by written notice.

G: LIABILITY OF CARRIERS

42 Introduction

Part II of the Immigration and Asylum Act 1999 (ss.32 to 43, as amended by the 2002 Act) contains provisions which impose civil penalties on those responsible for the transport of clandestine entrants to the UK.

Part II of the 1999 Act also contains some amendments to those parts of the 1971 Act that dealt with criminal sanctions against those who assist persons to enter the UK illegally.

43 Civil penalty for carrying clandestine entrants

Note.—The provisions described in this paragraph are at present only in force in relation to vehicles and rail freight wagons, but not ships, aircraft, passenger trains or the Channel Tunnel Shuttle.

Ss.32 to 37 of the Immigration and Asylum Act 1999 introduce a new civil penalty for "carriers" who bring clandestine entrants into the UK. A person is a clandestine entrant for these purposes if—

(a) he arrives in the UK concealed in a vehicle, ship, aircraft (including hovercraft), or rail freight wagon; or

(b) he passes, or attempts to pass, through immigration control concealed in a vehicle; or

(c) he arrives in the UK on a ship or aircraft, having embarked concealed in a vehicle at a time when the ship or aircraft was outside the UK,

and, in any of these cases, he claims asylum or evades, or tries to evade, immigration control.

The person responsible for a clandestine entrant is liable to pay a penalty of £2,000 for each clandestine entrant and each other person concealed with the clandestine entrant in the same transporter, subject to a maximum aggregate penalty of £4,000 (Carriers Liability Regulations 2002). The penalty must be paid within 60 days.

In the case of clandestine entrants to whom (a) above applies, the "responsible person" is the owner, hirer, or driver (in the case of a vehicle); the owner or captain (in the case of a ship or aircraft); or, in the case of a rail freight wagon, the railway operator who at the last scheduled stop before arrival in the UK certified the train as fit to travel. If the entrant arrived concealed in a detached trailer, the responsible person is the owner, hirer, or operator of the trailer. In the case of clandestine entrants to whom (b) or (c) above applies, the owner, hirer or driver of the vehicle is responsible, except where the transporter is a detached trailer in which case the owner, hirer, or operator is responsible.

Subject to any defence provided by s.34 (see below), it is immaterial whether the responsible person knew or suspected that anyone was concealed in the transporter.

S.33 allows the Secretary of State to issue a code of practice to be followed by anyone operating a system to prevent the carriage of clandestine entrants.

Under s.34, it will be a defence for a carrier to show that—

(i) he did not know, and had no reasonable grounds for suspecting, that a clandestine entrant was, or might be, concealed in the transporter; and

(ii) he had an effective system to prevent the carriage of clandestine entrants and on the occasion in question the person responsible for operating the system did so properly.

In the case of a rail freight wagon, it is also a defence to show that—

(iii) it was known or suspected that a clandestine entrant was or might be concealed in the wagon, having boarded after the wagon's journey began, but the train could not be stopped without endangering safety; and

(iv) there was an effective system to prevent the carriage of clandestine entrants and on the occasion in question the person responsible for operating the system did so properly.

In determining whether a particular system is effective, regard is to be had to the codes of practice issued under s.33. The Carriers' Liability (Clandestine Entrants) (Code of Practice for Rail Freight) Order 2001, the Carriers' Liability (Clandestine Entrants) (Code of Practice for Freight Shuttle Wagons) Order 2001, and the Carriers' Liability (Clandestine Entrants) (Revised Code of Practice for Vehicles) Order 2004 prescribe the *Immigration and Asylum Act 1999: Civil Penalty: Code of Practice for vehicles*, the *Civil Penalty: Code of Practice for Rail Freight Wagons*, the *Civil Penalty: Code of Practice for Channel Tunnel Freight Shuttle Wagons*, and the *Immigration and Asylum Act 1999: Prevention of Clandestine Entrants: Revised Code of Practice for Vehicles* for this purpose.

It is also a defence for the carrier to show that—

(v) he, or an employee directly responsible for allowing the concealment of the clandestine entrant, was acting under duress.

If the Secretary of State decides that a person is liable for a penalty under s.32, a penalty notice must be issued stating his reasons for the decision and the amount of the penalty. The person receiving the notice may in turn serve a "notice of objection" which the Secretary of State must consider (s.35).

Ss.36 and 36A allows any relevant vehicle, small ship, small aircraft, or rail freight wagon to be detained if no alternative satisfactory security has been given or if a penalty is not paid. S.37 provides for a procedure to obtain the release of a transporter detained under s.36. If a penalty is not paid, the Secretary of State may apply to the court for the vehicle to be sold with the proceeds being applied towards payment of the penalty, his costs and any outstanding duty (s.37, Sch. I and the Carriers Liability Regulations 2002).

44 Criminal penalties for assisting illegal entry

Note.—The provisions described in this paragraph are at present only in force in relation to vehicles and rail freight wagons.

Under s.25 of the Act (as amended by the Immigration and Asylum Act 1999 s.38), it is a criminal offence for any person to be knowingly concerned in making or carrying out arrangements for securing or facilitating the entry into the UK of anyone who he knows or has reasonable cause for believing to be an illegal entrant. A person convicted of such an offence who is the owner of a ship, aircraft or vehicle used to carry out the offence, or the captain of any such ship or aircraft, or the driver of any vehicle, risks having his ship, aircraft or vehicle forfeited by a court.

45 Passengers without proper documents

S.40 of the Immigration and Asylum Act 1999 re-enacts provisions previously contained in the Immigration (Carriers' Liability) Act 1987. S.40 is concerned with passengers who travel openly (rather than clandestinely), but without the correct documents. Under this section the owner of a ship or aircraft may be charged a £2,000 penalty if he carries a person who requires leave to enter the UK but who fails to produce a valid visa (if one is required) or a valid passport with a photograph or some other document satisfactorily establishing his identity, nationality, or citizenship. No penalty will be charged if the person concerned had the required document at the time of embarkation. Where false documents were shown, a carrier will only be liable where a document's falsity, or the fact that it did not belong to the person who showed it, was reasonably apparent.

The Secretary of State may, by Order, extend the provisions to individuals who require leave to enter the UK and arrive by train.

46 Passenger information

Immigration officers may require carriers to provide "passenger or service information" relating to passengers carried or expected to be carried by them (Immigration Act 1971, Sch. 2 para 27B, as inserted by the Immigration and Asylum Act 1999, s.18). The provision applies to ships and aircraft, but has been extended to trains using the Channel Tunnel by the Channel Tunnel (International Arrangements) (Amendment) Order 2000. The information required is set out in the Immigration and Police (Passenger, Crew and Service Information) Order 2008 to include various details given or shown by the passenger's passport or other travel document, together with other information, to the extent that it is known by the carrier, such as the name of the person who made the reservation, method of payment, travel itinerary, date and place of issue of ticket, etc. the information may be required as to all passengers, not just those subject to immigration control.

47 Transit visas

S.41 of the Immigration and Asylum Act 1999 provides that the Secretary of State may by order require persons of specified descriptions who on arrival in the UK pass through to another country or territory without entering the UK to hold a visa for that purpose (a transit visa).

The Immigration (Passenger Transit Visa) Order 2014 provides that a national of one or more of the under-mentioned countries (specified in the Schedule to the Order) who on arrival in the UK passes through to another country or territory without entering the UK must hold a transit visa (obtainable from any British High Commission, Embassy, or Consulate which accepts such applications). This provision does not apply to such a person if–

    (a) he is also an EU or EEA state national; or

    (b) he has the right of abode in the UK; or

    (c) in the case of a national or citizen of China, he holds a passport issued by the Hong Kong or Macao Special Administrative Regions; or

    (d) is a citizen or national of the territory of Taiwan.

The countries specified in the Schedule to the Order are: Afghanistan, Albania, Algeria, Angola, Bangladesh, Belarus, Burma, Burundi, Cameroon, Congo, Democratic Republic of the Congo, Egypt, Eritrea, Ethiopia, Gambia, Ghana, Guinea, Guinea-Bissau, India, Iran, Iraq, Ivory Coast, Jamaica, Kenya, Kosovo, Lebanon, Lesotho, Liberia, Libya, Former Yugoslav Republic of Macedonia, Malawi, Moldova, Mongolia, Nepal, Nigeria, Pakistan, Palestinian Territories, People's Republic of China, Rwanda, Senegal, Serbia, Sierra Leone, Somalia, South Africa, South Sudan, Sri Lanka, Sudan, Swaziland, Syria, Tanzania, Turkey, Uganda, Venezuela (if the passport does not contain biometric information contained in an electronic chip), Vietnam, Yemen and Zimbabwe.

In addition, transit visas are also needed by people holding travel documents issued by the Turkish Republic of

Northern Cyprus and by anyone who holds a passport; or another document that can be used (in some or all circumstances) instead of a passport; which does not establish citizenship or nationality

However, transit visas are not required by nationals of any of the above countries if they hold certain other specified documents, such as (Reg. 4)–

(1) a valid visa for entry into Australia, Canada, New Zealand, or the United States; or an expired visa provided it is less than six months since the transit passenger last entered that country with a valid visa (but this exception does not apply to a Syrian national holding a valid or expired US visa);

(2) a valid Australian or New Zealand Permanent Resident Visa, or US or Canadian Permanent Resident Card;

(3) an expired US Permanent Resident Card provided it is accompanied by a valid letter authorising an extension of the period of permanent residency; a valid temporary USA I-551 machine readable immigrant visa; a valid standalone US Immigration Form 155A/155B attached to a brown sealed envelope;

(4) certain common format EEA/Swiss entry visas or residence permits;

(5) a valid biometric visa issued by the Republic of Ireland;

(6) a valid visa issued by a Schengen Acquis State (i.e., Switzerland or an EEA State, excluding the UK and Republic of Ireland) under the Approved Destination Status Scheme where the transit passenger is undertaking a journey via the UK to that Schengen Acquis State;

(7) a valid airline ticket for travel via the UK as part of a journey from a Schengen Acquis State to another country or territory, provided that the transit passenger does not seek to travel via the UK on a date more than 30 days from the date on which he last entered a Schengen Acquis State with a valid visa issued by a Schengen Acquis State under the Approved Destination Status Scheme;

(8) a valid diplomatic or official/service passport issued by the People's Republic of China, India, South Africa, Turkey or Vietnam;

(9) valid alien's passport issued by Estonia or Latvia;

(10) a valid Convention Travel Document (i.e., for a refugee or stateless person); or

(11) a valid laissez-passer issued by the United Nations or the International Committee of the Red Cross.

If a person arrives in the UK without a required transit visa (or other required documentation such as a passport), the carrier may be fined (see **45 Passengers without proper documents**, above) (s.40(4) and (6)).

48 Extension to the Islands

The provisions of the 1987 Act (now superseded by the Immigration and Asylum Act 1999) have been extended to the Channel Islands and the Isle of Man by Orders in Council.

PART II: FEES AND FORMS

H: FEES

49 Immigration fees: leave to remain

The Immigration Act 2014 ss.68 and 74 allows the Secretary of State to prescribe fees in connection with immigration and nationality applications. The following fees have been prescribed by the Immigration and Nationality (Fees) Regulations 2016 (Reg. 4, Sch. 2)–

General fee for applications for limited leave to remain in the UK

(a) for limited leave to remain where the fee is not specified elsewhere in the 2016 Regulations   £811

Fees for and in connection with applications for limited leave to remain in the UK under the Points-Based System

(a) to the Home Office for an approval letter from a designated competent body in respect of a proposed application for entry clearance as a Tier 1 (Exceptional Talent) Migrant   £287

(b) for limited leave to remain as a Tier 1 (Exceptional Talent) Migrant where (a) above applies   £287

(c) for limited leave to remain as a Tier 1 (Exceptional Talent) Migrant where (a) above does not apply   £574

(d) for limited leave to remain as a Tier 1 (Entrepreneur) Migrant   £1,204

(e) for limited leave to remain as a Tier 1 (Graduate Entrepreneur) Migrant   £465

(f) for limited leave to remain as a Tier 1 (Investor) Migrant   £1,530

(g) for limited leave to remain as a Tier 2 (General) Migrant, a Tier 2 (Intra-Company Transfer) Long Term Staff Migrant, a Tier 2 (Sportsperson) Migrant or a Tier 2 (Minister of Religion) Migrant where a certificate of sponsorship has been issued for a period of three years or less, and (i) below does not apply   £664

(h) for limited leave to remain as a Tier 2 (General) Migrant or Tier 2 (Intra-   £1,328

Company Transfer) Long Term Staff Migrant where a certificate of sponsorship has been issued for a period of more than three years, and (j) below does not apply

(i)	for limited leave to remain as a Tier 2 (General) Migrant where a shortage occupation certificate of sponsorship has been issued for a period of three years or less	£437
(j)	for limited leave to remain as a Tier 2 (General) Migrant where a shortage occupation certificate of sponsorship has been issued for a period of more than three years	£873
(k)	for limited leave to remain as a Tier 2 (Intra-Company Transfer) Short Term Staff Migrant, a Tier 2 (Intra-Company Transfer) Graduate Trainee Migrant or a Tier 2 (Intra-Company Transfer) Skills Transfer Migrant	£454
(l)	for limited leave to remain as a Tier 4 Migrant	£448
(m)	for limited leave to remain as a Tier 5 (Temporary Worker) Migrant	£230

Other applications for limited leave to remain in the UK

(a)	for limited leave to remain as a representative of an overseas business under Part 5 of the immigration rules	£664
(b)	for limited leave to remain as a retired person of independent means under Part 7 of the immigration rules	£1,530

Fees for applications for leave to remain in the UK as the dependant of a main applicant

(a)	for limited leave to remain as the dependant of a Tier 1 (Exceptional Talent) Migrant	£574
(b)	for limited leave to remain as the dependant of a Tier 1 (General) Migrant	£1,771

Fee for applications for indefinite leave to remain in the UK

(a)	for indefinite leave to remain	£1,875

The fee for an application for leave to remain made by a dependant of a main applicant is the fee specified in respect of the main applicant's application, with certain exceptions which are listed above.

No fee is payable in respect of applications for leave to remain made (Sch.2, Table 9)–

(1) in respect of a person seeking variation of leave to remain in the UK for a period of up to six months where the application is made on arrival at the port of entry;

(2) in respect of a person, who, at the time of making the application, is a child who is being provided with assistance by a local authority;

(3) in respect of an Article 3 or Refugee Convention application (for the meaning of which see Schedule 2 to the Immigration and Nationality (Fees) Regulations 2016);

(4) under the Destitution Domestic Violence concession operated outside the immigration rules by the Home Office;

(5) as a victim of domestic violence under para 289A or Appendix FM of the immigration rules, where at the time of making the application the applicant appears to the Secretary of State to be destitute;

(6) in respect of a specified human rights Application where to require payment of the fee would be incompatible with the applicant's Convention rights;

(7) under the terms of the EC Association Agreement with Turkey;

(8) in respect of an application for an initial period of limited leave to remain as a stateless person or the family member of a stateless person under Part 14 of the immigration rules; or

(9) in respect of an application for variation of limited leave to remain in the UK to allow recourse to public funds in certain circumstances;

(10) by an individual with a positive conclusive grounds decision if the application is for a Trafficking Convention reason; or

(11) as a domestic worker who is the victim of slavery or human trafficking.

Where two or more applications for leave to remain are made at the same time by the same person a single fee will be payable. The fee payable will be the highest of the fees specified, if those fees are different (Sch. 2, para 5).

Note that an additional fee of £375 will be payable in respect of the fees stated below for using the expediting postal route. The expedited processing of an application not made under the super premium service incurs a fee of £400 if not otherwise specified (2016 Regulations, Reg. 8, Sch. 6).

Certain applications for limited leave to remain from applicants (who must be the main applicant) from a country which has ratified the European Social Charter are reduced by £55. The fee reduction will apply in respect of applications as a Tier 1 (Entrepreneur) Migrant, a Tier 1 (Graduate Entrepreneur) Migrant, a Tier 1 (Exceptional Talent) Migrant, a Tier 2 Migrant, or a Tier 5 (Temporary Worker) Migrant (Sch. 2, para 4).

50 Immigration fees: entry clearance

The fees for applications for entry clearance are contained in the Immigration and Nationality (Fees)

Regulations 2016, Reg. 3, Sch. 1.

The fee for an application for leave to remain made by a dependant of a main applicant (whether or not that application is made at the same time as that of the main applicant) is the fee specified in respect of the main applicant's application, with certain exceptions which are listed below.

Certain applications for entry clearance from applicants (who must be the main applicant) from a country which has ratified the European Social Charter are reduced by £55. The fee reduction will apply in respect of applications as a Tier 1 (Entrepreneur) Migrant, a Tier 1 (Graduate Entrepreneur) Migrant, a Tier 1 (Exceptional Talent) Migrant, a Tier 2 Migrant, or a Tier 5 (Temporary Worker) Migrant.

Note that an additional fee of £375 will be payable in respect of the fees stated below for using the expediting postal route. The expedited processing of an application not made under the super premium service incurs a fee of £400 if not otherwise specified (2016 Regulations, Reg. 8, Sch. 6).

The fees are—

Applications for entry clearance to enter the UK as a visitor

(a) for a visit visa under the immigration rules for six months or less	£87
(b) for a visit visa for two years	£330
(c) for a visit visa for five years	£600
(d) for a visit visa for ten years	£752
(e) for a visit visa as an academic under the immigration rules for a period of more than six months but not more than twelve months	£170
(f) for a visit visa for private medical treatment for a period of more than six months but not more than eleven months	£170
(g) for a transit visit visa	£59
(h) for a visit visa for a period of two years where the applicant is a Chinese national applying under the Chinese visa scheme	£87

Applications for entry clearance to enter the UK as a short term student

(a) as a short term student for a period of six months or less	£89
(b) as a short term student studying an English language course for a period of more than six months but not more than eleven months	£170
(c) as a short term student (child) for a period of six months or less	£89

Applications for entry clearance to enter the UK, and connected applications, under the Points-Based System

(a) to the Home Office for an approval letter from a designated competent body in respect of a proposed application for entry clearance as a Tier 1 (Exceptional Talent) Migrant	£287
(b) for entry clearance as a Tier 1 (Exceptional Talent) Migrant where (a) above applies	£287
(c) for entry clearance as a Tier 1 (Exceptional Talent) Migrant where (a) above does not apply	£574
(d) for entry clearance as a Tier 1 (Entrepreneur) Migrant	£963
(e) for entry clearance as a Tier 1 (Graduate Entrepreneur) Migrant	£342
(f) for entry clearance as a Tier 1 (Investor) Migrant	£1,530
(g) for entry clearance as a Tier 2 (General) Migrant, a Tier 2 (Intra-Company Transfer) Long Term Staff Migrant, a Tier 2 (Sportsperson) Migrant or a Tier 2 (Minister of Religion) Migrant where a certificate of sponsorship has been issued for a period of three years or less, and (i) below does not apply	£575
(h) for entry clearance as a Tier 2 (General) Migrant or Tier 2 (Intra-Company Transfer) Long Term Staff Migrant where a certificate of sponsorship has been issued for a period of more than three years, and (j) below does not apply	£1,151
(i) for entry clearance as a Tier 2 (General) Migrant where a shortage occupation certificate of sponsorship has been issued for a period of three years or less	£437
(j) for entry clearance as a Tier 2 (General) Migrant where a shortage occupation certificate of sponsorship has been issued for a period of more than three years	£873
(k) for entry clearance as a Tier 2 (Intra-Company Transfer) Short Term Staff Migrant, a Tier 2 (Intra-Company Transfer) Graduate Trainee Migrant or a Tier 2 (Intra-Company Transfer) Skills Transfer Migrant	£454
(l) for entry clearance as a Tier 4 Migrant	£328
(m) for entry clearance as a Tier 5 (Temporary Worker) Migrant or a Tier 5 (Youth Mobility) Temporary Migrant	£230

Other applications for entry clearance to enter or leave to enter the UK

(a) under paras 319V to 319VB of the immigration rules; or Appendix FM to the immigration rules, for entry clearance as a parent, grandparent or other dependant relative of a person with limited leave to enter or remain in the UK as a refugee or beneficiary of humanitarian protection; or under paras 319X to319XB for entry clearance as the child of a relative, who is not a parent, and who has limited leave to enter or remain in the UK as a refugee or beneficiary of humanitarian protection	£472
(b) for entry clearance for the purposes of obtaining a replacement biometric immigration document	£189
(c) for entry clearance for the purposes of joining a ship or aircraft as a member of the crew of that ship or aircraft	£59
(d) for entry clearance on a route to settlement in the UK where the fee is not specified elsewhere in these Regulations	£1,195
(e) for entry clearance as a parent, grandparent, or other dependant relative of a person present and settled in the United Kingdom under Appendix FM to the immigration rules	£2,676
(f) for entry clearance as a representative of an overseas business under Part 5 of the immigration rules	£546
(g) for leave to enter the UK made by a person physically present in the UK but liable to immigration detention	£811

General fee for applications for entry clearance to enter the UK

(a) for entry clearance (other than a transit visit visa) where the fee is not specified elsewhere in these Regulations	£405

Applications for entry clearance to enter the UK as the dependant of a main applicant

(a) for entry clearance as the dependant of a Tier 1 (Exceptional Talent) Migrant	£574
(b) for entry clearance as the dependant of a Tier 1 (Post-Study Work) Migrant	£570
(c) for entry clearance as the dependant of a Tier 1 (General) Migrant	£963
(d) for entry clearance as the dependant of a student granted leave under paragraphs 76 to 81 of the immigration rules	£328

Applications for indefinite leave to enter the UK: dependants of members of HM Forces

(a) for indefinite leave to enter the UK as the dependant of a member of HM Forces under Appendix Armed Forces to the immigration rules	£1,875

Application for administrative review (Schedule 10)

(a) for review of a single decision; or two (or more) decisions relating to applications or claims made by a main applicant and a dependant (or dependants) of that person	£80

Note.–If the outcome of the administrative review is that the decision in relation to the connected application is withdrawn, the fee will be refunded. No fee is payable for the administrative review of a decision if the applicant was exempt from payment of the fee for the application or claim to which that decision related, or if that fee was waived.

No fee is payable where the Secretary of State determines that it should be waived. No fee is payable in respect of dependants of refugees or persons granted humanitarian protection, applications under the EC Association Agreement with Turkey or officials of HM Government. Officials determining an application for entry clearance also have discretion to waive or reduce fees in respect of applications for entry clearance for scholarships funded by HM Government, as a matter of international courtesy, or for visitors under a Foreign and Commonwealth Office Bilateral or Strategic Programme.

51 Fees–health charges

Type of Application	Annual amount
(a) application for entry clearance or leave to remain as a student	£150
(b) application for entry clearance or leave to remain as the dependant of a person within (a)	£150
(c) application for entry clearance as a Tier 5 (Youth Mobility Scheme) Temporary Migrant	£150
(c) all other applications for entry clearance or leave to remain	£200

Note.–the applicant must pay the specified annual amount for *each* year of the *maximum* period of leave to remain which could be granted pursuant to their application Where a period would be less than a year, or includes part of a year, the amount payable for that part is either half of the specified annual amount for a period of up to 6 months, or the whole specified annual amount if the part of the year is more than 6 months. Where the applicant applies for entry clearance or leave to remain outside the immigration rules then they must pay the specified annual amount multiplied by 2.5 (Immigration (Health Charge) Order 2015, Reg. 4).

52 Immigration fees: biometric immigration documents

An application for a transfer of conditions onto a biometric immigration document where the application is made within the UK by post or courier or via the public website (known as www.gov.uk), and the applicant has limited leave to enter or remain in the UK is £223 and £308 where the applicant has indefinite leave to enter or remain. Where the application is made outside the UK the fee is £189. The fee for a mandatory application for a replacement biometric immigration document is £56. The fee for taking a record of biometric information for the purposes of an application for a biometric immigration document is £19.20 (Immigration and Nationality (Fees) Regulations 2016, Reg. 5, Sch. 3). However, no fee is payable for an application for a biometric immigration document–

(i) if the applicant has made a claim for asylum which has been granted, or has been granted humanitarian protection under the immigration rules or has leave to remain in the UK under the immigration rules paragraphs 352A to 352FI;

(ii) if the applicant is a child who was born in the UK to a person who had made a claim for asylum which had been granted or had been granted humanitarian protection under the immigration rules;

(iii) for the process used to take a record of a person's biometric information for the purposes of an application for a biometric immigration document to which exceptions (a) and (b) above apply;

(iv) if that person is a child who is being provided with assistance by a local authority;

(v) if that person has leave to remain in the UK under the terms of the EC Association Agreement with Turkey;

(vi) following an application for leave to remain in the UK and the application for leave to remain is exempt from any application fee or that fee has been waived;

(vii) where the person has applied for variation of limited leave to enter or remain in the UK to allow recourse to public funds in certain circumstances; or

(viii) where the person has paid for a fee for an application for a letter or document confirming a person's identity and immigration or nationality status.

53 Immigration fees: Life in the UK Test

A fee of £50 is payable for the administration of the Life in the UK Test, as provided for in Appendix KoLL (Knowledge of Language and Life) to the Immigration Rules (Immigration and Nationality (Fees) Regulations 2016, Reg. 12, Sch. 10).

I: IMMIGRATION FORMS

54 Application forms

Where an application form is specified for a particular purpose, then its use is compulsory (para 34). Forms are "specified" by an announcement on the website of UK Visas and Immigration <https://www.gov.uk/visas-immigration>, which manages applications for people who want to visit, work, study or settle in the UK.

55 Authorities

Statutes–

Asylum and Immigration Act 1996

Asylum and Immigration (Treatment of Claimants, etc.) Act 2004

British Nationality Act 1981

Immigration Acts 1971, 1988, and 2014

Immigration and Asylum Act 1999

Nationality, Immigration and Asylum Act 2002

Special Immigration Appeals Commission Act 1997

UK Borders Act 2007

Statutory Instruments, etc–

Asylum (Designated States) Orders 2003 to 2010 (S.I. 2003 Nos. 970 and 1919, 2005 Nos. 330, 1016, and 3306, 2006 Nos. 3215 and 3275, and 2010 No. 561)

Carriers' Liability Regulations 2003, as amended (S.I. 2003 No. 2817 and 2004 No. 244)

Carriers' Liability (Clandestine Entrants) (Application to Rail Freight) Regulations 2001, as amended (S.I. 2001 Nos. 280 and 3232)

Carriers' Liability (Clandestine Entrants) (Code of Practice for Freight Shuttle Wagons) Order 2001 (S.I. 2001 No. 3233)

Carriers' Liability (Clandestine Entrants) (Code of Practice for Rail Freight) Order 2001 (S.I. 2001 No. 312)

Carriers' Liability (Clandestine Entrants) (Revised Code of Practice for Vehicles) Order 2004 (S.I. 2004 No. 250)

Channel Tunnel (International Arrangements) Order 1993, as amended (S.I. 1993 No. 1813, 2000 No. 913, 2001 Nos. 178, 418, 1544, and 3707, 2003 No. 2799, 2006 No. 2626, 2007 Nos. 2907 and 3579, 2008 No. 2366, 2009 No. 2081, 2012 Nos. 1264 and 1547, 2014 No. 1814, and 2015 No. 856)

Immigration and Nationality (Fees) Regulations 2016 (S.I. 2016 No. 226)

Immigration (Biometric Registration) Regulations 2008, as amended (S.I. 2008 No. 3048, 2009 Nos. 819 and 3321, 2010 No. 2958, 2012 No. 594, and 2015 Nos. 433 and 897)

Immigration (Certificate of Entitlement to Right of Abode in the United Kingdom) Regulations 2006, as amended (S.I. 2006 No. 3145 and 2011 No. 2682)

Immigration (Control of Entry through the Republic of Ireland) Order 1972, as amended (S.I. 1972 No. 1610, 1979 No. 730, 1980 No. 1859, 1982 No. 1028, 1985 No. 1854, 1987 No. 2092, 2000 No. 1776, and 2014 No. 2475)

Immigration (Designation of Travel Bans) Order 2000, as amended (S.I. 2000 No. 2724 and 2015 No. 1994)

Immigration (European Economic Area) Regulations 2006, as amended (S.I. 2006 No. 1003, 2007 No. 3224, 2009 No. 1117, 2010 Nos. 21 and 1593, 2011 Nos. 544 and 1247, 2012 No. 2560, 2013 Nos. 1391 and 3032, 2014 Nos. 1976 and 2761, and 2015 No. 694)

Immigration (Exemption from Control) Order 1972, as amended (S.I. 1972 No. 1613, 1975 No. 617, 1977 No. 693, 1982 No. 1649, 1985 No. 1809, 1997 Nos. 1402 and 2207, 2004 No. 3171, and 2015 No. 1866)

Immigration (Health Charge) Order 2015, as amended (S.I. 2015 No. 792, and 2016 No. 400)

Immigration (Hotel Records) Order 1972, as amended (S.I. 1972 No. 1689, and 1982 No. 1025)

Immigration (Leave to Enter and Remain) Order 2000, as amended (S.I. 2000 No. 1161, 2004 No. 475, 2005 No. 1159, 2010 No. 957, 2013 No. 1749, and 2015 No. 434)

Immigration (Leave to Enter) Order 2001 (S.I. 2001 No. 2590)

Immigration (Notices) Regulations 2003, as amended (S.I. 2003 No. 658, 2006 Nos. 1003 and 2168, 2007 No. 3187, 2008 Nos. 684 and 1819, 2009 No. 1117, 2012 No. 1547, 2013 No. 793; and 2014 No. 2768)

Immigration (Passenger Transit Visa) Order 2014, as amended (S.I. 2014 No. 2702, and 2015 Nos. 657 and 1534)

Immigration (Provision of Physical Data) Regulations 2006, as amended (S.I. 2006 No. 1743, 2011 No. 1779, and 2015 No. 737)

Immigration (Registration with Police) Regulations 1972, as amended (S.I. 1972 No. 1758, 1982 No. 1024, 1990 No. 400, and 1995 No. 2928)

Immigration (Removal Directions) Regulations 2000 (S.I. 2000 No. 2243)

Immigration (Removal of Family Members) Regulations 2014 (S.I. 2014 No. 2816)

Immigration and Nationality (Fees) Regulations 2015, as amended (S.I. 2015 Nos. 768 and 1424)

Immigration and Police (Passenger, Crew and Service Information) Order 2008 (S.I. 2008 No. 5)

Nationality, Immigration and Asylum Act 2002 (Specification of Particularly Serious Crimes) Order 2004, as amended (S.I. 2004 No. 1910 and 2015 No. 800)

Refugee or Person in Need of International Protection (Qualification) Regulations 2006 (S.I. 2006 No. 2525)

Tribunal Procedure (First-tier Tribunal) (Immigration and Asylum Chamber) Rules 2014 (S.I. 2014 No. 2604)

THE IMMIGRATION RULES: ASYLUM, REFUGEES ETC

1 Introduction

This Note deals with those provisions of the Statement of Changes in Immigration Rules ("the Rules") which relate to asylum claimants, refugees and those seeking humanitarian protection.

The Home Secretary is the Secretary of State generally responsible for the control of immigration. The Home Office includes an Immigration and Nationality Directorate, at Lunar House, Wellesley Road, Croydon, Surrey CR9 2BY which handles most questions in this field on the Home Secretary's behalf.

S.4 of, and Schedule 2 to, the 1971 Act confer on immigration officers (aided by medical inspectors) power to give or refuse leave to enter, and various ancillary powers for the enforcement of control at points of entry. S.4 also empowers the Secretary of State to give leave to remain in the UK and to vary the terms on which limited leave to enter has been granted.

2 Definition of asylum applicant

Under the Rules, an asylum applicant is a person who either (a) makes a request to be recognised as a refugee under the Geneva Convention on the basis that it would be contrary to the UK's obligations under that Convention for him to be removed from or required to leave the UK; or (b) otherwise makes a request for international protection. "Application for asylum" is to be construed accordingly (para 327).

Every person has the right to make an application for asylum on his own behalf (para 327A).

Where the Secretary of State is considering a claim for asylum or humanitarian protection she will consider any Article 8 elements of that claim in line with the provisions of Appendix FM (family life) which are relevant to those elements and in line with paras 276ADE to 276DH (private life) of the Rules, which are relevant to those elements unless the person is someone to whom Part 13 of the Rules (deportation) applies (para 326B).

Note.– An EU asylum application will be declared inadmissible and will not be considered unless the applicant satisfies the Secretary of State that there are exceptional circumstances which require the application to be admitted for full consideration (para 326E). An "EU asylum applicant" is a national of a Member State of the European Union who either (para 326C)–

  (a) makes a request to be recognised a refugee under the Geneva Convention on the basis that it would be contrary to the UK's obligations under the Geneva Convention for him to be removed from or required to leave the UK, or

  (b) otherwise makes a request for international protection.

3 Applications for asylum

Every asylum application made at a port or airport in the UK will be referred by the immigration officer for determination by the Secretary of State in accordance with the UK's obligations under the Geneva Convention (para 328). The Secretary of State must ensure that authorities which are likely to be addressed by someone who wishes to make an application for asylum are able to advise that person how and where such an application may be made (para 328A). Until an asylum application has been determined by the Secretary of State or the Secretary of State has issued a certificate under Part 2, 3, 4 or 5 of Schedule 3 to the Asylum and Immigration (Treatment of Claimants, etc.) Act 2004 (see the Note on **Control of Immigration** at para **41 Protection of claimants from deportation**) no action will be taken to require the departure of the asylum applicant or his dependants from the UK. If refugee status is granted the immigration officer will grant limited leave to enter if he has not already done so (paras. 329 and 330). If asylum is refused or the claim is withdrawn or treated as withdrawn, the immigration officer will then resume his examination to determine whether or not to grant the applicant leave to enter under any other provision of the Rules and if an asylum-seeker fails at any time to comply with a requirement to report to an immigration officer for examination, the immigration officer may treat the person's application as concluded (para 331).

Written notice of decisions on applications for asylum must be given in reasonable time. Where the applicant is legally represented, notice may instead be given to the representative. Where the applicant has no legal representative and free legal assistance is not available, he must be informed of the decision on his asylum application and, if the application is rejected, how to challenge the decision, in a language that he may reasonably be supposed to understand (para 333).

A decision on an asylum application must be taken as soon as possible, without prejudice to an adequate and complete examination. Where a decision on an asylum application cannot be taken within six months of the date it was recorded, the Secretary of State must either (para 333A)–

  (a) inform the applicant of the delay; or

  (b) if the applicant has made a specific written request for it, provide information on the timeframe within which the decision on his application is to be expected. The provision of such information does not oblige the Secretary of State to take a decision within the stipulated time-frame.

Applicants for asylum must be allowed an effective opportunity to consult, at their own expense or at public expense in accordance with provision made by the Legal Aid Agency or otherwise, a person who is authorised to give immigration advice (see the Note on **Immigration Advisors and Immigration Service Providers**). This also applies where the Secretary of State is considering revoking a person's refugee status (para 333B).

If an application for asylum is withdrawn either explicitly or implicitly, consideration of it may be discontinued. An application will be treated as explicitly withdrawn if the applicant signs the relevant form provided by the Secretary of State. An application may be treated as impliedly withdrawn if an applicant leaves the UK without authorisation at any time prior to the conclusion of his or her asylum claim, or fails to complete an asylum questionnaire as requested by the Secretary of State, or fails to attend the personal interview as provided in para 339NA of the Rules (see **7 Consideration of cases**, below) unless he demonstrates within a reasonable time that that failure was due to circumstances beyond his control. The Secretary of State will indicate on the applicant's asylum file that the application for asylum has been withdrawn and consideration of it has been discontinued (para 333C).

4 Grant of refugee status

An asylum applicant will be granted refugee status in the UK if the Secretary of State is satisfied that (para 334)–
  (i) he is in the UK or has arrived at a port of entry;
  (ii) he is a refugee, as defined in the Refugee or Person in Need of International Protection (Qualification) Regulations 2006, Reg. 2;
  (iii) there are no reasonable grounds for regarding him as a danger to the security of the UK;
  (iv) having been convicted by a final judgment of a particularly serious crime, he does not, constitute danger to the community of the UK; and
  (v) refusing his application would result in his being required to go (whether immediately or after the time limited by an existing leave to enter or remain), in breach of the Geneva Convention, to a country in which his life or freedom would be threatened on account of his race, religion, nationality, political opinion, or membership of a particular social group.

Where the Secretary of State decides to grant refugee status to a person who has previously been given leave to enter (whether or not the leave has expired) or to a person who has entered without leave, he will vary the existing leave or grant limited leave to remain (para 335).

Where a person is granted leave in accordance with the provisions set out in Part 11 of the Immigration Rules (Asylum), that leave will, in addition to any other conditions which may apply, be granted subject to a condition that the applicant not study unless they have a valid Academic Technology Approval Scheme clearance certificate from the Counter-Proliferation Department of the Foreign Office (para 352H).

5 Refusal of asylum

An application which does not meet the criteria set out in paragraph 334 (see above) will be refused. Where an application for asylum is refused, the reasons in fact and law must be stated in the decision and information provided in writing on how to challenge the decision. (para 336).

When a person is notified that his asylum application has been refused he may, if liable to removal as an illegal entrant, removal under s.10 of the 1999 Act (see the Note on **Control of Immigration** at para **29 Administrative removal and deportation**), or to deportation, at the same time be notified of removal directions, or served with a notice of intention to make a deportation order, or with a deportation order, as appropriate (para 338).

A person's grant of refugee status under paragraph 334 will be revoked or not renewed if the Secretary of State is satisfied that (paras 338A, 339A-339AB)–
  (i) he has voluntarily re-availed himself of the protection of the country of nationality;
  (ii) having lost his nationality, he has voluntarily re-acquired it;
  (iii) he has acquired a new nationality, and enjoys the protection of the country of his new nationality;
  (iv) he has voluntarily re-established himself in the country which he left or outside which he remained owing to a fear of persecution;
  (v) he can no longer, because the circumstances in connection with which he has been recognised as a refugee have ceased to exist, continue to refuse to avail himself of the protection of the country of nationality;
  (vi) being a stateless person with no nationality, he is able, because the circumstances in connection with which he has been recognised a refugee have ceased to exist, to return to the country of former habitual residence;
  (vii) the Secretary of State is satisfied that the person should have been or is excluded from being a refugee in accordance with the Refugee or Person in Need of International Protection (Qualification) Regulations 2006, Reg. 7;
  (viii) the Secretary of State is satisfied that the person has instigated or otherwise participated in the crimes or acts mentioned in Article 1F of the Refugee Convention;
  (ix) the Secretary of State is satisfied that the person's misrepresentation or omission of facts, including the use of false documents, were decisive for the grant of refugee status;
  (x) the Secretary of State is satisfied that–
    (i) there are reasonable grounds for regarding the person as a danger to the security of the United Kingdom; or
    (ii) having been convicted by a final judgment of a particularly serious crime, the person constitutes a danger to the community of the United Kingdom.

In considering (v) and (vi), the Secretary of State must have regard to whether the change of circumstances is of such a significant and non-temporary nature that the refugee's fear of persecution can no longer be regarded as well-founded.

When a person's refugee status is revoked or not renewed any limited or indefinite leave which they have may be curtailed or cancelled (para 339B).

Where the Secretary of State is considering revoking refugee status, the person concerned must be informed in writing that the Secretary of State is reconsidering his qualification for refugee status and the reasons for the reconsideration. That person must be given the opportunity to submit, in a personal interview or in a written statement, reasons as to why his refugee status should not be revoked. If there is a personal interview, it must be subject to the safeguards set out in the Immigration Rules (para 339BA). If the person leaves the UK, the procedure may be initiated, and completed, while they are outside the UK (para 339BC).

Where a person acquires British citizenship status, his refugee status is automatically revoked without the need to follow the procedure set out above. Where refugee status is revoked, or if the person has unequivocally renounced his recognition as a refugee, his refugee status may be considered to have lapsed by law without the need to follow the above procedure (para 339BB).

6 Humanitarian protection

A person will be granted humanitarian protection in the UK if the Secretary of State is satisfied that (para 339C)–
  (i) he is in the UK or has arrived at a port of entry in the UK;
  (ii) he does not qualify as a refugee as defined in the Refugee or Person in Need of International Protection (Qualification) Regulations 2006, reg. 2;
  (iii) substantial grounds have been shown for believing that the person concerned, if he returned to the country of return, would face a real risk of suffering serious harm and is unable, or, owing to such risk, unwilling to avail himself of the protection of that country; and
  (iv) he is not excluded from a grant of humanitarian protection.
Serious harm consists of–
  (v) the death penalty or execution;
  (vi) unlawful killing;
  (vii) torture or inhuman or degrading treatment or punishment of a person in the country of return; or
  (viii) serious and individual threat to a civilian's life or person by reason of indiscriminate violence in situations of international or internal armed conflict.

A person is excluded from a grant of humanitarian protection under (iv) above where the Secretary of State is satisfied that (para 339D)–
  (a) there are serious reasons for considering that he has committed a crime against peace, a war crime, a crime against humanity, or any other serious crime or instigated or otherwise participated in such crimes;
  (b) there are serious reasons for considering that he is guilty of acts contrary to the purposes and principles of the United Nations or has committed, prepared or instigated such acts or encouraged or induced others to commit, prepare or instigate instigated such acts;
  (c) there are serious reasons for considering that he constitutes a danger to the community or to the security of the United Kingdom; or
  (d) prior to his admission to the UK he committed a crime outside the scope of (a) and (b) that would be punishable by imprisonment were it committed in the UK and he left his country of origin solely in order to avoid sanctions resulting from the crime.

If the Secretary of State decides to grant humanitarian protection and the person has not yet been given leave to enter, the Secretary of State or an Immigration Officer will grant limited leave to enter. If the Secretary of State decides to grant humanitarian protection to a person who has been given limited leave to enter (whether or not that leave has expired) or a person who has entered without leave, the Secretary of State will vary the existing leave or grant limited leave to remain (para 339E).

Where the criteria set out in paragraph 339C is not met humanitarian protection will be refused (para 339F).

A person's humanitarian protection *will* be revoked or not renewed if the Secretary of State is satisfied that at least one of the following applies (para 339G)–
  (1) the circumstances which led to the grant of humanitarian protection have ceased to exist or have changed to such a degree that such protection is no longer required (para 339GA);
  (2) the person granted humanitarian protection should have been or is excluded from humanitarian protection because there are serious reasons for considering that he (para 339GB)–
      (i) has committed a crime against peace, a war crime, a crime against humanity, or any other serious crime or instigated or otherwise participated in such crimes;
      (ii) is guilty of acts contrary to the purposes and principles of the United Nations or has committed, prepared or instigated such acts or encouraged or induced others to commit, prepare or instigate such acts;
      (iii) constitutes a danger to the community or to the security of the United Kingdom; or
  (3) prior to his admission to the UK the person granted humanitarian protection committed a crime outside the scope of (2)(i) and (ii) above that would be punishable by imprisonment had it been committed in the UK and the person left his country of origin solely in order to avoid sanctions resulting from the crime (para 339GC).

A person's humanitarian protection *may* be revoked or not renewed if the Secretary of State is satisfied that (para 339GD)–

(4) the person granted humanitarian protection misrepresented or omitted facts, including the use of false documents, which were decisive to the grant of humanitarian protection.

In applying (1) the Secretary of State must have regard to whether the change of circumstances is of such a significant and non-temporary nature that the person no longer faces a real risk of serious harm;

When a person's humanitarian protection is revoked or not renewed any limited or indefinite leave which they have may be curtailed or cancelled (para 339H).

7 Consideration of cases

Personnel examining applications for asylum and taking decisions must have the knowledge with respect to the relevant standards applicable in the field of asylum and refugee law Para 339HA).

When the Secretary of State considers a person's asylum claim, eligibility for a grant of humanitarian protection or human rights claim it is the duty of the person to submit to him as soon as possible all material factors needed to substantiate the asylum claim or establish that he is a person eligible for humanitarian protection or substantiate the human rights claim, which the Secretary of State will assess in co-operation with the person (para 339I).

The material factors include (para 339I)–

(i) the person's statement on the reasons for making an asylum claim or on eligibility for a grant of humanitarian protection or for making a human rights claim;

(ii) all documentation at the person's disposal regarding their age, background (including background details of relevant relatives), identity, nationality(ies), country(ies) and place(s) of previous residence, previous asylum applications, travel routes; and

(iii) identity and travel documents.

For the purposes of examining individual applications for asylum (para 339IA)–

(a) information provided in support of an application and the fact that an application has been made must not be disclosed to the alleged actor(s) of persecution of the applicant, and

(b) information must not be obtained from the alleged actor(s) of persecution that would result in their being directly informed that an application for asylum has been made by the applicant in question and would jeopardise the physical integrity of the applicant and his dependants, or the liberty and security of his family members still living in the country of origin. This also applies where the Secretary of State is considering revoking a person's refugee status.

The assessment by the Secretary of State of an asylum claim, eligibility for a grant of humanitarian protection or a human rights claim will be carried out on an individual, objective and impartial basis. This will include taking into account in particular (para 339J)–

(iv) all relevant facts as they relate to the country of origin or country of return at the time of taking a decision on the grant; including laws and regulations of the country of origin or country of return and the manner in which they are applied;

(v) relevant statements and documentation presented by the person including information on whether they have been or may be subject to persecution or serious harm;

(vi) the individual position and personal circumstances of the person, including factors such as background, gender and age, so as to assess whether, on the basis of their personal circumstances, the acts to which they have been or could be exposed would amount to persecution or serious harm;

(vii) whether the person's activities since leaving the country of origin or country of return were engaged in for the sole or main purpose of creating the necessary conditions for making an asylum claim or establishing that they are a person eligible for humanitarian protection or a human rights claim, so as to assess whether these activities will expose them to persecution or serious harm if they returned to that country; and

(viii) whether the person could reasonably be expected to avail himself of the protection of another country where he could assert citizenship.

Reliable and up-to-date information must be obtained from various sources as to the general situation prevailing in the countries of origin of applicants for asylum and, where necessary, in countries through which they have transited. Such information must be made available to the personnel responsible for examining applications and taking decisions and may be provided to them in the form of a consolidated country information report. This also applies where the Secretary of State is considering revoking a person's refugee status (para 339JA).

The fact that a person has already been subject to persecution or serious harm, or to direct threats of such persecution or such harm, will be regarded as a serious indication of their well-founded fear of persecution or real risk of suffering serious harm, unless there are good reasons to consider that such persecution or serious harm will not be repeated (para 339K).

It is the duty of the person to substantiate the asylum claim or establish that he is a person eligible humanitarian protection or substantiate his human rights claim. Where aspects of the person's statements are not supported by documentary or other evidence, those aspects will not need confirmation when all of the following conditions are met (para 339L)–

(a) they have made a genuine effort to substantiate their asylum claim or establish that they are a person eligible for humanitarian protection or to substantiate their human rights claim;

(b) all material factors at their disposal have been submitted, and a satisfactory explanation regarding any lack of other relevant material has been given;

(c) their statements are found to be coherent and plausible and do not run counter to available specific and general information relevant to the their case;

(d) they have made an asylum claim or sought to establish that they are a person eligible for humanitarian protection or made a human rights claim at the earliest possible time, unless they can demonstrate good reason for not having done so; and

(e) their general credibility has been established.

The Secretary of State may consider that a person has not substantiated his asylum claim or established that he is a person eligible for humanitarian protection or substantiated his human rights claim and thereby reject his application for asylum, determine that he is not eligible for humanitarian protection or reject his human rights claim, if he fails, without reasonable explanation, to make a prompt and full disclosure of material facts, either orally or in writing, or otherwise to assist the Secretary of State in establishing the facts of the case; this includes, for example, failure to report to a designated place to be fingerprinted, failure to complete an asylum questionnaire or failure to comply with a requirement to report to an immigration officer for examination (para 339M). Applications for asylum shall be neither rejected nor excluded from examination on the sole ground that they have not been made as soon as possible (para 339MA). In determining whether the general credibility of a person has been established the Secretary of State will apply the provisions in s.8 of the Asylum and Immigration (Treatment of Claimants, etc.) Act 2004 (para 339N).

Before a decision is taken on the application for asylum, the applicant shall be given the opportunity of a personal interview on his application for asylum with a representative of the Secretary of State who is legally competent to conduct such an interview (para 339NA). The personal interview may be omitted where–

(i) the Secretary of State is able to take a positive decision on the basis of evidence available;

(ii) the Secretary of State has already had a meeting with the applicant for the purpose of assisting him with completing his application and submitting the essential information regarding it;

(iii) the applicant, in submitting his application and presenting the facts, has only raised issues that are not relevant or of minimal relevance to the examination of whether he is a refugee, as defined in the Refugee or Person in Need of International Protection (Qualification) Regulations 2006, reg. 2;

(iv) the applicant has made inconsistent, contradictory, improbable or insufficient representations which make his claim clearly unconvincing in relation to his having been the object of persecution;

(v) the applicant has submitted a subsequent application which does not raise any relevant new elements with respect to his particular circumstances or to the situation in his country of origin;

(vi) the applicant is making an application merely in order to delay or frustrate the enforcement of an earlier or imminent decision which would result in his removal;

(vii) it is not reasonably practicable, in particular where the Secretary of State is of the opinion that the applicant is unfit or unable to be interviewed owing to enduring circumstances beyond his control; or

(viii) the applicant is an EU national whose claim the Secretary of State has nevertheless decided to consider substantively.

The omission of a personal interview does not prevent the Secretary of State from taking a decision on the application. Where the personal interview is omitted, the applicant and dependants must be given a reasonable opportunity to submit further information.

The personal interview must normally take place without the presence of the applicant's family members unless the Secretary of State considers it necessary for an appropriate examination to have other family members present (para 339NB). The personal interview must take place under conditions which ensure appropriate confidentiality.

A written report must be made of every personal interview containing at least the essential information regarding the asylum application as presented by the applicant. The Secretary of State must ensure that the applicant has timely access to the report and that access is possible as soon as necessary for allowing an appeal to be prepared and lodged in due time (para 339NC).

The Secretary of State must provide, at public expense, an interpreter for the purpose of allowing the applicant to submit his case, wherever necessary. An interpreter must be selected who can ensure appropriate communication between the applicant and the representative of the Secretary of State who conducts the interview (para 339ND).

The Secretary of State will not make–

(a) a grant of refugee status if in part of the country of origin the person would not have a well founded fear of being persecuted, and they can reasonably be expected to stay in that part of the country; or

(b) a grant of humanitarian protection if in part of the country of return the person would not face a real risk of suffering serious harm, and they can reasonably be expected to stay in that part of the country (para 339O).

In examining whether a part of the country of origin or country of return meets the requirements in (a) the Secretary of State, when making his decision on whether to grant asylum or humanitarian protection, will have regard to the general circumstances prevailing in that part of the country and to the personal circumstances of the person. Para (a) applies notwithstanding technical obstacles to return to the country of origin or country of return

A person may have a well-founded fear of being persecuted or a real risk of suffering serious harm based on events which have taken place since they left the country of origin or country of return and/or activates which they have engaged in since leaving the country of origin or country of return, in particular where it is established that the activities relied upon constitute the expression and continuation of convictions or orientations held in the country of origin or country of return (para 339P).

8 Grant of residence permits, etc

The Secretary of State will issue to a person granted refugee status or humanitarian protection in the UK a UK Residence Permit (UKRP) as soon as possible after the grant of refugee status. The UKRP may be valid for five years and renewable, unless compelling reasons of national security or public order otherwise require, or where there are reasonable grounds for considering that the applicant is a danger to the security of the UK or, having been convicted by a final judgment of a particularly serious crime, the applicant constitutes a danger to the community of the UK or the person's character, conduct or associations otherwise require (para 339Q).

The Secretary of State will issue a UKRP to a family member (provided they are treated as a dependant) of a person granted refugee status or humanitarian protection where the family member does not qualify for such status. A UKRP may be granted for a period of five years on the same terms set out above.

The Secretary of State may revoke or refuse to renew a person's UKRP where their grant of refugee status or humanitarian protection is revoked under the provisions in the immigration rules.

The requirements for indefinite leave to remain for a person who has been granted refugee status or humanitarian protection, or their dependants granted refugee status or humanitarian protection in line with the main applicant, or any dependant granted in accordance with the requirements of paras 352A to 352FJ of the Rules (Family Reunion) are that (para 339R)—

 (i) the applicant has held a UK Residence Permit (UKRP) issued under para 339Q for a continuous period of five years in the UK; and
 (ii) the applicant's UKRP has not been revoked or not renewed under paras 339A or 339G of the Rules; and
 (iii) the applicant has not—
   (a) been convicted of an offence for which they have been sentenced to imprisonment for at least 4 years; or
   (b) been convicted of an offence for which they have been sentenced to imprisonment for at least 12 months but less than 4 years, unless a period of 15 years has passed since the end of the sentence; or
   (c) been convicted of an offence for which they have been sentenced to imprisonment for less than 12 months, unless a period of 7 years has passed since the end of the sentence; or
   (d) within the 24 months prior to the date on which the application has been decided, been convicted of or admitted an offence for which they have received a non-custodial sentence or other out of court disposal that is recorded on their criminal record; or
   (e) in the view of the Secretary of State caused serious harm by their offending or persistently offended and shown a particular disregard for the law; or
   (f) in the view of the Secretary of State, at the date on which the application has been decided, demonstrated the undesirability of granting settlement in the UK in light of their conduct (including convictions which do not fall within paras (a)-(e)), character or associations; or the fact that they represents a threat to national security.

A person refused indefinite leave to remain may apply to have their UK Residence Permit extended in accordance with para 339Q (para 339T).

If a person who makes an asylum application is also eligible for temporary protection (see 11 **Temporary protection**, below), the Secretary of State may decide not to consider the asylum application until the applicant ceases to be entitled to temporary protection (para 355G).

The Secretary of State will not impose conditions restricting the employment or occupation in the UK of a person granted refugee status or humanitarian protection (para 344B).

A person who is granted refugee status or humanitarian protection will be provided with access to information in a language that they may reasonably be supposed to understand which sets out the rights and obligations relating to that status. The Secretary of State will provide the information as soon as possible after the grant of refugee status or humanitarian protection (para 344C).

9 Travel documents

After having received a complete application for a travel document, the Secretary of State will issue to a person granted refugee status in the UK, and their family members, travel documents in the form set out in the Schedule to the Geneva Convention, for the purpose of travel outside the UK, unless compelling reasons of national security or public order otherwise require.

After having received a completed application for a travel document, the Secretary of State will issue to a person granted humanitarian protection in the UK and their family members a travel document where they are unable to obtain a national passport or other identity documents which enable them to travel, unless compelling reasons of national security or public order otherwise require. Where such a person referred can obtain a national passport or identity documents but has not done so, a travel document will only be issued where he can show that he has made reasonable attempts to obtain a national passport or identity document and there are serious humanitarian reasons for travel (para 344A).

10 Third country cases

If the Secretary of State is satisfied that the conditions set out in Paragraphs 4 and 5(1), 9 and 10(1), 14 and 15(1) or 17 of Schedule 3 to the Asylum and Immigration (Treatment of Claimants, etc.) Act 2004 are fulfilled, he will normally decline to examine the asylum application substantively and issue a certificate under Part 2, 3, 4 or 5 of Schedule 3 to that Act, as appropriate.

The conditions are: (i) the applicant is not a national or citizen of the country or territory ("third country") to which he is to be sent; (ii) the applicant's life and liberty would not be threatened in that country for one of the "Convention reasons"; and (iii) the government of the third country would not send him elsewhere otherwise than in accordance with the Refugee Convention (para 345(1)).

A certificate will not be issued if (para 345(2))–

(i) the asylum applicant has not arrived in the UK directly from the country in which he claims to fear persecution and he has had an opportunity at the border or within that third country to make contact with the authorities of the country in order to seek protection; or

(ii) there is other clear evidence of his admissibility to a third country.

Provided that he is satisfied that the case meets these criteria, the Secretary of State is under no obligation to consult the authorities of the third country before the removal of the applicant (para 345).

11 Temporary protection

Temporary protection may be given in the event of a mass influx of displaced persons (para 355).

An applicant will be granted temporary protection if the Secretary of State is satisfied that–

(i) the applicant is in the UK or has arrived at a port of entry in the UK; and

(ii) the applicant is a person entitled to temporary protection as defined by, and in accordance with, the Temporary Protection Directive; and

(iii) the applicant does not hold an extant grant of temporary protection entitling him to reside in another EU Member State. This requirement is subject to the provisions relating to dependants set out in paras 356 to 356B and to any agreement to the contrary with the Member State in question; and

(iv) the applicant is not excluded from temporary protection under the provisions in para 355A.

An applicant or a dependant may be excluded from temporary protection if (para 355A)–

(i) there are serious reasons for considering that:

(a) he has committed a crime against peace, a war crime, or a crime against humanity, as defined in the international instruments drawn up to make provision in respect of such crimes; or

(b) he has committed a serious non-political crime outside the UK prior to his application for temporary protection; or

(c) he has committed acts contrary to the purposes and principles of the United Nations, or

(ii) there are reasonable grounds for regarding the applicant as a danger to the security of the UK or, having been convicted by a final judgment of a particularly serious crime, to be a danger to the community of the UK.

Consideration under this paragraph must be based solely on the personal conduct of the applicant concerned. Exclusion decisions or measures must be based on the principle of proportionality.

A person to whom temporary protection is granted will be granted limited leave to enter or remain, which is not to be subject to a condition prohibiting employment, for a period not exceeding 12 months. On the expiry of this period, he will be entitled to apply for an extension of this limited leave for successive periods of 6 months thereafter (para 355C).

12 Information for asylum seekers

Asylum seekers must be informed within a reasonable time (not exceeding 15 days their claim for asylum has been recorded) of the benefits and services that they may be eligible to receive and of the rules and procedures with which they must comply relating to them. The Secretary of State must also provide information on non-governmental organisations and persons that provide legal assistance to asylum applicants and which may be able to help asylum applicants or provide information on available benefits and services (para 358).

An asylum seeker must notify the Secretary of State of his current address and of any change to it (para 359).

The Secretary of State must ensure that, within three working days of recording an asylum application, a document is made available to that asylum applicant, issued in his own name, certifying his status as an asylum applicant or testifying that he is allowed to remain in the UK while his asylum application is pending (para 359). This does not apply where the asylum applicant is held in detention (para 359A).

13 Taking up of work by asylum seekers

An asylum applicant may apply for permission to take up employment (but not permission to become self employed or to engage in a business or professional activity) if a decision at first instance has not been taken on the applicant's asylum application within one year of the date on which it was recorded. The Secretary of State shall only consider such an application if, in his opinion, any delay in reaching a decision at first instance cannot be attributed to the applicant. Where permission is given, employment may only be taken up in a post which is, at the time an offer of employment is accepted, included on the list of shortage occupations published by UK

Visas and Immigration (paras 360, 360A).

If permission is granted it will only last until such time as his asylum application has been finally determined (para 360B).

14 Dependants

If a principal applicant is granted refugee status or humanitarian protection, a spouse/civil partner, unmarried/same sex partner, or minor child of that applicant, who has been included in the principal application, may be granted leave of the same duration to enter or remain. If a dependant claims asylum in his own right and would otherwise be refused leave to enter or remain, his case will be also considered individually under paragraph 334 (see **4 Grant of asylum**, above). If the dependant has a claim in his own right, it should be made at the earliest opportunity. Any failure to do so will be taken into account and may damage credibility if no reasonable explanation for it is given. Where an asylum or humanitarian protection application is unsuccessful, at the same time that asylum or humanitarian protection is refused the applicant may be notified of removal directions or served with a notice of the Secretary of State's intention to deport him, as appropriate (para 349). Unaccompanied children may apply for asylum and particular priority is to be given to their cases. A "child" means a person who is under 18 or who in the absence of documentary proof appears to under that age (para 350). If it is necessary to interview a child, special care must be taken and certain specified safeguards observed (paras. 351 to 352ZB).

15 Unaccompanied asylum-seeking children

Limited leave to remain should be granted to an unaccompanied asylum seeking child for a period of 30 months (or until the child is 17½ years of age whichever is shorter), provided specified requirements are met (para 352ZE). The requirements are (para 352ZC)–

(a) the applicant is an unaccompanied asylum seeking child under the age of 17½ years throughout the duration of leave to be granted in this capacity;

(b) the applicant must have applied for asylum and been granted neither refugee status nor and Humanitarian Protection;

(c) there are no adequate reception arrangements in the country to which they would be returned if leave to remain was not granted;

(d) the applicant must not be excluded from being a refugee under Regulation 7 of the Refugee or Person in Need of International Protection (Qualification) Regulations 2006 or excluded from a grant of Humanitarian Protection under para 339D or both;

(e) there are no reasonable grounds for regarding the applicant as a danger to the security of the UK;

(f) the applicant has not been convicted by a final judgment of a particularly serious crime, and the applicant does not constitute a danger to the community of the UK; and

(g) the applicant is not, at the date of their application, the subject of a deportation order or a decision to make a deportation order.

An unaccompanied asylum seeking child is a person who is under 18 years of age when the asylum application is submitted; is applying for asylum in their own right; and is separated from both parents and is not being cared for by an adult who in law or by custom has responsibility to do so (para 352ZD).

Limited leave granted under this provision will cease if any one or more of the above requirements cease to be met, or a misrepresentation or omission of facts, including the use of false documents, were decisive for the grant of (para 352ZF).

16 Spouses/civil partners and children of refugees

The requirements to be met by a person seeking leave to enter or remain as the spouse/civil partner of a refugee are that (para 352A)–

(i) the applicant is married to or the civil partner of a person who currently has refugee status under UK immigration rules;

(ii) the marriage/civil partnership did not take place after the person granted refugee status left the country of his former habitual residence in order to seek asylum;

(iii) the applicant would not be excluded from protection by virtue of Article 1F of the UN Convention and Protocol relating to the status of refugees were he to seek asylum in his own right;

(iv) each of the parties intends to live permanently with the other as his or her spouse or civil partner and the marriage is subsisting; and

(v) the parties are not involved in a consanguineous relationship with one another; and

(vi) if seeking leave to enter, the applicant holds a valid UK entry clearance for entry in this capacity.

Similar provisions apply to unmarried/same sex partners (para 352AA).

Limited leave to enter/remain in the UK as the spouse/civil partner or unmarried/same sex partner of a refugee may also be granted (paras 352B, 352BA).

The requirements for a child of a refugee are that the applicant (para 352D)–

(v) is the child of a parent who currently has refugee status under UK immigration rules;

   (vi) is under 18;

   (vii) is not leading an independent life, is unmarried and not a civil partner, and has not formed an independent family unit;

(viii) was part of the family unit of the person granted asylum at the time that person left his country of habitual residence in order to seek asylum;

   (ix) would not be excluded from protection by virtue of Article 1F of the UN Convention and Protocol relating to the status of refugees were he to seek asylum in his own right;

   (x) if seeking leave to enter, the applicant holds a valid UK entry clearance for entry in this capacity.

The requirements to be met by a person seeking leave to enter or remain as the spouse/civil partner of a person who has been granted humanitarian protection are that (para 352FA)–

   (i) the applicant is married to or the civil partner of a person who currently has humanitarian protection granted under UK immigration rules;

   (ii) the marriage/civil partnership did not take place after the person granted humanitarian protection left the country of his former habitual residence in order to seek asylum in the UK;

   (iii) the applicant would not be excluded from protection by virtue of any of the reasons in para 339D (see **6 Humanitarian protection**, above);

   (iv) each of the parties intend to live permanently with the other as his or her spouse/civil partner and the marriage or civil partnership is subsisting;

   (v) the parties are not involved in a consanguineous relationship with one another; and

   (vi) if seeking leave to enter, the applicant holds a valid UK entry clearance for entry in this capacity.

Similar provisions apply to unmarried/same sex partners (para 352FD) and to children (para 352FG).

Limited leave to enter/remain in the UK as the spouse/civil partner, unmarried/same sex partner, or child of a person who has been granted humanitarian protection may also be granted (paras 352FB, 352FE, 352FH).

17 Fresh claims

When a human rights or protection claim has been refused or withdrawn, or treated as withdrawn, and any appeal relating to that claim is no longer pending, the decision maker will consider any further submissions and, if rejected, will then determine whether they amount to a fresh claim. The submissions will amount to a fresh claim if they are significantly different from the material that has previously been considered. The submissions will only be significantly different if the content (para 353)–

   (i) had not already been considered; and

   (ii) taken together with the previously considered material, creates a realistic prospect of success, notwithstanding its rejection.

This does not apply to claims made overseas.

An applicant who has made further submissions must not be removed before the Secretary of State has considered those submissions (para 353A). This does not apply to submissions made overseas.

Where further submissions have been made and the decision maker has established whether or not they amount to a fresh claim under para 353 of the Rules, or in cases with no outstanding further submissions whose appeal rights have been exhausted and which are subject to a review, the decision maker will also have regard to the migrant's–

   (i) character, conduct and associations including any criminal record and the nature of any offence of which the migrant concerned has been convicted;

   (ii) compliance with any conditions attached to any previous grant of leave to enter or remain and compliance with any conditions of temporary admission or immigration bail where applicable;

   (iii) length of time spent in the United Kingdom spent for reasons beyond the migrant's control after the human rights or asylum claim has been submitted or refused;

in deciding whether there are exceptional circumstances which mean that removal from the UK is no longer appropriate. This does not apply to submissions made overseas or where the person is liable to deportation (para 353B).

18 Information to be provided

These provisions only apply to asylum applicants who are not nationals of an EU Member State.

The Secretary of State must inform asylum applicants in a language they may reasonably be supposed to understand and within a reasonable time after their claim for asylum has been recorded of the procedure to be followed, their rights and obligations during the procedure, and the possible consequences of non-compliance and non-co-operation. They must be informed of the likely timeframe for consideration of the application and the means at their disposal for submitting all relevant information (para 357).

The Secretary of State must inform asylum applicants within a reasonable time (not exceeding 15 days) after their claim for asylum has been recorded of the benefits and services that they may be eligible to receive and of the rules and procedures with which they must comply relating to them. He must also provide information on non-governmental organisations and persons that provide legal assistance to asylum applicants and which may be able to help asylum applicants or provide information on available benefits and services (para 358).

The Secretary of State must ensure that the information is available in writing and, to the extent possible, will provide the information in a language that asylum applicants may reasonably be supposed to understand. Where appropriate, he may also arrange for this information to be supplied orally (para 358A).

An asylum applicant must notify the Secretary of State of his current address and of any change to his address or residential status. If not notified beforehand, any change must be notified to the Secretary of State without delay after it occurs (para 358B).

The Secretary of State must ensure that, within three working days of recording an asylum application, a document is made available to that asylum applicant, issued in his own name, certifying his status as an asylum applicant or testifying that he is allowed to remain in the UK while his asylum application is pending. Where the Secretary of State declines to examine an application it will no longer be pending for the purposes of this rule (para 359). This obligation does not apply where the asylum applicant is detained under the Immigration Acts, the Immigration and Asylum Act 1999 or the Nationality, Immigration and Asylum Act 2002 (para 359A). A document issued to an asylum applicant under these provisions does not constitute evidence of the asylum applicant's identity (para 359B). In specific cases the Secretary of State or an Immigration Officer may provide an asylum applicant with evidence equivalent to that provided under para 359. This might be, for example, in circumstances in which it is only possible or desirable to issue a time-limited document (para 359C).

19 UNHCR

A representative of the United Nations High Commissioner for Refugees (UNHCR) or an organisation working in the UK on behalf of the UNHCR shall (para 358C)–
- (a) have access to applicants for asylum, including those in detention;
- (b) have access to information on individual applications for asylum, on the course of the procedure and on the decisions taken on applications for asylum, provided that the applicant for asylum agrees thereto;
- (c) be entitled to present his views, in the exercise of his supervisory responsibilities under Article 35 of the Geneva Convention, to the Secretary of State regarding individual applications for asylum at any stage of the procedure.

These provisions also apply where the Secretary of State is considering revoking a person's refugee status.

20 Stateless persons

A stateless person is someone who (para 401)–
- (a) satisfies the requirements of Article 1(1) of the 1954 United Nations Convention relating to the Status of Stateless Persons, as a person who is not considered as a national by any State under the operation of its law;
- (b) is in the UK; and
- (c) is not excluded from recognition as a Stateless person.

A person is excluded from recognition as a stateless person if there are serious reasons for considering that they (para 402)–
- (a) are at present receiving from organs or agencies of the United Nations, other than the United Nations High Commissioner for Refugees, protection or assistance, so long as they are receiving such protection or assistance;
- (b) are recognised by the competent authorities of the country of their former habitual residence as having the rights and obligations which are attached to the possession of the nationality of that country;
- (c) have committed a crime against peace, a war crime, or a crime against humanity, as defined in the international instruments drawn up to make provisions in respect of such crimes;
- (d) have committed a serious non-political crime outside the UK prior to their arrival in the UK;
- (e) have been guilty of acts contrary to the purposes and principles of the United Nations.

The requirements for leave to remain in the UK as a stateless person are that the applicant (para 403)–
- (a) has made a valid application for limited leave to remain as a stateless person;
- (b) is recognised as a stateless person by the Secretary of State in accordance with para 401;
- (c) is not admissible to their country of former habitual residence or any other country; and
- (d) has obtained and submitted all reasonably available evidence to enable the Secretary of State to determine whether they are stateless.

An applicant will be refused leave to remain in the UK as stateless person if they do not meet the above requirements or if there are reasonable grounds for considering that they are a danger to the security or public order of the UK; or if their application would fall to be refused under any of the grounds set out in para 322 of the Rules (see the Note on **The Immigration Rules: Refusal of entry, leave to remain etc and Deportation** at para **5 Refusal of leave or curtailment of leave**, above) (para 404). Where limited leave to remain in the UK is granted, it will be for a period not exceeding 30 months (para 405) and may be curtailed where the stateless person is a danger to the security or public order of the UK or where leave would be curtailed under para 323 of the Rules (para 406).

The requirements for indefinite leave to remain as a stateless person are that the applicant (para 407)–
- (a) has made a valid application for indefinite leave to remain as a stateless person;
- (b) was last granted limited leave to remain as a stateless person in accordance with para 405 (see above);
- (c) has spent a continuous period of five years in the UK with lawful leave, except that any period of overstaying for a period of 28 days or less will be disregarded; and
- (d) continues to meet the requirements of para 403 (see above).

Leave will be refused on the same grounds as in para 404 (para 409).

Similar rules apply to family members of stateless persons (paras 410-416). A family member of a stateless person means their (para 410)–

(a) spouse;

(b) civil partner;

(c) unmarried or same sex partner with whom they have lived together in a subsisting relationship akin to marriage or a civil partnership for two years or more;

(d) child under 18 who is not leading an independent life; is not married or a civil partner; and has not formed an independent family unit.

21 Authorities

Statutory Instruments, etc–

Refugee or Person in Need of International Protection (Qualification) Regulations 2006 (S.I. 2006 No. 2525)

Statement of Changes in Immigration Rules (HC 395–23rd May 1994 as amended by Cmnd 2663, HC 797, Cmnd 3073, HC 274, HC 329, Cmnd 3365, HC 31, HC 338, Cmnd 3369, HC 26, HC 161, Cmnd 3953, Cmnd 4065, HC 22, HC 704, Cmnd 4851, Cmnd 5253, HC 735, Cmnd 5597, HC 1301, HC 104, HC 180, HC 489, HC 538, Cmnd 5829, Cmnd 5949, HC 1224, HC 95, HC 176, HC 370, HC 464, HC 523, Cmnd 6297, Cmnd 6339, HC 1112, HC 164, HC 194, HC 302, HC 346, HC 486, HC 104, HC 299, HC 582, HC 645, HC 697, HC 769, HC 819, HC 949, HC 974, HC 1016, HC 1053, HC 1337, Cmnd 6918, HC 1702, HC 130, HC 398, Cmnd 7074, Cmnd 7075, HC 28, HC 40, HC 82, HC 321, HC 420, HC 607, HC 951, HC 971, HC 1113, HC 227, HC 314, HC413, Cmnd 7701, Cmnd 7711, HC 120, HC 367, HC 439, HC 59, HC 96, HC 382, Cmnd 7929, Cmnd 7944, HC698, HC863, HC908, HC1148, HC1436, HC 1511, HC1622, HC1693, HC1719, HC1733, HC1888, Cmnd 8337, HC194, Cmnd 8423, HC514, HC565, HC760, 820, HC847, HC943, HC967, HC1038, HC1039, Cmnd 8599, HC244, HC628, HC803, HC887, HC901, HC938, HC1130, HC1138, HC1201, HC198, HC532. HC693, HC1025, HC1116, HC297, HC 437, HC535, HC877)

THE IMMIGRATION RULES: FAMILY MEMBERS

1 Introduction

This Note deals with those provisions of the Statement of Changes in Immigration Rules ("the Rules") which relate to family members.

2 Rules from July 2012

A number of changes to the Immigration Rules came into effect from 9th July 2012 and affect non-European Economic Area nationals applying to enter or remain in the UK as family members.

There are transitional provisions so that family members who had leave to enter or remain in the UK before 9th July 2012, on the basis of being the spouse or partner of a settled person, will still need to satisfy the Immigration Rules as they were before that date if they apply for settlement.

The main changes are (Appendix FM)—

(a) there is a new minimum income threshold of £18,600 for sponsoring the settlement in the UK of a spouse, partner, fiancé(e) or proposed civil partner of non-European Economic Area (EEA) nationality, with an additional £3,800 for one child; and an additional £2,400 for each further child.

(b) the minimum probationary period for settlement for non-EEA spouses and partners is increased from two years to five years. The ability to apply for immediate settlement for a migrant spouses and partner where a couple have been living together overseas for at least 4 years, has been abolished.

(c) from October 2013, all applicants for settlement must pass the Life in the UK Test and present an English language speaking and listening qualification at B1 level or above of the Common European Framework of Reference for Languages unless they are exempt.

(d) adult and elderly dependants can settle in the UK only where they can demonstrate that, as a result of age, illness or disability, they require a level of long-term personal care that can only be provided by a relative in the UK. Application must be made from overseas (i.e., an applicant cannot come to the UK as a visitor and then apply to stay as a dependant).

Immigration Directorate Instructions lists the factors looked at to assess whether a relationship is genuine or not, see—

<https://www.gov.uk/government/uploads/system/uploads/attachment_data/file/263237/section-FM2.1.pdf>.

3 Spouses

Nothing in the immigration rules is to be construed as allowing a person to be granted entry clearance or leave to enter or remain as a spouse/civil partner of another, if either party to the marriage/civil partnership, or the sponsor, is aged under 18 either on arrival in the UK or when the leave would be granted (para 277).

A person will not be granted entry clearance or leave to enter or remain as a spouse/civil partner of a man or woman (the sponsor), if his or her marriage/civil partnership to the sponsor is polygamous and there is another person living who is the husband, wife or civil partner of the sponsor and who either is or has been in the UK at any time since his or her marriage/civil partnership to the sponsor, or has been granted a certificate of entitlement in respect of the right of abode (see the Note on **Control of Immigration** at para 12 **Certificate of entitlement to right of abode**), or an entry clearance as the sponsor's husband or wife. A marriage/civil partnership may be polygamous for these purposes even though neither party had any other spouse/civil partner at the beginning of the marriage/civil partnership (para 278).

Paragraph 278 does not apply to a person seeking entry clearance or leave to enter or remain where he or she has been in the UK before 1st August 1988, having been admitted for settlement as the sponsor's husband or wife, or where he or she has since their marriage to the sponsor been in the UK at any time when there was no such other spouse living as the sponsor's husband or wife. The burden of proof lies on the spouse to show that paragraph 278 does not apply (para 279).

The presence of any wife or husband in the UK as a visitor, illegal entrant or under s.11(1) of the 1971 Act is to be disregarded for the purposes of paragraphs 278 and 279 (para 280).

Nothing in the Rules is to be construed as allowing a child to be granted entry clearance or leave to enter or remain where his parent is party to a polygamous marriage and would be refused entry clearance or leave under paragraph 278 (para 296).

4 Spouses or civil partners of persons present and settled in the UK or being admitted on the same occasion for settlement

The requirements for a person seeking leave to enter in this category are that (para 281)—

(i) (a)(i) the applicant is married to or the civil partner of a person present and settled in the UK or who is on the same occasion being admitted for settlement; and

(a)(ii) the applicant provides an original English language test certificate in speaking and listening from an approved English language test provider which clearly shows their name and the qualification obtained (which must meet or exceed level A1 of the Common European Framework of Reference) unless: (a) the applicant is aged 65 or over at the time he makes his application; or (b) he has a physical or mental condition that would prevent him from meeting the requirement; or (c) there are exceptional compassionate circumstances that would prevent him from meeting the requirement; or

(a)(iii) the applicant is a national of one of the following countries: Antigua and Barbuda; Australia; the Bahamas; Barbados; Belize; Canada; Dominica; Grenada; Guyana; Jamaica; New Zealand; St Kitts and Nevis; St Lucia; St Vincent and the Grenadines; Trinidad and Tobago; United States of America; or

(a)(iv) the applicant has obtained an academic qualification (not a professional or vocational qualification), which is deemed to meet the recognised standard of a Bachelor's or Master's degree or PhD in the UK, from an educational establishment in one of the above countries or Ireland or the UK; and provides specified documents; or

(a)(v) the applicant has obtained an academic qualification (not a professional or vocational qualification) which is deemed to meet the recognised standard of a Bachelor's or Master's degree or PhD in the UK, and either (a) provides specified evidence to show he has the qualification, and (b) UK NARIC has confirmed that the qualification was taught or researched in English, or (c) provides specified evidence to show he has the qualification and that it was taught or researched in English;

(a)(vi) the applicant has obtained an academic qualification (not a professional or vocational qualification) which is deemed by UK NARIC to meet the recognised standard of a Bachelor's or Master's degree or PhD in the UK, and provides the specified evidence to show: he has the qualification and that the qualification was taught or researched in English; or

(b)(i) the applicant is married to or the civil partner of a person who has a right of abode in the UK or indefinite leave to enter or remain and is on the same occasion seeking admission to the UK for the purposes of settlement and the parties were married or formed a civil partnership at least 4 years ago, since which time they have been living together outside the UK; and

(b)(ii) the applicant has sufficient knowledge of the English language and sufficient knowledge about life in the UK, in accordance with Appendix KoLL;

(ii) the parties to the marriage/civil partnership have met;

(iii) the parties have a subsisting marriage/civil partnership and each of the parties intend to live permanently with the other as his or her spouse/civil partner;

(iv) there will be adequate accommodation for the parties and any dependants, without recourse to public funds in accommodation which they own or occupy exclusively;

(v) the parties will be able to maintain themselves and any dependants adequately without recourse to public funds;

(vi) the applicant holds a valid entry clearance for entry in this capacity; and

(vii) the applicant does not fall for refusal under the general grounds for refusal

Leave to enter may be granted for an initial period of not more than 27 months (for a person within (i)(a)(i) above who meets one of the requirements of (i)(a)(ii) to (v) above), or indefinitely (for a person within (i)(b) above) provided the requirements of para 281 are met (para 282); and will be refused if they are not (para 283). If a person would be within (i)(b) above, but fail the English language and life test, they may be admitted for an initial 27 month period.

An extension of stay for a period of 2 years may be granted (para 285) if the following requirements have been met (para 284)–

(i) he has or was last granted limited leave to enter or remain in the UK under any provision of the Rules and the grant was for a period of 6 months or more (except where granted as a fiancé or proposed civil partner) and was not granted to the applicant as the spouse, civil partner, unmarried or same-sex partner of a relevant points based system migrant;

(ii) he is married to or the civil partner of a person present and settled in the UK;

(iii) he is not in breach of the immigration laws disregarding any period of overstaying for a period of 28 days or less;

(iv) the marriage/civil partnership has not taken place after a decision has been taken to deport the applicant or he has been recommended for deportation, given notice under s.6(2) of the 1971 Act or given directions for removal under s.10 of the 1999 Act; and

(v) requirements (i) to (v) of para 281 above have been met.

The applicant will be refused an extension of stay if each of the above requirements is not met (para 286).

Indefinite leave to remain may be granted if the applicant was admitted or given an extension of stay for a period of 2 years and has completed a period of 2 years as the spouse/civil partner of a person present and settled in the UK, and conditions (iii) to (v) above (para 281) and the English language and life test are met (paras. 287 and 288); indefinite leave to remain will be refused if each of the above requirements is not met (para 289).

Persons seeking leave to enter in this category must hold a biometric immigration document: see the Note on **Control of Immigration** at para **6 Biometric registration**.

5 Family members of refugees, etc

The provisions of the previous paragraph only apply to spouses and partners of person present and settled in the UK; they do not therefore apply to spouses and partners of refugees or beneficiaries of humanitarian protection who have only limited rather than indefinite leave to remain in the UK. Such spouses and partners can however seek leave to enter under paras 319L to 319U which operate on a similar basis to paras 281-289. It should be noted that this means that the spouse or partner must be maintained by the refugee or beneficiary of humanitarian protection without recourse to public funds and must satisfy the English language requirements.

Similar provisions also apply to minor children and parents (paras 319R to 319U), grandparents and other dependent relatives (paras 319V to 319Y) of refugees or beneficiaries of humanitarian protection.

6 Victims of domestic violence

Indefinite leave to remain as the victim of domestic violence may be granted provided the Secretary of State is satisfied that each of the requirements of paragraph 289A is met (para 289B). Those requirements are that the applicant—

(i) (a) the applicant was last admitted to the UK for a period not exceeding 27 months in accordance with sub-paras 282(a), 282(c), 295B(a) or 295B(c) of the Rules; or

(b) the applicant was last granted leave to remain as the spouse or civil partner or unmarried partner or same-sex partner of a person present and settled in the UK in accordance with paras 285 or 295E of the Rules, except where that leave extends leave originally granted to the applicant as the partner of a Relevant Points Based System Migrant; or

(c) the applicant was last granted leave to enable access to public funds pending an application under para 289A and the preceding grant of leave was given in accordance with paras 282(a), 282(c), 285, 295B(a), 295B(c) or 295E of the Rules, except where that leave extends leave originally granted to the applicant as the partner of a Relevant Points Based System Migrant; and

(ii) the relationship with their spouse or civil partner or unmarried partner or same-sex partner, as appropriate, was subsisting at the beginning of the last period of leave granted in accordance with paras 282(a), 282(c), 285, 295B(a), 295B(c) or 295E of the Rules; and

(iii) is able to produce such evidence as may be required by the Secretary of State to establish that the relationship was caused to permanently break down before the end of that period as a result of domestic violence.

There is no fee for applications for leave to remain in the UK as a victim of domestic violence where at the time of making the application the applicant appears to the Secretary of State to be destitute (Immigration and Nationality (Fees) Regulations 2014, Sch. 1, para. 4.3). As to fees in respect of applications for limited leave to remain see the Note on **Control of Immigration** at para **49 Immigration fees: leave to remain**.

If a person does not meet these requirements for indefinite leave to remain only because paragraph 322(1C)(iii) or (iv) applies (see the Note on **The Immigration Rules: Refusal of entry, leave to remain etc and Deportation** at para **5 Refusal of leave or curtailment of leave**), the applicant may be granted limited leave to remain for a period not exceeding 30 months (para 289D).

7 Unmarried/same sex partners

Leave to enter the UK with a view to settlement as the unmarried or same sex partner of a person present and settled in the UK or being admitted on the same occasion for settlement will be considered where specific requirements are met. These requirements are that (para 295A)—

(i) (a)(i) the applicant is the unmarried or same sex partner of a person present and settled in the UK or who is on the same occasion being admitted for settlement and the parties have been living together in a relationship akin to marriage or civil partnership which has subsisted for two years or more; and (a)(ii) the applicant provides an original English language test certificate in speaking and listening from an approved English language test provider which clearly shows their name and the qualification obtained (which must meet or exceed level A1 of the Common European Framework of Reference) unless: (a) the applicant is aged 65 or over at the time he makes his application; or (b) the applicant has a physical or mental condition that would prevent him from meeting the requirement; or; (c) there are exceptional compassionate circumstances that would prevent the applicant from meeting the requirement; or (a)(iii) the applicant is a national of one of the following countries: Antigua and Barbuda; Australia; the Bahamas; Barbados; Belize; Canada; Dominica; Grenada; Guyana; Jamaica; New Zealand; St Kitts and Nevis; St Lucia; St Vincent and the Grenadines; Trinidad and Tobago; United States of America; or (a)(iv) the applicant has obtained an academic qualification (not a professional or vocational qualification), which is deemed to meet the recognised standard of a Bachelor's or Master's degree or PhD in the UK, from an educational establishment in one of the above countries or Ireland or the UK; and provides specified documents; or (a)(v) the applicant has obtained an academic qualification (not a professional or vocational qualification) which is deemed to meet the recognised standard of a Bachelor's or Master's degree or PhD in the UK, and either (a) provides specified evidence to show he has the qualification, and (b) UK NARIC has confirmed that the degree was taught or researched in English, or (c) provides specified evidence to show he has the qualification and that it was taught or researched in English; or (a)(vi) the applicant has obtained an academic qualification (not a professional or vocational qualification) which is deemed by UK NARIC to meet the recognised standard of a Bachelor's or Master's degree or PhD in the UK, and provides the specified evidence to show: he has the qualification and that the qualification was taught or researched in English; or (b) a person who has a right of abode in the UK or indefinite leave to enter or remain in the UK and is on the same occasion seeking admission to the UK for the purposes of settlement and the parties have been living together outside the UK in a relationship akin to marriage which has subsisted for 4 years or more; and the applicant has sufficient knowledge of the English language and sufficient knowledge about life in the UK, in accordance with Appendix KoLL; and

(ii) any previous marriage/civil partnership (or similar relationship) by either partner has permanently broken down;

(iii) the parties are not involved in a consanguineous relationships with one another;

(iv) *deleted*;

(v) there will be adequate accommodation for the parties and any dependants without recourse to public funds in accommodation which they own or occupy exclusively;

(vi) the parties will be able to maintain themselves and any dependants adequately without recourse to public funds;

(vii) the parties intend to live together permanently;

(viii) the applicant holds a valid UK entry clearance for entry in this capacity; and

(ix) the applicant does not fall for refusal under the general grounds for refusal

Admission will be for a period of 27 months (for a person within (i)(a)(i) and one of (i)(a)(ii) to (v) above), or indefinitely (for a person within (i)(b) above). A person within (i)(b) above but who fails the English language and life test will also be admitted for an initial period of 27 months.

Leave to remain after the initial two year period will be granted provided that the applicant is the unmarried or same sex partner of a person who is present and settled in the UK; has or was last granted limited leave to enter or remain in the UK which was given in accordance with any of the provisions of the Rules (unless as a result of that leave he would not have been in the UK beyond 6 months from the date on which he was admitted to the UK; or the leave was granted as the unmarried or same-sex partner of a Relevant Points Based System Migrant); has not remained in breach of immigration laws (disregarding any period of overstaying for a period of 28 days or less); the parties relationship pre-dates any decision or recommendation as to deportation or removal; and the requirements of paragraphs (ii) to (vii) above are satisfied, and English language requirements are met. An extension of stay will initially be granted for a period of two years (paras 295D, 295E).

Indefinite leave to remain will be granted if the applicant was admitted for a period of 27 months or given a two year extension (which has been completed) as the unmarried or same sex partner of a person settled here; is still the unmarried or same sex partner of that person and the relationship is still subsisting; and the requirements of paragraphs (v) to (vii) and (ix) above are still satisfied and the English language and life test is also satisfied (para 295G).

Nothing in the Rules will be construed as permitting a person to be granted entry clearance, leave to enter or variation of leave as an unmarried or same sex partner if the applicant will be aged under 16 or the sponsor will be aged under 18 on the date of arrival of the applicant in the UK or (as the case may be) on the date on which the leave to enter or variation of leave would be granted (para 295AA).

Persons seeking leave to enter in this category must hold a biometric immigration document: see the Note on **Control of Immigration** at para **6 Biometric registration**.

8 Bereaved unmarried/same sex partners

A bereaved unmarried or same sex partner of a person present and settled in the UK may seek indefinite leave to remain if they satisfy the following requirements (para 295M)—

(i) they were admitted to the UK for a period of 27 months, or given a two year extension of stay, as the unmarried or same sex partner of a person present and settled in the UK;

(ii) the person who the applicant was admitted or granted an extension of stay to join died during that two year period;

(iii) the applicant was still the unmarried or same sex partner of that person at the time of the death;

(iv) each of the parties intended to live with the other as his partner and the relationship was subsisting at the time of the death; and

(v) the applicant does not fall for refusal under the general grounds for refusal.

9 Fiancé(e)s and proposed civil partners

The requirements for a person seeking leave to enter in this category are very similar to those in paragraph 281 (see **4 Spouses or civil partners of persons present and settled in the UK or being admitted on the same occasion for settlement**, above), with the additional requirement that adequate maintenance and accommodation without recourse to public funds must be available to the applicant until the date of the marriage/civil partnership (para 290).

Leave to enter, with a prohibition on employment, may be granted for not more than six months to enable the marriage/civil partnership to take place (para 291).

An extension of stay, with a prohibition on employment, may be granted for an appropriate period to enable the marriage/civil partnership to take place, provided that the following requirements are met (para 294): the applicant had a valid entry clearance as a fiancé(e)/proposed civil partner on entry, there is a good reason why the marriage/civil partnership did not take place in the initial six months and evidence that it will take place at an early date, and the requirements of paragraph 290 have been met (para 293).

Leave to enter in this capacity will be refused if a valid entry clearance in this capacity is not produced, on arrival (para 292). Leave for an extension of stay will be refused if the applicant does not meet each of the requirements of paragraph 293 (see above) (para 295).

Nothing in the Rules will be construed as permitting a person to be granted entry clearance, leave to enter or variation of leave as a fiancé(e)/proposed civil partner if either the applicant or the sponsor will be aged under 18 on the date of arrival of the applicant in the UK or (as the case may be) on the date on which the leave to enter or variation of leave would be granted (para 289AA).

10 Child of a parent(s) or a relative settled or being admitted for settlement

Indefinite leave to enter.–The requirements to be met by a person in this category seeking indefinite leave to enter are that he (para 297)–

    (i) is seeking leave to enter to accompany or join a parent(s) or relatives in one of the following circumstances–
        (a) both parents are present and settled in the UK;
        (b) both parents are being admitted on the same occasion for settlement;
        (c) one parent is present and settled in the UK and the other is being admitted for settlement on the same occasion;
        (d) one parent is either settled or being admitted for settlement and the other parent is dead;
        (e) the parent who has had sole responsibility for the child's upbringing is either settled or being admitted for settlement;
        (f) one parent or a relative is settled in the UK or being admitted for settlement on the same occasion, there are serious and compelling family or other reasons which make exclusion of the child undesirable and suitable arrangements have been made for the child's care;
    (ii) is aged under 18;
    (iii) is unmarried, not a civil partner and not leading an independent life;
    (iv) can and will be maintained and accommodated by the parent, parents, or relative he is seeking to join without recourse to public funds in accommodation which the parent, parents or relative own or occupy exclusively;
    (v) can, and will, be maintained adequately by the parent, parents or relative without recourse to public funds;
    (vi) has a valid entry clearance in this capacity (para 297). Leave to enter will be refused if a valid entry clearance for entry in this capacity is not produced on arrival; and
    (vii) the applicant does not fall for refusal under the general grounds for refusal.

Indefinite leave to remain.–The requirements to be met by a person in this category seeking indefinite leave to remain are broadly similar to para 297(i)(a), (d), (e), (f), (ii) to (v) and (vii) except that instead of being aged under 18, the child may show either that he was given leave to enter or remain under para 302 (see below) or that he has limited leave to enter or remain in the UK in accordance with para 319X, as the child of a relative with limited leave to remain as a refugee or beneficiary of humanitarian protection in the UK and who is now present and settled here (paras 298 and 299). Leave to remain in this capacity will be refused if the applicant does not meet each of the requirements of paragraph 298 (para 300).

If a person does not meet these requirements for indefinite leave to remain only because para 322(1C)(iii) or (iv) applies (see the Note on **The Immigration Rules: Refusal of entry, leave to remain etc and Deportation** at para 5 **Refusal of leave or curtailment of leave**), or because he does not meet English language requirements, or has a specified unspent conviction, the applicant may be granted limited leave to remain for a period not exceeding 30 months (para 298A).

11 Child of a parent(s) given limited leave to enter or remain with a view to settlement

The requirements to be met by a child in this category who is seeking limited leave to enter or remain with a view to settlement are similar to paragraph 297(ii) to (vi) (see above). Additionally, he must show that he is seeking leave to enter to accompany or join or remain with a parent(s) in the following circumstances (para 301(i))–

    (a) one parent is present and settled in the UK or being admitted for settlement on the same occasion and the other parent is being given limited leave to enter or remain with a view to settlement; or
    (b) the parent with sole responsibility for the child's upbringing is being or has been given limited leave to enter or remain with a view to settlement; or
    (c) one parent is being or has been given limited leave to enter or remain with a view to settlement, and there are serious and compelling family or other reasons which make exclusion of the child undesirable and arrangements have been made for his care.;

and that he does not qualify for limited leave to enter as a child of a parent or parents given limited leave to enter or remain as a refugee or beneficiary of humanitarian protection under paragraph 319R.

Leave to enter in this category may be given for not more than 27 months provided that a valid entry clearance in this capacity is produced, on arrival, and will be refused if not so produced. The applicant will be granted leave to remain in the UK for a period not exceeding 27 months provided that each of the requirements of paragraph 301 (see above) is met; and will be refused if not met (para 302).

12 Children of fiancées or proposed civil partners

The requirements to be met by a child in this category who is seeking limited leave to enter or remain with a view to settlement are (para 303A)–

- (i) he is seeking to accompany or join a parent who is, on the same occasion, being admitted as a fiancée/proposed civil partner, or who has been admitted as a fiancée/proposed civil partner;
- (ii) he is under 18;
- (iii) he is not leading an independent life, is unmarried and not a civil partner, and has not formed an independent family unit;
- (iv) he can and will be maintained and accommodated adequately without recourse to public funds by the parent admitted or being admitted as a fiancée;
- (v) there are serious and compelling family or other considerations which make the child's exclusion undesirable, that suitable arrangements have been made for his care in the UK, and there is no other person outside the UK who could reasonably be expected to care for him;
- (vi) he holds a valid UK entry clearance for entry in this category.

Limited leave to enter will be granted for a period not in excess of that granted to the fiancée/proposed civil partner. Where the period of limited leave granted to the fiancée/proposed civil partner expires in more than six months, the leave for the child should be for a period not exceeding six months (para 303B).

An extension of stay may be granted if the requirements in (i) to (iv) above continue to be met (para 303E).

13 Children born in the United Kingdom who are not British citizens

Paragraphs 304 to 309 of the Rules apply only to dependent children aged under 18 who are unmarried and are not civil partners who were born in the UK after 1st January 1983, but who are not British citizens, and so are subject to immigration control, because neither of their parents was a British citizen or settled in the UK at the time of the birth. Such a child requires leave to enter or remain. If he qualifies for entry clearance or leave to enter or remain under any other part of the Immigration Rules, such a child may be granted entry clearance or leave to enter or remain under that other part (para 304).

The requirements to be met by a child in this category who is seeking leave to enter or remain are that he (para 305)–

- (i) (a) is accompanying or seeking to join or remain with a parent or parents who have leave to enter or remain; or (b) is accompanying or seeking to join or remain with a parent(s) one of whom is a British citizen or has the right of abode in the UK; or (c) is a child in respect of whom parental rights and duties are vested solely in a local authority;
- (ii) is aged under 18;
- (iii) was born in the UK;
- (iv) is unmarried and not a civil partner, not leading an independent life, and has not formed an independent family unit;
- (v) (where the application is for leave to enter) has not been away from the UK for more than two years.

Where paragraph 305(i)(a) applies, a child may be given leave to enter or remain for the same period as his parents provided that each of the requirements of paragraph 305(ii) to (v) is met. Where parents have different periods of leave the child may be given leave for the longer period except where the parents are living apart; the child must then be granted the same period of leave as the parent having day to day responsibility for him (para 306).

If a child does not qualify for leave to enter or remain because neither of his parents has a current leave, and neither is a British citizen nor has the right of abode, he will normally be refused leave even if the requirements of paragraph 305(ii) to (v) are met. However, leave for not more than three months may be granted, if both parents are in the UK and it is unlikely that they will be removed during that time and there is no other person outside the UK to care for him (para 307).

Indefinite leave to enter may be granted to a child who falls within paragraph 304 if paragraph 305(i)(b) or (c) applies provided that each of the requirements (ii) to (v) of paragraph 305 is met (para 308); and will be refused if they are not (para 309); where an application is for indefinite leave to remain, it will be granted provided that all of the above requirements are met, and will be refused if they are not (para 309).

14 Adopted children

Certain of the requirements to be met by a child seeking indefinite leave to enter as the adopted child of a parent(s) present and settled or being admitted for settlement in the UK at the same time are the same as those specified in paragraph 297 (see **10 Child of a parent(s) or a relative settled or being admitted for settlement,** above) (para 310(i) to (v) and (xii)). The following requirements must also be met, namely that he (para 310)–

- (vi) was adopted in accordance with a decision of the competent authority in his country of origin or residence;
- (vii) was adopted when (a) both adoptive parents were resident together abroad; or (b) either or both adoptive parents were settled in the UK;
- (viii) has the same rights and obligations as any other child of the adoptive parent's or parents' family;

(ix) was adopted due to the inability of the original parent(s) or current carer(s) to care for him and there has been a genuine transfer of parental responsibility to the adoptive parents;

(x) has lost or broken his ties with his family of origin;

(xi) the adoption is not one of convenience, arranged to facilitate his admission to or remaining in the UK;

(xii) holds a valid UK entry clearance for entry in this capacity; and

(xiii) the applicant does not fall for refusal under the general grounds for refusal.

The requirements to be met by an adopted child in this category seeking indefinite leave to remain are basically the same as those specified in paragraph 310 (see above), except that the child must already have limited leave to enter or remain and the parent(s) must already be present and settled in the UK. The condition that the child must be aged under 18 need not be met if the child was given leave to enter or remain with a view to settlement under paragraph 315 or 316B (see below) (para 311).

The requirements to be met by a child seeking indefinite leave to enter or remain with a view to settlement as the adopted child of a parent(s) given limited leave to enter or remain with a view to settlement are similar to those specified in paragraph 310(ii) to (xi) above (para 314(ii) to (x) and (xii)). Additionally, he must be: (i) seeking leave to enter to accompany or join or remain with a parent(s) in the following circumstances: (a) one parent is present and settled in the UK or being admitted on the same occasion for settlement, and the other parent is being or has been given limited leave to enter or remain with a view to settlement; or (b) one parent is being or has been given limited leave to enter or remain with a view to settlement and has had sole responsibility for the child's upbringing; or (c) one parent is being or has been given limited leave to enter or remain with a view to settlement and there are serious and compelling reasons which make exclusion of the child undesirable and arrangements have been made for his care (para 314(i)). Where a child makes an application for limited leave to remain with a view to settlement, he must have limited leave to enter or remain (para 314(xi)).

A child who falls within paragraph 314 may be granted leave to enter for not more than 12 months so provided that he can a valid entry clearance in this capacity on arrival (para 315) and will be refused if not so produced (para 316). If seeking limited leave to remain, this may be granted for a period of not more than 12 months provided that each of the requirements (i) to (xi) of paragraph 314 is met (para 315) and will be refused if they are not met (para 316).

Persons requiring the application form (RON 117) and further information may contact the Home Office, Lunar House (as above), or Community Services Division of the Department of Health, Wellington House, 133 Waterloo Road, SE1 8UG, (tel. 020 7972 4347).

15 Children to be adopted

The requirements to be met by a child in this category who is seeking limited leave to enter with a view to being adopted are that he (para 316A)–

(i) is seeking limited leave to enter to accompany or join a person or persons who wish to adopt him (the prospective parents) where either–

   (a) both prospective parents are present and settled in the UK;

   (b) both prospective parents are being admitted for settlement at the same time as the child;

   (c) one prospective parent is present and settled in the UK and the other is being admitted for settlement at the same time as the child;

   (d) one prospective parent is present and settled in the UK and the other is being given limited leave to enter or remain with a view to settlement on the same occasion as the child or previously;

   (e) one prospective parent is being admitted for settlement at the same time as the other is being given limited leave to enter or remain with a view to settlement which is also on the same occasion as the child is seeking admission;

   (f) one prospective parent is present and settled in the UK or is being admitted for settlement on the same occasion as the child, and has had sole responsibility for the child's upbringing; or

   (g) one prospective parent is present and settled in the UK or is being admitted for settlement on the same occasion as the child, and there are serious and compelling family or other considerations which make exclusion of the child undesirable and suitable arrangements have been made for the child's care.

(ii) is under 18;

(iii) is not leading an independent life, is unmarried and not a civil partner, and has not formed an independent family unit;

(iv) can and will be maintained and accommodated adequately without recourse to public funds in accommodation which the prospective parent(s) own or occupy exclusively;

(v) will have the same rights and obligations as any other child of the marriage/civil partnership;

(vi) is being adopted due to the inability of the original parent(s) or current carer(s) (or those looking after him immediately prior to him being physically transferred to the prospective parent(s)) to care for him, and there has been a genuine transfer of parental responsibility to the prospective parent(s);

(vii) has lost or broken or intends to break his ties with his family of origin; and

(viii) will be adopted in the UK by the prospective parent(s), but the proposed adoption is not one of convenience arranged to facilitate his admission to the UK.

If the above requirements are satisfied, limited leave will be granted for a period not exceeding 24 months (para 316B).

The requirements to be satisfied in the case of a child seeking limited leave to enter the UK for the purpose of being adopted under the Hague Convention are that he (para 316D)–

(i) is seeking limited leave to enter to accompany one or two people each of whom are habitually resident in the UK and who wish to adopt him under the Hague Convention ("the prospective parents");

(ii) is the subject of an agreement made under Article 17(c) of the Hague Convention; and

(iii) has been entrusted to the prospective parents by the competent administrative authority of the country from which he is coming to the UK for adoption under the Hague Convention; and

(iv) is under the age of 18; and

(v) can, and will, be maintained and accommodated adequately without recourse to public funds in accommodation which the prospective parent or parents own or occupy exclusively; and

(vi) holds a valid UK entry clearance for entry in this capacity.

16 Parents, grandparents and other dependent relatives of persons present and settled

Indefinite leave to enter may be granted to a person in this category provided that a valid entry clearance in this capacity is produced on arrival (para 318) and will be refused if not so produced (para 319). Indefinite leave to enter or remain may be granted if certain requirements are met (para 318). The requirements are that the person (para 317)–

(i) is related to a person present and settled in the UK in one of the following ways–

(a) as a parent or grandparent who is divorced, widowed, single or separated and aged 65 or over;

(b) as parents or grandparents travelling together of whom at least one is aged 65 or over;

(c) as a parent or grandparent aged 65 or over who has entered into a second marriage/civil partnership but cannot look to the spouse/civil partner or children of the second relationship for financial support. In this case the person settled in the UK must be able to support the parent or grandparent and any spouse/civil partner or child of the second relationship admissible as a dependant;

(d), (e), (f) as a parent or grandparent aged under 65, or a son, daughter, sister, brother, uncle or aunt aged over 18, in either case, living alone outside the UK in the most exceptional compassionate circumstances; and

(ii) is joining or accompanying a person present and settled in the UK or being admitted for settlement on the same occasion;

(iii) is financially wholly or mainly dependent on the relative in the UK;

(iv) will be adequately maintained and accommodated without recourse to public funds in accommodation which the sponsor owns or occupies exclusively;

(iva) can and will be maintained adequately, together with any dependants, without recourse to public funds;

(v) has no other close relatives in his own country to whom he can turn for financial support;

(vi) has a valid entry clearance in this capacity if seeking leave to enter; and

(vii) the applicant does not fall for refusal under the general grounds for refusal.

17 Family members of relevant points based system migrants

Partners

Subject as described below, all migrants arriving in the UK and wishing to enter as the Partner of a Tier 1, Tier 2 Tier 4 Migrant, or Tier 5 (Temporary Worker) Migrant ("relevant points based system migrants ") must have a valid entry clearance. If they do not, entry will be refused (para 319B). A migrant arriving in the UK and wishing to enter as a partner of a Tier 5 (Temporary Worker) Migrant, who does not have a valid entry clearance will not be refused entry if they–

(i) are not a visa national,

(ii) are accompanying an applicant who at the same time is being granted leave to enter under para 245ZN(b) (see the Note on **The Immigration Rules: The points based system** at para **24 Tier 5 (Temporary Workers)**), and

(iii) they meets the requirements of entry clearance in para 319C (see below).

To qualify for entry clearance or leave to remain as the Partner of a relevant points based system migrant, an applicant must meet the requirements listed below. If he does, entry clearance or leave to remain will be granted. If he does not, the application will be refused.

The requirements are (para 319C)–

(a) the applicant must not fall for refusal under the general grounds for refusal, and if applying for leave to remain, must not be an illegal entrant;

(b) the applicant must be the spouse or civil partner, unmarried or same-sex partner of a person who–

(i) has valid leave to enter or remain as a relevant points based system migrant;

(ii) is, at the same time, being granted entry clearance or leave to remain as a relevant points based system migrant; or

(iii) has indefinite leave to remain as a relevant points based system migrant, or is, at the same time being granted indefinite leave to remain as a relevant points based system migrant, where the applicant is applying for further leave to remain, or has been refused indefinite leave to remain solely because the applicant has not met the requirements of para 319E(g), and was last granted leave–

      (1) as the partner of that same relevant points based system migrant or

      (2) as the spouse or civil partner, unmarried or same-sex partner of that person at a time when that person had leave under another category of these Rules;

   (iv) has become a British Citizen where prior to that they held indefinite leave to remain as a relevant points based system migrant and where the applicant is applying for further leave to remain, or has been refused indefinite leave to remain solely because the application has not met the requirements of para 319E(g), and was last granted leave—

      (1) as the partner of that same relevant points based system migrant, or

      (2) as the spouse or civil partner, unmarried or same-sex partner of that person at a time when that person had leave under another category of the Rules.

(c) an applicant who is the unmarried or same-sex partner of a relevant points based system migrant must also meet the following requirements—

   (i) any previous marriage or civil partnership or similar relationship by the applicant or the relevant points based system migrant with another person must have permanently broken down;

   (ii) the applicant and the relevant points based system migrant must not be so closely related that they would be prohibited from marrying each other in the UK; and

   (iii) the applicant and the relevant points based system migrant must have been living together in a relationship similar to marriage or civil partnership for a period of at least 2 years;

(d) the marriage or civil partnership, or relationship similar to marriage or civil partnership, must be subsisting at the time the application is made;

(e) the applicant and the relevant points based system migrant must intend to live with the other as their spouse or civil partner, unmarried or same-sex partner throughout the applicants stay in the UK;

(f) the applicant must not intend to stay in the UK beyond any period of leave granted to the relevant points based system migrant;

(g) unless the relevant points based system migrant is a Tier 1 (Investor) Migrant or a Tier 1 (Exceptional Talent) Migrant, there must be a sufficient level of funds available to the applicant (as set out in Appendix E to the Immigration Rules: see the Note on **The Immigration Rules: The points based system** at para **28 Maintenance Funds for families (Appendix E)**);

(h) an applicant who is applying for leave to remain must not have last been granted—

entry clearance or leave as a (a) visitor, including where they entered the United Kingdom from the Republic of Ireland to stay under the terms of articles 3A and 4 of the Immigration (Control of Entry through the Republic of Ireland) Order 1972 (as amended by the Immigration (Control of Entry through Republic of Ireland) (Amendment) Order 2014) on the basis of a visa issued by the Republic of Ireland authorities endorsed with the letters "BIVS" for the purpose of travelling and staying in the Republic for a period of 90 days or fewer; or (b) short-term student or short term student (child); or (c) parent of a Tier 4 (child) student unless the Relevant Points Based System Migrant has, or is being granted, leave to remain as a Tier 5 (Temporary Worker) Migrant in the creative and sporting subcategory on the basis of having met the requirement at paragraph 245ZQ(b)(ii);

temporary admission; or

temporary release;

(i) if the applicant is a Tier 4 (General) Student—

   (1) the relevant points based system migrant must be a Government Sponsored student who is applying for or has entry clearance or leave to remain for a course of study that is longer than six months; or

   (2) the relevant points based system migrant must be undertaking a course which is 12 months or longer in duration, and is of post-graduate level study, sponsored by a Sponsor which is a UK recognised body or a body in receipt of State funding as a higher education institution; or

   (3) he relevant Points Based System Migrant must be applying for, or have been granted leave to remain as a Tier 4 (General) Student on the doctorate extension scheme; or

   (4) the relevant points based system migrant must be applying for a course of study of more than six months duration and must have or have last had entry clearance, leave to enter or leave to remain as a Tier 4 (General) Student or Student for a course of more than six months duration within the three months immediately preceding the date of the application; and

   (5) the Partner must have or have last had entry clearance, leave to enter or leave to remain as the Partner of a Tier 4 (General) Student or Student with leave for a course of more than six months duration within the three months immediately preceding the date of the application; and

   (6) the relevant points based system migrant and Partner must be applying at the same time; or

(j) the applicant must not be in the UK in breach of immigration laws except that any period of overstaying for a period of 28 days will be disregarded.

Entry clearance and leave to remain will be granted for a period which expires on the same day as the leave granted to the relevant points based system migrant or, if the relevant points-based system migrant has indefinite leave to remain as a relevant points-based system migrant, or is, at the same time being granted indefinite leave to remain as a relevant points-based system migrant, or where the relevant points-based system migrant has since become a British Citizen, leave to remain will be granted to the applicant for a period of 3 years.

Entry clearance and leave to remain under this route is subject to the following conditions (para 319D)–

    (i) no recourse to public funds;

    (ii) registration with the police, if this is required under para 326 of the Rules;

    (iii) no employment as a Doctor or Dentist in training, unless the applicant has either obtained a primary degree in medicine or dentistry at bachelor's level or above from a UK institution that is a UK recognised or listed body, or which holds a sponsor licence under Tier 4 of the Points Based System; or is applying for leave to remain and has, or has last been granted, entry clearance, leave to enter or leave to remain that was not subject to any condition restricting their employment, and has been employed during that leave as a Doctor or Dentist in Training;

    (iv) no employment at all if they are a Tier 4 (General) Student applying for leave for less than 12 months or for a course below degree level and the Partner meets the requirements of Para 319C(i)-(iv)(1), (2) and (3);

    (v) no employment as a professional sportsperson (including as a sports coach).

To qualify for indefinite leave to remain as the Partner of a relevant points based system migrant, an applicant must meet the requirements listed below. If he does, indefinite leave to remain will be granted. If he does not, the application will be refused unless the applicant qualifies for leave to remain by virtue of paras 33E to 33F of the Rules.

The requirements are (para 319E)–

    (a) the applicant must not fall for refusal under the general grounds for refusal, and must not be an illegal entrant;

    (b) the applicant must be the spouse or civil partner, unmarried or same-sex partner of a person who is being, or has been, granted indefinite leave to remain as a relevant points based system migrant or has become a British Citizen where prior to that they held indefinite leave to remain as a relevant points based system migrant;

    (c) the applicant must have, or have last been granted, leave as the Partner of the relevant points based system migrant who is being, or has been, granted indefinite leave to remain or has become a British Citizen where prior to that they held indefinite leave to remain as a relevant points based system migrant;

    (d) the applicant and the Relevant Points Based System Migrant must have been living together in the UK in a marriage or civil partnership, or in a relationship similar to marriage or civil partnership, for at least the period specified in (i) or (ii):

        (i) if the applicant was granted leave as: (a) the Partner of that Relevant Points Based System Migrant, or (b) the spouse or civil partner, unmarried or same-sex partner of that person at a time when that person had leave under another category of the Rules in place before 9th July 2012, and since then has had continuous leave as the Partner of that Relevant Points based System Migrant, the specified period is 2 years

        (ii) if (i) does not apply, the specified period is a continuous period of 5 years, during which the applicant must (a) have been in a relationship with the same Relevant Points Based System Migrant for this entire period, (b) have spent the most recent part of the 5 year period with leave as the Partner of that Relevant Points Based System Migrant, and during that part of the period have met all of the requirements of para 319C(a) to (e), and (c) have spent the remainder of the 5 year period, where applicable, with leave as the spouse or civil partner, unmarried or same-sex partner of that person at a time when that person had leave under another category of the Rules;

    (e) the marriage or civil partnership, or relationship similar to marriage or civil partnership, must be subsisting at the time the application is made;

    (f) the applicant and the relevant points based system migrant must intend to live permanently with the other as their spouse or civil partner, unmarried or same-sex partner;

    (g) the applicant has demonstrated sufficient knowledge of the English language and sufficient knowledge about life in the UK, in accordance with Appendix KoLL;

    (h) *deleted*;

    (i) the applicant must not be in the UK in breach of immigration laws except that any period of overstaying for a period of 28 days will be disregarded.

Children

Subject as described below, all migrants arriving in the UK and wishing to enter as the child of a Tier 1, Tier 2 or Tier 5 (Temporary Worker) Migrant must have a valid entry clearance. If they do not, entry will be refused (para 319G). However, a migrant arriving in the UK and wishing to enter as a child of a Tier 5 (Temporary Worker) Migrant, who does not have a valid entry clearance will not be refused entry if they are not a visa national, they are accompanying an applicant who at the same time is being granted leave to enter under para 245ZN(b), and they meet the requirements of entry clearance in para 319H.

To qualify for entry clearance or leave to remain, an applicant must meet the requirements listed below. If he does, entry clearance or leave to remain will be granted. If he does not, the application will be refused.

The requirements are (para 319H)–

    (a) the applicant must not fall for refusal under the general grounds for refusal, and if applying for leave to remain, must not be an illegal entrant;

    (b) the applicant must be the child of a parent who has, or is at the same time being granted, valid entry clearance, leave to enter or remain, or indefinite leave to remain, as either a Relevant Points Based

System Migrant, or the partner of a Relevant Points Based System Migrant, or who has obtained British citizenship having previously held indefinite leave to remain as above;

(c) the applicant must be under the age of 18 on the date the application is made, or if over 18 and applying for leave to remain, must have, or have last been granted, leave as the child of a relevant points based system migrant;

(d) the applicant must not be married or in a civil partnership, must not have formed an independent family unit, must not be leading an independent life, and, if he is over the age of 16 on the date the application is made, he must provide specified documents as evidence;

(e) the applicant must not intend to stay in the UK beyond any period of leave granted to the relevant points based system migrant parent;

(f) both of the applicant's parents must either be lawfully present in the UK, or being granted entry clearance or leave to remain at the same time as the applicant, or one parent must be lawfully present in the UK and the other is being granted entry clearance or leave to remain at the same time as the applicant, unless—

(i) the relevant points based system migrant is the applicant's sole surviving parent; or

(ii) the relevant points based system migrant parent has and has had sole responsibility for the applicant's upbringing; or

(iii) there are serious and compelling family or other considerations which would make it desirable not to refuse the application and suitable arrangements have been made in the UK for the applicant's care;

(g) unless the relevant points based system migrant is a Tier 1 (Investor) Migrant or a Tier 1 (Exceptional Talent) Migrant, there must be a sufficient level of funds available to the applicant, as set out in Appendix E to the Immigration Rules: see the Note on **The Immigration Rules: The points based system** at para **28 Maintenance Funds for families (Appendix E),** above;

(h) an applicant who is applying for leave to remain must not have last been granted—

(i) entry clearance or leave as a—

(a) visitor, including where they entered the United Kingdom from the Republic of Ireland to stay under the terms of articles 3A and 4 of the Immigration (Control of Entry through the Republic of Ireland) Order 1972 (as amended by the Immigration (Control of Entry through Republic of Ireland) (Amendment) Order 2014) on the basis of a visa issued by the Republic of Ireland authorities endorsed with the letters "BIVS" for the purpose of travelling and staying in the Republic for a period of 90 days or fewer; or

(b) short-term student (child) unless the Relevant Points Based System Migrant has, or is being granted, leave to remain as a Tier 5 (Temporary Worker) Migrant in the creative and sporting subcategory on the basis of having met the requirement at paragraph 245ZQ(b)(ii);

unless the Relevant Points Based System Migrant has, or is being granted, leave to remain as a Tier 5 (Temporary Worker) Migrant in the creative and sporting subcategory on the basis of having met the requirement at paragraph 245ZQ(b)(ii);

(ii) temporary admission; or

(iii) temporary release

(i) for an applicant who is a Tier 4 (General) Student, the course must be for longer than 6 months and he must have or have last had similar leave within the preceding 3 months, the child must have last had leave within the preceding 3 months, both must be applying at the same time, or the student must be Government sponsored, or be sponsored and undertaking a 12 month or longer postgraduate course;

(j) A child whose parent is a relevant points based system migrant, who is a Tier 4 (General) Student or Student, and who does not otherwise meet the requirements of (i) above—

(1) must have been born during the migrant's most recent grant of entry clearance, leave to enter or leave to remain as a Tier 4 (General) Student or Student with leave for a course of more than six months duration; or

(2) where the migrant's most recent grant of entry clearance, leave to enter or leave to remain was to re-sit examinations or repeat a module of a course, must either have been born during a period of leave granted for the purposes of re-sitting examinations or repeating a module of a course or during the migrant's grant of leave for a course of more than six months, where that course is the same as the one for which the most recent grant of leave was to re-sit examinations or repeat a module; or

(3) must have been born no more than three months after the expiry of that most recent grant of leave;

(4) must be applying for entry clearance;

(k) if the applicant is a child born in the UK to a Relevant Points Based System migrant and their partner, the applicant must provide a full UK birth certificate showing the names of both parents;

(l) all arrangements for the child's care and accommodation in the UK must comply with relevant UK legislation and regulations; and

(m) the applicant must not be in the UK in breach of immigration laws except that any period of overstaying for a period of 28 days will be disregarded.

Entry clearance and leave to remain will be granted for a period which expires on the same day as the leave granted to the relevant points based system migrant parent, or where both parents have or are at the same time being granted, indefinite leave to remain, or have since become British citizens, leave to remain will be granted to the applicant for a period of 3 years. Entry clearance and leave to remain under this route is subject to the following conditions (para 319I)–

(i) no recourse to public funds;

(ii) registration with the police, if this is required under para 326 of the Rules;

(iii) no employment if the relevant points based system migrant is a Tier 4 (General) Student applying for leave for less than 12 months or for a course of below degree level and the child meets the requirements of paras 319H(i)(iv)(1), (2) and (3) or 319H(j); and

(iv) no employment as a professional sportsperson (including as a sports coach).

To qualify for indefinite leave to remain, an applicant must meet the requirements listed below. If he does, indefinite leave to remain will be granted. If he does not, the application will be refused, unless he qualifies for leave to remain by virtue of paras 33E to 33F of the Rules.

The requirements are (para 319J)–

(a) the applicant must not fall for refusal under the general grounds for refusal, and must not be an illegal entrant;

(b) the applicant must be the child of a parent who has, or is at the same time being granted, indefinite leave to remain, as either a Relevant Points Based System Migrant, or the partner of a Relevant Points Based System Migrant,

(c) the applicant must have, or have last been granted, leave as the child of, or have been born in the UK to, the relevant points based system migrant or partner who is being granted indefinite leave to remain;

(d) the applicant must not be married or in a civil partnership, must not have formed an independent family unit, and must not be leading an independent life, and if he is over 16 on the date the application, he must provide the specified documents and information to show that this requirement is met;

(e) both of an applicant's parents must either be lawfully present in the UK, or being granted indefinite leave to remain at the same time as the applicant, unless–

(i) the relevant points based system migrant is the applicant's sole surviving parent; or

(ii) the relevant points based system migrant parent has and has had sole responsibility for the applicant's upbringing;

(iii) there are serious and compelling family or other considerations which would make it desirable not to refuse the application and suitable arrangements have been made for the applicant's care; or

(iv) one parent is, at the same time, being granted indefinite leave to remain as a relevant points-based system migrant, the other parent is lawfully present in the UK or being granted leave at the same time as the applicant, and the applicant was granted leave as the child of a Relevant Points Based System Migrant under the Rules in place before 9 July 2012;

(f) the applicant must have sufficient knowledge of the English language and sufficient knowledge about life in the UK, in accordance with Appendix KoLL of the Rules, unless he is under 18 at the time of the application;

(g) if the applicant is a child born in the UK to a Relevant Points Based System migrant and their partner, the applicant must provide a full UK birth certificate showing the names of both parents;

(h) all arrangements for the child's care and accommodation in the UK must comply with relevant UK legislation and regulations;

(i) the applicant must not be in the UK in breach of immigration laws except that any period of overstaying for a period of 28 days will be disregarded.

18 Authorities

Statutory Instruments, etc–

Statement of Changes in Immigration Rules (HC 395–23rd May 1994 as amended by Cmnd 2663, HC 797, Cmnd 3073, HC 274, HC 329, Cmnd 3365, HC 31, HC 338, Cmnd 3369, HC 26, HC 161, Cmnd 3953, Cmnd 4065, HC 22, HC 704, Cmnd 4851, Cmnd 5253, HC 735, Cmnd 5597, HC 1301, HC 104, HC 180, HC 489, HC 538, Cmnd 5829, Cmnd 5949, HC 1224, HC 95, HC 176, HC 370, HC 464, HC 523, Cmnd 6297, Cmnd 6339, HC 1112, HC 164, HC 194, HC 302, HC 346, HC 486, HC 104, HC 299, HC 582, HC 645, HC 697, HC 769, HC 819, HC 949, HC 974, HC 1016, HC 1053, HC 1337, Cmnd 6918, HC 1702, HC 130, HC 398, Cmnd 7074, Cmnd 7075, HC 28, HC 40, HC 82, HC 321, HC 420, HC 607, HC 951, HC 971, HC 1113, HC 227, HC 314, HC413, Cmnd 7701, Cmnd 7711, HC 120, HC 367, HC 439, HC 59, HC 96, HC 382, Cmnd 7929, Cmnd 7944, HC698, HC863, HC908, HC1148, HC1436, HC 1511, HC1622, HC1693, HC1719, HC1733, HC1888, Cmnd 8337, HC194, Cmnd 8423, HC514, HC565, HC760, 820, HC847, HC943, HC967, HC1038, HC1039, Cmnd 8599, HC244, HC628, HC803, HC887, HC901, HC938, HC1130, HC1138, HC1201, HC198, HC532. HC693, HC1025, HC1116, HC297, HC 437, HC535, HC877)

THE IMMIGRATION RULES:
INTRODUCTION AND LEAVE TO ENTER THE UK (OUTSIDE THE POINTS BASED SYSTEM)

1 Introduction

This Note deals with those provisions of the Statement of Changes in Immigration Rules ("the Rules") which are of a general nature, and those which relate to leave to enter the UK outside of the points-based system.

The Home Secretary is the Secretary of State generally responsible for the control of immigration. The Home Office includes an Immigration and Nationality Directorate, at Lunar House, Wellesley Road, Croydon, Surrey CR9 2BY which handles most questions in this field on the Home Secretary's behalf.

S.4 of, and Schedule 2 to, the Immigration Act 1971 confer on immigration officers (aided by medical inspectors) power to give or refuse leave to enter, and various ancillary powers for the enforcement of control at points of entry. S.4 also empowers the Secretary of State to give leave to remain in the UK and to vary the terms on which limited leave to enter has been granted.

2 The Immigration Rules

The Immigration Rules govern the entry and stay of people coming to the UK. They specify the categories in which leave to enter or remain in the UK may be granted. Where advising on a case where there is no immigration rule applicable, expert advice should be sought. For each category, there are specified requirements. The applicant must meet each of the requirements of the category in question.

In all cases, the immigration officer is the official empowered under the Act to give leave to enter; and the Secretary of State, to give leave to remain in the UK.

In each of the categories described below, there is a statement to the effect that a person may be given leave to enter (or refused leave to enter) if the immigration officer is satisfied (or not satisfied) that the applicant meets the specified requirements for entry in the category in which he seeks entry. There is a similar statement relating to the Secretary of State's power to grant leave to remain or his refusal to grant such leave.

3 General

The Immigration Rules govern the entry and stay of anyone coming to the UK who is not a British citizen or a Commonwealth citizen with right of abode in the UK.

Unless expressly stated, the Rules also do not apply to an EEA national who is entitled to enter or remain in the UK by virtue of the EEA Regulations (see the Note on **Control of Immigration** at para **10 Nationals of the European Economic Area**). EEA nationals and their family members who are not subject to these Regulations, however, are subject to the Rules (para 5).

For the purposes of the Rules, the following general definitions apply. A parent includes (para 6)–
- the stepfather, or, as the case may be, stepmother of a child (including relationships arising through civil partnership) whose father or mother is dead;
- the mother and proven father of an illegitimate child;
- an adoptive parent where the adoption was made by the competent authority in a country whose orders are recognised by the UK (but see the Note on **The Immigration Rules: Family members** at para **14 Adopted children**) or the child is the subject of a *de facto* adoption (as defined by para 309A);
- a person to whom there has been a genuine transfer of parental responsibility on the ground of the original parents' inability to care for a child who was born in the UK but is not a British citizen.

"Public funds" includes (para 6)–
- housing (including homelessness) provision (Pt II Housing Act 1985, Pts VI or VII Housing Act 1996, Pt I or II Housing (Scotland) Act 1987);
- attendance allowance, severe disablement allowance, carer's allowance and disability living allowance;
- income support, council tax benefit, housing benefit, social fund payments, child benefit, state pension credit, child and working tax credit, universal credit, personal independence payment, and council tax reduction; and
- income-based jobseeker's and employment and support allowances.

No child benefit is payable to a person who is "subject to immigration control" within the meaning of the Asylum and Immigration Act 1996 (1996 Act, s.10). This means any person who requires leave to enter or remain in the UK, whether or not such leave has been given (1996 Act, s.13(2)).

A person who wishes to sponsor another to come to the UK to settle must either be British or settled in the UK, and "settled" means ordinarily resident and free from any restriction on the period for which he may remain (para 6).

Immigration and entry clearance officers and all staff of the Home Office Immigration and Nationality Directorate must carry out their duties without regard to race, colour, or religion (para 2).

4 Requirement of leave to enter

A person who is neither a British citizen nor a Commonwealth citizen with the right of abode (see the Note on **Control of Immigration** at para 2 **Right of abode in the United Kingdom**) nor an EEA national or the family member of such a national who is entitled to enter or remain in the UK by virtue of the EEA Regulations (see the Note on **Control of Immigration** at para 10 **Nationals of the European Economic Area**) requires leave to enter the UK (para 7).

Under ss.3 and 4 of the Act (see the Note on **Control of Immigration** at para 3 **Leave to enter or remain in the United Kingdom**), an immigration officer, when admitting to the UK a person subject to control under that Act, may give leave to enter for a limited period and, if he does, may impose conditions (para 8)–
  (a) restricting or prohibiting employment or occupation in the UK;
  (b) requiring him to maintain and accommodate himself, and any dependants of his, without recourse to public funds;
  (c) requiring him to register with the police;
  (d) restricting his studies in the UK.
He may also require him to report to the Medical Officer of Environmental Health. Under s.24 of the Act, it is an offence knowingly to remain beyond the time limit or to fail to comply with such a condition or requirement (para 8). The time limit and any condition attached will be made known to the person concerned either by a written notice, which will normally be given to him or be endorsed by the immigration officer in his passport or travel document, or in any other manner permitted by the Immigration (Leave to Enter and Remain) Order 2000 (para 9). An immigration officer may authorise a person in advance to enter the UK through an automated gate. Where such a person passes through the gate in accordance with the authorisation, they will automatically be given leave to enter for six months. In such cases, no notice of the leave is given to the person concerned (2000 Order, Art. 8A).

A person who has been examined for the purpose of immigration control at the point at which he entered the common travel area (see the Note on **Control of Immigration** at para 16 **Common travel area**) does not normally require leave to enter any other part of it. However, certain persons who are subject to the Immigration (Control of Entry through the Republic of Ireland) Order 1972 who enter the UK through the Republic of Ireland do require leave to enter. Included in the 1972 Order are the following persons: (i) persons who merely passed through the Republic of Ireland; (ii) persons requiring visas; (iii) persons who entered the Republic of Ireland unlawfully; (iv) persons who are subject to directions given by the Secretary of State for their exclusion from the UK on the ground that their exclusion is conducive to the public good; and (v) persons who entered the Republic of Ireland from the UK and Islands after entering there unlawfully or overstaying their leave (para 15). The 1972 order does not apply to a person who arrives in the United Kingdom from the Republic of Ireland having already obtained leave to enter or remain in the UK.

A British Dependent Territories citizen, a British National (Overseas), a British Overseas citizen, a British protected person, and a British subject by virtue of the British Nationality Act 1981, s.30(a) (see the Note on **British Nationality**) may be admitted freely to the UK on production of a UK passport issued in the UK and Islands or, as the case may be, the Republic of Ireland prior to 1st January 1973, so long as his passport is not endorsed to show him to be subject to immigration control (para 16).

A British Overseas citizen who holds a UK passport, wherever issued, and who satisfies the immigration officer that, since 1st March 1968, he has been given indefinite leave to enter or remain in the UK, may be given indefinite leave to enter (para 17).

5 Refusal of leave to enter

The power to refuse leave to enter the UK must not be exercised by an immigration officer acting on his own. The authority of a chief immigration officer or immigration inspector must always be obtained (para 10).

Where a person arrives in the United Kingdom with leave to enter or remain in the United Kingdom which is already in force, an Immigration Officer may suspend that leave until he has completed an examination, or cancel the leave (paras 10A and 10B).

6 Evidence of identity and nationality

On arrival in the UK, or when seeking entry through the Channel Tunnel, a person must produce on request by the immigration officer a valid national passport or other document satisfactorily establishing his identity and nationality; and such other information as may be required to establish whether he requires leave to enter the UK and, if so, whether and on what terms leave to enter should be granted (para 11).

7 Proof of right of abode

A person claiming to be a British citizen must prove he has the right of abode in the UK by producing either a UK passport describing him as a British citizen or as a citizen of the UK and Colonies having the right of abode in the UK, or a certificate of entitlement certifying that he has the right of abode issued by or on behalf of the UK government (para 12). A person claiming to be a Commonwealth citizen with the right of abode must prove that he has that right by producing a certificate of entitlement as described above (para 13). A Commonwealth citizen given limited leave to enter may have the time limit on his stay removed if he is later able to establish a claim to the right of abode (para 14).

8 Returning residents

A returning resident will be admitted for settlement so long as he can satisfy the immigration officer that—
 (i) he had indefinite leave to enter or remain in the UK when he last left,
 (ii) has not been away from the UK for more than two years;
 (iii) received no assistance from public funds towards the cost of his leaving, and
 (iv) now seeks admission for the purpose of settlement (para 18).

Note (ii) and (iii) above do not apply to a person with indefinite leave to enter or remain in the UK who is returning after having accompanied a spouse, civil partner, unmarried or same-sex partner on an overseas armed forces, diplomatic or similar posting (para 19A).

Those who qualify for admission to the UK as returning residents do not need a visa to enter the UK (para 18A). If a person does not come within para 18 only because they have been away from the UK too long (i.e., more than two years) they may nevertheless be admitted as a returning resident if, for example, they has lived here for most of their life (para 19). Immigration Directorate's Instructions Annex K gives guidance on the factors that should be considered in assessing whether a person will qualify for admission under the discretion contained in para 19. These include—
 (a) the length of his original residence here;
 (b) the time the applicant has been outside the UK;
 (c) the reason for the delay beyond the 2 years – was it through his own wish or no fault of his own? Could he reasonably have been expected to return within 2 years?
 (d) why did he go abroad when he did, and what were his intentions?
 (e) the nature of his family ties to the UK – how close are they, and to what extent has he maintained them in his absence?
 (f) whether he has a home in the UK and, if admitted, would resume his residency.

The longer a person has remained outside the UK over two years, the more difficult it will be for him to qualify for admission under the para 19 discretion. Other more specific circumstances listed in Annex K which might apply in favour of an individual include whether the applicant has been undertaking a prolonged period of study abroad and now wishes to rejoin his family in the UK at the end of his studies; or has been undergoing prolonged medical treatment abroad of a kind not available in the UK.

Where a person has leave to stay in the UK which has a time limit, it will lapse on his going to a country or territory outside the common travel area if the leave was given for a period of six months or less or conferred by a visit visa. Such a person who returns after a temporary absence abroad has no claim to admission as a returning resident. His application to re-enter the UK will be considered in the light of all the relevant circumstances. If he meets the requirements of the Rules, the same time limit and any conditions attached will normally be re-imposed; unless he seeks admission in a different capacity from the one in which he was last given leave to enter or remain (para 20).

If a person is seeking to enter within the time limit of an earlier leave, and for the same purpose as that earlier leave, no visa is required, unless the leave was—
 (a) for a period of six months or less, or
 (b) extended by statutory instrument or by the Immigration Act 1971, s3C (para 20B).

Under the Immigration (Leave to Enter and Remain) Order 2000, Art. 13, the leave of a person going outside the common travel area will not lapse where it was given for a period exceeding six months or where it was conferred by means of an entry clearance (other than a visit visa) (para 20A).

9 Restricted travel documents and passports

The holder of a passport or travel document, whose permission to enter another country must be exercised before a given date, will have his leave to enter or remain in the UK restricted so as to terminate at least two months before that date (para 21). Where such a document is endorsed with a restriction on the period for which he may remain outside his country of normal residence, his leave to enter or remain in the UK will be limited so as not to extend beyond the period of authorised absence (para 22). The holder of a Home Office travel document will be given leave to enter or remain for the period of its validity (para 23).

Paragraphs 21 to 23 do not apply to a person eligible for admission for settlement, or to a spouse/civil partner eligible for admission under paragraph 282 (see the Note on **The Immigration Rules: Family members** at para **4 Spouses/civil partners of persons present and settled in the United Kingdom or being admitted on the same occasion for settlement**), or to a person who qualifies for the removal of the time limit on his stay (para 23).

10 Entry clearance

A person who—
 (a) is not a visa national can seek leave to enter the UK on arrival for a period not exceeding 6 months for a purpose for which prior entry clearance is not required under the Immigration Rules (para 23A).
 (b) A person who is a British National (Overseas), a British overseas territories citizen, a British Overseas citizen, a British protected person, or a person who under the British Nationality Act 1981 is a British subject can seek leave to enter on arrival in the UK for a purpose for which prior entry clearance is not

required under the Rules ands can be granted such leave, irrespective of the period of time for which he seeks entry, for a period not exceeding 6 months (para 23B).

A "visa national" (i.e., a national or citizen of a country specified in Appendix 2 to Appendix V to the Rules) and any other person not within (b) above must produce to the Immigration Officer a valid passport or other identity document endorsed with a UK entry clearance issued to him for the purpose for which he seeks entry or leave to enter will be refused (para 24). Entry clearance takes the form of a visa (for visa nationals) or an entry certificate (for non-visa nationals). These documents are to be taken as evidence of the holder's eligibility for entry into the UK, and accordingly are accepted as "entry clearances" within the meaning of the Immigration Act 1971 (para 25). An entry clearance which satisfies the requirements set out in the Immigration (Leave to Enter and Remain) Order 2000, Art. 3, will have effect as leave to enter the UK. The requirements are that the entry clearance must specify the purpose for which the holder wishes to enter the UK and should be endorsed with the conditions to which it is subject or with a statement that it has effect as indefinite leave to enter the UK. The holder of such an entry clearance will not require leave to enter on arrival in the UK and, for the purposes of the Immigration Rules, will be treated as a person who has arrived in the UK with leave to enter which is in force but which was given to him before his arrival (para 25A).

An application for entry clearance will be considered in accordance with the provisions of the Rules governing the grant or refusal of leave to enter; and will be decided in the light of the circumstances existing at the time of the decision (paras. 26 and 27). However, an applicant will not be refused an entry clearance where entry is sought in one of the categories contained in paras 296 to 316 (see H: FAMILY MEMBERS, below) or para EC-C of Appendix FM, solely on account of attaining the age of 18 between the receipt of the application and the date of decision (para 27).

An applicant for an entry clearance must be outside the UK and Islands at the time of the application. Such an applicant who is seeking entry as a short-term student must apply to a post designated to accept such applications by the Secretary of State. Any other application must be made to the post designated to accept such applications by the Secretary of State in the country or territory where the applicant is living. Where there is no such post, an applicant must apply to the appropriate designated post outside the country or territory where he is living (para 28). For these purposes "post" means a British diplomatic mission, British consular post, or the office of any person outside the UK and Islands authorised by the Secretary of State to accept applications for entry clearance. A list of designated posts is published by the Foreign and Commonwealth Office (para 29). The address of the Foreign and Commonwealth Office is King Charles Street, London SW1A 2AH (tel. 020 7270 1500).

As to the finger printing of applicants from certain countries, see the Note on **Control of Immigration** at para **5 Fingerprints and other physical data.**

An application for an entry clearance is not "made" until any fee required to be paid has been paid (see the Note on **Control of Immigration** at **PART II: FEES AND FORMS**) (para 30).

An entry clearance may be revoked if an Entry Clearance Officer is satisfied that false representations were made or material facts were not disclosed (whether knowingly or not) for the purpose of obtaining the entry clearance, a change of circumstances (other than exceeding an age limit) since the entry clearance was issued has removed the holder's claim to be admitted to the UK, or the holder's exclusion from the UK would be conducive to the public good (para 30A).

An Immigration Officer may cancel an entry clearance which is capable of having effect as leave to enter if the holder arrives in the UK before the day on which the entry clearance becomes effective or if the holder seeks to enter the UK for a purpose other than the purpose specified in the entry clearance (para 30C).

11 Variation of leave to enter or remain

When leave to enter or remain is varied under s.3(3) of the Act (see the Note on **Control of Immigration** at para **3 Leave to enter or remain in the United Kingdom**), an entry must be made in the applicant's passport or travel document, and his registration certificate where appropriate, or the decision may be made known in writing in some other appropriate way (para 31).

An application for variation of leave will be treated as withdrawn if the applicant requests the return of his passport for travel outside the common travel area (para 34J) unless the applicant is applying as a Tier 2 Migrant or a Tier 5 Migrant and their application is supported by a Certificate of Sponsorship from a Premium Sponsor (para 34K).

12 Knowledge of English language and life

An applicant for leave to enter or remain must demonstrate sufficient knowledge of the English language and about life in the UK where it is a requirement of the Rules to demonstrate this. Appendix KoLL to the Rules sets out the requirements and the general exemptions on grounds of age. It also allows the decision maker to waive the requirement in light of special circumstances in any particular case.

If the decision-maker has reasonable cause to doubt (on examination or interview or on any other basis) that any document submitted by an applicant for the purposes of satisfying the requirements of Appendix KoLL was genuinely obtained, that document may be discounted. In such a case the decision-maker may give the applicant a further opportunity to demonstrate sufficient knowledge of the English language and about life in the United Kingdom (para 39C).

13 Undertakings

A sponsor of a person seeking leave to enter or remain may be asked to give an undertaking in writing to be responsible for that person's maintenance, accommodation and (as appropriate) personal care for the period of leave granted, including any further variation, or for a period of 5 years from date of grant where indefinite leave to enter or remain is granted. The Department for Work and Pensions may seek to recover from the sponsor any income support and any support for asylum seekers paid to meet the sponsored person's needs (para 35). However, see now Regulations made under the Social Security Administration Act 1992, which preclude from receiving any benefits, persons who have been sponsored by a person giving an undertaking, for a period of five years, or until the death of the person giving the undertaking.

Under the Immigration and Asylum Act 1999, the Home Office may also seek to recover from a person giving an undertaking any amount given to or in respect of the person for whom the undertaking has been given which is attributable to support for asylum seekers under s.95 of the 1999 Act (see the Note on **Support for Asylum Seekers and Displaced Persons**).

Failure by the sponsor to maintain a person in accordance with an undertaking, may also be an offence under the Social Security Administration Act 1992, s.105 and/or the Immigration and Asylum Act 1999, s.108 if, as a consequence, asylum support and/or income support is provided to, or in respect of, that person.

14 Medical examination

A person intending to remain in the UK for more than six months should normally be referred to the medical inspector for examination. If he produces a medical certificate, he will be advised to hand it to the medical inspector. Any person mentioning health or medical treatment as a reason for his visit, or a person who appears not to be in good mental or physical health, should also be referred to the medical inspector for examination. An immigration officer has discretion to refer a person for medical examination in any other case (para 36).

Where the medical officer advises that a person seeking entry is suffering from a specified disease or condition which may interfere with his ability to support himself or his dependants, account will be taken of this, in conjunction with other factors, in deciding whether to admit that person. The means of a person seeking entry for private medical treatment may similarly be taken account of in the light of the likely course of treatment needed (para 37). (A person seeking to enter or remain for private medical treatment must also meet the requirements of Appendix V, see **18 Types of visit visa**, below.)

A returning resident should not be refused leave to enter on medical grounds. But where such a person would be refused leave to enter on medical grounds if he were not a returning resident, or in any case where it is decided on compassionate grounds not to exercise the power to refuse leave to enter, or in any other case where the medical officer so recommends, the immigration officer will give the person concerned a notice requiring him to report to a medical officer of environmental health designated by the medical inspector with a view to examination and treatment (para 38).

An entry clearance officer has the same discretion as the immigration officer to refer applicants for entry clearance (see **10 Entry clearance**, above) for medical examination. The same principles will apply for the decision whether or not to issue an entry clearance as obtain under the preceding paragraphs (para 39).

Anyone making an application for entry clearance to come to the UK for more than six months, or as a fiance(e) or proposed civil partner applying for leave to enter having been present in a country listed in Appendix T for more than six months immediately prior to their application, must present at the time of application, a valid medical certificate issued by a specified medical practitioner confirming that they have undergone screening for active pulmonary tuberculosis and that this tuberculosis is not present in them (para A39). Applicants seeking leave to enter as a returning resident, having been absent from the UK for more than two years must also satisfy this requirement (para B39).

Where a person has lawfully been present in a country not mentioned in Appendix T for more than six months and they are applying for entry clearance as in para A39 in a country in Appendix T but have not been in that country or any other country mentioned in Appendix T for more than six months immediately before making their application, they will not be required to produce a medical certificate showing they are free from active pulmonary TB. This does not alter the discretionary powers to require a medical examination contained in para 39 (para C39).

15 Interviews

An applicant for indefinite leave to enter or remain must, unless he provides a reasonable explanation, comply with any request made by the Secretary of State to attend an interview (para 39C).

A person with limited leave to enter or remain may be required to provide additional information and evidence to the Home Office within 28 calendar days and/or attend an interview to assess whether there are any grounds to curtail their leave (para 39D).

16 Registration with the police

A condition requiring registration with the police should normally be imposed on a "relevant foreign national" (i.e., a person over 16 from a country listed in Appendix 2 to the Rules (see below), or who is a stateless person, or a person holding a non-national travel document) (para 325) who is given (para 326)–

(i) limited leave to enter for longer than six months; or

(ii) limited leave to remain which has the effect of allowing him to remain in the UK for longer than six months, reckoned from the date of his arrival (whether or not such a condition was imposed when he arrived).

However, such a condition should not normally be imposed where the leave is given–

(iii) as a seasonal agricultural worker;

(iv) as a Tier 5 (Temporary Worker) Migrant, provided the Certificate of Sponsorship Checking System reference for which points were awarded records that the applicant is being sponsored as an overseas government employee or a private servant is a diplomatic household;

(v) as a Tier 2 (Minister of Religion) Migrant;

(vi) on the basis of marriage/civil partnership to a person settled in the UK or as the unmarried or same sex partner of a person settled in the UK;

(vii) as a person exercising access rights to a child resident in the UK;

(viii) as the parent of a Tier 4 (child) student; or

(ix) following the grant of asylum.

Such a condition should also be imposed on any foreign national given limited leave to enter the UK where, exceptionally, the Immigration Officer considers it necessary to ensure that he complies with the terms of the leave.

Appendix 2 lists 42 countries, including Brazil, China, Egypt, Iran, Iraq, Israel, Kuwait, Russia, Saudi Arabia, Turkey and other countries in South America, North Africa, the Middle East and the former Soviet Union.

17 Visitors–introduction

A visitor is a person who is coming to the UK, usually for up to six months, for a temporary purpose, for example as a tourist, to visit friends or family or to carry out a business activity.

Visitors cannot work or study in the UK unless this is allowed by the permitted activities that are set out in the Visitor Rules.

Each visitor must meet the requirements of the Visitor Rules, even if they are travelling as, for example, a family group, a tour group or a school party (Appendix V).

A person who wishes to enter the UK as a visitor must have either a visit visa or leave to enter (Appendix V, para VI.1).

A visa national (as defined in Appendix 2) must obtain a visit visa before they arrive in the UK. A visa national who arrives in the UK without a visit visa will be refused leave to enter.

A non-visa national may apply for a visit visa, but is not required to unless they are–

(a) visiting the UK to marry or to form a civil partnership, or to give notice of this; or

(b) seeking to visit the UK for more than 6 months.

Unless (a) or (b) applies, a non-visa national may apply for leave to enter as a visitor on arrival at the UK border (para VI).

An application for a visit visa must be made while the applicant is outside the UK.

To apply for a visit visa the applicant must–

(a) complete the online application process on the visas and immigration pages of the gov.uk website;

(b) pay any fee that applies;

(c) provide their biometrics if required; and

(d) provide a valid travel document.

Where the online application process is not available, the applicant must follow the instructions provided by the local visa post or application centre on how to make an application (para V2).

18 Types of visit visa

There are four types of visitor routes which depend on the purpose of the visit (Appendix V, para VI.5).

Within the period for which the visit visa is valid, a visitor may enter and leave the UK multiple times, unless the visit visa is endorsed as a single-or dual-entry visa (para VI.6)

Visit (standard)

This allows a stay for up to 6 months, except–

(i) a visitor who is coming to the UK for private medical treatment may be granted a visit visa of up to 11 months;

(ii) an academic, who is employed by an overseas institution and is carrying out specific permitted activities (set out in Appendix 3 para 12 of the Rules), along with their spouse or partner and children, may be granted a visit visa of up to 12 months;

(iii) a visitor under the Approved Destination Status Agreement (i.e., the ADS Agreement which relates to tour groups from China) may be granted a visit visa for a period of up to 30 days.

Visit visas, leave to enter or an extension of stay as a visitor will be subject to the following conditions (V4.23)–

(a) no recourse to public funds;

(b) no study (which does not prohibit the incidental study allowed by the permitted activities);

(c) no work (which does not prohibit the permitted activities in (ii) above).

Marriage/civil partnership visit
This allows a stay for up to 6 months.

Permitted Paid Engagements (PPE) visit
This allows a stay for up to 1 month.

Transit visit
This allows a stay for up to 48 hours, except for leave to enter as a transit visitor under the Transit Without Visa Scheme which may be granted until 23:59 hours on the next day after the day the applicant arrived.

19 Suitability requirements for visit visas–all cases

Public good: exclusion, deportation, and criminal convictions (V3.2-3.5)
An application for a visit visa *will* be refused if–
(a) the applicant's exclusion from the UK is conducive to the public good;
(b) the applicant is currently the subject of a deportation order or a decision to make a deportation order;
(c) the applicant has been convicted of a criminal offence for which they have been sentenced to a period of imprisonment of–
    (i) at least 4 years; or
    (ii) between 12 months and 4 years, unless at least 10 years have passed since the end of the sentence; or
    (iii) less than 12 months, unless at least 5 years has passed since the end of the sentence.
Where this paragraph applies, it will only be in exceptional circumstances that the public interest in maintaining refusal will be outweighed by compelling factors.
An application *will normally* be refused if–
(d) within the period of 12 months before the application is decided, the applicant has been convicted of or admitted an offence for which they received a non-custodial sentence or out of court disposal that is recorded on their criminal record (except for an application for an extension of stay as a visitor); or
(e) in the view of the Secretary of State the applicant's offending has caused serious harm; or
(f) in the view of the Secretary of State the applicant is a persistent offender who shows a particular disregard for the law.

False information in relation to an application (V3.6)
An applicant *will* be refused where–
(a) false representations have been made or false documents or information have been submitted (whether or not material to the application, and whether or not to the applicant's knowledge); or
(b) material facts have not been disclosed, in relation to their application or in order to obtain documents from the Secretary of State or a third party provided in support of their application.

Breaches of UK immigration laws (V3.7-3.11)
An applicant *will* be refused–
(a) if the applicant previously breached UK immigration laws by overstaying (except where this was for 90 days or less and they left the UK voluntarily and not at public expense); by breaching a condition attached to their leave; by being an illegal entrant; or if deception was used in relation to an application or documents used in support of an application (whether successful or not); and
(b) the applicant is outside the UK and the application is made within the relevant re-entry ban time period.
The re-entry time period ban varies depending on the manner in which the applicant left the UK (para V3.10)–

Manner of Leaving	Re-entry Ban
voluntarily at own expenses	12 months
voluntarily at public expense within 6 months of being given notice of liability for removal or when they no longer had a pending appeal or administrative review, whichever is later	2 years
voluntarily at public expense more than 6 months after being given notice of liability for removal or when they no longer had a pending appeal or administrative review, whichever is later	5 years
left or was removed from the UK as a condition of a caution (issued in accordance with the Criminal Justice Act 2003 s.22) and providing that any condition prohibiting their return to the UK has itself expired	5 years
was deported or removed from the UK at public expense	10 years
used deception in an application for entry clearance (including a visit visa)	10 years

Failure to produce satisfactory documentation (V3.12)
If the applicant has previously breached UK immigration laws but is outside the relevant re-entry ban time period the application *will normally* be refused if there are other aggravating circumstances, such as a failure to

cooperate with immigration control or enforcement processes. This applies even where the applicant has overstayed for 90 days or less and left voluntarily and not at public expense (para V3.8).

An application *will* be refused where the applicant fails to produce a valid travel document that satisfies the decision maker as to their identity and nationality.

An application *will* be refused where the applicant fails without reasonable excuse to comply with a requirement to attend an interview; provide information; provide biometrics; or undergo a medical examination or provide a medical report.

Medical (V3.13)

An applicant *will normally* be refused where, on the advice of the medical inspector, it is undesirable to grant the application for medical reasons

Debt to NHS or Home Office (V3.14, 14A)

An applicant *will normally* be refused where a relevant NHS body has notified the Secretary of State that the applicant has failed to pay charges under relevant NHS regulations on charges to overseas visitors and the outstanding charges have a total value of at least £500.

An applicant will normally be refused where they have failed to pay litigation costs awarded to the Home Office.

Admission to Common Travel Area or other countries (V3.15-3.16)

An applicant *will* be refused where they are seeking entry to the UK with the intention of entering another part of the Common Travel Area, and fails to satisfy the decision maker that they are acceptable to the immigration authorities there.

An applicant *will normally* be refused where they fail to satisfy the decision maker that they will be admitted to another country after a stay in the UK.

20 Eligibility criteria– Visit visa (standard)

The applicant must satisfy the decision maker that they are a genuine visitor i.e., that they (V4.2-4.4)–
(a) will leave the UK at the end of their visit;
(b) will not live in the UK for extended periods through frequent or successive visits, or make the UK their main home;
(c) is genuinely seeking entry for a purpose that is permitted by the visitor routes (these are listed in Appendix V, Appendices 3, 4 and 5);
(d) will not undertake any prohibited activities;
(e) must have sufficient funds to cover all reasonable costs in relation to their visit without working or accessing public funds. This includes the cost of the return or onward journey, any costs relating to dependants, and the cost of planned activities such as private medical treatment.

A visitor's travel, maintenance and accommodation may be provided by a third party where the decision maker is satisfied that they have a genuine professional or personal relationship with the visitor; are legally present in the UK, or will be at the time of the visitor's entry to the UK; and can and will provide support to the visitor for the intended duration of their stay. The third party may be asked to give an written undertaking to this effect.

Prohibited activities

Work (V4.5-4.6)

The applicant must not intend to work in the UK, which includes the following–
(a) taking employment in the UK;
(b) doing work for an organisation or business in the UK;
(c) establishing or running a business as a self-employed person;
(d) doing a work placement or internship;
(e) direct selling to the public;
(f) providing goods and services;
unless expressly allowed by the permitted activities in Appendix V, Appendices 3, 4 or 5.

Payment (V4.7)

The applicant must not receive payment from a UK source for any activities undertaken in the UK, except–
(a) reasonable expenses to cover the cost of their travel and subsistence, including fees for directors attending board-level meetings;
(b) prize money; or
(c) billing a UK client for their time in the UK, where the applicant's overseas employer is contracted to provide services to a UK company, and the majority of the contract work is carried out overseas. Payment must be lower than the amount of the applicant's salary; or
(d) multi-national companies who, for administrative reasons, handle payment of their employees' salaries from the UK; or
(e) where the applicant is engaged in Permitted Paid Engagements (PPE) as listed at Appendix 4, provided the applicant holds a visa or leave to enter as a PPE visitor; or
(f) paid performances at a permit free festival as listed in Appendix V, Appendix 5.

Study (V4.8)

The applicant must not intend to study in the UK, except where they are undertaking a maximum of 30 days incidental study as permitted by Appendix V, Appendix 3.

Medical (V4.9)

The applicant must not intend to access medical treatment other than private medical treatment or to donate an organ (for either of these activities they must meet the relevant additional requirements).

Marriage or civil partnership (V4.10)

The applicant must not intend to marry or forma civil partnership, or to give notice of this, in the UK, except where they have a visit visa endorsed for marriage or civil partnership

Additional eligibility requirements for children (4.11-4.13)

Adequate arrangements must have been made for a child's travel to, reception and care in the UK. If the child is not applying or travelling with a parent or guardian based in their home country or country of ordinary residence who is responsible for their care; that parent or guardian must confirm that they consent to the arrangements for the child's travel to, and reception and care in the UK. Where requested, this consent must be given in writing.

A visit visa held by a child must either state that they are accompanied and will be travelling with an adult identified on that visa; or state they are unaccompanied. If neither applies, the child may be refused entry.

Additional eligibility requirements for visitors coming to the UK to receive private medical treatment (V4.14-4.16)

If the applicant is suffering from a communicable disease, they must have satisfied the medical inspector that they are not a danger to public health. The applicant must have arranged their private medical treatment before they travel to the UK, and must provide a letter from their doctor or consultant detailing–
   (a) the medical condition requiring consultation or treatment; and
   (b) the estimated costs and likely duration of any treatment which must be of a finite duration; and
   (c) where the consultation or treatment will take place.

If the applicant is applying for an 11 month visit visa for the purposes of private medical treatment they must also provide evidence from their medical practitioner in the UK that the proposed treatment is likely to exceed 6 months but not more than 11 months; and if required, provide a valid medical certificate issued by a specified medical practitioner confirming that they have undergone screening for active pulmonary tuberculosis and that this tuberculosis is not present in the applicant.

Additional eligibility requirements for visitors coming to the UK to donate an organ (V4.17-4.20)

An applicant must satisfy the decision maker that they genuinely intend to donate an organ, or be assessed as a potential organ donor, to an identified recipient in the UK with whom they have a genetic or close personal relationship.

The applicant must provide written confirmation of medical tests to show that they are a donor match to the identified recipient, or that they are undergoing further tests to be assessed as a potential donor to the identified recipient.

The applicant must provide a letter, dated no more than three months prior to the intended date of arrival in the UK from either the lead nurse or coordinator of the UK's NHS Trust's Living Donor kidney Transplant team; or a UK registered medical practitioner who holds an NHS consultant post or who appears in the Specialist Register of the General Medical Council; which confirms that the visitor meets the above requirements and confirms when and where the planned organ transplant or medical tests will take place.

The applicant must be able to demonstrate, if required to do so, that the identified recipient is legally present in the United Kingdom, or will be at the time of the planned organ transplant.

Additional eligibility requirements for visitors coming under the ADS agreement (V4.21)

An applicant under the Approved Destination Status (ADS) Agreement with China must be a national of the People's Republic of China; and intend to enter, leave and travel within the UK as a member of a tourist group under the ADS agreement.

Additional eligibility requirements for academics (V4.22)

An academic applying for a 12 month visit visa (standard) must intend to do one (or more) of the following permitted activities–
   (a) take part in formal exchange arrangements with UK counterparts (including doctors);
   (b) carry out research for their own purposes if they are on sabbatical leave from their home institution;
   (c) if they are an eminent senior doctor or dentist, take part in research, teaching or clinical practice provided this does not amount to filling a permanent teaching post,
and–
   (d) be highly qualified within their own field of expertise; and
   (e) currently working in that field at an academic institution or institution of higher education overseas; and
   (f) if required, provide a valid medical certificate issued by a specified medical practitioner confirming that they have undergone screening for active pulmonary tuberculosis and that this tuberculosis is not present in the applicant

21 Eligibility criteria– Visit visa (PPE)

An applicant for permitted paid engagements must satisfy the decision maker that they meet the standard eligibility requirements at V4.2 -V4.10 (see above) (V5.1).

Additional eligibility requirements for a permitted paid engagements visit visa or leave to enter (V5.2-5.3)

An applicant must intend to do one (or more) of the permitted paid engagements set out in Appendix 4 to the Rules, which must–

(a) be arranged before the applicant travels to the UK; and
(b) be declared as part of the application for a visit visa or leave to enter; and
(c) be evidenced by a formal invitation; and
(d) relate to the applicant's area of expertise and occupation overseas.

An applicant must not be a child.

22 Eligibility requirements for a marriage or civil partnership visit visa

An applicant for a marriage or civil partnership visit visa must satisfy the decision maker that they meet the standard eligibility requirements at V4.2 -V4.10 (see above) and must be aged 18 or over (V6.1)..

On arrival in the UK a visitor coming to marry or form a civil partnership, or give notice of this, in the UK must have a valid visit visa endorsed with this purpose and the name of the holder's fiancé(e) or proposed civil partner (V6.2).

Additional eligibility requirements for a marriage or civil partnership visit visa (V6.3)

An applicant seeking to come to the UK as a visitor
who wishes to give notice of marriage or civil partnership, or marry or forma civil partnership, in the UK during that visit must satisfy the decision maker that they–

(a) intend to give notice of marriage or civil partnership; or
(b) intend to marry or form a civil partnership; and
(c) do not intend to give notice of or enter into a sham marriage or sham civil partnership, within the validity period covered by their visit visa.

23 Eligibility requirements for a transit visit visa

A transit visitor is a person who seeks to travel via the UK en route to another destination country outside the common travel area. Individuals seeking to transit the UK without passing through the UK border may need a Direct Airside Transit Visa. These are provided for by the Immigration (Passenger Transit Visa) Order 2014.

These provisions do not apply to crew members.

A visa national must either hold a transit visit visa or, if they meet the requirements for admission under the transit without visa scheme (see V7.6 –V7.8, below), they may seek leave to enter at the UK border (V7.1-7.4).

An applicant must satisfy the decision maker that they (V7.5)–

(a) are genuinely in transit to another country outside the common travel area, meaning the main purpose of their visit is to transit the UK and that the applicant is taking a reasonable transit route; and
(b) will not access public funds or medical treatment, work or study in the UK; and
(c) genuinely intend and are able to leave the UK within 48 hours after their arrival; and
(d) are assured entry to their country of destination and any other countries they are transiting on their way there.

To be granted leave to enter under the transit without visa scheme a visa national must (V7.6-7.8)–

(a) have arrived by air and will be departing by air; and
(b) be genuinely in transit to another country, meaning the purpose of their visit is to transit the UK and that the applicant is taking a reasonable transit route; and
(c) will not access public funds or medical treatment, work or study in the UK; and
(d) genuinely intend and be able to leave the UK before 23:59 hours on the day after the day when they arrived; and
(e) have a confirmed booking on a flight departing the UK before 23:59 hours on the day after the day when they arrived; and
(f) be assured entry to their country of destination and any other countries they are transiting through on their way there.
(g) be travelling to or from (or on part of a reasonable journey to or from) Australia, Canada, New Zealand or the USA and have a valid visa for that country; or
(h) be travelling from (or on part of a reasonable journey from) Australia, Canada, New Zealand or the USA and it is less than 6 months since he last entered that country with a valid entry visa; or
(i) hold a valid permanent residence permit issued by either Australia; Canada, issued after 28 June 2002; New Zealand; or
(j) hold a valid USA, I-551 permanent resident card issued on or after 21 April 1998; or
(k) hold a valid USA I-551 temporary immigrant visa (a wet-ink stamp version will not be accepted); or
(l) hold an expired USA I-551 permanent resident card issued on or after 21 April 1998, provided it is accompanied by a valid I-797 letter authorising extension of the period of permanent residency; or

(m) hold a valid standalone US immigration form 155A/155B attached to a sealed brown envelope; or

(n) hold a valid common format residence permit issued by an EEA state (pursuant to Council Regulation (EC) No. 1030/2002) or Switzerland; or

(o) hold a valid uniform format category D visa for entry to a state in the European Economic Area or Switzerland; or

(p) be travelling on to the Republic of Ireland and have a valid Irish biometric visa; or

(q) be travelling from the Republic of Ireland and it is less than three months since the applicant was last given permission to land or be in the Republic by the Irish authorities with a valid Irish biometric visa.

Paragraph (g) and (h) above do not apply where the transit passenger is a citizen or national of Syria holding a B1 or B2 category visa for entry to the United States of America (V7.8.1).

Electronic versions of any documents listed in paras (g)-(q), such as electronic visas (including printed versions), will not be accepted (V7.9).

24 Extension of stay as a visitor

Note.– It is not possible to switch to become a visitor while in the UK where a person is in the UK in breach of immigration laws or has entry clearance or leave to
enter or remain for another purpose (V8.1).

An applicant must be in the UK as a visitor. Visitors for permitted paid engagements and transit visitors may not apply for an extension of stay as a visitor (V8.3).

An application for an extension of stay as a visitor must satisfy the decision maker that they continue to meet all the suitability and eligibility requirements for a visit visa (V8.4).

The applicant must not be in the UK in breach of immigration laws, except for any period of overstaying of 28 days or less which will be discounted (V8.5).

If the applicant is applying for an extension of stay
as a visitor for the purpose of receiving private medical treatment they must also satisfy the decision maker that they have met the costs of any medical treatment received so far; and provide a letter from a registered medical practitioner, at a private practice or NHS hospital, who holds an NHS consultant post or who appears in the Specialist Register of the General Medical Council, detailing the medical condition requiring further treatment (V8.6).

Length of visa extension (V8.7-8.11)

A visitor (standard) and a visitor for marriage or civil partnership, who was granted a visit visa or leave to enter for less than 6 months may be granted an extension of stay as a visitor so that the total period they can remain in the UK (including both the original grant and the extension of stay) does not exceed 6 months.

A visitor (standard) who is in the UK for private medical treatment may be granted an extension of stay
as a visitor for a further 6 months, provided this is for
private medical treatment

A visitor (standard) who is an academic on sabbatical leave and is in the UK undertaking their own research, or the spouse, partner or child accompanying such an academic, can be granted an extension of stay as a visitor so that the total period they can remain in the UK (including both the original grant and the extension of stay) does not exceed 12 months.

A visitor (standard) may be granted an extension of stay as a visitor for up to 6 months in order to resit the Professional and Linguistic Assessment Board (PLAB) Test, provided they meet the requirements at Appendix 3, paragraph 22(b)(i) of the Rules.

A visitor (standard) who is successful in the Professional and Linguistic Assessment Board Test may be granted an extension of stay as a visitor to undertake an unpaid clinical attachment, provided they meet the requirements of Appendix 3, paragraph 22(a) of the Rules so that the total period they can remain in the UK (including both the original grant and the extension of stay) does not exceed 18 months.

25 Cancellation of a visit visa or leave to enter or remain as a visitor on or before arrival at the UK border

A current visit visa or leave to enter or remain as a visitor may be cancelled whilst the person is outside the UK or on arrival in the UK, if (V9.1-9.7)–

Change of circumstances

Where there has been such a change in the circumstances of the case since the visit visa or leave to enter or remain was granted that the basis of the visitor's claim to admission or stay has been removed and the visa or leave should be cancelled.

Change of purpose

Where the visitor holds a visit visa and their purpose
in arriving in the United Kingdom is different from the purpose specified in the visit visa.

False information or failure to disclose a material fact

Where false representations were made or false documents or information submitted (whether or not material to the application, and whether or not to the applicant's knowledge); or material facts were not disclosed, in relation to the application for a visit visa or leave to enter or remain as a visitor, or in order to obtain documents from the Secretary of State or a third party provided in support of their application.

Medical.

Where it is undesirable to admit the visitor to the UK for medical reasons, unless there are strong compassionate reasons justifying admission.

Not conducive to the public good

Where the criteria in V3.2 -V3.5 apply (see above).

Failure to supply information

Where the person is outside the UK and there is a failure to supply any information, documents, or medical reports requested by a decision maker.

26 Curtailment of a visit visa or leave to enter or remain as a visitor

A visit visa or leave to enter or remain as a visitor may be curtailed while the person is in the UK if (V9.8-V9.13)–

False information or failure to disclose a material fact

Where false representations were made or false documents or information were submitted (whether or not material to the application, and whether or not to the applicant's knowledge); or material facts were not disclosed, in relation to any application for an entry clearance or leave to enter or remain, or for the purpose of obtaining either a document from the Secretary of State or third party required in support of the application, or a document from the Secretary of State that indicates the person has a right to reside in the UK.

Requirements of the Rules

If the visitor ceases to meet the requirements of the Visitor Rules.

Failure to comply with conditions

If the visitor fails to comply with any conditions of their leave to enter or remain.

Not conducive to the public good

Where either–

(a) the visitor has, within the first 6 months of being granted a visit visa or leave to enter, committed an offence for which they are subsequently sentenced to a period of imprisonment; or

(b) in the view of the Secretary of State the applicant's offending has caused serious harm; or

(c) in the view of the Secretary of State the applicant is a persistent offender who shows a particular disregard for the law; or

(d) it would be undesirable to permit the visitor to remain in the UK in light of their conduct, character, associations, or the fact that they represent a threat to national security

27 Short-term studies

The following rules are for persons who wish to study in the UK as a short-term student for up to and including 6 months or, for persons aged 18 and over, for up to and including 11 months for English language study *only* (paras A57A-A57H).

Requirements for entry clearance or leave to enter –Short-Term Student

All applicants for entry clearance or leave to enter the UK as a short-term student must (A57C)–

(a) not fall for refusal under the general grounds for refusal; and,

(b) meets all of the following requirements–

(i) be aged 18 or over;

(ii) not intend to study at a state-maintained school or institution;

(iii) not intend to study in the UK for extended periods through frequent or successive periods as a short-term student;

(iv) not intend to take employment, including paid or unpaid work, a work placement or work experience in the UK.;

(v) not intend to undertake self-employment or engage in business activities or any professional activity in the UK;

(vi) have enough funds to meet the cost of his return or onward journey from the UK;

(vii) be maintained and accommodated adequately out of funds available to him;

(viii) not have recourse to public funds;

(ix) is genuinely seeking entry as a short-term student

Applicants for entry clearance or leave to enter the UK as a short-term student for up to and including 6 months must meet the requirements in A57C (see above) and (A57D)–

(a) Either;

(i) has been accepted on a course of study of no more than 6 months, which is to be provided by an accredited institution; or

(ii) is enrolled on a course of study abroad equivalent to at least degree level study in the UK and has been accepted by a UK recognised body or a body in receipt of public funding as a higher education institution from the Department for Employment and Learning in Northern Ireland, the Higher Education Funding Council for England, the Higher Education Funding Council for Wales or the Scottish Funding Council to undertake research or be taught about research (research tuition) at the UK institution, provided that the overseas course provider confirms that the research or research tuition is part of or relevant to the course of study that they are enrolled on overseas, and the student is not to be employed as a sponsored researcher under the relevant Tier 5 Government Authorised Exchange scheme, or under Tier 2 of the Points-Based System, at the UK institution; and

(b) intends to leave the UK at the end of the study or at the end of 6 months whichever is sooner;

(c) holds a valid entry clearance as a short-term student for 6 months unless he is a non-visa national.

Applicants for entry clearance or leave to enter the UK as a short-term student for up to and including 11months must meet the requirements in A57C (see above) and (A57E)–

(a) have been accepted on a course of study in English language of no more than 11 months which is to be provided by an accredited institution; and

(b) intend to leave the UK at the end of the study or at the end of 11 months whichever is sooner; and

(c) hold a valid entry clearance as a short-term student for a period not exceeding 11 months.

Requirements for entry clearance or leave to enter –Short-term student (child)

The requirements for entry clearance or leave to enter for short-term students (child) are that the applicant does not fall for refusal under the general grounds for refusal and meets all of the following requirements (A57G)–

(i) is aged under 18;

(ii) has been accepted on a course of study which is to be provided by an accredited institution which is not a state-maintained school or institution;

(iii) does not intend to study at a state-maintained school or institution;

(iv) intends to leave the UK at the end of 6 months;

(v) does not intend to study in the UK for extended periods through frequent or successive periods as a short-term student;

(vi) does not intend to take employment, including paid or unpaid work, work placements or work experience in the UK;

(vii) does not intend to undertake self-employment or engage in business or any professional activities in the UK;

(viii) has enough funds to meet the cost of his return or onward journey from the UK;

(ix) will be maintained and accommodated adequately out of funds available to him

(x) will not have recourse to public funds;

(xi) can demonstrate that suitable arrangements have been made for his travel to, and reception and care in the UK;

(xii) has a parent or guardian in his home country or country of habitual residence who is responsible for his care and who confirms that they consent to the arrangements for the applicant's travel, reception and care in the UK; and

(xiii) if a visa national–

(a) holds a valid UK entry clearance for entry as an accompanied short-term student (child) and is travelling in the company of the adult identified on the entry clearance, who is on the same occasion being admitted to the UK; or

(b) holds a valid UK entry for entry as an unaccompanied short-term student (child).

Entry clearance or leave to enter as a short-term student (child) will be granted for a period not exceeding 6 months (A57H).

28 Spouses or civil partners of students

The spouse/civil partner of a student seeking leave to enter or remain in the UK may be admitted or allowed to remain for the same period of time as the student, provided that each of the requirements of para 76 (see below) is met. Employment may be permitted where the period of leave being granted is 12 months or more (para 77). The requirements are that the applicant is married to or the civil partner of a person allowed to enter or remain under paras 57 to 75 (now deleted) but not A57A to A57H and intend to live with each other as spouses/civil partners during the applicant's stay; have adequate accommodation and funds (without recourse to public funds) for themselves and any dependants; the applicant does not intend to take employment except as permitted under para 77 (see above); intends to leave the UK at the end of any period of leave granted to him; and if seeking leave to remain must not be in the UK in breach of immigration laws except that any period of overstaying for a period of 28 days or less will be disregarded (para 76).

29 Children of students

A person seeking leave to enter or remain in the UK as the child of a student may be allowed to enter or remain for the same period of time as the student, provided that each of the requirements of para 79 (see below) is met and will be so refused if they are not (paras 80 and 81). Employment is prohibited except where the period of leave being granted is 12 months or more (para 80). The requirements to be met are that the child is the child of a parent allowed to enter or remain under paras 57 to 75 (now deleted) but not A57A to A57H; is aged under 18 or has current leave to enter or remain in this capacity; is not married or in a civil partnership, has not formed an independent family unit and is not leading an independent life; can, and will be maintained and accommodated adequately without recourse to public funds, will leave the UK when his parent's leave expires, meets the requirements of para 79A; and if seeking leave to remain must not be in the UK in breach of immigration laws except that any period of overstaying for a period of 28 days or less will be disregarded (para 79).

Para 79A provides that both of the applicant's parents must either be lawfully present in the UK, or being granted entry clearance or leave to remain at the same time as the applicant (or one parent must be lawfully present in the UK and the other being granted entry clearance or leave to remain at the same time as the applicant), unless–

(i) the student is the applicant's sole surviving parent, or
(ii) the student parent has and has had sole responsibility for the applicant's upbringing, or
(iii) there are serious or compelling family or other considerations which would make it desirable not to refuse the application and suitable arrangements have been made in the UK for the applicant's care.

30 Closed categories

A number of entry categories have been closed as they have been superseded by the Points Based System (see the Note on **Control of Immigration: The points based system**). These superseded categories are however still relevant in so far as those already admitted under them can apply for indefinite leave to remain in the UK.

The superseded categories are–
– Highly skilled migrants (replaced by Highly Skilled Worker, Tier 1 (General) Migrants));
the following categories, all replaced by Tier 2 Migrants–
– Work permit employment;
– Representatives of overseas newspapers, news agencies and broadcasting organisations;
– Private servants in diplomatic households;
– Overseas government employees;
– Ministers of religion, missionaries and members of religious orders;
– Airport-based operational ground staff of overseas-owned airlines.

In relation to those already admitted under these categories, indefinite leave to remain may in general be granted after five continuous years in the UK provided specified requirements have been met, principally, that the applicant–

(a) is still employed within the category, or in the case of highly skilled migrants, is still economically active;
(b) has not had recourse to public funds,
(c) has sufficient knowledge of the English language and about life in the UK;
(d) does not fall for refusal under the general grounds for refusal; and
(e) is not in the UK in breach of immigration laws except that any period of overstaying for a period of 28 days or less will be disregarded.

The following paragraphs of the Rules contain the detailed provisions for those seeking indefinite leave to remain under these superseded categories: paras 134-135 (work permit employment); 135G, GA, H, HA (highly skilled migrants); 142-143 (press representatives etc); 158-159 (diplomatic households); 167-168 (overseas government employees); 169, 175-177 (ministers of religion etc); 184-185 (airport ground staff).

Note.–In the case of Highly skilled migrants, application for indefinite leave to remain must be made before 6 April 2018 (para 135G(h)).

31 Business representatives

The requirements to be met by a person seeking leave to enter in this category are that he (para 144)–
(i) has been recruited and taken on as an employee outside the UK of a business which has its headquarters and principal place of business outside the UK; and
(ii) is seeking entry to the UK–
    (a) as a senior employee of an overseas business which has no branch, subsidiary or other representative in the UK with full authority to take operational decisions on behalf of the business for the purpose of representing it in the UK by establishing and operating a registered branch or wholly owned subsidiary of that overseas business, the branch or subsidiary of which will be concerned with same type of business activity as the overseas business; or
    (b) as an employee of an overseas newspaper, news agency or broadcasting organisation being posted on a long-term assignment as a representative of their overseas employer.
(iii) where entry is sought under (ii)(a), the person–
    (a) will be the sole representative of the employer present in the UK under the terms of this paragraph;
    (b) intends to be employed full time as a representative of that overseas business;
    (c) is not a majority shareholder in that overseas business; and
    (d) must supply from his employer:
        (1) a full description of the company's activities, including details of the company's assets and

accounts and the company share distribution for the previous year;

(2) a letter which confirms the overseas company will establish a wholly-owned subsidiary or register a branch in the UK in the same business activity as the parent company;

(3) a job description, salary details and contract of employment for the applicant;

(4) a letter confirming the applicant is fully familiar with the company's activities and has full powers to negotiate and take operational decisions without reference to the parent company; and

(5) a notarised statement which confirms the applicant will be their sole representative in the UK; the company has no other branch, subsidiary or representative in the UK; its operations will remain centred overseas; and the applicant will not engage in business of their own nor represent any other company's interest;

(iv) where entry is sought under (ii)(b), the person intends to work full-time as a representative of their overseas employer;

(v) does not intend to take employment except within the terms of this paragraph;

(vi) has competence in the English language to the required standard as set out in the Rules;

(vii) can maintain and accommodate himself and any dependants adequately without recourse to public funds; and

(viii) holds a valid UK entry clearance for entry in this capacity.

Such a person may be admitted for no more than three years so long as a valid entry clearance for entry in this capacity is produced on arrival (para 145); and will be refused entry if an entry clearance is not so produced (para 146). Leave may be subject to requirements not to have recourse to public funds, to register with the police where required, not to take employment other than for the business the person has been admitted to represent, and not to study unless they have a valid Academic Technology Approval Scheme clearance certificate from the Counter-Proliferation Department of the Foreign Office.

An extension of stay not exceeding two years (three years if the last leave was granted before 1st October 2009) may be granted to a sole representative if each of the following requirements have been met (para 148). The requirements (for someone admitted under para 144(ii)(a)) are that he entered with a valid entry clearance; he can show that the headquarters and principal place of business of the firm is still overseas; he is still employed full-time as a representative of that overseas firm and has established and is in charge of its registered branch or wholly-owned subsidiary; he is still required for the employment in question, as certified by the employer and is in receipt of a salary from his employer, he has generated business, principally with firms in the UK, on behalf of his employer since his last grant of leave, he can show a Companies House certificate of registration as a UK establishment (for a branch), and a certificate of incorporation (for a subsidiary) with either a copy of the share register or a letter from the company's accountants confirming that all shares are held by the parent company, and he must not be in the UK in breach of immigration laws except that any period of overstaying for a period of 28 days or less will be disregarded. (paras. 147 and 148). There are different requirements for someone admitted under para 144(ii)(b). An extension of stay will be refused if the above requirements have not been met (para 149).

Indefinite leave to remain may be granted if he has: been lawfully in the UK for five years continuously; met the requirements of para 147 throughout that time; has a certificate from his employer that he is still required for that employment; has sufficient knowledge of the English language and about life in the UK (unless he is under the age of 18 or aged 65 or over at the time he makes his application); he does not fall for refusal under the general grounds for refusal; and is not in the UK in breach of immigration laws except that any period of overstaying for a period of 28 days or less will be disregarded (para 150). Such leave will be refused each of the requirements of para 150 is not met (para 151).

Persons seeking leave to enter in this category must hold a biometric immigration document: see the Note on **Control of Immigration** at para **6 Biometric registration**.

32 Domestic worker in a private household

A person seeking leave to enter in this category must (para 159A)—

(i) be aged 18 to 65;

(ii) have been employed as a domestic worker for one year or more immediately prior to application for entry clearance under the same roof as his employer or in a household that the employer uses for himself on a regular basis and where there is evidence that there is a connection between employer and employee;

(iii) intend to work for the employer whilst the employer is in the UK and intend to travel in the company of either (a) a British or EEA national employer, or that employer's British or EEA national spouse, civil partner or child, where the employer's usual place of residence is outside the UK and where the employer does not intend to remain in the UK beyond six months; or (b) a British or EEA national employer's foreign national spouse, civil partner or child where the employer does not intend to remain in the UK beyond six months; or (c) a foreign national employer or the employer's spouse, civil partner or child where the employer is seeking or has been granted entry clearance or leave to enter under Part 2 of the Immigration Rules;

(iv) intends to leave the UK at the end of six months or at the same time as the employer, whichever is the earlier;

(v) have agreed in writing terms and conditions of employment in the UK with the employer, including specifically that the applicant will be paid in accordance with the National Minimum Wage Act 1998 and any Regulations made under it, and provides evidence of this as specified by Appendix 7 to the Rules, with the entry clearance application;

(va) satisfies the Entry Clearance Officer or Immigration Officer that, throughout their employment in the UK, the employer intends to pay them at least the then current National Minimum Wage;

(vb) provides a written and signed statement from the employer confirming that the applicant is an employee and the work that will be carried out by the applicant will not constitute work within the meaning of Reg. 57 of the National Minimum Wage Regulations 2015 (which relates to work in an employer's family home by a resident of that home);

(vi) not take employment other than as a domestic worker in a private household;

(vii) be able to maintain and accommodate themselves adequately without recourse to public funds; and

(viii) hold a valid entry clearance for entry in this capacity,

and will be refused if such an entry clearance is not produced on arrival (para 159C). Leave may be given to such a person to enter for no longer than 6 months (para 159B).

An extension of stay for no more than 6 months less the period already spent in the UK in this capacity may be granted (para 159E), if the applicant: last entered the UK with a valid entry clearance in this capacity; was granted less than 6 months leave to enter in this capacity; is still engaged full-time in that capacity and is still required for that employment in question, as certified by the employer; meets the requirements of para 159A(i), (va), (vb), (vi) and (vii) (see above); and is not in the UK in breach of immigration laws except that any period of overstaying for a period of 28 days or less will be disregarded (para 159D). An extension of stay will be refused if each of the requirements of paragraph 159D is not met (para 159F). In the case of a domestic worker in a private household who entered the UK under the Rules in place before 6 April 2012, the reference to 6 months in para 159E is replaced by 12 months (para 159EA).

Indefinite leave to remain may be granted to a person if he entered the UK with a valid entry clearance as a domestic worker in a private household under the Rules in place before 6 April 2012; has lawfully spent five continuous years in the UK in that category of employment; has met the requirements of paragraph 159A(vi) and (vii) throughout that time; his employer certifies that he is still required for the employment in question; he has sufficient knowledge of the English language and about life in the UK (unless he is under the age of 18 or aged 65 or over at the time he makes his application); he does not fall for refusal under the general grounds for refusal; and is not in the UK in breach of immigration laws except that any period of overstaying for a period of 28 days or less will be disregarded (para 159G). Leave will be refused if the above requirements are not met (para 159H).

Persons seeking leave to enter in this category must hold a biometric immigration document: see the Note on **Control of Immigration** at para **6 Biometric registration**.

33 Victims of slavery or human trafficking

A person who has previously been granted leave to enter or remain as a domestic worker in a private or diplomatic household may be granted leave to remain for up to six months where they have been the subject of a positive conclusive grounds decision under the National Referral Mechanism (the framework for identifying victims of human trafficking or modern slavery and ensuring they receive the appropriate support). Where the initial period of leave granted is for less than six months, a subsequent extension of stay may be granted to allow the individual to complete the maximum period of two years in this category (paras 159I, 159J).

Leave to remain granted subject to the following conditions (para 159J)–

(i) no recourse to public funds; and

(ii) no employment except as a domestic worker in a private household; or as a private servant in a diplomatic household working only in the household of the employer recorded by the Certificate of Sponsorship Checking Service in the Tier 5 (International Agreement) sub-category before the employment commences.

If the requirements are not met, leave will be refused (para 159K).

34 Persons with United Kingdom ancestry

The requirements to be met by a person seeking leave to enter the UK in this capacity are that he (para 186)–

(i) is a Commonwealth citizen;

(ii) is aged 17 or over;

(iii) is able to prove that one of his blood grandparents (or a grandparent by reason of a UK recognised adoption) was born in the UK and Islands;

(iv) is able to work and intends to take or seek employment in the UK;

(v) is able to maintain and accommodate himself and any dependants adequately without recourse to public funds; and

(vi) holds a valid entry clearance in this capacity.

Leave to enter may be granted for not more than five years in this capacity provided that the applicant is able to produce, on arrival, a valid entry clearance for entry in this capacity, and subject to a condition that the applicant not study unless they have a valid Academic Technology Approval Scheme clearance certificate from the Counter-Proliferation Department of the Foreign Office (para 187); leave to enter will be refused if such an entry clearance is not produced (para 188).

The requirements to be met by a person seeking an extension of stay in this capacity are that he is able to meet each of the requirements of paragraph 186(i) to (v), he was admitted to the UK on the grounds of UK ancestry in accordance with paras 186 to 188 or has been granted an extension of stay in that capacity; and is not in the UK in breach of immigration laws except that any period of overstaying for a period of 28 days or less will be disregarded (para 189). An extension of stay, for not more than five years, may be granted (subject to the same study condition as above) if the applicant meets each of the requirements of paragraph 189 (para 190); and will be refused if they are not met (para 191).

Indefinite leave to stay may be granted if the applicant meets the requirements of paragraph 186(i) to (v), has lawfully spent five years in the UK continuously; has sufficient knowledge of the English language and about life in the UK (unless he is under the age of 18 or aged 65 or over at the time he makes his application); he does not fall for refusal under the general grounds for refusal; and is not in the UK in breach of immigration laws except that any period of overstaying for a period of 28 days or less will be disregarded (para 192); and will be refused if each of these requirements is not met (para 193).

Persons seeking leave to enter in this category must hold a biometric immigration document: see the Note on **Control of Immigration** at para **6 Biometric registration.**

35 Partners of persons who have or had limited leave to enter or remain under paras 128 to 193 (but not 135I to 135K)

Leave to enter the UK under this category may be granted to a person if (paras 194 and 195)–

  (i) the applicant is the spouse, civil partner, unmarried or same-sex partner of a person with limited leave to enter the UK under paras 128-193 (but not paras 135I-135K); and
  (ii) if an unmarried or same-sex partner, any previous marriage or civil partnership (or similar relationship) by either partner has permanently broken down; the parties are not involved in a consanguineous relationship with one another; and have been living together in a relationship akin to marriage or civil partnership which has subsisted for 2 years or more;
  (iii) each of the parties intends to live with the other as his or her partner during the applicant's stay and the relationship is subsisting; and
  (iv) there will be adequate accommodation for the parties and any dependants without recourse to public funds which they own or occupy exclusively; and
  (v) the parties will be able to maintain themselves and any dependants adequately without recourse to public funds; and
  (vi) the applicant does not intend to stay in the UK beyond any period of leave granted to his partner;
  (vii) the applicant does not fall for refusal under the general grounds for refusal; and
  (viii) the applicant holds a valid UK entry clearance for entry in this capacity.

Leave to enter or remain in this category may be granted for a period not in excess of that granted to the spouse/civil partner and will be subject to a condition that the applicant not study unless they have a valid Academic Technology Approval Scheme clearance certificate from the Counter-Proliferation Department of the Foreign Office.

Indefinite leave to remain may be granted if the applicant had a valid entry clearance, meets the appropriate requirements of para 194; has sufficient knowledge of the English language and about life in the UK (unless he is under the age of 18 or aged 65 or over at the time he makes his application); he does not fall for refusal under the general grounds for refusal; and is not in the UK in breach of immigration laws except that any period of overstaying for a period of 28 days or less will be disregarded (para 196D).

Nothing in paras 194-196F is to be construed as allowing a person to be granted entry clearance, leave to enter, leave to remain or variation of leave as the partner of a person granted entry clearance or leave to enter under para 159A (domestic worker in a private household) where that entry clearance or leave to enter was granted under 159A on or after 6 April 2012 (para 193A).

36 Children of persons with limited leave to enter or remain under paras 128 to 193 (but not 135I to 135K)

Leave to enter the UK under this category may be granted to a person if (para 197)–

  (i) he is the child of a parent with limited leave to enter or remain in the UK under paras 128-193 (but not paras 135I-135K) or, in respect of applications for leave to remain only, of a parent who has indefinite leave to remain in the UK but who immediately before that grant had limited leave to enter or remain under those paragraphs; and
  (ii) he is under the age of 18 or has current leave to enter or remain in this capacity; and
  (iii) he is unmarried and is not a civil partner, has not formed an independent family unit and is not leading an independent life; and
  (iv) he can and will be maintained and accommodated adequately without recourse to public funds in accommodation which his parent(s) own or occupy exclusively; and
  (v) he will not stay in the UK beyond any period of leave granted to his parent(s); and
  (vi) both parents are being or have been admitted to or allowed to remain in the UK save where–
      (a) the parent he is accompanying or joining is his sole surviving parent; or
      (b) the parent he is accompanying or joining has had sole responsibility for his upbringing; or

(c) there are serious and compelling family or other considerations which make exclusion from the UK undesirable and suitable arrangements have been made for his care;

(vii) if seeking leave to enter, he holds a valid UK entry clearance for entry in this capacity or, if seeking leave to remain, he was not last granted (1) entry clearance or leave as a visitor, short-term student or short-term student (child), (2) temporary admission, or (3) temporary release; and

(viii) if seeking leave to remain, must not be in the UK in breach of immigration laws except that any period of overstaying for a period of 28 days or less will be disregarded.

Leave to enter or remain in this category may be granted for a period not in excess of that granted to the parent. (para 198).

A person seeking leave to remain as the child of a parent who has indefinite leave to remain in the UK and who had limited leave under paras 128–93 (but not paras 135I–135K) immediately before being granted indefinite leave may be given leave to remain in the UK for a period of 30 months provided he is in the UK with valid leave under para 198 and is able to satisfy the Secretary of State that each of the requirements of para 197(i)-(vi) and(viii) is met. Where the applicant is 18 or over at the time their leave is granted, or will be 18 before their period of limited leave expires, such leave will be subject to a condition that they do not study unless they have a valid Academic Technology Approval Scheme clearance certificate from the Counter-Proliferation Department of the Foreign Office.

Leave to enter or remain in the UK as the child of a person with limited leave to enter or remain in the UK under paras 128-193 (but not paras 135I-135K) will be refused if (para 198A)–

(i) in relation to an application for leave to enter, a valid UK entry clearance for entry in this capacity is not produced to the Immigration Officer on arrival; or

(ii) in the case of an application for limited leave to remain, if the applicant was last granted entry clearance or leave as a visitor, temporary admission, or temporary release; or

(iii) he is unable to satisfy the Secretary of State that each of the requirements of para197(i)-(vi) and (viii) is met.

The requirements to be met by a person seeking indefinite leave to remain in the UK as the child of a person who has or has had leave to enter or remain in the UK under paras 128-193 (but not paras 135I-135K) are that he (paras 199, 199A)–

(i) is the child of a person who has limited leave to enter or remain in the UK under paras 128-193 (but not paras 135I-135K) and who is being granted indefinite leave to remain at the same time; or has indefinite leave to remain in the UK and who had limited leave to enter or remain in the UK under paras 128-193 (but not paras 135I-135K) immediately before being granted indefinite leave to remain; and

(ii) meets the requirements of para 197(i) - (vi) and (viii); and

(iii) was not last granted (1) entry clearance or leave as a visitor, short-term student or short-term student (child), (2) temporary admission, or (3) temporary release; and

(iv) does not fall for refusal under the general grounds for refusal;

(v) must not be in the UK in breach of immigration laws except that any period of overstaying for a period of 28 days or less will be disregarded; and

(vi) has demonstrated sufficient knowledge of the English language and sufficient knowledge about life in the UK, in accordance with Appendix KoLL, unless he is under 18 at the date on which the application is made.

Nothing in paras 197-199 is to be construed as allowing a person to be granted entry clearance, leave to enter, leave to remain or variation of leave as the child of a person granted entry clearance or leave to enter under para 159A (domestic worker in a private household) where that entry clearance or leave to enter was granted under 159A on or after 6 April 2012 (para 196G).

37 Persons exercising rights of access to a child resident in the United Kingdom

This category applies only to a person who made an application before 9 July 2012 for leave to enter or remain or indefinite leave to remain as a person exercising rights of access to a child resident in the UK, or who before 9 July 2012 has been granted leave to enter or remain as a person exercising rights of access to a child resident in the UK (para A246).

Application for leave to enter or remain made on or after 9 July 2012 by a person exercising rights of access to a child resident in the UK are made under Appendix FM (para AB246)

A person in this category may be granted leave to enter for 12 months in the first instance, providing that he is able to produce, on arrival, a valid entry clearance for entry in this capacity (para 247) and provided that he fulfils the following requirements (para 246)–

(i) he is the parent of a child resident in the UK;

(ii) the parent or carer with whom the child permanently resides is resident in the UK;

(iii) he can produce evidence that he has access rights to the child in the form of a Residence or Contact Order granted by a UK court or a certificate issued by a district judge confirming the applicant's intention to maintain contact with the child;

(iv) he intends to take an active role in the child's upbringing;

(v) the child is under 18;

(vi) there will be adequate accommodation for the applicant and any dependants without recourse to public funds in accommodation which the applicant owns or occupies exclusively;

(vii) he will maintain himself and any dependants adequately without recourse to public funds; and

(viii) he holds a valid entry clearance in this capacity.

Where a person is seeking leave to remain as a person exercising a right of access to a child in the UK, the requirements are as (i) to (vii) above plus requirements that the child visits or stays with the applicant on a frequent and regular basis and that the applicant intends this to continue, that the applicant has limited leave to remain in the UK as the spouse/civil partner, unmarried/same sex partner of a person present and settled in the UK who is the other parent of the child, and the applicant has not remained in the UK in breach of immigration laws. In addition, a statement from the child's other parent (or if contact is supervised, the supervisor) that the applicant is maintaining contact with the child may be produced as evidence for (iii) above (para 248A).

Where it is not possible to meet these requirements, it may be that the UK still has an obligation under Art 8 European Convention on Human Rights to allow a parent access to a child.

Note.–A primary carer of a self sufficient EEA national child has a directly enforceable EU right to enter and reside in the UK to facilitate the child's free movement rights. This EU right is not subject to any restrictions imposed by the Immigration Rules.

38 Retired persons of independent means

Paragraph deleted. This category was closed in November 2008 as being irreconcilable with the immigration policy that citizenship should be earned. An extension of stay for a person already in the UK as a retired person of independent means could only be granted so as to bring the person's stay in this category up to a maximum of 5 years in aggregate (para 267) i.e., to November 2013. Indefinite leave to stay could be granted to a person already admitted under this category, provided that he had spent a continuous period of five years lawfully in the UK in this capacity, had met specified requirements throughout that period, did not fall for refusal under the general grounds for refusal; and was not in the UK in breach of immigration laws, except that any period of overstaying for a period of 28 days or less would be disregarded (para 269).

The routes for partners (paras 271-273F) and children paras 274-276) of retired persons of independent means have also now been closed.

39 Long residence

Indefinite leave to remain on the ground of long residence in the UK may be granted provided that the Secretary of State is satisfied that each of the requirements of paragraph 276B is met (para 276C). Those requirements are that the applicant–

(i) he has had at least ten years continuous lawful residence in the UK; or

(ii) having regard to the public interest there are no reasons why it would be undesirable for him to be given indefinite leave to remain on the ground of long residence, taking into account his–

(a) age;

(b) strength of connections in the UK;

(c) personal history, including character, conduct, associations and employment record;

(d) domestic circumstances;

(e) compassionate circumstances; and

(f) any representations received on the person's behalf;

(iii) does not does not fall for refusal under the general grounds for refusal;

(iv) has sufficient knowledge of the English language and about life in the, in accordance with Appendix KoLL; and

(v) must not be in the UK in breach of immigration laws except that any period of overstaying for a period of 28 days or less will be disregarded, as will any period of overstaying between periods of entry clearance, leave to enter or leave to remain of up to 28 days and any period of overstaying pending the determination of an application made within that 28 day period

"Continuous residence" means residence in the UK for an unbroken period. A period will not be considered to have been broken where an applicant is absent from the UK for a period of six months or less at any one time, provided that the applicant in question has existing limited leave to enter or remain upon their departure and return, but will be considered to have been broken if the applicant (para 276A)–

(a) has been removed under Schedule 2 of the 1971 Act, s.10 of the 1999 Act, has been deported, or has left the UK having been refused leave to enter or remain here;

(b) has left the UK and, on doing so, evidenced a clear intention not to return;

(c) left the UK in circumstances in which he could have had no reasonable expectation at the time of leaving that he would lawfully be able to return;

(d) has been convicted of an offence and was sentenced to a period of imprisonment or was directed to be detained in an institution other than a prison (including, in particular, a hospital or an institution for young offenders), provided that the sentence in question was not a suspended sentence; or

(e) has spent a total of more than 18 months absent from the UK during the period in question.

If requirements (i) and (ii), but not (iii) above, are met, an extension of stay on the ground of long residence in the UK may be granted for a period not exceeding 2 years (para 276A2). In such a case, if the applicant has spent less than 14 years in the UK, the grant of leave should be subject to the same conditions attached to his last period of lawful leave, and if he has spent 14 years or more in the UK, the grant of leave should not contain any restriction on employment (para 276A3).

40 Private life

Limited leave to remain on the grounds of private life in the UK may be granted for a period not exceeding 30 months provided that the Secretary of State is satisfied that the requirements in para 276ADE are met. Such leave will be given subject to a condition of no recourse to public funds unless the Secretary of State considers that the person should not be subject to such a condition (para 276BE), and if the requirements are not met, leave will be refused (para 276CE).

The requirements are that at the date of application, the applicant (para 276ADE)–

(i) does not fall for refusal under any of the grounds in Section S-LTR 1.2 to S-LTR 2.3 and 3.1 to S-LTR.4.4 in Appendix FM; and

(ii) has made a valid application for leave to remain on the grounds of private life in the UK; and

(iii) has lived continuously in the UK for at least 20 years (discounting any period of imprisonment); or

(iv) is under the age of 18 years and has lived continuously in the UK for at least 7 years (discounting any period of imprisonment) and it would not be reasonable to expect the applicant to leave the UK; or

(v) is aged 18 years or above and under 25 years and has spent at least half of his life living continuously in the UK (discounting any period of imprisonment); or

(vi) is aged 18 years or above, has lived continuously in the UK for less than 20 years (discounting any period of imprisonment) but there would be very significant obstacles to the applicant's integration into the country to which he would have to go if required to leave the UK (however this sub-para does not apply, and may not be relied upon, where it is proposed to return a person to a third country under the Asylum and Immigration (Treatment of Claimants, etc) Act 2004, Sch. 3).

Note.–para (vi) does not apply, and may not be relied upon where it is proposed to return a person to a third country under Schedule 3 to the Asylum and Immigration (Treatment of Claimants, etc) Act 2004 (safe countries: see the Note on **Control of Immigration** at para **41 Protection of claimants from deportation**).

Where an applicant does not meet the requirements in para 276ADE but the Secretary of State grants leave to remain outside the rules on Article 8 grounds, the applicant will normally be granted leave for a period not exceeding 30 months and subject to a condition of no recourse to public funds unless the Secretary of State considers that the person should not be subject to such a condition (para 276BE(2)).

Indefinite leave to remain on the grounds of private life in the UK may be granted provided that the Secretary of State is satisfied that each of the requirements of paragraph 276DE is met (para 276DF). Indefinite leave to remain on the grounds of private life in the UK will be refused if the Secretary of State is not satisfied that each of the requirements of paragraph 276DE is met unless the applicant does not meet the requirements for indefinite leave to remain on the grounds of private life in the UK only for one or both of the following reasons–

(a) paragraph S-ILR.1.5. or S-ILR.1.6. in Appendix FM applies (certain past convictions);

(b) the applicant has not met the requirements of paragraphs 33B to 33G of the Rules,

in which case the applicant may be granted further limited leave to remain on the grounds of private life in the UK for a period not exceeding 30 months, and subject to a condition of no recourse to public funds unless the Secretary of State considers that the person should not be subject to such a condition (paras 276DG, 276DH).

The requirements to be met for the grant of indefinite leave to remain on the grounds of private life in the UK are that (para 276DE)–

(a) the applicant has been in the UK with continuous leave on the grounds of private life for a period of at least 120 months;

(b) the applicant meets the requirements of para 276ADE(1), or, in respect of the requirements in para 276ADE(1)(iv) and (v), the applicant met the requirements in a previous application which led to a grant of limited leave to enter or remain under para 276BE(1);

(c) the applicant does not fall for refusal under any of the grounds in Section S-ILR: Suitability- indefinite leave to remain in Appendix FM;

(d) the applicant has sufficient knowledge of the English language and sufficient knowledge about life in the UK, in accordance with Appendix KoLL; and

(e) there are no reasons why it would be undesirable to grant the applicant indefinite leave to remain based on the applicant's conduct, character or associations or because the applicant represents a threat to national security.

41 Former members of HM Forces

From 1 December 2013, Appendix Armed Forces applies to all new applications for leave to enter or remain in the UK.

A person will be refused leave to enter the UK unless (Appendix para 6)–

(a) they have a valid entry clearance for entry in a route under Appendix Armed Forces unless they are–

(i) a non-visa national;

(ii) not seeking entry for a period exceeding 6 months; and

(iii) applying for leave to enter under paras 56, 61B or 64 of Appendix Armed Forces; and

(b) they produce to the Immigration Officer on arrival a valid national passport or other document satisfactorily establishing their identity and nationality.

An application *will* be refused on the grounds of suitability if–

(a) in respect of applications for entry clearance, the Secretary of State has personally directed that the exclusion of the applicant from the UK is conducive to the public good;

(b) the applicant is currently the subject of a deportation order;

(c) subject to (d) below, permitting the applicant to enter, or remain in, the UK is not conducive to the public good because the applicant has been convicted of an offence for which they have been sentenced to a period of imprisonment of–

    (i) at least 4 years; or

    (ii) at least 12 months, but less than 4 years, unless either 10 years (entry clearance) or 15 years (indefinite leave to remain) has passed since the end of the sentence; or

    (iii) less than 12 months, unless: either 5 years (entry clearance) or 7 years (indefinite leave to remain) has passed since the end of the sentence

(d) in respect of applications for entry clearance, where para (c) applies, unless refusal would be contrary to the Human Rights Convention or the Convention and Protocol Relating to the Status of Refugees, it will only be in exceptional circumstances that the public interest in maintaining refusal will be outweighed by compelling factors;

(e) in respect of applications for limited leave to remain or indefinite leave to remain, in the view of the Secretary of State, the applicant's offending has caused serious harm; or he is a persistent offender who shows a particular disregard for the law;

(f) in respect of applications for indefinite leave to remain, the applicant has, within the 24 months prior to the date on which the application is decided, been convicted of or admitted an offence for which they received a non-custodial sentence or other out of court disposal that is recorded on their criminal record;

(g) permitting the applicant to enter, or remain in, the UK is not conducive to the public good because e.g., their conduct (including convictions which do not fall within paras (c) or (f)), character, associations, or other reasons, make it undesirable to grant them entry clearance or allow them to remain in the UK;

(h) in respect of applications for entry clearance, the applicant left or was removed from the UK pursuant to a condition attached to a conditional caution given under the Criminal Justice Act 2003, s.22 less than 5 years before the date on which the application is decided;

(i) the applicant has failed without reasonable excuse to comply with a requirement to attend an interview; provide information or physical data; or undergo a medical examination or provide a medical report; or

(j) it is undesirable to grant entry clearance to the applicant for medical reasons.

An application will *normally* be refused on the grounds of suitability if–

(a) whether or not to the applicant's knowledge, false information, representations or documents have been submitted in relation to the application (including false information submitted to any person to obtain a document used in support of the application); or there has been a failure to disclose material facts in relation to the application;

(b) one or more relevant NHS bodies has notified the Secretary of State that the applicant has failed to pay charges of at least £1,000 in accordance with the relevant NHS regulations on charges to overseas visitors; and

(c) a maintenance and accommodation undertaking has been requested or required and has not been provided;

(d) in respect of applications for entry clearance, the exclusion of the applicant from the UK is conducive to the public good because within the 12 months prior to the date on which the application is decided, the person has been convicted of or admitted an offence for which they received a non-custodial sentence or other out of court disposal that is recorded on their criminal record; or in the view of the Secretary of State the applicant's offending has caused serious harm; or (they are a persistent offender who shows a particular disregard for the law.

An applicant may be refused on grounds of suitability if they have failed to pay litigation costs awarded to the Home Office (Appendix Armed Forces, para 10).

The general eligibility requirements to be met as a discharged member of HM Forces are (Appendix Armed Forces, para 11)–

(a) the applicant has completed at least 4 years' reckonable service in HM Forces; or meets specified medical discharge criteria; and

(b) on the date on which the application is made–

    (i) the applicant has been discharged from HM Forces for a period of less than 2 years; or

    (ii) in the case of an applicant who was medically discharged more than 2 years before, new information regarding his or her prognosis is being considered by the Secretary of State; or

    (iii) the applicant has been granted his or her most recent period of limited leave under Rules or concessions which previously applied; and

(c) in relation to an application made by a Gurkha, he is a citizen or national of Nepal.

The detailed requirements are set out in paras 12 to 19 of Appendix Armed Forces.

The general eligibility requirements to be met by the partner of a member of HM Forces are that on the date the application is made (para 20)–

(a) their sponsor is a member of HM Forces who:
   (i) is exempt from immigration control; or
   (ii) has leave to enter or remain under paras 13-19 of the Appendix or under Rules or concessions which previously applied; or
   (iii) is being granted leave to enter or remain at the same time as the applicant; or
   (iv) is a British Citizen;
(b) the parties are both aged 18 or over; not within a prohibited degree of relationship; intend to live together permanently; and have met in person;
(c) the relationship between them is genuine and subsisting; and
(d) any previous relationship of either of them must have broken down permanently (unless it is polygamous).

The detailed requirements are set out in paras 21 to 33 of the Appendix.

Special provision for bereaved partners of HM forces are contained in paras 34 to 38; and for partners who are the victims of domestic abuse in paras 39 to 41.

The general eligibility requirements to be met by the child of a member of HM Forces are that they are the child of a parent who is (para 42)–
   (i) a foreign or Commonwealth citizen who is a serving member of HM Forces; or
   (ii) a discharged member of HM Forces who has been granted, or who is being granted at the same time as the applicant, leave to enter or remain under paras 13-19 of the Appendix or Rules or concessions which previously applied; or
   (iii) a member of HM Forces who is a British Citizen; and
   they meet one of the following criteria–
   (iv) the applicant's other parent must also come within (i)-(iii) above, or have been granted leave to enter or remain under paras 23-33 of the Appendix or Rules or concessions which previously applied; or be being granted leave to enter or remain under those provisions at the same time as the applicant; or have died; or
   (v) the parent under (i)-(iii) above has sole responsibility for the applicant's upbringing; or
   (vi) there are serious and compelling family or other considerations which make the applicant's exclusion from the UK undesirable and suitable arrangements have been made for their care.

The detailed requirements are set out in paras 43 to 50 of the Appendix; with special provision for bereaved children of members of HM forces in paras 51 to 54.

Provision for members of foreign armed forces invited to undergo training in the UK are contained in paras 55 to 61; and for civilian staff in paras 61A to 61D. Dependants of these two categories are dealt with by paras 62 to 67.

Where English language or financial requirements apply, these are set out in paras 68 to 81.

42 Relevant Afghan citizens

Limited leave to enter the UK for a period not exceeding 5 years may be granted to relevant Afghan citizens i.e., a person who is in Afghanistan, is an Afghan citizen; is aged 18 years or over; was employed in Afghanistan directly by the Ministry of Defence, the Foreign and Commonwealth Office or the Department for International Development, was made redundant on or after 19 December 2012; and who the relevant Ministry or Department has determined should qualify for the resettlement redundancy package as described in the written Ministerial statement of the Secretary of State for Defence dated 4th June 2013.

See further paras 276BA1 to 276BV1 of the Rules.

43 Authorities

Statutory Instruments, etc–

Statement of Changes in Immigration Rules (HC 395–23rd May 1994 as amended by Cmnd 2663, HC 797, Cmnd 3073, HC 274, HC 329, Cmnd 3365, HC 31, HC 338, Cmnd 3369, HC 26, HC 161, Cmnd 3953, Cmnd 4065, HC 22, HC 704, Cmnd 4851, Cmnd 5253, HC 735, Cmnd 5597, HC 1301, HC 104, HC 180, HC 489, HC 538, Cmnd 5829, Cmnd 5949, HC 1224, HC 95, HC 176, HC 370, HC 464, HC 523, Cmnd 6297, Cmnd 6339, HC 1112, HC 164, HC 194, HC 302, HC 346, HC 486, HC 104, HC 299, HC 582, HC 645, HC 697, HC 769, HC 819, HC 949, HC 974, HC 1016, HC 1053, HC 1337, Cmnd 6918, HC 1702, HC 130, HC 398, Cmnd 7074, Cmnd 7075, HC 28, HC 40, HC 82, HC 321, HC 420, HC 607, HC 951, HC 971, HC 1113, HC 227, HC 314, HC413, Cmnd 7701, Cmnd 7711, HC 120, HC 367, HC 439, HC 59, HC 96, HC 382, Cmnd 7929, Cmnd 7944, HC698, HC863, HC908, HC1148, HC1436, HC 1511, HC1622, HC1693, HC1719, HC1733, HC1888, Cmnd 8337, HC194, Cmnd 8423, HC514, HC565, HC760, 820, HC847, HC943, HC967, HC1038, HC1039, Cmnd 8599, HC244, HC628, HC803, HC887, HC901, HC938, HC1130, HC1138, HC1201, HC198, HC532. HC693, HC1025, HC1116, HC297, HC 437, HC535, HC877)

THE IMMIGRATION RULES: REFUSAL OF ENTRY, LEAVE TO REMAIN ETC AND DEPORTATION

1 Introduction

This Note deals with those provisions of the Statement of Changes in Immigration Rules ("the Rules") which relate to refusal of leave to enter or remain the UK, and deportation.

A: GENERAL GROUNDS FOR REFUSAL OF ENTRY CLEARANCE, LEAVE TO ENTER OR VARIATION OF LEAVE TO ENTER OR REMAIN

2 Exclusions

Part 9 of the Rules (paras A320-324) (except for paragraph 322(1)) does not apply to an application for leave to remain on the grounds of private life under paragraphs 276ADE-276DH (para B320).

Paras 320 (except subparagraph (3), (10) and (11)) and 322 do not apply to an application for entry clearance, leave to enter or leave to remain as a Family Member under Appendix FM (para A320).

3 Refusal of entry clearance or leave to enter

Visa nationals will need to obtain a visa or entry clearance before arrival; non-visa nationals may request entry on arrival. This Paragraph deals with a refusal to issue a visa or entry clearance before arrival and refusal of leave to enter which is requested on arrival.

In addition to grounds for refusal of entry clearance or leave to enter set out above and subject to paragraph 321 (see below), the following grounds for refusal of entry clearance or leave to enter apply (para 320).

Grounds on which entry clearance or leave to enter must be refused.–

(1) entry is being sought for a purpose not covered by the Rules;

(2) the fact that the person seeking entry to the UK is currently the subject of a deportation order or has been convicted to an offence and been imprisoned and less than a specified time has passed since the end of that sentence (where this paragraph applies, unless refusal would be contrary to the Human Rights Convention or the Convention and Protocol Relating to the Status of Refugees, it will only be in exceptional circumstances that the public interest in maintaining refusal will be outweighed by compelling factors);

(2A) failure, if required to do so, by a person seeking entry to the UK to provide a criminal record certificate from the relevant authority in any country in which they have been resident for 12 months or more, in the past 10 years. Such evidence will not normally be required where. the applicant is aged 17 years old or under at the date the application is made; or it is not reasonably practicable for the applicant to obtain such evidence from the relevant authorities;

(3) failure by the person seeking entry to produce a valid national passport or other document satisfactorily establishing his identity and nationality (unless stateless);

(4) failure to satisfy the Immigration Officer, in the case of a person arriving in the UK or seeking entry through the Channel Tunnel with the intention of entering any other part of the common travel area, that he is acceptable to the immigration authorities there;

(5) failure, in the case of a visa national, to produce to the Immigration Officer a passport or other identity document endorsed with a valid and current UK entry clearance issued for the purpose for which entry is sought;

(6) where the Secretary of State has personally directed that the exclusion of a person from the UK is conducive to the public good;

(7) save in relation to a person settled in the UK or where the immigration Officer is satisfied that there are strong compassionate reasons justifying admission, confirmation from the Medical Inspector that, for medical reasons, it is undesirable to admit a person seeking leave to enter the UK;

(7A) where false representations have been made or false documents or information have been submitted (whether or not material to the application, and whether or not to the applicant's knowledge), or material facts have not been disclosed, in relation to the application, or in order to obtain documents from the Secretary of State or a third party required in support of the application.

(7B) where the applicant has previously breached the UK's immigration laws (and was 18 or over at the time of his most recent breach) by–

    (a) overstaying;

    (b) breaching a condition attached to his leave;

    (c) being an illegal entrant;

    (d) using deception in an application for entry clearance, leave to enter or remain, or in order to obtain documents from the Secretary of State or a third party required in support of the application (whether successful or not);

unless the applicant–

(i) overstayed for 90 days or less and left the UK voluntarily, not at the expense (directly or indirectly) of the Secretary of State;

(ii) used deception in an application for entry clearance more than 10 years ago;

(iii) left the UK voluntarily, not at the expense (directly or indirectly) of the Secretary of State, more than 12 months ago;

(iv) left the UK voluntarily, at the expense (directly or indirectly) of the Secretary of State, more than 2 years ago; and the date the person left the UK was no more than 6 months after the date on which he was given notice of liability for removal, or no more than 6 months after the date on which he no longer had a pending appeal or administrative review; whichever is the later;

(v) left the UK voluntarily, at the expense (directly or indirectly) of the Secretary of State, more than 5 years ago;

(vi) was removed or deported from the UK more than 10 years ago; or

(vii) left or was removed from the UK as a condition of a caution issued in accordance with s.22 of the Criminal Justice Act 2003 more than five years ago.

Where more than one breach of the UK's immigration laws has occurred, only the breach which leads to the longest period of absence from the UK is relevant.

(7C) *deleted*

(7D) failure, without providing a reasonable explanation, to comply with a request made on behalf of the Entry Clearance Officer to attend for interview.

Grounds on which entry clearance or leave to enter should normally be refused.–

(8) failure by a person arriving in the UK to provide the information necessary to decide whether he needs leave to enter and if so, on what terms;

(8A) where the person seeking leave is outside the UK, failure by him to supply any information, documents, copy documents or medical report requested by an Immigration Officer;

(9) failure by a person seeking leave to enter as a returning resident to satisfy an immigration officer that he meets the requirements of paragraph 18 or that he seeks leave to enter for the same purpose as that for which his earlier leave was granted (see the Note on **The Immigration Rules: Introduction and Leave to enter the UK (outside the points based system)** at para **8 Returning residents**, above);

(10) production of a passport or travel document issued by an authority which the British government does not recognise or which does not accept valid UK passports for its own immigration control, or a passport or travel document which does not comply with international practice;

(11) where the applicant has previously contrived in a significant way to frustrate the intentions of the Rules by–

(i) overstaying; or

(ii) breaching a condition attached to his leave; or

(iii) being an illegal entrant; or

(iv) using deception in an application for entry clearance, leave to enter or remain or in order to obtain documents from the Secretary of State or a third party required in support of the application (whether successful or not); and

there are other aggravating circumstances, such as absconding, not meeting temporary admission/reporting restrictions or bail conditions, using an assumed identity or multiple identities, switching nationality, making frivolous applications or not complying with the re-documentation process;

(12) *deleted*

(13) failure, except by a person eligible for admission for settlement, to prove that he will be admitted to another country after his stay in the UK;

(14) refusal by a sponsor to give a written undertaking to be responsible for the applicant's maintenance and accommodation;

(15) *deleted*

(16) failure, in the case of a child aged under 18, to provide written consent from his parents to his application, except in the case of an asylum seeker;

(17) failure to undergo a medical examination if requested, unless the applicant is settled in the UK;

(18) *deleted;*

(18A) within the 12 months prior to the date on which the application is decided, the person has been convicted of or admitted an offence for which they received a non-custodial sentence or other out of court disposal that is recorded on their criminal record;

(18B) in the view of the Secretary of State (a) the person's offending has caused serious harm; or (b) the person is a persistent offender who shows a particular disregard for the law.

(19) the immigration officer deems the exclusion of the person from the UK to be conducive to the public good e.g., because the person's conduct (including convictions which do not fall within paragraph 320(2)), character, associations, or other reasons, make it undesirable to grant them leave to enter;

(20) failure to comply with any requirement as to the provision of physical data (see the Note on **Control of Immigration** at para **5 Fingerprints and other physical data**);

(21) *deleted.*

(22) where an NHS body has notified the Secretary of State that the person seeking entry or leave to enter has failed to pay a charge or charges with a total value of at least £500 in accordance with the relevant

NHS regulations on charges to overseas visitors;

(23) failure to pay litigation costs awarded to the Home Office.

4 Refusal of leave to enter in relation to a person in possession of an entry clearance

A person seeking leave to enter on arrival who already holds a current entry clearance may be refused leave to enter only where the immigration officer is satisfied that (para 321)–

(1) whether or not to the holder's knowledge, false representations were made or false documents were submitted or material facts were not disclosed in relation to the application for entry clearance, or in order to obtain documents from the Secretary of State or a third party required in support of the application;

(2) a change of circumstances since it was issued has removed the holder's claim for admission (except where that change amounts solely to the person becoming over age for entry in one of the categories mentioned n paragraphs 296 to 316 of the Rules (children and adopted children seeking leave to enter or remain, see above); or

(3) refusal is justified on grounds of restricted returnability; on medical grounds; on grounds of criminal record; because the person seeking leave to enter is the subject of a deportation order, or because exclusion would be conducive to the public good.

In addition, leave to enter or remain will be cancelled at a port or whilst the holder is outside the UK if (para 321A)–

(1) there has been such a change in the circumstances of that person's case since the leave was given, that it should be cancelled; or

(2) false representations were made or false documents or information were submitted (whether or not material to the application, and whether or not to the holder's knowledge), or material facts were not disclosed, in relation to the application for leave, or in order to obtain documents from the Secretary of State or a third party required in support of the application;

(3) save in relation to a person settled in the UK or where the Immigration Officer or the Secretary of State is satisfied that there are strong compassionate reasons justifying admission, where it is apparent that, for medical reasons, it is undesirable to admit that person to the UK;

(4) where the Secretary of State has personally directed that the exclusion of that person from the UK is conducive to the public good;

(4A) grounds which would have led to a refusal under paras 320(2), 320(6), 320(18A), 320(18B) or 320(19) if the person concerned were making a new application for leave to enter or remain;

(5) the Immigration Officer or the Secretary of State deems the exclusion of the person from the UK to be conducive to the public good e.g., because the person's conduct (including convictions which do not fall within paragraph 320(2)), character, associations, or other reasons, make it undesirable to grant them leave to enter the UK; or

(6) where that person is outside the UK, failure by that person to supply any information, documents, copy documents or medical report requested by an Immigration Officer or the Secretary of State.

5 Refusal of leave or curtailment of leave

In addition to the grounds for refusal set out in the previous parts of the Rules, the following provisions apply in relation to an application for leave to remain, variation of leave to enter or remain or, where appropriate, the curtailment of leave.

[*Note* that only paras 322(1A), (1B), (5), (5A), (9) and (10) apply in the case of an application made under para 159I of the Rules – victims of slavery or human trafficking].

Variation of leave to enter or remain *must* be refused if–

(a) it is being sought for a purpose not covered by the Rules (para 322(1));

(b) where false representations have been made or false documents or information have been submitted (whether or not material to the application, and whether or not to the applicant's knowledge), or material facts have not been disclosed, in relation to the application or in order to obtain documents from the Secretary of State or a third party required in support of the application (para 322(1A));

(c) the applicant is, at the date of application, the subject of a deportation order or a decision to make a deportation order (para 322(1B)); or

(d) where the person is seeking indefinite leave to enter or remain (para 322(1C))–

(i) has been convicted of an offence for which they have been sentenced to imprisonment for at least 4 years; or

(ii) has been convicted of an offence for which they have been sentenced to imprisonment for at least 12 months but less than 4 years, unless a period of 15 years has passed since the end of the sentence; or

(iii) has been convicted of an offence for which they have been sentenced to imprisonment for less than 12 months, unless a period of 7 years has passed since the end of the sentence; or

(iv) has, within the 24 months prior to the date on which the application is decided, been convicted of or admitted an offence for which they have received a non-custodial sentence or other out of court disposal that is recorded on their criminal record

Variation of leave to enter or remain *should normally* be refused for (para 322(2)-(12))–

(1) false representations or failure to disclose material facts;

(2) failure to comply with conditions attached to the leave;

(3) failure by the person concerned to maintain or accommodate himself and any dependants without recourse to public funds;

(4) the undesirability of permitting the person concerned to remain in the UK in the light of his character, conduct or associations, the fact that he represents a threat to national security; because his offending has caused serious harm, or because they are a persistent offender who shows a particular disregard for the law;

(5) refusal by a sponsor to give a written undertaking to be responsible for maintenance and accommodation, or a failure to honour such an undertaking, once given;

(6) failure by the person concerned to honour a declaration or undertaking as to the intended duration and/or purpose of his stay;

(7) failure, except by a person who qualifies for settlement in the UK or by the spouse/civil partner of a person settled in the UK, to prove that he will be returnable to another country after the stay in the UK;

(8) failure to produce evidence, within a reasonable time, establishing a claim to remain;

(9) failure to attend for interview without reasonable excuse;

(10) failure of a child aged under 18 seeking a variation of his leave to produce written consent from his parents to the application, except in the case of an asylum seeker;

(11) where an NHS body has notified the Secretary of State that the person seeking leave has failed to pay a charge or charges with a total value of at least £500 in accordance with the relevant NHS regulations on charges to overseas visitors;

(12) failure to pay litigation costs awarded to the Home Office.

Leave may be curtailed on any of grounds (1) to (4) above or if the applicant (para 323)–

(ia) uses deception in seeking (whether successfully or not) leave to remain or a variation of leave to remain;

(i) ceases to meet the requirements under which the leave was granted;

(ii) is the dependent of an asylum claimant whose claim has been refused and whose leave has been curtailed and who does not qualify for leave to remain in his own right or on any of the grounds set out in paragraphs 339A(i)-(vi) and 339G(i)-(vi);

(iii) within the first 6 months of being granted leave to enter, commits an offence for which they are subsequently sentenced to a period of imprisonment;

(iv) was granted his current period of leave as the dependent of a person and that person leave to enter or remain is being, or has been, curtailed; or

(v) if, without a reasonable explanation, he fails to comply with a request made by or on behalf of the Secretary of State.

In addition, the leave to enter or remain of a Tier 2, Tier 4, or Tier 5 Migrant will be curtailed (para 323A)–

(a) in the case of a Tier 2 or Tier 5 Migrant–

(1) the migrant fails to commence, or

(2) the migrant ceases, or will cease, before the end date recorded on the Certificate of Sponsorship Checking Service, the employment, volunteering, training or job shadowing (as the case may be) that the migrant has been sponsored to do.

(b) in the case of a Tier 4 Migrant:

(1) the migrant fails to commence studying with the sponsor, or

(2) the sponsor has excluded or withdrawn the migrant, or the migrant has withdrawn, from the course of studies, or

(2A) the migrant's course of study has ceased, or will cease, before the end date recorded on the Certificate of Sponsorship Checking Service, or

(3) the sponsor withdraws their sponsorship of a migrant on the doctorate extension scheme, or

(4) the sponsor withdraws their sponsorship of a migrant who, having completed a pre-sessional course as provided in paragraph 120(b) (i) of Appendix A, does not have a knowledge of English equivalent to level B2 of the Council of Europe's Common European Framework for Language Learning in all four components (reading, writing, speaking and listening) or above.

Leave to enter or remain of a Tier 2, Tier 4, or Tier 5 Migrant may be curtailed if (para 323A)–

(a) the migrant's sponsor ceases to have a sponsor licence (for whatever reason);

(b) the migrant's sponsor transfers the business for which the migrant works or at which the migrant is studying to another person who does not have a sponsor licence and who fails to apply for a licence within 28 days of the date of the transfer of the business, or applies for a sponsor licence but is refused, or applies for a licence and is granted one, but not in a category that would allow it to issue a Certificate of Sponsorship to the migrant;

(c) the migrant fails to commence or ceases working for the sponsor; or

(d) in the case of a Tier 2 or Tier 5 Migrant, if the employment that the Certificate of Sponsorship Checking Service records that the migrant is being sponsored to do undergoes a prohibited change as specified in para 323AA; or

(e) (iv) above applies but–

(1) the migrant is under the age of 18;

(2) the migrant has a dependant child under the age of 18;

(3) leave is to be varied such that when the variation takes effect the migrant will have leave to enter or remain and the migrant has less than 60 days extant leave remaining;

(4) the migrant has been granted leave to enter or remain with another Sponsor or under another immigration category; or

(5) the migrant has a pending application for leave to remain, or variation of leave, with the Home Office, or has a pending appeal under s.82 of the Nationality, Immigration and Asylum Act 2002.

For the purposes of (d) above the prohibited changes (unless a further application for leave to remain is granted which expressly permits the changes) are (para 323AA)–

(a) The migrant is absent from work without pay for 30 days or more in total (whether over a single period or more than one period), during any calendar year (1 January to 31 December), unless the absence from work is due solely to–

(i) maternity leave,

(ii) paternity leave,

(iii) adoption leave, or

(iv) long term sick leave of one calendar month or more during any one period.

(b) The employment changes such that the migrant is working for a different employer or Sponsor, unless:

(i) the migrant is a Tier 5 (Temporary Worker) Migrant in the Government Authorised Exchange sub-category and the change of employer is authorised by the Sponsor and under the terms of the work, volunteering or job shadowing that the Certificate of Sponsorship Checking Service records that the migrant is being sponsored to do,

(ii) the migrant is working for a different Sponsor under arrangements covered by the Transfer of Undertakings (Protection of Employment) Regulations 2006 or similar protection to continue in the same job, or

(iii) the migrant is a Tier 2 (Sportsperson) Migrant or a Tier 5 (Temporary Worker) Migrant in the creative and sporting sub-category and the following conditions are met–

(1) The migrant's sponsor is a sports club;

(2) The migrant is sponsored as a player only and is being temporarily loaned as a player to another sports club;

(3) Player loans are specifically permitted in rules set down by the relevant sports governing body listed in Appendix M;

(4) The migrant's sponsor has made arrangements with the loan club to enable the sponsor to continue to meet its sponsor duties; and

(5) The migrant will return to working for the sponsor at the end of the loan.

(c) The employment changes to a job in a different Standard Occupational Classification (SOC) code to that recorded by the Certificate of Sponsorship Checking Service.

(d) If the migrant is a Tier 2 (Intra-Company Transfer) Migrant or a Tier 2 (General) Migrant, the employment changes to a different job in the same Standard Occupational Classification code to that recorded by the Certificate of Sponsorship Checking Service, and the gross annual salary (including such allowances as are specified as acceptable for this purpose in Appendix A) is below the appropriate salary rate for that new job as specified in the Codes of Practice in Appendix J.

(e) If the migrant was required to be Sponsored for a job at a minimum National Qualification Framework level in the application which led to his last grant of entry clearance or leave to remain, the employment changes to a job which the Codes of Practice in Appendix J record as being at a lower level.

(f) If the migrant is a Tier 2 (General) Migrant and scored points from the shortage occupation provisions of Appendix A, the employment changes to a job which does not appear in the Shortage Occupation List in Appendix K.

(g) Except where (h) applies, the gross annual salary (including such allowances as are specified as acceptable for this purpose in Appendix A) reduces below–

(i) any minimum salary threshold specified in Appendix A of the Rules, where the applicant was subject to or relied on that threshold in the application which led to his current grant of entry clearance or leave to remain, or

(ii) the appropriate salary rate for the job as specified in the Codes of Practice in Appendix J, or

(iii) in cases where there is no applicable threshold in Appendix A and no applicable salary rate in Appendix J, the salary recorded by the Certificate of Sponsorship Checking Service.

(h) Other reductions in salary are permitted if the reduction coincides with a period of:

(i) maternity leave,

(ii) paternity leave,

(iii) adoption leave,

(iv) long term sick leave of one calendar month or more,

(v) working for the sponsor's organisation while the migrant is not physically present in the UK, if the migrant is a Tier 2 (Intra-Company Transfer) Migrant, or

(vi) undertaking professional examinations before commencing work for the sponsor, where such examinations are a regulatory requirement of the job the migrant is being sponsored to do, and providing the migrant continues to be sponsored during that period.

In addition, leave to enter or remain as a Tier 1 (Exceptional Talent) Migrant may be curtailed if the Designated Competent Body that endorsed the application which led to the migrant's current grant of leave withdraws its endorsement (para 323B).

In addition leave to enter or remain as a Tier 1 (Graduate Entrepreneur) Migrant may be curtailed if the endorsing institution that endorsed the application which led to the migrant's current grant of leave (para 323C)—

(a) loses its status as an endorsing institution for Tier 1 (Graduate Entrepreneur) Migrants,

(b) ceases to be a sponsor with Tier 4 Sponsor status,

(c) ceases to be an A-rated Sponsor under Tier 2 or Tier 5 of the Points-Based System because its Tier 2 or Tier 5 Sponsor licence is downgraded or revoked by the Home Office, or

(d) withdraws its endorsement of the migrant.

6 Crew members

A person who has been given leave to enter to join a ship, aircraft, hovercraft, hydrofoil, or international train service as a crew member, or a crew member given leave to enter for hospital treatment, repatriation, or transfer to another of the above-mentioned passenger-carrying vehicles, will be refused leave to remain unless an extension of stay is necessary to fulfil the purpose for which he was given leave to enter or he meets the requirements for an extension of stay as a spouse/civil partner in paragraph 284 (see the Note on **The Immigration Rules: Family Members** at para **4 Spouses and civil partners of persons present and settled in the UK or being admitted on the same occasion for settlement**) (para 324).

7 Service of notices

Notices of appealable immigration decisions are served under the Immigration (Notices) Regulations 2003. Notices of non-appealable immigration decisions which grant or refuse leave to remain, vary leave to remain or refuse to vary leave to remain are served under the Immigration (Leave to Enter and Remain) Order 2000.

A notice in writing (Appendix SN)—

(a) that an application for entry clearance, leave to enter or leave to remain in the UK is invalid;

(b) that an application for entry clearance, leave to enter or leave to remain in the UK is void;

(c) that an application for administrative review is invalid; or

(d) notifying a person of the outcome of an administrative review application,

may be given to the person affected by hand; by fax; by post to an address provided for correspondence by the person or their representative; sent electronically to an e-mail address provided for correspondence by the person or their representative; sent by document exchange to a document exchange number or address; or sent by courier. Where no postal or e-mail address for correspondence has been provided, the notice may be sent by post to the last-known or usual place of abode, place of study or place of business of the person; or the last-known or usual place of business of their representative; or electronically to the last-known e-mail address for the person (including at their last-known place of study or place of business); or the last-known e-mail address of their representative.

Where it is not possible to give notice as above, or where an attempt to do so has failed, and the decision-maker records the reason for this and places the notice on file, the notice is deemed to have been given on the day that it is placed on file (if the person is subsequently located, they must as soon as is practicable be given a copy of the notice).

B: DEPORTATION AND ADMINISTRATIVE REMOVAL

8 Deportation Orders

A deportation order requires the person to leave the UK and authorises his detention until he is removed. It also prohibits him from re-entering the country for as long as it is in force and invalidates any leave to enter or remain (para 362).

Where Article 8 is raised in the context of deportation, the claim under Article 8 will only succeed where the requirements of the Immigration Rules are met (para A362)

The circumstances in which a person is liable to deportation include (para 363)—

(i) where the Secretary of State deems the person's deportation to be conducive to the public good;

(ii) where the person is a spouse/civil partner or child under 18 of the person to be deported; and

(iii) where a court recommends deportation in the case of a person over the age of 17 who has been convicted of an offence punishable with imprisonment.

A deportation order will not be made against any person if his removal under the order would be contrary to the United Nations Convention and Protocol relating to the Status of Refugees or the European Convention on Human Rights (para 380).

Where deportation or removal is a possibility, expert advice should be sought regarding the current Home Office policies on deportation, which are not published, but have been circulated, and to which the Home Office must have regard when considering a deportation or removal (*R v SSHD ex p Amankwah* [1993] CO/2114/92). These policies may be more generous than the immigration rules appear.

9 Family members

The Secretary of State will not normally deport the spouse/civil partner of a deportee under the Immigration Act 1971, s.5 where he or she has qualified for settlement in his or her own right or has been living apart from the deportee (para 365), nor will he normally deport a child under that provision where he and his mother or father are living apart from the deportee, or he has left home and has established himself on an independent basis, or has married/formed a civil partnership before deportation came into prospect (para 366).

10 Procedure

When a decision to make a deportation order has been taken (otherwise than on the recommendation of a court), a notice must be given to the person concerned informing him of the (para 381).

Following the issue of such a notice the Secretary of State may authorise detention, or make an order restricting a person as to residence, employment, or occupation and requiring him to report to the police, pending the making of a deportation order (para 382).

11 Arrangements for removal

Normally, a deportee will be returned to the country of which he is a national or which has most recently provided him with a travel document unless he can show that another country will receive him. In considering any departure from the normal arrangements, regard will be had to the public interest generally, and to any additional expense that may fall on public funds (para 385). A person who returns to the UK whilst a deportation order is in force against him may be deported under the original order. The Secretary of State will consider every such case in the light of the relevant circumstances before deciding whether to enforce the order (para 388).

12 Returned family members and revocation of order

If family members are deported with a principal deportee, a deported wife/civil partner may return if the marriage/civil partnership comes to an end and a deported child may return when he reaches age 18 (para 389).

An application for revocation of a deportation order will be considered in the light of all the relevant circumstances, including, the grounds on which the order was made and any compassionate grounds.

In the case of an applicant who has been deported following conviction for a criminal offence continued exclusion–

(i) in the case of a conviction which is capable of being spent under the Rehabilitation of Offenders Act 1974, unless the conviction is spent within the meaning of that Act or, if the conviction is spent in less than 10 years, 10 years have elapsed since the making of the deportation order when, if an application for revocation is received, consideration will be given on a case by case basis to whether the deportation order should be maintained; or

(ii) in the case of a conviction not capable of being spent under that Act, at any time, unless refusal to revoke the deportation order would be contrary to the Human Rights Convention or the Convention and Protocol Relating to the Status of Refugees

will normally be the proper course. In other cases, unless the situation has materially altered, the order will not usually be revoked, and except in the most exceptional circumstances, revocation will not be ordered until at least three years have passed since the deportation order was made. Revocation does not entitle the person to re-enter the UK; it renders him eligible to apply for admission under the Rules. Application for revocation of the order may be made to the Home Office (paras. 390 to 392).

13 Administrative removal

A person is now liable to administrative removal in certain circumstances in which he would previously have been liable to deportation. These circumstances are set out in s.10 of the 1999 Act, as to which see the Note on **Control of Immigration** at para **29 Administrative removal and deportation**.

14 Article 8 of the Human Rights Convention

Where a foreign criminal liable to deportation claims that his deportation would be contrary to the UK's obligations under Article 8 of the Human Rights Convention; or a foreign criminal applies for a deportation order made against him to be revoked, and in either case the deportation is conducive to the public good and in the public interest because (paras A398 and 398) –

(A) they have been convicted of an offence for which they have been sentenced to a period of imprisonment of at least 4 years;

(B) they have been convicted of an offence for which they have been sentenced to a period of imprisonment of less than 4 years but at least 12 months; or

(C) in the view of the Secretary of State, their offending has caused serious harm or they are a persistent offender who shows a particular disregard for the law, then the Secretary of State in assessing that claim will consider whether either para 399 or 399A applies and, if it does not, the public interest in deportation will only be outweighed by other factors where there are very compelling circumstances over and above those described in paras 399 and 399A

Para 399 applies where (B) or (C) above applies and the person to be deported has—

(a) a genuine and subsisting parental relationship with a child under the age of 18 years who is in the UK, and either the child is a British Citizen; or has lived in the UK continuously for at least the 7 years immediately preceding the date of the immigration decision; and in either case—

    (i) it would be unduly harsh for the child to live in the country to which the person is to be deported; and

    (ii) it would be unduly harsh for the child to remain in the UK without the person who is to be deported; or

(b) a genuine and subsisting relationship with a partner who is in the UK and is a British Citizen or settled in the UK, and—

    (i) the relationship was formed at a time when the person (deportee) was in the UK lawfully and their immigration status was not precarious; and

    (ii) it would be unduly harsh for that partner to live in the country to which the person is to be deported, because of compelling circumstances over and above those described in paragraph EX.2. of Appendix FM; and

    (iii) it would be unduly harsh for that partner to remain in the UK without the person who is to be deported.

Para 399A applies where (B) or (C) above applies and the person to be deported has—

(a) been lawfully resident in the UK for most of his life; and

(b) is socially and culturally integrated in the UK; and

(c) there would be very significant obstacles to his integration into the country to which it is proposed he is deported

Where an Article 8 claim from a foreign criminal is successful then (para 399B)—

(a) in the case of a person who is in the UK unlawfully or whose leave to enter or remain has been cancelled by a deportation order, limited leave may be granted for periods not exceeding 30 months and subject to such conditions as the Secretary of State considers appropriate;

(b) in the case of a person who has not been served with a deportation order, any limited leave to enter or remain may be curtailed to a period not exceeding 30 months and conditions may be varied to such conditions as the Secretary of State considers appropriate;

(c) indefinite leave to enter or remain may be revoked under s.76 of the 2002 Act and limited leave to enter or remain granted for a period not exceeding 30 months subject to such conditions as the Secretary of State considers appropriate;

(d) revocation of a deportation order does not confer entry clearance or leave to enter or remain or re-instate any previous leave.

Where a foreign criminal who has previously been granted a period of limited leave under these provisions applies for further limited leave or indefinite leave to remain, his deportation remains conducive to the public good and in the public interest notwithstanding the previous grant of leave (para 399C).

Where a foreign criminal has been deported and enters the UK in breach of the order, enforcement of the deportation order is in the public interest and will be implemented unless there are very exceptional circumstances (para 399D)

Where a person claims that their removal under paras 8 to 10 of Schedule 2 to the Immigration Act 1971, s.10 of the Immigration and Asylum Act 1999 or s.47 of the Immigration, Asylum and Nationality Act 2006 would be contrary to the UK's obligations under Article 8 of the Human Rights Convention, the Secretary of State may require an application under para 276ADE(1) (private life) or under para R-LTRP.1.1.(a), (b) and (d), R-LTRPT.1.1.(a), (b) and (d) and EX.1.of Appendix FM (family life as a partner or parent) of the rules. Where an application is not required, in assessing that claim the Secretary of State or an immigration officer will, subject to para 353, consider that claim against the requirements to be met (except the requirement to make a valid application) under those paragraph of the rules as appropriate and if appropriate the removal decision will be cancelled (para 400).

C: ADMINISTRATIVE REVIEW

15 Introduction

Administrative Review is a process whereby an applicant whose application for entry clearance or leave to remain has been refused can request that the refusal be reconsidered on the grounds that it was not in accordance with the relevant facts and laws i.e., there has been a case working error. The procedure for making an application is set out in paras 34N-34S of the Rules.

An application for administrative review cannot be made if an administrative review waiver form has previously been signed (para 34N(3)), or if, after receiving notice of the eligible decision, an application for entry clearance, leave to enter or leave to remain is made during the time within which an application for administrative review could have been brought (para 34N(4)).

16 Decisions eligible for administrative review in the UK

Administrative review is only available in relation to a decision to–
- refuse an application for leave to remain; or
- grant leave to remain where the review is of the period or conditions of leave granted.

The decisions for which a review can be requested are decisions (Appendix AR, para AR3)–

(a) for leave to remain as a Tier 4 Migrant under the Points Based System; or the partner or child of a Tier 4 Migrant;

(b) for leave to remain, as a Tier 1, 2 or 5 Migrant or the partner or child of such a migrant;

(c) on an application for leave to remain unless–
- it is an application as a visitor, or
- it is an application or human rights claim made under–
    - para 276B (long residence);
    - paras 276ADE(1) or 276DE (private life);
    - paras 276U and 276AA (partner or child of a member of HM Forces);
    - paras 276AD and 276AG (partner or child of a member of HM Forces) where the sponsor is a foreign or Commonwealth member of HM Forces and has at least 4 years' reckonable service in HM Forces at the date of application;
    - Part 8 (family members) where the sponsor is present and settled in the UK (unless the application is made under paras 319AA to 319J or paras 284, 287, 295D or 295G where the sponsor was granted settlement as a Points Based System Migrant) or has refugee or humanitarian protection status in the UK;
    - Part 11 (asylum);
    - Part 4 or Part 7 of Appendix Armed Forces (partner or child of a member of HM Forces) where the sponsor is a British Citizen or has at least 4 years' reckonable service in HM Forces at the date of application;
    - Appendix FM (family members), but not where an application is made under section BPILR (bereavement) or section DVILR (domestic violence), in which case the appropriate remedy is an appeal under s.82 of the Nationality, Immigration and Asylum Act 2002 rather than an application for administrative review.

(d) on applications for leave to remain made by a Turkish national or their family member pursuant to the UK's obligations under the Additional Protocol to the European Community Association Agreement (ECAA) with Turkey.

An application for an administrative review must be made within 14 days of getting the decision letter (7 days if the applicant is in detention). If the application for review is as to the amount or conditions of leave, it must be made within 14 days of getting a biometric residence permit.

17 Decisions eligible for administrative review outside the UK

Administrative review is only available in relation to a decision to refuse an application for entry clearance.

Administrative review is not available in the following cases (where the appropriate remedy is an appeal under s.82 of the Nationality, Immigration and Asylum Act 2002 instead): where the application was made (Appendix AR, para AR5)–

(a) under Part 3 (short-term students);

(b) as a visitor;

(c) under
- paras 276R and 276X (partner or child of a member of HM Forces);
- paras276AD and 276AG (partner or child of a member of HM Forces) where the sponsor is a foreign or Commonwealth member of HM Forces and has at least 4 years' reckonable service in HM Forces at the date of application;
- Part 8 (family members) where the sponsor is present and settled in the UK (unless the application is made under paras 319AA to 319J) or has refugee or humanitarian protection status in the UK;
- Part 4 or Part 7 of Appendix Armed Forces (partner or child of a member of HM Forces) where the sponsor is a British Citizen or has at least 4 years' reckonable service in HM Forces at the date of application;
- Appendix FM (family members),

Application for administrative review may also be made in relation to a refusal of an application for entry clearance made by a Turkish national or their family member pursuant to the UK's obligations under the Additional Protocol to the European Community Association Agreement (ECAA) with Turkey.

An application for an administrative review must be made within 28 days of getting the decision letter.

18 Decisions eligible for administrative review on arrival in the UK

Administrative review is only available against a decision to cancel a leave to enter or remain with the result that the applicant has no leave to enter or remain, and the reason for cancellation is that (Appendix AR, para AR4)–

(a) there has been such a change of circumstances in the applicant's case since leave was given that it should be cancelled; or

(b) the leave was obtained as a result of false information given by the applicant or the applicant's failure to disclose material facts.

19 Withdrawn applications

An application for administrative review which may only be brought from within the UK and which has not been determined will be treated as withdrawn if the applicant requests the return of their passport for the purpose of travel outside the UK.

An application which may only be brought from within the UK and which has not been determined will be treated as withdrawn if the applicant leaves the UK.

An application for administrative review which has not been determined will be treated as withdrawn if the applicant makes an application for entry clearance, leave to enter or leave to remain (para 34X).

20 Authorities

Statutory Instruments, etc–

Immigration (Leave to Enter and Remain) Order 2000, as amended (S.I. 2000 No. 1161, 2004 No. 475, 2005 No. 1159, 2010 No. 957,2013 No. 1749, and 2015 No. 434)

Immigration (Notices) Regulations 2003, as amended (S.I. 2003 No. 658, 2006 No. 2168, 2007 No. 3187, 2008 Nos. 684 and 1819, 2009 No. 1117, 2012 No. 1547, 2013 No. 793, and 2014 No. 2768

Statement of Changes in Immigration Rules (HC 395–23rd May 1994 as amended by Cmnd 2663, HC 797, Cmnd 3073, HC 274, HC 329, Cmnd 3365, HC 31, HC 338, Cmnd 3369, HC 26, HC 161, Cmnd 3953, Cmnd 4065, HC 22, HC 704, Cmnd 4851, Cmnd 5253, HC 735, Cmnd 5597, HC 1301, HC 104, HC 180, HC 489, HC 538, Cmnd 5829, Cmnd 5949, HC 1224, HC 95, HC 176, HC 370, HC 464, HC 523, Cmnd 6297, Cmnd 6339, HC 1112, HC 164, HC 194, HC 302, HC 346, HC 486, HC 104, HC 299, HC 582, HC 645, HC 697, HC 769, HC 819, HC 949, HC 974, HC 1016, HC 1053, HC 1337, Cmnd 6918, HC 1702, HC 130, HC 398, Cmnd 7074, Cmnd 7075, HC 28, HC 40, HC 82, HC 321, HC 420, HC 607, HC 951, HC 971, HC 1113, HC 227, HC 314, HC413, Cmnd 7701, Cmnd 7711, HC 120, HC 367, HC 439, HC 59, 11C 96, HC 382, Cmnd 7929, Cmnd 7944, HC698, HC863, HC908, HC1148, HC1436, HC 1511, HC1622, HC1693, HC1719, HC1733, HC1888, Cmnd 8337, HC194, Cmnd 8423, HC514, HC565, HC760, 820, HC847, HC943, HC967, HC1038, HC1039, Cmnd 8599, HC244, HC628, HC803, HC887, HC901, HC938, HC1130, HC1138, HC1201, HC198, HC532. HC693, HC1025, HC1116, HC297, HC 437, HC535, HC877)

THE IMMIGRATION RULES: THE POINTS BASED SYSTEM

1 Introduction

This Note deals with those provisions of the Statement of Changes in Immigration Rules ("the Rules") which relate to the points-based system.

2 The points-based system

The points-based system is the main route for migrants from outside the EEA wanting to work, study, or invest in the UK. There are 5 "Tiers" for different types of applicant and each tier has a different points-based assessment.

Tier 1 consists of–

Tier 1 (General) (for highly skilled migrants: now closed to new applicants);

Tier 1 (Investor);

Tier 1 (Entrepreneur);

Tier 1 (Post-Study Work); and

Tier 1 (Exceptional Talent)

Tier 2 consists of–

Tier 2 (General);

Tier 2 (Intra-company transferee);

Tier 2 (Minister of Religion); and

Tier 2 (Sportsperson).

Tier 3 was for low skilled workers, but has been removed;

Tier 4 is for students and consists of–

Tier 4 (General) Student; and

Tier 4 (Child) Student.

Tier 5 is for youth mobility and temporary workers. Temporary workers are subdivided into the following categories–

creative and sporting;

charity workers;

religious;

Government authorised exchange; and

international agreement.

To be successful, an applicant must satisfy the general requirements for the particular Tier they are applying under, and also achieve the required number of points for that Tier. Points are awarded under Appendix A (aptitude), Appendix B (language skills), and Appendix C (maintenance funds).

3 Tier 1 (Exceptional Talent) Migrants

This route is for exceptionally talented individuals in particular fields who wish to work in the UK. These individuals are those who are already internationally recognised at the highest level as world leaders in their particular field, or who have already demonstrated exceptional promise and are likely to become world leaders in their particular area (para 245B).

Every initial application must include an endorsement from a "designated competent body". There is a limit of 1,000 per year (500 available each April and October). The endorsements are assigned to the designated competent bodies as follows–

Designated competent body	Total endorsements per year
Royal Society	250
Arts Council England	250
British Academy	150
Royal Academy of Engineering	150
Tech City UK	200

All migrants wishing to enter the UK as a Tier 1 (Exceptional Talent) Migrant must have a valid entry clearance for entry under this route. If they do not, entry will be refused (para 245BA).

To qualify for entry clearance or leave to remain as a Tier 1 (Exceptional Talent) Migrant, an applicant must meet the requirements listed below. The requirements are (para 245BB, 245BD)–

(a) the applicant must not fall for refusal under the general grounds for refusal, and if applying for leave to remain, must not be an illegal entrant;

(b) for entry clearance or leave to remain the applicant must have a minimum of 75 points under Appendix A (see **4 The points system: Tier 1 (Exceptional Talent) Migrants**, below);

(c) for entry clearance an applicant who has, or was last granted, leave as a student or a Postgraduate Doctor or Dentist, a Student Nurse, a Student Writing-Up a Thesis, a Student Re-Sitting an Examination or as a Tier 4 Migrant and (i) is currently being sponsored by a government or international scholarship agency, or (ii) was being sponsored by a government or international scholarship agency, and that sponsorship came to an end 12 months ago or less, must provide the unconditional written consent of the sponsoring Government or agency to the application and must provide specified documents as set out in the Tier 1 (Exceptional Talent) guidance published on the UK Visas and Immigration website, to show that this requirement has been met;

(d) for leave to remain, the applicant must have, or have last been granted, entry clearance, leave to enter or remain as a Tier 1 Migrant, a Tier 2 Migrant, or as a Tier 5 (Temporary Worker) Migrant, sponsored in the Government Authorised Exchange sub-category in an exchange scheme for sponsored researchers.

(e) for leave to remain, the applicant must not be in the UK in breach of immigration laws except that any period of overstaying for a period of 28 days or less will be disregarded.

Entry clearance will be granted for a period of between 1 year and 5 years and 4 months, as requested by the applicant (para 245BC) and leave to remain will be granted for a period of between 1 and 5 years, as requested (para 245BE).

Entry clearance and leave to remain under this route are subject to the following conditions–

(i) no recourse to public funds;

(ii) registration with the police, if this is required by para 326 of the Immigration Rules;

(iii) no employment as a Doctor or Dentist in Training, except in specified circumstances;

(iv) no employment as a professional sportsperson (including as a sports coach);

(v) where the applicant is 18 or over at the time their leave is granted, or will be 18 before their period of limited leave expires, that that they do not study unless they have a valid Academic Technology Approval Scheme clearance certificate from the Counter-Proliferation Department of the Foreign Office.

To qualify for indefinite leave to remain, a Tier 1 (Exceptional Talent) Migrant must meet the requirements listed below. If he does, leave to remain will be granted. If he does not, the application will be refused. The requirements are that the applicant must (para 245BF)–

(a) *deleted*;

(b) not fall for refusal under the general grounds for refusal, and must not be an illegal entrant;

(c) have lawfully spent a continuous period of 5 years lawfully in the UK as follows–

    (i) the applicant must have, or have last been granted, leave as a Tier 1 (Exceptional Talent) Migrant;

    (II) the 5 years must have been spent with leave as a Tier 1 Migrant (excluding as a Tier 1 (Graduate Entrepreneur) Migrant or Tier 1 (Post-Study Work) Migrant), or as a Tier 2 Migrant (excluding as a Tier 2 (Intra-Company Transfer) Migrant); and

    (iii) the applicant must have had absences from the UK of no more than 180 days in any 12 calendar months during the 5 years;

(d) have a minimum of 75 points under paras 1 to 6 of Appendix A;

(e) have sufficient knowledge of the English language and sufficient knowledge about life in the UK, in accordance with Appendix KoLL of the Rules; and

(f) not be in the UK in breach of immigration laws except that any period of overstaying for a period of 28 days or less will be disregarded.

4 The points system: Tier 1 (Exceptional Talent) Migrants

Attributes (Appendix A)

An applicant applying for entry clearance, leave to remain or indefinite leave to remain as a Tier 1 (Exceptional Talent) Migrant must score 75 points for attributes.

Criterion	Points
For entry clearance–	
Endorsed by a Designated Competent Body according to that Body's criteria as published on the UK Visas and Immigration website	75
For leave to remain–	
The applicant is economically active in his expert field as previously endorsed by a Designated Competent Body, is in employment, self-employment or both; and that endorsement has not been withdrawn.	75

Language skills (Appendix B)

There are no language qualifications for entry clearance, but an applicant must score 10 points for leave to remain. See **26 Language Skills (Appendix B)**, below.

Maintenance Funds (Appendix C)

There are no maintenance fund requirements in this category.

5 Tier 1 (General) Migrants

This route is now closed except for indefinite leave to remain applications.

To qualify for indefinite leave to remain, a Tier 1 (General) Migrant must meet the requirements listed below. If he does, indefinite leave to remain will be granted, if he does not the application will be refused. The requirements are that he (para 245CD)–

    (a) *deleted*

    (b) the applicant must not fall for refusal under the general grounds for refusal (except that para 322(1C) will not apply if the applicant meets the conditions in (f)(i)-(iii) below), and must not be an illegal entrant.

    (c) the applicant must have spent a continuous period as specified in (d) lawfully in the UK, of which the most recent period must have been spent with leave as a Tier 1 (General) Migrant, in any combination of the following categories: as a Tier 1 (General) Migrant, a Highly Skilled Migrant, a Work Permit Holder, an innovator, a Self-Employed Lawyer, as a Writer, Composer or Artist, a Tier 2 (General) Migrant, a Tier 2 (Minister of Religion) Migrant or a Tier 2 (Sportsperson) Migrant, or as a Tier 2 (Intra-Company Transfer) Migrant, provided the continuous period of 5 years spent lawfully in the UK includes a period of leave as a Tier 2 (Intra-Company Transfer) Migrant granted under the Rules in place before 6 April 2010, or as a Work Permit Holder where the work permit was granted because the applicant was the subject of an Intra-Company Transfer.

    (d) the continuous period in (c) is 4 years, if the applicant received a Highly Skilled Migrant Programme approval letter issued on the basis of an application made before 3 April 2006, was subsequently granted entry clearance or leave to remain on the basis of that letter, and has not since been granted entry clearance or leave to remain in any category other than as a Highly Skilled Migrant or Tier 1 (General) Migrant; or 5 years, in all other cases.

    (e) if the applicant has or has had leave as a Highly Skilled Migrant, a writer, composer or artist, a self-employed lawyer or as a Tier 1 (General) Migrant under the Rules in place before 19 July 2010, and has not been granted leave in any categories other than these under the Rules in place since 19 July 2010, the applicant must have 75 points under Appendix A (see **6 The points system: Tier 1 (General) Migrants**, below).

    (f) where the applicant received a Highly Skilled Migrant Programme approval letter issued on the basis of an application made before 7 November 2006, was subsequently granted entry clearance or leave to remain on the basis of that letter, and has not since been granted entry clearance or leave to remain in any category other than as a Highly Skilled Migrant or Tier 1 (General) Migrant, the applicant must be economically active in the UK, in employment or self-employment or both.

    (g) in all cases other than those referred to in (e) or (f) above, the applicant must have 80 points under Appendix A.

    (h) the applicant must have sufficient knowledge of the English language and sufficient knowledge about life in the UK, in accordance with Appendix KoLL of the Rules, unless the applicant meets the conditions in (f)(i)-(iii) above.

    (i) the applicant must not be in the UK in breach of immigration laws except that any period of overstaying for a period of 28 days or less will be disregarded, unless the applicant meets the conditions in (f)(i)-iii) above;

    (j) the applicant must provide specified documents;

(k), (l) where time has been spent in the Channel Islands or Isle of Man, special rules must be complied with;

    (m) The application for indefinite leave to remain must have been made before 6 April 2018.

6 The points system: Tier 1 (General) Migrants

Attributes (Appendix A)

An applicant applying for leave to remain or indefinite leave to remain as a Tier 1 (General) Migrant must score–

    (i) if the applicant has, or has had, leave as a Highly Skilled Migrant, as a Writer, Composer or Artist, Self-employed Lawyer, or as a Tier 1 (General) Migrant under the rules in place before 19 July 2010, and has not been granted leave in any categories other than these under the rules in place since that date, 75 points; or

    (ii) in any other case, 80 points.

An applicant applying for indefinite leave to remain as a Tier 1 (General) Migrant whose application is being made under terms of the HSMP ILR Judicial Review Policy Document is not required to score points for attributes.

Points are awarded on the basis of–

  – qualifications: from 30 points for a Batchelor's degree to 45 points for a PhD'

  – previous earnings: from 5 points for earnings under £25,999.99 to 80 points for £150,000+

  – UK experience: if £25,000+ of the previous earnings were earned in the UK: 5 points; and

  – age: under 30, 20 points; 30 to 34, 10 points, 35 to 39, 5 points.

Different points apply for applications for leave to remain and indefinite leave to remain where the applicant has, or has had, leave as a Highly Skilled Migrant, as a Writer, Composer or Artist, Self-employed Lawyer, or as a Tier 1 (General) Migrant under the rules in place before 6 April 2010, and has not been granted leave in any categories other than those since 6 April 2010.

Language skills (Appendix B)

An applicant applying for entry clearance or leave to remain as a Tier 1 Migrant (other than as a Tier 1 (Exceptional Talent) or (Investor) Migrant), must have 10 points for English language. See **26 Language Skills (Appendix B)**, below.

Maintenance Funds (Appendix C)

An applicant applying for entry clearance or leave to remain as a Tier 1 Migrant (other than as a Tier 1 (Exceptional

Talent) or (Investor) Migrant) must score 10 points for funds. See **27 Maintenance Funds (Appendix C)**, below

An applicant applying as the partner or child of a Tier 1 Migrant must also have a sufficient level of funds available to them. See **27 Maintenance Funds for families (Appendix E)**, below.

7 Tier 1 (Entrepreneur) Migrants

This route is for migrants who wish to establish, join or take over one or more businesses in the UK (para 245D). "Business" means an enterprise as (i) a sole trader, (ii) a partnership, or (iii) a company registered in the UK.

All migrants arriving in the UK and wishing to enter as a Tier 1 (Entrepreneur) Migrant must have a valid entry clearance for entry under this route. If they do not, entry will be refused (para 245DA).

To qualify for entry clearance as a Tier 1 (Entrepreneur) Migrant, an applicant must meet the requirements listed below. If he meets those requirements, entry clearance will be granted. If he does not, the application will be refused (para 245DB).

The requirements are that the applicant–

(a) must not fall for refusal under the general grounds for refusal;

(b) must have a minimum of 75 points under Appendix A (see **8 The points system: Tier 1 (Entrepreneur) Migrants**, below);

(c) must have a minimum of 10 points under Appendix B. See **26 Language Skills (Appendix B)**, below;

(d) must have a minimum of 10 points under Appendix C. See **27 Maintenance Funds (Appendix C)**;

(e) an applicant who has, or was last granted, leave as a student or a postgraduate doctor or dentist, a student nurse, a student writing up a thesis a student re-sitting an examination or as a Tier 4 Migrant and (i) is currently being sponsored by a government or international scholarship agency, or (ii) was being sponsored by a government or international scholarship agency, and that sponsorship came to an end 12 months ago or less, must provide the unconditional written consent of the sponsoring Government or agency to the application and must provide specified documents to show that this requirement has been met;

(f) where the applicant is being assessed under Table 4 of Appendix A, the Entry Clearance Officer must be satisfied that–

    (i) the applicant genuinely intends and is able to establish, take over or become a director of one or more businesses in the UK within the next six months;

    (ii) the applicant genuinely intends to invest the money referred to in Table 4 of Appendix A in the business or businesses referred to in (i);

    (iii) that the money referred to in Table 4 of Appendix A is genuinely available to the applicant, and will remain available to him until such time as it is spent by his business or businesses;

    (iv) if the applicant is relying on one or more previous investments to score points, they have genuinely invested all or part of the investment funds required in Table 4 of Appendix A into one or more genuine businesses in the UK;

    (v) that the applicant does not intend to take employment in the UK other than under the terms of para 245DC;

(g) provides a business plan, setting out his proposed business activities in the UK and how he expects to make his business succeed;

(h) in making the assessment in (f), the Entry Clearance Officer will assess the balance of probabilities, taking into account the following factors–

    (i) the evidence the applicant has submitted;

    (ii) the viability and credibility of the source of the money referred to in Table 4 of Appendix A;

    (iii) the viability and credibility of the applicant's business plans and market research into their chosen business sector;

    (iv) the applicant's previous educational and business experience (or lack thereof);

    (v) the applicant's immigration history and previous activity in the UK; and

    (vi) any other relevant information;

(i) Where the applicant has had entry clearance, leave to enter or leave to remain as a Tier 1 (Entrepreneur) Migrant, a Businessperson or an Innovator in the 12 months immediately before the date of application, and is being assessed under Table 5 of Appendix A, the Entry Clearance Officer must be satisfied that–

    (i) the applicant has established, taken over or become a director of one or more genuine businesses in the UK, and has genuinely operated that business or businesses while he had leave as a Tier 1 (Entrepreneur) Migrant, a Businessperson or an Innovator; and

    (ii) the applicant has genuinely invested the money referred to in Table 5 of Appendix A into one or more genuine businesses in the UK to be spent for the purpose of that business or businesses; and

    (iii) the applicant genuinely intends to continue operating one or more businesses in the UK; and

    (iv) the applicant does not intend to take employment in the United Kingdom other than under the terms of paragraph 245DE.

(j) In making the assessment in (i), the Entry Clearance Officer will assess the balance of probabilities. The Entry Clearance Officer may take into account the following factors–

    (i) the evidence the applicant has submitted;

    (ii) the viability and credibility of the source of the money referred to in Table 5 of Appendix A;

    (iii) the credibility of the financial accounts of the business or businesses;

    (iv) the credibility of the applicant's business activity in the UK, including when he had leave as a Tier 1 (Entrepreneur) Migrant, a Businessperson or an Innovator;

    (v) the credibility of the job creation for which the applicant is claiming points in Table 5 of Appendix A;

    (vi) if the nature of the business requires mandatory accreditation, registration and/or insurance, whether that accreditation, registration and/or insurance has been obtained; and

    (vii) any other relevant information.

(k) the Entry Clearance Officer reserves the right to request additional information and evidence to support the assessment in (f) or (i), and to refuse the application if the information or evidence is not provided. Any requested documents must be received by the Home Office at the address specified in the request within 28 calendar days of the date of the request;

(l) if the Entry Clearance Officer is not satisfied with the genuineness of the application in relation to a points-scoring requirement in Appendix A, those points will not be awarded;

(m) the Entry Clearance Officer may decide not to carry out the assessment in (f) or (i) if the application already falls for refusal on other grounds, but reserves the right to carry it out in any reconsideration of the decision;

(n) the applicant must, unless he provides a reasonable explanation, comply with any request made by the Entry Clearance Officer to attend for interview;

(o) the applicant must be at least 16 years old;

(p) where the applicant is under 18 years of age, the application must be supported by his parents or legal guardian or by one parent if that parent has sole legal responsibility for the child;

(q) where the applicant is under 18 years of age, their parents or legal guardian, or one parent if that parent has sole legal responsibility for the child, must confirm that they consent to the arrangements for the applicant's care in the UK

Entry clearance will be granted for a period of 3 years and four months and will be subject to the following conditions (para 245DC)–

    (i) no recourse to public funds;

    (ii) registration with the police, if this is required by para 326 of the Rules; and

    (iii) no employment other than working for the business(es) the applicant has established, joined or taken over;

    (iv) no employment as a professional sportsperson (including as a sports coach); and

    (v) where the applicant is 18 or over at the time their leave is granted, or will be 18 before their period of limited leave expires, that that they do not study unless they have a valid Academic Technology Approval Scheme clearance certificate from the Counter-Proliferation Department of the Foreign Office.

To qualify for leave to remain as a Tier 1 (Entrepreneur) Migrant, an applicant must meet the requirements listed below. If he does, leave to remain will be granted. If he does not, the application will be refused. The requirements are (para 245DD)–

(a) the applicant must not fall for refusal under the general grounds for refusal (except that para 322(10) does not apply), and must not be an illegal entrant;

(b) the applicant must have a minimum of 75 points under Appendix A. See **8 The points system: Tier 1 (Entrepreneur) Migrants**, below;

(c) the applicant must have a minimum of 10 points under Appendix B. See **26 Language Skills (Appendix B)**, below;

(d) the applicant must have a minimum of 10 points under Appendix C. See **27 Maintenance Funds (Appendix C)**, below;

(e) the applicant who is applying for leave to remain must have, or have last been granted, entry clearance, leave to enter or remain–

    (i) as a Highly Skilled Migrant;

    (ii) as a Tier 1 (General) Migrant;

    (iii) as a Tier 1 (Entrepreneur) Migrant;

    (iv) as a Tier 1 (Investor) Migrant;

    (v) as a Tier 1 (Graduate Entrepreneur) Migrant;

    (vi) as a Tier 1 (Post-Study Work) Migrant;

    (vii) as a Businessperson;

    (viii) as an Innovator;

    (ix) as an Investor;

    (x) as a Participant in the Fresh Talent: Working in Scotland Scheme;

    (xi) as a Participant in the International Graduates Scheme (or its predecessor, the Science and Engineering Graduates Scheme);

    (xii) as a Postgraduate Doctor or Dentist;

    (xiii) as a Self-employed Lawyer;

    (xiv) as a Student;

    (xv) as a Student Nurse;

    (xvi) as a Student Re-sitting an Examination;

    (xvii) as a Student Writing Up a Thesis;

    (xviii) as a Work Permit Holder;

    (xix) as a Writer, Composer or Artist;

    (xx) as a Tier 2 Migrant;

(xxi) as a Tier 4 (General) Student and, in respect of such leave, is or was last sponsored by a UK recognised body or a body in receipt of public funding as a higher education institution; an overseas higher education institution to undertake a short-term study abroad programme in the UK; an Embedded College offering Pathway Courses; or an independent school;

(xxii) as a Tier 4 (Child) Student, or

(xxiii) a visitor who has been undertaking permitted activities as a prospective entrepreneur;

(f) an applicant who has, or was last granted, leave as a student or a postgraduate doctor or dentist, a student nurse, a student writing up a thesis a student re-sitting an examination or as a Tier 4 Migrant, and–

    (i) is currently being sponsored by a government or international scholarship agency; or

    (ii) was being sponsored by a government or international scholarship agency, and that sponsorship came to an end 12 months ago or less,

must provide the unconditional written consent of the sponsoring Government or agency to the application and must provide the specified documents to show that this requirement has been met;

(g) the applicant must not be in the UK in breach of immigration laws except that any period of overstaying for a period of 28 days or less will be disregarded;

(h) where the applicant is being assessed under Table 4 of Appendix A (see **8 The points system: Tier 1 (Entrepreneur) Migrants**, below), the Secretary of State must be satisfied that–

    (i) the applicant genuinely intends and is able to establish, take over or become a director of one or more businesses in the UK within the next six months, or has established, taken over or become a director of one or more businesses in the UK and continues to operate that business or businesses; and

    (ii) the applicant genuinely intends to invest the money referred to in Table 4 of Appendix A (see **8 The points system: Tier 1 (Entrepreneur) Migrants**, below) in the business or businesses referred to in (i);

    (iii) the money referred to in Table 4 of Appendix A is genuinely available to the applicant, and will remain available to him until such time as it is spent for the purposes of his business or businesses;

    (iv) if the applicant is relying on one or more previous investments to score points, they have genuinely invested all or part of the investment funds required in Table 4 of Appendix A into one or more genuine businesses in the UK;

    (v) that the applicant does not intend to take employment in the UK other than under the terms of para 245DE;

(i) the applicant must provide a business plan, setting out his proposed business activities in the UK and how he expects to make his business succeed;

(j) In making the assessment in (h), the Secretary of State will assess the balance of probabilities. The Secretary of State may take into account the following factors–

    (i) the evidence the applicant has submitted;

    (ii) the viability and credibility of the source of the money referred to in Table 4 of Appendix A;

    (iii) the viability and credibility of the applicant's business plans and market research into their chosen business sector;

    (iv) the applicant's previous educational and business experience (or lack thereof);

    (v) the applicant's immigration history and previous activity in the UK;

    (vi) where the applicant has already registered in the UK as self-employed or as the director of a business, and the nature of the business requires mandatory accreditation, registration and/or insurance, whether that accreditation, registration and/or insurance has been obtained; and

    (vii) any other relevant information;

(k) Where the applicant has, or was last granted, leave as a Tier 1 (Entrepreneur) Migrant, a Businessperson or an Innovator and is being assessed under Table 5 of Appendix A, the Secretary of State must be satisfied that–

    (i) the applicant has established, taken over or become a director of one or more genuine businesses in the UK, and has genuinely operated that business or businesses while he had leave as a Tier 1 (Entrepreneur) Migrant, a Businessperson or an Innovator; and

    (ii) the applicant has genuinely invested the money referred to in Table 5 of Appendix A into one or more genuine businesses in the UK to be spent for the purpose of that business or businesses; and

    (iii) the applicant genuinely intends to continue operating one or more businesses in the UK; and

    (iv) the applicant does not intend to take employment in the United Kingdom other than under the terms of paragraph 245DE.

(l) In making the assessment in (k), the Secretary of State will assess the balance of probabilities. The Secretary of State may take into account the following factors–

    (i) the evidence the applicant has submitted;

    (ii) the viability and credibility of the source of the money referred to in Table 5 of Appendix A;

    (iii) the credibility of the financial accounts of the business or businesses;

    (iv) the credibility of the applicant's business activity in the UK, including when he had leave as a Tier 1 (Entrepreneur) Migrant, a Businessperson or an Innovator;

    (v) the credibility of the job creation for which the applicant is claiming points in Table 5 of Appendix A;

(vi) if the nature of the business requires mandatory accreditation, registration and/or insurance, whether that accreditation, registration and/or insurance has been obtained; and

(vii) any other relevant information.

(m) the Secretary of State reserves the right to request additional information and evidence to support the assessment in (h) or (k), and to refuse the application if the information or evidence is not provided. Any requested documents must be received by the Secretary of State at the address specified in the request within 28 calendar days of the date of the request;

(n) if the Secretary of State is not satisfied with the genuineness of the application in relation to a points-scoring requirement in Appendix A, those points will not be awarded;

(o) the Secretary of State may decide not to carry out the assessment in (h) or (k) if the application already falls for refusal on other grounds, but reserves the right to carry it out in any reconsideration of the decision;

(p) the applicant must, unless he provides a reasonable explanation, comply with any request made by the Secretary of State to attend for interview;

(q) the applicant must be at least 16 years old;

(r) where the applicant is under 18 years of age, the application must be supported by his parents or legal guardian or by one parent if that parent has sole legal responsibility for the child;

(s) where the applicant is under 18 years of age, his parents or legal guardian, or one parent if that parent has sole legal responsibility for the child, must confirm that they consent to the arrangements for the applicant's care in the UK.

Leave to remain will be granted (i) for a period of 2 years, to an applicant who has, or was last granted, leave as a Tier 1 (Entrepreneur) Migrant, or (ii) for a period of 3 years, to any other applicant.

Leave to remain under this route will be subject to the following conditions (para 245DE)–

(i) no recourse to public funds;

(ii) registration with the police, if this is required by para 326 of the Rules; and

(iii) no employment, other than working for the business or businesses which he has established, joined or taken over,

(iv) no employment as a professional sportsperson (including as a sports coach); and

(v) where the applicant is 18 or over at the time their leave is granted, or will be 18 before their period of limited leave expires, that that they do not study unless they have a valid Academic Technology Approval Scheme clearance certificate from the Counter-Proliferation Department of the Foreign Office.

Leave to enter or remain granted to a Tier 1 (Entrepreneur) Migrant may be curtailed if, within 6 months of the specified date (see below) the applicant has not done one or more of the following things (para 245DE(c)–

(vi) registered with HM Revenue and Customs as self-employed;

(vii) registered a new business in which he is a director; or

(viii) registered as a director of an existing business; or if

(ix) the funds referred to in the relevant sections of Appendix A cease to be available to him, except where they have been spent for the purposes of his business or businesses.

The date referred to above is (where there is evidence to establish it) the date of entry to the UK, or (where there is no such evidence) the date of the grant of entry clearance, or (in any other case) the date of the grant of leave to remain to the applicant. Para 245DE(c) does not apply where the applicant's last grant of leave prior to the grant of the leave that he currently has was as a Tier 1 (Entrepreneur) Migrant, a Businessperson or an Innovator.

To qualify for indefinite leave to remain as a Tier 1 (Entrepreneur) Migrant, an applicant must meet the requirements listed below. If he meets these requirements, indefinite leave to remain will be granted. If he does not, the application will be refused. The requirements are the applicant (para 245DF)–

(a) *deleted*;

(b) must have a minimum of 75 points under Appendix A (see **8 The points system: Tier 1 (Entrepreneur) Migrants**, below);

(c) must be engaged in business activity at the time of his application and the applicant must provide specified evidence to show this;

(d) must have sufficient knowledge of the English language and sufficient knowledge about life in the UK, in accordance with Appendix KoLL;

(e) must not be in the UK in breach of immigration laws except that any period of overstaying for a period of 28 days or less will be disregarded;

(f) the Secretary of State must be satisfied that–

(i) the applicant has established, taken over or become a director of one or more genuine businesses in the UK, and has genuinely operated that business or businesses while he had leave as a Tier 1 (Entrepreneur) Migrant, a Businessperson or an Innovator; and

(ii) the applicant has genuinely invested the money referred to in Table 6 of Appendix A into one or more businesses in the UK to be spent for the purpose of that business or businesses; and

(iii) the applicant genuinely intends to continue operating one or more businesses in the UK.

(g) in making the assessment in (f), the Secretary of State will assess the balance of probabilities. The

Secretary of State may take into account the following factors–

    (i) the evidence the applicant has submitted;

    (ii) the viability and credibility of the source of the money referred to in Table 6 of Appendix A;

    (iii) the credibility of the financial accounts of the business or businesses;

    (iv) the credibility of the applicant's business activity in the UK, including when he had leave as a Tier 1 (Entrepreneur) Migrant, a Businessperson or an Innovator;

    (v) the credibility of the job creation for which the applicant is claiming points in Table 6 of Appendix A;

    (vi) if the nature of the business requires mandatory accreditation, registration and/or insurance, whether that accreditation, registration and/or insurance has been obtained; and

    (vii) any other relevant information.

(h) The Secretary of State reserves the right to request additional information and evidence to support the assessment in (f), and to refuse the application if the information or evidence is not provided. Any requested documents must be received by the Secretary of State at the address specified in the request within 28 calendar days of the date of the request.

(i) If the Secretary of State is not satisfied with the genuineness of the application in relation to a points-scoring requirement in Appendix A, those points will not be awarded.

(j) The Secretary of State may decide not to carry out the assessment in (f) if the application already falls for refusal on other grounds, but reserves the right to carry out this assessment in any reconsideration of the decision.

(k) The applicant must, unless he provides a reasonable explanation, comply with any request made by the Secretary of State to attend for interview.

8 The points system: Tier 1 (Entrepreneur) Migrants

An applicant applying for entry clearance or leave to remain as a Tier 1 (Entrepreneur) Migrant must score 75 points for attributes.

Attributes (Appendix A)

Subject as described below, the available points for applications for entry clearance or leave to remain are set out in Table 4–

Table 4

Investment	Points
(a) The applicant has access to not less than £200,000; or	25
(b) not less than £50,000 from–	
(i) one or more registered venture capitalist firms regulated by the Financial Services Authority,	
(ii) one or more UK Entrepreneurial seed funding competitions which is listed as endorsed on the UK Trade & Investment website, or	
(iii) one or more UK Government Departments, and made available by the Department(s) for the specific purpose of establishing or expanding a UK business; or	
(c) not less than £50,000 and is applying for leave to remain, and has, or was last granted, leave as a Tier 1 (Graduate Entrepreneur) Migrant, or	
(d) not less than £50,000 and is applying for leave to remain, has, or was last granted, leave as a Tier 1 (Post-Study Work) Migrant, and was, on a date falling within the three months immediately prior to the date of application–	
(i) registered with HM Revenue and Customs as self-employed, or	
(ii) registered a new business in which he is a director, or	
(iii) registered as a director of an existing business;	
and is engaged in business activity, other than the work necessary to administer his business, in an occupation which appears on the list of occupations skilled to National Qualifications Framework level 4 or above, as stated in the codes of practice for Tier 2 Sponsors in Appendix J	
The money is held in one or more regulated financial institutions	25
The money is disposable in the UK	25
If the applicant is applying for leave to remain, the money must be held in the UK	

Available points for an applicant applying for leave to remain who has, or has last been granted entry clearance, leave to enter or remain as–

  (i) a Tier 1 (Entrepreneur);

  (ii) a Businessperson;

  (iii) an Innovator,

are shown in Table 5–

Table 5

Investment and business activity	*Points*
(a) The applicant has invested, or had invested on his behalf, not less than £200,000 (or £50,000–see Table 4) in cash directly into one or more businesses in the UK.	20

(b) The applicant has–

    (a) registered with HM Revenue and Customs as self-employed; or   20

    (b) registered a new business in which he is a director; or

    (c) registered as a director of an existing business.

Where the applicant's last grant of entry clearance, leave to enter or leave to remain was as a Tier 1 (Entrepreneur) Migrant, the above condition must have been met within 6 months entry into the UK (if he was granted entry clearance as a Tier 1 (Entrepreneur) Migrant and there is evidence to establish his date of arrival to the UK), or, in any other case, the date of the grant of leave to remain.

(c) On a date no earlier than three months prior to the date of   15
application, the applicant was:

    (i) registered with HM Revenue and Customs as self-employed, or

    (ii) registered a new business in which he is a director, or

    (iii) registered as a director of an existing business.

(d) The applicant has–   20

    (a) established a new business or businesses that has or have created the equivalent of at least two new full time jobs for persons settled in the UK; or

    (b) taken over or joined an existing business or businesses and his services or investment have resulted in a net increase in the employment provided by the business or businesses for persons settled in the UK by creating the equivalent of at least two new full time jobs.

Where the applicant's last grant of entry clearance or leave to enter or remain was as a Tier 1 (Entrepreneur) Migrant, the jobs must have existed for at least 12 months of the period for which the previous leave was granted.

Available points for an applicant applying for indefinite leave to remain are shown in Table 6–

Table 6

(a) as (a) of Table 5. The applicant will not need to provide evidence of   20
this investment if he was awarded points for it, as set out in Table 5, in his previous grant of entry clearance or leave to remain as a Tier 1 (Entrepreneur) Migrant.

(b) as (c) of Table 5   20

(c) as (d) of Table 5

(d) The applicant has spent the "specified continuous period" lawfully   15
in the UK, with absences of no more than 180 days in any 12 calendar months during that period. The specified period must have been spent with leave as a Tier 1 (Entrepreneur) Migrant, as a Businessperson and/or as an Innovator, of which the most recent period must have been spent with leave as a Tier (1) (Entrepreneur) Migrant.

    The "specified continuous period" is–

    (a) 3 years if the number of new full time jobs in (b) above is at least 10;

    (b) 3 years if the applicant has: (i) established a new UK business that has had an income from business activity of at least £5 million during a 3 year period in which the applicant has had leave as a Tier 1 (Entrepreneur) Migrant, or (ii) taken over or invested in an existing UK business and his services or investment have resulted in a net increase in income from business activity to that business of £5 million during a 3 year period in which the applicant has had leave as a Tier 1 (Entrepreneur) Migrant, when compared to the immediately preceding 3 year period, or

    (c) 5 years in all other cases.

For language qualifications, see **26 Language Skills (Appendix B)**, below; and for maintenance qualifications see **27 Maintenance Funds (Appendix C)**, below.

9 Tier 1 (Investor) Migrants

This route is for high net worth individuals making a substantial financial investment to the UK (para 245E).

All migrants arriving in the UK and wishing to enter as a Tier 1 (Investor) Migrant must have a valid entry clearance for entry under this route. If they do not, entry will be refused (para 245EA).

To qualify for entry clearance as a Tier 1 (Investor) Migrant, an applicant must meet the requirements listed below. If he does, entry clearance will be granted. If he does not, the application will be refused. The requirements are (para 245EB)–

(a) the applicant must not fall for refusal under the general grounds for refusal;

(b) the applicant must have a minimum of 75 points under Appendix A (see **10 The points system: Tier 1 (Investor) Migrants**, below);

(c) an applicant who has, or was last granted, leave as a student or a postgraduate doctor or dentist, a student nurse, a student writing up a thesis a student re-sitting an examination or as a Tier 4 Migrant and who is currently being sponsored by a government or international scholarship agency, or was being so sponsored and that sponsorship came to an end 12 months ago or less, must provide the unconditional written consent of the sponsoring Government or agency to the application and must provide specified documents to show that this requirement has been met;

(d) the applicant must be at least 18 years old and the assets and investment he is claiming points for must be wholly under his control;

(e) the Entry Clearance Officer must not have reasonable grounds to believe that the applicant is not in control of and at liberty to freely invest the money specified in their application, or that any of the money has been obtained by unlawful means, or that where any of the money has been provided by another party, the character, conduct or associations of that party are such that approval of the application would not be conducive to the public good.

Entry clearance will be granted for a period of 3 years and four months and will be subject to the following conditions para 245EC)–

(i) no recourse to public funds;

(ii) registration with the police, if this is required by para 326 of the Rules;

(iii) no employment as a Doctor or Dentist in Training unless specified conditions are met;

(iv) no employment as a professional sportsperson (including as a sports coach);

(v) no study without a valid Academic Technology Approval Scheme clearance certificate from the Counter-Proliferation Department of the Foreign Office.

To qualify for leave to remain as a Tier 1 (Investor) Migrant, an applicant must meet the requirements listed below. If he does, leave to remain will be granted. If he does not, the application will be refused. The requirements are that the applicant (para 245ED)–

(a) must not fall for refusal under the general grounds for refusal, and must not be an illegal entrant;

(b) must have a minimum of 75 points under Appendix A (see **10 The points system: Tier 1 (Investor) Migrants**, below);

(c) must have, or have last been granted, entry clearance, leave to enter or remain–

(i) as a Highly Skilled Migrant;

(ii) as a Tier 1 (General) Migrant;

(iii) as a Tier 1 (Entrepreneur) Migrant;

(iv) as a Tier 1 (Investor) Migrant;

(v) as a Tier 1 (Post-Study Work) Migrant;

(vi) as a Businessperson;

(vii) as an Innovator;

(viii) as an Investor;

(ix) as a Student;

(x) as a Student Nurse;

(xi) as a Student Re-Sitting an Examination;

(xii) as a Student Writing Up a Thesis;

(xiii) as a Work Permit Holder;

(xiv) as a Writer, Composer or Artist;

(xv) as a Tier 2 Migrant;

(xvi) as a Tier 4 (General) Student and, in respect of such leave, is or was last sponsored by a UK recognised body or a body in receipt of public funding as a higher education institution; or by an overseas higher education institution to undertake a short-term study abroad programme in the UK; by an Embedded College offering Pathway Courses; or an independent school; or

(xvi) as a Tier 4 (Child) Student.

(d) who has, or was last granted, leave as a student, student nurse, a student re-sitting an examination, a student writing up a thesis, or as a Tier 4 Migrant and–

(i) is currently being sponsored by a government or international scholarship agency; or

(ii) was being sponsored by a government or international scholarship agency, and that sponsorship came to an end 12 months ago or less;

must provide the unconditional written consent of the sponsoring Government or agency to the application and must provide specified documents to show that this requirement has been met.

(e) the applicant must be at least 18 years old and the assets and investment he is claiming points for must be wholly under his control;

(f) must not be in the UK in breach of immigration laws except that any period of overstaying for a period of 28 days or less will be disregarded.

(g) the Entry Clearance Officer must not have reasonable grounds to believe that the applicant is not in control of and at liberty to freely invest the money specified in their application, or that any of the money has been obtained by unlawful means, or that where any of the money has been provided by another party, the character, conduct or associations of that party are such that approval of the application would not be conducive to the public good.

Leave to remain will be granted (i) for a period of 2 years, to an applicant who has, or was last granted, leave as a Tier 1 (Investor) Migrant, or (ii) for a period of 3 years, to any other applicant (para 245EE).

Leave to remain under this route will be subject to the following conditions—

(i) no recourse to public funds;

(ii) registration with the police, if this is required by para 326 of the Rules;

(iii) subject to exceptions, no employment as a Doctor or Dentist in Training;

(iv) no employment as a professional sportsperson (including as a sports coach); and

(v) no study without a valid Academic Technology Approval Scheme clearance certificate from the Counter-Proliferation Department of the Foreign Office.

Leave to enter or remain as a Tier 1 (Investor) Migrant may be curtailed if within 3 months of the specified date (see below) the applicant has not invested, or had invested on his behalf, at least £750,000 of his capital (£2 million if last granted leave after 6th November 2014) in the UK by way of UK Government bonds, share capital or loan capital in active and trading UK registered companies other than those principally engaged in property investment, or does not maintain that investment throughout the remaining period of his leave (para 245EE(c). The date referred to above is (where there is evidence to establish it) the date of entry to the UK, or (where there is no such evidence) the date of the grant of entry clearance, or (in any other case) the date of the grant of leave to remain to the applicant. Para 245EE(c) does not apply where the applicant's two most recent grants of leave were either as a Tier 1 (Investor) Migrant or as an Investor.

To qualify for indefinite leave to remain, a Tier 1 (Investor) Migrant must meet the requirements listed below. If he does, indefinite leave to remain will be granted. If he does not, the application will be refused. The requirements are that the applicant (para 245EF)—

(a) *deleted*;

(b) must not fall for refusal under the general grounds for refusal, and must not be an illegal entrant;

(c) must have a minimum of 75 points under Appendix A (see **10 The points system: Tier 1 (Investor) Migrants**, below);

(d) must have sufficient knowledge of the English language and sufficient knowledge about life in the UK, in accordance with Appendix KoLL;

(e) must not be in the UK in breach of immigration laws except that any period of overstaying for a period of 28 days or less will be disregarded.

10 The points system: Tier 1 (Investor) Migrants

An applicant applying for entry clearance or leave to remain as a Tier 1 (Investor) Migrant must score 75 points for attributes.

Attributes (Appendix A)

Subject as described below, the available points for applications for entry clearance or leave to remain are set out in Table 7.

Table 7

Assets	Points
The applicant—	
(a) has money of his own held in a regulated financial institution and disposable in the UK amounting to not less than £2 million; and	75
(b) has opened an account with a UK regulated bank for the purposes of investing not less than £2 million in the UK	

Available points for an applicant who—

(a) has had entry clearance, leave to enter or leave to remain as a Tier 1 (Investor) Migrant or an Investor in the 12 months immediately before the date of application, or

(b) is applying for leave to remain and has, or was last granted, entry clearance, leave to enter or leave to remain as a Tier 1 (Investor) Migrant or an Investor,

are shown in Table 8A (Note different provisions apply where the initial application to enter in this category was made before 6th November 2014 (see Table 8B).

Table 8A

Assets and Investments	*Points*
The applicant has invested not less than £2 million in the UK by way of UK Government bonds, share capital or loan capital in active and trading UK registered companies, subject to the restrictions set out in para 65.	75

This investment was made:
(1) within 3 months of the applicant's entry to the UK, if he was granted entry clearance as a Tier 1 (Investor) Migrant and there is evidence to establish his date of entry to the UK, unless there are exceptionally compelling reasons for the delay in investing, or
(2) where there is no evidence to establish his date of entry in the UK or where the applicant was granted entry clearance in a category other than Tier 1 (Investor) Migrant, within 3 months of the date of the grant of entry clearance or leave to remain as a Tier 1 (Investor) Migrant, unless there are exceptionally compelling reasons for the delay in investing, or
(3) where the investment was made prior to the application which led to the first grant of leave as a Tier 1 (Investor) Migrant, no earlier than 12 months before the date of such application,

and in each case the level of investment has been at least maintained for the whole of the remaining period of that leave.

"Compelling reasons for the delay in investing" must be unforeseeable and outside of the applicant's control. Delays caused by the applicant failing to take timely action will not be accepted. Where possible, the applicant must have taken reasonable steps to mitigate such delay.

The available points for application for indefinite leave to remain are set out in Table 9. Points are awarded for assets, investments and time spent in the UK. The greater the assets and investments, the shorter the time required to have been spent in the UK.

There are no language or maintenance qualifications in this category.

11 Tier 1 (Graduate Entrepreneur) Migrants

This route is for graduates who have been identified by Higher Education Institutions as having developed world class innovative ideas or entrepreneurial skills to extend their stay in the UK after graduation to establish one or more businesses here, and for It is also for overseas graduates who have been identified by UK Trade and Investment as elite global graduate entrepreneurs to establish one or more businesses in the UK. (para 245F).

All migrants arriving in the UK and wishing to enter as a Tier 1 (Graduate Entrepreneur) Migrant must have a valid entry clearance for entry under this route. If they do not have a valid entry clearance, entry will be refused (para245FA).

To qualify for entry clearance or leave to remain as a Tier 1 (Graduate Entrepreneur) Migrant, an applicant must meet the requirements listed below. If he does, entry clearance will be granted. If he does not, the application will be refused (para 245FB). The requirements are that the applicant–
(a) must not fall for refusal under the general grounds for refusal;
(b) must have a minimum of 75 points under Appendix A (see **12 The points system: Tier 1 (Graduate Entrepreneur) Migrants**, below);
(c) must have a minimum of 10 points under Appendix B, see **26 Language Skills (Appendix B)**, below;
(d) must have a minimum of 10 points under Appendix C, see **27 Maintenance Funds (Appendix C)**, below;
(e) if applying for leave to remain must have, or have last been granted, entry clearance, leave to enter or remain as a Tier 4 Migrant (and, in respect of such leave, is or was last sponsored by a UK recognised body or a body in receipt of public funding as a higher education institution; or by an overseas higher education institution to undertake a short-term study abroad programme in the UK), Student, Student Nurse, Student Re-sitting an Examination, Student Writing Up a Thesis, Postgraduate Doctor or Dentist, as a Tier 1 (Graduate Entrepreneur) Migrant, or as a Tier 2 (General) Migrant
(f) if applying for leave to remain has, or was last granted, entry clearance or leave to remain as a Tier 2 (General) Migrant must have been granted leave to work as a post-doctoral researcher for the same institution which is endorsing his application as a Tier 1 (Graduate Entrepreneur) Migrant;
(g) must not have previously been granted entry clearance, leave to enter or remain as a Tier 1 (Post-Study Work) Migrant, a Participant in the Fresh Talent: Working in Scotland Scheme, or a Participant in the International Graduates Scheme (or its predecessor, the Science and Engineering Graduates Scheme);
(h) must not previously have been granted leave to remain as a Tier 1 (Graduate Entrepreneur) Migrant on more than one occasion;
(i) must, where an applicant does not have, or was not last granted, leave to remain as a Tier 1 (Graduate Entrepreneur) Migrant and (i) is currently being sponsored in his studies by a government or international scholarship agency, or (ii) was so being sponsored in his studies and that sponsorship came to an end 12

months ago or less, provide the unconditional written consent of the sponsoring government or agency to the application and must provide specified documents to show that this requirement has been met; and

(j) must not be in the UK in breach of immigration laws, except that any period of overstaying for a period of 28 days or less will be disregarded.

Entry clearance will be granted for a period of 1 year and will be subject to the following conditions (para 245FC)–

(i) no recourse to public funds;

(ii) registration with the police, if this is required by para 326 of the Rules;

(iii) no employment except working for the business(es) the applicant has established and other employment of no more than 20 hours per week;

(iv) no employment as a Doctor or Dentist in Training or as a professional sports person (including as a sports coach); and

(v) where the applicant is 18 years of age or over at the time their leave is granted, or will be aged 18 before their period of limited leave expires, no study without a valid Academic Technology Approval Scheme clearance certificate from the Counter-Proliferation Department of the Foreign Office.

12 The points system: Tier 1 (Graduate Entrepreneur) Migrants

Attributes (Appendix A)

An applicant applying for entry clearance or leave to remain as a Tier 1 (Graduate Entrepreneur) Migrant must score 75 points for attributes.

The available points are shown in Table 10.

Table 10–

Qualification	Points
The applicant has been endorsed by a UK Higher Education Institution which–	25
(a) is a sponsor status with Tier 4 Sponsor status,	
(b) is an A-rated Sponsor under Tier 2 of the Points-Based System if a Tier 2 licence is held,	
(c) is an A-rated Sponsor under Tier 5 of the Points-Based System if a Tier 5 licence is held,	
(d) has degree awarding powers, and	
(e) has established processes and competence for identifying, nurturing and developing entrepreneurs among its undergraduate and postgraduate population; or	
The applicant has been endorsed by UK Trade and Investment	
The applicant has been awarded a degree qualification (not a qualification of equivalent level which is not a degree) which meets or exceeds the recognised standard of a Bachelor's degree in the UK. For overseas qualifications, the standard must be confirmed by UK NARIC	25
The endorsement must confirm that the institution has assessed the applicant and considers that–	25
(a) the applicant has a genuine, credible and innovative business idea, and	
(b) the applicant will spend the majority of his working time on developing business ventures, and	
(c) if the applicant's previous grant of leave was as a Tier 1 (Graduate Entrepreneur), he has made satisfactory progress in developing his business since that leave was granted	
The endorsement must also confirm the applicant's intended business sector or business intention. Points will not be awarded if this business will be mainly engaged in property development or property management. The principle is that business income must be generated from the supply of goods and/or services and not derived from the increased value of property or any income generated through property, such as rent.	

For language qualifications, see **26 Language Skills (Appendix B)**, below; and for maintenance qualifications see **27 Maintenance Funds (Appendix C)**, below.

13 Tier 2 (Intra-Company Transfer) Migrants

This route enables multinational employers to transfer their existing employees from outside the EEA to their UK branch for training purposes or to fill a specific vacancy that cannot be filled by a British or EEA worker. There are four sub-categories in this route (para 245G)–

(i) Short Term staff: for established employees of multi-national companies who are being transferred to a skilled job in the UK for 12 months or less that could not be carried out by a new recruit from the resident workforce;

(ii) Long Term staff: for established employees of multi-national companies who are being transferred to a skilled job in the UK which will, or may, last for more than 12 months and could not be carried out by a new recruit from the resident workforce;

(iii) Graduate Trainee: for recent graduate recruits of multi-national companies who are being transferred to the UK branch of the same organisation as part of a structured graduate training programme, which clearly defines progression towards a managerial or specialist role;

(iv) Skills Transfer: for overseas employees of multi-national companies who are being transferred to the UK branch of the same organisation in a graduate occupation to learn the skills and knowledge they will need to perform their jobs overseas, or to impart their specialist skills to the UK workforce.

All migrants wishing to enter the UK as a Tier 2 (Intra-Company Transfer) Migrant must have a valid entry clearance for entry under this route. If they do not, entry will be refused (para 245GA).

To qualify for entry clearance as a Tier 2 (Intra-Company Transfer) Migrant, an applicant must meet the requirements listed below. If the requirements are met, entry clearance will be granted. If they are not, the application will be refused (para 245GB).

The requirements are–

(a) the applicant must not fall for refusal under the general grounds for refusal;

(b) the applicant must have a minimum of 50 points under Appendix A (see 15 **The points system: Tier 2 (Intra-Company Transfer) Migrants and Tier 2 (General) Migrants**, below);

(c) the applicant must have a minimum of 10 points under Appendix C, see 27 **Maintenance Funds (Appendix C)**, below;

(d) except where the period of engagement recorded by the Certificate of Sponsorship used in support of the entry clearance or leave to remain was granted for a period of three months or less, the applicant must not have had entry clearance or leave to remain as a Tier 2 Migrant at any time during the 12 months immediately before the date of the application;

(e) para (d) above does not apply to an applicant who was not in the UK with leave as a Tier 2 migrant at any time during the above 12-month period, and provides evidence to show this; or is applying under the Long Term Staff sub-category and who has, or last had entry clearance or leave to remain as a Tier 2 (Intra-Company Transfer) Migrant in the Short Term staff, Graduate Trainee or Skills Transfer sub-categories, or under the Rules in place before 6 April 2011; or will be paid a gross annual salary (including such allowances as are specified as acceptable) of £155,300 or higher;

(f) an applicant who has, or was last granted, leave as a Student, a Student Nurse, a Student Re-Sitting an Examination, a Student Writing up a Thesis, a Postgraduate Doctor or Dentist, or a Tier 4 Migrant and–

    (i) is currently being sponsored by a government or international scholarship agency; or

    (ii) was being so sponsored and that sponsorship came to an end 12 months ago or less,

must provide the unconditional written consent of the sponsoring Government or agency to the application and must provide specified documents to show that this requirement has been met;

(g) the applicant must be at least 16 years old;

(h) where the applicant is under 18, the application must be supported by the applicant's parents or legal guardian, or by one parent if that parent has sole legal responsibility for the child;

(i) where the applicant is under 18, the applicant's parents or legal guardian, or just one parent if that parent has sole responsibility for the child, must confirm that they consent to the arrangements for the applicant's travel to, and reception and care in, the UK.

Entry clearance will be granted with effect from (para 245GC)–

(i) 14 days before the start date of the applicant's employment in the UK, as recorded by the Certificate of Sponsorship Checking Service,

(ii) 7 days before the intended date of travel recorded by the applicant either through the relevant online application process or in the specified application form, providing this is not more than 14 days after the start date of the applicant's employment in the UK, as recorded by the Certificate of Sponsorship Checking Service, or

(iii) the date entry clearance is granted,

whichever is the latest. Entry clearance will be granted for a period ending:

(i) 14 days after the end date of the applicant's employment in the UK, as recorded by the Certificate of Sponsorship Checking Service, or

(ii) at the end of the maximum time available for the Tier 2 (Intra-Company Transfer) subcategory, as set out in (c), from the date entry clearance was granted,

whichever is the earlier. The maximum time referred to in (b)(ii) is–

(i) 6 months, if the applicant is applying in the Skills Transfer subcategory,

(ii) 12 months, if the applicant is applying in either of the Graduate Trainee or Short Term Staff sub-categories, or

(iii) 5 years and 1 month, if the applicant is applying in the Long Term Staff sub-category.

To qualify for leave to remain as a Tier 2 (Intra-Company Transfer) Migrant, an applicant must meet the requirements listed below. If they do, leave to remain will be granted. If they do not, the application will be refused (para 245GD). The requirements are–

(a) the applicant must not fall for refusal under the general grounds for refusal, and must not be an illegal entrant;

(b) to (e) the applicant must have, or have last been granted, entry clearance, in the appropriate category as set out in para 245GD; and

(f) must have a minimum of 50 points under Appendix A, see 15 **The points system: Tier 2 (Intra-Company Transfer) Migrants and Tier 2 (General) Migrants**, below;

(g) *deleted*;

(h) the applicant must have a minimum of 10 points under Appendix C, see 27 **Maintenance Funds (Appendix C)**, below;

(i) the applicant must be at least 16 years old;

(j) where the applicant is under 18 years of age, the application must be supported by their parents or legal guardian, or by just one parent if that parent has sole legal responsibility for the child;

(k) where the applicant is under 18 years of age, the applicant's parents or legal guardian, or just one parent if that parent has sole legal responsibility for the child, must confirm that they consent to the arrangements for the applicant's care in the UK.

(l) the applicant must not be in the UK in breach of immigration laws except that any period of overstaying for a period of 28 days or less will be disregarded.

The period for which leave to remain will be granted varies according to the Tier 2 (Intra-Company Transfer) sub-category which applies to the applicant and to their job (see para 245GE) and will be subject to the same conditions as entry clearance (see above).

To qualify for indefinite leave to remain as a Tier 2 (Intra-Company Transfer) Migrant an applicant must (para 245GF)–

(a) *deleted*

(b) not fall for refusal under the general grounds for refusal, and must not be an illegal entrant;

(c) have spent a continuous period of 5 years lawfully in the UK, of which the most recent period must have been spent with leave as a Tier 2 (Intra-Company Transfer) Migrant, Qualifying Work Permit Holder or Representative of an Overseas Business

(d) the continuous period of 5 years in (c) above must include a period of leave as a Tier 2 (Intra-Company Transfer) Migrant granted under the Rules in place before 6 April 2010, or a Qualifying Work Permit Holder, provided that the work permit was granted because the applicant was the subject of an Intra-Company Transfer

(e) the sponsor that issued the certificate of sponsorship that led to the applicant's last grant of leave must still hold, or have applied for a renewal of, a Tier 2 (Intra-Company Transfer) Sponsor licence and must certify in writing that he still requires the applicant for employment and that the applicant is paid at or above the appropriate rate for the job (as stated in the codes of practice for Tier 2 in Appendix J to the Rules) or where the applicant is not paid at that rate only due to maternity, paternity, shared parental or adoption leave, the date that leave started and that the applicant was paid at the appropriate rate immediately before the leave;

(f) the applicant must provide the documents specified in para 245GF-SD to evidence the sponsor's certification in subsection (e) and to evidence the reason for the absences set out in para 245AAA;

(g) the applicant must have sufficient knowledge of the English language and sufficient knowledge about life in the UK, in accordance with Appendix KoLL;

(h) the applicant must not be in the UK in breach of immigration laws except that any period of overstaying for a period of 28 days or less will be disregarded; and

(i) where time has been spent in the Channel Islands or Isle of Man, special rules must be complied with.

14 Tier 2 (General), (Minister of Religion) and (Sportsperson) Migrants

These routes enable UK employers to recruit workers from outside the EEA to fill a particular vacancy that cannot be filled by a British or EEA worker. All migrants arriving in the UK and wishing to enter as a Tier 2 (General) Migrant, Tier 2 (Minister of Religion) Migrant or Tier 2 (Sportsperson) Migrant must have a valid entry clearance for entry under the relevant one of these routes. If they do not have a valid entry clearance, entry will be refused (para 245HA).

To qualify for entry clearance under one of these categories, an applicant must meet the requirements listed below. If the requirements are met, entry clearance will be granted. If they are not, the application will be refused (para 245HB).

The requirements are–

(a) the applicant must not fall for refusal under the general grounds for refusal;

(b) if applying as a Tier 2 (General) Migrant, the applicant must have a minimum of 50 points under Appendix A, see 15 **The points system: Tier 2 (Intra-Company Transfer) Migrants and Tier 2 (General) Migrants**, below;

(c) if applying as a Tier 2 (Minister of religion) Migrant, the applicant must have a minimum of 50 points under Appendix A, see 16 **The points system: Tier 2 (Ministers of Religion)**, below;

(d) if applying as a Tier 2 (sportsperson) Migrant, the applicant must have a minimum of 50 points under Appendix A, see 17 **The points system: Tier 2 (Sportsperson)**. below;

(e) the applicant must have a minimum of 10 points under Appendix B, see 26 **Language Skills (Appendix B)**, below;

(f) the applicant must have a minimum of 10 points under Appendix C, see **27 Maintenance Funds (Appendix C)**, below;

(g) except where the period of engagement recorded by the Certificate of Sponsorship used in support of the entry clearance or leave to remain was granted for a period of three months or less, the applicant must not have had entry clearance or leave to remain as a Tier 2 Migrant at any time during the 12 months immediately before the date of the application, unless the applicant was not in the UK with leave as a Tier 2 Migrant during this period, and provides evidence to show this, or will be paid a gross annual salary (including such allowances as are specified as acceptable) of £155,300 or higher;

(h) an applicant who has, or was last granted, leave as a Student, a Student Nurse, a Student Re-Sitting an Examination, a Student Writing-Up a Thesis, a Postgraduate Doctor or Dentist or a Tier 4 Migrant and who (i) is currently being sponsored by a government or international scholarship agency, or (ii) was being sponsored by a government or international scholarship agency, and that sponsorship came to an end 12 months ago or less, must provide the unconditional written consent of the sponsoring Government or agency to the application and must provide the specified documents to show that this requirement has been met;

(i) the applicant must be at least 16 years old;

(j) where the applicant is under 18 years of age, the application must be supported by the applicant's parents or legal guardian, or by one parent if that parent has sole legal responsibility for the child;

(k) where the applicant is under 18 years of age, the applicant's parents or legal guardian, or one parent if that parent has sole responsibility for the child, must confirm that they consent to the arrangements for the applicant's travel to, and reception and care in, the UK; and

(l) if the sponsor is a limited company, the applicant must not own more than 10% of its shares, unless the gross annual salary including such allowances as are specified as acceptable for this purpose in para 79 of Appendix A) is £153,500 or higher;

(m) if the applicant is applying as a Tier 2 (Minister of Religion) Migrant, the Entry Clearance Officer must be satisfied that the applicant genuinely intends to undertake, and is capable of undertaking, the role and will not undertake employment in the UK other than under the terms of para 245HC(e)(iii);

(n) to support the assessment in para (m), the Entry Clearance Officer may (i) request additional information and evidence, and refuse the application if it is not provided. Any requested documents must be received by the Home Office within 28 calendar days of the date the request is sent, and (ii) may request the applicant attends an interview, and refuse the application if he fails to do so without providing a reasonable explanation.

(o) if the Entry Clearance Officer is not satisfied following the assessment in para (m), no points will be awarded under paras 85 to 92A of Appendix A.

(p) the Entry Clearance Officer may decide not to carry out the assessment in para (m) if the application already falls for refusal on other grounds, but reserves the right to carry it out in any reconsideration of the decision.

Entry clearance will be granted with effect from (para 245HC)–

(i) 14 days before the start date of the applicant's employment in the UK, as recorded by the Certificate of Sponsorship Checking Service,

(ii) 7 days before the intended date of travel recorded by the applicant either through the relevant online application process or in the specified application form, providing this is not more than 14 days after the start date of the applicant's employment in the UK, as recorded by the Certificate of Sponsorship Checking Service, or

(iii) the date entry clearance is granted,

whichever is the latest.

Entry clearance will be granted for a period ending–

(i) 14 days after the end date of the applicant's employment in the UK, as recorded by the Certificate of Sponsorship Checking Service, or

(ii) at the end of the maximum time available for the applicable Tier 2 (General), Tier 2 (Minister of Religion) or Tier 2 (Sportsperson) category, as set below, from the date entry clearance was granted,

whichever is the earlier.

The maximum time referred to in (b)(ii) is–

(i) 5 years and 1 month, if the applicant is applying as a Tier 2 (General) Migrant; or

(ii) 3 years and 1 month, if the applicant is applying as a Tier 2 (Minister of Religion) Migrant or a Tier 2 (Sportsperson) Migrant.

Entry clearance will be subject to the following conditions (para 245HC(d))–

(i) no recourse to public funds;

(ii) registration with the police, if this is required by para 326 of the Immigration Rules; and

(iii) no employment except–

(1) working for the Sponsor in the employment that the Certificate of Sponsorship Checking Service records that the migrant is being sponsored to do;

(2) supplementary employment;

(3) voluntary work; and

(4) if the applicant is applying as a Tier 2 (Sportsperson) Migrant, employment as a sportsperson for his national team while his national team is in the UK and temporary engagement as a sports broadcaster.

(iv) where the applicant is 18 years of age or over at the time their leave is granted, or will be aged 18 before their period of limited leave expires, no study without a valid Academic Technology Approval Scheme clearance certificate from the Counter-Proliferation Department of the Foreign Office.

To qualify for leave to remain as a Tier 2 (General), (Minister of Religion) or (Sportsperson) Migrant, an applicant must meet the requirements listed below. If he does, leave to remain will be granted. If he does not, the application will be refused (para 245HD).

The requirements are—

(a) the applicant must not fall for refusal under the general grounds for refusal, and must not be an illegal entrant;

(b) the applicant must have, or have last been granted, entry clearance, leave to enter or leave to remain as a–
  (i) Tier 1 Migrant;
  (ii) Tier 2 Migrant;
  (iii) Highly Skilled Migrant,
  (iv) Innovator,
  (v) Jewish Agency Employee,
  (vi) Member of the Operational Ground Staff of an Overseas-owned Airline,
  (vii) Minister of Religion, Missionary or Member of a Religious Order,
  (viii) participant in the Fresh Talent: Working in Scotland Scheme,
  (ix) participant in the International Graduates Scheme (or its predecessor, the Science and Engineering Graduates Scheme),
  (x) Qualifying Work Permit Holder,
  (xi) Representative of an Overseas Business
  (xii) Representative of an Overseas Newspaper, News Agency or Broadcasting Organisation,
  (xiii) Tier 5 (Temporary Worker) Migrant, or
  (xiv) partner of a Relevant Points Based System Migrant if the relevant Points Based System Migrant is a Tier 4 Migrant;
  (xv) a Tier 4 Migrant (and, in respect of such leave, is or was last sponsored by a UK recognised body or a body in receipt of public funding as a higher education institution; or an overseas higher education institution to undertake a short-term study abroad programme in the UK),
  (xvi) a Student,
  (xvii) a Student Nurse,
  (xviii) a Student Re-Sitting an Examination,
  (xix) a Person Writing Up a Thesis,
  (xx) an Overseas Qualified Nurse or Midwife,
  (xxi) a Postgraduate Doctor or Dentist, or
  (xxii) a Student Union Sabbatical Officer.

(c) an applicant who has, or was last granted leave as a Tier 2 (Intra-Company Transfer) Migrant must (i) have previously had leave in that category under the Rules in place before 6 April 2010, or in the Established Staff sub-category under the Rules in place before 6 April 2011, (ii) not have been granted entry clearance in this or any other route since the grant of leave referred to in (i) above; and (iii) not be applying to work for the same Sponsor as sponsored him when he was last granted leave;

(d) an applicant under (b)(xv)-(xxii) above–
  (i) must have completed and passed a UK recognised bachelor's or master's degree (not a qualification of equivalent level which is not a degree), a UK Postgraduate Certificate in Education or Professional Graduate Diploma of Education (not a qualification of equivalent level), or must have completed a minimum of 12 months study in the UK towards a UK PhD;
  (ii) this study must (except for an applicant sponsored by a UK institution under (b)(xv) above) have been at a UK institution that is a UK recognised or listed body, or which holds a sponsor licence under Tier 4 of the Points Based System;
  (iii) the applicant must have studied the course referred to in (i) during his last grant of leave, or a period of continuous leave which includes his last grant of leave, (for these purposes continuous leave will not be considered to have been broken in specified circumstances);
  (iv) the applicant's periods of UK study and/or research towards the course in (i) must have been undertaken whilst he had entry clearance, leave to enter or leave to remain in the UK that was not subject to a restriction preventing him from undertaking that course of study and/or research;
  (v) *deleted*,
  (vi) If the applicant is currently being sponsored by a government or international scholarship agency, or was being so sponsored and that sponsorship came to an end 12 months ago or less, the applicant must provide the unconditional written consent of the sponsoring Government or agency to the application and must provide specified documents to show that this requirement has been met;
  (vii) the applicant must provide an original degree certificate, academic transcript or an academic

reference on official headed paper of the institution, which clearly shows his name, the course title/award, the course duration (except in the case of a degree certificate), and unless the course is a PhD course, the date of course completion and pass (or the date of award in the case of a degree certificate);

(e) an applicant who was last granted leave as a Tier 5 (Temporary Worker) Migrant must have been granted such leave in the Creative and Sporting sub-category of Tier 5 in order to allow the applicant to work as a professional footballer, and the applicant must be applying for leave to remain as a Tier 2 (Sportsperson) Migrant;

(f) if applying as a Tier 2 (General) Migrant, the applicant must have a minimum of 50 points under Appendix A, see **15 The points system: Tier 2 (Intra-Company Transfer) Migrants and Tier 2 (General) Migrants,** below;

(g) if applying as a Tier 2 (Minister of Religion) Migrant, the applicant must have a minimum of 50 points under Appendix A, see **16 The points system: Tier 2 (Ministers of Religion)**, below;

(h) if applying as a Tier 2 (Sportsperson) Migrant, the applicant must have a minimum of 50 points under Appendix A, see **17 The points system: Tier 2 (Sportsperson)**. below;

(i) the applicant must have a minimum of 10 points under Appendix B, see **26 Language Skills (Appendix B)**, below;

(j) the applicant must have a minimum of 10 points under Appendix C, see **17 Maintenance Funds (Appendix C)**, below;

(k) except where the period of engagement recorded by the Certificate of Sponsorship used in support of such entry clearance or leave to remain was three months or less, the applicant must not have had entry clearance or leave to remain as a Tier 2 Migrant at any time during the 12 months immediately before the date of the application, unless his last grant of leave was as a Tier 2 Migrant, or he was not in the UK with leave as a Tier 2 Migrant during this period, and provides evidence to show this, or he will be paid a gross annual salary (as recorded by the Certificate of Sponsorship Checking Service entry, and including such allowances as are specified as acceptable for this purpose) of £155,300 or higher;

(l) the applicant must be at least 16 years old;

(m) where the applicant is under 18 years of age, the application must be supported by the applicant's parents or legal guardian, or by just one parent if that parent has sole legal responsibility for the child;

(n) where the applicant is under 18 years of age, the applicant's parents or legal guardian, or just one parent if that parent has sole legal responsibility for the child, must confirm that they consent to the arrangements for the applicant's care in the UK;

(o) if the sponsor is a limited company, the applicant must not own more than 10% of its shares unless the gross annual salary (including such allowances as are specified as acceptable for this purpose) is £155,300 or higher;

(p) the applicant must not be in the UK in breach of immigration laws except that any period of overstaying for a period of 28 days or less will be disregarded;

(q) if the applicant is applying as a Tier 2 (Minister of Religion) Migrant, the Secretary of State must be satisfied that the applicant genuinely intends to undertake, and is capable of undertaking, the role and will not undertake employment in the UK other than under the terms of para 245HE(d)(iii);

(r) to support the assessment in para 245HD(q), the Secretary of State may request additional information and evidence, and refuse the application if it is not provided. Any requested documents must be received by the Home Office within 28 calendar days of the date the request is sent, and request the applicant attends an interview, and refuse the application if the applicant fails to comply with any such request without providing a reasonable explanation;

(s) if the Secretary of State is not satisfied following the assessment in para 245HD(q), no points will be awarded under Appendix A;

(t) the Secretary of State may decide not to carry out the assessment in para 245HD(q) if the application already falls for refusal on other grounds, but reserves the right to carry it out in any reconsideration of the decision.

Leave to remain will be granted for whichever of the following is the shortest–

(i) the length of the period of engagement plus 14 days,

(ii) 5 years if the applicant is applying as a Tier 2 (General) Migrant, or

(iii) 3 years if the applicant is applying as a Tier 2 (Minister of Religion) Migrant or a Tier 2 (Sportsperson) Migrant, or

(iv) except where (b) applies, the difference between the continuous period of leave that the applicant has already been granted (notwithstanding any breaks between periods of leave of up to 28 days) as a Tier 2 Migrant (other than as a Tier 2 (Intra-Company Transfer) Migrant), and 6 years.

If the calculation of period of leave comes to zero or a negative number, leave to remain will be refused. (para 245HE).

The 6 year restriction set out in (a)(iv) does not apply if the applicant previously had leave under the Rules in place before 6 April 2011 as (i) a Tier 2 (General) Migrant, a Tier 2 (Minister of Religion) Migrant, a Tier 2 (Sportsperson) Migrant, a Jewish Agency Employee, a Member of the Operational Ground Staff of an Overseas-owned Airline, a Minister of Religion, Missionary or Member of a Religious Order, a Qualifying Work Permit Holder, or a Representative of an Overseas Newspaper, News Agency or Broadcasting Organisation, and (ii) has not been granted entry clearance as a Tier 2 (General) Migrant, Tier 2 (Minister of Religion) Migrant or Tier 2 (Sportsperson) Migrant under the Rules in place from 6 April 2011, and (iii) has not been granted entry clearance, leave to enter or leave to remain in any other category since the grant of leave referred to in (i) above.

Leave to remain will be granted subject to the following conditions—
 (i) no recourse to public funds;
 (ii) registration with the police, if this is required by para 326 of the Rules; and
 (iii) no employment except—
    (1) working for the sponsor in the employment that the Certificate of Sponsorship Checking Service records that the migrant is being sponsored to do, subject to any notification of a change to the details of that employment, other than prohibited changes as defined in para 323AA,
    (2) supplementary employment,
    (3) voluntary work,
    (4) until the start date of the period of engagement, any employment which the applicant was lawfully engaged in on the date of his application, and
    (5) if the applicant is applying as a Tier 2 (Sportsperson) Migrant, employment as a sports person for his national team while his national team is in the UK, playing in British University and College Sport (BUCS) competitions and temporary engagement as a sports broadcaster;
 (iv) where the applicant is 18 years of age or over at the time their leave is granted, or will be aged 18 before their period of limited leave expires, no study without a valid Academic Technology Approval Scheme clearance certificate from the Counter-Proliferation Department of the Foreign Office.

To qualify for indefinite leave to remain as a Tier 2 (General), or (Sportsperson) Migrant, an applicant must meet the requirements listed below. If he does, indefinite leave to remain will be granted. If he does not, the application will be refused (para 245HF).

The requirements are that—
 (a) the applicant must not fall for refusal under the general grounds for refusal, and must not be an illegal entrant;
 (b) The applicant must have spent a continuous period of 5 years lawfully in the UK, of which the most recent period must have been spent with leave as a Tier 2 (General) Migrant or Tier 2 (Sportsperson) Migrant, in any combination of the following categories—
    (i) as a Tier 1 Migrant, other than a Tier 1 (Post Study Work) Migrant or a Tier 1 (Graduate Entrepreneur) Migrant,
    (ii) as a Tier 2 (General) Migrant, a Tier 2 (Minister of Religion) Migrant or a Tier 2 (Sportsperson) Migrant,
    (iii) as a Tier 2 (Intra-Company Transfer) Migrant, provided the continuous period of 5 years spent lawfully in the UK includes a period of leave as:—
        (1) a Tier 2 (Intra-Company Transfer) Migrant granted under the Rules in place before 6 April 2010, or
        (2) a Qualifying Work Permit Holder, provided that the work permit was granted because the applicant was the subject of an Intra-Company Transfer,
    (iv) as a Representative of an Overseas Business,
    (v) as a Highly Skilled Migrant,
    (vi) as an innovator,
    (vii) as a Qualifying Work Permit Holder,
    (viii) as a Member of the Operational Ground Staff of an Overseas-owned Airline,
    (ix) as a Minister of Religion, Missionary or Member of a Religious Order, or
    (x) as a Representative of an Overseas Newspaper, News Agency or Broadcasting Organisation.
 (c) the Sponsor that issued the Certificate of Sponsorship that led to the applicant's last grant of leave must still hold, or have applied for a renewal of, a Tier 2 Sponsor licence in the relevant category; and must certify in writing that—
    (1) he still requires the applicant for the employment in question for the foreseeable future,
    (2) the gross annual salary paid by the Sponsor, and that this salary will be paid for the foreseeable future,
    (3) if the applicant is currently on maternity, paternity, shared parental or adoption leave, the date that leave started, confirmation of what the applicant's salary was immediately before the leave, and what it will be on the applicant's return, and
    (4) if the applicant is paid hourly, the number of hours per week the salary in (2) or (3) is based on;
 (d) the salary paid must comply with the requirements set out in para 245HF(d)-(g) of the Rules;
 (e) the applicant must provide specified documents to evidence any absences that break their continuous presence in the UK;
 (f) the applicant must have sufficient knowledge of the English language and sufficient knowledge about life in the United Kingdom, in accordance with Appendix KoLL;
 (g) the applicant must not be in the UK in breach of immigration laws except that any period of overstaying for a period of 28 days or less will be disregarded; and
 (h) where time has been spent in the Channel Islands or Isle of Man, special rules must be complied with.

Similar provisions apply to qualifying for indefinite leave to remain as a Tier 2 (Minister of Religion) Migrant (para 245HG).

15 The points system: Tier 2 (Intra-Company Transfer) Migrants and Tier 2 (General) Migrants

Attributes

An applicant applying for entry or leave to remain as a Tier 2 (Intra-Company Transfer) or (General) Migrant must score 50 points for attributes.

Available points for (Intra-Company Transfer) Migrants are shown in Table 11 as follows–

Table 11

Criterion	Points
Certificate of Sponsorship	30
Appropriate salary	20

Available points for (General) Migrants are shown in Table 11A as follows–

Table 11A

Certificate of Sponsorship	Points
Either	
Job offer passes Resident Labour Market Test (see the Note on **Employment of Persons From Abroad**), or	30
Resident Labour Market Test exemption applies, or	30
Continuing to work in the same job for the same Sponsor and	30
Appropriate salary	20

Note.–In general, no points will be awarded if the salary is less than £20,500 (Appendix A, para 79A). No points will be awarded for salary if it is less than the appropriate rate for the job as stated in the codes of practice in Appendix J, unless the applicant is an established entertainer (para 79B).

There is an annual limit of 20,700 Certificates of Sponsorship available to sponsors under Tier 2 (General), although the limit does not apply to certain applications, including those who will earn more than £153,500 a year (Appendix A, para 80A and Guidance). A Sponsor must apply to the Secretary of State for a Certificate of Sponsorship and an application will not granted unless it scores a minimum of 20 points for Type of Job and a minimum of 1 point for salary, as set out in Table 11D.

Table 11D–

Type of Job	Points	Salary	Points
Shortage Occupation	130	£75,000– £99,999.99	55
		£100,000– £155,299.99	60
PhD-level occupation code and job passes Resident Labour Market Test	75	£50,000– £54,999.99 and then on a sliding scale up to–	30
		£70,000–£74,999.99	50
Job passes Resident Labour Market Test or an exemption applies	20	£20,800–£21,999.99 and then on a sliding scale up to–	41
		£45,000–£49,999.99	25

16 The points system: Tier 2 (Ministers of Religion)

An applicant applying for entry clearance or leave to remain as a Tier 2 (Ministers of Religion) Migrant must score 50 points for attributes. The available points are shown in Table 12 which simply states–

Criterion	Points
Certificate of sponsorship	50

For language qualifications, see **26 Language Skills (Appendix B)**, below; and for maintenance qualifications see **27 Maintenance Funds (Appendix C)**, below.

17 The points system: Tier 2 (Sportsperson)

An applicant applying for entry clearance or leave to remain as a Tier 2 (Sportsperson) Migrant must score 50 points for attributes. The available points are shown in Table 13 which simply states–

Criterion	Points
Certificate of sponsorship	50

For language qualifications, see **26 Language Skills (Appendix B)**, below; and for maintenance qualifications see **27 Maintenance Funds (Appendix C)**, below.

18 Tier 4 (General) Students

This route is for migrants aged 16 or over who wish to study in the UK at an institution that is not an Academy or a school maintained by a local authority (para 245ZT). All migrants arriving in the UK and wishing to enter as a Tier 4 (General) Student must have a valid entry clearance for entry under this route. If they do not have a valid entry clearance, entry will be refused (para 245ZU).

To qualify for entry clearance as a Tier 4 (General) Student, an applicant must meet the requirements listed below. If the requirements are met, entry clearance will be granted. If they are not, the application will be refused (para 245ZV).

The requirements are—

(a) the applicant must not fall for refusal under the general grounds for refusal;

(b) the applicant must have a minimum of 30 points under Appendix A;

(c) the applicant must have a minimum of 10 points under Appendix C, see **27 Maintenance Funds (Appendix C)**, below;

(ca) the applicant must, if required to do so on examination or interview, be able to demonstrate without the assistance of an interpreter English language proficiency of a standard to be expected from an individual who has reached the standard specified in a Confirmation;

(d) *deleted*

(da) if the applicant wishes to undertake—

    (i) undergraduate or postgraduate studies leading to a Doctorate or Masters degree by research in one of the disciplines listed in para 1 of Appendix 6 to; or

    (ii) undergraduate or postgraduate studies leading to a taught Masters degree in one of the disciplines listed in para 2 of Appendix 6; or

    (iii) a period of study or research in excess of 6 months in one of the disciplines listed in paras 1 or 2 of Appendix 6 of the Rules at an institution of higher education where this forms part of an overseas postgraduate qualification;

then he must hold a valid Academic Technology Approval Scheme clearance certificate from the Counter-Proliferation Department of the Foreign and Commonwealth Office which relates to the course, or area of research, that he will be taking and at the institution at which he wishes to undertake it and must provide specified documents to show that these requirements have been met.

(e) if the applicant wishes to be a postgraduate doctor or dentist on a recognised Foundation Programme—

    (i) he must have successfully completed a recognised UK degree in medicine or dentistry from an institution with a Tier 4 Sponsor Licence, or a UK publicly funded institution of further or higher education, or a UK bona fide private education institution which maintains satisfactory records of enrolment and attendance;

    (ii) he must have previously been granted leave as a Tier 4 (General) Student, or as a Student, for the final academic year of the studies referred to in paragraph (i) above, and as a Tier 4 (General) Student, or as a Student, for at least one other academic year (aside from the final year) of the studies referred to in paragraph (i) above;

    (iii) if he has previously been granted leave as a Postgraduate Doctor or Dentist, he must not be seeking entry clearance or leave to enter or remain to a date beyond 3 years from the date on which he was first granted leave to enter or remain in that category; and

    (iv) if he has previously been granted leave as a Tier 4 (General) Student to undertake a course as a postgraduate doctor or dentist, he must not be seeking entry clearance or leave to enter or remain to a date beyond 3 years from the date on which the applicant was first granted leave to undertake such a course;

(f) if he is currently being sponsored by a Government or international scholarship agency, or within the last 12 months has come to the end of such a period of sponsorship, he must provide the written consent of the sponsoring Government or agency to the application and must provide specified documents to show that this requirement has been met;

(g) if the course is below degree level, the grant of entry clearance he is seeking must not lead to his having been granted more than 2 years in the UK as a Tier 4 Migrant since the age of 18 studying courses that did not consist of degree level study;

(ga) if the course is at degree level or above, the grant of entry clearance the applicant is seeking must not lead to the applicant having been granted more than 5 years in the UK as a Tier 4(General) Migrant, or as a Student, studying courses at degree level or above unless—

    (i) the applicant has successfully completed a course at degree level in the UK of a minimum duration of 4 academic years, and will follow a course of study at Master's degree level sponsored by a UK recognised body or a body in receipt of public funding as a higher education institution from the Department of Employment and Learning in Northern Ireland, the Higher Education Funding Council for England, the Higher Education Funding Council for Wales or the Scottish Funding Council, and the grant of entry clearance must not lead to the applicant having spent more than 6 years in the UK as a Tier 4 (General) Migrant, or as a Student, studying courses at degree level or above; or

    (ii) the grant of entry clearance is to follow a course leading to the award of a PhD, and the applicant is sponsored by a UK recognised body or a body in receipt of public funding as a higher education institution from the Department of Employment and Learning in Northern Ireland, the Higher Education Funding Council for England, the Higher Education Funding Council for Wales or the Scottish Funding Council; or

(iii) the applicant is following a course of study in Architecture; Medicine; Dentistry; Law (where the applicant has completed a course at degree level in the UK and is progressing to a law conversion course, an accelerated graduate LLB in Scotland, the Legal Practice Course in England and Wales, a Diploma in Professional Legal Practice in Scotland; or the Bar Professional Training Course); Veterinary Medicine & Science; or Music at a music college that is a member of Conservatoires UK (CUK).

(gb) If the applicant has completed a course leading to the award of a PhD, postgraduate research qualification or a Masters degree by research in the UK, the grant of entry clearance the applicant is seeking must not lead to the applicant having spent more than 8 years in the UK as a Tier 4 (General) Migrant, or as a Student,.

(h) he must be at least 16 years old;

(i) where he is under 18 years of age, the application must be supported by the applicant's parents or legal guardian, or by just one parent if that parent has sole legal responsibility for the child;

(j) where he is under 18 years of age, the applicant's parents or legal guardian, or just one parent if that parent has sole responsibility for the child, must confirm that they consent to the arrangements for the applicant's travel to, and reception and care in, the UK;

(k) the Entry Clearance Officer must be satisfied that the applicant is a genuine student.

Entry clearance will be granted for the duration of the course. In addition, entry clearance will also be granted for the following periods (para 245ZW)–

Type of course	Period before course	Period after course
12 months or more	1 month before the course starts or 7 days before the intended date of travel, whichever is later	4 months
6-12 months	as above	2 months
Pre-sessional course (less than 6 months)	as above	1 month
Non pre-sessional course (less than 6 months)	7 days	7 days
Postgraduate Doctor or Dentist	1 month before the course starts or 7 days before the intended date of travel, whichever is later	1 month

If the grant of entry clearance is made less than 1 month or, in the case of a course of less than 6 months that is not a pre-sessional course, less than 7 days before the start of the course, entry clearance will be granted with immediate effect.

A pre-sessional course is a course which prepares a student for his main course of study in the UK.

Entry clearance will be granted subject to the following conditions (para 245ZW(c))–

(i) no recourse to public funds;

(ii) registration with the police, if this is required by para 326 of the Rules;

(iii) no employment except–

(1) employment during term time of no more than 20 hours per week and employment (of any duration) during vacations where the student is studying a degree level course and is sponsored (i) by a Recognised Body in receipt of public funds or (ii) by an overseas higher education institution to undertake a short-term Study Abroad Programme in the UK;

(2) employment during term time of no more than 10 hours per week or of any duration during vacations where the student is following a course of study below degree level study and is sponsored as in (1)(i) above;

(3) *deleted*;

(4) as part of a course-related work placement which forms an assessed part of the course and provided that any period that the applicant spends on that placement does not exceed one third of the total length of the course undertaken in the UK (unless a statutory requirement provides otherwise and in other limited cases);

(5) as a Student Union Sabbatical Officer, for up to 2 years, provided the post is elective and is at the institution which is the applicant's Sponsor or they must be elected to a National Union of Students position;

(6) as a postgraduate doctor or dentist on a recognised Foundation Programme,

(7) until such time as a decision is received from the Home Office on an application which is supported by a Certificate of Sponsorship assigned by a licensed Tier 2 Sponsor and which is made following successful completion of course at degree level or above at a Recognised Body or a body in receipt of public funding as a higher education institution from the Department of Employment and Learning in Northern Ireland, the Higher Education Funding Council for England, the Higher Education Funding Council for Wales or the Scottish Funding Council and while the applicant has

extant leave, and any appeal or administrative review against that decision has been determined, employment with the Tier 2 Sponsor, in the role for which they assigned the Certificate of Sponsorship to the Tier 4 migrant;

(8) self-employment, providing the migrant has made an application for leave to remain as a Tier I (Graduate Entrepreneur) Migrant which (a) is supported by an endorsement from a qualifying Higher Education Institution, (b) is made following successful completion of a UK recognised Bachelor degree, Masters degree or PhD (not a qualification of equivalent level which is not a degree) course at a Recognised Body or a body in receipt of public funding as a higher education institution, and (c) is made while the applicant has extant leave, until such time as a decision is received from the Home Office on that application and any appeal or administrative review against that decision has been determined,

provided that the migrant is not self employed, or employed other than under the conditions of (8) above, or as a Doctor or Dentist in Training other than under the conditions of (v) below, professional sportsperson (including a sports coach) or an entertainer, and provided that their employment would not fill a permanent full time vacancy other than under the conditions of (7) above, or a vacancy on a recognised Foundation Programme or as a sabbatical officer;

(iv) no study except–

    (1) study at the institution that the Confirmation of Acceptance for Studies Checking Service records as the migrant's Sponsor unless–

        (a) the migrant is studying at an institution which is a partner institution of the migrant's sponsor; or

        (b) until such time as a decision is received from the Home Office on an application which is supported by a Confirmation of Acceptance for Studies assigned by a sponsor with Tier 4 Sponsor status and which is made while the applicant has extant leave, and any appeal or administrative review against that decision has been determined, the migrant is studying at the sponsor with Tier 4 Sponsor status that the Confirmation of Acceptance for Studies Checking Service records as having assigned such Confirmation of Acceptance for Studies to the migrant; or

        (c) the study is supplementary study; and

    (2) study on the course, or courses where a pre-sessional is included, for which the Confirmation of Acceptance for Studies was assigned, unless the student:

        (a) has yet to complete the course for which the Confirmation of Acceptance for Studies was assigned; and

        (b) begins studying a new course at their sponsor institution, instead of the course for which the Confirmation of Acceptance for Studies was assigned, and the new course is either at a higher or the same level as the course for which the Confirmation of Acceptance for Studies was assigned; and specified conditions are met;

    (3) subject to (1) and (2) above, study on a course (or period of research) to which paragraph 245ZV(da) applies only if the migrant holds a valid Academic Technology Approval Scheme certificate issued prior to the commencement of the course (or period of research) that specifically relates to the course (or area of research) and to the institution at which the migrant undertakes such course (or period of research). Where–

        (a) the migrant's course (or research) completion date reported on the Confirmation of Acceptance for Studies is postponed or delayed for a period of more than three calendar months, or if there are any changes to the course contents (or the research proposal), the migrant must apply for a new Academic Technology Approval Scheme certificate within 28 calendar days; and

        (b) the migrant begins studying a new course (or period of research) as permitted in (2) above and the new course (or area of research) is of a type specified in para 245ZV(da), the migrant must obtain an Academic Technology Approval Scheme clearance certificate relating to the new course (or area of research) prior to commencing it.

(v) no employment as a Doctor or Dentist in Training unless–

    (1) the course that the migrant is being sponsored to do is a recognised Foundation Programme, or

    (2) the migrant has made an application as a Tier 4 (General) Student which is supported by a Confirmation of Acceptance for Studies assigned by a assigned by a sponsor with Tier 4 Sponsor status to do a recognised Foundation Programme, and this study satisfies the requirements of (iv)(2) above, or

    (3) the migrant has made an application as a Tier 2 (General) Migrant which is supported by a Certificate of Sponsorship assigned by a licensed Tier 2 Sponsor to sponsor the applicant to work as a Doctor or Dentist in Training, and this employment satisfies the conditions of (iii)(7) above.

(vi) no study at Academies or schools maintained by a local authority, except as specified.

To qualify for leave to remain as a Tier 4 (General) Student, an applicant must meet the requirements listed below. If they do, leave to remain will be granted. If they do not, the application will be refused (para 245ZX). The requirements are–

(l) the applicant must not fall for refusal under the general grounds for refusal and must not be an illegal entrant;

(m) the applicant must have, or have last been granted, entry clearance, leave to enter or leave to remain–

    (i) as a Tier 4 (General) Student and, in respect of such leave, is or was last sponsored by a UK recognised body or a body in receipt of public funding as a higher education institution; or by an overseas higher education institution to undertake a short-term study abroad programme in the UK; by an Embedded College offering Pathway Courses; or an independent school;

    (ii) as a Tier 4 (Child) Student;

    (iii) as a Tier 1 (Post-study Work) Migrant;

    (iv) as a Tier 2 Migrant;

    (v) as a participant in the International Graduates Scheme (or its predecessor, the Science and Engineering Graduates Scheme);

    (vi) as a participant in the Fresh Talent: Working in Scotland Scheme;

    (vii) as a postgraduate doctor or dentist;

    (viii) *deleted*;

    (ix) as a student;

    (x) as a student nurse;

    (xi) as a student re-sitting an examination;

    (xii) as a student writing-up a thesis;

    (xiii) as a student union sabbatical officer; or

    (xiv) as a work permit holder;

(n) requirements (b) to (j) above must be satisfied;

(o) the applicant must not be applying for leave to remain for the purpose of studies which would commence more than 28 days after the his current entry clearance or leave to remain expires;

(p) the applicant must not be in the UK in breach of immigration laws except that any period of overstaying for a period of 28 days or less will be disregarded.

(q) where the applicant is applying for leave to remain as a Tier 4 (General) Student on the doctorate extension scheme, leave to remain as a Tier 4 (General) Student on the doctorate extension scheme must not have previously been granted; the applicant must have leave to remain as a Tier 4 (General) Student and must be following a course leading to the award of a PhD; the applicant must be sponsored by a Sponsor that is a Recognised Body or a body in receipt of public funding as a higher education institution and that sponsor will be the sponsor awarding the PhD; and the date of the application must be within 60 days of the expected end date of a course leading to the award of a PhD; and

(r) the Secretary of State must be satisfied that the applicant is a genuine student.

The period for which leave to remain will be granted is the same as the period of the course plus a period before and after which varies between 7 days and 4 months depending on the length of the course (para 245ZY).

Persons seeking leave to enter in this category must hold a biometric immigration document: see the Note on **Control of Immigration** at para **6 Biometric registration**.

19 The points system: Tier 4 (General) Students

Attributes

An applicant applying for entry clearance or leave to remain as a Tier 4 (General) Student must score 30 points for attributes. The available points are shown in Table 16 as follows–

Criterion	Points
Confirmation of Acceptance for Studies	30

A Confirmation of Acceptance for Studies (CAS) will only be considered to be valid if–

(a) it was issued no more than 6 months before the application is made;

(b) the application for entry clearance or leave to remain is made no more than 3 months before the start date of the course of study as stated on the CAS;

(c) the sponsor has not withdrawn the offer since the CAS was issued;

(d) it was issued by an institution with a Tier 4 (General) Student Sponsor Licence;

(e) the institution still holds such a licence at the time the application for entry clearance or leave to remain is determined;

(f) it contains such information as is specified as mandatory in guidance published by the United Kingdom Border Agency; and

(g) if it was not issued for a course of studies, it was issued for a full-time, salaried, elected executive position as a student union sabbatical officer to an applicant who is part-way through their studies or who is being sponsored to fill the position in the academic year immediately after their graduation.

A CAS reference number will only be valid if it links to a CAS Checking Service entry that names the applicant as the migrant and confirms that the Sponsor is sponsoring him in the Tier 4 category indicated by the migrant in his application for leave to remain (that is, as a Tier 4 (General) Student or a Tier 4 (Child) Student), and that reference number has not been cancelled by the Sponsor or by UK Visas and Immigration since it was assigned. The applicant must supply, as evidence of previous qualifications, specified documents that he used to obtain the offer of a place on a course from the Sponsor and the course must meet specified requirements, or the applicant must come from a specified country or meet English language requirements.

If the applicant is re-sitting examinations or repeating a module of a course, the applicant must not previously have re-sat the same examination or repeated the same module more than once, unless the Sponsor is a Highly Trusted Sponsor. If this requirement is not met then no points will be awarded for the CAS, unless the Sponsor is a Highly Trusted Sponsor. Points will only be awarded for a CAS (even if all the above requirements are met) if the course in respect of which it is issued meets each of the following requirements–

    (a) he course must meet minimum academic requirements;

    (b) must lead to an approved qualification;

    (c) other than when the applicant is actually on a work placement, all study that forms part of the course must take place on the premises of the sponsoring educational institution;

    (d) the course must also meet one of the following requirements–

        (i) be a full time course of study that leads to a UK recognised bachelor or postgraduate degree;

        (ii) be an overseas course of degree level study that is recognised as being equivalent to a UK higher education course and is being provided by an overseas higher education institution;

        (iii) involve a minimum of 15 hours per week organised daytime study;

    (e) if the course contains a course-related work placement, any period that the applicant will be spending on that placement must not exceed half of the total length of the course spent in the UK (unless statutory provisions require otherwise).

Where the student is following a course of study below degree level study (excluding a foundation degree course), the course can only be offered if the Sponsor meets specified requirements.

Maintenance Funds

A Tier 4 (General) Student must score 10 points for funds. Points will only be awarded if the funds are available to the applicant and the applicant provides the specified documents to show this. See **27 Maintenance Funds (Appendix C)**, below.

20 Tier 4 (Child) Students

This route is for children at least 4 years old and under the age of 18 who wish to be educated in the UK at an Independent School. Academies and schools maintained by a local authority are not permitted to sponsor students under this route (para 245ZZ). All migrants arriving in the UK and wishing to enter as a Tier 4 (Child) Student must have a valid entry clearance for entry under this route. If they do not, entry will be refused.

To qualify for entry clearance as a Tier 4 (Child) Student, an applicant must meet the requirements listed below. If the requirements are met, entry clearance will be granted. If they are not, the application will be refused (para 245ZZA).

The requirements are–

    (a) the applicant must not fall for refusal under the general grounds for refusal;

    (b) the applicant must have a minimum of 30 points under Appendix A, see **21 The points system: Tier 4 (Child) Students**, below;

    (c) the applicant must have a minimum of 10 points under Appendix C, see **27 Maintenance Funds (Appendix C)**, below);

    (d) the applicant must be at least 4 years old and under the age of 18;

    (e) the applicant must have no children under the age of 18 who are either living with the applicant or for whom the applicant is financially responsible;

    (f) if a foster carer or a relative (not a parent or guardian) of the applicant will be responsible for the care of the applicant–

        (i) the arrangements for the care of the applicant by the foster carer or relative must meet the requirements laid down in para 245ZZE and the applicant must provide specified documents to show that this requirement has been met; and

        (ii) the applicant must provide details of the care arrangements as specified in para 245ZZE;

    (g) the application must be supported by the applicant's parents or legal guardian, or by just one parent if that parent has sole legal responsibility for the child;

    (h) the applicant's parents or legal guardian, or just one parent if that parent has sole responsibility for the child, must confirm that they consent to the arrangements for the applicant's travel to, and reception and care in, the UK;

    (i) if the applicant is currently being sponsored by a Government or international scholarship agency, or within the last 12 months has come to the end of such a period of sponsorship, the applicant must provide the written consent of the sponsoring Government or agency to the application and must provide the specified documents to show that this requirement has been met.

Where the applicant is under the age of 16, entry clearance will be granted for (para 245ZZB)–

    (ai) a period of no more than 1 month before the course starts or 7 days before the intended date of travel, whichever is later; plus

    (aii) a period (1) requested by the applicant, (2) equal to the length of the programme the applicant is following, or (3) of 6 years, whichever is the shorter; plus

    (aiii) 4 months.

Where the applicant is aged 16 or over, entry clearance will be granted for–

    (bi) a period of no more than 1 month before the course starts or 7 days before the intended date of travel, whichever is later; plus

(bii) a period (1) requested by the applicant, (2) equal to the length of the programme the applicant is following, or (3) of 3 years whichever is the shorter; plus

(biii) 4 months.

Entry clearance will be granted subject to the following conditions (para 245ZZB(c))–

  (i) no recourse to public funds;

  (ii) registration with the police, if this is required by para 326 of the Rules;

  (iii) no employment whilst the migrant is aged under 16;

  (iv) no employment whilst the migrant is aged 16 or over except–

      (1) during term time of no more than 10 hours per week;

      (2) (of any duration) during vacations;

      (3) as part of a course-related work placement which forms an assessed part of the applicant's course and provided that any period that he spend on that placement does not exceed half of the total length of the course undertaken in the UK (unless a statutory requirement provides otherwise);

      (4) as a Student Union Sabbatical Officer for up to 2 years provided the post is elective and is at the institution which is the applicant's sponsor or they must be elected to a National Union of Students position,

provided that the migrant is not self employed, or engaged in business activity, or employed as a Doctor or Dentist in Training, a professional sportsperson (including a sports coach) or an entertainer, and provided that the migrant's employment would not fill a full time vacancy;

  (v) no study except–

      (1) study at the institution that the Confirmation of Acceptance for Studies Checking Service records as the migrant's Sponsor unless–

         (a) the migrant is studying at an institution which is a partner institution of the migrant's sponsor; or

         (b) until such time as a decision is received from the Home Office on an application which is supported by a Confirmation of Acceptance for Studies assigned by a sponsor with Tier 4 Sponsor status and which is made while the applicant has extant leave, and any appeal or administrative review against that decision has been determined, the migrant is studying at the sponsor with Tier 4 Sponsor status that the Confirmation of Acceptance for Studies Checking Service records as having assigned such Confirmation of Acceptance for Studies to the migrant; or

         (c) the study is supplementary study; and

      (2) study on the course, or courses where a pre-sessional is included, for which the Confirmation of Acceptance for Studies was assigned, unless the student–

         (a) has yet to complete the course for which the Confirmation of Acceptance for Studies was assigned; and

         (b) begins studying a new course at their sponsor institution and the new course is at a higher or the same level as the course for which the Confirmation of Acceptance for Studies was assigned and is not a foundation course intended to prepare the student for entry to a higher education institution; and

  (vi) no study at Academies or schools maintained by a local authority except as provided by the Rules.

To qualify for leave to remain as a Tier 4 (Child) Student, an applicant must meet the requirements listed below. If they do, leave to remain will be granted. If they do not, the application will be refused (para 245ZZC). The requirements are–

  (a) the applicant must not fall for refusal under the general grounds for refusal and must not be an illegal entrant;

  (b) the applicant must have, or have last been granted, entry clearance, leave to enter or leave to remain–

      (i) as a Tier 4 Migrant; or

      (ii) as a student; or

  (c) requirements (b) to (i) above must be satisfied; and

  (d) the applicant must not be applying for leave to remain for the purpose of studies which would commence more than one month after the applicant's current entry clearance or leave to remain expires.

The period for which leave to remain will be granted is the same as the period for which entry clearance will be granted, and subject to the same requirements (para 245ZZD).

Persons seeking leave to enter in this category must hold a biometric immigration document: see the Note on **Control of Immigration** at para **6 Biometric registration**.

21 The points system: Tier 4 (Child) Students

An applicant applying for entry clearance or leave to remain as a Tier 4 (Child) Student must score 30 points for attributes. The available points are shown in Table 17 as follows–

Criterion	*Points*
Confirmation of Acceptance for Studies	30

A CAS will be considered to be valid only if–

(a) where the applicant is under 16, it was issued by an independent, fee paying school;

(b) it was issued no more than 6 months before the application is made;

(c) the application for entry clearance or leave to remain is made no more than 3 months before the start date of the course of study as stated on the CAS;

(d) the Sponsor has not withdrawn the offer since the CAS was issued;

(e) it was issued by an institution with a Tier 4 (Child) Student Sponsor Licence;

(f) the institution must still hold such a licence at the time the application for entry clearance or leave to remain is determined; and

(g) it contains such information as is specified as mandatory in guidance published by UK Visas and Immigration.

Points will not be awarded unless the course that the student will be pursuing meets one of the following requirements—

(h) be taught in accordance with the National Curriculum;

(i) be taught in accordance with the National Qualification Framework (NQF);

(j) be accepted as being of equivalent academic status to (a) or (b) above by Ofsted (England), the Education and Training Inspectorate (Northern Ireland), Education Scotland or Estyn (Wales);

(k) be provided as required by prevailing independent school education inspection standards.

A CAS reference number will only be valid if it links to a CAS Checking Service entry that names the applicant as the migrant and confirms that the Sponsor is sponsoring him in the Tier 4 category indicated by the migrant in his application for leave to remain (that is, as a Tier 4 (General) Student or a Tier 4 (Child) Student), and that reference number has not been cancelled by the Sponsor or by UK Visas and Immigration since it was assigned.

Maintenance Funds

For maintenance qualifications, see **27 Maintenance Funds (Appendix C)**, below.

22 Tier 5 (Youth Mobility Scheme)

This route is for sponsored young people from participating countries and territories who wish to live and work temporarily in the UK (para 245ZI). All migrants arriving in the UK and wishing to enter as a Tier 5 (Youth Mobility Scheme) Temporary Migrant must have a valid entry clearance for entry under this route. If they do not, entry will be refused (para 245ZJ).

To qualify for entry clearance as a Tier 5 (Youth Mobility Scheme) Temporary Migrant, an applicant must meet the requirements listed below. However, whether or not the requirements listed below are met, if a citizen of a country listed in Appendix G (see below) makes an application for entry clearance which, if granted, would mean that the annual allocation of places under this route for citizens of that country or territory would be exceeded, the application will be refused. The requirements are that the applicant (para 245ZK)—

(a) must not fall for refusal under the general grounds for refusal;

(b) must be (i) a citizen of a country/territory listed in Appendix G (see below), or (ii) a British Overseas Citizen, British Overseas Territories Citizen or British National (Overseas), as defined by the British Nationality Act 1981, and must provide a valid passport to show that this requirement has been met;

(c) must be sponsored by his country/territory as follows—

(i) if the applicant is a citizen of a country or territory that does not have Deemed Sponsorship Status, the applicant must hold a valid Certificate of Sponsorship issued by that country/territory and must use that Certificate of Sponsorship in support of an application lodged in the country/territory of issue; or

(ii) if the applicant is a citizen of a country or territory that does have Deemed Sponsorship Status, his valid passport issued by the country/territory holding such status will be evidence of sponsorship and the application for leave may be made at any post worldwide;

(ca) a Certificate of Sponsorship will only be considered to be valid if it was issued no more than 3 months before the application for entry clearance is made, and has not been cancelled;

(d) must have a minimum of 40 points under Appendix A, see **23 The points system: Tier 5 (Youth Mobility Scheme)**, below;

(e) must have a minimum of 10 points under Appendix C, see **27 Maintenance Funds (Appendix C)**, below;

(f) must have no children under the age of 18 who are either living with him or for whom he is financially responsible; and

(g) must not previously have spent time in the UK as a Working Holidaymaker or a Tier 5 (Youth Mobility Scheme) Temporary Migrant.

Appendix G countries with Deemed Sponsorship Status and their annual allocations are Australia (45,500), Canada (5,000), Japan (1,000), New Zealand (12,000) and Monaco (1,000); and without such status: Taiwan, South Korea and Hong Kong (1,000 each).

Entry clearance will be granted for a period of 2 years subject to the following conditions (para 245ZL)—

(a) no recourse to public funds;

(b) registration with the police, if this is required by para 326 of the Immigration Rules;

(c) no employment as a professional sportsperson (including as a sports coach);

(d) subject to exceptions, no employment as a Doctor or Dentist in Training;

(e) no self employment, except where the following conditions are met–

    (i) the migrant has no premises which he owns, other than his home, from which he carries out his business;

    (ii) the total value of any equipment used in the business does not exceed £5,000; and

    (iii) the migrant has no employees; and

(f) no study without a valid Academic Technology Approval Scheme clearance certificate from the Counter-Proliferation Department of the Foreign Office.

23 The points system: Tier 5 (Youth Mobility Scheme)

An applicant applying for entry clearance or leave to remain as a Tier 2 (Youth Mobility Scheme) Migrant must score 40 points for attributes. The available points are shown in Table 14 as follows–

Table 14–

Criterion	Points
Is Citizen of a country in Appendix G (see **60 Tier 5 (Youth Mobility Scheme)**, above); or Is a British Overseas Citizen, British Territories Overseas Citizen or British National (Overseas)	30
Will be 18 or over when his entry clearance becomes valid for use and was under the age of 31 on the date his application was made	10

Maintenance Funds

For maintenance qualifications, see **27 Maintenance Funds (Appendix C)**, below.

24 Tier 5 (Temporary Workers)

This route is for certain types of temporary worker whose entry helps to satisfy cultural, charitable, religious or international objectives, including volunteering and job shadowing (para 245ZM).

Except as described below, all migrants arriving in the UK and wishing to enter as a Tier 5 (Temporary Worker) Migrant must have a valid entry clearance for entry under this route. If they do not, entry will be refused (para 245ZN). A migrant arriving in the UK and wishing to enter as a Tier 5 (Temporary Worker) Migrant who does not have a valid entry clearance will not be refused entry if the following conditions are met (para 245ZN(b))–

    (i) he is not a visa national;

    (ii) the Certificate of Sponsorship reference number provided by the migrant leading to points being obtained under Appendix A links to an entry in the Certificate of Sponsorship Checking Service recording that their Sponsor has sponsored them in the creative and sporting subcategory of the Tier 5 (Temporary Worker) Migrant route;

    (iii) if he has consecutive engagements, the total length of all the periods of engagement, together with any gap between those engagements, is 3 months or less;

    (iv) if he does not have consecutive engagements, the total length of the period of engagement is 3 months or less; and

    (v) the migrant meets the requirements in paragraph 245ZO (see below).

To qualify for entry clearance or, as the case may be, leave to enter, as a Tier 5 (Temporary Worker) Migrant, an applicant must meet the following requirements. If he does, entry clearance will be granted. If he does not, the application will be refused. The requirements are that the applicant (para 245ZO)–

(a) must not fall for refusal under the general grounds for refusal;

(b) must have a minimum of 30 points under Appendix A, see **25 The points system: Tier 5 (Temporary Workers)**, below;

(c) must have a minimum of 10 points under Appendix C, see **27 Maintenance Funds (Appendix C)**, below;

(d) where the applicant is under 18 years of age, the application must be supported by their parents or legal guardian, or by just one parent if that parent has sole legal responsibility for the child;

(e) where the applicant is under 18 years of age, their parents or legal guardian, or just one parent if that parent has sole responsibility for the child, must confirm that they consent to the arrangements for the applicant's travel to, and reception and care in, the UK;

(f) if being sponsored in the international agreement sub-category of Tier 5 (Temporary Workers) as a private servant in a diplomatic household, must be no less than 18 years of age at the time of application, provide evidence of agreed written terms and conditions of employment in the UK with his employer including specifically that he will be paid in accordance with the National Minimum Wage Act 1998 and regulations made under that Act, in the form set out in Appendix 7, satisfy the Entry Clearance Officer or Immigration Officer that, throughout their employment in the UK, the employer intends to pay them at least the National Minimum Wage rate to which they are entitled by the law in force at the relevant time; and provide a written and signed statement from the employer confirming that the applicant is an employee and the work that will be carried out by the applicant will not constitute work within the meaning of Reg. 57 of the National Minimum Wage Regulations 2015 (as amended from time to time);

(g) the employer referred to in (f) must be either a diplomat or an employee of an international organisation enjoying certain privileges or immunity under UK or international law;

(h) where the applicant is being sponsored as a Contractual Service Supplier or Independent Professional in the International Agreement sub-category of the Tier 5 (Temporary Worker) Migrant route, the grant of leave to enter will not result in the applicant being granted leave to enter or remain in that sub-category for a cumulative period exceeding 6 months in any 12 month period ending during the period of leave to enter requested;

(i) the Entry Clearance Officer must be satisfied that the applicant genuinely intends to undertake, and is capable of undertaking, the role recorded by the Certificate of Sponsorship Checking Service, will not undertake employment in the UK other than under the terms of para 245ZP(f)(iii), and where the Certificate of Sponsorship Checking Service records the applicant as being sponsored in the international agreement sub-category of Tier 5 (Temporary Workers) to work as a private servant in a diplomatic household, the applicant's employer intends to pay the applicant, throughout their employment in the UK, at least the National Minimum Wage rate to which they are entitled by the law in force at the relevant time;

(j) to support the assessment in para (i), the Entry Clearance Officer may request additional information and evidence, and refuse the application if it is not provided. Any requested documents must be received by the Home Office within 28 calendar days of the date the request is sent, and request the applicant attends an interview, and refuse the application if the applicant fails to comply with any such request without providing a reasonable explanation;

(k) if the Entry Clearance Officer is not satisfied following the assessment in (i), no points will be awarded under Appendix A;

(l) the Entry Clearance Officer may decide not to carry out the assessment in para (i) if the application already falls for refusal on other grounds, but reserves the right to carry it out in any reconsideration of the decision.

Where para 245ZN(b) applies, and the applicant has consecutive engagements, leave to enter will be granted for a period starting not more than 14 days before the beginning of the first period of engagement and ending 14 days after the end of the last period of engagement, or for 3 months, whichever is the shorter. Where the applicant does not have consecutive engagements, leave to enter will be granted for: a period starting not more than 14 days before the beginning of the period of engagement and ending 14 days after it ends, or 3 months whichever is the shorter (para 245ZP).

Where para 245ZN(b) does not apply and the applicant is being sponsored in the Creative and Sporting subcategory, the Government Authorised Exchange subcategory for a Work Experience Programme, or the Charity Workers sub-category of the Tier 5 (Temporary Worker) Migrant route, entry clearance or leave to enter will be granted for a period starting 14 days before the beginning of the period of engagement (or of the first period of engagement, where the applicant has consecutive engagements) and ending 14 days after the end of that period of engagement (or of the last period of engagement, where the applicant has consecutive engagements), or 12 months, whichever is the shorter.

Where para 245ZN(b) does not apply and the applicant is being sponsored in the religious workers, the Government Authorised Exchange subcategory for a Research Programme, Training Programme or Overseas Government Language Programme, or other than as a Contractual Service Supplier, or Independent Professional, in the international agreement subcategory of the Tier 5 (Temporary Worker) Migrant route, entry clearance will be granted for: a period starting 14 days before the beginning of the period of engagement and ending 14 days after the end of that period of engagement, or 2 years, whichever is the shorter.

Where paragraph 245ZN(b) does not apply and the applicant is being sponsored as a Contractual Service Supplier, or Independent Professional in the International Agreement sub-category of the Tier 5 (Temporary Worker) Migrant route, entry clearance will be granted for a period starting 14 days before the beginning of the period of engagement and ending 14 days after the end of that period of engagement, or 6 months, whichever is the shorter.

To qualify for leave to remain as a Tier 5 (Temporary Worker) Migrant, an applicant must meet the requirements below. If the applicant meets these requirements, leave to remain will be granted, if not, the application will be refused (para 245ZQ). The requirements are—

(a) the applicant must not fall for refusal under the general grounds for refusal, and must not be an illegal entrant.

(b) the applicant must have, or have last been granted—

(i) entry clearance or leave to remain as a Tier 5 (Temporary Worker) Migrant, or

(ii) entry clearance, leave to enter or leave to remain as a visitor who has been in the UK undertaking permitted activities in the sports or creative sectors, provided he is being sponsored in the creative and sporting subcategory; and the Certificate of Sponsorship reference number was allocated to the applicant before he entered the UK as a visitor (excluding visitors for permitted paid engagements, marriage or civil partnership or transit), or

(iii) entry clearance, leave to enter or leave to remain as an Overseas Government Employee, provided (a) the Certificate of Sponsorship Checking Service reference for which he is being awarded points in this application shows he is being sponsored in the international agreement sub-category, and (b) the applicant is continuing employment with the same overseas government or international organisation for which earlier leave was granted, or

(iv) entry clearance, leave to enter or leave to remain as a Qualifying Work Permit Holder, provided (a) the applicant was previously issued with a work permit for the purpose of employment by an overseas government, and (b) the Certificate of Sponsorship Checking Service reference for which he is being awarded points in this application shows he is being sponsored in the international agreement sub-category, and (c) the applicant is continuing employment with the same overseas government or international organisation for which earlier leave was granted;

(v) entry clearance, leave to enter or leave to remain as a Qualifying Work Permit Holder, provided (a) the applicant was previously issued with a work permit for the purpose of employment as a sponsored researcher, and (b) the Certificate of Sponsorship Checking Service reference for which he is being awarded points in this application shows he is being sponsored in the government authorised exchange sub-category, and (c) the applicant is continuing employment with the same organisation for which his most recent period of leave was granted, or

(vi) entry clearance, leave to enter or leave to remain as a Student, a Student Re-Sitting an Examination, a Person Writing Up a Thesis, a Postgraduate Doctor or Dentist, a Student Nurse, a Student Union Sabbatical Officer, or a Tier 4 (General) Migrant (who, in respect of such leave, is or was last sponsored either by a UK recognised body or a body in receipt of public funding as a higher education institution; or by an overseas higher education institution to undertake a short-term study abroad programme in the UK), provided the Certificate of Sponsorship Checking Service reference for which he is being awarded points in this application confirms (1) he is being sponsored in the government authorised exchange sub-category, and (2) he lawfully obtained a UK recognised bachelor or postgraduate degree (not a qualification of equivalent level which is not a degree) during his last grant of leave, and (3) he is being sponsored to (a) undertake a period of postgraduate professional training or work experience which is required to obtain a professional qualification or professional registration in the same professional field as the qualification in (2) above, and will not be filling a permanent vacancy, such that the employer he is directed to work for by the Sponsor does not intend to employ him in the UK once the training or work experience for which he is being sponsored has concluded, or (b) undertake an internship for up to 12 months which directly relates to the qualification in (2) above, and will not be filling a permanent vacancy, such that the employer he is directed to work for by the Sponsor does not intend to employ him in the UK once the training or work experience for which he is being sponsored has concluded;

(c) the applicant must have a minimum of 30 points under Appendix A, see **25 The points system: Tier 5 (Temporary Workers)**, below.

(d) the applicant must have a minimum of 10 points under Appendix C, see **27 Maintenance Funds (Appendix C)**, below.

(e) the Certificate of Sponsorship Checking Service entry to which the Certificate of Sponsorship reference number for which points under Appendix A were awarded relates must–

(i) record that the applicant is being sponsored in the same subcategory of the Tier 5 (Temporary Worker) Migrant route as the one in which he was being sponsored to work for when he was last granted entry clearance or leave to remain as a Tier 5 (Temporary Worker) Migrant, and

(ii) in the case of an applicant who the Certificate of Sponsorship Checking Service records as being sponsored in the international agreement sub-category of Tier 5 (Temporary Workers), to work as a private servant in a diplomatic household, who entered the UK with a valid entry clearance in that capacity under the Rules in place from 6 April 2012, record that the applicant is being sponsored to work for the same employer as set out in paragraph 245ZO(g) who he was being sponsored to work for when he was last granted entry clearance or leave to remain as a Tier 5 (Temporary Worker) Migrant, and the applicant must have continued to work for that employer throughout his period of leave and must provide evidence of agreed written terms and conditions of employment in the UK with his employer in the form set out in Appendix 7.

(f) where the applicant is under 18 years of age, the application must be supported by his parents or legal guardian, or by just one parent if that parent has sole legal responsibility for the child.

(g) where the applicant is under 18 years of age, the applicant's parents or legal guardian, or just one parent if that parent has sole legal responsibility for the child, must confirm that they consent to the arrangements for the applicant's care in the UK.

(h) an applicant who has, or was last granted, leave as a Student, a Student Re-Sitting an Examination, a Person Writing Up a Thesis, a Postgraduate Doctor or Dentist, a Student Nurse, a Student Union Sabbatical Officer, or a Tier 4 (General) Migrant and (i) is currently being sponsored by a government or international scholarship agency, or (ii) was being sponsored by a government or international scholarship agency, and that sponsorship came to an end 12 months ago or less, must provide the unconditional written consent of the sponsoring Government or agency to the application and must provide the specified documents as set out in para 245A, to show that this requirement has been met.

(i) the applicant must not be in the UK in breach of immigration laws except that any period of overstaying for a period of 28 days or less will be disregarded.

(j) where the Certificate of Sponsorship Checking Service reference number for which the applicant was awarded points under Appendix A records that the applicant is being sponsored as a Contractual Service Supplier or Independent Professional in the International Agreement subcategory of the Tier 5 (Temporary Worker) Migrant route, the grant of leave to remain will not result in the applicant being granted leave to enter or remain as a Contractual Service Supplier, or Independent Professional under the international agreement sub-category of the Tier 5 (Temporary Worker) Migrant route for a cumulative period exceeding 6 months in any 12 month period ending during the period of leave to remain requested.

(k) the Secretary of State must be satisfied that the applicant genuinely intends to undertake, and is capable of undertaking, the role recorded by the Certificate of Sponsorship Checking Service; will not undertake employment in the United Kingdom other than under the terms of para 245ZR(h)(iii); and where the Certificate of Sponsorship Checking Service records the applicant as being sponsored in the international agreement sub-category of Tier 5 (Temporary Workers) to work as a private servant in a diplomatic household, the applicant's employer intends to pay the applicant, throughout their employment in the UK, at least the National Minimum Wage rate to which they are entitled by the law in force at the relevant time.

(l) to support the assessment in para 245ZQ(k), the Secretary of State may (i) request additional information and evidence, and refuse the application if the information or evidence is not provided. Any requested documents must be received by the Home Office within 28 calendar days of the date the request is sent, and (ii) request the applicant attends an interview, and refuse the application if the applicant fails to comply with any such request without providing a reasonable explanation.

(m) if the Secretary of State is not satisfied following the assessment in para 245ZQ(k), no points will be awarded under paragraphs 105 to 112 of Appendix A.

(n) the Secretary of State may decide not to carry out the assessment in para 245ZQ(k) if the application already falls for refusal on other grounds, but reserves the right to carry it out in any reconsideration of the decision.

(o) where the Certificate of Sponsorship Checking Service records the applicant as being sponsored in the international agreement sub-category of Tier 5 (Temporary Workers) to work as a private servant in a diplomatic household, the applicant must provide a written and signed statement from the employer confirming that the applicant is an employee and the work that will be carried out by the applicant will not constitute work within the meaning of Reg. 57 of the National Minimum Wage Regulations 2015 (as amended from time to time).

The period of leave granted will be a maximum of the period of he engagement plus 14 days (para 245ZR), but may be less depending on time already spent in the UK and the sub-category of temporary worker under which leave is applied for.

Leave to remain will be granted subject to there being no recourse to public funds, registration with the police if required by para 326 of the Rules, and no employment other than with the Sponsor (or supplementary employment).

To qualify for indefinite leave to remain as a Tier 5 (Temporary Worker) Migrant, an applicant must meet the requirements in para 245ZS. If they do, indefinite leave to remain will be granted; if they do not, the application will be refused. The requirements are–

(a) the applicant must not fall for refusal under the general grounds for refusal and must not be an illegal entrant.

(b) the applicant must have spent a continuous period of 5 years lawfully in the UK with leave in the international agreement sub-category of Tier 5 and working as a private servant in a diplomatic household and have last been granted entry clearance in that capacity under the Rules in place before 6 April 2012.

(c) the applicant must have demonstrated sufficient knowledge of the English language and sufficient knowledge about life in the UK, in accordance with Appendix KoLL.

(d) the applicant must not be in the UK in breach of immigration laws except that any period of overstaying for a period of 28 days or less will be disregarded.

(e) the applicant must provide a letter from their employer detailing the purpose and period of absences in connection with the employment, including periods of annual leave. Where the absence was due to a serious or compelling reason, the applicant must provide a personal letter which includes full details of the reason for the absences and all original supporting documents in relation to those reasons, e.g. medical, birth or death certificates, information about the reasons which led to the absence from the UK.

25 The points system: Tier 5 (Temporary Workers)

An applicant applying for entry clearance or leave to remain as a Tier 2 (Temporary Worker) Migrant must score 30 points for attributes. The available points are shown in Table 15 as follows–

Table 15

Criterion	Points
Holds a Tier 5 (Temporary Worker) Certificate of Sponsorship	30

Maintenance Funds

For maintenance qualifications, see **27 Maintenance Funds (Appendix C)**, below.

26 Language Skills (Appendix B)

An applicant applying for entry clearance or leave to remain as a Tier 1 Migrant or Tier 2 Migrant must have 10 points for English language, unless applying–
- (i) as a Tier 1 (Exceptional Talent) Migrant;
- (ii) as a Tier 1 (Investor) Migrant;
- (iii) as a Tier 2 (Intra-Company Transfer) Migrant.

The level of English required is–

Table 1

Category	Application	Level of English Language
Tier 1 (Entrepreneur)	Entry clearance and leave to remain	A knowledge of English equivalent to level B1 or above of the Council of Europe's Common European Framework for Language Learning
Tier 1 (Graduate Entrepreneur)	Entry clearance and leave to remain	As above
Tier 2 (Minister of Religion)	Entry clearance and leave to remain	As above, but to level B2
Tier 2 (General)	Entry clearance and leave to remain, except where* below applies	As above, but to level B1
Tier 2 (General)	Leave to remain where* below applies	As above, but to level A1
Tier 2 (Sportsperson)	Entry clearance and leave to remain	As above, but to level A1

*An applicant applying for leave to remain as a Tier 2 (General) Migrant must have competence of English to a level A1 or above if–
- (i) he previously had leave as a Tier 2 (General) Migrant under the rules in place before 6 April 2011, or as a Qualifying Work Permit Holder, a representative of an overseas newspaper, news agency or Broadcasting organisation, a Member of the Operational Ground Staff of an Overseas-owned Airline, or a Jewish Agency Employee; and
- (ii) he has not been granted leave to remain in any other routes, or entry clearance or leave to enter in any route, since the grant of leave referred to in (i) above.

Points will only be awarded if the applicant–

Factor	Points
(a) is a national of a majority English speaking country	10
(b) has a degree taught in English	10
(c) has passed an English language test	10
(d) met the English language requirement in a previous grant of leave	10

For the purposes of (a), the majority English speaking countries are: Antigua and Barbuda, Australia, The Bahamas, Barbados, Belize, Dominica, Grenada, Guyana, Ireland, Jamaica, New Zealand, St Kitts and Nevis, St Lucia, St Vincent and the Grenadines, Trinidad and Tobago, or USA. A current valid original passport or travel document must generally be produced to show that this requirement is met.

For the purposes of (b), the academic qualification (not a professional or vocational qualification) must either–
- (1) is a UK Bachelor's degree, Master's degree or PhD;
- (2) is a qualification awarded by an educational establishment outside the UK, which is deemed by UK NARIC to meet the recognised standard of a Bachelor's degree, a Master's degree or a PhD in the UK, and UK NARIC has confirmed that the degree was taught or researched in English to level C1 of the Council of Europe's Common European Framework for Language learning or above; or
- (3) be deemed by UK NARIC to meet or exceed the recognised standard of a Bachelor's or Master's degree or a PhD in the UK, and be from an educational establishment in one of the above majority English speaking countries.

and specified documentation must be provided as evidence.

For the purposes of (c), the 10 points will only be awarded for passing an English language test if the applicant has the required level of English language and provides specified documents from an English language test provider approved by the Secretary of State.

For the purposes of (d), the 10 points will be given if the applicant met the English language requirement in a previous grant of leave as set out in Appendix B.

27 Maintenance Funds (Appendix C)

An applicant applying for entry clearance or leave to remain as a Tier 1 Migrant must score 10 points for funds, unless applying as a Tier 1 (Exceptional Talent) Migrant or a Tier 1 (Investor) Migrant.

10 points will only be awarded if an applicant applying for entry clearance or leave to remain, has the level of funds shown in the table below and provides specified documents as proof.

Category	Application	Level of funds
Tier 1 (Entrepreneur)	Entry clearance	£3,310
Tier 1 (Graduate Entrepreneur)	Entry clearance	£1,890
Tier 1	Leave to remain	£945

Note.–a Tier 1 (Entrepreneur) Migrant applicant cannot use the same funds to score points for attributes under Appendix A and to score points for maintenance funds for himself or his dependants under Appendix C or Appendix E.

An applicant applying for entry clearance or leave to remain as a Tier 2 Migrant must score 10 points for funds. 10 points will only be awarded if the applicant–

(a) has funds of £945 and provides specified documents as proof; or

(b) has entry clearance, leave to enter or leave to remain as–

    (i) a Tier 2 Migrant

    (ii) a Jewish Agency employee

    (iii) a member of the operational ground staff of an overseas-owned airline,

    (iv) a minister of religion, missionary or member of a religious order,

    (v) a representative of an overseas newspaper, news agency or broadcasting organisation, or

    (vi) a work permit holder, or

(c) has a sponsor who is A rated and provides a written undertaking that, should it become necessary, it will maintain and accommodate the migrant up to the end of the first month of his employment. The sponsor may limit the amount of the undertaking but any limit must be at least £945.

An applicant applying for entry clearance as a Tier 5 (Youth Mobility) Migrant must score 10 points for funds. 10 points will only be awarded if an applicant has funds of £1,890.

An applicant applying for entry clearance or leave to remain as a Tier 5 (Temporary Worker) Migrant must score 10 points for funds. 10 points will only be awarded if an applicant has–

(a) £945; or

(b) an A rated Sponsor and the Certificate of Sponsorship Checking Service confirms that the Sponsor has certified maintenance and so confirmed that the applicant will not claim public funds during his period of leave as a Tier 5 (Temporary Worker) Migrant. Points will only be awarded if the applicant provides a valid Certificate of Sponsorship reference number with his application.

An applicant applying for entry clearance or leave to remain as a Tier 4 (General) Student Migrant must score 10 points for funds. 10 points will only be awarded if an applicant has–

(a) if studying in London–

    (i) Where the applicant is applying for leave to remain as a postgraduate doctor or dentist on a recognised Foundation Programme, Student Union Sabbatical Officer or on the doctorate extension scheme, the applicant must have £1,265 for each month remaining of the course up to a maximum of two months;

    (ii) in all other circumstances, funds amounting to the full course fees for the first academic year of the course, or for the entire course if it is less than a year long, plus £1,265 for each month of the course up to a maximum of nine months;

(b) if studying outside London–

    (iii) Where the applicant is applying for leave to remain as a postgraduate doctor or dentist on a recognised Foundation Programme, Student Union Sabbatical Officer or on the doctorate extension scheme, the applicant must have £1,015 for each month remaining of the course up to a maximum of two months;

    (iv) in all other circumstances, the applicant must have funds amounting to the full course fees for the first academic year of the course, or for the entire course if it is less than a year long, plus £1,015 for each month of the course up to a maximum of nine months.

An applicant applying for entry clearance or leave to remain as a Tier 4 (Child) Student Migrant must score 10 points for funds. 10 points will only be awarded if an applicant has–

(a) where the child is (or will be) studying at a residential Independent school, sufficient funds are available to the applicant to pay boarding fees (being course fees plus board/lodging fees) for an academic year;

(b) where the child is (or will be) studying at a non-residential Independent School and is in a private foster care arrangement or staying with and cared for by a close relative, sufficient funds available to pay school fees for an academic year, and the foster carer or relative must undertake to maintain and accommodate the child for the duration of the course, and that foster carer or relative must have funds equivalent to at least £570 per month, for up to a maximum of nine months, to support the child while he is in the UK;

(c) Where the child is (or will be) studying at a non-residential Independent School, is under the age of 12 and is (or will be) accompanied by a parent, sufficient funds to pay school fees for an academic year, plus if no other children are accompanying the applicant and the parent, £1,560 per month of stay up to a maximum of nine months; or if other children are accompanying the applicant and the parent, £1,560 per month, plus £625 per month for each additional child, up to a maximum of nine months;

(d) where the child is aged 16 or 17 years old and is living independently and studying at a non-residential Independent School in London–

(i) funds amounting to the full course fees for the first academic year of the course, or for the entire course if it is less than a year long, plus £1,265 for each month of the course up to a maximum of nine months;

(e) where the child is aged 16 or 17 years old, is living independently and studying at a non-residential Independent School outside London—

(ii) funds amounting to the full course fees for the first academic year of the course, or for the entire course if it is less than a year long, plus £1,015 for each month of the course up to a maximum of nine months.

Where the applicant is sponsored by a Highly Trusted Sponsor, or is a national of one of the countries listed in Appendix H, and is applying for entry clearance in his country of nationality, or leave to remain in the UK, he must confirm that the funds are available to him in the specified manner (rather than show the specified documents). UK Visas and Immigration reserves the right to request specified documents from these applicants to support this confirmation and an application will be refused if they are not provided in accordance with the request made. Appendix H countries are: Argentina, Australia, Botswana, Brunei, Canada, Chile, Croatia, Japan, Malaysia, New Zealand, Singapore, South Korea, Trinidad and Tobago, and the United States. The same applies to an applicant who is the rightful holder of one of the following passports, which has been issued by the relevant competent authority, and where he is applying for leave to remain in the UK or for entry clearance in the territory related to the passport he holds: British National (Overseas), Hong Kong, and Taiwan (where the passport issued by Taiwan includes the number of the identification card issued by the competent authority in Taiwan).

Note.– In all cases where an applicant is required to obtain points under Appendix C (Maintenance funds), he must (para 1A)–

(a) have the funds specified in the relevant part of Appendix C at the date of the application;

(b) if applying for entry clearance, leave to enter or leave to remain as a Tier 1 Migrant (other than a Tier 1 (Exceptional Talent) or (Investor) Migrant), a Tier 2 Migrant or a Tier 5 (Temporary Worker) Migrant, must have had the funds referred to in (a) above for a consecutive 90-day period of time;

(c) if applying for entry clearance or leave to remain as a Tier 4 Migrant, must have had the funds referred to in (a) above for a consecutive 28-day period of time, and must confirm that they are and will remain (unless used to pay course fees or living costs) available for his use;

(d) if the funds were obtained when he was in the UK, they must have been obtained while he had valid leave and was not acting in breach of any conditions attached to that leave;

(e) where the funds are in a foreign currencies, the applicant must have the specified level of funds when converted at a specified rate;

(f) where the applicant is applying as a Tier 1 Migrant, a Tier 2 Migrant or a Tier 5 Migrant, the funds must have been under his own control on the date of the application and for the period specified in (b) above;

(g) where the application is made at the same time as applications by the partner or child of the applicant (such that the applicant is a Relevant Points Based System Migrant for the purposes of paragraph 319AA), each applicant must have the total requisite funds. If each applicant does not individually meet the funds requirements, all the applications (the application by the relevant points based system migrant and applications as his partner or child) will be refused.

(h) the end date of the 90-day and 28-day periods referred to in (b) and (c) above will be taken as the date of the closing balance on the most recent of the specified documents (where specified documents from two or more accounts are submitted, this will be the end date for the account that most favours the applicant), and must be no earlier than 31 days before the date of application;

(i) no points will be awarded where the specified documents show that the funds are held in a financial institution listed in Appendix P as being an institution with which the Home Office is unable to make satisfactory verification checks;

(j) maintenance must be in the form of cash funds. Other accounts or financial instruments such as shares, bonds, credit cards, pension funds etc, regardless of notice period are not acceptable;

(k) if the applicant wishes to rely on a joint account as evidence of available funds, the applicant (or for children under 18 years of age, the applicant's parent or legal guardian who is legally present in the UK) must be named on the account as one of the account holders; and

(l) overdraft facilities will not be considered towards funds that are available or under an applicant's own control.

28 Maintenance Funds for families (Appendix E)

A sufficient level of funds must be available to an applicant applying as the Partner or Child of a Relevant Points Based System Migrant. A sufficient level of funds will only be available if the requirements below are met.

Note.–where the application is connected to a Tier 1 (Entrepreneur) Migrant, the applicant cannot use the same funds to score points for maintenance funds under Appendix E as the Tier 1 (Entrepreneur) Migrant used to score points under Appendix A.

(a) where the application is connected to a Tier 1 Migrant (other than a Tier 1 (Investor) Migrant or a Tier 1 (Exceptional Talent) Migrant) who is outside the UK or who has been in the UK for a period of less than 12 months, there must be–

    (i) £1,260 in funds, where the application is connected to a Tier 1 (Graduate Entrepreneur) Migrant; or

    (ii) £1,890 in funds in other cases;

(b) where para (a) does not apply, and the application is connected to a Relevant Points Based System Migrant who is not a Tier 1 (Investor) Migrant a Tier 1 (Exceptional Talent) Migrant or a Tier 4 (General) Student there must be £630 in funds;

(ba) where the application is connected to a Tier 4 (General) Student—

    (1) if the Tier 4 (General) Student is studying in London, there must be £845 in funds for each month for which the applicant would, if successful, be granted leave under para 319D(a), up to a maximum of nine months, or

    (2) if the Tier 4 (General) Student is not studying in London (as defined in Appendix C, para 12) , there must be £680 in funds for each month for which the applicant would, if successful, be granted leave under para 319D(a), up to a maximum of nine months, and in each case—

    (3) the applicant must confirm that the funds referred to in (1) or (2) above are—

        (i) available in the manner specified in paragraph (f) below for use in living costs in the UK; and

        (ii) that the funds will remain available in the manner specified in paragraph (f) below unless used to pay for living costs;

(c) where the applicant is applying as the Partner of a Relevant Points Based System Migrant the relevant amount of funds must be available to either the applicant or the Relevant Points Based System Migrant.

(d) where the applicant is applying as the Child of a Relevant Points Based System Migrant, the relevant amount of funds must be available to the applicant, the Relevant Points Based System Migrant, or the applicant's other parent who is Lawfully present in the UK or being granted entry clearance, or leave to enter or remain, at the same time.

(e) where the Relevant Points Based System Migrant is applying for entry clearance or leave to remain at the same time as the applicant, the amount of funds available to the applicant must be in addition to the level of funds required separately of the Relevant Points Based System Migrant.

(f) in all cases, the funds in question must be available to—

    (i) the applicant, or

    (ii) where he is applying as the partner of a Relevant Points Based System Migrant, either to him or to that Relevant Points Based System Migrant, or

    (iii) where he is applying as the child of a Relevant Points Based System Migrant, either to him, to the Relevant Points Based System Migrant or to the child's other parent who is lawfully present in the UK or being granted entry clearance, or leave to enter or remain, at the same time;

(g) the funds in question must have been available to the person referred to in (f) above on the date of the application and for:

    (i) a consecutive 90-day period of time, if the applicant is applying as the Partner or Child of a Tier 1 Migrant (other than a Tier 1 (Investor) Migrant) or a Tier 1 (Exceptional Talent) Migrant, a Tier 2 Migrant or a Tier 5 (Temporary Worker) Migrant;

    (ii) a consecutive 28-day period of time, if the applicant is applying as the Partner or Child of a Tier 4 (General) Student;

(h) if the funds in question were obtained when the person referred to in (f) above was in the UK, the funds must have been obtained while that person had valid leave and was not acting in breach of any conditions attached to that leave; and

(i) in the following cases, sufficient funds will be deemed to be available where all of the following conditions are met—

    (1) the Relevant Points Based System Migrant to whom the application is connected has, or is being granted, leave as a Tier 2 Migrant,

    (2) the Sponsor of that Relevant Points Based System Migrant is A-rated, and

    (3) that Sponsor has certified on the Certificate of Sponsorship that, should it become necessary, it will maintain and accommodate the dependants of the relevant Points Based System Migrant up to the end of the first month of the dependant's leave, if granted. The undertaking may be limited provided the limit is at least £630 per dependant. If the relevant Points Based System Migrant is applying at the same time as the applicant, points will only be awarded if the Relevant Points Based System Migrant provides a valid Certificate of Sponsorship reference number with his application.

(ia) sufficient funds will not be deemed to be available to the Partner or Child if the specified documents, as set out in paragraph 1B of Appendix C, show that the funds are held in a financial institution listed in Appendix P as being an institution with which the Home Office is unable to make satisfactory verification checks.

(ib) sufficient funds will be deemed to be available where the application is connected to a Tier 1 (Graduate Entrepreneur) Migrant who scores, or scored, points from Appendix A for an endorsement from UK Trade and Investment, and UK Trade and Investment has confirmed in the endorsement letter that it has awarded funding that is at least sufficient to cover the required maintenance funds for the Tier 1 (Graduate Entrepreneur) Migrant, the applicant and any other dependants.

(j) in all cases the applicant must provide the specified documents as set out in paragraph 1B of Appendix C, unless the applicant is applying at the same time as the Relevant Points Based System Migrant who is a

Tier 4 (General) Student sponsored by a Highly Trusted Sponsor, is a national of one of the countries or the rightful holder of a qualifying passport issued by one of the relevant competent authorities, as appropriate, listed in Appendix H, and is applying for entry clearance in his country of nationality or in the territory related to the passport he holds, as appropriate, or leave to remain in the UK and the applicant is also a national of the same country, and confirms these requirements are met, in which case the specified documents shall not be required. The Home Office reserves the right to request the specified documents from these applicants. The application will be refused if the specified documents are not provided in accordance with the request made.

(k) where the funds are in one or more foreign currencies, the applicant must have the specified level of funds when converted to pound sterling (£) using the spot exchange rate which appears on www.oanda.com* for the date of the application.

(l) where the application is one of a number of applications made at the same time as a partner or child of a Relevant Points Based System Migrant (as set out in paragraphs 319A and 319F) each applicant, including the Relevant Points Based System Migrant if applying at the same time, must have the total requisite funds specified in the relevant parts of appendices C and E. if each applicant does not individually meet the requirements of Appendices C and/or E, as appropriate, all the applications (the application by the Relevant Points Based System Migrant and applications as the partner or child of that Relevant Points Based System Migrant) will be refused.

(m) the end date of the 90-day and 28-day periods referred to in (g) above will be taken as the date of the closing balance on the most recent of the specified documents (where specified documents from two or more accounts are submitted, this will be the end date for the account that most favours the applicant), as set out in paragraph 1B of Appendix C, and must be no earlier than 31 days before the date of application.

(n) if—
   (i) the Relevant Points-Based System Migrant is a Tier 4 (General) Student who has official financial sponsorship as set out in paragraph 13(iii) of Appendix C, and
   (ii) this sponsorship is intended to cover costs of the Relevant Points-Based System Migrant's family member(s),

the applicant must provide a letter of confirmation from the Tier 4 (General) Student's official financial sponsor which satisfies the requirements in paragraph 13D of Appendix C, and confirms that the sponsorship will cover costs of the applicant in addition to costs of the Relevant Points-Based System Migrant.

(o) where the Relevant Points Based System Migrant is applying for entry clearance or leave to remain at the same time as the applicant, and is not required to provide evidence of maintenance funds because of the provisions in paragraph 5(b) of Appendix C, the applicant is also not required to provide evidence of maintenance funds.

(p) Where the applicant—
   (i) is not applying at the same time as the Relevant Points Based System Migrant, and
   (ii) in the application which led to his most recent grant of entry clearance or leave to remain, the Relevant Points Based System Migrant was not required to provide evidence of maintenance funds because of the provisions in para 5(b) of Appendix C,

the applicant is also not required to provide evidence of maintenance funds.

(q) overdraft facilities will not be considered towards funds that are available or under an applicant's own control.

Note.– In all cases where an applicant is required to obtain points under Appendix E (Maintenance funds), the general rules in Appendix C, para 1A (see **27 Maintenance Funds (Appendix C)**, above) apply.

29 Authorities

Statutory Instruments, etc–

Statement of Changes in Immigration Rules (HC 395–23rd May 1994 as amended by Cmnd 2663, HC 797, Cmnd 3073, HC 274, HC 329, Cmnd 3365, HC 31, HC 338, Cmnd 3369, HC 26, HC 161, Cmnd 3953, Cmnd 4065, HC 22, HC 704, Cmnd 4851, Cmnd 5253, HC 735, Cmnd 5597, HC 1301, HC 104, HC 180, HC 489, HC 538, Cmnd 5829, Cmnd 5949, HC 1224, HC 95, HC 176, HC 370, HC 464, HC 523, Cmnd 6297, Cmnd 6339, HC 1112, HC 164, HC 194, HC 302, HC 346, HC 486, HC 104, HC 299, HC 582, HC 645, HC 697, HC 769, HC 819, HC 949, HC 974, HC 1016, HC 1053, HC 1337, Cmnd 6918, HC 1702, HC 130, HC 398, Cmnd 7074, Cmnd 7075, HC 28, HC 40, HC 82, HC 321, HC 420, HC 607, HC 951, HC 971, HC 1113, HC 227, HC 314, HC413, Cmnd 7701, Cmnd 7711, HC 120, HC 367, HC 439, HC 59, HC 96, HC 382, Cmnd 7929, Cmnd 7944, HC698, HC863, HC908, HC1148, HC1436, HC 1511, HC1622, HC1693, HC1719, HC1733, HC1888, Cmnd 8337, HC194, Cmnd 8423, HC514, HC565, HC760, 820, HC847, HC943, HC967, HC1038, HC1039, Cmnd 8599, HC244, HC628, HC803, HC887, HC901, HC938, HC1130, HC1138, HC1201, HC198, HC532. HC693, HC1025, HC1116, HC297, HC 437, HC535, HC877)

PASSPORTS AND VISAS FOR NATIONALS AND OTHERS

A: PASSPORTS

1 Types of passport and fees for issue

United Kingdom passports and travel documents are of the following kinds—

(a) The Standard Passport

The Standard Passport is valid for ten years and is generally valid for travel to all countries-subject to a visa or permit being obtained where required, and to the immigration regulations of the country to be visited.

The fee for issue of a 32 page passport for applications made by post is £72.50 which includes applications for replacing an expired passport, replacing a passport of restricted validity with a new passport of full validity, issuing a new passport with amended personal details and replacing a lost or stolen passport.

The fee for issue of a 48 page passport for applications made by post, and in the circumstances listed above for applications for a 32 page passport, is £85.

The fee for issuing a Standard Passport to a person under 16 years of age (which is valid for five years) is £46.

Applicants born on or before 2nd September 1929 are entitled to free 32-page passport if they apply by post, and pay only the uplift if they apply by the fast-track, fast-track collect or premium services, but continue to pay the full fee for a 48 page passport.

For administering applications made abroad, with the exception of diplomatic, official or armed forces passports, the fees are—

32 page passport–	£83.00
48 page passport–	£91.00
Children's passport–	£53.00

No fees are payable by persons born on or after 2nd September 1929.

(b) The Collective Passport

The Collective Passport is issued for approved groups of British students or recognised youth organisations, all the members of which are under 18 years of age, going abroad in the charge of a responsible adult. The fee for issue is £39 or £54 if the application is made in person.

(c) Amending passports

Issuing a new passport with amended personal details costs the same as issuing a new passport. Higher fees are payable if the application is made abroad.

The appropriate "fast track" or "premium" fee is payable where the application is made in person (see below).

(d) Emergency Passports

The fee for administering an application for and providing an Emergency Travel Document is £95.

The fee for administering an application for and providing an Emergency Passport where it is not possible to provide an Emergency Travel Document is £75. The Consular Fees Regulations 1981, as amended, allow for consular fees to be paid in Sterling by debit or credit card at the discretion of a consular officer. Payment can still be made in the currency circulating at the place of payment (Reg. 3(1)).

In the case of emergency assistance, the following fees apply in respect of arranging, exceptionally, for currency to be made available against the deposit of funds (Consular Fees Order 2012, as amended)—

£0.01-£99.99–	£10.00
£100.00-£499.99–	£25.00
£500.00 or more–	£50.00

Note.—The fees set out in (a) to (c) above are for applications made by post in the UK. Applications made in person attract an additional charge as follows.

There are three levels of service—
  (a) where an application is made in person and the applicant wishes it to be processed within seven days ("fast-track" service);
  (b) where the application is made in person and the applicant wishes it to be processed in seven days and wishes to collect it in person ("fast-track collect" service); and
  (c) where the application is to be processed within 24 hours ("premium" service).
These services are not available for collective passports.
The fees for these services are as follows—
  (a) fast-track service for an adult 32 page passport £103 (or, if the applicant was born on or before 2nd September 1929, £30.50); for a child passport £87; for an adult 48 page passport (whenever born) £111;
  (b) fast-track collect service for an adult 32 page passport £123.00 (or, if the applicant was born on or before 2nd

September 1929, £50.50); for a child passport £103.50; for an adult 48 page passport (whenever born) £123;

(c) premium service for an adult 32 page passport £128 (or, if the applicant was born on or before 2nd September 1929, £55.50); for a child passport £106; for an adult 48 page passport (whenever born) £137.

The main conditions applicable to each type of passport are summarised below.

2 Applications for a Standard British Passport

British citizens, British Dependent Territories citizens, British Overseas citizens, British subjects, and British protected persons applying in the United Kingdom for passports or for the extension of, or addition of children to, existing passports may obtain application forms from one of the passport offices (addresses given below) or at any main post office, branch of Lloyds Bank or travel agent. When possible, at least four weeks' notice should be given.

Applications may be handed in at main post offices, and Worldchoice travel agents. For a fee of £5.00 the application is checked for accuracy, the passport fee paid, and the application sent by registered post to the passport office dealing with the application. The customer is given a reference number for the application and the telephone number of the passport office.

Where a woman who is about to be married wishes to travel abroad under her married name immediately after the wedding, a passport may be issued in advance, post-dated to the date of marriage. Alternatively, if she has a valid passport in her maiden name or a previous married name, it is open to her to have it amended to show her new married name upon production of her marriage certificate. If she wishes to travel immediately after her wedding, she may have the existing passport amended, with post-dated effect. The appropriate forms are obtainable on request.

Applications for passports for persons who have been adopted or who have changed their name (otherwise than by marriage) should be submitted direct to one of the passport offices.

The addresses and areas covered by the passport offices are as follows–

(a) London–Globe House, 89 Eccleston Square, London, SW1V 1PN (for Greater London, including Middlesex–personal callers only. Postal applications from residents of these areas should be sent to Peterborough);

(b) Liverpool–5th Floor, India Buildings, Water Street, Liverpool L2 0QZ (for Cheshire, Greater Manchester, Lancashire, Merseyside, Yorkshire, Shropshire, Staffordshire, and the unitary authorities of Blackburn with Derwent, Blackburn, Halton and Warrington, Telford and Wrekin);

(c) Newport–Olympia House, Upper Dock Street, Newport, Gwent NP20 1XA (for Wales, Cornwall and the Isles of Scilly, Devon, Dorset, Gloucestershire, Hampshire, Hereford, Isle of Wight, Oxfordshire, Somerset, Wiltshire, Worcestershire, and the unitary authorities of Portsmouth, Reading, Southampton, Bristol, North Somerset, Plymouth, Poole, South Gloucestershire, Swindon and Torbay);

(d) Peterborough–Aragon Court, Northminster Road, Peterborough PE1 1QQ (for Bedfordshire, Buckinghamshire, Cambridgeshire, Essex, Hertfordshire, Kent, East Sussex, Surrey, Inner London, Outer London, and the unitary authorities of Luton, Peterborough, Bracknell Forest, Brighton and Hove, Medway, Milton Keynes, Slough, Thurrock and Windsor and Maidenhead);

(e) Glasgow–3 Northgate, 96 Milton Street, Cowcaddens, Glasgow G4 0BT (for all Scotland, Cumbria, and postal applications from Essex County and Southend on Sea Unitary Authority);

(f) Belfast–Hampton House, 47-53 High Street, Belfast BT1 2QS (for Northern Ireland);

(g) Durham–Millburngate House, Durham DH97 1PA (for Durham County, Northumberland, Tyne and Wear, the counties of North, South and West Yorkshire, Derbyshire, Leicestershire, Lincolnshire, Northamptonshire, Nottinghamshire, Warwickshire, West Midlands, and the unitary authorities of Darlington, Hartlepool, Middlesbrough, Redcar and Cleveland, Stockton-on-Tees, East Riding of Yorkshire, Kingston Upon Hull, North East Lincolnshire, North Lincolnshire, York, Derby, Leicester, Nottingham, Rutland, and Stoke on Trent).

3 Authentication of applications

When completed, the application form should be counter-signed by a member of parliament, justice of the peace, minister of religion, lawyer, bank officer, established civil servant, school teacher, police officer, doctor, or any person of similar standing (not a member of the applicant's immediate family) who is a British citizen, a British subject, or a citizen of a Commonwealth country and who has been personally acquainted with the applicant for at least two years. It is important to submit with the application all the documents specified on the form, including evidence of birth, adoption, registration, or naturalisation (as the case may be), two copies of a recent photograph of the applicant properly endorsed, and evidence of any change of name otherwise than by marriage or adoption.

The above-mentioned documents need not be produced if the applicant is surrendering an unrestricted standard British passport and all details remain the same. Photographic copies of birth, marriage, or naturalisation certificates are not acceptable.

4 Family passports

The issue of Family Passports whereby the spouse of a passport holder and any children of the holder who were in the UK and under the age of 16 could be included in a family passport (without extra charge), provided that they did not hold a separate valid UK passport has been discontinued. Existing Family Passports may continue to be used until they expire.

5 Lost passports

Passport holders whose passports are lost or stolen while they are in the UK should apply to the passport office for a replacement. If the loss occurs abroad, they should apply to the British Embassy or High Commission in the country they are in. The usual fee and documentation should be submitted if available. A replacement passport may be issued initially for a one year period to enable enquiries to be made about the lost passport.

6 Persons under 18

Children under 16 (including babies) need their own individual passports. Passport applications of young persons over 16 but under 18 (except married persons, who must produce their marriage certificates, and members of H.M. Forces) must be signed by, or accompanied by a letter of consent from one of their parents or a person acting *in loco parentis*. If a passport is needed for a child who is five years of age or over but under 16 in his own name, application must be made on his behalf by his parent, or a person acting *in loco parentis*, on a special form. Such a passport will be valid initially for five years only but can subsequently be extended, at no extra charge, for a further five years.

Note.–Visas are required for visits to certain countries–see below.

7 Collective passports

Collective passports, in lieu of separate passports, are issued by a passport office for approved parties of British students, members of the Scout and Guide movements, and other recognised youth organisations, all of whom are under the age of 18 years, and are British citizens, British Dependent Territories citizens, British Overseas citizens, or British protected persons, and who are travelling abroad under a responsible leader. The leader (and, if there is one, the deputy leader) must be over 21 years of age and hold a valid standard British passport. No person who will have attained the age of 18 on the date of departure of the party may be included in a Collective passport. Not less than five or more than 50 persons may normally be included in a Collective passport; for travel to Finland and Sweden, the minimum is ten. Foreign, Commonwealth, and Irish citizens should obtain passports (and visas, if necessary) from their own authorities.

Applications for Collective passports should be made, at least four weeks before the passport is required, on the appropriate form, accompanied by the appropriate fee, a supporting letter (from the Board of Governors or headmaster of a school or from the national headquarters of the recognised youth organisation), and identity cards, if any (see below). The written consent of parents or legal guardians must be obtained. Every member of the party aged 16 years or over on the date of re-entry into the United Kingdom must carry a personal identity card, bearing a photograph, endorsed by the passport office.

For visits to Austria, Bulgaria, Cyprus, Denmark, Finland, Germany, Romania, Spain, Sweden, or Tunisia, members of the party who are under 16 years of age must also carry such an identity card. For visits to Belgium or the Netherlands, each child of the party must have an identity card if the party is staying in separate households; in France, children over 12 years of age need an identity card and each child needs a copy of the passport if the party is not staying together at the same hotel. For visits to Switzerland, a Collective passport is not acceptable if the children are staying in individual households.

Application forms for Collective passports, and blank identity cards, may be obtained from the appropriate passport office at the address given above, together with a note of guidance indicating particular conditions and requirements which apply in certain countries.

B: VISAS

8 When visas are required

Visas are required by holders of Standard British or Collective passports for travel to certain countries; they may be obtained from the consulates of the countries concerned, the addresses of which are obtainable from any passport office.

Person's proposing to travel abroad should make enquiries as to whether or not a visa is required in respect of the countries they intend to visit.

Note.–British citizens born in any Commonwealth country, and possessing United Kingdom passports issued in that country, must have their passports stamped with a re-entry permit before they go abroad.

C: TRAVEL DOCUMENTS

9 Non-nationals

A person who is not a British national, but who has the right to reside in the UK can apply for a travel document in certain special circumstances. There are four types of travel document, depending on the circumstances and the person's status in the UK–

  (a) a refugee can apply for a convention travel document;
  (b) a stateless person can apply for a stateless person's document;
  (c) a citizen of any country who is currently in the UK, can apply for a one-way document of identity; and
  (d) a person who has been refused a passport by their own country can apply for a certificate of travel.
  An application must be made on Form TD112 BRP, for the form go to:
<https://www.gov.uk/government/publications/application-for-home-office-travel-document-form-td112-brp>.

Convention travel documents

  A person with permission to stay in the UK as a refugee can apply for a convention travel document under the terms of the 1951 United Nations Convention Relating to the Status of Refugees. There are limited grounds for refusal, such as to protect national security. An applicant must be legally resident in the UK, be able to prove their refugee status, and have permission to stay in the UK for at least six months from the date when the application is made.

  Except in exceptional circumstances a Home Office convention travel document cannot be used to travel to a person's country of origin, or the country from which they sought asylum. It will normally be valid for travel to all other countries.

  A convention travel document issued to an adult will usually be valid for 10 years if they have indefinite leave to remain in the UK. An applicant with limited leave to remain will usually be granted a convention travel document valid for the same period as their permission to stay in the UK, up to a maximum of five years. Children cannot be named on the travel document of their parent or guardian. A convention travel document issued to a child will usually be valid for five years if the child has indefinite leave to remain, or for the same period as their permission to stay, up to a maximum of five years, otherwise.

Stateless persons' travel documents

  A person may apply for a stateless persons' travel document if they have been recognised as a stateless person under the terms of the 1954 United Nations Convention Relating to the Status of Stateless Persons. This convention defined a stateless person as someone who is not considered as a national by any country under the terms of its laws. An applicant for a travel document will need to provide a letter from UK Visas and Immigration confirming their status.

  A person cannot be recognised as stateless if–

  (a) they are receiving help or protection from agencies of the United Nations (except the UN High Commissioner for Refugees);
  (b) they are recognised by the competent authorities of the country in which they are resident (i.e., the UK) as having the rights and obligations attached to having nationality of that country; or
  (c) there are serious reasons for considering that they have committed a crime against peace, a war crime, a crime against humanity, or a serious non-political crime outside the UK before they started living here, or acts contrary to the purposes and principles of the United Nations.
  The period of issue of a stateless persons' travel document is as for a Convention travel document.

One-way travel documents

  A one-way document of identity allows travel for one journey out of the UK only. It cannot be used to return to the UK. If a person is currently in the UK and is a national of any other country, they may apply for a one-way document. Children cannot be named on the travel document of their parent or guardian. They must apply for their own document.

Certificates of travel

  If a person has not been given refugee status in the UK and has not been recognised as a stateless person, they may be able to apply for a certificate of travel, which will give permission to travel abroad and return to the UK. An applicant must first prove that they have been formally and unreasonably refused a passport by the authorities of the country of which they are a national.

  Except in exceptional circumstances a Home Office certificate of travel cannot be used to travel to a person's country of origin, or to the country from which they sought asylum.

  Some countries do not accept certificates of travel as valid travel documents. At present, countries that do *not* accept them include: Austria, Belgium, Denmark, France, Germany, Greece, Iceland, Italy, Luxembourg, the Netherlands, Portugal, South Africa, Spain, and Switzerland.

  The period of issue of a certificate of travel is as for a Convention travel document except that the maximum period for an adult is five years.

Fees and application process

  The application fee for a Convention travel document, stateless person's travel document or one-way document of identity is £72, except where the applicant is under the age of 16 when the fee is £46 (Immigration and Nationality (Fees) Regulations 2016). The fee for a certificate of travel is £218, except where the applicant is under the age of 16 when the fee is £109. However, no fee is payable under the 2016 Regulations in respect of an application for a travel document–

  (a) for a body that is being taken abroad for the purposes of burial or cremation;

(b) in order to enable the applicant to participate in a project operated or approved by the Secretary of State for the purposes of enabling a person in the UK to make a single trip to a country outside the UK in order to assist the reconstruction of that country or to decide whether to resettle there;

(c) where the applicant was born on or before 2nd September 1929; or

(d) in respect of an application for a document of identity for the purposes of the Assisted Voluntary Returns programme operated by the Home Office

All applicants for a travel document must also apply for a biometric residence permit (also known as a biometric immigration document). There is no revalidation of such documents: a new application and full fee must be paid each time the document expires. Where personal details have to be amended a new application will have to be made, accompanied by the full fee.

D: SEIZURE OF PASSPORTS ETC

10 Power to seize passports

The police have the power to seize a passport which has been cancelled by the Secretary of State (in practice, the Home Secretary) on grounds of involvement in activities so undesirable that it is contrary to the public interest for the person to have access to passport facilities. The Secretary of State must have specified the passport in an authorisation for these purposes (Anti-Social Behaviour, Crime and Policing Act 2014, Sch. 8, para 3).

A policeman, immigration officer, or customs official at a port (air or sea and including a rail station from where international departures leave) has the power to–

(a) require a person to hand over all travel documents;

(b) search for travel documents;

(c) inspect travel documents for the purpose of checking their validity and retain it whilst its validity is checked,

and to retain any travel document believed to be invalid (Sch. 8, para 2). For these purposes, "travel documents" are generally passports (issued by any state), but also includes other documents such as emergency travel documents. These powers may be exercised when the officer believes a person is entering or leaving Great Britain or Northern Ireland, or travelling by air within Great Britain or within Northern Ireland. A document that is retained whilst its validity is investigated must be checked as soon as possible. If it is found to be valid, or invalid only because it has expired, it must be returned straight away. A passport cannot be retained for checks for longer than seven days unless it has already been found to be invalid for a reason other than expiry. This is because there may be legitimate uses for an expired passport, for example, if it incorporated an extant visa issued by another country. However, a requirement to return an expired travel document does not apply if the officer concerned reasonably believes it to have been intended for use for purposes for which it is no longer valid.

11 Authorities

Anti-Social Behaviour, Crime and Policing Act 2014

Consular Fees Order 2012, as amended (S.I. 2012 Nos. 798 and 1752, 2013 Nos. 535 and 1720, 2014 No. 509, and 2016 No. 373)

Consular Fees Regulations 1981, as amended (S.I. 1981 No. 476, 2000 No. 1017, and 2013 No. 762)

Immigration and Nationality (Fees) Regulations 2016 (S.I. 2016 No. 226)

SUPPORT FOR ASYLUM SEEKERS, REFUGEES, AND DISPLACED PERSONS

A: ASYLUM SEEKERS

1 Introduction

Arrangements for the accommodation and support of asylum seekers over 18 while their asylum application is being considered are contained in Part VI (ss.94 to 127) of the Immigration and Asylum Act 1999. Part VI has been supplemented by the Asylum Support Regulations 2000 which contain detailed provisions about who is to receive support from the National Asylum Support Service (NASS); what support may be provided; and how an application for support should be made.

The provisions of Part VI and of the Regulations are set out in this Note.

2 The National Asylum Support Service

In April 2000, responsibility for the support of asylum seekers was transferred to the National Asylum Support Service (NASS) which was set up by the Home Office. NASS is responsible for the provision of support for destitute asylum seekers and their dependants during the period while their claim for asylum is being considered. Support takes the form of accommodation and cash support to meet essential living costs. NASS provides support either directly or through arrangements with local authorities and others. At the same time, asylum seekers and some others "subject to immigration control" cannot claim social security benefits and are excluded from local authority housing allocation and assistance under the homelessness legislation.

Children of asylum seekers supported by NASS are entitled to school places and qualify for free school meals and milk. The provision of assistance with transport costs and uniform is at the discretion of the local authority.

Asylum seekers supported by NASS are also entitled to health care under the NHS and to free prescriptions on the same basis as nationals. Asylum seekers with special needs (e.g., because they are disabled) may be entitled to help with those needs from local authority social services.

Asylum seekers under 18 are not covered by NASS and continue to receive help directly from local authorities under the Children Act 1989 or the Children (Scotland) Act 1995.

3 Refusal and discontinuance of support

Support under the Immigration and Asylum Act 1999 will be refused if the person claiming support–
(a) is able to support themselves; or
(b) is intentionally destitute.
Support will be discontinued once a person's asylum claim is decided (or once any appeal has been disposed of). However, where an asylum seeker's family includes a child under 18, support will continue while the asylum seeker and his child remain in the UK.

Under the UK Borders Act 2007, a person remains an asylum-seeker, despite the fact that their claim for asylum has been determined, during any period when they can bring an in-country appeal, or such an appeal is pending (s.17). Their status as an asylum-seeker will also continue for a prescribed period after the appeal ceases to be pending. This prescribed period is 28 days (if the appeal has been allowed) or 21 days (in all other cases) (Asylum Support (Prescribed Period Following Appeal) Regulations 2007 (S.I. No. 3102).

Asylum seekers who are granted refugee status or exceptional leave to remain will be able to start claiming social security benefits and will then qualify for local authority housing assistance.

Failed asylum seekers can receive only very limited support pending their removal from the country: see **21 Failed asylum applicants**, below.

NASS has the power to determine the age of anyone claiming support (this being necessary since some asylum seekers may claim to be under 18, when in fact they are over 18).

4 Refusal of support to people who make late claims for asylum

Support will not be provided or arranged for people who do not satisfy the Secretary of State that their claim for asylum was made "as soon as reasonably practicable" after their arrival in the UK (Nationality, Immigration and Asylum Act 2002, s.55).

Support will still be provided so as to prevent a breach of a person's right under the European Convention on Human Rights, and to families with children under the age of 18.

5 People for whom support may be provided

Under s.95 of the Immigration and Asylum Act 1999 and the Asylum Support Regulations 2000, NASS may arrange for support to be provided for asylum seekers and their dependants who appear to be destitute or likely to become destitute within 14 days (Reg. 7). The term "dependant" includes an asylum seeker's spouse or civil partner, child, or other member of his close family or member of his household who is under 18; anyone with whom he has lived as man and wife or as a same-sex couple for at least two years of the last three years; and any disabled member of his family or household who requires care from the asylum seeker or another member of his household (Reg. 2).

Support will not be provided for anyone except asylum seekers and their dependants and will not be provided for anyone entitled to claim universal credit, income-based jobseeker's allowance, income-related employment and support allowance, income support, housing benefit or council tax benefit (but most asylum seekers will be excluded from claiming these benefits–see **18 Exclusion from benefits**, below) (Reg. 4).

6 When a person is "destitute"

For the purposes of s.95 of the Immigration and Asylum Act 1999, a person is "destitute" if he (together with any dependants)–

(a) does not have adequate accommodation or any means of obtaining it (whether or not his essential living needs are met); or

(b) he has adequate accommodation or the means of obtaining it but cannot meet his other essential living needs.

Where an application is for support for the applicant and at least one dependant, a decision must be made as to whether the applicant and all his dependants, taken together, are destitute or likely to become destitute within the prescribed 14 day period (Asylum Support Regulations 2000, Reg. 5).

In deciding whether a person is destitute, or likely to become destitute, account must be taken of–

(i) any income available to the applicant or his dependants;

(ii) any other support available to them;

(iii) any assets (in the form of cash, savings, investments, land, cars or vehicles, and goods held for trade or business) whether held in the United Kingdom or elsewhere, which are available to the applicant or any of his dependants. Other assets must be ignored (Reg. 6).

In deciding whether a person's existing accommodation is adequate, NASS must take account of–

(i) the fact that the person has no enforceable right to occupy the accommodation;

(ii) the fact that it is temporary or emergency accommodation only;

(iii) its location and affordability;

(iv) whether the person can gain entry to it;

(v) whether the accommodation can be occupied by the person's dependants as well; and

(vi) whether it is probable that a person's continued occupation of the accommodation will lead to domestic violence against him or any of his dependants.

In deciding whether a person's existing accommodation is affordable, regard must be had to the claimant's income and assets, the cost of the accommodation; and his other reasonable living expenses (s.95 and Reg. 8).

In providing or arranging for the provision of accommodation, regard must be had to family unity and, so far as is reasonably practicable, family members should be housed together (Asylum Seekers (Reception Conditions) Regulations 2005, Reg. 3). If the asylum seeker or a member of their family is a "vulnerable person", their special needs must be taken into account. A person is "vulnerable" if they are a minor, disabled, elderly, pregnant, a lone parent with a minor child, or a person who has been subjected to torture, rape or other serious form of psychological, physical, or sexual violence (Reg. 4).

In deciding whether a person's essential living needs (apart from accommodation) are met, no account may be taken of a person's personal preferences as to clothing (although his individual circumstances as to clothing can be taken account of). Certain items and expenses, including the cost of faxes, computer facilities and photocopying, travel expenses (except the cost of the initial journey to the accommodation provided by NASS), toys, and other recreational items and entertainment expenses will not be treated as essential living needs (Asylum Support Regulations 2000, Reg. 9).

If it transpires that, at any time during which asylum support has been provided, a person was not destitute, then the Secretary of State can require the monetary value of the support given to be refunded (Reg. 17A).

7 Ways in which support may be provided

Support under s.95 of the Immigration and Asylum Act 1999 may be given by–

(a) the provision of accommodation;

(b) help with essential living needs; and

(c) payment of expenses (other than legal expenses) in connection with an asylum claim or in connection with attending bail proceedings (in cases where an asylum seeker or his dependants have been detained under the Immigration Acts (see the Note on **Control of Immigration**).

In exceptional circumstances, support may be provided in other ways as well (s.96). The provision which prevented support being given by way of cash payments except in exceptional circumstances has been repealed.

The Secretary of State has the power to restrict support under (b) to those who are provided with accommodation under (a), either generally or in a particular geographic area (Nationality, Immigration and Asylum Act 2002, s.43). Accordingly, help with essential living needs will be dependant on living in accommodation provided by the Secretary of State.

When exercising its power to provide accommodation, NASS must have regard to the fact that the accommodation is to be temporary pending determination of the asylum seeker's claim and to the desirability of providing accommodation in areas where there is a ready supply. No account will be taken of any preference that the supported person or a dependant may have as to the locality in which the accommodation is to be provided, or as to the nature of the accommodation provided or the nature or standard of fixtures and fittings (although account may be taken of a person's individual circumstances insofar as they affect his accommodation needs) (s.97 and the Asylum Support Regulations 2000, Reg. 13).

Asylum seekers in receipt of support may also be provided with educational services (including English lessons) and sporting or other developmental activities, but only for the purpose of maintaining good order among such persons (Reg. 14).

8 Accommodation centres

The Secretary of State may arrange for the provision of accommodation centres to house asylum seekers (Nationality, Immigration and Asylum Act 2002, s.16). Local authorities have a discretion to assist in the provision of such centres, to make premises available for use as such a centre, and to provide services in connection with centres (s.38). Before establishing a centre in Scotland, Wales or Northern Ireland, the Scottish Ministers, Welsh Assembly and First and deputy First Minister of Northern Ireland must be consulted (ss.40 to 42).

9 Amount of support

Where support is being provided for essential living needs that support will, as a general rule, be provided weekly in the form of a cash payment of £36.95 for each supported person (of whatever age) (Asylum Support Regulations 2000, Reg. 10).

Additional weekly amounts are payable in respect of (Reg. 10A)–

A pregnant mother	£3.00
A baby aged under 1	£5.00
A child aged at least 1 but under 3	£3.00

A one-off £300 maternity payment is payable if the mother has a baby which is due in 8 weeks or less, or if the baby is under 6 weeks old. The specified amount will be reduced where any accommodation is provided on a full board, half board or bed and breakfast basis.

In deciding what level or kind of support is to be provided for a person applying for asylum support, account will be taken of–

(a) any income which the claimant or any dependant of his might reasonably be expected to have;

(b) support which is or might reasonably be expected to be available to the claimant or any dependant of his; and any assets (i.e., cash, savings, investments, land, vehicles and goods held for business purposes), whether held in the United Kingdom or elsewhere, which are or might reasonably be expected to be available to the claimant or any dependant of his (Reg. 12).

10 Change of circumstances

Regulation 15 of the Asylum Support Regulations 2000 lists the types of change of circumstance that a supported person must report without delay, including becoming employed, getting married or divorced, forming or ending a civil partnership, becoming pregnant or leaving his accommodation.

11 Contributions and recovery of sums

In deciding the level of asylum support to be provided for a person under the support scheme, account will be taken of the person's income and assets. Support for a person may be set at a level which does not reflect his income, support or assets and that person may be required to make contributions towards the cost of the provision to him of asylum support (Asylum Support Regulations 2000, Reg. 16). In addition, where it appears that supported person had, at the time that he applied for support, assets of any kind (in the United Kingdom or elsewhere) which were not then capable of being realised, but which now can be, NASS may recover from that person the value of the support provided for that person up to the monetary value of the assets concerned (Reg. 17).

12 Suspension and discontinuance of support

Support may be provided subject to conditions which must be set out in writing and a copy of which must be given to the supported person (Immigration and Asylum Act 1999, s.95(9) to (11)). In particular, a condition may relate to the use of the support provided, or compliance with any restrictions which apply to someone who is at liberty (as opposed to being held in a detention centre) (s.95(9A)). When deciding whether to continue to provide support, account may be taken of the extent to which a relevant condition has been complied with (Asylum Support Regulations 2000, Reg. 19). A "relevant" condition for these purposes is one which makes support subject to actual residence in a specific place or location.

Support for a person and/or his dependants may be suspended or discontinued if (Reg. 20)–

(a) NASS has reasonable grounds to suspect that, where a person is in collective accommodation, he or any of his dependants has committed a serious breach of the rules of that accommodation;

(b) NASS has reasonable grounds to suspect that the person or any of his dependants has committed an act of seriously violent behaviour;

(c) NASS has reasonable grounds to suspect that the person or any of his dependants has committed an offence under Part VI (see 17 Offences, below); or

(d) NASS discovers that the supported person has abandoned or, without permission, left his authorised address (see below);

(e) the supported person does not comply with a request for information relating to his eligibility for, or receipt of, support within five working days;

(f) the supported person fails, without reasonable excuse to attend an interview relating to his eligibility for, or receipt of, support;

(g) the supported person or, if he is an asylum seeker, his dependant, does not comply with a request for information relating to his claim for asylum, within ten working days;

(h) NASS has reasonable grounds for believing that the supported person, or a dependant, has concealed financial resources and has therefore unduly benefited from asylum support;

(i) the supported person or a dependant have not complied with a reporting requirement;

(j) NASS has reasonable grounds for believing that the supported person, or a dependant, has made a prior claim for asylum in the same or a different name, and the current claim has been made before the prior claim has been determined; or

(k) the supported person or a dependant have without reasonable excuse failed to comply with a "relevant" condition (i.e., one which makes support subject to actual residence in a specific place or location).

For the above purposes, a person intentionally makes himself destitute if he becomes destitute as a result of an act or omission deliberately done by him or any dependant without reasonable excuse while in the UK.

A person's "authorised address" is the accommodation provided for him under the support scheme, or, if accommodation is not provided, the address notified by him (Asylum Support Regulations 2000, Reg. 20).

Where a person's support has been suspended or discontinued, no new application for support from him will be considered unless there has been a material change of circumstances since the suspension or discontinuation or unless NASS considers that there are exceptional circumstances (Reg. 21).

If a person is given a tenancy or licence to occupy accommodation under the asylum support scheme, he may be given notice to quit that accommodation if–

(i) his support is suspended or discontinued under Regulation 20 (see above);

(ii) his claim for asylum is determined (see below);

(iii) he ceases to be destitute; or

(iv) he is to be moved elsewhere.

A notice to quit must give a notice period of at least seven days (Reg. 22). For the purposes of Regulation 22, a claim for asylum is treated as having been determined at the expiry of a 14 day period following notification of NASS's decision to the claimant or, where the claimant has appealed against that decision, 14 days after the date on which the appeal is disposed of.

13 Applications for support

An asylum seeker himself or any dependant of his (see 5 People for whom support may be provided, above) may apply for asylum support (Asylum Support Regulations 2000, Reg. 3). The application must be made by completing in English a copy of the official application form (Asylum Support Application Form ASF1). The form can be downloaded from <https://www.gov.uk/government/publications/application-for-asylum-support-form-asf1>. Once the application is complete, the form and other documents required should be collated together and posted to the regional asylum team. A list of regional asylum support teams and their contact details can be found on the Home Office website at <http://www.ukba.homeoffice.gov.uk/asylum/helpandadvice/asylum-support-teams/>.

The telephone number of the Asylum Support Customer Contact Centre is 0300 123 2235. If an application is successful, the claimant will be issued with a certificate (HC2) entitling him to free NHS prescriptions, dental treatment and sight tests.

14 Temporary support

S.98 of the Immigration and Asylum Act 1999 allows temporary support to be provided for asylum seekers or their dependants who may be destitute, while a decision is made as to whether support should be provided under s.95.

The provisions as to keeping families together and taking account of those with special needs set out in the Asylum Seekers (Reception Conditions) Regulations 2005 (see 6 When a person is "destitute", above) also apply to temporary support.

If a decision is made not to provide asylum support, any temporary support that has been provided will be discontinued (Asylum Support Regulations 2000, Reg. 3(5C)).

Temporary support can be discontinued for breach of condition under the Asylum Support Regulations 2000, Regulations 19 and 20 (see **12 Suspension and discontinuance of support**, above).

15 Appeals

Under s.103 of the Immigration and Asylum Act 1999, an applicant may appeal against a decision by NASS to refuse or terminate support under s.95. Any such appeal should be made to the First-tier Tribunal which has taken over the functions of the Asylum Support Adjudicators (Transfer of Tribunal Functions Order 2008/2833).

16 Support and assistance by local authorities

S.99 of the Immigration and Asylum Act 1999 provides for asylum support to be provided by local authorities in accordance with agreements made with NASS. In particular, local authorities may provide services jointly with other bodies; tender for contracts; and provide services outside their own area. Local authorities and registered social landlords (in Scotland, registered housing associations) are also required to assist in the provision of accommodation under s.95 (s.100). If necessary, the Secretary of State may designate areas consisting of one or more local authorities as "reception zones". Authorities in such areas will then be required to make available currently unoccupied accommodation for the purposes of s.95 (s.101).

17 Offences

Ss.105 to 108 of the Immigration and Asylum Act 1999 list a number of offences in connection with the provision of support for asylum seekers. It is an offence for a person to make false representations or to produce false documents with a view to obtaining support, or for any other person to make dishonest statements with a view to obtaining any payment or advantage under the support scheme. It is also an offence to delay, obstruct or fail to provide information to a person exercising functions under the scheme (s.107).

S.112 allows proceedings to be taken in the county court (in Scotland, the sheriff's court) to recover the monetary value of any support provided as a result of misrepresentation or failure to disclose material facts. The value of any support provided in error may also be recovered (s.114).

The Secretary of State may require employers and financial institutions to provide information about those reasonably suspected of having fraudulently obtained asylum seeker support (Nationality, Immigration and Asylum Act 2002, ss.134 and 135).

18 Exclusion from benefits

Non-EEA nationals who are subject to immigration control (including asylum seekers) are excluded from the following means-tested benefits (Immigration and Asylum Act 1999, s.115)–

- universal credit;
- income-based jobseeker's allowance;
- state pension credit;
- income support;
- income-related employment and support allowance;
- child benefit;
- housing benefit;
- attendance allowance;
- severe disablement allowance;
- carer's allowance;
- disability living allowance;
- health in pregnancy grant; and
- social fund payments.

The term "subject to immigration control" includes persons who require leave to enter or remain in the UK but who do not have it, and those whose leave to remain in the UK is subject to a condition that they do not have recourse to public funds (i.e., claim social security benefits). All asylum seekers with undetermined claims are therefore excluded from claiming benefits, but those who are granted refugee status or exceptional leave to remain are no longer excluded and may start to claim benefits.

Some people may be exempted from the effects of s.115 by regulations. The Immigration (Eligibility for Assistance) (Scotland and Northern Ireland) Regulations 2000 provide that s.115 does not apply to certain people who, up until 3rd April 2000 were not entitled to means-tested benefits but were eligible for assistance under the Social Work (Scotland) Act 1968, the Mental Health (Scotland) Act 1984 or the Health and Personal Social Services (Northern Ireland) Order 1972 (S.I. No. 1265). For more details of other exemptions from s.115 (e.g., in the case of nationals from non-EEA countries which are parties to the European Convention on Social an Medical Assistance or the European Social Charter, or in the case of persons who are temporarily without funds because remittances from abroad have been disrupted) see the individual notes on the above benefits in the Social Security Section.

Those excluded from claiming benefits are also excluded from receiving help from local authorities under s.45 of the Health Services and Public Health Act 1968 (local authority services for the elderly) and from help under Schedule 20 to the National Health Service Act 2006 (arrangements by local authorities for the prevention of illness and for care and after-care) (s.117). However, the exclusions under ss.116 and 117 do not apply to those who have need of the services wholly or partly for reasons other than destitution (e.g., because they are disabled).

S.120 contains equivalent provisions for Scotland to those contained in ss.116 and 117.

19 Housing authority accommodation

Asylum seekers and others excluded from claiming benefits are also excluded from the allocation of long-term local authority housing accommodation and from assistance under the homelessness legislation. Housing authorities are also prohibited from granting tenancies or licences to persons "subject to immigration control" unless they are of a class specified by order or the accommodation is provided under the support scheme (see **16 Support and assistance by local authorities**, above) (s.118).

S.119 of the Immigration and Asylum Act 1999 contains equivalent provision for Scotland.

20 Support for children

Where the household of someone who is eligible for support under the scheme includes a child under 18, NASS must exercise its powers so as to ensure that adequate accommodation is provided for that child part of the eligible person's household and that the child's essential living expenses are met, again as part of the eligible person's household. Where support for a child is available under the scheme, local authorities may not provide assistance for that child under the Children Act 1989 or the Children (Scotland) Act 1995 (s.122).

Where an unaccompanied minor makes a claim for asylum, the Secretary of State must endeavour to trace the members of the minor's family as soon as possible after the claim is made (Asylum Seekers (Reception Conditions) Regulations 2005, Reg. 6). Where there may be a threat to the life or integrity of the minor or is close family, care must be taken to ensure that the collection, processing and circulation of information concerning the minor or his close family is undertaken on a confidential basis so as not to jeopardise his or their safety.

21 Failed asylum applicants

Failed asylum applicants are among the classes of people who are not eligible for support under the 1999 Act. In addition, these people are not eligible for support under any community care legislation, such as local authority accommodation or welfare services. Along with others (see **18 Exclusion from benefits**, above) they are also excluded from all social security support. See also **22 Accommodation for failed asylum seekers**, below.

The full list of categories of excluded people is (Nationality, Immigration and Asylum Act 2002, s.54 and Sch. 3)–

(a) people (not being EEA nationals) who have refugee status in an EEA country, or are dependants of someone who has;

(b) EEA nationals and their dependants;

(c) failed asylum seekers who also fail to co-operate with removal directions;

(d) people unlawfully in the UK (i.e., in breach of immigration law and not seeking asylum);

These provisions do not prevent support being provided to children. However, the Asylum and Immigration (Treatment of Claimants etc) Act 2004 added a further category to the above, namely–

(e) failed asylum seekers with a dependent child who the Secretary of State certifies have failed without reasonable excuse to take reasonable steps to voluntarily leave the UK or place themselves in such a position that they are able to leave the UK voluntarily.

In the case of someone within (e), they will have 14 days from receiving a copy of the Secretary of State's certificate before support is withdrawn. Before a certificate is issued, the Government have indicated that the failed asylum seekers would be interviewed so that they can explain why they have not yet left the UK, and what steps they are taking to do so. A certificate would only be issued where there was no co-operation in taking steps to leave. Children could continue to receive help from local authorities under the Children Act 1989 or the Children (Scotland) Act 1995.

Where it is determined that a person has refugee status abroad (i.e., in another EEA country), a local authority may make travel arrangements to enable that person to travel to that country. If that person has a dependant child, interim accommodation arrangements may also be made pending implementation of the travel arrangements (Withholding and Withdrawal of Support (Travel Assistance and Temporary Accommodation) Regulations 2002, Reg. 3). Travel arrangements and accommodation cannot include cash payments to the person involved and must be secured at the lowest practicable cost to the local authority. The travel arrangements must be made so that the person leaves the UK as soon as practicable (Reg. 4). Where a person fails to implement or co-operate with travel arrangements, accommodation cannot be provided unless that failure was due to medical reasons or transport disruption (Reg. 6).

22 Accommodation for failed asylum seekers

The Secretary of State may provide, or arrange for the provision of, facilities for the accommodation of a person who was an asylum seeker but whose claim for asylum has been rejected, together with their dependants (Immigration and Asylum Act 1999, s.4).

Such accommodation may be provided subject to conditions. The Immigration and Asylum (Provision of Accommodation for Failed Asylum-Seekers) Regulations 2005 provide that, in order to be eligible for accommodation, a person must be destitute (see **6 When a person is "destitute"**, above), and must satisfy one or more of the following conditions, i.e., he (Reg. 3)–

(a) is taking all reasonable steps to leave the UK or place himself in a position in which he is able to leave the UK, which may include complying with attempts to obtain a travel document to facilitate his departure;

(b) is unable to leave the UK because of a physical impediment to travel or for some other medical reason;

(c) is unable to leave the UK because in the opinion of the Secretary of State there is currently no viable route of return available;

(d) has made an application for judicial review of a decision in relation to his asylum claim and been granted permission to proceed with it; or

(e) must be provided with accommodation in order to avoid a breach of his rights under the European Convention on Human Rights.

The Secretary of State may make accommodation conditional upon a person's performance of, or participation in, "community activities" for up to 35 hours a week if they are aged 18 or over (Reg. 4). These are defined as activities which are beneficial to the public or a section of the public (s.4(7)).

The continued provision of accommodation may also be made conditional on compliance with specified standards of behaviour, reporting requirements, residence at a specified address, and the taking of specified steps to facilitate a person's departure from the UK (Reg. 5).

The Secretary of State may make regulations permitting a person who is provided with accommodation under s.4 to be supplied also with services or facilities of a specified kind. The Immigration and Asylum (Provision of Services or Facilities) Regulations 2007 specify–

(a) the supply, or arrangement for the supply, of facilities for travel to receive healthcare or register a birth;

(b) the provision to a supported person of his child's full birth certificate;

(c) the supply of facilities to make telephone calls, and receive stationery and postage for correspondence, to certain specified persons regarding medical treatment or care;

(d) the one-off supply, on application, of additional vouchers to pregnant women and new mothers;

(e) the weekly supply, on application of additional vouchers to pregnant women and children under the age of three;

(f) the weekly supply, on application, of additional vouchers for clothing for children under the age of 16;

(g) if the Secretary of State is satisfied that a person has an exceptional need for certain specified services or facilities, provision for that need.

B: DISPLACED PERSONS

23 The Temporary Protection Directive

EC Council Directive 2001/55/EC, the "Temporary Protection Directive", lays down minimum standards for giving protection in the event of a mass influx of displaced persons from third countries who are unable to return to their country of origin. It provides for immediate and temporary protection to be given to such people, in particular if there is also a risk that the asylum system will be unable to process the influx without adverse effects for its efficient operation (Art. 2).

"Displaced persons" are defined as people who have had to leave their country or region of origin, or have been evacuated, and are unable to return in safe and durable conditions because of the prevailing situation. In particular, it includes those who have fled areas of armed conflict or endemic violence and those at serious risk of, or who have been the victims of, systematic or generalised violations of their human rights.

The Directive is triggered by an EC Council Decision establishing the existence of a mass influx of displaced people. Once that Decision has been made, the Directive will apply.

In the UK, the Directive is implemented, in part, by the Displaced Persons (Temporary Protection) Regulations 2005, as described in the following paragraphs.

As to the provisions of the Immigration Rules dealing with temporary protection, see the Note on **The Immigration Rules: Asylum, Refugees etc** at para **11 Temporary protection**.

24 Leave to enter and remain in the UK

The Displaced Persons (Temporary Protection) Regulations 2005 provide that any person who is given temporary protection in the UK because of the triggering of EC Directive 2001/55 will be deemed to have been granted exceptional leave to enter or remain in the UK outside of the Immigration Rules (Reg. 3). This status will last–so allowing support to be provided–for as long as the temporary protection lasts, plus 28 days (provided that during those 28 days the person is taking all reasonable steps to leave the UK, or place himself in a position in which he will be able to leave). Under EC Directive 2001/55, temporary protection last for a period of one year, although, if not specifically terminated it will automatically be extended (twice) for a further six months. A further Council Decision may extend protection for one more year (Art. 4).

25 Assistance for displaced persons

A person who is given temporary protection is entitled to receive "subsistence" under the (Displaced Persons (Temporary Protection) Regulations 2005, Reg. 4)–

(a) the Social Security Contributions and Benefits Act 1992, Part VII (i.e., the income-related benefits, namely income support, housing benefit and council tax benefit);

(b) the Jobseekers Act 1995; and

(c) the State Pension Credit Act 2002.

The Secretary of State may also provide or arrange accommodation. To this end he may ask local authorities and registered social landlords to assist him and they must co-operate. The Secretary of State must have regard to the desirability, in general, of providing accommodation in areas where there is a ready supply, and must not have regard to any preference of the displaced person as to locality (Regs 5 to 8).

The Secretary of State can, after consultation, direct a local authority which he considers has suitable accommodation to make that accommodation available. Accommodation is "suitable" if it is unoccupied and likely to remain so for the foreseeable future, and is appropriate for housing those with temporary protection, or capable of being made so with minor work (Regs 10 to 13).

A tenancy, licence or right of occupation under these provisions can be ended by a notice to vacate giving seven days' notice (Reg. 15).

26 Claims for asylum

Normally, support for an asylum seeker will not be considered unless the claim for asylum was made "as soon as reasonably practicable" after arrival in the UK (Nationality, Immigration and Asylum Act 2002, s.55). (see **4 Refusal of support to people who make late claims for asylum**, above). However, any time during which a person has benefited from a grant of temporary protection may be disregarded. Accordingly, if a claim for asylum is made whilst a person has temporary protection, support may continue when that temporary protection ends, even though the asylum claim was not made upon arrival (Displaced Persons (Temporary Protection) Regulations 2005, Reg. 16).

C: REFUGEES

27 Integration loans

The Secretary of State may make regulations enabling him to make loans ("integration loans") to refugees (Asylum and Immigration (Treatment of Claimants, etc.) Act 2004, s.13). A person is a refugee for these purposes if the Secretary of State has either recorded him as a refugee within the meaning of the 1951 Geneva Convention relating to the Status of Refugees or granted him indefinite leave to enter or remain in the UK.

The Integration Loans for Refugees and Others Regulations 2007 have been made for this purpose. They apply to refugees, those who have been granted leave to enter or remain as a consequence of being granted humanitarian protection (see the Note on **The Immigration Rules: Asylum, Refugees etc** at para **6 Humanitarian protection**), and dependants of people in these two categories. In deciding whether to make a loan, the Secretary of State will look at various factors, including–

(a) a person's financial position taking into account their income, assets, liabilities, outgoings and number of dependants;

(b) their likely ability to repay a loan;

(c) the length of time since they were granted leave to enter or remain in the UK;

(d) the information they have provided as to their intended use of the loan; and

(e) the available budget for integration loans.

A person will not be able to receive a loan if they–

(f) are under the age of 18;

(g) are insolvent;

(h) have already received a loan; or

(i) were granted leave to enter or remain in the UK before 11th June 2007.

Where the recipient of a loan is receiving benefits, repayment of the loan will be by way of deduction from those benefits (Reg. 9).

D: THE INDEPENDENT ANTI-SLAVERY COMMISSIONER

28 Establishment and functions

The Modern Slavery Act 2015 s.40 provides for the establishment of an Independent Anti-slavery Commissioner, an independent office holder appointed by the Secretary of State. The Commissioner must encourage good practice in the prevention, detection, investigation and prosecution of slavery and human trafficking offences and the identification of victims of those offences. These offences include all current slavery and trafficking offences in the UK (s.41(1)). In practice the Commissioner will focus on improving the identification of victims as well as the effectiveness of the law enforcement response in the UK, to both encourage effective investigations leading to successful convictions of modern slavery offences and prevent future offences. The Commissioner can consider the provision of assistance and support to victims of slavery and human trafficking offences in relation to the functions set out in s.41(1) (s.41(4)).

The Commissioner must not exercise any function in relation to an individual case, however, this does not prevent the Commissioner considering individual cases and drawing conclusions about them for the purpose of, or in the context of, considering a general issue (s.44).

The Commissioner may request a specified public authority to co-operate with the Commissioner in any way that the Commissioner considers necessary for the purposes of the Commissioner's functions (s.43(1)). A public authority must so far as reasonably practicable comply with a request made to it (s.43(2)). A public authority which discloses information to the Commissioner in pursuance of a request does not breach any obligation of confidence owed by the public authority in relation to that information; but this does not apply in relation to patient information (s.43(3)). The public authorities are contained in Schedule 3 to the Act and include law enforcement, border security and local government authorities, and health bodies.

29 Authorities

Statutes–

Asylum and Immigration (Treatment of Claimants etc) Act 2004

Immigration and Asylum Act 1999

Modern Slavery Act 2015

Nationality, Immigration and Asylum Act 2002

UK Borders Act 2007

Statutory Instruments, etc

Asylum Seekers (Reception Conditions) Regulations 2005 (S.I. 2005 No. 7)

Asylum Support Regulations 2000, as amended (S.I. 2000 No. 704, 2002 Nos. 472 and 3110, 2003 No. 241, 2004 No. 1313, 2005 Nos. 11 and 2114, 2008 No. 1879, 2009 No. 641, 2013 No. 630, and 2015 Nos. 643, 645, and 1501)

Displaced Persons (Temporary Protection) Regulations 2005, as amended (S.I. 2005 No. 1379, 2010 No. 671, 2012 No. 700, and 2013 No. 630)

Immigration and Asylum (Provision of Accommodation for Failed Asylum-Seekers) Regulations 2005 (S.I. 2005 No. 930)

Immigration and Asylum (Provision of Services or Facilities) Regulations 2007 (S.I. 2007 No. 3627)

Immigration (Eligibility for Assistance) (Scotland and Northern Ireland) Regulations 2000 (S.I. 2000 No. 705)

Integration Loans for Refugees and Others Regulations 2007 (S.I. 2007 No. 1598)

Withholding and Withdrawal of Support (Travel Assistance and Temporary Accommodation) Regulations 2002, as amended (S.I. 2002 No. 3078 and 2005 No. 2114)

EC Council Directive 2001/55/EC, the Temporary Protection Directive

TAXATION

TAXATION

ADMINISTRATION OF TAXES

1 Introduction

This Note deals with the administration of the taxes with which other Notes in this Section are concerned, namely, income tax, corporation tax, capital gains tax, inheritance tax, and value added tax. It also explains the powers of Revenue Scotland in relation to devolved taxes.

A: INCOME TAX, CORPORATION TAX AND CAPITAL GAINS TAX

2 The Commissioners

The main provisions for the administration of income tax, corporation tax, and capital gains tax are contained in the Taxes Management Act 1970, as amended from time to time by the annual Finance Acts. Under s.1 of the 1970 Act, income tax, corporation tax, and capital gains tax are under the care and management of the Commissioners of Revenue and Customs, referred to as "the Commissioners". The Commissioners, who are civil servants, are required to appoint inspectors and collectors of taxes who act under their direction. They operate in accordance with a Charter which sets out the standards of behaviour and values to which they aspire when dealing with people and in the exercise of their functions (Commissioners for Revenue and Customs Act 2005, s.16A).

3 Returns of income and gains: self-assessment

The following summaries explain the position as to self-assessment which has been in operation for individuals since the tax year 1996/97.

The system in relation to a person's liability to income tax and capital gains tax now depends on whether he has received a notice under the Taxes Management Act 1970 s.8 requiring a return of his total income and chargeable gains. If a person is chargeable to income tax or capital gains tax for any year of assessment, and he has not received a notice under s.8, then unless all his income is within certain categories (including income taxed under PAYE) and he has no chargeable gains, he must within six months of the end of the year give notice that he is so chargeable (s.7).

Under s.8 a person may be required by a notice given for the purpose of establishing the amounts in which he is chargeable to income tax and capital gains tax to make and deliver a return, together with relevant accounts, statements and documents. Notices may require different information, accounts and statements in relation to different periods, different descriptions of source of income, and different descriptions of person.

The return must be delivered either by the 31st January (for electronic returns) or 31st October (non-electronic returns) next following the year of assessment. However, where the notice is given after the 31st July but before 31st October of the next following year, the return must be delivered within three months of the date the notice is given (non-electronic returns) or by 31st January (electronic returns). Where the notice is given after 31st October, the return must be delivered within three months (whether electronic or not).

Similar provisions apply to trustees of a settlement, with notices being given under s.8A. Notices may be given to one trustee or separate notices may be given separately to each trustee or to such trustees as the inspector may think fit.

The basic rule is that every return under ss.8 or 8A must include a self-assessment, that is an assessment of the income tax and capital gains tax payable on the basis of the information in the return, and reliefs and allowances claimed in the return (s.9(1)).

However, under s.9(2), a person's return need not state the income tax and capital gains tax payable if it is delivered either on or before 31st October next following the year of assessment or, where the notice under ss.8 or 8A is given after the 31st August following the year, if the return is delivered within two months after the notice is given. Where, in making and delivering his return, a person does not comply with s.9(1), the inspector must make the assessment if s.9(2) applies, and may make the assessment in any other case (s.9(3)).

A person may amend their return within 12 months of the filing date (s.9ZA). The Board may correct an obvious error or omission in a return (whether the error is of principle, arithmetic or otherwise), or anything else in the return that the officer has reason to believe is incorrect in the light of information available to him, within 9 months of it being filed (s.9ZB).

The inspector's powers to enquire into returns are set out in s.9A. Partnership returns are dealt with in ss.12AA and 12AB.

4 Dates for payment of tax on income and gains

S.59A of the Taxes Management Act 1970 applies only to a taxpayer who in any year of assessment is assessed under s.9 in respect of the preceding tax year for an amount of income tax which exceeds income tax already deducted at source. Where the amount of the excess is over a prescribed amount (currently £1,000: Income Tax (Payment on Account) Regulations 1996) he then must make two payments, each of 50% of the excess tax, the first on or before 31st January of that year and the second on or before the next following 31st July.

S.59B is more general and covers capital gains tax as well as income tax. If the person gave notice under s.7 within six months from the end of the tax year, but was not given notice under ss.8 or 8A until after the 31st October following that year, he must pay the tax three months after the notice under ss.8 or 8A. In any other case the tax is due on or before the 31st January next following the year of assessment.

5 Corporation tax: self-assessment

The main provisions relating to self-assessment for companies are contained in FA 1998 Schedule 18 which provides, *inter alia*, that every company tax return must include an assessment of the amount of tax that is payable by the company for the period covered by the return. To arrive at a figure for the self-assessment, the company must (Sch. 18, para 8)–

(1) calculate the corporation tax payable on the company's profits (i.e., apply the applicable rate of corporation tax to the chargeable profits for the period);

(2) give effect to any reliefs or set-offs against corporation tax (e.g., marginal small companies relief, double taxation relief);

(3) add any amounts assessable or chargeable as if they were corporation tax, reduced by any reliefs applicable to them (e.g., tax on a loan or advance made by a close company, sums chargeable as profits of a controlled foreign company);

(4) deduct any amount to be set off against the company's tax liability for the period.

A company's tax return must be filed by the last day of whichever of the following periods is last to end (Sch. 18, para 14)–

(a) 12 months from the end of the period for which the return is made;

(b) if the period for which the company makes up its accounts is not longer than 18 months, 12 months from the end of that period;

(c) if the period for which the company makes up its accounts is longer than 18 months, 30 months from the start of that period;

(d) 3 months from the date on which HM Revenue and Customs served notice requiring the return.

Every company which is chargeable to corporation tax for any accounting period and has not received a notice requiring a company return must within 12 months from the end of that period give notice to HM Revenue and Customs that it is so chargeable (FA 1998 Sch. 10, para 2). Failure to do so renders it liable to a penalty not exceeding the amount of the corporation tax for which it is liable in respect of its profits for that period that remains unpaid 12 months after the end of the period (FA 1998 Sch 18, para 2(3)).

Further requirements as to returns may be imposed by regulations made by the HMRC under s.17(5) (as inserted by the FA 1990, s.92).

6 Dates for payment of corporation tax

Corporation tax is due nine months after the end of the accounting period (Taxes Management Act 1970, s.59D). However, for large companies, i.e., those with profits of £1.5 million (or less if the company is in a group with others), tax is payable in instalments during the current year. If the amount payable is exceeded by amounts previously paid by instalment, the excess will be repaid. The amount payable is the amount calculated under self assessment in accordance with FA 1998 Schedule 18 para 8 (see **5 Corporation tax: self-assessment**, above).

7 Appeals against assessments

A taxpayer has a right of appeal if he is dissatisfied with a notice of assessment or the amendment of a self-assessment, or may ask for a determination to be reviewed (see **8 Reviews of assessments**, below). The appeal should be made in writing to the inspector or other officer who issued the notice, within 30 days after the date of the notice (Taxes Management Act 1970, ss.31, 31A). Late appeals may be admitted if there is reasonable cause for the delay in appealing (s.49).

An appeal will usually be to the First-tier Tribunal, but in certain circumstances it may be to the Upper Tribunal.

Many of the rules governing hearings before the tribunal are contained in the Tribunal Procedure (First-tier Tribunal) (Tax Chamber) Rules 2009. The taxpayer may be represented by any person, whether legally qualified or not.

On receiving a notice of appeal, application notice or notice of reference, the Tribunal will allocate the case to one of the following categories (Reg. 23)–

(i) default paper cases, which will usually be disposed of without a hearing;

(ii) basic cases, which will usually be disposed of after a hearing, with minimal exchange of documents before the hearing;

(iii) standard cases, which will usually be subject to more detailed case management and be disposed of after a hearing; and

(iv) complex cases, which may be transferred to the Upper Tribunal.

Tribunal hearings are generally public, although in each case the tribunal may direct that all or part of a hearing be in private (Reg. 32)–

(a) in the interests of public order or national security;

(b) for the protection of the private or family life of a party;

(c) in order to maintain the confidentiality of sensitive information;

(d) in order to avoid serious harm to the public interest; or

(e) if it considers that publicity would prejudice the interests of justice.

Either party to a hearing before the First-tier Tribunal may apply for permission to appeal within 56 days, on the basis that the decision was wrong in law (Reg. 39).

8 Reviews of assessments

If notice of appeal has been given to HMRC, then (Taxes Management Act 1970, s.49A)–

(a) the appellant may notify HMRC that he requires it to review the matter in question;

(b) HMRC may notify the appellant of an offer to review the matter in question; or

(c) the appellant may notify the appeal to the tribunal.

The nature and extent of any review will be such as appear appropriate to HMRC in the circumstances. HMRC must, in particular, have regard to steps taken before the beginning of the review by them in deciding the matter in question, and by any person in seeking to resolve disagreement about the matter in question. The review must take account of any representations made by the appellant at a stage which gives HMRC a reasonable opportunity to consider them. The review may conclude that HMRC's view of the matter in question is to be either upheld, varied, or cancelled and HMRC must notify the appellant of the conclusions of the review and their reasoning within 45 days (s.49E), after which the appellant has 30 days to notify the appeal to the tribunal (s.49G).

If HMRC have offered to review the matter in question (see (b) above), and the appellant does not accept the offer, he has 30 days in which to notify the appeal to the tribunal (s.49H).

9 Collection and recovery

When tax becomes due and payable, the collector of taxes (a permanent civil servant) is required to issue a demand for the sum due from the person(s) charged, and, on receiving payment, to issue a receipt if so requested (Taxes Management Act 1970, s.60). The collector may distrain on the property of a person who neglects or refuses to pay the sum charged. A justice of the peace, if satisfied by information on oath that there is reasonable ground for believing that a person is neglecting or refusing to pay a sum charged, may issue a warrant in writing authorising a collector to break open in the daytime any house or premises for this purpose (s.61, as amended by the Finance Act 1989, s.152). A claim for tax takes priority over any other execution (except at the suit of the landlord for rent) (s.62).

Ss.65 to 68 deal with court proceedings for recovery of tax. Ss.86 to 92, as amended, provide for the payment of interest on tax which is overdue (see also the Note on Income Tax: General Provisions at para **24 Interest on unpaid tax**). Penalties for failure to make correct returns are prescribed by the Finance Act 2009 (see **23 Penalties for failure to pay tax**, below).

HMRC may also collect amounts owed to it through the PAYE system (ITEPA 2003, s.684). The maximum amount that can be collected in this way over the course of a year ranges from £3,000 (for individuals with an annual PAYE income of less than £30,000) to £17,000 (for individuals with an annual PAYE income of more than £90,000), subject to a maximum limit of 50% of income (Income Tax (Pay As You Earn) Regulations 2003, Regs. 2 and 14D).

An officer of Revenue and Customs has certain data-gathering powers and may, by notice in writing, require a "relevant data-holder" (as defined in the Finance Act 2011, Sch. 23) to provide data relating to particular persons or matters. The meaning of "relevant data-holder" is wide-ranging and includes employers and persons who are concerned with making payments to or in respect of another person's employees and persons by or through whom interest is paid or credited. It also includes persons who, in whatever capacity, are in receipt of money or value of or belonging to another. Relevant data may not be specified in a notice unless an officer of Revenue and Customs has reason to believe that the data could have a bearing on chargeable or other periods ending on or after the applicable day, being the first day of the period of four years ending with the day on which the notice is given. The Data-gathering Powers (Relevant Data) Regulations 2012 specifies the data that data-holders may be required to provide and includes employment-related payments such as salaries, fees and commission, interest paid on money received or retained in the UK, data relating to credit and debit card payments, and rent or other payments arsing from land.

10 Compliance

The Finance Act 2000 makes it a criminal offence for a person to be knowingly concerned in the fraudulent evasion of income tax by themselves or any other person (s.144). A person guilty of an offence will be liable on summary conviction to imprisonment for a term not exceeding six months, or a fine (unlimited in England and Wales, not exceeding the statutory maximum in Scotland), or both; and on conviction on indictment to imprisonment for a term not exceeding seven years, or an unlimited fine, or both.

Where tax is owed by a person, and HMRC reasonably require contact details in order to be able to collect it, they may serve notice on a third party to provide those details where the third party is a business and HMRC reasonably believe that they have obtained the defaulters details in the course of business (Finance Act 2009, Sch.49).

HMRC may publish the names of any persons who deliberately evade tax of at least £25,000 (Finance Act 2009, s.94).

See also, **23 Penalties for failure to pay tax**, below.

11 Managed payment plans

A taxpayer may volunteer to enter into a managed payment plan with HMRC (FA 2009, s.111). Under such a plan, income and capital gains tax payable under self-assessment (and in certain cases corporation tax) may be paid by instalments balanced equally before and after the normal due date for payment, without any interest or penalties being incurred for payment after the due date. Failure to keep to the agreed payments means the plan lapses and the normal consequences for late payment will arise, however HMRC may reschedule payments.

B: INHERITANCE TAX

12 Introduction

Part VIII (ss.215 to 261) of the Inheritance Tax Act 1984, makes provision for the administration and collection of inheritance tax and, in relation to a liability to tax arising before 25th July 1986, capital transfer tax.

The provisions of the 1984 Act which relate to management, the delivery of accounts, the power of HMRC to require information and inspect property, payment of tax, and certificates of discharge are dealt with in the Note on **Inheritance Tax**.

13 Appeals against notices of determination

Where it appears to HMRC that a transfer of value has been made, or where a claim under the 1984 Act is made to them in connection with a transfer of value, they may give notice in writing to any person who appears to be the transferor or claimant, or to be liable for any of the tax chargeable on the value transferred, stating that they have determined the matters specified in the notice. *Inter alia*, the notice may state the amount of tax chargeable and the person liable to pay it. Such a notice must state the time within which and the manner in which an appeal against any determination may be made (Inheritance Tax Act 1984, s.221).

A person on whom such a notice is served may, within 30 days of service, appeal against any determination specified in it by giving notice in writing and specifying the grounds of appeal or may ask for the determination to be reviewed (see **14 Reviews of determinations**, below). Generally, an appeal is to the First-tier Tribunal, but where it is so agreed between the appellant and HMRC, or where the High Court (in Scotland, the Court of Session), on an application made by the appellant, is satisfied that the matters to be decided on appeal will be substantially confined to questions of law and gives leave for that purpose, the appeal may be to the High Court (in Scotland, the Court of Session) (s.222). Any question as to the value of land must be determined by the Upper Tribunal or the Lands Tribunal for Scotland (s.222). Appeals may be brought out of time, with consent of HM Revenue and Customs or the Tribunal, where there is a reasonable excuse for the delay (s.223).

Many of the rules governing hearings before the tribunal are contained in the Tribunal Procedure (First-tier Tribunal) (Tax Chamber) Rules 2009. The taxpayer may be represented by any person, whether legally qualified or not.

14 Reviews of determinations

If notice of appeal has been given to HMRC, then (Inheritance Tax Act 1984, s.223A)–
(a) the appellant may notify HMRC that he requires it to review the matter in question;
(b) HMRC may notify the appellant of an offer to review the matter in question; or
(c) the appellant may notify the appeal to the tribunal.

The nature and extent of any review will be such as appear appropriate to HMRC in the circumstances. HMRC must, in particular, have regard to steps taken before the beginning of the review by them in deciding the matter in question, and by any person in seeking to resolve disagreement about the matter in question. The review must take account of any representations made by the appellant at a stage which gives HMRC a reasonable opportunity to consider them. The review may conclude that HMRC's view of the matter in question is to be either upheld, varied, or cancelled and HMRC must notify the appellant of the conclusions of the review and their reasoning within 45 days (s.223E), after which the appellant has 30 days to notify the appeal to the tribunal (s.223G).

If HMRC have offered to review the matter in question (see (b) above), and the appellant does not accept the offer, he has 30 days in which to notify the appeal to the tribunal (s.223H).

15 Recovery of tax

HMRC must not take any legal proceedings for the recovery of tax or any interest on tax unless the amount has been agreed in writing with the person from whom the amount is due or that amount has been determined and specified in a notice of determination. HMRC may not take such proceedings in respect of any amount which is the subject of an appeal under s.222 (Inheritance Tax Act 1984, s.242).

16 Penalties

Ss.245 to 253 of the Inheritance Tax Act 1984, prescribe penalties *inter alia* for failure to comply with the duties imposed by the 1984 Act, e.g., for failure to deliver accounts or make a return.

See also, **23 Penalties for failure to pay tax,** below.

C: VALUE ADDED TAX

17 Introduction

The Value Added Tax Act 1994 includes provision relating to the administration, collection, and enforcement of the tax (s.58, Sch. 11), offences and penalties (ss.59–72), and appeals (ss.83, 84). The main provisions of the 1994 Act are dealt with in the Note on **Value Assed Tax.**

Schedule 11 provides that VAT is under the care and management of HMRC. HMRC are empowered *inter alia* to assess tax due to the best of their judgment where a person has failed to keep any documents or make any returns required under the Act and to require security and the production of documents as a condition of allowing or repaying input tax. Schedule 11 also gives persons acting under the authority of HMRC power to enter and search business premises in certain circumstances.

18 Appeals

An appeal lies to the First-tier Tribunal against the decision of HMRC with respect to any of the matters specified in s.83 of the Value Added Tax Act 1994. An appeal will not be entertained unless the appellant has made all the returns which he was required to make under paragraph 2(1) of Schedule 11 and has paid the amounts shown in those returns as payable by him (s.84(2)). In certain circumstances, an appeal will not be entertained unless the appellant has paid or deposited with HMRC the amount of tax which HMRC have determined to be payable (s.84(3)).

Many of the rules governing hearings before the tribunal are contained in the Tribunal Procedure (First-tier Tribunal) (Tax Chamber) Rules 2009. The taxpayer may be represented by any person, whether legally qualified or not.

The penalty for failure to comply with a VAT tribunal direction or summons is a fine of up to £1,000 (Sch. 12, para 10).

D: GENERAL MATTERS

19 Incentives for electronic communication

HMRC have the power to make regulations providing incentives for the use of electronic communications (FA 2000, s.143 and Sch. 38) for–

(a) delivery of information and making of payments; and

(b) any other communications with the tax authorities or in connection with tax matters.

Incentives may take the form of (Sch. 38, para 2)–

(i) discounts;

(ii) the allowing of additional time for complying with obligations under tax legislation; and

(iii) the facility to deliver information or make payments at more convenient intervals.

20 Disclosure of tax avoidance schemes

The Finance Act 2004 introduced a disclosure regime initially limited in scope to tax arrangements concerning employment, certain financial products and VAT (ss.306-319 and Sch. 2). It has since been extended to the whole of income tax, corporation tax, capital gains tax, and inheritance tax and since May 2007 it has also covered National Insurance contributions (Social Security Administration Act 1992, s.132A).

A tax arrangement must be disclosed when–

(a) it will, or might be expected to, enable any person to obtain a tax advantage;

(b) that tax advantage is, or might be expected to be the main benefit or one of the main benefits of the arrangement; and

(c) it is a tax arrangement that falls within any description ("hallmarks") prescribed by regulations.

In most situations where a disclosure is required it must be made by the scheme *promoter* within 5 days of it being made available. However, the scheme *user* may need to make the disclosure where–

(d) the promoter is based outside the UK;

(e) the promoter is a lawyer and legal privilege applies; or

(f) there is no promoter.

The "hallmarks" are–
- wishing to keep the arrangements confidential either from a competitor or from HMRC;
- arrangements–
  - for which a premium fee could reasonably be obtained;
  - that include off market terms;
  - that are standardised tax products;
  - that are loss schemes; and
  - that are certain leasing arrangements.

On disclosure, HMRC will issue the promoter with an 8-digit scheme reference number for the disclosed scheme. By law the promoter must provide this number to each client who uses the scheme, and they in turn must include the number on their tax return.

A person who designs and implements their own scheme must disclose it within 30 days of implementation.

In relation to VAT, disclosure is limited to listed VAT avoidance schemes (i.e., schemes that are designated by Order) and hallmarked schemes (i.e., schemes that include or are associated with a prescribed "hallmark" of avoidance).

The Tax Avoidance Schemes (Information) Regulations 2012 prescribe *inter alia* the information to be provided and the time limits for doing so.

The Finance Act 2014 Part 5 (ss.234-283) contains further provisions applying to certain promoters of tax avoidance schemes. It identifies when a promoter has triggered "threshold" conditions targeting specified behaviours, and provide for a "conduct" notice to be applied to these promoters. Those who fail to comply with a conduct notice may be issued with a "monitoring" notice, which requires pre-approval by a Tribunal. Names of promoters subject to a monitoring notice will be published by HMRC, including details of how the conduct notice was breached, and the promoter will be required to publish its monitored status to clients.

21 The general anti-abuse rule

The Finance Act 2013 introduced a general anti-abuse rule (GAAR) to counteract any tax advantages arising from tax arrangements that are "abusive". The GAAR applies to income tax, corporation tax, capital gains tax, petroleum revenue tax, inheritance tax, and stamp duty land tax. Tax arrangements are "abusive" if entering into them or carrying them out cannot reasonably be regarded as a reasonable course of action in relation to the relevant tax provisions having regard to all the circumstance (s.207).

Tax advantages that are found to arise from abusive tax arrangements are counteracted by the making of just and reasonable adjustments, whether in respect of the tax in question or any other tax to which the GAAR applies (e.g., an abusive arrangement which attempts to reduce or eliminate a person's charge to capital gains tax, may be counteracted by an adjustment to their income tax) (s.209).

If HMRC consider that a tax advantage has arisen from abusive tax arrangements, and that the advantage ought to be counteracted, they must give the taxpayer a written notice to that effect setting out (Sch. 43)–
(a) the arrangements concerned and the tax advantage;
(b) why HMRC considers that a tax advantage has arisen to the taxpayer from tax arrangements that are abusive;
(c) the counteraction that HMRC considers ought to be taken;
(d) the period within which the taxpayer may make representations;
(e) that if no representations are made HMRC will refer the matter to the GAAR Advisory Panel, and that if representations are made HMRC must consider them before deciding whether or not to refer the matter.

The notice may set out steps that the taxpayer may take to avoid the proposed counteraction. The taxpayer has 45 days beginning with the day on which the notice is given to send written representations.

If the matter is referred to the GAAR Advisory Panel, HMRC must at the same time give the taxpayer a notice advising that the matter has been referred. The taxpayer has 21 days beginning with the day on which a notice is given to send written representations to the GAAR Advisory Panel. The panel will then decide whether or not the entering into and carrying out of the tax arrangements was a reasonable course of action in relation to the relevant tax provisions, or that it is not possible, on the information available, to reach a view on the matter. If the Panel decides the tax arrangements are not reasonable, HMRC must give the taxpayer a written notice setting out whether the tax advantage is to be counteracted under the general anti-abuse rule and, if so, set out the adjustments required to give effect to the counteraction, and if relevant, any steps that the taxpayer must take to give effect to it.

As to the anti-avoidance rule in relation to devolved taxes, see **26 Devolved taxes**, below.

22 Time limits for assessments, etc

The Finance Act 2008 has aligned the time limits within which Revenue and Customs may make assessments to correct the amount of tax due from taxpayers, and for taxpayers to make claims, in relation to a range of taxes.

The time limits are–

Income tax and capital gains tax

Time limit for Revenue and Customs to make a determination of the amount of tax due where no tax return has been submitted–three years (Taxes Management Act 1970, s.28C).

Time limit for taxpayer to make a claim that too much tax has been paid because of an error or mistake in a tax return–four years (Sch. 1AB, para 3).

Time limit for Revenue and Customs to make an assessment to income tax or capital gains tax in ordinary cases–four years after the end of the year of assessment in question (s.34).

Time limit for Revenue and Customs to make an assessment to income tax or capital gains tax where a loss has arisen due to the taxpayer's carelessness–six years after the end of the year of assessment in question (s.36(1)).

Time limit for Revenue and Customs to make an assessment to income tax or capital gains tax where a loss has arisen due to deliberate action on the part of the taxpayer–twenty years after the end of the year of assessment in question (s.36(1A)).

Value added tax

Time limit for Revenue and Customs to make an assessment to value added tax in ordinary cases–four years after the end of the year of assessment in question (Value Added Tax Act 1994, s.77(1)).

Time limit for Revenue and Customs to make an assessment to value added tax where a loss has arisen due to deliberate action on the part of the taxpayer–twenty years after the end of the year of assessment in question (s.77(4)).

Inheritance tax

Claims for reductions in tax must generally be made within four years of the event giving rise to the claim, e.g.–

Time limit for claim for reduction of tax where value of an asset has decreased between the transfer and the death which gave rise to the charge (Inheritance Tax Act 1984, s.131)–four years.

Time limit in which to claim that a relevant transfer has been set aside (s.150)–four years.

Claims for underpayment (s.240) or overpayment (s.241) must also generally be made within four years.

23 Penalties for failure to pay tax

The Finance Act 2009 creates a new penalty regime for late payment of many taxes, levies and duties, including income tax; corporation tax; PAYE; National Insurance Contributions; the Construction Industry Scheme; stamp duty land tax; and stamp duty reserve tax; inheritance tax; VAT, insurance premium tax, pension schemes; petroleum revenue tax, and air passenger, gaming, tobacco and alcohol duties (s.107, and Sch. 56).

Taxpayers have a right of appeal against all penalties. The Schedule provides that if a taxpayer enters into a time to pay arrangement with HMRC, any late payment penalties that they would become liable to after the agreement is reached will be removed if the taxpayer keeps to the terms of the agreement. Generally–

- (a) a penalty of 5% of the amount of tax unpaid will be incurred if the tax has not been paid within 30 days of the date it should have been paid;
- (b) if the tax is still unpaid after another five months, a further 5% penalty will be incurred;
- (c) if it is still unpaid after 11 months, a further 5% penalty will be incurred.

For corporation tax, the first penalty is incurred if the tax is not paid by the day after the filing date, with further 5% penalties after three and nine months.

Penalties under the construction industry scheme and in respect of PAYE depend on the number of defaults in a tax year. The first failure does not count as a default. The penalty for the first, second and third defaults is 1% of the total amount of the defaults and it rises after that. In addition there is a 5% penalty if the tax is unpaid six months after the penalty date, with a further 5% penalty after 12 months.

HMRC may reduce penalties in special circumstances and no penalty is payable if a taxpayer satisfies HMRC (or a tribunal) that there is a reasonable excuse for the failure to pay on time.

Interest is also payable from the tax due date until the date payment is received (s.101 and Sch. 53). There are also penalties for failure to make returns relating to tax liabilities (s.106 and Sch. 55).

24 Penalties for incorrect returns

Where a person makes an incorrect return in relation to income tax, corporation tax, PAYE or VAT, a penalty is payable if the inaccuracy amounts to, or leads to (FA 2007, Sch 24)–

- (a) an understatement of their liability to tax;
- (b) a false or inflated statement of a loss; or
- (c) a false or inflated claim to repayment of tax.

Where a document contains more than one inaccuracy, a penalty is payable for each inaccuracy. The size of the penalty will vary depending on whether the inaccuracy is careless (penalty: 30% of the lost revenue), deliberate but not concealed (70%), or deliberate and concealed (100%).

A penalty (30% of the lost revenue) is also payable by a person where an assessment is issued to them by HMRC which understates their liability to income tax, corporation tax, VAT or capital gains tax and they fail to take reasonable steps to notify HMRC, within 30 days of the date of the assessment, that it is an under-assessment. In deciding what steps (if any) were "reasonable" HMRC must consider whether the person knew, or should have known, about the under-assessment, and what steps it would have been reasonable to take to notify HMRC.

The penalties may be reduced where a person discloses an inaccuracy, or a failure to disclose an under-assessment, by–

(d) informing HMRC about it;

(e) giving HMRC reasonable help in quantifying the inaccuracy or under-assessment; and

(f) allowing HMRC access to records for the purpose of ensuring that the inaccuracy or under-assessment is fully corrected.

The size of the penalty reduction will depend on whether the disclosure is prompted or unprompted.

25 Fees for online or telephone payments

Where a taxpayer pays HMRC an amount of tax using a credit card, either online or by telephone, a fee must be added to the payment (Fees for Payment of Taxes, etc. by Credit Card Regulations 2016). The fees for the use of personal credit cards are set out below. Higher fees apply for the use of corporate credit cards.

Type of card	Rate
VISA Personal Credit Card	0.415%
MasterCard Personal Credit Card	0.386%
MasterCard World Premium Credit Card	0.374%
MasterCard Signia Premium Credit Card	0.606%
MasterCard Elite Premium Credit Card	0.606%

Where a payment is made by credit card to Revenue Scotland in respect of a devolved tax (see **26 Devolved taxes**, below), a fee of 1.4% must be added to the payment (Revenue Scotland and Tax Powers Act (Fees for Payment) Regulations 2015, Reg. 3).

26 Devolved taxes

The Revenue Scotland and Tax Powers Act 2014 establishes Revenue Scotland as the tax authority responsible for collecting Scotland's devolved taxes, which are currently the Land and Buildings Transaction Tax and the Scottish Landfill Tax.

The 2014 Act also establishes the First-tier Tax Tribunal for Scotland and the Upper Tax Tribunal for Scotland to hear appeals and exercise other functions in relation to devolved taxes.

In relation to the devolved taxes, Revenue Scotland has the power to counteract tax advantages that arise from a tax avoidance arrangement that is artificial (s.66). An arrangement (or series of arrangements) is a tax avoidance arrangement if, having regard to all the circumstances, it would be reasonable to conclude that obtaining a tax advantage is the main purpose, or one of the main purposes, of the arrangement (s.63). An arrangement will be artificial if either (s.64)–

(a) it is not a reasonable course of action in relation to the tax legislation in question; or

(b) it lacks economic or commercial substance.

A "tax advantage" could include, but is not limited to, a reduction in tax paid, an increase in a tax repayment, a deferral in the payment of tax, or avoidance of payment of tax altogether (s.65).

Revenue Scotland has similar powers to HMRC (in relation to the general anti-abuse rule: see **21 The general anti-abuse rule**, above), in that any tax advantages that are found to arise may be counteracted by the making of just and reasonable adjustments, whether in respect of the tax in question or any other tax, following notice to the taxpayer concerned (ss.66-71).

Where a devolved tax is paid late, Revenue Scotland may charge interest at the Bank of England rate plus 2.5%. Where tax is to be repaid by Revenue Scotland, it will include interest at the higher of 0.5% and the Bank of England rate. Any change of Bank of England rate does not apply within three working days of its announcement (Revenue Scotland and Tax Powers Act (Interest on Unpaid Tax and Interest Rates in General) Regulations 2015, S.S.I. No. 128).

27 Authorities

Statutes–

Commissioners for Revenue and Customs Act 2005

Finance Acts 2000, 2009, 2013, and 2014

Income Tax (Earnings and Pensions) Act 2003 (ITEPA)

Inheritance Tax Act 1984

Revenue Scotland and Tax Powers Act 2014

Taxes Management Act 1970

Value Added Tax Act 1994

Statutory Instruments–

Data-gathering Powers (Relevant Data) Regulations 2012, as amended (S.I. 2012 No. 847, 2013 No. 1811, and 2015 No. 672)

Fees for Payment of Taxes, etc. by Credit Card Regulations 2016 (S.I. 2016 No. 333)

Income Tax (Pay As You Earn) Regulations 2003, as amended (S.I. 2003 No. 2682, 2004 No. 851, 2005 No. 2691, 2006 Nos. 243, 745, and 777, 2007 Nos. 1077, 2069, 2296, and 2969, 2008 Nos. 782 and 2601, 2009 Nos. 56, 588 and 2029, 2010 Nos. 668 and 2496, 2011 Nos. 729, 1054, and 1584, 2012 Nos. 822 and 1895, 2013 Nos. 521, 630 and 2300, and 2014 Nos. 472, 474, 1017, 2396, and 2689)

Income Tax (Payment on Account) Regulations 1996, as amended (S.I. 1996 No. 1654, 1997 No. 2491, and 2008 No. 838)

Revenue Scotland and Tax Powers Act (Fees for Payment) Regulations 2015 (S.S.I. No. 36)

Tax Avoidance Schemes (Information) Regulations 2012, as amended (S.I. 2012 No. 1836, 2013 No. 2592, and 2015 No. 948)

Tribunal Procedure (First-tier Tribunal) (Tax Chamber) Rules 2009 (S.I. 2009 No. 273)

CAPITAL GAINS TAX

A: GENERAL

1 Introduction

The Taxation of Chargeable Gains Act 1992 has consolidated the capital gains tax (commonly referred to as CGT) provisions. The 1992 Act has been amended by subsequent Finance Acts. Bracketed references to a Finance Act are abbreviated to read "FA" followed by the year, e.g., "F(No. 2)A 1992" is a reference to the Finance (No. 2) Act 1992. "Taxes Act" refers to the Income and Corporation Taxes Act 1988.

2 Taxation of chargeable gains

By virtue of the Taxation of Chargeable Gains Act 1992 s.1, capital gains tax is charged in respect of chargeable capital gains, computed in accordance with the Act, which accrue to a person on the disposal of assets (see below).

S.1(2) makes provision for tax upon the chargeable gains accruing to companies to be charged to corporation tax in accordance with s.6 of the Taxes Act. The effect of this provision is to exempt from capital gains tax gains accruing to entities liable to corporation tax on those gains, thus making capital gains tax normally applicable only to individuals (including trustees). However, the provisions of the Act, except where otherwise stated, are relevant in ascertaining and computing those chargeable gains of companies which are chargeable to corporation tax.

3 Persons chargeable

Subject to any exception provided by the Act, any person who is resident or ordinarily resident in the UK during any part of a year of assessment (i.e., a year beginning on 6th April and ending on 5th April in the following calendar year) (Taxation of Chargeable Gains Act 1992, s.288) is liable to capital gains tax in respect of the total amount of chargeable gains accruing to him in that year of assessment after deducting any allowable losses (see 15 **Losses**, below) (s.2). Any person who is not resident and not ordinarily resident in the UK in the year of assessment, but who is carrying on a trade in the UK through a branch or agency is chargeable in respect of chargeable gains accruing to him in that year and on chargeable gains accruing on the disposal of assets situated in the UK, and (a) used in or for the purposes of the trade at or before the time when the gain accrued or (b) used or held for the purposes of the branch or agency at or before that time or acquired for use by or for the purposes of the branch or agency (s.10(1)).

In the case of individuals resident or ordinarily resident but not domiciled in the UK, capital gains tax is not chargeable on gains accruing to them from the disposal of assets situate outside the UK, except that the tax will be charged on any amounts received in the UK in respect of those chargeable gains (s.12(1)); however, losses accruing on the disposal by such persons of assets situate outside the UK are not allowable losses (s.16).

Note.–By virtue of the Constitutional Reform and Governance Act 2010, Members of both Houses of Parliament are treated as resident, ordinarily resident, and domiciled in the UK for tax purposes, even if they have, for example, non-domiciled status (s.41).

4 Gains chargeable to tax

Where a disposal is made of an asset which was held on 31st March 1982 by the person making the disposal then, in computing the gain or loss accruing on the disposal, it is assumed that the asset was sold on that date by the person making the disposal, and immediately reacquired by them, at its market value on that date (Taxation of Chargeable Gains Act 1992, s.35(2)). However, s.35(2) does not apply where–
  (a) a gain would accrue if it did apply and either a smaller gain or a loss would so accrue if it did not;
  (b) a loss would accrue if it did apply and either a smaller loss or a gain would accrue if it did not;
  (c) either on the facts of the case or by virtue of Schedule 2 to the Act, neither a gain nor a loss would accrue if it did not apply; or
  (d) neither a gain nor a loss would accrue by virtue of any of the no gain/no loss provisions.
Where the application of s.35(2) would result in substituting a loss for a gain or *vice versa* but its application is precluded by (a) to (d) above, it is assumed that on the disposal neither a gain nor a loss accrues (s.35(4)).

A person may elect that any disposals made by him, including any made before the election, shall fall outside s.35(3) (and thus not be excluded from s.35(2)), but any such election is irrevocable and must be made by notice in writing to HM Revenue and Customs at any time before 6th April 1990, or at any time during the period beginning with the day of the first relevant disposal (i.e., the first disposal made by the person so electing to which s.35 applies) and ending two years after the end of the accounting period in which the disposal was made, or such later time as the Commissioners of Revenue and Customs may allow (s.35(5) and (6), as amended by FA 1996, Sch. 21 and FA 2008, Sch. 2).

The range of disposals in relation to which the Commissioners will exercise their discretion to extend the time limit for such elections is set out in Statement of Practice SP4/92.

5 Rate of tax

Each individual has an annual exempt amount of capital gains which are not taxable (see **7 Annual exempt amount of gains**, below). The exempt amounts for 2016/17 are—

Individuals	£11,100
Trustees (most)	£5,550

Capital gains tax on disposals between 6th April and 22nd June 2010 is charged at a flat rate of 18% (Taxation of Chargeable Gains Act 1992, s.4, as substituted by FA 2008, s.8).

For disposals between 23rd June 2010 and 5th April 2016, there are two rates. A lower rate of 18% applies where an individuals total taxable gains and income are less than the upper limit of the basic rate income tax band. A higher rate of 28% applies to gains (or any part of gains) above that limit.

For disposals from 6th April 2016, the lower rate is 10% and the higher rate is 20%, but in each case with an 8% surcharge for carried interest and for gains on residential property.

The rate of tax for trustees and personal representatives up to 22nd June 2010 was 18%, and from 23rd June to 5th April 2016 was 28%, and from 6th April 2016 is 20%.

Worked example

X has taxable income, after all deductions and the personal allowance, of £30,500. The upper limit of the basic rate income tax band is £32,000, so X's taxable income is £1,500 less than the upper limit.

In July 2014, X sells an asset realising a chargeable gain of £20,000. He has no allowable losses to set against this gain. The annual exempt amount is £11,100, which leaves £8,900 taxable.

The first £1,500 is taxable at 18%, the remaining £7,685 is taxable at 28%.

If the gain had been realised after 5th April 2016, the taxable gain would have been taxed at 10% on the first £1,500 and 20% on the balance.

An entrepreneur's relief is available for gains made on the disposal of certain business assets. The first £10 million of gains that qualify for relief are taxable at an effective rate of 10%. The £10 million is a lifetime limit (prior to 6th April 2011, the limit was £5 million and prior to 23rd June 2010, the limit was £2 million).

6 Trusts with a vulnerable beneficiary

The Finance Act 2005 introduced an alternative capital gains tax regime for trusts with a "vulnerable" beneficiary. Broadly, the trusts which qualify for this treatment are those with a beneficiary who is either mentally incapacitated, in receipt of attendance allowance or the care component of disability living allowance at the highest or middle rate, or a minor who has lost at least one parent. The effect of the alternative regime is that trust will be treated as if it were a settlement with the gains taxable on the beneficiary (FA 2005, ss.23-45).

7 Annual exempt amount of gains

S.3 of the Taxation of Chargeable Gains Act 1992 provides that an individual will not be chargeable to capital gains tax in respect of so much of his taxable amount for any year of assessment as does not exceed the exempt amount for that year. The exempt amount is subject to indexation each year, unless Parliament otherwise determines, if the retail prices index for the month of September preceding the year of assessment is higher than it was for the previous December (s.3(2) and (3)). Married couples and civil partners can each claim the full exempt amount.

For the purposes of s.3, an individual's taxable amount for a year of assessment is the amount on which he is chargeable under s.2 (see above) for that year, but (a) where the amount of chargeable gains less allowable losses in any year of assessment does not exceed the exempt amount for that year, no deduction will be made for that year in respect of allowable losses carried forward from a previous year or carried back from a subsequent year in which the individual dies, and (b) where that same amount exceeds the exempt amount for the year, the deduction from that amount for that year of allowable losses carried forward from a previous year or carried back from a subsequent year in which the individual dies must not be greater than the excess (s.3(5)).

Schedule 1 makes provision, *inter alia* as respects the application of s.3 to personal representatives and trustees, as follows.

Personal Representatives.–For the year of assessment in which an individual dies and for the next two following years of assessment, s.3(1) to (5C) applies to his personal representatives as it applies to an individual (s.3(7)).

Trustees of Settlements for the Disabled.–S.3(1) to (5C) will apply to the trustees of a settlement as it applies to an individual for any year of assessment during the whole or part of which settled property is held on trusts which secure that, during the lifetime of a mentally disabled person or a person in receipt of attendance allowance (both as defined), (a) not less than half of the property which is applied is applied for the benefit of that person, and (b) that person is entitled to not less than half of the income arising from the property, or no such income may be applied for the benefit of any other person (Sch. 1, para. 1).

Trustees of other Settlements.–S.3(1) to (5C) applies to the trustees of a settlement other than a settlement for the disabled which qualifies for separate treatment for any year of assessment during the whole or part of which any property is settled property as it applies to individuals but with modifications (Sch. 1, para. 2). The general rule in such cases is that for the exempt amount for the year there is substituted one-half of that amount (i.e., £5,500 for 2014/15).

8 Simplified tax returns

Where (Taxation of Chargeable Gains Act 1992, s.3A)–

(a) a taxpayer's chargeable gains for a year do not exceed the annual exempt amount; and

(b) his total consideration for all chargeable disposals in the year does not exceed four times the annual exempt amount,

then on his tax return the taxpayer only needs to state this fact, rather than having to complete the capital gains tax pages in full.

If a taxpayer has losses to take into account, his "chargeable gains" for these purposes means his gains before such losses are taken into account (see **15 Losses**, below).

Personal representatives can take advantage of this provision for the year of death and the next two years. Trustees can also use this provision, in which case the annual exempt amount used for the "four times rule" is that applicable to an individual, rather than the usual trustee annual exempt amount.

9 Time for payment of tax

From 1996/97 (following the introduction of self-assessment) capital gains tax is normally payable on or before 31st January following the year of assessment in which the gain accrues (Taxes Management Act 1970 (TMA 1970) s.59B, inserted by FA 1994, s.193 and amended by FA 1995, s.115 and FA 1996, ss.122 and 125 to 127). Where a person has given notice of his liability to tax under TMA 1970, s.7 within six months of the end of the year of assessment, but no notice requiring him to make a return (under TMA 1970, ss.8 or 8A) is sent to him until after 31st October following that year, the tax is due three months after the return is sent to him (TMA 1970, s.59B(3)). If a self-assessment is amended or a determination is superseded by a self-assessment, or if an assessment other than a self-assessment is made, and the relevant notice is given within 30 days of the due date, the amount payable by virtue of the amendment, etc., is due 30 days after the notice is given (TMA 1970, s.59B (5), (5A), and (6)).

B: GAINS AND LOSSES

10 Disposal of assets

All forms of property are assets for the purposes of the Act, whether situated in the United Kingdom or not, including (Taxation of Chargeable Gains Act 1992, s.21(1))–

(a) options, debts, and incorporeal property generally,

(b) any currency other than sterling, and

(c) any form of property created by the person disposing of it, or otherwise coming to be owned without being acquired.

11 Hire-purchase

A hire-purchase or other transaction under which the use and enjoyment of an asset is obtained by a person for a period at the end of which the property in the asset will or may pass to that person is treated, for the purposes of the Act and in relation to both parties to the transaction, as if it amounted to an entire disposal of the asset to that person at the beginning of the period for which he obtains the use and enjoyment of the asset. This treatment is subject to such adjustments of tax as may be required where the period for which that person has the use and enjoyment of the asset terminates without the property in the asset passing to him (Taxation of Chargeable Gains Act 1992, s.27).

12 Married persons and civil partners

If, in any year of assessment, an individual is living with his spouse or civil partner and one of them disposes of an asset to the other, both are treated as if the asset was acquired from the one making the disposal for a consideration of such amount as would secure that on the disposal neither a gain nor loss would accrue to the one making the disposal (Taxation of Chargeable Gains Act 1992, s.58). However, this does not apply–

(a) if the asset in question, until its disposal, formed part of the trading stock of the party making the disposal or if the asset is acquired as trading stock for the purposes of a trade carried on by the party acquiring the asset, or

(b) if the disposal is by way of *donatio mortis causa* (i.e., by way of a gift not taking effect until after the death of the donor or a third party).

13 Chargeable gains

Chargeable gains are to be computed in accordance with the rules set out in Part II of the Act (Taxation of Chargeable Gains Act 1992, ss.15 to 57 and Sch. 3). Schedule 2 has effect with respect to certain chargeable gains accruing on the disposal of assets owned on 6th April 1965 (s.35(9)).

The Act declares that gains from certain transactions are non-chargeable gains and exempts the transactions of certain types of organisations from capital gains tax; a list of these is set out in the section of this Note entitled C: EXEMPTIONS AND RELIEFS, below.

14 Disposals and acquisitions treated as made at market value

S.17 of the Taxation of Chargeable Gains Act 1992 provides that, subject to certain exceptions (which include the acquisition of an asset where there is no corresponding disposal of it and there is no consideration in money or money's worth, or the consideration is of an amount lower than the market value), a person's acquisition or disposal of an asset shall be deemed to be for a consideration equal to the market value of the asset–

(a) where he acquires (or disposes) of the asset otherwise than by way of a bargain made at arm's length, and in particular where he acquires or disposes of it by way of gift or on a transfer into settlement by a settlor or by way of distribution from a company in respect of shares in the company, or

(b) where he acquires (or disposes) of the asset wholly or partly for a consideration that cannot be valued, or in connection with his own or another's loss of employment or diminution of emoluments, or otherwise in consideration for or recognition of his or another's services or past services in any office or employment or of any service rendered or to be rendered by him or another (s.17(1)).

However, s.17(1) will not apply to the acquisition of an asset if (a) there has been no corresponding disposal of it, and (b) there is no consideration in money or money's worth or the consideration is of an amount or value lower than the market value of the asset (s.17(2)).

Note.–Subject to certain qualifications, s.17(1) will not apply in calculating the consideration for the acquisition of shares under an employee trust (s.239(2)).

15 Losses

The amount of a loss accruing on the disposal of an asset is to be computed in the same way as is the amount of a gain accruing on a disposal (Taxation of Chargeable Gains Act 1992, s.16), but may be subject to indexation (see below).

A loss is not allowable if it accrues to a company in such circumstances that, if a gain accrued, the company would be exempt from corporation tax in respect of it (s.8(2)). A loss accruing to a person during a year of assessment during no part of which he is resident or ordinarily resident in the United Kingdom is not an allowable loss unless he would be chargeable to tax under s.10 (see above) if there had been a gain instead of a loss on that occasion (s.16(3)).

A loss is also not allowable if it accrues directly or indirectly to a person in consequence of, or otherwise in connection with, any arrangements the main purpose (or one of the main purposes) of which is to secure a tax advantage (s.16A).

16 Indexation allowance on certain disposals

The provisions outlined in this paragraph apply only for the purposes of corporation tax.

S.53(1) of the Taxation of Chargeable Gains Act 1992 (as amended by FA 1994 s.93, and FA 1998 s.122), provides for an indexation allowance to be set against the unindexed gain when a disposal to which the section applies takes place so as to give the gain for the purposes of the Act, as follows. If, on the disposal of an asset, there is an unindexed gain (see below) an indexation allowance will be allowed against the unindexed gain–

(a) so as to give the gain for the purposes of the Act, or

(b) if the indexation allowance equals or exceeds the unindexed gain, so as to extinguish it (in which case the disposal shall be one on which, after taking account of the indexation allowance, neither a gain nor a loss accrues).

Unindexed gain means the amount of the gain on the disposal computed in accordance with Part II, and if there is no gain on the disposal as so computed, the unindexed gain or loss will be nil (s.53(2)).

S.54 provides for the calculation of the indexation allowance by reference to the movement in the retail prices index, taking the index for March 1982 as the base. Where the asset disposed of was held by the disponor on 31st March 1982, that date is used (s.55).

17 Consideration chargeable to tax on income

S.37 of the Taxation of Chargeable Gains Act 1992 provides for the exclusion from the computation of capital gains tax of any part consisting of money or money's worth of the consideration for a disposal of assets which is to be included in a computation for income tax of the person making the disposal, but this does not preclude the taking into account in a computation for capital gains tax purposes, as consideration for the disposal of an asset, of the capitalised value of a rentcharge, or the capitalised value of a ground rent, or a right of any other description to income or to payments in the nature of income over a period, or to a series of payments in the nature of income.

18 Expenditure: general

Except as otherwise expressly provided, the sums allowable as a deduction from the consideration in the computation of the gain accruing to a person on the disposal of an asset will be restricted to (Taxation of Chargeable Gains Act 1992, s.38(1))–

(a) the amount or value of the consideration, in money or money's worth, given by him or on his behalf wholly and exclusively for the acquisition of the asset, together with the incidental costs to him of the acquisition or, if the asset was not acquired by him, any expenditure wholly and exclusively incurred by him in providing the asset,

(b) the amount of any expenditure wholly and exclusively incurred on the asset by him or on his behalf for the purpose of enhancing the value of the asset, being expenditure reflected in the state or nature of the asset at the time of disposal, and any expenditure wholly and exclusively incurred by him in establishing, preserving, or defending his title to, or to a right over the asset,

(c) the incidental costs to him of making the disposal.

Incidental costs of the acquisition of the asset or of its disposal are defined in s.38. No payment of interest (except as provided by s.40 (companies; interest charged to capital) is allowable under s.38.

19 Exclusion of expenditure by reference to tax on income

There is to be excluded from the sums allowable under s.38 as a deduction in the computation of a gain any expenditure allowable as a deduction in computing the profits or losses of a trade, profession, or vocation for the purposes of income tax; or in computing any other income for the purposes of the Income Tax Acts, and any expenditure which, although not so allowable as a deduction in computing any losses, would be so allowable but for an insufficiency of income or profits or gains (Taxation of Chargeable Gains Act 1992, s.39(1)).

Without prejudice to s.39(1), there is also to be excluded from the sums allowable under s.38 as a deduction in the computation any expenditure which, if the assets, or all of them to which the computation relates, were, and had at all times been, held or used as part of the fixed capital of a trade the profits of which were chargeable to income tax, would be allowable as a deduction in computing the profits or gains or losses of the trade for the purposes of income tax (s.39(2)).

20 Expenses in administration of estates

In the case of a gain accruing to a person on the disposal of, or of a right or interest in or over, an asset to which he became absolutely entitled as legatee or as against the trustees of settled property (Taxation of Chargeable Gains Act 1992, s.64)–

(a) any expenditure within s.38 (see **18 Expenditure: general**, above) incurred by him in relation to the transfer of the asset to him by the personal representatives or trustees, and

(b) any such expenditure incurred in relation to the transfer of the asset by the personal representatives or trustees,

will be allowable as a deduction in computing the gain accruing to that person on the disposal.

21 Trustees of a settlement

Under s.80 of the Taxation of Chargeable Gains Act 1992, where trustees of a settlement become at any time neither resident nor ordinarily resident in the United Kingdom, they are deemed to have disposed of the defined assets immediately before that time and immediately to have re-acquired them at current market value. The defined assets are all assets constituting settled property of the settlement immediately before the relevant time, except the following–

(a) Where the trustees carry on a trade in the UK through a branch or agency and the assets are situated in the UK and are either used in or for the purposes of the trade or used or held for the purposes of the branch or agency.

(b) Where the assets are of a description specified in any double taxation agreement and where, if the trustees were to dispose of them immediately before the relevant time, they would not be liable to capital gains tax on them in the UK. Special rules apply where s.80 applies as a result of the death of a trustee (s.81), in the case of past trustees (s.82) or trustees ceasing to be liable to UK tax (s.83), and in various other special cases (ss.84 to 86).

Special rules apply in respect of non-UK settlements and settlements which migrate between being UK resident and non-resident (ss.87 to 89).

22 Death

For the purposes of capital gains tax, the assets of which a deceased person was competent to dispose are deemed to have been acquired on his death by the personal representatives or other person on whom they devolve for a consideration equal to their market value at the date of the death but they are not deemed to have been disposed of by him on his death (whether or not they were the subject of a testamentary disposition) (Taxation of Chargeable Gains Act 1992, s.62(1)).

Allowable losses sustained by an individual in the year of assessment in which he dies may, so far as they cannot be deducted from chargeable gains accruing in that year, be deducted from chargeable gains accruing to the deceased in the three years of assessment preceding the year of assessment in which the death occurs. Chargeable gains accruing in a later year are taken before those accruing in an earlier year (s.62(2)).

On a person acquiring an asset as legatee, no chargeable gain accrues to the personal representatives and the legatee is treated as if the personal representatives' acquisition of the asset had been his acquisition of it (s.62(4)).

S.62(5) provides that, notwithstanding s.17(1) (see above), no chargeable gain will accrue to any person on his making a disposal by way of *donatio mortis causa*.

In Scotland, on the death of an heir of entail in possession of any property subject to an entail, whether *sui juris* or not, or of a proper liferenter of any property, the heir of entail next entitled to the entailed property under the entail or, as the case may be, the person (if any) who, on the death of the liferenter, becomes entitled to possession of the property as fiar will be deemed to have acquired all the assets forming part of the property at the date of the deceased's death for a consideration equal to their market value (s.63).

23 Gift recovery of capital gains tax from donee

If in any year of assessment a chargeable gain accrues to any person or persons on the disposal of an asset by way of gift and any amount of capital gains tax assessed on that person or persons for that year of assessment is not paid within 12 months from the date when the tax becomes payable, the donee may, by an assessment made not later than two years from the date when the tax became payable, be assessed and charged (in the name of the donor or, as the case may be, donors) to tax on the amount of the gain accruing to the donor(s). A person paying the tax owing is entitled to recover the amount from the donor(s), and where there is more than one donor payment of the tax may be apportioned between them (Taxation of Chargeable Gains Act 1992, s.282).

24 Partnerships

Where two or more persons carry on a trade or business in partnership, tax in respect of chargeable gains accruing to them on the disposal of partnership assets is assessed and charged on them separately, and any partnership dealings are treated as dealings by the partners and not by the firm (Taxation of Chargeable Gains Act 1992, s.59). Similar provisions apply for limited liability partnerships (s.59A).

25 Insolvents' assets

S.66 of the Taxation of Chargeable Gains Act 1992 makes provision with respect to the assets held by a person as trustee in bankruptcy. Broadly, the transfer of the assets is not to be regarded as a disposal. A subsequent disposal by the trustee is treated as a disposal by the bankrupt, but any tax due upon the disposal is payable by the trustee.

C: EXEMPTIONS AND RELIEFS

26 Annual exemption

For the annual exemption for individuals, personal representatives and trustees, see **7 Annual exempt amount of gains**, above.

27 Winnings from betting

Winnings from betting, including pool betting, lotteries, and games with prizes, are not chargeable gains and no chargeable gains or allowable losses accrue on the disposal of rights to winnings obtained by participating in pool betting, lotteries, or games with prizes (Taxation of Chargeable Gains Act 1992, s.51(1)).

28 Sums obtained as compensation

Sums obtained by way of compensation or damage for any wrong or injury suffered by an individual in his person or in his profession or vocation are not chargeable gains (s.51(2)).

29 Employee trusts

Where a trust set up for the benefit of employees transfers assets to a beneficiary for no payment there is normally a charge to capital gains tax on the trustees, and there may also be a charge to income tax under Schedule E on an employee. Where the employee is liable to income tax on the full market value of the assets transferred, the trustees will, as an extra-statutory concession, not be charged to capital gains tax on any gain arising on the transfer of those assets (IR1, D35).

30 Gilt-edged securities and qualifying corporate bonds

Under s.115 of the Taxation of Chargeable Gains Act 1992, a gain accruing from the disposal by any person of gilt-edged securities or qualifying corporate bonds, or from the disposal of any option or contract to acquire or dispose of such securities or bonds, is not a chargeable gain. For this purpose, a corporate bond is a security falling within s.132(3)(b) (i.e., any loan stock or similar security, whether of the Government of the United Kingdom or of any other government, or of any public or local authority in the United Kingdom or elsewhere, or of any company, and whether secured or unsecured), the debt on which represents and has at all times represented, a normal commercial loan, and which is expressed in sterling with no provision for conversion into, or redemption in, another currency (s.117(1)). In order to be a qualifying corporate bond, it must have been issued either after 13th March 1984, or, if issued on or before that date, acquired by any person after that date other than as a result of a disposal excluded (a) for the purposes of s.117(7) or (b) for the purposes of s.64(4) of the Finance Act 1984. Under (a) a disposal is excluded if by virtue of any enactment it is treated for purposes of the Act as one on which neither a gain nor a loss accrues to the disponor, or the consideration for the disposal is reduced by an amount equal to the held-over gain on the disposal under s.165 (gifts of business assets) or s.260 (gifts on which inheritance tax is chargeable) (s.117(8)).

For relief in respect of irrecoverable loans in the form of qualifying corporate bonds, see below.

Gilt-edged securities for the purposes of the Act means the securities specified in Part I of Schedule 9 to the Act, and such stocks and bonds issued under s.12 of the National Loans Act 1968 denominated in sterling and issued after 15th April 1969, as may be specified by order made by the Treasury. The Capital Gains Tax (Gilt-edged Securities) Orders 1993 to 2014 specify gilt-edged securities disposals of which are exempt from tax on capital gains in accordance with s.115 of the Act.

For companies only, the rules on corporate debt and "loan relationships" have been substantially changed by FA 1996, which means that many transactions previously chargeable to capital gains tax are now chargeable to income tax.

31 Irrecoverable losses on loans

Under s.253 of the Taxation of Chargeable Gains Act 1992, relief is allowed for a loss incurred by a claimant who has made a qualifying loan and satisfies the inspector that any outstanding amount of the principal has become irrecoverable, provided that (a) he has not assigned his right to recover the amount; and (b) he was not, at the time of making the loan or at any subsequent time, the spouse/civil partner of the borrower or a company in the same group as the borrower. A qualifying loan is a loan in which the money lent is used by a borrower resident in the UK wholly for the purposes of a trade carried on by him, other than a trade which consists of, or includes, lending money, and the debt is not a debt on a security as defined in s.132.

A claim for relief under s.253 may also be made for a loss arising in an earlier year of assessment (or accounting period in the case of a company), provided that–
  (a) the amount was also irrecoverable at the earlier time;
  (b) the earlier time is not more than two years before the beginning of the year of assessment in which the claim is made (or a similar period in relation to the accounting period of a claimant company) (s.253(3A), inserted by FA 1996 Sch. 39, enacting extra-statutory concession D36).

32 Savings certificates and non-marketable securities

Savings certificates and non-marketable securities (both as defined) issued under the National Loans Acts 1968 and 1939 are not chargeable assets, and accordingly no chargeable gains accrue on their disposal (Taxation of Chargeable Gains Act 1992, s.121).

33 Unit trusts for exempt unit holders

If throughout a year of assessment all the issue units in a unit trust scheme are assets such that any gain accruing if they were disposed of by the unit holder (for example, a charity) would be wholly exempt from capital gains tax or corporation tax (otherwise than by reason of residence), gains accruing to the unit trust scheme in that year of assessment will not be chargeable gains (Taxation of Chargeable Gains Act 1992, s.100).

34 Investment trusts

Gains accruing to an investment trust are not chargeable gains (Taxation of Chargeable Gains Act 1992, s.100). An investment trust is a company (other than a close company) which is approved by HM Revenue and Customs under s.842 of the Taxes Act. A company will not be approved unless, *inter alia*, its income consists wholly or mainly of eligible investment income, i.e., income deriving from shares or securities, or eligible rental income as defined.

35 Venture capital trusts

Gains or losses arising out of a disposal of shares in a venture capital trust are not chargeable to capital gains tax provided that the disposal is a qualifying disposal. To qualify, the disposal must be made by an individual over the age of 18 who has not spent more than the permitted maximum on the shares in the year of assessment and who acquired them *bona fide* for commercial reasons (i.e., not as part of a scheme or arrangement a main purpose of which is the avoidance of tax) (Taxation of Chargeable Gains Act 1992, s.100, as amended and s.151A, as inserted by FA 1995, s.72).

36 Disposal of shares to an employee share ownership trust or plan

Under ss.227 to 236A of the Taxation of Chargeable Gains Act 1992, relief is available to a claimant disposing of shares to the trustees of a qualifying employee share ownership trust or plan established by a company which immediately after the disposal was a trading company or a holding company of a trading group. In the case of a disposal to an employee share ownership trust, the relief is only available in relation to disposals made before 6th April 2001.

In relation to a disposal to an employee share ownership plan the following conditions must be met–

(a) the plan must be approved under the Finance Act 2000, Schedule 8;

(b) the shares must be eligible shares within the meaning of Finance Act 2000, Schedule 8, Part VIII (i.e., they must form part of the company's ordinary share capital, be fully paid up, not be redeemable, and not be subject to any restrictions other than those permitted);

(c) the trustees must be beneficially entitled to not less than 10% of (a) the ordinary share capital of the company, (b) any profits available for distribution to its shareholders, and (c) any assets available for such a distribution on a winding up; and

(d) there must be no unauthorised arrangements at any time during the proscribed period under which the claimant or a person connected with him may be entitled to acquire any of the shares, or an interest or right deriving from any of the shares, which are the subject of the disposal by the claimant. The proscribed period is that beginning with the disposal and ending on the date of acquisition or, if later, that date on which the trustees first become beneficially entitled as in (c) above.

Disposals to employee share ownership trusts are subject to similar conditions (see s.228).

If the claimant obtains consideration for the disposal and, within six months, all of the consideration is reinvested in replacement assets (other than shares in the company) then, if the above conditions are fulfilled, the claimant, on making a claim within two years of the acquisition, will be treated for purposes of capital gains tax as if (Sch. 7C, para. 5)–

(i) the consideration for the disposal were of such amount as would secure that neither a gain nor a loss accrues to him, and

(ii) the amount or value of the consideration for the acquisition were reduced by the excess of the amount of the actual consideration for the disposal over that which the claimant is treated as receiving under (a) above.

Special provisions apply where only part of the consideration for the disposal is reinvested (see Sch. 7C, para. 5(2)).

Special provisions also apply where the replacement asset is a dwelling-house or land (Sch. 7C, para. 6).

37 Disposal of private residence

S.222 of the Taxation of Chargeable Gains Act 1992 applies to a gain accruing from a disposal by an owner of a dwelling-house which is, or has at any time in his period of ownership been, his only or main residence together with a garden and grounds up to 0.5 of a hectare, or such larger area as the Commissioners determine to be appropriate in a particular case. If the dwelling-house in question has been the individual's only or main residence throughout the period of ownership (which period does not include any period before 31st March 1982), or throughout that period except for all or any part of the last 18 months of that period, no part of a gain to which s.222 applies will be a chargeable gain (s.223(1)). This 18 month relief allows people 18 months to sell a previous only or main residence after moving to a new one without losing private residence relief for the property they are no longer living in. For those who are disabled or in a care home and who have no other property on which they can claim private residence relief, the 18 month period is extended to 36 months (s.225E).

If s.223(1) does not apply, a fraction of the gain will not be a chargeable gain, and that fraction will be the length of the part or parts of the period of ownership during which the dwelling-house was the individual's only or main residence, but inclusive of the last 36 months of the period of ownership in any event, divided by the length of the period of ownership (s.223(2)). The Treasury may by order amend the period of 36 months, in respect of either s.223(1) or s.223(2), to 24 months in relation to disposals on or after such date as may be specified in the order.

If Conditions A and B (see below) are met, the following periods of absence from the dwelling-house are treated as periods during which the dwelling-house was the individual's only or main residence (s.223(3))–

(a) Periods of absence which do not exceed three years (or which in aggregate do not exceed three years).

(b) Periods of absence throughout which (i) all the individual's duties in an employment or office were performed outside the United Kingdom, or (ii) he lived with a spouse or civil partner who worked in such an employment or office.

(c) Periods of absence not exceeding four years (or, in aggregate, not exceeding four years) throughout which the individual was prevented from residing in the dwelling-house or part of it in consequence of the reasonable requirement of his employment that he live elsewhere.

(d) Periods of absence not exceeding four years (or, in aggregate, not exceeding four years) throughout which the individual lived with a spouse or civil partner in respect of whom (c) above applied.

Condition A is that before the period of absence there was a time when the dwelling-house was the individual's only or main residence.

Condition B is that after the period of absence–

(i) in any of cases (a) to (d), there was a time when the dwelling-house was the individual's only or main residence; or

    (ii) in a case falling within (b), (c) or (d), the individual was prevented from resuming residence in the dwelling-house in consequence of the situation of the individual's place of work or a condition imposed by the terms of his employment requiring him to reside elsewhere, being a condition reasonably imposed to secure the effective performance by the employee of his duties; or

    (iii) in a case falling within (b), (c) or (d), the individual lived with a spouse or civil partner to whom (ii) above applied.

A period of absence means a period during which the dwelling-house or part of it was not the individual's only or main residence and throughout which he had no residence or main residence eligible for relief under s.223.

Any period during which the dwelling-house was occupied by a person under an adult placement scheme (or the Scottish equivalent) will be treated as a period during which it was occupied as an only or main residence and will not be treated as occupied for the purposes of a business (s.225D).

Extra-statutory concession D49 permits a delay of up to one year where the individual purchases a house or has a house built for use as his only or main residence, but postpones moving in until alterations or redecorations have been completed or until the previous residence is sold. The period of delay is treated as one of occupation for the purposes of s.223. (The permitted period may be extended to a total of two years in exceptional circumstances.)

Where an individual's only or main residence, or part of it, has at any time in his period of ownership been wholly or partly let by him as residential accommodation, the part of the gain, if any, which would be a chargeable gain by reason of the letting will be a gain only to the extent, if any, to which it exceeds whichever is the lesser of–

    (a) the part of the gain which is not a chargeable gain by virtue of s.223 or that section as applied by s.225 (see below); and

    (b) £40,000 (s.223(5)).

If the gain accrues for the disposal of a dwelling-house part of which is used exclusively for the purposes of a trade or business, or of a profession or vocation (business purposes), the gain will be apportioned and s.223 will apply in relation to the part of the gain apportioned to the part which is not used exclusively for business purposes (s.224(1)). If on account of a reconstruction or conversion of the building or for any other reason there have been at any time during the period of ownership changes in the use of part of the dwelling-house for business purposes, the relief given by s.223 may be adjusted in such manner as the Commissioners concerned consider just and reasonable (s.224(3)).

The relief provided by s.223 does not apply to a gain if the acquisition of, or of the interest in, the dwelling-house was made wholly or partly for the purpose of realising a gain from the disposal of it, nor will it apply in relation to a gain so far as attributable to any expenditure which was incurred after the beginning of the period of ownership wholly or partly for the purpose of realising a gain from the disposal (s.224(3)).

38 Disposal of private residence in other situations

Trustees under a settlement

Ss.222 to 224 apply in relation to a gain accruing to a trustee on the disposal of a dwelling-house held under a settlement where during the period of the trustee's ownership of the property it has been the only or main residence of a person entitled to occupy it under the terms of the settlement (s.225).

Personal representatives

Sections 222 to 224 also apply in relation to a gain accruing to the personal representatives of a deceased person on a disposal of a dwelling-house if the following conditions are satisfied–

    (a) immediately before and immediately after the death of the deceased person, the dwelling-house or part of the dwelling-house was the only or main residence of one or more individuals; and

    (b) (i) that individual or one of those individuals has a relevant entitlement, or two or more of those individuals have relevant entitlements, and (ii) the relevant entitlement accounts for, or the relevant entitlements together account for, 75% or more of the net proceeds of disposal;

and for this purpose "relevant entitlement" means an entitlement as legatee of the deceased person to, or to an interest in possession in, the whole or any part of the net proceeds of disposal (s.225A).

Divorce etc.,

Where an individual (s.225B)–

    (a) ceases to live with his spouse or civil partner in a dwelling-house or part of a dwelling-house which is their only or main residence, and

    (b) subsequently disposes of, or of an interest in, the dwelling-house or part to the spouse or civil partner,

then, if conditions A to C are met, ss.222 to 224 will apply as if the dwelling-house or part continued to be the individual's only or main residence until the disposal.

Condition A is that the disposal mentioned in (b) is pursuant to (i) an agreement between the individual and his spouse or civil partner made in contemplation of or otherwise in connection with the dissolution or annulment of the marriage or civil partnership, their judicial separation or the making of a separation order in respect of them, or their separation in other circumstances such that the separation is likely to be permanent, or (ii) an order of a court in specified family proceedings.

Condition B is that in the period between the individual ceasing to reside in the dwelling-house or part of the dwelling-house and the disposal to the spouse or civil partner, the dwelling-house or part continues to be the only or main residence of the spouse or civil partner.

Condition C is that the individual has not given notice under section 222(5) that another dwelling-house or part of a dwelling-house is to be treated as their main residence for any part of that period.

Employee to employer disposals

Where (s.225C)–

(a) an individual disposes of, or of an interest in, a dwelling-house or a part of a dwelling-house which is their only or main residence ("the initial disposal");

(b) they do so as a consequence of a change to the situation of their place of work or that of a co-owner of the dwelling-house or the interest, being a change that is required by the employer of the individual or the co-owner; and

(c) the initial disposal is under a home purchase agreement,

then, if–

(d) under the terms of the agreement the individual receives, within three years of the initial disposal, a share of any profit made by the purchaser upon the purchaser's disposal of, or of an interest in, the dwelling-house or part of the dwelling-house, and

(b) the receipt of that sum would be treated (apart from this provision) as a disposal falling within s.22 (disposal where capital sums derived from assets),

that receipt will be treated as a gain attributable to the initial disposal but accruing to the individual at the time the sum is received.

Dependent relatives

Ss.222 to 224 also apply in respect of the gain accruing to an individual on his disposal of a dwelling-house which is provided rent-free and without any other consideration as the sole residence of a dependent relative (as defined) of the owner or his spouse/civil partner where the relative was the occupier before 6th April 1988. This concession is available only in respect of one dependent relative for each individual and spouses/civil partners are counted as one person for the purposes of the concession (s.226). On the meaning of "rent-free and without any other consideration", see extra-statutory concession IR 1, D20.).

39 Entrepreneur Relief

An entrepreneur's relief is available for gains made on the disposal of certain business assets. The first £10 million of gains that qualify for relief are taxable at an effective rate of 10% (rather than 18% or 28%). The £10 million is a lifetime limit (Taxation of Chargeable Gains Act 1992, ss.169H-169S, as uprated by the Budget Statement of 23rd March 2011). Gains in excess of the lifetime limit are taxed at the normal rate.

The relief is intended to apply to the disposal of a business rather than the disposal of an asset. Accordingly, the disposal must be (s.1611)–

(a) of the whole or part of a business;

(b) of (or of interests in) one or more assets in use, at the time at which a business ceases to be carried on, for the purposes of the business; or

(c) of one or more assets consisting of (or of interests in) shares in or securities of a company.

In addition, the disposal must be "material". A disposal within (a) is a material disposal if the business is owned by the individual throughout the period of 1 year ending with the date of the disposal. A disposal within (b) is a material disposal if–

(i) the business is owned by the individual throughout the period of 1 year ending with the date on which the business ceases to be carried on, and

(ii) that date is within the period of 3 years ending with the date of the disposal.

A disposal within (c) is a material disposal if condition A or B is met. Condition A is that, throughout the period of 1 year ending with the date of the disposal the company is the individual's personal company and is either a trading company or the holding company of a trading group, and the individual is an officer or employee of the company or (if the company is a member of a trading group) of one or more companies which are members of the trading group. Condition B is that the same conditions are met throughout the period of 1 year ending with the date on which the company ceases to be a trading company without continuing to be or becoming a member of a trading group, or ceases to be a member of a trading group without continuing to be or becoming a trading company, and that date is within the period of 3 years ending with the date of the disposal.

40 Gifts of business assets

Where assets used for the purposes of a trade, profession or vocation are transferred, otherwise than under a bargain at arm's length, then relief may be obtained where both the transferee and the transferor make a claim (or, where the trustees of a settlement is the transferee, only the transferor need make the claim) (Taxation of Chargeable Gains Act 1992, s.165). Shares of a trading company, or of the holding company of a trading company, qualify as an asset where they are not listed, or dealt with on the Unlisted Securities Market, or where the company is a personal company.

41 Movable property which is a wasting asset

Subject to a number of exceptions, no chargeable gain will accrue on the disposal of, or of an interest in, an asset which is tangible movable property and which is a wasting asset (Taxation of Chargeable Gains Act 1992, s.45). A wasting asset is defined in s.44. Generally, a wasting asset means an asset with a predictable useful life not exceeding 50 years. Plant and machinery are to be regarded as having a predictable life of less than 50 years. A life interest in settled property is not a wasting asset until the predictable expectation of life of the life tenant is 50 years or less, and the predictable life of life interests in settled property and of annuities is to be ascertained from actuarial tables approved by the Commissioners. Freehold land, whatever its nature, is not a wasting asset (s.44).

42 Chattels

A gain accruing on a disposal of an asset which is tangible movable property is not a chargeable gain if the amount or value of the consideration for the disposal does not exceed £6,000. Where the amount or value of the consideration exceeds £6,000, the chargeable gain accruing on the disposal will be restricted to five-thirds of the amount of the excess.

In computing the amount of a loss accruing on the disposal of tangible movable property the consideration for the disposal will, if less than £6,000, be deemed to be £6,000 and the amount of the allowable losses will be restricted accordingly (Taxation of Chargeable Gains Act 1992, s.262).

43 Passenger vehicles

Private passenger motor vehicles are not chargeable assets (Taxation of Chargeable Gains Act 1992, s.263).

44 Decorations for valour or gallant conduct

A gain accruing on the disposal by any person of a decoration awarded for valour or gallant conduct which is acquired otherwise than for consideration in money or money's worth is not a chargeable gain (Taxation of Chargeable Gains Act 1992, s.268).

45 Foreign currency for personal expenditure

A gain accruing on the disposal by an individual of currency of any description acquired by him for his or his family's personal expenditure outside the UK (including expenditure on the provision or maintenance of any residence outside the UK) is not a chargeable gain (Taxation of Chargeable Gains Act 1992, s.269).

46 Debts

Subject to certain qualifications and exceptions, no chargeable gain or allowable loss accrues to a creditor or his personal representative or legatee on the disposal of a debt (Taxation of Chargeable Gains Act 1992, s.251).

47 Life assurance and deferred annuities

No chargeable gain accrues on the disposal of, or of an interest in, the rights under any policy of assurance or contract for a deferred annuity on the life of any person except where the person making the disposal is not the original beneficial owner and acquired the rights or interest for a consideration in money or money's worth (Taxation of Chargeable Gains Act 1992, s.210).

48 Superannuation funds, annuities, and annual payments

No chargeable gain accrues to any person on the disposal of a right to, or to any part of (Taxation of Chargeable Gains Act 1992, s.237)–
  (a) any allowance, annuity, or capital sum payable out of a superannuation fund or under any superannuation scheme, established solely or mainly for persons employed in a profession, trade, undertaking, or employment, and their dependants; or
  (b) an annual covenanted payment which is not secured on any property.

49 Business Expansion Scheme and Enterprise Investment Scheme

Where an individual to whom relief has been given in respect of eligible shares under a business expansion scheme disposes of those shares and the relief has not been withdrawn, any gain or loss which accrues to him on that disposal is not a chargeable gain (Taxation of Chargeable Gains Act 1992, s.150).

Similar provisions apply in relation to eligible shares under the Enterprise Investment Scheme, the Seed Enterprise Investment Scheme, and the Social Investment Tax Relief Scheme (Taxation of Chargeable Gains Act 1992, ss.150A, 150E, 255B).

50 Charities

Subject to certain qualifications, a gain will not be a chargeable gain if it accrues to a charity and is applicable and is applied for charitable purposes (Taxation of Chargeable Gains Act 1992, s.256).

51 Gifts to charities, etc.

Where a disposal is made otherwise than under a bargain at arm's length to a charity or to one of the bodies mentioned in Schedule 3 to the Inheritance Tax Act 1984 (see the Note on **Inheritance Tax** at para **5 Exempt transfers**), s.17(1) will not apply, but if the disposal is by way of gift or for a consideration not exceeding the sums allowable as a deduction under s.38 for acquisition and disposal costs, then the disposal and acquisition will be treated as taking place on a no gain no loss basis (Taxation of Chargeable Gains Act 1992, s.257).

52 Works of art, etc.

A gain will not be a chargeable gain if it accrues on the disposal of an asset which is property which has been or could be designated under s.31 of the Inheritance Tax Act 1984 and (s.258(2))–
   (a) the disposal is by way of sale by private treaty to a body mentioned in Schedule 3 to the 1984 Act (museums, etc), or is to such a body otherwise than by sale; or
   (b) the disposal is to the Board in pursuance of s.230 of the 1984 Act (acceptance of property in satisfaction of tax).
In the case of the disposal of any asset which has been or could be designated under s.31 of the 1984 Act, being (s.258(3) and (4))–
   (a) a disposal by way of gift, including a gift in settlement, or
   (b) a disposal of settled property by the trustee on an occasion when, under s.71(1), the trustee is deemed to dispose of and immediately reacquire settled property (other than any disposal on which by virtue of s.73 no chargeable gain or allowable loss accrues to the trustee),
then, if the requisite undertaking described in s.31 of the 1984 Act (maintenance, preservation and access) is given by such person as the Board think appropriate in the circumstances of the case, the person making the disposal and the person acquiring the asset on the disposal will be treated for all the purposes of this Act as if the asset was acquired from the one making the disposal for a consideration of such an amount as would secure that on the disposal neither a gain nor a loss would accrue to the one making the disposal.

53 Gifts to the nation

FA 2012 makes provision for a person's capital gains tax liability to be reduced where they make a gift of a "pre-eminent object" to the nation in accordance with a scheme set up by the Secretary of State (s.49 and Sch. 19). A donor must be acting in their own personal capacity: the tax reduction scheme does not extend to those who are acting as trustees or personal representatives.

The amount of the reduction is equivalent to 30% of the value of the gift.

See the Note on **Income Tax: General provisions** at para **31 Gifts to the nation**.

D: SUPPLEMENTAL

54 Valuation

Generally, "market value" in relation to any assets means the price which those assets might reasonably be expected to fetch on a sale in the open market (Taxation of Chargeable Gains Act 1992, s.272(1)). No reduction is made on account of the estimate being made on the assumption that the whole of the assets is to be placed on the market at one and the same time (s.272(2)).

Special provisions apply for calculating the market value of shares or securities listed in the Stock Exchange Daily Official List (s.272(3)).

Market value in relation to any rights of unit holders in any unit trust scheme the buying and selling prices of which are published regularly by the managers of the scheme means an amount equal to the buying price (i.e., the lower price) so published on the relevant date; or if none were published on that date, on the latest date before (s.272(5)).

55 Authorities

Income and Corporation Taxes Act 1988

Taxation of Chargeable Gains Act 1992

Taxes Management Act 1970

Capital Gains Tax (Gilt-edged Securities) Orders 1993 to 2013 (S.I. 1993 No. 950, 1994 No. 2656, 1996 No. 1031, 2001 No. 1122, 2002 No. 2849, 2004 No. 438, 2005 No. 276, 2006 Nos. 184 and 3170, 2008 No. 1588, 2010 No. 416, 2011 No. 1295, 2012 No. 1843, 2013 Nos. 13 and 2983, and 2014 No. 1120)

COUNCIL TAX: ENGLAND AND WALES

I The legislation and Contents

The Local Government Finance Act 1992 introduced the council tax which replaced the former community charge.
This Note is arranged as follows–
PART I: Council Tax
      A: General provisions
      B: Liability and discounts
      C: Administrative provisions
      D: Valuation
PART II Contracting out
Council tax reduction schemes are dealt with in the Note on **Council Tax Reduction Schemes**.

PART I: COUNCIL TAX

A: GENERAL PROVISIONS

2 Introduction

Part I of the Local Government Finance Act 1992 makes provision, in England and Wales, for the levying and collection of council tax, and for the abolition of community charges.

S.1(1) provides that, as regards each financial year beginning in 1993 and subsequent financial years, each billing authority must levy and collect council tax, which will be payable in respect of dwellings situated in their area. Billing authority means a district or London borough council, a county council in England which is a unitary authority, the Common Council, or the Council of the Isles of Scilly; or in Wales, a county or county borough council (s.1(2)).

Liability to pay council tax is determined on a daily basis and it is assumed that any state of affairs subsisting at the end of the day has subsisted throughout the day (s.2).

3 Meaning of dwelling

A dwelling is any property which–
(a) by virtue of the definition of hereditament in s.115(1) of the General Rate Act 1967, would have been a hereditament for the purposes of that Act, had it remained in force; and
(b) is not for the time being shown or required to be shown in a local or a central non-domestic rating list in force at that time; and
(c) is not for the time being exempt from local non-domestic rating for the purposes of Part III of the 1988 Act (see below) (Local Government Finance Act 1992, s.3(2)).

A hereditament which is a composite hereditament (i.e., part only of it consists of domestic property) for the purposes of Part III of the 1988 Act is also a dwelling for the purposes of Part I of the 1992 Act.

None of the following property is in itself a dwelling, except in so far as it forms part of a larger property which is itself a dwelling (s.3(4), (4A))–
(i) a yard, garden, outhouse, or other appurtenance belonging to or enjoyed with property used wholly for the purposes of living accommodation;
(ii) a private garage having a floor area of not more than 25 square metres or which is used wholly or mainly for the housing of a motor vehicle; or
(iii) private storage premises used wholly or mainly for the storage of articles of domestic use;
(iv) property used for the purpose of microgeneration installed on or within domestic properties.

The Secretary of State may by order provide that in prescribed cases anything which would (apart from the order) be one dwelling will be treated as two or more dwellings and anything which would be treated as two or more dwellings will be treated as one dwelling (s.3(5)). The Council Tax (Chargeable Dwellings) Order 1992 contains the following provisions–
(1) where a single property (i.e., a property which would, apart from the Order, be one dwelling within the meaning of s.3 of the Act) contains more than one self-contained unit (i.e., a building or part of a building constructed or adapted for use as separate living accommodation), it will be treated as comprising as many dwellings as there are such units included in it, and each such unit will be treated as a dwelling;
(2) where a multiple property (i.e., a property which would (apart from the Order) be two or more dwellings within the meaning of s.3 of the Act) consists of a single self-contained unit, or such a unit together with or containing premises constructed or adapted for non-domestic purposes and is occupied as more than one unit of separate living accommodation, the listing officer may treat the property as one dwelling;
(3) a care home is to be treated as comprising the number of dwellings equal to the number of self-contained units, plus one, occupied by the person registered in respect of it under the Care Standards Act 2000 or the Health

and Social Care Act 2008;

(4) in Wales, a refuge (definition contained in S.I. 2014 No. 2653) is to be treated as one dwelling, even if the property comprises more than one self-contained unit.

4 Dwellings chargeable to council tax

Council tax will be payable in respect of any dwelling which is not an exempt dwelling (Local Government Finance Act 1992, s.4(1)). Exempt dwelling means any dwelling of a class prescribed by order made by the Secretary of State and a class of dwellings may be prescribed by reference to one or more of the following factors–

(a) the physical characteristics of the dwellings;

(b) the fact that the dwellings are unoccupied or are occupied for prescribed purposes or are occupied or owned by persons of prescribed descriptions (s.4(4)).

The Council Tax (Exempt Dwellings) Order 1992 prescribes the following classes of dwellings for which no council tax is payable–

Class A

Class revoked by the Council Tax (Exempt Dwellings) (Amendment)(England) Order 2012.

Class B

A dwelling owned by a body established for charitable purposes only, which is unoccupied and has been so for a period of less than six months and was last occupied in furtherance of the objects of the charity.

Class C

Class revoked by the Council Tax (Exempt Dwellings) (Amendment)(England) Order 2012.

Class D

An unoccupied dwelling which either–

(a) would be the sole or main residence of a person who is an owner or tenant of the dwelling and is detained elsewhere in the circumstances specified in paragraph 1 of Schedule 1 to the Act (as added to by the Council Tax (Discount Disregards) Order 1992, Art. 1) but for his detention, or

(b) was previously his sole or main residence, if he had been a relevant absentee for the whole period since it last ceased to be such.

For the purposes of (a) and (b), a dwelling will be regarded as unoccupied if its only occupant or occupants are persons detained elsewhere in the circumstances there mentioned.

Note.–"Relevant absentee" in relation to a dwelling means a person who is detained elsewhere in the circumstances mentioned in Class D(a) above or who has his sole or main residence elsewhere in any of the circumstances mentioned in Class E(a), Class I(a), or Class J(a) (see below).

Class E

An unoccupied dwelling which was previously the sole or main residence of a person who is an owner or tenant of a dwelling and who–

(a) has his sole or main residence elsewhere in the circumstances specified in paragraphs 6, 7 of Schedule 1 to the Act (sole or main residence in a hospital, residential care home, nursing home, or hostel where he is receiving care and/or treatment), or in care home accommodation provided by a Scottish care home service under the Regulation of Care (Scotland) Act 2001; and

(b) has been a relevant absentee (see *Note* above) for the whole of the period since the dwelling last ceased to be his sole or main residence.

Class F

An unoccupied dwelling which has been unoccupied since a person's death and in relation to which one of the following conditions is satisfied–

(a) at the date of his death, the deceased had a freehold interest in the building or a leasehold interest granted for a term of six months or more *and* either no person is a qualifying person (see below) in relation to the building *or* a person is only a qualifying person in relation to the building in his capacity as executor or administrator; or

(b) the deceased was a tenant of the dwelling when he died and an executor is liable for rent or, as the case may be, licence fee.

For the purposes of Class F, a "qualifying person" is a person who would, but for the provisions of the Order, be liable for council tax in respect of the dwelling as owner.

Class G

An unoccupied dwelling–

(a) the occupation of which is restricted by a condition which prevents occupancy, and is imposed by any planning permission granted or deemed to be granted under Part 3 of the Town and Country Planning Act 1990; or

(b) the occupation of which is otherwise prohibited by law; or

(c) which is kept unoccupied by reason of action taken under powers conferred by or under any Act of Parliament, with a view to prohibiting its occupation or to acquiring it.

Class H

An unoccupied dwelling which is held for the purpose of being available for occupation by a minister of any religious denomination as a residence from which to perform the duties of his office.

Class I

An unoccupied dwelling which was previously the sole or main residence of a person who is an owner or tenant of the dwelling and who–

(a) has his sole or main residence in another place (not being a hospital, care home, independent hospital or hostel within the meaning of paragraphs 6 or 7 of Schedule 1 to the Act, or care home accommodation provided by a Scottish care home service under the Regulation of Care (Scotland) Act 2001; and

(b) has been a relevant absentee (see *Note* above) for the whole of the period since the dwelling last ceased to be his residence.

Class J

An unoccupied dwelling which was previously the sole or main residence of a person who is an owner or tenant of the dwelling and who–

(a) has his sole or main residence in another place for the purpose of providing, or better providing, personal care for a person who requires such care by reason of old age, disablement, illness, past or present alcohol or drug dependence, or past or present mental disorder; and

(b) has been a relevant absentee (see *Note* above) for the whole of the period since the dwelling last ceased to be his residence.

Class K

An unoccupied dwelling–

(a) which was last occupied as the sole or main residence of a qualifying person ("the last occupier"); and

(b) in relation to which every qualifying person is a student and either–

(i) has been a student throughout the period since the last occupier ceased to occupy the dwelling as his sole or main residence; or

(ii) has become a student within six weeks of that day.

Class L

An unoccupied dwelling where a mortgagee is in possession under the mortgage.

Class M

A dwelling comprising a hall of residence provided predominantly for the accommodation of students which is either–

(a) owned or managed by an institution within the meaning of paragraph 5 of Schedule 1 to the Act (as added to by S.I. 1992/548, Art. 5) or is owned or managed by a body established for charitable purposes only; or

(b) the subject of an agreement allowing such an institution to nominate the majority of the persons who are to occupy the accommodation so provided.

Class N

A dwelling which is either–

(a) occupied by one or more residents all of whom are relevant persons; or

(b) occupied only by one or more relevant persons as term time accommodation.

"Relevant person" means a student, a student's spouse/civil partner or dependant being in either case a person who is not a British citizen and who is prevented, by the terms of his leave to enter or remain in the UK, from taking paid employment or from claiming benefits or a person to whom Class C (school and college leavers) of the Council Tax (Additional Provision for Discount Disregards) Regulations 1992 Reg. 3(1) applies (see **17 Discount disregards**, below).

A dwelling is to be regarded as occupied by a relevant person as term time accommodation during any vacation in which he–

(i) holds a freehold or leasehold interest in or licence to occupy the whole or any part of the dwelling; and

(ii) has previously used or intends to use the dwelling as term time accommodation.

Class O

A dwelling of which the Secretary of State for Defence is the owner, held for the purposes of armed forces accommodation, other than accommodation for visiting forces within the meaning of Part I of the Visiting Forces Act 1952.

Class P

A dwelling in respect of which at least one person, who would be liable to pay council tax but for the Order, satisfies the following condition. He has a relevant association, within the meaning of Part I of the Visiting Forces Act 1952, with a body, contingent or detachment of the forces of a country, to which any provision in that Part applies on that day.

Class Q

An unoccupied dwelling in relation to which a person is a qualifying person in his capacity as a trustee in bankruptcy under the Bankruptcy Act 1914 or the Insolvency Act 1986.

Class R

A dwelling consisting of a pitch or mooring which is not occupied by a caravan or, as the case may be, a boat.

Class S

A dwelling occupied only by a person or persons aged under 18.

Class T

An unoccupied dwelling which–

(a) forms part of a single property (as defined by Articles 2 and 3 of the Council Tax (Chargeable Dwellings) Order 1992 (S.I. No. 549), see **3 Meaning of dwelling**, above) which includes another dwelling; and

(b) may not be let separately from that other dwelling without a breach of planning control within the meaning of s.171A of the Town and Country Planning Act 1990.

Class U

A dwelling occupied only by a person or persons who is or are severely mentally impaired within the meaning given in paragraph 2 of Schedule 1 to the Local Government Finance Act 1992 and who would otherwise be liable to pay council tax, or by one or more severely mentally impaired persons and one or more relevant persons as defined in Class N, above (i.e., students).

Class V

A dwelling occupied as his main residence by a diplomat or other person entitled to diplomatic privileges, where such a person is not a British citizen or British subject, or a permanent resident in the UK.

Class W

A dwelling which forms part of a single property including at least one other dwelling and which is the sole or main residence of a "dependent" relative of a person who is resident in that other dwelling, or as the case may be, one of those other dwellings (this exemption therefore includes "granny flats").

A person is dependent if they are aged 65 or over or are severely mentally impaired, or substantially and permanently disabled.

5 Different amounts for dwellings in different valuation bands

The amounts of tax payable in respect of dwellings situated in the same billing authority's area (or the same part of such an area) and listed in different valuation bands will be in the proportion–6: 7: 8: 9: 11: 13: 15: 18: [21: Wales only, from 2005] where 6 is for dwellings listed in valuation band A, 7 is for dwellings listed in valuation band B, and so on (Local Government Finance Act 1992, s.5(1)). The Secretary of State may by order substitute another proportion for that shown above (s.5(4)) or may increase the number of bands (s.5(4A)).

S.5(2) and (3) prescribe the following bands of values for England and Wales–

A Not exceeding £40,000
B Exceeding £40,000 but not exceeding £52,000
C Exceeding £52,000 but not exceeding £68,000
D Exceeding £68,000 but not exceeding £88,000
E Exceeding £88,000 but not exceeding £120,000
F Exceeding £120,000 but not exceeding £160,000
G Exceeding £160,000 but not exceeding £320,000
H Exceeding £320,000

The bands for Wales from 1st April 2005 are as follows–
A Not exceeding £44,000
B Exceeding £44,000 but not exceeding £65,000
C Exceeding £65,000 but not exceeding £91,000
D Exceeding £91,000 but not exceeding £123,000
E Exceeding £123,000 but not exceeding £162,000
F Exceeding £162,000 but not exceeding £223,000
G Exceeding £223,000 but not exceeding £324,000
H Exceeding £324,000, but not exceeding £424,000
I Exceeding £424,000.

The Secretary of State may by order substitute other valuation bands for those which are for the time being effective for the purposes of s.5(2) and (3) (s.5(4)).

For transitional reductions in liability to smooth the introduction of new valuation bands, see **19 Transitional reductions**, below.

6 Setting of council tax

For each financial year and each category of dwellings in their area, a billing authority must set an amount of council tax (Local Government Finance Act 1992, s.30(1)). An amount so set will be calculated by taking the aggregate of (a) the amount which, in relation to the year and the category of dwellings, has been calculated by the authority in accordance with ss.31A, 31B and 34 to 36 (in Wales, ss.32 to 36), and (b) any amounts which, in relation to the year and the category of dwellings, have been calculated in accordance with ss.42A, 42B and 45 to 47 (in Wales, ss.43 to 47) and have been stated in accordance with s.40 in precepts issued to the authority by major precepting authorities (s.30(2)). Where the aggregate amount given by s.30(2) is a negative amount, the amount set will be nil (s.30(3)).

Any amount must be set before 11th March in the financial year preceding that for which it is set, but is not invalid merely because it is set on or after that date (s.30(6)).

7 Substituted amounts

Where a billing authority have set amounts for a financial year under s.30 (see above) and at any later time make substitute calculations under ss.36A, 37, 52I or 52T, or are issued with a precept for the year by a major precepting authority, they must as soon as reasonably practicable after that time, set amounts in substitution so as to give effect to those calculations or to that precept (Local Government Finance Act 1992, ss.31(1)). If the old amount exceeds the new amount and has been paid, the difference must be repaid if the person by whom it was paid so requires and in any other case, it must either be repaid or credited against any subsequent liability of the person to pay council tax (s.31(4)).

8 Limitation of council tax–capping (Wales)

In any financial year the Welsh Ministers may either "designate" or "nominate" a Welsh authority if, in their opinion, the amount calculated by them as their budget requirement for the year is excessive (Local Government Finance Act 1992, s.52D).

A decision to designate or nominate must be made in accordance with principles determined by the Welsh Ministers (s.52B). If the Welsh Ministers decide to designate an authority, they must notify them *inter alia* of the amount which they propose should be the maximum for their budget requirement for the year (s.52E). A "target" amount must also be set (s.52E(e)). This will generally be the same as the maximum amount, however, if the Welsh Ministers believe that the authority will need more than one year to bring its budget requirements down to a level which is not excessive, then a lower target amount may be set as a target for the authority to reach within a specified time period. If this target is exceeded, the authority may be designated again the following year (s.52P).

The authority may either accept the maximum amount, or challenge it (s.52E(5)). If an authority challenges the proposed maximum, the Welsh Ministers will, after considering any relevant information, make an order stating the amount which the amount calculated by the authority as their budget requirement for the year is not to exceed (which may be the same as, or greater or smaller than, that stated in the notice under s.52E (s.52F). The authority must then make substitute calculations in relation to the year (s.52I).

Instead of designating an authority immediately, the Welsh Ministers may nominate it instead (s.52L). If an authority is nominated, the Welsh Ministers may either designate that authority in the following year (s.52M), or set a notional budget requirement for it for the current year (which will be used in determining whether or not the authority's budget for the following year is excessive (s.52N).

9 Council tax increase referendums (England)

The Secretary of State has the power to determine a principle based on a comparison of an authority's level of council tax with the level in the previous year (and additional principles if he so wishes) (s.52ZC, as added by the Localism Act 2011). For 2016-17, the principle provides that any increase in council tax in excess of 4% (comprising 2% for expenditure on adult social care and 2% for other expenditure) is excessive. Any authority in England planning an excessive council tax increase is required to prepare a "shadow budget" based on the maximum non-excessive council tax increase allowed by the principles. If it wants to breach the principle, the authority must hold a referendum (no later than the first Thursday in May) of all registered local electors to seek approval for the higher increase. The authority proposing the excessive increase must prepare supporting factual material setting out the proposed council tax increase and budget, the comparative non-excessive council tax rise and shadow budget, and the estimated cost of holding the referendum. At the same time that bills are sent to council taxpayers, the billing authority will send this information, together with polling cards, to every registered local elector. Local councillors may make the case for an excessive increase, but the authority itself is prohibited from campaigning on the issue. If the proposed rise in council tax is rejected, the relevant authority must immediately adopt the shadow budget. The billing authority may then issue new bills immediately, offer refunds at the end of the year or allow credits against liability in the following year. However, billing authorities must refund (and re-bill) any local resident who requests this.

The Local Authorities (Conduct of Referendums) (Council Tax Increases) (England) Regulations 2012 set out the question to be asked at a referendum as follows–

"Part of the council tax in your area goes to *[Council X]*.
For the financial year beginning on 1st April *[2016]* *[Council X]* has set an increase of *[Y percent]* in the amount it charges.
If most voters choose 'yes', the increase will be *[Y percent]*.
If most voters choose 'no', the increase will be *[Z percent]*.
Do you want *[Council X]* to increase the amount it charges by *[Y percent]*?"

B: LIABILITY AND DISCOUNTS

10 Liability to tax

The person who is liable to pay council tax in respect of any chargeable dwelling and any day is the person who falls within the first paragraph of s.6(2) (see below) to apply, taking paragraph (a) first, paragraph (b) next, and so on (Local Government Finance Act 1992, s.6(1)). Section 6(2) provides that a person falls within this subsection in relation to any chargeable dwelling and any day if, on that day–

(a) he is a resident of the dwelling and has a freehold interest in the whole or any part of it;

(b) he is such a resident and has a leasehold interest in the whole or any part of the dwelling which is not inferior to another such interest held by another such resident;

(c) he is both such a resident and a statutory, secure or introductory tenant of the whole or any part of the dwelling;

(d) he is such a resident and has a contractual licence to occupy the whole or any part of the dwelling;

(e) he is such a resident; or

(f) he is the owner of the dwelling.

Where, in relation to any chargeable dwelling and any day, two or more persons come within the first of any of paragraphs (a) to (f) above to apply, they will each be jointly and severally liable to pay the tax due (s.6(3)). S.6(3) will not apply as respects any day on which one or more of the persons there mentioned fall to be disregarded for the purpose of discount by virtue of paragraphs 2 or 4 of Schedule I to the Act (the severely mentally impaired and students) and one or more of them do not; and liability to pay the council tax in respect of the dwelling and that day will be determined as follows–

(a) if only one of those persons does not fall to be so disregarded, he will be solely liable;

(b) if two or more of those persons does not fall to be so disregarded, they will each be jointly and severally liable (s.6(4)).

Owner in relation to a dwelling means the person as regards whom the following conditions are fulfilled–

(a) he has a material interest in the whole or any part of the dwelling; and

(b) at least part of the dwelling, or as the case may be, of the part concerned is not subject to a material interest inferior to his interest.

Resident in relation to any dwelling means an individual who has attained the age of 18 years and has his sole or main residence in the dwelling.

Material interest means a freehold interest or a leasehold interest which was granted for a term of six months or more (s.6(5) and (6)).

S.6 does not apply in relation to any chargeable dwelling which consists of a pitch occupied by a caravan, or a mooring occupied by a boat. Instead, the owner of such a dwelling will normally be liable to pay any tax due, except that, where on any day the owner of such a dwelling is not, but some other person is, a resident of it, that other person will be liable to pay the tax due (s.7(2) and (3)). Where two or more persons fall into either s.7(2) or 7(3), they will each be jointly and severally liable to pay the council tax in respect of the dwelling on that day (s.7(4)) and s.6(4) (see above) will apply for the purposes of s.7(4) as it applies for the purposes of s.6(3).

Any reference to the owner of a caravan or boat in s.7 will be construed–

(a) in relation to a caravan or boat which is subject to an agreement for hire-purchase or conditional sale, as a reference to the person in possession under the agreement;

(b) in relation to a caravan or boat which is subject to a bill of sale or mortgage, as a reference to the person entitled to the property in it apart from the bill or mortgage.

In relation to any chargeable dwelling (including a boat or caravan) of a class prescribed by regulations (subject to the exceptions specified in Classes C and E below), the owner of the dwelling will be the person liable to pay the tax due in respect of that dwelling (s.8). The Council Tax (Liability for Owners) Regulations 1992 specify the following classes of dwelling for the purposes of s.8.

Class A

A care home in respect of which a person is registered under the Care Standards Act 2000 or the Health and Social Care Act 2008; a building (or part) in which residential accommodation is provided under the National Assistance Act 1948, s.21 or the Care Act 2014, ss.18 or 19; or a hostel within the meanings given by paragraph 7 of Schedule I to the Act, (as read with the Council Tax (Discount Disregards) Order 1992).

Class B

A dwelling inhabited by a religious community whose principal occupation consists of prayer, contemplation, education, the relief of suffering, or any combination of these.

Class C

A dwelling which–

(a) was originally constructed or subsequently adapted for occupation by persons who do not constitute a single household; or

(b) is inhabited by a person who, or by two or more persons each of whom either–

(i) is a tenant of, or has a licence to occupy, part only of the dwelling; or

(ii) has a licence to occupy, but is not liable (whether alone or jointly with other persons) to pay rent or a licence fee in respect of, the dwelling as a whole.

For the purposes of this Class, the person responsible for paying the tax is the person who has a relevant material interest (i.e., a freehold or leasehold interest in the whole of the dwelling) which is not subject to a relevant material interest inferior to it; or if there is no such person, then the person who has a freehold interest in the whole or any part of the dwelling.

Class D

A dwelling–

(a) in which at least one of the residents is employed in domestic service and resides in the dwelling wholly or mainly for the purposes of his employment;

(b) in which any other resident is either so employed or is a member of the family of a resident so employed; and

(c) which is from time to time occupied by the employer of that person.

Class E

A dwelling which is inhabited by a minister of any religious denomination as a residence from which he performs the duties of his office. However, where a minister of the Church of England is the inhabitant and the owner of the dwelling and is in receipt of a stipend, the person liable to pay the tax will be the Diocesan Board of Finance of the diocese in which the dwelling is situated.

Note.–For the purposes of these Regulations, "tenant" includes a secure, introductory or statutory tenant.

Class F

A dwelling provided to an asylum seeker under s.95 of the Immigration and Asylum Act 1999 (accommodation provided for destitute asylum seekers).

11 Liability of spouse/civil partner

Where a person who is liable to pay council tax in respect of any chargeable dwelling of which he is a resident is married to or is the civil partner of another person who is also a resident of the dwelling on that day but who would not otherwise be so liable, those persons will be jointly and severally liable to pay the tax (s.9(1)), except where on any day the other person falls to be disregarded for the purposes of discount by virtue of paragraphs 2 and 4 of Schedule 1 to the Act (the severely mentally impaired and students) (s.9(2)).

S.9(1) also applies to two persons living together as husband and wife or as civil partners (s.9(3)).

12 Basic amounts payable

A person who is liable to pay council tax in respect of any chargeable dwelling and any day must pay to the billing authority for the area in which the dwelling is situated an amount calculated in accordance with the formula–

A divided by D

where–

A is the amount which, for the financial year in which the day falls and for dwellings in the valuation band listed for the dwelling, has been set by the authority for their area, and

D is the number of days in the financial year (Local Government Finance Act 1992, s.10(1)).

13 Discounts to council tax

The amount of council tax payable in respect of any chargeable dwelling and any day will be subject to a discount equal to the appropriate percentage (see below) of that amount if on that day (Local Government Finance Act 1992, s.11(1))–

(a) there is only one resident of the dwelling who does not fall to be disregarded for the purposes of discount (see **17 Discount disregards,** below); or

(b) there are two or more residents of the dwelling and each of them except one falls to be disregarded for those purposes.

The "appropriate percentage" for these purposes is 25%, or such other percentage as the Secretary of State may by order provide (Local Government Finance Act 1992, s.11(3)).

The amount of council tax payable in respect of any chargeable dwelling and any day will be subject to a discount of twice the appropriate percentage (i.e., 50%) if on that day (s.11(2))–

(c) there is no resident of the dwelling, or

(d) there are one or more residents of the dwelling and each of them falls to be disregarded for the purposes of discount.

In Wales, the discount where there is no-one resident in the property may be reduced to 10% (s.12(3)).

As to different levels of discount, see **14 Discounts: special provision,** below.

As to empty homes, see however **15 Increases to council tax,** below.

14 Discounts: special provision

Under ss.11A (England) and 12 (Wales), where any class of dwellings is prescribed for the purposes of those sections for any financial year, a billing authority may prescribe a different level of discount.

The Council Tax (Prescribed Classes of Dwellings) (England) Regulations 2003 prescribe four classes of dwelling for the purposes of s.11A namely—

(A) every furnished dwelling which is not the sole or main residence of any individual, the occupation of which *is* restricted by a planning condition preventing occupancy for a continuous period of at least 28 days in the relevant year and which is not excluded (see below);

(B) every furnished dwelling which is not the sole or main residence of any individual, the occupation of which is *not* restricted by a planning condition preventing occupancy for a continuous period of at least 28 days in the relevant year and which is not excluded (see below);

For these classes, the discount may either be reduced or disapplied altogether (i.e., the discount may be set anywhere between 0% and 50%). The other classes are—

(C) every chargeable dwelling which is unoccupied and substantially unfurnished; and

(D) every chargeable dwelling which is unoccupied and substantially unfurnished and which is undergoing, or has undergone within the last six months, major repairs (but only for a maximum period of 12 months).

For these classes, billing authorities have a discretion to either determine that the empty homes discount should not apply at all, or should be set at any percentage up to 100%.

The exceptions for Classes A and B are—

(i) any dwelling which consists of a pitch occupied by a caravan, or a mooring occupied by a boat;

(ii) any dwelling where a qualifying person is a qualifying person in relation to another dwelling and one of those dwellings is for him job-related (as defined in the Schedule to the Regulations) (i.e., the discount cannot be reduced under s.11A for a dwelling owned by someone liable for council tax for another property if they have to live in one of the properties because of their job, e.g., service personnel and ministers of religion).

The Council Tax (Prescribed Classes of Dwellings) (Wales) Regulations 1998 make similar provision for Wales.

15 Increases to council tax

England

S.11B (added by the Local Government Finance Act 2012) makes provision for an empty homes premium of up to 150% to be charged in England in relation to such classes of long term empty dwelling as billing authorities choose, subject to exceptions prescribed by the Secretary of State. The premium can be levied on properties that have been unoccupied and substantially unfurnished for two years. Periods of no more than six weeks where a property has been occupied, regardless of whether it was furnished or not, and periods of no more than six weeks where a property has been furnished but not occupied, are disregarded for these purposes.

Two classes are prescribed as exceptions for the purposes of s.11B (the empty homes premium), meaning that the premium cannot be charged where they apply. These classes are—

(a) dwellings which would be the sole or main residence of a person but which are empty while that person resides in accommodation provided by the Ministry of Defence by reason of their employment i.e., service personnel posted away from home; and

(b) dwellings which form an annex to another property and which are being used by a resident of that other property as part of their sole or main residence.

Wales

In Wales, billing authorities may charge a higher amount to "long-term empty dwellings" (s.12A) ie., a dwelling which has been unoccupied and substantially unfurnished for a continuous period of at least one year (section 12A(11)). Billing authorities may also charge the higher amount to dwellings that are occupied periodically but where there is no resident and the dwelling is substantially furnished (s.12B). In both cases the billing authority may increase the amount of council tax payable in respect of the dwellings by up to 100%. In respect of long-term empty homes, different percentages may be set for different dwellings based on the length of time for which they have been empty. Certain dwellings, prescribed by the Council Tax (Exceptions to Higher Amounts) (Wales) Regulations 2015 cannot be charged the higher amount. These excepted dwellings are—

(a) Classes 1 and 2: for a maximum of one year, dwellings that are on the market for sale or let. Where a dwelling has benefitted from an exception under Class 1 (for sale) it will not be entitled to a further period of exception until the dwelling has been sold. Where a dwelling has benefitted from an exception under Class 2 (to let), it will not be eligible for a further period of exception unless it has been subject to a tenancy that was granted for a term of six months or more;

(b) Class 3: annexes that are being used as part of the main residence or dwelling;

(c) Class 4: dwellings that would be a person's sole or main residence but which are unoccupied because that person resides in armed forces accommodation;

In relation to dwellings occupied periodically, the excepted dwellings are—

(d) Class 5: pitches occupied by caravans and moorings occupied by boats;

(e) Class 6: dwellings the occupation of which is restricted by a planning condition preventing occupancy for a continuous period of at least 28 days in a year (e.g., purpose built holiday homes or chalets that are subject to planning condition restricting year-round occupancy);

(f) Class 7: job-related dwellings and dwellings that are occupied periodically when the usual resident is residing in job-related accommodation.

16 Annexes

An annexe is generally a separate chargeable dwelling, however the Council Tax (Exempt Dwellings) Order 1992, which prescribes the classes of dwellings for which no council tax is payable, provides exemptions for (a) empty annexes which are subject to planning restrictions which means that they cannot be let separately from the main property (Class T), and (b) annexes occupied by a "dependent" relative of the main property (Class W) (see **4 Dwellings chargeable to council tax**, above).

In addition, the Council Tax (Reductions for Annexes) (England) Regulations 2013 provide a 50% discount for people living in properties with annexes as long as the annexe is either in use by a resident of the property with the annexe, or occupied by a relative (non-dependent) of the person who pays the council tax for the property with the annexe. The discount is on top of any discounts under ss.11 or 11A and/ or any premiums under s.11B–see **14 Discounts: special provision** and **15 Increases to council tax**, above).

17 Discount disregards

Schedule 1 to the Local Government Finance Act 1992, together with the Council Tax (Discount Disregards) Order 1992 and the Council Tax (Additional Provisions for Discount Disregards) Regulations 1992, have effect for determining who will be disregarded for the purposes of discount under ss.11 and 12 (see above). Under these provisions, the following persons are to be disregarded–

  (a) a person detained in a prison (including military detention in specified circumstances), hospital, or any other place by virtue of a court order;
  (b) a person who is severely and permanently mentally impaired and who is entitled to one of the qualifying social security benefits listed in Article 3 of the 1992 Order;
  (c) a person aged 18 or over in respect of whom another person is entitled to child benefit;
  (d) a person who is a student, student nurse, apprentice, or (England only) a youth training trainee within the definitions prescribed by Schedule 1 to the 1992 Order;
  (e) a patient whose sole or main residence is in a hospital;
  (f) a person whose sole or main residence is in a care home, independent hospital, or hostel and who is receiving care or treatment (or both) in the home, hospital or hostel;
  (g) a care worker, who provides care or support (or both) to another person or persons where the care worker is either (i) providing the care and support in question on behalf of a local authority, the Crown, or a charity (a relevant body), or as an employee of the person concerned to whom he was introduced by a relevant body, and in either case works for at least 24 hours a week for remuneration of not more than £44 and resides on premises provided by his employer or by the relevant body, or (ii) is providing care for at least 35 hours a week on average to a person who is in receipt of one of the qualifying social security benefits listed in the Schedule to the Council Tax (Additional Provisions for Discount Disregards) Regulations 1992 and resides in the same dwelling as that person, and is not a disqualified relative of that person (i.e., that person's spouse/civil partner or cohabitee or (where that person is aged under 18) his or her parent);
  (h) a person whose sole or main residence is in a dwelling providing residential accommodation, whether as a hostel, night shelter, or otherwise provided that the accommodation is predominantly provided–
      (i) otherwise than in separate and self-contained sets of premises,
      (ii) for persons of no fixed abode and no settled way of life, and
      (iii) under licences to occupy not constituting tenancies;
  (i) a person who is a member (or the dependant of a member) of certain international and defence organisations;
  (j) a person who is a member of a religious community the principal occupation of which consists of prayer, contemplation, education, the relief of suffering, or any combination of these, and who is dependent on his community to provide for his material needs;
  (k) a person aged under 20 who has within a relevant period (i.e., the period after 30th April and before 1st November in any year), ceased to undertake a qualifying course of education or a full time course of education (as defined by the 1992 Order). (The day in question must be within the same relevant period as that in which the cessation takes place.);
  (l) a member of a visiting force and any dependant of his who is neither a British citizen nor ordinarily resident in the UK;
  (m) a person who is the spouse/civil partner or dependant of a student within the meaning of paragraph 4 of Schedule 1 to the Act; and not a British citizen, and who is prevented by the terms of his leave to enter and remain in the UK, from taking paid employment or from claiming benefits; and
  (n) a diplomat or other person entitled to diplomatic privileges, provided that that person is not a British citizen or British subject and is not permanently resident in the UK.

18 Reduced amounts

A billing authority may reduce the amount a person is liable to pay in respect of council tax in accordance with its council tax reduction scheme (Local Government Finance Act 1992, s.13A, added by the Local

Government Finance Act 2012 s.10). This includes the power to reduce a person's liability to nil.

The Secretary of State may make regulations as regards any case where a person is liable to pay an amount to a billing authority in respect of council tax for any financial year which is prescribed; and prescribed conditions are fulfilled (s.13(1)). The regulations may provide that the amount he is liable to pay will be a lesser amount than the amount it would be, apart from the regulations, and is determined in accordance with prescribed rules (s.13(2)). S.13 applies whether the amount mentioned in s.13(1) (see above) is determined under s.10 (see **12 Basic amounts payable**, above) or under that section as read with ss.11 and 12 (see **13 Discounts to council tax**, above, and see **14 Discounts: special provision**, above). The Council Tax (Reductions for Disabilities) Regulations 1992, made for the purposes of s.13 provide that a liable person will be entitled to a reduction in the amount of council tax payable as regards a dwelling which is the sole or main residence of at least one person who is substantially and permanently disabled (a qualifying individual) and in which there is provided within the dwelling (i) a room (other than a bathroom, kitchen or lavatory) which is predominantly used by and is required for meeting the needs of any qualifying individual resident in the dwelling; or (ii) an additional bathroom or kitchen which is required for meeting the needs of any qualifying individual resident in the dwelling; or (iii) sufficient floor space to permit the use of a wheelchair required for meeting the needs of any qualifying individual resident in the dwelling; and as regards the financial year in question, an application is made in writing by him or on his behalf to that authority.

References in (i), (ii), and (iii) above to anything being required for meeting the needs of a qualifying individual are references to its being essential or of major importance to his well-being by reason of the nature and extent of his disability.

A wheelchair is not required for meeting an individual's needs if he does not need to use it within the living accommodation comprising or included in the dwelling concerned.

The Regulations specify the formula for calculating the reduction. The effect of which is that the council tax bill of a person to whom the Regulations apply will be calculated as if the dwelling in respect of which his liability arises was in a lower valuation band than is in fact the case. If the dwelling is in valuation band A, the bill is reduced by the same proportion as in the case of dwellings in valuation bands B to D. If the eligible person would otherwise have been entitled to a discount under s.11 or s.12 of the Act (see **13 Discounts to council tax**, above and **14 Discounts: special provision**, above) or if he is entitled to council tax benefit, the amount payable is calculated accordingly.

19 Transitional reductions

When a new range of valuation bands is introduced, transitional arrangements may be introduced to smooth changes in council tax liability for properties which would otherwise have a large rise in council tax.

New valuation bands were introduced in Wales in April 2005 and the Council Tax (Transitional Arrangements) (Wales) Regulations 2004 have been made to help smooth their introduction over a period of three years. Where a property increased by two or more valuation bands between the old and new bandings then, provided the person liable to pay the council tax is unchanged, the increase in bands, and thus the increase in liability, is phased in.

C: ADMINISTRATIVE PROVISIONS

20 Administration

Schedule 2 to the Act contains provisions relating to the administration and collection of the tax. Schedule 3 contains provisions for civil penalties and Schedule 4 provisions for the recovery of sums due, including sums due as penalties. The Council Tax (Administration and Enforcement) Regulations 1992 make further provision for the administration of the Act.

Part V of the Regulations makes provision for the billing of persons liable to the tax. Each financial year a billing authority is required to serve a notice in writing (a demand notice) on every liable person as soon as practicable after the day the billing authority first sets an amount of council tax for the relevant year for the category of dwelling within which the chargeable dwelling to which the notice relates falls. Where the billing authority requires the payment of instalments, the notice must be served at least 14 days before the day on which the first instalment is due (Regs. 18 and 19). For English billing authorities, the matters to be contained in a demand notice are set out in the Council Tax (Demand Notices) (England) Regulations 2011 (in Wales: the Council Tax (Demand Notices) (Wales) Regulations 1993, as amended). The general matters that must be included are the name (if any) of the person to whom the notice is issued, the date the notice is issued, the period to which the notice relates, the address of the dwelling, and the applicable valuation band. The notice must also contain information regarding the amount of council tax (such as amounts for different categories of dwellings), the amount attributable (in England) to the adult social care precept, whether the total amount is excessive and requires a referendum to be held (see **9 Council tax increase referendums (England)**, above), comparisons with preceding years, premiums, discounts and reductions, and amounts to be paid under the notice. The Regulations also specify information which must be supplied with a notice when it is served. This information includes the gross expenditure and budget requirements of the billing authority and certain precepting authorities for the relevant year and the preceding year, as well as statements of the ground on which any penalty has been imposed and (in England) about the purpose of the 2% adult social care precept.

No payment on account of the chargeable amount (whether interim, final, or sole) need be made unless a notice served under Part V requires it (1992 Regulations, Reg. 22). Normally payment is made by 10 instalments, but a person may by notice in writing request there to be 12 monthly instalments (Reg. 21).

Where a demand notice has been served on a liable person, instalments in respect of the council tax to which the notice relates are payable, and if any such instalment is not paid, the billing authority must serve a notice (a reminder notice) on the liable person stating (a) the total of the instalments due under the notice and the instalment due within the next seven days; (b) that the above amount is required to be paid within seven days of the date of issue of the notice; (c) if the required amount is not paid within the seven day period, the unpaid balance of the estimated (or, as the case may be, chargeable) amount will become payable at the expiry of a further period of seven days beginning with the date of failure; and (d) where the notice is the second such notice as regards the relevant year, if the liable person fails to pay any subsequent instalment as regards that year on or before the day on which it falls due, the unpaid balance of the estimated (or, as the case may be, chargeable) amount will become payable by him on the day following the day of the failure (Reg. 23).

By virtue of Regulation 25, a billing authority may agree to accept lump sum payments of at least two instalments, being a lump sum which is of an amount determined by the authority and less than the estimated amount. Lump sum payments cannot be accepted unless (a) the determination as to the cases where a lump sum will be accepted and as to the amount of the sum in those cases was made by the authority before the day on which they first set an amount for the relevant year, (b) under those determinations persons liable to pay the same number of instalments in the relevant year are treated alike, and (c) the single lump sum payment must be made on or before the day on which the first instalment falls due under the notice.

A billing authority may also accept a discounted amount in such cases as they may determine and in satisfaction of any liability of a person to pay to them any instalment or other payment due under the demand notice provided that the discounted amount is paid to the authority otherwise than by either bank notes or coin; and the determinations as to the cases where a discounted amount will be accepted and as to the proportion that the amount is to bear to the amount of the instalment or other payment due must be made by the authority on or before the day on which they first set an amount for the relevant year (Reg. 26).

Under the provisions relating to joint and several liability, an amount will not be payable by a person unless a notice has been served on him by the billing authority stating the amount; and it will be due from him to the authority at the expiry of such period (being not less than 14 days) after the day of issue of the notice as is specified in it (Reg. 28).

21 Appeals

Part 13 of the Local Government and Public Involvement in Health Act 2007 establishes the Valuation Tribunal for England, abolishes existing valuation tribunals in England and transfers their jurisdiction to the Valuation Tribunal for England.

The procedure on appeals relating to England is contained in the Valuation Tribunal for England (Council Tax and Rating Appeals) (Procedure) Regulations 2009.

A person may appeal to the Valuation Tribunal for England if he is aggrieved by–

(a) any decision of a billing authority that a dwelling is a chargeable dwelling or that he is liable to pay council tax in respect of such a dwelling; or

(b) any calculation made by such an authority of an amount which he is liable to pay to the authority in respect of council tax (s.16(1)).

No appeal may be made under s.16 unless the aggrieved person serves a written notice on the billing authority concerned, stating the matter by which and the grounds on which he is aggrieved and one of the following conditions is fulfilled–

(i) the aggrieved person is notified in writing by that authority that they believe the grievance is not well-founded, but the person is still aggrieved;

(ii) the aggrieved person is notified in writing by the authority that steps have been taken by them to deal with the grievance but he is still aggrieved; or

(iii) two months have passed since the date of service of the aggrieved person's notice with-out his being notified under (i) or (ii) above.

The Valuation Tribunal for England must dismiss an appeal by a person to whom the condition in (i) or (ii) is fulfilled unless the appeal is initiated within two months of the date of service of the billing authority's notice. Where the condition in (iii) is fulfilled, the Valuation Tribunal for England must dismiss an appeal by an aggrieved person unless the appeal is initiated within four months of the date of service of the person's notice. The President of the Valuation Tribunal for England may authorise an appeal to be entertained where he is satisfied that the failure of the person aggrieved to initiate the appeal within the time limits has arisen by reason of circumstances beyond that person's control (Valuation Tribunal for England (Council Tax and Rating Appeals) (Procedure) Regulations 2009, Reg. 21).

Similar provisions for Wales are contained in the Valuation Tribunal for Wales Regulations 2010.

For appeals relating to the alteration of valuation lists, see **28 Alteration of lists**, below.

22 Enforcement

Schedule 4 to the Local Government Finance Act 1992 and Part VI of the Council Tax (Administration and

Enforcement) Regulations 1992 are concerned with the recovery of sums due by way of council tax (under Part V of the Regulations—see above).

Before the authority concerned can make use of the wide variety of remedies open to them, they must apply to a magistrates' court for a liability order against the person concerned, but as a first step, the billing authority must serve on the person against whom the application for a liability order is to be made a notice (a final notice), which is to be in addition to any notice required to be served under Part V of the Regulations, and which must state every amount in respect of which the authority is to make the application. However, a final notice need not be served on a person who has been served with a reminder notice in the circumstances outlined in (c) of Regulation 23 (see **20 Administration**, above). If the amount stated in the final notice is wholly or partly unpaid at the expiry of the period of seven days beginning with the day on which the notice was issued or if an amount which has fallen due under (c) of Regulation 23 (see **20 Administration**, above) is wholly or partly unpaid, the authority may apply to a magistrates' court for an order against the person by whom it is payable. The application is to be instituted by making complaint to a justice of the peace, and requesting the issue of a summons directed to that person to appear before the court to show why he has not paid the sum which is outstanding. An interval of at least 14 days must elapse after the service of a summons before a liability order may be made. The court will make the order if it is satisfied that the sum has become payable by the defendant and has not been paid. The order will be made in respect of an amount equal to the aggregate of the sum payable and a sum of an amount equal to the costs reasonably incurred by the applicant in obtaining the order.

If after a summons has been issued but before the application is heard, there is paid or tendered to the authority an amount equal to the aggregate of the sum specified in the summons as outstanding or so much of it as remains outstanding (as the case may be) and a sum of an amount equal to the costs reasonably incurred by the authority in connection with the application up to the time of the payment or tender, the authority must accept the amount and the application will not be proceeded with.

Where the sum payable is paid after a liability order has been applied for but before it is made, the court will nonetheless (if so requested by the billing authority) make the order in respect of a sum of an amount equal to the costs reasonably incurred by the authority in making the application (Reg. 34).

Where the court has made a liability order against a person (the debtor), if that person is an individual, the authority concerned may—

(a) make an attachment of earnings order to secure the payment of any outstanding sum (and the costs of any unsuccessful attempt to take control of goods and any abortive application to commit the debtor to prison) which is or forms part of the amount in respect of which the liability order was made;

(b) take control of goods (and sell them to recover a sum of money) (this remedy also applies in the case of a company);

(c) apply to a magistrates' court for the issue of a warrant committing the debtor to prison where they have previously sought to take control of goods and the enforcement agent is unable to find any or sufficient goods of the debtor on which to enforce a payment (but a court will only commit a debtor to prison where it is of the opinion that his failure to pay is due to wilful refusal or culpable neglect);

(d) petition for the bankruptcy of the debtor, or, in the case of a company, for the winding up of the business.

Where a magistrates' court has made a liability order in respect of unpaid council tax, and prescribed conditions are fulfilled, the authority concerned may apply to a court for a charging order imposing, on any interest held by the debtor beneficially in the relevant dwelling, a charging order for securing the due amount.

The Council Tax (Deductions from Income Support) Regulations 1993 provide for deductions to be made from income support (and jobseeker's allowance, employment and support allowance and state pension credit) where a liability order has been obtained against a person to meet unpaid council tax. Where an application to make such deductions is received from a billing authority, the application will be referred to an adjudication officer, who will determine whether there is sufficient income support to allow such deductions to be made. Provision is made for appeals by the debtor from the decision of the adjudication officer to the Social Security Appeal Tribunal.

Once a liability order has been made, the remedies of attachment of earnings, deductions under the income support regulations, and taking control of goods may be resorted to more than once and each of those remedies may be resorted to in any order or alternately (or both); but steps by way of attachment, taking control of goods, commitment, bankruptcy, winding up or charging may not be taken while steps by way of another of those methods are being taken and, where deductions from income support or jobseeker's allowance (see above) are being made, no other method of enforcement can be resorted to.

Where a warrant of commitment is issued against (or a term of imprisonment is fixed in the case of) the person concerned, no steps or no further steps by way of attachment, taking control of goods, bankruptcy, or charging may be taken.

The provisions of Part VI apply, with modifications, to cases where persons are jointly and severally liable to pay tax.

23 Completion of new dwellings

Schedule 4A to the Local Government Finance Act 1988 (which makes provision with respect to the determination of a day as the completion day in relation to a new building) will apply for the purposes of Part I of the Local Government Finance Act 1992, as it applies for the purposes of Part III of the 1988 Act (Local Government Finance Act 1992, s.17(1)). Where a completion notice is served under the Schedule and the building to which the notice relates is not completed on or before the relevant day, any dwelling in which the building or any part of it will be comprised will be deemed to have come into existence on that day (s.17(3)). The relevant day means, where an appeal against the completion notice is brought, the day stated in the notice and, where no appeal is brought, the day determined under the Schedule as the completion day in relation to the building to which the notice relates (s.17(4)). The procedure to be followed in connection with an appeal against a completion notice is governed by the Valuation Tribunal for England (Council Tax and Rating Appeals) (Procedure) Regulations 2009 or the Valuation Tribunal for Wales Regulations 2010. For appeals see **21 Appeals**, above.

24 Death of persons liable

The Secretary of State may make such regulations as he thinks fit to deal with the death of persons liable for council tax (Local Government Finance Act 1992, s.18(1)). In particular, the regulations may provide for council tax to be paid by a deceased person's executor or administrator (s.18(3)).

D: VALUATION

25 Valuation lists

The Commissioners of Inland Revenue must appoint a listing officer for each billing authority (Local Government Finance Act 1992, s.20).

The Commissioners must-

(a) carry out such valuations of dwellings in England and Wales;

(b) furnish listing officers with such information obtained in carrying out the valuations; and

(c) disclose to such officers such contents of particulars delivered documents,

as they consider necessary or expedient for the purpose of facilitating the compilation and maintenance by these officers of valuation lists (s.21(1)).

Unless new lists have been compiled, the valuations will be carried out by reference to 1st April 1991 and on such assumptions and in accordance with such principles as may be prescribed (s.21(2)). The Council Tax (Situation and Valuation of Dwellings) Regulations 1992 provide that, for the purposes of valuations under s.21, the value of any dwelling will be taken to be the amount which, on the following assumptions, the dwelling might reasonably have been expected to realise if it had been sold in the open market by a willing vendor on 1st April 1991. In Wales, where new lists have been compiled, the relevant date is 1st April 2003.

The assumptions are(Reg.6(2))–

(a) that the sale was with vacant possession;

(b) that the interest sold was the freehold or, in the case of a flat, a lease for 99 years at a nominal rent;

(c) that the dwelling was sold free from any rent charge or other incumbrance;

(d) except in the cases described below, that the size, layout and character of the dwelling, and the physical state of its locality, were the same as at the date on which the valuation was made (the relevant date);

(e) that the dwelling was in a state of reasonable repair;

(f) in the case of a dwelling the owner or occupier of which is entitled to use common parts, that those parts were in a like state of repair and the purchaser would be liable to contribute towards the cost of keeping them in such a state;

(g) in the case of a dwelling which contains certain fixtures designed to make the dwelling suitable for use by a disabled person and add to the value of the dwelling, that the fixtures were not included in the dwelling;

(h) that the use of the dwelling would be permanently restricted to use as a private dwelling; and

(i) that the dwelling had no development value other than value attributable to permitted development.

The exceptions in relation to (d) above are that in the case of a valuation carried out for the purposes of an alteration of the valuation list resulting from a material reduction in the value of the dwelling, it will be assumed that (Reg.6(3))–

(a) the physical state of the locality of the dwelling was the same as on the date from which the alteration of the list would have effect; and

(b) the size, layout, and character of the dwelling were the same–

(i) in the case of an alteration resulting from a change to the physical condition of the dwelling, as on the date from which the alteration of the list would have effect;

(ii) in a case where there has been a previous alteration of the valuation list in relation to the dwelling, as on the date from which that alteration had effect;

(iii) in a case where in relation to the dwelling, there has been a relevant transaction within the meaning of s.24 (see **28 Alteration of lists**, below), not resulting in an alteration of the valuation list, on the date of that transaction;

(iv) in a case where more than one of paragraphs (i) to (iii) applies, as on whichever is the latest dates there mentioned; and

(v) in any other case, as on 1st April 1993.

In the case of a valuation carried out for the purposes of an alteration of the valuation list resulting from an improvement to and subsequent sale of the property, or where a property has become or ceased to be a composite hereditament (or where the domestic use element has changed), or because of the splitting of a dwelling into more than one property, the valuation will be on the basis of the size, layout, and character of the property and the physical state of the locality on the date of sale, or the date the new unit of accommodation is created (Reg. 6(5A)).

In the case of a dwelling which is a composite hereditament or is part of a single property which is a composite hereditament, the value of the dwelling, for the purposes of s.21, will be taken to be that portion of the relevant amount which can reasonably be attributed to domestic use of the dwelling.

"Relevant amount" means the amount which the composite hereditament might reasonably have been expected to realise on the assumptions (a) to (g) and (i) mentioned above if for the references to dwelling throughout those paragraphs there were substituted references to the composite hereditament.

26 Compilation and maintenance of lists

The valuation lists for each authority were originally compiled as at 1st April 1993 (Local Government Finance Act 1992, s.22(2)). The listing officer must keep this list up to date.

In England, a new list must be compiled by 1st April in such year as the Secretary of State by order specifies (the revaluation planned for 1st April 2015 has been postponed). In Wales, a new list was compiled on 1st April 2005 and new lists must be compiled there on 1st April in each year specified by order made by the Welsh Ministers (Local Government Finance Act 1992, s.22B, added by the Local Government Act 2003 s.77, and amended by the Council Tax (New Valuation Lists for England) Act 2006 and the Localism Act 2011, s.80).

27 Contents of lists

A valuation list must show, for each day for which it is in force, each dwelling situated in the billing authority's area and, for each day on which a dwelling is shown in the list, the list must also show which of the valuation bands applies to the dwelling (Local Government Finance Act 1992, s.23(1) and (2)). A list must also contain such information about dwellings shown in it as may be prescribed (s.23(3)). The Council Tax (Contents of Valuation Lists) Regulations 1992 make additional provision in connection with valuation lists. *Inter alia* they provide for lists to show a reference number for each dwelling.

28 Alteration of lists

S.24 of the Local Government Finance Act 1992 and, in respect to England only, the Council Tax (Alteration of Lists and Appeals) (England) Regulations 2009 provide for the alteration of Council Tax valuation lists. In particular, the Regulations impose the following restrictions on alteration of valuation bands (Reg. 3). No alteration will be made to the valuation band applicable to any dwelling unless–

(a) since the valuation was made–
   (i) there has been a material increase in the value of the dwelling and a relevant transaction has been subsequently carried out in relation to the whole or any part of it;
   (ii) there has been a material reduction in the value of the dwelling;
   (iii) the dwelling has become or ceased to be a composite hereditament for the purposes of Part III of the 1988 Act (non-domestic rating); or
   (iv) in the case of a dwelling which continues to be such an hereditament, there has been an increase or reduction in its domestic use; or
(b) the listing officer is satisfied that–
   (i) a different valuation band should have been determined by him as applicable to the dwelling; or
   (ii) the band shown in the list is not that determined by him as so applicable; or
(c) an order of the Valuation Tribunal for England, or of the High Court requires the alteration to be made.
Provision for Wales is made by the Council Tax (Alteration of Lists and Appeals) Regulations 1993.

S.24(10) provides that "material increase", in relation to the value of a dwelling, means any increase which is caused (in whole or in part) by any building, engineering, or other operation carried out in relation to the dwelling, whether or not constituting development for which planning permission is required.

"Relevant transaction" means a transfer on sale of the fee simple, a grant of a lease for a term of seven years or more, or a transfer on sale of such a lease.

"Material reduction", in relation to the value of a dwelling, means any reduction which is caused (in whole or in part) by the demolition of any part of the dwelling, any change in the physical state of the dwelling's locality, or any adaptation of the dwelling to make it suitable for use by a physically disabled person. However, where a material reduction in the value of a dwelling is caused wholly by the demolition of any part of the dwelling, the valuation band will not be altered if the works of demolition are part of, or connected with, a building, engineering, or other operation (not including repair of any damage caused to the dwelling in the course of demolition) carried out, in progress, or proposed to be carried out in relation to the dwelling.

Regulation 4 prescribes the circumstances and periods in which proposals may be made. In general, the authority or an interested person may make a proposal for the alteration of a list where there is an inaccuracy on the list or if one or more of the events mentioned in (a)(i) to (iv) above has occurred, or if in relation to a matter shown in it, account has not been taken (whether as regards a particular dwelling or a class of dwelling) of a relevant decision of the Valuation Tribunal for England or the High Court. With respect to this latter circumstance, no proposal may be made after the expiry of the period of six months beginning on the day on which the decision in question was made.

An application on the grounds that the listing officer has determined the wrong valuation band for the property must be made not later than the end of the period of six months beginning on the day on which the list is compiled. However, a person who on any day during the period in which a list is in force becomes the taxpayer in respect of a particular dwelling shown in the list may make a proposal for the alteration of the list in respect of that dwelling where he has not during that period previously been the taxpayer in respect of that dwelling, but no proposal may be made where *inter alia* six months has expired since the day on which that person first became the taxpayer.

The Valuation Tribunal for England (Council Tax and Rating Appeals) (Procedure) Regulations 2009 and the Valuation Tribunal for Wales Regulations 2010 specify the procedure in relation to appeals to the Valuation Tribunals for England and for Wales where there is a disagreement about a proposed alteration to a council tax valuation list. An appeal against a decision of a Valuation Tribunal may be made on a point of law to the High Court. With the agreement of the persons concerned, disputes which would otherwise be the subject of an appeal to a Valuation Tribunal may be referred to arbitration (England, Reg. 4; Wales, Reg. 45).

29 Powers of entry, etc.

In England, if a valuation officer needs to value a dwelling for the purpose of carrying out any of the officer's functions, the officer and any servant of the Crown authorised by the officer in writing may enter on, survey and value the dwelling if approval is obtained from the First-tier Tribunal prior to exercising the power. The Tribunal must not give its approval unless it is satisfied that the valuation officer needs to value the dwelling. Having received approval the valuation officer must give three working days' notice, in writing, before exercising the power. A person who intentionally delays or obstructs a person in the exercise of a power under these provisions is liable on summary conviction to a fine not exceeding level one on the standard scale (as to which see Administration of Justice: Treatment of Offenders, Maximum fines: the "standard scale") (Local Government Finance Act 1992, s.25A). In Wales, if a valuation officer needs to value a dwelling, he may enter on, survey and value the dwelling, provided that he gives at least three clear days' written notice of his intention to do so (Local Government Finance Act 1992, s.26(1) and (2)). It is an offence to intentionally delay or obstruct a person in the exercise of these powers (s.26(4)).

In England and Wales, a valuation officer may, for the purpose of carrying out any of his functions, serve on a person who is or has been an owner or occupier of any dwelling a notice requesting him to supply information of a description specified in the notice. The notice must also state that the officer believes the information requested will assist him in carrying out his functions (s.27(2)). A person on whom such a notice is served must supply the information requested if it is in his possession or control, and must do so in such form and manner as is specified in the notice, within 21 days beginning with the day on which the notice is served (s.27(3)). It is an offence to fail to comply with such a notice or to supply false information (s.27(4) and (5)).

30 Use of information

A billing authority has specific power to use information it has obtained for council tax purposes for the purpose of identifying vacant dwellings or taking steps to bring vacant dwellings back into use. So far as personal information is concerned, only a person's name or an address or number for communicating with him may be so used (Local Government Finance Act 1992, Sch. 2 para 18A, added by the Local Government Act 2003, s.85).

31 Information

A person may require a listing officer to give him access to such information as will enable him to establish the state of a list and any such requirement must be complied with at a reasonable time and place and free of charge (Local Government Finance Act 1992, s.28). A person may also, at a reasonable time and free of charge, inspect any proposal made or notice of appeal given under regulations made under s.24 (see **28 Alteration of lists**, above) (s.29).

PART II: CONTRACTING OUT

32 Introduction

The functions of a local authority in relation to the administration and enforcement of council tax, and the collection and enforcement of non-domestic rates may be contracted out to the extent provided by the Local Authorities (Contracting Out of Tax Billing, Collection and Enforcement Functions) Order 1996.

33 Council tax

Part II of the Local Authorities (Contracting Out of Tax Billing, Collection and Enforcement Functions) Order 1996 provides that, *inter alia*, the following functions may be contracted out so as to be exercised by, or by an employee of such a person, as the local authority authorise—

(a) supplying information requested under s.17(1);

(b) requesting information for the purpose of identifying the person liable to pay council tax in respect of a dwelling house and identifying that person;

(c) requesting information from a public body or public officer under the Administration and Enforcement Regulations;

(d) ascertaining whether dwellings are exempt dwellings and exercising certain functions relating to such properties;

(e) ascertaining entitlements to discounts and reduced amounts;

(f) identifying the liable person in respect of any dwelling on any day;

(g) preparing and serving demand notices and making adjustments in respect of them;

(h) adjusting instalments, revising estimates and repaying overpayments;

(i) serving reminder notices;

(j) making adjustments with regard to payments including the preparation and serving of joint taxpayers' notices;

(k) requiring the payment of penalties and collecting the same;

(l) dealing with executors and administrators;

(m) functions in relation to liability orders, attachment of earnings orders, allowance orders, and charging orders;

(n) exercising functions in relation to taking control of goods and insolvency;

(o) giving notification of a decision about an application for a reduction of council tax;

(p) payment of a reduction, the function;

(q) ascertaining liability to a premium; and

(r) collection of penalties under the Council Tax Reduction Schemes (Detection of Fraud and Enforcement) (England) Regulations 2013.

34 Non-domestic rates

Part VI of the Local Authorities (Contracting Out of Tax Billing, Collection and Enforcement Functions) Order 1996 provides that, *inter alia*, the following functions may be contracted out so as to be exercised by, or by an employee of such a person, as the local authority authorise—

(a) identifying ratepayers;

(b) preparing and serving demand notices;

(c) adjusting instalments;

(d) preparing and serving notices in respect of unpaid rates;

(e) preparing and serving demand notices and making adjustments in respect of them;

(f) calculating and paying interest due to ratepayer;

(g) dealing with executors and administrators;

(h) functions in relation to liability orders;

(i) exercising functions in relation to taking control of goods and insolvency;

(j) entering into agreements to provide security for unpaid rates.

35 General conditions in relation to contracting out

Any demand notice served by a contractor must comply with the Council Tax and Non-Domestic Rating (Demand Notices) (England) Regulations 2003 (or the Welsh equivalents: Council Tax (Demand Notices) (Wales) Regulations 1993/255, Non-Domestic Rating (Demand Notices) (Wales) Regulations 1993/252, as amended) and any agreements for payment must be made in the name of the authority rather than in the name of the contractor, as must any application for a liability order. All enforcement proceedings must be taken or brought in the name of the authority.

36 Authorities

Statutes—

Local Government Act 2003

Local Government and Public Involvement in Health Act 2007

Local Government and Rating Act 1997

Localism Act 2011

Statutory Instruments—

Council Tax (Additional Provisions for Discount Disregards) Regulations 1992, as amended (S.I. 1992 Nos. 552 and 2942, 1993 No. 149, 1994 No. 540, 1995 No. 620, 1996 No. 637, 1997 No. 657, 1998 No. 294, 2005 Nos. 2866 and 3302, 2006 No. 3395, 2007 No. 581, and 2013 Nos. 388, 591, 639 and 725)

Council Tax (Administration and Enforcement) (Attachment of Earnings Order) (Wales) Regulations 1992 (S.I. 1992 No. 1741)

Council Tax (Administration and Enforcement) Regulations 1992, as amended (S.I. 1992 Nos. 613 and 3008, 1993 Nos. 196 and 773, 1994 No. 505, 1995 No. 22, 1996 Nos. 1880 and 2405, 1997 No. 393, 1998 No. 295, 1999 No. 534, 2000 No. 2026, 2001 Nos. 362 and 1076, 2003 Nos. 522, 768, 1715, 2211, and 2604, 2004 Nos. 785, 927, and 1013, 2005 Nos. 617, 2866 and 3302, 2006 No. 3395, 2007 Nos. 501 and 582, 2009 No. 2706, 2010 No. 752, 2011 No. 528, 2012 Nos. 672 and 3086, 2013 Nos. 62, 570, 590, and 630, and 2014 Nos. 129 and 600)

Council Tax (Alteration of Lists and Appeals) Regulations 2009, as amended (S.I. 2009 No. 2270 and 2013 No. 467)

Council Tax and Non-Domestic Rating (Demand Notices) (England) Regulations 2003, as amended (S.I. 2003 Nos. 2613 and 3081, 2004 No. 3389, 2006 Nos. 492 and 3395, 2008 Nos. 387 and 3264, 2009 Nos. 355 and 1597, 2010 Nos. 140 and 187, 2012 Nos. 538 and 994, 2013 No. 694, 2015 No. 427, and 2016 No. 316)

Council Tax (Chargeable Dwellings) Order 1992, as amended (S.I. 1992 No. 549, 1997 No. 656, 2003 No. 3121, 2004 No. 2921, 2012 No. 1915, and 2014 No. 2653)

Council Tax (Contents of Valuation Lists) Regulations 1992, as amended (S.I. 1992 No. 553 and 1996 No. 619)

Council Tax (Deductions from Income Support) Regulations 1993, as amended (S.I. 1993 No. 494 1996 No. 2344, and 2008 No. 1554)

Council Tax (Demand Notices)(England) Regulations 2011, as amended (S.I. 2011 No. 3038, 2012 No. 3087, and 2016 No. 188)

Council Tax (Discount Disregards) Order 1992, as amended (S.I. 1992 No. 548, 1994 No. 543, 1995 No. 619, 1996 Nos. 636 and 3143, 1997 No. 656, 1998 No. 291, 2003 Nos. 673 and 3121, 2004 No. 2921, 2006 No. 3396, 2007 No. 580, 2010 Nos. 677, 1941, and 2448, 2011 No. 948, 2012 No. 956, 2013 Nos. 630, 638, and 1048, and 2015 No. 971)

Council Tax (Exceptions to Higher Amounts) (Wales) Regulations 2015 (S.I. 2015 No. 2068)

Council Tax (Exempt Dwellings) Order 1992, as amended (S.I. 1992 Nos. 558 and 2941, 1993 No. 150, 1994 No. 539, 1995 No. 619, 1997 No. 656, 1998 No. 291, 1999 No. 536, 2000 Nos. 424 and 1025, 2003 No. 3121, 2004 No. 2921, 2005 Nos. 2865 and 3302, 2006 No. 2318, and 2012 No. 2965)

Council Tax (Liability for Owners) Regulations 1992, as amended (S.I. 1992 No. 551, 1993 No. 151, 1995 No. 620, 2000 Nos. 537 and 1024, 2003 No. 3125, 2004 No. 2920, 2012 No. 1915, and 2015 No. 643)

Council Tax (Prescribed Classes of Dwellings) (England) Regulations 2003, as amended (S.I. 2003 No. 3011, 2004 No. 926, 2005 Nos. 416 and 2866, and 2012 No. 2964)

Council Tax (Prescribed Classes of Dwellings) (Wales) Regulations 1998, as amended (S.I. 1998 No. 105, 2004 Nos. 452 and 3094, 2005 No. 3302, 2010 No. 612, and 2014 No. 107)

Council Tax (Reductions for Annexes) (England) Regulations 2013 (S.I. 2013 No. 2977)

Council Tax (Reductions for Disabilities) Regulations 1992, as amended (S.I. 1992 No. 554, 1993 No. 195, 1995 No. 3150, 1999 No. 1004, and 2005 No. 702)

Council Tax (Situation and Valuation of Dwellings Regulations 1992, as amended (S.I. 1992 No. 550, 1994 No. 1747, 2005 No. 701, and 2008 No. 315)

Council Tax (Transitional Arrangements) (Wales) Regulations 2004 (S.I. 2004 No. 3142)

Council Tax (Valuation Bands) (Wales) Order 2003 (S.I. 2003 No. 3046)

Local Authorities (Conduct of Referendums) (Council Tax Increases) (England) Regulations 2012, as amended (S.I. 2012 No. 444, 2013 No. 409, and 2014 Nos. 231 and 925)

Local Authorities (Contracting Out of Tax Billing, Collection and Enforcement Functions) Order 1996, as amended (S.I. 1996 No. 1880, 2013 Nos. 502 and 695, and 2014 Nos. 600 and 856)

Valuation Tribunal for England (Council Tax and Rating Appeals) (Procedure) Regulations 2009, as amended (S.I. 2009 No. 2270, 2011 No. 434, and 2013 No. 465)

Valuation Tribunal for Wales Regulations 2010, as amended (S.I. 2010 No. 713, 2013 No. 547, and 2014 No. 544)

COUNCIL TAX: SCOTLAND

Contents

This Note is structured as follows–

1 The legislation

The Local Government Finance Act 1992 introduced council tax.

Council tax reduction is dealt with in the Note on **Council Tax Reduction**.

2 Domestic subjects

Under the 1987 Act, with effect from 1st April 1989, existing entries in the valuation roll relating to domestic subjects were required to be deleted (s.2(2)). Domestic subjects are defined, broadly, as dwelling-houses (but excluding a caravan which is not a person's sole or main residence) (s.2(3), as amended by the Caravans (Standard Community Charge and Rating) Act 1991); the definition may be varied, by regulations, so as to include or exclude prescribed lands and heritages (s.2(4), as substituted by the Local Government Finance Act, 1988). The Abolition of Domestic Rates (Domestic and Part Residential Subjects) (Scotland) Regulations 1988 have been made *inter alia* for this purpose.

There is a right of appeal to the valuation appeal committee in respect of the deletion or retention of an entry in the roll (s.2(6)).

A: GENERAL PROVISIONS

3 Introduction

Part II of the Local Government Finance Act 1992 introduced the council tax which, since 1st April 1993, has been payable in respect of chargeable dwellings.

Each local authority in Scotland must impose a council tax payable in respect of dwellings situated in that authority's area (s.70). Liability to pay council tax is determined on a daily basis and it is assumed that any state of affairs subsisting at the end of the day has subsisted throughout the day (s.71).

4 Dwellings chargeable to council tax

Council tax is payable in respect of any dwelling which is not an exempt dwelling (s.72(1)) (see **7 Exempt dwellings**, below) and the term "dwelling" means–

    (1) any land and heritages (i) consisting of one or more dwelling-houses with any garden, yard, garage, outhouse, or pertinent belonging to, and occupied with, such dwelling-house or houses, and (ii) which would, but for the provisions of s.73(1) (see **8 Alterations to valuation roll**, below) be entered separately in the valuation roll, and

        (a) includes the residential part of part residential subjects (see below); but

        (b) does not include a caravan which is not a person's sole or main residence or any lands and heritages which are timeshare accommodation within the meaning of the Timeshare Act 1992 (s.72(2) and the Council Tax (Dwellings) (Scotland) Regulations 1993),

and by virtue of the Council Tax (Dwellings) (Scotland) Regulations 1992–

    (2) any lands and heritages which are a garage, a car port or, as the case may be, a car parking stance; (i) the use of which is ancillary to, and which is used wholly in connection with, another dwelling; and (ii) which is used wholly or mainly for the accommodation of one or more private motor vehicles (i.e., a mechanically propelled vehicle not falling within Schedule 1 to the Vehicle Excise and Registration Act 1994); and

    (3) lands and heritages (i) the use of which is ancillary to, and which are used wholly in connection with, another dwelling; and (ii) which are used wholly or mainly for the storage of articles of domestic use (including cycles and other similar vehicles).

Lands and heritages which are not in use will nevertheless be treated as falling within paragraphs (2)(i) and (ii) or (3).

The Council Tax (Dwellings) (Scotland) Regulations 2010 determine whether certain parts of a combined heat and power station are included or excluded from the definition of "dwelling" for the purpose of liability to non-domestic rates.

5 Statutory and other references to rateable values

S.5 of the 1987 Act makes provision in relation to references in deeds, documents, and legislation to gross annual, net annual, or rateable value of properties which consist wholly or partly of domestic subjects. In the case of references in any enactment (including a subordinate instrument), then, unless the context otherwise requires, the reference is to be construed as a reference to the gross annual value, net annual value, or rateable value which appears in the valuation roll in force immediately before 1st April 1989 or, in the case of such property which does not come into existence or occupancy as domestic subjects until after that date, which would have so appeared had it then existed or been in such occupancy. There is provision for material changes of circumstances to be taken into account.

6 Definitions for the purposes of council tax

Under the Council Tax (Dwellings and Part Residential Subjects) (Scotland) Regulations 1992, the term dwelling also includes certain bed and breakfast accommodation, student halls, barracks, communal residential establishments, and school boarding accommodation, but excludes certain huts, sheds, bothies, self-catering holiday accommodation, and women's refuges.

"Part residential subjects" means lands and heritages which are used partly as the sole or main residence of any person, other than—
(i) dwellings (except the residential part of part residential subjects); and
(ii) such other class or classes of lands and heritages as may be prescribed.

The Council Tax (Dwellings and Part Residential Subjects) (Scotland) Regulations 1992 provide that the classes of land and heritages which are prescribed for the purposes of (ii) are—
(a) any lands and heritages or parts thereof excluded from the definition of dwelling under paragraph 3 of Schedule 2 to the Regulations (women's refuges); and
(b) any part of (a) any building in which a care home service provides accommodation; or (b) a private hospital, which is not used wholly or mainly as the sole or main residence of a person employed there.

Schedule 5 to the Act has effect in relation to part-residential subjects.

"Qualifying person" means a person who would be liable (either solely or jointly and severally with another person or persons) for council tax in respect of the dwelling concerned, but for the provisions of the above-mentioned Order.

"Last occupation day" with respect to an unoccupied dwelling means the day on which the dwelling concerned was last occupied, save that where a dwelling which was unoccupied becomes occupied on any day and becomes unoccupied again at the expiry of a period of less than six weeks beginning with that day, for the purpose of determining the last occupation day (and only for that purpose) the dwelling will be treated as having remained unoccupied during that period.

7 Exempt dwellings

An exempt dwelling means any dwelling of a class prescribed by order of the Scottish Ministers and a class of dwelling may be prescribed by reference to (a) the physical characteristics of dwellings; (b) the fact that dwellings are unoccupied or occupied for prescribed purposes or are occupied or owned by people of prescribed descriptions; or (c) such other factors as the Scottish Ministers thinks fit (s.72(6) and (7)).

The Council Tax (Exempt Dwellings) (Scotland) Order 1997 prescribes the following classes of dwelling for which no council tax is payable.
1. An unoccupied and unfurnished dwelling in respect of which (i) less than six months have elapsed since the effective date for the first entry in the valuation list; and (ii) there was no entry in the valuation roll immediately prior to that effective date.
2. A dwelling which is undergoing major repair work to render it habitable or structural alteration (or which has recently undergone such work or alteration). The exemption lasts for a period of 12 months from the date the building was last occupied, or if sooner, six months from substantial completion of the works or alterations;
3. An unoccupied dwelling in respect of which (i) a body established for charitable purposes only is a qualifying person (see **6 Definitions for the purposes of council tax**, above); and (ii) less than six months have elapsed since the last occupation day (see above); and which was on that day occupied in furtherance of the objects of the body in question.
4. A dwelling which is both unoccupied and unfurnished and in respect of which less than six months have elapsed since the end of the last period of three months or more throughout which it was continually occupied.
5. An unoccupied dwelling which on the last occupation day (see above) was the sole or main residence of a person who is, and has throughout the period since that day, been a relevant person (i.e., a person who (i) is disregarded for the purposes of discount by virtue of paragraphs 1, 6, 7, or 8 of Schedule 1 to the Act (people in detention by virtue of a court order, hospital patients, patients in homes in England and Wales, and patients in homes in Scotland); (ii) has his sole or main residence in a place (other than the dwelling concerned or a place referred to in paragraphs 6(1) (a hospital), 7(1)(a) or 8(1)(a) of that Schedule (residential care home, nursing home, private hospital, or a hostel) for the purpose of receiving personal care which he requires by reason of old age, disablement, illness, past or present alcohol or drug dependence, or past or present mental disorder; or (iii) has his sole or main residence in a place (other

than the dwelling concerned) for the purpose of providing, or better providing care for a person of the kind described in (ii)); and is a qualifying person (see above).

6. A dwelling which is not the sole or main residence of any person and in respect of which any liability to pay council tax (but for the terms of the Order) would fall to be met solely out of the estate of a deceased person and either (i) no grant of confirmation to that person's estate has been made; or (ii) no more than six months have passed since such a grant was made.

7. A dwelling the occupation of which is prohibited by law; or which is kept unoccupied by reason of action taken under powers conferred by or under any Act of Parliament, with a view to prohibiting its occupation or to acquiring it.

8. A dwelling which is owned by a local authority, a registered social landlord, or Scottish Homes and is kept unoccupied with a view to having it demolished.

9. A dwelling which is not the sole or main residence of any person and is held by or on behalf of a religious body for the purpose of being available for occupation by a minister of religion as a residence from which to perform the duties of his office.

10. A dwelling which is occupied by at least one person who is either a student; a student's spouse or dependant, being in either case a person who is not a British citizen and who is prevented by the terms of his leave to enter or remain in the United Kingdom from taking paid employment or from claiming benefits; a person under the age of 18; a person who is severely mentally impaired; or a person aged under 20 on the day he is liable for council tax, where that day falls no earlier than 1st May and no later than 31st October in a year, and on 30th April in the year in question he was a student undertaking a qualifying course of education in respect of which the relevant number of hours per week exceed 12 or two or more such qualifying courses in respect of which the aggregate of the relevant number of hours per week for all those courses exceeds 12 and who has since ceased to be a student; and which is not the sole or main residence of any person other than the people mentioned above.

11. An unoccupied dwelling which is not the sole or main residence of any person other than a student or his spouse or dependant as described in paragraph 10 above, which, when last occupied, was occupied by at least one student, and in respect of which less than four months have passed since the last occupation day (see above).

12. A dwelling which is not the sole or main residence of any person and in respect of which each qualifying person (see above) is a student.

13. A dwelling which is not the sole or main residence of any person; in respect of which the qualifying person (see above) (or, where there is more than one such person, one or more of them) is a debtor, or one of the joint debtors, in a heritable security secured over the dwelling; and lawful possession of which has been entered into by the creditor in that heritable security.

14. An unoccupied and unfurnished dwelling which—
    (a) is situated on lands and heritages used for agricultural or pastoral purposes only, or as woodlands, market gardens, orchards, allotments or allotment gardens, or on lands exceeding one-tenth of an hectare used for the purpose of poultry farming; and
    (b) when last occupied and used, was occupied together with and used in connection with the lands and heritages on which the dwelling is situated.

15. A dwelling which is not the sole or main residence of any person, falls within the description mentioned in s.61(4)(a) of the Housing (Scotland) Act 1987 (one of a group of houses with facilities (including a call system and the services of a warden) specially designed or adapted for the needs of people of pensionable age or disabled people); and is held by a registered housing association for the purpose of being available for occupation by such people who are likely in future to have their sole or main residences in other dwellings falling within the same description which are provided by the association.

16. A dwelling which is, or is part of, a hall of residence provided predominantly for the accommodation of students, and which—
    (a) is owned and managed either by an institution within the meaning of paragraph 5(4) of Schedule 1 to the Act (i.e., any educational establishment or other body prescribed by order of the Scottish Ministers) or by a body established for charitable purposes only; or
    (b) is the subject of an agreement allowing such an institution to nominate the majority of the people who are to occupy all the accommodation so provided.

17. A dwelling of which the Secretary of State for Defence is the owner and which is held for the purposes of armed forces accommodation.

18. A dwelling which is the sole or main residence of one or more people under the age of 18 years and of no other person.

19. An unoccupied dwelling which forms part of premises which include another dwelling, or is situated within the curtilage of another dwelling, which is difficult to let separately from that other dwelling, and in respect of which a qualifying person (see above) has his sole or main residence in that other dwelling.

20. A dwelling which falls within either of the classes of lands and heritages specified in Regulation 2(2) and (3) of the Council Tax (Dwellings) (Scotland) Regulations 1992 (broadly, private garages, carports, car parking stances and storage premises, the use of which is ancillary to, and used wholly in connection with, another dwelling).

21. A dwelling (i) which is not the sole or main residence of any person; (ii) an interest in which is vested in a permanent trustee by virtue of s.31(1) or (10) or s.32(6) of the Bankruptcy (Scotland) Act 1985; and (iii) in respect of which that trustee is the only qualifying person (see above).

22. A dwelling in respect of which any of the qualifying persons (see above) is a person who has a relevant association, within the meaning of Part I of the Visiting Forces Act 1952, with a body, contingent, or detachment of the forces of a country to which any provision in that Part applies (other than a dependant who is a British citizen or is ordinarily resident in the UK).

23. A dwelling which is occupied only by one or more people who are disregarded for the purposes of discount by virtue of paragraph 2 of Schedule I to the Act (the severely mentally impaired).

24. A dwelling falling within the scope of Regulation 2(1) of the Council Tax (Dwellings) (Scotland) Regulations 1997 (the cells and communal areas of a prison).

25. a dwelling that is the residence of one or more people who are licensees, tenants or sub-tenants; where a registered prescribed housing support service is being provided to at least one resident; and in respect of which every resident has the right to share the use of a kitchen, bathroom, shower-room or toilet-room, and where such use is shared with at least one other person who is not resident in the dwelling (unless every licensee, tenant and sub-tenant of that dwelling also has the exclusive right to use a kitchen and either a bathroom or shower-room, and where either the bathroom or shower-room contains a toilet, or there is a separate toilet-room which every such licensee, tenant or sub-tenant also has a right to use).

8 Alterations to valuation roll

Dwellings must not be entered in the valuation roll [i.e., the roll reserved for non-domestic subjects] in respect of the financial year 1993-94, or any subsequent financial year, and dwellings in respect of which there is an entry in the valuation roll immediately before 1st April 1993 must, with effect from that date, be deleted from the roll (s.73(1) and (2)). Land and heritages in respect of which there is no entry on the roll because they are domestic subjects within the meaning of s.2(3) of the 1987 Act (see **2 Domestic subjects**, above) and which are not dwellings within the meaning of s.72(2) (see **4 Dwellings chargeable to council tax**, above), are to be entered on the roll with effect from 1st April 1993 (s.73(3)). Where, after that date, any lands or heritages, or any parts thereof, cease to be a dwelling, they must be entered in the valuation role on the date on which they so cease (s.73(4)).

Nothing in s.73 affects the entering in the valuation roll of part residential subjects (s.73(7)).

9 Different amounts for dwellings in different valuation bands

The amounts of council tax payable in respect of dwellings situated in any local authority's area and listed in the different valuation bands will be in the proportion–

$$6: 7: 8: 9: 11: 13: 15: 18$$

where 6 is for dwellings listed in band A, 7 is for dwellings listed in band B, and so on (s.74(1)). This proportion may from time to time be altered by order of the Scottish Ministers (s.74(3)).

S.74(2) prescribes the following valuation bands for dwellings–

A   Not exceeding £27,000
B   Exceeding £27,000 but not exceeding £35,000
C   Exceeding £35,000 but not exceeding £45,000
D   Exceeding £45,000 but not exceeding £58,000
E   Exceeding £58,000 but not exceeding £80,000
F   Exceeding £80,000 but not exceeding £106,000
G   Exceeding £106,000 but not exceeding £212,000
H   Exceeding £212,000

These bands may from time to time be altered by order of the Scottish Ministers (s.74(3)).

B: LIABILITY AND DISCOUNTS

10 Liability to tax

S.75(1) provides that the person who is liable to pay council tax in respect of any chargeable dwelling and any day is the person who falls within the first paragraph of s.75(2) (see below) to apply, taking paragraph (a) first, paragraph (b) next, and so on.

S.75(2) provides that a person falls within the sub-section in relation to any chargeable dwelling and any chargeable day if, on that day–
(a) he is the resident owner of the whole or any part of the dwelling;
(b) he is a resident tenant of the whole or any part of the dwelling;
(c) he is a resident statutory tenant, resident statutory assured tenant, or resident secure tenant of the whole or any part of the dwelling;
(d) he is a resident sub-tenant of the whole or any part of the dwelling;
(e) he is a resident of the dwelling; or

(f) he is any of the following–
    (i) a sub-tenant of the whole or any part of the dwelling under a sub-lease granted for six months or more;
    (ii) the tenant, under a lease granted for a term of six months or more, of any part of the dwelling which is not subject to a sub-lease granted for a term of six months or more; and
    (iii) the owner of any part of the dwelling which is not subject to a lease granted for a term of six months or more.

Where, in relation to any chargeable dwelling and any day, two or more people fall within the first paragraph of s.75(2) to apply, they will be jointly and severally liable to pay the tax payable in respect of the dwelling and that day (s.75(3)).

S.75(3) will not apply as respects any day on which one or more of the people there mentioned fall to be disregarded for the purpose of discount by virtue of either of paragraphs 2 or 4 of Schedule 1 to the Act (the severely mentally impaired and students) and one or more of them do not; and liability to pay the council tax in respect of the dwelling and that day will be determined as follows–
    (a) if only one of those people does not fall to be so disregarded, he will be solely liable;
    (b) if two or more of those people does not fall to be so disregarded, they will each be jointly and severally liable (s.75(4)).

"Resident" in relation to any dwelling means an individual who has attained the age of 18 years and has his sole or main residence in the dwelling; and cognate expressions will be construed accordingly.

S.76(3) and (4) (see below) will have effect in substitution for s.75 in relation to any chargeable dwelling of a class prescribed (s.76(1); see 11 **Chargeable dwellings**, below), and also in cases where the local authority so determines in relation to all dwellings of that class which are situated in their area (s.76(2)). On any day that s.76(3) has effect in relation to a dwelling, the owner of the dwelling will be liable to pay the council tax in respect of the dwelling and that day (s.76(3)) and where on any day two or more people fall within s.76(3), s.75(4) (joint and several liability, see above) will apply as it applies for the purposes of s.75(3) (s.76(4)).

Regulations prescribing a class of chargeable dwellings for the purposes of s.76(1) or (2) may provide that, in relation to any dwelling of that class, s.76(3) will have effect as if for the reference to the owner of the dwelling there were substituted a reference to the person falling within such description as may be prescribed. Further, s.72(7) (see 7 **Exempt dwellings**, above) will apply for the purposes of s.76(1) and (2) as it applies for the purposes of s.72(6).

11 Chargeable dwellings

The following classes of chargeable dwellings have been prescribed for the purposes of s.76(1) by the Council Tax (Liability of Owners) (Scotland) Regulations 1992.

Residential care homes, etc.
1. A dwelling which constitutes all or part of a residential care home, nursing home, private hospital, or hostel (within the meanings of paragraph 8 of Schedule 1 to the 1992 Act (patients in homes in Scotland)).

Religious communities
2. A dwelling occupied by a religious community whose principal occupation is prayer, contemplation, education, or the relief of suffering or consists of two or more of these occupations.

Houses in multiple occupation
3. A dwelling occupied, or which could be occupied, by people who do not constitute a single household and which is occupied by one or more people each of whom–
    (a) is a tenant of, or has a licence to occupy, only a part of the dwelling; or
    (b) has a licence to occupy, but is not liable (alone or jointly with others) to pay rent or a licence fee in respect of the dwelling as a whole.

Resident staff
4. A dwelling–
    (a) in which at least one of the residents is employed in domestic service and resides in the dwelling wholly or mainly for the purposes of his employment;
    (b) any other resident of which is either so employed or is a member of the family of a resident so employed; and
    (c) which is from time to time occupied by the employer of the person referred to in (a).

Ministers of religion
5. A dwelling, which is the sole or main residence of a minister for whose remuneration a person is liable, and from which the minister performs the duties of his office.
    However, in this case the owner is not liable for the tax but the person liable for the remuneration of the minister is so liable.

School boarding accommodation
6. Premises which fall to be treated as a dwelling by virtue of Regulation 4 of, and paragraph 5 of Schedule 1, to the Council Tax (Dwellings and Part Residential Subjects) (Scotland) Regulations 1992 (see 4 **Dwellings chargeable to council tax**, above).

Asylum seekers

7. A dwelling provided to an asylum seeker under, or under arrangements made under, section 95 of the Immigration and Asylum Act 1999 (provision of accommodation and other essential living needs to asylum seekers who appear destitute)

Notes.–

1. For the purposes of these Regulations, tenant includes a secure tenant, statutory tenant or statutory assured tenant (within the meanings assigned by s.75(5) of the Act).
2. Minister means a minister of any religious denomination.

12 Liability of spouses and civil partners

Where a person who is liable to pay council tax in respect of any chargeable dwelling of which he is a resident on any day is married to or in a civil partnership with another person who is also a resident of the dwelling on that day but who would not otherwise be so liable, those persons will be jointly and severally liable to pay the tax (s.77(1)), except where on any day the other person falls to be disregarded for the purposes of discount by virtue of paragraphs 2 or 4 of Schedule 1 to the Act (the severely mentally impaired and students) (s.77(2)).

S.77 also applies to two people living together as husband and wife or as civil partners (s.77(3), (4)).

13 Basic amounts payable

A person who is liable to pay tax in respect of any chargeable dwelling and any day must pay to the local authority for the area in which the dwelling is situated an amount calculated in accordance with the formula–

$$A \text{ divided by } D$$

where–

A   is the amount which, for the financial year in which the day falls and for dwellings in the valuation band listed for the dwelling, has been imposed by the local authority in whose area the dwelling is situated;

D   is the number of days in the financial year (s.78).

14 Discounts

The amount of tax payable in respect of a chargeable dwelling on any day will be subject to a discount equal to the appropriate percentage (see below) of that amount if on that day (s.79(1))–

(a) there is only one resident of the dwelling and he does not fall to be disregarded for the purposes of discount; or

(b) there are two or more residents and each of them except one falls to be disregarded for those purposes.

The amount of tax payable in respect of a chargeable dwelling and any day will be subject to a discount equal to twice the appropriate percentage (see below) of that amount if on that day there are one or more residents of the dwelling and each of them falls to be disregarded for the purposes of discount (s.79(2)).

The appropriate percentage is 25%, or such other percentage as the Scottish Ministers may from time to time prescribe by order (s.79(3)).

Dwellings in which no-one is resident qualify for a 50% discount under the Council Tax (Variation for Unoccupied Dwellings (Scotland) Regulations 2013 (Reg. 3). However, this is a maximum level of discount and local authorities may reduce it to not less than 10% in the case of empty dwellings and second homes. Different provision may be made for different parts of an authority's area. The 50% discount cannot be reduced in the case of certain types of dwelling such as purpose-built holiday homes subject to a planning condition preventing habitation throughout the year, and job-related dwellings. The 50% discount also cannot be modified during the period of 6 months beginning with the day on which the dwelling was purchased by the person who is liable to pay council tax where it is undergoing or requires major repair work to render it habitable, or which is undergoing structural alteration. No discount, or an increase of up to 100% may be imposed where a dwelling has been unoccupied for over a year (unless it is actively being marketed for sale or to let). In determining whether a dwelling has been unoccupied for over a year short periods of occupation as a sole or main residence are ignored and any period when a property has been a second home is regarded as a period of occupation. See also **7 Exempt dwellings**, above, at point 4.

Unoccupied properties owned by a local authority or a registered social landlord cannot be treated more favourably than other unoccupied dwellings solely due to the fact they are owned by a social landlord (s.33(2A) and Reg. 5).

The Council Tax (Administration and Enforcement) (Scotland) Regulations 1992 impose a duty on owners to notify their local authority where their dwelling is unoccupied in cases where they are not paying sufficient council tax due to the authority being unaware of the fact that the dwelling is unoccupied. An authority may impose a penalty, not exceeding £500, on any person who fails to notify it within the period prescribed in regulations.

15 Discount disregards

Under Schedule 1 to the Act and the Council Tax (Discounts) (Scotland) Consolidation and Amendment

Order 2003 as read with the Council Tax (Discounts) (Scotland) Regulations 1992, the following people are to be disregarded for the purposes of discount–

    (a) a person detained in prison (including military detention in specified circumstances), a hospital, or any other place by virtue of a court order;

    (b) a person who is severely and permanently mentally impaired and who (i) is in receipt of one or more of the following benefits (or, had he not reached retirement age, would have been entitled to one of those benefits): short-term or long-term incapacity benefit; attendance allowance; severe disablement allowance; the care component of disability living allowance at the highest or middle rate; an increase in the rate of disablement pension; unemployability supplement; the daily living component of personal independence payment; armed forces independence payment; constant attendance allowance; or an unemployability allowance under the Service Acts or income support, where the applicable amount includes a disability premium on grounds which include incapacity for work, employment and support allowance, or universal credit; or (ii) has a partner who is in receipt of jobseeker's allowance, which is increased on grounds of that person's incapacity for work;

    (c) a person aged 18 or over in respect of whom another person is entitled to child benefit;

    (d) a person who is a student, student nurse, apprentice, or youth training trainee within the definitions prescribed in Articles 5, 6, 7, 8, and 9 of the 2003 Order;

    (e) a patient whose sole or main residence is in a hospital;

    (f) a person whose sole or main residence is in a residential care home, nursing home, private hospital, or a hostel being a hostel (i) in which residential accommodation is provided and which is managed by a housing association registered under s.3 of the Housing Associations Act 1985; or (ii) operated other than on a commercial basis, the funds for which are provided wholly or in part by a Government department or agency or a local authority; or (iii) managed by a voluntary organisation, and where the sole or main function of any of the above-mentioned establishments is to provide personal care or support to people having their sole or main residence in the establishment (For this purpose personal care includes the provision of appropriate help with physical and social needs, and support means counselling or other help provided as part of a planned programme of care.);

    (g) a care worker who provides care or support (or both) to another person or persons where the carer is either (a) providing the care and support in question on behalf of a local authority the Crown, or a charity (a relevant body), or as an employee of the person concerned to whom he was introduced by the relevant body, and in either case works for at least 24 hours a week for remuneration of not more than £44 and resides on premises provided by the employer or by the relevant body for the better performance of his work; or (b) is providing care or support (or both) for an average of at least 35 hours a week to a person who is entitled to one of the qualifying social security benefits specified, is not that person's spouse, civil partner, or cohabitee or (where that person is aged under 18) his or her parent), and resides in the same dwelling as the person for whom he is providing care or support (or both);

    (h) a person whose sole or main residence is in a dwelling providing residential accommodation, whether as a hostel, night shelter, or otherwise, and the accommodation is predominantly provided–

        (i) otherwise than in separate and self-contained sets of premises;

        (ii) for people of no fixed abode and no settled way of life; and

        (iii) under licences to occupy not constituting tenancies;

    (i) people who are members (or dependants of members) of certain international and defence organisations;

    (j) a person who is a member of a religious community the principal occupation of which consists of prayer, contemplation, education, the relief of suffering, or any combination of these, and who is dependent on his community to provide for his material needs;

    (k) a person aged under 20 who has within a relevant period (i.e., the period after 30th April and before 1st November in any year), ceased to undertake a qualifying course of education or a full time course of education (as defined by he 2003 Order). (The day in question must be within the same relevant period as that in which the cessation takes place);

    (l) members of visiting forces and their dependants who are neither British citizens nor ordinarily resident in the United Kingdom; and

    (m) the spouse, civil partner, or dependant of a student who is not a British citizen and who is prevented by the terms of his leave to enter and remain in the United Kingdom from taking paid employment or from claiming benefits.

16 Reduced amounts

The Scottish Ministers may make regulations as regards any case where a person is liable to pay an amount to a local authority in respect of council tax for any financial year which is prescribed; and prescribed conditions are fulfilled (s.80(1)). The regulations may provide that the amount he is liable to pay shall be an amount which is less than the amount it would be, apart from the regulations, and is determined in accordance with prescribed rules (s.80(2)). S.80 applies whether the amount mentioned in s.80(1) (see above) is determined under s.78 (see **13 Basic amounts payable**, above) or under that section as read with s.79 (see **14 Discounts**, above).

Retrospective changes in valuation band–The Council Tax (Reduction of Liability) (Scotland) Regulations 1994 provide for the reduction of amounts payable by way of council where, on or after 12th January 1995, a local assessor alters a valuation list so as to place a dwelling retrospectively in a more expensive valuation band (and that alteration has not been made to reflect a material increase in the value of the dwelling since the inception of the council tax regime). Liability in respect of the dwelling will in most cases be calculated as if the alteration did not have effect until the first day of the month following that in which it is made. Accordingly, s.79 of the Act (see **14 Discounts**, above); the Council Tax (Reduction for Disabilities) (Scotland) Regulations 1992 (see below); the Council Tax Reduction (Scotland) Regulations 2012; and the Council Tax Reduction State Pension Credit) (Scotland) Regulations 2012 all have effect as if the band had been shown on the list for that day (Reg. 4).

Disability—The Council Tax (Reductions for Disabilities) (Scotland) Regulations 1992, made for the above mentioned purpose, provide that a liable person will be entitled to a reduction in the amount of council tax payable as regards a dwelling if he is the liable person as regards a dwelling which is the sole or main residence of at least one person who is substantially and permanently disabled (whether by illness, injury, congenital deformity, or otherwise) (a qualifying individual) and in which there is provided within the dwelling (i) a room (other than a bathroom, kitchen or lavatory) required for meeting the needs of any qualifying individual resident in the dwelling; or (ii) an additional bathroom or kitchen which is required for meeting the needs of any qualifying individual resident in the dwelling; or (iii) sufficient floor space to permit the use of a wheelchair required for meeting the needs of any qualifying individual resident in the dwelling; and as regards the financial year in question, an application is made in writing to the local authority.

References in (i), (ii), and (iii) above to anything being required for meeting the needs of a qualifying individual are references to its being essential or of major importance to his well-being by reason of the nature and extent of his disability.

A wheelchair is not required for meeting an individual's needs if he does not need to use it within the living accommodation comprising or included in the dwelling concerned.

17 Energy efficiency discounts

Local authorities must establish schemes for reducing the amounts which persons are liable to pay in respect of council tax where improvements are made to the energy efficiency of chargeable dwellings (Local Government Finance Act 1992, s.80A). Authorities have a discretion to design schemes as they see fit but a discount may only be given where–

    (a) person is liable to pay council tax in respect of a chargeable dwelling and any day;

    (b) improvements are made to the energy efficiency of that dwelling (whether by the person liable to pay or not);

    (c) those improvements are made during the same financial year to which the reduction of the amount which the person is liable to pay in respect of council tax relates;

    (d) the amount which the person is liable to pay in respect of that year has not already been reduced under the scheme in respect of those improvements; and

    (e) the amount which any other person is liable to pay in respect of council tax in respect of that dwelling and that year has not been reduced under the scheme in respect of those improvements.

The minimum reduction which may be provided for under an energy efficiency discount scheme is £50 (or where the amount which the person is liable to pay in respect of council tax is less than £50, an amount equal to that person's liability).

C: VALUATION

18 Appeal to valuation appeal committee

A person may appeal to a Valuation Appeal Committee if he is aggrieved by–

    (a) any decision of a local authority that a dwelling is chargeable, or that he is liable to pay council tax in respect of such a dwelling; or

    (b) any calculation (or estimate) made by a local authority of an amount which he is liable to pay to the authority in respect of council tax,

and the committee will make such decision as they think just (s.81(1)).

S.81(1) will not apply where the grounds on which the person concerned is aggrieved fall within such category or categories as may be prescribed (s.81(3)). Part III of the Council Tax (Alteration of Lists and Appeals) (Scotland) Regulations 1993 provides (Reg. 21) that s.81(1) of the Act will not apply where the grounds on which the person concerned is aggrieved are that any assumption as to the future that is required by Part V of the Administration Regulations to be made in the calculation of an amount payable as council tax or council water charge may prove to be inaccurate.

An appeal under s.81(1) may not be made unless the aggrieved person has served a written notice on the local authority, and one of the following conditions is then fulfilled (s.81(4))–

    (i) the authority have notified the aggrieved person that they believe the grievance to be ill-founded, but the person is still aggrieved;

    (ii) the authority have notified the aggrieved person that steps have been taken to deal with the grievance, but the person is still aggrieved;

(iii) two months have passed since the date of service of the aggrieved person's notice, but he has received no notification from the authority (s.81(7)).

The Scottish Ministers may, by regulations make provision for the procedure to be followed in appeals under s.81 (s.82). Part III of the above-mentioned Regulations (Reg. 22) provides that an appeal under s.81(1) must be initiated by serving a written notice of appeal on the local authority containing the grounds on which the appeal is made and the date on which the aggrieved person's notice under s.81(4) of the Act was served on the local authority. A notice of appeal must be served within four months of the date of service by him of the first notice under s.81(4) bringing the grievance in question to the attention of the local authority. On receipt of a notice of appeal the local authority must transmit it to the secretary or assistant secretary of the relevant local valuation panel.

19 New dwellings

S.83(1) introduces Schedule 6 to the Act which makes provision with respect to the determination of a day as the completion day in relation to a new building which, or any part of which, will constitute or constitutes a dwelling.

S.83(2) provides that a dwelling in a new building shall be deemed for the purposes of council tax to have come into existence on the day determined under that Schedule as the completion day in respect of that building, whether or not the building is completed on that day.

Where a day is determined under that Schedule as the completion day in relation to a new building, and the building is one produced by the structural alteration of a building which consists of one or more existing dwellings, the existing dwelling or dwellings will be deemed for the purposes of council tax to have ceased to exist on that day (s.83(3)).

Any reference in s.83 or Schedule 6 to a new building includes a reference to a building produced by the structural alteration of an existing building where—

(a) the existing building constitutes a dwelling which, by virtue of the alteration, becomes, or becomes part of, a different dwelling or different dwellings; or

(b) the existing building does not, except by virtue of the alteration, constitute a dwelling.

Building includes a reference to a part of a building (s.83(4) and (5)).

Paragraph 1 of Schedule 6 provides that where a local assessor is of the opinion that the erection of a new building has been completed, or the work remaining to be done on a building is such that its erection can reasonably be expected to be completed within three months and that the building constitutes, or when completed will constitute, a dwelling, he may serve on the owner of the building a notice (a completion notice) stating that the erection of the building is to be treated for the purposes of the Schedule as completed on the date of service of the notice or on such later date as may be specified by the notice.

A person on whom a completion notice is served may either agree in writing that the building has been completed, or may appeal against the notice within 21 days to a valuation appeal tribunal, on the ground that the building has not been or, as the case may be, cannot reasonably be expected to be, completed by the specified date.

If a completion notice is not withdrawn or no appeal is brought against the notice or such an appeal is abandoned or dismissed, the erection of the building will be treated as completed on the date specified by the notice; and if such an appeal is brought and is not abandoned or dismissed and the completion notice in question is not withdrawn, the erection of the building will be treated as completed on such date as the valuation appeal committee shall determine (para. 2).

20 Compilation and maintenance of valuation lists

The local assessor for each new local authority must compile for the council for that area, from the existing valuation lists, a valuation list as at 1st April 1996 (1994 Act, s.26(1)). The provisions of s.84 of the 1992 Act (compilation and maintenance of valuation lists) will apply, with any necessary modifications, to a valuation list compiled under s.26(1) of the 1994 Act as they apply to a valuation list compiled under s.84. S.84(1) and (2) of the 1992 Act provides for a local assessor to maintain the valuation list so compiled for that new authority, which, for each day that it is in force, must show each dwelling which is situated in the local authority's area and which of the valuation bands is applicable to the dwelling (s.84(1) and (2)). A list must also contain such information about dwellings shown in it as may be prescribed. The Council Tax (Contents of Valuation Lists) (Scotland) Regulations 1992 provide that the valuation list must contain, in addition to the matters required to be shown by s.84(2), the following matters, namely, (a) the reference number ascribed to the dwelling by the local assessor; (b) where the list is altered as regards the dwelling, a note from the day from which the alteration has effect and, if it be the case, a note that the alteration was made pursuant to an order of a valuation appeal committee or the Court of Session; and (c) where the dwelling falls within either of the classes of land and heritages specified in paragraphs (2) and (3) of Regulation 2 of the Council Tax (Dwellings) (Scotland) Regulations 1992 (see **4 Dwellings chargeable to council tax**, above, paragraphs (2) and (3)), a note that that is the case.

A list had to be compiled on 1st April 1993 and will come into force on that day (s.84(6)). S.26(6) provides that a local assessor shall compile a list under s.26 by extrapolating from the existing valuation lists and, accordingly, except to the extent that valuation may be required to be carried out under any provision of the 1992 Act, must not carry out any valuation of property for the purposes of a list compiled under s.26.

The assessor must send to each council for which he acts as assessor a copy of this list for that council's area and, as soon as practicable after the receipt of that list, each council must deposit a copy of the list at their office and take such steps as they think fit for giving notice of it (s.85).

Article 2 of the Rating Valuation and Council Tax (Miscellaneous Provisions) (Scotland) Order 1996 make provision so as to ensure *inter alia* continuity in the transition to the new assessors.

21 Valuation of dwellings

In order to enable him to compile a valuation list under s.84 (see above), a local assessor must carry out a valuation of such of the dwellings in his area as he considers necessary or expedient for the purpose of determining which of the valuation bands applies to each dwelling (s.86(1)). The valuation will be carried out by reference to 1st April 1991 and on such assumptions and in accordance with such principles as may be prescribed (s.86(2)). The Council Tax (Valuation of Dwellings) (Scotland) Regulations 1992 provide that for the purpose of valuations under s.86(2) and valuations carried out in connection with proposals to the alteration of a valuation list (see below), the value of any dwelling will be taken to be the amount which the dwelling might reasonably have been expected to realise if it had been sold in the open market by a willing seller on that date and on the assumptions specified in Regulation 2(2) and, where applicable, the additional assumption mentioned in Regulation 3(1)(a), (b), or (c), as the case may be. Regulation 3 sets out additional assumptions which are to be applied in respect of a dwelling occupied in connection with agriculture or fish farming.

The assumptions are–
(a) that the sale was with vacant possession;
(b) that the dwelling was sold free from any heritable security;
(c) that the size and layout of the dwelling, and the physical state of its locality, were the same as at the time when the valuation of the dwelling is made or, in the case of a valuation carried out in connection with a proposal for the alteration of a valuation list, as at the date from which that alteration would have effect;
(d) that the dwelling was in a state of reasonable repair;
(e) in the case of a dwelling the owner or occupier of which is entitled to use common parts, that those parts were in a like state of repair and the purchaser would be liable to contribute towards the cost of keeping them in such a state;
(f) in the case of a dwelling which contains certain fixtures designed to make the dwelling suitable for use by a disabled person and add to the value of the dwelling, that the fixtures were not included in the dwelling;
(g) that the use of the dwelling would be permanently restricted to use as a private dwelling; and
(h) that the dwelling had no development value other than value attributable to permitted development.

In determining what is reasonable repair in relation to a dwelling for the above purposes, the age and character of the dwelling and its locality will be taken into account.

Where it appears to an assessor that, having regard to the above-mentioned principles and assumptions, a dwelling clearly falls within a particular band, an individual valuation need not be carried out (s.86(3)).

22 Alteration of lists

S.87 and the Council Tax (Alteration of Lists and Appeals) (Scotland) Regulations 1993 provide for the alteration of council tax valuation lists and for appeals to a valuation appeal committee where there is a disagreement about an alteration between an assessor and another person making a proposal for the alteration of a list. In particular, the Regulations impose the following restrictions on alteration of valuation bands (Reg. 4). No alteration will be made of a valuation band shown in the list as applicable to any dwelling unless–
(a) since the valuation band was first shown in the list as applicable to the dwelling–
    (i) there has been a material increase in the value of the dwelling and it, or any part of it, has subsequently been sold; or
    (ii) subject to what is said below, there has been a material reduction in the value of the dwelling;
(b) the local assessor is satisfied that–
    (i) a different valuation band should have been determined by him as applicable to the dwelling, or
    (ii) the band shown in the list is not that determined by him as so applicable; or
(c) the assessor has, under Schedule 5 to the Act, added, amended, or deleted an apportionment note relating to any lands and heritages included in the valuation roll; or
(d) there has been a successful appeal under the Act against the valuation band shown in the list.

Where a material reduction in the value of a dwelling is caused wholly by the demolition of any part of the dwelling, the valuation band will not be altered if–
(a) the works of demolition are part of, or connected with, a building, engineering, or other operation which has been carried out, is in progress, or is proposed to be carried out in relation to the dwelling, and
(b) the market value of the dwelling immediately before the commencement of the relevant works is less than it would have been had the dwelling then been in the same physical state as it is in immediately after completion of those works.

For this purpose, market value means the amount which the dwelling might reasonably have been expected to realise if it had been sold in the open market by a willing seller, and relevant works means the works of demolition and the building, engineering, or other operation of which those works of demolition are part or with which they are connected.

Where a dwelling is shown on the list as compiled, no proposal for alteration of the valuation band first shown in respect of the dwelling on the grounds that it is not the band which should have been so shown may be made after 30th November 1993; however, *inter alia* where a person first becomes a taxpayer in respect of a dwelling after 31st May 1993, the person may, in general, make a proposal in relation to that dwelling within six months of becoming a taxpayer.

Part IV of the Regulations specifies the procedure in relation to appeals *inter alia* with respect to alteration of valuation lists.

23 Valuation lists: supplemental

S.89 of the Act gives local assessors power to enter properties for valuation purposes, provided that at least three days' clear notice in writing has been given to the occupier. It is an offence to wilfully delay or obstruct a person in the exercise of this power.

Under s.90, a local assessor may serve a notice on the owner or occupier of any dwelling in his area, requesting that person to supply to the assessor, within 21 days, information of a nature prescribed in the notice. It is an offence to fail to provide such information, or to supply false information.

A person may require a local assessor or local authority to give him access to such information as will enable him to establish the state of a valuation list. Any such requirement must be complied with at a reasonable time and place without payment being sought (s.91).

A person may, at a reasonable time and free of charge, inspect any proposal made, or notice of appeal given, under regulations made under s.87 (see above)) (s.92).

D: ADMINISTRATIVE PROVISIONS

24 Setting of council tax

In respect of the financial year 1993-94, and each subsequent year, a local authority must set an amount of council tax, as appropriate, to be paid in respect of a chargeable dwelling in their area listed in valuation band D, and determine the amount of tax to be paid in respect of a chargeable dwelling in each of the other valuation bands in accordance with the proportion mentioned in s.74(1) (see **9 Different amounts for dwellings in different valuation bands**, above (s.93(1)).

A local authority must set its tax before 11th March in the financial year preceding that for which it is set, but it is not invalid if set at a later date (s.93(2)).

The amounts set by an authority under s.93(1) must be such as will provide sufficient money to meet such part of the total estimated expenses to be incurred by that authority during the financial year in respect of which the amount is set as falls to be met out of their council tax together with such additional sum as is, in their opinion required–
(a) to cover expenses previously incurred;
(b) to meet contingencies;
(c) to meet any expenses which may fall to be met before the money to be received in respect of their council tax for the next financial year will become available (s.93(3)).

25 Substituted and reduced settings

A local authority may set, in substitution for an amount of tax already set, a lesser amount of tax for the same financial year (s.94(1)). Schedule 7 to the Act provides for the reduction of tax where the Scottish Ministers are satisfied, in accordance with that Schedule, that the total estimated expenses mentioned in s.93(3) (see above) of a local authority are excessive or that an increase in those expenses is excessive (s.94(2)).

Where a person has paid by reference to one setting of tax more tax than is due under a substituted or reduced setting, the balance will be repaid to that person if he so requires or, if he does not, the balance will either be repaid to him or credited against subsequent liability to council tax (s.94(8)).

26 Information

Within 21 days of setting a tax, a local authority must publish notice of the fact in at least one newspaper circulating in their area. The notice must include the amounts payable in respect of chargeable dwellings in each valuation band (s.96).

27 Levying and collection of tax

A local authority must levy and collect the council tax set by them in respect of their area (s.97(1)).

28 Administration

Schedule 2 to the 1992 Act contains provisions relating to the administration and collection of council tax. Schedule 3 (para. 6) contains provision for civil penalties, and Schedule 8 for the recovery of sums due, including sums due as penalties. The Council Tax (Administration and Enforcement) (Scotland) Regulations 1992 make further provision for the administration and enforcement of the 1992 Act.

Part V of the Regulations makes provision for the billing of people liable to the tax. Each financial year a local authority is required to serve a demand notice on every liable person as soon as practicable after they have set an amount of council tax for the relevant year. A demand notice must require the amount shown therein to be paid by instalments in accordance with Part I of Schedule I to the Regulations (Regs. 17 to 21).

No payment on account of the chargeable amount (whether interim, final, or sole) need be made unless a notice served under Part V requires it.

Where a notice under Part V is addressed to a liable person or liable persons, any other person who is jointly and severally liable with that person or those persons for payment of council tax and the council water charge in respect of the dwelling and the period to which the notice relates will be jointly and severally liable to make any payments required by the notice (Reg. 18).

A demand notice having been served on a liable person, instalments in respect of the council tax to which the notice relates are payable, and any such instalment is not paid, the local authority must serve a notice (a reminder notice) on the liable person stating (a) the instalments required to be paid; (b) if they are not paid within the period of seven days beginning with the day on which a reminder notice is issued, the unpaid balance of the estimated amount will become payable by him at the expiry of a further period of seven days beginning with the day of the failure; and (c) where the notice is the second such notice as regards the relevant year, if the liable person fails to pay any subsequent instalment as regards that year on or before the day on which it falls due, the unpaid balance of the estimated amount will become payable by him on the day following the day of the failure (Reg. 22).

By virtue of Regulation 24, a local authority may agree to accept lump sum payments of at least two instalments, being a lump sum which is of an amount determined by the authority and less than the estimated amount. Further provision is made for lump sum payments as follows. Lump sum payments cannot be accepted unless (a) the determination as to the cases where a lump sum will be accepted and as to the amount of the sum in those cases was made by the authority before the day on which they first set an amount for the relevant year; (b) under those determinations people liable to pay the same number of instalments in the relevant year are treated alike; and (c) the single lump sum payment must be made on or before the day on which the first instalment falls due under the notice.

A local authority may also accept a discounted amount in such cases as they may determine and in satisfaction of any liability of a person to pay to them any instalment or other payment due under the demand notice provided that the discounted amount is paid to the authority otherwise than by either bank notes or coin; and the determinations as to the cases where a discounted amount will be accepted and as to the proportion that the amount is to bear to the amount of the instalment or other payment due must be made by the authority on or before the day on which they first set an amount for the relevant year (Reg. 25).

29 Enforcement

Schedule 8 to the Act and Part VII of the Council Tax (Administration and Enforcement) (Scotland) Regulations 1992 are concerned with the recovery of sums due by way of council tax (under Part V of the Regulations—see above).

Where any or all of the above-mentioned sums have not been paid, they may be recovered by the local authority by diligence authorised by a summary warrant or in pursuance of a decree granted in an action of payment. The sheriff, on an application by the authority accompanied by a certificate from them, must grant a summary warrant authorising the recovery, by either of the following diligences: (a) an earnings arrestment; or (b) an arrestment and action of furthcoming or sale of the amount of the sum remaining due and unpaid along with a surcharge of 10% of that amount. The certificate from a local authority accompanying their application for a summary warrant must contain specified particulars. Broadly these particulars are—

(a) a statement that the people specified in the application have not paid the sums to which the application relates;

(b) the authority have served a reminder notice on each such person;

(c) a period of 14 days has expired without full payment of the sums due, or the notice required under s.81 (see **18 Appeal to valuation appeal committee**, above) being served on the authority by any of the people concerned or that such notice having been served, the authority have notified him in writing as specified in s.81(7)(a) or (b) or the period of two months as specified in s.81(7)(c) has expired; and

(d) specification of the amount due and unpaid by each person.

It will be incompetent for a sheriff to grant a summary warrant for recovery of any of the above-mentioned sums if an action has already been raised for the recovery of that sum, and, on the raising of an action for the recovery of any such sum, any existing summary warrant in so far as it relates to the recovery of that sum will cease to have effect. It will also be incompetent to raise an action in Scotland for the recovery of any of the above-mentioned sums if, in pursuance of a summary warrant, any of the above-mentioned diligences for the recovery of that sum has been executed.

Where a levying authority have obtained a summary warrant or a decree against a debtor in respect of arrears of sums payable under paragraph 1(1) of Schedule 8 to the Act or by virtue of an order made under s.79 of the Local Government etc. (Scotland) Act 1994 and the debtor is entitled to income support, the levying authority may, without prejudice to its right to pursue any other means of recovering such arrears, apply to the

Scottish Ministers asking them to deduct sums from any amounts payable to the debtor by way of income support in order to secure the payment of any outstanding sum which is or forms part of the amount in respect of which the summary warrant or decree was granted.

30 Supply of information

A local authority may supply relevant information to any person who requests it (Local Government Finance Act 1992, Sch. 2 para 17). "Relevant information" is information which has been obtained by the authority for the purpose of carrying out its council tax functions and which is not "personal information". "Personal information" is information which relates to an individual (living or dead) who can be identified from that information or from that and other information supplied to any person by the authority; and personal information includes any expression of opinion about the individual and any indication of the intentions of any person in respect of the individual. The Council Tax (Supply of Information) (Scotland) Regulations 2003 provide that a fee of up to £500 may be charged for the supply of such information.

HM Revenue and Customs may supply information held by them to a Scottish local authority, a person authorised to exercise any function of such an authority relating to council tax, and a person providing services to such an authority relating to council for the purposes of (Council Tax (Information-sharing in relation to Council Tax Reduction) (Scotland) Regulations 2013, S.I. No. 87)–

(a) determining applications for a council tax reduction;

(b) review of and appeals against such determinations;

(c) the prevention or detection of fraud or error in reductions that are awarded; and

(d) action as a result of a fraudulent application.

31 Authorities

Statutes–

Caravans (Standard Community Charge and Rating) Act 1991

Local Government etc. (Scotland) Act 1994

Local Government Finance Acts 1988 and 1992

Local Government (Financial Provisions etc.)

Statutory Instruments–

Abolition of Domestic Rates (Domestic and Part Residential Subjects) (Scotland) Regulations 1988, (No. 2) Regulations 1989, and 1990 Regulations (S.I. 1988 No. 1477, 1989 No. 1477, and 1990 No. 630)

Council Tax (Administration and Enforcement) (Scotland) Regulations 1992, as amended (S.I. 1992 Nos. 1332 and 3290, 1994 No. 3170, 1996 Nos. 430 and 746, S.S.I. 2000 No. 261, 2006 No. 402, and 2012 Nos. 303 and 332)

Council Tax (Alteration of Lists and Appeals) (Scotland) Regulations 1993, as amended (S.I. 1993 No. 355, 1996 No. 580, and S.S.I. 2012 No. 303)

Council Tax (Contents of Valuation Lists) (Scotland) Regulations 1992 (S.I. 1992 No. 1330)

Council Tax (Deductions from Income Support) Regulations 1993, as amended (S.I. 1993 No. 494 and 1996 No. 712)

Council Tax (Variation for Unoccupied Dwellings) (Scotland) Regulations 2013 (S.S.I. 2013 No. 45)

Council Tax (Discounts) (Scotland) Consolidation and Amendment Order 2003, as amended (S.S.I. 2003 No. 176, 2007 No. 214, and S.I. 2008 No. 1879, 2013 Nos. 65, 137, and 142, 2014 No. 37, and 2015 No. 153)

Council Tax (Discounts) (Scotland) Regulations 1992, as amended (S.I. 1992 No. 1409, 1993 No. 342, 1994 No. 629, 1995 No. 597, 1996 No. 580, 1997 No. 587, 2005 No. 572, 2007 No. 213, and 2013 Nos. 65 and 142)

Council Tax (Dwellings and Part Residential Subjects) (Scotland) Regulations 1992, as amended (S.I. 1992 No. 2955 and S.S.I. 2002 No. 102)

Council Tax (Dwellings) (Scotland) Regulations 1992, 1993, and 1997 (S.I. 1992 No. 1334, 1993 No. 526, 1997 No. 673, and 2010 No. 35)

Council Tax (Exempt Dwellings) (Scotland) Order 1997, as amended (S.I. 1997 No. 728, 1998 No. 561, 1999 No. 757, S.S.I. 2000 No. 140, 2002 No. 101, 2006 No. 402, 2007 No. 215, and 2012 No. 339)

Council Tax (Liability of Owners) (Scotland) Regulations 1992, as amended (S.I. 1992 No. 1331, 1993 No. 344, 2000 No. 715, and 2003 No. 137)

Council Tax (Reductions for Disabilities) (Scotland) Regulations 1992, as amended (S.I. 1992 No. 1335, 1996 No. 580, 1999 No. 756, and S.S.I. 2012 No. 303)

Council Tax (Reduction of Liability) (Scotland) Regulations 1994, as amended (S.I. 1994 No. 3170 and S.S.I. 2012 No. 303)

Council Tax (Supply of Information) (Scotland) Regulations 2003 (S.S.I. 2003 No. 147)

Council Tax (Valuation of Dwellings) (Scotland) Regulations 1992, as amended (S.I. 1992 No. 1329 and 1993 No. 354)

INCOME TAX: EMPLOYMENT INCOME

Contents

This Note covers the main rules as to the taxation of employment income. It has been arranged as follows–

A: INTRODUCTION

1 Introduction

In addition to employees, the provisions relating to income tax apply to apprentices, those in the service of the Crown, and office holders (ITEPA, ss.4 and 5).

The current rates of reliefs and allowances are given in the Note on **Income Tax: General provisions** at para **19 Personal allowances**.

2 Taxable earnings

There are two types of "income" chargeable to income tax. These are known as "general earnings" and "specific employment income" (s.7). General earnings are salaries, wages, fees, etc. Specific employment income is any other amount which counts as employment income (e.g., share-related income and payments to pension schemes, etc: as to which see the Note on **Income Tax: Other Income subject to Income Tax**).

Income tax is paid on "taxable earnings" and "taxable specific income", that is the total of earnings and specific income less any allowable deductions.

There are special rules where an employee–
(a) is resident and ordinarily resident but not domiciled in the UK (see ss.20-24);
(b) is resident, but not ordinarily resident in the UK (see ss.25, 26, and 28);
(c) is not resident in the UK (see ss.27 and 28); or
(d) earns earnings abroad, but remits them to the UK (see ss.33 and 34),
but these rules are not covered here.

Under s.6(5), the duties of divers and diving supervisors working on the seabed are treated as a trade or profession falling under ITTOIA, Part 2, above.

Under s.684, the Commissioners have made regulations with respect to the assessment, charge, collection, and recovery of income tax under ITEPA, which provide, in particular, for the deduction of the tax by the person paying the earnings, the accounting for it, and the production of wages sheets and other records (Pay As You Earn–see the Note on **Income Tax: Pay As You Earn**).

3 Occasional residence abroad

A person who has been both a UK resident and ordinarily resident in the UK, and who has left for the purpose only of occasional residence abroad will be treated as UK resident for the purpose of determining their income tax liability in any tax year (ITA, s.829).

4 Employment abroad

Where a person works full-time in a foreign trade, profession or vocation and/or employment or office, no part of which is carried on in the UK, and his duties are performed wholly abroad, the question of his residence is decided without regard to any place of abode maintained in the UK for his use (ITA, s.830).

As an extra-statutory concession, for the income tax year in which a person comes to the UK to take up permanent residence or stay for at least two years, his income from abroad is not assessed on the basis of the income for a full income tax year but is computed by reference to the period of his residence here during the year. A similar practice is adopted for the income tax year in which a person ceases to reside in this country if he has left here for permanent residence abroad. The concession extends to where a person goes abroad under a contract of employment provided that the absence abroad and the employment both extend over a period covering a complete tax year and interim visits to the UK during the period do not exceed 183 days in any tax year (or an average of 91 days over up to 4 years) (IRI, A11).

No relief of any kind is given to a person who is not resident in the UK unless the Commissioners are satisfied that he or she (ITA, s.56)–
(a) is a present or former servant of the Crown, or an employee of a missionary society or in the service of a protected territory; or

(b) is resident in the Isle of Man or the Channel Islands; or

(c) has previously resided within the UK and is resident abroad for health reasons; or

(d) is a person whose late spouse/civil partner was in Crown service.

As to the situation where income which is subject to tax has already been taxed under the laws of another country, see the Note on **Income Tax: Other Income subject to Income Tax** at para **28 Double taxation**.

5 Agency workers

Where a person, through an agency, personally provides, or is under an obligation to personally provide services to another and is subject to supervision, direction or control as to the manner in which the services are provided, then any earnings received in consequence of the agency contract are taxed as earnings from that employment (ITEPA, s.44).

Certain agency arrangements are excluded from this provision, in particular where the services provided are "entertainment" services (singing, acting, modelling) or are provided at the worker's own home or on premises neither controlled or managed by the client nor prescribed by the nature of the services (s.47). In such cases, the earnings are treated as self-employed earnings.

6 Intermediaries

Similar provisions apply to services provided through intermediaries as apply to services provided through agencies. The worker will generally be regarded as receiving earnings from employment and will be liable to income tax on those earnings (ss.48 to 61).

7 Profit sharing schemes

Special tax provisions apply with regard to profit sharing schemes, profit related pay, and share option schemes (including enterprise management incentives), but these are beyond the scope of this work.

8 Employment income provided by third parties

Where trusts and other intermediate vehicles are used in arrangements aimed at providing value to an individual for what is in substance a reward or recognition in connection with their employment, or a loan in connection with their employment, there will be a charge to tax (ITEPA, Part 7A (ss.554A to 554Z21). In effect, the following will be treated as PAYE income and taxed accordingly–

(a) sums or assets earmarked for employees by trusts or other intermediaries;

(b) loans provided to employees by trusts and other intermediaries;

(c) assets provided to employees by trusts and other intermediaries;

(d) sums or assets that are earmarked by the employer with a view to a trust or other intermediary providing retirement benefits to the employee.

There are numerous exceptions for arrangements that cannot be used for tax avoidance purposes, including the protection of rewards provided by group companies, share incentive arrangements and genuine deferred remuneration arrangements.

ITEPA Part 7A does not apply to payments chargeable to tax as pension income.

B: TAXABLE BENEFITS

9 Introduction

Certain benefits received during the course of employment are treated as income and so are taxable. These taxable benefits are known as the "Benefits Code" (ITEPA, s.63).

If a job is (s.216)–

(a) classed as "lower paid employment"; and

(b) either (i) the employee is not employed as a director of a company; or (ii) the company is non-profit making (i.e., non-trading and not established primarily for holding investments or property), or established only for charitable purposes,

then certain provisions of the Benefits Code do not apply, with the result that such benefits are not taxable.

"Lower paid employment" is employment with earnings of less than £8,500 per year (s.217).

The only provisions of the Benefits Code which do apply to such lower paid jobs are Chapter 4 (vouchers and credit tokens: see **11 Vouchers and credit tokens**, below), and Chapter 5 (living accommodation: see **12 Living accommodation**, below).

As an extra-statutory concession, the provision of board and lodging to certain lower paid agricultural workers is also disregarded for the purposes of income tax (IR1, A60).

10 Expenses

The general rule is that expenses payments will be taxable if (ITEPA, s.70)–

(a) they are paid to an employee by way of expenses and are paid to him by reason of his employment; or

(b) they are paid away (i.e., spent) by an employee and the sum paid away was put at the employee's disposal by his employer in respect of expenses for which they were used.

In many cases, although the expenses are taxable, there will be a corresponding deduction allowed from taxable income under ss.336-8, 340-44, 346, 351, or 353 (see D: ALLOWABLE DEDUCTIONS, below) (s.72).

11 Vouchers and credit tokens

Cash Vouchers

A cash voucher provided to an employee (or a member of his family) by his employer will be taxable if it is provided by reason of his employment unless the employer is an individual and the voucher is provided in the normal course of the employer's domestic, family or personal relationships (ITEPA, ss.73 and 74).

A "cash voucher" is a voucher, stamp or similar document capable of being exchanged for a sum of money which is not substantially less than that incurred by the person who paid for it (s.75). A voucher is still a cash voucher even if it can also be exchanged for goods or services, whether it can be exchanged on its own or only with other vouchers and irrespective of when it can be exchanged. The voucher will be taxed on it exchange value (s.81).

The provision does not apply to a voucher if it is of a kind made available to the public generally and is not made available to the employee on more favourable terms (s.78). Nor does the provision apply to schemes "approved" by HM Revenue and Customs which come within the PAYE regulations (s.79).

Non-cash vouchers

Similar rules apply to non-cash vouchers. A non-cash voucher is a voucher which does not come within the definition of a cash voucher and which is (i) capable of being exchanged for money, goods or services; (ii) a childcare voucher; (iii) a transport voucher; or (iv) a cheque voucher (s.84).

Where the non-cash voucher is a meal voucher, then the first 15p of any voucher for each day is not chargeable to tax, if (s.89) (*repealed from 1st April 2013*)–

(a) the voucher is non-transferable and can only be used for meals;

(b) they are available to all the employer's staff in lower paid employment (as to which see **9 Introduction**, above); and

(c) they are not otherwise exempt under s.317 (see **55 Meals**, below).

Credit tokens

Similar rules apply to credit tokens. A "credit token" is a credit or debit card or similar card, token or document which enables the holder to obtain money, goods or services on credit and which does not fall within the definitions of either cash vouchers or non-cash vouchers (s.92).

If the cash equivalent of the money, goods or services obtained by a cash or non-cash voucher or a credit token is treated as earnings, then the actual money, goods or services are disregarded for income tax purposes (s.95).

As to deductions from taxable income in respect of vouchers and credit tokens, see **77 Deductions from taxable benefits**, below.

12 Living accommodation

Under s.97, where living accommodation is provided for an employee or for members of his family or household by reason of his employment, he is treated for income tax purposes as receiving earnings of an amount equal to the cash equivalent of the accommodation, less any payments attributable to it that he may make to those at whose cost it is provided. The cash equivalent is calculated in different ways depending on whether the cost of providing the accommodation does or does not exceed £75,000.

However, there is no charge where (ss.97 to 100)–

(a) the accommodation is provided by a local authority for one of its employees and it can be shown that the terms on which it is provided are no more favourable than those on which similar accommodation is provided by the authority to persons who are not their employees but are otherwise similarly circumstanced; or

(b) it is necessary for the proper performance of the employee's duties that he should reside in the accommodation; or

(c) the accommodation is provided for the better performance of his duties and is customarily provided in the kind of employment in question;

Note.–There are limited exceptions to (b) and (c) in the case of company directors.

(d) the accommodation is provided as part of special security arrangements for the employee's safety; or

(e) the employer is an individual and provides the accommodation in the normal course of his domestic, family, or personal relationships (in which case the accommodation is not regarded as provided "in the course of employment").

As to limited exemptions from liability to tax in respect of accommodation, see **53 Repairs, accommodation expenses, etc,** below; and as to deductions from taxable income in respect of accommodation, see **77 Deductions from taxable benefits**, below.

13 Cars and vans

Where a car or van is—
(a) made available to an employee (or a member of their family or household);
(b) is made available by reason of their employment; and
(c) is available for the employee's (or member's) private use,

then, the cash equivalent of the car, any fuel provided for it, or the van are treated as earnings and taxed as such (ITEPA, ss.114-166). There are exceptions for pooled cars and vans (which are treated as not being available for private use: ss.167, 168). Where two members of a family work for the same employer, only one of them is generally liable in respect of a single car (s.169).

A car or van will be treated as "available for private use" unless the terms on which it is provided prohibit such use and it is not so used (s.118). There is no link to mileage and therefore no need to keep records of business miles travelled. Where an employee pays his employer for the private use of a car then that payment is deducted from the cash equivalent of the car, but any such private use payment must be made in the tax year in which private use was undertaken (s.144).

Cars (s.139)

The starting point for calculating the charge is the list price of the car, with additions for any accessories, and deductions for any contribution made by the employee. This figure is then multiplied by the appropriate percentage which corresponds to the CO_2 emissions figure for the car. These percentages are—

For 2016/2017, the figures are—

CO_2 emissions figure	%
up to 50 g/km	7
up to 75 g/km	11
76-94 g/km	15
95 g/km	16
for each additional 5/g/km (or part)	+1%
Maximum: 200 g/km	37%

From 2017/2018, the figures will be—

CO_2 emissions figure	%
up to 50 g/km	9
up to 75 g/km	13
76-94 g/km	17
for each additional 5/g/km (or part)	+1%
Maximum: 190 g/km	37%

Cars for disabled employees (s.138)

The CO_2 emissions figure for an automatic car is generally higher than for its manual equivalent. So as not to penalise a disabled employee whose disablement means that the car he or she drives must have an automatic gearbox, the CO_2 emissions figure to be used is that of the nearest equivalent manual version of the car.

Cars with no CO_2 emissions figure (s.140)

If a car has an internal combustion engine with one or more reciprocating pistons, the appropriate percentage for the year is 16% for cars with an engine size up to 1,400cc, 27% for cars with an engine size between 1,400 and 2,000cc, and 35% for cars with an engine size exceeding 2,000cc.

From 2017/18 the percentages will increase from 16 to 18% and from 27 to 29%.

For cars which cannot in any circumstances emit CO_2 by being driven (e.g., electric cars), the percentage was 0% until 2014-15, 5% in 2015/16 and 7% from 2016/17.

Different percentages apply to cars first registered before 1st January 1998 (see below).

Diesel cars (s.141)

Deleted. Provision repealed from 6th April 2016.

Older cars (s.142)

For older cars (i.e., those first registered before January 1998) for which there are no reliable sources of carbon dioxide emissions data, the tax charge is based on engine size. The charge is 15% for cars with an engine size up to 1,400cc, 22% for cars with an engine size between 1,400 and 2,000cc, and 32% for cars with an engine size exceeding 2,000cc. From 2016/17, these percentages will increase to 16%, 27% and 37%.

Free fuel (s.149)

Where an employer provides an employee with free fuel for private mileage, that free fuel is taxable. The cash equivalent of the free fuel is taken to be the "appropriate percentage" of £22,100 for the tax year 2015/16 (£22,200 from tax year 2016/17). The appropriate percentage is generally the same as that used for calculating the cash equivalent of the car for which the fuel is provided (i.e., a starting point of 15%, varied according to the car's carbon dioxide emissions) (s.150).

Classic cars (s.147)

Different rules apply to cars which are over 15 years old and which have a market value of £15,000+.

Vans

What is the cash equivalent of the benefit of a van for a tax year depends on whether or not the "restricted private use" condition is met in relation to the van for the year. The restricted private use condition is met in relation to a van for a tax year if (s.155)–

(a) the "commuter use" requirement is satisfied throughout the year (or part year during which it is available to the employee) or the extent to which it is not satisfied during that period is insignificant; and

(b) the business travel requirement is satisfied throughout that year (or part year).

The commuter use requirement is satisfied if–

(c) the terms on which the van is available prohibit its private use otherwise than for the purposes of ordinary commuting or travel between two places that is for practical purposes substantially ordinary commuting; and

(d) neither the employee nor a member of the employee's family or household makes private use of the van at the time otherwise than for those purposes.

The cash equivalent of the benefit of the van for the year is–

(e) nil if the restricted private use condition is met in relation to the van for the tax year; and

(f) £3,150 if it is not (£3,170 from tax year 2016/17).

The cash equivalent of the van may be reduced for any periods when the van is unavailable (s.156), where the van is shared (s.157), and in respect of payments by the employee for the private use of the van (s.158).

If in a tax year–

(g) fuel is provided for a van by reason of an employee's employment;

(h) that person is chargeable to tax in respect of the van, and

(i) the cash equivalent of the van for that year is the amount under (f) above,

the cash equivalent of the benefit of the fuel is to be treated as earnings from the employment for that year. That cash equivalent is £594 for the tax year 2015/16 (£598 from tax year 2016/17), or nil if either (ss.160-162)–

(j) the employee is required to make good to the person providing the fuel the whole of the expense incurred in connection with its provision for the employee's private use, and the employee does make good that expense; or

(k) the fuel is made available only for business travel.

If a reduction of the cash equivalent of the benefit of the van for which the fuel is provided is made because the van is shared, a corresponding reduction is made in relation to the cash equivalent of the benefit of the fuel (s.164).

14 Loans

Ss.173 to 191 make provision in regard to beneficial loans. Where an employee derives benefit from a loan (made to him or to a relative of his) by reason of his employment, and, during the whole or part of any year, no interest is paid for that year, or interest is paid at less than the official rate (currently 3%: Taxes (Interest Rate) Regulations 1989, Reg. 5), the cash equivalent of the benefit is treated as taxable earnings, and where this occurs the employee is to be treated as having paid interest on the loan of that amount (ss.175, 184). Where such a loan is released or written off, that amount is normally treated as earnings for that year (s.188). There is however no charge to tax where–

(a) at no time in the year does the amount outstanding on the loan or loans, exceed £10,000 (s.180);

(b) the loan is made on ordinary commercial terms, i.e., where a loan is made to an employee by an employer whose normal business includes the making of loans to members of the public, and the loan to the employee was made on the same terms as comparable loans made to the public (s.176);

(c) the amount of interest paid on the loan is not less than interest at the official rate at the time the loan was made and the loan is for a fixed and unvariable period and at a fixed and unvariable rate and the benefit arises by virtue of an increase in the official rate (s.177).

Special rules apply where an employee acquires shares in a company at an under-value by reason of his employment. In such a case he is treated as having the benefit of an interest-free notional loan, and the provisions of ss.192 to195 apply.

15 Disposal of shares for more than market value

Where an employee (or a person connected with him) acquires shares by reason of his employment then, if the shares are disposed of for more than their market value (otherwise than on the death of the employee), the amount by which the disposal value exceeds the market value is treated as earnings from the employee's employment and treated as such (ss.198 and 199).

16 Residual liability

Where an employee (or member of his family or household) receives a benefit from his employer by reason of his employment which is not chargeable to tax under any other provision, then it is caught by the residual liability to charge in s.201.

In these cases, the cash equivalent of the benefit is treated as earnings (s.202). The cash equivalent is the cost of providing the benefit, less any part of that cost made good by the employee.

If the benefit consists of an asset being made available to an employee, but without ownership of it passing to him, the "cost" of providing that benefit is the higher of (a) the annual value of the use of the asset, and (b) the annual amount of the sums paid by those providing it by way of rent, hire or charge. The annual value of the use of an asset is 20% of its market value at the time it is first used, or in the case of land, its rental value (s.205).

If the benefit consists of the transfer to the employee of a used or depreciated asset, the starting point is that the cost of the benefit is its market value at the time it is transferred (s.206). However, if the asset is not an excluded asset and has previously been used in the provision of an employment-related benefit (and was first so used after April 1980), then the cost will be the higher of (a) the market value at the time of the transfer, and (b) the market value at the time it was first used to provide an employee benefit less the cost of providing the benefit for each year since then (s.206). Excluded assets for these purposes are cars, computer equipment, and cycles and cycle safety equipment (s.206(6)).

As to allowable deductions from taxable income in respect of employment related benefits, see **77 Deductions from taxable benefits**, below.

17 Minor benefits

HM Revenue and Customs can, by regulations, exempt minor benefits from the charge to tax. Such exemptions are conditional on their being made available to the employer's employees generally on similar terms (s.210).

See **26 Bus services**, and see **27 Cycles and cyclists safety equipment**, below.

18 Scholarships, bursaries, etc.

Income from a scholarship, exhibition, bursary, or similar educational endowment held by a person receiving full-time instruction at a university, college, school, or other educational establishment is exempt from income tax. However, no exemption from tax as a benefit in kind is conferred on any person other than the holder of the scholarship (ITEPA, s.215).

Where a scholarship is provided to a member of the family or household of an employee by reason of the latter's employment, payments are treated as emoluments and are taxable (ITEPA, s.212). Where payments come from a trust fund, the cost of the benefit is the total of the payments made from the fund to the person holding the scholarship (s.214).

Certain scholarships, which are provided from trust funds not more than 25% of whose scholarship payments in the tax year concerned are provided to people because of their employment, are excepted from these rules (s.213).

19 Welfare counselling

The Income Tax (Benefits in Kind) (Exemption for Welfare Counselling) Regulations 2000 exempt from income tax welfare counselling that is made available to an employer's employees generally on similar terms other than medical treatment or advice on tax, leisure or recreation, legal advice, or advice on finance (other than debt problems).

20 Sick pay

Sick pay from an employer during periods of sickness is chargeable to income tax (ITEPA, s.221). Lump sums received under a life, accident, or sickness insurance policy are not normally regarded as income for tax purposes (see ITTOIA Part 6, Chapter 8), but continuing sickness benefit paid under insurance policies taken out by individual taxpayers on their own behalf is taxable.

Statutory sick pay under s.1 of the Social Security and Housing Benefits Act 1982 is chargeable to income tax as social security income under s.660 (see the Note on **Income Tax: Other Income subject to Income Tax** at B: SOCIAL SECURITY INCOME, below).

C: EXEMPT INCOME

21 Introduction

Certain types of employment income are exempt from income tax. These are described in the following paragraphs.

22 Mileage allowance and passenger payments

There is no charge to tax in respect of mileage allowance payments paid to an employee in respect of expenses in connection with the use by him of a qualifying vehicle for business travel (up to an approved amount).

A qualifying vehicle is one in which the employee is not a passenger and which is not a company vehicle (ITEPA, s.229).

Similarly, there is no charge to tax if an employee in receipt of a mileage allowance also receives a payment for carrying another employee for business purposes (up to an approved amount), even if the vehicle is a company vehicle (s.233).

Where an employee uses a qualifying vehicle for business travel but does not receive a mileage allowance payment, or the total paid to him is less than the approved amount, he will be entitled to mileage allowance relief equal to the difference between the amount he is paid, if any, and the approved amount (s.231).

The "approved amount" is given in s.230. For a car or van, the amount is the number of business miles travelled multiplied by 45p per mile for the first 10,000 miles or 25p per mile after that. For a passenger payment, the approved amount is the number of business miles travelled multiplied by 5p (s.234).

23 Parking facilities

An employee is not liable to tax on the benefit of facilities for the parking of cars, motorbikes or bicycles provided by an employer (ITEPA, s.237). Nor will liability to income tax arise from the paying or reimbursing of expenses in connection with the provision of a parking space for an employee.

Non-cash vouchers and credit tokens used by employees to obtain car parking spaces are also not taxable (ss.266(1) and 267).

24 Lorries

S.238 provides that, where a heavy goods vehicle (i.e., a vehicle constructed for the conveyance of goods and which has a design weight exceeding 3,500 kilograms) is made available to an employee, no liability to income tax will arise provided the employee's use of the vehicle is not wholly or mainly private use.

25 Incidental overnight expenses

Payments to cover an employee's incidental expenses during a business trip which includes at least one night away are not taxable up to a limit of £5 per night in the UK, and £10 per night overseas (ITEPA, ss.240, 241). This exemption is intended to cover expenses such as telephone calls.

26 Bus services

There is no charge to tax in respect of the provision of a works bus or minibus service, i.e., a service provided by means of a bus with nine seats or more for conveying employees of one or more employers on a journey between their homes and workplace or between one workplace and another (ITEPA, s.242). The service must be made available to employees generally and must be used substantially only by employees or their children.

There is a similar exemption in respect of financial or other support for a public transport road service used by employees of one or more employers for such journeys (s.243). If the service is not a bus service, the terms on which employees use the service must be no more favourable than those available to other passengers.

There is also no charge to tax in respect of the provision by an employer of a bus or minibus for taking employees on a single journey of not more than 10 miles between the workplace and shops or other amenities on a working day (ITEPA, s.210 and the Income Tax (Exemption of Minor Benefits) Regulations 2002).

27 Cycles and cyclists safety equipment

The provision by an employer to an employee of a cycle or cyclist's safety equipment (without any transfer of property) is not a taxable benefit (ITEPA, s.244). The benefit must be available generally to employees of the employer and the cycle or equipment must be used mainly for journeys between the employee's home and workplace, or between workplaces.

28 Strikes

Where public transport normally used by an employee is disrupted by a strike or other industrial action, no liability to income tax will arise from the provision of overnight accommodation at or near the employee's permanent workplace, or a payment to the employee in respect of expenses incurred in connection with such accommodation (s.245). Similarly, no liability to tax will arise in connection with the provision for an employee of transport for ordinary commuting during a strike, or the payment of expenses in connection with such transport.

29 Travel expenses for severely disabled employees

The provision of transport for a disabled employee, or the payment of expenses in connection with it, where that transport is used for the purposes of ordinary commuting is not liable to income tax (s.246). Where a car is made available to a disabled employee (without any transfer of ownership) no liability to income tax will arise in connection with the car, or the provision of fuel or reimbursement of expenses in connection with it if (s.247)–

(a) the car is adapted for the employee's special needs or, in the case of an employee who because of disability can only drive an automatic car, is such a car;

(b) the car is made available on terms which prohibit its use other than for business travel or ordinary commuting; and

(c) the car is actually used only in accordance with those terms.

30 Employment costs resulting from disability

No liability to tax arises from the provision of any benefit provided to a disabled employee the main purpose of which is to enable him to perform the duties of his employment and which consists of a hearing aid or other equipment, services or facilities. The benefit must be provided under or within the terms of the Access to Work programme or another statutory provision or arrangement and must be available to all employees generally on similar terms (Income Tax (Benefits in Kind) (Exemption for Employment Costs resulting from Disability) Regulations 2002).

31 Late night working

No liability to tax arises from the provision of transport, or the payment or reimbursement of expenses in connection with it, if (s.248)–

(a) the transport is from the workplace to the employee's home;

(b) the number of journeys is less than 60 in a tax year; and either

(c) the journey is made because the employee has been required to work after 9pm, such occasions arise irregularly, public transport is not available or it would not be reasonable to expect the employee to use it, and the journey is made by taxi or similar private road transport; or

(d) the employee regularly travels to work in a car share arrangement with another employee but is unable to do so because of unforeseen and exceptional circumstances.

32 Work-related training

No liability to income tax arises where an employee attends a work-related training course or other activity designed to impart, instil, improve or reinforce any knowledge, skills or personal qualities which (s.250)–

(a) are likely to prove useful to the employee when performing his duties or those of a related employment; or

(b) will qualify or better qualify the employee to perform those duties or participate in any charitable or voluntary activities that are available to be performed in association with the employment or any related employment.

Where an employee receives education and training of a kind that qualifies for a grant under the Learning and Skills Act 2000 ss.108 or 109 (individual learning account training), or regulations made under the Training (Scotland) Act 2000 s.1, any costs of the employer in making payments to the education and training provider, or in reimbursing any directly related costs, are not treated as a taxable emolument provided that all employees have a fair opportunity to undertake the education and training. Education and training funded by third parties (i.e., other than the employer) is also covered (ss.255 to 260).

S.311 relates to expenditure incurred by an employer in connection with a qualifying course of training which is undertaken by an employee (or former employee) with a view to retraining. No liability to tax arises in respect of such a course. A qualifying course is one which is designed to impart or improve skills or knowledge relevant to, and intended to be used in the course of, gainful employment (including self-employment); is entirely devoted to the teaching or practical application of the skills or knowledge; is of not more than one year's duration; and which the employee attends on a full-time or substantially full-time basis. The employee must have been employed by the employer for two years, begin the course whilst still employed by the employer or within one year after he ceases to be so employed, must cease to be so employed not more than two years after the end of the course, and must not be re-employed by the employer within the two years.

33 Sporting and recreational facilities

Under ITEPA s.261 there is no charge to tax where an employer makes available to his employees, or to members or their families and households, the right or opportunity to make use of sporting or recreational facilities, provided that the facilities are available generally for all the employees of the employer in question, are not available to members of the public, and are used wholly or mainly be people whose right to use them is employment-related. This exemption does not apply to (s.262)–

(a) an interest in a mechanically propelled vehicle (including boats and planes), a holiday or other overnight accommodation, or facilities which include, or are provided in association with, a right or opportunity to make use of holiday or overnight accommodation;

(b) facilities provided on domestic premises; or

(c) a right or opportunity to make use of facilities within (a) or (b).

Under the Income Tax (Exemption of Minor Benefits) Regulations 2002 there is no income tax payable in respect of the provision of recreational benefits to persons (other than employees) who work on the employer's premises even though the conditions set out in ITEPA s.261 may not be met (Reg. 6).

34 Staff parties and small gifts to employees

Any benefit to an employee arising from a staff annual party or similar annual function is not charged to tax provided that the function is open to staff generally and the cost is modest (up to £75 per head per annum is regarded as modest). This amount may be split between more than one annual event provided that the total is £150 or less (s.264, as amended by the Income Tax (Exemption of Minor Benefits) (Increase in Sums of Money) Order 2003).

Small gifts to an employee consisting of goods or vouchers only exchangeable for goods incur no income tax liability as a benefit, voucher or credit token provided that (s.270)–

(a) the donor is not the employer or a person connected with him, and the gift is not procured by the employer;

(b) the gift is not made in recognition or anticipation of particular services;

(c) the total cost of gifts made by the same donor to the employee in the income tax year does not exceed £250.

35 Childcare vouchers

Under ITEPA s.270A, employers can offer their employees tax-free childcare vouchers up to the value of £55 per week (basic rate taxpayers), £28 per week (higher rate taxpayers), or £25 per week (additional rate taxpayers). Such vouchers are tax and National Insurance-free in the hands of the employee and also have no adverse tax effects for the employer.

The child must be a child or stepchild of the employee maintained (wholly or partly) at the employee's expense or else must be resident with the employee who must have parental responsibility for him. The £55/£28/£25 limit applies irrespective of the number of children.

The childcare must be provided by someone who is registered or approved (see the Note on **Child Minding and Day Care for Young Children**). Accordingly, care by a relative will not qualify unless the relative is also approved or registered and looking after the child as part of their business.

In order to give a voucher of the correct value, the employer must estimate the employee's relevant earnings amount for the tax year in respect of which the voucher is provided. The Employer Supported Childcare (Relevant Earnings and Excluded Amounts) Regulations 2011 (S.I. No. 1798) make provision as to what must be included in calculating a person's earnings, and what may be excluded.

36 Removal expenses

Under ITEPA s.271 certain removal expenses and benefits paid to an employee are exempt from tax up to a limit of £8,000.

Removal benefits and expenses are those reasonably provided or incurred (s.272)–

(a) in connection with a change of residence upon an employee becoming employed, having his duties altered, or having his place of employment changed, provided the change of residence is necessary in order to enable him to live within a reasonable daily travelling distance of his work and that his former place of residence is not within a reasonable distance;

(b) on or before the last day of the tax year after that in which the employment change occurred;

(c) in the case of a removal expense, one of the following expenses; in the case of a removal benefit, a benefit provided in the form of a non-cash voucher, cash voucher or credit token to obtain goods or services or money to obtain one of the following goods or services–

(i) s.277 (acquisition benefits and expenses) e.g., legal services, survey fees, utility connection charges etc;

(ii) s.278 (abortive acquisition benefits and expenses) where the failure to acquire the premises is because of circumstances outside the control of the person seeking to acquire them or because that person has reasonably declined to proceed;

(iii) s.279 (disposal benefits and expenses) e.g., legal services, estate agents services etc);

(iv) s.280 (transporting belongings) i.e., removal expenses including insurance;

(v) s.281 (travelling and subsistence) e.g., for the employee and members of his family for temporary visits to the area in connection with the move, or for the employee to get to his new place of work from his old place of residence;

(vi) s.285 (replacement of domestic goods) e.g., to replace goods from the old home which are unsuitable for the new home; and

(vii) only in the case of money to obtain goods or services, s.284 (bridging loan expenses).

37 Paid or reimbursed expenses

There is no liability to tax in respect of an amount of paid or reimbursed expenses which if not paid would be treated as earnings for which a deduction would be due (see **69 Employee expenses–general**, below) e.g., costs necessarily incurred in travel for the performance of an employee's duties.

Payments of expenses that are calculated in an "approved way" (i.e., "scale rate" or "flat rate" payments) rather than for the exact amount also generally incur no liability to tax, although there are exceptions (see ITEPA, s.289A, 289B).

For the purpose of s.289A, a reimbursement of expenses in respect of meals will be "approved" if it does not exceed–

(a) £5 where the duration of the qualifying travel in that day is 5 hours or more;

(b) £10 where the duration of the qualifying travel in that day is 10 hours or more; or

(c) £25 where the duration of the qualifying travel in that day is 15 hours or more and is ongoing at 8pm.

An additional meal allowance not exceeding £10 per day is allowed where a meal allowance within (a) or (b) above is paid and the qualifying travel in respect of which that allowance is paid is ongoing at 8pm (Income Tax (Approved Expenses) Regulations 2015).

38 Ministers of religion–accommodation

There is no liability to tax in respect of benefits arising in connection with accommodation provided for a full-time minister in premises owned by a charity or ecclesiastical corporation (ITEPA, s.290).

39 Termination payments to MPs and others

MPs, MEPs and certain other political office-holders are entitled to termination payments (e.g., when Parliament is dissolved). That entitlement, established prior to termination, makes the payments chargeable to tax as earnings. The payments are in fact compensation for loss of office. If it were not for the predetermined entitlement they would normally fall within ITEPA Part 6 Chapter 3 and tax would be chargeable on an amount above the £30,000 threshold (see **50 Payments on termination of employment**, below). ITEPA s.291 ensures that such payments are not treated as earnings and are instead taxed as termination payments subject to the £30,000 threshold.

40 Member of Parliament's and others' expenses etc.

Allowances paid to Members of Parliament pursuant to a resolution of the House of Commons to cover expenses incurred by overnight stays in the pursuance of parliamentary duties are not regarded as income for tax purposes (ITEPA, s.292). In addition, transport and subsistence allowances paid to Government ministers and opposition leaders and whips and their families are not taxable (s.295). Similar provisions apply in relation to members of the Scottish Parliament, Welsh Assembly and Northern Ireland Assembly. Travel by members to European Union institutions or to the parliament of another member State is also exempt (s.294).

Note.–By virtue of the Constitutional Reform and Governance Act 2010, Members of both Houses of Parliament are treated as resident, ordinarily resident, and domiciled in the UK for tax purposes, even if they have, for example, non-domiciled status (s.41).

Certain travel expenses made to local authority members are also exempt from income tax (s.295A and the Income Tax (Travel Expenses of Members of Local Authorities etc.) Regulations 2016).

41 Armed forces

Travel facilities provided for members of the armed forces going on or returning from leave are not chargeable to tax (ITEPA, s.296).

Food, drink and mess allowances for the armed forces are also exempt (s.297) as are operational allowances (s.297A) and council tax relief (s.297B).

Training expenses allowances to members of the reserve and auxiliary forces, and bounties paid in consideration of training and attaining a particular standard are also exempt (s.298).

42 Crown service

There is no liability to tax for payments to those in the service of the Crown where the payment is certified to represent compensation for the extra cost of being obliged to live outside the UK (ITEPA, s.299).

43 Diplomats and visiting forces

There is no liability to tax in respect of the income of a consul in the UK in the service of a foreign state (ITEPA, s.300). Similarly, there is no liability to tax in respect of the income of an official agent of a foreign state, provided they are not Commonwealth or Irish citizens) and the functions are not exercised in connection with a trade, business or other profit making undertaking (s.301). In certain circumstances, the income of consular employees is also exempt (see s.302).

In certain circumstances, the earnings of visiting forces and staff of designated allied headquarters are also exempt from income tax (s.303).

44 Detached national experts

Expenses paid by the European Commission to employees seconded to the Commission are not taxable (ITEPA, s.304).

No liability to income tax arises in respect of any subsistence allowances paid by certain specified EU bodies to persons who, because of their expertise have been seconded to it by their employers (s.304A).

45 Offshore workers

Where a person has a permanent workplace at an offshore installation, no tax is payable on (or on the reimbursement of expenses incurred by the employee on) transfer transport, related accommodation and subsistence, or local transport (ITEPA, s.305).

46 Miners' coal allowance

No income tax is payable on a coal or smokeless fuel allowance (or payment in lieu) which is provided for personal use to a colliery worker (other than in clerical, administrative or technical work) (ITEPA, s.306).

47 Carers: board and lodging

There is no income tax payable in respect of the provision of board or lodging (or both) to an individual employed as a home care worker if the provision is (ITEPA, s.306A)–

(a) on a reasonable scale

(b) at the recipient's home; and

(c) by reason of the individual's employment as a home care worker.

48 Pension provisions

No income tax liability arises in respect of provision made by an employee's employer for a retirement or death benefit, or for payments made by an employer to an employee's approved personal pension (ITEPA, ss.307 and 308).

49 Pensions advice

There is no income tax payable on the provision to an employee of pensions advice as long as the cost to the employer of providing the advice does not exceed £150 in any year of assessment (Income Tax (Exemption of Minor Benefits) Regulations 2002, Reg. 5).

Where an employer pays for an employee to receive independent advice where rights to "safeguarded" pension benefits are being given up for flexible benefits or an uncrystallised funds pension lump sum, no liability to income tax arises either from the provision of such advice, or the payment to or reimbursement of an employee or former employee, for the cost of such advice, provided specified conditions are met (Income Tax (Earnings and Pensions) Act 2003, s.308B) (see the Note on **Occupational Pension Schemes** at para **43 Independent advice**).

50 Statutory redundancy payments

No liability to income tax in respect of earnings arises in respect of a redundancy payment or approved contractual payment, unless the approved contractual payment exceeds the amount which would have been due if a redundancy payment had been payable (in which case the excess is taxable) (ITEPA, s.309). There may still be a charge to income tax in respect of employment income other than earnings (see **50 Payments on termination of employment**, below).

51 Payments on termination of employment

Under ITEPA, ss.401 to 403, relief may be claimed in respect of the first £30,000 of any payment to a person (or his executor or administrator) following the termination of his employment or any change in his duties or emoluments. Payments to a person's spouse/civil partner, dependant, or any relative are treated as payments to the person concerned. Any amount in excess of £30,000 is chargeable to tax as employment income for the year in which the payment or other benefit is actually received.

Payments made on the death, or retirement due to injury or disability, of an employee are entirely exempt from tax (also, see **83 Retirement benefit schemes**, below, and the Note on **Income Tax: Other Income subject to Income Tax** at **7 Pensions of disabled employees**, below).

As to statutory redundancy payments, also see **49 Statutory redundancy payments**, above.

Where an employee incurs legal cost in a court action to recover compensation for loss of employment the Commissioners will not normally charge tax on the payment of such costs (s.413A).

52 Counselling services for employees

Under ITEPA, s.310 no charge to tax arises in respect of the provision of services to employees in connection with the termination of any office or employment held by them, or the payment or reimbursement of fees or travelling expenses in connection with the provision of such services, provided–
(a) their main purpose is to enable an employee to adjust to the termination of his employment and/or to find other gainful employment (including self-employment);
(b) the services consist wholly of any or all of the following, namely, giving advice and guidance, imparting or improving skills, and providing or making available office equipment or similar facilities;
(c) the employee in question has been employed for at least two years; and
(d) the opportunity to receive such services is available generally to employees of the employer in question, or to a particular class or classes of employees.

53 Retraining

No liability to income tax arises in connection with the payment or reimbursement of retraining course expenses by an employer if (ITEPA, s.311)–
(a) the course expenses consist of attendance and travelling expenses, examination fees, and the cost of any essential books;
(b) the course lasts no more than two years, the course provides training designed to impart or improve skills or knowledge relevant to, and intended to be used in the course of, gainful employment (including self-employment); and the course is entirely devoted to the teaching or practical application of those skills or knowledge;
(c) the course begins while the employee is still employed by the employer or within one year of the employee leaving the employer, the employee cease to be employed by the employer within two years of the end of the course and is not re-employed by him within two years, the employee was employed by the employer for two years before beginning the course or leaving the employment, and the course is available generally to all fellow employees or a particular class or classes of them.

54 Repairs, accommodation expenses, etc

Where living accommodation is provided by reason of employment (see **12 Living accommodation**, above), alterations and additions to the premises which are of a structural nature and repairs which would be the obligation of the landlord if the premises were let under a lease to which s.11 of the Landlord and Tenant Act 1985 applies are not treated as benefits to be included in their emoluments (ITEPA, s.313).

In the case of those whose accommodation is necessary for the proper performance, or provided for the better performance, of their duties, or provided as a result of security threats, there is also an exemption from liability to income tax in respect of any payment or reimbursement of council tax on the premises (s.314).

In the case of those whose accommodation is necessary for the proper performance, or provided for the better performance, of their duties, or provided as a result of security threats there is a limited exemption for certain expenses connected with living accommodation (s.315). Expenditure incurred on heating, lighting, or cleaning; on repairs to the premises, or their maintenance or decoration; or on the provision of furniture and other effects normal for domestic occupation is limited to 10% of the net earnings for the year (reduced proportionately where the accommodation is provided for a shorter period), with a deduction, where the expenditure is incurred by a person other than the employee, of so much of any sum made good to that person by the employee as is properly attributable to the expenditure.

Generally, there is no charge to tax in respect of the provision of accommodation, supplies or services provided to an employee performing the duties of his employment provided that any use for private purposes by the employee or his family or household is "not significant". This exemption does not include the provision of a vehicle, boat or aircraft or alterations to living accommodation (s.316). Motor vehicles, boats and aircraft are excluded from this provision, as is the extension, conversion or alteration of living accommodation or works to a building or other structure on land adjacent to or enjoyed with such accommodation.

55 Homeworker's additional expenses

Where an employer makes a payment to an employee in respect of "reasonable additional household expenses" which the employee incurs because he works from home, then no income tax liability arises in respect of the payment (ITEPA, s.316A). "Household expenses" are defined as expenses connected with the day to day running of the employee's home, and "homeworking arrangements" are arrangements whereby the employee regularly performs some or all of his employment duties at home. There is no definition as to what is meant by "reasonable". By an HM Revenue and Customs concession, employer contributions of up to £2 per week (£104 per year) will not need to be supported by evidence but above that figure, records will need to be kept to show that the additional household costs were incurred as a result of working at home (see REV BN 3: Payments by Employers towards the incidental costs of homeworking).

It should be noted that only employer payments are exempt, there is no relief for additional expenditure incurred by the employee.

56 Meals

Income tax is not charged on the benefit to employees of free or subsidised meals provided by an employer on his business premises or in a staff canteen, or on the use of vouchers or tickets to obtain such meals, provided that the meals are provided on a reasonable scale to all employees or the employer provides free or subsidised meal vouchers for staff for whom meals are not provided (ITEPA, s.317). If the meals are provided in a restaurant open to the public (e.g., in a hotel), at a time when meals are being served to the public, the meals must be taken in an area designated for use by employees only.

Under the Income Tax (Exemption of Minor Benefits) Regulations 2002 there is no income tax payable in respect of the provision of subsidised meals to persons (other than employees) who work on the employer's premises even though the conditions set out in ITEPA s.317 may not be met (Reg. 6).

57 Care of children

Employer provided childcare

No liability to income tax arises from the provision to an employee of care for a child (including a stepchild) provided (ITEPA, s.318, as substituted by the Finance Act 2004, Sch. 13, para. 1)–

- (a) the child is (i) one for whom the employee has parental responsibility, (ii) resident with the employee, or (iii) a child of the employee and maintained at his expense;
- (b) the care must be provided on non-domestic premises and where there is a registration requirement applying to the premises under Part 3 of the Childcare Act 2006, Part 2 of the Children and Families (Wales) Measure 2010, Part 5 of the Public Services Reform (Scotland) Act 2010, or s.118 of the Children (Northern Ireland) Order 1995, such requirement must be met;
- (c) the care must either–
    - (i) be provided on premises which are made available by the employer alone, or
    - (ii) be provided under arrangements made by persons who include the employer, on premises made available by one or more of those persons, and under arrangements by which the employer is wholly or partly responsible for financing and managing the provision of the care;
- (d) the scheme must be open to the employer's employees generally, or generally to the employer's employees at a particular location.

For the purposes of s.318 and ss.318A-D (see below) tax relief is available until a child is 15 years old, or 16 years old if they are disabled (s.318B(2)). A child is disabled if a disability living allowance is payable in respect of him, or has ceased to be payable solely because he is a patient (i.e. receiving free in-patient treatment) or he is certified as severely sight impaired or blind by a consultant ophthalmologist or ceased to be so certified within the previous 28 weeks.

Other childcare

Liability to income tax from the provision to an employee of care for a child (including a stepchild) only arises in so far as the cash equivalent of the benefit exceeds an exempt amount if (ITEPA, ss.318A-D, as substituted by the Finance Act 2004, Sch. 13, para. 1)–

- (a) the child is maintained (wholly or partly) by the employee, or is resident with the employee and the employee has parental responsibility for him;
- (b) the scheme must be open to the employer's employees generally, or generally to the employer's employees at a particular location;
- (c) the employer has made an estimate of the employee's relevant earnings amount for the tax year in respect of which the care is provided (see below); and
- (d) the care is "qualifying child care" i.e., provided by a person who is registered or approved i.e.,–

    In England–
    - (i) by a person registered under Part 3 of the Childcare Act 2006;
    - (ii) by or under the direction of the proprietor of a school on the school premises (except if provided during school hours for a child who has reached compulsory school age, or in breach of a requirement to register under Part 3 of the Childcare Act 2006); or
    - (iii) by a domiciliary care worker under the Domiciliary Care Agencies Regulations 2002,

    In Wales–
    - (i) by a person registered under Part 2 of the Children and Families (Wales) Measure 2010;
    - (ii) by a person in circumstances where, but for article 11, 12 or 14 of the Child Minding and Day Care Exceptions (Wales) Order 2010, the care would be day care for the purposes of Part 2 of the Children and Families (Wales) Measure 2010;
    - (iii) in the case of care provided for a child out of school hours, by a school on school premises or by a

local authority;

(iv) by a child care provider approved by an organisation accredited under the Tax Credit (New Category of Child Care Provider) Regulations 1999;

(v) by a domiciliary care worker under the Domiciliary Care Agencies (Wales) Regulations 2004;

(vi) by a child care provider approved under the Tax Credits (Approval of Child Care Providers) (Wales) Scheme 2007; or

(vii) by a foster parent in relation to a child (other than one whom the foster parent is fostering) in circumstances where, but for the fact that the child is too old, the care would be child minding, or day care, for the purposes of Part 2 of the Children and Families (Wales) Measure 2010, or qualifying child care for the purposes of the Tax Credits (Approval of Child Care Providers) (Wales) Scheme 2007,

In Scotland–

(i) by a local authority or other person in circumstances where the care service provided consists of child minding or day care of children, as defined by the Public Services Reform (Scotland) Act 2010, Sch. 12, paras 12 and 13, and is registered under Chapter 3 or 4 of Part 5 of that Act.

Note.–care is excluded from being qualifying child care if it is provided by the partner of the employee or by a relative of the child wholly or mainly in the child's home or that of someone having parental responsibility for the child.

The exempt amount is–

(1) where the employee's estimated relevant earnings amount for the tax year (see (c) above) exceeds the higher rate limit, £25;

(2) where the employee's estimated relevant earnings amount for the tax year exceed the basic rate limit but not the higher rate limit, £28;

(3) in any other case, £55 per week.

Any amount payable under the Up-Front Childcare Fund is wholly exempt from income tax (Taxation of Benefits under Government Pilot Schemes (Up-Front Childcare Fund) Order 2008/1464).

58 Mobile telephones

No charge to tax arises on the benefit to an employee from the private use of one mobile phone provided by an employer (ITEPA, s.319). A second phone is subject to tax as a benefit in the normal way.

59 Computer equipment

Where computer equipment was made available to an employee or a member of his household before 6th April 2006, it is only chargeable to tax under ITEPA, s.201 (see **16 Residual liability**, above) to the extent that the cash equivalent of the benefit exceeds £500 (s.320). The exemption does not apply where the benefit is only available to directors (or members of their households) or is made available to them on more favourable terms than to other employees. "Computer equipment" includes printers, scanners, modems, discs, and other peripheral devices. The exemption does not apply to computer equipment first made available after 5th April 2006.

60 Eye tests and glasses, etc

No liability to income tax arises in respect of the provision for an employee of an eye and eyesight test or special corrective appliances that an eye and eyesight test shows are necessary provided (s.320A)–

(a) the provision of the test or appliances is required by regulations made under the Health and Safety at Work etc. Act 1974 (e.g., for people using VDUs at work); and

(b) the tests and appliances are made available generally to those employees for whom they are required to be provided.

Non-cash vouchers and credit tokens used by employees to obtain eye tests and glasses, etc are also not taxable (ss.266(1) and 267).

61 Health screening and medical treatment etc

No liability to income tax arises in respect of the provision for an employee on behalf of an employer of one health screening assessment and one medical check-up per year (s.320B).

Non-cash vouchers and credit tokens used by employees to obtain such assessments or check-ups are also not taxable (ss.266 and 267).

The funding by an employer of medical treatment which is recommended to an employee as part of an occupational health service for the purposes of assisting the employee to return to work after a period of absence due to injury or ill health is also exempt from income tax (s.320C). The exemption applies to expenditure up to a cap of £500 per tax-year per employee, provided the recommendation for treatment meets specified conditions set out in s.320C(3)(a) and (b) and the Income Tax (Recommended Medical Treatment) Regulations 2014 (S.I. 2014 No. 3227). The period of absence from work must have been at least 28 days.

62 Staff suggestion schemes

An award to an employee under a staff suggestion scheme is not taxed as income provided that (ITEPA, s.321)–
- (a) there is a formal scheme open to all employees on equal terms, or to a particular description of them;
- (b) the suggestion relates to activities carried on by the employer, and is made by an employee who could not reasonably be expected to make it in the course of his duties, having regard to his experience;
- (c) the suggestion is not made at a meeting held for the purpose of proposing suggestions;
- (d) an encouragement award, which is made in respect of a suggestion that shows intrinsic merit or special effort by the person making it, but which is not a financial benefit award, must not exceed £25;
- (e) a financial benefit award, which relates to an improvement in efficiency or effectiveness which the employer has decided to adopt and reasonably expects to result in a financial benefit must not exceed 50% of the expected net financial benefit during the first year of implementation, or 10% of the expected net financial benefit over a period of five years, subject to a maximum of £5,000 (any excess over £5,000 will be taxed).

63 Long service awards

No charge to tax arises in respect of a long service award marking 20 years' service or more with the same employer which takes the form of (s.323, as amended by the Income Tax (Exemption of Minor Benefits) (Increase in Sums of Money) Order 2003)–
- (a) tangible moveable property;
- (b) shares in the employee's company or one in the same group;
- (c) the provision of any other benefit except a payment, cash voucher, credit-token, securities, shares not within (b), or an interest in or rights over securities or shares.

A second tax-free award cannot be made within 10 years of a first award. The permitted maximum is £50 for each year of service.

64 Small gifts

No charge to tax arises in respect of a gift to an employee or a member of their family or household (ITEPA, s.324, as amended by the Income Tax (Exemption of Minor Benefits) (Increase in Sums of Money) Order 2003) provided–
- (a) the donor is not the employer or a person connected with him, and the gift is not procured by the employer;
- (b) the gift is not made in recognition or anticipation of particular services;
- (c) the gift is not in cash or securities or the use of a service;
- (d) the total cost of gifts made by the same donor to the employee in the income tax year does not exceed £250.

See also **34 Staff parties and small gifts to employees**, above.

65 Overseas medical treatment

No charge to tax arises in respect of the provision to an employee of medical treatment outside the UK when the need for it arises while the employee is abroad for the purposes of his job, or in respect of providing an employee with insurance to cover the cost of providing such treatment (ITEPA, s.325).

66 Asset transfers

No charge to tax arises in respect of the payment or reimbursement of expenses in connection with an employment-related asset transfer where those expenses are normally met by the transferor (s.326). An "employment-related asset transfer" is one where an asset is transferred to the employer and the right or opportunity to make the transfer arose by reason of the employment.

67 Fees relating to monitoring schemes

No liability to income tax arises by virtue of the payment or reimbursement of a fee in respect of (s.326A)–
- (a) an application to join the scheme administered under the Protection of Vulnerable Groups (Scotland) Act 2007, s.44 (scheme to collate and disclose information about individuals working with vulnerable persons);
- (b) fees payable for up-dating certificates from the Disclosure and Barring Scheme, and fees for criminal record and enhanced criminal record certificates where the application is made at the same time the employee applies to join the up-date service or where a person already holds a certificate that is subject to up-dating arrangements.

D: ALLOWABLE DEDUCTIONS

68 Introduction

Whereas ITEPA Part 4 (ss.227 to 326) deals with items which are exempt from income tax, ITEPA Part 5 (ss.327 to 385) deals with items which are allowable deductions from taxable earnings.

These allowable deductions relate to–

(a) employee expenses;

(b) deductions from those benefits which are otherwise taxable;

(c) fixed allowances for employee expenses;

(d) deductions for earnings which represent benefits or reimbursed expenses; and

(e) deductions from seafarers' earnings.

In general, deductions are allowed up to a limit of the amount of earnings from which they are deductible (i.e., there is no provision for refunds) (ITEPA, s.329).

69 Payments to adopters and foster carers

Certain payments to adopters are not treated as income for any purpose of the Income Tax Acts (ITTOIA, ss.744-745). These include–

(a) payments authorised by a court to an adopter or intending adopter;

(b) payments by adoption agencies of legal or medical expenses of intending adopters;

(c) payment of allowances to an adopter or intending adopter;

(d) payments of financial support made in the course of providing adoption support services;

(e) payments to a person as a child's special guardian;

(f) payments made to a person by reason of their being named in a child arrangements order as a person with whom a child is to live;

(g) local authority contributions to a child's maintenance made to a person with whom the child is living, or is to live, as a result of a child arrangements order; and

(h) payments made to a special guardian or person named in a child arrangements order as a person with whom the child is to live under an order for financial relief against a parent or under a maintenance agreement.

Paragraphs (e) to (h) do not apply where the payment is made to an excluded relative of the child, or where an excluded relative is also a special guardian or person named in a child arrangements order as a person with whom the child is to live. An "excluded relative" is a parent or a current or former spouse/civil partner of a parent.

Payments to foster carers and shared lives carers are also exempt from income tax up to a limit of £10,000 per household plus £200 per week for each cared for/fostered child aged under 11 and £250 for older children and adults (ITTOIA, Part 7, Chapter 2 and the Qualifying Care Relief (Specified Social Care Schemes) Order 2011, S.I. No. 712, as amended by SIs 2012/794 and 2014/582). Where payments in excess of these figures are received, foster carers must choose either to pay tax on the excess as receipts of a trade (under ITTOIA, Part 2) or income not otherwise charged (under ITTOIA, Part 5, Chapter 8) (ITTOIA, ss.816-817).

70 Employee expenses–general

From tax year 2016-17, most expenses will be paid or reimbursed through payroll and so there will ne no need for a claim for an allowable deduction to be made (see **37 Paid or reimbursed expenses**, above). Some expenses, such as those covered by a salary sacrifice agreement cannot be paid through payroll under the new statutory exemption.

Where an expense is not paid/reimbursed through payroll then a deduction is allowed from an employee's taxable earnings only if the amount to be deducted is paid by that employee, or by someone on his behalf and it is included in his earnings (ITEPA, s.333).

The general rule (except for travel expenses) is that a deduction is allowed if (s.336)–

(a) the employee is obliged to incur and pay it as holder of the employment; and

(b) the amount is incurred wholly, exclusively and necessarily in the performance of the duties of the employment.

There are additional rules either allowing or preventing deductions in particular cases, as described in the following paragraphs.

71 Travel expenses

If not paid/reimbursed by the employer, a deduction from taxable earnings is allowed for any sum incurred necessarily on travelling in the performance of the duties of the employment which the employee is obliged to incur and pay as holder of that employment (ITEPA, s.337).

A deduction is also allowed for any amount which the employee is obliged to incur and pay as holder of that employment and which is due to the employee's necessary attendance at any place in the performance of his duties, but not for the expenses of "ordinary commuting" or "private travel" (s.338). "Ordinary commuting" is defined as travel between the employee's home (or place that is not his workplace) and his permanent workplace. "Private travel" is defined as travel between the employee's home and a place that is not a workplace or between two places neither of which is a workplace.

An area-based employee may have a permanent workplace consisting of an area; and depots and bases may also be treated as permanent workplaces for these purposes (s.339).

There are special rules for–
(a) travel between group employments (see s.340);
(b) travel at the start or finish of overseas employment (see s.341); and
(c) travel between employments where duties are performed abroad (see s.342).

72 Annual subscriptions

If not paid/reimbursed by the employer, a deduction from taxable earnings is allowed for annual subscriptions and fees to certain professional bodies if the fees or contributions are paid in respect of a qualification which is a condition of carrying on the duties of the claimant's employment or if the subscriptions are to approved bodies whose activities are relevant to the employment (ITEPA, ss.343 and 344 and the Income Tax (Professional Fees) Orders 2003/1652, 2004/1360, 2005/1091, 2008/836, 2012/3004, 2013/1126, 2014/859, and 2015/886).

73 Employee liabilities

If not paid/reimbursed by the employer, a deduction from taxable earnings is allowed for (ITEPA, s.346)–
(a) a payment in or towards the discharge of a liability related to the employment;
(b) payment of any costs or expenses incurred in connection with a claim, or proceedings related to a claim, that the employee is subject to a liability related to the employment; or
(c) payment of an insurance premium for the employee to be indemnified against (a) or (b).

74 Ministers of religion

If not paid/reimbursed by the employer, a deduction from taxable earnings is allowed for ministers of a religious denomination for amounts incurred by them wholly, exclusively and necessarily in the performance of their duties of employment (ITEPA, s.351). If a minister pays rent for his home, part of which is used mainly and substantially for the purposes of his duties, he is allowed a deduction of one quarter of the rent, or, if less, that part of the rent which, on a just and reasonable apportionment, is attributable to that part of the home. If the premises belong to a charity or ecclesiastical corporation, a deduction is also allowed for a part of the expenses of maintenance. repair, insurance and management borne by the minister.

75 Entertainers' expenses

If not paid/reimbursed by the employer, a deduction from taxable earnings is allowed for actors, singers, musicians, dancers, and theatrical artists in respect of agency fees, provided that the fees (ITEPA, s.352)–
(a) are paid by the employee under a contract with another person who carries on an employment agency with a view to profit under the Employment Agencies Act 1973 at the time of any payment of the fees; and
(b) are calculated as a percentage of the net taxable earnings of the employment not exceeding 17.5% in the tax year.

76 Business entertainment

No deduction from taxable earnings is allowed for the cost of business entertainment except in limited circumstances (see ITEPA, ss.356 to 358).

77 Travel expenses

No deduction from taxable earnings is allowed in respect of travel allowances for the use by an employee of a vehicle which is not a company vehicle (e.g., the employee's own car) if either mileage allowance payments are made in respect of the use of the vehicle or mileage allowance relief is available: see **22 Mileage allowance and passenger payments**, above (s.359).

78 Deductions from taxable benefits

Where an employee's taxable earnings include an amount in respect of a taxable benefit, a deduction is allowed in the following cases (ITEPA, ss.361 to 365)–
(a) where the taxable benefit is a voucher or credit token (see **11 Vouchers and credit tokens**, above) which is used to pay for goods and services which, had the employee paid for them himself would have been deductible, then a deduction is allowed of the lesser of (i) the amount treated as earnings and (ii) the amount that would have been so deductible (ITEPA, ss.362 and 363);
(b) where the taxable benefit is living accommodation (see **12 Living accommodation**, above) and had the employee incurred and paid an amount equal to the benefit the whole or part of it would have been deductible, a deduction of that amount is allowed;

TAXATION

(c) where the taxable benefit arises under the residual liability to charge (see **16 Residual liability**, above) and had the employee incurred and paid the cost of the benefit the whole or part of it would have been deductible, a deduction of that amount is allowed.

79 Fixed allowances for employee expenses

The Treasury may by Order prescribe fixed amounts to be allowed as deductions from earnings by reference to an employee's employment (ITEPA, s.366). An Order may cover–
(a) the average annual expenses incurred in a particular occupation for the repair and maintenance of work equipment (s.367);
(b) the average annual expenses of an employee whose earnings are payable out of the public revenue which the employee is obliged to pay wholly, exclusively and necessarily in the performance of his duties (s.368).

80 Overseas travel costs and duties, etc

In certain circumstances, deductions are allowed from taxable earnings where those earnings include an amount in respect of an employee's travel costs where his duties are performed abroad, or travel costs of a visiting spouse/civil partner or child (ss.369 to 371). A deduction may also be allowed in respect of foreign accommodation and subsistence costs (s.376). Similar provisions apply to non-domiciled employees working in the UK (see ss.373 to 375).

81 Security assets and services

Where an asset or service is provided for or is used by an employee by reason of his employment, in order to improve his personal security (i.e., to meet a threat which is a special threat to his personal physical security and which arises wholly or mainly because of his job) and the cost is borne wholly or partly by a person other than the employee, a deduction can be made from his taxable earnings of an amount equal to so much of the cost so borne as falls to be included in his earnings (ITEPA, s.377). Similarly, in computing the profits or gains of an individual or partnership of individuals for purposes of ITTOIA, Part 2 (trading income: see above), a deduction may be made, notwithstanding the provisions of s.74, in respect of expenditure incurred on or after 6th April 1989 on such assets or services, provided that–
(i) they are used to meet a special threat or one which arises wholly or partly by virtue of the particular trade;
(ii) the expenditure is incurred with the sole object of meeting that threat;
(iii) in the case of a service, the benefit resulting to the individual consists wholly or mainly of an improvement to his personal physical security; and
(iv) in the case of an asset, the person incurring the expenditure does so with the intention that the asset should be used solely to improve his personal physical security. Where this is only part of the intention the expenditure will be appropriately apportioned (ITTOIA, 81).
In certain cases where expenditure is incurred by an individual or partnership of individuals on a security asset, a capital allowance may be made under s.33 of the Capital Allowances Act 2001.

82 Seafarer's earnings

Various deductions are allowed from the taxable earnings of seafarers, but these are beyond the scope of this work. See ITEPA ss.378 to 385.

83 Former employees

When an employee changes jobs, certain deductions may be made from his taxable earnings in respect of liabilities relating to his former employment. These are known as "deductible payments" and must be made within six years of leaving the former employment (ss.555 to 564).

84 Retirement benefit schemes

From April 2006, the Finance Act 2004 provides for a single set of rules to apply to all tax registered pension schemes. There are two key controls–
(a) the lifetime allowance; and
(b) the annual allowance.
The lifetime allowance is the amount of a person's pension contributions that can benefit from tax relief. It was initially set at £1.5m (FA 2004, s.218) rising to £1.6m in 2007, £1.65m in 2008, £1.75m in 2009 and £1.8m in 2010 (HM Revenue and Customs 2004 Budget press release). The amount of this allowance will be reviewed every five years. The rate for each of the years 2011-12 to 2015-16 has also been set at £1.8m (Registered Pension Schemes (Standard Lifetime and Annual Allowances) Order 2010). Funds in excess of these figures will attract a lifetime allowance charge of 25%. Excess funds may be taken as a lump sum, in which case the charge will be 55%.

The annual allowance is the amount an individual can put into a pension scheme during a year. The initial annual allowance for 2006-07 was £215,000 with no limit on the percentage of a person's earnings that could be contributed. The annual allowance for tax year 2007-08 was £225,000 and has in subsequent years so that by 2010 it is £255,000 for contributions to Defined Contribution schemes or increases in accrued benefits in Defined Benefit schemes. The level of the annual allowance is also reviewed every five years. For the years 2011-2012 to 2015-2016 the level will remain at £255,000 (Registered Pension Schemes (Standard Lifetime and Annual Allowances) Order 2010).

Contributions in excess of these figure will attract an annual allowance charge of 40% (FA 2004, s.227). Contributions (up to the age of 75) are deducted from income for the purposes of calculating income tax (FA 2004, s.188-192).

Non-registered pension schemes may continue, but will not have any tax advantages.

For these benefits to apply, the pension scheme must be registered with HM Revenue and Customs (under FA 2004, s.153).

E: EMPLOYMENT INCOME OTHER THAN EARNINGS

85 Benefits from employer-financed retirement benefits schemes

Where a person receives a benefit provided under an employer-financed retirement benefits scheme, the amount of the benefit (provided it exceeds £100) counts as employment income of the individual for the relevant tax year (ITEPA, s.394). Certain specified non-cash benefits are excluded from the charge to tax. These are set out in the Employer-Financed Retirement Benefits (Excluded Benefits for Tax Purposes) Regulations 2007, as amended (S.I. Nos. 2007/3537, 2009/2886, and 2011/2281) and include living accommodation and associated benefits, recreational benefits, annual parties, provision of equipment for the disabled, welfare counselling, and will writing.

86 Share-related income

Special rule apply to share-related income but these are beyond the scope of this work.

87 Authorities

Statutes–

The Finance Acts

Income Tax (Earnings and Pensions) Act 2003

Statutory Instruments–

Income Tax (Approved Expenses) Regulations 2015 (S.I. 2015 No. 1948)

Income Tax (Benefits in Kind) (Exemption for Employment Costs resulting from Disability) Regulations 2002 (S.I. 2002 No. 1596)

Income Tax (Exemption of Minor Benefits) (Increase in Sums of Money) Order 2003 (S.I. 2003 No. 1361)

Income Tax (Exemption of Minor Benefits) Regulations 2002, as amended (S.I. 2002 No. 205, 2003 No. 1434, 2004 No. 3087, 2009 No. 695, and 2012 No. 1808)

Income Tax (Travel Expenses of Members of Local Authorities etc.) Regulations 2016 (S.I. 2016 No. 350)

Taxes (Interest Rate) Regulations 1989, as amended (S.I. 1989 No.1297, 1994 Nos. 1307 and 1567, 2009 No. 199, 2014 No 496, and 2015 No. 411)

INCOME TAX: GENERAL PROVISIONS

Contents

This Note gives an introduction to Income Tax and the way in which it is levied and administered and covers–
A: The income on which income tax is payable
B: Rates of tax
C: Administration of income tax and personal reliefs

A: THE INCOME ON WHICH INCOME TAX IS PAYABLE

1 Interpretation

In this Note–
- ICTA means the Income and Corporation Taxes Act 1988
- ITTOIA means the Income Tax (Trading and Other Income) Act 2005
- ITEPA means the Income Tax (Earnings and Pensions) Act 2003, and
- ITA means the Income Tax Act 2007

Bracketed references to Finance Acts are abbreviated to read "FA" followed by the year e.g., FA 1988. "The Commissioners" means the Commissioners of Revenue and Customs.

2 Liability to income tax

ITA provides that income tax is charged under (ITA, s.3)–
(a) Parts 2 (employment income), 9 (pension income), and 10 (social security income) of ITEPA;
(b) Parts 2 (trading income), 3 (property income), 4 (savings and investment income), and 5 (miscellaneous income) of ITTOIA;
(c) certain other provisions, such as FA 2004, Part 4 Chapter 5 (registered pension schemes); F (No.2) A 2005, s.7 (social security pension lump sums); and ITA Parts 10 (charitable trusts), 12 (accrued income profits), and 13 (tax avoidance).

Income tax is charged for a year (a "tax year") only if an Act so provides. A tax year starts on 6th April and ends on the following 5th April (s.4).

3 Trading income: the charge to tax

ITTOIA Part 2 (ss.3-259) is concerned with the taxation of the profits of a trade, profession or vocation.

In particular, farming and market gardening are treated for income tax purposes as the carrying on of a trade and so income is taxable under Part 2 (rather than under Part 3 as income from land). The same applies to income from the commercial occupation of land (other than woodlands), mines and quarries, and fishing rights (ss.9 to 12).

Income arising from the commercial occupation of woodlands is not chargeable to income tax (ss.11 and 768).

Income from employment as a diver or diving supervisor working on the seabed is also treated as taxable under this Part rather than as employment income under ITEPA (s.15).

As to profits averaging, which is available for farmers and creative artists with fluctuating incomes, see the Note on **Income Tax: Other Income subject to Income Tax** at para **19 Profits averaging**.

There are detailed rules in Part 2 as to the calculation of the profits of a trade, profession or vocation for income tax purposes, and as to the deductions which can and cannot be made. These are beyond the scope of this work.

4 Property income: the charge to tax

ITTOIA Part 3 (ss.260-364) is basically concerned with the taxation of income from property. Income tax is charged on the profits of a property business (s.268). Generally, profits of a UK property business are chargeable to tax whether the business is carried on by a UK resident or a non-resident. Profits of an overseas property business are chargeable to tax only if the business is carried on by a UK resident.

A person's UK property business consists of every business they carry on for generating income from land in the UK, together with every transaction which they enter into for that purpose otherwise than in the course of business (s.264). If the land is outside the UK, then it is classed as overseas property business (s.265).

These provisions have replaced the old "Schedule A", although that Schedule continues to apply so as to charge corporation tax to the income of companies derived from land.

5 Income generated from land

Income tax is charged under ITTOIA on the annual profits or gains arising from any business carried on for the exploitation, as a source of rents or other receipts, of any estate, interest or rights in or over land in the UK (s.266).

Rents includes payments by a tenant for work to maintain or repair leased premises which the lease does not require the tenant to carry out. Receipts include payments in respect of a licence to occupy or otherwise use land; payments to exercise rights over land; and rentcharges and other annual payments reserved in respect of, or charged on or issuing out of, land (s. 266).

Specified activities are treated as not generating income from land (s.267). These include farming and market gardening (which are treated as generating trading income instead); any other occupation of land (although, again, commercial occupation will give rise to income tax on trading income); and activities connected with mines and quarries (which, again, give rise to trading income rather than property income).

The person liable for any income tax on property income is the person receiving or entitled to receive the profits (s.271).

6 Premiums

Tax is chargeable under ITTOIA on premiums, and certain other sums received by a landlord in respect of a lease granted for a term not exceeding 50 years (ss.277-279). These other sums include (ss.278-285)–
(a) surrender payments;
(b) variation and waiver fees;
(c) sums payable instead of rent;
(d) sums received on an assignment for profit of a lease granted at an undervalue;
(e) sums received on a sale with a right to re-conveyance where the sale price exceeds the re-conveyance price; and
(f) certain sale and leaseback transactions.
In each case, the amount of such a premium (or other sum), reduced by one-fiftieth for each full year of the duration of the lease after the first, is treated as additional rent chargeable to tax in the chargeable period in which it is received.

7 Energy-saving expenditure

Where a person carries on a property business in relation to land which consists of or includes a dwelling-house, then expenditure incurred before 6th April 2015 in acquiring and installing certain energy-saving items may be deducted from their tax liability (ITTOIA, s.312). Energy saving items include solid wall and floor insulation, hot water system insulation and draught proofing. The maximum deduction that can be claimed in any tax year is £1,500 per dwelling (Energy-Saving Items (Income Tax) Regulations 2007/3278).

The relief is not available if the business consists of or includes the commercial letting of furnished holiday accommodation or if the rent-a-room scheme is being used (s.313).

8 Wear and tear allowance

A person carrying on a property business which includes furnished lettings (*not* including the commercial letting of furnished holiday accommodation) can claim an allowance of 10% of the net rental income for "wear and tear" (ss.308A-C). The allowance takes the form of a deduction from the profits of the business.

9 Furnished holiday lettings

For the purposes of income and corporation tax, any income arising from the commercial letting of furnished holiday accommodation in the UK is taxable under ITTOIA as income from a trade rather than as income from property (ITA s.127).

10 Rent-a-room scheme

ITTOIA continues a relief (originally contained in the Finance (No. 2) Act 1992, Schedule 10) which gives an exemption from income tax on rent received from the letting of a furnished room in the taxpayer's only or main residence (ITTOIA, Part 7). The exemption applies to rent received up to a specified limit (£4,250 for 1997/98 and subsequent years; £7,500 from 2016/17: ITTOIA, s.789, as amended by the Income Tax (Limit for Rent-a-Room Relief) Order 2015/1539). If the rent received exceeds the specified limit, the taxpayer can choose either to have the excess taxed without any deduction for expenses, or to have expenses set against the full amount of the rent received with tax being calculated on the whole amount. The excess will be taxed as either trading income, property income, or income not otherwise charged to tax, as appropriate. The letting of a furnished room as office accommodation does not qualify for the relief.

11 Savings and Investment income: the charge to tax

ITTOIA Part 4 (ss.365-573) is concerned with the taxation of savings and investment income. This includes–
(a) interest, including building society dividends;
(b) dividends from UK and non-UK companies;

(c) stock dividends from UK companies;

(d) release of loan to a participator in a close company;

(e) purchased life annuity payments;

(f) profits from deeply discounted securities;

(g) gains from contracts for life insurance etc;

(h) distributions from unauthorised unit trusts;

(i) transactions in deposits;

(j) disposals of futures and options involving guaranteed returns; and

(k) sales of foreign dividend coupons.

These provisions have replaced the old "Schedule F", although that Schedule continues to apply so as to charge corporation tax to the income of companies in the above categories.

12 Miscellaneous income: the charge to tax

ITTOIA Part 5 (ss.574-689) is concerned with the taxation of income from various miscellaneous sources including–

(a) intellectual property;

(b) film and sound recordings: non-trade business;

(c) certain telecommunications rights: non-trade income;

(d) settlements: amounts treated as the income of the settlor;

(e) beneficiaries income from estates in administration;

(f) annual payments not charged to tax under any other provision; and

(g) any other income not charged to tax under any other provision.

These provisions have replaced the old "Schedule D", although that Schedule continues to apply so as to charge corporation tax to the income of companies in the above categories.

13 Exemptions from tax under ITTOIA

Part 6 of ITTOIA (ss.690-783) provides for exemptions from income tax for certain categories of income which would otherwise be chargeable under that Act. These exemptions are for–

(a) income from national savings;

(b) income from individual investment plans;

(c) SAYE interest;

(d) venture capital trust dividends;

(e) income from free of tax to residents abroad (FOTRA) securities;

(f) purchased life annuity payments;

(g) other annual payments; and

(h) other income.

For these, see the Note on **Income Tax: Other Income subject to Income Tax**.

14 The charge to tax under ITEPA

Tax is charged under ITEPA on (s.1)–

(a) employment income;

(b) pension income; and

(c) social security income.

15 Employment income

Employment income means (s.7)–

(a) earnings;

(b) any amount treated as earnings; and

(c) any other amount which counts as employment income.

An amount will be "treated as earnings" in the case of agency workers and those employed through an intermediary. Certain benefits of employment (such as vouchers, cars, loans etc) are also treated as earnings.

Income may also be counted as employment income if it comes within Parts 6 (income which is not earnings or share related) or 7 (share related income) of ITEPA.

See the Note on **Income Tax: Employment Income**.

16 Pension income

Pension income means (s.566)–

(a) income from UK and foreign pensions;

(b) annuities; and

(c) voluntary annual payments.

See the Note on **Income Tax: Other Income subject to Income Tax**.

17 Social security income

Social security income is divided into that which is taxable, and that which is not taxable. Taxable social security income means, subject to exemptions (s.657)–

   (a) income from bereavement allowance, carer's allowance, incapacity benefit, income support, jobseeker's allowance, and, to the extent that they are not taxed under any other provision, (i.e., as employment income) statutory adoption, maternity, paternity and sick pay; and

   (b) foreign benefits payable to a person resident in the UK which are substantially similar in character to a benefit listed in (a) and which are not taxed as pension income.

See the Note on **Income Tax: Other Income subject to Income Tax.**.

B: RATES OF TAX

18 The lower, basic and higher rates

There are three main rates of tax: the starting rate, which applies to so much of an individual's taxable income as does not exceed a determined level (the starting rate limit); the basic rate, which applies to so much of his taxable income as exceeds the starting rate limit but does not exceed a determined basic rate limit; and a higher rate which applies to any taxable income in excess of the basic rate limit (ITA s.6). The rates for any tax year are determined annually by Parliament. The starting and basic rate limits are linked to the retail prices index for the month of September and adjusted annually (ITA, s.21). The current limits and rates are as follows–

The basic rate of income tax for the year 2016/17 is 20%. Where an individual's total *taxable* income exceeds £32,000, the excess over that figure will be charged at the higher rate of 40%. For 2017/18 the limit will be £33,500.

There is an additional rate of 45% for taxable income in excess of £150,000.

Note.–Taxable income is income over and above an individual's personal allowance.

Savings income which falls within the basic rate band is also taxed at the 20% basic rate, with savings income above the basic rate being taxed at 40%.

There is a starting rate for savings of 0% on savings up to £5,000.

The rate of income tax on dividend income is 10% for income up to the basic rate limit, and 32.5% above it. A 10% tax credit is set against the tax due on dividend income. There is an additional rate of 37.5% for dividends which form part of an individual's taxable income in excess of £150,000.

19 Personal allowances

The following Tables show personal allowances and certain other reliefs which will be allowed for the year 2016/17 and 2017/18.

Where a person's adjusted net income (i.e., taking into account pensions contributions and Gift Aid payments) exceeds £100,000, their personal allowance is reduced by £1 for every £2 of excess income.

Personal allowances for 2016/17–

Personal Allowance	£11,000

Personal allowances for 2017/18–

Personal Allowance	£11,500

If a couple are married or in a civil partnership and one of them was born before 6 April 1935, they may be entitled to married couple's allowance (MCA), part of which is means-tested. Married couple's allowance doesn't increase the amount of income that can be received before tax is payable but it reduces the tax bill by 10% of the allowance that the couple are entitled to.

The full married couple's allowance of £8,355 applies if income is below £27,700 (so giving a tax reduction of £835.50). Where total income exceeds £37,970, the minimum married couple's allowance of £3,220 applies (giving a tax reduction of £322). Between those income figures, the allowance is reduced by £1 for every £2 above £27,700 (see **27 Personal allowance and married couple's allowance**, below).

A person who is registered blind with a local authority in England and Wales is entitled to an additional amount of tax-free income. In Scotland a person qualifies for the allowance if their eyesight is such that they are unable to perform any work where eyesight is essential. The amount of the allowance is–

Blind person's allowance	£2,290

A blind person who does not have enough income to use their allowance can transfer it, or part of it, to their spouse or civil partner.

Transfer of personal allowance

A spouse or civil partner who is not liable to income tax because their income is below their personal allowance, or who is liable to income tax at the basic rate, dividend ordinary rate or the starting rate for savings, can elect to transfer £1,100 of their personal allowance to their spouse or civil partner. There is a corresponding reduction to the transferring spouse's personal allowance (Income Tax Act 2007, ss.55A-55E, added by Finance Act 2014, s.11).

A spouse or civil partner who is liable to income tax at the basic rate, dividend ordinary rate or the starting rate for savings will receive the transferred personal allowance. The transferred allowance will be given effect as a reduction to their income tax liability at the basic rate of tax.

From 2016-17 the transferable amount is 10% of the basic personal allowance.

Note.– Married couples or civil partners entitled to claim the married couple's allowance are not entitled to make a transfer.

20 The Scottish rate of income tax

The Income Tax Act 2007, s.6A provides for a Scottish rate of income tax (to be introduced in April 2016). The basic, higher and additional rates of income tax on non-savings income set annually by the UK Government will be reduced by 10p in the pound for Scottish taxpayers, and the Scottish rate, set by the Scottish Parliament, added across the (reduced) rates.

The effect of this will be that if the Scottish Parliament sets a Scottish rate of 10%, the rates of income tax paid by Scottish taxpayers would be the same as elsewhere in the UK, a rate of 9% would mean the rates were 1% lower, and a rate of 11% would mean they were 1% higher, than elsewhere in the UK.

C: ADMINISTRATION OF INCOME TAX AND PERSONAL RELIEFS

21 Independent taxation

ITA Part 3 Chapter 3 (ss.42-58), make provision in regard to married couples and civil partners. These provisions are as follows–

   (a) under s.45 a married man whose wife is living with him and whose marriage was entered into before 5th December 2005 is entitled to a married couple's allowance if either of them was born before 6th April 1935 (see **27 Personal allowance and married couple's allowance,** below);

   (b) under s.46, an individual whose spouse/civil partner is living with him and whose marriage/civil partnership was entered into on or after 5th December 2005 is entitled to an income tax reduction if either of them was born before 6th April 1935 and the claimant's income for the year exceeds that of his spouse/civil partner (this section also applies to marriages before that date if an election has been made);

   (c) where an individual marries or becomes a civil partner in the course of a year of assessment and has not previously been entitled to an income tax reduction under s.45/s.46, the amount of such reduction is reduced by one twelfth for each month of the year ending before the date of the marriage (for this purpose a month begins on the 6th day of a month of the calendar year) (s.54).

   (d) the married couple's allowance/income tax reduction may be allocated in a number of ways–

      (i) an individual may claim one-half of the married couple's allowance/income tax reduction (s.47);

      (ii) an individual and their spouse/civil partner may jointly elect that the wife/civil partner shall be entitled to the whole married couple's allowance/income tax reduction (s.48);

      (iii) for a year in which an election in accordance with (ii) has been made, an individual may effectively claim back one half of the allowance (s.49); and

      (iv) where the relief an individual has under s.45/s.46 exceeds his/her income, the other spouse/civil partner is entitled to claim the unused part of the relief (s.51).

Individuals who are married to or who are civil partners of each other are treated for income tax purposes as living together unless (s,1011)–

   (a) they are separated by a court order or deed of separation; or

   (b) they are in fact separated in such circumstances that the separation is likely to be permanent.

Income (subject to exceptions, including earned income and income to which ITTOIA Part 9 (partnership assessments to income tax) applies) arising from property held jointly by a husband and wife or civil partners is to be regarded as income to which they are beneficially entitled in equal shares unless (ss.836, 837)–

   (i) it is income to which neither of them is beneficially entitled; or

   (ii) it is income to which either beneficiary is entitled to the exclusion of the other or they are beneficially entitled to the income in unequal shares and, in either case, a joint declaration has been made by both of them of their beneficial interest in that income and in the property from which it arises. Notice of such a declaration must be given to the Inspector, in such form and manner as the Commissioners may prescribe, within the period of 60 days beginning with the date of the declaration. Such a declaration does not have effect if the beneficial interests of the husband and wife/civil partners in the property itself do not accord with their beneficial interests in the income from it.

22 Trusts with a vulnerable beneficiary

The Finance Act 2005 introduced an alternative income tax regime for trusts with a "vulnerable" beneficiary. Broadly, the trusts which qualify for this treatment are those with a beneficiary who is either mentally incapacitated, in receipt of attendance allowance or the care component of disability living allowance at the highest or middle rate, or a minor who has lost at least one parent. The effect of the alternative regime is that the liability of the trustees to income tax will be the same as the beneficiary's would have been had they received the income direct (FA 2005, ss.23-45).

23 Overpaid tax

Under s.43 of the Taxes Management Act 1970, a claim to a repayment of tax overpaid (by deduction at source, or otherwise) must, subject to any specific provisions of the Taxes Acts, be made within four years of the tax year in which the overpayment occurred (Taxes Management Act 1970, Sch. 1AB).

Under an extra-statutory concession (IR1, B41), repayments of tax may be made outside the statutory time limit where an overpayment of tax has arisen because of an error by HM Revenue and Customs or another Government department where there is no dispute or doubt as to the facts.

24 Interest on unpaid tax

FA 2009 provides that interest is payable on unpaid tax from the payment due date until the date that payment is received by HMRC (s.101). Where there is an appeal against an assessment, payment is postponed pending the determination of the appeal, but the late payment interest start date in respect of that amount is the date which would have been the late payment interest start date if there had been no appeal.

The late payment interest rate is the Bank of England base rate + 2.5% (Taxes and Duties, etc (Interest Rate) Regulations 2011). In addition to any interest that may be payable, penalties are also charged if tax is not paid on time: see the Note on **Administration of Taxes** at para **16 Penalties for failure to pay tax**.

25 Interest on delayed repayments of tax

FA 2009 provides that interest is payable on overpaid tax (s.102) from the late payment interest start date, which is the 31st January next following the tax year in respect of which the assessment giving rise to the overpayment was made. If tax is repaid before that date, no interest is payable.

The repayment interest rate is the Bank of England base rate - 1%, but subject to a minimum of 0.5% (Taxes and Duties, etc (Interest Rate) Regulations 2011).

26 Remission of arrears

Where arrears of tax arise due to failure of the Commissioners to make proper and timely use of relevant information supplied by the taxpayer, they may, as an extra-statutory concession (see below), in certain circumstances, be wholly or partly waived. The proportion of the remission depends on the amount of gross income and the date on which the taxpayer or his agent was first notified of the arrears. No remission is normally allowed where the arrears are notified to the taxpayer by the end of the tax year following that in which they arose (IR1, A19).

27 Personal allowance and married couple's allowance

Under ITA ss.35-37, an individual may claim a personal allowance by way of an income tax reduction.

The former married couples allowance was abolished with effect from April 2000 for couples under the age of 65. The allowance remains for couples (and also includes civil partners) where at least one of the spouses/civil partners was born before 6th April 1935, with a higher rate where at least one of them is aged 75 or more. From 1999/2000 the rate has been 10%. Where, however, the claimant's income exceeds a specified limit the amount of the allowance is reduced by one-half of the amount of the excess but so that the claimant receives not less than £3,220 (the "minimum amount"). An individual cannot claim more than one allowance, and where he marries/enters into a civil partnership in the course of a year of assessment and has not previously in the year been entitled to an allowance under this section his allowance is based on the length of the unexpired period of the year of assessment in which the marriage/civil partnership takes place (s.54).

The current rates of allowances are given in **19 Personal allowances**, above.

28 Index linking of personal reliefs

Under ITA s.57, the personal allowance, married couple's allowance, and married couples/civil partners income tax reduction will, unless Parliament otherwise determines for any year of assessment, be increased by the same percentage as the percentage increase, if any, in the retail prices index for the September preceding the year of assessment over that for the previous September.

29 Blind person's allowance

Under ITA s.38, an allowance may be claimed, subject to conditions, by any person who is a registered as a severely sight-impaired adult or a blind person for the whole or part of the year of assessment. Where the claimant is a person whose spouse or civil partner is living with him and the amount of the person's allowance exceeds what is left of his total income after all other deductions have been made, his spouse or civil partner is entitled to deduct the amount of the excess from his/her total income.

For the current rate of allowance, see **19 Personal allowances**, above.

30 Payroll deduction scheme

ITEPA ss.713 to 715 provide for relief from income tax on donations made to charities in accordance with approved schemes by way of deductions from pay under the PAYE scheme. The Charitable Deductions (Approved Schemes) Regulations 1986 prescribe the circumstances in which the Commissioners may approve schemes for this purpose and may approve agents to whom employers will pay the sums withheld under PAYE. The sums must be withheld in accordance with a request by the employee, must constitute a gift to the charity or charities concerned, must not be a payment under a covenant, and must be paid to the charities specified by the employee within 35 days (extended to 60 days in certain circumstances, such as where the employer has made no payments to the specified charity within the previous 12 months).

Where an employer voluntarily makes reasonable payments to an approved agency towards administrative costs, the amount may, be deducted from the employer's profits for tax purposes if it would not otherwise be deductible as expenses incurred wholly and exclusively for the purposes of his trade or profession or as management expenses (ITTOIA, s.72).

31 Gifts to the nation

FA 2012 makes provision for a person's income tax liability to be reduced where they make a gift of a "pre-eminent object" to the nation in accordance with a scheme set up by the Secretary of State (s.49 and Sch. 19). A donor must be acting in their own personal capacity: the tax reduction scheme does not extend to those who are acting as trustees or personal representatives.

An object or collections of objects may be "pre-eminent" if it has an especially close association with the country's history and national life; or is of especial artistic or art-historical interest; especial importance for the study of some particular form of art, learning or history; or has an especially close association with a particular historic setting. The decision as to whether an object is pre-eminent rests with the relevant Minister, who will be the Secretary of State, the Scottish or Welsh Ministers or a combination of those Ministers acting jointly, depending on the object. The scheme does not cover land or buildings.

The effect of the scheme is that if a person makes a qualifying gift then part of their tax liability is treated as having been paid, leading to a reduction in the amount of tax they still have to pay for that period. A person may apply the tax reduction against their income tax and/or capital gains tax liabilities in the tax year in which the offer was registered under the scheme or any of the succeeding four tax years. The total tax reduction for an individual is 30% of the value of the qualifying gift. The individual may then agree, pursuant to the scheme, that this total tax reduction amount is to be allocated across the five relevant tax years in whatever amounts they wish, including nil amounts for any year.

If the donor does not express any preference, the tax reduction will be applied first to their income tax liability and thereafter to any capital gains tax liability.

Note.– There is no obligation for an offer of a gift under the scheme to be accepted, even if it meets all of the qualifying circumstances under the scheme.

32 Authorities

Statutes–

The Finance Acts

Income and Corporation Taxes Act 1988

Income Tax Act 2007

Income Tax (Earnings and Pensions) Act 2003

Income Tax (Trading and Other Income) Act 2005

Taxes Management Act 1970

Statutory Instruments–

Charitable Deductions (Approved Schemes) Regulations 1986, as amended (S.I. 1986 No. 2211, 2000 Nos. 759 and 2083, 2003 No. 1745, 2009 No. 56, and 2014 No. 584)

Taxes and Duties, etc (Interest Rate) Regulations 2011 (S.I. 2011 No. 2446)

INCOME TAX: OTHER INCOME SUBJECT TO INCOME TAX

Contents

This Note covers the types of income – other than from employment – on which income tax is payable, and some of the reliefs which are available.. It is set out as follows–

A: Pension Income
B: Social Security Income
C: Wholly exempt income
D: Miscellaneous allowances and reliefs
E: Charities and charitable giving
F: Settlements
G: Covenants and Dispositions
H: Income from investments

A: PENSION INCOME

1 Introduction

ITEPA Part 9 (ITEPA, ss.564 to 654) provides for the taxation of pension income. Tax is charged on–

(a) UK pensions;
(b) foreign pensions paid to a UK resident;
(c) UK social security pensions (i.e., the State pension, graduated retirement benefit, industrial death benefit, widowed mother's allowance, widowed parent's allowance and widow's pension);
(d) pensions or annuities from approved schemes;
(e) unauthorised payments from–
(i) approved schemes;
(ii) former approved superannuation funds;
(f) annuities paid under–
(i) former approved superannuation funds;
(ii) approved personal pension schemes;
(iii) retirement annuity contracts;
(iv) sponsored superannuation schemes;
(g) income withdrawals under approved personal pension schemes;
(h) unauthorised personal pension payments;
(i) annuities for the benefit of dependants;
(j) annuities in recognition of another's services;
(k) certain overseas government pensions paid in the UK;
(l) the house of Commons Members' Fund;
(m) return of surplus employee additional voluntary contributions;
(n) pre-1973 pensions paid under the Overseas Pensions Act 1973; and
(o) voluntary annual payments.

2 Exemptions for lump sums under certain pension schemes

No liability to income tax arises on a lump sum paid under a registered pension scheme if it is (ITEPA, s.636A-636C)–

(a) a pension commencement lump sum;
(b) a serious ill-health lump sum;
(c) a refund of contributions lump sum;
(d) a defined benefits lump sum death benefit; or
(e) an uncrystallised funds lump sum death benefit.
In the case of–
(f) a trivial commutation lump sum;
(g) a winding-up lump sum; or
(h) an equivalent pension benefits commutation lump sum,
the member is treated as having taxable pension income equivalent to the amount of the lump sum, but if the member has uncrystallised rights under the pension scheme that taxable amount is reduced. If a lump sum is paid to a person (not a member) under (f) to (h) above, it is fully taxable.

3 Award for gallantry

Annuities and/or additional pensions paid to holders of certain awards for gallantry by virtue of the award are exempt from income tax (ITEPA, s.638).

4 War service pensions and early departure payments

Pensions payable in respect of death due to war service or war injuries or peace-time service in the armed forces (including pensions paid by foreign governments) are exempt from income tax (ITEPA, s.639).

No liability to income tax arises on a lump sum provided under a scheme established by the Armed Forces Early Departure Payments Scheme Order 2005 or the Armed Forces Early Departure Payments Scheme Regulations 2014 (s.640A).

5 Wounds and disability pensions

Wounds and disability pensions granted to members of the naval, military, or air forces of the Crown, and injury and disablement pensions granted to members of the Mercantile Marine on account of war, are exempt from income tax (ITEPA, s.641).

6 Victims of National-Socialist persecution

Annuities and pensions payable under any special provision for victims of National-Socialist persecution which is made under the laws of Germany or Austria will not be treated as income (ITEPA, s.642).

In addition compensation paid to the heirs of a dormant foreign bank account of a holocaust victim is exempt from tax (s.268A).

7 Pensions of disabled employees

Where an employee retires on account of disability caused by injury on duty or by work-related illness, or by war wounds, and receives an enhanced pension on that account, the amount by which such pension exceeds the pension that would have been awarded if retirement had been on ordinary ill-health grounds is, not treated as income for income tax purposes (ITEPA, s.644).

No liability to income tax arises in respect of a pension or annuity payment which would be exempt from income tax under ITTOIA s.735 (see **18 Sick pay and proceeds of insurance against sickness**, below) provided that the payments are made to (a) a person ("the pensioner") who made payments or contributions in respect of premiums under an insurance policy which another person took out wholly or partly for the pensioner's benefit, or (b) to the pensioner's spouse or civil partner (s.644A).

8 Increases in respect of children

No liability to income tax arises on a part of a social security pension or an equivalent foreign pension which is attributable to an increase in respect of a child (ITEPA, s.645).

9 Non-UK resident taxpayers

No liability to income tax arises on certain kinds of pension if the recipient meets a "foreign residence condition", i.e., the pension is payable to someone who is not resident in the UK (s.647).

B: SOCIAL SECURITY INCOME

10 Taxable social security income

There are exemptions as follows (ITEPA, ss.663-676)–

Incapacity benefit
Long-term incapacity benefit is usually taxable, however, no liability to income tax arises on long-term incapacity benefit if the period of incapacity for work for which it is paid began before 13th April 1995 and the person to whom it is paid was entitled to the benefit before that date (s.663).

No liability to income tax arises on short-term incapacity benefit unless it is payable at the higher rate (s.664).

Income Support
Income support is generally exempt from income tax, unless paid to a member of a couple involved in a trade dispute (and the other member of the couple is not so involved) (s.665). Only the part of the income support which is attributable to the person on strike is taxable (s.667).

The child maintenance bonus element of income support is not taxable (s.666).

Jobseeker's Allowance
The child maintenance bonus element of jobseeker's allowance is not taxable (s.670).

Both income and contribution-based jobseeker's allowance are only taxable up to a "taxable maximum". For a single person the taxable maximum for income-based JSA is the amount of contribution-based allowance which would have been payable to them (s.673); and the taxable maximum for contribution-based JSA is the age-related amount applicable to them (s.674). For couples, the taxable amount of income-based JSA is their applicable amount (i.e., the age related amount, less some earnings and pensions); and of contribution-based JSA is the amount of income-based allowance which would have been payable to them. The amount of any allowance which relates to child or adult dependants is excluded.

Increases in respect of children

Any increases in respect of children are not taxable (s.676).

11 Wholly exempt social security income

Social security benefits which are always tax free are listed in s.677. They include–
- (a) attendance allowance;
- (b) back to work bonus;
- (c) bereavement payments;
- (d) child benefit;
- (e) child's special allowance;
- (f) child tax credit;
- (g) council tax benefit;
- (h) disability living allowance;
- (i) guardian's allowance;
- (j) health in pregnancy grant;
- (k) housing benefit;
- (l) income-related employment and support allowance;
- (m) industrial injuries benefit*;
- (n) in-work and return to work credit;
- (o) in-work emergency discretion fund payments;
- (p) pensioner's Christmas bonus;
- (q) personal independence payment;
- (r) social fund payments;
- (s) severe disablement allowance;
- (t) state maternity allowance;
- (u) state pension credit;
- (v) universal credit;
- (w) working tax credit;
- (x) payments to reduce under-occupation by housing benefit claimants.

*Note.–*Industrial death benefit is taxable as pension income.

C: WHOLLY EXEMPT INCOME

12 Introduction

Income from certain sources is wholly exempt from income tax. Such sources include those outlined in the following paragraphs.

13 Damages awarded for personal injuries

Any interest included in a sum awarded in judgment or (in Scotland) interlocutor for damages for personal injuries or death is not counted as income (ITTOIA, s.751). There is also an exemption from income tax for–
- (a) a settlement on a court order providing for periodic or annual payments of damages for personal injury (s.731);
- (b) annuity payments under an award of compensation made under the Criminal Injuries Compensation Scheme (s.732);
- (c) payments from trusts for injured persons (s.734).

14 Mis-sold personal pensions, etc

Compensation for financial loss caused by reliance on bad investment advice, at least some of which was given between 29th April 1988 and 30th June 1994 inclusive, is exempt from income tax (FA 1996, s.148).

Authorised payments under the Equitable Life (Payments) Act 2010 are disregarded for tax purposes including for income tax (Taxation of Equitable Life (Payments) Order 2011 (S.I. No. 1502)).

15 Payments relating to job finding

By ITTOIA, s.781, a payment to a person as a participant in the New Deal 50 plus by way of an employment credit or training grant is exempt from income tax. By s.782 of that Act, a payment to a person as a participant in an employment zone programme established under the Welfare Reform and Pensions Act 1999 is also exempt from income tax. By virtue of the Taxation of Benefits under Government Pilot Schemes (Return to Work Credit and Employment Retention and Advancement Schemes) Order 2003 (S.I. No. 2339), any amount paid under those two schemes is also wholly exempt from income tax.

16 Save as you earn (SAYE) schemes

Any interest (including any bonus) payable under a certified contractual SAYE savings scheme in respect of–
(a) money raised under s.12 of the National Loans Act 1968,
(b) shares in a building society,
(c) money paid to an institution authorised under the Banking Act 1987, or
(d) money paid to a relevant European institution (as defined),
does not give rise to an income tax liability (ITTOIA, ss.702-708).

17 Savings certificates and Government securities

Income arising from savings certificates is not liable to tax, except where certificates are purchased by or on behalf of a person in excess of the authorised maximum holding for any issue (ITTOIA, s.692).

18 Sick pay and proceeds of insurance against sickness

ITTOIA ss.735-743 make detailed provision for payments under a variety of insurance policies, including mortgage protection policies, to be exempt from tax, for so long as the person entitled to the benefits of the policy is sick, disabled or unemployed.

D: MISCELLANEOUS ALLOWANCES AND RELIEFS

19 Profits averaging

Profits averaging is available to taxpayers who have been carrying on a qualifying trade, profession or vocation (alone or in partnership) and whose profits fluctuate from one year to the next.
Qualifying trades, professions and vocations are (ITTOIA, s.221)–
(a) farming and market gardening;
(b) intensive rearing of stock or fish on a commercial basis for the production of food for human consumption; and
(c) occupations where the taxpayer's profits are derived wholly or mainly from creative works (i.e., literary, dramatic, musical or artistic works or designs personally created by the taxpayer or a partner).
In brief, the system allows for "profits averaging" over two or more consecutive years where the profits in the lower year are less than 75% of the profits in the higher year, or the profits in one, but not both, of the tax years is nil (s.222).
(For performing artists' expenses, see **83 Entertainers' expenses**, above.)

20 Enterprise Investment Scheme

The Enterprise Investment Scheme is now regulated by ITA Part 5 (ss.156-257).
Under the Scheme, an individual is eligible for relief if (ITA, s.157)–
(a) shares are issued to him;
(b) he is a qualifying investor;
(c) certain general requirements are met; and
(d) the company is a qualifying company.

Qualifying investors
The requirements to be met by an investor are contained in ss.162-171. In particular, an individual will not be eligible for relief in respect of any shares unless those shares are subscribed and issued for genuine commercial reasons and not as part of a scheme or arrangement, a main purpose of which is tax avoidance (s.165). In general, the investor must not be "connected" with the company during a period starting two years before the issue of the shares, and ending immediately before their termination date, be an employee of the company or of any subsidiary, or a director or partner of the company or of any subsidiary. However, a person will not be treated as being connected with an issuing company if he is an unpaid director of it, or if any payment that he receives is reasonable and necessary remuneration for services rendered in the course of a trade or profession (not being secretarial or management services or services of a kind provided by the person to whom they are rendered) (s.169).
Where a husband and wife (or civil partners) both subscribe for eligible shares, relief is given to them separately.

Amount of relief
Where an eligible individual claims relief under the EIS scheme, the amount of his tax liability will be reduced by an amount equal to tax at the EIS rate (30% for 2011-12 and subsequent tax years) for the current year on

the amount subscribed for eligible shares issued in that year, in respect of which he is eligible for relief (to a maximum of £1m) (s.158).

Where a person disposes of shares within three years then, if the disposal is not at arm's length, any relief attributable to those shares is withdrawn and, in any other case, relief may be reduced (s.209: this does not apply to a disposal between spouses/civil partners living together (s.209(4)).

An individual will not be entitled to relief if there is a loan made by any person to that individual, or any associate of his, which would not have been made, or would not have been made on the same terms, if that individual had not subscribed for those shares (s.164). Similarly, no relief will be available if there is a pre-arranged exit (as defined) e.g., where arrangements are made for the shares to be repurchased at a future date (s.177).

General requirements

General requirements are contained in ss.172-179. A claim for relief will not be allowed unless the company or subsidiary, as the case may be, has carried on a qualifying business activity for at least four months (176).

A "qualifying business activity means (s.179)–
  (i) the company or any qualifying subsidiary is carrying on a "qualifying trade" (see below), or is preparing to carry on such a trade, which it then begins to carry on within two years; or
  (ii) the company or any qualifying subsidiary is carrying on research and development (i.e., any activity intended to result in a patentable invention or in a computer program) from which it is intended that a "qualifying trade" will be derived.

A trade is a qualifying trade if it is conducted on a commercial basis and with a view to profit (s.189). It must not consist to any substantial extent of excluded activities. Excluded activities are (s.192)–
  (a) dealing in land, commodities, futures or shares, securities or other financial instruments;
  (b) dealing in goods otherwise than in the course of an ordinary trade of wholesale or resale distribution;
  (c) banking and insurance;
  (d) leasing and letting on hire, and receiving royalties and licence fees;
  (e) receiving royalties or licence fees;
  (f) providing legal or accounting services;
  (g) property development;
  (h) farming or market gardening;
  (i) holding, managing or occupying woodlands, any other forestry activities or timber production;
  (ia) shipbuilding or coal or steel production;
  (j) operating or managing hotels or comparable establishments or managing property used as an hotel or comparable establishment;
  (k) operating or managing nursing homes or residential care homes, or managing property used as a nursing home or residential care home;
  (ka) the subsidised generation or export of electricity, or the subsidised generation of heat or subsidised production of gas or fuel;
  (l) providing services or facilities for any trade carried on by another person (other than a parent company of the company concerned) which consists to any substantial extent of such excluded activities where one person has a controlling interest in both trades.

To come within the EIS schemes, shares must be "relevant shares" i.e., new ordinary shares which do not at any time carry any present or future preferential rights to dividends, or to a company's assets on winding up and no present or future rights of redemption (s.173).

Qualifying companies

To be a qualifying company, the requirements of ss.180-200 must be met. The assets of the company must not exceed £15 million immediately before the issue of the shares, and £16 million afterwards (s.186); it must, throughout the relevant period, be an unquoted company (s.184); must satisfy certain conditions as to its independence (s.185); must have a permanent establishment in the UK (s.180A); and must not be in financial difficulty (s.180B).

21 Seed Enterprise Investment Schemes (SEIS)

ITA Part 5A (ss.257A-257HJ) (added by FA 2012, s.38, Sch.6) provides entitlement to tax reductions in respect of amounts subscribed by individuals for shares in companies carrying on new businesses.

SEIS is intended to recognise the particular difficulties which very early stage companies face in attracting investment, by offering tax relief at a higher rate than that offered by the Enterprise Investment Scheme and its rules mirror that scheme (see **20 Enterprise Investment Scheme**, above). The amount of relief is 50% up to a maximum of £100,000 (s.257AB).

22 Social Investment Tax Relief (SITR)

A social enterprise is a commercial business that helps people or communities. SITR is a tax relief that investors can claim in respect of investments made in social enterprises (ITA Part 5B (ss.257J-257TE) (added by FA 2014 s.57, Sch. 11). The rules are similar to those for the Enterprise Investment Scheme (see **20 Enterprise Investment Scheme**, above)

The social enterprise must meet specified requirements including having fewer than 500 employees (s.257MH) and assets not exceeding £15 million immediately before the issue of the shares, and £16 million afterwards (s.257MC). Enterprises undertaking the following trades are excluded (s.257MQ)–

(a) dealing in land, in commodities or futures, in shares, securities or other financial instruments;

(b) banking, insurance, money-lending, debt-factoring, hire-purchase financing or other financial activities (with the exception of lending money to another social enterprise);

(c) property development;

(d) activities in the fishery and aquaculture sector that are covered by EU rules on the common organisation of the markets in fishery and aquaculture products;

(e) the primary production of products listed in Annex I to the Treaty on the Functioning of the European Union (agricultural products);

(f) generating or exporting electricity which will attract a Feed-in-Tariff;

(g) road freight transport for hire or reward; and

(h) providing services to another person where that person's trade substantially consists of excluded activities, and the person controlling that trade also controls the company providing the services.

Where an eligible individual claims relief under the SITR scheme, the amount of his tax liability will be reduced by an amount equal to 30% of his investment (to a maximum of £1m) (s.257JA) and claims may be made up to 5 years after the 31 January following the tax year in which the investment was made, provided the investment is held for at least 3 years.

23 Interest payments

Where a person pays interest in any tax year, that person, if he makes a claim for relief, will for that tax year, be entitled to relief in accordance with the provisions of ITA, s.383 in respect of so much of that interest as is eligible for relief under ss.388 to 405 (see below).

Loans for which interest relief may be available include loans

(1) to buy plant or machinery for partnership or employment use (ss.388-391);

(2) to buy an interest in a close company or an employee-controlled company (ss.392-397);

(3) to invest in a co-operative or partnership (ss.398-402); and

(4) to pay inheritance tax (ss.403-405).

In respect of loans taken out before 9th March 1999 by persons aged 65 or more to buy annuities (under ICTA s.365), relief will consist of an income tax reduction for the year of assessment concerned, whereby income tax liability will be reduced by the 23% of the interest paid (ICTA s.353(1AA)).

Note.–For interest on beneficial loans, see the Note on **Income Tax: Employment Income** at para **14 Loans**.

24 Life assurance relief

(a) *Policies made on or before 13th March 1984.*

In the case of insurance policies made on or before 13th March 1984, relief is given under ICTA, s.266 in respect of premiums on qualifying life assurance policies (as defined in Schedule 15), up to certain limits, provided that the individual is resident in the UK (or is serving abroad in the armed forces of the Crown or in specified women's services), that the policy is on his own or his spouse/civil partner's life, and that the insurance or contract was made by one of them. The amount of the relief is normally deducted from the premium by the insurance company, who recover it from the Commissioners.

(b) *Policies made after 13th March 1984.* No relief is granted in respect of premiums payable under insurance policies made after 13th March 1984.

Where a policy issued in respect of an insurance made before 13th March 1984 is varied after that date so as to increase the benefits secured or to extend the term of the insurance, the insurance will be treated as made after that date. Any change made in the terms of a policy, which was issued in respect of an insurance made before the date and which conferred an option to have its terms changed or to have another policy substituted, will be deemed to be a variation.

S.268 provides that where, within four years of the making of the insurance, a qualifying policy is wholly or partly surrendered, or a sum payable in pursuance of a right conferred by the policy to participate in profits falls due, or the policy is converted into a paid-up or partly paid-up policy, there is a "clawback" of the relief and the issuing body must pay to the Commissioners a sum calculated in accordance with s.268(2) to (6). Under paragraph 20 of Schedule 15, however, exemption is granted from this clawback where one qualifying policy is replaced by another in consequence of a variation in the life or lives assured, provided that the later policy was made on or after 25th March 1982 and certain other conditions are satisfied.

Where the individual is not resident (or treated as resident) in the UK, he must pay the premium on a qualifying policy in full but may be entitled to claim appropriate relief (under s.278).

Note.–Certain life assurance policies (whenever made) which are linked with other policies on unusually beneficial terms are disqualified for the purpose of relief under s.266 (Sch. 15, para. 14).

25 Losses

Provision is made for any loss sustained in a trade, profession, vocation, or employment to be set off against other income for the year of assessment, or against any income for the last preceding year. A claim must be made within 12 months of the normal self-assessment filing date for the loss-making year (ITA, s.64). Relief is given only where the activities in respect of which the loss was suffered are conducted on a commercial basis with a reasonable expectation of profit (s.68). Where losses have been incurred in farming or market gardening for five successive years, further losses in subsequent years will not (subject to certain exceptions) qualify for relief (s.67).

Losses sustained in the early years of a business may be carried back and set off against the general income of the individual in the preceding three years (s.72) and losses sustained in the 12 months before the permanent discontinuance of a business may be set off against profits in that business charged to tax for the three years of assessment prior to discontinuance (s.89).

26 Foreign maintenance payments

No liability to income tax arises in respect of an annual payment if it is a maintenance payment which arises outside the UK and, had it arisen in the UK, it would have been exempt as an annual payment (ITTOIA, s.730).

27 Patentees

Where a royalty or other sum is paid in respect of the user of a patent, and that user extended over a period of two or more years, the person receiving the payment may on the making of a claim require that the income tax (or corporation tax) payable by him by reason of the receipt of that sum be reduced so as not to exceed the total amount of tax which would have been payable by him if that royalty or sum had been paid in equal yearly instalments, the last of which was paid on the date on which the payment was in fact made (ITA, s.461).

28 Double taxation

Relief against double taxation, in the form of income tax or corporation tax, and taxes of a similar nature imposed by the laws of another territory, is provided under international agreements made operative in the UK by Orders in Council (ICTA, s.788, and FA 1989, s.115). Ss.792 to 806 set out rules which apply where the agreed arrangements provide for tax payable in the overseas territory to be allowed as a credit against tax payable in the UK. *Inter alia* a person claiming such relief must normally be resident in the UK for the chargeable period concerned.

Where no such arrangements are in force unilateral relief may be available on a similar basis under s.790.

E: CHARITIES AND CHARITABLE GIVING

29 Charities

Under ITA, Part 10 (ss.518-564), exemption is granted, to charities claiming it, from tax arising on—
(a) property income etc. i.e., income chargeable to tax under Parts 2 and 3 of ITTOIA in respect of any profits or gains arising in respect of rents or other receipts from an estate, interest or right in or over land vested in any person for charitable purposes, so far as they are applied to charitable purposes only (ITA s.531);
(b) savings and investment income i.e., income chargeable to as interest, annuities, dividends, distributions, and annual payments where the income belongs to a charity or is applicable to charitable purposes only, and so far as it is so applied (ITA s.532);
(c) public revenue dividends on securities which are in the name of trustees, to the extent that the dividends are applicable and applied only for the repair of (i) any cathedral, college, church or chapel, or (ii) any building used only for the purpose of divine worship (ITA s.533);
(d) profits etc of charitable trades i.e., in respect of the profits of any trade carried on by a charity; where the profits are applied solely to the work of the charity *and* either (i) the trade is exercised in carrying out a primary purpose of the charity, or (ii) the work in connection with the trade is mainly carried out by beneficiaries of the charity (ITA ss.524-525);
(e) profits from fund-raising events if they are VAT exempt (see VAT Act 1994, Sch.9, Group 12). (ITA s.529);
(f) profits from lotteries where the profits are applied solely to the charity's purposes (ITA s.530);
(g) small-scale trades (ITA s.526); certain other miscellaneous income listed in ITA s.1016 (including e.g., intellectual property royalties, interest, wayleaves, etc) (ITA ss.527-528).

Where a payment is received by one charity from another charity in the UK, which is not made for full consideration in money or money's worth, is not otherwise chargeable to tax, and is not such as would otherwise be eligible for tax relief under (a) to (g) above, it will be chargeable to tax under ITA s.523, except in so far as it is applied to charitable purposes only.

TAXATION

Under ITA, for every £1 of non-charitable expenditure incurred by a charity, there is a corresponding restriction of the income and gains that attract tax exemption. Where there is an excess of non-charitable expenditure over total income in the current year, the excess can be carried back by Revenue and Customs to an earlier period (ITA ss.539-564).

Where a payment is made to a body outside the UK, it will not be charitable expenditure unless the charity has taken reasonable steps to ensure that the payment will be applied for charitable purposes. Where such expenditure is not actually incurred in a particular chargeable period but properly falls to be charged against the income of that period, it will be treated as incurred in that period (s.547).

If a charity makes an investment or a loan which is not an approved charitable investment or loan, as defined, the expenditure incurred will be treated as non-charitable expenditure, but if during the chargeable period such an investment or loan is in whole or part realised or repaid, as the case may be, any further investment or lending in that period of the sum realised or repaid will be discounted in determining the amount of non-charitable expenditure so long as it does not exceed the sum originally invested or lent (ss.543, 548).

There are rules to prevent abuse of these provisions by the making of "tainted" donations. If a charitable donation is considered a "tainted donation", then the donor and any advantaged person are jointly and severally liable, and if an officer of HMRC is satisfied that the charity was knowingly party to the agreement then they will also be liable to penalties (ITA 2007, Part 13, Chapter 8, ss.809ZH-809ZR). For a charitable donation to be deemed "tainted" it must meet three conditions–

(a) the donor or a person connected with them enters into an arrangement where it is reasonable to assume that the donations and arrangements would not be entered into separately;

(b) one of the main purposes of the arrangements is to obtain a direct or indirect financial advantage from the charity;

(c) the donor is not a qualifying charity owned company or relevant housing provider linked with the charity to which the donation is made.

(For the provisions relating to donations to charity, see **31 Donations to charity (Gift Aid)**, and Part G: COVENANTS AND DISPOSITIONS, below; and see the Note on **Income Tax: General Provisions** at para **30 Payroll deduction scheme.**)

30 Definition of "charity" for taxation purposes

For taxation purposes, a charity is a company or body of persons or trust that (Finance Act 2010, s.30 and Sch. 6)–

(a) is established for charitable purposes only;

(b) meets the jurisdiction condition (i.e., is subject to the control of a UK court in the exercise of its jurisdiction with respect to charities, or of any other court in the exercise of a corresponding jurisdiction under the law of an EU Member State or other relevant territory;

(c) meets the registration condition (i.e., is registered as a charity in England and Wales or in an equivalent register outside England and Wales); and

(d) meets the management condition (i.e., it's managers are fit and proper persons to be managers of the body or trust).

For these purposes, Iceland, Liechtenstein and Norway are relevant territories (Taxes (Definition of Charity) (Relevant Territories) Regulations 2010).

31 Donations to charity (Gift Aid)

Under ITA s.414 a qualifying donation to a charity made by an individual is treated as if, in relation to him, the gift had been made after deduction of income tax at the basic rate and the basic rate limit were increased by an amount equal to the grossed up amount of the gift.

The requirements for qualification are that (s.416)–

(a) the gift takes the form of a payment of a sum of money;

(b) it is not subject to a condition as to repayment;

(c) it does not fall under the Payroll Deduction Scheme (see below);

(d) it is not deductible in calculating the individual's income from any source;

(e) neither the donor nor any person connected with him receives any benefit in consequence of making it which exceeds a prescribed limit (see below);

(f) the gift is not conditional on or associated with the acquisition of property by the charity from the donor, or any person connected with him, otherwise than by way of a gift;

(g) the donor is resident in the UK at the time the gift is made (some gifts from overseas do qualify for gift aid: see ss.422, 427).

When making the donation the donor must supply an appropriate declaration confirming *inter alia* that these conditions are fully met. The declaration may be given in advance, at the time of, or after the donation (subject to the normal time limits for reclaiming tax), and may cover one or any number of donations. It may be given in writing or orally (in which case either a written record must be sent to the donor or the charity must keep a sufficient record of the declaration for it to be audited by HM Revenue and Customs). A declaration must contain the donor's name and address, the charity's name, a description of the donation(s) to which it relates

TAXATION

and a declaration that the donation(s) are to be treated as Gift Aid donations. Except in the case of oral declarations, it must also contain a note explaining the requirement that the donor must pay an amount of income tax (or capital gains tax) equal to the tax deducted from the donation, and the date of the declaration (Donations to Charity by Individuals (Appropriate Declarations) Regulations 2000).

The permissible limits for donor benefits (see (e) above) are (s.418))–

Aggregate Donations	Limit of Benefits
Up to £100	25%
£101 to £1,000	£25
£1,001 +	5%
	Subject to a maximum of £2,500 in any tax year

These figures are adjusted where the benefits are received over a period of less than a year.

Where a donor receives a right of admission in return for a sum of money, the donation will only qualify for gift-aid if it is either an unlimited right of admission for at least a year or the donation is at least 10% more than the normal admission price (s.420).

Note.– If a donor is a higher or additional rate taxpayer, they can claim relief equal to the difference between the higher rate of tax at 40% or 45% and the basic rate of tax at 20% on the total value of the donation – a total of 20% and/or 25%. So if £1 was donated, the "grossed up" donation would be £1.25 and a donor liable at the 40% tax rate could claim relief of 25 pence (20% of £1.25).

As to the Payroll Deduction Scheme, see the Note on **Income Tax: General Provisions** at para **30 Payroll deduction scheme**.

32 Gifts in kind to charities

Where a donor gives a charity, a registered club, the National Heritage Memorial Fund, the Historic Buildings and Monuments Commission for England, or the National Endowment for Science, Technology and the Arts, new or second-hand equipment which is of a class manufactured, sold or used by the donor in the course of his trade, profession or vocation, then no amount needs to be brought into account in consequence of a disposal from trading stock (ITTOIA, s.108).

If the donor or a connected person receives a benefit attributable to the gift, an amount equal to the value of the benefit is taken into account in calculating the profits of the trade, as a receipt of the trade, on the date on which the benefit is received, or, if the donor has ceased to trade, as a post-cessation receipt (s.109).

See also **34 Gifts to educational establishments**, below.

33 Gifts of shares, etc to charities

Where a donor disposes of the whole of his beneficial interest in shares or securities listed on a recognised stock exchange, or units in a unit trust, to a charity either by way of gift or sale at an undervalue, he may deduct from his income tax liability for that tax year an amount equal to the market value of the shares plus any incidental costs of disposal (e.g., broker's fees), less any consideration received (including the value of any benefits received by the donor or a connected person in consequence of the disposal) (ITA, s.431).

34 Gifts to educational establishments

Where a donor gives a designated educational institution new or second-hand equipment which is of a class manufactured, sold or used by the donor in the course of his trade, profession or vocation, then no amount needs to be brought into account in consequence of a disposal from trading stock (ITTOIA, s.108). The Taxes (Relief for Gifts) (Designated Educational Establishments) Regulations 1992 define what is an educational institution for these purposes.

As to the situation where the donor receives a benefit from the gift, see **32 Gifts in kind to charities**, above.

F: SETTLEMENTS

35 Income from settlements

Any income, unless it does not exceed £100, paid in any year under a settlement to or for the benefit of a child of the settlor who is aged under 18 years and not married or in a civil partnership at the date of payment is treated as the income of the settlor (ITTOIA, s.629).

In the case of a settlement under which the income arising is, during the life of the settlor, payable to or applicable for the benefit of a person other than the settlor, the income will, with certain exceptions, be treated as the income of the settlor for all the purposes of the Income Tax Acts unless it is income from property of which the settlor has divested himself absolutely by the settlement. The exceptions include annual payments made by an individual for *bona fide* commercial reasons connected with his trade, profession, or vocation, payments by one party to a marriage under a settlement made after the marriage has been terminated, and covenanted payments to charity (s.627).

References to a settlement does not include an outright gift (as defined) by one spouse/civil partner to the other of property from which income arises unless (a) the gift does not carry a right to the whole of that income, or (b) the property given is wholly or substantially a right to income (s.626).

Under s.151 of the Finance Act 1989, tax on income arising to the trustees of a settlement or to the personal representatives of a deceased person may be assessed and charged on and in the name of any one or more of the relevant trustees or personal representatives.

G: COVENANTS AND DISPOSITIONS

36 Income from annuities

Under ITA ss.447-452, where any annuity or other annual payment charged with tax under ITTOIA, Part 4, Chapters 7, Part 5, Chapters 4 or 7, or s.579 (or Case III of Schedule D for corporation tax) (other than interest and certain payments under discretionary trusts), is payable wholly out of profits or gains brought into charge to income tax, the payer is taxed on the whole of those profits or gains but may deduct from each payment a sum representing the amount of income tax thereon. The deduction is treated as income tax paid by the recipient which the payer may retain so far as it is covered by his own taxed income.

Under ITTOIA s.624, income arising under a settlement during the life of the settlor is treated as the income of the settlor unless the income arises from property in which the settlor has no interest. Settlement is widely defined to include any disposition, trust, covenant, agreement, arrangement, or transfer of assets (s.620). This does not however apply to income which is payable as a qualifying donation to charity i.e., one which satisfies ITA s.414 (see **31 Donations to charity (Gift Aid)**, above).

H: INCOME FROM INVESTMENTS

37 The personal savings allowance

From 6th April 2016, a new personal savings allowance is being introduced. This will allow a basic rate taxpayer to earn up to £1,000 in savings income tax-free. Higher rate taxpayers will be able to earn up to £500 in savings interest tax free, but additional-rate tax payers do not qualify for a personal savings allowance. From that date, banks and building societies will no longer deduct tax from account interest. Instead, tax will be collected either through PAYE or through self-assessment.

Savings income includes account interest from—
(1) bank and building society accounts;
(2) accounts with providers like credit unions or National Savings and Investments;
(3) interest distributions (but not dividend distributions) from authorised unit trusts, open-ended investment companies and investment trusts;
(4) income from government or company bonds; and
(5) most types of purchased life annuity payments.

Interest from Individual Savings Accounts (ISAs) will not count towards the Personal Savings Allowance as it is already tax-free.

38 Individual savings accounts: introduction

Note.–From 6th April 2016, see also **37 The personal savings allowance**, above.

Individual savings accounts (ISAs) superseded Personal Equity Plans and Tax-exempt Special Savings Accounts with effect from 6th April 1999, although PEPs and TESSAs then current could continue to run their course.

ITTOIA s.694 empowers the Treasury to make regulations providing for introducing an investment scheme, whereby an individual investing under an individual investment plan (IIPs) may be entitled to relief from income tax in respect of his investments.

ITTOIA ss.694 to 698, s.151 of the Taxation of Chargeable Gains Act and ss.75 and 76(3) of the Finance Act 1998 empower the Treasury to make regulations to provide for the setting up of IIPs by account managers to which an individual may make subscriptions and through which those subscriptions are invested. The Individual Savings Account Regulations 1998 specify the individuals who may invest, the permitted investments and maximum investment levels, and provide for accounts to be managed by account managers. The Regulations also provide for relief from tax in respect of accounts, withdrawal of relief and modifications to income tax and capital gains tax legislation in relation to accounts.

From 1st July 2014 ISAs have become New ISAs (NISA) which may be held entirely in cash, entirely in stocks and shares, or a mixture of the two.

39 Types of ISA and investment limits

An ISA must consist of one or a combination of three components, namely–
(a) stocks and shares;
(b) cash; and
(c) innovative finance (see below).

Those under 18 can open an adult cash ISA at the age of 16, but cannot open an adult stocks and shares or innovative finance ISA until they turn 18.

The annual subscription limits for a qualifying individual (see **41 Qualifying ISA investors**, below) from 6th April 2015 are as follows—

For an individual aged 18 or over	£15,240 which may be held entirely in cash, entirely in stocks and shares, entirely in innovative finance or a mixture of the three
For an individual aged 16 but under 18	£15,240 (cash ISA only)
For a Junior ISA (see below)	£4,080 which may be held entirely in cash, entirely in stocks and shares, or a mixture of the two

Note.–From 6th April 2016, an ISA (other than a Junior ISA) may be a "flexible account" which will allow a saver to replace cash they have withdrawn from their ISA earlier in the tax year, without this replacement money counting towards the annual ISA subscription limit. Savers may also replace cash withdrawn from a previous year's ISA savings in the account from which it was withdrawn, without breaching the condition that an individual can only subscribe to one ISA in a tax year.

A junior ISA can be set up by a person with parental responsibility for a child. It can also be set up by a qualifying child who is aged 16 or over. See **41 Qualifying ISA investors**, below.

An Innovative Finance ISA allows an individual (the lender) to include loans they make through P2P (Peer to Peer) lending platforms to be held within an ISA, up to the ISA allowance threshold. As a result, the interest paid by borrowers on the money loaned will be tax free.

40 Lifetime ISAs

From April 2017 people under the age of 40 will be able to open a new "Lifetime ISA" and pay in up to £4,000 in each tax year, with an annual government bonus of 25% to help buy a first home or save for retirement.

A Lifetime ISAs can be opened from the age of 18 and payments can continue to be made into it until the age of 50. The funds can be used either–

(a) to buy a first home worth up to £450,000 at any time after 12 months from opening the account; or

(b) can be taken out from age 60.

The savings can be taken out before the age of 60 but, except in the case of terminal illness, there will be a 5% charge and any government bonus will be lost.

41 Qualifying ISA investors

An individual may invest in an ISA if they are a "qualifying individual". A qualifying individual is someone who is resident in the UK (or who is a Crown employee serving overseas (for example a member of the armed forces)) and who (Individual Savings Account Regulations 1998, Reg. 10, as amended)–

(a) in the case of a cash account, is 16 years of age or over and, in the case of a stocks and shares account, is 18 years of age or over;

(b) in the case of a stocks and shares account, has not subscribed, and will not subscribe, to any other stocks and shares account, in the year in which the subscription is made;

(c) in the case of a cash account, has not subscribed, and will not subscribe, to any other cash account, in the year in which the subscription is made;

(d) has not exceeded the overall subscription limit (see para **39 Types of ISA and investment limits**, above).

An individual who ceases to be resident may retain the benefits of an account outstanding at that time, but cannot subscribe further to the account until he becomes resident again (Reg. 11).

A "junior ISA" may be opened for a child if they (ITTOIA s.695A and Reg. 2)–

(a) are under 18;

(b) live in the UK; and

(c) do not already have a Child Trust Fund account.

Each child can have one cash and one stocks and shares junior ISA at any one time. Anybody can put money into a junior ISA. The money in a junior ISA belongs to the child, but cannot be withdrawn until they are 18 when they can either take the money out, or let it remain in which case it will automatically become an adult ISA. Withdrawals may also be made where a child is terminally ill or has died.

42 Tax credit on dividend payments

Tax payable on dividend distributions on company shares is dealt with by way of tax credit, but is not covered in detail here.

43 Venture capital trusts

Relief for investment in a venture capital trust (VCT) was introduced by the Finance Act 1995 and is now contained in ITA.

Income from an investment in an approved VCT is granted relief from income tax by ITA s.258. An approved VCT is one which (ITA, s.259)–

    (i) is not close company; and

which, in relation to it most recent complete accounting period, has (ITA s.274)–

    (ii) its income derived wholly or mainly from shares or securities;

    (iii) at least 70% by value of its investments in qualifying holdings (as defined by s.280);

    (iv) at least 70% by value of its shares in ordinary shares;

    (v) no more than 15% by value of its investments outside the VCT area;

    (vi) its shares admitted to trading on a regulated market;

    (vii) not retained more than 15% of its income from investments;

and which HM Revenue and Customs are satisfied will also meet these requirements for the accounting period for which the application relates. Provisional approval may be granted where some but not all of these conditions are met and HM Revenue and Customs are satisfied that the other conditions will be met.

The maximum relief for any given year of assessment is £200,000 (s.262).

44 Interest on deposits

Note.–From 6th April 2016, see **37 The personal savings allowance**, above.

Under ITA s.851, interest on deposits with banks and certain other deposit-takers (which term is defined to include banks, the Post Office, and any person or class of person who receives deposits in the course of his business or activities and is prescribed by Treasury order for this purpose) is taxable at source. A deposit-taker is liable to account for and pay income tax on any payment of interest made in respect of any relevant deposit. A deposit is relevant for this purpose only if the person beneficially entitled to any interest on it is an individual or, where two or more persons are so entitled, all of them are individuals, the person entitled to any such interest receives it in the capacity of personal representative, or, in Scotland, the person who is so entitled is a partnership all the partners of which are individuals, and the deposit is not specifically excepted under ITA or by a Treasury order made thereunder (s.856).

Any tax deducted under ITA s.851 will be at the savings rate for the year in which the payment is made. However, s.852 empower Revenue and Customs to make regulations enabling a deposit-taker on prescribed conditions to make gross payments of interest without deduction of tax, thereby disapplying s.851. Under the Income Tax (Deposit-takers and Building Societies) (Interest Payments) Regulations 2008 gross payments may be made in respect of relevant deposits to persons beneficially entitled to the payments provided a certificate of non-tax liability on savings income has been supplied to the deposit-taker and it has not ceased to be valid. A certificate of non-tax liability must–

    (a) certify that the person beneficially entitled to the payment is unlikely to be liable to pay any amount by way of income tax on savings income, for the year beginning on 6th April in which the payment is made;

    (b) be given by–

        (i) a depositor who was aged 16 or over at the beginning of the year in which the payment is made and who is beneficially entitled to the payment,

        (ii) the parent or guardian of a person beneficially entitled to it who is under the age of 16 at the beginning of the year,

        (iii) a person beneficially entitled to it who is under the age of 16 at the beginning of that year, but will attain that age during the year,

        (iv) the donee of a power of attorney authorising him to administer the affairs of a person beneficially entitled to the payment,

        (v) a parent or guardian, spouse or civil partner, or son or daughter of a person who lacks capacity to make a decision for himself for the purposes of the Mental Capacity Act 2005, s.2; or

        (vi) a receiver or other person appointed to manage and administer the affairs of a person who lacks capacity to make a decision for himself;

        (vii) a person appointed by the Secretary of State under Reg. 33 para 1 of the Social Security (Claims and Payments) Regulations 1987 (see the Note on **Social Security Benefits: General and Common Provisions** at para **19 Third parties**), or Reg. 28 para 2 of the Child Benefit and Guardian's Allowance (Administration) Regulations 2003, whose appointment has not been revoked or terminated, or who has not resigned his office.

    (c) not be given or supplied where ITTOIA s.629 applies to the payment, or where Revenue and Customs have given notice requiring the deposit-taker to deduct tax from payments made in respect of a specified account, having reason to believe that the person beneficially entitled is or has become liable to pay income tax on savings income, and the notice has not been cancelled;

    (d) be given and supplied to the deposit-taker before the end of the year in which the payment is made or, in the case of (b)(iii) above, before the end of the year in which the person beneficially entitled attains the age of 16;

    (e) be in the prescribed form, and contains the information specified in the Reg. 9 and also an undertaking to inform Revenue and Customs should the person beneficially entitled to the payment become liable to pay income tax on savings income during the year.

Part 4 of the Regulations provide for the furnishing of information to, and inspection of documents by, officers of Revenue and Customs in connection with payments of interest made without deduction of tax, and connected provisions.

The Income Tax (Interest Payments) (Information Powers) Regulations 1992 make further requirements as to the provision of information.

45 Dividends and interest

Note.–From 6th April 2016, see **37 The personal savings allowance**, above.

ITA s.889 requires building societies to deduct out of any dividend or interest paid or credited in any year in respect of shares in, deposits with, or loans to, the society a sum representing the amount of income tax on it for the year in which the payment is made, and to account for and pay the amount deducted to the Commissioners.

See also **42 Interest on deposits**, above.

46 Authorities

Statutes–

The Finance Acts

Income Tax Act 2007

Income Tax (Trading and Other Income) Act 2005

Statutory Instruments–

Donations to Charity by Individuals (Appropriate Declarations) Regulations 2000, as amended (S.I. 2000 No. 2074 and 2005 No. 2790)

Income Tax (Deposit-takers and Building Societies) (Interest Payments) Regulations 2008, as amended (S.I. 2008 No. 2682, 2010 No. 22, and 2015 No. 653)

Income Tax (Interest Payments) (Information Powers) Regulations 1992, as amended (S.I. 1992 No. 15, 2001 No. 405, 2008 No. 2688, and 2011 No. 22)

Individual Savings Accounts Regulations 1998, as amended (S.I. 1998 Nos. 1870 and 3174, 2000 Nos. 809, 2079 and 3112, 2001 Nos. 908, 3629, and 3778, 2002 Nos. 453, 1409, 1974, and 3158, 2003 No. 2747, 2004 Nos. 1677 and 2996, 2005 Nos. 609, 2561, 3230, and 3350, 2006 No. 3194, 2007 No. 2119, 2008 Nos. 704, 1934, and 3025, 2009 Nos. 56, 1550 and 1994, 2010 Nos. 835 and 2957, 2011 Nos. 22, 782, and 1780, 2012 Nos. 705, 1871, and 2404, 2013 Nos. 267, 472, 605, 623, 1743, and 1765, 2014 Nos. 654 and 1450, 2015 Nos. 608, 869, 941, and 1370, and 2016 Nos. 16 and 364)

Taxes (Definition of Charity) (Relevant Territories) Regulations 2010, as amended (S.I. 2010 No. 1904 and 2014 No. 1807)

Taxes (Relief for Gifts) (Designated Educational Establishments) Regulations 1992, as amended (S.I. 1992 No. 42, 1993 No. 561, 2010 No. 1172, and 2012 No. 979)

INCOME TAX: PAY AS YOU EARN

1 Introduction

The Pay As You Earn (PAYE) scheme of income tax collection is operated under the Income Tax (Pay As You Earn) Regulations 2003, made under the Income Tax (Earnings and Pensions) Act 2003 (ITEPA). It applies to all "PAYE income", that is all employment, pension and social security income (ITEPA, s.682).

Unless otherwise stated, any references to a numbered regulation of, or Part of, any Regulations is a reference to the 2003 Regulations.

Essentially, the scheme provides for the deduction by an employer, at the time of payment to his employee(s), of the tax due in respect of each such payment and for payment of the amount deducted by the employer to HM Revenue and Customs. Regulation 98 enables employers to set up separate schemes for different groups of employees.

2 Real time information

From April 2013 HM Revenue and Customs (HMRC) introduced a new way of reporting PAYE, known as Real Time Information, or RTI.

Using RTI, employers and pension providers tell HMRC about PAYE payments at the time they are made as part of their payroll process. Payroll software collects the necessary information and sends it to HMRC Online. Information about PAYE payments is therefore submitted throughout the year as part of the payroll process, rather than at the end of the year as previously.

Most employers were required to use RTI from April 2013 with all employers submitting RTI by October 2013. On or before making a relevant payment to an employee, an RTI employer must deliver to HMRC the information specified in Schedule A1 to the Income Tax (Pay As You Earn) Regulations 2003 (a real time return of information) unless the employer is not required by Regulation 66 (deductions working sheets) to maintain a deductions working sheet for an employee (Reg. 67B(1)).

There was a two year relaxation to the RTI reporting requirements for existing micro employers (i.e., until 6th April 2016). From 6th April 2014 all new employers, regardless of size, need to report each time they pay their employees.

Where an employer fails to deliver an RTI return when required he will be liable to a penalty which varies according to the size of the employer from £100 (under 10 employees) to £400 (250 or more employees) (Reg. 67I).

3 Meaning of payments

In determining whether anything constitutes a payment for the purposes of the 2003 Act and the PAYE regulations, a payment of, or on account of, any PAYE income is treated as made at the time found in accordance with the following rules, taking the earlier or earliest time where more than one rule applies—
  (a) the time when the payment is actually made;
  (b) the time when a person becomes entitled to the payment;
  (c) in the case of income of a director of a company from an office or employment with that company—
      (i) where sums on account of the income are credited in the company's accounts, the time when they are so credited;
      (ii) where the amount of the income for a period is determined before the period ends, the time when the period ends;
      (iii) where the amount of the income for a period is not known until it is determined after the period has ended, the time when the amount is determined.

Rules (c)(i), (ii), and (iii) apply whether or not the office or employment concerned is that of director, provided that the holder of the office or employment is a director of the company at any time in the year of assessment in which the time mentioned in the paragraph concerned falls (ITEPA, s.686).

4 Persons responsible for deduction of tax

Generally, the employer is the person responsible for the deduction of tax, but where any payment of PAYE income is made to an employee by an intermediary of an employer, the employer will be treated as having made that payment, unless the intermediary himself deducts tax from the payment and accounts for it in accordance with the 1993 Regulations (ITEPA, s.687). An "intermediary" is defined to mean a person acting on behalf of, or at the expense of, an employer, or a trust holding property for the employee (ITEPA, s.687(4)). ITEPA ss.688-691 make special provision for agency workers, employees of non-United Kingdom employers, non-resident employees, and mobile workforces.

Where organised arrangements (a tronc) exist for gratuities or service charges to be shared among two or more employees by any person, that person (the tronc-master) is responsible for the deduction of tax on any payments made in accordance with the arrangements. But where the tronc-master fails to observe the requirements of the Regulations, then the principal employer will be deemed to be the employer and thus will be responsible for deducting the tax in accordance with the Regulations (ITEPA, s.692, and Reg. 100).

5 Coding

An employee's code number is determined by the Inspector of Taxes having regard to (Regs. 14 to 14B)–

(a) the reliefs from income tax to which the employee is entitled (these include allowances and deductions but not allowable superannuation contributions);

(b) any PAYE income of the employee (other than the relevant payments in relation to which the code is being determined);

(c) any tax overpaid for any previous tax year which has not been repaid;

(d) any tax remaining unpaid for any previous tax year which is not otherwise recovered;

(e) any tax repaid to the employee in excess of the amount properly due to the employee which may be recovered as if it were unpaid tax under the Taxes Management Act 1970, s.30(1) (recovery of overpayment of tax etc.) and which is not otherwise recovered;

(f) unless the employee objects, any other income of the employee which is not PAYE income;

(g) any relevant debt owed to HMRC;

(h) unless the employee objects, the collection of the high income child benefit charge; and

(i) such other adjustments as may be necessary to secure that, so far as possible, the tax in respect of the employee's income in relation to which the code is determined will be deducted from the relevant payments made during that tax year.

The deduction includes the income tax on any benefits in kind. The coding system contains an overriding limit on the amount of tax which may be deducted from a payment of income to ensure that the tax liability does not exceed 50% of the employee's pay (Regs 2(1) and 23).

The Inspector must notify the employee of any alteration in his tax code other than one arising from a general alteration in personal reliefs, or where the employee's PAYE income is not chargeable to tax, or where the employee has no liability to tax in respect of any PAYE income (Reg. 17). There are provisions enabling employees to object to and appeal against coding and in relation to the amendment of coding.

6 Meaning of "net PAYE income"

"Net PAYE income", for the purposes of the scheme, means PAYE income (as defined by ITEPA s.683) less any–

(a) allowable pension contributions, and

(h) allowable donations to charity.

7 Deduction of tax

An employer is required to operate the PAYE scheme in respect of any employee to whom he pays emoluments in any week or month exceeding the amount of a single person's annual tax allowance expressed as a weekly or monthly rate, as appropriate. Generally, the employer ascertains the amount of tax to be deducted by reference to the employee's coding and the tax tables supplied by the tax office.

Regulations 46 to 49 set out the procedure to be followed by an employer in respect of an employee for whom the appropriate code is not known. *Inter alia* these Regulations have the effect of requiring an employer to operate the scheme in respect of any employee who is in receipt of PAYE income in any week or month exceeding the PAYE threshold (i.e., the amount of a single person's annual tax allowance expressed as a weekly or monthly rate: Reg. 9).

8 Termination of employment

If an employer ceases to employ an employee in respect of whom a code has been, or is deemed to have been, issued to him, he is required to notify the Inspector in the prescribed form (P45) (Reg. 36). He is also required to deliver three copies of the P45 to the employee on the day the employment ceases. On commencing his next employment the employee must deliver two copies of the P45 to his new employer (Reg. 40(1)). Retirement on a pension paid by the former employer is not a cessation of employment for these purposes (Reg. 36(3)).

See also **10 Return by employer**, below.

Note.–For employers using Real Time Information (see **2 Real time information**, above), and their employees, P45s will no longer be needed.

9 Payment of tax

Employers are normally required to pay any tax due to HM Revenue and Customs (i.e., amounts liable to be deducted less the amount of any repayments due) within 14 days of the end of every income tax month (or within 17 days after the end of the tax month, where payment is made by an approved method of electronic communications) (Reg. 69). Where, however, an employer has reasonable grounds for believing that the average monthly total amount to be paid to HM Revenue and Customs by way of–

(a) PAYE; plus

(b) National Insurance Contributions; plus

(c) student loan repayments; plus

(d) any statutory deductions under s.559 on payments to sub-contractors in the building; less

(e) any amount payable by the employer by way of statutory sick, maternity, paternity, shared parental and adoption pay; and

(f) if the employer is a company, the amount which others would deduct from payments to it, in its position as a sub-contractor,

will be less than £1,500, payment may be allowed quarterly instead of monthly (Reg. 70).

Regulations 77, 78, and 84 make provision for the recovery of tax from an employer. Regulation 78 provides inter *alia* that if, after 17 days following the end of any income tax period, HM Revenue and Customs has reason to believe that an amount or a further amount of tax is due from the employer, HM Revenue and Customs may specify the amount or further amount that they consider the employer liable to pay, and serve notice to him of that amount. If on the expiration of the period of seven days allowed in the notice, the employer either fails to pay the amount specified or the actual amount for which he is liable, or to satisfy HM Revenue and Customs that no such amount is due, the specified amount must be certified by HM Revenue and Customs and will then be recoverable from the employer.

There is a payment tolerance of £100 with real time information, so that where an employer pays over a sum that is within £100 of the total sum due to HMRC from all sources for the tax period in question, no late payment default will be due (Reg. 69A).

10 Return by employer

Note.–For employers using Real Time Information (see **2 Real time information**, above), the following provisions no longer apply.

Paper returns are still allowed by (Reg. 67D)–

(a) an individual who is a practising member of a religious society or order whose beliefs are incompatible with the use of electronic communications;

(b) a partnership, if all the partners fall within (a);

(c) a company, if all the directors and the company secretary fall within (a), and

(d) a care and support employer.

11 Repayment of tax

Regulations 63, 64, and 65 deal with repayment of tax during absence from work through sickness, or in consequence of a trade dispute, and during periods of unemployment. Regulation 63 provides that, where an employee is absent from work through sickness or other similar cause (or is absent from work in circumstances other than where Regulation 64 applies) and consequently loses his right to be paid on his usual pay day, his employer must, on application being made in person by or on behalf of the employee, make an appropriate repayment of tax to him.

Regulation 64 provides *inter alia* that an employer must not make a repayment of tax due to an employee who is absent from work in consequence of a trade dispute in which he is participating or directly interested until–

(a) the employee is no longer absent;

(b) the employer ceases to employ the employee;

(c) the employee has become *bona fide* employed elsewhere in his usual occupation or has become regularly engaged in some other occupation; or

(d) the employee dies.

Where a person has ceased to be employed and has not made, or has ceased to make, a claim for jobseeker's allowance or incapacity benefit, any repayment of tax must be made to him by HM Revenue and Customs, who will require the production *inter alia* of a certificate that he is not a claimant and evidence of his unemployment (Reg. 65).

An employer is also required to give each of his employees in respect of whom he has deducted tax during the year a certificate (P60) showing *inter alia* the total emoluments in respect of which deductions have been made, the total net tax deducted, and the appropriate code (Reg. 67).

12 Repayment of overpayment of tax

Where the amount of tax deducted by the employer is more than the amount which is due for the tax year, HM Revenue and Customs will, unless the employee objects, rectify the situation by adjusting the employee's code for the subsequent year (Reg. 187).

13 Recovery of underpayment of tax

Where the amount of tax deducted is less than the amount which is due, HM Revenue and Customs may require the employee to pay the balance to it; alternatively, it may adjust the employee's code for the subsequent year so as to produce a balancing overpayment (Reg. 186). HM Revenue and Customs may, if they consider the deduction of tax by reference to tax tables to be impracticable (e.g., in cases of casual employment), employ the method of direct collection specified in Regulation 141 (direct collection involving deductions working sheets).

See also the Note on **Administration of Taxes** at para **6 Collection and recovery**.

14 Taxation of social security benefits

Part 8 of the 2003 Regulations, deals with the taxation of taxable benefits under the Social Security Contributions and Benefits Act 1992 paid to those who are wholly unemployed or, as the case may be, to employed persons. *Inter alia*, a claimant who is wholly unemployed must deliver to the Department for Work and Pensions the two copies of the certificate of tax deduction supplied by his previous employer (P45). On each occasion that the Department pays benefit (jobseeker's allowance) to a claimant, it must determine and record the amount of taxable benefit included in that payment. At the end of a person's period of claim (or at the end of the tax year if that occurs first), the Department is required to calculate the claimant's tax position, make any repayment of tax due to him, and notify the claimant and HM Revenue and Customs of the details.

Special provisions apply to the deduction of tax from payments of incapacity benefit (see below).

Chapter 2 of Part 8 deals with jobseeker's allowance paid in special cases to employed persons. It provides that, where benefit is paid direct to an employed claimant, the paying Department must determine and record the amount of taxable benefit, pay the benefit in full without deduction or repayment of tax, and, on termination of the claim to benefit, notify both HM Revenue and Customs and the claimant of the total benefit and taxable benefit paid.

Where the benefit is paid by the employer on behalf of the Department and the employer calculates the benefit payable by reference to instructions supplied by the Department, he must also calculate the taxable benefit; if the employer does not calculate the benefit payable, the Department must notify the employer of the amount of benefit and of taxable benefit. In either event, the Department must pay the full amount of benefit to the employer (for payment by him to the employee) without deduction of tax and the normal arrangements in regard *inter alia* to coding and deduction of tax (see above) apply unless that appears to HM Revenue and Customs to be impracticable.

Chapter 3 of Part 8 deals with the payment of incapacity benefit. Such a payment is to be treated as if it were a payment of emoluments from the claimant's employment. Where on the cessation of employment, a claimant has received from his employer copies of his P45, and he is not entitled to receive (in addition to payments of incapacity benefit) any payments of emoluments or is so entitled but has failed to furnish any details relating to those emoluments when making his claim, he must deliver the copies of the P45 to the Department for Work and Pensions when making the claim, and the Department must forthwith send the copies to the Inspector by whom code authorisations are ordinarily issued to the Department. [The Department will deduct (or refund) the tax payable in respect of the benefit, but in cases where the claimant is in receipt of other income which is subject to tax under the PAYE system (for example, an occupational pension), the Inspector will adjust the code in respect of the occupational pension and the tax payable on the incapacity benefit will then be deducted by the occupational pension scheme; the claimant being paid the full amount of the incapacity benefit by the Department.]

Chapter 4 of Part 8 deals with the payment if income support which must be paid in full without any deduction or repayment of income tax.

Chapter 5 of Part 8 deals with the payment of Employment and Support Allowance. Whenever a payment of allowance is made, the Department for Work and Pensions must record the taxable amount (if any) included in the payment. If taxable allowance is paid, the claimant must be given an annual certificate showing, *inter alia* the amount of taxable allowance which has been paid to him in the tax year.

15 Social security lump sums

Chapter 2A of Part 7 of the Regulations deals with social security pension lump sums. The normal provisions as to codes do not apply to such a lump sum but the remainder of the Regulations apply as if a basic rate code had been issued in respect of it (Reg. 133B). The amount of income tax to be deducted from the lump sum will be either the rate notified by the recipient of the lump sum or, in the absence of a notification, the basic rate (Regs. 133C and 133D).

16 Holiday pay

Chapter 3 of Part 7 of the Regulations deals with holiday pay. It provides that, where holiday pay is paid to a participant in a voucher, stamp, or similar holiday scheme, tax must be deducted by the manager of the scheme at the basic rate in force at the time the payment is made; the normal provisions of the Regulations as to coding, repayment, and deduction do not apply (Reg. 135). On each occasion where holiday pay is paid under the scheme, the employee must be given a certificate showing *inter alia* the amount of the payment and the tax deducted in making it (Reg. 137).

17 Marketable assets

ITEPA ss.693 to 700, contain measures to prevent employers avoiding the PAYE provisions by paying employees in marketable assets or with assets which are not immediately marketable, but where the employer arranges for the employee to convert them into cash. That is to say, the employer will be treated as having made a notional payment of income and PAYE must be operated where employees are provided with–

(a) readily convertible assets (excluding shares in an employer company or in a company controlling an employer company) (s.696);

(b) anything which enhances the value of an asset which they, or a member of their family or household, already owns (s.697);

(c) a share option which the employee exercises where the shares obtained can readily be converted into cash (this does not include HM Revenue and Customs approved share options or shares in an employee's own company where the option was granted before 27th November 1996) (ss.698-700);

(d) non-cash vouchers capable of being sold or exchanged for saleable goods (s.694);

(e) certain credit-tokens exchangeable for money or saleable goods (s.695); or

(f) certain cash vouchers (s.693).

18 Councillors and members of the reserve and auxiliary forces

Chapter 1 of Part 7 of the Regulations relates to the collection of income tax in respect of the attendance allowances paid to councillors and others under the Local Government Acts 1972 and 2000, the Local Government (Scotland) Act 1973, and regulations made under the Local Government and Housing Act 1989, or the Local Government (Payments to Councillors) (Northern Ireland) Regulations 1999 (SR (NI) No. 449). It provides an option for the payee to have income tax deducted from the attendance allowance at the basic rate in force at the time of the payment, after the taking into account of expenses wholly, exclusively, and necessarily incurred in performing his duties as a councillor (the amount of which is determined by HM Revenue and Customs and notified to the authority concerned).

Chapter 2 of Part 7 provides for the payment of reserve pay and requires the Ministry of Defence to deduct tax at the basic rate from such pay unless notified by HM Revenue and Customs not to do so. The Regulations also make provision for objections and appeals by reservists against the deducting of tax from their reserve pay, and for the repayment of tax by HM Revenue and Customs where appropriate, on application being made by the reservist.

19 Guidance and booklets

A booklet, *Employer's Further Guide to PAYE (CWG2)* explaining the scheme, is issued by the HMRC and is available from tax offices and <www.hmrc.gov.uk>.

20 Authorities

Income Tax (Earnings and Pensions) Act 2003

Income Tax (Pay As You Earn) Regulations 2003, as amended (S.I. 2003 No. 2682, 2004 No. 851, 2005 No. 2691, 2006 Nos. 243, 745, and 777, 2007 Nos. 1077, 2069, 2296, and 2969, 2008 Nos. 782 and 2601, 2009 Nos. 56, 588 and 2029, 2010 Nos. 668 and 2496, 2011 Nos. 729, 1054, and 1584, 2012 Nos. 822 and 1895, 2013 Nos. 521, 630 and 2300, 2014 Nos. 472, 474, 1017, 2396, and 2689, 2015 Nos. 2, 125, 171, 1667, and 1927, and 2016 No. 329)

INHERITANCE TAX

1 Introduction

The Finance Act 1986 introduced inheritance tax, a tax on certain transfers of value, to replace capital transfer tax. Inheritance tax applies to—

(a) gratuitous dispositions (e.g., gifts) of property made by an individual in his lifetime; and

(b) the value of a person's estate on his death,

where the transfer on death occurs on or after 18th March 1986. Transfers occurring before 19th March 1986 remain subject to capital transfer tax under the Capital Transfer Tax Act 1984, and are not dealt with in this Note.

The inheritance tax threshold for 2007/08 was £300,000. For 2008/09 it was £312,000; and for 2009/10 to 2017/18, it is £325,000. Up to that amount, the rate of tax is nil. Above that amount, the rate is 40% although a lower rate applies where at least 10% of the deceased's estate is left to charity.

From 2017/18 there will be an additional extra nil-rate band when a residence is passed on death to a direct descendant (see **13 Rates of tax**, below).

The 1986 Act provided for the Capital Transfer Tax Act 1984 to be renamed the Inheritance Tax Act 1984. Unless the context otherwise requires, references in this Note to a section or Schedule are references to a section of, or Schedule to, the 1984 Act, as amended by the 1986 Act and subsequent Finance Acts.

Bracketed references to a Finance Act are abbreviated to read FA followed by the year, e.g., FA 1997 is a reference to the Finance Act 1997.

2 Administration

Inheritance tax is administered by the Commissioners of Revenue and Customs (HMRC) at the Capital Taxes Office. In England and Wales, accounts and enquiries should be addressed to Ferrers House, P.O. Box 38, Castle Meadow Road, Nottingham NG2 1BB (tel: 0115 974 2400). In Scotland, the address is Mulberry House, 16 Picardy Place, Edinburgh EH1 3NB (tel: 0131 556 8511). However, Scottish enquiries should also be made to Ferrers House (see above).

3 General principles

Inheritance tax is charged on the value transferred by a *chargeable transfer*, which is defined as a transfer of value made by an individual, other than an exempt transfer (ss.1 and 2). A transfer of value is a disposition made by a person (the transferor) as a result of which the value of his estate immediately after the disposition is less than it would be but for the disposition; and it includes a deliberate omission by a person to exercise a right (such as a failure to exercise an option) whereby there is a diminution in the value of that person's estate (or of settled property with no subsisting interest in possession) (s.3). Certain transfers of value which would otherwise be chargeable transfers are potentially exempt transfers and become wholly exempt transfers if made seven or more years before the transferor's death (see **6 Potentially exempt transfers**, below).

On the death of any person, tax is charged as if, immediately before his death, the deceased had made a transfer of value equal to the value of his estate immediately before death (s.4(1)). For both lifetime transfers and those on death, a person's estate is the aggregate of all property to which he is beneficially entitled (s.5), except that the estate of a person immediately before his death does not include excluded property (see below).

4 Dispositions that are not transfers of value

A disposition is not a transfer of value if it is shown that it was not intended to confer any gratuitous benefit on any person and either that it was made in a transaction at arm's length between people not connected with each other, or that it was such as might be expected to be made in such a transaction (s.10(1)). S.10(1) will not apply to a sale of unquoted shares or unquoted debentures unless it is shown that the sale was at a price freely negotiated at the time of the sale, or at a price such as might be expected to have been freely negotiated at the time of sale (s.10(2)).

In addition to dispositions made at arm's length, referred to above, the following dispositions are also not transfers of value—

(a) dispositions made by one party to a marriage or civil partnership in favour of the other party, or of a child (including a step-child or adopted child) of either party, or in favour of an illegitimate child of the transferor, which is for the maintenance, education, or training of the child for a period ending not later than the year in which that child attains the age of 18, or, after attaining that age, ceases to undertake full-time education or training (s.11(1) and (4));

(b) dispositions in favour of a child who is not in the care of either of his parents, for his maintenance, education, or training, as described in (a) above, provided that he has been in the care of the transferor for substantial periods before he attained the age of 18 (s.11(2));

(c) dispositions in favour of a dependent relative of the transferor which make reasonable provision for his care and maintenance (s.11(3));

(d) dispositions allowable for income tax, or conferring retirement benefits, including contributions under approved personal pensions arrangements (s.12, as amended by Finance (No. 2) Act 1987 (the 1987 Act), s.98);

(e) certain dispositions to trustees by close companies for the benefit of employees (s.13);

(f) certain waivers of remuneration which would be earnings, or would be treated as earnings, and would constitute employment income (see section 7(2)(a) or (b) of the Income Tax (Earnings and Pensions) Act 2003) (s.14);

(g) waivers of dividends on shares of a company made within 12 months before any right to the dividend has accrued (s.15);

(h) a grant of a tenancy of agricultural property if made for full consideration in money or money's worth (s.16);

(j) certain changes in the distribution of a deceased person's estate (s.17).

5 Exempt transfers

The following exemptions apply to lifetime transfers only.

(a) Transfers not exceeding £3,000 in any year (i.e., the period of 12 months ending with 5th April). Any unused part of the exemption may be carried forward for one year (s.19).

(b) Small gifts made by the transferor in any one fiscal year not exceeding £250 to each donee (s.20).

(c) Transfers made as part of the normal expenditure out of the transferor's income, provided that it can be shown that, after allowing for all transfers of value forming part of his normal expenditure, the transferor was left with sufficient income to maintain his usual standard of living (s.21).

(d) Gifts in consideration of marriage or civil partnership made to a party to the marriage or civil partnership and not exceeding (a) £5,000 by a parent of a party to the marriage or civil partnership, (b) £2,500 by a grandparent or remoter ancestor outright, or by one party to the marriage or civil partnership to the other outright or by way of settlement, or (c) £1,000 in the case of any other gift to a party to the marriage or civil partnership (s.22).

The following exemptions which are subject to certain provisos, apply to lifetime transfers, transfers on death, and settlements.

(a) Transfers between spouses/civil partners, but where the transferee is domiciled outside the United Kingdom the exemption is limited to a cumulative total of £55,000 (s.18).

(b) Gifts to charities in the United Kingdom (s.23).

(c) Gifts to qualifying political parties (s.24).

(d) Gifts of land in the United Kingdom made on or after 14th March 1989 to registered housing associations (s.24A, inserted by FA 1989, s.171).

(e) Gifts for national purposes, where property is transferred to a body which comes within Schedule 3 (e.g., the British Museum, the National Trust, a university), or which qualifies as a gift to the Nation under FA 2012, Sch. 14 (s.25).

(f) Gifts for public benefit, to the extent that property is transferred to a non-profit-making body before 17th March 1998 (this relief has effectively been superseded by (b) above) (s.26).

(g) A potentially exempt transfer (see below) which would, but for s.26A, have proved to be a chargeable transfer will be an exempt transfer to the extent that the value transferred by it is attributable to property which has been or could be designated under s.31(1) (see paragraph (j) below) and which, during the period beginning with the date of the transfer and ending with the death of the transferor, has been disposed of by sale by private treaty or otherwise than by sale to a body mentioned in Schedule 3, has been gifted to the Nation (under FA 2012, Sch. 14), or has been disposed of in pursuance of s.230 (acceptance of property in satisfaction of tax) (s.26A).

(h) Gifts to a settlement for the maintenance of historic buildings, etc., for which a direction made by HMRC under paragraph 1 of Schedule 4 has effect at the time of the transfer, or is subsequently given having been claimed within two years of the transfer (s.27) and certain dispositions relating to settled property which enters such a maintenance fund after the death of the person beneficially entitled to possession of the property (s.57A).

(i) Transfers of shares or securities made by an individual to a trust for the benefit of all or most of the employees of a company, made after 10th April 1978 by a shareholder in that company, are exempt from the tax (and are also exempt from the ten-year anniversary charge (see below)), provided that the trustees *inter alia* hold more than one-half of the voting shares in the company (s.28).

(j) A claim for a conditional exemption from tax may be made under s.30 where the property transferred has been designated by HMRC under s.31(1) and where an undertaking has been given under s.31(2) (s.30(1)). In the case of a lifetime transfer, the conditions of s.30(3) must be satisfied. Property which may be so designated includes works of art, scientific collections of national, scientific, or historic interest, and land and buildings of outstanding scenic or historical interest (s.31(1)). Tax becomes chargeable on the failure to observe an undertaking (s.32(2)) or (except in the circumstances specified by s.32(4) and (5)) on the death of the person beneficially entitled, or on a disposal of the property (s.32).

The provisions of s.30 must be disregarded in determining whether a transfer of value is a potentially exempt transfer (see below). No claim may be made under s.30 with respect to such a transfer until the transferor has died and no claim may be made under s.30(1) in respect of a potentially exempt transfer to the extent that the value transferred by it is attributable to property disposed of by sale during the period beginning with the date of the transfer and ending with the death of the transferor. Where a transfer of value in relation to which a claim for designation under s.31 is made is a potentially exempt transfer which (apart from s.30) proves to be a chargeable transfer, the question whether any property is appropriate for such designation will be determined by reference to the circumstances existing after the death of the transferor. In such a case, if at the time of the transferor's death an undertaking given under the terms of Schedule 4 (maintenance funds for historic buildings) or s.258 of the Taxation of Chargeable Gains Act 1992 is in force with respect to any property to which the value transferred by the transfer is attributable, that undertaking will be treated for the purposes of conditional exemption from inheritance tax as an undertaking given under s.30 (ss.30(3A) to (3C) and 31(1A) and (4G)).

6 Potentially exempt transfers

A potentially exempt transfer of value is a transfer of value (s.3A(1) and (1A))–
- (a) (i) which is made by an individual on or after 18th March 1986 but before 22nd March 2006, and (ii) which would otherwise be a chargeable transfer (or to the extent to which, apart from this provision, it would be such a transfer), and (iii) to the extent that it constitutes either a gift to another individual or a gift into an accumulation and maintenance trust or a disabled trust; but not a disposition or transfer of value of a particular description which is declared not to be a potentially exempt transfer by any provision of the 1984 Act; or
- (b) (i) which is made by an individual on or after 22nd March 2006, and (ii) which would otherwise be a chargeable transfer (or to the extent to which, apart from this provision, it would be such a transfer), and (iii) to the extent that it constitutes either a gift to another individual or a disabled trust or a gift into a bereaved minor's trust on the coming to an end of an immediate post-death interest; but not a disposition or transfer of value of a particular description which is declared not to be a potentially exempt transfer by any provision of the 1984 Act

A potentially exempt transfer becomes an exempt transfer where it is made seven years or more before the death of the transferor (s.3A(4)).

Subject to s.3A(6), a transfer of value qualifies as a gift to an individual falling within (iii) above–
- (a) to the extent that the value transferred is attributable to property which, by virtue of the transfer, becomes comprised in the estate of that individual; or
- (b) so far as that value is not attributable to property which becomes comprised in the estate of another person, to the extent that, by virtue of the transfer, the estate of that other individual is increased.

In the case of transfers made before 17th March 1987, (a) and (b) above apply with the exclusion of transfers where the property becomes comprised in the estate of the other individual as settled property (see **12 Settlements**, below) (s.3A(2), as amended by the 1987 Act, s.96).

Subject to s.3A(6), a transfer of value qualifies under (iii) above if it is a gift into an accumulation and maintenance trust or a disabled trust to the extent that the value transferred is attributable to property which, by virtue of the transfer, becomes settled property to which s.71 (accumulation and maintenance trusts) or s.89 (trusts for disabled people) applies (s.3A(3), (3B)).

S.3A(6), as amended by the 1987 Act, provides that where, under any provision of the 1984 Act other than any provision in relation to settlements where there is an interest in possession (see **12 Settlements**, below), tax is in any circumstances to be charged as if a transfer of value had been made, that transfer is to be taken to be a transfer which is not a potentially exempt transfer.

During the period beginning on the date of the transfer and ending before the seventh anniversary of that date or, if it is earlier, the death of the transferor, it will be assumed that the transfer will prove to be an exempt transfer (s.3A(5)).

A gift with reservation (see below) may also be treated as a potentially exempt transfer and, in the special circumstances dealt with by s.103 of the 1986 Act (treatment of certain debts and incumbrances), a person may be treated as having made a transfer qualifying as a potentially exempt transfer when he pays or applies money or money's worth in or towards the discharge of a debt previously incurred by him.

7 Voidable transfers

Where by virtue of any enactment or rule of law a chargeable transfer (the relevant transfer) has been set aside as voidable or otherwise defeasible–
- (a) tax (including interest) paid or payable which would not have been payable if the relevant transfer had been void *ab initio* is repayable or not payable as the case may be; and
- (b) tax on any chargeable transfer made after the relevant transfer has been set aside is determined as if that transfer had been void (s.150).

8 Gifts with reservation

S.102 of the 1986 Act applies where, on or after 18th March 1986, an individual disposes of any property by way of gift and either–

(a) possession and enjoyment of the property is not *bona fide* assumed by the donee at or before the beginning of the relevant period, i.e., the period ending on the date of the donor's death and beginning seven years before that date or, if it is later, on the date of the gift; or

(b) at any time in the relevant period the property is not enjoyed to the entire exclusion, or virtually to the entire exclusion, of the donor and of any benefit to him by contract or otherwise.

If and so long as condition (a) or (b) applies to the gift, the property concerned is referred to as "property subject to a reservation" both in relation to the gift and the donor. Further, if immediately before the death of the donor, there is any property which, in relation to him, is property subject to a reservation, then, to the extent that the property would not, apart from this provision (s.102(3)), form part of the donor's estate immediately before his death, that property will be treated for the purposes of the 1984 Act as property to which he was beneficially entitled immediately before his death. But if at any time before the end of the relevant period the property ceases to be property subject to a reservation, the donor will be treated as having at that time made a disposition of the property by a disposition which is a potentially exempt transfer (s.102(4)).

Ss.102A to 102C (inserted by FA 1999, s.104) further provide that if, at any time after 9th March 1999 and within the relevant period (i.e., the seven years before the donor's death), the donor or his spouse/civil partner enjoy a significant right or interest or are party to a significant arrangement, in relation to the gifted property, then the interest disposed of is to be referred to as "property subject to a reservation" and s.102(3) and (4) will apply. A right, interest or arrangement will be "significant" if, and only if, it entitles or enables the donor to occupy all or part of the land, or to enjoy some right in relation to it, otherwise than for full consideration in money or money's worth. These provisions were introduced to reverse the case of *Ingram and another v IRC* where the House of Lords had decided that the creation by the donor of a rent-free lease in favour of herself prior to a gift of the freehold did not amount to a reservation of benefit in relation to the gift.

S.102 does not apply *inter alia* if or, as the case may be, to the extent that, the disposal of property by way of gift is an exempt transfer by virtue of any of the following provisions of the 1984 Act, namely, ss.18, 20, and 22 to 28 (see **5 Exempt transfers**, above) (s.102(5)). However, in the case of a transfer exempted by s.18 (transfers between spouses/civil partners), s.102 *will* still apply if the gift by the donor is to a trust, the spouse gets an interest in possession, that interest in possession ends before the donor dies, and when that interest ends the spouse/civil partner does not become beneficially entitled to the property or to another interest in possession in it (s.102(5A)-(5C)).

Schedule 20 to the 1986 Act contains detailed rules for the purpose of supplementing the provisions of s.102 of that Act.

9 Reliefs

The 1984 Act provides for relief from tax in the case of certain transfers of value.

(1) *Business property relief* (ss.103 to 114) may be available where the whole or part of the value transferred includes relevant business property (as defined by s.105) (which must, as a general rule, have been owned by the transferor for the two years immediately preceding the transfer). The value of the transfer is treated as reduced—

(a) by 100% in the case of a business or interest in a business;

(b) by 100%, in the case of shares in or securities of a company which are unquoted (the 50% relief in respect of certain unquoted shares was abolished by FA 1996, s.184 in relation to transfers of value on or after 6th April 1996);

(c) by 50%, in the case of shares in or securities of a company which are quoted and which, either by themselves or together with other shares or securities owned by the transferor, gave the transferor control of the company immediately before the transfer;

(d) by 50%, in the case of any land or building, machinery or plant which, immediately before the transfer, was used wholly or mainly for the purposes of a business carried on by a company of which the transferor had control or by a partnership of which the transferor was then a partner;

(e) by 50%, in the case of any land or building, machinery or plant which, immediately before the transfer, was used wholly or mainly for the purposes of a business carried on by the transferor and was settled property in which he was then beneficially entitled to an interest in possession. (Where the transferor succeeded to the shares less than two years before the transfer, he must have owned the shares throughout that lesser period.)

Business relief is not available in respect of any property if the business consists wholly or mainly of dealing in securities, stocks or shares, land or buildings, or making or holding investments unless it is—

(a) wholly that of a market maker or is that of a discount house, as defined in s.105 of the 1984 Act, as substituted by the 1986 Act, s.106; or

(b) that of a holding company of one or more companies whose business does qualify.

There are special rules for calculating business relief on transfers within seven years before the death of the transferor (s.113A). Provided that certain conditions are met, then—

(a) any part of the value transferred by a potentially exempt transfer which proves to be a chargeable transfer will qualify for business relief; and

(b) where, because the transfer is made within seven years before the transferor's death, additional tax becomes chargeable in respect of the value of a chargeable transfer (other than a potentially exempt transfer) which has been reduced by the application of business relief, the additional tax will be calculated on the basis of the reduced value.

The conditions (s.113A(3)) are that–

(i) the property which was the subject of the relevant transfer was owned by the transferee throughout the period from the date of the chargeable transfer to the death of the transferor; and

(ii) except to the extent that the business property consists of certain shares or securities (categorised in s.113A(3A)), that property would be relevant business property in relation to a notional transfer of the value made by the transferee immediately before his death.

S.113B, as amended by s.247 of the Finance Act 1994, makes special provision for a case where the transferee replaces the relevant business property with other property. Relief will not be forfeited if a qualifying property is purchased within three years of the disposal of the original property.

(2) *Agricultural property relief* is available where the conditions set out in ss.115 to 124B are satisfied.

The agricultural property must have been occupied by the transferor for the purposes of agriculture throughout the period of two years ending with the date of transfer, or owned by him and occupied (by him or another) for the purposes of agriculture throughout the period of seven years ending with that date (s.117). Occupation by a company which is controlled by the transferor will be treated as occupation by the transferor (s.119).

By virtue of s.116, the relief consists of reducing the value transferred–

(a) by 100%, if (i) the transferor at the time of the transfer has the right to vacant possession or has the right to obtain it within 12 months; or (ii) does not have that right (other than by his own act or deliberate omission) but has been beneficially entitled to the land since before 10th March 1981 and would have qualified for 50% relief by a claim made under paragraph 1 of Schedule 8 to the Finance Act 1975 within the limits prescribed by paragraph 5 of that Schedule (i.e., maximum aggregate of all transfers to date not to exceed £250,000 in value or 1,000 acres in extent) had he transferred the land immediately before that date; or (iii) the interest of the transferor in the property immediately before the transfer does not carry either of the rights in (i) above because the property is let on a tenancy beginning on or after 1st September 1995 (s.116(2)(c), inserted by FA 1995, s.155(1), with effect in relation to transfers of value made, and other events occurring, after 31st August 1995). S.185 of the Finance Act 1996 inserts new subsections (5A) to (5E) inclusive to s.116 in relation to successions to tenancies following a death on or after 1st September 1995.

(b) by 50% in any other case (including the excess of any value transferred over the limits of paragraph 5 of Schedule 8).

S.124A disallows relief under s.116 for agricultural property (as defined by s.115) in the same two cases as are dealt with by s.113A (see above). In those two cases, relief will nevertheless be available if specified conditions as to the ownership of the property are satisfied.

If those conditions are satisfied only with respect to part of the original property, partial agricultural relief will be available. S.124B, as amended by s.247 of the Finance Act 1994, makes special provision for a case where the transferee replaces the original property with other property. Relief will not be forfeited if a qualifying replacement property is purchased within three years of the disposal of the original property.

S.124C (inserted by FA 1997, s.94) extends agricultural property relief to land taken completely out of farming use under a habitat scheme (which must be for a minimum of 20 years).

(3) *Woodland relief* is available where the conditions set out in ss.125 to 130 are satisfied.

The value of the trees or underwood growing on non-agricultural property owned by a person for the five years before his death is to be left out of account in establishing the value of his estate, provided that the person liable for the tax so elects within two years of the death. When the whole or any part of the timber is subsequently disposed of (whether together with or apart from the land), tax may be charged on the net proceeds of sale or the net value of the timber at the time of disposal (subject to business property relief, if applicable).

(4) *Quick succession relief* under s.141 is available where the value of a person's estate was increased by a chargeable transfer (the first transfer) made not more than five years before (a) his death or (b) a chargeable transfer made by him otherwise than on his death which satisfies conditions specified in s.141(2) (which refers to interests in possession in settled property). In such circumstances, the tax chargeable on the value transferred by the transfer made on his death or referred to in (b) above is reduced. The reduction is the following percentage of the tax charged on the first transfer–

(a) 100%, if the period beginning with the first transfer and ending with the date of the last does not exceed one year;

(b) 80%, if it exceeds one year but does not exceed two years;

(c) 60%, if it exceeds two years but does not exceed three years;

(d) 40%, if it exceeds three years but does not exceed four years; and

(e) 20%, if it exceeds four years.

(5) *Double charges relief* is available where liability for tax would arise, on or after 18th March 1986, within the United Kingdom in the following circumstances (1986 Act, s.104 and the Inheritance Tax (Double Charges Relief) Regulations 1987)–

(a) where property given by a potentially exempt transfer is subsequently returned by the donee to the transferor for less than full consideration and the property becomes again chargeable as result of the transferor's death;

(b) where property is transferred by way of gift and the transfer is, or subsequently becomes, a chargeable transfer, and the property is then subject to a further transfer (by virtue of the provisions relating to gifts with reservation) which is chargeable as a result of the transferor's death;

(c) where a transfer of value is or subsequently becomes a chargeable transfer, and at the transferor's death his estate owes to the transferee a debt which falls to be abated or disallowed in determining the value of the estate chargeable on death; and

(d) where property is given by a transfer of value which is chargeable when made, is returned by the donee to the transferor for less than full consideration, and subsequently becomes chargeable as part of the transferor's estate on his death;

(e) in certain circumstances (for deaths on or after 6th April 2005) where both an income tax and an inheritance tax charge arise in relation to the benefit enjoyed by a taxpayer from continuing to enjoy an asset they formerly owned (Charge to Income Tax by Reference to Enjoyment of Property Previously Owned Regulations 2005);

(f) where there are transfers of both property and a debt owed to the deceased, the debt is written off and, on the deceased's death (on or after 6th April 2005), both the property and the debt are chargeable (Inheritance Tax (Double Charges Relief) Regulations 2005).

10 Excluded property

For the purposes of inheritance tax, including the provisions relating to settlements, no account is to be taken of the value of excluded property which is the subject of the lifetime transfer or of a transfer on death (ss.6, 48, and 53). Excluded property comprises *inter alia*–

(a) property situated outside the UK, if the person beneficially entitled to it is domiciled outside the UK;

(b) certain government securities, where the beneficial owner is neither domiciled nor ordinarily resident in the UK;

(c) a decoration or other award for valour or gallant conduct provided it has never been disposed of for money or money's worth;

(d) a reversionary interest, unless it has been acquired for money or money's worth, or it is one to which the settlor or his spouse/civil partner is beneficially entitled, or it is an interest expectant on the determination of a lease for life or lives or for a period, or subject to termination at a date ascertainable only by reference to a death.

11 Double taxation relief

Double taxation relief is available where a person domiciled in the UK makes a chargeable transfer of value of property which is subject in another country to a tax of a similar character to inheritance tax. Double taxation agreements under s.158 have been made with certain countries; in other cases, unilateral double taxation relief may be obtained under s.159.

12 Settlements

The transfer of property to the trustees of a settlement will normally be treated as a chargeable transfer of value made by the settlor. Ss.49 to 57 make additional provision in relation to settlements where there is a qualifying interest in possession and ss.58 to 85 make provision for settlements where there is no such interest.

The Finance Act 2006 severely restricted the types of trusts created on or after 22nd March 2006 which have a qualifying interest in possession for these purposes. The only trusts which come within the definition after that date are "immediate post-death interests" (i.e., where the settlement is effected by a will or intestacy (not therefore interests in possession created during a settlor's lifetime)); "transitional serial interests" (which relates to certain existing settlements where the interest in possession ends before 6th April 2008); and "disabled persons' interests" (which allow an interest in possession for a disabled person).

For inheritance tax purposes, a person beneficially entitled to an interest in possession is treated as the owner of the settled property, and, with a few exceptions, on the termination (whether during life or on death) or disposal of the interest in possession, tax is charged as if he has made a transfer of value of that property. *Inter alia* tax is not chargeable if, when the interest come to an end, the property reverts to the settlor, or if the beneficiary becomes beneficially entitled to it (ss.49 and 51 to 55).

Settlements without a qualifying interest in possession (e.g., discretionary trusts) are subject to a ten-year anniversary charge on the tenth anniversary of the date on which the settlement commenced and at subsequent ten-year intervals (ss.61 and 64). The charge is normally 30% of the effective rate (i.e., the rate found by expressing the tax chargeable as a percentage of the amount on which it is charged) at which tax would be charged on the value transferred by a chargeable transfer of a specified description. Tax is also charged where all or any part of the settled property ceases to be relevant property (e.g., because it ceases to be part of the settlement as a result of a capital distribution) (s.65). Ss.66 to 69 set out the method of calculating the rate at which tax is to be charged.

Accumulation and maintenance settlements created on or after 22nd March 2006 will generally be treated as discretionary trusts. The only exception is a bereaved minor's trust (see below). Until 5th April 2008, accumulation and maintenance settlements created before 22nd March 2006 are dealt with by s.71.

S.71 applies to settled property if–

(a) no interest in possession subsists in it and the income is to be accumulated so far as not applied for the maintenance, education, or benefit of a beneficiary; and

(b) one or more beneficiaries will, on or before attaining a specified age (not exceeding 25), become beneficially entitled to an interest in possession; and

(c) either (i) not more than 25 years have elapsed since the commencement of the settlement or, if later, since the latest time when conditions stated in paragraphs (a) and (b) were satisfied, or (ii) all the persons who are or were beneficiaries are or were either grandchildren of a common grandparent or children, widows, or widowers or surviving civil partners of such grandchildren who were beneficiaries but died before the time when, had they survived, they would have become entitled to an interest in possession.

From 6th April 2008, these s.71 rules will continue to apply only if under the terms of the trust the beneficiaries are entitled to the capital outright at age 18. Where beneficiaries become absolutely entitled after the age of 18 but before the age of 25 tax will be charged, but at a reduced rate. Where there is no absolute entitlement the full ten-yearly charge will apply.

A bereaved minor's trust is one where the beneficiary is under 18, at least one of his parents has died and the trust arises from a will, intestacy, or a criminal injuries compensation payment. The minor must become absolutely entitled by the age of 18. In such cases there are no ten-yearly or exit charges and no charge when the minor becomes absolutely entitled or when funds are applied for his benefit (s.71A).

13 Rates of tax

Inheritance tax is chargeable in accordance with s.7 and Schedule 1, as amended from time to time. The current nil rate band extends to £325,000. Above that amount, the rate of tax is 40% unless at least 10% of the deceased's estate is left to charity in which case a lower rate of 36% applies.

During the lifetime of an individual tax may be charged and become payable on any particular transfer of value made by him which is a chargeable transfer when it is made. Whether or not tax is payable on that transfer is determined by adding together all the chargeable transfers made by that individual in the period of seven years ending with the date of the making of the transfer under consideration, the first £325,000 of the value of the aggregate so found bearing the tax at the nil rate and the balance (if any) bearing tax at 50% of the rate for the time being (currently 40%). Once a transferor has survived the making of a chargeable transfer by him by at least seven years, no further tax is payable in respect of that transfer and its value is ignored in calculating any subsequent seven-year total of chargeable transfers of his.

Upon the death of the transferor, the chargeable transfers made by him during the period of seven years ending with his death, potentially exempt transfers made by him during that period, and the transfer of value deemed to be made on his death under s.4 (see above) are aggregated. A lifetime transfer which was made during this period and which attracted tax as a transfer chargeable at the time it was made will be aggregated with those other transfers at the transferor's death, but credit will be given for any tax paid in respect of it. Subject to s.7(5) (see below), any chargeable transfers made by the transferor during the period of three years ending with his death will be charged at 100% of the rate for the time being (currently 40%); and any such transfers made outside that period but within seven years of his death will be charged at the following percentage of that rate–

(a) where the transfer is made more than three but not more than four years before his death, 80%;

(b) where the transfer is made more than four years but not more than five years before his death, 60%;

(c) where the transfer is made more than five years but not more than six years before his death, 40%; and

(d) where the transfer is made more than six years but not more than seven years before his death, 20%.

If the tax so payable is less than the amount of tax payable by applying the lifetime rates, no additional tax is payable but no part of the tax paid on the lifetime transfer is refundable (s.7(5)).

The rate bands for inheritance tax are increased annually by order in line with the rise in the retail price index, unless Parliament otherwise determines (s.8).

14 Extra nil-rate band on death if interest in home goes to descendants etc

There is an additional main residence nil-rate band for an estate if the deceased's interest in a residential property, which has been their residence at some point and is included in their estate, is left to one or more direct descendants on death. The value of the main residence nil-rate band for an estate will be the lower of the net value of the interest in the residential property (after deducting any liabilities such a mortgage) or the maximum amount of the band. The maximum amount will be will be phased in as follows (Inheritance Tax Act 1984, ss.8D-8M)–

2017/18	£100,000
2018/19	£125,000
2019/20	£150,000
2020/21	£175,000

It will then increase in line with the Consumer Prices Index for subsequent years.

The qualifying residential interest will be limited to one residential property but personal representatives will be able to nominate which residential property should qualify if there is more than one in the estate. A property which was never a residence of the deceased, such as a buy-to-let property, will not qualify.

A direct descendant will be a child (including a step-child, adopted child or foster child) of the deceased and their lineal descendants. A claim will have to be made on the death of a person's surviving spouse or civil partner to transfer any unused proportion of the additional nil-rate band unused by the person on their death, in the same way that the ordinary nil-rate band can be transferred.

If the net value of the estate (after deducting any liabilities but before reliefs and exemptions) is above £2 million, the additional nil-rate band will be tapered away by £1 for every £2 that the net value exceeds that amount. The taper threshold at which the additional nil-rate band is gradually withdrawn will rise in line with the Consumer Prices Index from 2021-22 onwards.

15 Transfer of unused nil-rate band

On the death of a surviving spouse or civil partner, any unused proportion of the inheritance tax nil-rate band from the death of the first spouse/civil partner can be used on the second death (Inheritance Tax Act 1984, s.8A, added by FA 2008, Sch. 4).The amount that can be transferred is based on the unused proportion of the nil-rate band at the time of the first death, applied in the same proportion to the nil-rate band current at the date of the second death.

As an example–

J and K are married and the nil-rate band is £300,000 at the date J dies.

J leaves taxable legacies amounting to £75,000 with the remainder to his spouse, K. Therefore, 25% of J's nil-rate band has been used (the remainder to K benefiting from the spouse exemption).

When K dies, she will be entitled to an additional 75% of the nil-rate band current at the date she dies.

If the nil-rate band at the time of K's death is £320,000, she will be entitled to a total nil-rate band of £320,000 + £240,000 = £560,000.

The maximum nil-rate band that can be claimed on the second death is twice the individual nil-rate band for that year. Claims for transfer of the nil-rate band are made on submitting the IHT return by the personal representatives at the time of the second death and must be made within two years of that second death (although there is discretion to extend this period) (s.8B).

16 Powers of HMRC

For the purpose of inheritance tax, property is valued at the open market value, and HMRC have powers of inspection for valuation purposes (ss.160 and FA 2008, Sch.36, para 12A). HMRC also have power, by notice in writing, to–

(a) request any person to furnish them with such information as they require for the purposes of the Act; and

(b) require any person who has delivered or is liable to deliver an inheritance tax account to produce documents, or furnish accounts or particulars, to enable HMRC to enquire into or determine whether an account is incorrect or incomplete, or to make a determination under s.221 (see **22 Notices of determination**, below).

17 Who must submit an account

Transferors have a duty to submit an account of chargeable transfers to HMRC within 12 months of the end of the month in which a transfer is made, or within three months of the date on which they first become liable for tax, whichever is the later. Trustees of relevant property settlements must deliver the IHT account six months after the end of the month in which the chargeable event arises.

Personal representatives must submit an account of–

(i) all property forming part of the deceased's estate; and

(ii) details of any chargeable transactions made by the deceased within seven years of the death;

within 12 months of the end of the month in which the deceased died or within three months of the date on which they first begin to act, whichever is the later (s.216, as amended by FA 1999, s.105).

A transferee must deliver an account within 12 months of the death of the transferor–

(a) if he is the transferee under a transfer made by the deceased which has become a chargeable transfer, whether or not he is subject to a personal liability to pay the tax (if any) due by virtue of s.199 (see below), or

(b) if he is the transferee under a chargeable transfer of value made on death, if and so far as any tax due as a result of the death is attributable to the value of property which is deemed to form part of the deceased's estate as a gift with reservation, whether or not he would be liable to payment of the tax on that transfer under s.200(1)(c) as a person in whom the property has vested (whether beneficially or otherwise) at any time after the deceased's death (s.216).

18 Liability for payment

HMRC may require payment of tax due from either transferor or the transferee, or, in the case of settlements, from the trustees or the beneficiaries (ss.199 and 201). A transferor's personal representative is liable to pay the tax on the value transferred by a potentially exempt transfer which proves to be a chargeable transfer and so much of the tax on the value transferred by any other chargeable transfer made within seven years of the transferor's death as exceeds what it would have been had the transferor died more than seven years after the transfer (s.199(2)). But his liability under s.199(2) is subject to the limit imposed by or by virtue of s.204(8). Although personal representatives are generally liable for payment of tax, their liability is limited (ss.200 and 204).

19 Excepted accounts

No account need be delivered of a chargeable lifetime transfer made after 5th April 2007 if it is an excepted transfer or an excepted termination. An excepted transfer is one where–

(a) the value transferred is attributable to either cash or quoted shares or securities and that value, together with the transferor's chargeable transfers in the previous seven years, does not exceed the threshold for payment of inheritance tax for the year in which the transfer was made ("the inheritance tax threshold"); or

(b) the value of the chargeable transfer, together with the transferor's chargeable transfers in the previous seven years, does not exceed 80% of the inheritance tax threshold, and the value of the transfer of value does not exceed that threshold less the value of the transferor's chargeable transfers in the previous seven years.

No account need be delivered of a chargeable lifetime transfer made before 6th April 2007 where the value of the transfer, together with any others made in the same period of one year ending with 5th April, does not exceed £10,000, and which, together with any other made in the previous 10 years, does not exceed £40,000 (S.I. 2002 No. 1731).

Similar rules apply to the termination of an interest in possession in the settled property of certain trusts.

20 Excepted settlements

In a limited category of small discretionary trusts, no account need be delivered. This will be the case where there is no interest in possession in the settled property (which must consist solely of cash), the trustees are resident in the UK, the settlor has not added to the settled property since the settlement was set up, there are no related settlements, and the value of the settled property at the time of the chargeable event does not exceed £1,000 (Inheritance Tax (Delivery of Accounts) (Excepted Settlements) Regulations 2008).

Other trusts are also excepted provided the settlor was domiciled in the UK at the time the settlement was set up and has remained so domiciled throughout the existence of the settlement until either the occasion of charge or the settlor's earlier death; the trustees of the settlement have been resident in the UK throughout the existence of the settlement; and there are no related settlements for IHT purposes. The exception is generally limited to chargeable transfers that do not exceed 80% of the inheritance tax threshold.

21 Excepted estates

On the death of any person on or after 6th April 2004 who died domiciled in the United Kingdom, an account need *not* be delivered by the personal representatives where (Inheritance Tax (Delivery of Accounts) (Excepted Estates) Regulations 2004)–

First category

(a) the estate comprises only property which has passed by will or intestacy, under a nomination, under a single settlement, or by survivorship;

(b) of that property not more than £150,000 represented value attributable to settled property, and not more than £100,000 represented value attributable to property which is situated outside the United Kingdom;

(c) the deceased made no chargeable transfers during the last seven years other than "specified transfers" the aggregate value of which did not exceed £150,000; and

(d) the aggregate gross value of the estate, any "specified transfers", and any "specified exempt transfers" does not exceed the inheritance tax nil rate band for the previous year (if the death occurred and an application for a grant of representation (in Scotland, an application for confirmation) is made between 6th April and 6th August), or the year of death (in any other case).

Second category

(a) paragraphs (a), (b), and (c) of the *First category* above apply;

(b) the aggregate gross value of the estate, any "specified transfers", and any "specified exempt transfers" does not exceed £1,000,000;

(c) at least part of the estate passes to the deceased's spouse/civil partner or to a charity; and

(d) that aggregate value of the estate after the deduction of–

(i) the total value transferred on that person's death by a spouse/civil partner or charity transfer, and

(ii) the total liabilities of the estate,

does not exceed the inheritance tax nil rate band.

Third category
(a) the deceased was never domiciled or treated as domiciled in the UK; and
(b) the value of the estate situated in the UK is wholly attributable to cash or quoted shares or securities, the gross value of which does not exceed £150,000.

For the above purposes, a "specified transfer" is one made within the seven years of the death where the value transferred is attributable to cash, personal chattels or moveable property, quoted shares or securities, or an interest in land (and furnishings etc disposed of to the same person at the same time unless they become settled property on the transfer), except where the Finance Act 1986 ss.102 or 102A apply (gifts of land with reservation). In valuing specified transfers business property relief and agricultural property relief do not apply. A "specified exempt transfer" is one which is exempt only by reason of being made between spouses/civil partners or to a charity, political party, housing association, maintenance fund for historic buildings, or an employee trust.

Transfers within seven years prior to the death which are exempt as being normal expenditure out of income (under s.21: see **5 Exempt transfers**, above at (c)) will be treated as chargeable transfers if they total more than £3,000.

The Inheritance Tax (Delivery of Accounts) (Excepted Estates) Regulations 2004 also prescribe the circumstances in which the personal representatives of an estate benefiting from an unused nil rate band which has been transferred to a surviving spouse or civil partner (see **15 Transfer of unused nil-rate band**, above) may submit an excepted estate return as opposed to having to complete a full IHT account. Where these provisions apply, the IHT threshold for the purposes of delivering an account is doubled. This will be the case where (Reg. 5A)–
(a) the nil-rate band on the death of the survivor is treated as increased by 100%; and
the first deceased spouse/civil partner–
(b) died domiciled in the UK;
(c) had an estate whose value was attributable wholly to property passing under their will or intestacy (or by survivorship);
(d) had property outside the UK which represented no more than £100,000;
(e) had made no chargeable transfers in the seven years before their death; and
(f) had an estate where the value of any chargeable transfer on the their death was not reduced by business or agricultural property relief.

Trustees need not deliver an account in the case of an excepted termination, that is upon the termination of an interest in possession in settled property which is wholly covered by an annual or marriage/civil partnership gift exemption which is made available to them.

22 Notices of determination

Where it appears to HMRC that a transfer of value has been made, they may issue a "notice of determination" to any person who appears to them to be the transferor or to be liable for any of the tax; if an appeal is not made, the notice becomes conclusive against the person on whom it is served (s.221).

The procedure relating to notices of determination and appeals against them is dealt with in the Note on **Administration of Taxes**.

23 Penalties

If a taxpayer fails to deliver an account he will be liable to a fixed penalty of £100 (unless the tax is due is less than that amount, in which case the penalty is the amount due), plus not more than £60 for every day on which he fails to deliver it after the day on which the failure has been declared by a court or tribunal (s.245, as substituted by FA 1999, s.108 and amended by the Finance Act 2004, s.295). If the return is more than 12 months late and there is tax to pay, an additional fine of up to £3,000 may be imposed.

If a person fails to comply with a notice issued–
(a) under s.218 (non-resident trustees), he will be liable to a penalty of not more than £300, plus £60 per day thereafter;
(b) under s.218A (post-death variation), he will be liable to a penalty of not more than £100, plus £60 per day thereafter, and a fine of £3,000 after 6 months continued failure; (s.245A(1), (1A), (1B) as substituted by FA 1999, s.108 and amended by FA 2002).

If incorrect information is provided, a person will be liable to a penalty not exceeding–
(c) the difference by which the amount of tax for which he is liable exceeds the amount he would have paid based on the incorrect account, information or document; and
(d) in the case of fraud or negligence by a person not liable for the tax (e.g., an adviser), an additional penalty of up to £3,000 (s.247, as amended by FA 1999, s.108 and the Finance Act 2004, s.295).

A person who assists or induces the delivery, furnishing or production of an incorrect account, information or document will be liable to a penalty not exceeding £3,000.

24 Payment of tax

Inheritance tax is normally payable six months after the end of the month in which a chargeable transfer is made, but in the case of a lifetime transfer made between 6th April and 30th September in any year, payment is due on 30th April in the following year. Personal representatives must pay all tax for which they are liable on delivery of their account, otherwise probate or letters of administration will not be granted. Additional tax is chargeable, by virtue of a transfer of value having taken place within seven years of death or by virtue of a potentially exempt transfer which has proved to be a chargeable transfer, is due six months after the end of the month in which death occurs (s.226).

Where tax is payable on death, or it consists of the ten-year anniversary charge on settled property, or the tax is to be paid by a beneficiary, the person liable may, by notice in writing, elect to pay in ten equal yearly instalments, provided that the tax is attributable to a transfer of one of the following categories of qualifying property: land; shares and securities to which s.228 applies; or a business or interest in a business. This right is not however exercisable in relation to (i) tax payable on the value transferred by a potentially exempt transfer which proves to be a chargeable transfer, or (ii) additional tax becoming payable on the value transferred by any chargeable transfer by reason of the transferor's death within seven years of the transfer, except to the extent permitted by s.227(1A), as substituted by the Finance Act 1987, Schedule 8 (s.227).

Interest is charged on any tax which is due but unpaid and is calculated from the due date of payment; where ss.227 or 229 (payment of tax by instalments) applies, interest charged on an instalment which is in arrears is added to the next instalment (ss.233 and 234). Rates change from time to time. The current rate is the Bank of England base rate + 2.5% (Taxes and Duties etc (Interest Rate) Regulations 2011. Old rates and the dates for which they were applicable can be found at <http://www.hmrc.gov.uk/rates/iht-interest-rates.htm>.

Where HMRC agree to accept property in satisfaction of inheritance tax on terms that the value to be attributed to the property for this purpose is determined at a date earlier than that on which the property is actually accepted, the terms may provide that the amount of tax satisfied by the acceptance shall not carry interest from that date (s.233(1A) inserted by FA 1987, s.60).

When tax has been paid, the person liable for tax may apply to HMRC for a certificate of discharge, stating that tax has been paid, and discharging the property from any charge. Such a certificate must be given where the property is transferred on death, but in the case of a potentially exempt transfer which has proved to be a chargeable transfer, HMRC may decide not to entertain an application for a certificate until the expiration of two years from the death of the transferor (s.239).

25 Authorities

Statutes–

Finance Acts 1986 and 1999

Inheritance Tax Act 1984

Statutory Instruments–

Charge to Income Tax by Reference to Enjoyment of Property Previously Owned Regulations 2005 (S.I. 2005 No. 724)

Inheritance Tax (Delivery of Accounts) (Excepted Estates) Regulations 2004, as amended (S.I. 2004 No. 2543, 2005 No. 3230, 2006 No. 2141, 2011 Nos. 214 and 2226, and 2014 No. 488)

Inheritance Tax (Delivery of Accounts) (Excepted Settlements) Regulations 2008 (S.I. 2008 No. 606)

Inheritance Tax (Delivery of Accounts) (Excepted Transfers and Excepted Terminations) Regulations 2008 (S.I. 2008 No. 605)

Inheritance Tax (Double Charges) Relief Regulations 1987 and 2005 (S.I. 1987 No. 1130 and 2005 No. 3441)

Taxes and Duties, etc (Interest Rate) Regulations 2011 (S.I. 2011 No. 2446)

THE JUSTICE SYSTEM

THE JUSTICE SYSTEM

ANTI-SOCIAL BEHAVIOUR IN ENGLAND AND WALES

1 Contents

Anti-social behaviour in England and Wales is dealt with largely by the Anti-social Behaviour Act 2003 and the Anti-Social Behaviour, Crime and Policing Act 2014, often by way of amending other statutes. This Note explains the key provisions as follows–
- A: Introduction
- B: Closure of premises
- C: Housing
- D: Parental responsibilities
- E: Dispersal of groups
- F: Firearms
- G: The environment
- H: Public order and trespass
- I: High hedges
- J: CBO and other court orders
- K: Community remedies and case reviews

A: INTRODUCTION

2 Preliminary

The Anti-social Behaviour Act 2003 and Anti-Social Behaviour, Crime and Policing Act 2014 aim to give to the police the appropriate powers to deal with serious anti-social behaviour in England and Wales. They contain powers to tackle: premises used for anti-social purposes, dispersal of intimidating groups, nuisance caused by air weapons, the possession of imitation guns, the conversion of air weapons for use with conventional ammunition, public assemblies, illegal raves and unauthorised encampments.

The Acts also provide local authorities with powers to tackle anti-social behaviour in local communities and extends landlords' powers. Parental responsibilities are also covered as well as clearing land and high hedges.

This Note outlines those provisions and other related provisions which deal with anti-social behaviour.

B: CLOSURE OF PREMISES ASSOCIATED WITH NUISANCE, DISORDER, ETC

3 Closure of premises–introduction

The Anti-Social Behaviour, Crime and Policing Act 2014 provides for closure notice and closure orders which can be used to close premises (both licensed and non-licensed) which are causing, or are likely to cause, anti-social behaviour. These provisions replace separate provisions in the Anti-social Behaviour Act 2003 and the Licensing Act 2003 which related to the closure of premises used in connection with drugs, associated with persistent disorder or nuisance, or noise.

4 Closure notices

The police or a local authority may issue a closure notice if satisfied on reasonable grounds that (Anti-Social Behaviour, Crime and Policing Act 2014, s.76)–
- (a) the use of particular premises has resulted, or (if the notice is not issued) is likely soon to result, in nuisance to members of the public; or
- (b) there has been, or (if the notice is not issued) is likely soon to be, disorder near those premises associated with their use,

and that the notice is necessary to prevent the nuisance or disorder from continuing, recurring or occurring.

A notice can be issued for a maximum of 48 hours, and cannot prohibit access by the owner of the premises or people who habitually live there. If the notice is not issued by a police officer of at least the rank of superintendent or, in the case of a notice issued by a local authority, is not signed by the chief executive officer of the authority or a person designated by him, then it will have effect only for 24 hours but may be extended by a further 24 hours on authorisation by one of those two persons (s.77).

A closure notice must (s.76(5))–
- (a) identify the premises;
- (b) explain the effect of the notice;
- (c) state that failure to comply with the notice is an offence;
- (d) state that an application will be made for a closure order;
- (e) specify when and where the application will be heard;
- (f) explain the effect of a closure order;

(g) give information about the names of, and means of contacting, persons and organisations in the area that provide advice about housing and legal matters.

A closure notice may be issued only if reasonable efforts have been made to inform people who live on the premises (whether habitually or not), and any person who has control of or responsibility for the premises or who has an interest in them, that the notice is going to be issued (s.76(6)).

The police or local authority representative must if possible (s.79)–

(a) fix a copy of the notice to at least one prominent place on the premises;

(b) fix a copy of the notice to each normal means of access to the premises;

(c) fix a copy of the notice to any outbuildings that appear to them to be used with or as part of the premises;

(d) give a copy of the notice to at least one person who appears to them to have control of or responsibility for the premises; and

(e) give a copy of the notice to the people who live on the premises and to anyone who does not live there but was informed that the notice was going to be issued.

5 Closure orders

If a closure notice has been issued (see **4 Closure notices**, above) the police or local authority must apply to a magistrates' court for a closure order. The application must be heard by the court within 48 hours of the service of the closure notice (Anti-Social Behaviour, Crime and Policing Act 2014, s.80).

An order may prohibit access for up to 3 months–

(a) by all persons, or by all persons except those specified, or by all persons except those of a specified description;

(b) at all times, or at all times except those specified;

(c) in all circumstances, or in all circumstances except those specified.

The magistrates may make a closure order if it is satisfied that–

(d) a person has engaged, or (if the order is not made) is likely to engage, in disorderly, offensive or criminal behaviour on the premises; or

(e) the use of the premises has resulted, or (if the order is not made) is likely to result, in serious nuisance to members of the public; or

(f) there has been, or (if the order is not made) is likely to be, disorder near those premises associated with their use,

and that the order is necessary to prevent the behaviour, nuisance or disorder from continuing, recurring or occurring.

An application may be adjourned for up to 14 days to allow an occupier, or anyone else with an interest in the premises, to show why an order should not be made. If it does so, the court can continue the closure notice for the period of the adjournment. If the court ultimately does not make a closure order, it can continue the closure notice for up to another 48 hours (s.81).

A closure order may be made in respect of all or any part of the premises specified in the closure notice. If the premises are licensed, the licensing authority must be notified.

6 Enforcement of closure orders

If a magistrates' court makes a closure order the police or local authority on whose application it was made, or any person authorised by them, may enter the premises, using reasonable force, and do anything reasonably necessary to secure the premises against entry by anyone else (Anti-Social Behaviour, Crime and Policing Act 2014, s.85). They may also enter the premises to carry out essential maintenance or repairs.

If asked to do so, they must produce evidence of their identity and authority before entering the premises (s.85(4)).

7 Offences, extensions, costs and compensation

It is an offence to remain in or enter premises in contravention of a closure notice or order without reasonable excuse. A person guilty of this offence is liable on summary conviction to imprisonment for up to three months (breach of a notice) or 51 weeks (breach of an order) or a fine, or both (Anti-Social Behaviour, Crime and Policing Act 2014, s.86).

At any time before it expires, application can be made by the police or local authority (having consulted each other) for an extension of the period for which the order has effect up to a maximum period of six months (including the period for which the original order had effect) (s.82).

Where costs have been incurred by either the police or a local authority in clearing, securing or maintaining premises in respect of which a closure order has effect, they may apply to the court for reimbursement of those costs from anyone served with the application for the order (s.s8). Application for costs must be made within 3 months of the date the closure order ceases to have effect.

Where a person who has no connection with the unlawful use of the premises (and, if they are the owner or occupier of the premises, they took reasonable steps to prevent the unlawful use) suffers financial loss as a result of a closure notice or order then, if it is appropriate, the court may award them compensation for that loss (s.90). Application for compensation must be made within 3 months of the date the closure order was refused, cancelled or ceased to have effect.

8 Appeals against closure notices

Where a closure order or an extension to a closure order is made, an appeal may be made to the Crown Court within 21 days by someone on whom the closure notice was served or a person who has an interest in the closed premises.

An appeal against a decision not to make such an order may be brought by the police or a local authority (Anti-Social Behaviour, Crime and Policing Act 2014, s.84).

9 Premises used for prostitution, etc

There are similar powers giving the courts the power to close, on a temporary basis, premises being used for activities related to certain sexual offences for a period of up to three months. An application can be made for the closure order to be extended but the total period for which a closure order has effect may not exceed six months (Sexual Offences Act 2003, ss.136A-136R, inserted by the Policing and Crime Act 2009, s.21 and Sch. 2 and extended by the Anti-Social Behaviour, Crime and Policing Act 2014, s.115).

C: HOUSING

10 Landlords' obligations and powers

Anti-social behaviour policy and procedures must be prepared by (Housing Act 1996, s.218A, inserted by the Anti-social Behaviour Act 2003, s.12)–
  (a) local housing authorities;
  (b) housing action trusts; and
  (c) registered social landlords.
This provision is not yet in force in Wales.

There are also provisions allowing certain social landlords to apply for injunctions to prohibit anti-social behaviour which relates to or affects their management of their housing stock.

These measures include an anti-social behaviour injunction (Anti-social Behaviour, Crime and Policing Act 2014, ss.1 and 5).

As to these provisions, see the Note on **Secure Tenancies**.

11 Security of tenure and anti-social behaviour

A local authority, a housing action trust or a registered social landlord can apply to the county court for a demotion order. Both a secure tenancy and an assured tenancy can be brought to an end by a demotion order. The court may only make the order if the tenant, another resident of or visitor to the tenant's home has behaved in a way which is capable of causing nuisance or annoyance or if such a person has used the premises for illegal purposes. In addition, the court must be satisfied that it is reasonable to make the order.

The intent is that they act as a warning against anti-social behaviour without going so far as evicting the tenant.

As to demotion orders in respect of secure tenancies, see the Note on **Secure Tenancies** at para **9 Demotion orders for anti-social behaviour**.

As to demotion orders in respect of assured tenancies, see the Note on **Assured Tenancies** at para **17 Demotion orders for anti-social behaviour**, and para **44 Action short of possession: demotion**.

12 Proceedings for possession

A court is required to grant possession of a secure tenancy (i.e., without consideration of reasonableness or the availability of alternative accommodation) if any one of five anti-social behaviour conditions is met and the proper procedures are followed: see the Note on **Secure Tenancies** at para 10 Absolute ground for possession (s.84A); and as to assured tenancies see the Note on **Assured Tenancies** at para 36 Mandatory grounds for possession, Ground 7A.

When a court is considering whether it is reasonable to grant a possession order against a secure or assured tenant under one of the non-mandatory nuisance grounds for possession, the court must give particular consideration to the actual or likely effect which the anti-social behaviour has had or could have on others (Housing Act 1985, s.85A; Housing Act 1988, s.9A, both inserted by the Anti-social Behaviour Act 2003, s.16).

As to the non-mandatory nuisance grounds in relation to secure tenancies, see the Note on **Secure Tenancies** at para **15 Discretionary grounds and orders for possession (s.84)**; and as to assured tenancies, see the Note on **Assured Tenancies** at para **37 Discretionary grounds for possession (Part II of Schedule 2, as amended by the Housing Act 1996)**.

D: PARENTAL RESPONSIBILITIES

13 Parenting orders

The power to make parenting orders was originally introduced by s.8 of the Crime and Disorder Act 1998, s.8. The situations when parenting orders can be made has since been extended by the Anti-social Behaviour Act 2003 and the Police and Justice Act 2006.

Orders can now be made under the 1998 Act when–
(a) a child safety order is made in respect of a child;
(aa) a parental compensation order is made in relation to a child's behaviour;
(b) an anti-social behaviour injunction, criminal behaviour order or sexual harm prevention order is made in respect of a child or young person;
(c) a child or young person is convicted of an offence; or
(d) a person is convicted under s.443 of the Education Act 1996 (failure to comply with a school attendance order) or s.444 (failure to secure regular attendance at school).

There are conditions to be fulfilled before a court can make an Order and these are detailed in the Note on **Treatment of Offenders: Children and Young Persons** para **45 When a parenting order may be made**.

Orders can also be made on the application of a local authority under the Anti-social Behaviour Act 2003, s.20, and the Education (Parenting Orders) (England) Regulations 2004, when a pupil has–
(e) been excluded from school on disciplinary grounds for a fixed period or permanently; and
(f) in the case of a fixed period exclusion it is the second such exclusion in a 12 month period; and
(g) application is made within the relevant period,

See further the Note on **Schools: Discipline and Exclusion** at para **11 Parenting orders**.

In addition, a parenting order may also be made (Anti-social Behaviour Act 2003, ss.26-26B)–
(h) where a child or young person has been referred to a youth offending team and a member of the team applies to a magistrates' court for such an order to be made. In deciding whether to make such an order, the court will take into account any refusal by a parent to enter into a parenting contract or any failure to comply with the requirements of such a contract (see **14 Parenting contracts**, below) or
(i) against a parent because of anti-social behaviour by his or her children, on the application of a local authority or a registered social landlord to a magistrates' court.

Parenting Orders can require parents or guardians to attend guidance and counselling sessions. Such programmes may consist of or include a residential course provided the court is satisfied that this is likely to be more effective than a non-residential course and that any interference with family life is proportionate. See further the paragraphs cited above.

An appeal against the making of a parenting order lies to the Crown Court (Anti-social Behaviour Act 2003, ss.22, 28; Crime and Disorder Act 1998, s.10).

14 Parenting contracts

Parenting contracts were introduced by the Anti-social Behaviour Act 2003. Signing parenting contracts is voluntary for parents. Contracts can be made where a pupil has–
(a) been excluded from school for a fixed period or permanently; or
(b) failed to attend regularly at the school at which he is registered.

Local authorities and schools may make parenting contracts with parents. A parenting contract is defined as a document containing–
(c) a statement by the parent that he agrees to comply with the requirements laid down by the contract for the specified period; and
(d) a statement by the local authority or school governing body that they will provide or arrange support to the parent to help them comply with the requirements.

The requirements must include attendance at counselling or guidance sessions. The purpose of the requirements is to improve the pupil's behaviour and/or secure his regular attendance at school. Parenting contracts must not result in actions for breach of contract or for civil damages (s.19). See also the Note on **Schools: Discipline and Exclusion** at para **10 Parenting contracts**.

Local authorities may also arrange parenting contracts for parents where it has reason to believe that their child or young person has engaged, or is likely to engage, in anti-social behaviour and where that child or the young person resides, or appears to reside, in the authority's area. Registered social landlords have a similar power where the child's behaviour directly or indirectly relates to, or affects, the landlord's housing management functions or, in the case of likely behaviour, would do so (ss.25A, 25B).

Youth offending teams may also arrange parenting contracts for parents of children who have engaged or are likely to engage in criminal conduct or anti-social behaviour (s.25) (see the Note on **Treatment of Offenders: Children and Young Persons** at para **48 Parenting contracts**.

15 Penalty notices for parents in cases of truancy

Parents of registered pupils whose child fails to attend school regularly are guilty of an offence (s.444 of the Education Act 1996). Fixed penalty notices are an alternative to prosecution. Authorised local authority and school staff, the police and community support officers, may issue such notices, although there is no requirement for them to do so (Education Act 1996, s.444A, as inserted by the Anti-social Behaviour Act 2003, s.23).

A penalty notice offers the parent the opportunity of discharging any liability to conviction for the offence by paying a penalty in accordance with the notice (the notice will specify the amount to be paid and deadlines for payment). The parent is prevented from being prosecuted until after the final deadline for payment has passed and from being convicted of that offence if he pays a penalty in accordance with the notice. Penalties are to be paid to local authorities.

See further the Note on **Schools: Admission and Attendance** at para **24 Penalty notices**.

At present, these provisions only apply to England, but the National Assembly for Wales may make an order applying them to Wales. If such an order is made, regulations for Wales will be made and guidance issued by the National Assembly (s.23(9)).

E: DISPERSAL OF GROUPS

16 The power to disperse groups

The Anti-Social Behaviour, Crime and Policing Act 2014 gives the police the power to direct a person who has committed, or is likely to commit, anti-social behaviour to leave a specified area and not return for a specified period of up to 48 hours. Before doing so, an officer must be satisfied on reasonable grounds that the behaviour of the person in the locality has contributed or is likely to contribute to (s.35)–

(a) members of the public in the locality being harassed, alarmed or distressed, or

(b) the occurrence in the locality of crime or disorder; and

(c) that giving a direction to the person is necessary for the purpose of removing or reducing the likelihood of (a) or (b) occurring.

The dispersal power can only be used where an officer of at least the rank of inspector has authorised its use in a specified locality, and cannot last longer than a maximum of 48 hours (s.34).

A direction must be given in writing, unless that is not reasonably practicable (in which case it may be given orally); must specify the area to which it relates; and may impose requirements as to the time by which the person must leave the area and the manner in which the person must do so (including the route). If the police reasonably believe that the person to whom a direction is given is under the age of 16, they may remove him to his home or a place of safety. A direction may not be given to (s.36)–

(a) someone who appears to be under the age of 10;

(b) prevent someone from having access to their home, place of work, school etc;

(c) someone engaged in peaceful picketing (under the Trade Union and Labour Relations (Consolidation) Act 1992, s.220); or

(d) someone taking part in a public procession for which written notice has been given (where required) under the Public Order Act 1986, s.11.

A direction may also require a person to surrender to the police any item in their possession or control that the police reasonably believe has been or is likely to be used in behaviour that harasses, alarms or distresses members of the public. Unless it is not reasonably practicable such a direction must be in writing, tell the person that failing without reasonable excuse to comply with the direction is an offence, and give information about when and how the surrendered item can be recovered. It must not be returned before the end of the exclusion period but if within 28 days after the end of that period the person asks for the item to be returned, it must be returned (unless there is power to retain it under another enactment). If it appears to the police that the person is under the age of 16, they need not return the surrendered item unless that person is accompanied by a parent or other responsible adult (s.37).

In deciding whether to give an authorisation (under s.34) or a direction (under s.35), an officer must have particular regard to the rights of freedom of expression and freedom of assembly set out in articles 10 and 11 of the European Convention on Human Rights (see the Note on **The Human Rights Act 1998**).

F: FIREARMS

17 The possession of weapons

Part 5 of the Anti-social Behaviour Act 2003 relates to firearms and applies to England, Wales and Scotland and principally amends the Firearms Act 1968.

It is an offence to carry an air weapon (whether loaded or not) or an imitation firearm in a public place without lawful authority or reasonable excuse (Firearms Act 1968, s.19 and Sch.6, as amended by the Anti-social Behaviour Act 2003, s.37). It is an arrestable offence which is subject to a maximum penalty of six months' imprisonment.

It is an offence for a young person under the age of 17 to own an air weapon; it is also an offence for anybody to give an air weapon to a person under 17. This means no-one under 17 can have an air weapon in their possession unless supervised by someone who is aged at least 21 or as part of an approved target shooting club or shooting gallery. However, 14 to 16 year olds are permitted to have air weapons unsupervised when on private land, provided they have the consent of the occupier. It is an offence for them to shoot beyond the boundaries of that land (Firearms Act 1968, ss.22-24 and Sch.6, as amended by the Anti-social Behaviour Act 2003, s.38).

As to firearms generally, see the Note on **Offensive Weapons and Firearms**.

18 Prohibition of certain air weapons

There is a ban on air weapons that use the self-contained gas cartridge system, which are vulnerable to conversion to fire conventional ammunition (Firearms Act 1968, s.5(1), as amended by the Anti-social Behaviour Act 2003, s.39). This means that these weapons cannot be possessed, purchased, acquired, manufactured, sold or transferred without the authority of the Secretary of State. Existing owners of the weapons may keep them, provided they obtain a firearms certificate from the police.

As to firearms generally, see the Note on **Offensive Weapons and Firearms.**.

G: THE ENVIRONMENT

19 Community protection notices–introduction

Community protection notice are intended to deal with unreasonable, ongoing problems or nuisances which negatively affect a community's quality of life, such as litter, noise or graffiti. They may be issued by (Anti-social Behaviour, Crime and Policing Act 2014, s.53)–

(a) the police;

(b) a local authority; or

(c) a person designated by a local authority (only a person specified in an order made by the Secretary of State may be designated in this way: the Anti-social Behaviour (Authorised Persons) Order 2015, S.I. No. 749, specifies housing providers).

These community protection notices have replaced litter clearing notices, defacement removal notices, street litter control notices and other similar notices bur are of wider effect in that they can also be used to combat other anti-social behaviour affecting a community, such as noise.

Note.– Community protection notices are not meant to replace the statutory nuisance regime, although they can be used to combat behaviour which is such as to amount to a statutory nuisance. Local authorities have a duty to investigate complaints of statutory nuisance from people living within their area and the issue of a community protection notice will not relieve the local authority of its obligation to serve an abatement notice where a statutory nuisance exists: see the Note on **Public Health: Nuisance, Diseases etc.**

20 Issue and content of community protection notices

A notice can be issued to an individual over the age of 16, or to a body (such as a business), if there are reasonable grounds to be satisfied that (s.43)–

(a) the conduct of the individual or body is having a detrimental effect, of a persistent or continuing nature, on the quality of life of those in the locality; and

(b) the conduct is unreasonable.

A community protection notice may require the person or body on whom it is served to do, or stop doing, specified things; or to take reasonable steps to achieve specified results, but a requirement can only be imposed if it is reasonable to impose it in order to either prevent the detrimental effect referred to in (a) from continuing or recurring, or to reduce that detrimental effect or to reduce the risk of its continuance or recurrence.

Before issuing a notice, the person issuing it must–

(c) give a written warning and allow the person "enough time to deal with the matter" (s.43(5)). This is to ensure that the perpetrator is aware of their behaviour and to give them time to rectify the situation;

(d) inform whatever agencies or persons he or she considers appropriate (e.g., the landlord of the person in question, or the local authority), This is partly in order to avoid duplication (s.43(6)).

It is for the person issuing the written warning to decide how long is "enough time" before serving a notice. For example, if a fence needs to be mended to stop a dog escaping, several days or weeks may be appropriate; if the warning notice relates to the persistent playing of loud music in a park, it could be only minutes or hours before the notice is issued.

Note that conduct which is on or affecting premises is treated as conduct of the person who owns, leases, occupies, controls, operates, or maintains them, but not so as to treat an individual's conduct as that of another person if that person cannot reasonably be expected to control or affect it (s.44).

Where a community protection notice needs to be issued because of a detrimental effect arising from the condition of premises or the use to which premises have been put, but after reasonable enquiries the name or proper address of the occupier of the premises (or, if the premises are unoccupied, the owner) cannot be found, the community protection notice may be posted on the premises, which may be entered to the extent reasonably necessary for that purpose (s.45).

21 Appeal against a community protection notice

Within 21 days of being issued with it, a person may appeal to a magistrates' court against a notice on any of the following grounds that (Anti-social Behaviour, Crime and Policing Act 2014, s.46)–

(a) the conduct specified in the community protection notice–

(i) did not take place,

(ii) has not had a detrimental effect on the quality of life of those in the locality,

(iii) has not been of a persistent or continuing nature,

(iv) is not unreasonable, or

(v) is conduct that the person cannot reasonably be expected to control or affect;

(b) any of the requirements in the notice, or any of the periods within which or times by which they are to be complied with, are unreasonable;

(c) there is a material defect or error in, or in connection with, the notice;

(d) the notice was issued to the wrong person.

While an appeal is pending, any requirements in the notice for the person to stop doing certain things will have effect, but any positive requirements to do certain things will not. For example, where rubbish has accumulated in someone's front garden and a notice has been issued to the owner, a requirement to stop adding to the rubbish would continue in effect pending the hearing of the appeal, but a requirement to clear the garden would not.

22 Effect of a community protection notice

Where a person issued with a community protection notice fails to comply with its requirements, the local authority may, if it relates to land that is open to the air (e.g., a garden), carry out works to ensure that the failure is remedied. In any other case, the local authority may issue the defaulter with a notice (Anti-social Behaviour, Crime and Policing Act 2014, s.47)–

(a) specifying work it intends to have carried out to ensure that the failure is remedied;

(b) specifying the estimated cost of the work; and

(c) inviting the defaulter to consent to the work being carried out,

but may carry out the work only if the consent of the defaulter and (if different) the owner of the property is given. The cost can then be recovered from the defaulter, subject to any appeal to the magistrates' court as to the amount.

If no consent is given, and the necessary remedial works are not carried out by the defaulter, then an offence is committed unless all reasonable steps have been taken to comply with the notice, or there is some other reasonable excuse for the failure to comply with it (s.48).

On summary conviction (i.e., in the magistrates' court) an individual would be liable to a fine not exceeding Level 4 on the standard scale (as to the standard scale, see the Note on **Treatment of Offenders** at para **68 Maximum fines: the "standard scale".**); and an organisation such as a company to an unlimited fine (s.48). The magistrates' court would also have the power to order forfeiture and destruction of any item used in the commission of the offence e.g., noise equipment (s.50). Where necessary, the court can also issue a warrant allowing the police or local authority to seize such items (s.51).

As an alternative to court proceedings, a fixed penalty notice may be issued in an amount not exceeding £100 which, if paid, will prevent court action being taken(s.52).

23 Noise at night

The Noise Act 1996 gives powers to local authorities in England and Wales to deal with noise at night. Under these provisions, local authorities have a discretionary power to investigate a complaint and take steps in response to a complaint.

For further detail on these provisions, see the Note on **Control of Noise**.

24 Use of vehicle in an anti-social manner

Where the use of a vehicle is causing or is likely to cause alarm, distress, or annoyance to members of the public, the police have the power to order the driver to stop driving, and to seize and remove the vehicle: see the Note on **Road Traffic Offences** at para **4 Use of vehicle in an anti-social manner**.

25 Fireworks

The Fireworks Regulations 2004 prohibit the use of "adult" fireworks during "night hours" i.e., between 11 p.m. and 7 am.. There are exceptions in that fireworks are allowed for extended hours on a "permitted fireworks night", namely from 11 pm–

(a) on the first day of the Chinese year until 1 a.m. the next day;

(b) on the 5th November, until midnight;

(c) on the day of Diwali, until 1 a.m. the next day; and

(d) on New Year's Eve, until 1 a.m. the following day.

There is also an exemption for any local authority employee using fireworks at a local authority organised fireworks display or national public celebration of commemorative event.

An "adult firework" is basically any firework other than a cap, cracker snap, novelty match, party popper, serpent, sparkler or throwdown.

The Regulations also prohibit excessively loud fireworks (as defined in the Regulations).

The Regulations also prohibit persons under 18 from possessing such fireworks in a public place, and prohibit anyone from possessing certain more dangerous fireworks (known as category 4 fireworks) at all. There are exceptions e.g., for professional fireworks organisers, manufacturers and traders.

26 Penalty notices for graffiti and fly-posting

An authorised local authority official can issue a fixed penalty notice to a person he has reason to believe has committed a relevant graffiti or fly posting offence. The penalties are levied on the people actually committing these acts and not, in the case of fly-posting, on the person whose goods or services are advertised on the poster. Offenders have 14 days in which to pay the penalty, after which prosecution for the offence may be initiated. No proceedings may be brought where payment of the fixed penalty has been made within the 14 days. In issuing a fixed penalty, a local authority officer must provide a written statement setting out the particulars of the offence. This must state: that legal proceedings will not be initiated until after 14 days; the amount of the fixed penalty; and details of where and to whom the penalty should be paid. Payment of a penalty may be made by pre-paying and posting a letter containing the full amount of the penalty (in cash or otherwise) to the person named on the notice (Anti-social Behaviour Act 2003, ss.43-47).

The amount of penalty is fixed by each local authority at between £50 and £80 (in Wales, £75 and £150), but where an authority has not specified an amount the default penalty is £75. A local authority may provide for a lesser amount (but not less than £50) to be accepted as full payment if early payment is made within a specified period. Parish and community councils (by way of their qualifying as "litter authorities" under s.88(9)(f) of the Environmental Protection Act 1990, and therefore as "local authorities"" under the Clean Neighbourhoods and Environment Act 2005) are also given the power to issue fixed penalty notices for the graffiti and fly-posting offences. However, they must adopt the amount of penalty specified by the local authority for their area (s.43A, inserted by the Clean Neighbourhoods and Environment Act 2005, s.28).

If an authorised officer of a local authority plans to give a person a notice under s.43, the officer may require them to give their name and address. It is an offence punishable on summary conviction to a fine not exceeding level 3 on the standard scale to fail to do so or to give false or inaccurate information (s.43B, inserted by the Clean Neighbourhoods and Environment Act 2005, s.29). As to the standard scale, see the Note on **Treatment of Offenders** at para **68 Maximum fines: the "standard scale"**.

The relevant graffiti and fly-posting offences in respect of which fixed penalty notices may be issued are (s.44)–

    (a) s.54(10) of the Metropolitan Police Act 1839 (affixing posters, etc.);

    (b) s.20(1) of the London County Council (General Powers) Act 1954 (defacement of streets with slogans, etc.);

    (c) s.1(1) of the Criminal Damage Act 1971 (damaging property, etc., which involves only the painting or writing on, or the soiling, marking or other defacing of, any property by whatever means);

    (d) s.131(2) of the Highways Act 1980 (including that provision as applied by s.27(6) of the Countryside Act 1968 which involves only an act of obliteration);

    (e) s.132(1) of the Highways Act 1980 (painting or affixing things on structures on the highway, etc.); and

    (f) s.224(3) of the Town and Country Planning Act 1990 (displaying advertisements in contravention of regulations).

A penalty notice may not be given for certain more serious types of offence, for which there can be no avoidance of a prosecution. These offences are graffiti and fly posting offences which amount to racially aggravated criminal damage, and any of the above offences which are motivated wholly or partly by hostility towards a person based on their racial or religious group, or by hostility to members of a racial or religious group based on their membership of that group (s.43(2)).

27 Penalty receipts

The penalties are payable to the local authority and may be used by it only for the purposes of its "qualifying functions" (these are functions under s.43 and any subsequently specified as such in regulations made by the Secretary of State in England or the Welsh Assembly). The local authority must provide the Secretary of State (or Welsh Assembly) with information relating to the use of the penalty receipts. Regulations may make provision as to what local authorities must do with receipts if they are not being spent, and may make provision for appropriate accounting arrangements (Anti-social Behaviour Act 2003, s.45).

The Environmental Offences (Use of Fixed Penalty Receipts) Regulations 2007 (S.I. No. 901) provide that a local authority rated as "excellent" or "good" or with 4, 3 or 2 "stars" may use such receipts for any function of that authority.

28 Powers of police civilians

Community support officers have the power to issue penalty notices in respect of graffiti and fly posting (in the same way as they can issue penalties for littering and dog fouling) (Police Reform Act 2002, Sch.4, as amended by the Anti-social Behaviour Act 2003, s.46).

Accredited people (i.e., employees of private companies who undertake specified functions in support of the police) may also issue fixed penalty notices in respect of graffiti and fly-posting (Police Reform Act 2002, Sch. 5, as amended by s.46 of the 2003 Act).

29 Advertisements

Displaying an advertisement in contravention of Regulations made under s.220 of the Town and Country

Planning Act 1990 (i.e., the Town and Country Planning (Control of Advertisements) Regulations 1992 (S.I. 1992 No. 666)) attracts a penalty of up to Level 4 on the standard scale.

As to the standard scale, see the Note on **Treatment of Offenders** at para **68 Maximum fines: the "standard scale"**.

30 Aerosol paints

It is an offence to sell aerosol spray paints to children aged under 16. The maximum penalty for the offence is a fine of up to Level 4 on the standard scale.

As to the standard scale, see the Note on **Treatment of Offenders** at para **68 Maximum fines: the "standard scale"**.

It is a defence that the person charged with the offence took all reasonable steps to determine the purchaser's age and reasonably believed he was 16 or over. There is also a defence for someone who is charged with an offence but did not carry out the sale themselves (such as a shopkeeper) if he took all reasonable steps to avoid the offence (Anti-social Behaviour Act 2003, s.54).

A programme of enforcement action must be contemplated at least annually by the local weights and measures authority (s.54A, inserted by the Clean Neighbourhoods and Environment Act 2005, s.32).

31 Waste and litter

The Secretary of State has the power to issue statutory directions to clarify the roles and responsibilities of the waste regulation authority (the Environment Agency) and waste collection authorities (local authorities) when dealing with illegally deposited waste (Control of Pollution (Amendment) Act 1989, ss.7 and 9; Environmental Protection Act 1990, ss.59 and 71; Environment Act 1995, s.108; all as amended by the Anti-social Behaviour Act 2003, s.55).

See also **19 Community protection notices–introduction**, above.

As to controls on litter and dumping generally, see the Note on **Waste on Land**.

32 Public space protection orders–introduction

Public spaces protection orders are intended to deal with a particular nuisance or problem in a particular area that is detrimental to a local community's quality of life, by imposing conditions on the use of that area. They have replaced designated public place orders, gating orders and dog control orders.

Orders are generally issued by a local authority, but the Secretary of State has power to designate other bodies to make orders in respect of land in England that they have a statutory power to regulate (Anti-social Behaviour, Crime and Policing Act 2014, ss.59, 71).

33 Making of public space protection orders

Before it can make an order, a local authority must be satisfied on reasonable grounds that (Anti-social Behaviour, Crime and Policing Act 2014, s.59)–
- (a) activities carried on in a public place within the authority's area have had a detrimental effect on the quality of life of those in the locality (or it is likely that such activities will be carried on and that they will have such an effect); and
- (b) the effect, or likely effect, of the activities–
   - (a) is, or is likely to be, of a persistent or continuing nature;
   - (b) is, or is likely to be, such as to make the activities unreasonable; and
   - (c) justifies the restrictions to be imposed.

An order will specify the area to which it applies and can prohibit specified things being done in the restricted area (e.g., drinking alcohol in public), require specified things to be done by persons carrying on specified activities in that area (e.g., keep dogs on a lead), or both of those things, but must be reasonable in order to prevent or reduce the detrimental effect referred to in (a) above from continuing, occurring or recurring.

In deciding whether to make a public spaces protection order, and if so what it should include, an authority must have particular regard to the rights of freedom of expression and freedom of assembly set out in Articles 10 and 11 of the European Convention on Human Rights (see the Note on **The Human Rights Act 1998**). Before making an order they must consult the police, such community representatives as they consider appropriate, and the owners or occupiers of land within the restricted area. The text of the proposed order must be publicised, and once made the order itself must be published on the council's website and a notice (or notices) must be erected on or adjacent to the public place to which the order relates so as to be sufficient to draw the attention of any member of the public using that place to the fact that the order has been made and its effect (s.72, and the Anti-social Behaviour, Crime and Policing Act 2014 (Publication of Public Spaces Protection Orders) Regulations 2014, Reg. 2). The notice provisions also apply if an order is extended, varied or discharged.

Once made, an order can have effect for up to three years, and may be extended for further three year periods if the authority is satisfied on reasonable grounds that doing so is necessary to prevent (s.60)–
- (a) an occurrence or recurrence of the activities identified in the order; or
- (b) an increase in the frequency or seriousness of those activities.

The validity of a public spaces protection order can challenged by anyone who lives in the area or regularly visits the area it covers, but must be made within six weeks of the order (or variation) being made (s.66). A challenge (to the High Court) may only be made on the grounds that the local authority did not have power to make the order (or variation), or to include particular prohibitions or requirements imposed by it, or that a procedural requirement has not been complied with.

34 Public space protection orders–alcohol

An order which prohibits the consumption of alcohol does not apply to licensed premises (Anti-social Behaviour, Crime and Policing Act 2014, s.62).

Consuming alcohol in breach of a public spaces protection order is not an offence unless an individual does not stop drinking or surrender the alcoholic drink when challenged by an enforcement officer (i.e., a police, police community support, or local authority officer) (ss.63(2), 67(4)). This gives officers a discretion in each situation. Where there is no threat of anti-social behaviour, they need not challenge the individual.

An offence will only be committed if the individual is told that failing without reasonable excuse to comply with the requirement is an offence, and the enforcement officer shows evidence of their authorisation if asked for it. The offence extends to anything which the enforcement officer reasonably believes to be alcohol. Anything surrendered may be disposed of in whatever way the enforcement officer thinks appropriate.

35 Public space protection orders–rights of way

A local authority may not make a public spaces protection order that restricts the public right of way over a highway without considering (Anti-social Behaviour, Crime and Policing Act 2014, s.64)–
   (a) the likely effect of making the order on the occupiers of premises adjoining or adjacent to the highway;
   (b) the likely effect of making the order on other persons in the locality;
   (c) in a case where the highway constitutes a through route, the availability of a reasonably convenient alternative route.

In any event, an order cannot restrict the access of occupiers of premises adjacent to or adjoining the affected highway, or for which it is the only or principal means of access. In the case of business or recreational premises, an order cannot restrict the public right of way over the highway during periods when the premises are normally in use.

36 Public space protection orders–penalties

Breach of an order, without reasonable excuse, is a criminal offence, subject to a fixed penalty notice (of up to £100) (Anti-social Behaviour, Crime and Policing Act 2014, s.68) or prosecution.

On summary conviction, an individual can be liable to a fine not exceeding level 3 on the standard scale (s.67), except in relation to failure to comply with a request to stop drinking or surrender alcohol in a controlled drinking zone which is punishable by a fine not exceeding level 2 (s.63).

As to the standard scale, see the Note on **Treatment of Offenders** at para **68 Maximum fines: the "standard scale"**.

37 Alcohol–young persons

The Confiscation of Alcohol (Young Persons) Act 1997 gives power to police constables to confiscate alcohol and alcohol containers from any person in a public place who is himself under the age of 18, or who intends to give the alcohol to a person under 18, or who is, or has been, accompanied by a person under 18 who has been drinking alcohol. A place is a "public place" if the public, or any section of the public, has access to it whether or not for payment (but not including licensed premises). The same police powers apply if the person concerned is in a non-public place to which he has unlawfully gained access. It is an offence for a person to fail to surrender alcohol when required to do so by a police constable acting in pursuance of his powers under the Act.

H: PUBLIC ORDER AND TRESPASS

38 Public assemblies

A senior police officer has the power to impose conditions on public assemblies under s.14 of the Public Order Act 1986 if he believes that serious public disorder, serious damage to property or serious disruption to the life of the community might result, or that the purpose of a demonstration is the intimidation of others with a view to compelling them to act in a particular way.

Conditions may include the location of the assembly, its duration, or the maximum number of people involved. A "public assembly" for these purposes is two or more people (Public Order Act 1986, s.16, as amended by the Anti-social Behaviour Act 2003, s.57).

39 Raves

Open air raves where 20 or more people are present are regulated by s.63 of the Criminal Justice and Public Order Act 1994. This provision also covers raves in buildings, if those attending the rave are trespassing.

40 Aggravated trespass

The offence of aggravated trespass results when a person is trespassing, whether in a building or in the open air, and does anything which is intended to intimidate or deter people from engaging in lawful activity, or to obstruct or disrupt that activity (Criminal Justice and Public Order Act 1994, ss.68 and 69, amended by the Anti-social Behaviour Act 2003, s.59).

41 Power to remove trespassers

Senior police officers have the power to direct a person to leave land and to remove any vehicle or other property with him on that land. At least two people must be trespassing on the land; they must have between them at least one vehicle; they must be present on the land with the intent of residing there; and the occupier of the land must have asked the police to remove them. In addition, it must appear to the senior police officer, after consultation with the local authority, that there are relevant caravan sites with suitable pitches available for the trespassers to move to (Criminal Justice and Public Order Act 1994, s.62A, as inserted by the Anti-social Behaviour Act 2003, s.60).

I: HIGH HEDGES

42 Introduction to high hedges

Part 8 of the Anti-social Behaviour Act 2003 gives local authorities the power to deal with complaints about high hedges which are having an adverse effect on a neighbour's property.

Complaints must be made by the owner or occupier of a domestic property on the grounds that his reasonable enjoyment of that property is being adversely affected by the height of a high hedge situated on land owned or occupied by another person. Even if the property is unoccupied, the owner may still bring a complaint. Complaints about roots are specifically excluded (s.65).

A "high hedge" is a barrier to light or access formed wholly or predominantly by a line of two or more evergreen or semi-evergreen trees or shrubs which rise more than two metres above ground level (s.66).

A "domestic property" is a dwelling or its associated garden or yard (s.67).

43 The complaints procedure

A complaint must be made to the local authority and must be accompanied by a fee (if the authority charges one), the maximum amount of which may be prescribed by regulations (Anti-social Behaviour Act 2003, s.68). The High Hedges (Fees) (Wales) Regulations 2004 set this maximum amount at £320 in relation to Wales. No maximum has been set for England.

The local authority may reject the complaint if it considers that the complainant has not taken all reasonable steps to resolve the matter without involving the authority, or if it considers that the complaint is frivolous or vexatious. If the local authority decides, on this basis, not to proceed with the complaint, it must inform the complainant as soon as is reasonably practicable and must explain the reasons for its decision.

Where the local authority proceeds with the complaint, it must decide in the first place whether the height of the high hedge is adversely affecting the complainant's reasonable enjoyment of his property. If so, the authority must then consider what, if any, action should be taken in relation to the hedge.

The authority must, as soon as is reasonably practicable, inform the parties of its decision and the reasons for it. If the authority decides that action should be taken, it must also issue a remedial notice (under s.69, see **44 Remedial notices**, below).

44 Remedial notices

The remedial notice must specify the hedge to which it relates; the action required to be taken and a timescale; the further action, if any, required to prevent recurrence of the adverse effect; the date the notice takes effect; and the consequences of failure to comply with the requirements of the notice.

The action specified in a remedial notice may not involve reducing the height of the hedge below 2 metres, or its removal.

While the remedial notice is in force, there is an obligation on the local authority to register it as a local land charge. In addition, the notice is binding not only on whoever is the owner or occupier of the neighbouring land at the time it is issued but also on their successors (Anti-social Behaviour Act 2003, s.69).

A local authority can withdraw a remedial notice or waive or relax its requirements. If it does so, it must notify the complainant and the owner/occupier of the neighbouring land (s.70).

45 Appeals against remedial notices

The appeal authority is the Secretary of State in relation to hedges in England, and the Welsh Assembly in respect of appeals relating to hedges in Wales (Anti-social Behaviour Act 2003, s.71).

The appeal authority may by regulations set out the procedure for dealing with such appeals, may appoint another person to hear and determine appeals, and may also require this person to carry out all or any of its appeals functions (s.72). The High Hedges (Appeals) (Wales) Regulations 2004 and (England) Regulations 2005 have been made for this purpose.

The appeal authority may allow or dismiss an appeal, either in total or in part. If the appeal authority decides to allow the appeal, it may quash or vary the remedial notice to which the appeal relates. It may also issue such a notice where the local authority had not done so in response to the original complaint. Whatever its decision on the appeal, the appeal authority may correct any defect, error or wrong description in the original remedial notice if it considers this will not cause injustice (s.73).

46 Powers of entry

Local authorities and the appeal authority (i.e., the Secretary of State or Welsh Assembly) have the power to enter the neighbouring land in order to carry out their functions. They must give 24 hours' notice of their intended entry and, if the land is unoccupied, leave it as effectively secured as they found it. Intentionally obstructing a person exercising these powers is an offence punishable on summary conviction by a fine not exceeding level 3 on the standard scale (Anti-social Behaviour Act 2003, s.74).

As to the standard scale, see the Note on **Treatment of Offenders** at para **68 Maximum fines: the "standard scale"**.

47 Enforcement powers

Failure to comply with a remedial notice is a criminal offence punishable on summary conviction by a fine not exceeding level 3 on the standard scale. Daily fines of one twentieth of that amount can be imposed if the work remains outstanding following a court order (Anti-social Behaviour Act 2003, s.75).

As to the standard scale, see the Note on **Treatment of Offenders** at para **68 Maximum fines: the "standard scale"**.

There is also the power to require an occupier to permit action to be taken by the owner through the application of s.289 of the Public Health Act 1936 (as applied by s.76 of the 2003 Act).

The local authority has power to enter the neighbouring land and carry out the works specified in the remedial notice, if the owner or occupier of the land fails to comply with its requirements (s.77). The costs of this work can then be recovered from the owner or occupier of the land. Any unpaid expenses will (until recovered) be registered as a local land charge. When exercising these powers, the local authority must give seven days' notice of its planned action.

Where offences are committed by companies, proceedings may, in certain circumstances, be taken against individual officers of the company as well as against the company itself (s.78).

48 Overhanging branches

A similar problem to that caused by high hedges can result from overhanging tree branches, but there are no statutory provisions to cover this situation. Instead, the matter is dealt with by the common law. In summary, if a tree owner is unwilling to cut back branches which overhang a neighbouring property, the neighbour can himself cut them back, but only so far as the boundary between the properties. Any branches cut off remain the property of the tree owner and must be offered to him before they are disposed of. Likewise any fruit on an overhanging branch is the property of the tree owner, not of the person whose land it overhangs. Windfall fruit also remain the property of the tree owner, but cannot be collected by him without the permission of the person on whose land they have fallen.

Note.—Before any tree branches are lopped a check should be made (with the local planning department) to ensure that the tree is not subject to a preservation order as a tree subject to such an order cannot be lopped without. Trees in conservation areas are automatically protected.

J: CBO AND OTHER COURT ORDERS

49 Criminal behaviour orders

S.22 of the Anti-social Behaviour, Crime and Policing Act 2014 provides for the making of "criminal behaviour orders" where a person has been convicted of an offence and either sentenced or conditionally discharged. They have replaced both "anti-social behaviour orders" and "drinking banning orders" in England and Wales. For further details, see the Note on **Treatment of Offenders** at para **34 Criminal Behaviour Orders**.

50 Civil injunctions

The High Court or county court (or a Youth Court where a person is aged under 18) may grant an injunction against anyone aged 10 or over if it (Anti-social Behaviour, Crime and Policing Act 2014, s.1)–

(a) is satisfied, on the balance of probabilities, that the person has engaged or threatens to engage in anti-social behaviour; and

(b) considers it just and convenient to grant the injunction for the purpose of preventing the person from engaging in anti-social behaviour.

An injunction may prohibit the respondent from doing anything, or require the respondent to do anything, described in the injunction, but any prohibitions or requirements must, so far as practicable, be such as to avoid any interference with works or school attendance. An injunction must either specify the period for which it has effect, or state that it has effect until further order, but an injunction in relation to a person under 18 must be for no more than 12 months. In cases of violence or risk of harm an injunction may exclude a person (if aged 18 or over) from the place where they normally live (s.13).

Application for an injunction may be made – depending on the circumstances – by a local authority, a housing provider, the police, Transport for London, the Environment Agency, the Natural Resources Body for Wales, or NHS Protect and its Welsh equivalent (s.5).

"Anti-social behaviour" means conduct (s.2)–

(a) that has caused, or is likely to cause, harassment, alarm or distress to any person;

(b) capable of causing nuisance or annoyance to a person in relation to that person's occupation of residential premises; or

(c) capable of causing housing-related nuisance or annoyance to any person.

51 Penalty notices for disorderly behaviour

The Criminal Justice and Police Act 2001 introduced a penalty notice scheme for disorderly behaviour. The scheme applies to anyone aged 18 or over: see the Note on **Treatment of Offenders** at para **73 Penalty notices**, et seq.

52 Other orders in respect of young people

In addition to criminal behaviour orders, other orders which courts can make in respect of children and young persons include youth rehabilitation orders, referral orders and reparation orders.

Youth rehabilitation orders can be made where a person under 18 is convicted of an offence and can impose on that person one or more requirements, such as an activity requirement, a curfew requirement, an exclusion requirement or a residence requirement. See further the Note on **Treatment of Offenders: Children and Young Persons** at para **13 Youth rehabilitation orders**.

The making of a referral order to a youth offending team can, and in certain circumstance must, be made where a youth court or other magistrates' court is dealing with a young person under the age of 18 for an offence punishable with imprisonment. See further the Note on **Treatment of Offenders: Children and Young Persons** at para **32 Referral orders**.

Reparation orders provide that where a child or young person is convicted of an offence other than one for which the sentence is fixed by law, the court may make a reparation order requiring that child or young person to make reparation, as specified in the order, to a specified person or persons or to the community at large. See further the Note on **Treatment of Offenders: Children and Young Persons** at para **42 Reparation orders**.

K: COMMUNITY REMEDIES AND CASE REVIEWS

53 The community remedy

Every Police and Crime Commissioner (or, in London, the Mayor's Office for Policing and Crime and the Common Council of the City of London), must prepare a "community remedy document" i.e., a list of actions that might be appropriate in a particular case to be carried out by a person who has carried out anti-social behaviour as a sanction without going to court (Anti-social Behaviour, Crime and Policing Act 2014, s.101).

The document could, for example, include actions such as paying compensation to the victim, making good any damage caused, or mediation to resolve a dispute. Any action included in the document must have one or more of the following objects (s.101(3))–

(a) assisting in rehabilitation;

(b) ensuring that a person makes reparation for the behaviour or offence in question;

(c) punishment.

In preparing a community remedy document the Commissioner must have regard to any guidance issued by the Secretary of State, consult the police, local authorities, and such community representatives as he thinks appropriate, and carry out appropriate public consultation. He must also have regard to the need to promote public confidence in the out-of-court disposal process.

54 When a community remedy is appropriate

A community remedy can only be used where (Anti-social Behaviour, Crime and Policing Act 2014, s.102)–

(a) there is enough evidence to apply for an anti-social behaviour injunction or to take other court proceedings;

(b) it is not considered that a caution or fixed penalty notice would be appropriate; and

(c) the behaviour has been admitted.

Before deciding what action to invite a person to carry out, reasonable efforts must be taken to obtain the views of the victim (if any) of the anti-social behaviour or the offence, and in particular the victim's views as to whether the person should carry out any of the actions listed in the community remedy document. If the victim expresses the view that they should carry out a particular action listed in the community remedy document, the person must be invited to carry out that action unless it seems that it would be inappropriate to do so. Where there is more than one victim and they express different views, those views must nevertheless take account in deciding what action to choose.

If the person refuses to carry out the community remedy, then more formal procedures (such as court proceedings) will be considered.

55 Anti-social behaviour case reviews

In every local government area the relevant authorities must set up review procedures for people resident in those areas to ask for case reviews about complaints they have made about anti-social behaviour (Anti-social Behaviour, Crime and Policing Act 2014, s.104).

A local government area for these purpose is generally a London borough, district council or unitary authority (in England), or the county or county borough council (in Wales). The "relevant authorities" are the local council, the police for that area, the clinical commissioning groups in that area, and such local providers of social housing as the local council has co-opted to be involved (s.105, Sch. 4).

Where a person has made a complaint about anti-social behaviour in a particular local government area, the relevant bodies in that area must carry out a review of the response to that behaviour if an application is made for a review and the threshold for a review is met. The threshold will be set by the relevant bodies but if at least three complaints have been made about the anti-social behaviour to which the application relates in a six-month period, then the relevant bodies must decide that the threshold for a review is met (s.104(4)). In any other situation where an application for a case review is made, the question whether the threshold for a review is met must be decided by the relevant bodies in accordance with their review procedures which may be framed by reference to the–

   (a) persistence of the anti-social behaviour about which the original complaint was made;
   (b) harm caused, or the potential for harm to be caused, by that behaviour; or
   (c) adequacy of the response to that behaviour.

Where the threshold is met, the relevant bodies must carry out a review of the response to the anti-social behaviour that was the subject of the original complaint. This will entail the relevant bodies sharing information in relation to the case, discussing what action has previously been taken, and collectively deciding whether any further action could be taken.

56 Authorities

Statutes–

Anti-social Behaviour Act 2003

Anti-Social Behaviour, Crime and Policing Act 2014

Clean Neighbourhoods and Environment Act 2005

Confiscation of Alcohol (Young Persons) Act 1997

Control of Pollution (Amendment) Act 1989

Crime and Disorder Act 1998

Criminal Justice and Police Act 2001

Criminal Justice and Public Order Act 1994

Criminal Justice and Immigration Act 2008

Education Act 1996

Environment Act 1995

Environmental Protection Act 1990

Firearms Act 1968

Football Spectators Act 1989

Housing Acts 1985, 1988 and 1996

Police Reform Act 2002

Public Order Act 1986

Sexual Offences Act 2003

Town and Country Planning Act 1990

Statutory Instruments–

Anti-social Behaviour, Crime and Policing Act 2014 (Publication of Public Spaces Protection Orders) Regulations 2014 (S.I. 2014 No. 2591)

Education (Parenting Orders) (England) Regulations 2004 (S.I. 2004 No. 182)

Fireworks Regulations 2004, as amended (S.I. 2004 Nos. 1836 and 3262)

High Hedges (Appeals) (England) Regulations 2005 (S.I. 2005 No. 711)

High Hedges (Appeals) (Wales) Regulations 2004 (S.I. 2004 No. 3240)

High Hedges (Fees) (Wales) Regulations 2004 (S.I. 2004 No. 3241)

ANTI-SOCIAL BEHAVIOUR IN SCOTLAND

1 Contents

Anti-social behaviour in Scotland is dealt with largely by the Antisocial Behaviour etc. (Scotland) Act 2004, often by way of amending other statutes. This Note explains the key provisions as follows–

A: ANTI-SOCIAL BEHAVIOUR STRATEGIES

2 Duty to prepare a strategy

The Antisocial Behaviour etc. (Scotland) Act 2004 gives the responsibility for preparing a strategy for dealing with anti-social behaviour in an authority's area jointly to the local authority concerned and the relevant chief constable (s.1).

The strategy must–

(a) assess the amount of anti-social behaviour in the authority's area;

(b) assess the types of anti-social behaviour;

(c) specify arrangements for consulting community bodies and other persons (particularly young people) in areas where there is antisocial behaviour; about how to deal with such behaviour;

(d) specify the range and availability in that area of any services for those under the age of 16, and for people generally, designed to deal with antisocial behaviour, or the consequences or prevention of such behaviour;

(e) specify the range and availability in that area of any services for victims of antisocial behaviour, witnesses of such behaviour; and for mediation in relation to disputes arising from such behaviour; and

(f) make provision in relation to the exchange of information.

In preparing, reviewing and revising a strategy, the principal reporter and registered social landlords with property in the area must be consulted, along with such community bodies and other persons as the local authority consider appropriate. The local authority must seek to include amongst those consulted representatives of those adversely affected by antisocial behaviour.

Reports on how the authority and chief constable have implemented the strategy and the results of that implementation must be published by each local authority (s.2)

The Scottish Ministers may make regulations in order to involve a registered social landlord in the preparation, review or revision of the anti-social behaviour strategy, rather than them simply being consulted (s.3).

B: ASBOS AND FURTHER CRIMINAL MEASURES

3 Anti-social behaviour orders

Part 2 of the Antisocial Behaviour etc. (Scotland) Act 2004 replaces existing provisions on anti-social behaviour orders (ASBOs) in the Crime and Disorder Act 1998.

A sheriff may make an ASBO if he is satisfied that (s.4)–

(a) the person specified in the application is at least 12 years of age;

(b) he has engaged in antisocial behaviour towards a relevant person; and

(c) the order is necessary for the purposes of protecting relevant people from further anti-social behaviour.

A "relevant person" is, in relation to an application by a local authority, a person within the authority's area, and, in relation to an application by a registered social landlord, a person living in or likely to be in a property provided by or managed by that landlord, or a person in or likely to be in the vicinity of that property.

Where the specified person is a child aged between 12 and 15, the sheriff must consider advice from a children's hearing as to whether the condition that the order is necessary to protect relevant persons is met.

Before making an ASBO the sheriff must explain to the person it is being made against–

(a) the effect of the order and the prohibitions proposed to be included in it;

(b) the consequences of failing to comply with the order;

(c) the powers of the sheriff under ss.5 and 6 of the Act (see **4 Variation and revocation of ASBOs**, below); and

(d) the entitlement of that person to appeal against the making of the order.

Before applying for an ASBO, a local authority must consult the police force for its area and, where the application relates to someone under 16, the Principal Reporter. Further, where the application is intended to protect an affected person who does not live within that local authority's area, the local authority must also consult the local authority and police for that area. A registered social landlord must consult the police for the area in which the person who is proposed to be subject to the order lives and, where the application relates to someone under 16, the Principal Reporter and the local authority for the area in which the child lives. Where a registered social landlord is making an application in relation to an adult, it is required to notify (rather than consult) the local authority for the area in which the adult resides (s.4).

4 Variation and revocation of ASBOs

A sheriff may vary or revoke an ASBO on the application of either the authority that obtained it, or the person subject to it. An authority must consult the following before making such an application (Antisocial Behaviour etc. (Scotland) Act 2004, s.5)–

(a) in relation to an ASBO originally sought or made on the application of a local authority–

    (i) the police for the area which includes the local authority's area;

    (ii) the police for any area where there is a person affected by the antisocial behaviour;

    (iii) each local authority in whose area there is a person affected by the antisocial behaviour; and

    (iv) if the person in respect of whom the order is sought or made is a child, the Principal Reporter;

(b) in relation to an ASBO originally sought or made on the application of a registered social landlord–

    (i) the police for the area where the person lives (and the local authority for that area must also be notified, though not consulted); and

    (ii) if the person is a child, the local authority where the child lives and the Principal Reporter.

A person appealing against the making or variation of an ASBO may not make another application to vary or revoke it before the first appeal is determined or abandoned (s.6).

5 Interim ASBOs

An interim ASBO prohibits, pending the determination of the application by the court, the person specified in the order from doing anything described in the order.

The sheriff must be satisfied that the person is aged 12 years or more, that there is a *prima facie* case that they have engaged in antisocial behaviour, and that an interim order is necessary for the purpose of protecting people from further anti-social behaviour (Antisocial Behaviour etc. (Scotland) Act 2004, s.7).

6 Breach of orders

Breach of an ASBO or an interim order without reasonable excuse is a criminal offence and a person will be liable (Antisocial Behaviour etc. (Scotland) Act 2004, s.9)–

(a) on summary conviction, to imprisonment for a term not exceeding six months or to a fine not exceeding the statutory maximum or both; or

(b) on conviction on indictment, to imprisonment for a term not exceeding five years or to a fine (unlimited), or to both.

If a separate offence is committed while breaching the ASBO or interim order, the person charged with the separate offence is not liable to proceedings for breach of the ASBO or interim order. However, if the person is convicted for the separate offence, the sheriff must have regard to the fact that they were subject to an ASBO at the time, the number of orders they were subject to, any previous convictions for breach of an ASBO or interim ASBO, and the extent to which the sentence or disposal for any previous breach differed because of this provision (i.e., breach of the ASBO is treated as an aggravating factor in deciding sentence for the new offence).

In the case of a child, (a) and (b) above are modified. Where a child (i.e., under the age of 16) is convicted of breach of an ASBO or interim order they cannot be detained for that breach (Criminal Procedure (Scotland) Act 1995, ss.44, 208).

There is a statutory power of arrest for breach of an ASBO or interim order (s.11).

As to the statutory maximum, see the Note on **Treatment of Offenders** at para **35 Maximum fines: the "standard scale"**.

7 ASBOs in respect of children

Where the sheriff makes an ASBO or an interim order in respect of a child, he may require the Principal Reporter to refer the child's case to a children's hearing (Antisocial Behaviour etc. (Scotland) Act 2004, s.12). Such a hearing may consider imposing a compulsory supervision order: see the Note on **Treatment of Offenders: Children and Young Persons** at para **10 The supervision requirement**.

Where a sheriff makes an ASBO in respect of a child, he must make a parenting order in respect of the child's parent where he is satisfied that the making of an order is desirable in the interests of preventing the child from engaging in further anti-social behaviour, and the local authority for the area in which the parent ordinarily lives has arrangements in place to provide the support and services required under such an order (s.13). As to parenting orders, see J: PARENTING ORDERS, below.

8 Provision of information, and records

Registered landlords must pass on to the local authority any notifications it receives in relation to the making, variation, revocation or recall of an ASBO or interim order (Antisocial Behaviour etc. (Scotland) Act 2004, s.14).

A local authority must keep a record of ASBOs and interim orders. Requests for disclosure of these records can be made by–
  (a) the Scottish Ministers;
  (b) the Principal Reporter;
  (c) any other local authority;
  (d) a chief constable; and
  (e) a registered social landlord.

C: DISPERSAL OF GROUPS

9 Authorisations and powers

Where a police officer of the rank of superintendent or above has reasonable grounds for believing that (Antisocial Behaviour etc. (Scotland) Act 2004, s.19)–
  (a) members of the public have been alarmed or distressed as a result of the presence or behaviour of groups of two or more people in public places in his police area; and
  (b) anti-social behaviour is a significant, persistent and serious problem there,
he may authorise a constable to give a direction (s.21)–
  (c) requiring those in the group to disperse;
  (d) requiring any of those people who do not live within the police area to leave; and
  (e) prohibiting any of those people who do not live within that area from returning for a specified period of time (not exceeding 24 hours).
Such a direction may not be given in respect of a group of people (s.21(5))–
  (f) who are engaged in conduct which is lawful under the Trade Union and Labour Relations (Consolidation) Act 1992, s.220 (industrial disputes); or
  (g) who are taking part in a procession in respect of which written notice has been given, or such notice is not required.
The exercise of these powers may be (s.19(2))–
  (h) during a specified period;
  (i) on specified days that fall within a specified period; or
  (j) between specified times that fall within a specified period.
Before issuing such an authorisation, the police must consult the local authority (s.19(4)). An authorisation notice must also be published in the press (s.20).

A person who, without reasonable excuse, knowingly contravenes a direction given to them under s. 21 of the Act is guilty of an offence and liable on summary conviction to a fine not exceeding level 4 on the standard scale, or imprisonment for a term not exceeding three months, or both. (s.22).

As to the standard scale, see the Note on **Treatment of Offenders** at para **35 Maximum fines: the "standard scale"**.

D: FIREARMS

10 Possession and prohibition of weapons

Part 5 of the Anti-social Behaviour Act 2003 relates to firearms and principally amends the Firearms Act 1968.

It is an offence to carry an air weapon (whether loaded or not) or an imitation firearm in a public place without lawful authority or reasonable excuse (Firearms Act 1968, s.19 and Sch.6, as amended by the Anti-social Behaviour Act 2003, s.37). It is an arrestable offence which is subject to a maximum penalty of six months' imprisonment.

It is an offence for a young person under the age of 17 to own an air weapon; it is also an offence for anybody to give an air weapon to a person under 17. This means no-one under 17 can have an air weapon in their possession unless supervised by someone who is aged at least 21 or as part of an approved target shooting club or shooting gallery. However, 14 to 16 year olds are permitted to have air weapons unsupervised when on private land, provided they have the consent of the occupier. It is an offence for them to shoot beyond the boundaries of that land (Firearms Act 1968, ss.22-24 and Sch.6, as amended by the Anti-social Behaviour Act 2003, s.38).

There is a ban on air weapons that use the self-contained gas cartridge system, which are vulnerable to conversion to fire conventional ammunition (Firearms Act 1968, s.5(1), as amended by the Anti-social Behaviour Act 2003, s.39). This means that these weapons cannot be possessed, purchased, acquired, manufactured, sold or transferred without the authority of the Secretary of State. Existing owners of the weapons may keep them, provided they obtain a firearms certificate from the police.

As to firearms generally, see the Note on **Offensive Weapons and Firearms.**

E: CLOSURE OF PREMISES

11 Introduction

Closure orders are intended to allow the temporary closure of premises which are associated with antisocial behaviour. This may be because, for example, they are being used for the sale or use of illegal drugs, as a brothel, or because they are the source of excessive noise. They also allow for the closure of premises associated with the commission of "exploitation offences" such as human trafficking and child sexual abuse.

12 Closure notices

A senior police officer may authorise the issue of a closure notice prohibiting access to specified premises by any person other than someone who usually lives on the premises or the owner of the premises. The Scottish Ministers may, by regulations, specify premises in respect of which an authorisation may not be given (Antisocial Behaviour etc. (Scotland) Act 2004, s.26). "Premises" for these purposes include any land or other place, whether enclosed or not (s.40).

A senior police officer may authorise the service of a closure notice only where he (s.26(3))–

(a) has reasonable grounds for believing that during the preceding three months a person has engaged in anti-social behaviour on the premises and the use of the premises is associated with the occurrence of relevant harm (i.e., significant and persistent disorder, or significant, persistent and serious nuisance to members of the public); and

(b) is satisfied that the local authority has been consulted and that reasonable steps have been taken to establish the identity of any person who lives on, has control of, has responsibility for, or has an interest in the premises.

The closure notice must be served by the police by (s.27)–

(a) fixing a copy of the notice to at least one prominent place on the premises, each normal means of access to the premises, and any outbuildings; and

(b) giving a copy of the notice to any person identified as or appearing to, live on, have control of, have responsibility for, or have an interest in the premises.

A copy of the notice must also be given to any occupant whose access to any other part of the those premises are impeded by the making of an order.

The closure notice must–

(a) specify the premises to which it relates;

(b) state that access to the premises by anyone other than a person who habitually resides there or the owner of the premises is prohibited;

(c) state that failure to comply with the notice amounts to an offence;

(d) state that an application is to be made under s.28 for the closure of the premises;

(e) specify such matters about that application as may be prescribed in rules of court;

(f) explain the effect of a closure order made under s.30 (see **13 Closure orders,** below); and

(g) give information about the names of, and means of contacting, people who, and organisations which, provide advice about housing and legal matters locally.

13 Closure orders

Once a closure notice has been served, a senior police officer can apply to the sheriff for a closure order in respect of the premises specified in the notice (Antisocial Behaviour etc. (Scotland) Act 2004, s.28).

The application must–

(a) specify the premises in respect of which the closure order is sought;

(b) state the grounds on which the application is made; and

(c) be accompanied by supporting evidence.

A closure order requires that the premises are closed for up to three months. It may be made in respect of all or any part of premises, and may include such provision as to access to other parts of the premises as the sheriff (or, on appeal, the sheriff principal) considers appropriate (s.29).

The sheriff may make a closure order if the following conditions are met (s.30)–

(a) a person has engaged in anti-social behaviour on the premises;

(b) the use of the premises is associated with the occurrence of relevant harm (as defined in **12 Closure notices,** above); and

(c) the making of the order is necessary to prevent the occurrence of such relevant harm for the period specified in the order.

The sheriff must have regard to the ability of any person living on the premises to find alternative accommodation and, where that person has not been engaged in antisocial behaviour at the premises, their vulnerability.

Generally, the sheriff must decide an application within two days, however he may postpone his decision for up to 14 days to enable the following people to show why a closure order should not be made–
    (a) the occupier of the premises specified in the closure notice;
    (b) any person who has control of or responsibility for those premises; and
    (c) any other person with an interest in those premises.

14 Enforcement of closure orders

The police, or a person authorised in writing by the chief constable for the area in which the premises are situated may, using reasonable force and producing evidence of identity and authorisation if asked to do so (Antisocial Behaviour etc. (Scotland) Act 2004, s.31)–
    (a) do anything necessary to secure closed premises against entry by any person;
    (b) carry out essential maintenance or repairs to closed premises; and
    (c) enter the premises for the purposes of (a) or (b).

15 Extension of a closure order

The sheriff may, under certain circumstances, on the application of a senior police officer and if satisfied that it is necessary to do so to prevent the occurrence of relevant harm (as defined in 12 **Closure notices**, above), make an order extending the period for which a closure order has effect provided that the total closure period does not exceed six months (Antisocial Behaviour etc. (Scotland) Act 2004, s.32).

16 Revocation of a closure order

The sheriff may, if satisfied that a closure order is no longer necessary to prevent the occurrence of relevant harm (as defined in 12 **Closure notices**, above), revoke a closure order. Application may be made by (Antisocial Behaviour etc. (Scotland) Act 2004, s.33)–
    (a) a senior police officer;
    (b) the appropriate local authority;
    (c) a person on whom the closure notice was served; and
    (d) a person who has an interest in the closed premises but on whom the closure notice was not served.

17 Access to premises

The sheriff may, on the application of a person who occupies or owns any part of a building or structure in which closed premises are situated but which is not itself closed, make an order making such provision as the sheriff considers appropriate in relation to access while the closure order has effect (Antisocial Behaviour etc. (Scotland) Act 2004, s.34).

18 Reimbursement of expenditure

A sheriff may, on the application of a police authority or a local authority, make such order as he considers appropriate for the reimbursement by the owner of the closed premises of expenditure incurred by the applicant for the purpose of clearing, securing or maintaining the premises in respect of which the closure order has (or had) effect (Antisocial Behaviour etc. (Scotland) Act 2004, s.35).

19 Appeals

An appeal may be made against (Antisocial Behaviour etc. (Scotland) Act 2004, s.36)–
    (a) a closure order or order extending a closure order;
    (b) a decision to refuse to make a closure order or an order extending a closure order;
    (c) a decision to revoke a closure order;
    (d) a decision to refuse to revoke a closure order;
    (e) an order in relation to access to premises or reimbursement of expenditure; and
    (f) a decision to refuse to make an order mentioned in (e) above.
An appeal must be made to the sheriff principal within 21 days from the day on which the order or decision appealed against was made. The decision of the sheriff principal on an appeal is final.

20 Offences

A person is guilty of an offence if, without reasonable excuse, he remains on or enters premises in contravention of a closure notice or in respect of which a closure order has effect (Antisocial Behaviour etc. (Scotland) Act 2004, s.37(1)).
It is also an offence to obstruct an authorised person enforcing a closure order under s.31(1) (s.37(2)).
A person guilty of these offences is liable on summary conviction–

(a) where the person has not, within two years, been convicted of a previous offence under the same subsection, to a fine not exceeding level 4 on the standard scale or imprisonment for a term not exceeding three months, or to both;

(b) where the person has, within two years, been convicted of a previous offence under the same subsection, to a fine not exceeding the statutory maximum or imprisonment for a term not exceeding nine months, or to both.

Where a constable reasonably believes that a person is committing or has committed an offence under s.37, he may arrest the person without warrant (s.38).

As to the standard scale and the statutory maximum, see the Note on **Treatment of Offenders** at para **35 Maximum fines: the "standard scale"**.

F: NOISE NUISANCE

21 Application of noise control provisions

A local authority may adopt the noise control provisions in Part 5 of the Antisocial Behaviour etc. (Scotland) Act 2004 if it so chooses. If a local authority decides to apply these provisions to its area, it must adopt them by resolution and there must be a period of two months before they take effect. The resolution must specify the periods of the week for which noise is to be controlled. It may decide to specify the whole week as a noise control period, or different noise control periods for different areas, times of the year, or other circumstances (Antisocial Behaviour etc. (Scotland) Act 2004, s.41).

A local authority may, by a further resolution, revoke or vary a noise control period (s.42).

The following paragraphs deal with the provisions of the 2004 Act. For other provisions as to noise control, see Note on **Control of Noise**.

22 Noise control provisions

Where a local authority receives a complaint from an individual that excessive noise is coming from a "relevant property" during a noise control period, an officer of the authority must investigate it (Antisocial Behaviour etc. (Scotland) Act 2004, s.43).

If the officer is satisfied that–

(a) noise is coming from a relevant property during a noise control period; and

(b) the noise, if it were measured, would or might, exceed the permitted level,

the officer may serve a notice about the noise under s.44 (see **23 Warning notices**, below).

Where a local authority receives a complaint about noise and the property from which the noise is coming is situated within another local authority's area, the first local authority may act under the noise control provisions as if the property were within its area, whether or not the noise control provisions apply to the other local authority's area.

A "relevant property" for these purposes is–

(i) a building or other structure used or intended to be used as a separate unit of accommodation;

(ii) any land belonging to or enjoyed exclusively with the property in (i);

(iii) any land not within (ii) to which at least two people have rights in common and which is used by them as a private garden;

(iv) a common passage, stair, yard etc to a tenement or group of separately owned houses; or

(v) any other place as the Scottish Ministers may prescribe.

23 Warning notices

A warning notice must (Antisocial Behaviour etc. (Scotland) Act 2004, s.44)–

(a) state that an officer considers that noise is coming from the property during a noise control period and that the noise exceeds, or may exceed, the permitted level; and

(b) state that any person who is responsible for noise which exceeds the permitted level during the period specified in the notice may be guilty of an offence.

If it is not reasonably practicable to identify someone responsible for the noise on whom the notice may reasonably be served, a warning notice is served by leaving it at the property.

The period specified in the warning notice must not begin less than 10 minutes after the notice is served and will end at the end of the noise control period during which it is served (or when the permitted noise level during a control period changes i.e., 7 pm, 11 pm, or 7 am: see **27 The permitted level of noise**, below).

24 Offence after service of the notice

If a warning notice has been served, any person who is responsible for noise which comes from the relevant property and which exceeds the permitted level is guilty of an offence and is liable on summary conviction to a fine not exceeding level 3 on the standard scale.

It is a defence to show that there was a reasonable excuse for the act, failure or sufferance which resulted in the noise.

A measurement of noise by a device is not admissible as evidence unless the device has been approved (Antisocial Behaviour etc. (Scotland) Act 2004, ss.45 and 49).

As to the standard scale, see the Note on **Treatment of Offenders** at para **35 Maximum fines: the "standard scale"**.

25 Fixed penalty notices

Where an officer has reason to believe that a person is committing or has just committed an offence under s.45, the officer may give that person a fixed penalty notice instead of starting proceedings for that offence.

A fixed penalty notice must state (Antisocial Behaviour etc. (Scotland) Act 2004, s.46)–

(a) the period during which the penalty must be paid if proceedings are not be started for the offence (currently, 28 days);

(b) the amount of the fixed penalty; and

(c) the person to whom, and the address at which, the fixed penalty may be paid.

The fixed penalty payable under this section is £100 (ss.46 and 51).

26 Powers of entry and seizure of equipment

Where–

(a) a noise warning notice has been served; and

(b) an officer has reason to believe that the noise has exceeded the permitted level during the period specified in the notice,

an officer, or a person authorised by the authority, may seize and remove any equipment which appears to be causing or to have caused the noise (Antisocial Behaviour etc. (Scotland) Act 2004, s.47).

A sheriff or justice of the peace may grant a warrant under certain circumstances for the purpose of entering a property and seizing and removing any equipment which appears to be causing or to have caused the noise.

Anyone who wilfully obstructs a person exercising powers under s.47 is guilty of an offence and is liable on summary conviction to a fine not exceeding level 3 on the standard scale (s.47 and Sch.1). As to the standard scale, see the Note on **Treatment of Offenders** at para **35 Maximum fines: the "standard scale"**.

Any equipment seized may be retained for 28 days or, if it is related equipment in proceedings for a noise offence, until the person against whom proceedings are brought is sentenced or acquitted or the proceedings are discontinued. Where a person is convicted of a noise offence, the court may make an order for forfeiture of any related equipment.

The sheriff may deliver the forfeited equipment to anyone who claims it (except to the person on whom the forfeiture order was made) if the sheriff is satisfied that the applicant is the owner of the equipment.

The court may give directions to return, retain or dispose of the equipment, depending upon the circumstances (Sch.1).

27 The permitted level of noise

The Scottish Ministers may, by regulations, prescribe the "permitted level" of noise which may be emitted from a relevant property.

Different permitted levels may be prescribed for different periods of the week, areas or times of the year (s.48).

The Antisocial Behaviour (Noise Control) (Scotland) Regulations 2005 prescribe the maximum levels of noise which may be made at specified times of the day from property which is subject to the noise provisions (Part 5) of the Act, and the way in which noise may be measured. The permitted levels change at 7 pm, 11 pm, and 7 am, and vary according to the underlying level of noise.

28 Fireworks

The Fireworks (Scotland) Regulations 2004 (made under the Fireworks Act 2003) prohibit the use of "adult" fireworks during "night hours" i.e., between 11pm and am. There are exceptions in that fireworks are allowed for extended hours on a "permitted fireworks night", namely from 11pm–

(a) on the first day of the Chinese year until 1 am the next day;

(b) on the 5th November, until midnight;

(c) on the day of Diwali, until 1 am the next day; and

(d) on New Year's Eve, until 1am the following day.

There is also an exemption for any local authority employee using fireworks at a local authority organised fireworks display or national public celebration of commemorative event.

An "adult firework" is basically any firework other than a cap, cracker snap, novelty match, party popper, serpent, sparkler or throwdown.

G: THE ENVIRONMENT

29 Alcohol–young persons

The Crime and Punishment (Scotland) Act 1997 gives power to police constables to confiscate alcohol from any person in a public place who is himself under the age of 18, or who has or intends to give the alcohol to a person under 18. A place is a "public place" if the public, or any section of the public, has access to it whether or not for payment (but not including licensed premises). The same police powers apply if the person concerned is in a non-public place to which he has unlawfully gained access. It is an offence for a person to fail to surrender alcohol when required to do so by a police constable acting in pursuance of his powers under the Act (s.61).

30 Fly-tipping

The Environmental Protection Act 1990 makes provision for the offence of fly-tipping, i.e., depositing waste, or knowingly causing or permitting the depositing of waste, without a licence to do so, and to treating, keeping or disposing of controlled waste in a manner likely to cause pollution of the environment or harm to human health (Environmental Protection Act 1990, s.33). The Antisocial Behaviour etc. (Scotland) Act 2004 provides for a fixed penalty to be given as an alternative to prosecution.

31 Litter and fixed penalty notices

Fixed penalty notices may also be given in respect of littering offences (Environmental Protection Act 1990, s.88, as amended).

These provisions are dealt with in the Note on **Waste on Land** at para **3 Fixed penalty notices for litter**.

32 Graffiti removal notices

A local authority has the power to serve a "graffiti removal notice where it appears to it that the graffiti is either offensive or detrimental to the locality. The people on whom a graffiti removal notice can be served are those responsible for "relevant surfaces" (Antisocial Behaviour etc. (Scotland) Act 2004, s.58).

A relevant surface is defined as the surface of a public road and certain objects physically on the road (or pavement), and surfaces belonging to an educational institution or a statutory undertaker which are visible to members of the public from land owned by such a body, or from public land.

A "statutory undertaker" means (Environmental Protection Act 1990, s.98(6))–

(a) any person authorised by any enactment to carry on any railway, light railway, tramway or road transport undertaking, or operate a railway asset;

(b) any person authorised by any enactment to carry on any canal, inland navigation, dock, harbour or pier undertaking; or

(c) any relevant airport operator.

Where a local authority is unable to ascertain the name or address of the person on whom a graffiti removal notice may be served, the local authority may enter any land and affix the notice to the surface to which it relates (s.60).

In the event that a graffiti removal notice is not complied with, the local authority may enter any land and remove the graffiti itself. Any expenditure reasonably incurred may be recovered (an appeal by the person from whom costs are sought may be made under s.64) (s.61).

33 Appeal against graffiti notices

There are 21 days in which the person on whom the graffiti notice is served can appeal against it. A notice may be revoked by the sheriff if he is satisfied that–

(a) the surface was not defaced;

(b) the defacement was neither detrimental to the amenity of the locality nor offensive; or

(c) the applicant was not a responsible person.

Alternatively, if the sheriff is satisfied that there is a material defect in, or in connection with, the notice, he may make an order revoking or amending it (Antisocial Behaviour etc. (Scotland) Act 2004, s.63).

H: HIGH HEDGES

34 Introduction

The High Hedges (Scotland) Act 2013 gives local authorities powers to settle disputes between neighbours related to high hedges. If the local authority, having taken all views into account, finds that a hedge is having an adverse effect, it can issue a high hedge notice requiring the hedge owner to take action to remedy the problem and prevent it recurring. Failure to comply with such a notice allows the local authority to do the work itself, recovering the costs from the hedge owner.

A hedge is a "high hedge" if it is formed wholly or mainly by a row of two or more trees or shrubs which exceed two metres in height and which forms a barrier to light. However, a hedge is not to be regarded as forming a barrier to light when the row of trees or shrubs contains gaps, which significantly reduce its overall effect as a barrier to light at heights of over two metres. In calculating the height of a hedge, its roots are not relevant (s.1).

35 High hedge notices

An owner or occupier of a domestic property may apply to their local authority for a high hedge notice if they feel that the reasonable enjoyment of their property is adversely affected by the height of a hedge on land occupied by another person (which need not be domestic property or share a boundary with the affected property) High Hedges (Scotland) Act 2013, s.2). A fee may be charged (s.4).

Before making an application a person must take all reasonable steps to resolve the high hedge dispute. In doing so they must have regard to any guidance published by their local authority which may, for example, require applicants to have attempted to resolve matters through mediation before making an application (s.3). If the local authority considers that the applicant has not taken all reasonable steps to resolve the high hedge dispute without involving them, or that the application is frivolous or vexatious, it must dismiss the application (s.5).

Where it does not dismiss an application the authority must give a copy of it to every owner and occupier of the neighbouring land, advise them of their right to make representations within 28 days, and that a copy of any such representations will be given to the applicant (s.6).

After 28 days, the local authority must take a decision on the application and decide whether the height of the high hedge is adversely affecting the enjoyment of the property that an occupant of the property could reasonably expect to have (s.7). If the local authority concludes that there is an adverse effect, it must then decide what, if any, action should be required to be taken (the "initial action"), and by when (the "compliance period"), in order to remedy the adverse effect or to prevent it recurring. It must also decide whether or not any preventative action should be taken following the end of the compliance period so as to prevent the recurrence of the adverse effect e.g., annual maintenance of the hedge.

In considering whether any action is required, the local authority must have regard to all the circumstances of the case, including in particular, the effect of the high hedge on the amenity of the area and whether the high hedge is of cultural or historical significance.

As reasonably practicable after reaching a decision, the local authority must either notify the parties that no action is to be taken (s.7), or issue a high hedge notice specifying the initial action and the compliance period for that action and any preventative action following that period required to be carried out (s.8). The Notice must also outline the right of appeal to the Scottish Ministers (under s.12), and that if the notice is not complied with the local authority has power to go in and take action itself, recovering the expenses of that action from the hedge owner (under s.25).

Where a high hedge notice relates to a high hedge which includes a tree or forms part of a group of trees subject to a tree preservation order, the tree preservation order has no effect in relation to any initial or preventative action done to any tree or group of trees specified in the high hedge notice (s.11).

I: HOUSING AND ANTI-SOCIAL BEHAVIOUR NOTICES

36 Antisocial behaviour notices

A local authority may serve an anti-social behaviour notice on the landlord of a relevant house if–
(a) any person who occupies the house under a tenancy or occupancy agreement; or
(b) any person who visits the house,
is engaging in anti-social behaviour which causes or is likely to cause alarm, distress, nuisance or annoyance at or in the locality of the house. The relevant house must be in the local authority's area but houses which are owned by a local authority, a registered social landlord or Scottish Homes are excluded (Antisocial Behaviour etc. (Scotland) Act 2004, ss.68 and 81).

The anti-social behaviour notice must describe the anti-social behaviour which has led to the serving of the notice and require the landlord to take specified action within a set period. It must also state the consequences of a failure to take the action, and inform the landlord of the right to request a review.

The landlord has the right to request that the notice be reviewed by the local authority provided he applies for a review within 21 days of the service of the notice (or such longer period as is allowed by the local authority: s.69). The local authority's review must be carried out independently of the initial decision (s.70).

Where an authority propose to serve an antisocial behaviour notice on a landlord it must give him advice and assistance. This includes general advice on such notices, relevant advice on the management of the antisocial behaviour at issue, and advice on the consequences of not managing that antisocial behaviour (Antisocial Behaviour Notice (Advice and Assistance) (Scotland) Regulations 2005).

These provisions have been extended so that they also apply to property used for holiday purposes where an occupant or visitor engages in antisocial behaviour (s.68(1A), added by the Antisocial Behaviour Notices (Houses Used for Holiday Purposes) (Scotland) Order 2011).

37 Failure to comply with the notice

If a landlord fails to take the action required by an anti-social behaviour notice the local authority may make an application to the sheriff. If the sheriff is satisfied both that the landlord has failed to comply with the anti-social behaviour notice and that it would not have been unreasonable for him to have done so, he may make an order that no rent is payable for occupation of the house. The sheriff can also make incidental orders if necessary (s.71).

An appeal against a decision by a sheriff on an application for an order as to rental income must be made to the sheriff principal within 21 days; the sheriff principal's decision is final. Where a landlord appeals against a decision to make an order, the landlord must give notice to the tenant of any matters which are prescribed by the Scottish Ministers in regulations (s.72). The Antisocial Behaviour Notice (Appeals against Order as to Rent Payable) (Scotland) Regulations 2005 provide that the matters prescribed for this purpose are: a statement that an appeal against the Order has been made, and that the tenant may be required by the sheriff to pay any sums due from the date of the order to the date the appeal is decided. This notice must be served on the tenant at the same time as the appeal is lodged or as soon as reasonably practicable afterwards.

If the sheriff is satisfied either that the action specified in the anti-social behaviour notice has been taken, or that it is otherwise unreasonable for the order to continue, he may revoke or suspend an order as to rental income on an application by either the local authority or the landlord (s.73).

38 Management control orders

If the sheriff is satisfied that a landlord has failed to comply with an anti-social behaviour notice and that it would not have been unreasonable for him to have done so, and that it is necessary in order for the anti-social behaviour to be dealt with to do so, the sheriff may make a management control order. This is an order which transfers to the local authority for up to 12 months the rights and obligations of the landlord under the tenancy or occupancy arrangements existing at the time of the order (Antisocial Behaviour etc. (Scotland) Act 2004, s.74).

There are detailed provisions in connection with management control orders as to the effect on tenants and occupants, the keeping of accounts, the making of regulations to govern expenditure recoverable by the local authority from the landlord, the recovery of rent arrears from the tenant, the delegation by the local authority of management functions to third parties and the requirement to obtain the local authority's approval to re-let accommodation (see Sch. 3). For these purposes, the Antisocial Behaviour Notice (Management Control Orders) (Scotland) Regulations 2005 prescribe that a local authority may incur expenditure which is necessary and reasonable for the purposes of the operation of the management control order and which is—
(a) relative to the management of the tenancy, the collection of rent and any other sums due under the tenancy, or the taking of certain court proceedings;
(b) incurred for meeting repair and maintenance obligations of the landlord; or
(c) necessary to ensure that the house meets the tolerable standard (i.e., is habitable).

The local authority must inform both the landlord and the tenant (or the occupant under any occupancy arrangement) of the making of the order, and give a copy to any known agent of the landlord (s.75).

The sheriff may revoke a management control order if either the action specified in the anti-social behaviour notice has been carried out by the landlord or the local authority or it would in all the circumstances be unreasonable for the notice to continue to have effect (s.76). When a management control order is revoked, the party which applied for the revocation must notify the other party and the occupiers as soon as practicable (s.77).

Where a landlord fails to comply with an anti-social behaviour notice, the local authority may take the steps that it feels are necessary to deal with the anti-social behaviour described in the notice. The landlord will be liable for the local authority's expenditure in so doing provided that the expenditure is of a description prescribed by the Scottish Ministers by regulation (s.78). The Antisocial Behaviour Notice (Landlord Liability) (Scotland) Regulations 2005 prescribes for these purposes—
(a) payments to other parties for services which deal with or contribute to dealing with the antisocial behaviour; and
(b) the costs of the local authority directly connected with dealing with it,
provided that the authority has first given the landlord—
(c) notice of its intention to take the steps it considers necessary to deal with the antisocial behaviour; and
(d) that notice contains a statement that the authority will seek to recover its expenditure from the landlord and an estimate of the expenditure it will seek to recover.

A landlord who has failed without reasonable excuse to comply with an antisocial behaviour notice is guilty of an offence and liable on summary conviction to a fine not exceeding level 5 on the standard scale (as to the standard scale, see the Note on **Treatment of Offenders** at para **35 Maximum fines: the "standard scale".**) (s.79).

J: PARENTING ORDERS

39 Applications for parenting orders

A court may make a parenting order only if it has been notified by the Scottish Ministers that the local authority has put in place the necessary arrangements for the operation of parenting orders in that area.

A court may make a parenting order on the application of the Principal Reporter or the local authority (Antisocial Behaviour etc. (Scotland) Act 2004, s.102).

A local authority or the Principal Reporter may apply for a parenting order on the following grounds—
(a) the child has engaged in anti-social behaviour and the order is desirable in the interests of preventing further behaviour of this kind; or
(b) the child has engaged in criminal conduct and the order is desirable in the interests of preventing further conduct of this kind.

In addition, the Principal Reporter may apply for a parenting order on the following ground–

(c) that the making of the order is desirable in the interests of improving the welfare of the child.

A child engages in criminal conduct if that conduct constitutes a criminal offence (or would do so if the child had attained the age of eight years).

An application for a parenting order must be made by summary application to the sheriff of the sheriffdom where the parent ordinarily resides. Before an application is made by a local authority, it must consult the Principal Reporter. Before an application is made by the Principal Reporter, he must consult the appropriate local authority (i.e., the local authority for the area in which the child lives).

When a Children's Hearing is satisfied that it might be appropriate for a parenting order to be made in respect of a parent of a child it may require the Principal Reporter to consider making an application to the sheriff for a parenting order (Children's Hearings (Scotland) Act 2011, s.128).

40 Parenting orders

The effect of a parenting order is to direct a parent as to how he or she should behave in respect of their child. It may last for up to 12 months during which time the parent must comply with the requirements of the order. An order will also include a requirement to attend counselling or guidance for a maximum of three months unless the parent has previously been the subject of a parenting order in respect of the same child (Antisocial Behaviour etc. (Scotland) Act 2004, s.103).

The order can either be given to the parent or sent to them by registered post or recorded delivery (s.104).

On an application for a review of the order by the parent, the child or the local authority, the court may revoke it or vary it (although variation of the time during which a parent must undertake counselling or guidance is subject to the maximum period of three months). Before making an application to vary or revoke a parenting order, the local authority must consult the Principal Reporter (s.105).

An appeal against a parenting order, or a decision to vary or refuse to vary a parenting order, may be made to the sheriff principal.

41 Failure to comply with a parenting order

Failure without reasonable excuse to comply with a parenting order is an offence, the penalty for which is a fine not exceeding level 3 on the standard scale (as to the standard scale, see the Note on **Treatment of Offenders** at para **35 Maximum fines: the "standard scale"**). The court must take into account the welfare of any child of the parent subject to the order in determining what sentence to impose for failure to comply with a parenting order (Antisocial Behaviour etc. (Scotland) Act 2004, s.107).

42 Procedural requirements

Before making, varying or revoking a parenting order the court must, having regard to the child's age and maturity, so far as practicable give the child an opportunity to express its views; give the parent an opportunity to be heard; and obtain information as to the family circumstances and the likely effect of the order on those circumstances (Antisocial Behaviour etc. (Scotland) Act 2004, s.108).

The paramount consideration when deciding whether to make, vary, or revoke a parenting order is the welfare of the child (s.109). In determining whether to vary or revoke a parenting order a court must also have regard to any parental behaviour that appears to be relevant, including the taking of voluntary steps by the parent intended to be in the interests of preventing the child from engaging in anti-social behaviour.

As far as practicable, a court must ensure the requirements of a parenting order avoid conflict with the religious beliefs of the person specified in the order and any interference with their work or educational commitments (s.110).

It is a criminal offence to publish, anywhere in the world, matters in respect of proceedings relating to parenting orders which are intended, or likely to, identify the parent, their address, the child concerned or any other child (s.111).

The Scottish Ministers have the power to make regulations empowering a children's reporter to conduct proceedings before a sheriff in respect of applications for the making, variation or revocation of a parenting order. The reporter can also be empowered to conduct proceedings before a sheriff principal in respect of an appeal (s.112).

The Principal Reporter has the power to make such investigations as he or she considers appropriate to determine whether to make an application for a parenting order (s.113).

In any proceedings, except applications for ASBOs or for a parenting order itself, a court may require the Principal Reporter to consider whether to apply for a parenting order (s.114).

K: FURTHER CRIMINAL MEASURES

43 Anti-social behaviour orders

Where a person is convicted of an offence involving anti-social behaviour a court may impose an ASBO on conviction instead of, or in addition to, any other sentence.

The court must be satisfied, on the balance of probabilities, that the making of an ASBO is necessary for the purpose of protecting others from further anti-social behaviour by the offender (Criminal Procedure (Scotland) Act 1995, s.234AA, inserted by the Antisocial Behaviour etc. (Scotland) Act 2004, s.118).

A person engages in anti-social behaviour if he—

(a) acts in a manner that causes or is likely to cause alarm or distress; or

(b) pursues a course of conduct that causes or is likely to cause alarm or distress,

to at least one person who is not of the same household as he is (s.234AA(3)).

Where an ASBO is made or varied, the court must arrange for a copy of the order to be served on the person in respect of whom the ASBO was made and given to the local authority it considers most appropriate (Criminal Procedure (Scotland) Act 1995, s.234AB, as inserted).

Local authorities must keep records of ASBOs made under these provisions (Antisocial Behaviour etc. (Scotland) Act 2004, s.119).

44 Restriction of liberty orders

A court may impose a restriction of liberty order which may require an offender to be restricted to a specified place for up to 12 hours per day or prohibited from a specified place for up to 24 hours per day, or both, for a maximum period of 12 months (Criminal Procedure (Scotland) Act 1995, s.245A, amended by the Antisocial Behaviour etc. (Scotland) Act 2004, s.121).

See the Note on **Treatment of Offenders** at para **36 Restriction of liberty orders**.

45 Offence of selling spray paint to a child

It is a criminal offence to sell a spray paint device to a person under the age of 16. The maximum penalty for a person guilty of this offence is a fine not exceeding level 3 on the standard scale. The offence is dealt with on a summary basis and it is a defence for a person charged with the offence to show they took all reasonable precautions and exercised all due diligence to avoid committing of the offence (Antisocial Behaviour etc. (Scotland) Act 2004, s.122).

Retailers must display a notice stating: "It is illegal to sell a spray paint device to anyone under the age of 16". The maximum penalty for the offence is a fine not exceeding level 2 on the standard scale. The offence is dealt with on a summary basis (s.123).

As to the standard scale, see the Note on **Treatment of Offenders** at para **35 Maximum fines: the "standard scale"**.

Local authorities have a duty to enforce, within their areas, the ban on the sale of spray paint to under 16s and the requirement to display warning statements in premises at which spray paint devices are sold (s.124).

Authorised officers of a local authority have statutory powers of entry, inspection and seizure for the purpose of enforcing the offences under ss.122 and 123. An "authorised officer" means an officer of the authority authorised in writing by it for the purposes of s.124.

46 Vehicles used in manner causing alarm, distress or annoyance

The police have the power to deal with the anti-social use of motor vehicles on public roads or off-road. This includes powers to stop, seize and remove motor vehicles which are being or have been driven –

(a) off-road contrary to s.34 of the Road Traffic Act 1988; and

(b) on the public road or other public place without due care and attention or reasonable consideration for other road users, contrary to s.3 of the 1988 Act.

A constable must also, in both of these instances, have reasonable grounds for believing that a motor vehicle is being, or has been used, in a manner which is likely to cause alarm, distress or annoyance to members of the public (Antisocial Behaviour etc. (Scotland) Act 2004, s.126).

An officer may enter premises, other than a private dwelling house, for the purpose of exercising these powers.

It is an offence, punishable on summary conviction by a fine not exceeding level 3 on the standard scale, for a person to fail to stop a vehicle when required to do so by a police officer under this provision (as to the standard scale, see the Note on **Treatment of Offenders** at para **35 Maximum fines: the "standard scale"**) (s.126).

The Scottish Ministers may make regulations relating to the removal, retention, release or disposal of motor vehicles seized under these provisions (s.127). The Police (Retention and Disposal of Motor Vehicles) (Scotland) Regulations 2005 provide for the retention, safe keeping and disposal of vehicles by the police or anyone authorised by the chief constable. The Regulations also provide for the giving of notice in relation to the retention of a motor vehicle that is in the custody of an authority. Where a vehicle is sold, the proceeds of sale (less charges for removal and storage) must be paid to the owner if a claim is made by them within a year of the sale.

47 Trespass on designated sites

It is a specific criminal offence to trespass on a "designated site". Sites may be designated by the Secretary of State by Order, but only in the interests of national security (Serious Organised Crime and Police Act 2005, s.129). Public access rights do not apply if land has been designated (s.131).

The Serious Organised Crime and Police Act 2005 (Designated Sites) Order 2005 and the Serious Organised

Crime and Police Act 2005 (Designated Sites under Section 128) Order 2007 designate a number of RAF and naval bases around the UK, and various government, security service and defence establishments and royal residences.

L: FIXED PENALTIES

48 Fixed penalty offences

Certain types of anti-social behaviour can be dealt with by the police by means of a fixed penalty as an alternative to criminal proceedings. Fixed penalty offences comprises the following (Antisocial Behaviour etc. (Scotland) Act 2004, s.128)–
  (a) disorderly conduct while drunk in licensed and other relevant premises (Licensing (Scotland) Act 2005, s.115);
  (b) refusing to leave licensed and other relevant premises on being requested to do so (Licensing (Scotland) Act 2005, s.116);
  (c) urinating or defecating in circumstances causing annoyance to others (Civic Government (Scotland) Act 1982, s.47);
  (d) being drunk and incapable in a public place (Civic Government (Scotland) Act 1982, s.50(1));
  (e) being drunk in a public place in charge of a child (Civic Government (Scotland) Act 1982, s.50(2));
  (f) persisting, to the annoyance of others, in playing musical instruments, singing, playing radios etc. on being required to stop (Civic Government (Scotland) Act 1982, s.54(1));
  (g) vandalism (Criminal Law (Consolidation) (Scotland) Act 1995, s.52(1));
  (h) consuming alcoholic liquor in a public place (Local Government (Scotland) Act 1973, ss.201 and 203);
  (i) the common law offence of breach of the peace; and
  (j) the common law offence of malicious mischief.

49 Fixed penalty notices

A constable who believes that a person aged 16 or over has committed a fixed penalty offence (see **48 Fixed penalty offences**, above) in a prescribed area may give the person a fixed penalty notice. The whole of Scotland has been designated as a prescribed area (Antisocial Behaviour (Fixed Penalty Offences) (Prescribed Area) (Scotland) Regulations 2007).

A fixed penalty notice is a notice offering the opportunity, by paying a fixed penalty, to discharge any liability to be convicted of the offence to which the notice relates (Antisocial Behaviour etc. (Scotland) Act 2004, s.129).

The penalty payable is the amount the Scottish Ministers may specify by order which must not exceed level 2 on the standard scale (as to the standard scale, see the Note on **Treatment of Offenders** at para **35 Maximum fines: the "standard scale"**). The Antisocial Behaviour (Amount of Fixed Penalty) (Scotland) Order 2005 sets the fixed penalty payable at £40.

The fixed penalty notice must (s.130)–
  (a) state the alleged offence;
  (b) give particulars of the circumstances alleged to constitute the offence;
  (c) state the amount of the fixed penalty;
  (d) state the clerk of the district court to whom, and the address at which, the fixed penalty may be paid;
  (e) inform the person to whom it is given of the right to ask to be tried for the alleged offence and explain how that right may be exercised; and
  (f) include any other information the Scottish Ministers may by order prescribe. The Antisocial Behaviour (Fixed Penalty Notice) (Additional Information) (Scotland) Order 2005 requires that the additional information to be included on a fixed penalty notice should include–
      (i) the name, address and date of birth of the person to whom the fixed penalty notice has been given;
      (ii) the date and time on which the fixed penalty notice was given;
      (iii) the place at which the fixed penalty notice was given;
      (iv) the details of the constable that gave it;
      (v) administrative information; and
      (vi) the method of payment of the penalty.
Once a fixed penalty notice has been issued to a person, proceedings may not be brought against him unless he asks to be tried for the offence. Such a request must be made by a notice in the manner specified in the fixed penalty notice and within 28 days of the notice being given. If, by the end of this period, the fixed penalty has not been paid and no request has been made to be tried for the offence, then that person is liable to pay to the clerk of the district court specified in the fixed penalty notice a sum equal to one and a half times the amount of the fixed penalty. If it remains unpaid, it can be recovered in the same way as a fine imposed by a court (s.131).

Under usual circumstances, the fixed penalty stated in a fixed penalty notice is payable to the clerk of the district court specified in the notice (s.132).

50 Revocation of fixed penalty notices

If a fixed penalty notice has been given to a person and a constable determines that either of the following conditions is satisfied, the constable may revoke the notice (Antisocial Behaviour etc. (Scotland) Act 2004, s.133)–

(a) the offence to which the fixed penalty notice relates was not committed; and

(b) the notice ought not to have been issued to the person named.

When a fixed penalty notice is revoked, no payment is required and where payment has been made it must be repaid.

M: MISCELLANEOUS

51 Failure to provide for excluded pupils

Either the Reporter or a children's hearing may refer the case of a child who has been excluded from school to the Scottish Ministers if it appears that the local authority concerned has failed to comply with its duty (under the Education (Scotland) Act 1980, s.14(3)) to provide education to a pupil excluded from school (Antisocial Behaviour etc. (Scotland) Act 2004, s.137).

52 Proceedings held in private

Unless the court directs otherwise, the following court proceedings must be held in private (Antisocial Behaviour etc. (Scotland) Act 2004, s.138)–

(a) applications for an ASBO in respect of someone under 16 under s.4;

(b) applications for variation or revocation of such orders under s.5;

(c) applications for a parenting order under section 102(1); and, for variation or revocation of a parenting order under s.105(1);

(d) applications to determine whether to make an interim ASBO under s.7(2) in respect of someone under 16; or to recall such an interim ASBO;

(e) applications to require the Principal Reporter to refer a child's case to a children's hearing under s.12(1) where an ASBO or interim ASBO has been made in respect of that child;

(f) applications to make a parenting order under s.13(1) where an anti-social behaviour or interim ASBO has been made in respect of a child; and

(g) applications to make an order under s.105(5) to specify the sheriff of another sheriffdom as the court that may entertain an application for review of a parenting order under s.105(1).

An appeal arising from any of these proceedings is subject to the same privacy restriction.

53 Disclosure and sharing of information

There is legal protection for those who disclose information to a relevant authority where the disclosure of information is necessary or expedient for the purposes of any provision in connection with anti-social behaviour or its effects (s.139).

Where a person discloses information to a relevant authority which is confidential, and where they inform the authority of the breach of that confidentiality on disclosing the information, the authority must respect that confidentiality except where the disclosure by the recipient is permitted or required by law.

A relevant authority is a local authority, a chief constable, the Principal Reporter, a registered social landlord, any authority administering housing benefit and other specified person providing services relating to housing benefit.

54 Authorities

Statutes–

Anti-social Behaviour Act 2003

Antisocial Behaviour etc. (Scotland) Act 2004

Children (Scotland) Act 1995

Civic Government (Scotland) Act 1982

Crime and Punishment (Scotland) Act 1997

Criminal Procedure (Scotland) Act 1995

Environmental Protection Act 1990

High Hedges (Scotland) Act 2013

Serious Organised Crime and Police Act 2005

Statutory Instruments–

Antisocial Behaviour (Amount of Fixed Penalty) (Scotland) Order 2005 (S.S.I. 2005 No. 110)

Antisocial Behaviour (Fixed Penalty Notice) (Additional Information) (Scotland) Order 2005 (S.S.I. 2005 No. 130)

Antisocial Behaviour (Fixed Penalty Offences) (Prescribed Area) (Scotland) Regulations 2007 (S.S.I. 2007 No. 15)

Antisocial Behaviour (Noise Control) (Scotland) Regulations 2005 (S.S.I. 2005 No. 43)

Antisocial Behaviour Notice (Advice and Assistance) (Scotland) Regulations 2005, as amended (S.S.I. 2005 No. 563 and 2011 No. 201)

Antisocial Behaviour Notice (Appeals against Order as to Rent Payable) (Scotland) Regulations 2005 (S.S.I. 2005 No. 560)

Antisocial Behaviour Notice (Landlord Liability) (Scotland) Regulations 2005, as amended (S.S.I. 2005 No. 562 and 2011 No. 201)

Antisocial Behaviour Notice (Management Control Orders) (Scotland) Regulations 2005 (S.S.I. 2005 No. 561)

Antisocial Behaviour Notices (Houses Used for Holiday Purposes) (Scotland) Order 2011 (S.S.I. 2011 No. 201)

Fireworks (Scotland) Regulations 2004, as amended (S.S.I. 2004 No. 393 and 2005 No. 245)

Intensive Support and Monitoring (Scotland) Regulations 2008 (S.S.I 2008 No. 75)

Police (Retention and Disposal of Motor Vehicles) (Scotland) Regulations 2005 (S.S.I 2005 No 80)

ATTACHMENT OF EARNINGS: ENGLAND AND WALES

1 Introduction

The Attachment of Earnings Act 1971 provides for the enforcement of judgment debts of not less than a certain specified amount, and the payment of sums due under a maintenance order or an administration order, by the making of an attachment of earnings order. In addition, the 1971 Act *inter alia* specifies the courts in which these orders may be made and the purposes for which they may be made.

2 Enforcement by attachment of earnings

S.1 of the Attachment of Earnings Act 1971 provides that the following courts may make attachment of earnings orders for the following purposes.
 (1) The High Court, to secure payment under a High Court maintenance order.
 (1A) The family court may make an attachment of earnings order to secure payments under a High Court or family court maintenance order.
 (2) The county court, to secure (a) payment of a judgment debt (as defined by s.2) of not less than £15 (as prescribed by rules of court), or (c) payments under an administration order.
 (3) A magistrates' court, to secure payment of any sum required to be paid, by a legal aid contribution order in criminal cases.
The Courts Act 2003 provides that attachment of earnings orders can, and in certain cases must, be made where a person over the age of 18 is liable to pay a fine (see **9 Enforcement of fines by attachment,** below).

S.3(1) of the 1971 Act specifies the person who may apply for an attachment of earnings order. *Inter alia*, where the application is to the High Court or the family court for an order to secure maintenance payments or to a magistrates' court, the debtor may apply.

For an attachment of earnings order to be made on the application of any person other than the debtor, it must appear to the court that the debtor has failed to make one or more payments required by the relevant adjudication (s.3(3)). However, s.3(3A) (added by the Maintenance Enforcement Act 1991) provides that where the relevant adjudication is a maintenance order, s.3(3) will not apply.

Where proceedings are brought for the enforcement of a maintenance order by committal under s.5 of the Debtors Act 1869 the court may instead make an attachment of earnings order (s.3(4)).

3 Administration orders

Where, on application to the county court for an attachment of earnings order to secure the payment of a judgment debt, it appears to the court that the debtor also has other debts, the court is required *inter alia* to consider whether the case is one in which all the debtor's liabilities should be dealt with together and whether for that purpose an administration order should be made. If the court is satisfied that the debtor's total indebtedness does not exceed £5,000, it may make such an order in respect of the debtor's estate and may also make an attachment of earnings order to secure the payments required by the administration order (Attachment of Earnings Act 1971, ss.4 and 5).

(For the general provisions relating to administration orders, see the Note on **The County Court**)

4 Effect and contents of attachment of earnings order

An order will operate as an instruction to the debtor's employer to make periodical deductions from the debtor's earnings in accordance with Part 1 of Schedule 3 and pay them to the collecting officer of the court (Attachment of Earnings Act 1971, s.6). The order, except where it is made to secure maintenance payments, must specify the total amount outstanding, including any relevant costs.

An order must specify–
 (a) the normal deduction rate, i.e., the rate at which the court thinks it reasonable for the debtor's earnings to be applied to meeting his liability under the relevant adjudication; and
 (b) the protected earnings rate, i.e., the rate below which, having regard to the debtor's resources and needs, the court thinks it reasonable that the earnings actually paid to him should not be reduced (s.6(5)).
Where the order is made to secure payments under a maintenance order, not being an order for the payment of a lump sum, the normal deduction rate is to be determined after taking account of any right or liability of the debtor to deduct income tax when making payments, and is not to exceed the rate which the court considers necessary to secure payment of the sums falling due under the order from time to time and (within a reasonable period) of any such sums already due and unpaid under the order (s.6(6)).

5 Compliance with order by employer

An employer is required to comply with the terms of an attachment of earnings order but allows him seven days' grace after service, during which period he is under no liability for non-compliance. Where a person is served with an attachment of earnings order and the debtor (a) is not in his employment, or (b) subsequently ceases to be in his employment, he must notify that fact to the court, within 10 days of the service in case (a) or within 10 days of the cessation in case (b) (Attachment of Earnings Act 1971, s.7).

Whenever an employer makes a deduction from the debtor's earnings he may also deduct £1 towards his clerical and administrative costs and he must give the debtor a written statement of the total amount deducted. S.23(2) *inter alia* provides that a person commits an offence if he fails to comply with the requirements of s.7(1) or (2).

Part II of Schedule 3 regulates the priorities to be followed by the employer if he receives two or more orders in respect of the same debtor. Orders in respect of maintenance payments are given priority over judgment debts and administration orders.

6 Interrelation with other remedies open to creditor

Where an attachment of earnings order has been made to secure maintenance payments, no order or warrant of commitment may be issued in consequence of any proceedings for the enforcement of the related maintenance order. The same rule applies where the county court has made an attachment of earnings order to secure the payment of a judgment debt, but, in addition, no execution for the recovery of the debt shall issue against any property of the debtor without the leave of the county court (Attachment of Earnings Act 1971, s.8).

An attachment of earnings order made to secure maintenance payments, payment of a judgment debt, payment of a legal aid contribution order, or of a fine will cease to have effect upon the making of an order of commitment or the issue of a warrant of commitment for the enforcement of the related maintenance order or the judgment debt.

7 Subsequent proceedings

S.9 of the Attachment of Earnings Act 1971 makes provision for the variation, lapse, and discharge of attachment of earnings orders. If the debtor changes his employment or becomes unemployed, the order will not come to an end but will lapse until re-directed to a new employer.

S.10 empowers the court to reduce the deduction rate of certain attachment of earnings orders made to secure maintenance payments if it appears to the collecting officer of the court that the aggregate of the payments made for the purposes of the related maintenance order by the debtor exceeds the aggregate of the payments required up to that time by the maintenance order, and that the normal deduction rate, as specified by the attachment order, exceeds the rate of payments required by the maintenance order.

8 Administrative and miscellaneous provisions

S.13 of the Attachment of Earnings Act 1971 provides for the application of the sums received by the collecting officer under an attachment of earnings order.

S.14 empowers the court to order a debtor to give particulars of his employment, earnings, and commitments, and to order the employer to give particulars of the debtor's earnings.

The debtor, and any new employer who has the necessary knowledge of the attachment of earnings order, are required to keep the court informed of changes in the debtor's employment (s.15). The court by which an attachment of earnings order has been made also has power to determine any question whether payments of a particular description are earnings for the purposes of the order (s.16).

The consolidation of attachment orders by the county court in respect of judgment debts, or by a magistrates' court in respect of certain other debts, is authorised by s.17.

Jurisdiction is conferred on the family court to hear applications by or against persons residing outside England and Wales for the discharge or variation of attachment of earnings orders made by the family court to secure maintenance payments (s.20).

S.22 provides for the operation of the attachment of earnings system when the debtor is in the employment of the Crown. S.23 *inter alia* makes it an offence (subject to certain defences for employers) to fail to comply with the requirements of the 1971 Act.

S.24 defines earnings for the purposes of the 1971 Act. Broadly, they include any sums, other than excepted sums (see below), payable by way of wages or salary (including overtime, fees, bonuses, and commission), by way of pension (including an annuity in respect of past services and periodical payments by way of compensation for loss of office) but not a guaranteed minimum pension under the Pension Schemes Act 1993, or by way of statutory sick pay. The excepted sums specified by the Act include pay or allowances as a member of H.M. Forces (but see **10 Application to the forces**, below), and pension allowances or benefit payable under any enactment relating to social security.

9 Enforcement of fines by attachment

The Courts Act 2003 provides that attachment of earnings orders can, and in certain cases must, be made where a person over the age of 18 is liable to pay a fine. This includes a fixed penalty which has not been paid and has subsequently been registered as a fine.

Instructions for employers to enable them to calculate the attachable earnings in different circumstances are set out in Part 3, Regs. 5 to 15 of the Fines Collection Regulations 2006. For example, the employee may be paid, weekly, monthly, in multiples of weeks or months, in advance, for holidays or in various regular or irregular intervals.

An attachment of earnings order must be made where the offender is classed as an "existing defaulter" i.e., is currently in default, without adequate reason, on any fine or similar sum ordered to be paid by a court. Where a sum due includes a sum under a compensation order, an unlawful profit order or a slavery and trafficking reparation order an attachment or earnings order can also be made without consent. In any other case, an attachment of earnings order can only be made with his consent (Courts Act 2003, s.97 and Sch. 5).

If a fine is not to be paid immediately, or the offender has failed to pay, the court must make a collection order. The collection order gives the details of the sums due, and the payment terms if no attachment of earnings order has been made. If an attachment of earnings order has been made, the collection order will state the "reserve terms" which will apply if the attachment is not successful. Once a collection order has been made, enforcement is undertaken by a "fines officer" without the need to go back to court.

An attachment of earnings order will fail if either the employer fails to comply with the terms of the order or if the order is discharged whilst the offender still owes money (Sch. 5, para 16).

If the offender is not in default and asks for a variation, a fines officer may vary the payment terms set by the court in the collection order. As part of a variation, the fines officer may make an attachment of earnings order (and set reserve terms in case it fails) (Sch. 5, para 22). The offender may appeal to a magistrates' court against the fines officer's decision.

If an offender defaults in paying a fine, and no attachment of earnings order has so far been made, then provided that it is not impracticable or inappropriate, the fines officer must make an attachment of earnings order if the offender is in employment (Sch. 5, para 26).

If an attachment of earnings order is made, and fails, the reserve terms will have effect. Provided he is not in default, an offender can apply to the fines officer (and subsequently appeal to a magistrates' court) for the reserve terms to be varied.

A second default will lead to the fines officer taking further steps such as issuing a distress warrant or clamping a vehicle (and selling it if the need arises). The fines officer can also apply to the court for the fine to be increased in certain cases. Again at this stage an attachment of earnings can be made by the fines officer (Sch. 5, para 38).

Note.–If an offender is not in work, a deduction from benefits order can be made as an alternative to an attachment of earnings order. The benefits from which deductions can be made are income support, jobseekers allowance, income-related employment and support allowance, and state pension credit (Fines Collection (Disclosure of Information) (Prescribed Benefits) Regulations 2008).

As to enforcement of fines by attachment, see also the Note on **Treatment of Offenders** at para **67 New provisions from July 2006**.

10 Application to the forces

Although the Attachment of Earnings Act 1971 excepts pay and allowances paid to a person as a member of H.M. Forces, there are alternative procedures under the Armed Forces Act 2006, s.342, which apply, *inter alia*, to both maintenance orders and judgment debts. Broadly speaking, the Acts provide for a copy of the relevant order to be sent to the appropriate service authority, which will then make deductions from the serviceman's pay not exceeding the permitted proportion determined by the Defence Council.

11 Authorities
Statutes–
Armed Forces Act 2006

Attachment of Earnings Act 1971

Courts Act 2003

Magistrates' Courts Act 1980

Maintenance Enforcement Act 1991

Social Security Acts 1985 and 1986

Statutory Instruments–
Attachment of Earnings (Employer's Deduction) Order 1991 (S.I. 1991 No. 356)

Fines Collection (Disclosure of Information) (Prescribed Benefits) Regulations 2008 (S.I. 2008 No. 3242)

Fines Collection Regulations 2006, as amended (S.I. 2006 No. 501 and 2014 No. 879)

Magistrates' Courts (Attachment of Earnings) Rules 1971, as amended (S.I. 1971 No. 809, 2001 No. 615, 2003 No. 1236, 2005 No. 617, and 2014 No. 879)

ATTACHMENT OF EARNINGS: SCOTLAND

1 Diligence against earnings

In Scotland, Part III of the Debtors (Scotland) Act 1987 introduced new diligences against earnings, and replaced the remedies of diligence of arrestment and action of furthcoming against the earnings of a debtor contained therein. The 1987 Act has been amended by the Bankruptcy and Diligence etc. (Scotland) Act 2007.

S.46 of the 1987 Act provides for the following diligences against earnings of a debtor in the hands of his employer–
   (a) an earnings arrestment to enforce the payment of any ordinary debt which is due as at the date of execution of the diligence;
   (b) a current maintenance arrestment to enforce the payment of current maintenance; and
   (c) a conjoined arrestment order to enforce the payment of two or more debts owed to different creditors against the same earnings.

S.73(2) defines earnings in terms similar to those used by the 1971 Act in relation to England and Wales and s.73(3) excepts similar sums to those excepted in relation to England and Wales.

2 Earnings arrestments

An earnings arrestment will, subject to s.69, have the effect of requiring the employer of a debtor to deduct a sum calculated in accordance with ss.49 or 49A from the debtor's net-calculated earnings on every pay-day and as soon as is reasonably practicable, to pay any sum so deducted to the creditor (Debtors (Scotland) Act 1987, s.47(1)).

Subject to ss.59 (priority among arrestments–see below), 62 (relationship of conjoined arrestment order with other arrestments–see below), and 90 (provisions relating to charges for payment), an earnings arrestment–
   (a) comes into effect on the date of its execution, being the date on which a schedule (an earnings arrestment schedule) in the prescribed form is served on the employer; and
   (b) remains in effect until the debt recoverable has been paid or otherwise extinguished, the debtor has ceased to be employed by the employer, or the arrestment has been recalled or abandoned by the creditor or has for any other reason ceased to have effect (s.47(2)).

However, an earnings arrestment will not come into effect unless, no earlier than 12 weeks before the date on which the earnings arrestment schedule is served, the creditor has provided the debtor with a debt advice and information package (s.47(3)).

S.69 provides *inter alia* that an employer shall have seven days' grace after service, during which period he is under no liability for non-compliance.

S.48 provides that the debt recoverable by an earnings arrestment consists of–
   (a) any ordinary debt and any expenses due under the decree or other document on which the earnings arrestment proceeds;
   (b) any interest on those sums which has accrued at the date of execution of the earnings arrestment; and
   (c) the expenses incurred in executing the earnings arrestment and the charge which preceded it.

The sums to be deducted on any pay-day are specified in ss.49, 49A (where net earnings includes holiday pay), and Schedule 2. S.50 enables the debtor or the employer to apply to the sheriff for an order declaring that an earnings arrestment is invalid or has ceased to have effect.

3 Current maintenance arrestments

S.51 of the Debtors (Scotland) Act 1987 describes the effect of a current maintenance arrestment which is similar to that of an earnings arrestment (see above) and is subject to s.58(2) (see **12 Simultaneous operation of, and priority among, arrestments**, below) and s.69 (see **9 Earnings arrestments**, above). The sum to be deducted is calculated under s.53. S.52 makes provision for the making of a single current maintenance arrestment, where one or more maintenance orders are in effect for the payment by the same debtor to the same person of maintenance in respect of more than one individual. S.54 imposes a requirement that a current maintenance arrestment be preceded by a default payment; normally a sum of not less than the aggregate of three instalments of maintenance must remain unpaid before a current maintenance arrestment schedule may be served. S.55 provides for the review and termination of current maintenance arrestments.

As with an earnings arrestment, a current maintenance arrestment will not come into effect unless, no earlier than 12 weeks before the date on which the arrestment schedule is served, the creditor has provided the debtor with a debt advice and information package (s.51(2A)).

4 Conjoined arrestment orders

The sheriff must, subject to s.60(4), make a conjoined arrestment order where on the date of an application made by a qualified creditor (i.e., a creditor already enforcing a debt by an arrestment mentioned in paragraph

(a) below) (Debtors (Scotland) Act 1987, s.60(1) and (2))–

    (a) there is in effect against the earnings of a debtor in the hands of a single employer an earnings arrestment or a current maintenance arrestment or both (see **12 Simultaneous operation of, and priority among, arrestments,** below), and

    (b) a creditor, who may be a qualified creditor, would be entitled but for the rules of priority among arrestments under s.59(1) and (2) (see below) to enforce his debt by executing an earnings arrestment or a current maintenance arrestment.

S.60(3) provides that the effect of a conjoined arrestment order is to (i) recall and thus invalidate any existing arrestments and (ii) to require deductions under the order, calculated in accordance with s.63, to be paid to the sheriff's clerk as soon as is reasonably practicable.

As with an earnings arrestment, a conjoined arrestment will not come into effect unless, no earlier than 12 weeks before the date on which the arrestment schedule is served, the creditor has provided the debtor with a debt advice and information package (s.60(3A)).

S.60(4) provides that a conjoined arrestment order must not be made where s.52 could apply (see above), s.58(1) could apply (see below), or where the same person is the creditor or recipient of maintenance in respect of all debts. A conjoined arrestment order comes into effect seven days after a copy of it has been served on the employer and remains in effect until a copy of an order recalling it is served on him or the debtor ceases to be employed by him (s.60(5)).

S.61 specifies the amount recoverable under a conjoined arrestment order. Sums paid to the sheriff's clerk must be disbursed by him to the creditors whose debts are being enforced by the conjoined arrestment order in accordance with Schedule 3 (s.64). S.65 gives the sheriff the power to make an order determining any dispute on an application by the debtor, the creditor, the employer, or the sheriff clerk. S.66 makes provision for the recall and variation of conjoined arrestment orders.

5 Simultaneous operation of, and priority among, arrestments

One earnings arrestment and one current maintenance arrestment may be in effect simultaneously against earnings payable to the same debtor by the same employer ((Debtors (Scotland) Act 1987, s.58(1)). If on any pay-day the net earnings of the debtor are less than the total of the sums required to be paid under an earnings arrestment or a current maintenance arrestment, then both arrestments rank equally and the employer must calculate an equal proportion of the available net earnings to satisfy both creditors, in accordance with the formula set out in the section.

S.59 lays down certain rules for priority among arrestments. *Inter alia*, while an earnings arrestment or a current maintenance arrestment is in effect, any other earnings arrestment or current maintenance arrestment against the earnings of the same debtor payable by the same employer will not be competent. While a conjoined arrestment order is in effect it is not competent to execute any earnings arrestment or current maintenance arrestments, or for the sheriff to grant any other conjoined arrestment against the earnings of the same debtor payable by the same employer (s.62).

6 Non-compliance by employer

Subject to s.69(4) (one year time limit for claims to be brought in respect of deductions), where an employer fails to comply with an earnings arrestment or a current maintenance arrestment, he shall be liable to pay to the creditor any sum which he would have paid to him under either arrestment and he will not be entitled to recover any sum paid to the debtor in contravention of the arrestment (Debtors (Scotland) Act 1987, s.57(1)). In the case of a conjoined arrestment order, s.60(9) specifies similar consequences for the employer, but in addition, the sheriff may, on an application by the sheriff clerk, grant a warrant for diligence against the employer for recovery of the sums which appear to the sheriff to be due.

7 Employer's duty to provide information

Where an employer receives, in relation to a debtor (Debtors (Scotland) Act 1987, s.70A)–

    (a) an earnings arrestment schedule;

    (b) a current maintenance arrestment schedule; or

    (c) a copy of a conjoined arrestment order,

the employer must, as soon as is reasonably practicable, send to the creditor or, in the case of a conjoined arrestment order, the sheriff clerk, information as to–

    (d) how the debtor is paid (whether weekly, monthly or otherwise);

    (e) the date of the debtor's pay-day next following receipt of the schedule or order;

    (f) the sum deducted on that pay-day and the net earnings from which it is so deducted; and

    (g) any other information which the Scottish Ministers may, by regulations, prescribe.

The employer must also, provided the debt has not been extinguished, send such information, on or as soon as is reasonably practicable after the next 6th April (or the day falling 6 months after receiving the schedule or order), and every 6th April thereafter.

An employer must, if the debtor ceases for whatever reason to be employed by him, give notice of that fact, as soon as is reasonably practicable, to the creditor or, as the case may be, the sheriff clerk together with, in so far as he knows, the name and address of any new employer of the debtor.

Copies of any notice or information given by an employer must also be given to the debtor (s.70A(5)). Where an employer fails without reasonable excuse to do so, the sheriff may, on the application of any creditor, make an order requiring the employer (s.70B)–

  (i) to provide such information as he has as to the debtor's employment after ceasing to be employed by that employer;
  (ii) to pay to the creditor an amount not exceeding twice the sum which the employer would have been required to deduct on the debtor's next pay-day had the debtor still been employed by that employer.

Where a sum is paid by virtue of an order under (ii) above, the debt owed by the debtor to the creditor will be reduced by that sum; and the employer will not be entitled to recover that sum from the debtor.

8 Creditor's duty to provide information

A creditor who is receiving payment from a debtor by virtue of (Debtors (Scotland) Act 1987, s.70C)–
  (a) an earnings arrestment schedule;
  (b) a current maintenance arrestment schedule; or
  (c) a conjoined arrestment order,
must, provided the debt has not been extinguished, as soon as is reasonably practicable after the next 6th April (or the day falling 6 months after service of the schedule or order), and every 6th April thereafter, send to the employer or, in the case of a conjoined arrestment order, the sheriff clerk, information as to–
  (d) the sum owed by the debtor to the creditor;
  (e) the amounts received by the creditor by virtue of the arrestment or order; and
  (f) the dates of payment of those amounts.

9 Debtor's duty to provide information

Where a debtor ceases to be employed by an employer who is deducting sums from his wages by arrestment, the debtor must give notice to the creditor or, where those sums are being deducted by virtue of a conjoined arrestment order, the sheriff clerk, of that fact; and of the name and address of any new employer (Debtors (Scotland) Act 1987, s.70D).

10 Application to the forces

Although the Debtors (Scotland) Act 1987 excepts pay and allowances paid to a person as a member of H.M. Forces, there are alternative procedures under the Armed Forces Act 2006, s.342, which apply, *inter alia*, to both maintenance orders and judgment debts. Broadly speaking, the Acts provide for a copy of the relevant order to be sent to the appropriate service authority, which will then make deductions from the serviceman's pay not exceeding the permitted proportion determined by the Defence Council.

11 Authorities

Statutes–
Armed Forces Act 2006
Bankruptcy and Diligence etc. (Scotland) Act 2007
Debtors (Scotland) Act 1987

COMPENSATION FOR VICTIMS OF CRIMES OF VIOLENCE AND VICTIMS' RIGHTS: ENGLAND AND WALES

1 Scope of the Note

This Note deals with two distinct areas. Part A is concerned with compensation for victims of crimes of violence (primarily under the Criminal Injuries Scheme), including crimes committed in Europe. Part B covers the rights conferred on victims of crime under the Domestic Violence, Crime and Victims Act 2004.

A: THE CRIMINAL INJURIES SCHEME

2 Introduction

The Criminal Injuries Compensation Scheme (2008) has been made under the Criminal Injuries Compensation Act 1995. Applications received on or after 3 November 2008 for the payment of compensation are considered under this Scheme.

3 Administration of the Scheme

Claims officers in the Criminal Injuries Compensation Authority ("the Authority") determine claims for compensation in accordance with the Scheme. Appeals against decisions taken on reviews are determined by the First-tier Tribunal.

Claims officers are responsible for deciding what awards (if any) should be made in individual cases, and how they should be paid. Their decisions are open to review and then to appeal to the First-tier Tribunal. No decision is open to appeal to the Secretary of State.

The Accounting Officer for the Authority must submit a report to the Secretary of State and the Scottish Ministers as soon as possible after the end of each financial year (Scheme, paras 2 to 5).

4 Eligibility to apply for compensation

Compensation may be paid to an applicant who has sustained a criminal injury on or after 1 August 1964 or where the victim of a criminal injury sustained on or after 1 August 1964 has since died, who is a qualifying claimant (see **11 Compensation in fatal cases**, below). For the purposes of this Scheme, "applicant" means any person for whose benefit an application for compensation is made, even where it is made on his or her behalf by another person.

No compensation is payable where–
   (a) the applicant has previously lodged any claim for compensation for the same criminal injury under this or any other scheme for the compensation of the victims of violent crime in Great Britain; or
   (b) the criminal injury was sustained before 1 October 1979 and the victim and the assailant were living together at the time as members of the same family.

For the purposes of this Scheme, "criminal injury" means one or more personal injuries sustained in and directly attributable to an act occurring in Great Britain which is–
   (a) a crime of violence (including arson, fire-raising or an act of poisoning);
   (b) an offence of trespass on a railway; or
   (c) the apprehension or attempted apprehension of an offender or a suspected offender, the prevention or attempted prevention of an offence, or the giving of help to any constable who is engaged in any such activity.

For the purposes of this Scheme, personal injury includes physical injury (including fatal injury), mental injury (i.e., temporary mental anxiety, medically verified, or a disabling mental illness confirmed by psychiatric diagnosis) and disease (i.e., a medically recognised illness or condition). Mental injury or disease may either result directly from the physical injury or from a sexual offence or may occur without any physical injury. Compensation will not be payable for mental injury or disease without physical injury, or in respect of a sexual offence, unless the applicant–
   (a) was put in reasonable fear of immediate physical harm;
   (b) had a close relationship of love and affection with another person at the time that person sustained physical and/or mental injury (including fatal injury), where that relationship still subsists (unless the victim has since died), and the applicant either witnessed and was present when the other person sustained the injury, or was closely involved in its immediate aftermath;
   (c) in a claim arising out of a sexual offence, was the non-consenting victim of that offence (which does not include a victim who consented in fact but was deemed in law not to have consented); or
   (d) was a railway employee who either witnessed and was present when another person sustained physical (including fatal) injury directly attributable to an offence of trespass on a railway, or was closely involved in its immediate aftermath.

It is not necessary for the assailant to have been convicted of a criminal offence in connection with the injury. Moreover, even where the injury is attributable to conduct associated with certain offences where the assailant cannot be convicted of an offence by reason of age, insanity or diplomatic immunity, the conduct may nevertheless be treated as constituting a criminal act.

A personal injury is not a criminal injury for the purposes of this Scheme where it is attributable to the use of a vehicle, except where the vehicle was used to deliberately inflict, or attempt to inflict, injury on any person.

Where an injury is sustained accidentally by a person who is engaged in certain law-enforcement activities, compensation will not be payable unless the person injured was, at the time of injury, taking an exceptional risk which was justified in all the circumstances (Scheme, paras.6-12).

5 Eligibility to receive compensation

A claims officer may withhold or reduce an award where he considers that–

(a) the applicant failed to take, without delay, all reasonable steps to inform the police, or other body or person considered by the Authority to be appropriate for the purpose, of the circumstances giving rise to the injury;

(b) the applicant failed to co-operate with the police or other authority in attempting to bring the assailant to justice;

(c) the applicant has failed to give all reasonable assistance to the Authority or other body or person in connection with the application;

(d) the conduct of the applicant before, during or after the incident giving rise to the application makes it inappropriate that a full award or any award at all be made;

(e) the applicant's character, as shown by his or her criminal convictions or by evidence available to the claims officer, makes it inappropriate that a full award or any award at all be made.

In considering the issue of conduct under (d) above, a claims officer may withhold or reduce an award where he considers that excessive consumption of alcohol or use of illicit drugs by the applicant contributed to the circumstances which gave rise to the injury.

In considering the issue of character under (e) above, a claims officer must withhold or reduce an award to reflect unspent criminal convictions unless he considers that there are exceptional reasons not to do so.

Where the victim has died since sustaining the injury (whether or not in consequence of it), the above will apply in relation both to the deceased and to any other applicant for compensation (see 11 **Compensation in fatal cases**, below).

A claims officer will make an award only where he or she is satisfied that there is no likelihood that an assailant would benefit if an award were made; or, where the applicant is under 18 years of age when the application is determined, that it would not be against his or her interest for an award to be made.

Where a case is not ruled out but when the injury was sustained, the victim and any assailant were living in the same household as members of the same family, an award will be withheld unless the assailant has been prosecuted in connection with the offence, or a claims officer considers that there are practical, technical or other good reasons why a prosecution has not been brought; and in the case of violence between adults in the family, a claims officer is satisfied that the applicant and the assailant stopped living in the same household before the application was made and are unlikely to share the same household again.

A man and woman living together as husband and wife (whether or not they are married) or same sex partners living together (whether or not they are civil partners) will be treated as members of the same family (Scheme, paras 13-17).

6 Consideration of applications

An application for compensation in respect of a criminal injury must be made in writing on a form obtainable from the Authority. It should be made as soon as possible after the incident giving rise to the injury and must be received by the Authority within two years of the date of the incident. A claims officer may waive this time limit.

It is for the applicant to make out his or her case. Where an applicant is represented, the costs of representation will not be met by the Authority.

Where a claims officer considers that an examination of the injury is required before a decision can be reached, the Authority will make arrangements for such an examination by a qualified medical practitioner. A Guide to the operation of the Scheme will be published by the Authority and will set out the procedures for dealing with applications (Scheme, paras 18-22).

7 Types and limits of compensation

The compensation payable under an award is–

(a) a standard amount of compensation determined by reference to the nature of the injury (see 8 **Standard amount of compensation**, below);

(b) where the applicant has lost earnings or earning capacity for longer than 28 weeks as a direct consequence of the injury (other than injury leading to his or her death), an additional amount in respect of such loss of earnings (see 9 **Compensation for loss of earnings**, below);

(c) where the applicant has lost earnings or earning capacity for longer than 28 weeks as a direct consequence of the injury (other than injury leading to his or her death) or, if not normally employed, is incapacitated to a similar extent, an additional amount in respect of any special expenses (see

10 **Compensation for special expenses**, below);

(d) where the victim has died in consequence of the injury (see 11 **Compensation in fatal cases**, below and see 12 **Where victim died in consequence of injury**, below); and

(e) where the victim has died otherwise than in consequence of the injury, a supplementary amount (see 12 **Where victim died in consequence of injury**, below*).*

The maximum award that may be made (before any reduction) in respect of the same injury will not exceed £500,000 (Scheme, paras 23-25).

8 Standard amount of compensation

The standard amount of compensation is the amount shown in respect of the relevant description of injury in the Tariff to the Scheme, which sets out a scale of fixed levels of compensation; the level and corresponding amount of compensation for each description of injury; and qualifying notes. Level 1 represents the minimum award under this Scheme, and Level 25 represents the maximum award for any single description of injury. Where the injury has the effect of accelerating or exacerbating a pre-existing condition, the compensation awarded will reflect only the degree of acceleration or exacerbation.

The Scheme contains rules as to how compensation will be assessed for minor multiple injuries. The standard amount of compensation for more serious but separate multiple injuries will, unless expressly provided for otherwise in the Scheme, be calculated as–

(a) the Tariff amount for the highest-rated description of injury; plus

(b) 30 per cent of the Tariff amount for the second highest-rated description of injury; plus, where there are three or more injuries,

(c) 15 per cent of the Tariff amount for the third highest-rated description of injury.

Where the Authority considers that any description of injury for which no provision is made in the Tariff is sufficiently serious to qualify for at least the minimum award under this Scheme, it will, following consultation with the First-tier Tribunal, refer the injury to the Secretary of State. In doing so the Authority will recommend to the Secretary of State both the inclusion of that description of injury in the Tariff and also the amount of compensation for which it should qualify. Any such consultation with the First-tier Tribunal or reference to the Secretary of State must not refer to the circumstances of any individual application for compensation under this Scheme other than the relevant medical reports.

Where an application for compensation is made in respect of an injury for which no provision is made in the Tariff and the Authority decides to refer the injury to the Secretary of State, an interim award may be made of up to half the amount of compensation for which such an injury should qualify if subsequently included in the Tariff (paras 26-29).

9 Compensation for loss of earnings

Where the applicant has lost earnings or earning capacity for longer than 28 weeks as a direct consequence of the injury (other than injury leading to his or her death), no compensation in respect of loss of earnings or earning capacity is payable for the first 28 weeks of loss. The period of loss for which compensation may be payable begins after those 28 weeks and, subject to the paragraph below, continues for such period as a claims officer may determine.

Where an injury has resulted in a reduction in the life expectancy of the applicant to an age below the applicant's expected retirement age, the period of loss for which compensation may be payable must be restricted to reflect that fact. No compensation in respect of loss of earnings or earning capacity is payable in respect of any years of employment lost as a result of a reduction in life expectancy, subject to the right of a qualifying claimant to make an application for compensation (see 11 **Compensation in fatal cases,** below).

Loss of earnings or earning capacity for any period prior to the date of assessment (and, where appropriate, the date of the assessment itself) ("past loss"), is assessed by–

(a) calculating the applicant's earnings as they would have been during the period of loss had it not been for the injury; and

(b) deducting any earnings which have, or should have, been paid to the applicant during the period of loss, whether or not as a result of the injury.

Loss of earnings or earning capacity for any period of loss following the date of assessment ("future loss") is assessed by–

(a) calculating an annual rate of loss at the time of the assessment (the "multiplicand");

(b) calculating any further multiplicand; and

(c) multiplying each multiplicand by an appropriate multiplier (and applying any other relevant factor).

For the purposes of this Scheme, "earnings" includes any profit or gain payable in respect of an office or employment (including salary, benefits in kind, pensions benefits (whether or not paid as a lump sum), redundancy payments and other severance payments) and is calculated net of tax, national insurance and pension contributions.

The compensation payable in respect of each period of future loss is a lump sum, which is the product of the relevant multiplicand and an appropriate multiplier. When the loss does not start until a future date, the lump sum is discounted to provide for the present value of the money. The claims officer will assess the appropriate multiplier, discount factor, or life expectancy, and may make such adjustments as he considers appropriate to take account of any factors and contingencies which appear to him or her to be relevant.

Any rate of net loss of earnings or earning capacity (before any reduction in accordance with the Scheme) which is to be taken into account in calculating any compensation payable must not exceed one and a half times the median gross weekly earnings at the time of assessment according to the latest figures published by the Office for National Statistics (Scheme, paras 30-34).

10 Compensation for special expenses

Where the applicant has lost earnings or earning capacity for longer than 28 weeks as a direct consequence of the injury (other than injury leading to his or her death), or, if not normally employed, is incapacitated to a similar extent, additional compensation may be payable in respect of any special expenses incurred by the applicant from the date of the injury for–

    (a) loss of or damage to property or equipment belonging to the applicant on which they relied as a physical aid, where the loss or damage was a direct consequence of the injury;

    (b) costs (other than by way of loss of earnings or earning capacity) associated with NHS treatment for the injury;

    (c) the cost of private health treatment for the injury, but only where a claims officer considers that, in all the circumstances, both the private treatment and its cost are reasonable;

    (d) the reasonable cost of special equipment, and/or adaptations to the applicant's accommodation, and/or care and supervision, whether in a residential establishment or at home, which is not provided or available free of charge from the NHS, local authorities or any other agency, provided that a claims officer considers such expense to be necessary as a direct consequence of the injury;

    (e) fees payable to the Public Guardian or the Court of Protection, or to any sheriff court in respect of an application made under the Adults with Incapacity (Scotland) Act;

    (f) other costs associated with the administration of the applicant's affairs due to his or her lack of mental capacity provided that the claims officer considers that the costs were necessarily incurred as a result of the injury and are reasonable; and

    (g) the reasonable cost of setting up and administering a trust pursuant to a direction given by the claims officer.

In the case of (d) above, the expense of unpaid care provided at home by a relative or friend of the victim is compensated by having regard to the level of care required, the cost of a carer, assessing the carer's loss of earnings or earning capacity and/or additional personal and living expenses, as calculated on such basis as a claims officer considers appropriate in all the circumstances (Scheme, paras 35 to 36).

11 Compensation in fatal cases

Where the victim has died in consequence of the injury, no compensation other than funeral expenses is payable for the benefit of his or her estate. Such expenses will, subject to the eligibility criteria (see **5 Eligibility to receive compensation**, above), be payable up to an amount considered reasonable by a claims officer, even where the person bearing the cost of the funeral is otherwise ineligible to claim.

Where the victim has died, if the death was in consequence of the injury, compensation may be payable to a qualifying claimant (see **12 Where victim died in consequence of injury**, below); or if the death was otherwise than in consequence of the injury, and occurred before title to the award had been vested in the victim (see **13 Effect on awards of other payments**, below), compensation may be payable to a qualifying claimant (see **12 Where victim died in consequence of injury**, below), and no standard amount or other compensation is payable to the estate or to the qualifying claimant.

A "qualifying claimant" is a person who at the time of the deceased's death was–

    (a) the partner of the deceased who was living with them as husband and wife or as a same sex partner in the same household immediately before the date of death and who, unless married to or a civil partner of that person, had been so living throughout the two years before that date; or a spouse or civil partner or former spouse or civil partner of the deceased who was financially supported by the deceased immediately before the date of death;

    (b) a natural parent of the deceased, or a person who was not the natural parent but was accepted by the deceased as a parent within the deceased's family; or

    (c) a natural child of the deceased, or a person who was not the natural child but was accepted by the deceased as a child within the deceased's family or was dependent on the deceased.

But a person who was criminally responsible for the death of a victim may not be a qualifying claimant (Scheme, paras 37-38).

12 Where victim died in consequence of injury

A qualifying claimant may claim an award (a "bereavement award") unless they were a former spouse or civil partner of the deceased or otherwise estranged from them immediately before the date of death. In cases where only one person qualifies for a bereavement award, the standard amount of compensation is Level 13 of the Tariff, except that where a claims officer is aware of the existence of one or more other persons who would in the event of their making a claim qualify for a bereavement award, the standard amount of compensation is Level 10 of the Tariff. Where more than one person qualifies for a bereavement award, the standard amount of compensation for each claimant is Level 10 of the Tariff.

Additional compensation may be payable to a qualifying claimant where a claims officer is satisfied that the claimant was financially or physically dependent on the deceased. A financial dependency will not be established where the deceased's only normal income was from social security benefits.

For the purposes of the Scheme, "social security benefits" includes all UK social security benefits, other state or local authority benefits and all such benefits or similar payments paid from the funds of other countries.

The amount of compensation payable in respect of dependency is calculated on the basis of loss of earnings and the cost of care. The period of loss begins from the date of the deceased's death and continues for such period as a claims officer may determine, with no account being taken, where the qualifying claimant was married to or a civil partner of the deceased, of remarriage or prospects of remarriage or of a new civil partnership or the prospects of a new civil partnership.

In assessing the dependency, the claims officer takes account of the qualifying claimant's earnings and other income, if any. Where the deceased had been living in the same household as the qualifying claimant before death, the claims officer will, in calculating the multiplicand, make such proportional reduction as he or she considers appropriate to take account of the deceased's own personal and living expenses.

Where a qualifying claimant was under 18 years of age at the time of the deceased's death and was dependent on them for parental services, compensation may also be payable for loss of that parent's services at an annual rate of Level 5 of the Tariff; and such other payments as a claims officer considers reasonable to meet other resultant losses.

Application may be made even where an award had been made to the victim in respect of the same injury before his or her death. Any such application will be subject to the conditions for the re-opening of cases (see **17 Review of decisions**, below), and any compensation payable to the qualifying claimant or claimants, except funeral expenses and the standard amount of compensation, will be reduced by the amount paid to the victim.

Where a victim who would have qualified for additional compensation for loss of earnings and/or special expenses has died, otherwise than in consequence of the injury, before such compensation was awarded, supplementary compensation may be payable to a qualifying claimant who was financially dependent on the deceased, whether or not a relevant application was made by the victim before his or her death.

The amounts payable to the victim and the qualifying claimant or claimants may not in total exceed £500,000 (Scheme, paras 38 to 44).

13 Effect on awards of other payments

The compensation payable to an applicant, other than tariff-based amounts of compensation) (see **8 Standard amount of compensation**, above, and see **12 Where victim died in consequence of injury**, above), is reduced to take account of any social security benefits or insurance payments made by way of compensation for the same contingency.

No reduction is made to take account of an insurance payment if it is made under an insurance arrangement entered into and wholly funded by the victim personally (or by the parent or guardian of a victim who was under the age of 18 at the time of the injury), except where the reduction is made to compensation payable.

A reduction will be made irrespective of the period in respect of which the social security benefits or insurance payments have been, or will be paid. In particular, the reduction will be made whether or not any actual loss occurred or will occur in that period.

No reduction will be made to take account of any social security benefits or insurance payments paid in respect of the first 28 weeks of lost earnings.

The amount of the reduction is the full value of the social security benefits or insurance payments less the amount of any income tax which has been or may be charged in respect of them.

If the benefits or payments will be paid after the date of the assessment, the claims officer will calculate the amount of the reduction as he or she would calculate a lump sum to compensate for future loss.

For the purposes of the Scheme, disablement pension payable are be treated as a social security benefit payable to compensate for loss of earnings, loss of earning capacity or loss of pension benefits.

Where the victim is alive, any compensation payable for loss of earnings (see **9 Compensation for loss of earnings,** above) is reduced to take account of any pension benefits accruing as a result of the injury which have not already been taken into account. Where the victim has died in consequence of the injury, any compensation payable is similarly reduced to take account of any pension benefits which have not already been taken into account and which are payable, as a result of the victim's death, for the benefit of the applicant (see **12 Where victim died in consequence of injury**, above).

"Pension benefits" means any payment payable as a result of the injury or death in pursuance of pension or any other rights connected with the victim's employment, and includes any gratuity of that kind and similar benefits payable under insurance policies paid for by the victim's employers. Pension rights accruing solely as a result of payments by the victim or a dependant will be disregarded.

A reduction will be made irrespective of the period in respect of which the pension benefits have been, or will be paid. In particular, a reduction will be made whether or not any actual loss of earnings or earning capacity occurred or will occur in that period. However, no reduction will be made to take account of any pension benefits paid in respect of the first 28 weeks of lost earnings.

Where such pension benefits are taxable, one half of their gross value will be deducted, but they will otherwise be deducted in full (where, for example, a lump sum payment not subject to income tax is made). However, if the pension benefits will be paid after the date of the assessment, the claims officer will calculate the amount of the reduction as he or she would calculate a lump sum to compensate for future loss. In the case of taxable pension benefits the claims officer will assume for these purposes that the applicant will receive one half of their gross value.

Where, in the opinion of a claims officer, an applicant may be or may become eligible for any social security benefits, insurance payments or pension benefits, an award may be withheld until the applicant has taken such steps as the claims officer considers reasonable to claim them.

An award will be reduced by the full value of any payment in respect of the same injury which the applicant has received or to which he has any present or future entitlement.

A claims officer may require an applicant to provide details of any steps taken or planned to obtain damages or compensation in respect of the same injury and may decline to process an application further until those details have been provided or until the applicant's attempts to obtain such damages or compensation have been exhausted.

Where a person in whose favour an award is made subsequently receives any other payment in respect of the same injury, but the award was not reduced accordingly, the person will be required to repay the Authority in full up to the amount of the other payment (Scheme, paras 45-50).

14 Determination of applications and payment

An application for compensation under the Scheme will be determined by a claims officer, and written notification of the decision will be sent to the applicant or their representative. Written acceptance of an award must be received by the Authority within 90 days of the date the decision was issued. If such an acceptance is not received within that period, and no application for a review has been made, the Authority may withdraw the award. A claims officer may grant an extension to this time limit (whether or not it has already expired) and overturn any withdrawal.

The claims officer may make such directions and arrangements, including the imposition of conditions, in connection with the acceptance, settlement, or trust, payment, repayment and/or administration of an award as they consider appropriate in all the circumstances.

Compensation is normally paid as a single lump sum, but one or more interim payments may be made where a claims officer considers this appropriate (Scheme, paras 51-52).

15 Reconsideration of decisions

A decision made by a claims officer (other than a decision made in accordance with a direction by the First-tier Tribunal on determining an appeal–see **18 Appeals**, below) may be reconsidered at any time before actual payment of a final award where there is new evidence or a change in circumstances. In particular, the fact that an interim payment has been made does not preclude a claims officer from reconsidering issues of eligibility for an award.

Where an applicant has already been sent written notification of the decision on the application, they will be sent written notice that the decision is to be reconsidered, and any representations which they send to the Authority within 30 days of the date of such notice will be taken into account in reconsidering the decision. Whether or not any such representations are made, the applicant will be sent written notification of the outcome of the reconsideration, and where the original decision is not confirmed, such notification will include the revised decision.

Where a decision to make an award has been made by a claims officer in accordance with a direction by the First-tier Tribunal on determining an appeal, but before the award has been paid the claims officer considers that there is new evidence or a change in circumstances which justifies reconsidering whether the award should be withheld or the amount of compensation reduced, the Authority will refer the case to the First-tier Tribunal for rehearing (Scheme, paras 53-55).

16 Re-opening of cases

A decision made by a claims officer and accepted by the applicant, or a direction by the First-tier Tribunal, will normally be regarded as final, except where an appeal is reheard. A claims officer may, however, subsequently re-open a case where there has been such a material change in the victim's medical condition that injustice would occur if the original assessment of compensation were allowed to stand, or where the victim has since died in consequence of the injury.

A case will not be re-opened more than two years after the date of the final decision unless the claims officer is satisfied, on the basis of evidence presented in support of the application to re-open the case, that the renewed application can be considered without a need for further extensive enquiries (Scheme, paras 56-57).

17 Review of decisions

An applicant may seek a review of any decision by a claims officer under the Scheme–
(a) not to waive or extend the time limit for applications for compensation or applications for review;
(b) not to re-open a case;

    (c) to withhold an award, including such decision made on reconsideration of an award;

    (d) to make an award, including a decision to make a reduced award whether or not on reconsideration of an award;

    (e) to require repayment of an award; or

    (f) to withdraw an award.

An applicant may not, however, seek the review of any such decision where the decision was itself made on a review and either the applicant did not appeal against it or the appeal did not result in a direction from the First-tier Tribunal; or where the decision was made in accordance with a direction by the First-tier Tribunal on determining an appeal.

An application for the review of a decision by a claims officer must be made in writing to the Authority and must be supported by reasons together with any relevant additional information. It must be received by the Authority within 90 days of the date the decision to be reviewed was issued.

All applications for review will be considered by a different claims officer to the one who made the original decision. The officer conducting the review will reach a decision in accordance with the provisions of the Scheme applying to the original application, and will not be bound by any earlier decision either as to the eligibility of the applicant for an award or as to the amount of an award (Scheme, paras 58-60).

18 Appeals

An applicant who is dissatisfied with a decision taken on a review, or with a determination, may appeal against the decision to the First-tier Tribunal in accordance with Tribunal Procedure Rules.

19 European Convention on the Compensation of Victims of Violent Crimes

The United Kingdom has signed the European Convention on the Compensation of Victims of Violent Crimes which took effect in the UK on 1st June 1990. Under the terms of the Convention, citizens of the countries which are signatories to the Convention are entitled, if criminally injured in a signatory State, to compensation from the signatory State. Relatives of a person fatally injured in a signatory State are also able to claim compensation from that State. The Convention currently covers 21 European States. Notable exceptions include Greece, Hungary, Ireland, Italy, Poland and Russia. Compensation must at least cover loss of earnings and medical expenses and, in fatal cases, funeral expenses and loss of financial support suffered by dependants.

20 European Union co-operation

EC Council Directive 2004/80 requires Member States to set up a system of co-operation between the authorities in Member States to facilitate access to compensation where a crime is committed in a country other than that where the victim lives. The purpose is to allow the victim to turn to the authority in their own country, so easing practical and linguistic difficulties. Compensation will be paid by the authority in the Member Sate where the crime was committed.

The Victims of Violent International Crime (Arrangements for Compensation) (European Communities) Regulations 2005 designates the First-tier Tribunal as the "assisting authority" in the UK. A British resident who is a victim of a crime elsewhere in the EU will be provided by the Tribunal with essential information on the opportunities for making an application for compensation, including application forms and general guidance, and may submit such an application to the Tribunal who will transmit it the relevant authority in the Member State where the crime occurred.

B: VICTIMS' RIGHTS

21 Introduction

The Domestic Violence, Crime and Victims Act 2004 introduced new rights for victims of certain crimes. These are (s.35)–

    (a) a right to receive information about the release of an offender; and

    (b) a right to receive information about, and make representations before, the release on licence of an offender.

The rights only apply where a person is convicted of a serious sexual or violent offence for which a sentence of 12 months imprisonment; detention during Her Majesty's pleasure; a 12 month detention and training order; or a hospital direction and limitation order is imposed.

Similar provisions apply where a hospital order with or without a restriction order is imposed after a person is convicted of an offence; found not guilty by reason of insanity; or found to be under a disability [which would constitute a bar to his being tried] and also found to have done the act or made the omission with which he was charged (s.36). When considering whether to discharge a patient, the responsible clinician must notify the hospital managers who must inform the victim if the local probation board has established that they wish to receive such information. If the patient is to be subject to a community treatment order the victim must be informed of any conditions relating to contact with him or his family. The victim has a right to make representations to the hospital managers about the discharge and any conditions and these must be forwarded to the responsible clinician (ss.36A to 41A).

The local probation board for the area in which the sentence is imposed must take all reasonable steps to ascertain whether a person who appears to be a victim wishes to make use of these provisions.

Under the 2004 Act, the Secretary of State may also pay grants to such persons as he considers appropriate in connection with measures which appear to him to be intended to assist victims, witnesses or other persons affected by offences (s.56).

22 The right to make representations

A victim has the right to make representations as to (Domestic Violence, Crime and Victims Act 2004, s.35(4))–

(a) whether the offender should be subject to any licence conditions or supervision requirements in the event of his release from prison/discharge from hospital; and

(b) if so, what licence conditions or supervision requirements.

23 The right to receive information

A victim has the right to receive information as to any licence conditions or supervision requirements to which the offender is to be subject in the event of his release from prison/discharge from hospital (Domestic Violence, Crime and Victims Act 2004, ss.35(5), 36(4), and 39(4)). If they wish to receive such information, the probation board must take all reasonable steps (ss.35(7), 38(3), and 41(3))–

(a) to inform them whether or not the offender is to be subject to any licence conditions or supervision requirements in the event of his release/discharge;

(b) if he is, to provide them with details of any licence conditions or supervision requirements which relate to contact with the victim or his family;

(c) to inform them when any restriction order imposed on a patient is to end; and

(d) to provide them with such other information as the local probation board considers appropriate in all the circumstances of the case.

24 Code of Practice for Victims of Crime

The Domestic Violence, Crime and Victims Act 2004 requires the Secretary of State to produce a code of practice for victims of crime (s.32).

The Ministry of Justice has produced a Code of Practice for Victims of Crime (updated November 2015 by the Domestic Violence, Crime and Victims Act 2004 (Victims' Code of Practice) Order 2015, S.I. No. 1817) which sets out the services victims can expect to receive from the criminal justice system including–

(a) a right to information about their crime within specified time scales, including the right to be notified of any arrests and court cases and to be informed if the suspect is to be prosecuted or not or given an out of court disposal;

(b) a right to be informed about how to seek a review of CPS decisions not to prosecute, to discontinue or offer no evidence in all proceedings;

(c) a dedicated family liaison police officer to be assigned to bereaved relatives;

(d) clear information from the Criminal Injuries Compensation Authority on eligibility for compensation under the Scheme;

(e) a needs assessment to help work out what support is needed;

(f) a right to be referred to organisations supporting victims of crime;

(g) an enhanced service in the cases of victims of serious crime, persistently targeted victims and vulnerable or intimidated victims;

(h) a right to opt into the Victim Contact Scheme if the offender is sentenced to 12 months or more for a specified violent or sexual offence;

(i) a right to make a Victim Personal Statement to explain how the crime affected the victim and read the Statement aloud or have it read aloud on the victim's behalf, subject to the views of the court, if a defendant is found guilty; and

(j) information about Restorative Justice and how the victim can take part.

The Code is available at <www.gov.uk/government/consultations/revising-the-victims-code>. Leaflets summarising the key points for victims of crime, including young victims of crime, to help understand the support they can expect are also available from www.gov.uk.

Criminal justice bodies, including the Prison Service, the Criminal Injuries Compensation Authority and all police forces in England and Wales must ensure that victims of crime and their families receive information, protection and support. Failure to comply with the Code is not in itself an offence, but a court can take such a failure into account in determining any proceedings (s.34).

25 Commissioner for Victims and Witnesses

The Domestic Violence, Crime and Victims Act 2004 provides for the appointment of a Commissioner for

Victims and Witnesses (s.48) whose primary functions are to promote the interests of victims and witnesses of crime and anti-social behaviour, take steps to encourage good practice in their treatment and keep the code of practice for victims under review (s.49).

The Commissioner cannot exercise his functions on behalf of individual victims or witnesses (e.g., he cannot ask the police or Crown Prosecution Service to bring or reconsider a particular charge against an individual offender), or ask for the courts to impose a particular sentence; but he can comment on charging or sentencing policy, or any other wider policy issue relating to victims and witnesses (s.51).

For these purposes, a "victim" means (s.52)–

(a) a victim of an offence; or

(b) a victim of anti-social behaviour.

It is immaterial that no complaint has been made about the offence or that no person has been charged with or convicted of the offence.

A "witness" means a person (other than a defendant)–

(c) who has witnessed conduct in relation to which he may be or has been called to give evidence either in criminal proceedings or in proceedings of any other kind in respect of anti-social behaviour;

(d) who is able to provide or has provided anything which might be used or has been used as evidence in such proceedings; or

(e) who is able to provide or has provided anything which might (i) tend to confirm, has tended to confirm or might have tended to confirm evidence which may be, has been or could have been admitted in such proceedings; (ii) be, has been or might have been referred to in evidence given in such proceedings by another person; or (iii) be, has been or might have been used as the basis for any cross examination in the course of such proceedings (whether or not admissible in evidence in such proceedings).

26 Authorities

Criminal Injuries Compensation Act 1995

Domestic Violence, Crime and Victims Act 2004

Victims of Violent International Crime (Arrangements for Compensation) (European Communities) Regulations 2005, as amended (S.I. 2005 No. 3396 and 2008 No. 2683)

European Convention on the Compensation of Victims of Violent Crimes 24th November 1983

The Criminal Injuries Compensation Scheme 2008

EC Council Directive 2004/80

COMPENSATION FOR VICTIMS OF CRIMES OF VIOLENCE AND VICTIMS' RIGHTS: SCOTLAND

1 Scope of the Note

This Note deals with two distinct areas. Part A is concerned with compensation for victims of crimes of violence (primarily under the Criminal Injuries Scheme), including crimes committed in Europe. Part B covers the rights conferred on victims of crime by the Criminal Justice (Scotland) Act 2003 and the Victims and Witnesses (Scotland) Act 2014.

A: THE CRIMINAL INJURIES SCHEME

2 Introduction

The Criminal Injuries Compensation Scheme (2008) has been made under the Criminal Injuries Compensation Act 1995. Applications received on or after 3 November 2008 for the payment of compensation are considered under this Scheme.

3 Administration of the Scheme

Claims officers in the Criminal Injuries Compensation Authority ("the Authority") determine claims for compensation in accordance with the Scheme. Appeals against decisions taken on reviews are determined by the First-tier Tribunal established under the Tribunals, Courts and Enforcement Act 2007.

Claims officers are responsible for deciding what awards (if any) should be made in individual cases, and how they should be paid. Their decisions are open to review and then to appeal to the First-tier Tribunal. No decision is open to appeal to the Secretary of State.

The Accounting Officer for the Authority must submit a report to the Secretary of State and the Scottish Ministers as soon as possible after the end of each financial year (Scheme, paras 2 to 5).

4 Eligibility to apply for compensation

Compensation may be paid to an applicant who has sustained a criminal injury on or after 1 August 1964 or where the victim of a criminal injury sustained on or after 1 August 1964 has since died, who is a qualifying claimant (see **11 Compensation in fatal cases**, below). For the purposes of this Scheme, "applicant" means any person for whose benefit an application for compensation is made, even where it is made on his or her behalf by another person.

No compensation is payable where—
(a) the applicant has previously lodged any claim for compensation for the same criminal injury under this or any other scheme for the compensation of the victims of violent crime in Great Britain; or
(b) the criminal injury was sustained before 1 October 1979 and the victim and the assailant were living together at the time as members of the same family.

For the purposes of this Scheme, "criminal injury" means one or more personal injuries sustained in and directly attributable to an act occurring in Great Britain which is—
(a) a crime of violence (including arson, fire-raising or an act of poisoning);
(b) an offence of trespass on a railway; or
(c) the apprehension or attempted apprehension of an offender or a suspected offender, the prevention or attempted prevention of an offence, or the giving of help to any constable who is engaged in any such activity.

For the purposes of this Scheme, personal injury includes physical injury (including fatal injury), mental injury (i.e., temporary mental anxiety, medically verified, or a disabling mental illness confirmed by psychiatric diagnosis) and disease (i.e., a medically recognised illness or condition). Mental injury or disease may either result directly from the physical injury or from a sexual offence or may occur without any physical injury. Compensation will not be payable for mental injury or disease without physical injury, or in respect of a sexual offence, unless the applicant—
(a) was put in reasonable fear of immediate physical harm;
(b) had a close relationship of love and affection with another person at the time that person sustained physical and/or mental injury (including fatal injury), where that relationship still subsists (unless the victim has since died), and the applicant either witnessed and was present when the other person sustained the injury, or was closely involved in its immediate aftermath;
(c) in a claim arising out of a sexual offence, was the non-consenting victim of that offence (which does not include a victim who consented in fact but was deemed in law not to have consented); or
(d) was a railway employee who either witnessed and was present when another person sustained physical (including fatal) injury directly attributable to an offence of trespass on a railway, or was closely involved in its immediate aftermath.

It is not necessary for the assailant to have been convicted of a criminal offence in connection with the injury. Moreover, even where the injury is attributable to conduct associated with certain offences where the assailant cannot be convicted of an offence by reason of age, insanity or diplomatic immunity, the conduct may nevertheless be treated as constituting a criminal act.

A personal injury is not a criminal injury for the purposes of this Scheme where it is attributable to the use of a vehicle, except where the vehicle was used to deliberately inflict, or attempt to inflict, injury on any person.

Where an injury is sustained accidentally by a person who is engaged in certain law-enforcement activities, compensation will not be payable unless the person injured was, at the time of injury, taking an exceptional risk which was justified in all the circumstances (Scheme, paras.6-12).

5 Eligibility to receive compensation

A claims officer may withhold or reduce an award where he considers that–
  (a) the applicant failed to take, without delay, all reasonable steps to inform the police, or other body or person considered by the Authority to be appropriate for the purpose, of the circumstances giving rise to the injury;
  (b) the applicant failed to co-operate with the police or other authority in attempting to bring the assailant to justice;
  (c) the applicant has failed to give all reasonable assistance to the Authority or other body or person in connection with the application;
  (d) the conduct of the applicant before, during or after the incident giving rise to the application makes it inappropriate that a full award or any award at all be made;
  (e) the applicant's character, as shown by his or her criminal convictions or by evidence available to the claims officer, makes it inappropriate that a full award or any award at all be made.

In considering the issue of conduct under (d) above, a claims officer may withhold or reduce an award where he considers that excessive consumption of alcohol or use of illicit drugs by the applicant contributed to the circumstances which gave rise to the injury.

In considering the issue of character under (e) above, a claims officer must withhold or reduce an award to reflect unspent criminal convictions unless he considers that there are exceptional reasons not to do so.

Where the victim has died since sustaining the injury (whether or not in consequence of it), the above will apply in relation both to the deceased and to any other applicant for compensation (see **11 Compensation in fatal cases**, below).

A claims officer will make an award only where he or she is satisfied that there is no likelihood that an assailant would benefit if an award were made; or, where the applicant is under 18 years of age when the application is determined, that it would not be against his or her interest for an award to be made.

Where a case is not ruled out but when the injury was sustained, the victim and any assailant were living in the same household as members of the same family, an award will be withheld unless the assailant has been prosecuted in connection with the offence, or a claims officer considers that there are practical, technical or other good reasons why a prosecution has not been brought; and in the case of violence between adults in the family, a claims officer is satisfied that the applicant and the assailant stopped living in the same household before the application was made and are unlikely to share the same household again.

A man and woman living together as husband and wife (whether or not they are married) or same sex partners living together (whether or not they are civil partners) will be treated as members of the same family (Scheme, paras 13-17).

6 Consideration of applications

An application for compensation in respect of a criminal injury must be made in writing on a form obtainable from the Authority. It should be made as soon as possible after the incident giving rise to the injury and must be received by the Authority within two years of the date of the incident. A claims officer may waive this time limit.

It is for the applicant to make out his or her case. Where an applicant is represented, the costs of representation will not be met by the Authority.

Where a claims officer considers that an examination of the injury is required before a decision can be reached, the Authority will make arrangements for such an examination by a qualified medical practitioner. A Guide to the operation of the Scheme will be published by the Authority and will set out the procedures for dealing with applications (Scheme, paras 18-22).

7 Types and limits of compensation

The compensation payable under an award is–
  (a) a standard amount of compensation determined by reference to the nature of the injury (see **8 Standard amount of compensation**, below);
  (b) where the applicant has lost earnings or earning capacity for longer than 28 weeks as a direct consequence of the injury (other than injury leading to his or her death), an additional amount in respect of such loss of earnings (see **9 Compensation for loss of earnings**, below);
  (c) where the applicant has lost earnings or earning capacity for longer than 28 weeks as a direct

consequence of the injury (other than injury leading to his or her death) or, if not normally employed, is incapacitated to a similar extent, an additional amount in respect of any special expenses (see 10 **Compensation for special expenses**, below);

(d) where the victim has died in consequence of the injury (see 11 **Compensation in fatal cases**, below and see 12 **Where victim died in consequence of injury**, below); and

(e) where the victim has died otherwise than in consequence of the injury, a supplementary amount (see 12 **Where victim died in consequence of injury**, below).

The maximum award that may be made (before any reduction) in respect of the same injury will not exceed £500,000 (Scheme, paras 23-25).

8 Standard amount of compensation

The standard amount of compensation is the amount shown in respect of the relevant description of injury in the Tariff to the Scheme, which sets out a scale of fixed levels of compensation; the level and corresponding amount of compensation for each description of injury; and qualifying notes. Level 1 represents the minimum award under this Scheme, and Level 25 represents the maximum award for any single description of injury. Where the injury has the effect of accelerating or exacerbating a pre-existing condition, the compensation awarded will reflect only the degree of acceleration or exacerbation.

The Scheme contains rules as to how compensation will be assessed for minor multiple injuries. The standard amount of compensation for more serious but separate multiple injuries will, unless expressly provided for otherwise in the Scheme, be calculated as—

(a) the Tariff amount for the highest-rated description of injury; plus

(b) 30 per cent of the Tariff amount for the second highest-rated description of injury; plus, where there are three or more injuries,

(c) 15 per cent of the Tariff amount for the third highest-rated description of injury.

Where the Authority considers that any description of injury for which no provision is made in the Tariff is sufficiently serious to qualify for at least the minimum award under this Scheme, it will, following consultation with the First-tier Tribunal, refer the injury to the Secretary of State. In doing so the Authority will recommend to the Secretary of State both the inclusion of that description of injury in the Tariff and also the amount of compensation for which it should qualify. Any such consultation with the First-tier Tribunal or reference to the Secretary of State must not refer to the circumstances of any individual application for compensation under this Scheme other than the relevant medical reports.

Where an application for compensation is made in respect of an injury for which no provision is made in the Tariff and the Authority decides to refer the injury to the Secretary of State, an interim award may be made of up to half the amount of compensation for which such an injury should qualify if subsequently included in the Tariff (paras 26-29).

9 Compensation for loss of earnings

Where the applicant has lost earnings or earning capacity for longer than 28 weeks as a direct consequence of the injury (other than injury leading to his or her death), no compensation in respect of loss of earnings or earning capacity is payable for the first 28 weeks of loss. The period of loss for which compensation may be payable begins after those 28 weeks and, subject to the paragraph below, continues for such period as a claims officer may determine.

Where an injury has resulted in a reduction in the life expectancy of the applicant to an age below the applicant's expected retirement age, the period of loss for which compensation may be payable must be restricted to reflect that fact. No compensation in respect of loss of earnings or earning capacity is payable in respect of any years of employment lost as a result of a reduction in life expectancy, subject to the right of a qualifying claimant to make an application for compensation (see 11 **Compensation in fatal cases**, below).

Loss of earnings or earning capacity for any period prior to the date of assessment (and, where appropriate, the date of the assessment itself) ("past loss"), is assessed by—

(a) calculating the applicant's earnings as they would have been during the period of loss had it not been for the injury; and

(b) deducting any earnings which have, or should have, been paid to the applicant during the period of loss, whether or not as a result of the injury.

Loss of earnings or earning capacity for any period of loss following the date of assessment ("future loss") is assessed by—

(a) calculating an annual rate of loss at the time of the assessment (the "multiplicand");

(b) calculating any further multiplicand; and

(c) multiplying each multiplicand by an appropriate multiplier (and applying any other relevant factor).

For the purposes of this Scheme, "earnings" includes any profit or gain payable in respect of an office or employment (including salary, benefits in kind, pensions benefits (whether or not paid as a lump sum), redundancy payments and other severance payments) and is calculated net of tax, national insurance and pension contributions.

The compensation payable in respect of each period of future loss is a lump sum, which is the product of the relevant multiplicand and an appropriate multiplier. When the loss does not start until a future date, the lump sum is discounted to provide for the present value of the money. The claims officer will assess the appropriate multiplier, discount factor, or life expectancy, and may make such adjustments as he considers appropriate to take account of any factors and contingencies which appear to him or her to be relevant.

Any rate of net loss of earnings or earning capacity (before any reduction in accordance with the Scheme) which is to be taken into account in calculating any compensation payable must not exceed one and a half times the median gross weekly earnings at the time of assessment according to the latest figures published by the Office for National Statistics (Scheme, paras 30-34).

10 Compensation for special expenses

Where the applicant has lost earnings or earning capacity for longer than 28 weeks as a direct consequence of the injury (other than injury leading to his or her death), or, if not normally employed, is incapacitated to a similar extent, additional compensation may be payable in respect of any special expenses incurred by the applicant from the date of the injury for–

(a) loss of or damage to property or equipment belonging to the applicant on which they relied as a physical aid, where the loss or damage was a direct consequence of the injury;

(b) costs (other than by way of loss of earnings or earning capacity) associated with NHS treatment for the injury;

(c) the cost of private health treatment for the injury, but only where a claims officer considers that, in all the circumstances, both the private treatment and its cost are reasonable;

(d) the reasonable cost of special equipment, and/or adaptations to the applicant's accommodation, and/or care and supervision, whether in a residential establishment or at home, which is not provided or available free of charge from the NHS, local authorities or any other agency, provided that a claims officer considers such expense to be necessary as a direct consequence of the injury;

(e) fees payable to the Public Guardian or the Court of Protection, or to any sheriff court in respect of an application made under the Adults with Incapacity (Scotland) Act;

(f) other costs associated with the administration of the applicant's affairs due to his or her lack of mental capacity provided that the claims officer considers that the costs were necessarily incurred as a result of the injury and are reasonable; and

(g) the reasonable cost of setting up and administering a trust pursuant to a direction given by the claims officer.

In the case of (d) above, the expense of unpaid care provided at home by a relative or friend of the victim is compensated by having regard to the level of care required, the cost of a carer, assessing the carer's loss of earnings or earning capacity and/or additional personal and living expenses, as calculated on such basis as a claims officer considers appropriate in all the circumstances (Scheme, paras 35 to 36).

11 Compensation in fatal cases

Where the victim has died in consequence of the injury, no compensation other than funeral expenses is payable for the benefit of his or her estate. Such expenses will, subject to the eligibility criteria (see **5 Eligibility to receive compensation**, above), be payable up to an amount considered reasonable by a claims officer, even where the person bearing the cost of the funeral is otherwise ineligible to claim.

Where the victim has died, if the death was in consequence of the injury, compensation may be payable to a qualifying claimant (see **12 Where victim died in consequence of injury**, below); or if the death was otherwise than in consequence of the injury, and occurred before title to the award had been vested in the victim (see **13 Effect on awards of other payments**, below), compensation may be payable to a qualifying claimant (see **12 Where victim died in consequence of injury**, below), and no standard amount or other compensation is payable to the estate or to the qualifying claimant.

A "qualifying claimant" is a person who at the time of the deceased's death was–

(a) the partner of the deceased who was living with them as husband and wife or as a same sex partner in the same household immediately before the date of death and who, unless married to or a civil partner of that person, had been so living throughout the two years before that date; or a spouse or civil partner or former spouse or civil partner of the deceased who was financially supported by the deceased immediately before the date of death;

(b) a natural parent of the deceased, or a person who was not the natural parent but was accepted by the deceased as a parent within the deceased's family; or

(c) a natural child of the deceased, or a person who was not the natural child but was accepted by the deceased as a child within the deceased's family or was dependent on the deceased.

But a person who was criminally responsible for the death of a victim may not be a qualifying claimant (Scheme, paras 37-38).

12 Where victim died in consequence of injury

A qualifying claimant may claim an award (a "bereavement award") unless they were a former spouse or civil partner of the deceased or otherwise estranged from them immediately before the date of death. In cases where only one person qualifies for a bereavement award, the standard amount of compensation is Level 13 of the Tariff, except that where a claims officer is aware of the existence of one or more other persons who would in the event of their making a claim qualify for a bereavement award, the standard amount of compensation is Level 10 of the Tariff. Where more than one person qualifies for a bereavement award, the standard amount of compensation for each claimant is Level 10 of the Tariff.

Additional compensation may be payable to a qualifying claimant where a claims officer is satisfied that the claimant was financially or physically dependent on the deceased. A financial dependency will not be established where the deceased's only normal income was from social security benefits.

For the purposes of the Scheme, "social security benefits" includes all UK social security benefits, other state or local authority benefits and all such benefits or similar payments paid from the funds of other countries.

The amount of compensation payable in respect of dependency is calculated on the basis of loss of earnings and the cost of care. The period of loss begins from the date of the deceased's death and continues for such period as a claims officer may determine, with no account being taken, where the qualifying claimant was married to or a civil partner of the deceased, of remarriage or prospects of remarriage or of a new civil partnership or the prospects of a new civil partnership.

In assessing the dependency, the claims officer takes account of the qualifying claimant's earnings and other income, if any. Where the deceased had been living in the same household as the qualifying claimant before death, the claims officer will, in calculating the multiplicand, make such proportional reduction as he or she considers appropriate to take account of the deceased's own personal and living expenses.

Where a qualifying claimant was under 18 years of age at the time of the deceased's death and was dependent on them for parental services, compensation may also be payable for loss of that parent's services at an annual rate of Level 5 of the Tariff; and such other payments as a claims officer considers reasonable to meet other resultant losses.

Application may be made even where an award had been made to the victim in respect of the same injury before his or her death. Any such application will be subject to the conditions for the re-opening of cases (see **17 Review of decisions**, below), and any compensation payable to the qualifying claimant or claimants, except funeral expenses and the standard amount of compensation, will be reduced by the amount paid to the victim.

Where a victim who would have qualified for additional compensation for loss of earnings and/or special expenses has died, otherwise than in consequence of the injury, before such compensation was awarded, supplementary compensation may be payable to a qualifying claimant who was financially dependent on the deceased, whether or not a relevant application was made by the victim before his or her death.

The amounts payable to the victim and the qualifying claimant or claimants may not in total exceed £500,000 (Scheme, paras 38 to 44).

13 Effect on awards of other payments

The compensation payable to an applicant, other than tariff-based amounts of compensation) (see **8 Standard amount of compensation**, above, and see **12 Where victim died in consequence of injury**, above), is reduced to take account of any social security benefits or insurance payments made by way of compensation for the same contingency.

No reduction is made to take account of an insurance payment if it is made under an insurance arrangement entered into and wholly funded by the victim personally (or by the parent or guardian of a victim who was under the age of 18 at the time of the injury), except where the reduction is made to compensation payable.

A reduction will be made irrespective of the period in respect of which the social security benefits or insurance payments have been, or will be paid. In particular, the reduction will be made whether or not any actual loss occurred or will occur in that period.

No reduction will be made to take account of any social security benefits or insurance payments paid in respect of the first 28 weeks of lost earnings.

The amount of the reduction is the full value of the social security benefits or insurance payments less the amount of any income tax which has been or may be charged in respect of them.

If the benefits or payments will be paid after the date of the assessment, the claims officer will calculate the amount of the reduction as he or she would calculate a lump sum to compensate for future loss.

For the purposes of the Scheme, disablement pension payable are be treated as a social security benefit payable to compensate for loss of earnings, loss of earning capacity or loss of pension benefits.

Where the victim is alive, any compensation payable for loss of earnings (see **9 Compensation for loss of earnings**, above) is reduced to take account of any pension benefits accruing as a result of the injury which have not already been taken into account. Where the victim has died in consequence of the injury, any compensation payable is similarly reduced to take account of any pension benefits which have not already been taken into account and which are payable, as a result of the victim's death, for the benefit of the applicant (see **12 Where victim died in consequence of injury**, above).

"Pension benefits" means any payment payable as a result of the injury or death in pursuance of pension or any other rights connected with the victim's employment, and includes any gratuity of that kind and similar benefits payable under insurance policies paid for by the victim's employers. Pension rights accruing solely as a result of payments by the victim or a dependant will be disregarded.

A reduction will be made irrespective of the period in respect of which the pension benefits have been, or will be paid. In particular, a reduction will be made whether or not any actual loss of earnings or earning capacity occurred or will occur in that period. However, no reduction will be made to take account of any pension benefits paid in respect of the first 28 weeks of lost earnings.

Where such pension benefits are taxable, one half of their gross value will be deducted, but they will otherwise be deducted in full (where, for example, a lump sum payment not subject to income tax is made). However, if the pension benefits will be paid after the date of the assessment, the claims officer will calculate the amount of the reduction as he or she would calculate a lump sum to compensate for future loss. In the case of taxable pension benefits the claims officer will assume for these purposes that the applicant will receive one half of their gross value.

Where, in the opinion of a claims officer, an applicant may be or may become eligible for any social security benefits, insurance payments or pension benefits, an award may be withheld until the applicant has taken such steps as the claims officer considers reasonable to claim them.

An award will be reduced by the full value of any payment in respect of the same injury which the applicant has received or to which he has any present or future entitlement.

A claims officer may require an applicant to provide details of any steps taken or planned to obtain damages or compensation in respect of the same injury and may decline to process an application further until those details have been provided or until the applicant's attempts to obtain such damages or compensation have been exhausted.

Where a person in whose favour an award is made subsequently receives any other payment in respect of the same injury, but the award was not reduced accordingly, the person will be required to repay the Authority in full up to the amount of the other payment (Scheme, paras 45-50).

14 Determination of applications and payment

An application for compensation under the Scheme will be determined by a claims officer, and written notification of the decision will be sent to the applicant or their representative. Written acceptance of an award must be received by the Authority within 90 days of the date the decision was issued. If such an acceptance is not received within that period, and no application for a review has been made, the Authority may withdraw the award. A claims officer may grant an extension to this time limit (whether or not it has already expired) and overturn any withdrawal.

The claims officer may make such directions and arrangements, including the imposition of conditions, in connection with the acceptance, settlement, or trust, payment, repayment and/or administration of an award as they consider appropriate in all the circumstances.

Compensation is normally paid as a single lump sum, but one or more interim payments may be made where a claims officer considers this appropriate (Scheme, paras 51-52).

15 Reconsideration of decisions

A decision made by a claims officer (other than a decision made in accordance with a direction by the First-tier Tribunal on determining an appeal (see **18 Appeals**, below)) may be reconsidered at any time before actual payment of a final award where there is new evidence or a change in circumstances. In particular, the fact that an interim payment has been made does not preclude a claims officer from reconsidering issues of eligibility for an award.

Where an applicant has already been sent written notification of the decision on the application, they will be sent written notice that the decision is to be reconsidered, and any representations which they send to the Authority within 30 days of the date of such notice will be taken into account in reconsidering the decision. Whether or not any such representations are made, the applicant will be sent written notification of the outcome of the reconsideration, and where the original decision is not confirmed, such notification will include the revised decision.

Where a decision to make an award has been made by a claims officer in accordance with a direction by the First-tier Tribunal on determining an appeal, but before the award has been paid the claims officer considers that there is new evidence or a change in circumstances which justifies reconsidering whether the award should be withheld or the amount of compensation reduced, the Authority will refer the case to the First-tier Tribunal for rehearing (Scheme, paras 53-55).

16 Re-opening of cases

A decision made by a claims officer and accepted by the applicant, or a direction by the First-tier Tribunal, will normally be regarded as final, except where an appeal is reheard. A claims officer may, however, subsequently re-open a case where there has been such a material change in the victim's medical condition that injustice would occur if the original assessment of compensation were allowed to stand, or where the victim has since died in consequence of the injury.

A case will not be re-opened more than two years after the date of the final decision unless the claims officer is satisfied, on the basis of evidence presented in support of the application to re-open the case, that the renewed application can be considered without a need for further extensive enquiries (Scheme, paras 56-57).

17 Review of decisions

An applicant may seek a review of any decision by a claims officer under the Scheme—

(a) not to waive or extend the time limit for applications for compensation or applications for review;

(b) not to re-open a case;

(c) to withhold an award, including such decision made on reconsideration of an award;

(d) to make an award, including a decision to make a reduced award whether or not on reconsideration of an award;

(e) to require repayment of an award; or

(f) to withdraw an award.

An applicant may not, however, seek the review of any such decision where the decision was itself made on a review and either the applicant did not appeal against it or the appeal did not result in a direction from the First-tier Tribunal; or where the decision was made in accordance with a direction by the First-tier Tribunal on determining an appeal.

An application for the review of a decision by a claims officer must be made in writing to the Authority and must be supported by reasons together with any relevant additional information. It must be received by the Authority within 90 days of the date the decision to be reviewed was issued.

All applications for review will be considered by a different claims officer to the one who made the original decision. The officer conducting the review will reach a decision in accordance with the provisions of the Scheme applying to the original application, and will not be bound by any earlier decision either as to the eligibility of the applicant for an award or as to the amount of an award (Scheme, paras 58-60).

18 Appeals

An applicant who is dissatisfied with a decision taken on a review, or with a determination, may appeal against the decision to the First-tier Tribunal in accordance with Tribunal Procedure Rules.

19 European Convention on the Compensation of Victims of Violent Crimes

The United Kingdom has signed the European Convention on the Compensation of Victims of Violent Crimes which took effect in the UK on 1st June 1990. Under the terms of the Convention, citizens of the countries which are signatories to the Convention are entitled, if criminally injured in a signatory State, to compensation from the signatory State. Relatives of a person fatally injured in a signatory State are also able to claim compensation from that State. The Convention currently covers 21 European States. Notable exceptions include Greece, Hungary, Ireland, Italy, Poland and Russia. Compensation must at least cover loss of earnings and medical expenses and, in fatal cases, funeral expenses and loss of financial support suffered by dependants.

20 European Union co-operation

EC Council Directive 2004/80 requires Member States to set up a system of co-operation between the authorities in Member States to facilitate access to compensation where a crime is committed in a country other than that where the victim lives. The purpose is to allow the victim to turn to the authority in their own country, so easing practical and linguistic difficulties. Compensation will be paid by the authority in the Member Sate where the crime was committed.

The Victims of Violent International Crime (Arrangements for Compensation) (European Communities) Regulations 2005 designates the First-tier Tribunal as the "assisting authority" in the UK. A British resident who is a victim of a crime elsewhere in the EU will be provided by the Tribunal with essential information on the opportunities for making an application for compensation, including application forms and general guidance, and may submit such an application to the Tribunal who will transmit it the relevant authority in the Member State where the crime occurred.

B: VICTIMS' RIGHTS

21 Introduction

The Criminal Justice (Scotland) Act 2003 provides rights for victims of certain crimes. These are–

(a) the right to make a statement to be submitted to the court at any time after the prosecutor moves for sentence (or, in summary proceedings, at any time after the accused pleads guilty or is found guilty) and before sentence is passed about the effect which the crime has had upon them;

(b) a right to receive information about the release of an offender; and

(c) a right to receive information about, and make representations before, the release on licence of an offender.

The Victims and Witnesses (Scotland) Act 2014 gives victims additional rights. It provides for–

(d) victims to receive certain information about their case;

(e) a presumption that certain categories of victim are vulnerable, and so entitled to use certain special measures when giving evidence; and

(f) the court to be required to consider compensation to victims in relevant cases.

22 Victim statements

A victim of a prescribed offence (see 23 **Prescribed offences**, below) who is a natural person (i.e., not, for example, a company) has the right where proceedings are taken in prescribed courts to make a "victim statement". A victim statement is a statement as to the way in which, and degree to which, the offence has affected (and, as the case may be, continues to affect) them. If the offenders pleads, or is found, guilty, then a copy of the victim statement must be provided to the offender and will also be given to the court. In deciding on sentence, the court must have regard to so much of the statement as it considers relevant to the offence (Criminal Justice (Scotland) Act 2003, s.14). The Victim Statements (Prescribed Courts) (Scotland) Order 2009 prescribes the High Court and all sheriff courts as courts at which victim statements can be presented.

Where a statement has been made, a victim can make another statement supplementary to or in amplification to the original statement at any time before sentencing.

Where the victim has died, the statement can be made by any or all of the four highest listed of their–
- (a) spouse;
- (b) cohabitee (of either sex, provided they have been cohabiting for at least six months);
- (c) son or daughter (or person for whom they had parental responsibility);
- (d) parent (or person with parental responsibility for them);
- (e) brother or sister;
- (f) grandparent;
- (g) grandchild;
- (h) uncle or aunt;
- (i) nephew or niece.

If the victim died whilst under the age of 16 then, in addition to the four nearest relatives, the child's carer (if different) is also entitled to make a statement.

Where a victim is incapable of giving a statement because of mental or physical incapacity, their nearest relative from the above list can make the statement on their behalf. Where a victim is aged under 12, the right to make a statement lies with their carer.

23 Prescribed offences

The prescribed offences which gave rise to the right to make a victim statement are (Victim Statements (Prescribed Offences) (No. 2) (Scotland) Order 2009)–
- (a) non-sexual crimes of violence (e.g., assault, murder, culpable homicide, robbery, etc);
- (b) sexual crimes of violence and indecent crimes (e.g., rape, indecent assault, etc.);
- (c) theft by housebreaking;
- (d) racially aggravated crimes;
- (f) serious road traffic offences involving death, such as causing death by dangerous driving and causing death by careless driving whilst under the influence of drink or drugs;
- (g) fireraising;
- (h) conspiring or inciting any of the above offences, or aiding, abetting, counselling or procuring the commission of any of them.

24 Information as to the release of an offender

If they have asked to receive such information then, unless it is inappropriate because of exceptional circumstances, the Scottish Ministers must give any natural person against whom an offence has been committed information as to (Criminal Justice (Scotland) Act 2003, s.16, as amended by the Victim Notification Scheme (Scotland) Order 2008)–
- (a) the date on which the offender is released;
- (b) if the offender dies before release, the date of death;
- (c) the transfer of the offender to a place outside Scotland;
- (d) the first time the offender is entitled to be considered for temporary release;
- (e) the offender being unlawfully at large from a prison or young offender's institution;
- (f) where the convicted person (i) was released as in (a) above or was unlawfully at large as in (e) above, and (ii) subsequently has been returned to a prison or young offenders institution to continue serving the sentence, the date of the person's return.

The right to receive information only arises if the offender is–
- (i) sentenced to imprisonment or detention for a period of 18 months or more;
- (ii) sentenced to life imprisonment or detention for life; or
- (iii) sentenced to detention without time limit (which may be the case where a child is convicted of a serious offence).

Where the victim has died at the time the information is to be given, it is to be given instead to those entitled to make a statement (see **22 Victim statements**, above).

Where the offender was sentenced to imprisonment or detention for a period of less than 18 months, the Scottish Ministers must, if any person who is or appears to be a victim in relation to the offence so requests, notify them of any lawful release or escape from prison of the offender, unless .the Scottish Ministers consider that there is an identified risk of harm to victim if notification occurs (Victims and Witnesses (Scotland) Act 2014, s.27A).

25 Release on licence

If they have asked to do so, then a person entitled to receive information (see **24 Information as to the**

release of an offender, above) in respect of an offender must be given an opportunity to make written representations to the Scottish Ministers before any decision is taken to release the offender on licence (Criminal Justice (Scotland) Act 2003, s.17). The representations can be as to the release itself, or as to conditions which might be specified in the licence.

The right does not apply if the offender is under the age of 16 at the date on which the Scottish Ministers refer the case to the Parole Board. Similarly it does not apply if the release of the offender is ordered on compassionate grounds.

Whether or not the victim makes representations, the Parole Board (or Scottish Ministers if they set conditions on an offender's release) must notify him as to–

(a) whether or not it has recommended or directed the offender's release;

(b) if it has recommended or directed release, whether it has recommended any conditions;

(c) any conditions which relate to contact with the victim or their family;

(d) where release is automatic, whether any conditions have been recommended (and if so, whether any are within (iii) above); and

(e) such other information as the Board considers appropriate in the circumstances.

26 Right to case information

Victims (and witnesses) have a right to ask for and be given certain information about criminal proceedings (Victims and Witnesses (Scotland) Act 2014, s.6). The right applies to a person who–

(1) appears to be a victim of the offence or alleged offence;

(2) where the person in (a) has died because of, or apparently because of the offence or alleged offence, a prescribed relative of the person;

(3) a witness or potential witness in criminal proceedings;

(4) a person who has given a statement in relation to the offence or alleged offence to the police or the prosecutor.

The information which may be requested – from the police, the prosecutor or the Scottish Court Service – is information as to–

(a) a decision not to proceed with a criminal investigation and any reasons for it;

(b) a decision to end a criminal investigation and any reasons for it;

(c) a decision not to institute criminal proceedings against a person and any reasons for it;

(d) the place in which a trial is to be held;

(e) the date on which and time at which a trial is to be held;

(f) the nature of charges libelled against a person;

(g) the place in which the hearing of an appeal arising from a trial is to be held;

(h) the date on which and time at which the hearing of an appeal arising from a trial is to be held;

(i) the stage that criminal proceedings have reached;

(j) the final decision of a court in a trial or any appeal arising from a trial, and any reasons for it.

27 The Victims' Code for Scotland

The Scottish Ministers must prepare and publish a Victims' Code for Scotland, setting out the following information (or directing the reader as to where that information is set out) (Victims and Witnesses (Scotland) Act 2014, s.3B)–

(a) the types of support that victims may obtain and from whom that support can be obtained;

(b) the procedures for making complaints with regard to a criminal offence and the victim's role in connection with such procedures;

(c) how and under what conditions victims may obtain protection, including special measures;

(d) how and under what conditions victims may access legal advice, legal aid or any other sort of advice which the Scottish Ministers consider relevant to the needs of victims;

(e) how and under what conditions victims may obtain compensation;

(f) how and under what conditions victims are entitled to interpretation and translation;

(g) in relation to a criminal offence which was not committed in Scotland, any measures, procedures or arrangements, which are available to protect victims' interests in Scotland;

(h) the available procedures for making complaints against any competent authority in relation to a breach of victims' rights;

(i) the contact details for all competent authorities;

(j) the available restorative justice services; and

(k) how and under what conditions victims may be reimbursed for their reasonable expenses incurred as a result of their participation in criminal proceedings.

The Police must ensure that, as soon as reasonably practicable after they identify a person who is or appears to be a victim in relation to an offence or alleged offence, they inform them that they may request a copy of the Victims' Code for Scotland, and information relating to the rights of victims (s.3C).

Where a person who is or appears to be a victim in relation to an offence or alleged offence makes a complaint about the offence or alleged offence to the police, the police must as soon as reasonably practicable provide them with a written acknowledgement of the complaint which states the basic elements of the offence or alleged offence complained of (s.3G).

28 The right to understand and be understood

A competent authority (e.g., the police or the Scottish Courts and Tribunals Service) must take appropriate measures to ensure that a victim both understands and is understood in their dealings with them (Victims and Witnesses (Scotland) Act 2014, s.3E). A victim may also be assisted by someone of their choice on first contact with the competent authority where it is considered that the victim requires assistance to communicate; the onus being on the victim to identify and arrange for this support. This right to be assisted does not apply to a hearing in criminal proceedings where other general assistance for victims is available, or where it would be contrary to the interests of the person or prejudicial to any criminal proceedings.

There is also a right to translation and interpretation services where appropriate during an investigation or prosecution. (s.3F).

29 Victims' rights in relation to offences committed abroad

Where a person who is or appears to be a victim in relation to an offence or alleged offence committed in a Member State of the EU other than the United Kingdom makes a complaint about that offence to the police, and criminal proceedings cannot be raised in Scotland, the police must ensure that the complaint is transmitted without undue delay to the appropriate authority of the Member State in which the offence or alleged offence was committed (Victims and Witnesses (Scotland) Act 2014, s.3J).

30 Protection of victims during investigations

During criminal investigations, a victim may be accompanied by a person of their choice during interview, and may also be accompanied by their legal representative if they so choose (Victims and Witnesses (Scotland) Act 2014, s.9A).

The police must carry out an individual assessment of a victim to identify whether they are vulnerable to victimisation, intimidation or retaliation, and whether they would benefit from the use of certain special measures such as the use of specially designed interview rooms, specialist interviewers, or using the same interviewer throughout the process (ss.9B, 9C).

Reasonable steps (such as providing separate waiting rooms for victims in court buildings) must be taken to enable victims (and their families) to avoid contact with the person suspected, accused or convicted of the offence. This obligation only extends to places within the control of a competent authority, such as a police station, prosecutor's office or court building, and does not extend to public places (s.9D).

Reasonable steps must also be taken to protect the privacy of a victim, and where they or a family member is a child, to prevent disclosure of any information that could lead to the identification of the child, and to prevent the disclosure of any images of them or any their family (s.9E). This does not apply to the giving of evidence in a hearing in criminal proceedings.

31 Counselling

Where it appears to a constable that a person has been the victim of a crime he may, with their consent, give their details to a prescribed body which provides counselling or other support to victims of crime (Criminal Justice (Scotland) Act 2003, s.18). Where the victim has died, the constable may, with their consent, pass on the details of any other person who he considers would derive benefit from the counselling or support.

The Police must ensure that, as soon as reasonably practicable after they identify a person who is or appears to be a victim in relation to an offence or alleged offence, they inform them that they may request a referral, or contact providers of victim support services directly without referral (Victims and Witnesses (Scotland) Act 2014, s.3D).

The only bodies so far prescribed for these purposes are Rape Crisis Scotland and Victim Support Scotland (Victims' Rights (Prescribed Bodies) (Scotland) Order 2010).

32 Child victims and deceased victims

Where a victim is under the age of 18, they may still exercise their rights under the Victims and Witnesses (Scotland) Act 2014 if the competent authority (i.e., the police, prosecutor or court service) decides it is in their best interests to do so. Alternatively, the child's parents may in some cases exercise the rights of the child victim (s. 29A).

Where a victim's death has been caused by the offence in question, their rights under the 2014 Act may be transferred to their relatives (s.29B).

33 Authorities

Criminal Injuries Compensation Act 1995

Criminal Justice (Scotland) Act 2003

Victims and Witnesses (Scotland) Act 2014

Victim Notification Scheme (Scotland) Order 2008 (S.S.I. 2008 No. 185)

Victim Statements (Prescribed Courts) (Scotland) Order 2009 (S.S.I. 2009 No. 134)

Victim Statements (Prescribed Offences) (No. 2) (Scotland) Order 2009 (S.S.I. 2009 No. 71)

Victims of Violent International Crime (Arrangements for Compensation) (European Communities) Regulations 2005, as amended (S.I. 2005 No. 3396 and 2008 No. 2683)

Victims' Rights (Prescribed Bodies) (Scotland) Order 2010 (S.S.I. 2010 No. 165)

European Convention on the Compensation of Victims of Violent Crimes 24th November 1983

The Criminal Injuries Compensation Scheme 2008

EC Council Directive 2004/80

CRIMINAL RECORD CHECKS

1 Contents

This Note covers the criminal conviction and criminal record certificates which an employer can insist that a prospective employee provide.

Note.– Criminal Records Bureau (CRB) checks are now called Disclosure and Barring Service (DBS) checks.

2 Introduction

Part V of the Police Act 1997 provides for a system of registration for employers and licensing bodies in sensitive areas of work (e.g., work with children and young people or vulnerable adults) who can then obtain information about prospective employees through–

(a) criminal record certificates; and

(b) enhanced criminal record certificates.

The Act also provides for individuals to apply for criminal record certificates, enhanced criminal record certificates, and criminal conviction certificates.

Applications for disclosure can be made in England and Wales through the Criminal Records Agency to the Disclosure and Barring Service (see below); and in Scotland through Disclosure Scotland, an executive agency of the Scottish Government.

In England and Wales, the Criminal Records Bureau (CRB), an executive agency of the Home Office established under Part V of the Police Act 1997, enabled those to access criminal record checks. Provisions in the Protection of Freedoms Act 2012 have established the Disclosure and Barring Service (DBS). As a result, the CRB has merged with the Independent Safeguarding Authority to combine the criminal record functions of the CRB with the barring functions of the Independent Safeguarding Authority (as to which see the Note on **Protection of Children and Young Persons**), those functions now being the responsibility of the DBS (2012 Act, s.88 and the Protection of Freedoms Act 2012 (Disclosure and Barring Service Transfer of Functions) Order 2012). The Disclosure and Barring Service (Core Functions) Order 2012 specifies the core functions of the DBS under Part 5 of the Police Act 1997. Functions which are core functions of the DBS cannot be delegated to a person who is neither an appointed member nor a member of staff of the DBS. These functions include decision-making about what information needs to be submitted in an application for a certificate, setting conditions for the use of the electronic service and the up-date service, indentifying the chief officer of police for the purposes of providing information in relation to an application, verifying the identity of applicants (except in relation to an application for a criminal conviction certificate under the Police Act 1997, s.112) receiving police information and paying fees for that information and maintaining the register of persons able to countersign applications.

The Home Office has taken over the function of running the Police National Computer from the National Policing Improvement Agency. The Police National Computer is the names database of convictions, cautions, warnings and reprimands which are prescribed as "central records" for the purposes of ss.112(3) and 113A(6) of the Police Act 1997.

3 The ACPO Criminal Records Office

The Association of Chief Police Officers (ACPO) Criminal Records Office (ACRO) provides Subject Access disclosures from the Police National Computer (PNC) on behalf of most police forces in England and Wales, Northern Ireland, Jersey, the Isle of Man and the British Transport Police. It is a service for individuals who would like to know what information is held about them on the PNC. A Subject Access Request (SAR1) form, which is available at <http://www.acro.police.uk/subject_access.aspx>, will need to be completed.

ACRO are also able to issue police certificates, which are criminal records check issued to people who want to emigrate to a number of countries including Australia, Belgium, Canada, Cayman Islands, New Zealand, South Africa, and the United States of America. The certificate details whether or not the applicant has a criminal record in the UK and is required as part of the visa process. The certificate can also include foreign criminal history information where it has been disclosed to the UK.

*Note.–*ACRO does not provide Disclosure and Barring Service (DBS) checks for people who are applying to work with children or vulnerable adults in the UK (for which the DBS website should be used: see <https://www.gov.uk/government/organisations/disclosure-and-barring-service>), and is unable to provide PNC disclosures for UK employment purposes (for these services go to the Disclosure Scotland website <http://www.disclosurescotland.co.uk/about/index.htm>. It is not necessary to live in Scotland to use this service).

4 Types of criminal record check

There are various types of criminal record check, depending on the circumstances.

Basic DBS checks.

All employers are entitled to ask, and know, about any unspent convictions a person has – they are therefore entitled to request a basic check, which will provide details of unspent convictions.

Standard and Enhanced DBS checks

If a job is exempt from the Rehabilitation of Offenders Act 1974 (see the Note on **Rehabilitation of Offenders**), the employer is entitled to ask for a standard or enhanced Disclosure and Barring Service check (whether the check is Standard or Enhanced will depend on the job itself).

Note.– An employer can only apply for a check if the job or role is eligible for one.

Enhanced check with additional check of the DBS Barred Lists

Jobs that involve carrying out certain activities with children and/or adults may need an enhanced DBS check together with a check of the barred lists. This will check whether or not someone is included in the "barred lists" of individuals who are unsuitable for working with either children or adults.

Overview of the Types of DBS Check

Information included	Basic DBS check	Standard DBS check	Enhanced DBS check
Unspent convictions	YES	YES	YES
Spent convictions (unless protected)	NO	YES	YES
Cautions, reprimands and final warnings (unless protected)	NO	YES	YES
Inclusion on the children or adult barred list (where relevant to the job)	NO	NO	YES, but only if required by the job in question
*Other relevant information	NO	NO	YES

*i.e., any non-conviction information which the police might hold, such as about arrests, matters that resulted in no further action or not guilty verdicts. Such information will not be routinely disclosed, but the police may do so if they feel that it is relevant to the job in respect of which the application has been made.

5 Criminal record certificates

An individual may make an application for his or her criminal record certificate if (i) the applicant is aged 16 years or over at the time of the application, (ii) the application is countersigned by a "registered person" (see **6 Registered persons**, below), and (iii) accompanied by a statement by the registered person that the certificate is required for the purposes of an "exempted question" (Police Act 1997, s.113A). An application need not be countersigned if it is submitted electronically and the requirements and conditions for an electronic application are complied with. An application must be made in the prescribed manner and form and the prescribed fee paid. The form is prescribed by the Police Act 1997 (Criminal Records) Regulations 2002, as amended. For the payment of fees see **16 Fees for certificates**, below.

An "exempted question" is one which overrides the provisions as to the non-disclosure of spent convictions in the Rehabilitation of Offenders Act 1974 s.4(2) (see the Note on **Rehabilitation of Offenders**).

Where a person is seeking Crown employment, the application for a certificate need not be countersigned and the accompanying statement may be made by a government Minister rather than by a registered person (s.114).

The certificate is issued to the applicant only, so allowing him to make representations regarding the information released without the disputed information already having been seen by the registered person (who is generally the employer).

A criminal record certificate is a certificate which gives the prescribed details of every "relevant matter" relating to the applicant which is recorded in central records, or states that there is no such matter (s.113A(3)). In relation to a person who has one conviction only, a "relevant matter" means (s.113A(6))–

(a) a conviction of an offence within s.113A(6D) (see below);

(b) a conviction in respect of which a custodial sentence or a sentence of service detention was imposed; or

(c) a current conviction.

In relation to any other person, a "relevant matter" means–

(d) any conviction;

(e) a caution given in respect of an offence within s.113A(6D);

(f) a current caution.

For the purposes of the definition of "relevant matter" as it has effect in England and Wales (s.113A(6E))–

(g) "conviction" has the same meaning as in the Rehabilitation of Offenders Act 1974, and includes a spent conviction within the meaning of that Act;

(h) "caution" includes a caution which is spent for the purposes of Schedule 2 to that Act but excludes a disregarded caution within the meaning of Chapter 4 of Part 5 of the Protection of Freedoms Act 2012;

(i) a person's conviction is a current conviction if (i) the person was aged 18 or over on the date of the conviction and that date fell within the 11 year period ending with the day on which the certificate is issued, or (ii) the person was aged under 18 on the date of conviction and that date fell within the period of 5 years and 6 months ending with the day on which the certificate is issued;

(j) a caution given to a person is a current caution if (i) the person was aged 18 or over on the date it was given and that date fell within the 6 year period ending with the day on which the certificate is issued, or (ii) the person was aged under 18 on the date it was given and that date fell within the 2 year period ending with the day on which the certificate is issued;

(k) "custodial sentence" and "sentence of service detention" have the same meaning as in s.5(8) of the Rehabilitation of Offenders Act 1974.

The offences referred to in the definition of "relevant matter", as it has effect in England and Wales, are as follows (s.113A(6D))–

(i) murder;

(ii) an offence under s.67(1A) of the Medicines Act 1968 (prescribing, etc. a medicinal product in contravention of certain conditions);

(iii) an offence under any of ss.126 to 129 of the Mental Health Act 1983;

(iv) an offence specified in the Schedule to the Disqualification from Caring for Children (England) Regulations 2002;

(v) an offence specified in Schedule 15 to the Criminal Justice Act 2003 (specified offences for the purposes of Chapter 5 of Part 12 of that Act (dangerous offenders));

(vi) an offence under the following provisions of the Mental Capacity Act 2005: s.44 (ill-treatment or neglect); paragraph 4 of Schedule 1 (applications and procedure for registration); paragraph 4 of Schedule 4 (duties of attorney in event of incapacity of donor);

(vii) an offence under ss.7, 9 or 19 of the Safeguarding Vulnerable Groups Act 2006 (offences in respect of regulated activity);

(viii) an offence specified in s.17(3)(a), (b) or (c) of the Health and Social Care Act 2008 (cancellation of registration), apart from an offence under s.76 of that Act (disclosure of confidential personal information);

(ix) an offence specified in the Schedule to the Safeguarding Vulnerable Groups Act 2006 (Prescribed Criteria and Miscellaneous Provisions) Regulations 2009;

(x) an offence specified in Schedule 2 or 3 to the Childcare (Disqualification) Regulations 2009;

(xi) an offence which has been superseded (directly or indirectly) by an offence within paragraphs (i) to (x) above;

(xii) an offence of attempting or conspiring to commit any offence falling within paragraphs (i) to (xi) above, or inciting or aiding, abetting, counselling or procuring the commission of any such offence, or an offence under Part 2 of the Serious Crime Act 2007 (encouraging or assisting crime) committed in relation to any such offence;

(xiii) an offence under the law of Scotland or Northern Ireland or any territory outside the United Kingdom which corresponds to an offence under the law of England and Wales within any of paragraphs (i) to (xii) above;

(xiv) any offence under s.42 of the Armed Forces Act 2006 in relation to which the corresponding offence under the law of England and Wales (within the meaning of that section) is an offence within any of paragraphs (i) to (xii) above;

(xv) an offence under s.70 of the Army Act 1955, s.70 of the Air Force Act 1955 or s.42 of the Naval Discipline Act 1957 of which the corresponding civil offence (within the meaning of that Act) is an offence within any of paragraphs (i) to (xii) above.

6 Registered persons

A person can be registered if they are (Police Act 1997, s.120)–

(a) a corporate or unincorporated body;

(b) an office holder appointed under any enactment; or

(c) a person who employs others in the course of a business;

who is likely to ask exempted questions, or

(d) a body which is likely to countersign an application for a criminal record certificate at the request of a body or individual asking exempted questions (this allows for registration by a body acting as an umbrella organisation for a number of other registered bodies).

The Disclosure and Barring Service or Scottish Ministers may refuse to register a person, or remove them from the register, if it appears to them that the registration of that person is likely to make it possible for information to become available to an individual who, in their opinion, is not a suitable person to have access to it (s.120A, added by the Criminal Justice and Police Act 2001 and the Criminal Justice (Scotland) Act 2003). An organisation that has previously been removed from the register as a result of a breach of the CRB Conditions of Registration can also be refused registration (s.120AA).

The Police Act 1997 (Criminal Records) (Registration) Regulations 2006 make provision as to registration. A body applying for registration must supply details of those who will act as countersignatories or transmit applications electronically, together with a specimen of their signature and the nature of the questions that they are likely to ask (Reg. 3). Authorised countersignatories can also be added at a later date. The Disclosure and Barring Service can refuse to accept, or to continue to accept, the nomination of any person who in its opinion is not a suitable person to have access to the information which is likely to become available to him as a result of the registration of the nominating body (Reg. 3A). Registered persons who countersign applications for criminal record certificates and enhanced criminal record certificates must be aged 18 years or over (s.120(4)).

Similar provision is made for Scotland in the Police Act 1997 (Criminal Records) (Registration) (Scotland) Regulations 2010.

A fee of £300 is payable on an application for inclusion in the register. In the case of a registered body which wants to register more than one person, a fee of £5 is payable by for the inclusion of the second and each subsequent name entered in the register (Reg. 5).

The fees payable in Scotland are £75 and £10 respectively, and this includes up to four countersignatories (Reg. 8). For any additional countersignatories the fee is £15 each (Reg. 9).

Provisions allow registered persons to track the progress of an application for a criminal record certificate or an enhanced criminal record certificate, including whether it has been issued and for the registered person to be informed that the certificate does not contain any relevant information when that is the case (s.120AC, inserted by the Protection of Freedoms Act 2012, s.79).

7 Enhanced criminal record certificates

An individual can make an application for his or her enhanced criminal record certificate where the application is made in the prescribed manner and form and the prescribed fee is paid (Police Act 1997, s.113B(1)). The form is prescribed by the Police Act 1997 (Criminal Records) Regulations 2002, as amended. For the payment of fees see **16 Fees for certificates**, below. The applicant must be aged 16 years or over at the time of the application. An enhanced criminal record certificate will not only contain details of every "relevant matter" (for the meaning of which see **5 Criminal record certificates**, above) relating to the applicant, or state that there is no such matter or information, but also any information from local police records, Police Scotland, and information which any relevant chief officer of police "reasonably believes to be relevant" (s.113B(3)-(4)). This could include "non-conviction" information such as acquittals, decisions not to prosecute, and details of known associates of the applicant which give rise to concern. Where the police are engaged in an ongoing criminal investigation and the premature release of the relevant information to an applicant for an enhanced criminal record certificate might compromise that they may, using their common law powers to prevent crime and protect the public, pass such information to a potential employer where they consider it justified and proportionate without including it in the certificate.

S.50A of the Safeguarding Vulnerable Groups Act 2006 enables the police to use information given to them by the Disclosure and Barring Service (see the Note on **Protection of Children and Young Persons**) for prescribed purposes and the Safeguarding Vulnerable Groups Act 2006 (Miscellaneous Provisions) Regulations 2012, Reg. 29 provides that the police can use information given to them by the Disclosure and Barring Service for the purposes of disclosing it as relevant information on an enhanced criminal record certificate.

The application must be countersigned by a registered person and accompanied by a statement that the certificate is required for a prescribed purpose (s.113B(2)). An application need not be countersigned if it is submitted electronically and the requirements and conditions for an electronic application are complied with. In England and Wales, the prescribed purposes are set out in the Police Act 1997 (Criminal Records) Regulations 2002 as (Reg. 5A)–

    (a) considering the applicant's suitability to engage in any activity which is "work with children" (as defined in Reg. 5C, see **8 "Work with children"**, below);

    (b) considering the applicant's suitability to engage in any activity which is work with adults (as defined in Reg. 5B, see **9 "Work with adults"**, below);

    (c) obtaining or holding certain gaming licences;

    (d) considering a person's suitability for employment by the Gambling Commission;

    (e) obtaining or holding a licence under ss.5 or 6 of the National Lottery etc Act 1993 (running or promoting lotteries);

    (f) considering the suitability of any person appointed by the Commissioner for Older People in Wales to assist him in the discharge of his functions or authorised to discharge his functions on his behalf;

    (g) considering the applicant's suitability for work as a person who provides immigration advice or services as defined in the Immigration and Asylum Act 1999, s.82(1) and who is (i) a registered person under Part 5 of that Act, or (ii) a person who acts on behalf of and under the supervision of such a registered person, or (iii) a person who is exempt by s.84(4)(a) to (c) of that Act;

    (h) considering the applicant's suitability to obtain or retain a licence under the Misuse of Drugs Regulations 2001, Reg. 5 or under Article 3(2) of Regulation 2004/273/EC or under Article 6(1) of Regulation 2005/111/EC where the question relates to any person who as a result of his role in the body concerned is required to be named in the application for such a licence (or would have been so required if that person had had that role at the time the application was made);

    (i) considering an individual's suitability to possess, acquire and/or transfer prohibited weapons (within the meaning of s.5 of the Firearms Act 1968) and associated ammunition;

    (j) assessing the suitability of a person for any office or employment which relates to national security; and

    (k) considering the applicant's suitability to obtain or hold a taxi driver licence.

Similar provision for Scotland is contained in the Police Act 1997 (Criminal Records) (Scotland) Regulations 2010.

Where a person is seeking Crown employment or a judicial appointment, the application for a certificate need not be countersigned and the accompanying statement may be made by a government Minister or a person nominated by a Minister rather than by a registered person (s.116).

8 "Work with children"

For the purposes of enhanced criminal record certificates, "work with children" means (Criminal Records) Regulations 2002, Reg. 5C)–

- (a) considering the applicant's suitability to engage in any activity which is a regulated activity relating to children (within the meaning of the Safeguarding Vulnerable Groups Act 2006, Sch. 4, Pt 1), including as it had effect immediately before the coming into force of the Protection of Freedoms Act 2012, s.64 (which restricted the scope of regulated activity);
- (b) a decision made by an adoption agency as to a person's suitability to adopt a child or be a special guardian including obtaining information in respect of any person aged 18 years or over living in the same household as the prospective adopter/guardian;
- (c) registration for child minding or providing day care under the Children and Families (Wales) Measure 2010 Part 2, or Chapters 2, 3 or 4 of Part 3 of the Childcare Act 2006, including assessing the suitability of any person to have regular contact with children who are (i) aged 16 or over and living on the premises at which the child minding or day care is being or is to be provided, or (ii) aged 16 or over and working, or who will be working, on the premises at which the child minding or day care is being or is to be provided at times when such child minding or day care is being or is to be provided;
- (ca) registration as a childminder agency under the Childcare Act 2006, Part 3 Chapter 2A or 3A, considering the applicant's suitability to manage a childminder agency; and considering the applicant's suitability to work for a childminder agency in any capacity which requires them to enter childcare premises and enables them, in the normal course of duties, to have contact with children for whom childcare is provided, or access to sensitive or personal information about children for whom childcare is provided;
- (d) placing children with foster parents or the exercise of any duty as to the welfare of privately fostered children, including obtaining information in respect of any person who is (i) aged 18 or over and living in the same household as a person who is, or who wishes to be approved as, a foster parent within the meaning of the Safeguarding Vulnerable Groups Act 2006, s.53(7)(a) or (b), (ii) aged 16 or over and living in the same household as a person who fosters, or intends to foster, a child privately within the meaning of the Children Act 1989, s.66(1), or who is otherwise a private foster parent within the meaning of the Safeguarding Vulnerable Groups Act 2006, s.53(7)(c) and (8);
- (e) obtaining information in respect of persons who are aged 16 and over and who are members of the household of another person who is having or who has had their suitability assessed for the purposes of working closely with children (including persons engaging in regulated activity relating to children or working in a further education institution or 16 to 19 Academy where the normal duties of that work involve regular contact with persons aged under 18) where both of those persons live on the same premises as the work takes place (e.g., the spouse of a boarding school manager);
- (f) work done infrequently which, if done frequently, would be regulated activity relating to children within the meaning of the Safeguarding Vulnerable Groups Act 2006 Sch. 4, Pt 1, including as it had effect immediately before the coming into force of the Protection of Freedoms Act 2012, s.64 (which restricted the scope of regulated activity);
- (g) registration under Part II of the Care Standards Act 2000 (establishments and agencies);
- (h) registration under Part IV of the Care Standards Act 2000 (social care workers);
- (i) considering the applicant's suitability for work in a further education institution or a 16 to 19 Academy where the normal duties of that work involve regular contact with persons aged under 18.

9 "Work with adults"

For the purposes of enhanced criminal record certificates, "work with adults" means (Criminal Records) Regulations 2002, Reg. 5B)–

- (a) any employment or other work which is normally carried out in a hospital used only for the provision of high security psychiatric services;
- (b) the provision to an adult of a regulated activity relating to vulnerable adults within the meaning of the Safeguarding Vulnerable Groups Act 2006, Sch. 4, Pt. 2;
- (c) the provision of specified care, treatment etc (as set out in Reg. 5B(6)) to an adult who receives a health or social care service (as defined in Reg. 5B(9)) or a specified activity (as defined in Reg. 5B(10)), provided that the person carrying out the activity does so–
    - (i) at any time on more than three days in any period of 30 days;
    - (ii) at any time between 2 a.m. and 6 a.m. and the activity gives the person the opportunity to have face-to-face contact with the adult; or
    - (iii) at least once a week on an ongoing basis;
- (d) the regular day to day management or supervision of a person mentioned in (c) above;
- (e) the exercise of any of the functions of the Welsh Ministers relating to the inspection of specified bodies, so far as the function gives the person exercising it the opportunity to have contact with an adult who receives a health or social care service or a specified activity (both as defined) in so far as the inspection relates to social services, care, treatment or therapy provided for adults who receive a health or social care service or a specified activity;

(f) the exercise of a specified function of the Care Quality Commission in so far as it involves the provision of social services, care, treatment or therapy for adults who receive a health or social care service or a specified activity, and gives the person exercising the function the opportunity, in consequence of anything they are permitted or required to do in the exercise of that function, to have contact with an adult who receives a health or social care service or a specified activity;

(g) the exercise of a function of a person who is a—

(i) a member of a body such as a local authority which discharges any social services functions which relate wholly or mainly to adults who receive a health or social care service or a specified activity;

(ii) a chief executive or a director of adult social services/social services of a local authority that has any social services functions;

(iii) a Commissioner or deputy Commissioner for older people in Wales;

(iv) a charity trustee of a charity whose workers normally engage in any activity which is work with adults;

(v) a person who is required to register to carry out a regulated activity within the meaning of the Health and Social Care Act 2008 where that activity will be carried out in relation to an adult who receives a health or social care service.

10 Employment with children and vulnerable adults

If an application for a criminal record certificate (or enhanced certificate) is accompanied by a statement from the registered person that it is required for the purpose of assessing the applicant's suitability—

(a) for a child care or teaching position;

(b) for work with vulnerable adults (paid or unpaid);

(c) for work involving the provision of care or advocacy services to vulnerable adults, or

(d) as the Commissioner for Older People in Wales or working for him,

then the certificate will also state whether the applicant is included on the lists of people prohibited from taking such positions kept under the Protection of Children Act 1999, the Care Standards Act 2000, the Education Act 2002, the Safeguarding Vulnerable Groups Act 2006 (as to which see the Note on **Protection of Children and Young Persons**) or the equivalent Scottish or Northern Irish provisions (Police Act 1997, ss.113C and 113D). Only one application is therefore needed to search all the lists and obtain a criminal record certificate.

11 Suitability information

In prescribed cases an enhanced criminal record certificate must also contain "suitability information" relating to the children or vulnerable adults (Police Act 1997, ss.113BA, 113BB). "Suitability information" is information as to whether a person is barred from or subject to monitoring in relation to a regulated activity and, if he is barred, the circumstances as to the barring; whether the Disclosure and Barring Service is considering barring (not Scotland); or whether a person is prohibited from participating in the management of an independent school.

The Police Act 1997 (Criminal Records) (No. 2) Regulations 2009, as amended, prescribes the cases in which suitability information in relation to children and vulnerable adults must be included on an enhanced criminal record certificate. The prescribed cases are, generally, those which involve regular contact with children and vulnerable adults (children's and adults' barred list information).

12 Criminal conviction certificates

S.112 of the Police Act 1997 makes provision for a person to apply for a criminal conviction certificate. The applicant must be aged 16 years or over at the time of the application. Such a certificate will give details of that person's convictions and conditional cautions or state that there are none. For these purposes, a conviction/conditional caution does not include a spent conviction/conditional caution which will not therefore appear on the certificate. Any employer will be able to ask a potential employee to provide a criminal conviction certificate.

13 Evidence of identity

An application for a certificate must be accompanied by such evidence as to identity as the Disclosure and Barring Service may require. This may include fingerprints and such information as he thinks is appropriate from data held by (a) the UK Passport Agency; (b) the Driver and Vehicle Licensing Agency; (c) the Secretary of State in connection with keeping records of national insurance numbers; and (d) such other persons or for such purposes as may be prescribed (Police Act 1997, s.118).

The disclosure application form for England and Wales (prescribed by the Police Act 1997 (Criminal Records) Regulations 2002) provides for an applicant to give details of his national insurance number, marital status, number of financially dependent children under 18, mother's maiden name, occupancy and employment status, and a referee; and for the registered person to give details of the evidence of the applicant's identity seen by him (e.g., passport, driving licence, birth or marriage certificate details, etc).

14 Challenging a certificate

Where an applicant believes that the information contained in a certificate is inaccurate, he can apply for a new certificate (Police Act 1997, s.117). S.117A allows a person other than an applicant to make such an application where that person believes that information provided in accordance with s.113B (see **7 Enhanced criminal record certificates**, above) and included in a certificate under ss.113B or 116 is not relevant or ought not to be included in the certificate. The Disclosure and Barring Service could consider fingerprint evidence where, for example, there is a dispute as to identity (s.118).

15 Up-dating information

In certain circumstances the Secretary of State must, on the request of a "relevant person" give up-date information to that person about a criminal conviction certificate, a criminal record certificate, or an enhanced criminal record certificate which is subject to up-date arrangements (Police Act 1997 s.116A, as inserted by the Protection of Freedoms Act 2012, s.83). "Relevant person" means the individual whose certificate it is or any person who is authorised by the individual (and, if relevant, is seeking the information for the purposes of an exempted question) (s.116A(11)). "Up-date information" means information that there is no information recorded in central records which would be included in a new certificate but is not included in the current certificate, or advice to apply for a new certificate or (as the case may be) request another person to apply for such a certificate (s.116A(8)). A certificate is subject to up-date arrangements if condition A, B or C below is met and the arrangements have not ceased to have effect. The conditions are (s.116A(4) to (6)):

Condition A.
Condition A is that–
  (a) the individual who applied for the certificate made an application at the same time to the Secretary of State for the certificate to be subject to up-date arrangements;
  (b) the individual has paid the prescribed fee (see **16 Fees for certificates**, below);
  (c) the Secretary of State has granted the application for the certificate to be subject to up-date arrangements; and
  (d) the period of 12 months beginning with the date on which the grant comes into force has not expired.

Condition B.
Condition B is that–
  (a) the individual whose certificate it is has made an application to the Secretary of State to renew or (as the case may be) further renew unexpired up-date arrangements in relation to the certificate;
  (b) the individual has paid the prescribed fee;
  (c) the Secretary of State has granted the application;
  (d) the grant has come into force on the expiry of the previous up-date arrangements; and
  (e) the period of 12 months beginning with the date on which the grant has come into force has not expired.

Condition C.
Condition C is that–
  (a) the certificate was issued under s.117(2) or s.117A(5)(b) (disputes about accuracy of certificates); and
  (b) the certificate which it superseded was subject to up-date arrangements immediately before it was superseded, and would still be subject to those arrangements had it not been superseded.

When the updating service advises that a new certificate should be applied for, such a certificate is applied for, and the applicant does not, within a prescribed period, send a copy of it to "the relevant person" (to be prescribed), the Disclosure and Barring Service must send a copy to the registered body if it makes a request within a prescribed period and no prescribed circumstances apply (s.120AD).

16 Fees for certificates

In England and Wales, an application for a criminal record certificate must be accompanied by a fee of £26 and that for an enhanced criminal record certificate by a fee of £44, unless in either case the application is made by someone seeking to become a volunteer, in which case no fee is payable (Police Act 1997 (Criminal Records) Regulations 2002, Regs 4 and 4A). If an urgent preliminary response is sought, there is an additional fee of £6 (except in the case of volunteers). The fee for a criminal conviction certificate is £25. The fee for requesting up-date information about a person's criminal conviction certificate, criminal record certificate or enhanced criminal record certificate under the Police Act 1997 s.116A is £13, except in the case of volunteers or where the person making the request already holds any such certificate that is subject to up-date arrangements (Police Act 1997 (Criminal Records) Regulations 2002, Reg. 6).

In Scotland, the fee for a criminal record certificate, an enhanced criminal record certificate, or a criminal conviction certificate is £25, with no concessions (Police Act 1997 (Criminal Records) (Scotland) Regulations 2010, Reg. 3).

17 Offences

Unauthorised disclosure of the information provided in a criminal record or enhanced criminal record certificate is an offence punishable with a term of imprisonment of up to three months, a fine not exceeding level 3 on the standard scale, or both. As to the standard scale, see the Note on **Treatment of Offenders** (Police Act 1997, s.124).

It is also an offence (punishable in the same way) for a person to make a false certificate, alter a certificate, use somebody else's certificate, or allow their certificate to be used by someone else, or to make a false statement to obtain or allow someone else to obtain a certificate (s.123).

18 Authorities

Statutes–

Children Act 1989

Criminal Justice and Court Services Act 2000

Police Act 1997

Protection of Freedoms Act 2012

Statutory Instruments–

Disclosure and Barring Service (Core Functions) Order 2012, as amended (S.I. 2012 No. 2522 and 2014 No. 238)

Police Act 1997 (Criminal Records) (Registration) Regulations 2006, as amended (S.I. 2006 No. 750 and 2009 No. 203)

Police Act 1997 (Criminal Records) (Registration) (Scotland) Regulations 2010 (S.S.I. 2010 No. 383)

Police Act 1997 (Criminal Records) Regulations 2002, as amended (S.I. 2002 No. 233, 2003 Nos. 137, 520, and 1418, 2004 Nos. 367, 1759 and 2592, 2005 No. 347, 2006 Nos. 748 and 2181, 2007 Nos. 700, 1892, and 3224, 2008 No. 2143, 2009 Nos. 460, 1882, and 2428, 2010 Nos. 817 and 2702, 2011 No. 719, 2012 Nos. 979, 2114, 2669 and 3016, 2013 Nos. 1194, 1198, and 2669, 2014 Nos. 239, 955, 2103, and 2122, and 2015 No. 643)

Police Act 1997 (Criminal Records) (No. 2) Regulations 2009, as amended (S.I. 2009 No. 1882, 2010 No. 817, 2012 Nos. 523 and 2114, and 2013 No. 2669)

Police Act 1997 (Criminal Records) (Scotland) Regulations 2010, as amended (S.S.I. 2010 Nos. 168 and 383, 2011 Nos. 157 and 211, 2012 No. 354, and 2013 No. 2318)

Protection of Freedoms Act 2012 (Disclosure and Barring Service Transfer of Functions) Order 2012 (S.I. 2012 No. 3006)

DEBTS: PROTECTION OF DEBTORS AND RECOVERY OF DEBTS: ENGLAND AND WALES

A: HARASSMENT OF DEBTORS

1 Harassment of debtors

S.40 of the Administration of Justice Act 1970 provides that a person in England and Wales commits an offence if, with the object of coercing another person to pay money claimed from the other as a debt due under contract, he–

(a) harasses the other with demands for payment which by their frequency, or the manner or occasion of their making, or any accompanying threat or publicity are calculated to subject him or his family or household to alarm, distress, or humiliation;

(b) falsely represents, in relation to the money claimed, that criminal proceedings lie for failure to pay it;

(c) falsely represents himself to be authorised in some official capacity to claim or enforce payment;

(d) utters a document falsely represented by him to have some official character or purporting to have some official character which he knows it has not.

S.40(3) provides that paragraph (a) above does not apply to anything done by a person which is reasonable (and otherwise permissible in law) for the purpose–

(1) of securing the discharge of an obligation due, or believed by him to be due, to himself or to persons for whom he acts, or protecting himself or them from future loss; or

(2) of the enforcement of any liability by legal process.

It is also provided that a person may be guilty of an offence under paragraph (a) above if he concerts with others in the taking of such action as is described in that paragraph, notwithstanding that his own course of conduct does not by itself amount to harassment.

S.40(3A) provides that paragraphs (a) to (d) do not apply where what is done is a "commercial practice".

A "commercial practice" is any act, omission, course of conduct, representation or commercial communication (including advertising and marketing) by a trader, which is directly connected with the promotion, sale or supply of a product to consumers, whether occurring before, during or after a commercial transaction (if any) in relation to a product (Consumer Protection from Unfair Trading Regulations 2008, Reg. 2). If however a commercial practice is unfair, it will be prohibited under the 2008 Regulations. As to what amounts to an unfair commercial practice, see the Note on **Fair Trading and Consumer Protection**.

B: TAKING CONTROL OF DEBTORS' GOODS

2 Taking control of goods–introduction

Part 3 of the Tribunals, Courts and Enforcement Act 2007 (ss. 62 to 90) replaces the laws relating to the seizure and sale of goods for most purposes, and the common law right to distrain for arrears of rent which has been abolished, with a unified procedure to be followed by enforcement agents when taking control of and selling goods to recover a debt. Schedule 12 of the 2007 Act sets out the new procedure and provides for various matters relating to the operation of the procedure to be prescribed in regulations. The provisions in the 2007 Act replace the common law rules about how the powers to take control of, and sell, goods are exercised (s.65). In this regard, writs of fieri facias, except writs of fieri facias de bonis ecclesiasticis, are re-named writs of control, and warrants of execution and warrants of distress, unless the power they confer is exercisable only against specific goods, are re-named warrants of control (s.62(4)).

The Taking Control of Goods Regulations 2013 supplement Part 3 of the Tribunals, Courts and Enforcement Act 2007 by setting out a comprehensive code for operation of the procedure which enforcement agents must follow when acting under powers conferred by enactment, or under a warrant or writ of control or under instructions from a landlord of commercial premises who is owed rent arrears.

Note that the High Court has power to stay the execution of any writ of control issued in proceedings, for whatever period and on whatever terms it thinks fit, if satisfied that a party to proceedings is unable to pay a sum recovered against him (by way of satisfaction of the claim or counterclaim in the proceedings or by way of costs or otherwise), or any instalment of such a sum (s.70).

3 Acting as an enforcement agent

An individual may act as an enforcement agent only if one of the following applies (Tribunals, Courts and Enforcement Act 2007, s.63(2))–

(a) he acts under a certificate under s.64 of the 2007 Act;

(b) he is exempt;

(c) he acts in the presence and under the direction of a person to whom paragraphs (a) or (b) above applies.

An individual is exempt if he acts in the course of his duty as a constable, an officer of Revenue and Customs, or a person appointed under s.2(1) of the Courts Act 2003 (court officers and staff). An individual is also exempt if he acts in the course of his duty as an officer of a government department and, for the purposes of an enforcement power conferred by a warrant, an individual is exempt if in relation to the warrant he is a civilian enforcement officer as defined in s.125A of the Magistrates' Courts Act 1980 (s.63(3)).

A certificate to act as an enforcement agent may be issued by a judge of the county court. The Lord Chancellor must make regulations about certificates under these provisions (s.64) and the Certification of Enforcement Agents Regulations 2014 have been made for this purpose. They provide for the process by which a person who requires a certificate in order to act as an enforcement agent is issued with a certificate, including the requirements which must be satisfied for such a certificate to be issued, the duration of a certificate and how it may be suspended or cancelled. The Regulations also make provision concerning the making of complaints that a person issued with a certificate is not a fit and proper person to hold such a certificate. *Inter alia*, the Regulations provide a certificate has effect, unless cancelled, for two years from the date on which it was issued (Reg. 7). Certificates are to be issued by a judge of the county court and the court is required to keep and publish certain information about certificated persons (Reg. 4). Any person who considers that a certificated person is by reason of the person's conduct in acting as an enforcement agent, or for any other reason, not a fit person to hold a certificate, may submit a complaint in writing to the court. No fee is payable for submitting a complaint (Reg. 9).

A person is guilty of an offence if, knowingly or recklessly, he purports to act as an enforcement agent without being authorised to do so and is liable on summary conviction to an unlimited fine (s.63(6), (7)).

4 Procedure for taking control of goods

A notice of enforcement prior to taking control of goods must be given to the debtor not less than seven clear days before the enforcement agent takes control of the debtor's goods. A Sunday, bank holiday, Good Friday or Christmas Day does not count in calculating the period. A court may order that a specified shorter period of notice may be given to the debtor (Taking Control of Goods Regulations 2013, Reg. 6). Notice of enforcement must be given in writing to the debtor by, *inter alia*, post, fax or hand delivery and must be given by the enforcement agent or the enforcement agent's office (Reg. 8). The notice must include the following information (Reg. 7)–

(a) the name and address of the debtor;

(b) the reference number or numbers;

(c) the date of notice;

(d) details of the court judgment or order or enforcement power by virtue of which the debt is enforceable against the debtor;

(e) the following information about the debt: (i) sufficient details of the debt to enable the debtor to identify the debt correctly; (ii) the amount of the debt including any interest due as at the date of the notice; (iii) the amount of any enforcement costs incurred up to the date of notice; and (iv) the possible additional costs of enforcement if the sum outstanding should remain unpaid as at the date mentioned in (h) below;

(f) how and between which hours and on which days payment of the sum outstanding may be made;

(g) a contact telephone number and address at which, and the days on which and the hours between which, the enforcement agent or the enforcement agent's office may be contacted; and

(h) the date and time by which the sum outstanding must be paid to prevent goods of the debtor being taken control of and sold and the debtor incurring additional costs.

5 Exempt goods

Certain debtors' goods are classed as exempt goods and as such an enforcement officer may not take control of them. Where any goods of the debtor are also premises and are occupied by the debtor or another person as the debtor's or that person's only or principal home, they are also classed as exempt goods (Reg. 5). The following goods are exempt goods (Reg. 4)–

(a) items or equipment (for example, tools, books, telephones, computer equipment and vehicles) which are necessary for use personally by the debtor in the debtor's employment, business, trade, profession, study or education, except that the aggregate value of the items or equipment shall not exceed £1,350;

(b) clothing, bedding, furniture, household equipment, items and provisions as are reasonably required to satisfy the basic domestic needs of the debtor and every member of the debtor's household, including (but not restricted to) (i) a cooker or microwave; (ii) a refrigerator; (iii) a washing machine; (iv) a dining table large enough, and sufficient dining chairs, to seat the debtor and every member of the debtor's household; (v) beds and bedding sufficient for the debtor and every member of the debtor's household; (vi) one landline telephone, or if there is no landline telephone at the premises, a mobile or internet telephone which may be used by the debtor or a member of the debtor's household; (vii) any item or equipment reasonably required for the medical care of the debtor or any member of the debtor's household, safety in the dwelling-house; or the security of the dwelling-house (for example, an alarm system) or security in the dwelling-house; (viii) sufficient lamps or stoves, or other appliance designed to provide lighting or heating facilities, to satisfy the basic heating and lighting needs of the debtor's household; and (ix) any item or equipment reasonably required for the care of a person under the age of 18, a disabled person or an older person;

(c) assistance dogs (including guide dogs, hearing dogs and dogs for disabled persons), sheep dogs, guard dogs or domestic pets;

(d) a vehicle on which a valid disabled person's badge is displayed because it is used for, or in relation to which there are reasonable grounds for believing that it is used for, the carriage of a disabled person;

(e) a vehicle (whether in public ownership or not) which is being used for, or in relation to which there are reasonable grounds for believing that it is used for, police, fire or ambulance purposes; and

(f) a vehicle displaying a valid British Medical Association badge or other health emergency badge because it is being used for, or in relation to which there are reasonable grounds for believing that it is used for, health emergency purposes.

6 Taking control of controlled goods

An enforcement agent may not take control of goods of the debtor after the expiry of a period of 12 months beginning with the date of notice of enforcement. A court may order, on one occasion only, that the 12 month period be extended by a further 12 months. Where after giving notice of enforcement the enforcement agent enters into an arrangement with the debtor for the repayment, by the debtor, of the sum outstanding by instalments (a repayment arrangement); and the debtor breaches the terms of the repayment arrangement, the period begins with the date of the debtor's breach of the repayment arrangement (Taking Control of Goods Regulations 2013, Reg. 9).

An enforcement agent may not take control of goods of the debtor where (Reg. 10(1))–

(a) the debtor is a child;

(b) a child or vulnerable person (whether more than one or a combination of both) is the only person present in the premises in which the goods are located; or

(c) the goods are also premises in which a child or vulnerable person (whether more than one or a combination of both) is the only person present.

Where an item which belongs to the debtor is in use by any person at the time at which the enforcement agent seeks to take control of it, the enforcement agent may not do so if such action is in all the circumstances likely to result in a breach of the peace (Reg. 10(2)).

Specific rules apply where an enforcement officer proposes to take control of goods found on a highway: see Regulation 11.

The days for taking control of goods, and the prohibited hours for taking control, are contained in Regulations 12 and 13 and are the same as for entry or re-entry to premises (see **7 Entry or re-entry to premises**, below).

7 Entry or re-entry to premises

An enforcement agent may enter or re-enter premises only by any door, or any usual means by which entry is gained to the premises (for example, a loading bay to premises where a trade or business is carried on) or any usual means of entry, where the premises are a vehicle, vessel, aircraft, hovercraft, a tent or other moveable structure (Taking Control of Goods Regulations 2013, Reg. 20) and may enter, re-enter or remain on the premises on any day of the week (Reg. 21). He may only enter, re-enter or remain on the premises after 6 am and before 9 pm (or in the case of a business when the premises are open for the conduct of that business), except that where he has already entered the premises he may remain there outside of permitted hours if it is reasonably necessary for him to continue to search for and take control of goods, inspect controlled goods or remove controlled goods for storage or sale, provided the duration of time spent is reasonable (Reg. 22). An enforcement agent may enter, re-enter or remain on the premises only if the debtor is not a child or a child or vulnerable person (whether more than one or a combination of both) is not the only person present in the premises which the enforcement agent proposes to enter or re-enter (Reg. 23). There are also restrictions on repeated entry to premises. Where the enforcement agent, having previously entered premises, has determined that there are no or insufficient goods of the debtor on the premises of which control may be taken that will pay the sum outstanding he may enter the premises on a second or subsequent occasion only (Reg. 24)–

(a) if the enforcement agent has reason to believe that, since the occasion of the enforcement agent's last entry, there have been brought on to the premises further goods of the debtor of which control has not yet been, but may be, taken; or

(b) where the enforcement agent was prohibited from taking control of particular goods at the time of the original entry by virtue of Regulation 10 (control not to be taken of goods if those goods are in use and the enforcement agent considers that a breach of the peace would be likely if an attempt were made to take control of them).

Notice of the enforcement agent's intention to re-enter premises must be given to the debtor not less than 2 clear days before the enforcement agent re-enters the premises. A day that includes a Sunday, bank holiday, Good Friday or Christmas Day does not count in calculating the period (Reg. 25). The form and contents of notice of re-entry are contained in Regulation 26.

In certain circumstances a court may issue a warrant authorising an enforcement agent to use reasonable force to enter premises. The conditions of which the court must be satisfied before it issues a warrant are (Reg. 28)–

(c) either (i) the enforcement agent is attempting to recover a debt enforceable under s.127 of the Finance Act 2008; or (ii) the premises are premises to which the goods have been deliberately removed in order to avoid control being taken of them;

(d) there are, or are likely to be, goods of the debtor on the premises of which control can be taken;

(e) the enforcement agent has explained to the court (i) the likely means of entry, and the type and amount of force that will be required to make the entry; (ii) how, after entry, the enforcement agent proposes to leave the premises in a secure state; and

(f) in all the circumstances it is appropriate for the court to give an authorisation, having regard (among other matters) to (i) the sum outstanding; and (ii) the nature of the debt.

8 Dealing with controlled goods

Where an enforcement agent removes controlled goods, other than securities, from premises or a highway where the enforcement agent has found them (Taking Control of Goods Regulations 2013, Reg. 34)–

(a) the enforcement agent must keep the controlled goods, so long as they remain in the enforcement agent's control, in a similar condition to that in which the enforcement agent found them immediately prior to taking control of them;

(b) the goods must be removed to storage, unless the goods are removed for sale; and

(c) the storage must be secure and the conditions of that storage such as to prevent damage to or deterioration of the goods for so long as they remain in the enforcement agent's control.

The enforcement agent must not remove controlled goods to a place where there would be at any time a contravention of any prohibition or restriction imposed by or under any enactment.

Valuation of controlled goods must be carried out in accordance with Regulation 35. Where the enforcement agent makes the valuation it must be in writing, signed by the enforcement agent and set out the enforcement agent's name, the reference number or numbers and the date of the valuation, and where appropriate, a separate value for each item of goods of which control has been taken. The enforcement agent must provide a copy of the written valuation to the debtor and any co-owner. Where the enforcement agent obtains the valuation the enforcement agent must only instruct a qualified, independent valuer. Again, the written valuation must be provided to the debtor and any co-owner.

Detailed provision as to sale of controlled goods, including the form and contents of notice of sale, are contained in Regulations 36 to 43.

9 National Standards for Enforcement Agents

The Ministry of Justice has produced guidance for enforcement agents in England and Wales which, although not legally binding, is intended to set out minimum standards. The guidance covers matters such as professionalism and conduct, training and certification, complaints, the hours during which enforcement should take place, and protection of the vulnerable. It also includes a section on the responsibilities of creditors, both to debtors and to enforcement agents.

C: DEBT RELIEF ORDERS

10 Debt relief orders–introduction

Debt relief orders have been available since April 2009 and were introduced by the Tribunals, Courts and Enforcement Act 2007 which inserted new provisions into the Insolvency Act 1986. They are an alternative to bankruptcy and are intended to provide immediate relief from creditor action for debtors who have relatively low liabilities, little surplus income and few assets (Insolvency Act 1986, s.251A). The effect of an order (a DRO) will be to prevent creditors from enforcing their debts and the debtor will be discharged from those debts after a period of one year. Creditors will be notified of the making of an order and have a right to make objections on certain grounds if they believe the order should not have been made. An application can only be made online with the help of an approved intermediary, who will be a debt adviser, and the application will be sent to the official receiver (s.251B). The debtor must pay a fee to cover the administration costs but at £90 this is significantly less than the deposit required for bankruptcy proceedings to be begun. As to bankruptcy see the Note on **Bankruptcy: England and Wales**.

An approved intermediary is approved to give advice on DROs by one of the competent authorities. Details of the competent authorities can be found on The Insolvency Service website at–

<www.bis.gov.uk/insolvency/personal-insolvency/dro-debtors>

11 Eligibility for a debt relief order

To be eligible to apply for an order, the debtor must–

(a) have debts not exceeding £20,000 (the maximum amount of debt);

(b) have disposable income, following deduction of normal household expenses, not exceeding £50 per month (the monthly surplus income);

(c) have total gross assets not exceeding £1,000 (the asset limit or maximum total value of property which a person may have);

(d) live in England or Wales, or have been resident or carrying on business there in the last three years;

(e) not have previously been subject to a DRO within the last six years;

(f) not be involved in another formal insolvency procedure at the time of application for a DRO, such as–

    (i) being an undischarged bankrupt;

    (ii) having a current Individual Voluntary Arrangement; Bankruptcy Restrictions Order or Undertaking; Debt Relief Restrictions Order or Undertaking;

    (iii) having an interim order;

    (iv) a current pending debtor's bankruptcy petition in relation where they have not been referred to the DRO procedure by the court as a more suitable method of debt relief;

    (v) a current pending creditor's bankruptcy petition where they have not obtained the creditor's permission for entry into the DRO process.

The monetary conditions in paragraphs (a) to (c) above are contained in Part 2 of the Schedule to the Insolvency Proceedings (Monetary Limits) Order 1986, as amended.

12 Effect of a debt relief order

During the period that a DRO is in force, the debtor will be (Insolvency Act 1986, ss.251G-251J)–

(a) protected from enforcement action by his creditors (except those creditors whose debts cannot be scheduled in the DRO and those whose debts are included in the DRO but who have successfully obtained leave from the court to pursue their debts);

(b) free from those debts at the end of the period (normally 12 months from the making of the DRO);

(c) obliged to provide information to and co-operate with the official receiver;

(d) expected to make arrangements to repay their creditors should their financial circumstances improve.

During the period of the DRO the debtor must carry on paying ongoing commitments, such as rent and utility bills.

The official receiver may revoke or amend a DRO during the moratorium period to correct errors and omissions (s.251L). Revocation may take place when information provided by the debtor turns out to be incomplete or misleading, or where the debtor fails to comply with his duties to provide information or attend on the official receiver. The order may also be revoked if the official receiver ought not have made the order because he ought not have been satisfied the criteria were met and also if the debtor's income and property levels change (e.g., following a windfall) after the order has been made and the debtor would no longer meet the criteria for obtaining an order.

As with other forms of personal insolvency, a DRO debtor's credit rating will be affected and there are civil and criminal penalties for those who abuse the system.

For the duration of a DRO, a debtor will be subject to similar restrictions as in bankruptcy, and their details will be on the publicly available Individual Insolvency Register (available at <www.insolvency.gov.uk>).

These restrictions include that the debtor (s.251S)–

(e) must not obtain credit of £500 or more, either alone or jointly with another person, without disclosing that they are subject to a DRO to the lender;

(f) may not carry on a business (directly or indirectly) in a name that is different from the name under which they were granted a DRO, without telling all those with whom they do business the name under which they were granted a DRO;

(g) may not be involved (directly or indirectly) with the promotion, management or formation of a limited company, and may not act as a company director, without the court's permission; and

(h) will only be able to obtain a DRO once every six years.

Furthermore the official receiver will be able to apply for a Debt Relief Restrictions Order, similar to the bankruptcy restriction order, which will extend the period of restriction for up to fifteen years for debtors who are dishonest or culpable (s.251V).

13 Authorities

Statutes–

Administration of Justice Act 1970

Insolvency Act 1986

Tribunals, Courts and Enforcement Act 2007

Statutory Instruments–

Certification of Enforcement Agents Regulations 2014 (S.I. 2014 No. 421)

Insolvency Proceedings (Monetary Limits) Order 1986, as amended (S.I. 1986 No. 1996, 2004 No. 547, 2009 No. 465 and 2015 No. 26)

Taking Control of Goods Regulations 2013 (S.I. 2013 No. 1894)

DEBTS: PROTECTION OF DEBTORS AND RECOVERY OF DEBTS: SCOTLAND

1 The debt arrangement scheme

In Scotland a national debt arrangement scheme has been created by Part 1 of the Debt Arrangement and Attachment (Scotland) Act 2002, to enable individuals and sole traders, with the support of a money adviser, to arrange for their debts to be paid over time under a debt payment programme (s.1).

A debt payment programme is a programme which provides for the payment of money owed by a debtor (s.2(1)). The Scottish Ministers may, on an application by a debtor, approve any debt payment programme set out in an application (s.2(2)). This power may be delegated to another body (s.8, see **2 Administration of the scheme**, below). The programme must specify the arrangements proposed for the payment of debts, giving details of the amounts, periods and manner in which debts are to be paid, according to the debtor's knowledge and belief (s.2(3)). An application form must incorporate the consent of all the debtor's creditors (s.2(4)).

The Scottish Ministers may, by regulations, make provision in relation to debt payment programmes to provide an element of debt relief. Such programmes may be set up in such a way that debtors do not have to pay off the whole amounts due to creditors under the programmes, and for the writing-off at the end of the programme of any debts outstanding (s.7A, added by the Bankruptcy and Diligence etc. (Scotland) Act 2007, s.211).

The debtor must seek the assistance of a money adviser before applying for approval of a debt payment programme, or its variation (s.3(1)). The debtors' application to enter into a debt payment programme must contain a signed declaration by the money adviser that money advice has been given (s.3(2)).

When a debt payment programme has been approved or varied, the debts specified in the application for the approval or the variation must be paid in accordance with the programme (s.4(1)). Creditors are prohibited from executing any form of diligence against or seeking to sequestrate a person who has debts which are being paid by way of an approved debt payment programme under the scheme (s.4(2) and (3)). This stay on debt enforcement proceedings extends not only to those creditors whose debts are covered by the debt payment programme, but also any other creditor who has been given notice of the approval of such a programme (s.4(5)). Any interest, fees, penalties or other charges which are not owed as at the date on which a debtor applies for a debt payment programme (which is subsequently approved) and which would, in relation to a debt included in the programme, become payable after that date, are not payable unless and until the debt payment programme is revoked and cease to be owed or payable if and when the debt payment programme is completed (Debt Arrangement Scheme (Interest, Fees, Penalties and Other Charges) Regulations 2011, Reg. 4).

Both creditors and debtors may apply for a variation of a debt payment programme (s.5). An approved debt payment programme may require sums to be paid by way of deduction from the debtor's earnings. It is the duty of the employer to comply with any instruction along these lines (s.6).

Debt payment programmes can also be entered into by partnerships, limited partnerships, corporate bodies other than companies registered under the Companies Act 2006, trusts, and unincorporated bodies of persons.

2 Administration of the scheme

The Debt Arrangement Scheme (Scotland) Regulations 2011 provide a scheme for the repayment of debts under the Debt Arrangement and Attachment (Scotland) Act 2002. They provide the procedure and forms to be used in respect of a repayment arrangement under the scheme which, on approval, is described as a debt payment programme.

The debt arrangement scheme (DAS) administrator has the main responsibility for approval or rejection of applications for approval of a programme. The Scottish Ministers have delegated their functions as DAS administrator to the Accountant in Bankruptcy of 1, Pennyburn Road, Kilwinning KA13 6SA (Debt Arrangement and Attachment (Scotland) Act 2002 (Transfer of Functions to the Accountant in Bankruptcy) Order 2004). Certain debts are excluded from the DAS. These are (Debt Arrangement Scheme (Scotland) Regulations 2011, Reg. 3)–

(i) a debt secured by a standard security, other than to the extent that the sum is arrears of a periodic payment due to be paid under a loan agreement so secured;

(ii) a liability for the purpose of s.17(2B) of the Legal Aid (Scotland) Act 1986 (liability of a party to pay the Scottish Legal Aid Board);

(iii) a fee charged by a money adviser for the money adviser's services in the debt payment programme in respect of which the services are provided; and

(iv) student loan debt.

The Debt Arrangement Scheme (Scotland) Regulations 2011 deal with the following areas–

(a) money advisers;

Anyone whose debts are being repaid under a programme must at all times have a money adviser; who can and cannot be a money adviser; that a fee may not be charged unless information about free advice is given to the client; changing advisers.

(b) payments distributors;

A payment distributor assists a money adviser with payments distribution including distributing sums received in accordance with the debt payment programme; who can and cannot be a distributor; when an administration fee for distribution services may be charged to a creditor (but not a debtor).

(c) debt arrangement scheme register;

The keeping of a register of programmes; the information to be held on that register; and who can have access to it.

(d) approval of debt payment programmes;

Only individuals habitually resident in Scotland may apply for approval of a programme; when the consent of a creditor can be dispensed with; the procedure for giving approval and the conditions to which approval is subject.

(e) debt payment programmes;

The methods of payment under a programme, including through an employer, by direct debit, payment card or key, or electronic banking.

(f) variation of debt payment programmes;

The procedure for varying a programme.

(g) revocation of debt payment programmes;

When a programme may, or must, be revoked.

(h) completion of a debt payment programme;

The notices required when a programme is completed, and

(i) appeals;

When appeals about a programme can be made on a point of law.

Two debtors may apply together for a joint debt payment programme if they are joint and severally liable for a debt which the programme would provide for the payment of and they are (i) husband and wife to each other; (ii) civil partners of each other; (iii) living together as husband and wife; or (iv) living together in a relationship with the characteristics of the relationship between a husband and wife except that they are of the same sex. Both debtors must consent to any application for approval of a joint debt payment programme (2011 Regulations, Reg. 22).

For more information, and to find a money adviser, see <http://www.dasscotland.gov.uk/home>.

3 Attachment of possessions

Part 2 of the Debt Arrangement and Attachment (Scotland) Act 2002 introduces a method of enforcement for the recovery of corporeal moveable property. This is property which is tangible, is not fixed like land or buildings and can be moved. The recovery of legally constituted debt in this way is known as attachment (s.10).

Attachment is only possible where the debtor has either (s.10(3) and (4))–

(a) been charged to pay the sum owed together with interest and the creditor has provided the debtor with a debt advice and information package; or

(b) in summary warrant cases, the creditor has provided the debtor with a debt advice and information package (without a charge to pay) before taking any steps to carry out an attachment.

The debt advice and information package must contain such information as may be determined by the Scottish Ministers (s.10(5)).

Certain property is exempt from attachment, such as articles which are reasonably required for the debtor's profession, trade or business, and which do not exceed an aggregate value of £1,000 (s.11).

Attachment may not take place on a Sunday, a day which is a public holiday in the area in which the attachment is to be executed, or any other day prescribed by rules of court. Times during which attachment may take place are restricted to between 8am and 8pm unless prior authority has been obtained from the sheriff (s.12).

There is a presumption that articles in the possession of a debtor are owned by the debtor, either solely or in common with a third party (s.13).

4 Attachment outwith dwellinghouses

The attachment of articles kept outwith dwellinghouses is dealt with by the Debt Arrangement and Attachment (Scotland) Act 2002, ss.14 to 19. Entry into premises which are not a home (dwellinghouse) for the purpose of attachment and valuation is allowed and locked premises may be opened if necessary (s.15). A caravan, houseboat or other moveable structure used as a dwellinghouse, which is the only or principal residence of a third party, may be released from an attachment (s.16). A report of the attachment must be made to the sheriff within 14 days of its execution (s.17). Attached articles may be redeemed by the debtor within 14 days of the date on which the article was attached (s.18). Arrangements for the removal and auction of attached articles may be made (s.19) and an article may be removed without notice if that is considered necessary for its security or preservation of its value (s.19A, added by the Bankruptcy and Diligence etc. (Scotland) Act 2007, s.212). In these circumstances an article will be taken to the nearest convenient premises of the debtor or the person in possession of the item but if the debtor or person does not have any premises which are convenient or the court officer thinks those premises are unsuitable for storing the article the officer can take the articles to other secure premises.

5 Attachment: further provisions

The sheriff may make an order for the security of attached articles and for the immediate sale of perishable articles so that they will not deteriorate and lose value. The proceeds of sale are then consigned in court (Debt Arrangement and Attachment (Scotland) Act 2002, s.20).

The removal, sale, gifting or other disposal of attached articles and their wilful destruction or damage is prohibited. To do so is in breach of the attachment and may be dealt with as a contempt of court (s.21).

There is provision for the protection of vehicles where auction would be unduly harsh in the circumstances (s.22).

Where a sheriff is satisfied that the aggregate value of the attached articles is substantially below market value, the sheriff may, until the date of their auction, order the attachment to cease (s.23).

An attachment will cease to have effect if no further action is taken within six months of the attachment or 28 days of the removal of the attached article from the place at which it was attached, whichever is the earlier. An extension of the period may be permitted only by order of the sheriff (s.24).

A second attachment may not be undertaken at the same premises to enforce the same debt unless other articles have been brought onto the premises after the first attachment took place (s.25).

At any time before the auction of attached articles, the sheriff may, on his own initiative or on an application by the debtor, make an order declaring the attachment to be invalid or to have ceased to have effect. The sheriff may also make such other order as is considered necessary in the circumstances (s.26).

6 Auction of attached articles

An auction of attached articles must be held by public auction in an auction room unless it is impractical to do so in which event the auction may be held in an alternative location that the officer considers appropriate other than in a debtor's home (Debt Arrangement and Attachment (Scotland) Act 2002, s.27).

The date of auction or date of removal of the articles must not be varied, unless due to circumstances beyond the creditor's or court officer's control. In the event of a new date being set, it must be intimated to the debtor and to any other person in possession of the attached articles (s.28).

An auction may be cancelled to enable the debtor to repay the debt in the event of an agreement having been reached with the creditor but an auction may be cancelled on not more than two occasions (s.29).

The auction must be attended by the court officer and a witness and a record must be made of the articles sold specifying the amount which each achieved (s.30).

The proceeds of the auction must be used firstly to meet the expenses of the procedure and then to pay the creditor to meet the debt; any surplus is payable to the debtor (s.31).

Where an article is sold at auction at less than the value assigned to it when it was attached, the difference between that price and the value will be credited against the sum owed i.e., the debtor benefits from having the debt reduced by the amount the item was valued at even if it does not actually sell for that value at auction (s.31(1A), added by the Bankruptcy and Diligence etc. (Scotland) Act 2007, s.212). Where an article has been damaged and revalued and the damage was not caused by the fault of the debtor and no sum has been consigned into the court by a third party to compensate for the damage, the revaluation is disregarded and the original value is the value that is credited against the debt after the sale even if the sale price of the item was less than that (s.31(1B), as so added).

A report must be made to the sheriff within 14 days of the date of auction (s.32). The sheriff must remit the report of the auction to the auditor of court for him to tax the expenses charged, certify the balance due to or by the debtor and make a report to the sheriff (s.33).

7 Attachment: miscellaneous provisions

Articles, prior to auction, can be released from attachment where a third party claims ownership and either the court officer is satisfied as to the validity of the claim or the sheriff grants an order (Debt Arrangement and Attachment (Scotland) Act 2002, s.34). Articles commonly owned by a debtor and a third party can be attached and sold to cover the debtor's debt (s.35).

Where assets in common ownership are sold at auction, the third party is entitled to a proportion of the proceeds of sale corresponding to his/her interest in them (s.36). An attachment ceases to be effective where the full amount owing to the creditor is paid (s.37).

The sheriff's clerk must, if requested by the debtor, provide assistance in explaining the procedure involved or in completing any forms which may be necessary in connection with any of the procedures in the 2002 Act (s.38).

Liability as between the debtor and creditor for the expenses of the procedures in the Act is determined according to s.39 and Sch.1. A list of expenses of attachment which are recoverable from the debtor regardless of whether an attachment takes place within or outwith a dwellinghouse has been drawn up (Sch.1).

The situations in which the expenses of an attachment chargeable against the debtor may be recovered otherwise than from the proceeds of auction are specified in s.40. The order in which amounts recovered by attachment are to be applied is firstly towards the cost of attachment, then to interest payable which had accrued by the date of the attachment, then to the debt due including expenses (s.41).

A debtor may not be charged a fee for any application made by him under the Act in relation to attachment, any objections made by him to an application made by another party, or in relation to any hearing (s.42).

Lay representation may be permitted in proceedings concerning attachment (s.43). Legal aid is not available for proceedings under Parts 2 and 3 of the Act. Third parties are not prevented from obtaining legal aid in connection with those proceedings (s.44).

8 Attachment of articles kept in dwellinghouses

The attachment of articles kept in a dwellinghouse is prohibited except in accordance with the provisions of the Debt Arrangement and Attachment (Scotland) Act 2002 Part 3 under an exceptional attachment order (s.46).

An order of court authorising the attachment of non-essential assets within dwellinghouses may be granted on an exceptional basis (s.47). Before making an order, the court will take into account a number of factors (set out in s.47(4)) such as the nature of the debt, whether money advice has been given, etc. The sheriff must be satisfied when deciding whether to grant an exceptional attachment order that there are exceptional circumstances for doing so. S.48 sets out what constitutes exceptional circumstances–

(a) the creditor must have taken reasonable steps to negotiate a settlement;

(b) the creditor must have tried other methods of recovery (such as earnings arrestment); and

(c) there must be a reasonable prospect that the amount recovered will equal the costs of the procedure plus £100.

A dwellinghouse may not be entered unless there is a person present who is over 16 years of age and is able to understand the proceedings, or the debtor has been given four days' notice of the intended entry. The sheriff may dispense with the requirement to give notice in certain circumstances (s.49).

The removal, sale, gifting or relinquishment of non-essential assets known to be subject to an exceptional attachment order or their wilful destruction or damage by anyone amounts to the breach of the order (s.50).

Assets being attached under an exceptional attachment order should be valued by the court officer at the price which they would be likely to fetch on the open market (s.51).

The attachment of assets of sentimental value to the debtor not exceeding an aggregate value of £150, according to the values attributed by the court officer under s.51, is prohibited (s.52).

Unless the court officer considers that it is impractical to do so, non-essential assets must be removed immediately in execution of an exceptional attachment order once an attachment schedule has been completed (s.53).

The court officer, if he considers it appropriate, can arrange for an article, attached under an exceptional attachment order, to be valued by a professional valuer or other suitable skilled person (s.54).

A period of seven days is allowed from the removal of non-essential assets during which the debtor may apply to the sheriff for the return of an asset on the grounds that attachment was incompetent or that auction would be unduly harsh (s.55).

The redemption of non-essential assets within seven days of the date on which they were attached is allowed. Redemption is at an amount which the asset is likely to fetch if sold on the open market, according to the values attributed by the court officer under s.51 or by the specialist valuer under s.54 (s.56).

There is an appeal against any decision in relation to proceedings concerning an exceptional attachment order to be made to the sheriff principal with the leave of the sheriff and on a point of law only; the decision of the sheriff principal is final (s.57).

9 Authorities

Statutes–

Bankruptcy and Diligence etc. (Scotland) Act 2007

Debt Arrangement and Attachment (Scotland) Act 2002

Statutory Instruments–

Debt Arrangement and Attachment (Scotland) Act 2002 (Transfer of Functions to the Accountant in Bankruptcy) Order 2004 (S.S.I 2004 No. 448)

Debt Arrangement Scheme (Interest, Fees, Penalties and Other Charges) (Scotland) Regulations 2011, as amended (S.S.I. 2011 No. 238, 2013 No. 225 and 2015 No. 216)

Debt Arrangement Scheme (Scotland) Regulations 2011, as amended (S.S.I. 2011 No. 141, 2013 No. 225, 2014 No. 294 and 2015 No. 216)

LEGAL AID (CIVIL): ENGLAND AND WALES

A: INTRODUCTION

1 Provision of legal aid: introduction

The Lord Chancellor has overall responsibility for legal aid and he must secure that civil legal services (civil legal aid) is made available in accordance with Part 1 of the Legal Aid, Sentencing and Punishment of Offenders Act 2012. The 2012 Act abolishes the Legal Services Commission (s.38) which had previous responsibility for the Community Legal Service (which replaced civil legal aid) and the Criminal Defence Service (which replaced criminal legal aid). The Legal Aid Agency, an executive agency within the Ministry of Justice, replaces the Legal Services Commission and now manages the processing of legal aid applications and payments.

The Lord Chancellor is required to designate a civil servant as the Director of Legal Aid Casework whose function is to make decisions on legal aid in individual cases (s.4). The Director is required to comply with directions given by the Lord Chancellor and to have regard to guidance issued by the Lord Chancellor. However, the Lord Chancellor may not give a direction or guidance in relation to an individual case. The Lord Chancellor is under a duty to ensure that the Director acts independently of the Lord Chancellor when applying directions or guidance in relation to an individual case. The *Lord Chancellor's Guidance under section 4 of Legal Aid, Sentencing and Punishment of Offenders Act 2012* has been issued by the Lord Chancellor to the Director which the Director must have regard to in determining whether civil legal services are to be made available under s.11 of the 2012 Act: see **7 Qualifying for civil legal aid: introduction**, below.

This Note relates to civil legal aid in England and Wales and is set out as follows—
  A: Introduction
  B: Description of civil legal services
  C: Qualifying for civil legal aid
  D: Financial eligibility
  E: Contributions and costs
  F: Providers of services
For criminal legal aid in England and Wales see the Note on **Legal Aid (Criminal): England and Wales**.

B: DESCRIPTION OF CIVIL LEGAL SERVICES

2 The meaning of "civil legal aid"

"Civil legal aid" means civil legal services required to be made available under s.9 (see **3 Funding of general cases**, below), s.10 (funding of exceptional cases) or paragraph 3 of Schedule 3 to the Legal Aid, Sentencing and Punishment of Offenders Act 2012 (civil legal services made available to a legal person) (see **6 Funding of exceptional cases**, below). "Legal services" are further defined to mean the following types of services (s.8(1))—
  (a) providing advice as to how the law applies in particular circumstances;
  (b) providing advice and assistance in relation to legal proceedings;
  (c) providing other advice and assistance in relation to the prevention of disputes about legal rights or duties ("legal disputes") or the settlement or other resolution of legal disputes; and
  (d) providing advice and assistance in relation to the enforcement of decisions in legal proceedings or other decisions by which legal disputes are resolved.
The services described above include, in particular, advice and assistance in the form of representation, and mediation and other forms of dispute resolution (s.8(2)). Civil legal services are all legal services other than those services that are required to be made available under the provisions about criminal legal aid, thereby avoiding any overlap between civil and criminal legal aid (s.8(3)).

3 Funding of general cases

Civil legal services are to be available to an individual if they are civil legal services described in Part 1 of Schedule 1 to the Legal Aid, Sentencing and Punishment of Offenders Act 2012, and the Director of Legal Aid Casework has determined that the individual qualifies for the services and has not withdrawn the determination (s.9). Services not described in Part 1 of Schedule 1 can only be provided through exceptional funding: see **6 Funding of exceptional cases**, below.

In order to be described in Part 1 of Schedule 1 the services must both fall within the description of services in a paragraph of Part 1 and must not fall within an exclusion either set out in that paragraph itself (a specific exclusion) or listed by Part 2 of Schedule 1 (types of case that are excluded (see **4 Types of cases that are excluded**, below)) or Part 3 of Schedule 1 (advocacy services excluded other than in certain venues (see **5 Advocacy services excluded**, below)). Each paragraph of Part 1 Schedule 1 states which of the exclusions listed in Parts 2 and Part 3 apply to the relevant services. The types of services described in Part 1 are civil legal services provided in relation to—
  (1) care, supervision and protection of children;

(2) special educational needs;

(3) abuse of a child or vulnerable adult;

(4) working with children and vulnerable adults;

(5) mental health and mental capacity;

(6) community care services;

(7) facilities for disabled persons;

(8) appeals on a point of law in relation to welfare benefits;

(9) appeals on a point of law to the High Court, the Court of Appeal or the Supreme Court relating to a council tax reduction scheme;

(10) inherent jurisdiction of the High Court in relation to children and vulnerable adults;

(11) unlawful removal of children;

(12) family homes and domestic violence (and "domestic violence" means any incident, or pattern of incidents, of controlling, coercive or threatening behaviour, violence or abuse (whether psychological, physical, sexual, financial or emotional) between individuals who are associated with each other);

(13) a matter arising out of a family relationship concerning domestic violence (see also the Civil Legal Aid (Family Relationship) Regulations 2012 which provide that a matter arising out of a family relationship includes applications under s.14 of the Trusts of Land and Appointment of Trustees Act 1996 where the subject of the application is or includes the home or former home of the individuals);

(14) protection of children;

(15) a matter arising out of a family relationship concerning mediation in family disputes (see (12), above);

(16) children who are parties to family proceedings;

(17) forced marriage;

(18) EU and international agreements concerning children;

(19) EU and international agreements concerning maintenance including in relation to an application under Article 10 of the 2007 Hague Convention on the international recovery of child support and other forms of family maintenance and to an individual for proceedings in England and Wales in relation to recognition and enforcement of a maintenance decision where the individual makes a request directly to a competent authority for recognition and enforcement of the decision;

(20) judicial review;

(21) a writ of habeas corpus;

(22) abuse of position or powers by public authority;

(23) breach of Convention rights by public authority;

(24) clinical negligence causing neurological injury as a result of which an infant is severely disabled;

(25) proceedings before the Special Immigration Appeals Commission;

(26) detention under immigration legislation;

(27) temporary admission under immigration legislation;

(28) residence restrictions imposed under immigration legislation;

(29) victims of domestic violence and indefinite leave to remain applications;

(30) victims of domestic violence and residence cards applications;

(31) rights to enter and remain under immigration legislation (and see the Civil Legal Aid (Immigration Interviews) (Exceptions) Regulations 2012 which allow civil legal aid to be made available to cover attendance at any immigration interview where the individual being interviewed is under the age of 18, such services not being included for those over 18);

(32) accommodation for asylum-seekers;

(32A) victims of slavery, servitude or forced or compulsory labour;

(33) victims of trafficking in human beings;

(34) loss of home due to court order, eviction or bankruptcy;

(35) homeless or threatened homelessness;

(36) serious risk to health or safety in a rented home;

(37) anti-social behaviour;

(38) protection from harassment;

(39) gang-related violence;

(40) victims of sexual offences or their personal representatives;

(41) orders or directions under proceeds of crime legislation;

(42) inquests into the death of a member of an individual's family;

(43) injunctions in respect of nuisance arising from prescribed types of pollution of the environment (see the Civil Legal Aid (Prescribed Types of Pollution of the Environment) Regulations 2012 which prescribes pollution of the air, water or land that causes harm to the health of human beings or other living organisms or the quality of the air, water or land);

(44) contraventions of equality legislation;

(45) cross-border disputes;

(46) terrorism prevention and investigation measures;

(47) prescribed civil legal services provided in connection with the provision of services described above.

Where a paragraph of Part I of Schedule I describes services that consist of or include services provided in relation to proceedings, the description is to be treated as including in particular services provided in relation to, *inter alia*, preliminary or incidental proceedings. The Civil Legal Aid (Preliminary Proceedings) Regulations 2013 specify the proceedings that are not to be regarded as preliminary for these purposes.

For the purposes of paragraph (46) above, the Civil Legal Aid (Connected Matters) Regulations 2013 prescribe both the civil legal services and the circumstances in which they may be made available. The effect is that where an individual qualifies for civil legal services described in a paragraph of Part I of Schedule I, further civil legal services in relation to the identification of a proposed defendant or respondent may be made available in connection with the provision of services.

4 Types of cases that are excluded

The services described in Part I of Schedule I to the Legal Aid Sentencing and Punishment of Offenders Act 2012 (see **3 Funding of general cases**, above) do not include the services listed below. Some paragraphs in Part I provide exceptions from the exclusions, so that one or more of the general exclusions are disapplied. Those exceptions are outside the scope of this Note. The services are civil legal services provided in relation to (Sch. I, Pt. 2)–

- (a) personal injury or death;
- (b) a claim in tort in respect of negligence;
- (c) a claim in tort in respect of assault, battery or false imprisonment;
- (d) a claim in tort in respect of trespass to goods;
- (e) a claim in tort in respect of trespass to land;
- (f) damage to property;
- (g) defamation or malicious falsehood;
- (h) a claim in tort in respect of breach of statutory duty;
- (i) conveyancing;
- (j) the making of wills;
- (k) matters of trust law;
- (l) a claim for damages in respect of a breach of Convention rights within the meaning of the Human Rights Act 1998 by a public authority to the extent that the claim is made in reliance on s.7 of that Act;
- (m) matters of company or partnership law;
- (n) matters arising out of or in connection with (i) a proposal by that individual to establish a business, (ii) the carrying on of a business by that individual (whether or not the business is being carried on at the time the services are provided), or (iii) the termination or transfer of a business that was being carried on by that individual;
- (o) a benefit, allowance, payment, credit or pension under (i) a social security enactment, (ii) the Vaccine Damage Payments Act 1979, or (iii) Part 4 of the Child Maintenance and Other Payments Act 2008;
- (p) compensation under the Criminal Injuries Compensation Scheme;
- (q) changing an individual's name; and
- (r) judicial review of an enactment, decision, act or omission.

5 Advocacy services excluded

The services described in Part I of Schedule I to the Legal Aid Sentencing and Punishment of Offenders Act 2012 (see **3 Funding of general cases**, above) do not include advocacy unless the type of advocacy in question is listed below, except to the extent that Part I of Schedule I provides otherwise; or Part I of Schedule I makes specific provision bringing other types of advocacy within scope for that particular matter which are not listed (which are outside the scope of this Note). The exceptions are advocacy in proceedings in (Sch. I, Pt. 3)–

- (a) the Supreme Court;
- (b) the Court of Appeal;
- (c) the High Court;
- (d) the Court of Protection to the extent that they concern a person's right to life; a person's liberty or physical safety; a person's medical treatment (within the meaning of the Mental Health Act 1983); a person's capacity to marry, to enter into a civil partnership or to enter into sexual relations, or a person's right to family life;
- (e) the county court;
- (ea) the family court;
- (f) the Crown Court in proceedings for the variation or discharge of an order under ss.5 or 5A of the Protection from Harassment Act 1997, proceedings under certain matters listed in the Proceeds of Crime Act 2002, appeals from youth court decisions relating to injunctions under Part I of the Anti-social Behaviour, Crime and Policing Act 2014, appeals under s.46B of the Policing and Crime Act 2009 (appeal to the Crown Court against a decision of a youth court), and appeals under s.10(1)(b) of the Crime and Disorder Act 1998 relating to parenting orders where an injunction is granted under s.1 of the Anti-social Behaviour, Crime and Policing Act 2014 Act;
- (g) a magistrates' court that falls within the description of certain civil legal services: see **3 Funding of general cases**, above (paras (1), (12) to (14) and (16) to (19)) and, additionally, injunctions to prevent gang-related

violence under Part 4 of the Policing and Crime Act 2009 and injunctions under Part 1 of the Anti-social Behaviour, Crime and Policing Act 2014 (engagement in anti-social behaviour);

(h) a magistrates' court in proceedings under s.47 of the National Assistance Act 1948; proceedings in relation to bail or arrest under Schedules 2 and 3 to the Immigration Act 1971; proceedings for the variation or discharge of an order under ss.5 or 5A of the Protection from Harassment Act 1997; and proceedings in relation to certain matters under the Proceeds of Crime Act 2002;

(i) the Mental Health Review Tribunal for Wales;

(j) the First-tier Tribunal under certain proceedings contained, *inter alia*, in the Mental Health Act 1983, the Repatriation of Prisoners Act 1984, the Immigration Act 1971, the Nationality, Immigration and Asylum Act 2002, the British Nationality Act 1981, the Protection of Children Act 1999, the Care Standards Act 2000, the Criminal Justice and Court Services Act 2000, the Education Act 2002, or that falls within the description of certain civil legal services (see **3 Funding of general cases**, above (paras (29), (30), (32A) or (33));

(k) the Upper Tribunal arising out of proceedings within paragraphs (i) and (j) above;

(l) the Upper Tribunal under certain proceedings contained, *inter alia*, in the Safeguarding Vulnerable Groups Act 2006, the Tribunals, Courts and Enforcement Act 2007 (appeals on a point of law) from decisions made by the First-tier Tribunal or the Special Educational Needs Tribunal for Wales), to exercise its judicial review jurisdiction under the Tribunals, Courts and Enforcement Act 2007 and the Senior Courts Act 1981, and appeals under Part 3 of the Children and Families Act 2014 (provisions concerning children and young people with special educational needs or disabilities);

(m) the Employment Appeal Tribunal, but only to the extent that the proceedings concern contravention of the Equality Act 2010;

(n) the Special Immigration Appeals Commission;

(o) the Proscribed Organisations Appeal Commission;

(p) legal proceedings before any person to whom a case is referred (in whole or in part) in any proceedings within any other paragraph of this Part of this Schedule;

(q) bail proceedings before any court which are related to proceedings within any other paragraph of this Part of this Schedule; and

(r) proceedings before any person for the enforcement of a decision in proceedings within any other paragraph of this Part of this Schedule.

6 Funding of exceptional cases

The Director of Legal Aid Casework has the power to provide individuals with civil legal services not included in Part 1 of Schedule 1 to the Legal Aid, Sentencing and Punishment of Offenders Act 2012 in exceptional circumstances subject to certain conditions. The Director must first make an exceptional case determination and, secondly, determine that the individual qualifies for those services. Neither determination must have been withdrawn (s.10(2)). The Director can make an exceptional case determination where it is necessary to make legal services available to an individual because the failure to do so would amount to a breach of the individual's Convention rights (as defined in s.1(1) of the Human Rights Act 1998) or any rights of the individual to the provision of legal services that are enforceable EU rights (as defined in s.2(1) of the European Communities Act 1972). A determination may also be made where the Director considers that the failure to provide legal services would not necessarily amount to a breach of an individual's rights, but that it is nevertheless appropriate for the services to be made available, having regard to the risk of such a breach occurring (2012 Act, s.10(3)).

Under the exceptional cases provisions, advocacy services are to be made available to an individual for the purposes of an inquest under the Coroners Act 1988 into the death of a member of that individual's family if the Director makes a wider public interest determination in relation to the individual and the inquest and determines that the individual qualifies for the services (s.10(4)).

Civil legal services are to be available to a legal person (i.e. a person other than an individual) only if the Director has made an exceptional case determination in relation to the person and the services; has determined that the person qualifies for the services; and has not withdrawn either determination (Sch. 3, para. 3).

C: QUALIFYING FOR CIVIL LEGAL AID

7 Qualifying for civil legal aid: introduction

The Director of Legal Aid Casework must determine whether an individual qualifies for civil legal services in accordance with s.21 (financial resources) of the Legal Aid, Sentencing and Punishment of Offenders Act 2012 and regulations under that section and other criteria set out in regulations made under s.11(1) of the 2012 Act. The regulations made under s.11(1) are the Civil Legal Aid (Merits Criteria) Regulations 2013. In setting the criteria, the Lord Chancellor must consider the circumstances in which it is appropriate to make civil legal services available and must, in particular, consider the extent to which the criteria ought to reflect the following factors (s.11(3))–

(a) the likely cost of providing the services and the benefit which may be obtained by the services being provided;

(b) the availability of resources to provide the services;

(c) the appropriateness of applying those resources to provide the services, having regard to present and likely future demands for the provision of civil legal services;

(d) the importance for the individual of the matters in relation to which the services would be provided;

(e) the nature and seriousness of the act, omission, circumstances or other matter in relation to which the services are sought;

(f) the availability to the individual of services provided other than under the Act and the likelihood of the individual being able to make use of such services;

(g) if the services are sought by the individual in relation to a dispute, the individual's prospects of success in the dispute;

(h) the conduct of the individual in connection with services made available under the Act or an application for such services;

(i) the conduct of the individual in connection with any legal proceedings or other proceedings for resolving disputes about legal rights or duties; and

(j) the public interest.

The procedure in relation to determinations under ss.9 and 10 and Schedule 3 are governed by s.12 and regulations under that section. A determination by the Director that an individual qualifies must specify the type of services and the matters in relation to which the services are to be available (s.12(1)). Regulations may make provision about the making and withdrawal of determinations (s.12(2)). The regulations made under s.12(2) are the Civil Legal Aid (Procedure) Regulations 2013: see **19 Procedure for applying for civil legal aid**, below.

8 Qualifying for legal services

Regulation 11 of the Civil Legal Aid (Merits Criteria) Regulations 2013 provides the framework for the determination of whether the applicant qualifies for legal services in relation to the merits criteria. The Director of Legal Aid Casework is required to apply the merits criteria which are relevant to the forms of civil legal services set out in Part 2 of the Regulations (forms of civil legal services (see **9 Forms of civil legal service,** below)) and must consider which form of civil legal services is appropriate in accordance with Part 3 of the Regulations (availability of forms of civil legal services) (Reg. 11(5)). Regulations 21 to 31 set out restrictions on the forms of service available for particular types of case (see **18 Restrictions on the forms of service,** below). Where more than one form of service is in principle available the Director must choose the most appropriate (Reg. 20). In determining whether an individual qualifies for civil legal services, the Director must apply the general merits criteria contained in the Regulations except to the extent that they are disapplied, modified or supplemented by the specific merits criteria (see **17 Merits criteria,** below) (Reg. 11(2)).

In addition to the relevant general and specific merits criteria, two further criteria have to be satisfied before an applicant can qualify for legal services. First, the Director must decide, for all applications, if it is reasonable to provide civil legal services in the light of the conduct of the individual or legal person (Reg. 11(6)). Additionally, if the likely costs of the case exceed £250,000 or, if the case forms part of a multi-party action, the likely costs of the multi-party action exceed £1,000,000, the Director must be satisfied, having regard to the present and future likely demands for civil legal aid, it is reasonable to provide the individual or legal person with civil legal services in all the circumstances of the case. This criterion does not apply to cases relating to the life or liberty of the individual or their family or to public law children cases (Reg. 11(7), (8)).

9 Forms of civil legal service

The Civil Legal Aid (Merits Criteria) Regulations 2013 describes the forms of civil legal service which may be granted following an application for legal aid. The forms of civil legal service each have their own merits criteria which will be applied in order to determine whether legal aid should be granted. There are seven forms of civil legal service as follows (Reg. 12)–

(a) legal help;

(b) help at court;

(c) family help;

(d) family mediation;

(e) help with family mediation;

(f) legal representation; and

(g) other legal services.

Each of the forms of civil legal service is described below.

10 "Legal help"

"Legal help" means the provision of civil legal services other than (Civil Legal Aid (Merits Criteria) Regulations 2013, Reg. 13)–

(a) acting as a mediator or arbitrator;

(b) issuing or conducting court proceedings;

(c) instructing an advocate in proceedings;

(d) preparing to provide advocacy in proceedings; or

(e) advocacy in proceedings.

11 "Help at court"

"Help at court" means the provision of any of the following civil legal services at a particular hearing (Civil Legal Aid (Merits Criteria) Regulations 2013, Reg. 14)–

(a) instructing an advocate;
(b) preparing to provide advocacy; or
(c) advocacy.

This allows the provision of advocacy at a particular hearing but not generally in the proceedings. It is not available in family cases or certain immigration cases (Regs. 22 to 24).

12 "Family help"

Family help may be provided in a family dispute as either family help (lower) or family help (higher) (Civil Legal Aid (Merits Criteria) Regulations 2013, Reg. 15). "Family help (lower)" means–

(a) civil legal services provided in relation to the negotiation of a family dispute before the issuing of proceedings; or
(b) civil legal services provided in relation to the issuing of proceedings in order to obtain a consent order following the settlement of a family dispute.

"Family help (higher)" means such civil legal services as are available under legal representation but does not include preparation for, or representation at, a contested final hearing or appeal. It is available in family cases except for public law children cases and special Children Act 1989 cases (Reg. 26).

13 "Family mediation"

"Family mediation" means the provision of any of the following civil legal services in a family dispute (Civil Legal Aid (Merits Criteria) Regulations 2013, Reg. 16)–

(a) an assessment by a mediator of whether, in the light of all the circumstances, a case is suitable for mediation; or
(b) acting as a mediator.

14 "Help with family mediation"

"Help with family mediation" means the provision of any of the following civil legal services in relation to a family dispute (Civil Legal Aid (Merits Criteria) Regulations 2013, Reg. 17)–

(a) civil legal services provided in relation to family mediation; or
(b) civil legal services provided in relation to the issuing of proceedings to obtain a consent order following the settlement of the dispute following family mediation.

This form of civil legal service allows civil legal services to be provided in relation to ongoing or recently completed family mediation.

15 "Legal representation"

"Legal representation" means the provision of civil legal services, other than acting as a mediator or arbitrator, to an individual or legal person in particular proceedings where that individual or legal person (Civil Legal Aid (Merits Criteria) Regulations 2013, Reg. 18)–

(a) is a party to those proceedings;
(b) wishes to be joined as a party to those proceedings; or
(c) is contemplating issuing those proceedings.

Legal representation may be provided as either investigative representation or full representation. "Investigative representation" means legal representation which is limited to the investigation of the strength of the contemplated proceedings and includes the issuing and conducting of proceedings but only so far as necessary to–

(d) obtain disclosure of information relevant to the prospects of success of the proceedings;
(e) protect the position of the individual or legal person applying for investigative representation in relation to an urgent hearing; or
(f) protect the position of the individual or legal person applying for investigative representation in relation to the time limit for the issue of the proceedings.

It cannot be granted to a person who considers that proceedings may be brought against them.

16 "Other legal services"

"Other legal services" means the provision of any of the following civil legal services (Civil Legal Aid (Merits Criteria) Regulations 2013, Reg. 19)–

(a) instructing an advocate;
(b) preparing to provide advocacy; or
(c) advocacy,

in proceedings in relation to which the Director of Legal Aid Casework, having applied the relevant merits criteria in accordance with Regs. 48 to 50 (application of the merits criteria in exceptional cases), has made a determination under s.10(2)(b) or (4)(c) (exceptional cases) of the Legal Aid, Sentencing and Punishment of Offenders Act 2012. See **6 Funding of exceptional cases**, above.

17 Merits criteria

The Civil Legal Aid (Merits Criteria) Regulations 2013, Part 4 set out the general merits criteria which apply to all applications for services other than to the extent that specific criteria state otherwise. The general merits criteria cover all forms of service under Part 2 of the Regulations (see **9 Forms of civil legal service**, above). The criterion that, in order to qualify for legal representation, a case should not be suitable for a conditional fee agreement now applies to all applications for legal aid in non-family proceedings other than Mental Health First-tier Tribunal cases. "Conditional fee agreement" is given an extended meaning to include damages-based agreements and litigation funding agreements under the amended Courts and Legal Services Act 1990 (2013 Regulations, Reg. 2). Additionally, in respect of determinations for legal help, help at court and legal representation (excluding family proceedings) the individual must not have access to other potential sources of funding from which it would be reasonable to fund the case such as insurance or where another body could be expected to fund the case. Standard criteria for determinations in respect of legal representation also mean the following conditions must be met (Reg. 39)–

(a) there is no person other than the individual, including a person who might benefit from the proceedings, who can reasonably be expected to bring the proceedings;

(b) the individual has exhausted all reasonable alternatives to bringing proceedings including any complaints system, ombudsman scheme or other form of alternative dispute resolution;

(c) there is a need for representation in all the circumstances of the case including (i) the nature and complexity of the issues, (ii) the existence of other proceedings, and (iii) the interests of other parties to the proceedings; and

(d) the proceedings are not likely to be allocated to the small claims track.

Part 6 of the Regulations set out criteria for specific categories of case and which include criteria for determinations (Regs. 51 to 75)–

(i) for full representation in relation to mental health or mental capacity proceedings;

(ii) for legal representation in relation to public law claims;

(iii) for investigative and full representation in relation to claims against public authorities;

(iv) for full representation in relation to immigration;

(v) for representation in relation to court orders for possession or unlawful eviction cases;

(vi) for full representation in relation to certain family disputes including cases relating to EU and international agreements, public law and private law children cases and domestic violence;

(vii) in relation to cross-border disputes; and

(viii) for legal help and legal representation in relation to legal persons.

18 Restrictions on the forms of service

Regulations 21 to 31 of the Civil Legal Aid (Merits Criteria) Regulations 2013 set out restrictions on the forms of service available for particular types of case, as follows–

Mental Health

Investigative representation is not appropriate in relation to any matter described in paragraph 5(1)(a) or (b) of Part 1 of Schedule 1 to the Legal Aid, Sentencing and Punishment of Offenders Act 2012 (mental health), to the extent that it relates to proceedings before the First-tier Tribunal or the Mental Health Review Tribunal for Wales.

Immigration and terrorism prevention and investigation measures

Help at court and investigative representation are not appropriate in relation to any matter described in any of the following paragraphs of Part 1 of Schedule 1 to the 2012 Act (civil legal services)–

(a) paragraphs 25 to 30 of Part 1 of Schedule 1 to the 2012 Act (immigration), to the extent they relate to proceedings before the First-tier Tribunal or the Upper Tribunal;

(b) paragraphs 32(1) (victims of trafficking in human beings) and 32A(1) (victims of slavery, servitude or forced or compulsory labour); and

(c) paragraph 45 of Part 1 of Schedule 1 to the 2012 Act (terrorism prevention and investigation measures etc.).

Special Immigration Appeals Commission, immigration: accommodation for asylum-seekers etc. and victims of trafficking in human beings

Help at court is not appropriate in relation to any matter described in any of the following paragraphs of Part 1 of Schedule 1 to the 2012 Act (civil legal services)–

(a) paragraph 24 (Special Immigration Appeals Commission); and

(b) paragraph 31 (immigration: accommodation for asylum-seekers etc.).

Family disputes

Help at court and investigative representation are not appropriate in relation to a family dispute and full representation is not appropriate in relation to any matter described in paragraph 14 of Part 1 of Schedule 1 to the 2012 Act (mediation in family disputes).

Victims of domestic violence and family matters: family help (lower)

Family help (lower) is not appropriate in relation to any matter described in paragraph 12 of Part 1 of Schedule 1 to the 2012 Act (victims of domestic violence and family matters) to the extent that it relates to a petition for divorce under s.1 of the Matrimonial Causes Act 1973 or an application for a dissolution order under s.44 of the Civil Partnership Act 2004.

Public law children cases and special Children Act 1989 cases

Family help (higher) is not appropriate in public law children cases or special Children Act 1989 cases.

Victims of domestic violence and family matters: help with family mediation

Help with family mediation in relation to the issuing of proceedings to obtain a consent order following the settlement of the dispute following family mediation is not appropriate in relation to certain matters arising under paragraph 12(9) (victims of domestic violence and family matters) of Part 1 of Schedule 1 to the 2012 Act.

Emergency representation

Legal representation and family help (higher) are the only forms of civil legal services which are appropriate for an individual who qualifies for emergency representation.

Civil legal services which do not include advocacy

Legal representation, family help (higher) and help at court are not appropriate forms of civil legal services in relation to any matter in which the civil legal services available under Part 1 of the 2012 Act do not include advocacy.

Inquests

Legal help is the only form of civil legal services which is appropriate in relation to any matter described in paragraph 41 of Part 1 of Schedule 1 to the 2012 Act (inquests).

Cross-border disputes

Legal help and legal representation are the only forms of civil legal services which are appropriate in relation to any matter described in paragraph 44 of Part 1 of Schedule 1 to the 2012 Act (cross-border disputes).

19 Procedure for applying for civil legal aid

The Civil Legal Aid (Procedure) Regulations 2012 make provision about the making and withdrawal of determinations that an individual qualifies for civil legal services under the Legal Aid, Sentencing and Punishment of Offenders Act 2012.

In accordance with Part 2 of the Regulations any individual intending to apply for legal help in certain categories of law (defined as "Gateway Work") must, in most circumstances, do so through "the Gateway". The Civil Legal Advice ("CLA") advice line acts as the Gateway. The areas of work to which this Part applies are applications for legal help in the discrimination, education and debt categories. In most cases it is anticipated legal help will be provided by telephone, e-mail or post. In other cases the Gateway may determine that the case is not suitable for such advice and that face to face advice may be required. In these circumstances the Gateway will inform the person that they may seek advice from a face to face provider (see **26 Arrangements by the Lord Chancellor,** below) and will confirm that they have been assessed and are eligible for face to face advice.

An application for legal help in Gateway Work cannot be made to a provider with a face to face contract in the first instance and providers cannot. make determinations in these matters except in certain circumstances

Certain persons are exempt from the requirement to seek advice through the Gateway and may choose either to contact the Gateway or to seek face to face advice. These are (i) persons who have been deprived of their liberty, (ii) children under the age of 18, and (iii) persons who have been previously assessed by the Gateway as being eligible for face to face advice and who now have a linked problem. Unless the person is an exempted person, a provider cannot provide legal help unless the matter has been assessed by the Gateway as requiring face to face advice. Advice is available through CLA in two other areas of law: family and housing. These are known as non-Gateway areas and the person will have a choice as to whether to access advice via CLA or by attending at a face to face provider.

An applicant has a right of a review in respect of determinations, refusals or withdrawals of legal help. The applicant has 14 days from the decision to apply to the Director of Legal Aid Casework and include written representations supporting the application (Reg. 69).

Part 2 of the Regulations do not apply to applications for licensed work (i.e. work carried out under the authority of a certificate). A provider will therefore be able to make an application for licensed work in Gateway areas of law on behalf of a client. However, an application for licensed work should not be made until work which could have been carried out under legal help has been completed. Part 4 of the Regulations set out the procedure for making and withdrawing determinations about licensed work which include requirements concerning evidence to be provided with applications for particular services.

Note that Part 7 of the Regulations sets out the procedure for making and withdrawing determinations about whether an individual qualifies for family mediation which remain outside the scope of licensed work provisions.

An individual applying for family mediation must attend the mediator's premises in person and complete the specified application form.

Part 5 of the Regulations sets out the procedure for making and withdrawing determinations about emergency representation (civil legal services provided on an urgent basis). An individual may make an application for emergency representation by such method as the Director of Legal Aid Casework has agreed to accept given the urgency of the particular circumstances. The application must specify whether the emergency representation is to be provided as licensed work or under an individual case contract.

Specific rules apply concerning the evidence requirements relating to victims of, or persons at risk of, domestic violence and persons with a child who has experienced, or is at risk of, child abuse: Regs. 33 and 34.

D: FINANCIAL ELIGIBILITY

20 Introduction

The basic rule is that legal aid will only be granted to an individual who is determined to be financially eligible for the services (Legal Aid, Sentencing and Punishment of Offenders Act 2012, s.21(1)). The financial eligibility rules are contained in regulations made by the Lord Chancellor (see 21 **Financial eligibility for civil legal services**, below). The Regulations may provide for exceptions from the basic rule, so that an individual may receive certain services regardless of their financial means (s.21(2)) (see 22 **Financial eligibility: exceptions**, below).

S.22 provides that the Director of Legal Aid Casework may make an information request to the Secretary of State or the Commissioners for Her Majesty's Revenue and Customs for the purposes of facilitating a determination about an individual's financial resources for the purpose of legal aid available under Part 1 of the Act. The Legal Aid (Information about Financial Resources) Regulations 2013 specify, *inter alia*, the particular benefits in relation to which an individual's benefit status may be requested.

21 Financial eligibility for civil legal services

The Civil Legal Aid (Financial Resources and Payment for Services) Regulations 2013 make provision about the rules the Director of Legal Aid Casework must apply to determine whether a individual's financial resources are such that the individual is eligible for civil legal services under Part 1 of the Legal Aid, Sentencing and Punishment of Offenders Act 2012. The Legal Aid (Financial Resources and Payment for Services) (Legal Persons) Regulations 2013 make provision in relation to determinations of a legal person's financial eligibility for such services. The following rules set out the provisions concerning an individual's eligibility for civil legal aid.

Gross income

Where the gross monthly income of the individual exceeds £2,657 the Director must determine that the individual's financial resources are such that the individual is not eligible for civil legal services. However, where the individual has more than four dependent children in respect of whom the individual receives child benefit, that sum must be increased by £222 in respect of the fifth and each subsequent child (Reg. 7).

Disposal income and disposal capital

Where an individual's monthly disposable income does not exceed £733 and the individual's disposable capital does not exceed £8,000, the Director must determine that the individual's financial resources are such that the individual is eligible for civil legal services (Reg. 8(1)). Where an individual's monthly disposable income does not exceed £733 and the individual's disposable capital does not exceed £3,000, the Director must determine that the individual's financial resources are such that the individual is eligible for legal representation in respect of any matters described in Part 1 of Schedule 1 of the 2012 Act relating to immigration and victims of trafficking in human beings before the Immigration and Asylum Chamber of the First-tier Tribunal and the Immigration and Asylum Chamber of the Upper Tribunal in relation to an appeal or review from the Immigration and Asylum Chamber of the First-tier Tribunal (Reg. 8(2)).

Certain payments are disregarded in calculating disposal income including disability living allowance, attendance allowance, constant attendance allowance, payments made out of the social fund, carer's allowance, council tax benefit, direct payments made under the Health and Social Care Act 2001, the Children and Families Act 2014, or the Care Act 2014, severe disablement allowance, back to work bonus received under the Jobseekers Act 1995, financial support paid for the care of a foster child, any payment made out of the Independent Living Fund 2006, and any personal or armed forces independence payment (Reg. 24). Deductions will also be made in respect of the following (Regs. 23, 25 to 29)–

   (a) national insurance contributions and income tax;
   (b) a partner and dependants of the individual;
   (c) maintenance;
   (d) employment expenses and child care costs;
   (e) rent or cost of living accommodation; and
   (f) contribution orders made under the Criminal Legal Aid (Contribution Orders) Regulations 2013.

In calculating the disposable capital of the individual, certain sums are disregarded including any back to work bonus received under s.26 of the Jobseekers Act 1995, any payment made out of the social fund under the

Social Security Contributions and Benefits Act 1992, any arrears of direct payments, and any payment made out of the Independent Living Fund 2006 (Reg. 40). There are also capital disregards for individuals aged over 60 depending on their monthly disposal income (Reg. 41). The individual's interest in the main or only dwelling in which the individual resides must be disregarded in calculating their disposal capital. The total amount to be disregarded must not exceed £100,000 (Reg. 39). Additionally, in calculating the disposable capital of the individual, the amount or value of the subject matter of the dispute to which the application relates must be disregarded. The total amount to be disregarded must not exceed £100,000 (Reg. 38).

Individuals in receipt of certain support

Subject to exceptions noted below, where the Director is satisfied that the individual is properly in receipt, directly or indirectly, of (i) income support; (ii) income-based jobseeker's allowance; (iii) guarantee credit; (iv) income-related employment and support allowance; or (v) universal credit, the Director must determine that the individual's financial resources are such that the individual is eligible for all forms of civil legal services without paying any contributions (Reg. 6(2)). However, if the individual's disposable capital exceeds £8,000 the Director must determine that the individual's financial resources are such that the individual is not eligible for civil legal services. If the individual's disposable capital exceeds £3,000 but does not exceed £8,000, the individual must pay a contribution out of capital in accordance with the Regulations (Reg. 6(4)) (see **23 Payment for services**, below).

Where an individual is in receipt, directly or indirectly, of support provided under ss.4(14) or 95(15) of the Immigration and Asylum Act 1999, that individual will be eligible for legal help and help at court and legal representation in relation to immigration and asylum and victims of trafficking in human beings proceedings in the Immigration and Asylum Chamber of the First-tier Tribunal and the Immigration and Asylum Chamber of the Upper Tribunal in relation to an appeal or review from the Immigration and Asylum Chamber of the First-tier Tribunal (Reg. 6(1)).

Waiver of eligibility limits

Provisions concerning the waiver of financial eligibility limits are as follows (Regs. 9 to 12)–

(a) where an application is made for legal representation in a multi-party action which the Director considers has a significant wider public interest, the Director may, if the Director considers it equitable to do so, disapply the eligibility limits concerning gross income and disposal income and capital or waive all or part of any contributions payable under the Regulations;

(b) where an application is made for legal help in relation to inquests the Director may, if the Director considers it equitable to do so, disapply the eligibility limits concerning gross income and disposal income and capital or waive all or part of any contributions payable under the Regulations;

(c) the Director must disapply the eligibility limits concerning gross income and disposal income and capital or any contributions payable if the individual proves that they are unable to pay the cost of proceedings in England and Wales in relation to a cross-border dispute as a result of differences in the cost of living between the individual's Member State of domicile or habitual residence and England and Wales; and

(d) where an application is in respect of legal representation concerning family homes and domestic violence or forced marriage to the extent that the individual is seeking an injunction or other order for protection from harm to the person or committal for breach of any such order, the Director may, if the Director considers it equitable to do so, disapply the eligibility limits concerning gross income and disposal income and capital.

Further determinations

Where an individual is eligible to receive civil legal services and the circumstances of the individual may have changed so that (i) their normal disposable income may have increased by an amount greater than £60 or decreased by an amount greater than £25, or (ii) their disposable capital may have increased by an amount greater than £750 the Director must make a further determination in respect of the individual's financial resources. The Director may, however, decide not to make a further determination if the Director considers such a determination inappropriate, having regard in particular to the period during which civil legal services are likely to continue to be provided to the individual (Reg. 20).

Provision of information

An individual must provide the Director with the information necessary to enable a determination to be made and for the individual's disposable income and disposable capital to be calculated (Reg. 13). An individual is also under a duty to report a change in financial circumstances (Reg. 18).

22 Financial eligibility: exceptions

There are some forms of civil legal services which are available without a determination in respect of an individual's financial resources and these include (Civil Legal Aid (Financial Resources and Payment for Services) Regulations 2013, Reg. 5)–

(a) such legal help and help at court as is authorised, under the provider's arrangement with the Lord Chancellor under s.2 (arrangements) of the Legal Aid, Sentencing and Punishment of Offenders Act 2012, to be provided without a determination in respect of an individual's financial resources;

(b) such forms of civil legal services as are provided through grants under s.2 of the 2012 Act where the terms of the grant provide that the services are available without a determination in respect of an individual's financial resources;

(c) legal representation in a special Children Act 1989 case and related proceedings;

(d) family help (lower) in matters concerning the care, supervision and protection of children to the extent that the matter concerns contemplated proceedings in relation to care and supervision orders and the individual to whom the family help (lower) may be provided is the parent of a child, or the person with parental responsibility for a child or, in the case of an unborn child, will be the parent of the child and will have parental responsibility for the child;

(e) legal help in contemplated proceedings or legal representation in proceedings or contemplated proceedings in relation to the mental health and repatriation of prisoners;

(f) legal representation in relation to mental capacity to the extent that the legal representation is in proceedings in the Court of Protection under s.21A of the Mental Capacity Act 2005 and the individual to whom legal representation may be provided is the individual in respect of whom an authorisation is in force under that Act, or an appointed representative of that individual;

(fa) such family mediation as is a Mediation Information and Assessment meeting (i.e. an assessment of whether a case is suitable for mediation) for an individual ("A") in relation to any mediation in family disputes matter described in paragraph 14 of Part 1 of Schedule 1 to the 2012 Act if A is a party to the Mediation Information and Assessment meeting and the Director of Legal Aid Casework has made a determination that the financial resources of another individual who is a party to that meeting ("B") are such that B is eligible, for that meeting, for such family mediation as is a Mediation Information and Assessment meeting;

(g) legal representation in relation to international agreements concerning children to the extent that the matter relates to an applicant under the 1980 European Convention on Child Custody or the 1980 Hague Convention;

(ga) family mediation in relation to any matter described in paragraph 17(1)(b) (EU and international agreements concerning children) of Part 1 of Schedule 1 to the 2012 Act to the extent that the matter relates to an applicant under the 1980 Hague Convention;

(gb) family mediation for the initial mediation session following a Mediation Information and Assessment Meeting (whether or not the mediation proceeds beyond that initial session) if the individual is a party to the mediation and another party to that mediation has already been assessed as financially eligible for family mediation;

(h) legal representation in a case in which the applicant is an individual who, in the State of origin, has benefited from complete or partial legal aid, or exemption from costs or expenses, in relation to any matter concerning international agreements and children or international agreements concerning maintenance;

(i) family help (higher) or legal representation in relation to parties who benefited from free legal aid in a Member State of origin including in relation to cases where Art.17(b) of the 2007 Hague Convention applies, which provides for free legal assistance if the individual previously received legal aid for the matter in the State of origin;

(j) legal help, family help (lower), family help (higher) and legal representation in relation to EU and international agreements concerning maintenance to the extent that the matter relates to any application under Art.56(1) of the EU Maintenance Regulation and is an application made by a creditor concerning maintenance obligations arising from a parent-child relationship towards a person under the age of 21;

(k) legal help, family help (lower), family help (higher) and legal representation in relation to any matter described in paragraph 18(3A) (applications under Art.10 of the 2007 Hague Convention) of Part 1 of Schedule 1 to the Act where the matter is an application made by a creditor under the 2007 Hague Convention concerning maintenance obligations arising from a parent-child relationship towards a person under the age of 21; and

(l) civil legal services in relation to a matter concerning terrorism prevention and investigation measures to the extent that the services consist of legal help or legal representation for an individual who is the subject of an application for permission under s.6 of the Terrorism Prevention and Investigation Measures Act 2011, including legal help and legal representation for advice in connection with a Terrorism Prevention and Investigation Measures Act 2011 notice.

E: CONTRIBUTIONS AND COSTS

23 Payment for services

An individual to whom services are made available is not to be required to make a payment in connection with the provision of the services, except where regulations provide otherwise. The regulations may, in particular, provide that in prescribed circumstances an individual must do one or more of the following (Legal Aid, Sentencing and Punishment of Offenders Act 2012, s.23)–

(a) pay the cost of the services;

(b) pay a contribution in respect of the cost of the services of a prescribed amount;

(c) pay a prescribed amount in respect of administration costs.

Regulations must provide for repayment to the individual of any amount paid by the individual that exceeds the amount required to be paid (see the Civil Legal Aid (Financial Resources and Payment for Services) Regulations 2013, Reg. 46). Those Regulations also provide that where an application is made for (i) legal representation, except legal representation before the Immigration and Asylum Chamber of the First-tier

Tribunal and the Immigration and Asylum Chamber of the Upper Tribunal in relation to an appeal or review from the First-tier Tribunal; (ii) family help (higher); or (iii) such other legal services as are the subject of a determination under s.10 (funding of exceptional cases) of the 2012 Act, and the individual's monthly disposable income exceeds £315, the individual must pay the following contributions (Reg. 44(2))–

(d) 35% of any such income between £311 and £465;
(e) 45% of any such income between £466 and £616;
(f) 70% of any remaining disposable income.

In similar circumstances described above and where the individual's disposable capital exceeds £3,000, the individual must pay a contribution of the lesser of the excess and the sum which the Director considers to be the likely maximum cost of the civil legal services provided to the individual (Reg. 44(3)).

Regulations may provide for the enforcement of a requirement to make a payment in connection with the provision of services under s.23. Regulations will be able to provide that overdue sums are recoverable summarily as a civil debt, i.e. through a magistrates' court. The regulations will also be able to provide that overdue sums are recoverable, if the county court or High Court so orders, as if they were payable under an order of the High Court or county court, thereby making it unnecessary to begin fresh proceedings in respect of the debt (Legal Aid, Sentencing and Punishment of Offenders Act 2012, s.24).

24 Costs in civil proceedings

The Legal Aid, Sentencing and Punishment of Offenders Act 2012 sets out the general principle that costs ordered against a legally aided individual in civil proceedings must be reasonable, having regard to all the circumstances, including the financial resources and conduct of the parties to the proceedings ("cost protection") (s.26(1)). The Civil Legal Aid (Costs) Regulations 2013 make provision about costs orders in civil proceedings in favour of or against a legally aided party. The Regulations makes exceptions to the general principle of cost protection in relation to certain forms of civil legal aid and in certain family proceedings. Cost protection does not apply in relation to (Reg. 6)–

(a) parts of proceedings for which civil legal services are provided in the form of (i) help at court or (ii) legal help, help with family mediation or family help (lower), except in the circumstances described below;
(b) parts of family proceedings for which civil legal services are provided in the form of (i) family help (higher) or (ii) legal representation.

Cost protection applies where a legally aided party receives legal help, help with family mediation or family help (lower) in relation to proceedings (other than family proceedings) and later receives, in respect of the same proceedings, family help (higher) or legal representation (Reg. 7). Subject to certain exceptions, cost protection applies in respect of costs incurred by the receiving party during the period in which civil legal services are being provided, whether before or after the commencement of proceedings (Reg. 8).

Part 3 of the Regulations makes provision in relation to the procedure, determination and enforcement of costs orders against a legally aided party. Where, for the purpose of enforcing a costs order against a legally aided party who is not a legal person, a charging order is made under s.1 of the Charging Orders Act 1979 in respect of that party's interest in the main or only dwelling in which that party resides (Reg. 11)–

(c) that charging order must operate to secure the amount payable under the costs order (including, without limitation, any interest) only to the extent of the amount (if any) by which the proceeds of sale of the legally aided party's interest in the dwelling (having deducted any mortgage debts) exceed £100,000; and
(d) an order for the sale of the dwelling must not be made in favour of the person in whose favour the charging order is made.

Where an assessment of an individual's resources is made, the first £100,000 of the value of the legally aided party's interest in the main or only dwelling in which the legally aided party resides must not be taken into account in having regard to that party's resources for the purposes of s.26(1). Further, the court may not take into account the legally aided party's clothes or household furniture, or the implements of that party's trade, unless, and if so only to the extent that, the court considers the circumstances of the case are exceptional, having regard in particular to the quantity or value of the items concerned. The resources of the party's partner are to be treated as the resources of the party to the proceedings unless the partner has a contrary interest in the proceedings (Reg. 13). Where the court is considering whether to make a s.26(1) costs order, it must consider whether (i) but for cost protection, it would have made a costs order against the legally aided party; and (ii) if so, whether, on making the costs order, it would have specified the amount to be paid under that order (Reg. 15). A determination under Regulation 15 will be final, except that any party with a financial interest in an assessment of the full costs may appeal against that assessment if, and to the extent that, the party would but for the Regulations be entitled to appeal against an assessment of costs by the court in which the relevant proceedings are taking place (Reg. 18). Further, where the amount which the legally aided party is required to pay under the s.26(1) costs order is less than the full costs, the receiving party may, on the ground there has been a significant change in the legally aided party's circumstances since the date of the order, apply to the court for an order varying the amount which the legally aided party is required to pay (Reg. 19).

Where the court makes a s.26(1) costs order but does not specify the amount which the legally aided party is to pay under it, and has sufficient information before it to decide the minimum amount which that party is likely to be ordered to pay on a determination, the court may order that party to pay an amount on account of the costs which are the subject of the order (Reg. 17). Where a legally aided party is required to give security for costs, the amount of that security must not exceed the amount (if any) which is reasonable having regard to all the circumstances, including the legally aided party's resources and the legally aided party's conduct in connection with the dispute (Reg. 12).

25 The statutory charge

S.25 of the Legal Aid, Sentencing and Punishment of Offenders Act 2012 provides for a statutory charge to arise on any property recovered or preserved by an individual in receipt of civil legal aid, including costs payable to the individual, whether the property or costs are recovered, preserved or payable following legal proceedings or as part of a compromise or settlement of a dispute. The amounts of money to which the statutory charge relate are—
  (a) amounts expended by the Lord Chancellor in securing the provision of the civil legal services (except to the extent that they are recovered by other means), and
  (b) other amounts payable by the individual in connection with the services under ss.23 or 24 (see **23 Payment for services**, above).

The Civil Legal Aid (Statutory Charge) Regulations 2013 make provision about the calculation and operation of the charge which arises over money and other property preserved or recovered by a legally aided party in civil proceedings and over costs payable to the legally aided party by another party to the proceedings.

Generally, the amount of the statutory charge does not include the cost of providing legal help, help at court, family help (lower), family mediation; or help with family mediation. Where a legally aided party receives family help (higher) or legal representation, the amount of the statutory charge will includes such costs where they are made available (Reg. 4).

There are exceptions to the statutory charge where it will not apply to certain property recovered or preserved, including (Reg. 5)—
  (c) any periodical payment of maintenance;
  (d) any sum or sums ordered to be paid under (i) s.25B(4) (pensions) or s.25C (pensions: lump sums) of the Matrimonial Causes Act 1973, (ii) s.5 of the Inheritance (Provision for Family and Dependants) Act 1975 (interim orders), (iii) Part 4 of the Family Law Act 1996 (family homes and domestic violence), or (iv) para. 25(2) or 26 of Sch. 5 to the Civil Partnership Act 2004 (financial relief in the High Court or the county court);
  (e) half of any redundancy payment within the meaning of Part 11 of the Employment Rights Act 1996.

Additionally, except in exceptional circumstances, the statutory charge does not apply to a legally aided party's clothes or household furniture or the implements of a legally aided party's trade.

Where the statutory charge is in favour of a provider, that provider may be granted authority to waive all or part of the amount of the statutory charge where its enforcement would cause grave hardship or distress to a legally aided party or be unreasonably difficult because of the nature of the property (Reg. 8). Waiver may also occur in cases of significant wider public interest (Reg. 9).

F: PROVIDERS OF SERVICES

26 Arrangements by the Lord Chancellor

The Lord Chancellor may make such arrangements as he considers appropriate for the purposes of carrying out his functions concerning the provision of civil legal aid. The Lord Chancellor may, in particular, make arrangements by (Legal Aid, Sentencing and Punishment of Offenders Act 2012, s.2)—
  (a) making grants or loans to enable persons to provide services or facilitate the provision of services;
  (b) making grants or loans to individuals to enable them to obtain services; and
  (c) establishing and maintaining a body to provide services or facilitate the provision of services.

The Civil Legal Aid (Remuneration) Regulations 2013 make provision about the payment to persons who provide civil legal services under arrangements made for the purposes of the 2012 Act. The Regulations as amended deal with, *inter alia*, the fees paid in respect of remuneration for matters before the family court, inquests, expert services, applications for judicial review, immigration and asylum cases, mental health proceedings, housing matters, debt and payments on account direct to barristers in independent practice.

The Lord Chancellor's duty to secure that legal aid is made available in accordance with the Act does not include a duty to secure that, where services are made available to an individual, they are made available by the means selected by the individual (s.28(1)).

27 Position of providers of services

The fact that services provided for an individual are or could be provided under arrangements made for the purposes of the Legal Aid, Sentencing and Punishment of Offenders Act 2012 does not affect (i) the relationship between the individual and the person by whom the services are provided, (ii) any privilege arising out of that relationship, or (iii) any right which the individual may have to be indemnified by another person in respect of expenses incurred by the individual, except to the extent that regulations provide otherwise (s.28(1)). The Legal Aid (Disclosure of Information) Regulations 2013 make provision for providers of services under Part 1 of the 2012 Act to disclose relevant information to the Lord Chancellor or the Director of Legal Aid Casework for the purposes of enabling or assisting them to carry out their functions under the Act notwithstanding the usual rules of privilege regarding the disclosure of client information.

A person who provides services under arrangements made for the purposes of the 2012 Act must not take any payment in respect of the services apart from payment made in accordance with the arrangements, and payment authorised by the Lord Chancellor to be taken (s.28(2)).

28 Authorities

Statutes–

Legal Aid, Sentencing and Punishment of Offenders Act 2012

Statutory Instruments–

Civil Legal Aid (Connected Matters) Regulations 2013 (S.I. 2013 No. 451)

Civil Legal Aid (Costs) Regulations 2013 (S.I. 2013 No. 611)

Civil Legal Aid (Family Relationship) Regulations 2012 (S.I. 2012 No. 2684)

Civil Legal Aid (Financial Resources and Payment for Services) Regulations 2013, as amended (S.I. 2013 Nos. 480 and 753, 2014 Nos. 812 and 2701, and 2015 Nos. 643, 838, and 1416)

Civil Legal Aid (Immigration Interviews) (Exceptions) Regulations 2012 (S.I. 2012 No. 2683)

Civil Legal Aid (Merits Criteria) Regulations 2013, as amended (S.I. 2013 Nos. 104, 772, and 3195, 2014 No. 131, and 2015 Nos. 1414, 1571, and 2005)

Civil Legal Aid (Preliminary Proceedings) Regulations 2013 (S.I. 2013 No. 265)

Civil Legal Aid (Prescribed Types of Pollution of the Environment) Regulations 2012 (S.I. 2012 No. 2687)

Civil Legal Aid (Procedure) Regulations 2012, as amended (S.I. 2012 No. 3098, 2014 Nos. 814 and 1824, 2015 Nos. 1416 and 1678, and 2016 No. 516)

Civil Legal Aid (Remuneration) Regulations 2013, as amended (S.I. 2013 Nos. 422, 2877, 2014 Nos. 7, 586, 1389, and 1824, and 2015 Nos. 325, 898, 1416, and 1678)

Civil Legal Aid (Statutory Charge) Regulations 2013, as amended (S.I. 2013 No. 503, 2014 No. 1824, and 2015 No. 1678)

Legal Aid (Disclosure of Information) Regulations 2013 (S.I. 2013 No. 457)

Legal Aid (Financial Resources and Payment for Services) (Legal Persons) Regulations 2013, as amended (S.I. 2013 Nos. 512 and 754)

Legal Aid (Information about Financial Resources) Regulations 2013, as amended (S.I. 2013 Nos. 628 and 2726, 2014 No. 901, and 2015 Nos. 643, 1408, 1985, and 2005)

LEGAL AID (CRIMINAL): ENGLAND AND WALES

A: INTRODUCTION

1 Provision of criminal legal aid: introduction

The Lord Chancellor has overall responsibility for legal aid and he must secure that legal aid is made available in accordance with Part 1 of the Legal Aid, Sentencing and Punishment of Offenders Act 2012. The 2012 Act abolishes the Legal Services Commission (s.38) which had previous responsibility for the Community Legal Service and the Criminal Defence Service. The Legal Aid Agency, an executive agency within the Ministry of Justice, replaces the Legal Services Commission and now manages the processing of legal aid applications and payments.

The Lord Chancellor is required to designate a civil servant as the Director of Legal Aid Casework whose function is to make decisions on legal aid in individual cases (s.4). The Director is required to comply with directions given by the Lord Chancellor and to have regard to guidance issued by the Lord Chancellor. However, the Lord Chancellor may not give a direction or guidance in relation to an individual case. The Lord Chancellor is under a duty to ensure that the Director acts independently of the Lord Chancellor when applying directions or guidance in relation to an individual case.

This Note relates to criminal legal aid in England and Wales and is set out as follows–
   A: Introduction
   B: Individuals held in custody
   C: Advice and assistance
   D: Representation
   E: Financial eligibility
   F: Providers of services
For civil legal aid in England and Wales see the Note on **Legal Aid (Civil): England and Wales**.

2 Arrangements to secure the provision of legal aid

The Lord Chancellor may make such arrangements as he considers appropriate for the purposes of carrying out his functions under Part 1 of the Legal Aid, Sentencing and Punishment of Offenders Act 2012. The Lord Chancellor may, in particular, make arrangements by–
   (a) making grants or loans to enable persons to provide services or facilitate the provision of services;
   (b) making grants or loans to individuals to enable them to obtain services; and
   (c) establishing and maintaining a body to provide services or facilitate the provision of services.
The Lord Chancellor may by regulations make provision about the payment of remuneration to persons who provide services under arrangements made. The Criminal Legal Aid (Remuneration) Regulations 2013 make provisions for the funding and remuneration of advice, assistance and representation made available under the Legal Aid Sentencing and Punishment of Offenders Act 2012.

3 Qualifying for criminal legal aid: general

The Criminal Legal Aid (General) Regulations 2013 make provision for determinations in relation to whether an individual qualifies for criminal legal aid under Part 1 of the Legal Aid, Sentencing and Punishment of Offenders Act 2012. A person with whom the Lord Chancellor has made an arrangement under s.2 of the Act for the provision of criminal legal aid is known as a "provider". A reporting duty requires providers to report misrepresentation by individuals receiving criminal legal aid (2013 Regulations, Reg. 5).

4 The meaning of "criminal proceedings"

For the purposes of Part 1 of the Legal Aid, Sentencing and Punishment of Offenders Act 2012 "criminal proceedings" means proceedings (s.14)–
   (a) before a court for dealing with an individual accused of an offence;
   (b) before a court for dealing with an individual convicted of an offence (including proceedings in respect of a sentence or order);
   (c) for dealing with an individual under the Extradition Act 2003;
   (d) for binding an individual over to keep the peace or to be of good behaviour (or failing to comply with such an order);
   (e) on an appeal brought by an individual under s.44A of the Criminal Appeal Act 1968 (appeals brought or continued after the appellant has died);
   (f) for contempt or alleged contempt of court;
   (g) on a reference under s.36 of the Criminal Justice Act 1972 on a point of law following the acquittal of an individual on indictment; and
   (h) before any court or other body as may be prescribed.

For the purposes of (h) above, Part 3 of the Criminal Legal Aid (General) Regulations 2013 sets out civil proceedings prescribed as criminal for the purposes of legal aid which are included due to the gravity of the potential sentence. The following proceedings have been prescribed (Reg. 9)–

 (i) civil proceedings in a magistrates' court arising from a failure to pay a sum due or to obey an order of that court where such failure carries the risk of imprisonment;

 (ii) proceedings under the Crime and Disorder Act 1998 s.8(1)(b) (relating to parenting orders made where a criminal behaviour order or sexual harm prevention order is made in respect of a child);

 (iii) proceedings under the Crime and Disorder Act 1998 s.8(1)(c) (relating to parenting orders made on the conviction of a child);

 (iv) proceedings under the Crime and Disorder Act 1998 s.9(5) (to discharge or vary a parenting order) or s.10 (to appeal against a parenting order);

 (v) proceedings under the Football Spectators Act 1989 (relating to banning orders and references to a court);

 (vi) proceedings under s.13 of the Tribunals, Court and Enquiries Act 2007 on appeal against a decision of the Upper Tribunal in relation to a decision of the Financial Conduct Authority, Prudential Regulation Authority, Bank of England, or a person assessing compensation or consideration under the Banking (Special Provisions) Act 2008 or Banking Act 2009;

 (vii) proceedings under ss.80, 82, 83 and 84 of the Anti-social Behaviour, Crime and Policing Act 2014 relating to closure orders made where a person has engaged in, or is likely to engage in behaviour that constitutes a criminal offence on the premises;

 (viii) proceedings under ss.20, 22, 26 and 28 of the Anti-social Behaviour Act 2003 relating to parenting orders in cases of exclusion from school or criminal conduct and anti-social behaviour;

 (ix) proceedings under ss.97, 100 and 101 of the Sexual Offences Act 2003 relating to notification orders and interim orders;

 (x) proceedings under ss.103A, 103E, 103F and 103H of the Sexual Offences Act 2003 relating to sexual harm prevention orders;

 (xi) proceedings under ss.122A, 122D, 122E and 122G of the Sexual Offences Act 2003 relating to risk of sexual risk orders;

 (xii) proceedings under Part 1A of Schedule 1 to the Powers of Criminal Courts (Sentencing) Act 2000 relating to parenting orders for failure to comply with an order under s.20 of that Act to attend a youth offender panel;

 (xiii) proceedings under the Protection from Harassment Act 1997, s.5A relating to restraining orders on acquittal;

 (xiv) proceedings in the Crown Court or Court of Appeal relating to serious crime prevention orders under the Serious Crime Act 2007, ss.19-21 or 24;

 (xv) proceedings under the Criminal Justice and Immigration Act 2008, ss.100, 101, 103, 104 and 106 relating to violent offender orders and interim orders;

 (xvi) proceedings relating to domestic violence protection notices and orders under the Crime and Security Act 2010 ss.26, 27 and 29;

 (xvii) proceedings that involve the determination of a criminal charge for the purposes of Article 6(1) (right to a fair trial) of the European Convention on Human Rights;

 (xviii) proceedings in a youth court (or on appeal from such a court) in relation to the breach or potential breach of a provision of an injunction under the Anti-social Behaviour, Crime and Policing Act 2014, Part 1 where the person who is subject to the injunction is aged under 14;

 (xix) proceedings under the Female Genital Mutilation Act 2003, Sch.2, para 3 in relation to female genital mutilation protection orders made other than on conviction and related appeals, and under Sch. 2, para 6 in relation to orders made under para 3;

 (xx) proceedings under the Modern Slavery Act 2015, ss.14(1)(b), (c), 15, 20-22 in relation to slavery and trafficking prevention orders, and under ss.23 and 27-29 in relation to slavery and trafficking risk orders.

B: INDIVIDUALS HELD IN CUSTODY

5 Individuals arrested and held in custody

Initial advice and assistance is required to be made available to individuals who are arrested and held in custody at a police station or other premises if the Director of Legal Aid Casework has determined that the individual qualifies for advice and assistance and has not withdrawn that determination (Legal Aid, Sentencing and Punishment of Offenders Act 2012 s.13(1)). In making a determination the Director must have regard, in particular, to the interests of justice (s.13(2)). "Initial advice" means advice as to how the law in relation to a matter relevant to the individual's arrest applies in particular circumstances and as to the steps that might be taken having regard to how it applies and "initial assistance" means assistance in taking any of those steps which the individual might reasonably take while in custody, including assistance in the form of advocacy (s.13(7)).

Part 2 of the Criminal Legal Aid (General) Regulations 2013 sets out the process for making an application for initial advice and initial assistance at a police station or other premises. All applications (whether made by the appropriate adult or by the individual making a request to the custody officer) must be made to the Defence Solicitor Call Centre established by the Lord Chancellor under s.2 of the 2012 Act and in accordance with the requirements set out in the 2010 Standard Crime Contract (i.e. the contract between the Lord Chancellor and providers for the provision of criminal legal aid) for the unit of work which is the subject of the application (Reg. 8).

C: ADVICE AND ASSISTANCE

6 Advice and assistance for criminal proceedings

Regulations provide that advice and assistance for criminal proceedings is to be available under Part 1 of the Legal Aid, Sentencing and Punishment of Offenders Act 2012 to an individual if prescribed conditions are met (see below), and the Director of Legal Aid Casework has determined that the individual qualifies for such advice and assistance in accordance with the regulations and has not withdrawn the determination. These are individuals who (s.15)–

(a) are involved in investigations which may lead to criminal proceedings (other than individuals arrested and held in custody at a police station or other premises);

(b) are before a court, tribunal or other person in criminal proceedings; and

(c) have been the subject of criminal proceedings.

Part 4 of the Criminal Legal Aid (General) Regulations 2013 sets out the provisions for making and withdrawing determinations about advice and assistance for criminal proceedings. The Regulations require the Director to have regard to the interests of justice when making a determination (Reg. 13).

The prescribed conditions for the purposes of s.15 of the Act are that an individual must (Reg. 12)–

(i) be the subject of an investigation which may lead to criminal proceedings;

(ii) be the subject of criminal proceedings;

(iii) require advice and assistance regarding an appeal or potential appeal against the outcome of any criminal proceedings or an application to vary a sentence;

(iv) require advice and assistance regarding a sentence where the calculation of the date on which they are entitled to be released or become eligible for consideration by the Parole Board for a direction to be released, is disputed;

(v) require advice and assistance regarding an application or potential application to the Criminal Cases Review Commission;

(vi) require advice and assistance regarding the individual's treatment or discipline in a prison, young offender institution or secure training centre (other than in respect of actual or contemplated proceedings regarding personal injury, death or damage to property) where the proceedings engage Article 6(1) of the European Convention on Human Rights (the right to a fair trial), or where the governor has exercised his discretion to allow advice and assistance in relation to the hearing;

(vii) be the subject of proceedings before the Parole Board where the Parole Board has the power to direct the individual's release;

(viii) be a witness in criminal proceedings and require advice and assistance regarding self-incrimination;

(ix) be a volunteer; or

(x) be detained under Schedule 7 to the Terrorism Act 2000.

The Director must determine whether an individual qualifies for advice and assistance in accordance with s.21 of the Act (financial resources (see **10 Financial eligibility: introduction**, below)) and regulations made under that section and the qualifying criteria set out in the 2010 Standard Crime Contract (i.e. the contract between the Lord Chancellor and providers for the provision of criminal legal aid). A determination must specify any limitations and conditions to which the determination is subject (Reg. 15).

It is possible to appeal to an Independent Funding Adjudicator following a determination that an individual does not qualify for advice and assistance for criminal proceedings (Reg. 17).

D: REPRESENTATION

7 Representation for criminal proceedings

Ss. 16 to 20 of the Legal Aid, Sentencing and Punishment of Offenders Act 2012 and Part 5 of the Criminal Legal Aid (General) Regulations 2013 makes provision for individuals to be provided with representation for criminal proceedings and for determinations in respect of such representation.

Representation is to be available if the individual is a specified individual in relation to the proceedings (see **4 The meaning of "criminal proceedings"**, above, paras. (a) to (h)) and the Director of Legal Aid Casework or, as the case may be, a court has determined, provisionally or otherwise, that the individual qualifies for representation (s.16(1) (see **8 Qualifying for representation**, below)). Where an individual qualifies for representation for the purposes of criminal proceedings, representation is also to be made available for the purposes of any related bail proceedings as well as any preliminary or incidental proceedings (s.16(3)). Proceedings which are, and which are not, to be regarded as incidental proceedings are set out in Regs. 19 and 20 of the Criminal Legal Aid (General) Regulations 2013. Representation for the purposes of criminal proceedings is to be made available on appeal to the Crown Court to private prosecutors whom the Director or court has determined, provisionally or otherwise, qualify for such representation (s.16(3)).

8 Qualifying for representation

The Director of Legal Aid Casework or a court is required to determine whether an individual qualifies for representation by applying the means testing provisions contained in s.21 of the Legal Aid, Sentencing and

Punishment of Offenders Act 2012 (see **10 Financial eligibility: introduction,** below) and the interests of justice test (s.17(1)). The Director may determine whether an individual is eligible for representation for criminal proceedings unless a court is authorised to do so under s. 19 of the Act (s.18(1)). In deciding what the interests of justice consist of for the purposes of such a determination, the following factors must be taken into account (s.17(2))–

(a) whether, if any matter arising in the proceedings is decided against the individual, the individual would be likely to lose his or her liberty or livelihood or to suffer serious damage to his or her reputation;

(b) whether the determination of any matter arising in the proceedings may involve consideration of a substantial question of law;

(c) whether the individual may be unable to understand the proceedings or to state his or her own case;

(d) whether the proceedings may involve the tracing, interviewing or expert cross-examination of witnesses on behalf of the individual; and

(e) whether it is in the interests of another person that the individual be represented.

For the purposes of a determination, making representation available to an individual for the purposes of criminal proceedings is taken to be in the interests of justice when the proceedings are before (2013 Regulations, Reg. 21)–

(f) the Crown Court, to the extent that such proceedings do not relate to an appeal to the Crown Court;

(g) the High Court;

(h) the Court of Appeal; or

(i) the Supreme Court.

An individual may apply for a review of a determination by the Director that the interests of justice do not require representation to be made available (Reg. 27). If the individual remains dissatisfied with the review, then that individual may appeal (Regs. 29 and 30).

A determination which is made in relation to an individual for proceedings in the magistrates' court includes representation in the Crown Court in relation to those proceedings except this does not include representation for any appeal to the Crown Court in the proceedings to which the determination relates (Reg. 24). The Director must consider an application for legal aid in the Crown Court by an individual determined to be financially ineligible for legal aid in relation to proceedings in the magistrates' court, where those proceedings continue in the Crown Court other than on appeal (Reg. 25).

The Director must withdraw a determination if satisfied that the interests of justice no longer require representation. A determination may also be withdrawn where (Reg. 26)–

(i) the individual declines to accept the determination in the terms which are offered;

(ii) the individual requests that the determination is withdrawn; or

(iii) the provider named in the representation order which recorded the original determination declines to continue to represent the individual.

The Criminal Legal Aid (Determinations by a Court and Choice of Representative) Regulations 2013 make provision in relation to the power of the Crown Court, High Court and Court of Appeal to make a determination under s.16 of the Act as to whether an individual qualifies for representation for criminal proceedings.

9 Provisional determinations

The Lord Chancellor has the power to make regulations to allow the Director of Legal Aid Casework or a court to make a provisional determination about whether an individual qualifies for representation where (Legal Aid, Sentencing and Punishment of Offenders Act 2012, s.20)–

(a) the individual is involved in an investigation which may result in criminal proceedings;

(b) the determination is made for the purposes of criminal proceedings that may result from the investigation; and

(c) any prescribed conditions are met.

E: FINANCIAL ELIGIBILITY

10 Financial eligibility: introduction

S.21 of the Legal Aid, Sentencing and Punishment of Offenders Act 2012 provides that a determination that an individual qualifies for services may not be made unless it is determined that the individual's financial resources are such that the individual is eligible for the services. The Criminal Legal Aid (Financial Resources) Regulations 2013 make provision in relation to the circumstances in which an individual's financial resources are such that they are eligible for criminal legal aid under Part 1 of the 2012 Act. See **11 financial eligibility for advice and assistance,** below and **12 Financial eligibility for representation,** below.

11 Financial eligibility for advice and assistance

Exceptions from requirement to make a determination in respect of financial resources

The Director of Legal Aid Casework must make a determination in respect of an individual's application for certain advice and assistance *without* making a determination in respect of that individual's financial resources. Such advice and assistance is as follows (Criminal Legal Aid (Financial Resources) Regulations 2013, Reg. 5)–

(a) advocacy assistance before a magistrates' court or the Crown Court;

(b) advice and assistance provided by a duty solicitor acting as such in accordance with an arrangement with the Lord Chancellor under the Legal Aid, Sentencing and Punishment of Offenders Act 2012;

(c) advice and assistance provided to a volunteer during voluntary attendance;

(d) advice and assistance provided to an individual being interviewed in connection with a serious service offence; and

(e) advice and assistance provided to an individual who is the subject of an identification procedure carried out by means of a video recording, in connection with that procedure.

"Volunteer" means an individual who, for the purpose of assisting with an investigation, without having been arrested attends voluntarily at a police station, customs office or any other place where a constable is present or accompanies a constable to a police station, customs office or any other such place.

Advocacy assistance for individuals in prison

In relation to the individual's discipline in a prison, young offender institution or secure training centre (other than in respect of actual or contemplated proceedings regarding personal injury, death or damage to property), or in relation to proceedings before the Parole Board, where the individual is the subject of the proceedings, an individual's financial resources are such that he is eligible for advocacy assistance in respect of criminal proceedings if his (Reg. 7)–

weekly disposable income does not exceed	£209
disposable capital does not exceed	£3,000

Other advice and assistance

An individual's financial resources are such that he is eligible for advice and assistance under s.15 of the Act (see **6 Advice and assistance for criminal proceedings**, above) if his (Reg. 8)–

weekly disposable income does not exceed	£99
disposable capital does not exceed	£1,000

Calculating disposable income and disposal capital

The financial resources of the individual's partner will be treated as the individual's financial resources unless the partner has a contrary interest in the matter in respect of which the individual is seeking advice and assistance, or it is considered that, in all the circumstances of the case, it would be inequitable or impractical to do so (Reg. 9). Where the individual applying for a determination is a child, the financial resources of any maintaining adult will be treated as that child's financial resources unless, having regard to all the circumstances of the case, including the age and financial resources of the child and any conflict of interest between the child and the maintaining adult, it appears to be inequitable to do so (Reg. 10).

In calculating disposal income maintenance payments will be deducted. A sum in respect of the maintenance of an individual's partner and any dependant child or dependant relative of the individual that is a member of the individual's household will also be deducted (Reg. 12). In calculating disposal income, tax and national insurance payments are deducted as are certain benefit payments such as attendance allowance, disability living allowance and payments out of the social fund (Reg. 11). In calculating capital, deductions must be made, *inter alia*, in respect of household furniture and effects, clothes and tools and implements of the individual's trade. In assessing the value of any interest in land, the amount of mortgage debt will be deducted up to £100,000 and, after any such deduction, the first £100,000 of the value of the individual's interest (if any) in the main or only dwelling in which the individual resides will be disregarded (Reg. 13).

Where an individual directly or indirectly deprives themselves of any financial resources, which includes the transfer of any financial resources to another person, the Director will treat such financial resources as part of the individual's resources (Reg. 4).

Deemed eligibility: qualifying benefits

Where an individual is, directly or indirectly, properly in receipt of a qualifying benefit his disposable income and disposal capital will be treated as not exceeding the specified sums set out in Regulations 7 and 8 (see above). For these purposes, "benefit" also includes any working tax credit claimed together with child tax credit or any working tax credit with a disability element or severe disability element where the individual's total income from all sources for the year ending with the date on which the application is made is not more than £14,213 (Reg. 14).

12 Financial eligibility for representation

Exceptions from requirement to make a determination in respect of financial resources

In magistrates' court proceedings, the Director of Legal Aid Casework must make a determination in respect of an individual's application for representation without making a determination in respect of that individual's financial resources where that determination relates to any criminal proceedings *not* listed as follows (Criminal Legal Aid (Financial Resources) Regulations 2013, Reg. 17)–

(i) proceedings referred to in s.14(a) to (g) of the Legal Aid, Sentencing and Punishment of Offenders Act 2012 (see **4 The meaning of "criminal proceedings"**, above paras. (a) to (g)) and in Regulation 9 of the Criminal Legal Aid (General) Regulations 2013 (see **4 The meaning of "criminal proceedings"**, above paras. (i) to (xx), excepting para (xii)), but only to the extent that such proceedings take place in the magistrates' court; and

(ii) proceedings in which an individual has been committed to the Crown Court for sentence, but only where that individual did not apply for, or was not granted, representation for the proceedings that took place in the magistrates' court.

Additionally, no determination of financial resources is required where the individual has made an application for a determination in proceedings in a magistrates' court and (should the proceedings continue there) in the Crown Court and the proceedings continue to the Crown Court other than on appeal.

Financial eligibility

In magistrates' court proceedings, an individual's financial resources are such that they are eligible for representation where (Reg. 18)–

(a) their gross annual income (see below) does not exceed £12,475; or
(b) their gross annual income is more than £12,475 and less than £22,325, if their annual disposable income (see below) does not exceed £3,398.

An individual is not eligible for representation where their gross annual income is £22,325 or greater. Resources and income of a partner are to be treated as resources and income of the individual making the application unless the partner has a contrary interest in the proceedings (Reg. 19).

In Crown Court proceedings, an individual's financial resources are such that they are eligible for representation where (Reg. 31)–

(a) their gross annual income (see below) does not exceed £12,475;
(b) their gross annual income is more than £12,475 and their annual disposable income (see below) does not exceed £37,500;
(c) the individual is a child; or
(d) the Director is satisfied that the individual is, directly or indirectly, properly in receipt of a qualifying benefit.

An individual is not eligible for representation where their disposable annual income is £37,500 or greater. Again, resources and income of a partner are to be treated as resources and income of the individual making the application unless the partner has a contrary interest in the proceedings (Reg. 32).

Assessment of gross annual income

Certain deductions are made in calculating the gross annual income of an individual if they are paid during the period of calculation including (Regs. 20, 33)–

(a) financial support paid under an agreement for the care of a foster child;
(b) any payments paid out of the Independent Living Fund;
(c) any exceptionally severe disablement allowance;
(d) certain benefits and allowances including attendance allowance, severe disablement allowance, carer's allowance, disability living allowance, constant attendance allowance, housing benefit, council tax benefit, payments made out of the social fund and personal and armed forces independence payments;
(e) personal budgets and direct payments made under e.g., the Children and Families Act 2014.

Where an individual making an application for a determination has a partner, or a child of the individual, living as a member of their household, paragraphs 2 and 2A of the Schedule to the Regulations have effect (which divide the individual's gross annual income by a certain factor depending on, for example, ages of the children).

Assessment of annual disposable income

The following amounts must be deducted from the individual's gross annual income in arriving at annual disposable income if they are paid or payable by the individual during the period of calculation (Regs. 21, 34)–

(a) any income tax;
(b) any estimated national insurance contributions;
(c) any council tax;
(d) either (i) any annual rent or annual payment (whether of interest or capital) in respect of a mortgage debt or hereditable security, in respect of the individual's only or main dwelling, or (ii) the annual cost of the individual's living accommodation;
(e) any child care costs;
(f) the amount of any maintenance payment, provided that such amount is considered reasonable;
(g) an amount representing cost of living expenses, being either (i) £5,676, or (ii) if the individual has a partner, or a child of the individual, living as a member of their household, the amount calculated in accordance with paragraphs 3 or 3A of the Schedule to the Regulations (i.e. by multiplying £5,676 by a certain factor depending on ages of children).

Deemed eligibility: children

If the individual making an application for a determination is a child, then it must be determined that the individual's financial resources are such that the individual is eligible for representation (Regs. 22, 31(c)).

Deemed eligibility: qualifying benefits

Where an individual is, directly or indirectly, properly in receipt of a qualifying benefit (see **11 Financial eligibility for advice and assistance**, above), that individual's gross annual income will be treated as not exceeding the amount specified in *Financial eligibility*, para (a), above (Regs. 23, 31(d)).

Duty to report changes in circumstances

An individual must inform the Director of Legal Aid Casework of any change in their financial circumstances which might affect whether or not they are eligible for representation in the magistrates' court (Reg. 26).

Renewal of an application

Where the Director makes a determination that an individual's financial resources are such that they are not eligible for representation, that individual may renew the application if there is a change in their financial circumstances which might affect whether or not they are eligible (Regs. 27, 36).

Review of decision

Where it has been determined that an individual's financial resources are such that the individual is not eligible for representation, that individual may apply for a review of the decision on the grounds that (Regs. 28, 37)–

(a) there has been a miscalculation of the individual's financial resources or an administrative error; or

(b) the individual does not have sufficient financial resources to pay for the cost of legal assistance, notwithstanding the determination concerning financial resources that the individual is not eligible for representation.

Other criminal proceedings

In criminal proceedings other than in the magistrates' or Crown court, the authority determining an individual's application for legal aid must deem the individual to be financially eligible (Reg. 39).

Recovery of defence costs

Where a defendant in the Crown Court who was denied criminal legal aid because their annual disposable household income exceeded £37,500 (see *Financial eligibility*, above) is acquitted, they can apply for a defendant's costs order to recoup their costs from central funds at legal aid rates (Prosecution of Offences Act 1985, s.16A(5A)).

13 Contribution orders

The Criminal Legal Aid (Contribution Orders) Regulations 2013 make provision in relation to the liability of individuals who are in receipt of representation for criminal proceedings in the Crown Court to make a payment in connection with the provision of such representation, based on an assessment of their financial resources. The Regulations provide that an individual may be liable to pay a contribution of up to 100% towards their defence costs either from income or capital assets. While proceedings are ongoing, an individual may be liable to make contributions from income under an income contribution order. If they are acquitted, these contributions will be repaid to them. Once proceedings have concluded, if they are convicted, then they may be liable make a contribution from their capital assets up to the full amount of the their defence costs, under a capital contribution order.

Calculation of gross annual income and disposable annual income are similar to those contained in the Criminal Legal Aid (Financial Resources) Regulations 2013 (see **12 Financial eligibility for representation**, above). Generally, where it is calculated that an individual's disposable annual income is £3,398 or less they are not liable to make a payment out of income. Where it is calculated that an individual's disposable annual income exceeds £3,398, a determination must be made that the individual is liable to make six payments of one twelfth of 90 per cent of their disposable annual income (Reg. 12). There are specified maximum amounts payable under an income contribution order for classes of offences (Reg. 15).

Where the recoverable costs of representation exceed the amount of any payment already made by an individual under an income contribution order; or an individual was not liable to make a payment, an assessment of the individual's capital must be made. In calculating capital, £30,000 will be deducted from the total value unless, for example, an individual fails without reasonable excuse to provide documentary evidence in relation to his capital and there are reasonable grounds for believing he has capital in excess of this amount (Reg. 28).

If an individual fails to pay a contribution as required, then enforcement action may be taken and the costs of enforcement may be added to the amount payable by them. Any overdue sums are recoverable summarily as a civil debt (Regs. 45, 46). The Criminal Legal Aid (Motor Vehicles Orders) Regulations 2013 authorise a court to make motor vehicle orders in respect of an individual for the purpose of enabling certain sums required to be paid to be recovered from the individual, where those sums are overdue.

14 Information about financial resources

S.22 of the Legal Aid, Sentencing and Punishment of Offenders Act 2012 provides that the Director of Legal Aid Casework may make an information request to the Secretary of State or the Commissioners for Her Majesty's Revenue and Customs for the purposes of facilitating a determination about an individual's financial resources for the purpose of legal aid available under Part 1 of the Act. The Legal Aid (Information about Financial Resources) Regulations 2013 specify, *inter alia*, the particular benefits in relation to which an individual's benefit status may be requested.

15 Recovery of defence costs

The Criminal Legal Aid (Recovery of Defence Costs Orders) Regulations 2013 provide that where an individual receives legal aid for representation under Part 1 of the Legal Aid, Sentencing and Punishment of

Offenders Act 2012 in relation to criminal proceedings before any court other than a magistrates' court or the Crown Court, the court hearing the proceedings must, unless an exception applies (see below), make a determination at the conclusion of the proceedings requiring the individual to pay some or all of the cost of their representation. Such determinations are known as "recovery of defence costs orders". The maximum amount payable in respect of a determination is the full cost of the represented individual's representation in the proceedings before the court (Reg. 5). A determination may provide for immediate payment of the full amount payable, or for periodic payment of specified instalments (Reg. 6). A determination cannot be made in respect of an individual under the age of 18 (Reg. 7) and cannot usually be made in respect of an acquitted individual where that person was before the court to appeal a conviction and the appeal was allowed unless the court considers in all the circumstances of the case it is reasonable to do so (Reg. 8). Further, a determination cannot be made in respect of a represented individual who is, directly or indirectly, properly in receipt of a qualifying benefit unless they fail to provide information on time (Reg. 9) and cannot be made in relation to a represented individual who has none of the following (Reg. 10)–

    (a) capital exceeding £3,000;
    (b) equity in the individual's main dwelling exceeding £100,000; and
    (c) gross annual income exceeding £22,325.

The court must not make a determination if it is satisfied that it would not be reasonable to make such a determination, on the basis of the information and evidence available, or that requiring a represented individual to make a payment in respect of the cost of their representation would involve undue financial hardship (Reg. 11).

Any overdue amounts payable in respect of a determination may be recovered summarily as a civil debt (Reg. 20).

Note.– Where a defendant in criminal proceedings who has received legal aid is the subject of a restraint order made under the Proceeds of Crime Act 2002, that restraint order will remain in place until either the obligation to make legal aid payments has been satisfied, or until it is discharged by a court (Restraint Orders (Legal Aid Exception and Relevant Legal Aid Payments) Regulations 2015, SI No. 868).

F: PROVIDERS OF SERVICES

16 Choice of provider

The Lord Chancellor's duty to secure the provision of legal aid does not include a duty to secure that legal aid is made available by the means selected by the individual or that they are made available by a person selected by the individual. The Lord Chancellor may, in particular, discharge the duty by arranging for some services to be provided by telephone or by other electronic means (Legal Aid, Sentencing and Punishment of Offenders Act 2012, s.27(1) to (3)). However, an individual who qualifies for representation for the purposes of criminal proceedings by virtue of a determination under s.16 of the Act (see **7 Representation for criminal proceedings**, above) may select any representative or representatives willing to act for the individual, subject to regulations (s.27(4)). Such regulations may, *inter alia*, limit the choice to a specified group of providers or may limit the number of legal representatives who can act for any individual at any one time. They may also restrict the right of the individual to appoint a new legal representative in place of one previously chosen (s.27(6)). The Criminal Legal Aid (Determinations by a Court and Choice of Representative) Regulations 2013 make provision in relation to the selection of a provider. The Regulations specify the types of provider (persons who have entered into arrangements with the Lord Chancellor to provide legal aid under Part 1 of the 2012 Act) that an individual may select to represent them in criminal proceedings (Reg. 12). The Regulations require co-defendants to select the same provider unless there is, or is likely to be, a conflict of interest (Reg. 13). The circumstances in which an individual may change providers are also specified. These include (i) a determination by the court that there is a breakdown in the relationship between the individual and the original provider such that effective representation can no longer be provided, or (ii) the original provider considers there to be a duty to withdraw from the case in accordance with the provider's professional rules of conduct (Reg. 14). Where an individual has a determination withdrawn and there is a subsequent determination in respect of the same proceedings, the individual must select the same provider unless the relevant court considers that there are good reasons not to do so (Reg. 15).

The Regulations also make provision in relation to the selection of advocates. Generally, an individual in criminal proceedings before a magistrates' court may not select an advocate, except that in certain specified circumstances a Queen's Counsel or more than one advocate may be selected, for example in the case of an extradition hearing or an indictable offence and there are circumstances which make the proceedings unusually grave or difficult (Regs. 16, 17). Provision is also made that an individual in criminal proceedings before a court other than a magistrate's court may only select a single junior advocate. However, in specified circumstances the court may permit a Queen's Counsel or more than one advocate to be selected by the individual, for example where the case involves substantial novel or complex issues of law or fact and certain other specified conditions are met (Reg. 18).

17 Authorities

Statutes–
Legal Aid, Sentencing and Punishment of Offenders Act 2012

Statutory Instruments–
Criminal Legal Aid (Contribution Orders) Regulations 2013, as amended (S.I. 2013 Nos. 483 and 2792, and 2015

Nos. 643, 710, 838, and 1678)

Criminal Legal Aid (Determinations by a Court and Choice of Representative) Regulations 2013, as amended (S.I. 2013 Nos. 614, 1765, and 2814, and 2015 No. 1678)

Criminal Legal Aid (General) Regulations 2013, as amended (S.I. 2013 Nos. 9, 472, and 2790, and 2015 Nos. 326, 838, 1416, and 1678)

Criminal Legal Aid (Financial Resources) Regulations 2013, as amended (S.I. 2013 Nos. 471, 591, and 2791, and 2015 Nos. 643 and 838)

Criminal Legal Aid (Motor Vehicles Orders) Regulations 2013 (S.I. 2013 No. 1686)

Criminal Legal Aid (Recovery of Defence Costs Orders) Regulations 2013 (S.I. 2013 No. 511)

Criminal Legal Aid (Remuneration) Regulations 2013, as amended (S.I. 2013 Nos. 435, 862, and 2803, 2014 Nos. 415 and 2422, 2015 Nos. 325, 800, 882, 1369, 1416, and 1678, and 2016 No. 313)

Legal Aid (Information about Financial Resources) Regulations 2013, as amended (S.I. 2013 Nos. 628 and 2726, 2014 No. 901, and 2015 Nos. 643, 1408, 1985, and 2005)

LEGAL AID: SCOTLAND

Contents
This Note has been arranged as follows—
A: Preliminary
B: Legal advice and assistance (The Pink Form Scheme)
C: Legal aid in civil proceedings
D: Legal aid in criminal proceedings
E: Legal aid in special cases
F: Financial conditions
G: Employment of solicitors by the Board

A: PRELIMINARY

1 Introduction

The Legal Aid (Scotland) Act 1986 (the 1986 Act), and the regulations made under it, make provision for the legal aid scheme in Scotland.

The Act creates three types of legal aid—
(a) advice and assistance,
(b) civil legal aid, and
(c) criminal legal aid.

These are available, in accordance with the provisions of the 1986 Act, for the provision of services by legal representatives and, where appropriate, by advocates. Legal representation is also available from people who have acquired rights to conduct litigation or, as the case may be, rights of audience by virtue of the Law Reform (Miscellaneous Provisions) (Scotland) Act 1990.

The legal advice and assistance scheme is also available for clients who seek advice on the provision of executry services from executry practitioners and recognised financial institutions offering executry services, and for clients who seek advice on conveyancing services from independent qualified conveyancers, these being the different types of practitioner created by the 1990 Act.

2 The Scottish Legal Aid Board

The Scottish Legal Aid Board was established by Part I of the Legal Aid (Scotland) Act 1986 and is appointed by the Scottish Ministers. It administers the Scottish legal aid scheme.

B: LEGAL ADVICE AND ASSISTANCE
(THE PINK FORM SCHEME)

3 Advice and assistance

Part II of the Legal Aid (Scotland) Act 1986 and the Advice and Assistance (Scotland) Regulations 1996 make provision for legal advice and assistance in Scotland under the Pink Form Scheme.

Under the 1996 Regulations it is for the solicitor to determine whether the subject matter of an application for advice and assistance relates to civil, criminal or children's matters (Reg. 8), and that solicitor is required not to approve it where the applicant has available rights and facilities which make it unnecessary for them to receive assistance (Reg. 10).

A legal representative is required, within 14 days of his having begun to give advice and assistance, to send a copy of his client's application to the Board.

A legally assisted person must not be required to pay his legal representative any charge or fee except where his financial resources are such as make him liable to pay a contribution. For the current contribution payable, see **32 Maximum contributions in respect of advice and assistance and assistance by way of representation,** below.

4 Assistance by way of representation

Assistance may be provided by way of representation. S.6 of the Legal Aid (Scotland) Act 1986 defines assistance by way of representation as advice and assistance provided to a person by taking on his behalf any step in instituting, conducting, or defending any proceedings (a) before a court or tribunal or (b) in connection with a statutory inquiry, whether by representing him in those proceedings or by otherwise taking any step on his behalf.

5 Scope of advice and assistance

By virtue of the Advice and Assistance (Assistance by Way of Representation) (Scotland) Regulations 2003, assistance by way of representation is available in relation to (Reg. 3)–

(a) summary criminal proceedings (see **6 Advice and assistance in summary criminal proceedings**, below);

(b) petitions for the appointment of an executor to a deceased person under the Act of Sederunt (Confirmation of Executors) 1964;

(c) proceedings under s.17 of the Matrimonial Homes (Family Protection) (Scotland) Act 1981;

(d) proceedings before the Mental Health Tribunal for Scotland;

(e) petitions by a debtor for the sequestration of his estate under the Bankruptcy (Scotland) Act 1985;

(f) disciplinary proceedings before a governor in relation to a prisoner, where the prisoner has been permitted by the governor to be legally represented;

(g) proceedings in Parole Board cases;

(h) proceedings on an application for removal of a driving disqualification;

(i) proceedings under s.66 of the Criminal Justice and Public Order Act 1994 for the return of sound equipment (see Note **[15]** 48, E: RAVES);

(j) civil proceedings arising from a person's failure to pay a fine or other sum or obey a court order where there is a risk of imprisonment and it is reasonable for assistance to be made available;

(k) applications made by people (other than the accused) under the Criminal Law (Consolidation) (Scotland) Act 1995, s.31(6) (proceedings relating to, and discharge and variation of, court orders relating to drug trafficking);

(l) *deleted*;

(m) proceedings before an employment tribunal where the case is arguable, it is reasonable for assistance to be given, and the case is too complex to allow the applicant to present it in person to a minimum standard of effectiveness;

(n) proceedings in connection with an application for a warrant of further detention (or for an extension) made under the Terrorism Act 2000;

(na) proceedings under the Counter-Terrorism and Security Act 2015 relating to the review of decisions relating to temporary exclusion orders (under s.11 of the 2015 Act) and proceedings relating to an application by a senior police officer under paragraph 8 of Schedule 1 to the 2015 Act (seizure of passports etc.) for an extension of the 14-day period during which a travel document may be retained;

(o) proceedings involving existing life prisoners who are the subject of a hearing to specify a notional punishment part;

(p) proceedings under s.5 of the Protection from Abuse (Scotland) Act 2001;

(q) *deleted*;

(r) applications in relation to the variation or termination of a football banning order under the Police, Public Order and Criminal Justice (Scotland) Act 2006, s.51;

(s) any disability discrimination in schools case heard by an Additional Support Needs Tribunal for Scotland; and

(t) proceedings under the Double Jeopardy (Scotland Act 2011 where an application has been made to bring a new prosecution where (a) a person has been acquitted of an offence; (b) a person has been acquitted of an offence involving the physical injury of another person and the injured person has since died; or (c) on the basis that the previous proceedings were a nullity.

The assistance by way of representation which may be provided under (b) above (appointment of an executor) will be for representation of the petitioner in all stages of an unopposed petition until the petitioner be decerned executor and extract decree dative obtained (Reg. 8).

The prior approval of the Board is not required except in respect of proceedings under (h), (k), (m) and (s) above (Reg. 13).

Assistance by way of representation is also available in relation to children's hearings and some proceedings in the sheriff court involving children (Reg. 3A). See **25 Proceedings relating to children**, below.

Assistance by way of representation is also available in relation to certain proceedings under the Criminal Procedure (Scotland) Act 1995, namely (Reg. 4)–

(t) in relation to a probation progress review or failure to comply with the requirements of a probation order, community service order, or supervised attendance order;

(ta) in relation to a periodic review of a community payback order, breach of such an order, or application to vary, revoke or discharge an order;

(u) proceedings relating to the amendment or revocation of a community service order or supervised attendance order; the revocation or variation of a non-harassment order; the revocation, variation, review of, or failure to comply with any requirement of, a drug treatment and testing order; or the revocation or variation of, or failure to comply with any requirement of, a restriction of liberty order;

(v) proceedings relating to the conviction of a probationer of an offence committed during his probation period;

(w) proceedings for failure to appear as a witness.

Assistance by way of representation is also available (with the prior approval of the Board) in relation to certain proceedings under the Proceeds of Crime (Scotland) Act 1995 and Proceeds of Crime Act 2002, namely (Reg. 5)–

(x) applications under s.25 (recall or variation of suspended forfeiture order) or s.26 (property wrongly forfeited: return or compensation) of the Proceeds of Crime (Scotland) Act 1995 and appeals under s.27 of that Act (appeal against court decision under ss.25(1) and 26(1));

(y) applications and appeals in relation to property not being treated as a gift for the purposes of the Proceeds of Crime (Scotland) Act 1995;

(z) applications made by people (other than the accused) under the Proceeds of Crime (Scotland) Act 1995, s.18(7) (discharge and variation of order to make material available for the purposes of investigation into whether a person has benefited from a crime;

(za) representations made by someone other than the accused in relation to an application for disposal of the family home made under the Proceeds of Crime (Scotland) Act 1995, s.45(2)(b);

(zb) representations made by someone other than the accused who is likely to be affected by an order under the Proceeds of Crime Act 2002, s.92 (confiscation orders).

Note.—Assistance by way of representation may not be available where the proceedings take place in a court which has been designated a drug court (Reg. 4(3)). Where assistance by way of representation is not available, criminal legal aid may be (see **18 Availability of legal aid**, below).

Where the solicitor to whom application has been made is satisfied that the Tribunal deciding the case will do so sitting in Scotland (and any permission needed from the Upper Tribunal has been given or the solicitor is satisfied that the case is arguable, it is reasonable for assistance to be given, and the case is too complex to allow the applicant to present it in person to a minimum standard of effectiveness), assistance by way of representation is also available in relation to proceedings before the (Regs. 5A, 5B)–

(zc) Immigration and Asylum chambers of the First-tier and Upper Tribunals,

and before the First-tier and Upper Tribunals on appeals against–

(zd) penalties imposed under the Value Added Tax Act 1984, s.60, or for evasion of excise duty, for penalties for errors in returns, or failures to notify;

(ze) a decision of the Pensions Regulator,

and before the Upper Tribunal on appeals against various decisions made under or by virtue of–

(ze) the Pensions Appeal Tribunal Act 1943, Vaccine Damage Payments Act 1979, Child Support Act 1991, Social Security (Recovery of Benefits) Act 1997, Social Security Act 1998, Child Support, Pensions and Social Security Act 2000, Tax Credits Act 2002, Health and Social Care (Community Health and Standards) Act 2003, Chid Trust Funds Act 2004 or the Child Maintenance and Other Payments Act 2008.

6 Advice and assistance in summary criminal proceedings

The assistance by way of representation in summary criminal proceedings that may be provided is representation of an accused person who is not in custody (Advice and Assistance (Assistance by Way of Representation) (Scotland) Regulations 2003, Reg. 6)–

(a) at any diet (not preceded by a plea of not guilty) at which a plea to the competency or relevancy of the complaint or proceedings, or a plea in bar of trial, is tendered, and thereafter until that plea has been determined by the court and any related appeal therefrom has been disposed of;

(b) at any diet (not preceded by a plea of not guilty) at which a question within the meaning of the Act of Adjournal (Criminal Procedure Rules) 1996 is raised, and thereafter until that question has been determined by the court;

(ba) in relation to any diet to which the case has been adjourned without plea;

(c) at any diet at which there is tendered on his behalf a plea of guilty to the charges or part of them (his partial plea being accepted by the prosecutor) and he has not previously tendered a plea of not guilty, and thereafter until his case has been finally disposed of;

(d) at any diet at which the court is considering the accused's plea of guilty to the charges and where there has been no change of plea, and thereafter until final disposal of the case;

(e) at any diet at which the court is considering the accused's changed plea of guilty to the charges, provided that no application for criminal legal aid has been made, and thereafter until final disposal of the case; and

(f) at any diet where the judge orders a proof in mitigation, and thereafter until final disposal of the case.

The assistance by way of representation is to be provided only if the solicitor to whom the application has been made is satisfied that it is in the interests of justice for it to be provided. The factors to be taken into account in determining whether it is in the interests of justice for the assistance to be provided include those listed in s.24(3)(a) to (c) of the Act (see **20 Other circumstances when legal aid is available**, below). (Reg. 7).

The assistance by way of representation in summary criminal proceedings that may be provided in a sheriff court which is a youth court or a domestic abuse court, includes, where legal aid has not been granted under s.24, representation after a finding of guilt (Reg. 6(2)).

The assistance by way of representation in summary criminal proceedings that may be provided in any court includes attending upon, advising and acting for any person who appears from custody on the day when that person is first brought to a court to answer to any complaint and thereafter until the conclusion of the first diet at which he is called upon to plead and in connection with any application for liberation following upon that diet and, where he has tendered a plea of guilty at that diet, until his case is finally disposed of (Reg. 6A).

For custody cases, a solicitor other than the duty solicitor may provide the representation only if available to act immediately (whether in person or, in certain circumstances, through another solicitor) and where instructed directly in the context of a demonstrable solicitor and client relationship. Otherwise, it is to be the duty solicitor only (as part of the duty solicitor scheme) who may provide the representation (Reg. 6A).

7 Prospective cost

S.10 of the Legal Aid (Scotland) Act 1986 provides for a limit on the cost of advice and assistance and assistance by way of representation which a legal representative may provide without obtaining the prior approval of the Board. This provision is supplemented by the Advice and Assistance (Financial Limit) (Scotland) Regulations 1993 which provide (Regs 3 and 4) for differing limits to apply to different types of summary and solemn criminal case.

See **28 Prospective cost limits**, below.

8 Financial eligibility

As to the eligibility limits for advice and assistance, see **29 Eligibility for advice and assistance**, below. A person's disposable income and capital for these purposes is calculated in accordance with the Advice and Assistance (Scotland) Regulations 1996, Schedule 2. The resources of a person's spouse or unmarried partner (including a same sex partner) are generally taken into account (s.42 and Reg. 7, Sch. 2, para. 5(c)). However, in calculating a person's capital and income, the following are not included (Sch. 2, para. 5)–

    (a) the value of the subject matter of the claim for which advice and assistance is being applied for;

    (b) any community care direct payment;

    (c) the resources of a spouse who has a contrary interest in the matter in respect of which advice and assistance is being applied for, or who is separated for the applicant, or whose resources it would be inequitable or impracticable to include;

    (d) social security benefits and allowances (except statutory sick pay), tax credits, child maintenance bonus and child support maintenance, contribution-based jobseeker's allowance, contributory employment and support allowance, severe disablement allowance, universal credit, personal or armed forces independence payment, retirement and war pensions, sums payable to holders of the Victoria or George Cross, Welfare Fund payments, and state pension credit.

In addition, in calculating a person's capital, the value of his home, household furniture and effects, personal clothing and the tools of his trade are not included (Sch. 2, para. 6).

People of pensionable age (i.e., for these purposes, the age of 60) are allowed an additional disregard of capital by reference to a sliding scale where their disposable income (excluding any net income derived from capital) is below the limit for making a contribution to legal aid costs. For the amounts of capital to be disregarded and the amounts of disposable income, see **33 Amount of capital to be disregarded in the case of people of pensionable age**, below (Advice and Assistance (Scotland) Regulations 1996, Sch. 2, para. 10).

In computing the capital of the person concerned, there will be wholly disregarded any capital payment received from any source which is made in relation to the subject matter of the dispute (e.g., disaster fund payments) in respect of which the legal aid application has been made (Sch. 2, para. 11).

Assistance is available without reference to financial limits, and there are no client contributions, in the case of–

    (i) proceedings within paragraphs (c) (matrimonial home), (d) (mental health), (n) (terrorism), (o) (life prisoner applications), and (p) (protection from abuse) of see **5 Scope of advice and assistance**, above;

    (ii) where representation is provided under Reg. 6A (see **6 Advice and assistance in summary criminal proceedings**, above);

    (iii) in relation to criminal matters, where the Scottish Ministers so prescribe. Consultations with suspects who have been detained, arrested, or who have voluntarily attended at an HMRC office in connection with a revenue and customs offence, and with persons detained in connection with certain drug smuggling offences, have been prescribed (s.8A and the Criminal Procedure (Legal Assistance, Detention and Appeals) (Scotland) Act 2010 (Consequential Provisions) Order 2011).

9 Payment for advice and assistance

Any person who receives advice and assistance is required to submit to the Board any information requested by the Board, and failure to do so entitles the Board to recover from that person any sum paid out of the Scottish Legal Aid Fund to that person's solicitors (Advice and Assistance (Scotland) Regulations 1996, Reg. 15A).

Regulation 16 specifies the property against which the right to recover costs is not to apply. *Inter alia* money paid under a decree following an action for aliment or by way of periodical allowance, child support maintenance under the Child Support Act 1991, council tax reduction, income support, income-based jobseeker's allowance, personal or armed forces independence payment, income-related employment and support allowance, incapacity benefit or housing benefit, any Welfare Fund payment, any payment of money in accordance with an order of an employment tribunal, the Social Security Commissioners or the Upper Tribunal, and the first £5,338 of any money, or the value of any property, recovered or preserved in certain family proceedings are so specified. It also provides that the Board may give authority for the right not to be enforced if to do so would cause grave hardship or distress to the client or if it could only be exercised with unreasonable difficulty because of the nature of the property.

Where the Board has paid a solicitor for advice and assistance given to a person and, either before or after such payment, the person or any solicitor acting on their behalf obtains expenses or property in connection with the matter in question which is not disclosed to the Board, the Board can recover from the person the sum already paid (Reg. 21). Payments may also be recovered or withheld where a solicitor has not correctly applied the relevant tests for eligibility in relation to a non-criminal matter (Reg. 22).

10 Costs

The Legal Aid (Scotland) Act 1986 makes no provision for limits on awards of costs against assisted persons or for costs of successful unassisted parties to be paid by the Board.

C: LEGAL AID IN CIVIL PROCEEDINGS

11 Introduction

Part III of the Legal Aid (Scotland) Act 1986 and the Civil Legal Aid (Scotland) Regulations 2002 make provision for legal aid in civil proceedings.

12 Scope of legal aid

By virtue of Part I of Schedule 2 to the Legal Aid (Scotland) Act 1986 and Regulation 4 of the Civil Legal Aid (Scotland) Regulations 2002, civil legal aid is available for civil proceedings before the–
- Supreme Court of the United Kingdom (in relation to applications under the Scotland Act 1998 and appeals from the Court of Session);
- Court of Session;
- Lands Valuation Appeal Court;
- Scottish Land Court;
- sheriff court;
- Lands Tribunal for Scotland;
- Employment Appeal Tribunal;
- Social Security Commissioners, but only where–
  - any onward appeal would lie to the Court of Session (Reg. 47)); or
  - the proceedings to the commissioners are themselves by way of an appeal;
- judicial review proceedings before the Upper Tribunal which have been transferred from the Court of Session; and
- Proscribed Organisations Appeal Commission,

except those proceedings specified in Schedule 2, Pt II.

Part II excepts proceedings which are wholly or partly concerned with defamation or verbal injury unless additional criteria prescribed by the Scottish Ministers are met (but legal aid may be granted for defending a counterclaim for defamation or verbal injury) or which relate to election petitions, and simplified divorce applications. First instance small claims processes and certain debt actions are also excluded.

Council Directive 2003/8 establishes common rules for legal aid in relation to cross border disputes.

13 Proceedings under the Child Abduction and Custody Act 1985 and for registration of foreign orders

Regulations 45 and 46 of the Civil Legal Aid (Scotland) Regulations 2002 provide for legal aid to be made available–
(a) in proceedings under the Child Abduction and Custody Act 1985;
(b) on an application to the Court of Session for the registration of a foreign judgment under s.4 of the Civil Jurisdiction and Judgments Act 1982 (judgments other than maintenance orders);
(c) on an application to the sheriff for the enforcement of a maintenance order under s.5 of the 1982 Act.

A person who qualifies for legal aid under paragraph (a) is to be granted legal aid without enquiry into his resources, without requiring him to make a contribution, without requiring him to show that he has *probabilis causa litigandi* or that it is reasonable for him to receive legal aid and without requiring him to make a contribution and the statutory charge will not apply to any property recovered or preserved for him. A person who qualifies for legal aid under paragraph (b) or paragraph (c) is to be granted legal aid without enquiry into his resources and without requiring him to make a contribution and the statutory charge will not apply to any property recovered or preserved for him.

14 Application for legal aid

The Civil Legal Aid (Scotland) Regulations 2002 govern applications for legal aid.

Application is made to the Board; the Board must send to any opponent (or his legal representative) notification that application for legal aid has been made and copies of specified supporting documents, and the opponent has the right to make representations to the Board as to the application (Regs 5, 7, and 8).

The Board may suspend the availability of legal aid for up to 90 days when the applicant has failed without reasonable cause to comply with any condition or duty to pay any contribution (or instalment thereof), or where, in certain cases, the Board requires to consider information which might merit termination of legal aid, or where the nominated legal representative has ceased to act. At the end of that period the Board must either restore legal aid, suspend it for one further period of 90 days, or terminate it (Reg. 29).

The Board may request from any applicant or assisted person (or their solicitors or counsel) any information relating to a change in circumstances, financial or otherwise, (Reg. 23A) and if that information is not forthcoming, the Board has the right to recover from that person any funds paid already and further legal aid may be withdrawn or suspended (Reg. 31A).

The Board may make legal aid available for specially urgent work undertaken before an application is determined, if it is satisfied that at the time the work was undertaken there was *probabilis causa litigandi* and it appears to the Board to be reasonable in the circumstances of the case that the applicant should receive legal aid in either of the following sets of circumstances–

(a) where any of certain specified steps has been required to be taken as a matter of special urgency to protect the applicant's position; or

(b) subject to exceptions, where steps are required to be taken as a matter of special urgency to protect the applicant's position. The exceptions include where, in the same proceedings, an application has already been refused or treated as abandoned or the Board has ceased to make legal aid available.

Where (b) applies, the Board may limit the steps to be taken in such a way as it considers appropriate in the circumstances and, if an application for legal aid has not already been submitted, the solicitor must submit an application within 28 days of commencement of the urgent work (Reg. 18).

Legal aid made available to a person may be subject to such conditions as the Board considers expedient; and such conditions may be imposed at any time (Legal Aid (Scotland) Act 1986, s.14).

15 Assessment of resources

The assessment of income is carried out by officers of the Board. In certain cases, where the applicant is acting on behalf of an incapable adult, the resources of the incapable adult will be assessed rather than those of the applicant (Civil Legal Aid (Scotland) Regulations 1996, Reg. 14(3)).

16 Determination in case of urgency

There is no provision for the granting of legal aid based on an estimate, but legal aid may be granted in cases of special urgency (see **14 Application for legal aid**, above).

17 Financial contributions by assisted persons

Regulation 33 of the Civil Legal Aid (Scotland) Regulations 2002 specifies the property in respect of which the statutory charge will *not* apply. Money payable by way of child support maintenance, income support, income-based jobseeker's allowance, income-related employment and support allowance, housing benefit, personal or armed forces independence payment, State pension or universal credit, and any Welfare Fund payment are specifically excluded from the statutory charge.

D: LEGAL AID IN CRIMINAL PROCEEDINGS

18 Availability of legal aid

Part IV of the Legal Aid (Scotland) Act 1986 provides for legal aid in criminal proceedings. S.21 of the Act provides that Part IV applies to criminal legal aid in connection with the following–

(a) criminal proceedings before any of the following: (i) the High Court of Justiciary, (ii) the sheriff, (iii) the district court;

(b) any case the referral of which is required, under s.2(6) of the Prisoners and Criminal Proceedings (Scotland) Act 1993, by a designated life prisoner and any reference in connection with such proceedings under Article 177 of the EEC Treaty;

(c) any reference, appeal or application for special leave to appeal to the Judicial Committee of the Privy Council under paragraph 11 or 13(a) of Schedule 6 to the Scotland Act 1998; and

(d) any reference, appeal or application for permission to appeal to the Supreme Court under s.288ZB or 288AA of the Criminal Procedure (Scotland) Act 1995.

Under s.22, criminal legal aid is automatically available to every accused person, without enquiry into his means–

(a) where he is given representation by a legal representative at an identification parade held in connection with or in contemplation of criminal proceedings against him;

(b) where his case is being prosecuted under solemn procedure until either his application to the Board for legal aid under s.23 (see below) has been determined or he is admitted to bail or he is committed until liberated in due course of law, whichever first occurs;

(c) where he is being prosecuted under summary procedure, and either is in custody or has been liberated (under s.22(1)(a) of the Criminal Procedure (Scotland) Act 1995) on his undertaking to appear (i) until the conclusion of the first diet at which he tenders a plea of guilty or not guilty or (ii) where he has tendered a plea of guilty at that diet, until his case is finally disposed of;

(d) where he is in custody and is being prosecuted under summary procedure and he has (i) tendered a plea of not guilty and (ii) has applied to the Board for legal aid, until his application has been determined by the Board;

(e) where he is being prosecuted under ss.119 or 185 of the 1995 Act (new prosecution for same or similar offence), until his case is finally disposed of;

(f) where the proceedings are for the court to determine whether the accused is unfit for trial under s.53F of the Criminal Procedure (Scotland) Act 1995 or, following a decision that a trial cannot proceed for that reason, consist of an examination of facts under s.55 of the 1995 Act;

(g) in relation to an examination of the facts held under s.55 of the 1995 Act and the disposal of the case following such an examination;

(h) where the proceedings consist of an appeal under ss.62 or 63 of the 1995 Act (appeal by, respectively, accused or prosecutor where accused found not criminally responsible or unfit for trial); and

(i) where a solicitor has been appointed by the court under s.288D of the 1995 Act (for those accused of sexual offences and therefore prohibited from conducting their own defence).

Where legal aid is made available under (c)(i) above, it will also be available in connection with any steps taken in the making of, and representation in connection with, any application for liberation following upon the diet there mentioned.

Under ss.23 and 23A, criminal legal aid will be available on an application to the Scottish Legal Aid Board–

(a) where a person is being prosecuted under solemn procedure; or

on an application made to the appropriate court–

(b) where a person who has not previously been sentenced to imprisonment or detention has been convicted in summary proceedings and the court is considering a sentence of imprisonment or detention or the imposition of imprisonment under s.214(2) of the 1995 Act (failure to pay a fine when no time for payment is allowed),

if the Board or court is satisfied that the expenses of the case cannot be met without undue hardship to the applicant or his dependants.

19 Proceedings where legal aid is not available

Criminal legal aid is not available in connection with certain prescribed proceedings, i.e., (Criminal Legal Aid (Scotland) (Prescribed Proceedings) Regulations 1997)–

(a) on an application for removal of a driving disqualification;

(b) for failure to comply with the requirements of a probation order, community service order, or supervised attendance order;

(c) relating to a conviction of a probationer of an offence committed during his probation period;

(d) relating to the amendment or revocation of a community service order or supervised attendance order; the revocation or variation of a non-harassment order; the revocation, variation, review of, or failure to comply with any requirement of, a drug treatment and testing order; or the revocation or variation of, or failure to comply with any requirement of, a restriction of liberty order;

(e) for an application for an order declaring that a gift should not be confiscated under the Proceeds of Crime (Scotland) Act 1995, ss.5(3) or 6(3);

(f) relating to applications for the return of property wrongly forfeited, or for compensation for the non-return of such property under the Proceeds of Crime (Scotland) Act 1995, ss.25(1) or 26(1);

(g) certain hearings involving life prisoners who are the subject of a hearing to specify a notional punishment part;

(h) the variation or termination of a football banning order under the Police, Public Order and Criminal Justice (Scotland) Act 2006, s.51.

Assistance by way of representation may be available in such cases (see **4 Assistance by way of representation**, above). Note also that criminal legal aid may still be available where the proceedings take place before a court which has been designated as a drug court (see Reg. 4).

20 Other circumstances when legal aid is available

Criminal legal aid is available on application to the Board by an accused person in summary proceedings, if the Board is satisfied, after considering his financial circumstances, that the expenses of the case cannot be met without undue hardship to him or his dependants and that in all the circumstances of the case it is in the interests of justice that legal aid should be made available to him. The factors which the Board must take into account in determining whether it is in the interests of justice that legal aid be granted include (Legal Aid (Scotland) Act 1986, s.24)–

(a) the likelihood that the court would impose a sentence which would deprive the accused of his liberty or lead to loss of his livelihood;

(b) the complexity of the case;

(c) the accused's age, inadequate knowledge of English, or mental or physical disability;

(d) whether it is in the interests of someone other than the accused that the accused be legally represented;

(e) the fact that the accused has been remanded in custody pending trial.

Legal aid made available to a person in such circumstances may be subject to such conditions as the Board considers expedient; and such conditions may be imposed at any time.

Under s.25, as amended, legal aid is available on application to the Board in connection with an appeal against conviction, sentence, other disposal, or acquittal in criminal proceedings other than proceedings under ss.62 or 63 of the 1995 Act (see **19 Proceedings where legal aid is not available**, above, para. (g))–

    (a) except where criminal legal aid was made available under ss.23 or 24 in connection with the original proceedings, if the Board is satisfied that the expenses of the appeal cannot be met without undue hardship to the applicant or his dependants; and

    (b) either, where the appeal is under ss.106(1) or 175(2) of the 1995 Act, leave to appeal is granted or, in any other case where the applicant is the appellant, the Board is satisfied that in the circumstances of the case it is in the interests of justice that the applicant should receive criminal legal aid.

The same principles apply to the consideration of applications for legal aid in connection with an application for leave to appeal (s.25(5)).

Where an application for criminal legal aid for an appeal has been refused or terminated by the Board on the basis that it is not satisfied that it is (or continues to be) in the interests of justice for it to made available, the High Court can determine that legal aid should be made available, or continue to be made available, if it thinks that it is in the interests of justice for it to do so (s.25(2A), (2B)).

Where it appears to the court or to the Board that an applicant for legal aid under ss.23, 23A, 24, or 25 has available to him rights and facilities making it unnecessary for him to obtain legal aid, or has a reasonable expectation of receiving financial or other help from a body of which he is a member, the court, or as the case may be, the Board must not, unless it is satisfied that there is special reason for doing so, make legal aid available to him. The court or Board must, before making legal aid available under any of those sections to a person who is a member of a body which might reasonably have been expected to give him financial help towards his defence, require from the applicant an undertaking to pay to the Board any sum received from that body on account of those expenses (Criminal Legal Aid (Scotland) Regulations 1996, Regs 7 and 10).

21 When legal aid must be stopped

The Board must cease to make criminal legal aid available where it is satisfied, taking into account any explanation offered by the assisted person, that he (Criminal Legal Aid (Scotland) Regulations 1996, Reg. 18)–

    (a) has wilfully failed to supply information in accordance with the regulations;

    (b) knowingly made a false statement or representation in providing such information;

    (c) conducted himself in connection with the proceedings in such a way as to make it appear to the board unreasonable that he should continue to receive legal aid;

    (d) wilfully or deliberately given false information for the purpose of misleading the Board when they consider his financial circumstances; or

    (e) failed to comply with any condition to which his receipt of legal aid is subject.

When the Board ceases to make criminal legal aid available, it also has the right to recover legal aid already paid out.

Note.–Reg. 18 does not apply where criminal legal aid is made available automatically under s.22(1)(dd) of the 1986 Act on the appointment of a solicitor by a court for a person accused of a sexual offence.

22 Public defence solicitors

The Scottish Legal Aid Board has the power to directly employ solicitors to provide criminal legal assistance (Legal Aid (Scotland) Act 1986, s.28A, as inserted by the Crime and Punishment (Scotland) Act 1997, s.50) and may require applicants for legal aid to instruct one of these employed solicitors who operate, independently of the Board, from a Public Defence Solicitors Office (Scottish Legal Aid Board (Employment of Solicitors to Provide Criminal Legal Assistance) Regulations 1998).

23 Choice of representative

In general, a person receiving legal aid or advice and assistance can choose who is to represent him (Legal Aid (Scotland) Act 1986, s.31). However, the right to select a solicitor or counsel is subject to (s.31(1A))–

    (a) criminal legal assistance must be provided by a solicitor whose name appears on the Criminal Legal Assistance Register maintained by the Scottish Legal Aid Board (s.25A(3));

    (b) in contempt cases, the court may assign any counsel or solicitor who is within the court precincts at the time the order is made (s.30(2));

    (c) in pilot areas, the Scottish Legal Aid Board has the power to directly employ solicitors to provide criminal legal assistance (see **22 Public defence solicitors**, above);

    (d) where the Scottish Legal Aid Board has entered into contracts in any area under s.33A(4) for firms to provide criminal legal assistance, a solicitor connected with one of the contracted firms must be selected;

    (e) in prescribed circumstances, the Board may specify a solicitor (s.31(8) and (9)); and

    (f) where a defendant is precluded from conducting his own defence (i.e., in sexual offence cases) and the court is satisfied that he has not engaged and does not intend to engage his own solicitor, then the court will appoint one for him (1995 Act, s.288D(2)).

24 Duty solicitors

The Board is required by the Criminal Legal Assistance (Duty Solicitor) (Scotland) Regulations 2011 to make arrangements for duty solicitors to be available in the district of each sheriff court and district court, where required, for the following purposes–

(a) attending on any person at an identification parade held in connection with or in contemplation of criminal proceedings against that person at which the services of the duty solicitor are required;

(b) attending on any person who has been taken into custody on a charge of murder, attempted murder, or culpable homicide and who requires the services of the duty solicitor, and to advise and act for such a person until he is admitted to bail or is committed until liberated in due course of law;

(c) advising and acting for any person in custody whose case is being prosecuted under solemn procedure on his first examination by the sheriff and thereafter until he is admitted to bail or committed until liberated in due course of law;

(d) advising and acting for any person who is being prosecuted under summary procedure and who is either in custody or has been liberated on his undertaking to appear on his first appearance in court to answer a complaint and thereafter (i) until the end of the first diet at which he is called upon to plead and in connection with any application for liberation following upon that diet and (ii) where he has tendered a plea of guilty at that diet, until his case is finally disposed of;

(e) providing advice and assistance to any person suspected of having committed an offence who attends a police station or other place voluntarily for questioning, and any person detained for questioning at a police station, and any person arrested but not charged who is detained for questioning.

Unless the proceedings are taking place in a youth court or a domestic abuse court, criminal legal aid in cases within (d) may be provided only by a duty solicitor. The duty solicitor scheme is not available in proceedings which take place in a court which has been designated as a drug court.

E: LEGAL AID IN SPECIAL CASES

25 Proceedings relating to children

Under Part 5A of the Legal Aid (Scotland) Act 1986, legal aid is available for proceedings (s.28B)–

(a) before a sheriff for variation or termination of a child protection order;

(b) before a Children's Hearing or Pre-Hearing Panel–

(i) following the making of a child protection order;

(ii) where the hearing or Pre-Hearing Panel considers it might be necessary to make a compulsory supervision order including a secure accommodation authorisation;

(iii) following the arrest of a child and his or her detention in a place of safety; and

(c) before a sheriff, the sheriff principal or the Court of Session in connection with a Children's Hearing.

Legal aid is available to a child automatically (i.e., without application of the merits and means tests) where (s.28C)–

(a) there are proceedings before a sheriff for variation or termination of a child protection order;

(b) the hearing follows the making of a child protection order;

(c) a hearing or Pre-Hearing Panel considers it may be necessary to authorise the placement of the child in secure accommodation; or

(d) the hearing follows the child being apprehended by the police if it has been decided that criminal proceedings are not going to be pursued.

Legal aid is available to a child in respect of proceedings before a sheriff where the Scottish Legal Aid Board is satisfied that (s.28D)–

(a) it is in the best interests of the child that children's legal aid be made available;

(b) it is reasonable in the particular circumstances of the case that the child should receive legal aid; and

(c) after consideration of the disposable income and disposable capital of the child, the expenses of the case cannot be met without undue hardship to the child.

In relation to an appeal to the sheriff principal or the Court of Session, the Board must also be satisfied that–

(d) the child has substantial grounds for making or responding to the appeal.

Legal aid is also available to a "relevant person" (i.e., the child's parent, guardian or other person with parental responsibility) where (b) and (c) above are satisfied in relation to them. For an appeal to the sheriff principal of Court of Session, they must have substantial grounds for making or responding to the appeal (s.28E).

Legal aid is also available for court proceedings in which an individual is seeking deemed relevant person status, or where such status may be ended (s.28F).

The Children's Legal Assistance (Scotland) Regulations 2013 make provision for children's legal aid setting out how to apply for it; making provision for review or changes of circumstances; and when it can be terminated. Depending on the financial circumstances of the applicant, a contribution may be payable by those in receipt of children's legal aid. The Board may grant children's legal aid for court proceedings (not for children's hearings) in matters of special urgency, even though the eligibility tests have not yet been shown to be met (Reg. 18).

In certain urgent situations assistance by way of representation is available to a child without a financial test and can be granted by a solicitor without prior approval from the Board. In all other cases there is a financial eligibility test, and the Board must be satisfied that representation is necessary to allow the child to participate effectively. In limited circumstances, assistance by way of representation can also be granted to a relevant person, subject to a financial test, if the solicitor is satisfied that representation is necessary to allow them to participate effectively. In all other cases, prior approval of the Board is required.

The "effective participation" test requires the solicitor or the Board to take account of (Advice and Assistance (Assistance By Way Of Representation) (Scotland) Regulations 2003, Reg. 14)–

    (i) the complexity of the case, including the existence and difficulty of any points of law in issue;

    (ii) the nature of the legal issues involved;

    (iii) the ability of the person to consider and challenge any document or information in the hearings or proceedings without the assistance of a solicitor; and

    (iv) the ability of the person to present his or her views in an effective manner without the assistance of a solicitor.

26 Legal aid in contempt proceedings

S.30 of the Legal Aid (Scotland) Act 1986 provides for legal aid to be granted by the court in contempt proceedings if, after consideration of the applicant's financial resources, it is satisfied that the expenses of the proceedings cannot be met without undue hardship to him or his dependants and that in all the circumstances of the case it is in the interests of justice that legal aid should be made available.

The Legal Aid in Contempt of Court Proceedings (Scotland) Regulations 1992 (S.I. No. 1227, as amended) make further provision for contempt of court proceedings. *Inter alia* they provide for the manner of making applications for legal aid in such proceedings (Reg. 4).

F: FINANCIAL CONDITIONS

I: ADVICE AND ASSISTANCE

27 Introduction

The Legal Aid (Scotland) Act 1986 and the Regulations made under it impose various financial conditions on the availability of legal aid. These are set out in this Part.

28 Prospective cost limits

S.10 of the Legal Aid (Scotland) Act 1986 provides that a solicitor may not provide (or continue to provide) advice and assistance without the approval of the Board when it appears to him that the cost of giving it is likely to exceed specified limits. The current limits are (S.I. 1993 No. 3187, as amended)–

(a) In a special case (see below)– where the advice and assistance or assistance by way of representation relates to a civil matter which is a distinct matter or to a civil matter which is not distinct but following application to the Scottish Legal Aid Board is to be treated as if it were so	£180
(b) In a case which is not a special case– (i) where the advice and assistance or assistance by way of representation relates to a children's matter, a civil matter which is a distinct matter or a civil matter which is not distinct but following application to the Scottish Legal Aid Board is to be treated as if it were so	£95
(ii) where the advice and assistance or assistance by way of representation relates to a civil matter not falling within sub para (i)	£35
(c) in other cases– (i) where the advice and assistance relates to a criminal matter as regards which a summary complaint has been served	£90
(ii) where the advice and assistance relates to a criminal matter as regards which a fixed penalty, compensation or work offer has been made under section 302, 302A or 303ZA of the Criminal Procedure (Scotland) Act 1995, and the offer or any resulting measure occurring under that section is to be challenged (including by non-acceptance of the offer or by disputing whether the offer has been accepted)	£90
(iii) where the advice and assistance relates to any other summary criminal matter	£35
(iv) where in relation to criminal proceedings before a stipendiary magistrate, or the sheriff sitting summarily, the assistance by way of representation is as described in reg. 6(1) or (2) of the Advice and Assistance (Assistance by Way of Representation) (Scotland) Regulations 2003, or reg. 6A of those	£550

Regulations otherwise than in connection with a plea of not guilty

(v) where in relation to criminal proceedings in the justice of the peace court (other than before a stipendiary magistrate) the assistance by way of representation is as described as referred to in (iv) above £185

(vi) where the assistance by way of representation relates to any other summary criminal matter £90

(vii) where the advice and assistance or assistance by way of representation relates to a solemn criminal matter £90

(viii) despite (vi) and (vii) above, where the assistance by way of representation involves a second or subsequent diet that has been ordered by the court £165

(ix) where the assistance by way of representation relates to Parole Board proceedings £165

A "special case" is one–

(a) where assistance by way of representation is provided when a second or subsequent diet has been ordered by the court; or

(b) where advice and assistance is provided and the solicitor is satisfied that –

(i) the matter on which advice and assistance is provided is likely to be resolved only by preparing for proceedings in a civil court for which legal aid is available; and

(ii) it is likely, on the information provided to him, that the applicant will qualify on financial grounds for civil legal aid; and

(iii) it is reasonable in the circumstances of the case.

29 Eligibility for advice and assistance

Advice and Assistance is available under the Legal Aid (Scotland) Act 1986 provided certain disposable income and disposable capital limits are met (s.8). The current maximums are (S.S.I. 2011 No. 217, Reg. 4)–

Maximum amount of weekly disposable income	£245
Maximum amount of disposable capital	£1,716

Note.–a person will automatically qualify on grounds of income if he is in receipt of universal credit (or until replaced, income support or income-based Jobseeker's or employment and support allowance), but may still not qualify on grounds of capital (1986 Act, s.8).

As to allowable deductions when calculating income and capital, see the following paragraphs.

Assistance by way of representation is available without reference to the financial limits in the case of proceedings or applications (Advice and Assistance (Assistance by Way of Representation) (Scotland) Regulations 2003, Reg. 9)–

(a) under the Matrimonial Homes (Family Protection) (Scotland) Act 1981, s.17;

(b) before the Mental Health Tribunal for Scotland;

(c) for a warrant of further detention, or for an extension of such a warrant, made to the sheriff under to the Terrorism Act 2000, Sch. 8, paras 29 or 36;

(d) before a hearing established under–

(i) the Convention Rights (Compliance) (Scotland) Act 2001, Sch, paras 12 or 59; or

(ii) the Prisoners and Criminal Proceedings (Scotland) Act 1993, s.10(2F);

(e) under the Protection from Abuse (Scotland) Act 2001, s.5;

(f) under the Criminal Procedure (Scotland) Act 1995, ss.90B to 90E;

(g) under the Double Jeopardy (Scotland) Act 2011, ss.2(2), 3(3)(b), 4(3)(b), 11(3) and 12(3).

30 Deductions when calculating income

When calculating a person's income for the purpose of assessing their eligibility for advice and assistance, there are certain allowable deductions which may be made. These include deductions for dependants in the same household, as follows (S.I. 1996 No. 2447, Sch. 2 para. 7(c))–

Partner	£32.65
Other dependants	
under 16	£45.58
aged 16 or older	£45.58

31 Capital allowances for dependants

When calculating a person's capital for the purpose of assessing their eligibility for advice and assistance, there are certain allowable deductions which may be made. Deductions, which are made only in respect of dependants, are in the following amounts (S.I. 1996 No. 2447, Sch. 2 para. 6(d))–

First dependant	£335
Second dependant	£200
Each further dependant	£100

32 Maximum contributions in respect of advice and assistance and assistance by way of representation

Where a legally assisted person's income exceeds £102 per week they will have to make a contribution towards the cost of their assistance. The contributions are set on a sliding scale as follows (1986 Act, s.11(2))–

Disposable Weekly Income	Maximum Contribution
Exceeding £105 but not exceeding £112	£7
Exceeding £112 but not exceeding £119	£14
Exceeding £119 but not exceeding £126	£21
Exceeding £126 but not exceeding £133	£28
Exceeding £133 but not exceeding £140	£35
Exceeding £140 but not exceeding £147	£42
Exceeding £147 but not exceeding £154	£49
Exceeding £154 but not exceeding £161	£56
Exceeding £161 but not exceeding £168	£63
Exceeding £168 but not exceeding £175	£70
Exceeding £175 but not exceeding £182	£77
Exceeding £182 but not exceeding £189	£84
Exceeding £189 but not exceeding £196	£91
Exceeding £196 but not exceeding £203	£98
Exceeding £203 but not exceeding £210	£105
Exceeding £210 but not exceeding £217	£112
Exceeding £217 but not exceeding £224	£119
Exceeding £224 but not exceeding £231	£126
Exceeding £231 but not exceeding £245	£135
Exceeding £245	£142

Where the advice and assistance is approved by a solicitor, the contributions are set on a sliding scale as follows–

Disposable Weekly Income	Maximum Contribution
Exceeding £105 but not exceeding £134	£7
Exceeding £134 but not exceeding £163	£14
Exceeding £163 but not exceeding £193	£21
Exceeding £193 but not exceeding £222	£28
Exceeding £222 but not exceeding £245	£35

Note.– In relation to a criminal matter, the above reference to advice and assistance is to advice and assistance to which the sum specified in paragraph 3(c)(iii) of the Advice and Assistance (Financial Limit) (Scotland) Regulations 1993 applies (see **28 Prospective cost limits**, above). In relation to a civil matter, the reference above to advice and assistance is to advice and assistance by way of a diagnostic interview where the work undertaken is made up solely of a diagnostic interview.

33 Amount of capital to be disregarded in the case of people of pensionable age

Where a person aged 60 or over has a weekly disposable income which is less than £86 (excluding any net income derived from capital) then in calculating their disposable capital, the following amounts may be disregarded (S.I. 1996 No. 2447, Sch. 2 para 10)–

Disposable Weekly Income (excluding net income derived from capital)	Amount of capital disregarded
Up to £10	£25,000
£11 to £22	£20,000
£23 to £34	£15,000
£35 to £46	£10,000
£47 to £74.99	£5,000

2: CIVIL LEGAL AID

34 Eligibility for legal aid in civil proceedings

An applicant for civil legal aid will not be entitled to legal aid if (a) his disposable income exceeds £26,239 per annum, or (b) if his disposable capital exceeds £13,017 and it appears to the Area Director that he could afford to proceed without legal aid (Legal Aid (Scotland) Act 1986, s.15). This provision is modified in relation to cross border disputes by Council Directive 2003/8 which establishes common rules for legal aid in such cases.

As to allowable deductions when calculating income and capital, see the following paragraphs.

35 Amount of capital to be disregarded in the case of people of pensionable age

Where a person aged 60 or over has an annual disposable income which is less than £3,085 (excluding any net income derived from capital) then, the following amounts of capital may be disregarded (S.S.I. 2002 No. 494, Sch. 3, para. 15)–

Annual Disposable Income (excluding net income derived from capital)	*Amount of Capital Disregarded*
Up to £350	£35,000
£351 to £800	£30,000
£801 to £1,200	£25,000
£1,201 to £1,600	£20,000
£1,601 to £2,050	£15,000
£2,051 to £2,450	£10,000
£2,451 and above	£5,000

36 Deductions from income

Deductions from annual income include deductions for a spouse or other dependant living in the same household at an annual rate equivalent to the weekly rates for dependants, as to which see **30 Deductions when calculating income**, above.

37 Financial contributions payable by assisted person

Where the applicant's disposable income exceeds £3,521, or disposable capital exceeds £7,853, he may be called upon to pay a contribution of an amount (Legal Aid (Scotland) Act 1986, s.17, as amended)–
(a) equal to one third of the excess where his disposable income exceeds £3,521 per annum, and
(b) not greater than the amount by which his disposable capital exceeds £7,853.
For children and relevant persons in receipt of children's legal aid (see **25 Proceedings relating to children**, above), the figures are £3,355 and £7,504 respectively (s.28K).

38 Further assessments on change of circumstances

Where a person's disposable income or capital changes after a determination of their income, capital, or the amount of contribution for which they are liable is determined, the Board may require that amount to be re-determined. This will be the case where (S.S.I. 2002 No. 494, Reg. 28)–

Annual disposable income increases by an amount greater than	£750
Annual disposable income decreases by an amount greater than	£300
Disposable capital increases by an amount greater than	£750

G: EMPLOYMENT OF SOLICITORS BY THE BOARD

39 Employment of solicitors by the Board

Ss.26 to 28 of the Legal Aid (Scotland) Act 1986 make provision for the employment of solicitors by the Scottish Legal Aid Board. The Legal Aid (Employment of Solicitors) (Scotland) Regulations 2001 set out the circumstances when solicitors may be so employed. The Regulations provide that a solicitor may be employed by the Board if it receives a written request from a local organisation concerned in the giving of advice or guidance for the services of a solicitor and the Board is satisfied, having regard to the arrangements proposed by the organisation, that the services of such a solicitor would enhance the services provided by the organisation.
An employed solicitor may–
(a) help the organisation in its function of giving advice and guidance;
(b) promote contacts between the organisation and local solicitors;
(c) give oral advice to applicants instead of referring them to other solicitors in cases which can be readily disposed of by such advice;
(d) give advice and assistance under the pink form scheme;
(e) provide legal aid; and
(f) provide criminal legal assistance to an accused person who is eligible to receive it and would otherwise be unable to secure the services of a solicitor to provide such assistance.

40 Authorities

Statutes–
Law Reform (Miscellaneous Provisions) (Scotland) Act 1990
Legal Aid (Scotland) Act 1986

Statutory Instruments–

Advice and Assistance and Civil Legal Aid (Financial Conditions and Contributions) (Scotland) Regulations 2011, as amended (S.S.I. 2011 No. 217 and S.I. 2011 No. 1739)

Advice and Assistance (Assistance by Way of Representation) (Scotland) Regulations 2003, as amended (S.S.I. 2003 No. 179, 2004 Nos. 307 and 500, 2005 Nos. 165 and 482, 2006 Nos. 345 and 615, 2008 No. 251, 2010 No. 239, 2011 Nos. 13 and 216, 2012 No. 84, 2013 No. 200, 2014 No. 366, and 2015 Nos. 13, 155 and 2015 No. 279)

Advice and Assistance (Financial Limit) (Scotland) Regulations 1993, as amended (S.I. 1993 No. 3187, 2004 No. 308, 2007 No. 248, and 2008 No. 251)

Advice and Assistance (Scotland) (Consolidation and Amendment) Regulations 1996, as amended (S.I. 1996 No. 2447, 1997 No. 726, 1998 No. 724, S.S.I. 2000 Nos. 181 and 399, 2002 No. 495, 2003 Nos. 163 and 421, 2004 Nos. 262, 305, and 492, 2005 Nos. 111, 171, and 339, 2007 No. 60, S.I. 2008 No. 1879, S.S.I. 2008 No. 240, 2010 Nos. 57, 166, 312, and 462, 2011 Nos. 134 and 161, 2013 Nos. 65, 137, 142, 144, 200 and 250, and 2014 No. 90)

Children's Legal Assistance (Scotland) Regulations 2013, as amended (S.S.I. 2013 No. 200 and 2014 No. 90)

Civil Legal Aid (Scotland) Regulations 2002, as amended (S.S.I. 2002 No. 494, 2003 Nos. 49 and 486, 2004 Nos. 282 and 491, 2005 Nos. 112 and 448, 2006 No. 325, 2007 Nos. 59 and 425, S.I. 2008 No. 1879, S.S.I 2008 No. 50, and 2009 Nos. 312, and 429, 2010 Nos. 57, 166, and 461, 2011 Nos. 134 and 161, 2012 No. 64, 2013 Nos. 65 and 137, 2014 No. 90, and 2015 No. 380)

Criminal Legal Aid (Scotland) (Prescribed Proceedings) Regulations 1997, as amended (S.I. 1997 No. 3069, 1998 No. 969, 2001 No. 381, and 2006 No. 616)

Criminal Legal Aid (Scotland) Regulations 1996, as amended (S.I. 1996 No. 2555, 1999 No. 1042, S.S.I. 2001 No. 306, 2002 No. 441, 2003 No. 249, 2005 No. 450, 2009 No. 312, 2010 No. 377, 2011 No. 161 and 163, S.I. 2013 No. 7, and S.S.I. 2015 No. 337)

Criminal Legal Assistance (Duty Solicitor) (Scotland) Regulations 2011, as amended (S.S.I. 2011 No. 163 and S.I. 2011 No. 1739)

Criminal Procedure (Legal Assistance, Detention and Appeals) (Scotland) Act 2010 (Consequential Provisions) Order 2011 (S.S.I. 2011 No. 1739)

Legal Aid (Employment of Solicitors) (Scotland) Regulations 2001 (S.I. 2001 No. 392)

Legal Aid (Scotland) Act 1986 Amendment Regulations 1988, 2002, and 2004 (S.I. 1988 No. 2289, 2002 No. 532, and 2004 No. 493)

Scottish Legal Aid Board (Employment of Solicitors to Provide Criminal Legal Assistance) Regulations 1998 (S.I. 1998 No. 1938 as amended by S.S.I. 2003 No. 511)

OFFENSIVE WEAPONS AND FIREARMS: ENGLAND AND WALES

1 Introduction

The Acts and instruments listed in **35 Authorities**, below, contain provisions which apply restrictions of various kinds on the acquisition, possession, supply, use, manufacture, conversion, repair, and testing of offensive weapons and firearms. Except where otherwise stated, the provisions apply throughout Great Britain.

This Note covers the law relating to—

A: Offensive Weapons
B: Firearms, and
C: Imitation Firearms

A: OFFENSIVE WEAPONS

2 Possession of offensive weapon in a public place

The Prevention of Crime Act 1953 makes it an offence for any person, without lawful authority or reasonable excuse, to have with him in any public place any offensive weapon. The burden of proving lawful authority or reasonable excuse is placed on the person alleging that he has such authority or excuse. The court may order the forfeiture or disposal of any weapon in respect of which an offence is committed. Public place includes any highway and any other premises to which, at the material time, the public have or are permitted to have access, whether on payment or otherwise; and offensive weapon means any article made or adapted for use for causing injury to the person, or intended by the person having it with him for such use by him or by some other person.

Powers of search and arrest which arise where a constable suspects a person of committing the offence of carrying an offensive weapon are contained in the Police and Criminal Evidence Act.

It is a separate offence for a person to use an offensive weapon to unlawfully and intentionally threaten another person in a public place creating an immediate risk of serious physical harm to them (s.1A).

Note.—The inclusion of the word "unlawfully", allows defences such as self-defence, defence of others or property, and the prevention of crime.

3 Articles with blades or points

It is also an offence (under s.139 of the Criminal Justice Act 1988) for any person to have with him in a public place any article which has a blade or is sharply pointed except a folding pocket-knife the blade of which has a cutting edge of three inches or less. It is a defence for a person charged with such an offence to prove that he had good reason or lawful authority for having the article with him in a public place or that he had the article with him for use at work, for religious reasons, or as part of any national costume. For this purpose, public place includes any place to which, at the material time, the public have or are permitted access, whether on payment or otherwise.

It is a separate offence for a person to use an article with a blade or point to unlawfully and intentionally threaten another person in a public place creating an immediate risk of serious physical harm to them (s.139AA).

Note.—The inclusion of the word "unlawfully", allows defences such as self-defence, defence of others or property, and the prevention of crime.

4 Weapons on school premises

S.139A of the Criminal Justice Act 1988 (inserted by the Offensive Weapons Act 1996) make it an offence for any person to have with him on school premises an article with a blade or point to which s.139 of the 1988 Act applies, or to have with him another type of offensive weapon to which s.1 of the Prevention of Crime Act 1953 applies.

It is a defence for a person charged with an offence under s.139A show that he had a good reason or lawful authority for having the article or weapon with him on the premises. In particular, it is a defence for a person to show that he had it with him for use at work, for educational or religious reasons, or as part of a national costume. S.139B gives police officers powers to enter and search school premises and any person on those premises for offensive weapons. The police constable must have reasonable grounds for suspecting there is a weapon on the school premises (Criminal Justice Act 1988, s.139B, as amended by the Violent Crime Reduction Act 2006).

It is a separate offence for a person to use an article with a blade or point to unlawfully and intentionally threaten another person on school premises creating an immediate risk of serious physical harm to them (s.139AA).

Note.—The inclusion of the word "unlawfully", allows defences such as self-defence, defence of others or property, and the prevention of crime.

5 Manufacture, sale, or distribution of flick knives and gravity knives

The Restriction of Offensive Weapons Act 1959, as amended by the corresponding Act of 1961, makes it an offence for any person to manufacture, sell, hire, offer for sale or hire, expose or have in his possession for the purposes of sale or hire, or lend or give to any other person, any flick knife (sometimes known as a flick gun) or any gravity knife.

A flick knife is described, in the 1959 Act, as any knife having a blade which opens automatically by hand pressure applied to a button, spring, or other device in or attached to the handle of the knife. A gravity knife is described as any knife having a blade which is released from the handle or sheath by the force of gravity or the application of centrifugal force and which, when released, is locked in place by means of a button, spring, lever, or other device.

The importation of any flick knife or gravity knife is also prohibited.

6 Sale of knives to persons under 18

S.141A of the Criminal Justice Act 1988 (as inserted by the Offensive Weapons Act 1996, s.6 and amended by the Violent Crime Reduction Act 2006, s.43) makes it an offence for any person to sell to a person under 18 any knife, knife blade or razor blade, axe, or other article which has a blade or is sharply pointed and which is made or adapted to cause injury. S.141A does not apply to articles already covered by the Restriction of Offensive Weapons Act 1959 (see above). In addition, the Criminal Justice Act 1988 (Offensive Weapons) (Exemption) Order 1996 exempts from the scope of s.141A the sale of folding pocket-knives which have a blade of less than three inches (7.62 cm) and razor blades which are permanently enclosed in a cartridge or housing.

It is a defence for a person charged with an offence under s.141A to prove that he took all reasonable precautions and exercised all due diligence to avoid the commission of the offence.

7 Unlawful marketing of knives

S.1 of the Knives Act 1997 makes it an offence for a person to market a knife in a way which indicates or suggests that it is suitable for combat (suitable for use as a weapon for inflicting injury) or which is otherwise likely to stimulate or encourage violent behaviour involving the use of the knife as a weapon. An indication or suggestion that a knife is suitable for combat may in particular be given by a name or description (a) applied to the knife; or (b) included on the knife or its packaging; or (c) included in any advertisement relating to it. A person "markets" a knife for the purposes of s.1 if he sells or hires it; offers it for sale or hire; or possesses it for the purpose of sale or hire.

Under s.2 of the 1997 Act, a person is also guilty of an offence if he publishes any written, pictorial or other material in connection with the marketing of any knife suggesting that it is suitable for combat, or which is likely to stimulate or encourage violent behaviour. It is a defence for a person charged under the 1997 Act to show that the knife was marketed for use by the armed forces of any country; as an antique or curio; or for use for a prescribed purpose (s.3). No purposes have as yet been prescribed. It is also a defence for a person to show that he did not know or suspect and had no reasonable ground for suspecting that the way in which the knife was marketed constituted a breach of s.1 (s.4). S.5 of the Act contains powers of entry and search similar to those contained in the Criminal Justice Act 1988 s.142 (see **9 Powers of entry and search**, below).

A person convicted of an offence under either s.1 or s.2 may be ordered by the court to forfeit any knives or written or other material in his possession (s.6).

8 Weapons to which s.141 of the Criminal Justice Act 1988 applies

S.141 of the Criminal Justice Act 1988 provides that any person who manufactures, sells, hires, offers for sale or hire, exposes or possesses for the purpose of sale or hire, or lends or gives to any other person a weapon to which the section applies commits an offence. The Criminal Justice Act 1988 (Offensive Weapons) Orders 2002 to 2008 specify the descriptions of weapons to which s.141 is to apply. *Inter alia* knuckledusters, swordsticks, the death star, telescopic truncheons, batons and knives disguised as everyday objects, and "Samurai" type swords except those made before 1954 or made at any time according to traditional methods of making swords by hand, are so specified. There are exceptions for historical re-enactments, sporting activities, and religious ceremonies. S.141 does not apply to weapons of the specified descriptions which are antiques.

The importation of a weapon to which s.141 applies is also prohibited.

S.141 (as amended by the Violent Crime Reduction Act 2006, s.43(4)) specifies certain defences including *inter alia*–

   (a) it is a defence to show that the conduct in question was only for the purposes of making the weapon available to a museum or gallery;

   (b) it is a defence for a person acting on behalf of such a museum or gallery who is charged with hiring or lending a weapon to which s.141 applies to show that he had reasonable grounds for believing that the person to whom he lent or hired it would use it only for cultural, artistic, or educational purposes;

   (c) it is also a defence for a person to show that his conduct in lending, hiring, etc., the weapon was for the purpose of theatrical performances and rehearsals, the production of films or the production of television programmes.

9 Powers of entry and search

A justice of the peace may, subject to certain conditions, authorise the entry and search of premises if there are reasonable grounds for believing that flick knives, gravity knives, or weapons to which s.141 of the Criminal Justice Act 1988 applies are on the premises and that an offence under that provision is being committed in relation to them (Criminal Justice Act 1988, s.142).

S.60 of the Criminal Justice and Public Order Act 1994, as amended by s.8 of the Knives Act 1997, *inter alia*, allows a police officer of or above the rank of inspector to authorise, for a specified period of up to 24 hours, the stopping and searching of persons in any locality within his police area who are suspected of carrying dangerous instruments or offensive weapons.

10 Crossbows

The Crossbows Act 1987 (amended by the Violent Crime Reduction Act 2006, s.44) makes it an offence for a person—

(a) to sell or let on hire a crossbow or part of a crossbow to a person aged under 18 without reasonable grounds for believing him to be 18 years of age or older (s.1);

(b) being under the age of 18, to buy or hire a crossbow or part of a crossbow (s.2); or

(c) being under the age of 18, and not under the supervision of a person aged 21 or over, to be in possession of a crossbow which is, or parts of a crossbow which when assembled without other parts are, capable of discharging a missile (s.3).

None of the above offences is committed if the crossbow in question has a draw weight of less than 1.4 kg (s.5).

By s.4 of the Act, a constable who suspects with reasonable cause that a person is or has been committing an offence under s.3 of the Act may detain and search that person for a crossbow or part of a crossbow, may detain and search any vehicle and its contents for a crossbow or part of a crossbow connected with the offence, may seize anything appearing to be a crossbow or part of a crossbow, and may, for any of the above purposes, enter any land other than a dwelling-house.

11 Power of staff to search school pupils for weapons

A head teacher, or other member of staff in a school in Wales may, with the authority of the head teacher, search a pupil who they have reason to suspect is carrying a knife or other offensive weapon and search his possessions. The power is exercisable whenever the member of staff is in lawful control of the pupil, so as to include a time when the pupil is not on school premises, for example on a school trip. A head teacher cannot require a person other than a member of the security staff to carry out a search. A person who carries out a search may not require the pupil to remove any clothing other than outer clothing, must be of the same sex as the pupil, and cannot search without the presence of another member of staff who is of the same sex as the pupil. The pupils' possessions may not be searched except in the presence of the pupil and another member of staff. The member of staff can seize and retain any articles found, but, must deliver them to the police as soon as is reasonably practicable. The member of staff may use reasonable force if necessary in exercising this power (Education Act 1996, s.550AA inserted by the Violent Crime Reduction Act 2006, s.45).

In England the power of search is wider and includes other items such as controlled drugs, alcohol, and stolen property. There is also a power to make regulations to add to the list of prohibited items for which a search may be made ((Education Act 1996, s.550ZA, inserted by the Apprenticeships, Skills, Children and Learning Act 2009, s.242).

12 Power to search further education students for weapons

Students at institutions in the further education sector in Wales may be searched for weapons in the same way as school children (see 11 **Power of staff to search school pupils for weapons**, above). A search can only be carried out by the principal of the institution or by a member of staff authorised by the principal (Further and Higher Education Act 1992, s.85B inserted by the Violent Crime Reduction Act 2006, s.46).

Again, in England the power of search is wider and includes other items such as controlled drugs, alcohol (for students under 18), and stolen property. There is also a power to make regulations to add to the list of prohibited items for which a search may be made (Education Act 1996, ss.85AA to 85AD, inserted by the Apprenticeships, Skills, Children and Learning Act 2009, s.244).

13 power to search people in attendance centres

There is a power equivalent to that above (see 11 **Power of staff to search school pupils for weapons,** above) to search people in attendance centres for weapons. A search can only be carried out by the officer in charge of the attendance centre or a person authorised by that officer and can only be carried out on the premises of the centre (Violent Crime Reduction Act 2006, s.47).

14 Using someone to mind a weapon

It is an offence for a person to use someone else to hide or carry a dangerous weapon so as to make the weapon available to the first person for an unlawful purpose (Violent Crime Reduction Act 2006, s.28(1)).

"Dangerous weapon" for these purposes means a firearm, knife or other specified offensive weapon (s.28(3)).

The penalties for this offence are determined according to the type of dangerous weapon involved and are in line with penalties for possession of the particular weapon (s.29). In some circumstances the offence will attract a minimum sentence. The courts must take the ages of the offender and the person used to hide or carry the weapon into account when considering sentencing. If the offender is 18 or over and the person used is under 18, this will be regarded as an aggravating factor increasing the seriousness of the offence (s.29(11)). The court must state that the person's age is an aggravating factor (s.29(12)). If either person turns 18 during the period that the weapon is being held, the offence is still liable to be treated as aggravated if at some point in that period the offender was 18 or over and the other person was under 18.

B: FIREARMS

15 The legislation

The Firearms Act 1968 regulates the possession and distribution of firearms. In addition, the possession of certain types of firearms, and the possession of firearms by certain persons or under certain circumstances, are altogether prohibited. By virtue of the Firearms Act 1982, the 1968 Act also applies to imitation firearms.

The 1968 Act has been substantially amended by the Firearms Acts listed in **35 Authorities**, below.

For all the purposes of the 1968 Act, a "firearm" means a lethal barrelled weapon of any description from which any shot, bullet, or other missile can be discharged and includes–

(a) any prohibited weapon (see **25 Prohibited weapons and ammunition**, below), whether it is such a lethal weapon as aforesaid or not; and

(b) any component part of such a lethal or prohibited weapon; and

(c) any accessory to any such weapon designed or adapted to diminish the noise or flash caused by firing the weapon (s.57).

16 Firearm certificates

Subject to certain exemptions, s.1 of the Firearms Act 1968 provides that it is an offence to possess, purchase, or acquire a firearm or ammunition to which the section applies without a firearm certificate, or otherwise than as authorised by such a certificate. It is also an offence to fail to comply with a condition subject to which the certificate is held.

S.1 applies to every firearm except a shot gun and an air weapon, and to any ammunition for a firearm except cartridges containing five or more shot, none of which exceeds .36 inch in diameter, ammunition for an air gun, air rifle, or air pistol, and blank cartridges not more than one inch in diameter.

A shot gun means a smooth-bore gun (not being an air gun) which–

(a) has a barrel not less than 24 inches in length and does not have a barrel with a bore exceeding two inches in diameter;

(b) either has no magazine or has a non-detachable magazine incapable of holding more than two cartridges; and

(c) is not a revolver gun (s.1(3)(a)).

An air weapon means an air rifle, air gun, or air pistol which is not subject to a general prohibition (see **25 Prohibited weapons and ammunition**, below) and which is not of a type declared to be specially dangerous.

The Firearms (Dangerous Air Weapons) Rules 1969 declare as specially dangerous an air rifle, air gun, or air pistol which (a) is capable of discharging a missile with kinetic energy (i.e., its force of impact on hitting an object) in excess, in the case of an air pistol, of 6ft./lb, or in the case of an air rifle or air gun, of 12ft./lb., or (b) is disguised as another object. The declaration does not apply to a weapon which only falls within paragraph (a) above and which is designed for use under water.

A firearm certificate must be granted by the chief officer of police if he is satisfied that the applicant is a fit person to be entrusted with a firearm and is not prohibited by the 1968 Act from possessing a firearm and has a good reason for having in his possession, or for purchasing or acquiring the firearm or ammunition in respect of which the application is made, and can be permitted to have it in his possession without danger to the public safety or to the peace (s.27).

17 Shot gun certificates

Subject to certain exemptions, it is an offence to possess, purchase, or acquire a shot gun without a shot gun certificate. It is also an offence to fail to comply with a condition subject to which the certificate is held (Firearms Act 1968, s.2).

A shot gun certificate must be granted or, as the case may be, renewed by the chief officer of police if he is satisfied that the applicant for a certificate can be permitted to possess a shot gun without danger to the public safety or to the peace. However, it must not be granted or renewed if the chief officer of police has reason to believe that the applicant is prohibited by the 1968 Act from possessing a shot gun or is satisfied that the applicant does not have a good reason for possessing, purchasing, or acquiring one. An applicant is to be regarded as having a good reason if the gun is intended to be used for sporting or competition purposes or for shooting vermin, and the application is not to be refused merely because the applicant intends neither to use the gun himself nor to lend it for anyone else to use (s.28).

S.5 of the 1988 Act provides that it is an offence to sell to another person in the United Kingdom any ammunition to which s.1 of the 1968 Act does not apply and which is capable of being used in a shot gun or a smooth bore gun to which that section applies unless that other person–
(a) is a registered firearms dealer or a person who sells ammunition by way of trade or business;
(b) produces a certificate authorising him to possess such a gun;
(c) shows that he is entitled to have possession of such a gun without holding a certificate; or
(d) produces a certificate authorising another person to possess such a gun, together with that person's written authority to purchase the ammunition on his behalf.

18 Register of holders of certificates

S.39 of the Firearms (Amendment) Act 1997 provides for the establishment of a central register of all persons who have applied for a firearm or shotgun certificate or to whom a certificate has been granted or whose certificate has been renewed. The register is kept by means of a computer which provides access on-line to all police forces.

19 Revocation of certificates

A firearm certificate may be revoked by a chief officer of police if he has reason to believe that the holder is of intemperate habits, unsound mind, or is otherwise unfitted to have a firearm or can no longer be permitted to have the firearm and ammunition to which the certificate relates without danger to public safety or to the peace. A certificate may also be revoked if the holder is prohibited by the Firearms Act 1968 from possessing a firearm or no loner has a good reason for having the firearm or ammunition to which the certificate relates (s.30A). A certificate may also be partially revoked if the chief officer of police is satisfied that the holder no longer has a good reason for possessing the firearm or ammunition to which the partial revocation relates (s.30B).

A shot gun certificate may be revoked by the chief officer of police if he is satisfied that the holder is prohibited by the Act from possessing a shot gun, or cannot be permitted to possess one without danger to the public safety or to the peace (s.30C).

An appeal against the revocation of a firearm or shot gun certificate lies to the Crown Court (s.44).

20 Duration of certificates and appeals

A certificate will, unless previously revoked or cancelled, continue in force for a period of five years, but is renewable for a further five year period by the chief officer of police for the area in which the holder resides (s.28A of the Firearms Act 1968).

An appeal against a decision of a chief officer of police to refuse to grant, or renew, a certificate lies to the crown Court (s.44).

21 Exemptions

Under ss.7 to 13 of the Firearms Act 1968, there are certain circumstances under which possession of a firearm or shot gun does not require a certificate, as follows.
(i) A person holding a permit from the local chief officer of police may possess a firearm and ammunition in accordance with the terms of the permit (s.7).
(ii) Registered firearms dealers (see below) and their servants, and auctioneers, carriers, warehousemen, and their servants may possess firearms or ammunition in the ordinary course of business (ss.8 and 9). (An auctioneer may sell firearms by auction without being registered as a firearms dealer, but he must obtain a permit to do so from the local chief officer of police.)
(iii) Persons licensed to slaughter animals may possess slaughtering instruments at slaughter-houses or knackers' yards where they are employed. Similarly, the proprietor of a slaughterhouse or knacker's yard, or a person appointed by him, may hold a slaughtering instrument and ammunition therefor for the purpose of storing them in safe custody at the slaughterhouse or yard (s.10).
(iv)
    (a) A person may carry a firearm or ammunition belonging to another person who does hold a certificate, under instructions from, and for the use of, that other person for sporting purposes only (*Note.*–where the person carrying the firearm is under 18, the certificate holder must be 18 or over) (s.11(1)).
    (b) A person aged 18 or over may possess a firearm at an athletic meeting for starting races at that meeting (s.11(2)).
    (c) A member of a cadet corps approved by the Secretary of State may possess a fire-arm and ammunition when engaged as a member of the corps on, or in connection with, drill or target shooting (s.11(3)).
    (d) A person conducting or carrying on a miniature rifle range or shooting gallery at which only air weapons or miniature rifles not exceeding .23 inch calibre are used may possess, purchase, or

acquire such miniature rifles and ammunition suitable for them; and any person may use such miniature rifles at such a range or gallery (s.11(4)).

    (e) A person may borrow a shot gun from the occupier of private premises and use it on those premises in the occupier's presence (*Note.*–where the borrower of the firearm is under 18, the occupier must be 18 or over) (s.11(5)).

    (f) A person may use a shot gun to shoot at artificial targets at a time and place approved by the local chief of police (s.11(6)).

  (v) A person may have a firearm in his possession for a theatrical performance or rehearsal or a film production. For such purposes, the Ministry of Defence may authorise the use of firearms which are prohibited weapons (s.12).

  (vi) A person may have in his possession a firearm or ammunition on board a ship, or signalling apparatus or ammunition therefor on board an aircraft or at an aerodrome, as part of the equipment of the ship, aircraft, or aerodrome (s.13).

The Criminal Justice Act 1988 provides for the following further exemptions.

  (vii) A member of a rifle club, miniature rifle club, or muzzle-loading pistol club approved by the Secretary of State may have in his possession a firearm and ammunition when engaged as a member of the club in connection with target shooting (1988 Act, s.15).

    Note.– Guidance published by the Home Office, *Approval of rifle and muzzle loading-loading pistol clubs* (April 2012) available at <https://www.gov.uk/government/publications/approval-of-rifle-and-muzzle-loading-pistol-clubs> provides information on approval means and how clubs can apply for it and explains the criteria and conditions which clubs must meet in order to obtain approval and remain approved by the Home Secretary. It also gives the addresses of national shooting organisations.

  (viii) A person of, or over, the age of 17 may borrow a rifle from the occupier of private premises and use it on those premises in the presence either of the occupier or of a servant of the occupier if the occupier or servant in whose presence it is used holds a firearm certificate in respect of that rifle and the borrower's possession and use of it complies with any conditions as to those matters specified in the certificate (and, if the borrower is aged 17, the occupier or servant is aged 18 or over). A person who is so entitled may also purchase or acquire ammunition for use in the rifle and have it in his possession during the period for which the rifle is borrowed subject to compliance with the conditions of the firearm certificate which relate to that rifle (1988 Act, s.16).

  (ix) The holder of a visitor's firearm permit may have in his possession any firearm, and have in his possession, purchase, or acquire any ammunition to which s.1 of the 1968 Act applies; the holder of a visitor's shot gun permit may have shot guns in his possession and purchase or acquire shot guns (1988 Act, s.17).

  (x) A person may purchase a firearm from a registered firearms dealer provided that he has not been in Great Britain for more than 30 days in the preceding 12 months and the firearm is purchased for the purpose only of being exported from Great Britain without first coming into that person's possession (1988 Act, s.18).

  (xi) Firearms and ammunition in certain museums are exempted from certain provisions of the 1968 Act in accordance with the provisions of the Schedule to the 1988 Act (1988 Act, s.19).

Note also that nothing in the Firearms Act 1968 relating to firearms applies to an antique firearm which is sold, transferred, purchased, acquired or possessed "as a curiosity or ornament" (s.58). That phrase, and the definition of what is "antique" are questions of fact, not law, and consequently it is for a jury to decide. The Home Office has produced a *Guide on Firearms Licensing Law* (November 2013) which, for the benefit of prosecutors, states that "evidence of antique status may include an indication of date of manufacture, details of technical obsolescence, a lack of commercial availability of suitable ammunition, or a written opinion by an accredited expert".

22 Firearms dealers

A person who, by way of trade or business *inter alia* (Firearms Act 1968, s.3, as amended by the Violent Crime Reduction Act 2006, s.31(1))–

  (a) manufactures, sells, transfers, repairs, tests, or proves firearms (including shot guns) or ammunition to which s.1 applies; or

  (b) sells or transfers an air weapon,

must be registered as a firearms dealer. A dealer must not sell or transfer firearms or ammunition within (a) above to, or undertake to repair, test, or prove them for, a person unless that person produces the appropriate certificate or shows his authority to hold the firearm or ammunition without a certificate (1968 Act, s.3(2)). A person must not sell air weapons by way of trade or business other than face to face (2006 Act, s.32).

Dealers must keep a register of transactions, including those involving air weapons (1968 Act, s.40(2) as amended by the 2006 Act, s.31(2)).

23 Applications and fees

Applications for firearm or shot gun certificates must be made to the chief officer of police of the area in which the applicant resides. The Firearms Rules 1998 require persons applying for a certificate to provide two referees (only one for a shotgun), who must have known the applicant personally for at least two years, and who are required to give statements to the effect that they know of no reason why the applicant should not be permitted to possess a firearm, or shot gun, as the case may be. Applicants are also required to give permission for the police to obtain information from their doctors about their medical history, including details of mental health problems.

The fee for the grant of a firearm certificate is £88, and for a shotgun certificate it is £79.50. The fee for the renewal of a firearm certificate is £62, and for the renewal of or shot gun certificate is £49. The fee for the replacement of a lost or destroyed certificate is £4. Where a shotgun certificate is granted at the same time as a firearm certificate, the fee is £28, and where a shotgun certificate is renewed at the same time as a firearm certificate, the fee is £2. Certificates are valid for five years or for such other period as may be specified by order. The fee for a visitors' permit is £20.

No fee is payable for the grant, variation, or renewal of firearm certificates *inter alia* related solely to signalling devices (such as flare signal pens used by yachtsmen or mountaineers in case of emergency), provided that they do not exceed eight inches in length when assembled and ready to fire, or to ammunition for such devices.

The fee for the grant or renewal of registration as a firearms dealer is £200.

24 Conversion of weapons

Otherwise than by a registered firearms dealer in the course of repair, it is an offence to shorten to less than 24 inches the barrel of any exempted shot gun (see **16 Firearm certificates**, above) or of any other smooth bore gun not being one which has a barrel exceeding two inches in diameter (s.4(1) and (2) and 1988 Act, s.6). It is also an offence for any person other than a registered dealer to convert a dummy weapon into a firearm (s.4(3) of the Firearms Act 1968).

25 Prohibited weapons and ammunition

A person commits an offence if, without the written authority of the Secretary of State, he has in his possession, purchases, or acquires any of the under-mentioned weapons and ammunition (known as "prohibited" weapons and ammunition) (Firearms Act 1968, s.5(1), (1A), (2))–

(a) any firearm which is so designed or adapted that two or more missiles can be successively discharged without repeated pressure on the trigger;

(b) any self-loading or pump-action rifled gun other than one which is chambered for .22 non-fire cartridges;

(c) any firearm which either has a barrel less than 30cm in length or is less than 60cm in length overall, other than an air weapon, a muzzle-loading gun or a firearm designed as signalling apparatus;

(d) any self-loading or pump-action smooth bore gun which is not an air weapon or chambered for .22 non-fire cartridges and either has a barrel less than 24 inches in length or (excluding any detachable, folding, retractable or other movable butt-stock) is less than 40 inches in length overall;

(e) any smooth-bore revolver gun other than one which is chambered for 9mm non-fire cartridges or a muzzle-loading gun;

(ea) any air rifle, air gun or air pistol which uses, or is designed or adapted for use with, a self-contained gas cartridge system;

(f) any rocket launcher, or any mortar, for projecting a stabilised missile, other than a launcher or mortar designed for line-throwing or pyrotechnic purposes or as signalling apparatus;

(g) any weapon of whatever description designed or adapted for the discharge of any noxious liquid, gas, or other thing;

(h) any cartridge with a bullet designed to explode on or immediately before impact, any ammunition containing or designed or adapted to contain any such noxious thing as is mentioned in (g), and, if capable of being used with a firearm of any description, any grenade, bomb (or other like missile), or rocket or shell designed to explode on or immediately before impact;

(i) any firearm which is disguised as another object;

(j) any rocket or ammunition not falling within paragraph (h) which consists in or incorporates a missile designed to explode on or immediately before impact and is for military use;

(k) any launcher or other projecting apparatus not falling within paragraph (f) which is designed to be used with any rocket or ammunition falling within paragraph (h);

(l) any ammunition for military use which consists in or incorporates a missile designed so that a substance contained in the missile will ignite on or immediately before impact;

(m) any ammunition for military use which consists in or incorporates a missile designed, on account of its having a jacket and hard-core, to penetrate armour plating, armour screening, or body armour;

(n) any ammunition which incorporates a missile designed or adapted to expand on impact; or

(o) anything which is designed to be projected as a missile from any weapon and is designed to be, or has been, incorporated in any ammunition falling within any of the preceding paragraphs.

A person also commits an offence if without authority he–

(p) manufactures any weapon or ammunition specified in (a) to (h) above;

(q) sells or transfers any prohibited weapon or ammunition;

(r) has in his possession for sale or transfer any prohibited weapon or ammunition; or

(s) he purchases or acquires for sale or transfer any prohibited weapon or ammunition.

The general prohibition contained in (c) above is subject to a number of special exemptions, which are set out in ss.2 to 8 of the Firearms (Amendment) Act 1997. The effect of these exemptions is that it is not an offence to possess, purchase, acquire, sell or transfer, without the authority of the Secretary of State, a firearm of the type prohibited by (c) above if the firearm in question is required for the purposes of slaughtering, or humanely killing, or tranquillising animals; shooting vermin; or starting races at athletics meetings. Trophies of war acquired before 1st January 1946 and firearms of historic interest manufactured before 1919 and kept as part of a collection are also exempt. The Firearms Amendment Act 1997 (Firearms of Historic Interest) Order 1997 specifies the description of historic firearms which are covered by this exemption. Firearms permitted by the above exemptions must still be covered by a firearms certificate or permit. Museums who hold a museum firearms licence (granted under the Firearms (Amendment) Act 1988, s.1, Schedule 1) do not also need to hold firearm or shot gun certificates and, if the licence so provides, may hold prohibited weapons without the consent of the Secretary of State.

Any authority may be issued subject to conditions (s.5(3)). However, an authority will not be required for any person to have in his possession, or to purchase, acquire, sell, or transfer any of the weapons and ammunition described in paragraphs (i) to (o) above if he is authorised by a certificate under the 1968 Act to possess, purchase, or acquire that weapon or ammunition subject to a condition that he does so only for the purpose of its being kept or exhibited as part of a collection (1968 Act, s.5A(1)). But no sale or transfer may be made under s.5A(1) except to a person who–

(a) produces the authority of the Secretary of State under s.5(1) for his purchase or acquisition; or

(b) shows that he is, under s.5A or a licence under the Schedule to the Firearms (Amendment) Act 1988 (museums etc.), entitled to make the purchase or acquisition without such authority.

The authority of the Secretary of State is not required–

(a) for any person to have in his possession, or to purchase or acquire, any of the prohibited weapons, ammunition or missiles described in paragraphs (i) to (o) above if his possession, purchase, or acquisition is exclusively in connection with the carrying on of activities in respect of which that person, or the person on whose behalf he has possession, or makes the purchase or acquisition, is recognised, for the purposes of the law of another Member State relating to firearms, as a collector of firearms or a body concerned in the cultural or historical aspects of weapons (s.5A(3));

(b) for any person to have in his possession any expanding ammunition or the missile for any such ammunition if–

   (i) he is authorised by a firearm certificate to possess, purchase, acquire, sell or transfer such ammunition; and

   (ii) the certificate or permit contains a condition restricting the use of expanding ammunition to the lawful shooting of deer or vermin; the humane killing of animals; or the shooting of animals for the protection of people or other animals (s.5A(4));

(c) for any person to have in his possession any expanding ammunition or the missile for any such ammunition if–

   (i) he is entitled, under s.10 of the 1968 Act, to have a slaughtering instrument and the ammunition for it in his possession; and

   (ii) the ammunition or missile in question is designed to be capable of being used with a slaughtering instrument (s.5A(5));

(d) for the sale or transfer of any expanding ammunition or the missile for any such ammunition to any person who produces a certificate by virtue of which he is authorised under paragraph (b) above to purchase or acquire it without the authority of the Secretary of State (s.5A(6));

(e) for a person carrying on the business of a firearms dealer, or any servant of his, to have in his possession, or to purchase, acquire, sell, or transfer any expanding ammunition or the missile for any such ammunition in the ordinary course of his business (s.5A(7)).

26 Restriction on sale and purchase of primers

There are restrictions on the purchase and sale of primers to people who hold a relevant firearms certificate or who otherwise have lawful authority for having them. Primers are components of ammunition which contain a chemical compound that detonates on impact (Violent Crime Reduction Act 2006, s.35).

27 Transfers of firearms and ammunition

Ss. 32 to 36 of the Firearms (Amendment) Act 1997 contain strict requirements relating to the transfer of firearms, shotguns and ammunition. Except where the transferee is a registered dealer or a person who is exempted from the need to have a certificate (see above), all transfers must be made in person and the transferee must produce to the transferor the certificate or permit entitling him to acquire the firearm or ammunition in question. The details of any transfer of a weapon must be notified to a chief officer of police within seven days. Notification must also be given whenever a firearm is de-activated, destroyed, lost or stolen, or whenever ammunition is lost or stolen.

28 Young people

Ss.22 to 24ZA of the Firearms Act 1968 impose a number of prohibitions in relation to the possession of firearms by young people under the age of 17. It is an offence under s.22–

  (a) for a person under the age of eighteen to purchase or hire any firearm or ammunition (s.22(1));
  (b) where a person under the age of eighteen is entitled, as the holder of a certificate under the 1968 Act to have a firearm in his possession, for that person to use that firearm for a purpose not authorised by the European weapons directive (s.22(1A), inserted by S.I. 1992 No. 2823, reg.4(1));
  (c) for a person under the age of fourteen to have in his possession any firearm or ammunition to which s.1 of the 1968 Act or s.15 of the Firearms (Amendment) Act 1988 applies, except in circumstances where under s.11(1), (3) or (4) of the 1968 Act he is entitled to have possession of it without holding a firearm certificate (s.22(2), amended by s.23(4) of the 1988 Act);
  (d) for a person under the age of fifteen to have with him an assembled shot gun except while under the supervision of a person of or over the age of twenty-one, or while the shot gun is so covered with a securely fastened gun cover that it cannot be fired (s.22(3)); and
  (e) subject to s.23 below, for a person under the age of eighteen to have with him an air weapon or ammunition for an air weapon (s.22(4), amended by the Violent Crime Reduction Act 2006, s.33(1) and (3)).

Exceptions to s.22(4) of the 1968 Act are provided in s.23 of that Act–

  (f) it is not an offence under s.22(4) of the 1968 Act for a person to have with him an air weapon or ammunition while he is under the supervision of a person of or over the age of twenty-one; but where a person has with him an air weapon on any premises in circumstances where he would be prohibited from having it with him but for this provision, it is an offence for the person under whose supervision he is to allow him to use it for firing any missile beyond those premises (s.23(1), amended by the Violent Crime Reduction Act 2006, s.34(1), (3)(a));
  (g) in proceedings against a person for an offence under s.22(1) it will be a defence for him to show that the only premises into or across which the missile was fired were premises the occupier of which had consented to the firing of the missile (whether specifically or by way of a general consent) (s.23(1A), inserted by the Violent Crime Reduction Act 2006, s.34(1), (3)(b));
  (h) it is not an offence under s.22(4) of the 1968 Act for a person to have with him an air weapon or ammunition at a time when he is a member of a rifle club or miniature rifle club approved by the Secretary of State and is engaged as such a member in connection with target shooting or he is using the weapon or ammunition at a shooting gallery where the only firearms used are either air weapons or miniature rifles not exceeding .23 inch calibre (s.23(2) of the 1968 Act, amended by the Firearms (Amendment) Act 1997, s.52, Sch.2 and Sch.3); and
  (i) it is not an offence under s.22(4) of the 1968 Act for a person of or over the age of fourteen to have with him an air weapon or ammunition on private premises with the consent of the occupier (s23(3), inserted by the Anti-social Behaviour Act 2003, s.38(3)(b)).

It is, however, an offence under s.24 of the 1968 Act–

  (j) to sell or let on hire any firearm or ammunition to a person under the age of eighteen (1968 Act, s.24(1));
  (k) to make a gift of or lend any firearm or ammunition to which s.1 of the 1968 Act applies to a person under the age of fourteen, or to part with the possession of any such firearm or ammunition to a person under that age, except in circumstances where that person is entitled under s.11(1), (3) or (4) of the 1968 Act or s.15 of the Firearms (Amendment) Act 1988 (see 21 **Exemptions**, above) to have possession thereof without holding a firearm certificate (1968 Act, s.24(2) amended by the Firearms (Amendment) Act 1988, s.23(4));
  (l) to make a gift of a shot gun or ammunition for a shot gun to a person under the age of fifteen (1968 Act, s.24(3));
  (m) to make a gift of an air weapon or ammunition for an air weapon to a person under the age of 18 or to part with the possession of an air weapon or ammunition for an air weapon to a person under the age of 18 except where by virtue of s.23 the person is not prohibited from having it with him (1968 Act, s.24(4) amended).

In proceedings for an offence under any provision of s.24 of the 1968 Act, it is a defence to prove that the person charged with the offence believed the other person to be of or over the age mentioned in that provision and had reasonable ground for that belief (1968 Act, s.24(5)).

Under s.24ZA (added by the Crime and Security Act 2010, s.46), it is an offence for a person in possession of an air weapon to fail to take reasonable precautions to prevent any person under the age of eighteen from having the weapon with him (unless that young person is not prohibited from having the weapon with him by virtue of s.23). It is a defence to show that the person charged believed the other person to be aged eighteen or over; and had reasonable ground for that belief.

29 Preservation of the public safety and prevention of crime

Ss.16 to 21 and 25 of the Firearms Act 1968 prohibit the possession of firearms in certain circumstances. *Inter alia* an offence is committed by–

  (a) a person who has in his possession any firearm or imitation firearm with intent (i) by means thereof to cause, or (ii) to enable another person by means thereof to cause, any person to believe that unlawful violence will be used against him or another person (s.16A, inserted by Firearms (Amendment) Act 1994);

(b) a person who has with him a firearm or imitation firearm with intent to commit an indictable offence, or to resist arrest or prevent the arrest of another (s.18);

(c) a person who, without lawful authority or reasonable excuse (the proof whereof lies on him), has with him in a public place a loaded shot gun, an air weapon (whether loaded or not), any other firearm (whether loaded or not) together with ammunition suitable for use in that firearm, or an imitation firearm (s.19, as amended by the Anti-social Behaviour Act 2003);

(d) a person who is in any building or on any land, as a trespasser and without reasonable excuse (the proof whereof lies on him), and has a firearm or imitation firearm with him (s.20); and

(e) a person who supplies a firearm or ammunition to, or repairs, tests, or proves, a firearm or ammunition for, another person whom he knows, or has reasonable cause to believe, to be drunk or of unsound mind (s.25).

It is an offence for a person of any age to fire an air weapon beyond the boundary of premises. A defence is provided to cover the situation where the person shooting has the consent of the occupier of the land over or into which he shoots (1968 Act, s.21A inserted by the Violent Crime Reduction Act 2006, s.34).

30 Possession of firearms by persons previously convicted of crime

Anyone convicted of a crime and sentenced to custody for life, or detention, imprisonment, corrective training, or youth custody for a term of three years or more, is permanently prohibited from possessing, using, or carrying firearms or ammunition at any time following their release (Firearms Act 1968, s.21(1)).

Those sentenced to imprisonment or youth custody for between three months and three years, are prohibited from possessing, using, or carrying firearms or ammunition at any time during the five years after their release (s. 21(2)).

A person given a suspended sentence of three months or more is also prohibited for five years, the prohibition starting on the second day after the date on which sentence was passed (s.21(2C)).

Children and young persons convicted of serious crime and discharged on licence must not possess, use, or carry a firearm or ammunition during the period of the licence. It may be made a condition of a recognisance to keep the peace or be of good behaviour, or a requirement of a community rehabilitation order or a probation order, that the person subject to the recognisance or the order shall not possess, use, or carry a firearm or ammunition. It is an offence for a person to supply a firearm or ammunition to, or to repair, test, or prove a firearm or ammunition for, another person whom he knows, or has reasonable cause to believe, to be thus prohibited from possessing firearms or ammunition. A person subject to one of the above prohibitions may apply to the Crown Court for the prohibition to be removed (s.21).

The prohibition under s.21 extends to antique firearm owned "as a curiosity or ornament" under s.58 (as to which, see **22 Exemptions**, above).

31 Powers of arrest and search

S. 46 of the Firearms Act 1968 contains a power of arrest with a warrant

Where a constable has reasonable cause to suspect that a person has a firearm, with or without ammunition, in a public place, or is committing or about to commit an offence under ss.18 or 20 (see **30 Preservation of the public safety and prevention of crime**, above), he may require that person to hand over the weapon for examination, or require him to submit to search (s.47(1) and (3)). Similarly, he may search a vehicle in a public place if he suspects that the vehicle contains a firearm or is being used or is about to be used in connection with an offence under ss.18 or 20 elsewhere than in a public place, and may stop the vehicle for this purpose (s.47(4)).

A constable may require the production of a firearm or shot gun certificate by a person he believes to be carrying a firearm or ammunition, or a shot gun, as the case may be (s.48(1)). If the person concerned fails to produce the certificate or permit or to permit the constable to read it, or to show that he is entitled to have the firearm, ammunition, or shot gun without holding a certificate, the constable may seize and detain the firearm, ammunition, or shot gun, and require the person to give his name and address (s.48(2)).

32 Prosecution and punishment of offences

The way in which firearms offences are punishable upon conviction is set out in s.51 and Sch.6 to the Firearms Act 1968.

Minimum sentences for offences under s.5 of the 1968 Act (prohibition of certain weapons and control of arms traffic: see **25 Prohibited weapons and ammunition**, above) are set by s.51A (inserted by the Criminal Justice Act 2003, s.287). This section applies only to the simple offence of possession of a prohibited weapon. The minimum sentence, other than in exceptional circumstances, is five years' imprisonment for people aged 18 or over and three years' imprisonment for a person aged between 16 and 18 S.51A is amended (by s.30 of the Violent Crime Reduction Act 2006) so as to extend it to other serious offences involving the possession of prohibited weapons, to ensure that offenders do not escape the minimum sentence where they are not also charged with the simple possession offence. The additional offences all appear in the 1968 Act and are the offences under:

(a) s.16 (possession of firearm with intent to injure);

(b) s.16A (possession of firearm with intent to cause fear of violence);

(c) s.17 (use of firearm to resist arrest);
(d) s.18 (carrying firearm with criminal intent);
(e) s.19 (carrying a firearm in a public place); and
(f) s.20(1) (trespassing in a building with firearm).

As to ss.16-20, see **30 Preservation of the public safety and prevention of crime,** above.

The minimum sentences apply in these offences only where a prohibited weapon is involved.

C: IMITATION FIREARMS

33 Imitations convertible into firearms

The Firearms Act 1982 applies the provisions of the Firearms Act 1968 (subject to exceptions) to an imitation firearm which has the appearance of being a firearm to which s.1 of the 1968 Act applies (see **16 Firearm certificates,** above) and which is so constructed or adapted as to be readily convertible into a firearm to which that section applies (s.1). The provisions of the 1982 Act do not apply to imitation component parts of firearms or to imitations of accessories to firearms such as are described in s.57 of the 1968 Act. The 1982 Act also provides that an imitation air weapon, including an imitation of a type of weapon declared by the Firearms (Dangerous Air Weapons) Rules 1969 to be specially dangerous, is excluded from the provisions of the Act.

An imitation firearm will be regarded as readily convertible into a firearm to which s.1 of the 1968 Act applies if—

(a) it can be so converted without any special skill in the construction or adaptation of firearms of any description on the part of the person converting it; and
(b) the work involved in converting it does not require equipment or tools other than such as are in common use by persons carrying out works of construction and maintenance in their own homes.

It is a defence for a person accused of an offence under the 1968 Act involving an imitation firearm to which the 1982 Act applies to show that he did not know and had no reason to suspect that the imitation firearm was so constructed or adapted as to be readily convertible into a firearm to which s.1 of the 1968 Act applies.

The following provisions of the 1968 Act do not apply to imitation firearms to which the 1982 Act applies.

(a) S.4(3) and (4) (conversion of dummy weapon–see **25 Conversion of weapons,** above–and aggravated offence under s.1 in relation to illegally shortened shot gun or illegally converted dummy weapon).
(b) Ss.16 to 20 (see **30 Preservation of the public safety and prevention of crime,** above), but without prejudice to the application of any of those provisions to an imitation firearm apart from the 1982 Act (i.e., ss.17 and 18).
(c) S.47 (see **32 Powers of arrest and search,** above), but again without prejudice to its application to an imitation firearm apart from the 1982 Act.

34 Manufacture, import and sale of realistic imitation firearms

It is an offence to manufacture, import or sell a realistic imitation firearm. The Secretary of State has a power to make regulations to provide for exceptions, exemptions and defences to this offence. Realistic imitation firearms are defined by as anything which has the appearance of being a firearm whether or not it is capable of discharging any shot, bullet or other missile (Violent Crime Reduction Act 2006, ss.36, 38).

The Violent Crime Reduction Act 2006 (Realistic Imitation Firearms) Regulations 2007, provides defences to the offences of the manufacture, import and sale of realistic imitation firearms in the 2006 Act, s.36. These defences operate where a person who is charged with such an offence can show that his conduct was for the purpose only of making the imitation firearm in question available for one or more of the purposes specified in the Regulations. These are the organisation and holding of permitted activities for which public liability insurance is held in relation to liabilities to third parties arising from or in connection with the organisation and holding of those activities; and the purposes of display at a permitted event.

It is also a defence to show that the sale of a realistic imitation firearm was for the purposes of a museum or gallery; for theatre, film or television productions; for specified historical re-enactments; or for Crown service. It is also a defence for business to import realistic imitation firearms for the purposes of modifying them so that they cease to be realistic imitations. For a defence to be shown, a person must adduce sufficient evidence of it and the contrary must not be proved beyond reasonable doubt (Violent Crime Reduction Act 2006, s.37).

Where imitation firearms are still permitted to be manufactured, imported or sold, they must be constructed in accordance with specifications laid down in regulations by the Secretary of State (Violent Crime Reduction Act 2006, s.39). The Violent Crime Reduction Act 2006 (Specification for Imitation Firearms) Regulations 2011 sets out specifications for blank firing imitation firearms and revolvers. The regulations also provide a defence for a person charged with importing an imitation firearm which does not conform to the specifications if they did so only for the purpose of a museum or gallery, a theatrical performance, film of television production, the organisation of historical enactments, or Crown service.

It is also an offence to sell an imitation firearm to a person under the age of 18, or for a person under 18 to purchase one. In relation to the selling offence, it is a defence for the vendor to show that he believed that the purchaser was 18 or over and that he had reasonable grounds for that belief (Firearms Act 1968, s.24A, inserted by the Violent Crime Reduction Act 2006, s.40).

35 Authorities

Statutes–

Criminal Justice Act 1988

Criminal Justice and Public Order Act 1994

Crossbows Act 1987

Firearms Acts 1968 and 1982

Firearms (Amendment) Acts 1988, 1992, 1994, and 1997, and (Amendment) (No. 2) Act 1997

Knives Act 1997

Offensive Weapons Act 1996

Police and Criminal Evidence Act 1984

Prevention of Crime Act 1953

Public Order Act 1986

Restriction of Offensive Weapons Acts 1959 and 1961

Violent Crime Reduction Act 2006

Statutory Instruments–

Criminal Justice Act 1988 (Offensive Weapons) (Exemption) Order 1996 (S.I. 1996 No. 3064)

Criminal Justice Act 1988 (Offensive Weapons) Orders 2002, 2004 and 2008 (S.I. 2002 No. 1668, 2004 No. 1271, and 2008 Nos. 973 and 2039)

Firearms Acts (Amendment) Regulations 1992 (S.I. 1992 No. 2823)

Firearms (Dangerous Air Weapons) Rules 1969, as amended (S.I. 1969 No. 47 and 1993 No. 1490)

Firearms Rules 1998, as amended (S.I. 1998 No. 1941, 2005 No. 3344, 2007 No. 2605, 2010 No. 1759, 2013 Nos. 1945 and 2970, 2014 No. 1239, and 2016 No. 425)

Firearms (Variation of Fees) Orders 2015 (S.I. 2015 No. 611)

Transfer of Functions (Prohibited Weapons) Order 1968 (S.I. 1968 No. 1200)

Violent Crime Reduction Act 2006 (Realistic Imitation Firearms) Regulations 2007 (S.I. 2007 No. 2606)

Violent Crime Reduction Act 2006 (Specification for Imitation Firearms) Regulations 2011 (S.I. 2011 No. 1754)

OFFENSIVE WEAPONS AND FIREARMS: SCOTLAND

1 Introduction

The Acts and instruments listed in **34 Authorities**, below, contain provisions which apply restrictions of various kinds on the acquisition, possession, supply, use, manufacture, conversion, repair, and testing of offensive weapons and firearms. Except where otherwise stated, the provisions apply throughout Great Britain.

This Note covers the law relating to–

A: Offensive Weapons
B: Firearms, and
C: Imitation Firearms

A: OFFENSIVE WEAPONS

2 Possession of offensive weapon in a public place

The Criminal Law (Consolidation) (Scotland) Act 1995 makes it an offence for any person, without lawful authority or reasonable excuse, to have with him in any public place any offensive weapon (s.47). The burden of proving lawful authority or reasonable excuse is placed on the person alleging that he has such authority or excuse. The court may order the forfeiture or disposal of any weapon in respect of which an offence is committed. Public place includes any highway (or, in Scotland, road) and any other premises to which, at the material time, the public have or are permitted to have access, whether on payment or otherwise; and offensive weapon means any article made or adapted for use for causing injury to the person, or intended by the person having it with him for such use by him or by some other person.

The police have powers of search and arrest which arise where they suspect a person of committing the offence of carrying an offensive weapon (s.48).

3 Articles with blades or points

It is also an offence (under s.49 of the Criminal Law (Consolidation) (Scotland) Act 1995) for any person to have with him in a public place any article which has a blade or is sharply pointed except a folding pocket-knife the blade of which has a cutting edge of three inches or less. It is a defence for a person charged with such an offence to prove that he had reasonable excuse or lawful authority for having the article with him in a public place or that he had the article with him for use at work, for religious reasons, or as part of any national costume. For this purpose public place includes any place to which, at the material time, the public have or are permitted access, whether on payment or otherwise.

4 Weapons on school premises

S.49A of the Criminal Law (Consolidation) (Scotland) Act 1995 (inserted by the Offensive Weapons Act 1996) make it an offence for any person to have with him on school premises an article with a blade or point to which s.49 of the 1995 Act applies, or to have with him another type of offensive weapon to which s.47 of the 1995 Act applies.

It is a defence for a person charged with an offence under s.49A to show that he had a reasonable excuse or lawful authority for having the article or weapon with him on the premises. In particular, it is a defence for a person to show that he had it with him for use at work, for educational or religious reasons, or as part of a national costume. Police officers have powers to enter and search school premises and any person on those premises for offensive weapons. The police constable must have reasonable grounds for suspecting there is a weapon on the school premises (Criminal Law (Consolidation) (Scotland) Act 1995, s.49B).

5 Manufacture, sale, or distribution of flick knives and gravity knives

The Restriction of Offensive Weapons Act 1959 (as amended by the corresponding Act of 1961), makes it an offence for any person to manufacture, sell, hire, offer for sale or hire, expose or have in his possession for the purposes of sale or hire, or lend or give to any other person, any flick knife (sometimes known as a flick gun) or any gravity knife.

A flick knife is described, in the 1959 Act, as any knife having a blade which opens automatically by hand pressure applied to a button, spring, or other device in or attached to the handle of the knife. A gravity knife is described as any knife having a blade which is released from the handle or sheath by the force of gravity or the application of centrifugal force and which, when released, is locked in place by means of a button, spring, lever, or other device.

The importation of any flick knife or gravity knife is also prohibited.

6 Sale of knives to persons under 18

S.141A of the Criminal Justice Act 1988 (as inserted by the Offensive Weapons Act 1996, s.6 and amended by the Police, Public Order and Criminal Justice (Scotland) Act 2006, s.75 and the Criminal Justice and Licensing (Scotland) Act 2010, s.35) makes it an offence for any person to sell, let on hire to a person under 18 any knife, knife blade or razor blade, axe, sword or other article which has a blade or is sharply pointed and which is made or adapted to cause injury. S.141A does not apply to articles already covered by the Restriction of Offensive Weapons Act 1959 (see above). In addition, the Criminal Justice Act 1988 (Offensive Weapons) (Exemption) Order 1996 exempts from the scope of s.141A the sale of folding pocket-knives which have a blade of less than three inches (7.62 cm) and razor blades which are permanently enclosed in a cartridge or housing.

It is not an offence to sell or let on hire a knife or knife blade to a person if the person is aged 16 or over and the knife or blade is designed for domestic use (s.141A(3A) of the Criminal Justice Act 1988, inserted by s.75 of the Police, Public Order and Criminal Justice (Scotland) Act 2006).

It is a defence for a person charged with an offence under s.141A to show that he believed the buyer or hirer to be aged 18 or over, and that either he had taken reasonable steps to establish the purchaser or hirer's age, or no reasonable person could have suspected from their appearance that they were under the age of 18. A person is to be treated as having taken reasonable steps to establish the purchaser or hirer's age if and only if (s.141A(4) and the Sale and Hire of Crossbows, Knives and certain other Articles to Children and Young Persons (Scotland) Order 2011)—

(a) they were shown a passport, European Union photocard driving licence, or a photographic identity card bearing the national Proof of Age Standards Scheme hologram, and

(b) the document would have convinced a reasonable person.

7 Unlawful marketing of knives

S.1 of the Knives Act 1997 makes it an offence for a person to market a knife in a way which indicates or suggests that it is suitable for combat (suitable for use as a weapon for inflicting injury) or which is otherwise likely to stimulate or encourage violent behaviour involving the use of the knife as a weapon. An indication or suggestion that a knife is suitable for combat may in particular be given by a name or description (a) applied to the knife; or (b) included on the knife or its packaging; or (c) included in any advertisement relating to it. A person "markets" a knife for the purposes of s.1 if he sells or hires it; offers it for sale or hire; or possesses it for the purpose of sale or hire.

Under s.2 of the 1997 Act, a person is also guilty of an offence if he publishes any written, pictorial or other material in connection with the marketing of any knife suggesting that it is suitable for combat, or which is likely to stimulate or encourage violent behaviour. It is a defence for a person charged under the 1997 Act to show that the knife was marketed for use by the armed forces of any country; as an antique or curio; or for use for a prescribed purpose (s.3). No purposes have as yet been prescribed. It is also a defence for a person to show that he did not know or suspect and had no reasonable ground for suspecting that the way in which the knife was marketed constituted a breach of s.1 (s.4). S.5 of the Act contains powers of entry and search similar to those contained in the Criminal Justice Act 1988 s.142 (see **10 Powers of entry and search**, below).

A person convicted of an offence under either s.1 or s.2 may be ordered by the court to forfeit any knives or written or other material in his possession (s.6).

8 Licensing of knife dealers

A "knife dealer's licence" is required to carry on business as a "dealer" in knives and other specified articles (it is not required for private sales between individuals) (Civic Government (Scotland) Act 1982, s.27A, added by the Custodial Sentences and Weapons (Scotland) Act 2007, s.58). The items for which a licence is required are—

(a) knives and knife blades (other than folding pocket knives whose blades do not exceed 3.5 inches (8.91 cm) in length or knives designed for domestic use);

(aa) daggers (other than kirpans or skean dhus whose blades do not exceed 3.5 inches (8.91cm) in length);

(b) swords;

(c) any other article which has a blade or which is sharply pointed, and which is made or adapted for use for causing injury to the person (e.g., arrows and crossbow bolts).

"Dealing" is defined widely, to include those whose business involves not only selling knives etc., but also hiring, lending, giving, and offering for sale or exposing for sale or hire such items. The provision only applies to businesses which sell to private purchasers and not to sales etc to those acting in the course of a business or profession. Auction sales are not covered (s.27A(6)). There are also specific exceptions for the hiring or lending of a sword or arrow in connection with the teaching of, or in connection with a competition in, the sports of fencing or archery, or for a historical re-enactment event (Knife Dealers (Exceptions) Order 2009, Art. 3; Knife Dealer's Licence (Miscellaneous) (Scotland) Order 2010, Art. 2; Knife Dealer's Licence (Historical Re-enactment Events) (Scotland) Order 2011, Art.2). A similar exception applies to the hiring, lending or giving of a knife used in a water sport by a teacher to a pupil, but only where the purposes is the safety of the pupil whilst undertaking the sport (2010 Order, Art. 3).

Application for a licence is made to the local authority and each licence will include certain mandatory conditions. These are that a detailed record is kept of (Knife Dealers (Licence Conditions) Order 2013)—

(d) the identity of the customer and the means by which the customer's identity was verified;

(e) the proof that the customer was at least eighteen years of age at the time of the transaction and the means by which the customer's age was established or an explanation why it was considered unnecessary for proof of age to be established; and

(f) a full description of the article which was sold, hired, lent or given to the customer.

Additionally, in relation to swords, the dealer must take all reasonable steps to establish from the customer, and confirm, the intended use of any sword, and a record must be kept of–

(g) the enquiries made of the customer or other persons or bodies as to that intended use.

The records must be kept for 3 years.

A dealer must also display a notice visible to customers both at the entry to the premises and at the point of sale or counter containing the wording–

(i) it is an offence to sell to a person under the age of 18 any knife or knife blade (except if the person is aged 16 or over and the knife or blade is designed for domestic use);

(ii) it is also an offence to sell to a person under the age of 18 any razor blade, axe, sword or other article which has a blade or which is sharply pointed and which is made or adapted for use for causing injury; and

(iii) a customer may be asked to provide details of his/her age and identity (which may be recorded or copied and kept for inspection for up to 3 years).

9 Weapons to which s.141 of the Criminal Justice Act 1988 applies

S.141 of the Criminal Justice Act 1988 provides that any person who manufactures, sells, hires, offers for sale or hire, exposes or possesses for the purpose of sale or hire, or lends or gives to any other person a weapon to which the section applies commits an offence. The Criminal Justice Act 1988 (Offensive Weapons) (Scotland) Order 2005 specifies the descriptions of weapons to which s.141 is to apply. *Inter alia* knuckledusters, swordsticks, the death star, telescopic truncheons, batons and knives disguised as everyday objects are so specified. There are exceptions for historical re-enactments, sporting activities, and religious ceremonies. S.141 does not apply to weapons of the specified descriptions which are antiques.

The importation of a weapon to which s.141 applies is also prohibited.

S.141 (as amended by the Custodial Sentences and Weapons (Scotland) Act 2007) specifies certain defences including *inter alia*–

(a) it is a defence to show that the conduct in question was only for the purposes of making the weapon available to a museum or gallery;

(b) it is a defence for a person acting on behalf of such a museum or gallery who is charged with hiring or lending a weapon to which s.141 applies to show that he had reasonable grounds for believing that the person to whom he lent or hired it would use it only for cultural, artistic, or educational purposes;

(c) it is also a defence for a person to show that his conduct in lending, hiring, etc., the weapon was for the purpose of theatrical performances and rehearsals, the production of films or the production of television programmes.

10 Powers of entry and search

A sheriff may, subject to certain conditions, authorise the entry and search of premises if there are reasonable grounds for believing that flick knives, gravity knives, or weapons to which s.141 of the Criminal Justice Act 1988 applies are on the premises and that an offence under that provision is being committed in relation to them (Criminal Justice Act 1988, s.142).

S.60 of the Criminal Justice and Public Order Act 1994, as amended by s.8 of the Knives Act 1997, *inter alia*, allows a police officer of or above the rank of inspector to authorise, for a specified period of up to 24 hours, the stopping and searching of persons in any locality within his police area who are suspected of carrying dangerous instruments or offensive weapons.

11 Crossbows

The Crossbows Act 1987 (amended by the Violent Crime Reduction Act 2006, s.44) makes it an offence for a person–

(a) to sell or let on hire a crossbow or part of a crossbow to a person aged under 18 without reasonable grounds for believing him to be 18 years of age or older (s.1);

(b) being under the age of 18, to buy or hire a crossbow or part of a crossbow (s.2); or

(c) being under the age of 18, and not under the supervision of a person aged 21 or over, to be in possession of a crossbow which is, or parts of a crossbow which when assembled without other parts are, capable of discharging a missile (s.3).

None of the above offences is committed if the crossbow in question has a draw weight of less than 1.4 kilograms (s.5).

By s.4 of the Act, a constable who suspects with reasonable cause that a person is or has been committing an offence under s.3 of the Act may detain and search that person for a crossbow or part of a crossbow, may detain and search any vehicle and its contents for a crossbow or part of a crossbow connected with the offence, may seize anything appearing to be a crossbow or part of a crossbow, and may, for any of the above purposes, enter any land other than a dwelling-house.

It is a defence for a person charged with an offence under s.1 to show that he believed the person to whom the crossbow or part was sold or let on hire to be aged 18 or over, and that either he had taken reasonable steps to establish the purchaser or hirer's age, or no reasonable person could have suspected from their appearance that they were under the age of 18. A person is to be treated as having taken reasonable steps to establish the purchaser or hirer's age if and only if (s.1A(2) and the Sale and Hire of Crossbows, Knives and certain other Articles to Children and Young Persons (Scotland) Order 2011)–

(a) they were shown a passport, European Union photocard driving licence, or a photographic identity card bearing the national Proof of Age Standards Scheme hologram, and

(b) the document would have convinced a reasonable person.

12 Using someone to mind a weapon

It is an offence for a person to use someone else to hide or carry a dangerous weapon so as to make the weapon available to the first person for an unlawful purpose (Violent Crime Reduction Act 2006, s.28(1)). "Dangerous weapon" for these purposes means a firearm (s.28(4)).

The penalties for this offence are determined according to the type of dangerous weapon involved and are in line with penalties for possession of the particular weapon (s.29). In some circumstances the offence will attract a minimum sentence. The courts must take the ages of the offender and the person used to hide or carry the weapon into account when considering sentencing. If the offender is 18 or over and the person used is under 18, this will be regarded as an aggravating factor increasing the seriousness of the offence (s.29(11)). The court must state that the person's age is an aggravating factor (s.29(12)). If either person turns 18 during the period that the weapon is being held, the offence is still liable to be treated as aggravated if at some point in that period the offender was 18 or over and the other person was under 18.

B: FIREARMS

13 The legislation

The Firearms Act 1968 regulates the possession and distribution of firearms. In addition, the possession of certain types of firearms, and the possession of firearms by certain persons or under certain circumstances, are altogether prohibited. By virtue of the Firearms Act 1982, the 1968 Act also applies to imitation firearms.

The 1968 Act has been substantially amended by the Firearms Acts listed in **34 Authorities**, below.

For all the purposes of the 1968 Act, a "firearm" means a lethal barrelled weapon of any description from which any shot, bullet, or other missile can be discharged and includes–

(a) any prohibited weapon (see **24 Prohibited weapons and ammunition**, below), whether it is such a lethal weapon as aforesaid or not; and

(b) any component part of such a lethal or prohibited weapon; and

(c) any accessory to any such weapon designed or adapted to diminish the noise or flash caused by firing the weapon (s.57).

Air weapons are regulated either by the Firearms Act 1968 or by the Air Weapons and Licensing (Scotland) Act 2015, depending on the type of weapon concerned.

14 Firearm certificates

Subject to certain exemptions, the Firearms Act 1968 provides that it is an offence to possess, purchase, or acquire a firearm or ammunition to which the section applies without a firearm certificate, or otherwise than as authorised by such a certificate. It is also an offence to fail to comply with a condition subject to which the certificate is held (s.1).

S.1 applies to every firearm except a shot gun and an air weapon, and to any ammunition for a firearm except cartridges containing five or more shot, none of which exceeds .36 inch in diameter, ammunition for an air gun, air rifle, or air pistol, and blank cartridges not more than one inch in diameter.

A shot gun means a smooth-bore gun (not being an air gun) which–

(a) has a barrel not less than 24 inches in length and does not have a barrel with a bore exceeding two inches in diameter;

(b) either has no magazine or has a non-detachable magazine incapable of holding more than two cartridges; and

(c) is not a revolver gun (s.1(3)(a)).

An air weapon for these purposes means an air rifle, air gun, or air pistol which is not subject to a general prohibition (see **24 Prohibited weapons and ammunition**, below) and which is not of a type declared to be specially dangerous.

The Firearms (Dangerous Air Weapons) (Scotland) Rules 1969 declare as specially dangerous an air rifle, air gun, or air pistol which–

(d) is capable of discharging a missile with kinetic energy (i.e., its force of impact on hitting an object) in excess, in the case of an air pistol, of 6ft./lb, or in the case of an air rifle or air gun, of 12ft./lb.; or

(e) is disguised as another object.

The declaration does not apply to a weapon which only falls within paragraph (d) above and which is designed for use under water.

For other air weapons, see **17 Air weapon certificates**, below.

A firearm certificate must be granted by the chief officer of police if he is satisfied that the applicant is a fit person to be entrusted with a firearm and is not prohibited by the 1968 Act from possessing a firearm and has a good reason for having in his possession, or for purchasing or acquiring the firearm or ammunition in respect of which the application is made, and can be permitted to have it in his possession without danger to the public safety or to the peace (s.27).

15 Shot gun certificates

Subject to certain exemptions, it is an offence to possess, purchase, or acquire a shot gun without a shot gun certificate. It is also an offence to fail to comply with a condition subject to which the certificate is held (Firearms Act 1968, s.2).

A shot gun certificate must be granted or, as the case may be, renewed by the chief officer of police if he is satisfied that the applicant for a certificate can be permitted to possess a shot gun without danger to the public safety or to the peace. However, it must not be granted or renewed if the chief officer of police has reason to believe that the applicant is prohibited by the 1968 Act from possessing a shot gun or is satisfied that the applicant does not have a good reason for possessing, purchasing, or acquiring one. An applicant is to be regarded as having a good reason if the gun is intended to be used for sporting or competition purposes or for shooting vermin, and the application is not to be refused merely because the applicant intends neither to use the gun himself nor to lend it for anyone else to use (s.28).

S.5 of the 1988 Act provides that it is an offence to sell to another person in the United Kingdom any ammunition to which s.1 of the 1968 Act does not apply and which is capable of being used in a shot gun or a smooth bore gun to which that section applies unless that other person—
(a) is a registered firearms dealer or a person who sells ammunition by way of trade or business;
(b) produces a certificate authorising him to possess such a gun;
(c) shows that he is entitled to have possession of such a gun without holding a certificate; or
(d) produces a certificate authorising another person to possess such a gun, together with that person's written authority to purchase the ammunition on his behalf.

16 Register of holders of certificates

S.39 of the Firearms (Amendment) Act 1997 provides for the establishment of a central register of all persons who have applied for a firearm or shotgun certificate or to whom a certificate has been granted or whose certificate has been renewed. The register is kept by means of a computer which provides access on-line to all police forces.

17 Air weapon certificates

The Firearms (Dangerous Air Weapons) (Scotland) Rules 1969 require certain air weapons to be covered by a firearms certificate (see **14 Firearm certificates**, above). Some air weapons are also caught by the general prohibition contained in the Firearms Act 1968, s.5(1) (see **24 Prohibited weapons and ammunition**, below).

In addition, from 31st December 2016, air weapons which are not covered by the requirement to have a firearms certificate under the 1969 Rules, and are not prohibited by s.5(1), must have an air weapon certificate. The only exceptions are (Air Weapons and Licensing (Scotland) Act 2015, s.1)—
(a) low power air weapons with a muzzle energy of one joule or below;
(b) air weapons (such as paint ball guns) which are not within the definition of a firearm i.e., a lethal barrelled weapon of any description from which any shot, bullet, or other missile can be discharged (see **13 The legislation**, above); and
(c) air weapons designed for use only under water.

It is an offence for a person to use, possess, purchase or acquire an air weapon without holding an air weapon certificate where one is required (Air Weapons and Licensing (Scotland) Act 2015, s.2). The minimum age for holding an air weapon certificate is 14 (s.3) but those under 18 must have the consent of their parent or guardian (s.7).

An air weapon certificate will only be granted if the chief constable is satisfied that the applicant (s.5)—
(a) is fit to be entrusted with an air weapon;
(b) is not prohibited from possessing an air weapon or other firearm;
(c) has a good reason for using, possessing, purchasing or acquiring an air weapon; and
(d) in all the circumstances, can be permitted to possess an air weapon without danger to the public safety or to the peace.

Visitors to Scotland may apply to the Chief Constable for a permit to use, possess, purchase or acquire air weapons while in Scotland, without holding an air weapon certificate (s.13). Such a permit can last up to 12 months.

Provision is also made for air weapon event permits which will be required where an event is to take place at which people may borrow, hire, use or possess an air weapon for a short timescale, without holding individual air weapon certificates (s.17).

There are various exemptions from the requirement to hold an air weapons licence. These are contained in

Schedule 1 to the 2015 Act and include members of approved air weapons clubs for the purpose of possessing or using an air weapon for target shooting at that club; registered firearms dealers; auctioneers, museums, and artistic performers. It is also permissible for a person without an air weapon certificate to borrow an air weapon from an individual who holds a certificate, and to possess and use it while on private land and under the supervision of the certificate holder, or their employee. Any use must be in line with the conditions attached to the relevant air weapon certificate and if the borrower is under 14, then the supervisor must be aged 21 or over. There is no lower age limit to the application of this exemption.

18 Revocation of certificates

A firearm certificate may be revoked by a chief officer of police if he has reason to believe that the holder is of intemperate habits, unsound mind, or is otherwise unfitted to have a firearm or can no longer be permitted to have the firearm and ammunition to which the certificate relates without danger to public safety or to the peace. A certificate may also be revoked if the holder is prohibited by the Firearms Act 1968 from possessing a firearm or no loner has a good reason for having the firearm or ammunition to which the certificate relates (Firearms Act 1968, s.30A). A certificate may also be partially revoked if the chief officer of police is satisfied that the holder no longer has a good reason for possessing the firearm or ammunition to which the partial revocation relates (s.30B).

A shot gun certificate may be revoked by the chief officer of police if he is satisfied that the holder is prohibited by the Act from possessing a shot gun, or cannot be permitted to possess one without danger to the public safety or to the peace (s.30C).

Similar provisions apply to air weapon certificates (Air Weapons and Licensing (Scotland) Act 2015, s.11).

An appeal against the revocation of a firearm, shot gun or air weapon certificate lies to the Sheriff (Firearms Act 1968, s.44; Air Weapons and Licensing (Scotland) Act 2015, s.34).

19 Duration of certificates and appeals

A certificate will, unless previously revoked or cancelled, continue in force for a period of five years, but is renewable for a further five year period by the chief officer of police for the area in which the holder resides (s.28A of the Firearms Act 1968).

An air weapon certificate lasts for 5 years (or for those under 18, until the age of 18) (Air Weapons and Licensing (Scotland) Act 2015, s.8).

An appeal against a decision of a chief officer of police to refuse to grant, or renew, a certificate lies to the sheriff (Firearms Act 1968, s.44; Air Weapons and Licensing (Scotland) Act 2015, s.34).

20 Exemptions

Under ss.7 to 13 of the Firearms Act 1968, there are certain circumstances under which possession of a firearm or shot gun does not require a certificate, as follows.

(i) A person holding a permit from the local chief officer of police may possess a firearm and ammunition in accordance with the terms of the permit (s.7).

(ii) Registered firearms dealers (see below) and their servants, and auctioneers, carriers, warehousemen, and their servants may possess firearms or ammunition in the ordinary course of business (ss.8 and 9). (An auctioneer may sell firearms by auction without being registered as a firearms dealer, but he must obtain a permit to do so from the local chief officer of police.)

(iii) Persons licensed to slaughter animals may possess slaughtering instruments at slaughter-houses or knackers' yards where they are employed. Similarly, the proprietor of a slaughterhouse or knacker's yard, or a person appointed by him, may hold a slaughtering instrument and ammunition therefor for the purpose of storing them in safe custody at the slaughterhouse or yard (s.10).

(iv)

(a) A person may carry a firearm or ammunition belonging to another person who does hold a certificate, under instructions from, and for the use of, that other person for sporting purposes only (*Note.*–where the person carrying the firearm is under 18, the certificate holder must be 18 or over) (s.11(1)).

(b) A person aged 18 or over may possess a firearm at an athletic meeting for starting races at that meeting (s.11(2)).

(c) A member of a cadet corps approved by the Secretary of State may possess a fire-arm and ammunition when engaged as a member of the corps on, or in connection with, drill or target shooting (s.11(3)).

(d) A person conducting or carrying on a miniature rifle range or shooting gallery at which only air weapons or miniature rifles not exceeding .23 inch calibre are used may possess, purchase, or acquire such miniature rifles and ammunition suitable for them; and any person may use such miniature rifles at such a range or gallery (s.11(4)).

(e) A person may borrow a shot gun from the occupier of private premises and use it on those premises in the occupier's presence (*Note.*–where the borrower of the firearm is under 18, the occupier must be 18 or over) (s.11(5)).

(f) A person may use a shot gun to shoot at artificial targets at a time and place approved by the local chief of police (s.11(6)).

(v) A person may have a firearm in his possession for a theatrical performance or rehearsal or a film production. For such purposes, the Ministry of Defence may authorise the use of firearms which are prohibited weapons (s.12).

(vi) A person may have in his possession a firearm or ammunition on board a ship, or signalling apparatus or ammunition therefor on board an aircraft or at an aerodrome, as part of the equipment of the ship, aircraft, or aerodrome (s.13).

The Criminal Justice Act 1988 provides for the following further exemptions.

(vii) A member of a rifle club, miniature rifle club, or muzzle-loading pistol club approved by the Secretary of State may have in his possession a firearm and ammunition when engaged as a member of the club in connection with target shooting (1988 Act, s.15).

    Note.– Guidance published by the Home Office, *Approval of rifle and muzzle loading-loading pistol clubs* (April 2012) available at <https://www.gov.uk/government/publications/approval-of-rifle-and-muzzle-loading-pistol-clubs> provides information on approval means and how clubs can apply for it and explains the criteria and conditions which clubs must meet in order to obtain approval and remain approved by the Scottish Ministers. It also gives the addresses of national shooting organisations.

(viii) A person of, or over, the age of 17 may borrow a rifle from the occupier of private premises and use it on those premises in the presence either of the occupier or of a servant of the occupier if the occupier or servant in whose presence it is used holds a firearm certificate in respect of that rifle and the borrower's possession and use of it complies with any conditions as to those matters specified in the certificate (and, if the borrower is aged 17, the occupier or servant is aged 18 or over). A person who is so entitled may also purchase or acquire ammunition for use in the rifle and have it in his possession during the period for which the rifle is borrowed subject to compliance with the conditions of the firearm certificate which relate to that rifle (1988 Act, s.16).

(ix) The holder of a visitor's firearm permit may have in his possession any firearm, and have in his possession, purchase, or acquire any ammunition to which s.1 of the 1968 Act applies; the holder of a visitor's shot gun permit may have shot guns in his possession and purchase or acquire shot guns (1988 Act, s.17).

(x) A person may purchase a firearm from a registered firearms dealer provided that he has not been in Great Britain for more than 30 days in the preceding 12 months and the firearm is purchased for the purpose only of being exported from Great Britain without first coming into that person's possession (1988 Act, s.18).

(xi) Firearms and ammunition in certain museums are exempted from certain provisions of the 1968 Act in accordance with the provisions of the Schedule to the 1988 Act (1988 Act, s.19).

Note also that nothing in the Firearms Act 1968 relating to firearms applies to an antique firearm which is sold, transferred, purchased, acquired or possessed "as a curiosity or ornament" (s.58). That phrase, and the definition of what is "antique" are questions of fact, not law, and consequently it is for a jury to decide. The Home Office has produced a *Guide on Firearms Licensing Law* (November 2013) which, for the benefit of prosecutors, states that "evidence of antique status may include an indication of date of manufacture, details of technical obsolescence, a lack of commercial availability of suitable ammunition, or a written opinion by an accredited expert".

As to the exemptions in relation to air weapons, see **17 Air weapon certificates**, above.

21 Firearms dealers

A person who, by way of trade or business *inter alia* (Firearms Act 1968, s.3, as amended by the Violent Crime Reduction Act 2006, s.31(1); Air Weapons and Licensing (Scotland) Act 2015, s.24)–

(a) manufactures, sells, transfers, repairs, tests, or proves firearms (including shot guns) or ammunition to which s.1 applies; or

(b) sells or transfers an air weapon,

must be registered as a firearms dealer. A dealer must not sell or transfer firearms or ammunition within (a) above to, or undertake to repair, test, or prove them for, a person unless that person produces the appropriate certificate or shows his authority to hold the firearm or ammunition without a certificate (1968 Act, s.3). A person must not sell air weapons by way of trade or business other than face to face (2015 Act, s.25).

Dealers must keep a register of transactions, including those involving air weapons (1968 Act, s.40(2) as amended by the 2006 Act, s.31(2)).

22 Applications and fees

Applications for firearm or shot gun certificates must be made to the chief officer of police of the area in which the applicant resides. The Firearms Rules 1998 require persons applying for a certificate to provide two referees (only one for a shotgun), who must have known the applicant personally for at least two years, and who are required to give statements to the effect that they know of no reason why the applicant should not be permitted to possess a firearm, or shot gun, as the case may be. Applicants are also required to give permission for the police to obtain information from their doctors about their medical history, including details of mental health problems.

The fee for the grant of a firearm certificate is £88, and for a shotgun certificate it is £79.50. The fee for the renewal of a firearm certificate is £62, and for the renewal of or shot gun certificate is £49. The fee for the replacement of a lost or destroyed certificate is £4. Where a shotgun certificate is granted at the same time as a firearm certificate, the fee is £28, and where a shotgun certificate is renewed at the same time as a firearm certificate, the fee is £2. Certificates are valid for five years or for such other period as may be specified by order. The fee for a visitors' permit is £20.

No fee is payable for the grant, variation, or renewal of firearm certificates *inter alia* related solely to signalling devices (such as flare signal pens used by yachtsmen or mountaineers in case of emergency), provided that they do not exceed eight inches in length when assembled and ready to fire, or to ammunition for such devices.

The fee for the grant or renewal of registration as a firearms dealer is £200.

As to applications for air weapon certificates, see **17 Air weapon certificates**, above.

23 Conversion of weapons

Otherwise than by a registered firearms dealer in the course of repair, it is an offence to shorten to less than 24 inches the barrel of any exempted shot gun (see **14 Firearm certificates**, above) or of any other smooth bore gun not being one which has a barrel exceeding two inches in diameter (s.4(1) and (2) and 1988 Act, s.6). It is also an offence for any person other than a registered dealer to convert a dummy weapon into a firearm (s.4(3) of the Firearms Act 1968).

24 Prohibited weapons and ammunition

A person commits an offence if, without the written authority of the Scottish Ministers, he has in his possession, purchases, or acquires any of the under-mentioned weapons and ammunition (known as "prohibited" weapons and ammunition) (Firearms Act 1968, s.5(1), (1A), (2))–

  (a) any firearm which is so designed or adapted that two or more missiles can be successively discharged without repeated pressure on the trigger;
  (b) any self-loading or pump-action rifled gun other than one which is chambered for .22 non-fire cartridges;
  (c) any firearm which either has a barrel less than 30cm in length or is less than 60cm in length overall, other than an air weapon, a muzzle-loading gun or a firearm designed as signalling apparatus;
  (d) any self-loading or pump-action smooth bore gun which is not an air weapon or chambered for .22 non-fire cartridges and either has a barrel less than 24 inches in length or (excluding any detachable, folding, retractable or other movable butt-stock) is less than 40 inches in length overall;
  (e) any smooth-bore revolver gun other than one which is chambered for 9mm non-fire cartridges or a muzzle-loading gun;
  (ea) any air rifle, air gun or air pistol which uses, or is designed or adapted for use with, a self-contained gas cartridge system;
  (f) any rocket launcher, or any mortar, for projecting a stabilised missile, other than a launcher or mortar designed for line-throwing or pyrotechnic purposes or as signalling apparatus;
  (g) any weapon of whatever description designed or adapted for the discharge of any noxious liquid, gas, or other thing;
  (h) any cartridge with a bullet designed to explode on or immediately before impact, any ammunition containing or designed or adapted to contain any such noxious thing as is mentioned in (g), and, if capable of being used with a firearm of any description, any grenade, bomb (or other like missile), or rocket or shell designed to explode on or immediately before impact;
  (i) any firearm which is disguised as another object;
  (j) any rocket or ammunition not falling within paragraph (h) which consists in or incorporates a missile designed to explode on or immediately before impact and is for military use;
  (k) any launcher or other projecting apparatus not falling within paragraph (f) which is designed to be used with any rocket or ammunition falling within paragraph (h);
  (l) any ammunition for military use which consists in or incorporates a missile designed so that a substance contained in the missile will ignite on or immediately before impact;
  (m) any ammunition for military use which consists in or incorporates a missile designed, on account of its having a jacket and hard-core, to penetrate armour plating, armour screening, or body armour;
  (n) any ammunition which incorporates a missile designed or adapted to expand on impact; or
  (o) anything which is designed to be projected as a missile from any weapon and is designed to be, or has been, incorporated in any ammunition falling within any of the preceding paragraphs.

A person also commits an offence if without authority he–
  (p) manufactures any weapon or ammunition specified in (a) to (h) above;
  (q) sells or transfers any prohibited weapon or ammunition;
  (r) has in his possession for sale or transfer any prohibited weapon or ammunition; or
  (s) he purchases or acquires for sale or transfer any prohibited weapon or ammunition.

The general prohibition contained in (c) above is subject to a number of special exemptions, which are set out in ss.2 to 8 of the Firearms (Amendment) Act 1997. The effect of these exemptions is that it is not an offence to possess, purchase, acquire, sell or transfer, without the authority of the Secretary of State, a firearm of the type prohibited by (c) above if the firearm in question is required for the purposes of slaughtering, or humanely killing, or tranquillising animals; shooting vermin; or starting races at athletics meetings. Trophies of war acquired before 1st January 1946 and firearms of historic interest manufactured before 1919 and kept as part of a collection are also exempt. The Firearms Amendment Act 1997 (Firearms of Historic Interest) Order 1997 specifies the description of historic firearms which are covered by this exemption. Firearms permitted by the above exemptions must still be covered by a firearms certificate or permit. Museums who hold a museum firearms licence (granted under the Firearms (Amendment) Act 1988, s.1, Schedule 1) do not also need to hold firearm or shot gun certificates and, if the licence so provides, may hold prohibited weapons without the consent of the Secretary of State.

Any authority may be issued subject to conditions (s.5(3)). However, an authority will not be required for any person to have in his possession, or to purchase, acquire, sell, or transfer any of the weapons and ammunition described in paragraphs (i) to (o) above if he is authorised by a certificate under the 1968 Act to possess, purchase, or acquire that weapon or ammunition subject to a condition that he does so only for the purpose of its being kept or exhibited as part of a collection (1968 Act, s.5A(1)). But no sale or transfer may be made under s.5A(1) except to a person who—

(a) produces the authority of the Scottish Ministers under s.5(1) for his purchase or acquisition; or

(b) shows that he is, under s.5A or a licence under the Schedule to the Firearms (Amendment) Act 1988 (museums etc.), entitled to make the purchase or acquisition without such authority.

The authority of the Scottish Ministers is not required—

(a) for any person to have in his possession, or to purchase or acquire, any of the prohibited weapons, ammunition or missiles described in paragraphs (i) to (o) above if his possession, purchase, or acquisition is exclusively in connection with the carrying on of activities in respect of which that person, or the person on whose behalf he has possession, or makes the purchase or acquisition, is recognised, for the purposes of the law of another Member State relating to firearms, as a collector of firearms or a body concerned in the cultural or historical aspects of weapons (s.5A(3));

(b) for any person to have in his possession any expanding ammunition or the missile for any such ammunition if—

(i) he is authorised by a firearm certificate to possess, purchase, acquire, sell or transfer such ammunition; and

(ii) the certificate or permit contains a condition restricting the use of expanding ammunition to the lawful shooting of deer or vermin; the humane killing of animals; or the shooting of animals for the protection of people or other animals (s.5A(4));

(c) for any person to have in his possession any expanding ammunition or the missile for any such ammunition if—

(i) he is entitled, under s.10 of the 1968 Act, to have a slaughtering instrument and the ammunition for it in his possession; and

(ii) the ammunition or missile in question is designed to be capable of being used with a slaughtering instrument (s.5A(5));

(d) for the sale or transfer of any expanding ammunition or the missile for any such ammunition to any person who produces a certificate by virtue of which he is authorised under paragraph (b) above to purchase or acquire it without the authority of the Secretary of State (s.5A(6));

(e) for a person carrying on the business of a firearms dealer, or any servant of his, to have in his possession, or to purchase, acquire, sell, or transfer any expanding ammunition or the missile for any such ammunition in the ordinary course of his business (s.5A(7)).

25 Restriction on sale and purchase of primers

There are restrictions on the purchase and sale of primers to people who hold a relevant firearms certificate or who otherwise have lawful authority for having them. Primers are components of ammunition which contain a chemical compound that detonates on impact (Violent Crime Reduction Act 2006, s.35).

26 Transfers of firearms and ammunition

Ss. 32 to 36 of the Firearms (Amendment) Act 1997 contain strict requirements relating to the transfer of firearms, shotguns and ammunition. Except where the transferee is a registered dealer or a person who is exempted from the need to have a certificate (see above), all transfers must be made in person and the transferee must produce to the transferor the certificate or permit entitling him to acquire the firearm or ammunition in question. The details of any transfer of a weapon must be notified to a chief officer of police within seven days. Notification must also be given whenever a firearm is de-activated, destroyed, lost or stolen, or whenever ammunition is lost or stolen.

27 Young people

Ss.22 to 24ZA of the Firearms Act 1968 impose a number of prohibitions in relation to the possession of firearms by young people under the age of 17. It is an offence under s.22–

(a) for a person under the age of eighteen to purchase or hire any firearm or ammunition (s.22(1));

(b) where a person under the age of eighteen is entitled, as the holder of a certificate under the 1968 Act to have a firearm in his possession, for that person to use that firearm for a purpose not authorised by the European weapons directive (s.22(1A), inserted by S.I. 1992 No. 2823, reg.4(1));

(c) for a person under the age of fourteen to have in his possession any firearm or ammunition to which s.1 of the 1968 Act or s.15 of the Firearms (Amendment) Act 1988 applies, except in circumstances where under s.11(1), (3) or (4) of the 1968 Act he is entitled to have possession of it without holding a firearm certificate (s.22(2), amended by s.23(4) of the 1988 Act);

(d) for a person under the age of fifteen to have with him an assembled shot gun except while under the supervision of a person of or over the age of twenty-one, or while the shot gun is so covered with a securely fastened gun cover that it cannot be fired (s.22(3)).

It is an offence under s.24 of the 1968 Act–

(e) to sell or let on hire any firearm or ammunition to a person under the age of eighteen (1968 Act, s.24(1));

(f) to make a gift of or lend any firearm or ammunition to which s.1 of the 1968 Act applies to a person under the age of fourteen, or to part with the possession of any such firearm or ammunition to a person under that age, except in circumstances where that person is entitled under s.11(1), (3) or (4) of the 1968 Act or s.15 of the Firearms (Amendment) Act 1988 (see **20 Exemptions**, above) to have possession thereof without holding a firearm certificate (1968 Act, s.24(2) amended by the Firearms (Amendment) Act 1988, s.23(4));

(g) to make a gift of a shot gun or ammunition for a shot gun to a person under the age of fifteen (1968 Act, s.24(3));

(h) to make a gift of an air weapon or ammunition for an air weapon to a person under the age of eighteen or to part with the possession of an air weapon or ammunition for an air weapon to a person under the age of eighteen except where the person holds an air weapon certificate granted under s.5 of the Air Weapons and Licensing (Scotland) Act 2015 or the possession is otherwise in accordance with Part 1 of that Act (1968 Act, s.24(4) as amended by the 2015 Act).

In proceedings for an offence under any provision of s.24 of the 1968 Act, it is a defence to prove that the person charged with the offence believed the other person to be of or over the age mentioned in that provision and had reasonable ground for that belief (1968 Act, s.24(5)).

Under s.24ZA (added by the Crime and Security Act 2010, s.46), it is an offence for a person in possession of an air weapon to fail to take reasonable precautions to prevent any person under the age of eighteen from having the weapon with him (unless that young person is not prohibited from having the weapon with him by virtue of the Air Weapons and Licensing (Scotland) Act 2015). It is a defence to show that the person charged believed the other person to be aged eighteen or over; and had reasonable ground for that belief.

28 Preservation of the public safety and prevention of crime

Ss.16 to 21 and 25 of the Firearms Act 1968 prohibit the possession of firearms in certain circumstances. *Inter alia* an offence is committed by–

(a) a person who has in his possession any firearm or imitation firearm with intent (i) by means thereof to cause, or (ii) to enable another person by means thereof to cause, any person to believe that unlawful violence will be used against him or another person (s.16A, inserted by Firearms (Amendment) Act 1994);

(b) a person who has with him a firearm or imitation firearm with intent to commit an indictable offence, or to resist arrest or prevent the arrest of another (s.18);

(c) a person who, without lawful authority or reasonable excuse (the proof whereof lies on him), has with him in a public place a loaded shot gun, an air weapon (whether loaded or not), any other firearm (whether loaded or not) together with ammunition suitable for use in that firearm, or an imitation firearm (s.19, as amended by the Anti-social Behaviour Act 2003);

(d) a person who is in any building or on any land, as a trespasser and without reasonable excuse (the proof whereof lies on him), and has a firearm or imitation firearm with him (s.20); and

(e) a person who supplies a firearm or ammunition to, or repairs, tests, or proves, a firearm or ammunition for, another person whom he knows, or has reasonable cause to believe, to be drunk or of unsound mind (s.25).

It is an offence for a person of any age to fire an air weapon beyond the boundary of premises. A defence is provided to cover the situation where the person shooting has the consent of the occupier of the land over or into which he shoots (1968 Act, s.21A inserted by the Violent Crime Reduction Act 2006, s.34).

It is also an offence for a person supervising the use and possession of an air weapon on private premises by a person under 18 to allow the supervised person to fire any missile beyond those premises (s.21A(1A)).

29 Possession of firearms by persons previously convicted of crime

Anyone convicted of a crime and sentenced to custody for life, or detention, imprisonment, corrective training, or youth custody for a term of three years or more, is permanently prohibited from possessing, using, or carrying firearms or ammunition at any time following their release (Firearms Act 1968, s.21(1)).

Those sentenced to imprisonment or youth custody for between three months and three years, are prohibited from possessing, using, or carrying firearms or ammunition at any time during the five years after their release (s. 21(2)).

A person given a suspended sentence of three months or more is also prohibited for five years, the prohibition starting on the second day after the date on which sentence was passed (s.21(2C)).

Children and young persons convicted of serious crime and discharged on licence must not possess, use, or carry a firearm or ammunition during the period of the licence. It may be made a condition of a recognisance to keep the peace or be of good behaviour, or a requirement of a community rehabilitation order or a probation order, that the person subject to the recognisance or the order shall not possess, use, or carry a firearm or ammunition. It is an offence for a person to supply a firearm or ammunition to, or to repair, test, or prove a firearm or ammunition for, another person whom he knows, or has reasonable cause to believe, to be thus prohibited from possessing firearms or ammunition. A person subject to one of the above prohibitions may apply to the Crown Court (in Scotland, the sheriff) for the prohibition to be removed (s.21).

The prohibition under s.21 extends to antique firearm owned "as a curiosity or ornament" under s.58 (as to which, see **20 Exemptions**, above).

30 Powers of arrest and search

S. 46 of the Firearms Act 1968 contains a power of arrest with a warrant. Certain special powers of arrest are granted by s.50 of the 1968 Act.

Where a constable has reasonable cause to suspect that a person has a firearm, with or without ammunition, in a public place, or is committing or about to commit an offence under ss.18 or 20 (see **28 Preservation of the public safety and prevention of crime**, above), he may require that person to hand over the weapon for examination, or require him to submit to search (s.47(1) and (3)). Similarly, he may search a vehicle in a public place if he suspects that the vehicle contains a firearm or is being used or is about to be used in connection with an offence under ss.18 or 20 elsewhere than in a public place, and may stop the vehicle for this purpose (s.47(4)).

A constable may require the production of a firearm or shot gun certificate by a person he believes to be carrying a firearm or ammunition, or a shot gun, as the case may be (s.48(1)). If the person concerned fails to produce the certificate or permit or to permit the constable to read it, or to show that he is entitled to have the firearm, ammunition, or shot gun without holding a certificate, the constable may seize and detain the firearm, ammunition, or shot gun, and require the person to give his name and address (s.48(2)).

Search powers in relation to air weapon offences are contained in the Air Weapons and Licensing (Scotland) Act 2015, s.26. The police may also require a person whom they believe to be in possession of an air weapon to produce their air weapon certificate, or evidence that they are entitled to possess an air weapon under the 2015 Act without holding an air weapon certificate (s.27).

31 Prosecution and punishment of offences

The way in which firearms offences are punishable upon conviction is set out in s.51 and Sch.6 to the Firearms Act 1968.

Minimum sentences for offences under s.5 of the 1968 Act (prohibition of certain weapons and control of arms traffic: see **24 Prohibited weapons and ammunition**, above) are set by s.51A (inserted by the Criminal Justice Act 2003, s.287). This section applies only to the simple offence of possession of a prohibited weapon. The minimum sentence, other than in exceptional circumstances, is five years' imprisonment for people aged 21 or over and three years' imprisonment for a person aged between 16 and 21. S.51A is amended (by s.30 of the Violent Crime Reduction Act 2006) so as to extend it to other serious offences involving the possession of prohibited weapons, to ensure that offenders do not escape the minimum sentence where they are not also charged with the simple possession offence. The additional offences all appear in the 1968 Act and are the offences under:

(a) s.16 (possession of firearm with intent to injure);
(b) s.16A (possession of firearm with intent to cause fear of violence);
(c) s.17 (use of firearm to resist arrest);
(d) s.18 (carrying firearm with criminal intent);
(e) s.19 (carrying a firearm in a public place); and
(f) s.20(1) (trespassing in a building with firearm).

As to ss.16-20, see **28 Preservation of the public safety and prevention of crime**, above.

The minimum sentences apply in these offences only where a prohibited weapon is involved.

C: IMITATION FIREARMS

32 Imitations convertible into firearms

The Firearms Act 1982 applies the provisions of the Firearms Act 1968 (subject to exceptions) to an imitation firearm which has the appearance of being a firearm to which s.1 of the 1968 Act applies (see **14 Firearm certificates**, above) and which is so constructed or adapted as to be readily convertible into a firearm to which that section applies (s.1). The provisions of the 1982 Act do not apply to imitation component parts of firearms or to imitations of accessories to firearms such as are described in s.57 of the 1968 Act. The 1982 Act also provides that an imitation air weapon, including an imitation of a type of weapon declared by the Firearms (Dangerous Air Weapons) (Scotland) Rules 1969 to be specially dangerous, is excluded from the provisions of the Act.

An imitation firearm will be regarded as readily convertible into a firearm to which s.1 of the 1968 Act applies if–

(a) it can be so converted without any special skill in the construction or adaptation of firearms of any description on the part of the person converting it; and

(b) the work involved in converting it does not require equipment or tools other than such as are in common use by persons carrying out works of construction and maintenance in their own homes.

It is a defence for a person accused of an offence under the 1968 Act involving an imitation firearm to which the 1982 Act applies to show that he did not know and had no reason to suspect that the imitation firearm was so constructed or adapted as to be readily convertible into a firearm to which s.1 of the 1968 Act applies.

The following provisions of the 1968 Act do not apply to imitation firearms to which the 1982 Act applies.

(a) S.4(3) and (4) (conversion of dummy weapon–see **23 Conversion of weapons**, above–and aggravated offence under s.1 in relation to illegally shortened shot gun or illegally converted dummy weapon).

(b) Ss.16 to 20 (see **28 Preservation of the public safety and prevention of crime**, above), but without prejudice to the application of any of those provisions to an imitation firearm apart from the 1982 Act (i.e., ss.17 and 18).

(c) S.47 (see **30 Powers of arrest and search**, above), but again without prejudice to its application to an imitation firearm apart from the 1982 Act.

33 Manufacture, import and sale of realistic imitation firearms

It is an offence to manufacture, import or sell a realistic imitation firearm. The Secretary of State has a power to make regulations to provide for exceptions, exemptions and defences to this offence. Realistic imitation firearms are defined by as anything which has the appearance of being a firearm whether or not it is capable of discharging any shot, bullet or other missile (Violent Crime Reduction Act 2006, ss.36, 38).

The Violent Crime Reduction Act 2006 (Realistic Imitation Firearms) Regulations 2007, provides defences to the offences of the manufacture, import and sale of realistic imitation firearms in the 2006 Act, s.36. These defences operate where a person who is charged with such an offence can show that his conduct was for the purpose only of making the imitation firearm in question available for one or more of the purposes specified in the Regulations. These are the organisation and holding of permitted activities for which public liability insurance is held in relation to liabilities to third parties arising from or in connection with the organisation and holding of those activities; and the purposes of display at a permitted event.

It is also a defence to show that the sale of a realistic imitation firearm was for the purposes of a museum or gallery; for theatre, film or television productions; for specified historical re-enactments; or for Crown service. It is also a defence for business to import realistic imitation firearms for the purposes of modifying them so that they cease to be realistic imitations. For a defence to be shown, a person must adduce sufficient evidence of it and the contrary must not be proved beyond reasonable doubt (Violent Crime Reduction Act 2006, s.37).

Where imitation firearms are still permitted to be manufactured, imported or sold, they must be constructed in accordance with specifications laid down in regulations by the Secretary of State (Violent Crime Reduction Act 2006, s.39). The Violent Crime Reduction Act 2006 (Specification for Imitation Firearms) Regulations 2011 sets out specifications for blank firing imitation firearms and revolvers. The regulations also provide a defence for a person charged with importing an imitation firearm which does not conform to the specifications if they did so only for the purpose of a museum or gallery, a theatrical performance, film of television production, the organisation of historical enactments, or Crown service.

It is also an offence to sell an imitation firearm to a person under the age of 18, or for a person under 18 to purchase one. In relation to the selling offence, it is a defence for the vendor to show that he believed that the purchaser was 18 or over and that he had reasonable grounds for that belief (Firearms Act 1968, s.24A, inserted by the Violent Crime Reduction Act 2006, s.40).

34 Authorities

Statutes–

Air Weapons and Licensing (Scotland) Act 2015

Civic Government (Scotland) Act 1982

Criminal Justice Act 1988

Criminal Justice and Public Order Act 1994

Criminal Law (Consolidation) (Scotland) Act 1995

Crossbows Act 1987

Firearms Acts 1968 and 1982

Firearms (Amendment) Acts 1988, 1992, 1994, and 1997, and (Amendment) (No. 2) Act 1997

Knives Act 1997

Offensive Weapons Act 1996

Police, Public Order and Criminal Justice (Scotland) Act 2006

Public Order Act 1986

Restriction of Offensive Weapons Acts 1959 and 1961

Violent Crime Reduction Act 2006

Statutory Instruments–

Criminal Justice Act 1988 (Offensive Weapons) (Scotland) Order 2005 (S.S.I. 2005 No. 483)

Criminal Justice Act 1988 (Offensive Weapons) (Exemption) Order 1996 (S.I. 1996 No. 3064)

Criminal Justice Act 1988 (Offensive Weapons) Orders 2002, 2004 and 2008 (S.I. 2002 No. 1668, 2004 No. 1271, and 2008 Nos. 973 and 2039)

Firearms Acts (Amendment) Regulations 1992 (S.I. 1992 No. 2823)

Firearms (Dangerous Air Weapons) (Scotland) Rules 1969, as amended (S.I. 1969 No. 270 and 1993 No. 1541)

Firearms Rules 1998, as amended (S.I. 1998 No. 1941, 2005 No. 3344, 2007 No. 2605, 2010 No. 1759, 2013 Nos. 1945 and 2970, 2014 No. 1239, and 2016 No. 425)

Firearms (Variation of Fees) Orders 2015 (S.I. 2015 No. 611)

Knife Dealers (Exceptions) order 2009 (S.S.I. 2009 No. 218)

Knife Dealers (Licence Conditions) Order 2013 (S.S.I. 2013 No. 22)

Knife Dealer's Licence (Historical Re-enactment Events) (Scotland) Order 2011 (S.S.I. 2011 No. 263)

Knife Dealer's Licence (Miscellaneous) (Scotland) Order 2010 (S.S.I. 2010 No. 311)

Sale and Hire of Crossbows, Knives and certain other Articles to Children and Young Persons (Scotland) Order 2011 (S.S.I. 2011 No. 129)

Transfer of Functions (Prohibited Weapons) Order 1968 (S.I. 1968 No. 1200)

Violent Crime Reduction Act 2006 (Realistic Imitation Firearms) Regulations 2007 (S.I. 2007 No. 2606)

Violent Crime Reduction Act 2006 (Specification for Imitation Firearms) Regulations 2011 (S.I. 2011 No. 1754)

RACIAL HATRED: SCOTLAND

1 The legislation

Part III of the Public Order Act 1986, makes it an offence to commit certain acts intended or likely to stir up racial hatred, and to be in possession of racially inflammable material.

Provision as to discrimination against a person in respect of the protected characteristic of religion or belief is made by the Equality Act 2010. As to the provisions of the Equality Act 2010 see the Note on **Discrimination and Equality Law.**

2 The offence of racial hatred

Under Part III (ss.17 to 29) of the Public Order Act 1986, which applies to the whole of Great Britain, it is an offence to commit certain acts which are intended to stir up racial hatred or, having regard to all the circumstances and subject to certain defences, are likely to do so. Racial hatred means, for this purpose, hatred against a group of persons defined by reference to colour, race, nationality (including citizenship), or ethnic or national origins (s.17). These acts include–

- (a) using threatening, abusive, or insulting words or behaviour, or displaying written material which is threatening, abusive, or insulting (s.18);
- (b) publishing or distributing written material which is threatening, abusive or insulting (s.19);
- (c) presenting or directing the public performance of a play involving the use of threatening, abusive, or insulting words or behaviour (however this does not apply *inter alia* to performances given solely for the purpose of rehearsal or making a reading, and a person does not present a performance if he only takes part in it as a performer, provided that he performs in accordance with any directions) (s.20);
- (d) distributing, showing, or playing a recording of visual images or sounds which are threatening, abusive, or insulting (s.21). Further, if a programme involving threatening, abusive, or insulting visual images or sounds is broadcast, or included in a cable programme service, the person providing the broadcasting or cable programme service, any producer or director of the programme, and any person by whom offending words or behaviour are used are, subject to certain defences, guilty of an offence (s.22).

Note.–The group of persons against whom the hatred is directed need not be in Great Britain. The territorial restriction which previously applied was repealed by the Anti-terrorism, Crime and Security Act 2001, s.37.

3 Powers of entry, search, and forfeiture

A sheriff may issue a warrant to enter and search premises if he is satisfied that there are reasonable grounds for suspecting that a person is in possession of written material or a recording in breach of s.23 of the Public Order Act 1986 (s.24), and a court before which a person is convicted of displaying written material under s.18 of the 1986 Act or of an offence under ss.19, 21 or 23 of the 1986 Act may order the forfeiture of any written material or recording to which the offence relates (s.25).

4 Authorities

Statutes–
Public Order Act 1986

RACIAL, RELIGIOUS AND SEXUAL ORIENTATION HATRED: ENGLAND AND WALES

1 The legislation

Part III of the Public Order Act 1986, makes it an offence to commit certain acts intended or likely to stir up racial hatred, and to be in possession of racially inflammable material. The Racial and Religious Hatred Act 2006 amended the 1986 Act so as to include, in a new Part 3A, religious hatred, and the Criminal Justice and Immigration Act amended Part 3A to include hatred defined by reference to sexual orientation.

Provision as to discrimination against a person in respect of the protected characteristic of religion or belief is made by the Equality Act 2010. As to the provisions of the Equality Act 2010 see the Note on **Discrimination and Equality Law.**

A: RACIAL HATRED

2 The offence of racial hatred

Under Part III (ss.17 to 29) of the Public Order Act 1986, which applies to the whole of Great Britain, it is an offence to commit certain acts which are intended to stir up racial hatred or, having regard to all the circumstances and subject to certain defences, are likely to do so. Racial hatred means, for this purpose, hatred against a group of persons defined by reference to colour, race, nationality (including citizenship), or ethnic or national origins (s.17). These acts include–
  (a) using threatening, abusive, or insulting words or behaviour, or displaying written material which is threatening, abusive, or insulting (s.18);
  (b) publishing or distributing written material which is threatening, abusive or insulting (s.19);
  (c) presenting or directing the public performance of a play involving the use of threatening, abusive, or insulting words or behaviour (however this does not apply *inter alia* to performances given solely for the purpose of rehearsal or making a reading, and a person does not present a performance if he only takes part in it as a performer, provided that he performs in accordance with any directions) (s.20);
  (d) distributing, showing, or playing a recording of visual images or sounds which are threatening, abusive, or insulting (s.21). Further, if a programme involving threatening, abusive, or insulting visual images or sounds is broadcast, or included in a cable programme service, the person providing the broadcasting or cable programme service, any producer or director of the programme, and any person by whom offending words or behaviour are used are, subject to certain defences, guilty of an offence (s.22).
Note.–The group of persons against whom the hatred is directed need not be in Great Britain. The territorial restriction which previously applied was repealed by the Anti-terrorism, Crime and Security Act 2001, s.37.

3 Powers of entry, search, and forfeiture

A justice of the peace may issue a warrant to enter and search premises if he is satisfied that there are reasonable grounds for suspecting that a person is in possession of written material or a recording in breach of s.23 of the 1986 Act (s.24 of that Act), and a court before which a person is convicted of displaying written material under s.18 of the 1986 Act or of an offence under ss.19, 21 or 23 of the 1986 Act may order the forfeiture of any written material or recording to which the offence relates (1986 Act, s.25).

4 Enforcement

Proceedings under Part III of the 1986 Act may not be instituted in England and Wales except by or with the consent of the Attorney General (s.27).

B: RELIGIOUS HATRED

5 Introduction

The Racial and Religious Hatred Act 2006 amended the Public Order Act 1986 (which already dealt with racial hatred: see A: RACIAL HATRED, above) so as to include, in a new Part 3A, religious hatred.

There are two main differences between the racial and religious hatred offences. Firstly, the starting point for racial hatred is that the words or material are insulting, abusive or threatening. For an offence of religious hatred, insults and abuse is not sufficient, the words or material must be threatening. Secondly, for racial hatred there must either be an intention to stir up hatred or, subject to defences, the words or material must be likely to stir up such hatred. For religious hatred there must be a direct intention.

6 The offences of religious hatred

It is an offence–

(a) to use words or behaviour which are, or display written material which is, threatening *and* which is intended to stir up religious hatred. There is an exception for behaviour or a display entirely within a dwelling or which it is reasonably believed cannot be seen from outside the dwelling (Public Order Act 1986, s.29B);

(b) to publish or distribute written material which is threatening *and* which is intended to stir up religious hatred (Public Order Act 1986, s.29C);

(c) to perform in public a play which involves the use of threatening words or behaviour *and* which is intended to stir up religious hatred (*Note.*–the offence is committed by the person presenting or directing the performance, not by the actors, unless they create the offence by performing otherwise than as directed) (Public Order Act 1986, s.29D);

(d) to distribute, show or play a recording which involves the use of threatening words or images *and* which is intended to stir up religious hatred (Public Order Act 1986, s.29E);

(e) to include a programme in any service (including broadcast and cable) which involves the use of threatening words or images *and* which is intended to stir up religious hatred (Public Order Act 1986, s.29F);

(f) to possess religiously inflammatory material (i.e., written material or recordings of images or sounds, with a view to its display, broadcast, distribution, etc) *if* it is intended thereby to stir up religious hatred (Public Order Act 1986, s.29G).

Proceedings under Part 3A of the 1986 Act may not be instituted except by or with the consent of the Attorney General (s.29L).

It is expressly provided that nothing in Part 3A is to be read or given effect in a way which prohibits or restricts discussion, criticism or expressions of antipathy, dislike, ridicule, insult or abuse of particular religions or the beliefs or practices of their adherents, or of any other belief system or the beliefs or practices of its adherents, or proselytising or urging adherents of a different religion or belief system to cease practising their religion or belief system (s.29J).

7 The Commission for Racial Equality

The Commission for Racial Equality has been abolished and replaced by the Commission for Equality and Human Rights (CEHR) established by s.1 of the Equality Act 2006. For details of the Commission see the Note on **Discrimination and Equality Law**. It has a general duty to champion equality, diversity and human rights (s.3). As to the enforcement powers of the Commission see the Note on **Discrimination and Equality Law**.

C: SEXUAL ORIENTATION HATRED

8 The offence of sexual orientation hatred

The Criminal Justice and Immigration Act 2008 extends the Public Order Act 1986 Part 3A to include hatred on the grounds of sexual orientation. This is defined as hatred against a group of persons defined by reference to sexual orientation (whether towards persons of the same sex, the opposite sex or both) (1986 Act, s.29AB).

The offence is committed in the same circumstances as for the offence of religious hatred: see **6 The offences of religious hatred**, above (ss.29B to 29G, as amended).

It is expressly provided that any discussion or criticism of (s.29JA)–

(a) sexual conduct or practices, or the urging of persons to refrain from or modify such conduct or practices; or

(b) marriage which concerns the sex of the parties to marriage,

is not to be taken by itself to be threatening or as intended to stir up hatred.

9 Authorities
Statutes–
Equality Act 2006
Equality Act 2010
Public Order Act 1986
Racial and Religious Hatred Act 2006

REHABILITATION OF OFFENDERS: ENGLAND AND WALES

1 Contents

This Note covers the provisions of the Rehabilitation of Offenders Act 1974 which allows certain convictions and cautions to become "spent" after a fixed period of time, but which also sets out circumstances when such spent convictions and cautions must be disclosed.

2 Introduction

The Rehabilitation of Offenders Act 1974, which applies throughout Great Britain, makes provision for the rehabilitation of offenders who have not been reconvicted of any serious offence for periods of years and for penalising the unauthorised disclosure of their previous convictions or cautions. The Act provides for the exclusion of certain categories of sentence from these provisions (see **6 Excluded categories of sentence**, below) and for certain exceptions and limitations.

3 Convictions treated as spent

A person is to be treated as rehabilitated in respect of a conviction and that conviction is to be treated as spent where (Rehabilitation of Offenders Act 1974, s.1)–

(a) the sentence which was imposed upon him is not in an excluded category (see **6 Excluded categories of sentence**, below) (s.1(11));

(b) during the rehabilitation period applicable to the sentence (see **7 Rehabilitation period**, below) he has not had imposed upon him a further sentence which is in an excluded category; and

(c) he has served or otherwise undergone or complied with any sentence imposed upon him in respect of the conviction (s.1(2)).

"Sentence" means any order made in respect of a conviction for an offence other than a surcharge, criminal courts charge, an order relating to non-payment of a fine, or in respect of a suspended sentence (s.1(3)). "Conviction" includes a conviction by a court outside England and Wales, or Scotland (as the case may be), a finding (not being linked with a finding of insanity or a finding that a person is not criminally responsible under the Criminal Procedure (Scotland) Act 1995, s.51A) in any criminal proceedings that a person has committed an offence or done the act or made the omission charged, and convictions in respect of which a community rehabilitation order (previously known as a probation order) or an order for absolute or conditional discharge is made (s.1(4)).

4 Cautions treated as spent

The Rehabilitation of Offenders Act 1974 has been amended (by the Criminal Justice and Immigration Act 2008, s.49 and Sch. 10) so as to provide for the protection of spent cautions.

A caution means–

(a) a conditional caution i.e., a caution given under the Criminal Justice Act 2003, s.22 (conditional cautions for adults) or under the Crime and Disorder Act 1998, s.66A (conditional cautions for children and young persons);

(b) any other caution given to a person in England or Wales in respect of an offence which, at the time the caution is given, that person has admitted; and

(c) anything corresponding to a caution falling within paragraphs (a) or (b) above (however described) which is given to a person in respect of an offence under the law of a country outside England and Wales (Rehabilitation of Offenders Act 1974, s.8A).

For the rehabilitation period relating to spent cautions see **7 Rehabilitation period**, below. The unauthorised disclosure of spent cautions is also an offence, see **10 Unauthorised disclosure of a spent conviction or caution etc**, below.

5 Service disciplinary proceedings

For the purposes of the Rehabilitation of Offenders Act 1974, any finding of guilt in service disciplinary proceedings is to be treated as a conviction, and any punishment awarded as a result of such a finding is to be treated as a sentence. Accordingly, any such conviction will become spent in accordance with the Act (s.2, as amended by the Armed Forces Act 1996 s.13). Schedule One to the Act (as inserted by the Armed Forces Act 1996 s.13) lists various minor offences which, if committed during a rehabilitation period, may be disregarded for the purpose of extending the rehabilitation period under s.6 (see **8 Subsequent conviction during rehabilitation period**, below).

If a service person (or former service person) applies for any of the positions covered by the (Exceptions) Order, they must disclose previous convictions for all service offences other than non-recordable service offences (i.e., those offences which do not correlate to conduct which would be criminal in the civilian sphere e.g., being absent without leave or disobeying a superior). Non-recordable service offences once spent, do not need to be disclosed regardless of the position being applied for.

6 Excluded categories of sentence

Rehabilitation under the Rehabilitation of Offenders Act 1974 does not apply to a sentence of (s.5)–
(a) life imprisonment or custody for life;
(b) imprisonment, youth custody, detention in a young offender institution, or corrective training for a term exceeding 48 months (in Scotland, 30 months);
(c) preventive detention;
(d) detention during Her Majesty's pleasure or for life;
(e) detention for a term exceeding 48 months (in Scotland, 30 months) (young offenders convicted of grave crimes and children convicted on indictment); or
(f) imprisonment or detention for public protection, or an extended sentence.

7 Rehabilitation period

The rehabilitation period applicable to sentences is calculated from the date of conviction. The sentence to which rehabilitation applies and the rehabilitation period applicable to each such sentence is set out in the following tables. The rehabilitation period is reduced by half for people aged under 18 at the date of the conviction.

Sentence	Rehabilitation period
–Imprisonment, youth custody, detention in a young offender institution, borstal or corrective training–	
for a term exceeding 30 months but not exceeding 48 months.	7 years
for a term exceeding 6 months, but not exceeding 30 months	4 years
for a term up to an including 6 months	2 years
–A fine or a community or youth rehabilitation order*	12 months from the last day the order has effect
–A relevant* order**	the last day the order has effect
–A compensation order	when paid in full

*Where no provision is made by or under a community or youth rehabilitation order or a relevant order for the last day on which it is to have effect, the rehabilitation period is 24 months beginning with the date of conviction.
** A relevant order includes a conditional discharge, binding over order, hospital order, and any other order which imposes a disqualification, disability, prohibition or other penalty which is not otherwise dealt with in the Table (except a reparation order).

There are special rehabilitation periods relating to sentences imposed in service disciplinary proceedings.
There is no rehabilitation period for an absolute discharge or any other sentence not dealt with above.
Where more than one sentence is imposed in respect of a conviction, the rehabilitation period is the longer or longest of the periods applicable to the sentences imposed (s.6(2)).
Where a disqualification order is made under ss.28 or 29 of the Criminal Justice and Court Services Act 2000 disqualifying a person from working with children, the rehabilitation period is to be determined as if the disqualification order had not been made (2000 Act, s.38).
Rehabilitation periods in respect of cautions are given in Schedule 2 to the 1974 Act as follows–

Type of Caution	Rehabilitation period
–"Simple" police cautions, reprimands and warnings, and cautions given in a jurisdiction outside England and Wales.	Spent at the time they are given.
–adult and youth conditional cautions	3 months.
–a conditional caution where the offender is subsequently prosecuted and convicted for the offence in respect of which the conditional caution was given	The same as the rehabilitation period for the offence.

8 Subsequent conviction during rehabilitation period

Where during a rehabilitation period a person is convicted of a further offence (other than a summary offence or a scheduled offence within the meaning of s.22 of the Magistrates' Courts Act 1980 (certain offences to be tried summarily if value is small) tried summarily, or, in Scotland, an offence not excluded from the jurisdiction of inferior courts of summary jurisdiction) and a sentence is imposed which is not excluded from rehabilitation, the rehabilitation period (if any) which is shorter is extended so that it ends at the same time as the other period (Rehabilitation of Offenders Act 1974, s.6(4) and (6)).

9 Treatment of the rehabilitated offender

An offender who has become a rehabilitated person in respect of a spent conviction is to be treated for all purposes of law as a person who has not committed or been charged with, prosecuted for or convicted of, or sentenced for the offence or offences which were the subject of the conviction. No evidence to the contrary effect is to be admissible in any proceedings before a judicial authority in England and Wales, or Scotland (as the case may be) and no question is to be asked in such proceedings which cannot be answered without referring to a spent conviction or any circumstances ancillary thereto (Rehabilitation of Offenders Act 1974, s.4(1)). Proceedings before a judicial authority include the ordinary courts of law and also any tribunal or body having power to determine questions affecting the rights, privileges, obligations, or liabilities of any person (e.g., arbitration tribunals and professional associations).

Where a question seeking information with respect to a person's previous convictions is put otherwise than in judicial proceedings (e.g., in application forms for employment or proposal forms for insurance), the question is to be treated as not relating to spent convictions and the answer may be framed accordingly. The person questioned may not be subjected to any liability or be otherwise prejudiced in law by reason of his failure to disclose a spent conviction (s.4(2)). Any obligation of disclosure imposed by a rule of law, agreement, or arrangement is not to extend to the disclosure of a spent conviction (s.4(3)(a)).

The fact of a spent conviction or a failure to disclose it is not to be a proper ground for dismissing or excluding a person from any office, profession, occupation, or employment, or for prejudicing him in any occupation or employment (s.4(3)(b)).

The Secretary of State may exclude or modify these provisions as regards disclosure outside judicial proceedings in such circumstances and in such cases as may be specified by order (see **8 Exceptions and limitations: general**, below). Section 4(1), (2), and (3) have been excluded in relation to immigration decisions relating to "good character" (UK Borders Act 2007, s.56A).

The same protection is also extended to spent cautions i.e., adult and youth conditional cautions, other cautions (e.g., "simple" cautions issued by the police), reprimands and warnings given to children and young people, and cautions given in a jurisdiction outside England and Wales (Sch. 2, para 3, added by the Criminal Justice and Immigration Act 2008, s.49).

Note.—The fact that a caution is spent does not affect the operation of the caution itself (e.g., if conditions attached to a conditional caution apply for a period longer than 3 months) or the operation of any enactment (e.g., the Crime and Disorder Act 1998, s.65 which prevents the police from giving a child or young person more than two warnings and/or reprimands).

10 Unauthorised disclosure of a spent conviction or caution

A person who, in the course of his official duties, has or at any time has had custody of or access to any official record (as defined) or the information contained therein commits an offence (subject to statutory defences) if he discloses specified information (i.e., information relating to spent convictions in respect of a living person) to another person other than in the course of his duties, and a person who obtains such information by means of any fraud, dishonesty, or bribe also commits an offence (Rehabilitation of Offenders Act 1974, s.9(2)).

Protection is also extended to the disclosure of "caution information" i.e., information about adult and youth conditional cautions, other cautions (e.g., "simple" cautions issued by the police), reprimands and warnings given to children and young people, and cautions given in a jurisdiction outside England and Wales (s.9A, added by the Criminal Justice and Immigration Act 2008, s.49).

11 Exceptions and limitations: general

Limitations of the effect of the Rehabilitation of Offenders Act 1974, and exceptions to the above rules on rehabilitation, arise as follows—

(1) under s.7 (see **12 S.7 of the Rehabilitation of Offenders Act 1974**, below) and s.8 (defamation actions) of the Act;
(2) under the Rehabilitation of Offenders Act 1974 (Exceptions) Order;
(3) under the Financial Services Act 1986; and
(4) under the Gambling Act 2005.

12 S.7 of the Rehabilitation of Offenders Act 1974

By s.7(1), nothing in s.4(1) is to affect any prerogative of the Crown in regard to the granting of a free pardon or the quashing or commutation of any sentence; the enforcement of any fine or other sum in respect of a spent conviction; any proceedings in respect of a breach of condition or requirement in respect of a spent conviction; or the operation of any enactment imposing any disability, disqualification, prohibition, or other penalty other than by way of sentence for a period extending beyond that of the rehabilitation period applicable to the sentence.

The Act does not prevent the admission of evidence relating to a person's previous convictions/cautions in criminal proceedings before a court, in service disciplinary proceedings, or in proceedings relating to minors, including any proceedings brought under the Children Act 1989.

In the case of other proceedings before a judicial authority, the admission of evidence relating to a person's spent convictions/cautions may be allowed if the authority is satisfied that justice cannot otherwise be done. The Secretary of State also has power to make an order allowing the admission of evidence as to spent convictions/cautions in proceedings before a judicial authority to such extent and for such purposes as may be specified in the order.

13 The (Exceptions) Orders

The Rehabilitation of Offenders Act 1974 (Exceptions) Order 1975 lays down exceptions from the Act with regard to certain–
(a) professions;
(b) employments, offices and work (including unpaid work);
(c) regulated occupations;
(d) kinds of licences, certificates, and permits;
(e) proceedings; and
(e) other cases.

In each case the exception means that spent convictions must be disclosed, but the exception only applies if the person being questioned is informed at the time that the question is asked that, by virtue of the Exceptions Order, those spent convictions must be disclosed. References to a conviction include references to a caution, and a caution includes any caution, conditional caution, reprimand or final warning.

The (Exceptions) Order does not apply to "protected" cautions and convictions – with the effect that they do not have to be disclosed when they would otherwise have to be – except in specified circumstances. The circumstances when a protected conviction or caution must still be disclosed are set out in Arts 3ZA and 4ZA and relate to particular employment, offices and work. A conviction is a "protected conviction" if–
(i) it was given otherwise than for an offence listed in Art. 2A(5) (i.e., serious violent and sexual offences and other offences of specific relevance for posts concerned with safeguarding children and vulnerable adults);
(ii) a sentence other than custody or service detention was imposed;
(iii) the person has not been convicted of any other offence at any time and; and
(iv) 11 years or more have passed since the date of conviction (5 and a half years if under 18 at the time of conviction).

A caution is a "protected caution" if it was given otherwise than for an offence listed in Art. 2A(5) (see above) and was given, six years ago or more (2 years if under 18 when given).

The following paragraphs describe the exceptions set out in the (Exceptions) Order.

14 Protected convictions and cautions

The Supreme Court has held that the blanket disclosure of *all* spent convictions was incompatible with Article 8 (the right to respect for private and family life) of the European Convention on Human Rights (as to which see the Note on **The Human Rights Act 1998**) as it meant that even historic and minor convictions and cautions (even if irrelevant to the position applied for) had to be disclosed and could be taken into account by a prospective employer.

The Supreme Court decided that a conviction would usually become part of someone's private life once it became spent (as set out in the 1974 Act) and should therefore be filtered out from disclosure, but that some spent convictions were so serious that they could still be disclosed. Those spent convictions which are filtered out and are *not* to be disclosed are known as "protected" convictions and cautions.

A conviction or caution will *never* be protected if it is one of a range of offences which are so serious, relate to sexual or violent offending, or are relevant in the context of safeguarding, that it would never be appropriate to filter them. The current list of such offences can be seen at–
www.gov.uk/government/publications/dbs-list-of-offences-that-will-never-be-filtered-from-a-criminal-record-check

A conviction will also *never* be protected if it resulted in a custodial sentence or if the individual has more than one conviction.

A person's conviction or caution is a "protected" conviction or caution if it is spent and either–
(a) 11 years have elapsed since the date of conviction in the case of an adult;
(b) 5 and a half years have elapsed since the date of conviction in the case of a juvenile;
(c) it is an adult caution and six years have elapsed; or
(d) it is a youth caution, reprimand or final warning and 2 years have elapsed.

15 Excepted professions

The excepted professions, where spent convictions (including cautions) *must*, unless protected, be disclosed to a person assessing the suitability of someone to be admitted to that profession are (Rehabilitation of Offenders Act 1974 (Exceptions) Order 1975, Sch. 1, Pt I)–
– health care professionals (i.e. persons who are members of a profession regulated by a body mentioned in s.25(3) of the National Health Service Reform and Health Care Professions Act 2002);
– solicitors, barristers,
– registered European or foreign lawyers, and legal executives;
– chartered or certified accountants;
– veterinary surgeons;
– actuaries;
– receivers appointed by the Court of Protection;
– home inspectors.

16 Excepted employment, offices and work

The excepted employment, offices and work, where spent convictions (including cautions) *must*, unless protected, be disclosed to a person assessing the suitability of someone for any office or employment, are (Rehabilitation of Offenders Act 1974 (Exceptions) Order 1975, Sch. 1, Pt II)–
- Judicial appointments and designated officers for magistrates' courts, for justices of the peace or for local justice areas, justices' clerks and their assistants, also members of various judicial tribunals and appointments boards;
- approved legal services body manager;
- employment in the office of the Director of Public Prosecutions, or in the Crown Prosecution Service or Crown Office;
- constables, police cadets, military, naval, and air force police; prison service employees, including appointment to a board of prison visitors;
- officers of providers of probation services;
- traffic wardens;
- any employment by the RSPCA which involves the humane killing of animals;
- any office or employment in the Serious Fraud Office, or National Crime Agency;
- any office or employment in HM Revenue and Customs;
- any employment which is concerned with the monitoring, for the purposes of child protection, of internet communications;
- any employment or other work) concerned with the provision of health services and which is of such a kind as to enable a person to have access to those in receipt of such services in the course of his normal duties;
- employment or other work connected with the provision of care services to vulnerable adults (within the meaning of the Safeguarding Vulnerable Groups Act 2006, s.59, the definition of which is unaffected by the restriction on the definition of "vulnerable adult" contained in the Protection of Freedoms Act 2012 s.65 (see SI 2012 No. 1957)) which is of such a kind as to allow a person to have access to vulnerable adults in the course of his normal duties (this includes representation of or advocacy services for vulnerable adults);
- employment or other work concerned with the investigation of fraud, corruption or other unlawful activity affecting the NHS, or security management in the NHS;
- any work which is a regulated activity relating to children or vulnerable adults;
- any employment or other work that is carried out at a children's home or residential family centre;
- any employment or other work for the purposes of an adoption service, an adoption support agency, a voluntary adoption agency, a fostering service or a fostering agency and which is of such a kind as to allow a person, in the course of his normal duties, to have contact with children or access to sensitive or personal information about children;
- Any employment or office which is concerned with the management of a childminder agency or any work for a childminder agency which is of such a kind as to require a person to enter day care premises or premises on which child minding is provided and as to allow the person, in the course of his normal duties, to have contact with children for whom child minding or day care is provided or access to sensitive or personal information about such children;
- any employment or other work normally carried out in a bail or probation hostel or a hospital used only for the provision of high security psychiatric services;
- any work which is a regulated position for the purposes of the Criminal Justice and Court Services Act 2000 Part II (basically employment where the normal duties involve working with children) or which is work in a further education institution where the normal duties of that work involve regular contact with people aged under 18;
- persons elected to the office of police and crime commissioner;
- traffic officers designated under the Traffic Management Act 2004;
- judges' clerks, secretaries and legal secretaries;
- court officers and court contractors, who in the course of their work, have face to face contact with judges of the Senior Courts, or access to such judges' lodgings;
- persons who in the course of their work have regular access to personal information relating to an identified or identifiable member of the judiciary;
- court officers and court contractors, who, in the course of their work, attend either the Royal Courts of Justice or the Central Criminal Court;
- court security officers, and tribunal security officers;
- court contractors, who, in the course of their work, have unsupervised access to court-houses, offices and other accommodation used in relation to the courts;
- contractors, sub-contractors, and any person acting under the authority of such a contractor or sub-contractor, who, in the course of their work, have unsupervised access to tribunal buildings, offices and other accommodation used in relation to tribunals;
- the following persons–
    (a) court officers who execute county court warrants;
    (b) High Court enforcement officers;

   (c) sheriffs and under-sheriffs;

   (d) tipstaffs;

   (e) any other persons who execute High Court writs or warrants who act under the authority of a person listed at (a) to (d);

   (f) persons who execute writs of sequestration;

   (g) civilian enforcement officers as defined in the Magistrates' Courts Act 1980 s.125A;

   (h) persons who are authorised to execute warrants under s.125B(1) of the Magistrates' Courts Act 1980, and any other person, (other than a constable), who is authorised to execute a warrant under s.125(2) of that Act;

   (i) persons who execute clamping orders, as defined in the Courts Act 2003, Sch. 5 para 38;

– The Official Solicitor and his deputy;

– persons appointed to the office of Public Trustee or deputy Public Trustee, and officers of the Public Trustee;

– court officers and court contractors who exercise functions in connection with the administration and management of funds in court including the deposit, payment, delivery and transfer in, into and out of any court of funds in court and regulating the evidence of such deposit, payment, delivery or transfer and court officers and court contractors, who receive payments in pursuance of a conviction or order of a magistrates' court.;

– people working in the Department for Education, the Office for Standards in Education, Children's Services and Skills with access to sensitive or personal information about children;

– any office, employment or other work which is concerned with the establishment or operation of a database under the Children Act 2004 s.12, and which is of such a kind as to enable the holder of that office or employment, or the person engaged in that work, to have access to information included in the database, or which may permit or require them to be given access;

– the chairman, other members, and members of staff (including any person seconded to serve as a member of staff) of the Disclosure and Barring Service;

– staff working within the Office of the Public Guardian with access to data relating to children and vulnerable adults;

– the Commissioner for Older People in Wales, and his deputy, and any person appointed by the Commissioner to assist him in the discharge of his functions or authorised to discharge his functions on his behalf;

– the Commissioners for the Gambling Commission and any office or employment in their service.

– individuals seeking authorisation from the Secretary of State for the Home Department to become authorised search officers.

– any employment or other work where the normal duties involve caring for, training, supervising, or being solely in charge of, persons aged under 18 serving in the naval, military or air forces of the Crown, or supervising or managing a person so employed.

17 Regulated occupations

The regulated occupations, where spent convictions (including cautions) *must*, unless protected, be disclosed to a person assessing the suitability of someone to pursue it subject to a particular condition or restriction, are (Rehabilitation of Offenders Act 1974 (Exceptions) Order 1975, Sch. 1, Pt III)–

– firearms dealers;

– any occupation requiring a licence from the Gambling Commission;

– director, controller or manager of an insurer;

– dealer in securities;

– a regulated immigration advisor;

– manager or trustee under a unit trust scheme;

– management of an abortion clinic, a private hospital, or nursing home;

– any occupation for which a certificate to keep explosives is required;

– a head of finance and administration or a head of legal services of a body licensed under the Legal Services Act 2007 (i.e., as an alternative business structure for providing legal services); and any Chartered Institute of Legal Executives approved manager.

18 Licences, certificates, and permits

The excepted licences, certificates, and permits where spent convictions (including cautions) *must*, unless protected, be disclosed to a person assessing the suitability of someone to hold such a licence, certificate or permit are (Rehabilitation of Offenders Act 1974 (Exceptions) Order 1975, Sch. 2)–

– firearm and shotgun certificates;

– licences relating to the employment of children abroad;

– certificates as to fitness to keep explosives for private use;

– taxi driver licences (including private hire care licences in London);

– licences granted under the Private Security Industry Act 2001;

19 Excepted proceedings

The excepted proceedings, where spent convictions (including cautions) *must* be disclosed, are (Rehabilitation of Offenders Act 1974 (Exceptions) Order 1975, Sch. 3)–

- admission or disciplinary (and similar) proceedings relating to an excepted professions, see **15 Excepted professions,** above;
- police disciplinary proceedings;
- proceedings as to excepted licences, certificates, and permits, see **18 Licences, certificates, and permits,** above;
- certain mental health proceedings;
- certain proceedings before the Gambling Commission;
- certain proceedings under the Financial Services and Markets Act 2000;
- certain proceedings as to a direction that a person be prohibited from teaching (including being involved in the management of an independent school);
- proceedings as to the cancellation of a registration as an abortion clinic or a nursing home;
- proceedings in respect of an application for, or suspension or cancellation of, registration in respect of a regulated activity under Part 1 of the Health and Social Care Act 2008;
- proceedings as to registration under the Care Standards Act 2000 or the Public Services Reform (Scotland) Act 2010;
- proceedings before the Parole Board;
- proceedings under the Proceeds of Crime Act 2002–
    - (a) Chapter 2 of Part 5;
    - (b) pursuant to a notice under s.317(2); or
    - (c) pursuant to an application under Part 8 in connection with a civil recovery investigation (within the meaning of s.341);
- proceedings brought before the Football Association, Football League or Football Association Premier League against a decision taken by the body before which the proceedings are brought to refuse to approve a person as able to undertake, in the course of acting as a steward at a sports ground at which football matches are played or as a supervisor or manager of such a person, licensable conduct within the meaning of the Private Security Industry Act 2001 without a licence issued under that Act, in accordance with regulations made under s.4 of that Act.
- proceedings under the Criminal Injuries Compensation Act 1995, s.7D (not yet in force).
- proceedings under s the Private Security Industry Act 2001, s.11.
- appeals or reviews of decisions taken under the (Exceptions) Orders.

20 Other cases

The other cases, where spent convictions *must* be disclosed are where the question is asked (Rehabilitation of Offenders Act 1974 (Exceptions) Order 1975, Arts. 3, 4A)–

- of a person to assess his suitability to work with children where he would live on the premises where his work would normally take place and the question relates to a person living in his household or who regularly works in those premises;
- of a person to assess his suitability as a child minder and the question relates to a person who lives on the premises where the child minding would take place or who regularly works in those premises;
- in order to assess a person's suitability for the purposes of safeguarding national security, by the Crown, UK Atomic Energy Authority, Financial Conduct Authority, Prudential Regulation Authority, or the Civil Aviation Authority;
- to assess a person's suitability to adopt and the question relates to them or a member of their household aged over 18;
- of a person seeking appointment as a member of an adoption or fostering panel in Scotland;
- to assess a person's suitability to provide day care and the question relates to them or a person who lives on the premises where the day care will be provided;
- in various situations, by the Financial Conduct Authority and Prudential Regulation Authority;
- by the Gambling Commission in relation to the grant or revocation of a National Lottery licence;
- by or on behalf of a contracting authority or utility for the purpose of determining whether or not to treat a person as ineligible under specified provisions of the Public Contracts Regulations 2015, the Concession Contracts Regulations 2016, or the Utilities Contracts Regulations 2016;
- by or on behalf of the Care Council for Wales for the purpose of determining whether or not to grant an application for registration under Part IV of the Care Standards Act 2000;
- by or on behalf of the Football Association, Football League or Football Association Premier League in order to assess the suitability of a person to be approved as able to undertake, in the course of acting as a steward at a sports ground at which football matches are played or as a supervisor or manager of such a person, licensable conduct within the meaning of the Private Security Industry Act 2001 without a licence issued under that Act;
- by the Disclosure and Barring Service for the purpose of considering the suitability of an individual to

have access to information released under the Police Act 1997, ss.113A or 113B (criminal and enhanced criminal record certificates);

- by or on behalf of the Master Locksmiths Association for the purposes of assessing the suitability of any person who has applied to be granted membership of that Association;
- by or on behalf of the Secretary of State for the purpose of assessing the suitability of any person or body to obtain or retain a licence under the Misuse of Drugs Regulations 2001;
- of any person to assess their suitability to hold a restricted interest in a licensed body providing restricted legal services through an alternative business structure;
- by or on behalf of any person, in the course of their duties in order to assess whether the person to whom the question relates is disqualified from being elected as, or being, a police and crime commissioner.

21 Consequences of an exception

In the case of any of the exceptions, none of the provisions of s.4(2) (questions as to convictions to be treated as not applying to spent convictions, see **9 Treatment of the rehabilitated offender**, above) applies where a question is asked in the course of duties of an office or employment in order to assess a person's suitability, provided that in all cases the person questioned is informed at the time the questions are asked that, by virtue of the Order, spent convictions must be disclosed (Rehabilitation of Offenders Act 1974 (Exceptions) Order 1975, Art. 3).

S.4(3)(b) (spent conviction not to be grounds for dismissal) does not apply in relation to–
(a) the dismissal or exclusion of any person from any of the excepted professions;
(b) any office, employment or occupation excepted by the Order (see above);
(c) any action taken for the purpose of safeguarding national security;
(d) various specified decisions of the Financial Conduct Authority or Prudential Regulation Authority and other specified bodies in relation to financial services or Lloyds;
(e) any decision by the Care Council for Wales to refuse to grant an application for registration under Part IV of the Care Standards Act 2000 or to suspend, remove or refuse to restore a person's registration;
(f) any decision to refuse to grant a taxi driver licence, to grant such a licence subject to conditions or to suspend, revoke or refuse to renew such a licence;
(g) any decision by the Security Industry Authority to refuse to grant a licence under the Private Security Industry Act 2001, s.8, to grant such a licence subject to conditions, or to modify or revoke such a licence;
(h) any decision by the Football Association, Football League, or Football Association Premier League to refuse to approve a person as able to undertake, in the course of acting as a steward at a sports ground at which football matches are played or as a supervisor or manager of such a person, licensable conduct within the meaning of the Private Security Industry Act 2001 without a licence issued under that Act;
(i) the disqualification of a person from being elected as, or being, a police and crime commissioner.

22 The Gambling Act 2005

The provisions as to rehabilitation do not apply in relation to "relevant" offences for the purposes of, or in connection with, an application for an operating licence (Gambling Act 2005, s.125).

A "relevant" offence is one listed in Schedule 7 to the Act. These include offences under legislation relating to gambling, theft, fraud, sexual and violent offences, and firearms and drugs offences.

23 Authorities

Statutes–

Children Act 1989

Criminal Justice Act 1991

Criminal Justice and Court Services Act 2000

Criminal Justice and Immigration Act 2008

Criminal Justice and Public Order Act 1994

Financial Services Act 1986

Gambling Act 2005

Rehabilitation of Offenders Act 1974

Statutory Instruments–

Rehabilitation of Offenders Act 1974 (Exceptions) Order 1975, as amended (S.I. 1975 No. 1023, 1986 Nos. 1249 and 2268, 2001 Nos. 1192 and 3816, 2002 No. 441, 2003 Nos. 965 and 1590, 2005 No. 617, 2006 Nos. 594, 2143, and 3290, 2007 No. 3224, 2008 Nos. 2683 and 3259, 2009 No. 1818, 2010 No. 1153, 2011 Nos. 99, 1800, and 2865, 2012 Nos. 979, 1479, 1957 and 3006, 2013 Nos. 472, 1198 and 2329, 2014 Nos. 834, 1638 and 1707, 2015 Nos. 317 and 968, and 2016 No. 275)

REHABILITATION OF OFFENDERS: SCOTLAND

1 Contents

This Note covers the provisions of the Rehabilitation of Offenders Act 1974 which allows certain convictions and cautions to become "spent" after a fixed period of time, but which also sets out circumstances when such spent convictions and cautions must be disclosed.

2 Introduction

The Rehabilitation of Offenders Act 1974, which applies throughout Great Britain, makes provision for the rehabilitation of offenders who have not been reconvicted of any serious offence for periods of years and for penalising the unauthorised disclosure of their previous convictions or cautions. A conviction may become "spent" if a certain length of time has elapsed since the date of conviction.

Once a conviction is spent, the 1974 Act provides that an individual is not normally required to disclose it and cannot be prejudiced by its existence. This allows an individual to move away from their past criminal activity so that they can contribute effectively to society while also ensuring that people with a legitimate interest, such as employers, are able to understand an individual's background. Broadly speaking, the 1974 Act permits individuals not to disclose spent convictions when asked to do so, (e.g., by a prospective employer), prevents others from asking about those spent convictions, and prohibits reliance on spent convictions in certain legal proceedings or to prejudice an individual in an employment context.

The 1974 Act provides for the exclusion of certain categories of sentence from these provisions (see **6 Excluded categories of sentence,** below) and for certain exceptions and limitations (see **13 The (Exceptions) Orders,** et seq. below).

3 Convictions treated as spent

A person is to be treated as rehabilitated in respect of a conviction and that conviction is to be treated as spent where (Rehabilitation of Offenders Act 1974, s.1)–

(a) the sentence which was imposed upon him is not in an excluded category (see **6 Excluded categories of sentence,** below) (s.1(11));

(b) during the rehabilitation period applicable to the sentence (see **7 Rehabilitation period,** below) he has not had imposed upon him a further sentence which is in an excluded category; and

(c) he has served or otherwise undergone or complied with any sentence imposed upon him in respect of the conviction (s.1(2)).

"Sentence" means any order made in respect of a conviction for an offence other than a surcharge, criminal courts charge, an order relating to non-payment of a fine, or in respect of a suspended sentence (s.1(3)). "Conviction" includes a conviction by a court outside England and Wales, or Scotland (as the case may be), a finding (not being linked with a finding of insanity or a finding that a person is not criminally responsible under the Criminal Procedure (Scotland) Act 1995, s.51A) in any criminal proceedings that a person has committed an offence or done the act or made the omission charged, and convictions in respect of which a community rehabilitation order (previously known as a probation order) or an order for absolute or conditional discharge is made (s.1(4)).

4 Alternatives to prosecution treated as spent

The Rehabilitation of Offenders Act 1974 has been amended (by the Criminal Justice and Licensing (Scotland) Act 2010, s.109) so as to provide for the protection of alternatives to prosecution. These provisions extend to Scotland only.

An alternative to prosecution means (s.8B)–

(a) a warning by the police or a procurator fiscal;

(b) acceptance or deemed acceptance of a conditional offer to pay a fixed penalty, or a compensation offer (or a combination of the two);

(c) a work order, which offers the individual the opportunity of undertaking unpaid work;

(d) a fixed penalty notice under the Antisocial Behaviour etc. (Scotland) Act 2004; or

(e) acceptance of an offer from a procurator fiscal to undertake an activity or treatment or to receive services.

The unauthorised disclosure of an alternative to prosecution is also an offence, see **10 Unauthorised disclosure of spent conviction, etc,** below.

5 Service disciplinary proceedings

For the purposes of the Rehabilitation of Offenders Act 1974, any finding of guilt in service disciplinary proceedings is to be treated as a conviction, and any punishment awarded as a result of such a finding is to be treated as a sentence. Accordingly, any such conviction will become spent in accordance with the Act (s.2, as

THE JUSTICE SYSTEM

amended by the Armed Forces Act 1996 s.13). Schedule One to the Act (as inserted by the Armed Forces Act 1996 s.13) lists various minor offences which, if committed during a rehabilitation period, may be disregarded for the purpose of extending the rehabilitation period under s.6 (see **8 Subsequent conviction during rehabilitation period**, below).

If a service person (or former service person) applies for any of the positions covered by the (Exceptions) Order, they must disclose previous convictions for all service offences other than non-recordable service offences (i.e., those offences which do not correlate to conduct which would be criminal in the civilian sphere e.g., being absent without leave or disobeying a superior). Non-recordable service offences once spent, do not need to be disclosed regardless of the position being applied for.

6 Excluded categories of sentence

Rehabilitation under the Rehabilitation of Offenders Act 1974 does not apply to a sentence of (s.5)–
(a) life imprisonment or custody for life;
(b) imprisonment, youth custody, detention in a young offender institution, or corrective training for a term exceeding 48 months (in Scotland, 30 months);
(c) preventive detention;
(d) detention during Her Majesty's pleasure or for life;
(e) detention for a term exceeding 48 months (in Scotland, 30 months) (young offenders convicted of grave crimes and children convicted on indictment); or
(f) imprisonment or detention for public protection, or an extended sentence.

7 Rehabilitation period

The rehabilitation period applicable to sentences is calculated from the date of conviction. The sentence to which rehabilitation applies and the rehabilitation period applicable to each such sentence is set out in the following tables. In the case of sentences in Table A, the rehabilitation period is reduced by half for people aged under 18 at the date of the conviction. Sentences in Table B are confined to young offenders.

TABLE A

Sentence	Rehabilitation period
–Imprisonment, youth custody, detention in a young offender institution, or corrective training for a term exceeding 6 months but not exceeding 30 months.	10 years
–Imprisonment or youth custody for a term not exceeding 6 months.	7 years
–A fine or any other sentence subject to a rehabilitation, not being a sentence to which Table B or certain other provisions (see (a) to (h) below) apply.	5 years

TABLE B

Sentence	Rehabilitation period
Borstal training	7 years
Detention for a term exceeding 6 months but not exceeding 30 months.	5 years
Detention for a term not exceeding 6 months.	3 years
Order for detention in a detention centre made under s.4 of the Criminal Justice Act 1961 or s.4 of the Criminal Justice Act 1982.	3 years

There are special rehabilitation periods relating to sentences imposed in service disciplinary proceedings. For other sentences, the rehabilitation periods are–
(a) an absolute discharge: six months;
(b) a conditional discharge or binding over: one year from the date of conviction or the period during which the conditional discharge or binding over is in force, whichever is the longer;
(c) a community order: five years from the date of conviction or, in the case of a person under the age of 18 two and a half years from the date of the conviction or the period during which the order is in force, whichever is the longer;
(d) a referral order, with or without a youth offender contract: the period beginning with the date of conviction and ending on the date when the contract ceases (or would cease if there had been one) to have effect;
(e) orders under various Acts committing a child or young person to care or to undergo residential training, an approved school order, an attendance centre order, secure training order, or care order: one year from the date of conviction or the period during which the order or requirement remains in force, whichever is the longer;

(f) a detention and training order: in the case of a person aged 15 or over at the date of conviction, five years if the order was, and three and a half years if the order was not, for a term exceeding six months; in the case of a person aged under 15 at the date of his conviction, a period beginning with that date and ending one year after the date on which the order ceases to have effect;

(g) a hospital order with or without a restriction order: five years from the date of conviction or the period starting with that date and ending two years after the hospital order ceases to have effect, whichever is the longer;

(h) an order imposing any disqualification, disability, prohibition, or other penalty is the period during which the order has effect.

Where more than one sentence is imposed in respect of a conviction, the rehabilitation period is the longer or longest of the periods applicable to the sentences imposed (s.6(2)).

Where a disqualification order is made under ss.28 or 29 of the Criminal Justice and Court Services Act 2000 disqualifying a person from working with children, the rehabilitation period is to be determined as if the disqualification order had not been made (2000 Act, s.38).

The rehabilitation period in respect of alternatives to prosecution (see **4 Alternatives to prosecution treated as spent**, above) is generally three months unless there is a subsequently prosecution and conviction of the offence, except that warnings issued by a procurator fiscal or the police and fixed penalty notices issued under the Antisocial Behaviour etc. (Scotland) Act 2004 become spent at the time they are given.

8 Subsequent conviction during rehabilitation period

Where during a rehabilitation period a person is convicted of a further offence (other than a summary offence or a scheduled offence within the meaning of s.22 of the Magistrates' Courts Act 1980 (certain offences to be tried summarily if value is small) tried summarily, or, in Scotland, an offence not excluded from the jurisdiction of inferior courts of summary jurisdiction) and a sentence is imposed which is not excluded from rehabilitation, the rehabilitation period (if any) which is shorter is extended so that it ends at the same time as the other period (Rehabilitation of Offenders Act 1974, s.6(4) and (6)).

9 Treatment of the rehabilitated offender

An offender who has become a rehabilitated person in respect of a spent conviction is to be treated for all purposes of law as a person who has not committed or been charged with, prosecuted for or convicted of, or sentenced for the offence or offences which were the subject of the conviction. No evidence to the contrary effect is to be admissible in any proceedings before a judicial authority in England and Wales, or Scotland (as the case may be) and no question is to be asked in such proceedings which cannot be answered without referring to a spent conviction or any circumstances ancillary thereto (Rehabilitation of Offenders Act 1974, s.4(1)). Proceedings before a judicial authority include the ordinary courts of law and also any tribunal or body having power to determine questions affecting the rights, privileges, obligations, or liabilities of any person (e.g., arbitration tribunals and professional associations).

Where a question seeking information with respect to a person's previous convictions is put otherwise than in judicial proceedings (e.g., in application forms for employment or proposal forms for insurance), the question is to be treated as not relating to spent convictions and the answer may be framed accordingly. The person questioned may not be subjected to any liability or be otherwise prejudiced in law by reason of his failure to disclose a spent conviction (s.4(2)). Any obligation of disclosure imposed by a rule of law, agreement, or arrangement is not to extend to the disclosure of a spent conviction (s.4(3)(a)).

The fact of a spent conviction or a failure to disclose it is not to be a proper ground for dismissing or excluding a person from any office, profession, occupation, or employment, or for prejudicing him in any occupation or employment (s.4(3)(b)).

The Secretary of State may exclude or modify these provisions as regards disclosure outside judicial proceedings in such circumstances and in such cases as may be specified by order (see **11 Exceptions and limitations: general**, below). Section 4(1), (2), and (3) have been excluded in relation to immigration decisions relating to "good character" (UK Borders Act 2007, s.56A).

The same protection is also extended to spent cautions i.e., adult and youth conditional cautions, other cautions (e.g., "simple" cautions issued by the police), reprimands and warnings given to children and young people, and cautions given in a jurisdiction outside England and Wales (Sch. 2, para 3, added by the Criminal Justice and Immigration Act 2008, s.49).

Note.–The fact that a caution is spent does not affect the operation of the caution itself (e.g., if conditions attached to a conditional caution apply for a period longer than 3 months) or the operation of any enactment (e.g., the Crime and Disorder Act 1998, s.65 which prevents the police from giving a child or young person more than two warnings and/or reprimands).

10 Unauthorised disclosure of spent conviction, etc

A person who, in the course of his official duties, has or at any time has had custody of or access to any official record (as defined) or the information contained therein commits an offence (subject to statutory defences) if he discloses specified information (i.e., information relating to spent convictions in respect of a living person) to another person other than in the course of his duties, and a person who obtains such information by means of any fraud, dishonesty, or bribe also commits an offence (Rehabilitation of Offenders Act 1974, s.9(2)).

Protection is also extended to the unauthorised disclosure of alternatives to prosecution (s.9B, added by the Criminal Justice and Licensing (Scotland) Act 2010, s.109).

11 Exceptions and limitations: general

Limitations of the effect of the Rehabilitation of Offenders Act 1974, and exceptions to the above rules on rehabilitation, arise as follows–
(1) under ss.7 and 8 of the Act;
(2) under the Rehabilitation of Offenders Act 1974 (Exceptions) Order, and the equivalent Scottish Order;
(3) under the Financial Services Act 1986; and
(4) under the Gambling Act 2005.

12 S.7 of the Rehabilitation of Offenders Act 1974

By s.7(1), nothing in s.4(1) is to affect any prerogative of the Crown in regard to the granting of a free pardon or the quashing or commutation of any sentence; the enforcement of any fine or other sum in respect of a spent conviction; any proceedings in respect of a breach of condition or requirement in respect of a spent conviction; or the operation of any enactment imposing any disability, disqualification, prohibition, or other penalty other than by way of sentence for a period extending beyond that of the rehabilitation period applicable to the sentence.

The Act does not prevent the admission of evidence relating to a person's previous convictions/cautions in criminal proceedings before a court, in service disciplinary proceedings, or in proceedings relating to minors, including any proceedings brought under the Children Act 1989 and the Children (Scotland) Act 1995.

In the case of other proceedings before a judicial authority, the admission of evidence relating to a person's spent convictions/cautions may be allowed if the authority is satisfied that justice cannot otherwise be done. The Secretary of State also has power to make an order allowing the admission of evidence as to spent convictions/cautions in proceedings before a judicial authority to such extent and for such purposes as may be specified in the order.

13 The (Exceptions) Orders

The Rehabilitation of Offenders Act 1974 (Exclusions and Exceptions) (Scotland) Order 2013 lay down exceptions from the Act with regard to certain–
(a) professions;
(b) employments, offices and work (including unpaid work);
(c) regulated occupations;
(d) kinds of licences, certificates, and permits;
(e) proceedings; and
(e) other cases.

In each case the exception means that spent convictions must be disclosed, but the exception only applies if the person being questioned is informed at the time that the question is asked that, by virtue of the Exceptions Order, those spent convictions must be disclosed. References to a conviction include references to a caution, and a caution includes any caution, conditional caution, reprimand or final warning.

The (Exceptions) Order does not apply to "protected" convictions – with the effect that they do not have to be disclosed when they would otherwise have to be – except in specified circumstances–see **14 Protected convictions**, below..

14 Protected convictions

The Supreme Court has held that the blanket disclosure of *all* spent convictions was incompatible with Article 8 (the right to respect for private and family life) of the European Convention on Human Rights (as to which see the Note on **The Human Rights Act 1998**) as it meant that even historic and minor convictions and cautions (even if irrelevant to the position applied for) had to be disclosed and could be taken into account by a prospective employer.

The Supreme Court decided that a conviction would usually become part of someone's private life once it became spent (as set out in the 1974 Act) and should therefore be filtered out from disclosure, but that some spent convictions were so serious that they could still be disclosed. Those spent convictions which are filtered out and are *not* to be disclosed are known as "protected" convictions

A person's conviction is a "protected" conviction if it is a spent conviction and either (Rehabilitation of Offenders Act 1974 (Exclusions and Exceptions) (Scotland) Order 2013, Reg. 2A)–
(i) it is not a conviction for an offence listed in Schedule A1 or B1 to the Order; or
(ii) it is a conviction for an offence listed in Schedule B1 *and* at least one of the following conditions is satisfied–

    (a) the sentence imposed in respect of the conviction was an admonition or an absolute discharge;

    (b) the person was aged under 18 on the date of conviction and at least 7 years and 6 months have passed since the date of conviction; and

    (c) the person was aged 18 or over on the date of conviction and at least 15 years have passed since the date of conviction.

If a convictions falls within the above definition it does *not* need to be self-disclosed once spent, even if the Rehabilitation of Offenders Act 1974 (Exclusions and Exceptions) (Scotland) Order 2013 would otherwise require it to be disclosed.

Schedule A1 contains serious offences which will never be "protected" no matter how long has passed, including serious violent and sexual offences, terrorism and other offences of specific relevance for posts concerned with safeguarding children and vulnerable adults.

Schedule B1 contains less serious offences which will be protected after a period of time (see above).

If a conviction is not yet protected (e.g., because although spent the allotted period of time has not yet passed), then before making the disclosure the individual must be informed of that fact and he then has 10 days in which to notify Disclosure Scotland that he intends to make an application to the Sheriff for the conviction to be removed from the disclosure. Such an application must then be made within 3 months. The Sheriff's decision is final.

15 Excepted professions

The excepted professions, where spent convictions (including cautions) *must*, unless protected, be disclosed to a person assessing the suitability of someone to be admitted to that profession are (Rehabilitation of Offenders Act 1974 (Exclusions and Exceptions) (Scotland) Order 2013, Sch. 4, Pt 1)–

– health care professionals (i.e. persons who are members of a profession regulated by a body mentioned in s.25(3) of the National Health Service Reform and Health Care Professions Act 2002);

– advocates and in registered European or foreign lawyers, and legal executives;

– chartered or certified accountants;

– veterinary surgeons;

– registered teachers;

– actuaries;

– social workers and social service workers; and

16 Excepted employment, offices and work

The excepted employment, offices and work, where spent convictions (including cautions) *must*, unless protected, be disclosed to a person assessing the suitability of someone for any office or employment, are (Rehabilitation of Offenders Act 1974 (Exclusions and Exceptions) (Scotland) Order 2013, Sch. 4, Pt 2)–

– Judicial appointments and designated officers for magistrates' courts, for justices of the peace or for local justice areas, justices' clerks and their assistants, also members of various judicial tribunals and appointments boards;

– approved legal services body manager;

– employment in the office of the Director of Public Prosecutions, or in the Crown Prosecution Service or Crown Office;

– constables, police cadets, military, naval, and air force police; prison service employees, including appointment to a board of prison visitors;

– officers of providers of probation services;

– traffic wardens;

– any employment by the RSPCA or SSPCA which involves the humane killing of animals;

– any office or employment in the Serious Fraud Office, or National Crime Agency;

– any office or employment in HM Revenue and Customs;

– any employment which is concerned with the monitoring, for the purposes of child protection, of internet communications;

– any employment concerned with the provision of health services and which is of such a kind as to enable a person to have access to those in receipt of such services in the course of his normal duties;

– employment or work–

    – concerned with the provision of a care service;

    – concerned with the provision of health services where the holder would have access to people in receipt of such services in the normal course of their duties;

    – which is regulated work with children;

    – which is regulated work with adults.

– any office or employment concerned with the provision to people under 18 of accommodation, care, leisure, recreational facilities, schooling, social services, supervision or training, which in the normal course of duties allows access to such people, and any other office or employment on premises where such provision takes place;

– any office or employment in the Scottish Social Services Council or Social Care and Social Work Improvement Scotland;

- school inspectors or any office or employment in the General Teaching Council for Scotland;
- members of the panels for curators *ad litem*, reporting officers and safeguarders established under the Children (Scotland) Act 1995;
- any office or employment in the Risk Management Authority;
- any office or employment in the Scottish Criminal Cases Review Commission;
- any office or employment in a relevant authority under the Fire (Scotland) Act 2005;
- social work inspectors;
- any employment or work in a body primarily providing counselling or support for victims or witnesses of offences and which involves having access to personal information;
- a Head of Practice or member of a practising committee of a licensed legal services provider.

17 Regulated occupations

The regulated occupations, where spent convictions (including cautions) *must*, unless protected, be disclosed to a person assessing the suitability of someone to pursue it subject to a particular condition or restriction, are (Rehabilitation of Offenders Act 1974 (Exclusions and Exceptions) (Scotland) Order 2013, Sch. 4, Pt 3)–
- firearms dealers;
- any occupation requiring a licence from the Gambling Commission;
- management of an abortion clinic;
- any occupation for which a certificate to keep explosives is required;
- taxi drivers and private hire drivers;
- any occupation which requires an application for a licence under the Private Security Industry Act 2001;
- any occupation which involves visiting persons detained in police stations to examine and report on the conditions under which they are held;
- any occupation in respect of which a licence or registration is needed under the Road Traffic Act 1988 Pt V (driving instruction).

18 Licences, certificates, and permits

The excepted licences, certificates, and permits where spent convictions (including cautions) *must*, unless protected, be disclosed to a person assessing the suitability of someone to hold such a licence, certificate or permit are (Rehabilitation of Offenders Act 1974 (Exclusions and Exceptions) (Scotland) Order 2013, Sch. 3, para 3(3))–
- firearm and shotgun certificates;
- air weapon certificates and permits;
- licences relating to the employment of children abroad;
- certificates as to fitness to keep explosives for private use;
- licences granted under the Private Security Industry Act 2001;
- a licence required by or under Part V (driving instruction) of the Road Traffic Act 1988.

Note.–There are no protected convictions in relation to firearm licence applications and explosive certificates: *all* spent convictions must be self-disclosed if asked (Art. 4(3)).

19 Excepted proceedings

The excepted proceedings, where spent convictions (including cautions) *must*, unless protected, be disclosed, are (Rehabilitation of Offenders Act 1974 (Exclusions and Exceptions) (Scotland) Order 2013, Sch. 1)–
- admission or disciplinary (and similar) proceedings relating to an excepted professions, see **15 Excepted professions**, above;
- police disciplinary proceedings;
- proceedings as to excepted licences, certificates, and permits, see **18 Licences, certificates, and permits**, above;
- certain mental health proceedings;
- certain proceedings before the Gambling Commission;
- certain proceedings under the Financial Services and Markets Act 2000;
- certain proceedings as to a direction that a person be prohibited from teaching (including being involved in the management of an independent school);
- proceedings as to the cancellation of a registration as an abortion clinic;
- proceedings as to registration under the Care Standards Act 2000 or the Public Services Reform (Scotland) Act 2010;
- proceedings in respect of a decision by a local authority to refuse to enter a person in, or remove a person from, the register of landlords maintained under the Antisocial Behaviour (Scotland) Act 2004;
- proceedings in respect of accreditation under the Criminal Justice (Scotland) Act 2003, s.11 (risk management accreditation);
- proceedings before the Scottish Parole Board;
- proceedings under the Proceeds of Crime Act 2002–
    (a) Chapters 2 and 3 of Part 5;

(b) pursuant to a notice under s.317(2); or

(c) pursuant to an application under Part 8 in connection with a civil recovery investigation (within the meaning of s.341);

– proceedings under the Criminal Injuries Compensation Act 1995, s.7D (not yet in force).
– proceedings under s the Private Security Industry Act 2001, s.11.
– proceedings in connection with a decision of the Scottish Social Services Council under the Regulation of Care (Scotland) Act 2001, Part 3;
– appeals or reviews of decisions taken under the (Exceptions) Order.
– proceedings before the Sheriff in respect of intervention or guardianship orders under the Adults with Incapacity (Scotland) Act 2000.
– proceedings before the Scottish Criminal Case Review Commission or in connection with compensation for wrongful conviction or charge.
– proceedings before the NHS Tribunal under The National Health Service (Scotland) Act 1978, Part II.
– proceedings before the Court of Session or sheriff in respect of a guardianship order made under the Children (Scotland) Act 1995, s.11.
– proceedings under the Protection of Vulnerable groups (Scotland) Act 2007 Part 1 (considerations as to listing).
– proceedings before the Court of Session or the sheriff to determine the suitability of a person to become a lay representative in court proceedings.
– proceedings under the Children's Hearings (Scotland) Act 2011.

20 Other cases

The other cases, where spent convictions *must*, unless protected, be disclosed are where the question is asked (Rehabilitation of Offenders Act 1974 (Exclusions and Exceptions) (Scotland) Order 2013, Scotland Sch. 3)–

– of a person to assess his suitability to work with children where he would live on the premises where his work would normally take place and the question relates to a person living in his household or who regularly works in those premises;
– of a person to assess his suitability as a child minder and the question relates to a person who lives on the premises where the child minding would take place or who regularly works in those premises;
– in order to assess a person's suitability for the purposes of safeguarding national security, by the Crown, UK Atomic Energy Authority, Financial Conduct Authority, Prudential Regulation Authority, or the Civil Aviation Authority (*Note.*–There are no protected convictions in relation to questions about spent convictions asked in the interest of national security: *all* spent convictions must be self-disclosed if asked (Art.4(3)));
– to assess a person's suitability to adopt and the question relates to them or a member of their household aged over 18;
– of a person seeking appointment as a member of an adoption or fostering panel;
– to assess a person's suitability to provide day care and the question relates to them or a person who lives on the premises where the day care will be provided;
– in various situations, by the Financial Conduct Authority and Prudential Regulation Authority;
– by the Gambling Commission in relation to the grant or revocation of a National Lottery licence;
– of a registered person, or a nominee, to assess their suitability to be supplied with information under the Protection of Vulnerable Groups (Scotland) Act 2007;
– by or on behalf of a personnel supplier in order to assess the suitability of a person to be supplied by them under the Protection of Vulnerable Groups (Scotland) Act 2007 to do regulated work with adults or children for another person;
– by or on behalf of a contracting authority or contracting entity for the purpose of determining whether or not to treat a person as ineligible under specified provisions of the Public Contracts Regulations 2006 or the Utilities Contracts Regulations 2006;
– of a person seeking to become an economic operator under the Public Contracts (Scotland) Regulations 2012 where the spent conviction relates to fraud, money laundering or other specified offences;
– by the Risk Management Authority in relation to its functions relating to risk management plans;
– of a person to assess his fitness to be a non-solicitor investor in a licensed legal services provider;
– in order to assess the suitability of a person to act as a lay representative in court proceedings;
– by the Disclosure and Barring Service for the purpose of considering the suitability of an individual to have access to information released under the Police Act 1997, ss.113A or 113B (criminal and enhanced criminal record certificates);
– of a person to be registered as a private sector landlord.

21 Consequences of an exception

In the case of any of the exceptions, none of the provisions of s.4(2) (questions as to convictions to be treated as not applying to spent convictions, see **9 Treatment of the rehabilitated offender**, above) applies where a question is asked in the course of duties of an office or employment in order to assess a person's suitability, provided that in all cases the person questioned is informed at the time the questions are asked that, by virtue of the Order, spent convictions must be disclosed (Rehabilitation of Offenders Act 1974 (Exclusions and Exceptions) (Scotland) Order 2013, Art. 3).

S.4(3)(b) (spent conviction not to be grounds for dismissal) does not apply in relation to–

(a) the dismissal or exclusion of any person from any of the excepted professions;

(b) any office, employment or occupation excepted by the Order (see above);

(c) any action taken for the purpose of safeguarding national security;

(d) various specified decisions of the Financial Conduct Authority or Prudential Regulation Authority and other specified bodies in relation to financial services or Lloyds;

(e) any decision to refuse to grant a taxi driver licence, to grant such a licence subject to conditions or to suspend, revoke or refuse to renew such a licence; or

(f) any decision by the Security Industry Authority to refuse to grant a licence under the Private Security Industry Act 2001, s.8, to grant such a licence subject to conditions, or to modify or revoke such a licence.

22 The Gambling Act 2005

The provisions as to rehabilitation do not apply in relation to "relevant" offences for the purposes of, or in connection with, an application for an operating licence (Gambling Act 2005, s.125).

A "relevant" offence is one listed in Schedule 7 to the Act. These include offences under legislation relating to gambling, theft, fraud, sexual and violent offences, and firearms and drugs offences.

23 Authorities

Statutes–

Criminal Justice and Court Services Act 2000

Criminal Justice and Immigration Act 2008

Criminal Justice and Licensing (Scotland) Act 2010

Financial Services Act 1986

Gambling Act 2005

Rehabilitation of Offenders Act 1974

Statutory Instruments–

Rehabilitation of Offenders Act 1974 (Exclusions and Exceptions) (Scotland) Order 2013, as amended (S.S.I. 2013 Nos. 50 and 204, S.I. 2013 No. 2329, S.S.I. 2015 Nos. 150 and 329, S.I. 2015 No. 968, and S.S.I. 2016 Nos. 91 and 147)

THE COUNTY COURT

1 Introduction

The County Court is the main court dealing with civil (i.e., non-criminal) matters. For further detail as to its jurisdiction, see the Note on **The Court System**.

2 Procedure

The procedure for the conduct of cases in the County Court is contained in the Civil Procedure Rules 1998 (the Rules). Part 1 of the Rules sets out their overriding objective as being to enable the court to deal with cases jointly, which means, so far as possible–

  (i) ensuring that the parties are on an equal footing;
  (ii) saving expense;
  (iii) dealing with cases in ways which are proportionate to the–
     (a) amount of money involved;
     (b) importance of the case;
     (c) complexity of the issues; and
     (d) the financial position of each party.
  (iv) ensuring that cases are dealt with expeditiously and fairly; and
  (v) allotting to a case an appropriate share of the court's resources, taking into account the need to allot resources to other cases.
The parties are required to help the court to further the overriding objective (Rule 1.3).

The overriding objective is modified in respect of financial restrictions proceedings under the Counter-Terrorism Act 2008 and terrorism prevention and investigation measures under the Terrorism Prevention and Investigation Measures Act 2011. In these case, a duty is placed on the court to ensure that information is not disclosed contrary to the public interest, and the court is required to read and give effect to the overriding objective in a way which is compatible with this duty.

As to court fees, see **20 County Court fees**, below.

As to offers to settle, see **22 The effect of an offer to settle**, below.

3 Court management powers

The court must actively manage each case with a view to achieving the overriding objective (see **2 Introduction**, above). This includes amongst other things–

  (a) encouraging co-operation between the parties in the conduct of the proceedings;
  (b) identifying the issues at an early stage, deciding which need full investigation and trial and which can be dealt with summarily;
  (c) encouraging the use of alternative dispute resolution; and
  (d) helping the parties to settle the whole or part of the case.
The court will allocate each case to one of three "tracks", described in the following paragraphs, taking into account the following factors (Civil Procedure Rules 1998, Rule 26.8)–

  (i) the financial value, if any, of the claim;
  (ii) the nature of the remedy sought;
  (iii) the likely complexity of the facts, law or evidence;
  (iv) the number of the parties or likely parties;
  (v) the value of any counterclaim or additional claim and the complexity of any matters relating to it;
  (vi) the amount of oral evidence which may be required;
  (vii) the importance of the claim to persons who are not parties to the proceedings;
  (viii) the views expressed by the parties; and
  (ix) the circumstances of the parties.

4 The small claims track

Part 26 of the Civil Procedure Rules 1998 defines which cases will normally be allocated to the small claims track. These are (Rule 26.6)–

  (a) claims for personal injuries where the financial value of the claim is less than £10,000 and the financial value of any claim for damages for personal injuries is not more than £1,000;
  (b) claims by tenants against landlords where the cost of repairs is estimated to be not more than £1,000 and the financial value of any other claim for damages is not more than £1,000, but not including any case which includes a claim for a remedy for harassment or unlawful eviction; and
  (c) any other claims which have a financial value of not more than £10,000.
The procedure for dealing with a case subject to the small claims track is laid down in Part 27. The court may

adopt any method of proceeding at a hearing that it considers to be fair. Hearings are informal, the strict rules of evidence do not apply, the court need not take evidence on oath, it may limit cross-examination, and it must give reasons for its decisions. No expert evidence may be given except with the court's permission and no solicitor's costs may be recovered.

An intellectual property claim (except as to patents or registered designs) the value of which is less than £10,000 will also be allocated to the small claims track if the parties agree; if one party does not agree the court will decide whether to allocate to the small claims or multi-track: Rule 63.27.

5 Low value personal injury claims

A streamlined process applies to—
(a) road traffic accident personal injury claims;
(b) employers liability personal injury claims; and
(c) public liability personal injury claims,
where the accident occurs in England and Wales and the claim is between £1,000 (i.e., over the small claims limit) and £25,000.

For this purpose, the value of the claim is based on the level of general damages and special damages, excluding damage to the vehicle and hire costs. It also takes into account any deduction for failure to wear a seat belt, but not other forms of contributory negligence.

Claims must be brought using an online claims portal which incorporates strict time limits and fixed legal fees at each stage.

Claims where there are complicating factors (such as the death of either party, or which involve contributory negligence) are outside the scope of this procedure, as are employer's liability claims which have more than one defendant, and mesothelioma and clinical negligence claims.

6 The fast track

Rule 26.6 of the Civil Procedure Rules 1998 provides that the fast track will be the normal track for—
(i) any claim which does not come within the small claims track and which
(ii) has a financial value of not more than £25,000,
provided that the court considers—
(iii) that the trial is likely to take no more than one day, and
(iv) that oral expert evidence will be limited to one expert per party in not more than two expert fields.

The procedure for dealing with fast track cases is set out in Part 28 of the Rules. When allocating a case to the fast track, the court will give directions for the management of the case and set a timetable for the steps to be taken between the giving of directions and the trial. When giving directions the court will also either fix the trial date or a period (not exceeding three weeks) within which the trial will take place. The standard period between the giving of directions and the trial will be not more than 30 weeks.

The amount of costs recoverable in fast track cases is strictly limited. For example, the maximum basic trial costs that may be awarded is £1,650 for cases where the value of the claim exceeds £15,000, plus an additional £345 if the court considers it necessary for a party's legal representative to be present in addition to an advocate (Rule 45.38, 45.39).

Expert evidence will be given in a written report unless the court directs that it is in the interests of justice for oral evidence to be given (Rule 35.5).

7 The multi-track

Rule 26.6 of the Civil Procedure Rules 1998 also provides that the multi-track is the normal track for all claims for which the small claims and fast tracks are not the normal track. The procedure for dealing with multi-track cases is set out in Part 29 of the Rules. The court will be responsible for the management of multi-track cases and must fix a trial date, or a period within which the trial is to take place, as soon as possible.

The multi-track will be the usual track where the value of a claim exceeds £25,000, or where it is expected that a trial will last longer than a day, or where more than two experts per party will be needed.

8 European small claims

EC Regulation 861/2007 establishes a European small claims procedure to simplify and speed up cross-border small claims procedures. The procedure applies where the claimant is in the UK and the defendant resides in another EU Member State (except Denmark).

Claims are treated as if they were allocated to the small claims track (see **4 The small claims track**, above), but with a lower maximum claim of 2,000 (EC Reg. 861/2007, Art. 2). A number of types of claim are excluded, including all claims relating to divorce, wills, bankruptcy, social security, tenancies and employment.

The procedure for dealing with a case subject to the European small claims track is laid down in the EC Regulation, as supplemented by Part 78 of the Civil Procedure Rules 1998. There is a standard form which must be completed in English and the court has 30 days from receipt of a claim to decide whether it is within the scope of the procedure. If the claim is outside the scope of the procedure, the claimant will have 21 days to decide whether to withdraw it or continue as a normal (non-small) claim.

Once it has accepted a claim under the European small claims procedure, the court will forward it to the defendant. If the defendant refuses it because it is either not in an official language of his Member State or in a language he understands, the court will inform the claimant so that he may provide a translation. Generally, a claim will proceed by written procedure, but where an oral hearing is necessary, it will be held by video conference. The other procedural requirements and time limits are set out in EC Regulation 861/2007.

9 European order for payment

EC Regulation 1896/2006 allow creditors to recover uncontested cross-border debts using standard forms submitted to their own national courts. The procedure can only be used for monetary claims and there is no limit on the amount for which a claim may be issued. As with other debts, a claim worth £15,000 or less must be made in the County Court, but a claim worth more than £15,000 can be started in either the High Court or the County Court.

The procedure for dealing with a case is laid down in the EC Regulation, as supplemented by Part 78 of the Civil Procedure Rules 1998. There is a standard form which must be completed in English. If the claim is accepted by the court, and not contested by the defendant within 30 days, it becomes automatically enforceable in every EU Member State (except Denmark). If the defendant challenges the amount due, the claimant may either drop the case or else proceed using normal procedures.

10 Inquiry and report

S.65 of the County Courts Act 1984 provides that, subject to rules of court, a judge of the County Court may refer to another judge of the County Court for inquiry and report certain types of proceedings, including (a) any proceedings which require any prolonged examination of documents or any scientific or local investigation which cannot, in the judge's opinion, conveniently be made before him, (b) any proceedings where the question in dispute consists wholly or in part of matters of account, (c) with the consent of the parties, any other proceedings, and (d) any question arising in any proceedings, subject to any right to have particular cases tried with a jury.

11 Capacity to sue

In general, any individual, partner, firm or company, or trustee may, in appropriate cases, institute proceedings in the County Court and likewise may be sued therein. However, Part 21 of the Civil Procedure Rules 1998 makes special provision in relation to proceedings involving a child (i.e., a person who is under the age of 18) or a patient (i.e., a person who, by reason of a mental disorder within the meaning of the Mental Health Act 1983, is incapable of administering his own affairs). A patient must have a litigation friend to conduct proceedings on his behalf. A child must have a litigation friend to conduct proceedings on his behalf unless the court orders otherwise.

Subject to the provisions of any enactment limiting the jurisdiction of the County Court, proceedings by the Crown may be instituted in the County Court. All rules of law and enactment regulating the removal or transfer of proceedings from the County Court to the High Court and *vice versa* will apply to Crown proceedings (County Courts Act 1984, s.46), except that the transfer to the County Court of any proceedings by or against the Crown in the High Court cannot be made without the consent of the Crown (s.40(5)).

12 Witnesses

S.55 of the County Courts Act 1984 provides that any person duly summoned as a witness who has paid or tendered to him at the time of the service of the summons the prescribed sum in respect of his expenses and who refuses or neglects without sufficient cause to appear or produce any documents required by the summons to be produced, or who refuses to be sworn or give evidence, will forfeit such fine, up to £1,000, as the judge directs.

13 Right of audience

In any proceedings in the County Court, the following are included among the persons who may address the court (County Courts Act 1984, ss.60 and 61)—
(a) any party to the proceedings;
(b) a barrister retained by or on behalf of any party;
(c) a solicitor on the record (i.e., a solicitor acting generally in the proceedings for a party to them);
(d) any solicitor employed by a solicitor on the record, or any solicitor engaged as an agent by a solicitor on the record, and any solicitor employed by a solicitor so engaged;
(e) any other person allowed by leave of the court to appear instead of any party;
(f) persons in relevant legal employment, as defined, who may be granted limited rights of audience by the Lord Chancellor.

Under the Courts and Legal Services Act 1990 (s.11), the Lord Chancellor may by order provide that there shall be no restriction on the persons who may exercise rights of audience, or rights to conduct litigation, in relation to County Court proceedings of a kind specified in the order. An order may be made only in relation to proceedings (a) for the recovery of amounts due under contracts for the supply of goods or services; (b) for the enforcement of any judgment or order of any court or the recovery of any sum due under any such judgment or order; (c) in any application under the Consumer Credit Act 1974; (d) in relation to domestic premises; or (e) allotted to the small claims track.

The Lay Representatives (Rights of Audience) Order 1999 gives lay representatives rights of audience in small claims cases dealt with under the small claims track in the County Court.

14 Appeals to the Court of Appeal

If any party to any proceedings in the County Court is dissatisfied with the determination of a judge or jury he may, subject to rules of court and the following provisions, appeal from it to the Court of Appeal (County Courts Act 1984, s.77). The Access to Justice Act 1999 provides that rules of court may make provision as to the classes of case in which a right to appeal may only be exercised with permission, the courts which my give permission, and the considerations to be taken into account in deciding whether permission should be given (s.54 of the 1999 Act).

An appeal on a question of fact does not lie in cases where either the claimant or the defendant claims possession of residential premises if, by virtue of *inter alia* the Rent Act 1977 or the Landlord and Tenant Act 1954, the court can only grant possession on being satisfied that it is reasonable to do so (s.77(6) of the 1984 Act). S.77 has effect subject to any other enactment; it does not confer or take away any right of appeal where a right of appeal is conferred by some other enactment.

On the hearing of an appeal, the Court of Appeal may draw any inference of fact and may either order a new trial, or order judgment to be entered for any party, or make a final or other order on such terms as the court thinks fit (s.81).

In addition to the above procedure for appeals to the Court of Appeal, certain statutes make special provision for appeals on points of law to the High Court. Under s.57 of the Access to Justice Act 1999, where an appeal would be to a court other than the Court of Appeal or the Supreme Court of the United Kingdom, the Master of the Rolls or the court from which an appeal is made, or from which permission to appeal is sought, may direct that the appeal be heard instead by the Court of Appeal.

15 Online claims

A claimant may start a claim to recover a sum of money by requesting the issue of a claim form electronically (Rule 7.12). This can be done using the Court Service Money Claim Online, which is available at <www.moneyclaim.gov.uk/csmco2/index.jsp>. Online claims are limited to claims for fixed amounts up to £99,999 and are only suitable for simple claims as there is limited space to enter details of the claim online. More complex claims will need to be filed at court using a paper form.

The court fees for online claims are lower than for issuing proceedings through a court, but there are no fee exemptions, remissions or reductions. As to the fees, see **20 County Court fees**, below.

16 Enforcement of judgment

A judgment or order of the County Court for the payment of a sum of money which it is sought to enforce wholly or partially by execution against goods must be enforced (High Court and County Court Jurisdiction Order 1991, Art. 8)–

    (a) only in the High Court where the sum it is sought to enforce is £5,000 or more and the proceedings in which the judgment or order was obtained did not arise out of an agreement regulated by the Consumer Credit Act 1974;

    (b) only in the County Court where the sum it is sought to enforce is less than £600; and

    (c) in any other case, either in the High Court or the County Court.

These rules also apply to sums of money recoverable as if payable under an order of the County Court except those payable under employment tribunal decisions. A sum of money under an employment tribunal decision, or a compromise sum, payable as if under an order of the County Court must be enforced in the High Court if it is for £5,000 or more, and may be enforced in either the High Court or the County Court if it is under that sum (Art. 8).

Traffic penalties are enforced through the County Court (Art. 8A).

A judgment or order of a County Court for possession of land made in a possession claim against trespassers may be enforced in either the High Court or the County Court (Art. 8B).

In the County Court a judgment may be enforced in a number of ways, including the following–

    (1) where the order is for order for the payment of money then, subject to Article 8 of the High Court and County Courts Jurisdiction Order 1991 (see above), by warrant of execution issued by the district judge against the debtor's goods and chattels (s.85, as amended); however, by virtue of s.89 (as amended) such tools, books, vehicles and other items of equipment as are necessary to that person for use personally by him in his employment, business or vocation, and such clothing, bedding, furniture, household equipment and provisions as are necessary for satisfying the basic domestic needs of that person and his family, are protected from seizure;

(2) by making a charging order imposing a charge on any such property of the debtor as may be specified in the order (Charging Orders Act 1979, s.1). Where a debtor is required by the County Court (or High Court) order to pay a sum by instalments, a charging order may be made even though there has been no default in payment, but the court must take the fact that there has been no default into account in deciding whether to make the order. An order for sale to enforce the charging order may not be made where there has been no default in payment. The Lord Chancellor has the power by regulations to set financial thresholds for the making of charging orders and for the enforcement of such orders by an order for sale (s.3A, as inserted by the Tribunals, Courts and Enforcement Act 2007, s.94);

(3) by the appointment of a receiver (County Courts Act 1984, s.107);

(4) by an attachment of earnings order;

(5) by making a third party debt order whereby a third party is ordered to pay to the judgment creditor a debt he owes to the judgment debtor (Civil Procedure Rules, Part 72).

By ss.105 and 106 of the County Courts Act 1984, a High Court judgment for the payment of money may be enforced in the County Court and, in certain specified circumstances, *vice versa.*

17 Administration orders

Where a debtor is unable to pay forthwith the amount of a judgment obtained against him, and alleges that his whole indebtedness amounts to a sum not exceeding the County Court limit (see **16 Enforcement of judgment,** above), inclusive of the debt for which the judgment was obtained; the County Court may make an order [an administration order] providing for the administration of his estate (County Courts Act 1984, s.112(1)).

Before an administration order is made the County Court must, in accordance with court rules, send to every person whose name the debtor has notified to it as being a creditor of his, a notice that that person's name has been so notified (s.112(3)). So long as an administration order is in force, a creditor whose name has been included in the schedule to the order will not, without the leave of the appropriate court, be entitled to present, or join in, a bankruptcy petition against the debtor unless his name was so notified and the debt by virtue of which he presents, or joins in, the petition exceeds £1,500, and the notice given under s.112(3) (see above) was received by the creditor within 28 days immediately preceding the day on which the petition is presented (s.112(4)).

Under an administration order, the debtor may be required to pay his debts by instalments or otherwise, and either in full or to such extent as appears to the court in the circumstances of the case to be practicable, and subject to any conditions as to his future earnings or income as the court may think just (s.112(6)).

Subject to ss.115 and 116 (see below), when an administration order is made, no creditor will have any remedy against the person or property of the debtor in respect of any debt of which the debtor notified the County Court before the order was made or which has been scheduled to the order, except with the leave of the County Court, and on such terms as that court may impose (s.114).

Where it appears to the court at any time while an administration order is in force, that property of the debtor exceeds in value £50, it must, at the request of any creditor, and without fee, issue execution against the debtor's goods, but subject to the protection under s.89 (see **16 Enforcement of judgment,** above) (s.115). S.116 provides that a person to whom rent is due from a debtor subject to an administration order may distrain upon the debtor's goods for six months rent due before the date of the order notwithstanding the making of the order.

Money paid into court under an administration order will be appropriated first, in satisfaction of the costs of administration (which must not exceed 10p in the pound of the total amount of the debts) and then, in liquidation of debts in accordance with the order. Where the amount received is sufficient to pay (a) each creditor scheduled to the order to the extent provided by the order; (b) the costs of the claimant in the action in respect of which the order was made; and (c) the costs of the administration, the order will be superseded, and the debtor will be discharged from his debts to the scheduled creditors (s.117).

For the provision of ss.4 and 5 of the Attachment of Earnings Act 1971 relating to administration orders, see the Note on **Attachment of Earnings.**

18 Committal under Debtors Act 1869

Under s.5 of the Debtors Act 1869, as restricted by s.11 of the Administration of Justice Act 1970, the County Court may commit to prison a person making default in the payment of a debt or instalment of a debt due to be paid by him under a High Court or County Court maintenance order or a judgment or order for the payment of certain taxes or contributions (e.g., income tax).

19 Restriction on enforcement of certain arrears

A person cannot enforce through the High Court or the County Court without leave of the court (which may be refused or granted subject to such restrictions and conditions as the court thinks fit) any arrears under a maintenance order which became due more than 12 months before the commencement of the enforcement proceedings. The court also has the power to remit payment of all or any part of the arrears (Matrimonial Causes Act 1973, s.32).

20 County Court fees

County Court fees are prescribed by the Civil Proceedings Fees Order 2008. To issue a claim form where the claim is solely for money, the following fees are payable (effective 9th March 2015)–

Where the amount claimed is not more than	Fee	Fee if claim issued online
£300	£35	£25
£500	£50	£35
£1,000	£70	£60
£1,500	£80	£70
£3,000	£115	£105
£5,000	£205	£185
£10,000	£455	£410
£10,000-£200,000	5%	4.5%*
£200,000+ (or not limited)	£10,000	n/a

*Online claims are limited to £99,999, see 15 **Online claims,** above.

Where the claim is for something other than money, the fee is £355 (or, for a possession claim made online, £325) (effective from 21st March 2016).

Additional fees may become payable during the court process.

Note.–Claims can also be filed with the County Court Money Claims Centre, if they are for a specified amount and are in computer readable form. There is a discount on the standard court issue fee where claims are made through the CCBC.

21 Fee remissions and reductions

Fee remissions are now standardised for all courts and tribunals. For the County Court, the remission system is contained in the Civil Proceedings Fees Order 2008, Schedule 2.

Eligibility for remission or part remission of a fee is based on a disposable capital test and a gross monthly income test. Parties who satisfy the disposable capital test will either receive a full fee remission, pay a contribution to the fee, or have to pay the fee in full, as determined by the gross monthly income test.

The Disposable Capital Test.

A party satisfies the disposable capital test if–

  (i) the fee for which an application for remission is made, falls within a fee band set out in column 1 of TABLE 1 below; and

  (ii) the party's disposable capital is less than the amount in the corresponding row of column 2.

TABLE 1

Fee band.	Disposable capital.
Up to and including £1,000	£3,000
£1,001 to £1,335	£4,000
£1,336 to £1,665	£5,000
£1,666 to £2,000	£6,000
£2,001 to £2,330	£7,000
£2,331 to £4,000	£8,000
£4,001 to £5,000	£10,000
£5,001 to £6,000	£12,000
£6,001 to £7,000	£14,000
£7,001 or more	£16,000

"Disposable capital" is the value of every resource of a capital nature belonging to the party on the date on which the application for remission is made, unless it is treated as income or it is disregarded as excluded disposable capital (see (f) below).

Note that–

  (a) if a party or their partner is aged 61 or over, they satisfy the disposable capital test if their disposable capital is less than £16,000, whatever the fee band;

  (b) the value of a resource of a capital nature that does not consist of money is calculated as the amount which it would realise if sold, less 10% of the sale value and the amount of any borrowing secured against it that would be repayable on sale;

  (c) capital resources in a country outside the UK count towards disposable capital. If there is no prohibition in that country against the transfer of a resource into the UK, the value of that resource is the amount which it would realise if sold in that country (calculated as in (b) above). If there is a prohibition against the transfer of a resource into the UK, its value is the amount it would realise if sold to a buyer in the UK;

  (d) where disposable capital is held in currency other than sterling, the cost of any banking charge or commission that would be payable if that amount were converted into sterling, is deducted from its value;

(e) where any resource of a capital nature is owned jointly or in common, there is a presumption that it is owned in equal shares, unless evidence to the contrary is produced;
(f) the following are excluded disposable capital–
  – a property which is the main or only dwelling occupied by the party;
  – the household furniture and effects of the main or only dwelling occupied by the party;
  – articles of personal clothing;
  – any vehicle, the sale of which would leave the party, or their partner, without motor transport;
  – tools and implements of trade, including vehicles used for business purposes;
  – the capital value of the party's or their partner's business, where the party or their partner is self-employed;
  – the capital value of any funds or other assets held in trust, where the party or their partner is a beneficiary without entitlement to advances of any trust capital;
  – a jobseeker's back to work bonus;
  – a payment made as a result of a determination of unfair dismissal by a court or tribunal, or by way of settlement of a claim for unfair dismissal;
  – any compensation paid as a result of a determination of medical negligence or in respect of any personal injury by a court, or by way of settlement of a claim for medical negligence or personal injury;
  – the capital held in any personal or occupational pension scheme;
  – any cash value payable on surrender of a contract of insurance;
  – any capital payment made out of the Independent Living Funds;
  – any bereavement payment;
  – any capital insurance or endowment lump sum payments that have been paid as a result of illness, disability or death;
  – any student loan or student grant;
  – any payments under the criminal injuries compensation scheme.

The Gross Monthly Income Test.
If a party satisfies the disposable capital test, no fee is payable if they or their partner has the number of children specified in column 1 of TABLE 2 below and–
  (i) if they are single, their gross monthly income does not exceed the amount set out in the appropriate row of column 2; or
  (ii) if they are one of a couple, their joint gross monthly income does not exceed the amount set out in the appropriate row of column 3.

TABLE 2

Number of children.	Gross Monthly Income.	
	Single Person.	Couple.
none	£1,085	£1,245
1 child	£1,330	£1,490
2 children	£1,575	£1,735

If a party or their partner has more than 2 children, the gross monthly income figure given above is increased by £245 for each additional child.
"Gross monthly income" is total monthly income, for the month preceding that in which the application for remission is made, from all sources, other than receipt of any excluded benefits (see below). Income from a trade, business or gainful occupation other than an occupation at a wage or salary is calculated as the profits which have accrued or will accrue to the party, and their drawings, in the month preceding that in which the application for remission is made. All sums necessarily expended to earn those profits are deducted.
Parties are required to pay a contribution of £5 towards their fee for every £10 of gross monthly income they earn over the threshold applicable to them. Parties with income in excess of £4,000 above the threshold (the "gross monthly income cap") will not be eligible for any remission or part remission of a fee.
The excluded benefits (which are not counted as income) are–
(a) any of the following benefits–
  – attendance allowance;
  – severe disablement allowance;
  – carer's allowance;
  – disability living allowance;
  – constant attendance allowance as an increase to a disablement pension;
  – any payment made out of the social fund;
  – housing benefit;
  – widowed parents allowance;
(b) under the Tax Credits Act 2002–
  – any disabled child element or severely disabled child element of the child tax credit;
  – any childcare element of the working tax credit;
(c) any direct payment made under the Community Care, Services for Carers and Children's Services (Direct Payments) (England) Regulations 2009, the Community Care, Services for Carers and Children's Services (Direct Payments) (Wales) Regulations 2011, or the Social Care (Self-directed Support) (Scotland) Act 2013;

(d) a back to work bonus payable under the Jobseekers Act 1995;

(e) any exceptionally severe disablement allowance paid under the Personal Injuries (Civilians) Scheme 1983;

(f) any payments from the Industrial Injuries Disablement Benefit;

(g) any pension paid under the Naval, Military and Air Forces etc. (Disablement and Death) Service Pension Order 2006;

(h) any payment made from the Independent Living Funds;

(i) any payment made from the Bereavement Allowance;

(j) any financial support paid under an agreement for the care of a foster child;

(k) any housing credit element of pension credit;

(l) any armed forces independence payment;

(m) any personal independence payment payable under the Welfare Reform Act 2012;

(n) any payment on account of benefit as defined in the Social Security (Payments on Account of Benefit) Regulations 2013;

(o) any of the following amounts that make up an award of universal credit–

  – an additional amount to the child element in respect of a disabled child;
  – a housing costs element;
  – a childcare costs element;
  – a carer element;
  – a limited capability for work or limited capacity for work and work -related activity element.

An application for remission of a fee must be made at the time when the fee would otherwise be payable.

Application for a refund of a fee may also be made after a fee has been paid, and will be granted if the Lord Chancellor would have granted a reduction or remission had he known the circumstances at the time the fee was paid. Application should normally be made within 3 months of payment of the fee.

A party is not entitled to a fee remission if they are in receipt of the following civil legal services: Legal representation; Family help (higher); or Family help (lower) in respect of applying for a consent order.

No remissions or refunds are available in respect of the fee payable for copy or duplicate documents or for searches.

22 The effect of an offer to settle

If an offer to settle a civil claim is made – by either a claimant or a defendant – but refused by the other party, then if the subsequent court decision is at least as favourable as the offer, the court may penalise the party which refused it.

Offer made by a defendant

If a claimant fails to beat the defendant's offer (i.e., the court award is less than or equal to the defendant's pre-hearing offer to settle), the claimant must pay the defendant's costs from the last date the offer could have been accepted, plus interest of up to 10% above base rate on those costs.

Offer made by a claimant

If a defendant fails to beat the claimant's offer at trial (i.e., the court awards the claimant an amount equal to or more than the claimant's offer), the defendant must pay (Offers to Settle in Civil Proceedings Order 2013)–

  – interest on the whole or part of the damages awarded from the last date the offer could have been accepted at a rate of up to 10% above base rate;
  – the claimant's costs on an indemnity basis from the last date the offer could have been accepted; and interest on costs at a rate of up to 10% above base rate;
  – in damages only claims and mixed claims, an additional amount of up to 10% of the value of the damages awarded to the claimant; and
  – in non-damages claims, an amount of up to 10% of the costs ordered by the court to be paid by the defendant to the claimant.

There is a taper on the amount that might be paid under these provisions and, in mixed damages/non-damages, and solely non-damages claims there is a cap on the amount that may be awarded (whether as a percentage of damages or costs) of £75,000. In respect of damages only claims, there is no cap but a nominal percentage increase in respect of damages over £1 million has the same effect. The tapers are as follows–

Damages only claims

Amount awarded by the court	Prescribed percentage
Up to £500,000	10% of the amount of damages awarded.
Above £500,000, up to £1,000,000	10% of the first £500,000 and 5% of the damages awarded above that figure.
Above £1,000,000	7.5% of the first £1,000,000 and 0.001% of the damages awarded above that figure

Mixed claims

Amount awarded by the court	Amount to be paid by the defendant
Up to £500,000	10% of the amount awarded.
Above £500,000, up to £1,000,000	10% of the first £500,000 and 5% of the amount awarded above that figure

Non-damages claims

Costs ordered to be paid to the claimant	Amount to be paid by the defendant
Up to £500,000	10% of the costs awarded
Above £500,000, up to £1,000,000	10% of the first £500,000 and 5% of any costs ordered to be paid above that figure

23 Authorities

Statutes–

Access to Justice Act 1999

Administration of Justice Act 1970

County Courts Acts 1984

Courts and Legal Services Act 1990

Statutory Instruments–

Civil Procedure Rules 1998, as amended (S.I. 1998 No. 3132, 1999 No. 1008, 2000 Nos. 221, 940, 1317, and 2092, 2001 Nos. 1388, 1769, and 2792, 2004 Nos. 1306, 3129 and 3419, 2005 Nos. 352, 656, 2292 and 2515, 2006 Nos. 1689, 3232 and 3435, 2007 Nos. 2204 and 3543, 2008 Nos. 2178, 3085 and 3327, 2009 Nos. 2092 and 3390, 2010 Nos. 621, 1953, 2577 and 3038, 2011 Nos. 88, 1045, 1979, 2970, and 3103, 2012 Nos. 505 and 2208, 2013 Nos. 262, 515, 789, 1412, 1571, 1695, 1974, and 3112, 2014 Nos. 407, 482, 610, 867, 879, 1233, 2044, 2948, and 3299, 2015 Nos. 406, 670, 877, 1569, and 1881, and 2016 No. 234)

Civil Proceedings Fees Order 2008, as amended (S.I. 2008 Nos. 1053 and 2853, 2009 No. 1498, 2011 No. 586, 2013 Nos. 534, 591, 734, 1410, and 2302, 2014 Nos. 513, 590, 874, 1834, and 2059, 2015 No. 576, and 2016 No. 402)

County Court Jurisdiction Order 2014 (S.I. 2014 No. 503)

High Court and County Courts Jurisdiction Order 1991, as amended (S.I. 1991 No. 724, 1993 No. 1407, 1995 No. 205, 1996 No. 3141, 1999 No. 1014, 2001 Nos. 1387 and 2685, 2005 No. 587, 2008 No. 2934, 2009 No. 577, 2014 Nos. 821 and 2947, and 2015 No. 1641)

Lay Representatives (Rights of Audience) Order 1999 (S.I. 1999 No. 1225)

Offers to Settle in Civil Proceedings Order 2013 (S.I. 2013 No. 93)

EC Regulation 1896/2006 creating a European order for payment procedure

EC Regulation No. 861/2007 establishing a European Small Claims Procedure

THE COURT SYSTEM IN ENGLAND AND WALES

A: INTRODUCTION

1 Introduction

Different types of case are dealt with in specific courts. All criminal cases start in the magistrates' court, but the more serious criminal matters are sent to the Crown Court which has greater sentencing powers. Appeals from the Crown Court go to the High Court, and possibly on to the Court of Appeal and finally the Supreme Court.

Civil cases will sometimes be dealt with by magistrates, but many civil cases will start in the county court. Again, appeals will go to the High Court and then to the Court of Appeal.

Collectively, the Court of Appeal, the High Court, and the Crown Court are known as the Senior Courts.

B: MAGISTRATES' COURTS

2 Magistrates' Courts–criminal jurisdiction

The jurisdiction of magistrates' courts in criminal matters is twofold (Magistrates' Courts Act 1980 s.6)–

(a) they hear and determine criminal cases in summary proceedings (i.e., cases which can be dealt with only in a magistrates' court), or which are triable either way (i.e., summarily in a magistrates' court or on indictment in the Crown Court) and which are tried summarily with the consent of the defendant;

(b) they act as "examining justices" in respect of offences triable either way, in which case their task is to conduct preliminary enquiries to decide whether a *prima facie* case has been made out against a person to justify his committal to the Crown Court for trial.

If an offence is triable *only* on indictment (which will be the case for more serious offences), the magistrates must send the defendant to the Crown Court for trial (Crime and Disorder Act 1998, s.51).

3 Reporting restrictions

As a rule, criminal proceedings before magistrates' courts are held in public, but when magistrates sit as examining justices (i.e., in committal proceedings) evidence given at the proceedings must not be reported until the case is disposed of, except at the request of the accused (or any one of several accused) (s.8). Where there are two or more accused, and one of them objects to the making of an order permitting the reporting of committal proceedings, the court must make the order only if it is satisfied, after hearing the representation of the accused, that it is in the interests of justice to do so (Magistrates' Courts Act 1980, s.8(2A), as added by the Criminal Justice (Amendment) Act 1981).

Similar reporting restrictions apply where magistrates send a case to the Crown Court without a committal hearing (1998 Act, Sch.3 para 3).

As a rule it is not lawful to publish in the UK a written report of any allocation or sending proceedings in England and Wales; or to include in a relevant programme for reception in the UK a report of any such proceedings (Crime and Disorder Act 1998, s.52A(1)). However, a magistrates' court may, with reference to any allocation or sending proceedings, order that s.52A(1) does not apply to reports of those proceedings. The court must make the order if, and only if, it is satisfied, after hearing the representations of the accused, that it is in the interests of justice to do so (s.52A(2) to (4)). If a report is published or included in a relevant programme in contravention of s.52A an offence will have been committed by the person who publishes it, which can include a proprietor, editor or publisher of a newspaper or periodical in which such a report is published or a body corporate which is engaged in providing the service in which a programme is included (s.52B).

Reporting restrictions may also be imposed in pre-trial hearings (as to the admissibility of evidence and questions of law) in cases which magistrates are to hear summarily (ss.8A to 8D, added by the Courts Act 2003).

4 Reporting restrictions–minors

Courts also have a discretion to impose prohibitions on reporting information leading to the identification of witnesses, complainants or defendants under the age of 18 once proceedings have started (Youth Justice and Criminal Evidence Act 1999, s.45). The restrictions apply until the person reaches the age of 18 unless, in the meantime, the court has lifted or relaxed them. This power does not apply to proceedings in youth courts where automatic restrictions have effect (see **10 Restrictions on attendance and publicity,** below). The factors to be taken into account by the court in deciding whether to exercise its discretion include (s.52)–

(a) the interest in the open reporting of crime, and of matters relating to human health or safety; and the prevention and exposure of miscarriages of justice;

(b) the welfare of any person in relation to whom the restrictions apply or would apply (or, as the case may be, applied); and

(c) any views expressed by an appropriate person on behalf of a person within paragraph (b) who is under the age of 16, or of that person themselves if they have reached the age of 16.

All criminal courts (not just magistrates' courts) also have power to make a "reporting direction" in relation to any witness or victim who was under 18 when proceedings commenced. The direction will provide that no matter relating to the person may be included in a publication if it is likely to lead to members of the public identifying him as being concerned in the proceedings. Such a direction can last for the lifetime of the victim or witness and can be made if the court is satisfied that the quality of evidence, or the level of co-operation, given to any party to the proceedings in connection with the preparation of their case, is likely to be diminished by reason of fear or distress at being identified as a person concerned in the proceedings (s.45A). In deciding whether to make a reporting direction the court must have regard to the welfare of the person, whether it would be in the interests of justice to make the reporting direction, and the public interest in avoiding the imposition of a substantial and unreasonable restriction on the reporting of the proceedings.

5 Sentencing powers

The sentencing power of magistrates is limited, the maximum sentence which they may impose for any one offence (except certain offences under the Misuse of Drugs Act 1971) being six months' imprisonment or a fine or both (Magistrates' Courts Act 1980, s.32, as amended). The previous £5,000 limit on fines has been removed in most cases by the Legal Aid, Sentencing and Punishment of Offenders Act 2012, s.85 which provides that where an offence would, be punishable on summary conviction by a fine or maximum fine of £5,000 or more (however expressed), the offence is punishable on summary conviction by a fine of any amount.

Where, after summary trial, a person of not less than 18 years is convicted of an offence triable either way and the court is of the opinion, having regard to the seriousness or nature of the offence, that greater punishment should be inflicted than it has power to inflict, it may commit him to the Crown Court for sentence (s.38, as substituted by the Criminal Justice Act 1991 s.25).

6 Special measures directions

Where a witness in a magistrates' court is—

(a) aged under 18; or

(b) the court considers that the quality of their evidence is likely to be diminished because they are—

    (i) suffering from a mental disorder;

    (ii) otherwise have significant impairment of intelligence and social functioning;

    (iii) have a physical disorder or disability; or

(c) the court considers that the quality of their evidence is likely to be diminished because of their fear or distress in connection with testifying (taking into account various factors such as the nature and circumstances of the offence, the age, background, ethnicity, domestic and employment circumstances, and religious and political beliefs of the witness);

then the court may make a "special measures direction". Such a direction may allow a witness to be screened from the accused; to give evidence by a live link, in private or by video recording; for a witness to be examined through an intermediary; or for the wearing of wigs and gowns to be dispensed with whilst the witness gives evidence (Youth Justice and Criminal Evidence Act 1999, ss.16 to 33). The Magistrates' Courts (Special Measures Directions) Rules 2002 make further provision as to such directions, and include a form of application.

Witnesses in cases involving sexual offences and certain gun and knife crimes are given automatic eligibility for special measures without the court having to be satisfied that the quality of their evidence would otherwise be diminished.

7 Magistrates' Courts—civil jurisdiction

In the absence of any express provision in any Act or in the rules specifying which magistrates' court has jurisdiction to hear a complaint, magistrates' courts have jurisdiction to deal with any complaint (s.52, as substituted by the Courts Act 2003, s.47).

The civil jurisdiction of magistrates' courts includes summary proceedings for the recovery of certain civil debts and family proceedings (see below).

8 Appeals and cases stated

In criminal cases, a person has a right of appeal against conviction by, or against a sentence imposed by, a magistrates' court to the Crown Court (Magistrates' Courts Act 1980, s.108).

An appeal to the Crown Court can also be made in licensing matters.

On a point of law or jurisdiction arising in any proceedings before a magistrates' court, an appeal may lie by way of case stated to the High Court (s.111).

C: YOUTH COURTS

9 Youth Courts—Introduction

Youth courts are a special category of magistrates' courts, composed of justices specially qualified to deal with juvenile cases. They sit for the purpose of (Children and Young Persons Act 1933, s.45, as substituted by the Courts Act 2003)–

(a) hearing any charge against a child or young person; or

(b) exercising any other jurisdiction which may be conferred on them.

Youth courts deal with all cases concerned with children (i.e., persons under the age of 14) or young persons (i.e., persons who have attained the age of 14 but are under 18), whether accused of an offence or alleged to be in need of care and control.

Where a person charged with an offence who appears or is brought before a youth court subsequently attains the age of 18, the youth court may at any time before the start of the trial, or after conviction and before sentence, remit that person for trial or sentence to a magistrates' court (Crime and Disorder Act 1998, s.47).

For details of proceedings before youth courts, see the Note on **Treatment of Offenders: Children and Young Persons**.

10 Restrictions on attendance and publicity

Arrangements must be made to segregate children and young persons from accused adults (unless jointly charged) (Children and Young Persons Act 1933, s.31). There are restrictions on attendance at, and reporting of, proceedings in, or on an appeal from, youth courts; no matter relating to any child or young person concerned in proceedings may while he is under 18 be included in any publication if it is likely to lead members of the public to identify him as someone concerned in the proceedings (s.49). These automatic reporting restrictions do not apply in relation to proceedings for anti-social behaviour injunctions or criminal behaviour order under the Anti-social Behaviour, Crime and Policing Act 2014.

For non-youth court proceedings, see **3 Reporting restrictions**, above.

11 Procedure

Procedure in youth courts is governed by the Magistrates' Courts (Children and Young Persons) Rules 1992. Parents or guardians may be required to attend. Appeals from decisions of youth courts and committals for sentence are heard by special benches of the Crown Court, which include justices authorised to sit as members of a youth court.

D: THE COUNTY COURT

12 The County Court–Introduction

The County Court is the main court dealing with civil (i.e., non-criminal) matters.

The County Court can deal with contract and tort (civil wrong) cases and recovery of land actions. Some County Court offices can also deal with bankruptcy and insolvency matters, as well as cases relating to wills and trusts (equity and contested probate actions) where the value of the trust, fund or estate does not exceed £30,000, matters under the Equality Act 2010, and actions which all parties agree to have heard in a county court (e.g. defamation cases).

Some civil matters e.g., liquor licensing, can also be dealt with by magistrates. More complex cases or those involving large amounts of money will be dealt with by the High Court.

For the procedure of the County Court (e.g., to bring a small claim) and the fees involved, see the Note on **The County Court**.

13 Jurisdiction of the County Court

Within certain prescribed limits (which are set by the County Courts Act 1984, s.147 and the County Courts Jurisdiction Order 1981, as amended by the High Court and County Courts Jurisdiction Orders, see **36 Authorities**, below), the County Court has jurisdiction *inter alia* in proceedings in equity, probate, attachment of debts, and actions by minors for wages.

The Courts and Legal Services Act 1990 makes provision for the allocation and transfer of business between the High Court and the County Court (s.1). The Lord Chancellor has the power to allocate different types of proceedings between those courts and the High Court and County Courts Jurisdiction Order 1991 makes detailed provision for this.

(a) the County Court has jurisdiction, whatever the monetary amount involved and whatever the value of any fund or asset connected with the proceedings, in actions under the County Courts Act 1984 (Art. 2)–

(i) actions founded in contract and tort under the 1984 Act, s.15;

(ii) any action under the 1984 Act, s.16 for money recoverable by virtue of any enactment for the time being in force (unless it is expressly provided by that or any other enactment that such sums shall only be recoverable in the High Court or shall only be recoverable summarily);

(iii) actions for the recovery of land under the 1984 Act, s.21; and actions in which the title to any hereditament is in question;

(iv) applications for an order under s.2 of the Inheritance (Provision for Family and Dependants) Act 1975 (under the 1984 Act, s. 25); and

    (v) under specified provisions of various other statutes;

(b) the County Court also has jurisdiction in proceedings under s.10 of the Local Land Charges Act 1975 and s.10(4) of the Rent Charges Act 1977 up to a limit of £5,000; and under various provisions of the Law of Property Act 1925 up to a limit of £30,000 (Art. 2).

Proceedings in which both the County Court and the High Court have jurisdiction may be commenced either in the County Court or in the High Court however–

(c) except in relation to personal injury claims under Article 5 (see below), a claim for money must be commenced in the County Court unless the value of the claim is more than £100,000 (Art. 4A);

(d) actions in respect of personal injuries must be commenced in the County Court unless the value of the action is £50,000 or more (Art. 5), although this does not apply to proceedings which include a claim for damages in respect of an alleged breach of duty of care committed in the course of the provision of clinical or medical services (including dental or nursing services);

(e) applications and appeals under the Audit Commission Act 1998, ss.17 and 18 must be commenced in the High Court (Art. 6);

(f) applications under the Access to Neighbouring Land Act 1992 must be commenced in the County Court (Art. 6A);

(g) small claims must be commenced in the County Court (Art. 6B);

(h) proceedings to wind up a company registered in England and Wales may be commenced only in the High Court if its registered office during the previous six months has been situated mainly in London;

(i) proceedings under the Variation of Trusts Act 1958, s.1 must be commenced only in the High Court; and

(j) proceedings under the Companies Act 2006, ss.98, 641(1)(b) and 645-651 must be commenced only in the High Court.

14 Other jurisdictions

The County Court also has the equity jurisdiction of the High Court in cases where the amount or value involved does not exceed £350,000 (County Court Act 1984, s.23 and the County Courts Jurisdiction Order 2014, Art. 3). This applies *inter alia* to proceedings for–

(a) the administration of a deceased person's estate;

(b) the execution of any trust;

(c) foreclosure or redemption of a mortgage or enforcing any charge or lien;

(d) the maintenance of an infant;

(e) the dissolution of a partnership; and

(f) relief against fraud or mistake.

The County Court has jurisdiction in respect of any contentious probate matter arising in connection with an application for the grant or revocation of probate or administration where the grant or application is made through the principal registry of the Family Division or a district probate registry, if the value of the deceased's estate at the time of death was less than £30,000 (exclusive of what he was possessed of as a trustee and after making allowances for funeral expenses and for debts and liabilities).

The County Court's jurisdiction under the Settled Land Act 1925, various provisions of the Trustee Act 1925, and of the Administration of Estates Act 1925 is £30,000. The County Court jurisdiction under the Charging Orders Act 1979 is £5,000 (County Courts Jurisdiction Order 2014, Art. 3).

Except where s.18 (see below) applies, the County Court has no jurisdiction to hear and determine *inter alia* actions for libel or slander (s.15(2)).

If a claim is for more than the County Court limit, the claimant may abandon the excess in order to bring his action within the jurisdiction of the County Court (s.17).

A claimant may not divide a cause of action to bring the County Court (s.35).

S.18 provides that parties to an action may, by a memorandum signed by them or their respective solicitors specify the County Court as having jurisdiction to hear the action, except where the action, if commenced in the High Court, would have been assigned to the Chancery Division or Family Division or would have involved the exercise of the High Court's Admiralty jurisdiction.

E: THE FAMILY COURT

15 The Family Court

The Crime and Courts Act 2013 establishes a Family Court for England and Wales replacing the previous three tier High Court/county court/magistrates' court structure for family proceedings. The High Court retains exclusive jurisdiction in just a limited number of areas.

The Family Court generally sits at the county or magistrates court for an area.

16 Composition

A family court should be composed of one of the following (Family Court (Composition and Distribution of Business) Rules 2014, Rule 3)–

(a) a judge of district judge level;

(b) a judge of circuit judge level;

(c) a judge of High Court judge level; or

(d) two or three lay justices.

Cases are allocated to a judge according to the type of proceedings, whether they are emergency applications; ongoing proceedings etc. Schedule 1 to the Rules makes the following provision—

Cases to be heard by lay justices

Cases under the—

- Maintenance Orders (Facilities for Enforcement) Act 1920;
- Marriage Act 1949;
- Maintenance Orders Acts 1950 and 1958;
- Maintenance Orders (Reciprocal Enforcement) Act 1972;
- Domestic Proceedings and Magistrates' Courts Act 1978;
- Civil Jurisdiction and Judgments Act 1982;
- Family Law Act 1986, s.55A (declarations of parentage);
- Child Support Act 1991, except s.32L or appeals;
- Crime and Disorder Act 1998, s.11 (child safety order);
- Council Regulation (EC) No.44/2001 (known as the Judgments Regulation);
- s.34 of the Children and Families (Wales) Measure 2010;
- Schedule 6 to the Civil Partnership Act 2004;
- Childcare Act 2006, except s.79;
- Human Fertilisation and Embryology Act 2008, s.54, where the child's place of birth was in England and Wales and where all respondents agree to the making of the order;
- Council Regulation (EC) No. 4/2009 (known as the Maintenance Regulation);

(q) Council and EU Parliament Regulation (EU) No. 606/2013 (the Protection Measures Regulation for enforcement of an incoming protection measure).

Cases to be heard by a judge of district judge level

Cases under the—

- Married Women's Property Act 1882;
- Matrimonial Causes Act 1973;
- Matrimonial and Family Proceedings Act 1984 ss.13 and 12 (permission and substantive application) where the parties consent to permission being granted and to the substantive order sought;
- Children Act 1989, Schedule 1;
- Gender Recognition Act 2004, except appeals under s.8(1) and referrals to the court under s.8(5);
- Civil Partnership Act 2004, except under (i) Schedule 6 (financial provision corresponding to provision made by the Domestic Proceedings and Magistrates' Courts Act 1978); or (ii) Schedule 7 (financial relief after overseas dissolution), unless the parties consent to permission being granted and to the substantive order sought.

Cases to be heard by judge of circuit judge level

Cases under the—

- Family Law Act 1986 ss.55 (declarations as to marital status), 56 (declarations as to legitimacy or legitimation) or 57 (declarations as to adoptions effected overseas);
- Child Support Act 1991 under s.32L (orders preventing avoidance);
- Human Fertilisation and Embryology Act 2008, s.54, where the child's place of birth was in England and Wales but where not all respondents agree to the making of the order.

Cases to be heard by a judge of High Court judge level

Cases under the—

- Matrimonial and Family Proceedings Act 1984, sections 13 and 12 (permission and substantive application) where (i) the parties do not consent to permission being granted; or (ii) the parties consent to permission being granted but do not consent to the substantive order sought;
- Adoption and Children Act 2002, s.60(3) (order to disclose or to prevent disclosure of information to an adopted person);
- Adoption and Children Act 2002, s.79(4) (order for Registrar General to give information);
- Civil Partnership Act 2004, Schedule 7 paras 45 and 9 (permission and substantive application) where (i) the parties do not consent to permission being granted; or (ii) the parties consent to permission being granted but do not consent to the substantive order sought;
- referrals to the court under s.8(5) of the Gender Recognition Act 2004;
- the Human Fertilisation and Embryology Act 2008, s.54, where the child's place of birth was outside of England and Wales;
- Article 13 of Council and EU Parliament Regulation (EU) No. 606/2013 (the Protection Measures Regulation).

Other matters will be dealt with by the level of judge who is dealing with, or has dealt with, proceedings relating to the same child or, if there are or were no such proceedings, by lay justices or a judge of district judge level.

F: THE CROWN COURT

17 The Crown Court

The Crown Court forms part of the Senior Courts of England and Wales.

All proceedings on indictment must be brought before the Crown Court (Senior Courts Act 1981, s.46).

The Crown Court also has power to deal with–

(a) a summary offence where the person charged has been committed for trial to the Crown Court for a more serious offence (Criminal Justice Act 1988, s.41); and

(b) appeals and committals for sentence from magistrates' courts where the magistrates feel that their sentencing powers are not great enough for the particular case (1981 Act, s.74 and the Powers of Criminal Courts (Sentencing) Act 2000, s.5).

18 Special measures directions etc

Special measures directions can be made by the Crown Court for the benefit of young or vulnerable witnesses in the same circumstances as they can be made in the magistrates' court (see **6 Special measures directions**, above). The Crown Court (Special Measures Directions and Directions Prohibiting Cross-examination) Rules 2002 make further provision as to such directions, and include a form of application.

Where it is considered to be in the interests of efficient or effective administration of justice, a court may direct that a witness (other than a defendant) may give evidence by a live link, rather than be physically present in court. This is only available in certain sexual offences cases, and only in courts which have the appropriate facilities (Criminal Justice Act 2003, s.51).

G: THE HIGH COURT

19 The High Court–Introduction

The High Court sits in three Divisions: the Chancery Division, the Queen's Bench Division, and the Family Division.

The Queen's Bench Division has within it a number of specialised courts, namely the Technology and Construction Court, the Commercial Court, the Admiralty Court, the Mercantile Court and the Planning Court. As part of the Chancery Division there is a Patents Court.

20 Jurisdiction

The High Court exercises an original, an appellate, and a supervisory jurisdiction. Its original jurisdiction extends to all causes of action and is unlimited in amount. Its appellate jurisdiction has been extended by numerous statutes conferring jurisdiction, either exclusively or concurrently with other courts, in relation to particular subjects. The High Court's jurisdiction is dealt with in ss.19-31A of the Senior Courts Act 1981.

Schedule 1 to the Senior Courts Act 1981 allocates business between the High Court's Divisions as follows–

Paragraph 1 provides for the matters which are to be assigned to the Chancery Division. These include all causes and matters relating to the administration of estates of deceased persons; probate business other than non-contentious or common form business; the redemption or foreclosure of mortgages; the rectification, setting aside, or cancellation of deeds or other instruments; the dissolution of partnerships or the taking of partnership or other accounts; bankruptcy; patents, trademarks, registered designs, or copyright; and all causes and matters involving the exercise of the High Court's jurisdiction under the enactments relating to companies. Proceedings relating to patents and such other matters as may be prescribed are dealt with by the Patents Court.

Paragraph 2 provides for the assignment of certain proceedings to the Queen's Bench Division, including applications for writs of *habeas corpus* and applications for judicial review but, by virtue of the Rules, most matters not specifically assigned to the other Divisions will be dealt with in the Queen's Bench Division. The Queen's Bench Division also has jurisdiction in all causes which formerly came within the High Court's Admiralty jurisdiction and its jurisdiction as a prize court (ss.20 and 27) and in all matters entered on the commercial list, but these cases will be taken by the Admiralty Court or the Commercial Court, as the case may be (s.62(2) and (3)).

Paragraph 3 specifies the proceedings assigned to the Family Division. Included in those proceedings are all matrimonial causes and matters; proceedings relating to legitimacy, wardship, and most other matters relating to minors; and non-contentious or common form probate business.

21 Appellate jurisdiction

The appellate jurisdiction of the High Court is exercisable by divisional courts as follows–

(a) the Chancery Division hears appeals from the county court on bankruptcy and land registration matters;

(b) the Queen's Bench Division hears appeals from, inferior courts or tribunals, Government departments, and certain appeals from decisions of a judge of the Queen's Bench Division sitting in chambers.

(c) the Family Division hears appeals from the Crown Court, and from a magistrates' court on applications for variation of maintenance agreements, or the enforcement of maintenance orders, or other payments ordered under various enactments, including the Domestic Proceedings and Magistrates' Courts Act 1978 and the Children Act 1989. It also hears appeals from a magistrates' court in relation to the making of, or the refusal to make, adoption orders and orders under the Children Act 1989 Act, and certain appeals against the exercise of a magistrates' court's jurisdiction to punish for contempt of court in matrimonial proceedings.

22 Supervisory jurisdiction

In addition to its appellate jurisdiction, the Queen's Bench Division has a supervisory jurisdiction, which includes, by virtue of the Rules of the Supreme Court, proceedings for committal for contempt in certain cases, and proceedings directed by any Act of Parliament to be heard in the High Court and in which the court's decision is final.

23 Appeals from the High Court

An appeal from the High Court will generally be to the Court of Appeal, however a "leapfrog" appeal may be made direct to the Supreme Court where the judge is satisfied that there is a point of law of general public importance involved in the decision (Administration of Justice Act 1969, s.12)–

(a) which either (i) relates wholly or mainly to legislative construction, or (ii) as to which the judge is bound by a decision of the Court of Appeal or of Supreme Court in previous proceedings; or

(b) (i) the proceedings entail a decision relating to a matter of national importance or consideration of such a matter, (ii) the result of the proceedings is so significant (whether considered on its own or together with other proceedings or likely proceedings) that, in the opinion of the judge, a hearing by the Supreme Court is justified, or (iii) the judge is satisfied that the benefits of earlier consideration by the Supreme Court outweigh the benefits of consideration by the Court of Appeal.

No appeal may be made from the High Court to the Court of Appeal from a decision of the High Court exercising its appellate jurisdiction (i.e., there may be no second appeal) unless the Court of Appeal itself considers that the appeal would raise an important point of principle or practice, or there is some other compelling reason for the Court of Appeal to hear it (Access to Justice Act 1999, s.55).

24 The effect of an offer to settle

As to offers to settle, see the Note on **The County Court** at para **22 The effect of an offer to settle**.

H: THE COURT OF APPEAL

25 The Court of Appeal

The Court of Appeal consists of two divisions, a civil division and a criminal division.

Generally, the civil division has jurisdiction to hear appeals from any judgment or order of the High Court, except where leave is granted to appeal direct from the High Court to the Supreme Court (Senior Courts Act 1981, s.16). Under s.17, Applications for a new trial of a matter heard in the High Court are also heard by the Court of Appeal (s.17). The civil division also hears certain appeals from the county court as well as any matters in which jurisdiction is specifically given to it by statute (e.g., an appeal on a point of law from the Pensions Regulator Tribunal under the Pensions Act 2004, s.104).

No second appeal may be made to the Court of Appeal from an appeal heard by the county court or the High Court unless the Court of Appeal considers that the appeal would raise an important point of principle or practice or that there is some other compelling reason for it to hear the case (Access to Justice Act 1999, s.55).

The criminal division of the Court of Appeal has jurisdiction to entertain–

(a) under s.1 of the Criminal Appeal Act 1968 (as amended by the Criminal Appeal Act 1995, s.1), an appeal by a person convicted on indictment by the Crown Court against his conviction–
 (i) with the leave of the Court of Appeal; or
 (ii) if the judge of the court of trial grants a certificate that the case is fit for appeal.

(b) with the leave of the Court of Appeal, under s.9 of the 1968 Act, an appeal by a person who has been convicted of an offence on indictment against any sentence (not being a sentence fixed by law) passed on him for the offence, whether passed on his conviction or in subsequent proceedings, and for a summary offence for which he was convicted by the Crown Court;

(c) with the leave of the Court of Appeal, under s.10 of the 1968 Act, an appeal by a person against sentence where the offender has been convicted by a magistrates' court and–
 (i) is committed to the Crown Court for sentence;
 (ii) having been made the subject of a community rehabilitation or community punishment order (previously known as probation and community service orders), or an order for conditional

discharge or given a wholly or partly suspended sentence, appears before the Crown Court to be further dealt with for his offence; or

    (iii) having been released early after serving part of a sentence of imprisonment or detention is ordered by the Crown Court to be returned to prison or detention;

(d) under ss.12 and 16A of the 1968 Act (as amended by the 1995 Act, s.1 and the Domestic Violence, Crime and Victims Act 2004), an appeal by a person against a verdict of not guilty by reason of insanity, or against the making of a hospital or supervision order, in either case–

    (i) with the leave of the Court of Appeal; or

    (ii) if the judge of the court of trial grants a certificate that the case is fit for appeal.

(e) under s.15 of the 1968 Act (as amended by the 1995 Act, s.1), an appeal by a person against a finding that he is under a disability on the question of his fitness to be tried–

    (i) with the leave of the Court of Appeal; or

    (ii) if the judge of the court of trial grants a certificate that the case is fit for appeal.

(f) with the leave of the Court of Appeal, under Part IV of the Criminal Justice Act 1988, a reference from the Attorney General for the review of a sentence imposed on a person in respect of an offence–

    (i) triable only on indictment; or

    (ii) triable either way, and of a description specified by order,

where it appears to the Attorney General that the sentencing by the Crown Court has been unduly lenient. The Criminal Justice Act 1988 (Review of Sentencing) Order 2006 specifies certain serious fraud cases, people trafficking, slavery, sexual offences and other miscellaneous offences.

(g) under s.24 of the Serious Crime Act 2007, an appeal in relation to a serious crime prevention order–

    (i) with the leave of the Court of Appeal; or

    (ii) if the judge whose decision is being appealed grants a certificate that the case is fit for appeal.

26 Reference to the Court of Appeal by the Criminal Cases Review Commission

The Criminal Cases Review Commission may at any time refer to the Court of Appeal the conviction or sentence (not being a sentence fixed by law) of a person convicted on indictment (1995 Act, s.9). Any such reference will be treated as an appeal under s.1 (conviction) or s.9 (sentence) of the 1968 Act (see Paragraph 5 (a) and (b), above) as appropriate. The Commission may also refer a verdict or finding on a trial on indictment relating to a person suffering from a mental disorder, which will be treated as an appeal under s.12 or s.15 of the 1968 Act, as appropriate (see Paragraph 5 (d) and (e), above).

27 Broadcast of proceedings

The recording and broadcasting of hearings in the Court of Appeal is permitted provided that certain conditions are satisfied (Court of Appeal (Recording and Broadcasting) Order 2013). Recording and broadcast is only allowed of (Regs. 6, 8)–

(a) submissions of a legal representative;

(b) exchanges between a legal representative and the court; and

(c) the court giving judgment.

The Crime and Courts Act 2013 allows discretion for the judge in any case to prevent broadcasting to protect the interests of justice or prevent undue prejudice to anyone involved (s.32(3)). There is no appeal against a judge's exercise (or non-exercise) of this discretion (s.32(4)).

I: THE SUPREME COURT

28 The Supreme Court

The Constitutional Reform Act 2005 created a Supreme Court of the United Kingdom, essentially taking over the judicial role of the House of Lords and abolishing its appellate jurisdiction.

The Supreme Court considers English, Welsh, Scots and Northern Ireland law and is the Supreme Court of Appeal in the United Kingdom. Its practice and procedure is regulated by the Supreme Court Rules 2009.

29 Jurisdiction

Inter alia an appeal lies to the Supreme Court–

(a) from any order or judgment of the Court of Appeal in England, by leave of that court or the Supreme Court (Appellate Jurisdiction Act 1876, s.3(1)), subject to restrictions imposed by statute or by practice in respect of specific matters;

(b) in civil actions tried in the Inner House of the Court of Session in Scotland;

(c) subject to statutory restrictions, direct from a decision of the High Court in England (Administration of Justice Act 1969, ss.12 to 16).

In certain civil proceedings, an appeal may be brought direct to the Supreme Court from a decision of the High Court if the trial judge grants a certificate for this purpose and if leave is granted by the Supreme Court. Before granting a certificate, the judge must be satisfied that a point of law of general public importance is involved and that it either relates to the construction of an enactment or of a statutory instrument, or is one in respect of which he was bound by a previous decision of the Court of Appeal or the Supreme Court; that a sufficient case has been made out to bring such an appeal; and that all the parties to the proceedings consent to the grant of the certificate (1969 Act, ss.12 and 13).

The judge may grant a certificate only in cases where in the usual way an appeal would lie from his decision to the Court of Appeal and then to the Supreme Court. No certificate may be granted when the decision of the judge, or any order made by him in pursuance of the decision, is made in the exercise of jurisdiction to punish for contempt of court (1969 Act, s.15).

30 Criminal appeals

An appeal lies, with the leave of the Supreme Court, at the instance of the defendant or prosecutor, *inter alia*–
   (i) from any decision of the Court of Appeal on an appeal to that court only with the leave of the Court of Appeal or the Supreme Court (Criminal Appeal Act 1968, s.33);
   (ii) from any decision of the High Court in a criminal cause or matter (Administration of Justice Act 1960, s.1 (as amended by the Access to Justice Act 1999, s.63)).

Leave will not be granted unless it is certified by the Court of Appeal or the High Court that a point of law of general public importance is involved in the decision and it appears to that court or to the Supreme Court (as the case may be) that the point is one which ought to be considered by the Supreme Court (1960 Act, s.1 and 1968 Act, s.33).

31 General

In England and Wales, an appeal lies to the Supreme Court only with the permission of the Court of Appeal or the Supreme Court (2005 Act, s.40(6)).

In Scotland, an appeal may be taken to the Supreme Court only with the permission of the Inner House of the Court of Session or, if the Inner House has refused permission, with the permission of the Supreme Court and the decision to be appealed (Court of Session Act 1988, s.40)–
   (a) constitutes final judgment in any proceedings;
   (b) is a decision in an exchequer cause;
   (c) is a decision on an application to grant or refuse a new trial in any proceedings; or
   (d) is any other decision in any proceedings if (i)there is a difference of opinion among the judges making the decision, or (ii)the decision is one sustaining a preliminary defence and dismissing the proceedings.

Cases not within (a) to (d) are appealable to the Supreme Court only with the permission of the Inner House.

The Supreme Court has power to determine any question necessary to be determined for the purposes of doing justice in an appeal to it under any enactment (2005 Act, s.40(5)).

The rules governing the practice and procedure to be followed in the Supreme Court are contained in the Supreme Court Rules 2009 (the 2009 Rules). This includes the rules governing applications for permission to appeal and the documents that are to be filed when making such applications. An application for permission to appeal must first be made to the court from which an appeal is made, and an application may be made to the Supreme Court only after the court from which an appeal is made has refused to grant permission to appeal (2009 Rules, r.10(2)). An admissible application for permission to appeal will be considered on paper without a hearing by a panel of Justices. The panel may direct an oral hearing (2009 Rules, r.16).

J: COMMON PROVISIONS

32 Closed material procedures

The Justice and Security Act 2013 makes provision for "closed material procedures" to be adopted in civil proceedings to allow relevant national security-sensitive material to be relied upon in those proceedings without its being disclosed in a way which would be damaging to national security (s.6). Where such procedures are adopted, the sensitive material is disclosed to the court and a special advocate representing the interests of the other party, but not directly to the other party (s.9). Closed material procedures may be adopted in civil cases before the High Court, Court of Appeal, Court of Session and the Supreme Court.

Part 82 of the Civil Procedure Rules 1998 make provision in this regard.

The court may make a declaration that the proceedings are proceedings in which a "closed material application" may be made either of its own motion or on application by one of the parties. The court may make such a declaration if it considers that–
   (a) a party to the proceedings would be required to disclose material in the course of the proceedings to another person (whether or not another party to the proceedings);
   (b) that such a disclosure would be damaging to the interests of national security; and
   (c) that a declaration would be in the interests of the fair and effective administration of justice.

The effect of a declaration is not that the proceedings as a whole are closed, but that closed material procedure may be used where necessary in the proceedings, but with those parts of the proceedings where sensitive material is not in issue being conducted in "open" procedure as normal.

If permission is given for material to be disclosed in closed session, the court must consider whether a summary should be provided in open session (s.8 and Rule 82.14). The court must ensure that any such summary would not itself be damaging to the interests of national security.

Nothing in these provisions is to be read as requiring a court to act in a manner inconsistent with Article 6 of the Human Rights Convention (the Right to a Fair Trial: see the Note on **The Human Rights Act 1998**), and if that right requires that a damaging summary must be provided, the party seeking to disclose the material in closed session will have the option of either declining to provide the damaging summary and instead being unable to rely on the material, or having to make concessions in the proceedings.

33 Third party costs orders

The Lord Chancellor may by regulations make provision for a magistrates' court, the Crown Court and the Court of Appeal to have the power to make a third party costs order, i.e., an order as to the payment of the costs incurred by a party to criminal proceedings by a person who is not a party (Prosecution of Offences Act 1985, s.19B). Before doing so, the court must be satisfied that there has been serious misconduct (whether or not amounting to contempt) by the third party and that as a consequence it is appropriate to make the order.

34 Witness anonymity orders

A a magistrates' court, the Crown Court or the criminal division of the Court of Appeal may make a witness anonymity order authorising measures to be taken to ensure that the identity of a witness is not disclosed in or in connection with court proceedings (Coroners and Justice Act 2009, s.86). This may mean that—
  (a) the witness's name and other identifying details may be withheld, or removed from materials disclosed to any party to the proceedings;
  (b) the witness may use a pseudonym;
  (c) the witness is not asked questions of any specified description that might lead to their identification;
  (d) the witness is screened to any specified extent;
  (e) the witness's voice is subjected to modulation to any specified extent.
An order may only be made where the court is satisfied that (s.88)—
  (f) the measures are necessary in order to protect the safety of the witness or another person or to prevent any serious damage to property, or in order to prevent real harm to the public interest;
  (g) having regard to all the circumstances, the taking of the measures would be consistent with the defendant receiving a fair trial; and
  (h) it is necessary to make the order in the interests of justice by reason of the fact that it appears to the court that it is important that the witness should testify, and the witness would not testify if the order were not made or there would be real harm to the public interest if the witness were to testify without the proposed order being made.
There are a number of matters which the court must consider before making an order (s.89) and the jury must be given a warning to the effect that the fact that an order has been made does not prejudice the defendant (s.90).

35 Register of judgments, orders and fines

The Register of Judgments Orders and Fines Regulations 2005 provide for the keeping of a register of—
  (a) High court judgments;
  (b) County court judgments;
  (c) administration orders made under s the County Courts Act 1984, s.112; and
  (d) unpaid magistrates' court fines.
A fine is entered in the register if, and only if, the court fines officer notifies the keeper of the register that it should be included. He will do this if the fine is unpaid and further steps for its recovery are being taken. An entry in the register can be cancelled if it is paid in full within one month of registration. If the fine is paid after that date, the entry in the register remains, but a note will be added recording that that it has been paid and the date of payment. All entries relating to fines are removed after five years; other entries are removed after six years.
The regulations exempt from being registered (Reg. 9)—
  (i) judgments in family proceedings;
  (ii) judgments made by the Administrative or Technology and Construction courts;
  (iii) judgments subject to appeal;
  (iv) judgments (other than a liability order under the Child Support Act 1991) where the hearing was contested, until such time as the creditor takes steps to enforce it;
  (v) an order for the payment of money arising from an action for the recovery of land, until such time as the creditor takes steps to enforce it;
  (vi) a County Court order for recovery of a parking fine or increased penalty charge; and
  (vii) a tribunal decision until such time as a copy of the decision is filed with the High Court or County Court (as appropriate).
The Register can be searched upon payment of a fee (Reg. 27). A registered debtor can apply, in writing and

upon payment of a fee of £15, for a "certification of satisfaction" that a debt has been paid (Reg. 17 and the Civil Proceedings Fees Order 2008).

36 Authorities

Statutes–

Access to Justice Act 1999

Administration of Justice Acts 1960, 1969, and 1985

Children Act 1989

Children and Young Persons Act 1933

Civil Procedure Act 1997

Constitutional Reform Act 2005

Coroners and Justice Act 2009

County Courts Acts 1984

Court of Session Act 1988

Courts Act 2003

Courts and Legal Services Act 1990

Crime and Courts Act 2013

Crime and Disorder Act 1998

Criminal Appeal Acts 1968 and 1995

Criminal Justice Acts 1988 and 1991

Criminal Justice (Amendment) Act 1981

Insolvency Act 1985

Justice and Security Act 2013

Magistrates' Courts Act 1980

Senior Courts Act 1981

Youth Justice and Criminal Evidence Act 1999

Statutory Instruments–

Civil Procedure Rules 1998, as amended (S.I. 1998 No. 3132, 1999 No. 1008, 2000 Nos. 221, 940, 1317, and 2092, 2001 Nos. 1388, 1769, and 2792, 2004 Nos. 1306, 3129 and 3419, 2005 Nos. 352, 656, 2292 and 2515, 2006 Nos. 1689, 3232 and 3435, 2007 Nos. 2204 and 3543, 2008 Nos. 2178, 3085 and 3327, 2009 Nos. 2092 and 3390, 2010 Nos. 621, 1953, 2577 and 3038, 2011 Nos. 88, 1045, 1979, 2970, and 3103, 2012 Nos. 505 and 2208, 2013 Nos. 262, 515, 789, 1412, 1571, 1695, 1974, and 3112, 2014 Nos. 407, 482, 610, 867, 879, 1233, 2044, 2948, and 3299, 2015 Nos. 406, 670, 877, 1569, and 1881, and 2016 No. 234)

Civil Proceedings Fees Order 2008, as amended (S.I. 2008 Nos. 1053 and 2853, 2009 No. 1498, 2011 No. 586, 2013 Nos. 534, 591, 734, 1410, and 2302, 2014 Nos. 513, 590, 874, 1834, and 2059, and 2015 No. 576)

County Court Jurisdiction Order 2014 (S.I. 2014 No. 503)

Court of Appeal (Recording and Broadcasting) Order 2013 (S.I. 2013 No. 2786)

Criminal Justice Act 1988 (Review of Sentencing) Order 2006, as amended (S.I. 2006 No. 1116, 2012 No. 1833, 2013 No. 862, 2014 No. 1651, and 2015 No. 800)

Crown Court (Special Measures Directions and Directions Prohibiting Cross-examination) Rules 2002, as amended (S.I. 2002 No. 1688 and 2004 No. 185)

Family Court (Composition and Distribution of Business) Rules 2014, as amended (S.I. 2014 Nos. 840 and 3297, and 2015 No. 1421)

High Court and County Courts Jurisdiction Order 1991, as amended (S.I. 1991 No. 724, 1993 No. 1407, 1995 No. 205, 1996 No. 3141, 1999 No. 1014, 2001 Nos. 1387 and 2685, 2005 No. 587, 2008 No. 2934, 2009 No. 577, 2014 Nos. 821 and 2947, and 2015 No. 1641)

Magistrates' Courts (Children and Young Persons) Rules 1992, as amended (S.I. 1992 No. 2071, 1997 No. 2420, 1998 No. 2167, 1999 No. 1343, and 2014 No. 879)

Magistrates' Courts (Special Measures Directions) Rules 2002, as amended (S.I. 2002 No. 1687 and 2004 No. 184)

Offers to Settle in Civil Proceedings Order 2013 (S.I. 2013 No. 93)

Register of Judgments, Orders and Fines Regulations 2005, as amended (S.I. 2005 No. 3595 and 2009 No. 474)

Supreme Court Rules 2009 (S.I. 2009, No. 1603)

THE SCOTTISH COURT SYSTEM

A: JUSTICE OF THE PEACE COURTS

1 Introduction

Justice of the peace courts (or "JP courts") may be established by the Scottish Ministers under the Criminal Proceedings etc. (Reform) (Scotland) Act 2007 by reference to a particular sheriff court district (s.59).

2 Area and constitution

There is a presumption that there will be at least one JP court established for each sheriff court district, except where the Scottish Ministers determine that a JP court is not necessary. In deciding whether a JP court is necessary, the Scottish Ministers must take account of the amount of summary criminal business and the capacity of other JP or sheriff courts in the sheriffdom (Criminal Proceedings etc. (Reform) (Scotland) Act 2007, s.59).

3 Jurisdiction and powers

The responsibility for the efficient administration of JP courts is the sheriff principal for the sherrifdom in which they are situated (Criminal Proceedings etc. (Reform) (Scotland) Act 2007, s.61).

A JP court may try offences committed within the sheriff court district in which it is located, or in any other sheriff court district within the sheriffdom. This is similar to the territorial jurisdiction of the sheriff court (s.62).

The jurisdiction and powers of a JP court are exercisable by a stipendiary magistrate or by one or more justices. Any objection to the constitution of the court must be taken no later than the time the proceedings or the alleged irregularity began (Criminal Procedure (Scotland) Act 1995, s.6(2), as amended by the 2007 Act, Sch. para. 9). The Scottish Ministers may by order amend s.6(2) so that it provides that a JP court (when not constituted by a stipendiary magistrate) is to be constituted by one JP only (2007 Act, s.63(2)).

Except in so far as any enactment otherwise provides, it is competent for a JP court to—
(a) try any common law or statutory offence which is triable summarily;
(b) make such orders and grant such warrants as are appropriate to a court of summary jurisdiction;
(c) do anything else (by way of procedure or otherwise) as is appropriate to such a court.
It is competent for any of the following offences to be tried in a JP court—
(a) theft or reset of theft;
(b) falsehood, fraud or wilful imposition;
(c) breach of trust or embezzlement,
where (in any such case) the amount concerned does not exceed level 4 on the standard scale [currently £2,500] (1995 Act s.7(3), (4), as so amended).

When a JP court is constituted by a stipendiary magistrate, it has, under s.7(5) (as so amended), the summary criminal jurisdiction and powers of a sheriff (see below).

Under s.7(8) (as so amended), a JP court does not have jurisdiction to try or pronounce sentence in the case of any person who is brought before it charged within certain serious offences specified in s.7(8)(b).

Without prejudice to any other or wider powers conferred by statute, a JP court may—
(i) impose imprisonment for any period not exceeding 60 days;
(ii) impose a fine not exceeding level 4 on the standard scale [currently £2,500];
(iii) ordain the accused to find caution for good behaviour for up to six months and to any amount not exceeding level 4 on the standard scale [currently £2,500]; and
(iv) impose imprisonment for failure to pay such fine or to find such caution.
In no case, however, may the total period of imprisonment imposed by a JP court under its powers to punish common law offences exceed 60 days (s.7(6)). A stipendiary magistrates in a JP court may—
(v) impose fines of up to £10,000 and imprisonment of up to 1 year.

4 Clerk of the court

Each JP court has a clerk of the court (Criminal Proceedings etc. (Reform) (Scotland) Act 2007, s.63(3)), who must be a solicitor or advocate (s.63(4)). The clerk provides legal advice to the court. Clerks of court and other staff are appointed and employed by the Scottish Ministers (in practice they will be employees of the Scottish Courts Service).

5 Drugs courts

The Scottish Ministers may prescribe a JP court as a drugs court (Criminal Justice (Scotland) Act 2003, s.42, as amended by the Criminal Proceedings etc. (Reform) (Scotland) Act 2007, Sch. para. 30). A drugs court is one which is especially appropriate to deal with cases involving people dependent on, or with a propensity to misuse, drugs. Where a court is designated as a drugs court it has additional sentencing powers in relation to breach of drug treatment and testing orders.

B: SHERIFF AND SHERIFF APPEAL COURTS

6 Introduction

The sheriff court in Scotland has both a civil and a criminal jurisdiction. It deals with the overwhelming majority of civil cases and almost all criminal cases that are not disposed of in the district courts. The country is divided into six sheriffdoms, each of which has a sheriff principal and a number of sheriffs appointed from amongst qualified lawyers. The Scottish Ministers, who are under a duty to secure the efficient organisation and administration of the sheriff courts, may, by order, alter the boundaries of sheriffdoms, form new sheriffdoms, or abolish any existing sheriffdom (Courts Reform (Scotland) Act 2014, s.2). Each sheriffdom is divided into districts the area of which may be determined by the Scottish Ministers (s.1).

7 Civil jurisdiction

The sheriff court has a wide civil jurisdiction (extending to all actions of debt or damages without any upper pecuniary limit). S.39 of the Courts Reform (Scotland) Act 2014 provides that all causes not exceeding £100,000 in value, competent in the sheriff court, are to be brought in that court only. There is however an exception for family proceedings unless the only order sought in the proceedings is an order for payment of aliment (s.39(3)).

On the application of any of the parties to the proceedings, the sheriff may, at any stage, request the Court of Session to allow the proceedings to be remitted to that Court if the sheriff considers that the importance or difficulty of the proceedings makes it appropriate to do so (s.92(4)).

Actions of a kind specified in s.72(3) of the 2014 Act where the amount in dispute does not exceed £5,000 are subject to the form of process known as "simple procedure". Aliment claims which do not exceed £100 per week in respect of a child under the age of 18 years, or £200 per week in any other case, may also use the simple procedure (s.74). The Scottish Ministers may be order provide that no award of expenses may be made in prescribed types of simple procedure claim (s.81).

The Small Claims (Scotland) Order 1988 provides that no award of expenses may be made in such a small claim as is specified above where the value of the claim does not exceed £200 and that in the case of any other small claim the sheriff may award expenses not exceeding £150 where the value of the claim is £1,500 or less or not exceeding 10% of the claim where the value of the claim exceeds £1,500.

In most cases tried by a sheriff, an appeal lies to the sheriff appeal court and thereafter to the Court of Session. An appeal lies in cases tried by the sheriff appeal court directly to the Court of Session.

The sheriff court also has an administrative function in respect of adoption, bankruptcy, and inventories of estates.

The Scottish Ministers may by order provide for certain types of civil proceedings in the sheriff court to be tried by jury (s.63).

In relation to civil proceedings in the sheriff court, the Scottish Civil Justice Council has been established by the Scottish Civil Justice Council and Criminal Legal Assistance Act 2013. The Council's functions are to keep the civil justice system under review and to review the practice and procedure followed in proceedings in the Court of Session and in civil proceedings in the sheriff court.

8 Criminal jurisdiction

The criminal jurisdiction of the sheriff court consists of a solemn and a summary jurisdiction. In the case of the solemn procedure (cases prosecuted on indictment), the sheriff sits with a jury of 15 and, in the case of summary proceedings (cases prosecuted on complaint), the sheriff sits alone. The sheriff has power to remit the accused to the High Court of Justiciary for sentencing where the accused (Criminal Procedure (Scotland) Act 1995, s.195(1) and (2))—

(i) has been convicted on indictment and the sheriff holds that any sentence he may give is inadequate and that the question of punishment should be disposed of by the High Court; and

(ii) has been convicted on indictment of an offence punishable by imprisonment for a term exceeding five years, but the sheriff's power to impose a sentence of imprisonment for a term exceeding five years is restricted by statute.

Where under any enactment an offence is punishable on conviction on indictment by imprisonment for a term exceeding two years (enactments passed or made before 1st January 1988) or three years (enactments passed or made on or after that date) but the enactment restricts the power of the sheriff to impose such a sentence, the sheriff may impose a sentence of imprisonment for a term exceeding two (or three, as the case may be) but not exceeding five years, provided that the sentence does not exceed the maximum sentence which may be imposed on conviction of the offence (s.3(4), (4A) and (5)).

In summary proceedings, the sheriff, without prejudice to any other or wider powers conferred by statute, has power on convicting any person of a common law offence *inter alia* to impose imprisonment for a period not exceeding twelve months and to impose a fine not exceeding £5,000 or such sum as may be prescribed (s.5(2)).

Appeals from the sheriff are by way of stated case to the sheriff appeal court in summary proceedings (s.175), and to the High Court in its capacity as Court of Criminal Appeal in solemn proceedings (s.106). In the latter case, a person may appeal, with leave of a judge of the High Court, against his conviction or sentence (except any sentence fixed by law).

9 The Sheriff Appeal Court

The Sheriff Appeal Court deals with all civil appeals from the sheriff court, and all summary criminal appeals by an accused on conviction or sentence; appeals by the Crown on acquittal or sentence; and bail appeals.

The Sheriff Appeal Court has the power to remit or transfer a particularly important or complex appeal to the Inner House (civil matters) or the High Court (criminal matters) (Courts Reform (Scotland) Act 2014, s.113; Criminal Procedure (Scotland) Act 1995, s.194ZB).

An onward appeal to either the Inner House or High Court requires their permission, and in the case of the High Court will only be granted where there are clearly arguable grounds of appeal, on a point of law.

10 The Sheriff Personal Injury Court

The Edinburgh Sheriff Court has been designated as the Sheriff Personal Injury Court and exercises an all-Scotland jurisdiction in personal injuries cases above £5,000 (the sum below which proceedings are subject to simple procedure) and also in cases below £5,000 for specific cases designated by Order. The All-Scotland Sheriff Court (Sheriff Personal Injury Court) Order 2015 designates for this purpose workplace related personal injury cases–
  (a) above £1,000; and
  (b) below £1,000 if a local sheriff considers that they are of sufficient importance or difficulty.

11 Drugs courts

The Scottish Ministers may prescribe a sheriff court as a drugs court (Criminal Justice (Scotland) Act 2003, s.42). A drugs court is one which is especially appropriate to deal with cases involving people dependent on, or with a propensity to misuse, drugs. Where a sheriff court is designated as a drugs court it has additional sentencing powers in relation to breach of drug treatment and testing orders.

12 European order for payment

EC Regulation 1896/2006 allow creditors to recover uncontested cross-border debts using standard forms submitted to their own national courts. The procedure can only be used for monetary claims and there is no limit on the amount for which a claim may be issued.

The procedure for dealing with a case is laid down in the EC Regulation, as supplemented by Part 78 of the Civil Procedure Rules 1998. There is a standard form which must be completed in English. If the claim is accepted by the court, and not contested by the defendant within 30 days, it becomes automatically enforceable in every EU Member State (except Denmark). If the defendant challenges the amount due, the claimant may either drop the case or else proceed using normal procedures.

An application in Scotland for a European order for payment must be made to the sheriff court (European Communities (European Order for Payment) (Scotland) Regulations 2009).

C: SUPERIOR AND APPEAL COURTS

13 The Court of Session and the High Court of Judiciary

The Supreme Court in Scotland is known as the College of Justice. It is divided into a civil branch, known as the Court of Session, and a criminal branch, known as the High Court of Justiciary; the same judges serve in both.

The Court of Session is itself subdivided into the Inner House, presided over by the Lord President of the Court of Session, and the Outer House, composed of judges of the Court sitting singly (Lords Ordinary) and is a court of first instance. An interlocutor of the Lord Ordinary may be reviewed by the Inner House in accordance with the Act. An appeal lies from the Inner House to the Supreme Court.

If the Lord President is incapacitated, or the office is vacant, his functions may be carried out by the Lord Justice Clerk (who is the next senior judge). If the Lord Justice Clerk is incapacitated, or the office is vacant, his functions may be carried out by a senior judge of the Inner House (Senior Judiciary (Vacancies and Incapacity) (Scotland) Act 2006, ss.1 and 2).

The Court of Session comprises the Lord President, the Lord Justice Clerk and 32 other judges. The two senior judges plus ten of the other judges form the Inner House. In relation to civil proceedings in the Court of Session, the Scottish Civil Justice Council has been established by the Scottish Civil Justice Council and Criminal Legal Assistance Act 2013. The Council's functions are to–
  (a) keep the civil justice system under review;
  (b) review the practice and procedure followed in proceedings in the Court of Session (and in civil proceedings in the sheriff court;
  (c) prepare and submit to the Court of Session draft civil procedure rules;
  (d) provide advice and make recommendations to the Lord President on the development of, and changes to, the civil justice system; and
  (e) provide such advice on any matter relating to the civil justice system as may be requested by the Lord President.

The High Court of Justiciary is a criminal court of first instance in cases which lie outside the jurisdiction of the sheriff court and in certain other cases involving serious offences. For this purpose, the High Court goes on circuit as well as sitting in Edinburgh. Cases are always heard with a jury of 15 laymen, who may reach a decision by a simple majority. Appeals from the sheriff court lie to the High Court of Justiciary sitting as the Court of Criminal Appeal. There is no right of appeal to the Supreme Court in Scottish criminal cases. As to the special measures which may be taken in relation to vulnerable witnesses in the High Court, see **16 Special measures for vulnerable witnesses**, below.

14 Scottish Criminal Cases Review Commission

S.25 of the Crime and Punishment (Scotland) Act 1997 inserts a new Part (Part XA) into the Criminal Procedure (Scotland) Act 1995, so as to provide for the establishment of a Scottish Criminal Cases Review Commission. The function of the Commission is to consider alleged miscarriages of justice and to refer cases to the High Court of Judiciary. The Commission consists of at least three members, at least a third of whom must be legally qualified and at least two-thirds of whom must have knowledge and experience of the investigation of offences and the treatment of offenders (s.194A). Initially, the Commission could only consider convictions on indictment, but the Scottish Criminal Cases Review Commission (Application to Summary Proceedings) Order 1999 extended the Commission's remit from 1st April 1999 to include convictions, sentences and findings in summary proceedings.

A case may be referred to the Commission at any time, whether or not an appeal against conviction or sentence has previously been heard or determined by the High Court. A reference may be made even if the person convicted has since died (s.194B). The Commission will refer a case on to the High Court if they believe that a miscarriage of justice may have occurred and that it is in the interests of justice that reference should be made (s.194C). The appeal arising from a reference can only be based on a ground relating to one or more of the reasons given by the Commission for the reference unless the High Court has, where it considers it is in the interests of justice to do so, given leave for the appellant to found the appeal on additional grounds (s.194D).

15 Closed material procedures

The Justice and Security Act 2013 makes provision for "closed material procedures" to be adopted in civil proceedings to allow relevant national security-sensitive material to be relied upon in those proceedings without its being disclosed in a way which would be damaging to national security (s.6). Where such procedures are adopted, the sensitive material is disclosed to the court and a special advocate representing the interests of the other party, but not directly to the other party (s.9). Closed material procedures may be adopted in civil cases before the High Court, Court of Appeal, Court of Session and the Supreme Court.

Part 82 of the Civil Procedure Rules 1998 make provision in this regard.

The court may make a declaration that the proceedings are proceedings in which a "closed material application" may be made either of its own motion or on application by one of the parties. The court may make such a declaration if it considers that—

(a) a party to the proceedings would be required to disclose material in the course of the proceedings to another person (whether or not another party to the proceedings);

(b) that such a disclosure would be damaging to the interests of national security; and

(c) that a declaration would be in the interests of the fair and effective administration of justice.

The effect of a declaration is not that the proceedings as a whole are closed, but that closed material procedure may be used where necessary in the proceedings, but with those parts of the proceedings where sensitive material is not in issue being conducted in "open" procedure as normal.

If permission is given for material to be disclosed in closed session, the court must consider whether a summary should be provided in open session (s.8 and Rule 82.14). The court must ensure that any such summary would not itself be damaging to the interests of national security.

Nothing in these provisions is to be read as requiring a court to act in a manner inconsistent with Article 6 of the Human Rights Convention (the Right to a Fair Trial: see the Note on **The Human Rights Act 1998**), and if that right requires that a damaging summary must be provided, the party seeking to disclose the material in closed session will have the option of either declining to provide the damaging summary and instead being unable to rely on the material, or having to make concessions in the proceedings.

D: COMMON PROVISIONS

16 Special measures for vulnerable witnesses

Special measures may be taken for the hearing of evidence to be given by vulnerable witnesses in any hearing in the course of criminal proceedings in the High Court, a Sheriff court, or a Justice of the Peace court. These measures apply in relation to witnesses who are (Criminal Procedure (Scotland) Act 1995, s.271(1))—

(1) children under the age of 18;

(2) adult witnesses whose quality of evidence is at significant risk of being diminished either as a result of a mental disorder or due to fear or distress in connection with giving evidence;

(3) victims of alleged sexual offences, human trafficking, or an offence the commission of which involves domestic abuse or stalking, and who are giving evidence in proceedings which relate to that particular offence; and

(4) witnesses who are considered by the court to be at significant risk of harm by reason of them giving evidence.

In relation to (2) and (4) various factors will be taken into account including the nature and circumstances of the alleged offence; the nature of the evidence which the witness is likely to give; the relationship (if any) between the witness and the accused; the witness's age and maturity; any behaviour towards the witness on the part of the accused, his family or associates, or others likely to be accused; and such other matters as appear to the court to be relevant (e.g., social and cultural background, ethnic origins, sexual orientation, domestic and employment circumstances, religious beliefs or political opinions, or physical disability or other physical impairment) (s.271(2)). In determining whether a person is a vulnerable witness the court must have regard to the best interests of the witness, and take account of any views expressed by them (s.271(4A)).

Vulnerable witnesses are entitled to give their evidence with the aid of at least one special measure (Criminal Procedure (Scotland) Act 1995, ss.271A, 271C). The special measures are (s.271H)–

(a) the taking of evidence by a court-appointed commissioner;

(b) the giving of evidence via a live television link;

(c) the use of a screen to conceal the accused from the witness;

(d) the use of a supporter to be present alongside the witness during the giving of evidence;

(e) giving evidence in chief in the form of a prior statement;

(ea) excluding the public during the taking of the evidence; and

(f) such other measures as the Scottish Ministers may prescribe.

Note.–These provisions were extended to justice of the peace courts in December 2015 by the Justice of the Peace Courts (Special Measures) (Scotland) Order 2015 (S.S.I. No. 447).

17 Witness anonymity orders

Courts have an order-making power to secure anonymity for witnesses when giving evidence but may not make a witness anonymity order which prevents the judge or jury either from seeing the witness or from hearing the witness's natural voice. The judge and jury must always be able to see and hear the witness. (Criminal Procedure (Scotland) Act 1995, ss.271N-271Z).

An order may only be made if–

(a) it is necessary in order to protect the safety of the witness or another person or to prevent any serious damage to property, or to prevent real harm to the public interest (whether affecting the carrying on of any activities in the public interest or the safety of a person involved in carrying on such activities or otherwise);

(b) having regard to all the circumstances, the effect of the proposed order would be consistent with the accused receiving a fair trial;

(c) the importance of the witness's testimony is such that in the interests of justice the witness ought to testify; and

(d) the witness would not testify if the proposed order were not made, or there would be real harm to the public interest if the witness were to testify without the proposed order being made.

In deciding whether the above conditions are met, the court must consider–

(e) the general right of an accused in criminal proceedings to know the identity of a witness in the proceedings;

(f) the extent to which the credibility of the witness concerned would be a relevant factor when the witness's evidence comes to be assessed;

(g) whether evidence given by the witness might be material in implicating the accused;

(h) whether the witness's evidence could be properly tested (whether on grounds of credibility or otherwise) without their identity being disclosed;

(i) whether there is any reason to believe that the witness (i) has a tendency to be dishonest, or (ii)has any motive to be dishonest in the circumstances of the case, having regard in particular to any previous convictions of the witness and to any relationship between the witness and the accused or any associates of the accused;

(j) whether it would be reasonably practicable to protect the witness's identity by any means other than by making a witness anonymity order specifying the measures that are under consideration by the court.

18 Authorities

Statutes–

Court of Session Act 1988

Courts Reform (Scotland) Act 2014

Crime and Punishment (Scotland) Act 1997

Criminal Justice (Scotland) Act 2003

Criminal Procedure (Scotland) Act 1995

Criminal Proceedings etc. (Reform) (Scotland) Act 2007

Scottish Civil Justice Council and Criminal Legal Assistance Act 2013

Statutory Instruments–

All-Scotland Sheriff Court (Sheriff Personal Injury Court) Order 2015 (S.S.I. 2015 No. 213)

European Communities (European Order for Payment) (Scotland) Regulations 2009 (S.S.I. 2009 No. 99)

Scottish Criminal Cases Review Commission (Application to Summary Proceedings) Order 1999 (S.I. 1999 No. 1181)

Senior Judiciary (Vacancies and Incapacity) (Scotland) Act 2006

Small Claims (Scotland) Order 1988, as amended (S.I. 1988 No. 1999 and S.S.I. 2007 No. 496)

TREATMENT OF OFFENDERS: CHILDREN AND YOUNG PERSONS: ENGLAND AND WALES

1 Introduction

This Note is concerned with the provisions of the above Acts and Orders which relate to the treatment of children and young persons who commit offences. Except where otherwise specified, a child is a person under the age of 14 and a young person is a person who has attained the age of 14 but is under the age of 18.

This Note is structured as follows—
A: Arrest and prosecution
B: Youth cautions and conditional cautions
C: Youth rehabilitation orders
D: Remand, etc.
E: Punishment of children: first time offenders
F: Punishment of children: repeat offenders
G: Parenting orders and contracts
H: Child safety orders

A: ARREST AND PROSECUTION

2 Age of criminal responsibility

By virtue of s.50 of the Children and Young Persons Act 1933, it is conclusively presumed that no child under the age of 10 years can be guilty of any offence. The previously rebuttable presumption that a child aged 10 or over but under 14 was incapable of committing an offence has been abolished (Crime and Disorder Act 1998, s.34).

3 Arrest and detention

The Police and Criminal Evidence Act 1984 contains provisions which govern the law relating to the treatment of suspects (see the Note on **Treatment of Suspects**).

Where a child or young person is in police detention, or has been detained under the terrorism provisions (as defined), all practicable steps must be taken to ascertain the identity of a person responsible for his welfare, i.e., his parent or guardian or any other person who has for the time being assumed such responsibility (which will include, if the child is in care, the local authority concerned). That person must then be informed as soon as practicable—
(a) that the child or young person has been arrested,
(b) why he has been arrested, and
(c) where he is being detained.

Where the child or young person is subject to a supervision order made under Part IV of the Children Act 1989, or a youth rehabilitation order made under s.1 of the Criminal Justice and Immigration Act 2008 the supervisor or responsible officer as the case may be must also be informed as above (Children and Young Persons Act 1933, s.34(2) to (11), as substituted by the 1984 Act, s.57, and as amended by the 1989 Act, Sch. 13 and the Criminal Justice and Immigration Act 2008, Sch. 4 para. 2). If it appears that at the time of his arrest the child or young person is being provided with accommodation by or on behalf of a local authority under s.20 of the 1989 Act, the local authority must also be informed as above, as soon as it is reasonably practicable to do so (s.34(7A), added by the 1989 Act). For the purposes of s.34, a young person is a person who has attained the age of 14 but is under the age of 17 (1933 Act, s.31(2), as amended by the Criminal Justice Act 1991 (the 1991 Act), Sch. 8).

All the above rights conferred on a child or young person by s.34 of the 1933 Act are in addition to his rights under s.56 of the 1984 Act (see the Note on **Treatment of Suspects**).

4 Separation from other accused persons

Arrangements must be made for preventing a child or young person, whilst waiting in a police station or on being conveyed from a criminal court, from associating with an adult (not being a relative) who is charged with any offence other than an offence with which a child or young person is jointly charged, and for ensuring that a female child or young person, whilst so detained or being conveyed or waiting, is under the care of a woman (Children and Young Persons Act 1933, s.31). For the purposes of s.31, a young person is a person who has attained the age of 14 but is under the age of 17 (1933 Act, s.31(2), as amended by the 1991 Act, Sch. 8).

5 Summary trial of young persons

S.24 of the Magistrates' Courts Act 1980 prohibits the trial by jury of a young person accused of an indictable offence, other than homicide, and requires that he be tried summarily, except when charged with certain grave crimes (see **38 Restriction on imposing imprisonment on young offenders**, below) or jointly charged with a person over the age of 18. In cases where the young person is being tried with another person over the age of 18, the court may also commit him for trial for any other indictable offence with which he is charged at the same time (whether jointly with the person who has attained that age or not), provided that the offence arose out of the same circumstances as gave rise to the first-mentioned offence or circumstances connected therewith.

In the local justice areas of Bath and Wansdyke, Berkshire, Bristol, Liverpool and Knowsley, North Avon, North Hampshire, North Somerset, Ormskirk, Sefton, St Helens, Wigan and Leigh, and Wirral the provisions in the 1980 Act by which children and young persons are ordinarily tried summarily for an offence which is triable on indictment are modified and provisions are also introduced by which children and young persons may indicate intention as to plea in certain cases (Criminal Justice Act 2003, Sch. 3, paras. 9, 10).

6 Time limits

The Secretary of State may (Prosecution of Offences Act 1985, s.22A, as inserted by the Crime and Disorder Act 1998, s.44), by regulation, make provision as to the maximum time to be allowed–
  (a) for the completion of the stage beginning with the arrest of a person under the age of 18 and ending with the date fixed for his first appearance in court; and
  (b) between conviction and sentencing of a person aged under 18 at the time of his arrest (or the laying of the information charging him).

A magistrates' court may extend the time limit in (a) above, at any time before its expiry, if it is satisfied that there is a good and sufficient cause and that the investigation has been conducted, and (where applicable) the prosecution has acted, with all due diligence and expedition (s.22A(3)).

Where the time limit expires before a person is charged, he may not be charged with the offence unless further evidence relating to it is obtained and if he is under arrest he must be released or if he is on bail it must be discharged (s.22A(4)). Where the time limit expires after a person has been charged but before the time fixed for his first court appearance, the court must stay the proceedings (s.22A(5)). Stayed proceedings may be re-instituted within three months (s.22B).

7 Attendance of parent or guardian at court

S.34A of the Children and Young Persons Act 1933, as inserted by s.56 of the 1991 Act, provides that, where a child or young person is charged with an offence or is for any other reason brought before a court, any parent or guardian of his may be required to attend at the court before which the case is heard or determined during all the stages of the proceedings, and must be required to attend in the case of a child or young person under the age of 16, unless the court is satisfied that it would be unreasonable to require his attendance.

8 General welfare of children and young persons

S.44 of the Children and Young Persons Acts 1933, as amended by s.72(4) of the Children and Young Persons Act 1969, provides that a court, when dealing with a child or young person brought before it as an offender, must have regard to his welfare and must, in a proper case, take steps for removing him from undesirable surroundings, and for securing that proper provision is made for his education and training.

9 Notice to and investigations by local authorities

Where a local authority bring proceedings for an offence alleged to have been committed by a young person, or are notified that any such proceedings are to be brought, it is their duty to make investigations, unless they are of opinion that it is unnecessary to do so, and to provide the court before which the proceedings are heard with information relating to the home surroundings, school record, health, and character of the young person (Children and Young Persons Act 1969, s.9(1)). If the court requests the local authority to make such investigations, the authority must comply with such a request (1969 Act, s.9(2)).

S.34(2) and (3) of the 1969 Act and the Children and Young Persons Act 1969 (Transitional Modifications of Part I) Orders provide that where criminal proceedings are brought in the case either of a child over the age of 13 years or of a young person, prior notice must be given to a probation officer, and that, where arrangements have been made for the probation officer to make enquiries into the child's or young person's home surroundings, the local authority will be relieved of their duty under s.9(1) to make enquiries.

B: YOUTH CAUTIONS AND CONDITIONAL CAUTIONS

10 Youth cautions

The police can give a child or young person a youth caution if they decide that there is sufficient evidence to charge them with an offence, they admit the offence, and the police do not consider that they should be prosecuted or given a youth conditional caution (see **11 Youth conditional cautions**, below) in respect of the offence (Crime and Disorder Act 1998, s.66ZA, added by the Legal Aid, Sentencing and Punishment of Offenders Act 2012).

A youth caution given to a person under the age of 18 must be given in the presence of an appropriate adult.

When a young person receives a youth caution then the police must as soon as is practicable refer them to a youth offending team who *may* assess the young person and put in place a rehabilitation programme for them. If a young person receives a second or subsequent referral to them they *must* be assessed and a rehabilitation programme *must* be put in place, unless this is deemed inappropriate (s.66ZB).

11 Youth conditional cautions

A youth conditional caution means a caution which is given in respect of an offence committed by an offender aged between 10 and 17 and which has conditions attached to it with which the offender must comply (Crime and Disorder Act 1998 s.66A(2), as added by the Criminal Justice and Immigration Act 2008 s.48(1)(a), Sch.9). Such a caution can be given by an authorised person which in this case means a constable, an investigating officer, or a person authorised by a relevant prosecutor (for example the Director of Public Prosecutions). The following requirements must also be satisfied (ss.66A(1), 66B)–

(a) the authorised person has evidence that the offender has committed an offence;
(b) the authorised person decides that there is sufficient evidence to charge the offender with the offence and that a youth conditional caution should be given to the offender in respect of the offence;
(c) the offender admits to the authorised person that he committed the offence;
(d) the authorised person explains the effect of the youth conditional caution to the offender and warns him that failure to comply with any of the conditions attached to the caution may result in his being prosecuted for the offence (the explanation and warning must be given in the presence of an appropriate adult); and
(e) the offender signs a document which contains (i) details of the offence; (ii) an admission by him that he committed the offence; (iii) his consent to being given the youth conditional caution; and (iv) the conditions attached to the caution.

The conditions which may be attached to such a caution are those which have one or more of the following objectives (s.66A(3))–

(a) facilitating the rehabilitation of the offender;
(b) ensuring the offender makes reparation for the offence;
(c) punishing the offender.

The conditions that may be attached to a youth conditional caution include (ss.66A(4), 66(C)(3))–

(d) a condition that the offender pay a financial penalty, such amount in respect of any offence not to exceed £100;
(e) a condition that the offender attend at a specified place at specified times.

Before deciding what conditions to attach to a youth conditional caution, reasonable efforts must be made to obtain the views of the victim (if any) of the offence, and in particular the victim's views as to whether the offender should carry out any of the actions listed in a community remedy document (see the Note on **Anti-Social Behaviour** at para **53 The community remedy**). If the victim expresses the view that they should carry out a particular action listed in the community remedy document, that action must be attached as a condition unless it seems that it would be inappropriate to do so. Where there is more than one victim and they express different views, those views must nevertheless be taken account in deciding what conditions to attach to the conditional caution (s.66BA).

The Crime and Disorder Act 1998 (Youth Conditional Cautions: Financial Penalties) Order 2013 prescribes the offences and descriptions of offences in relation to which a financial penalty condition may be attached, and the maximum penalties–

(a) any summary offence: £30;
(b) any offence triable either way: £50;
(c) any offence triable only on indictment: £75.

The maximum penalties are reduced to £15, £25, and £35 respectively if the offender is aged 10 or over but under 14.

If the offender fails, without reasonable excuse, to comply with any of the conditions attached to the youth conditional caution, criminal proceedings may be instituted against the person for the offence in question (s.66E(1)).

A young person who is given a youth conditional caution must be referred to a youth offending team as soon as is practicable so that they can consider assessment to identify rehabilitative programmes and decide whether to apply for a parenting order (see **46 When a parenting order may be made**, below).

The Secretary of State is under a duty to prepare a code of practice in relation to youth conditional cautions which may make provision, *inter alia*, as to the circumstances in which youth conditional cautions may be given, the procedure to be followed in connection with the giving of such cautions, and the conditions which may be attached. The *Code of Practice for Youth Conditional Cautions* has been made (Crime and Disorder Act 1998 (Youth Conditional Cautions: Code of Practice) Order 2013 (S.I. No. 613).

12 Effect on a subsequent conviction

If–

(a) a person who has received two or more youth cautions is convicted of an offence committed within two years beginning with the date of the last of those cautions; or
(b) a person who has received a youth conditional caution followed by a youth caution is convicted of an offence committed within two years beginning with the date of the youth caution,

then in sentencing him the court must not give a conditional discharge in respect of the offence unless it is of the opinion that there are exceptional circumstances relating to the offence or the person that justify it doing so, in which case it must state in open court that it is of that opinion and its reasons for that opinion (Crime and Disorder Act 1998, s.66ZB).

C: YOUTH REHABILITATION ORDERS

13 Youth rehabilitation orders

Where a person aged under 18 is convicted of an offence, the court by or before which the person is convicted may make a youth rehabilitation order imposing on the person any one or more of the following requirements (Criminal Justice and Immigration Act 2008, s.1)–

    (a) an activity requirement;
    (b) a supervision requirement;
    (c) in a case where the offender is aged 16 or 17 at the time of the conviction, and unpaid work requirement;
    (d) a programme requirement;
    (e) an attendance centre requirement;
    (f) a prohibited activity requirement;
    (g) a curfew requirement;
    (h) an exclusion requirement;
    (i) a residence requirement;
    (j) a local authority residence requirement;
    (k) a mental health treatment requirement;
    (l) a drug treatment requirement;
    (m) a drug testing requirement;
    (n) an intoxicating substance treatment requirement; and
    (o) an education requirement.

A court must not make a youth rehabilitation order on an offender unless it is of the opinion that the offence, or the combination of the offence and one or more offences associated with it, was serious enough to warrant such a sentence. Such an order is not available where the sentence is fixed by law (s.1(6)).

A youth rehabilitation order may also impose an electronic monitoring requirement and must do so where an order imposes a curfew or exclusion requirement, unless in the particular circumstances of the case the court is satisfied it would be inappropriate to do so, or the court is prevented from including such a requirement e.g., because arrangements for electronic monitoring are not available or a person (other than the offender) whose co-operation is required to the monitoring has not consented to that requirement (s.1(2)).

A youth rehabilitation order may also be made with intensive supervision or surveillance and such an order can also be made with a fostering requirement. However, a youth rehabilitation order with intensive supervision or surveillance may not impose a fostering requirement (Sch. 1, para. 5). A court can only make an order with an intensive supervision or surveillance requirement or a fostering requirement if (s.1(3), (4))–

    (a) the court is dealing with the offender for an offence which is punishable with imprisonment;
    (b) the court is of the opinion that the offence, or a combination of the offence and one or more offences associated with it, was so serious that, but for the supervision or surveillance requirement or the fostering requirement, a custodial sentence would be appropriate (or, if the offender was aged under 12 at the time of conviction, would be appropriate if the offender had been aged 12); and
    (c) if the offender was aged under 15 at the time of the conviction, the court is of the opinion that the offender is a persistent offender.

If the conditions in (a) to (c) are met, the court may also impose an extended activity requirement for between 90 and 180 days and, if it does, it must include a supervision requirement, a curfew requirement and (if practicable, see above) an electronic monitoring requirement (Sch. 1, para. 3).

The court may only make a youth rehabilitation order which imposes a fostering requirement if the court is satisfied that–

    (a) the behaviour which constituted the offence was due to a significant extent to the circumstances in which the offender was living; and
    (b) the imposition of a fostering requirement would assist in the offender's rehabilitation.

The court must also consult the local authority and, unless it is impracticable to do so, the parents or guardians of the offender prior to imposing a fostering requirement. A youth rehabilitation order with fostering must also impose a supervision requirement. (Sch. 1, para. 4). A court may not include a fostering requirement unless it has been notified by the Secretary of State that arrangements for implementing such a requirement are available in the area of the local authority which is to place the offender (Sch. 1, para. 18(7)). The offender must also be given the opportunity of legal representation (Sch. 1, para. 19).

14 The activity requirement

An "activity requirement", in relation to a youth rehabilitation order, is a requirement that the offender must do

819

any or all of the following (Criminal Justice and Immigration Act 2008, Sch. 1, paras 6–8)–

    (a) participate on such number of days as may be specified in the order, in activities at a specified place or places;

    (b) participate in an activity, or activities, specified in the order on such number of days as may be specified;

    (c) participate in one or more residential exercises for a continuous period or periods comprising such number or numbers of days as may be specified in the order (each period must not comprise more than 7 days);

    (d) engage in activities in accordance with instructions of the responsible officer on such number of days as may be specified in the order

The number of days specified in the order must not in aggregate be more than 90 unless an extended activity requirement is imposed (see **13 Youth rehabilitation orders**, above).

For the purposes of the activity requirement, the "responsible officer" means a member of a youth offending team or an officer of the local probation board (s.4(2)). In giving instructions, the responsible officer is under a duty to avoid any conflict with the offender's religious beliefs; any interference with the times, if any, at which the offender normally works or attends school or any other educational establishment; and, any conflict with the requirements of any other youth rehabilitation order to which the offender is subject. It is also the duty of the responsible officer to make any arrangements that are necessary in connection with the requirements imposed by the order and to promote the offender's compliance with those requirements. If appropriate, the officer must take steps to enforce the requirements. The offender is under an obligation to keep in touch with the responsible officer in accordance with instructions given and must notify the officer of any change of address (s.5).

15 The supervision requirement

A "supervision requirement", in relation to a youth rehabilitation order, is a requirement that during the period for which the order remains in force, the offender must attend appointments with the responsible officer or another person determined by the responsible officer, at such times and places as may be determined (Criminal Justice and Immigration Act 2008, Sch. 1, para. 9). For the meaning of "responsible officer" and his duties, including the duties of the offender in relation to that officer, see **14 The activity requirement**, above.

16 The unpaid work requirement

The number of hours which a person may be required to work under an unpaid work requirement in relation to a youth rehabilitation order must be specified in the order and must in aggregate be not less than 40 and not more than 240. A court may not impose such a requirement unless it is satisfied that the offender is a suitable person to perform work under that requirement and that arrangements exist in the local justice area for persons to perform work under the requirement. The work must be performed during the period of 12 months beginning with the day on which the order takes effect (Criminal Justice and Immigration Act 2008, Sch. 1, para. 10). For the meaning of "responsible officer" and his duties, including the duties of the offender in relation to that officer, see **14 The activity requirement**, above.

17 The programme requirement

A "programme requirement", in relation to a youth rehabilitation order, is a requirement that the offender must participate in a systematic set of activities specified in the order at a place or places so specified on such number of days as may be specified. A programme requirement may require the offender to reside at any place in order to participate in the programme. A court may not include a programme requirement in an order unless–

    (a) the programme has been recommended to the court by a member of a youth offending team, an officer of a local probation board or an officer of a provider of probation services as being suitable for the offender; and

    (b) the court is satisfied that the programme is available at the place proposed.

A court cannot impose a programme requirement if compliance involves the co-operation of a person other than the offender and the offender's responsible officer, unless that person consents to its inclusion. A requirement to participate operates to require the offender to participate in the programme at the place, and on the number of days, specified and to comply with instructions given by the person in charge of the programme (Criminal Justice and Immigration Act 2008, Sch. 1, para. 11). For the meaning of "responsible officer" and his duties, including the duties of the offender in relation to that officer, see **14 The activity requirement**, above.

18 The attendance centre requirement

An "attendance centre requirement", in relation to a youth rehabilitation order, is a requirement that the offender must attend at an attendance centre specified in the order for such number of hours as may be so specified. The aggregate number of hours for which the offender may be required to attend must–

    (a) if the offender is aged 16 or over at the time of conviction, be not less than 12 and not more than 36;

    (b) if the offender is aged 14 or over but under 16 at the time of conviction, be not less than 12 and not more than 24;

    (c) if the offender is aged under 14 at the time of the conviction, be not more than 12.

A court may not include an attendance centre requirement unless an attendance centre is available for a person of the offender's description and provision can be made at the centre for the offender (Criminal Justice and Immigration Act 2008, Sch. 1, para. 12).

19 The prohibited activity requirement

A "prohibited activity requirement", in relation to a youth rehabilitation order, is a requirement that the offender must refrain from participating in activities specified in the order on a day or days specified or during a period so specified. A court may not include such a requirement unless it has consulted (Criminal Justice and Immigration Act 2008, Sch. 1, para. 13)–
(a) a member of a youth offending team;
(b) an officer of a local probation board; or
(c) an officer of a provider of probation services.

20 The curfew requirement

A "curfew requirement", in relation to a youth rehabilitation order, is a requirement that the offender must remain, for periods specified in the order, at a place so specified. An order imposing a curfew requirement may specify different places or different periods for different days, but may not specify periods which amount to less than 2 hours or more than 16 hours in any day. Such a requirement must not specify periods which fall outside the period of 12 months beginning with the day on which the requirement first takes effect. Before imposing such a requirement the court must obtain and consider information about the place proposed to be specified, including information as to the attitude of persons likely to be affected by the enforced presence there of the offender (Criminal Justice and Immigration Act 2008, Sch. 1, para. 14).

21 The exclusion requirement

An "exclusion requirement", in relation to a youth rehabilitation order, is a provision prohibiting the offender from entering a place or area for a period not exceeding three months. An exclusion requirement may provide for the prohibition to operate during specified periods and may specify different places for different periods or days (Criminal Justice and Immigration Act 2008, Sch. 1, para. 15).

22 The residence requirement

A "residence requirement", in relation to a youth rehabilitation order, is a requirement that, during a specified period, the offender must reside with a specified individual or at a specified place (in the latter case it is called a "place of residence requirement"). A court cannot include a place of residence requirement in an order that the offender reside with an individual unless that individual has consented to the requirement. For such a requirement to be included, the offender must be aged 16 or over at the time of conviction. If the order so provides, a place of residence requirement does not prohibit the offender from residing, with the prior approval of the responsible officer, at a place other than that specified in the order. Before making a place of residence requirement the court must consider the home surroundings of the offender. A court may not specify a hostel or other institution as a place where the offender must reside except on the recommendation of a member of a youth offending team, an officer of a local probation board, an officer of a provider of probation services or a social worker of a local authority (Criminal Justice and Immigration Act 2008, Sch. 1, para. 16). For the meaning of "responsible officer" and his duties, including the duties of the offender in relation to that officer, see **14 The activity requirement**, above.

23 The local authority residence requirement

A "local authority residence requirement", in relation to a youth rehabilitation order, is a requirement that, during the period specified in the order, the offender must reside in accommodation provided by or on behalf of a specified local authority. A local authority residence requirement may also stipulate that the offender is not to reside with a specified person. Before imposing a local authority residence requirement the court must be satisfied that–
(a) the behaviour which constituted the offence was due to a significant extent to the circumstances in which the offender was living; and
(b) the imposition of that requirement would assist in the offender's rehabilitation.
A court may not include a local authority residence requirement unless it has consulted a parent or guardian of the offender (unless it is impracticable to do so) and the local authority which is to receive the offender. Any period specified in a youth rehabilitation order as the period for which the offender must reside in local authority accommodation must not be longer than six months and must not include any period after the offender has reached the age of 18 (Criminal Justice and Immigration Act 2008, Sch. 1, para. 17).

24 The mental health treatment requirement

A "mental health treatment requirement", in relation to a youth rehabilitation order, is a requirement that the offender must submit for a specified period to treatment by or under the direction of a registered medical practitioner or a chartered psychologist (or both) with a view to the improvement of the offender's mental condition. A court may not include such a requirement in a youth rehabilitation order unless it is satisfied that the mental condition of the offender—

(a) requires and may be susceptible to treatment; and is not such as to warrant the making of a hospital order or guardianship order;

(b) the court is also satisfied that arrangements have been made or can be made for the treatment intended; and

(c) the offender has expressed willingness to comply with the requirement.

The medical practitioner or psychologist has the power to make arrangements for the offender to be treated at an institution or a place other than that specified in the order where that person is of the opinion that part of the treatment can be better or more conveniently given there (Criminal Justice and Immigration Act 2008, Sch. 1, paras 20, 21)

25 The drug treatment requirement

A "drug treatment requirement", in relation to a youth rehabilitation order, is a requirement that the offender must submit for a specified period to treatment by or under the direction of a person having the necessary qualifications or experience with a view to the reduction or elimination of the offender's dependency on, or propensity to misuse, drugs. A court may not include a drug treatment requirement in a youth rehabilitation order unless it is satisfied that (Criminal Justice and Immigration Act 2008, Sch. 1, para. 22)—

(a) the offender is dependent on, or has a propensity to misuse, drugs; and

(b) the offender's dependency or propensity is such as requires and may be susceptible to treatment.

The treatment must be as a resident or non-resident at an institution or a place specified in the order but the order must not otherwise specify the nature of the treatment. A court may not include a drug treatment requirement unless—

(c) arrangements for implementing drug treatment requirements are in force in the local justice area;

(d) the court is satisfied that arrangements have been or can be made for the treatment intended to be specified in the order;

(e) the requirement has been recommended as suitable for the offender by a member of a youth offending team, an officer of a local probation board or an officer of a provider of probation services; and

(f) the offender has expressed willingness to comply with the requirement.

26 The drug testing requirement

A "drug testing requirement", in relation to a youth rehabilitation order, is a requirement that, for the purposes of ascertaining whether there is any drug in the offender's body during any treatment period, the offender must during that period, provide samples in accordance with instructions given by the responsible officer or the treatment provider (see **25 The drug treatment requirement**, above).

A court may not include a drug testing requirement unless (Criminal Justice and Immigration Act 2008, Sch. 1, para. 23)—

(a) arrangements for implementing the drug testing requirements are in force in the local justice area;

(b) the order also imposes a drug treatment requirement; and

(c) the offender has expressed willingness to comply with the requirement.

An order which imposes a drug testing requirement—

(d) must specify for each month the minimum number of occasions on which samples are to be provided; and

(e) may specify times at which and circumstances in which the responsible officer or treatment provider may require samples to be provided and descriptions of the samples which may be required.

For the meaning of "responsible officer" and his duties, including the duties of the offender in relation to that officer, see **14 The activity requirement**, above.

27 The intoxicating substance treatment requirement

An "intoxicating substance treatment requirement", in relation to a youth rehabilitation order, is a requirement that the offender must submit, during periods specified in the order, to treatment by or under the direction of a person having the necessary qualifications or experience with a view to the reduction or elimination of the offender's dependency on, or propensity to misuse, intoxicating substances. "Intoxicating substance" means alcohol or any other substance or product (other than a controlled drug) which is, or the fumes of which are, capable of being inhaled or otherwise used for the purpose of causing intoxication. A court may not include an intoxicating substance treatment requirement in a youth rehabilitation order unless it is satisfied that (Criminal Justice and Immigration Act 2008, Sch. 1, para. 24)—

(a) the offender is dependent on, or has a propensity to misuse, intoxicating substances; and

(b) the offender's dependency or propensity is such as requires and may be susceptible to treatment.

The treatment must be as a resident or non-resident at an institution or a place specified in the order but the order must not otherwise specify the nature of the treatment. A court may not include an intoxicating treatment requirement in a youth rehabilitation order unless—

(a) arrangements have been or can be made for the treatment intended to be specified in the order;

(b) the requirement has been recommended to the court as suitable for the offender by a member of a youth offending team, an officer of a local probation board or an officer of a provider of probation services; and

(c) the offender has expressed willingness to comply with the requirements.

28 The education requirement

An "education requirement", in relation to a youth rehabilitation order, means a requirement that the offender must comply, during a period or periods specified in the order, with approved education arrangements. "Approved education arrangements" means arrangements for the offender's education–

(a) made for the time being by the offender's parent or guardian; and

(b) approved by the local authority specified in the order.

A court may not include an education requirement in a youth rehabilitation order unless–

(a) it has consulted the local authority proposed to be specified in the order with regard to the proposal to include the requirement; and

(b) it is satisfied that (i) in the view of that local authority, arrangements exist for the offender to receive efficient full-time education suitable to the offender's age, ability, aptitude and special educational needs (if any), and (ii) having regard to the circumstances of the case, the inclusion of the education requirement is necessary for securing the good conduct of the offender or for preventing the commission of further offences.

Any period specified in an order as a period during which the offender must comply with such arrangements must not include any period after the offender has ceased to be of compulsory school age (Criminal Justice and Immigration Act 2008, Sch. 1, para. 25).

29 Breach, revocation and amendment of youth rehabilitation orders

If a responsible officer (see **14 The activity requirement**, above) is of the opinion that an offender has failed without reasonable excuse to comply with a youth rehabilitation order he must give the offender a warning. A warning will last the duration of the "warned period", which is a period of 12 months beginning with the date on which the warning was given. A warning must–

(a) describe the circumstances of the failure and state that the failure is unacceptable; and

(b) state that the offender will be liable to be brought before a court (i) in a case where the warning is given during the warned period relating to a previous warning, if during that period the offender again fails to comply with the order or (ii) in any other case, if during the warned period relating to the warning, the offender fails on more than one occasion to comply with the order (Criminal Justice and Immigration Act 2008, s.2, Sch. 2, para. 3).

If the responsible officer has given another warning during a warned period relating to the first warning, and is of the opinion that during that period the offender has again failed to comply with the order he must, unless there are exceptional circumstances, cause an information to be laid before a justice of the peace. A justice of the peace has the power to issue a summons or warrant where it appears that an offender has failed to comply with an order. The court may deal with the offender by ordering the payment of a fine of up to £2,500 or by amending the terms of the order so as to impose any requirement which could have been included in the order when it was made (Sch. 2, paras 5, 6). A magistrates' court has, in certain circumstances, the power to commit the offender in custody or release the offender on bail in order to refer the offender to the Crown Court (Sch. 2, para. 7).

A court has the power, where it appears to be in the interests of justice to do so, to revoke a youth rehabilitation order or both revoke the order and deal with offender for the offence in respect of which the order was made in any way the court could have dealt with the offender for that offence. In dealing with an offender the court must take account of the extent to which he has complied with the requirements of the order. A person sentenced for an offence may appeal to the Crown Court against sentence. An order may also be revoked where the offender is making good progress or responding satisfactorily to supervision or treatment (Sch. 2, para. 11).

On an application by the responsible officer or the offender a court may amend a youth rehabilitation order, for example where the offender proposes to reside, or is residing, in a local justice area other than the area specified in the order. A court may also amend an order by cancelling any of the requirements of the order or replacing those requirements with a requirement of the same kind which could have been included in the order when it was made (Sch. 2, para. 13).

D: REMAND, ETC.

30 Remand to care of local authorities

Where a court deals with a child (i.e., anyone under-18) charged with or convicted of one or more offences by remanding them, and the child is not released on bail, then the court must either remand the child to local authority accommodation or to youth detention accommodation (Legal Aid, Sentencing and Punishment of Offenders Act 2012, s.91).

Normally the remand will be to local authority accommodation, but it may be to youth detention if either (ss.91, 98, and 99)–

   (a) the child has reached the age of twelve; and

   (b) the offence is either a violent or sexual offence or one that is punishable if committed by an adult with a sentence of imprisonment of fourteen years or more; and

   (c) the court is of the opinion, after considering all the options for the remand of the child, that only remanding the child to youth detention accommodation would be adequate to protect the public from death or serious personal injury (whether physical or psychological) occasioned by further offences committed by the child, or to prevent the commission by the child of imprisonable offences; and

   (d) either

      (i) the child is legally represented before the court; or

      (ii) the child is not legally represented before the court and (1) representation was provided to the child but was withdrawn because of the child's conduct or because it appeared that the child's financial resources were such that he was not eligible for such representation; (2) the child applied for such representation and the application was refused because it appeared that the child's financial resources were such that the child was not eligible for such representation, or (3) having been informed of the right to apply for such representation and having had the opportunity to do so, the child refused or failed to apply,

or

   (e) the child has reached the age of twelve; and

   (f) it appears to the court that there is a real prospect that the child will be sentenced to a custodial sentence; and

   (g) the offence is an imprisonable offence; and

   (h) the child has a recent history of absconding while subject to a custodial remand and the offence is alleged to be, or has been found to have been, committed while the child was remanded to local authority accommodation or youth detention accommodation and/or the offence, together with any other imprisonable offences of which the child has been convicted in any proceedings, amount or would if the child were convicted amount, to a recent history of committing imprisonable offences while on bail or subject to a custodial remand; and

   (i) the necessity condition (see (c) above), and the legal representation condition (see (d) above), apply.

A remand to youth detention accommodation is a remand a secure children's home, a secure training centre, a young offender institution, or accommodation specified by order.

A local authority designated by the court must receive the child and provide or arrange suitable accommodation for them. The powers and duties of a local authority to place a child that is remanded to their care are set out in the Children Act 1989, s.22C (see the Note on **Local Authority Support for Children and Families** at para **23 Provision of accommodation and maintenance by local authorities for children they are looking after**).

Where a child is remanded to local authority accommodation, the court may attach conditions, which may in certain cases include electronic tagging. The police may arrest without a warrant a child who they have reasonable grounds for suspecting has breached any of the conditions imposed upon him. They have a duty to bring the child before a court as soon as reasonably practicable and in any event within 24 hours. If the court decides that the child has broken any of the conditions imposed under the original remand it can remand the child on new conditions or, if it thinks the test for remand to youth detention accommodation is met, remand the child to such accommodation. If it is not satisfied that the conditions have been breached then the child must be remanded to local authority accommodation again, subject to the same conditions as those originally imposed (ss.93-97).

31 Restriction on reports of proceedings

S.49 of the Children and Young Persons Act 1933 (as substituted by s.49 of the Criminal Justice and Public Order Act 1994 (the 1994 Act) and amended by s.45 of the Crime (Sentences) Act 1997) provides that no report of any proceedings in a youth court must reveal the name, address, or school of, or include any particulars calculated to lead to the identification of, any child or young person concerned in those proceedings either as being the person against or in respect of whom the proceedings are taken, or as being a witness, nor may the picture of such a child or young person be published or included in any programme service. The prohibitions may be dispensed with by a court where–

   (a) it is satisfied that it is appropriate to do so in order to avoid injustice to the child or young person; or

   (b) in the case of a child or young person who has been charged with or convicted of a violent or sexual offence or an offence punishable in the case of an adult with imprisonment for 14 years or more and who is unlawfully at large, it is necessary to do so for the purpose of apprehending him; or

   (c) the court is satisfied that it is in the public interest to do so (although the court must first consider any representations made by the parties to the proceedings).

S.49 also applies in respect of proceedings on appeal from a youth court, proceedings for breach, revocation or amendment of a youth rehabilitation order, or appeals arising out of such proceedings, provided that the court carries out its duty to announce, in the course of the proceedings, that s.49 applies to them.

E: PUNISHMENT OF CHILDREN AND YOUNG PERSONS: FIRST TIME OFFENDERS

32 Referral orders

The Powers of Criminal Courts (Sentencing) Act 2000 makes provision for referral orders. If a youth court or other magistrates' court is dealing with a young person under the age of 18 for an offence punishable with imprisonment, they must make a referral order if the young person has (s.17)–

(a) pleaded guilty to the offence and any associated offence; and

(b) never been convicted of an offence before (and never received a conditional discharge) in the UK or any EU Member State;

and

(c) the offence is not one for which the sentence is fixed by law;

(d) the court is not proposing to impose a custodial sentence or make a hospital order; and

(e) the court is not proposing to grant an absolute or conditional discharge.

In these circumstances, the sentence of a referral order is mandatory in those areas where the courts have been notified that it is available (it will be tested in pilot areas before extending to the whole of England and Wales).

The court has a discretion to make a referral order if–

(f) the compulsory referral conditions are not satisfied in relation to the offence; and

(g) the offender pleaded guilty to the offence or if the offender is being dealt with by the court for the offence and any connected offence, the offender pleaded guilty to at least one of those offences.

Where a court makes a referral order in respect of an offender who is already subject to such an order it may direct that the new youth offender contract should not take effect until the earlier order has been revoked or completed (s.18(3A)).

33 Content of a referral order

A referral order must specify the youth offending team responsible for implementing the order, require the offender to attend meetings of the youth offender panel established by the team, and specify the length of any youth offender contract (which must be between 3 and 12 months: Powers of Criminal Courts (Sentencing) Act 2000, s.18(1)).

Local authorities are required to set up youth offending teams (by the Crime and Disorder Act 1998, s.39) and these teams will establish a youth offender panel for each young offender referred to them (2000 Act, s.21). Panels will conduct their proceedings and discharge their functions in accordance with guidance given by the Secretary of State.

34 Attendance at panel meetings

The young offender must attend at each meeting of the panel (Powers of Criminal Courts (Sentencing) Act 2000, s.22). If he does not, the panel may refer him back to the court (see **37 Referral back to the court,** below). In addition, the court must require at least one parent or guardian (or local authority representative where the child is being looked after by a local authority) of an offender under the age of 16 to attend meetings unless the court is satisfied that it would be unreasonable to do so. If the offender is aged 16 or over, the court has a discretion as to whether to order attendance by a parent (s.20).

35 Youth offender contracts

At its first meeting, the youth offender panel must seek to reach agreement with the offender on a programme of behaviour the aim (or principal aim) of which is the prevention of re-offending by him (Powers of Criminal Courts (Sentencing) Act 2000, s.23).

The programme may include the offender (s.23(2))–

(a) making financial or other reparation to anyone who appears to the panel to be a victim or otherwise affected by the offence(s) for which the offender has been referred;

(b) attending mediation sessions with any such victim or other person;

(c) carrying out unpaid work or service in or for the community;

(d) being at home at specified times;

(e) attending at school or a place of work;

(f) participating in specified activities (e.g., drug or alcohol rehabilitation sessions, education or training, or activities to address offending behaviour);

(g) presenting himself to specified persons at specified times and places;

(h) staying away from specified persons or places;

(i) enabling supervision and recording of his compliance with the programme.

Physical restriction on the offender's liberty and electronic monitoring are specifically excluded (s.23(3)). For (a) or (b) above, the consent of the victim or other person must be obtained.

Once agreed, the programme becomes the "youth offender contract". If a programme cannot be agreed, the panel may refer the offender back to the court (see **37 Referral back to the court,** below) (s.25).

36 Progress meetings

Progress meetings may be held at any time and must be held if (Powers of Criminal Courts (Sentencing) Act

2000, s.26)–

(a) the offender wishes to seek a variation to the terms of his contract or to have the matter referred back to the court with a view to the referral order being revoked because a change of circumstances makes compliance impractical (as an example, the Act cites where the offender is to be taken to live abroad); or

(b) it appears to the panel that the offender is in breach of his contract.

The panel will review the offender's progress, discuss with him any breaches of the contract, and consider any variations to the contract or requests for referral back to the court. if there has been a breach of contract, the panel may refer the offender back to the court (see **37 Referral back to the court**, below).

Before the end of the contract, the panel will hold a "final meeting" to review the offender's compliance with his contract and decide whether he has satisfactorily completed it. If they decide he has, they must give him written confirmation of that decision, which has the effect of discharging the referral order. If they decide he has not, they must refer the offender back to the court (see **37 Referral back to the court**, below) (s.27).

The panel may also refer the offender back to court for revocation of the order where the offender is making good progress (see **37 Referral back to the court**, below).

37 Referral back to the court

A youth offender panel may refer an offender back to court if–

(a) he fails to attend a panel meeting (Powers of Criminal Courts (Sentencing) Act 2000, s.22(2));

(b) he fails to agree a contract (s.25(2));

(c) he fails to sign a contract or an agreed variation(ss.25(3) and 26(8));

(d) he breaches his contract (s.26(5));

(e) his overall compliance is such that the panel cannot discharge the order at the end of the contract period (s.27(4)); or

(f) the offender requests a referral back to the court (s.26(10)).

If the court considers the referral back to it to be justified, it may sentence the offender as if the requirement in section 16 of the Act to make a referral order did not apply, with account being taken of the extent of the offender's compliance with the order (Sch. 1, para. 5).

Where an offender has been referred back to the court because (a), (d) or (e) above applies, the court may impose a fine up to a maximum of £2,500 on the offender, or extend the youth offender contract up to a maximum overall length of 12 months (Sch. 1, para 6A).

The court has the power to adjourn the hearing and remand the offender (Sch. 1, para. 9).

Where an offender is convicted of a further offence whilst subject to a referral order the court may, if the offence was committed before the referral order was made, extend the order (to a maximum of 12 months). In exceptional circumstances the court may also extend a referral order in respect of an offence committed after the order was made.

If the court decides against either an extension of the referral order or an absolute or conditional discharge then, whenever the further offence was committed, the court may revoke the referral order if it appears to it to be in the interests of justice to do so and the court will sentence the offender for both offences, taking into account his compliance up to that time with the terms of his contract (Sch. 1, para. 14).

The youth offender panel has the power to refer the offender back to the appropriate court where they consider it is in the interests of justice for the period of the referral order to be extended. The court has the power to extend the period of the order by up to three months subject to the maximum period of a referral order of twelve months. In deciding to make an order the court will have regard to the extent of the offender's compliance with the terms of the contract (s.27B).

If a parent or guardian fails to comply with a requirement to attend at a panel meeting, the panel can refer them to a youth court (s.22(2A)). If it is satisfied that there was no reasonable excuse for the non-attendance, the youth court can make a parenting order to run for up to 12 months (see G: PARENTING ORDERS AND CONTRACTS, below).

A youth offender panel has the power to refer an offender back to the appropriate court where it appears to the panel to be in the interests of justice for the referral order revoked. This provision allows a court to revoke early a referral order where the offender is making good progress or where there are other reasons for revoking the order (s.27A).

F: PUNISHMENT OF CHILDREN AND YOUNG PERSONS: REPEAT OFFENDERS

38 Restriction on imposing imprisonment on young offenders

No court may pass a sentence of imprisonment on a person under 21 years of age or commit such a person to prison for any reason. However, this provision does not prevent the committal to prison of a person under 21 years of age who is remanded or committed in custody for trial or sentence (Powers of Criminal Courts (Sentencing) Act 2000 s.89).

S.90 provides that any person under the age of 18 must not, if convicted of murder, be sentenced to imprisonment for life; he must instead be sentenced to be detained during Her Majesty's pleasure and, if so sentenced, he is liable to be detained in such place and under such conditions as the Secretary of State may direct or arrange.

Where a child or young person is convicted on indictment of any offence punishable in the case of an adult with imprisonment for 14 years or more (other than a sentence fixed by law) or an offence of indecent assault on a man or woman, then if the court is of the opinion that no other method of dealing with the case is suitable it may sentence him to be detained for a specified period in such place and on such conditions as the Secretary of State may direct or arrange. The period specified must not exceed the maximum term with which the offence is punishable in the case of an adult (2000 Act, s.91).

Subject to s.90, a court must sentence any person to custody for life where that person is under the age of 21 and has been convicted of murder or any other offence the sentence for which is fixed by law as life imprisonment (s.93). The court must, if it considers that a custodial sentence for life would be appropriate, sentence any person to custody for life where that person is over 18 but under 21 years of age and is convicted of any other offence for which a person aged 21 years or over would be liable to imprisonment for life (s.94).

Where a person aged under 18 is convicted of a serious offence and the court is of the opinion that there is a significant risk to members of the public of serious harm occasioned by the commission by him of further specified offences then, if the offence is one in respect of which the offender could be given a life sentence under s.91 of the 2000 Act, and the court considers that the seriousness of the offence, or of the offence and one or more offences associated with it, is such as to justify the imposition of a life sentence, then the court *must* impose a sentence of detention for life (Criminal Justice Act 2003, s.226).

Where an offender is convicted of certain violent or sexual offences and the court considers that there is a significant risk to members of the public of serious harm occasioned by the commission by the offender of further offences but the court is not *required* (see above) to impose a sentence of detention for life, it may impose on the offender an extended sentence of detention. The court can do so only where, if it were to impose an extended sentence of detention, the term that it would specify as the appropriate custodial term would be at least four years. An extended sentence of detention is one where the term is equal to the normal custodial term he would receive, together with a further period ("the extension period") for which the offender is to be subject to a licence and which is of such length as the court considers necessary for the purpose of protecting members of the public from serious harm occasioned by the commission by the offender of further offences. The maximum extension period is five years for a violent offence and eight years for a sexual offence (s.226B).

Where an offender sentenced to a term of detention in a young offender institution, to be detained under ss.90 or 91 of the 2000 Act, or to custody for life under s.94 (see above) has attained the age of 21, or has attained the age of 18 and has been reported to the Secretary of State by the board of visitors to an institution as exercising a bad influence on the other inmates of the institution or as behaving in a disruptive manner, the Secretary of State may direct that he be treated as if he had been sentenced to imprisonment for the same term (s.99).

39 Young offender institutions

S.96 of the Powers of Criminal Courts (Sentencing) Act 2000 provides for a court, subject to ss.90, 93 and 94 (see **38 Restriction on imposing imprisonment on young offenders**, above), to pass a sentence of detention in a young offender institution where an offender aged under 21 but not less than 15 is convicted of an offence which is punishable with imprisonment in the case of a person aged 21 or over and the court is of the opinion that—

    (a) the offence or the combination of the offence and one or more associated offences was so serious that only a custodial sentence can be justified; and/or

    (b) the offence is a violent or sexual one and only a custodial sentence would be adequate to protect the public from serious harm.

The maximum term of detention in a young offender institution that a court may impose for an offence is the same as the maximum term of imprisonment that it may impose for that offence; and the minimum term of detention is 21 days (s.97(1), (2)).

Where an offender aged over 21 is serving a sentence of detention and is convicted of one or more further offences for which he is liable to imprisonment, the court has the power to pass one or more sentences of imprisonment to run consecutively upon the sentence of detention in a young offender institution (s.97(5)).

An offender who is released from a term of detention in a young offender institution where the term was for less than 12 months and who is under 18 at the time of release will be subject to supervision by a member of the youth offending team for a period of three months (Criminal Justice Act 2003, s.256B).

While a person is under such supervision, he must comply with such requirements as may be specified in a notice from the Secretary of State e.g., relating to drug testing or electronic monitoring. If, without reasonable excuse, he fails to comply with those requirements he will be guilty of an offence (s.256C) and may be detained in prison or youth detention accommodation for a period not exceeding 30 days, or given a fine not exceeding level 3 on the standard scale (see the Note on **Treatment of Offenders** at para **68 Maximum fines**, for the current amount).

Where an offender is aged 18 or over at the time of release, they will be subject to the adult licence and supervision requirements: see the Note on **Treatment of Offenders** at para **27 Supervision on release**.

40 Attendance centres

S.60 of the Powers of Criminal Courts (Sentencing) Act 2000 provides that, where the Crown Court or a magistrates' court would have power to—

    (a) pass a sentence of imprisonment on a person who is under 21 years of age; or

(b) but for s.89 of the 2000 Act (see **38 Restriction on imposing imprisonment on young offenders**, above) to commit such a person to prison in default of payment of any sum of money, or for failing to do or abstain from doing anything required to be done or left undone; or

(c) commit a person aged 21 but under 25 to prison in default of payment of any sum of money,

the court may, if it has been notified by the Secretary of State that an attendance centre reasonably accessible to the offender is available for the reception of persons of his description, order him to attend at the centre specified in the order.

So far as is practicable, the times at which the offender is required to attend a centre must not interfere with his school or working hours and he may not be required to attend on more than one occasion on each day or for more than three hours on any one occasion. The aggregate number of hours of attendance will be 12 hours, but this may be reduced where the offender is under 14 years of age and the court is of the opinion that 12 hours' attendance would be excessive and may be increased where the court is of the opinion that 12 hours' attendance is inadequate, to a maximum of 24 hours where the offender is under 16 years of age, or 36 hours where the offender is under 21 (or 25, as the case may be) but not less than 16 years of age.

Under Schedule 5 to the 2000 Act there is power to discharge or vary an order for attendance at an attendance centre and a power to deal with an offender for failing to attend, or for breach of the rules while attending at a centre. The power to discharge the order includes power to deal with the offender for the offence in respect of which the order was made in any manner in which he could have been dealt with by the court which made the order and includes the power to impose a fine.

41 Detention and training orders

S.100 of the Powers of Criminal Courts (Sentencing) Act 2000 provides for the making of detention and training orders (which have superseded secure training orders). Subject to ss.90, 91 and 93 (see **38 Restriction on imposing imprisonment on young offenders**, above) a court must impose a detention and training order where a child or young person is—

(a) convicted of an offence which is punishable with imprisonment in the case of a person aged 21 or over; and

(b) the offence is so serious that only such a sentence can be justified or would be adequate (in the case of violent or sexual offences) to protect the public from serious harm.

A court cannot however make a detention and training order in the case of an offender under the age of 15 unless it is of the opinion that he is a persistent offender; and cannot make an order in the case of an offender under the age of 12 unless it is of the opinion that only a custodial sentence would be adequate to protect the public from further offending by him and the offence was committed after a date to be appointed by the Secretary of State (s.100(2)).

A detention and training order is an order that an offender be subject to a specified term of detention followed by supervision. An order may be made for 4, 6, 8, 10, 12, 18 or 24 months. The term of an order cannot exceed the maximum term of imprisonment that a Crown court could have imposed in the case of an offender aged 21 or over (s.101).

The period of detention under a detention and training order is half of the term of the order and will be served in secure accommodation, e.g., a secure training centre, a young offender institution, or local authority accommodation provided for the purpose of restricting the liberty of children and young persons (s.102). The remainder of the term of the order will be the supervision period (s.103). Supervision is carried out by either (i) a probation officer, (ii) a local authority social worker, or (iii) a member of a youth offending team.

If an offender breaches the supervision requirements of his order, he may be detained in secure accommodation for such period, not exceeding the shorter of 3 months or the remainder of the term of the order, or be subject to an additional period of supervision, or be fined a sum not exceeding level 3 on the standard scale (see the Note on **Treatment of Offenders** at para **68 Maximum fines**, for the current amount) (s.104).

Where an offender commits a further offence before the end of the term of his detention and training order the court may, in addition to any other sentence, order him to be detained in secure accommodation for a period equal to the time between when the new offence was committed and the end of the original order (s.105). This additional period must be disregarded in determining the appropriate length of sentence for the new offence.

Where an offender is aged 18 or over at the halfway point of a detention and training order (i.e., when they are released) of less than 24 months, then they will be subject to supervision beginning at the end of their detention and training order and ending 12 months after the halfway point of the order (s.106B). For example, an offender serving a detention and training order of 10 months will spend half of the sentence (i.e., 5 months) in custody and half subject to supervision in the community, with an additional supervision period (to start after the 10 month sentence has ended) of 7 months.

42 Reparation orders

S.73 of the Powers of Criminal Courts (Sentencing) Act 2000 provides that where a child or young person is convicted of an offence other than one for which the sentence is fixed by law, the court may make a reparation order requiring that child or young person to make reparation, as specified in the order, to a specified person or persons or to the community at large.

A court must not make a reparation order if it proposes to pass a custodial sentence, or one of detention at

Her Majesty's pleasure, or if it proposes to make a youth rehabilitation order or referral order in respect of him. A court must not make a reparation order at a time when a youth rehabilitation order is in force in respect of the offender unless when it makes the reparation order it revokes the youth rehabilitation order (for youth rehabilitation orders see **13 Youth rehabilitation orders**, above).

A reparation order must not require an offender to work for more than 24 hours in aggregate or to make reparation to any person without that person's consent. Subject to this, the requirements specified in the order must be (a) commensurate with the seriousness of the offence(s); (b) avoid conflict with the offender's religious beliefs or with the requirements of any youth community order to which he may be subject; and (c) avoid interference with the offender's work or schooling.

Reparation must be made within three months of the date of the order.

Failure to comply with an order is punishable by the court who may impose a fine of up to £1,000 (Sch. 8, para. 2).

If the order was made by a magistrates' court the court may discharge the order and deal with the offender for the offence in any manner in which it could have dealt with him if the order had not been made.

If the order was made by a crown court the court may commit the offender in custody or release him on bail until he can be dealt with by the crown court who may then deal with him in any manner in which it could have dealt with him for the offence had the order not been made.

Before making a reparation order the court must consider a written report from a probation officer, social worker, or member of a youth offending team indicating the type of work that is suitable for the offender, and the attitude of the victim(s) to the proposed reparation (s.73(5)).

43 Payments of fines by parents and guardians

Where a child or young person is found guilty of an offence for the commission of which a fine or an order for the payment of costs may be imposed or a compensation order may be made under s.141 of the 2000 Act (see the Note on **Treatment of Offenders** at M: FINES, and P: COMPENSATION ORDERS, respectively) and the court is of the opinion that the case would be best met by the imposition of a fine, costs, or the making of a compensation order, whether with or without any other punishment, the court is under a duty to order the parent or guardian of the child or young person to pay the fine, surcharge, costs, or compensation awarded unless the court is satisfied (i) that the parent or guardian cannot be found or (ii) that it would by unreasonable to make an order for payment having regard to the circumstances of the case (Powers of Criminal Courts (Sentencing) Act 2000, s.137(1)).

S.137(2) imposes a similar duty on a court where it would otherwise impose a fine upon a child or young person for failure to comply with a requirement included in an attendance order, or for breach of a youth rehabilitation order, breach of a reparation order, or of the requirements of supervision under a detention and training order or secure training order.

S.137(3), provides that, in the case of a young person aged 16 or over, the court merely has a power, rather than a duty, to order the parent or guardian to pay the fine, costs, or compensation awarded.

44 Binding over of parent or guardian

Where a child or young person is convicted of an offence, the court by which he is sentenced may, with the consent of his parent or guardian, order that parent or guardian to enter into a recognisance to take proper care of him and exercise proper control over him. In the case of a child aged under 16, it is the duty of the court to exercise this power if it is satisfied, having regard to the circumstances of the case, that it would be desirable to do so in the interests of preventing the commission of further offences by the child concerned. Where the court has passed a sentence which consists of or includes a youth rehabilitation order, it may include in the recognisance a provision that the parent or guardian ensure that the minor complies with the requirements of that sentence (2000 Act, s.150).

An order under s.150 cannot require the parent or guardian to enter into a recognisance for an amount exceeding £1,000 or for a period exceeding three years (or, where the young person concerned will reach the age of 18 in less than three years, that shorter period).

If a parent or guardian unreasonably refuses to consent to enter into a recognisance the court may order him to pay a fine of up to £1,000.

G: PARENTING ORDERS AND CONTRACTS

45 When a parenting order may be made

S.8 of the Crime and Disorder Act 1998 (amended by the Violent Crime Reduction Act 2006, s.60) provides that where in any court proceedings–
  (a) a child safety order is made in respect of a child;
  (aa) a parental compensation order is made in relation to a child's behaviour;
  (b) an anti-social behaviour injunction, criminal behaviour order or sexual harm prevention order is made in respect of a child or young person;
  (c) a child or young person is convicted of an offence;

(d) a person is convicted under s.443 of the Education Act 1996 (failure to comply with a school attendance order) or s.444 (failure to secure regular attendance at school);

then the court may make a parenting order if it is satisfied that the relevant condition has been fulfilled.

The "relevant condition" is that the order would be desirable in the interests of preventing (s.8(6))–

(i) any repetition of the behaviour that led to the order/injunction in (a), (aa), or (b) above; or

(ii) the commission of any further offences by the child;

(iii) the commission of any further offences under ss.443 or 444 of the Education Act 1996.

Where a person under 16 is convicted of an offence, or an anti-social behaviour injunction or criminal behaviour order is made in respect of them, the court, if satisfied that the relevant condition is fulfilled, must make a parenting order. If it is not satisfied that the condition is fulfilled it must state in open court that it is not and why not (s.9(1)).

A "sexual harm prevention order" means an order under s.103A of the Sexual Offences Act 2003 (see the Note on **Treatment of Offenders** at para **30 Sexual harm prevention orders–England and Wales**).

A court may not make a parenting order unless it has been notified that arrangements are in place for implementing such orders in its area (s.8(3)).

In addition, a parenting order may also be made where a child or young person has been referred to a youth offending team and a member of the team applies to a magistrates' court for such an order to be made (Anti-social Behaviour Act 2003, s.26). In deciding whether to make such an order, the court will take into account any refusal by a parent to enter into a parenting contract or any failure to comply with the requirements of such a contract (see **48 Parenting contracts**, below).

46 Terms of a parenting order

A parenting order may require a parent (or guardian) of a child to (Crime and Disorder Act 1998, s.8(4))–

(a) comply with such requirements as are specified in the order, for a period not exceeding 12 months; and

(b) attend, for a concurrent period not exceeding three months, a counselling or guidance programme. This may be residential if the court is satisfied that this would be more effective than a non-residential course, provided that any interference to family life which would result from the attendance is proportionate in all the circumstances.

The requirements referred to in (a) are those which the court considers desirable in the interests of preventing any repetition of behaviour or commission of the offence (s.8(7)). For a second or subsequent order, the requirement in (b) need not be included.

Before making an order, the court must explain to the parent the effect of the order, the consequences of failure to comply with it, and that any order may be reviewed. So far as practicable, an order will be made so as to avoid any conflict with a parent's religious beliefs and any interference with their work or attendance at an educational establishment (s.9(3) and (4)).

Failure by a parent to comply with any requirement of a parenting order is punishable with a fine not exceeding level 3 on the standard scale (see the Note on **Treatment of Offenders** at para **68 Maximum fines**) (s.9(7)).

47 Appeals against parenting orders

An appeal may be made as follows (Crime and Disorder Act 1998, s.10)–

(1) against an order made under (a) of **45 When a parenting order may be made**, above: to the county court;

(2) against an order made under (b) of **45 When a parenting order may be made**, above: to the Crown Court;

(3) against an order made under (c) of **45 When a parenting order may be made**, above: as if the offence had been committed by the parent and the order were a sentence passed on him; and

(4) against an order made under (d) of **45 When a parenting order may be made**, above: as if the order were a sentence passed on the parent for the offence that led to the making of the order.

48 Parenting contracts

Parenting contracts are intended to prevent children and young persons from engaging in further criminal conduct or anti-social behaviour. Where a child has been referred to a youth offending team and a member of that team has reason to believe that the child will engage in such behaviour, they may enter into a parenting contract with the child's parent (Anti-social Behaviour Act 2003, s.25).

A parenting contract will contain–

(a) a statement by the parent that he agrees to comply with such requirements as may be specified; and

(b) a statement by the youth offending team that they agree to provide support to the parent for the purpose of complying with those requirements.

The purpose of the requirements (which may include attendance on a counselling or guidance programme) is to prevent the child (or young person) from engaging in criminal conduct or anti-social behaviour, or further such conduct or behaviour.

H: CHILD SAFETY ORDERS

49 Circumstances when an order may be made

S.11 of the Crime and Disorder Act 1998 provides that a magistrates' court may make a child safety order where–

(a) a child under the age of ten has committed an act which, if he had been ten or over would have constituted an offence;

(b) a child safety order is necessary for the purpose of preventing the commission by the child of an offence within (a) above;

(c) a child has contravened a ban imposed by a curfew notice; or

(d) a child has acted in a manner that caused, or was likely to cause, harassment, alarm or distress to one or more persons not of his household.

Application for an order is made to the magistrates' court by a local authority. A court may not make an order unless it has been notified by the Secretary of State that arrangements for implementing such an order are available in its area.

50 Contents of an order and consequences of non-compliance

A child safety order is an order which places a child for a period (not exceeding three months or, in exceptional cases, 12 months) under the supervision of a "responsible officer" i.e., a social worker of a local authority social services department or a member of a youth offending team, and requires the child to comply with specified requirements (Crime and Disorder Act 1998, s.11(1)). The requirements that may be specified are those which the court considers desirable in the interests of–

(a) securing that the child receives appropriate care, protection and support and is subject to proper control; or

(b) preventing any repetition of the kind of behaviour which led to the child safety order being made.

Requirements included in an order must, so far as practicable, avoid any conflict with the parent's religious beliefs and any interference with the child's schooling (s.12(3)).

Before making an order, the court must consider the child's family circumstances and the likely effect of the order on those circumstances, and must explain to the parent or guardian of the child the effect of the order, the consequences if the child fails to comply with it, and the power of the court to review the order (s.12(2)).

Where a court is satisfied that a child has failed to comply with a requirement included in an order, the court may discharge the order and make a care order under s.31 of the Children Act 1989 or vary the provisions of the child safety order (1998 Act, s.12(6)).

51 Authorities

Statutes–

Anti-social Behaviour Act 2003

Children Act 1989

Children and Young Persons Acts 1933 to 1969

Children and Young Persons (Amendment) Act 1986

Courts and Legal Services Act 1990

Crime and Disorder Act 1998

Crime (Sentences) Act 1997

Criminal Justice Acts 1982, 1988, 1991, and 1993

Criminal Justice and Immigration Act 2008

Criminal Justice and Police Act 2001

Criminal Justice and Public Order Act 1994

Legal Aid, Sentencing and Punishment of Offenders Act 2012

Magistrates' Courts Act 1980

Police and Criminal Evidence Act 1984

Powers of Criminal Courts (Sentencing) Act 2000

Youth Justice and Criminal Evidence Act 1999

Statutory Instruments–

Children and Young Persons Act 1969 (Transitional Modifications of Part I) Orders 1970, 1979, and 1981, and (Amendment) Orders 1973 and 1974 (S.I. 1970 No. 1882, 1979 No. 125, 1981, No. 81, 1973 No. 485, and 1974 No. 1083)

Crime and Disorder Act 1998 (Youth Conditional Cautions: Financial Penalties) Order 2013 (S.I. 2013 No. 608)

Secure Remands and Committals (Prescribed Description of Children and Young Persons) Order 1999 (S.I. 1999 No. 1265)

TREATMENT OF OFFENDERS: CHILDREN AND YOUNG PERSONS: SCOTLAND

1 Introduction

The above Acts make provision for the treatment of young offenders who commit offences. S.93(2)(b) of the Children (Scotland) Act 1995 defines a child for the purposes of the Acts to mean–

(a) a child who has not attained the age of 16 years;

(b) a child over the age of 16 years who has not attained the age of 18 years and in respect of whom a supervision requirement of a children's hearing (see below) is in force under Part II of the 1995 Act (children in need of compulsory measures of care);

(c) a child under 18 years of age who has been referred to a children's hearing in pursuance of s.33 of the 1995 Act (return or removal of children within the United Kingdom); and

(d) for the purposes of the application of Chapters 2 and 3 of Part II of the 1995 Act to a person who has failed to attend school regularly without reasonable excuse, a person who is over the age of 16 years but not over school age.

Where a child attains the age of 16 years after the date on which a children's hearing first sits to consider his case but before the date of the conclusion of the proceedings of his case, the provisions of Part II of the 1995 Act and of any statutory instrument made thereunder will continue to apply to him in relation to that case as if he had not attained that age (1995 Act, s.93(3)).

A: ARREST AND PROSECUTION

2 Age of criminal responsibility

It is conclusively presumed that no child under the age of eight years can be guilty of any offence (Criminal Procedure (Scotland) Act 1995, s.41). Furthermore, no child under the age of 12 may be prosecuted, and. no-one over the age of 12 may be prosecuted for an offence they committed under that age (s.41A).

A child who has done anything which, in respect of an older child, would constitute an offence may be subject to the provisions of Part II of the 1995 Act (compulsory measures of care–see below).

3 Restrictions on prosecution of children for offences

No child aged between 12 and 16 may be prosecuted for any offence except at the instance of the Lord Advocate, and only the sheriff court and the High Court of Justiciary have jurisdiction in such cases (Criminal Procedure (Scotland) Act 1995, s.42).

4 Right to have someone informed when arrested or detained

Where a person held for questioning in a police station, or arrested and in custody in a police station or other premises, appears to be a child, the police must notify his parent or guardian of the child's custody and whereabouts. Subject to any restriction essential for the furtherance of the investigation or the well-being of the child, the parent must be permitted access to the child unless there is reasonable cause to suspect that he has been involved in the alleged offence in respect of which the child has been arrested or detained; in the latter case, the police have discretion as to whether or not to permit the parent access (Criminal Procedure (Scotland) Act 1995, s.15(4)).

The Terrorism Act 2000, Sch. 8, makes special provision for cases where children are detained in connection with terrorism.

5 Release and arrangements following arrest

Where a person who is apparently a child is arrested and cannot be brought forthwith before a sheriff, a police officer of or above the rank of inspector or the officer in charge of the police station must inquire into the case and, subject to certain exceptions, may release him either unconditionally or on a written undertaking entered into by him or his parent or guardian that he will attend at the hearing of the charge (Criminal Procedure (Scotland) Act 1995, s.43(1)). The exceptions apply where (s.43(3))–

(a) the charge is one of homicide or other grave crime;

(b) it is necessary in his interest to remove him from association with any reputed criminal or prostitute; or

(c) the officer has reason to believe that his release would defeat the ends of justice.

Where the child is not released, he must be kept in a place of safety, other than a police station, until he can be brought before a sheriff unless the police officer certifies that it is impracticable to do so, that he is of so unruly a character that he cannot safely be so detained, or that it is inadvisable to so detain him because of his state of health or his bodily or mental condition (s.43(4)).

Where a child has been detained by the police in a place of safety and it is decided not to proceed with criminal charges against him the police must inform the Principal Reporter of this (s.43(5)). The Reporter may either direct that the child be released from the place of safety or that the child is kept in there until the Reporter has determined whether the ground(s) for referral apply to the child (see **8 Functions of the Principal Reporter**, below) and whether it is necessary for a compulsory supervision order to be made (Children's Hearings (Scotland) Act 2011, s.65). The Children's Hearing must be arranged to take place no later than the third working day after the Principal Reporter receives notice from the police (2011 Act, s.69).

Any person who, without reasonable excuse, is in breach of an undertaking given under s.43(1) is guilty of an offence and liable on summary conviction in addition to any other penalty which the court can impose on him, to a fine not exceeding level 3 on the standard scale (1995 Act, s.43(6)).

6 References and remit of children's cases by courts for children's hearings

Where a child who is not subject to a supervision requirement is charged with an offence (other than one the sentence for which is fixed by law) and pleads guilty to, or is found guilty of, that offence, the court may, instead of making an order on that plea or finding, remit the case to the Principal Reporter (see B: CHILDREN'S PANELS AND CHILDREN'S HEARINGS, below) to arrange for the disposal of the case by a children's hearings. Alternatively, the court may request the Principal Reporter to arrange a children's hearing for the purpose of obtaining their advice as to the treatment of the child; the court, after the consideration of the advice so received, may, as it thinks proper, itself dispose of the case or remit it. In a case where the child is subject to a supervision requirement, the High Court may and the sheriff court must request the Principal Reporter to arrange a children's hearing for the purpose of obtaining their advice as to the treatment of the child, and after consideration of that advice may, as it thinks proper, itself dispose of the case or remit the case for disposal by a children's hearing. Where the court remits a case in the above circumstances, the jurisdiction of the court in respect of the child ceases and his case stands referred to the children's hearing (1995 Procedure Act, s.49(1) to (4)).

A court may also take similar action where the person concerned is over 16 but not over $17\frac{1}{2}$ years of age, provided that he is not subject to a supervision requirement (1995 Procedure Act, s.49(6) and (7)).

B: CHILDREN'S PANELS AND CHILDREN'S HEARINGS

7 Formation and constitution

The National Convener has a duty to appoint members of the Children's Panel for Scotland and to ensure that it includes people from all local authority areas (Children's Hearings (Scotland) Act 2011, s.4).

Such hearings consist of a chairman and two members, and must not consist solely of men or women (ss.5 and 6). There are strict rules to ensure the privacy of hearings (s.182).

The Principal Reporter is the person responsible for arranging all Children's Hearings, assisted by the Scottish Children's Reporter Administration (ss.14 and 15).

8 Functions of the Principal Reporter

The Principal Reporter must investigate a child's circumstances whenever he considers that the child might be in need of protection, guidance, treatment or control. This includes, but is not limited to, circumstances where information is passed on to him on the making of a child protection order, or by the courts, the police or by a local authority or any other person (Children's Hearings (Scotland) Act 2011, s.66).

The Reporter must investigate and assess (s.66(2))–
(1) whether there is sufficient evidence to support a referral to a hearing; and
(2) if so, whether compulsory measures of supervision are necessary for the child.

If he determines that both tests are satisfied, the Reporter must refer the child to a hearing. The Reporter may make further investigations as necessary and require the local authority to submit a report on the child. The grounds for referral, as set out in s.67, are–
(a) the child is likely to suffer unnecessarily, or the health or development of the child is likely to be seriously impaired, due to a lack of parental care;
(b) a sexual or violent offence has been committed against the child (a "schedule 1 offence");
(c) the child has, or is likely to have, a close connection with a person who has committed a schedule 1 offence;
(d) the child is, or is likely to become, a member of the same household as a child in respect of whom a schedule 1 offence has been committed;
(e) the child is being, or is likely to be, exposed to persons whose conduct is (or has been) such that it is likely that–
    (i) the child will be abused or harmed; or
    (ii) the child's health, safety or development will be seriously adversely affected;
(f) the child has, or is likely to have, a close connection with a person who has carried out domestic abuse;
(g) the child has, or is likely to have, a close connection with a person who has committed a serious offence under the Sexual Offences (Scotland) Act 2009;
(h) the child is being provided with accommodation by a local authority under the Children (Scotland) Act

1995, s.25 (child lost or abandoned or for whom no-one has parental responsibility) and special measures are needed to support the child;

(i) a permanence order is in force in respect of the child and special measures are needed to support the child;
(j) the child has committed an offence;
(k) the child has misused alcohol;
(l) the child has misused a drug (whether or not a controlled drug);
(m) the child's conduct has had, or is likely to have, a serious adverse effect on his health, safety or development or that of another person;
(n) the child is beyond the control of a relevant person (i.e., their parent, guardian or other person with parental responsibility);
(o) the child has failed without reasonable excuse to attend regularly at school; or
(p) the child is being, or is likely to be, subjected to physical, emotional or other pressure to enter into a marriage or civil partnership, or is, or is likely to become, a member of the same household as such a child.

When a child has pled guilty to or been convicted of an offence in a criminal court and is not already subject to a compulsory supervision order, the grounds for referral are deemed to be established. Similarly, where a sheriff refers a case to the Principal Reporter under the Antisocial Behaviour etc. (Scotland) Act 2004, s.12A, the grounds are treated as established (ss.69 and 70).

The Principal Reporter must prepare a statement of grounds setting out which of the above grounds he believes applies in relation to the child, and the facts on which that belief is based (s.89).

The Principal Reporter must ensure that, so far as practicable, a children's hearing takes place in the local authority area of the child to whom the hearing relates (s.17).

9 Procedure at a children's hearing

A child whose case has been referred to a children's hearing must attend unless the children's hearing excuses them for limited reasons, such as where attendance may be damaging to their physical, mental or moral welfare (Children's Hearings (Scotland) Act 2011, s.73). The parent, guardian or other person with parental responsibility for the child must also attend (s.74).

The Principal Reporter is responsible for ensuring the child's attendance at a children's hearing. On his application a children's hearing may issue a warrant to secure the child's attendance (s.123).

The chairman must explain to the child and his parent the grounds stated by the Principal Reporter for the referral of the case and ask whether they accept those grounds in whole or in part. If at least one ground is accepted, and they are satisfied that it is necessary to do so for the protection, guidance, treatment or control of the child, the hearing may make a compulsory supervision order, or if they are not so satisfied, discharge the referral. If the child or parent do not accept the grounds, the case must be referred to the sheriff for his decision on the contested points (s.91).

In any proceedings either before a children's hearing or a sheriff, consideration must be given as to whether it is necessary to appoint a person to safeguard the child's interests (a safeguarder), and if it is considered necessary to make such an appointment (2011 Act, ss.30, 31).

10 The supervision requirement

A compulsory supervision order is an order made by a Children's Hearing or sheriff that requires a child to comply with specified conditions and requires the local authority to perform duties in relation to the child's needs (Children's Hearings (Scotland) Act 2011, s.83).

The specified conditions can include—
(a) a requirement that the child reside at a specified place (and a direction granting authority to the person in charge of that place to restrict the child's liberty to the extent that they considers appropriate taking account of the measures included in the order);
(b) a prohibition on the disclosure (whether directly or indirectly) of the place specified under (a) above;
(c) a movement restriction condition (see 11 **Movement restrictions**, below);
(d) a secure accommodation authorisation;
(e) a requirement that specified medical or other examinations or treatment of the child be undertaken;
(f) a direction regulating contact between the child and a specified person or class of person;
(g) a requirement that the child comply with any other specified condition;
(h) a requirement that the local authority carry out specified duties in relation to the child.

Where a local authority receives information suggesting that compulsory measures of supervision may be necessary in respect of a child, it must, unless it is satisfied that it is unnecessary, make inquiries into the case and inform the Principal Reporter about the child if such measures may be required (s.60). The police must also give information to the Principal Reporter about a child whom they believe to be in need of such measures, and any other person may do so (ss.61, 64).

Where in any family proceedings (e.g., an action for divorce or judicial separation; proceedings relating to parental rights and responsibilities; and adoption etc), it appears to the court that one of the grounds for referral (other than that the child has committed an offence) is satisfied, it may refer the matter to the Principal Reporter, specifying the ground (s.62).

The Lord Advocate may direct that in any specified criminal case or class of case evidence lawfully obtained in the investigation of a crime or suspected crime must be given to the Principal Reporter (s.63).

A supervision requirement will cease to have effect after one year but may, after review, be continued for further yearly periods. It must cease when the child attains the age of 18 (ss.83, 133).

A local authority may instigate a review by the Principal Reporter and must do so e.g., where they are satisfied that the requirement ought to cease, or be varied; that a condition of the requirement is not being complied with; where they intend to apply for a parental responsibility order or an order freeing a child for adoption or they intend to place the child for adoption; or where they become aware that an adoption application has been or is about to be made (s.131).

A child or his parent may require a review at any time after the end of three months from the start or most recent continuation or variation of the order (s.132). Reviews will also be carried out when a child is subject to an existing compulsory supervision order and—

(i) a sheriff directs the Principal Reporter to arrange a hearing for the child under the Antisocial Behaviour etc. (Scotland) Act 2004, s.12;

(ii) a court remits a case relating to the child for disposal to a Children's Hearing under the Criminal Procedure (Scotland) Act 1995, s.49;

(iii) there plans to take the child to live outwith Scotland where removing the child from Scotland is not in accordance with the order or with an order under the Children (Scotland) Act 1995, s.11 (parental responsibility orders);

(iv) when a child is required to stay in a specified place as a condition of their order and they are transferred from that accommodation in their own interests or those of another child in that accommodation as a matter of urgent necessity. In such a case, a hearing to review the compulsory supervision order must be held within 3 days.

The Principal Reporter will also initiate a review where a compulsory supervision order is due to expire within 3 months and no other arrangements exist to review the order before the end of that period.

11 Movement restrictions

Children's hearings may impose, as a condition of a supervision requirement, a movement restriction condition i.e., a condition imposed as an alternative to keeping the child in secure accommodation and which (Children's Hearings (Scotland) Act 2011, s.84)—

(a) restricts the child's movements in such ways as may be specified in the supervision requirement; and

(b) requires the child to comply with such arrangements for monitoring compliance with the restriction as may be so specified.

The Children's Hearings (Scotland) Act 2011 (Movement Restriction Conditions) Regulations 2013 regulate the arrangements for monitoring compliance with supervision requirements which have a movement restriction attached and provide that the monitoring arrangements must include the preparation by the implementation authority of a child's plan which must, so far as is practicable, address the immediate and longer term needs of the child with a view to safeguarding and promoting his welfare (Reg. 3). The movement restriction condition must set out (Reg. 6)—

(a) the place at which the child is required to reside;

(b) the days of the week during which the child is required to remain at that place, and the period or periods when the child is required to remain there (which must not exceed 12 hours in any one day); and

(c) the period for which the movement restriction condition is to have effect (which must not exceed 6 months).

12 Appeals and legal aid

A child or his parent or safeguarder has a right of appeal to the sheriff against the decision of a children's hearing and may appeal from the sheriff's decision to either the sheriff principal or the Court of Session where a point of law or any irregularity in the conduct of the case is involved. If the sheriff allows the appeal, he may (Children's Hearings (Scotland) Act 2011, Part 15)

Legal aid is available to a child or his parent in proceedings before the sheriff or subsequent appeal to the principal sheriff or Court of Session (Legal Aid (Scotland) Act 1986, Part 5A—see the Note on **Legal Aid**).

13 Miscellaneous provisions

A children's hearing must be conducted in private and apart from the child, their parent and representatives, the only others allowed to be present are a member of the Administrative Council on Tribunals or of the Scottish Committee of that Council, and a member of an area support team. Journalists also have a right to attend but may be excluded where their presence either inhibits the child from expressing his views or is causing or is likely to cause significant distress to the child (Children's Hearings (Scotland) Act 2011, s.78).

Where a child might be required to give evidence in a sheriff court (i.e., on an appeal against a decision of a children's hearing, or on an application to establish the grounds of a referral to a children's hearing or for a review of a referral), then special measures for the hearing of the child's evidence will be used (Vulnerable

Witnesses (Scotland) Act 2004, ss.11 and 18). These special measures are as set out in the Note on **The Court System** at para **16 Special measures for vulnerable witnesses**, only without para (e).

The Children (Scotland) Act 1995 requires the parents of a child in the care of a local authority or subject to a supervision requirement to keep the person responsible for the care or supervision informed of their address (s.18).

Where the Principal Reporter is satisfied that the provision of information would not be detrimental to the interests of the child concerned (or any other child connected with the case), and that it is appropriate in the circumstances, he must provide to a victim of an offence who requests it, information as to the action that he has taken in the case and of any disposal of the case, in so far as the information relates to the offence (Criminal Justice (Scotland) Act 2003, s.53).

14 Children who abscond

Where a child absconds from or fails to return to a particular place in which they are required to be kept by virtue of an order or warrant e.g., a place of safety or residential establishment, they may be arrested without a warrant and returned there (Children's Hearings Act 2011, s.169).

A court may grant a warrant authorising the police to enter premises and search for the child where there are reasonable grounds for believing he is within the premises. The use of reasonable force is expressly permitted. Where a child cannot be returned to the place at which they are required to reside because the occupier is unwilling or unable to take the child back, the police must inform the Principal Reporter immediately and the child must be kept in a place of safety.

Similar provisions apply where a child absconds from a particular person, such as a foster carer or relative, with who me is required to reside (s.170).

It is an offence for a person to knowingly help or induce a child to abscond, to knowingly harbour or conceal a child, or to knowingly prevent a child from returning to a place of safety or person (a.171).

C: CHILDREN'S HEARINGS RULES

15 Scope of the Rules

The Scottish Ministers are empowered to make procedural rules for children's hearings (Children's Hearings (Scotland) Act 2011, s.177).

The Children's Hearings (Scotland) Act 2011 (Rules of Procedure in Children's Hearings) Rules 2013 provide for *inter alia* the arrangement, constitution, and conduct of children's hearings; the procedure at hearings; the issue of warrants to ensure attendance; and requirements concerning documents, reports of proceedings, and the payment of travelling and subsistence expenses to persons attending a hearing.

Where the Principal Reporter arranges a children's hearing he must, wherever practicable at least seven days (and no later than three days) before the hearing, notify the chairman and members of the children's hearing of the time and place of the hearing. Seven days notice must also be given to the child, their parent, safeguarder, and the chief social work officer of the relevant local authority (Rules 21-26).

The Rules also make detailed provisions as to the documents that must be supplied and the timescales in which they must be given.

A child or their parent may have a representative with them at children's hearings or pre-hearing panels to assist them with any matter that may arise. They may also have a legal representative in attendance (Rule 11).

16 Safeguarders

Safeguarders are appointed by children's hearings and sheriffs in certain cases to provide an independent assessment at hearings or in court of what is in a child's best interest. They are independent from all other agencies involved in the children's hearings system.

Safeguarders must seek the views of the child when preparing any report or making any recommendation to the children's hearing or sheriff (Children's Hearings (Scotland) Act 2011 (Safeguarders: Further Provision) Regulations 2012, Reg. 7).

The Scottish Ministers have a duty to establish a national Safeguarders Panel (s.32). The Children's Hearings (Scotland) Act 2011 (Safeguarders Panel) Regulations 2012 make provision in relation to the Safeguarder Panel, including the establishment and management of the Panel and the appointment, qualifications and training of its members.

17 Views of the child

Where any document is to be given to members of the children's hearing or pre-hearing panel, the document must contain any views expressed by the child which have been given to the person who has prepared that document (Rule 8). The chair of the children's hearing must ask the child whether the documents accurately reflect his views (Children's Hearings (Scotland) Act 2011, s.121) and if they do not he must endeavour to clarify the child's views on the relevant matter (Rule 58).

D: GENERAL PROVISIONS FOR THE PROTECTION OF CHILDREN AND YOUNG PERSONS IN CRIMINAL PROCEEDINGS

18 Welfare of child

Every court in dealing with a child who is brought before it as an offender must have regard to the welfare of the child and must, in a proper case, take steps for removing him from undesirable surroundings (Criminal Procedure (Scotland) Act 1995, s.50(6)).

19 Children under 14 years of age not to be in court during trial of another person

No child under 14 (other than an infant in arms) is allowed to be present in court during any proceedings against any other person charged with an offence unless his presence is required as a witness or otherwise for the purposes of justice (Criminal Procedure (Scotland) Act 1995, s.50(1)).

20 Separation of children from adults at courts, etc.

Arrangements must be made for preventing a child, while detained in a police station or while being conveyed to or from any criminal court, from associating with an adult (not being a relative) who is charged with any offence other than an offence with which the child is jointly charged and for ensuring that a female child, while so detained, being conveyed, or waiting, will be under the care of a woman (Criminal Procedure (Scotland) Act 1995, s.42(9) and (10)).

Where summary proceedings are brought in respect of an offence alleged to have been committed by a child, the sheriff must sit either in a different building or room from that in which he normally sits or on different days from those on which other courts in the building are engaged in criminal proceedings (1995 Procedure Act, s.142(1)).

21 Restrictions on reports of proceedings involving persons under 16 years of age

No newspaper report or sound or television broadcast of any proceedings in a court must reveal the name, address, or school of, or include any particulars calculated to lead to the identification of, any person under the age of 16 years concerned in the proceedings, either as being a person against or in respect of whom the proceedings are taken or as being a witness therein; nor must any picture which is, or includes, a picture of such a person be published in any newspaper or shown on television (Criminal Procedure (Scotland) Act 1995, s.47(1), (2), and (4)).

The restrictions on reporting do not apply where a person under the age of 16 is concerned as a witness only and no one against whom the proceedings are taken is under that age unless the court so directs. At any stage in the proceedings, the court may, where it is satisfied that it is in the public interest to do so, dispense with the restrictions to a specified extent; the Scottish Ministers may also, after completion of the proceedings, dispense with the restrictions to a specified extent if they are satisfied that it is in the public interest to do so (1995 Procedure Act, s.47(3)).

22 Attendance at court of parent of child charged with an offence

Where a child is charged with an offence, the child's parent or guardian may, and, if he can be found and resides within a reasonable distance, must, be required to attend at the court before which the case is heard or determined during all the stages of the proceedings, unless the court is satisfied that it would be unreasonable to require his attendance.

Where a child is arrested, the parent or guardian must be warned to attend at the court before which the child is to appear. The parent or guardian whose attendance must be required is the parent having parental responsibilities or rights in relation to the child, or the guardian having actual possession of the child. If, before the proceedings, the child had been removed from the care or charge of his parent by court order, then the parent's presence will not be required (Criminal Procedure (Scotland) Act 1995, s.42(2) to (6)).

23 Power to order parent to give security for the child's good behaviour

Where a child has been charged with any offence, the court may order his parent or guardian to give security for his co-operation in securing the child's good behaviour. No such order may be made without giving the parent or guardian an opportunity of being heard, unless the parent or guardian, having been required to attend, fails to do so (Criminal Procedure (Scotland) Act 1995, s.45).

24 Committal of children to place of safety and certificate of unruly character

S.51 of the Criminal Procedure (Scotland) Act 1995 (as amended by the Crime and Punishment (Scotland) Act 1997 s.56 and the Criminal Justice (Scotland) Act 2003 s.23) makes provision for a court to remand or commit for trial or for sentence a person under 21 years of age who is charged with or convicted of an offence and is not released on bail. In such a case—

    (a) a person aged 14 or 15 must be committed to the local authority who will have the duty of placing him, where the court requires, in secure accommodation or, in any other case, in a place of safety;

    (b) a person aged 16 or over who is subject to a supervision requirement (see **10 The supervision requirement**, above) may be committed to a prison, a young offenders institution, or to a local authority;

    (c) a person aged 16 or over who is not subject to a supervision requirement, must be committed to a remand centre, provided that the court has been notified by the Scottish Ministers that a remand centre is available for persons of his class or description, or to a prison or young offenders institution if the court has not been so notified.

E: PUNISHMENT OF CHILDREN AND YOUNG PERSONS

25 Detention

A person convicted of murder who is under the age of 18 years must not be sentenced to imprisonment for life but must be sentenced to be detained without limit of time in such place and under such conditions as the Scottish Ministers may direct (1995 Procedure Act, s.205(2)). Where a person convicted of murder has attained the age of 18 but is under the age of 21, he must not be sentenced to imprisonment for life but to be detained in a young offenders' institution and will be liable to be detained for life (Criminal Procedure (Scotland) Act 1995, s.205(3)).

Subject to the provisions of s.205 of the 1995 Procedure Act, where a child is convicted on indictment and the court is of the opinion that no other method of dealing with him is appropriate, it may sentence him to be detained for the period specified in the sentence in such place and on such conditions as the Scottish Ministers may direct (1995 Procedure ct, s.208).

No court must impose imprisonment on a person under 21 years of age. However, subject to the power to impose detention on a person under s.205 of the 1995 Procedure Act (see above), the court may impose detention on a person aged 16 but under 21 where, but for the fact that he is under age, a period of imprisonment might otherwise have been imposed. A sentence of detention may not be imposed unless the court is of the opinion that no other method of dealing with the offender is appropriate, having obtained such information as it can about the offender's circumstances and it must also take into account any information before it concerning the offender's character, and physical and mental condition. A sentence of detention imposed under s.207 is to be treated as a sentence of detention in a young offenders institution (1995 Procedure Act, s.207).

26 Substitution of custody for imprisonment where a child defaults on fine

Where a child would, if he were an adult, be liable to be imprisoned in default of payment of any fine, the court may, if it considers none of the other methods by which the case may legally be dealt with is suitable, order the child to be detained, for such period not exceeding one month as may be specified in the order, in a place chosen by the local authority for the area (Criminal Procedure (Scotland) Act 1995, s.216(7)).

For community payback order in respect of persons over 16 years of age, which may be imposed in default of payment of a fine or instead of imposing a fine, see the Note on **Treatment of Offenders**.

27 Detention in residential care

Under s.44 of the Criminal Procedure (Scotland) Act 1995, where a child pleads guilty to, or is found guilty of, an offence in summary proceedings before the sheriff and the offence is one in respect of which a sentence of imprisonment may be imposed on a person of the age of 21 or more, the sheriff may order that he be detained in residential accommodation by the appropriate local authority in such place (in any part of the United Kingdom) as the local authority may consider appropriate for a period not exceeding one year. Where a child is so detained he must be released from such detention not later than the date by which half the period specified in the order has (following commencement of the detention) elapsed, but, until the entire such period has elapsed, he may be required by the local authority to submit to supervision in accordance with such conditions as they consider appropriate. The local authority may, at any time, review the case of a child detained under the above provision and may, in consequence of such review and after having regard to the best interests of the child and the need to protect the public, release the child either conditionally or unconditionally. If, while released early from detention (and before the entire period specified in the order has elapsed), a child commits an offence in respect of which a person aged 21 or over could be imprisoned a court may order that he be returned to residential accommodation for the whole or any part of the period which (a) begins with the date of the order for his return and (b) is equal in length to the period between the date on which the new offence was committed and the date on which that entire period elapses. An order for return to residential care will, as the court may direct, either be for a period of detention before and to be followed by, or to be concurrent with, any period of detention to be imposed in respect of the new offence.

The Secure Accommodation (Scotland) Regulations 2013 make provision restricting the use of secure accommodation in respect of children detained under s.44. *Inter alia* they provide that such a child can be detained in secure accommodation only where the chief social work officer of the local authority and the person in charge of the establishment concerned are satisfied that–

    (a) the child has a history of absconding, he is likely to abscond unless kept in secure accommodation, and, if he absconds, it is likely that his physical, mental, or moral welfare will be at risk; or

    (b) he is likely to injure himself or other persons unless he is kept in secure accommodation;

and it is in the child's best interests that he be kept in secure accommodation (Reg. 9).

The Regulations also make provision relating to the review of the use of secure accommodation and the welfare of children kept therein (Reg. 13).

28 Release on licence

Under s.7 of the Prisoners and Criminal Proceedings (Scotland) Act 1993, where a child is detained under s.208 of the 1995 Act (see **25 Detention**, above) and the period specified in the sentence–

    (a) is less than four years, he must be released on licence by the Scottish Ministers as soon as half of the period so specified has elapsed;

    (b) is of four or more years, he must be so released as soon as two-thirds of the period so specified has elapsed.

If a child is released on licence, either under s.208 or s.7 and, before the date on which the entire period specified in the sentence elapses, he commits an offence in respect of which a person aged 21 or over could be sent to prison, a court may order that he be returned to detention for the whole or any part of the period which (a) begins with the date of the order for his return and (b) is equal in length to the period between the date on which the new offence was committed and the date on which the entire period so elapses. The period for which a child is ordered to be returned to detention will, as the court directs, either be served before and be followed by, or be served concurrently with, any sentence imposed for the new offence.

29 Authorities

Statutes–

Children (Scotland) Act 1995

Children's Hearings (Scotland) Act 2011

Criminal Justice (Scotland) Act 2003

Criminal Procedure (Scotland) Act 1995

Prisoners and Criminal Proceedings (Scotland) Act 1993

Vulnerable Witnesses (Scotland) Act 2004

Statutory Instruments–

Children's Hearings (Scotland) Act 2011 (Movement Restriction Conditions) Regulations 2013 (S.S.I. 2013 No. 210)

Children's Hearings (Scotland) Act 2011 (Safeguarders: Further Provision) Regulations 2012, as amended (S.S.I. 2012 No 336 and 2013 No. 203)

Children's Hearings (Scotland) Act 2011 (Safeguarders Panel) Regulations 2012 (S.S.I. 2012 No. 54)

Children's Hearings (Scotland) Act 2011 (Rules of Procedure in Children's Hearings) Rules 2013, as amended (S.S.I. 2013 No. 194 and 2015 No. 21)

Secure Accommodation (Scotland) Regulations 2013, as amended (S.I. 2013 No. 205, and 2015 No. 20)

TREATMENT OF OFFENDERS: ENGLAND AND WALES

1 Introduction

The powers of the criminal courts to deal with offenders are largely contained in the Powers of Criminal Courts (Sentencing) Act 2000, and the Criminal Justice Act 2003.

This Note is structured as follows–

A: General factors affecting sentencing
B: Discharge
C: Deferment of sentence or prosecution
D: Imprisonment
E: Early release of prisoners
F: Sex offenders
G: Criminal behaviour orders
H: Violent offender orders
I: Slavery and trafficking prevention and risk orders
J: Disqualification orders
K: Travel restriction orders (drug trafficking offenders)
L: Community orders
M: Fines and surcharges
N: Simple and conditional cautions
O: On-the-spot penalties
P: Compensation orders
Q: Confiscation and restraint orders
R: Miscellaneous powers
S: Miscarriage of justice

A: GENERAL FACTORS AFFECTING SENTENCING

2 Race and other aggravating factors

When a court is considering the seriousness of an offence (other than specifically for racially or religiously aggravated assault, criminal damage, public order offences or harassment) then, if the offence was racially or religiously aggravated the court must treat that as an aggravating factor and state in open court that the offence was so aggravated (Criminal Justice Act 2003, s.145). Similar provisions apply where an offence is aggravated by hostility based on sexual orientation, transgender identity, or disability (s.146). The sentence passed will reflect the aggravating factor.

When a court is considering the seriousness of certain offences connected with explosives, hostage taking, soliciting murder, safety of the channel tunnel and offences involving chemical, biological or nuclear weapons, it must consider whether the offence has or may have a terrorist connection. If it decides that it does, it must treat that as an aggravating factor when determining sentence (Counter-Terrorism Act 2008, ss.30 and 31).

3 Immunity from prosecution

A specified prosecutor may, if he thinks it appropriate for the purposes of the investigation or prosecution of any offence give a person an "immunity notice" (Serious Organised Crime and Police Act 2005, s.71). The effect of such a notice is that that person cannot be prosecuted for an offence of a type described in the notice except in specified circumstances. A notice will generally be subject to conditions and will cease to have effect if those conditions are not complied with.

Specified prosecutors include the Director of Public Prosecutions, and of the Serious Fraud Office (s.71(4)).

4 Restriction on use of evidence

A specified prosecutor (see **3 Immunity from prosecution**, above) may, if he thinks it appropriate for the purposes of the investigation or prosecution of any offence give a person a "restricted use undertaking" to the effect that any evidence given by that person will not be used against them in criminal proceedings except in specified circumstances (Serious Organised Crime and Police Act 2005, s.72). An undertaking will generally be subject to conditions and will cease to have effect if those conditions are not complied with.

5 Reduction in sentence for assistance by defendant

In deciding what sentence to pass on an offender who has pleaded guilty, a court must take into account the stage in the proceedings at which the offender indicated his intention to plead guilty, and the circumstances in which this indication was given (Criminal Justice Act 2003, s.144).

If a defendant who has pleaded guilty is (Serious Organised Crime and Police Act 2005, s.73)–

(a) convicted by a Crown Court, or committed to a Crown Court for sentence; and

(b) has, pursuant to a written agreement made with a specified prosecutor (see **3 Immunity from prosecution**, above), assisted or offered to assist the investigator or prosecutor in relation to that or any other offence,

then, in determining what sentence to pass the Court may take into account the extent and nature of the assistance given or offered. If the court passes a sentence which is less than it would have passed but for the assistance given or offered, it must (unless it would not be in the public interest to do so) state in open court that it has done so and what the greater sentence would have been. This provision does not however affect any requirements as to minimum sentences or minimum periods which must be served.

If he thinks that it is in the interests of justice to do so, a prosecutor can refer a case back to the court for a review of a sentence where (2005 Act, s.74)–

(c) a person who received a discounted sentence after having offered in a written agreement to give assistance to the prosecutor or investigator of an offence has knowingly failed to any extent to give assistance in accordance with the agreement;

(d) a person who received a discounted sentence after giving assistance to the prosecutor or investigator of an offence under a written agreement, gives or offers to give further assistance under another written agreement; or

(e) a person received a sentence which was not discounted but under a written agreement he has subsequently given or offered to give assistance to the prosecutor or investigator of an offence.

B: DISCHARGE

6 Absolute and conditional discharge

Where a court by or before which a person is convicted of an offence (not being an offence the sentence for which is fixed by law and certain other very serious offences) is of the opinion, having regard to the circumstances, including the nature of the offence and the offender's character, that punishment is inexpedient, it may make an order either discharging the person absolutely or discharging him subject to the condition that he commits no offence during such period, not exceeding three years, as may be specified in the order (Powers of Criminal Courts (Sentencing) Act 2000, s.12).

If it appears to the competent court (i.e., the Crown Court or a magistrates' court, as the case may be), that a person in whose case an order for conditional discharge has been made has been convicted and dealt with by a court in any part of Great Britain in respect of an offence committed during the period of discharge, the court may deal with him for the offence for which the order was made in any manner in which it could deal with him if it had just convicted him of that offence. In certain cases, if a person is convicted by another court of an offence committed during the relevant period, that court may deal with him in respect of the offence for which the order was made, in the above-mentioned manner (2000 Act, s.13).

C: DEFERMENT OF SENTENCE OR PROSECUTION

7 Circumstances when sentence may be deferred

Under ss.1 to 1D of the Powers of Criminal Courts (Sentencing) Act 2000, the Crown Court or a magistrates' court may defer passing sentence on an offender, with his consent, on one occasion only and for a period not exceeding six months from the date on which the deferment is announced by the court. The power to defer sentence may be exercised e.g., to allow for restorative justice activities to take place. The court may then have regard to the offender's engagement (or lack of engagement) in those activities when it passes sentence. However, the participation of the offender in restorative justice activities does not automatically affect the sentence given which is for the court to decide.

The court must be satisfied, having regard to the nature of the offence and the character and circumstances of the offender, that deferment would be in the interests of justice. An offender may be sentenced by the court before the expiration of the period of deferment only if, during that time, he is convicted in Great Britain of a subsequent offence.

8 Deferred prosecution agreements

In the case of certain alleged corporate economic or financial offences specified in the Crime and Courts Act 2013 s.45, Sch. 17 such as theft, false accounting and conspiracy to defraud an agreement between a designated prosecutor and an organisation facing prosecution for such an offence may be reached whereby the organisation agrees to comply with a range of terms and conditions and the prosecutor agrees to institute but then defer criminal proceedings for the alleged offence. Such an agreement is known as a deferred prosecution agreement. "Designated prosecutors" are the Director of Public Prosecutions and the Director of the Serious Fraud Office or any prosecutor designated by an order made by the Secretary of State (Sch. 17, para. 3). Those organisations that may enter into a deferred prosecution agreement may be a body corporate, a partnership or an unincorporated association, but may not be an individual (Sch. 17, para. 4). The effect of a deferred prosecution agreement is that proceedings instituted in respect of the alleged offence are automatically suspended. The suspension may only be lifted on an application to the Crown Court by the prosecutor, and no such application may be made at any time when the deferred prosecution agreement is in force. No other person (including a private prosecutor) may bring charges against the organisation for the same alleged offence whilst the prosecution is deferred (Sch. 17, para. 2). The requirements that an agreement may impose on an organisation include, but are not limited to, the following (Sch. 17, para. 5(3))–

(a) to pay to the prosecutor a financial penalty;

(b) to compensate victims of the alleged offence;

(c) to donate money to a charity or other third party;

(d) to disgorge any profits made by the organisation from the alleged offence;

(e) to implement a compliance programme or make changes to an existing compliance programme relating to the organisation's policies or to the training of the organisation's employees or both;

(f) to co-operate in any investigation related to the alleged offence;

(g) to pay any reasonable costs of the prosecutor in relation to the alleged offence or the deferred prosecution agreement.

Every agreement must contain a statement of facts relating to the alleged offence which may include admissions made by the organisation, and each agreement must specify an expiry date upon which it will cease to have effect (Sch. 17, para 5(1), (2)).

Where the prosecutor believes there has been a breach of an agreement the prosecutor may seek a factual determination from the court as to whether or not there has been a breach. The court must decide whether the organisation has failed to comply with the terms of the agreement. If the court determines that a breach has occurred, the court may either invite the parties to agree proposals to remedy the breach or decide to terminate the agreement. If the agreement is terminated, the prosecutor may seek to have the suspension of the criminal proceedings against the organisation lifted (Sch. 17, para 9).

If a deferred prosecution agreement remains in force until its expiry date, then after its expiry the proceedings instituted are to be discontinued by the prosecutor giving notice to the Crown Court that the prosecutor does not want the proceedings to continue. Where proceedings are discontinued, fresh criminal proceedings may not be instituted against the organisation for the alleged offence (Sch. 17, para. 11).

Schedule 17, para. 6 provides for a deferred prosecution agreement Code of Practice for prosecutors setting out guidance on the deferred prosecution agreement process. The Code must be Issued jointly by the Director of Public Prosecutions and the Director of the Serious Fraud Office.

D: IMPRISONMENT

9 Introduction

The most severe form of punishment normally available to the courts is imprisonment. A prison term may vary from a few days to a sentence for life. Most statutes creating an offence specify a limit to the term of imprisonment which may be imposed on a person convicted of the offence but, where they do not, s.77 of the Powers of Criminal Courts (Sentencing) Act 2000 prescribes a maximum term of two years. A person convicted of murder must be sentenced to life imprisonment.

By virtue of s.4 of the Criminal Attempts Act 1981, a person convicted on indictment under the Act of attempting to commit murder or any other offence the sentence for which is fixed by law is liable to imprisonment for life and a person so convicted of any other indictable offence or one triable either way is liable to the same penalty as for the completed crime.

10 General restrictions on imposing custodial sentences

Under s.152 of Criminal Justice Act 2003 where a person is convicted of an offence punishable with a custodial sentence (other than one fixed by law and certain other very serious offences (see **15 Sentences fixed by law and extended sentences**, below)) the court must not pass a custodial sentence unless it is of the opinion that the offence, or the combination of the offence and one or more associated offences, is so serious that neither a fine alone nor a community sentence can be justified.

A custodial sentence may also be passed on an offender who refuses to give his consent to a proposed community sentence (see below) or who fails to comply with a pre-sentence drug-testing requirement.

11 Procedural requirements for custodial sentences

Before forming an opinion as to the need for a custodial sentence, a court must normally obtain and consider a pre-sentence report, except that this need not be done where the court considers the obtaining of a report to be unnecessary. Where the offender is aged under 18 then, except where the offence or any associated offence is triable only on indictment, the court must not consider a pre-sentence report unnecessary, unless there exists a previous pre-sentence report on the offender and it has regard to that report (Criminal Justice Act 2003, s.156).

A pre-sentence report is a written report made, or submitted by a probation officer or social worker, containing such information as may be prescribed by rules (s.158). The failure of a court to obtain such a report does not invalidate any custodial sentence passed, but an appeal court may obtain and consider a report if none was obtained by the lower court (s.156(6)).

12 Restriction on imprisonment of persons not legally represented

S.83 of the Powers of Criminal Courts (Sentencing) Act 2000 provides that a magistrates' court or the Crown Court may not impose a sentence of imprisonment or of detention in a young offenders' institution (see the Note on **Treatment of Offenders: Children and Young Persons** at para **39 Young offender institutions**) on an offender who has not previously been sentenced to that form of punishment and who has not been legally represented in that court, unless–

(a) representation was made available to him for the purposes of the proceedings under Part 1 of the Legal Aid, Sentencing and Punishment of Offenders Act 2012 but this has been withdrawn because of his conduct or because it appeared that his financial resources were such that he was not eligible for such representation;

(b) he applied for such representation and the application was refused because it appeared that his financial resources were such that he was not eligible to be granted such representation; or

(c) having been informed of his right to apply for such representation and having had the opportunity to do so, he refused or failed to apply.

13 Restriction on imprisonment of mentally disordered offenders

S.157 of the Criminal Justice Act 2003 provides that, in a case where the court has obtained and considered a pre-sentence report (see 11 **Procedural requirements for custodial sentences**, above), it appears that an offender is mentally disordered, the court, must (unless they consider it unnecessary to do so) obtain and consider a medical report before passing any custodial sentence, other than one fixed by law. In addition, a court must consider (i) any information before it relating to the offender's medical condition (whether given in a medical report, a pre-sentence report, or otherwise); and (ii) the likely effect of a custodial sentence on that condition and on any available treatment.

Although no custodial sentence will be invalidated by a failure to comply with s.157, an appeal court may itself obtain and consider a medical report if none was obtained by the lower court (s.157(4)).

For further provision in relation to mentally disordered offenders, see **94 Hospital and guardianship orders**, below.

14 Length of custodial sentence

Where a court passes a custodial sentence it must be for the shortest term (not exceeding the permitted maximum) as is in the opinion of the court commensurate with the seriousness of the offence, or the combination of the offence and one or more associated offences (Criminal Justice Act 2003, s.153). This provision does not however apply where the sentence is fixed by law or where a minimum sentence is fixed by law (for certain dangerous offenders).

15 Sentences fixed by law and extended sentences

For certain offences, the sentence is fixed by law (e.g., a life sentence for murder). For other offences, there are "required" custodial sentences for offences which are not first offences. These required sentences are as follows–

(a) a minimum sentence of seven years for a third Class A drug trafficking offence (Powers of Criminal Courts (Sentencing) Act 2000, s.110);

(b) a minimum sentence of three years for a third domestic burglary (2000 Act, s.111).

(c) a life sentence where a person aged 18 or over is convicted of a violent or sexual offence (as listed in the Criminal Justice Act 2003, Sch. 15B) which is serious enough to justify a sentence of imprisonment of 10 years or more, if that person has previously been convicted of such an offence and was sentenced to imprisonment for life or for a period of 10 years or more in respect of that previous offence. However, the court is not obliged to impose a life sentence under this provision where it is of the opinion that there are particular circumstances which relate to the offence, the previous offence or the offender which would make it unjust to do so in all the circumstances (2003 Act, s.224A).

(d) unless it would be unjust to do so in all the circumstances, a minimum 6 months sentence for a second (or further) conviction in England and Wales for possession of a knife or offensive weapon where aged 18 or over at the time of the second conviction. A previous conviction for threatening with a knife or offensive weapon also counts as a "first strike". There is also a minimum 4 month Detention and Training Order for those aged 16 or over but under 18 when convicted of the second offence (Prevention of Crime Act 1953, s.1).

Where a person aged 18 or over is convicted of a serious offence and the court is of the opinion that there is a significant risk to members of the public of serious harm occasioned by the commission by him of further offences then, if the offence is one in respect of which the offender can be sentenced to life imprisonment and the court considers that the seriousness of the offence, or of the offence and one or more offences associated with it, is such as to justify the imposition of a sentence of life imprisonment then the court *must* impose a sentence of life imprisonment (s.225).

Where an offender is convicted of certain violent or sexual offences and the court considers that there is a significant risk to members of the public of serious harm occasioned by the commission by the offender of further offences but the court is not *required* (see above) to impose a sentence of imprisonment for life, it may impose on the offender an extended sentence of imprisonment. The court can do so only if, at the time the offence was committed, the offender had a previous conviction for a specified violent or sexual offence or, if the court were to impose an extended sentence of imprisonment, the term that it would specify as the appropriate custodial term would be at least four years. An extended sentence of imprisonment is one where the term is equal to the normal custodial term he would receive, together with a further period ("the extension period") for which the offender is to be subject to a licence and which is of such length as the court considers necessary for the purpose of protecting members of the public from serious harm occasioned by the commission by the offender of further offences. The extension period must be at least one year and the maximum extension period is five years for a violent offence and eight years for a sexual offence (s.226A).

The effect of the extension period is that the offender will remain on licence, and therefore liable to recall to custody, up to the end of the extension period.

16 Offenders of particular concern

Where an adult offender has been convicted of an offence listed in Schedule 18A to the Criminal Justice Act 2003 and been given a sentence of imprisonment (but not a life sentence or an extended determinate sentence under s.226A), the sentence must consist of a custodial term and a one year period of licence.

The offences listed in Schedule 18A are mainly terrorism connected offences and child sex offences.

Where the offender is aged 18-20, the sentence will be for detention in a young offender institution (Sch. 18A, para 10).

17 Intermittent custody

The Criminal Justice Act 2003 introduced intermittent custody orders whereby a court, with the consent of the offender, may make an order that the offender serve intermittent periods of his sentence in custody and the remainder of the sentence on licence (s.183). This power is only available to the court if the sentence is not less than 28 and not more than 51 weeks in respect of any one offence. The minimum number of days served in custody must be at least 14 and must not exceed 90 in respect of any one offence.

In the case of consecutive sentences, the aggregate length of the terms of imprisonment must not exceed 65 weeks, and the aggregate number of custodial days must not exceed 180.

Before making an order the court must have been notified by the Secretary of State that such orders are available for use in its area. The court must also consult the local probation board. It must have been notified that suitable prison accommodation will be available during the custodial periods and must be satisfied that the offender will have suitable accommodation available to him during the licence periods (s.184).

The licence may be granted subject to conditions requiring the offender to perform unpaid work or a specified activity, attend a specified programme, not perform specified activities, comply with a curfew, not enter a specified place, attend appointments for supervision, or, if aged under 25, attend at an attendance centre (s.182). As to the standard conditions applicable to such licences, see **26 Licence conditions**, below.

18 Suspended sentences

Under the Criminal Justice Act 2003, a court has the power to suspend a sentence of imprisonment which is at least 14 days but not more than 2 years long (including consecutive sentences) (s.189). Such a sentence may be suspended on condition that the offender–
  (i) complies with a supervision requirement and/or;
  (ii) does not commit another offence during the period for which the sentence is suspended.
The periods for each of (i) and (ii) must be between six months and two years.
The requirements which can be imposed under (i) above, are (s.190)–
  (a) an unpaid work requirement;
  (b) a rehabilitation activity requirement;
  (c) a programme requirement;
  (d) a prohibited activity requirement;
  (e) a curfew requirement;
  (f) an exclusion requirement;
  (g) a residence requirement;
 (ga) a foreign travel prohibition requirement;
  (h) a mental health treatment requirement;
  (i) a drug rehabilitation requirement;
  (j) an alcohol treatment requirement;
  (k) an alcohol abstinence and monitoring requirement;
  (l) in a case where the offender is aged under 25, an attendance centre requirement.

Suspended sentences can be reviewed periodically and amended where necessary (ss.191 and 192).

If, during the period of suspension, the offender fails to comply with a requirement, or commits a further offence punishable with imprisonment, the court before which the offender is then brought is required to order either that–

- the suspended sentence is to take effect;
- the suspended sentence will take effect with the substitution of a lesser term;
- the suspended order be amended to provide more onerous requirements or by extending its term; or
- the offender pay a fine not exceeding £2,500.

E: EARLY RELEASE OF PRISONERS

19 Introduction

Part 12 of the Criminal Justice Act 2003 (fixed-term prisoners) and Part II of the Crime (Sentences) Act 1997 (life sentence prisoners) provide for the early release of prisoners. For the purpose of advising the Secretary of State on any matter relating to the early release or recall of prisoners, the Parole Board (the Board), consisting of a chairman and four other members appointed by the Secretary of State has been established (Criminal Justice Act 2003, s.239 and Sch. 19).

20 Fixed-term prisoners: short terms

A fixed-term prisoner who is serving a sentence which is–
(a) for a term of one day; or
(b) for a term of less than twelve months and who is aged under 18 on the last day of the "requisite custodial period,

will be released unconditionally after having served the requisite custodial period: i.e., one-half of the sentence (Criminal Justice Act 2003, s.243A).

Consecutive sentences which add up to 12 months or more, are treated as a single sentence of 12 months or more. This means that where a sentence of less than 12 months is served consecutively with another sentence and either (i) the other sentence is 12 months or more, or (ii) the two sentences together add up to 12 months or more, then release for the sentence of less than 12 months will be on licence for the remainder of the sentence (see **21 Fixed-term prisoners**, below). However, where consecutive sentences add up to less than 12 months, release will be unconditional if (b) above applies (s.264).

21 Fixed-term prisoners

Requirement to release early

As soon as a fixed-term prisoner, other than one to whom s.243A applies (see **20 Fixed-term prisoners: short terms**, above), has served the "requisite custodial period", it is the duty of the Secretary of State to release him on licence (Criminal Justice Act 2003, ss.244).

The requisite custodial period is generally one half of the sentence. The licence period runs until the end of the original sentence.

Power to release early

A fixed-term prisoner may be released on licence (under the home detention early release scheme) up to 135 days before he has served half of his sentence provided that he has served a "requisite custodial period" (s.246). This will not apply unless–

(a) the requisite custodial period is at least 6 weeks;
(b) he has served at least four weeks of that period; and
(c) he has served at least one half of that period.
   In effect this means that the original sentence must have been at least three months as the requisite custodial period is one half of the original sentence: s.244.

The provisions do not apply to certain categories of prisoner including: those serving sentences of 4 years or more, sex offenders, those liable to deportation (see below), prisoners subject to a hospital order or direction, those serving an extended sentence (see below), and those previously released and recalled under the scheme for breach of licence conditions (during a previous or current sentence), and those previously returned to prison for committing a further offence before the expiry of a previous sentence.

Any licence under s.246 must contain curfew conditions requiring the offender to remain at specified places at specified times (not less than nine hours a day) and provision for electronic monitoring (i.e., "tagging") (s.250).

Prisoners serving extended sentences

Where a prisoner is serving an extended sentence: (see **15 Sentences fixed by law and extended sentences**, above), they will be considered for release on licence by the Parole Board once they have served two-thirds of the appropriate custodial term, and will be released automatically at the end of the appropriate custodial term if the Parole Board has not already directed release (s.246A). Different provisions apply to those sentenced before 13th April 2015 – those sentenced prior to that date for less serious offences (i.e., those not listed in Sch. 15B) are subject to automatic release at the two thirds point of their sentence.

Any licence must contain curfew conditions requiring the offender to remain at specified places at specified times (not less than nine hours a day), and provision for electronic monitoring (i.e., "tagging") (s.250).

Prisoners to be removed from the UK

Shorter periods apply where a prisoner is to be removed from the UK (s.260). Such a prisoner can be released (and removed) up to 270 days earlier than their normal release date

22 Discretionary life prisoners

Under s.28 of the Crime (Sentences) Act 1997, the Secretary of State has a duty to release on licence certain life prisoners in respect of whom a minimum term order has been made. As soon as the prisoner has served the minimum term and the Board has directed his release under s.28, it is the duty of the Secretary of State to release him. The Board must not direct a prisoner's release under s.28 unless his case has been referred to them by the Secretary of State and they are satisfied that it is no longer necessary for the protection of the public that the prisoner be confined. A prisoner may require the Secretary of State to refer his case to the Board once he has served his minimum term.

A prisoner whose case has been refused by the Board under s.28 may require the Secretary of State to refer his case back to the Board after two years.

23 Mandatory life prisoners

A mandatory life sentence is one where that sentence is fixed by law, e.g., murder. If the offender was 21 or over when the offence was committed and the court is of the opinion that the offence (or the offence in combination with other offences) is so serious that the early release provisions should not apply it must make an order to that effect (Criminal Justice Act 2003, s.269). In any other case, the court must order that the early release provisions will apply after he has served a specified part of his sentence. As to the early release provisions, see **22 Discretionary life prisoners**, above. In specifying the part of the sentence which must be served, the court is fixing a minimum term which must be served before the parole board can consider the prisoner for release. It must have regard to the following general principles (set out in Sch. 21)–

(a) where the seriousness of the offence (or the combination of the offence and one or more offences associated with it) is exceptionally high, and the offender was aged 21 or over when he committed the offence, the appropriate starting point is a whole life order;

(b) where the case does not fall within (a) above but the court considers that the seriousness of the offence (or combination of offences) is particularly high, and the offender was aged 18 or over when he committed the offence, the appropriate starting point, in determining the minimum term, is 30 years;

(c) where an offender aged 18 or over takes a knife or other weapon to the scene of the crime with the intention of using it to commit any offence or to use it as a weapon and does use it in committing a murder, the appropriate starting point, in determining the minimum term, is 25 years.

The Home Secretary no longer has any role in determining the minimum term which must be served or in deciding whether to release a prisoner serving a mandatory life sentence on licence.

24 Offenders of particular concern

Offenders who are of particular concern because of the offence they committed (see **16 Offenders of particular concern**, above) are subject to discretionary release by the Parole Board between the halfway and end point of the custodial term (Criminal Justice Act 2003, s.244A).

25 Release on compassionate grounds

The Secretary of State may, at any time, release a prisoner on licence on compassionate grounds. (2003 Act, s.248). S.30 of the Crime (Sentences) Act 1997 contains a similar provision in respect of life prisoners.

26 Licence conditions

Where a prisoner is released on licence, the licence will normally remain in force until the prisoner would (but for his release) have served his sentence (Criminal Justice Act 2003, s.249).

Any licence in respect of a prisoner serving one or more sentences of imprisonment of less than twelve months and no sentence of twelve months or more must include the conditions required by the relevant court order and, so far as not inconsistent with them, the standard conditions, and may also include, so far as compatible, conditions as to electronic monitoring and drug testing (see below) and such other prescribed conditions as the Secretary of State may for the time being consider to be necessary for the protection of the public and specify in the licence.

Any licence in respect of a prisoner serving a sentence of imprisonment for a term of twelve months or more must include the standard conditions, provision for electronic monitoring ("tagging"), and such other conditions as the Secretary of State may prescribe (s.250).

The Secretary of State may revoke a licence and recall a prisoner released on licence to prison (s.254). A person recalled to prison may make written representations with respect to his recall and these must be referred to the Board.

S.32 of the Crime (Sentences) Act 1997 contains similar provisions in relation to life prisoners.

The Criminal Justice (Sentencing) (Licence Conditions) Order 2015 provides that the standard licence conditions are (Art. 2)–

(a) to be of good behaviour and not behave in a way which undermines the purpose of the licence period (i.e., to protect the public, prevent re-offending, and promote successful re-integration);

(b) not commit any offence;

(c) keep in touch with the responsible officer in accordance with instructions;

(d) receive visits from the responsible officer in accordance with instructions;

(e) reside permanently at a specified address and obtain prior permission to stay overnight elsewhere;

(f) undertake work only with approval, and give advance notice of any proposal to undertake work or a particular type of work;

(g) not to travel abroad without prior permission unless for the purposes of immigration deportation or removal;

When preparing for the release of a determinate sentenced offender, supervising officers will consider whether to recommend any additional condition which must in turn be approved by the Governor of the releasing prison. These other conditions concern (Art. 7)–

(h) residence at a certain place;

(i) restriction of residency;

(j) making or maintaining contact with a person;

(k) participation in, or co-operation with, a programme or set of activities;

(l) possession, ownership, control or inspection of specified items or documents;

(m) disclosure of information;

(n) a curfew arrangement;

(o) freedom of movement;

(p) supervision in the community by the supervising officer, or other responsible officer, or organisation.

Other standard conditions where relevant relate to electronic monitoring, drug testing and polygraph testing.

A drug testing requirement can only be imposed as part of a licence if the Secretary of State is satisfied that–

(1) the misuse of a specified Class A or B drug by the offender caused or contributed to a past offence or is likely to cause or contribute to further offending; and

(2) the offender is dependent on, or has a propensity to misuse, a specified Class A or Class B drugs.

The specified drugs are cocaine and diamorphine (Class A); cannabis, cannabis resin, and amphetamine (Class B) (Criminal Justice (Specified Class A Drugs) Order 2001 No. 1816; Criminal Justice (Specified Class B Drugs) Order 2015 No. 9).

27 Supervision on release

Where a person is given a custodial sentences of more than 1 day but less than 2 years they will be liable to supervision on release Criminal Justice Act 2003, s.256AA). The supervision period begins at the end of the sentence and ends on the expiry of 12 months from the date of release. This means that an offender serves half of their custodial sentence in custody, the second half under licence in the community, with the post-sentence supervision period then applying until the offender has spent 12 months in the community since their automatic release date.

For example, if a person is given an 10 month sentence, they will serve 5 months in prison, 5 months on licence, and then have 7 months post-sentence supervision.

During the supervision period the offender must comply with any of the following requirements as may be specified to him (s.256AB)–

(a) to be of good behaviour and not to behave in a way which undermines the purpose of the supervision period;

(b) not to commit any offence;

(c) to keep in touch with the supervisor in accordance with instructions given by the supervisor;

(d) to receive visits from the supervisor in accordance with instructions given by the supervisor;

(e) to reside permanently at an address approved by the supervisor and to obtain the prior permission of the supervisor for any stay of one or more nights at a different address;

(f) not to undertake work, or a particular type of work (paid or unpaid), unless it is approved by the supervisor and to notify the supervisor in advance of any proposal to undertake work or a particular type of work;

(g) not to travel outside the British Islands, except with the prior permission of the supervisor or in order to comply with a legal obligation;

(h) to participate in activities in accordance with any instructions given by the supervisor;

(i) a drug testing requirement;

(j) a drug appointment requirement

Where it is proved to the satisfaction of the court that a person has failed without reasonable excuse to comply with a supervision requirement the court may (s.256AC)–

(k) order the person to be committed to prison for a period of up to 14 days (or a young offender institution if aged under 21),

(l) order the person to pay a fine not exceeding level 3 on the standard scale (see **68 Maximum fines: the "standard scale"**, below), or

(m) make a "supervision default order" imposing either an unpaid work requirement or an electronically monitored curfew requirement.

F: SEX OFFENDERS

28 Notification requirements

The Sexual Offences Act 2003 contains notification requirements for persons (s.80)—

(a) convicted of specific sex offences;

(b) found not guilty of such an offence by reason of insanity;

(c) found to be under a disability and to have done the act charged in respect of such an offence; or

(d) cautioned in respect of such an offence.

Such persons must notify the police within three days of their release (from custody or remand), and annually thereafter (or such other period as may be prescribed where the offender has no residence), of their (ss.83 and 85)—

(i) name (all names used), both at the time of conviction and the time of release;

(ii) home address, both at the time of conviction and the time of release, and the address of any other premises where he regularly resides or stays;

(iii) date of birth;

(iv) National Insurance number;

(v) passport details (added by the Sexual Offences Act 2003 (Travel Notification Requirements) Regulations 2004);

(vi) any information prescribed by regulations made by the Secretary of State. The Sexual Offences Act 2003 (Travel Notification Requirements) Regulations 2004 require that a relevant offender notify the police as to whether he has a bank or building society account, or a debit or credit card.

This is commonly known as the "sex offenders register" although the requirement is to "notify" rather than to "register".

An offender must also notify the police of any changes in the above information within three days (s.84).

The police must also be notified if he stays away from his usual home address for a period of seven days, or a total of seven days in any 12 month period. Failure to do so Is an offence punishable on summary conviction to imprisonment for six months or an unlimited fine, or both; and on conviction on indictment to a term not exceeding five years (s.91). A person giving a notification must also allow the police to take his fingerprints, his photograph or both (s.87(4)). These checks are to allow the police to verify a person's identity.

A person subject to the notification requirements must also, in accordance with regulations made by the Secretary of State, notify police if he intends to leave the UK, giving specified details as to the date of his departure and travel plans (s.86). The Sexual Offences Act 2003 (Travel Notification Requirements) Regulations 2004 provide that where a person intends to be abroad he must notify police at least seven days before his departure, unless that is not reasonably practicable, and in any event within 12 hours of departure. Where known, details must be given of the (first) country to which he will be travelling, his point of arrival in each country he is to visit, the carriers he intends to travel with, accommodation arrangements outside the UK, date of intended return and intended point of arrival on his return. Within three days of returning he must disclose his point of arrival and date of return to the police (if he hasn't already done so). Notices must be given by attendance in person at a local police station. It should be noted here that if a UK National does an act in a country outside the UK, being an act which if done in England and Wales, or in Northern Ireland, would constitute an offence specified in Schedule 2 to the Sexual Offences Act 2003 that person is guilty in that part of the UK of that sexual offence (Sexual Offences Act 2003 s.72 as amended).

A magistrate may, on application from a senior police officer, issue a warrant to allow a constable to enter and search the home of a relevant offender for the purposes of assessing the risks that the offender may pose to the community. The address must be one that the offender has notified to the police as his home address or one in respect of which there is a reasonable belief that the offender can be regularly found there or resides there. The offender must not be in custody, detained in a hospital or outside the UK at the time. A constable must have tried on at least two previous occasions to gain entry to the premises for the purpose of conducting a risk assessment and been unable to gain entry for that purpose. The warrant must specify each address to which it relates and a constable may use reasonable force if it is necessary to do so to enter and search the premises. The warrant can authorise as many visits as the magistrate considers to be necessary for the purposes of assessing the risks posed by the offender (s.96B, inserted by the Violent Crime Reduction Act 2006, s.58).

The police may apply for a notification order in respect of a person if paragraphs (a) to (d) above apply to that person in respect of an offence committed abroad. Application can be made retrospectively in respect of any conviction since 1 September 1997, with the notification period running from the date of conviction abroad (Sexual Offences Act 2003, s.97).

29 Period of notification

The length of the notification period varies according to the length of the sentence. If a person was sentenced to imprisonment for public protection or for 30 months or more, the notification period is an indefinite period (i.e., for life, but see *Note* below). For sentences of less than 30 months, the notification period varies from 10 years (sentences between 6 and 30 months) to 2 years (cautions) or the length of a conditional discharge or period of probation (s.82, as amended by the Violent Crime Reduction Act 2006, s.57).

For persons under 18 at the date of conviction or caution, these periods are halved (s.82(2)). The court may direct the parent of an offender under the age of 18 to comply with the notification requirements (s.89).

Note.–On the 21st April 2010 in the case of *R (on the application by JF (by his litigation friend OF)) v Secretary of State for the Home Department* the Supreme Court held that an indefinite notification period constituted a disproportionate interference with Article 8 of the European Convention of Human Rights (right to respect for a private and family life: see the Note on **The Human Rights Act 1998**) as there was no procedure for reviewing requirements in individual cases. This has been remedied by providing a mechanism for periodic review of the justification for continuing notification in individual cases. Reviews will be held 15 years (8 years for offenders under 18 at the date of conviction) after release from prison. At a review, a chief constable will decided whether to discharge the notification requirement or, if satisfied that the offender still poses a risk of sexual harm, make a notification continuation order which can last for up to 15 years, after which period another review will be carried out (ss.91A to 91G added by the Sexual Offences Act 2003 (Remedial) Order 2012, S.I. No. 1883).

30 Sexual harm prevention orders

Where a court deals with a person in respect of an offence listed in Schedules 3 or 5 to the Sexual Offences Act 2003 (which cover most sexual offences), they may make a sexual harm prevention order. An order may also be made if a court is satisfied that the defendant's behaviour since conviction (including conviction overseas) or caution for such an offence, makes it necessary to make an order for the purpose of–

 (i) protecting the public or any particular members of the public from sexual harm from the defendant, or
 (ii) protecting children or vulnerable adults generally, or any particular children or vulnerable adults, from sexual harm from the defendant outside the UK.

A magistrates' court (or youth court, where the defendant is under 18) may also make such an order when an application is made to it by the police or the National Crime Agency (s.103A), and an interim order can be made until the main application is considered (s.103F).

An order will prohibit the defendant from doing anything described in the order that the court considers necessary for the purpose of (i) and (ii) above and will have effect either for a fixed period, specified in the order, of at least five years, or until further order (s.103C). An order can include a prohibition on foreign travel to a specified country or countries (or to all foreign countries). Where the order prevents the person from any travel outside the UK, they must surrender their passport to the police for the duration of the prohibition (s.103D). A foreign travel prohibition cannot be for more than five years, but can be renewed.

A person made subject to a sexual harm prevention order will also be made subject to the notification requirements for registered sex offenders, if they are not already so subject (see **28 Notification requirements**, above).

31 Sexual risk orders

The police and the National Crime Agency may apply to a magistrates' court for a sexual risk order where a person has done an act of a sexual nature (whether or not they have a conviction) and, as a result, the police or NCA have reasonable cause to believe that an order is necessary to (s.122A)–

 (a) protect the public or any particular members of the public from harm from the defendant; or
 (b) protect children or vulnerable adults generally, or any particular children or vulnerable adults, from harm from the defendant outside the UK.

An order can include any prohibition the court considers necessary for the purposes of (a) and (b),, including the prevention of foreign travel (on the same basis as for sexual harm prevention orders) (s.122C), and will have effect either for a fixed period, specified in the order, of at least two years, or until further order. A foreign travel prohibition cannot be for more than five years, but can be renewed (ss.122A, 122C).

An interim order can be made until the main application is considered (s.122E).

A person subject to an order (or an interim order) must notify to the police, within three days, of their name and address (and any subsequent changes to this information) (s.122F).

Note.– The sexual risk order differs from the risk of sexual harm order (applicable in Scotland) in that it can be made after the defendant has committed only one act of a sexual nature, rather than two.

32 Forfeiture and detention of vehicles etc.

When a person is convicted on indictment of an offence under s.2 of the Modern Slavery Act 2015 (human trafficking) the court may order the forfeiture of a land vehicle, ship or aircraft used or intended to be used in connection with the offence (s.11). If a person has been arrested for an offence under s.2, a constable or senior immigration officer may detain a relevant land vehicle, ship or aircraft. A land vehicle, ship or aircraft is relevant if the constable or officer has reasonable grounds to believe that an order for its forfeiture could be made under s.11 if that person were convicted of the offence (s.12).

33 Release on licence—lie detector tests

When offenders convicted of certain sexual offences are released on licence, a "polygraph condition" may be imposed (Offender Management Act 2007, s.28). Such a condition will require the offender to (s.29) participate in polygraph (i.e., lie detector) sessions conducted with a view to (a) monitoring his compliance with the other conditions of his licence; or (b) improving the way in which he is managed during his release on licence. The procedure for carrying out the tests is prescribed by the Polygraph Rules 2009.

G: CRIMINAL BEHAVIOUR ORDERS

34 Criminal behaviour orders

S.22 of the Anti-social Behaviour, Crime and Policing Act 2014 provides for the making of "criminal behaviour orders" where a person has been convicted of an offence and either sentenced or conditionally discharged. They have replaced both "anti-social behaviour orders" and "drinking banning orders".

A court may make a criminal behaviour order against an offender only if the prosecutor applies for it and the court—
- (a) is satisfied, beyond reasonable doubt, that the offender has engaged in behaviour that caused or was likely to cause harassment, alarm or distress to any person; and
- (b) considers that making the order will help in preventing the offender from engaging in such behaviour.

An order may prohibit the offender from doing anything described in the order and/or require him to do anything described in the order. An order must, so far as practicable, avoid any interference with either the times, if any, at which the offender normally works or attends school or any other educational establishment; and any conflict with the requirements of any other court order or injunction to which the offender may be subject.

Where the offender is aged under 18, the prosecution must find out the views of the local youth offending team before applying for an order.

In considering making an order, the court can consider evidence which was inadmissible in the criminal proceedings (such as hearsay or bad character evidence (s.23(2)). The automatic reporting restrictions on certain information (such as the name, address or school of a child or young person) that normally apply in respect of legal proceedings in relation to a person under 18 do not apply to proceedings in which a CBO is made, however, the court has a discretion to prohibit the publication of certain information that would identify a child or young person (s.23(7) and (8)).

Where a criminal behaviour order is made against a person aged under 18 it must be for a fixed period of between one and three years. In the case of an adult, a criminal behaviour order must be for either a fixed period of two years or more or for an indefinite duration – there is no maximum length (s.25).

In the case of offenders under the age of 18, the order must be reviewed every 12 months (s.28). The review must consider the offender's compliance with the order and the support provided to help him or her comply with it, and give consideration to whether an application should be made to vary or discharge the order. The review should be carried out by the police with the local authority and any other relevant person or body (s.29)

H: VIOLENT OFFENDER ORDERS

35 Violent offender orders

Part 7 of the Criminal Justice and Immigration Act 2008 has introduced the violent offender order, a civil order designed to protect the public from the risk of serious harm from a "qualifying offender". Such an order may contain prohibitions, restrictions or conditions preventing the offender from (2008 Act, s.102)–
- (a) going to any specified premises or any other specified place;
- (b) attending any specified event;
- (c) having any contact with a specified individual.

A chief officer of police may by complaint to a magistrates' court apply for a violent offender order to be made in respect of a person who resides in the chief officer's police area or who the chief officer believes is in, or is intending to come to, that area, if it appears the following conditions are met (2008 Act, s.100)–
- (d) that the person is a qualifying offender (see below);
- (e) that the person has acted in such a way, since he became a qualifying offender (referred to as the "appropriate date"), as to give reasonable cause to believe that it is necessary for a violent offender order to be made in respect of the person.

An order will have effect for not less than two, nor more than five, years. The "public" is defined as either the general public or a particular member of public in the UK (2008 Act, s.98). A "qualifying offender" means a person aged 18 or over who has been convicted of murder or a specified offence and either (2008 Act, s.99)–
- (f) a custodial sentence of at least 12 months was imposed for the offence or a hospital order was made in respect of it (with or without a restriction order); or
- (g) the person has been found not guilty of a specified offence by reason of insanity and the court made in respect of the offence a hospital order (with or without a restriction order) or a supervision order; or
- (h) the person has been found to be under a disability and to have done the act charged in respect of a specified offence and the court made in respect of the offence a hospital order (with or without a restriction order) or a supervision order.

The provisions also apply to offences committed outside England and Wales by providing that if the criteria set out in (i) to (iii) above apply in respect of equivalent sentences or findings of court (and that a relevant order has been made if applicable) that person will fall within these provisions (2008 Act, s.99(4)).

A "specified offence" means (2008 Act, s.98(3))–

  (i) manslaughter;

  (ii) soliciting murder;

  (iii) wounding with intent to cause grievous bodily harm;

  (iv) malicious wounding;

  (v) attempting to commit murder or conspiracy to commit murder;

  (vi) a relevant service offence.

There is a procedure for making an interim violent offender order where it appears to the court desirable to act with a view to securing the immediate protection of the public from the risk of serious violent harm (2008 Act, s.104). An offender subject to either a full or interim violent offender order will be subject to notification requirements (2008 Act, s.108). A person, including the offender, may apply for an order varying or discharging a violent offender order (2008 Act, s.103).

All offenders subject to violent offender orders (full or interim) are also be subject to notification requirements meaning that they must provide the police with a home address or place where they can be regularly found. If they have no sole or main residence, notification must be given weekly. An offender must also notify the police, within 3 days, of the address of any premises in the UK at which he has stayed for a "qualifying period" and, which he has not already notified to them. This place might be a friend or relative's house or a hotel where he has stayed. A "qualifying period" is any period of 7 days, or two or more periods, in any twelve months, which taken together amount to 7 days. Notification must also be given if the offender wants to leave the UK for 3 days or more, and again on his return (Criminal Justice and Immigration Act 2008 (Violent Offender Orders) (Notification Requirements) Regulations 2009 (S.I. 2019).

Notification is given by attending any police station in the offender's local police area and giving an oral notification to any police officer or other authorised person at that station.

I: SLAVERY AND TRAFFICKING PREVENTION, RISK AND REPARATION ORDERS

36 Slavery and trafficking prevention orders

Where an offender is convicted for a slavery or human trafficking offence (as defined), the court may make a slavery and trafficking prevention order if it is satisfied that there is a risk that he may commit another such offence and that it is necessary to make an order for the purposes of protecting persons generally, or particular persons, from physical or psychological harm which would be likely to occur if the defendant did commit such an offence (Modern Slavery Act 2015, s.14).

An order may prohibit the person in respect of whom it is made from doing anything described in it, such as participating in a particular type of business, operating as a gangmaster, visiting a particular place, working with children, or travelling to a specified country and will last for a fixed period of at least five years, or until further order (s.17). A prohibition on foreign travel (which involves surrendering any passport the offender has to the police) cannot exceed five years, but may be renewed at the end of that period (s.18). A person subject to an order may also be required to notify specified people of their address and of any change of address (s.19).

An interim order can be made whilst the court considers the making of a full order (s.21).

37 Slavery and trafficking risk orders

A magistrates' court may make a slavery and trafficking risk order on an application by the police, an immigration officer or the National Crime Agency if it is satisfied there is a risk that the defendant may commit a slavery or human trafficking offence and that it is necessary to make an order for the purpose of protecting persons generally, or particular persons, from physical or psychological harm which would be likely to occur if the defendant committed such an offence. There is no requirement for the person in respect of whom an order is sought to have previously been convicted or cautioned in relation to a criminal offence (Modern Slavery Act 2015, s.23).

The restrictions that an order can contain are similar to those for slavery and trafficking prevention orders (see **36 Slavery and trafficking prevention orders**, above) save that, except for a ban on foreign travel (which must be for a fixed period of not more than 5 years), the maximum term is two years, with renewals thereafter.

38 Slavery and trafficking reparation orders

The court may make a slavery and trafficking reparation order against a person under s.8(1) of the Modern Slavery Act 2015 if–

  (a) the person has been convicted of an offence under s.1 of that Act (slavery, servitude and forced or compulsory labour), s.2 (human trafficking) or s.4 (committing offence with intent to commit offence under s.2); and

  (b) a confiscation order is made against the person in respect of the offence.

The court may also make such an order against a person if (s.8(2))–

(c) by virtue of s.28 of the Proceeds of Crime Act 2002 (defendants who abscond during proceedings) a confiscation order has been made against a person in respect of an offence under ss.1, 2 or 4 of the 2015 Act; and

(d) the person is later convicted of the offence.

A slavery and trafficking reparation order is an order requiring the person against whom it is made to pay compensation to the victim of a relevant offence for any harm resulting from that offence (s.9(1)). "Relevant offence" means the offence under ss.1, 2 or 4 of which the person is convicted and any other offence under ss. 1, 2 or 4 which is taken into consideration in determining the person's sentence (s.9(2)).

J: DISQUALIFICATION ORDERS

39 Nature of disqualification orders

Disqualification orders were introduced by the Criminal Justice and Court Services Act 2000 Part II. They are mandatory in certain circumstances and have the effect of prohibiting a person from working with children (see **43 Effect of a disqualification order**, below). They apply when a person is convicted of an "offence against a child", as defined in Schedule 4 to the Act. The listed offences include most sexual offences as well as murder, manslaughter, serious assaults, kidnapping and false imprisonment.

For these purposes, a "child" is a person under the age of 18 (s.42).

Note, however, that where a person is barred from regulated activity (which includes work involving certain close contact with children) under the Safeguarding Vulnerable Groups Act 2006 no disqualification order can be made in relation to that person. For the provisions of the Safeguarding Vulnerable Groups Act 2006 regarding barring of individuals see the Note on **Protection of Children and Young Persons** at B: EMPLOYMENT TO WORK WITH CHILDREN.

40 When orders must be made

S.28 of the Criminal Justice and Court Services Act 2000 provides that a court must make a disqualification order against an individual convicted of an offence committed against a child, unless having regard to all the circumstances it considers that it is unlikely that the individual will commit any further offences against a child, if either–

(a) a "qualifying sentence" has been imposed by a "superior court" in respect of the conviction; or

(b) a "relevant order" has been made by a senior court in respect of the act or omission charged against him as the offence.

In this context, a "qualifying sentence" is a sentence of 12 months or more of–

(a) imprisonment (including a suspended sentence);

(b) detention in a young offender institution;

(c) detention under s.91 of the Powers of Criminal Courts (Sentencing) Act (under 18 offenders convicted of serious offences);

(d) a detention and training order;

(e) detention (including a suspended sentence) imposed by a court-martial;

or a sentence of detention during Her Majesty's pleasure, a hospital order or a guardianship order.

A "relevant order" means an order made by the Crown Court, the Court of Appeal, or a court-martial that the individual in question be admitted to hospital; or a guardianship order.

A "superior court" means one of the above courts.

Where the court does not make a disqualification order in circumstances where it is obliged to do so, the prosecutor may apply to it for one to be made (s.29B).

Where the offender was under 18 at the time of the commission of the offence, the court must only make a disqualification order if it is satisfied, having regard to all the circumstances, that it is likely that the individual will commit a further offence against a child. If it does make an order it must state its reasons for so doing.

Note.–A Youth Court may not impose a disqualification order as it is not a "senior court".

41 When orders may be made

Where an offender (adult or child) is sentenced by a senior court for an offence against a child, but the sentence imposed is not a qualifying sentence, the court still has a discretion to make a disqualification order if it satisfied, having regard to all the circumstances, that it is likely that the individual will commit a further offence against a child. If it does make such an order it must give its reasons for doing so and they must be included in the record of the proceedings (Criminal Justice and Court Services Act 2000, s.29A).

42 Review of disqualification orders

An individual subject to a disqualification order may make an application to the Tribunal established under the Protection of Children Act 1999 for it to determine whether or not he is to continue to be subject to the disqualification. If the Tribunal is satisfied that the individual is suitable to work with children, it must direct that the order is to cease to have effect, otherwise it must dismiss the application (Criminal Justice and Court Services Act 2000, s.32).

An application may only be made with the leave of the Tribunal. No application may be made unless ten years has elapsed since the offender was released from custody or hospital (or in the case of a suspended sentence, ten years from the making of the order) and no application may be made within ten years of a previous application (s.33). In the case of an individual under 18 at the time of the commission of the offence, the ten year periods are reduced to five years. The Tribunal may not grant an application unless it is satisfied that the individual's circumstances have changed since the order was made (or the last application was made) and that the change is such that the application should be granted.

If a disqualification order is no longer in force, but an individual has acted in such a way as to give reasonable cause to believe that an order is necessary to protect children in general, or any children in particular, from serious harm from him, the police or social services may apply to the High Court for the order to be restored (s.34).

43 Effect of a disqualification order

An individual who is the subject of a disqualification order will be guilty of an offence if he knowingly applies for, offers to do, accepts or does any work in a "regulated position" (Criminal Justice and Court Services Act 2000, s.35).

A "regulated position" is one where the normal duties include (s.36)–
(a) work at a specified establishment (including schools, children's homes and hospital and care homes exclusively or mainly for children);
(b) work on day care premises;
(c) caring for, training, supervising, or being in sole charge of children;
(d) unsupervised contact with children under arrangements made with a responsible person (e.g., a parent, guardian, head teacher, registered day care provider, etc.);
(e) caring for children under the age of 16 in the course of the children's employment;
(f) to a substantial degree, supervising or training children under the age of 16 in the course of the children's employment.

The Act also prescribes as "regulated positions": a member of an educational institution's governing body, a member of a local authority who discharges education or social service functions, a director of social services or chief education officer, a charity trustee of a children's charity (i.e., a charity whose workers normally include individuals who work in regulated positions), a member of the Youth Justice Board, the Children's Commissioner for Wales (and his deputy), and a member of the Children and Family Court Advisory and Support Service.

An individual will also be guilty of an offence if he knowingly offers work in a regulated position to, or procures wok in a regulated position for, an individual who is disqualified from working with children; or fails to remove such an individual from such work (s.35(2)).

Persons subject to certain disqualification orders are excluded from the scope of s.35 where they are or have been at any time barred from regulated activity under the Safeguarding Vulnerable Groups Act 2006 or have been included in the children's barred list but are removed from that list by the Disclosure and Barring Service (previously introduced in the 2006 Act as the Independent Barring Board and subsequently renamed by the Policing and Crime Act 2009 as the Independent Safeguarding Authority). For a person to be excluded from the scope of s.35, that person must be subject to a disqualification order immediately before the Disclosure and Barring Service included him in the children's barred list and at that time the Disclosure and Barring Service was aware that the person was subject to the disqualification order. For the provisions of the Safeguarding Vulnerable Groups Act 2006 regarding barring of individuals see the Note on **Protection of Children and Young Persons** at B: EMPLOYMENT TO WORK WITH CHILDREN.

A disqualification order is disregarded when determining a person's rehabilitation period under the Rehabilitation of Offenders Act 1974, which is calculated according to the sentence (see the Note on **Rehabilitation of Offenders**).

K: TRAVEL RESTRICTION ORDERS (DRUG TRAFFICKING OFFENDERS)

44 Introduction

The Criminal Justice and Police Act 2001 introduced powers to impose overseas travel restrictions on offenders convicted of certain drug trafficking offences. The "trigger" offences covered by this provision are listed in s.34 and include the production and supply of controlled drugs.

45 When an order may be made

A travel restriction order may be made by a court if a person has been convicted of one of the specified drug trafficking offences and has been sentenced to a term of imprisonment of four years or more (Criminal Justice and Police Act 2001, s.33). In every such case the court must consider whether to make an order, and if it decides not to it must state the reasons why.

46 Effect of a travel restriction order

A travel restriction order has the effect of prohibiting an offender who has a United Kingdom passport from leaving the UK at any time specified in the order (which will be not less than two years) beginning with the date of the offender's release from custody. The offender may be required to hand over his passport for the duration of the travel ban period (Criminal Justice and Police Act 2001, s.33).

47 Revocation and suspension of orders

An offender may apply for a travel restriction order to be revoked after a minimum period has passed. The minimum period varies according to the length of the ban that has been imposed. A four-year ban may not be revoked until two years have passed, a ban of more than four and less than ten years may not be revoked until four years have passed, and any other ban may not be revoked until five years have passed (Criminal Justice and Police Act 2001, s.35). In deciding whether to revoke an order the court must take into account the offender's character, his conduct since the making of the order and the offences for which he was originally convicted.

An offender may apply for an order to be suspended and the court may do so if it is satisfied that there are exceptional circumstances which justify a suspension on compassionate grounds (s.35(3)). If an order is suspended, the offender has a duty to be in the United Kingdom at the time when the suspension ends. Where an order is suspended, the total length of the travel ban imposed by the order is extended for the length of the suspension period.

48 Offences

A person who leaves the United Kingdom in breach of a travel ban, or who is not in the UK at the end of a period during which the ban has been suspended, will be guilty of an offence. An offence is punishable on summary conviction to a term of imprisonment not exceeding six months, or an unlimited fine, or both; and on conviction on indictment to imprisonment for a term not exceeding five years or a fine, or both (Criminal Justice and Police Act 2001, s.36).

L: COMMUNITY ORDERS

49 General

Under s.177 of the Criminal Justice Act 2003, a court may impose a community order on a person aged 18 or over who is convicted of an offence. A community order is an order imposing on an offender any one or more of the following requirements—
  (a) an unpaid work requirement;
  (b) a rehabilitation activity requirement;
  (c) a programme requirement;
  (d) a prohibited activity requirement;
  (e) a curfew requirement;
  (f) an exclusion requirement;
  (g) a residence requirement;
 (ga) a foreign travel prohibition requirement;
  (h) a mental health treatment requirement;
  (i) a drug rehabilitation requirement;
  (j) an alcohol treatment requirement;
  (k) an alcohol abstinence and monitoring requirement;
  (l) in a case where the offender is aged under 25, an attendance centre requirement.
Where a court makes a community order, it must (unless there are exceptional circumstances relating to the offence or to the offender which would make it unjust in all the circumstances) include in the order at least one requirement imposed for the purpose of punishment, or impose a fine for the offence in respect of which the community order is made, or both (s.177(2A), (2B)).

Before making a community order imposing two or more different requirements the court must consider whether, in the circumstances of the case, the requirements are compatible with each other.

If an offender breaches a community order, a court may either vary the order to make its requirements more onerous (e.g., by extending the duration of a requirement or adding a new one), or revoke the order and re-sentence the offender as if he had just been convicted. The court must take into account the extent to which the offender has already complied with the order. If he has wilfully and persistently failed to comply with a community order the court can re-sentence the offender to custody even if the original offence was not serious enough to justify a custodial sentence. A court may also fine an offender up to £2,500 in relation to a breach (and in that case the order will continue in force).

50 The unpaid work requirement

An offender in respect of whom an unpaid work requirement of a community order is in force must perform for the number of hours specified in the order such work at such times as he may be instructed by the responsible officer (Criminal Justice Act 2003, s.200). Unless revoked, a community order imposing an unpaid work requirement remains in force until the offender has worked under it for the number of hours specified in it.

The number of hours which a person may be required to work under an unpaid work requirement must be specified in the relevant order and must be in the aggregate not less than 40 nor more than 300 (s.199).

A court may not impose an unpaid work requirement in respect of an offender unless after hearing (if the courts thinks necessary) an officer of a local probation board or an officer of a provider of probation services, the court is satisfied that the offender is a suitable person to perform work under such a requirement.

51 The rehabilitation activity requirement

An offender in respect of whom a rehabilitation activity requirement of a community order is in force must comply with any instructions to attend appointments or participate in activities or both (Criminal Justice Act 2003, s.200A).

The specified activities may consist of or include activities whose purpose is that of reparation, such as activities involving contact between offenders and persons affected by their offences. The court imposing the requirement must specify in the order the maximum number of days for which the offender may be instructed to participate in activities, and any instructions must be given with a view to promoting the rehabilitation of the offender, although they may also serve other purposes.

A court may not include an activity requirement in an order if compliance with it would involve the co-operation of a person other than the offender and the offender's responsible officer, unless that other person consents to its inclusion.

52 The programme requirement

An offender in respect of whom a programme requirement of a community order is in force must participate in an accredited programme on such number of days as may be specified in the order (Criminal Justice Act 2003, s.202).

53 The prohibited activity requirement

An offender in respect of whom a prohibited activity requirement of a community order is in force must refrain from participating in activities specified in the order on a day or days so specified or during a period so specified (Criminal Justice Act 2003, s.203).

A court may not include a prohibited activity in an order unless it has consulted an officer of a local probation board or an officer of a provider of probation services.

It is expressly provided that a requirement that may be included in an order includes a requirement that the offender does not possess, use or carry a firearm.

54 The curfew requirement

An offender in respect of whom a curfew requirement of a community order is in force must remain, for periods specified in the relevant order, at a place so specified (Criminal Justice Act 2003, s.204). The curfew requirement may specify different places or different periods for different days, but may not specify periods which amount to less than two hours or more than sixteen hours in any day and may not specify periods beyond the period of twelve months beginning with the day on which the order is made.

Before making an order imposing a curfew requirement, the court must obtain and consider information about the place proposed to be specified in the order (including information as to the attitude of persons likely to be affected by the enforced presence there of the offender).

55 The exclusion requirement

An offender in respect of whom an exclusion requirement of a community order is in force must not enter a place (which includes an "area") specified in the order for a period (not exceeding two years) so specified (Criminal Justice Act 2003, s.205).

An exclusion requirement may provide for the prohibition to operate only during the periods specified in the order and may specify different places for different periods or days.

56 The residence requirement

An offender in respect of whom a residence requirement of a community order is in force must, during a period specified in the order, reside at a place specified in the order (Criminal Justice Act 2003, s.206). If the order so provides, a residence requirement does not prohibit the offender from residing, with the prior approval of the responsible officer, at a place other than that specified in the order.

Before making a community order or suspended sentence order containing a residence requirement, the court must consider the home surroundings of the offender and may not specify a hostel or other institution as the place where an offender must reside, except on the recommendation of an officer of a local probation board.

57 The mental health treatment requirement

An offender in respect of whom a mental health treatment requirement of a community order is in force must submit, during a period or periods specified in the order, to treatment by or under the direction of a registered medical practitioner or a chartered psychologist (or both, for different periods) with a view to the improvement of the offender's mental condition (Criminal Justice Act 2003, s.207).

The treatment required must be such one of the following and must be specified in the order–

(a) treatment as a resident patient in an independent hospital or care home or a hospital, but not in hospital premises where high security psychiatric services are provided;

(b) treatment as a non-resident patient at such institution or place as may be specified in the order;

(c) treatment by or under the direction of such registered medical practitioner or chartered psychologist (or both) as may be so specified;

The nature of the treatment is not to be specified in the order except as mentioned in (a), (b) or (c) above.

A court may not include a mental health treatment requirement unless it is satisfied that the mental condition of the offender is such as requires and may be susceptible to treatment, but is not such as to warrant the making of a hospital order or guardianship order; that arrangements have been or can be made for the treatment intended to be specified in the order; and that the offender has expressed his willingness to comply with such a requirement.

58 The drug rehabilitation requirement

An offender in respect of whom a residence requirement of a community order is in force must (Criminal Justice Act 2003, s.209)–

(a) submit to treatment by or under the direction of a specified person having the necessary qualifications or experience with a view to the reduction or elimination of the offender's dependency on or propensity to misuse drugs, and

(b) for the purpose of ascertaining whether he has any drug in his body during that period, provide samples, at such times or in such circumstances as may (subject to the provisions of the order) be determined by the responsible officer or by the person specified as the person by or under whose direction the treatment is to be provided.

A court may not impose a drug rehabilitation requirement unless it is satisfied that–

(i) the offender is dependent on, or has a propensity to misuse, drugs and that his dependency or propensity is such as requires and may be susceptible to treatment;

(ii) arrangements have been or can be made for the treatment intended to be specified in the order;

(iii) the requirement has been recommended to the court as being suitable for the offender by an officer of a local probation board or an officer of a provider of probation services; and

(iv) the offender expresses his willingness to comply with the requirement.

Treatment may be resident or non-resident.

A community order or suspended sentence order imposing a drug rehabilitation requirement may (and must if the treatment and testing period is more than 12 months) provide for the requirement to be reviewed periodically at intervals of not less than one month (s.210). At a review hearing, the court may amend the community order or suspended sentence order, so far as it relates to the drug rehabilitation requirement if the offender expresses his willingness to comply with the requirement as amended, but may not reduce the period for which the drug rehabilitation requirement has effect below six months (s.211). If the offender fails to express his willingness to comply with the drug rehabilitation requirement as proposed to be amended by the court, the court may revoke the community order, or the suspended sentence order and the suspended sentence to which it relates and deal with him, for the offence in respect of which the order was made, in any way in which he could have been dealt with for that offence by the court which made the order if the order had not been made.

59 The alcohol treatment etc requirements

An offender in respect of whom an alcohol treatment requirement of a community order is in force must submit during a period (of not less than six months) specified in the order to treatment by or under the direction of a specified person having the necessary qualifications or experience with a view to the reduction or elimination of the offender's dependency on alcohol (Criminal Justice Act 2003, s.212).

A court may not impose an alcohol treatment requirement in respect of an offender unless it is satisfied that he is dependent on alcohol, that his dependency is such as requires and may be susceptible to treatment, and that arrangements have been or can be made for the treatment intended to be specified in the order.

A court may not impose an alcohol treatment requirement unless the offender expresses his willingness to comply with its requirements.

Treatment may be resident or non-resident.

An offender in respect of whom an alcohol abstinence and monitoring requirement of a community order is in force must (for a maximum of 120 days) either abstain from consuming alcohol for a period specified in the order, or not consume an amount of alcohol during a specified period such they have a level of alcohol in their body higher than that specified by the order. An offender on whom such a requirement is imposed must submit to monitoring for the purposes of ascertaining whether they are complying with the requirement (s.212A–in force only in the South London local justice area, comprising Croydon, Lambeth, Southwark and Sutton for a trial period until 31st January 2016–see S.I. 2014 No. 1777, as amended by S.I. 2015 No. 1480).

60 The attendance centre requirement

An offender in respect of whom an attendance centre requirement of a community order is in force must attend at a specified attendance centre for such number of hours as may be so specified, being not less than 12 or more than 36 (Criminal Justice Act 2003, s.214).

A court may not impose an attendance centre requirement unless it is satisfied that an attendance centre is available for persons of the offender's description which is reasonably accessible to him, having regard to the means of access available to him and any other circumstances. An offender may not be required to attend at an attendance centre on more than one occasion on any day, or for more than three hours on any occasion.

61 The foreign travel prohibition requirement

An offender in respect of whom a foreign travel prohibition requirement of a community order is in force is prohibited from travelling to a country or countries (or territory or territories) outside the British Islands (i.e., the UK, the Channel Islands and the Isle of Man) for a specified period of up to 12 months (Criminal Justice Act 2003, s.206A).

62 Pre-sentence reports

Unless in the circumstances it considers it unnecessary to do so, a court must obtain and consider a pre-sentence report before forming an opinion as to as to the suitability for the offender of the particular requirement or requirements to be imposed by a community order (Criminal Justice Act 2003, s.156). The court may accept a report given orally in open court, except in relation to an offender under 18, where a report must be in writing (2003 Act, ss.157, 158).

Where a pre-sentence report is made by a probation officer to any court the offender, or his counsel or solicitor, must be given a copy of it as must the prosecutor (2003 Act, s.159).

63 Pre-sentence drug testing

Where a person is convicted of an offence and the court is considering passing a community sentence or a suspended sentence, it may make an order requiring the offender to undergo pre-sentence drug testing to ascertain whether he has any specified Class A drug in his body (Criminal Justice Act 2003, s.161). Failure to comply with the order is punishable by a fine not exceeding level 4 on the standard scale (see **68 Maximum fines: the "standard scale"**, below).

64 Electronic monitoring

S.215 of the Criminal Justice Act 2003 provides for the electronic monitoring of an offender's compliance with the requirements of a community sentence. A requirement for electronic monitoring may only be included in an order in those areas where suitable arrangements are in place to cope with such an order.

M: FINES AND SURCHARGES

65 Circumstances in which fines may be imposed

Under s.163 of the Criminal Justice Act 2003, where a person is convicted on indictment of any offence (other than one for which the sentence is fixed by law or for which a minimum sentence is prescribed), the court, if not precluded from sentencing him by the exercise of some other power, may impose a fine instead of, or in addition to, dealing with him in any other way in which the court has power to deal with him, subject, however, to any enactment requiring the offender to be dealt with in any particular way.

Subject to its jurisdictional limits, a magistrates' court has power to impose a fine in respect of any offence (Magistrates' Courts Act 1980, s.34). Under s.164 of the 2003 Act a court is required to inquire into the assets and other financial circumstances of any individual offender before fixing the amount of any fine. The amount of the fine must reflect the seriousness of the offence and take into account the circumstances of the case, including the financial circumstances of the offender so far as they are known or appear to the court. The maximum level of a fine may be fixed by law by reference to "the standard scale" (see **68 Maximum fines: the "standard scale"**, below).

A court may, before sentencing an individual offender, order him to furnish to the court, within a specified period, a statement of his means, and it is an offence to fail to provide such a statement or to provide false information.

The Register of Fines Regulations 2003 establish a register of unpaid fines imposed by magistrates' courts. The register is kept by the Lord Chancellor. An entry will be cancelled if the fine is paid in full within 28 days of it being entered in the register, otherwise an entry will remain in the register for five years.

66 Consequences of default

Under s.139 of the Powers of Criminal Courts (Sentencing) Act 2000 where the Crown Court imposes a fine on any person, the court may make an order allowing time for payment or directing payment by specified instalments on specified dates. In addition, the court must make an order fixing the term of imprisonment (or of detention, in the case of persons aged between 17 and 20 years) appropriate to the amount of the fine imposed, as set out in the Table to the section, which that person is to undergo if any sum which he is liable to pay is not duly paid or recovered. A person must not, on the occasion when a fine is imposed, be committed to prison in pursuance of such an order unless–

(a) in the case of an offence punishable with imprisonment, he appears to have sufficient means to pay forthwith; or

(b) it appears to the court that he is unlikely to remain long enough at a place of abode in the UK to enable payment of the sum to be enforced by other methods; or

(c) on the occasion when the order is made, the court sentences him to immediate imprisonment or detention in a detention centre for that or another offence, or he is already serving a term of imprisonment or detention.

Under the Magistrates' Courts Act 1980, a magistrates' court has a similar power to dispense with immediate payment of a fine (s.75) and is similarly restricted from imposing imprisonment in default of payment (s.82). A magistrates' court imposing a fine is empowered to impose a term of imprisonment in default of payment of the fine only in the circumstances set out at (a), (b), and (c) above; the maximum term which may be so specified is 12 months. *Inter alia*, a magistrates' court may remit fines if the court thinks it just to do so having regard to any change in the offender's circumstances (1980 Act, s.85). A court may also in the case of a defaulter under the age of 25, commit them to an attendance centre (2000 Act, s.60).

Under s.24 of the 1991 Act the Secretary of State may by regulations provide that, where a fine or surcharge is imposed by a magistrates' court or a compensation or unlawful profit order or a slavery and trafficking reparation order is made against an offender by such a court and the offender is entitled to universal credit, income support, jobseeker's allowance, employment and support allowance or state pension credit, the court may apply for the deduction at source of sums due by way of fine or compensation from the offender's benefit payments. The Fines (Deduction from Income Support) Regulations 1992 have been made in exercise of this power (and relate to all the above benefits).

67 New provisions from July 2006

The Courts Act 2003 introduced new provisions as to the payment and enforcement of fines (s.97, and Schs. 5 and 6).

Discharge of fines by unpaid work

Where a person aged 18 or over is fined by a magistrates' court, the court may, either of its own motion or on the application of a fines officer, make a "work order" (Courts Act 2003, Sch. 6). Such an order may be made where–

(a) considering the offender's financial circumstances, the normal methods of enforcing payment of the fine are likely to be impracticable or inappropriate;

(b) it appears to the court that the offender is a suitable person to perform unpaid work; and

(c) the offender consents.

The order must specify the number of hours which need to be worked, the date by which the work must be performed, and must specify a supervisor.

The Discharge of Fines by Unpaid Work (Prescribed Hourly Sum) Regulations 2004 (S.I. No. 2196) prescribe that one hour's unpaid work is equivalent to £6 of a fine.

Attachment of Earnings and Benefit Deduction Orders

Where a court imposes a fine without a requirement for immediate payment, or with such a requirement but the defendant has failed to pay it, then the court may impose an Attachment of Earnings Order or a Benefit Deduction Order. Where the defendant is an existing defaulter, such an order can be made without his consent, otherwise he must consent.

Where the sum due includes a sum under a compensation order, the court must make an attachment of earnings/benefit deduction order unless it is impracticable or inappropriate, whether or not the defendant consents.

In order to assist a magistrates' court in deciding whether to make an application for benefit deductions, the Secretary of State is permitted to disclose details of whether a person is in receipt of prescribed benefits to a designated officer of the court. The benefits prescribed for these purposes are universal credit, contribution-based jobseeker's allowance, income-based jobseeker's allowance, income-related employment and support allowance, income support and state pension credit.

Collection Orders

Where a court imposes a fine without a requirement for immediate payment, or with such a requirement but the defendant has failed to pay it, then the court, whether or not it has made an Attachment of Earnings Order or a Benefit Deduction Order, may make a Collection Order. The Order will state the amount due and the "payment terms". Where an Attachment or Benefit Deduction Order has been made, these are reserve terms to come into effect if that Order fails (e.g. because an employer fails to comply with it or Secretary of State decides not to make benefit deductions). If a person defaults on the payment terms then, if no Attachment or Benefit Deduction Order has been made, such an Order can be made by the fines officer. If the fine remains unpaid, further steps are available (see below).

Further steps

The further steps which may be taken include–

(a) issuing a warrant of distress;

(b) registering the sum due in the register of judgments and orders;

(c) making an Attachment or Benefit Deduction Order if not already made;

(d) making a clamping order in respect of a motor vehicle of the defendant's, and subsequently selling it (not applicable to vehicles displaying disabled badges); or

(e) taking proceedings for enforcement in the county court or the High Court (e.g., for a third part debt order or charging order to secure payment).

Where a person is in default on a collection order due to his wilful refusal or culpable neglect, the fines officer can refer the case back to the magistrates' court who have the power to increase the fine by up to 50%.

The Fines Collection Regulations 2006, as amended (S.I. 2006 No. 501) contain detailed requirements as to these provisions.

68 Maximum fines: the "standard scale"

Frequently, the maximum level of a fine for a particular offence will be fixed by law by reference to a particular level on the "standard scale". This scale, which applies only to summary offences, is contained in the Criminal Justice Act 1982 s.37 as substituted by the Criminal Justice Act 1991 s.17.

The current levels on the standard scale are–

Level 1	£200
Level 2	£500
Level 3	£1,000
Level 4	£2,500
Level 5	unlimited

The maximum fine that may be imposed on a child (i.e., under the age of 14) is £250; and on a young person (i.e., under the age of 18) is £1,000 (Magistrates Court Act 1980 ss.24 and 36).

69 Surcharges

When a court is dealing with an offender, in addition to the sentence it passes, it must also impose a surcharge. For these purposes a court does not "deal with" a person if it discharges the person absolutely or makes an order under the Mental Health Act 1983 in respect of that person (Criminal Justice Act 2003, s.161A). The Secretary of State has the power to prescribe further exceptions (see below). It is intended that the surcharge will be paid into a fund to provide practical and emotional support to a range of victims of crime. Where a court considers it appropriate that an offender pay one or more of a compensation order (see **76 Compensation orders**, below), an unlawful profit order and a slavery and trafficking reparation order to a victim, that order takes priority over the surcharge, and if the court considers that the offender should pay such an order and has insufficient means to pay the surcharge as well, it must reduce the surcharge accordingly, if necessary, to nil (s.161A(3)).

The Criminal Justice Act 2003 (Surcharge) Order 2012 prescribes the amount of surcharge where one is payable. The amount of surcharge payable in relation to offences committed by individuals under 18 is set out in Table 1 of the Schedule to the Order as follows (Art.3)–

A conditional discharge	£15
A fine	£20
A youth rehabilitation order	£20
A referral order	£20
A community order	£20
A suspended sentence of imprisonment	£30
A custodial sentence	£30

In respect of offences committed by individuals who were 18 or over at the time the offence was committed the surcharge amount is to be determined by reference to Table 2 of the Schedule to the Order as follows (Art.4)–

A conditional discharge	£20
A fine	10% of the value of the fine, rounded up or down to the nearest pound, which must be no less than £30 and no more than £170

A community order	£85
A suspended sentence of imprisonment where the sentence of imprisonment or detention in a young offender institution is for a period of 6 months or less	£115
A suspended sentence of imprisonment where the sentence of imprisonment or detention in a young offender institution is for a determinate period of more than 6 months	£140
A sentence of imprisonment or detention in a young offender institution imposed for a determinate period of up to and including 6 months	£115
A sentence of imprisonment or detention in a young offender institution imposed for a determinate period of more than 6 months and up to and including 24 months	£140
A sentence of imprisonment or detention in a young offender institution for a determinate period exceeding 24 months	£170
A sentence of imprisonment or custody for life	£170

Where a court imposes more than one disposal the surcharge amount, where the corresponding amounts specified are the same, is that amount; where the corresponding amounts are not the same, the surcharge amount is the highest of those amounts.

A court's duty to order payment of surcharge does not apply in cases in which a court deals with a person for one or more offences and does not impose any disposal described in the Schedule to the 2012 Order. The 2012 Order also specifies the amount of surcharge for offences committed by a person who is not an individual (i.e. a legal person): Art. 6, Schedule, Table 3.

70 Criminal courts charges

Where a person aged 18 or over is convicted of an offence the court must order them to pay a charge in respect of relevant court costs (Prosecution of Offences Act 1985, s.21A). The charge has however been suspended pending a review: see the Prosecution of Offences Act 1985 (Criminal Courts Charge) Regulations 2015 as amended by S.I. 2015 No. 1970.

N: SIMPLE AND CONDITIONAL CAUTIONS

71 Simple cautions

A simple caution provides a means for the police to deal with a person aged 18 or over who has admitted committing a criminal offence and agrees to be given a caution. It does not involve any court or tribunal process or the imposition of any condition or sanction. There are restrictions which mean that a caution may not be given (Criminal Justice and Courts Act 2015, s.17)

  (a) for an offence triable only on indictment, unless there are exceptional circumstances and the Director of Public Prosecutions consents;

  (b) for an offence that is triable either way and which is specified in an Order made by the Secretary of State, unless there are exceptional circumstances;

  (c) for a summary or a non specified either-way (i.e., any other offence not within (a) or (b)) if the person has, in the two years before the commission of the current offence, received a caution (including a youth caution, youth conditional caution and an adult conditional caution), or conviction for a similar offence, unless there are exceptional circumstances.

Whether there are "exceptional circumstances" for the purposes of (a) is not to be determined by a police officer below the rank of Superintendent; and whether there are "exceptional circumstances" for the purposes of (b) or (c) and whether a previous offence is "similar" to the current offence is not to be determined by a police officer below the rank of Inspector (Criminal Justice and Courts Act 2015 (Simple Cautions) (Specification of Police Ranks) Order 2015). The "specified" offences for the purposes of (b) above are set out in the Criminal Justice and Courts Act 2015 (Simple Cautions) (Specification of Either-Way Offences) Order 2015 and are mainly those serious violent and sexual offences that would ordinarily attract a custodial sentence were the offender convicted.

72 Conditional cautions

A conditional caution is a caution to which conditions are attached which the offender must comply with. The conditions attached must have the object of facilitating the rehabilitation of the offender, punishing the offender, and/or ensuring that he makes reparation for the offence and may require him to attend at a specified place at specified times or pay a financial penalty (Criminal Justice Act 2003, s.22). In the case of a an offender who is a foreign national and who does not have leave to enter or remain in the UK, the object of the conditional caution can be to bring about their departure from the UK and ensure that they do not return to the UK for a period.

Conditional cautions may be given to offenders if (s.23)–

(a) there is evidence that the offender has committed an offence;

(b) an authorised person decides that there is sufficient evidence to charge the offender but that a conditional caution should be given;

(c) the offender admits the offence;

(d) the effect of a conditional caution is explained to the offender including that failure to comply with the conditions may result in the offender being prosecuted for the offence; and

(e) the offender signs a document containing details of the offence, an admission that he committed the offence, his consent to being given a conditional caution, and the conditions attached to the caution (which may include a financial condition–see below). If he fails to comply with the conditions, this document may be used in subsequent proceedings for the original offence (s.24).

Before deciding what conditions to attach to a conditional caution, reasonable efforts must be made to obtain the views of the victim (if any) of the offence, and in particular the victim's views as to whether the offender should carry out any of the actions listed in a community remedy document (see the Note on **Anti-Social Behaviour** at para **53 The community remedy**). If the victim expresses the view that they should carry out a particular action listed in the community remedy document, that action must be attached as a condition unless it seems that it would be inappropriate to do so. Where there is more than one victim and they express different views, those views must nevertheless be taken account in deciding what conditions to attach to the conditional caution (s.23ZA).

A conditional caution may be given by an authorised person i.e., a constable, an investigating officer, or a person authorised by a relevant prosecutor. A Code of Practice in relation to conditional cautions is brought into force by the Criminal Justice Act 2003 (Conditional Cautions: Code of Practice) Order 2013 (S.I. No. 801).

For these purposes a "relevant prosecutor" means the Attorney General, the Director of the Serious Fraud Office, the Director of Public Prosecutions, a Secretary of State, or a person who is specified in an order made by the Secretary of State as being a relevant prosecutor (s.27).

The police have the power to arrest and detain a person suspected of breaching a conditional caution (s.24A).

The Criminal Justice Act 2003 (Conditional Cautions: Financial Penalties) Order 2013 provides for the following maximum financial penalty conditions to be attached to a conditional caution–

(a) for any summary offence: £50;

(b) for any offence triable either way: £100; and

(c) for any offence triable only on indictment: £150.

O: ON-THE-SPOT PENALTIES

73 Penalty notices

A police officer may issue a penalty notice to any person aged 18 or over who appears to him to have committed a penalty offence (Criminal Justice and Police Act 2001, s.2). A penalty notice gives that person an opportunity to discharge any liability to conviction for the offence by payment of a fixed penalty. There is thus no conviction and no admission of guilt. If the alleged offender does not want to pay the penalty, he has the option to opt for a trial (s.4).

74 Penalty offences

A penalty notice may only be issued in respect of a penalty offence. These are listed in s.1 of the Criminal Justice and Police Act 2001 (as extended by the Criminal Justice and Police Act 2001 (Amendment) Orders 2002/1934, 2009/110, 2012/1430, and 2014/1365 and the Criminal Justice and Police Act 2001 (Amendment) and Police Reform Act 2002 (Modification) Order 2004/2540) and relate primarily to theft, criminal damage, alcohol-related offences and other disorder offences such as behaviour likely to cause harassment, alarm or distress, throwing objects at trains, throwing fireworks, trespassing on a railway, wasting police time or giving a false report, giving a false alarm to a fire brigade, possession of cannabis or khat and litter offences.

Penalty notices are discretionary, the police may instead arrest and charge an alleged offender if they believe that the offence is such that it should be dealt with by the courts.

75 Amount of penalty and effect of non-payment

The maximum amount of a penalty notice is one quarter of the maximum amount which a person could be fined on summary conviction for the offence plus a half of the relevant surcharge payable under s.161A of the Criminal Justice Act 2003 (see **69 Surcharges**, above) (Criminal Justice and Police Act 2001, s.3). The Penalties for Disorderly Behaviour (Amount of Penalty) Order 2002 sets penalties of either £90 (including sale of tobacco etc to persons under 18 years, wasting police time or giving false report, disorderly behaviour while drunk in a public place, possession of cannabis etc., theft, destroying or damaging property, making off without payment, behaviour likely to cause harassment, alarm or distress, touting for hire car services, using a public electronic communications network in order to cause annoyance, inconvenience or needless anxiety, and throwing fireworks in a thoroughfare) or £60 (any other penalty offence).

A penalty must be paid within 21 days, failing which the police may register a fine of one and half times the penalty with the local magistrates' court. The fine will be enforced by the magistrates' court as if it had imposed it (s.4).

P: COMPENSATION ORDERS

76 Compensation orders

Under s.130 of the Powers of Criminal Courts (Sentencing) Act 2000 a court must consider whether to make a compensation order against a convicted person. A court may make such an order, on application or otherwise, and in addition to dealing with him in any other way, so as to require him to pay compensation for any personal injury, loss, or damage resulting from the offence of which he is convicted, or any other offence taken into consideration in determining sentence, or to make payments for funeral expenses or bereavement in respect of a death resulting from any such offence, other than a death due to an accident arising out of the presence of a motor vehicle on a road; and a court must give reasons, on passing sentence, if it does not make such an order in a case where it has the power to do so. In the case of an offence under the Theft Act 1968, where the property in question is recovered, any damage to the property occurring while it was out of the owner's possession is to be treated for the purposes of compensation order as having resulted from the offence, however and by whomsoever it was caused (s.130(5)). A compensation order may only be made in respect of injury, loss, or damage (other than loss suffered by a person's dependants in consequence of his death) which was due to an accident arising out of the presence of a motor vehicle on a road, if–

(a) it is in respect of damage which is treated by s.130(5) above as resulting from an offence under the Theft Act 1968, or

(b) it is in respect of injury, loss, or damage as respects which–
  (i) the offender is uninsured in relation to the use of the vehicle; and
  (ii) compensation is not payable under any arrangements to which the Secretary of State is a party (see the Note on **Accidents and Insurance**);

and, where a compensation order is made in respect of injury, loss, or damage due to such an accident, the amount to be paid may include an amount representing the whole or part of any loss of or reduction in preferential rates of insurance attributable to the accident. For these purposes, a vehicle the use of which is exempted from insurance by s.144 of the Road Traffic Act 1988 is not uninsured. A compensation order in respect of funeral expenses may be made for the benefit of anyone who incurred the expenses. A compensation order in respect of bereavement may be made only for the benefit of a person for whose benefit a claim for damages for bereavement could be made under s.1A of the Fatal Accidents Act 1976 and such an amount must not exceed the amount specified in s.1A of the 1976) (s.130(6) to (10)).

In deciding whether to make a compensation order against a convicted person and in determining the amount to be paid if such an order is made, the court must have regard to the means of the convicted person so far as known. Where the court considers that it would be appropriate both to impose a fine and to make a compensation order but the offender has insufficient means to pay both, the court must give preference to compensation (though it may impose a fine as well) (s.130(11) and (12)).

There is no limit on the value of a compensation order handed down to an adult offender by a magistrates' court, but in the case of an order imposed on a young offender (i.e., an offender under the age of 18) the maximum compensation amount is £5,000 (s.131).

There is provision for the suspension of a magistrates' court compensation order pending the result of an appeal and for the effect of an appeal on a compensation order (s.132).

77 Review of compensation orders

S.133 of the Powers of Criminal Courts (Sentencing) Act 2000 enables a magistrates' court responsible for enforcing a compensation order to review it, on the application of the person against whom it was made, at any time before the whole of the compensation has been paid into court, but at a time when (disregarding any power of a court to grant leave to appeal out of time) there is no further possibility of appeal, and it appears to the court that–

(a) the injury, loss, or damage has been held in civil proceedings to be less than it was taken to be for the purposes of the order; or

(b) in the case of an order in respect of the loss of any property, that the property has been recovered; or

(c) that the means of the person against whom the order was made are insufficient to satisfy both the order and any or all of the following made against him in the same proceedings (i) a confiscation order under Part 6 of the Criminal Justice Act 1988 or Part 2 of the Proceeds of Crime Act 2002, (ii) an unlawful profit order under s.4 of the Prevention of Social Housing Fraud Act 2013, or (iii) a slavery and trafficking reparation order under s.8 of the Modern Slavery Act 2015; or

(d) that the person against whom the order was made has suffered a substantial reduction in his means which was unexpected at the time when the order was made and that his means seem unlikely to increase for a considerable period.

Where the order was made by the Crown Court, a magistrates' court must not exercise any of its powers under s.133 in a case where it is satisfied as mentioned in paragraph (c) or (d) above unless it has first obtained the consent of the Crown Court. S.134 provides for the amount of a compensation order to be taken into account in the award of damages in any subsequent civil proceedings.

78 Application of proceeds of forfeited property

S.145 of the Powers of Criminal Courts (Sentencing) Act 2000 enables a court making an order under s.143 (see **88 Deprivation of property used for crime (forfeiture orders)**, below) to make an order applying the proceeds of the disposal of forfeited property (not exceeding a specified sum) for the benefit of a person who has suffered personal injury, loss, or damage. Such an order may be made only if the court is satisfied that but for the inadequacy of the means of the offender it would have made a compensation order requiring the offender to pay compensation of an amount not less than the specified amount.

79 Restitution orders

Under s.148 of the Powers of Criminal Courts (Sentencing) Act 2000, where goods have been stolen and a person is convicted of any offence (whether or not the passing of the sentence is in other respects deferred) related to their theft, the court may order that restitution of the goods be made to any person entitled to recover them, or may order payment of a sum, not exceeding the value of the original goods, to that person out of money found in the possession of the convicted person on his arrest, or may order the delivery of any other goods directly or indirectly representing the stolen goods.

Q: CONFISCATION AND RESTRAINT ORDERS

80 The Proceeds of Crime Act 2002

The confiscation of assets of those convicted of a criminal offence is provided for in the Proceeds of Crime Act 2002. The 2002 Act also provides for the issue of restraint orders to prohibit dealing in property which has been the subject of a crime.

Asset recovery is undertaken by the National Crime Agency, the Director of Public Prosecutions, and the Director of the Serious Fraud Office.

81 Confiscation orders

Part 2 of the Proceeds of Crime Act 2002 provides for the making of confiscation orders (replacing with some changes earlier provisions).

Confiscation orders are made in the Crown Court which can exercise the power to make a confiscation order if the following two conditions are met (s.6(1))–
   (a) the defendant is convicted of an offence in the Crown Court, is committed for sentencing to the Crown Court, or is committed to the Crown Court with a view to a confiscation order being made (s.6(2)); and
   (b) the prosecutor asks the court to consider a confiscation order and the Court believes it is appropriate to do so (s.6(3)).
In considering the making of a confiscation order, the court must decide (s.6(4))–
   (c) whether the defendant has a criminal lifestyle;
   (d) if so, whether the defendant has benefited from his general criminal conduct, defined as all his criminal conduct whether before or after the passing of the 2002 Act (s.76(2)); and
   (e) if not, whether he has benefited from his particular criminal conduct, defined as all his criminal conduct which is connected with the offence or offences for which he appears before the court (s.76(3)).
If the court decides that the defendant has so benefited, it must then decide a "recoverable amount" and make a confiscation order requiring him to pay that amount (s.6(5)).

The Secretary of State can extend the power to make such orders to magistrates' courts (Serious Organised Crime and Police Act 2005, s.97).

82 A criminal lifestyle

A defendant has a criminal lifestyle if–
   (a) he engages in drug trafficking, money laundering, directing terrorism, people trafficking, offences connected with slavery, servitude and forced or compulsory labour, arms trafficking, counterfeiting, intellectual property offences, offences in relation to gangmasters or acting as a pimp or running brothels, and blackmail; or he attempts, conspires or incites the commission of one of those offences or aids, abets, counsels or procures the commission of such an offence (Proceeds of Crime Act 2002, s.75(2)(a), Sch.2);
   (b) the offence forms part of a "course of criminal activity" and the benefit resulting from that course is more than £5,000. A "course of criminal activity" means that the defendant must have been convicted in the same proceedings of three or more offences in addition to the principal offence and he has benefited from each of the additional offences, or he has been convicted on at least two occasions of an offence

from which he has benefited during the previous six years (s.75(2)(b), (3), (4)); or

(c) the offence is committed over a period of at least six months and the defendant has benefited from it by more than £5,000 (s.75(2)(c), (4)).

83 The recoverable amount

If a confiscation order is made by the Crown Court under the Proceeds of Crime Act 2002, s.6, the recoverable amount is an amount equal to the defendant's benefit from his conduct (s.7(1)). If the available amount is less than the benefit, the recoverable amount becomes either the available amount or a nominal amount (s.7(2)). If the victim of the offence has started or intends to start civil proceedings against the defendant, or if the defendant shows that the available amount is less than the benefit, the court may use its discretion under s.6(6) to determine the recoverable amount. If s.6(6) applies, the recoverable amount is an amount the court thinks is just but is not more than the sum under s.7(1) or (2).

84 Appeals

The prosecutor may appeal to the Court of Appeal against a decision by the Crown Court to either make, or not make, a confiscation order (s.31).

On appeal, the Court of Appeal may confirm, quash or vary the confiscation order (s.21(1)) or, if the appeal is against the decision not to make a confiscation order, the Court of Appeal may confirm the decision or, if it believes the Crown Court's decision was wrong–

(a) make a confiscation order itself; or

(b) direct the Crown Court to make a confiscation order.

An appeal lies to the Supreme Court of the United Kingdom from a decision of the Court of Appeal (s.33). The Proceeds of Crime Act 2002 (Appeals under Part 2) Order 2003 sets out the procedure to be followed under ss.31 to 33.

85 Restraint orders and seizure and sale of property

The Crown Court may make a restraint order prohibiting a specified person from dealing with property held by him (Proceeds of Crime Act 2002, ss.40 and 41). Restraint orders are usually made before criminal proceedings end in anticipation of a confiscation order.

If a restraint order is in force, a constable or officer of HM Revenue and Customs may seize any property to which it relates to prevent its removal from England and Wales (s.45).

The police may seize any realisable property (other than cash or exempt property such as work equipment or household bedding or furniture) if they have reasonable grounds for suspecting that either (s.47C)–

(a) the property may otherwise be made unavailable for satisfying any confiscation order that has been or may be made against the defendant, or

(b) the value of the property may otherwise be diminished as a result of conduct by the defendant or any other person.

There are accompanying powers to search premises, people and vehicles in order to find property to be seized (ss.47D-F). These powers must usually only be exercised with the approval of a justice of the peace or (if that is not practicable in any case) of a senior police officer. If a search is carried out without the approval of a JP, or if any seized property is held for less than 48 hours, a report must be made to an independent person appointed by the Secretary of State (ss.47G-H).

The Proceeds of Crime Act 2002 (Search, Seizure and Detention of Property: Code of Practice) (England and Wales) Order 2016 relates to the operation of these powers by the police.

A magistrates' court may authorise the sale of seized property to satisfy a confiscation order, if the seized property belongs to a person against whom a confiscation order has been made, the time to pay that order has expired, and provided that an enforcement receiver has not been appointed in relation to the property (s.67A).

86 Civil recovery of the proceeds of crime

The Proceeds of Crime Act 2002 Part 5 provides two schemes for the civil recovery of the proceeds of unlawful conduct.

Chapters 1 and 2 of Part 5 provide the first scheme which allows the enforcement authority (i.e., the National Crime Agency, the Director of Public Prosecutions, or the Director of the Serious Fraud Office) to make an application to the High Court for the civil recovery of–

(a) property (not just cash) that is or represents property obtained through unlawful conduct; and

(b) cash which is intended to be used in unlawful conduct.

Proceedings for a recovery order cannot be started unless the enforcement authority reasonably believe that the value of the property to be the subject of the order is not less than £10,000 (s.287, and the Proceeds of Crime Act 2002 (Financial Threshold for Civil Recovery) Order 2003).

Chapters 1 and 3 of Part 5 provide the second scheme under which the police, immigration officers and officers of HM Revenue and Customs may recover cash through summary proceedings before a magistrates' court. If a police, immigration or HM Revenue and Customs officer who is lawfully on any premises has reasonable grounds for suspecting that there is cash on the premises which is recoverable property or is intended for use in unlawful conduct he may search for cash there (s.289(1)). However, in order to do this, there must be not less than £1,000 on the premises (s.289(1)(b) and the Proceeds of Crime Act 2002 (Recovery of Cash in Summary Proceedings: Minimum Amount) Order 2006). Any cash found may be seized and detained, initially for 48 hours but extendable by a magistrates' court for up to three months (and further extended up to a maximum of two years) (s.295). To extend the detention period the court or sheriff must be satisfied that either–

(a) there are reasonable grounds for suspecting that the cash is recoverable property and that either its continued detention is justified while its derivation is further investigated or consideration is given to proceedings against any person for an offence with which the cash is connected, or proceedings against any person for an offence with which the cash is connected have been started and have not been concluded; or

(b) there are reasonable grounds for suspecting that the cash is intended to be used in unlawful conduct and that either its continued detention is justified while its intended use is further investigated or consideration is given to bringing proceedings against any person for an offence with which the cash is connected, or proceedings against any person for an offence with which the cash is connected have been started and have not been concluded.

It will only be released if the court is satisfied, on an application by the person from whom the cash was seized, that the conditions for it seizure are no longer met. Where seized cash has been detained under a magistrates' court's order, a senior police officer may give a forfeiture notice to the person from whom the cash was seized to advise them that the police intend to forfeit the cash without a hearing before a magistrates' court unless that person objects, in which case the forfeiture can only take place by way of proceedings before a magistrates' court. If the owner of the cash is not known, notice can be given in the London Gazette (ss.297A-G). The form of forfeiture notice is prescribed by the Administrative Forfeiture of Cash (Forfeiture Notices) (England and Wales) Regulations 2015 (S.I. No. 857).

Property which has already been seized or forfeited under other provisions (e.g., the Obscene Publications Act 1959, the Misuse of Drugs Act 1971, or the Terrorism Act 2001) cannot be forfeited under the 2002 Act (Proceeds of Crime (Exemptions from Civil Recovery) Order 2003 (S.I. No. 336).

The Secretary of State must draw up a code of practice in connection with the exercise of the power to recover cash under Chapter 3 (ss.292 and 293). The Proceeds of Crime Act 2002 (Cash Searches: Code of Practice) Order 2016 brings these codes of practice into operation.

There is a right of appeal against forfeiture of cash (or a refusal of a court to order forfeiture) to the Crown Court (s.299).

In order to preserve the property before a recovery order is made, the enforcement authority can apply for an interim order, allowing to take the property and manage it pending the making of a full order. Alternatively, they can apply for a freezing order under s.245A.

R: MISCELLANEOUS POWERS

87 Deportation orders

A court may recommend for deportation a person who is not a British citizen aged 17 or over who has been convicted of an offence punishable with imprisonment.

88 Deprivation of property used for crime (forfeiture orders)

Under s.143(1) of the Powers of Criminal Courts (Sentencing) Act 2000 a person convicted of an offence may be deprived by the court of property where that property was used, or intended to be used, for the purpose of committing a crime or where the offence with which the person is charged consists of unlawful possession of that property.

The court also has power, under s.145, to make an order applying the proceeds of the sale of the forfeited property for the benefit of the victim (see P: COMPENSATION ORDERS, above).

89 Financial reporting orders

Where an offender is convicted of certain offences, the court can make a financial reporting order in respect of him (Serious Organised Crime and Police Act 2005, ss.76 and 77, as extended by the Serious Organised Crime and Police Act 2005 (Amendment of Section 76(3)) Order 2007 (S.I. 2007 No. 1392)). The effect of such an order is to require the defendant to report specified particulars of his financial affairs to a specified person for a specified period.

The offences in respect of which financial reporting orders can be made include various deception and fraud offences, terrorism, corruption, drug trafficking, and lifestyle offences (as to which, see **82 A criminal lifestyle**, above).

90 Disqualification from driving

Under s.147 of the Powers of Criminal Courts (Sentencing) Act 2000, where a person is convicted before the Crown Court (or is committed to that Court for sentence) in respect of an offence punishable on indictment with not less than two years' imprisonment, the court may disqualify him for holding or obtaining a licence to drive a motor vehicle, for such period as the court thinks fit, if a motor vehicle was used, whether by that person or anyone else, in connection with the commission of the offence.

S.146 of the 2000 Act gives both Crown courts and Magistrates' courts power to disqualify an offender from driving on conviction for any offence, either in addition to any other sentence or instead of any other sentence, except in the case of an offence for which the sentence is fixed by law or where the court is required to impose a sentence. In those cases, the court may impose a disqualification in addition to the sentence. S.146 may be used only by courts notified by the Secretary of State that the power may be exercised by that court. Similarly, s.40 of the Crime (Sentences) Act 1997 Act empowers a magistrates' court to impose a disqualification from driving on an offender who has defaulted with the payment of a fine or other financial order. The maximum period of disqualification is 12 months. Again, this power may not be exercised unless the court has been notified that it may exercise it.

S.147A provides for an extension in the length of the period of a driving disqualification imposed under ss.146 or 147 where a custodial sentence is also imposed for the same offence. The court must determine the appropriate discretionary period of disqualification and then add on the appropriate extension period.

The appropriate extension period takes account of that part of the sentence which the offender will serve in prison. Where a life sentence or an indeterminate sentence for public protection is imposed the extension period is the period of the minimum tariff set by the court. Where an extended sentence is imposed the extension period is half the custodial term i.e., the period of the sentence to be served in prison. Where a detention and training order is imposed, the extension period is half the term of the order. In all other cases, the extension period is equal to one half of the custodial sentence (at which point the offender will be released either automatically or on licence in the community until the end of sentence). The extension period will be reduced to reflect any reduction in the custodial sentence as a result of the court taking into account time already served on remand, or periods of remand on bail in a case where the offender was subject to a curfew condition which was electronically monitored.

Where the court imposes a suspended sentence, or a life sentence to which no early release provisions apply (i.e., where the offender must spend the rest of their life in prison), the extension period does not apply.

Where an offender is disqualified at the same time as they are imprisoned for another offence, or at a time when they are already in prison for another offence, the court must, so far as appropriate, have regard to the diminished effect of disqualification as a distinct punishment where the person who is disqualified Is also imprisoned (s.147B). For example, the more that the beginning of a driving disqualification overlaps with the end of the period of detention under an earlier sentence, the more a court might extend the disqualification to compensate for the diminished effect during the overlap.

The Road Traffic Offenders Act 1988 includes further provision for the disqualification of drivers and endorsement of licences (see the Note on **Penalty Points, Revocation, Disqualification, and Endorsement**).

91 Drunken offenders

S.34 of the Criminal Justice Act 1972 gives a constable the power, as an alternative to arresting a person for drunken behaviour under specified statutory powers, to take that person to an approved treatment centre for alcoholics. A person may not be detained against his will in such a centre but he will remain liable to be charged with an offence.

92 Exclusion zones

A policeman may direct a person to leave a place if he believes, on reasonable grounds, that the person is in the place at a time when (Serious Organised Crime and Police Act 2005, s.112)–
   (a) he is prohibited from being there by virtue of an order made following his conviction for an offence which prohibits him from entering the place or from doing so during a period specified in the order; or
   (b) his presence there contravenes a condition of his release from a prison which prohibits him from entering the place or from doing so during a period specified in the condition.
A person who fails to leave when asked to do so can be arrested.

93 Football banning orders

The Football Spectators Act 1989 (as amended by the Football (Disorder) Act 2000) makes detailed provision for the making and enforcement of football banning orders in relation to offences connected with football at prescribed matches both in England and Wales and abroad. These provisions are beyond the scope of this work.

94 Hospital and guardianship orders

Under s.5 of the Criminal Procedure (Insanity) Act 1964 (as substituted by the Domestic Violence, Crime and Victims Act 2004, s.24) where a special verdict is returned that the accused is not guilty by reason of insanity, or findings are recorded that the accused is under a disability [which would constitute a bar to his being tried] and that he did the act or made the omission charged against him, the court must either make–
   (a) a hospital order under the Mental Health Act 1983, with or without a restriction order;

866

(b) a supervision order within the meaning of Schedule 1A to the 1964 Act; or

(c) an order for his absolute discharge.

Note.– Where the offence to which the special verdict or finding relates is an offence the sentence for which is fixed by law (e.g., murder), the court must make a hospital order with a restriction order (1964 Act, s.5(3)). A restriction order gives the Secretary of State certain powers in relation to the management of the person whilst in hospital, such as that the Secretary of State's consent is required before he is given leave or discharged. Supervision orders enable treatment to be given to a person under supervision. A person cannot be required to undergo in-patient treatment and there is no sanction for breach of a supervision order.

Under the Mental Health Act 1983, the Crown Court and a magistrates' court have the following powers–

(a) to remand an accused person to a hospital for a report on his mental condition (s.35);

(b) to order that a person convicted of an offence punishable by imprisonment, other than an offence for which there is a fixed sentence, be admitted to and detained in hospital (a hospital order) or be placed under the guardianship of a local social services authority or a person specified by such an authority (a guardianship order) (s.37);

(c) to make an interim order for detaining a person referred to in (b) in hospital before deciding whether to make a full hospital order or to deal with him in some other way (s.38);

(d) to make a hospital and limitation direction ordering a convicted offender to be sent to a hospital, rather than to prison, for treatment for a mental disorder (only the Crown court can make such a direction (s.45A, inserted by s.46 of the Crime (Sentences) Act 1997)).

The Crown Court may also remand an accused person to hospital for medical treatment (s.36).

In cases where powers are exercised under ss.35 to 38, the court must be satisfied on medical evidence of certain matters relating to the mental health of the person concerned.

S: MISCARRIAGE OF JUSTICE

95 Compensation for miscarriage of justice

S.133 of the Criminal Justice Act 1988 places a duty on the Secretary of State, upon application by a person, or, if he is dead, his personal representatives, to pay compensation for a miscarriage of justice to that person where he has suffered punishment as a result of being convicted of a criminal offence and his conviction has been reversed or he has been pardoned on the ground that a new or newly discovered fact shows beyond reasonable doubt that there has been a miscarriage of justice, unless the non-disclosure of the unknown fact was wholly or partly attributable to the person convicted. The question whether there is a right to compensation is to be determined by the Secretary of State; the amount of compensation is to be determined by an assessor appointed by him.

Compensation will only be paid where the new or newly discovered fact (on the basis of which the conviction was reversed) shows beyond reasonable doubt that the person did not commit the offence of which they were convicted (s.133(1ZA)).

96 Authorities

Statutes–

Crime and Courts Act 2013

Crime and Disorder Act 1998

Crime (Sentences) Act 1997

Criminal Attempts Act 1981

Criminal Justice Acts 1982, 1988, 1991, and 2003

Criminal Justice and Court Services Act 2000

Criminal Justice and Courts Act 2015

Criminal Justice and Immigration Act 2008

Criminal Justice and Police Act 2001

Criminal Procedure (Insanity) Act 1964

Criminal Procedure (Insanity and Unfitness to Plead) Act 1991

Football Spectators Act 1989

Magistrates' Courts Act 1980

Mental Health Act 1983

Modern Slavery Act 2015

Offender Management Act 2007

Powers of Criminal Courts (Sentencing) Act 2000

Proceeds of Crime Act 2002

Serious Organised Crime and Police Act 2005

Safeguarding Vulnerable Groups Act 2006

Sexual Offences Act 2003

Violent Crime Reduction Act 2006

Statutory Instruments—

Criminal Justice Act 2003 (Conditional Cautions: Financial Penalties) Order 2013 (S.I. 2013 No. 615)

Criminal Justice Act 2003 (Surcharge) Order 2012, as amended (S.I. 2012 Nos. 1696 and 2824, and 2014 No. 2120, and 2016 No. 389)

Criminal Justice and Courts Act 2015 (Simple Cautions) (Specification of Either-Way Offences) Order 2015, as amended (S.I. 2015 Nos. 790 and 1472)

Criminal Justice and Courts Act 2015 (Simple Cautions) (Specification of Police Ranks) Order 2015 (S.I. 2015 No. 830)

Criminal Justice (Sentencing) (Licence Conditions) Order 2015 (S.I. 2015 No. 337)

Criminal Justice (Specified Class A Drugs) Order 2001 (S.I. 2001 No. 1816)

Fines (Deduction from Income Support) Regulations 1992, as amended (S.I. 1992 No. 2182, 1993 No. 495, 1996 No. 2344, 2002 No. 1397, 2003 No. 1360, 2004 No. 2889, and 2008 No. 1554)

Penalties for Disorderly Behaviour (Amount of Penalty) Order 2002, as amended (S.I. 2002 No. 1837, 2004 Nos. 316, 2468 and 3371, 2005 No. 3048, 2008 No. 3297, 2009 No. 83, 2012 No. 1431, 2013 Nos. 903 and 1579, and 2014 No. 1383)

Polygraph Rules 2009 (S.I. 2009 No. 619)

Proceeds of Crime Act 2002 (Appeals under Part 2) Order 2003, as amended (S.I. 2003 No. 82 and 2015 No. 1855)

Proceeds of Crime Act 2002 (Cash Searches: Code of Practice) Order 2016 (S.I. 2016 No. 208)

Proceeds of Crime Act 2002 (Financial Threshold for Civil Recovery) Order 2003 (S.I. 2003 No. 175)

Proceeds of Crime Act 2002 (Recovery of Cash in Summary Proceedings: Minimum Amount) Order 2006 (S.I. 2006 No. 1699)

Proceeds of Crime Act 2002 (Search, Seizure and Detention of Property: Code of Practice) (England and Wales) Order 2016 (S.I. 2016 No. 207)

Prosecution of Offences Act 1985 (Criminal Courts Charge) Regulations 2015, as amended (S.I. 2015 Nos. 796 and 1970)

Register of Fines Regulations 2003 (S.I. 2003 No. 3184)

Sexual Offences Act 2003 (Travel Notification Requirements) Regulations 2004, as amended (S.I. 2004 No. 1220 and 2012 No. 1876)

TREATMENT OF OFFENDERS: SCOTLAND

I Introduction

In Scotland, the Criminal Procedure (Scotland) Act 1995 consolidated most of the enactments relating to the powers of criminal courts. Part XI of the Act (ss.195 to 254) deals with sentencing.

This Note is structured as follows—

A: General factors affecting sentencing
B: Discharge
C: Deferment of sentence or prosecution
D: Imprisonment
E: Early release of prisoners
F: Sex offenders
G: Criminal and Anti-social behaviour orders
H: Travel restriction orders (drug trafficking offenders)
I: Drug treatment and testing orders
J: Fines and surcharges
K: Curfew and restriction of liberty orders
L: Community payback orders
M: Compensation orders
N: Confiscation and restraint orders
O: Miscellaneous powers
P: Miscarriage of justice

A: GENERAL FACTORS AFFECTING SENTENCING

2 Race and other aggravating factors

Where it is libelled in an indictment or specified in a complaint and, in either case, proved that an offence has been racially or religiously aggravated, the court must take that aggravation into account in deciding the appropriate sentence (Crime and Disorder Act 1998, s.96 (race); and Criminal Justice (Scotland) Act 2003, s.74 (religion)).

When a court is considering the seriousness of certain offences connected with explosives, hostage taking, soliciting murder, safety of the channel tunnel and offences involving chemical, biological or nuclear weapons, it must consider whether the offence has or may have a terrorist connection. If it decides that it does, it must treat that as an aggravating factor when determining sentence (Counter-Terrorism Act 2008, ss.30 and 31).

Where it is libelled in an indictment or specified in a complaint and, in either case, proved that an offence is aggravated by a connection with serious organised crime (because the person committing the offence is motivated, wholly or partly, by the objective of committing or conspiring to commit serious organised crime), the court must take that aggravation into account in deciding the appropriate sentence (Criminal Justice and Licensing (Scotland) Act 2010, s. 29).

3 Reduction in sentence for assistance by defendant

When sentencing a person who pleaded guilty in proceedings on indictment and who entered into a written agreement with a prosecutor (an "assistance agreement") to provide assistance in relation to any investigation or prosecution, the court must take account the nature and extent of that assistance and may pass a lower sentence on account of it (Police, Public Order and Criminal Justice (Scotland) Act 2006, s.91).

If the court passes a sentence which is less than it would have passed but for the assistance given or offered, it must (unless it would not be in the public interest to do so) state in open court that it has done so and what the greater sentence would have been. This provision does not however affect any requirements as to minimum sentences or minimum periods which must be served.

If he thinks that it is in the interests of justice to do so, a prosecutor can refer a case back to the court for a review of a sentence where (s.92)—

(a) a person who received a discounted sentence after having offered in a written agreement to give assistance to the prosecutor or investigator of an offence has knowingly failed to any extent to give assistance in accordance with the agreement;

(b) a person who received a discounted sentence after giving assistance to the prosecutor or investigator of an offence under a written agreement, gives or offers to give further assistance under another written agreement; or

(c) a person received a sentence which was not discounted but under a written agreement he has subsequently given or offered to give assistance to the prosecutor or investigator of an offence.

Assistance otherwise than in pursuance of an assistance agreement may also be taken into account by the court in passing sentence (2006 Act, s.95).

4 Conditional immunity

A prosecutor may grant a person conditional immunity from prosecution by giving that person a notice in writing known as a conditional immunity notice. If a conditional immunity notice is given to a person, that person may not be prosecuted for the offence or any offence of a description specified in the notice, and any proceedings for those offences which have already commenced when the notice is given must be discontinued (Police, Public Order and Criminal Justice (Scotland) Act 2006, s.97).

5 Voluntary intoxication

In sentencing an offender in respect of an offence it is specifically provided that a court must not take into account by way of mitigation the fact that, at the time of the offence, the offender was under the influence of alcohol as a result of having voluntarily consumed it (Criminal Justice and Licensing (Scotland) Act 2010, s. 26).

B: DISCHARGE

6 Admonition and absolute discharge

Where a court by or before which a person is convicted of an offence (not being an offence the sentence for which is fixed by law and certain other very serious offences) is of the opinion, having regard to the circumstances, including the nature of the offence and the offender's character, that punishment is inexpedient, it may make an order discharging the person absolutely (Criminal Procedure (Scotland) Act 1995, s.246(2), (3)).

A court may also, if it appears to meet the justice of the case, dismiss with an admonition any person convicted by the court of any offence (Criminal Procedure (Scotland) Act 1995, s.246(1)).

C: DEFERMENT OF SENTENCE OR PROSECUTION

7 Circumstances when sentence may be deferred

Under s.202 of the Criminal Procedure (Scotland) Act 1995, a court may defer sentence after conviction for such period and on such conditions as the court may determine.

D: IMPRISONMENT

8 General restrictions on imposing custodial sentences

A court may not pass a sentence of imprisonment on a person aged 21 or more who has not previously received a sentence of imprisonment or detention in any part of the UK or EU, unless the court considers that no other method of dealing with him is appropriate, taking into account all the information available about the relevant circumstances, and his character and physical and mental condition (Criminal Procedure (Scotland) Act 1995, s.204(2)). Also, a court must not pass a sentence of imprisonment for a term of 3 months or less on a person unless the court considers that no other method of dealing with the person is appropriate (s.204(3A)).

9 Procedural requirements for custodial sentences

S.201 of the Criminal Procedure (Scotland) Act 1995 provides that the powers of the court to adjourn the hearing of a case include power, after a person has been convicted or the court has found that he committed the offence and before he has been sentenced or otherwise dealt with, to adjourn the case for the purpose of enabling enquiries to be made or for determining the most suitable method of dealing with the case. No such adjournment must, where the accused is remanded in custody, exceed three weeks (six weeks in the case of sex offences) on a single occasion. In particular, under s.200 of the 1995 Act, the court may adjourn to enable an enquiry to be made into the physical or mental condition of an offender found guilty of an offence punishable with imprisonment.

A copy of any report made to a court by an officer of a local authority, with a view to assisting the court in determining the most suitable method of dealing with an offender, must be given to the offender, his solicitor (if any) and the prosecutor (1995 Act, s.203(3)).

10 Restriction on imprisonment of persons not legally represented

S.204(1) of the Criminal Procedure (Scotland) Act 1995 provides that a court may not impose a sentence of imprisonment or detention on an offender who has not previously been sentenced to that form of punishment in the UK or elsewhere in the EU and who has not been legally represented in that court, unless the accused either–
(a) applied for legal aid and the application was refused on the ground that he was not financially eligible; or
(b) having been informed of his right to apply for legal aid, and having had the opportunity, failed to do so.

11 Length of custodial sentence

Where a person already serving a life sentence is convicted of a further offence, the sentence for the further offence may be framed so as to take effect from the date when that person would be entitled to be released (if the second sentence is another life sentence) or when the punishment part of the original sentence expires (if the second sentence is a determinate sentence) (Criminal Procedure (Scotland) Act 1995, ss.167(7A), 204B).

The High Court, after considering a risk assessment, may impose either a compulsion order (for mentally disordered offenders) or an order for lifelong restriction where it considers, on a balance of probabilities, that the nature or circumstances of the offence either in themselves or as part of a pattern of behaviour are such as to demonstrate that there is a likelihood that the offender, if at liberty, will seriously endanger the lives, or physical or psychological well-being, of members of the public at large (Criminal Procedure (Scotland) Act 1995, s.210F).

12 Sentences fixed by law and extended sentences

For certain offences, the sentence is fixed by law (e.g., a life sentence for murder). For other offences, there are "required" custodial sentences for offences which are not first offences. These required sentences are as follows–

(a) where a person is convicted on indictment in the High Court of a class A drug trafficking offence and at the time when that offence was committed he was aged at least 18 years and had two previous convictions for relevant offences then, except in special circumstances, if he is aged at least 21 he must be sentenced to a term of imprisonment of at least seven years; and if aged at least 18 years but under 21, to detention in a young offenders institution for a period of at least seven years (Criminal Procedure (Scotland) Act 1995, s.205B);

Where an offender is convicted of certain violent or sexual offences, the court may, if it intends, in relation to–

(b) a sexual offence, to pass a determinate sentence of imprisonment; or

(c) a violent offence, to pass such a sentence for a term of four years or more;

and the court considers that the period (if any) for which the offender would be subject to a licence would not be adequate for the purpose of protecting the public from serious harm from the offender, it may pass an extended sentence on him.

An extended sentence of imprisonment is one where the term is equal to the normal custodial term he would receive, together with a further period ("the extension period") for which the offender is to be subject to a licence. The extension period may be up to ten years (five years if the sentence is passed by a sheriff) (s.210A).

The effect of the extension period is that the offender will remain on licence, and therefore liable to recall to custody, up to the end of the extension period.

Where a person is convicted of more than one offence on the same indictment for which the court must or would impose a life sentence, only one life sentence may be imposed (Criminal Procedure (Scotland) Act 1995, s.205D) (but see **11 Length of custodial sentence**, above, where an existing life prisoner is convicted of a further offence).

E: EARLY RELEASE OF PRISONERS

13 Release on licence–Introduction

The Criminal Justice Act 1967 (ss.61 to 64) contains provisions relating to the release on licence of prisoners in Scotland. There is a separate Parole Board for Scotland and consultation before release on licence is with the Lord Justice General.

Part I of the Prisoners and Criminal Proceedings (Scotland) Act 1993 (the 1993 Act), as amended by the Crime and Punishment (Scotland) Act 1997, the Convention Rights (Compliance) (Scotland) Act 2001, and the Management of Offenders etc. (Scotland) Act 2005 makes arrangements for the early release of prisoners serving determinate sentences and for their supervision and liabilities after release; and for the review and release of life sentence prisoners.

Among the conditions which may be included in a licence is the remote monitoring of a person's whereabouts or compliance with any other conditions of the licence (i.e., electronic tagging) (Criminal Justice (Scotland) Act 2003, s.40).

14 Release on licence–short and long-term prisoners

As soon as a short-term prisoner (other than a sex offender) has served one-half of his sentence, the Scottish Ministers must release him unconditionally, and, as soon as a long-term prisoner has served two-thirds of his sentence, the Scottish Ministers must release him on licence (Prisoners and Criminal Proceedings (Scotland) Act 1993, s.1). Short-term prisoners who are sex offenders are released on licence after they have served one-half of their sentence (s.1AA).

Where a long-term prisoner has served half his sentence, the Scottish Ministers must release him on licence if recommended to do so by the Parole Board (unless he is liable to deportation, in which case the Scottish Ministers have a discretion as to whether to release him).

There is a discretionary power to release prisoners on what is commonly known as Home Detention Curfew. This allows the release of prisoners on licence a short time before they would be eligible for automatic release or, in the case of long-term prisoners, (i.e., those serving a sentence of 4 or more years), for release on licence on the direction of the Parole Board. The length of the Home Detention Curfew period varies according to the sentence length, but cannot be less than 14 days nor more than 180 days. The prisoner must be serving a sentence of at least 3 months, and must have spent at least 4 weeks in custody. Certain classes of prisoner are excluded entirely. Release on Home Detention Curfew must be subject to a curfew condition and other standard conditions, and further conditions may also be added on a case-by-case basis. The curfew condition requires the offender to remain at a specified place for at least 9 hours each day, and compliance with this is monitored remotely using electronic tagging technology (s.3AA). The standard conditions which must be attached to a licence are contained in the Home Detention Curfew Licence (Prescribed Standard Conditions) (Scotland) No. 2) Order 2008 (S.S.I. No. 125).

15 Release on licence– discretionary life prisoners

S.2 of the Prisoners and Criminal Proceedings (Scotland) Act 1993, as amended, provides for the release of discretionary life prisoners. A discretionary life prisoner is one who is (s.2(1))–

(a) sentenced to life imprisonment for an offence which, subject to (d) below, such a sentence is not the sentence fixed by law; or

(b) sentenced to life imprisonment for murder or for any other offence for which that sentence is fixed by law; or

(c) subject to an order for lifelong restriction in respect of an offence (i.e. an order under s.210F of the Criminal Procedure (Scotland) Act 1995); or

(d) whose sentence was imposed under s.205A(2) of the 1995 Act (imprisonment for life on further conviction for certain offences); and

in respect of whom the sentencing court ordered that s.2(2) should apply to him (if a life sentence is imposed the court must order that s.2(2) applies to him: s.2(3)). S.2(2) provides that the sentencing court must make an order specifying the "punishment part" of the sentence, i.e., that part which must be served before the parole provisions in sub-sections (4) and (6) will apply. The period must be specified in years and months with no account being taken of the fact that such a period may exceed the remainder of the prisoner's natural life (s.2(3A)). The punishment part of a sentence is that part which the court considers appropriate to satisfy the requirements for retribution and deterrence, taking into account–

(1) the seriousness of the offence, and any other offences which the life prisoner is convicted of at the same time;

(2) any previous convictions;

(3) where appropriate, whether and at what point a guilty plea was tendered (i.e., the matters mentioned in s.196(1)(a) and (b) of the 1995 Act); and

(4) in the case of a life prisoner to whom paragraph (a) or (c) above applies (i.e. a non-mandatory life sentence), the matters mentioned in s.2A(1) (see below).

The matters mentioned in (1) to (3) above (taken together) are for the case of a life prisoner to whom paragraph (b) above applies; and, as respects the punishment part in the case of such a prisoner, the court is to ignore any period of confinement which may be necessary for the protection of the public (s.2(2A)). The rules by which the court is to set the punishment part for cases within (4) above are (s.2A(1), (2))–

(i) an assessment of the period of imprisonment which the court considers would have been appropriate for the offence had the prisoner not been sentenced to a non-mandatory life sentence (ignoring any period of confinement which may be necessary for the protection of the public);

(ii) an assessment of the part of that period of imprisonment which would represent an appropriate period to satisfy the requirements of retribution and deterrence; and

(iii) where appropriate, the matters mentioned in s.196(1)(a) and (b) of the 1995 Act.

The consideration by the court as to whether and at what level any sentence discount for an early guilty plea is appropriate in paragraph (iii) above is to be left until after the court has made the assessment under paragraphs (i) and (ii) (s.2A(2)(c)). Paragraph (ii) above is subject to the requirements of s.2B. S.2B provides that the part of the period of imprisonment is to be either one-half of the period specified under paragraph (i) above or a greater proportion of the period specified under that paragraph. The court can specify a greater proportion of the period up to and including the whole of that period (s.2B(3)). Again, the court is to ignore any period of confinement which may be necessary for the protection of the public (s.2B(4)). However, a greater proportion than one-half can only be specified if the court considers it appropriate to do so having considered, in particular, the following matters (continuing to ignore any period of confinement which may be necessary for the protection of the public) (s.2B(2), (5))–

(iv) the seriousness of the offence, or of the offence combined with other offences of which the prisoner is convicted of at the same time;

(v) where the offence was committed when the prisoner was serving a period of imprisonment for another offence, that fact; and

(vi) any previous convictions of the prisoner.

S.2(4) provides that the Scottish Ministers must, if directed by the Parole Board release a life prisoner on licence. However the Parole Board must not give a direction under s.2(4) unless the Scottish Ministers have referred the prisoner's case to the Board and it is satisfied that it is no longer necessary for the protection of the public that the prisoner should be confined (s.2(5)). A life prisoner may require the Scottish Ministers to refer his case to the Parole Board, but where he is serving a determinate term in addition to the life term, he cannot require that his case be referred before he has served half of the determinate term (s.2(6) and (7)). A prisoner cannot require the Scottish Ministers to refer his case to the Parole Board if he has already required them to do so, or the Scottish Ministers have already referred his case without his requiring them to do so, or the Parole Board has previously declined to direct his release on licence (s.2(6A)).

Where the Parole Board refuses to direct a prisoner's release on licence it must give the prisoner written reasons for its decision and fix a date, not more than two years later, when it will next consider the prisoner's case (s.2(5A)). If a prisoner is sentenced for another offence, the date of the review may be put back beyond the two year maximum to a date when he will also be eligible for review for that other offence (s.2(5AB) to (5AD)). The Scottish Ministers must refer the case on the date fixed by the Board, and the Board, at the request of the prisoner, may request the Scottish Ministers to refer the case to them before that date (s.2(5B) and (5C)).

Where a long-term prisoner is released on licence, the licence must (unless revoked) remain in force until the entire period specified in his sentence has elapsed and, where a life prisoner is released, the licence shall remain in force until his death (s.11). A person released on licence must comply with such conditions (including conditions as to supervision by a probation officer) as may be specified in the licence by the Scottish Ministers (s.12).

16 Supervised release

Under s.209 of the Criminal Procedure (Scotland) Act 1995, where a person is sentenced to imprisonment for between one and four years, the court on passing sentence may, if it considers that it is necessary to do so to protect the public from serious harm from the offender on his release, make a supervised release order requiring the person to be under the supervision of a probation officer or other relevant person for a specified period not exceeding 12 months (or the period until the date by which the entire term of imprisonment specified in his sentence has elapsed, if this is shorter). A person who breaches a requirement of a supervised release order may be returned to prison for the whole or any part of his sentence (Prisoners and Criminal Proceedings (Scotland) Act 1993, s.18).

17 Further offences

S.16 of the Prisoners and Criminal Proceedings (Scotland) Act 1993 contains provisions relating to the commission of offences by released prisoners and provides that, instead of or in addition to making any other order, a court may order the person to be returned to prison.

S.17 provides that the Scottish Ministers must revoke the licence of a long-term or life prisoner and recall him to prison if recommended to do so by the Parole Board (and in urgent cases the recommendation of the Board may be dispensed with).

F: SEX OFFENDERS

18 Notification requirements

The Sexual Offences Act 2003 contains notification requirements for persons (s.80)–
(a) convicted of specific sex offences;
(b) found not guilty of such an offence by reason of insanity; or
(c) found to be under a disability and to have done the act charged in respect of such an offence.

Such persons must notify the police within three days of their release (from custody or remand), and annually thereafter (or such other period as may be prescribed where the offender has no residence), of their (ss.83 and 85)–
(i) name (all names used), both at the time of conviction and the time of release;
(ii) home address, both at the time of conviction and the time of release, and the address of any other premises where he regularly resides or stays;
(iii) date of birth;
(iv) National Insurance number;
(v) passport details (added by the Police, Public Order and Criminal Justice (Scotland) Act 2006, s.78);
(vi) any information prescribed by regulations made by the Scottish Ministers. The Sexual Offences Act 2003 (Notification Requirements) (Scotland) Regulations 2007 require that a relevant offender notify the police as to whether he has a bank or building society account, or a debit or credit card.

This is commonly known as the "sex offenders register" although the requirement is to "notify" rather than to "register".

An offender must also notify the police of any changes in the above information within three days (s.84).

The police must also be notified if he stays away from his usual home address for a period of seven days, or a total of seven days in any 12 month period. Failure to do so is an offence punishable on summary conviction to imprisonment for six months or a fine (unlimited in England and Wales, not exceeding the statutory maximum in Scotland: see **35 Maximum fines: the "standard scale"**, below), or both; and on conviction on indictment to a term not exceeding five years (s.91). A person giving a notification must also allow the police to take his fingerprints, his photograph or both (s.87(4)). These checks are to allow the police to verify a person's identity.

A person subject to the notification requirements must also, in accordance with regulations made by the Scottish Ministers, notify police if he intends to leave the UK, giving specified details as to the date of his departure and travel plans (s.86). The Sexual Offences Act 2003 (Travel Notification Requirements) (Scotland) Regulations 2004 provide that where a person intends to be abroad for three days or longer he must notify police at least seven days before his departure, unless that is not reasonably practicable, and in any event within 24 hours of departure. Where known, details must be given of the (first) country to which he will be travelling, his point of arrival in each country he is to visit, the carriers he intends to travel with, accommodation arrangements outside the UK, date of intended return and intended point of arrival on his return. Within three days of returning he must disclose his point of arrival and date of return to the police (if he hasn't already done so). Notices must be given by attendance in person at a local police station. It should be noted here that if a UK National does an act in a country outside the UK, being an act which if done in England and Wales, or in Northern Ireland, would constitute an offence specified in Schedule 2 to the Sexual Offences Act 2003 that person is guilty in that part of the UK of that sexual offence (Sexual Offences Act 2003 s.72 as amended).

A sheriff may, on application from a senior police officer, issue a warrant to allow a constable to enter and search the home of a relevant offender for the purposes of assessing the risks that the offender may pose to the community. The address must be one that the offender has notified to the police as his home address or one in respect of which there is a reasonable belief that the offender can be regularly found there or resides there. The offender must not be in custody, detained in a hospital or outside the UK at the time. A constable must have tried on at least two previous occasions to gain entry to the premises for the purpose of conducting a risk assessment and been unable to gain entry for that purpose. The warrant must specify each address to which it relates and a constable may use reasonable force if it is necessary to do so to enter and search the premises. The warrant can authorise as many visits as the magistrate considers to be necessary for the purposes of assessing the risks posed by the offender (s.96A, inserted by the Police, Public Order and Criminal Justice (Scotland) Act 2006 s.80).

The police may apply for a notification order in respect of a person if paragraphs (a) to (d) above apply to that person in respect of an offence committed abroad. Application can be made retrospectively in respect of any conviction since 1 September 1997, with the notification period running from the date of conviction abroad (Sexual Offences Act 2003, s.97).

19 Period of notification

The length of the notification period varies according to the length of the sentence. If a person was sentenced to imprisonment for public protection or for 30 months or more, the notification period is an indefinite period (i.e., for life, but see *Note* below). For sentences of less than 30 months, the notification period varies from 10 years (sentences between 6 and 30 months) to 2 years (cautions) or the length of a conditional discharge or period of probation (s.82, as amended by the Management of Offenders etc. (Scotland) Act 2005, ss.17 and 24).

For persons under 18 at the date of conviction or caution, these periods are halved (s.82(2)). The court may direct the parent of an offender under the age of 18 to comply with the notification requirements (s.89).

Note.—On the 21st April 2010 in the case of *R (on the application by JF (by his litigation friend OF)) v Secretary of State for the Home Department* the Supreme Court held that an indefinite notification period constituted a disproportionate interference with Article 8 of the European Convention of Human Rights (right to respect for a private and family life: see the Note on **The Human Rights Act 1998**) as there was no procedure for reviewing requirements in individual cases. This has been remedied by providing a mechanism for periodic review of the justification for continuing notification in individual cases. Reviews will be held 15 years (8 years for offenders under 18 at the date of conviction) after release from prison. At a review, a chief constable will decided whether to discharge the notification requirement or, if satisfied that the offender still poses a risk of sexual harm, make a notification continuation order which can last for up to 15 years, after which period another review will be carried out (ss.88A to 88H, added by the Sexual Offences Act 2003 (Remedial) (Scotland) Order 2010, S.S.I. No. 370).

20 Sexual offences prevention orders

If it appears to a chief constable that a person who is in his area, or is intending to come there—
(a) is a "qualifying offender" (see below); and
(b) has acted, since the "appropriate date" (see below), in such a way as to give reasonable cause to believe that such an order is necessary,
then he may apply to a sheriff's court for a sexual offences prevention order prohibiting that person from doing anything described in the order. An order will have effect for such period of not less than five years as is specified in the order or until a further order is made (Sexual Offences Act 2003, ss.104 to 106).

A "qualifying offender" is defined as a person who (s.106(5))—
(a) has been convicted of an offence listed in Schedules 3 or 5 of the Sexual Offences Act 2003 (which cover most sexual and violent offences); or
(b) has been found not guilty by reason of insanity or found to be under a disability and to have done the act charged in respect of such an offence; or
(c) has been punished abroad for an act which if committed in the United Kingdom would have been such an offence.
The "appropriate date" is the date of the first conviction (or finding, caution or punishment abroad), (s.106(8)).
Where appropriate the sheriff may grant an application for an interim order prior to making a full order (s.109).

A court may also issue an order when dealing with an offender for a Schedule 3 or 5 offence without an application from the police.

21 Effect of a sexual offences prevention order

Where a sexual offences prevention order is made, the person to whom it relates is treated as being subject to the notification requirements of the Sexual Offences Act 2003. Accordingly such a person must, *inter alia*, notify the police of any name which he uses, any change of his home address, and any address at which he will be staying in the UK for a period of 14 days (or for two periods in any 12 months which total 14 days) (s.107).

Breach of a sexual offences prevention order is punishable on summary conviction to imprisonment for six months or a fine (not exceeding the statutory maximum: see **35 Maximum fines: the "standard scale"**, below), or both; and on conviction on indictment to a term not exceeding five years (s.113).

22 Foreign travel orders

The police may apply to a sheriff court for a foreign travel order in respect of any person living in their area, or who they believe is in or intending to come to their area, and who (s.114 of the Sexual Offences Act 2003)–
    (a) is a "qualifying offender"; and
    (b) has since the day he was convicted (or found not guilty by reason of insanity, or cautioned) acted in such a way as to give reasonable cause to believe that it is necessary for an order to be made.

A qualifying offender for these purposes is in general anyone who has committed an offence against a child under the age of 18 and who has been sentenced to a term of 12 months or more (but not including an offence of possession of indecent images). The offence may have been committed either in the UK or abroad.

The court may make a foreign travel order if it is satisfied that the defendant is a qualifying offender and that his behaviour makes it necessary for such an order to be made for the purpose of protecting children generally, or any child, from serious sexual harm from the defendant outside the UK. Sexual harm is defined as physical or psychological harm caused by the defendant doing anything which, if done in the UK would constitute one of certain specified offences (most sexual offences are specified).

The effect of an order, which has effect for a fixed period of not more than 5 years, is to prohibit the defendant from travelling either to any specified country, or to any country other than a specified country, or from travelling abroad at all (s.117). An order may be renewed or varied (e.g., to impose additional prohibitions) (s.118). An appeal against an order may be made to the Crown Court (s.119).

Offenders who are subject to a foreign travel order that prohibits them from travelling anywhere in the world, must surrender their passport. Such offenders must also surrender any new passports which they acquire throughout the duration of a foreign travel order (s.117A, 117B)

Breach of a foreign travel order is punishable on summary conviction to imprisonment for six months or a fine not exceeding the statutory maximum: see **35 Maximum fines: the "standard scale"**, below), or both; and on conviction on indictment to a term not exceeding five years (s.122).

23 Risk of sexual harm orders

The police may apply a sheriff court for a risk of sexual harm order in respect of any person living in their area, or who they believe is in or intending to come to their area, who (Protection of Children and Prevention of Sexual Offences (Scotland) Act 2005, s.2)–
    (a) has on at least two occasions done one of the following acts–
        (i) engaged in sexual activity involving a child or in the presence of a child;
        (ii) caused or incited a child to watch a person engaging in a sexual activity or to look at a moving or still image that is sexual;
        (iii) given a child anything which relates to a sexual activity or contains a reference to such an activity; or
        (iv) communicated with a child where any part of the communication is sexual; and
    (b) as a result of those acts there is reasonable cause to believe that it is necessary to make the order.

The person in respect of whom an order is applied for need not have been convicted of any offence.

The court may make a risk of sexual harm order if it is satisfied that the defendant has on at least two occasions done one of the above acts and that it is necessary for such an order to be made for the purpose of protecting children generally, or any child, from harm from the defendant (i.e., physical or psychological harm caused by him doing one of the above acts: s.3).

An order will prohibit that person from doing anything described in the order and have effect for such period of not less than two years as is specified in the order or until a further order is made (s.2(7)).

Orders may be renewed and varied and interim orders may be made (ss.4 and 5). Appeals against orders may be made to the High Court (s.6).

Breach of a risk of sexual harm order is punishable on summary conviction to imprisonment for six months or a fine not exceeding the statutory maximum: see **35 Maximum fines: the "standard scale"**, below), or both; and on conviction on indictment to a term not exceeding five years (s.7). Breach of an order will also make the defendant subject to the notification requirements of the 2003 Act if they are not already subject to them (see **18 Notification requirements**, above) (s. 8).

G: CRIMINAL AND ANTI-SOCIAL BEHAVIOUR ORDERS

24 Who may apply for an Order

In Scotland, a "relevant" authority may apply to the sheriff for an anti-social behaviour order against any person aged 16 or over on the ground that—

(a) that person has—
  (i) acted in an anti-social manner, that is to say in a manner that caused or was likely to cause alarm or distress, or
  (ii) pursued a course of anti-social conduct, that is to say a course of conduct that caused or was likely to cause alarm or distress,
  to one or more persons not of the same household as himself in the local authority's area, and
(b) an order is necessary to protect person's in the authority's area from further anti-social acts and conduct by him (Crime and Disorder Act 1998 s.19).

A "relevant" authority can be either the local authority or a registered social landlord (s.19(8)).

An order under s.19 will prohibit the person concerned from doing anything described in the order. Application for an order is made to the sheriff within whose sheriffdom the alarm or distress was alleged to have been caused or to have been likely to be caused. Nothing in s.19 prevents a local authority from instituting any legal proceedings otherwise than under that section against any person in relation to any anti-social act or conduct (e.g., eviction proceedings).

Where an application is made for an anti-social behaviour order, the sheriff may if he considers that it is just to do so make an interim order before the full order is made (s.19(2A)).

Before making an application under s.19, the local authority must consult the chief constable for the area concerned. An order under s.19 has effect either for such period as is specified in it or indefinitely, and may be revoked or varied on an application either by the applicant for the order or the person subject to it (s.21).

If, without reasonable excuse, a person breaches an order by doing anything prohibited by it, he will be guilty of an offence punishable by a fine or imprisonment or both (s.22).

Anti-social behaviour orders can also be made under the Criminal Procedure (Scotland) Act 1995, s.234AA (as inserted by the Antisocial Behaviour (Scotland) Act 2004, s.118) where—

(c) the offender is convicted of an offence;
(d) at the time when he committed the offence, the offender was at least 12 years of age;
(e) in committing the offence he engaged in antisocial behaviour; and
(f) the court is satisfied, on a balance of probabilities, that the making of an antisocial behaviour order is necessary for the purpose of protecting other persons from further antisocial behaviour by the offender.

Anti-social behaviour is defined in similar terms as in (a) above.

H: TRAVEL RESTRICTION ORDERS (DRUG TRAFFICKING OFFENDERS)

25 Introduction

The Criminal Justice and Police Act 2001 introduced powers to impose overseas travel restrictions on offenders convicted of certain drug trafficking offences. The "trigger" offences covered by this provision are listed in s.34 and include the production and supply of controlled drugs.

26 When an order may be made

A travel restriction order may be made by a court if a person has been convicted of one of the specified drug trafficking offences and has been sentenced to a term of imprisonment of four years or more (Criminal Justice and Police Act 2001, s.33). In every such case the court must consider whether to make an order, and if it decides not to it must state the reasons why.

27 Effect of a travel restriction order

A travel restriction order has the effect of prohibiting an offender who has a United Kingdom passport from leaving the UK at any time specified in the order (which will be not less than two years) beginning with the date of the offender's release from custody. The offender may be required to hand over his passport for the duration of the travel ban period (Criminal Justice and Police Act 2001, s.33).

28 Revocation and suspension of orders

An offender may apply for a travel restriction order to be revoked after a minimum period has passed. The minimum period varies according to the length of the ban that has been imposed. A four-year ban may not be revoked until two years have passed, a ban of more than four and less than ten years may not be revoked until four years have passed, and any other ban may not be revoked until five years have passed (Criminal Justice and Police Act 2001, s.35). In deciding whether to revoke an order the court must take into account the offender's character, his conduct since the making of the order and the offences for which he was originally convicted.

An offender may apply for an order to be suspended and the court may do so if it is satisfied that there are exceptional circumstances which justify a suspension on compassionate grounds (s.35(3)). If an order is suspended, the offender has a duty to be in the United Kingdom at the time when the suspension ends. Where an order is suspended, the total length of the travel ban imposed by the order is extended for the length of the suspension period.

29 Offences

A person who leaves the United Kingdom in breach of a travel ban, or who is not in the UK at the end of a period during which the ban has been suspended, will be guilty of an offence. An offence is punishable on summary conviction to a term of imprisonment not exceeding six months, or a fine (unlimited in England and Wales, not exceeding the statutory maximum in Scotland: see **35 Maximum fines: the "standard scale"**, below, or both; and on conviction on indictment to imprisonment for a term not exceeding five years or a fine, or both (Criminal Justice and Police Act 2001, s.36).

I: DRUG TREATMENT AND TESTING ORDERS

30 When orders may be made

A drug treatment and testing order is a non-custodial order which may be imposed on a person aged 16 or over who is convicted of an offence other than one for which the sentence is fixed by law (Criminal Procedure (Scotland) Act 1995, s.234B).

Before making an order, the court must be satisfied that the offender—
(a) is dependent on or has a propensity to misuse drugs and is a suitable person to be subject to such an order;
(b) the dependency or propensity is such as requires and may be susceptible to treatment; and
(c) the court must explain the effect and requirements of the order to the offender, the consequences if he fails to comply with it, and that it will be reviewed periodically.

An order may not be made unless the offender expresses a willingness to comply with its requirements.

A court may not make an order unless it has been informed that arrangements for implementing such orders are available in its area.

31 Terms of orders

An order will have effect for a period, specified in the order, of between six months and three years (Criminal Procedure (Scotland) Act 1995, s.234B) and must include a requirement that the offender submit, during the whole of the period, to treatment by or under the direction of a specified person with a view to the reduction or elimination of the offender's dependency on or propensity to misuse drugs (s.234C). Treatment may be either residential or non-residential and the treatment provider must be specified in the order. The offender must agree to submit to mandatory drug tests as part of the treatment. During the term of an order, the offender will be under the supervision of a probation officer. Orders must be reviewed periodically at intervals of not less than one month and, after a review, the court may amend any requirement or provision of the order (s.234F). If the offender fails to express his willingness to comply with the order as amended, the court may revoke it and deal with him for the original offence as if he had just been convicted, taking into account the extent to which he has complied with the order.

Where the court considers it expedient, an offender may be made subject to both a drug treatment and testing order and a community payback order (1995 Act, s.234J). A restriction of liberty order may also be attached (see **36 Restriction of liberty orders**, below) where these are available and the offender consents (s.234CA).

32 Breach of an order

Where an offender on whom a drug treatment and testing order has been imposed fails to comply with a requirement imposed by the order, the court may issue a warrant for his arrest, or issue a citation requiring him to appear before the court (and a warrant if he fails to do so) (Criminal Procedure (Scotland) Act 1995, s.234G).

Where the court is satisfied that an offender has failed without reasonable excuse to comply with a requirement imposed by an order, it may—
(a) impose a fine not exceeding level 3 on the standard scale; or
(b) vary or revoke the order.

In addition, where a drug treatment and testing order is breached and the court is satisfied that the person in breach has a dependency on or a propensity to misuse drugs, a drugs court (but not any other court) has additional powers. It may, on one or more than one occasion—
(a) sentence the person in breach to a term of imprisonment or detention not exceeding 28 days (in total) (*Note.*–the minimum custody period of five days does not apply in these circumstances); or
(b) make a community payback order imposing a level 1 unpaid work or other activity requirement (*Note.*–the usual minimum of 80 hours does not apply in these circumstances).

Where the drugs court uses either of these powers, the drug treatment and testing order is unaffected and remains in force (Criminal Justice (Scotland) Act 2003, s.42).

33 Fines

Under the Criminal Procedure (Scotland) Act 1995 (ss.211 to 226), provision is made for the imposition of fines on offenders by Scottish courts. *Inter alia* the courts may allow time for payment or allow payment to be made by instalments. Provision is also made for the imposition of a period of imprisonment in the event of failure to pay the fine.

Under Sections 226A to 226I of the Criminal Procedure (Scotland) Act 1995, fines enforcement officers ("FEOs") have the functions of providing information and advice to offenders regarding the payment of relevant penalties and of securing compliance with enforcement orders. These orders provide general information to the offender regarding the amount of the penalty, the arrangements for repayment and their effect. FEOs have a wide range of powers, including the power to execute civil diligence to execute arrestment of earnings and arrestment of funds held in a bank or other financial institution, and to seize an offender's vehicle and (with the court's approval) dispose of it.

Under s.227M, where a fine has been imposed on an offender and he fails to pay the fine (or an instalment of it) then, if he is not serving a sentence of imprisonment and the court (other than the High Court) would have imposed a period of imprisonment on him for the failure to pay the fine or instalment, it must where the amount of the fine or the instalment does not exceed level 2 on the standard scale, impose instead a community payback order on the offender imposing a level 1 unpaid work or other activity requirement Where the amount of the fine or the instalment exceeds that level, the court may impose such a community payback order (see **37 Community payback orders—introduction**, below). Failure to comply with a community payback order can lead to either an increase in the hours of unpaid work to be completed, or imprisonment for up to 60 days (justice of the peace court) or 3 months (any other court) (s.227ZC).

Where a person is convicted of a "relevant offence" (i.e., one of the environmental offences specified by the Environmental Regulation (Relevant Offences) (Scotland) Order 2014, Sch. 2) then, in determining the amount of the fine, the court must in particular have regard to any financial benefit which has accrued or is likely to accrue to the person in consequence of the offence (Regulatory Reform (Scotland) Act 2014, s.35).

34 Consequences of default

Under s.24 of the Criminal Justice Act 1991 the Secretary of State may by regulations provide that, where a fine or surcharge is imposed by a magistrates' court or a compensation or unlawful profit order or a slavery and trafficking reparation order is made against an offender by such a court and the offender is entitled to universal credit, income support, jobseeker's allowance, employment and support allowance or state pension credit, the court may apply for the deduction at source of sums due by way of fine or compensation from the offender's benefit payments. The Fines (Deduction from Income Support) Regulations 1992 have been made in exercise of this power (and relate to all the above benefits).

35 Maximum fines: the "standard scale"

Frequently, the maximum level of a fine for a particular offence will be fixed by law by reference to a particular level on the "standard scale". This scale, which applies only to summary offences, is contained in the Criminal Justice Act 1982 s.37 as substituted by the Criminal Procedure (Scotland) Act 1995 s.225.

The current levels on the standard scale are—

Level 1	£200
Level 2	£500
Level 3	£1,000
Level 4	£2,500
Level 5	£5,000

Sometimes, the maximum fine that may be imposed for an offence in Scotland is stated to be "not exceeding the statutory maximum". The statutory maximum is £10,000 (Criminal Procedure (Scotland) Act 1995 s.225(8) as amended).

The maximum fine that may be imposed on a child (i.e., under the age of 14) is £250; and on a young person (i.e., under the age of 18) is £1,000 (Magistrates Court Act 1980 ss.24 and 36).

K: RESTRICTION OF LIBERTY ORDERS

36 Restriction of liberty orders

Under s.245A of the Criminal Procedure (Scotland) Act 1995, where a person is convicted of an offence punishable by imprisonment (other than an offence the sentence for which is fixed by law) the court may, instead of imprisonment or any other form of detention, make a restriction of liberty order in respect of him. A restriction of liberty order is an order requiring the offender to remain in a specified place for a specified period (or not to be in a specified place at a specified time). The power to make such an order is available only to courts which have been notified by the Scottish Ministers that arrangements for monitoring the whereabouts of offenders are available in the area concerned. The High Court of Justiciary, the Sheriff Appeal Court and all Sheriff Courts have been prescribed (Restriction of Liberty etc (Scotland) Regulations 2013). An order can only be made in respect of a person under the age of 16 if having obtained a report on the offender from the local authority in whose area he resides, the court is satisfied as to the services which the authority will provide for his support and rehabilitation during the period when he is subject to the order.

The maximum time for which a person can be required to be in a particular place is 12 hours in any one day, and the maximum length of an order is 12 months. Before making an order, a court must obtain and consider information about the place to be specified in the order, including information as to the attitude of any persons likely to be affected by the offender's enforced presence there. It must also explain the order's effect in ordinary language, as well as the consequences of any breach and the court's power to review the order. An order cannot be made unless the offender expresses his willingness to comply with its requirements.

Compliance with the restriction of liberty order may be monitored remotely (i.e., by electronic tagging). An order may be made concurrently with a community payback order.

L: COMMUNITY PAYBACK ORDERS

37 Community payback orders–introduction

Section 227A of the Criminal Procedure (Scotland) Act 1995 (inserted by the Criminal Justice and Licensing (Scotland) Act 2010, s.14) makes provision for community payback orders.

A community payback order is an order imposing one or more of the following requirements as an alternative to a prison sentence–

(a) an offender supervision requirement;
(b) a compensation requirement;
(c) an unpaid work or other activity requirement at level 1 or level 2;
(d) a programme requirement;
(e) a residence requirement;
(f) a mental health treatment requirement;
(g) a drug treatment requirement;
(h) an alcohol treatment requirement;
(i) a conduct requirement.

Where imprisonment is an option, but the court decides to impose a fine instead, it may also impose a community payback order in addition, but only one within (a), (c) level 1, or (i) above.

A justice of the peace court may only impose community payback orders with requirements within (a), (b), (c) level 1, (e) or (i) above.

An order may include a requirement for it to be reviewed periodically, at which time it may be varied, revoked or discharged (s.227X). Application to the court for variation, revocation or discharge can also be made (227Y).

38 The requirements

(a) Offender supervision

A requirement that, during a specified period of between 6 months and 3 years, the offender must attend appointments, at such time and place as may be determined, for the purpose of promoting his rehabilitation (Criminal Procedure (Scotland) Act 1995, s.227G). A community payback order must include an offender supervision requirement if the offender is under the age of 18 or if any of requirements (b), or (d) to (h) below are imposed.

(b) Compensation

A requirement that the offender must pay compensation (in a lump sum or by instalments) for any personal injury, loss, damage or other matter in respect of which a compensation order could be made against him, to the person who would have benefited under such a compensation order (s.227H).

(c) Unpaid work or other activity

A requirement that the offender aged at least 16 must, for a specified number of hours, undertake unpaid work, or unpaid work and other activity. Whether the offender must undertake other activity as well as unpaid work is for the officer supervising the payback order to determine, as is the nature of the unpaid work and any other activity. The number of hours that may be specified in the requirement must be (in total) at least 20 hours, but not more than 300 hours. Up to 100 hours is known as level 1, over that is known as level 2. The "other activity" must not amount to more than the lower of 30% of the hours specified in the requirement or 30 hours (s.227K).

A level 1 requirement must be completed within 3 months, a level 2 within 6 months, or such longer period as the court specifies.

(d) Programmes

A requirement that the offender must participate in a specified programme (i.e., a course or other planned set of activities, taking place over a period of time, and provided to individuals or groups of individuals for the purpose of addressing offending behavioural needs), at a specified place and on a specified number of days. A court may impose a programme requirement only if the specified programme is one which has been recommended by an officer of a local authority as being suitable for the offender to participate in (s.227P).

(e) Residence
A requirement that, for a specified period, the offender must reside at a specified place. The court may require an offender to reside at a hostel or other institution only if it has been recommended as a suitable place for the offender to reside in by an officer of a local authority (s.227Q).

(f) Mental health treatment
A requirement that the offender submit to treatment by or under the direction of a registered medical practitioner or a registered psychologist (or both) with a view to improving his mental condition. The nature of the treatment will not to be specified in the order, but it must be treatment (i) as a resident patient in a hospital (other than a State hospital) within the meaning of the Mental Health (Care and Treatment) (Scotland)Act 2003; (ii) as a non-resident patient at such institution or other place as may be specified, or (iii) by or under the direction of such registered medical practitioner or registered psychologist as may be specified (s.227R).

A mental health treatment requirement can only be imposed if certain medical conditions are met.

(g) Drug treatment
A requirement that the offender submit to treatment with a view to reducing or eliminating his dependency on, or propensity to misuse, drugs. The nature of the treatment will not to be specified in the order, but it must be treatment (i) as a resident in a specified institution or other place, or (ii) as a non-resident at such institution or other place, and at such intervals, as are specified in the order.

A drug treatment requirement can only be imposed if the court is satisfied that the offender is dependent on, or has a propensity to misuse, any controlled drug, the dependency or propensity requires, and may be susceptible to, treatment, and arrangements have been, or can be, made for the proposed treatment (s.227U).

(h) Alcohol treatment
A requirement that the offender submit to treatment with a view to the reduction or elimination of his dependency on alcohol. The nature of the treatment will not to be specified in the order, but it must be treatment (i) as a resident in such institution or other place as is specified, (ii) as a non-resident at such institution or other place, and at such intervals, as is specified, or (iii) by or under the direction of such person as is specified.

An alcohol treatment requirement can only be imposed if the court is satisfied that the offender is dependent on alcohol, the dependency requires, and may be susceptible to, treatment, and arrangements have been, or can be, made for the proposed treatment (s.227V).

(i) Conduct
A requirement that the offender, during a specified period (of not more than 3 years), do or refrain from doing specified things. A court may impose a conduct requirement only if it is satisfied that the requirement is necessary with a view to securing or promoting good behaviour by the offender, or preventing further offending by him (s.227W).

39 Breach of a community payback order
Where an offender on whom a community payback order has been imposed fails to comply with a requirement imposed by the order, the court may issue a warrant for his arrest, or issue a citation requiring him to appear before the court (and a warrant if he fails to do so) (Criminal Procedure (Scotland) Act 1995, s.227ZC).

Where the court is satisfied that an offender has failed without reasonable excuse to comply with a requirement imposed by an order, it may–
  (a) impose a fine not exceeding level 3 on the standard scale;
  (b) where the original offence was punishable by imprisonment, revoke the order and deal with the offender in respect of the offence in relation to which the order was imposed as it could have dealt with the offender had the order not been imposed;
  (c) where the original offence was punishable by imprisonment or a fine, revoke the order and impose on the offender a sentence of imprisonment for a term not exceeding (i) where the court is a justice of the peace court, 60 days, (ii)in any other case, 3 months;
  (d) vary the order so as to impose a new requirement, vary any requirement imposed by the order or revoke or discharge any requirement imposed by the order; or
  (e) both impose a fine under (a) above and vary the order under (d) above.

A requirement under (d) above can include a restricted movement requirement requiring the offender to be in a specified place at a specified time or during specified periods (not exceeding 12 hours in any one day), or not to be in a specified place, or a specified class of place, at a specified time or during specified periods (s.227ZF). Such restrictions can be imposed for between 14 days and 12 months. Where the offender is aged under 18 or the requirement breached was a level 1 unpaid work or activity requirement, the maximum restricted movement period is 3 months (60 days if imposed by a justice of the peace court). The power to make such an order is available only to courts which have been notified by the Scottish Ministers that arrangements for monitoring the whereabouts of offenders are available in the area concerned. The High Court of Justiciary, all Sheriff Courts and all Justice of the Peace courts have been prescribed (Restriction of Liberty Order and Restricted Movement Requirement (Scotland) Regulations 2011).

M: COMPENSATION ORDERS

40 Compensation orders (Scotland)

Similar provision for Scotland is made by ss.249 to 253 of the Criminal Procedure (Scotland) Act 1995, except that no compensation orders may be made in respect of funeral expenses or bereavement nor in respect of any injury, loss, or damage due to any accident involving a motor vehicle (except where it involves dishonest appropriation or the unlawful taking and using of the vehicle). A court which makes an order discharging a person absolutely, makes a community payback order or defers sentence may not also make a compensation order (s.249(2)). A "victim" is defined as a person against whom or a person against whose property the acts which constituted the offence were directed (s. 249(1A)).

Where a person is convicted of a "relevant offence" (i.e., one of the environmental offences specified by the Environmental Regulation (Relevant Offences) (Scotland) Order 2014, Sch. 1), compensation of up to £50,000 can also be ordered to be paid to a relevant person (e.g., SEPA, a local authority or landowner) for the costs incurred or to be incurred by them in preventing, reducing, remediating or mitigating the effects of any harm to the environment resulting directly or indirectly from the offence, and any other harm, loss, damage or adverse impacts so resulting from the offence (Regulatory Reform (Scotland) Act 2014, s.34).

Under s.21(9) of the Proceeds of Crime (Scotland) Act 1995, there is power to order that the proceeds of sale of forfeited property be first directed towards satisfaction of a compensation order made in the same proceedings as the order for forfeiture.

N: CONFISCATION AND RESTRAINT ORDERS

41 The Proceeds of Crime Act 2002

The confiscation of assets of those convicted of a criminal offence is provided for in the Proceeds of Crime Act 2002. The 2002 Act also provides for the issue of restraint orders to prohibit dealing in property which has been the subject of a crime.

Asset recovery is undertaken by the National Crime Agency, the Director of Public Prosecutions, and the Director of the Serious Fraud Office.

42 Confiscation orders

Part 3 of the Proceeds of Crime Act 2002 substantially replaces the Proceeds of Crime (Scotland) Act 1995 and other money laundering legislation.

The High Court in Scotland or a sheriff must make a confiscation order where the accused (s.92(2)-(4))–
- (a) is convicted of an offence or offences;
- (b) the prosecutor asks the court to act; and
- (c) the court decides to order a disposal in respect of the accused.

A confiscation order can be made if the court decides that the accused has a criminal lifestyle (s.142, and Sch. 4) – see **43 A criminal lifestyle**, below. If it decides that the accused does have a criminal lifestyle, the court must decide whether he has benefited from either his general criminal conduct (s.143(2)) or his particular criminal conduct (s.143(3)).

If the court decides that the accused has benefited from his conduct, it must decide a recoverable amount (s.93(1)) and must make a confiscation order requiring him to pay that amount (s.92(6)), although the court may use its discretion if the victim of the crime has already started civil proceedings (s.92(7)).

43 A criminal lifestyle

A defendant has a criminal lifestyle if–
- (a) he engages in drug trafficking, money laundering, directing terrorism, people trafficking, arms trafficking, offences related to slavery, servitude and forced or compulsory labour, counterfeiting, intellectual property offences, offences in relation to gangmasters or acting as a pimp or running brothels, traffic in prostitution, blackmail, distribution of obscene material, possession and supply of unclassified videos, using an unlicensed security operative, and being involved in, or directing, serious organised crime; or he attempts, conspires or incites the commission of one of those offences or aids, abets, counsels or procures the commission of such an offence (Proceeds of Crime Act 2002, s.142(1)(a), Sch.4);
- (b) the offence forms part of a "course of criminal activity" and the benefit resulting from that course is more than £5,000. A "course of criminal activity" means that the defendant must have been convicted in

the same proceedings of three or more offences in addition to the principal offence and he has benefited from each of the additional offences, or he has been convicted on at least two occasions of an offence from which he has benefited during the previous six years (s.142(1)(b), (2), (3)); or

(c) the offence is committed over a period of at least six months and the defendant has benefited from it by more than £5,000 (s.142(1)(c), (3)).

44 Appeals

The prosecutor has the power to appeal against any decision of the court to make a confiscation order and also against any confiscation order where it considers that the amount to be paid is too low (Proceeds of Crime Act 2002, s.115).

45 Restraint orders

The court may make a restraint order prohibiting a specified person from dealing with property held by him (Proceeds of Crime Act 2002, ss.119 and 120).

The police may seize any realisable property (other than cash or exempt property such as work equipment or household bedding or furniture) if they have reasonable grounds for suspecting that either (s.127C)–

(a) the property may otherwise be made unavailable for satisfying any confiscation order that has been or may be made against the accused, or

(b) the value of the property may otherwise be diminished as a result of conduct by the accused or any other person.

There are accompanying powers to search premises, people and vehicles in order to find property to be seized (ss.127D-F). These powers must usually only be exercised with the approval of a sheriff or (if that is not practicable in any case) of a senior police officer. If a search is carried out without the approval of a sheriff, or if any seized property is held for less than 48 hours, a report must be made to an independent person appointed by the Scottish Ministers (ss.127G-H).

A sheriff may authorise the sale of seized property to satisfy a confiscation order, if the seized property belongs to a person against whom a confiscation order has been made, the time to pay that order has expired, and provided that an enforcement receiver has not been appointed in relation to the property (s.131A).

46 Civil recovery of the proceeds of crime

The Proceeds of Crime Act 2002 Part 5 provides two schemes for the civil recovery of the proceeds of unlawful conduct.

Chapters 1 and 2 of Part 5 provide the first scheme which allows the enforcement authority (i.e., the National Crime Agency, the Director of Public Prosecutions, or the Director of the Serious Fraud Office, and the Scottish Ministers) to make an application to the Court of Session in Scotland for the civil recovery of–

(a) property (not just cash) that is or represents property obtained through unlawful conduct; and

(b) cash which is intended to be used in unlawful conduct.

Proceedings for a recovery order cannot be started unless the enforcement authority reasonably believe that the value of the property to be the subject of the order is not less than £10,000 (s.287, and the Proceeds of Crime Act 2002 (Financial Threshold for Civil Recovery) Order 2003).

Chapters 1 and 3 of Part 5 provide the second scheme under which the police, immigration officers and officers of HM Revenue and Customs may recover cash through summary proceedings before a magistrates' court. If a police, immigration or HM Revenue and Customs officer who is lawfully on any premises has reasonable grounds for suspecting that there is cash on the premises which is recoverable property or is intended for use in unlawful conduct he may search for cash there (s.289(1)). However, in order to do this, there must be not less than £1,000 on the premises (s.289(1)(b) and the Proceeds of Crime Act 2002 (Recovery of Cash in Summary Proceedings: Minimum Amount) Order 2006). Any cash found may be seized and detained, initially for 48 hours but extendable by a sheriff for up to three months (and further extended up to a maximum of two years) (s.295). To extend the detention period the sheriff must be satisfied that either–

(a) there are reasonable grounds for suspecting that the cash is recoverable property and that either its continued detention is justified while its derivation is further investigated or consideration is given to proceedings against any person for an offence with which the cash is connected, or proceedings against any person for an offence with which the cash is connected have been started and have not been concluded; or

(b) there are reasonable grounds for suspecting that the cash is intended to be used in unlawful conduct and that either its continued detention is justified while its intended use is further investigated or consideration is given to bringing proceedings against any person for an offence with which the cash is connected, or proceedings against any person for an offence with which the cash is connected have been started and have not been concluded.

It will only be released if the sheriff is satisfied, on an application by the person from whom the cash was seized, that the conditions for it seizure are no longer met.

Property which has already been seized or forfeited under other provisions (e.g., the Obscene Publications Act 1959, the Misuse of Drugs Act 1971, or the Terrorism Act 2001) cannot be forfeited under the 2002 Act

(Proceeds of Crime (Exemptions from Civil Recovery) Order 2003 (S.I. No. 336).

The Scottish Ministers must draw up a code of practice in connection with the exercise of the power to recover cash under Chapter 3 (ss.292 and 293). The Proceeds of Crime Act 2002 (Cash Searches: Constables in Scotland: Code of Practice) Order 2015 bring this code of practice into operation in relation to the police. Searches by Revenue and Customs are covered by the Proceeds of Crime Act 2002 (Cash Searches: Code of Practice) Order 2016.

There is a right of appeal against forfeiture of cash (or a refusal of a court to order forfeiture) to the Sheriff Principal (s.299).

In order to preserve the property before a recovery order is made, the enforcement authority can apply for an interim order, allowing to take the property and manage it pending the making of a full order. Alternatively, they can apply for a prohibitory property order under s.255A.

O: MISCELLANEOUS POWERS

47 Deportation orders

A court may recommend for deportation a person who is not a British citizen aged 17 or over who has been convicted of an offence punishable with imprisonment.

48 Deprivation of property used for crime (forfeiture orders)

Under ss.21 to 27 of the Proceeds of Crime (Scotland) Act 1995, a court may make a suspended forfeiture order where a person is convicted of an offence or is given an absolute discharge. The court must be satisfied that property, which was at the time of the offence or of the accused's apprehension in his ownership or possession or under his control, has been used, or was intended to be used, for the purpose of committing, or facilitating the commission of, any offence. The district court's power to order forfeiture is limited to moveable property.

49 Disqualification from driving

Under s.248 of the Criminal Procedure (Scotland) Act 1995, where a person is convicted of an offence (other than a summary offence), the court may disqualify him for holding or obtaining a licence to drive a motor vehicle, for such period as the court thinks fit, if a motor vehicle was used, whether by that person or anyone else, in connection with the commission of the offence.

S.248A of the 1995 Act (added by s.15 of the Crime and Punishment (Scotland) Act 1997) gives courts power to disqualify an offender from driving on conviction for any offence, either in addition to any other sentence or instead of any other sentence, except in the case of an offence for which the sentence is fixed by law or where the court is required to impose a sentence. In those cases, the court may impose a disqualification in addition to the sentence. These powers may be used only by courts notified by the Secretary of State that the power may be exercised by that court. Similarly, s.248B empowers a court to impose a disqualification from driving on an offender who has defaulted with the payment of a fine or other financial order. The maximum period of disqualification is 12 months. Again, this power may not be exercised unless the court has been notified that it may exercise it.

S.248D provides for an extension in the length of the period of a driving disqualification imposed under ss.248 or 248A where a custodial sentence is also imposed for the same offence. The court must determine the appropriate discretionary period of disqualification and then add on the appropriate extension period.

The appropriate extension period takes account of that part of the sentence which the offender will serve in prison. Where a life sentence or an indeterminate sentence for public protection is imposed the extension period is the period of the minimum tariff set by the court. Where an extended sentence is imposed the extension period is half the custodial term i.e., the period of the sentence to be served in prison. Where a detention and training order is imposed, the extension period is half the term of the order. In all other cases, the extension period is equal to one half of the custodial sentence (at which point the offender will be released either automatically or on licence in the community until the end of sentence). The extension period will be reduced to reflect any reduction in the custodial sentence as a result of the court taking into account time already served on remand, or periods of remand on bail in a case where the offender was subject to a curfew condition which was electronically monitored.

Where the court imposes a suspended sentence, or a life sentence to which no early release provisions apply (i.e., where the offender must spend the rest of their life in prison), the extension period does not apply.

Where an offender is disqualified at the same time as they are imprisoned for another offence, or at a time when they are already in prison for another offence, the court must, so far as appropriate, have regard to the diminished effect of disqualification as a distinct punishment where the person who is disqualified is also imprisoned (s.248E). For example, the more that the beginning of a driving disqualification overlaps with the end of the period of detention under an earlier sentence, the more a court might extend the disqualification to compensate for the diminished effect during the overlap.

The Road Traffic Offenders Act 1988 includes further provision for the disqualification of drivers and endorsement of licences (see the Note on **Penalty Points, Revocation, Disqualification, and Endorsement**).

50 Drunken offenders

A constable has the power, as an alternative to arresting a person for drunken behaviour under specified statutory powers, to take that person to an approved treatment centre for alcoholics. A person may not be detained against his will in such a centre but he will remain liable to be charged with an offence (Criminal Procedure (Scotland) Act 1995, s.16).

51 Fixed penalty – conditional offer

A procurator fiscal may, on receiving a report that a relevant offence has been committed, give the alleged offender a conditional offer to accept a fixed penalty in respect of the offence. A relevant offence is one which could be tried summarily other than specified offences under the Road Traffic Offenders Act 1988 (which are subject to a separate fixed penalty or conditional offer regime: see the Note on **Fixed Penalties**) (Criminal Procedure (Scotland) Act 1995, s.302).

A conditional offer must–

(a) give such particulars of the circumstances alleged to constitute the offence to which it relates as are necessary for giving reasonable information about the alleged offence;

(b) state the amount of the fixed penalty and, if the penalty is to be payable in instalments, the amount of the instalments and the intervals at which they must be paid (for these purposes, the Criminal Procedure (Scotland) Act 1995 Fixed Penalty Order 2008 prescribes the scale of fixed penalties);

(c) indicate that if, within 28 days of the date on which the conditional offer was issued, or such longer period as may be specified in the conditional offer, the alleged offender accepts the offer by making payment in respect of the fixed penalty to the clerk of the court specified in the offer at the address therein mentioned, any liability to conviction of the offence will be discharged;

(d) indicate (i) that the alleged offender may refuse the conditional offer by giving notice to the clerk of court in the manner specified in the conditional offer before the expiry of 28 days, or such longer period as may be specified in the offer, beginning on the day on which the offer is made; (ii) that unless the alleged offender gives such notice, he will be deemed to have accepted the conditional offer (even where no payment is made in respect of the offer); (iii) that where the alleged offender is deemed to have accepted the conditional offer as described above any liability to conviction of the offence will be discharged except where the offer is recalled under s.302C of the 1995 Act (see **54 Recall of fixed penalty or compensation offer**, below);

(e) state that proceedings against the alleged offender will not be commenced in respect of that offence until the end of a period of 28 days from the date on which the conditional offer was issued, or such longer period as may be specified in the conditional offer;

(f) state (i) that acceptance of the offer in the manner described in paragraph (c) above or deemed acceptance of the offer as described in paragraph (d) above will not be a conviction nor recorded as such; (ii) that the fact that the offer has been accepted, or deemed to have been accepted, may be disclosed to the court in any proceedings for an offence committed by the alleged offender within the period of two years beginning on the day of acceptance of the offer; (iii) that if the offer is not accepted, that fact may be disclosed to the court in any proceedings for the offence to which the conditional offer relates;

(g) state that refusal of a conditional offer under paragraph (d) above will be treated as a request by the alleged offender to be tried for the offence;

(h) explain the right to request a recall of the fixed penalty under s.302C of the 1995 Act.

The clerk of the court must, without delay, notify the procurator fiscal who issued the conditional offer when notice given by the alleged offender refusing the offer has been received or, following the expiry of 28 days or such longer period as may be specified in the offer (see paragraph (d)), notify the procurator fiscal that no notice accepting the offer has been received. A conditional offer is accepted by the alleged offender making any payment in respect of the appropriate fixed penalty. Where an alleged offender to whom a conditional offer of a fixed penalty is made does not give notice refusing the offer, he is deemed to have accepted such offer. Where an alleged offender accepts a conditional offer or is deemed to have accepts a conditional offer and the fixed penalty is not recalled no proceedings will be brought against the alleged offender for the offence.

For the purpose of these provisions, the alleged offender will be presumed to have received a conditional offer if the offer is sent to the address given by the alleged offender in a request for recall under s.302C of the 1995 Act of an earlier offer in the same matter, or any address given by the alleged offender to the clerk of the court specified in the offer, or to the procurator fiscal, in connection with the offer.

Where an alleged offender accepts a fixed penalty offer, any amount of the penalty which is outstanding at any time must, under s.303, be treated as if the penalty were a fine imposed by the court (see J: FINES, above). No action will be taken to enforce a fixed penalty which an alleged offender is deemed to have accepted unless the offender is sent a notice of the intention to take enforcement action and which explains the right to request a recall of the penalty (as to which see para 80C, below). Any request for recall must also have been finally disposed of.

52 Compensation offer

Under s.302A of the Criminal Procedure (Scotland) Act 1995, a procurator fiscal may, on receiving a report that a relevant offence has been committed, send to the alleged offender a notice known as a "compensation offer". The provisions are in near identical terms to those in respect of conditional offers, see **51 Fixed penalty**

– **conditional offer**, above. A relevant offence is any offence in respect of which an alleged offender could be tried summarily and on conviction of which it would be competent for the court to make a compensation order under s.249 of the 1995 Act.

A compensation offer must–

(a) give such particulars of the circumstances alleged to constitute the offence to which it relates as are necessary for giving reasonable information about the alleged offence;

(b) state the amount of compensation payable and, if compensation is to be payable by instalments, the amount of the instalments, and the intervals at which they must be paid;

(c) indicate that if, within 28 days of the date on which the offer was issued, or such longer period as may be specified in the offer, the alleged offender accepts the offer by making payment in respect of the offer to the clerk of the court specified in the offer, any liability to conviction of the offence will be discharged;

(d) indicate (i) that the alleged offender may refuse the conditional offer by giving notice to the clerk of court in the manner specified in the offer before the expiry of 28 days, or such longer period as may be specified in such offer, beginning on the day on which the offer is made; (ii) that unless the alleged offender gives such notice, he will be deemed to have accepted the offer (even where no payment is made in respect of the offer); (iii) that where the alleged offender is deemed to have accepted the offer as described above any liability to conviction of the offence shall be discharged except where the offer is recalled under s.302C of the 1995 Act (see **54 Recall of fixed penalty or compensation offer**, below);

(e) state that proceedings against the alleged offender will not be commenced in respect of that offence until the end of a period of 28 days from the date on which the offer was issued, or such longer period as may be specified in the offer;

(f) state (i) that acceptance of the offer in the manner described in paragraph (c) above or deemed acceptance of the offer as described in paragraph (d) above, will not be a conviction nor recorded as such; (ii) that the fact that the offer has been accepted, or deemed to have been accepted, may be disclosed to the court in any proceedings for an offence committed by the alleged offender within the period of two years beginning on the day of acceptance of the offer; (iii) that if the offer is not accepted, that fact may be disclosed to the court in any proceedings for the offence to which the offer relates;

(g) state that refusal of an offer under paragraph (d) above will be treated as a request by the alleged offender to be tried for the offence;

(h) explain the right to request a recall of the offer under s.302C of the 1995 Act.

The clerk of the court must, without delay, notify the procurator fiscal who issued the compensation offer when notice given by the alleged offender refusing the offer has been received or, following the expiry of 28 days or such longer period as may be specified in the offer (see paragraph (d)), notify the procurator fiscal that no notice accepting the offer has been received. A compensation offer is accepted by the alleged offender making any payment in respect of the offer. Where an alleged offender to whom a compensation offer is made does not give notice refusing the offer, he is deemed to have accepted such offer. Where an alleged offender accepts an offer or is deemed to have accepted an offer and the offer is not recalled no proceedings will be brought against the alleged offender for the offence.

The clerk of court must account for the amount paid under a compensation offer to the person entitled thereto.

The Scottish Ministers have prescribed the maximum amount of a compensation offer. It is currently £5,000 (Criminal Procedure (Scotland) Act 1995 Compensation Offer (Maximum Amount) Order 2008).

Where an alleged offender accepts a compensation offer, any amount which is outstanding at any time must, under s.303, be treated as if the offer were a fine imposed by the court (see L: FINES, above). No action will be taken to enforce a compensation offer which an alleged offender is deemed to have accepted unless the offender is sent a notice of the intention to take enforcement action and which explains the right to request a recall of the offer (as to which see para 80C, below). Any request for recall must also have been finally disposed of.

53 Combined fixed penalty and compensation offer

The procurator fiscal may, under s.302B of the Criminal Procedure (Scotland) Act 1995, send to an alleged offender a notice containing a combined fixed penalty and compensation offer (a "combined offer"). For the provisions dealing with fixed penalty offers and compensation offers see **51 Fixed penalty – conditional offer**, and see **52 Compensation offer** above.

A combined offer must be contained in one notice. In addition to the information required to be provided in respect to fixed penalty and compensation offers, a combined offer must state–

(a) that the combined offer consists of both a fixed penalty offer and a compensation offer;

(b) the whole amount of the combined offer; and

(c) that liability to conviction will not be discharged unless the whole of the combined offer is accepted.

Any acceptance or deemed acceptance of part of a combined offer will be treated as applying to the whole of the offer.

54 Recall of fixed penalty or compensation offer

Where an alleged offender is deemed to have accepted a fixed penalty offer (see para 80, above) or a compensation offer (see para 80A, above), the alleged offender may request that it be recalled under s.302C of the Criminal Procedure (Scotland) Act 1995. A request for recall is valid only if–

(a) the alleged offender claims that he did not receive the offer concerned and would (if he had received it) have refused the offer; or

(b) the alleged offender claims that although he received the offer concerned, it was not practicable by reason of exceptional circumstances for him to give notice of refusal of the offer, and he would (but for those circumstances) have refused the offer.

A request for recall of a fixed penalty offer or compensation offer is required to be made to the clerk of court concerned. It is required to be made no later than seven days after the end of the period specified in the offer for payment of the fixed penalty or compensation offer or, where a notice of intention to take enforcement action is sent, no later than seven days after that notice is sent. The clerk of court may, on cause shown, consider a request for recall despite it being made outside such time limits. On receipt of a request, the clerk of court may uphold the fixed penalty offer or compensation offer, or recall it. The alleged offender can apply to the court specified in the offer for a review of the clerk's decision. In such a review, the court may confirm or quash the decision and give such direction to the clerk of court as the court considers appropriate. Such decision will be final. The clerk of court must notify the procurator fiscal of a request for recall, an application for review by the court, and any decision of the clerk or court.

55 Work orders

The Criminal Procedure (Scotland) Act 1995 has been amended by the Criminal Proceedings etc. (Reform) (Scotland) Act 2007 by the insertion of a new s.303ZA enabling work orders to be made offering an alleged offender the opportunity of performing unpaid work. The power to make work orders currently applies where an alleged offence in relation to which the work order is to be made was committed in the local authority areas of Highland, South Lanarkshire, West Dunbartonshire or West Lothian and in respect of which arrangements have been made by a local authority within those areas for the supervision of any such work order.

Where a procurator fiscal receives a report that a relevant offence has been committed he may send the alleged offender a notice known as a work offer. The total number of hours of unpaid work will not be less than ten or more than fifty. A relevant offence means any offence in respect of which an alleged offender could be tried summarily.

A work offer must–

(a) give such particulars of the circumstances alleged to constitute the offence to which it relates as are necessary for giving reasonable information about the alleged offence;

(b) state the number of hours of unpaid work which the alleged offender is required to perform and the date by which that work is required to be completed;

(c) indicate that if the alleged offender accepts the work offer and completes the work to the satisfaction of the supervising officer any liability to conviction of the offence will be discharged;

(d) state that proceedings against the alleged offender will not be commenced in respect of that offence until the end of a period of 28 days from the date no which the offer was issued, or such longer period as may be specified in the offer;

(e) state that (i) acceptance of a work offer will not be a conviction nor be recorded as such; (ii) the fact that the offer has been accepted may be disclosed to the court in any proceedings for an offence committed by the alleged offender within the period of two years beginning on the day of acceptance of the offer; (iii) if a work order that has been made is not completed, that fact may be disclosed to the court in any proceedings for the offence to which the order relates.

An alleged offender accepts a work offer by giving notice to the procurator fiscal specified in the order before the end of 28 days, or such longer period as may be specified in the offer, beginning on the day on which the offer is made. If the alleged offender accepts a work offer, the procurator fiscal may make a work order against the alleged offender. Notice of a work order must be sent to the alleged offender as soon as reasonably practicable after its acceptance, and must contain the information set in (b) above and the name and contact details of the person who is to act as supervisor (the supervising officer) in relation to the alleged offender. The procurator fiscal will notify the local authority which will be responsible for supervision of an alleged offender of the terms of any work order. It is for the supervising officer to determine the nature of the work which the alleged offender is required to perform, the times and places at which such work is to be performed and to give directions to the alleged offender in relation to that work. In giving directions, the supervising officer must, so far as practicable, avoid any conflict with the alleged offender's religious beliefs or any interference with times at which he works (including voluntary work) or attends an educational establishment. As soon as practicable after the date on which the work is required to be completed, the supervising officer must notify the procurator fiscal whether or not the work has been performed to the supervising officer's satisfaction. Where the alleged offender completes the work specified in the work order to the satisfaction of the supervising officer, no proceedings will be brought against the alleged offender for the offence.

56 Setting aside of offers and orders

Under s.303ZB of the 1995 Act, the procurator fiscal may, where the provisions set out below apply, set aside a–

(a) fixed penalty offer (see para 51, above);

(b) compensation offer (see para 52, above);

(c) work order (see para 55, above).

These provisions apply where, on the basis of information which comes to the procurator fiscal's attention after the offer or (as the case may be) order has been made, the procurator fiscal considers that the offer or order should not have been made. The procurator fiscal may act even where an offer has been accepted or deemed to have accepted. Where the procurator fiscal decides to act, he must give the alleged offender notice of the setting aside of the offer or order (as the case may be), and indicate that any liability of the alleged offender to conviction of the alleged offence is discharged.

57 Publicity orders

Where a person is convicted of a "relevant offence" (i.e., one of the environmental offences specified by the Environmental Regulation (Relevant Offences) (Scotland) Order 2014, Sch. 3) then the court may, instead of or in addition to dealing with the person in any other way, make an order (a "publicity order") requiring the person to publicise in a specified manner (Regulatory Reform (Scotland) Act 2014, s.36)–
    (a) the fact that they have been convicted of the relevant offence;
    (b) specified particulars of the offence; and
    (c) specified particulars of any other sentence passed by the court in respect of the offence.
Failure to comply with a publicity order is itself an offence (s.36(8)).

58 Vicarious liability etc

Where a person commits a "relevant offence" (i.e., one of the environmental offences specified by the Environmental Regulation (Relevant Offences) (Scotland) Order 2014, Sch. 4) whilst acting as the employee or agent of another person, then that other person also commits the relevant offence and is liable to be proceeded against and punished accordingly (Regulatory Reform (Scotland) Act 2014, s.38). There will be a defence if the other person did not know that the relevant offence was being committed, no reasonable person could have suspected that the relevant offence was being committed, and he took all reasonable precautions and exercised all due diligence to prevent the offence being committed.

Where, in the course of carrying on a "regulated activity" (i.e., one of the environmental activities specified by the Environmental Regulation (Liability where Activity Carried Out by Arrangement with Another) (Scotland) Order 2014 (S.S.I. 2014 No. 323)) a person committed a relevant offence (as specified, see above) whilst carrying on the activity for another person who managed or controlled its carrying on, then that other person also commits the relevant offence and is liable to be proceeded against and punished accordingly (Regulatory Reform (Scotland) Act 2014, s.39). The same due diligence defence applies.

59 Assessment, treatment and compulsion orders

Criminal proceedings for people with mental disorders are dealt with by Part VI and ss.200 and 230 of the Criminal Procedure (Scotland) Act 1995, as amended by Part 8 of the Mental Health (Care and Treatment) (Scotland) Act 2003. Part 8 amends the 1995 Act, adding ss.52A to 52U to provide for two new pre-sentence disposals–
    (a) assessment orders; and
    (b) treatment orders.
Where an offender has been convicted a court may make–
    (c) an interim compulsion order (1995 Act, ss.53, 53A to 53D); or
    (d) a compulsion order (1995 Act, ss.57A to 57D).
These orders have replaced hospital (and interim hospital) orders.

The courts also have a power to detain acquitted people for medical treatment where they have a mental disorder which, if untreated, would lead to a significant risk to their health, safety or welfare or to the safety of others (ss.60C and 60D). In addition, Part 8 provides for the transfer of mentally disordered prisoners to hospital (2003 Act, s.136).

Compulsion orders made under s.57A of the 1995 Act are dealt with extensively by Part 9 of the 2003 Act (ss.137 to 180) which includes provision for their review, variation, extension and revocation, transfer of patients subject to them and suspension of measures authorised by them. The care plan must record the medical treatment to be given while the patient is subject to a compulsory treatment order and any other information relating to the care of the patient as may be prescribed. The Mental Health (Content and amendment of Part 9 care plans) (Scotland) Regulations 2005 prescribe this information (Reg. 2) and also the circumstances in which the patient's responsible medical officer is required to amend the patient's Part 9 care plan (Reg. 3).

A compulsion orders made under s.57A of the 1995 Act may be combined with a restriction order made under s.59 of the 1995 Act where there is a risk that as a result of his mental disorder a person would commit offences if set at large and it is necessary for the protection of the public from serious harm that such restrictions be imposed. The regime for these combined orders is contained in Part 10 of the 2003 Act (ss.181 to 204).

Part 11 (ss.205 to 217) provides for the regime which governs the effect of hospital directions made under s.59A of the 1995 Act and transfer for treatment directions made under s.136 of the 2003 Act. This regime is similar to the regime for compulsion orders combined with restriction orders set out in Part 10 of the 2003 Act.

The transfer of patients between hospitals is provided for in Part 12 (ss.218 to 220) while Part 13 (ss.221 to 226) provides for the temporary release from detention of patients subject to assessment orders, treatment orders, interim compulsion orders, compulsion orders combined with restriction orders, hospital directions and transfer for treatment directions. Provision for patients subject to compulsion orders is made by s.179.

Part 14 (ss.227 and 228) is concerned with the assessment of needs for community care services (s.227) and the duty on local authorities and health boards. The designation of the mental health officer responsible for a patient's case (s.229), the appointment of a patient's responsible medical officer (s.230) and a mental health officer's duty to prepare a social circumstances report (s.331) come under Part 15 of the 2003 Act (ss.229 to 232).

Under the Mental Health (Social Circumstances Reports) (Scotland) Regulations 2005, a social circumstances report must set out a list of specified information where it is relevant to the care of the patient.

P: MISCARRIAGE OF JUSTICE

60 Compensation for miscarriage of justice

S.133 of the Criminal Justice Act 1988 places a duty on the Scottish Ministers, upon application by a person, or, if he is dead, his personal representatives, to pay compensation for a miscarriage of justice to that person where he has suffered punishment as a result of being convicted of a criminal offence and his conviction has been reversed or he has been pardoned on the ground that a new or newly discovered fact shows beyond reasonable doubt that there has been a miscarriage of justice, unless the non-disclosure of the unknown fact was wholly or partly attributable to the person convicted. The question whether there is a right to compensation is to be determined by the Scottish Ministers; the amount of compensation is to be determined by an assessor appointed by them.

The Scottish Ministers may by order provide for further circumstances in respect of which a person (or, if dead, their representatives) may be paid compensation for a miscarriage of justice, or for wrongful detention prior to acquittal or a decision by the prosecutor to take no proceedings (or to discontinue proceedings) (s.133(1A)).

61 Authorities

Statutes–

Convention Rights (Compliance) (Scotland) Act 2001

Crime and Disorder Act 1998

Crime and Punishment (Scotland) Act 1997

Criminal Justice Acts 1967, 1982, 1988, and 1991

Criminal Justice and Licensing (Scotland) Act 2010

Criminal Justice and Police Act 2001

Criminal Procedure (Insanity) Act 1964

Criminal Procedure (Scotland) Act 1995

Criminal Proceedings etc. (Reform) (Scotland) Act 2007

Police, Public Order and Criminal Justice (Scotland) Act 2006

Prisoners and Criminal Proceedings (Scotland) Act 1993

Proceeds of Crime Act 2002

Proceeds of Crime (Scotland) Act 1995

Safeguarding Vulnerable Groups Act 2006

Sexual Offences Act 2003

Statutory Instruments–

Criminal Procedure (Scotland) Act 1995 Compensation Offer (Maximum Amount) Order 2008 (S.I. 2008, No. 7)

Criminal Procedure (Scotland) Act 1995 Fixed Penalty Order 2008 (S.S.I. 2008 No. 108)

Environmental Regulation (Relevant Offences) (Scotland) Order 2014 (S.S.I. 2014 No. 319)

Fines (Deduction from Income Support) Regulations 1992, as amended (S.I. 1992 No. 2182, 1993 No. 495, 1996 No. 2344, 2002 No. 1397, 2003 No. 1360, 2004 No. 2889, and 2008 No. 1554)

Proceeds of Crime Act 2002 (Cash Searches: Code of Practice) Order 2016 (S.I. 2016 No. 208)

Proceeds of Crime Act 2002 (Cash Searches: Constables in Scotland: Code of Practice) Order 2015 (S.S.I. 2015 No. 220)

Proceeds of Crime Act 2002 (Financial Threshold for Civil Recovery) Order 2003 (S.I. 2003 No. 175)

Proceeds of Crime Act 2002 (Recovery of Cash in Summary Proceedings: Minimum Amount) Order 2006 (S.I. 2006 No. 1699)

Prisoners and Criminal Proceedings (Scotland) Act 1993 (Release of Prisoners etc.) Order 1995 (S.I. 1995 No. 911)

Restriction of Liberty etc (Scotland) Regulations 2013, as amended (S.S.I. 2013 No. 6 and 2016 No.89)

Sexual Offences Act 2003 (Notification Requirements) (Scotland) Regulations 2007 (S.S.I. 2007 No. 246)

Sexual Offences Act 2003 (Travel Notification Requirements) (Scotland) Regulations 2004 (S.S.I. 2004 No. 205)

TREATMENT OF SUSPECTS: ENGLAND AND WALES

Contents

This Note is set out as follows—

A: INTRODUCTION

1 The legislation

Parts I to VI of the Police and Criminal Evidence Act 1984 (PACE) contain the main statutory provisions governing the powers and duties of the police in relation to the treatment of persons who are suspected of committing offences in England and Wales. The Children and Young Persons Acts 1933 and 1969, as amended by the 1984 Act, make additional provision in relation to children and young persons who are suspected offenders.

Certain PACE powers (such as powers of arrest, search and seizure) are extended to customs officials and immigration officers carrying out criminal immigration investigations by the Police and Criminal Evidence Act 1984 (Application to Immigration Officers and Designated Customs Officials in England and Wales) Order 2013, S.I. No. 1542.

Part III of the Police Act 1997 deals with the surveillance of suspects and covert searches of their property, and the Interception of Communications Act 1985 deals with telephone bugging. These are both dealt with in the Note on **Covert Surveillance, Searches, and Telephone Tapping, etc..**

2 Codes of Practice

The Secretary of State is required to issue Codes of Practice in connection with the exercise by the police of their powers under the Police and Criminal Evidence Act 1984 (ss.60(1)(a) and 66).

The following Codes have been published (Police and Criminal Evidence Act 1984 (Codes of Practice) Orders)—

Code (A): Exercise by Police Officers of Statutory Powers of Stop and Search; and the exercise by Police Officers and Police Staff of Requirements to Record Public Encounters

Code (B): Searching of Premises by Police Officers and the Seizure of Property found by Police Officers on Persons or Premises

Code (C): Detention, Treatment and Questioning of Persons by Police Officers

Code (D): Identification of Persons by Police Officers

Code (E): Tape Recording of Interviews with Suspects

Code (F): Visual Recording with Sound of Interviews with Suspects

Code (G): Exercise by Police Officers of Statutory Powers to Arrest a Person

Code (H): Detention, treatment and questioning by police officers of persons under s.41 of, and Sch.8 to, the Terrorism Act 2000 and s.22 of the Counter-Terrorism Act 2008.

Persons other than police officers (e.g., officers of HM Revenue and Customs) who are charged with the duty of investigating offences or charging offenders are also to have regard to the Codes (s.67(9)). A failure by a police officer or other person bound by the Codes to comply with any provision of a Code does not of itself render him liable to any criminal or civil proceedings (s.67(10)). However, a police officer is liable to disciplinary proceedings for failure to comply with any such provision unless he has been convicted or acquitted of a criminal offence and the charge of an offence against discipline would be in substance the same as that offence (ss.67(8) and 104(1)).

The Codes are admissible in civil or criminal proceedings and are to be taken into account in determining any question in the proceedings to which they appear to the court or tribunal to be relevant (s.67(11)).

The Codes of Practice are available at all police stations for consultation by police officers, detained persons, and members of the public. In this Note, they are referred to where they clarify statutory provisions or where they make provision for the treatment of suspects which is not made by statute. The Codes of Practice are available from the Stationery Office.

3 Police complaints and discipline

Part IX of the Police and Criminal Evidence Act 1984 contains provisions relating to the Police Complaints Authority and the handling of complaints. These are beyond the scope of this work.

4 Power of constable to use reasonable force

Where any provision of the Police and Criminal Evidence Act 1984 confers a power on a constable and does not provide that the power may only be exercised with the consent of some person, other than a police officer, the officer may use reasonable force, if necessary, in the exercise of the power (Police and Criminal Evidence Act 1984, s.117).

B: DEFINITIONS

5 Indictable offences

Whether an offence is indictable or not is important in that—
  (a) the power to make a citizens' arrest applies only to indictable offences (see **25 Citizens' powers of arrest**, below);
  (b) certain police powers which are contingent on arrest are triggered only if the offence for which a person has been arrested is an indictable offence.

An "indictable" offence is one which is triable only on indictment (i.e., by the Crown Court rather than in a magistrates' court) or which is triable either way (i.e., in the Crown Court or a magistrates' court). An offence which is triable only summarily (i.e., by the magistrates' court) is not an indictable offence (Interpretation Act 1978, s.5 and Sch. 1).

The police powers referred to in (b) above include the power to—
  (a) set up road blocks;
  (b) authorise entry and searches;
  (c) obtain a warrant for further detention of a suspect;
  (d) delay the right of a suspect to have someone informed of his arrest or have access to legal advice.

6 Arrestable and serious arrestable offences

The concept of the "arrestable" and "serious arrestable" offence no longer exists. All offences are now "arrestable" (see **26 Additional powers of arrest of constables**, below) but the criteria for arrest is no longer related to the "seriousness" of the offence, but rather whether an arrest is "necessary" in the context of the police investigation.

7 Police detention

A person is in police detention if—
  (a) he has been taken to a police station after being arrested for an offence or after being arrested under the Terrorism Act 2000, s.41 by an examining officer who is a constable; or
  (b) he is arrested at a police station after attending voluntarily at the station or accompanying a constable to it,
and is detained there or is detained elsewhere in the charge of a constable, but a person who is at a court after being charged is not in police detention (Police and Criminal Evidence Act 1984, s.118(2)).

C: POWERS TO STOP AND SEARCH

8 The legislation

Part I of the Police and Criminal Evidence Act 1984 (ss.1 to 7) contains the principal powers of stop and search. Additional powers of stop and search are contained in the Criminal Justice and Public Order Act 1994 (s.60) and the powers of stop and search in connection with acts of terrorism are contained in ss.43, 43A and 47A of the Terrorism Act 2000.

9 Power of constable to stop and search

S.1 of the Police and Criminal Evidence Act 1984 empowers a constable—
  (a) to search any person or vehicle (which includes vessels, aircraft, and hovercraft), or anything which is in or on a vehicle, for stolen or prohibited articles (see below), or prohibited fireworks, and
  (b) to detain a person or vehicle for the purpose of such a search in any place to which the public has access, on payment or otherwise, as of right or by virtue of express or implied permission, or in any other place to which people have ready access but which is not a dwelling,
provided that he has reasonable grounds for suspecting (see **11 Reasonable grounds for suspicion**, below) that he will find stolen or prohibited articles, or any article in relation to which a person has committed, is committing, or is going to commit an offence under s.139 of the Criminal Justice Act 1988 (offence of having article with blade or point in a public place) (s.1(1) to (3)).

If a person (or vehicle) is in a garden or yard occupied with and used for the purposes of a dwelling or on other land so occupied and used, a constable may not search him (or the vehicle or anything in or on it) in exercise of the powers conferred by s.1 unless the constable has reasonable grounds for believing (a) that he (or the person in charge of the vehicle) does not reside in the dwelling and (b) that he (or the vehicle) is not in the place in question with the express or implied permission of a person who resides in the dwelling (s.1(4) and (5)).

A constable may seize an article which he discovers in the course of such a search and has reasonable grounds for suspecting it to be a stolen or prohibited article, or an article in relation to which an offence under s.139 of the Criminal Justice Act 1988 has been, is being, or will be committed (s.1(6)).

An article is prohibited if it is–

(a) an offensive weapon (i.e., made or adapted for use for causing injury to persons or intended by the person having it with him for such use by him or by some other person), or

(b) an article made or adapted for use in the course of or in connection with any one of the following offences, namely burglary, theft, taking a motor vehicle or other conveyance without authority, or obtaining property by deception, or intended by the person having it with him for such use by him or by some other person (s.1(7) to (9)).

A constable who detains a person or vehicle in the exercise of the power conferred by s.1, or of any other power to search a person or vehicle without making an arrest (these powers are listed in Annex A of Code (A)), need not conduct a search if it appears to him subsequently that no search is required or that a search is impracticable (s.2(1)).

Before commencing a search (other than a search of an unattended vehicle) in the exercise of the power conferred by s.1 or (with certain exceptions) of any other power to search a person or vehicle without making an arrest, a constable is under a duty to take reasonable steps to bring to the attention of the appropriate person (i.e., the person he is proposing to search or the person in charge of the vehicle he is proposing to search), if he is not in uniform, documentary evidence that he is a constable, and whether he is in uniform or not, his name and the name of the station to which he is attached, the object and grounds for the proposed search, and the entitlement of the person concerned to request a copy of the record of the search under s.3(7) or (8) (see **12 Duty to record searches**, below), unless it appears that it will not be practicable to make the record (s.2(2) to (5)).

On completing a search of an unattended vehicle or anything in or on such a vehicle, a constable must leave a notice stating that he has searched it, giving the name of the station to which he is attached, stating that an application for compensation for any damage caused by the search may be made to that station, and stating the effect of s.3(8). The notice must be left inside the vehicle unless it is not reasonably practicable to do so without damaging the vehicle (s.1(6) and (7)).

A person or vehicle may be detained for such time as is reasonably required to permit a search to be carried out either at the place where the person or vehicle was first detained or nearby (s.1(8)).

The Terrorism Act 2000 contains additional stop and search powers: see the Note on **Prevention of Terrorism** at para **22 Search of premises, persons and vehicles**.

10 Removal of clothing and disguises

A constable exercising the above powers is not authorised to require a person to remove any of his clothing in public other than an outer coat, jacket, or gloves, nor is a constable authorised to stop a vehicle if he is not in uniform (Police and Criminal Evidence Act 1984, s.2(9)).

Paragraph 3.6 of Code (A) provides inter alia that where it is thought necessary to conduct a more thorough search (e.g., by requiring someone to take off a T-shirt or headgear), this should be done out of public view (e.g., in a police van or police station, if there is one nearby).

By virtue of s.60 of the Criminal Justice and Public Order Act 1994, where a suitably qualified police officer reasonably believes that–

(a) incidents involving serious violence may take place in any locality in his area, and it is expedient to do so to prevent their occurrence;

(b) an incident involving serious violence has taken place in his area, a dangerous instrument or offensive weapon used in the incident is being carried in any locality in that area by a person, and it is expedient to find the instrument or weapon; or

(c) that persons are carrying dangerous instruments or offensive weapons in any locality in his area without good reason,

he may authorise the exercise of the powers in that locality for a period not exceeding 24 hours (s.60(1)). The authorisation may in certain circumstances be extended for a further 24 hours (s.60(3)).

S.60 confers power on a constable in uniform to stop and search pedestrians and vehicles and search the pedestrian or anything carried by him, or the vehicle, its driver, and any passenger for offensive weapons and dangerous instruments. The constable is not required to have grounds for suspecting that weapons or articles of that kind are being carried. He may seize any dangerous instrument or article which he has reasonable grounds for suspecting to be an offensive weapon (s.60(4) to (6)).

Where an authorisation under s.60 is in force, or where a suitably qualified police officer reasonably believes that activities which are likely to involve the commission of offences may take place, a police officer may require a person to remove any item he believes a person is wearing wholly or mainly for the purpose of concealing their identity (s.60AA).

Note.–S.60(4) is limited to incidents involving "serious violence". S.60AA is not so limited.

11 Reasonable grounds for suspicion

Paragraphs 2.2–2.11 of Code (A) to the Police and Criminal Evidence Act 1984 provides guidance as to the meaning of "reasonable grounds for suspicion" which includes the following. Reasonable suspicion can never be supported on the basis of personal factors alone. For example, a person's race, age, appearance, or the fact that he is known to have a previous conviction, cannot be used alone or in combination with each other as the sole basis on which to search that person. Nor may it be founded on the basis of stereotyped images of certain persons or groups as more likely to be committing offences.

However, Paragraph 2.6 of the Code provides that where there is reliable information or intelligence that members of a group or gang who habitually carry knives unlawfully or weapons or controlled drugs and wear a distinctive item of clothing or other means of identification (such as distinctive jewellery or a tattoo) to indicate membership then members may be identified by that item.

12 Duty to record searches

Subject to certain exceptions, where a constable has carried out a search he is under a duty to make a record of it in writing unless it is not practicable to do so. He must make the record as soon as practicable after the completion of the search if it is not practicable to make it on the spot. Where a person is arrested as a result of a stop and search and taken to a police station, the constable who carried out the search must ensure that the search record forms part of the person's custody record (rather than completing a separate form). The record of a search of a person or a vehicle must state (i) the object of the search, (ii) the grounds for making it, (iii) the date and time when it was made, (iv) the place where it was made; and (v) the ethnic origin of the person searched, or whose vehicle is searched. It must also identify the constable who made the search (Police and Criminal Evidence Act 1984, s.3(1) to (6)).

If a constable who conducted a search of a person made a record of it, the person who was searched is entitled to a copy of the record if he asks for one before the end of the period of 3 months beginning with the date of the search (s.3(7)). Similar provision is made by s.3(8) in respect of a vehicle where either the owner or the person in charge of the vehicle when it was searched requests a copy of the record of the search.

Constables are no longer required to record all encounters not governed by statutory powers (Code A, Paragraph 4.12).

13 Road checks

A road check may be carried out by police officers for the purpose of ascertaining whether a vehicle is carrying–
(a) a person who has committed an offence other than a road traffic offence or a vehicle excise offence;
(b) a person who is a witness to such an offence;
(c) a person intending to commit such an offence; or
(d) a person who is unlawfully at large (Police and Criminal Evidence Act 1984, s.4(1)).
A road check consists of the exercise in a locality of the power conferred by s.163 of the Road Traffic Act 1988 in such a way as to stop, during the period for which its exercise in that way in the locality continues, all vehicles or vehicles selected by any criterion (s.4(2)).

Except in cases of urgency, a suitably qualified officer must authorise a road check in writing (s.4(3)).

Such an officer may authorise a road check–
(1) for the purpose specified in paragraph (a) or (c) above, only if he has reasonable grounds for believing that the offence is or would be an indictable offence (see **5 Indictable offences**, above) and for suspecting that the person sought is, or is about to be, in the relevant locality;
(2) for the purpose specified in paragraph (b) above, only if he has reasonable grounds for believing that the offence is an indictable offence; and
(3) for the purpose specified in paragraph (d) above, only if he has reasonable grounds for suspecting that the person is, or is about to be, in the relevant locality.

A suitably qualified officer who gives an authorisation under s.4 must specify a period, not exceeding seven days, during which the road check may continue and may direct that the road check be continuous or be conducted at specified times, during that period (s.4(11)). He may from time to time specify in writing a further period, not exceeding seven days, during which the road check may continue (s.4(12)).

An officer who is not a suitably qualified officer may authorise the setting up of a road check if it appears to him that it is required as a matter of urgency for one of the purposes specified in paragraphs (a) to (d) above. Where such an authorisation has been given, the authorising officer must make a written record of the time at which he gives the authorisation and cause a suitably qualified officer to be informed that it has been given as soon as it is practicable to do so (s.4(5), (6), and (7)). The suitably qualified officer to whom such a report is made may, in writing, authorise the road check to continue or, if he considers that it should not continue, he must record in writing the fact that it took place and the purpose for which it took place (s.4(8) and (9)). Every written authorisation must specify the name of the officer giving it, the purpose of the road check, and the locality in which vehicles are to be stopped (s.4(13)). The person in charge of a vehicle which is stopped is entitled to obtain a written statement of the purpose of the road check if he applies for such a statement not later than the end of the period of 12 months from the day on which the vehicle was stopped (s.4(15)).

Nothing in s.4 affects the exercise by police officers of any power to stop vehicles for purposes other than those specified in s.4(1)–see above (s.4(10)).

D: POWERS OF ENTRY, SEARCH AND SEIZURE

14 Introduction

Part II of the Police and Criminal Evidence Act 1984 (ss.8 to 23) deals with the powers of entry, search, and seizure, described in the following paragraphs.

15 Search warrants

A justice of the peace may, upon application by a constable, issue a warrant authorising a constable to enter and search premises (on one or more occasions, as specified in the warrant), if he is satisfied that there are reasonable grounds for believing–

(a) that an indictable offence (see **5 Indictable offences**, above) has been committed, and

(b) that there is material on premises (specified in the application or all premises occupied or controlled by a person specified in the application) which is likely to be of substantial value (whether by itself or together with other material) to the investigation of the offence; and

(c) that the material is likely to be relevant evidence (i.e., in relation to any offence, anything that would be admissible in evidence at a trial for the offence (Police and Criminal Evidence Act 1984, s.8(4)); and

(d) that it does not consist of or include items subject to legal privilege, excluded material, or special procedure material (these expressions are defined in ss.10, 11, and 14, respectively); and

(e) that any of the conditions specified in s.8(3) applies (s.8(1)).

S.8(3) specifies the following conditions–

(i) that it is not practicable to communicate with any person entitled to grant entry to the premises;

(ii) that it is practicable to communicate with a person entitled to grant entry to the premises but it is not practicable to communicate with any person entitled to grant access to the evidence;

(iii) that entry to the premises will not be granted unless a warrant is produced;

(iv) that the purpose of the search may be frustrated or seriously prejudiced unless a constable arriving at the premises can secure immediate entry to them.

A constable may seize and retain anything for which a search has been authorised under s.8(1) (s.8(2)).

The power to issue a warrant conferred by s.8 is additional to any such power otherwise conferred (s.8(5)).

S.9 and Schedule 1 make provision *inter alia* for a constable to obtain access to excluded material or special procedure material for the purposes of any criminal investigation by order of a Circuit judge.

16 Search, etc. for material relevant to overseas investigation

S.16 of the Crime (International Co-operation) Act 2003 provides that Part II of the 1984 Act (powers of entry, search, and seizure) is to have effect as if references in s.8 and Schedule 1 (see above) included any conduct which is an offence under the law of a country or territory outside the UK and would constitute an indictable offence if it had occurred in any part of the UK. However, in order to issue a warrant to enter and search premises and seize any evidence found there under s.16, a justice of the peace must be satisfied–

(a) that criminal proceedings have been instituted against the person in a country or territory outside the UK or that he has been arrested in the course of a criminal investigation carried out there;

(b) that the conduct constituting the offence which is the subject of the proceedings or investigation would constitute an indictable (in Scotland, imprisonable) offence within the meaning of the 1984 Act if it had occurred in any part of the UK; and

(c) (England and Wales only) that there are reasonable grounds for suspecting that there is on premises in the UK occupied or controlled by the person evidence relating to the offence other than items subject to legal privilege within the meaning of the 1984 Act.

Further, no application for a warrant or order under s.7 can be made except in pursuance of a direction given by the Secretary of State in response to a request received–

(i) from a court or tribunal exercising criminal jurisdiction in the overseas country or territory in question or a prosecuting authority in that country or territory; or

(ii) through any other authority in that country or territory which appears to him to have the function of making requests for the purposes of s.7,

and any evidence seized by a constable under s.7 must be furnished by him to the Secretary of State for transmission to that court, tribunal, or authority.

17 Search warrants–safeguards

Ss.15 and 16 of the Police and Criminal Evidence Act 1984 apply in relation to the issue to constables under any enactment of warrants to enter and search premises. An entry or a search of premises under a warrant is unlawful unless it complies with ss.15 and 16 (s.15(1)).

18 Entry and search without search warrant for purpose of arrest, etc.

S.17 empowers a constable to enter and search any premises without a search warrant for the purpose—
  (a) of executing—
      (i) a warrant of arrest issued in connection with or arising out of criminal proceedings; or
      (ii) a warrant of commitment issued under s.76 of the Magistrates' Courts Act 1980;
  (b) of arresting a person for an indictable offence (see **5 Indictable offences**, above);
  (c) of arresting a person for an offence under—
      (i) s.1 of the Public Order Act 1936 (prohibition of uniforms in connection with political objects);
      (ii) any enactment contained in ss.6 to 8 or s.10 of the Criminal Law Act 1977 (offences relating to entering and remaining on the property) (only exercisable by a constable in uniform);
      (iii) s.4 of the Public Order Act 1986 (fear of provocation of violence);
      (iv) s.76 of the Criminal Justice and Public order Act 1994 (failure to comply with interim possession order);
  (ca) of arresting and child or young person who has been remanded or committed to local authority accommodation under the Children and Young Persons Act 1969, s.23(1);
  (cb) of recapturing any person who is, or is deemed to be, unlawfully at large while liable to be detained in a prison, remand centre, young offender institution, secure training centre or in pursuance of the Children and Young Persons Act 1933, s.53;
  (d) of recapturing any person who is unlawfully at large and whom he is pursuing; or
  (e) of saving life or limb or preventing serious damage to property (s.17(1) and (3), as amended).

Except for the purpose specified in (e), the powers of entry and search are exercisable only if the constable has reasonable grounds for believing that the person whom he is seeking is on the premises, and are limited, in relation to premises consisting of two or more separate dwellings, to powers to enter and search (i) any parts of the premises which the occupiers of any dwelling comprised in the premises use in common with the occupiers of any other such dwelling and (ii) any such dwelling in which the constable has reasonable grounds for believing that the person whom he is seeking may be (s.17(2)). A constable may conduct a search only to the extent that is reasonably required for the purpose for which the power of entry is exercised (s.17(4)). All common law powers to enter premises without a warrant are abolished by s.17 except the power of entry to deal with or prevent a breach of the peace (s.17(5) and (6)).

19 Search with consent

Paragraphs 5.1 to 5.4 of Code (B) to the Police and Criminal Evidence Act 1984 state that, if it is proposed to search premises with the consent of a person entitled to grant entry to the premises, the consent must, if practicable, be given in writing on the Notice of Powers and Rights before the search takes place. Before seeking consent, the officer in charge of the search must state the purpose of the proposed search and its extent, inform the person concerned that he is not obliged to consent, and that anything seized may be produced in evidence, and if at the time the person is not suspected of an offence, the officer must tell him so. However, it is unnecessary to seek the above-mentioned consent where, in the circumstances, this would cause disproportionate inconvenience to the person concerned. For example, where a suspect has fled from the scene of a crime or to evade arrest and it is necessary quickly to check surrounding gardens and readily accessible places to see where he is hiding.

20 Entry and search after arrest

S.18 of the Police and Criminal Evidence Act 1984 empowers a constable who has written authorisation from a suitably qualified officer to enter and search any premises occupied or controlled by a person who is under arrest for an indictable offence (see **5 Indictable offences**, above), if he has reasonable grounds for suspecting that there is on the premises evidence, other than items subject to legal privilege, that relates to the offence or to some other indictable offence which is connected with or similar to that offence (s.18(1)). A constable may seize and retain anything for which he may search; his power to search is limited to the extent that is reasonably required for the purpose of discovering such evidence (s.18(2) and (3)). S.32 deals with a constable's powers of search or arrest (see **33 Search upon arrest**, below).

A constable may conduct a search under s.18(1) before taking the person to a police station and without obtaining the required authorisation, if the presence of that person at a place other than a police station is necessary for the effective investigation of the offence. He must inform a suitably qualified officer that he has made the search as soon as practicable after he has made it (s.18(5) and (6)). An officer who authorises, or is informed of, a search must make a record in writing of the grounds for the search and of the nature of the evidence that was sought (s.18(7)). If the person who was in occupation or control of the premises at the time of the search is in police detention at the time the record is to be made, the officer must make the record as part of his custody record (see **67 Custody records**, below) (s.18(8)).

21 Seizure

In addition to any power otherwise conferred, s.19 of the Police and Criminal Evidence Act 1984 empowers a constable who is lawfully on any premises to seize anything (other than an item which the constable has reasonable grounds for believing to be subject to legal privilege) which is on the premises if he has reasonable grounds for believing that it has been obtained in consequence of the commission of an offence, or that it is evidence in relation to an offence which he is investigating or any other offence, and that it is necessary to seize it in order to prevent it being concealed, lost, altered, or destroyed.

This power of seizure and any power of seizure under any other enactment also applies to any information which is stored in any electronic form and is accessible from the premises. A constable may require such information to be produced in a form in which it can be taken away and in which it is visible and legible (ss.19(4) and 20).

Where the police are lawfully on premises and discover something but it is not reasonably practicable for them to determine there and then whether they are entitled to seize it, or whether it contains something that they are entitled to seize, then they are entitled to seize so much of what they have found as it is necessary to remove to enable that to be determined (Criminal Justice and Police Act 2001, s.50). Similarly, where they discover something that they are entitled to seize, but it is not reasonably practicable to separate it from something they have no power to seize, then they may nevertheless seize the whole item. This might be the case for example with a computer disk or hard drive. Where what has been seized turns out to contain legally privileged, special procedure or excluded material, it must be returned, unless it is inextricably linked to seizable material (ss.54 and 55).

Note.–The extended powers of seizure in the 2001 Act are not limited to the police, but extend to all persons lawfully on premises who have a power of seizure, such as HM Revenue and Customs.

22 Access and copying

A constable who seizes anything in exercise of a power conferred by any enactment, including an enactment contained in an Act passed after the 1984 Act, must, if so requested by a person showing himself (a) to be the occupier of premises on which it was seized or (b) to have had custody or control of it immediately before the seizure, provide that person with a record of what he seized (Police and Criminal Evidence Act 1984, s.21(1)). He must provide the record within a reasonable time from the making of the request for it (s.21(2)). If a request for access to anything seized and retained for the purpose of investigating an offence is made by the person who had custody and control of it immediately before it was seized or by someone acting on his behalf, access to it must be allowed under the supervision of a constable. A request for a photograph or copy of it will be similarly allowed, either by granting access for that purpose or by supplying a photograph or copy within a reasonable time from the making of the request. No such duty arises, however, if the officer in charge of the investigation has reasonable grounds for believing that to grant access to, or to supply a photograph or copy of, anything which was seized would prejudice (a) that investigation, (b) the investigation of an offence other than the offence for the purposes of investigating which the thing was seized, or (c) any criminal proceedings which may be brought as a result of either (a) or (b) (s.21(3) to (8)).

23 Retention

S.22 of the Police and Criminal Evidence Act 1984 provides that, as a general rule, anything which has been seized by a constable or taken away by a constable following a requirement under ss.19 or 20 may be retained so long as is necessary in all the circumstances. In particular (a) anything seized for the purposes of a criminal investigation may be retained, except where a photograph or copy would be sufficient (i) for use as evidence at a trial for an offence, or (ii) for forensic examination or for investigation in connection with an offence; and (b) anything may be retained in order to establish its lawful owner, where there are reasonable grounds for believing that it has been obtained in consequence of an offence. Nothing seized on the ground that it may be used to cause personal injury to any person, to damage property, to interfere with evidence, or to assist in escape from police detention or lawful custody may be retained when the person from whom it was seized is no longer in police detention or the custody of a court or is in the custody of a court but has been released on bail. Nothing in s.22 precludes a person from applying to a magistrates' court for an order to return property under s.1 of the Police (Property) Act 1987.

E: ARREST

24 Introduction

Part III of the Police and Criminal Evidence Act 1984 (ss.24 to 33) deals with the general powers of arrest in the following paragraphs.

25 Citizens' powers of arrest

Any person may arrest without a warrant anyone who is in the act of committing, or anyone whom he has reasonable grounds for suspecting to be committing, an indictable offence (see 5 **Indictable offences**, above). Where an indictable offence has been committed, a person may arrest without a warrant anyone who is guilty of the offence or anyone whom he has reasonable grounds for suspecting to be guilty of it (Police and Criminal Evidence Act 1984, s.24A(1) and (2)).

26 Additional powers of arrest of constables

Where a constable has reasonable grounds for suspecting that an offence (any offence) has been committed, he may arrest without a warrant anyone whom he has reasonable grounds for suspecting to be guilty of the offence. He may also arrest without a warrant anyone who is about to commit, or anyone whom he has reasonable grounds for suspecting to be about to commit, an offence (Police and Criminal Evidence Act 1984, s.24(1) and (2)).

This power of arrest is however subject to the limitation that an arrest may only be made if there are reasonable grounds for believing that because of a prescribed reason it is necessary to arrest that person. As to the prescribed reasons, see **27 General arrest conditions**, below.

Designated immigration officers have the power to detain a person where they considers him someone who the police could arrest without a warrant under s.24, or where a warrant is outstanding for the individual. This detention will be pending the arrival of the police and is subject to a maximum detention period of three hours (UK Borders Act 2007, ss.1-2).

27 General arrest conditions

Before a constable can arrest someone he must reasonable believe that the arrest is necessary because of one of the following reasons (Police and Criminal Evidence Act 1984, s.24(5))–

- (a) that the name of the relevant person is unknown to, and cannot be readily ascertained by, the constable or the constable has reasonable grounds for doubting whether a name furnished by the relevant person as his name is his real name;
- (b) correspondingly as regards the person's address;
- (c) to prevent the relevant person–
    - (i) causing physical injury to himself or any other person;
    - (ii) suffering physical injury;
    - (iii) causing loss of or damage to property;
    - (iv) committing an offence against public decency (but only where members of the public going about their normal business cannot reasonably be expected to avoid the person to be arrested); or
    - (v) causing an unlawful obstruction of the highway;
- (d) to protect a child or other vulnerable person from the relevant person;
- (e) to allow prompt and effective investigation of the offence or of the conduct of the person in question; or
- (f) to prevent any prosecution for the offence from being hindered by disappearance of the person in question.

28 Other powers of summary arrest

By virtue of s.26 of the Police and Criminal Evidence Act 1984, all other previous statutory powers to arrest without a warrant, including those contained in local Acts, but with the exception of those listed in Schedule 2, are repealed.

29 Information to be given on arrest

Where a person is arrested, otherwise than by being informed that he is under arrest, the arrest is not lawful unless the person arrested is informed that he is under arrest as soon as is practicable after his arrest, and no arrest is lawful unless the person arrested is informed of the ground for the arrest at the time of, or as soon as is practicable after, the arrest. Where a person is arrested by a constable these requirements apply regardless of whether the fact of, or the ground for, the arrest is obvious but do not apply if it was not reasonably practicable for the person to be so informed by reason of his having escaped from arrest before the information could be given (Police and Criminal Evidence Act 1984, s.28).

30 Voluntary attendance at police station, etc.

Where for the purpose of assisting with an investigation a person attends voluntarily at a police station or any other place where a constable is present or accompanies a constable to a police station or any such other place without having been arrested–

- (a) he is entitled to leave at will unless he is placed under arrest;
- (b) he must be informed at once that he is under arrest if a decision is taken by a constable to prevent him from leaving at will (Police and Criminal Evidence Act 1984, s.29).

31 Arrest elsewhere than at police station

Where a person is arrested (a) by a constable for an offence or (b) is taken into custody by a person other than a constable, at any place other than a police station, he must be taken to a police station by a constable as soon as practicable after the arrest. This does not apply in relation to arrests and detentions under certain provisions of Schedule 2 to the Immigration Act 1971, under s.34 of the Criminal Justice Act 1972 (see the

Note on **Treatment of Offenders**), or under any provision of the Terrorism Act 2000 (see the Note on **Prevention of Terrorism**) (Police and Criminal Evidence Act 1984, s.30(1) and (12)).

A person arrested by a constable at a place other than a police station must be released, if the constable is satisfied, before the person arrested reaches a police station, that there are no grounds for keeping him under arrest. He must as soon as is practicable after releasing him make a record of the fact that he has done so (s.30(7) to (9)).

A constable may delay taking a person who has been arrested to a police station if the presence of that person elsewhere is necessary in order to carry out such investigations as it is reasonable to carry out immediately. The reasons for such a delay must be recorded when that person first arrives at a police station (s.30(10) and (11)).

32 Arrest for further offence

Where a person has been arrested for an offence and is at a police station in consequence, and it appears to a constable that, if he were released from that arrest, he would be liable to arrest for some other offence, he must be arrested for that other offence (Police and Criminal Evidence Act 1984, s.31). S.41(4) provides that the time for which the period of detention is to be calculated (see **39 Limits on period of detention without charge**, below) is the time of the arrest for the first offence.

Note.—For the purposes of s.30 (subject to s.46A(2)—see **44 Powers of arrest for failure to answer police bail**, below) and s.31, an arrest under s.46A will be treated as an arrest for any offence (s.46A(3)).

33 Search upon arrest

A constable may search an arrested person, in any case where the person to be searched has been arrested at a place other than a police station, if he has reasonable grounds for believing that the arrested person may present a danger to himself or others, and may seize and retain anything he finds, if he has reasonable grounds for believing that the person searched might use it to cause physical injury to himself or to any other person (Police and Criminal Evidence Act 1984, s.32(1) and (8)).

A constable is also empowered in such a case—

(a) to search the arrested person for anything which he might use to assist him to escape from lawful custody or which might be evidence relating to an offence (and any item so found (other than one subject to legal privilege) may be seized and retained, if the constable has reasonable grounds for believing that he might use it to assist him to escape, or that it is evidence of an offence or has been obtained in consequence for the commission of an offence); and

(b) to enter and search any premises in which he was when arrested, or immediately before he was arrested, for evidence relating to the offence for which he has been arrested (s.32(2) and (9)).

A power to search under (a) and (b) above may be exercised only if the constable has reasonable grounds for believing that the person to be searched may have concealed on him anything for which such a search is permitted, or that there is evidence for which such a search is permitted on the premises. The power to search is limited to the extent that is reasonably required for the purpose of discovering any such thing or any such evidence (s.32(3), (5), and (6)).

Nothing in s.32 is to be construed as authorising a constable to require a person to remove any of his clothing in public other than an outer coat, jacket, or gloves, but it does authorise a search of a person's mouth (s.32(4)).

S.32 does not affect the power to stop and search conferred by s.43 of the Terrorism Act 2000 (see the Note on **Prevention of Terrorism**) (s.32(10)).

Where during a lawful search of a person after arrest, the police discover something but it is not reasonably practicable for them to determine there and then whether they are entitled to seize it, or whether it contains something that they are entitled to seize, then they are entitled to seize so much of what they have found as it is necessary to remove to enable that to be determined (Criminal Justice and Police Act 2001, s.51). Similarly, where they discover something that they are entitled to seize, but it is not reasonably practicable to separate it from something they have no power to seize, then they may nevertheless seize the whole item. This might be the case for example with a computer disk.

F: DETENTION

34 Introduction

Part IV of the Police and Criminal Evidence Act 1984 (ss.34 to 52) deals with the conditions and duration of detention of suspected persons. In summary, once a person is arrested and brought to a police station they must not be detained for longer than 96 hours without being charged with an offence. The detention of a person within the overall maximum permitted 96-hour period is subject to various safeguards which require an on-going detention to be subject to review after 6 hours and then every 9 hours, and for continued detention to be subject to a further authorisation, by a police officer of at least the rank of superintendent after the initial 24 hours, and by a magistrate after the initial 36 hours.

If a person is released from pre-charge detention on bail, then the clocks on review and overall detention are paused. If they are subsequently arrested for failing to answer bail at the appointed time and place, or for breach of bail conditions, or they return to the police station in accordance with their bail, they are treated as having been arrested for the original offence and the detention clock and the review clock resume at the point they were paused at on their release.

These provisions are dealt with in detail in the following paragraphs.

35 Limitations on police detention

A person arrested for an offence (which includes a person arrested under s.6D of the Road Traffic Act 1988 (failing a breath test) and a person who returns to a police station to answer to bail or is arrested under s.46A for failure to answer to police bail–see **44 Powers of arrest for failure to answer police bail**, below) must not be kept in police detention (see B: DEFINITIONS, above) except in accordance with the Act (Police and Criminal Evidence Act 1984, s.34(1), (6), and (7)).

A custody officer (i.e., an officer of at least the rank of sergeant who is so appointed, or other officer performing that role) is under a duty to order the immediate release of a person in police detention when he becomes aware that the grounds for the detention of that person have ceased to apply and he is not aware of any other grounds on which the continued detention of that person could be justified under the Act (s.34(2)). There is no duty to release a person if it appears to the custody officer that the person arrested was unlawfully at large when arrested (s.34(4)).

No person in police detention is to be released except on the authority of a custody officer at the police station where his detention was authorised or, if it was authorised at more than one station, a custody officer at the station where it was last authorised (s.34(3)). A person whose release is ordered under s.34(2) must be released without bail unless it appears to the custody officer (a) that there is need for further investigation of any matter in connection with which he was detained at any time during the period of his detention, or (b) that proceedings may be taken against him in respect of any matter and if it so appears, he must be released on bail (s.34(4) and (5)). For the purposes of Part IV of the 1984 Act, a person who returns to a police station to answer bail or is arrested under s.46A (failure to answer bail) will be treated as arrested for an offence and the offence in connection with which he was granted bail will be deemed to be that offence (s.34(7)).

36 Duties of custody officer before charge

Where a person is arrested for an offence without a warrant or under a warrant not endorsed for bail (as defined), the custody officer at each police station where he is detained after his arrest must determine whether he has before him sufficient evidence to charge that person with the offence for which he was arrested and may detain him at the police station for such period as is necessary to enable him to do so (Police and Criminal Evidence Act 1984, s.37(1)). The custody officer must carry out this duty as soon as practicable after an arrested person arrives at the station, or in the case of a person arrested at the police station, after his arrest (s.37(10)). Code (C) provides further guidance as to the treatment of persons in custody; for example, it provides that all persons in custody must be dealt with expeditiously, (see **65 Treatment of persons in custody**, below).

If the custody officer determines that he does not have such evidence before him, the person arrested must be released on bail or without bail, unless the officer has reasonable grounds for believing that his detention without being charged is necessary to secure or preserve evidence relating to an offence for which he is under arrest or to obtain such evidence by questioning him; and if he so believes, he may authorise the person arrested to be kept in police detention, and he must, as soon as is practicable, make a written record of the grounds for detention in the presence of the arrested person who must at that time be informed of the grounds for his detention. An arrested person need not be so informed, if at that time, he is incapable of understanding what is said to him, is violent or likely to become violent, or is in urgent need of medical attention (s.37(2) to (6)). Code (C) provides further guidance as to the treatment of persons incapable of understanding what is said to them and in urgent need of medical attention (see **65 Treatment of persons in custody**, below, and see **68 Treatment of detained persons**, below).

Subject to s.41(7) (see **39 Limits on period of detention without charge**, below), if a custody officer determines that he has before him sufficient evidence to charge the person arrested with the offence for which he was arrested, the person arrested must be either charged or must be released without charge, either on bail or without bail. Where he is released, the custody officer is under a duty, if at the time of his release no decision has been taken whether to prosecute him for the offence for which he was arrested, so to inform him. If the person arrested is not in a fit state to be charged or released, he may be kept in police detention until he is (s.37(7) to (9)).

37 Duties of custody officer after charge

Where a person arrested for an offence otherwise than under a warrant endorsed for bail is charged with an offence, the custody officer must (subject to the restrictions on the granting of bail in the case of charges relating to homicide or rape imposed by s.25 of the Criminal Justice and Public Order Act 1994) order his release from police detention, either on bail or without bail, unless–

(a) if the person arrested is not an arrested juvenile (see below)–

(i) his name or address cannot be ascertained or the custody officer has reasonable grounds for doubting whether a name or address furnished by him as his name and address is his real name and address;

(ii) the custody officer has reasonable grounds for believing that the person arrested will fail to appear in court to answer to bail;

(iii) in the case of a person arrested for an imprisonable offence, the custody officer has reasonable grounds for believing that the detention of the person arrested is necessary to prevent him from committing an offence;

(iv) in the case of a person arrested for an offence which is not an imprisonable offence, the custody officer has reasonable grounds for believing that the detention is necessary to prevent him from causing physical injury to any other person or from causing loss of or damage to property;

(v) the custody officer has reasonable grounds for believing that the detention of the person is necessary to prevent him from interfering with the administration of justice or with the investigation of offences or of a particular offence;

(vi) the custody officer has reasonable grounds for believing that the detention of the person arrested is necessary for his own protection;

(b) if he is an arrested juvenile—

(i) any of the requirements of (a) above is satisfied; or

(ii) the custody officer has reasonable grounds for believing that he ought to be detained in his own interest (s.38(1), as amended).

An arrested juvenile is a person arrested with or without a warrant who appears to be under the age of 17 (s.37(15), as amended).

Where a person arrested is not required to be released, the custody officer may authorise him to be kept in police detention (s.38(2)). Where he is so detained, s.38(3) to (5) makes provision for information to be given to him which is similar to that required to be given under s.37(4) to (6) (see above). Where an arrested juvenile is to be kept in police detention, the custody officer must, unless he certifies (a) that it is impracticable to do so, or (b) in the case of an arrested juvenile who has attained the age of 12 years, that no secure accommodation is available and that keeping him in other local authority accommodation would not be adequate to protect the public from serious harm from him, secure that the arrested juvenile is moved to local authority accommodation, i.e., accommodation provided by or on behalf of a local authority within the meaning of the Children Act 1989; any reference, in relation to an arrested juvenile charged with a violent or sexual offence, to protecting the public from serious harm from him is to be construed as a reference to protecting members of the public from death or serious personal injury, whether physical or psychological, occasioned by further such offences committed by him (s.38(6) and (6A), as substituted by the Criminal Justice Act 1991, s.59). After the arrested juvenile has been moved to such accommodation, it will be lawful for any person acting on behalf of the authority to detain him (s.38(6B), as amended by the 1989 Act).

38 Review of police detention

S.40 of the Police and Criminal Evidence Act 1984 makes provision for the periodic review by a review officer of the detention of each person in police detention in connection with the investigation of an offence. It provides that the first review must be not later than six hours after the detention was first authorised, the second review must be not later than nine hours after the first, and subsequent reviews must be at intervals of not more than nine hours. However, a review may be postponed (a) if, having regard to all the circumstances prevailing at the latest time for it, it is not practicable to carry out the review at that time or (b) without prejudice to (a) if at any time the person in detention is being questioned by a police officer and the review officer is satisfied that an interruption of the questioning for the purpose of carrying out the review would prejudice the investigation in connection with which he is being questioned, or if at that time no review officer is readily available. A review which is postponed must be carried out as soon as practicable after the latest time specified for it. The fact that a review is postponed does not affect any requirement as to the time at which any subsequent review is to be carried out. The review officer is under a duty to record the reasons for any postponement in the custody record (see below) (s.40(1) to (7)).

Where the person whose detention is under review has not been charged before the time of the review, s.37(1) to (6) (see above) is to apply to him, but with the substitution of references to the person whose detention is under review for references to the person arrested and of references to the review officer for references to the custody officer (s.40(8)). Where a person has been kept in police detention by virtue of s.37(9) (person not in a fit state to be dealt with), s.37(1) to (6) will not apply but the review officer is under a duty to determine whether he is yet in a fit state (s.40(9)).

Where the person whose detention is under review has been charged before the time of the review, s.38(1) to (6) above is to apply to him, but with the substitution of references to the person whose detention is under review for references to the person arrested (s.40(10)).

Before determining whether to authorise a person's continued detention the review officer must give that person (unless he is asleep) or any solicitor representing him who is available at the time of the review, an opportunity to make representations to him about the detention. Such representations may be made orally or in writing, but the review officer may refuse to hear oral representations from the person whose detention is under review if he considers that he is unfit to make such representations by reason of his condition or behaviour (s.40(12) to (14)).

Any reference in ss.40 to 52 to a period or a time of day is to be treated as approximate only (s.45(2)).

39 Limits on period of detention without charge

Subject to ss.42 and 43 of the Police and Criminal Evidence Act 1984 (which provide for extensions of the period of detention–see below) a person must not be kept in police detention for more than 24 hours without being charged (s.41(1)).

The time from which the period of detention of a person must be calculated (the relevant time) is as follows–
(1) in the case of a person whose arrest is sought in one police area in England and Wales, is arrested in another police area, and is not questioned in the area in which he is arrested in order to obtain evidence in relation to an offence for which he is arrested either (a) the time at which that person arrived at the relevant police station (i.e., the first police station to which he is taken in the police area in which his arrest was sought), or (b) the time 24 hours after the time of that person's arrest, whichever is the earlier;
(2) in the case of a person arrested outside England and Wales (a) the time at which that person arrives at the first police station to which he is taken in the police area in England and Wales in which the offence for which he was arrested is being investigated, or (b) the time 24 hours after the time of that person's entry into England and Wales, whichever is the earlier;
(3) in the case of a person who attends voluntarily at a police station or accompanies a constable to a police station, and is arrested at the police station, the time of his arrest;
(4) in any other case, except where paragraph (5) below applies, the time at which the person arrested arrives at the first police station to which he is taken after his arrest (s.41(2));
(5) if (a) a person is in police detention in a police area in England and Wales (the first area), (b) his arrest for an offence is sought in some other police area in England and Wales (the second area), and (c) he is taken to the second area for the purposes of investigating that offence, without being questioned in the first area in order to obtain evidence in relation to it, (i) the time 24 hours after he leaves the place where he is detained in the first area, or (ii) the time at which he arrives at the first police station to which he is taken in the second area, whichever is the earlier (s.41(5)).

When a person who is in police detention is removed to hospital because he is in need of medical treatment, any time during which he is being questioned in hospital or on the way there or back by a police officer for the purpose of obtaining evidence relating to an offence must be included in calculating the period of detention, but any other time which he is in hospital or on his way there or back must not be so included (s.41(6)).

A person who at the expiry of 24 hours after the relevant time is in police detention and has not been charged must be released at that time either on bail or without bail (s.41(7)), unless the period of detention has been extended in accordance with ss.42 or 43 (see below) (s.41(8)). A person so released must not be re-arrested without a warrant for the offence for which he was previously arrested unless new evidence justifying a further arrest has come to light since his release, except where the arrest is for failure to answer to police bail (s.41(9), as amended).

40 Authorisation of continued detention

A suitably qualified officer may authorise the keeping of a detained person in police detention for a period expiring at or before 36 hours after the relevant time, if he has reasonable grounds for believing that–
(a) the detention of that person without charge is necessary (i) to secure or preserve evidence relating to an offence for which he is under arrest, or (ii) to obtain such evidence by questioning him;
(b) an offence for which he is under arrest is an indictable offence (see B: DEFINITIONS, above); and
(c) the investigation is being conducted diligently and expeditiously (Police and Criminal Evidence Act 1984, s.42(1)).

However no such authorisation is to be given more than 24 hours after the relevant time or before the second review of his detention under s.40 (see above) has been carried out (s.42(4)). If it is proposed to transfer the person to another police area, regard must be had to the distance and the time the journey would take (s.42(3)).

Where the officer has authorised the keeping of a person in police detention for a period expiring less than 36 hours after the relevant time, he may authorise the detention of that person for a further period expiring not more than 36 hours after that time if the conditions specified in s.42(1) are still satisfied when he gives the authorisation (s.42(2)).

An opportunity to make representations about the detention similar to that provided during the review procedure under s.40(12) to (14) (see above) must be given before an authorisation of continued detention is made (s.42(6) to (8)).

An officer who authorises the keeping of a person in detention under s.42(1) before that person has exercised a right conferred on him by ss.56 or 58 (see **51 Right to have someone informed when arrested,** below, and see **53 Access to legal advice**, below) must inform him of that right, decide whether he should be permitted to exercise it, and record the decision in his custody record, and, if the decision is to refuse to permit the exercise of the right, also record the grounds for that decision (s.42(9)).

Where an officer has authorised the keeping of a person who has not been charged in detention under s.42(1) or (2), he must be released from detention, either on bail or without bail, not later than 36 hours after the relevant time, unless he has been charged with an offence or his continued detention is authorised or otherwise permitted in accordance with s.43 (see below). A person so released must not be re-arrested without a warrant for the offence for which he was previously arrested unless new evidence justifying a further arrest has come to light since his release, except were the arrest is for failure to answer police bail (s.42(10) and (11)).

41 Warrants of further detention

A magistrates' court consisting of two or more justices of the peace sitting otherwise than in open court may issue a warrant of further detention authorising the keeping of a person in police detention if it is satisfied that there are reasonable grounds for believing that the further detention of that person is justified (Police and Criminal Evidence Act 1984, s.43(1)).

A court may not hear an application for a warrant of further detention unless the person to whom the application relates has been furnished with a copy of the information and has been brought before the court for hearing (s.43(2)). He is entitled to be legally represented at the hearing, and if he is not so represented but wishes to be, the court must adjourn to enable him to obtain representation; during the adjournment he may be kept in police detention (s.43(3)).

A person's further detention is justified only if it satisfies three conditions, laid down by s.43(4), which are similar to those laid down by s.42(1) in relation to the authorisation of continued detention by a suitably qualified officer (see above).

An application for a warrant of further detention may be made (a) at any time before the expiry of 36 hours after the relevant time, or (b) in a case where it is not practicable for the magistrates' court to which the application will be made to sit, at the expiry of 36 hours after the relevant time but the court will sit, during the six hours following the end of that period, at any time before the expiry of the said six hours. In the latter case, the person may be kept in police detention until the application is heard, and the custody officer must make a note in that person's custody record of the fact of, and the reasons for, the detention (s.43(5) and (6)). A magistrates' court must dismiss the application for a warrant of further detention made after the expiry of 36 hours after the relevant time, if it appears to the court that it would have been reasonable for the police to have made it before the expiry of that period (s.43(7)).

A magistrates' court must refuse an application for a warrant of further detention of a person, or adjourn the hearing of it until a time not later than 36 hours after the relevant time, if it is not satisfied that there are reasonable grounds for believing that further detention of that person is justified. During such an adjournment the person may be kept in police detention (s.43(8) and (9)).

A warrant of further detention must state the time at which it is issued and authorise the keeping in police detention of the person to whom it relates for the period stated on it (s.43(10)). A warrant will authorise further detention of a person for such period as the magistrates' court thinks fit, not exceeding 36 hours. If it is proposed to transfer the person to another police area, the court must have regard to the distance and the time the journey would take (s.43(11) to (13)).

Where an application is refused, the person to whom the application relates must forthwith be charged or released, either on bail or without bail. However, a person need not be released before the expiry of 24 hours after the relevant time or before the expiry of any longer period for which continued detention is or has been authorised under s.42 (see above). No further application for a warrant of further detention may be made unless supported by evidence which has come to light since the refusal (s.43(15) to (17)).

Where a warrant of further detention is issued, the person to whom it relates must be released from police detention, either on bail or without bail, upon or before the expiry of the warrant unless he is charged. He must not be re-arrested without a warrant for the offence for which he was previously arrested unless new evidence justifying a further arrest has come to light since his release, except where the arrest is for failure to answer police bail (s.43(18) and (19)).

Provision is made by s.44 for the extension of warrants of further detention issued under s.43. A magistrates' court may, if it is satisfied that there are reasonable grounds for believing that the further detention of a person is justified, extend a warrant of further detention for such period as it thinks fit, but the period must not exceed 36 hours nor end later than 96 hours after the relevant time (s.44(1) to (3)). S.44(4) makes provision for further applications to be made, but any period of further extension must not exceed 36 hours nor end later than 96 hours after the relevant time.

A warrant of further detention must be endorsed with a note of the period of extension (s.43(5)). *Inter alia* s.43(2) and (3) (see above) applies to an application made under s.44 as it applies to an application made under s.43 (s.44(6)).

Where an application for an extension is refused, the person to whom the application relates must forthwith be charged or released, either on bail or without bail. However, a person need not be released before the expiry of any period for which a warrant of further detention issued in relation to him has been extended or further extended (s.44(7) and (8)).

Note.–Where a person is charged with an offence under the Misuse of Drugs Act 1971, s.5(2) (possession of a controlled drug), or a drug trafficking offence, magistrates may commit a person to detention for up to 192 hours. This is to increase the likelihood of evidence being recovered where, for example, suitably wrapped drugs have been swallowed (Criminal Justice Act 1988, s.152, as amended by the Drugs Act 2005, s.8).

42 Detention after charge

Where a person is charged with an offence and after being charged is kept in police detention, or detained by a local authority in pursuance of arrangements made under s.38(6) of the Police and Criminal Evidence Act 1984 above (i.e., an arrested juvenile), he must be brought before a magistrates' court as soon as practicable and in any event not later than the first sitting after he is charged with the offence (s.46(1)). A person in hospital who is not well enough to attend is not to be brought before the court (s.46(9)).

43 Responsibilities in relation to persons detained

The custody officer at a police station must ensure that all persons in police detention at that station are treated in accordance with the Act and Code (C) and where the custody officer transfers a person to the custody of another officer, that officer is under a similar duty. All matters relating to such persons which are required by the Act or the Codes to be recorded must be recorded in their custody records (see below) (Police and Criminal Evidence Act 1984, s.39(1) and (2)).

44 Powers of arrest for failure to answer police bail

A constable may arrest without a warrant any person who, having been released on bail under Part IV subject to a duty to attend at a police station, fails to attend at the police station at the time appointed for him to do so (Police and Criminal Evidence Act 1984, s.46A). A person arrested under s.46A must be taken to the police station appointed as the place at which he is to surrender to custody as soon as practicable after the arrest (s.46A(2)).

G: QUESTIONING AND TREATMENT OF PERSONS BY THE POLICE

45 Introduction

Part V of the Police and Criminal Evidence Act 1984 (ss.53 to 65) deals with the questioning and treatment of persons by the police, as described in the following paragraphs.

46 Abolition of certain powers of constables to search persons

S.53 of the Police and Criminal Evidence Act 1984 abolishes all previous statutory and all common law powers, including those contained in local Acts, to search a person in police detention at a police station or to carry out an intimate search (see below).

47 Searches of detained persons

The custody officer at a police station is under a duty to ascertain and to record (in the case of an arrested person, in his custody records) everything which a person has with him when (a) he is brought to the station after being arrested elsewhere or after being committed to custody by an order or sentence of a court, or (b) he is arrested at the station or, being a person arrested for an offence who was released on bail subject to a duty to attend a station, he is detained there when so attending in accordance with s.37 (see **37 Duties of custody officer before charge**, above) (Police and Criminal Evidence Act 1984, s.54(1) as amended, s.147, and s.54(2)).

A custody officer may seize and retain any such thing, but clothes and personal effects (defined by Code (C), paragraph 4.3, as those items which a person may lawfully need, use or refer to while in detention, but not cash and other items of value) may be seized only if the officer–

- (a) believes that the person from whom they are seized may use them to cause physical injury to himself or any other person, to damage property, to interfere with evidence, or to assist him to escape, or
- (b) has reasonable grounds for believing that they may be evidence relating to an offence (s.54(3) and (4)).

    A person from whom anything is seized must be told of the reason for the seizure, unless he is violent or likely to become violent, or is incapable of understanding what is said to him. (s.54(3) to (5)). Code (C) provides guidance as to the treatment of persons incapable of understanding what is said to them (see **68 Treatment of detained persons**, below).

A person may be searched if the custody officer considers it necessary to enable him to carry out his duty under s.54(1) and (2), though he may be searched only to the extent that the officer considers necessary for that purpose. S.54(6A) to (6C), inserted by s.147 of the 1988 Act, provides that a person who is in custody at a police station or is in police detention otherwise than at a police station may at any time be searched in order to ascertain whether he has with him anything which he could use for any of the four purposes specified in paragraph (a) above. A constable may seize and retain anything found on such a search, but may seize clothes and personal effects only where paragraph (a) or (b) above applies. A search must be carried out by a constable of the same sex as the person searched. An intimate search (see below) may not be carried out under s.54 (s.54(6) to (9)). Annex A to Code (C) states that a strip search (i.e., a search involving the removal of more than outer clothing) may take place only if the custody officer considers it to be necessary to remove an article which the detained person would not be allowed to keep, and the officer reasonably believes that the person might have concealed such an article. The officer must record the reasons for, and the result of, the search and those present during it. A police officer carrying out a strip search must be of the same sex as the person searched and the search should take place in an area where the person being searched cannot be seen by anyone who does not need to be present. In general, whenever a strip search involves exposure of intimate parts of the body, there must be at least two people present other than the person searched. Persons who are searched should not normally be required to have all their clothes removed at the same time.

48 Search and examination to ascertain identity

On the authority of a police officer of the rank of inspector or above, a suspect may be searched and/or examined for marks which would either (Police and Criminal Evidence Act 1984, s.54A added by the Anti-terrorism, Crime and Security Act 2001, s.90)–
  (a) assist in identifying him; or
  (b) identify him as being involved in an offence.
For the purposes of (a) above, a search may only be authorised if the suspect refuses to identify himself, or the police have reasonable grounds for suspecting that he is not who he claims to be.

Any identifying marks which are found may be photographed. Reasonable force may be used, but an intimate search may not be carried out for the purposes of s.54A.

49 Intimate searches

A suitably qualified officer may authorise an intimate search of a person (i.e., a search which consists of the physical examination of a person's body orifices, other than the mouth or the taking of a genital swab (Police and Criminal Evidence Act 1984, s.65)) if he has reasonable grounds for believing–
  (a) that a person who has been arrested and is in police detention may have concealed on him anything which he could use to cause physical injury to himself or others and which he might so use while he is in police detention or in the custody of a court; or
  (b) that such a person may have a Class A drug (as defined) concealed on him, and was in possession of it with the appropriate criminal intent (as defined) before his arrest.
However, the officer may not authorise such a search of a person for anything unless he has reasonable grounds for believing that it cannot be found without his being intimately searched (s.55(1) and (2)). An authorisation may be given orally or in writing, but if given orally, must be confirmed in writing as soon as is practicable (s.55(3)). Annex A to Code (C) provides that the reasons why an intimate search is considered necessary must be explained to the person before the search begins. If the search is a drug offence search, the suspect must give his consent in writing (s.55(3A)), however, if consent is refused without good cause then, in any subsequent proceedings, a court can draw such inferences from the refusal as appear proper (s.55(13A)).

An intimate search must be carried out by a registered medical practitioner or registered nurse unless an officer of at least the rank of inspector considers that this is not practicable, in which case, where it is believed that there has been concealed an article which could cause physical injury to the detained person or others at the police station, the search must be carried out by a constable of the same sex as the person to be searched. An intimate search for a concealed article must take place only at a hospital, surgery, other medical premises, or police station. A minimum of two people, other than the person searched, must be present during the search. No person of the opposite sex who is not a medical practitioner or nurse can be present, nor shall anyone whose presence is unnecessary.

Such a search, where it is believed that the person has concealed a Class A drug which he intended to supply to another person or to export, may take place only at a hospital, surgery, or other medical premises and it must be carried out by a registered medical practitioner or a registered nurse.

Annex A to Code (C) also states that an intimate search at a police station of a juvenile, 17 year old, or mentally disordered or mentally vulnerable person may take place only in the presence of an appropriate person of the same sex to the person searched, unless the person searched requests a particular person of the opposite sex who is readily available.

The custody record of a person searched must state which parts of his body were searched and why they were searched; the information must be recorded as soon as is practicable after the completion of the search. In the case of a drugs search, the custody record must also state the authorisation by virtue of which the search was carried out, the grounds for giving the authorisation, and that consent to the search was given (s.55(4) to (11)).

S.55(12) and (13) make provision for the seizure and retention, and the information required to be given on the seizure, of anything found on an intimate search similar to that made by s.54(4) and (5) (see above) in relation to searches which are not intimate searches.

50 X-rays and ultrasound scans

If an officer of at least the rank of inspector has reasonable grounds for believing that a person who has been arrested for an offence and is in police detention may have swallowed a Class A drug, and was in possession of it with the appropriate criminal intent before his arrest, the officer may authorise that an x-ray is taken of the person or an ultrasound scan is carried out on the person (or both) (Police and Criminal Evidence Act 1984, s.55A).

The suspect must give his consent in writing to the x-ray or scan(s.55A(2)), however, if consent is refused without good cause then, in any subsequent proceedings, a court can draw such inferences from the refusal as appear proper (s.55A(9)). An x-ray or scan may only be carried out be a suitably qualified person and may only take place at a hospital, surgery or other place used for medical purposes. The custody record must state the authorisation by virtue of which the x-ray or scan was carried out, the grounds for giving the authorisation, and that consent was given (s.55A(5)).

51 Right to have someone informed when arrested

Where a person has been arrested and is being held in custody in a police station or other premises, he is entitled, if he so requests, to have one friend or relative or other person who is known to him or who is likely to take an interest in his welfare told, as soon as is practicable except to the extent that a delay is permitted (see below) that he has been arrested and is being detained there (Police and Criminal Evidence Act 1984, s.56(1)). In any case, he must be permitted to exercise this right within 36 hours from the relevant time as defined in s.41(2) (see **39 Limits on period of detention without charge**, above), and is also entitled to exercise it on each occasion that he is transferred from one place to another within the said 36 hours (s.56(3) and (8)).

Delay is permitted only in the case of a person who is in police detention for an indictable offence, and if a suitably qualified officer authorises it (s.56(2)). That officer may authorise delay only in the following circumstances–

  (a) where he has reasonable grounds for believing that telling the named person of the arrest will–
      (i) lead to interference with or harm to evidence connected with an indictable offence or interference with or physical injury to other persons, or
      (ii) lead to the alerting of other persons suspected of having committed such an offence but not yet arrested for it, or
      (iii) hinder the recovery of any property obtained as a result of such an offence (s.56(5)); or
  (b) where the indictable offence is a drug trafficking offence (see below), or an offence to which Part VI of the 1988 Act applies (confiscation orders–see the Note on **Treatment of Offenders**) and the officer has reasonable grounds for believing–
      (i) where the offence is a drug trafficking offence, that the detained person has benefited from drug trafficking and that the recovery of the value of that person's proceeds of drug trafficking will be hindered by telling the named person of the arrest; and
      (ii) where the offence is one to which Part VI of the 1988 Act applies, that the detained person has benefited from the offence and that the recovery of the value of the property obtained by that person from or in connection with the offence or of the pecuniary advantage derived by him from or in connection with it will be hindered by telling the named person of the arrest (s.56(5A), inserted by the Drug Trafficking Offences Act 1986 (the 1986 Act), s.32, and amended by the 1988 Act, s.99).

References to drug trafficking and drug trafficking offence have the same meaning as in the Drug Trafficking Act 1994 and references to any person's proceeds of drug trafficking are to be construed in accordance with that Act (s.65, as amended by the 1986 Act, s.32).

Any authorisation for delay may be given orally or in writing, but if given orally, must be confirmed in writing as soon as is practicable (s.56(4)).

If a delay is authorised, the detained person must be told of the reason for it and the reason must be noted on his custody record as soon as is practicable (s.56(6) and (7)). No further delay is permitted once the reason for authorising delay ceases to subsist (s.56(9)).

S.56 does not apply to a person who has been detained under the terrorism provisions (i.e., the Terrorism Act 2000 s.41 and Sch. 7) (s.56(10)).

Paragraph 5.7 of Code (C) states that before any letter or message is sent, or telephone call made, the person must be informed that what he says in a letter, call, or message (other than in the case of a communication to a solicitor) may be read or listened to as appropriate and may be given in evidence. A telephone call may be terminated if the right to make it is being abused. The costs can be at public expense at the discretion of the custody officer. Paragraph 5.4 states that a person may receive visits at the custody officer's discretion.

52 Additional rights of children and young persons

In addition to the rights granted under s.56 of the Police and Criminal Evidence Act 1984, where a child (i.e., someone under the age of 14), or young person (i.e., someone who has attained the age of 14 but is under the age of 17) is in police detention, or has been detained under the terrorism provisions, all practicable steps must be taken to ascertain the identity of a person responsible for his welfare (i.e., his parent or guardian or any other person who has for the time being assumed such responsibility, including, if the child is in the care of a local authority, that authority). That person must then be informed, as soon as practicable–

  (a) that the child or young person has been arrested;
  (b) why he has been arrested; and
  (c) where he is being detained.

If it appears that at the time of his arrest the child or young person is being accommodated by or on behalf of a local authority under s.20 of the Children Act 1989 (the 1989 Act), the local authority must similarly be informed. Where the child or young person is subject to a supervision order under s.11 of the Children and Young Persons Act 1969 (the 1969 Act) (see the Note on **Treatment of Offenders: Children and Young Persons**) or Part IV of the 1989 Act, the supervisor must also be informed (Children and Young Persons Act 1933, s.34(2) to (11), as substituted by the 1984 Act, s.57, and amended by the 1989 Act).

A child or young person arrested in pursuance of a warrant must not be released unless he or his parent or guardian (with or without sureties) enters into a recognisance for such amount as the custody officer considers will secure his attendance at the hearing of the charge and, if the officer thinks fit, the recognisance may be conditioned for the attendance of the parent or guardian at the hearing in addition to the child or young person (1969 Act, s.29, as substituted by the 1984 Act, Sch. 6 and amended by the Criminal Justice Act 1991).

53 Access to legal advice

A person who is in police detention is entitled, if he so requests, to consult a solicitor privately at any time. The consultation must be permitted as soon as is practicable after the request is made except to the extent that delay is permitted (see below); in any case it must be permitted within 36 hours from the relevant time as defined in s.41(2) of the Police and Criminal Evidence Act 1984 (see **39 Limits on period of detention without charge**, above). The request and the time of the request must be recorded in the custody record unless the request is made at a time while the person making the request is at a court after being charged with an offence (s.58(1) to (5)).

Delay in compliance with a request is permitted only in the case of a person who is in police detention for an indictable offence and if a suitably qualified officer authorises it (s.58(6)). S.58(8) and (8A) specifies the grounds on which such an authorisation may be made in terms similar to those specified by s.56(5) and (5A) (see **51 Right to have someone informed when arrested**, above, paras. (a) and (b)).

S.58(7), (9), and (10) makes provision for the manner of authorisation, the information required to be given to a person whose consultation with a solicitor is delayed, and the duty to record information in his custody records similar to that made by s.56(4), (6), and (7) (see **51 Right to have someone informed when arrested**, above). No further delay is permitted once the reason for authorising delay ceases to subsist (s.58(11)).

If a suitably qualified officer has reasonable grounds for believing that, unless he directs that a consultation with a solicitor must be within the sight and hearing of a qualified uniformed officer, any of the consequences specified in s.58(8) and (8A) (see above) will result, he may give such a direction. A direction ceases to have effect once the reason for giving it ceases to subsist (s.58(14) and (18)).

S.58 does not apply to a person who has been detained under the terrorism provisions (i.e., the Terrorism Act 2000 s.41 and Sch. 7) (s.58(12)).

Paragraph 6 of Code (C) amplifies the above statutory provisions *inter alia* as follows. Consultation with a solicitor may be in person, in writing, or on the telephone. A person who wants legal advice may not be interviewed or continue to be interviewed until he has received it unless (1) a delay is permitted under s.58(6)—see above; or (2) a suitably qualified officer has reasonable grounds for believing that (i) delay will lead to interference with evidence, involve an immediate risk of harm to persons or serious loss of, or damage to, property, lead to alerting other people suspected of committing an offence, or hinder the recovery of property; or (ii) where a solicitor, including a duty solicitor, has been contacted and has agreed to attend the interview, awaiting his arrival would cause unreasonable delay to the process of investigation; or (3) where the solicitor nominated by the person, or selected by him from a list, cannot be contacted, has previously indicated that he does not wish to be contacted, or having been contacted, has declined to attend, and the person has been advised of the duty solicitor scheme but has declined to ask for the duty solicitor, or the duty solicitor is unavailable, or (4) the person who wanted the legal advice has changed his mind. In these circumstances, the interview may be started or continued without further delay provided that the person has given his agreement in writing or on tape that the interview may be started at once. A person who has been permitted to consult a solicitor must be allowed to have his solicitor present while he is interviewed provided that the solicitor is available (i.e., present at the station, on his way to the station, or easily contactable by telephone) at the time the interview begins or is in progress. The solicitor may be required to leave the interview only if his conduct is such that the investigating officer is unable properly to put questions to the suspect.

54 Tape-recording of interviews

S.60 of the Police and Criminal Evidence Act 1984 provides that it is the Secretary of State's duty (a) to issue a code of practice in connection with the tape-recording of interviews of persons suspected of the commission of criminal offences which are held by police officers at police stations; and (b) to make an order requiring the tape-recording of interviews of persons suspected of the commission of criminal offences, or of such descriptions of criminal offences as may be specified in the order, which are so held, in accordance with the Code as it has effect for the time being. Code (E) has been issued for this purpose.

55 Visual recording of interviews

S.60A of the Police and Criminal Evidence Act 1984 provides that it is the Secretary of State's duty (a) to issue a code of practice in connection with the visual recording of interviews held by police officers at police stations; and (b) to make an order requiring the visual recording of interviews in such cases or police stations in such areas, or both, as he may specify. Code (F) has been issued for this purpose.

56 Fingerprinting

No person's fingerprints (which term includes a record of the skin pattern and any other physical characteristics of any of a person's fingers or either of his palms) may be taken without appropriate consent (see below) unless (Police and Criminal Evidence Act 1984, s.61(1), (3), (4), (6) to (6A))–

   (a) a suitably qualified officer authorises them to be taken where he has reasonable grounds for suspecting the involvement of the person whose fingerprints are to be taken in a criminal offence, and for believing that his fingerprints will tend to confirm or disprove his involvement or his identity; or

   (b) (i) he has been charged with a recordable offence (i.e., an offence specified by the National Police Records (Recordable Offences) Regulations 2000, which includes an offence punishable with imprisonment, loitering or soliciting for the purposes of prostitution, paying for sexual services of a prostitute subjected to force, drunkenness in a public place, throwing missiles at a football match, going on to the pitch or indecent or racialist chanting, certain offences in relation to football banning orders, failing to provide a specimen of breath, kerb crawling, taking part in a prohibited public procession, tampering with a motor vehicle, touting for hire car services or designated football matches, begging and persistent begging, and various offences under the Licensing Act 2003), or informed that he will be reported for such an offence; and (ii) he has not had his fingerprints taken in the course of the investigation of the offence by the police; or

   (c) a constable reasonably suspects that the person whose fingerprints are to be taken is committing or attempting to commit, or has committed or attempted to commit, an offence and either the name of the person is unknown to, and cannot be readily ascertained by, the constable, or the constable has reasonable grounds for doubting whether a name furnished by the person as his name is his real name; or

an officer of at least the rank of inspector is satisfied that taking them is necessary to assist in the prevention or detection of crime and–

   (d) he has been convicted of a recordable offence (or been given a caution in respect of such an offence which has been admitted); or

   (e) he has been convicted of a qualifying offence outside England and Wales, has not had his fingerprints taken previously or, if such data has been taken previously, it must have proved inadequate for analysis and/or loading onto the national database (s.61(6)).

Where fingerprints have been taken, but they are incomplete or of poor quality, they may be retaken (s.61(3A)). Where biometric data (fingerprints and non-intimate samples) has not been taken from someone who has been arrested for a recordable offence and released on bail, or their biometric data was taken and has subsequently proved inadequate for analysis and/or loading onto the national fingerprint or DNA database, it may be taken (s.61(5A)). Where a persons was fingerprinted, the investigation was discontinued and the fingerprints destroyed, and the investigation is then resumed, he may be fingerprinted again (s.61(5C)).

Where a person who has previously had his fingerprints taken answers bail at a court or police station, his fingerprints may be taken without the appropriate consent if there are reasonable grounds for believing that he is not the same person as the one whose fingerprints were previously taken, or if he claims to be a different person to the one whose fingerprints were previously taken (s.61(4A), (4B)).

"Appropriate consent" means, in relation to a person who has attained 17 years, the consent of that person; in relation to a person who is under 17 years of age, but has attained the age of 14 the consent of that person and his parent or guardian; and in relation to a person who has not attained the age of 14 years, the consent of his parent or guardian (s.65).

Consent must be given in writing if it is given at a time when the person is at a police station (s.61(2)). Where an officer gives an authorisation for fingerprints to be taken, it may be given orally or in writing, but if given orally, must be confirmed in writing as soon as is practicable (s.61(5)). A person must be told the reason for taking his fingerprints before they are taken without his consent, and the reason must be recorded as soon as is practicable after they are taken and if he is detained at a police station when the fingerprints are taken, the reason for taking them must be recorded on his custody record. Before the fingerprints are taken, the person from whom they are taken must be informed that they may be the subject of a speculative search and the fact that the person has been so informed must be recorded (s.61(7), (7A), and (8)). Speculative search in relation to a person's fingerprints or samples means such a check against other fingerprints or samples or against information derived from other samples as is referred to in s.63A(1) (see **61 Fingerprints and samples: supplementary provisions**, below).

Nothing in s.61 affects any power conferred by paragraph 18(2) of Schedule 2 to the Immigration Act 1971 or applies to a person arrested or detained under the terrorism provisions (i.e., the Terrorism Act 2000 s.41 and Sch. 7) or under an extradition arrest power.

Where a person–

   (a) has been convicted of a recordable offence (or been given a caution in respect of such an offence which has been admitted);

(b) has not at any time been in police detention for the offence; and

(c) has not had his fingerprints taken in the course of the investigation of the offence by the police or since the conviction,

a constable may, not more than one month after the date of his conviction, require him to attend at a police station in order that his fingerprints may be taken. Where a person who has been convicted of (or cautioned for) a recordable offence has already had his fingerprints taken, but they are incomplete or of poor quality, a second set may be taken.

A person must be given a period of at least seven days within which he must attend to have his fingerprints taken (or retaken), and he may be directed so to attend at a specified time of day or between specified times of day. Any constable may arrest without a warrant a person who has failed to so attend (Sch. 2A, para 16).

57 Intimate samples

S.62 of the Police and Criminal Evidence Act 1984, which was amended by the Criminal Justice and Public Order Act 1994, governs the taking of intimate samples.

An "intimate sample" (i.e., a sample of blood, semen, or any other tissue fluid, urine, or pubic hair, a dental impression, or a swab taken from a person's body orifice other than the mouth (s.65, as amended)), may be taken from a person in police detention only if a suitably qualified officer authorises it and the appropriate consent is given in writing (s.62(1)). An intimate sample may be taken from a person who is not in police detention but from whom, in the course of the investigation of an offence, two or more intimate samples suitable for the same means of analysis have been taken which have proved insufficient, provided that a suitably qualified officer authorises the taking and the appropriate consent (see **56 Fingerprinting**, above) is given (s.62(1A)). Authorisation may be given only if the officer has reasonable grounds for suspecting the involvement of the person in a recordable offence and for believing that the sample will tend to confirm or disprove his involvement (s.62(2), and (4)). An authorisation under s.62(1) or (1A) may be given orally or in writing, but if given orally, must be confirmed in writing as soon as is practicable (s.62(3)). The officer must inform the person from whom the sample is to be taken of the giving of the authorisation and of the grounds for giving it and must warn him that it may be the subject of a speculative search (as defined, see **56 Fingerprinting**, above). As soon as is practicable after the sample has been taken, the authorisation by virtue of which it was taken, the grounds for giving it, and the fact that the appropriate consent and warning was given must be recorded (if at a police station, in a person's custody record) (s.62(5) to (8)). An intimate sample, other than a sample of urine or a dental impression may be taken only by a registered medical practitioner or a registered health care professional (e.g., a registered nurse), and a dental impression may only be taken by a registered dentist (s.62(9)). In any proceedings against a person for an offence, a court or jury may draw such inferences as appear proper from the refusal of that person to give appropriate consent to the taking of an intimate sample without good cause (s.62(10)). Paragraph 6.3 of Code (D) provides *inter alia* that a person must be warned about the treatment of such a refusal before he is asked to provide an intimate sample.

The police may also take an intimate sample from a person convicted of a qualifying offence outside England and Wales where two or more non-intimate samples have been but have proved insufficient and that person consents. The taking of the sample must be authorised by an officer of at least the rank of inspector who must be satisfied that taking the sample is necessary to assist in the prevention or detection of crime (s.62(2A)).

Nothing in s.62 affects ss.4 to 11 of the Road Traffic Act 1988 (see the Note on **Road Traffic Offences**). S.62 does not apply in respect of terrorist investigations under the Terrorism Act 2000 s.41 and Schedule 7.

58 Non-intimate samples

S.63 of the Police and Criminal Evidence Act 1984, as amended by the Criminal Evidence (Amendment) Act 1997, governs the taking of non-intimate samples. A "non-intimate sample" is (s.65)–

(1) a sample of hair other than pubic hair;

(2) a sample taken from, or from under, a nail;

(3) a swab taken from any part of a person's body including the mouth but not from any other body orifice;

(4) saliva; or

(5) a skin impression i.e., a record (other than a fingerprint) of the skin pattern and other physical characteristics of the whole or any part of the foot or any other body part.

A non-intimate sample may not be taken from a person without appropriate consent in writing (see **56 Fingerprinting**, above). However, a non-intimate sample may be taken from a person without the appropriate consent if–

(a) (i) he is in police detention or is being held in custody by the police on the authority of the court, and (ii) a suitably qualified officer authorises it provided that the officer has reasonable grounds for suspecting the involvement of that person in a recordable offence and for believing that the sample will tend to confirm or disprove his involvement (s.63(1) to (3), and (4));

(b) he has been charged with a recordable offence (i.e., any offence to which regulations under s.27 of the 1984 Act apply) or informed that he will be reported for such an offence and either (i) has not had a non-intimate sample taken from him in the course of the investigation of the offence by the police or (ii) has had such a sample taken from him which was not suitable for the same means of analysis or which proved insufficient, or (iii) has had a sample taken previously, from which a DNA profile has been created, but the sample has since been destroyed and the person now claims that the DNA profile did not come from his sample (s.63(3A));

(c) he is a person to whom s.2 of the 1997 Act applies i.e., he is a person who has at any time been detained following acquittal for an offence on grounds of insanity or who has been found unfit to plead;

(d) he has been arrested for a recordable offence and released and, in the case of a person who is on bail, he has not had a non-intimate sample of the same type and from the same part of the body taken from him in the course of the investigation of the offence by the police; or, in any case, he has had a non-intimate sample taken from him in the course of that investigation but it was not suitable for the same means of analysis, or it proved insufficient (s.63(3ZA)).

an officer of at least the rank of inspector is satisfied that taking them is necessary to assist in the prevention or detection of crime and–

(e) he has been convicted of a recordable offence on or after 10th April 1995, or at any time if he was convicted of a recordable offence listed in Schedule 1 to the 1997 Act (see below) (s.63(3B) and (9A));

(f) has been given a caution (after 10th April 1995) in respect of a recordable offence which, at the time of the caution, he has admitted) for a recordable offence (s.63(3B)); or

(g) he has been convicted of a qualifying offence outside England and Wales, has not had a sample taken previously or, if such data has been taken previously, it must have proved inadequate for analysis and/or loading onto the national database (s.63(3E)).

Authorisation for a non-intimate sample consisting of a skin impression may not be given if one sample of the same part of the body has already been taken, unless that sample has proved insufficient (s.63(5A)). A sample will be "insufficient" if the whole or any part of it is lost, destroyed, contaminated or damaged, or if the whole or part of the sample is used for analysis which produces no results or results some or all of which must in the circumstances be regarded as unreliable (s.65(2)). Where a persons has had a non-intimate sample taken, the investigation was discontinued and the sample destroyed, and the investigation is then resumed, another sample may be taken (s.63(3AA)).

Schedule 1 to the 1997 Act lists a number of sexual offences and offences of indecency; violent and other offences, including murder, manslaughter, grievous bodily harm, burglary, cruelty to children, and possession of firearms; and offences of conspiracy, incitement, and attempting to commit any of these offences.

S.63(5) to (9) makes provision relating to the manner of authorisation, the information required to be given to a person before a sample is taken, and the duty to record such information similar to that made in relation to intimate samples by s.62(3) and (5) to (8) (see above).

S.63 does not apply, to persons arrested or detained under terrorism provisions (i.e., s.41 of and Schedule 7 to the Terrorism Act 2000: s.63(10)).

59 Testing for Class A drugs

S.63B of the Police and Criminal Evidence Act 1984 (added by the Criminal Justice and Court Services Act 2000) provides that a sample of urine or a non-intimate sample may be taken from a detained person and tested for the presence of a Class A drug, provided that the person–

(a) has either–
   (i) been arrested in connection with or charged with a "trigger" offence; or
   (ii) been arrested in connection with or charged with any offence and a police officer (of the rank of inspector or above) who has reasonable grounds for suspecting that the misuse by the person of any specified Class A drug caused or contributed to the offence has authorised the taking of the sample; and

(b) (i) if he has been charged, that he is aged 14, or in some areas, 18 or over (see below); or
   (ii) he has been arrested, that he is aged 18 or over; and

(c) has been requested by a police officer to give the sample (and been warned that failure to do so without good cause is an offence punishable by imprisonment for up to 3 months and/or a fine not exceeding level 4 on the standard scale (as to which see the Note on **Treatment of Offenders** at para **68 Maximum fines**)). In the case of (ii) above, the person must, at the time of the request, also be told of the authorisation and of the grounds in question.

The age limit was originally 18, but was reduced to 14 by the Criminal Justice Act 2003, s.5. In the case of children age under 17, the request, warning and taking of the sample must take place in the presence of an appropriate adult (s.63B(5A)).

Under Schedule 6 of the Criminal Justice and Court Services Act 2000 (as extended by the Criminal Justice and Court Services Act 2000 (Amendment) Order 2004), the "trigger" offences are various offences under the Theft Act 1968 (and the Criminal Attempts Act 1981 in relation to offences under the 1968 Act), and the Misuse of Drugs Act 1971, together with begging and persistent begging under the Vagrancy Act 1824. Where a person has been charged with an offence, they may be detained for up to 6 hours in order to allow for a sample to be taken (s.38).

Information obtained from a sample may be disclosed in bail applications; to inform decisions about supervision whilst in detention, on remand, in custody or on bail; to inform decisions about an appropriate sentence and about supervision or release; and for the purpose of ensuring that appropriate advice and treatment is available to that person.

60 Initial and follow-up assessments

If an analysis of a sample taken under s.63B of the Police and Criminal Evidence Act 1984 (see **59 Testing for Class A drugs**, above) reveals that a specified Class A drug may be present in a person's body then, if that person is aged 18 or over a police officer may, at any time before releasing them from detention, require them to attend an initial assessment and remain for its duration (Drugs Act 2005, s.9).

An initial assessment is an appointment with an assessor for the purpose of–
(a) establishing whether the person is dependent upon or has a propensity to misuse any specified Class A drug;
(b) if so, establishing whether the person might benefit from further assessment or from assistance or treatment; and
(c) if so, providing him with advice, including an explanation of the types of assistance or treatment which are available.

Note.–The Secretary of State may, by order, extend the provisions to those under 18.

At the same time as requiring attendance at an initial assessment, the police officer must also require the person to attend a follow-up assessment, unless at the initial assessment he is informed that he need not do so (s.10). A follow-up assessment will be for any of the purposes which were not fulfilled at the initial assessment and also, if appropriate, to draw up a care plan setting out the nature of the assistance or treatment which is appropriate.

Failure to attend an assessment and to remain for its duration is an offence (ss.11 to 14).

61 Fingerprints and samples: supplementary provisions

The information derived from samples taken under any powers conferred by Part V of the Police and Criminal Evidence Act 1984 from a person who has been arrested on suspicion of being involved in a recordable offence may be checked against other fingerprints, footwear impressions or samples or the information derived from other samples contained in records held by the police or held in connection with or as a result of an investigation of an offence (s.63A(1)).

Where fingerprints have been taken by a constable in order to verify a person's identity, they may be checked against other fingerprints which are held by or on behalf of any relevant law-enforcement authority or which are held in connection with or as a result of an investigation of an offence (s.63A(1ZA)).

Where fingerprints, footwear impressions or samples have been taken from any person who has not been arrested or charged and that person has given his consent in writing to their use in a speculative search, then the fingerprints, footwear impressions or samples may be checked in the same way as if they had been arrested or charged. A consent given for these purposes cannot be withdrawn (s.63A(1C)).

Where a sample of hair other than pubic hair is to be taken, it may be taken by cutting hairs or by plucking hairs with their roots, provided that no more are plucked than the person taking the sample reasonably considers to be necessary for a sufficient sample (s.63A(2)).

Where a non-intimate sample under s.63(3B) or (3C) is taken (see above), the sample may be taken in the hospital or other place where the person is detained (s.63(3A) and (3B)).

Under Sch. 2A, a constable may require a person who is neither in police detention nor held in custody by the police on the authority of a court to attend a police station in order to have a sample taken.

In cases where fingerprints or samples of a person arrested or charged are being taken because the previous ones were inadequate in some way, the power must be exercised within six months of the day on which the relevant police officer learnt of the inadequacy. There are also time limits where fingerprints or samples are to be taken from a person charged (6 months), where fingerprints are to be taken from person convicted (2 years), and where a non-intimate sample is to be taken from a person charged or convicted (2 years). The time limits do not apply and the power to compel attendance may be exercised at any time in cases where a person has been convicted of a qualifying offence (i.e., a serious violent, sexual, terrorist or human trafficking offence listed in s.65A) or, in the case of non-intimate samples, where the person is convicted of an offence prior to 10 April 1995 and he is a person to whom the Criminal Evidence (Amendment) Act 1997, s.1 applies (see **58 Non-intimate samples**, above). In the case of a persons convicted of an offence outside England and Wales, there is no time limit.

Where a person's fingerprints or a non-intimate sample have been taken on two occasions in relation to any offence, he may not be required to attend a police station to have them taken again in relation to that offence without the authorisation of an officer of at least the rank of inspector.

62 Destruction of fingerprints or samples

The retention or destruction of fingerprints and DNA profiles is dealt with by the Police and Criminal Evidence Act 1984, ss.63D to 63U. In certain cases, retention is subject to authorisation by the Commissioner for the Retention and Use of Biometric Material, appointed under the Protection of Freedoms Act 2012, s.20. The permitted periods of retention are as follows–

	Period of Retention
ADULT—on conviction—all crimes	Indefinite
ADULT—charged but not convicted – serious crime	3 Years + possible single 2-year extension by Court
ADULT—arrested but not charged or convicted –serious crime	Only where authorised by the Commissioner –3 years + possible single 2-year extension by Court
ADULT—non-conviction – minor crime	None*
UNDER 18s –on conviction – serious crime	Indefinite
UNDER 18s—on conviction – minor crime	1st Conviction–5 Years (plus length of any custodial sentence); 2nd Conviction—indefinite
UNDER 18s—charged but not convicted – serious crime	3 Years + possible single 2-Year extension by Court
UNDER 18s—arrested but not charged or convicted – serious crime	Only where authorised by the Commissioner – 3 Years + possible single 2-year extension by Court
UNDER 18s—non-conviction – minor crime	None*
Penalty Notice for disorder	2 Years
Terrorist suspects	3 Years plus renewable 2-year period(s) on national security grounds (Commissioner will review all determinations)
Biological DNA samples	Within six months of sample being taken

* In all cases, a speculative search of the DNA and fingerprint databases may be conducted before the destruction.

Where a DNA profile derived from a DNA sample is retained, it must be recorded on the National DNA Database (s.63AA).

Fingerprints or a DNA profile taken in connection with the investigation of one offence are treated as if they were taken in connection with the investigation of any other offence that the person is subsequently arrested for, charged with, convicted of or given a penalty notice for. This means that the above provisions for the retention of fingerprints or DNA profiles where there is a criminal conviction apply in such cases, without the need for a causal link between the arrest in respect of which the fingerprints and DNA profiles were taken and the subsequent offence (s.63P).

Note.–For these purposes, any reference to a person who is "convicted" of an offence includes a person who has been (s.65B)–
(a) given a caution in respect of the offence which, at the time of the caution, the person has admitted;
(b) warned or reprimanded (under the Crime and Disorder Act 1998, s.65) for the offence;
(c) found not guilty of the offence by reason of insanity; or
(d) found to be under a disability and to have done the act charged in respect of the offence.

63 Photographing of suspects

A person who has been–
(a) detained at a police station or elsewhere;
(b) issued with a fixed penalty notice, or
(c) made subject to a requirement to wait by a community support officer;
may be photographed with or without his consent (Police and Criminal Evidence Act 1984, s.64A added by the Anti-terrorism, Crime and Security Act 2001 s.92 and amended by the Serious Organised Crime and Security Act 2005). If a person whose photograph is to be taken refuses to remove any item or substance worn on or over the whole or any part of the head or face, reasonable force may be used to remove it. Any photographs taken in these circumstances may be used or disclosed to anyone for the purpose of the prevention or detection of crime, the investigation of an offence, or the conduct of a prosecution.

For these purpose, "photograph" includes a moving image.

64 Footwear impressions

An impression of a person's footwear may be taken with their written consent, or without consent if they are detained at a police station having been arrested, charged with, or informed that they will be reported for, a recordable offence (Police and Criminal Evidence Act 1984, s.61A added by the Serious Organised Crime and Security Act 2005).

65 Treatment of persons in custody

Paragraphs 1 and 3 of Code (C) to the Police and Criminal Evidence Act 1984 make general provision relating to persons in custody, as follows. Paragraph 1 provides *inter alia* that all persons in custody must be dealt with expeditiously and released as soon as the need for detention ceases to apply. Paragraph 3 provides *inter alia* that when a person is brought to a police station under arrest or is arrested at the police station, having attended there voluntarily, the custody officer must inform him of his rights under ss.56 and 58 (see **51 Right to have someone informed when arrested**, above, and see **53 Access to legal advice**, above) and his right to consult the Codes of Practice, and he must also give the person a written notice setting out the above three rights, the arrangements for obtaining legal advice, the right to a copy of the custody record and the prescribed caution (see **69 Cautions**, below) and an additional written notice briefly setting out his entitlements while in custody. The person must acknowledge receipt of the notice by signing the custody record. If such a person does not understand English or appears to be deaf and the custody officer cannot communicate with him, the officer must as soon as practicable call an interpreter, and ask him to provide the information required above. If the person is a juvenile, 17 year old, is mentally handicapped or is suffering from mental illness, or is blind or seriously visually handicapped or is unable to read, the custody officer is under a duty to ensure that an appropriate adult or some other person likely to take an interest in him is available to help him. Further provision relating to the treatment of mentally disordered and mentally vulnerable people is made by Annex E to the Code.

66 Interpreters

Paragraph 13 of Code (C) to the Police and Criminal Evidence Act 1984 provides for appropriately qualified independent persons to act as interpreters and to provide translations of essential documents for both detained suspects and suspects who are not under arrest but are cautioned. The arrangements must comply with the minimum requirements set out in EU Directive 2010/64 on the right to interpretation and translation in criminal proceedings and are provided at public expense. The arrangements made and the quality of interpretation and translation provided must be sufficient to "safeguard the fairness of the proceedings, in particular by ensuring that suspected or accused persons have knowledge of the cases against them and are able to exercise their right of defence".

Similar provisions apply where assistance is needed in court proceedings.

67 Custody records

Paragraph 2 of Code (C) to the Police and Criminal Evidence Act 1984 provides *inter alia* that a separate custody record must be opened as soon as practicable for each person who is brought to a police station under arrest or is arrested at a police station having attended there voluntarily. In the case of any action requiring the authority of an officer of a specified rank, his name and rank must be noted in the custody record. The custody officer is responsible for the accuracy and completeness of the custody record and for ensuring that the record or a copy of the record accompanies a detained person if he is transferred to another police station. The record must show the time of, and reason for, the transfer and the time a person is released from detention. All entries in custody and written interview records (see below) must be timed and signed by the maker (a computerised record must be timed and contain the operator's identification). Any refusal by a person to sign either a custody or an interview record must itself be recorded.

The detainee's solicitor and appropriate adult must be permitted to inspect the whole of the custody record as soon as practicable after their arrival at the station and at any other time on request, whilst the person is detained.

68 Treatment of detained persons

Paragraph 9 of Code (C) to the Police and Criminal Evidence Act 1984 makes provision for *inter alia* the treatment of detained persons as follows. If a complaint is made by or on behalf of a detained person about his treatment since his arrest, or it comes to the notice of any officer that he may have been treated improperly, a report must be made to a suitably qualified officer. If the matter concerns a possible assault or the possibility of the unnecessary or unreasonable use of force then an appropriate health care professional must also be called as soon as practicable.

The custody officer must make sure a detainee receives appropriate clinical attention as soon as reasonably practicable if they–
    (a) appear to be suffering from physical or mental illness;
    (b) are injured;
    (c) appear to be suffering from a mental disorder; or
    (d) otherwise appears to need clinical attention.

In urgent cases, the nearest health care professional or an ambulance must be called (this will be the case if the detainee does not show sign of sensibility and awareness or fails to respond normally to questions or conversation, other than through drunkenness alone). This applies even if the person makes no request for medical attention and whether or not he has recently had medical treatment elsewhere (unless brought to the station direct from hospital). If a detained person requests a medical examination an appropriate health care professional must be called as soon as practicable. If a safe and appropriate care plan cannot be provided, the police surgeon's advice must be sought. The detained person may in addition be examined by a medical practitioner of his own choice at his own expense.

Paragraph 7 makes special provision for the treatment of citizens of independent Commonwealth countries or foreign nationals *inter alia* as follows. A citizen of an independent Commonwealth country or a national of a foreign country (including the Republic of Ireland) may communicate at any time with his High Commission, Embassy, or Consulate. If a citizen of an independent Commonwealth country or a national of a foreign country with which a bilateral consular convention or agreement requiring notification of arrest is in force is detained, the appropriate High Commission, Embassy, or Consulate must be informed as soon as practicable. Visits by consular officers, under the provisions of Paragraph 7, will take place out of the hearing of a police officer. Where the detained person claims to be a refugee, or has or intends to apply for asylum, then notwithstanding consular conventions, the UK Border Agency must be informed as soon as practicable of the claim and they will then determine whether compliance with relevant international obligations requires notification of the arrest to be sent to the appropriate embassy/consulate and will inform the custody officer as to what action the police need to take.

69 Cautions

Paragraph 10 of Code (C) to the Police and Criminal Evidence Act 1984 provides *inter alia* that a person whom there are grounds for suspecting of an offence must be cautioned before any questions about it (or further questions if it is his answers to previous questions that provide grounds for suspicion) are put to him regarding his involvement or suspected involvement in that offence if his answers or his silence (i.e., failure or refusal to answer a question or to answer satisfactorily) may be given in evidence to a court in a prosecution. He therefore need not be cautioned if questions are put for other purposes, e.g., solely to establish his identity, his ownership of, or responsibility for, any vehicle, to obtain information in accordance with any statute, to search him in the exercise of powers of stop and search, or to verify a written record. When a person who is not under arrest is initially cautioned or reminded that he is under caution, he must at the same time be told that he is not under arrest and is not obliged to remain with the officer. A person must be cautioned upon arrest for an offence unless he has already been cautioned immediately prior to arrest as described above or it is impracticable to do so by reason of his condition or behaviour at the time. A record must be made when a caution is given either in the officer's pocket book or in the interview record as appropriate. Annex D of the Code makes provision for written statements under caution.

70 Interviews and recording

Paragraph 11 of Code (C) to the Police and Criminal Evidence Act 1984 makes provision relating to the conduct and recording of interviews.

Code (E) makes provision relating to the tape recording of interviews. Paragraph 3 of Code (E) provides *inter alia* that, subject to certain exceptions, a tape recording must be used at police stations for any interview–

(a) with a person cautioned in respect of any indictable offence, which includes any offence triable either way (except where that person has been arrested and the interview takes place elsewhere than at a police station in accordance with Code C for which a written record would be required);

(b) which takes place as a result of a police officer exceptionally putting further questions to a suspect about an offence under (a) above after he has been charged with, or informed he may be prosecuted for, that offence; or

(c) in which a police officer wishes to bring to the notice of a person, after he has been charged with, or informed he may be prosecuted for, an offence under (a) above, any written statement made by another person, or the content of an interview with another person.

Paragraph 3.3A makes an exception in the case of faulty equipment or lack of facilities if there are reasonable grounds for considering that the interview should not be delayed. There are also exemptions from the requirement to audio record – subject to conditions – where the interview relates to possession of cannabis or khat, shoplifting or criminal damage (Annex A).

Paragraph 4 of Code (E) makes provision for the conduct of the interview and for objections and complaints by the suspect. In certain circumstances, the recorder may be turned off because of the suspect's objections. Paragraph 5 of Code (E) provides *inter alia* that, after the interview, the police officer must make a note in his notebook of the fact that the interview has taken place and has been recorded on tape, its time, duration, and date, and the identification number of the master tape.

Failure by a police officer to comply with the Code will render him liable to disciplinary proceedings. Interviews about certain offences connected with terrorism are dealt with under the Terrorism Code (see the Note on **Prevention of Terrorism** at para 21 **Post-charge questioning**) rather than Code (E).

Code (F) makes provision for the visual recording of interviews. The provisions of Code (F) are similar to those of Code (E).

71 Arrest or detention in connection with terrorism

Special provisions apply to terrorist suspects under the Terrorism Act 2000 and the Anti-terrorism, Crime and Security Act 2001. These provisions apply throughout the United Kingdom.

Where the police reasonably suspect someone to be a terrorist, they may arrest him without a warrant (Terrorism Act 2000, s.41).

For these purposes, a "terrorist" is a person who has committed a terrorist offence or has been concerned in the commission, preparation or instigation of acts of terrorism. Terrorist offences include membership of or support for a proscribed organisation, fund-raising for terrorism, money laundering of terrorist property, weapons training, and inciting terrorism overseas.

Where a person is arrested for terrorism, they may initially be detained for 48 hours (s.41(3)), although this may be extended for up to 14 days (Sch. 8 para 36, as amended by the Criminal Justice Act 2003, s.306 and the Terrorism Act 2006, s.23). The arrest and detention procedures are governed by Schedule 8 to the 2000 Act (as amended by the Anti-terrorism, Crime and Security Act 2001 and the Terrorism Act 2006) instead of by the provisions of the 1984 Act. Provisions is made for the audio recording of interviews and the taking of fingerprints and samples. The right of a detained person to have someone informed of his detention and the right to consult a solicitor may both be delayed.

72 Authorities

Statutes–

Anti-terrorism, Crime and Security Act 2001

Children Act 1989

Children and Young Persons Acts 1933 and 1969

Crime and Punishment (Scotland) Act 1997

Crime (International Co-operation) Act 2003

Criminal Evidence (Amendment) Act 1997

Criminal Justice Acts 1988 and 1991

Criminal Justice and Court Services Act 2000

Criminal Justice and Public Order Act 1994

Drug Trafficking Act 1994

Drugs Act 2005

Police Act 1997

Police and Criminal Evidence Act 1984

Public Order Act 1986

Terrorism Act 2000

Statutory Instruments–

Criminal Justice and Court Services Act 2000 (Amendment) Order 2004 (S.I. 2004 No. 1892)

National Police Records (Recordable Offences) Regulations 2000, as amended (S.I. 2000 No. 1139, 2003 No. 2823, 2005 No. 3106, 2007 No. 2121, and 2012 No. 1713)

Police and Criminal Evidence Act 1984 (Codes of Practice) Orders 2005 to 2015 (S.I. 2005 No. 3503 2008 No. 167, and 2011 No. 412, 2013 No. 1798, 2013 No. 2685, 2014 No. 1237, 2015 No. 418, and 2016 No. 35)

TREATMENT OF SUSPECTS: SCOTLAND

1 Introduction

The Criminal Procedure (Scotland) Act 1995 contains the main statutory provisions governing police powers in relation to detention and questioning at police stations prior to arrest and sets out certain rules relating to the treatment of persons following their arrest.

2 Police powers in relation to suspects and potential witnesses

Under s.13(1) and (1A) of the Criminal Procedure (Scotland) Act 1995 (amended by the Police, Public Order and Criminal Justice (Scotland) Act 2006, s.81), where a constable has reasonable grounds for suspecting that a person has committed or is committing an offence at any place, he may require–

(a) that person, if the constable finds him at that place or at any place where the constable is entitled to be, to give his name, address, date and place of birth and nationality, and may ask him for an explanation of the circumstances which have given rise to the constable's suspicion;

(b) any other person whom the constable finds at that place or at any place where the constable is entitled to be and who the constable believes has information relating to the offence, to give his name, address, date and place of birth and nationality.

The constable may require the person to provide their fingerprints or a record, created by a device approved by the Scottish Ministers, of the skin on their fingers (s.13(1B), inserted by the Police, Public Order and Criminal Justice (Scotland) Act 2006, s.82(2) – not yet in force).

Fingerprints or a record provided by a person under a requirement under s.13(1B) may be used only for the purposes verifying the name and address given by the them, or establishing whether they may be a person who is suspected of having committed any other offence, and all record of such fingerprints or record must be destroyed as soon as possible after they have fulfilled those purposes (s.13(1C), inserted by the Police, Public Order and Criminal Justice (Scotland) Act 2006, s.82 – not yet in force).

The constable may require the suspected person to remain with him while he verifies any of the above information given by them (provided that it appears to the constable that the verification can be obtained quickly), establishes whether the person may be suspected of having committed any other offence, and notes any explanation proffered by the suspected person, and he may use reasonable force to ensure that the suspected person remains with him. The constable may only establish whether the person may be a person who is suspected of having committed any other offence where the person has given a name and address and it appears to the constable that establishing the matter can be achieved quickly (s.13(2) to (4), amended by the Police, Public Order and Criminal Justice (Scotland) Act 2006, s.82 – not yet in force). A constable imposing any requirement under s.13 must explain his reasons and that failure to comply with his requirement may constitute an offence under s.13(6).

A constable may arrest without warrant any person who he has reasonable grounds for suspecting has committed an offence under s.13(6).

The Scottish Ministers may, by order, approve a device for the purposes of creating records (s.13(8), inserted by the Police, Public Order and Criminal Justice (Scotland) Act 2006, s. 82 – not yet in force).

3 Detention and questioning at police stations

S.14 of the Criminal Procedure (Scotland) Act 1995 empowers a constable to detain a person and take him as quickly as is reasonably practicable to a police station or other premises for the purpose of facilitating the carrying out of investigations (a) into an offence and (b) as to whether criminal proceedings should be instigated against that person. The power is exercisable where the constable has reasonable grounds for suspecting that a person has committed or is committing an offence punishable by imprisonment (s.14(1)). The constable may use reasonable force in exercising his power under s.14(1) (s.14(8)). At the time when a constable detains a person under s.14(1), he must inform the person of his suspicion, of the general nature of the offence which he suspects has been or is being committed and of the reason for the detention (s.14(6)).

The Right to Interpretation and Translation in Criminal Proceedings (Scotland) Regulations 2014, which extend to anyone in police custody or attending voluntarily at a police station or other premises or place for the purpose of being questioned by the police about an offence which the police have reasonable grounds to suspect they have committed, require the provision of interpreters where needed and for the translation of essential documents. Such services must be provided free of charge.

Under s.14(2), detention under s.14(1) must (unless extended, see below) be terminated not more than 12 hours after it begins or (if earlier)–

(a) when the person is arrested;

(b) when the person is detained under any other enactment;

(c) where the grounds for detention no longer apply.

Where a person is detained under s.14(1) and the detention under that power is terminated, the person must be informed immediately of the termination.

Where a person has been released at the end of a period of detention under s.14(1), he must not thereafter be detained, under that provision, on the same grounds or on any grounds arising out of the same circumstances (s.14(3)). Subject to the exception set out in s.14(5) (which concerns detention in relation to the introduction into a prison of prohibited articles), where a person has previously been detained under any other enactment and is detained under s.14(1) on the same grounds or on grounds arising from the same circumstances, the period of 12 hours is reduced by the length of that earlier detention (s.14(4)).

Where a person is detained under s.14(1), a constable may put questions to him in relation to the suspected offence, and exercise the same powers of search as are available following an arrest. The power to put questions does not prejudice any rule of law as to the admissibility in evidence of any answer given (s.14(7)).

A person detained under s.14(1) is under no obligation to answer any question other than to give his name, address, date and place of birth and nationality, and the constable must so inform him both on detaining him and on arrival at the police station or other premises (s.14(9) and (10) (inserted by the Police, Public Order and Criminal Justice (Scotland) Act 2006, s.81).

Before the expiry of the 12 hour detention period, a custody review officer (i.e., an officer of the rank of inspector or above who has not been involved in the investigation in connection with which the person is detained) may authorise that period to be extended by a further 12 hours (s.14A). The further period of 12 hours starts from the time when the period of detention would have expired but for the authorisation. A custody review officer may authorise such an extension only if he is satisfied that—

(a) the continued detention of the detained person is necessary to secure, obtain or preserve evidence (whether by questioning the person or otherwise) relating to an offence in connection with which the person is being detained;

(b) an offence in connection with which the detained person is being detained is an indictable one; and

(c) the investigation is being conducted diligently and expeditiously.

Before deciding whether to authorise an extension, the custody review officer must give either the detained person or the solicitor representing them, if available, the opportunity to make representations on the decision to extend the period. If the detained person is unfit to make representation either through condition or behaviour the officer may refuse to hear any oral representations from that person (s.14B).

Every suspect who is in police custody must be given a "letter of rights", giving information about the right of access to a lawyer and assisting in ensuring they are informed of essential information (Right to Information (Suspects and Accused Persons) (Scotland) Regulations 2014, Reg. 3). The information may be given verbally rather than in a letter if e.g., the suspect cannot read, or there are safety concerns.

Special provisions apply where the detention is in connection with suspected terrorism (see 12 **Arrest or detention in connection with terrorism**, below).

Designated immigration officers have the power to detain a person where a warrant is outstanding for the individual. This detention will be pending the arrival of the police and is subject to a maximum detention period of three hours (UK Borders Act 2007, ss.1-2).

4 Access to solicitor following arrest

By virtue of s.17 of the Criminal Procedure (Scotland) Act 1995, a person who is arrested for an offence is entitled to have intimation sent immediately to a solicitor that his professional assistance is required. The intimation must inform the solicitor of the place where the person is being detained, whether the person is to be liberated and, if not, the court to which he is to be taken and the date when he is to be so taken. The accused and the solicitor are entitled to have a private interview before the examination or, as the case may be, first appearance.

Upon request, suspects or their solicitors must be provided free of charge with access to any documents held by Police Scotland related to their specific case which are essential to challenging effectively the lawfulness of their arrest and detention (Right to Information (Suspects and Accused Persons) (Scotland) Regulations 2014, Reg. 4).

Special provisions apply where the detention is in connection with suspected terrorism (see 12 **Arrest or detention in connection with terrorism**, below).

5 Right to have someone informed when arrested or detained

Without prejudice to the right to have arrest intimated to a solicitor in accordance with s.17 of the Criminal Procedure (Scotland) Act 1995, a person is entitled to have intimation of his custody or detention and of the place where he is being held or detained sent to a person reasonably named by him. The intimation must be sent without delay or, where some delay is necessary in the interest of the investigation or the prevention of crime or the apprehension of offenders, with no more delay than is so necessary. The person arrested or detained must be told of his entitlement on arrival at the police station or other premises or, where he is not arrested or detained until after such arrival, on such arrest or detention. The time at which a request for such intimation to be sent is made, and the time at which it is complied with, must be recorded (1995 Act, s.15(1) to (3)).

Where the person arrested or detained appears to a constable to be a child (i.e., under 16 years of age), he must send without delay such intimation to that person's parent (if known). The parent must be permitted access to the arrested or detained person, unless there is reasonable cause to suspect that the parent has been involved in the alleged offence, in which case access may be permitted. The nature and extent of any access is subject to any restriction essential for the furtherance of the investigation or the well-being of the child. The term "parent" includes the child's guardian and any person who has the actual custody of the child (1995 Act, s.15(4) to (6)).

Special provisions apply where the detention is in connection with suspected terrorism (see **12 Arrest or detention in connection with terrorism**, below).

6 Prints and samples etc. in criminal investigations

The provisions of s.18 of the Criminal Procedure (Scotland) Act 1995 (as amended by s.47 of the Crime and Punishment (Scotland) Act 1997 and s.83 of the Police, Public Order and Criminal Justice (Scotland) Act 2006), apply to the taking of prints, samples etc. where a person has been arrested and is in custody or is detained under s.14(1) (see **3 Detention and questioning at police stations**, above), but nothing in s.18 prejudices any power of search, any power to take possession of evidence where there is imminent danger of it being lost or destroyed, or any power to take prints, impressions or samples under the authority of a warrant.

Under s.18(2), a constable may take from the person or require the person to provide him with such relevant physical data as the constable may, having regard to the circumstances of the suspected offence, reasonably consider it appropriate to take from him or require him to provide, and the person so required must comply with that requirement. "Relevant physical data" includes fingerprints, palm prints, other prints, impressions of an external part of the body, and a record of a person's skin created by an approved device (s.18(7A)). With the authority of an officer of a rank no lower than inspector, a constable may, under s.18(6), take from the person–

(a) from the hair of an external part of the body, other than pubic hair, by means of cutting, combing or plucking, a sample of hair or other material;

(b) from a fingernail or toenail or from under any such nail, a sample of nail or other material;

(c) from an external part of the body, by means of swabbing or rubbing, a sample of blood or other body fluid, of body tissue or of other material.

A constable (or at a constable's direction a police custody and security officer) may take from the inside of the mouth, by means of swabbing, a sample of saliva or other material. The consent of a senior officer is not required unless reasonable force will be needed to take the sample (ss.18(6A), 19B(2)).

Where a decision is taken not to institute proceedings against a person from whom samples have been taken, or where that person is not convicted or is merely made the subject of an absolute discharge by a court of summary jurisdiction, physical data and samples, and all information derived from such data or samples, must be destroyed as soon as possible. There is an exception to the duty to destroy which applies in respect of samples taken under s.18(6) and information derived therefrom–

(a) where the destruction would have the effect of destroying a sample or information lawfully held in relation to some other person; or

(b) where the record, sample or information is of the same kind as one lawfully held by or on behalf of the police in relation to the person sampled (s.18(3) and (4)).

7 Retention of samples

The retention or destruction of fingerprints and DNA profiles is dealt with by the Criminal Procedure (Scotland) Act 1995 ss.18-20 as follows–

	Period of Retention
ADULT–on conviction–all crimes	Indefinite
ADULT–charged but not convicted –serious crime	3 Years + possible 2 year extension(s) by Court
ADULT– arrested but not charged or convicted –serious crime	None
ADULT – non-conviction – minor crime	None
UNDER 18s –on conviction – serious crime	Indefinite
UNDER 18s –on conviction – minor crime	Indefinite
UNDER 18s –charged but not convicted – serious crime	3 Years + possible 2 year extension(s) by Court
UNDER 18s – arrested but not charged or convicted – serious crime	None
UNDER 18s –non-conviction – minor crime	None
Penalty Notice for disorder	2 Years
Terrorist suspects	Not covered (reserved matter so as for England and Wales)
Biological DNA samples	As per destruction of profiles

8 Supplementary provisions

S.19 of the Criminal Procedure (Scotland) Act 1995 provides for a constable to exercise similar powers to those set out in s.18(2) and (6) (see above), where a person has been convicted of an offence and either has not had any relevant physical data or had any impression or sample taken from him since the conviction, or has (whether before or after conviction) had taken from him, or been required to provide, any relevant physical data or had any impression or sample taken from him but it has proved unsuitable or insufficient for the intended analysis. The powers are exercisable within the period of one month following conviction or, in the case of an unsuitable or insufficient sample, within one month of the police force receiving written intimation of the inadequacy of the data or sample. A convicted person may be required to attend a police station so that these powers may be exercised; a minimum of seven days' notice of the date of attendance must be given.

S.19A (inserted by s.48 of the Crime and Punishment (Scotland) Act 1997) allows a constable to take from persons convicted of and imprisoned for certain sexual and violent offences, or to require such persons to provide, such physical data as the constable reasonably considers appropriate. In addition, with the authority of an inspector, a constable may take from such persons any sample of the type mentioned in s.18(6) (see above). The power conferred by s.19A cannot be exercised where a person has previously supplied such data or samples, unless the data or samples previously taken have been lost or destroyed.

Where a person volunteers a sample (e.g., in the course of a mass screening of members of the public), such a sample may be retained only if the person giving the sample consents in writing. Consent may be given generally, or limited to the investigation and prosecution of the offence for which the sample was given. Consent may be withdrawn at any time, but evidence derived from the sample before consent was withdrawn can still be used. A sample must be destroyed as soon as possible after consent is withdrawn (Criminal Justice (Scotland) Act 2003, s.56).

9 Use of prints and samples

Prints, impressions, samples and information lawfully held by or on behalf of any police force or in connection with or as a result of an investigation of an offence may be checked against other prints, impressions, samples and information (Criminal Procedure (Scotland) Act 1995, s.20).

10 Arrested people: testing for drugs

The police may test a person for a relevant Class A drug if he or she has been arrested under suspicion of committing a relevant offence provided certain conditions are met, including that the person is held in custody in a police station which is located in a prescribed area (Criminal Procedure (Scotland) Act 1995, ss.20A and 20B inserted by the Police, Public Order and Criminal Justice (Scotland) Act 2006, s.84). The Testing of Arrested Persons for Class A Drugs (Prescribed Area) (Scotland) Order 2007 prescribes the local government areas of the City of Aberdeen, City of Edinburgh and City of Glasgow for these purposes.

A "relevant offence" is theft, assault, robbery, fraud, reset, uttering a forged document, embezzlement or an attempt, conspiracy or incitement to commit any of these offences (s.20A(8)).

A person who has been arrested under suspicion of committing any other offence, which is not a relevant offence, can also be tested at the discretion of a senior police officer if he or she believes that misuse of a Class A drug caused or contributed to the offence. The Class A drugs that will be tested for are cocaine and diamorphine (heroin) (s.20A(1)).

The police cannot test a person for a relevant Class A drug if that person has already given a sample for testing after they have been brought to a police station (s.20A(2)). A further sample can be taken if the original is not suitable for analysis, was insufficient or was destroyed during the testing process (s.20A(5)).

The conditions which must be met before a person is tested for a relevant Class A drug are set out in s.20A(3)). A sample must be taken or provided within six hours of a person being brought to a police station.

It is an offence for a person arrested to refuse to comply with a drugs test under these powers if required to do so (s.20A(7)).

The procedures that must be followed where a senior police officer decides that a person should be tested for a class A drug are set out in s.20B(4) and (5). There is a requirement to destroy a sample which has been taken under s.20A as soon as possible after analysis (s.20B(7)) unless the sample is to be retained for the purposes of prosecution under s.88 of the Police, Public Order and Criminal Justice (Scotland) Act 2006 (for failing to attend and stay for the duration of assessments: see 11 **Assessment following positive test,** below) (s.20B(8)). In this case, the sample needs to be retained to be produced in court, but must be destroyed as soon as possible once it is not longer needed for any proceedings.

11 Assessment following positive test

An individual who has tested positive for a relevant Class A drug will be required to attend a drugs assessment with a suitably qualified drugs assessor (Police, Public Order and Criminal Justice (Scotland) Act 2006, s.85).

The duties imposed on the police when a person is required to attend a mandatory assessment into their drug misuse are set out in s.86.

A drugs assessor is required to notify the person in writing of the date, time and place of the drugs assessment (s.87).

A person will have committed an offence if they fail to attend the assessment location to obtain details of their appointment, or fail to attend or to stay for the duration of a drugs assessment. A drugs assessor must notify the police if an offence has been committed (s.88).

12 Arrest or detention in connection with terrorism

Special provisions apply to terrorist suspects under the Terrorism Act 2000 and the Anti-terrorism, Crime and Security Act 2001. These provisions apply throughout the United Kingdom.

Where the police reasonably suspect someone to be a terrorist, they may arrest him without a warrant (Terrorism Act 2000, s.41).

For these purposes, a "terrorist" is a person who has committed a terrorist offence or has been concerned in the commission, preparation or instigation of acts of terrorism. Terrorist offences include membership of or support for a proscribed organisation, fund-raising for terrorism, money laundering of terrorist property, weapons training, and inciting terrorism overseas.

Where a person is arrested for terrorism, they may initially be detained for 48 hours (s.41(3)), although this may be extended for up to 14 days (Sch. 8 para 36, as amended by the Criminal Justice Act 2003, s.306 and the Terrorism Act 2006, s.23). The arrest and detention procedures are governed by Schedule 8 to the 2000 Act (as amended by the Anti-terrorism, Crime and Security Act 2001 and the Terrorism Act 2006) instead of by the provisions of the 1984 Act. Provisions is made for the audio recording of interviews and the taking of fingerprints and samples. The right of a detained person to have someone informed of his detention and the right to consult a solicitor may both be delayed.

13 Authorities

Statutes–

Anti-terrorism, Crime and Security Act 2001

Crime and Punishment (Scotland) Act 1997

Criminal Justice (Scotland) Act 2003

Criminal Procedure (Scotland) Act 1995

Law Reform (Miscellaneous Provisions) (Scotland) Act 1985

Police, Public Order and Criminal Justice (Scotland) Act 2006

Terrorism Act 2000

Statutory Instruments–

Right to Information (Suspects and Accused Persons) (Scotland) Regulations 2014 (S.S.I. 2014 No. 159)

Right to Interpretation and Translation in Criminal Proceedings (Scotland) Regulations 2014 (S.S.I. 2014 No. 95)

Testing of Arrested Persons for Class A Drugs (Prescribed Area) (Scotland) Order 2007 (S.S.I. 2007 No. 131)